1st EDITION

POWER PACK

SSC MATHS

CHAPTERWISE 7000+ TCS MCQ

All SSC Exams PYQs Till Jan. 2025

SSC CGL, CHSL, CPO, MTS, GD, Selection Post, etc.

Authors
Rishabh Khurana, Mohd. Mustakeem
Anubhav Singh, Sanni Kumar

arihant
SUCCESS AND NOTHING LESS

AF819697

arihant
SUCCESS AND NOTHING LESS

ARIHANT PUBLICATIONS (INDIA) LIMITED

Administrative & Production Offices

Regd. Office
'Ramchhaya' 4577/15, Agarwal Road, Darya Ganj, New Delhi -110002
Tele: 011- 47630600, 43518550

Head Office
Kalindi, TP Nagar, Meerut (UP) - 250002
Tel: 0121-7156203, 7156204

Sales & Support Offices
Agra, Ahmedabad, Bengaluru, Bareilly, Chennai, Delhi, Guwahati, Hyderabad, Jaipur, Jhansi, Kolkata, Lucknow, Nagpur & Pune.

PRICE ₹695.00

PO No : TXT-XX-XXXXXXX-X-XX

Published by Arihant Publications (India) Ltd.

For further information about the books published by Arihant, log on to www.arihantbooks.com or e-mail at info@arihantbooks.com

PRODUCTION TEAM

Publishing Manager
Mahendra Singh Rawat

Project Head
Shahid Saifi

Cover Designer
Bilal Hashmi

Inner Designer
Ankit Prajapati

Page Layouting
Ravindra Kumar
Sonu Kumar

Proof Readers
Sagar Sharma, Nishi, Rashid, Ravi, Guljar

CHAPTER INDEX

POWER PACK

POWER PACK

POWER PACK

SSC Cutoff 2023-24

Exam	Tier	Year	SC	ST	EWS	OBC	UR	ESM
SSC CGL	TIER I	2024	126.45554	111.8893	142.01963	146.26291	153.18981	69.92674
		2023	126.68201	118.16655	143.44441	145.93743	150.04936	100.29326
	TIER II	2024	-	-	-	-	-	-
		2023	252	241	265	271	287	223
SSC CHSL	TIER I	2024	139.68408	129.44568	150.51731	156.61665	157.36168	78.23008
		2023	136.41166	124.52592	151.09782	152.26953	153.91142	102.47651
	TIER I	2024	89.8581	82.6568	111.4352	113.50911	119.80335	40.07024
		2023	79.3189	78.13852	103.97465	102.9603	115.04762	40
SSC CPO	Grade C	2024	-	-	-	-	-	-
		2023	136.08122	128.04746	-	145.03097	147.45086	147.45086
SSC STENO	Grade D	2024	-	-	-	-	-	-
		2023	109.41004	88.71217	40.15035	125.02167	131.32184	126.29805
SSC GD	Tier I	2024	148.21914	143.65896	151.15627	152.28771	153.56851	94.65261
		2023	129.75	126.45	139.16	140.75	142.03	75.01

01

Number System

The system of writing or representing numbers using certain rules is called number system

- **Face value** In a numeral, the face value of a digit is the value of digit itself. e.g. In a numeral 4321, the face value of 3 is 3 and 2 is 2
- **Place value** (Local value) In a numeral, the position of a digit is called its place value e.g. In the number, 2897, place value of $8 = 8 \times 100 = 800$ and 9 is $9 \times 10 = 90$

Types of Number

- **Natural numbers (N)** All positive counting numbers excluding zero (0). i.e. $N = \{1, 2, 3, ...\}$
- **Whole numbers (W)** All the natural numbers including zero (0) forms the set of whole numbers. i.e., $W = \{0, 1, 2, 3......\}$
- **Integer (Z)** All the negative natural numbers and whole numbers form the set of integers. i.e. $Z = \{..... -4, -3, -2, -1, 0, 1, 2, 3, ...\}$
- **Even numbers** Completely divisible by 2 i.e., 2, 4, 6, ...etc.
- **Odd numbers** Not completely divisible by 2 i.e., 1, 3, 5, 7,...... etc.
- **Prime numbers** Which are exactly divisible by 1 and itself i.e. 2, 3, 5, 7, 11, 13, 17, ...etc.
- **Composite numbers** Which have atleast one factor other than 1 and number itself. i.e 4, 6, 8, 9, 10, ...etc.
- **Coprime numbers** The natural numbers are said to be coprimes, if their HCF is 1. i.e (7,9), (15, 16), (17, 18), etc.
- **Rational numbers** Which can be expressed in the form of $\frac{p}{q}$, and $q \neq 0$ i.e. $\frac{3}{5}, \frac{7}{9}, \frac{8}{9}$, ... etc.
- **Irrational numbers** The numbers that cannot be expressed in the form of $\frac{p}{q}$ i.e $\sqrt{2}, \sqrt{3}, \sqrt{7}$,.....etc.
- **Real numbers (R)** The set of real numbers that include both rational and irrational numbers. i.e, $\frac{7}{9}, \sqrt{2}, \sqrt{5}, \pi, \frac{8}{9}$, etc

Results on Divisibility

- $(x^n - a^n)$ is divisible by $(x - a)$ for all values of n.
- $(x^n - a^n)$ is divisible by $(x + a)$ for even values of n.
- $(x^n + a^n)$ is divisible by $(x + a)$ for odd values of n.

Divisibility Test

By	Rule
2	If the last digit of a number is either zero (0) or even e.g. 12, 472, 52, etc.
3	Sum of digits of a number is divisible by 3 e.g. 156, 1233, etc.
4	When the last two digits of a number are divisible by 4 e.g. 6428, 4300 etc.
5	When the last digit is 0 or 5. e.g 45, 4350, etc.
6	When the number is divisible by both 2 and 3. e.g 36 and 72
7	When the difference between twice the digits at unit place and the number formed by the other digits is either 0 or a multiple of 7 e.g. 658 is divisible by 7 e.g. $65 - 2 \times 8 = 65 - 16 = 49$
8	When the last three digits are divisible by 8 e.g. 2256, 4362000
9	When the sum of digits of a number is divisible by 9 e.g. 4356, 936819, etc.
10	When a number ends with zero e.g, 20, 40, 150, ..etc.
11	When the difference between the sum of odd and even place digits is equal to 0 or multiple of 11. e.g, 2865423 Sum of digits at odd places $(A) = 2 + 6 + 4 + 3 = 15$ Sum of digits at even places $(B) = 8 + 5 + 2 = 15$ $\therefore A - B = 15 - 15 = 0$ $\therefore$ 2865423 s divisible by 11.

Ex. 1 If a number is divided by 3 and the remainder is 5, then what will be remainder when twice of the same number is divided by 3.

Sol. Let the number be n.

By Division Algorithm, we know

$\therefore \quad n = 3q + 5$

Also, $\quad 2n = 2(3q + 5)$

$\Rightarrow \quad 2n = 6q + 10 = 6q + 9 + 1 = 3(2q + 3) + 1$

$\therefore$ Required remainder = 1

Unit Digit of an Expression

- To find the unit's digit in the product of two or more numbers, take unit's digit of every number and multiply them.

e.g. $\quad 207 \times 781 \times 39 \times 94$

$$= 7 \times 1 \times 9 \times 4 = 7 \times 36 = 7 \times 6 = 42$$

$\therefore$ Required unit digit = 2

- If a number is of the form a^b, where a and b are natural numbers. Then, following cases are possible.

Case I If b is a Multiple of 4.

(i) If a is an even number, i.e. 2, 4, 6......, then unit's digit is 6.

(ii) If a is an odd number, except 5 i.e. 1, 3, 7.........then unit's digit is 1.

e.g. Unit's digit in $(4137)^{756}$ is 1 as 756 divisible by 4 and 4137 is odd.

Case II If b is not a multiple of 4.

Let r be the remainder when b is divided by 4, i.e. $b = 4q + r$, then unit's place digit of a^b is equal to unit's place digit of a^r.

e.g. Consider 7^{105}. Here, 105 is not a multiple of 4, so when 105 is divided by 4, we get remainder as 1.

$\therefore$ Unit's digit in 7^{105} = Unit's digit in $7^1 = 7$

Case III If the unit's digit of a is 0, 1, 5 or 6, then the resultant unit's digit of a^b remains same.

e.g. (i) Unit's digit of $(576)^{1151} = 6$

(ii) Unit's digit of $(155)^{120} = 5$

Case IV If unit's digit of a is 9 and the power of a is even, then unit's digit will be 1 and if the power of a is odd, then unit's digit will be 9.

e.g. $(539)^{140}$ Since, the power is even and unit's digit is 9.

$\therefore$ Unit's digit in $(539)^{140} = 1$

Number of Divisors and Number of Factors

- Number of factors of $a^p b^q c^r d^s = (p+1)\times(q+1)\times(r+1)\times(s+1)$ where, a, b, c and d are prime numbers.
- Number of prime factors of $a^p b^q c^r d^s = p + q + r + s$ where, a, b, c and d are prime numbers.

Some Important Formulae

- Sum of first n natural numbers $= \dfrac{n(n+1)}{2}$
- Sum of first n odd numbers $= n^2$
- Sum of first n even numbers $= n(n+1)$
- Sum of squares of first n natural numbers $= \dfrac{n(n+1)(2n+1)}{6}$
- Sum of cubes of first n natural numbers $= \left[\dfrac{n(n+1)}{2}\right]^2$

Arithmetic Progression (AP)

- A sequence which either continuously decreases or increases by a fixed quantity is called an arithmetic progression.
- This fixed quantity is difference of two consecutive terms and is called common difference.
- The general form of AP is $a, a+d, a+2d, \ldots, a+(n-1)d$

  In the AP, first term $= a$, common difference $= d$ and number of terms $= n$
- nth term $(T_n) = a + (n-1)d$
- Sum of n terms $(S_n) = \dfrac{n}{2}[2a + (n-1)d] = \dfrac{n}{2}[a + T_n]$

Arithmetic Mean (AM)

If a, b, c are in AP, then b will be Arithmetic Mean (AM) of a and c

i.e. $b = \dfrac{a+c}{2}$

Ex. 2 Find the sum of the given series: 2, 4, 6, 8, ..., 98.

Sol. Given, AP 2, 4, 6, 8, ..., 98

First term $(a) = 2$, common difference $(d) = 2$, $T_n = 98$

$\therefore \quad T_n = a + (n-1)d \Rightarrow 98 = 2 + (n-1)(2)$

$\Rightarrow \quad \dfrac{96}{2} + 1 = n \Rightarrow n = 49$

$\Rightarrow \quad S_n = \dfrac{n}{2}[a + T_n]$

$\Rightarrow S_{49} = \dfrac{49}{2}[2 + 98] \Rightarrow S_{49} = \dfrac{49}{2}[100] = 2450$

Geometric Progression (GP)

- If in a sequence, the ratio of two consecutive terms is fixed, then it is called a Geometric Progression (GP).
- The general form of GP is, $a, ar, ar^2, \ldots, ar^{n-1}$.

  In the GP, first term $= a$, common ratio $= r$ and number of terms $= n$
- nth term$(T_n) = ar^{n-1}$
- Sum of n terms $= \begin{cases} \dfrac{a(1-r^n)}{1-r}; & r<1 \\ \dfrac{a(r^n-1)}{(r-1)}; & r>1 \end{cases}$
- Sum of infinite GP $(S_\infty) = \dfrac{a}{1-r}$

Geometric Mean (GM)

If a, b, c are in GP, then b will be Geometric Mean (GM) of a and c i.e. $b^2 = ac$ or $b = \sqrt{ac}$.

Ex. 3 Find the sum of first 9 terms in the given series 3, 6, 12, ...

Sol. Given, GP 3, 6, 12, ...

First term $(a) = 3$, Common ratio $(r) = 2 > 1$, $n = 9$

$\therefore \quad S_n = \dfrac{a(r^n - 1)}{(r-1)}$

$\Rightarrow \quad S_9 = \dfrac{3(2^9 - 1)}{2-1} = 3(512 - 1) = 1533$

Fraction

Fraction is a number that represents a part of a whole or a group of equal parts.

- **Simple Fraction** The fraction which has denominator other than power of 10.
- **Proper Fractions** When numerator < denominator e.g. $\dfrac{1}{2}, \dfrac{15}{17}, \dfrac{21}{43}$, etc.
- **Improper Fractions** When numerator > denominator e.g. $\dfrac{17}{13}, \dfrac{18}{14}$, etc.
- **Equivalent Fractions** The fractions whose values are same, is called equivalent fractions e.g. $\dfrac{2}{3} = \dfrac{4}{6} = \dfrac{6}{9}$.
- **Inverse Fractions** The reciprocal of the original fraction is called the inverse of the fraction.

  e.g. If fraction $= \dfrac{3}{8}$, then its inverse fraction $= \dfrac{8}{3}$

SSC Exam Scanner

SSC CGL 2024 (Tier I & II)

1. Which number among 38211, 38121, 32118 and 31128 is divisible by 24? SSC CGL (Tier II) 20/01/2025 Shift-I
(a) 32118 (b) 31128
(c) 38121 (d) 38211

2. $7^{15} + 7^{16} + 7^{17}$ is divisible by which of the following given numbers? SSC CGL (Tier I) 26/09/2024 Shift-III
(a) 3 (b) 5 (c) 2 (d) 4

3. The five-digit number $45yz0$ is divisible by 40. What is the maximum possible value of $(y + z)$? SSC CGL (Tier I) 26/09/2024 Shift-II
(a) 15 (b) 18 (c) 16 (d) 17

4. The sum of two consecutive even numbers is 174. Find the smaller number. SSC CGL (Tier I) 26/09/2024 Shift-II
(a) 84 (b) 90 (c) 86 (d) 88

5. In a room, there are some chairs and some people. If on each chair, only one person is seated, then there is no chair for exactly one person. If on each chair, two persons sit, then there is one vacant chair. What is the number of chairs in the room? SSC CGL (Tier I) 26/09/2024 Shift-I
(a) 7 (b) 4
(c) 3 (d) 6

6. Find the remainder when $9^{20} + 2$ is divided by 4. SSC CGL (Tier I) 26/09/2024 Shift-I
(a) 1 (b) 3 (c) 0 (d) 2

7. Which of the following numbers is divisible by 6? SSC CGL (Tier I) 25/09/2024 Shift-III
(a) 128530 (b) 12581
(c) 438750 (d) 62233

8. If m is even, then $(8^m - 1)$ is divisible by SSC CGL (Tier I) 25/09/2024 Shift-II
(a) 63 (b) 42 (c) 68 (d) 8

9. Which of the following fractions is the largest? SSC CGL (Tier I) 25/09/2024 Shift-I
$\frac{3}{7}, \frac{7}{53}, \frac{41}{80}, \frac{29}{79}$
(a) $\frac{29}{79}$ (b) $\frac{7}{53}$ (c) $\frac{3}{7}$ (d) $\frac{41}{80}$

10. Which composite number can divide the sum of the first 12 natural numbers? SSC CGL (Tier I) 24/09/2024 Shift-III
(a) 6 (b) 12 (c) 4 (d) 8

11. If $436P5$ is divisible by 3, then the largest value of P is SSC CGL (Tier I) 24/09/2024 Shift-III
(a) 12 (b) 6 (c) 8 (d) 9

12. On dividing a number by 55, we get 28 as the remainder. On dividing the same number by 11, what is the remainder? SSC CGL (Tier I) 24/09/2024 Shift-II
(a) 5 (b) 8 (c) 7 (d) 6

13. Find the greatest value of 'k' in a 6-digit number $6745k2$ such that the number is divisible by 3. SSC CGL (Tier I) 24/09/2024 Shift-I
(a) 8 (b) 6 (c) 9 (d) 7

14. The number 429714 is divisible by SSC CGL (Tier I) 23/09/2024 Shift-III
(a) 3 and 5 (b) 6 and 5
(c) 4 and 6 (d) 3 and 6

15. A customer pays ₹ 975 in installments. The payment is done each month ₹ 5 less than the previous month. If the first installment is ₹ 100, how much time will be taken to pay the entire amount? SSC CGL (Tier I) 23/09/2024 Shift-III
(a) 14 months (b) 15 months
(c) 27 months (d) 26 months

16. The least number which must be subtracted from 7278745 so as to obtain a sum that is divisible by 11 is SSC CGL (Tier I) 23/09/2024 Shift-II
(a) 3 (b) 1
(c) 5 (d) 2

17. For what least value of n, $2^{2n} + 2n$ is completely divided by 6, where n is an integer? SSC CGL (Tier I) 23/09/2024 Shift-I
(a) 3 (b) 1 (c) 0 (d) 2

18. Which of the following numbers is not divisible by 8? SSC CGL (Tier I) 19/09/2024 Shift-III
(a) 7344 (b) 5544
(c) 7497 (d) 4608

19. From the given numbers A, B, C and D, which number is not divisible by 11? SSC CGL (Tier I) 19/09/2024 Shift-II
$A = 712712$ $B = 177210$
$C = 64614$ $D = 756148$
(a) C (b) D
(c) B (d) A

20. At a school building, there is an overhead tank. To fill this tank 50 buckets of water are required. Assume that the capacity of the bucket is reduced to two-fifth of the present. How many buckets of water are required to fill the same tank? SSC CGL (Tier I) 19/09/2024 Shift-II
(a) 62.5 (b) 20
(c) 125 (d) 60

21. If the 9-digit number $5x79856y6$ is divisible by 36, then what is the negative value of $\sqrt{(2x + y)}$ for the largest possible value of y, given x and y are natural numbers? SSC CGL (Tier I) 18/09/2024 Shift-III
(a) – 7 (b) – 2
(c) – 4 (d) – 5

22. Which of the following fractions is the largest? SSC CGL (Tier I) 18/09/2024 Shift-II
$\frac{2}{3}, \frac{6}{53}, \frac{79}{90}, \frac{33}{44}$
(a) $\frac{2}{3}$ (b) $\frac{33}{44}$
(c) $\frac{6}{53}$ (d) $\frac{79}{90}$

23. Find the remainder, if 19^{200} is divided by 20. SSC CGL (Tier I) 18/09/2024 Shift-II
(a) 2 (b) – 1
(c) 1 (d) 3

24. The sum of five consecutive numbers is 80. Find the largest number. SSC CGL (Tier I) 18/09/2024 Shift-I
(a) 18 (b) 15 (c) 19 (d) 14

25. A number r when divided by 8 leaves remainder 3. What will be the remainder, when $(r^2 + 6r + 7)$ is divided by 8? SSC CGL (Tier I) 18/09/2024 Shift-I
(a) 2 (b) 3
(c) 1 (d) 4

26. If P is a digit such that $6954P$ is divisible by 11, then P equals SSC CGL (Tier I) 17/09/2024 Shift-III
(a) 2 (b) 8
(c) 6 (d) 7

27. Find the least value of x for which $57x716$ is divisible by 9. SSC CGL (Tier I) 17/09/2024 Shift-II
(a) 1 (b) 9
(c) 0 (d) 8

28. Find the least value of k for which a 7-digit number $249k876$ is divisible by 6. SSC CGL (Tier I) 17/09/2024 Shift-I
(a) 1 (b) 0
(c) 5 (d) 7

29. Find the remainder $(17^{13} - 21) \div 18$
SSC CGL (Tier I) 13/09/2024 Shift-III
(a) 15 (b) 17
(c) 14 (d) 21

30. Which digits should come in the place of x and y, respectively, if the number 62684xy is divisible by both 8 and 5?
SSC CGL (Tier I) 13/09/2024 Shift-II
(a) 5 and 0 (b) 4 and 0
(c) 2 and 0 (d) 0 and 5

31. If 321y72 is a multiple of 6, where y is a digit, what is the least value of y? SSC CGL (Tier I) 13/09/2024 Shift-I
(a) 3 (b) 0
(c) 7 (d) 2

32. Find the smallest value that must be assigned to number 'a' in order for 91876a2 to be divisible by 8.
SSC CGL (Tier I) 12/09/2024 Shift-III
(a) 3 (b) 0
(c) 1 (d) 2

33. Which of the following numbers is divisible by 2, 5, 10 and 11?
SSC CGL (Tier I) 12/09/2024 Shift-III
(a) 203467 (b) 830942
(c) 589270 (d) 1234560

34. In a garden, there are 6 daisy plants the first year. Each year, a gardener adds 3 new daisy plants. He has 26 jasmine plants the first year and loses 2 each year. When will the number of daisy plants equal to the number of jasmine plants after the first year?
SSC CGL (Tier I) 12/09/2024 Shift-II
(a) 5 yr (b) 4 yr
(c) 2 yr (d) 6 yr

35. Which of following numbers is not divisible by 11?
SSC CGL (Tier I) 12/09/2024 Shift-II
(a) 109153 (b) 5445
(c) 128041 (d) 80124

36. Which digits should come in place * and $, respectively, if the number 72864*$ is divisible by both 8 and 5? SSC CGL (Tier I) 12/09/2024 Shift-I
(a) 4 and 0 (b) 2 and 0
(c) 2 and 5 (d) 4 and 5

37. Replace * by the smallest digit so that 723*56* is divisible by 6.
SSC CGL (Tier I) 11/09/2024 Shift-III
(a) 4 (b) 3
(c) 2 (d) 1

38. Which of the following numbers is divisible by both 2 and 5?
SSC CGL (Tier I) 11/09/2024 Shift-II
(a) 63840 (b) 20792
(c) 37915 (d) 37254

39. In a division problem, the divisor is 4 times the quotient and 2 times the remainder. If the remainder is 32, then find the dividend.
SSC CGL (Tier I) 11/09/2024 Shift-I
(a) 1056 (b) 1650
(c) 3240 (d) 1065

40. Find the smallest number to be added to 999, so that 99 divides the sum exactly.
SSC CGL (Tier I) 11/09/2024 Shift-I
(a) 99 (b) 0
(c) 90 (d) 9

41. If the number 6484y6 is divisible by 8, then find the least value of y?
SSC CGL (Tier I) 10/09/2024 Shift-III
(a) 7 (b) 3
(c) 1 (d) 4

42. If $(77^{77} + 77)$ is divided by 78, then the remainder will be
SSC CGL (Tier I) 10/09/2024 Shift-II
(a) 76 (b) 77
(c) 78 (d) 1

43. Which of the following is the largest 5-digit number divisible by 47? SSC CGL (Tier I) 10/09/2024 Shift-I
(a) 99999 (b) 98888
(c) 99969 (d) 10000

44. If 7845K854 is divisible by 11, then what is the value of K?
SSC CGL (Tier I) 09/09/2024 Shift-III
(a) 6 (b) 9
(c) 7 (d) 8

45. Without doing the actual division, find the remainder when 28735429 is divided by 9.
SSC CGL (Tier I) 09/09/2024 Shift-II
(a) 4 (b) 2
(c) 8 (d) 9

46. Which of the following can be the value of 'k' so that the number 217924k is divisible by 6?
SSC CGL (Tier I) 09/09/2024 Shift-I
(a) 4 (b) 6
(c) 2 (d) 0

SSC CGL 2023 (Tier I & II)

47. Which of the following numbers is divisible by 11?
SSC CGL (Tier-II) 07/03/2023 Shift-II
(a) 6598321 (b) 5214341
(c) 2378965 (d) 5648741

48. If the four-digit number 463y is divisible by 7, then what is the value of y?
SSC CGL (Tier-II) 07/03/2023 Shift-I
(a) 6 (b) 3
(c) 5 (d) 4

49. The number 1254216 is divisible by which of the following numbers?
SSC CGL (Tier-II) 06/03/2023 Shift-II
(a) 5 (b) 11
(c) 16 (d) 8

50. The cost of 3 kg of rice is ₹ 180. The cost of 8 kg of rice is equal to that of 5 kg of pulse. The cost of 15 kg of pulses is equal to that of 2 kg of tea. The cost of 3 kg of tea is equal to that of 6 kg of walnuts. What is the cost (in ₹) of 10 kg of walnuts?
SSC CGL (Tier-II) 03/03/2023 Shift-II
(a) 2400 (b) 3200
(c) 2800 (d) 3600

51. The number 2918245 is divisible by which of the following numbers?
SSC CGL (Tier-II) 03/03/2023 Shift-I
(a) 3 (b) 11
(c) 12 (d) 9

52. The number 5769116 is divisible by which of the following numbers?
SSC CGL (Tier-II) 02/03/2023 Shift-I
(a) 4 (b) 5
(c) 12 (d) 8

53. Which number among 11368, 11638, 11863 and 12638 is divisible by 11? SSC CGL (Tier-I) 27/07/2023 Shift-III
(a) 11368 (b) 12638
(c) 11638 (d) 11863

54. How many of the following numbers are divisible by 3 but not by 9?
5826, 5964, 6039, 6336, 6489, 6564, 6867 and 6960
SSC CGL (Tier-I) 27/07/2023 Shift-III
(a) 5 (b) 4
(c) 6 (d) 3

55. A 6-digit number has digits as consecutive natural numbers. The number is always divisible by .... SSC CGL (Tier-I) 27/07/2023 Shift-II
(a) 4 (b) 5
(c) 2 (d) 3

56. When a number is divided by 45, the remainder is 21. What will be the remainder when the number is divided by 15?
SSC CGL (Tier-I) 26/07/2023 Shift-III
(a) 6 (b) 5
(c) 3 (d) 0

57. A 9-digit number 846523X7Y is divisible by 9, and $Y - X = 6$. Find the value of $\sqrt{2X + 4Y}$.
SSC CGL (Tier-I) 26/07/2023 Shift-II
(a) 4 (b) 2
(c) 6 (d) 8

58. A 4-digit number *abba* is divisible by 4 and $a < b$. How many such numbers are there? **SSC CGL (Tier-I) 26/07/2023 Shift-I**

(a) 10 (b) 8
(c) 12 (d) 6

59. Which of the following numbers is divisible by 44? **SSC CGL (Tier-I) 25/07/2023 Shift-IV**

(a) 32802 (b) 54736
(c) 93472 (d) 27048

60. What is the remainder when $(x^{17} + 1)$ is divided by $(x + 1)$? **SSC CGL (Tier-I) 25/07/2023 Shift-III**

(a) x (b) $x - 1$
(c) 0 (d) 1

61. Which of the following numbers is divisible by 8? **SSC CGL (Tier-I) 25/07/2023 Shift-II**

(a) 18718 (b) 18716
(c) 18712 (d) 18714

62. Which of the following numbers is divisible by 99? **SSC CGL (Tier-I) 25/07/2023 Shift-II**

(a) 31548 (b) 60687
(c) 44775 (d) 84456

63. Find the remainder when $8^8 + 6$ is divided by 7. **SSC CGL (Tier-I) 25/07/2023 Shift-I**

(a) 0 (b) 2
(c) 3 (d) 1

64. In a division sum, the divisor is 13 times the quotient and 6 times the remainder. If the remainder is 39, then the dividend is **SSC CGL (Tier-I) 25/07/2023 Shift-I**

(a) 4240 (b) 4576
(c) 4251 (d) 4800

65. Find the value of *'a'* to make 6234*a*6 divisible by 9. **SSC CGL (Tier-I) 21/07/2023 Shift-IV**

(a) 8 (b) 7
(c) 10 (d) 6

66. What is the smallest number which can be added to 9454351626 so that it becomes divisible by 11? **SSC CGL (Tier-I) 21/07/2023 Shift-IV**

(a) 1 (b) 6
(c) 5 (d) 4

67. Which number among 34936, 35508, 35580 and 36508 is divisible by 33? **SSC CGL (Tier-I) 20/07/2023 Shift-IV**

(a) 35508 (b) 35580
(c) 36508 (d) 34936

68. The square of 72 is equal to the product of 216 and a number. Find the number. **SSC CGL (Tier-I) 20/07/2023 Shift-III**

(a) 36 (b) 18
(c) 24 (d) 48

69. Which of the following numbers is divisible by 9? **SSC CGL (Tier-I) 20/07/2023 Shift-II**

(a) 83061 (b) 29568
(c) 78432 (d) 47695

70. Which of the following numbers is divisible by 11? **SSC CGL (Tier-I) 20/07/2023 Shift-I**

(a) 97174 (b) 56923
(c) 63962 (d) 17295

71. What is the sum of the divisors of 484 that are perfect squares? **SSC CGL (Tier-I) 20/07/2023 Shift-I**

(a) 125 (b) 35
(c) 610 (d) 13

72. Which number among 98984, 98992, 98998 and 99008 is not divisible by 8? **SSC CGL (Tier-I) 19/07/2023 Shift-IV**

(a) 98998 (b) 98992
(c) 98984 (d) 99008

73. When *m* is divided by 7, the remainder is 5. When 3 *m* is divided by 7, the remainder is **SSC CGL (Tier-I) 19/07/2023 Shift-IV**

(a) 3 (b) 2
(c) 1 (d) 0

74. Which of the numbers 9592450, 9592330, 9592885 and 9592741 is divisible by 11? **SSC CGL (Tier-I) 19/07/2023 Shift-III**

(a) 9592885
(b) 9592741
(c) 9592450
(d) 9592330

75. Which number among 34623, 34716, 34782 and 34783 is not divisible by 3? **SSC CGL (Tier-I) 19/07/2023 Shift-II**

(a) 34716 (b) 34783
(c) 34623 (d) 34782

76. While solving a question, Suhas mistakenly took a number is dividend which was 10% less than the original dividend. He also mistakenly took as divisor a number which was 20% less than the original divisor. If the correct quotient of the original question of division was 24 and the remainder was 0, then what quotient did Suhas obtain, assuming there was no error in his calculations? **SSC CGL (Tier-I) 19/07/2023 Shift-I**

(a) 27 (b) 21.6
(c) 26.4 (d) 30

77. Which of the following numbers is divisible by 36? **SSC CGL (Tier-I) 19/07/2023 Shift-I**

(a) 8840 (b) 1542
(c) 96272 (d) 55512

78. The smallest number added to 888 so that it is exactly divisible by 35 is **SSC CGL (Tier-I) 18/07/2023 Shift-III**

(a) 22 (b) 21
(c) 23 (d) 20

79. Which of the following numbers is divisible by 36? **SSC CGL (Tier-I) 18/07/2023 Shift-II**

(a) 47502 (b) 29412
(c) 54732 (d) 87064

80. Which number among 24963, 24973, 24983 and 24993 is divisible by 7? **SSC CGL (Tier-I) 18/07/2023 Shift-II**

(a) 24973 (b) 24983
(c) 24963 (d) 24993

81. Which of the following numbers will completely divide $4^{12} + 4^{13} + 4^{14} + 4^{15}$? **SSC CGL (Tier-I) 18/07/2023 Shift-I**

(a) 3 (b) 7
(c) 11 (d) 17

82. A six-digit number is divisible by 33. If 54 is added to the number, then the new number formed will also be divisible by **SSC CGL (Tier-I) 17/07/2023 Shift-IV**

(a) 3 (b) 5
(c) 7 (d) 2

83. During a division, Pranjal mistakenly took as the dividend a number that was 10% more than the original dividend. He also mistakenly took as the divisor a number that was 25% more than the original divisor. If the correct quotient of the original division problem was 25 and the remainder was 0, what was the quotient that Pranjal obtained, assuming his calculations had no error? **SSC CGL (Tier-I) 17/07/2023 Shift-IV**

(a) 28.75 (b) 21.25
(c) 21.75 (d) 22

84. How many of the following numbers are divisible by 132? 660, 754, 924, 1452, 1526, 1980, 2045 and 2170 **SSC CGL (Tier-I) 17/07/2023 Shift-III**

(a) 3 (b) 6
(c) 5 (d) 4

85. The largest 5-digit number exactly divisible by 88 is **SSC CGL (Tier-I) 17/07/2023 Shift-II**

(a) 99968 (b) 99984
(c) 99990 (d) 99978

86. Find the sum of $3 + 3^2 + 3^3 + ... + 3^8$. **SSC CGL (Tier-I) 17/07/2023 Shift-II**

(a) 6561 (b) 9840
(b) 3280 (d) 6560

87. Find the smallest number that can be subtracted from 148109326, so that it becomes divisible by 8.
SSC CGL (Tier-I) 17/07/2023 Shift-I

(a) 4 (b) 8
(c) 6 (d) 10

88. $6^{25} + 6^{26} + 6^{27} + 6^{28}$ is divisible by **SSC CGL (Tier-I) 14/07/2023 Shift-I**

(a) 256 (b) 259
(c) 254 (d) 255

89. What will be the remainder when $(265)^{4081} + 9$ is divided by 266?
SSC CGL (Tier-I) 14/07/2023 Shift-I

(a) 1 (b) 6
(c) 8 (d) 9

SSC CGL 2022 (Tier I)

90. If the nine-digit number 3422213*AB* is divisible by 99, then what is the value of $2A + B$?
SSC CGL (Tier-I) 13/12/2022 Shift-IV

(a) 11 (b) 12
(c) 10 (d) 13

91. If the number 6788934*a*4 is divisible by 11,then find the smallest whole number in the place of *a*.
SSC CGL (Tier-I) 13/12/2022 Shift-III

(a) 3 (b) 4
(c) 5 (d) 2

92. Choose the option in which the numbers are in correct ascending order. **SSC CGL (Tier-I) 13/12/2022 Shift-II**

(a) $\frac{4}{5}, \frac{2}{3}, \frac{1}{11}$ and $\frac{2}{9}$

(b) $\frac{1}{11}, \frac{2}{9}, \frac{2}{3}$ and $\frac{4}{5}$

(c) $\frac{2}{3}, \frac{4}{5}, \frac{1}{11}$ and $\frac{2}{9}$

(d) $\frac{2}{9}, \frac{1}{11}, \frac{4}{5}$ and $\frac{2}{3}$

93. A four-digit pin, say *abcd*, of a lock has different non-zero digits. The digits satisfy $b = 2a$, $c = 2b$, $d = 2c$. The pin is divisible by.......... .
SSC CGL (Tier-I) 13/12/2022 Shift-II

(a) 2, 3, 11 (b) 2, 3, 7
(c) 2, 3, 5 (d) 2, 3, 13

94. If a 7-digit number 54*p*3987 is divisible by 11, then *p* is equal to
SSC CGL (Tier-I) 12/12/2022 Shift-IV

(a) 5 (b) 9
(c) 4 (d) 1

95. If the seven-digit number 52*A*6*B*7*C* is divisible by 33 and *A*, *B*, *C* are primes, then the maximum value of $2A + 3B + C$ is
SSC CGL (Tier-I) 12/12/2022 Shift-III

(a) 32 (b) 23
(c) 27 (d) 34

96. Any six-digit number that is formed by repeating a three-digit number, is always divisible by
SSC CGL (Tier-I) 12/12/2022 Shift-II

(a) 111 (b) 1001
(c) 19 (d) 101

97. The remainder when $19^{19} + 20$ is divided by 18 is
SSC CGL (Tier-I) 09/12/2022 Shift-IV

(a) 3 (b) 2
(c) 1 (d) 0

98. In a 7-digit number 89476*x*2, what is the smallest possible value of *x* such that the number is divisible by 8? **SSC CGL (Tier-I) 09/12/2022 Shift-III**

(a) 2 (b) 1
(c) 4 (d) 3

99. If the number 123456789 is divided by 9, then the remainder is
SSC CGL (Tier-I) 09/12/2022 Shift-II

(a) 0 (b) 1
(c) 2 (d) 3

100. The sum of the greatest and smallest number of six digits is
SSC CGL (Tier-I) 09/12/2022 Shift-I

(a) 199999 (b) 100000
(c) 1099999 (d) 999999

101. If 7-digit number 678*p*37*q* is divisible by 75 and *p* is not composite, then the values of *p* and *q* are **SSC CGL (Tier-I) 08/12/2022 Shift-IV**

(a) $p = 5, q = 5$
(b) $p = 3, q = 0$
(c) $p = 3, q = 5$
(d) $p = 2, q = 5$

102. 7 is added to a certain number and the sum is multiplied by 5. The product is then divided by 3 and 4 is subtracted from the quotient. If the result comes to 16, then what is the original number?
SSC CGL (Tier-I) 08/12/2022 Shift-III

(a) 3 (b) 1
(c) 5 (d) 4

103. In a division sum, the divisor is 10 times the quotient and four times the remainder. What is the dividend if the remainder is 45?
SSC CGL (Tier-I) 08/12/2022 Shift-II

(a) 4123 (b) 3285
(c) 2895 (d) 5412

104. A number when divided by 221, leaves a remainder 30. If the same number is divided by 13, the remainder will be
SSC CGL (Tier-I) 08/12/2022 Shift-I

(a) 4 (b) 3
(c) 2 (d) 1

105. 9435 is added to 7593, then 2607 is subtracted from the sum. The result is divisible by
SSC CGL (Tier-I) 07/12/2022 Shift-III

(a) 4 (b) 10
(c) 3 (d) 5

106. How many numbers from 1 to 430 are divisible by 7 and 11 both?
SSC CGL (Tier-I) 07/12/2022 Shift-II

(a) 5 (b) 11
(c) 9 (d) 7

107. If a number $K = 42 \times 25 \times 54 \times 135$ is divisible by 3^a, then find the maximum value of *a*.
SSC CGL (Tier-I) 07/12/2022 Shift-I

(a) 6 (b) 7 (c) 4 (d) 5

108. What should be subtracted from 246837 to make it divisible by 13?
SSC CGL (Tier-I) 06/12/2022 Shift-IV

(a) 4 (b) 5 (c) 3 (d) 6

109. Numbers divisible by 9 between 43 and 481 are
SSC CGL (Tier-I) 06/12/2022 Shift-III

(a) 51 (b) 49
(c) 48 (d) 50

110. $3^{50} + 9^{26} + 27^{18} + 9^{28} + 9^{29}$ is divisible by which of the following integers? **SSC CGL (Tier-I) 06/12/2022 Shift-II**

(a) 11 (b) 5
(c) 7 (d) 2

111. A number *n* when divided by 6, leaves a remainder 3. What will be the remainder when $(n^2 + 5n + 8)$ is divided by 6?
SSC CGL (Tier-I) 06/12/2022 Shift-I

(a) 1 (b) 3
(c) 5 (d) 2

112. If the 9-digit number 83P93678 *Q* is divisible by 72, then what is the value of $\sqrt{P^2 + Q^2 + 12}$?
SSC CGL (Tier-I) 05/12/2022 Shift-IV

(a) 6 (b) 7 (c) 8 (d) 9

113. Find the greatest 5-digit number which is divisible by 11, 33, 99 and 121. **SSC CGL (Tier-I) 05/12/2022 Shift-III**

(a) 90099 (b) 99990
(c) 99099 (d) 90909

114. What is the value of
$100^2 - 99^2 + 98^2 - 97^2 + 96^2 - 95^2 + 94^2 - 93^2 + ...12^2 - 11^2$?
SSC CGL (Tier-I) 05/12/2022 Shift-III

(a) 5050 (b) 4985
(c) 4995 (d) 4950

115. What is the smallest number that should be added to 4567, so that the sum is divisible by 7?
SSC CGL (Tier-I) 05/12/2022 Shift-III

(a) 7 (b) 5
(c) 6 (d) 4

116. Find the two-digit number such that the sum of its digits is 8 and the digits of the number get reversed, when 36 is added to it.
SSC CGL (Tier-I) 05/12/2022 Shift-II

(a) 35 (b) 26
(c) 71 (d) 62

117. On dividing a certain number by 363, we get 17 as the remainder. What will be the remainder when the same number is divided by 11?
SSC CGL (Tier-I) 05/12/2022 Shift-II

(a) 7 (b) 8
(c) 6 (d) 9

118. Which of the following pairs of non-zero values of p and q make 6-digit number $674pq0$ divisible by both 3 and 11?
SSC CGL (Tier-I) 05/12/2022 Shift-I

(a) $p = 4$ and $q = 2$
(b) $p = 5$ and $q = 2$
(c) $p = 5$ and $q = 4$
(d) $p = 2$ and $q = 2$

119. If the 8-digit number $123456xy$ is divisible by 8, then the total possible pairs of (x, y) are
SSC CGL (Tier-I) 03/12/2022 Shift-IV

(a) 8 (b) 13
(c) 10 (d) 11

120. A number when divided by 7 leaves remainder of 4. If the square of the same number is divided by 7, then what is the remainder?
SSC CGL (Tier-I) 03/12/2022 Shift-III

(a) 3 (b) 1
(c) 4 (d) 2

121. What will be the remainder when 7^{42} is divided by 48?
SSC CGL (Tier-I) 03/12/2022 Shift-II

(a) 2 (b) 3
(c) 1 (d) 0

122. The nearest number which is greater to 87501, and is completely divisible by 765 is
SSC CGL (Tier-I) 03/12/2022 Shift-I

(a) 88975 (b) 87975
(c) 87966 (d) 87775

123. Which of the following numbers are divisible by 2, 3 and 5?
SSC CGL (Tier-I) 02/12/2022 Shift-IV

(a) 5467760 (b) 1345678
(c) 2345760 (d) 2456732

124. The difference of two numbers is 1564. After dividing the larger number by the smaller, we get 6 as quotient and 19 as remainder. What is the smaller number?
SSC CGL (Tier-I) 02/12/2022 Shift-III

(a) 456 (b) 287 (c) 623 (d) 309

125. In a class of students, the first student has 2 toffees, second has 4 toffees, third has 6 toffees and so on. If the number of students in the class is 25, then the total number of toffees are divisible by ....
SSC CGL (Tier-I) 02/12/2022 Shift-II

(a) 5 and 7 (b) 5 and 13
(c) 11 and 13 (d) 7 and 11

126. If the 4-digit number $x67y$ is exactly divisible by 9, then the least value of $(x + y)$ is
SSC CGL (Tier-I) 02/12/2022 Shift-I

(a) 9 (b) 0 (c) 5 (d) 3

127. A truck runs 492 km on 36 L of diesel. How many (approx.) kilometres can it run on 33 L of diesel? **SSC CGL (Tier-I) 01/12/2022 Shift-IV**

(a) 454 km (b) 453 km
(c) 451 km (d) 452 km

128. If the 5-digit number $750PQ$ is divisible by 3, 7 and 11, then what is the value of $P + 2Q$?
SSC CGL (Tier-I) 01/12/2022 Shift-IV

(a) 17 (b) 15
(c) 18 (d) 16

129. What will be the remainder, when $27^{27} + 27$ is divided by 28?
SSC CGL (Tier-I) 01/12/2022 Shift-III

(a) 28 (b) 27 (c) 25 (d) 26

130. What is the remainder, when 8127 is divided by 8?
SSC CGL (Tier-I) 01/12/2022 Shift-II

(a) 5 (b) 7
(c) 4 (d) 6

131. Which of the following numbers is a divisor of $(49^{15} - 1)$?
SSC CGL (Tier-I) 01/12/2022 Shift-I

(a) 46 (b) 14
(c) 8 (d) 50

SSC CGL 2021 & 2020 (Tier I)

132. If a nine-digit number $7698x138y$ is divisible by 72, then the value of $\sqrt{4x + y}$ is
SSC CGL (Tier-I) 24/08/2021 Shift-III

(a) 8 (b) 6 (c) 9 (d) 5

133. Find the sum of all the possible values of $(a + b)$, so that the number $4a067b$ is divisible by 11.
SSC CGL (Tier-I) 24/08/2021 Shift-II

(a) 21 (b) 11
(c) 16 (d) 5

134. The sum of 3-digit numbers abc, cab and bca is not divisible by
SSC CGL (Tier-I) 24/08/2021 Shift-I

(a) 37 (b) 3
(c) 31 (d) $a + b + c$

135. If the six-digit number $5z3x4y$ is divisible by 7, 11 and 13, then what is the value of $(x + y - z)$?
SSC CGL (Tier-I) 23/08/2021 Shift-II

(a) 3 (b) 6
(c) 5 (d) 4

136. What is the value of k such that number $72k460k$ is divisible by 6?
SSC CGL (Tier-I) 20/08/2021 Shift-I

(a) 4 (b) 7
(c) 9 (d) 8

137. If a number P is divisible by 2 and another number Q is divisible by 3, then which of the following is true?
SSC CGL (Tier-I) 18/08/2021 Shift-III

(a) $P + Q$ is divisible by 6
(b) $P + Q$ is divisible by 5
(c) $P \times Q$ is divisible by 6
(d) $P \times Q$ is divisible by 5

138. If the 8-digit number $888x53y4$ is divisible by 72, then what is the value of $(7x + 2y)$, for the maximum value of y?
SSC CGL (Tier-I) 18/08/2021 Shift-II

(a) 19 (b) 23
(c) 27 (d) 15

139. Find the sum of squares of the greatest value and the smallest value of k in the number so, that the number $45082k$ is divisible by 3.
SSC CGL (Tier-I) 17/08/2021 Shift-III

(a) 100 (b) 68
(c) 50 (d) 64

140. If the seven-digit number $94x29y6$ is divisible by 72, then what is the value of $(2x + 3y)$ for $x \neq y$?
SSC CGL (Tier-I) 17/08/2021 Shift-I

(a) 35 (b) 37
(c) 23 (d) 21

141. Find the difference between squares of the greatest value and the smallest value of P, if the number $5306P2$ is divisible by 3.
SSC CGL (Tier-I) 16/08/2021 Shift-III

(a) 6 (b) 36
(c) 68 (d) 60

142. If the 6-digit number $5x423y$ is divisible by 88, then what is the value of $(5x - 8y)$?
SSC CGL (Tier-I) 16/08/2021 Shift-I

(a) 16 (b) 28
(c) 24 (d) 14

143. Find the greatest value of b so that $30a68b$ $(a > b)$ is divisible by 11.
SSC CGL (Tier-I) 13/08/2021 Shift-III

(a) 4 (b) 6
(c) 3 (d) 9

144. If 7 divided a positive integer n, the remainder is 2. Which of the following numbers gives a remainder of '0' when divided by 7? **SSC CGL (Tier-I) 07/03/2020 Shift-II**

(a) $n + 2$ (b) $n + 5$
(c) $n - 5$ (d) $n + 1$

145. If the given number 925x85 is divisible by 11, then the smallest value of x is **SSC CGL (Tier-I) 07/03/2020 Shift-I**

(a) 1 (b) 2 (c) 3 (d) 4

146. The largest number which should replace * in the number 2365*4 to make the number divisible by 4 is **SSC CGL (Tier-I) 06/03/2020 Shift-II**

(a) 9 (b) 0 (c) 2 (d) 8

147. If the number 687x29 is divisible by 9, then the value of 2x is **SSC CGL (Tier-I) 06/03/2020 Shift-I**

(a) 8 (b) 3
(c) 2 (d) 4

148. The greatest number which should be replace '*' in the number 146*48 to make it divisible by 8 is **SSC CGL (Tier-I) 05/03/2020 Shift-III**

(a) 2 (b) 0 (c) 9 (d) 8

149. When a positive integer is divided by d, the remainder is 15. When ten times of the same number is divided by d, the remainder is 6. The least possible value of d is **SSC CGL (Tier-I) 05/03/2020 Shift-II**

(a) 9 (b) 16 (c) 18 (d) 12

150. If the nine-digit number 708x6y8z9 is divisible by 99, then what is the value of $x+y+z$? **SSC CGL (Tier-I) 05/03/2020 Shift-I**

(a) 27 (b) 5 (c) 16 (d) 9

151. How many numbers are there from 200 to 800 which are neither divisible by 5 nor by 7? **SSC CGL (Tier-I) 04/03/2020 Shift-III**

(a) 407 (b) 410
(c) 413 (d) 411

SSC CPO SI 2023 - 2020

152. The sum of five consecutive number is 240. The sum of the first and last number is **SSC CPO 03/10/2023 Shift-II**

(a) 96 (b) 126
(c) 106 (d) 116

153. If each digit of the number 72514368 is subtracted from 9. How many even digits will be there in the newly formed number? **SSC CPO 03/10/2023 Shift-I**

(a) 3 (b) 5 (c) 6 (d) 4

154. Ramu had to select a list of numbers between 1 and 1000 (including both), which are divisible by both 2 and 7. How many such numbers are there? **SSC CPO 11/11/2022 Shift-I**

(a) 142 (b) 71
(c) 97 (d) 642

155. The sum of the odd divisors of 216 is **SSC CPO 11/11/2022 Shift-I**

(a) 16 (b) 14
(c) 40 (d) 600

156. If the 9-digit number 97x4562y8 is divisible by 88, what is the value of $(x^2 + y^2)$ for the smallest value of y, given that x and y are natural numbers ? **SSC CPO 11/11/2022 Shift-I**

(a) 64 (b) 68
(c) 76 (d) 80

157. Find the least value of p so that 246p48 is divisible by 8. **SSC CPO 11/11/2022 Shift-I**

(a) 2 (b) 1
(c) 4 (d) 0

158. What are the values of R and M, respectively, if the given number is perfectly divisible by 16 and 11 ? 34R05030M6 **SSC CPO 10/11/2022 Shift-I**

(a) 4 and 6 (b) 7 and 5
(c) 5 and 5 (d) 5 and 7

159. If a 4 digit number x58y is exactly divisible by 9, then the least value of $(x + y)$ is **SSC CPO 10/11/2022 Shift-I**

(a) 4 (b) 5
(c) 3 (d) 2

160. The number 150328 is divisible by 23. If the digits are rearranged in descending order and five times of 13 is subtracted from the new number thus formed, then the resultant number will be divisible by **SSC CPO 10/11/2022 Shift-I**

(a) 3 (b) 5
(c) 11 (d) 2

161. When a number is successively divided by 3, 4 and 7, the remainder obtained is 2, 3 and 5, respectively. What will be the remainder when 42 divides the same number? **SSC CPO 25/11/2020 Shift-II**

(a) 41 (b) 30
(c) 29 (d) 31

162. If a nine-digit number 785x3678y is divisible by 72, then the value of $(x + y)$ is **SSC CPO 25/11/2020 Shift-I**

(a) 20 (b) 12
(c) 10 (d) 5

163. If $14331433 \times 1422 \times 1425$ is divided by 10, then what is the remainder? **SSC CPO 25/11/2020 Shift-I**

(a) 3 (b) 9
(c) 0 (d) 8

164. The students of a class donated a sum of ₹ 2809 to the fund. Each student donated as many rupees as the number of students in the class. The number of student in the class is **SSC CPO 24/11/2020 Shift-I**

(a) 49 (b) 53
(c) 51 (d) 47

165. If six-digit number 5x2y6z is divisible by 7, 11 and 13, then the value of $(x - y + 3z)$ is **SSC CPO 24/11/2020 Shift-I**

(a) 7 (b) 4
(c) 0 (d) 9

166. The remainder when $72 \times 73 \times 78 \times 76$ is divided by 35 is **SSC CPO 24/11/2020 Shift-I**

(a) 12 (b) 15
(c) 22 (d) 8

167. What is the least number which when divided by 15, 18 and 36 leaves the same remainder 9 in each case and is divisible by 11? **SSC CPO 23/11/2020 Shift-I**

(a) 1269 (b) 1071
(c) 1089 (d) 1080

168. If $1433 \times 1433 \times 1422 \times 1425$ is divided by 12, then what is the remainder? **SSC CPO 23/11/2020 Shift-I**

(a) 3 (b) 6
(c) 9 (d) 8

169. If a nine-digit number 785x3678y is divisible by 72, then the value of $(x - y)$ is **SSC CPO 23/11/2020 Shift-I**

(a) – 2 (b) 0
(c) 2 (d) – 1

SSC CHSL 2024 (Tier I & II)

170. A number 37 is divided into two parts such that 5 times one part and 11 times the other is together equal to 227. Find the value of 9 times the smaller number. **SSC CHSL (Tier-II) 18/11/2024**

(a) 62 (b) 60
(c) 61 (d) 63

171. The number 611611611611 is
1. divisible by both 6 and 11
2. neither divisible by 6 nor by 11
3. divisible by 6 only
4. divisible by 11 only
SSC CHSL (Tier-I) 11/07/2024 Shift-IV

(a) (4) (b) (3) (c) (2) (d) (1)

172. On dividing a certain number by 459, we get 19 as remainder. What will be the remainder, when the same number is divided by 17?
SSC CHSL (Tier-I) 11/07/2024 Shift-II

(a) 13 (b) 2
(c) 11 (d) 1

173. The sum of the digits of a two-digit number is 9. The number obtained by interchanging its digits exceeds the given number by 45, then the original number is
SSC CHSL (Tier-I) 11/07/2024 Shift-II

(a) 18 (b) 27
(c) 36 (d) 54

174. What is the value of a so that the seven-digit number $4645a52$ is divisible by 72?
SSC CHSL (Tier-I) 11/07/2024 Shift-II

(a) 3 (b) 2
(c) 0 (d) 1

175. The sum of two numbers is 76. Three times the larger number is 46 more than four times the smaller one. Find the two numbers.
SSC CHSL (Tier-I) 11/07/2024 Shift-I

(a) 35 and 41 (b) 40 and 36
(c) 44 and 32 (d) 50 and 26

176. If the number $6p5157q$ is divisible by 88, then $p \times q =$ ...., where p and q are single digit numbers.
SSC CHSL (Tier-I) 11/07/2024 Shift-I

(a) 15 (b) 18
(c) 20 (d) 12

177. A number is divisible by 11, if and only if the difference of the sum of the digits in the even and odd positions in the number is
SSC CHSL (Tier-I) 10/07/2024 Shift-IV

(a) 0
(b) 1
(c) 0 or multiple of 11
(d) 11

178. When 2^{256} is divided by 17, the remainder would be
SSC CHSL (Tier-I) 10/07/2024 Shift-IV

(a) 2 (b) 5
(c) 0 (d) 1

179. The sum of the digits of a two-digit number is 9. If the digits are reversed, then the number is increased by 27. Find the number.
SSC CHSL (Tier-I) 10/07/2024 Shift-I

(a) 36 (b) 63
(c) 54 (d) 45

180. $(8^6 + 1)$ when divided by 7, would leave a remainder of
SSC CHSL (Tier-I) 10/07/2024 Shift-I

(a) 4 (b) 6
(c) 1 (d) 2

181. A natural number n divides 732 and leaves 12 as a remainder. How many values of n are possible?
SSC CHSL (Tier-I) 09/07/2024 Shift-I

(a) 18 (b) 20
(c) 16 (d) 22

182. If $6428A83$ is divisible by 9, then the value of A is equal to
SSC CHSL (Tier-I) 09/07/2024 Shift-I

(a) 6 (b) 7
(c) 5 (d) 3

183. 8 apples and 10 oranges weight 5 kg. 12 apples and 20 oranges weight 9 kg. What is the weight (in kg, rounded off to the nearest integer) of 15 apples and 24 oranges?
SSC CHSL (Tier-I) 08/07/2024 Shift-III

(a) 13 (b) 10
(c) 16 (d) 11

184. The two-digits number is 12 more than five times the sum of its digits. The number formed by reversing the digits is 9 less than the original number. The number is
SSC CHSL (Tier-I) 08/07/2024 Shift-II

(a) 96 (b) 78 (c) 69 (d) 87

185. When the integer n is divided by 5, the remainder is 3. What is the remainder, if $6n$ is divided by 5?
SSC CHSL (Tier-I) 08/07/2024 Shift-II

(a) 2 (b) 1 (c) 3 (d) 0

186. Identify a single-digit number other than 1, which may exactly divide the number $17^3 + 18^3 - 16^3 - 15^3$.
SSC CHSL (Tier-I) 08/07/2024 Shift-II

(a) 2 (b) 3
(c) 5 (d) 7

187. How many numbers between 10 and 65 are divisible by 2, 3 and 4?
SSC CHSL (Tier-I) 08/07/2024 Shift-I

(a) 3 (b) 7 (c) 9 (d) 5

188. How many factors of 14400 are divisible by 18 but not by 36?
SSC CHSL (Tier-I) 05/07/2024 Shift-IV

(a) 5 (b) 2 (c) 4 (d) 3

189. k being any odd number greater than 1, $k^{33} - k$ is always divisible by
SSC CHSL (Tier-I) 05/07/2024 Shift-IV

(a) 24 (b) 13 (c) 5 (d) 15

190. After the division of a number successively by 2,3 and 5, the remainders are 1,2 and 3, respectively. What will be the remainder, if 13 divides the same number (if the last quotient is 1)?
SSC CHSL (Tier-I) 05/07/2024 Shift-III

(a) 1 (b) 2
(c) 0 (d) 3

191. Write the smallest digit in the blank space of a number 7... 7624, so that the number formed is divisible by 3.
SSC CHSL (Tier-I) 05/07/2024 Shift-II

(a) 1 (b) 2 (c) 0 (d) 3

192. The sum of two-digit number and the number obtained by interchanging the digit is 77. If the difference of digits is 1, then the number is
SSC CHSL (Tier-I) 05/07/2024 Shift-II

(a) 67 (b) 45
(c) 34 (d) 12

193. If $3c2933k$ is divisible by both 5 and 11, where c and k are single digit natural numbers, then $c + k =$ ....
SSC CHSL (Tier-I) 05/07/2024 Shift-I

(a) 7 (b) 8
(c) 6 (d) 5

194. What is the smallest number that must be added to 19487161, so that it is divisible by 11?
SSC CHSL (Tier-I) 04/07/2024 Shift-IV

(a) 11 (b) 5
(c) 16 (d) 10

195. If two numbers are each divided by the same divisor, then the remainders are 6 and 7, respectively. If the sum of the two numbers be divided by the same divisor, then the remainder is 5. The divisor is
SSC CHSL (Tier-I) 04/07/2024 Shift-II

(a) 6 (b) 8
(c) 13 (d) 4

196. The number nearest to 7658 and exactly divisible by 45 is
SSC CHSL (Tier-I) 04/07/2024 Shift-I

(a) 7645 (b) 7660
(c) 7650 (d) 7640

197. Which of the following numbers is divisible by 22?
SSC CHSL (Tier-I) 04/07/2024 Shift-I

(a) 893002 (b) 645372
(c) 602351 (d) 654320

198. When the integer n is divided by 18, the quotient is x and the remainder is 6. When the integer n is divided by 25, the quotient is y and the remainder is 15. Which of the following is true?
SSC CHSL (Tier-I) 03/07/2024 Shift-IV

(a) $25y + 18x = 9$ (b) $25y - 18x = 9$
(c) $18x + 25y = 9$ (d) $18x - 25y = 9$

199. A seven digit number $489y5z6$ is divisible by 72. Which of the options gives the highest possible product of y and z?
SSC CHSL (Tier-I) 03/07/2024 Shift-III

(a) 21 (b) 30 (c) 42 (d) 3

200. Find the remainder, when $179 \times 172 \times 173$ is divided by 17.
SSC CHSL (Tier-I) 03/07/2024 Shift-II
(a) 3 (b) 6 (c) 9 (d) 2

201. The 8-digits number is divisible by 99. If the digits are shuffled, then the number is always divisible by ....
SSC CHSL (Tier-I) 03/07/2024 Shift-I
(a) 6 (b) 9
(c) 5 (d) 11

202. When a number is divided by 512 it leaves a remainder 67. If the same number is divided by 32, then what will be the remainder?
SSC CHSL (Tier-I) 03/07/2024 Shift-I
(a) 4 (b) 0
(c) 5 (d) 3

203. What is the number of digits required for numbering a book with 428 pages?
SSC CHSL (Tier-I) 02/07/2024 Shift-IV
(a) 1176 (b) 1500
(c) 2000 (d) 988

204. On dividing a certain number by 304, we get 43 as the remainder. If the same number is divided by 16, what will be the remainder?
SSC CHSL (Tier-I) 02/07/2024 Shift-II
(a) 8 (b) 11
(c) 15 (d) 12

205. The sum of the five consecutive even numbers is 2720. The sum of the third and fifth numbers is
SSC CHSL (Tier-I) 02/07/2024 Shift-II
(a) 1192 (b) 1292
(c) 1092 (d) 1392

206. How many numbers lie between 2000 and 2020 that are divisible by 8?
SSC CHSL (Tier-I) 02/07/2024 Shift-I
(a) 2 (b) 5 (c) 3 (d) 4

207. Find the lowest positive value of $(c-b)$ such that the 7-digits number $1738b9c$ is divisible by 12.
SSC CHSL (Tier-I) 01/07/2024 Shift-IV
(a) 4 (b) 2
(c) 1 (d) 7

208. Successive division of a number by 2, 3, 5 and 7 gives remainders 1,4,0 and 5, respectively. What will be the sum of the remainders, if the same number is divided by 7, 5,3 and 2 successively?
SSC CHSL (Tier-I) 01/07/2024 Shift-IV
(a) 8 (b) 9
(c) 10 (d) 17

209. If $1234567y$ is divisible by 11, then what is the value of y?
SSC CHSL (Tier-I) 01/07/2024 Shift-III
(a) 3 (b) 1
(c) 4 (d) 2

210. Find the number when successively divided by 3,5 and 7 leaves remainder 2,1and 3, respectively, and the last quotient is 3.
SSC CHSL (Tier-I) 01/07/2024 Shift-II
(a) 360 (b) 362
(c) 365 (d) 367

211. What will be the least value of x, so that the 5-digits number $627x5$ becomes divisible by 9?
SSC CHSL (Tier-I) 01/07/2024 Shift-I
(a) 7 (b) 4 (c) 3 (d) 9

SSC CHSL 2023-2021 (Tier I & II)

212. Which of the numbers amongst 25560, 35751, 48168 and 49608 is not divisible by 24?
SSC CHSL (Tier-I) 14/08/2023 Shift-IV
(a) 35751 (b) 48168
(c) 25560 (d) 49608

213. Find the least value for * in the number 3*7440 such that it is divisible by 12.
SSC CHSL (Tier-I) 11/08/2023 Shift-I
(a) 0 (b) 2
(c) 1 (d) 4

214. Find the smallest number to be added to 1000, so that 55 divides the sum exactly.
SSC CHSL (Tier-I) 10/08/2023 Shift-III
(a) 25 (b) 45
(c) 35 (d) 10

215. If 7 divides the integer n, then the remainder is 2. What will be the remainder if $9n$ is divided by 7?
SSC CHSL (Tier-I) 09/08/2023 Shift-I
(a) 3 (b) 5
(c) 1 (d) 4

216. What is the remainder, when 3^8 is divided by 7?
SSC CHSL (Tier-I) 08/08/2023 Shift-II
(a) 5 (b) 4
(c) 6 (d) 2

217. In a division sum, the divisor is 11 times the quotient and 5 times the remainder. If the remainder is 44, then the dividend is
SSC CHSL (Tier-I) 07/08/2023 Shift-IV
(a) 8888 (b) 4448
(c) 8444 (d) 4444

218. Which of the following numbers is not divisible by 11 ?
SSC CHSL (Tier-I) 02/08/2023 Shift-I
(a) 1735624 (b) 752563
(c) 1661308 (d) 1904529

219. What is the sum of all two digit numbers, which are divisible by 9 ?
SSC CHSL (Tier-I) 21/03/2023 Shift-IV
(a) 565 (b) 535
(c) 585 (d) 475

220. Which of the following statement is true ?
SSC CHSL (Tier-I) 21/03/2023 Shift-Iv
I. $\frac{5}{11} > \frac{5}{6}$ II. $\frac{5}{9} > \frac{8}{9}$
III. $\frac{5}{6} > \frac{4}{5}$
(a) Only III
(b) Both I and II
(c) Only II
(d) Only I

221. What is the sum of all three digit numbers which are divisible by 20?
SSC CHSL (Tier-I) 21/03/2023 Shift-II
(a) 19400 (b) 20500
(c) 24300 (d) 21800

222. $6m61$ is divisible by 11. What is the value of m?
SSC CHSL (Tier-I) 17/03/2023 Shift-II
(a) 0 (b) 4
(c) 3 (d) 5

223. How many numbers are there between 501 and 701 which are divisible by 10 but are not divisible by 3?
SSC CHSL (Tier-I) 16/03/2023 Shift-I
(a) 20 (b) 14
(c) 15 (d) 13

224. What is the sum of the largest and the smallest of the given fractions?
$\frac{6}{5}, \frac{11}{15}, \frac{4}{7}, \frac{5}{13}$
SSC CHSL (Tier-I) 14/03/2023 Shift-I
(a) $\frac{97}{65}$ (b) $\frac{61}{65}$
(c) $\frac{94}{65}$ (d) $\frac{103}{65}$

225. How many composite numbers are there between 23 and 43?
SSC CHSL (Tier-I) 14/03/2023 Shift-I
(a) 7 (b) 14
(c) 15 (d) 18

226. How many prime numbers are there between 20 and 50?
SSC CHSL (Tier-I) 10/03/2023 Shift-II
(a) 8 (b) 5 (c) 6 (d) 7

227. The largest six-digit number exactly divisible by 81 is
SSC CHSL (Tier-I) 02/06/2022 Shift-I
(a) 999876 (b) 999945
(c) 999989 (d) 999991

228. How many numbers between 100 and 1000 are divisible by 17?
SSC CHSL (Tier-I) 01/06/2022 Shift-I
(a) 51 (b) 53
(c) 52 (d) 54

229. What is the remainder, when 8127 is divided by 8 ?
SSC CHSL (Tier-I) 31/05/2022 Shift-I
(a) 7 (b) 5
(c) 4 (d) 6

230. When two numbers are separately divided by 44, the remainders are 11 and 38, respectively. If the sum of the two numbers is divided by 44, then the remainder will be
SSC CHSL (Tier-I) 30/05/2022 Shift-I
(a) 16 (b) 44
(c) 33 (d) 5

231. Which of the following numbers is divisible by 33?
SSC CHSL (Tier-I) 27/05/2022 Shift-I
(a) 178750 (b) 164461
(c) 185592 (d) 171116

232. If the nine-digit number '8475639*AB*' is divisible by 99, then what is the value of *A* and *B*?
SSC CHSL (Tier-I) 12/08/2021 Shift-III
(a) $A = 4, B = 6$ (b) $A = 5, B = 3$
(c) $A = 3, B = 9$ (d) $A = 4, B = 8$

233. What is the sum of all the possible values of *k* for which a seven-digit number 23*k*567*k* is divisible by 3?
SSC CHSL (Tier-I) 10/08/2021 Shift-I
(a) 15 (b) 3
(c) 109 (d) 16

234. On dividing 12401 by a certain number, we get 76 as quotient and 13 as remainder. What is the divisor? **SSC CHSL (Tier-I) 04/08/2021 Shift-I**
(a) 947 (b) 948
(c) 163 (d) 136

235. When a number *M* is divided by 7, the remainder is 6. What is the remainder if the square of *M* is divided by 7?
SSC CHSL (Tier-I) 19/04/2021 Shift-I
(a) 4 (b) 1 (c) 3 (d) 2

236. If the number *A*9257*B*684 is divisible by 11, then what is the least value of $A - B$?
SSC (CHSL) (Tier-I) 12/04/2021 Shift-II
(a) 14 (b) 0 (c) –8 (d) 3

SSC MTS 2024

237. Reduce $\frac{374}{418}$ to the lowest term.
SSC MTS 16/10/2024 Shift-II
(a) $\frac{17}{19}$ (b) $\frac{11}{19}$ (c) $\frac{12}{13}$ (d) $\frac{11}{13}$

SSC GD Constable 2024 & 2023

238. Which of the following number is divisible by 4? **SSC GD 24/02/2024 Shift-I**
(a) 2342 (b) 4348
(c) 1734 (d) 1570

239. Which of the following number is not divisible by 8?
SSC GD 23/02/2024 Shift-II
(a) 5968 (b) 5896
(c) 6032 (d) 6044

240. How many two digit numbers are there which are divisible by 8?
SSC GD 22/02/2024 Shift-IV
(a) 11 (b) 13
(c) 12 (d) 10

241. Which of the following number is divisible by 9? **SSC GD 22/02/2024 Shift-IV**
(a) 4131 (b) 1474
(c) 4124 (d) 1254

242. For what value of *M*, 58524*M* is divisible by 9? **SSC GD 22/02/2024 Shift-II**
(a) 3 (b) 2
(c) 8 (d) 7

243. Which of the following number is not divisible by 9?
SSC GD 22/02/2024 Shift-I
(a) 3789 (b) 7857
(c) 1845 (d) 3658

244. What is the remainder when 58^{23} is divided by 5? **SSC GD 21/02/2024 Shift-IV**
(a) 2 (b) 4
(c) 3 (d) 7

245. Which of the following number is divisible by 11?
SSC GD 21/02/2024 Shift-III
(a) 8962 (b) 6589
(c) 9164 (d) 4857

246. Which of the following number is not divisible by 11?
SSC GD 21/02/2024 Shift-II
(a) 2728 (b) 2763
(c) 2651 (d) 2563

247. What is the remainder, when 35^{29} is divided by 10?
SSC GD 20/02/2024 Shift-IV
(a) 5 (b) 0
(c) 6 (d) 4

248. If '*a*' and '*b*' are prime numbers, which of the following cannot be the sum of '*a*' and '*b*' ? (Where *a* and *b* are distinct prime numbers)
SSC GD 09/02/2023 Shift-I
(a) 6 (b) 10
(c) 28 (d) 14

249. What is the least value of *x* so that the 5-digit number 725*x*3 becomes divisible by 9? **SSC GD 06/02/2023 Shift-I**
(a) 0 (b) 6
(c) 3 (d) 1

250. Find the absolute difference between the greatest 3-digit number and the smallest 4-digit number divisible by 12, 25 and 18.
SSC GD 01/02/2023 Shift-I
(a) 900
(b) 300
(c) 600
(d) 1200

SSC Selection Post 2024-2022

251. Which of the following numbers are divisible by 11?
Matric Level 20/06/2024 Shift-IV
(i) 29435417 (ii) 57463828
(iii 57463824 (iv) 29435416
(a) (iii) and (iv) (b) (ii) and (iii)
(c) (i) and (ii) (d) (i) and (iii)

252. A 4-digit number '34PQ' divisible by 3,5 and 7. Find the value of P+Q.
Matric Level 20/06/2024 Shift-IV
(a) 11 (b) 12
(c) 10 (d) 13

253. If a 9-digit number 389*x*6378*y* is divisible by 72, then the value of $6x + 7y$ is **Graduate Level 20/06/2024 Shift-III**
(a) 64 (b) 32
(c) 16 (d) 28

254. Which of the following numbers is divisible by 9?
Graduate Level 20/06/2024 Shift-III
(a) 553986 (b) 350846
(c) 941201 (d) 132490

255. In a division sum, the divisor is 13 times the quotient and 6 times the remainder. If the remainder is 39, then the dividend is
Higher Secondary Level 20/06/2024 Shift-II
(a) 4800 (b) 4576
(c) 4251 (d) 4240

256. A six digits number is divisible by 33. If 21 is added to the number, then the new number which formed is also divisible by
Higher Secondary Level 20/06/2024 Shift-II
(a) 5 (b) 4
(c) 2 (d) 3

257. Find the least value of *K* for which 7864*K*3 is divisible by 7.
Graduate Level 27/06/2023 Shift-IV
(a) 4 (b) 5
(c) 2 (d) 1

258. In 46.5 weeks, Ram raised ₹ 2170 for science research. How much money will he raise in 30 weeks?
Graduate Level 27/06/2023 Shift-IV
(a) ₹ 1500 (b) ₹ 1700
(c) ₹ 1600 (d) ₹ 1400

259. Find the remainder when $11^7 + 9$ is divided by 10.
Graduate Level 27/06/2023 Shift-IV
(a) 1 (b) 0
(c) 3 (d) 2

260. Which of the following is not divisible by 4?
Higher Secondary Level 27/06/2023 Shift-III
(a) 67547172 (b) 56783294
(c) 73568916 (d) 80936292

261. Mohan divides 18935 by a certain number. If the quotient and the remainder he gets are 102 and 65, respectively, then the divisor is
Higher Secondary Level 27/06/2023 Shift-III

(a) 155 (b) 165
(c) 175 (d) 185

262. Which of the following numbers is not divisible by 72?
Metric Level 27/06/2023 Shift-I

(a) 359784 (b) 426816
(c) 486280 (d) 754344

263. The sum of two numbers 10373 + 24871 is divisible by
Metric Level 27/06/2023 Shift-I

(a) 7 (b) 8
(c) 6 (d) 13

264. If arithmetic and geometric mean of x and y is 8 and $3\sqrt{7}$, respectively, then the value of $x^3 + y^3$ is **Graduate Level 01/08/2022 Shift-IV**

(a) 559 (b) 1072
(c) 855 (d) 945

265. Which of the following is not a pair of co-prime numbers?
Graduate Level 01/08/2022 Shift-IV

(a) 1, 4 (b) 21, 22
(c) 22, 24 (d) 3, 7

266. A number is divided by 49 leaves a remainder 9. If the same number is divided by 7, then the remainder will be
Higher Secondary Level 01/08/2022 Shift-II

(a) 1 (b) 3 (c) 2 (d) 0

267. A five-digit number 58828 is divisible by 77. If we add 5 more than twice of 11 to the number, then the resultant number will be divisible by **Matric Level 01/08/2022 Shift-I**

(a) 5 (b) 11
(c) 7 (d) 33

268. A seven-digit number 5702718 is divisible by 147. If we rearrange the digits of the number in descending order and subtract 4 more than three times of 17 from the new number which is formed, then the resultant number will be divisible by **Matric Level 01/08/2022 Shift-I**

(a) 17 (b) 11
(c) 7 (d) 5

Right Answers

1 (b)	2 (a)	3 (c)	4 (c)	5 (c)	6 (b)	7 (c)	8 (a)	9 (d)	10 (a)
11 (d)	12 (d)	13 (c)	14 (d)	15 (b)	16 (b)	17 (b)	18 (c)	19 (b)	20 (c)
21 (d)	22 (d)	23 (c)	24 (a)	25 (a)	26 (a)	27 (a)	28 (b)	29 (c)	30 (b)
31 (b)	32 (a)	33 (c)	34 (b)	35 (c)	36 (a)	37 (c)	38 (a)	39 (a)	40 (c)
41 (c)	42 (a)	43 (c)	44 (b)	45 (a)	46 (c)	47 (b)	48 (d)	49 (d)	50 (d)
51 (b)	52 (a)	53 (c)	54 (b)	55 (d)	56 (a)	57 (c)	58 (b)	59 (b)	60 (c)
61 (c)	62 (b)	63 (a)	64 (c)	65 (d)	66 (b)	67 (a)	68 (c)	69 (a)	70 (a)
71 (c)	72 (a)	73 (c)	74 (d)	75 (b)	76 (a)	77 (d)	78 (a)	79 (b)	80 (b)
81 (d)	82 (a)	83 (d)	84 (d)	85 (a)	86 (b)	87 (c)	88 (b)	89 (c)	90 (a)
91 (d)	92 (b)	93 (d)	94 (a)	95 (b)	96 (b)	97 (a)	98 (d)	99 (a)	100 (c)
101 (c)	102 (c)	103 (b)	104 (a)	105 (c)	106 (a)	107 (b)	108 (d)	109 (b)	110 (a)
111 (d)	112 (c)	113 (c)	114 (c)	115 (d)	116 (b)	117 (c)	118 (b)	119 (b)	120 (d)
121 (c)	122 (b)	123 (c)	124 (d)	125 (b)	126 (c)	127 (c)	128 (a)	129 (d)	130 (b)
131 (c)	132 (b)	133 (a)	134 (c)	135 (d)	136 (a)	137 (c)	138 (b)	139 (b)	140 (b)
141 (d)	142 (c)	143 (c)	144 (b)	145 (d)	146 (d)	147 (a)	148 (d)	149 (b)	150 (c)
151 (d)	152 (a)	153 (d)	154 (b)	155 (c)	156 (d)	157 (d)	158 (c)	159 (b)	160 (b)
161 (c)	162 (c)	163 (c)	164 (b)	165 (a)	166 (d)	167 (c)	168 (b)	169 (c)	170 (d)
171 (a)	172 (b)	173 (b)	174 (d)	175 (d)	176 (b)	177 (c)	178 (d)	179 (a)	180 (d)
181 (b)	182 (c)	183 (d)	184 (d)	185 (c)	186 (a)	187 (d)	188 (d)	189 (d)	190 (a)
191 (a)	192 (c)	193 (c)	194 (d)	195 (b)	196 (c)	197 (a)	198 (d)	199 (c)	200 (a)
201 (b)	202 (d)	203 (a)	204 (b)	205 (c)	206 (a)	207 (c)	208 (b)	209 (c)	210 (c)
211 (a)	212 (a)	213 (a)	214 (b)	215 (d)	216 (d)	217 (d)	218 (b)	219 (c)	220 (a)
221 (c)	222 (a)	223 (d)	224 (d)	225 (c)	226 (d)	227 (b)	228 (b)	229 (a)	230 (d)
231 (c)	232 (d)	233 (a)	234 (c)	235 (b)	236 (c)	237 (a)	238 (b)	239 (d)	240 (a)
241 (a)	242 (a)	243 (d)	244 (c)	245 (b)	246 (b)	247 (a)	248 (a)	249 (d)	250 (a)
251 (d)	252 (a)	253 (a)	254 (a)	255 (c)	256 (d)	257 (a)	258 (d)	259 (b)	260 (b)
261 (d)	262 (c)	263 (c)	264 (b)	265 (c)	266 (c)	267 (a)	268 (d)		

Solutions

1. (b) For a number to be divisible by 24, it should be divisible by both 8 and 3.

Rule of 8 Last three digits should be divisible by 8.

Rule of 3 Sum of all digits will be divisible by 3.

By checking the options and applying the divisibility rules, we get 31128 is divisible by 24.

2. (a) We have, $7^{15}+7^{16}+7^{17}$

$=7^{15}(1+7^1+7^2)=7^{15}\ [1+7+49]$

$=7^{15}(57)=7^{15}(3\times 19)$

$\therefore (7^{15}+7^{16}+7^{17})$ is divisible by 3.

3. (c) For a number to be divisible by 40, it should be divisible by 8 and 5.

Rule of 5 Unit digit of a number should be either '0' or '5'.

Rule of 8 Last three digits of a number should be divisible by 8.

$\therefore$ Maximum possible value of y and z is 8.

i.e., Last three digits = 880 is divisible by 8.

Also unit digit is '0'.

$\therefore$ Given number is divisible by 40

$\Rightarrow$ Max value of $(y+z)=8+8=16$

4. (c) Let the two consecutive numbers be x and $(x+2)$.

According to the question,

$x+(x+2)=174 \Rightarrow 2x=172 \Rightarrow x=86$

5. (c) Let number of people be 4.

i.e. P_1, P_2, P_3, P_4

Also, assume number of chair be 3 i.e.,

C_1, C_2, C_3

Case-1 Exactly one person on each chair

$\frac{P_1}{C_1}\ \frac{P_2}{C_2}\ \frac{P_3}{C_3}\ P_4 \rightarrow$ Exactly one person left

Case-2 Two persons sit on each chair.

$\frac{P_1P_2}{C_1}\ \frac{P_3P_4}{C_2}\ \frac{\ }{C_3} \rightarrow$ Exactly one chair left

Hence, number of chairs has to be 3.

Speedy Method

Let the chair be C and person be P.

According to the question,

$(C-1)\times 2 = C\times 1 + 1 = P$

$2C-2 = C+1 = P$

$C=3$ and $P=2$

$\therefore$ Chair = 3

6. (b) According to the question,

$$\frac{9^{20}+2}{4}=\frac{(9)^{20}}{4}+\frac{2}{4}$$

$\therefore$ Remainder when $9 \div 4 = 1$

$$\therefore \frac{(9)^{20}}{4}+\frac{2}{4}=\frac{(1)^{20}+2}{4}=\frac{1+2}{4}=\frac{3}{4}$$

$\therefore$ Required remainder = 3

7. (c) For option (c) - 438750 $\quad 6=2\times 3$

Divisible by 2 $\rightarrow$ Last digit is even number or zero.

Divisible by 3 $\rightarrow$ Sum of digit is divisible by 3

$$\frac{4+3+8+7+5+0}{3}=\frac{27}{3}\ (\text{Rem}=0)$$

Hence, option (c) is correct.

8. (a) Let $m=2n$, where $(n\in N)$

$\therefore (8^{2n}-1)$ is divisible by $(8^2-1)=63$.

9. (d) $\frac{3}{7}=0.4285,\ \frac{7}{53}=0.1320,$

$\frac{41}{80}=0.5125$ and $\frac{29}{79}=0.3670$

Thus, the largest fraction is $\frac{41}{80}$.

10. (a) As we know, sum of n natural number

$$=\frac{n(n+1)}{2}$$

Sum of first 12 natural number

$$=\frac{12\times 13}{2}=6\times 13$$

Thus, (6×13) is divisible by 6.

Thus, option (a) is correct.

11. (d) 436P5 is divisible by 3

then $4+3+6+P+5$ is divisible by 3

$18+P$ is divisible by 3

For maximum value of P

We must take $P=9$ to make $(18+P)$ divisible by 3

Hence, value of P is 9.

12. (d) Let the number be 28 remainder when divided by 55.

Number = 28 + 55 = (28 as reminder)

Again on dividing by 11 to same number

$$\frac{28}{11}=(6 \text{ as remainder})$$

Thus, required remainder is 6.

13. (c) Divisibility by 3

If sum of the digits of a number is divisible by 3 then the whole number is divisible by 3.

i.e., for 6745k2

Sum of the digits $=6+7+4+5+k+2$

$=24+k$

for $k=9 \Rightarrow 24+k=24+9=33$

which is divisible by 3.

$\therefore$ Maximum value of $k=9$

14. (d) Number 429714 is divisible by

$=4+2+9+7+1+4$

$=27$ is divisible by 3

and 429714 last digit is divisible by 2.

So the number is divisible by 3 and 6.

15. (b) Total amount = ₹ 975

First installment = ₹ 100

$a=100,\ d=-5$

Now, $S_n=\frac{n}{2}[2a+(n-1)d]$

$\Rightarrow 975=\frac{n}{2}[2\times 100+(n-1)\times -5]$

$\Rightarrow 975=\frac{n}{2}[200-5n+5]$

$\Rightarrow 1950=205n-5n^2 \Rightarrow 390=41n-n^2$

$\Rightarrow n^2-41n+390=0$

$\Rightarrow (n-15)(n-26)=0$

$\Rightarrow n=15$ or $n=26 \Rightarrow n=15$

$\therefore$ Time = 15 months

16. (b) 7278745

$7+7+7+5=26$ (Sum of odd place digits)

$2+8+4=14$ (Sum of even place digits)

Now, $\quad 26-14=12$

In place of 26, if it were 25 then

$25-14=11$

$\therefore$ Given number is divisible by 11.

1 should be subtracted from 7278745.

17. (b) $\frac{2^{2n}+2n}{6}$

Put $n=0$, $\frac{2^0+0}{6}=\frac{1+0}{6}=\frac{1}{6}$

Put $n=1$, $\frac{2^2+2}{6}=\frac{4+2}{6}=\frac{6}{6}$

(Remainder = 0)

Hence, min. value of n is 1.

18. (c) Divisible by 8 $\rightarrow$ Last three digit should be divisible by 8

Hence, option (c) 7497 is not divisible by 8. It's last three digits are not divisible by 8.

19. (b) Divisibility rule by 11,

Difference of the sum of the digits at odd and even place should be 0 or divisible by 11.

$\therefore$ From the given numbers.

$D=756148$

$\therefore (7+6+4)-(5+1+8)=17-14=3$

$\therefore$ Number D is not divisible by 11.

20. (c) Let the total capacity of bucket be x L.

$\therefore$ Total capacity of tank $=50\times x$ L

$\therefore$ New capacity of bucket $=\frac{2}{5}\times x=\frac{2x}{5}$ L

Let the number of bucket required be 'n'.

$\therefore \quad \frac{2x}{5}\times n=50x \Rightarrow n=125$ buckets

21. (d) Given, number = $5x79856y6$

$36=4\times 9$

Divisible by 4 $\rightarrow$ Last two digit divisible by 4

$\frac{16}{4},\frac{36}{4},\frac{56}{4},\frac{76}{4},\frac{96}{4}$

$\therefore \quad y=1,3,5,7,9$

Divisible by 9 $\rightarrow$ Digit sum is divisible by 9

$$\frac{5+x+7+9+8+5+6+y+6}{9}=\frac{46+x+y}{9}$$

$\frac{46+x+9}{9}$ [$\because y$ is largest]

$\therefore \quad x = 8$

$\sqrt{2x+y} = \sqrt{2\times 8+9} = \sqrt{25} = +5$

$\therefore$ Required negative value $= -5$

22. (d) $\frac{2}{3} = 0.666\ldots$

$\frac{6}{53} = 0.113, \frac{79}{90} = 0.877, \frac{33}{44} = 0.75$

$\therefore \quad 0.877 > 0.75 > 0.666\ldots > 0.113$

$\therefore \frac{79}{90}$ is the largest.

23. (c) 19^{200} is divided by 20

$19^{200} = (20-1)^{200} = 20K + (-1)^{200} = 20K+1$

When $20K+1$ is divided by 20 it will give remainder 1.

24. (a) Let five consecutive number be $(x-2), (x-1), x, (x+1), (x+2)$.

According to the question,

$\therefore \quad (x-2)+(x-1)+x+(x+1)+(x+2) = 80$

$\Rightarrow \quad 5x = 80 \Rightarrow x = 16$

$\therefore$ Largest number $= x+2 = 18$

25. (a) According to the question,

$r = 8q+3$

$\therefore \quad (r^2+6r+7) = (8q+3)^2 + 6(8q+3)+7$

$= 64q^2 + 9 + 48q + 48q + 18 + 7$

$= 64q^2 + 96q + 34$

$= (64q^2 + 96q + 32) + 2$

$= 8(8q^2 + 12q + 4) + 2$

$\therefore$ Required remainder $= 2$

26. (a) 6954P is divisible by 11

Then, $(9+4)-(6+5+P) = 0$

$\Rightarrow \quad 13-(11+P) = 0 \Rightarrow 13-11-P = 0$

$\Rightarrow \quad 2-P = 0 \Rightarrow P = 2$

27. (a) Number $= 57X716$

(Divisibility of 9 = Sum of digits should be divisible by 9)

$5+7+X+7+1+6 = 26+x = 26+1$

$= 27$ is divisible by 9

$x = 1$

28. (b) Given, number $= 249K876$

Number is divisible by 6, So, number will be divisible by 2 and 3.

Unit digit is '6', so number is already divisible by '2'.

Now, for divisibility by 3,

Sum of digits $= 2+4+9+K+8+7+6$

$= 36+K$

This should be divisible by 3,

So, minimum/least value of $K = 0$

$\left(\text{Because, } \frac{36}{3} = 12\right)$

29. (c) Remainder of $[(17)^{13} - 21] \div 18$

$= [(-1)^{13} - (3)] = -1-3 = -4$

Now, add 18 and get the remainder

$-4+18 = 14$ is remainder.

30. (b) Number $= 62684xy$

Divisible by 5 $\rightarrow$ unit digits 5, 0

unit digit $(y) = 0$

[$\because$ Number divisible by 8]

Divisible by 8 $\rightarrow$ last three digit divisible by 8

$\therefore \quad \frac{4xy}{8}$

$\Rightarrow \quad \frac{4x0}{8}$

$\therefore \quad x = 4 \quad \left[\frac{440}{4} = \text{Rem}(0)\right]$

$\therefore \quad x = 4$ and $y = 0$

31. (b) $6 = 2\times 3$

Divisibility of 2 $= \frac{\text{Last digit}}{2}$

$\therefore \quad \frac{321y72}{2}$ (Rem = 0)

Divisibility of 3 $= \frac{\text{Sum of digit}}{3}$

$\therefore \quad \frac{3+2+1+y+7+2}{3} = \frac{15+y}{3}$

$\therefore$ Possible value of $y = 0, 3, 6, 9$

$\therefore \quad$ Least value of $y = 0$

32. (a) Number $= 91876a2$

Divisible by 8 $= \frac{6a2}{8}$

[Divisibility of 8 $\rightarrow$ last 3 digit should be divisible by 8]

$a = 3, \left[\frac{632}{8}, \text{ Remainder} = 0\right]$

Hence, $a = 3$

33. (c) Divisibility by 10,

Last digit of the number should be '0'.

Divisibility by 11, Absolute value of (sum of digits at even places – sum of digits at odd places) should be either 0 or multiple of 11.

Hence, 589270 is divisible by 2, 5, 10 and 11.

34. (b) In the first year,

Number of daisy plants = 6

and in subsequent years daisy plants increases by 3 each year.

$\therefore$ Progression is-

6, 9, 12, 15, 18, 21, 24, 27, ...

Number of Jasmine plants = 26

and in subsequent years jasmine plants decreases by 2 each year.

$\therefore$ Progression is-

26, 24, 22, 20, 18, 16, 14, 12, ...

Comparing these two plants,

6, 9, 12, 15, 18, 21, 24, 27, ...

26, 24, 22, 20, 18, 16, 14, 12, ...

Clearly in the 4th yr after 1st yr.

Number of daisy plants = number of jasmine plants.

35. (c) Divisibility by 11, Absolute value of (Sum of digits at even places - sum of digits at odd places) Should be either 0 or multiple of 11.

For 128041-

Sum of digits at even places $= 4+8+1 = 13$

Sum of digits at odd places $= 1+0+2 = 3$

Difference $= 13-3 = 10$

$\therefore$ 128041 is not divisible by 11.

For 109153,

Difference $= |(3+1+0)-(5+9+1)| = 11$

for 5445,

Difference $= |(5+4)-(4+5)| = 0$

for 80124,

Difference $= |(4+1+8)-(2+0)| = 11$

36. (a) Divisibility Rule of 5 Last digit of a number should be either 0 or 5.

Divisibility Rule of 8 Last three digits of a number must be divisible by 8.

Using the options, * and $ should be 4 and 0.

i.e. last three digits, 440 is divisible by 8.

$\therefore$ Option (a) is correct.

37. (c) Given, Number = 723 * 56 *

Divisible by 2 $\rightarrow$ Unit digit is always even.

$\therefore \quad * = \text{Even}$

Divisible by 3 $\rightarrow$ Digit sum divisible by 3.

$\frac{7+2+3+*+5+6+*}{3} = \frac{23+2*}{3}$

$\therefore \quad * = 2$

$\frac{23+2\times 2}{3} = \frac{27}{3}$ (Rem = 0)

38. (a) If a number is divisible by 2 and 5

A number is also divisible by 10.

$\therefore$ A number should have a unit digit as '0'.

$\therefore$ Option (a) i.e., 63840 is the only option with unit digit '0'.

39. (a) Give remainder = 32

$\therefore$ Divisor $= 2\times 32 = 64$

and quotient $= \frac{64}{4} = 16$

$\therefore$ Dividend = Divisor × Quotient + Remainder

$= 64\times 16 + 32 = 1056$

40. (c) We can write, $999 = 99\times 10 + 9$

So, the remainder = 9

We have to add 90 to 9 to be it divisible by 99

41. (c) We know that, divisibility rule of 8-last 3 digits must be divisible by 8.

Given number $= 6484y6$

$\therefore \quad 4y6$ is divisible by 8.

Now, put the value of y is 1.

So, $\frac{416}{8} = 52$

$\therefore$ Least value = 1

42. (a) $(77^{77} + 77)$ is divided by 78.

We know, $(A+1)^n = AK + (1)^n$

Where K is a natural n.

Let $S = (77^{77}+77) = (78-1)^{77} + 77$

$S = 78K + (-1)^{77} + 77$

When S is divided by 78.

78K will give remainder 0

$(-1)^{77} = -1$ will given remainder -1

and 77 will given remainder 77

$\therefore$ Sum of the remainder $= 0 - 1 + 77 = 76$

Which is less than 78

$\therefore$ Final remainder = 76

43. (c) Largest 5 digit number = 99999

$$\frac{99999}{47} = 2127\frac{30}{47}$$

$\therefore$ Required number $= 99999 - 30 = 99969$

44. (b) $7845K854$ is divisible by 11.

Sum of even place digits – Sum of odd place digits = 0

$\Rightarrow (8+5+8+4)-(7+4+K+5)=0$

$\Rightarrow \quad 25-(16+K)=0$

$\Rightarrow 25-16-K=0 \Rightarrow 9-K=0 \Rightarrow K=9$

45. (a) We know, Divisibility Rule of 9,

Sum of the digits of a number should be divisible by 9.

$\therefore \quad 2+8+7+3+5+4+2+9=40$

Required remainder when $40 \div 9 = 4$

46. (c) $217924k$ is divisible by 6.

As we know, if a number is divisible by 2 and 3 then the number is divisible by 6 it is very clear that k must be an even number if we put $k = 2$, then the number is divisible by 2.

and $2179242 = 2+1+7+9+2+4+2 = 27$

Sum of digit is also divisible by 3.

Then it is sure that value of k is 2.

47. (b) Divisibility test of 11.

= (Sum of odd place value) – (Sum of even place value) is divisible by 11 or it should be 0.

From option (b),

$(5+1+3+1)-(2+4+4) = 10-10 = 0$

Hence, number 5214341 is divisible by 11.

48. (d) Given number = $463y$

$$7)\,463y\,(662$$
$$\underline{-42}$$
$$43$$
$$\underline{-42}$$
$$1y$$
$$\underline{-14}$$
$$\underline{0}$$

$\therefore \quad y = 4$

49. (d) Number = 1254216

According to the option, given number is divisible by 8.

As last three digit is divisible by 8.

50. (d) Cost of 3 kg rice = ₹180

Cost of 1 kg rice = ₹60

$\because$ Cost of 5 kg of pulse = Cost of 8 kg of rice

Cost of 1 kg of pulse $= \dfrac{60 \times 8}{5} = 12 \times 8 =$ ₹96

$\because$ Cost of 2 kg of tea = Cost of 15 kg of pulse

Cost of 1 kg of tea $= \dfrac{15 \times 96}{2} = 15 \times 48 =$ ₹720

$\because$ Cost of 6 kg of walnuts = Cost of 3 kg of tea

Cost of 1 kg of walnuts $= \dfrac{3 \times 720}{6}$

Cost of 1 kg of walnuts = ₹360

$\therefore$ Cost of 10 kg of walnuts $= 360 \times 10 =$ ₹3600

51. (b) From the given options,

Applying divisibility rule of 11, we get

$(2+1+2+5) \sim (9+8+4)$

$10 \sim 21$

$11 \div 11$

So, given number is divisible by 11.

52. (a) Number = 5769116

Divisibility rule of 4 $\rightarrow$ last 2 digits of a number must be divisible by 4.

Here, 16 is divisible by 4.

So, number 5769116 is divisible by 4.

53. (c) Using the divisibility rule of 11, we get

Here, $11638 = (1+6+8)-(1+3)$

$= 15 - 4 = 11$

So, 11638 is divisible by 11.

54. (b) To be divisible by 3 and 9, sum of all the digits of a number should be divisible by 3 and 9.

So, $5+8+2+6 = 21$, divisible by 3 not by 9.

$5+9+6+4 = 24$, divisible by 3 not by 9.

$6+0+3+9 = 18$, divisible by 3 and 9.

$6+3+3+6 = 18$, divisible by 3 and 9.

$6+4+8+9 = 27$, divisible by 3 and 9.

$6+5+6+4 = 21$ divisible by 3 not by 9.

$6+8+6+7 = 27$, divisible by 3 and 9.

$6+9+6+0 = 21$, divisible by 3 not by 9.

Hence, 4 numbers are divisible by 3 but not by 9.

55. (d) Let digits if a 6 digit number be $x, (x+1), (x+2), (x+3), (x+4)$ and $(x+5)$.

Sum of the number $= x + x + 1 + x + 2 + x + 3 + x + 4 + x + 5$

$= 6x + 15 = 3(2x+5)$

Hence, the number always divisible by 3.

56. (a) When a number is divided by 45 remainder is 21.

When the number is divided by 15

$21 = 15 \times 1 + 6$

$\therefore$ The remainder will be 6.

57. (c) The number is 846523 X 7Y, is divisible by 9

$8+4+6+5+2+3+X+7+Y$

For divisible by 9, $35 + X + Y = 45$

$\therefore \quad X + Y = 10$

and $\quad Y - X = 6 \quad$ (given)

$2Y = 16$

$\Rightarrow \quad Y = 8$

$\therefore \quad X = 10 - 8 = 2$

$\therefore \quad \sqrt{2X+4Y} = \sqrt{2\times 2 + 4 \times 8} = \sqrt{36} = 6$

58. (b) To be divisible by 4, last two digits number should be divisible by 4.

So, the number 'abba' to be divisible by 4,

ba = 32, 52, 64, 72, 76, 84, 92 and 96

($\because a \neq 0$ and $b > a$)

Hence, total 8 numbers are there.

59. (b) For a number to be divisible by 44, it should be divisible by both 4 and 11.

Using the divisibility rule of 4, we know that, 54736 is divisible by 4.

Also, from the divisibility rule of 11,

$(5+7+6)-(4+3) = 18 - 7 = 11$

$\therefore$ 54736 is divisible by 11.

60. (c) $(x^{\text{odd number}} + 1)$ is always divisible by $(x+1)$.

$\therefore (x^{17}+1)$ is divisible by $(x+1)$

$\therefore$ The remainder is 0.

61. (c) For a number to be divisible by 8, Last three digits of a number must be divisible by 8.

$\therefore$ Out of the given options,

Let us take, 18712

$\therefore$ Last three digits i.e., 712 is divisible by 8.

$\therefore$ 18712 is divisible by 8.

62. (b) Divisible by 99 means that the number must be divisible by both 9 and 11.

From the option (b), 60687

Sum of odd place digits $= 6+6+7 = 19$

Even place digits $= 0+8 = 8$

Difference $= 19 - 8 = 11$

$\Rightarrow$ Multiple of 11

$\therefore$ 60687 is divisible by 11.

Also, sum of digits $= 6+0+6+8+7 = 27$

$\Rightarrow$ Multiple of 9

$\therefore$ The number is divisible by 9

$\therefore$ 60687 is divisible by 99.

63. (a) Given number $= 8^8 + 6$

When divided by 7 leaves remainder

$$= \frac{\{(7+1)^8 + (7-1)\}}{7}$$

$= 1^8 - 1 = 0$ (remainder)

64. (c) Remainder = 39,

Divisor $= 6 \times 39 = 234$

Quotient $= \dfrac{234}{13} = 18$

$\therefore$ Dividend = Divisor × Quotient + Remainder

$= 18 \times 234 + 39 = 4251$

65. (d) Given, number = $6234\,a\,6$

Using divisibility test of 9 i.e.

Sum of digits of a number must be divisible by 9.

$\therefore$ Sum of digits of given number

$= 6+2+3+4+a+6 = 21+a$

For the sum of this number to be divisible by 9.

It should be a multiple of 9.

∴ Nearest multiple of 9 to $21 + a$ is 27.

∴ $21 + a = 27 \Rightarrow a = 6$

66. (b) If 6 is added then the number will become $9454351626 + 6 = 9454351632$

Sum of odd place's digits
$= 9 + 5 + 3 + 1 + 3 = 21$

Sum of even place's digits
$= 4 + 4 + 5 + 6 + 2 = 21$

Difference $= 21 - 21 = 0$

⇒Number is multiple of 11

∴ Minimum 6 has to be added.

67. (a) For a number to be divisible by 33, it must be divisible by both 3 and 11.

From the option (a),

For a number, 35508

Applying divisibility test of 3, we get

∴ $3 + 5 + 5 + 0 + 8 = 21$ and 21 is divisible by 3.

∴ 35508 is divisible by 3.

Now, apply divisibility test of 11.

i.e., $(3 + 5 + 8) - (5 + 0) = 11$ and 35508 is divisible by 11.

∴ 35508 is divisible by 33.

68. (c) Let the other number be x.

According to the question,

$$216 \times x = (72)^2$$

$$\Rightarrow 216 \times x = 72 \times 72$$

$$\Rightarrow x = \frac{72 \times 72}{216} = 24$$

69. (a) For a number to be divisible by 9

Sum of all digits of a number should be divisible by 9.

From option (a),

$83061 = 8 + 3 + 0 + 6 + 1$
$= 18$ is divisible by 9

Hence, 83061 is divisible by 9.

70. (a) Divisibility rule of 11 : Difference between sum of digits in odd place and sum of digits in even place must be a multiple of 11 or 0.

∴ For the number 97174,

Sum of digits at odd place $= 9 + 1 + 4 = 14$

Sum of digits at even place $= 7 + 7 = 14$

Difference $= 14 - 14 = 0 = 0 \times 11$

∴ 97174 is divisible by 11.

71. (c) Divisors of 484 that are perfect squares are 1, 4, 121, 484.

∴ Sum of these numbers

$= 1 + 4 + 121 + 484 = 610$

72. (a) We know, for a number to be divisible by 8, the last three digits of the number must be divisible by 8.

So, out of the given numbers, the last three digits of 98998 i.e. 998 is not divisible by 8.

Hence, 98998 is not divisible by 8.

73. (c) Let quotient be Q and remainder be R.

Given, dividend $= m$, divisor $= 7$

According to the question,

$$m = 7Q + 5 \quad \ldots(i)$$

Also, $3m = 7Q + R$

∴ From Eq. (i),

∴ $3m = 3(7Q + 5) = 7Q + R$

⇒ $21Q + 15 = 7Q + R$

⇒ $14Q + 15 = R$

Now, $14\,Q$ is completely divisible by 7, When 15 is divided by 7, gives Remainder 1.

∴ $R = 1$

Speedy Method

$$\frac{3 \times 5}{7} = \frac{15}{7} = 2\frac{1}{7}$$

∴ Rem = 1

74. (d) Divisibility rule of 11

Sum of odd places digits – Sum of even places digits is equal to a multiple of 11 or 0.

$(9 + 9 + 3 + 0) - (5 + 2 + 3)$
$= 21 - 10 = 11 = 11 \times 1$

∴ 9592330 is divisible by 11.

75. (b) For a number to be divisible by 3, the sum of digits of a number must be divisible by 3.

From the option (b), 34783 is not divisible by 3.

∵ $3 + 4 + 7 + 8 + 3 = 25$ is not divisible by 3.

76. (a) Quotient = 24 and remainder = 0

Let divisor $= 20x$

Dividend $= 24 \times 20x = 480x$

New divisor $= 20x \times \frac{80}{100} = 16x$

Dividend $= 480x \times \frac{90}{100} = 432x$

∴ New quotient $= \frac{432x}{16x} = 27$

77. (d) If a number is divisible by 36 a number is divisible by both 4 and 9.

Taking from option (d)

∴ For a number to be divisible by 4, last two digits of the number must be divisible by 4.

i.e., 12 is exactly divisible by 4.

Also, for a number to be divisible by 9 sum of digits must be divisible by 9.

i.e., $5 + 5 + 5 + 1 + 2 = 18$, it is divisible by 9.

∴ The number 55512 is divisible by 36.

78. (a) Find the remainder when 888 is divided by 35.

⇒$888 \div 35 = 25$ with a remainder of 13

⇒ Subtract the remainder 13 from 35

$35 - 13 = 22$

So, the smallest number that needs to be added to 888 to make it exactly divisible by 35 is 22.

79. (b) For a number to be divisible by 36 ⇒ number is divisible by both 9 and 4.

From option (b), $29412 = 2 + 9 + 4 + 1 + 2$
$= 18$ (divisible by 9)

And last two digits = 12 (divisible by 4)

So, 29412 is also divisible by 36.

80. (b) For divisibility by 7, we double the unit digit $= 3 \times 2 = 6$

And difference by the number
$= 2498 - 6 = 2492 \div 7 = 356$

So, 24983 is divisible by 7.

81. (d) Given, $4^{12} + 4^{13} + 4^{14} + 4^{15}$

$= 4^{12}[1 + 4 + 4^2 + 4^3]$

$= 4^{12}[1 + 4 + 16 + 64] = 4^{12} \times 85$

Hence, 17 will completely divided this number.

82. (a) Let six-digit number = 333333 is divisible by 33.

According to the question,

New number $= 333333 + 54 = 333387$

We can observe that the above number is not divisible by 2, 5 and 7.

∴ Number is divisible by 3.

[∵ $3 + 3 + 3 + 3 + 8 + 7 = 27$ which is divisible by 3]

83. (d) Let dividend and divisor be $100y$ and $100x$, respectively.

According to the question,

$$\frac{100y}{100x} = 25 \text{ (Quotient)}$$

$$\Rightarrow \frac{y}{x} = 25 \quad \ldots(i)$$

Also, if dividend is 10% more and divisor is 25% more.

$$\frac{110y}{125x} = \text{Quotient}$$

$$\Rightarrow \frac{110}{125}\left(\frac{y}{x}\right) = \text{Quotient}$$

$$\Rightarrow \text{Quotient} = \frac{110}{125}(25) = 22$$

84. (d) Divisible by 132 means it will be also divisible by 4, 3 and 11.

We can see 754, 1526, 2045 and 2170 are not divisible by 11, 4 or 3.

∴ Remaining numbers are 660, 924, 1452, 1980

$660 = 132 \times 5$; $924 = 132 \times 7$;

$1452 = 132 \times 11$; $1980 = 132 \times 15$

∴ 4 numbers are divisible by 132.

85. (a) For a number to be divisible by 88, it must be divisible by 8 and 11.

From option (a),

Number = 99968

Divisibility by 11, the difference between the sum of odd and even placed digit should be divisible by 11 or 0.

i.e., $(9 + 9 + 8) - (9 + 6) = 26 - 15 = 11$

Hence, number is divisible by 11.

Divisibility by 8, the last three digits should be divisible by 8.

i.e., last three digits are 968, which is divisible by 8

$\therefore$ 99968 is divisible by 88.

86. (b) Given, $3 + 3^2 + 3^3 + \dots\dots + 3^8$

Here the series in GP.

Then, $a = 3, n = 8, r = \frac{3^2}{3} = 3 > 1$

Sum of GP $= S_n = \frac{a(r^n - 1)}{r - 1}$ $[\because r > 1]$

$= \frac{3(3^8 - 1)}{3 - 1} = \frac{3 \times 6560}{2} = 9840$

87. (c) For a number to be divisible by 8, last three digits must be divisible by 8.

Last 3 digit are 326.

On dividing 326 by 8, remainder is 6.

$\therefore$ We subtract 6 from the given number.

88. (b) Given, $6^{25} + 6^{26} + 6^{27} + 6^{28}$

$= 6^{25} \times [1 + 6 + 6^2 + 6^3]$

$= 6^{25} \times [7 + 36 + 216] \Rightarrow 6^{25} \times 259$

Hence, it is divisible by 259.

89. (c) $(265)^{4081} + 9 = (265)^{4081} + (1)^{4081} + 8$

$\because x^n + a^n$ is divisible by $(x + a)$ for all odd values of n.

$\therefore (265)^{4081} + (1)^{4081}$ is completely divisible by $(265 + 1)$ or 266.

$\therefore$ Required remainder = 8

90. (a) Nine-digit number = 3422213 AB

This number is divisible by 99, then this number will be divisible by both 9 and 11.

$\because$ The number is divisible by 9, then the sum of digits of number will be divisible by 9.

$\Rightarrow \quad 3 + 4 + 2 + 2 + 2 + 1 + 3 + A + B$ will be divisible by 9

$\Rightarrow 17 + A + B$, will be divisible by 9

$\therefore$ The possible value of $A + B = 1, 10$ ...(i)

$\because$ The number is divisible by 11, then the difference of the sum of digits at odd places and the sum of digits of even places will be 0 or divisible by 11.

$\Rightarrow (3 + 2 + 2 + 3 + B) - (4 + 2 + 1 + A)$ = 0 or divisible by 11.

$\Rightarrow 10 + B - 7 - A$ = 0 or divisible by 11

$\Rightarrow \quad 3 + B - A$ = 0 or divisible by 11

If $3 + B - A = 0 \Rightarrow A - B = 3$

(The values of A and B will be not possible)

If $\quad 3 + B - A = 11$

$\Rightarrow \quad B - A = 8$ ...(ii)

From relation Eq. (i),

$A + B = 10$ ...(iii)

From Eqs. (ii) and (iii), $B = 9, A = 1$

$\therefore \quad 2A + B = 2 \times 1 + 9 = 11$

91. (d) Given number = 6788934a4

Sum of digit at odd places

$= (6 + 8 + 9 + 4 + 4) = 31$

Sum of digit at even places

$= (7 + 8 + 3 + a) = 18 + a$

Applying divisibility rule of 11, we have

$31 - (18 + a) = 0$

[Not possible because a is single digit no.]

Now, take $a = 2$, then

$31 - (18 + 2) = 31 - 20 = 11$, which is divisible by 11. So, $a = 2$

92. (b) $\frac{2}{3} = 0.666\dots\dots$

$\frac{4}{5} = 0.8$

$\frac{1}{11} = 0.0909\dots\dots$

$\frac{2}{9} = 0.222\dots\dots$

$\therefore$ Correct ascending order is $\frac{1}{11}, \frac{2}{9}, \frac{2}{3}$ and $\frac{4}{5}$.

93. (d) Given, four digit pin of a lock = $abcd$

$b = 2a, c = 2b = 4a, d = 2c = 8a$

We can write it as,

$abcd = 1000a + 100b + 10c + d$

$abcd = 1000a + 200a + 40a + 8a$

$abcd = 1248a$

$abcd = (2^5 \times 3 \times 13)a$

The pin is divisible by 2, 3 and 13.

94. (a) Given number = 54p3987

Using divisibility rule of 11, we get

Sum of digits at the odd places

$= 5 + p + 9 + 7 = 21 + p$

Sum of digits at the even places

$= 4 + 3 + 8 = 15$

Now, $\quad 21 + p - 15 = 0$ (Not possible)

Then, $21 + p - 15 = 11$

$p = 11 - 6 = 5$

So, value of p is 5.

95. (b) The number 52A6B7C is divisible by 33.

So, it is also divisible by both 11 and 3.

By divisibility rule of 3,

Sum of the digits of the given number

$= 5 + 2 + A + 6 + B + 7 + C$

$= 20 + A + B + C$

So, sum $(20 + A + B + C)$ should be divisible by

3 .... (i)

By divisibility rule of 11,

Sum of the digits at odd places

$= 5 + A + B + C$

Sum of the digits at even places

$= 2 + 6 + 7 = 15$

Here, A, B and C are prime number less than 9.

Possible values of A, B and C are 2, 3, 5, 7.

So, $5 + A + B + C = 15$

$\Rightarrow \quad A + B + C = 15 - 5 = 10$ ....(ii)

It also satisfy the Eq. (i).

As, we need to find the maximum value of the given expression

$\therefore \quad A = 3, B = 5, C = 2$

$\therefore$ Maximum value of $2A + 3B + C$

$= 2 \times 3 + 3 \times 5 + 2 = 6 + 15 + 2 = 23$

96. (b) Let any three digit number = xyz

Six-digit number formed by repeating three digit number $xyz = xyzxyz$

Here, $xyzxyz = 100000x + 10000y + 1000z + 100x + 10y + z$

$= 100100x + 10010y + 1001z$

$= 1001 \times 100x + 1001 \times 10y + 1001 \times z$

$= 1001(100x + 10y + z)$

The number $xyzxyz$ is multiple of 1001. So, any six-digit number that is formed by repeating three digit number is always divisible by 1001.

97. (a) $(19^{19} + 20) \div 18$

$= (19^{19} - 1^{19} + 1^{19} + 20) \div (19 - 1)$

$= (19^{19} - 1^{19} + 21) \div (19 - 1)$

$\because x^m - a^m$ is divisible by $(x - a)$ for all value of m.

$\therefore \quad 21 \div 18$

Remainder = 3

98. (d) Divisible rule of 8 is last three digits of a number must be divisible by 8.

So, 6x2 should be divisible by 8.

$\therefore$ 632 and 672 both can be divisible by 8 so, there are 2 possible values of $x = 3, 7$

But we have to find the smallest possible value of x i.e. 3.

99. (a) We know, a number is completely divisible by 9 if the sum of its digits is also divisible by 9.

$\therefore$ Given number = 123456789

Sum of its digits

$= 1 + 2 + 3 + 4 + 5 + 6 + 7 + 8 + 9 = 45$

Since 45 is completely divisible by 9, therefore the given number is also completely divisible by 9. So, remainder = 0

100. (c) We know that,

Six digits greatest number = 999999

and six digits smallest numbers = 100000

$\therefore$ The sum of both six digits = 1099999

101. (c) Given, 7 digit number is 678p37q.

For a number to be divisible by 75, it should be divisible by 3 and 5.

Now, for a number to be divisible by 5, the ones place should be either 0 or 5.

$\Rightarrow \quad q = 0$ or $q = 5$

Now, for a number to be divisible by 3, the sum of its digit should be divided by 3.

$\Rightarrow \quad 6 + 7 + 8 + p + 3 + 7 + q = 31 + p + q$

Should be divisible by 3.

Now, if $q = 0$

$\Rightarrow 31 + p + 0 = 31 + p$ should be divisible by 3.

$\Rightarrow$ Here, $p = 2$, so that $31 + 2 = 33$ is divisible by 3.

But, $p = 2$ and $q = 0$ is not an option.

Now, if $q = 5$

$\Rightarrow 31 + p + 5 = 36 + p$ should be divisible by 3.

$\Rightarrow$ Here, $p = 0$, so that $36 + 0 = 36$ is divisible by 3.

But again, $p = 0$ and $q = 5$ is not an option.

Now, if $p = 3$, then $36 + p$

$= 36 + 3 = 39$ is divisible by 3.

$\therefore$ $p = 3$ and $q = 5$ is the correct values of p and q.

102. (c) Let the number is x.

Then, $\frac{(7+x)5}{3} - 4 = 16$

$\Rightarrow (7+x)5 = (16+4)\times 3$

$\Rightarrow 7 + x = \frac{20\times 3}{5} = 4\times 3$

$\therefore x = 12 - 7 = 5$

103. (b) Divisor $= 4 \times$ remainder

$= 4 \times 45 = 180$ [$\because$ Remainder $= 45$]

Also, divisor $= 10 \times$ quotient

$\Rightarrow 180 = 10 \times$ quotient

$\Rightarrow$ Quotient $= \frac{180}{10} = 18$

Now, Dividend

= Divisor × Quotient + Remainder

$= 180 \times 18 + 45 = 3240 + 45 = 3285$

104. (a) Since 221 is also divisible by 13.

According to the question,

When 30 is divided by 13, the remainder will be 4.

$\therefore$ Required number = 4

105. (c) Here, the result is

$7593 + 9435 - 2607 = 14421$

14421 is not divisible by 4, 10 and 5.

Here, the sum of digits

$= 1 + 4 + 4 + 2 + 1 = 12$

(12 is divisible by 3)

Hence, 14421 is divisible by 3.

106. (a) Number divisible by 7 and 11,

$7 \times 11 = 77$ and its multiple

Now, multiples of 77 between 1 to 430

$= 77, 154, 231, 308, 385$

Hence, there are 5 numbers from 1 to 430 which are divisible by 7 and 11 both.

107. (b) $K = 42 \times 25 \times 54 \times 135$

$\Rightarrow K = (2\times 3\times 7)\times(5\times 5)$

$\times(2\times 3\times 3\times 3)\times(3\times 3\times 3\times 5)$

$\Rightarrow K = 2^2 \times 3^7 \times 5^3 \times 7$

Since, K is divisible by 3^a

Hence, maximum value of $a = 7$

108. (d) To find it, firstly we have to find out the remainder, when we divide 246837 by 13.

```
13)246837(18987
   13
   116
   104
    128
    117
     113
     104
      97
      91
       6  Remainder
```

So, we have to subtract 6 from number to make it divisible by 13.

109. (b) Between 43 and 481, first number divisible by 9 = 45

last number divisible by 9 = 477,

These numbers will form an AP, which is 45, 54, 63, ..., 477

$a = 45, d = 9$

$a_n = 477$

$\Rightarrow a + (n-1)d = 477$

$\Rightarrow 45 + (n-1)(9) = 477$

$\Rightarrow 45 + 9n - 9 = 477$

$\Rightarrow 9n + 36 = 477$

$\Rightarrow 9n = 441$

$\Rightarrow n = \frac{441}{9} \Rightarrow n = 49$

Hence, there are total 49 numbers between 43 and 481, which are divisible by 9.

110. (a) $3^{50} + 9^{26} + 27^{18} + 9^{28} + 9^{29}$

$= 3^{50} + (3^2)^{26} + (3^3)^{18} + (3^2)^{28} + (3^2)^{29}$

$[\because (a^m)^n = a^{mn}]$

$= 3^{50} + 3^{52} + 3^{54} + 3^{56} + 3^{58}$

$= 3^{50}(1 + 3^2 + 3^4 + 3^6 + 3^8)$

$= 3^{50}(1 + 9 + 81 + 729 + 6561)$

$= 3^{50} \times 7381$

Here, the number 7381 is divisible by 11 as difference between the even and odd places digits sum is 11 (multiple of 11)

So, $3^{50} + 9^{26} + 27^{18} + 9^{28} + 9^{29}$ is divisible by 11.

111. (d) Let quotient be q when n is divided by 6 and remainder is 3.

$\therefore n = 6q + 3$

$n^2 + 5n + 8 = (6q+3)^2 + 5(6q+3) + 8$

$= 36q^2 + 9 + 36q + 30q + 15 + 8$

$= 36q^2 + 66q + 32$

$= 36q^2 + 66q + 30 + 2$

$= 6(6q^2 + 11q + 5) + 2$

$\therefore$ Remainder when $(n^2 + 5n + 8)$ is divided by $6 = 2$

112. (c) Given, 9-digit number = $83P93678Q$

For a number to be divisible by 72, the number should be divisible by both 8 and 9.

Now, for a number to be divisible by 8, the number formed by last 3-digit of a number is divisible by 8.

$\because$ $78Q$ should be divisible by 8.

$\therefore Q = 4$, as $\frac{784}{8} = 98$

Now, for a number to be divisible by 9, the sum of its digits should be divisible by 9,

$\therefore 8 + 3 + P + 9 + 3 + 6 + 7 + 8 + Q = 44 + Q + P$

$= 44 + 4 + P = 48 + P$

Now, $48 + P$ to be divisible by 9

$\therefore P = 6$

Hence, $\sqrt{P^2 + Q^2 + 12}$

$= \sqrt{6^2 + 4^2 + 12} = \sqrt{36 + 16 + 12}$

$= \sqrt{64} = 8$

113. (c) We know, LCM of 11, 33, 99, 121

$= 3\times 3\times 11\times 11 = 1089$

Greatest 5- digit number = 99999

On dividing 99999 by 1089;

Remainder = 900

$\therefore$ Required number $= 99999 - 900 = 99099$

114. (c) Given, $100^2 - 99^2 + 98^2 - 97^2 + 96^2 - 95^2 + ...12^2 - 11^2$

Since, $(a^2 - b^2) = (a-b)(a+b)$

$\therefore (100-99)(100+99) + (98-97)(98+97) + ...+(12-11)(12+11)$

$= 199 + 195 + ...+ 23$

Since, difference of two consecutive number is same here. Therefore this is an AP

$\therefore 199 = 23 + (n-1)\times 4$

$\therefore$ Number of terms $(n) = 45$

Now, sum of all 45 terms.

$S_{45} = \frac{45}{2}\times(23 + 199) = 4995$

115. (d) According to the question,

$4567 \div 7 = 652 + 3$ (Remainder)

So, smallest number should be added to 4567 for divisible by $7 = 7 - 3 = 4$

116. (b) Let the number $= 10x + y$ ...(i)

Given, $x + y = 8$ ...(ii)

and $10y + x = 10x + y + 36$

$\Rightarrow 10y - y = 10x - x + 36$

$\Rightarrow 9y = 9x + 36$

$\Rightarrow y - x = 4$ ...(iii)

On solving Eqs. (ii) and (iii), we get

$x = 2$ and $y = 6$

$\therefore$ From Eq. (i) the number $= 10\times 2 + 6 = 26$

117. (c) Since 363 is completely divisible by 11.

So, if we divide the same number by 11, the remainder will be $17 - 11 = 6$.

118. (b) Given, 6-digit number = $674pq0$.

If this number is divisible by 3.

Then, the sum of its digits will be divisible by 3.

$\Rightarrow 6 + 7 + 4 + p + q + 0$, is divisible by 3.

$\Rightarrow 17 + p + q$, is divisible by 3.

$\Rightarrow p + q = 1, 4, 7$ ...(i)

$\because$ The number is also divisible by 11, then

$\therefore$ Sum of digits odd places – Sum of digits even places = 0 or divisible by 11.

$\Rightarrow (6 + 4 + q) - (7 + p + 0) = 0$ or divisible by 11

$\Rightarrow 10 + q - 7 - p = 0$ or divisible by 11

$\Rightarrow 3 + q - p = 0$ or divisible by 11

If $3 + q - p = 0$

$\Rightarrow q - p = -3$

$\Rightarrow p - q = 3$ ...(ii)

From Eq. (i),

$$p+q=7 \quad ...(iii)$$

$$[\because p+q \geq 4]$$

To solve Eqs. (ii) and (iii),

$$p=5, q=2$$

Hence, $p=5$ and $q=2$.

119. (b) For 1 2 3 4 5 6 xy to be divisible by 8, then 6 xy should be divisible by 8.

Now, numbers between 600 and 699 divisible by 8 are

→ 600, 608, 616, 624, 632, 640, 648, 656, 664, 672, 680, 688, 696.

Hence, there are 13 total possible pairs of (x,y).

120. (d) Let n be a number which is divided by 7 leaving remainder 4 and quotient q.

$$\Rightarrow \quad n=7q+4$$

$$\text{Now, } \frac{n^2}{7}=\frac{(7q+4)^2}{7}=\frac{49q^2+16+56q}{7}$$

$$[\because (a+b)^2=a^2+b^2+2ab]$$

$$=\frac{49q^2}{7}+\frac{56q}{7}+\frac{16}{7}=7q^2+8q+\frac{16}{7}$$

Now, when, 16 is divided by 7 remainder is 2.

Hence, remainder = 2

121. (c) We know, $7^{42}=(7^2)^{21}=(49)^{21}$

Now, when 49 is divided by 48.

Remainder = 1

$$\therefore \quad \frac{(49)^{21}}{48}=\frac{(1)^{21}}{48}=1 \text{ (Remainder)}$$

122. (b) According to the question,

```
765)87501(114
    765
    1100
     765
    3351
    3060
     291→ Remainder
```

$\therefore$ Required number $=87501+(765-291)$

$=87501+474=87975$

123. (c) If a number is divisible by 2 and 5, then it is also divisible by $2\times5=10$. *i.e.*, unit digit of the number should be zero. Also, a number is divisible by 3, only if sum of the digits of the number is divisible by 3.

From option (c),

Sum of digits of 2345760

$=2+3+4+5+7+6+0=27$

Here, 27 is divisible by 3 and unit digit is also zero.

So, the number 2345760 is divisible by 2, 3 and 5.

124. (d) Let the two numbers be x and $y (x>y)$.

According to the question,

$$x=6y+19 \quad ...(i)$$

$$\text{Also,} \quad x-y=1564 \quad ...(ii)$$

From Eqs. (i) and (ii), we get

$$6y+19-y=1564$$

$$\Rightarrow \quad 6y-y=1564-19$$

$$\Rightarrow \quad 5y=1545$$

$$\Rightarrow \quad y=\frac{1545}{5}=309$$

So, smaller number $y=309$.

125. (b) The number of toffees forms an AP, 2,4,6....25 terms.

Where, $a=2$, $d=2$

Total number of toffees

$$S_{25}=\frac{25}{2}[2\times2+(24)\times2]=\frac{25}{2}(4+48)$$

$$=\frac{25}{2}\times52=25\times26=650$$

$$=5\times13\times10$$

Hence, the total number of toffees is divisible by 5 and 13 both.

126. (c) $x67y$ is exactly divisible by 9, then sum of the digits of the number must be divisible by 9,

Sum of digits $=x+6+7+y=x+y+13$

If $x+y=5$, then

$13+5=18$ (exactly divisible by 9)

$\therefore$ The least value of $x+y=5$

127. (c) On 36 L, truck runs 492 km.

So, on 33 L, truck will run

$$=\frac{492}{36}\times33=451 \text{ km}$$

128. (a) If a number is divisible by 3, 7 and 11, then it will be also divisible by (LCM)

LCM of 3, 7 and 11 = 231

Let the number is 75099 as $PQ \leq 99$

Here, $75099=231\times325+24$

So, the actual number $=231\times325=75075$

By comparing, $P=7$ and $Q=5$

Now, $P+2Q=7+2\times5=17$

129. (d) $27^{27}+27=27^{27}+1+26$

$$=(27)^{27}+(1)^{27}+26$$

We know that, x^n+a^n is completly divisible by $x+a$, for n is an odd number.

So, $(27)^{27}+(1)^{27}$ is divisible by $(27+1)=28$

$\therefore$ Required remainder = 26

130. (b) Given number = 8127

Using divisibility rule of 8,

Last three digits of a number should be divisible by 8.

$$\therefore \quad \frac{127}{8}=7 \text{ (Remainder)}$$

131. (c) We know that, (x^n-a^n) is always completely divisible by $(x-a)$ for all value of n.

$\therefore$ $(49^{15}-1)$, is divisible by $(49-1)=48$

Since, 48 is completely divisible by 8.

$\therefore$ $(49^{15}-1)$ will also be divisible by 8.

132. (b) $7698x138y$ is divisible by 72

$$72=8\times9.$$

So, if the number is divisible by 8 and 9 both, the number is divisible by 72.

Divisibility of 8,

Last 3 digit of number is divisible by 8, $\frac{38y}{8}$

If we put $y=4$ the number 384 will divisible by 8.

Divisibility of 9,

If sum of digit is divisible by 9

$$\Rightarrow \quad 7+6+9+8+x+1+3+8+4=\frac{46+x}{9}$$

Put $x=8$ we get, the number 54 will divisible by 9.

$$x=8, y=4.$$

$$\therefore \quad \sqrt{4x+y}=\sqrt{4\times8+4}=\sqrt{36}=6$$

133. (a) Divisiblity rule of 11,

Sum of odd place digit – Sum of even place digit equal 0 or 11.

$$=(4+0+7)-(a+6+b)$$

$$=11-6-(a+b)=5-(a+b)$$

So, only 2 possible value we will get

$$(a+b)=5 \text{ and } (a+b)=16$$

So, sum of all possible value of $(a+b)$ is

$$16+5=21$$

134. (c) Let the 3 digit number is 123.

Where $a=1$, $b=2$, $c=3$

Then, $abc=123$, $cab=312$ and $bca=231$

Sum of all digits $=123+312+231=666$

So, 666 is divisible by all options, except option (c).

135. (d) According to the question,

$7\times11\times13=1001$, when any 3 digit number is multiplied by 1001 then it repeat itself and always completely divisible by 7, 11, 13.

Let 3 digit number are pqr

$$pqr\times1001=5z\,3x\,4y$$

$$pqrpqr=5z3x4y$$

Compare both sides,

$\Rightarrow \quad p=5, r=3, q=4$

So, $\quad p=5=x, q=4=z, r=3=y$

$\therefore$ $(x+y-z)=(5+3-4)=4$

136. (a) A number is divisible by 6.

If it divisible by 2 and 3 also.

Using divisibility rule of 2 and 3.

Number $=7+2+k+4+6+0+k=19+2k$

If we put $k=4$, $19+2\times4=19+8=27$ is divisible by 3 and is also divisible by 2.

$\therefore$ The value of $k=4$

137. (c) If any number P is divisible by 2 and any number Q is divisible by 3.

For divisibility of 2, last digit should be even number.

For divisibility of 3, sum of digits divided by 3

Let put $P=4$ and $Q=3$

$\therefore$ $P\times Q$ is divisible by 6.

$$P\times Q=4\times3=12.$$

138. (b) Number $888x53y4$ is divisible by 72 we can write 72 as 8×9.

Divisiblity of 8 → If last 3 digit is divisible by 8 then given number is also divisible by 8.

$\frac{3y4}{8}$ put $y = 8$ (maximum)

$\Rightarrow \quad \frac{384}{8} \Rightarrow 48$

The value of y is 8.

Divisibility of 9 ⇒ If sum of digit is divisible by 9, so the number will be divisible by 9.

$\Rightarrow \quad 888x5384$

$\Rightarrow 8+8+8+x+5+3+8+4 \Rightarrow 44+x$

If we put $x = 1$

So, 45 will be divisible by 9.

Put value of $x = 1$ and $y = 8$ in $(7x + 2y)$

$\therefore \ (7x + 2y) = (7\times 1 + 2\times 8) = 7 + 16 = 23$

139. (b) Divisibility of 3,

If the sum of all number is divided by 3, so that number will be divisible by 3.

$\Rightarrow \quad 45082k$

$\Rightarrow 4+5+0+8+2+k = \frac{19+k}{3}$

If we put $k = 2$ (smallest value)

$= \frac{19+2}{3} = \frac{21}{3}$

If we put $k = 8$ (greatest value)

$\Rightarrow \quad \frac{19+8}{3} = \frac{27}{3}$

So, the value of k are 2 and 8.

According to the question,

$\therefore$ Sum of square of greatest value and smallest value $= (8)^2 + (2)^2 = 64 + 4 = 68$

140. (b) Given, number $94x\ 29y\ 6$ is divisible by 72 then it is also divisible by 8 and 9

Divisibility of 8, last 3 digits of the number should be divisibile by 8.

$\therefore$ Last 3-digits of number $= 9y6$

for $y = 3, 7$, $9y6$ is divisible by 8

Divisibility of 9, sum of digits of the number should be divisible by 9.

$\therefore$ Sum of digits $= 9+4+x+2+9+y+6$

$= 30 + x + y$

for $y = 3$, then $x = 3$.

$\Rightarrow \quad 30 + 3 + 3 = 36$

(which is divisible by 9)

for $y = 7$, then $x = 8 \Rightarrow 30 + 8 + 7 = 45$

(which is divisible by 9)

According to the question,

$x \neq y$

$\therefore \quad x = 8$ and $y = 7$

$\therefore \ 2x + 3y = 2\times 8 + 3\times 7$

$= 16 + 21 = 37$

141. (d) $5306P2$ divisible by 3.

Divisibility of 3,

Sum of all number should be divisible by 3.

$\Rightarrow \quad \frac{5+3+0+6+P+2}{3} \Rightarrow \frac{(16+P)}{3}$

Put $P = 2$ (smallest value)

$\frac{18}{3} = 6$

Again put $P = 8 \Rightarrow \frac{16+8}{3} = 8$

The greatest value of $P = 8$ and smallest value of $P = 2$

Difference between square of greatest value of P and smallest value of P

$\Rightarrow \quad (8)^2 - (2)^2 \Rightarrow 64 - 4 = 60$

142. (c) $5x423y$ divided by 88, then the digit is also divisible by 8 and 11.

Divisibility of 8 → Last 3 digit divisible by 8.

For 8 → $\frac{23y}{8}$,

If we put $y = 2$, it will divided by 8.

$\frac{232}{8} = 29 \Rightarrow y = 2$

Divisibility of 11 → Difference of sum of odd place digit and even place digit is 0 or divisible by 11.

For 11 → $5\ x423y$

$\Rightarrow \quad (5+4+3)-(x+2+2)$

$\Rightarrow \quad 12-4-x \Rightarrow (8-x)$

If we put $x = 8$, we get, $8 - 8 = 0$

Value of $x = 8$ and $y = 2$ put in given expression.

$\therefore (5x - 8y) = (5\times 8 - 8\times 2) = 40 - 16 = 24$

143. (c) Divisibility rule of 11, difference of odd place sum and even place sum is equal to 0 or divisible by 11.

$= (3 + a + 8) - (0 + 6 + b)$

$= 11 + a - 6 - b = 5 + (a - b)$

$\because a$ is greater than b,

So, $\quad a = 9, b = 3$

$\Rightarrow \quad 5 + (9-3) = 5 + 6 = 11$

$\therefore$ The greatest value of b is 3.

144. (b) If 7 divided by positive number n, the remainder is 2.

We know that,

Dividend = Divisor × Quotient + Remainder

$\therefore \quad n = 7a + 2$ (quotient $= a$ (let)

On adding 5 in both sides,

$n + 5 = 7a + 2 + 5 = 7(a+1)$

Hence, $n + 5$ gives a remainder of '0' when divided by 7.

145. (d) Given number $= 925x85$

Using divisibility rule of 11, we get

(Sum of digit of odd place) – (Sum of digit at even place) is equal to or divisible by 11.

$= (9 + 5 + 8) - (2 + x + 5)$

$= 22 - (7 + x) = 22 - 7 - x$

$= 15 - x$

If we put 4 in place of x that number is divisible by 11.

$= 15 - 4 = \frac{11}{11} = 1$

So, the minimum value of $x = 4$.

146. (d) Divisibility of 4 → Last 2 digits of number are divisible by 4

Last two digits = * 4

Then, $\quad * = 0, 2, 4, 6, 8$

So, the largest value of * = 8

147. (a) Divisibility of 9 ⇒ A number is divisible by 9 if sum of its digit is divisible by 9.

If the number $687x29$ is divisible by 9

$\Rightarrow \ 6+8+7+x+2+9 = 32+x$

If we put $x = 4$, the number become

$32 + 4 = 36$

36 is divisible by 9.

Now, we have to find $2x$.

$\Rightarrow \quad 2x = 2\times 4 = 8$

148. (d) Divisibility condition of 8, last 3 digit should be divisible by 8.

By option, if we put largest number which is 9.

$= 948/8 =$ Not perfectly divisible.

If we choose 8 in place of *

$848/8 \Rightarrow 106$

$\therefore$ 8 is the greatest number.

149. (b) According to the question,

When a positive integer is divided by d, remainder is 15.

$\Rightarrow \quad d > 15$

Now, the minimum value for 15 to be remainder is 15.

$\therefore$ Assuming the required number to be 15.

As, $\quad d > 15 \Rightarrow d = 16$

$\therefore$ 10 times of a number $= 10(15) = 150$

$\therefore$ Remainder when 150 is divided by 16 is 6.

i.e., $\frac{150}{16} = 6$ (Remainder)

As, $d = 16$ satisfies all the conditions.

$\therefore$ Least value of d is 16.

150. (c) Given, $708x6y8z9$ is divisible by 99, then it is also divisible by 9 and 11 (factors of 99).

For divisibility by 9 → The sum of digits of the number should be divisible by 9.

$\therefore$ Sum of digits

$= 7+0+8+x+6+y+8+z+9$

$= 38 + (x+y+z)$

For divisibility by 11 → The difference of sum of odd and even digits should be zero or divisible by 11.

$\therefore$ Difference

$= (7+8+6+8+9) - (0+x+y+z)$

$= 38 - (x+y+z)$

From option (c), $x + y + z = 16$

Sum of digits $= 38 + 16 = 54$ (which is divisible by 9)

And difference $= 38 - 16 = 22$ (which is divisible by 11)

$\therefore \quad x + y + z = 16$

151. (d) Total numbers from 200 to 800 (including 200) $= (800 - 200) + 1 = 601$

Total numbers from 1 to 800 (including 800) which are divisible by $5 = \frac{800}{5} = 160$

Total numbers, from 1 to 200 (excluding 200) which are divisible by $5 = \frac{199}{5} \approx 39$

Total numbers from 200 to 800 which are divisible by 5 = 160 − 39 = 121

Total numbers from 1 to 800 (including 800) which are divisible by 7 = $\frac{800}{7} \approx 114$

Total numbers from 1 to 200 (excluding 200) which are divisible by 7 = $\frac{199}{7} \approx 28$

Total numbers from 200 to 800 which are divisible by 7 = 114 − 28 = 86

Similarly, we can write, total numbers from 200 to 800 which are divisible by

$$35 = \frac{800}{35} - \frac{200}{35} \approx 17$$

Numbers neither divisible by 5 nor 7

$= 601 - (121 + 86 - 17) = 601 - 190 = 411$

∴ There are 411 numbers between 200 and 800 which are neither divisible by 5 nor 7.

152. (a) We know that,

Average of the five consecutive number

$$= \frac{240}{5} = 48$$

and

Average of consecutive number

$$= \frac{\text{First number} + \text{Last number}}{2}$$

∴ First number + Last number = 48 × 2 = 96

153. (d) Given number = 72514368

Number obtained by subtracting each digit of the number from 9 = 2 7 4 8 5 6 3 1

Even digit will be 4 in namely formed number.

154. (b) A number which are divisible by both 2 and 7 is multiple of 14.

Total number of such numbers between 1 and 1000 = Quotient of (1000 ÷ 14) = 71

155. (c) Factors of 216 = 1, 2, 3, 4, 6, 8, 9, 12, 18, 24, 27, 36, 54, 72, 108 and 216.

Sum of odd divisors = 1 + 3 + 9 + 27 = 40

156. (d) A number to be divisible by 88, must be divisible by 8 and 11.

The number $97x4562y8$ to be divisible by 8, the number formed by last three digits of number must be divisible by 8.

So, $2y8$ is divisible by 8, if $y = 4$ $(\because y \le 9)$

Also, the number $97x4562y8$ will be divisible by 11 only if difference of sum of odd and even places digits is multiple of 11 or 0.

Now, $(9 + x + 5 + 2 + 8)$

$- (7 + 4 + 6 + y) = 11$

$\Rightarrow \quad 24 + x - 17 - y = 11$

$\Rightarrow \quad x = y + 4 = 8 \quad (\because y = 4)$

Now, $(x^2 + y^2) = (8^2 + 4^2) = 64 + 16 = 80$

157. (d) As per divisibility rule of 8, $p48$ divisible by 8. Therefore, least possible value of p is 0.

158. (c) Given number is $34R05030M6$.

When the number is divisible by 16.

Then the number formed by last 4 digits is divisible by 16.

∴ Only possible value of $M = 5$

[∵ 30M6 = 3056 ÷ 16 = 0 (Remainder)]

Now,

Using divisibility rule of 11,

$(3 + R + 5 + 3 + M) - (4 + 0 + 0 + 0 + 6)$

$= 11 + R + M - 10 = 1 + R + 5 = 6 + R$

$(\because M = 5)$

Now, as $6 + R$ is exactly divisible by 11

∴ $6 + R = 11 \Rightarrow R = 5$

159. (b) Given, number $x58y$.

For divisible by 9.

∴ $(x + 5 + 8 + y)$ is divisible by 9.

⇒ $13 + x + y$ is divisible by 9.

For the least value of $(x + y) = 5$

$$\left[\because \frac{13 + 5}{9} = 2\right]$$

160. (b) Given, number is 150328.

After rearranged,

Then number is 853210.

According to the question,

853210 − 65 = 853145

Which is divisible by 5.

161. (c) The number give remainder 5 When its divided by 7, then the number must be $7x + 5$.

The same give remainder 3 when its divided by 4.

So, the number must be in the form of

$$4(7x + 5) + 3$$

The number when divided by 3 given remainder 2.

Thus, number must be in the form of

$[3\{4(7x + 5) + 3\} + 2]$

$\Rightarrow [3\{28x + 20 + 3\} + 2]$

$\Rightarrow [84x + 60 + 9 + 2]$

$\Rightarrow 84x + 71$ ...(i)

Now, if we divide the Eq. (i) by 42, we will get remainder 29.

162. (c) If it is divisible by 72,

Then it should be divisible by both 8 and 9.

Divisibility by 8 → The last three digits should be divisible by 8.

∴ 78y are last three digits.

```
8) 78y (9
   72
   ---
   6y
```

There should be $y = 4$

Because 64 is divisible by 8.

Rule of divisibility by 9.

The sum of all digits should be divisible by 9.

So, $7 + 8 + 5 + x + 3 + 6 + 7 + 8 + y$

$= 20 + x + 24 + 4 = 48 + x \quad (\because y = 4)$

There should be $x = 6$

Because 48 + 6 = 54 is divisible by 9.

Hence, $x = 6$ and $y = 4$

So, $x + y = 6 + 4 = 10$

163. (c) If we multiply only the last digit's of every number, we will get 3 × 2 × 5 = 30.

That means, after multiplication of all three numbers, the last digit will be '0'.

Therefore, if 14331433 × 1422 × 1425 is divided by 10, it doesn't have any remainder, the number is completely divisible by 10.

164. (b) Let the number of students in the class is x.

So, each student donated ₹ x.

Total find value = $x \times x = x^2$

According to the question,

$x^2 = 2809$

$\Rightarrow \quad x = 53$

∴ The number of students in the class is 53.

165. (a) Given 6 digit number is = $5x2y6z$

If a six digit number combinedly divisible by 7, 11 and 13, then the number must be in the form of $ABCABC$

Hence, number is $5x2y6z$.

$ABCABC \quad x = B = 6$

$y = A = 5$

$z = C = 2$

So, $x - y + 3z = 6 - 5 + 6 = 7$

166. (d) Remainder in

$$\frac{72 \times 73 \times 78 \times 76}{35} = \frac{2 \times 3 \times 8 \times 6}{35}$$

$$= \frac{288}{35} = \frac{35 \times 8 + 8}{35} \Rightarrow 8$$

So required remainder is 8.

167. (c) LCM of 15, 18 and 36

$= 2 \times 3 \times 3 \times 5 \times 1 \times 2 = 180$

The required number which is exactly divisible by 11 = $180x + 9$

Put $x = 6$

$= 180 \times 6 + 9$

1089 is divisible by 11.

Hence, the required number is 1089.

168. (b) Required remainder

$= (1433 \times 1433 \times 1422 \times 1425) \div 12$

Remainder in

$= (1433 \div 12) \times (1433 \div 12)$

$\times (1422 \div 12) \times (1425 \div 12)$

$$= \frac{(5 \times 5 \times 6 \times 9)}{12} = \frac{1350}{12} = 6$$

Hence, the remainder is 6.

169. (c) If a number is divided by 72, then the number will be divisible by 8 and 9.

As, the number $785x3678y$ is divisible by 8, $78y$ is divisible by 8.

For $y = 4$, the number is divisible by 8.

As, the number $785x3678y$ is divisible by 9,

$7 + 8 + 5 + x + 3 + 6 + 7 + 8 + y$ is divisible by 9.

$44 + x + y$ is divisible by 9.

$48 + x$ is divisible by 9. $(\because y = 4)$

Nearest integer to 48 is 54 which is divisible by 9.

$$48 + x = 54$$
$$x = 6$$
$$x - y = 6 - 4 = 2$$

170. (d) Let first number be x.

Second number $= (37 - x)$

According to the question,

$$5 \times x + 11(37 - x) = 227$$
$$\Rightarrow \quad 5x + 407 - 11x = 227$$
$$\Rightarrow \quad 6x = 180$$
$$\therefore \quad x = 30$$

Smaller part $= (37 - 30) = 7$

Required number $= 7 \times 9 = 63$

171. (a) A number is divisible by 6 if it divisible by both 2 and 3. As, the number is odd, it cannot divisible by 2. So, it is also not divisible by 6.

The number is divisible by 11 only if the difference between 'sum of digits at even place' and 'sum of digits at odd place' must be either zero or divisible by 11.

Number = 611611611611

Sum of digits at odd places (A)
$$= 6 + 1 + 1 + 6 + 1 + 1 = 16$$

Sum of digits at even places (B)
$$= 1 + 6 + 1 + 1 + 6 + 1 = 16$$

$\because \; A - B = 16 - 16 = 0$

$\therefore$ Number is divisible by only 11.

172. (b) Given, divisor = 459

Remainder = 19

Let quotient be x.

$\therefore$ Number (Dividend)

= Divisor × Quotient + Remainder

Number $= 459 \times x + 19$

According to the question,

$$\therefore \quad \frac{\text{Number}}{17} = \frac{459x + 19}{17} = 27x + \frac{19}{17}$$

Hence, remainder = 2

173. (b) Let the number be $10x + y$.

Given, sum of digit = 9

$$\therefore \; x + y = 9 \quad \text{...(i)}$$

According to the question,

$$(10y + x) - (10x + y) = 45$$
$$\Rightarrow \quad 9y - 9x = 45$$
$$\Rightarrow \quad y - x = 5 \quad \text{...(ii)}$$

On solving Eqs. (i) and (ii),

$$2y = 14$$
$$\therefore \quad y = 7 \text{ and } x = 2$$

$\therefore$ Original number $= 10x + y = 20 + 7 = 27$

174. (d) Given number $= 4645a52$

If a number is divisible by 72 then, it must be divisible by 9 and 8.

as $\quad 72 = 9 \times 8$

Divisibility by 8 If the number formed by last three digits is divisible by 8, then the number is also divisible by '8'.

So, '$a52$' should be divisible by 8.

Possible value of a = 1 or 3

Divisibility by 9 If the sum of the digits of a number is divisible by 9, then the number is also divisible by 9.

$$4 + 6 + 4 + 5 + a + 5 + 2 = 26 + a$$

Out of the given options if we put $a = 1$, then,

$26 + 1 = 27$ (is divisible by 9)

and 152 is divisible by 8.

Therefore, the value of a should be '1' to make it divisible by 72.

175. (d) Let the larger number be x.

Then, smaller number be $(76 - x)$.

According to the question,

$$3x - 4 \times (76 - x) = 46$$
$$\Rightarrow \quad 3x - 304 + 4x = 46$$
$$\Rightarrow \quad 7x = 46 + 304 \Rightarrow 7x = 350$$
$$\therefore \quad x = 50$$

Then, other number $= 76 - 50 = 26$

176. (b) Number $6p5157q$ is divisible by 88, it means number is divisible by 8 and 11.

By rule of divisibility of 8, if last three digits are divisible by 8, then whole number is divisible by 8.

$57q$ is divisible by 8, when $q = 6$

and by rule of divisibility of 11.

"Difference of alternate digits sum of number is 0 or multiple of 11".

Thus, $\quad 6\,p\,5\,1\,5\,7\,q$

Sum of odd digits $= 6 + 5 + 5 + 6 = 22$

$[\because q = 6]$

Sum of even digits $= p + 1 + 7 = 8 + p$

Difference $= 22 - (8 + p) = 0$ or multiple of 11

$$14 - p = 0 \text{ or multiple of } 11$$

Possible value of $p = 3$

Then, required value of $p \times q = 3 \times 6 = 18$

177. (c) Divisibility rule of 11 → A number is divisible by 11 if and only if the difference of the sum of the digits at the even and odd positions in the number is 0 or multiple of 11.

178. (d) We need to find the remainder when, 2^{256} is divided by 17.

$$\therefore \quad \frac{2^{256}}{17} = \frac{(2^4)^{64}}{17} = \frac{(16)^{64}}{17}$$

Now, when 16 is divided by 17, remainder is -1

$$\therefore \quad \frac{(16)^{64}}{17} = \frac{(-1)^{64}}{17} = \frac{1}{17}$$

$\therefore$ Remainder = 1

179. (a) Let the two digit numbers $= 10x + y$

After reversing the digit,

New number $= 10y + x$

According to question,

$$27 + (10x + y) = 10y + x$$
$$\Rightarrow \quad 9(y - x) = 27$$
$$\therefore \quad y - x = 3 \quad \text{...(i)}$$

Again, $x + y = 9$ ...(ii) (given)

From Eqs. (i) and (ii)

$$x = 3 \text{ and } y = 6$$

Required number $= 10x + y = 10 \times 3 + 6 = 36$

180. (d) $\dfrac{8^6 + 1}{7} = \dfrac{8^6}{7} + \dfrac{1}{7}$

Remainder $= 1 + 1 = 2$

181. (b) According to the question,

$$732 - 12 = 720$$
$$720 = 2 \times 2 \times 2 \times 2 \times 3 \times 3 \times 5$$
$$= 2^4 \times 5^1 \times 3^2$$

Total factors $= (4 + 1) \times (2 + 1) \times (1 + 1)$
$$= 5 \times 3 \times 2 = 30$$

Now, factors of 720 up to 12.

$(\because$ Remainder $= 12)$

1, 2, 3, 4, 5, 6, 8, 9, 10 and 12 $\quad (\because n > 12)$

Then, total factors upto 12 = 10

Required number $(n) = 30 - 10 = 20$

182. (c) By divisibility rule of 9, the sum of digits of number must be divisible by 9.

Number $= 6428A83$

Then, $\dfrac{6 + 4 + 2 + 8 + A + 8 + 3}{9} = \dfrac{31 + A}{9}$

Put $\quad A = 5$

Thus, $\dfrac{31 + 5}{9} = 4$ (divisible)

Thus, value of A is 5.

183. (d) Let the weight of each apple be x kg and weight of each orange be y kg.

According to the question,

$$8x + 10y = 5 \text{ kg} \quad \text{...(i)}$$
$$\text{and} \quad 12x + 20y = 9 \text{ kg} \quad \text{...(ii)}$$

Multiplying Eq. (i) by 2 and subtract Eq. (ii),

$$4x = 1 \Rightarrow x = \frac{1}{4}$$

Now, put value of x in Eq. (i)

$$8 \times \frac{1}{4} + 10y = 5$$
$$\Rightarrow \quad 2 + 10y = 5 \Rightarrow y = \frac{3}{10}$$

Hence, required weight of 15 apples and 24 oranges

$$= 15x + 24y$$
$$= 15 \times \frac{1}{4} + 24 \times \frac{3}{10}$$
$$= \frac{15}{4} + \frac{72}{10} = 10.95 \text{ kg} \approx 11 \text{ kg}$$

184. (d) Let two digit number $= 10x + y$

Number when digits are reversed $= 10y + x$

According to the question,

$$10x + y = 5(x + y) + 12$$
$$\Rightarrow \quad 10x + y = 5x + 5y + 12$$
$$\Rightarrow \quad 5x - 4y = 12 \quad \text{...(i)}$$

Also, $10y + x + 9 = 10x + y$

$$\Rightarrow \quad 9x - 9y = 9$$
$$\Rightarrow \quad x - y = 1$$
$$\Rightarrow \quad x = 1 + y \quad \text{...(ii)}$$

From Eqs.(i) and (ii),

$5(1+y)-4y=12$

$\Rightarrow \quad 5+5y-4y=12$

$\Rightarrow \quad y=7$

$\therefore \quad x=1+7=8$

∴ Required original number

$= 10\times 8+7=87$

185. (c) As, integer n is divided by 5, remainder is 3.

$\therefore \quad n=5q+3$

When $6n$ is divided by 5, then

Now, $6n=6(5q+3)$

$=30q+18$

$=(30q+15)+3$

$=5(6q+3)+3$

$6n=5k+3$ [Here, $k=6q+3$]

∴ Required remainder = 3

186. (a) Given,

$17^3+18^3-16^3-15^3$

$=(17^3+18^3)-(16^3+15^3)$

$=(17+18)(17^2-17\times 18+18^2)$

$-(16+15)(16^2-16\times 15+15^2)$

$[\because a^3+b^3=(a+b)(a^2-ab+b^2)]$

$=35(289-306+324)-31(256-240+225)$

$=35\times 307-31\times 241$

$=10745-7471=3274$

∵ Unit digits of the number 3274 is 4.

∴ The number is divisible by single digit 2.

187. (d) LCM of 2, 3 and 4 = 12

Thus, numbers between 10 and 65 which divisible by 12 are 12, 24, 36, 48, 60

Thus, there are 5 numbers.

188. (d) $14400=2^6\times 3^2\times 5^2$

Now, $14400=2^1\times 3^2\times(2^5\times 5^2)$

$=18\times(2^5\times 5^2)$

Number of factors divisible by

$18=(5+1)(2+1)=18$

and $14400=2^2\times 3^2\,(2^4\times 5^2)=36(2^4\times 5^2)$

Number of factors divisible by

$36=(4+1)(2+1)=15$

∴ Number of factors which are divisible by 18 but not by 36 is = 18 − 15 = 3

189. (a) Given number,

$k^{33}-k=k(k^{32}-1)$

We know that,

x^n-a^n is always divisible by $(x-a)$.

∴ $k(k^{32}-1)$ is always divisible by $(k-1)$.

Here, k = odd number

$\therefore \quad k-1=$ even number

∴ $k^{32}-1$ is always divisible by even number. i.e., 24 only from option.

190. (a) Let the original number be n.

We know, by Division Algorithm,

Dividend = Divisor × Quotient + Remainder

When divided by 5, remainder is 3

$n=5q+3$

When further divided by 3, remainder is 2

$\therefore \quad n=3(5q+3)+2$

$n=15q+9+2=15q+11$

When further divided by 2, remainder is 1

$\therefore \quad n=2(15q+11)+1$

$=30q+22+1=30q+23$

If Quotient $(q)=1$

$\therefore \quad n=30(1)+23=53$

Now, $\frac{53}{13}=4\frac{1}{13}$

∴ When divided by 13, remainder = 1

191. (a) Let the number at blank space be x.

∴ $7x7624$ must be divisible by 3.

To check divisibility by 3, sum of digits of number must be divisible by 3.

$\therefore\ 7+x+7+6+2+4=x+26$

Possible value of $x=1, 4, 7$

∴ Least value of $x=1$

192. (c) Let the two digits number be $(10y+x)$.

According to the question,

$10y+x+10x+y=77$

$\Rightarrow \quad 11x+11y=77$

$\Rightarrow \quad 11(x+y)=77$

$\Rightarrow \quad x+y=7$ ...(i)

Also, given $\quad x-y=1$ ...(ii)

Solving Eqs. (i) and (ii), we get

$x=4,\ y=3$

∴ Required number $=10y+x$

$=10(3)+4=34$

193. (c) If number $3c2933k$ is divisible by 5.

Then, k must be 5. $(\because K\in N)$

The number becomes = $3c29335$

Now, to check the divisiblity by 11, difference between sum of odd place digits and sum of even place digit must be multiple of 11 or 0.

$\therefore\ (3+2+3+5)-(c+9+3)=11$ or 0

$\Rightarrow \quad 13-(12+c)=11$ or 0

$\Rightarrow \quad c=1$

Now, $\quad c+k=1+5=\boxed{6}$

194. (d) Given number = 19487161

Sum of digits at odd place

$=1+4+7+6=18$

Sum of digits at even place

$=9+8+1+1=19$

Thus, difference = 19 − 18 = 1

We add 10 i.e.1 + 10 = 11 to make it divisible by 11.

195. (b) Let divisor be x and numbers are y and z.

Then, $\quad y=x\times n+6$ ...(i)

$z=x\times m+7$ ...(ii)

$\therefore \quad (y+z)=(x\times n+x\times m+6+7)$

Now, $\frac{(y+z)}{x}=\frac{(x\times n+x\times m+13)}{x}=\frac{13}{x}$

∴ Remainder = 5

∴ Divisor = 8

196. (c) On dividing 7658 by 45,

As, $\frac{7658}{45}=8$ (remainder)

∴ Required number = 7658 − 8 = 7650

197. (a) A number which is divisible by 22, it must be divisible by 11 and 2 both.

From option (a),

Number 893002 is an even number.

Hence, it is divisible by 2.

Now, the check the divisibility with 11

$\Rightarrow \quad (8+3+0)-(9+0+2)=0$ or 11

$\Rightarrow \quad 11-11=0$

Hence, it is also divisible by 11.

∴ Required number = 893002.

198. (d) When n is divided by 18, the quotient is x and the remainder is 6.

$\Rightarrow \quad n=18x+6$ ...(i)

When n is divided by 25, the quotient is y and remainder is 15

$n=25y+15$ ...(ii)

From Eqs. (i) and (ii),

$18x+6=25y+15$

$\Rightarrow \quad 18x-25y=9$

199. (c) According to the question,

Given number = $489y5z6$

This number is divisible by 72.

$(72=9\times 8)$

∴ Last three digits of the given number $5z6$, to be divided by 8

$\frac{5z6}{8}$,

Putting $z=7$ number is divisible by 8.

[By taking the maximum value of z]

∴ Number = $489y576$.

Now, in order to divide the number by 9, sum of digits of number will be divided by 9.

$\therefore \quad 4+8+9+y+5+7+6=y+39$

Putting $y=6$ number is divisible by 9.

$\therefore \quad y\times z=7\times 6=42$

200. (a) Remainder of $\frac{179\times 172\times 173}{17}$

$=$ Remainder of $\frac{9\times 2\times 3}{17}$

$=$ Remainder of $\frac{54}{17}=3$

201. (b) Divisibility by 9 A number is divisible by 9, if the sum of its digits is divisible by 9.

Divisibility by 11 A number is divisible by 11 if the difference between the sum of the digits in the odd position and the sum of the digits in the even position is divisible by 11 or 0.

∴ Now that the shuffled number will always be divisible by 9, but not necessarily by 11.

202. (d) Let the number be N and the quotient be x.

$$N = 512x + 67$$

Now, $\frac{512x + 67}{32} = \frac{512x + 64 + 3}{32}$

$$= (16x + 2) + 3$$

Hence, the required remainder = 3

203. (a) According to the question,

Digits from 1 to 9 $\rightarrow 1 \times 9 = 9$

Digits from 10 to 99 $\rightarrow 2 \times 90 = 180$

Digits from 100 to 428 $\rightarrow 3 \times 329 = 987$

$\therefore$ Total number of digits from 1 to 428

$$= 9 + 180 + 987 = 1176$$

204. (b) Let the number is N.

Then, $N = 304K + 43$

when, $K = 1$, then $N = 347$

$\therefore \quad \frac{N}{16} = \frac{347}{16} = 11$ (remainder)

205. (c) Let the five consecutive even numbers are $a-4, a-2, a, a+2, a+4$

According to the question,

$$a - 4 + a - 2 + a + a + 2 + a + 4 = 2720$$

$\Rightarrow \quad 5a = 2720$

$\Rightarrow \quad a = 544$

The sum of third and fifth numbers

$$= a + a + 4 = 2a + 4 = 2 \times 544 + 4 = 1092$$

206. (a) Divisibility rule of 8 is its last three digits is divisible by 8.

Now, numbers between 2000 to 2020, which is divisible by 8 is *i.e.*, 2008 and 2016.

Hence, only two number is divisible by 8.

207. (c) Given number = $1738b9c$

By divisibility rule of 4,

$\frac{9c}{4}$ = completely divisible

$\therefore \quad c = 6$ [For maximum value]

To check divisibility of 3, the sum of digits of number

$$= 1 + 7 + 3 + 8 + b + 9 + 6 = 34 + b$$

$\therefore \quad b = 5 \Rightarrow \frac{34 + 5}{3} = 13$ (Quotient)

So, the lowest positive value of $(c - b)$

$$= 6 - 5 = 1$$

208. (b) According to the question,

$$[\{(7 \times 1 + 5) \times 5 + 0\} \times 3 + 4] \times 2 + 1$$

$$= (60 \times 3 + 4) \times 2 + 1$$

$$= (184 \times 2) + 1 = 369$$

Now, on dividing 369 by 7,

quotient = 52 and remainder = 5

On dividing 52 by 5, quotient = 10 and remainder = 2

On dividing 10 by 3, quotient = 3 and remainder = 1

On dividing 3 by 2, quotient = 1 and remainder = 1

$\therefore$ Required remainder

$$= 5 + 2 + 1 + 1 = 9$$

Speedy Method

By remainder theorem,

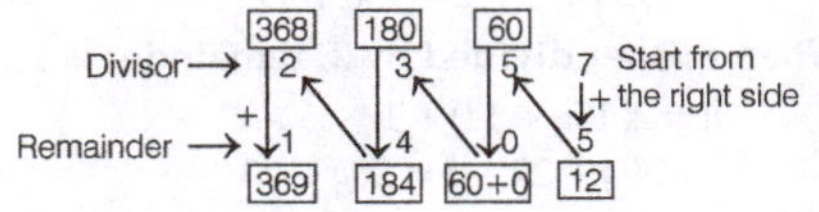

Dividend is 369

Now,

7	369	R
5	52	5
3	10	2
2	3	1
	1	

$\therefore$ Sum of remainder = 5 + 2 + 1 + 1 = 9

209. (c) Divisibility of 11 the sum of even place digit – sum of odd place digit = 0 or 11

$\therefore$ Number = $1234567y$

Difference

$$= 1 + 3 + 5 + 7 - (2 + 4 + 6 + y) = 0$$

$\Rightarrow \quad 16 - 12 - y = 0$

$\therefore \quad y = 4$

210. (c) Given, last quotient = 3

Remainder when divided by 7 is 3.

$\therefore$ Dividend = Divisor $\times$ Quotient + Remainder

Dividend = $7 \times 3 + 3 = 24$

$\because$ 24 is the result of division by 5 leaving a remainder of 1.

$\therefore$ The number before division

$\Rightarrow \quad 5 \times 24 + 1 = 121$

$\because$ 121 is the result of division by 3 leaving a remainder of 2.

$\therefore \quad 121 \times 3 + 2 = 363 + 2 = 365$

Hence, the original number = 365

211. (a) Given number = $627x5$

We know that, if the sum of digits of a number is divisible by 9, then the number is also divisible by 9.

Sum of digits = $6 + 2 + 7 + x + 5 = 20 + x$

If we put $x = 7$, then $20 + 7 = 27$, which is divisible by 9.

$\therefore$ The required least value of x is 7.

212. (a) If a number is divisible by 8 and 3, then it is also divisible by 24.

In number = 25560

Last 3 digits of number 25560 be multiple of 8.

Sum of digits = $2 + 5 + 5 + 6 + 0 = 18$, divisible by 3.

So, number is divisible by 24.

In number 35751

Last 3 digits of number is not a multiple of 8.

So, the number is not divisible by 24.

Hence, option (a) is the correct answer.

213. (a) Factor of 12 = 4×3

Divisibility rule of 4-A number divisible by 4 if its last two digit is divisible by 4.

Divisiblity rule of 3 - A number divisible by 3 if its digits sum is divisible by 3.

Given number = 3 * 7440

It's last two digit is completely divisible by $4 = \frac{40}{4} = 10$

To check divisibility by 3

$$= 3 + * + 7 + 4 + 4 + 0 = 18 + *$$

18 is completely divisible by 3 then least possible given options only value of * is 0.

Hence, the least value of * is 0 .

214. (b) 55) 1000 (18

```
55
450
440
 10
```

Remainder = 10

Number = 1000 + (55 – 10) = 1000 + 45

$$= 1045$$

$$\frac{1045}{55} = 19$$

Hence, smallest number = 45

215. (d) Let quotient be a.

$\therefore \quad n = 7a + 2$

[$\because$ Dividend = Divisor $\times$ Quotient + Remainder]

$\Rightarrow \quad 9n = 9 \times 7a + 9 \times 2$

$$= 9 \times 7a + 18$$

$\Rightarrow \quad 9n = 9 \times 7a + 14 + 4$

$\Rightarrow \quad 9n = 7(9a + 2) + 4$

$\therefore$ When $9n$ is divided by 7, then remainder is 4.

216. (d) $\frac{3^8}{7} = \frac{3^6 \cdot 3^2}{7}$

$$= \frac{3^2}{7}$$

$\left[\because \frac{a^{p-1}}{p} = 1 \text{ (remainder)} \quad \text{when}, a, p \text{ are co-prime}\right]$

$$= \frac{9}{7} = 2 \text{ (remainder)}$$

217. (d) According to the question,

Divisor = $5 \times$ Remainder = $5 \times 44 = 220$

Then, quotient = $\frac{\text{divisor}}{11} = \frac{220}{11} = 20$

$\therefore$ Dividend = Divisor $\times$ Quotient + Remainder

$$= 220 \times 20 + 44$$

$$= 4400 + 44 = 4444$$

218. (b) Apply divisibility rule of 11 on options.

Taking option (b) i.e,

$752563 = (7 + 2 + 6) - (5 + 5 + 3)$

$$= 15 - 13 = 2$$

Whereas, as per divisibility it should be either 0 or 11.

219. (c) All two digit numbers which are divisible by 9, are

18, 27, 36 .... 90, 99

Here, 27 – 18 = 36 – 27 = ... = 9

∴ It is an AP.

$a = 18, d = 9, a_n = 99$

Let number of terms be n.

∵ $a_n = a + (n-1)d$

∴ $99 = 18 + (n-1)9$

⇒ $81 = (n-1)9$

⇒ $9 = n - 1 \Rightarrow n = 10$

∵ $S_n = \frac{n}{2}\{2a + (n-1)d\}$

$S_n = \frac{10}{2}[2(18) + (10-1)(9)]$

$= 5[36 + 81] = 5(117) = 585$

220. (a) For Statement I,

$\frac{5}{11} = 0.45;\ \frac{5}{6} = 0.83$

Then, $\frac{5}{11} < \frac{5}{6}$

So, Statement I is wrong.

For Statement II,

$\frac{5}{9} = 0.55;\ \frac{8}{9} = 0.88$

Then, $\frac{8}{9} > \frac{5}{9}$

So, Statement II is wrong.

For Statement III,

$\frac{5}{6} = 0.83;\ \frac{4}{5} = 0.8$

Then, $\frac{5}{6} > \frac{4}{5}$

So, Statement III is true.

Hence, option (a) is correct.

221. (c) The three digit numbers divisible by 20 are 100, 120, 140, ..., 980.

Here, $a = 100, d = 20, a_n = 980$

∴ $a_n = a + (n-1)d$

$\Rightarrow 980 = 100 + (n-1) \times 20 \Rightarrow \frac{880}{20} = (n-1)$

⇒ $n = 45$

∴ $S_n = \frac{n}{2}[a + a_n] = \frac{45}{2}[100 + 980]$

$= \frac{45}{2}[1080] = 24300$

222. (a) Using divisibility rule of 11, we get

Sum of the digits in odd places = 6 + 6 = 12

And sum of digits in even places = $m + 1$

Now, $12 - (m + 1) = 11 (0 \le m \le 9)$

⇒ $12 - m - 1 = 11$

⇒ $11 - m = 11 \Rightarrow m = 11 - 11 = 0$

∴ Required value of m is 0.

223. (d) Number divisible by '10' between '501' and '701'.

510, 520, 530, ..., 700

It is an AP.

Here, $l = 700, d = 10, a = 510$

∴ $l = a + (n-1)d$

⇒ $700 = 510 + (n-1)10$

⇒ $(n-1)10 = 190$

⇒ $n - 1 = 19 \Rightarrow n = 20$

Number divisible by 10 and 3 between '501' and '701'.

510, 540, 570, ..., 690

It is an AP.

Here, $l = 690, a = 510, d = 30$

∴ $l = a + (n-1)d$

⇒ $690 = 510 + (n-1)30$

$\Rightarrow (n-1)30 = 180 \Rightarrow n - 1 = 6 \Rightarrow n = 7$

Number divisible by only 10 not by 3 = Number divisible by 10 – Number divisible by 10 and 3 = 20 – 7 = 13

224. (d) $\frac{6}{5}, \frac{11}{15}, \frac{4}{7}, \frac{5}{13}$

↓ ↓ ↓ ↓

1.2, 0.73, 0.57, 0.38

Largest fraction $= \frac{6}{5}$

And smallest fraction $= \frac{5}{13}$

∴ Sum of largest and smallest fraction

$= \frac{6}{5} + \frac{5}{13} = \frac{78 + 25}{65} = \frac{103}{65}$

225. (c) Composite number between 23 and 43 are 24, 25, 26, 27, 28, 30, 32, 33, 34, 35, 36, 38, 39, 40, 42

So, total composite numbers = 15

226. (d) Prime number between 20 and 50 are 23, 29, 31, 37, 41, 43, 47.

Hence, there are 7 prime numbers between 20 and 50.

227. (b) Largest six-digit number = 999999

```
81)999999(12345
   81
   189
   162
    279
    243
     369
     324
      459
      405
       54 = Remainder
```

Required largest six-digit number exactly divisible by 81 = 999999 – 54 = 999945

228. (b) Numbers between 100 to 1000 which are divisible by 17

102, 119, ..., 986

Here, $a = 102, d = 17, l = 986$

Let the number of terms in this series be n.

∴ $l = a + (n-1)d$

⇒ $986 = 102 + (n-1)(17)$

⇒ $884 = (n-1) \times 17$

⇒ $52 = n - 1 \Rightarrow n = 52 + 1 = 53$

229. (a)

```
8)8127(1015
  8
   12
    8
    47
    40
     7 = Remainder
```

∴ Required remainder = 7

Speedy Method

According to divisibility rule of 8 "last three digit should be divisible by 8"

$\frac{127}{8}$ = remainder is 7.

230. (d) Let the two numbers are x and y.

Given, $x = 44m + 11$ $[m = 0, 1, 2, 3, ...]$

$y = 44n + 38$ $[n = 0, 1, 2, 3 ...]$

Now, $x + y = 44m + 11 + 44n + 38$

$= 44(m + n) + 49$

Hence, $44(m + n)$ is completely divisible by 44.

So, required remainder = Remainder of (49 ÷ 44) = 5

231. (c) Out of the given options only 185592 is divisible by 33 because it is divisible by both 3 and 11.

232. (d) Given, number 8475639AB is divisible by 99, then it also divisible by 9 and 11.

A number is divisible by 9, if the sum of the digit of that number is divisible by 9.

Now, $8 + 4 + 7 + 5 + 6 + 3 + 9 + A + B$

$= 42 + A + B$

Here, the possible value of $A + B$ = 3 and 12

Now, a number is divisible by 11 if the difference of the sum of the even and odd places digits is equal to zero or the multiple of 11.

Then, $(8 + 7 + 6 + 9 + B) - (4 + 5 + 3 + A)$

$= 30 + B - 12 - A = 18 + B - A$

Here, the possible value of $B - A = 4$.

So, the value of $A + B$ can not be equal to 3.

Hence, $A = 4, B = 8$

233. (a) For divisibility by 3, sum of digits must be divisible by 3,

∴ $2 + 3 + k + 5 + 6 + 7 + k = 23 + 2k$

Since, $(23 + 2k)$ is divisible by 3

∴ $23 + 2k = 27$

⇒ $27 - 23 = 2k$

⇒ $2k = 4 \Rightarrow k = 2$

∴ Possible value of $k = 2$

Next possible values of k = 5, 8.

∴ Now sum of all possible values of

$k = 2 + 5 + 8 = 15.$

234. (c) Here, Dividend = 12401,

Quotient = 76 and remainder = 13

We know that,

Dividend = Divisor × Quotient + Remainder

$\Rightarrow$ Divisor $= \dfrac{\text{Dividend} - \text{Remainder}}{\text{Quotient}}$

$= \dfrac{12401 - 13}{76} = 163$

235. (b) Let $M = 7k + 6$

$\therefore \quad M^2 = (7k + 6)^2 = (49k^2 + 36 + 84k)$

$= [7(7k^2 + 12k) + 7 \times 5] + 1$

If it is divided by 7, the remainder will be 1.

> **Speedy Method**
>
> $\text{Rem}\left(\frac{6}{7}\right) = 6 \Rightarrow \text{Rem}\ \frac{(6)^2}{7} = \frac{36}{7} = 1$

236. (c) We know, if the difference between the sum of the digits at the odd and even places equal 0 or divisible by 11, then the number is divisible by 11.

Given number = A9257B684

Difference $= (A + 2 + 7 + 6 + 4) - (9 + 5 + B + 8)$

$= A + 19 - B - 22 = A - B - 3$

Now, $A - B - 3 = -11$ or 11.

$\therefore \quad A - B - 3 = -11 \Rightarrow A - B = -8$

or $\quad A - B - 3 = 0 \Rightarrow A - B = 3$

and $\quad A - B - 3 = 11 \Rightarrow A - B = 14$

(which is not possible)

$\therefore$ Least value of $A - B = -8$

237. (a) We have, $\dfrac{374}{418} = \dfrac{34}{38} = \dfrac{17}{19}$

238. (b) A number is said to be divisible by 4, if the number formed by its last two digits is divisible by 4.

$\therefore$ 4348 is divisible by 4 because it's last two digits 48 is divisible by 4.

239. (d) When the last three digits of any number is divisible by 8. then, the whole number is also divisible by 8.

So, the option (d), the number is that 6044.

By rule of 8, $\dfrac{044}{8} = \dfrac{44}{8} = 5.5$

(not completely divided)

So, the following number 6044 is not divisible by 8.

240. (a) According to the question,

2 digit numbers divisible by 8 are 16, 24, 32, ..., 96 respectively.

This is AP series

$a = 16, d = 8$ and $a_n = 96$,

So, $\quad a_n = a + (n - 1)d$

$\Rightarrow \quad 96 = 16 + (n - 1)8$

$\Rightarrow \quad 80 = (n - 1)8$

$\Rightarrow \quad 10 = n - 1$

$\therefore \quad n = 11$

So, 11 two digit numbers are there which are divisible by 8.

241. (a) From the divisibility rule of 9

By option (a), the number 4131.

Sum of digits = 4 + 1 + 3 + 1 = 9

Which is divisible by 9.

242. (a) We know that, if the sum of digits of a number is divisible by 9, then the number is also divisible by 9.

Sum of the digits of 58524 M

$= 5 + 8 + 5 + 2 + 4 + M = 24 + M$

($\therefore$ least value of $M = 3$ for the number divisible by 9.)

243. (d) If the sum of the digits is multiple of 9 then, the number is divisible by 9.

From option (d), 3658 = 3 + 6 + 5 + 8 = 22 and 22 is not divisible by 9.

244. (c) When $(58)^{29}$ is divided by 5, then remainder,

$R\left[\dfrac{(58)^{29}}{5}\right] = R\left[\dfrac{((58)^4)^7 \cdot 58}{5}\right]$

$\left[\because \dfrac{a^{P-1}}{P} = 1 \text{ where } a \text{ and } p \text{ are co-prime}\right]$

$= R\left[\dfrac{((3)^4)^7 \cdot 58}{5}\right]$

$= R\left[\dfrac{(1)^7 \cdot 58}{5}\right] = R\left[\dfrac{3}{5}\right] = \boxed{3}$

245. (b) Using divisibility rule of 11 and taking option (b), we get

$6589 = (6 + 8) - (5 + 9) = 0$

$\therefore$ 6589 is divisible by 11.

246. (b) Divisibility rule of 11 If the difference between the sum of the digits at an even place and the sum of the digits at an odd place is divisible by 11 or 0, then the number is divisible by 11.

From option (b), the number : 2763

$(7 + 3) - (2 + 6) = 2 \neq 0$

$\therefore$ 2763 is not divisible by 11.

247. (a) We know, if a number having 5 as its unit digit and the number is divided by 10 then remainder will always be 5.

$\therefore \quad \dfrac{(35)^{29}}{10} = 5$ (Remainder)

248. (a) According to the question,

Option (b) 10 Let $a = 7$ and $b = 3$

$\Rightarrow \quad 7 + 3 = 10$

Option (c) 28

Let $a = 23$ and $b = 5$

$\Rightarrow \quad 23 + 5 = 28$

Option (d) 14

Let $a = 11$ and $b = 3$

$\Rightarrow 11 + 3 = 14$

Hence, only 6 cannot be the sum of 'a' and 'b'.

249. (d) Divisibility rule of 9 $\rightarrow$ When the sum of all the digits of a number is divisible by 9, then the number is said to be divisible by 9.

Now, sum of digits $= 7 + 2 + 5 + x + 3$

$= 17 + x$

Put $x = 1$, then

$\Rightarrow 17 + 1 = 18$ is completely divided by 9.

$\therefore$ So, the least value of x is 1.

250. (a) Greatest 3-digit number divisible by 12, 25, 18 = 900

Smallest 4-digit number divisible by 12, 25, 18 = 1800

$\therefore$ Absolute difference = Smallest 4-digit number − Greatest 3-digit number

$= 1800 - 900 = 900.$

251. (d) By divisibility of 11.

(i) 2 9 4 3 5 4 1 7

$\left.\begin{array}{l} 2 + 4 + 5 + 1 = 12 \\ 9 + 3 + 4 + 7 = 23 \end{array}\right\rangle 23 - 12 = 11,$

It is divisible by 11.

(iii) 5 7 4 6 3 8 2 4

$\left.\begin{array}{l} 5 + 4 + 3 + 2 = 14 \\ 7 + 6 + 8 + 4 = 25 \end{array}\right\rangle 25 - 14 = 11,$

It is divisible by 11.

252. (a) Number = $34PQ$

Since, $34PQ$ is divisible by 3, 5 and 7.

Hence, it will be also divisible by 105.

(LCM of 3, 5 and 7)

$\therefore \quad \dfrac{3499}{105} = 33\dfrac{34}{105}$

Hence, if we substract 34 from 3499. It will be divisible by 105.

$34PQ = 3499 - 34 = 3465$

The value of $P + Q = 6 + 5 = 11$

253. (a) Given, number = $389x6378y$

$\therefore$ This number will be divisible by 9 and 8.

$\therefore$ This number is divisible by 72.

For divisible by 8, $78y$ will be divisible by 8.

$\therefore \quad y = 4 \quad (\because 784$ is divisible by 8)

For divisible by 9,

Sum of digits

$= 3 + 8 + 9 + x + 6 + 3 + 7 + 8 + y$, will be divisible by 9

$= 44 + x + 4$, will be divisible by 9.

$(\because y = 4)$

$= 48 + x$, will be divisible by 9.

$\therefore \quad x = 6$

Now, $6x + 7y = 6(6) + 7(4) = 36 + 28 = 64$

254. (a) From option (a), number = 553986

Divisibility of 9,

Sum of digits = 5 + 5 + 3 + 9 + 8 + 6

= 36, is divisible by 9.

So, the number 553986 is divisible by 9.

255. (c) Given, remainder = 39

Divisor $= 6 \times 39$

Quotient $= \dfrac{6 \times 39}{13} = 6 \times 3$

$\therefore$ Dividend = Divisor × Quotient + Remainder

$= 6 \times 39 \times 6 \times 3 + 39 = 4212 + 39 = 4251$

256. (d) Let six digits number = x

We know that,

Dividend = Divisor × Quotient + Remainder

$x = 33 \times q + 0 \Rightarrow x = 33q$

If 21 is added to the number, then

New number = $33q + 21 = 3(11q + 7)$

Hence, we can clearly say that the new number is divisible by 3.

257. (a) Given number = 7864K3

After checking all option, we put $K = 4$

Then, number = 786443

Now, $\frac{786443}{7} = 112349$

Number is divisible by 7.

$\therefore$ The value of $K = 4$

258. (d) Total amount raised by Ram in 30 weeks $= \frac{2170}{46.5} \times 30 =$ ₹ 1400

259. (b) $(11^7 + 9) \div 10$

According to the question,

Remainder when $\frac{11}{10} = 1$

$\therefore \frac{((1)^7 + 9)}{10} = \frac{10}{10}$

$\therefore$ Remainder = 0

260. (b) From option (b), number = 56783294

Divisibility of 4 $= \frac{94}{4}$ (Remainder $\neq 0$)

Hence, 56783294 is not divisible by 4.

261. (d) Let divisor be x.

$\therefore$ Dividend = Quotient × Divisor + Remainder

$\Rightarrow 18935 = x \times 102 + 65$

$\Rightarrow x = \frac{18870}{102} = 185$

262. (c) If the number is not divisible by 72, then it is also not divisible by 9 and 8 both.

From option (3), Number = 486280

There are sum of digits of number

$= 4 + 8 + 6 + 2 + 8 + 0 = 28$, it is not divisible by 9

The number formed by last three digits = 280, it is divisible by 8.

Hence, the number 486280 is not divisible by 72.

263. (c) Sum of two numbers

$= 10373 + 24871 = 35244$

Sum of digits of the number

$= 3 + 5 + 2 + 4 + 4$

$= 18$, it is divisible by 3.

$\therefore$ The number is divisible by 3.

The last digit of the number is 4 (even)

$\therefore$ The number is divisible by 2.

Hence, the number is divisible by 6.

264. (b) Arithmetic mean of x and $y = \frac{x + y}{2}$

$\Rightarrow 8 = \frac{x + y}{2}$

$\Rightarrow x + y = 16$ ... (i)

Geometric mean of x and $y = \sqrt{xy}$

$\Rightarrow 3\sqrt{7} = \sqrt{xy}$

$\Rightarrow xy = 63$ ... (ii)

$\because x - y = \sqrt{(x + y)^2 - 4xy}$

$= \sqrt{256 - 252} = \sqrt{4}$

$\therefore x - y = 2$ ...(iii)

From Eqs. (i) and (iii), we get

$x = 9, y = 7$

Now, $x^3 + y^3 = (9)^3 + (7)^3$

$= 729 + 343 = 1072$

265. (c) Co-prime numbers are the numbers which do not have any common factor other than 1.

From option (c), $22 = 2 \times 11$

and $24 = 2 \times 2 \times 2 \times 3$

Here, 2 is the common factor of these numbers

$\therefore$ 22, 24 is not pair of co-prime numbers

266. (c) According to the question,

Let number be x.

Dividend = Divisor × Quotient + Remainder

$x = 49q + 9 = 49q + 7 + 2$

$x = 7(7q + 1) + 2$

Therefore, when the number 'x' is divided by '7' then remainder will be '2'.

Speedy Method

Required remainder

$= \text{Remainder of} \left(\frac{\text{First remainder}}{\text{New divisor}}\right)$

$= \text{Remainder of} \left(\frac{9}{7}\right) = 2$

267. (a) New number $= 58828 + (5 + 2 \times 11)$

$= 58828 + 5 + 22 = 58855$

We know that a number is divisible by 5. When last digit of the number is either 0 or 5.

268. (d) Given, number = 5702718

Rearrange number = 8775210

Resultant number $= 8775210 - (4 + 3 \times 17)$

$= 8775210 - 55 = 8775155$

$\because$ Last digit of resultant number is 5.

$\therefore$ Resultant number will be divisible by 5.

02

HCF and LCM

Highest Common Factor (HCF)

HCF of two or more numbers is the greatest number which divides each of them exactly. e.g. HCF of 12, 18 and 24 is 6.

Least Common Multiple (LCM)

The LCM of two or more numbers is the least number which is exactly divisible by each of them. e.g. LCM of 4, 6 and 12 = 12

LCM and HCF of Fraction

(i) LCM of fractions $= \dfrac{\text{LCM of numerator}}{\text{HCF of denominator}}$

(ii) HCF of fractions $= \dfrac{\text{HCF of numerator}}{\text{LCM of denominator}}$

e.g. LCM of $\dfrac{1}{22}$ and $\dfrac{1}{16} = \dfrac{\text{LCM of 1 and 1}}{\text{HCF of 22 and 16}} = \dfrac{1}{2}$

Relation Between Two Numbers and Their HCF and LCM

Product of two numbers = HCF × LCM

i.e. If two numbers are a and b, then $a \times b = \text{HCF}(a,b) \times \text{LCM}(a,b)$

Word Problems Based on HCF and LCM

- The greatest number that will divides x, y and z, leaving remainder k in each case, is given by $= \text{HCF}\,[(x-k),(y-k),(z-k)]$
- The greatest number which divides the number x, y and z, leaving remainders a, b and c, respectively, is given by

$$= \text{HCF}\,[(x-a),(y-b),(z-c)]$$

Ex. 1 Find the greatest number which divides 1657 and 2037 leaving remainders 6 and 5, respectively .

Sol. Here, $x = 1657$, $y = 2037$ and $a = 6$, $b = 5$

Required number = HCF of $\{(x-a),(y-b)\}$

$= \text{HCF of } \{(1657-6),(2037-5)\} = \text{HCF of } (1651, 2032)$

Now, using prime factorisation method,

$1651 = 13 \times 127;\ 2032 = 2 \times 2 \times 2 \times 2 \times 127 = 2^4 \times 127$

$\therefore$ HCF of (1651, 2032) = 127

Hence, required number = 127

- The greatest number that will divides x, y, z .... leaving the same remainder in each case, is given by

$$= \text{HCF}(|x-y|,|y-z|,|z-x|,\ldots)$$

- The least number which when divided by x, y and z, leaves the same remainder k in each case, is given by $= [\text{LCM}(x,y,z) + k]$
- The least number which when divided by x, y and z, leaves the remainders a, b and c, respectively, is given by $= [\text{LCM}(x,y,z)] - k$ where, $k = (x-a) = (y-b) = (z-c)$
- The greatest n-digit number is completely divisible by x, y, z.

$$= N - \text{Remainder obtained from } \frac{N}{\text{LCM of } x, y, z}$$

[where, N = greatest n-digit number]

Ex. 2 Find the greatest four digit number which is completely divisible by 17 and 36.

Sol. LCM of 17 and 36 = 612

$\therefore$ Required number = 9999 − Remainder of $\dfrac{9999}{612}$

$= 9999 - 207 = 9792$

- The smallest n-digit number which is completely divisibly by x, y, z

$$= N + L - \text{Remainder obtained from } \frac{N}{L}$$

[where, N = Smallest n-digit number and L = LCM of x, y, z]

Ex. 3 What is the smallest five digits number which is completely divisible by 9, 12, 15, 25 and 27.

Sol. LCM of 9, 12, 15, 25, 27 = 2700

Required number $= 10000 + 2700 - \text{Remainder}\left(\dfrac{10000}{2700}\right)$

$R = 10000 - 8100 = 1900$

$\therefore$ Required number $= 10000 + 2700 - 1900 = 10800$

SSC Exam Scanner

SSC CGL 2024-2020 (Tier I & II)

1. The LCM of $2^3 \times 9^2 \times 13$, $2^2 \times 13^2 \times 19$ and $9^3 \times 13^2 \times 19^2$ is
SSC CGL (Tier-II) 20/01/2025 Shift-I
(a) $2^3 \times 9^2 \times 13^2 \times 19$
(b) $2^3 \times 9^3 \times 13^2 \times 19^2$
(c) $2^2 \times 9^2 \times 13^2 \times 19^3$
(d) $2^2 \times 9^3 \times 13 \times 19^2$

2. The largest three-digit number that gives the same remainder 2 when divided by 3, 5 and 9 is ....
SSC CGL (Tier-II) 07/03/2023
(a) 999 (b) 998
(c) 992 (d) 984

3. The product of the two numbers is 1500 and their HCF is 10. The number of such possible pairs is/are **SSC CGL (Tier-II) 2/03/2023**
(a) 1 (b) 3 (c) 4 (d) 2

4. Find the least number divisible by 2, 3, 5, 6, 9 and 18 which is a perfect square.
SSC CGL (Tier-I) 24/07/2023 Shift II
(a) 900 (b) 400 (c) 144 (d) 3600

5. The ratio of two numbers is 6 : 7 and their HCF is 3. Their LCM is .... **SSC CGL (Tier-I) 13/12/2022 Shift IV**
(a) 124 (b) 128
(c) 122 (d) 126

6. The HCF of three numbers 72, 108 and 2010 is
SSC CGL (Tier-I) 13/12/2022 Shift III
(a) 18 (b) 6 (c) 12 (d) 5

7. The HCF of two numbers is 17 and the other two factors of their LCM are 11 and 19. The smaller of the two numbers is **SSC CGL (Tier-I) 13/12/2022 Shift II**
(a) 187 (b) 209
(c) 323 (d) 306

8. Determine the LCM of two numbers if their HCF is 9 and their ratio is 14 : 19.
SSC CGL (Tier-I) 13/12/2022 Shift I
(a) 2394 (b) 3990
(c) 1596 (d) 3192

9. Find the HCF of 60, 148 and 382.
SSC CGL (Tier-I) 12/12/2022 Shift IV
(a) 2 (b) 6 (c) 4 (d) 24

10. The HCF of three numbers 98, 175 and 210 will be
SSC CGL (Tier-I) 12/12/2022 Shift III
(a) 6 (b) 3 (c) 5 (d) 7

11. The LCM of 1.2 and 2.7 is
SSC CGL (Tier-I) 12/12/2022 Shift II
(a) 5.4 (b) 10.8 (c) 1.08 (d) 32.4

12. The least number that should be added to 35460, so that the sum is exactly divisible by 3, 4, 5 and 7 is
SSC CGL (Tier-I) 12/12/2022 Shift I
(a) 84 (b) 420 (c) 240 (d) 180

13. The HCF of two numbers is 21 and their LCM is 840. If one of the numbers is 49, then the other number is **SSC CGL (Tier-I) 12/12/2022 Shift I**
(a) 650 (b) 540
(c) 810 (d) 360

14. The LCM of $\frac{3}{8}, \frac{5}{16}$ and $\frac{7}{2}$ is
SSC CGL (Tier-I) 09.12.2022 Shift IV
(a) $101\frac{1}{2}$ (b) $52\frac{1}{2}$
(c) $28\frac{1}{2}$ (d) $25\frac{1}{4}$

15. The HCF of $\frac{1}{2}, \frac{3}{4}, \frac{5}{6}$ and $\frac{7}{8}$ is
SSC CGL (Tier-I) 09/12/2022 Shift III
(a) $\frac{105}{2}$ (b) $\frac{1}{24}$ (c) $\frac{7}{24}$ (d) $\frac{1}{48}$

16. The LCM of 144,360 and 450 is
SSC CGL (Tier-I) 09.12.2022 Shift II
(a) 4800 (b) 3600
(c) 7200 (d) 2400

17. The LCM of 96, 136 and 504 is
SSC CGL (Tier-I) 09/12/2022 Shift I
(a) 34272 (b) 36548
(c) 25872 (d) 28564

18. Find the HCF of 4.08 and 6.63.
SSC CGL (Tier-I) 08/12/2022 Shift III
(a) 0.50 (b) 0.52
(c) 0.51 (d) 0.53

19. The HCF of 222, 642 and 1062 is .... **SSC CGL (Tier-I) 08/12/2022 Shift II**
(a) 6 (b) 8
(c) 4 (d) 2

20. The HCF of three numbers 105, 335 and 465 will be
SSC CGL (Tier-I) 08/12/2022 Shift I
(a) 11 (b) 5
(c) 7 (d) 3

21. If the HCF of two numbers is 8, then which of the following can never be their LCM?
SSC CGL (Tier-I) 07/12/2022 Shift IV
(a) 56 (b) 48
(c) 42 (d) 40

22. Find the LCM of 186.6 and 373.2 .
SSC CGL (Tier-I) 07/12/2022 Shift III
(a) 373.2 (b) 398.2
(c) 186.6 (d) 276.6

23. Find the least number exactly divisible by 9, 24 and 36.
SSC CGL (Tier-I) 07/12/2022 Shift II
(a) 72 (b) 36 (c) 24 (d) 9

24. The sum of two numbers is 18 and their HCF and LCM are 3 and 54, respectively. What will be the sum of their reciprocals?
SSC CGL (Tier-I) 06/12/2022 Shift IV
(a) $\frac{1}{7}$ (b) $\frac{1}{11}$ (c) $\frac{1}{6}$ (d) $\frac{1}{9}$

25. What is the smallest perfect square which is completely divisible by each of 16, 18 and 36?
SSC CGL (Tier-I) 06/12/2022 Shift III
(a) 144 (b) 81
(c) 196 (d) 169

26. Choose the correct statement from the following.
SSC CGL (Tier-I) 06/12/2022 Shift II
(a) HCF is the least common multiple of the given numbers
(b) HCF of two or more numbers is the highest number which perfectly divides all the given numbers
(c) HCF is also called the least common divisor.
(d) In prime factorisation method of HCF, the multiples of all the given numbers are listed

27. Find the greatest number that will divide 49, 147 and 322 to leave the same remainder in each case.
SSC CGL (Tier-I) 06/12/2022 Shift I
(a) 9 (b) 5
(c) 7 (d) 8

28. The LCM of the two numbers is 4104 and the HCF is 9. If one of the numbers is 171, find the other.
SSC CGL (Tier-I) 05/12/2022 Shift IV
(a) 218 (b) 215
(c) 220 (d) 216

29. The HCF of two numbers 110 and 1980 is **SSC CGL (Tier-I) 05/12/2022 Shift I**
(a) 180 (b) 110
(c) 140 (d) 120

30. Find the largest number of 3 digits divisible by 4 and 7.
SSC CGL (Tier-I) 03/12/2022 Shift IV
(a) 960 (b) 980
(c) 990 (d) 970

31. The LCM of two numbers is 120 and the numbers are in the ratio 3 : 8. The sum of the numbers will be
SSC CGL (Tier-I) 03/12/2022 Shift III
(a) 48 (b) 55 (c) 45 (d) 60

32. What is the HCF of 36 and 198?
SSC CGL (Tier-I) 03/12/2022 Shift II
(a) 36 (b) 22 (c) 18 (d) 9

33. Calculate the HCF of $\frac{12}{5}, \frac{14}{15}$ and $\frac{16}{17}$.
SSC CGL (Tier-I) 03/12/2022 Shift I
(a) $\frac{4}{255}$ (b) $\frac{3}{255}$ (c) $\frac{2}{255}$ (d) $\frac{1}{255}$

34. Three numbers are in the ratio of 2 : 3 : 5 and their LCM is 90. Find their HCF. SSC CGL (Tier-I) 02/12/2022 Shift IV
(a) 9 (b) 1
(c) 6 (d) 3

35. The HCF of two numbers 2040 and 391 is SSC CGL (Tier-I) 02/12/2022 Shift III
(a) 17 (b) 21
(c) 16 (d) 18

36. What will be the least number which when doubled will be exactly divisible by 15, 18, 25 and 32 ? SSC CGL (Tier-I) 02/12/2022 Shift II
(a) 3600 (b) 7200
(c) 6400 (d) 3200

37. What is the largest common divisor of the numbers 1026, 2268 and 2430?
SSC CGL (Tier-I) 02/12/2022 Shift I
(a) 108 (b) 54 (c) 81 (d) 27

38. The ratio of two numbers is 5 : 4 and their HCF is 4. What is their LCM? SSC CGL (Tier-I) 01/12/2022 Shift IV
(a) 80 (b) 48 (c) 36 (d) 60

39. Two numbers are in the ratio of 6 : 5. If their HCF is 3, then what is the LCM of the two numbers?
SSC CGL (Tier-I) 01/12/2022 Shift III
(a) 64 (b) 110
(c) 90 (d) 80

40. What is the ratio between the HCF and LCM of the numbers whose LCM is 48 and the product of the numbers is 384?
SSC CGL (Tier-I) 01/12/2022 Shift II
(a) 1 : 4 (b) 1 : 6
(c) 1 : 3 (d) 2 : 5

41. The HCF of two numbers is 12. Which one of the following can never be their LCM?
SSC CGL (Tier-I) 01/12/2022 Shift I
(a) 72 (b) 60
(c) 90 (d) 84

42. What is the sum of the digits of the largest five digit number which is divisible by 5, 35, 39 and 65?
SSC CGL (Tier-I) 20/08/2021 Shift II
(a) 30 (b) 33
(c) 27 (d) 35

43. What is the smallest integer, that is divisible by 3, 7 and 18?
SSC CGL (Tier-I) 06/03/2020 Shift III
(a) 72 (b) 252
(c) 63 (d) 126

SSC CPO SI 2023-2020

44. Find the HCF of 125, 250 and 750.
SSC CPO 05/10/2023 Shift III
(a) 50 (b) 25 (c) 125 (d) 75

45. The LCM of two numbers is five times their HCF. If the product of the two numbers is 20480, then find their HCF and LCM, respectively.
SSC CPO 05/10/2023 Shift III
(a) 46 and 230 (b) 48 and 240
(c) 64 and 320 (d) 56 and 280

46. The least number of five digits which is exactly divisible by 9, 12, 15, 25 and 27 is
SSC CPO 05/10/2023 Shift III
(a) 10800 (b) 10250
(c) 10700 (d) 10600

47. The HCF and LCM of two numbers are 9 and 126, respectively. Find the larger number, if the ratio between the numbers is 2 : 7.
SSC CPO 05/01/2023 Shift III
(a) 42 (b) 63
(c) 77 (d) 21

48. Which of the following is the greatest four-digit number that is divisible by 15, 25, 40, and 75?
SSC CPO 05/10/2023 Shift III
(a) 9200 (b) 9500
(c) 9600 (d) 9000

49. The LCM of 8, 12 and 18 is
SSC CPO 05/10/2023 Shift III
(a) 24 (b) 80 (c) 72 (d) 36

50. If the sum of two numbers is 60 and their HCF and LCM are 5 and 60, respectively, then the sum of the reciprocals of the numbers will be
SSC CPO 05/10/2023 Shift III
(a) $\frac{1}{11}$ (b) $\frac{1}{6}$ (c) $\frac{1}{4}$ (d) $\frac{1}{5}$

51. Find the HCF of 240, 280 and 560.
SSC CPO 04/10/2023 Shift II
(a) 30 (b) 10
(c) 20 (d) 40

52. The HCF of 3888 and 3969 is
SSC CPO 04/10/2023 Shift II
(a) 81 (b) 73
(c) 83 (d) 71

53. The LCM and HCF of two numbers are 1105 and 5. If the LCM is 17 times the first number, then find the two numbers.
SSC CPO 04/10/2023 Shift II
(a) 65 and 85 (b) 55 and 85
(c) 65 and 75 (d) 60 and 80

54. A person has three iron bars whose lengths are 20 m, 30 m and 40 m, respectively. He wants to cut pieces of the same length from each of the three bars. What is the least number of total pieces if he cuts without any wastage ?
SSC CPO 04/10/2023 Shift II
(a) 8 (b) 10 (c) 9 (d) 11

55. Which is the smallest natural number that is exactly divisible by each of 96, 108 and 144?
SSC CPO 04/10/2023 Shift II
(a) 864 (b) 2592
(c) 1296 (d) 1728

56. The LCM of two numbers is 660 and their HCF is 5. If one of the numbers is 55, find the other.
SSC CPO 04/10/2023 Shift II
(a) 275 (b) 12 (c) 110 (d) 60

57. The HCF and the LCM of two numbers are 5 and 175, respectively. If the ratio of the two numbers is 5 : 7, the larger of the two numbers is SSC CPO 03/10/2023 Shift I
(a) 35 (b) 25
(c) 45 (d) 75

58. Two numbers are in the ratio 3 : 4. The product of their HCF and LCM is 2700. The sum of the numbers is
SSC CPO 03/10/2023 Shift I
(a) 60 (b) 105
(c) 15 (d) 45

59. Find the LCM of 15, 24, 35 and 54.
SSC CPO 03/10/2023 Shift I
(a) 5670 (b) 7560
(c) 7650 (d) 6570

60. The product of two numbers is 726 and their HCF is 11, then their LCM is SSC CPO 03/10/2023 Shift I
(a) 58 (b) 68
(c) 66 (d) 76

61. Find the HCF of 69, 96 and 99.
SSC CPO 11/11/2022
(a) 3 (b) 9
(c) 1 (d) 6

62. Find the LCM of 28 and 92. SSC CPO 11/11/2022
(a) 464 (b) 644
(c) 161 (d) 322

63. The sides of a triangular field are 62 m, 186 m and 279 m. Find the greatest length of tape that would be able to exactly measure each of them without any fractions. SSC CPO 10/11/2022
(a) 62 m (b) 93 m
(c) 31 m (d) 30 m

64. The HCF and LCM of two numbers are 126 and 9, respectively. If one of the number is 18, then what is the other number ? SSC CPO 10/11/2022
(a) 63 (b) 36
(c) 84 (d) 24

65. The least common multiple of 48 and 64 is ...... times the highest common factor of 12 and 18. SSC CPO 10/11/2022
(a) 28 (b) 32 (c) 24 (d) 16

66. Find the HCF of 238 and 832. SSC CPO 10/11/2022
(a) 16 (b) 8 (c) 2 (d) 14

67. The HCF of two numbers is 29 and the other two factors of their LCM are 15 and 13. The smaller of the two numbers is SSC CPO 25/11/2020 Shift II
(a) 377 (b) 406
(c) 435 (d) 464

68. How many numbers between 300 and 700 are divisible by 5, 6 and 8? SSC CPO 25/11/2020 Shift II
(a) 3 (b) 2 (c) 5 (d) 20

69. What is the sum of the digits of the least number which when divided by 15, 18 and 36 leaves the same remainder 9, in each case and is divisible by 11? SSC CPO 25/11/2020 Shift II
(a) 15 (b) 16
(c) 18 (d) 17

70. Two numbers are in the ratio 7 : 11. If their HCF is 28, then the sum of the two numbers is SSC CPO 25/11/2020 Shift II
(a) 504 (b) 196
(c) 308 (d) 112

71. Five bells ring together at the intervals of 3, 5, 8, 9 and 10 sec. All the bells ring simultaneously at the same time. They will again ring simultaneously after SSC CPO 25/11/2020 Shift II
(a) 6 min (b) 8 min
(c) 9 min (d) 4 min

72. The least number which is exactly divisible by 4, 5, 8, 10 and 12 is SSC CPO 24/11/2020 Shift I
(a) 150 (b) 120
(c) 180 (d) 240

73. Two numbers are in the ratio 7 : 11. If their HCF is 28, then the difference between the two numbers is SSC CPO 23/11/2020 Shift I
(a) 28 (b) 308
(c) 112 (d) 196

SSC CHSL 2024 (Tier I & II)

74. Three numbers are in the ratio 5 : 7 : 9 and their LCM is 1260. What is the difference between the largest and the smallest number? SSC CHSL (Tier II) 18/11/2024
(a) 20 (b) 32
(c) 16 (d) 24

75. A milk vendor has 75 litres of cow milk, 45 litres of toned milk and 30 litres of full cream milk. These should be placed in different trays such that each tray contains the same quantity of milk and two kinds of milk should not be mixed in a tray. What is the least number of trays required to place all the milk? SSC CHSL (Tier II) 18/11/2024
(a) 25 (b) 20
(c) 15 (d) 10

SSC MTS 2024

76. What is the HCF of 513,1134 and 1215? SSC MTS 14/11/2024 Shift III
(a) 27 (b) 81 (c) 3 (d) 19

77. The product of LCM and HCF of two numbers is 24. If the difference between the two numbers is 2, then find the numbers. SSC MTS 13/11/2024 Shift III
(a) 5 and 3 (b) 6 and 4
(c) 2 and 4 (d) 8 and 6

78. Using the factor method of HCF, which of the following is the HCF of 160 and 256? SSC MTS 12/11/2024 Shift III
(a) 40 (b) 32 (c) 16 (d) 64

79. The greatest number which exactly divides the numbers 38, 95 and 171 is SSC MTS 11/11/2024 Shift III
(a) 19 (b) 21 (c) 9 (d) 13

80. The ratio of two numbers is 3:4 and their HCF is 4. Then, their LCM is SSC MTS 05/11/2024 Shift III
(a) 24 (b) 28 (c) 38 (d) 48

81. The HCF and LCM of two numbers are 11 and 3465, respectively. If one of the two numbers is 693, what is the other number? SSC MTS 04/11/2024 Shift III
(a) 315 (b) 75 (c) 55 (d) 65

82. Three bells toll at intervals of 12, 15 and 18 minutes, respectively. If all the three bells toll together at 8 a.m., when will they toll together next? SSC MTS 30/10/2024 Shift III
(a) 8 am (b) 11 am
(c) 3 pm (d) 10 am

83. Find the HCF of $2^3 \times 3^3 \times 5^2 \times 7^2$, $2^4 \times 3^2 \times 5^3 \times 7^2$ and $3 \times 5 \times 7 \times 11$. SSC MTS 29/10/2024 Shift III
(a) 1260 (b) 360
(c) 105 (d) 1155

84. If the HCF of 156 and 96 is expressible in the form of $156 \times 12 + 96$ A, then the value of A is SSC MTS 23/10/2024 Shift II
(a) –19.735 (b) 19.735
(c) –19.375 (d) 19.375

85. Which of the following is equal to the LCM of 12, 36, 72, 144, 288 and 576? SSC MTS 22/10/2024 Shift II
(a) 72 (b) 576 (c) 144 (d) 288

86. Find the HCF of 576,324 and 360 SSC MTS 21/10/2024 Shift II
(a) 72 (b) 108
(c) 144 (d) 36

87. Find the HCF of 36 and 84. SSC MTS 18/10/2024 Shift II
(a) 6 (b) 4 (c) 18 (d) 12

88. The greatest number of four digits which is divisible by each one of the numbers 15, 25, 40 and 75 is SSC MTS 17/10/2024 Shift II
(a) 9500 (b) 9600
(c) 9400 (d) 9800

89. The greatest possible length of a scale that can exactly measure a cloth of lengths 250 cm, 420 cm and 710 cm is SSC MTS 15/10/2024 Shift I
(a) 71 cm (b) 10 cm
(c) 460 cm (d) 170 cm

90. Find the LCM of $\frac{1}{7}, \frac{2}{5}$ and $\frac{3}{15}$. SSC MTS 09/10/2024 Shift I
(a) 6 (b) 4 (c) 5 (d) 3

91. Find the HCF of 70 and 90. SSC MTS 08/10/2024 Shift I
(a) 2 (b) 5
(c) 7 (d) 10

92. The highest common factor of 84 and 108 is SSC MTS 07/10/2024 Shift I
(a) 16 (b) 8 (c) 12 (d) 6

93. The least number of square tiles required to pave the ceiling of a room 525 cm long and 378 cm broad is SSC MTS 01/10/2024 Shift I
(a) 178 (b) 150 (c) 380 (d) 450

94. Three numbers are in the ratio of 6 : 7 : 3 and their LCM is 3654. Their HCF is SSC MTS 30/09/2024 Shift I
(a) 28 (b) 87 (c) 29 (d) 27

SSC MTS 2023-2021

95. The ratio of two numbers is 7 : 11 and their LCM is 462. What is the difference between these two numbers? SSC MTS 14/09/2023 Shift I
(a) 24 (b) 26 (c) 30 (d) 28

96. Two numbers are in the ratio of 13 : 15. If their HCF is 3, then what is the difference between these two numbers? SSC MTS 13/09/2023 Shift I
(a) 4 (b) 2 (c) 8 (d) 6

97. Sanjay wants to exactly measure the lengths 7000 mm, 3850 mm and 12950 mm using a single measuring tape. What will be the greatest possible length (in cm) of the measuring tape?
SSC MTS 11/09/2023 Shift II
(a) 40 (b) 45 (c) 35 (d) 30

98. Find the LCM of 1288, 230, 276.
SSC MTS 11/09/23 Shift I
(a) 19320 (b) 19230
(c) 9660 (d) 6440

99. Find the HCF of 230, 276 and 322.
SSC MTS 08/09/2023 Shift II
(a) 23 (b) 12 (c) 46 (d) 14

100. Two numbers are in the ratio of 2 : 5. Their LCM is 80. Find the numbers. SSC MTS 06/09/2023 Shift I
(a) 18,38 (b) 14,36
(c) 16,40 (d) 16,38

101. The HCF of three numbers is 57. If they are in the ratio of 4 : 5 : 6, then find the numbers.
SSC MTS 05/09/2023 Shift II
(a) 228, 285, 342 (b) 236, 295, 354
(c) 240, 300, 360 (d) 232, 290, 348

102. The least common multiple (LCM) of p and q is r. The LCM of p^2q and pq^2 is SSC MTS 04/09/2023 Shift II
(a) pqr^3 (b) pqr
(c) pq (d) pqr^2

103. Find the greatest two digit number which on dividing 219, 365, 511 leaves the remainders 3, 5, 7, respectively. SSC MTS 01/09/2023 Shift III
(a) 63 (b) 82
(c) 53 (d) 72

104. Two persons take steps of 77 cm and 88 cm, respectively. If they start in step, then what is the minimum distance (in cm) they should cover so that both of them can cover the distance in complete steps? SSC MTS 01/09/2023 Shift I
(a) 968 (b) 828
(c) 616 (d) 560

105. $P = 2^5 \times 3^8$ and $Q = 2^3 \times 3^K$. If the highest common factor of P and Q is $2^3 \times 3^3$, then what is the value of K? SSC MTS 15/07/2022 Shift I
(a) 1 (b) 2
(c) 3 (d) 5

106. The ratio of the LCM of two numbers to the sum of the same two numbers is 12 : 7. If their HCF is 4, what is the product of these two numbers ? SSC MTS 14/07/2022 Shift I
(a) 192 (b) 172
(c) 196 (d) 169

107. What is the LCM of two numbers, whose product is 432 and HCF is 6? SSC MTS 13/07/2022 Shift I
(a) 68 (b) 48
(c) 78 (d) 72

108. What is the greatest number which on dividing 342 and 480 leaves remainders of 6 and 4, respectively? SSC MTS 11/07/2022 Shift I
(a) 14 (b) 4
(c) 7 (d) 28

109. The HCF of 2-digit numbers is 19 and their sum is 152. What is their difference? SSC MTS 02/11/2021 Shift III
(a) 19 (b) 38
(c) 57 (d) 76

110. Which is the largest number that will divide 1992 and 233 leaving remainders 12 and 13, respectively?
SSC MTS 02/11/2021 Shift II
(a) 242 (b) 220
(c) 246 (d) 186

111. Find the smallest number such that, when it is divided by 5, 6 and 8, it leaves a remainder 3 in each case. SSC MTS 02/11/2021 Shift I
(a) 243 (b) 123
(c) 117 (d) 792

SSC GD Constable 2024

112. Find the LCM of 18, 24 and 36.
SSC GD 26/02/2024 Shift I
(a) 24 (b) 36
(c) 64 (d) 72

113. Find the numbers if the HCF of two numbers is 47 and their sum is 188. SSC GD 26/02/2024 Shift I
(a) 141 and 138 (b) 47 and 141
(c) 215 and 211 (d) 47 and 51

114. The least common multiple of three different numbers is 120. Which of the following cannot be their highest common factor?
SSC GD 26/02/2024 Shift I
(a) 15 (b) 40
(c) 20 (d) 16

115. Find the greatest number which on dividing 60 and 90 leaves remainders 2 and 3, respectively.
SSC GD 24/02/2024 Shift III
(a) 29 (b) 19
(c) 17 (d) 23

116. Find the HCF of $\frac{27}{50}, \frac{9}{20}, \frac{6}{25}$.
SSC GD 24/02/2024 Shift III
(a) $\frac{68}{7}$ (b) $\frac{47}{5}$
(c) $\frac{56}{5}$ (d) $\frac{3}{100}$

117. What is the Least Common Multiple (LCM) of 120, 240 and 480? SSC GD 24/02/2024 Shift III
(a) 240 (b) 960
(c) 480 (d) 1800

118. Which among the following is divisible by 4, 7 and 23?
SSC GD 24/02/2024 Shift II
(a) 6457 (b) 6440
(c) 6245 (d) 6490

119. Find the HCF of 84, 126, and 168.
SSC GD 24/02/2024 Shift I
(a) 44 (b) 40 (c) 49 (d) 42

120. The Least Common Multiple (LCM) of two prime numbers x and y, $(x < y)$ is 141. Then, what is the value of $(y - 5x)$? SSC GD 24/02/2024 Shift I
(a) 40 (b) 32
(c) 38 (d) 30

121. HCF of the two numbers is 14 and their LCM is 490. If one number is 70, then find the another number.
SSC GD 23/02/2024 Shift III
(a) 78 (b) 65
(c) 74 (d) 98

122. What is that smallest number which, if added to 140, will make it completely divisible by both 5 and 6? SSC GD 23/02/2024 Shift III

(a) 12 (b) 15
(c) 20 (d) 10

123. Find LCM of $\frac{9}{4}, \frac{21}{10}, \frac{63}{20}$.
SSC GD 23/02/2024 Shift I

(a) $\frac{2}{63}$ (b) $\frac{21}{2}$
(c) $\frac{85}{7}$ (d) $\frac{63}{2}$

124. The least common multiple of two prime numbers x and y, $(x < y)$ is 145. Then, what is the value of $(10x - y)$?
SSC GD 22/02/2024 Shift IV

(a) 21 (b) 11
(c) 18 (d) 27

125. What is the Highest Common Factor (HCF) of 12, 8 and 24?
SSC GD 22/02/2024 Shift II

(a) 12 (b) 6
(c) 4 (d) 8

126. The least number which is exactly divisible by 27, 36, 56, 12 and 10?
SSC GD 22/02/2024 Shift II

(a) 7694
(b) 8584
(c) 7560
(d) 5953

127. Find the HCF of 258, 301 and 387.
SSC GD 22/02/2024 Shift I

(a) 29 (b) 27
(c) 22 (d) 43

128. The product of two numbers is 1408 and their LCM is 352. Find the HCF. SSC GD 22/02/2024 Shift I

(a) 4 (b) 2
(c) 3 (d) 7

129. What is the Least Common Multiple (LCM) of $2^4 \times 3^3$, $2^5 \times 3^2$ and $2^5 \times 3^6$? SSC GD 21/02/2024 Shift IV

(a) $2^3 \times 3^5$
(b) $2^5 \times 3^5$
(c) 2^5
(d) $2^5 \times 3^6$

130. 4 bells ring at intervals of 6, 8, 9 and 10 sec. All the bells ring at the same time. After how many minutes will they ring together again? SSC GD 21/02/2024 Shift IV

(a) 6 min (b) 10 min
(c) 8 min (d) 15 min

131. What is the Highest Common Factor (HCF) of $2^3 \times 3^5$ and $2^4 \times 3^6$? SSC GD 21/02/2024 Shift III

(a) 2×3^2 (b) $2^3 \times 3^5$
(c) $2^2 \times 3^2$ (d) $2^3 \times 3^3$

132. Two numbers are in the ratio of 11 : 13. If their HCF is 7, find the numbers. SSC GD 20/02/2024 Shift III

(a) 21 and 28 (b) 63 and 70
(c) 77 and 91 (d) 70 and 80

133. Find the maximum number of students among whom 1003 chocolates and 2703 candies can be distributed, such that each student gets the same number of each.
SSC GD 20/02/2024 Shift II

(a) 19 (b) 29 (c) 17 (d) 33

134. The product of two numbers is 720 and their Highest Common Factor (HCF) is 4. What is the Least Common Multiple (LCM) of these numbers? SSC GD 20/02/2024 Shift II

(a) 120 (b) 480 (c) 180 (d) 240

135. There are 44 mangoes, 121 bananas and 11 apples, they have to be arranged in several rows in such a way that every row contains equal number of fruits and each row contains fruit of one type. What is the minimum number of rows?
SSC GD 20/02/2024 Shift I

(a) 16 (b) 14 (c) 13 (d) 15

SSC GD Constable 2023

136. Find the HCF of 0.25, 2.08 and 8.1.
SSC GD 13/02/2023 Shift IV

(a) 0.01 (b) 0.1 (c) 0.05 (d) 0.02

137. Find the greatest number by which when numbers 47, 95 and 187 are divided, leave the same remainder in each case. SSC GD 13/02/2023 Shift IV

(a) 6 (b) 8 (c) 2 (d) 4

138. Find the difference between the digits of the greatest number that can exactly divide 144 and 216 ?
SSC GD 13/02/2023 Shift II

(a) 2 (b) 4 (c) 3 (d) 5

139. The traffic lights at two different road crossings change after every 54 sec and 76 sec, respectively. If they change simultaneously at 10 : 15 : 00 h, then find the time at which they will change again simultaneously. SSC GD 09/02/2023 Shift II

(a) 10 : 34 :12 h
(b) 10 : 59 :12 h
(c) 10 : 52 : 34 h
(d) 10 : 49 : 12 h

140. The greatest 4 digit number divisible by 36 and 45 is subtracted from 10000. Find the result.
SSC GD 09/02/2023 Shift II

(a) 150 (b) 100
(c) 180 (d) 120

141. Sum of 2 natural numbers is 140 and their HCF and LCM are 28 and 168, respectively. Find the difference between the numbers.
SSC GD 09/02/2023 Shift I

(a) 21 (b) 14
(c) 7 (d) 28

142. What is the largest number which can divide 187, 233 and 279, leaving the same remainder in each case? SSC GD 08/02/2023 Shift I

(a) 30 (b) 36
(c) 46 (d) 56

143. Find the HCF of the cube of 16 and the square of 48. SSC GD 07/02/2023 Shift I

(a) 256
(b) 768
(c) 512
(d) 128

144. Find the LCM of the greatest 2-digit number divisible by 12 and the smallest 2-digit number divisible by 8. SSC GD 02/02/2023 Shift I

(a) 96 (b) 192
(c) 48 (d) 384

SSC Selection Post 2024

145. If the sum of two numbers is 126 and their HCF and LCM are 7 and 180, respectively then the sum of the reciprocals of the two numbers is Higher Secondary Level 01/08/2024 Shift II

(a) $\frac{1}{11}$ (b) $\frac{1}{9}$
(c) $\frac{1}{10}$ (d) $\frac{1}{12}$

Right Answers

1 (b)	2 (c)	3 (d)	4 (a)	5 (d)	6 (b)	7 (a)	8 (a)	9 (a)	10 (d)
11 (b)	12 (c)	13 (d)	14 (b)	15 (b)	16 (b)	17 (a)	18 (c)	19 (a)	20 (b)
21 (c)	22 (a)	23 (a)	24 (d)	25 (a)	26 (b)	27 (c)	28 (d)	29 (b)	30 (b)
31 (b)	32 (c)	33 (c)	34 (d)	35 (a)	36 (a)	37 (b)	38 (a)	39 (c)	40 (b)
41 (c)	42 (b)	43 (d)	44 (c)	45 (c)	46 (a)	47 (b)	48 (c)	49 (c)	50 (d)
51 (d)	52 (a)	53 (a)	54 (c)	55 (a)	56 (d)	57 (a)	58 (b)	59 (b)	60 (c)
61 (a)	62 (b)	63 (c)	64 (a)	65 (b)	66 (c)	67 (a)	68 (a)	69 (c)	70 (a)
71 (a)	72 (b)	73 (c)	74 (c)	75 (d)	76 (a)	77 (b)	78 (b)	79 (a)	80 (d)
81 (c)	82 (b)	83 (c)	84 (c)	85 (b)	86 (d)	87 (d)	88 (b)	89 (b)	90 (a)
91 (d)	92 (c)	93 (d)	94 (b)	95 (a)	96 (d)	97 (c)	98 (a)	99 (c)	100 (c)
101 (a)	102 (b)	103 (d)	104 (c)	105 (c)	106 (a)	107 (d)	108 (d)	109 (b)	110 (b)
111 (b)	112 (d)	113 (b)	114 (d)	115 (a)	116 (d)	117 (c)	118 (b)	119 (d)	120 (b)
121 (d)	122 (d)	123 (d)	124 (a)	125 (c)	126 (c)	127 (d)	128 (a)	129 (d)	130 (a)
131 (b)	132 (c)	133 (c)	134 (c)	135 (a)	136 (a)	137 (d)	138 (d)	139 (d)	140 (b)
141 (d)	142 (c)	143 (a)	144 (a)	145 (c)					

Solutions

1. (b) Let $x = 2^3 \times 9^2 \times 13$

$y = 2^2 \times 13^2 \times 19$

$z = 9^3 \times 13^2 \times 19^2$

LCM of x, y and z = Product of highest power factors $= 2^3 \times 9^3 \times 13^2 \times 19^2$

2. (c) According to the question,

The highest three digit number = 999

LCM of 3, 5, and 9 = 45

$\therefore$ 999 ÷ 45

Remainder = 9

So, the greatest number divisible by 3, 5 and 9 = 999 − 9 = 990

The required number that will leave the remainder 2 = 990 + 2 = 992

3. (d) Product of the two number = 1500

HCF = 10

Let two numbers are $10a$ and $10b$.

According to the question,

$10a \times 10b = 1500$

$\Rightarrow a \times b = \frac{1500}{100} \Rightarrow a \times b = 15$

So, two possible pairs are (1, 15) (3, 5).

4. (a) LCM of 2, 3, 5, 6, 9, 18 $= 2 \times 3^2 \times 5$

Then, least perfect square which is divisible by given numbers $= 2 \times 2 \times 3^2 \times 5 \times 5 = 900$

5. (d) Let two numbers be $6x$ and $7x$,

and HCF of the numbers = 3

$\therefore \quad x = 3$

$\therefore$ LCM of the numbers $= 6 \times 7 \times x = 42 \times 3 = 126$

6. (b) Since,

$72 = 2 \times 2 \times 2 \times 3 \times 3 = 2^3 \times 3^2$

$108 = 2 \times 2 \times 3 \times 3 \times 3 = 2^2 \times 3^3$

$2010 = 2 \times 3 \times 5 \times 67$

$\therefore$ HCF $= 2 \times 3 = 6$

7. (a) Given, HCF of two numbers = 17

Other two factors of their LCM = 11 and 19

$\therefore$ The smaller number $= 17 \times 11 = 187$

8. (a) Let the numbers be $14x$ and $19x$.

$\therefore$ HCF of numbers $= x$

$\Rightarrow x = 9$

$\therefore$ LCM of numbers $= 14 \times 19 \times x = 14 \times 19 \times 9 = 2394$

9. (a) Since, $60 = 2 \times 2 \times 3 \times 5$,

$148 = 2 \times 2 \times 37$

and $382 = 2 \times 191$

$\therefore$ Highest common factor = 2

10. (d) We know that,

$98 = 2 \times 7 \times 7$

$175 = 5 \times 5 \times 7$

and $210 = 2 \times 3 \times 5 \times 7$

So, HCF of 98, 175 and 210 = 7

11. (b) Here, $1.2 = \frac{12}{10}$ and $2.7 = \frac{27}{10}$

$12 = 2 \times 2 \times 3$

$27 = 3 \times 3 \times 3$

LCM of 12 and 27 $= 2 \times 2 \times 3 \times 3 \times 3 = 108$

LCM of 1.2 and 2.7 = LCM of $\frac{12}{10}$ and $\frac{27}{10}$

$= \frac{\text{LCM of 12 and 27}}{\text{HCF of 10 and 10}}$

$= \frac{108}{10} = 10.8$

12. (c) LCM of 3, 4, 5 and 7 $= 3 \times 4 \times 5 \times 7 = 420$

Now, 420) 35460 (84

3360

1860

1680

180 = Remainder

$\therefore$ The least number that should be added $= 420 - 180 = 240$

13. (d) Second number $= \frac{21 \times 840}{49} = 360$

14. (b) LCM of $\frac{3}{8}, \frac{5}{16}$ and $\frac{7}{2}$

$= \frac{\text{LCM (3, 5, 7)}}{\text{HCF (8, 16, 2)}} = \frac{105}{2} = 52\frac{1}{2}$

15. (b) HCF of $\frac{1}{2}, \frac{3}{4}, \frac{5}{6}, \frac{7}{8}$

$= \frac{\text{HCF (1, 3, 5, 7)}}{\text{LCM (2, 4, 6, 8)}} = \frac{1}{24}$

16. (b) Since,

$144 = 2 \times 2 \times 2 \times 2 \times 3 \times 3 = 2^4 \times 3^2$

$360 = 2 \times 2 \times 2 \times 3 \times 3 \times 5 = 2^3 \times 3^2 \times 5$

and $450 = 2 \times 3 \times 3 \times 5 \times 5 = 2^1 \times 3^2 \times 5^2$

$\therefore$ LCM of 144, 360 and 450

$= 2^4 \times 3^2 \times 5^2 = 16 \times 9 \times 25$

$= 3600$

17. (a) LCM of 96, 136 and 504

2	96, 136, 504
2	48, 68, 252
2	24, 34, 126
2	12, 17, 63
2	6, 17, 63
3	3, 17, 63
3	1, 17, 21
	1, 17, 7

$\therefore$ LCM of 96, 136, 504

$= 2 \times 2 \times 2 \times 2 \times 2 \times 3 \times 3 \times 17 \times 7 = 34272$

18. (c) Here, $4.08 = \frac{408}{100}$ and $6.63 = \frac{663}{100}$

Then, $408 = 2 \times 2 \times 2 \times 3 \times 17$

$663 = 3 \times 13 \times 17$

So, HCF of 408 and 663 = $3 \times 17 = 51$

$\therefore$ HCF of 4.08 and 6.63 = $\frac{51}{100} = 0.51$

19. (a) Since, $222 = 2 \times 3 \times 37$

$642 = 2 \times 3 \times 107$

$1062 = 2 \times 3 \times 3 \times 59$

So, the HCF of 222, 642

and 1062 = $2 \times 3 = 6$

20. (b) Since, $105 = 3 \times 5 \times 7$, $335 = 5 \times 67$,

and $465 = 3 \times 5 \times 31$

$\therefore$ HCF = 5

21. (c) Given, HCF of 2 numbers = 8

LCM of two numbers must be completely divisible by their HCF.

Here, $56 = 8 \times 7$, $48 = 8 \times 6$

and $40 = 8 \times 5$

but 42 is not completely divisible by 8.

So, 42 can never be their LCM.

22. (a) LCM of 186.6 and 373.2 = LCM of $\frac{1866}{10}$ and $\frac{3732}{10} = \frac{3732}{10} = 373.2$

23. (a) LCM of 9, 24 and 36

2	9, 24, 36
2	9, 12, 18
2	9, 6, 9
3	9, 3, 9
3	3, 1, 3
	1, 1, 1

$\therefore$ LCM = $2 \times 2 \times 2 \times 3 \times 3 = 72$

Hence, 72 is the least number exactly divisible by 9, 24 and 36.

24. (d) Let first number = a

Second number = b

$a \times b = 3 \times 54$

$ab = 162$

Sum of two numbers = 18 (Given)

$a + b = 18$

$\therefore$ Sum of their reciprocals = $\frac{1}{a} + \frac{1}{b}$

$= \frac{a+b}{ab} = \frac{18}{162} = \frac{1}{9}$

25. (a) $\because 16 = 2^4$, $18 = 2 \times 3^2$ and $36 = 2^2 \times 3^2$

LCM of (16, 18, 36) = $2^4 \times 3^2 = 144$

$\therefore$ Smallest perfect square is 144 (12^2).

Which is exactly divisible by 16, 18 and 36.

26. (b) HCF or Highest Common Factor is the highest number which divides perfectly each of the two or more given numbers. It is also called Greatest Common Divisor (GCD). In prime factorisation method of HCF, only common multiples of all the given numbers are listed.

27. (c) Here, $x = 49$, $y = 147$ and $z = 322$

$\therefore$ Required HCF

$= \text{HCF of } |x - y|, |y - z|, |z - x|$

$= \text{HCF of } |49 - 147|, |147 - 322|, |322 - 49|$

$= \text{HCF of } 98, 175, 273$

Now, $98 = 2 \times 7 \times 7$

$175 = 5 \times 5 \times 7$

$273 = 3 \times 7 \times 13$

$\therefore$ HCF of 98, 175 and 273 = 7

28. (d) Let the two numbers be a and b.

$\therefore$ $a = 171$

Also, LCM $(a, b) = 4104$

HCF $(a, b) = 9$

$\Rightarrow$ $171 \times b = 4104 \times 9$

$\Rightarrow$ $b = \frac{4104 \times 9}{171} \Rightarrow b = 216$

29. (b) Here, $110 = 2 \times 5 \times 11$

$1980 = 2 \times 2 \times 3 \times 3 \times 5 \times 11$

$\therefore$ HCF of 110 and 1980 = $2 \times 5 \times 11 = 110$

30. (b) LCM of 4 and 7 = $4 \times 7 = 28$

If the number is divisible by 4 and 7, that it will be divisible by 28.

Now, largest 3-digit number = 999

Now, $999 = 28 \times 35 + 19$

$\therefore$ $999 = 980 + 19$

Hence, 980 is the largest 3-digit number divisible by 4 and 7.

31. (b) Let the number be $3x$ and $8x$.

HCF of these number = x

And given LCM of these numbers = 120

$\therefore$ $3x \times 8x = 120 \times x$

$\Rightarrow$ $24x^2 = 120x \Rightarrow 24x = 120$

$\Rightarrow$ $x = \frac{120}{24} = 5$

Hence, sum of numbers = $3x + 8x$

$= 11x = 11 \times 5 = 55$

32. (c) $\because 36 = 2^2 \times 3^2$ and $198 = 2 \times 3^2 \times 11$

Then, HCF of (36, 198) = $2 \times 3^2 = 18$

33. (c) HCF of $\left(\frac{12}{5}, \frac{14}{15}, \frac{16}{17}\right)$

$= \frac{\text{HCF of}(12, 14, 16)}{\text{LCM of } (15, 5, 17)} = \frac{2}{15 \times 17} = \frac{2}{255}$

34. (d) Let the numbers are $2x$, $3x$ and $5x$.

So, their HCF = x

LCM of $2x$, $3x$ and $5x$ = 90

$\Rightarrow$ $2 \times 3 \times 5 \times x = 90$

$\therefore$ $x = \frac{90}{30} = 3$

35. (a) Here, $2040 = 2 \times 2 \times 2 \times 3 \times 5 \times 17$

$391 = 17 \times 23$

So, HCF of 2040 and 391 = 17

36. (a) $15 = 3 \times 5$, $18 = 2 \times 3^2$, $25 = 5^2$

and $32 = 2^5$

LCM (15, 18, 25, 32) = $2^5 \times 3^2 \times 5^2 = 7200$

So, if 3600 is doubled i.e.

LCM (15, 18, 25, 32 = $2 \times 3600 = 7200$

Then, it will be exactly divisible by 15, 18, 25 and 32.

$\therefore$ Required number = $\frac{7200}{2} = 3600$

37. (b) HCF (1026, 2268, 2430)

```
2268) 2430 (1
      2268
      ----
       162) 2268 (14
            2268
            ----
              ×

162) 1026 (6
      972
      ---
       54) 162 (3
           162
           ---
            ×
```

$\therefore$ HCF (largest common divisor) = 54

38. (a) Given, ratio of two numbers = 5 : 4

and their HCF = 4

So, the numbers are $5 \times 4 = 20$

and $4 \times 4 = 16$

$\therefore$ LCM of 20 and 16 = $5 \times 4 \times 4 = 80$

39. (c) Let the numbers be $6x$ and $5x$.

$\therefore$ HCF = x

Given, HCF = $3 \Rightarrow x = 3$

$\therefore$ LCM = $\frac{6x \times 5x}{3} = \frac{6 \times 3 \times 5 \times 3}{3} = 90$

40. (b) According to the question,

HCF = $\frac{384}{48} = 8$

$\therefore$ Ratio of HCF and LCM = $\frac{8}{48} = \frac{1}{6} = 1 : 6$

41. (c) We know that, LCM of two number will always be completely divisible by their HCF.

$\therefore$ Here, 90 can never be their LCM because 90 is not completely divisible by 12.

42. (b) Let the five digit largest number is 99999.

Take LCM of 5, 35, 39, 65 = 1365

Now,

```
1365) 99999 (73
     -9555
     -----
      4449
     -4095
     -----
       354
```

The largest 5 digit number

$= 99999 - 354 = 99645$

$\therefore$ Sum of digit = $9 + 9 + 6 + 4 + 5 = 33$

43. (d) For finding the smallest integer that is divisible by 3, 7, 18 we take

LCM of (3, 7, 18) = $(3 \times 6 \times 7) = 126$

$\therefore$ Smallest integer that is divisible by 3, 7, 18 is 126 .

44. (c) Here,

$125 = 5 \times 5 \times 5 = 5^3$

$250 = 2 \times 5 \times 5 \times 5 = 2 \times 5^3$

$750 = 2 \times 3 \times 5 \times 5 \times 5 = 2 \times 3 \times 5^3$

$\therefore$ HCF $= 5^3 = 125$

45. (c) Let HCF $= x$

Then, LCM $= 5x$

According to question $\Rightarrow$ $20480 = x \times 5x$

$\Rightarrow x^2 = 4096$

$\therefore$ $x = 64$

Hence, HCF $= 64$

and LCM $= 5 \times x = 5 \times 64 = 320$

46. (a) For least number divisible, we have to find LCM of 9, 12, 15, 25 and 27.

Then, $9 = 3^2$

$12 = 3 \times 2^2$

$15 = 3 \times 5$

$25 = 5^2$

$27 = 3^3$

$\therefore$ LCM $= 3 \times 3 \times 3 \times 4 \times 5 \times 5 = 2700$

From option (a), 10800 is multiple of 2700. So, it is a least number which is divisible by 9, 12, 15, 25 and 27.

47. (b) Let the numbers be $2x$ and $7x$.

$\therefore$ $2x \times 7x = 9 \times 126$

$\Rightarrow$ $14x^2 = 9 \times 126$

$\Rightarrow$ $x^2 = 9 \times 9$

$\Rightarrow$ $x^2 = 81$

$\therefore$ $x = 9$

Hence, larger number $= 7x = 7 \times 9 = 63$

48. (c) According to the question,

Largest number which is divisible by 15, 25, 40, 75 = LCM (15, 25, 40, 75)

$15 = 3 \times 5$

$25 = 5^2$

$40 = 2^3 \times 5$

$75 = 3 \times 5^2$

LCM (15, 25, 40, 75) $= 2^3 \times 3^1 \times 5^2 = 600$

Now, we check the option, whose completely divisible by 600. 9000 and 9600 are completely divisible by 600.

$\therefore$ Required number $= 9600$

49. (c) LCM of 8, 12 and 18

$8 = 2^3$

$12 = 3 \times 2^2$

$18 = 2 \times 3^2$

$\therefore$ LCM $= 2 \times 2 \times 2 \times 3 \times 3 = 72$

50. (d) Let the numbers be a and b.

Then, according to the question,

$\Rightarrow$ $a + b = 60$ ...(i)

and, $a \times b = 5 \times 60$ [I × II = HCF × LCM]

$\Rightarrow$ $ab = 300$ ...(ii)

Now, $\frac{1}{a} + \frac{1}{b} = \frac{b + a}{ab} = \frac{60}{300} = \frac{1}{5}$

Hence, sum of the reciprocals of the numbers will be $\frac{1}{5}$.

51. (d) Here, $240 = 4 \times 6 \times 10$

$280 = 4 \times 7 \times 10$

$560 = 4 \times 2 \times 7 \times 10$

$\therefore$ HCF $= 4 \times 10 = 40$

52. (a) Here,

$3888 = 2 \times 2 \times 2 \times 2 \times 3 \times 3 \times 3 \times 3 \times 3$

$3969 = 3 \times 3 \times 3 \times 3 \times 7 \times 7$

$\therefore$ HCF $= 3 \times 3 \times 3 \times 3 = 81$

53. (a) Let the first number be x.

Then, LCM $= 17x$.

According to the question,

$17x = 1105 \Rightarrow x = 65$

So, first number is 65

$\therefore$ Second number $= \frac{1105 \times 5}{65} = 85$

54. (c) Here, $20 = 2 \times 2 \times 5$

$30 = 2 \times 3 \times 5$

$40 = 2 \times 2 \times 2 \times 5$

HCF (20, 30, 40) $= 2 \times 5 = 10$

He wants to cut pieces of the same length = 10 m

Hence, the least number of total pieces

$= \frac{20}{10} + \frac{30}{10} + \frac{40}{10} = 2 + 3 + 4 = 9$

55. (a) Smallest number which is exactly divisible by each of 96, 108 and 144 = LCM of 96, 108 and 144

$96 = 2^5 \times 3$

$108 = 3^3 \times 4$

$144 = 2^4 \times 9$

LCM of 96, 108 and 144 $= 2^5 \times 3^3 = 864$

56. (d) Let the second number is x.

$\therefore$ $x \times 55 = 5 \times 660$

$\Rightarrow$ $x = \frac{5 \times 660}{55} \Rightarrow x = \frac{660}{11}$

$\therefore$ $x = 60$

57. (a) Let numbers be $5x$ and $7x$.

$\therefore$ $5x \times 7x = 5 \times 175$

$\Rightarrow$ $x^2 = \frac{5 \times 175}{5 \times 7}$

$\Rightarrow$ $x^2 = 25$

$\therefore$ $x = 5$

Then, larger number $= 7x = 7 \times 5 = 35$

58. (b) Let the numbers be $3x$ and $4x$.

$\therefore$ $3x \times 4x = 2700$

$\Rightarrow$ $x^2 = \frac{2700}{12}$

$\Rightarrow$ $x^2 = 225$

$\Rightarrow$ $x = 15$

Now, sum of the numbers $= 3x + 4x$

$= 7x = 7 \times 15 = 105$

59. (b) Factor of $15 = 3 \times 5$

$24 = 2 \times 2 \times 2 \times 3$

$35 = 5 \times 7$

$54 = 2 \times 3 \times 3 \times 3$

Then, LCM $= 2 \times 3 \times 5 \times 2 \times 2 \times 7 \times 3 \times 3$

$= 7560$

60. (c) According to the question,

$726 = 11 \times \text{LCM}$

$\therefore$ LCM $= \frac{726}{11} = 66$

61. (a) Here, $69 = 3 \times 23$

$96 = 2^5 \times 3$

$99 = 3 \times 3 \times 11$

So, HCF $= 3$

62. (b) Here, $28 = 2 \times 2 \times 7$

$92 = 2 \times 2 \times 23$

$\therefore$ LCM of 28 and 92 $= 2 \times 2 \times 7 \times 23 = 644$

63. (c) $\because$ $62 = 2 \times 31$

$186 = 2 \times 3 \times 31$

and $279 = 3 \times 3 \times 31$

$\therefore$ The greatest length of tap = HCF of 62, 186 and 279 = 31 m

64. (a) According to formula,

$18 \times$ II number $= 126 \times 9$

$\therefore$ II number $= 7 \times 9 = 63$

65. (b) The least common multiple of 48 and 64 = 192 and the highest common factor of 12 and 18 = 6

So, LCM of (48 and 64) is 32 times of HCF of (12 and 18).

66. (c) Here, $238 = 2 \times 119$

$832 = 2 \times 2 \times 2 \times 2 \times 2 \times 2 \times 13$

$\therefore$ HCF of (238, 832) = 2

67. (a) HCF of two numbers is 29.

HCF will be always a factor of LCM.

So, 29 is a factor of LCM.

Other two factors of LCM are 13 and 15.

So, numbers can be taken as

(13×29) and $(15 \times 29) = 377$ and 435

$\therefore$ Smallest number is 377.

68. (a) The LCM of 5, 6, 8 = 120

$\therefore$ Numbers between 300 and 700 are divisible by 120 is 3 i.e. 360, 480, 600.

69. (c) The least number which is divided by 15, 18 and 36 = LCM (15, 18, 36) = 180

$\therefore$ Required number $N = 180 \times x + 9$ ...(i)

It is also given that N should be multiple of 11.

$N = (176 + 4)x + 9 = 176x + 4x + 9$

So, $4x + 9$ should be multiple of 11.

If we calculate, we get that, at $x = 6$, $4x + 9$ will be multiple of 11.

Putting $x = 6$ in Eq. (i), we get

$N = 180 \times 6 + 9 = 1080 + 9 = 1089$

Thus, sum of digits $= 1 + 0 + 8 + 9 = 18$

70. (a) Let's take the two numbers as $7x$ and $11x$.

HCF $(7x, 11x) = x$

According to the question,

$x = 28$

$\therefore$ Sum of two numbers

$= 7x + 11x = 18x = 18 \times 28 = 504$

71. (a) Given, five bells ring together at the interval of 3, 5, 8, 9, 10 sec.

By taking LCM of 3, 5, 8, 9, 10

$3 = 3$
$5 = 5$
$8 = 2^3$
$9 = 3^2$
$10 = 2 \times 5$

$LCM = 2 \times 2 \times 2 \times 3 \times 3 \times 5 = 360.$

They will again ring simultaneously after

$= \frac{360}{60} = 6 \text{ min}$ [∵ 1 min = 60 sec]

∴ All the bells ring together in 6 min.

72. (b) To find the least number exactly divisible by 4, 5, 8, 10 and 12 we, need to find the LCM of the given number.

$4 = 2^2$
$5 = 5$
$8 = 2^3$
$10 = 2 \times 5$
$12 = 3 \times 2^2$

∴ LCM of (4, 5, 8, 10, 12)

$= 2 \times 2 \times 5 \times 2 \times 3 = 120$

73. (c) Let the number be $7x$ and $11x$.

HCF of those number is x.

Difference between two numbers is

$(11x - 7x) = 4x$

∴ The difference between the numbers is

$= 4 \times 28 = 112$

74. (c) Let the number are $5x$, $7x$ and $9x$

LCM of numbers $= 5 \times 7 \times 9 \times x$

∴ $5 \times 7 \times 9 \times x = 1260$

⇒ $x = 4$

∴ Difference of largest and smallest $= 9x - 5x$

$= 4 \times 4 = 16$

75. (d) Least number of trays

$= \frac{75 + 45 + 30}{\text{HCF of 75,45 and 30}}$

$= \frac{150}{15} = 10$ tray

76. (a) HCF of 513, 1134 and 1215

$513 = 3 \times 3 \times 3 \times 19$
$1134 = 2 \times 3 \times 3 \times 3 \times 3 \times 7$
$1215 = 3 \times 3 \times 3 \times 3 \times 3 \times 5$

∴ HCF $= 3 \times 3 \times 3 = 27$

77. (b) Let the first number be x.

second number $= x + 2$

By formula,

HCF × LCM = Product of number

$24 = x \times (x + 2)$

⇒ $x^2 + 2x - 24 = 0$

⇒ $(x + 6)(x - 4) = 0$ ⇒ $x = 4$

Second number $= 4 + 2 = 6$

Thus, numbers are 4 and 6.

78. (b) $160 = 2^5 \times 5$

$256 = 2^8$

∴ HCF of 160 and 256 $= 2^5 = 32$

79. (a) The greatest number is the HCF of 38,95 and 171.

$$\begin{array}{l} 38)\overline{95}(\\ \quad\ \ 76 \\ \quad\ \ 19)\overline{171}(9 \\ \qquad\ \ \ 171 \\ \qquad\ \ \ \ \times \end{array}$$

∴ The greatest number is 19.

80. (d) Ratio of two numbers = 3 : 4

HCF = 4

∴ LCM $= 3 \times 4 \times 4 = 48$

81. (c) Let the other number be x.

Using Formula,

HCF × LCM = Product of two numbers

$11 \times 3465 = 693 \times x$

⇒ $x = \frac{11 \times 3465}{693}$ ⇒ $x = 55$

∴ The other number is 55.

82. (b) LCM of 12, 15, 18 = 180 min = 3 h

They will toll together next

$= 8:00 + 3:00$

$= 11:00$ am

83. (c) $(2)^3 \times (3)^3 \times (5)^2 \times (7)^2$

$= (2)^4 \times (3)^2 \times (5)^3 \times (7)^2$

$= 3 \times 5 \times 7 \times 11$

Thus, HCF $= 3 \times 5 \times 7 = 105$

84. (c) HCF of 156 and 96 = 12

According to the question,

$12 = 156 \times 12 + 96A$ ⇒ $-12 \times 155 = 96A$

⇒ $A = -19.375$

85. (b) $12 = 2^2 \times 3$

$36 = 2^2 \times 3^2$
$72 = 2^3 \times 3^2$
$144 = 2^4 \times 3^2$
$288 = 2^5 \times 3^2$
$576 = 2^6 \times 3^2$

∴ LCM of these numbers = 576

86. (d) $576 = 2^6 \times 3^2$

$324 = 2^2 \times 3^4$
$360 = 2^3 \times 3^2 \times 5^1$

∴ HCF of 576, 324 and 360 $= 2^2 \times 3^2 = 36$

87. (d) $36 = 2^2 \times 3^2$

$84 = 2^2 \times 3 \times 7$

∴ HCF of 36 and 84 $= 2^2 \times 3 = 12$

88. (b) LCM of 15, 25, 40 and 75 is 600.

Greatest four digit number = 9999

$$\begin{array}{r} 600)\ 9999\ (16 \\ -600 \\ \hline 3999 \\ -3600 \\ \hline 399 \end{array}$$

∴ Required number = 9999 − 399

= 9600

89. (b) Greatest possible length of scale

= HCF of 250, 420 and 710 = 10 cm

90. (a) LCM of $\frac{1}{7}, \frac{2}{5}$ and $\frac{3}{15}$

$= \frac{\text{LCM of Numerator}}{\text{HCF of Denominator}}$

$= \frac{\text{LCM (1, 2, 3)}}{\text{HCF (7, 5, 15)}}$

$= \frac{1 \times 2 \times 3}{1} = 6$

91. (d) $70 = 7 \times 10$

$90 = 9 \times 10$

∴ HCF of 70 and 90 is 10 (common factor).

92. (c) HCF of 84 and 108

$84 = 12 \times 7$

$108 = 12 \times 9$

Thus, HCF of 84 and 108 = 12 (common factor)

93. (d) HCF of 525 and 378 = 21

Size of square tile $= 21 \times 21$

∴ Number of square tiles $= \frac{525 \times 378}{21 \times 21} = 450$

94. (b) Let numbers be $6x$, $7x$ and $3x$.

According to the question,

LCM of these numbers = 3654

$6x = 2 \times 3 \times x$
$7x = 7 \times x$
$3x = 3 \times x$

∴ LCM of $(6x, 7x, 3x) = 2^1 \times 3^1 \times 7^1 \times x$

Thus, $2 \times 3 \times 7 \times x = 3654$

⇒ $x = \frac{3654}{2 \times 3 \times 7} = 87$

Hence, required HCF = 87

95. (a) Let the both number be $7x$ and $11x$.

HCF of these two numbers $= x$

According to the question,

$7x \times 11x = 462 \times x$ ⇒ $(7 \times 11) \times x^2 = 462 \times x$

∴ $x = \frac{462}{77} = 6$

∴ Difference between both numbers

$= 11x - 7x = 4x = 4 \times 6 = 24$

96. (d) Given, ratio of numbers = 13:15

HCF of numbers = 3

Let number be $13x$ and $15x$.

x is the multiple of 3.

Let $x = 3$

∴ Numbers are 39 and 45.

∴ Required difference = 45 − 39 = 6

97. (c) Given, lengths

7000 mm = 700 cm

3850 mm = 385 cm

12950 mm = 1295 cm

∴ Prime factorisation,

$700 = 2 \times 2 \times 5 \times 5 \times 7$
$385 = 7 \times 5 \times 11$
$1295 = 5 \times 7 \times 37$

∴ HCF (700, 385, 1295) = 35 cm

∴ The greatest possible length of measuring tape = 35 cm

98. (a) Prime factorisation of

$1288 = 2 \times 2 \times 2 \times 7 \times 23 = 2^3 \times 7 \times 23$

$230 = 2 \times 5 \times 23 = 2^1 \times 5^1 \times 23$

$276 = 2 \times 2 \times 3 \times 23 = 2^2 \times 3 \times 23$

$\therefore$ LCM (1288, 230, 276)

$= 2^3 \times 3 \times 5 \times 7 \times 23 = 19320$

99. (c) Prime factorisation of

$230 = 2 \times 5 \times 23$

$276 = 2 \times 2 \times 3 \times 23$

$322 = 2 \times 7 \times 23$

$\therefore$ HCF (230, 276, 322) $= 2 \times 23 = 46$

100. (c) Let the numbers are $2x$ and $5x$.

LCM of $2x$ and $5x = 10x$

Given, $10x = 80 \Rightarrow x = 8$

$\therefore$ The numbers are $2x = 2 \times 8 = 16$

and $5x = 5 \times 8 = 40$

101. (a) The numbers are 57×4, 57×5 and 57×6 i.e, 228, 285 and 342.

102. (b) Given, LCM of p and q is r.

$\Rightarrow p \times q = r$

Factors of $p^2q = p \times p \times q$

Factors of $pq^2 = p \times q \times q$

$\therefore$ LCM of p^2q and $pq^2 = p^2q^2 = pqr$

103. (d) The number divides 219, 365 and 511 leaving the remainder 3, 5 and 7.

So, that number will divide (219–3), (365 – 5) and (511 – 7).

Now, the greatest number that will divide 216, 360 and 504 completely is the HCF of these numbers.

$216 = 2^3 \times 3^3$

$360 = 2^3 \times 3^2 \times 5$

$504 = 2^3 \times 3^2 \times 7$

$\therefore$ Required HCF $= 2^3 \times 3^2 = 8 \times 9 = 72$

104. (c) Given, two persons take steps of 77 cm and 88 cm.

So, the minimum distance they should cover

$=$ LCM of (77 and 88) $\Rightarrow 77 = 7 \times 11$, $88 = 8 \times 11$

$\therefore$ LCM $= (7 \times 8 \times 11) = 616$

$\therefore$ So, they both cover 616 cm.

105. (c) Given, $P = 2^5 \times 3^8$ and $Q = 2^3 \times 3^K$

Highest common factor of P and $Q = 2^3 \times 3^K$, where, K may be equal to or less than 8.

Given, HCF of P and $Q = 2^3 \times 3^3$

$\therefore$ Value of $K = 3$

106. (a) Given, HCF = 4

Let the two numbers be $4a$ and $4b$.

LCM $= 4ab$

Now, according to the question,

$$\frac{4(a+b)}{4ab} = \frac{7}{12}$$

$\therefore a + b = 7$

and $ab = 12$

From these two equations, $a = 3$ or 4 and $b = 4$ or 3

$\therefore$ Product of two numbers

$= (4 \times 3) \times (4 \times 4) = 192$

107. (d) According to the question,

LCM of given two numbers $= \dfrac{432}{6} = 72$

108. (d) Here, $342 - 6 = 336$ and $480 - 4 = 476$

HCF of 336 and 476,

```
      336)476(1
          336
          140)336(2
              280
               56)140(2
                  112
          HCF→ 28)56(2
                  56
                   ×
```

Hence, the required largest number is 28.

109. (b) Let the two numbers be $19x$ and $19y$, respectively,

Then, $19x + 19y = 152$

$\Rightarrow x + y = 8$

Possible value of (x, y) are (1, 7) (2,6) (3, 5) but the numbers are 2-digits, then

$x = 3, y = 5$

$\therefore$ Numbers are, $19 \times 3 = 57$

and $19 \times 5 = 95$

Hence, required difference $= 95 - 57 = 38$

110. (b) According to the question,

Largest number

$=$ HCF of $(1992 - 12), (233 - 13)$

HCF of 1980 and 220

Since, $1980 = 9 \times 220$

$\therefore$ HCF of 1980 and 220 will be 220.

111. (b) LCM (5, 6, 8) = 120

$\therefore$ Required number $= 120 + 3 = 123$.

112. (d) Factors of numbers

$18 = 2 \times 3 \times 3$

$24 = 2 \times 2 \times 2 \times 3$ and $36 = 2 \times 2 \times 3 \times 3$

$\therefore$ LCM $= 2^3 \times 3^2 = 9 \times 8 = 72$

113. (b) Given that, sum of numbers = 188 and HCF of numbers = 47

Let number be x and y.

HCF $(x, y) = 47$

Let $x = 47p, y = 47q$

Here, p and q are co-prime numbers to each other.

According to the question,

$x + y = 188$

$\Rightarrow 47p + 47q = 188$

$\Rightarrow p + q = \dfrac{188}{47} = 4$

The possible pair is (1, 3).

$x = 47 \times 1 = 47$

$y = 47 \times 3 = 141$

$\therefore$ Numbers are 47 and 141.

114. (d) It is given that, LCM of 3 different numbers is 120. Thus, HCF of those numbers must be a factor of that LCM too.

From the given options, only 16 is not a factor of 120 and therefore it can't be the HCF.

115. (a) The greatest number which on dividing 60 and 90 leaves remainders 2 and 3, respectively.

$\therefore$ Greatest number

$=$ HCF of $(60 - 2$ and $90 - 3)$

$=$ HCF of (58 and 87)

$=$ HCF of $(2 \times 29$ and $3 \times 29) = 29$

116. (d) HCF of $\left(\dfrac{27}{50}, \dfrac{9}{20}, \dfrac{6}{25}\right)$

$$= \frac{\text{HCF of } (27, 9, 6)}{\text{LCM of } (50, 20, 25)} = \frac{3}{100}$$

117. (c) Here, $120 = 2 \times 2 \times 2 \times 3 \times 5$

$240 = 2 \times 2 \times 2 \times 2 \times 3 \times 5$

and $480 = 2 \times 2 \times 2 \times 2 \times 2 \times 3 \times 5$

$\therefore$ LCM of (120, 240, 480) $= 2^5 \times 3 \times 5 = 480$

118. (b) We know that a number which is divisible by 4, 7, and 23. It is also divisible by their LCM i.e, $4 \times 7 \times 23 = 644$

From the option (b), we can easily see that 6440 is divisible by 644. It means 6440 is divisible by 4, 7 and 23.

119. (d) Here, $168 = 2 \times 2 \times 2 \times 3 \times 7$

$126 = 2 \times 3 \times 3 \times 7$

and $84 = 2 \times 2 \times 3 \times 7$

$\therefore$ HCF $= 2 \times 3 \times 7 = 42$

120. (b) Prime factors of 141 are 3 and 47.

Therefore, we can say that LCM of 3 and 47 will be 141.

We can write, $141 = 3 \times 47$

$y = 47$ and $x = 3$

[$\because$ given $= x < y$]

Now, the value of $y - 5x$

$= 47 - 5(3) = 47 - 15 = \boxed{32}$

121. (d) According to the question,

$14 \times 490 = 70 \times$ IInd number

$\therefore$ IInd number $= \dfrac{14 \times 490}{70} = 98$

122. (d) According to the question,

LCM of 5 and 6 is 30.

Multiples of 30 are 30, 60, 90, 120, 150 number which is nearest to 140 is 150.

$\therefore$ Required number $= 150 - 140 = 10$

123. (d) LCM of $\dfrac{9}{4}, \dfrac{21}{10}, \dfrac{63}{20}$

$$= \frac{\text{LCM of } (9, 21, 63)}{\text{HCF of } (4, 10, 20)} = \frac{63}{2}$$

124. (a) $\because$ LCM of two prime number = 145

Product of two number

$145 = x \times y$

$\Rightarrow x = 5$ or $y = 29$

5 and 29 both are prime numbers. [$\because x < y$]

So, the value of $(10x - y)$

$= 10 \times (5) - 29 = 50 - 29 = \boxed{21}$

125. (c) The HCF is as follows,

$12 = 2 \times 2 \times 3$

$8 = 2 \times 2 \times 2$

and $24 = 2 \times 2 \times 2 \times 3$

$\therefore$ HCF $= 2 \times 2 = 4$

126. (c) Given numbers,

$27 = 3^3, 36 = 2^2 \times 3^2$

$56 = 2^3 \times 7, 12 = 2^2 \times 3$

$10 = 2 \times 5$

$\because$ LCM (27, 36, 56,12,10)

$= 2^3 \times 3^3 \times 7 \times 5 = 7560$

$\therefore$ Least number that is divisible by 27, 36, 56 , 12 and 10 is 7560.

127. (d) The factors of the given numbers are as follows,

$258 = 2 \times 3 \times 43$

$301 = 7 \times 43$

and $387 = 3 \times 3 \times 43$

$\therefore$ HCF $= 43$

128. (a) $\because$ Product of two numbers = 1408

and LCM of two numbers = 352

$\because$ HCF $= \frac{1408}{352} = 4$

129. (d) Given,

$2^4 \times 3^3 = 2 \times 2 \times 2 \times 2 \times 3 \times 3 \times 3$

$2^5 \times 3^2 = 2 \times 2 \times 2 \times 2 \times 2 \times 3 \times 3$

and $2^5 \times 3^6 = 2 \times 2 \times 2 \times 2 \times 2$
$\times 3 \times 3 \times 3 \times 3 \times 3 \times 3$

$\therefore$ LCM $= 2 \times 2 \times 2 \times 2 \times 2 \times 3 \times 3 \times 3 \times 3 \times 3 \times 3$

$= 2^5 \times 3^6$

130. (a) Given, 4 bells rings at the intervals of

= 6, 8, 9 and 10 sec

The bells will ring together again i.e.

$\therefore$ LCM of 6, 8, 9 and 10 = 360 sec or 6 min.

131. (b) Highest common factor of $2^3 \times 3^5$ and $2^4 \times 3^6$ is $2^3 \times 3^5$.

132. (c) Let the numbers are $11x$ and $13x$.

and their HCF is 7.

So, HCF of $11x$ and $13x$ is x.

$\therefore$ $x = 7$

Hence, required number $= 11 \times 7$ and 13×7

= 77 and 91

133. (c) Given, maximum number of students who get the same number of chocolates and same number of candies

= HCF (1003, 2703)

$=$ HCF $(17 \times 59, 3 \times 17 \times 53) = 17$

$\therefore$ 17 students get same number of chocolates and candies.

134. (c) According to the question,

$720 = 4 \times$ LCM

$\therefore$ LCM = 180

135. (a) 44 mangoes, 121 bananas and 11 apples.

First we have to find HCF of 44, 121 and 11.

HCF of 44, 121 and 11 = 11

$(44 = 4 \times 11, 121 = 11 \times 11,$ and $11 = 1 \times 11)$

Number of rows

$= \frac{44 \text{ mangoes}}{11} + \frac{121 \text{ bananas}}{11} + \frac{11 \text{ apples}}{11}$

$= 4 + 11 + 1 = 16$

So, minimum 16 rows are there.

136. (a) $\because$ $0.25 = \frac{25}{100}, 2.08 = \frac{208}{100}, 8.1 = \frac{81}{10}$

HCF (0.25, 2.08, 8.1)

$= \frac{\text{HCF of 25, 208, 81}}{\text{LCM of 100, 100, 10}} = \frac{1}{100} = 0.01$

137. (d) Given, numbers = 47, 95 and 187

Greatest divisor

$=$ HCF of $[(a-b),(b-c),(a-c)]; a > b > c$

$=$ HCF $[(187-95),(95-47),(187-47)]$

$=$ HCF $[140, 48, 92] = 4$

Hence, 4 is the greatest number by which when numbers 47, 95 and 187 are divided, leave the same remainder in each case.

138. (d) Here, $144 = 2 \times 2 \times 2 \times 2 \times 3 \times 3$

$216 = 2 \times 2 \times 2 \times 3 \times 3 \times 3$

HCF of 144 and 216 $= 2 \times 2 \times 2 \times 3 \times 3 = 72$

So, the greatest number that can exactly divide 144 and 216 = 72

$\therefore$ Required difference $= 7 - 2 = 5$

139. (d) The time at which they will change again simultaneously

= LCM of 54 and 76 = 2052 sec

= 34 min and 12 sec

Hence, required time

= 10 : 15 : 00 + 00 : 34 : 12 = 10 : 49 : 12 h

140. (b) LCM of 36 and 45 = 180

$\therefore$ The greatest 4-digit number divisible by 36 and 45 = 9900

[as 9900 is multiple of 180]

Hence, required result = 10000 − 9900 = 100

141. (d) Given, Sum of 2 natural number is 140.

Their HCF and LCM are 28 and 168.

Let the two number is $28a$ and $28b$

$\Rightarrow$ $28(a + b) = 140$

$\Rightarrow$ $a + b = 5$ ...(i)

and $28ab = 168$

$\Rightarrow$ $ab = 6$ ...(ii)

On solving Eqs (i) and (ii)

$a = 3, b = 2$

So, the difference between that number

$= 28(a - b) = 28(3 - 2) = 28$

142. (c) Here, $233 - 187 = 46$; $279 - 233 = 46$

and $279 - 187 = 92$

HCF of 46, 46 and 92 = 46

So, 46 is the largest number which can divide 187, 233 and 279, leaving the same remainder in each case.

143. (a) $\because$ Cube of 16 = 4096

and square of 48 = 2304

$\therefore$ HCF of 4096 and 2304 = 256

144. (a) The greatest 2-digit number divisible by 12 = 96

The smallest 2-digit number divisible by 8 = 16

Now, LCM of (96 and 16) = 96

145. (c) Let two numbers be x and y.

$\therefore$ $x + y = 126$ ...(i)

and $xy =$ HCF $\times$ LCM

$\Rightarrow$ $xy = 7 \times 180$ ...(ii)

From Eqs. (i) and (ii), we get

$\frac{x + y}{xy} = \frac{126}{7 \times 180}$

$\Rightarrow$ $\frac{1}{x} + \frac{1}{y} = \frac{1}{10}$

03

Simplification

Simplification is a process of reducing a complex arithmetical expression into a simple expression.

BODMAS Rule

The operations have to be carried out in the order, in which they appear in the word BODMAS, where different letters of the word stand for following operations.

B = Brackets '[{(–)}]'
O = of '×'
D = Division '÷'
M = Multiplication '×'
A = Addition '+'
S = Subtraction '–'

Note Order of removing the brackets,

First → Bar bracket '–'
Second → Small bracket (circular bracket) '()'
Third → Middle bracket (curly bracket) '{}'
Fourth → Square bracket (big bracket) '[]'

Ex. 1 $\left(2\frac{6}{7}\text{ of }4\frac{1}{5}\div\frac{2}{3}\right)\times5\frac{1}{9}\div\left(\frac{3}{4}\times2\frac{2}{3}\text{ of }\frac{1}{2}\div\frac{1}{4}\right)$

Sol. $\left(2\frac{6}{7}\text{ of }4\frac{1}{5}\div\frac{2}{3}\right)\times5\frac{1}{9}\div\left(\frac{3}{4}\times2\frac{2}{3}\text{ of }\frac{1}{2}\div\frac{1}{4}\right)$

Applying BODMAS, we get

$$\left(\frac{20}{7}\times\frac{21}{5}\div\frac{2}{3}\right)\times\frac{46}{9}\div\left(\frac{3}{4}\times\frac{8}{3}\times\frac{1}{2}\div\frac{1}{4}\right)$$

$$=\left(12\div\frac{2}{3}\right)\times\frac{46}{9}\div\left(\frac{3}{4}\times\frac{4}{3}\div\frac{1}{4}\right)$$

$$=\left(12\times\frac{3}{2}\right)\times\frac{46}{9}\div\left(\frac{3}{4}\times\frac{16}{3}\right)=18\times\frac{46}{9}\div4=18\times\frac{46}{9}\times\frac{1}{4}=23$$

Algebraic Formulae

- $(a+b)^2=a^2+2ab+b^2$
- $(a-b)^2=a^2-2ab+b^2$
- $(a+b)^2+(a-b)^2=2(a^2+b^2)$
- $(a+b)^2-(a-b)^2=4ab$
- $a^2-b^2=(a+b)(a-b)$
- $(a+b+c)^2=a^2+b^2+c^2+2(ab+bc+ca)$
- $(a+b)^3=a^3+b^3+3ab(a+b)$
- $(a-b)^3=a^3-b^3-3ab(a-b)$
- $a^3+b^3=(a+b)^3-3ab(a+b)=(a+b)(a^2-ab+b^2)$
- $a^3-b^3=(a-b)^3+3ab(a-b)=(a-b)(a^2+ab+b^2)$
- $a^3+b^3+c^3-3abc=(a+b+c)(a^2+b^2+c^2-ab-bc-ca)$

If $a+b+c=0$, then $a^3+b^3+c^3=3abc$

Ex. 2 Simplify the given expression $\frac{108\times108\times108-92\times92\times92}{108\times108+92\times92+108\times92}$

Sol. Given, $\frac{108\times108\times108-92\times92\times92}{108\times108+92\times92+108\times92}$

Let $a=108$ and $b=92$

$$=\frac{(108)^3-(92)^3}{(108)^2+(92)^2+108\times92}$$

$$=\frac{(108-92)[(108)^2+(92)^2+108\times92]}{[(108)^2+(92)^2+108\times92]}$$

$[\because a^3-b^3=(a-b)(a^2+b^2+ab)]$

$=(108-92)=16$

Square

If a number is multiplied with itself, then the result of this multiplication is called the square of that number.

e.g. Square of $100=100\times100=10000$

Note The square of any number always ends with 0, 1, 4, 5, 6, 9 but will never end with 2, 3, 7 and 8.

Square Root

The square root of a number is the number, the square of which is equal to the given number. e.g., $\sqrt{49}=\sqrt{7\times7}=7$

Square Root by Factorisation Method

Ex. 3 Find square root of 1089

3	1089
3	363
11	121
	11

$\therefore\quad 1089=\overline{3\times3}\times\overline{11\times11}\Rightarrow\sqrt{1089}=3\times11=33$

Square Root by Division Method

Ex. 4 Find square root of 18769

	137
1	18769
+1	1
23	87
+3	69
267	1869
	1869
	×

∴ $\sqrt{18769} = 137$

Cube

If a number is multiplied two times with itself, then the result of this multiplication is called the cube of that number.

e.g. Cube of $6 = 6^3 = 6 \times 6 \times 6 = 216$

Cube Root

The cube root of a given number is the number whose cube is the given number. e.g. $\sqrt[3]{512} = \sqrt[3]{8 \times 8 \times 8} = 8$

Cube Root by Factorisation Method

Ex. 5 Find the cube root of 9261

Sol. Prime factor of $9261 = \underline{3 \times 3 \times 3} \times \underline{7 \times 7 \times 7}$

∴ Cube root of $9261 = 3 \times 7 = 21$

Important Formulae

1. $\sqrt{x\sqrt{x\sqrt{x \ldots n}}} = (x)^{\frac{2^n - 1}{2^n}}$

e.g. find the value of $\sqrt{2\sqrt{2\sqrt{2}}}$

Here, $n = 3$, then $\sqrt{2\sqrt{2\sqrt{2}}} = (2)^{\frac{2^3 - 1}{2^3}} = 2^{\frac{7}{8}}$

2. $\sqrt{x\sqrt{x\sqrt{x \ldots \infty}}} = x$

e.g. $\sqrt{5\sqrt{5\sqrt{5 \ldots \infty}}} = 5$

3. To find the value of $\sqrt{x + \sqrt{x + \sqrt{x + \ldots \infty}}}$, find the factors of x, such that the difference between the factors is 1 and product is x, then the larger factor will be the result.

e.g. Find the value of $\sqrt{20 + \sqrt{20 + \sqrt{20 + \ldots \infty}}}$

Co-prime factor of 20 = (5, 4)

In case of (+ ve) sign larger number is the right answer.

Hence, required answer = 5

4. To find the value of $\sqrt{x - \sqrt{x - \sqrt{x \ldots \infty}}}$, find the factors of x, such that the difference between the factors is 1 and product is x, then the smaller factor will be the result.

e.g. Find the value of $\sqrt{12 - \sqrt{12 - \sqrt{12 - \ldots \infty}}}$

Co-prime factor of 12 = (4, 3)

In case of (– ve) sign smaller number is the right answer.

Hence, required answer = 3

SSC Exam Scanner

SSC CGL 2024 (Tier I & II)

1. $\frac{\sqrt[3]{6859}}{\sqrt[4]{1296}} \times \frac{3}{57} \times 42 = ?$

SSC CGL (Tier II) 18/01/2025 Shift -I

(a) 7 (b) 16
(c) –3 (d) 17

2. The value of

$4^3 - 0^2 + \left(\frac{22}{2}\right)^2 - 8 + 7 \times 6 = \ldots\ldots$

SSC CGL (Tier II) 18/01/2025 Shift -I

(a) 224 (b) 229
(c) 219 (d) 218

3. Simplify $626 \times 2912 \div 8138$

SSC CGL (Tier I) 26/09/2024 Shift -III

(a) 285 (b) 224
(c) 364 (d) 310

4. Simplify the following expression.

SSC CGL (Tier I) 26/09/2024 Shift -II

$(60 + 64 \div 4 \text{ of } 4) \times \{1000 \div ((10 \text{ of } (3 + 2)) \times 2 \text{ of } 5)\} - 28 + (100 \times 3 \text{ of } 3)$.

(a) 600 (b) 1000
(c) 100 (d) 500

5. The value of N in the equation $9 \times N$ of $4 \div 4 - 15 \times 4 = 12$ is

SSC CGL (Tier I) 25/09/2024 Shift -III

(a) 9 (b) 0 (c) 12 (d) 8

6. Simplify: $[25 - 48 \div 6 + 12 \times 2] + 78 - [5 + 3 \text{ of } (25 - 2 \times 10)]$

SSC CGL (Tier I) 25/09/2024 Shift -II

(a) 98 (b) 90
(c) 99 (d) 89

7. $9 \div \left[1 + \left\{4 \times \left(\frac{5}{6} - \frac{1}{3} + \frac{1}{2}\right)\right\}\right]$ is equal to **SSC CGL (Tier I) 25/09/2024 Shift -I**

(a) 1 (b) $\frac{9}{5}$ (c) 0 (d) 9

8. Simplify the following expression.

SSC CGL (Tier I) 24/09/2024 Shift -II

$133 \div 19 \times 3 - 48 \times 2 \div 24 + 841 \div [\{\overline{45 - 16}\}]$

(a) 46 (b) 21 (c) 12 (d) 42

9. Find the value of $\frac{(453 \times 453 \times 453 - 383 \times 383 \times 383)}{(453 \times 383 + 383 \times 383 + 453 \times 453)}$.

SSC CGL (Tier I) 24/09/2024 Shift -II

(a) 60 (b) 50
(c) 80 (d) 70

10. Find the value of $11 - [(3 + 4) \text{ of } (8 - \overline{4 - 8})]$. **SSC CGL (Tier I) 24/09/2024 Shift -I**

(a) 2 (b) 3
(c) 1 (d) – 1

11. Simplify the following expression.

$0.07 \times 0.28 \div 0.04 + 0.64 - 1.64 \div 0.04$

SSC CGL (Tier I) 23/09/2024 Shift -III

(a) 38.56 (b) –39.87
(c) – 46.48 (d) 36.78

12. Simplify

$\frac{(232)^3 + (140)^3 + (353)^3 - 3 \times 232 \times 140 \times 353}{(232)^2 + (140)^2 + (353)^2 - 232 \times 140 - 140 \times 353 - 353 \times 232}$

SSC CGL (Tier I) 23/09/2024 Shift -I

(a) 261 (b) 725 (c) 445 (d) 596

13. Simplify

$6 \times [28 \div 84 \times \{36 \times 49 \div (6 \times 7)\}]$

SSC CGL (Tier I) 23/09/2024 Shift -I

(a) 84 (b) 74 (c) 64 (d) 94

14. Simplify $\frac{(25)^4 + 1250 + 1 - (25)^2}{(25)^2 + 25 + 1}$.
SSC CGL (Tier I) 19/09/2024 Shift -III
(a) 602 (b) 601 (c) 603 (d) 604

15. Simplify the following expression.
$25 \div 5 + 3$ of $2 - 4 + 6$ of $3 \div 2 - 8 + 4$
SSC CGL (Tier I) 19/09/2024 Shift -II
(a) 16 (b) 4
(c) 8 (d) 12

16. The value of $4\frac{1}{6} \div 25 \times 75 \div \frac{1}{5}$ of 125 is
SSC CGL (Tier I) 19/09/2024 Shift -I
(a) $\frac{1}{3}$ (b) $\frac{1}{4}$ (c) $\frac{1}{6}$ (d) $\frac{1}{2}$

17. The value of $9 - 5 \times 6 + \{29 - (7 - 2)\} \div 8$ is
SSC CGL (Tier I) 18/09/2024 Shift -III
(a) – 8 (b) 18
(c) – 18 (d) 8

18. Simplify the following
$\left[\left(5\frac{1}{2} - 3\frac{1}{3}\right) \text{ of } 1\frac{5}{13} + 1 - 2 \times 3\frac{5}{2} \div 2\frac{3}{4}\right]$
SSC CGL (Tier I) 18/09/2024 Shift -I
(a) 0 (b) $\frac{11}{2}$ (c) – 2 (d) $3\frac{1}{2}$

19. Simplify: $\left[\left(\frac{1}{6} \div \frac{1}{9} \times \frac{2}{3}\right) \times 18 + 5\right]$
SSC CGL (Tier I) 17/09/2024 Shift -I
(a) 9 (b) 23 (c) 27 (d) 15

20. Simplify
$$\frac{1.5 \times 1.5 + 2.5 \times 2.5 + 3.5 \times 3.5 + 2 \times 1.5 \times 2.5 + 2 \times 2.5 \times 3.5 + 2 \times 1.5 \times 3.5}{1.5 + 2.5 + 3.5}$$
SSC CGL (Tier I) 13/09/2024 Shift -III
(a) 9.5 (b) 6.5
(c) 8.5 (d) 7.5

21. Simplify the following
$16 \div 2 - 7 \times 15 \div 3 + 5 \times 5 + 4 \times 3 - 10$
SSC CGL (Tier I) 13/09/2024 Shift -III
(a) 1 (b) 2
(c) 0 (d) – 1

22. Simplify : $1\frac{1}{3} + 1\frac{3}{4} \times 1\frac{2}{3} \div 3\frac{1}{2}$
SSC CGL (Tier I) 13/09/2024 Shift -II
(a) $2\frac{1}{3}$ (b) $2\frac{1}{6}$ (c) $2\frac{1}{5}$ (d) $3\frac{1}{4}$

23. Simplify the following expression.
$[\{70 - 60 \div 2 \text{ of } 6\} + (20 - 10) \div 10] + 600 \div 25 \text{ of } (2 \times 3) \times (2 \text{ of } 3) + 2 \text{ of } 5.$
SSC CGL (Tier I) 13/09/2024 Shift -I
(a) 90 (b) 100
(c) 99 (d) 110

24. Solve the following
$\left[(2.5 + 1.5)^2 + 4 \text{ of } \frac{1}{2} \times 8 - 1\right]$
SSC CGL (Tier I) 12/09/2024 Shift -I
(a) 0 (b) 81
(c) 27.1 (d) 63

25. Simplify $4\frac{4}{5} \times \frac{3}{8} + \left(3\frac{1}{2} + \frac{2}{3}\right) \times \frac{4}{5}$
SSC CGL (Tier I) 11/09/2024 Shift -III
(a) $\frac{15}{77}$ (b) $\frac{77}{15}$ (c) $\frac{3}{10}$ (d) $\frac{10}{3}$

26. The value of the expression $(1.55^2 + 0.55^2 + 1.55 \times 0.55)$ is equal to
SSC CGL (Tier I) 11/09/2024 Shift -II
(a) $1.55^2 - 0.55^2$ (b) $1.55^3 - 0.55^3$
(c) $1.55^3 + 0.55^3$ (d) $1.55^2 + 0.55^2$

27. Simplify $\frac{(4.2)^3 - (1.2)^3}{(4.2)^2 + 5.04 + (1.2)^2}$
SSC CGL (Tier I) 11/09/2024 Shift -II
(a) 2 (b) 3
(c) 1 (d) 5

28. Simplify
$1020 \div \left[\frac{4}{3} \text{ of } (26 + 4) - 11\frac{2}{3}\right]$
SSC CGL (Tier I) 11/09/2024 Shift -II
(a) 28 (b) 36
(c) 17 (d) 31

29. If $45 \div 3 + 4 \times A - 48 \div 24 + 4 = 1$, then the value of A is
SSC CGL (Tier I) 10/09/2024 Shift -III
(a) –2 (b) 4
(c) 2 (d) –4

30. Simplify
$21 - [6 + 7 - \{3.22 - (1.1 \times 0.2)\}]$
SSC CGL (Tier I) 10/09/2024 Shift -II
(a) 13 (b) 12
(c) 11 (d) 10

31. Simplify $\frac{0.58 \times 0.58 \times 0.58 - 0.001}{0.58 \times 0.58 + 0.058 + 0.01}$
SSC CGL (Tier I) 10/09/2024 Shift -II
(a) 0.48 (b) 0.28
(c) 0.37 (d) 0.42

32. Simplify
$13 - [7 - (4 + 7) - \{7 - (7 - 4 + 7)\} + 14]$
SSC CGL (Tier I) 09/09/2024 Shift -III
(a) 13 (b) 9 (c) 0 (d) 26

33. Simplify the following:
$21 - 4.9 \div 7 + 3.9 \times 0.4 + 0.9$
SSC CGL (Tier I) 09/09/2024 Shift -II
(a) 18.23 (b) 24.12
(c) 26.32 (d) 22.76

34. Simplify
$$\frac{(8.3)^3 + (9.2)^3 + (6.1)^3 - 3 \times 8.3 \times 9.2 \times 6.1}{(8.3)^2 + (9.2)^2 + (6.1)^2 - 8.3 \times 9.2 - 9.2 \times 6.1 - 6.1 \times 8.3}$$
SSC CGL (Tier I) 09/09/2024 Shift -II
(a) 30.2 (b) 23.6
(c) 28.7 (d) 25.5

35. Which of the following can be the value of k, if $\frac{(88 \div 8 \times k - 3 \times 3)}{(6^2 - 7 \times 5 + k^2)} = 1$?
SSC CGL (Tier I) 09/09/2024 Shift -I
(a) 1,10 (b) 4,7
(c) 3,10 (d) 2,7

SSC CGL 2023 (Tier I & II)

36. What is the value of
$$\left[\frac{1}{8} + \left\{\frac{1}{6} \times \left(\frac{36}{45} \div \frac{24}{25}\right) - \left(\frac{12}{21} \times \frac{14}{15} \div \frac{24}{45}\right)\right\} + \frac{27}{36}\right]?$$
SSC CGL (Tier-II) 26/10/2023 Shift-I
(a) $\frac{1}{36}$ (b) $\frac{1}{72}$ (c) $\frac{1}{108}$ (d) $\frac{1}{27}$

37. Find the value of $\frac{\sqrt{124} \times \sqrt{2.79}}{\sqrt{2.64} \times \sqrt{5.94}}$.
SSC CGL (Tier-II) 26/10/2023 Shift-I
(a) $\frac{31}{66}$ (b) $\frac{31}{44}$
(c) $\frac{33}{64}$ (d) $\frac{33}{31}$

38. The value of $\frac{0.7 \times 0.7 \times 0.7 + 0.3 \times 0.3 \times 0.3}{0.7 \times 0.7 - 0.7 \times 0.3 + 0.3 \times 0.3}$ is
SSC CGL (Tier-II) 07/03/2023 Shift-I
(a) 1 (b) 2
(c) 3 (d) – 1

39. If $x = \sqrt{64} + \sqrt{121} - \sqrt{169}$, then find the value of x^2.
SSC CGL (Tier-II) 07/03/2023 Shift-I
(a) 49 (b) 36
(c) 25 (d) 16

40. Find the value of given expression.
$3 - (-6)\{-2 - 9 - 3\} \div 7\{1 + (-2)(-1)\}$
SSC CGL (Tier-II) 06/03/2023 Shift-I
(a) –1 (b) 15 (c) 7 (d) 1

41. Simplify the following.
$$\frac{\sqrt{10 + \sqrt{25 + \sqrt{108 + \sqrt{154 + \sqrt{225}}}}}}{\sqrt{16 + 19.25 \times 4^2}}$$
SSC CGL (Tier-II) 06/03/2023 Shift-I
(a) $\frac{7}{18}$ (b) $\frac{2}{9}$
(c) $\frac{5}{18}$ (d) $\frac{1}{9}$

42. Find the value of the given expression.
$\sqrt{20 - \sqrt{20 - \sqrt{20 - \sqrt{20 - \ldots\ldots\infty}}}}$.
SSC CGL (Tier-II) 03/03/2023 Shift-I
(a) 4 (b) 6
(c) 5 (d) 2

43. Find the value of given expression.
$[76 - \{90 \div 5 \times (24 - 36 \div 3) \div 3\}]$
SSC CGL (Tier-II) 03/03/2023 Shift-I
(a) 71.5 (b) 75.5
(c) 4 (d) 77.5

44. Find the value of the given expression
$30 - [40 - \{56 - (25 - 13 - 12)\}]$
SSC CGL (Tier-II) 02/03/2023 Shift-I
(a) 38 (b) 22
(c) 14 (d) 46

45. The value of
$1\frac{3}{4} + 1\frac{5}{7} \div 2\frac{3}{7} \times 2\frac{3}{7} = ?$
SSC CGL (Tier-I) 27/07/2023 Shift-II
(a) $1\frac{11}{28}$ (b) $2\frac{13}{28}$ (c) $3\frac{13}{28}$ (d) $4\frac{23}{28}$

46. Simplify the given expression.
$\frac{[120 \times 120 \times 120 - 100 \times 100 \times 100]}{[120 \times 120 + 120 \times 100 + 100 \times 100]}$
SSC CGL (Tier-I) 27/07/2023 Shift-II
(a) 20 (b) 25
(c) 10 (d) 15

47. Find the value.
$80.40 \div 20 - (-4.02) + 2.06 = ...$
SSC CGL (Tier-I) 27/07/2023 Shift-I
(a) 9.8 (b) 10.2
(c) 10.1 (d) 8.2

48. Find the value of the given expression.
$14 \div 7 \times 1 + 3 - [18 - \{15 - (7 - 7 - 2)\}]$
SSC CGL (Tier-I) 26/07/2023 Shift-IV
(a) 5 (b) 6 (c) 4 (d) 3

49. The value of $\frac{2}{3} - \frac{5}{6} \times \frac{4}{5} \div \frac{4}{3} + \frac{1}{2}$ is
SSC CGL (Tier-I) 26/07/2023 Shift-III
(a) $\frac{2}{3}$ (b) $\frac{2}{5}$
(c) $-\frac{11}{60}$ (d) 0

50. What is the value of
$6 - (6 \div 2 - 3 + 7 - 2) \times [\{3 - 2 \div 2\} \times 5 - 6]$?
SSC CGL (Tier-I) 26/07/2023 Shift-II
(a) – 4 (b) – 14
(c) – 12 (d) – 16

51. $100 \div 10 - [-2 + \{-9 + (3 - 6 \text{ of } 2)\}] = ...$.
SSC CGL (Tier-I) 25/07/2023 Shift-III
(a) – 6 (b) 20 (c) 30 (d) 0

52. Find the value of k if
$13 - [10 - \{16 + 8 \div (k - 2)\} + 2] = 20$
SSC CGL (Tier-I) 24/07/2023 Shift-IV
(a) $\frac{14}{3}$ (b) $\frac{31}{3}$ (c) $\frac{40}{13}$ (d) $\frac{23}{13}$

53. Simplify
$220 + 80 \div [63 - \{7 \times 8 + (13 - 2 \times 4)\}]$
SSC CGL (Tier-I) 24/07/2023 Shift-IV
(a) 260 (b) 270
(c) 240 (d) 250

54. Simplify the following expression.
$2 + (30 - 26)^2 \div 8^{3-2} \times 0.5$
SSC CGL (Tier-I) 24/07/2023 Shift-III
(a) 2 (b) 1
(c) 3 (d) 0

55. Simplify the given expression.
$15 - (-5) \times \{4 - (7 - 3)\} \div [3 \times \{5 + (-3) \times (-6)\}]$
SSC CGL (Tier-I) 24/07/2023 Shift-III
(a) 21 (b) 15
(c) 88 (d) 125

56. Simplify the following.
$\frac{0.01 \times 0.01 \times 0.01 + 0.003 \times 0.003 \times 0.003}{0.05 \times 0.05 - 0.015 \times 0.05 + 0.015 \times 0.015}$
SSC CGL (Tier-I) 24/07/2023 Shift-III
(a) $\frac{13}{25} \times 10^3$ (b) $\frac{13}{15} \times 10^{-3}$
(c) $\frac{13}{15} \times 10^3$ (d) $\frac{13}{25} \times 10^{-3}$

57. If $720 \div 8 + 915 \div 15 - m + 32 \times 5 = 1104 \div 16 \times 111 \div 37$, then the value of m is **SSC CGL (Tier-I) 24/07/2023 Shift-I**
(a) 104 (b) 518 (c) 207 (d) 311

58. Solve the following
$22 - [9 - \{6 - (10 - 4 + 3)\}] + 2 \times 3$
SSC CGL (Tier-I) 24/07/2023 Shift-I
(a) 12 (b) 4 (c) 3 (d) 20

59. The value of $(16 + 14) \div 2 - 12 + 16 \times 4 - 28 + 13(-16 + 13)$ is
SSC CGL (Tier-I) 21/07/2023 Shift-III
(a) 6 (b) 0 (c) –3 (d) 3

60. The value of
$\frac{3}{2} \div \frac{1}{7} \times \left[\left(\frac{1}{2} - \frac{1}{3}\right) \div \frac{1}{42}\right] = ?$
SSC CGL (Tier-I) 21/07/2023 Shift-III
(a) $72\frac{1}{3}$ (b) $73\frac{1}{2}$
(c) $72\frac{1}{2}$ (d) $71\frac{2}{3}$

61. The value of $(3^2)^2 + 3 \times 3 \div 3 - 3$ is
SSC CGL (Tier-I) 21/07/2023 Shift-II
(a) 3^2 (b) 9^2
(c) 2^3 (d) 3^0

62. Simplify
$264 - \left[142 - \left\{75 + \left(38 - \left(\frac{5}{4} + \frac{11}{4}\right)\right)\right\}\right]$
SSC CGL (Tier-I) 21/07/2023 Shift-II
(a) 231 (b) 230
(c) 232 (d) 234

63. Find the value of the given expression,
$10 \div 5 \times 1 + 3 - [8 - \{5 - (7 - 7 - 9)\}]$
SSC CGL (Tier-I) 21/07/2023 Shift-I
(a) 11 (b) 10
(c) 9 (d) 8

64. Simplify $[0.08 - \{3.5 - 4.9 - (12.5 - 7.8 - 4.6)\}]$
SSC CGL (Tier-I) 20/07/2023 Shift-IV
(a) 1.58 (b) 0.08
(c) 2.58 (d) 12.58

65. Solve the following expression.
$8 + (-9 - 3) - (-12 - 5)$
SSC CGL (Tier-I) 20/07/2023 Shift-III
(a) 14 (b) 13 (c) 16 (d) 15

66. Simplify.
$325 + 276 \div [150 - \{9 \times 9 + (83 - 4 \times 15)\}]$
SSC CGL (Tier-I) 20/07/2023 Shift-III
(a) 332 (b) 333 (c) 334 (d) 331

67. $7.5 \times 17.2 \div 8.6 + (59.5) \text{ of } \frac{1}{17} - \frac{7}{2} \text{ of } 5 = ?$ **SSC CGL (Tier-I) 20/07/2023 Shift-II**
(a) 1 (b) 3
(c) 4 (d) 2

68. Simplify the following expression
$\frac{\left(12 + 5 - \frac{48}{16} + 71\right) + \left(\frac{\frac{72}{36} + 6 \times 7}{11}\right) \times [(51 + 4 - 13) + (13 - 12 \times 7)]}{232}$
SSC CGL (Tier-I) 19/07/2023 Shift-II
(a) $\frac{-31}{233}$ (b) $\frac{31}{232}$ (c) $\frac{41}{232}$ (d) $\frac{-31}{232}$

69. Simplify the given expression
$\frac{432 \times 432 + 247 \times 247 - 432 \times 247}{432 \times 432 \times 432 + 247 \times 247 \times 247}$
SSC CGL (Tier-I) 19/07/2023 Shift-I
(a) $\frac{1}{259}$ (b) $\frac{1}{185}$ (c) $\frac{1}{679}$ (d) $\frac{1}{450}$

70. Simplify the following expression
$[\sqrt{25} + 12 \div 3 - \{20 + (16 \text{ of } 8 \div 16) - (54 \div 18 \text{ of } 1/2)\}]$
SSC CGL (Tier-I) 18/07/2023 Shift-IV
(a) 22 (b) – 13
(c) 12 (d) 0

71. The value of
$51 \div \{25 + (25 \text{ of } 12 \div 30) - (5^4 \div 5 \text{ of } 125)\}$ is
SSC CGL (Tier-I) 18/07/2023 Shift-III
(a) $\frac{2}{3}$ (b) $-\frac{3}{2}$
(c) $\frac{3}{2}$ (d) $-\frac{2}{3}$

72. Simplify the given expression.
$$\frac{(326+222)^2-(326-222)^2}{(326\times 222)}$$
SSC CGL (Tier-I) 18/07/2023 Shift-I

(a) 1 (b) 4
(c) 3 (d) 2

73. $18\div\{(6 \text{ of } 2-4)\}\times 5\,(6-3)=$.........
SSC CGL (Tier-I) 17/07/2023 Shift-IV

(a) $\frac{145}{4}$ (b) $\frac{153}{4}$ (c) $\frac{154}{4}$ (d) $\frac{135}{4}$

74. Simplify the expression.
$$\frac{3.35^2-1.25^2}{3.35+1.25}=?$$
SSC CGL (Tier-I) 17/07/2023 Shift-IV

(a) 4.60 (b) 3.10
(c) 4.10 (d) 2.1

75. The product of 277 and 323 is
SSC CGL (Tier-I) 17/07/2023 Shift-III

(a) 89471 (b) 88471
(c) 91371 (d) 89391

76. Solve the following expression.
$(-25)\times 8+(-25)\times 2$
SSC CGL (Tier-I) 17/07/2023 Shift-III

(a) –210 (b) 250
(c) –250 (d) 210

77. Simplify $2.5\times[144\div 198\times\{121\times 81\div(11\times 9)\}]$
SSC CGL (Tier-I) 17/07/2023 Shift-I

(a) 180 (b) 175
(c) 185 (d) 190

78. Simplify the following expression.
$(2\times 7-5+9\div 3)\div(4+2)^2\times 2$
SSC CGL (Tier-I) 14/07/2023 Shift-IV

(a) 2 (b) $\frac{3}{2}$
(c) $\frac{2}{3}$ (d) 1.5

79. Simplify the given expression
$18\div 3 \text{ of } 2\times 5+72\div 18 \text{ of } 2\times 3-4\div 8\times 2$
SSC CGL (Tier-I) 14/07/2023 Shift-IV

(a) 20 (b) $\frac{20}{3}$
(c) $\frac{25}{3}$ (d) 25

80. Simplify the following expression.
$$\left[\frac{85}{34}\times\frac{1}{18}-\left\{\left(\frac{46}{69}\div\frac{27}{135}\right)-\left(\frac{86}{129}\times\frac{91}{14}\right)\right\} \text{ of } \frac{112}{36}\right]$$
SSC CGL (Tier-I) 14/07/2023 Shift-III

(a) $3\frac{1}{5}$ (b) $3\frac{3}{4}$
(c) $3\frac{1}{2}$ (d) $3\frac{1}{4}$

81. Find the simplified value of the given expression.
$$4\frac{4}{5}\div\frac{3}{5} \text{ of } 5+\frac{4}{5}\times\frac{3}{10}-\frac{1}{5}$$
SSC CGL (Tier-I) 14/07/2023 Shift-II

(a) $1\frac{16}{25}$ (b) 6 (c) 5 (d) $1\frac{4}{5}$

SSC CGL 2022-2020 (Tier I)

82. The value of $\frac{1.6\times 1.6\times 1.6-0.6\times 0.6\times 0.6}{1.6\times 1.6+1.6\times 0.6+0.6\times 0.6}$ is
SSC CGL (Tier-I) 12/12/2022 Shift-III

(a) 0 (b) 1 (c) –1 (d) 2

83. Simplify the following
$25^3-75^3+50^3$
SSC CGL (Tier-I) 05/12/2022 Shift-III

(a) 281350 (b) –281450
(c) –281250 (d) 271250

84. The value of $\frac{428\times 428\times 428+348\times 348\times 348}{428\times 428-428\times 348+348\times 348}$ is
SSC CGL (Tier-I) 01/12/2022 Shift-IV

(a) 776 (b) 62080
(c) 80 (d) 40

85. If $\frac{(17)^3+(7)^3}{(17^2+7^2-k)}=24$, then what is the value of k?
SSC CGL (Tier-I) 01/12/2022 Shift-I

(a) 119 (b) 128
(c) 24 (d) 109

86. Simplify the following expression.
$$\left(\frac{3}{4}-\frac{1}{4}\div\frac{1}{4} \text{ of } \frac{2}{5}\right)\div\left(\frac{3}{4}\div\frac{2}{3} \text{ of } \frac{3}{5}\right)$$
SSC CGL (Tier-I) 24/08/2021 Shift-III

(a) $\frac{14}{75}$ (b) $\frac{32}{75}$ (c) $-\frac{70}{27}$ (d) $-\frac{14}{15}$

87. The value of $3\frac{1}{5}\div 4\frac{1}{2} \text{ of } 5\frac{1}{3}-\frac{1}{8}\div\frac{1}{2} \text{ of } \frac{1}{4}+\frac{1}{4}\left(\frac{1}{2}+\frac{1}{8}\times\frac{1}{4}\right)$ is
SSC CGL (Tier-I) 24/08/2021 Shift-I

(a) $-\frac{37}{60}$ (b) $-\frac{17}{60}$ (c) $\frac{17}{60}$ (d) $\frac{37}{60}$

88. Simplify the following expression
$7\times 4\div 21 \text{ of } 4-5\div 4\times(9-13)+2-2\div 8$
SSC CGL (Tier-I) 23/08/2021 Shift-I

(a) $5\frac{1}{16}$ (b) $7\frac{1}{12}$
(c) $5\frac{1}{3}$ (d) $12\frac{1}{2}$

89. Simplify the following expression:
$3\times 8\div 9 \text{ of } 6-2\div 3\times(5-2)\times 2+18\div 3 \text{ of } 3$
SSC CGL (Tier-I) 20/08/2021 Shift-I

(a) $-1\frac{5}{9}$ (b) $2\frac{12}{13}$
(c) –4 (d) $2\frac{1}{3}$

90. Simplify the expression
$$441\div\left[270\div\frac{3}{7}+\left(17\div\frac{1}{3}\right)-\left(8\frac{1}{2}-\frac{5}{2}\right)\right]$$
SSC CGL (Tier-I) 18/08/2021 Shift-III

(a) $\frac{39}{75}$ (b) $\frac{29}{75}$ (c) $\frac{19}{75}$ (d) $\frac{49}{75}$

91. The value of
$18\div[26-\{25-(15-5)\div 2\}] \text{ of } 12+2-2\div 4\times 16$ is
SSC CGL (Tier-I) 18/08/2021 Shift-I

(a) $-\frac{23}{4}$ (b) $\frac{3}{2}$
(c) $\frac{9}{4}$ (d) $-\frac{25}{2}$

92. Simplify the following expression.
$$\frac{(375+125)^2-(125-375)^2}{375\times 375-125\times 125}$$
SSC CGL (Tier-I) 18/08/2021 Shift-I

(a) $\frac{15}{8}$ (b) $\frac{3}{2}$
(c) $\frac{27}{28}$ (d) $\frac{3}{4}$

93. Simplify the following expression.
$$\left(\frac{7}{16}\div\frac{1}{2} \text{ of } \frac{1}{5}\right)\times\frac{4}{5}-\frac{1}{3}\times\frac{5}{8}\div\frac{1}{2}+\frac{3}{4}$$
SSC CGL (Tier-I) 17/08/2021 Shift-III

(a) $\frac{23}{6}$ (b) $\frac{10}{3}$ (c) $\frac{317}{96}$ (d) $\frac{71}{150}$

94. The value of $32\div 12$ of $3\times[5-(15-12)\div 9] \text{ of } \frac{3}{7}+4-8\div 2$ of 4 is
SSC CGL (Tier-I) 17/08/2021 Shift-I

(a) $3\frac{1}{3}$ (b) $4\frac{7}{9}$
(c) $3\frac{1}{6}$ (d) $1\frac{7}{9}$

95. The value of $\frac{52-1170\div 26+13\times 2}{2+1\frac{1}{8} \text{ of } 2-1\frac{1}{4}}$ is
SSC CGL (Tier-I) 16/08/2021 Shift-I

(a) 12 (b) 41
(c) 27 (d) 11

96. The value of $90\div 20$ of $6\times[11\div 4 \text{ of } \{3\times 2-(3-8)\}]\div(9\div 3\times 2)$ is
SSC CGL (Tier-I) 13/08/2021 Shift-III

(a) $\frac{9}{8}$ (b) $\frac{3}{8}$ (c) $\frac{1}{36}$ (d) $\frac{1}{32}$

97. The value of $1\frac{1}{8}\div\left(4\frac{1}{4}\div\frac{3}{5} \text{ of } 8\frac{1}{2}\right)-\frac{2}{5}\times 1\frac{1}{3}\div\frac{4}{5} \text{ of } 1\frac{2}{3}+\frac{11}{20}$ is
SSC CGL (Tier-I) 07/03/2020 Shift-II

(a) $1\frac{1}{2}$ (b) $1\frac{1}{4}$ (c) $3\frac{1}{8}$ (d) $3\frac{1}{2}$

98. The value of 151^2-149^2 is
SSC CGL (Tier-I) 07/03/2020 Shift-I
(a) 600 (b) 300
(c) 2^2 (d) 400

99. The value of $3-(9-3\times8\div2)$ is
SSC CGL (Tier-I) 07/03/2020 Shift-I
(a) – 21 (b) 6
(c) 0 (d) $\frac{21}{2}$

100. The value of $=\frac{[54-(5\div2)\times8]+13}{48-4\div3\times8-2}$ is
SSC CGL (Tier-I) 06/03/2020 Shift-III
(a) $\frac{89}{127}$ (b) $\frac{89}{106}$
(c) $\frac{141}{127}$ (d) $\frac{141}{106}$

101. Solve the following
$\frac43\div\frac16\times2-1=?$
SSC CGL (Tier-I) 06/03/2020 Shift-II
(a) –2 (b) 8
(c) 3 (d) 15

102. What is the value of
$40-[3-\{4-(6-6-4)\}]$
SSC CGL (Tier-I) 06/03/2020 Shift-I
(a) 47 (b) 100
(c) 300 (d) 37

103. The value of $-1+\frac14\div\frac12\times2+5$ is
SSC CGL (Tier-I) 05/03/2020 Shift-III
(a) 5 (b) 2
(c) $\frac{17}{4}$ (d) $-\frac72$

104. The value of $\frac35\times1\frac78\div1\frac13$ of $\frac{3}{16}-\left(3\frac15\div4\frac12\text{ of }5\frac13\right)\times2\frac12+\frac12+\frac18\div\frac14$ is
SSC CGL (Tier-I) 05/03/2020 Shift-II
(a) $4\frac13$ (b) $5\frac56$ (c) $5\frac16$ (d) $4\frac18$

SSC CPO SI 2024

105. Find the value of
$[16\div2-7\times15\div3+\{(1+4)\times5\}+4\times3-10]$
SSC CPO 29/06/2024 Shift-III
(a) 2 (b) 0 (c) 4 (d) –2

106. Simplify the given expression.
$55\frac13\div\left[3\frac15+\left\{2\frac12-\left(2\frac13+\frac35\right)\right\}\right]$
SSC CPO 29/06/2024 Shift-III
(a) 25 (b) 15 (c) 20 (d) 35

107. Simplify : $45\div5\times5+10-5$.
SSC CPO 29/06/2024 Shift-III
(a) 60 (b) 30 (c) 50 (d) 40

108. Simplify
$8.16\times5.35+17.9-19.5\text{ of }\frac{1}{15}+\frac15$
SSC CPO 29/06/2024 Shift-III
(a) 60.456 (b) 70.225
(c) 57.426 (d) 65.234

109. Simplify the following expression :
$3\frac17\div1\frac47+3\text{ of }2\frac23+2.5\times2.4\div3\frac13-4$ of 3
SSC CPO 29/06/2024 Shift-III
(a) $-\frac45$ (b) $-\frac35$ (c) $-\frac15$ (d) $-\frac25$

110. Simplify the given expression.
$\frac{53-\frac27\text{ of }63-9}{72-\frac25\text{ of }(96-31)}$
SSC CPO 29/06/2024 Shift-III
(a) $\frac{13}{23}$ (b) $\frac{7}{23}$ (c) $\frac{11}{23}$ (d) $\frac{26}{23}$

111. The value of
$264\div8-1-32\times2+80\div5\times40\div20$ is
SSC CPO 29/06/2024 Shift-II
(a) 0 (b) 1 (c) 3 (d) 2

112. Simplify $63-[15+\{17-(9-7+1)\}]$.
SSC CPO 29/06/2024 Shift-II
(a) 44 (b) 40 (c) 34 (d) 30

113. The value of
$(12+18)\div2-11+16\times4-28+13(-18+15)$ is
SSC CPO 29/06/2024 Shift-II
(a) 3 (b) 0
(c) 1 (d) 2

114. The value of
$\frac{(275\times275\times275+725\times725\times725)}{(275\times275+725\times725-725\times275)}\times\frac{(275\times275\times275-725\times725\times725)}{(275\times275+725\times725+725\times275)}$
is
SSC CPO 29/06/2024 Shift-II
(a) –45000 (b) 450000
(c) 45000 (d) –450000

115. The value of
$\frac{7+8\times8\div8\text{ of }8+8\div8\times5}{4\div4\text{ of }4+4\times4\div4-4\div4}$ is
SSC CPO 29/06/2024 Shift-II
(a) 4 (b)3
(c) 2 (d)1

116. If $x+\frac{1}{1+\frac{1}{3+\frac12}}=1$, then the value of x is equal to
SSC CPO 29/06/2024 Shift-II
(a) $\frac29$ (b) $\frac17$
(c) $\frac79$ (d) $\frac37$

117. Simplify the given expression.
$12.3-[7+0.8\text{ of }(5.6-3.8\times1.03)]$
SSC CPO 29/06/2024 Shift-II
(a) 1.2368 (b) 7.8539
(c) 5.2314 (d) 3.9512

118. The value of
$\frac{1}{2^2}+\frac{1}{2^3}\div\left(\frac12+\frac12\div1\right)+3\frac13\div\frac52\times\frac34\div6\frac23\times\frac76$ is
SSC CPO 29/06/2024 Shift-II
(a) $\frac{7}{40}$ (b) $\frac{21}{20}$ (c) $\frac{11}{20}$ (d) $\frac{11}{30}$

119. Simplify
$\left(\frac34+\frac54\right)\times\left(\frac95-\frac45\right)\div\left(\frac32+\frac12\right)$.
SSC CPO 29/06/2024 Shift-I
(a) 1 (b) – 1
(c) 2 (d) – 2

120. Simplify the given expression
$\left(7.2\times4.1\div12.3+22.5\text{ of }\frac{1}{25}-\frac{1}{10}\right)$
SSC CPO 29/06/2024 Shift-I
(a) 4.9 (b) 9.6
(c) 7.4 (d) 3.2

121. If $m\times7+4-6\div3-7+45\div5\times4+49=87$, then the value of m is
SSC CPO 29/06/2024 Shift-I
(a) 0 (b) 14
(c) 1 (d) 7

122. Simplify
$\left[\left(7\frac14\right)^2-\left(5\frac45\right)^2\right]\div5\frac45\times\frac{16}{9}$
SSC CPO 29/06/2024 Shift-I
(a) 9.3 (b) 7.4 (c) 5.8 (d) 3.1

123. Simplify the given expression
$\frac{\left(2\frac17+6\frac17\right)\div\frac97}{1\frac19\div\left\{\frac79+\left(\frac49\div\frac43\right)\right\}}$
SSC CPO 29/06/2024 Shift-I
(a) $\frac{56}{9}$ (b) $\frac{55}{9}$ (c) $\frac{58}{9}$ (d) $\frac{53}{9}$

124. The value of $\left(2\frac12+1\frac34-\frac16\right)\times16\div49$ is
SSC CPO 29/06/2024 Shift-I
(a) $\frac47$ (b) $\frac39$
(c) $1\frac13$ (d) $2\frac34$

125. Simplify $13.5-[5+0.5\times(9-3\times2)]$
SSC CPO 28/06/2024 Shift-III
(a) 5 (b) 7 (c) 6 (d) 8

126. Simplify
$22.0625-[15+0.25\times(4.78-15\times3.02)]$
SSC CPO 28/06/2024 Shift-III
(a) 7.1 (b) 7.3
(c) 7.2 (d) 7.0

127. The value of
$72\div8-210\div15-5+2\times5$ is
SSC CPO 28/06/2024 Shift-III
(a) 3 (b) 0 (c) 1 (d) 2

128. Simplify the following
$$\frac{2\left\{3+3\left(\frac{1}{4}\div\frac{15}{20}+2\right)-18\times\frac{1}{3}\right\}}{2(4+20\div4)}$$
SSC CPO 28/06/2024 Shift-III
(a) $\frac{7}{18}$ (b) $\frac{11}{18}$ (c) $\frac{4}{9}$ (d) $\frac{5}{9}$

129. Find the value of $\frac{3\div3\times2-6\div3+7}{5\div5\times6\div6+3+3}$.
SSC CPO 28/06/2024 Shift-III
(a) 1 (b) $\frac{6}{7}$ (c) $\frac{8}{7}$ (d) 2

130. If $56\div4+p\times3-24\div12+4$ $=21\div3+3$, then the value of p is
SSC CPO 28/06/2024 Shift-III
(a) 2 (b) 1 (c) –1 (d) –2

131. Find the value of
$\left[9+3-2\times\left\{\left(4\div\frac{1}{4}\right)-4\right\}\right.$
$\left.+81\div9+81\div9+3-9\right]+9$
SSC CPO 28/06/2024 Shift-III
(a) 3 (b) 9
(c) 6 (d) 0

132. Simplify the given expression
$$\frac{13\div\{6-6\div(7-9)\times8+9\}}{5+5\times5\div5\text{ of }5}$$
SSC CPO 28/06/2024 Shift-III
(a) $\frac{1}{18}$ (b) 13 (c) 39 (d) $\frac{1}{2}$

133. Simplify the following expression.
$(4.2\text{ of }2.5\div3.5)-(3.6\div2.4+2.5\text{ of }3\div7.5)$
$+(6-3\text{ of }2+4\text{ of }3\div6)$
SSC CPO 28/06/2024 Shift-III
(a) 4.5 (b) 3.5 (c) 1.5 (d) 2.5

134. Simplify the given expression.
$[\{9\times81+(142\div2)\}+350$
$-155+5]\div[(25\times25)-125]$
SSC CPO 28/06/2024 Shift-II
(a) 1 (b) –1 (c) –2 (d) 2

135. Simplify the given expression.
$1000\times100-1000+4000\div200$
SSC CPO 28/06/2024 Shift-II
(a) 99235 (b) 99980
(c) 99020 (d) 99999

136. Simplify the following expression.
$(6+6\text{ of }5\div5)\div6\text{ of }5+(24\div2$
$\text{of }3-6\text{ of }5+4)$
SSC CPO 28/06/2024 Shift-II
(a) $-26\frac{2}{5}$ (b) $-21\frac{3}{5}$
(c) $-17\frac{2}{5}$ (d) $-23\frac{1}{5}$

137. The value of
$66\div[34-(32\text{ of }2-4)\div(4\times15)]$ is equal to
SSC CPO 28/06/2024 Shift-II
(a) 3 (b) 2
(c) 0 (d) 1

138. Simplify
$$\left[3\frac{2}{5}\times\left\{2\frac{3}{4}+3.3\left(5\frac{1}{3}+3\frac{1}{3}-2\frac{1}{3}\right)\right\}\right]$$
SSC CPO 28/06/2024 Shift-II
(a) 46.29 (b) 80.41
(c) 70.25 (d) 53.25

139. Find the simplified value of
$5055-(1002\div20.04)$.
SSC CPO 28/06/2024 Shift-II
(a) 50.05 (b) 4050
(c) 5050 (d) 5005

140. If $855\div15-K+32\times5=1152\div16\times111\div37$, then the value of K is
SSC CPO 28/06/2024 Shift-II
(a) 0 (b) 3
(c) 2 (d) 1

141. If $x[-5\{-4(-a)\}]+6[-3\{-3(-a)\}]=6a$, then the value of x is
SSC CPO 28/06/2024 Shift-I
(a) –3 (b) –1
(c) 2 (d) 0

142. The value of
$29-[(48\div12)+2\times(8\div4+4)]$ is equal to
SSC CPO 28/06/2024 Shift-I
(a) 15 (b) 21
(c) 19 (d) 13

143. Simplify the following expression
$$\frac{3.2\times3.2-0.2\times0.2}{0.2\times0.2-2\times0.2\times3.2+3.2\times3.2}$$
SSC CPO 28/06/2024 Shift-I
(a) $\frac{13}{15}$ (b) $\frac{19}{15}$
(c) $\frac{17}{15}$ (d) $\frac{11}{15}$

144. Simplify : $20\div5\text{ of }4\times8+6\div24\text{ of }3\times48-6\div18\times9$.
SSC CPO 28/06/2024 Shift-I
(a) 6 (b) 4
(c) 9 (d) 1.125

145. Find the value of
$[\{(82+48\div8\times3)+5\times6\}-7.5\times2]$
SSC CPO 28/06/2024 Shift-I
(a) 115 (b) 125 (c) 121 (d) 130

146. Simplify
$$1898\div\left[\frac{13}{4}\times(35+45)-\frac{91}{4}\right]$$
SSC CPO 28/06/2024 Shift-I
(a) 4 (b) 8
(c) 12 (d) 16

147. Simplify $[25-(-4)\{9-(6-2)\}]$
$\div[3\times\{6+(-3)\times(-3)\}]$
SSC CPO 28/06/2024 Shift-I
(a) 1 (b) 6
(c) 4 (d) 2

148. The value of $1-\cfrac{1}{1+\cfrac{1}{2-\cfrac{1}{2+\cfrac{1}{3}}}}$ is
SSC CPO 28/06/2024 Shift-I
(a) $\frac{7}{18}$ (b) $\frac{3}{11}$
(c) $\frac{7}{15}$ (d) $\frac{3}{16}$

149. The value of
$$5\frac{1}{4}-\left[3\frac{1}{2}-\left\{\frac{5}{6}-\left(\frac{3}{5}\times\frac{1}{10}\div\frac{4}{5}\right)\right\}\right]\text{ is}$$
SSC CPO 28/06/2024 Shift-I
(a) $2\frac{43}{120}$ (b) $1\frac{18}{120}$
(c) $1\frac{97}{120}$ (d) $2\frac{47}{120}$

150. The value of
$64\div[44-(8\text{ of }3-16)\div4\times20]$ is equal to
SSC CPO 28/06/2024 Shift-I
(a) 15 (b) 16
(c) 18 (d) 12

151. The value of $9\times9+9\div9-9\times9$
$+9+9\times9-9-9\times9$ is
SSC CPO 27/06/2024 Shift-III
(a) 9 (b) 81
(c) 1 (d) 0

152. Simplify : $22\times10\div5\times2+12$
SSC CPO 27/06/2024 Shift-III
(a) 101 (b) 103
(c) 100 (d) 102

153. The value of
$$\frac{1}{4}+\frac{2}{5}\div\left[\left\{2\frac{1}{5}-2\right\}\times5\right]-\frac{2}{3}\text{ of }\frac{3}{5}\text{ is}$$
SSC CPO 27/06/2024 Shift-III
(a) $\frac{2}{3}$ (b) $\frac{1}{4}$ (c) $\frac{3}{5}$ (d) $\frac{5}{6}$

154. Simplify : $[\{38-(-6)\}\times\{9-(8-1)\}]$
$\div[4\times\{6+(-4)\}]$ SSC CPO 27/06/2024 Shift-III
(a) 14 (b) 18 (c) 11 (d) 22

155. The value of $(4^2)^2+4\times4\div4-4$ is
SSC CPO 27/06/2024 Shift-III
(a) 4^0 (b) 4^2
(c) 4^3 (d) 4^4

156. The value of $5 + [6 + (3 + 5) \div 2] \div 2$ is equal to **SSC CPO 27/06/2024 Shift-III**

(a) 8 (b) 12
(c) 10 (d) 14

157. Simplify the following expression.

$$\frac{(525+175)^2-(525-175)^2}{(525\times 175)}$$

SSC CPO 27/06/2024 Shift-III

(a) 700 (b) 4
(c) 2 (d) 350

158. Simplify
$35 - [30 + \{10 + (12 - 10 - 4)\}]$ **SSC CPO 27/06/2024 Shift-III**

(a) –3 (b) 2
(c) –2 (d) 3

159. Simplify : $\dfrac{92736}{(274+830) \text{ of } \frac{7}{4}} + 513$

SSC CPO 27/06/2024 Shift-III

(a) 574 (b) 546
(c) 561 (d) 526

160. Simplify: $8.2 + 2.6 + 3.2 - 4.5 \div 0.9 \times 1.2$ **SSC CPO 27/06/2024 Shift-II**

(a) 6 (b) 10
(c) 4 (d) 8

161. Simplify the following expression
$25 \times 25 + 9 \times 9 + 6 \times 6 + 2 \times 25 \times 9 + 2 \times 9 \times 6 + 2 \times 25 \times 6$ **SSC CPO 27/06/2024 Shift-II**

(a) 2500 (b) 1200
(c) 1600 (d) 900

162. Find the value of

$$\frac{12+3\frac{2}{3}\div\left[1\frac{3}{4}\div\left\{5\frac{1}{4}\times\left(3\frac{3}{5}\div 4\frac{1}{2}\right)\right\}\right]}{1\frac{1}{3}\times 5\frac{1}{5}}$$

SSC CPO 27/06/2024 Shift-II

(a) 1 (b) 3
(c) 5 (d) 2

163. The value of
$30 + 180 \div 30 \times 6 - 15 - 16 - 60 \div 3 - 15$ is **SSC CPO 27/06/2024 Shift-II**

(a) 2 (b) 1
(c) 0 (d) 3

164. The value of $1-\dfrac{7}{1-\dfrac{1}{1+\dfrac{1}{1-7}}}$ is

SSC CPO 27/06/2024 Shift-II

(a) –1 (b) 2 (c) 1 (d) 0

165. Find the value of $(13.49 + 12.51) \times 13$. **SSC CPO 27/06/2024 Shift-II**

(a) 438 (b) 238
(c) 138 (d) 338

166. Simplify : $9^{18} \div 3^{14} \text{ of } 27^3 \times \sqrt{6561}$ **SSC CPO 27/06/2024 Shift-II**

(a) 3^{16} (b) 3^{18}
(c) 3^{15} (d) 3^{17}

167. Simplify
$5 \times [14 \div 13 \times \{13 \times 14 \div (14 \times 14)\}]$ **SSC CPO 27/06/2024 Shift-II**

(a) 10 (b) 15
(c) 5 (d) 20

168. Simplify the following expression.
$3\frac{1}{5} \text{ of } 2\frac{3}{4} \div \frac{11}{3} + \left(2\frac{1}{5} \div 1\frac{2}{5} \text{ of } 1\frac{3}{7} - 2\frac{1}{3}\right)$ **SSC CPO 27/06/2024 Shift-I**

(a) $2\frac{1}{6}$ (b) $4\frac{1}{6}$ (c) $1\frac{1}{6}$ (d) $3\frac{1}{6}$

169. Simplify the given expression.
$25 \div 5 \times 7 \text{ of } (5 + 7) - 13(6 \times 4)$ **SSC CPO 27/06/2024 Shift-I**

(a) 108 (b) 138
(c) 126 (d) 112

170. Find the value of
$12 + 24 \div 2 - 7 \times 30 \div 6 + (5 + 4) \times 8 + 8 \div 8 - 8$. **SSC CPO 27/06/2024 Shift-I**

(a) 45 (b) 54
(c) 85 (d) 58

171. The value of

$$3\frac{2}{3}\div 2\frac{1}{5}\times\frac{1}{4}\times\left(1+\frac{3}{1-\frac{2}{5}}\right) \text{ is}$$

SSC CPO 27/06/2024 Shift-I

(a) $2\frac{1}{4}$ (b) $1\frac{3}{4}$ (c) $3\frac{1}{2}$ (d) $2\frac{1}{2}$

172. Find the value of

$$\left[18-3\times\left\{3-3\times\left(3\div\frac{1}{3}-3\right)+3\div\frac{1}{3}+3\right\}-4\times 2\right]$$

SSC CPO 27/06/2024 Shift-I

(a) 18 (b) 15
(c) 12 (d) 19

173. The value of
$35 - [28 - (60 \div 4 + 26 \div 13)]$ is equal to **SSC CPO 27/06/2024 Shift-I**

(a) 22 (b) 24
(c) 27 (d) 26

SSC CPO SI 2023-2020

174. The value of $\dfrac{(157\times 157)+(157\times 133)+(133\times 133)}{(157\times 157\times 157)-(133\times 133\times 133)}$ is **SSC CPO 04/10/2023 Shift-II**

(a) $\frac{1}{24}$ (b) 24 (c) 290 (d) $\frac{1}{290}$

175. Simplify the following.
$19 \div 5 \text{ of } (27 - 15 - 21) + 37$ **SSC CPO 04/10/2023 Shift-II**

(a) $\frac{6124}{165}$ (b) $\frac{19}{165}$ (c) $\frac{6142}{165}$ (d) $\frac{37}{165}$

176. Evaluate $\dfrac{0.04}{0.05} \text{ of } \dfrac{\left(3\frac{1}{3}-2\frac{1}{2}\right)\div\frac{1}{2} \text{ of } 1\frac{1}{4}}{\frac{1}{3}+\frac{1}{5} \text{ of } \frac{1}{9}}$

SSC CPO 03/10/2023 Shift-I

(a) 0.3 (b) 5 (c) 3 (d) 0.03

177. Find the value of the following expression.

$$\frac{\left[\frac{5}{8}-\left\{\frac{3}{8}-\left(\frac{5}{8}-\frac{3}{8}\right)\right\}\right] \text{ of } 8.8-1.2}{4\frac{1}{6}\div 2.5\times 2\div\frac{1}{6} \text{ of } 60+\left(\frac{3}{4}-\frac{3}{8}\right)}$$

SSC CPO 11/11/2022 Shift-II

(a) $5\frac{22}{43}$ (b) $3\frac{23}{67}$ (c) $4\frac{44}{85}$ (d) $4\frac{4}{5}$

178. The simplified value of
$(0.2)^3 \times 400 \div 2000 \text{ of } (0.2)^2$ is **SSC CPO 10/11/2022 Shift-II**

(a) $\frac{1}{25}$ (b) $\frac{3}{25}$ (c) $\frac{2}{25}$ (d) $\frac{1}{50}$

179. What is the simplified value of $(0.00243)^{0.2}$? **SSC CPO 10/11/2022 Shift-II**

(a) 0.3 (b) 0.03
(c) 0.003 (d) 0.0003

180. The value of $\frac{2}{3} \div \frac{3}{10}$ of $\frac{4}{9} - \frac{4}{5} \times 1\frac{1}{9} \div \frac{8}{15} + \frac{3}{4} \div \frac{1}{2}$ is **SSC CPO 25/11/2020 Shift-II**

(a) $\frac{29}{6}$ (b) $\frac{17}{9}$
(c) $\frac{14}{3}$ (d) $\frac{49}{12}$

181. The value of $\dfrac{427\times 427\times 427+325\times 325\times 325}{42.7\times 42.7+32.5\times 32.5-42.7\times 32.5}$ is **SSC CPO 25/11/2020 Shift-II**

(a) 75.2 (b) 752
(c) 75200 (d) 7520

182. The value of
$7 \div [5 + 1 \div 2 - \{4 + (4 \text{ of } 2 \div 4\} + (5 \div 5 \text{ of } 2)\}]$ is **SSC CPO 25/11/2020 Shift-II**

(a) 7 (b) $\frac{7}{2}$ (c) –7 (d) $-\frac{7}{2}$

183. The value of

$$\frac{0.325\times 0.325+0.175\times 0.175+25\times 0.00455}{5\times 0.0065\times 3.25-7\times 0.175\times 0.025}+\frac{0.5}{1.5} \text{ is}$$

SSC CPO 24/11/2020 Shift-I

(a) 3 (b) 0 (c) $\frac{7}{3}$ (d) $\frac{11}{3}$

184. The value of $2\frac{1}{3} \div 2\frac{1}{2}$ of $1\frac{3}{5} + \left(\frac{3}{8} + \frac{1}{7} \times 1\frac{3}{4}\right)$ is

SSC CPO 24/11/2020 Shift-I

(a) $\frac{25}{24}$ (b) $\frac{29}{24}$ (c) $\frac{35}{24}$ (d) $\frac{5}{24}$

185. The value of $\dfrac{40 - \frac{3}{4} \text{ of } 32}{37 - \frac{3}{4} \text{ of } (34 - 6)}$ is

SSC CPO 23/11/2020 Shift-I

(a) $\frac{1}{2}$ (b) 1 (c) $-\frac{1}{2}$ (d) 0

186. The value of $8 - 3 \div 6$ of $2 + \left(4 \div 4 \text{ of } \frac{1}{4}\right) \div 8 + \left(4 \times 8 \div \frac{1}{4}\right) \times \frac{1}{8}$ is

SSC CPO 23/11/2020 Shift-I

(a) $\frac{7}{4}$ (b) $-\frac{97}{4}$ (c) $-\frac{7}{4}$ (d) $\frac{97}{4}$

SSC CHSL 2024 (Tier I & II)

187. The value of $5 + 24 \times 8 \div 8$ of $8 - 8 \div 8 \times 4$ of 4 is equal to

SSC CHSL (Tier II) 18/11/2024

(a) –9 (b) 9
(c) –8 (d) 8

188. If $\frac{15}{8} + \left[\left\{\frac{4}{5} \text{of} \frac{5}{12} \div \left(1\frac{1}{15}\right)\right\} \times 1\frac{7}{12}\right]$ is expressed in the form of $\frac{a}{b}$, where a and b are integers and relatively prime to each other, the value $4b - a$ is

SSC CHSL (Tier I) 11/07/2024 Shift-IV

(a) 313 (b) 225 (c) 164 (d) 189

189. If $640 \div 8 + 930 \div 15 - k + 32 \times 5 = 1104 \div 16 \times 148 \div 37$, then the value of k is

SSC CHSL (Tier I) 11/07/2024 Shift-III

(a) 276 (b) 26 (c) 35 (d) 302

190. The value of $[3^3\{(40 \times 5) + (7 \times 6)\} \div 11] + (2^3 \times 15 \div 24)$ is

SSC CHSL (Tier I) 10/07/2024 Shift-III

(a) 959 (b) 595
(c) 599 (d) 559

191. If $42 \div 3 + k \times 3 - 22 \div 11 + 4 = 28$, then the value of k is

SSC CHSL (Tier I) 10/07/2024 Shift-III

(a) 0 (b) 1 (c) 4 (d) 2

192. If $A = 60\left[\frac{6}{25} \div \left(\frac{16}{15} \text{ of } \frac{3}{8}\right) + 5 - \left(1 - 2\frac{1}{12}\right)\right]$, then the sum of the digits of A is

SSC CHSL (Tier I) 10/07/2024 Shift-II

(a) 7 (b) 3
(c) 5 (d) 6

193. If $A = \frac{9}{16} \div \frac{25}{36}$, $B = 9 \div [(16 \div 25) \div 36]$, $C = [9 \div (16 \div 25)] \div 36$, $D = (9 \div 16) \div (25 \div 36)$, then which of the following is true?

SSC CHSL (Tier I) 10/07/2024 Shift-II

(a) B and D are equal
(b) C and D are equal
(c) A and B are equal
(d) A and D are equal

194. Simplify the following.
$12 \div 4$ of $3 \times 6 + 8 \div 16$ of $4 \times 8 - 4 \div 6 \times 9$

SSC CHSL (Tier I) 10/07/2024 Shift-I

(a) 13 (b) –1 (c) 1 (d) $6\frac{1}{4}$

195. Simplify
$\left[6 - 2\left\{3 - 4\left(4 \div \frac{1}{4} - 1\right) + 2 \div \frac{1}{3}\right\} - 3 \times 2\right]$

SSC CHSL (Tier I) 09/07/2024 Shift-IV

(a) 102 (b) 98
(c) 96 (d) 92

196. The value of $\dfrac{5 + 7 \times 5 \div 8 \text{ of } 5 + 3 \div 3 \times 5}{6 \div 6 \text{ of } 4 + 9 \times 9 \div 3 \times 2 \times 2}$ is

SSC CHSL (Tier I) 09/07/2024 Shift-III

(a) $\frac{77}{861}$ (b) $\frac{97}{881}$ (c) $\frac{67}{859}$ (d) $\frac{87}{866}$

197. What is the value of the following expression?
$\left(24 \div 3 \text{ of } \frac{1}{6}\right) \times \left(\frac{4}{5} \div \frac{9}{8} \times \frac{3}{5}\right) \div \left(\frac{4}{7} \div \frac{3}{14} \text{of} \frac{3}{14}\right)$

SSC CHSL (Tier I) 09/07/2024 Shift-II

(a) $\frac{579}{459}$ (b) $\frac{288}{175}$ (c) $\frac{379}{179}$ (d) $\frac{363}{553}$

198. Simplify the expression :
$720 + 48 \div 8 \times 5 - 6 \times 3$

SSC CHSL (Tier I) 08/07/2024 Shift-IV

(a) $\frac{112}{5}$ (b) 732
(c) 161 (d) 242

199. Solve $\dfrac{2 \times 2 + 2}{2 \div 2 \times 2} \div \dfrac{\frac{1}{2} \div \frac{1}{2} \text{ of } \frac{1}{2}}{\frac{1}{2} + \frac{1}{2} \text{ of } \frac{1}{2}}$.

SSC CHSL (Tier I) 08/07/2024 Shift-IV

(a) $4\frac{1}{8}$ (b) $3\frac{1}{8}$ (c) $2\frac{1}{8}$ (d) $1\frac{1}{8}$

200. What is the value of the following expression?
$420 \div \left[\frac{4}{9} \times \left(1 + \frac{4}{5}\right) \times 5\right] + \left[\frac{5}{7} \text{ of } \frac{21}{25} \div \frac{3}{4} \text{ of } \frac{2}{5}\right]$

SSC CHSL (Tier I) 08/07/2024 Shift-III

(a) 127 (b) 139 (c) 107 (d) 89

201. Simplify the following expression.
$4 \times 7 - 3\{7 \times 4 + (6 \times 2)\}$

SSC CHSL (Tier I) 08/07/2024 Shift-I

(a) 21 (b) 4 (c) 19 (d) 12

202. Simplify
$\dfrac{\frac{1}{2} \div \frac{3}{4} \text{ of } \frac{5}{6}}{\frac{1}{2} \div \frac{3}{4} \times \frac{5}{6}} + \dfrac{2 + 2 \times 2}{2 \div 2 \times 2}$

SSC CHSL (Tier I) 05/07/2024 Shift-II

(a) $\frac{121}{25}$ (b) 4 (c) $\frac{111}{25}$ (d) $\frac{75}{36}$

203. Simplify the following expression.
$99 - [169 \div (13 \times 13) - (-4) - \{3 - 17 + 10\}]$

SSC CHSL (Tier I) 05/07/2024 Shift-I

(a) 80 (b) 87 (c) 107 (d) 90

204. Simplify the given expression.
$\left[3 \times 6 - 3\left\{2\left(2 \div \frac{1}{2} - 2\right) + 2 \div \frac{1}{2}\right\} - 18\right]$

SSC CHSL (Tier I) 04/07/2024 Shift-IV

(a) 24 (b) 18
(c) –24 (d) –18

205. The value of $10 + 3\frac{3}{5} \div \left[2\frac{2}{3} \div \left\{7\frac{1}{6} - \left(2\frac{1}{2} + \frac{2}{3}\right)\right\}\right]$ is equal to

SSC CHSL (Tier I) 04/07/2024 Shift-II

(a) $\frac{77}{5}$ (b) $\frac{5}{77}$ (c) $\frac{55}{27}$ (d) $\frac{27}{55}$

206. Simplify the given expression.
$8 - 5 \div 2^3 \times 3 + (7 \div 7 \times 7) \div 7 + \left(3 \times 6 \div \frac{1}{3}\right) \times \frac{1}{3^3}$

SSC CHSL (Tier I) 03/07/2024 Shift-III

(a) $\frac{73}{9}$ (b) $\frac{73}{21}$ (c) $\frac{73}{27}$ (d) $\frac{73}{8}$

207. The value of $(17 + 15) \div 2 - 11 + 16 \times 4 - 28 + 13(-16 + 13)$ is

SSC CHSL (Tier I) 03/07/2024 Shift-II

(a) 3 (b) 1 (c) 0 (d) 2

208. Simplify the following expression.
$[40 - 48 \div 4 \text{ of } 3] \div \{(6 + 4) - 4 \text{ of } 4 + 4 + (6 - 4) + (4 \times 4) \div 4\} \times 3$

SSC CHSL (Tier I) 02/07/2024 Shift-III

(a) 25 (b) 27
(c) 30 (d) 26

209. Simplify $\left\{(3^3 + 2^3) \times \frac{22}{7}\right\} \times \left\{(6^2 + 3^2 - 4^2) \div \left(14\frac{1}{2}\right)\right\}$

SSC CHSL (Tier I) 02/07/2024 Shift-III

(a) 220 (b) 198 (c) 110 (d) 145

210. Simplify the following expression.
$(3 - 3 \times 3 + 3 \div 3 + 3 \times 5) \times 2$ of $5 + (2 + 2 \div 2 + 2 \times 2 - 2)$
SSC CHSL (Tier I) 02/07/2024 Shift-II
(a) 102 (b) 100 (c) 106 (d) 105

211. Simplify :
$18 \div (7 \times 2 - 5) \times 5 \times 24 \div 30$
SSC CHSL (Tier I) 02/07/2024 Shift-I
(a) 8 (b) 0.5
(c) 10 (d) 6

212. What is the value of the following expression?
$\frac{4}{7} \times 4\frac{1}{2} \div 5\frac{1}{3}$ of $2\frac{1}{2} - \left(7\frac{7}{8} \div 5\frac{1}{9} \text{ of } 9\frac{9}{20}\right) + \frac{1}{2}$
SSC CHSL (Tier I) 01/07/2024 Shift-II
(a) $\frac{853}{1610}$ (b) $\frac{1093}{111}$ (c) $\frac{1113}{856}$ (d) $\frac{1759}{3250}$

213. Simplify the following expression.
$3 + 28 \div 35 \times 15 + 4 - 3 \times 4$
SSC CHSL (Tier I) 01/07/2024 Shift-I
(a) 10 (b) 26 (c) 64 (d) 7

214. Find the value of
$\sqrt{625} + \sqrt{\frac{625}{100}} + \sqrt{\frac{625}{10000}} + \sqrt{\frac{625}{1000000}}$.
SSC CHSL (Tier II) 10/01/2024 Shift-I
(a) 27.075 (b) 27.775
(c) 27.75 (d) 27.025

215. Simplify $(\sqrt[3]{\sqrt[3]{343}})^3 \times (\sqrt[3]{\sqrt[3]{216}})^3$
SSC CHSL (Tier-II) 10/01/2024 Shift-I
(a) 56 (b) 42 (c) $\sqrt[3]{42}$ (d) 42^3

SSC CHSL 2023-2021 (Tier I & II)

216. The value of
$\left(\frac{2 + 7 \times 7 \div 9 \text{ of } 9 + 6 \div 6 \times 2}{4 \div 4 \text{ of } 5 + 7 \times 7 \div 7 - 6 + 4}\right)$ is
SSC CHSL (Tier-I) 17/08/2023 Shift-I
(a) $\frac{1734}{2407}$ (b) $\frac{1865}{2106}$ (c) $\frac{1857}{2507}$ (d) $\frac{1664}{2305}$

217. Simplify the following expression.
$\frac{(0.96 \times 0.96 \times 0.96 + 0.04 \times 0.04 \times 0.04)}{(0.96 \times 0.96 - 0.96 \times 0.04 + 0.04 \times 0.04)}$
SSC CHSL (Tier-I) 07/08/2023 Shift-II
(a) 0 (b) 0.82
(c) 2 (d) 1

218. If $(2^2 + 4)^2 \times (3 - 5) + 20\%$ of $400 + x\%$ of $30 = 30\%$ of 30, find the value of x.
SSC CHSL (Tier-I) 04/08/2023 Shift-I
(a) 150 (b) 120
(c) 190 (d) 160

219. What is the value of
$\frac{\frac{3}{4} \div \frac{9}{64} + \frac{7}{11} \times \frac{121}{14} - \frac{9}{13} \times \frac{65}{36}}{\frac{1}{2} \div \frac{4}{5} + \frac{3}{4} \times \frac{16}{15}}$?
SSC CHSL (Tier-I) 21/03/2023 Shift-II
(a) $\frac{1169}{143}$ (b) $\frac{1150}{171}$ (c) $\frac{1413}{157}$ (d) $\frac{1216}{141}$

220. The value of
$[(24 - 12) \div 4] + [81 - 48 \div 12 \text{ of } 2]$ is
SSC CHSL (Tier-I) 20/03/2023 Shift-III
(a) 67 (b) 73 (c) 35 (d) 82

221. What is the value of
$\frac{8 \times 5 \div 25}{7 \div 14 \times 2} - \frac{14 \div 7 - 5}{7 \div 14 - 25}$?
SSC CHSL (Tier-I) 16/03/2023 Shift-I
(a) $\frac{362}{245}$ (b) $\frac{115}{245}$ (c) $\frac{306}{245}$ (d) $\frac{106}{245}$

222. What is the value of
$2160 \times 3 \div 144 + 13 - 2$?
SSC CHSL (Tier-I) 15/03/2023 Shift-IV
(a) 56 (b) 57 (c) 59 (d) 54

223. What is the value of
$\frac{\frac{5}{3} \text{ of } \frac{1}{4} \times \frac{24}{5} - \frac{1}{5} \text{ of } \frac{25}{8} \times \frac{24}{5}}{\frac{5}{12} \text{ of } \frac{3}{4} \times \frac{4}{3} + \frac{3}{4} \text{ of } \frac{12}{5} \times \frac{5}{6}}$?
SSC CHSL (Tier-I) 15/03/2023 Shift-IV
(a) – 24/23 (b) – 12/23
(c) – 25/46 (d) – 28/23

224. What is the value of
$(1665 \div 37) + (42 \times 5)$?
SSC CHSL (Tier-I) 13/03/2023 Shift-III
(a) 285 (b) 255 (c) 270 (d) 295

225. What is the value of x, if
$x = 0.05 \times 0.36 \div 0.4 + 0.055 + 1.50 \div 0.03$
SSC CHSL (Tier-I) 13/03/2023 Shift-III
(a) 55.1 (b) 49.9 (c) 50.1 (d) 45.9

226. Find the value of
$1200 \div 15 \times [45 \div (17 - 2)]$ of $2 + [-2(1 + 2)]$.
SSC CHSL (Tier-I) 10/03/2023 Shift-II
(a) 486 (b) 0 (c) 484 (d) 474

227. What is the value of
$44 \times 12 - (25 + 13 \times 10)$?
SSC CHSL (Tier-I) 09/03/2023 Shift-I
(a) 613 (b) 633
(c) 573 (d) 373

228. Simplify the following expression.
Given expression
$= \frac{(777 \times 777 \times 777) + (423 \times 423 \times 423)}{(777 \times 777) - (777 \times 423) + (423 \times 423)} \times \frac{1}{(77 - 47)}$
SSC CHSL (Tier-I) 02/06/2022 Shift-I
(a) 40 (b) 400 (c) 1200 (d) 30

229. Simplify :
$178.01 - [86.23 - \{40.22 + (28 - 24)\}]$
SSC CHSL (Tier-I) 02/06/2022 Shift-I
(a) 125 (b) 120 (c) 130 (d) 136

230. Find the value of
$\left(\frac{9^3 + 9^4 + 9^5 + 9^6 + 9^7}{9^1 + 9^2 + 9^3 + 9^4 + 9^5}\right)^{\frac{1}{2}}$.
SSC CHSL (Tier-I) 01/06/2022 Shift-I
(a) 9 (b) 3 (c) 729 (d) 81

231. $8 + [16 - \{7 + 4 - (9 \text{ of } 3 + 6 - 4 \times 7)\}] = ?$
SSC CHSL (Tier-I) 31/05/2022 Shift-I
(a) 21 (b) 16 (c) 18 (d) 23

232. The value of $\frac{[(5.4)^3 - 0.064]}{[(5.4)^2 + 2.16 + 0.16]}$ is
SSC CHSL (Tier-I) 30/05/2022 Shift-I
(a) 5 (b) 7 (c) 3 (d) 1

233. $9 \div [5 + 7 \div \{9 + 9 \div (9 + 9 \div 4)\}] = ?$
SSC CHSL (Tier-I) 27/05/2022 Shift-I
(a) $\frac{48}{40}$ (b) $\frac{63}{40}$ (c) $\frac{59}{40}$ (d) $\frac{37}{40}$

234. $16\frac{1}{4} \div \left[2\frac{1}{6} + \left\{4\frac{1}{3} - \left(2\frac{1}{2} + \frac{3}{4}\right)\right\}\right]$ is equal to **SSC CHSL (Tier-I) 10/08/2021 Shift-I**
(a) 6 (b) 4 (c) 5 (d) 3

235. The value of $[\{(232 \div 29 \text{ of } 2) + 77 \times 10\} \div 18] - \frac{18 \times 8 \div 4 \text{ of } 3 - 4}{2 \times (8 - 6) + 1 - 2 \times 3 \div 4 \text{ of } \frac{1}{2}}$ is
SSC CHSL (Tier-I) 04/08/2021 Shift-I
(a) 39 (b) 44 (c) 33 (d) 47

SSC MTS 2024-2021

236. Simplify the following expression.
$(5 \times 5 + 5 - 5 \times 5 + 5 - 5 \times 5) + (5 \times 5) \div 5(2 + 3)$
SSC MTS 28/10/2024 Shift-II
(a) 25 (b) 10 (c) 20 (d) 5

237. Find the value of
$5 + 32 \div 2 + 6 \times 2.5$.
SSC MTS 14/10/2024 Shift-I
(a) 40 (b) 36 (c) 15 (d) 34

238. If $6\frac{1}{2} \times 2\frac{4}{5} \div x = \frac{7}{10}$, then find x.
SSC MTS 13/09/2023 Shift-I
(a) 26 (b) 6 (c) 32 (d) 12

239. What is the value of R, if
$10(8 + 4R) \div (12 \times 5) - 5 \times 2^3 = 6$?
SSC MTS 11/09/2023 Shift-II
(a) 86 (b) 68 (c) 76 (d) 67

240. Evaluate
$3\frac{1}{2} - \left[2\frac{1}{4} \div \left\{1\frac{1}{4} - \frac{3}{4}\left(1\frac{1}{2} - \frac{1}{2} - 2\frac{1}{2}\right)\right\}\right]$
SSC MTS 11/09/2023 Shift-I

(a) $1\frac{21}{38}$ (b) $2\frac{19}{18}$ (c) $2\frac{21}{38}$ (d) $\frac{47}{38}$

241. On simplifying the following expression, we get
$$\frac{24\sqrt{45}-16\sqrt{20}+\sqrt{245}-47\sqrt{5}}{3\frac{1}{5}+1\frac{2}{5}-2\frac{1}{6}-2\frac{1}{5}-5\frac{2}{5}+3\frac{1}{6}}$$
SSC MTS 08/09/2023 Shift-II

(a) 0 (b) 3 (c) 1 (d) 2

242. Simplify the following expression.
$45-22\div2+12+70\div35+0.4\div0.8+1.5\div3+1$
SSC MTS 06/09/2023 Shift-I

(a) 50 (b) 50.5
(c) 48.5 (d) 54.5

243. Which of the following expressions has value equal to 0 ?
SSC MTS 04/09/2023 Shift-II

(a) $(2\times3+5-(1-2(3-2\times2)))$
(b) $(2\times3-5-(1+2(3-2\times2)))$
(c) $(2\times3-5+(1+2(3-2\times2)))$
(d) $(2\times3-5-(1-2(3-2\times2)))$

244. Simplify
$24\div6\times\left(\frac{3}{4}\text{ of }\frac{1}{3}+\frac{5}{3}\text{ of }\frac{3}{4}\right)=?$
SSC MTS 01/09/2023 Shift-III

(a) 9 (b) 6 (c) 3 (d) 8

245. Simplify $\frac{(13\div13\text{ of }13+13)}{(13\div13\times13+13)}$
SSC MTS 01/09/2023 Shift-I

(a) $\frac{1}{26}$ (b) $\frac{15}{26}$ (c) $\frac{13}{96}$ (d) $\frac{85}{169}$

246. The value of
$(256)^{\frac{1}{2}}-(1331)^{\frac{1}{3}}+23\times13$ is
SSC MTS 15/07/2022 Shift-I

(a) 304 (b) 305 (c) 309 (d) 302

247. What should come in place of the question mark (?) in the following mathematical statement ?
$\sqrt{19\times650\div13+18.5\times4}\times13=?$
SSC MTS 14/07/2022 Shift-I

(a) 416 (b) 418
(c) 413 (d) 415

248. If $A=3+7\times2$, $B=12\div4-6$ and $C=6\times5+2$, then what is the value of $A\times B+C$? SSC MTS 14/07/2022 Shift-I

(a) –22 (b) –19 (c) –25 (d) –26

249. What is the value of $\frac{7}{8}+\frac{8}{11}$ of
$\left[\frac{33}{16}-\frac{5}{12}+\left(\frac{6}{11}-\frac{5}{12}+\frac{7}{22}\right)\right]$?
SSC MTS 13/07/2022 Shift-I

(a) $\frac{6871}{3605}$ (b) $\frac{6805}{2987}$ (c) $\frac{6907}{3971}$ (d) $\frac{6961}{2904}$

250. What is the value of
$[7\div14\times8+(5\div15\times6-4\times3)]$?
SSC MTS 12/07/2022 Shift-I

(a) –4 (b) –2 (c) –6 (d) –5

251. Find the value of P, when
$P=(5\div6)$ of $54-40\div10-41-22$.
SSC MTS 12/07/2022 Shift-I

(a) –11 (b) –22 (c) –18 (d) –23

252. What should come in place of the question mark (?) in the following mathematical statement ?
$8^2+16^2-19^2=?^3-257$
SSC MTS 11/07/2022 Shift-I

(a) 9 (b) 2 (c) 6 (d) 8

253. What should come in place of the question mark (?) for the following mathematical statement to be true ?
$(9576\div21)\times(462\div42)-563\times8=(?)^3$
SSC MTS 11/07/2022 Shift-I

(a) 5 (b) 7 (c) 8 (d) 3

254. The value of $120\div\left[\frac{2}{3}\times\left(1-\frac{2}{5}\right)\times5\right]+\left[\frac{9}{8}\text{ of }\frac{4}{3}\div\frac{3}{4}\text{ of }\frac{2}{3}\right]$ is
SSC MTS 02/11/2021 Shift-III

(a) 62 (b) 65 (c) 63 (d) 60

255. What is the value of the following expression?
$108\div18\times3-64\times2\div32+80\div5$ of 4
SSC MTS 02/11/2021 Shift-I

(a) 78 (b) 62 (c) 2 (d) 18

256. The value of $16+[0.2\div0.004+5.2$ of $2\div(0.7\times2+0.84\div0.7)]$ is
SSC MTS 02/11/2021 Shift-I

(a) 75 (b) 65 (c) 60 (d) 70

SSC GD Constable 2024 & 2023

257. What is the value of
$750-350\div7+43\times5$?
SSC GD 26/02/2024 Shift-I

(a) 812 (b) 915 (c) 935 (d) 795

258. What is the value of
$\frac{2}{1\times3}+\frac{2}{3\times5}+\frac{2}{5\times7}.....+\frac{2}{45\times47}$?
SSC GD 24/02/2024 Shift-III

(a) $\frac{45}{46}$ (b) $\frac{46}{47}$ (c) $\frac{49}{50}$ (d) $\frac{47}{48}$

259. What is the value of
$1100\div5+420\div2+550\div5$
SSC GD 24/02/2024 Shift-II

(a) 460 (b) 500 (c) 540 (d) 510

260. What is the value of
$3[4+2\{42-4(9-1)\}]$?
SSC GD 24/02/2024 Shift-II

(a) 48 (b) 72 (c) 81 (d) 69

261. Find the value of
$12\times5\times3\div[129-69]$.
SSC GD 23/02/2024 Shift-IV

(a) 9 (b) 3 (c) 6 (d) 2

262. What is the value of $\frac{144}{33}$ of $\frac{11}{12}-\frac{132}{13}$ of $\frac{52}{12}$? SSC GD 23/02/2024 Shift-IV

(a) 44 (b) –40 (c) –44 (d) 40

263. What is the value of
$1.4\times1.4+1.2\times1.2+1.3\times1.3$?
SSC GD 23/02/2024 Shift-IV

(a) 8.19 (b) 5.09 (c) 9.29 (d) 2.19

264. Find the value of
$58-25\div5+\{55+25-(30+20-10+30)\}$.
SSC GD 23/02/2024 Shift-III

(a) 66 (b) 56 (c) 63 (d) 68

265. Evaluate $14-3\times(5+2)\div4$.
SSC GD 23/02/2024 Shift-II

(a) 8.75 (b) 5.72
(c) 6.29 (d) 11.36

266. What is the value of $0.\overline{5}+0.\overline{3}$?
SSC GD 23/02/2024 Shift-II

(a) $\frac{8}{9}$ (b) $\frac{2}{3}$ (c) $\frac{3}{4}$ (d) $\frac{7}{9}$

267. What is the value of
$[36-(48\times7\div16)-(19+3-24)]$?
SSC GD 23/02/2024 Shift-I

(a) 13 (b) 17 (c) 15 (d) 11

268. What is the value of
$\frac{2}{1\times3}+\frac{2}{3\times5}+\frac{2}{5\times7}+....+\frac{2}{99\times101}$?
SSC GD 22/02/2024 Shift-IV

(a) 99/100 (b) 100/101
(c) 99/101 (d) 101/102

269. What is the value of
$4500\div9+1800\times2-310\times7$?
SSC GD 22/02/2024 Shift-III

(a) 1941 (b) 1825
(c) 1930 (d) 1935

270. What is the value of $\frac{0.5\div(0.5\times0.5)}{(0.5\div0.5)\times0.5}$?
SSC GD 22/02/2024 Shift-III

(a) 0.2 (b) 2 (c) 4 (d) 0.4

271. What is the value of
$13\times12+12\times11-14\times15-9\times13+19\times15$?
SSC GD 22/02/2024 Shift-III

(a) 246 (b) 346 (c) 546 (d) 146

272. Convert $0.4\overline{1}$ into fraction.
SSC GD 22/02/2024 Shift-I

(a) $\frac{5}{9}$ (b) $\frac{3}{7}$ (c) $\frac{37}{90}$ (d) $\frac{4}{9}$

273. What is the value of $\sqrt{0.000081}$?
SSC GD 21/02/2024 Shift-IV

(a) 0.09 (b) 0.009 (c) 0.9 (d) 9.9

274. What is the value of $[289 \div \{68 \div 4 \times (14 + 2 \times 6 - 9)\}]$? **SSC GD 21/02/2024 Shift-III**

(a) 1 (b) 0 (c) 289 (d) 17

275. What is the value of $4400 - (3200 \div 16) + 32 \times 4$? **SSC GD 21/02/2024 Shift-II**

(a) 4164 (b) 4328 (c) 3924 (d) 4068

276. What is the value of $2.\overline{3} + 4.\overline{3}$? **SSC GD 21/02/2024 Shift-I**

(a) $\frac{21}{4}$ (b) $\frac{20}{3}$ (c) $\frac{22}{7}$ (d) $\frac{18}{7}$

277. What is the value of $(0.5)^2 + (0.05)^2$? **SSC GD 21/02/2024 Shift-I**

(a) 2.5 (b) 0.2525
(c) 0.255 (d) 0.5025

278. Find the value of $(27 \times 50) \div 25 \times 5(15 - 14) + 800 \div 25$. **SSC GD 21/02/2024 Shift-I**

(a) 302 (b) 312 (c) 420 (d) 366

279. What is the value of $443 - 226 \div 2 \times 5$? **SSC GD 20/02/2024 Shift-IV**

(a) −127 (b) −121 (c) −119 (d) −122

280. What is the value of $2016 \div 4 + 32 \times 6 - 26 \times 3$? **SSC GD 20/02/2024 Shift-IV**

(a) 626 (b) 628 (c) 618 (d) 624

281. What is the value of $[19 \times \{24 \div 4 \text{ of } (24 \times 4 \div 16)\}]$? **SSC GD 20/02/2024 Shift-III**

(a) 1 (b) 19 (c) 76 (d) 38

282. What is the value of $\frac{16 \times (9 + 4) - 13 \times 14}{50 - (12 + 12)}$? **SSC GD 20/02/2024 Shift-III**

(a) 1 (b) 2 (c) 13 (d) 26

283. What is the value of $[41 \times \{36 \text{ of } 4 \div (96 \text{ of } 2 \div 24)\}]$? **SSC GD 20/02/2024 Shift-I**

(a) 779 (b) 738
(c) 697 (d) 656

284. If $\frac{5}{8}$ of $184 \times 15 \div 5 + k = 513 \div 9 + 435$, then the value of k is **SSC GD 13/02/2023 Shift-II**

(a) 192 (b) 147
(c) 239 (d) 136

285. Simplify the following.
30% of [{ (820% of 40) − 28}] % of 600 **SSC GD 07/02/2023 Shift-I**

(a) 540 (b) 200
(c) 500 (d) 250

286. Simplify the following.
$15.2625 - [5.2 + 0.25 \times (4.78 - 1.5 \times 3.02)]$ **SSC GD 06/02/2023 Shift-I**

(a) 9 (b) 10
(c) 8 (d) 11

287. If $3\frac{1}{3} \div 6\frac{3}{7} \times 1\frac{1}{2} \times 3\frac{1}{7} = (p)^{1/2}$, then the value of '$p$' is **SSC GD 02/02/2023 Shift-I**

(a) $\frac{22}{9}$ (b) $\frac{22}{3}$ (c) $\frac{484}{3}$ (d) $\frac{484}{81}$

288. The simplified value of $\frac{5}{16}$ of $\frac{7}{8} \times 6 + 15 - 10$ is **SSC GD 01/02/2023 Shift-I**

(a) $\frac{425}{64}$ (b) $\frac{850}{64}$ (c) $\frac{425}{128}$ (d) $\frac{525}{64}$

SSC Selection Post 2024-2022

289. Simplify the following expression $\frac{0.7^2 + (0.4 + 0.2)(0.7) + (0.4 \times 0.2)}{(0.7 + 0.4)}$. **Graduate Level 20/06/2024 Shift-III**

(a) 0.9 (b) 0.7 (c) 0.3 (d) 0.4

290. Simplify the expression.
$(0.3 - 0.2)(0.3^2 + 0.3 \times 0.2 + 0.2^2)$ **Graduate Level 20/06/2024 Shift-III**

(a) 0.035 (b) 0.027
(c) 0.019 (d) 0.053

291. If $\frac{9^m \times 3^5 \times 27^3}{3 \times 81^4} = 3^9$, then the value of m is . **Higher Secondary Level 20/06/2024 Shift-II**

(a) 5 (b) 7 (c) 6 (d) 12

292. Simplify $52 \times 52 - 48 \times 48$. **Higher Secondary Level 27/06/2023 Shift-III**

(a) 386 (b) 400 (c) 424 (d) 326

293. Find the value of $13^3 + (-8)^3 + (-5)^3$. **Higher Secondary Level 20/06/2022 Shift-II**

(a) 1560 (b) 1052 (c) 1152 (d) 1562

Right Answers

1	(a)	2	(c)	3	(b)	4	(b)	5	(d)	6	(c)	7	(d)	8	(a)	9	(d)	10	(c)
11	(b)	12	(b)	13	(a)	14	(b)	15	(d)	16	(d)	17	(c)	18	(a)	19	(b)	20	(d)
21	(c)	22	(b)	23	(b)	24	(d)	25	(b)	26	(b)	27	(b)	28	(b)	29	(d)	30	(c)
31	(a)	32	(c)	33	(d)	34	(b)	35	(a)	36	(b)	37	(a)	38	(a)	39	(b)	40	(a)
41	(b)	42	(a)	43	(c)	44	(d)	45	(c)	46	(a)	47	(c)	48	(c)	49	(a)	50	(b)
51	(c)	52	(a)	53	(a)	54	(c)	55	(b)	56	(d)	57	(a)	58	(b)	59	(b)	60	(b)
61	(b)	62	(a)	63	(a)	64	(a)	65	(b)	66	(d)	67	(a)	68	(d)	69	(c)	70	(b)
71	(c)	72	(b)	73	(d)	74	(d)	75	(a)	76	(c)	77	(a)	78	(c)	79	(a)	80	(d)
81	(a)	82	(b)	83	(c)	84	(a)	85	(a)	86	(d)	87	(a)	88	(b)	89	(a)	90	(d)
91	(a)	92	(b)	93	(a)	94	(b)	95	(d)	96	(d)	97	(a)	98	(a)	99	(b)	100	(d)
101	(d)	102	(d)	103	(a)	104	(c)	105	(b)	106	(c)	107	(c)	108	(a)	109	(c)	110	(a)
111	(a)	112	(c)	113	(c)	114	(d)	115	(a)	116	(a)	117	(d)	118	(c)	119	(a)	120	(d)
121	(c)	122	(c)	123	(c)	124	(c)	125	(b)	126	(d)	127	(b)	128	(c)	129	(a)	130	(d)
131	(b)	132	(a)	133	(d)	134	(d)	135	(c)	136	(b)	137	(b)	138	(b)	139	(d)	140	(d)
141	(a)	142	(d)	143	(c)	144	(c)	145	(a)	146	(b)	147	(a)	148	(a)	149	(a)	150	(b)
151	(c)	152	(c)	153	(b)	154	(c)	155	(d)	156	(c)	157	(b)	158	(a)	159	(c)	160	(d)
161	(c)	162	(b)	163	(c)	164	(d)	165	(d)	166	(d)	167	(c)	168	(c)	169	(a)	170	(b)
171	(d)	172	(d)	173	(b)	174	(a)	175	(a)	176	(c)	177	(c)	178	(a)	179	(a)	180	(a)
181	(c)	182	(c)	183	(d)	184	(b)	185	(b)	186	(d)	187	(c)	188	(a)	189	(b)	190	(c)
191	(c)	192	(c)	193	(d)	194	(c)	195	(a)	196	(d)	197	(b)	198	(b)	199	(d)	200	(c)
201	(a)	202	(c)	203	(d)	204	(c)	205	(a)	206	(d)	207	(d)	208	(b)	209	(a)	210	(d)
211	(a)	212	(a)	213	(d)	214	(b)	215	(b)	216	(b)	217	(d)	218	(c)	219	(b)	220	(d)
221	(a)	222	(a)	223	(b)	224	(b)	225	(c)	226	(d)	227	(d)	228	(a)	229	(d)	230	(a)
231	(c)	232	(a)	233	(b)	234	(c)	235	(a)	236	(b)	237	(b)	238	(a)	239	(d)	240	(c)
241	(a)	242	(a)	243	(c)	244	(b)	245	(d)	246	(a)	247	(a)	248	(b)	249	(d)	250	(c)
251	(b)	252	(c)	253	(c)	254	(c)	255	(d)	256	(d)	257	(b)	258	(b)	259	(c)	260	(b)
261	(b)	262	(b)	263	(b)	264	(c)	265	(a)	266	(a)	267	(b)	268	(b)	269	(c)	270	(c)
271	(a)	272	(c)	273	(b)	274	(a)	275	(b)	276	(b)	277	(b)	278	(a)	279	(d)	280	(c)
281	(b)	282	(a)	283	(b)	284	(b)	285	(a)	286	(b)	287	(d)	288	(a)	289	(a)	290	(c)
291	(c)	292	(b)	293	(a)														

Solutions

1. (a) $\frac{\sqrt[3]{6859}}{\sqrt[4]{1296}} \times \frac{3}{57} \times 42 = \frac{19}{6} \times \frac{3}{57} \times 42 = 7$

2. (c) $4^3 - 0^2 + \left(\frac{22}{2}\right)^2 - 8 + 7 \times 6$

$= 64 - 0 + 121 - 8 + 42$

$= 227 - 8 = 219$

3. (b) We have,

$626 \times 2912 \div 8138 = 626 \times \frac{2912}{8138} = 224$

4. (b) We have, $(60 + 64 \div 4 \text{ of } 4) \times \{1000 \div ((10 \text{ of } (3+2)) \times 2 \text{ of } 5)\} - 28 + (100 \times 3 \text{ of } 3)$

$= (60 + 64 \div 4 \times 4) \times \{1000 \div ((10 \times (3+2) \times 2 \times 5)\} - 28 + (100 \times 3 \times 3)\}$

$= \left(60 + \frac{64}{16}\right) \times \{1000 \div (10 \times 5 \times 2 \times 5)\} - 28 + (900)$

$= 64 \times \{1000 \div (500)\} - 28 + 900$

$= 64 \times \frac{1000}{500} - 28 + 900 = 128 - 28 + 900$

$= 1000$

5. (d) $9 \times N \text{ of } 4 \div 4 - 15 \times 4 = 12$

$\Rightarrow \quad 9 \times 4N \div 4 - 15 \times 4 = 12$

$\Rightarrow \quad 9 \times N - 15 \times 4 = 12$

$\Rightarrow \quad 9N - 60 = 12 \Rightarrow 9N = 72 \Rightarrow N = 8$

6. (c) $[25 - 48 \div 6 + 12 \times 2] + 78 - [5 + 3 \text{ of } (25 - 2 \times 10)]$

$= [25 - 48 \div 6 + 12 \times 2] + 78 - [5 + 3 \times (25 - 20)]$

$= [25 - 48 \div 6 + 12 \times 2] + 78 - [5 + 3 \times 5]$

$= [25 - 8 + 12 \times 2] + 78 - [5 + 15]$

$= [25 - 8 + 24] + 78 - 20$

$= [49 - 8] + 78 - 20$

$= 41 + 78 - 20 = 99$

7. (d) $9 \div \left[1 + \left\{4 \times \left(\frac{5}{6} - \frac{1}{3} + \frac{1}{2}\right)\right\}\right]$

$= 9 \div \left[1 + \left\{4 \times \left(\frac{5}{6} - \frac{5}{6}\right)\right\}\right] = 9 \div [1 + \{4 \times 0\}]$

$= 9 \div [1 + 0]$ [By BODMAS Rule]

$= \frac{9}{1} = 9$

8. (a) $133 \div 19 \times 3 - 48 \times 2 \div 24 + 841 \div [\{\overline{45 - 16}\}]$

$= 133 \div 19 \times 3 - 48 \times 2 \div 24 + [841 \div 29]$

$= 133 \div 19 \times 3 - 48 \times 2 \div 24 + 29$

$= 7 \times 3 - \frac{48 \times 2}{24} + 29$ [By BODMAS rule]

$= 21 - 4 + 29 = 46$

9. (d) Here, $\frac{(453)^3 - (383)^3}{(453)^2 + (383)^2 + 453 \times 383}$

By algebraic identity

$[\because a^3 - b^3 = (a-b)(a^2 + b^2 + ab)]$

$= \frac{(453 - 383)[(453)^2 + (383)^2 + 453 \times 383]}{[(453)^2 + (383)^2 + 453 \times 383]}$

$= 453 - 383 = 70$

10. (c) $11 - \{(3 \div 4) \text{ of } 8 - \overline{4 - 8}\}$

$= 11 - \{(3 \div 4) \text{ of } 8 - (-4)\}$

$= 11 - \{(3 \div 4) \text{ of } 8 + 4\}$

$= 11 - \left\{\frac{3}{4} \times 8 + 4\right\}$

$= 11 - \{6 + 4\} = 11 - 10 = 1$

11. (b) $0.07 \times 0.28 \div 0.04 + 0.64 - 1.64 \div 0.04$

$= 0.07 \times \frac{0.28}{0.04} + 0.64 - \frac{1.64}{0.04}$

$= 0.07 \times 7 + 0.64 - 41 = 0.49 + 0.64 - 41$

$= 1.13 - 41 = -39.87$

12. (b) $\frac{(232)^3 + (140)^3 + (353)^3 - 3 \times 232 \times 140 \times 353}{(232)^2 + (140)^2 + (353)^2 - 232 \times 140 - 140 \times 353 - 353 \times 232}$

$= 232 + 140 + 353$

$\left[\because \frac{a^3 + b^3 + c^3 - 3abc}{a^2 + b^2 + c^2 - ab - bc - ca} = a + b + c\right]$

$= 725$

13. (a) $6 \times [28 + 84 \times \{36 \times 49 \div (6 \times 7)\}]$

$= 6 \times [28 + 84 \times \{36 \times 49 \div 42\}]$

$= 6 \times [28 + 84 \times \{42\}]$

$= 6 \times [28 + 84 \times 42] = 6 \times \left[\frac{42}{3}\right] = 84$

14. (b) $\frac{(25)^4 + 1250 + 1 - (25)^2}{(25)^2 + 25 + 1}$

$= \frac{[(25)^2]^2 + (1)^2 + 2 \times (25)^2 \times 1 - (25)^2}{(25)^2 + 25 + 1}$

$= \frac{[(25)^2 + 1]^2 - (25)^2}{(25)^2 + 25 + 1}$

$[\because (a+b)^2 = a^2 + b^2 + 2ab]$

$= \frac{((25)^2 + 1 + 25)((25)^2 + 1 - 25)}{((25)^2 + 25 + 1)}$

$[\because a^2 - b^2 = (a+b)(a-b)]$

$= (25)^2 + 1 - 25 = 601$

15. (d) We have,

$25 \div 5 + 3 \text{ of } 2 - 4 + 6 \text{ of } 3 \div 2 - 8 + 4$

$= 25 \div 5 + 3 \times 2 - 4 + 6 \times 3 \div 2 - 8 + 4$

$= 5 + 6 - 4 + \frac{18}{2} - 8 + 4$ [Using BODMAS]

$= 11 - 4 + 9 - 8 + 4 = 12$

16. (d) $4\frac{1}{6} \div 25 \times 75 \div \frac{1}{5} \text{ of } 125$

$= \frac{25}{6} \div 25 \times 75 \div \frac{1}{5} \times 125$

$= \frac{25}{6} \div 25 \times \frac{75}{25} = \frac{25}{6} \times \frac{1}{25} \times 3 = \frac{1}{2}$

17. (c) $9 - 5 \times 6 + \{29 - (7 - 2)\} \div 8$

$= 9 - 5 \times 6 + \{29 - 5\} \div 8$

$= 9 - 5 \times 6 + 24 \div 8 = 9 - 30 + 3 = -18$

18. (a) We have,

$\left[\left(5\frac{1}{2} - 3\frac{1}{3}\right) \text{ of } 1\frac{5}{13} + 1 - 2 \times 3\frac{5}{2} \div 2\frac{3}{4}\right]$

$= \left[\left(\frac{11}{2} - \frac{10}{3}\right) \times \frac{18}{13} + 1 - 2 \times \frac{11}{2} \times \frac{4}{11}\right]$

$= \left[\left(\frac{33 - 20}{6}\right) \times \frac{18}{13} + 1 - 4\right]$

[Using VBODMAS]

$= \left[\frac{13}{6} \times \frac{18}{13} - 3\right] = (3 - 3) = 0$

19. (b) Expression $= \left[\left(\frac{1}{6} \div \frac{1}{9} \times \frac{2}{3}\right) \times 18 + 5\right]$

Applying BODMAS rule,

We have, $\left[\left(\frac{1}{6} \times 9 \times \frac{2}{3}\right) \times 18 + 5\right] = [1 \times 18 + 5]$

$= 23$

20. (d) $\frac{1.5 \times 1.5 + 2.5 \times 2.5 + (3.5)^2 + 2 \times 1.5 \times 2.5 + 2 \times 2.5 \times 3.5 + 2 \times 1.5 \times 3.5}{1.5 + 2.5 + 3.5}$

$= \frac{(1.5)^2 + (2.5)^2 + (3.5)^2 + 2 \times 1.5 \times 2.5 + 2 \times 2.5 \times 3.5 + 2 \times 1.5 \times 3.5}{1.5 + 2.5 + 3.5}$

$[\therefore (a + b + c)^2 = a^2 + b^2 + c^2 + 2ab + 2bc + 2ca]$

$= \frac{(1.5 + 2.5 + 3.5)^2}{(1.5 + 2.5 + 3.5)} = 1.5 + 2.5 + 3.5 = 7.5$

21. (c) $16 \div 2 - 7 \times 15 \div 3 + 5 \times 5 + 4 \times 3 - 10$

$= 8 - 7 \times 5 + 25 + 12 - 10$

$= 8 - 35 + 25 + 2 = 0$

22. (b) $1\frac{1}{3} + 1\frac{3}{4} \times 1\frac{2}{3} \div 3\frac{1}{2} = \frac{4}{3} + \frac{7}{4} \times \frac{5}{3} \div \frac{7}{2}$

$= \frac{4}{3} + \frac{7}{4} \times \frac{5}{3} \times \frac{2}{7} = \frac{4}{3} + \frac{5}{6} = \frac{8 + 5}{6}$

$= \frac{13}{6} = 2\frac{1}{6}$

23. (b) $[\{70 - 60 \div 2 \text{ of } 6\} + (20 - 10) \div 10] + 600 \div 25 \text{ of } (2 \times 3) \times (2 \text{ of } 3) + 2 \text{ of } 5$

$= [\{70 - 60 \div 12\} + (20 - 10) \div 10] + 600 \div (25 \times 6) \times 6 + 10$

$= [\{70 - 5\} + 1] + 4 \times 6 + 10$

$= [65 + 1] + 24 + 10 = 66 + 24 + 10 = 100$

24. (d) $\left[(2.5 + 1.5)^2 \div 4 \text{ of } \frac{1}{2} \times 8 - 1\right]$

$= [(4)^2 \div 2 \times 8 - 1] = [16 \div 2 \times 8 - 1]$

$= [8 \times 8 - 1] = 64 - 1 = 63$

25. (b) $4\frac{4}{5} \times \frac{3}{8} + \left(3\frac{1}{2} + \frac{2}{3}\right) \times \frac{4}{5}$

$= \frac{24}{5} \times \frac{3}{8} + \left(\frac{7}{2} + \frac{2}{3}\right) \times \frac{4}{5}$

$= \frac{24}{5} \times \frac{3}{8} + \frac{25}{6} \times \frac{4}{5} = \frac{9}{5} + \frac{10}{3}$

$= \frac{27 + 50}{15} = \frac{77}{15}$

26. (b) We have,

$[(1.55)^2 + (0.55)^2 + (1.55 \times 0.55)]$

$= (1)[(1.55)^2 + (0.55)^2 + (1.55 \times 0.55)]$

$= [1.55 - 0.55][(1.55)^2 + (0.55)^2 + (1.55 \times 0.55)]$

$= (1.55)^3 - (0.55)^3$

$[\because (a - b)(a^2 + b^2 + ab) = a^3 - b^3]$

27. (b) We have, $\dfrac{(4.2)^3-(1.2)^3}{(4.2)^2+5.04+(1.2)^2}$

$=\dfrac{(4.2-1.2)[(4.2)^2+5.04+(1.2)^2]}{(4.2)^2+5.04+(1.2)^2}$

$[\because a^3-b^3=(a-b)(a^2+ab+b^2)]$

$=4.2-1.2=3$

28. (b) We have, $1020\div\left[\dfrac{4}{3}\text{ of }(26+4)-11\dfrac{2}{3}\right]$

$=1020\div\left[\dfrac{4}{3}\times(26+4)-\dfrac{35}{3}\right]$ [using BODMAS]

$=1020\div\left[\dfrac{4}{3}\times 30-\dfrac{35}{3}\right]$

$=1020\div\dfrac{85}{3}=1020\times\dfrac{3}{85}=36$

29. (d) We have,

$45\div3+4\times A-48\div24+4=1$

$\Rightarrow 15+4A-2+4=1$ [∴ By using BODMAS]

$\therefore 4A=-16\Rightarrow A=\dfrac{-16}{4}=-4$

30. (c) $21-[6+7-\{3.22-(1.1\times0.2)\}]$

$=21-[13-\{3.22-0.22\}]$

$=21-[13-3]=21-10=11$

31. (a) $\dfrac{0.58\times0.58\times0.58-0.001}{0.58\times0.58+0.058+0.01}$

$=\dfrac{(0.58)^3-(0.1)^3}{(0.58)^2+(0.58)\times(0.1)+(0.1)^2}$

$=\dfrac{(0.58-0.1)((0.58)^2+(0.58)\times(0.1)+(0.1)^2)}{[(0.58)^2+(0.58)\times(0.1)+(0.1)^2]}$

$(\because a^3-b^3=(a-b)(a^2+ab+b^2))$

$=0.58-0.1=0.48$

32. (c) By the rule of BODMAS,

$13-[7-(4+7)-\{7-(7-4+7)\}+14]$

$=13-[7-(11)-\{7-(10)\}+14]$

$=13-[7-11-\{-3\}+14]$

$=13-[-4+3+14]$

$=13-[13]=13-13=0$

Hence, option (c) is correct.

33. (d) We have,

$21-4.9\div7+3.9\times0.4+0.9$

Using BODMAS, we get

$=21-0.7+3.9\times0.4+0.9$

$=21-0.7+1.56+0.9$

$=23.46-0.7=22.76$

34. (b) We have,

$\dfrac{(8.3)^3+(9.2)^3+(6.1)^3-3\times8.3\times9.2\times6.1}{[(8.3)^2+(9.2)^2+(6.1)^2-8.3\times9.2-9.2\times6.1-6.1\times8.3]}$

$=\dfrac{(8.3+9.2+6.1)[(8.3)^2+(9.2)^2+(6.1)^2-8.3\times9.2-9.2\times6.1-6.1\times8.3]}{[(8.3)^2+(9.2)^2+(6.1)^2-8.3\times9.2-9.2\times6.1-6.1\times8.3]}$

$[\because a^3+b^3+c^3-3abc=(a+b+c)(a^2+b^2+c^2-ab-bc-ca)]$

$=(8.3+9.2+6.1)=23.6$

35. (a) $\dfrac{(88\div8\times k-3\times3)}{(6^2-7\times5+k^2)}=1$

$\Rightarrow \dfrac{\left(\dfrac{88k}{8}-9\right)}{(36-35+k^2)}=1$

$11k-9=k^2+1$

$\Rightarrow k^2-11k+10=0$

$\Rightarrow k^2-10k-k+10=0$

$\Rightarrow (k-10)(k-1)=0$

$k=1, 10$

Thus, value of k is (1, 10).

36. (b) Given expression,

$\left[\dfrac{1}{8}+\left\{\dfrac{1}{6}\times\left(\dfrac{36}{45}\div\dfrac{24}{25}\right)-\left(\dfrac{12}{21}\times\dfrac{14}{15}\div\dfrac{24}{45}\right)\right\}+\dfrac{27}{36}\right]$

$=\left[\dfrac{1}{8}+\left\{\dfrac{1}{6}\times\dfrac{5}{6}-\left(\dfrac{12}{21}\times\dfrac{7}{4}\right)\right\}+\dfrac{27}{36}\right]$

$=\left[\dfrac{1}{8}+\left\{\dfrac{5}{36}-1\right\}+\dfrac{27}{36}\right]$

$=\dfrac{1}{8}-\dfrac{31}{36}+\dfrac{27}{36}=\dfrac{9-62+54}{72}=\dfrac{1}{72}$

37. (a) $\dfrac{\sqrt{1.24}\times\sqrt{2.79}}{\sqrt{2.64}\times\sqrt{5.94}}=\sqrt{\dfrac{1.24\times2.79}{2.64\times5.94}}$

$=\sqrt{\dfrac{31\times31}{66\times66}}=\dfrac{31}{66}$

38. (a) $\dfrac{0.7\times0.7\times0.7+0.3\times0.3\times0.3}{0.7\times0.7-0.7\times0.3+0.3\times0.3}$

$[\because a^3+b^3=(a+b)(a^2-ab+b^2)]$

$=\dfrac{(0.7)^3+(0.3)^3}{(0.7)^2-0.7\times0.3+(0.3)^2}$

$=0.7+0.3=1$

39. (b) $x=\sqrt{64}+\sqrt{121}-\sqrt{169}$

$=8+11-13 \quad x=6$

Squaring on both sides,

$x^2=36$

40. (a) $3-(-6)\{-2-9-3\}\div7\{1+(-2)(-1)\}$

$=3+6\{-14\}\div7\{1+2\}$

$=3+\dfrac{6\times(-14)}{7\times3}=3-4=-1$

41. (b) $\dfrac{\sqrt{10+\sqrt{25+\sqrt{108+\sqrt{154+\sqrt{225}}}}}}{\sqrt{16+19.25\times4^2}}$

$=\dfrac{\sqrt{10+\sqrt{25+\sqrt{108+\sqrt{154+15}}}}}{\sqrt{16(1+19.25)}}$

$=\dfrac{\sqrt{10+\sqrt{25+\sqrt{108+13}}}}{\sqrt{16\times20.25}}$

$=\dfrac{\sqrt{10+\sqrt{25+11}}}{4\times4.5}=\dfrac{\sqrt{10+6}}{4\times4.5}=\dfrac{4\times10}{4\times45}=\dfrac{2}{9}$

42. (a) Let

$x=\sqrt{20-\sqrt{20-\sqrt{20-\sqrt{20-\ldots\ldots\infty}}}}$ ...(i)

Squaring on both sides,

$x^2=20-\sqrt{20-\sqrt{20-\sqrt{20-\ldots\ldots\infty}}}$

$x^2=20-x$ (∵ from Eq. (i))

$x^2+x-20=0$

$x^2+5x-4x-20=0$

$x(x+5)-4(x+5)=0$

$(x+5)(x-4)=0$

$x=-5$ and $x=4$

So, required solution is 4.

Speedy Method

Co-prime factors of 20 = (4, 5)

In case of (– ve) sign, smaller number is the right answer.

Hence, required answer = 4

43. (c) $[76-\{90\div5\times(24-36\div3)\div3\}]$

$=\left[76-\left\{\dfrac{90}{5}\times(24-12)\div3\right\}\right]$

$=[76-\{18\times12\div3\}]$

$=[76-\{18\times4\}]=76-72=4$

44. (d) $30-[40-\{56-(25-13-12)\}]$

$=30-[40-\{56-(25-25)\}]$ [By BODMAS rule]

$=30-[40-\{56-0\}]$

$=30-[40-56]$

$=30-(-16)=30+16=46$

45. (c) $1\dfrac{3}{4}+1\dfrac{5}{7}\div2\dfrac{3}{7}\times2\dfrac{3}{7}$

$=\dfrac{7}{4}+\dfrac{12}{7}\div\dfrac{17}{7}\times\dfrac{17}{7}$

$=\dfrac{7}{4}+\dfrac{12}{7}\times\dfrac{7}{17}\times\dfrac{17}{7}=\dfrac{7}{4}+\dfrac{12}{7}$

$=\dfrac{49+48}{28}=\dfrac{97}{28}=3\dfrac{13}{28}$

46. (a) $\dfrac{120\times120\times120-100\times100\times100}{120\times120+120\times100+100\times100}$

$[\because a^3-b^3=(a-b)(a^2+b^2+ab)]$

$=\dfrac{(120)^3-(100)^3}{(120)^2+(120\times100)+(100)^2}$

$=\dfrac{(120-100)[(120)^2+(100)^2+(120\times100)]}{(120)^2+120\times100+(100)^2}=(120-100)$

$=20$

47. (c) $80.40\div20-(-4.02)+2.06$

$=4.02+4.02+2.06=10.1$

48. (c) $14\div7\times1+3-[18-\{15-(7-7-2)\}]$

$=2\times1+3-[18-\{15+2\}]$

$=2+3-[18-17]=5-1=4$

49. (a) $\dfrac{2}{3}-\dfrac{5}{6}\times\dfrac{4}{5}\div\dfrac{4}{3}+\dfrac{1}{2}$

$=\dfrac{2}{3}-\dfrac{5}{6}\times\dfrac{4}{5}\times\dfrac{3}{4}+\dfrac{1}{2}=\dfrac{2}{3}-\dfrac{1}{2}+\dfrac{1}{2}=\dfrac{2}{3}$

50. (b) $6-(6\div 2-3+7-2)\times[\{3-2\div 2\}\times 5-6]$

$=6-(3-3+7-2)\times[\{3-1\}\times 5-6]$

$=6-5\times[10-6]=6-20=-14$

51. (c) $100\div 10-[-2+\{-9+(3-6\text{ of }2)\}]$

$=10-[-2+\{-9+(3-12)\}]$

$=10-[-2+\{-9-9\}]$

$=10-[-2-18]=10+20=30$

52. (a) $13-[10-\{16+8\div(k-2)+2\}]=20$

$\Rightarrow\ 13-\left[10-\left\{16+\frac{8}{k-2}\right\}+2\right]=20$

$\Rightarrow\ 13-\left[10-\frac{16k-32+8}{k-2}+2\right]=20$

$\Rightarrow\ 13-\left[\frac{10k-20-16k+24+2k-4}{k-2}\right]=20$

$\Rightarrow\ \frac{13k-26-10k+20+16k-20-2k}{k-2}=20$

$\Rightarrow\ \frac{17k-26}{k-2}=20$

$\Rightarrow\ 17k-26=20k-40$

$\Rightarrow\ 3k=14\Rightarrow k=\frac{14}{3}$

$\therefore$ Value of $k=\frac{14}{3}$

53. (a) $220+80\div[63-\{7\times 8+(13-2\times 4)\}]$

$=220+80\div[63-\{56+5\}]$

$=220+80\div[63-61]$

$=220+80\div 2=260$

54. (c) $2+(30-26)^2\div 8^{3-2}\times 0.5$

$=2+4^2\div 8\times\frac{5}{10}=2+\frac{16}{8}\times\frac{1}{2}$

$=2+1=3$

55. (b) $15-(-5)\times\{4-(7-3)\}\div[3\times\{5+(-3)\times(-6)\}]$

$=15+5\times\{4-4\}\div[3\times\{5+18\}]$

$=15+5\times\{0\}\div[3\times(5+18)]$

$=15+0=15$

56. (d) $\frac{0.01\times 0.01\times 0.01+0.003\times 0.003\times 0.003}{0.05\times 0.05\times -0.015\times 0.05+0.015\times 0.015}$

$=\frac{(0.01)^3+(0.003)^3}{25\times(0.01)^2-5\times 5(0.003\times 0.01)+25(0.003)^2}$

$=\frac{(0.01+0.003)\{(0.01)^2-0.003\times 0.01+(0.003)^2\}}{25\{(0.01)^2-0.003\times 0.01+(0.003)^2\}}$

$=\frac{\frac{1}{100}+\frac{3}{1000}}{25}=\frac{13}{25}\times 10^{-3}$

57. (a) $720\div 8+915\div 15-m+32\times 5=1104\div 16\times 111\div 37$

$\Rightarrow\ 90+61-m+160=69\times 3$

$\Rightarrow\ 311-m=207\ \therefore\ m=104$

58. (b) $22-[9-\{6-(10-4+3)\}]\div 2\times 3$

$=22-[9-\{6-9\}]\div 2\times 3$

$=22-[9+3]\div 2\times 3$

$=22-12\div 2\times 3=22-6\times 3=22-18=4$

59. (b) $(16+14)\div 2-12+16\times 4-28+13(-16+13)$

$=30\div 2-12+64-28+13(-3)$

$=15-12+64-28-39=79-79=0$

60. (b) $\frac{3}{2}\div\frac{1}{7}\times\left[\left(\frac{1}{2}-\frac{1}{3}\right)\div\frac{1}{42}\right]$

$=\frac{3}{2}\div\frac{1}{7}\times\left[\frac{3-2}{6}\div\frac{1}{42}\right]$

$=\frac{3}{2}\times 7\times\frac{1}{6}\times 42=\frac{147}{2}=73\frac{1}{2}$

61. (b) $(3^2)^2+3\times 3\div 3-3$

$=9^2+3\times 1-3=9^2+0=9^2$

62. (a) $264-\left[142-\left\{75+\left(38-\left(\frac{5}{4}+\frac{11}{4}\right)\right)\right\}\right]$

$=264-\left[142-\left\{75+\left(38-\frac{16}{4}\right)\right\}\right]$

$=264-[142-\{75+34\}]$

$=264-[142-109]=264-33=231$

63. (a) $10\div 5\times 1+3-[8-\{5-(7-7-9)\}]$

$=2+3-[8-\{5+9\}]$

$=2+3-[-6]=5+6=11$

64. (a) $[0.08-\{3.5-4.9-(12.5-7.8-4.6)\}]$

$=[0.08-\{3.5-4.9-0.1\}]$

$=[0.08-\{-1.5\}]=[0.08+1.5]=1.58$

65. (b) $8+(-9-3)-(-12-5)$

$=8-12+17=13$

66. (d) $325+276\div[150-\{9\times 9+(83-4\times 15)\}]$

$=325+276\div[150-\{81+83-60\}]$

$=325+276\div[150-104]$

$=325+276\div 46=325+6=331$

67. (a) $7.5\times 17.2\div 8.6+(59.5)\text{ of }\frac{1}{17}-\frac{7}{2}\text{ of }5$

$=7.5\times 2+3.5-\frac{35}{2}$

$=15+3.5-17.5=18.5-17.5=1$

68. (d) $\frac{\left(12+5-\frac{48}{16}+71\right)+\left(\frac{\frac{72}{36}+6\times 7}{11}\right)\times[(51+4-13)+(13-12\times 7)]}{232}$

$=\frac{(12+5-3+71)+\left(\frac{2+42}{11}\right)\times[(55-13)+(13-84)]}{232}$

$=\frac{85+4\times[42-71]}{232}=\frac{85+4\times(-29)}{232}$

$=\frac{85-116}{232}=\frac{-31}{232}$

69. (c) $\frac{432\times 432+247\times 247-432\times 247}{432\times 432\times 432+247\times 247\times 247}$

[Using $a^3+b^3=(a+b)(a^2+b^2-ab)$]

$=\frac{432^2-432\times 247+247^2}{(432+247)(432^2-247\times 432+247^2)}=\frac{1}{679}$

70. (b) $[\sqrt{25}+12\div 3-\{20+(16\text{ of }8\div 16)-(54\div 18\text{ of }1/2)\}]$

$=5+4-[(20+8)-6]$

$=9-(28-6)=-13$

71. (c) $51\div\{25+(25\text{ of }12\div 30)-(5^4\div 5\text{ of }125)\}$

$=51\div\{25+(300\div 30)-(5^4\div 5^4)\}$

$=51\div\{25+10-1\}=51\div 34=\frac{51}{34}=\frac{3}{2}$

72. (b) Let, $326=a,\ 222=b$

$\therefore\ \frac{(326+222)^2-(326-222)^2}{326\times 222}$

$=\frac{(a+b)^2-(a-b)^2}{ab}=\frac{4ab}{ab}=4$

73. (d) $18\div\{(6\text{ of }2-4)\}\times 5(6-3)$

$=18\div\{(6\times 2-4)\}\times 5\times 3$

$=18\div\{(12-4)\}\times 5\times 3$

$=18\div 8\times 15=\frac{18}{8}\times 15=\frac{135}{4}$

74. (d) Given expression,

$\frac{(3.35)^2-(1.25)^2}{3.35+1.25}=\frac{(3.35+1.25)(3.35-1.25)}{3.35+1.25}$

$[\because a^2-b^2=(a-b)(a+b)]$

$=3.35-1.25=2.1$

75. (a) The product of 277 and 323

$=277\times 323=(300-23)(300+23)$

$[\because a^2-b^2=(a-b)(a+b)]$

$=300^2-23^2=90000-529=89471$

76. (c) $(-25)\times 8+(-25)\times 2$

$=(-25)(8+2)=-250$

77. (a) $2.5\times[144\div 198\times\{121\times 81\div(11\times 9)\}]$

$=2.5\left[\frac{144}{198}\times\{121\times 81\div 99\}\right]$

$=2.5\times\left[\frac{144}{198}\times\left\{121\times\frac{81}{99}\right\}\right]$

$=2.5\times\left[\frac{144}{198}\times 99\right]=2.5\times 72=180$

78. (c) $(2\times 7-5+9\div 3)\div(4+2)^2\times 2$

$=(14-5+3)\div(6)^2\times 2=\frac{12}{36}\times 2=\frac{2}{3}$

79. (a) $18\div 3\text{ of }2\times 5+72\div 18\text{ of }2\times 3-4\div 8\times 2$

$=18\div 6\times 5+72\div 36\times 3-\frac{1}{2}\times 2$

$=3\times 5+2\times 3-1=15+6-1=20$

80. (d) $\left[\frac{85}{34}\times\frac{1}{18}-\left\{\left(\frac{46}{69}\div\frac{27}{135}\right)-\left(\frac{86}{129}\times\frac{91}{14}\right)\right\}\text{ of }\frac{112}{36}\right]$

$=\left[\frac{85}{34}\times\frac{1}{18}-\left\{\left(\frac{46}{69}\times\frac{135}{27}\right)-\left(\frac{13}{3}\right)\right\}\times\frac{112}{36}\right]$

$=\left[\frac{5}{36}-\left\{\left(\frac{10}{3}\right)-\left(\frac{13}{3}\right)\right\}\times\frac{112}{36}\right]$

$=\left[\frac{5}{36}+\frac{112}{36}\right]=\frac{117}{36}=\frac{39}{12}=\frac{13}{4}=3\frac{1}{4}$

81. (a) $4\frac{4}{5}\div\frac{3}{5}\text{ of }5+\frac{4}{5}\times\frac{3}{10}-\frac{1}{5}$

$=4\frac{4}{5}\div 3+\frac{6}{25}-\frac{1}{5}$

$=\frac{24}{5}\times\frac{1}{3}+\frac{6-5}{25}=\frac{8}{5}+\frac{1}{25}=\frac{41}{25}=1\frac{16}{25}$

82. (b) $\dfrac{1.6\times1.6\times1.6-0.6\times0.6\times0.6}{1.6\times1.6+1.6\times0.6+0.6\times0.6}$

$=\dfrac{(1.6)^3-(0.6)^3}{(1.6)^2+1.6\times0.6+(0.6)^2}$

$[\because a^3-b^3=(a-b)(a^2+ab+b^2)]$

$=\dfrac{(1.6-0.6)[(1.6)^2+1.6\times0.6+(0.6)^2]}{(1.6)^2+1.6\times0.6+(0.6)^2}$

$=1.6-0.6=1$

83. (c) $25^3-75^3+50^3$

$=15625-421875+125000=-281250$

> **Speedy Method**
>
> We know that, if $a+b+c=0$
>
> Then, $a^3+b^3+c^3=3abc$
>
> Here, $a=25$, $b=-75$, $c=50$
>
> $\therefore\ a+b+c=25-75+50=0$
>
> $\therefore\ 25^3-75^3+50^3=3(25)(-75)(50)$
>
> $=-281250$

84. (a) $\dfrac{428\times428\times428+348\times348\times348}{428\times428-428\times348+348\times348}$

$=\dfrac{(428)^3+(348)^3}{(428)^2-428\times348+(348)^2}$

$[\because a^3+b^3=(a+b)(a^2-ab+b^2)]$

$=\dfrac{(428+348)[(428)^2-428\times348+(348)^2]}{(428)^2-428\times348+(348)^2}$

$=428+348=776$

85. (a) $\dfrac{4[(17)^3-(7)^3]}{(17^2+7^2+p)}=40$

$\Rightarrow\ \dfrac{4\times[(17-7)(17^2+7^2+17\times7)]}{(17^2+7^2+p)}=40$

$[\because a^3-b^3=(a-b)(a^2+b^2+ab)]$

$\Rightarrow\ 40\times(17^2+7^2+119)$

$=40\times(17^2+7^2+p)$

$\Rightarrow\ 17^2+7^2+119=17^2+7^2+p$

$p=119$

86. (d) $\left[\dfrac34-\dfrac14\div\dfrac14\text{ of }\dfrac25\right]\div\left[\dfrac34\div\dfrac23\text{ of }\dfrac35\right]$

$=\left[\dfrac34-\left(\dfrac14\div\dfrac1{10}\right)\right]\div\left[\dfrac34\div\dfrac25\right]$

$=\left[\dfrac34-\dfrac14\times10\right]\div\left[\dfrac34\times\dfrac52\right]$

$=\left[\dfrac34-\dfrac52\right]\div\left[\dfrac{15}{8}\right]=\left[\dfrac{(3-10)}{4}\times\dfrac{8}{15}\right]$

$=\dfrac{-7}{4}\times\dfrac{8}{15}=-\dfrac{14}{15}.$

87. (a) $3\dfrac15\div4\dfrac12\text{ of }5\dfrac13-\dfrac18\div\dfrac12\text{ of }$

$\dfrac14+\dfrac14\left(\dfrac12\div\dfrac18\times\dfrac14\right)$

$=\dfrac{16}{5}\div\dfrac92\text{ of }\dfrac{16}{3}-\dfrac18\div\dfrac12\text{ of }\dfrac14+\dfrac14(1)$

$=\dfrac{16}{5}\div\left(\dfrac92\times\dfrac{16}{3}\right)-\dfrac18\div\left(\dfrac12\times\dfrac14\right)+\dfrac14$

$=\dfrac{16}{5}\div24-\dfrac18\div\dfrac18+\dfrac14$

$=\dfrac{16}{5}\times\dfrac1{24}-\dfrac18\times8+\dfrac14$

$=\dfrac2{15}-1+\dfrac14=\dfrac{8-60+15}{60}=-\dfrac{37}{60}.$

88. (b) $7\times4\div21\text{ of }$

$4-5\div4\times(9-13)+2-2\div8$

$=7\times4\div(21\times4)-5\div4\times(9-13)$

$+2-2\div8$

$=7\times4\times\dfrac1{84}-\dfrac54\times(-4)+2-\dfrac28$

$=\dfrac13-(-5)+2-\dfrac14=\dfrac13+5+2-\dfrac14$

$=\dfrac{4+60+24-3}{12}=\dfrac{85}{12}=7\dfrac1{12}$

89. (a) $3\times8\div9\text{ of }$

$6-2\div3\times(5-2)\times2+18\div3\text{ of }3$

$=3\times8\div(9\times6)-(2\div3)\times(3)\times2$

$+18\div(3\times3)$

$=3\times\left(8\times\dfrac1{54}\right)-\dfrac23\times3\times2+18\times\dfrac19$

$=\dfrac49-4+2=\dfrac49-2=-\dfrac{14}{9}=-1\dfrac59$

90. (d) $441\div\left[270\div\dfrac37+\left(17\div\dfrac13\right)-\left(8\dfrac12-\dfrac52\right)\right]$

$=441\div\left[270\times\dfrac73+(17\times3)-\left(\dfrac{17}{2}-\dfrac52\right)\right]$

$=441\div\left[90\times7+51-\dfrac{(17-5)}{2}\right]$

$=441\div\left[630+51-\dfrac{12}{2}\right]$

$=441\div[630+51-6]=441\div675$

$=\dfrac{441}{675}=\dfrac{49}{75}$

91. (a) $18\div[26-\{25-(15-5)\div2\}]$ of $12+2-2\div4\times16$

$=18\div[26-\{25-(10/2)\}]$ of $12+2-\dfrac24\times16$

$=18\div[26-\{25-5\}]$ of $12+2-8$

$=18\div[26-20]$ of $12+2-8$

$=18\div[6]$ of $12+2-8$

$=18\div(6\times12)+2-8$

$=\dfrac{18}{6\times12}+2-8=\dfrac14+2-8=\dfrac94-8=\dfrac{-23}{4}$

92. (b) $\dfrac{(375+125)^2-(125-375)^2}{375\times375-125\times125}$

$=\dfrac{(375)^2+(125)^2+2\times375\times125-[(125)^2+(375)^2-2\times125\times375]}{(375)^2-(125)^2}$

$=\dfrac{(375)^2+(125)^2+2\times375\times125-(125)^2-(375)^2+2\times125\times375}{(375-125)(375+125)}$

$[\because a^2-b^2=(a-b)(a+b)]$

$=\dfrac{4\times125\times375}{250\times500}=\dfrac{375}{250}=\dfrac32$

93. (a) $\left(\dfrac7{16}\div\dfrac12\text{ of }\dfrac15\right)\times\dfrac45-\dfrac13\times\dfrac58\div\dfrac12+\dfrac34$

$=\left[\dfrac7{16}\div\left(\dfrac12\times\dfrac15\right)\right]\times\dfrac45-\dfrac13\times\left(\dfrac58\times2\right)+\dfrac34$

$=\left[\dfrac7{16}\div\dfrac1{10}\right]\times\dfrac45-\dfrac13\times\dfrac{10}8+\dfrac34$

$=\dfrac7{16}\times10\times\dfrac45-\dfrac5{12}+\dfrac34$

$=\dfrac72-\dfrac5{12}+\dfrac34=\dfrac{42-5+9}{12}=\dfrac{46}{12}=\dfrac{23}6$

94. (b) $32\div12\text{ of }3\times[5-(15-12)\div9]\text{ of }$

$\dfrac37+4-8\div2\text{ of }4$

$=32\div(12\times3)\times\left[5-\left(\dfrac39\right)\right]$

$\text{of }\dfrac37+4-8\div(2\times4)$

$=32\div36\times\left[5-\dfrac13\right]\text{of }\dfrac37+4-\dfrac88$

$=\dfrac{32}{36}\times\left(\dfrac{14}3\times\dfrac37\right)+4-1$

$=\dfrac89\times2+3=\dfrac{16}9+3=\dfrac{16+27}{9}$

$=\dfrac{43}9=4\dfrac79.$

95. (d) $\dfrac{52-1170\div26+13\times2}{2+1\frac18\text{ of }2-1\frac14}$

$=\dfrac{52-\frac{1170}{26}+26}{2+\left(\frac98\times2\right)-\frac54}=\dfrac{52-45+26}{2+\frac94-\frac54}=\dfrac{33}{3}=11$

96. (d) $90\div20\text{ of }6\times[11\div4\text{ of }\{3\times2-(3-8)\}]$

$\div(9\div3\times2)$

$=90\div(20\times6)\times[11\div4\text{ of }(6-(-5))]\div\left(\dfrac93\times2\right)$

$=90\div(120)\times[11\div4\text{ of }\{11\}\div6]$

$=\dfrac{90}{120}\times[11\div(4\times11)\div6]=\dfrac34\times\dfrac{11}{4\times11}\div6$

$=\dfrac{3}{4\times4\times6}=\dfrac1{32}$

97. (a) $1\dfrac18\div\left(4\dfrac14\div\dfrac35\text{ of }8\dfrac12\right)$

$-\dfrac25\times1\dfrac13\div\dfrac45\text{ of }1\dfrac23+\dfrac{11}{20}$

$=\dfrac98\div\left(\dfrac{17}4\div\dfrac35\text{ of }\dfrac{17}2\right)-\dfrac25\times\dfrac43\div\dfrac45\text{ of }\dfrac53+\dfrac{11}{20}$

$=\dfrac98\div\left(\dfrac{17}4\div\dfrac{51}{10}\right)-\dfrac25\times\dfrac43\div\dfrac43+\dfrac{11}{20}$

$=\dfrac98\div\left(\dfrac{17}4\times\dfrac{10}{51}\right)-\dfrac25\times\dfrac43\times\dfrac34+\dfrac{11}{20}$

$=\dfrac98\div\dfrac56-\dfrac25+\dfrac{11}{20}=\dfrac98\times\dfrac65-\dfrac25+\dfrac{11}{20}$

$=\dfrac{27}{20}-\dfrac25+\dfrac{11}{20}=\dfrac{38}{20}-\dfrac25=\dfrac{38-8}{20}=\dfrac{30}{20}=1\dfrac12$

98. (a) $151^2-149^2=(151-149)(151+149)$

$=2\times300=600$

$[\because a^2-b^2=(a-b)(a+b)]$

99. (b) $3-(9-3\times 8\div 2)=3-(9-3\times 4)$
$=3-(9-12)=3-(-3)=3+3=6$

100. (d) Given, $\dfrac{[54-(5\div 2)\times 8]+13}{48-4\div 3\times 8-2}$

$$=\frac{54-\left(\frac{5}{2}\times 8\right)+13}{48-\frac{4}{3}\times 8-2}=\frac{54-20+13}{48-\frac{32}{3}-2}$$

$$=\frac{47}{46-\frac{32}{3}}=\frac{47}{\frac{138-32}{3}}=\frac{47}{\frac{106}{3}}$$

$$=\frac{47\times 3}{106}=\frac{141}{106}$$

101. (d) $\frac{4}{3}\div\frac{1}{6}\times 2-1=\frac{4}{3}\times 6\times 2-1$
$=8\times 2-1=15$

102. (d) $40-[3-\{4-(6-\overline{6-4})\}]$
$=40-[3-\{4-(6-2)\}]$
$=40-[3-\{4-6+2)\}]$
$=40-[3-0]=40-3=37$

103. (a) $-1+\frac{1}{4}\div\frac{1}{2}\times 2+5$
$=-1+\frac{1}{4}\times 2\times 2+5=-1+1+5=5$

104. (c) $\dfrac{\frac{3}{5}\times 1\frac{7}{8}\div 1\frac{1}{3}\text{ of }\frac{3}{16}-\left(3\frac{1}{5}\div 4\frac{1}{2}\text{ of }5\frac{1}{3}\right)\times 2\frac{1}{2}+\frac{1}{2}+\frac{1}{8}\div\frac{1}{4}}{}$

$$=\frac{3}{5}\times\frac{15}{8}\div\left(\frac{4}{3}\times\frac{3}{16}\right)-\left[\frac{16}{5}\div\left(\frac{9}{2}\times\frac{16}{3}\right)\right]\times\frac{5}{2}+\frac{1}{2}+\frac{1}{8}\times 4$$

$$=\frac{3}{5}\times\frac{15}{8}\times\frac{3\times 16}{4\times 3}-\left(\frac{16}{5}\times\frac{2\times 3}{9\times 16}\right)\times\frac{5}{2}+\frac{1}{2}+\frac{1}{2}$$

$$=\frac{9}{2}-\left(\frac{2}{15}\right)\times\frac{5}{2}+\frac{1}{2}+\frac{1}{2}=\frac{9}{2}-\frac{1}{3}+\frac{1}{2}+\frac{1}{2}$$

$$=\frac{27-2+3+3}{6}=\frac{31}{6}=5\frac{1}{6}$$

105. (b) Using BODMAS rule,
$[16\div 2-7\times 15\div 3+\{(1+4)\times 5\}+4\times 3-10]$
$=[16\div 2-7\times 15\div 3+\{5\times 5\}+4\times 3-10]$
$=[16\div 2-7\times 15\div 3+25+4\times 3-10]$
$=[8-7\times 5+25+4\times 3-10]$
$=[8-35+25+12-10]$
$=[45-35-10]=45-45=0$

106. (c) $55\frac{1}{3}\div\left[3\frac{1}{5}+\left\{2\frac{1}{2}-\left(2\frac{1}{3}+\frac{3}{5}\right)\right\}\right]$

$$=\frac{166}{3}\div\left[\frac{16}{5}+\left\{\frac{5}{2}-\left(\frac{7}{3}+\frac{3}{5}\right)\right\}\right]$$

Using BODMAS rule,

$$\frac{166}{3}\div\left[\frac{16}{5}+\left\{\frac{5}{2}-\left(\frac{35+9}{15}\right)\right\}\right]$$

$$=\frac{166}{3}\div\left[\frac{16}{5}+\left\{\frac{5}{2}-\frac{44}{15}\right\}\right]$$

$$=\frac{166}{3}\div\left[\frac{16}{5}+\left\{\frac{75-88}{30}\right\}\right]$$

$$=\frac{166}{3}\div\left[\frac{16}{5}-\frac{13}{30}\right]=\frac{166}{3}\div\left(\frac{96-13}{30}\right)$$

$$=\frac{166}{3}\times\frac{30}{83}=20$$

107. (c) $45\div 5\times 5+10-5$
$=9\times 5+10-5=45+10-5=50$

108. (a) $8.16\times 5.35+17.9-19.5\text{ of }\frac{1}{15}+\frac{1}{5}$
$=8.16\times 5.35+17.9-1.3+\frac{1}{5}$
$=43.656+17.9-1.3+0.2$
$=61.756-1.3=60.456$

109. (c) $\dfrac{3\frac{1}{7}\div 1\frac{4}{7}+3\text{ of }}{}\;2\frac{2}{3}+2.5\times 2.4\div 3\frac{1}{3}-4\text{ of }3$

$$=\frac{22}{7}\div\frac{11}{7}+3\text{ of }\frac{8}{3}+2.5\times 2.4\div\frac{10}{3}-12$$

$$=\frac{22}{7}\times\frac{7}{11}+8+2.5\times 2.4\times\frac{3}{10}-12$$

$$=2+8+2.5\times\frac{7.2}{10}-12$$

$$=2+8+\frac{18}{10}-12=10+1.8-12$$

$$=11.8-12=-0.2=-\frac{2}{10}=-\frac{1}{5}$$

110. (a) $\dfrac{53-\frac{2}{7}\text{ of }63-9}{72-\frac{2}{5}\text{ of }(96-31)}=\dfrac{53-2\times 9-9}{72-\frac{2}{5}\times 65}$

$$=\frac{53-18-9}{72-2\times 13}=\frac{26}{72-26}=\frac{26}{46}=\frac{13}{23}$$

111. (a) $264\div 8-1-32\times 2+80\div 5\times 40\div 20$

$$=\frac{264}{8}-1-32\times 2+\frac{80}{5}\times\frac{40}{20}$$

$=33-1-64+16\times 2=32-64+32$
$=64-64=0$

112. (c) $63-[15+\{17-(9-7+1)\}]$
$=63-[15+\{17-3\}]$
$=63-[15+14]=63-29=34$

113. (c) $(12+18)\div 2-11+16\times 4-28+13(-18+15)$
$=30\div 2-11+16\times 4-28+13(-3)$
$=15-11+64-28-39$
$=79-78=1$

114. (d) Let $275=a$ and $725=b$
∴ Value of given expression

$$\frac{a^3+b^3}{(a^2+b^2-ab)}\times\frac{a^3-b^3}{(a^2+b^2+ab)}$$

$$=\frac{(a+b)(a^2+b^2-ab)}{(a^2+b^2-ab)}\times\frac{(a-b)(a^2+b^2+ab)}{(a^2+b^2+ab)}$$

$=(a+b)(a-b)=a^2-b^2$
$=(275)^2-(725)^2=75625-525625$
$=-450000$

115. (a) $\dfrac{7+8\times 8\div 8\text{ of }8+8\div 8\times 5}{4\div 4\text{ of }4+4\times 4\div 4-4\div 4}$

$$=\frac{7+8\times 8\div 64+8\div 8\times 5}{4\div 4\text{ of }4+4\times 4\div 4-4\div 4}$$

$$=\frac{7+\frac{8\times 8}{64}+1\times 5}{\frac{4}{16}+4\times 1-1}=\frac{7+1+1\times 5}{\frac{1}{4}+4-1}$$

$$=\frac{13\times 4}{1+16-4}=\frac{13\times 4}{13}=4$$

116. (a) $x+\dfrac{1}{1+\dfrac{1}{3+\frac{1}{2}}}=1$

$$\Rightarrow\quad x+\frac{1}{1+\frac{1}{\frac{7}{2}}}=1\Rightarrow x+\frac{1}{1+\frac{2}{7}}=1$$

$$\Rightarrow\quad x+\frac{7}{9}=1\Rightarrow x=1-\frac{7}{9}$$

$$\therefore\quad x=\frac{2}{9}$$

117. (d) $12.3-[7+0.8\text{ of }(5.6-3.8\times 1.03)]$
$=12.3-[7+0.8\text{ of }(5.6-3.914)]$
$=12.3-[7+0.8\text{ of }1.686]$
$=12.3-[7+1.3488]$
$=12.3-8.3488=3.9512$

118. (c) Using BODMAS rule for simplification,

$$\frac{1}{2^2}+\frac{1}{2^3}\div\left(\frac{1}{2}+\frac{1}{2}\div 1\right)+3\frac{1}{3}\div\frac{5}{2}\times\frac{3}{4}\div 6\frac{2}{3}\times\frac{7}{6}$$

$$=\frac{1}{4}+\frac{1}{8}\div\left(\frac{1}{2}+\frac{1}{2}\div 1\right)+\frac{10}{3}\div\frac{5}{2}\times\frac{3}{4}\div\frac{20}{3}\times\frac{7}{6}$$

$$=\frac{1}{4}+\frac{1}{8}\div\left(\frac{1}{2}+\frac{1}{2}\right)+\frac{10}{3}\div\frac{5}{2}\times\frac{3}{4}\div\frac{20}{3}\times\frac{7}{6}$$

$$=\frac{1}{4}+\frac{1}{8}\div(1)+\frac{10}{3}\div\frac{5}{2}\times\frac{3}{4}\div\frac{20}{3}\times\frac{7}{6}$$

$$=\frac{1}{4}+\frac{1}{8}+\frac{10}{3}\times\frac{2}{5}\times\frac{3}{4}\times\frac{3}{20}\times\frac{7}{6}$$

$$=\frac{1}{4}+\frac{1}{8}+\frac{7}{40}=\frac{10+5+7}{40}=\frac{22}{40}=\frac{11}{20}$$

119. (a) $\left(\frac{3}{4}+\frac{5}{4}\right)\times\left(\frac{9}{5}-\frac{4}{5}\right)\div\left(\frac{3}{2}+\frac{1}{2}\right)$

$$=\left(\frac{8}{4}\right)\times\left(\frac{5}{5}\right)\div\left(\frac{4}{2}\right)=\left(\frac{8}{4}\right)\times\left(\frac{5}{5}\right)\times\left(\frac{2}{4}\right)=\frac{80}{80}=1$$

120. (d) By using BODMAS rule,

$$7.2\times 4.1\div 12.3+22.5\text{ of }\frac{1}{25}-\frac{1}{10}$$

$$=7.2\times 4.1\div 12.3+22.5\times\frac{1}{25}-\frac{1}{10}$$

$$=7.2\times\frac{1}{3}+\frac{9}{10}-\frac{1}{10}=\frac{24}{10}+\frac{9}{10}-\frac{1}{10}$$

$$=\frac{32}{10}=3.2$$

121. (c) $m \times 7 + 4 - 6 \div 3 - 7 + 45 \div 5 \times 4 + 49 = 87$

$\Rightarrow m \times 7 + 4 - 2 - 7 + 9 \times 4 + 49 = 87$

$\Rightarrow m \times 7 + 4 - 2 - 7 + 36 + 49 = 87$

$\Rightarrow m \times 7 + 89 - 9 = 87$

$\Rightarrow m \times 7 + 80 = 87 \Rightarrow m \times 7 = 7 \Rightarrow m = 1$

122. (c) $\left[\left(7\frac{1}{4}\right)^2 - \left(5\frac{4}{5}\right)^2\right] \div 5\frac{4}{5} \times \frac{16}{9}$

$= \left[\left(\frac{29}{4}\right)^2 - \left(\frac{29}{5}\right)^2\right] \div \frac{29}{5} \times \frac{16}{9}$

$= \left[(29)^2\left(\frac{1}{16} - \frac{1}{25}\right)\right] \div \frac{29}{5} \times \frac{16}{9}$

$= (29)^2 \times \frac{9}{16 \times 25} \times \frac{5}{29} \times \frac{16}{9} = \frac{29}{5} = 5.8$

123. (c) $\frac{\left(2\frac{1}{7} + 6\frac{1}{7}\right) \div \frac{9}{7}}{1\frac{1}{9} \div \left\{\frac{7}{9} + \left(\frac{4}{9} \div \frac{4}{3}\right)\right\}}$

$= \frac{\left(\frac{15}{7} + \frac{43}{7}\right) \div \frac{9}{7}}{\frac{10}{9} \div \left\{\frac{7}{9} + \left(\frac{4}{9} \times \frac{3}{4}\right)\right\}}$

$= \frac{\frac{58}{7} \times \frac{7}{9}}{\frac{10}{9} \div \left\{\frac{7}{9} + \frac{1}{3}\right\}} = \frac{\frac{58}{9}}{\frac{10}{9} \div \frac{10}{9}}$

$= \frac{\frac{58}{9}}{\frac{10}{9} \times \frac{9}{10}} = \frac{58}{9}$

124. (c) $\left(2\frac{1}{2} + 1\frac{3}{4} - \frac{1}{6}\right) \times 16 \div 49$

$= \left(\frac{5}{2} + \frac{7}{4} - \frac{1}{6}\right) \times 16 \div 49$

$= \left(\frac{30 + 21 - 2}{12}\right) \times \frac{16}{49}$

$= \frac{49}{12} \times \frac{16}{49} = \frac{16}{12} = \frac{4}{3} = 1\frac{1}{3}$

125. (b) $13.5 - [5 + 0.5\,(9 - 3 \times 2)]$

$= 13.5 - [5 + 0.5\,(9 - 6)]$

$= 13.5 - [5 + 0.5 \times 3] = 13.5 - [5 + 1.5]$

$= 13.5 - 6.5 = 7$

126. (d) $22.0625 - [15 + 0.25 \times (4.78 - 1.5 \times 3.02]$

$= 22.0625 - [15 + 0.25 \times (4.78 - 4.53)]$

$= 22.0625 - [15 + 0.25 \times 0.25]$

$= 22.0625 - [15 + 0.0625]$

$= 22.0625 - 15.0625 = 7$

127. (b) $72 \div 8 - 210 \div 15 - 5 + 2 \times 5$

$= 9 - 14 - 5 + 10 = 19 - 19 = 0$

128. (c) $\frac{2\left\{3 + 3\left(\frac{1}{4} \div \frac{15}{20} + 2\right) - 18 \times \frac{1}{3}\right\}}{2(4 + 20 \div 4)}$

$= \frac{2\left\{3 + 3\left(\frac{1}{4} \times \frac{20}{15} + 2\right) - 6\right\}}{2(4 + 5)}$

$= \frac{2\left\{3 + 3\left(\frac{1}{3} + 2\right) - 6\right\}}{2 \times 9} = \frac{2\left\{3 + 3 \times \frac{7}{3} - 6\right\}}{18}$

$= \frac{2\{3 + 7 - 6\}}{18} = \frac{2 \times 4}{18} = \frac{4}{9}$

129. (a) $\frac{3 \div 3 \times 2 - 6 \div 3 + 7}{5 \div 5 \times 6 \div 6 + 3 + 3} = \frac{1 \times 2 - 2 - 7}{1 \times 1 + 3 + 3}$

$= \frac{2 - 2 + 7}{1 + 3 + 3} = \frac{7}{7} = 1$

130. (d) $56 \div 4 + p \times 3 - 24 \div 12 + 4 = 21 \div 3 + 3$

$\Rightarrow 14 + 3p - 2 + 4 = 7 + 3$

$\Rightarrow 16 + 3p = 10 \Rightarrow 3p = -6$

$\therefore p = -2$

131. (b) $\left[9 + 3 - 2 \times \left\{\left(4 \div \frac{1}{4}\right) - 4\right\} + 81 \div 9 + 81 \div 9 + 3 - 9\right] + 9$

$= [9 + 3 - 2 \times \{16 - 4\} + 9 + 9 + 3 - 9] + 9]$

$= [9 + 3 - 2 \times 12 + 9 + 9 + 3 - 9] + 9$

$= [9 + 3 - 24 + 9 + 9 + 3 - 9] + 9 = 9$

132. (a) $\frac{13 \div \{6 - 6 \div (7 - 9) \times 8 + 9\}}{5 + 5 \times 5 \div 5 \text{ of } 5}$

$= \frac{13 \div \{6 - 6 \div (-2) \times 8 + 9\}}{5 + 5 \times 5 \div 25}$

$= \frac{13 \div \{6 - (-3) \times 8 + 9}{5 + 5 \times \frac{1}{5}}$

$= \frac{13 \div \{6 + 24 + 9\}}{5 + 1} = \frac{13 \div (39)}{6}$

$= \frac{13}{39 \times 6} = \frac{1}{3 \times 6} = \frac{1}{18}$

133. (d) $(4.2 \text{ of } 2.5 \div 3.5) - (3.6 \div 2.4 + 2.5 \text{ of } 3 + 7.5) + (6 - 3 \text{ of } 2 + 4 \text{ of } 3 \div 6)$

$= (10.5 \div 3.5) - (1.5 + 7.5 \div 7.5) + (6 - 6 + 12 \div 6)$

$= 3 - (1.5 + 1) + 2$

$= 3 - 2.5 + 2 = 2.5$

134. (d) $[\{9 \times 81 + (142 \div 2)\} + 350 - 155 + 5] \div [(25 \times 25) - 125)]$

$= [\{729 + 71\} + 200] \div [625 - 125]$

$= 1000 \div 500 = 2$

135. (c) $1000 \times 100 - 1000 + 4000 \div 200$

$= 100000 - 1000 + 20 = 99020$

136. (b) $(6 + 6 \text{ of } 5 \div 5) \div 6 \text{ of } 5 + (24 \div 2 \text{ of } 3 - 6 \text{ of } 5 \div 4)$

$= (6 + 30 \div 5) \div 30 + (24 \div 6 - 30 + 4)$

$= (6 + 6) \div 30 + (4 - 30 + 4)$

$= \frac{12}{30} + (-30 + 8) = \frac{12}{30} - 22 = \frac{2}{5} - 22$

$= \frac{2 - 110}{5} = -\frac{108}{5} = -21\frac{3}{5}$

137. (b) $66 \div [34 - (32 \text{ of } 2 - 4) \div (4 \times 15)]$

$= 66 \div [34 - (64 - 4) \div (60)]$

$= 66 \div [34 - 60 \div 60]$

$= 66 \div (34 - 1) = 66 \div 33 = 2$

138. (b) $\left[3\frac{2}{5} \times \left\{2\frac{3}{4} + 3.3\left(5\frac{1}{3} + 3\frac{1}{3} - 2\frac{1}{3}\right)\right\}\right]$

$= \left[\frac{17}{5} \times \left\{\frac{11}{4} + 3.3\left(\frac{16}{3} + \frac{10}{3} - \frac{7}{3}\right)\right\}\right]$

$= \left[\frac{17}{5} \times \left\{\frac{11}{4} + 3.3 \times \frac{19}{3}\right\}\right]$

$= \left[\frac{17}{5} \times \left\{\frac{11}{4} + 1.1 \times 19\right\}\right]$

$= [3.4 \times \{2.75 + 20.9\}] = 3.4 \times 23.65$

$= 80.41$

139. (d) $5055 - (1002 \div 20.04)$

$= 5055 - 50 = 5005$

140. (d) $855 \div 15 - K + 32 \times 5 = 1152 \div 16 \times 111 \div 37$

$\Rightarrow 57 - K + 160 = 72 \times 3$

$\Rightarrow 217 - K = 216$

$\therefore K = 1$

141. (a) $x[-5\{-4(-a)\}] + 6[-3\{-3(-a)\}] = 6a$

$\Rightarrow x[-5\{4a\}] + 6[-3\{3a\}] = 6a$

$\Rightarrow x[-20a] + 6[-9a] = 6a$

$\Rightarrow -20ax - 54a = 6a$

Dividing it by a, we get

$-20x - 54 = 6$

$\Rightarrow -20x = 60$

$\Rightarrow x = -3$

142. (d) $29 - [(48 \div 12) + 2 \times (8 \div 4 + 4)]$

$= 29 - [4 + 2 \times (2 + 4)]$

$= 29 - [4 + 2 \times 6]$

$= 29 - [4 + 12]$

$= 29 - 16 = 13$

143. (c) $\frac{3.2 \times 3.2 - 0.2 \times 0.2}{0.2 \times 0.2 - 2 \times 0.2 \times 3.2 + 3.2 \times 3.2}$

$= \frac{(3.2)^2 - (0.2)^2}{(0.2)^2 - 2 \times 0.2 \times 3.2 + (3.2)^2}$

Let $a = 3.2$ and $b = 0.2$

$\therefore \frac{a^2 - b^2}{b^2 - 2 \times b \times a + a^2} = \frac{a^2 - b^2}{(a - b)^2}$

$= \frac{(a - b)(a + b)}{(a - b)^2}$

$= \frac{a + b}{a - b} = \frac{3.2 + 0.2}{3.2 - 0.2} = \frac{3.4}{3} = \frac{34}{30} = \frac{17}{15}$

144. (c) $20 \div 5 \text{ of } 4 \times 8 + 6 \div 24 \text{ of } 3 \times 48 - 6 \div 18 \times 9$

$= 20 \div 20 \times 8 + 6 \div 72 \times 48 - \frac{1}{3} \times 9$

$= 1 \times 8 + \frac{1}{12} \times 48 - 3$

$= 8 + 4 - 3 = 9$

145. (a) $[\{(82 + 48 \div 8 \times 3) + 5 \times 6\} - 7.5 \times 2]$

$= [\{(82 + 6 \times 3) + 30\} - 15]$

$= [\{(82 + 18) + 30\} - 15]$

$= [\{100 + 30\} - 15]$

$= [130 - 15] = 115$

146. (b) $1898 \div \left[\frac{13}{4}\times(35+45)-\frac{91}{4}\right]$

$=1898\div\left[\frac{13}{4}\times 80-\frac{91}{4}\right]$

$=1898\div\left[13\times20-\frac{91}{4}\right]$

$=1898\div\left[260-\frac{91}{4}\right]=1898\div\frac{949}{4}$

$=1898\times\frac{4}{949}=2\times4=8$

147. (a) $[25-(-4)\{9-(6-2)\}]\div[3\times\{6+(-3)\times(-3)\}]$

$=[25-(-4)\{9-4\}]\div[3\times\{6+9\}]$

$=[25-(-4)(5)]\div[3\times15]$

$=[25+20]\div[3\times15]=45\div45=1$

148. (a) $1-\cfrac{1}{1+\cfrac{1}{2-\cfrac{1}{2+\cfrac{1}{3}}}}$

$=1-\cfrac{1}{1+\cfrac{1}{2-\cfrac{1}{\frac{7}{3}}}}=1-\cfrac{1}{1+\cfrac{1}{2-\frac{3}{7}}}$

$=1-\cfrac{1}{1+\cfrac{1}{\frac{11}{7}}}=1-\cfrac{1}{1+\frac{7}{11}}$

$=1-\cfrac{1}{\frac{18}{11}}=1-\frac{11}{18}=\frac{7}{18}$

149. (a) $5\frac{1}{4}-\left[3\frac{1}{2}-\left\{\frac{5}{6}-\left(\frac{3}{5}\times\frac{1}{10}\div\frac{4}{15}\right)\right\}\right]$

$=\frac{21}{4}-\left[\frac{7}{2}-\left\{\frac{5}{6}-\left(\frac{3}{5}\times\frac{1}{10}\times\frac{15}{4}\right)\right\}\right]$

$=\frac{21}{4}-\left[\frac{7}{2}-\left\{\frac{5}{6}-\left(\frac{9}{40}\right)\right\}\right]$

$=\frac{21}{4}-\left[\frac{7}{2}-\frac{73}{120}\right]=\frac{21}{4}-\left[\frac{420-73}{120}\right]$

$=\frac{21}{4}-\frac{347}{120}=\frac{630-347}{120}=\frac{283}{120}=2\frac{43}{120}$

150. (b) $64\div[44-(8\text{ of }3-16)\div4\times20]$

$=64\div[44-(24-16)\div4\times20]$

$=64\div[44-(8\div4)\times20]$

$=64\div[44-2\times20]$

$=64\div[44-40]=64\div4=16$

151. (c) $9\times9+9\div9-9\times9+9+9\times9-9-9\times9$

$=81+1-81+9+81-9-81=1$

152. (c) $22\times10\div5\times2+12$

$=22\times2\times2+12$

$=22\times4+12=88+12=100$

153. (b) $\frac{1}{4}+\frac{2}{5}\div\left[\left\{2\frac{1}{5}-2\right\}\times5\right]-\frac{2}{3}\text{ of }\frac{3}{5}$

$=\frac{1}{4}+\frac{2}{5}\div\left[\left\{\frac{11}{5}-2\right\}\times5\right]-\frac{2}{5}$

$=\frac{1}{4}+\frac{2}{5}\div\left[\frac{1}{5}\times5\right]-\frac{2}{5}$

$=\frac{1}{4}+\left(\frac{2}{5}\div1\right)-\frac{2}{5}$

$=\frac{1}{4}+\frac{2}{5}-\frac{2}{5}=\frac{1}{4}$

154. (c) $[\{38-(-6)\}\times\{9-(8-1)\}]\div[4\times\{6+(-4)\}]$

$=[\{38+6\}\times\{9-7\}]\div[4\times\{6-4\}]$

$=[44\times2]\div[4\times2]$

$=88\div8=11$

155. (d) $(4^2)^2\div4\times4\div4-4$

$=4^4\div4\times1-4=4^4\div4-4=4^4$

156. (c) $5+[6+(3+5)\div2]\div2$

$=5+[6+8\div2]\div2$

$=5+[6+4]\div2$

$=5+10\div2=5+5=10$

157. (b) We know that,

$(a+b)^2=a^2+b^2+2ab$

And $(a-b)^2=a^2+b^2-2ab$

$=\frac{[(525)^2+(175)^2+2\times525\times175]-[(525)^2+(175)^2-2\times525\times175]}{525\times175}$

$=\frac{4\times525\times175}{525\times175}=4$

158. (a) $35-[30+\{10+(12-10-4)\}]$

$=35-[30+\{10+(-2)\}]$

$=35-[30+8]$

$=35-38=-3$

159. (c) $\frac{92736}{(274+830)\text{ of }\frac{7}{4}}+513$

$=\frac{92736}{1104\times\frac{7}{4}}+513=\frac{92736}{276\times7}+513$

$=48+513=561$

160. (d) $8.2+2.6+3.2-4.5\div0.9\times1.2$

$=8.2+2.6+3.2-5\times1.2$

$=8.2+2.6+3.2-6$

$=14-6=8$

161. (c) We know that,

$(a+b+c)^2=a^2+b^2+c^2+2((ab+bc+ca))$

Required answer $=(25+9+6)^2$

$=40^2=1600$

162. (b) $\frac{12+3\frac{2}{3}\div\left[1\frac{3}{4}\div\left\{5\frac{1}{4}\times\left(3\frac{3}{5}\div4\frac{1}{2}\right)\right\}\right]}{1\frac{1}{3}\times5\frac{1}{5}}$

$=\frac{12+\frac{11}{3}\div\left[\frac{7}{4}\div\left\{\frac{21}{4}\times\left(\frac{18}{5}\div\frac{9}{2}\right)\right\}\right]}{\frac{4}{3}\times\frac{26}{5}}$

$=\frac{12+\frac{11}{3}\div\left[\frac{7}{4}\div\left\{\frac{21}{4}\times\frac{4}{5}\right\}\right]}{\frac{4}{3}\times\frac{26}{5}}$

$=\frac{12+\frac{11}{3}\div\left[\frac{7}{4}\times\frac{5}{21}\right]}{\frac{4}{3}\times\frac{26}{5}}=\frac{12+\frac{11}{3}\times\frac{12}{5}}{\frac{4}{3}\times\frac{26}{5}}$

$=\frac{104}{\frac{104}{3}}=3$

163. (c) $30+180\div30\times6-15-16-60\div3-15$

$=30+6\times6-15-16-20-15$

$=30+36-15-16-20-15$

$=30+36-30-36=0$

164. (d) $1-\cfrac{7}{1-\cfrac{1}{1+\cfrac{7}{1-7}}}=1-\cfrac{7}{1-\cfrac{1}{1+\cfrac{7}{(-6)}}}$

$=1-\cfrac{7}{1-\cfrac{1}{\frac{(-6+7)}{-6}}}=1-\cfrac{7}{1-\cfrac{1}{\frac{1}{(-6)}}}$

$=1-\frac{7}{1-(-6)}=1-\frac{7}{7}=1-1=0$

165. (d) $(13.49+12.51)\times13=(26.00)\times13$

$=26\times13=338$

166. (d) $9^{18}\div3^{14}\text{ of }27^3\times\sqrt{6561}$

$=(3^2)^{18}\div(3)^{14}\text{ of }(3^3)^3\times81$

$=(3)^{36}\div(3)^{14}\text{ of }(3)^9\times(3)^4$

$=(3)^{36}\div(3)^{23}\times(3)^4$

$=(3)^{13}\times(3)^4=(3)^{17}$

167. (c) $5\times[14\div13\times\{13\times14\div(14\times14)\}]$

$=5\times\left[14\div13\times\left\{\frac{13}{14}\right\}\right]$

$=5\times\left[\frac{14}{13}\times\frac{13}{14}\right]=5\times1=5$

168. (c) $3\frac{1}{5}\text{ of }2\frac{3}{4}\div\frac{11}{3}+\left(2\frac{1}{5}\div1\frac{2}{5}\text{ of }1\frac{3}{7}-2\frac{1}{3}\right)$

$=\frac{16}{5}\text{ of }\frac{11}{4}\div\frac{11}{3}+\left(\frac{11}{5}\div\frac{7}{5}\text{ of }\frac{10}{7}-\frac{7}{3}\right)$

$=\frac{44}{5}\times\frac{3}{11}+\left(\frac{11}{5}\div2-\frac{7}{3}\right)$

$=\frac{12}{5}+\left(\frac{11}{5}\times\frac{1}{2}-\frac{7}{3}\right)=\frac{12}{5}+\frac{11}{10}-\frac{7}{3}$

$=\frac{35}{10}-\frac{7}{3}=\frac{105-70}{30}=\frac{35}{30}=\frac{7}{6}=1\frac{1}{6}$

169. (a) $25\div5\times7\text{ of }(5+7)-13(6\times4)$

$=25\div5\times7\text{ of }12-13\times24$

$=5\times7\text{ of }12-13\times24$

$=5\times84-13\times24$

$=420-312=108$

170. (b) $12+24\div2-7\times30\div6+(5+4)\times8+8\div8-8.$

$=12+12-7\times5+9\times8+1-8$

$=12+12-35+72+1-8=97-43=54$

171. (d) $3\frac{2}{3} \div 2\frac{1}{5} \times \frac{1}{4} \times \left(1+\frac{3}{1-\frac{2}{5}}\right)$

$= \frac{11}{3} \div \frac{11}{5} \times \frac{1}{4} \times \left(1+\frac{3}{\frac{3}{5}}\right)$

$= \frac{11}{3}\times\frac{5}{11}\times\frac{1}{4}\times(1+5)$

$= \frac{11}{3}\times\frac{5}{11}\times\frac{1}{4}\times 6 = \frac{5}{2} = 2\frac{1}{2}$

172. (d) $\left[18 - 3\times\left\{3-3\times\left(3\div\frac{1}{3}-3\right)+3\div\frac{1}{3}+3\right\}-4\times 2\right]$

$=[18-3\times\{3-3\times(3\times3-3)+3\times3+3\}-4\times2]$

$=[18-3\times\{3-(3\times6)+9+3\}-8]$

$=[18-3\times\{3-18+9+3\}-8]$

$=[18-3\times(-3)-8]=[18+9-8]=19$

173. (b) $35-[28-(60\div4+26\div13)]$

$=35-[28-(15+2)]=35-[28-17]$

$=35-11=24$

174. (a)

$$\frac{(157\times157)+(157\times133)+(133\times133)}{(157\times157\times157)-(133\times133\times133)}$$

Let $a=157,\ b=133$

Then, $\frac{(a\times a)+(a\times b)+(b\times b)}{(a\times a\times a)-(b\times b\times b)}=\frac{a^2+ab+b^2}{a^3-b^3}$

$\because a^3-b^3=(a-b)(a^2+ab+b^2)$

Then, $\frac{(a^2+ab+b^2)}{(a-b)(a^2+ab+b^2)}=\frac{1}{a-b}$

Putting a and b value,

$=\frac{1}{(157-133)}=\frac{1}{24}$

175. (a) $19\div5 \text{ of } (27-\overline{15-21})+37$

$=19\div5 \text{ of } [27-(15-21)]+37$

$=19\div5 \text{ of } [27-(-6)]+37$

$=19\div5 \text{ of } [27+6]+37$

$=19\div5 \text{ of } 33+37$

$=19\div(5\times33)+37=19\div165+37$

$=\frac{19}{165}+37=\frac{19+37\times165}{165}$

$=\frac{19+6105}{165}=\frac{6124}{165}$

176. (c) $\frac{0.04}{0.05}$ of $\frac{\left(3\frac{1}{3}-2\frac{1}{2}\right)\div\frac{1}{2}\text{ of }1\frac{1}{4}}{\frac{1}{3}+\frac{1}{5}\text{ of }\frac{1}{9}}$

$=\frac{4}{5}\times\frac{\left(\frac{10}{3}-\frac{5}{2}\right)\div\frac{1}{2}\times\frac{5}{4}}{\frac{1}{3}+\frac{1}{5}\times\frac{1}{9}}$

$=\frac{4}{5}\times\frac{\left(\frac{20-15}{6}\right)\div\frac{5}{8}}{\frac{1}{3}+\frac{1}{45}}=\frac{4}{5}\times\frac{\frac{5}{6}\times\frac{8}{5}}{\frac{15+1}{45}}$

$=\frac{4}{5}\times\frac{5}{6}\times\frac{8}{5}\times\frac{45}{16}=3$

177. (c) $\frac{\left[\frac{5}{8}-\left\{\frac{3}{8}-\left(\frac{5}{8}-\frac{3}{8}\right)\right\}\right]\text{ of } 8.8-1.2}{4\frac{1}{6}\div2.5\times2\div\frac{1}{6}\text{ of }60+\left(\frac{3}{4}-\frac{3}{8}\right)}$

$=\frac{\left[\frac{5}{8}-\left\{\frac{3}{8}-\frac{2}{8}\right\}\right]\text{ of }8.8-1.2}{\frac{25}{6}\div2.5\times2\div10+\frac{3}{8}}$

$=\frac{\left[\frac{5}{8}-\frac{1}{8}\right]\text{ of }8.8-1.2}{\frac{25}{6}\times\frac{1}{2.5}\times2\times\frac{1}{10}+\frac{3}{8}}$

$=\frac{\frac{4}{8}\times8.8-1.2}{\frac{1}{3}+\frac{3}{8}}=\frac{4.4-1.2}{\frac{8+9}{24}}=3.2\times\frac{24}{17}$

$=\frac{16\times24}{5\times17}=\frac{384}{85}=4\frac{44}{85}$

178. (a) $(0.2)^3\times400\div2000\text{ of }(0.2)^2$

$=(0.2)^3\times400\div[2000\times(0.2)^2]$

$=(0.2)^3\times\frac{400}{2000\times(0.2)^2}=(0.2)\times\frac{1}{5}=\frac{1}{25}$

179. (a) $(0.00243)^{0.2}=(0.00243)^{\frac{2}{10}}$

$=[(0.3)^5]^{\frac{1}{5}}=(0.3)^{5\times\frac{1}{5}}=0.3$

180. (a) $\frac{2}{3}\div\frac{3}{10}\text{ of }\frac{4}{9}-\frac{4}{5}\times1\frac{1}{9}\div\frac{8}{15}+\frac{3}{4}\div\frac{1}{2}$

$=\frac{2}{3}\div\frac{2}{15}-\frac{4}{5}\times\frac{25}{12}+\frac{3}{2}=5-\frac{5}{3}+\frac{3}{2}$

$=\frac{30-10+9}{6}=\frac{29}{6}$

181. (c) $\frac{427\times427\times427+325\times325\times325}{42.7\times42.7+32.5\times32.5-42.7\times32.5}$

From formula,

$(a^3+b^3)=(a+b)(a^2+b^2-ab)$,

Here, apply this formula in above expression

$=\frac{(427)^3+(325)^3}{\left[\left(\frac{427}{10}\right)^2+\left(\frac{325}{10}\right)^2-\left(\frac{427}{10}\times\frac{325}{10}\right)\right]}$

$=\frac{(427)^3+(325)^3}{[(427)^2+(325)^2-(427\times325)]\frac{1}{100}}$

$=(427+325)/\frac{1}{100}=(752)100=75200$

182. (c) $7\div[5+1\div2-\{4+(4\text{ of }2\div4)+(5\div5\text{ of }2)\}]$

$=7\div[5+0.5-\{4+(8\div4)+(5\div10)\}]$

$=7\div[5+0.5-\{4+2+1/2\}]$

$=7\div(5.5-6.5)=7\div(-1)=-7$

183. (d) $\frac{0.325\times0.325+0.175\times0.175+25\times0.00455}{5\times0.0065\times3.25-7\times0.175\times0.025}+\frac{0.5}{1.5}$

$=\frac{(0.325)^2+(0.175)^2+25\times0.00455}{0.0325\times3.25-0.175\times0.175}+\frac{1}{3}$

$=\frac{(0.325)^2+(0.175)^2+2\times0.325\times0.175}{(0.325)^2-(0.175)^2}+\frac{1}{3}$

$=\frac{(0.325+0.175)^2}{(0.325+0.175)(0.325-0.175)}+\frac{1}{3}$

$[\because (a+b)^2=a^2+b^2+2ab]$

$=\frac{(0.325+0.175)}{(0.325-0.175)}+\frac{1}{3}$

$[\because a^2-b^2=(a-b)(a+b)]$

$=\frac{0.5}{0.15}+\frac{1}{3}=\frac{50}{15}+\frac{1}{3}=\frac{10}{3}+\frac{1}{3}=\frac{11}{3}$

184. (b) $2\frac{1}{3}\div2\frac{1}{2}\text{ of }1\frac{3}{5}+\left(\frac{3}{8}+\frac{1}{7}\times1\frac{3}{4}\right)$

$=\frac{7}{3}\div\frac{5}{2}\text{ of }\frac{8}{5}+\left(\frac{3}{8}+\frac{1}{7}\times\frac{7}{4}\right)$

$=\frac{7}{3}\div4+\left(\frac{3}{8}+\frac{1}{4}\right)$

$=\frac{7}{3}\div4+\left(\frac{3+2}{8}\right)=\frac{7}{3}\times\frac{1}{4}+\frac{5}{8}$

$=\frac{7}{12}+\frac{5}{8}=\frac{14+15}{24}=\frac{29}{24}$

185. (b) $\frac{40-\frac{3}{4}\text{ of }32}{37-\frac{3}{4}\text{ of }(34-6)}$

$=\frac{40-\frac{3}{4}\times32}{37-\frac{3}{4}\times(28)}=\frac{40-3\times8}{37-3\times7}$

$=\frac{40-24}{37-21}=\frac{16}{16}=1$

186. (d) $8-3\div6\text{ of }2+\left(4\div4\text{ of }\frac{1}{4}\right)\div8+\left(4\times8\div\frac{1}{4}\right)\times\frac{1}{8}$

$=8-3\div12+(4\div1)\div8+\left(4\times8\times4\times\frac{1}{8}\right)$

$=8-\frac{3}{12}+\frac{4}{8}+16=24-\frac{1}{4}+\frac{1}{2}$

$=\frac{96-1+2}{4}=\frac{97}{4}$

187. (c) Given,

$5+24\times8\div8\text{ of }8-8\div8\times4\text{ of }4$

$=5+24\times8\div64-8\div8\times16$

[By BODMAS Rule]

$=5+3-16=-8$

188. (a) $\frac{15}{8}+\left[\left\{\frac{4}{5}\text{ of }\frac{5}{12}\div\left(1\frac{1}{15}\right)\right\}\times1\frac{7}{12}\right]=\frac{a}{b}$

Applying VBODMAS,

$\frac{15}{8}+\left[\left\{\frac{1}{3}\times\frac{15}{16}\right\}\times\frac{19}{12}\right]=\frac{a}{b}$

$\Rightarrow \quad \frac{15}{8} + \left[\frac{5}{16} \times \frac{19}{12}\right] = \frac{a}{b}$

$\Rightarrow \frac{15}{8} + \frac{95}{192} = \frac{a}{b} \Rightarrow \frac{360 + 95}{192} = \frac{a}{b} \Rightarrow \frac{455}{192} = \frac{a}{b}$

Hence, $a = 455$, $b = 192$

(Here a and b are coprime numbers)

$\therefore \quad 4b - a = 4 \times 192 - 455$
$= 768 - 455 = 313$

189. (b) $640 \div 8 + 930 \div 15 - k + 32 \times 5$
$= 1104 \div 16 \times 148 \div 37$

$\Rightarrow \frac{640}{8} + \frac{930}{15} - k + 160 = \frac{1104}{16} \times \frac{148}{37}$

$\Rightarrow 80 + 62 - k + 160 = 69 \times 4$

$\Rightarrow \quad 302 - k = 276$

$\Rightarrow \quad k = 302 - 276$

$\therefore \quad k = 26$

190. (c) $[3^3 \{(40 \times 5) + (7 \times 6)\} \div 11]$
$+ (2^3 \times 15 \div 24)$

By using BODMAS rule,

$= [3^3 \{(200) + 42\} \div 11] + \left(\frac{8 \times 15}{24}\right)$

$= [3^3 \times 22] + \left(\frac{120}{24}\right) = 594 + 5 = 599$

191. (c) Given equation as,

$42 \div 3 + k \times 3 - 22 \div 11 + 4 = 28$

Using BODMAS rule,

$\Rightarrow \quad 14 + 3k - 2 + 4 = 28 \Rightarrow 14 + 3k + 2 = 28$

$\Rightarrow \quad 3k = 12 \;\therefore\; k = 4$

192. (c)

$A = 60\left[\frac{6}{25} \div \left(\frac{16}{15} \text{ of } \frac{3}{8}\right) + 5 - \left(1 - 2\frac{1}{12}\right)\right]$

$= 60\left[\frac{6}{25} \div \left(\frac{16}{15} \times \frac{3}{8}\right) + 5 - \left(1 - \frac{25}{12}\right)\right]$

$= 60\left[\frac{6}{25} \div \frac{2}{5} + 5 + \frac{13}{12}\right]$

$= 60\left[\frac{6}{25} \times \frac{5}{2} + 5 + \frac{13}{12}\right]$

$= 60 \times \left[\frac{3}{5} + \frac{5}{1} + \frac{13}{12}\right]$

$= 60 \times \left[\frac{36 + 300 + 65}{60}\right] = 60 \times \frac{401}{60} = 401$

Thus, sum of digits $= 4 + 0 + 1 = 5$

193. (d) Given, $A = \frac{9}{16} \div \frac{25}{36}$

$= \frac{9}{16} \times \frac{36}{25} = \frac{81}{100}$

$B = 9 \div [(16 \div 25) \div 36]$

$= 9 \div \left[\frac{16}{25} \times \frac{1}{36}\right] = 9 \div \left[\frac{4}{25 \times 9}\right]$

$= \frac{9}{4} \times 25 \times 9 = \frac{2025}{4}$

$C = [9 \div (16 \div 25)] \div 36$

$= \left[9 \div \frac{16}{25}\right] \div 36 = \left(\frac{9}{16} \times 25\right) \div 36$

$= \frac{9}{16} \times 25 \times \frac{1}{36} = \frac{75}{12 \times 16} = \frac{25}{64}$

$D = (9 \div 16) \div (25 \div 36)$

$= \frac{9}{16} \div \left(\frac{25}{36}\right) = \frac{9}{16} \times \frac{36}{25} = \frac{81}{100}$

Thus, $A = D$

194. (c) $12 \div 4 \text{ of } 3 \times 6 + 8 \div 16 \text{ of } 4 \times 8 - 4 \div 6 \times 9$

[Using BODMAS rule]

$= 12 \div 12 \times 6 + 8 \div 64 \times 8 - \frac{4}{6} \times 9$

$= 1 \times 6 + \frac{1}{8} \times 8 - \frac{2}{3} \times 9 = 6 + 1 - 6 = 1$

195. (a)

$\left[6 - 2\left\{3 - 4\left(4 \div \frac{1}{4} - 1\right) + 2 \div \frac{1}{3}\right\} - 3 \times 2\right]$

Using BODMAS,

$\left[6 - 2\left\{3 - 4\left(4 \times \frac{4}{1} - 1\right) + 2 \times \frac{3}{1}\right\} - 3 \times 2\right]$

$= [6 - 2\{3 - 60 + 6\} - 6] = [6 + 102 - 6]$

$= 102$

196. (d) Given expression,

$\frac{5 + 7 \times 5 \div 8 \text{ of } 5 + 3 \div 3 \times 5}{6 \div 6 \text{ of } 4 + 9 \times 9 \div 3 \times 2 \times 2}$

$= \frac{5 + 7 \times 5 \div 40 + 3 \div 3 \times 5}{6 \div 24 + 9 \times 9 \div 3 \times 2 \times 2}$

$= \frac{5 + 7 \times \frac{5}{40} + \frac{3}{3} \times 5}{\frac{6}{24} + 9 \times \frac{9}{3} \times 2 \times 2} = \frac{5 + \frac{7}{8} + 5}{\frac{1}{4} + 9 \times 3 \times 4}$

$= \frac{\frac{40 + 7 + 40}{8}}{\frac{433}{4}} = \frac{87 \times 4}{8 \times 433} = \frac{87}{866}$

197. (b) The given expression,

$\left(24 \div 3 \text{ of } \frac{1}{6}\right) \times \left(\frac{4}{5} \div \frac{9}{8} \times \frac{3}{5}\right) \div \left(\frac{4}{7} \div \frac{3}{14} \text{ of } \frac{3}{14}\right)$

By using BODMAS rule,

$\left(24 \div \frac{1}{2}\right) \times \left(\frac{4}{5} \times \frac{8}{9} \times \frac{3}{5}\right) \div \left(\frac{4}{7} \div \frac{9}{196}\right)$

$= 48 \times \frac{32}{75} \div \frac{112}{9} = 48 \times \frac{32}{75} \times \frac{9}{112}$

$= \frac{288}{175}$

198. (b) Given expression,

$720 + 48 \div 8 \times 5 - 6 \times 3$

(using BODMAS rule,)

$= 720 + 6 \times 5 - 6 \times 3$

$= 720 + 30 - 18 = 732$

199. (d) Given expression,

$\frac{2 \times 2 + 2}{2 \div 2 \times 2} \div \frac{\frac{1}{2} \div \frac{1}{2} \text{ of } \frac{1}{2}}{\frac{1}{2} + \frac{1}{2} \text{ of } \frac{1}{2}}$

(By using BODMAS rule)

$= \frac{4 + 2}{1 \times 2} \div \frac{\frac{1}{2} \div \frac{1}{4}}{\frac{1}{2} + \frac{1}{4}} = \frac{6}{2} \div \frac{\frac{1}{2} \times 4}{\frac{2 + 1}{4}}$

$= 3 \div \frac{2 \times 4}{3} = 3 \div \frac{8}{3} = 3 \times \frac{3}{8} = \frac{9}{8} = 1\frac{1}{8}$

200. (c) $420 \div \left[\frac{4}{9} \times \left(1 + \frac{4}{5}\right) \times 5\right]$
$+ \left[\frac{5}{7} \text{ of } \frac{21}{25} \div \frac{3}{4} \text{ of } \frac{2}{5}\right]$

$= 420 \div \left[\frac{4}{9} \times \frac{9}{5} \times 5\right] + \left[\frac{5}{7} \times \frac{21}{25} \div \frac{3}{4} \times \frac{2}{5}\right]$

$= 420 \div [4] + \left[\frac{3}{5} \div \frac{3}{10}\right]$

$= 420 \div 4 + \left[\frac{3}{5} \times \frac{10}{3}\right] = 420 \div 4 + 2$

$= 105 + 2 = 107$

201. (a) $4 \times 7 - 3 \{7 \times 4 \div (6 \times 2)\}$

By using BODMAS rule,

$28 - 3 \{7 \times 4 \div 12\}$

$= 28 - 3\left(\frac{7}{3}\right) = 28 - 7 = 21$

202. (c) Given, $\frac{\frac{1}{2} \div \frac{3}{4} \text{ of } \frac{5}{6}}{\frac{1}{2} \div \frac{3}{4} \times \frac{5}{6}} + \frac{2 + 2 \times 2}{2 \div 2 \times 2}$

$= \frac{\frac{1}{2} \div \frac{5}{8}}{\frac{1}{2} \times \frac{4}{3} \times \frac{5}{6}} + \frac{6}{2} = \frac{\frac{1}{2} \times \frac{8}{5}}{\frac{5}{9}} + 3$

$= \frac{4}{5} \times \frac{9}{5} + 3 = \frac{36}{25} + 3$

$= \frac{36 + 75}{25} = \frac{111}{25}$

203. (d) Given expression,

$99 - [169 \div (13 \times 13) - (-4) - \{3 - 17 + 10\}]$

$= 99 - [169 \div 169 + 4 - \{-4\}]$

$= 99 - (1 + 4 + 4) = 90$

204. (c) Given expression,

$\left[3 \times 6 - 3\left\{2\left(2 \div \frac{1}{2} - 2\right) + 2 \div \frac{1}{2}\right\} - 18\right]$

$= [18 - 3\{2(4 - 2) + 4\} - 18]$

$= [18 - 3\{4 + 4\} - 18]$

$= [18 - 24 - 18] = -24$

205. (a) According to the question,

$10 + 3\frac{3}{5} \div \left[2\frac{2}{3} \div \left\{7\frac{1}{6} - \left(2\frac{1}{2} + \frac{2}{3}\right)\right\}\right]$

$= 10 + \frac{18}{5} \div \left[\frac{8}{3} \div \left\{\frac{43}{6} - \left(\frac{5}{2} + \frac{2}{3}\right)\right\}\right]$

$= 10 + \frac{18}{5} \div \left[\frac{8}{3} \div \left\{\frac{43}{6} - \left(\frac{15 + 4}{6}\right)\right\}\right]$

$= 10 + \frac{18}{5} \div \left[\frac{8}{3} \div \left\{\frac{43}{6} - \frac{19}{6}\right\}\right]$

$= 10 + \frac{18}{5} \div \left[\frac{8}{3} \div \left\{\frac{24}{6}\right\}\right] = 10 + \frac{18}{5} \div \left[\frac{8}{3} \times \frac{6}{24}\right]$

$= 10 + \frac{18}{5} \div \frac{2}{3} = 10 + \frac{18}{5} \times \frac{3}{2} = 10 + \frac{27}{5} = \frac{77}{5}$

206. (d) Given expression,

$8 - 5 \div 2^3 \times 3 + (7 \div 7 \times 7) \div 7$
$+ \left(3 \times 6 \div \frac{1}{3}\right) \times \frac{1}{3^3}$

$= 8 - 5 \div 2^3 \times 3 + \left(\frac{7}{7} \times 7\right) \div 7 + (3 \times 6 \times 3) \times \frac{1}{3^3}$

$= 8 - \frac{5}{8} \times 3 + 1 \times \frac{7}{7} + 2 = 8 - \frac{15}{8} + 3$

$= 11 - \frac{15}{8} = \frac{73}{8}$

207. (d) $(17 + 15) \div 2 - 11 + 16 \times 4 - 28 + 13(-16 + 13)$

$= 32 \div 2 - 11 + 64 - 28 + 13 \times (-3)$

$= 16 - 11 + 64 - 28 - 39$

$= 80 - 78 = 2$

208. (b) $[40 - 48 \div 4 \text{ of } 3] \div [(6+4) - 4 \text{ of } 4 + 4 + (6-4) + (4 \times 4) \div 4] \times 3$

$= [40 - 48 \div 12] \div [10 - 16 + 4 + (6-4) + 16 \div 4] \times 3$

$= \left(40 - \frac{48}{12}\right) \div (10 - 16 + 4 + 2 + 4) \times 3$

$= \left(\frac{36}{4}\right) \times 3 = 27$

209. (a) Given equation,

$\left\{(3^3 + 2^3) \times \frac{22}{7}\right\} \times \left\{(6^2 + 3^2 - 4^2) \div \left(14\frac{1}{2}\right)\right\}$

$= \left\{(27 + 8) \times \frac{22}{7}\right\} \times \left\{(36 + 9 - 16) \div \frac{29}{2}\right\}$

$= \{5 \times 22\} \times \left\{(29) \div \frac{29}{2}\right\} = 110 \times 2 = 220$

210. (d) $(3 - 3 \times 3 + 3 \div 3 + 3 \times 5) \times 2 \text{ of } 5 + (2 + 2 \div 2 + 2 \times 2 - 2)$ (using BODMAS rule)

$= (3 - 9 + 1 + 15) \times 10 + (2 + 1 + 4 - 2)$

$= (19 - 9) \times 10 + (7 - 2)$

$= 10 \times 10 + 5 = 105$

211. (a) Given, $18 \div (7 \times 2 - 5) \times 5 \times 24 \div 30$

$= 18 \div (14 - 5) \times 5 \times 24 \div 30$

$= 18 \div 9 \times 5 \times 24 \div 30 = 18 \div 9 \times 5 \times \frac{24}{30}$

$= 18 \div 9 \times 4 = 2 \times 4 = 8$

212. (a) $\frac{4}{7} \times 4\frac{1}{2} \div 5\frac{1}{3} \text{ of } 2\frac{1}{2} - \left(7\frac{7}{8} \div 5\frac{1}{9} \text{ of } 9\frac{9}{20}\right) + \frac{1}{2}$

$= \frac{4}{7} \times \frac{9}{2} \div \left(\frac{16}{3} \times \frac{5}{2}\right) - \left(\frac{63}{8} \div \frac{46}{9} \text{ of } \frac{189}{20}\right) + \frac{1}{2}$

$= \frac{4}{7} \times \frac{9}{2} \div \frac{40}{3} - \left(\frac{63}{8} \div \frac{483}{10}\right) + \frac{1}{2}$

$= \frac{4}{7} \times \frac{9}{2} \times \frac{3}{40} - \left(\frac{63}{8} \times \frac{10}{483}\right) + \frac{1}{2}$

$= \frac{27}{140} - \frac{15}{92} + \frac{1}{2} = \frac{27 + 70}{140} - \frac{15}{92}$

$= \frac{97}{140} - \frac{15}{92} = \frac{2231 - 525}{3220} = \frac{1706}{3220} = \frac{853}{1610}$

213. (d) Given expression,

$3 + 28 \div 35 \times 15 + 4 - 3 \times 4$

Applying BODMAS rule, we get

$3 + \frac{28}{35} \times 15 + 4 - 3 \times 4$

$= 3 + 12 + 4 - 12 = 7$

214. (b) $\sqrt{625} + \sqrt{\frac{625}{100}} + \sqrt{\frac{625}{10000}} + \sqrt{\frac{625}{1000000}}$

$= 25 + \frac{25}{10} + \frac{25}{100} + \frac{25}{1000}$

$= 25 + 2.5 + 0.25 + 0.025 = 27.775$

215. (b) $(\sqrt[3]{\sqrt[3]{343}})^3 \times (\sqrt[3]{\sqrt[3]{216}})^3$

$= (\sqrt[3]{7})^3 \times (\sqrt[3]{6})^3$

$= 7 \times 6 = 42$

216. (b) $\left(\frac{2 + 7 \times 7 \div 9 \text{ of } 9 + 6 \div 6 \times 2}{4 \div 4 \text{ of } 5 + 7 \times 7 \div 7 - 6 + 4}\right)$

$= \left(\frac{2 + 7 \times 7 \div 81 + 1 \times 2}{4 \div 20 + 7 \times 1 - 6 + 4}\right) = \left(\frac{2 + 7 \times \frac{7}{81} + 2}{\frac{4}{20} + 7 - 2}\right)$

$= \frac{\left(2 + \frac{49}{81} + 2\right)}{\left(\frac{4}{20} + 5\right)} = \frac{\frac{(162 + 49 + 162)}{81}}{\left(\frac{104}{20}\right)}$

$= \frac{373}{81} \times \frac{20}{104} = \frac{1865}{2106}$

217. (d)

$\frac{(0.96 \times 0.96 \times 0.96 + 0.04 \times 0.04 \times 0.04)}{(0.96 \times 0.96 - 0.96 \times 0.04 + 0.04 \times 0.04)}$

$= \frac{(0.96)^3 + (0.04)^3}{(0.96)^2 - (0.96 \times 0.04) + (0.04)^2}$

$= 0.96 + 0.04 = 1.00$

$[\because a^3 + b^3 = (a + b)(a^2 + b^2 - ab)]$

218. (c) $(2^2 + 4)^2 \times (3 - 5) + 20\% \text{ of } 400 + x\%$ of $30 = 30\%$ of 30

$\Rightarrow \quad 64 \times (-2) + 80 + \frac{30x}{100} = 9$

$\Rightarrow \quad -128 + 80 + \frac{30x}{100} = 9$

$\Rightarrow \quad \frac{30x}{100} = 9 + 48 \Rightarrow \frac{30x}{100} = 57$

$\therefore \quad x = \frac{57 \times 100}{30} = 190$

219. (b) $\frac{\frac{3}{4} \div \frac{9}{64} + \frac{7}{11} \times \frac{121}{14} - \frac{9}{13} \times \frac{65}{36}}{\frac{1}{2} \div \frac{4}{5} + \frac{3}{4} \times \frac{16}{15}}$

$= \frac{\frac{3}{4} \times \frac{64}{9} + \frac{7}{11} \times \frac{121}{14} - \frac{9}{13} \times \frac{65}{36}}{\frac{1}{2} \times \frac{5}{4} + \frac{3}{4} \times \frac{16}{15}}$

$= \frac{\frac{16}{3} + \frac{11}{2} - \frac{5}{4}}{\frac{5}{8} + \frac{4}{5}} = \frac{\frac{64 + 66 - 15}{12}}{\frac{25 + 32}{40}}$

$= \frac{\frac{115}{12}}{\frac{57}{40}} = \frac{115 \times 40}{12 \times 57} = \frac{1150}{171}$

220. (d) $[(24 - 12) \div 4] + [81 - 48 \div 12 \text{ of } 2]$

$= [12 \div 4] + [81 - 48 \div 24]$

$= 3 + [81 - 2] = 3 + 79 = 82$

221. (a) $\frac{8 \times 5 \div 25}{7 \div 14 \times 2} - \frac{14 \div 7 - 5}{7 \div 14 - 25}$

$= \frac{8 \times \frac{5}{25}}{\frac{7}{14} \times 2} - \frac{\frac{14}{7} - 5}{\frac{7}{14} - 25}$

$= \left(\frac{\frac{8}{5}}{1}\right) - \left(\frac{2 - 5}{\frac{1}{2} - 25}\right) = \left(\frac{8}{5}\right) - \left(\frac{-3}{\frac{1 - 50}{2}}\right)$

$= \left(\frac{8}{5}\right) - \left(\frac{-6}{-49}\right) = \frac{8}{5} - \frac{6}{49}$

$= \frac{392 - 30}{245} = \frac{362}{245}$

222. (a) $2160 \times 3 \div 144 + 13 - 2$

$= 2160 \times \frac{1}{48} + 13 - 2$

$= 45 + 13 - 2 = 58 - 2 = 56$

223. (b) $\frac{\frac{5}{3} \text{ of } \frac{1}{4} \times \frac{24}{5} - \frac{1}{5} \text{ of } \frac{25}{8} \times \frac{24}{5}}{\frac{5}{12} \text{ of } \frac{3}{4} \times \frac{4}{3} + \frac{3}{4} \text{ of } \frac{12}{5} \times \frac{5}{6}}$

$= \frac{\frac{5}{12} \times \frac{24}{5} - \frac{5}{8} \times \frac{24}{5}}{\frac{5}{16} \times \frac{4}{3} + \frac{9}{5} \times \frac{5}{6}}$

$= \frac{2 - 3}{\frac{5}{12} + \frac{3}{2}} = \frac{2 - 3}{\frac{5 + 18}{12}} = \frac{-1}{\frac{23}{12}} = -\frac{12}{23}$

224. (b) $(1665 \div 37) + (42 \times 5) = 45 + 210 = 255$

225. (c) $x = 0.05 \times 0.36 \div 0.4 + 0.055 + 1.50 \div 0.03$

$= 0.05 \times 0.9 + 0.055 + 50$

$= 0.045 + 0.055 + 50 = 50.1$

226. (d) $1200 \div 15 \times [45 \div (17 - 2)] \text{ of } 2 + [-2(1 + 2)]$

$= \frac{1200}{15} \times [45 \div 15] \text{ of } 2 + [-2 \times 3]$

$= 80 \times 3 \text{ of } 2 + (-6)$

$= 80 \times 6 - 6 = 480 - 6 = 474$

227. (d) $44 \times 12 - (25 + 13 \times 10)$

$= 44 \times 12 - (25 + 130)$

$= 528 - 155 = 373$

228. (a) $\frac{(777 \times 777 \times 777) + (423 \times 423 \times 423)}{(777 \times 777) - (777 \times 423) + (423 \times 423)} \times \frac{1}{(77 - 47)}$

$= \frac{(777)^3 + (423)^3}{(777)^2 - 777 \times 423 + (423)^2} \times \frac{1}{(77 - 47)}$

$= \frac{(777 + 423)((777)^2 + (423)^2 - 777 \times 423)}{(777)^2 - 777 \times 423 + (423)^2} \times \frac{1}{30}$

$= \frac{1200}{30} = 40$

229. (d) $178.01 - [86.23 - \{40.22 + (28 - 24)\}]$

$= 178.01 - [86.23 - \{40.22 + 4\}]$

$= 178.01 - [86.23 - 44.22]$

$= 178.01 - 42.01 = 136$

230. (a) $\left(\dfrac{9^3+9^4+9^5+9^6+9^7}{9^1+9^2+9^3+9^4+9^5}\right)^{\frac{1}{2}}$

$=\left[\dfrac{9^3(1+9+9^2+9^3+9^4)}{9(1+9+9^2+9^3+9^4)}\right]^{\frac{1}{2}}=[9^2]^{\frac{1}{2}}=9$

231. (c) $8+[16-\{7+4-(9 \text{ of } 3+6-4\times 7)\}]$

$=8+[16-\{7+4-(27+6-28)\}]$

$=8+[16-\{11-5\}]=8+[16-6]$

$=8+10=18$

232. (a) $\dfrac{[(5.4)^3-0.064]}{[(5.4)^2+2.16+0.16]}$

$=\dfrac{[(5.4)^3-(0.4)^3]}{[(5.4)^2+5.4\times 0.4+(0.4)^2]}$

$=\dfrac{(5.4-0.4)[(5.4)^2+5.4\times 0.4+(0.4)^2]}{[(5.4)^2+5.4\times 0.4+(0.4)^2]}$

$=5.4-0.4=5$

233. (b) $9\div[5+7\div\{9+9\div(9+9\div4)\}]$

$=9\div\left[5+7\div\left\{9+9\div\left(9+\frac{9}{4}\right)\right\}\right]$

$=9\div\left[5+7\div\left\{9+9\div\frac{45}{4}\right\}\right]$

$=9\div\left[5+7\div\left\{9+9\times\frac{4}{45}\right\}\right]$

$=9\div\left[5+7\div\left\{9+\frac{4}{5}\right\}\right]$

$=9\div\left[5+7\div\left\{\frac{45+4}{5}\right\}\right]=9\div\left[5+7\times\frac{5}{49}\right]$

$=9\div\left[5+\frac{5}{7}\right]=9\div\left[\frac{40}{7}\right]=\frac{9\times 7}{40}=\frac{63}{40}$

234. (c) $16\frac{1}{4}\div\left[2\frac{1}{6}+\left\{4\frac{1}{3}-\left(2\frac{1}{2}+\frac{3}{4}\right)\right\}\right]$

$=\frac{65}{4}\div\left[\frac{13}{6}+\left\{\frac{13}{3}-\left(\frac{5}{2}+\frac{3}{4}\right)\right\}\right]$

$=\frac{65}{4}\div\left[\frac{13}{6}+\left\{\frac{13}{3}-\frac{13}{4}\right\}\right]=\frac{65}{4}\div\left[\frac{13}{6}+\frac{13}{12}\right]$

$=\frac{65}{4}\div\frac{39}{12}=\frac{65}{4}\times\frac{12}{39}=5$

235. (a) $[\{(232\div 29 \text{ of } 2)+77\times 10\}\div 18]-\dfrac{18\times 8\div 4 \text{ of } 3-4}{2\times(8-6)+1-2\times 3\div 4 \text{ of } \frac{1}{2}}$

$=[\{(232\div 58)+770\}\div 18]-\dfrac{18\times 8\div 12-4}{2\times(2)+1-2\times 3\div 2}$

$=[\{774\div 18\}]-\dfrac{12-4}{4+1-3}=43-\dfrac{8}{2}=43-4=39$

236. (b) $(5\times 5+5-5\times 5+5-5\times 5)+(5\times 5)\div 5(2+3)$

$=25+5-25+5-25+\frac{25}{5}\times 5$

$=10-25+25=10$

237. (b) Given expression,

$5+32\div 2+6\times 2.5$

Using BODMAS $=5+16+15=36$

238. (a) $6\frac{1}{2}\times 2\frac{4}{5}\div x=\frac{7}{10}$

$\Rightarrow \dfrac{\frac{13}{2}\times\frac{14}{5}}{x}=\frac{7}{10}$

$\Rightarrow 2\times 5\times 7\times x=13\times 14\times 10 \Rightarrow x=26$

239. (d) $10(8+4R)\div(12\times 5)-5\times 2^3=6$

$\Rightarrow \dfrac{10(8+4R)}{60}-40=6\Rightarrow \dfrac{8+4R}{6}=46$

$\Rightarrow 8+4R=276\Rightarrow R=\dfrac{268}{4}=67$

240. (c) $3\frac{1}{2}-\left[2\frac{1}{4}\div\left\{1\frac{1}{4}-\frac{3}{4}\left(1\frac{1}{2}-\frac{1}{2}-2\frac{1}{2}\right)\right\}\right]$

$=\frac{7}{2}-\left[\frac{9}{4}\div\left\{\frac{5}{4}-\frac{3}{4}\left(\frac{3}{2}-\frac{1}{2}-\frac{5}{2}\right)\right\}\right]$

$=\frac{7}{2}-\left[\frac{9}{4}\div\left\{\frac{5}{4}-\frac{3}{4}\left(-\frac{3}{2}\right)\right\}\right]$

$=\frac{7}{2}-\left[\frac{9}{4}\div\left(\frac{5}{4}+\frac{9}{8}\right)\right]=\frac{7}{2}-\left[\frac{9}{4}\times\frac{8}{19}\right]=\frac{7}{2}-\frac{18}{19}$

$=\frac{133-36}{38}=\frac{97}{38}=2\frac{21}{38}$

241. (a) $\dfrac{24\sqrt{45}-16\sqrt{20}+\sqrt{245}-47\sqrt{5}}{3\frac{1}{5}+1\frac{2}{5}-2\frac{1}{6}-2\frac{1}{5}-5\frac{2}{5}+3\frac{1}{6}}$

$=\dfrac{24\times 3\sqrt{5}-16\times 2\sqrt{5}+7\sqrt{5}-47\sqrt{5}}{\frac{16}{5}+\frac{7}{5}-\frac{13}{6}-\frac{11}{5}-\frac{27}{5}+\frac{19}{6}}$

$=\dfrac{72\sqrt{5}-32\sqrt{5}-40\sqrt{5}}{\frac{23}{5}+1-\frac{38}{5}}=0$

242. (a) $45-22\div 2+12+70\div 35+0.4\div 0.8+1.5\div 3+1$

$=45-11+12+2+0.5+0.5+1$

$=61-11=50$

243. (c) From option (a), we get

$2\times 3+5-[1-2(3-2\times 2)]$

$=6+5-[1-2(-1)]=11-1-2=8\neq 0$

From option (b), we get

$2\times 3-5-[1+2(3-2\times 2)]$

$=6-5-[1+2(-1)]=1-1+2=2\neq 0$

From option (c), we get

$2\times 3-5+[1+2(3-2\times 2)]$

$=6-5+[1+2(-1)]=1+1-2=0$

Hence, option (c) is the correct answer.

244. (b) $24\div 6\times\left(\frac{3}{4}\text{ of }\frac{1}{3}+\frac{5}{3}\text{ of }\frac{3}{4}\right)=?$

$\Rightarrow 4\times\left(\frac{3}{4}\times\frac{1}{3}+\frac{5}{3}\times\frac{3}{4}\right)$

$\Rightarrow 4\times\left(\frac{1}{4}+\frac{5}{4}\right)\Rightarrow 4\times\frac{6}{4}=6$

245. (d) $\dfrac{(13\div 13 \text{ of } 13+13)}{(13\div 13\times 13+13)}$

$=\dfrac{\left(\frac{13}{13\times 13}+13\right)}{(1\times 13+13)}=\dfrac{\left(\frac{1+169}{13}\right)}{26}=\dfrac{170}{13\times 26}$

$=\dfrac{85}{169}$

246. (a) $(256)^{1/2}-(1331)^{1/3}+23\times 13$

$=(16\times 16)^{1/2}-(11\times 11\times 11)^{1/3}+23\times 13$

$=16-11+299=315-11=304$

247. (a) $(\sqrt{19\times 650\div 13+18.5\times 4})\times 13=?$

$?=\sqrt{19\times 50+18.5\times 4}\times 13$

$?=(\sqrt{950+74})\times 13=(\sqrt{1024})\times 13$

$?=32\times 13=416$

248. (b) $A=3+7\times 2=17$

$B=12\div 4-6=-3$

and $C=6\times 5+2=32$

$\therefore A\times B+C=17\times(-3)+32$

$=-51+32=-19$

249. (d) $\frac{7}{8}+\frac{8}{11}$ of $\left[\frac{33}{16}-\frac{5}{12}+\left(\frac{6}{11}-\frac{5}{12}+\frac{7}{22}\right)\right]$

$=\frac{7}{8}+\frac{8}{11}$ of $\left[\frac{33}{16}-\frac{5}{12}+\left(\frac{72-55+42}{132}\right)\right]$

$=\frac{7}{8}+\frac{8}{11}$ of $\left[\frac{33}{16}-\frac{5}{12}+\frac{59}{132}\right]$

$=\frac{7}{8}+\frac{8}{11}$ of $\left[\frac{1089-220+236}{528}\right]$

$=\frac{7}{8}+\frac{8}{11}$ of $\frac{1105}{528}=\frac{7}{8}+\frac{1105}{726}$

$=\dfrac{(2541+4420)}{2904}=\dfrac{6961}{2904}$

250. (c) $[7\div 14\times 8+(5\div 15\times 6-4\times 3)]$

$=\frac{7}{14}\times 8+\left(\frac{5}{15}\times 6-4\times 3\right)$

$=4+(2-12)=4-10=-6$

251. (b) $P=(5\div 6)$ of $54-40\div 10-41-22$

$=\frac{5}{6}\times 54-\frac{40}{10}-41-22$

$=45-4-41-22=-22$

252. (c) $8^2+16^2-19^2=?^3-257$

$\Rightarrow 64+256-361+257=?^3$

$\Rightarrow ?^3=216 \Rightarrow ?=\sqrt[3]{216}\Rightarrow ?=6$

253. (c) $(9576\div 21)\times(462\div 42)-563\times 8=?^3$

$\Rightarrow 456\times 11-4504=?^3\Rightarrow 5016-4504=?^3$

$\Rightarrow 512=?^3\Rightarrow ?=\sqrt[3]{512}$

$\therefore ?=8$

254. (c) $120\div\left[\frac{2}{3}\times\left(1-\frac{2}{5}\right)\times 5\right]+\left[\frac{9}{8}\text{ of }\frac{4}{3}\div\frac{3}{4}\text{ of }\frac{2}{3}\right]$

$=120\div\left[\frac{2}{3}\times\frac{3}{5}\times 5\right]+\left[\left(\frac{9}{8}\times\frac{4}{3}\right)\div\left(\frac{3}{4}\times\frac{2}{3}\right)\right]$

$=120\div 2+\left[\frac{3}{2}\div\frac{1}{2}\right]=120\div 2+\left[\frac{3}{2}\times 2\right]$

$=\frac{120}{2}+3=60+3=63$

255. (d) $108\div 18\times 3-64\times 2\div 32+80\div 5$ of $4=\frac{108}{18}\times 3-64\times\frac{2}{32}+80\div 20$

$=6\times 3-64\times\frac{1}{16}+4=18-4+4=18$

256. (d) $16+[0.2\div 0.004+5.2 \text{ of } 2\div(0.7\times 2+0.84\div 0.7)]$

$= 16+[50+5.2\times 2\div(1.4+1.2)]$

$= 16+[50+5.2\times 2\div 2.6]$

$= 16+\left[50+\dfrac{5.2\times 2}{2.6}\right]$

$= 16+[50+4]=16+54=70$

257. (b) $750-350\div 7+43\times 5$

$= 750-\dfrac{350}{7}+43\times 5$

$= 750-50+215=965-50=915$

258. (b) Here, $d=2;\ a_1=1;\ a_n=47$

$\therefore$ Required answer

$= 2\left[\dfrac{1}{1\times 3}+\dfrac{1}{3\times 5}+\ldots\ldots\dfrac{1}{45\times 47}\right]$

$= 2\left\{\dfrac{1}{d}\left[\dfrac{1}{a_1}-\dfrac{1}{a_n}\right]\right\}=2\left\{\dfrac{1}{2}\left[\dfrac{1}{1}-\dfrac{1}{47}\right]\right\}$

$= \dfrac{1}{1}-\dfrac{1}{47}=\dfrac{46}{47}$

259. (c) $\dfrac{1100}{5}+\dfrac{420}{2}+\dfrac{550}{5}$

$= 220+210+110=540$

260. (b) $3[4+2\{42-4(9-1)\}]$

$= 3[4+2\{42-4(8)\}]=3[4+2\{10\}]$

$= 3[4+2\times 10]=3[4+20]=3\times 24=72$

261. (b) $12\times 5\times 3\div(129-69)$

$= 12\times 5\times 3\div(60)=12\times 5\times\dfrac{3}{60}=3$

262. (b) $\dfrac{144}{33}$ of $\dfrac{11}{12}-\dfrac{132}{13}$ of $\dfrac{52}{12}$

$= \left(\dfrac{144}{33}\times\dfrac{11}{12}\right)-\left(\dfrac{132}{13}\times\dfrac{52}{12}\right)=4-44=-40$

263. (b) $14\times 14+1.2\times 1.2+1.3\times 1.3$

$= 1.4\times 1.4+1.2\times 1.2+1.3\times 1.3$

$= 1.96+1.44+1.69=5.09$

264. (c) $58-25\div 5+\{55+25-(30+20-10+30)\}$

$= 58-5+\{80-70\}=53+10=63$

265. (a) $14-3\times(5+2)\div 4$

$= 14-3\times 7\div 4$

$= 14-\dfrac{21}{4}=14-5.25=8.75$

266. (a) $0.5+0.\bar{3}=\dfrac{5}{9}+\dfrac{3}{9}=\dfrac{8}{9}$

267. (b) $[36-(48\times 7\div 16)-(19+3-24)]$

$= [36-(3\times 7)-(19+3-24)]$

$= [36-21-(-2)]=[36-21+2]=38-21=17$

268. (b) $\dfrac{2}{1\times 3}+\dfrac{2}{3\times 5}+\dfrac{2}{5\times 7}+\ldots\ldots\dfrac{2}{99\times 101}$

$= \left[\dfrac{1}{1}-\dfrac{1}{3}+\dfrac{1}{3}-\dfrac{1}{5}+\dfrac{1}{5}-\dfrac{1}{7}+\dfrac{1}{99}\ldots\ldots-\dfrac{1}{101}\right]$

$= \left(1-\dfrac{1}{101}\right)=\dfrac{100}{101}$

269. (c) $4500\div 9+1800\times 2-310\times 7$

$= 500+3600-2170=4100-2170=1930$

270. (c) $\dfrac{0.5\div(0.5\times 0.5)}{(0.5\div 0.5)\times 0.5}=\dfrac{\dfrac{0.5}{(0.5\times 0.5)}}{(0.5\div 0.5)\times 0.5}$

$= \dfrac{\dfrac{0.5}{(0.5\times 0.5)}}{\left(\dfrac{0.5}{0.5}\right)\times 0.5}=\dfrac{\dfrac{0.5}{0.25}}{1\times 0.5}=\dfrac{1}{0.25}=\dfrac{100}{25}=4$

271. (a) $13\times 12+12\times 11-14\times 15-9\times 13+19\times 15$

$= 156+132-210-117+285$

$= 573-327=246$

272. (c) Let $X=0.4\bar{1}=0.4111\ldots\ldots$

$10x=4.1111\ldots\ldots$ ...(i)

$\Rightarrow\ 100x=41.111\ldots\ldots$ ... (ii)

Subtract Eq. (i) from Eq. (ii),

$90x=37\ \Rightarrow x=\dfrac{37}{90}$

Speedy Method

$0.4\bar{1}=\dfrac{41-4}{90}=\dfrac{37}{90}$

273. (b) $\sqrt{0.000081}=\sqrt{\dfrac{81}{1000000}}$

$= \dfrac{9}{1000}=0.009$

274. (a) $[289\div\{68\div 4\times(14+2\times 6-9)\}]$

$= 289\div\{17\times(17)\}=1$

275. (b) $4400-(3200\div 16)+32\times 4$

$= 4400-200+128$

$= 4200+128=4328$

276. (b) $2.\bar{3}+4.\bar{3}=\dfrac{23-2}{9}+\dfrac{43-4}{9}$

$= \dfrac{21}{9}+\dfrac{39}{9}=\dfrac{7}{3}+\dfrac{13}{3}=\dfrac{20}{3}$

277. (b) $(0.5)^2+(0.05)^2=0.25+0.0025$

$= 0.2525$

278. (a) $(27\times 50)\div 25\times 5\,(15-14)+800\div 25$

$= 1350\div 25\times 5\times 1+800\div 25$

$= 54\times 5+32=270+32=302$

279. (d) $443-226\div 2\times 5=443-113\times 5$

$= 443-565=-122$

280. (c) $2016\div 4+32\times 6-26\times 3$

$= 504+192-78=696-78=618$

281. (b) $[19\times\{24\div 4 \text{ of } (24\times 4\div 16)\}]$

$= \left[19\times\left\{24\div 4 \text{ of }\left(24\times\dfrac{4}{16}\right)\right\}\right]$

$= [19\times\{24\div 24\}]=[19\times 1]=19$

282. (a) $\dfrac{16\times(9+4)-13\times 14}{50-(12+12)}$

$= \dfrac{16\times 13-182}{50-24}=\dfrac{208-182}{26}=\dfrac{26}{26}=1$

283. (b) $[41\times\{36 \text{ of } 4\div(96 \text{ of } 2\div 24)\}]$

$= \left[41\times\left\{36\times 4\div\left(96\times\dfrac{2}{24}\right)\right\}\right]$

$= \left[41\times\left\{36\times\dfrac{4}{8}\right\}\right]=[41\times 18]=738$

284. (b) $\dfrac{5}{8}$ of $184\times 15\div 5+k=513\div 9+435$

$\Rightarrow\ 115\times 15\div 5+k=57+435$

$\Rightarrow\ 115\times 3+k=492\Rightarrow 345+k=492$

$\Rightarrow\ k=492-345=147$

285. (a) 30% of [{(820% of 40) − 28}] % of 600

$= 30\%$ of $\left[\left(\dfrac{820}{100}\times 40\right)-28\right]\%$ of 600

$= 30\%$ of 300% of $600=\dfrac{30}{100}\times\dfrac{300}{100}$ of 600

$= 90\times\dfrac{600}{100}=540$

286. (b) $15.2625-[5.2+0.25\times(4.78-1.5\times 3.02)]$

$= 15.2625-[5.2+0.25\times(4.78-4.53)]$

$= 15.2625-[5.2+0.25\times 0.25]$

$= 15.2625-[5.2+0.0625]$

$= 15.2625-5.2625=10$

287. (d) $3\dfrac{1}{3}\div 6\dfrac{3}{7}\times 1\dfrac{1}{2}\times 3\dfrac{1}{7}=(p)^{\frac{1}{2}}$

$\Rightarrow\ \dfrac{10}{3}\div\dfrac{45}{7}\times\dfrac{3}{2}\times\dfrac{22}{7}=(p)^{\frac{1}{2}}$

$\Rightarrow\ \dfrac{14}{27}\times\dfrac{3}{2}\times\dfrac{22}{7}=(p)^{\frac{1}{2}}$

$\Rightarrow\ \dfrac{22}{9}=(p)^{\frac{1}{2}}\Rightarrow p=\dfrac{484}{81}$

288. (a) $\dfrac{5}{16}$ of $\dfrac{7}{8}\times 6+15-10$

$= \dfrac{35}{128}\times 6+15-10=\dfrac{425}{64}$

289. (a) $\dfrac{0.7^2+(0.4+0.2)(0.7)+(0.4\times 0.2)}{(0.7+0.4)}$

$= \dfrac{0.49+0.28+0.14+0.08}{1.1}=\dfrac{0.99}{1.1}=0.9$

290. (c) $(0.3-0.2)(0.3^2+0.3\times 0.2+0.2^2)$

$= (0.3)^3-(0.2)^3$

$[\because a^3-b^3=(a-b)(a^2+ab+b^2)]$

$= 0.027-0.008=0.019$

291. (c) $\dfrac{9^m\times 3^5\times 27^3}{3\times 81^4}=3^9$

$\Rightarrow\ \dfrac{3^{2m}\times 3^5\times 3^9}{3\times 3^{16}}=3^9\Rightarrow\dfrac{3^{14+2m}}{3^{17}}=3^9$

$\Rightarrow\ 3^{14+2m}=3^{26}$

On comparing both sides, we get

$14+2m=26$

$2m=12$

$m=6$

292. (b) $52\times 52-48\times 48=(52+48)(52-48)$

$[\because a^2-b^2=(a+b)(a-b)]$

$= 100\times 4=400$

293. (a) $13^3+(-8)^3+(-5)^3=3(13)(-8)(-5)$

$[\because a^3+b^3+c^3=3abc, \text{ if } a+b+c=0]$

$= 1560$

04

Average

An average or an arithmetic mean of given quantities is the sum of the given quantities divided by number of quantities.

$$\text{Average } (A) = \frac{\text{Sum of all quantities } (S)}{\text{Number of quantities } (N)}$$

Important Properties and Formulae

- If all the quantities get increased/decreased by a, then their average is also increased / decreased by a.
- If all the quantities are multiplied / divided by a, then their average is also multiplied / divided by a.
- Average of first n natural numbers $= \left(\frac{n+1}{2}\right)$
- Average of first n even numbers $= (n+1)$
- Average of first n odd numbers $= n$
- Average of 1 to n odd numbers $= \frac{\text{Last odd number} + 1}{2}$
- Average of 1 to n even numbers $= \frac{\text{Last even number} + 2}{2}$
- Average of consecutive numbers $= \frac{\text{First number} + \text{Last number}}{2}$
- Average of squares of first n natural numbers $= \frac{(n+1)(2n+1)}{6}$
- Average of cubes of first n natural numbers $= \frac{n(n+1)^2}{4}$
- Average of n multiples of any number $= \frac{\text{Number } \times (n+1)}{2}$

Question Based on Average of Group

If the average of n_1 quantities is a_1, the average of n_2 quantities is a_2 and so on, then average of all the quantities $= \frac{n_1a_1 + n_2a_2 + \ldots\ldots}{n_1 + n_2 + \ldots}$

Question Based on if a Person/Quantity Included in a Group

- If the average of n quantities is a but the average becomes b, when one quantity is eliminated, then value of eliminated observation
$$= n(a-b) + b$$
- If average of n quantities is a but the average become b, when a new quantity is added, then value of added observation $= n(b-a) + b$

Ex. 1 The average runs scored by a batsman in 20 innings is 32. After 21st innings, the average runs becomes 34. How much runs does the batsman score in his 21st inning?

Sol. Here, $n = 20$, initial average, $a = 32$ and last average, $b = 34$

$\therefore$ Runs scored in 21st inning $= n(b-a) + b = 20(34-32) + 34$
$= 20 \times 2 + 34 = 74$

Question Based on if a Person/Quantity is Excluded in a Group

Ex. 2 The average of 15 numbers is 55. One number is removed and the average of 14 numbers now becomes 57. Which number is removed.

Sol. Removed number $= 15(55-57) + 57 = -30 + 57 = 27$

Question Based on if a Person or Some Quantities Replaced in a Group

Ex. 3 The average age of 8 men is increased by 4 yr when one of them whose age is 30 yr is replaced by a new man. What is the age of new man?

Sol. Here, $n = 8, a = 30, b = 4$

$\therefore$ Age of new man $= a + nb = 30 + 8 \times 4 = 30 + 32 = 62$ yr

Important Formulae Related to Batting/Bowling Questions

- Run rate $= \frac{\text{Total runs scored}}{\text{Number of overs played}}$
- Bowling average $= \frac{\text{Total runs given by bowler}}{\text{Total number of wickets taken}}$
- Batting average $= \frac{\text{Total runs scored by batsman}}{\text{Total numbers of innings}}$

Ex. 4 In a cricket game opposition team scored 290 runs in 40 over find run rate.

Sol. Run rate $= \frac{290}{40} = 7.25$

Ex. 5 If a bowler has taken 5 wickets by giving 60 runs. Find his bowling average.

Sol. Bowling average $= \frac{60}{5} = 12$ runs/wicket

Ex. 6 If a batsman scored 340 runs in 17 innings find his batting average.

Sol. Batting average $= \frac{340}{17} = 20$ runs/inning

SSC Exam Scanner

SSC CGL 2024 (Tier I & II)

1. The average of first 92 even numbers is SSC CGL (Tier II) 20/01/2025 Shift-I
(a) 94 (b) 91 (c) 92 (d) 93

2. The average of first 91 even numbers is SSC CGL (Tier II) 18/01/2025 Shift-I
(a) 92 (b) 90 (c) 91 (d) 93

3. In a class of 150 students (boys and girls only), the girls are 60. The average weight of boys is 52 kg and that of girls is 48 kg. What is the average weight (in kg) of the whole class? SSC CGL (Tier I) 26/9/2024 Shift-III
(a) 50.4 (b) 48.8
(c) 49.6 (d) 51.2

4. A class of 30 students appeared in a test. The average score of 12 students is 60, and that of the rest is 80. What is the average score of the class? SSC CGL (Tier I) 25/9/2024 Shift-III
(a) 73 (b) 70
(c) 71 (d) 72

5. In the 8th class, consisting of 30 students, a Mathematics test was taken. 10 students had an average score of 90. The other students had an average score of 75. What is the average score of the whole class? SSC CGL (Tier I) 25/9/2024 Shift-II
(a) 78 (b) 80 (c) 76 (d) 74

6. The average of the squares of the first 48 natural numbers is SSC CGL (Tier I) 25/9/2024 Shift-I
(a) 793.17 (b) 791.17
(c) 794.17 (d) 792.17

7. A class of 30 students appeared in a test. The average score of 12 students is 62 and that of the rest is 78. What is the average score of the class? SSC CGL (Tier I) 24/9/2024 Shift-III
(a) 72.6 (b) 69.6
(c) 70.6 (d) 71.6

8. A class of 30 students appeared in a test. The average score of 12 students is 62, and that of the rest is 60. What is the average score of the class? SSC CGL (Tier I) 23/9/2024 Shift-III
(a) 58.8 (b) 61.8
(c) 60.8 (d) 59.8

9. In a team of seven members, the average age of six of the members is 42 yr while the age of the seventh member of the team is 36 yr more than the average age of all the seven members taken together. Find the age (in years) of the seventh member of the team. SSC CGL (Tier I) 23/9/2024 Shift-III
(a) 90 (b) 84 (c) 80 (d) 78

10. A class of 30 students appeared in a test. The average score of 12 students is 62 and that of the rest is 68. What is the average score of the class? SSC CGL (Tier I) 19/9/2024 Shift-III
(a) 63.6 (b) 65.6 (c) 66.6 (d) 64.6

11. The average score of a batsman in twenty matches is 15 and in twenty-five other matches is 24. Find the average score in all the forty-five matches. SSC CGL (Tier I) 19/9/2024 Shift-II
(a) 21 (b) 20 (c) 19.5 (d) 22

12. Find the average of first 125 natural numbers. SSC CGL (Tier I) 18/9/2024 Shift-III
(a) 62.5 (b) 63 (c) 62 (d) 63.5

13. The average weight of 10 students is increased by half a kg when one of the students weighing 51 kg is replaced by a new student. Find the weight of the new student. SSC CGL (Tier I) 18/9/2024 Shift-II
(a) 56 kg (b) 75 kg
(c) 45 kg (d) 66 kg

14. A group of 30 students appeared in a test. The average score of 12 students is 62, and that of the rest is 76. What is the average score of the group? SSC CGL (Tier I) 17/9/2024 Shift-II
(a) 71.4 (b) 68.4 (c) 69.4 (d) 70.4

15. The average of the squares of the first 47 natural numbers is SSC CGL (Tier I) 17/9/2024 Shift-I
(a) 760 (b) 761
(c) 759 (d) 762

16. A class of 30 students appeared in a test. The average score of 12 students is 62, and that of the rest is 72. What is the average score of the class? SSC CGL (Tier I) 13/9/2024 Shift-III
(a) 66 (b) 68
(c) 67 (d) 69

17. The average of the squares of the first 46 natural numbers is SSC CGL (Tier I) 12/9/2024 Shift-II
(a) 729.5 (b) 728.5
(c) 727.5 (d) 730.5

18. The average of 12 numbers is 48. The average of the first 5 numbers is 45 and the average of next 4 numbers is 52. If the 10th number is 10 less than the 11th number and is 5 more than the 12th number, then the average of the 11th and 12th numbers is: SSC CGL (Tier I) 12/9/2024 Shift-I
(a) 50.5 (b) 46.5
(c) 47.5 (d) 48.5

19. A class of 30 students appeared in a test. The average score of 12 students is 62, and that of the rest is 74. What is the average score of the class? SSC CGL (Tier I) 11/9/2024 Shift-III
(a) 70.2 (b) 69.2
(c) 68.2 (d) 67.2

20. Find the average of the prime numbers lying between 50 and 76. SSC CGL (Tier I) 11/9/2024 Shift-II
(a) 66 (b) 60 (c) 62 (d) 64

21. A group of 30 students appeared in a test. The average score of 12 students is 62, and that of the rest is 62. What is the average score of the group? SSC CGL (Tier I) 11/9/2024 Shift-I
(a) 62 (b) 63 (c) 60 (d) 61

22. The average of the squares of the first 45 natural numbers is SSC CGL (Tier I) 10/9/2024 Shift-III
(a) 698.67 (b) 699.67
(c) 697.67 (d) 696.67

23. The average temperature of a city for the first sixteen days of January is 22°C, and the average temperature for the last sixteen days of the same month is 26°C. If the average temperature for the entire month is 24°C, what is the temperature on the sixteenth day? SSC CGL (Tier I) 09/9/2024 Shift-II
(a) 24°C (b) 25°C
(c) 23°C (d) 22°C

SSC CGL 2023 (Tier I & II)

24. The average weight of the first thirteen persons among fourteen persons is 78 kg. The weight of the 14th person is 39 kg more than the average weight of all the fourteen persons. Find the weight of the 14th person. SSC CGL (Tier-II) 26/10/2023 Shift-I
(a) 118 kg (b) 98 kg
(c) 110 kg (d) 120 kg

25. Find the average of the following sets of numbers.
693, 456, 876, 532, 934, 691, 596, 398, 682
SSC CGL (Tier-II) 07/03/2023 Shift-I
(a) 650.89 (b) 550.50
(c) 750.80 (d) 725.90

26. The average marks obtained by Saloni in four papers is 51, and in the fifth paper she gets 56 marks. Find her new average in all five papers. SSC CGL (Tier-II) 06/03/2023 Shift-I
(a) 51 (b) 52 (c) 49 (d) 50

27. The average weight of three men is increased by 4 kg when one of them, whose weight is 100 kg, is replaced by another man. What is the weight of the new man?
SSC CGL (Tier-II) 03/03/2023 Shift-I
(a) 107 kg (b) 103 kg
(c) 104 kg (d) 112 kg

28. The average of 20 numbers is 32. If two numbers are 29 and 31, then what is the average of the remaining numbers (correct up to two decimals)?
SSC CGL (Tier-II) 03/03/2023 Shift-I
(a) 31.24 (b) 30.22
(c) 34.44 (d) 32.22

29. Find the average of the cubes of the first five natural numbers.
SSC CGL (Tier-II) 02/03/2023 Shift-I
(a) 35 (b) 40
(c) 45 (d) 50

30. The average of all prime numbers between 32 and 69 is
SSC CGL (Tier-I) 27/07/2023 Shift-I
(a) 52.5 (b) 60 (c) 51 (d) 56.5

31. In an examination of 7 papers of 100 marks each, there were 3 Mathematics papers, 2 English papers and 2 Hindi papers. D gets average marks of 45, 55 and 60 in Mathematics, English and Hindi, respectively. What are the average marks per paper?
SSC CGL (Tier-I) 26/07/2023 Shift-IV
(a) 56.5 (b) 52.1
(c) 55.6 (d) 54.1

32. In a class of 60 students, there are 35 boys. The average weight of boys is 42 kg and the average weight of the full class is 46.5 kg. Find the average weight of girls in the class. SSC CGL (Tier-I) 26/07/2023 Shift-II
(a) 48.7 kg (b) 49.7 kg
(c) 52.8 kg (d) 56.7 kg

33. Ram has an average score of 65 runs in 19 innings in cricket matches. Find out how many runs are to be scored by him in the 20th innings to raise the average score to 67? SSC CGL (Tier-I) 25/07/2023 Shift-I
(a) 135 (b) 105 (c) 115 (d) 195

34. In a class of 60 students, 20 are girls. The average weight of the boys in the class is 40 kg, while that of all the girls is 35 kg. What is the average weight (in kg) of the entire class (correct to two decimal places)? SSC CGL (Tier-I) 24/07/2023 Shift-II
(a) 36.67 (b) 38.33
(c) 33.33 (d) 40.67

35. During a school excursion each student of junior school was charged ₹ 325 and each student of senior school was charged ₹ 400. If there were 80 students from junior school and the combined average amount charged per student was ₹ 352, then how many students from senior school went for the excursion?
SSC CGL (Tier-I) 24/07/2023 Shift-I
(a) 55 (b) 45 (c) 50 (d) 40

36. College *P* has 180 students scoring average marks of 88 and college *Q* has 320 students scoring average marks of 72. Find the average marks of both the colleges together.
SSC CGL (Tier-I) 21/07/2023 Shift-IV
(a) 82.00 (b) 75.25
(c) 77.76 (d) 80.00

37. There are 15 students in a class. Their average weight is 40 kg. When one student leaves the class, the average weight is 39.5 kg. What is the weight of the student who left the class (where kg means kilogram)?
SSC CGL (Tier-I) 21/07/2023 Shift-III
(a) 47 kg (b) 42 kg
(c) 52 kg (d) 48 kg

38. The weight (in kg) of five girls of a class are 49, 42, 61, 55 and 58. What is the average weight (in kg) of these five girls?
SSC CGL (Tier-I) 21/07/2023 Shift-I
(a) 53 (b) 54 (c) 51 (d) 52

39. The average monthly income of the father and mother is ₹ 5000. The average monthly income of the mother and her son is ₹ 6000. The average monthly income of the father and his son is ₹ 10000. Find the monthly income (in ₹) of the father. SSC CGL (Tier-I) 20/07/2023 Shift-IV
(a) 9000 (b) 8000
(c) 12000 (d) 10000

40. The average weight of 15 persons is increased by 1.2 kg when one of them whose weight is 51 kg is replaced by a new man. The weight of the new man is
SSC CGL (Tier-I) 20/07/2023 Shift-II
(a) 69 kg (b) 70 kg
(c) 65 kg (d) 59 kg

41. The average age of a group of friends is 27 yr. If 4 new friends whose average age is 25 yr join them, the average age of the entire group becomes 26 yr. How many people were there in the group initially ? SSC CGL (Tier-I) 20/07/2023 Shift-I
(a) 3 (b) 4 (c) 5 (d) 6

42. The average of 8 numbers is 18. If one of the numbers is excluded, the average becomes 20. Find the excluded number.
SSC CGL (Tier-I) 19/07/2023 Shift-IV
(a) 6 (b) 10 (c) 8 (d) 4

43. In ₹ 150, *B* buys 10 pens for ₹ 8 each, 10 erasers for ₹ 5 each and some sharpeners for ₹ 4 each. What is the average price per item in ₹ ?
SSC CGL (Tier-I) 19/07/2023 Shift-III
(a) 8 (b) 7 (c) 10 (d) 6

44. In a group of 32 students, the average weight was 18.5 kg. When 4 students left the group, the average came down to 15.5 kg. What was the average weight (in kg) of those 4 students?
SSC CGL (Tier-I) 19/07/2023 Shift-II
(a) 39.5 (b) 37.5 (c) 27.5 (d) 36.5

45. According to Raghav, his weight is more than 64 kg but less than 74 kg. His sister does not agree with Raghav and she thinks that his weight is more than 60 kg but less than 69 kg. His mother's view is that his weight cannot be more than 68 kg. His father's view is that his weight cannot be more than 67 kg. If all of them are correct in their estimation, then what is the average of different probable weights of Raghav measured (in kg)? SSC CGL (Tier-I) 18/07/2023 Shift-III
(a) 68 (b) 66 (c) 65 (d) 67

46. The average weight of a team of 20 people was calculated to be 59.8 kg and it was later discovered that one weight was misread as 68 kg instead of 77 kg. The correct average weight is
SSC CGL (Tier-I) 18/07/2023 Shift-I
(a) 70.25 kg (b) 61.25 kg
(c) 60.25 kg (d) 60.50 kg

47. 20 students of a college went to a hotel. 19 of them spent ₹ 175 each on their meal and the 20th student spent ₹19 more than the average of all the 20. Find the total money spent by them.
SSC CGL (Tier-I) 17/07/2023 Shift-IV
(a) ₹ 3540 (b) ₹ 3490
(c) ₹ 3500 (d) ₹ 3520

48. The average of 36 numbers was found to be 45. Later, it was detected that 84 was misread as 48. Find the correct average of the given numbers.
SSC CGL (Tier-I) 14/07/2023 Shift-III
(a) 58 (b) 48
(c) 46 (d) 56

SSC CGL 2022 (Tier I)

49. In nine innings of cricket, the average of a batsman is 58 runs. How many runs does he need to make in the tenth innings to get the average score 61?
SSC CGL (Tier-I) 13/12/2022 Shift-IV
(a) 88 (b) 69 (c) 79 (d) 100

50. Ram, Shyam, Rohan, Reeta and Mukesh are five members of a family who are weighed consecutively and their average weight is calculated after each member is weighed. If the average weight increases by 2 kg each time, how much heavier is Mukesh than Ram? **SSC CGL (Tier-I) 13/12/2022 Shift-I**
(a) 14 kg (b) 18 kg
(c) 16 kg (d) 12 kg

51. The average age of six members of a family is 40 yr. If the age of a guest is included, then the average age increases by 12.5%. What is the age (in years) of the guest?
SSC CGL (Tier-I) 12/12/2022 Shift-IV
(a) 59 (b) 65
(c) 75 (d) 69

52. The average of six numbers is 3.52. The average of two of them is 3.7, while the average of other two is 2.5. What is the average of the remaining two?
SSC CGL (Tier-I) 12/12/2022 Shift-I
(a) 3.7 (b) 2.5
(c) 4.36 (d) 3.52

53. If the average of s numbers is r^4 and the average of r numbers is s^4, then find the average of all $r+s$ numbers?
SSC CGL (Tier-I) 09/12/2022 Shift-IV
(a) $rs(r^2+s^2-rs)$ (b) rs
(c) r^2+s^2 (d) $rs(r^2+s^2)$

54. In a hotel, there is 120 staff members. Their average weight is 62.5 kg. When one of the staff members leaves the hotel, the average weight is reduced by 250 g. Find the weight of the staff member who left the hotel.
SSC CGL (Tier-I) 09/12/2022 Shift-I
(a) 64.25 kg (b) 78.75 kg
(c) 90.50 kg (d) 92.25 kg

55. While finding the average marks of a class, Vikas's marks were wrongly entered as 98 in place of 89. Due to this error, the average marks of the class were 0.25 more than the actual average. What is the number of students in the class? **SSC CGL (Tier-I) 08/12/2022 Shift-IV**
(a) 32 (b) 38
(c) 34 (d) 36

56. A student's marks were wrongly entered as 65 instead of 45. Due to this, the average marks for the class got increased by $\frac{1}{3}$. The number of students in the class is
SSC CGL (Tier-I) 08/12/2022 Shift-III
(a) 40 (b) 20
(c) 60 (d) 30

57. The average weight of apples in a basket is 50 kg. 6 more apples with the average weight of 60 kg are added in the basket. If the average weight of the basket is increased by 5 kg, then find the number of apples in the basket originally.
SSC CGL (Tier-I) 07/12/2022 Shift-IV
(a) 4 (b) 6 (c) 2 (d) 8

58. The average of the first 7 non-zero multiples of 17 is
SSC CGL (Tier-I) 07/12/2022 Shift-III
(a) 67 (b) 68
(c) 69 (d) 66

59. The average weight of 12 persons increases by 3.5 kg when a new person comes in place of one of them weighting 58 kg. The weight of the new person is
SSC CGL (Tier-I) 07/12/2022 Shift-II
(a) 100 kg (b) 16 kg
(c) 70 kg (d) 42 kg

60. The average of eight consecutive odd numbers is 48. Find the sum of the fifth and seventh numbers.
SSC CGL (Tier-I) 06/12/2022 Shift-III
(a) 102 (b) 86 (c) 89 (d) 90

61. Sonali applied for a job of Science teacher in a school. In the test for job, she scored 8 in Physics, 8 in Chemistry, 6 in Biology and 6.5 in the interview. For calculating the final score, weightage of 2, 3, 3 and 4 were assigned to Physics, Chemistry, Biology and interview, respectively. What is the weighted average score of Sonali?
SSC CGL (Tier-I) 06/12/2022 Shift-I
(a) 7 (b) 8.4 (c) 7.2 (d) 21

62. The average weight of 5 men decreases by 3 kg when one of them weighting 150 kg is replaced by another person. Find the weight of the new person.
SSC CGL (Tier-I) 05/12/2022 Shift-II
(a) 125 kg (b) 100 kg
(c) 120 kg (d) 135 kg

63. A company employed 700 men and 300 women and the average wage was 450 per day. If a man got ₹50 more than a woman, then the daily wage of the woman is
SSC CGL (Tier-I) 03/12/2022 Shift-III
(a) ₹ 350 (b) ₹375 (c) ₹415 (d) ₹ 435

64. The average marks of 60 students in a class are 62. The average marks of boys and girls in that subject are 60 and 65, respectively. The number of boys in the class is
SSC CGL (Tier-I) 3/12/2022 Shift-I
(a) 36 (b) 25 (c) 41 (d) 31

65. The average of the marks of 25 students in a class, in an examination was calculated to be 19. Later, the teacher realized that the marks of two students were taken as 18 and 19 respectively, instead of 14 and 15. Find the new actual average marks of the class.
SSC CGL (Tier-I) 01/12/2022 Shift-II
(a) 17.43 (b) 16.56
(c) 18.68 (d) 17.65

66. The batting average for 27 innings of a cricket player is 47 runs. His highest score in an innings exceeds his lowest score by 157 runs. If these two innings are excluded, the average score of the remaining 25 innings is 42 runs. Find his highest score in an innings.
SSC CGL (Tier-I) 01/12/2022 Shift-I
(a) 176 (b) 188 (c) 186 (d) 174

SSC CGL 2021 & 2020 (Tier I)

67. What is the average of numbers from 1 to 50 which are multiples of 2 or 5? (correct to one decimal place). **SSC CGL (Tier-I) 24/08/2021 Shift-III**
(a) 25.9 (b) 25.8 (c) 25.4 (d) 26.4

68. What is the product of the average of first ten positive odd numbers and the average of first fifteen positive even numbers?
SSC CGL (Tier-I) 24/08/2021 Shift-II

(a) 44 (b) 150 (c) 160 (d) 85.25

69. The average of 23 numbers is 51. The average of first 12 numbers is 49 and the average of last 12 numbers is 54. If the 12th number is removed, then the average of the remaining numbers (correct to two decimal places) is
SSC CGL (Tier-I) 24/08/2021 Shift-I

(a) 53.25 (b) 50.45
(c) 51.75 (d) 52.65

70. The average weight of students of Section *A* and *B* having 40 students each is 45.5 kg and 44.2 kg, respectively. Two students of Section *A* having average weight 48.75 kg were shifted to Section *B* and 2 students of Section *B* were shifted to Section *A*, making the average weight of both the sections equal. What is the average weight (in kg) of the students who were shifted from Section *B* to Section *A*?
SSC CGL (Tier-I) 23/08/2021 Shift-II

(a) 35.75 (b) 34.25
(c) 34.5 (d) 35

71. In an examination, the average score of a student was 67.6 . If he would have got 27 more marks in Mathematics, 10 more marks in Computer Science, 18 more marks in History and retained the same marks in other subjects, then his average score would have been 72.6. How many papers were there in the examination?
SSC CGL (Tier-I) 23/08/2021 Shift-I

(a) 10 (b) 11 (c) 12 (d) 9

72. The average monthly salary of 60 employees of a factory is ₹ 29900. If two officers are getting ₹ 90000 each and the average salary of 8 supervisors is ₹ 65000, then what is the average salary (in ₹) of the remaining employees?
SSC CGL (Tier-I) 20/08/2021 Shift-II

(a) 22680 (b) 29080
(c) 21080 (d) 21880

73. The average of squares of five consecutive odd natural numbers is 233. What is the average of the largest number and the smallest number? SSC CGL (Tier-I) 20/08/2021 Shift-I

(a) 15 (b) 17
(c) 11 (d) 13

74. The average daily production of toys in a factory in the month of December is 512. If the average production during first 20 days is 515 and that of the last 13 days is 510, then what is the average of production on 19 and 20 December?
SSC CGL (Tier-I) 18/08/2021 Shift-III

(a) 1058 (b) 513
(c) 529 (d) 512

75. The average of x occurring 5 times and y occurring 7 times is 37. Also, the average of x occurring 7 times and y occurring 5 times is 35. The value of y is
SSC CGL (Tier-I) 18/08/2021 Shift-I

(a) 45 (b) 42 (c) 30 (d) 27

76. The average score of 40 students in a class test is 45. Later on, it was found that at two places 25 was read as 35 and at one place 38 was read as 32. What is the actual average score of the class?
SSC CGL (Tier-I) 17/08/2021 Shift-III

(a) 43.80 (b) 39.69
(c) 45.35 (d) 44.65

77. The average of 8 consecutive even numbers written in ascending order is 17. What is the average of the last three numbers, 36 and 53?
SSC CGL (Tier-I) 17/08/2021 Shift-I

(a) 31 (b) 32.2 (c) 31.6 (d) 29.8

78. The average height of some students in a group is 156 cm. If 5 students of average height 160 cm join the group, then the average height of all the students in the group increases by 0.8 cm. What is the number of students in the group, initially?
SSC CGL (Tier-I) 16/08/2021 Shift-III

(a) 10 (b) 15 (c) 20 (d) 25

79. The average of 22 numbers is 37.5. The average of first 12 numbers is 40.6 and that of the last 12 numbers is 35.4. If 11th and 12th numbers are excluded, then what is the average of the remaining numbers?
SSC CGL (Tier-I) 16/08/2021 Shift-I

(a) 37.8 (b) 36.9 (c) 37.4 (d) 36.4

80. The average of eleven numbers is 56. The average of first three numbers is 52 and that of next five numbers is 60. The 9th and 10th number are 3 and 1 more than the 11th number respectively. What is the average of 9th and 11th numbers?
SSC CGL (Tier-I) 13/08/2021 Shift-III

(a) 53.5 (b) 54 (c) 52.5 (d) 52

81. The average of 28 numbers is 77. The average of first 14 numbers is 74 and the average of last 15 numbers is 84. If the 14th number is excluded, then what is the average of remaining numbers? (correct to one decimal place)
SSC CGL (Tier-I) 13/08/2021 Shift-I

(a) 76.9 (b) 77
(c) 73.1 (d) 74.7

82. The average of five consecutive odd numbers is m. If the next three odd numbers are also included, then what is the increase in the average? SSC CGL (Tier-I) 07/03/2020 Shift-I

(a) 3 (b) 0 (c) 17 (d) 8

83. The average of 60 student's result is 38. If the average of the first 22 students is 36, and that of the last 32 students is 32, then the average result of the remaining students is
SSC CGL (Tier-I) 06/03/2020 Shift-III

(a) 77.33 (b) 65.30
(c) 81.9 (d) 52.12

84. 24 students collected money for donation. The average contribution was ₹50. Later on, their teacher also contributed some money. Now, the average contribution is ₹56. The teacher's contribution is
SSC CGL (Tier-I) 06/03/2020 Shift-II

(a) ₹106 (b) ₹56
(c) ₹200 (d) ₹194

85. The average of the marks of 30 boys is 88, and when the top two scores were excluded, the average marks reduced to 87.5. If the top two scores differ by 2, then the highest mark is
SSC CGL (Tier-I) 06/03/2020 Shift-I

(a) 92 (b) 96 (c) 94 (d) 90

86. The average height of 5 boys is 175 cm. A sixth boy joined the group and the average height of all the boys in the group now increased by 1 cm. The height of the sixth boy is
SSC CGL (Tier-I) 05/03/2020 Shift-III

(a) 180 cm (b) 181 cm
(c) 179 cm (d) 175 cm

87. The average of some numbers is 54.6. If 75% of the numbers are increased by 5.6 each and the rest are decreased by 8.4 each, then what is the average of the numbers so obtained?
SSC CGL (Tier-I) 05/03/2020 Shift-II

(a) 55.6 (b) 55.8
(c) 56.7 (d) 56.3

88. The average of 24 numbers is 56. The average of the first 10 numbers is 71.7 and that of the next 11 numbers is 42. The next three numbers (i.e. 22nd, 23rd and 24th) are in the ratio $\frac{1}{2}:\frac{1}{3}:\frac{5}{12}$. What is the average of the 22nd and 24th numbers? SSC CGL (Tier-I) 05/03/2020 Shift-I

(a) 60.5 (b) 58
(c) 55 (d) 49.5

SSC CPO SI 2024-2020

89. In a class, there are 60 students. The average weight of the entire class is 42 kg. If there are 36 boys in the class and the average weight of all the boys is 50 kg, then what is the average weight (in kg) of all the girls? SSC CPO 28/06/2024 Shift-II

(a) 32 (b) 30 (c) 36 (d) 34

90. Anwesha's marks in a class text of Sanskrit were incorrectly entered as 99 instead of 66. If there are 55 students in the class, then what is the increment in the average marks of the class in Sanskrit because of this typing error? SSC CPO 28/06/2024 Shift-I

(a) 0.4 (b) 0.8
(c) 0.6 (d) 0.2

91. What is the average of the first six prime numbers? SSC CPO 05/10/2023 Shift-III

(a) $6\frac{1}{3}$ (b) $6\frac{5}{6}$
(c) $6\frac{2}{3}$ (d) $6\frac{1}{6}$

92. Rakesh runs a coaching institute having 50 faculty members. The average monthly salary of 35 faculty members is ₹ 37500. What will be the average monthly salary (in ₹) of the other 15 faculty members, if the average monthly salary of all the 50 faculty members is found to be ₹ 30000? SSC CPO 05/10/2023 Shift-III

(a) 13000 (b) 13500
(c) 12500 (d) 12000

93. The average of 12 numbers is 39. The average of the last five numbers is 35, and that of the first four numbers is 40. The fifth number is 6 less than the sixth number and 5 more than the seventh number. The average of the sixth and seventh numbers is SSC CPO 25/11/2020 Shift-I

(a) 47.5 (b) 50 (c) 39 (d) 44.5

94. The average weight of A, B and C is 65 kg. If the average weight of C and B is 61.5 kg and the average weight of A and C is 68.5 kg then the weight of C (in kg) is SSC CPO 25/11/2020 Shift-I

(a) 65 (b) 60 (c) 68 (d) 67

95. The average weight of a group of 3 people A, B and C is 70 kg. When D joins this group, the average becomes 60 kg. A man E, whose weight is 5 kg more than that of D, replaces A and the average weight of B, C, D and E now becomes 59 kg. What is the average weight (in kg) of A, D and E? (correct to the nearest integer) SSC CPO 24/11/2020 Shift-I

(a) 40 (b) 35
(c) 30 (d) 39

96. The average weight of A, B and C is 65 kg. If the average weight of A and B is 63.5 kg and the average weight of A and C is 67.5 kg, then the weight of A (in kg) is SSC CPO 23/11/2020 Shift-I

(a) 67 (b) 60
(c) 68 (d) 65

97. The average of twelve numbers is 39. The average of the last five numbers is 35, and that of the first four numbers is 40. The fifth number is 6 less than the sixth number and 5 more than the seventh number. The average of the fifth and sixth numbers is SSC CPO 23/11/2020 Shift-I

(a) 47 (b) 39
(c) 44 (d) 50

SSC CHSL 2024 (Tier I & II)

98. The average of 11 results is 59 and that of the first 10 is 58. The 11th result is SSC CHSL (Tier II) 18/11/2024

(a) 59 (b) 68 (c) 58 (d) 69

99. The average of 11 results is 60 and that of the first 10 is 59. The 11th result is SSC CHSL (Tier II) 18/11/2024

(a) 70 (b) 60 (c) 69 (d) 59

100. The average of five integers is 48. The average of the first four integers is 50% of the 5th integer. The 5th integer is SSC CHSL (Tier II) 18/11/2024

(a) 78 (b) 74 (c) 82 (d) 80

101. The average of 50 numbers is 23. If each number is multiplied by 13, then the new average is SSC CHSL (Tier I) 11/07/2024 Shift-IV

(a) 219 (b) 299 (c) 650 (d) 88

102. If the average weight of 40 apples is 33 kg and that of 32 apples is 60 kg, then the average weight (in kg) of all the apples is SSC CHSL (Tier I) 10/07/2024 Shift-IV

(a) 46.5 (b) 45 (c) 44 (d) 45.2

103. A public library has an average attendance of 410 on Sundays and 230 for the remaining days. The average attendance per day of a month of 30 days beginning with Sunday would be SSC CHSL (Tier I) 10/07/2024 Shift-III

(a) 230 (b) 254 (c) 320 (d) 260

104. In a class with a certain number of students, if one student weighing 30 kg is added, then the average weight of the class increases by 1 kg. If one more student weighing 30 kg is added, then the average weight of the class increases by 1.5 kg over the original average. What is the original average weight (in kg) of the class? SSC CHSL (Tier I) 09/07/2024 Shift-IV

(a) 27 (b) 26.5
(c) 25.5 (d) 24

105. The average salary of a group of 12 employees in an institution is ₹ 3950 per month and that of another group of employees is ₹ 1850. If the average salary of all employees is ₹ 2150, then the total number of employees is SSC CHSL (Tier I) 09/07/2024 Shift-II

(a) 100 (b) 88
(c) 84 (d) 72

106. The average weight of 35 students in a class is 40 kg. Five of the students of this class whose average weight is 42 kg left the class. Find the average weight of the remaining 30 students. SSC CHSL (Tier I) 08/07/2024 Shift-IV

(a) $39\frac{2}{3}$ kg (b) $19\frac{2}{3}$ kg
(c) $49\frac{2}{3}$ kg (d) $29\frac{2}{3}$ kg

107. The average of the first 10 natural numbers is SSC CHSL (Tier I) 08/07/2024 Shift-II

(a) 5.5 (b) 6.5
(c) 5 (d) 6

108. The weights of the five friends are 67 kg, 85 kg, 70 kg, 90 kg and 103 kg. Find the average of their weights in kg. SSC CHSL (Tier I) 08/07/2024 Shift-I

(a) 83 (b) 87
(c) 80 (d) 90

109. Abhishek's marks in Mathematics were incorrectly entered as 93 instead of 63. Due to this, the average marks of the class in Mathematics got increased by 0.5. How many students were there in class? SSC CHSL (Tier I) 05/07/2024 Shift-I

(a) 45 (b) 55 (c) 60 (d) 50

110. A man bought 4 books for ₹ 50 each, 5 books for ₹ 60 each and 6 books for ₹ 70 each. The average cost of a book for the man is (round up to two decimal places) SSC CHSL (Tier I) 04/07/2024 Shift-IV

(a) ₹ 36.33 (b) ₹ 50.33
(c) ₹ 61.33 (d) ₹ 60.33

111. In a college, the average weight of 40 boys in a section among 72 students is 33 kg and that of the remaining students is 15 kg. What is the average weight of all the students in the section? SSC CHSL (Tier I) 04/07/2024 Shift-II

(a) 18 kg (b) 25 kg (c) 24 kg (d) 22 kg

112. Find the average of natural numbers from 1 to 69. (both included) SSC CHSL (Tier I) 04/07/2024 Shift-I

(a) 37 (b) 31 (c) 35 (d) 33

113. A class of 25 students took an English test. 15 students had an average score of 80. The other students had an average score of 60. What is the average score of the whole class? SSC CHSL (Tier I) 03/07/2024 Shift-IV

(a) 80 (b) 76 (c) 74 (d) 72

114. If the average of 50 numbers $N_1, N_2, \ldots\ldots N_{50}$ is M. Then, the average of the numbers $N_1 - 100, N_2 - 100, \ldots\ldots N_{50} - 100$ will be SSC CHSL (Tier I) 03/07/2024 Shift-III

(a) $100\,M$ (b) $M - 50$
(c) $50\,M$ (d) $M - 100$

115. The salaries of T in twelve months of a year are ₹ 12000, ₹ 12000, ₹ 12000, ₹ 15000, ₹ 15000, ₹ 15000, ₹ 21000, ₹ 21000, ₹ 21000, ₹ 30000, ₹ 30000, ₹ 30000. The average salary of T per month in ₹ is SSC CHSL (Tier I) 03/07/2024 Shift-II

(a) 19500 (b) 18500
(c) 18000 (d) 19000

116. In June, Rohit's bank account balance is ₹ 5000 for 25 days, ₹ 20000 for 2 days and ₹ 1500 for 3 days. What is the average balance (in ₹) in Rohit's bank account in June? SSC CHSL (Tier I) 02/07/2024 Shift-IV

(a) 5575 (b) 5650 (c) 5200 (d) 6000

117. The average monthly expenditure of a family was ₹ 2500 during the first 4 months, ₹ 2750 during the next 5 months and ₹ 3550 during the last 3 months of a year. If the total saving during the year was ₹ 5500, what was the average monthly income of the family? SSC CHSL (Tier I) 02/07/2024 Shift-II

(a) ₹ 3325 (b) ₹ 4375
(c) ₹ 5790 (d) ₹ 7355

118. There are 12 workers in an office and the average age of all the workers is $35\frac{1}{2}$ yr. A new worker joins the office, the average becomes 37 yr. The current age of the newly joined worker is SSC CHSL (Tier I) 01/07/2024 Shift-IV

(a) $55\frac{1}{2}$ yr (b) $57\frac{1}{2}$ yr
(c) $47\frac{1}{2}$ yr (d) 55 yr

119. Find the average of the prime numbers lying between 69 and 92. SSC CHSL (Tier II) 10/01/2024 Shift-I

(a) 79 (b) 82 (c) 80 (d) 91

120. The average of the first eight multiples of 6 is SSC CHSL (Tier II) 10/01/2024 Shift-I

(a) 24 (b) 27 (c) 30 (d) 25

121. The average salary of all 40 employees, including 35 non- teaching staff members, of a school is ₹ 4000. If the average salary of the non-teaching staff members is ₹ 4200, find the average salary of the remaining staff of the school. SSC CHSL (Tier II) 10/01/2024 Shift-I

(a) ₹ 3600 (b) ₹ 2600
(c) ₹ 2800 (d) ₹ 2300

SSC CHSL 2023-2021 (Tier I & II)

122. The average weight of 40 students of a school is 52 kg. If the weight of the teacher is included, the average weight rises by 500 gm. Find the weight (in kg) of the teacher. SSC CHSL (Tier II) 02/11/2023 Shift-I

(a) 71.5 (b) 73.5
(c) 74.5 (d) 72.5

123. The average weight of 64 students is 48 kg and the average weight of another class of 32 students is 24 kg. Find the average weight of both classes combined. SSC CHSL (Tier I) 17/8/2023 Shift-I

(a) 34 kg (b) 36 kg
(c) 40 kg (d) 32 kg

124. The average weight of a class of 30 students is 45 kg. One of the students whose weight is 48.5 kg is replaced by another student and the average weight was increased by 200 gm. Find the weight of the new student. SSC CHSL (Tier I) 11/08/2023 Shift-I

(a) 54.5 kg (b) 50 kg
(c) 55 kg (d) 51 kg

125. The average marks obtained by 80 students in an examination is 50. If the average marks of passed students is 55 and the number of students who failed the examination are 30, then what is the average marks of students who failed the examination? SSC CHSL (Tier II) 21/03/2023 Shift-IV

(a) 41.66 (b) 46.66
(c) 40.33 (d) 52.33

126. The average of 5 consecutive even numbers is A. If next 5 even numbers are also included, then what is the average of these 10 numbers? SSC CHSL (Tier I) 21/03/2023 Shift-II

(a) $A + 7$ (b) $A + 2$
(c) $A + 9$ (d) $A + 5$

127. Average weight of 10 persons is 40 kg. A new person join the group and average weight of 11 person become 42 kg. What will be the weight of new person? SSC CHSL (Tier I) 21/03/2023 Shift-II

(a) 58 kg (b) 60 kg
(c) 62 kg (d) 64 kg

128. A man spends ₹ 2300 monthly on average for the first four months and ₹ 1800 monthly for the next eight months and saves ₹ 12400 a year. Find his monthly income. SSC CHSL (Tier I) 20/03/2023 Shift-III

(a) ₹ 3000 (b) ₹ 2400
(c) ₹ 2200 (d) ₹ 2100

129. Average of 15 numbers is 53. A number is removed and the average of 14 numbers now becomes 55. Which number was removed? SSC CHSL (Tier I) 16/03/2023 Shift-I

(a) 26 (b) 23 (c) 25 (d) 24

130. The average runs scored by a batsman in 7 matches is 49 and in other 9 matches the average is 27 what is the average runs scored by the batsman in these 16 matches? SSC CHSL (Tier I) 15/03/2023 Shift-IV

(a) 35.725 (b) 28.475
(c) 40.25 (d) 36.625

131. If in the sales department of a company, the average salary per employee is ₹ 350, average salary of 10 senior employees is ₹ 450 per employee and average salary of remaining staff is ₹ 250 per employee, then what is the total number of employees working in the sales department?
SSC CHSL (Tier I) 10/03/2023 Shift-II
(a) 30 (b) 20 (c) 15 (d) 25

132. The average of 32, 34, 38, 21, 26 and x is 30. What will be the value of x? SSC CHSL (Tier I) 09/03/2023 Shift-I
(a) 31 (b) 29 (c) 27 (d) 28

133. The average age of 30 students is 15 yr. It was observed that while calculating the average age, the age of a student was taken as 15 yr instead of 9 yr. What will be the correct average age?
SSC CHSL (Tier I) 09/03/2023 Shift-I
(a) 14.2 yr (b) 16.4 yr
(c) 15.6 yr (d) 14.8 yr

134. The average weight of A, B and C is 65 kg. If the average weight of A and B is 62 kg and that of B and C is 66 kg, then the weight (in kg) of B is SSC CHSL (Tier I) 30/05/2022 Shift-I
(a) 64 (b) 63 (c) 62 (d) 61

135. In a class of 45 students, there are 20 girls who scored an average of 42 marks in a test of 50 marks. If the class average is 36, what are the average marks of the boys?
SSC CHSL (Tier I) 27/05/2022 Shift-I
(a) 32.50 (b) 32.10 (c) 30.80 (d) 31.20

136. The average weight of 52 girls is 47 kg. What will be the sum of their weights?
SSC CHSL (Tier I) 27/05/2022 Shift-I
(a) 2544 kg (b) 2458 kg
(c) 2454 kg (d) 2444 kg

137. A, B, C and D are four positive numbers such that A is $\frac{3}{4}$ times of B, B is $\frac{4}{5}$ times of C and C is $\frac{3}{8}$ times of D. If the average of 4 times of A and 7 times of D is 316, then the average of all the four numbers A, B, C and D is
SSC CHSL (Tier I) 12/08/2021 Shift-III
(a) 36 (b) 38 (c) 28 (d) 34

138. There are 3 groups of persons male, female and children. There are 20 males and the number of females and children taken together is 4 more than that of the males. The average weight of males is 54 kg, that of females is 49 kg and that of children is 30 kg. If the average weight of the whole group is 48.25 kg, then what is the difference between the number of females and the number of children?
SSC CHSL (Tier I) 10/08/2021 Shift-I
(a) 17 (b) 10 (c) 7 (d) 14

139. The average of 5 numbers is 26.4. The first number is one-fifth of the sum of the remaining 4 numbers. What is the first number?
SSC CHSL (Tier I) 19/04/2021 Shift-I
(a) 20 (b) 21 (c) 23 (d) 22

140. 30 people went to a restaurant for a dinner party. 20 of them paid ₹ 880 each and each of the rest of them paid ₹ 110 more than the average of the total expenses. What was the total expense (in ₹) for the dinner?
SSC CHSL (Tier I) 12/04/2021 Shift-II
(a) 27840 (b) 29360
(c) 28050 (d) 24580

SSC MTS 2024

141. A school's 41 students weight an average of 52 kg. The mean weight increases by 500 grams when the teacher's weight is taken into an
SSC MTS 14/11/2024 Shift-III
(a) 72 kg (b) 71 kg
(c) 73 kg (d) 74 kg

142. The average of two numbers is 13.5 and the square root of their product is $6\sqrt{5}$. Find the numbers.
SSC MTS 14/11/2024 Shift-III
(a) 13 and 14 (b) 12 and 15
(c) 11 and 16 (d) 10 and 17

143. The average weight of a family of five members (in kg) whose weights are 40 kg, 49 kg, 56 kg, 68 kg and 38 kg is
SSC MTS 14/11/2024 Shift-III
(a) 50.2 (b) 49.2 (c) 51.2 (d) 52.2

144. In a group of sports persons, 20 wrestlers have an average weight of 90 kg, while some athletes have an average weight of 68 kg. If the average weight of all sports persons is 78 kg, then the number of athletes is SSC MTS 13/11/2024 Shift-III
(a) 24 (b) 52 (c) 39 (d) 30

145. The average weight of a family of five members (in kg) whose weights are 40 kg, 49 kg, 56 kg, 69 kg and 39 kg is
SSC MTS 13/11/2024 Shift-III
(a) 49.6 (b) 50.6 (c) 52.6 (d) 51.6

146. The average score of boys in an examination in a school is 71 and that of the girls is 73. The average score of the school is 71.8. The ratio of the number of boys to that of the girls that appeared in the examination is
SSC MTS 13/11/2024 Shift-III
(a) 4 : 3 (b) 3 : 2 (c) 3 : 4 (d) 2 : 3

147. The average weight of a family of five members (in kg) whose weights are 40 kg, 49 kg, 56 kg, 68 kg and 37 kg is
SSC MTS 13/11/2024 Shift-III
(a) 50 (b) 51 (c) 49 (d) 52

148. The average score of 30 students (boys and girls only) in a class test was 16.2 and that of 18 boys in the same test was 16. The average score of girls in the same test was
SSC MTS 13/11/2024 Shift-III
(a) 16.3 (b) 16.5 (c) 16.1 (d) 16.7

149. Harsha obtained 72, 63 and 81 marks (out of 100) in Maths, Physics and Chemistry, respectively. What is the average of his marks? SSC MTS 12/11/2024 Shift-III
(a) 84 (b) 81 (c) 63 (d) 72

150. In a hospital, 60% of the patients are men, 25% of the patients are women and 15% of the patients are children. If the average age of the men is 40 yr, that of the women is 36 yr and that of the children is 8 yr. What is the average age of all the patients? SSC MTS 12/11/2024 Shift-III
(a) 24.3 years (b) 34.2 years
(c) 32.4 years (d) 23.4 years

151. The average salary of all 50 employees including 5 officers of a company is ₹ 855. If the average salary of the officers is ₹ 2550. Find the average salary of the remaining staff of the company. (Rounded to the nearest integer.)
SSC MTS 12/11/2024 Shift-III
(a) ₹ 637 (b) ₹ 657 (c) ₹ 677 (d) ₹ 667

152. There are five baskets- A, B, C, D and E. Each basket has rings in it and the average number of rings in all five baskets is 42. If basket D is removed, the average number of rings in the remaining baskets is 38. How many rings are there in basket D? SSC MTS 11/11/2024 Shift-III
(a) 42 (b) 58 (c) 38 (d) 64

153. In an examination, the average marks of the student in class were 85.4. If the student had got 8 more marks in History, 12 more marks in

Science, 10 more marks in Computer Science, 15 less marks in Hindi and retained the same marks in other subjects, then the average would have been 87.9. How many subjects were there in the examination? **SSC MTS 11/11/2024 Shift-III**

(a) 8 (b) 6 (c) 5 (d) 7

154. The average marks of 60 students was found to be 48. Later on, it was discovered that a score of 68 was misread as 56. Find the correct average corresponding to the correct score. **SSC MTS 11/11/2024 Shift-III**

(a) 54.2 (b) 44.2 (c) 40.8 (d) 48.2

155. The sum of three consecutive odd numbers is 58 more than the average of these numbers. Find the largest number. **SSC MTS 11/11/2024 Shift-III**

(a) 33 (b) 27 (c) 37 (d) 31

156. In a factory, the average monthly salary of 25 unskilled workers is ₹ 11950, that of 20 mechanics is ₹ 24000 and that of 5 supervisors is ₹ 35000. The average monthly salary of all the employees is **SSC MTS 05/11/2024 Shift-III**

(a) ₹19180 (b) ₹19225
(c) ₹19055 (d) ₹19075

157. The average of a non-zero number and its square is 7 times the number. The number is **SSC MTS 05/11/2024 Shift-III**

(a) 14 (b) 91 (c) 7 (d) 13

158. A library has an average number of 768 visitors on Monday and 258 visitors on others day. Find the average number of visitors per day in a month of 30 days, beginning with Tuesday. **SSC MTS 05/11/2024 Shift-III**

(a) 362 (b) 263 (c) 236 (d) 326

159. The average of the first twelve multiples of 11 is **SSC MTS 05/11/2024 Shift-III**

(a) 68.5 (b) 71.5 (c) 69.5 (d) 70.5

160. The average weight of X, Y and Z is 67 kg. The average weight of X and Y is 64 kg and that of Y and Z is 52 kg. The weight of Y (in kg) is **SSC MTS 04/11/2024 Shift-III**

(a) 31 (b) 33 (c) 30 (d) 28

161. The marks obtained by A in Mathematics, English and Biology are 71 out of 100, 82 out of 150 and 177 out of 200, respectively. What is the average scores? **SSC MTS 04/11/2024 Shift-III**

(a) $\frac{13}{21}$ (b) $\frac{11}{16}$ (c) $\frac{12}{13}$ (d) $\frac{11}{15}$

162. In Class I there are 12 students of average age 20 yr, and in Class II there are 16 students of average age 23 yr. What is the average age (approximately) of both the classes? **SSC MTS 30/10/2024 Shift-III**

(a) 17.6 yr (b) 20.7 yr
(c) 21.7 yr (d) 15.3 yr

163. Two sections A and B of class VIII consist of 42 and 38 students, respectively. If the average marks of section A is 400 and that of section B is 320, find the average marks of the whole class. **SSC MTS 30/10/2024 Shift-III**

(a) 360 (b) 576 (c) 362 (d) 310

164. If the average of nine numbers is 360, then what is the sum of the nine numbers? **SSC MTS 30/10/2024 Shift-III**

(a) 3420 (b) 1620
(c) 40 (d) 3240

165. The average monthly pocket money of Ram and Shyam is ₹ 2460, Shyam and Manohar is ₹ 2380 and Manohar and Ram is ₹ 2760. Find the monthly pocket money of Ram alone. **SSC MTS 30/10/2024 Shift-III**

(a) ₹ 2048 (b) ₹ 2840
(c) ₹ 2408 (d) ₹ 2480

166. In the first 24 matches, a cricket player averages 60 runs. The overall average for all 32 matches is 80. Determine the average for the last 8 matches. **SSC MTS 29/10/2024 Shift-III**

(a) 140 (b) 110 (c) 120 (d) 130

167. In a math exam, two students scored 95, six students scored 90, three students scored 80, and one student scored 50. What was the average score of the class? **SSC MTS 29/10/2024 Shift-III**

(a) 85 (b) 82
(c) 96.25 (d) 78.75

168. A batsman scores 152 runs in his 15th inning, which increases his average score by 5 runs. Find the average score per inning of the batsman after the 15th innings. **SSC MTS 28/10/2024 Shift-II**

(a) 85 (b) 41 (c) 77 (d) 82

169. The average weight of a family of five members (in kg) whose weights are 40 kg, 49 kg, 56 kg, 71 kg and 37 kg is **SSC MTS 28/10/2024 Shift-II**

(a) 51.6 (b) 50.6 (c) 52.6 (d) 49.6

170. A student saves an average of ₹ 4000 per month for the first three months. How much should be saved (in ₹) on an average per month over the next 9 months to average ₹ 4375 per month over the whole year? **SSC MTS 23/10/2024 Shift-II**

(a) 4000 (b) 4500
(c) 4200 (d) 4187.5

171. If the average of the first 15 multiples of 9 is x, then x is **SSC MTS 23/10/2024 Shift-II**

(a) 72 (b) 68 (c) 114 (d) 78

172. The average weight of a family of five members (in kg) whose weights are 40 kg, 49 kg, 56 kg, 66 kg and 36 kg is **SSC MTS 23/10/2024 Shift-II**

(a) 49.4 (b) 50.4 (c) 48.4 (d) 51.4

173. The average height of 50 students in a class was 105 cm. A group of five students with an average height of 95 cm were admitted to this class. What is the average height (in cm) of the class of 55 students? (correct to the nearest integer) **SSC MTS 22/10/2024 Shift-II**

(a) 104 (b) 100 (c) 105 (d) 102

174. 15 kg rice costing ₹ 60 per kg and 8 kg rice costing ₹ 55 per kg are mixed with 7 kg rice costing ₹ 40 per kg. Find the average per kg price of mixed rice. **SSC MTS 22/10/2024 Shift-II**

(a) ₹ 56 (b) ₹ 45 (c) ₹ 54 (d) ₹ 48

175. John has scored 60% in statistics and 70% in mathematics. A weightage of 2 is given to statistics and a weightage of 4 is given to mathematics. Which of the following expressions represents the weighted average of the two scores? **SSC MTS 22/10/2024 Shift-II**

(a) $\frac{2 + 60\,\% \times 4 + 70\,\%}{2 + 4}$

(b) $\frac{2 \times 60\,\% \times 40 \times 70\,\%}{2 \times 4}$

(c) $\frac{2 \times 60\,\% + 4 \times 70\,\%}{2 \times 4}$

(d) $\frac{2 \times 60\,\% + 4 \times 70\,\%}{2 + 4}$

176. The average of nine consecutive numbers is 45. The largest number among these numbers is **SSC MTS 21/10/2024 Shift-II**

(a) 50 (b) 49 (c) 48 (d) 41

177. If the average of 53 consecutive even numbers is 1280. Find the difference between the smallest and the largest number. **SSC MTS 21/10/2024 Shift-II**

(a) 24 (b) 34 (c) 124 (d) 104

178. In a class, there are 30 boys and 20 girls. The average score of boys in Physics is 92, whereas the average score of girls in Physics is 83. Find the average score of the whole class in Physics. SSC MTS 18/10/2024 Shift-II
(a) 89.3 (b) 92.6 (c) 88.4 (d) 96.2

179. The average weight of a family of five members (in kg) whose weights are 40 kg, 49 kg, 56 kg, 72 kg and 36 kg is SSC MTS 18/10/2024 Shift-II
(a) 52.6 (b) 51.6 (c) 50.6 (d) 49.6

180. In an office, the average salary of 22 staff members was ₹81400. If the average salary of staff and the Vice-Chairman was ₹ 89600, then how much is the salary of the Vice-Chairman (in ₹)? SSC MTS 18/10/2024 Shift-II
(a) 197300 (b) 270000
(c) 217000 (d) 300000

181. The average weight of a family of five members (in kg) whose weights are 40 kg, 49 kg, 56 kg, 71 kg and 38 kg is SSC MTS 17/10/2024 Shift-II
(a) 50.8 (b) 49.8
(c) 52.8 (d) 51.8

182. Five athletes are weighed consecutively and after each measurement, their average weight is calculated. If the average weight increases by 1.5 kg each time, then how much heavier is the last player than the first player? SSC MTS 17/10/2024 Shift-II
(a) 18 kg (b) 15.5 kg
(c) 10 kg (d) 12 kg

183. The average age of a class of 39 students is 20 years. If the age of the teacher is included, then the average increases by 6 months. Find the age of the teacher (in years). SSC MTS 17/10/2024 Shift-II
(a) 30 (b) 50 (c) 40 (d) 45

184. Two classes took the same test. One class of 20 students made an average grade of 85%, the other class of 30 students made an average grade of 70%. The average grade for all students across both classes is SSC MTS 16/10/2024 Shift-II
(a) 74% (b) 72% (c) 76% (d) 75%

185. The average weight of 12 students and two teachers is 55 kg. When one teacher weighing 68 kg is included in the group, then the average weight of the group (in kg) is SSC MTS 16/10/2024 Shift-II
(a) 56 (b) 56.5 (c) 54.5 (d) 55

186. In a group of 260 people, one-fourth are women, two-fifth are men and the rest are children. The average age of women is five-sixth of the average age of men, average age of children is one-third of the average age of men. If the average age of men is 48 years, what is the average age of the group in years? SSC MTS 16/10/2024 Shift-II
(a) 42.7 (b) 34.8 (c) 38.4 (d) 32.7

187. The average age of 14 students and their teacher is 18 yr. If the teacher's age is excluded, the average reduces by 1 year. What is the teacher's age? SSC MTS 15/10/2024 Shift-I
(a) 32 (b) 35 (c) 37 (d) 34

188. When a class of 40 students took a science test, 25 students had an average score of 80 and the remaining students had an average score of 90. What was the average score of the whole class? SSC MTS 15/10/2024 Shift-I
(a) 82.75 (b) 80.75
(c) 81.75 (d) 83.75

189. The batting average of a cricket player for 40 innings is 60 runs. His highest score in an innings exceeds his lowest score by 110 runs. If these two innings are excluded, the average score of the remaining 38 innings is 58 runs. Find his highest score. SSC MTS 15/10/2024 Shift-I
(a) 290 (b) 153 (c) 220 (d) 310

190. If the average marks of three batches of 40, 50 and 60 students, respectively, is 50, 60 and 75, then the average marks of all the students is SSC MTS 15/10/2024 Shift-I
(a) 70.00 (b) 65.50
(c) 63.33 (d) 61.25

191. Find the average of the prime numbers lying between 68 and 91. SSC MTS 14/10/2024 Shift-I
(a) 76 (b) 77 (c) 78 (d) 79

192. The average weight of a family of five members (in kg) whose weights are 40 kg, 49 kg, 56 kg, 67 kg and 37 kg is SSC MTS 14/10/2024 Shift-I
(a) 51.8 (b) 50.8 (c) 49.8 (d) 48.8

193. In a school, the average salary of 12 teachers was ₹ 71400. If the average salary of the teachers, principal and vice principal was ₹ 89500, then what was the average salary of the principal and vice principal (in ₹)? SSC MTS 14/10/2024 Shift-I
(a) 176800 (b) 211000
(c) 198100 (d) 118900

194. The average of four girls age is 12 yr. The ages of three of them are 7, 12 and 13 years. Find the age of the fourth girl. SSC MTS 09/10/2024 Shift-I
(a) 16 yr (b) 14 yr
(c) 17 yr (d) 15 yr

195. The average weight of a family of five members (in kg) whose weights are 40 kg, 49 kg, 56 kg, 71 kg and 39 kg is SSC MTS 09/10/2024 Shift-I
(a) 52 (b) 53 (c) 51 (d) 50

196. The average age of 11 players of a cricket team is increased by 2 months, when two of them aged 20 yr and 21 yr, respectively, are replaced by two new players. Find the average age of the two new players (in yr). SSC MTS 08/10/2024 Shift-I
(a) $18\frac{5}{12}$ (b) $21\frac{5}{12}$ (c) $18\frac{1}{4}$ (d) $20\frac{1}{2}$

197. The average weight of a family of five members (in kg) whose weights are 40 kg, 49 kg, 56 kg, 70 kg and 39 kg is SSC MTS 08/10/2024 Shift-I
(a) 49.8 (b) 52.8 (c) 51.8 (d) 50.8

198. The average of the first six multiples of 7 is SSC MTS 08/10/2024 Shift-I
(a) 24.5 (b) 23.2 (c) 22.4 (d) 25.1

199. The average age of 12 men is increased by 6 yr when three of them, whose ages are 36, 40 and 44 yr are replaced by 3 persons. What is the average age of the 3 persons? SSC MTS 07/10/2024 Shift-I
(a) 58 yr (b) 64 yr (c) 67 yr (d) 50 yr

200. From every perfect square not exceeding 101. Rahul subtracts 5. What is the average of the numbers Rahul obtained? SSC MTS 07/10/2024 Shift-I
(a) 37.5 (b) 38 (c) 33.5 (d) –11.5

201. Find the average of 300, 129, 49, 120 and 102. SSC MTS 01/10/2024 Shift-I
(a) 130 (b) 120
(c) 150 (d) 140

202. The average of 9 numbers is 3. If the average of the first 8 of these numbers is 2, the 9th number is SSC MTS 01/10/2024 Shift-I
(a) 11 (b) 12
(c) 14 (d) 15

203. The average weight of a certain number of students in a group was 72 kg. If 11 students, with an average weight of 76 kg each, leave the group and 5 students, each with an average weight of 79 kg, join the group, the average weight

of the students in the group decreases by 0.6 kg. The number of students initially in the group was
SSC MTS 01/10/2024 Shift-I

(a) 21 (b) 25 (c) 17 (d) 19

204. The average monthly expenditure of a family was ₹8600 during the first three months, ₹ 9750 during the next four months and ₹ 9920 during the last five months of a year. If the total savings during the year was ₹ 65300, the average monthly income (in ₹) of the family was SSC MTS 30/09/2024 Shift-I

(a) 14975 (b) 15794
(c) 15479 (d) 14597

205. The average monthly income of A and B is ₹3590. The average monthly income of B and C is ₹ 4250. The average monthly income of A and C is ₹ 6500. What is the monthly income of C?
SSC MTS 30/09/2024 Shift-I

(a) ₹ 7545 (b) ₹ 6984
(c) ₹ 8190 (d) ₹ 7160

206. In a 100-marks test, the average of marks scored by 50 students was found to be 65. Later on, it was discovered that a score of 88 was misread as 68. Find the correct average. SSC MTS 30/09/2024 Shift-I

(a) 65.60 (b) 65.50
(c) 65.70 (d) 65.40

SSC MTS 2023-2021

207. The average weight of 20 students in a class is 55 kg. If the weight of the class teacher is included, the average is increased by 0.5 kg. The weight of the class teacher is
SSC MTS 13/09/2023 Shift-I

(a) 67.2 kg (b) 63.5 kg
(c) 65.5 kg (d) 68.4 kg

208. The average weight of 15 parcels is 20 kg. Addition of another new parcel increases the average weight by 250 gm. What is the weight of the new parcel?
SSC MTS 11/09/2023 Shift-II

(a) 28 kg (b) 24 kg
(c) 22 kg (d) 26 kg

209. The average weight of some students in class 12th was 56 kg. When seven students whose average weight was 58 kg joined the class, the average weight of all the students increased by 200 gm. Find the number of students in the class in the beginning?
SSC MTS 11/09/2023 Shift-I

(a) 56 (b) 77 (c) 49 (d) 63

210. If the average of two numbers is 12 and the product of the same two numbers is 119, then the difference of those two numbers is
SSC MTS 11/09/2023 Shift-I

(a) 7 (b) 6 (c) 10 (d) 8

211. The average of a batsman in 20 innings is 41 runs. In the next inning, he scored 41 runs. What will be his new average?
SSC MTS 08/09/2023 Shift-II

(a) 39 (b) 41 (c) 38 (d) 36

212. A batsman makes 96 runs in the 13th innings and thus his average increases by 3. Find his average after 13th innings. SSC MTS 06/09/2023 Shift-I

(a) 65 (b) 50 (c) 70 (d) 60

213. The average weight of 20 students of a class was 30.5 kg. After 6 new students joined the class, its average weight increased by 2 kg. Find the average weight of the 6 new students who joined the class (rounded off to one decimal place).
SSC MTS 06/09/2023 Shift-I

(a) 30.5 kg (b) 32.5 kg
(c) 39.2 kg (d) 38.5 kg

214. The average score of a cricketer for 10 matches is 40 runs. If the average for first six matches is 44, then the average runs of the last four matches is SSC MTS 06/09/2023 Shift-I

(a) 20 (b) 38 (c) 42 (d) 34

215. A school has two sections of a class. Section A has 30 students and Section B has 20 students. The average score of the students in Section A is 85 and the average score of the students in Section B is 70. What is the overall average score of the class ?
SSC MTS 05/09/2023 Shift-II

(a) 81 (b) 80 (c) 79 (d) 78

216. The average weight of 17 men is 63 kg and the average weight of 36 women is 54 kg. What is the average weight (in kg) of all the men and women together? (rounded off to the nearest integer)
SSC MTS 04/09/2023 Shift-II

(a) 59 (b) 62 (c) 57 (d) 52

217. In a class of 37 students, there are 22 girls. The average weight of these girls is 46 kg and the average weight of the whole class is 50 kg. What is the average weight (in kg) of the boys in that class ? (rounded off to 2 decimal places)
SSC MTS 01/09/2023 Shift-I

(a) 60.74 (b) 55.87
(c) 61.35 (d) 58.25

218. What is the average of the first 10 prime numbers ?
SSC MTS 15/07/2022 Shift-I

(a) 10.9 (b) 12.9 (c) 11.9 (d) 13.9

219. What will be the average of all the prime numbers between 9 and 22 ?
SSC MTS 15/07/2022 Shift-I

(a) 14 (b) 15 (c) 10 (d) 12

220. The average of a set of 15 numbers is 41. Five numbers 21, 24, 39, 47 and 97 are removed from the above set. What will the average of the remaining 10 numbers ?
SSC MTS 15/07/2022 Shift-I

(a) 39.2 (b) 37.6 (c) 38.7 (d) 36.4

221. The average of all the numbers between 14 and 61 which are divisible by 5 is
SSC MTS 14/07/2022 Shift-I

(a) 37.5 (b) 38 (c) 40 (d) 44

222. Rohit scored an average of 58 runs in his last five innings. The runs scored by Rohit in the last four innings are 42, 56, 72 and 40. How many runs did Rohit score in the first of these five innings ?
SSC MTS 14/07/2022 Shift-I

(a) 80 (b) 60 (c) 90 (d) 40

223. What is the average of the squares of the first five natural numbers ?
SSC MTS 14/07/2022 Shift-I

(a) 11.5 (b) 10 (c) 12.5 (d) 11

224. There are 32 consecutive natural numbers. The average of the first 13 numbers is x. What is the average of the next 19 numbers?
SSC MTS 13/07/2022 Shift-I

(a) $x + 15$ (b) $x + 16$
(c) $x + 17$ (d) $x + 18$

225. The average marks obtained in a test by three students is x. If the marks of a new student is also considered, then the average marks increases by 2. What is the marks secured by the new student in the test? SSC MTS 13/07/2022 Shift-I

(a) $x + 4$ (b) $x + 6$
(c) $x + 8$ (d) $x + 2$

226. There are two numbers such that the first number is four times of the second number. If their average is 65, then what is the second number? SSC MTS 12/07/2022 Shift-I

(a) 26 (b) 104 (c) 24 (d) 28

227. The average of ten numbers is 24. If each number is divided by 2, then what will be the new average ?
SSC MTS 11/07/2022 Shift-I

(a) 12 (b) 6 (c) 20 (d) 5

228. The average age of eight girls is y yr. 5 new girls having ages (in years) given by $(y+3)$, $y-6$, $y+15$, $y+8$ and $y+6$, join the class. What is the new average age of the class? **SSC MTS 11/07/2022 Shift-I**

(a) $(y+2)$ yr (b) $(y+6)$ yr
(c) $(y+3)$ yr (d) $(y+1)$ yr

229. In a family of six males and a few females, the average monthly consumption of grain per head is 14.4 kg. If the average monthly consumption per head is 20 kg in the case of males and 6 kg in the case of females, find the number of females in the family. **SSC MTS 11/07/2022 Shift-I**

(a) 8 (b) 4
(c) 6 (d) 7

230. The average of ten numbers is A. If C is subtracted from each number, except the tenth and $(C-1)$ is subtracted from the tenth number, then what will be the new average? **SSC MTS 02/11/2021 Shift-III**

(a) $A-C+0.1$ (b) $A-C$
(c) $A-C+1$ (d) $A-(0.1)C+0.1$

231. The average monthly expenditure of a family was ₹ 10000 during the first three months, ₹ 12500 during the next four months and ₹ 13500 during the last five months of a year. If the total savings during the year was ₹ 32500, then 70% of the average monthly income of the family (in ₹) was **SSC MTS 02/11/2021 Shift-II**

(a) 11250 (b) 12250
(c) 15000 (d) 10500

232. Ratio between average of first four prime numbers and first four composite numbers is **SSC MTS 02/11/2021 Shift-I**

(a) 13 : 10 (b) 17 : 27
(c) 11 : 27 (d) 17 : 19

233. The average of three numbers is 45. The first number is thrice the second and the second number is twice the third. Find the difference between the first number and the second number. **SSC MTS 02/11/2021 Shift-I**

(a) 75 (b) 45
(c) 60 (d) 15

234. The average of the square of first seven natural numbers is **SSC MTS 02/11/2021 Shift-I**

(a) 16 (b) 29
(c) 25 (d) 20

SSC GD Constable 2024

235. Average of 28 observations is 53. Average of first 11 observations is 54. Average of last 18 observations is 52.5. What is the value of 11th observation ? **SSC GD 26/02/2024 Shift-I**

(a) 59 (b) 63
(c) 57 (d) 55

236. The average of 25 numbers is 150. One more number is added and the new average became 160. What is that new number? **SSC GD 26/02/2024 Shift-I**

(a) 400 (b) 410 (c) 415 (d) 420

237. The average marks of 18 students was 190. But later it was found that the score of one student was wrongly entered as 46 instead of 64. What is the correct average of their score? **SSC GD 24/02/2024 Shift-III**

(a) 192.27 (b) 191.25
(c) 191 (d) 193.4

238. In 25 consecutive natural numbers, the average of last 13 numbers is 39. What is the average of all 25 numbers? **SSC GD 24/02/2024 Shift-III**

(a) 34 (b) 37 (c) 31 (d) 33

239. There are 120 hens in a poultry. Due to the addition of 140 more hens, the expenses of the poultry increases by ₹ 4050 while the average expenditure per hen diminishes by ₹ 3. What was the original expenditure of the poultry. **SSC GD 24/02/2024 Shift-II**

(a) ₹ 4780 (b) ₹ 4140
(c) ₹ 4540 (d) ₹ 4350

240. The average of 17 numbers is 47. If each of the numbers is multiplied by 6, then find the new average. **SSC GD 24/02/2024 Shift-II**

(a) 270 (b) 282 (c) 280 (d) 265

241. The average of 16.5, 9, 10.5, 12.5 and Y is 12.5. What is the value of Y? **SSC GD 23/02/2024 Shift-IV**

(a) 16 (b) 14 (c) 17 (d) 11

242. The average marks obtained by a group of 11 students is 53 and the average marks obtained by another group of 13 students is 48. What is the average marks obtained by all 24 students (approximately)? **SSC GD 23/02/2024 Shift-IV**

(a) 52.45 (b) 48.14
(c) 46.32 (d) 50.29

243. Out of 5 subjects, the average marks of Rakesh in first 3 subjects is 80 and the average marks in last 3 subjects is 92. If his marks in the third subject is 51, then what is his average marks in all the 5 subjects? **SSC GD 23/02/2024 Shift-III**

(a) 97 (b) 102 (c) 90 (d) 93

244. The average of 90 observations is 38. If 4 is subtracted from each observation, then what will be the new average of the observations? **SSC GD 23/02/2024 Shift-III**

(a) 37 (b) 36 (c) 32 (d) 34

245. If the average of 24, 28, 27, 23, D and E is 29, then what is the average of D and E ? **SSC GD 23/02/2024 Shift-II**

(a) 38 (b) 36
(c) 35 (d) 37

246. The average of the three numbers X, Y and Z is 54. X is 10 more than the average of Y and Z. Y is 12 more than the average of Y and Z. What is the difference between X and Z ? **SSC GD 23/02/2024 Shift-II**

(a) 22 (b) 26 (c) 18 (d) 24

247. The average of 28 numbers is 110. If we add a number 'B' in each number, then the average becomes 128. What is the value of B ? **SSC GD 23/02/2024 Shift-I**

(a) 18 (b) 24 (c) 12 (d) 14

248. A group of students has an average weight of 44 kg. One student of weight 40 kg leaves the group and another student of weight 34 kg joins the group. If the new average weight becomes 43.4 kg, then how many students are there in the group? **SSC GD 23/02/2024 Shift-I**

(a) 12 (b) 13 (c) 14 (d) 10

249. What is the average of squares of first 17 natural numbers? **SSC GD 22/02/2024 Shift-IV**

(a) 113 (b) 94 (c) 124 (d) 105

250. The average of mark obtained by S_1 and S_2 is 35 more than the average of marks obtained by S_2 and S_3. If the marks obtained by S_3 is 75. Then, what are the marks obtained by S_1? **SSC GD 22/02/2024 Shift-II**

(a) 155 (b) 170
(c) 165 (d) 145

251. Average of 12 numbers is 60. If 12 is subtracted from the first five numbers and 10 is added in the next seven numbers, then what will be the new average? **SSC GD 22/02/2024 Shift-III**

(a) 60.83 (b) 61.83
(c) 59.25 (d) 59.75

252. The average of P, Q and R is 40. If the average of P and Q is 35 and the average of Q and R is 45, what is the value of Q? SSC GD 22/02/2024 Shift-I
(a) 32 (b) 40 (c) 28 (d) 48

253. Average of five numbers is 36. The average of first two numbers is 1.5 times of the average of last three numbers. What is the sum of first two numbers? SSC GD 21/02/2024 Shift-IV
(a) 79 (b) 78 (c) 90 (d) 85

254. What is the average of first 31 odd numbers? SSC GD 21/02/2024 Shift-IV
(a) 32 (b) 37
(c) 31 (d) 33

255. The average weight of T, U and V is 42 kg. If the average weight of T and U is 40 kg and the average weight of U and V is 36 kg, then what is the weight of U? SSC GD 21/02/2024 Shift-III
(a) 26 kg (b) 29 kg (c) 24 kg (d) 22 kg

256. Average of 4 numbers is 24. Average of first 2 numbers is double of the average of last 2 numbers. What is the sum of last 2 numbers? SSC GD 21/02/2024 Shift-III
(a) 48 (b) 72 (c) 56 (d) 32

257. The average marks of a student in 6 subjects are 75. If the student scores 80 in one subject, what will be the total score in the remaining subjects. SSC GD 21/02/2024 Shift-II
(a) 380 (b) 350 (c) 340 (d) 370

258. There are two numbers such that the first number is half of the second number. If their average is 15, then what is the first number? SSC GD 21/02/2024 Shift-II
(a) 12 (b) 14
(c) 10 (d) 8

259. The average income of 35 employees is ₹ K. If the income of manager is also included, then the average income becomes ₹ 19000. If the income of the manager is ₹ 54000, then what is the value of K? SSC GD 21/02/2024 Shift-I
(a) ₹ 18800 (b) ₹ 17700
(c) ₹ 18000 (d) ₹ 19200

260. Average of 4 numbers is 52. Average of first two numbers is thrice the average of other two numbers. What is the sum of first two numbers? SSC GD 20/02/2024 Shift-III
(a) 148 (b) 147
(c) 156 (d) 174

261. Six friends have an average height of 144 cm. A boy with a height of 150 cm leaves the group. Find the new average height. SSC GD 20/02/2024 Shift-III
(a) 108.6 cm (b) 142.8 cm
(c) 155.5 cm (d) 160.5 cm

262. The average marks of 13 students was 130. But later, it was found that the score of one student was wrongly entered as 23 instead of 32. What is the correct average of their scores? SSC GD 20/02/2024 Shift-III
(a) 130.88 (b) 132.28
(c) 130.69 (d) 131.72

263. The average weight of a class of 22 students is 42 kg. If 2 new students of weight 33 kg and 39 kg are added to the class, then what will be the new average weight of 24 students? SSC GD 20/02/2024 Shift-II
(a) 39.5 kg (b) 43 kg
(c) 41.5 kg (d) 42 kg

264. The average of 5 numbers is 32. If one number is removed, then the average becomes 28. What is the removed number? SSC GD 20/02/2024 Shift-II
(a) 47 (b) 52 (c) 49 (d) 48

265. What will be the average of all the prime numbers before 32 ? SSC GD 20/02/2024 Shift-II
(a) 14.54 (b) 13.26 (c) 15.60 (d) 17.82

266. In one year, the average monthly expenditure of Sapna was ₹ 1100 for the first 3 months of the year, ₹ 1000 for the next 5 months and ₹ 1200 for the last 4 month. If the total annual saving was ₹ 1300, then what was Sapna's average monthly income? SSC GD 20/02/2024 Shift-I
(a) ₹ 1200 (b) ₹ 1250
(c) ₹ 1210 (d) ₹ 1270

SSC GD Constable 2023

267. The average weight of 34 persons is increased by 3 kg when one person weighing 90 kg replaced by a new person. Weight of the new person is SSC GD 13/02/2023 Shift-II
(a) 196 kg (b) 202 kg
(c)190 kg (d)192 kg

268. The average weight of eight persons is 40 kg. If one person is removed, then the average weight becomes 38 kg. The weight of the removed person is SSC GD 13/02/2023 Shift-II
(a) 38 kg (b) 54 kg
(c) 33.25 kg (d) 78 kg

269. In a class there are 80 students. Average weight of girls is 40 kg and average weight of boys is 50 kg. If number of boys is 50, then what will be the average weight of class? SSC GD 09/02/2023 Shift-II
(a) 46.25 kg (b) 45.5 kg
(c) 47.75 kg (d) 48.25 kg

270. There are 45 boxes which have an average weight of 52 g. Some boxes are blue, while others are green. If five boxed having average weight of 40 g and eight green boxed having average weight of 43 g, are added, then what is the average weight (in g) now? SSC GD 09/02/2023 Shift-II
(a) 49.72 (b) 51.25
(c) 52.5 (d) 52.25

271. If the average marks of two batches of 45 and 50 students, respectively, are 78 and 65, then the average marks of all the students are SSC GD 09/02/2023 Shift-I
(a) $\frac{1252}{13}$ (b) $\frac{1352}{19}$
(c) $\frac{1052}{13}$ (d) $\frac{1152}{19}$

272. 10 kg of superior quality of rice is mixed with 5 kg of inferior quality of rice. The prices of superior quality and inferior quality rice are ₹ 85 and ₹ 46, respectively. Find the average price per kg of the mixture. SSC GD 08/02/2023 Shift-I
(a) ₹ 72 (b) ₹ 73 (c) ₹ 75 (d) ₹ 74

273. The average marks of eight students is 7. It was found that marks of one student was taken as 10 instead of 6. Find the correct average. SSC GD 06/02/2023 Shift-I
(a) 6.5 (b) 7.5
(c) 7 (d) 6.8

SSC Selection Post 2024-2022

274. The average of v numbers is w^2 and that of w numbers is v^2. Then, the average of all the numbers is Matric Level 20/06/2024 Shift-IV
(a) vw^2 (b) $v + w$
(c) vw (d) $v^2 + w^2$

275. The average age of all the students of a class is 18 yr. The average age of the boys of the class is 19 yr and of the girls is 14 yr. If the number of girls in the class is 30, then what is the number of boys in the class? Matric Level 20/06/2024 Shift-IV
(a) 100 (b) 120
(c) 140 (d) 110

276. The average of 12 numbers is 47. The average of the first 5 numbers is 45 and the average of the next 4 numbers is 52. If the 10th number is 10 less than the 11th number and is 5 more than the 12th number, then what is the average value of the 11th and 12th numbers?
Graduate Level 20/06/2024 Shift-III

(a) 44.5 (b) 42.5
(c) 46.5 (d) 47.5

277. The average weight of 30 students in a class is 60 kg. If the weight of the class teacher is included, the average increases by 0.5 kg. The weight (in kg) of the teacher is
Graduate Level 27/06/2023 Shift-IV

(a) 76.5 (b) 75.5
(c) 72.5 (d) 74.5

278. The average score in a test for 50 students is 44. Out of the total students, 40% of the students are girls and the rest are boys. The average score of boys is 20% less than that of girls. What is the average score of girls?
Higher Secondary Level 27/06/2023 Shift-III

(a) 50 (b) 54
(c) 48 (d) 52

279. Class A has 20 students scoring average marks of 75 and class B has 30 students scoring average marks of 60. What is the average of both the classes together?
Matric Level 27/06/2023 Shift-I

(a) 64 (b) 66
(c) 68 (d) 62

280. The mean weight of 32 students in a school is 50 kg. If the weight of the teacher be included, the mean rises by 500 gm. Find the weight of the teacher. **Matric Level 27/06/2023 Shift-I**

(a) 63.5 kg (b) 66.5 kg
(c) 65.5 kg (d) 64.5 kg

281. The average of the first eight odd natural numbers is:
Graduate Level 1/08/2022 Shift-IV

(a) 8 (b) 11
(c) 9 (d) 10

282. If the average of P numbers is Q^2 and the average of Q numbers is P^2, then the average of $(P+Q)$ numbers will be **Graduate Level 1/08/2022 Shift-IV**

(a) $P+Q$ (b) $2PQ$
(c) $P-Q$ (d) PQ

283. For the past five months, a merchant has made sales of ₹ 6435, ₹ 6927, ₹ 6855, ₹ 7230 and ₹ 6562. What amount of sales does he need in the sixth month to achieve an average sale of ₹ 6500?
Higher Secondary Level 1/08/2022 Shift-II

(a) ₹ 4991
(b) ₹ 5021
(c) ₹ 4810
(d) ₹ 4781

Right Answers

1 (d)	2 (a)	3 (a)	4 (d)	5 (b)	6 (d)	7 (d)	8 (c)	9 (b)	10 (b)
11 (b)	12 (b)	13 (a)	14 (d)	15 (a)	16 (b)	17 (b)	18 (d)	19 (b)	20 (d)
21 (a)	22 (c)	23 (a)	24 (d)	25 (a)	26 (b)	27 (d)	28 (d)	29 (c)	30 (c)
31 (b)	32 (c)	33 (b)	34 (b)	35 (b)	36 (c)	37 (a)	38 (a)	39 (a)	40 (a)
41 (b)	42 (d)	43 (d)	44 (a)	45 (b)	46 (c)	47 (d)	48 (c)	49 (a)	50 (c)
51 (c)	52 (c)	53 (a)	54 (d)	55 (d)	56 (c)	57 (b)	58 (b)	59 (a)	60 (a)
61 (a)	62 (d)	63 (c)	64 (a)	65 (c)	66 (b)	67 (b)	68 (c)	69 (b)	70 (a)
71 (b)	72 (d)	73 (a)	74 (c)	75 (b)	76 (d)	77 (a)	78 (c)	79 (b)	80 (a)
81 (d)	82 (a)	83 (a)	84 (c)	85 (b)	86 (b)	87 (c)	88 (a)	89 (b)	90 (c)
91 (b)	92 (c)	93 (d)	94 (a)	95 (b)	96 (a)	97 (a)	98 (d)	99 (a)	100 (d)
101 (b)	102 (b)	103 (d)	104 (a)	105 (c)	106 (a)	107 (a)	108 (a)	109 (c)	110 (c)
111 (b)	112 (c)	113 (d)	114 (d)	115 (a)	116 (b)	117 (a)	118 (d)	119 (a)	120 (b)
121 (b)	122 (d)	123 (c)	124 (a)	125 (a)	126 (d)	127 (c)	128 (a)	129 (c)	130 (d)
131 (b)	132 (b)	133 (d)	134 (d)	135 (d)	136 (d)	137 (b)	138 (b)	139 (d)	140 (c)
141 (c)	142 (b)	143 (a)	144 (a)	145 (b)	146 (b)	147 (a)	148 (b)	149 (d)	150 (b)
151 (d)	152 (b)	153 (b)	154 (d)	155 (d)	156 (d)	157 (d)	158 (d)	159 (b)	160 (a)
161 (d)	162 (c)	163 (c)	164 (d)	165 (b)	166 (a)	167 (a)	168 (d)	169 (b)	170 (b)
171 (a)	172 (a)	173 (a)	174 (c)	175 (d)	176 (b)	177 (d)	178 (c)	179 (c)	180 (b)
181 (a)	182 (d)	183 (c)	184 (c)	185 (a)	186 (b)	187 (a)	188 (d)	189 (b)	190 (c)
191 (d)	192 (c)	193 (c)	194 (a)	195 (c)	196 (b)	197 (d)	198 (a)	199 (b)	200 (c)
201 (d)	202 (a)	203 (a)	204 (a)	205 (d)	206 (d)	207 (c)	208 (b)	209 (d)	210 (c)
211 (b)	212 (d)	213 (c)	214 (d)	215 (c)	216 (c)	217 (b)	218 (b)	219 (b)	220 (c)
221 (a)	222 (a)	223 (d)	224 (b)	225 (c)	226 (a)	227 (a)	228 (a)	229 (b)	230 (a)
231 (d)	232 (b)	233 (c)	234 (d)	235 (d)	236 (b)	237 (c)	238 (d)	239 (b)	240 (b)
241 (b)	242 (d)	243 (d)	244 (d)	245 (b)	246 (a)	247 (a)	248 (d)	249 (d)	250 (d)
251 (a)	252 (b)	253 (c)	254 (c)	255 (a)	256 (d)	257 (d)	258 (c)	259 (c)	260 (c)
261 (b)	262 (c)	263 (c)	264 (d)	265 (a)	266 (a)	267 (d)	268 (b)	269 (a)	270 (a)
271 (b)	272 (a)	273 (a)	274 (c)	275 (b)	276 (a)	277 (b)	278 (a)	279 (b)	280 (b)
281 (a)	282 (d)	283 (a)							

Solutions

1. (d) ∵ Average of first n even numbers

$= (n + 1)$

∴ The average of first 92 even numbers

$= 92 + 1 = 93$

2. (a) ∵ Average of first 'n' even numbers

$= n + 1$

∴ Average of first 91 even number

$= 91 + 1 = 92$

3. (a) Required average $= \dfrac{90 \times 52 + 60 \times 48}{150}$

$= \dfrac{4680 + 2880}{150} = \dfrac{7560}{150} = 50.4$

4. (d) Required average

$= \dfrac{12 \times 60 + (30 - 12) \times 80}{30}$

$= \dfrac{720 + 1440}{30} = \dfrac{2160}{30} = 72$

5. (b) Average $= \dfrac{10 \times 90 + (30 - 10) \times 75}{30}$

$= \dfrac{900 + 1500}{30} = 80$

6. (d) As we known, average of the square of n natural number $= \dfrac{(n+1)(2n+1)}{6}$

Here, $n = 48$

∴ Average $= \dfrac{(48 + 1) \times (2 \times 48 + 1)}{6}$

$= \dfrac{49 \times 97}{6} = 792.17$

7. (d) Let the average of class is x

Sum of scored of all 30 students $= 30x$

Sum of score of 12 student $= 62 \times 12 = 744$

Sum of scored of remaining students

$= 18 \times 78 = 1404$

∴ $30x = 744 + 1404$

$30x = 2148$

$x = \dfrac{2148}{30} = 71.6$

Hence, average of class is 71.6.

8. (c) Number of students in class = 30

Total score of 12 students $= 12 \times 62 = 744$

Total score of rest 18 students

$= 18 \times 60 = 1080$

Total score of class $= 744 + 1080 = 1824$

Average score of class $= \dfrac{1824}{30} = 60.8$

9. (b) Total age of six members of the group

$= 42 \times 6 = 252$

Let the age of seventh member $= x$

According to the question,

$x = \dfrac{252 + x}{7} + 36 \Rightarrow x = \dfrac{252 + x + 252}{7}$

$\Rightarrow 7x - x = 504$

$\Rightarrow 6x = 504 \Rightarrow x = 84$

Age of seventh member = 84 yr

10. (b) Average $= \dfrac{12 \times 62 + (30 - 12) \times 68}{30}$

$= \dfrac{744 + 1224}{30} = 65.6$

11. (b) Required average $= \dfrac{15 \times 20 + 24 \times 25}{45}$

$= \dfrac{300 + 600}{45} = \dfrac{900}{45} = 20$

12. (b) Average of first 125 natural numbers

$= \dfrac{n+1}{2} = \dfrac{125+1}{2} = 63$

13. (a) Let the weight of students are $a_1, a_2 \ldots, a_9$ and 51 (in kgs).

∴ $a_1 + a_2 + \ldots + a_9 + 51 = 10M$ …(i)

and according to question,

$a_1 + a_2 + \ldots + a_9 + a_{10} = 10\left(M + \dfrac{1}{2}\right)$ …(ii)

Where a_{10} is the new student

Eqs. (ii) and (i),

$a_{10} - 51 = 10M + 5 - 10M$

∴ $a_{10} = 51 + 5 = 56$ kg

14. (d) Average score of 12 students

$= 12 \times 62 = 744$

Average score of rest 18 students

$= 18 \times 76 = 1368$

Total score of the group $= 744 + 1368 = 2112$

Average score of the group $= \dfrac{2112}{30} = 70.4$

15. (a) Average of square of first 'n' natural numbers $= \dfrac{(n + 1)(2n + 1)}{6}$

∴ Average of square of first '47' natural numbers $= \dfrac{(47 + 1)(2 \times 47 + 1)}{6}$

$= \dfrac{48 \times 95}{6} = 760$

16. (b) Let the average of class be x.

Sum of all 30 student's marks $= 30x$

Sum of 12 student's marks $= 12 \times 62 = 744$

Sum of remaining student's marks

$= 18 \times 72 = 1296$

∴ $30x = 744 + 1296$

$30x = 2040$

$x = \dfrac{2040}{30} = 68$

17. (b) The average of the squares of the first n natural number $= \dfrac{(n + 1)(2n + 1)}{6}$

∴ The required average

$= \dfrac{(46 + 1)(2 \times 46 + 1)}{6} = \dfrac{46 \times 47 \times 93}{6 \times 46}$

$= 728.5$

18. (d) Let 10th term be x.

∴ 11th term $= x + 10$

12th term $= x - 5$

According to the question,

Average of 12 numbers

$48 = \dfrac{5 \times 45 + 4 \times 52 + x + x + 10 + x - 5}{12}$

$\Rightarrow 48 \times 12 = 225 + 208 + 3x + 5$

$\Rightarrow 576 = 433 + 3x + 5 \Rightarrow \dfrac{138}{3} = x \Rightarrow x = 46$

∴ Required average $= \dfrac{x + 10 + x - 5}{2}$

$= \dfrac{2x + 5}{2} = \dfrac{97}{2} = 48.5$

19. (b) Average score $= \dfrac{\text{Total score}}{\text{Number of student}}$

$= \dfrac{12 \times 62 + (30 - 12) \times 74}{30} = \dfrac{2076}{30} = 69.2$

20. (d) Prime numbers between 50 and 76 are 53, 59, 61, 67, 71, 73.

∴ Required average

$= \dfrac{53 + 59 + 61 + 67 + 71 + 73}{6} = \dfrac{384}{6} = 64$

21. (a) Let $a_1, a_2, \ldots, a_{30}$ are the students.

∴ According to the question,

$a_1 + a_2 + \ldots + a_{12} = 12 \times 62$

and $a_{13} + a_{14} + \ldots + a_{30} = 18 \times 62$

∴ Average $\dfrac{a_1 + a_2 + \ldots + a_{30}}{30} = \dfrac{12 \times 62 + 18 \times 62}{30}$

$= \dfrac{62 \times (12 + 18)}{30} = 62 \times \dfrac{30}{30} = 62$

22. (c) We know,

Average of squares of first n natural numbers

$= \dfrac{(n + 1)(2n + 1)}{6}$

∴ Required average $= \dfrac{(45 + 1)[2(45) + 1]}{6}$

$= \dfrac{46 \times 91}{6} = 697.67$

23. (a) Total temperature of first 16 days

$= 22° \times 16 = 352°$

Total temperature of last 16 days

$= 26° \times 16 = 416°$

Total temperature $= 352° + 416° = 768°$

Also, total temperature of the entire month

$= 24° \times 31 = 744°$

∴ Temperature on 16th day

$= 768° - 744° = 24°$

Speedy Method

Required temperature on 16th day

$= (22° + 26°) - (24°) = 48° - 24° = 24°$C

24. (d) Let average weight of 14 persons be x kg.

From alligation rule,

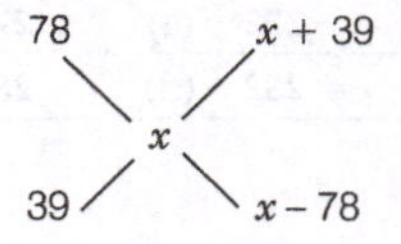

$\therefore \quad \frac{39}{x-78} = \frac{13}{1} \Rightarrow x - 78 = 3$

$\therefore \quad x = 81\text{ kg}$

Hence, weight of the 14th person

$= 81 + 39 = 120\text{ kg}$

25. (a) Average $= \frac{\text{Total sum of all numbers}}{\text{Total numbers}}$

$= \frac{693 + 456 + 876 + 532 + 934 + 691 + 596 + 398 + 682}{9}$

$= \frac{5858}{9} = 650.88 \approx 650.89$

26. (b) Sum of 4 paper marks $= 51 \times 4 = 204$

Total marks of 5 papers $= 204 + 56 = 260$

Average of 5 papers $= \frac{260}{5} = 52$

27. (d) Let the average of 3 men $= x$ kg

Total weight of 3 men $= 3x$ kg

Let the weight of new person $= P$ kg

According to the question,

$\frac{3x - 100 + P}{3} = x + 4$

$\Rightarrow \quad 3x - 100 + P = 3x + 12$

$\Rightarrow \quad P = 100 + 12 = 112\text{ kg}$

28. (d) Sum of 20 numbers $= 20 \times 32 = 640$

Average of 18 numbers

$= \frac{640 - (29 + 31)}{18} = \frac{580}{18} = 32.22$

29. (c) Required average $= \frac{n(n+1)^2}{4}$

$= \frac{5(5+1)^2}{4} = \frac{5 \times 36}{4} = 45$

30. (c) Average of all prime numbers between 32 and 69

$= \frac{37 + 41 + 43 + 47 + 53 + 59 + 61 + 67}{8}$

$= \frac{408}{8} = 51$

31. (b) Total marks in Mathematics

$= 45 \times 3 = 135$

Total marks in English $= 55 \times 2 = 110$

Total marks in Hindi $= 60 \times 2 = 120$

Then, average marks per paper

$= \frac{135 + 110 + 120}{7} = \frac{365}{7} = 52.14 \approx 52.1$

32. (c) Total weight of boys $= 42 \times 35$

$= 1470\text{ kg}$

Total weight of the class $= 46.5 \times 60 = 2790$ kg

$\therefore$ Total weight of girls $= 2790 - 1470 = 1320$ kg

$\therefore$ Average weight of girls $= \frac{1320}{25} = 52.8$ kg

33. (b) In 19 innings Ram scored

$= 65 \times 19 = 1235$ runs

In 20 innings average has to be $= 67$

Total runs $= 67 \times 20 = 1340$

$\therefore$ In 20th innings his score is

$= 1340 - 1235 = 105$

34. (b) Average weight of entire class

$= \frac{40 \times 40 + 20 \times 35}{60} = \frac{1600 + 700}{60}$

$= 38.33$ kg

35. (b) Let number of students in senior school $= x$

According to the question,

$\frac{325 \times 80 + 400 \times x}{80 + x} = 352$

$\Rightarrow \quad 26000 + 400x = 28160 + 352x$

$\Rightarrow \quad 48x = 2160$

$\therefore \quad x = 45$

> **Speedy Method**
>
> By alligation method,
>
> Junior students Senior students
>
> 325 400
>
> 352
>
> 48 27
>
> 16 : 9
>
> $\because$ 16 units $\rightarrow$ 80
>
> $\therefore$ 9 units $\rightarrow \frac{80}{16} \times 9 = 45$
>
> Hence, required answer is 45.

36. (c) Required average

$= \frac{180 \times 88 + 320 \times 72}{180 + 320}$

$= \frac{15840 + 23040}{500} = \frac{38880}{500} = 77.76$

37. (a) Total weight of 15 students

$= 15 \times 40 = 600$ kg

Total weight of 14 students

$= 39.5 \times 14 = 553$ kg

$\therefore$ Weight of the student who left the class

$= 600 - 553 = 47$ kg

> **Speedy Method**
>
> Weight of the student who left
>
> $= 40 + (40 - 39.5) \times 14$
>
> $= 40 + 7 = 47$ kg

38. (a) Average weight

$= \frac{49 + 42 + 61 + 55 + 58}{5} = \frac{265}{5}$

$= 53$ kg

39. (a) Let father's income be 'F', mother's income be 'M' and son's income be 'S'.

According to the question,

$F + M = 10000 \quad \text{... (i)}$

$S + M = 12000 \quad \text{...(ii)}$

And, $S + F = 20000 \quad \text{...(iii)}$

$\frac{1}{2}$ [Eqs. (i) + (ii) + (iii)] − Eq. (ii)

$\therefore$ Monthly income of father = ₹9000

40. (a) Actual weight increase

$= 1.2 \times 15 = 18.0$ kg

$\because$ New man was replaced by 51 kg man.

Hence, weight of new man $= 51 + 18 = 69$ kg

41. (b) Let total friends $= x$

Total age $= 27x$ yr

Age of 4 friends $= 4 \times 25 = 100$ yr

New average age $= 26$ yr

$27x + 100 = 26(x + 4)$

$\Rightarrow \quad 27x - 26x = 104 - 100 \Rightarrow x = 4$

$\therefore$ There were 4 people initially.

42. (d) Total sum of numbers $= 18 \times 8 = 144$

Let excluded number $= x$

Now, $\frac{144 - x}{7} = 20$

$\Rightarrow \quad 144 - x = 140$

$\Rightarrow \quad x = 144 - 140 = 4$

43. (d) Spend on pens and erasers

$= 10 \times 8 + 10 \times 5 =$ ₹130

Remaining amount $= 150 - 130 =$ ₹20

Number of sharpners $= \frac{20}{4} = 5$

Total items $= 10 + 10 + 5 = 25$

$\therefore$ Average price per items $= \frac{150}{25} =$ ₹ 6

44. (a) Total weight $= 32 \times 18.5 = 592$ kg

If 4 students left,

Weight of 28 students $= 15.5 \times 28 = 434$ kg

$\therefore$ Average weight of 4 students

$= \frac{592 - 434}{4} = \frac{158}{4} = 39.5$ kg

45. (b) According to Raghav's weight

$64 < R < 74$

But according to sister

$60 < R < 69$

But according to his mother

$64 < R \le 68$

And according to his father

$R \le 67$

Then, average of remaining possible weight

$= \frac{65 + 66 + 67}{3} = 66$ kg

46. (c) Total weight of 20 people

$= 59.8 \times 20 = 1196$ kg

The correct average weight

$= \frac{1196 + 77 - 68}{20}$

$= \frac{1205}{20} = 60.25$ kg

> **Speedy Method**
>
> Difference of misread weight $= 77 - 68 = 9$ kg
>
> $\therefore$ Correct average weight $= 59.8 + \frac{9}{20}$
>
> $= 59.8 + 0.45 = 60.25$ kg

47. (d) Let average of all 20 students $= x$

So, $19 \times 175 + x + 19 = 20x$

$\Rightarrow \quad 19 \times 175 + 19 = 20x - x$

$\Rightarrow \quad x = \frac{19 \times 175 + 19}{19}$

$= 175 + 1 = 176$

$\therefore$ Total money spent $= 20x = 20 \times 176 =$ ₹3520

48. (c) Correct average $= \frac{45 \times 36 - 48 + 84}{36}$

$= \frac{1656}{36} = 46$

49. (a) Total runs to make in nine innings

$= 58 \times 9 = 522$

Let he has to score x runs in 10th inning to get average of 61.

Then, $\frac{522 + x}{10} = 61$

$\Rightarrow \quad 522 + x = 610$

$\therefore \quad x = 610 - 522 = 88$ runs

50. (c) Let weight of Ram $= x$ kg

Total weight of Ram and Shyam

$= 2(x + 2) = 2x + 4$

$\therefore$ Weight of Shyam $= 2x + 4 - x = x + 4$

Total weight of Ram, Shyam and Rohan

$= 3(x + 2 + 2) = 3x + 12$

$\therefore$ Weight of Rohan $= 3x + 12 - 2x - 4 = x + 8$

Total weight of Ram, Shyam, Rohan and Rita

$= 4(x + 2 + 2 + 2) = 4x + 24$

$\therefore$ Weight of Rita $= 4x + 24 - 3x - 12 = x + 12$

Total weight of Ram, Shyam, Rohan, Rita and Mukesh.

$= 5(x + 2 + 2 + 2 + 2) = 5x + 40$

$\therefore$ Weight of Mukesh $= 5x + 40 - 4x - 24$

$= x + 16$

Mukesh heavier than Ram by

$= x + 16 - x = 16$ kg.

51. (c) Total age of the family

$= 6 \times 40 = 240$ yr

Let the age of the guest be x yr.

$\therefore$ According to the question,

$\frac{240 + x}{7} = \frac{40 \times 112.5}{100} = 45$

$\Rightarrow \quad 240 + x = 315$

$\Rightarrow \quad x = 315 - 240 = 75$ yr

52. (c) Sum of remaining two numbers

$= (6 \times 3.52) - (2 \times 3.7) - (2 \times 2.5)$

$= 21.12 - 7.4 - 5.0$

$= 21.12 - 12.4 = 8.72$

$\therefore$ Average of remaining two numbers

$= \frac{8.72}{2} = 4.36$

53. (a) $\therefore$ Sum of s numbers $= r^4 \times s$

$\therefore$ Sum of r numbers $= r \times s^4$

Average of $(r + s)$ numbers

$= \frac{r^4 s + r s^4}{r + s} = \frac{rs(r^3 + s^3)}{r + s}$

$= \frac{rs(r + s)(r^2 + s^2 - rs)}{r + s}$

$= rs(r^2 + s^2 - rs)$

54. (d) Sum of weight of 120 staff members

$= 120 \times 62.5$ kg $= 7500$ kg

Sum of weight of 119 staff members

$= 119 \times 62.25$ kg $= 7407.75$ kg

Hence, weight of staff who left the hotel

$= (7500 - 7407.75)$ kg $= 92.25$ kg

55. (d) Let 'n' be the number of students in the class and let actual average of marks of a class be x.

Sum of marks of a class wrongly

$= xn - 89 + 98 = xn + 9$

Now, wrong average = Actual average + 0.25

$\Rightarrow \quad \frac{xn + 9}{n} = \frac{xn}{n} + 0.25$

$\Rightarrow \quad \frac{9}{n} = 0.25 = 9 \times 4 = 36$

$\therefore$ Number of students in the class = 36.

56. (c) Increase in total marks of the class from actual marks $= 65 - 45 = 20$

Let the total number of students $= x$

Then, $\frac{1}{3} \times x = 20 \quad \therefore x = 20 \times 3 = 60$

57. (b) Let the number of apples be x in the basket originally.

$\therefore$ Weight of x apples $= 50x$ kg

Weight of 6 apples $= 6 \times 60 = 360$ kg

And total weight of $(x + 6)$ apples

$= (50x + 360)$ kg

New average $= 50 + 5 = 55$ kg

$\therefore \quad 55 = \frac{50x + 360}{x + 6}$

$\Rightarrow 55x + 330 = 50x + 360 \Rightarrow x = 6$

58. (b) First seven non-zero multiple of 17

$= 17, 34, 51, 68, 85, 102, 119$

Hence, average

$= \frac{17 + 34 + 51 + 68 + 85 + 102 + 119}{7}$

$= \frac{476}{7} = 68$

> **Speedy Method**
>
> $\therefore$ Required average $= \frac{17 \times (7 + 1)}{2} = 68$

59. (a) Let x be the weight of the new person and y be the old average of 12 persons.

Sum of weight of 12 persons

$= 12 \times y = 12y$

New average $= (y + 3.5)$ kg

Also, new average $= \frac{(12y + x - 58)}{12}$

$\Rightarrow \quad y + 3.5 = \frac{12y + x - 58}{12}$

$\Rightarrow (y + 3.5) \times 12 = 12y + x - 58$

$\Rightarrow \quad 12y + 42 = 12y + x - 58$

$\Rightarrow \quad x = 42 + 58 = 100$ kg

> **Speedy Method**
>
> Increase in total weight of 12 persons
>
> $= 12 \times 3.5$ kg $= 42$ kg
>
> Weight of the new person
>
> $= (58 + 42)$ kg $= 100$ kg

60. (a) Let the eight consecutive odd numbers be $x, x + 2, x + 4, x + 6, x + 8, x + 10, x + 12, x + 14$.

$\Rightarrow \frac{x + (x + 2) + (x + 4) + (x + 6) + (x + 8) + (x + 10) + (x + 12) + (x + 14)}{8} = 48$

$\Rightarrow \quad 8x + 56 = 48 \times 8$

$\Rightarrow \quad 8x = 328 \Rightarrow x = 41$

$\therefore$ Sum of fifth and seventh numbers

$= (x + 8 + x + 12)$

$= 2x + 20$

$= 2 \times 41 + 20$

$= 82 + 20 = 102$

61. (a) Here, weighted average score

$= \frac{8 \times 2 + 8 \times 3 + 6 \times 3 + 6.5 \times 4}{2 + 3 + 3 + 4}$

$= \frac{16 + 24 + 18 + 26}{12} = \frac{84}{12} = 7$

62. (d) Let the average weight of 5 persons be x kg.

Let the weight of the new person be N kg.

According to the question,

$\frac{5x - 150 + N}{5} = x - 3$

$\Rightarrow \quad 5x - 150 + N = 5x - 15$

$\Rightarrow \quad N = 150 - 15 = 135$ kg

63. (c) Let the women get ₹ x per day.

The man get = ₹$(x + 50)$ per day.

Now, according to the question,

$700(x + 50) + 300x = 450 \times 1000$

$\Rightarrow \quad 7(x + 50) + 3x = 4500$

$\Rightarrow \quad 7x + 350 + 3x = 4500$

$\Rightarrow \quad 10x = 4150$

$\Rightarrow \quad x = \frac{4150}{10} = 415$

Hence, the daily wage of the woman is ₹415.

64. (a) Total marks of 60 students

$= 60 \times 62 = 3720$

Let the boys will be x in the class then girls will be $(60 - x)$.

According to the question,

$60x + 65(60 - x) = 3720$

$\Rightarrow \quad (65 \times 60) - 5x = 3720$

$\Rightarrow \quad 5x = 3900 - 3720$

$\Rightarrow \quad 5x = 180$

$\therefore \quad x = 36$

Then, the number of boys in the class is 36.

> **Speedy Method**
>
> 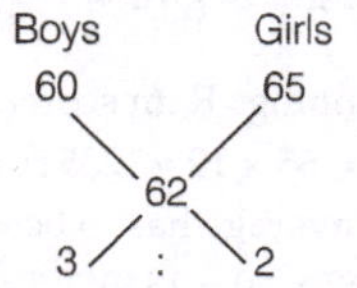
>
>
> Hence, number of boys $= \frac{60}{3 + 2} \times 3 = 36$

65. (c) Total marks of 25 students

$= 25 \times 19 = 475$

According to the question,

Actual average of marks of class

$$= \frac{475 - [(19 + 18 - (15 + 14)]}{25} = \frac{467}{25} = 18.68$$

66. (b) Total runs in 27 innings

$= 27 \times 47 = 1269$

Let the highest score be x runs.

$\therefore$ Lowest score $= x - 157$

According to the question,

$x + x - 157 = 1269 - 25 \times 42$

$\Rightarrow \quad 2x = 1269 - 1050 + 157 = 376$

$\Rightarrow \quad x = \frac{376}{2} = 188$

67. (b) Multiples of 2 = 2, 4, 6, 8 ⋯ 50

Sum of multiples of 2

$= 2 + 4 + 6 + 8 + \cdots + 50$

$= 2[1 + 2 + 3 + 4 + \cdots + 25]$

$= \frac{2 \times 25 \times (25 + 1)}{2} = 25 \times 26 = 650$

Multiples of 5 = 5, 10, 15, 20, 25, 30, 35, 40, 45, 50

But, 10, 20, 30, 40 and 50 are already taken as multiples of 2.

So, remaining multiples of 5 = 5, 15, 25, 35, 45

$\therefore$ Sum of multiples of 5

$= 5 + 15 + 25 + 35 + 45 = 125$

$\therefore$ Required average $= \frac{650 + 125}{25 + 5} = \frac{775}{30} = 25.8$

68. (c) Average of first ten odd numbers = 10

Average of first 15 even numbers

$= 15 + 1 = 16$

Thus, product $= 16 \times 10 = 160$

69. (b) Total sum of 23 numbers

$= 23 \times 51 = 1173$

Sum of first 12 numbers $= 12 \times 49 = 588$

Sum of last 12 numbers $= 54 \times 12 = 648$

$\therefore$ 12th number $= (588 + 648) - 1173$

$= 1236 - 1173 = 63$

$\therefore$ Average of remaining 22 numbers is

$$= \frac{1173 - 63}{22} = \frac{1110}{22} = 50.45$$

70. (a) Total weight of student in Section A

$= 40 \times 45.5 = 1820$ kg

Total weight of students in Section B

$= 40 \times 44.2 = 1768$ kg

Weight of two students of Section A shifted to $B = 48.75 \times 2 = 97.50$ kg

Now, students weight in section A

$= 1820 - 97.50 = 1722.5$ kg

And student weight in Section B

$= 1768 + 97.50 = 1865.5$ kg

According to the question,

Let x is weight of each student who shifted from B to A.

$1865.5 - 2x = 1722.5 + 2x$

$\Rightarrow \quad 4x = 1865.5 - 1722.5$

$\Rightarrow \quad 4x = 143$

$\Rightarrow \quad x = 35.75$

So, the average weight of student shifted to A from $B = \frac{2 \times 35.75}{2} = 35.75$ kg.

71. (b) Let total subjects are x.

According to the question,

$72.6x - 67.6x = 27 + 10 + 18$

$\Rightarrow \quad 5x = 55$

$\Rightarrow \quad x = 11$

So, the total number of subjects are 11.

72. (d) Total salary of 60 workers

$= 29900 \times 60 =$ ₹ 1794000

Total salary of 2 officers

$= 2 \times 90000 =$ ₹ 180000

Total salary of 8 supervisors

$= 8 \times 65000 =$ ₹ 520000

Total salary of 10 employees

$= 180000 + 520000 =$ ₹ 700000

Total remaining salary of 50 employees

$= 1794000 - 700000 =$ ₹ 1094000

$\therefore$ Average salary of 50 employee

$= \frac{1094000}{50} =$ ₹ 21880

73. (a) Let the 5 consecutive odd natural numbers are $(x - 4), (x - 2), x, (x + 2)$ and $(x + 4)$.

$(x - 4)^2 + (x - 2)^2 + x^2 + (x + 2)^2 + (x + 4)^2 = 233 \times 5$

$\Rightarrow x^2 + 16 - 8x + x^2 + 4 - 4x + x^2 + x^2 + 4 + 4x + x^2 + 16 + 8x = 1165$

$\Rightarrow \quad 5x^2 + 40 = 1165$

$\Rightarrow \quad 5x^2 = 1125 \Rightarrow x^2 = 225$

$\Rightarrow \quad x = 15$

Now, largest number $= (x + 4) = 15 + 4 = 19$

Smallest number $= (x - 4) = 15 - 4 = 11$

$\therefore$ Required average $= \frac{11 + 19}{2} = \frac{30}{2} = 15$

74. (c) Total production in December

$= 31 \times 512 = 15872$

Total production in first 20 days

$= 20 \times 515 = 10300$

Total production in last 13 days

$= 13 \times 510 = 6630$

Total production on 19 and 20 December

$= 6630 + 10300 - 15872 = 1058$

$\therefore$ Average production on 19 and 20 December

$= \frac{1058}{2} = 529$

75. (b) Given, average of x occurring 5 times and y occurring 7 times is 37.

$\Rightarrow \quad 5x + 7y = 37 \times (5 + 7)$

$\Rightarrow \quad 5x + 7y = 37 \times 12 \quad \ldots$ (i)

Average of x occurring 7 times and y occurring 5 times is 35

$\Rightarrow \quad 7x + 5y = 35(7 + 5) \quad \ldots$ (ii)

From Eq. (i) and Eq. (ii),

$\therefore \quad y = 42, x = 30$

76. (d) Total score $= 40 \times 45 = 1800$

Actual average score

$$= \frac{1800 + 2 \times 25 - 2 \times 35 + 38 - 32}{40}$$

$$= \frac{1786}{40} = 44.65$$

77. (a) Let 8 consecutive even numbers are $x, x + 2, x + 4, x + 6, x + 8, x + 10, x + 12$ and $x + 14$.

According to the question,

$$\frac{x + x + 2 + x + 4 + x + 6 + x + 8 + x + 10 + x + 12 + x + 14}{8} = 17$$

$\Rightarrow \quad 8x + 56 = 136$

$\Rightarrow \quad 8x = 136 - 56 = 80$

$\Rightarrow \quad x = \frac{80}{8} = 10$

$\therefore$ Average of last 3 numbers, 36 and 53

$$= \frac{x + 10 + x + 12 + x + 14 + 36 + 53}{5}$$

$$= \frac{3 \times 10 + 125}{5} = \frac{30 + 125}{5} = \frac{155}{5} = 31$$

78. (c) Let total students are x and average is 156.

Now, total height of students $= 156x$

Total height of 5 students $= 5 \times 160 = 800$ cm

According to the question,

$156x + 800 = (x + 5)156.8$

$\Rightarrow \quad 156x + 800 = 156.8x + 156.8 \times 5$

$\Rightarrow 156.8x - 156x = 800 - 784$

$\Rightarrow \quad 0.8x = 16$

$\therefore \quad x = 20$

79. (b) Total sum of 22 numbers

$= 37.5 \times 22 = 825$

Sum of first 12 numbers $= 40.6 \times 12 = 487.2$

Sum of last 12 numbers $= 12 \times 35.4 = 424.8$

11th and 12th numbers

$= (487.2 + 424.8) - 825 = 87$

If 11th and 12th number excluded.

Average of remaining number

$$= \frac{825 - 87}{20} = \frac{738}{20} = 36.9$$

80. (a) Total sum of 11 numbers

$= 11 \times 56 = 616$

Sum of first 3 numbers $= 3 \times 52 = 156$

Sum of next 5 numbers $= 5 \times 60 = 300$

9th, 10th number is 3 and 1 more then 11th number

Let 11th number is x,

9th number $= x + 3$

10th number $= x + 1$

According to the question,

$616 = 156 + 300 + (x + 3) + (x + 1) + x$

$\Rightarrow 616 - 456 = 3x + 4 \Rightarrow 160 = 3x + 4$

$\Rightarrow \quad 3x = 156 \Rightarrow x = 52$

9th number $= x + 3 = 52 + 3 = 55$

11th number = 52,

$\therefore$ Required average $= \frac{(52+55)}{2} = 53.5$

81. (d) Sum of 28 numbers $= 77 \times 28 = 2156$

Sum of first 14 numbers $= 74 \times 14 = 1036$

Sum of last 15 numbers $= 84 \times 15 = 1260$

14th number $= (1036 + 1260) - 2156 = 140$

$\therefore$ Required average $= \frac{2156 - 140}{27} = \frac{2016}{27}$

$= 74.67 \approx 74.7$

82. (a) Let five consecutive odd numbers be $x, x+2, x+4, x+6, x+8$.

$\therefore$ Average $= \frac{\text{Sum of terms}}{\text{Number of terms}}$

$\Rightarrow \quad m = \frac{x + x + 2 + x + 4 + x + 6 + x + 8}{5}$

$\Rightarrow \quad 5m = 5x + 20 \Rightarrow x = m - 4$ ... (i)

Average of eight odd numbers

$= \frac{x + x + 2 + x + 4 + x + 6 + x + 8 + x + 10 + x + 12 + x + 14}{8}$

$= \frac{8x + 56}{8} = x + 7$

$= m - 4 + 7$ [from Eq. (i)]

$= m + 3$

$\therefore$ Required increase $= m + 3 - m = 3$.

83. (a) The sum of total 60 students

$= 38 \times 60 = 2280$

The sum of total 22 students $= 36 \times 22 = 792$

The sum of total 32 students $= 32 \times 32 = 1024$

Sum of remaining 6 students

$= 2280 - 792 - 1024 = 464$

Average of remaining 6 students

$= 464 / 6 = 77.33$

84. (c) Total donation of 24 students

$= 50 \times 24 =$ ₹ 1200

Later on, teacher also contribute some money. (24 student + 1 teacher) average donation ₹ 56.

Sum of total donation (students + teacher)

$= 56 \times 25 =$ ₹ 1400

$\therefore$ Teacher's contribution

$= 1400 - 1200 =$ ₹ 200

85. (b) Total marks of 30 boys

$= 30 \times 88 = 2640$

Now the total marks of 28 boys

$= 28 \times 87.5 = 2450$

Total marks of 2 student $= 2640 - 2450 = 190$

$\therefore$ Let x, y = remaining student.

$x + y = 190$ ... (i)

$x - y = 2$ ... (ii)

From Eqs. (i) and (ii),

$x = 96$ and $y = 94$

The heighest mark is 96.

86. (b) Sum of height of 5 boys

= Average × Number of boys

$= 175 \times 5 = 875$ cm

Sum of height of 6 boys $= 176 \times 6 = 1056$ cm

Height of 6th boy $= 1056 - 875 = 181$ cm

87. (c) Let there are 4 numbers, each value $= 54.6$

Then, average of 4 numbers = 54.6

Sum of 4 numbers $= 54.6 \times 4 = 218.4$

According to the question,

New average of 4 numbers

$= \frac{3(54.6 + 5.6) + 1(54.6 - 8.4)}{4}$

$= \frac{180.6 + 46.2}{4} = \frac{226.8}{4} = 56.7$

Speedy Method

Let there are 4 numbers. $\left[\because 75\% = \frac{3}{4}\right]$

$\therefore$ New average of 4 numbers

$= 54.6 + \frac{(3 \times 5.6 - 1 \times 8.4)}{4}$

$= 54.6 + \frac{8.4}{4} = 54.6 + 2.1 = 56.7$

88. (a) The sum of 24 numbers

$= 24 \times 56 = 1344$

Sum of 10 numbers $= 71.7 \times 10 = 717$

Sum of 11 numbers $= 42 \times 11 = 462$

Sum of 22nd, 23rd, 24th numbers

$= 1344 - 717 - 462 = 165$

Ratio of 22nd, 23rd, 24th numbers

$= \frac{1}{2} : \frac{1}{3} : \frac{5}{12} = 6 : 4 : 5$

Let 22nd, 23rd and 24th numbers are $6x$, $4x$ and $5x$, respectively.

$6x + 4x + 5x = 165$

$\Rightarrow \quad 15x = 165$

$\Rightarrow \quad x = 165 / 15 = 11$

22nd number is $6x = 6 \times 11 = 66$

24th number is $5x = 5 \times 11 = 55$

Average of 22nd and 24th numbers

$= \frac{66 + 55}{2} = \frac{121}{2} = 60.5$

89. (b) Total number of students = 60

Number of boys = 36

$\therefore$ Number of girls $= 60 - 36 = 24$

Let the average weight of girls be 'x' kg.

Now, $\quad 60 \times 42 = 36 \times 50 + 24 \times x$

$\Rightarrow \quad 2520 - 1800 = 24x$

$\Rightarrow \quad 720 = 24x$

$\therefore \quad x = 30$ kg

90. (c) Difference or error in marks

$= 99 - 66 = 33$

Total number of students = 55

Hence, increasing in the average marks of the class because of typing error $= \frac{33}{55} = \frac{3}{5}$

$= 0.6$

91. (b) We know that,

The first six prime numbers = 2, 3, 5, 7, 11, 13

$\therefore$ Average $= \frac{\text{Total sum of numbers}}{\text{Total numbers}}$

$= \frac{2 + 3 + 5 + 7 + 11 + 13}{6}$

$= \frac{41}{6} = 6\frac{5}{6}$

92. (c) Required average

$= \frac{\text{50 faculty monthly salary} - \text{35 faculty monthly salary}}{15}$

$= \frac{50 \times 30000 - 35 \times 37500}{15}$

$= \frac{1500000 - 1312500}{15} = \frac{187500}{15} =$ ₹12500

93. (d) Sum of 12 numbers $= 39 \times 12 = 468$

Sum of first 4 numbers $= 40 \times 4 = 160$

Sum of last 5 numbers $= 35 \times 5 = 175$

Let's take the 5th number is x.

$\therefore \quad$ 6th number is $= x + 6$

$\therefore \quad$ 7th number is $= x - 5$

According to the question,

$468 = 160 + 175 + x + (x + 6) + (x - 5)$

$\Rightarrow 468 = 336 + 3x$

$\Rightarrow \quad x = \frac{468 - 336}{3} = \frac{132}{3} = 44$

The average of 6th and 7th number is

$= \frac{x + 6 + x - 5}{2} = \frac{2x + 1}{2}$

$= \frac{44 \times 2 + 1}{2} = \frac{89}{2} = 44.5$

94. (a) Total weight of

$A + B + C = 65 \times 3 = 195$ ...(i)

Average weight of C and B is 61.5 kg.

Total weight of $C + B = 61.5 \times 2 = 123$ kg

In the same way, total weight of

$A + C = 68.5 \times 2 = 137$ kg

$\therefore$ Total weight of

$C + B + A + C = A + B + 2C$

$= 123 + 137 = 260$ ...(ii)

From Eqs. (ii) – (i),

$C = 65$

95. (b) Total weight of A, B, C

$= 70 \times 3 = 210$ kg.

$\therefore$ Total weight of A, B, C and D

$= 60 \times 4 = 240$ kg

$\therefore$ Weight of $D = 240 - 210 = 30$ kg

Weight of $E = 30 + 5 = 35$ kg

Total weight of B, C, D and E

$= 59 \times 4 = 236$ kg

Now, weight of B and C is

$= 236 - (30 + 35) = 236 - 65 = 171$ kg

And weight of $A = 210 - 171 = 39$ kg

So, average weight of A, D and E is

$= \frac{39 + 30 + 35}{3} = \frac{104}{3} = 34.66 \approx 35$ kg

96. (a) $A + B + C = 65 \times 3 = 195$ kg ...(i)

$A + B = 63.5 \times 2 = 127$ kg ...(ii)

Substracting Eq. (ii) from (i), we'll get

$A + B + C - (A + B) = 195 - 127$

$C = 68$ kg

Also, $A + C = 67.5 \times 2 = 135$

$A + 68 = 135$

$A = 135 - 68 = 67$ kg

97. (a) The sum of the twelve numbers

$= 12 \times 39 = 468$

The sum of the last five numbers

$= 5 \times 35 = 175$

The sum of the first four numbers

$= 4 \times 40 = 160$

The sum of the fifth, sixth and seventh number $= (468 - 175 - 160) = 133$

Let, the fifth number is x.

Then, the sixth number is $(x + 6)$ and the seventh number is $(x - 5)$.

$x + (x + 6) + (x - 5) = 133$

$3x + 1 = 133$

$\Rightarrow \quad x = 44$

The fifth number is 44 and the sixth number is $(44 + 6) = 50$

Average of fifth and sixth number is

$\frac{(44 + 50)}{2} = 47$

98. (d) 11th result $= 11 \times 59 - 10 \times 58$

$= 649 - 580 = 69$

99. (a) 11th result $= 11 \times 60 - 10 \times 59$

$= 660 - 590 = 70$

100. (d) Let five integers are a,b,c,d and e respectively.

According to the question,

$\frac{a + b + c + d}{4} = \frac{e}{2}$

$\Rightarrow \quad a + b + c + d = 2e$

Sum of five integers $= 48 \times 5 = 240$

$a + b + c + d + e = 240$

$\Rightarrow \quad 3e = 240$

$\Rightarrow \quad e = 80$

101. (b) We know that, in averages, if each of the observations is multiplied by same number, then the new average will be equal to the old average multiplied by that same number.

Hence, new average $= 23 \times 13 = 299$

102. (b) We know, combined average

$= \frac{n_1 a_1 + n_2 a_2}{n_1 + n_2} = \frac{40 \times 33 + 32 \times 60}{40 + 32}$

$= \frac{1320 + 1920}{72} = \frac{3240}{72} = 45$

103. (d) Average attendance on Sunday $= 410$

Average attendance on remaining days $= 230$

5 Sunday in 30 days month

Remaining days $= 30 - 5 = 25$

$\therefore$ Required average $= \frac{5 \times 410 + 25 \times 230}{30}$

$= \frac{7800}{30} = 260$

104. (a) Let the weight of n number of students having an average weight (A) be $w_1, w_2, w_3 \ldots w_n$.

$\therefore$ Average $(A) = \frac{w_1 + w_2 + w_3 + \ldots + w_n}{n}$

$\Rightarrow \quad w_1 + w_2 + w_3 + \ldots + w_n = nA$ ...(i)

If one student having 30 kg weight is added, then

$A + 1 = \frac{w_1 + w_2 + \ldots + w_n + 30}{n + 1}$

$\Rightarrow \quad nA + n + A + 1 = w_1 + w_2 + \ldots + w_n + 30$

$\Rightarrow \quad nA + n + 1 + A = nA + 30$ [from Eq. (i)]

$\Rightarrow \quad n + A = 29$

$\Rightarrow \quad n = 29 - A$ ...(ii)

Now, if one more student of 30 kg is added, then

$A + 1.5 = \frac{w_1 + w_2 + \ldots + w_n + 30 + 30}{n + 2}$

$\Rightarrow \quad (A + 1.5)(n + 2) = nA + 60$ [$\because$ from Eq. (i)]

$\Rightarrow \quad nA + 2A + 1.5n + 3 = nA + 60$

$\Rightarrow \quad 2A + 1.5(29 - A) + 3 = 60$ [$\because$ from Eq. (ii)]

$\Rightarrow \quad 0.5A + 46.5 = 60$

$\Rightarrow \quad 0.5A = 13.5$

$\therefore \quad A = 27$

105. (c) Average salary of 12 employees group = ₹ 3950

Average salary of another group = ₹ 1850

Average salary of all employees = ₹ 2150

Let number of employees in another group $= x$

We know that,

Average salary $= \frac{\text{Total salary}}{\text{Number of employees}}$

$2150 = \frac{3950 \times 12 + x \times 1850}{(12 + x)}$

$\Rightarrow 25800 + 2150x = 47400 + 1850x$

$\Rightarrow \quad 21600 = 300x$

$x = 72$

$\therefore$ Total number of employees $= x + 12$

$= 72 + 12 = 84$

Speedy Method

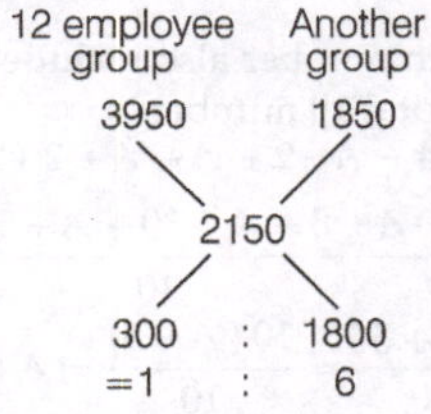

$\because \quad 1 \rightarrow 12 \quad \therefore \quad 7 \rightarrow 84$

106. (a) We know that,

Average weight $= \frac{\text{Total weight}}{\text{Total number of students}}$

$\therefore$ Average weight of remaining

30 students $= \frac{35 \times 40 - 42 \times 5}{35 - 5}$

$= \frac{1400 - 210}{30} = \frac{1190}{30} = 39\frac{2}{3}$ kg

107. (a) $\therefore$ Required average

$= \frac{1 + 2 + 3 + 4 + 5 + 6 + 7 + 8 + 9 + 10}{10}$

$= \frac{55}{10} = 5.5$

Speedy Method

Average of first 10 natural numbers

$= \frac{10 + 1}{2} = 5.5$

108. (a) Sum of weight of all the five friends

$= (67 + 85 + 70 + 90 + 103) = 415$ kg

$\therefore$ Average of their weight $= \frac{415}{5} = 83$ kg

109. (c) Increment in marks due to mistake

$(x) = 93 - 63 = 30$

Increase in average $(a) = 0.5$

$\therefore$ Total students in class $= \frac{x}{a} = \frac{30}{0.5} = 60$

110. (c) Average cost

$= \left[\frac{4 \times 50 + 5 \times 60 + 6 \times 70}{4 + 5 + 6}\right]$

$= \left[\frac{200 + 300 + 420}{15}\right] = \frac{920}{15} =$ ₹ 61.33

111. (b) Average weight of 40 boys = 33 kg

Total weight of 40 boys $= 40 \times 33 = 1320$ kg

$\therefore$ Average weight of 32 boys = 15 kg

Total weight of 32 boys $= 15 \times 32$ kg $= 480$ kg

$\therefore$ Average age of all students

$= \frac{(1320 + 480)}{72}$ kg $= \frac{1800}{72}$ kg $= 25$ kg

112. (c) Required average

$= \frac{\text{First number} + \text{Last number}}{2}$

$= \frac{1 + 69}{2} = 35$

113. (d) Average score of whole class

$= \frac{15 \times 80 + 10 \times 60}{25} = \frac{1200 + 600}{25} = \frac{1800}{25} = 72$

114. (d) Average of 50 numbers

$(N_1, N_2, \ldots, N_{50}) = M$

Sum of 50 numbers $= 50\,M$

Sum of 50 numbers

$(N_1 - 100, N_2 - 100, \ldots, N_{50} - 100)$

$= (N_1 + N_2 + N_3 \ldots N_{50}) -$

$(100 + 100 + 100 \ldots +$ up to 50 terms$)$

$= 50\,M - 50 \times 100 = 50M - 5000$

$\therefore$ Required average $= \frac{50M - 5000}{50} = M - 100$

115. (a) The average salary of T per month is

$$= \frac{12000 \times 3 + 15000 \times 3 + 21000 \times 3 + 30000 \times 3}{12}$$

$$= \frac{36000 + 45000 + 63000 + 90000}{12}$$

$$= \frac{234000}{12} = ₹\ 19500$$

116. (b) According to the question,

$$\text{Average} = \left[\frac{25 \times 5000 + 2 \times 20000 + 3 \times 1500}{30}\right]$$

$$= \left[\frac{125000 + 40000 + 4500}{30}\right]$$

$$= \left[\frac{169500}{30}\right] = ₹\ 5650$$

117. (a) Total yearly income of a family

$= (2500 \times 4 + 2750 \times 5 + 3550 \times 3 + 5500)$

$= (10000 + 13750 + 10650 + 5500) = 39900$

$\therefore$ Average monthly income $= \frac{39900}{12} = ₹\ 3325$

118. (d) Total age of 12 workers in an office

$= 12 \times \frac{71}{2} = 426$ yr

After joining the new worker, the total age of all the workers in an office $= 37 \times 13 = 481$ yr

$\therefore$ The current age of newly joined worker

$= (481 - 426) = 55$ yr

119. (a) Prime numbers between 69 and 92.

$= 71, 73, 79, 83, 89$ (5 numbers)

$$\therefore \text{Average} = \frac{71 + 73 + 79 + 83 + 89}{5}$$

$$= \frac{395}{5} = 79$$

120. (b) Average of the first eight multiple of 6

$$= \frac{\text{Number} \times (n+1)}{2} = \frac{6 \times (8+1)}{2} = 27$$

121. (b) Average salary of 40 employees

$= ₹\ 4000$

$\therefore$ Total salary of 40 employees

$= 40 \times 4000 = ₹\ 160000$

$\therefore$ Total salary of 35 non-teaching staff

$= 35 \times 4200 = ₹\ 147000$

$\therefore$ Total salary of remaining 5 members

$= 160000 - 147000 = ₹\ 13000$

$\therefore$ Average salary of remaining 5 members

$= \frac{13000}{5} = ₹\ 2600$

122. (d) Total weight of 40 students

$= 40 \times 52 = 2080$ kg

$\therefore$ Total weight of 41 (40 students + 1 teacher)

$= 41 \times 52.5 = 2152.5$ kg

$\therefore$ Weight of teacher $= 2152.5 - 2080$

$= 72.5$ kg

Speedy Method

$\therefore$ Required weight $= 52 + 41 \times 0.5$

$= 52 + 20.5 = 72.5$ kg

123. (c) The total weight of 64 students

$= 48 \times 64 = 3072$ kg

The total weight of 32 students

$= 24 \times 32 = 768$ kg

When, the both classes will be combined, them average weight of both classes

$$= \frac{(3072 + 768)}{64 + 32} = \frac{3840}{96} = 40 \text{ kg}$$

Speedy Method

Ratio of students of both classes

$= 64 : 32 = 2 : 1$

Let average weight of both classes $= x$ kg

By alligation rule,

48 24

x

2 : 1

$$\Rightarrow \frac{48 - x}{x - 24} = \frac{1}{2} \Rightarrow 96 - 2x = x - 24$$

$$\Rightarrow 3x = 120 \Rightarrow x = 40 \text{ kg}$$

124. (a) Total weight $= 30 \times 45 = 1350$ kg

One of the student whose weight is 48.5 kg is replaced by another student

$= 1350 - 48.5 = 1301.5$ kg

After replacing with new student average weight $= 45$ kg $+ 200$ gm $= 45.2$ kg

$\therefore$ Weight of new student

$= (45.2 \times 30) - 1301.5$

$= 1356 - 1301.5 = 54.5$ kg

Hence, weight of new student is 54.5 kg.

125. (a) Total marks of 80 students

$= 80 \times 50 = 4000$

Number of passed students $= (80 - 30) = 50$

Let, average marks obtained by failed students $= x$

Total marks obtained by failed students

$= 30 \times x = 30x$

Total marks obtained by passed students

$= 55 \times 50 = 2750$

$\therefore \quad 30x + 2750 = 4000$

$\Rightarrow \quad 30x = 4000 - 2750 \Rightarrow x = 41.66$

126. (d) Given, average of 5 consecutive even number is A.

Let 5 consecutive even number are

$x - 4, x - 2, x, x + 2, x + 4$

Then, $\frac{x - 4 + x - 2 + x + x + 2 + x + 4}{5} = A$

$\Rightarrow \frac{5x}{5} = A \Rightarrow x = A$

If 5 next even number also included then average of total 10 numbers

$$= \frac{A - 4 + A - 2 + A + A + 2 + A + 4 + A + 6 + A + 8 + A + 10 + A + 12 + A + 14}{10}$$

$$= \frac{10A + 50}{10} = \frac{10(A + 5)}{10} = A + 5$$

127. (c) Total weight of 10 persons

$= 40 \times 10 = 400$ kg

Total weight of 11 persons $= 42 \times 11 = 462$ kg

So, weight of new person

= Weight of 11 person – Weight of 10 person

$= 462 - 400 = 62$ kg

128. (a) Spends in first four months

$= 2300 \times 4 = ₹\ 9200$

Spends in last eight months

$= 1800 \times 8 = ₹\ 14400$

Total spend in a year $= 9200 + 14400 = ₹23600$

Saving $= ₹\ 12400$

Total income $= 23600 + 12400 = ₹\ 36000$

$\therefore$ Monthly income $= \frac{36000}{12} = ₹\ 3000$

129. (c) Sum of 15 numbers $= 53 \times 15 = 795$

Sum of 14 numbers $= 55 \times 14 = 770$

$\therefore$ Number which is removed $= 795 - 770 = 25$

130. (d) Total runs scored in 7 matches

$= 49 \times 7 = 343$

$\therefore$ Total run scored in other 9 matches

$= 27 \times 9 = 243$

Now, total runs scored in all 16 matches

$= 343 + 243 = 586$

$\therefore$ Average runs scored in 16 matches

$= \frac{586}{16} = 36.625$

131. (b) Let total number of employees in the sales department be x.

Total amount of salary of all employees

$= ₹\ 350x$

Total amount of salary of 10 senior employees

$= 450 \times 10 = ₹4500$

And total amount of salary of remaining employees $= 250 \times (x - 10) = ₹\ (250x - 2500)$

According to the question,

$350x = 4500 + 250x - 2500$

$\Rightarrow \quad 350x - 250x = 2000$

$\Rightarrow \quad 100x = 2000$

$\Rightarrow \quad x = \frac{2000}{100} = 20$

Speedy Method

By alligation rule,

Senior Employees Remaining Staff

450 250

350

100 : 100 $\Rightarrow$ 1 : 1

$\because \quad 1 \rightarrow 10$

$(1 + 1) \rightarrow 10 \times 2 = 20$

Hence, total employes is 20.

132. (b) $\because$ Average $= \frac{\text{Sum of terms}}{\text{Number of terms}}$

$$\Rightarrow 30 = \frac{32 + 34 + 38 + 21 + 26 + x}{6}$$

$\Rightarrow \quad 180 = 151 + x$

$x = 180 - 151 = 29$

133. (d) Sum of all observations

$= 30 \times 15 = 450$

Correct sum of observations

$= 450 + 9 - 15 = 444$

$\therefore$ Correct average $= \dfrac{444}{30} = 14.8$ yr

134. (d) Total weight of $(A + B + C)$

$= 3 \times 65$ kg $= 195$ kg

Weight of $(A + B) = 2 \times 62$ kg $= 124$ kg

Weight of $(B + C) = 2 \times 66$ kg $= 132$ kg

Weight of B

$= (A + B) + (B + C) - (A + B + C)$

$= (124 + 132 - 195)$ kg $= 61$ kg

135. (d) Let the average marks of boys be x.

Number of boys in class $= 45 - 20 = 25$

According to the question,

$$\frac{20 \times 42 + 25 \times x}{45} = 36$$

$\Rightarrow \quad 840 + 25x = 1620$

$\Rightarrow \quad 25x = 780 \Rightarrow x = \dfrac{780}{25}$

$\therefore \quad x = 31.2$

136. (d) Sum of weights of all the girls

$= 52 \times 47 = 2444$ kg

137. (b) Given, $A = \dfrac{3}{4}$ of B

$B = \dfrac{4}{5}$ of C and $C = \dfrac{3}{8}$ of D

$\therefore \quad A = \dfrac{3}{4}$ of $\dfrac{4}{5}$ of $\dfrac{3}{8}$ of D

$A = \dfrac{9}{40}$ of D ...(i)

Given, $\dfrac{4A + 7D}{2} = 316$

$\Rightarrow \quad 4A + 7D = 316 \times 2 = 632$

$\Rightarrow \quad 4 \times \dfrac{9}{40} \times D + 7D = 632$

[$\because$ from Eq. (i)]

$\Rightarrow \quad D = \dfrac{6320}{79} = 80,$

$\therefore \quad C = \dfrac{3}{8} \times 80 = 30,$

$B = \dfrac{4}{5}$ of $30 = 24$

and $\quad A = \dfrac{3}{4} \times 24 = 18$

Now, average of A, B, C and D

$$= \frac{18 + 24 + 30 + 80}{4} = \frac{152}{4} = 38$$

138. (b) Given, number of males = 20

Number of females and children

$= 20 + 4 = 24$

Let the number of females be x,

$\therefore$ Number of children $= 24 - x$.

Now, according to the question,

$x \times 49 + (24 - x) \times 30 = (44 \times 48.25) - (54 \times 20)$

$\Rightarrow \quad 19x = 323 \Rightarrow x = \dfrac{323}{19} = 17$

Number of females = 17

and number of children $= 24 - 17 = 7$

$\therefore$ Difference between number of females and children $= 17 - 7 = 10$.

139. (d) Sum of 5 numbers $= 26.4 \times 5 = 132$

Now, first number

$= \dfrac{1}{5} \times$ (Sum of four numbers)

$\Rightarrow$ First number $= \dfrac{1}{5} \times$

[Sum of 5 numbers – First number]

$\Rightarrow$ First number $+ \dfrac{1}{5}$ first number $= \dfrac{1}{5} \times 132$

$\therefore \quad$ First number $= \dfrac{1}{5} \times 132 \times \dfrac{5}{6} = 22$

140. (c) Let the total expense for the dinner be ₹ x.

According to the question,

$$(20 \times 880) + 10 \times \left(110 + \frac{x}{30}\right) = x$$

$\Rightarrow \quad 20 \times 880 + 1100 = x - \dfrac{x}{3} = \dfrac{2x}{3}$

$x = \dfrac{18700 \times 3}{2} =$ ₹ 28050

141. (c) Weight of teacher $= 52 + 0.5 \times 42$

$= 52 + 21.0 = 73$ kg

142. (b) Let the two numbers be a and b.

So, $\dfrac{a + b}{2} = 13.5$

$a + b = 27$ ... (i)

and $\sqrt{ab} = 6\sqrt{5}$

$ab = 180$

Now, $(a - b) = \sqrt{(a + b)^2 - 4ab}$

$(a - b) = \sqrt{(27)^2 - 4 \times 180}$

$(a - b) = \sqrt{729 - 720}$

$(a - b) = 3$ ... (ii)

By solving Eqs. (i) and (ii), we get

$a = 15, b = 12$

143. (a) Average weight of five members

$$= \frac{40 + 49 + 56 + 68 + 38}{5}$$

$$= \frac{251}{5} = 50.2 \text{ kg}$$

144. (a) By Alligation Method

Average of wrestlers		Average of Athletes
90		68
	78	
10	:	12
5	:	6

Here, 5 units $\rightarrow$ 20

1 units $\rightarrow$ 4

6 units $\rightarrow 4 \times 6 = 24$ athletes

145. (b) Average weight of family

$$= \frac{40 + 49 + 56 + 69 + 39}{5} = \frac{253}{5} = 50.6$$

146. (b) By alligation Method

Boys		Girls
71		73
	71.8	
1.2	:	0.8

$\therefore$ Required ratio = 3 : 2

147. (a) Average weight of family

$$= \frac{40 + 49 + 56 + 68 + 37}{5} = \frac{250}{5} = 50$$

148. (b) Average $= \dfrac{30 \times 16.2 - 18 \times 16}{30 - 18} = 16.5$

149. (d) Average $= \dfrac{72 + 63 + 81}{3} = \dfrac{216}{3} = 72$

150. (b) Average

$$= \frac{40 \times 60\,\% + 36 \times 25\,\% + 8 \times 15\,\%}{100\,\%}$$

$$= \frac{2400 + 900 + 120}{100} = \frac{3420}{100} = 34.2 \text{ yr}$$

151. (d) Let Average salary of staff = ₹ x

According to the question,

$$\frac{2550 \times 5 + 45x}{50} = \text{₹ } 855$$

$12750 + 45x = 42750$

$45x = 30000$

$x =$ ₹ 667

152. (b) Total number of rings in 5 baskets

$= 5 \times 42 = 210$

Total number of rings in 4 baskets, when D is removed $= 4 \times 38 = 152$

Rings in the basket $D = 210 - 152 = 58$

153. (b) Let the number of subjects be n

According to the question,

$85.4n + 8 + 12 + 10 - 15 = 87.9\,n$

$\Rightarrow \quad 2.5n = 15 \Rightarrow n = 6$

So, the number of subjects in the examination is 6.

154. (d) Total marks of 60 students

$= 60 \times 48 = 2880$

Correct score $= 2880 + 68 - 56 = 2892$

Correct average score $= \dfrac{2892}{60} = 48.2$

155. (d) Let the three consecutive add number be $x + 1$, $x + 3$, $x + 5$

According to the question,

$x + 1 + x + 3 + x + 5$

$= 58 + \dfrac{(x + 1 + x + 3 + x + 5)}{3}$

$3x + 9 = 58 + \dfrac{3(x + 3)}{3}$

$3x + 9 - x - 3 = 58$

$2x + 6 = 58 \Rightarrow x = 26$

So, the largest number $= x + 5 = 26 + 5 = 31$

156. (d) Average

$$= \frac{25 \times 11950 + 20 \times 24000 + 5 \times 35000}{50}$$

$$= \frac{953750}{50} = ₹\,19075$$

157. (d) Let number be x.

According to the question,

$$\Rightarrow \frac{x + x^2}{2} = 7x$$

$$\Rightarrow x + x^2 = 14x \Rightarrow x^2 - 13x = 0$$

$$\Rightarrow x(x - 13) = 0$$

$$\Rightarrow x = 13 \quad [\because x \neq 0]$$

158. (d)

Tue	Wed	Thu	Fri	Sat	Sun	Mon
5	5	4	4	4	4	4

∴ Average

$$= \frac{5 \times 258 + 5 \times 258 + 4 \times 258 + 4 \times 258 \; 4 \times 258 + 4 \times 258 + 768 \times 4}{30}$$

$$= \frac{258 \times 10 + 16 \times 258 + 4 \times 768}{30}$$

$$= \frac{2580 + 4128 + 3072}{30} = \frac{9780}{30} = 326$$

159. (b) Average

$$= \frac{11 \times (1 + 2 + 3 + 4 + 5 ......+12)}{12}$$

$$= \frac{11 \times 12 \times 13}{2 \times 12} = \frac{143}{2} = 71.5$$

160. (a) Total weight of X, Y and Z

$= 67 \times 3 = 201$ kg

Total weight of Y and Z $= 52 \times 2 = 104$ kg

Total weight of X and Y $= 64 \times 2 = 128$ kg

$\Rightarrow$ Weight of Z $= 201 - 128 = 73$ kg

$\Rightarrow$ Weight of X $= 201 - 104 = 97$ kg

∴ Weight of Y $= 201 - (73 + 97)$

$= 201 - 170 = 31$ kg

161. (d) Required average score

$$= \frac{71 + 82 + 177}{100 + 150 + 200} = \frac{330}{450} = \frac{11}{15}$$

162. (c) Average age of both class

$$= \frac{12 \times 20 + 16 \times 23}{12 + 16} = \frac{608}{28} = 21.7 \text{ yr}$$

163. (c) Average $= \dfrac{42 \times 400 + 38 \times 320}{42 + 38}$

$$= \frac{28960}{80} = 362$$

164. (d) Sum of nine numbers

$= 360 \times 9 = 3240$

165. (b) $\dfrac{R + S}{2} = ₹\,2460$

$R + S = ₹\,4920$ ...(i)

$\dfrac{S + M}{2} = ₹\,2380$

$S + M = ₹\,4760$ ...(ii)

$\dfrac{M + R}{2} = ₹\,2760$

$M + R = ₹\,5520$ ...(iii)

On adding these three equations, we get

$2(R + S + M) = ₹\,15200$

$R + S + M = ₹\,7600$ ...(iv)

From Eq. (ii) and Eq. (iv), we get

$R = ₹\,2840$

166. (a) Sum of run of 24 matches

$= 24 \times 60 = 1440$

Sum of run of 32 matches

$= 32 \times 80 = 2560$

Average of last 8 matches

$$= \frac{2560 - 1440}{8} = 140$$

167. (a) Total marks scored by all students

$= 2 \times 95 + 6 \times 90 + 3 \times 80 + 1 \times 50$

$= 190 + 540 + 240 + 50$

$= 1020$

Average score of the class $= \dfrac{1020}{12} = 85$

168. (d) Let average of 14 innings be x.

Sum of runs score in 14 innings $= 14x$

According to the question,

$$\frac{14x + 152}{15} = x + 5$$

$\Rightarrow \quad 14x + 152 = 15x + 75 \Rightarrow x = 77$

∴ New average after 15th inning

$= 77 + 5 = 82$

Speedy Method

∴ Required average $= 152 - 14 \times 5 = 82$

169. (b) Average weight of family

$$= \frac{40 + 49 + 56 + 71 + 37}{5} = \frac{253}{5} = 50.6$$

170. (b) Let x be the average saving for next 9 months.

According to the question,

$$\frac{4000 \times 3 + x \times 9}{12} = 4375$$

$\Rightarrow \quad 12000 + 9x = 52500$

$\Rightarrow \quad 9x = 40500 \Rightarrow x = ₹\,4500$

171. (a) Average of first n multiple

$$= \text{Multiplying factor} \times \left(\frac{n + 1}{2}\right)$$

∴ Average of first 15 multiples of 9

$$= 9 \times \left(\frac{15 + 1}{2}\right) = 72$$

172. (a) Average weight

$$= \frac{40 + 49 + 56 + 66 + 36}{5} = 49.4 \text{ kg}$$

173. (a) Average $= \dfrac{50 \times 105 + 5 \times 95}{55}$

$$= \frac{5250 + 475}{55} = 104.1 \sim 104$$

174. (c) Average price

$$= \frac{15 \times 60 + 8 \times 55 + 7 \times 40}{(15 + 8 + 7)}$$

$$= \frac{900 + 440 + 280}{30} = \frac{1620}{30} = ₹\,54/\text{kg}$$

175. (d) Weight Average

$$= \frac{2 \times 60\% + 4 \times 70\%}{2 + 4}$$

176. (b) Average of nine consecutive number is 45.

∴ 5th term = 45

∴ 9th term is largest number $= 45 + 4 = 49$

177. (d) Let numbers be

$a - 52, a - 50, \ldots\ldots, a, \ldots\ldots a + 50, a + 52$

∴ Required difference $= a + 52 - (a - 52) = 104$

178. (c) Average $= \dfrac{30 \times 92 + 20 \times 83}{30 + 20}$

$$= \frac{4420}{50} = 88.4$$

179. (c) Average $= \dfrac{40 + 49 + 56 + 72 + 36}{5}$

$$= \frac{253}{5} = 50.6 \text{ kg}$$

180. (b) Let salary of Vice-Chairman be ₹ x.

According to the question,

Average = ₹ 89600

$$\frac{22 \times 81400 + x}{23} = 89600 \Rightarrow x = ₹\,270000$$

181. (a) Average weight of family

$$= \frac{40 + 49 + 56 + 71 + 38}{5} = \frac{254}{5} = 50.8$$

182. (d) Assuming a, b, c, d and e are five athletes.

According to the question,

$$\frac{a + b}{2} = a + 1.5$$

$\Rightarrow \quad a + b = 2a + 3$ ...(i)

Again, $\dfrac{a + b + c}{3} = a + 3$

$\Rightarrow \quad a + b + c = 3a + 9$ ...(ii)

Again, $\dfrac{a + b + c + d}{4} = a + 4.5$

$\Rightarrow \quad a + b + c + d = 4a + 18$ ... (iii)

Again, $\dfrac{a + b + c + d + e}{5} = a + 6$

$\Rightarrow a + b + c + d + e = 5a + 30$ ...(iv)

Eq. (iv) – Eq. (iii), we get

$e = a + 12$

$e - a = 12$ kg

183. (c) The age of teacher

$= 20 \text{ yr} + 6 \text{ month} \times 40$

$= 20 \text{ yr} + 240 \text{ month} = 20 \text{ yr} + 20 \text{ yr}$

$= 40 \text{ yr}$

184. (c) Average grade for all students for both classes.

$$= \frac{20 \times 85\% + 30 \times 70\%}{20 + 30} = \frac{3800\%}{50} = 76\%$$

185. (a) Average weight of group including teacher $= \frac{55 \times 14 + 68}{15} = 55.86 \approx 56$

186. (b) Total People in group = 260

Number of women in group $= 260 \times \frac{1}{4} = 65$

Number of men $= 260 \times \frac{2}{5} = 104$

$\therefore$ Number of children = 260 – 65 – 104 = 91

Average age of women $= \frac{5}{6} \times 48 = 40$

Sum of age of women $= 40 \times 65 = 2600$

Sum of age of men $= 104 \times 48 = 4992$

Sum age of children $= 48 \times \frac{1}{3} \times 91 = 1456$

$\therefore$ Average age of group

$$= \frac{2600 + 4992 + 1456}{260} = \frac{9048}{260} = 34.8 \text{ yr}$$

187. (a) According to the question,

Age of teacher

$= 18 \times 15 - 14 \times 17 = 32$ yr

188. (d) Average $= \frac{\text{Sum of observation}}{\text{Number of observation}}$

$$= \frac{25 \times 80 + 15 \times 90}{40}$$

$$= \frac{2000 + 1350}{40} = \frac{3350}{40} = 83.75$$

189. (b) Let highest score be H and lowest score be L.

$H - L = 110$ ...(i)

According to the questions,

$40 \times 60 - 38 \times 58 = H + L$

$H + L = 196$ ...(ii)

From Eq. (i) and Eq. (ii), we get

$H = 153$

190. (c) Average marks of all students

$$= \frac{40 \times 50 + 50 \times 60 + 60 \times 75}{40 + 50 + 60}$$

$$= \frac{2000 + 3000 + 4500}{150}$$

$$= \frac{9500}{150} = 63.33$$

191. (d) Sum of prime number between 68 and 91 = 71 + 73 + 79 + 83 + 89 = 395

Average of prime numbers between 68 and 91 $= \frac{395}{5} = 79$

192. (c) Average weight of five members

$$= \frac{40 + 49 + 56 + 67 + 37}{5} = \frac{249}{5} = 49.8 \text{ kg}$$

193. (c) Sum of salary of 12 teachers

$= 71400 \times 12 =$ ₹ 856800

Sum of salary of 12 teachers, principal and vice principal $= 14 \times 89500 =$ ₹ 1253000

Average salary of principal and vice principal

$$= \frac{1253000 - 856800}{2} = ₹\,198100$$

194. (a) Let the age of fourth girl be x.

According to the question,

$$\frac{7 + 12 + 13 + x}{4} = 12$$

$32 + x = 48$

$x = 16$ yr

195. (c) Average weight of five members

$$= \frac{40 + 49 + 56 + 71 + 39}{5} = 51 \text{ kg}$$

196. (b) Average of two new player

$$= \frac{20 + 21}{2} + \frac{2\text{month} \times 11}{2}$$

$= \frac{41}{2} + 11$ month

= 20 yr + 6 month +11 month

= 20 yr +17 month

$= 21 \text{ yr } 5 \text{ month} = 21\frac{5}{12}$

197. (d) Average weight of family

$$= \frac{40 + 49 + 56 + 70 + 39}{5} = \frac{254}{5} = 50.8$$

198. (a) Average of six multiple of 7

$$= \frac{7 + 14 + 21 + 28 + 35 + 42}{6} = \frac{147}{6} = 24.5$$

199. (b) Average of 3 person

$$= \frac{(36 + 40 + 44)}{3} + \frac{12 \times 6}{3} = 40 + 24 = 64 \text{ yr}$$

200. (c) We know that,

Sum of squares of 'n' natural numbers

$$= \frac{n \times (n + 1)(2n + 1)}{6}$$

$\therefore$ Sum of squares of 1 to 10

$$= \frac{10 \times (10 + 1)(20 + 1)}{6}$$

$$= \frac{10 \times 11 \times 21}{6} = 385$$

Now, average $= \frac{385}{10} = 38.5$

When, Rahul subtract 5 from each number then average will also decreases by 5.

$\therefore$ Required average = 38.5 – 5 = 33.5

201. (d) Average $= \frac{300 + 129 + 49 + 120 + 102}{5}$

$$= \frac{700}{5} = 140$$

202. (a) Let 9th number be x.

$\because$ Average $= \frac{\text{Sum of observations}}{\text{Number of observations}}$

$\therefore$ $3 = \frac{8 \times 2 + x}{9}$

$\Rightarrow$ $27 = 16 + x \Rightarrow x = 11$

203. (a) Let initial number of student be x.

Average $= \frac{\text{Total weight}}{\text{Number of students}}$

$$71.4 = \frac{72 \times x - 11 \times 76 + 5 \times 79}{x - 11 + 5}$$

$\Rightarrow$ $71.4x - 428.4 = 72x - 836 + 395$

$\Rightarrow$ $0.6x = 441 - 428.4$

$\Rightarrow$ $0.6x = 12.6 \Rightarrow x = 21$

204. (a) Total expenditure

$= 3 \times 8600 + 4 \times 9750 + 5 \times 9920$

= ₹114400

Total saving = ₹ 65300

$\therefore$ Total income = 114400 + 65300 = ₹179700

$\therefore$ Monthly income $= \frac{179700}{12} =$ ₹14975

205. (d) The average monthly income of A and B = ₹3590 [$\because$ Sum $= n \times Avg.$]

$\therefore$ A + B = ₹ 7180 ...(i)

The average monthly income of B and C = ₹4250

$\therefore$ B + C = ₹8500 ...(ii)

The average monthly income of A and C = ₹6500

$\therefore$ A + C = ₹13000 ...(iii)

On adding Eqs. (i), (ii) and (iii)

2(A + B + C) = ₹28680

$\Rightarrow$ A + B + C = ₹14340 ...(iv)

From Eqs. (i) and (iv), we get

C = ₹7160

206. (d) Correct average

$$= \frac{50 \times 65 + 88 - 68}{50} = 65.40$$

207. (c) Total weight of 20 students

$= 55 \times 20 = 1100$ kg

Average weight of 20 students and 1 teacher

$= (55 + 0.5)$ kg = 55.5 kg

$\therefore$ Total weight of 20 students and 1 teacher

$= 55.5 \times 21 = 1165.5$ kg

$\therefore$ Weight of teacher = (1165.5 – 1100) kg

= 65.5 kg

208. (b) Sum of weight of parcels

$= 20 \times 15 = 300$ kg

Let the weight of new parcel be x kg.

$\therefore$ New average = 20 kg + 250gm

= 20.25 kg

According to the question,

$20.25 = \frac{300 + x}{16} \Rightarrow 324 = 300 + x$

$\therefore$ $x = 24$ kg

209. (d) Let total number of students be x.

Sum of weight of students = $56x$

$\therefore$ Sum of weight of seven students

$= 58 \times 7 = 406$ kg

According to the question,

$$56.2 = \frac{56x + 406}{x + 7}$$

$\Rightarrow$ $56.2x + 393.4 = 56x + 406$

$\Rightarrow$ $0.2x = 12.6 \Rightarrow x = 63$

210. (c) Let the two numbers be x and y.

$$\frac{x + y}{2} = 12 \Rightarrow x + y = 24$$

and $xy = 119$

$\therefore \quad (x + y)^2 = x^2 + y^2 + 2xy$

$\Rightarrow \quad (24)^2 = x^2 + y^2 + 2(119)$

$\Rightarrow \quad 576 = x^2 + y^2 + 238$

$\Rightarrow \quad x^2 + y^2 = 338 \quad \ldots(i)$

Now, $(x - y)^2 = x^2 + y^2 - 2xy$

$(x - y)^2 = 338 - 238$ [from Eq. (i)]

$\Rightarrow \quad (x - y)^2 = 100$

$\Rightarrow \quad x - y = 10$

211. (b) Sum of scores $= 41 \times 20 = 820$

$\therefore$ New average $= \dfrac{\text{Sum of scores}}{\text{Total number of innings}}$

$= \dfrac{820 + 41}{21} = \dfrac{861}{21} = 41$

212. (d) Let the average of 12 innings $= x$

According to the question,

$\dfrac{12x + 96}{13} = x + 3$

$\Rightarrow \quad 12x + 96 = 13x + 39$

$\Rightarrow \quad 13x - 12x = 96 - 39 \Rightarrow x = 57$

Average after 13th innings $= 57 + 3 = 60$

213. (c) Total weight of 20 students

$= 20 \times 30.5$ kg$= 610$ kg

Total weight of 26 students

$= (20 + 6) \times (30.5 + 2) = 26 \times 32.5 = 845$ kg

Average weight of 6 new students

$= \dfrac{845 - 610}{6} = \dfrac{235}{6} = 39.166 \text{ kg} \approx 39.2 \text{ kg}$

214. (d) The total sum of the score of 10 matches $= 40 \times 10 = 400$

and total sum of the scores of first 6 matches

$= 44 \times 6 = 264$

$\therefore$ Required average $= \dfrac{400 - 264}{4} = \dfrac{136}{4} = 34$

215. (c) The overall average score of the class

$= \dfrac{30 \times 85 + 20 \times 70}{30 + 20} = 79$

216. (c) Average weight of all men and women

$= \dfrac{17 \times 63 + 36 \times 54}{17 + 36} = \dfrac{1071 + 1944}{53}$

$= \dfrac{3015}{53} = 56.88 \approx 57$ kg

217. (b) Total weight of girls

$= 46 \times 22 = 1012$ kg

Total weight of whole class

$= 50 \times 37 = 1850$ kg

Now, the average weight of boys

$= \dfrac{1850 - 1012}{15} = \dfrac{838}{15} = 55.87$ kg

218. (b) Required average

$= \dfrac{2 + 3 + 5 + 7 + 11 + 13 + 17 + 19 + 23 + 29}{10}$

$= \dfrac{129}{10} = 12.9$

219. (b) Required average

$= \dfrac{(11 + 13 + 17 + 19)}{4} = \dfrac{60}{4} = 15$

220. (c) Required average

$= \dfrac{[(15 \times 41) - (21 + 24 + 39 + 47 + 97)]}{10}$

$= \dfrac{[615 - 228]}{10} = \dfrac{387}{10} = 38.7$

221. (a) Required average

$= \dfrac{(15 + 20 + 25 + 30 + 35 + 40 + 45 + 50 + 55 + 60)}{10}$

$= \dfrac{375}{10} = 37.5$

222. (a) Score of Rohit in the first inning

$= (5 \times 58) - (42 + 56 + 72 + 40)$

$= 290 - 210 = 80$

223. (d) Required average

$= \left[\dfrac{(1)^2 + (2)^2 + (3)^2 + (4)^2 + (5)^2}{5}\right]$

$= \dfrac{1 + 4 + 9 + 16 + 25}{5} = \dfrac{55}{5} = 11$

> **Speedy Method**
>
> Average of squares of first five natural numbers
>
> $= \dfrac{(5+1)(2 \times 5 + 1)}{6} = \dfrac{6 \times 11}{6} = 11$

224. (b) Let 32 consecutive natural numbers be $a, a + 1, a + 2, \ldots\ldots\ldots, a + 31$

According to the question,

Average of first 13 numbers $= x$

$\Rightarrow \quad \dfrac{a + a + 1 + \ldots\ldots\ldots + a + 12}{13} = x$

$\Rightarrow \quad 13a + \dfrac{12}{2}\{2 + (12 - 1)1\} = 13x$

$\Rightarrow \quad 13a + 6 \times 13 = 13x$

$\Rightarrow \quad a + 6 = x \Rightarrow a = x - 6$

$\therefore$ Average of next 19 numbers

$= \dfrac{a + 13 + a + 14 + \ldots\ldots\ldots\ldots + a + 31}{19}$

$= \dfrac{19a + \dfrac{19}{2}\{26 + 18\}}{19}$

$= a + 22 = x - 6 + 22 = x + 16$

225. (c) Average marks obtained by three students $= x$

$\therefore$ Total marks obtained by three students $= 3x$

According to the question,

$\Rightarrow \quad \dfrac{3x + \text{new student's marks}}{4} = (x + 2)$

$\Rightarrow 3x +$ New student's marks $= 4x + 8$

$\therefore$ New student's marks

$= 4x - 3x + 8 = x + 8$

226. (a) Let the first number is $4x$.

Then second number $= x$

$\dfrac{x + 4x}{2} = 65 \Rightarrow 5x = 65 \times 2$

$\Rightarrow \quad x = 13 \times 2 = 26$

227. (a) The new average

$= \dfrac{\text{Old average}}{2} = \dfrac{24}{2} = 12$

228. (a) Total age after adding the age of 5 new girls

$= 8y + y + 3 + y - 6 + y + 15 + y + 8 + y + 6$

$= 13y + 26$

Hence, new average age

$= \dfrac{13y + 26}{13} = (y + 2)$ yr

229. (b) Let the number of females in the family be x.

Then,

$\Rightarrow \quad 20 \times 6 + 6 \times x = 14.4(x + 6)$

$\Rightarrow \quad 120 + 6x = 14.4x + 86.4$

$\Rightarrow \quad 8.4x = 33.6$

$\therefore \quad x = 4$

230. (a) Sum of 10 numbers $= 10A$

New average $= \dfrac{10A - 9C - (C - 1)}{10}$

$= \dfrac{10A - 9C - C + 1}{10}$

$= \dfrac{10A - 10C + 1}{10} = A - C + 0.1$

231. (d) Total expenditure of the year

$= (10000 \times 3) + (12500 \times 4) + (13500 \times 5)$

$=$ ₹ 147500

$\therefore$ Total income of the year

$= 147500 + 32500 =$ ₹ 180000

$\therefore$ 70 % of average monthly income

$= \dfrac{70}{100} \times \dfrac{180000}{12} =$ ₹ 10500

232. (b) Average of first four prime numbers

$= \dfrac{2 + 3 + 5 + 7}{4} = \dfrac{17}{4}$

Average of first four composite numbers

$= \dfrac{4 + 6 + 8 + 9}{4} = \dfrac{27}{4}$

$\therefore$ Required ratio $= \dfrac{\left(\dfrac{17}{4}\right)}{\left(\dfrac{27}{4}\right)} = \dfrac{17}{27} = 17 : 27$

233. (c) Let third number be x.

$\therefore$ Second number $= 2x$

And first number $= 3 \times 2x = 6x$.

According to the question,

$\dfrac{6x + 2x + x}{3} = 45 \Rightarrow 9x = 45 \times 3$

$\Rightarrow \quad x = \dfrac{45 \times 3}{9} = 15$

$\therefore$ Required difference

$= 6x - 2x = 4x = 4 \times 15 = 60$

234. (d) We know that,

Average of square of first n natural numbers

$= \dfrac{(n + 1)(2n + 1)}{6}$

$= \dfrac{(7 + 1)(2 \times 7 + 1)}{6} \quad [\because n = 7]$

$= \frac{8 \times 15}{6}$

$\therefore$ Required average = 20

235. (d) Sum of 28 observations

$= 53 \times 28 = 1484$

Sum of first 11 observations $= 54 \times 11 = 594$

Sum of last 18 observations $= 52.5 \times 18 = 945$

Value of 11th observation $= 594 + 945 - 1484$

$= 1539 - 1484 = 55$

236. (b) Sum of 25 numbers $= 150 \times 25 = 3750$

Sum of 26 numbers $= 160 \times 26 = 4160$

$\therefore$ New number $= 4160 - 3750 = 410$.

237. (c) Wrong total of the class

= Average × Number of students

$= 190 \times 18 = 3420$

Correct total $= 3420 - 46 + 64$

$= 3484 - 46 = 3438$

$\therefore$ Correct average $= \frac{3438}{18} = 191$

Speedy Method

Correct average $= 190 + \left(\frac{64-46}{18}\right)$

$= 190 + \left(\frac{18}{18}\right) = 190 + 1 = 191$

238. (d) Let the first integer $= n$

And second integer $= n + 1$

According to the question,

$39 = \frac{(n+12)+(n+13)+\ldots\ldots+(n+24)}{13}$

$\Rightarrow \quad 13n + 234 = 39 \times 13$

$\Rightarrow \quad 13n + 234 = 507$

$\Rightarrow \quad 13n = 273$

$\Rightarrow \quad n = 21$

$\therefore$ Consecutive numbers are 21, 22, 23 ...... 45.

$\therefore$ Sum of 25 numbers $= \frac{25}{2}(21 + 45)$

$= \frac{25}{2}(66) = 25 \times 33$

$\therefore$ Required average $= \frac{25 \times 33}{25} = 33$

239. (b) Let the expense for 120 hens = ₹ x

and the expense for 260 hens = ₹$(x + 4050)$

The expense per hen = ₹ H (for 120 hens)

The expense per hen = ₹ $H - 3$ (for 260 hens)

According to the question,

$H \times 120 = x$ ...(i)

$(H - 3) \times 260 = x + 4050$ ...(ii)

From Eqs. (i) and (ii),

$260H - 780 = 120H + 4050$

$260H - 120H = 4050 + 780$

$\Rightarrow \quad H = \frac{4830}{140} = 34.5$

Now for x, $x = 120 \times H = 120 \times 34.5 = 4140$

Hence, original expenditure of the poultry

= ₹ 4140

240. (b) If all of the quantities multiplied by 6, then their average is also multiplied by 6.

According to the question,

The new average $= 47 \times 6 = 282$.

241. (b) $12.5 = \frac{16.5 + 9 + 10.5 + 12.5 + Y}{5}$

$62.5 = 48.5 + Y$

$\Rightarrow \quad Y = 62.5 - 48.5$

$\therefore \quad Y = 14$

242. (d) Required average $= \frac{53 \times 11 + 48 \times 13}{11 + 13}$

$= \frac{583 + 624}{24} = 50.29$

243. (d) Average marks of Rakesh in first 3 subjects is 80.

$\therefore \quad I + II + III = 80 \times 3 = 240$ ...(i)

Average marks of last 3 subjects is 92.

$III + IV + V = 92 \times 3 = 276$ ...(ii)

Given, marks in IIIrd subject is 51.

$\therefore \quad I + II = 189$ ...(iii)

and $IV + V = 225$ ...(iv)

$\therefore \quad I + II + III + IV + V$

$= 189 + 51 + 225 = 465$

Hence, average marks in all the 5 subjects

$= \frac{465}{5} = 93$

244. (d) Let the new average be x.

According to the question,

$90 \times 38 - 4 \times 90 = x \times 90$

$\Rightarrow \quad 3420 - 360 = x \times 90$

$\Rightarrow \quad 3060 = x \times 90$

$\therefore$ New average of observation (x)

$= \frac{3060}{90} = 34$

Speedy Method

If all observation subtract by 4 then their average is also subtract by 4.

So, new average $= 38 - 4 = 34$

245. ((b) The average of 24, 28, 27, 23 D and E is 29.

So, sum of $(24 + 28 + 27 + 23 + D + E) = 29 \times 6$

$\Rightarrow \quad (102 + D + E) = 174$

$\Rightarrow \quad D + E = 174 - 102$

$\Rightarrow \quad D + E = 72$

$\therefore$ Average of D and E is $\frac{D + E}{2} = \frac{72}{2} = 36$

246. (a) According to the question,

$X + Y + Z = 54 \times 3 = 162$ ...(i)

X is 10 more than average of $Y + Z$.

So, $\quad X = 10 + \left(\frac{Y + Z}{2}\right)$ ...(ii)

Again, Y is 12 more than average of Y and Z,

So, $\quad Y = 12 + \left(\frac{Y + Z}{2}\right)$

$\Rightarrow \quad 2Y = 24 + Y + Z$

$\Rightarrow \quad Y = 24 + Z$ ...(iii)

Put the value of Y in Eq. (ii),

$X = 10 + \frac{Z + 24 + Z}{2}$

$X = 10 + Z + 12$

$X - Z = 22$

247. (a) According to the question,

$28 \times 110 + 28B = 128 \times 28$

$\Rightarrow \quad 28B = 128 \times 28 - 110 \times 28$

$\Rightarrow \quad 28B = (128 - 110) \times 28$

$\Rightarrow \quad 28B = 28 \times 18$

$\therefore \quad B = 18$

Speedy Method

If a number x is added to the observations then average of the data also increases by x.

$\therefore$ New average = Original average + New number

$\therefore \quad 128 = 110 + B \Rightarrow B = 18$

248. (d) Let the total students be x.

According to the question,

$44x - 40 + 34 = 43.4x$

$\Rightarrow 44x - 43.4x = 6 \Rightarrow 0.6x = 6$

$\therefore \quad x = 10$

249. (d) The average of square of first n natural number $= \frac{(n+1)(2n+1)}{6}$

Here, $n = 17$

Average $= \frac{(17+1)(34+1)}{6} = \frac{18 \times 35}{6} = 105$

250. (d) Let the marks obtained by S_1, S_2 and S_3 be x, y and z, respectively.

Then, $\quad \frac{x + y}{2} = \frac{y + z}{2} + 35$

$\Rightarrow \quad x + y = y + z + 70$

$\Rightarrow \quad x - z = 70$

It is given that $z = 75$

$\therefore \quad x - 75 = 70 \Rightarrow x = 145$

So, marks obtained by S_1 is 145.

251. (a) Total sum of 12 numbers

$= 12 \times 60 = 720$

$\therefore$ Total deduction $= 5 \times 12 = 60$

and 10 is added to next 7 numbers

$\therefore$ Total addition $= 7 \times 10 = 70$

$\therefore$ New average $= \frac{720 - 60 + 70}{12} = 60.83$

252. (b) According to the question,

$P + Q + R = 40 \times 3$

$\Rightarrow \quad P + Q + R = 120$ ...(i)

And $\quad P + Q = 35 \times 2$

$P + Q = 70$ ...(ii)

Similarly, $Q + R = 45 \times 2$

$Q + R = 90$ ...(iii)

Subtract Eq. (i) from the sum of Eq. (ii) and (iii),

$P + Q + Q + R - (P + Q + R)$

$= 70 + 90 - 120$

$\therefore \quad Q = 40$

253. (c) ∵ Average of 5 numbers = 36
Let the last three numbers = a, b, c
and the first two numbers = x, y
According to the question,

$$\frac{(x+y)}{2} = 1.5 \times \frac{(a+b+c)}{3}$$

$$\Rightarrow \quad x + y = a + b + c \quad \ldots(i)$$

Now, $x + y + a + b + c = 36 \times 5$

$$2(x+y) = 180 \quad \text{[from Eq. (i)]}$$

∴ Sum of first two numbers

$$(x+y) = \frac{180}{2} = 90$$

254. (c) The first 31 odd numbers
1, 3, 5, 7, 9 .... a_{31}

$\therefore a_{31} = 1 + (31-1) \times 2 \Rightarrow a_{31} = 1 + 60 = 61$

So, the average of first 31 odd numbers

$$= \frac{1+3+5+7+9+\ldots\ldots+61}{31}$$

$$= \frac{\frac{31}{2}[1+61]}{31} = \frac{[1+61]}{2} = \frac{62}{2} = 31$$

Speedy Method

Average of first n odd numbers $= \frac{n^2}{n} = n$

∴ Average of first 31 odd numbers = 31

255. (a) According to the given information,

$$T + U + V = 42 \times 3 = 126 \text{ kg} \quad \ldots(i)$$

$$T + U = 40 \times 2 = 80 \text{ kg} \quad \ldots(ii)$$

and $U + V = 36 \times 2 = 72$ kg ...(iii)

Subtract Eq. (i) from the sum of Eq. (ii) and (iii),

$(T + U) + (U + V) - (T + U + V)$

$$\Rightarrow \quad = 80 + 72 - 126$$

$$\therefore \quad U = 26 \text{ kg}$$

256. (d) Sum of 4 numbers = 24 × 4 = 96.
Let the first two numbers are A and B.
And the last two numbers are C and D.
According to the question,

$$(A+B)/2 = 2(C+D)/2$$

$$\Rightarrow \quad (A+B) = 2(C+D)$$

Now, $A + B + C + D = 96$

$$\Rightarrow \quad 2(C+D) + C + D = 96$$

$$\Rightarrow \quad 3(C+D) = 96$$

$$\therefore \quad (C+D) = 32$$

257. (d) Total marks in 6 subjects = 75 × 6
∴ Total marks in remaining subjects

$$= 75 \times 6 - 80 = 450 - 80 = 370$$

258. (c) Let the first number = x
and the second number = $2x$
According to the question,

$$(x + 2x)/2 = 15 \Rightarrow 3x = 30$$

$$\therefore \quad x = 10$$

259. (c) Total income of 35 employees = 35 K
According to the question,

$$35K + 54000 = 36 \times 19000$$

$$\Rightarrow \quad 35K = 630000$$

$$\Rightarrow \quad K = ₹\ 18000$$

260. (c) Sum of 4 numbers = 52 × 4 = 208

$$\Rightarrow \quad a + b + c + d = 208 \quad \ldots(i)$$

According to the question,

$$\frac{a+b}{2} = 3 \times \left(\frac{c+d}{2}\right)$$

$$\Rightarrow \quad c + d = \frac{a+b}{3} \quad \ldots(ii)$$

From Eqs. (i) and (ii),

$$a + b + \frac{a+b}{3} = 208 \Rightarrow 3a + 3b + a + b = 624$$

$$\Rightarrow \quad 4(a+b) = 624$$

$$\therefore \quad a + b = 156$$

261. ((b) Sum of height of 6 friends

$$= 144 \times 6 = 864 \text{ cm}$$

Remaining sum of height of 5 person

$$= 864 - 150 = 714 \text{ cm}$$

$$\therefore \quad \text{New average} = \frac{714}{5} = 142.8 \text{ cm}$$

262. (c) Sum of marks of 13 students

$$= 130 \times 13 = 1690$$

But according to the question,
Correct sum of marks = 1690 − 23 + 32 = 1699
∴ Correct average marks of 13 students

$$= \frac{1699}{13} = 130.69$$

Speedy Method

Correct average $= 130 + \frac{32-23}{13}$

$= 130 + 0.68 = 130.69$

263. (c) Sum of weight of all 22 students

$$= 42 \times 22 = 924 \text{ kg}$$

Sum of 24 student's weight

$$= 924 + 33 + 39 = 996 \text{ kg}$$

New average weight of 24 students

$$= \frac{996}{24} = 41.5 \text{ kg}$$

264. (d) Sum of 5 numbers = 32 × 5 = 160
Sum of 4 numbers = 28 × 4 = 112
∴ Removed number = 160 − 112 = 48

265. (a) Required average

$$= \frac{2+3+5+7+11+13+17+19+23+29+31}{11}$$

$$= \frac{160}{11} = 14.54$$

266. (a) According to the question,
Sapna's expenditure for first three months

$$= 1100 \times 3 = ₹\ 3300$$

Sapna's expenditure for next 5 months

$$= 1000 \times 5 = ₹\ 5000$$

Sapna's expenditure for last 4 months

$$= 1200 \times 4 = ₹\ 4800$$

Total expenditure in years

$$= ₹\ 3300 + 5000 + 4800 = ₹\ 13100$$

Total saving = 1300
So, income of yearly

$$= \text{Expenditure} + \text{Saving}$$

$$= 13100 + 1300 = ₹\ 14400$$

So, average income monthly $= \frac{14400}{12}$

$$= ₹\ 1200$$

267. (d) Let the average weight of 34 persons $= x$ kg
Total weight of 34 persons = $34x$ kg
Let the weight of new person = y kg
According to the question,

$$\frac{34x - 90 + y}{34} = (x+3)$$

$$\Rightarrow \quad 34x - 90 + y = 34x + 102$$

$$\Rightarrow \quad y = 102 + 90 = 192 \text{ kg}$$

268. (b) Total weight of 8 persons

$$= 8 \times 40 = 320 \text{ kg}$$

Let the weight of removed person be x kg.
According to the question,

$$\frac{320 - x}{7} = 38$$

$$\Rightarrow \quad 320 - x = 266$$

$$x = 320 - 266 = 54 \text{ kg}$$

Speedy Method

Weight of the removed person

$= 40 \times 8 - 38 \times 7$

$= 320 - 266 = 54$ kg

269. (a) Total weight of boys = 50 × 50

$$= 2500 \text{ kg}$$

Numbers of girls = 80 − 50 = 30
∴ Total weight of girls = 30 × 40 = 1200 kg
Hence, average weight

$$= \frac{2500 + 1200}{80} = \frac{3700}{80} = 46.25 \text{ kg}$$

270. (a) Total weight of 45 boxes

$$= 52 \times 45 = 2340 \text{ g}$$

Total weight of 5 blue boxes

$$= 5 \times 40 = 200 \text{ g}$$

Total weight of 8 green boxes

$$= 8 \times 43 = 344 \text{ g}$$

Hence, required average

$$= \frac{2340 + 200 + 344}{45 + 5 + 8}$$

$$= \frac{2884}{58} = 49.72 \text{ g}$$

271. (b) Average marks of all students

$$= \frac{(45 \times 78) + (50 \times 65)}{45 + 50}$$

$$= \frac{3510 + 3250}{95} = \frac{6760}{95} = \frac{1352}{19}$$

272. (a) Total price of superior quality rice

$$= 10 \times 85 = ₹\ 850$$

Total price of inferior quality of rice

$$= 5 \times 46 = ₹\ 230$$

Total quantity of rice = (10 + 5) kg = 15 kg
Average price of mixture

$$= \frac{850 + 230}{15} = \frac{1080}{15} = ₹\ 72$$

273. (a) Sum of marks of eight students

$= 8 \times 7 = 56$

If found that marks of one student was taken as 10 instead of 6.

$\Rightarrow$ 56 – 10 (subtract wrong marks)

$\Rightarrow$ 46 + 6 = 52 (addition of correct marks)

$\therefore$ New average $= \frac{52}{8} = 6.5$

274. (c) Total sum of v number $= w^2 \times v$

Total sum of w number $= v^2 \times w$

$\therefore$ Required average $= \frac{w^2 \times v + v^2 \times w}{w + v}$

$= \frac{wv(w + v)}{w + v} = wv$

275. (b) According to the question,

Total age of girls = 30 × 14 = 420 yr

Now, (Boy + Girl) 18 = 19 Boy + 420

(Boy + 30) 18 = 19 Boy + 420

18 Boy + 540 = 19 Boy + 420

$\therefore$ Boy = 120

Speedy Method

Boys Girls

19 14

18

4 1

$\therefore$ Boys = 4 × 30 = 120

276. (a) Sum of 12 numbers = 12 × 47 = 564

Sum of first 5 numbers = 5 × 45 = 225

Sum of next 4 numbers = 4 × 52 = 208

Let 10th number $= x$

$\therefore$ 11th number $= x + 10$

12th number $= x - 5$

According to the question,

$564 = 225 + 208 + x + x + 10 + x - 5$

$\Rightarrow 564 = 438 + 3x \Rightarrow 3x = 126 \Rightarrow x = 42$

Average of 11 th and 12 th numbers

$= \frac{x + 10 + x - 5}{2} = \frac{2x + 5}{2} = \frac{2(42) + 5}{2}$

$= \frac{89}{2} = 44.5$

277. (b) Total weight of 30 students in class

= 60 × 30 = 1800 kg

After including teacher weight,

Total weight of class = (60 + 0.5) × (30 + 1)

= 60.5 × 31 = 1875.5 kg

$\therefore$ The weight of the teacher

= (1875.5 – 1800) = 75.5 kg

Speedy Method

$\therefore$ Weight of teacher = 60 + 31 × 0.5

= 60 + 15.5 = 75.5 kg

278. (a) Total score of 50 students

= 50 × 44 = 2200

Let average score of girls be x.

$\therefore$ Average score of boys $= x \times \frac{80}{100} = \frac{4x}{5}$

According to the question,

$50 \times \frac{40x}{100} + 50 \times \frac{60}{100} \times \frac{4x}{5} = 2200$

$\Rightarrow 20x + 24x = 2200 \Rightarrow 44x = 2200$

$\therefore x = 50$

279. (b) Required average $= \frac{20 \times 75 + 30 \times 60}{20 + 30}$

$= \frac{1500 + 1800}{50} = \frac{3300}{50} = 66$

280. (b) Total weight of 32 students

= 32 × 50 = 1600 kg

Let weight of teacher be x kg.

According to the question,

$1600 + x = 33 \times (50 + 0.5)$

$\Rightarrow x = 1666.5 - 1600 = 66.5$ kg

Speedy Method

Weight of teacher = 50 + 33 × 0.5 = 66.5 kg

281. (a) $\because$ Average of first n odd numbers $= n$

$\therefore$ Average of first 8 odd numbers = 8

282. (d) Average of $(P + Q)$ numbers

$= \frac{P \times Q^2 + Q \times P^2}{P + Q}$

$= \frac{PQ(Q + P)}{P + Q} = PQ$

283. (a) Let the amount of sales in the sixth month be ₹ x.

According to the question,

$\frac{6435 + 6927 + 6855 + 7230 + 6562 + x}{6} = 6500$

$\Rightarrow 34009 + x = 39000$

$\Rightarrow x = 39000 - 34009 = 4991$

05

Ratio & Proportion

Ratio

A ratio compares two similar quantities, showing how many times one quantity is compared to the other denoted by a colon (:).

- For non-zero numbers a and b, the ratio is written as $a : b$ and read as 'a ratio b'.
- The first term a is the antecedent and the second term b is the consequent.

Types of Ratio

1. **Duplicate Ratio** Duplicate ratio of $x : y$ will be $x^2 : y^2$.
2. **Sub-duplicate Ratio** Sub-duplicate ratio of $x : y$ will be $\sqrt{x} : \sqrt{y}$.
3. **Triplicate Ratio** Triplicate ratio of $x : y$ will be $x^3 : y^3$.
4. **Sub-triplicate Ratio** Sub- triplicate ratio of $x : y$ will be $\sqrt[3]{x} : \sqrt[3]{y}$.
5. **Inverse or Reciprocal Ratio** Inverse ratio of $x : y$ will be $y : x$.
6. **Compound Ratio** The ratio of the products of antecedent and consequent terms of two or more ratios is called compound ratio of their ratios.

   The compound ratio of three ratio $u : v$, $w : x$ and $y : z$ will be $uwy : vxz$.

Ex. 1 If $\frac{x}{2} = \frac{y}{3} = \frac{z}{8}$, then $x : y : z$ is equal to

Sol. Let $\frac{x}{2} = \frac{y}{3} = \frac{z}{8} = k$ and $x = 2k,\ y = 3k,\ z = 8k$

$\therefore$ Required ratio $= x : y : z = 2k : 3k : 8k = 2 : 3 : 8$

Division of Sum

- If m is divided in $a : b$, then

  1st part $= \frac{am}{a+b}$ and 2nd part $= \frac{bm}{a+b}$

- If m is divided in $a : b : c$, then

  1st part $= \frac{am}{a+b+c}$ and 2nd part $= \frac{bm}{a+b+c}$

  3rd part $= \frac{cm}{a+b+c}$

Proportion

Proportion is the equality of two ratios.

As, $w : x = y : z$, we write $w : x :: y : z$ and we say that w, x, y and z are in proportion.

Here, w and z are called extremes and x and y are means.

Essential Rules of Proportion

1. If $x \propto y$, then $x = ky$, where k is a constant.
2. If $x \propto \frac{1}{y}$, then $x = \frac{k}{y}$, where k is a constant.
3. Componendo and dividendo rule -

   If $w : x :: y : z$ or $\frac{w}{x} = \frac{y}{z}$, then $\frac{w+x}{w-x} = \frac{y+z}{y-z}$

4. If $\frac{a}{b} = \frac{c}{d} = \frac{e}{f} = k$, where k is constant, then $k = \frac{a+c+e}{b+d+f}$

Ex. 2 Find the third proportional of 8 and 4.

Sol. Let the third proportional be x.

$\therefore\ 8 : 4 :: 4 : x$

$\Rightarrow \frac{8}{4} = \frac{4}{x} \Rightarrow x = \frac{(4)^2}{8} = \frac{16}{8} = 2$

Ex. 3 $\frac{2+x}{4-x} = \frac{8-x}{1+x} = k$, find the value of k.

Sol. $k = \frac{2+x+8-x}{4-x+1+x} = \frac{10}{5} = 2$

Types of Proportion

- **Third proportional** If $w : x :: x : a$, then a is called the third proportional to w and x, then $a = \frac{x^2}{w}$.
- **Fourth proportional** If $w : x :: y : a$, then a is called the fourth proportional to w, x and y, then $a = \frac{xy}{w}$.
- **Mean proportional** If $w : a :: a : x$, then a is called the mean or second proportional between w and x, then $a = \sqrt{wx}$.

Questions Based on Word Problems

Ex. 4 Three numbers are in the ratio $2 : 3 : 5$. The sum of the numbers is 250. The difference of the first two numbers is

Sol. Let the numbers be $2x$, $3x$ and $5x$.

According to the question,

$$2x + 3x + 5x = 250$$

$$\Rightarrow \quad 10x = 250 \Rightarrow x = 25$$

$\therefore$ Required difference $= 3x - 2x = x = 25$

SSC Exam Scanner

SSC CGL 2024 (Tier I & II)

1. Adi and Dia together have ₹ 1440. If $\frac{3}{10}$ of Adi's amount is equal to $\frac{3}{5}$ of Dia's amount, how much amount does Dia have? **SSC CGL (Tier-II) 20/01/2025 Shift-I**

(a) ₹ 480 (b) ₹ 540
(c) ₹ 464 (d) ₹ 512

2. If $a:b=2:3$, $b:c=5:7$, then find the ratio $c:a$. **SSC CGL (Tier-II) 20/01/2025 Shift-I**

(a) 15 : 21 (b) 20 : 21
(c) 21 : 10 (d) 10 : 21

3. A sum of money is to be distributed among 3 friends *P*, *Q* and *R* in the proportion of 5: 3 : 4. If *P* gets ₹ 1500 more than *R*, what is *Q*'s share? **SSC CGL (Tier-II) 20/01/2025 Shift-I**

(a) ₹ 4950 (b) ₹ 4680
(c) ₹ 5100 (d) ₹ 4500

4. The monthly incomes of *A*, *B* and *C* are in the ratio 2 : 9 : 3 and their expenses are in the ratio 3 : 9 : 5. If *A*'s saving is half of his total income, then savings of *A*, *B* and *C* are, respectively, in the ratio of **SSC CGL (Tier-I) 26/09/2024 Shift-III**

(a) 3 : 9 : 2 (b) 2 : 5 : 2
(c) 3 : 18 : 4 (d) 1 : 2 : 1

5. If $a:b=c:d=e:f=5:7$, then what is the ratio $(3a+5c+11e):(3b+5d+11f)$? **SSC CGL (Tier-I) 26/09/2024 Shift-II**

(a) 7 : 11 (b) 3 : 7
(c) 5 : 7 (d) 11 : 7

6. If $A:B=6:8$ and $B:C=5:11$, then $A:B:C$ is **SSC CGL (Tier-I) 25/09/2024 Shift-II**

(a) 11 : 23 : 14 (b) 14 : 31 : 25
(c) 15 : 32 : 44 (d) 15 : 20 : 44

7. The salaries of *P* and *Q* together amount to ₹ 960000. *P* and *Q* save 64% and 44%, respectively of their individual salaries. If *P*'s expenditure is 1.5 times *Q*'s expenditure, then what is the ratio of *P*'s salary to *Q*'s salary? **SSC CGL (Tier-I) 25/09/2024 Shift-I**

(a) 2 : 3 (b) 7 : 3
(c) 3 : 7 (d) 3 : 2

8. The ratio of two numbers is 2 : 5 and their difference is 210. The smaller number is .... **SSC CGL (Tier-I) 24/09/2024 Shift-III**

(a) 60 (b) 150 (c) 140 (d) 350

9. If the mean proportional between *p* and *q* is 12, then the possible values of *p* and *q*, respectively, are **SSC CGL (Tier-I) 24/09/2024 Shift-II**

(a) 3, 38 (b) 3, 28 (c) 24, 6 (d) 24, 16

10. Find the fourth proportional to 4, 9 and 16. **SSC CGL (Tier-I) 23/09/2024 Shift-II**

(a) 18 (b) 27 (c) 36 (d) 16

11. 30 is the mean proportional of 18 and *A*. Find the value of *A*. **SSC CGL (Tier-I) 23/09/2024 Shift-I**

(a) 60 (b) 40 (c) 45 (d) 50

12. Initially the ratio of boys and girls in a college is 5 : 6. If 40 boys leave the college and 50 girls join the college, the ratio will become 8 : 11. Find the number of girls (initial) in the college. **SSC CGL (Tier-I) 19/09/2024 Shift-III**

(a) 740 (b) 860 (c) 720 (d) 640

13. The cost of a diamond varies directly as the square of its weight. Once, this diamond broke into four pieces with weights in the ratio of 4 : 3 : 2 : 1 .When the pieces were sold, the merchant got ₹ 63000 less than that of one piece. Find the original price of the diamond. **SSC CGL (Tier-I) 19/09/2024 Shift-I**

(a) ₹ 86000 (b) ₹ 80000
(c) ₹ 90000 (d) ₹ 75000

14. If $A:B=6:8$ and $B:C=7:12$, then $A:B:C$ is **SSC CGL (Tier-I) 18/09/2024 Shift-III**

(a) 14 : 31 : 20 (b) 21 : 32 : 40
(c) 11 : 23 : 40 (d) 21 : 28 : 48

15. The mean proportional of $4a^2$ and x is $\frac{1}{5a}$, where *a* is a positive number, then the value of *x* is .... **SSC CGL (Tier-I) 18/09/2024 Shift-II**

(a) $\frac{1}{100a^4}$ (b) $\frac{1}{100a^2}$
(c) $\frac{1}{25a^2}$ (d) $\frac{1}{25a^4}$

16. Find the mean proportional of 36 and 100. **SSC CGL (Tier-I) 18/09/2024 Shift-I**

(a) 65 (b) 60 (c) 55 (d) 70

17. In a company, the ratio of men and women is 5 : 3, respectively. When 150 additional women are employed in the company, the ratio becomes 5 : 4. How many men are employed in the company? **SSC CGL (Tier-I) 17/09/2024 Shift-II**

(a) 850 (b) 750 (c) 550 (d) 950

18. If $A:B=6:8$ and $B:C=7:10$, then $A:B:C$ is **SSC CGL (Tier-I) 17/09/2024 Shift-I**

(a) 21:28:40 (b) 21:23:40
(c) 23:32:40 (d) 14:31:20

19. In a collection of rare coins, there is one gold coin for every four non-gold coins. If 20 more gold coins are added to the collection, the ratio of the number of gold coins to that of non-gold coins will be 2 : 3. The total number of coins in the collection will now become .... **SSC CGL (Tier-I) 17/09/2024 Shift-I**

(a) 80 (b) 60 (c) 100 (d) 48

20. Find the mean proportional of 12.96 and 0.16. **SSC CGL (Tier-I) 13/09/2024 Shift-III**

(a) 1.21 (b) 1.96
(c) 1.44 (d) 1.69

21. If $A:B=6:8$ and $B:C=5:10$, then $A:B:C$ is **SSC CGL (Tier-I) 13/09/2024 Shift-I**

(a) 3 : 4 : 8 (b) 1 : 3 : 4
(c) 4 : 3 : 2 (d) 1 : 2 : 4

22. The mean proportional of 2 and 32 is .... **SSC CGL (Tier-I) 12/09/2024 Shift-III**

(a) 16 (b) 8 (c) 12 (d) 6

23. The ratio between male and female members in a club is 2 : 3. If the number of male members is increased by 200, the ratio becomes 5 : 6. How many female members are there in the club? **SSC CGL (Tier-I) 12/09/2024 Shift-II**

(a) 1200 (b) 900
(c) 1400 (d) 1000

24. If 28.9 : *x* :: *x* : 36.1, then find the value of *x*. **SSC CGL (Tier-I) 12/09/2024 Shift-I**

(a) 38.3 (b) 32.3
(c) 30.4 (d) 35

25. Raj divides ₹ 1200 in the ratio 2 : 1 : 3 among three of his friends. The amount equal to the sum of three times the largest share and two times the smallest share is **SSC CGL (Tier-I) 12/09/2024 Shift-I**

(a) ₹ 2400 (b) ₹ 1800
(c) ₹ 2200 (d) ₹ 2000

26. The incomes of *P*, *Q* and *R* are in the ratio 10 : 12 : 9 and their expenditures are in the ratio 12 : 15 : 8. If Q saves 25% of his income, then what is the ratio of the savings of *P*, *Q* and *R* ? **SSC CGL (Tier-I) 12/09/2024 Shift-I**

(a) 15 : 14 : 21 (b) 14 : 15 : 21
(c) 21 : 15 : 14 (d) 21 : 14 : 15

27. What is the ratio of the mean proportional of 1.21 and 0.09 with the mean proportional of 0.16 and 0.36? **SSC CGL (Tier-I) 11/09/2024 Shift-III**
(a) 11 : 8 (b) 13 : 8
(c) 13 : 12 (d) 11 : 13

28. Find the quotient, when the mean proportional of $7\frac{1}{5}$ and 245 is divided by an even prime number. **SSC CGL (Tier-I) 11/09/2024 Shift-II**
(a) 49 (b) 42 (c) 21 (d) 36

29. A sum of money is divided among P, Q, R and S in the proportion of 4 : 9 : 2 : 3. If Q gets ₹ 560 more than R, then the share of S is **SSC CGL (Tier-I) 11/09/2024 Shift-I**
(a) ₹ 140 (b) ₹ 340
(c) ₹ 240 (d) ₹ 440

30. If $A : B = 6 : 8$ and $B : C = 5 : 12$, then $A : B : C$ is **SSC CGL (Tier-I) 10/09/2024 Shift-II**
(a) 11:32:44 (b) 10:23:14
(c) 14:31:28 (d) 15:20:48

31. What is the value of D, if $A : C = B : D$ in the given table? **SSC CGL (Tier-I) 10/09/2024 Shift-I**

A	B	C	D
25	40	30	?

(a) 56 (b) 48
(c) 45 (d) 42

32. A money bag contains 1 rupee, 5 rupee and 10 rupee coins in the ratio of 3 : 5 : 7 respectively. If the total amount in the bag is ₹ 980, then find the number of coins of ₹ 10. **SSC CGL (Tier-I) 10/09/2024 Shift-I**
(a) 69 (b) 70 (c) 71 (d) 68

33. The mean proportional of $8a^2$ and $\frac{18}{a^4}$, where a is a positive number, is .... **SSC CGL (Tier-I) 09/09/2024 Shift-III**
(a) $\frac{12}{a^2}$ (b) $12a$ (c) $12a^2$ (d) $\frac{12}{a}$

34. If x varies inversely as y and $x = 2$ when $y = 6$, then the value of y when $x = 3$ is **SSC CGL (Tier-I) 09/09/2024 Shift-II**
(a) 2 (b) 3 (c) 4 (d) 6

35. The average marks (out of 100) of boys and girls in an examination are 75 and 80, respectively. If the average marks of all the students in that examination are 78. Find the ratio of the number of boys to the number of girls. **SSC CGL (Tier-I) 09/09/2024 Shift-I**
(a) 2 : 3 (b) 3 : 4
(c) 1 : 3 (d) 1 : 2

SSC CGL 2023 (Tier I & II)

36. The ratio of the number of coins of 25 paise, 50 paise, ₹ 2 and ₹ 5 is 5 : 4 : 3 : 1, respectively. If the total amount of the coins is ₹ 285, then the difference between the number of 25 paise and ₹ 5 coins is **SSC CGL (Tier-II) 06/03/2023 Shift-I**
(a) 80 (b) 30 (c) 40 (d) 60

37. The ratio of marks obtained by Rajesh, Rakesh and Ramesh in an exam is 2 : 4 : 9. What are the marks obtained by Rakesh and Ramesh, if Rajesh scored 30 marks in the exam? **SSC CGL (Tier-II) 03/03/2023 Shift-I**
(a) Rakesh = 40, Ramesh 90
(b) Rakesh = 60, Ramesh = 135
(c) Rakesh = 120, Ramesh = 180
(d) Rakesh = 90, Ramesh = 40

38. The ratio of the incomes of two employees is 7 : 4 and the ratio of their expenditures is 3 : 1. If each of them manages to save ₹ 4800 per month, find the sum of their monthly incomes (in ₹). **SSC CGL (Tier-II) 02/03/2023 Shift-I**
(a) 21120 (b) 20120
(c) 21150 (d) 18150

39. Two numbers are, respectively, 10% and 25% more than the third number. The ratio of the two numbers is **SSC CGL (Tier-II) 02/03/2023 Shift-I**
(a) 22 : 25 (b) 19 : 25
(c) 23 : 25 (d) 28 : 35

40. Avinash's monthly salary is ₹ 50000 and his monthly expenditure is ₹ 18000. Radha's monthly salary is ₹ 60000 and her monthly expenditure is ₹ 24000. Find the ratio of Radha's savings to Avinash's saving's. **SSC CGL (Tier-I) 27/07/2023 Shift-III**
(a) 9 : 8 (b) 9 : 7
(c) 6 : 5 (d) 8 : 7

41. The third proportional to 7 and 63 is **SSC CGL (Tier-I) 27/07/2023 Shift-III**
(a) 576 (b) 567
(c) 441 (d) 625

42. If the third proportional of $3x^2$ and $4xy$ is 48, then find the positive value of y. **SSC CGL (Tier-I) 27/07/2023 Shift-II**
(a) 3 (b) 5 (c) 2 (d) 4

43. What smallest positive number should be subtracted from 2 and 3 so that 4 is the third proportion to them? **SSC CGL (Tier-I) 26/07/2023 Shift-IV**
(a) 1 (b) 2 (c) 4 (d) 3

44. The ratio of the number of boys in a school to the total number of boys and girls in that school is 7 : 17. If the number of boys in that school is 1099, then how many girls are there in that school? **SSC CGL (Tier-I) 26/07/2023 Shift-II**
(a) 1570 (b) 1580
(c) 1560 (d) 1550

45. The fourth proportional to 8, 32 and 13 is **SSC CGL (Tier-I) 25/07/2023 Shift-III**
(a) 39 (b) 40 (c) 26 (d) 52

46. Which of the following is the lowest ratio? **SSC CGL (Tier-I) 25/07/2023 Shift-II**
(a) 8 :19 (b) 15 : 38
(c) 17 : 38 (d) 13 : 19

47. A pole is 9030 cm long. It is colored saffron, white and green in the ratio of 6 : 7 : 8. Find the length of the green part of the pole. **SSC CGL (Tier-I) 24/07/2023 Shift-IV**
(a) 3440 cm (b) 3010 cm
(c) 3480 cm (d) 2580 cm

48. Three numbers are in the ratio $\frac{4}{5}:\frac{5}{6}:\frac{9}{10}$. The difference between the smallest and the greatest numbers is 12. Find the number which is neither the smallest nor the greatest. **SSC CGL (Tier-I) 24/07/2023 Shift-II**
(a) 96 (b) 108
(c) 100 (d) 104

49. If 28 : 98 :: 98 : y, find the value of y. **SSC CGL (Tier-I) 21/07/2023 Shift-IV**
(a) 333 (b) 338
(c) 348 (d) 343

50. The fourth proportional of the numbers 8, 12 and 14 is **SSC CGL (Tier-I) 21/07/2023 Shift-III**
(a) 15 (b) 18
(c) 24 (d) 21

51. X, Y and Z completed a work costing ₹ 3400. X worked for 5 days, Y for 7 days and Z for 10 days. If their daily wages are in the ratio of 4 : 5 : 3, how much amount will be received by X? **SSC CGL (Tier-I) 20/07/2023 Shift-IV**
(a) ₹ 700 (b) ₹ 900
(c) ₹ 800 (d) ₹ 600

52. If $a : b :: b : c$ and $b = 96$, then which of the following can be a possible pair of values of a and c? **SSC CGL (Tier-I) 20/07/2023 Shift-II**
(a) $a = 24$; $c = 374$
(b) $a = 32$; $c = 288$
(c) $a = 48$; $c = 168$
(d) $a = 16$; $c = 586$

53. Radhika owns 2 dogs, 3 rabbits and 4 parrots as pets. What is the ratio of the number of rabbits to the total number of pets Radhika owns ?
SSC CGL (Tier-I) 20/07/2023 Shift-I
(a) 2 : 3 (b) 1 : 3
(c) 3 : 1 (d) 3 : 2

54. The third proportional between 25 and 35 is SSC CGL (Tier-I) 19/07/2023 Shift-III
(a) 35 (b) 49 (c) 40 (d) 25

55. The seats for Mathematics, English and Chemistry in a school are in the ratio of 6 : 4 : 7. If these seats are increased by 20%, 40% and 60% respectively, the ratio of the increased seats is
SSC CGL (Tier-I) 19/07/2023 Shift-II
(a) 9 : 7 : 8 (b) 9 : 7 : 14
(c) 1 : 2 : 3 (d) 7 : 9 : 14

56. *A* varies directly as $(B+18)$ and $A = 108$, when $B = 36$. Find the value of A when $B = 68$.
SSC CGL (Tier-I) 19/07/2023 Shift-I
(a) 75 (b) 86
(c) 127 (d) 172

57. Find the fourth proportional of 144, 192 and 216.
SSC CGL (Tier-I) 18/07/2023 Shift-IV
(a) 361 (b) 288
(c) 324 (d) 289

58. If $405 : y :: y : 125$, and $y > 0$, then find the value of y.
SSC CGL (Tier-I) 18/07/2023 Shift-II
(a) 225 (b) 205
(c) 215 (d) 235

59. In a factory, 48% of the number of male workers is equal to two-third of the number of female workers. What is the ratio of the number of males to that of the females in the factory? SSC CGL (Tier-I) 18/07/2023 Shift-II
(a) 25 : 12 (b) 12 : 25
(c) 18 : 25 (d) 25 : 18

60. The third proportional to $(x^2 - y^2)$ and $(x - y)$ is
SSC CGL (Tier-I) 18/07/2023 Shift-I
(a) $(x-y)$ (b) $\frac{x-y}{x+y}$
(c) $\frac{x+y}{x-y}$ (d) $(x+y)$

61. A bag contains ₹ 550 in the form of 50 paisa, 25 paisa and 20 paisa coins in the ratio 2 : 3 : 5. The difference between the amounts that are contributed by the 50 paisa and the 20 paisa coins is
SSC CGL (Tier-I) 17/07/2023 Shift-III
(a) ₹ 30 (b) ₹ 20 (c) ₹ 10 (d) ₹ 0

62. In a bag containing red, green and blue pens, the ratio of red, blue and green pens, in the given order, was 7 : 4 : 9. If the total number of pens in the bag was 320, how many of them were red?
SSC CGL (Tier-I) 17/07/2023 Shift-II
(a) 119 (b) 112
(c) 105 (d) 126

63. If the LCM and the HCF of two numbers are 12 and 2 respectively, then find the mean proportional of these numbers.
SSC CGL (Tier-I) 17/07/2023 Shift-I
(a) $2\sqrt{6}$ (b) $\sqrt{14}$
(c) 2 (d) $\sqrt{6}$

64. The ratio of the number of boys to that of the girls in a school is 11 : 15. If there are 200 more girls than boys in the school, what is the number of boys in that school ?
SSC CGL (Tier-I) 14/07/2023 Shift-IV
(a) 550 (b) 750
(c) 506 (d) 605

65. The mean proportion between 7 and 112 is SSC CGL (Tier-I) 14/07/2023 Shift-II
(a) 21 (b) 28
(c) 42 (d) 14

66. If the four numbers, 39, 117, 17 and y are in proportion, then find the value of y.
SSC CGL (Tier-I) 14/07/2023 Shift-I
(a) 49 (b) 51
(c) 85 (d) 57

SSC CGL 2022 (Tier I)

67. Find the mean proportional between 25 and 225.
SSC CGL (Tier-I) 13/12/2022 Shift-IV
(a) 65 (b) 25
(c) 75 (d) 85

68. X is directly proportional to the square of Y. When X is 12, then Y is 2. Find the value of X when Y is 3.
SSC CGL (Tier-I) 12/12/2022 Shift-IV
(a) 30 (b) 9 (c) 27 (d) 18

69. In a proportion, the 1st, 2nd and 4th terms are 51, 68 and 108 respectively. What is the 3rd term?
SSC CGL (Tier-I) 12/12/2022 Shift-III
(a) 84 (b) 83
(c) 82 (d) 81

70. What is the fourth proportional to 7, 15 and 21?
SSC CGL (Tier-I) 09/12/2022 Shift-IV
(a) 29 (b) 30
(c) 48 (d) 45

71. Three positive numbers are in the ratio of 4 : 5 : 7 and the sum of their squares is 15210. Find the sum of the three numbers.
SSC CGL (Tier-I) 09/12/2022 Shift-III
(a) 148 (b) 156
(c) 126 (d) 208

72. If 36 : 81 : : X : 63, what is the value of X ? SSC CGL (Tier-I) 09/12/2022 Shift-II
(a) 30 (b) 31
(c) 28 (d) 29

73. The third proportional of a and $\frac{b^4}{4a}$ is
SSC CGL (Tier-I) 09/12/2022 Shift-I
(a) $\frac{b^8}{16a^2}$ (b) $\frac{b^8}{8a^2}$
(c) $\frac{b^8}{8a^3}$ (d) $\frac{b^8}{16a^3}$

74. If $a : b = 4 : 5$ and $b : c = 3 : 10$, then $a : c$ is SSC CGL (Tier-I) 08/12/2022 Shift-IV
(a) 4 : 10 (b) 5 : 3
(c) 25 : 6 (d) 6 : 25

75. Find the fourth proportional to the numbers 17, 272 and 19.
SSC CGL (Tier-I) 08/12/2022 Shift-III
(a) 332 (b) 323
(c) 403 (d) 304

76. The fourth proportional to 16 and 26 and 32 is SSC CGL (Tier-I) 08/12/2022 Shift-II
(a) 16 (b) 52 (c) 54 (d) 24

77. Find the mean proportional between 27 and 300.
SSC CGL (Tier-I) 07/12/2022 Shift-IV
(a) 90 (b) 45 (c) 135 (d) 180

78. Find the fourth proportional to the numbers 24, 192 and 27.
SSC CGL (Tier-I) 07/12/2022 Shift-III
(a) 216 (b) 108
(c) 162 (d) 170.67

79. If 14 : 30 :: 7 : x, then what is the value of x?
SSC CGL (Tier-I) 07/12/2022 Shift-II
(a) 15 (b) 21 (c) 9 (d) 12

80. The mean proportional of 6 and 54 is .... more than 15.
SSC CGL (Tier-I) 07/12/2022 Shift-I
(a) 3 (b) 6 (c) 4 (d) 5

81. Rohan scored twice as many marks in English as he did in Science. His total marks in English, Science and Mathematics are 126. If the ratio of his marks in English and Mathematics is 2 : 3, his marks in English are
SSC CGL (Tier-I) 06/12/2022 Shift-IV
(a) 63 (b) 20 (c) 21 (d) 42

82. Find the mean proportion of $\frac{a^3+b^3}{a-b}$ and $\frac{a^2-b^2}{a^2-ab+b^2}$

SSC CGL (Tier-I) 06/12/2022 Shift-III

(a) 1 (b) $a+b$
(c) $\frac{a+b}{a-b}$ (d) $\sqrt{a+b}$

83. If x is the mean proportional between 12.8 and 64.8, then the value of x is

SSC CGL (Tier-I) 06/12/2022 Shift-II

(a) 32 (b) 34
(c) 28.8 (d) 26.4

84. The mean proportional of a and b is c. What is the mean proportional of a^2c and b^2c?

SSC CGL (Tier-I) 06/12/2022 Shift-I

(a) c (b) $3c$
(c) c^3 (d) c^2

85. Two numbers are in the ratio of 5 : 7. If 6 be added to each, the ratio becomes 3 : 4. Find the numbers.

SSC CGL (Tier-I) 05/12/2022 Shift-IV

(a) 30, 42 (b) 55, 88
(c) 10, 16 (d) 25, 40

86. The fourth proportion to 12, 24 and 27 is the same as the third proportion to A and 36. What is the value of A?

SSC CGL (Tier-I) 05/12/2022 Shift-III

(a) 22 (b) 24
(c) 26 (d) 20

87. A varies directly as the positive square root of B, and inversely as the cube of C. If $A = 15$, when $B = 27$ and $C = 2$, then find B when $A = 9$ and $C = 2$

SSC CGL (Tier-I) 05/12/2022 Shift-II

(a) $\frac{281}{42}$ (b) $\frac{243}{25}$
(c) $\frac{264}{37}$ (d) $\frac{275}{51}$

88. Which smallest positive number should be subtracted from each of 9 and 13 so that 18 is the third proportion to them?

SSC CGL (Tier-I) 03/12/2022 Shift-III

(a) 2 (b) 4 (c) 3 (d) 1

89. The cost of a piece of diamond varies with the square of its weight. A diamond of ₹ 6084 value is cut into 3 pieces whose weights are in the ratio 3 : 2 : 1. Find the loss involved in the cutting.

SSC CGL (Tier-I) 03/12/2022 Shift-II

(a) ₹ 3768 (b) ₹ 3718
(c) ₹ 3168 (d) ₹ 3518

90. Find the mean proportion between $(6+\sqrt{8})$ and $(3-\sqrt{2})$.

SSC CGL (Tier-I) 03/12/2022 Shift-II

(a) $2\sqrt{12}$ (b) $\sqrt{14}$
(c) $(6-\sqrt{8})$ (d) $\sqrt{15}-7$

91. If $a : b = c : d$, then which of the following ratio is equal to $a : c$?

SSC CGL (Tier-I) 03/12/2022 Shift-I

(a) $a : d$ (b) $b : c$
(c) $a + d : b + c$ (d) $a + b : c + d$

92. What is the ratio of the fourth proportional of 2, 5, 6 and the fourth proportional of 6, 8, 9?

SSC CGL (Tier-I) 02/12/2022 Shift-III

(a) 3 : 2 (b) 5 : 3
(c) 3 : 4 (d) 5 : 4

93. A, B, C and D share a property worth ₹ 93100. If $A : B = 1 : 2$, $B : C = 3 : 4$ and $C : D = 5 : 6$, then find the share of C.

SSC CGL (Tier-I) 02/12/2022 Shift-II

(a) ₹ 34000 (b) ₹ 28000
(c) ₹ 25000 (d) ₹ 31000

94. What is the ratio of the mean proportional between 1.6 and 3.6 and the third proportional of 5 and 8?

SSC CGL (Tier-I) 01/12/2022 Shift-II

(a) 2 : 15 (b) 5 : 16
(c) 3 : 16 (d) 4 : 15

95. The mean proportion of 169 and 144 is

SSC CGL (Tier-I) 01/12/2022 Shift-I

(a) 156 (b) 147
(c) 126 (d) 165

SSC CGL 2021 & 2020 (Tier I)

96. A certain sum is divided among A, B, C and D, such that the ratio of the shares is $A : B : C : D = 4 : 12 : 30 : 45$. If the difference between the shares of A and D is ₹5535, then the total sum (in ₹) is

SSC CGL (Tier-I) 24/08/2021 Shift-III

(a) 12785 (b) 13550
(c) 12285 (d) 11000

97. Monthly salaries of Anil and Kumud are in the ratio 19:17. If Anil and Kumud get salary hike of ₹2000 and ₹1000 respectively, then the ratio in their salaries become 8 : 7. What is the present salary of Kumud (in ₹)?

SSC CGL (Tier-I) 24/08/2021 Shift-II

(a) 38000 (b) 18000
(c) 34000 (d) 35000

98. If P is the third proportional to 3, 9, then what is the fourth proportional to 6, P, 4?

SSC CGL (Tier-I) 24/08/2021 Shift-I

(a) $\frac{3}{2}$ (b) 10 (c) 18 (d) $2\sqrt{3}$

99. If x is subtracted from each of 24, 40, 33 and 57, the numbers, so obtained are in proportion. The ratio of $(5x + 12)$ to $(4x + 15)$ is

SSC CGL (Tier-I) 23/08/2021 Shift-II

(a) 7 : 4 (b) 4 : 3
(c) 14 : 13 (d) 7 : 5

100. Fourth proportion to 12, 18, 6 is equal to the third proportion to 4, k. What is the value of k?

SSC CGL (Tier-I) 23/08/2021 Shift-I

(a) 6.5 (b) 4
(c) 6 (d) $4\sqrt{3}$

101. The ratio of monthly incomes of A and B is 4 : 5 and that of their monthly expenditures is 3 : 8. If the income of A is equal to the expenditure of B, then what is the ratio of savings of A and B?

SSC CGL (Tier-I) 20/08/2021 Shift-II

(a) 3 : 8 (b) 2 : 5
(c) 8 : 3 (d) 5 : 2

102. The ratio of two numbers A and B is 5 : 8. If 5 is added to each of A and B, then the ratio becomes 2 : 3. The difference in A and B is

SSC CGL (Tier-I) 20/08/2021 Shift-I

(a) 15 (b) 20
(c) 12 (d) 10

103. Find the ratio between the fourth proportional of 12, 16, 6 and the third proportional of 4, 6.

SSC CGL (Tier-I) 18/08/2021 Shift-I

(a) 4 : 3 (b) 3 : 2
(c) 11 : 5 (d) 8 : 9

104. A sum of ₹ 31866 is divided between A, B and C such that the ratio of shares A and B is 9 : 8 and that of A and C is 4 : 5. The share (in ₹) of B is

SSC CGL (Tier-I) 17/08/2021 Shift-I

(a) 9024 (b) 12690
(c) 10152 (d) 8460

105. Fourth proportion to 12, 18 and 6 is same as the third proportion to k and 6. What is the value of k?

SSC CGL (Tier-I) 16/08/2021 Shift-III

(a) $3\sqrt{6}$ (b) 4
(c) 13.5 (d) 3

106. Atul purchased bread costing ₹ 20 and gave a ₹ 100 note to the shopkeeper. The shopkeeper gave the balance money in coins of denomination ₹ 2, ₹ 5 and ₹ 10. If these coins are in the ratio 5 : 4 : 1, then how many ₹ 5 coins did the shopkeeper give?

SSC CGL (Tier-I) 13/08/2021 Shift-III

(a) 6 (b) 5 (c) 4 (d) 8

107. When x is subtracted from each of 19, 28, 55 and 91, the numbers so obtained in this order are in proportion. What is the value of x? **SSC CGL (Tier-I) 13/08/2021 Shift-I**

(a) 8 (b) 7
(c) 9 (d) 5

108. If $A : B = 3 : 5$, and $B : C = 2 : 3$, then $A : B : C$ is equal to **SSC CGL (Tier-I) 07/03/2020 Shift-I**

(a) 3 : 8 : 6 (b) 3 : 7 : 3
(c) 6 : 10 : 15 (d) 6 : 15 : 10

109. The sum of the squares of 3 natural numbers is 1029, and they are in the proportion 1 : 2 : 4. The difference between greatest number and smallest number is **SSC CGL (Tier-I) 06/03/2020 Shift-III**

(a) 21 (b) 18
(c) 15 (d) 31

110. In a wallet, there are notes of the denominations ₹ 10 and ₹ 50. The total number of notes is 12. The number of ₹ 10 and ₹ 50 notes are in the ratio of 1 : 2. Total money in the wallet is **SSC CGL (Tier-I) 06/03/2020 Shift-II**

(a) ₹ 440 (b) ₹ 280
(c) ₹ 360 (d) ₹ 110

111. If a sum of ₹ 1180 is to be divided among A, B and C, such that 2 times A's share, 5 times B's share and 7 times C's share, are equal, then A's share is **SSC CGL (Tier-I) 06/03/2020 Shift-I**

(a) ₹ 500 (b) ₹ 750
(c) ₹ 650 (d) ₹ 700

112. A certain amount is divided among Sunita, Amit and Vibha in the ratio of 2 : 3 : 4. If Vibha gets ₹ 14416, then the total amount is **SSC CGL (Tier-I) 05/03/2020 Shift-III**

(a) ₹ 16219 (b) ₹ 32436
(c) ₹ 3604 (d) ₹ 43248

113. When x is added to each of 10, 16, 22 and 32, the numbers so obtained in this order are in proportion? What is the mean proportional between the numbers $(x + 1)$ and $(3x + 1)$? **SSC CGL (Tier-I) 05/03/2020 Shift-II**

(a) 12 (b) 9
(c) 15 (d) 10

114. A sum of ₹x was divided between A, B, C and D in the ratio $\frac{1}{3}:\frac{1}{5}:\frac{1}{6}:\frac{1}{9}$.
If the difference between the shares of B and D is ₹ 832, then the value of x is **SSC CGL (Tier-I) 04/03/2020 Shift-III**

(a) ₹ 7592 (b) ₹ 7384
(c) ₹ 7696 (d) ₹ 7488

SSC CPO SI 2024 - 2020

115. If $\frac{5x + 3y}{5x - 3y} = \frac{7}{3}$, then find $x : y$. **SSC CPO 29/06/2024 Shift-II**

(a) 2 : 3 (b) 5 : 3
(c) 3 : 2 (d) 3 : 5

116. What is the ratio between S and T, if S is 75% of T? **SSC CPO 28/06/2024 Shift-III**

(a) 2 : 3 (b) 4 : 3
(c) 75 : 1 (d) 3 : 4

117. Arrange the following ratios in ascending order.
3 : 4, 3 : 5, 2 : 11, 7 : 2 **SSC CPO 28/06/2024 Shift-III**

(a) 3 : 5 < 2 : 11 < 3 : 4 < 7 : 2
(b) 2:11 < 3: 5 < 3 : 4 < 7 : 2
(c) 7 : 2 < 3 : 4 < 3 : 5 < 2 : 11
(d) 3 : 4 < 3 : 5 < 2 : 11 < 7: 2

118. Let a be a positive number and $b = \frac{4}{a}$.
What is the mean proportional of a and b? **SSC CPO 28/06/2024 Shift-III**

(a) a (b) 3
(c) 2 (d) 4

119. If four distinct positive numbers, a, b, c and d, in the order given are in proportion, then which of the following options is not correct? **SSC CPO 28/06/2024 Shift-II**

(a) b, a, d and c, in the order given are in proportion.
(b) c, d, b and a, in the order given are in proportion.
(c) a, c, b and d, in the order given are in proportion.
(d) d, c, b and a, in the order given are in proportion.

120. Find the natural number obtained when the number 13 is subtracted from the mean proportional of 75 and 12. **SSC CPO 28/06/2024 Shift-I**

(a) 14 (b) 27
(c) 17 (d) 30

121. A sum of ₹ 17600 was divided between Jeevan, Praveen and Kanan, such that the ratio of the sums received by Jeevan and Praveen was 5 : 8, while the ratio of the sums received by Praveen and Kanan was 3 : 2. How much money did Jeevan receive as his share? **SSC CPO 28/06/2024 Shift-I**

(a) ₹ 4850 (b) ₹ 4750
(c) ₹ 4800 (d) ₹ 4900

122. The ratio of marks of A and B is 3 : 4 and the ratio of marks of B and C is 4 : 5. If the difference in the marks of C and A is 30, then how much marks does B get? **SSC CPO 27/06/2024 Shift-III**

(a) 52 (b) 60
(c) 56 (d) 64

123. If 40 % of A = 60% of $B = \frac{1}{6}$ of C, then find the ratio of A: B: C. **SSC CPO 27/06/2024 Shift-III**

(a) 15 : 10 : 36 (b) 36 : 10 : 15
(c) 15 : 10 : 18 (d) 10 : 15 : 36

124. In a class, the numbers of boys and girls are in the ratio of 3 : 5. What is the percentage of boys in the class? **SSC CPO 27/06/2024 Shift-II**

(a) 60% (b) 12.5%
(c) 42.5% (d) 37.5%

125. Find the fourth proportion to 10, 12 and 15. **SSC CPO 27/06/2024 Shift-II**

(a) 20 (b) 22
(c) 16 (d) 18

126. Two numbers are in the ratio of 3 : 7. If 11 is subtracted from each, the ratio between the numbers becomes 7 : 20. Find the smaller number. **SSC CPO 27/06/2024 Shift-I**

(a) 39 (b) 27 (c) 36 (d) 21

127. The fourth proportional to 4, a and $16a$ is 81. What is the value of a? **SSC CPO 27/06/2024 Shift-I**

(a) $\frac{13}{2}$ (b) $\frac{5}{2}$
(c) $\frac{9}{2}$ (d) $\frac{11}{2}$

128. Find the fourth proportional of 22, 66 and 11. **SSC CPO 05/10/2023 Shift-III**

(a) 23 (b) 33
(c) 17 (d) 39

129. In a school of 720 students, the ratio of boys to girls is 3 : 5. Find how many new boys may be allowed to the school if 18 new girls are admitted, so that the ratio of boys to girls changes to 2 : 3. **SSC CPO 05/10/2023 Shift-III**

(a) 42 (b) 44
(c) 50 (d) 38

130. The ratio of monthly income and expenditure of a man is 7: 3. If his expenditure is ₹ 5400, find his monthly income. **SSC CPO 05/10/2023 Shift-III**

(a) ₹ 12600 (b) ₹ 13300
(c) ₹ 11500 (d) ₹ 10400

131. The fourth proportional to 0.3, 0.8 and 0.108 is **SSC CPO 04/10/2023 Shift-II**

(a) 0.144 (b) 0.124
(c) 0.288 (d) 0.482

132. Two numbers are in the ratio 5 : 3 and the difference between these two numbers is 34. Find the smaller of the two numbers. SSC CPO 03/10/2023 Shift-I

(a) 51 (b) 85
(c) 68 (d) 34

133. If 42, 36 and 35 are the first three terms of a proportion, then the fourth term is SSC CPO 03/10/2023 Shift-I

(a) 27 (b) 28
(c) 30 (d) 32

134. The third proportional of 0.024 and 0.12 is SSC CPO 11/11/2022 Shift-I

(a) 0.060 (b) 6.000
(c) 0.6 (d) 0.006

135. The ratio of the third proportional to 16 and 40 and the mean proportional between 10 and 40 is SSC CPO 11/11/2022 Shift-I

(a) 5 : 1 (b) 1 : 5
(c) 4 : 1 (d) 1 : 4

136. The average height of three kids is 56 cm and their heights are in the proportion of 7 : 8 : 9. Find the heights of all the three. SSC CPO 11/11/2022 Shift-I

(a) 42 cm, 48 cm, 54 cm
(b) 56 cm, 64 cm, 72 cm
(c) 35 cm, 40 cm, 45 cm
(d) 49 cm, 56 cm, 63 cm

137. Which of the following is the smallest ratio? SSC CPO 10/11/2022 Shift-I

(a) 41 : 92
(b) 33 : 41
(c) 42 : 49
(d) 35 : 47

138. If the total price of three chairs is ₹ 14014 and their prices are in the ratio of 3 : 4 : 7, then the highest price (in ₹) of chair is SSC CPO 24/11/2020 Shift-I

(a) 3003 (b) 1001
(c) 7007 (d) 5005

SSC CHSL 2024 (Tier I & II)

139. What should be added to each term of the ratio 5 : 11 so that the ratio becomes 3 : 5 ? SSC CHSL (Tier-I) 11/07/2024 Shift-IV

(a) 6 (b) 4
(c) 2 (d) 5

140. Find the mean proportion to 0.72 and 2.85 (round up to one decimal place). SSC CHSL (Tier-I) 11/07/2024 Shift-III

(a) 0.4 (b) 2.8
(c) 0.7 (d) 1.4

141. The ratio of red to green sweets in a bag is 3 : 4. How many red sweets are there in the bag, if the number of green sweets is 120? SSC CHSL (Tier-I) 11/07/2024 Shift-I

(a) 100 (b) 80 (c) 70 (d) 90

142. Which of the following ratios is greater? SSC CHSL (Tier-I) 10/07/2024 Shift-III

(a) 7 : 4 (b) 2 : 3 (c) 8 : 3 (d) 1 : 5

143. If $x : y = 5 : 6$, then $2x + 3y : 3x + 5y$ is SSC CHSL (Tier-I) 10/07/2024 Shift-II

(a) 28 : 48 (b) 28 : 45
(c) 18 : 45 (d) 18 : 35

144. Raju and Ramu have more land than Sonu by 15% and 25%, respectively. What is the ratio of land owned by Raju and Ramu? SSC CHSL (Tier-I) 10/07/2024 Shift-I

(a) 23 : 25 (b) 25 : 23
(c) 21 : 23 (d) 15 : 25

145. The strength of a school is 640, with the number of boys being 400. Find the ratio of girls to boys. SSC CHSL (Tier-I) 9/07/2024 Shift-IV

(a) 8 : 5 (b) 5 : 6 (c) 4 : 5 (d) 3 : 5

146. If $A : B = 5 : 8$ and $B : C = 7 : 8$, then find $A : C$. SSC CHSL (Tier-I) 9/07/2024 Shift-III

(a) 35 : 64 (b) 55 : 30
(c) 34 : 64 (d) 35 : 56

147. The age of a tree depends on the number of rings in the trunk. The value of a such tree is proportional to its age. If a tree with 40 rings and 50 yr of age has a value of ₹ 50000, then a tree with 30 rings is ...... yr of age and its value is ₹ .... SSC CHSL (Tier-I) 9/07/2024 Shift-II

(a) 37.5, 57500 (b) 37.5, 37500
(c) 57.5, 57500 (d) 57.5, 37500

148. If $A : B = 2 : 3$ and $B : C = 7 : 8$, find $A : C$. SSC CHSL (Tier-I) 08/07/2024 Shift-IV

(a) 12 : 7 (b) 7 : 12 (c) 4: 7 (d) 7 : 2

149. Find the mean proportional between 25 and 81. SSC CHSL (Tier-I) 08/07/2024 Shift-III

(a) 36 (b) 12 (c) 45 (d) 81

150. Two numbers are in the ratio 2 : 3. Their sum is 135. Find the numbers. SSC CHSL (Tier-I) 08/07/2024 Shift-II

(a) 50, 85 (b) 60, 75
(c) 54, 81 (d) 45, 90

151. Find the fourth proportion to 1.25, 5.75 and 3.5. SSC CHSL (Tier-I) 05/07/2024 Shift-IV

(a) 4.5 (b) 16.1 (c) 6.5 (d) 12.5

152. The mean proportion of 0.14 and 2.24 is SSC CHSL (Tier-I) 05/07/2024 Shift-III

(a) 1.02 (b) 1.12
(c) –2.39 (d) 0.56

153. R gives $\frac{3}{8}$ of the toffees, he has with him to S. If now R has k% of the toffies with S, then find the value of k. SSC CHSL (Tier-I) 05/07/2024 Shift-III

(a) $\frac{200}{3}$ (b) 200 (c) $\frac{500}{3}$ (d) 140

154. If $\frac{1}{M}:\frac{1}{N}:\frac{1}{O} = 3:4:5$, then $M : N : O$ is equal to SSC CHSL (Tier-I) 05/07/2024 Shift-II

(a) 12 : 15 : 20 (b) 15 : 20 : 12
(c) 20 : 12 : 15 (d) 20 : 15 : 12

155. If $a : b = 3 : 4$, $b : c = 2 : 3$ and $c : d = 5 : 6$, then $a : b : c : d$ is SSC CHSL (Tier-I) 05/07/2024 Shift-I

(a) 15 : 25 : 30 : 36 (b) 15 : 20 : 30 : 36
(c) 15 : 20 : 35 : 36 (d) 10 : 20 : 30 : 36

156. Find the third proportion to 36 and 48. SSC CHSL (Tier-I) 04/07/2024 Shift-III

(a) 36 (b) 54 (c) 64 (d) 48

157. Find the fourth proportional to 2, 6, 8. SSC CHSL (Tier-I) 04/07/2024 Shift-II

(a) 12 (b) 48 (c) 36 (d) 24

158. A box filled with gift articles weighs 25 kg. If the weight of the box and the gift articles, respectively, are in the ratio 1 : 9, then the weight of the articles (in grams) is SSC CHSL (Tier-I) 04/07/2024 Shift-I

(a) 21500 (b) 22500
(c) 24500 (d) 23500

159. When x is added to each of the numbers 7, 11, 18 and 23, then the number so obtained are in proportion. What is the mean proportional between the $(x - 1)$ and $(2x - 10)$? SSC CHSL (Tier-I) 03/07/2024 Shift-IV

(a) 68 (b) 78 (c) 98 (d) 48

160. Which is the greatest ratio among the following?

$\frac{8}{11}, \frac{4}{5}, \frac{1}{2}$ and $\frac{1}{11}$ SSC CHSL (Tier-I) 03/07/2024 Shift-III

(a) $\frac{4}{5}$ (b) $\frac{1}{2}$
(c) $\frac{1}{11}$ (d) $\frac{8}{11}$

161. If $a : b = 3 : 7$ and $b : c = 4 : 9$, then find $a : b : c$. SSC CHSL (Tier-I) 03/07/2024 Shift-II

(a) 12 : 28 : 63 (b) 3 : 28 : 63
(c) 12 : 28 : 9 (d) 3 : 28 : 9

162. Among the ratios 3 : 4, 5 : 8, 1 : 2, 6 : 9, which is the greatest?
SSC CHSL (Tier-I) 03/07/2024 Shift-I
(a) 5 : 8 (b) 3 : 4
(c) 6 : 9 (d) 1 : 2

163. Divide some money in the ratio between Ravi, Reeta and Rahul such that 5 (Part of Ravi) = 3 (Part of Reeta) = 11 (Part of Rahul). The money ratio of Ravi : Reeta : Rahul is equal to
SSC CHSL (Tier-I) 02/07/2024 Shift-IV
(a) 5 : 11 : 3 (b) 33 : 55 : 15
(c) 11 : 33 : 15 (d) 11 : 5 : 3

164. Two quantities are in the ratio 3 : 5. If the first quantity is 155 kg. Find the other quantity (approximately).
SSC CHSL (Tier-I) 02/07/2024 Shift-III
(a) 258.3 kg (b) 150.5 kg
(c) 200.4 kg (d) 240.6 kg

165. If 35 is the mean proportional of 25 and x, then what is value of x?
SSC CHSL (Tier-I) 02/07/2024 Shift-II
(a) 46 (b) 47 (c) 49 (d) 48

166. M varies inversely as $(N^2 + 3)$. If $M = 3$ when $N = 3$, then what will be the value of M, when $N^2 = 69$?
SSC CHSL (Tier-I) 01/07/2024 Shift-IV
(a) $\frac{1}{2}$ (b) 1 (c) $\sqrt{69}$ (d) $\frac{1}{4}$

167. The difference between two numbers is 48. The ratio of these two numbers is 7 : 3. What is the sum of the two numbers?
SSC CHSL (Tier-I) 01/07/2024 Shift-IV
(a) 110 (b) 90
(c) 100 (d) 120

168. P pays Q a sum of ₹ 150 using coins of ₹ 2, ₹ 5 and ₹ 10. He uses a total of 50 coins. If the ratio of ₹ 2 and ₹ 5 coins used is 5 : 2, then how many coins of ₹ 10 are used in the payment?
SSC CHSL (Tier-I) 01/07/2024 Shift-III
(a) 1 (b) 4 (c) 5 (d) 2

169. If $A : B = 3 : 7$ and $B : C = 2 : 5$, find $A : B : C$ **SSC CHSL (Tier-I) 01/07/2024 Shift-III**
(a) 10 : 3 : 4 (b) 4 : 10 : 3
(c) 4 : 3 : 10 (d) 6 : 14 : 35

170. If $2^3 : 8^{5.06} :: 8^{-4.06} : x$, find the value of x.
SSC CHSL (Tier-I) 01/07/2024 Shift-II
(a) $\frac{1}{2^3}$ (b) 1 (c) 2^3 (d) 0

171. Radhika requested the cashier of a bank to get her coins in lieu of her cheque worth ₹ 1845. Cashier gave her a packet containing ₹ 5, ₹ 10 and ₹ 20 coins in the ratio of 3 : 5 : 7. What is the total worth of the smallest coin received by her?
SSC CHSL (Tier-I) 01/07/2024 Shift-I
(a) ₹ 125 (b) ₹ 105 (c) ₹ 145 (d) ₹ 135

172. The ratio of prices of coffee and tea is 3 : 4 and the ratio of their quantities consumed by a family is 4 : 7. Find the ratio of expenditures on coffee and tea.
SSC CHSL (Tier II) 10/01/2024 Shift-I
(a) 3 : 7 (b) 7 : 3 (c) 7 : 4 (d) 4 : 7

173. The ratio of the expenditure to the savings of Richa is 2 : 1. If her income and expenditure increase by 20% and 15%, respectively, then find the percentage increase in her savings. **SSC CHSL (Tier II) 10/01/2024 Shift-I**
(a) 35% (b) 30% (c) 20% (d) 25%

SSC CHSL 2023-2021 (Tier I)

174. If $a : b = 3 : 7$, then $(2a + 3b) : (3a + 2b)$ is **SSC CHSL (Tier I) 17/08/2023 Shift-I**
(a) 27 : 23 (b) 23 : 29
(c) 21 : 29 (d) 21 : 23

175. What is the third proportional to 12 and $6\sqrt{5}$?
SSC CHSL (Tier I) 14/08/2023 Shift-IV
(a) 12 (b) 15 (c) 18 (d) 21

176. Find the fourth proportion of the numbers $\frac{1}{3}$rd of 15, $\frac{4}{5}$th of 25, $\frac{3}{7}$ th of 35. **SSC CHSL (Tier I) 09/08/2023 Shift-I**
(a) 65 (b) 55 (c) 60 (d) 50

177. If 2 : 9 :: 4 : x, then the value of x is
SSC CHSL (Tier I) 08/08/2023 Shift-II
(a) 42 (b) 18 (c) 36 (d) 22

178. The difference between 24 and the mean proportional of 7 and 63 is
SSC CHSL (Tier I) 07/08/2023 Shift-IV
(a) 3 (b) 2 (c) 5 (d) 4

179. Find the third proportional of 25 and 45 **SSC CHSL (Tier I) 02/08/2023 Shift-I**
(a) 85 (b) 65 (c) 81 (d) 76

180. In a school there are total 414 students. The ratio of boys and girls is 5 : 4. If 46 more boys gets admitted into the school, then what will be the new ratio of boys and girls? **SSC CHSL (Tier I) 21/03/2023 Shift-II**
(a) 3 : 1 (b) 4 : 3
(c) 5 : 2 (d) 3 : 2

181. If $A : B = 2 : 3, B : C = 6 : 7, C : D = 14 : 3$, then find $A : B : C : D$.
SSC CHSL (Tier I) 20/03/2023 Shift-III
(a) 12 : 12 : 4 : 6 (b) 7 : 2 : 10 : 4
(c) 8 : 12 : 14 : 3 (d) 8 : 5 : 14 : 6

182. ₹ 13000 is divided among X, Y and Z such that 2 times of X's share is equal to 3 times of Y's share which is equal to 4 times of Z's share. What is the share of Y?
SSC CHSL (Tier I) 17/03/2023 Shift-II
(a) ₹ 3200 (b) ₹ 4800
(c) ₹ 5600 (d) ₹ 4000

183. If $p : q = 3 : 5$ and $p : r = 2 : 3$, then what is the value of $3p : 4q : 3r$?
SSC CHSL (Tier I) 16/03/2023 Shift-II
(a) 12 : 8 : 9 (b) 18 : 40 : 27
(c) 10 : 5 : 4 (d) 9 : 5 : 4

184. 50% of A is equal to 80% of B. What is the ratio between A and B ?
SSC CHSL (Tier I) 13/03/2023 Shift-III
(a) 4 : 5 (b) 5 : 8 (c) 8 : 5 (d) 5 : 4

185. Find the fourth proportional to 7, 13 and 21. **SSC CHSL (Tier I) 02/06/2022 Shift-I**
(a) 14 (b) 26 (c) 39 (d) 21

186. A and B share a few marbles in the ratio 4 : 5. If B gets 10 marbles more than A, then what is A's share?
SSC CHSL (Tier I) 01/06/2022 Shift-I
(a) 8 marbles (b) 42 marbles
(c) 12 marbles (d) 40 marbles

187. If $a : b = 2 : 3$ and $b : c = 6 : 8$, then find $a : b : c$. **SSC CHSL (Tier I) 31/05/2022 Shift-I**
(a) 2 : 3 : 5 (b) 2 : 3 : 4
(c) 1 : 2 : 3 (d) 2 : 3 : 6

188. In a bag, black tablet covers and white tablet covers are in the ratio 5 : 9. If there are 450 white tablet covers, how many black tablet covers are there in the bag?
SSC CHSL (Tier I) 30/05/2022 Shift-I
(a) 200 (b) 275 (c) 225 (d) 250

189. The fourth proportional to 5, 8 and 30 is **SSC CHSL (Tier I) 27/05/2022 Shift-I**
(a) 50 (b) 60 (c) 48 (d) 90

190. Two numbers A and B are in the ratio 13 : 17. If A is increased by 15% and B is increased by 30%, then the new ratio of A to B will be
SSC CHSL (Tier I) 12/08/2021 Shift-III
(a) 21 : 29 (b) 21 : 31
(c) 23 : 34 (d) 23 : 33

191. If $A : B = 11 : 7$ and $B : C = 5 : 19$, then what is $A : B : C$?
SSC CHSL (Tier I) 04/08/2021 Shift-I
(a) 55 : 35 : 133 (b) 35 : 55 : 133
(c) 35 : 133 : 55 (d) 55 : 133 : 35

192. The ratio of boys and girls in a school is 6 : 7. If the total number of students in the school is 3289, then what is the number of girls?
SSC CHSL (Tier I) 19/04/2021 Shift-I
(a) 1771 (b) 1876 (c) 1984 (d) 1569

193. A's salary increases in the ratio 8 : 11. If his new salary is ₹ 33000, then what was his original salary (in ₹)? **SSC CHSL (Tier I) 12/04/2021 Shift-II**

(a) 20000 (b) 18000
(c) 22000 (d) 24000

SSC MTS 2024

194. The quantity of milk ordered on the first, second, third and fourth day of a four day ceremony is in the proportion of 30 litres, 24 litres, 35 litres and 'x' litres, respectively. Find the quantity of milk (in litres) ordered on the fourth day. **SSC MTS 14/11/2024 Shift-III**

(a) 30 (b) 32 (c) 28 (d) 26

195. If 49 : x :: x : 81 and 64 : y :: y : 169, where x and y are both natural numbers, then find the value of $2x + 3y$. **SSC MTS 13/11/2024 Shift-III**

(a) 312 (b) 126 (c) 348 (d) 438

196. What is the mean proportional between $(6 - 2\sqrt{2})$ and $(9 + 3\sqrt{2})$? **SSC MTS 12/11/2024 Shift-III**

(a) $\sqrt{54}$ (b) $\sqrt{52}$ (c) $\sqrt{66}$ (d) $\sqrt{42}$

197. The ratio between the monthly incomes of P and Q is 7 : 6 and the ratio between their expenditures is 6 : 5. If they save ₹ 480 each, then find P's monthly income. **SSC MTS 11/11/2024 Shift-III**

(a) ₹ 2880 (b) ₹ 2400
(c) ₹ 6240 (d) ₹ 3360

198. A person divided a certain sum among his three sons in the ratio 3 : 4 : 5. Had he divided the sum in the ratio $\frac{1}{3}:\frac{1}{4}:\frac{1}{5}$, the son, who got the least share earlier, would have got ₹ 1188 more. The sum (in ₹) was **SSC MTS 05/11/2024 Shift-III**

(a) 6768 (b) 6876
(c) 6678 (d) 6687

199. If $\sqrt{5} : \sqrt{42} :: \sqrt{7} : x$, then what is the value of x? **SSC MTS 05/11/2024 Shift-III**

(a) $\frac{7}{5}\sqrt{42}$ (b) $\frac{6}{5}\sqrt{42}$
(c) $\frac{6}{5}\sqrt{30}$ (d) $\frac{7}{5}\sqrt{30}$

200. A bag contains coins of 1 rupee, 0.5 rupee and 0.25 rupee in the ratio of 5 : 6 : 8. If the total amount of money in the bag is ₹ 420, find the number of coins of type1 rupee, 0.5 rupee and 0.25 rupee are **SSC MTS 30/10/2024 Shift-III**

(a) 212, 232, 312 (b) 210, 252, 336
(c) 216, 252, 292 (d) 208, 272, 352

201. If $P(P>0)$ is the least possible number that must be subtracted from 7, 9 and 12, so that the resulting numbers are in continued proportion then, find the value of $P^2 + 1$. **SSC MTS 29/10/2024 Shift-III**

(a) 10 (b) 12
(c) 3 (d) 8

202. The ratio of the I class and II class AC train coach fares between two stations is 5 : 3 and that of the number of passengers travelling between the two stations by I class and II classes AC coach is 3 : 10. If on a particular day ₹ 37080 is collected from passengers travelling between the two stations, then find the amount collected from second class AC coach passengers. **SSC MTS 28/10/2024 Shift-II**

(a) ₹ 24720 (b) ₹ 27420
(c) ₹ 20247 (d) ₹ 22047

203. If 30% of P = 0.6 of Q = $\frac{1}{3}$ of R, then P : Q : R is **SSC MTS 28/10/2024 Shift-II**

(a) 10 : 5 : 9 (b) 10 : 5 : 7
(c) 5 : 10 : 9 (d) 5 : 10 : 7

204. The price ratio between wheat and rice is 9 : 11, whereas the household consumption ratio is 11 : 13, Calculate the ratio of expenses **SSC MTS 23/10/2024 Shift-II**

(a) 13 : 9 (b) 9 : 13
(c) 7 : 13 (d) 13 : 7

205. Shankar comes to buy a T-shirt in a showroom. He purchases a shirt which costs ₹ 1020 after a discount. He pays his bill in the form of 50 paise, 20 paise and 10 paise coins in the ratio 2 : 3 : 4 (assume for the sake of the problem). What is the number of 10 paise coins he used to pay his bill? **SSC MTS 17/10/2024 Shift-II**

(a) 1530 (b) 510
(c) 1020 (d) 2040

206. If 12 : x :: x : 27 and 25 : y :: y : 36, where x and y are both positive numbers, then find $x : y$. **SSC MTS 16/10/2024 Shift-II**

(a) 7 : 9 (b) 3 : 5
(c) 5 : 6 (d) 4 : 7

207. In a college, 20% of the number of boys are equal to the three-fourth of the number of girls. What is the ratio of boys and girls in that college ? **SSC MTS 30/09/2024 Shift-I**

(a) 15 : 4 (b) 13 : 4
(c) 5 : 3 (d) 7 : 6

SSC MTS 2023-2021

208. In a class of boys and girls, the number of girls is twice the number of boys. If 20 more boys join the class, the ratio of girls and boys is 1 : 1. How many total students were there in the class initially? **SSC MTS 14/09/2023 Shift-I**

(a) 60 (b) 75 (c) 45 (d) 90

209. Three numbers are in the ratio 1 : 2 : 3. By adding 5 to each of the numbers, then the ratio changes to 2 : 3 : 4. The smallest number is **SSC MTS 14/09/2023 Shift-I**

(a) 5 (b) 15 (c) 12 (d) 20

210. The ratio of the number of boys to the number of girls in a school of 1650 students is 6 : 5. If 124 new boys are admitted and few new girls are admitted, the ratio changes to 4 : 3. What is the ratio of the newly admitted girls to the newly admitted boys? **SSC MTS 13/09/2023 Shift-I**

(a) 3 : 4 (b) 62 : 9
(c) 4 : 3 (d) 9 : 62

211. If $A : B = 3 : 4$ and $B : C = 6 : 5$, then $A : B : C$ is **SSC MTS 11/09/2023 Shift-I**

(a) 9 : 12 : 20 (b) 9 : 10 : 20
(c) 9 : 10 : 12 (d) 9 : 12 : 10

212. The fourth proportion of 2, a and $5a$ is .... . **SSC MTS 11/09/2023 Shift-I**

(a) $\frac{2a^2}{5}$ (b) $\frac{5a^2}{2}$ (c) $\frac{2a^2}{3}$ (d) $\frac{5a^2}{3}$

213. Among four numbers, the sum of the smallest and largest is 72 more than the sum of middle two numbers. If the numbers are in the ratio 6 : 7 : 15 : 19, then the smallest number is **SSC MTS 08/09/2023 Shift-II**

(a) 72 (b) 144 (c) 168 (d) 216

214. Three numbers are in the ratio 5 : 2 : 7. The sum of their squares is 3822. The biggest number is **SSC MTS 08/09/2023 Shift-II**

(a) 35 (b) 38 (c) 78 (d) 49

215. The fourth proportional to 1.5, 4.8 and 8 is **SSC MTS 06/09/2023 Shift-I**

(a) 25.6 (b) 26.5
(c) 22.6 (d) 24.5

216. A certain sum is to be divided between A, B and C in the ratio 2 : 5 : 7. But by mistake it was divided in the ratio 5 : 2 : 7. Thus, B loses by ₹ 150. Find the sum. **SSC MTS 06/09/2023 Shift-I**

(a) ₹ 700 (b) ₹ 850
(c) ₹ 900 (d) ₹ 625

217. The mean proportion of a and $\frac{a}{b^2}$ is .... SSC MTS 05/09/2023 Shift-II

(a) ab (b) $\frac{b}{a}$ (c) $\frac{a}{b}$ (d) $\frac{a}{2b}$

218. Two numbers are in the ratio of 6 : 7. If the difference between these numbers is 16, then find the numbers. SSC MTS 04/09/2023 Shift-II

(a) 96, 112 (b) 80, 96
(c) 120, 136 (d) 104, 120

219. If $A : B = 7 : 9$ and $B : C = 5 : 6$, then find the ratio of C and A, respectively. SSC MTS 04/09/2023 Shift-II

(a) 15 : 14 (b) 14 : 15
(c) 54 : 35 (d) 35 : 54

220. If $A : B = 3 : 4$ and $A : C = 9 : 8$, then $A : B : C$ is SSC MTS 01/09/2023 Shift-III

(a) 9 : 12 : 8 (b) 3 : 4 : 6
(c) 9 : 8 : 12 (d) 9 : 8 : 8

221. What is the mean proportional of 9.61 and 3.61? SSC MTS 01/09/2023 Shift-I

(a) 3.17 (b) 5.89 (c) 4.87 (d) 6.78

222. The ratio of two numbers is 3 : 7. The sum of the two numbers is 180. What is the positive difference between the two numbers ? SSC MTS 13/07/2022 Shift-I

(a) 80 (b) 72 (c) 85 (d) 78

223. If 16 : x :: x : 196, find the positive value of x ? SSC MTS 12/07/2022 Shift-I

(a) 60 (b) 62 (c) 56 (d) 64

224. If ₹ 1000 is divided into three parts in the ratio 2 : 3 : 5, find the value of the smallest part SSC MTS 12/07/2022 Shift-I

(a) ₹ 100 (b) ₹ 300 (c) ₹ 200 (d) ₹ 400

225. A bats woman missed her century by four runs in an innings, in which the scoring shorts in the form of sixes, fours, threes, twos and single, were in the proportion 1 : 3 : 2 : 7 : 10. How many runs did she score in single? SSC MTS 02/11/2021 Shift-III

(a) 20 (b) 16 (c) 10 (d) 12

226. The fourth proportional of 18, 27, 68 is SSC MTS 02/11/2021 Shift-III

(a) 136 (b) 170 (c) 204 (d) 102

227. The ratio of two numbers is 4 : 5. If one is subtracted from the first number and two is added to the second number, then the ratio becomes 3 : 4. What will be the ratio, when eight and four are respectively added to the first and the second number? SSC MTS 02/11/2021 Shift-III

(a) 2 : 3 (b) 8 : 9 (c) 6 : 7 (d) 1 : 5

228. In an examination, the ratio of the number of candidates who passed, to those who failed was 5 : 2. If the number of failed candidates had been 14 more, then the ratio of the number of passed candidates to those who failed would have been 4 : 3. How many candidates passed the examination? SSC MTS 02/11/2021 Shift-II

(a) 126 (b) 70 (c) 100 (d) 98

229. The ratio of the incomes of A and B is 1 : 2 and that of their expenditure is 2 : 3. If 80% of B's expenditure is equal to the income of A, then what is the ratio of the savings of B to the savings of A? SSC MTS 02/11/2021 Shift-II

(a) 2 : 9 (b) 9 : 2 (c) 7 : 3 (d) 3 : 7

230. If $x : y = 5 : 7$, then $(6x - y) : (5x + 3y)$ is equal to SSC MTS 02/11/2021 Shift-I

(a) 1 : 4 (b) 11 : 2 (c) 4 : 1 (d) 1 : 2

SSC GD Constable 2024 & 2023

231. ₹ 7400 is divided among A, B and C in the ratio of 9 : 12 : 16 respectively. What is the share of B ? SSC GD Constable 26/02/2024 Shift-I

(a) ₹ 2400 (b) ₹ 1800
(c) ₹ 9200 (d) ₹ 2600

232. The ratio of two numbers is 3 : 5. If their product is 3375, then what is the sum of both the numbers ? SSC GD Constable 26/02/2024 Shift-I

(a) 75 (b) 120 (c) 90 (d) 135

233. The ratio of incomes of Anil and Vikas is 8 : 5. If Vikas gets ₹ 3000 less than Anil, then what is the total income of Anil and Vikas? SSC GD Constable 24/02/2024 Shift-III

(a) ₹ 5000 (b) ₹ 13000
(c) ₹ 8000 (d) ₹ 14000

234. If $x : y = 3 : 5$ and $z : w = 2x : 5y$, then what is the value of $xz : yw$? SSC GD Constable 24/02/2024 Shift-III

(a) 18 : 75 (b) 19 : 75
(c) 18 : 125 (d) 18 : 65

235. In a bag, the ratio of black balls to white balls is 7 : 4. If there are 44 white balls, find the total number of balls in the bag. SSC GD Constable 24/02/2024 Shift-II

(a) 121 (b) 110 (c) 128 (d) 112

236. ₹ 9900 is divided among X, Y and Z in the ratio of 7 : 12 : 14, respectively. What is the share of Y ? SSC GD Constable 24/02/2024 Shift-I

(a) ₹ 900 (b) ₹ 4200 (c) ₹ 2100 (d) ₹ 3600

237. The cost of diamond is directly proportional to the square of its weight. The cost of diamond is ₹ 87880. It break into two pieces whose weight are in the ratio of 5 : 8. What is the loss incurred because of the breakage? SSC GD Constable 24/02/2024 Shift-I

(a) ₹ 41600 (b) ₹ 36400
(c) ₹ 52600 (d) ₹ 32600

238. If $P : Q = 6 : 5$ and $Q : R = 3 : 4$, then what is the value of $Q : (P + R)$? SSC GD Constable 23/02/2024 Shift-III

(a) 15 : 37 (b) 15 : 38
(c) 14 : 37 (d) 13 : 38

239. ₹ 17600 is divided among Raja, Ram and Mohan in the ratio of 6 : 7 : 9 respectively. What is the share of Mohan? SSC GD Constable 23/02/2024 Shift-II

(a) ₹ 7200 (b) ₹ 4800
(c) ₹ 5600 (d) ₹ 4000

240. If $x : y = 7 : 2$, then what is the value of $(7x + 4y) : (7x - 4y)$? SSC GD Constable 23/02/2024 Shift-I

(a) 39 : 29 (b) 40 : 31
(c) 54 : 43 (d) 57 : 41

241. Find the fourth proportional of $4x, x + 4, 3x - 1$, if $x = 2$ SSC GD Constable 23/02/2024 Shift-I

(a) 15/4 (b) 21/4 (c) 14/4 (d) 11/4

242. In a smoothie recipe, the ratio of Fruits to Yogurt is 5 : 2 and the ratio of Yogurt to Honey is 3 : 1. What is the ratio of Fruits to Honey in the recipe? SSC GD Constable 22/02/2024 Shift-IV

(a) 2 : 11 (b) 15 : 2 (c) 16 : 3 (d) 3 : 14

243. The ratio of P, Q and R is 6 : 5 : 9, respectively. If their sum is 400, then what is the difference between P and R? SSC GD Constable 22/02/2024 Shift-IV

(a) 80 (b) 70 (c) 100 (d) 60

244. The sum of the three numbers is 123. If the ratio between the first and second is 3 : 4 and that between the second and third is 3 : 5, then find the second number. SSC GD Constable 22/02/2024 Shift-II

(a) 42 (b) 33 (c) 46 (d) 36

245. The ratio of three numbers is 6 : 8 : 9. If the sum of the three numbers is 460, then what is the largest number among the three numbers? SSC GD Constable 22/02/2024 Shift-II

(a) 100 (b) 180 (c) 120 (d) 160

246. If $4T = 5U$, then what is the value of $(T + U)/T$? SSC GD Constable 22/02/2024 Shift-III

(a) 9/5 (b) 4/9 (c) 5/4 (d) 7/4

247. If the difference between the two numbers is 30% of their sum, then what is the ratio of larger number and smaller number?
SSC GD Constable 22/02/2024 Shift-I
(a) 14 : 3 (b) 12 : 5 (c) 13 : 7 (d) 15 : 7

248. If $X : Y = 11 : 5$, then what is the value of $(X - Y) : (X + Y)$?
SSC GD Constable 22/02/2024 Shift-I
(a) 6 : 15 (b) 3 : 8 (c) 5 : 16 (d) 8 : 3

249. If $M : N : P = 3 : 7 : 5$ and $P : Q = 1 : 2$, then what is the value of $M : Q$?
SSC GD Constable 22/02/2024 Shift-I
(a) 2 : 1 (b) 2 : 3 (c) 1 : 3 (d) 3 : 10

250. If ₹ 70000 is distributed among A, B and C such that $A : B = 2 : 3$ and $B : C = 4 : 5$, then find the share of A.
SSC GD Constable 21/02/2024 Shift-IV
(a) ₹ 15800 (b) ₹ 16000
(c) ₹ 18500 (d) ₹ 14500

251. If $4M = 5N = 20C$, then what is the value of $M : N : C$?
SSC GD Constable 21/02/2024 Shift-IV
(a) 9 : 3 : 1 (b) 5 : 4 : 1
(c) 7 : 5 : 4 (d) 5 : 4 : 3

252. In a school there are total 560 students. The ratio of boys and girls is 13 : 15. If 40 more boys gets admitted into the school, then what will be the new ratio of boys and girls?
SSC GD Constable 21/02/2024 Shift-III
(a) 2 : 1 (b) 3 : 1 (c) 2 : 3 (d) 1 : 1

253. If $\frac{4}{5}$th of A is equal to the $\frac{2}{5}$th of B, then find the value of A : B.
SSC GD Constable 21/02/2024 Shift-II
(a) 1 : 2 (b) 2 : 1 (c) 2 : 3 (d) 3 : 4

254. Determine the fourth proportion to 30, 120, and 15.
SSC GD Constable 21/02/2024 Shift-II
(a) 90 (b) 60 (c) 100 (d) 120

255. The ratio of the income to the expenditure of a family is 19 : 13. If the family's expenses are ₹ 29510, then find the savings of the family.
SSC GD Constable 21/02/2024 Shift-I
(a) ₹ 13620 (b) ₹ 15550
(c) ₹ 14440 (d) ₹ 12240

256. The ratio of copper and zinc in brass is 25 : 12. How much amount of copper will be there in 370 kg of brass? **SSC GD Constable 20/02/2024 Shift-III**
(a) 250 kg (b) 150 kg
(c) 350 kg (d) 50 kg

257. If $P : Q : R = 9 : 10 : 11$, then what is the value of $(P + Q) : (Q + R) : (R + P)$? **SSC GD Constable 20/02/2024 Shift-III**
(a) 19 : 21 : 20 (b) 19 : 21 : 19
(c) 19 : 21 : 23 (d) 19 : 21 : 22

258. Prithvi has pears and peaches in the ratio of 10 : 13. Celine has pears and peaches in the ratio of 7 : 9. Vikram has pears and peaches in the ratio of 5 : 7. Who has a greater ratio of pears to peaches? **SSC GD Constable 20/02/2024 Shift-II**
(a) Prithvi (b) Celine
(c) Vikram (d) All are equal

259. ₹ 8400 is divided among P, Q and R in the ratio of $\frac{2}{3} : 3 : \frac{1}{3}$, respectively. What is the share of R?
SSC GD Constable 20/02/2024 Shift-II
(a) ₹ 900 (b) ₹ 1400
(c) ₹ 700 (d) ₹ 18000

260. If $M : N = 9 : 6$, then what is the value of $(M + N) : (M - N)$?
SSC GD Constable 20/02/2024 Shift-I
(a) 5 : 2 (b) 5 : 4 (c) 5 : 1 (d) 1 : 5

261. ₹ 7200 is divided among P, Q and R in the ratio of 1/2 : 4 : 3/2, respectively. What is the share of R?
SSC GD Constable 20/02/2024 Shift-I
(a) ₹ 1800 (b) ₹ 2400 (c) ₹ 4800 (d) ₹ 600

262. There are 50 students in a class. If the ratio of the number of boys to the girls is 16 : 9, then what is the mean proportional between the number of boys and girls in the school? **SSC GD Constable 13/02/2023 Shift-IV**
(a) 16 (b) 22 (c) 36 (d) 24

263. The fourth proportional of 2 h 40 min, 1 h 20 min and 10 h is
SSC GD Constable 13/02/2023 Shift-II
(a) 4 h (b) 6 h (c) 5 h (d) 2 h

264. What is the mean proportional between 121 and 169?
SSC GD Constable 09/02/2023 Shift-II
(a) 143 (b) 157
(c) 153 (d) 147

265. Find the fourth proportional of $(a^4 - b^4), (a^2 - ab)$ and $(a^2 + b^2)$.
SSC GD Constable 09/02/2023 Shift-I
(a) $\frac{a}{a+b}$ (b) $(a - b)$
(c) $(a + b)$ (d) $\frac{b}{a+b}$

266. The fourth proportional to $a^3 + a^2b + ab^2, a + b$ and $a^2 + ab + b^2$ is **SSC GD Constable 09/02/2023 Shift-I**
(a) $\frac{b}{a+b}$ (b) $1 + \frac{a}{b}$
(c) $\frac{a}{a+b}$ (d) $1 + \frac{b}{a}$

267. ₹ 936 is divided among P, Q and R in the ratio 2 : 3 : 4 instead of $\frac{1}{2} : \frac{1}{3} : \frac{1}{4}$ by mistake. The gain of R in the distribution is
SSC GD Constable 07/02/2023 Shift-I
(a) ₹ 200 (b) ₹ 24 (c) ₹ 124 (d) ₹ 216

268. What is the smallest positive number that should be subtracted from each of 12 and 21 so that 36 is the third proportion to them?
SSC GD Constable 07/02/2023 Shift-I
(a) 5 (b) 3 (c) 4 (d) 2

269. A, B and C are three batsmen of a cricket team. Given is the ratio of the runs scored by them in a certain match, $A : B = 6 : 7$ and $B : C = 5 : 6$. At the end of the match, A, B and C together scored 856 runs. The number of runs scored by B is
SSC GD Constable 06/02/2023 Shift-I
(a) 265 (b) 280 (c) 216 (d) 224

270. If the third proportional to 8 and 24 is A and the mean proportional of 4 and 16 is B, then the value of $\frac{A}{B}$ is
SSC GD Constable 02/02/2023 Shift-I
(a) 10 (b) 12 (c) 8 (d) 9

271. The third proportional to 0.1 and 0.12 is **SSC GD Constable 02/02/2023 Shift-I**
(a) 0.24 (b) 0.124 (c) 0.122 (d) 0.144

272. Find the mean proportional of squares of $\frac{x}{y}$ and $\frac{y}{z}$.
SSC GD Constable 01/02/2023 Shift-I
(a) $\left(\frac{x}{z}\right)^{3/2}$ (b) $\sqrt{\frac{x}{z}}$ (c) $\frac{x}{z}$ (d) $\left(\frac{x}{z}\right)^2$

SSC Selection Post 2024-2022

273. If class A has 11 boys and 18 girls, class B has 13 boys and 17 girls and class C has 20 boys and 9 girls, which class has the biggest ratio(s) of boys to girls? **Matric Level 20/06/2024 Shift-IV**
(a) Class A
(b) Both class A and class B
(c) Class C
(d) Class B

274. If A:B = 8:13, B:C = 5:8 and C : D = 4 : 5, then A : B : C : D is equal to
Graduate Level 20/06/2024 Shift-III
(a) 20 : 50 : 105 : 119
(b) 38 : 65 : 111 : 120
(c) 40 : 60 : 103 : 112
(d) 40 : 65 : 104 : 130

275. Two numbers are in the ratio 4 : 5. If 3 is added to the smaller and 7 is subtracted from the larger number, they are in the ratio 1 : 1. Find the numbers.
Higher Secondary Level 20/06/2024 Shift-II

(a) 60, 75 (b) 40, 50
(c) 55, 44 (d) 20, 25

276. The ratio of cheese to sauce for a single pizza is 1 cup to 1/2 cup. If Rama used 15 cups of sauce to make a number of pizzas, then how many cups of cheese did she use on those pizzas? **Graduate Level 27/06/2023 Shift-IV**

(a) 20 cups (b) 10 cups
(c) 40 cups (d) 30 cups

277. Out of the total income, a family saves 15% and the rest of the amount is spent on three types of expenditure – health, education and food in the ratio of 1 : 2 : 2. The income is ₹ 300 less than thrice the expenditure incurred on education. What is the difference between the savings and the expenditure incurred on health?

Graduate Level 27/06/2023 Shift-IV

(a) ₹ 300 (b) ₹ 350 (c) ₹ 2250 (d) ₹ 500

278. Salaries of Rohan and Soham are in the ratio 2 : 3. If the salary of each is increased by ₹ 2000, the new ratio becomes 40 : 57. What is Soham's present salary?

Higher Secondary Level 27/06/2023 Shift-III

(a) ₹ 34000 (b) ₹ 25500
(c) ₹ 17000 (d) ₹ 20000

279. A varies directly with B. When $A = 52$, $B = 91$. Find the value of A when $B = 126$.

Higher Secondary Level 27/06/2023 Shift-III

(a) 76 (b) 84
(c) 72 (d) 70

280. The students in three batches of a dance class are in ratio 2 : 3 : 5. If 20 students increase in each batch the ratio changes to 4 : 5 : 7. Find the total number of students in the three batches before the increase.

Matric Level 27/06/2023 Shift-I

(a) 120 (b) 100
(c) 150 (d) 80

281. If $C = \frac{2}{3}$ of D and $D = \frac{3}{8}$ of E, then find the ratio of $C : E$.

Matric Level 27/06/2023 Shift-I

(a) 4 : 1 (b) 1 : 4
(c) 3 : 4 (d) 1 : 3

282. The third proportional of 16 and 24 will be .... **Matric Level 27/06/2023 Shift-I**

(a) 40 (b) 30
(c) 36 (d) 32

283. Find the third proportional of 0.9 and 1.5. **Graduate Level 01/08/2022 Shift-IV**

(a) 2.8 (b) 1.5
(c) 2.5 (d) 1.7

284. If $\frac{a}{2} = \frac{b}{3} = \frac{c}{4} = \frac{2a - 3b + 5c}{k}$, then find the value of k.

Higher Secondary Level 01/08/2022 Shift-II

(a) 15 (b) 18
(c) 10 (d) 12

285. The mean proportion between 5 and 125 is

Higher Secondary Level 01/08/2202 Shift-II

(a) 4.8 (b) 25
(c) 60 (d) 65

286. Find the mean proportional of 18 and 50. **Matric Level 01/08/2022 Shift-I**

(a) 40 (b) 30
(c) 33 (d) 35

287. 15 is the mean proportional of 30 and a. Find the value of a.

Matric Level 01/08/2022 Shift-I

(a) $\frac{15}{2}$ (b) $\frac{13}{2}$
(c) $\frac{15}{4}$ (d) $\frac{2}{15}$

288. Two numbers are in the ratio of 5 : 9. If 25 is subtracted from each, the ratio becomes 25 : 49. Find the numbers. **Matric Level 01/08/2022 Shift-I**

(a) 40, 56 (b) 55, 77
(c) 45, 63 (d) 150, 270

Right Answers

1	(a)	**2**	(c)	**3**	(d)	**4**	(c)	**5**	(c)	**6**	(d)	**7**	(b)	**8**	(c)	**9**	(c)	**10**	(c)
11	(d)	**12**	(c)	**13**	(c)	**14**	(d)	**15**	(a)	**16**	(b)	**17**	(b)	**18**	(a)	**19**	(a)	**20**	(c)
21	(a)	**22**	(b)	**23**	(a)	**24**	(b)	**25**	(c)	**26**	(b)	**27**	(a)	**28**	(c)	**29**	(c)	**30**	(d)
31	(b)	**32**	(b)	**33**	(d)	**34**	(c)	**35**	(a)	**36**	(a)	**37**	(b)	**38**	(a)	**39**	(a)	**40**	(a)
41	(b)	**42**	(a)	**43**	(a)	**44**	(a)	**45**	(d)	**46**	(b)	**47**	(a)	**48**	(c)	**49**	(d)	**50**	(d)
51	(c)	**52**	(b)	**53**	(b)	**54**	(b)	**55**	(b)	**56**	(d)	**57**	(b)	**58**	(a)	**59**	(d)	**60**	(b)
61	(d)	**62**	(b)	**63**	(a)	**64**	(a)	**65**	(b)	**66**	(b)	**67**	(c)	**68**	(c)	**69**	(d)	**70**	(d)
71	(d)	**72**	(c)	**73**	(d)	**74**	(d)	**75**	(d)	**76**	(b)	**77**	(a)	**78**	(a)	**79**	(a)	**80**	(a)
81	(d)	**82**	(b)	**83**	(c)	**84**	(c)	**85**	(a)	**86**	(b)	**87**	(b)	**88**	(d)	**89**	(b)	**90**	(b)
91	(d)	**92**	(d)	**93**	(b)	**94**	(c)	**95**	(a)	**96**	(c)	**97**	(c)	**98**	(c)	**99**	(c)	**100**	(c)
101	(d)	**102**	(a)	**103**	(d)	**104**	(a)	**105**	(b)	**106**	(d)	**107**	(b)	**108**	(c)	**109**	(a)	**110**	(a)
111	(d)	**112**	(b)	**113**	(c)	**114**	(a)	**115**	(c)	**116**	(d)	**117**	(b)	**118**	(c)	**119**	(b)	**120**	(c)
121	(c)	**122**	(b)	**123**	(a)	**124**	(d)	**125**	(d)	**126**	(a)	**127**	(c)	**128**	(b)	**129**	(a)	**130**	(a)
131	(c)	**132**	(a)	**133**	(c)	**134**	(c)	**135**	(a)	**136**	(d)	**137**	(a)	**138**	(c)	**139**	(b)	**140**	(d)
141	(d)	**142**	(c)	**143**	(b)	**144**	(a)	**145**	(d)	**146**	(a)	**147**	(b)	**148**	(b)	**149**	(c)	**150**	(c)
151	(b)	**152**	(d)	**153**	(c)	**154**	(d)	**155**	(b)	**156**	(c)	**157**	(d)	**158**	(b)	**159**	(d)	**160**	(a)
161	(a)	**162**	(b)	**163**	(b)	**164**	(a)	**165**	(c)	**166**	(a)	**167**	(d)	**168**	(a)	**169**	(d)	**170**	(b)
171	(d)	**172**	(a)	**173**	(b)	**174**	(a)	**175**	(b)	**176**	(c)	**177**	(b)	**178**	(a)	**179**	(c)	**180**	(d)
181	(c)	**182**	(d)	**183**	(b)	**184**	(c)	**185**	(c)	**186**	(d)	**187**	(b)	**188**	(d)	**189**	(c)	**190**	(c)
191	(a)	**192**	(a)	**193**	(d)	**194**	(c)	**195**	(d)	**196**	(d)	**197**	(d)	**198**	(a)	**199**	(d)	**200**	(b)
201	(a)	**202**	(a)	**203**	(a)	**204**	(b)	**205**	(d)	**206**	(b)	**207**	(a)	**208**	(a)	**209**	(a)	**210**	(d)
211	(d)	**212**	(b)	**213**	(b)	**214**	(d)	**215**	(a)	**216**	(a)	**217**	(c)	**218**	(a)	**219**	(c)	**220**	(a)
221	(b)	**222**	(b)	**223**	(c)	**224**	(c)	**225**	(a)	**226**	(d)	**227**	(b)	**228**	(b)	**229**	(b)	**230**	(d)
231	(a)	**232**	(b)	**233**	(b)	**234**	(c)	**235**	(a)	**236**	(d)	**237**	(a)	**238**	(b)	**239**	(a)	**240**	(d)
241	(a)	**242**	(b)	**243**	(d)	**244**	(d)	**245**	(b)	**246**	(a)	**247**	(c)	**248**	(b)	**249**	(d)	**250**	(b)
251	(b)	**252**	(d)	**253**	(a)	**254**	(b)	**255**	(a)	**256**	(a)	**257**	(a)	**258**	(b)	**259**	(c)	**260**	(c)
261	(a)	**262**	(d)	**263**	(c)	**264**	(a)	**265**	(a)	**266**	(d)	**267**	(a)	**268**	(b)	**269**	(b)	**270**	(d)
271	(d)	**272**	(c)	**273**	(c)	**274**	(d)	**275**	(b)	**276**	(d)	**277**	(a)	**278**	(c)	**279**	(c)	**280**	(b)
281	(b)	**282**	(c)	**283**	(c)	**284**	(a)	**285**	(b)	**286**	(b)	**287**	(a)	**288**	(d)				

Solutions

1. (a) According to the question,

$$\text{Adi} + \text{Dia} = ₹\,1440 \quad \ldots\text{(i)}$$

and $\frac{3}{10}\text{Adi} = \frac{3}{5}\text{Dia}$

$\Rightarrow \quad \text{Adi} = 2\,\text{Dia}$

$2\,\text{Dia} + \text{Dia} = 1440$ [from Eq. (i)]

$\therefore \quad \text{Dia} = \frac{1440}{3} = ₹\,480$

Speedy Method

$\frac{\text{Adi}}{\text{Dia}} = \frac{\frac{3}{5}}{\frac{3}{10}} = 2:1$

According to the question,

$3 \rightarrow ₹\,1440$

$1 \rightarrow ₹\,480$

2. (c) Given, $a:b = 2:3$ and $b:c = 5:7$

$\therefore \; a:b:c = 2\times5 : 3\times5 : 3\times7$

$= 10:15:21$

$\Rightarrow \; c:a = 21:10$

3. **(d)** Let the money distributed among P, Q and R be $5x$, $3x$ and $4x$.

According to the question,

$5x - 4x = 1500$

$\Rightarrow \quad x = 1500$

So, Q's share $= 3x = 3 \times 1500 = ₹\,4500$

Speedy Method

P : Q : R

5 : 3 : 4

(difference of P and R) 1

$1 \rightarrow 1500$

$\Rightarrow \; 3 \rightarrow 3 \times 1500 = ₹\,4500$

4. (c) Let the monthly income of A, B and C be ₹ $2x$, $9x$ and $3x$ respectively.

Also, let their expenditure be $3y$, $9y$ and $5y$ respectively.

As, Savings = Income − Expenditure

According to the question,

$2x - 3y = \frac{1}{2}(2x) \Rightarrow 2x - 3y = x$

$\Rightarrow \; x = 3y \Rightarrow \frac{x}{y} = \frac{3}{1}$

$\therefore$ Required ratio of savings

$= (2x - 3y) : (9x - 9y) : (3x - 5y)$

$= \{2(3) - 3(1)\} : \{9(3) - 9(1)\} : \{3(3) - 5(1)\}$

$= 3:18:4$

5. (c) According to the question,

$a = c = e = 5$ and $b = d = f = 7$

$\therefore$ Required ratio

$= (3a + 5c + 11e) : (3b + 5d + 11f)$

$= \{3(5) + 5(5) + 11(5)\} : \{3(7) + 5(7) + 11(7)\}$

$= 5(19) : 7(19) = 5:7$

6. (d) Given,

$A:B = 6:8$ and $B:C = 5:11$

$\therefore \quad A:B:C$

$6:8 \;\; 8$

$5 \;\; 5:11$

$30:40:88$

$\therefore \; A:B:C = 15:20:44$

7. (b) Let P's and Q's salary be $100x$ and $100y$.

$\Rightarrow 100x + 100y = 960000$

$\Rightarrow \; 100(x+y) = 960000 \Rightarrow x + y = 9600$

P's saving = 64 % of $100x = 64x$

P's Expenditure $= 100x - 64x = 36x$

Q's saving = 44% of $100y = 44y$

Q's Expenditure $= 100y - 44y = 56y$

According to the question,

$36 \times x = 56y \times 1.5 \Rightarrow \; 36x = 56y \times \frac{3}{2}$

$\Rightarrow \quad \frac{x}{y} = \frac{56}{36} \times \frac{3}{2} = \frac{7}{3}$

$\therefore$ Required ratio $= \frac{100 \times 7}{100 \times 3} = \frac{7}{3} = 7:3$

8. (c) Let the numbers be $2x$ and $5x$.

According to the question,

$\Rightarrow \; 5x - 2x = 210 \Rightarrow 3x = 210 \Rightarrow x = 70$

$\therefore$ Smaller number $= 2x = 2 \times 70 = 140$

9. (c) Mean proportional of p and $q = 12$

$\therefore$ Mean proportional of p and $q = \sqrt{p \times q}$

So, $\; 12 = \sqrt{pq} \;\Rightarrow\; pq = 144 \;\Rightarrow\; pq = 24 \times 6$

Thus, p, q are 24 and 6 respectively.

10. (c) Fourth proportional to 4, 9 and 16 is x.

$\Rightarrow \quad 4:9::16:x \Rightarrow 9 \times 16 = 4x$

$\Rightarrow \quad x = \frac{9 \times 16}{4} \Rightarrow x = 36$

11. (d) We know,

Mean proportion of a and $b = \sqrt{ab}$

Mean proportion $= \sqrt{18 \times A}$

$\therefore \quad 30 = \sqrt{18 \times A} \Rightarrow 900 = 18A \Rightarrow A = 50$

12. (c) Let initially number of boys $= 5x$ and girls $= 6x$

According to the question,

$\frac{5x - 40}{6x + 50} = \frac{8}{11} \;\Rightarrow\; 55x - 440 = 48x + 400$

$\Rightarrow \quad 7x = 840 \;\Rightarrow\; x = 120$

Initially number of girls $= 6x = 720$

13. (c) Cost = $(\text{Weight})^2$

Weight = 4 : 3 : 2 : 1

Cost $= 16:9:4:1 = 16 + 9 + 4 + 1 = 30$

Original weight $= 4 + 3 + 2 + 1 = 10$

Original cost $= (10)^2 = 100$

Difference between original cost of piece and cost of four pieces

$(100 - 30) \rightarrow 63000 \Rightarrow 70 \rightarrow 63000$

$\Rightarrow 1 \rightarrow 900 \Rightarrow 100 \rightarrow 900 \times 100 = ₹\,90000$

Original price of diamond ₹ 90000.

14. (d) Given, $A:B = 6:8$, $B:C = 7:12$

$A \; : \; B \; : \; C$

$6 \; : \; 8 : \; 8$

$7 \; : \; 7:12$

$42:56:96$

$\therefore \quad A:B:C = 21:28:48$

15. (a) Mean proportional of $4a^2$ and $x = \frac{1}{5a}$

$\Rightarrow \; \sqrt{4a^2 \times x} = \frac{1}{5a} \Rightarrow 4a^2 x = \frac{1}{25a^2} \Rightarrow x = \frac{1}{100a^4}$

16. (b) We know,

Mean proportion of a and $b = \sqrt{ab}$

$\therefore$ Mean proportion of 36 and 100

$= \sqrt{36 \times 100} = 6 \times 10 = 60$

17. (b) Ratio of men and women = 5: 3

Let the number of men and women is $5x$ and $3x$.

Women added = 150

Final ratio = 5 :4

So, $\frac{5x}{3x + 150} = \frac{5}{4} \Rightarrow 20x = 15x + 750$

$\Rightarrow \quad 5x = 750 \Rightarrow x = 150$

Men in the company $= 5 \times 150 = 750$

18. (a) $A:B$ and $B:C$

$(6:8)_{\times 7} \quad (7:10)_{\times 8}$

$42:56 \quad 56:80$

Thus, $A:B:C = 42:56:80 = 21:28:40$

19. (a) Given, there is one gold coin for every four non-gold coins.

Let number of gold coins $= x$

Number of non-gold coins $= 4x$

According to the question,

$\frac{x + 20}{4x} = \frac{2}{3} \Rightarrow 3x + 60 = 8x$

$\Rightarrow \quad 5x = 60 \Rightarrow x = 12$

Number of gold coins = 12

Number of non-gold coins $= 4 \times 12 = 48$

Total number of coins $= 12 + 48 = 60$

After adding 20 more gold coins,

Now, total number of coins $= 60 + 20 = 80$

20. (c) Mean proportional of 12.96 and 0.16

Here, $a = 12.96$ and $b = 0.16$

Mean proportional $= \sqrt{ab}$

$= \sqrt{12.96 \times 0.16} = \sqrt{\frac{1296}{100} \times \frac{16}{100}}$

$= \frac{36}{10} \times \frac{4}{10} = 1.44$

21. (a) Given, $A:B=6:8$

and $B:C=5:10$

Here, $A:B:C$

$6:8:8$

$5:5:10$

$30:40:80$

$\therefore\ A:B:C=3:4:8$

22. (b) Mean proportional of 2 and 32.

$=\sqrt{2\times32}=\sqrt{64}=8$

23. (a) Given, $\frac{M}{F}=\frac{2}{3}$

Let number of males $=2x$

Number of females $=3x$

According to the question,

$\frac{2x+200}{3x}=\frac{5}{6}\Rightarrow 12x+1200=15x$

$\Rightarrow\ 3x=1200$

$\Rightarrow\ x=400$

$\therefore$ Number of females $=3x=3\times400=1200$

24. (b) According to the question,

$28.9:x::x:36.1$

$\Rightarrow\ \frac{28.9}{x}=\frac{x}{36.1}$

$\Rightarrow\ x^2=28.9\times36.1$

$\Rightarrow\ x=\sqrt{1043.29}=32.3$

25. (c) Given ratio $=2:1:3$

According to the question,

Largest share $=\frac{3}{6}\times1200=₹\ 600$

Smallest share $=\frac{1}{6}\times1200=₹\ 200$

$\therefore$ Required amount $=3\times600+2\times200$

$=1800+400=₹\ 2200$

26. (b) Let incomes of P, Q and R be $10x$, $12x$ and $9x$, respectively.

Also, let their expenditures be $12y$, $15y$ and $8y$, respectively.

According to the question,

$12x-15y=\frac{25}{100}\times12x$

$\Rightarrow\ 12x-15y=3x$

$\Rightarrow\ 9x=15y\Rightarrow3x=5y\Rightarrow\frac{x}{y}=\frac{5}{3}$

$\Rightarrow\ x=5,\ y=3$

$\therefore$ Required ratio of savings

$=(10x-12y):(12x-15y):(9x-8y)$

$=[10(5)-12(3)]:[12(5)-15(3)]:[9(5)-8(3)]$

$=14:15:21$

27. (a) Mean proportional of 1.21 and 0.09

$=\sqrt{1.21\times0.09}=0.33$

Mean proportional of 0.16 and 0.36

$=\sqrt{0.16\times0.36}=0.24$

$\therefore$ Required ratio $=0.33:0.24=11:8$

28. (c) We know,

Mean proportional of a and $b=\sqrt{ab}$

$\therefore$ Mean proportional of $7\frac{1}{5}$ and 245

$=\sqrt{\frac{36}{5}\times245}=\sqrt{36\times49}=6\times7=42$

As, even prime number = 2

$\therefore$ Required quotient $=\frac{42}{2}=21$

29. (c) $P:Q:R:S=4:9:2:3$

$\therefore\ P=4x,\ Q=9x,\ R=2x,\ S=3x$

The difference between share of Q and

$R=9x-2x=7x$ and $7x=560\Rightarrow\ x=80$

$\therefore$ Share of $S=3x=3\times80=₹240$

30. (d) Given,

$A:B\Rightarrow\ 6\ :\ 8$

$B:C\Rightarrow\ 5\ :\ 12$

$30:40:96$

$\therefore\ A:B:C=30:40:96$

$=15:20:48$

31. (b) Given, $\frac{A}{C}=\frac{B}{D}\Rightarrow\ \frac{25}{30}=\frac{40}{D}\Rightarrow D=48$

32. (b) Volume of coin $\rightarrow1:5:10$

Number of coin $\rightarrow3:5:7$

Total value $\rightarrow3:25:70$

Let the value of each type of coin be $3x$, $25x$ and $70x$.

Then, $3x+25x+70x=980$

$\Rightarrow\ 98x=980\ \Rightarrow\ x=10$

Total value of ₹ 10 coin $=70\times10=₹\ 700$

$\therefore$ Number of coin $=\frac{700}{10}=70$

33. (d) The mean proportional of $8a^2$ and $\frac{18}{a^4}$

($\because$ Mean proportional of two numbers $=\sqrt{ab}$)

$=\sqrt{8a^2\times\frac{18}{a^4}}=\frac{12}{a}$

34. (c) According to the question,

$x\ \alpha\ \frac{1}{y}\Rightarrow x=\frac{k}{y}$

Now, if $x=2,\ y=6$

$\therefore\ 2=\frac{k}{6}\Rightarrow k=12$

If $x=3\Rightarrow\ 3=\frac{12}{y}\Rightarrow\ y=4$

35. (a) By Alligation Method,

Average marks of Boys		Average marks of Girls
75		80
	Average marks of all students 78	
2	:	3

$\therefore$ Ratio of the number of boys to the number of girls $=2:3$

36. (a) Let total number of 25 paise, 50 paise, ₹ 2 and ₹ 5 coins are $5x$, $4x$, $3x$ and $1x$, respectively.

According to the question,

$\frac{1}{4}\times5x+\frac{1}{2}\times4x+2\times3x+5\times1x=285$

$\Rightarrow\ \frac{5x+8x+24x+20x}{4}=285$

$\Rightarrow\ 57x=285\times4$

$\therefore\ x=5\times4=20$

Number of 25 paise coins $=5\times20=100$

Number of ₹ 5 coins = 20

$\therefore$ Required difference $=100-20=80$

37. (b) Let the marks of Rajesh, Rakesh and Ramesh are $2x$, $4x$ and $9x$, respectively.

According to the question,

Rajesh scored $=2x=30\Rightarrow\ x=15$

Rakesh scored $=4\times15=60$

Ramesh scored $=9\times15=135$

38. (a) Let the income of A and B are $7x$ and $4x$ and the expenditure of A and B are $3y$ and y.

Saving of each employee = ₹ 4800

According to the question,

$7x-3y=4800$ ...(i)

$4x-y=4800$

$y=4x-4800$ ...(ii)

Value of y putting in Eq. (i),

$7x-3(4x-4800)=4800$

$\Rightarrow\ 7x-12x+14400=4800$

$\Rightarrow-5x=4800-14400\Rightarrow-5x=-9600$

$\Rightarrow\ x=\frac{9600}{5}=1920$

$\because$ Sum of their income $=7x+4x=11x$

$=11\times1920=21120$

39. (a) Let the third number be x.

According to the question,

First number $=\frac{110\ x}{100}=\frac{11}{10}x$

Second number $=x\times\frac{125}{100}=\frac{5}{4}x$

$\therefore$ Required ratio $=\frac{11}{10}x:\frac{5}{4}x=22:25$

Speedy Method

1st number	2nd number	3rd number
110	125	100 (Assumed)

(3rd to 2nd: +25%; 3rd to 1st: +10%)

$\therefore$ Required ratio $=110:125=22:25$

40. (a) Avinash's savings $=50000-18000$

$=₹\ 32000$

Radha's savings $=60000-24000=₹\ 36000$

$\therefore$ Ratio of Radha to Avinash savings

$=\frac{36000}{32000}=\frac{9}{8}=9:8$

41. (b) Third proportional $=\frac{b^2}{a}=\frac{63\times63}{7}$

$=567$

42. (a) Given, $3x^2:4xy::4xy:48$

$\Rightarrow\ (4xy)^2=3x^2\times48$

$\Rightarrow \quad 16x^2y^2 = 3x^2 \times 48$

$\Rightarrow \quad y^2 = \frac{48 \times 3}{16} \Rightarrow y^2 = 9$

$\Rightarrow \quad y = 3$

43. (a) According to the question,

$(2-x):(3-x)::(3-x):4$

$\therefore$ Third proportional, $4 = \frac{(3-x)^2}{(2-x)}$

$\Rightarrow \quad 4(2-x) = (3-x)^2$

$\Rightarrow \quad 8-4x = 9+x^2-6x$

$\Rightarrow \quad x^2-2x+1=0 \Rightarrow (x-1)^2=0 \Rightarrow x=1$

44. (a) Let the number of boys = $7x$ and total students = $17x$

$\therefore$ Number of girls = $17x - 7x = 10x$

According to the question,

$7x = 1099 \Rightarrow x = \frac{1099}{7} = 157$

Hence, the number of girls = $157 \times 10 = 1570$

Speedy Method

Boys : Girls = 7 : (17 − 7) = 7 : 10

Here, $7 \rightarrow 1099$

$\therefore \quad 10 \rightarrow \frac{1099}{7} \times 10 = 1570$

$\therefore$ Number of girls = 1570

45. (d) Fourth proportional of 8, 32 and 13 is

$= \frac{32 \times 13}{8} = 52$

46. (b) $\frac{8}{19} = \frac{16}{38}, \frac{13}{19} = \frac{26}{38}$

$\frac{15}{38} < \frac{16}{38} < \frac{17}{38} < \frac{26}{38}$

$\therefore$ 15 : 38 is the lowest ratio.

47. (a) Given, length of the pole = 9030 cm

Ratio of saffron, white and green colours = 6:7:8

$\therefore$ Length of the green part

$= \frac{9030}{21} \times 8 = 3440$ cm

48. (c) Given, numbers are in the ratio

$\frac{4}{5}:\frac{5}{6}:\frac{9}{10} = 48:50:54$

Let smallest $=48x$, greatest $=54x$

$\therefore \quad 54x - 48x = 12$

$\Rightarrow \quad 6x = 12$

$\therefore \quad x = 2$

Then, neither smallest nor greatest

$= 50x = 50 \times 2 = 100$

49. (d) 28 : 98 :: 98 : y

$\frac{28}{98} = \frac{98}{y} \Rightarrow y = \frac{98 \times 98}{28} = 343$

50. (d) Fourth proportional of the numbers 8, 12 and 14 $= \frac{12 \times 14}{8} = 21$

51. (c) Daily wages of $X:Y:Z = 4:5:3$

Number of days $X:Y:Z = 5:7:10$

Amount of $X:Y:Z = 20:35:30$

$\therefore$ Amount of X $= \frac{3400}{85} \times 20 =$ ₹ 800

52. (b) Given, $a:b::b:c$ and $b = 96$

Then, $\quad b^2 = ac$

$96 \times 96 = a \times c$

From option (b),

$a = 32$ and $c = 288$

$96 \times 96 = 32 \times 288 = 9216$

Hence, possible values of $a = 32$ and $c = 288$.

53. (b) Radhika owns 2 dogs, 3 rabbits and 4 parrots.

Total number of pets = 2 + 3 + 4 = 9

$\therefore$ Number of rabbits : Total number of pets

= 3 : 9 = 1 : 3

54. (b) Let third proportional be x.

$\therefore \quad 25:35::35:x$

$\Rightarrow \quad \frac{25}{35} = \frac{35}{x} \Rightarrow x = \frac{35 \times 35}{25} = 49$

55. (b) Given, ratio of Mathematics, English and Chemistry = 6 : 4 : 7

These seats are increased by 20%, 40%, 60%

$= \frac{1}{5}, \frac{2}{5}, \frac{3}{5}$

Then, ratio of the increased seats

$= 6 \times \frac{6}{5} : 4 \times \frac{7}{5} : 7 \times \frac{8}{5} = 36:28:56 = 9:7:14$

56. (d) $A \propto (B+18) \Rightarrow A = k(B+18)$

When, $B = 36$

$\therefore \quad 108 = k(36+18) \Rightarrow k = \frac{108}{54} = 2$

When, $B = 68$

$\therefore \quad A = 2(68+18) = 2 \times 86 = 172$

57. (b) Let fourth proportional = x

144 : 192 :: 216 : x

So, $x = \frac{216 \times 192}{144} = 288$

58. (a) Given, 405 : y :: y : 125

Then, $\quad \frac{405}{y} = \frac{y}{125} \Rightarrow y^2 = 405 \times 125$

$\Rightarrow \quad y = 225$

59. (d) According to the question,

$m \times \frac{48}{100} = \frac{2}{3} w$

$\Rightarrow \quad \frac{m}{w} = \frac{200}{48 \times 3} = \frac{25}{18}$

Hence, required ratio of males and females.

= 25 : 18

60. (b) Let third proportional is z.

$(x^2-y^2):(x-y)::(x-y):z$

$\Rightarrow \quad z = \frac{(x-y)(x-y)}{x^2-y^2} \Rightarrow z = \frac{(x-y)(x-y)}{(x-y)(x+y)}$

$\Rightarrow \quad z = \frac{x-y}{x+y}$

Hence, third proportional is $\frac{x-y}{x+y}$.

61. (d) Given, total amount = ₹ 550

	50 p	25 p	20 p
Value →	10 :	5 :	4
Number →	2 :	3 :	5
Amount →	20 :	15 :	20

Total = 55 → ₹ 550, 1 → ₹ 10

$\therefore$ Difference of amount contributed by 50p and 20p = (20 − 20) × 10 = ₹0

62. (b) Number of red pens are

$= \frac{7}{7+4+9} \times 320 = \frac{7}{20} \times 320 = 112$

63. (a) Given, LCM and HCF of two numbers

= 12 and 2

Let two numbers be 'a' and 'b'.

We know that, $a \times b$ = LCM × HCF

$\therefore$ Mean proportional

$= \sqrt{ab} = \sqrt{\text{LCM} \times \text{HCF}}$

$= \sqrt{12 \times 2} = \sqrt{24} = 2\sqrt{6}$

64. (a) Let the number of boys = x

Then, number of girls = $x + 200$

According to the question,

$\frac{x}{x+200} = \frac{11}{15} \Rightarrow 15x = 11x + 2200$

$\Rightarrow \quad x = \frac{2200}{4} \Rightarrow x = 550$

Hence, number of boys = 550

65. (b) Mean proportion between 7 and 112

$= \sqrt{7 \times 112} = \sqrt{784} = 28$

66. (b) According to the question,

39 : 117 :: 17 : y

Then, $\frac{39}{117} = \frac{17}{y} \Rightarrow y = \frac{17 \times 117}{39} = 51$

67. (c) Let the mean proportional between 25 and 225 be x.

Then, 25 : x :: x : 225

$\Rightarrow \quad \frac{25}{x} = \frac{x}{225} \Rightarrow x^2 = 25 \times 225$

$\Rightarrow \quad x = \sqrt{25 \times 225} \Rightarrow x = 5 \times 15 = 75$

68. (c) Given, $X \propto Y^2 \Rightarrow X = k \times Y^2$

When $X = 12$ and $Y = 2$

$\Rightarrow \quad 12 = k \times (2)^2 \Rightarrow k = \frac{12}{4} = 3$

When $Y = 3$,

$\therefore \quad X = kY^2 = 3 \times (3)^2 = 27$

69. (d) Let the 3rd term = x

Then, 51 : 68 :: x : 108 $\Rightarrow 68 \times x = 51 \times 108$

$\Rightarrow \quad x = \frac{51 \times 108}{68} \Rightarrow x = 3 \times 27 = 81$

70. (d) 7 : 15 :: 21 : $x \Rightarrow x = \frac{15 \times 21}{7} \Rightarrow x = 45$

71. (d) Let three positive numbers are $4x$, $5x$ and $7x$.

Sum of their squares $= (4x)^2 + (5x)^2 + (7x)^2$

$= 16x^2 + 25x^2 + 49x^2 = 90x^2$

Given, $90x^2 = 15210 \Rightarrow x^2 = 169 \Rightarrow x = 13$

Then, sum of three numbers

$$= 4x + 5x + 7x = 16x = 16 \times 13 = 208$$

72. (c) Given, $36 : 81 : : X : 63$

$$\therefore \quad X = \frac{36 \times 63}{81} = 28$$

73. (d) Let the third proportional be x.

$$\text{Then,} \quad a : \frac{b^4}{4a} : : \frac{b^4}{4a} : x \Rightarrow \frac{a}{\frac{b^4}{4a}} = \frac{\frac{b^4}{4a}}{x}$$

$$\Rightarrow x = \frac{b^4}{4a} \times \frac{b^4}{4a} \times \frac{1}{a} \Rightarrow x = \frac{b^8}{16a^3}$$

74. (d) Given, $a : b = 4 : 5$ and $b : c = 3 : 10$

$\Rightarrow a : b : c = 4 \times 3 : 5 \times 3 : 10 \times 5 = 12 : 15 : 50$

$\therefore a : c = 12 : 50 = 6 : 25$

75. (d) Let the fourth proportional be x.

$\therefore \quad 17 : 272 : : 19 : x$

$$\therefore \quad x = \frac{272 \times 19}{17} = 16 \times 19 = 304$$

76. (b) Let the fourth proportional be x.

$$\therefore \quad 16 : 26 : : 32 : x \Rightarrow x = \frac{26 \times 32}{16} = 52$$

77. (a) Mean proportional between 27 and 300

$$= \sqrt{27 \times 300} = 3 \times 3 \times 10 = 90$$

78. (a) Let the fourth proportional be x.

$\Rightarrow \quad 24 : 192 : : 27 : x$

$$\Rightarrow \frac{24}{192} = \frac{27}{x} \Rightarrow x = \frac{27 \times 192}{24} = 216$$

79. (a) Given, $14 : 30 : : 7 : x$

$$\therefore \quad x = \frac{7 \times 30}{14} = 15$$

80. (a) Mean proportional between 6 and

$54 = \sqrt{6 \times 54} = 6 \times 3 = 18$

$\therefore$ Required answer $= 18 - 15 = 3$

81. (d) Let Rohan scored x marks in Science.

$\Rightarrow$ Marks in English $= 2x$

Let Rohan's marks in Mathematics be y.

$\Rightarrow \quad 2x + x + y = 126$

$\Rightarrow \quad 3x + y = 126 \quad \text{...(i)}$

According to the question,

$$\frac{2x}{y} = \frac{2}{3} \Rightarrow y = 3x$$

From Eq. (i),

$3x + 3x = 126 \Rightarrow 6x = 126$

$\Rightarrow \quad x = 21$

$\therefore$ Marks in English $= 2x = 2 \times 21 = 42$

Speedy Method

Given, Science (S) : English $(E) = 1 : 2$

English (E) : Maths $(M) = 2 : 3$

$\therefore \quad S : E : M = 1 : 2 : 3$

$\therefore \quad 1 + 2 + 3 = 6 \rightarrow 126$

$$\Rightarrow 2 \rightarrow \frac{126 \times 2}{6} = 42$$

82. (b) $\because$ Mean proportion between two numbers p and q is $\sqrt{pq}$.

$\therefore$ Required mean proportion

$$= \sqrt{\frac{a^3 + b^3}{a - b} \times \frac{a^2 - b^2}{a^2 - ab + b^2}}$$

$$= \sqrt{\frac{(a + b)(a^2 - ab + b^2)}{(a - b)} \times \frac{(a + b)(a - b)}{(a^2 - ab + b^2)}}$$

$$= \sqrt{(a + b)^2} = a + b$$

83. (c) Mean proportional x between 12.8 and $64.8 = \sqrt{12.8 \times 64.8} = 28.8$

84. (c) Given, $a : c : : c : b \Rightarrow \dfrac{a}{c} = \dfrac{c}{b} \Rightarrow c^2 = ab$

Now, let x be the mean proportion of a^2c and b^2c.

$$\therefore \quad a^2c : x : : x : b^2c \Rightarrow \frac{a^2c}{x} = \frac{x}{b^2c}$$

$$\Rightarrow \quad x^2 = a^2b^2c^2 \Rightarrow x = \sqrt{a^2b^2c^2}$$

$$\Rightarrow x = abc \Rightarrow x = c^2 \times c = c^3 \qquad (\because ab = c^2)$$

$\therefore$ c^3 is the mean proportional of a^2c and b^2c.

Speedy Method

$\therefore$ Required mean proportional $= \sqrt{a^2c \times b^2c}$

$$= \sqrt{a^2b^2c^2} = abc$$

$$= (c^2) \cdot c = c^3 \qquad [\because c = \sqrt{ab} \Rightarrow c^2 = ab]$$

85. (a) Let the two number be $5x$ and $7x$.

$$\therefore \quad \frac{5x + 6}{7x + 6} = \frac{3}{4} \Rightarrow (5x + 6) \times 4 = (7x + 6) \times 3$$

$\Rightarrow \quad 20x + 24 = 21x + 18$

$\Rightarrow \quad 24 - 18 = 21x - 20x \Rightarrow x = 6$

$\therefore$ Numbers are $5x = 5 \times 6 = 30$

and $\quad 7x = 7 \times 6 = 42$

86. (b) Fourth proportion to 12, 24 and 27

$$\Rightarrow \quad \frac{24 \times 27}{12} = 54$$

Since, 54 is also the third proportion to A and 36.

$$\therefore \quad \frac{A}{36} = \frac{36}{54} \Rightarrow A = \frac{36 \times 36}{54} = 24$$

87. (b) According to the question,

$$A \propto \frac{\sqrt{B}}{C^3} \Rightarrow A = \frac{k\sqrt{B}}{C^3}$$

If $A = 15$, $B = 27$ and $C = 2$, then

$$15 = \frac{k\sqrt{27}}{(2)^3} \Rightarrow 120 = k(3\sqrt{3}) \Rightarrow k = \frac{40}{\sqrt{3}} \quad \text{...(i)}$$

Now, if $A = 9$ and $C = 2$, then

$$9 = \frac{40}{\sqrt{3}} \cdot \frac{\sqrt{B}}{(2)^3} \Rightarrow \frac{9\sqrt{3}}{5} = \sqrt{B}$$

$$\therefore \text{Squaring both sides, } B = \frac{(9)^2 \times 3}{25} = \frac{243}{25}$$

88. (d) Let the required number to be subtracted be x.

$\therefore (9 - x) : (13 - x) : : (13 - x) : 18$

$$\Rightarrow \quad \frac{9 - x}{13 - x} = \frac{13 - x}{18}$$

$\Rightarrow \quad 18(9 - x) = (13 - x)^2$

$\Rightarrow \quad 162 - 18x = (13)^2 + (x)^2 - 2 \times 13 \times x$

$\Rightarrow \quad 162 - 18x = 169 + x^2 - 26x$

$\Rightarrow \quad x^2 - 8x + 7 = 0 \Rightarrow (x - 1)(x - 7) = 0$

$\therefore \quad x = 1, 7$

$\therefore$ Required smallest number $= 1$

89. (b) Given, the cost of a piece of diamond $\propto$ square of its weight

$\therefore$ Cost of a piece of diamond $= K \times (\text{weight})^2$

Let total weight of the pieces

$$= (3a + 2a + a) = 6a$$

$\therefore$ Initial cost of diamond

$$= (6a)^2 \times K = 36a^2K = 6084$$

After cutting, new cost of diamond

$$= K \times (9a^2 + 4a^2 + a^2) = 14a^2K$$

$$\therefore \text{New cost of diamond} = \frac{6084}{36} \times 14 = ₹\ 2366$$

$\therefore$ Loss occured $= 6084 - 2366 = ₹\ 3718$

90. (b) Let the mean proportion be x.

So, $6 + \sqrt{8} : x : : x : 3 - \sqrt{2}$

$\Rightarrow \quad x^2 = (6 + \sqrt{8}) \times (3 - \sqrt{2})$

$\Rightarrow \quad x^2 = 2(3 + \sqrt{2})(3 - \sqrt{2})$

$\Rightarrow \quad x^2 = 2(9 - 2) = 2 \times 7 = 14$

$\Rightarrow \quad x = \pm\sqrt{14} \qquad (-\text{ve impossible})$

$\therefore \quad x = \sqrt{14}$

91. (d) Given; $a : b = c : d$

$$\Rightarrow \quad \frac{a}{b} = \frac{c}{d} \quad \text{...(i)}$$

$$\Rightarrow \quad \frac{a}{c} = \frac{b}{d} \quad \text{...(ii)}$$

Adding $(+1)$ in Eq. (i),

$$\frac{a}{b} + 1 = \frac{c}{d} + 1 \Rightarrow \frac{a + b}{b} = \frac{c + d}{d}$$

$$\Rightarrow \quad \frac{a + b}{c + d} = \frac{b}{d}$$

$$\text{Using Eq. (ii),} \quad \frac{a + b}{c + d} = \frac{a}{c}$$

92. (d) Let the fourth proportional of 2, 5, 6. be x.

$$\text{Then, } 2 : 5 : : 6 : x \Rightarrow x = \frac{6 \times 5}{2} = 15$$

Also, let the fourth proportional of 6, 8, 9 be y.

$$\text{Then,} \quad 6 : 8 : : 9 : y \Rightarrow y = \frac{8 \times 9}{6} = 12$$

$\therefore$ Required ratio $= x : y = 15 : 12 = 5 : 4$

93. (b) $A : B = 1 : 2$, $B : C = 3 : 4$, $C : D = 5 : 6$

$\Rightarrow A : B : C : D = 15 : 30 : 40 : 48$

$$\therefore \text{Share of C} = \frac{40}{(15 + 30 + 40 + 48)} \times 93100$$

$$= \frac{40}{133} \times 93100 = ₹28000$$

94. (c) $\therefore$ Required ratio $= \dfrac{\sqrt{1.6 \times 3.6}}{\dfrac{8 \times 8}{5}}$

$$= \frac{2.4 \times 5}{64} = \frac{12}{64} = 3 : 16$$

95. (a) Mean proportion of 169 and 144

$= \sqrt{169 \times 144} = 13 \times 12 = 156$

96. (c) Let share of A, B, C and D are $4x$, $12x$, $30x$ and $45x$, respectively.

Difference between share of A and D

$45x - 4x = 5535 \Rightarrow 41x = 5535$

$\Rightarrow x = 135$

Total sum $= 4x + 12x + 30x + 45x$

$= 91x = 91 \times 135 = 12285$

97. (c) Let the salary of Anil = ₹ $19x$

and the salary of Kumud = ₹$17x$

According to the question,

$$\frac{19x + 2000}{17x + 1000} = \frac{8}{7}$$

$\Rightarrow 133x + 14000 = 136x + 8000$

$\Rightarrow 136x - 133x = 14000 - 8000$

$\Rightarrow 3x = 6000 \Rightarrow x = 2000$

Present salary of Kumud $= 17x = 17 \times 2000$

= ₹ 34000

98. (c) Given, P is third proportional to 3, 9

$\Rightarrow \frac{3}{9} = \frac{9}{P} \Rightarrow P = \frac{81}{3} = 27$

Now, let the fourth proportional to 6, P, 14 be x.

$\frac{6}{P} = \frac{4}{x} \Rightarrow \frac{6}{27} = \frac{4}{x} \Rightarrow x = \frac{27 \times 4}{6} = 18$

99. (c) According to the question,

$$\frac{(24 - x)}{(40 - x)} = \frac{(33 - x)}{(57 - x)}$$

$\Rightarrow (24 - x)(57 - x) = (40 - x)(33 - x)$

$\Rightarrow 24 \times 57 - 24x - 57x + x^2$

$= 40 \times 33 - 40x - 33x + x^2$

$\Rightarrow 1368 - 81x = 1320 - 73x$

$\Rightarrow 1368 - 1320 = 81x - 73x$

$\Rightarrow 48 = 8x \Rightarrow x = 6$

$\therefore$ Required ratio $\frac{5x + 12}{4x + 15} = \frac{5 \times 6 + 12}{4 \times 6 + 15}$

$= \frac{42}{39} = \frac{14}{13} = 14 : 13$

100. (c) Let fourth proportion of 12, 18 and 6 be x.

Then, $\frac{12}{18} = \frac{6}{x} \Rightarrow x = \frac{18}{2} = 9$

As, $x = 9$ is third proportion of 4 and k.

The value of k is $\frac{4}{k} = \frac{k}{x} \Rightarrow \frac{4}{k} = \frac{k}{9}$

$\Rightarrow k^2 = 36 \Rightarrow k = 6$

101. (d) Let monthly income of A and B

$= 4x : 5x$

Monthly expenditures of A and $B = 3y : 8y$

According to the question,

A's income = B expenditure

$\Rightarrow 4x = 8y \Rightarrow \frac{x}{y} = \frac{2}{1} \Rightarrow x = 2$ and $y = 1$

Now, saving of $A = 4x - 3y$

$= 4 \times 2 - 3 \times 1 = 8 - 3 = 5$

and saving of $B = 5x - 8y$

$= 5 \times 2 - 8 \times 1 = 10 - 8 = 2$

$\therefore$ Ratio of savings of A and $B = 5 : 2$

102. (a) Let A and B be $5x$ and $8x$.

According to the question,

$\frac{5x + 5}{8x + 5} = \frac{2}{3} \Rightarrow 15x + 15 = 16x + 10 \Rightarrow x = 5$

Now, $A = 5x = 5 \times 5 = 25$

and $B = 8x = 8 \times 5 = 40$

$\therefore$ Difference $= 40 - 25 = 15$

103. (d) Let fourth proportional of 12, 16, 6, be x.

Then, $\frac{12}{16} = \frac{6}{x} \Rightarrow x = \frac{16 \times 6}{12} \Rightarrow x = 8$

Let the third proportional of 4,6, be y.

Then, $\frac{4}{6} = \frac{6}{y} \Rightarrow y = \frac{6 \times 6}{4} \Rightarrow y = 9$

$\therefore$ Ratio $= x : y = 8 : 9$

104. (a) Given, $A : B = 9 : 8 = 36 : 32$

$A : C = 4 : 5 = 36 : 45$

$\therefore A : B : C = 36 : 32 : 45$

Share of $B = \frac{32}{113} \times 31866 =$ ₹ 9024

105. (b) Let the fourth proportional be x.

Fourth proportion to 12, 18 and 6 is same as third proportion to k and 6.

$\Rightarrow \frac{12}{18} = \frac{6}{x} \Rightarrow 2x = 18 \Rightarrow x = 9$

Now, $k, 6, 9 \Rightarrow \frac{k}{6} = \frac{6}{9}$

$\Rightarrow 9k = 36 \Rightarrow k = 4$

106. (d) Atul purchased bread costing ₹ 20 and gave ₹ 100.

In return he get ₹ 80.

Let number of ₹ 2, ₹ 5 and ₹ 10 coins be $5x$, $4x$, and x, respectively.

Then, $5x \times 2 + 4x \times 5 + x \times 10 = 80$

$\Rightarrow 10x + 20x + 10x = 80 \Rightarrow 40x =$ ₹$80 \Rightarrow x = 2$

$\therefore$ Number of ₹ 5 coins $= 4x = 4 \times 2 = 8$ coins

107. (b) According to the question,

$$\frac{(19 - x)}{(28 - x)} = \frac{(55 - x)}{(91 - x)}$$

$\Rightarrow (19 - x)(91 - x) = (55 - x)(28 - x)$

$\Rightarrow 19 \times 91 - 19x - 91x + x^2$

$= 55 \times 28 - 55x - 28x + x^2$

$\Rightarrow -110x + 91 \times 19 = 55 \times 28 - 83x$

$\Rightarrow 110x - 83x = 91 \times 19 - 55 \times 28$

$\Rightarrow 27x = 1729 - 1540$

$\Rightarrow 27x = 189 \Rightarrow x = 7$

108. (c) Given, $A : B = 3 : 5$ and $B : C = 2 : 3$

Then,

A : B : C

3 : 5

2 3

3×2 : 5×2 : 5×3

$\therefore A : B : C = 6 : 10 : 15$

109. (a) Let three numbers be x, $2x$ and $4x$.

According to the question,

$x^2 + (2x)^2 + (4x)^2 = 1029$

$\Rightarrow x^2 + 4x^2 + 16x^2 = 1029 \Rightarrow 21x^2 = 1029$

$\Rightarrow x^2 = 49 \Rightarrow x = 7$

The greatest number is $4x = 4 \times 7 = 28$

The smallest number is $x = 7$

The difference between greatest and smallest number is $28 - 7 = 21$

110. (a) Given, ₹ 10 notes : ₹ 50 notes = 1:2

$\therefore 1 + 2 = 3 \rightarrow 12$

$\Rightarrow$ ₹ 10 notes, $1 \rightarrow 4$

And ₹ 50 notes, $2 \rightarrow 8$

$\therefore$ Total money $= 4 \times 10 + 8 \times 50 =$ ₹440

111. (d) According to the question,

$2A = 5B = 7C$

Let $2A = 5B = 7C = k$

$A = \frac{k}{2}, B = \frac{k}{5}, C = \frac{k}{7}$

$A : B : C = \frac{k}{2} : \frac{k}{5} : \frac{k}{7} = \frac{1}{2} : \frac{1}{5} : \frac{1}{7}$

Take LCM of $2, 5, 7 = 2 \times 5 \times 7 = 70$

$= \frac{70}{2} : \frac{70}{5} : \frac{70}{7} = 35 : 14 : 10$

$\therefore A$'s share $= 1180 \times \frac{35}{(35 + 14 + 10)}$

$= \frac{1180 \times 35}{59} =$ ₹ 700

112. (b) Let the amount of Sunita, Amit and Vibha be ₹ $2x$, $3x$ and $4x$.

Amount of Vibha = ₹ 14416 $\Rightarrow 4x = 14416$

$\Rightarrow x = 3604$

$\therefore$ Total amount $= 2x + 3x + 4x$

$= 9x = 9 \times 3604$

= ₹ 32436

113. (c) When x is added to each of 10, 16, 22, 32, then ratio

$$\frac{(10 + x)}{(16 + x)} = \frac{(22 + x)}{(32 + x)}$$

$\Rightarrow 320 + 32x + 10x + x^2 = 352 + 22x + 16x + x^2$

$\Rightarrow 320 + 42x = 38x + 352$

$4x = 32 \Rightarrow x = 8$

We know that, mean proportional between a and $b = \sqrt{ab}$

Here, $a = (x + 1)$, $b = (3x + 1)$

$\therefore A = \sqrt{(x + 1)(3x + 1)} = \sqrt{9 \times 25} = \sqrt{225} = 15$

114. (a) Given, the ratio of shares of A, B, C and D is $\frac{1}{3} : \frac{1}{5} : \frac{1}{6} : \frac{1}{9}$

LCM of [3, 5, 6, 9] = 90

Then, $A : B : C : D = \frac{1}{3} \times 90 : \frac{1}{5} \times 90$

$: \frac{1}{6} \times 90 : \frac{1}{9} \times 90$

$\Rightarrow A : B : C : D = 30 : 18 : 15 : 10$

Let the shares of A, B, C and D are $30y$, $18y$, $15y$ and $10y$, respectively.

So, difference between the shares of B and D

$18y - 10y = 832$

$\Rightarrow \quad y = 104 \quad \ldots(i)$

Now, total sum $= 30y + 18y + 15y + 10y$

$= 73y = 73 \times 104 = ₹\,7592$

$\therefore \quad x = ₹\,7592$

115. (c) $\dfrac{5x+3y}{5x-3y} = \dfrac{7}{3} \Rightarrow 15x + 9y = 35x - 21y$

$\Rightarrow \quad 30y = 20x \Rightarrow \dfrac{x}{y} = \dfrac{30}{20} \Rightarrow x : y = 3 : 2$

116. (d) Given, $S = \dfrac{75}{100} \times T \Rightarrow S = \dfrac{3}{4} \times T$

$\Rightarrow \quad \dfrac{S}{T} = \dfrac{3}{4}$ or $S : T = 3 : 4$

117. (b) Given, $\dfrac{3}{4}, \dfrac{3}{5}, \dfrac{2}{11}, \dfrac{7}{2} = 0.75, 0.6, 0.18, 3.5$

$\therefore$ Ascending order $= 0.18 < 0.6 < 0.75 < 3.5$

$= \dfrac{2}{11} < \dfrac{3}{5} < \dfrac{3}{4} < \dfrac{7}{2}$

$= 2 : 11 < 3 : 5 < 3 : 4 < 7 : 2$

118. (c) Given, $b = \dfrac{4}{a}$

$\therefore$ Mean proportional of a and $b = \sqrt{ab}$

$= \sqrt{a \times \dfrac{4}{a}} = \sqrt{4} = 2$

119. (b) If a, b, c and d in the given order are in proportion, then

$\dfrac{a}{b} = \dfrac{c}{d}$ or $\dfrac{a}{c} = \dfrac{b}{d}$ or $\dfrac{d}{c} = \dfrac{b}{a}$

120. (c) Mean proportion of 75 and 12

$= \sqrt{75 \times 12} = 30$

Hence, required number $= 30 - 13 = 17$

121. (c)

$J : P : K$
$5 : 8 : 8$
$3 : 3 : 2$
$15 : 24 : 16$

Now, $15x + 24x + 16x = 17600$

$55x = 17600$

$\Rightarrow \quad x = \dfrac{17600}{55} = 320$

$\therefore$ Jeevan's share $= 15x = 15 \times 320 = ₹\,4800$

122. (b) Let the marks of A and B be $3x$ and $4x$ respectively.

Let the marks of B and C $= 4x$ and $5x$, respectively.

So, $A : B : C = 3x : 4x : 5x$

Difference of marks of C and $A = 5x - 3x = 2x$

$\Rightarrow \quad 2x = 30 \Rightarrow x = 15$

$\therefore$ B's marks $= 4x = 4 \times 15 = 60$

123. (a) Given, 40% of A = 60% of $B = \dfrac{1}{6}$ of C

$\Rightarrow \quad \dfrac{40}{100} A = \dfrac{60}{100} B \Rightarrow \dfrac{A}{B} = \dfrac{3}{2} \Rightarrow B = \dfrac{2}{3} A$

Now, $\dfrac{40}{100} A = \dfrac{1}{6} C \Rightarrow \dfrac{A}{C} = \dfrac{5}{12} \Rightarrow C = \dfrac{12}{5} A$

$\therefore \; A : B : C = A : \dfrac{2}{3} A : \dfrac{12}{5} A = 15 : 10 : 36$

124. (d) Let the number of boys and girls be $3x$ and $5x$ respectively.

$\therefore$ Percentage of boys in the class

$= \dfrac{3x}{8x} \times 100 = 37.5\%$

125. (d) Let fourth proportional to 10, 12 and 15 be x.

$\dfrac{10}{12} = \dfrac{15}{x} \Rightarrow x = \dfrac{15 \times 12}{10}$

$\Rightarrow \quad x = \dfrac{180}{10} \Rightarrow x = 18$

126. (a) Let the numbers be $3x$ and $7x$.

Now, $\dfrac{3x - 11}{7x - 11} = \dfrac{7}{20} \Rightarrow 60x - 220 = 49x - 77$

$\Rightarrow \quad 11x = 143 \Rightarrow x = 13$

$\therefore$ Smaller number $= 3x = 3 \times 13 = 39$

127. (c) $4 : a : : 16a : 81$

$\Rightarrow \quad \dfrac{4}{a} = \dfrac{16a}{81} \Rightarrow a^2 = \dfrac{81}{4} \Rightarrow a = \dfrac{9}{2}$

128. (b) Fourth proportional $= \dfrac{11 \times 66}{22}$

$= 11 \times 3 = 33$

129. (a) Let the number of boys and girls be $3x$ and $5x$, respectively.

According to the question,

$3x + 5x = 720 \Rightarrow 8x = 720 \Rightarrow x = 90$

So, number of boys $= 3 \times 90 = 270$

and number of girls $= 5x = 5 \times 90 = 450$

Let the number of new boys admitted be 'B'.

$\therefore \quad \dfrac{270 + B}{450 + 18} = \dfrac{2}{3} \Rightarrow 810 + 3B = 468 \times 2$

$\Rightarrow \quad 810 + 3B = 936 \Rightarrow 3B = 126 \Rightarrow B = 42$

130. (a) Let monthly income $= 7x$

and expenditure $= 3x$

Given, expenditure $= 5400$

$\Rightarrow \quad 3x = ₹\,5400$

$\Rightarrow \quad x = 1800$

Then, monthly income $= 7x = 7 \times 1800$

$= ₹\,12600$

131. (c) Fourth proportional

$= \dfrac{0.8 \times 0.108}{0.3} = 0.288$

132. (a) Let the numbers be $5x$ and $3x$, respectively.

According to the question,

$5x - 3x = 34 \Rightarrow x = 17$

Now, smaller number $= 3x = 3 \times 17 = 51$

133. (c) Given, $42 : 36 : : 35 : d$

Let fourth term is d.

Then, $\dfrac{42}{36} = \dfrac{35}{d} \Rightarrow d = \dfrac{35 \times 36}{42} = 30$

134. (c) Third proportional, $c = \dfrac{b^2}{a}$

Here, $a = 0.024$, $b = 0.12$

$\therefore \quad x = \dfrac{(0.12)^2}{0.024} \Rightarrow x = 0.6$

135. (a) $16 \times x = 40 \times 40 \Rightarrow x = \dfrac{40 \times 40}{16} = 100$

Also, let the mean proportional between 10 and 40 be y

Then, $10 : y : : y : 40 \Rightarrow y^2 = 400 \Rightarrow y = 20$

$\therefore$ Required ratio $= 100 : 20 = 5 : 1$

136. (d) Let the heights of the kids be $7x$, $8x$ and $9x$.

$\therefore \quad 7x + 8x + 9x = 56 \times 3 \Rightarrow x = \dfrac{56 \times 3}{24} = 7$

Then, heights of the kids are 49, 56 and 63 (in cm).

137. (a) From option (a), $41 : 92 = \dfrac{41}{92} = 0.45$

From option (b), $33 : 41 = \dfrac{33}{41} = 0.80$

From option (c), $42 : 49 = \dfrac{42}{49} = 0.86$

From option (d), $35 : 47 = \dfrac{35}{47} = 0.75$

Hence, the smallest ratio is 41 : 92 i.e. 0.45.

138. (c) According to the question,

Total price of three chairs $= ₹\,14014$

$\therefore$ The highest price of chair

$= 14014 \times \dfrac{7}{3 + 4 + 7} = 14014 \times \dfrac{7}{14} = ₹\,7007$

139. (b) Let x is added in each term, then

$\dfrac{5 + x}{11 + x} = \dfrac{3}{5} \Rightarrow 25 + 5x = 33 + 3x$

$\Rightarrow \quad 2x = 33 - 25 \Rightarrow x = 4$

140. (d) Required mean proportion

$= \sqrt{0.72 \times 2.85} = \sqrt{2.052} = 1.4$

(round upto one decimal place)

141. (d) Let the number of red and green sweets be $3x$ and $4x$.

According to the question,

$4x = 120 \Rightarrow x = 30$

Hence, number of red sweets

$= 3x = 3 \times 30 = 90$

142. (c) Given, $7 : 4 = 1.75$

$2 : 3 = 0.66$

$8 : 3 = 2.66$

$1 : 5 = 0.2$

Hence, greater ratio $= 2.66 = 8 : 3$

143. (b) Given, $\dfrac{x}{y} = \dfrac{5}{6} \Rightarrow \dfrac{2x + 3y}{3x + 5y} = \dfrac{2\dfrac{x}{y} + 3}{3\dfrac{x}{y} + 5}$

(Dividing numerator and denominator by y)

$= \dfrac{2 \times \dfrac{5}{6} + 3}{3 \times \dfrac{5}{6} + 5} = \dfrac{\dfrac{5}{3} + 3}{\dfrac{5}{2} + 5} = \dfrac{\left(\dfrac{14}{3}\right)}{\left(\dfrac{15}{2}\right)} = \dfrac{28}{45} = 28 : 45$

144. (a) Let Sonu has $100x$ land.

Then, Raju has $100x \times \dfrac{115}{100} = 115x$ land

and Ramu has $100x \times \frac{125}{100} = 125x$ land

∴ Required ratio of land by Raju and Ramu

$= \frac{115x}{125x} = \frac{23}{25}$

Hence, required ratio = 23 : 25

145. (d) Total strength of school = 640

Number of boys = 400

∴ Number of girls = 640 − 400 = 240

∴ Required ratio = 240 : 400 = 3 : 5

146. (a) $\frac{A}{C} = \frac{A}{B} \times \frac{B}{C}$

$A : C = \frac{5}{8} \times \frac{7}{8}$

$A : C = \frac{35}{64} = 35 : 64$

147. (b) According to the question,

Age of tree ∝ Number of rings

∴ Let age of tree = x yr

∴ $\frac{x}{50} = \frac{30}{40} \Rightarrow x = 37.5$ yr

∴ Age of tree having 30 rings = 37.5 yr

Now, value ∝ age

Let age of tree having 30 rings = ₹ y

∴ $\frac{y}{50000} = \frac{37.5}{50} \Rightarrow y = ₹\, 37500$

∴ Value of tree having 30 rings = ₹ 37500

148. (b) Given $\frac{A}{C} = \frac{A}{B} \times \frac{B}{C}$

$A : C = \frac{2}{3} \times \frac{7}{8}$

$A : C = \frac{14}{24} = \frac{7}{12} = 7 : 12$

149. (c) We know that,

Mean proportional $= \sqrt{ab} = \sqrt{25 \times 81}$

$= 5 \times 9 = 45$

150. (c) Let the two numbers be 2x and 3x, respectively.

According to the question,

$2x + 3x = 135 \Rightarrow 5x = 135$

$\Rightarrow x = \frac{135}{5} = 27$

∴ Required numbers are (2 × 27), (3 × 27)

= 54, 81

151. (b) Let x be the fourth proportional.

We can write 1.25 : 5.75 :: 3.5 : x

Here, $1.25 \times x = 5.75 \times 3.5 \Rightarrow x = 16.1$

152. (d) We know, mean proportion of a and $b = \sqrt{ab}$

∴ Mean proportion of 0.14 and 2.24

$= \sqrt{0.14 \times 2.24} = \sqrt{0.3136} = 0.56$

153. (c) Let R has 8 toffees initially.

R gives $\frac{3}{8}$ of toffees with him to S.

∴ Number of toffees with $S = \frac{3}{8} \times 8 = 3$

∴ Number of toffees left with R = 8 − 3 = 5

Toffees with R = k% toffees with S

$\Rightarrow 5 = \frac{k}{100} \times (3) \Rightarrow \frac{500}{3} = k$

154. (d) Given, $\frac{1}{M} : \frac{1}{N} : \frac{1}{O} = 3 : 4 : 5$

$M : N : O = \frac{1}{3} : \frac{1}{4} : \frac{1}{5}$

[∵ LCM = of 3, 4, 5, is 60]

$M : N : O = \frac{1}{3} \times 60 : \frac{1}{4} \times 60 : \frac{1}{5} \times 60$

M : N : O = 20 : 15 : 12

155. (b) Given,

a : b = (3 : 4) × 5 = (15 : 20)

b : c = (2 : 3) × 10 = (20 : 30)

c : d = (5 : 6) × 6 = (30 : 36)

∴ a : b : c : d = 15 : 20 : 30 : 36

156. (c) Let the third proportion to 36 and 48 is x.

∴ $36 : 48 :: 48 : x \Rightarrow \frac{36}{48} = \frac{48}{x}$

$\Rightarrow x = \frac{48 \times 48}{36} \Rightarrow x = 64$

157. (d) Let 2, 6, 8, a are in proportion.

∴ $\frac{2}{6} = \frac{8}{a} \Rightarrow a = \frac{8 \times 6}{2} = 24$

158. (b) Let the weight of box and gift articles are x : 9x.

According to the question,

$x + 9x = 25 \times 1000$ gm

$10x = 25 \times 1000$ gm

$x = 2500$ gm

∴ The weight of articles = 9x = 9 × 2500

= 22500 gm

159. (d) According to the question,

$\frac{7 + x}{11 + x} = \frac{18 + x}{23 + x}$

$(23 + x)(7 + x) = (11 + x)(18 + x)$

$\Rightarrow 161 + 7x + 23x + x^2 = 198 + 11x + 18x + x^2$

$\Rightarrow 161 + 30x = 198 + 29x$

$\Rightarrow x = 37$

Now, required mean proportional

$= \sqrt{(x-1)(2x-10)} = \sqrt{(37-1)(2 \times 37 - 10)}$

$= \sqrt{36 \times 64} = 6 \times 8 = 48$

160. (a) According to the question,

$\frac{8}{11} = 0.72, \frac{4}{5} = 0.8, \frac{1}{2} = 0.5, \frac{1}{11} = 0.09$

Clearly, 0.8 > 0.72 > 0.5 > 0.09

∴ Greatest ratio $= \left(\frac{4}{5}\right)$

161. (a) a : b = (3 : 7) × 4 = 12 : 28

b : c = (4 : 9) × 7 = 28 : 63

∴ a : b : c = 12 : 28 : 63

162. (b) $\frac{3}{4} = 0.75, \frac{5}{8} = 0.625$

$\frac{1}{2} = 0.5, \frac{6}{9} = 0.66$

Hence, $\frac{3}{4}$ is the greatest.

163. (b) Let 5 × Part of Ravi = 3 × Part of Reeta = 11 × Part of Rahul = k

∴ Part of Ravi $= \frac{k}{5}$

Part of Reeta $= \frac{k}{3}$

and part of Rahul $= \frac{k}{11}$

Ratio of Ravi : Reeta : Rahul $= \frac{k}{5} : \frac{k}{3} : \frac{k}{11}$

= 33 : 55 : 15

164. (a) Given, ratio of two quantity = 3 : 5

First quantity = 155 kg

∴ Other quantity $= \frac{5}{3} \times 155 = 258.3$ kg

165. (c) Given, a = 25, b = x

Mean proportion $= \sqrt{a \times b}$

According to the question,

$\sqrt{25 \times x} = 35$

Squaring both sides, we get

$\Rightarrow 25 \times x = 1225$

$\Rightarrow x = \frac{1225}{25} \Rightarrow x = 49$

166. (a) Given, $M \propto \frac{1}{N^2 + 3} \Rightarrow M = \frac{K}{N^2 + 3}$

Putting the value of M and N

$3 = \frac{K}{3^2 + 3} \Rightarrow K = 36$

Now, $M = \frac{K}{N^2 + 3} = \frac{36}{69 + 3} = \frac{36}{72} = \frac{1}{2}$

Hence, the value of $M = \frac{1}{2}$

167. (d) Let the two numbers be 7x and 3x.

According to the question,

$7x - 3x = 48 \Rightarrow 4x = 48$

∴ $x = 12$

Hence, the sum of two numbers is (7x + 3x)

= 10 × 12 = 120

168. (a) Let ratio of number of ₹ 2 and ₹ 5 coins = 5x : 2x

Let number of ₹ 10 coins = y

Then, 5x + 2x + y = 50

$7x + y = 50$ ...(i)

∴ Total amount = 150

$\Rightarrow 2 \times 5x + 5 \times 2x + y \times 10 = 150$

$\Rightarrow 10x + 10x + 10y = 150$

$\Rightarrow 2x + y = 15$ ...(ii)

Subtracting Eq. (ii) from Eq. (i),

$5x = 35 \Rightarrow x = 7$

From Eq. (ii),

$2 \times 7 + y = 15 \Rightarrow y = 1$

∴ Number of ₹ 10 coins = 1

169. (d) A : B = (3 : 7) × 2 = 6 : 14

B : C = (2 : 5) × 7 = 14 : 35

A : B : C = 6 : 14 : 35

170. (b) Given, $2^3 : 8^{5.06} :: 8^{-4.06} : x$

$\Rightarrow 2^3 \times x = 8^{5.06} \times 8^{-4.06}$

$\Rightarrow 2^3 \times x = 8^{5.06+(-4.06)}$

$\Rightarrow 2^3 \times x = 8^{5.06-4.06}$

$\Rightarrow 2^3 \times x = 8^1$

$\Rightarrow 2^3 \times x = 2^3$

$\therefore \quad x = \frac{2^3}{2^3} = 1$

171. (d) Let the number of ₹ 5, ₹ 10 and ₹ 20 coins be $3x$, $5x$ and $7x$, respectively.

Value of the all coins = ₹ 1845

$3x \times 5 + 5x \times 10 + 7x \times 20 = 1845$

$\Rightarrow \quad 15x + 50x + 140x = 1845$

$\Rightarrow \quad 205x = 1845 \Rightarrow x = \frac{1845}{205} \Rightarrow x = 9$

Worth of smallest coin $= 5 \times 3x = 5 \times 3 \times 9$

= ₹ 135

172. (a) Given, Coffee : Tea

Ratio of price = 3 : 4

Ratio of consumption = 4 : 7

$\therefore$ Ratio of expenditure = 12 : 28 = 3 : 7

[$\because$ Expenditure = Price × Consumption quantity]

173. (b) Ratio of Richa's $I = E + S = 2 + 1 = 3$

Suppose income is ₹ 300.

Expenditure is 200 and saving is ₹ 100.

Given, income and expenditure increases by 20% and 15%.

$\therefore$ Savings = Income − Expenditure

= 360 − 230 = ₹ 130

$\therefore$ Increase % in savings $= \frac{130-100}{100} \times 100$

= 30%

174. (a) Given, $a : b = 3 : 7 \Rightarrow \frac{a}{b} = \frac{3}{7}$

Then, $\frac{2a+3b}{3a+2b} = \frac{2\left(\frac{a}{b}\right)+3}{3\left(\frac{a}{b}\right)+2}$

$= \frac{2\left(\frac{3}{7}\right)+3}{3\left(\frac{3}{7}\right)+2} = \frac{\left(\frac{6}{7}+3\right)}{\left(\frac{9}{7}+2\right)} = \frac{27}{23}$

$\therefore (2a+3b) : (3a+2b) = 27 : 23$

$\therefore$ Required ratio is 27 : 23.

175. (b) Let third proportional be x.

According to the question,

$\frac{12}{6\sqrt{5}} = \frac{6\sqrt{5}}{x} \Rightarrow 12x = 180 \Rightarrow x = 15$

176. (c) $\frac{1}{3}$rd of 15 = 5, $\frac{4}{5}$th of 25 = 20,

and $\frac{3}{7}$th of 35 = 15

Let fourth proportion be x.

$5 : 20 :: 15 : x \Rightarrow \frac{5}{20} = \frac{15}{x}$

$\Rightarrow 5x = 20 \times 15 \Rightarrow x = 60$

177. (b) Given $2 : 9 :: 4 : x$

$\Rightarrow \quad \frac{2}{9} = \frac{4}{x} \Rightarrow x = \frac{4 \times 9}{2} \Rightarrow x = 18$

178. (a) Let the mean proportional of 7 and 63 be x.

$\Rightarrow 7 : x :: x : 63 \Rightarrow \frac{7}{x} = \frac{x}{63}$

$\Rightarrow x^2 = 7 \times 63$

$\Rightarrow \quad x = \sqrt{7 \times 63} \Rightarrow x = \sqrt{7 \times 7 \times 3 \times 3}$

$\Rightarrow \quad x = 7 \times 3 = 21$

Now, the difference between 24 and 21

= 24 − 21 = 3

179. (c) Let third proportional be x.

$\therefore$ 25 : 45 : : 45 : x

$\Rightarrow \frac{25}{45} = \frac{45}{x} \Rightarrow x = \frac{45 \times 45}{25} = 81$

180. (d) Let number of boys and girls be $5x$ and $4x$, respectively.

Total students = 414

$\therefore \quad 5x + 4x = 414 \Rightarrow 9x = 414$

$\Rightarrow \quad x = 46$

So, boys $= 5 \times 46 = 230$

Girls $= 4 \times 46 = 184$

New ratio $= \frac{230+46}{184} = \frac{276}{184} = \frac{3}{2} = 3 : 2$

181. (c) $A : B = 2 : 3 = 4 : 6$

$B : C = 6 : 7$

$\therefore \quad A : B : C = 4 : 6 : 7 = 8 : 12 : 14$

and $C : D = 14 : 3$

Hence, $A : B : C : D$

$\therefore$ Required ratio = 8 : 12 : 14 : 3

182. (d) $2 \times X$'s share $= 3 \times Y$'s share

$= 4 \times Z$'s share ...(i)

$\Rightarrow \quad X = \frac{3}{2}Y$ and $Z = \frac{3}{4}Y$

And $X + Y + Z =$ ₹ 13000 ...(ii)

$\frac{3}{2}Y + Y + \frac{3}{4}Y = 13000$ [From Eq. (i)]

$\Rightarrow \quad \frac{6Y + 4Y + 3Y}{4} = 13000 \Rightarrow \frac{13Y}{4} = 13000$

$\therefore \quad Y =$ ₹4000

$\therefore$ Required share of Y = ₹ 4000

183. (b) $p : q = 3 : 5$

$\Rightarrow \quad q : p = 5 : 3$

and $\quad p : r = 2 : 3$

$\therefore \quad q : p : r = 5 \times 2 : 3 \times 2 : 3 \times 3 = 10 : 6 : 9$

$\Rightarrow \quad p : q : r = 6 : 10 : 9$

$\therefore$ Required value $= 3p : 4q : 3r$

$= 3 \times 6 : 4 \times 10 : 3 \times 9$

= 18 : 40 : 27

184. (c) According to the question,

50% of A = 80% of B

$\Rightarrow \quad A \times \frac{50}{100} = B \times \frac{80}{100} \Rightarrow \frac{A}{B} = \frac{80}{50}$

$\therefore \quad A : B = 8 : 5$

185. (c) Let the fourth proportional be x.

Then, $7 : 13 :: 21 : x$

$\Rightarrow \quad 7 \times x = 13 \times 21 \Rightarrow x = 13 \times 3 = 39$

186. (d) Let A's and B's share be $4x$ and $5x$, respectively.

Given, $\quad 5x - 4x = 10$

$\Rightarrow \quad x = 10$

A's share $= 4x = 4 \times 10 = 40$ marbles

187. (b) Given, $a : b = 2 : 3 = 4 : 6$

and $\quad b : c = 6 : 8$

Then, $a : b : c = 4 : 6 : 8 = 2 : 3 : 4$

$\therefore$ Required ratio of $a : b : c$ is 2 : 3 : 4.

188. (d) Number of black tablet covers in the bag $= \frac{5}{9} \times 450 = 250$

189. (c) Let the fourth proportional be x.

$\therefore \quad \frac{5}{8} = \frac{30}{x} \Rightarrow x = \frac{30 \times 8}{5} \Rightarrow x = 48$

190. (c) Let the two numbers A and B are $13x$ and $17x$.

According to the question,

$\frac{A}{B} = \frac{13x \times 1.15}{17x \times 1.3} = \frac{13}{17} \times \frac{115}{130} = \frac{23}{34}$

= 23 : 34

$\therefore$ Required ratio is 23 : 34.

191. (a) Given, $A : B = 11 : 7$ ...(i)

and $\quad B : C = 5 : 19$ ...(ii)

To find $A : B : C$, multiply 5 in Eq. (i) and 7 in Eq. (ii),

$A : B = 55 : 35$

and $B : C = 35 : 133$

$\therefore \quad A : B : C = 55 : 35 : 133$

192. (a) Ratio of boys and girls is 6 : 7.

Total students = 3289

Number of girls $= \frac{3289}{(6+7)} \times 7 = 1771$

193. (d) Let the original and new salary of A is $8x$ and $11x$, respectively.

According to the question,

$11x = 33000 \Rightarrow x = \frac{33000}{11} =$ ₹ 3000

$\therefore$ A's original salary = ₹ $8x$ = ₹ 8×3000

= ₹ 24000

194. (c) Quantity of milk on fourth day, when qualities are in proportion = 30 : 24 :: 35 : x

$x = \frac{24 \times 35}{30} = 28$ litres

195. (d) $49 : x :: x : 81$

$\therefore \quad x^2 = 81 \times 49$

$\Rightarrow \quad x = 9 \times 7 = 63$

and $64 : y :: y : 169$

$\therefore y^2 = 169 \times 64 \Rightarrow y = 13 \times 8 = 104$

$\therefore$ Required value $= 2x + 3y = 2 \times 63 + 3 \times 104$

= 126 + 312 = 438

196. (d) Mean Proportional

$= \sqrt{(6-2\sqrt{2})(9+3\sqrt{2})}$

$= \sqrt{54+18\sqrt{2}-18\sqrt{2}-12} = \sqrt{42}$

197. (d)

	P	:	Q
Income	7	:	6
Expenditure	6	:	5
Saving	1	:	1

$1 \rightarrow 480$

$7 \rightarrow 7 \times 480 = ₹\,3360$

P's income = ₹ 3360

198. (a) First ratio of the sum, 3x, 4x and 5x respectively and second ratio of the sum 20y, 15y and 12y respectively.

According to the question,

$3x + 4x + 5x = 20y + 15y + 12y$

$\Rightarrow 12x = 47y$

$\Rightarrow x = \frac{47y}{12}$ ...(i)

and $20y - 3x = 1188$

$\Rightarrow 20y - \frac{3 \times 47y}{12} = 1188$ [From Eq. (i)]

$\Rightarrow 80y - 47y = 1188 \times 4$

$\Rightarrow y = 144$

$\therefore$ Sum $= 47y = 47 \times 144 = ₹\,6768$

Speedy Method

Initial Ratio – 3 : 4 : 5 = 12] × 47

141 : 188 : 235

Final Ratio – 20 : 15 : 12 = 47] × 17

240 : 180 : 144

According to the question,

$(240 - 141) \rightarrow ₹1188$

$99 \rightarrow ₹1188$

$12 \times 47 \rightarrow ₹6768$

199. (d) $\frac{\sqrt{5}}{\sqrt{42}} = \frac{\sqrt{7}}{x}$

$x = \frac{\sqrt{7} \times \sqrt{42}}{\sqrt{5}} = \frac{7\sqrt{6}}{\sqrt{5}} = \frac{7}{5}\sqrt{30}$

200. (b) Let number of ₹ 1, ₹ 0.5 and ₹ 0.25 coin be 5x, 6x and 8x, respectively.

According to the question,

$1 \times 5x + 0.5 \times 6x + 0.25 \times 8x = 420$

$5x + 3x + 2x = 420$

$\Rightarrow 10x = 420 \Rightarrow x = 42$

$\therefore$ Required number of coins = 42 × 5, 42 × 6 and 42 × 8 = 210, 252 and 336

201. (a) According to the question,

$\frac{7-P}{9-P} = \frac{9-P}{12-P}$

By componendo and dividendo rule,

$\frac{16-2P}{-2} = \frac{21-2P}{-3}$

$\Rightarrow 48 - 6P = 42 - 4P$

$\Rightarrow 2P = 6 \Rightarrow P = 3$

Hence, $P^2 + 1 = (3)^2 + 1 = 10$

202. (a)

	I Class	:	II Class
Ratio of fare	5	:	3
Ratio of Passenger	3	:	10

Ratio of collected amount = 15 : 30 = 1 : 2

$\therefore$ Required amount collected from II AC coach $= \frac{2}{3} \times 37080 = ₹\,24720$

203. (a) $30\% \times P = 0.6 \times Q = \frac{1}{3} \times R$

$\Rightarrow \frac{30}{100} \times P = 0.6 \times Q$

$\Rightarrow \frac{P}{Q} = \frac{60}{30} = \frac{2}{1} = \frac{10}{5}$

Again $0.6 \times Q = \frac{1}{3} \times R$

$\frac{Q}{R} = \frac{10}{18} = \frac{5}{9}$

$\therefore$ Required ratio of P : Q : R

10 : 5 : 9

204. (b) We know,

Expense = Price × Consumption

$\therefore$ Required ratio $= \frac{9}{11} \times \frac{11}{13} = 9 : 13$

205. (d) Let 50 paise, 20 paise and 10 paise coins are 2x, 3x and 4x.

According to the question,

$\frac{2x}{2} + \frac{3x}{5} + \frac{4x}{10} = ₹\,1020$

$\frac{10x + 6x + 4x}{10} = ₹\,1020 \Rightarrow x = 510$

Thus, 10 paise coins = 510 × 4 = 2040

206. (b) 12 : x :: x : 27

$\Rightarrow x^2 = 12 \times 27$

$\Rightarrow x = \sqrt{4 \times 3 \times (3)^3} = 9 \times 2 = 18$

and 25 : y :: y : 36

$\Rightarrow y^2 = 36 \times 25$

$\Rightarrow y = \sqrt{36 \times 25} = 30$

$\therefore$ Required Ratio $= \frac{18}{30} = \frac{3}{5} = 3 : 5$

207. (a) According to the question,

$20\% \times \text{Boys} = \frac{3}{4} \times \text{Girls}$

$\Rightarrow \frac{\text{Boys}}{\text{Girls}} = \frac{3}{4} \times \frac{100}{20} = \frac{15}{4}$

$\therefore \frac{\text{Boys}}{\text{Girls}} = 15 : 4$

208. (a) Let the number of boys be x, and the number of girls be 2x.

According to the question,

$\frac{x+20}{2x} = \frac{1}{1} \Rightarrow x + 20 = 2x \Rightarrow x = 20$

Total number of students in class (initially)

$= x + 2x = 3x = 3 \times 20 = 60$

209. (a) Let the three numbers are x, 2x and 3x.

According to the question,

$\frac{x+5}{2x+5} = \frac{2}{3} \Rightarrow 3x + 15 = 4x + 10$

$\Rightarrow x = 15 - 10 = 5$

Numbers are x, 2x and 3x.

i.e. 5 ; 2 × 5 = 10 and 3 × 5 = 15

$\therefore$ Smallest number = 5

210. (d) Let newly admitted girls be x.

Number of boys in class

$= 1650 \times \frac{6}{11} = 900$

Number of girls in class $= 1650 \times \frac{5}{11} = 750$

According to the question,

$\frac{900 + 124}{750 + x} = \frac{4}{3} \Rightarrow \frac{1024}{750 + x} = \frac{4}{3}$

$\Rightarrow 768 = 750 + x \Rightarrow x = 18$

$\therefore$ Ratio of newly admitted girls to newly admitted boys $= \frac{18}{124} = \frac{9}{62} = 9 : 62$

211. (d) Given, A : B = 3 : 4, B : C = 6 : 5

$\therefore$ A : B : C = 18 : 24 : 20 = 9 : 12 : 10

212. (b) Let the fourth proportional be x.

The fourth proportional of 2, a, 5a is

$\frac{2}{a} = \frac{5a}{x} \Rightarrow x = \frac{5a^2}{2}$

213. (b) Let the number be 6x, 7x, 15x, 19x.

According to the question,

$6x + 19x = 7x + 15x + 72 \Rightarrow 25x - 22x = 72$

$\Rightarrow 3x = 72 \Rightarrow x = 24$

$\therefore$ Smallest number = 6(24) = 144

214. (d) Let the numbers be 5x, 2x and 7x.

According to the question,

$(5x)^2 + (2x)^2 + (7x)^2 = 3822$

$\Rightarrow 25x^2 + 4x^2 + 49x^2 = 3822$

$\Rightarrow 78x^2 = 3822 \Rightarrow x^2 = 49 \Rightarrow x = 7$

$\therefore$ Biggest number = 7x = 7(7) = 49

215. (a) Let the fourth proportional to 1.5, 4.8 and 8 = x

According to the question,

$1.5 : 4.8 :: 8 : x \Rightarrow x = \frac{4.8 \times 8}{1.5} = 25.6$

216. (a) Let the sum be ₹ x.

According to the question,

$\frac{5x}{2+5+7} - \frac{2x}{5+2+7} = 150$

$\Rightarrow \frac{5x - 2x}{14} = 150 \Rightarrow x = \frac{150 \times 14}{3} = ₹\,700$

217. (c) The mean proportion of a and $\frac{a}{b^2} = \sqrt{a \times \frac{a}{b^2}} = \frac{a}{b}$

218. (a) Let two numbers be 6x and 7x.

According to the question,

$7x - 6x = 16 \Rightarrow x = 16$

Two numbers are 6x = 96 and 7x = 112.

219. (c) According to the question,

$\frac{A}{B} = \frac{7}{9} \times \frac{5}{5} = \frac{35}{45}$ and $\frac{B}{C} = \frac{5}{6} \times \frac{9}{9} = \frac{45}{54}$

Hence, C : A = 54 : 35

220. (a) According to the question,

$$A : B : C$$
$$(3 : 4 : \ ) \times 3$$
$$(9 : \ : 8) \times 1$$
$$9 : 12 : 8$$

∴ Required ratio i.e. $A : B : C = 9 : 12 : 8$

221. (b) Mean proportional of 9.61 and 3.61

$$= \sqrt{9.61 \times 3.61} = 5.89$$

222. (b) According to the question,

$$7x + 3x = 180 \Rightarrow x = \frac{180}{10} = 18$$

∴ Required difference $= 7x - 3x = 4x$

$$= 4 \times 18 = 72$$

223. (c) Given, $16 : x :: x : 196$

$$\Rightarrow \quad x^2 = 16 \times 196$$
$$\therefore \quad x = \sqrt{16 \times 196} = 4 \times 14 = 56$$

224. (c) Required part $= \frac{2}{2+3+5} \times 1000$

$$= ₹\,200$$

225. (a) Number of runs scored in singles

$$= \frac{1 \times 10}{6 \times 1 + 4 \times 3 + 3 \times 2 + 2 \times 7 + 1 \times 10} \times 96$$
$$= \frac{10}{6 + 12 + 6 + 14 + 10} \times 96 = \frac{10}{48} \times 96 = 20$$

226. (d) Let the fourth proportional be x.

$$\therefore \quad \frac{18}{27} = \frac{68}{x} \Rightarrow x = \frac{27 \times 68}{18} \Rightarrow x = 102$$

227. (b) Let the two numbers be $4x$ and $5x$, respectively.

According to the question,

$$\frac{4x - 1}{5x + 2} = \frac{3}{4} \Rightarrow 16x - 4 = 15x + 6 \Rightarrow x = 10$$

∴ Required ratio $= \frac{4x + 8}{5x + 4} = \frac{4 \times 10 + 8}{5 \times 10 + 4}$

$$= \frac{48}{54} = \frac{8}{9} = 8 : 9$$

228. (b) Let the number of candidates, who passed be $5x$ and who failed be $2x$.

∴ According to the question,

$$\frac{5x - 14}{2x + 14} = \frac{4}{3} \Rightarrow 15x - 42 = 8x + 56$$
$$\Rightarrow 15x - 8x = 98 \Rightarrow 7x = 98 \Rightarrow x = \frac{98}{7} = 14$$

∴ Number of passed candidates

$$= 5x = 5 \times 14 = 70$$

229. (b) Let the incomes of A and B be ₹ x and ₹ $2x$, respectively.

And let the expenditures of A and B be ₹ $2y$ and ₹ $3y$, respectively.

According to the question,

$$x = 80\% \text{ of } 3y = 0.8 \times 3y = 2.4y$$

∴ Ratio of saving B to $A = \frac{2x - 3y}{x - 2y}$

$$= \frac{2 \times 2.4y - 3y}{2.4y - 2y} = \frac{1.8y}{0.4y} = \frac{18}{4} = 9 : 2$$

230. (d) Let $x = 5k$ and $y = 7k$

Then, $\frac{6x - y}{5x + 3y} = \frac{6(5k) - 7k}{5(5k) + 3(7k)}$

$$= \frac{30k - 7k}{25k + 21k} = \frac{23k}{46k} = \frac{1}{2} = 1 : 2$$

231. (a) Given that, ₹ 7400 divided among A, B and C in ratio of 9 : 12 : 16.

Let the amount received by A, B and C is ₹ $9x$, ₹ $12x$ and ₹ $16x$, respectively.

According to the question,

$$9x + 12x + 16x = 7400 \Rightarrow 37x = 7400$$
$$\Rightarrow x = \frac{7400}{37} \Rightarrow x = 200$$

So, amount received by B

$$= 12x = 12 \times 200 = ₹\,2400$$

232. (b) Let the numbers be $3x$ and $5x$, respectively.

According to the question,

$$3x \times 5x = 3375 \Rightarrow 15x^2 = 3375 \Rightarrow x^2 = \frac{3375}{15}$$
$$\Rightarrow x^2 = 225 \Rightarrow x = 15$$

∴ Required sum $= 3x + 5x = 8x = 8(15) = 120$

233. (b) Let the incomes of Anil and Vikas are $8x$ and $5x$, respectively.

As, Vikas get 3000 less.

$$8x - 5x = 3000 \Rightarrow 3x = 3000 \Rightarrow x = \frac{3000}{3}$$
$$\Rightarrow \quad x = 1000$$

Income of Anil $= 8 \times 1000 = ₹\,8000$

and income of Vikas $= 5 \times 1000 = ₹\,5000$

∴ Total income $= 8000 + 5000 = ₹\,13000$

234. (c) Given, $\frac{x}{y} = \frac{3}{5}$ ...(i)

and $\frac{z}{w} = \frac{2x}{5y} \Rightarrow \frac{z}{w} = \frac{2}{5}\left(\frac{3}{5}\right)$ [By Eq. (i)]

$$\Rightarrow \quad \frac{z}{w} = \frac{6}{25}$$

So, the value of $xz : yw$

$$= \frac{xz}{yw} = \left(\frac{x}{y}\right) \times \left(\frac{z}{w}\right) = \frac{3}{5} \times \frac{6}{25} = \frac{18}{125}$$
$$= 18 : 125$$

235. (a) Let number of white balls $= 4x$

and number of black balls $= 7x$

Number of white balls = 44

According to the question,

$$4x = 44 \Rightarrow x = 11$$

Number of black balls $= 7 \times 11 = 77$

Total number of balls $= 44 + 77 = 121$

Speedy Method

So, according to the question,

4 units → 44

1 unit → 11

∴ (7 + 4) units → 11 × 11 = 121

Hence, total number of balls in the bag = 121

236. (d) Given, $X : Y : Z = 7 : 12 : 14$

Now, Share of $Y = \frac{12}{33} \times 9900 = ₹\,3600$

∴ Share of Y is 3600.

237. (a) Let the weight of first piece of diamond $= 5x$

and the weight of second piece of diamond $= 8x$

According to the question,

$$\because \quad (5x + 8x)^2 = 87880 \Rightarrow (13x)^2 = 87880$$
$$\Rightarrow \quad 169x^2 = 87880 \Rightarrow x^2 = 520 \quad \text{...(i)}$$

Now, loss incurred because of the breakage

$$= 87880 - \{(5x)^2 + (8x)^2\}$$
$$= 87880 - \{25x^2 + 64x^2\}$$
$$= 87880 - 89(520) \quad \text{[by Eq. (i)]}$$
$$= 87880 - 46280 = ₹\,41600$$

238. (b) According to the question,

$$P : Q \text{ and } Q : R$$
$$(6 : 5)_{\times 3} \text{ and } (3 : 4)_{\times 5}$$
$$18 : 15 \text{ and } 15 : 20$$

Thus, $P : Q : R$

$$18 : 15 : 20$$

∴ Ratio of $\frac{Q}{(P + R)} = \frac{15}{38}$

So, $Q : (P + R) = 15 : 38$

239. (a) Total amount = ₹ 17600

According to the question,

Mohan's share

$$= \frac{9}{(6 + 7 + 9)} \times 17600 = \frac{9}{22} \times 17600 = ₹\,7200$$

240. (d) Given, $\frac{x}{y} = \frac{7}{2}$

Now, $\frac{(7x + 4y)}{(7x - 4y)}$ [Divided by y]

$$\frac{\left(7 \times \frac{x}{y} + 4\right)}{\left(7 \times \frac{x}{y} - 4\right)} = \frac{\left(7 \times \frac{7}{2} + 4\right)}{\left(7 \times \frac{7}{2} - 4\right)} = \frac{(49 + 8)}{(49 - 8)} = \frac{57}{41}$$
$$= 57 : 41$$

241. (a) When $x = 2$ then,

numbers $4x = 8$, $x + 4 = 6$ and $3x - 1 = 5$.

Three proportionals are 8, 6, 5.

Let 4th proportional be a, then $8 : 6 :: 5 : a$

So, $\frac{8}{6} = \frac{5}{a} \Rightarrow a = \frac{15}{4}$

242. (b) According to the question,

Fruits : Yogurt : Honey

5 : 2

3 : 1

15 : 6 : 2

∴ Required ratio i.e. Fruits : Honey = 15 : 2

243. (d) Let the P, Q and R be $6x$, $5x$ and $9x$, respectively.

$$6x + 5x + 9x = 400 \Rightarrow 20x = 400 \Rightarrow x = 20$$

Now, difference between P and R

$= 9x - 6x = 3x = 3 \times 20 = 60$

244. (d) According to the question,

I : II : III

3 : 4

3 : 5

$(3 \times 3) : (4 \times 3) : (4 \times 5)$

$= 9 : 12 : 20$

$\therefore$ The second number $= \dfrac{12}{9 + 12 + 20} \times 123$

$= \dfrac{12}{41} \times 123 = 12 \times 3 = 36$

245. (b) Let the numbers be $6x$, $8x$ and $9x$, respectively.

According to the question,

$6x + 8x + 9x = 460 \Rightarrow 23x = 460$

$\Rightarrow \quad x = 20$

$\therefore$ Largest number $= 9 \times 20 = 180$

246. (a) Given, $4T = 5U \Rightarrow \dfrac{T}{U} = \dfrac{5}{4}$

Let $\quad T = 5k$ and $U = 4k$

Now, $\dfrac{(T + U)}{T} = \dfrac{(5 + 4)k}{5k} = \dfrac{9}{5}$

247. (c) Let the numbers be X and Y.

According to the question,

$\Rightarrow \dfrac{30}{100}(X + Y) = (X - Y)$

$\Rightarrow \quad 30X + 30Y = 100X - 100Y$

$\Rightarrow \quad 70X = 130Y$

$\therefore \quad X : Y = 13 : 7$

248. (b) Let $X = 11k$ and $Y = 5k$

According to the question,

$(X - Y) : (X + Y) = (11k - 5k) : (11k + 5k)$

$= 6K : 16K$

$\therefore \quad (X - Y) : (X + Y) = 3 : 8$

249. (d) According to the question,

$M : N : P : Q$

$(3 : 7 : 5 : \ \ ) \times 1$

$(\ \ : \ \ : 1 : 2) \times 5$

$3 : 7 : 5 : 10$

$\therefore$ Required ratio i.e. $M : Q = 3 : 10$

250. (b) Total money = ₹ 70000

$A : B = 2 : 3$

and $B : C = 4 : 5 \Rightarrow A : B : C = 8 : 12 : 15$

So, share of $A = \dfrac{[(70000) \times 8]}{35} =$ ₹16000

251. (b) $\because \ 4M = 20C, \Rightarrow M = 5C$

and $5N = 20C \Rightarrow N = 4C$

Hence, $M : N : C = 5C : 4C : C$

$M : N : C = 5 : 4 : 1$

252. (d) Let the number of boys and girls be $13x$ and $15x$, respectively.

According to the question,

$13x + 15x = 560 \Rightarrow 28x = 560 \Rightarrow x = 20$

Ratio of boys and girls after 40 more boys admitted $= (13 \times 20 + 40) : 15 \times 20 = 1 : 1$

253. (a) Given, $\dfrac{4}{5}A = \dfrac{2}{5}B \Rightarrow \dfrac{A}{B} = \dfrac{2}{5} \times \dfrac{5}{4}$

$\therefore \quad A : B = 1 : 2$

254. (b) Let the fourth proportion be x.

$\Rightarrow \ 30 : 120 :: 15 : x \Rightarrow x = \dfrac{120 \times 15}{30}$

$\Rightarrow \quad x = 60$

255. (a) Let income and expenditure be $19x$ and $13x$, respectively.

$\therefore$ Saving = Income − Expenditure

$= 19x - 13x = 6x$

and expenses of family = 29510

$\Rightarrow 13x =$ ₹ 29510 $\Rightarrow x = \dfrac{29510}{13}$

$\therefore$ Savings $= \dfrac{29510 \times 6}{13} =$ ₹ 13620

256. (a) Ratio of copper and zinc = 25 : 12

$\therefore$ Amount of copper in 370 kg of brass

$= \dfrac{25}{37} \times 370 = 250$ kg

257. (a) Given, $P : Q : R = 9 : 10 : 11$

Let, $P = 9k, Q = 10k, R = 11k$

Then value of $(P + Q) : (Q + R) : (R + P)$

$= (9k + 10k) : (10k + 11k) : (11k + 9k)$

$= 19k : 21k : 20k = 19 : 21 : 20$

258. (b) According to the question,

To compare the ratio, make the denominators equal.

Prithvi's ratio $= \dfrac{10 \times 9 \times 7}{13 \times 9 \times 7} = \dfrac{630}{819}$

Celine's ratio $= \dfrac{7 \times 13 \times 7}{9 \times 13 \times 7} = \dfrac{637}{819}$

Vikram's ratio $= \dfrac{5 \times 13 \times 9}{7 \times 13 \times 9} = \dfrac{585}{819}$

On comparing for Celine's, ratio is the greatest among them.

259. (c) According to the question,

$P : Q : R = \dfrac{2}{3} : 3 : \dfrac{1}{3} = 2 : 9 : 1$

$\therefore \ R$'s share $= \dfrac{1}{12} \times 8400 =$ ₹ 700

260. (c) Let $M = 9k$ and $N = 6k$

Then, $(M + N) : (M - N) = (9k + 6k) : (9k - 6k)$

$= 15k : 3k = 15 : 3 = 5 : 1$

261. (a) According to the question,

$P : Q : R = \dfrac{1}{2} : 4 : \dfrac{3}{2} = 1 : 8 : 3$

$\therefore R$'s share $= \dfrac{3}{12} \times 7200 =$ ₹ 1800

262. (d) Let the number of boys and girls be $16x$ and $9x$, respectively.

According to the question,

$16x + 9x = 50 \Rightarrow 25x = 50 \Rightarrow x = 2$

Number of boys = 16(2) = 32

Number of girls = 9(2) = 18

Mean proportional between number of boys and number of girls $= \sqrt{32 \times 18} = \sqrt{576} = 24$

263. (c) Given, 2 h 40 min $= 2\dfrac{40}{60} = \dfrac{8}{3}$ h

1 h 20 min $= 1\dfrac{20}{60} = \dfrac{4}{3}$ h and 10 h.

Let the fourth proportion be x.

Then, $\dfrac{\left(\frac{8}{3}\right)}{\left(\frac{4}{3}\right)} = \dfrac{10}{x} \Rightarrow x = \dfrac{\frac{4}{3} \times 10}{\frac{8}{3}} = \dfrac{40}{3} \times \dfrac{3}{8} = 5$ h

264. (a) Required mean proportional

$= \sqrt{121 \times 169} = 11 \times 13 = 143$

265. (a) Let the fourth proportional be x.

According to the question,

$\dfrac{(a^4 - b^4)}{a^2 - ab} = \dfrac{a^2 + b^2}{x}$

$\Rightarrow \ x = \dfrac{(a^2 - ab) \times (a^2 + b^2)}{(a^4 - b^4)}$

$\Rightarrow \ x = \dfrac{(a^2 - ab) \times (a^2 + b^2)}{(a^2 + b^2)(a + b)(a - b)}$

$\Rightarrow \ x = \dfrac{a^2 - ab}{(a + b)(a - b)} \Rightarrow x = \dfrac{a}{a + b}$

266. (d) Let the fourth proportional be x.

According to the question,

$\dfrac{a^3 + a^2b + ab^2}{a + b} = \dfrac{a^2 + ab + b^2}{x}$

$\Rightarrow \ x = \dfrac{(a + b)(a^2 + ab + b^2)}{(a^3 + a^2b + ab^2)}$

$\Rightarrow \ x = \dfrac{(a + b)(a^2 + ab + b^2)}{a(a^2 + ab + b^2)}$

$\Rightarrow \ x = \dfrac{a + b}{a} \Rightarrow x = \dfrac{a}{a} + \dfrac{b}{a} \Rightarrow x = 1 + \dfrac{b}{a}$

267. (a) According to the question,

Correct ratio $= \dfrac{1}{2} : \dfrac{1}{3} : \dfrac{1}{4} = 6 : 4 : 3$

Incorrect ratio = 2 : 3 : 4

$\therefore R$'s gain = (Incorrect share − Correct share) $\times 936$

$= \left(\dfrac{4}{9} - \dfrac{3}{13}\right) \times 936 = \dfrac{25}{117} \times 936 =$ ₹ 200

268. (b) Let the required number to be subtracted be x.

$(12 - x) : (21 - x) :: (21 - x) : 36$

$\Rightarrow \quad \dfrac{12 - x}{21 - x} = \dfrac{21 - x}{36}$

$\Rightarrow \quad 432 - 36x = x^2 - 42x + 441$

$\Rightarrow \quad x^2 - 6x + 9 = 0 \ \Rightarrow \ x = 3$

269. (b) According to the question,

A : B : C

6 : 7

5 : 6

$6 \times 5 : 7 \times 5 : 7 \times 6$

$= 30 : 35 : 42$

$\therefore$ Runs scored by $B = \dfrac{35}{107} \times 856 = 280$

270. (d) Given, third proportional to 8 and 24 is A.

$\therefore 8:24::24:A \Rightarrow A = \frac{(24)^2}{8} = 72$

Also, mean proportional between 4 and 16 is B.

$\therefore \quad B = \sqrt{4 \times 16} = 2 \times 4 = 8$

$\Rightarrow \quad \frac{A}{B} = \frac{72}{8} = 9$

271. (d) $\because$ Third proportional of a and $b = \frac{b^2}{a}$

$\therefore$ Third proportional of 0.1 and 0.12

$= \frac{(0.12)^2}{0.1} = 0.144$

272. (c) Mean proportional of squares of $\frac{x}{y}$ and $\frac{y}{z} = \sqrt{\frac{x^2}{y^2} \times \frac{y^2}{z^2}} = \sqrt{\frac{x^2}{z^2}} = \frac{x}{z}$

273. (c) Ratio of boys and girls

	Boys	Girls

Class A $11:18 = \frac{11}{18} < 1$

Class B $13:17 = \frac{13}{17} < 1$

Class C $20:9 = \frac{20}{9} > 2$

Hence, Class C has biggest ratio of boys to girls.

274. (d) $A:B = 8:13 = 40:65$ (multiplying by 5)

$B:C = 5:8 = 65:104$ (multiplying by 13)

$C:D = 4:5 = 104:130$ (multiplying by 26)

$\therefore A:B:C:D = 40:65:104:130$

275. (b) Let the two numbers are $4x$ and $5x$, respectively.

According to the question,

$\frac{4x+3}{5x-7} = \frac{1}{1} \Rightarrow 4x + 3 = 5x - 7$

$\Rightarrow \quad 5x - 4x = 3 + 7 \Rightarrow x = 10$

Hence, the numbers $= 4 \times 10$ and 5×10

$= 40, 50$

276. (d) The ratio of cheese to sauce

$= 1:\frac{1}{2} = 2:1$

Total number of cheese cup

$= \frac{15}{1} \times 2 = 30$ cups

277. (a) Let the total income of the family be ₹ $100x$.

Total saving $= 100x \times \frac{15}{100} = 15x$

$\therefore$ Total expenditure $= (100x - 15x) = 85x$

The ratio of expenditure on health, education and food $= 1:2:2$

$\therefore$ Expenditure on education $= 85x \times \frac{2}{5} = 34x$

According to the question,

$3 \times 34x - 300 = 100x$

$\Rightarrow \quad 102x - 100x = 300$

$\Rightarrow \quad 2x = 300 \Rightarrow x = \frac{300}{2} = 150$

$\therefore$ Income of the family $= 100x = 100 \times 150$ $=$ ₹ 15000

Expenditure incurred on health

$= 85 \times 150 \times \frac{1}{5} =$ ₹ 2550

$\therefore$ Total saving $= 15x = 15 \times 150 =$ ₹ 2250

$\therefore$ Required difference $= (2550 - 2250) =$ ₹ 300

278. (c) Let present salary of Rohan and Soham is $2x$ and $3x$, respectively.

According to the question,

$\frac{2x + 2000}{3x + 2000} = \frac{40}{57}$

$\Rightarrow 114x + 114000 = 120x + 80000$

$\Rightarrow \quad 6x = 34000 \Rightarrow x = \frac{34000}{6}$

Hence, present salary of Soham is

$= \frac{3 \times 34000}{6} =$ ₹ 17000

279. (c) According to the question,

$A \propto B \Rightarrow A = kB$

$\Rightarrow \quad 52 = k \times 91 \Rightarrow k = \frac{52}{91}$

when, $B = 126$, then $A = \frac{52}{91} \times 126 = 72$

280. (b) Let the number of students in three batches before the increase $2x$, $3x$ and $5x$.

Let the number of students in three batches after increase $4y$, $5y$ and $7y$.

According to the question,

$4y - 2x = 20 \quad \ldots(i)$

$5y - 3x = 20 \quad \ldots(ii)$

and $\quad 7y - 5x = 20 \quad \ldots(iii)$

From Eqs. (i) and (ii) (or any two of them)

$x = 10, y = 10$

$\therefore$ Required number of students

$= 2x + 3x + 5x = 10x$

$= 10 \times 10 = 100$

281. (b) $C = \frac{2}{3}$ of $D \Rightarrow C = \frac{2D}{3}$

and $D = \frac{3}{8}$ of $E \Rightarrow D = \frac{3E}{8} \Rightarrow E = \frac{8D}{3}$

Now, $C:E = \frac{2D}{3}:\frac{8D}{3} = 1:4$

282. (c) Third proportional of 16 and 24

$= \frac{24 \times 24}{16} = 36$

283. (c) Third proportional of 0.9 and 1.5

$= \frac{1.5 \times 1.5}{0.9} = \frac{15 \times 15}{90} = 2.5$

284. (a) $\frac{a}{2} = \frac{b}{3} = \frac{c}{4} = \frac{2a - 3b + 5c}{k} = m$ (let)

$\therefore \quad a = 2m, b = 3m, c = 4m$

and $\quad 2a - 3b + 5c = km$

$\therefore \quad 4m - 9m + 20m = km$

$\Rightarrow \quad 24 - 9 = k \Rightarrow k = 15$

285. (b) The mean proportion between 5 and $125 = \sqrt{5 \times 125} = 25$

286. (b) Given, $a = 18$ and $b = 50$

$\therefore$ Mean proportional $= \sqrt{ab}$

$= \sqrt{18 \times 50} = \sqrt{900} = 30$

287. (a) We know that,

Mean proportional $= \sqrt{xy}$

$15 = \sqrt{30 \times a}$

On squaring both sides, we get

$225 = 30 \times a \Rightarrow a = \frac{225}{30} = \frac{45}{6}$

$\Rightarrow \quad a = \frac{15}{2}$

288. (d) Let the two numbers are $5x$ and $9x$.

According to the question,

$\frac{5x - 25}{9x - 25} = \frac{25}{49}$

$\Rightarrow \quad 245x - 1225 = 225x - 625$

$\Rightarrow \quad 245x - 225x = 1225 - 625$

$\Rightarrow \quad 20x = 600 \Rightarrow x = 30$

Hence, numbers $= 5 \times 30$ and 9×30

$= 150, 270$

06

Problems Based On Age

Age is defined as a period of time that a person has lived or a thing has existed. Age is measured in months, years, decades and so on.

Question Based on Ratio

Ex. 1 At present, the ratio of the ages of Maya and Chhaya is 6 : 5 and 15 yr from now the ratio will get changed to 9 : 8. What is the present age of Maya?

Sol. Let the present ages of Maya and Chhaya be $6x$ yr and $5x$ yr, respectively.

According to the question,

$$\frac{6x+15}{5x+15}=\frac{9}{8}$$

$\Rightarrow \quad 48x+120=45x+135$

$\Rightarrow \quad 3x=15$

$\therefore \quad x=5$

Hence, present age of Maya $=5\times 6=30$ yr

Ex. 2 The ratio of the ages of Ram and Rahim 10 yr ago was 1 : 3. The ratio of their ages 5 yr hence will be 2 : 3. Then, the ratio of their present ages is

Sol. Let the ages of Ram and Rahim 10 yr ago be x yr and $3x$ yr respectively.

Then, present age of Ram $=(x+10)$ yr

and present age of Rahim $=(3x+10)$ yr

According to the question,

$$\frac{(x+10)+5}{(3x+10)+5}=\frac{2}{3}$$

$\Rightarrow \quad 3x+30+15=6x+20+10$

$\Rightarrow \quad 3x=15 \Rightarrow x=5$

$\therefore$ Required ratio $=\dfrac{5+10}{3\times 5+10}=\dfrac{15}{25}=3:5$

Question Based on *M* Times Ages

Ex. 2 The present age of Karan is 5 times the age of Shivam. After 10 yr, Karan will be 3 times as old as Shivam. What are the present ages of Karan and Shivam?

Sol. Let the present age of Shivam be x yr, then the present age of Karan be $5x$ yr.

After 10 yr, age of Shivam $=(x+10)$ yr

and age of Karan $=(5x+10)$ yr

According to the question,

$$5x+10=3(x+10) \Rightarrow 5x+10=3x+30$$

$\Rightarrow \quad 2x=20 \Rightarrow x=10$ yr

So, the present age of Shivam $=10$ yr

and the present age of Karan $=5\times 10=50$ yr

Ex. 3 4 yr ago, the age of Garvit was three times of Yuvansh, but 1 yr ago the age of Garvit was two times that of Yuvansh. What is the difference between the ages of Garvit and Yuvansh?

Sol. Let the present age of Garvit and Yuvansh be G yr and Y yr, respectively.

According to the question,

4 yr ago, $\quad (G-4)=3(Y-4) \Rightarrow G-3Y=-8 \quad$ ...(i)

1 yr ago, $\quad (G-1)=2(Y-1) \Rightarrow G-2Y=-1 \quad$ ...(ii)

On solving Eqs. (i) and (ii), we get

$$Y=7 \text{ yr and } G=13 \text{ yr}$$

$\therefore$ Required difference $=13-7=6$ yr

Important Facts

- If present age of a person is x yr, then his age after n yr $=(x+n)$ yr
- If present age of a person is x yr, then his age n yr ago $=(x-n)$ yr
- The difference in ages between two persons remains same either n yr after or n yr ago.

SSC Exam Scanner

SSC CGL 2024 (Tier I & II)

1. The present ages of Sweeta and Suman are in the ratio 4 : 5. Six years back, the ratio of their ages was 2 : 3. What is the present age of Sweeta?
SSC CGL (Tier-II) 20/01/2025 Shift-I

(a) 16 yr (b) 12 yr
(c) 8 yr (d) 20 yr

2. The ratio of the ages of two friends is 4 : 3, which will become 6 : 5 after 4 yr. What will be the sum of their ages (in years) after 22 yr from now?
SSC CGL (Tier-II) 20/01/2025 Shift-I

(a) 56 (b) 58 (c) 52 (d) 50

3. If the average age of three persons is 56 yr and their ages are in the ratio 2 : 5 : 7, then find the age of the youngest person.
SSC CGL (Tier-II) 18/01/2025 Shift-I

(a) 20 yr (b) 22 yr
(c) 24 yr (d) 26 yr

4. Anil and Beena are friends, and the difference between their ages is 5 yr. Anil's father Dinesh is three times as old as Anil, and Beena is twice as old as her sister Charu. The ages of Dinesh and Charu differ by 45 yr. If Beena is older than Anil, then find the sum of the present ages of both Dinesh and Charu. SSC CGL (Tier-II) 18/01/2025 Shift-I

(a) 78 yr (b) 69 yr
(c) 91 yr (d) 100 yr

5. Nihira is 25 yr old and Punith is 30 yr old. How many years ago was the ratio of their ages 3 : 4?
SSC CGL (Tier-I) 25/09/2024 Shift-I

(a) 20 yr (b) 15 yr
(c) 5 yr (d) 10 yr

6. 1 yr ago, the age of *B* was twice that of *A*. After 9 yr, if the ratio of the ages of *B* and *A* would be 4 : 3, then the sum of their present ages is .... years.
SSC CGL (Tier-I) 24/09/2024 Shift-III

(a) 30 (b) 15 (c) 17 (d) 21

7. Ghanshyam is thrice as old as Akash. 10 yr ago, Ghanshyam was four times as old as Akash. What is the difference between their current ages (in years)?
SSC CGL (Tier-I) 24/09/2024 Shift-II

(a) 65 (b) 50 (c) 55 (d) 60

8. Amit's father is aged five times more than Amit. After 6 yr, he would be three and a half times of Amit's age. After further 9 yr, how many times of Amit's age would he be? SSC CGL (Tier-I) 24/09/2024 Shift-I

(a) $2\frac{3}{4}$ times (b) $2\frac{1}{4}$ times
(c) $3\frac{2}{7}$ times (d) $2\frac{3}{7}$ times

9. The ratio of the ages of *A* and *B*, 3 yr ago was 5 : 7. The ratio of their ages, 13 yr from now, will be 9 : 11. If the present age of *C* is 11 yr less than that of *B*, then the present age of *C*, in years, is
SSC CGL (Tier-I) 23/09/2024 Shift-III

(a) 23 (b) 36 (c) 31 (d) 20

10. Hema is 20 yr old and her sister Neha is 30 yr old. How many years ago were their ages in the ratio of 3 : 5? SSC CGL (Tier-I) 23/09/2024 Shift-II

(a) 3 (b) 2 (c) 7 (d) 5

11. 10 yr ago, the age of Sunita was thrice the age of her daughter Tanya. 10 yr hence, the age of Sunita will be twice the age of Tanya. What is the ratio of their present ages?
SSC CGL (Tier-I) 23/09/2024 Shift-I

(a) 3 : 7 (b) 7 : 3
(c) 2 : 7 (d) 7 : 2

12. The sum of the ages of 6 children born at the interval of 2 yr each is 90 yr. What is the age (in years) of the eldest child?
SSC CGL (Tier-I) 19/09/2024 Shift-II

(a) 14 (b) 20
(c) 16 (d) 10

13. Three years ago, the age of a person was six times the age of his younger brother. Eight years later, the age of the person will be 3 yr less than twice the age of his younger brother. Find the present ages of the person and his younger brother. SSC CGL (Tier-I) 19/09/2024 Shift-II

(a) 15 yr and 5 yr (b) 5 yr and 15 yr
(c) 12 yr and 4 yr (d) 4 yr and 12 yr

14. In a family, the combined age of husband, wife and a son is 90 yr. The husband is the oldest. The difference in the ages of the husband and wife $\frac{1}{3}$rd the age of their son. After 10 yr, the age of the son would be half the age of his father. What is the present age of his mother (in years)?
SSC CGL (Tier-I) 19/09/2024 Shift-I

(a) 40 (b) 45
(c) 35 (d) 30

15. The present ages (in years) of *A* and *B* are in the ratio of 3 : 4. Five years back, the ratio of their ages was 2 : 3. What is the present age (in years) of *A*?
SSC CGL (Tier-I) 18/09/2024 Shift-II

(a) 15 (b) 28 (c) 20 (d) 21

16. The ages of two friends, Ram and Ravi, differ by 7 yr. Ram's mother Mayadevi is three times as old as Ram, and Ravi is four times as old as his brother Soham. The ages of Mayadevi and Soham differ by 65 yr. Find the age of Mayadevi (in years). SSC CGL (Tier-I) 10/09/2024 Shift-I

(a) 69 (b) 36 (c) 85 (d) 45

17. 7 yr ago, Prachi was four times as old as her daughter was at that time. 4 yr from now, Prachi will be two-and-a-half times as old as her daughter would then be. Find the sum of the present ages (in years) of Prachi and her daughter.
SSC CGL (Tier-I) 09/09/2024 Shift-II

(a) 69 (b) 77
(c) 49 (d) 72

18. At present, *A* is thrice as old as *B*. *C* is 5 yr elder than *B*. The sum of the ages of *A*, *B*, *C* is 75 yr. The ratio of the age of *B* 5 yr ago to the age of *A* three years from now is
SSC CGL (Tier-I) 09/09/2024 Shift-II

(a) 2 : 3 (b) 1 : 4
(c) 4 : 7 (d) 1 : 5

SSC CGL 2023-2020 (Tier I & II)

19. 6 yr ago, the ratio of ages of *A* to *B* was 7 : 5. After 4 yr from now, the ratio of their ages will be 11 : 9. What is *A*'s age at present?
SSC CGL (Tier-II) 06/03/2023 Shift-II

(a) $24\frac{1}{2}$ yr (b) $22\frac{1}{2}$ yr
(c) $23\frac{1}{2}$ yr (d) $21\frac{1}{2}$ yr

20. Meenu is 38 yr old. Her daughter is 8 yr old. In how many years will Meenu be double her daughter's age? SSC CGL (Tier-I) 18/07/2023 Shift-IV

(a) 20 (b) 24
(c) 22 (d) 25

21. The present current ages of Sudhir and Ashish are in the ratio 5 : 7. 12 yr ago, the ratio of their ages was 1 : 2. What will be the age of Sudhir after 5 yr from now?
SSC CGL (Tier-I) 14/07/2023 Shift-III
(a) 20 yr (b) 25 yr
(c) 33 yr (d) 28 yr

22. The present age of Rahim is five times the present age of his daughter, Savita. 7 yr from now, Rahim will be three times as old as Savita. What is the present age (in years) of Rahim?
SSC CGL (Tier-I) 14/07/2023 Shift-II
(a) 40 (b) 35
(c) 45 (d) 30

23. The ratio of the present age of father to that of his son is 7 : 2. If after 10 yr the ratio of their ages will become 9 : 4, then the present age of the father is
SSC CGL (Tier-I) 13/12/2022 Shift-III
(a) 43 yr (b) 35 yr
(c) 37 yr (d) 40 yr

24. The average age of a man and his son is 55 yr. The ratio of their ages is 7 : 4, respectively. What will be the ratio of their ages after 6 yr?
SSC CGL (Tier-I) 12/12/2022 Shift-II
(a) 1 : 2 (b) 12 : 7
(c) 25 : 17 (d) 38 : 23

25. Ratio between the present ages of *A* and *B* is 2 : 3, respectively. After 5 yr, the ratio between their ages will be 3 : 4. What is *B*'s age at present? SSC CGL (Tier-I) 02/12/2022 Shift-IV
(a) 20 yr (b) 15 yr
(c) 10 yr (d) 25 yr

26. The ratio of present ages of *A* and *B* is 7 : 8. After 6 yr from now, the ratio of their ages will be 8 : 9. If *C*'s present age is 10 yr more than the present age of *A*, then the present age (in years) of *C* is
SSC CGL (Tier-I) 17/08/2021 Shift-III
(a) 45 (b) 52
(c) 59 (d) 56

27. Ratio of the present age of a mother to that of the daughter is 7 : 1. After 5 yr the ratio will become 4 : 1. What is the difference (in years) in their present ages?
SSC CGL (Tier-I) 16/8/2021 Shift-I
(a) 29 (b) 30 (c) 28 (d) 31

28. The ratio of the ages of *A* and *B*, 8 yr ago was 2 : 3. 4 yr ago, the ratio of their ages was 5 : 7. What will be the ratio of their ages 8 yr from now? SSC CGL (Tier-I) 05/03/2020 Shift-I
(a) 4 : 5 (b) 3 : 4
(c) 7 : 8 (d) 5 : 6

29. The average age of a number of persons in a group was calculated as 35 yr, which was 2.5 yr more than the correct average as there was an error in recording the age of two persons as 38.5 yr and 40 yr instead of 29 yr and 22 yr, respectively. The number of persons in the group was
SSC CGL (Tier-I) 04/03/2020 Shift-III
(a) 11 (b) 12
(c) 15 (d) 13

SSC CPO SI 2024-2020

30. Three boys, on an average are 25 yr old and their age are in the ratio of 3 : 5 : 7. What is the age of youngest boy? SSC CPO 27/06/2024 Shift-II
(a) 21 yr (b) 12 yr
(c) 15 yr (d) 24 yr

31. 7 yr ago, the ratio of the ages of *A* and *B* was 4 : 5. 8 yr hence, the ratio of the ages of *A* and *B* will be 9 : 10. What is the difference between their present ages in years? SSC CPO 25/11/2020 Shift-I
(a) 3 (b) 2
(c) 4 (d) 6

32. 5 yr ago, Rohan's father's age was 8 times Rohan's age. After 5 yr the ratio of Rohan's father's age to Rohan's age will be 10 : 3. What is the present age of Rohan?
SSC CPO 25/11/2020 Shift-II
(a) 15 yr (b) 8 yr
(c) 10 yr (d) 12 yr

33. The average age of 40 students of a class is 16 yr. After admission of 10 new students to the class, the average becomes 15 yr. If the average age of 5 of the new students is 11 yr, then the average age (in years) of the remaining 5 new students is
SSC CPO 25/11/2020 Shift-II
(a) 10 (b) 15
(c) 16 (d) 11

34. 7 yr ago, the ratio of ages of *A* and *B* was 4 : 5. 8 yr hence, the ratio of the ages of *A* and *B* will be 9 : 10. What is the sum of their present ages in years? SSC CPO 23/11/2020 Shift-I
(a) 32 (b) 82
(c) 41 (d) 56

SSC CHSL 2024 (Tier I & II)

35. If a man's age is four times the sum of the ages of his three children and after 6 yr his age will be twice the sum of the ages of his three children, then what is the man's present age?
SSC CHSL (Tier-II) 18/11/2024 Shift-IV
(a) 56 yr (b) 30 yr
(c) 60 yr (d) 45 yr

36. My father is presently 25 yr older than me. The sum of our ages 5 yr ago was 39 yr. Find my present age. SSC CHSL (Tier-I) 11/07/2024 Shift-IV
(a) 13 yr (b) 12 yr
(c) 15 yr (d) 20 yr

37. The sum of the present ages of a father and son is 50 yr. If after 5 yr, the father's age will be 5 times the age of the son, then what was the father's age 5 yr ago?
SSC CHSL (Tier-I) 11/07/2024 Shift-III
(a) 36 (b) 47 (c) 43 (d) 40

38. The average age of Ruby and Soni is 40 yr. The ratio of their ages is 11 : 5, respectively. What is the age (in years) of Soni?
SSC CHSL (Tier-I) 11/07/2024 Shift-I
(a) 15 (b) 30
(c) 55 (d) 25

39. *P* got married 15 ys ago. Today her age is $1\frac{3}{5}$ times her age at the time of her marriage. At present her son's age is $\frac{1}{5}$ of her age. What was her son's age 4 yr ago as a fraction of *P*'s age at that time?
SSC CHSL (Tier-I) 10/07/2024 Shift-II
(a) $\frac{1}{9}$ (b) $\frac{1}{8}$
(c) $\frac{5}{9}$ (d) $\frac{1}{10}$

40. 4 yr ago, Ravi was 4 times as old as Kavya. 7 yr from now, Ravi will be 3 times as old as Kavya. Find the sum of their present ages.
SSC CHSL (Tier-I) 10/07/2024 Shift-I
(a) 118 yr (b) 122 yr
(c) 117 yr (d) 115 yr

41. Ram is 20 yr older than Rahul. '*n*' yr ago, Ram was thrice as old as Rahul. '2*n*' yr from now the ratio of the ages of Ram and Rahul will be 15 : 11. What is the value of '*n*'?
SSC CHSL (Tier-I) 08/07/2024 Shift-IV
(a) 15 (b) 10
(c) 30 (d) 20

42. A father is presently 3 times his daughter's age. After 10 yr, he will be twice as old as her. Find the daughter's present age.
SSC CHSL (Tier-I) 08/07/2024 Shift-I
(a) 5 yr (b) 10 yr
(c) 20 yr (d) 15 yr

43. The average age of 24 workers and their supervisor is 41 yr. If the supervisor's age is excluded, the average reduces by 0.75 yr. The age of the supervisor is
SSC CHSL (Tier-I) 05/07/2024 Shift-II
(a) 59 yr
(b) 41 yr 9 months
(c) 40 yr 9 months
(d) 49 yr

44. The age of a father will be double the age of his son 10 yr later. 10 yr ago, the father's age was 6 times the age of the son. How many years from now, the ratio of their ages will be 3 : 2?
SSC CHSL (Tier-I) 04/07/2024 Shift-III
(a) 35 (b) 30
(c) 20 (d) 25

45. 10 yr ago, a man's age was 5 times of his son's age. 2 yr hence, twice his age will be equal to 4 times the age of his son. What is the present age (in years) of the son?
SSC CHSL (Tier-I) 04/07/2024 Shift-II
(a) 20 (b) 16
(c) 18 (d) 14

46. In the year 2000, Monu was 3 times his sister's age. In 2010, he was 24 yr older than her. Find Monu's age in 2010.
SSC CHSL (Tier-I) 04/07/2024 Shift-I
(a) 46 yr (b) 52 yr
(c) 38 yr (d) 62 yr

47. The ratio of a father's age to his son's age is 7 : 4. The product of the numbers representing their ages is 1372. The ratio of their ages after 8 yr will be
SSC CHSL (Tier-I) 02/07/2024 Shift-I
(a) 19 : 11
(b) 19 : 12
(c) 19 : 13
(d) 19 : 14

48. The age of the older of two boys is thrice that of the younger. 9 yr ago, it was five times that of the younger. Find the present age of each. **SSC CHSL (Tier-I) 01/07/2024 Shift-II**
(a) 15 yr, 45 yr
(b) 12 yr, 36 yr
(c) 17 yr, 51 yr
(d) 18 yr, 54 yr

49. The sum of the ages of a son and father is 52 yr, after 4 yr the age of the father will be four times that of the son. What is the present age (in years) of the son?
SSC CHSL (Tier II) 10/01/2024 Shift-I
(a) 10 (b) 9 (c) 8 (d) 12

50. The age of the father 10 yr ago was thrice the age of his son. 10 yr hence, the father's age will be twice that of his son. What is the ratio of their present ages?
SSC CHSL (Tier II) 10/01/2024 Shift-I
(a) 3 : 2 (b) 7 : 3
(c) 5 : 3 (d) 5 : 2

SSC CHSL 2023 & 2022 (Tier I & II)

51. At a yoga center, 60% of the members are men and 40% of the members are women. If the average age of the men is 55 yr and the average age of the women is 45 yr, then what is the average age (in years) of all the members?
SSC CHSL (Tier II) 02/11/2023 Shift-I
(a) 49 (b) 48 (c) 50 (d) 51

52. The ratio of the father's age to his son's age is 5 : 3. The product of the numbers representing their ages is 960. The ratio of their ages after 6 yr will be
SSC CHSL (Tier I) 11/08/2023 Shift-I
(a) 23 : 15 (b) 23 : 17
(c) 21 : 15 (d) 21 : 17

53. The average age of 6 members of a family is 25 yr. If the youngest member is 4 yr old, then what was the average age of family just before the birth of the youngest member? **SSC CHSL (Tier I) 02/08/2023 Shift-I**
(a) 27.2 yr (b) 24.8 yr
(c) 32.8 yr (d) 25.2 yr

54. The average age of Rustam and Preetam is 30 yr. The average age of Preetam and Geetam is 20 yr. The average age of Rustam and Geetam is 26 yr. What will be the age of the youngest of the three after 5 yr?
SSC CHSL (Tier I) 10/03/2023 Shift-III
(a) 21 yr (b) 22 yr
(c) 26 yr (d) 25 yr

55. The average age of a husband, wife and child 2 yr ago was 28 yr and the average age of husband and child 5 yr ago was 21 yr. What is the present age of wife?
SSC CHSL (Tier I) 13/03/2023 Shift-III
(a) 38 yr (b) 36 yr
(c) 42 yr (d) 40 yr

56. A family consists of a father, mother and son. The ratio of their present ages is 8 : 5 : 2 and the present age of the father is 48 yr. What will be the average age of family after 3 yr?
SSC CHSL (Tier I) 10/03/2023 Shift-II
(a) 30 yr
(b) 31 yr
(c) 33 yr
(d) 35 yr

57. The average age of a group is increased by 6 yr when a person whose age is 24 yr was replaced by a person whose age is 66 yr. Find the number of persons in the group. **SSC CHSL (Tier-I) 02/06/2022 Shift-I**
(a) 8 (b) 9
(c) 6 (d) 7

58. The ratio of the ages of two friends is 7 : 9. After 10 yr, it will become 19 : 23. What will be the average age 7 yr from now?
SSC CHSL (Tier-I) 01/06/2022 Shift-I
(a) 33 yr (b) 35 yr
(c) 36 yr (d) 39 yr

59. A family consists of two grandparents, two parents and four grandchildren. The average age of the grandparents is 67 yr, that of the parents is 35 yr and that of the grandchildren is 9 yr. What is the average age of the family?
SSC CHSL (Tier-I) 30/05/2022 Shift-I
(a) 40 yr (b) 30 yr
(c) 36 yr (d) 45 yr

60. The average age of a man and his son is 56 yr. The ratio of their ages is 11 : 5. What is the son's age?
SSC CHSL (Tier-I) 27/05/2022 Shift-I
(a) 40 yr (b) 35 yr
(c) 30 yr (d) 32 yr

SSC MTS 2024-2021

61. The ratio of the present ages of Ram and Shyam is 3 : 4 and 4 yr ago the ratio was 2 : 3. What will be the ratio of the ages of Ram and Shyam 4 yr from now?
SSC MTS 01/10/2024 Shift-I
(a) 4 : 5 (b) 1 : 5
(c) 2 : 5 (d) 3 : 5

62. The ratio of the present age of *A* and *B* is 3 :1 Five years ago, the ratio of their ages was 5 : 1. The age of *A* (in yr) after eight years will be **SSC MTS 30/09/2024 Shift-I**
(a) 30 (b) 22
(c) 38 (d) 40

63. The average age of a family of three members (mother, father and son) is 44 yr. After the son's marriage, the average age of the family become 39 yr. What is the age of the daughter-in-law ? **SSC MTS 05/09/2023 Shift-II**

(a) 24 yr (b) 25 yr
(c) 23 yr (d) 22 yr

64. 5 yr from now, the ratio of the ages of *A*, *B* and *C* will be 3 : 5 : 2. The sum of the squares of their present ages is 525. What is the present age of *B* ? **SSC MTS 14/07/2022 Shift-I**

(a) 10 yr (b) 15 yr
(c) 25 yr (d) 20 yr

65. The present ages of *A* and *B* are in the ratio 3 : 5. If *A*'s present age is 33 yr, then what will be *B*'s age (in years) after 5 yr? **SSC MTS 14/07/2022 Shift-I**

(a) 65 (b) 60 (c) 50 (d) 55

66. The father of a girl is three years older than his mother. 6 yr ago, the average age of the girl and her parents was 32 yr and the age of the father was twice the present age of his daughter. What is the present age (in years) of the mother? **SSC MTS 02/11/2021 Shift-III**

(a) 48 (b) 42 (c) 45 (d) 49

SSC GD Constable 2024 & 2023

67. In a group of 22 men, two men whose average age is 58 yr are replaced by two new men. If the average age of the group decreases by 2 yr, then what is the average age of two new men? **SSC GD Constable 24/02/2024 Shift-I**

(a) 36 yr (b) 35 yr
(c) 37 yr (d) 32 yr

68. Average age of a group of 20 boys is 25 yr. A boy having age 15 yr leaves the group. A new boy joins the group and the average increases by 2 yr. What is the age of the new boy? **SSC GD Constable 24/02/2024 Shift-I**

(a) 52 yr (b) 57 yr
(c) 55 yr (d) 50 yr

69. The average age of a group of 11 men is 53 yr, 2 men leave the group and the average age of group increases by 1 yr. What is the average age of 2 men who left the group? **SSC GD Constable 22/02/2024 Shift-IV**

(a) 51 yr (b) 53 yr
(c) 49 yr (d) 48.5 yr

70. The average age of 19 students of a class is 22 yr. If a new student of age 42 yr joins the class, then what will be the average age of these 20 students? **SSC GD Constable 22/02/2024 Shift-III**

(a) 23 yr (b) 28 yr
(c) 26 yr (d) 24 yr

71. The average age of 14 students of a class is 17 yr. If a new student of age 32 yr joins the class, then what will be the average age of these 15 students? **SSC GD Constable 22/02/2024 Shift-II**

(a) 22 yr (b) 21 yr
(c) 18 yr (d) 19 yr

72. The average age of 30 students in a class is 20 yr. If each student's age is increased by 5 yr, then determine the number by which the average age is increased. **SSC GD Constable 22/02/2024 Shift-I**

(a) 8 (b) 7
(c) 5 (d) 3

73. Average age of 22 teachers is 64 yr. After involving a new teacher in that group the average increases by 1 yr. What is the age of the new teacher? **SSC GD Constable 21/02/2024 Shift-I**

(a) 93 yr (b) 91 yr
(c) 89 yr (d) 87 yr

74. The present ages of three people in proportions is 3 : 5 : 7, 6 yr ago, the sum of their ages was 87. Find their present ages (in years). **SSC GD Constable 20/02/2024 Shift-IV**

(a) 24 yr, 40 yr, 56 yr
(b) 18 yr, 30 yr, 42 yr
(c) 21 yr, 35 yr, 49 yr
(d) 27 yr, 45 yr, 63 yr

75. The sum of the present ages of a father and his daughter 80 yr. 8 yr ago, the father's age was 7 times the age of the daughter. 8 yr from now, what will be the daughter's age? **SSC GD Constable 20/02/2024 Shift-I**

(a) 18 yr (b) 20 yr
(c) 24 yr (d) 22 yr

76. The average age of 30 men is 25 yr 5 new men of an average age of 30 yr joined them. Find the average age of all the men put together. **SSC GD Constable 13/02/2023 Shift-IV**

(a) $26\frac{5}{7}$ yr (b) $27\frac{5}{7}$ yr
(c) $25\frac{5}{7}$ yr (d) $28\frac{5}{7}$ yr

77. John' and Tanvi's ages are in the ratio 8 : 15. After 9 yr, the ratio of their ages will be 11 : 18. What is the difference (in yr) between their ages? **SSC GD Constable 09/02/2023 Shift-II**

(a) 45 yr (b) 7 yr
(c) 21 yr (d) 24 yr

78. The average age of husband and wife is 24 yr. The age of their son is $\frac{1}{9}$th of the age of the husband. The wife is 6 yr younger to the husband. Find the average age of all three members of family. **SSC GD Constable 09/02/2023 Shift-I**

(a) 16 yr (b) 15 yr
(c) 18 yr (d) 17 yr

SSC Selection Post 2023

79. At present, Ritika's age is 3 times the age of Vipul. After 7 yr, Ritika will be 2 times as old as Vipul. What is the present age of Ritika (in years)? **Graduate Level 27/06/2023 Shift-IV**

(a) 42 (b) 35
(c) 53 (d) 21

80. The ratio of Rahul's age and his son Aman's age is 9 : 1 and the product of their ages is 144. What will be the sum of their ages after four years? **Higher Secondary Level 27/06/2023 Shift-III**

(a) 40 yr (b) 44 yr
(c) 48 yr (d) 46 yr

81. In Class I, there are 12 students of average age 20 yr and in class II, there are 16 students of average age 23 yr. What will be the approximate average age for all the students of these two classes? **Matric Level 27/06/2023 Shift-I**

(a) 20.7 yr (b) 1.53 yr
(c) 21.7 yr (d) 43 yr

Right Answers

1 (b)	2 (b)	3 (c)	4 (b)	5 (d)	6 (c)	7 (d)	8 (d)	9 (d)	10 (d)
11 (b)	12 (b)	13 (a)	14 (c)	15 (a)	16 (a)	17 (a)	18 (d)	19 (c)	20 (c)
21 (b)	22 (b)	23 (b)	24 (d)	25 (b)	26 (b)	27 (b)	28 (a)	29 (a)	30 (c)
31 (a)	32 (c)	33 (d)	34 (c)	35 (c)	36 (b)	37 (d)	38 (d)	39 (a)	40 (a)
41 (a)	42 (b)	43 (a)	44 (a)	45 (d)	46 (a)	47 (b)	48 (d)	49 (c)	50 (b)
51 (d)	52 (a)	53 (d)	54 (a)	55 (c)	56 (a)	57 (d)	58 (d)	59 (b)	60 (b)
61 (a)	62 (c)	63 (a)	64 (d)	65 (b)	66 (c)	67 (a)	68 (c)	69 (d)	70 (a)
71 (c)	72 (c)	73 (d)	74 (c)	75 (c)	76 (c)	77 (c)	78 (d)	79 (d)	80 (c)
81 (c)									

Solutions

1. (b) Let present ages of Sweeta and Suman be x yr and y yr respectively.

According to the question,

$$\frac{x}{y}=\frac{4}{5} \Rightarrow 5x=4y \quad \ldots(i)$$

and $$\frac{x-6}{y-6}=\frac{2}{3}$$

$\Rightarrow \quad 3x-18=2y-12$

$\Rightarrow \quad 3x-18=2\times\frac{5x}{4}-12 \quad$ [from Eq. (i)]

$\Rightarrow \quad 3x-18=2.5x-12$

$\Rightarrow \quad 0.5x=6$

$\Rightarrow \quad x=12$ yr

$\therefore$ The present age of Sweeta = 12 yr

Speedy Method

Sweeta : Suman

$2\begin{pmatrix}2 & : & 3\\ 4 & : & 5\end{pmatrix}6$

2 units ⟶ 6 years

1 unit ⟶ 3 years

$\therefore$ Present age of Sweeta = 4 unit → 12 yr

2. (b) Let ages of two friends be x yr and y yr.

According to the question,

$$\frac{x}{y}=\frac{4}{3}$$

$\Rightarrow \quad 3x=4y \quad \ldots(i)$

and $$\frac{x+4}{y+4}=\frac{6}{5} \quad \ldots(ii)$$

$\Rightarrow \quad 5x+20=6y+24$

$\Rightarrow \quad 5x+20=6\times\frac{3x}{4}+24 \quad$ [from Eq. (i)]

$\Rightarrow \quad 5x+20=4.5x+24$

$\Rightarrow \quad 0.5x=4$

$\Rightarrow \quad x=8$ yr

$\therefore \quad y=3\times\frac{8}{4}=6$ yr

So, sum of their ages after 22 yr

$=8+6+44=58$ yr

Speedy Method

$2\begin{pmatrix}4 & : & 3\\ 6 & : & 5\end{pmatrix}$

2 unit → 4

1 unit → 2

Present ages = 8, 6

After 22 yr = 30, 28

$\therefore$ Sum of their ages = 58 yr

3. (c) Let the age of three persons be $2x$, $5x$ and $7x$.

Average age of three persons = 56 yr

$\therefore \quad 56=\frac{2x+5x+7x}{3}$

$\Rightarrow \quad 14x=56\times3 \Rightarrow x=12$

$\therefore$ Age of the youngest person

$=2x=2\times12=24$ yr

4. (b) Let the age of Anil and Beena be x yr and y yr.

According to the question,

$$y-x=5 \quad \ldots(i)$$

Age of Dinesh = $3x$ yr

Age of Charu = $\frac{y}{2}$ yr

$\therefore \quad 3x-\frac{y}{2}=45 \Rightarrow 6x-y=90 \quad \ldots(ii)$

From Eqs. (i) and (ii),

$5x=95$

$\Rightarrow \quad x=19$ and $y=24$

$\therefore$ Sum of ages of Dinesh and Charu

$=3x+\frac{y}{2}=57+12=69$ yr

5. (d) Let x year ago their ratio is 3 : 4

According to the question,

$$\frac{25-x}{30-x}=\frac{3}{4} \Rightarrow 90-3x=100-4x$$

$\Rightarrow \quad x=10$ yr

$\therefore$ Required time = 10 yr

6. (c) 1 yr ago,

Let age of A be x.

Then, age of $B=2x$

According to the question,

$$\frac{x+10}{2x+10}=\frac{3}{4}$$

$\Rightarrow \quad 6x+30=4x+40$

$\Rightarrow \quad 2x=10$

$\Rightarrow \quad x=5$

Present age of $A=5+1=6$ yr

Present age of $B=5\times2+1=11$ yr

$\therefore \quad$ Sum $=11+6=17$ yr

7. (d) Let the age of Akash be x yr

Thus, age of Ghanshyam = $3x$ yr

According to the question,

$3x-10=4(x-10)$

$\Rightarrow \quad 3x-10=4x-40$

$\Rightarrow \quad x=30$ yr

Thus age of Akash = 30yr

and age of Ghanshyam = $3x=3\times30=90$ yr

$\therefore$ Required difference = $90-30=60$ yr

8. (d) Let Amit's present age = x yr

and Amit's father's present age = $6x$ yr

After 6 yr, $(6x+6)=3\frac{1}{2}(x+6)$

$\Rightarrow \quad 6x+6=\frac{7x}{2}+21$

$\Rightarrow \quad 6x-\frac{7x}{2}=21-6=15$

$\Rightarrow \quad \frac{5x}{2}=15 \Rightarrow x=6$

After further 9 yr

Amit's age = $(x+6+9)=6+15=21$ yr

Amit's father age = $(6x+6+9)$

$=6\times6+15=51$ yr

Now, $\frac{51}{21}=2\frac{3}{7}$ times

9. (d) Ratio of ages of A and B, 3 yr ago

$=5:7$

Let the ages of A and B, 3 yr ago = $5x$, $7x$

Present ages of A and $B=5x+3$, $7x+3$

Ages of A and B after 13 yr

$=(5x+3+13), (7x+3+13)$

According to the question,

$\Rightarrow \quad \dfrac{5x+16}{7x+16}=\dfrac{9}{11}$

$\Rightarrow \quad 55x+176=63x+144$

$\Rightarrow \quad 8x=32 \Rightarrow x=4$

Present age of $B = 7\times 4+3=31$

$\therefore$ Present age of $C = 31-11= 20$ yr

10. (d) Age of Hema = 20 yr

Age of Neha = 30 yr

Let x yr ago ratio of their ages was 3 : 5

$\Rightarrow \quad \dfrac{20-x}{30-x}=\dfrac{3}{5}$

$\Rightarrow \quad 100-5x=90-3x$

$\Rightarrow \quad 2x=10$

$\therefore \quad x=5$

11. (b) Let the present ages of Sunita and Tanya are S and T yr, respectively.

According to the question,

$S-10=3(T-10)$

$\Rightarrow \quad S-3T=-20 \quad \text{...(i)}$

Again, $\quad S+10=2(T+10)$

$\Rightarrow \quad S-2T=+10 \quad \text{...(ii)}$

Eqs. (ii) and (i), we get

$T=30,\ S=70$

$\therefore$ Ratio of their present ages $= 70:30=7:3$

12. (b) Let the age of children be

$(x-4), (x-2), x, (x+2), (x+4), (x+6)$ yr.

According to the question,

$(x-4)+(x-2)+x+(x+2)+(x+4)+(x+6)=90$

$\Rightarrow \quad 6x+6=90$

$\Rightarrow \quad 6x=84 \Rightarrow x=14$ yr

$\therefore$ Age of eldest child $=(x+6)$

$\Rightarrow \quad (14+6)=20$ yr

13. (a) Let the present age of the person and his younger brother be x and y, respectively.

According to the question,

3 yr ago, $\quad (x-3)=6(y-3)$

$\Rightarrow \quad x-3=6y-18$

$\Rightarrow \quad x-6y=-15 \quad \text{...(i)}$

Now, 8 yr later,

$(x+8)+3=2(y+8)$

$\Rightarrow \quad x+11=2y+16$

$\Rightarrow \quad x-2y=5 \quad \text{...(ii)}$

From Eqs. (i) and (ii),

$x-6y=-15$

$x-2y=5$

$-\quad +\quad -$

$-4y=-20$

$\Rightarrow \quad y=5$

$\therefore$ From Eq. (i),

$x=6(5)-15$

$\Rightarrow \quad x=15$ yr

$\therefore$ The present age of the person and his younger brother be 15 yr and 5 yr, respectively.

14. (c) Given, combined age of husband, wife and son = 90 yr

$H+W+S=90 \quad \text{...(i)}$

and $\quad H-W=\dfrac{S}{3} \quad \text{...(ii)}$

$\Rightarrow \quad S+10=\dfrac{H+10}{2}$

$\Rightarrow \quad 2S+20=H+10$

$\Rightarrow \quad H-2S=10 \quad \text{...(iii)}$

$\Rightarrow \quad H=2S+10$

Put the value of H in Eq. (ii),

$\Rightarrow \quad 2S+10-W=\dfrac{S}{3}$

$\Rightarrow \quad 6S+30-3W=S$

$\Rightarrow \quad \dfrac{5S+30}{3}=W$

Put the value of H and W in Eq. (i),

$\Rightarrow \quad 2S+10+\dfrac{5S+30}{3}+S=90$

$\Rightarrow \quad 3S+10+\dfrac{5S+30}{3}=90$

$\Rightarrow \quad 9S+30+5S+30=270$

$\Rightarrow \quad 14S=210$

$\Rightarrow \quad S=15$ yr

$\therefore$ Age of his mother $=\dfrac{5\times 15+30}{3}=35$ yr

15. (a) Let the present age of $A=3x$ and the present age of $B=4x$

According to the question,

$\dfrac{3x-5}{4x-5}=\dfrac{2}{3}$

$\Rightarrow \quad 9x-15=8x-10 \Rightarrow x=5$

$\therefore$ Present age of $A=3\times 5=15$

16. (a) Given,

Ram − Ravi = 7 ...(i)

Maya = 3 Ram ...(ii)

Ravi = 4 Sohan ...(iii)

Maya − Sohan = 65 ...(iv)

$3\text{ Ram}-\dfrac{\text{Ravi}}{4}=65$

12 Ram − Ravi = 260 ...(v)

From Eqs. (i) and (v),

Ram = 23

$\therefore$ Maya's age $=23\times 3=69$ yr

17. (a) Let the present age of Prachi be x yr. Also, her daughter's age be y yr.

7 yr ago,

$\Rightarrow \quad (x-7)=4(y-7)$

$\Rightarrow \quad x-7=4y-28$

$\Rightarrow \quad x=-21+4y \quad \text{...(i)}$

4 yr from now,

$\Rightarrow \quad (x+4)=2.5(y+4)$

$\Rightarrow \quad x+4=2.5y+10$

$\Rightarrow \quad x=2.5y+6 \quad \text{...(ii)}$

From Eqs. (i) and (ii)

$-21+4y=2.5y+6$

$\Rightarrow \quad 1.5y=27 \Rightarrow y=18$

$\therefore$ Prachi's age, $x=-21+4(18)=51$ [From Eq. (i)]

$\therefore$ Required sum = 51 + 18 = 69

18. (d) According to the question,

$A=3B$ and $C=B+5$

and $\quad A+B+C=75$

$\Rightarrow \quad 3B+B+(B+5)=75$

$\Rightarrow \quad 5B=70 \Rightarrow B=14$

$\therefore$ Age of B, 5 yr ago = 9 yr

Age of A, 3 yr from now $=3(14)+3=45$

$\therefore$ Required ratio = 9 : 45 = 1 : 5

19. (c) Let age of A and B in 6 yr ago be $7x$ yr and $5x$ yr, respectively.

According to the question,

$\dfrac{7x+6+4}{5x+6+4}=\dfrac{11}{9} \Rightarrow \dfrac{7x+10}{5x+10}=\dfrac{11}{9}$

$\Rightarrow \quad 63x+90=55x+110$

$\Rightarrow \quad x=\dfrac{5}{2}$

$\therefore$ Present age of $A=7\times\dfrac{5}{2}+6=23\dfrac{1}{2}$ yr

Speedy Method

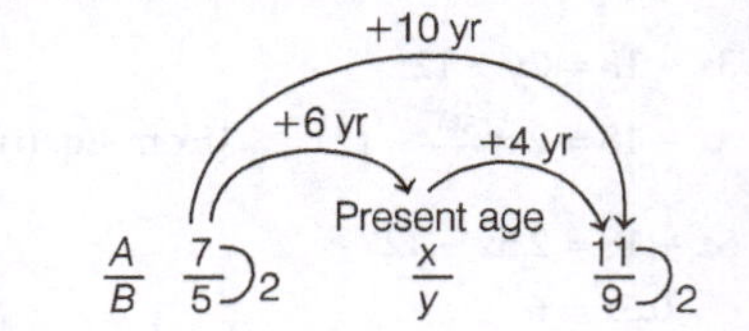

$(11-7)$ units $\rightarrow$ 10 yr

4 units $\rightarrow$ 10 yr

A's age $=\dfrac{10}{4}\times 7$ yr

$\therefore$ Present age of $A=\dfrac{10}{4}\times 7+4=23\dfrac{1}{2}$ yr.

20. (c) Let x yr will be double her daughter's age.

According to the question,

$38+x=2(8+x) \Rightarrow 38+x=16+2x$

$\therefore \quad x=22$ yr

21. (b) Let current age of Sudhir and Ashish are $5x$ yr and $7x$ yr, respectively.

$\dfrac{5x-12}{7x-12}=\dfrac{1}{2} \Rightarrow 10x-24=7x-12$

$\Rightarrow \quad 3x=12 \Rightarrow x=4$

Age of Sudhir after 5 yr $=5x+5$

$=20+5=25$ yr

Speedy Method

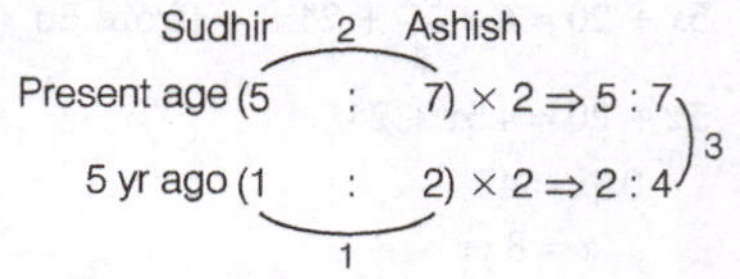

3 units $\rightarrow$ 12

5 units $\rightarrow \dfrac{12}{3}\times 5=20$ yr

Hence, age of Sudhir after 5 yr = 25 yr

22. (b) Let present age of Savita = x yr

$\therefore$ Rahim's present age = $5x$ yr

According to the question,

$$5x + 7 = 3(x + 7)$$

$$\Rightarrow \quad 5x + 7 = 3x + 21 \Rightarrow 2x = 14$$

$$\therefore \quad x = 7$$

$\therefore$ Present age of Rahim = $5x = 5 \times 7 = 35$ yr

23. (b) Let the present ages of father and son be $7x$ yr and $2x$ yr, respectively.

According to the question,

$$\frac{7x + 10}{2x + 10} = \frac{9}{4}$$

$$\Rightarrow \quad 28x + 40 = 18x + 90$$

$$\Rightarrow \quad x = 5$$

$\therefore$ Present age of father = $7x = 7 \times 5 = 35$ yr

24. (d) Let the age of the man and his son be $7x$ yr and $4x$ yr, respectively.

According to the question,

$$7x + 4x = 55 \times 2$$

$$\Rightarrow \quad x = \frac{110}{10} = 10$$

$\therefore$ Ratio of their ages after 6 yr

$$= \frac{7x + 6}{4x + 6} = \frac{7 \times 10 + 6}{4 \times 10 + 6} = 38:23$$

25. (b) Let the present age of A and B are $2x$ yr and $3x$ yr, respectively.

According to the question,

$$\frac{2x + 5}{3x + 5} = \frac{3}{4}$$

$$\Rightarrow \quad 8x + 20 = 9x + 15$$

$$\therefore \quad x = 5$$

So, B's present age $= 3x = 3 \times 5 = 15$ yr

26. (b) Given, present age of A and B are $7x$ and $8x$ yr, respectively.

According to the question,

$$\frac{7x + 6}{8x + 6} = \frac{8}{9} \Rightarrow 63x + 54 = 64x + 48$$

$$\Rightarrow \quad x = 6$$

Present age of $A = 7x = 7 \times 6 = 42$ yr

$\therefore$ Present age of $C = 42 + 10 = 52$ yr

27. (b) Let present age of mother is $7x$.

Present age of daughter = x yr

According to the question,

$$\frac{7x + 5}{x + 5} = \frac{4}{1} \Rightarrow 7x + 5 = 4x + 20$$

$$\Rightarrow \quad x = 5$$

$\therefore$ Difference of present ages of mother and daughter $= 7x - x = 6x = 6 \times 5 = 30$ yr.

28. (a) The ratio of age of A and B, 8 yr ago $= 2x : 3x$

According to the question,

$$\frac{(2x + 4)}{(3x + 4)} = \frac{5}{7}$$

$$\Rightarrow \quad 14x + 28 = 15x + 20 \Rightarrow x = 8$$

Ratio of age of A : B, after 8 yr

$$= 2 \times 8 + 8 + 8 : 3 \times 8 + 8 + 8$$

$$= 32 : 40 = 4 : 5$$

29. (a) Let total number of persons in the group = x

According to the question,

Wrong average = 35

$\therefore$ Total age for wrong average = $35x$

Again, according to the question,

Correct average = $35 - 2.5 = 32.5$

$\therefore$ Total correct age = $32.5x$

Wrong age of two persons

$$= (38.5 + 40) = 78.5 \text{ yr}$$

Correct age of two persons

$$= (29 + 22) = 51 \text{ yr}$$

Difference between correct age and wrong age of two persons = $(78.5 - 51) = 27.5$ yr

So, $\quad 35x - 32.5x = 27.5$

$$\Rightarrow \quad x = \frac{27.5}{2.5} = 11$$

30. (c) Sum of the ages of three boys

$$= 25 \times 3 = 75$$

Ratio of their ages = 3 : 5 : 7

Let their ages be $3x$, $5x$ and $7x$, respectively.

Now, $(3x + 5x + 7x) = 75$

$$\Rightarrow \quad 15x = 75$$

$$\Rightarrow \quad x = 5$$

$\therefore$ Age of youngest boy = $3x = 3 \times 5 = 15$ yr

31. (a) Let's take, seven year ago, the age of A and B is $4x$ yr and $5x$ yr.

According to the question,

$$\frac{4x + 7 + 8}{5x + 7 + 8} = \frac{9}{10}$$

$$\Rightarrow \quad 40x + 150 = 45x + 135$$

$$\Rightarrow \quad x = 3 \text{ yr}$$

$\therefore$ Present age of A is $(4x + 7) = 19$ yr

and present age of B is $(5x + 7) = 22$ yr

$\therefore$ Difference between their present ages is $(22 - 19) = 3$ yr

32. (c) Let 5 yr ago,

Age of Rohan = x yr

Then, age of Rohan's father = $8x$ yr

According to the question,

$$\frac{8x + 5 + 5}{x + 5 + 5} = \frac{10}{3} \Rightarrow \frac{8x + 10}{x + 10} = \frac{10}{3}$$

$$\Rightarrow \quad 24x - 10x = 100 - 30$$

$$\Rightarrow \quad 14x = 70 \Rightarrow x = 5$$

Hence, the present age of Rohan

$$= x + 5 = 5 + 5 = 10 \text{ yr}$$

33. (d) Total age of 40 students

$$= 40 \times 16 = 640 \text{ yr}$$

Total age of 50 students with 10 new students

$$= 50 \times 15 = 750 \text{ yr}$$

Total age of 5 new students = $5 \times 11 = 55$ yr

$\therefore$ Average age of remaining 5 students

$$= \frac{750 - 640 - 55}{5} = \frac{55}{5} = 11 \text{ yr}$$

34. (c) 7 yr ago, the ratio of ages of A and B is $4x : 5x$.

According to the question,

$$\frac{4x + 7 + 8}{5x + 7 + 8} = \frac{9}{10} \Rightarrow x = 3$$

$\therefore$ Sum of their present ages

$$= (4 \times 3 + 7) + (5 \times 3 + 7) = 41 \text{ yr}$$

35. (c) Let sum of age of three children be x.

Then, Man's age = $4x$

According to the question,

$$4x + 6 = 2(x + 18)$$

$$\Rightarrow \quad 4x + 6 = 2x + 36 \Rightarrow 2x = 30$$

$$\Rightarrow \quad x = 15$$

Thus, Man's age = $15 \times 4 = 60$ yr

36. (b) Let my present age is x yr.

$\therefore$ My father's present age = $(x + 25)$ yr

According to the question,

$(x - 5) + (x + 25 - 5) = 39$

$$\Rightarrow \quad x - 5 + x + 20 = 39$$

$$\Rightarrow \quad 2x = 39 - 15 = 24$$

$$\therefore \quad x = 12 \text{ yr}$$

37. (d) Let the present age of father be x yr, then the present age of son is $(50 - x)$ yr.

According to the question,

$$x + 5 = 5(50 - x + 5)$$

$$\Rightarrow \quad x + 5 = 5(55 - x)$$

$$\Rightarrow \quad x + 5 = 275 - 5x \Rightarrow 6x = 270$$

$$\Rightarrow \quad x = 45$$

$\therefore$ 5 yr ago father's age = $45 - 5 = 40$ yr

38. (d) Let the age of Rubi and Soni are $11x$ and $5x$.

According to the question,

$$\frac{11x + 5x}{2} = 40 \Rightarrow 8x = 40 \Rightarrow x = 5$$

Thus, age of Soni = $5x = 5 \times 5 = 25$ yr

39. (a) Let age of P at the time of marriage be x yr.

Thus, the present age of P

$$\Rightarrow \quad x + 15 = x \times \frac{8}{5}$$

$$\Rightarrow \quad \frac{8}{5}x - x = 15 \Rightarrow \frac{3x}{5} = 15$$

$$\Rightarrow \quad x = 25 \text{ yr}$$

$\therefore$ Present age of $P = x + 15 = 25 + 15 = 40$ yr

and age of son = $40 \times \frac{1}{5} = 8$ yr

$\therefore$ Required fraction $= \frac{8 - 4}{(40 - 4)} = \frac{4}{36} = \frac{1}{9}$

40. (a) Let age of Kavya 4 yr ago be x yr.

Then, age of Ravi 4 yr ago = $4x$ yr

According to the question,

$$3(x + 11) = (4x + 11)$$

$$\Rightarrow \quad 3x + 33 = 4x + 11 \Rightarrow 22 = x$$

Thus, present Age of Kavya = $22 + 4 = 26$ yr

and present Age of Ravi = $22 \times 4 + 4 = 92$ yr

$\therefore$ Required sum = $26 + 92 = 118$ yr

41. (a) Let the age of Rahul be x yr.

$\therefore$ Ram's age = $(x + 20)$ yr

According to the question,

$$(x + 20) - n = 3(x - n)$$

$\Rightarrow \quad x + 20 - n = 3x - 3n$

$\Rightarrow \quad x - n = 10 \quad \ldots(i)$

Again, $\dfrac{(x + 20) + 2n}{x + 2n} = \dfrac{15}{11}$

$\Rightarrow \quad 11x + 220 + 22n = 15x + 30n$

$\Rightarrow \quad x + 2n = 55 \quad \ldots(ii)$

On solving Eqs. (i) and (ii),

$\Rightarrow \quad 3n = 45 \Rightarrow n = 15$

42. (b) Let the daughter's age be x yr at present, then, father's age be $(3x)$ yr.

After 10 yr,

$\Rightarrow \quad (3x + 10) = 2(x + 10)$

$\Rightarrow \quad 3x + 10 = 2x + 20 \Rightarrow x = 10$ yr

Thus, present age of daughter is 10 yr.

43. (a) The total age of workers and supervisor $= (24 + 1) \times 41 = 25 \times 41 = 1025$ yr

If supervisor excluded, total age of workers becomes $= 24 \times [41 - 0.75]$

$= 24 \times 40.25 = 966$ yr

$\therefore$ Age of supervisor $= [1025 - 966]$ yr $= 59$ yr

44. (a) Let the present age of father $= x$ yr and the present age of son $= y$ yr

According to the question,

$(x + 10) = 2(y + 10)$

$\Rightarrow \quad x + 10 = 2y + 20$

$\Rightarrow \quad x - 2y = 10 \quad \ldots(i)$

and $\quad (x - 10) = 6(y - 10)$

$\Rightarrow \quad x - 10 = 6y - 60$

$\Rightarrow \quad x - 6y = -50 \quad \ldots(ii)$

From Eqs. (i) and (ii),

$x = 40$, and $y = 15$ yr

Assume 'a' yr from now, the ratio of their ages will be 3 : 2.

$\therefore \quad \dfrac{40 + a}{15 + a} = \dfrac{3}{2} \Rightarrow 80 + 2a = 45 + 3a$

$\Rightarrow \quad 80 - 45 = 3a - 2a \Rightarrow a = 35$ yr

45. (d) Let the present age of man $= y$ yr and the present age of son $= x$ yr

According to the question,

10 yr ago, $\quad y - 10 = 5(x - 10)$

$\Rightarrow \quad y - 10 = 5x - 50$

$\Rightarrow \quad 5x - y = 40 \quad \ldots(i)$

2 yr hence, $\quad 2(y + 2) = 4(x + 2)$

$\Rightarrow \quad y + 2 = 2x + 4$

$\Rightarrow \quad y - 2x = 2 \quad \ldots(ii)$

From Eqs. (i) and (ii),

$x = 14$ yr

Hence, present age of the son $= 14$ yr

46. (a) Let sister age be x yr and Monu's age be $3x$ yr.

According to the question,

$3x + 10 - (x + 10) = 24$

$\Rightarrow \quad 2x = 24$

$\Rightarrow \quad x = 12$

$\therefore$ Monu's age in 2010 $= 3x + 10 = 3 \times 12 + 10$

$= 46$ yr

47. (b) Let the age of father is $7x$ yr and the age of son is $4x$ yr.

According to the question,

$7x \times 4x = 1372$

$\Rightarrow \quad 28x^2 = 1372$

$\Rightarrow \quad x^2 = 49 \Rightarrow x = 7$

Present age of father and son are

$= (7 \times 7)$ and $(7 \times 4) = 49$ and 28

$\therefore$ Ratio of their ages after 8 yr

$= (49 + 8) : (28 + 8)$

$= 57 : 36 = 19 : 12$

48. (d) Let Present age of younger boy $= x$ yr.

Then, Present age of older boy $= 3x$ yr

According to the question

$$\frac{3x - 9}{x - 9} = \frac{5}{1}$$

$\Rightarrow \quad 3x - 9 = 5x - 45$

$\Rightarrow \quad 2x = 36$

$\Rightarrow \quad x = 18$

So, their present ages are 18 yr and 54 yr, respectively.

49. (c) Let age of father $= f$ yr

and $\quad$ age of son $= s$ yr

According to the question,

$f + s = 52 \quad \ldots(i)$

and $\quad (f + 4) = (s + 4)4$

$\Rightarrow \quad f - 4s = 12 \quad \ldots(ii)$

Solving Eqs. (i) and (ii), we get

$f = 44$ yr and $s = 8$ yr

50. (b) The present age of father and son is x yr and y yr, respectively.

According to the question,

Before 10 yr,

$x - 10 = 3(y - 10)$

$\Rightarrow \quad x - 3y = -20 \quad \ldots(i)$

And, after 10 yr, $x + 10 = 2(y + 10)$

$\Rightarrow \quad x - 2y = 10 \quad \ldots(ii)$

On subtracting Eq. (i) from Eq. (ii), we get

$y = 30$

From Eq. (ii), $x = 10 + 60 = 70$

$\therefore$ Required ratio $= \dfrac{70}{30} = 7 : 3$

51. (d) The ratio of men and women in yoga centre,

Men : Women

60% : 40%

3 : 2

or $\quad 3x : 2x$

Ratio of average age of men and women

$= 55 : 45$

$\therefore$ Total age of both $= 3x \times 55 + 2x \times 45$

$= 255x$

$\therefore$ Average age of all members $= \dfrac{255x}{5x} = 51$ yr

52. (a) Let the father's age and son's age be $5x$ yr and $3x$ yr, respectively.

According to the question,

$5x \times 3x = 960 \Rightarrow x^2 = \dfrac{960}{15}$

$\Rightarrow \quad x^2 = 64 \Rightarrow x = 8$

$\therefore$ Required ratio $= \dfrac{5x + 6}{3x + 6} = \dfrac{5 \times 8 + 6}{3 \times 8 + 6}$

$= \dfrac{46}{30} = \dfrac{23}{15} = 23 : 15$

53. (d) Sum of age of 6 members of family

$= 25 \times 6 = 150$

Age of youngest member $= 4$ yr

Sum of age of 5 members of family, just before the birth $= 150 - (6 \times 4) = 126$

$\therefore$ Required average $= \dfrac{126}{5} = 25.2$ yr

54. (a) Let age of Rustam, Preetam and Geetam be a, b and c yr, respectively.

According to the question,

$a + b = 60 \quad \ldots(i)$

$b + c = 40 \quad \ldots(ii)$

and $\quad a + c = 52 \quad \ldots(iii)$

Adding Eqs. (i), (ii) and (iii),

$2(a + b + c) = 152$

$\therefore \quad a + b + c = 76 \quad \ldots(iv)$

From Eqs. (i), (ii), (iii) and (iv),

$a = 36, b = 24, c = 16$

Hence, the youngest of the three is Geetam.

$\therefore$ Geetam's age after 5 yr $= 16 + 5 = 21$ yr

55. (a) Total age of husband, wife and child 2 yr ago $= 28 \times 3 = 84$ yr

Present age of husband, wife and child together $= 84 + (2 \times 3) = 90$ yr

Total age of husband and child 5 yr ago

$= 21 \times 2 = 42$ yr

Present age of husband and child together

$= 42 + (2 \times 5) = 52$ yr

$\therefore$ Present age of wife $= 90 - 52 = 38$ yr

56. (c) Let present age of father, mother and son be $8x$, $5x$ and $2x$ yr, respectively.

Also, $8x = 48$

$\therefore$ $x = 6$

Hence, average age of family after 3 yr

$$= \frac{8x+3+5x+3+2x+3}{3}$$

$$= \frac{15x+9}{3} = \frac{15\times6+9}{3}$$

$$= \frac{90+9}{3} = \frac{99}{3} = 33 \text{ yr}$$

57. (d) Total increase in the age of the group $= (66-24) = 42$ yr

Given, increase in average age of the group $= 6$ yr

$\therefore$ Number of person in the group $= \frac{42}{6} = 7$

58. (d) Let their present ages are $7x$ and $9x$ yr, respectively.

According to the question,

$$\frac{7x+10}{9x+10} = \frac{19}{23}$$

$\Rightarrow$ $161x + 230 = 171x + 190$

$\Rightarrow$ $10x = 40$

$\therefore$ $x = 4$

After 7 yr, their average age

$$= \frac{(7x+7)+(9x+7)}{2}$$

$= 8x + 7 = 8\times4+7 = 39$ yr

59. (b) According to the question,

Average age of the family

$$= \frac{2\times67+2\times35+4\times9}{8}$$

$$= \frac{67+35+18}{4} = \frac{120}{4} = 30 \text{ yr}$$

60. (b) Let the age of man and his son be $11x$ yr and $5x$ yr, respectively.

Then, $\frac{11x+5x}{2} = 56 \Rightarrow x = 7$

$\therefore$ Son's age $= 5x = 5\times7 = 35$ yr

Speedy Method

According to the question,

16 units $\rightarrow 56\times2$

5 units $\rightarrow \frac{112}{16}\times5 = 35$ yr

$\therefore$ Son's age $= 35$ yr

61. (a) Let ages of Ram and Shyam be $3x$ and $4x$ respectively.

According to the question,

$$\frac{3x-4}{4x-4} = \frac{2}{3}$$

$\Rightarrow$ $9x - 12 = 8x - 8$

$\Rightarrow$ $x = 4$

$\therefore$ Ratio of ages of Ram and Shyam after 4 years from now $= \frac{3\times4+4}{4\times4+4} = \frac{16}{20} = \frac{4}{5} = 4:5$

62. (c) Let the age of A be $3x$ yr and age of B be x yr.

According to the question,

$$\frac{3x-5}{x-5} = \frac{5}{1}$$

$\Rightarrow$ $3x - 5 = 5x - 25$

$\Rightarrow$ $2x = 20$

$\Rightarrow$ $x = 10$ yr

$\therefore$ Age of A after 8 yr $= 3\times10+8 = 38$ yr

63. (a) Total age of mother, father and son $= 3\times44 = 132$ yr

Then, age of daughter-in-law $= (4\times39-132) = (156-132) = 24$ yr

64. (d) 5 yr from now, let the ages of A, B and C be $3x$, $5x$ and $2x$ yr, respectively.

According to the question,

$(3x-5)^2 + (5x-5)^2 + (2x-5)^2 = 525$

$\Rightarrow 9x^2 + 25 - 30x + 25x^2 + 25 - 50x + 4x^2 + 25 - 20x = 525$

$\Rightarrow$ $38x^2 + 75 - 100x = 525$

$\Rightarrow$ $38x^2 - 100x = 525 - 75 = 450$

$\Rightarrow$ $38x^2 - 100x - 450 = 0$

$\Rightarrow$ $19x^2 - 50x - 225 = 0$

$\Rightarrow$ $19x^2 - 95x + 45x - 225 = 0$

$\Rightarrow$ $19x(x-5) + 45(x-5) = 0$

$\Rightarrow$ $(x-5)(19x+45) = 0$

$\therefore$ $x = 5$ $\left[\because x \neq -\frac{45}{19}\right]$

Hence, present age of $B = 5x - 5 = 5\times5-5 = (25-5) = 20$ yr

65. (b) According to the question,

B's age after 5 yr $= \left(\frac{33}{3}\times5\right) + 5 = 55 + 5 = 60$ yr

66. (c) Let the present age of mother be x yr.

Then, present age of father $= (x+3)$ yr

Now, 6 yr ago,

Age of father $= 2\times$ present age of daughter

$x + 3 - 6 = 2\times$ present age of daughter

$\Rightarrow$ $x - 3 = 2\times$ present age of daughter

$\therefore$ Present age of daughter $= \frac{x-3}{2}$ yr

According to the question,

Average of their ages 6 yr ago $= 32$

$$\Rightarrow \frac{(x-6)+(x+3-6)+\left(\frac{x-3}{2}-6\right)}{3} = 32$$

$$\Rightarrow x-6+x-3+\frac{x-3}{2}-6 = 96$$

$$\Rightarrow x+x+\frac{x-3}{2}-15 = 96$$

$$\Rightarrow \frac{4x+x-3-30}{2} = 96$$

$\Rightarrow 5x - 33 = 192 \Rightarrow 5x = 225 \Rightarrow x = 45$ yr

67. (a) Let the average of 22 men be x yr.

$$x = \frac{\text{Sum of 20 person's age} + 58\times2}{22}$$

$\Rightarrow$ $22x =$ Sum of 20 person's age $+ 116$

Sum of age of 20 persons $= 22x - 116$ ...(i)

Now, average got decreased because of 2 new men.

Let age of two new men $= (a+b)$

According to the question,

$$x - 2 = \frac{\text{Sum of 20 persons age} + (a+b)}{22}$$

$\Rightarrow 22x - 44 = 22x - 116 + (a+b)$

$\Rightarrow$ $a + b = 72$

$\therefore$ Average of $a + b = \frac{72}{2} = 36$ yr

68. (c) Average age of 20 boys $= 25$ yr

Sum of age of 20 boys $= 25\times20 = 500$

According to the question,

15 yr old leaves the group which means the sum of age of 19 boys $= 500 - 15 = 485$ yr and average age of 20 boys after new boy $= 27$ yr

Sum of age of 20 boys after new boy $= 27\times20 = 540$ yr

$\therefore$ The age of new boy $= 540 - 485 = 55$ yr

69. (d) Let average age of 2 men be x yr.

According to the question,

$11\times53 - 2\times x = 9\times(53+1)$

$\Rightarrow$ $583 - 2x = 486$

$\Rightarrow$ $583 - 486 = 2x \Rightarrow 97 = 2x$

$\therefore$ $x = 48.5$ yr

70. (a) According to the question,

Total age of 19 students $= 19\times22 = 418$ yr

$\therefore$ Average age of 20 students

$$= \frac{418+42}{20} = \frac{460}{20} = 23 \text{ yr}$$

71. (c) Average age of 14 students $= 17$ yr

$\therefore$ New average $= \frac{(14\times17+32)}{15} = \frac{238+32}{15} = 18$ yr

72. (c) According to the question,

Sum of ages of all students in a class $= 30\times20 = 600$

If each student's age is increased by 5 yr.
Then, total increase in average $= 5 \times 30 = 150$
$\therefore$ New sum of age of all students
$$= 600 + 150 = 750$$
So, increased average age
$$= \frac{750 - 600}{30} = \frac{150}{30} = 5$$

Speedy Method

$\therefore$ In question each student's age is increased by 5 yr, then average is also increased by 5.

73. (d) Total age of 22 teachers $= 22 \times 64$
$$= 1408 \text{ yr}$$
According to the question,
Involving 1 new teacher,
Average increased by 1 yr, then
Total age of 23 teachers $= 23 \times 65 = 1495$ yr
$\therefore$ Age of new teacher $= 1495 - 1408 = 87$ yr

74. (c) Let present ages of three people are $3x$, $5x$ and $7x$ yr respectively.
6 yr ago, sum of their ages = 87
$$3x + 5x + 7x - 18 = 87$$
$$\Rightarrow \quad 15x - 18 = 87$$
$$\Rightarrow \quad 15x = 105$$
$$\therefore \quad x = 7$$
So, present age of people are
$$3x = 3 \times 7 = 21 \text{ yr}$$
$$5x = 5 \times 7 = 35 \text{ yr}$$
$$7x = 7 \times 7 = 49 \text{ yr}$$

75. (c) Let the present age of daughter $= x$ yr
Then, the present age of her father $= (80 - x)$ yr
According to the question,
$$80 - x - 8 = 7(x - 8)$$
$$\Rightarrow \quad 72 - x = 7x - 56$$
$$\Rightarrow \quad 8x = 72 + 56 = 128 \Rightarrow x = 16$$
Now, after 8 yr the age of his daughter
$$= 16 + 8 = 24 \text{ yr}$$

76. (c) Required average $= \frac{30 \times 25 + 30 \times 5}{30 + 5}$
$$= \frac{750 + 150}{30 + 5} = \frac{900}{35} = 25\frac{5}{7} \text{ yr}$$

77. (c) Let, John's and Tanvi's ages are $8x$ yr and $15x$ yr respectively.
According to the question,
$$\frac{8x + 9}{15x + 9} = \frac{11}{18}$$
$$\Rightarrow \quad 144x + 162 = 165x + 99$$
$$\Rightarrow \quad 21x = 63$$
$$\therefore \quad x = 3$$
Hence, difference between their ages
$$= 15x - 8x = 7x = 7 \times 3 = 21 \text{ yr}$$

78. (d) Let the age of husband is x yr.
Then, the age of wife will be $(x - 6)$ yr.
According to the question,
$$\frac{x + x - 6}{2} = 24 \Rightarrow 2x - 6 = 48$$
$$\Rightarrow \quad 2x = 54$$
$$\therefore \quad x = 27 \text{ yr}$$
Age of son $= \frac{1}{9} \times 27 = 3$ yr
$\therefore$ Age of wife $= x - 6 = 27 - 6 = 21$ yr
So, average age of all three family members
$$= \frac{27 + 3 + 21}{3} = \frac{51}{3} = 17 \text{ yr}$$

79. (d) Let the present age of Vipul $= x$ yr
and the present age of Ritika $= 3x$ yr
After 7 yr, the age of Vipul $= (x + 7)$ yr
and the age of Ritika $= (3x + 7)$ yr.
According to the question,
$$3x + 7 = 2(x + 7) \Rightarrow 3x + 7 = 2x + 14$$
$$\therefore \quad x = 7 \text{ yr}$$
$\therefore$ The present age of Ritika
$$= 3x = 3 \times 7 = 21 \text{ yr}$$

80. (c) Let ages of Rahul and his son's be $9x$ and x, respectively.
According to the question,
$$(9x) \times (x) = 144$$
$$\Rightarrow \quad x^2 = 16 \Rightarrow x = 4$$
$\therefore$ Sum of their ages after 4 yr
$$= 9x + 4 + x + 4 = 10x + 8$$
$$= 10 \times 4 + 8 = 48 \text{ yr}$$

81. (c) Required average $= \frac{12 \times 20 + 16 \times 23}{12 + 16}$
$$= \frac{240 + 368}{28} = \frac{608}{28} = 21.7 \text{ yr}$$

07

Percentage

The term 'percentage' means for "every hundred" it can be defined as follows.

A percentage is a way of expressing a number as a fraction of 100. It is denoted by %.

e.g. 25% represents 25 out of 100 means $\frac{25}{100}=\frac{1}{4}$

Important Formulae Related to Percentage

- A% of B = B% of A

  e.g. 20% of $30=\frac{20}{100}\times 30=6$ and 30% of $20=\frac{30}{100}\times 20=6$
- If initial value is a and final value is b, then

  $$\text{Percentage change}=\frac{\text{Final value}-\text{Initial value}}{\text{Initial value}}\times 100=\frac{b-a}{a}\times 100$$
- If there are two number A and B, then A is what per cent of B

  $$=\left(\frac{A}{B}\times 100\right)\%$$
- Percentage point change means difference between two percentage value e.g. 40% and 60%, then percentage point change $=60\%-40\%=20\%$
- If the price of an article is increased/decreased by x%, then to keep expenditure same, the percentage decrease/increase in consumption

  $$=\frac{x}{100\pm x}\times 100$$

  where, + ve → price increase, − ve → price decrease
- If a number is first increased by a% and then decreased by a%, then the resultant change is always decrease by $\frac{a^2}{100}$%.
- If a number is increased /decreased x% and y% successively, then equivalent percentage change $=\left(\pm x\pm y+\frac{(\pm x)(\pm y)}{100}\right)$

  where, + ve → increase, − ve → decrease

Ex. 1 A number 1000 is increased successively by 15% and 25%. Find the overall increase in percentage.

Sol. Overall increase in percentage

$$=15+25+\frac{15\times 25}{100}=40+3.75=43.75\%$$

Quick Conversion Fraction to Percentage

Fraction	Percentage		Fraction	Percentage	
1	100%	100%	$\frac{1}{9}$	11.11%	$11\frac{1}{9}\%$
$\frac{1}{2}$	50%	50%	$\frac{1}{10}$	10%	10%
$\frac{1}{3}$	33.33%	$33\frac{1}{3}\%$	$\frac{1}{11}$	9.09%	$9\frac{1}{11}\%$
$\frac{1}{4}$	25%	25%	$\frac{1}{12}$	8.33%	$8\frac{1}{3}\%$
$\frac{1}{5}$	20%	20%	$\frac{1}{15}$	6.66%	$6\frac{2}{3}\%$
$\frac{1}{6}$	16.66%	$16\frac{2}{3}\%$	$\frac{1}{16}$	6.25%	$6\frac{1}{4}\%$
$\frac{1}{7}$	14.28%	$14\frac{2}{7}\%$	$\frac{1}{20}$	5%	5%
$\frac{1}{8}$	12.5%	$12\frac{1}{2}\%$	$\frac{1}{25}$	4%	4%

Question Based on Population/Depreciation

- The population of a town is P and it increases at the rate of R% per annum, then

  (i) Population after n yr $=P\left(1+\frac{R}{100}\right)^n$

  (ii) Population n yr ago $=\frac{P}{\left(1+\frac{R}{100}\right)^n}$
- The population of a town or value of an object is P and it decrease at the rate of R% per annum, then

  (i) Population/value of an object after n yr $=P\left(1-\frac{R}{100}\right)^n$

  (ii) Population/value of an object n yr ago $=\frac{P}{\left(1-\frac{R}{100}\right)^n}$
- If present population of a city is P and there is increment or decrement of r_1%, r_2% and r_3% in first, second and third year respectively, then

  Population of city after 3 yr $=P\times\left(1\pm\frac{r_1}{100}\right)\left(1\pm\frac{r_2}{100}\right)\left(1\pm\frac{r_3}{100}\right)$

Note Here, take '+' for increment and '−' for decrement.

Ex. 2 The population of a city increased by 30% in the first year and decreased by 15% in the next year. If the present population is 11050, then population 2 yr ago was

Sol. Present population = Initial population $\times \left(\frac{100+30}{100}\right) \times \left(\frac{100-15}{100}\right)$

$$11050 = \text{Initial population} \times \frac{130}{100} \times \frac{85}{100}$$

$\therefore$ Initial population = 10000

Question Based on Election

In this topic, we will study the question that ask about the total vote polled.

Ex. 3 In an election between two candidates one got 52% of total valid votes, 25% of the total votes were invalid. The total number of votes was 8400. How many valid votes did the other person get?

Sol. Total valid votes $= 8400 \times \frac{75}{100} = 6300$

According to the question,

Number of votes obtained by other person

$$= 6300 \times \frac{48}{100} = 3024$$

Question Based on Passing Marks

In this topic, we will study the question that ask about the passing marks of the student.

Ex. 4 The passing marks of an exam is 40% marks. A student gets 250 marks and yet fails by 38 marks. What is the maximum marks?

Sol. Let the maximum marks be x.

According to the question, $\frac{40x}{100} = 250 + 38 \Rightarrow x = \frac{288 \times 100}{40} \Rightarrow x = 720$

Question Based on Expenditure

In this topic, we will study the question that ask about the percentage decrease/increase in consumption and expenditure.

Ex. 5 The price of sugar is increased by 24%. A person wants to increase his expenditure by 18% only. By approximately what per cent should he decrease his consumption?

Sol. Let price be $100x$ and consumption be 100.

Price $\times$ Consumption = Expenditure

$\Rightarrow$ $100x \times 100 = 10000x \Rightarrow 124x \times 95.16 = 11800x$

$\therefore$ Per cent decrease $= \frac{100-95.16}{100} \times 100 = 4.84\%$

SSC Exam Scanner

SSC CGL 2024 (Tier I & II)

1. Amit gets 6% increase in his sale amount in the first year and 20% in the second year, with that his present sale is ₹ 254400, what was his sale (in ₹) two years ago? **SSC CGL (Tier II) 20/01/2025 Shift-I**

(a) 200000 (b) 180000
(c) 212000 (d) 240000

2. Two years ago, the population of a town was 9487500. Due to migration to big cities, it decreases every year at the rate of 8%. The present population of the town is **SSC CGL (Tier II) 20/01/2025 Shift-I**

(a) 9060110 (b) 7060320
(c) 8070120 (d) 8030220

3. By how much is 60% of 75 greater than $\frac{1}{5}$ of 25? **SSC CGL (Tier II) 18/01/2025 Shift-I**

(a) 37 (b) 38
(c) 40 (d) 34

4. The population of a place increased to 50000 from 2016 to 2018 at the rate of 6% per annum and continued the same trend for the next 3 yr. If A is the population in 2016 and B is the population in 2020, both are approximated to the next possible integers, then the value of $B-A$ is **SSC CGL (Tier II) 18/01/2025 Shift-I**

(a) 11680 (b) 16270
(c) 13220 (d) 12850

5. Ram's income is 2.5% more than Shyam's income. By what percentage is Shyam's income less than Ram's income? **SSC CGL (Tier I) 26/09/2024 Shift-III**

(a) 2.43% (b) 3.43%
(c) 1.43% (d) 4.43%

6. Suresh's expenditure and savings are in the ratio of 3 : 1. His income increases by 25%. If his savings increase by 20%, then by how much percentage does his expenditure increase? **SSC CGL (Tier I) 26/09/2024 Shift-II**

(a) $27\frac{2}{3}\%$ (b) $25\frac{2}{3}\%$
(c) $28\frac{2}{3}\%$ (d) $26\frac{2}{3}\%$

7. Two successive percentage decrease of 25% each is by what percentage less than two successive percentage increase of 25% each? (round to two decimal places.) **SSC CGL (Tier I) 26/09/2024 Shift-I**

(a) 50% (b) 43.75%
(c) 22.22% (d) 56.25%

8. The monthly income of Ramesh in year 2021 was ₹ 18600 and his monthly expenditure was ₹ 12400. In year 2022 his income increased by 15% and his expenditure increased by 8%. Find the percentage increase in his savings. **SSC CGL (Tier I) 25/09/2024 Shift-III**

(a) 29% (b) 32%
(c) 25% (d) 27%

9. The income of a person is ₹16500 and his expenditure is ₹12000. Next year his income increases by 24%, but his expenditure decreases by 10%. The percentage increase (rounded-off to the nearest integer) in his savings is **SSC CGL (Tier I) 24/09/2024 Shift-III**

(a) 90% (b) 120% (c) 115% (d) 95%

10. Vipul spends 30% of his monthly income on rent, 60% of the remaining on groceries, and 40% of the remaining on others. If he saves ₹ 7056 in a month, then how much (in ₹) does he spend on groceries? **SSC CGL (Tier I) 24/09/2024 Shift-II**

(a) 18323 (b) 15230
(c) 17640 (d) 22386

11. In an election between two candidates, 80% of the voters cast their votes, out of which 4% votes were declared invalid. A candidate got 15,360 votes which were 80% of the valid votes. Find the total number of votes. **SSC CGL (Tier I) 24/09/2024 Shift-I**

(a) 20000 (b) 18000
(c) 25000 (d) 23000

12. If an employee's income is ₹ 72000, the amount he spends is 40% higher than his savings. Therefore, his savings (in ₹) is **SSC CGL (Tier I) 23/09/2024 Shift-III**

(a) 30000 (b) 34000
(c) 32000 (d) 28000

13. In an election between two candidates, P received 42% of the valid votes and Q won by 45,360 votes. 20% people did not cast their vote. If 10% of the votes cast were found invalid, what is the total number of votes registered in the poll booth?
SSC CGL (Tier I) 23/09/2024 Shift-II

(a) 393750 (b) 359000
(c) 393600 (d) 353790

14. R targets to score 85% marks in exams. He scores 450 marks and misses the target by 35%. How much increment in percentage should be there in his scored marks to meet the target? **SSC CGL (Tier I) 23/09/2024 Shift-I**

(a) 70 (b) 35 (c) 53 (d) 45

15. Three candidates X, Y and Z participated in an election. X got 30% more votes than Y, whereas Z got 25% more votes than Y. X also overtook Z by 5000 votes. If 71% of the voters voted and no invalid votes were cast, then what was the total number of voters in the voting list? **SSC CGL (Tier I) 19/09/2024 Shift-III**

(a) 500000 (b) 405000
(c) 355000 (d) 450000

16. The price of an item is increased twice successively. The final price is ₹ 2295 and initial price was ₹ 1000. The percentage increment the second time was twice the percentage increment the first time. By what percentage was the price increased the second time?
SSC CGL (Tier I) 19/09/2024 Shift-II

(a) 35% (b) 65%
(c) 70% (d) 25%

17. The cost of tomatoes per kg is increased by 300%. A housewife reduces her consumption of tomatoes by 70%. By what percentage does her expenditure on tomatoes increase or decrease?
SSC CGL (Tier I) 19/09/2024 Shift-I

(a) Decreases, 30%
(b) Decreases, 20%
(c) Increases, 30%
(d) Increases, 20%

18. An investor, invested ₹ 200000 in shares. The shares rose by 18% on the first day, fell by 15% on the second day, and then fell by 3% on the third day. What is the net percentage increase or decrease in the value of the investor's shares? (rounded up to one decimal place)
SSC CGL (Tier I) 18/09/2024 Shift-III

(a) increase by 2.2%
(b) increase by 2.7%
(c) decrease by 2.7%
(d) decrease by 2.2%

19. In an election between two candidates, the one who gets 88% of the votes is elected by a majority of 684 votes. What is the total number of votes polled? (all polled votes are valid) **SSC CGL (Tier I) 18/09/2024 Shift-II**

(a) 900 (b) 800
(c) 850 (d) 750

20. In a constituency, 45% of the total number of voters are males and the rest are females. If 60% of the males are illiterate and 60% of the females are literate, then by what per cent is the number of illiterate females more than that of literate males? (rounded off to 2 decimal places.)
SSC CGL (Tier I) 18/09/2024 Shift-I

(a) 19.11% (b) 27.23%
(c) 30.24% (d) 22.22%

21. Ajay spends $66\frac{2}{3}\%$ of his income on different household items. If his income increases by 25% and expenditure increase by 20%, then the effect on his savings will be
SSC CGL (Tier I) 17/09/2024 Shift-III

(a) 28% (b) 61%
(c) 49% (d) 35%

22. Two candidates contested in an election. 80% of the voters cast their votes, out of which 5% of the polled votes were invalid. The winning candidate got 70% of valid votes and won by a majority of 36,480 votes. Find the total number of voters.
SSC CGL (Tier I) 17/09/2024 Shift-II

(a) 115000 (b) 120000
(c) 125000 (d) 118000

23. In a company, all employees are getting equal wages. If the number of employees is increased by 20% and their wages per head are decreased by 18%, what is the percentage decrease in total wages?
SSC CGL (Tier I) 17/09/2024 Shift-I

(a) 2.4% (b) 1%
(c) 1.6% (d) 1.4%

24. P and Q are two fixed points 10 cm apart and R is a point on PQ such that PR = 6 cm. By what percentage is the length of QR decreased when the length of PR is increased by 5%?
SSC CGL (Tier I) 13/09/2024 Shift-II

(a) 8.5% (b) 7.5%
(c) 7% (d) 8%

25. In an election between R and S, R gets 110% of the votes of S and beats S by 770 votes. If there were no invalid votes, then the total number of votes polled is: **SSC CGL (Tier I) 13/09/2024 Shift-I**

(a) 17610 (b) 17160
(c) 16170 (d) 16710

26. The proportion of Suresh's spending to saving is 3 : 1. His salary rises by 25%. What percentage of his expenditure will increase if his saving grows by 10%?
SSC CGL (Tier I) 12/09/2024 Shift-III

(a) 40% (b) 20%
(c) 10% (d) 30%

27. Every month, a man consumes 20 kg of rice and 8 kg of wheat. The price of rice is 20% of the price of wheat, resulting in a total expenditure of ₹ 300 per month for rice and wheat combined. If the price of wheat is increased by 20%, what percentage reduction in rice consumption is needed to maintain the same expenditure of ₹ 300? (given that price of rice and consumption of wheat is constant.)
SSC CGL (Tier I) 12/09/2024 Shift-II

(a) 40% (b) 38% (c) 24% (d) 22%

28. A woman spends $\frac{2}{3}$ of her income. If her income increase by 18% and the expenditure increases by 24%, then the percentage increase in her savings will be:
SSC CGL (Tier I) 11/09/2024 Shift-III

(a) 6% (b) 3%
(c) 5% (d) 4%

29. The salary of a worker is first increased by 25%, then it is decreased by 12%. The percentage change in his salary is
SSC CGL (Tier I) 11/09/2024 Shift-II

(a) 10% increase (b) 13% increase
(c) 10% decrease (d) 13% decrease

30. In an election between two candidates P and Q, P got 78% of the total valid votes. If the total votes of the electorate were 7560000, then what was the number of valid votes that Q got if 10% of the voters did not cast their vote and 15% of the votes polled were declared invalid?
SSC CGL (Tier I) 11/09/2024 Shift-I

(a) 141372 (b) 141732
(c) 1272348 (d) 147312

31. In an election between Sunita and Mamata, 85% of voters cast their votes but 2% of votes were invalid. If Sunita got 64974 votes which is

78% of valid votes, then the total number of voters enrolled in the election was

SSC CGL (Tier I) 10/09/2024 Shift-III

(a) 125000 (b) 100000
(c) 165000 (d) 180000

32. A number is first increased by 12% and then increased by 23%. The number, so obtained, is now decreased by 34%. What is the net increase or decrease percent in the original number (nearest to an integer)? **SSC CGL (Tier I) 09/09/2024 Shift-III**

(a) 10% increase (b) 9% decrease
(c) 10% decrease (d) 9% increase

33. A stock portfolio consists of four stocks. Stock *A* represents 20% of the portfolio and has a return of 6%. Stock *B* represents 30% of the portfolio and has a return of 8%. Stock *C* represents 20% of the portfolio and has a return of 4%. Stock *D* represents the remaining 30% of the portfolio and has a negative-return of 5%. What is the average return of the portfolio?

SSC CGL (Tier I) 09/09/2024 Shift-III

(a) 2.9% (b) 2.6%
(c) 3.2% (d) 3.4%

34. In an election between two candidates, *y*% of the voters did not vote. 10% of the votes cast were declared invalid, while all the valid votes were cast in favour of either of the two candidates. The candidate who got 59.375% of the valid votes cast was declared elected by 2484 votes. If the number of people eligible to vote in that election was 16000, what is the value of *y*?

SSC CGL (Tier I) 09/09/2024 Shift-I

(a) 7.2 (b) 8.4
(c) 8 (d) 7.5

SSC CGL 2023 (Tier I & II)

35. If 20% of $(A + B)$ = 30% of $(A - B)$, then what percentage of *B* is equal to *A*? **SSC CGL (Tier-II) 07/03/2023 Shift-I**

(a) 100% (b) 500%
(c) 300% (d) 400%

36. Mrs. Deepa Devi saves 30% of her salary. If she receives ₹ 42000 per month as her salary, what is her monthly expenditure?

SSC CGL (Tier-II) 06/03/2023 Shift-I

(a) ₹ 29200
(b) ₹ 29400
(c) ₹ 29300
(d) ₹ 29100

37. Two candidates contested an election. One of them got 64% of the votes and won by 434 votes. What was the total number of votes polled? **SSC CGL (Tier-II) 03/03/2023 Shift-I**

(a) 1550 (b) 1345
(c) 1680 (d) 1684

38. A basket contains 350 eggs. If 12% of the eggs are rotten, how many eggs are good enough to be sold?

SSC CGL (Tier-II) 02/03/2023 Shift-I

(a) 408 (b) 310
(c) 308 (d) 410

39. Soham's initial expenditure and savings were in the ratio of 5: 3. His income increases by 25%. If his initial savings were ₹ 4500, find his income (in ₹) after the increment.

SSC CGL (Tier-I) 27/07/2023 Shift-II

(a) 16000 (b) 15000
(c) 9375 (d) 12000

40. If the price of petrol is increased by 81%, by what percentage should the consumption of petrol be decreased by the consumer if the expenditure on petrol remains unchanged? (correct to two decimal places)

SSC CGL (Tier-I) 27/07/2023 Shift-I

(a) 40.45% (b) 41.25%
(c) 43.12% (d) 44.75%

41. A father gives 8% of his monthly income to both his sons as pocket money. The elder son gets 85% of the total amount given to both the sons. He spend 90% of the amount and saves ₹17. What is the monthly income of father?

SSC CGL (Tier-I) 26/07/2023 Shift-III

(a) ₹ 5000
(b) ₹ 4500
(c) ₹ 3500
(d) ₹ 2500

42. If in a competitive exam, the marks obtained by Sam are 19% less than those of Peter, then the marks obtained by Peter are how much percentage more than the marks obtained by Sam? (correct to two decimal places)

SSC CGL (Tier-I) 26/07/2023 Shift-II

(a) 28.64% (b) 22.25%
(c) 21.50% (d) 23.46%

43. Which of the following is the least?
12% of 625
15% of 555
10% of 720
9% of 845 **SSC CGL (Tier-I) 26/07/2023 Shift-I**

(a) 9% of 845 (b) 12% of 625
(c) 10% of 720 (d) 15% of 555

44. Ravi initially used to save 20% of his monthly income. Recently his monthly income was raised by 25%. His nominal savings also went up by 5%. What percentage of his present nominal income does Ravi currently save? **SSC CGL (Tier-I) 26/07/2023 Shift-I**

(a) 25% (b) 20% (c) 15% (d) 16.8%

45. In the first month, the income of Mohan increases by 30%. In the second month his income decreases by 30%. What will be percentage increase or decrease in the income after two months?

SSC CGL (Tier-I) 25/07/2023 Shift-III

(a) 15% increase (b) 9% increase
(c) 15% decrease (d) 9% decrease

46. The cost price of an article is decreased by 10% and then increased by 20%. If the final price is ₹ 540, then the original cost price is

SSC CGL (Tier-I) 25/07/2023 Shift-III

(a) ₹ 500 (b) ₹ 650 (c) ₹ 550 (d) ₹ 600

47. A family income is ₹ 35000 in a month. The family spends the income on various expenditures, viz., food, health, education, entertainment and rent. After incurring all the expenditures, 8% is saved every month. The expenditure on health is 50% more than that of food. While food is three times of the expenditure on entertainment, the expenditure on health is half of the expenditure on education. The expenditure on rent is one-third of the combined expenditure on food, health and education. How much expenditure (in ₹) is incurred on education?

SSC CGL (Tier-I) 25/07/2023 Shift-II

(a) 12600 (b) 8400
(c) 13200 (d) 7700

48. Out of the total toffees, $\frac{1}{10}$ are wasted. 35% of the rest are given to *S* and $\frac{1}{8}$ of the total are given to *N*. If the toffees with *N* are 10 more than the wasted toffees, then how many toffees were given to S?

SSC CGL (Tier-I) 25/07/2023 Shift-I

(a) 126 (b) 150 (c) 110 (d) 135

49. In an examination, a candidate had to sit for three paper *A*, *B* and *C*. The candidate secured 75% marks in paper *A*, 80% marks in Paper *B* and 60% marks in Paper *C*. If the weightage assigned to papers *A*, *B* and *C* were 40%, 50% and 10%

respectively then find the weighted percentage of marks obtained by the candidate, when all the three papers were taken together.
SSC CGL (Tier-I) 24/07/2023 Shift-IV

(a) 77% (b) 74% (c) 72% (d) 76%

50. A person spends 25% of his income on goods of daily uses. Furthermore, he spends 18% of the rest on house rent and 16% of the rest on travel. After that, only ₹861 is left with him. What is his salary?
SSC CGL (Tier-I) 24/07/2023 Shift-III

(a) ₹$1852\frac{1}{3}$ (b) ₹$1666\frac{2}{3}$
(c) ₹$1563\frac{1}{3}$ (d) ₹$1426\frac{1}{3}$

51. In a election between two candidates, 10% of the voters in the voter list did not cast their vote, whereas 10% of the votes cast were found to be invalid. The winning candidate got 56% of the valid votes and won the election by a margin of 1458 votes. What is the total number of voters enrolled in the voter list?
SSC CGL (Tier-I) 24/07/2023 Shift-II

(a) 14000 (b) 15000
(c) 16000 (d) 13000

52. In January 2022, Kriti paid an EMI, which was 22% of her monthly salary. She spent the remaining salary on shopping of groceries and clothes in the ratio 7 : 5. She spent ₹ 18200 on shopping of clothes. If , in February 2022, her salary increased by 16%, then what was her salary (in ₹) in February?
SSC CGL (Tier-I) 24/07/2023 Shift-I

(a) 66350 (b) 68520
(c) 70250 (d) 64960

53. John got 20% marks in an examination and failed by 10 marks. In the same examination, Jack got 35% marks which were 20 more than the minimum passing marks. Find the percentage of minimum marks required to pass.
SSC CGL (Tier-I) 21/07/2023 Shift-III

(a) 30 (b) 35
(c) 25 (d) 20

54. The monthly income of a person was ₹ 12000 and his monthly expenditure was ₹ 8000. Next year, his income increased by 10% and his expenditure by 8%. Find the percentage increase in his savings.
SSC CGL (Tier-I) 21/07/2023 Shift-I

(a) 10% (b) 14%
(c) 12% (d) 15%

55. Pass percentage of an examination is 35%. If a student who got 210 marks, failed by 14 marks, then what are the maximum marks of the examination?
SSC CGL (Tier-I) 20/07/2023 Shift-IV

(a) 600 (b) 660
(c) 620 (d) 640

56. The price of an article is increased by *r* %. The new price was decreased by *r* % later. Now the latest price is ₹ 1. What was the original price of the article?
SSC CGL (Tier-I) 20/07/2023 Shift-III

(a) $\frac{10000}{10000-r^2}$ (b) $\frac{10000-r^2}{10000}$
(c) $\frac{100}{100-r^2}$ (d) $\frac{100}{1-r^2}$

57. In a certain year, the population of a city was 18000. If in the next year, the population of males increased by 5% and that of females increased by 7% and the total population increased to 19200, then what was the ratio of the populations of males and females in that given year ?
SSC CGL (Tier-I) 20/07/2023 Shift-I

(a) 2 : 5 (b) 1 : 5
(c) 4 : 3 (d) 3 : 5

58. If 65% of 350 – ?% of 250 + 40% of 120 =158, then find the value of ?
SSC CGL (Tier-I) 19/07/2023 Shift-III

(a) 57 (b) 63 (c) 47 (d) 54

59. In a constituency, 85% of the total number of people on the electoral roll cast their votes during an election. 10% of the votes cast were declared invalid. If there were 300000 people on the electoral roll and Dharam secured 137700 valid votes, what percentage of the total number of valid votes did Dharam secure? **SSC CGL (Tier-I) 18/07/2023 Shift-III**

(a) 50.5% (b) 70.2%
(c) 45.9% (d) 60.0%

60. Raj's income is ₹ 45000 and his expenditure is ₹ 33000. If his income is increased by 20% and expenditure by 12%, then what will be the percentage increase in saving?
SSC CGL (Tier-I) 18/07/2023 Shift-I

(a) 48% (b) 56%
(c) 36% (d) 42%

61. In a constituency, 90% of the total number of people on the electoral roll cast their votes during an election. 15% of the votes cast were declared invalid. Jeeta secured 60% of the valid votes. If Jeeta secured 91800 valid votes, what was the total number of people on the electoral roll? **SSC CGL (Tier-I) 17/07/2023 Shift-III**

(a) 216000 (b) 225000
(c) 180000 (d) 200000

62. Suhani pays tax at the rate of 30% on her entire income of ₹ 90000 and Ritika pays tax at the rate of 40% on her entire income of ₹ *y*. If the overall tax rate on their combined income comes to 37%, then what is the value of *y*? **SSC CGL (Tier-I) 17/07/2023 Shift-II**

(a) ₹ 216000 (b) ₹ 213000
(c) ₹ 204000 (d) ₹ 210000

63. If *x*% of 280 = 15% of 240 + 20% of 310, then the value of *x* is
SSC CGL (Tier-I) 17/07/2023 Shift-I

(a) 38 (b) 35 (c) 30 (d) 40

64. The ratio between the monthly income and the expenditure of Vaidic is 8 : 5. If his income increases by 20% and his expenditure increases by 30%, then find the percentage increase or decrease in his monthly savings.
SSC CGL (Tier-I) 14/07/2023 Shift-IV

(a) $5\frac{2}{3}$% increase (b) $5\frac{2}{3}$% decrease
(c) $3\frac{1}{3}$% increase (d) $3\frac{1}{3}$% decrease

65. In an election, 2% persons enrolled in the voter list did not participate and 500 votes were invalid. Two candidates *A* and *B* fought the election and *A* defeated *B* by 200 votes. If 43% of the persons enrolled in the voter list casted their votes in favour of *A*, then what is the number of the total casted votes?
SSC CGL (Tier-I) 14/07/2023 Shift-II

(a) 2800 (b) 2450
(c) 3000 (d) 3250

66. In an election between three candidates, Arjun, Bhaskar and Saral contested for a post. Arjun got 50% votes more than Saral and Saral got 2% votes less than Bhaskar. The difference between the votes of Bhaskar and Saral is 1296. What is the half of the difference between the votes of Arjun and Bhaskar?
SSC CGL (Tier-I) 14/07/2023 Shift-I

(a) 3888 (b) 13988
(c) 7766 (d) 15228

67. If *A* is 95% of *B*, then what per cent of *A* is *B*? **SSC CGL (Tier-I) 14/07/2023 Shift-I**

(a) $104\frac{7}{19}$% (b) $105\frac{5}{19}$%
(c) $110\frac{3}{19}$% (d) $108\frac{17}{19}$%

SSC CGL 2022 (Tier I)

68. Shiva's monthly salary is ₹ 75000. He spends ₹ 12000 on household items, ₹ 14000 on LIC and mutual funds, ₹ 15000 on his children's education, and keeps ₹ 10000 for miscellaneous expenses. His savings are ₹ 21000 per month and he donates the rest of the amount to an orphanage. The percentage of his income that he donates is
SSC CGL (Tier-I) 13/12/2022 Shift-III

(a) 3% (b) 6% (c) 8% (d) 4%

69. The expenditure on the cost of living of a man and his family is 60% of his salary. He gets two increment of 30% and 60% in his salary. If his saving increases by 250% of his initial saving, then the new cost of living expenditure is what percentage (rounded off to the nearest integer) of the increased salary?
SSC CGL (Tier-I) 12/12/2022 Shift-IV

(a) 32.7% (b) 43.6%
(c) 29.5% (d) 36.6%

70. A number is decreased by 20% to get another number. The number so obtained is increased by 200% to get a third number. The difference of the third number and the original number is what percentage more or less than the difference of second and the third number?
SSC CGL (Tier-I) 12/12/2022 Shift-II

(a) More, 15.7 per cent
(b) Less 15.7 per cent
(c) More, 12.5 per cent
(d) Less, 12.5 per cent

71. During the first year, the strength of a school increased by 12%, in the second year it decreased by 12% and in the third year it increased by 10%. At the end of the third year its strength was nearly 10842. What was the strength at the beginning of the first year?
SSC CGL (Tier-I) 09/12/2022 Shift-III

(a) 8000 (b) 10000
(c) 6500 (d) 12000

72. In the first year the population of a town decreased by 5% due to the Corona virus first wave. In the next year it decreased again by 5% due to the second wave and in the third year it increased by 5%. At the end of the third year the population was 947625. What was the population at the beginning of the first year?
SSC CGL (Tier-I) 08/12/2022 Shift-III

(a) 700000 (b) 1000000
(c) 897993 (d) 992519

73. In an election between two candidates, a candidate who gets 76 % of the total votes polled is elected by a majority of 1480 votes. What is the total number of votes polled? (Consider integral part only)
SSC CGL (Tier-I) 08/12/2022 Shift-I

(a) 2800 (b) 1800
(c) 2846 (d) 1846

74. Three candidates were participating in an election. The person at third place got 20% of the total votes while the difference between the votes of the winner and the first runner up was 20% of the total votes. If the difference between the votes of the first runner up and the second runner up was 37000, how many votes did the winner receive?
SSC CGL (Tier-I) 07/12/2022 Shift-IV

(a) 180000 (b) 185000
(c) 175000 (d) 195000

75. 20% of the inhabitants of a village having died of malaria, a panic set in, during which 30% of the remaining inhabitants left the village. The population was then reduced to 12000. What was the number of inhabitants initially (Consider integral part only)
SSC CGL (Tier-I) 07/12/2022 Shift-II

(a) 21000 (b) 21428
(c) 21500 (d) 30428

76. A mask manufacturing company manufactured 'X' number of masks in 2018. If increased its manufacturing capacity by 30% in 2019 and further increased its manufacturing by 15% in 2020. In 2021, due to the machinery breakdown, its manufacturing declined by 40%. What is the value of 'X' if it manufactured 179400 masks in 2021? **SSC CGL (Tier-I) 07/12/2022 Shift-I**

(a) 180000 (b) 230000
(c) 200000 (d) 210000

77. The population of country A decreased by p% and the population of country B decreased by q% from the year 2020 to 2021. Here 'p' is greater than 'q'. Let 'x' be the ratio of the population of country A to the population of country B in the given year. What is the percentage decrease in 'x' from 2020 to 2021?
SSC CGL (Tier-I) 06/12/2022 Shift-II

(a) $\frac{100(p-q)}{100-q}$ (b) $\frac{100(p-q)}{100+p}$
(c) $\frac{100(p-q)}{100-p}$ (d) $\frac{100(p-q)}{100+q}$

78. Two candidates P and Q contested in an election. 70% of the registered voters are P supporters. If 60% of the P supporters and 30% of the Q supporters are expected to vote for candidate P, then what percentage of the registered voters are expected to vote for candidate P ?
SSC CGL (Tier-I) 06/12/2022 Shift-I

(a) 30% (b) 51% (c) 26% (d) 47%

79. Mr. X has a monthly income of $26500 and his monthly expenditure is $20500. The next year, his salary is increased by 12% and expenditure is increased by 6%. His savings increase by how much per cent?
SSC CGL (Tier-I) 05/12/2022 Shift-III

(a) 32.5% (b) 27.3%
(c) 32.0% (d) 34.7%

80. 0.5 is what percentage of 20?
SSC CGL (Tier-I) 05/12/2022 Shift-I

(a) 0.025% (b) 0.25%
(c) 25% (d) 2.5%

81. The cost of apples is increased by 20% and then decreased by 20%. What is the net pecentage decrease?
SSC CGL (Tier-I) 03/12/2022 Shift-IV

(a) 4% (b) 3% (c) 5% (d) 6%

82. If the price of salt decreases by 20%, then by what percentage should consumption be increased to keep the expenditure same?
SSC CGL (Tier-I) 03/12/2022 Shift-III

(a) 26% (b) 27%
(c) 25% (d) 24%

83. Number p is 15% more than 150. If k is 15% less than p, then k is equal to
SSC CGL (Tier-I) 03/12/2022 Shift-II

(a) 136.324 (b) 166.625
(c) 116.328 (d) 146.625

84. Ram loses $12\frac{1}{2}$% of his money and after spending 75% of the remainder, is left with ₹ 630. How much money did Ram have initially?
SSC CGL (Tier-I) 03/12/2022 Shift-I

(a) ₹ 2080 (b) ₹ 2880
(c) ₹ 2205 (d) ₹ 2808

85. In an election between two candidates, 12% of voters did not cast their votes. The winner by obtaining 68% of the total votes defeated his contestant by 2880 votes. What was the total number of voters who cast their votes in the election? **SSC CGL (Tier-I) 02/12/2022 Shift-III**

(a) 5280 (b) 8000
(c) 4000 (d) 6000

86. A district has 1024000 inhabitants. If the population increases at the rate 2.5% per annum, find the number of inhabitants at the end of three years.
SSC CGL (Tier-I) 02/12/2022 Shift-II
(a) 1120736 (b) 1102736
(c) 1075840 (d) 1064850

87. The reduction of 20% in the price of rice enables a person to obtain 50 kg more for ₹ 450. Find the original price of rice per kg.
SSC CGL (Tier-I) 02/12/2022 Shift-II
(a) ₹ 1 (b) ₹ 2
(c) ₹ 1.25 (d) ₹ 2.25

88. In an election between two candidates, the defeated candidate secured 42% of the valid votes polled and lost the election by 768400 votes. If 82560 votes were declared invalid and 20% people did not cast their vote, then the invalid votes were what percentage (rounded off to 1 decimal place) of the votes which people did not cast?
SSC CGL (Tier-I) 02/12/2022 Shift-II
(a) 10.6% (b) 9.8%
(c) 12.9% (d) 6.8%

89. In the election, 8% of the voters did not cast their votes. Two candidates contested the election in which the winning candidate got 48% of the total votes and won election by 1100 votes. Find the total number of voters in the election, given that all the votes cast were valid?
SSC CGL (Tier-I) 02/12/2022 Shift-I
(a) 25500 (b) 26500
(c) 27500 (d) 28500

90. Raju, Ravi and Ashok contested an election. 5% votes polled were invalid. Raju got 30% of the total votes. Ravi got 32% of the total votes. The winner got 5136 more votes than the person who received the least number of votes. Find the total number of votes polled.
SSC CGL (Tier-I) 01/12/2022 Shift-IV
(a) 171200
(b) 64200
(c) 171220
(d) 172100

91. The ratio of expenditure to savings of a woman is 5 : 1. If her income and expenditure are increased by 10% and 20% respectively, then find the percentage change in her savings. **SSC CGL (Tier-I) 01/12/2022 Shift-III**
(a) 55% (b) 60%
(c) 50% (d) 40%

SSC CGL 2021 & 2020 (Tier I)

92. Avinash has 20% less coins of different countries than Gaurav has. Gaurav has 40% more such coins than Chetan has. By what per cent the number of coins which Chetan has is less than the number of coins which Avinash has?(correct to one decimal place)
SSC CGL (Tier-I) 24/08/2021 Shift-II
(a) 10.7 (b) 10.6
(c) 10.5 (d) 12

93. The total number of students in a school is 1400, out of which 35% of the students are girls and the rest are boys. If 80% of the boys and 90% of the girls passed in an annual examination, then the percentage of the students who failed is
SSC CGL (Tier-I) 24/08/2021 Shift-II
(a) 16.5 (b) 21.5
(c) 17.4 (d) 15.8

94. Radha saves x% of her income. If her income increased by 28% and the expenditure increased by 20%, then her savings increased by 40%. What is the value of x ?
SSC CGL (Tier-I) 23/08/2021 Shift-I
(a) 25 (b) 40
(c) 50 (d) 35

95. The present population of a village is 15280. If the number of males increases by 25% and the number of females increases by 15%, then the population will become 18428. The difference between present population of males and females in the village is
SSC CGL (Tier-I) 20/08/2021 Shift-II
(a) 1840 (b) 920
(c) 2760 (d) 1380

96. Weight of A is 20% more than weight of B, whose weight is 30% more than weight of C. By how much percent weight of A is more than weight of C ?
SSC CGL (Tier-I) 20/08/2021 Shift-I
(a) 44 (b) 56
(c) 69 (d) 35.89

97. In an examination, 45% of all the students who appeared are boys and the rest are girls. If 60% of the boys and 70% of the girls passed. then what is the percentage of students who failed?
SSC CGL (Tier-I) 18/08/2021 Shift-I
(a) 36 (b) 40
(c) 35.4 (d) 34.5

98. A sports-goods shop has tennis balls of 3 colours-red, green and white. The number of white balls is 60% more than number of red balls and the number of green balls is 12.5% less than number of white balls. If total number of balls is 120, then how many green balls are there?
SSC CGL (Tier-I) 17/08/2021 Shift-III
(a) 48 (b) 40 (c) 42 (d) 30

99. A certain number of students from School X appeared in an examination and 20% students failed. From School Y, 130% more students than that from School X, appeared in the same examination. If 90% of the total number of students appeared from both the schools passed, then what is the percentage of students from School Y who failed (correct to one decimal place)? **SSC CGL (Tier-I) 17/08/2021 Shift-I**
(a) 6.4% (b) 10% (c) 5.7% (d) 8.3%

100. If a number is first increased by 15%, then reduced by 15%, it results is 782. If the same number is first reduced by 25%, then increased by 25% and again reduced by 20%, then what will be the resulting number?
SSC CGL (Tier-I) 16/08/2021 Shift-III
(a) 712 (b) 150 (c) 750 (d) 600

101. A, B and C divide a certain sum of money among themselves. The average of the amounts with them is ₹ 4520. Share of A is $10\frac{2}{3}$% more than share of B and $33\frac{1}{3}$% less than share of C. What is the share of B (in ₹)? **SSC CGL (Tier-I) 13/08/2021 Shift-III**
(a) 3500 (b) 3600 (c) 3984 (d) 5976

102. The income of A is 45% more than the income of B and the income of C is 60% less than the sum of the incomes of A and B. The income of D is 20% more than that of C. If the difference between the income of B and D is ₹13200, then the income (in ₹) of C is **SSC CGL (Tier-I) 13/08/2021 Shift-I**
(a) 72000 (b) 72500
(c) 73500 (d) 75000

103. In an examination, Anita scored 31% marks and failed by 16 marks. Sunita scored 40% marks and obtained 56 marks more than those required to pass. Find the minimum marks required to pass.
SSC CGL (Tier-I) 07/03/2020 Shift-I
(a) 3116 (b) 264
(c) 394 (d) 7100

104. In a school, 4% of the students did not appear for the annual exams. 10% of the students who appeared for the exams could not pass the exam. Out of the remaining students, 50% got distinction marks and 432 students passed the exam but could not get distinction marks. The total number of students in the school is
SSC CGL (Tier-I) 06/03/2020 Shift-II

(a) 878 (b) 1200 (c) 1000 (d) 960

105. The population of a city increased by 30% in the first year and decreased by 15% in the next year. If the present population is 11050, then the population 2 yr ago was
SSC CGL (Tier-I) 06/03/2020 Shift-I

(a) 10000 (b) 99500
(c) 99000 (d) 10050

106. The price of sugar is increased by 20%. By what percentage must one cut down on the consumption of sugar, so that no extra amount has to be incurred on sugar?
SSC CGL (Tier-I) 05/03/2020 Shift-III

(a) $16\frac{2}{3}\%$ (b) 20%
(c) $83\frac{1}{3}\%$ (d) 80%

107. A and B spend 60% and 75% of their incomes, respectively. If the savings of A are 20% more than that of B, then by what percentage is the income of A less than the income of B? **SSC CGL (Tier-I) 05/03/2020 Shift-II**

(a) 15 (b) 20
(c) 10 (d) 25

108. In an examination in which the full marks were 500, A scored 25% more marks than B. B scored 60% more marks than C and C scored 20% less marks than D. If A scored 80% marks. then the percentage of marks obtained by D is
SSC CGL (Tier-I) 05/03/2020 Shift-I

(a) 65% (b) 60%
(c) 50% (d) 54%

109. A, B and C donate 8%, 7% and 9% of their salaries, respectively to a charitable trust. The salaries of A and B are same and the difference between their donations is ₹259. The total donation of A and B is ₹ 1185 more than that of C. The total donation of A and C is what percentage of the total salaries of A, B and C? (Correct to one decimal place) **SSC CGL 04/03/2020 Shift-III**

(a) 6.2% (b) 5.8%
(c) 6.4% (d) 7.1%

SSC CPO SI 2024

110. In an election, 95% of the total voters cast their votes. In this election, there were only two candidates A and B. The Winner A, by obtaining 75% of the total votes, defeated his Contestant B by 5500 votes. Find the total number of voters in the election. **SSC CPO 29/06/2024 Shift-III**

(a) 12000 (b) 11000
(c) 13000 (d) 10000

111. The population of a town is 15000. If the population increases by 15% in the first year, by 25% in the second year and due to pollution it decreases by 6% in the third year, what will be its population after 3 yr? (round off number in answer)
SSC CPO 29/06/2024 Shift-III

(a) 20269 (b) 25269
(c) 28269 (d) 15269

112. In a sweet, one-third is sugar. If the price of sugar now is $\frac{7}{6}$ of the previous price, what is the effective percentage increase in the cost of the sweet? **SSC CPO 29/06/2024 Shift-III**

(a) $\frac{200}{9}\%$ (b) $\frac{100}{3}\%$
(c) $\frac{100}{18}\%$ (d) $\frac{100}{9}\%$

113. Swati earns a sum of ₹ 40000, out of which she saves 25%. She spends the remaining amount on food and education in the ratio of 3 : 2. What is the percentage of expenditure incurred on education to her total income? **SSC CPO 29/06/2024 Shift-II**

(a) 30% (b) 60%
(c) 40% (d) 20%

114. The population of a town increases annually by 20%. If the present population is 80 lakh, then what is the difference between the population 3 yr ago and 2 yr ago?
SSC CPO 29/06/2024 Shift-II

(a) 925925.93 (b) 85592.6
(c) 65592.6 (d) 75592.6

115. A is 25% more than B and B is 30% less than C. If C is 20% more than D, then by what percentage is A more than D? **SSC CPO 29/06/2024 Shift-I**

(a) 5% (b) 3% (c) 6% (d) 2%

116. 42% of Ranita's weekly income is equal to 56% of Bhaskar's weekly income. If Bhaskar's weekly income was raised by ₹ 200, while Ranita's weekly income did not change, the ratio of the weekly incomes of Ranita and Bhaskar, respectively, would have been 5 : 4. What is Ranita's weekly income (in ₹)?
SSC CPO 29/06/2024 Shift-I

(a) 3000 (b) 4000
(c) 3600 (d) 4200

117. In a school, the total number of boys is 20% more than the total number of girls. What is the ratio of the number of boys to that of girls in the school? **SSC CPO 29/06/2024 Shift-I**

(a) 6 : 5 (b) 4 : 5 (c) 5 : 3 (d) 5 : 6

118. If the number of school going children in a town is 64000 and it is increasing annually by 10%, then what will be the number of school going children in the town at the end of 3 yr? **SSC CPO 28/06/2024 Shift-III**

(a) 85000 (b) 85100
(c) 85184 (d) 80000

119. The cost of Compressed Natural Gas (CNG) per litre is increased by 65%. By what percentage must Manish reduce his consumption of CNG so as not to increase his expenditure? (correct up to two decimal places)
SSC CPO 28/06/2024 Shift-III

(a) 25.39% (b) 45.13%
(c) 39.39% (d) 30.13%

120. In an election between P, R and S, $\frac{1}{10}$ of the total votes polled are invalid. Votes polled in favour of R and S are half of the total votes polled and they get equal votes Due to a fault in the machine, half of the votes of S and half of the invalid votes are counted additionally in favour of R. What is the overall percentage of votes secured by R due to the fault ?
SSC CPO 28/06/2024 Shift-III

(a) 42.5% (b) 38.5%
(c) 41.55% (d) 37.55%

121. Ramnarayan's salary was reduced by $3\frac{1}{8}\%$ and then the reduced Salary was increased by $7\frac{2}{5}\%$. By what percentage (rounded off to two decimal places) is his new salary more/ less as compared to his original salary? **SSC CPO 28/06/2024 Shift-II**

(a) 4.04% less (b) 4.04% more
(c) 3.03% less (d) 3.03% more

122. Shiya invests ₹ 153000, which is 30% of her annual income, in mutual funds. What is her monthly income (in ₹)? **SSC CPO 28/06/2024 Shift-II**

(a) 45800 (b) 42500
(c) 55600 (d) 52300

123. The population of a city increases every year at the rate of 5%. If the population of the city is 16000, what will be the population after 2 yr?
SSC CPO 28/06/2024 Shift-II

(a) 17700 (b) 17600
(c) 17000 (d) 17640

124. In an election between *A* and *B*, every fifth vote polled was marked as invalid by the machine. In the remaining votes, *A* wins the election with a margin of 2500 votes or 10% of the total votes polled, over *B*. If 90% of the invalid votes would have been in favour of *B*, then which of the following would have been the result of the election?
SSC CPO 28/06/2024 Shift-II

(a) *A* would have won by 3%
(b) *A* would have won by 8%
(c) *B* would have won by 8%
(d) *B* would have won by 3%

125. A number is first decreased by 10%, then increased by 30% and then further it is decreased by 20%. What is the net decrease percentage in the number? **SSC CPO 28/06/2024 Shift-I**

(a) $4\frac{1}{5}$% (b) $3\frac{4}{5}$%
(c) $6\frac{2}{5}$% (d) $5\frac{3}{5}$%

126. Bhavani spends 68% of her income. Her income increases by 15% and her expenditure increases by 10%. How much is the increase in the percentage of saving? (use decimal up to 2 digits.) **SSC CPO 28/06/2024 Shift-I**

(a) 24.80% (b) 20.57%
(c) 28.42% (d) 25.62%

127. In an election, *A* received 27% of the votes and *B* received 125,982 votes. 19% did not cast their votes. Find the number of votes received by *A*.
SSC CPO 27/06/2024 Shift-III

(a) 188973 (b) 62991
(c) 57827 (d) 44327

128. On account of corona virus, 5% of the population of a village died. Out of the remaining population, 20% fled due to panic. If the present population is 4655, then what was the population of the village before the corona attack?
SSC CPO 27/06/2024 Shift-II

(a) 6000 (b) 6125 (c) 5995 (d) 5985

129. The strength of a school increases and decreases every alternate year by 15%. If it started with an increase in 2012, then the strength of the school in the beginning of 2015, as compared to that in 2012, had (correct to two decimal places).
SSC CPO 27/06/2024 Shift-II

(a) Decreased by 13.85 %
(b) Increased by 12.41 %
(c) Decreased by 12.41%
(d) Increased by 13.85 %

130. In an election, the winner was supported by 46% of all the voters in the list and he got 410 votes more than his only rival. 10% of the voters on the voters' list did not cast their votes, and 60 voters cast their ballot papers blank. How many voters were on the list?
SSC CPO 27/06/2024 Shift-II

(a) 17500 (b) 15750
(c) 17445 (d) 16550

131. In an election between two candidates, one got 60% of the total valid votes. 25% of the votes were invalid. If the total number of votes was 15000, then find the number of valid votes that the other candidate got. **SSC CPO 27/06/2024 Shift-I**

(a) 5000 (b) 4500
(c) 5550 (d) 6750

132. In an election, 12% of the voters in the voter list did not cast their votes, where as 84 voters cast their ballot papers blank. There were only two candidates, Ramagya and Shravan. The winner, Ramagya was supported by 54% of all the voters in the list. He got 1456 more votes than his rival, Shravan. Find the total number of voters in the list.
SSC CPO 27/06/2024 Shift-I

(a) 5690 (b) 6860
(c) 6670 (d) 7860

SSC CPO SI 2023 - 2020

133. The value of a washing machine depreciated from ₹ 40960 to ₹ 21970 in 3 yr. Find the yearly rate of depreciation.
SSC CPO 05/10/2023 Shift-III

(a) 25% (b) 16.25%
(c) 18.75% (d) 20%

134. Ayush spends 25% of an amount of money on an insurance policy, 26% on food, 23% on children's education and 19% on recreation. He deposits the remaining amount of ₹ 26600 in the bank. What is the total amount (in ₹) that he spends on food and recreation together?
SSC CPO 05/10/2023 Shift-III

(a) 195000 (b) 171000
(c) 162000 (d) 183000

135. The price of a stock increased by 30% in the first year and decreased by 20% in the second year. If an investor bought 100 shares of the stock for ₹ 1000, then what is the final value of the investment after 2 yr? **SSC CPO 04/10/2023 Shift-II**

(a) ₹ 960 (b) ₹ 1040
(c) ₹ 1400 (d) ₹ 1020

136. A number is first decreased by 28% and then increased by 28%. The number so obtained is 784 less than the original number. Find the value of the original number.
SSC CPO 04/10/2023 Shift-II

(a) 1000 (b) 15000
(c) 10000 (d) 1500

137. A man spends 72% of his salary and saves ₹ 5740 per month. What is 10% of his annual salary (in ₹)?
SSC CPO 03/10/2023 Shift-I

(a) ₹ 21600 (b) ₹ 24600
(c) ₹ 20500 (d) ₹ 28400

138. A number is first increased by 10% and then increased by 20%. The number, so obtained, is now decreased by 12%. What is the net increase or decrease per cent in the original number?
SSC CPO 03/10/2023 Shift-I

(a) 16.16% increase
(b) 14.14% decrease
(c) 11.11% decrease
(d) 12.12% increase

139. A man spends 65% of his income. His income increases by 20% and his expenditure also increases by 10%. The percentage of increase in his savings is...... **SSC CPO 11/11/2022**

(a) 38.5%
(b) 35.8%
(c) 10%
(d) 20%

140. Due to fall in manpower, the production in a company decreases by 35%. By what percentage should the working hours be increased to restore the original production?
SSC CPO 11/11/2022

(a) 58.35 % (b) 55.83 %
(c) 53.85 % (d) 55.38 %

141. Due to pandemic, the population of a city reduces at the rate of 2% per annum. What will be its total population after 2 yr if the present population of the city is 45000?
SSC CPO 11/11/2022

(a) 40538 (b) 44521
(c) 41568 (d) 43218

142. The income of Raju is 25% more than that of Manju. Raju got a 25% rise in his income, and Manju got a 40% rise in his income, the percentage increase in their combined incomes is **SSC CPO 11/11/2022**

(a) 51.72% (b) 31.67%
(c) 22.43% (d) 41.26%

143. If Ram's income exceeds Shyam's income by 70% and Shyam's income is less than Sohan's income by 30%, then find the ratio of the incomes of Ram and Sohan. **SSC CPO 10/11/2022**

(a) 119 : 100 (b) 121 : 102
(c) 120 : 101 (d) 118 : 99

144. The ratio of the number of boys to that of girls in a school is 5 : 2. If 87% of the boys and 80% of the girls passed in the annual exams, then find the percentage of students who failed in the annual exams. **SSC CPO 10/11/2022**

(a) 18 % (b) 16 %
(c) 15 % (d) 17 %

145. In an election, a candidate secures 42% of the votes polled but is defeated by his only opponent by a majority of 3080 votes, because of 1400 invalid votes. The percentage of invalid votes is .... **SSC CPO 10/11/2022**

(a) 5 % (b) 3 %
(c) 4 % (d) 6 %

146. In an entrance examination at different centres, a total of 25, 30, 40, 45, 60 and 100 students appeared. The pass percentages of the different centres are 20%, 30%, 35%, 40%, 50% and 75%, respectively. The pass percentage of the entrance examination is (correct to the nearest integer) **SSC CPO 25/11/2020 Shift-II**

(a) 59% (b) 43% (c) 53% (d) 50%

147. *A*'s salary is 35% more than *B*'s salary. How much percent is *B*'s salary less than that of *A*'s? (correct to the nearest integer) **SSC CPO 25/11/2020 Shift-II**

(a) 17.5%(b) 20% (c) 35% (d) 26%

148. If the numerator of a fraction is increased by 60% and the denominator is increased by 40%, then the resultant fraction is $\frac{16}{63}$. The original fraction is **SSC CPO 25/11/2020 Shift-II**

(a) $\frac{5}{9}$ (b) $\frac{2}{9}$
(c) $\frac{2}{11}$ (d) $\frac{4}{9}$

149. The price of diesel is increased by 26%. A person wants to increase his expenditure by 15% only. By what percentage, correct to one decimal place, should he decrease his consumption? **SSC CPO 25/11/2020 Shift-I**

(a) 7.2% (b) 9.5%
(c) 8.7% (d) 6.5%

150. If decreasing 110 by x% gives the same result as increasing 50 by x%, then x% of 650 is what percentage (correct to the nearest integer) more than $(x - 10)$% of 750? **SSC CPO 25/11/2020 Shift-I**

(a) 12% (b) 17% (c) 14% (d) 18%

151. The monthly salary of a person was ₹ 75000. He used to spend on Family Expenses (*E*), Taxes (*T*), Charity (*C*) and rest were his savings. *E* was 60% of the income. *T* was 20% of *E*, and *C* was 15% of *T*. When his salary got raised by 40%, he maintained the percentage level of *E*, but *T* became 30% of *E* and *C* became 20% of *T*. The ratio of the savings of his earlier salary to that of the savings of his present salary is **SSC CPO 24/11/2020 Shift-I**

(a) 655 : 644 (b) 325 : 337
(c) 644 : 655 (d) 337 : 325

152. A man spends 75% of his income. If his income increases by 28% and his expenditure increases by 20%, then what is the increase or decrease percentage in his savings? **SSC CPO 24/11/2020 Shift-I**

(a) 52% decrease (b) 52% increase
(c) 13% decrease (d) 13% increase

153. A person's salary has increased from ₹ 7000 to ₹ 12000. What is the percentage increase in his salary? **SSC CPO 24/11/2020 Shift-I**

(a) $61\frac{1}{7}$% (b) $69\frac{1}{7}$%
(c) $76\frac{4}{7}$% (d) $71\frac{3}{7}$%

154. The price of diesel increased by 16%. A person wants to increase his expenditure on diesel by 10% only. By what percentage, correct to one decimal place, should he reduce his consumption? **SSC CPO 23/11/2020 Shift-I**

(a) 6.5% (b) 5.2%
(c) 3.7% (d) 4.5%

155. If *A*'s salary is 60% more than *B*'s salary, then by what percentage is *B*'s salary less than that of *A*? **SSC CPO 23/11/2020 Shift-I**

(a) 45% (b) 37.5%
(c) 47.7% (d) 33.3%

156. If decreasing 110 by x% gives the same result as increasing 50 by x%, then x% of 650 is what percentage more than $(x + 20)$% of 180? (correct to nearest integer) **SSC CPO 23/11/2020 Shift-I**

(a) 136% (b) 90%
(c) 154% (d) 80%

SSC CHSL 2024 (Tier I & II)

157. The price of an electronic machine decreased by 5%, 10% and 15% during the first three years. What will be the price of the machine after three years if the value at the beginning was ₹ 8000? **SSC CHSL (Tier II) 18/11/2024 Shift-IV**

(a) ₹ 6721 (b) ₹ 5814
(c) ₹ 7000 (d) ₹ 5000

158. An election was held between two candidates. The winning candidate scored 54% of the valid votes and won by 88 votes. If 58 votes were declared invalid, then find the total number of votes polled in the election. **SSC CHSL (Tier I) 11/07/2024 Shift-IV**

(a) 1850 (b) 1158
(c) 1156 (d) 2000

159. The salary of employees in a factory was reduced by 20% due to economic crisis. In order to have their salary back to original amount, it must be raised by **SSC CHSL (Tier I) 11/07/2024 Shift-IV**

(a) 20% (b) 12.5%
(c) 40% (d) 25%

160. If the price of a commodity is increased by 36%, by what percentage (rounded off to 1 decimal place) should its consumption be decreased so that the expenditure of the commodity stays the same? **SSC CHSL (Tier I) 11/07/2024 Shift-IV**

(a) 26.5% (b) 36%
(c) 29.5% (d) 32%

161. The price of a product increases by 10% in the first year and 20% in the second year. What is the overall percentage increase in the price of the product over the two years? **SSC CHSL (Tier I) 11/07/2024 Shift-III**

(a) 30% (b) 32% (c) 28% (d) 36%

162. Shantanu's income decreased from ₹42800 to ₹37236. Find the percentage decrease in his income. **SSC CHSL (Tier I) 11/07/2024 Shift-III**

(a) 12% (b) 11%
(c) 14% (d) 13%

163. In two successive years, 75 and 50 employees of a company appeared at the departmental examination. Respectively, 84% and 52% of them passed. The average rate of pass percentage is
SSC CHSL (Tier I) 11/07/2024 Shift-III

(a) $41\frac{1}{5}\%$ (b) 41%
(c) 71% (d) $71\frac{1}{5}\%$

164. In an election between two candidates, 30% voters did not cast their votes and 200 votes were declared invalid. The winner got 65% of the valid votes. If he won by 1200 votes, then find the total votes.
SSC CHSL (Tier I) 11/07/2024 Shift-II

(a) 9000 (b) 6000 (c) 7000 (d) 8000

165. In an election, there were only two candidates. One of the candidates secured 44% of the votes and is defeated by the other candidate by 1440 votes. If there were no invalid votes, then the total number of votes polled is
SSC CHSL (Tier I) 11/07/2024 Shift-II

(a) 15000 (b) 12000
(c) 14000 (d) 13000

166. Shyam's income is 20% less than Ram's. How much is Ram's income more than Shyam's in percentage terms? **SSC CHSL (Tier I) 11/07/2024 Shift-II**

(a) 80% (b) 30%
(c) 25% (d) 20%

167. The population of a village was 400000. It increased by 20% in the first year and increased by 30% in the second year. Its population after two years is
SSC CHSL (Tier I) 11/07/2024 Shift-I

(a) 625000 (b) 624000
(c) 540000 (d) 520000

168. Two numbers are respectively 61% and 35% less than a third number. The first number is what percentage of the second number?
SSC CHSL (Tier I) 10/07/2024 Shift-IV

(a) 24% (b) 48%
(c) 30% (d) 60%

169. In an election between two candidates, Ananth and Aravind, Ananth got 55% of the total valid votes, and 20% of the votes were invalid. If the total number of votes was 30000, find the number of valid votes that Aravind got.
SSC CHSL (Tier I) 10/07/2024 Shift-IV

(a) 10800 (b) 1080
(c) 24000 (d) 13200

170. In an election between two candidates, 15% of the votes were invalid and one candidate got 52% of the total valid votes. If the total number of votes was 8000, what was the number of valid votes that the other candidate got?
SSC CHSL (Tier I) 10/07/2024 Shift-IV

(a) 3264 (b) 3536
(c) 3840 (d) 6800

171. In an election, a candidate secures 40% of the votes, but is defeated by the only other candidate with a majority of 298 votes. Find the total number of votes recorded.
SSC CHSL (Tier I) 10/07/2024 Shift-III

(a) 1470 (b) 1270
(c) 1490 (d) 1290

172. Two numbers are, respectively, 30% and 40% more than the third number. The ratio of the second number to the first number is
SSC CHSL (Tier I) 10/07/2024 Shift-III

(a) 26:28 (b) 14:13
(c) 39:42 (d) 13:14

173. After an increase of 9% in salary, a person received ₹6300. What was his salary before the increase (consider integral part only)?
SSC CHSL (Tier I) 10/07/2024 Shift-II

(a) ₹ 3879 (b) ₹ 5779
(c) ₹ 5000 (d) ₹ 4000

174. When 12 is subtracted from a number, it reduces to its 40%. Two-fifth of that number is
SSC CHSL (Tier I) 10/07/2024 Shift-II

(a) 20 (b) 12
(c) 8 (d) 50

175. Ram spends 30% of his salary on food, 10% on house rent, 7% on entertainment, and 6% on conveyance. If at the end of a month his savings are ₹ 1880, then his monthly salary is
SSC CHSL (Tier I) 10/07/2024 Shift-I

(a) ₹ 4500 (b) ₹ 4000
(c) ₹ 5000 (d) ₹ 5500

176. In an election between two candidates, *A* gets 63% of the total valid votes. If the total votes polled were 8750, what is the number of valid votes that the other candidate *B* gets, if 20% of the total votes were declared invalid?
SSC CHSL (Tier I) 10/07/2024 Shift-I

(a) 2590 (b) 3560
(c) 4410 (d) 6450

177. After decreasing 30%, an article costs ₹ 3500. Find its actual cost.
SSC CHSL (Tier I) 09/07/2024 Shift-IV

(a) ₹ 4500 (b) ₹ 6500
(c) ₹ 5000 (d) ₹ 5500

178. If 20% of 35% of a number is 240.8, then 18% of that number (rounded off to 1 decimal place) is
SSC CHSL (Tier I) 09/07/2024 Shift-IV

(a) 619.2 (b) 618.2
(c) 621.2 (d) 623.2

179. The price of an electronic watch is first reduced by 25% and then increased by 50%. If the resulting price of the electronic watch is ₹ 7650, then what was its original price (in ₹)?
SSC CHSL (Tier I) 09/07/2024 Shift-IV

(a) 6900 (b) 6500
(c) 6600 (d) 6800

180. If a person's salary increases from ₹ 200 per day to ₹ 234 per day, then the percentage increase in the person's salary is
SSC CHSL (Tier I) 09/07/2024 Shift-III

(a) 17% (b) 14%
(c) 15% (d) 16%

181. In an election, there were only two candidates. One of the candidates secured 35% of votes and is defeated by the other candidate by 381 votes. The total number of votes polled is.
SSC CHSL (Tier I) 09/07/2024 Shift-III

(a) 635 (b) 1028
(c) 1270 (d) 514

182. A car is sold for ₹ 500000, which is 20% less than its original price. What was the original price of the car ?
SSC CHSL (Tier I) 09/07/2024 Shift-III

(a) ₹ 625000 (b) ₹ 650000
(c) ₹ 675000 (d) ₹ 600000

183. If Ramu's salary is 30% less than Somu's salary, then by how much per cent is Somu's salary more than Ramu's salary?
SSC CHSL (Tier I) 09/07/2024 Shift-II

(a) 42.67% (b) 42.86%
(c) 45.47% (d) 34.56%

184. The total income of three families is ₹ 72000. Their expenditures are 80%, 85% and 75%, respectively. If the savings are in the ratio 8 : 9 : 20, then the income of the second family is **SSC CHSL (Tier I) 09/07/2024 Shift-II**

(a) ₹ 32000
(b) ₹ 16000
(c) ₹ 40000
(d) ₹ 24000

185. A number is first decreased by 18% and the resulting number is then increased by 25%. What is the overall percentage change in the original number?
SSC CHSL (Tier I) 09/07/2024 Shift-II

(a) Decrease by 2.5%
(b) Increase by 3.5%
(c) Increase by 2.5%
(d) Decrease by 3.5%

186. In an election between two candidates, 10% of the voters did not cast their votes and 5% of the votes polled were found invalid. The successful candidate got 52.5% of the valid votes and won by a majority of 1710 votes. The number of voters enrolled on the voters list was SSC CHSL (Tier I) 09/07/2024 Shift-I

(a) 36000 (b) 40000
(c) 42000 (d) 48000

187. A person saves 45% of his income. Next year, his income increases by 200%. He increases his savings by five times the previous year's savings. By what percentage (correct to one place of decimal) has he increased/decreased his expenditure?
SSC CHSL (Tier I) 9/07/2024 Shift-I

(a) Decreased, 63.4%
(b) Decreased, 36.4%
(c) Increased, 63.4%
(d) Increased, 36.4%

188. 5% of 2% of 3 is equal to
SSC CHSL (Tier I) 08/07/2024 Shift-IV

(a) 0.3 (b) 3
(c) 0.003 (d) 0.03

189. The value of a machine depreciates every year by 5%. If the present value of the machine is ₹ 80000, what will be its value after 2 yr?
SSC CHSL (Tier I) 08/07/2024 Shift-IV

(a) ₹ 72200 (b) ₹ 74400
(c) ₹ 74000 (d) ₹ 72000

190. In an election contested by two candidates, one candidate got 42% of the total votes and still lost by 800 votes. Find the total number of votes that were cast.
SSC CHSL (Tier I) 08/07/2024 Shift-IV

(a) 7000 (b) 2000 (c) 8000 (d) 5000

191. Ramesh's pocket money was reduced by 25% and then the reduced pocket money was increased by 20%. Find the net increase or decrease percentage in his original pocket money.
SSC CHSL (Tier I) 08/07/2024 Shift-III

(a) Decrease 12% (b) Increase 12%
(c) Increase 10% (d) Decrease 10%

192. At an election involving two candidates, 68 votes are declared invalid. The winning candidate gets 52% of the valid votes and wins by 98 votes. The total number of votes polled is
SSC CHSL (Tier I) 08/07/2024 Shift-III

(a) 2475 (b) 2518
(c) 2500 (d) 2250

193. Suresh studies the pattern of daily sale of a shop. He finds that on Monday, the sale was decreased by 10% in comparison to the sale on Sunday. On Tuesday, the sale was increased by 10% in comparison to the sale of Monday. If the sale on Tuesday was of ₹ 1485, how much was the sale on Sunday?
SSC CHSL (Tier I) 08/07/2024 Shift-II

(a) ₹ 1495 (b) ₹ 1475
(c) ₹ 1485 (d) ₹ 1500

194. Pranav gave 30% of the money, he had to his wife and 86% of the remaining to his two children. Half of the amount left was spent on other things and the remaining amount of ₹ 98000 was deposited in the bank. How much money did he have initially?
SSC CHSL (Tier I) 08/07/2024 Shift-II

(a) ₹ 2000000 (b) ₹ 4000000
(c) ₹ 1000000 (d) ₹ 3000000

195. *A*'s income is equal to 125% of the income of *B*, while *B*'s savings are 120% of the savings of *A*. If the expenditure of *B* is 75% of the expenditure of *A*, then how much are *B*'s savings as a percentage of her expenditure?
SSC CHSL (Tier I) 08/07/2024 Shift-II

(a) 20% (b) $22\frac{1}{2}$%
(c) $18\frac{3}{4}$% (d) $16\frac{2}{3}$%

196. The price of a car is decreased by 15% and 20% in two successive years respectively. What percentage of the price of the car is decreased after two years?
SSC CHSL (Tier I) 08/07/2024 Shift-I

(a) 32% (b) 25% (c) 46% (d) 15%

197. An interval of 2 h 25 min is wrongly estimated by 2 h 30.5 min. The error percentage is
SSC CHSL (Tier I) 08/07/2024 Shift-I

(a) $3\frac{23}{29}$% (b) $2\frac{27}{29}$%
(c) $3\frac{19}{29}$% (d) $2\frac{21}{29}$%

198. If the price of rice is reduced by 24%, it enables Alok to buy 10 kg more rice for ₹ 2500. The reduced rate of rice per kg is
SSC CHSL (Tier I) 08/07/2024 Shift-I

(a) ₹ 25 (b) ₹ 50
(c) ₹ 60 (d) ₹ 75

199. A person spends 60% of his salary on family expenses, 10% on medical expenses, 5% on charity and saves the remaining amount. If the amount on savings is ₹ 4000, find his monthly salary.
SSC CHSL (Tier I) 05/07/2024 Shift-IV

(a) ₹ 16000
(b) ₹ 12000
(c) ₹ 14000
(d) ₹ 15000

200. The price of a motorcycle was $750 last year. The price increased by 20% this year. What is the price of the motorcycle this year?
SSC CHSL (Tier I) 05/07/2024 Shift-IV

(a) $ 750 (b) $ 900
(c) $ 600 (d) $ 790

201. In an assembly election, a candidate got 60% of the total valid votes. 3% of the total votes were declared invalid. If the total number of voters is 240000, then find the number of valid votes polled in favour of the candidate.
SSC CHSL (Tier I) 05/07/2024 Shift-III

(a) 193680 (b) 139680
(c) 139860 (d) 139608

202. A quantity $\frac{4}{5}$ is changed to $\frac{5}{6}$.
How much percentage change is given to the quantity?
SSC CHSL (Tier I) 05/07/2024 Shift-III

(a) 4.71% (b) 4.73%
(c) 4.17% (d) 4.37%

203. A number is first increased by 44% and then decreased by 30%. The net percentage change (rounded off to the nearest integer) in the original number is SSC CHSL (Tier I) 05/07/2024 Shift-II

(a) increase by 1%
(b) decrease by 4%
(c) increase by 4%
(d) decrease by 1%

204. In an election between two candidates, one candidate gets 72% of the total votes cast. If the total votes are 1000, by how many votes does the winner win the election?
SSC CHSL (Tier I) 05/07/2024 Shift-II

(a) 360 (b) 250
(c) 720 (d) 440

205. The difference between 31% and 26% of votes for the same party at different places is 2350. What is 7% of those votes?

SSC CHSL (Tier I) 05/07/2024 Shift-I

(a) 2270 (b) 3090
(c) 4090 (d) 3290

206. Monthly salary of Jitvik in the month of December 2020 was ₹ 24800. Every year his salary increases by 5% from the month of January. What was his salary (in ₹) in the month of February 2022?

SSC CHSL (Tier I) 05/07/2024 Shift-I

(a) 27342 (b) 26485
(c) 27486 (d) 27180

207. If the income of Neha is 5% more than that of Monica, then the income of Monica is what percentage less than that of Neha?

SSC CHSL (Tier I) 04/07/2024 Shift-IV

(a) $4\frac{5}{21}\%$ (b) $4\frac{13}{21}\%$
(c) $4\frac{11}{21}\%$ (d) $4\frac{16}{21}\%$

208. If the price of tea is increased by 40%, by what percentage must the consumption of tea be decreased, so as not to increase the expenditure?

SSC CHSL (Tier I) 04/07/2024 Shift-IV

(a) $15\frac{2}{9}\%$ (b) $31\frac{3}{5}\%$
(c) $35\frac{9}{2}\%$ (d) $28\frac{4}{7}\%$

209. Ramu used to spend 72% of his income. His income has increased by 12% and he increases his expenditure by 5%. If Ramu earlier saved y and after the increases, now he saves x, then what is the value of $\left(\frac{x-y}{y}\times 100\right)\%$?

SSC CHSL (Tier I) 04/07/2024 Shift-IV

(a) 25% (b) 22% (c) 27% (d) 30%

210. Express the following as decimals, respectively. 20%, 0.5%, 0.03%

SSC CHSL (Tier I) 04/07/2024 Shift-III

(a) 0.02,0.005,0.0003
(b) 0.02,0.005,0.003
(c) 0.2,0.005,0.0003
(d) 0.2,0.0005,0.0003

211. Last year, Geeta's monthly salary was ₹ 12000 and Seeta's monthly salary was ₹ 10000. This year, Geeta's monthly salary is ₹ 14400, while Seeta's monthly salary is ₹ 12500. If the percentage increase in Seeta's monthly salary this year over her monthly salary last year is denoted by x% and the percentage increase in Geeta's monthly salary this year over her monthly salary last year is denoted by y%, then what is the value of $\left(\frac{x-y}{y}\times 100\right)\%$?

SSC CHSL (Tier I) 04/07/2024 Shift-III

(a) 24 (b) 20 (c) 22 (d) 25

212. The cost of rice is increased by 25% but its consumption is decreased by 30%. Find the percentage increase or decrease in the expenditure of money. **SSC CHSL (Tier I) 04/07/2024 Shift-II**

(a) Increase $12\frac{1}{2}\%$
(b) Increase $13\frac{1}{3}\%$
(c) Decrease $12\frac{1}{2}\%$
(d) Decrease $13\frac{1}{3}\%$

213. Rahul spends 70% of his income. His income increased by 15% and his expenditure increased by 7.5%. What is the percentage increase in his savings?

SSC CHSL (Tier I) 04/07/2024 Shift-II

(a) 25.5% (b) 30.5%
(c) 50% (d) 32.5%

214. Last year, Ranjan's monthly salary was ₹ 34500 and this year his monthly salary is ₹ 38640. What is the percentage increase in Ranjan's monthly salary this year over his monthly salary last year?

SSC CHSL (Tier I) 04/07/2024 Shift-II

(a) 15% (b) 12%
(c) 20% (d) 13%

215. In a state election between two parties, 83% of the voters cast their votes, out of which 4% of the votes were declared invalid. Party A got 156611 votes which were 83% of the total valid votes. Find the total number of votes enrolled in that election. (Consider integer part only)

SSC CHSL (Tier I) 04/07/2024 Shift-I

(a) 258233 (b) 234888
(c) 236807 (d) 2346807

216. A person spends 10% of his income on groceries, 10% on medicines, 20% on children's education, 15% on house rent, and he saves the remaining amount. If his monthly income is ₹ 30000, find his savings.

SSC CHSL (Tier I) 04/07/2024 Shift-I

(a) ₹ 15500
(b) ₹ 16500
(c) ₹ 13500
(d) ₹ 12500

217. Convert 28% into the form of ratio.

SSC CHSL (Tier I) 04/07/2024 Shift-I

(a) 25 : 7 (b) 18 : 7
(c) 7 : 25 (d) 7 : 18

218. In an election between two candidates, 10% of the registered voters did not cast their vote. The winning candidate got 60% of the total votes cast and defeated the other candidate by 1242 votes. Find the total number of registered voters. **SSC CHSL (Tier I) 03/07/2024 Shift-III**

(a) 9600 (b) 6200 (c) 8640 (d) 6900

219. 12.75% is equivalent to ....

SSC CHSL (Tier I) 03/07/2024 Shift-III

(a) $\frac{37}{400}$ (b) $\frac{51}{400}$ (c) $\frac{41}{400}$ (d) $\frac{17}{200}$

220. If the income of P is 40% less than Q, then the combined income of P and Q is how much per cent more than the income of P?

SSC CHSL (Tier I) 03/07/2024 Shift-III

(a) $164\frac{1}{3}$ (b) $166\frac{1}{3}$
(c) $166\frac{2}{3}$ (d) $164\frac{2}{3}$

221. A fraction $\frac{3}{5}$ is decreased by $\frac{2}{5}$. The resulting fraction is then increased by 20%. What is the percentage decrease/increase in the value of the original fraction ?

SSC CHSL (Tier I) 03/07/2024 Shift-II

(a) Increase, 60% (b) Decrease, 50%
(c) Increase, 50% (d) Decrease, 60%

222. Ramana spends 75% of his income. His income is increased by 25% and he increases his expenditure by 10%. By what percentage are his savings increased ?

SSC CHSL (Tier I) 03/07/2024 Shift-II

(a) 60% (b) 50% (c) 70% (d) 40%

223. A person wants to buy 10 chairs. The total cost of 10 chairs is ₹ 4500. After bargaining, the shopkeeper agrees to decrease the cost of each chair by 20%. Then, the person purchased 10% more chairs. What will be the cost of the chairs that he purchased ?

SSC CHSL (Tier I) 03/07/2024 Shift-II

(a) ₹ 4100 (b) ₹ 3960
(c) ₹ 3260 (d) ₹ 3900

224. Monthly expenditure of Ritvik decreases from ₹ 12800 to ₹ 11712. Find the percentage decrease in his expenditure.

SSC CHSL (Tier I) 03/07/2024 Shift-I

(a) 7.7% (b) 6.25%
(c) 8.5% (d) 9.25%

225. In an election between two candidates, a candidate who gets 78% of the votes is elected by a majority of 448 votes. What is the total number of votes polled?
SSC CHSL (Tier I) 03/07/2024 Shift-I

(a) 700 (b) 850
(c) 800 (d) 750

226. In an election between two candidates, the defeated candidate secured 42% of the valid votes polled and lost the election by 2545800 votes. If 365500 votes were declared invalid and 30% people did not cast their vote, what was the approximate number of people (in millions) in the electorate who did not cast their votes?
SSC CHSL (Tier I) 03/07/2024 Shift-I

(a) 5 (b) 6
(c) 8 (d) 7

227. In an election between two candidates, one got 65% of the total valid votes. 20% of the votes were invalid. If the total number of votes was 7500, the number of valid votes that the other candidate got was
SSC CHSL (Tier I) 02/07/2024 Shift-IV

(a) 1700 (b) 2100
(c) 4300 (d) 1900

228. A man spends 35% of his monthly income on food and four-thirteenths of the remaining income on transport. He incurs some other expenses, but also saves ₹ 6300 per month, the latter being equal to 20% of the balance remaining just after spending on food and transport. What is his monthly income (₹ in)?
SSC CHSL (Tier I) 02/07/2024 Shift-IV

(a) 67500 (b) 72000
(c) 70000 (d) 63000

229. At the beginning of day 1 of a month, Rajesh has 500 eggs. He sells 20% of the eggs by the end of the day and added b% of the eggs at the beginning of the next day and sold 20% of the eggs at the end of the next day. This pattern continued up to the end of the third day of the month when he is left with 1024 eggs. The value of b is equal to
SSC CHSL (Tier I) 02/07/2024 Shift-IV

(a) 20 (b) 10
(c) 500 (d) 100

230. The price of an article is first increased by 40% and then decreased by 45%, due to reduction in sales. Find the net percentage change in the final price of the article. **SSC CHSL (Tier I) 02/07/2024 Shift-III**

(a) –23% (b) 23%
(c) 13% (d) –13%

231. What is the number which needs to be added to 20% of 460 to have the sum as 70% of 920 ?
SSC CHSL (Tier I) 02/07/2024 Shift-III

(a) 926 (b) 762
(c) 552 (d) 335

232. When a number is increased by 8, it becomes 120% of itself. The number is **SSC CHSL (Tier I) 02/07/2024 Shift-II**

(a) 30 (b) 40
(c) 60 (d) 50

233. From the salary of a software engineer, if 15% is used as house rent, 25% of the remaining is spent on household items, 25% of the remaining as income tax and 15% of the remaining on clothing, then he is left with ₹10404. Find his total salary. **SSC CHSL (Tier I) 02/07/2024 Shift-II**

(a) ₹ 22600 (b) ₹ 24600
(c) ₹ 25600 (d) ₹ 23600

234. During the first year, the population of a village increased by 5% and during the second year it diminished by 5%. At the end of the second year its population was 47880. What was the population at the beginning of the first year?
SSC CHSL (Tier I) 02/07/2024 Shift-I

(a) 45000 (b) 48000
(c) 43500 (d) 53000

235. In a group of 250 persons, 40% are males and 60% are females. If 30 more females join the group, then what will be the percentage of females in the new group? (correct to 2 decimal places)
SSC CHSL (Tier I) 02/07/2024 Shift-I

(a) 62.58% (b) 72.25%
(c) 64.29% (d) 90.25%

236. Sumit's income in 2020 was ₹ 21000. He gets an increment of 10% every year. What was his income in 2022?
SSC CHSL (Tier I) 01/07/2024 Shift-IV

(a) ₹ 23100 (b) ₹ 25410
(c) ₹ 29100 (d) ₹ 26530

237. In an election, a candidate secured 41% of the votes polled and lost the election by 97632. What is the number of votes obtained by the winning candidate?
SSC CHSL (Tier I) 01/07/2024 Shift-IV

(a) 320016 (b) 542400
(c) 222384 (d) 360072

238. If the price of an article is raised by 35%, by how much per cent must a householder reduce his consumption of that article, so as not to increase his expenditure?
SSC CHSL (Tier I) 01/07/2024 Shift-III

(a) $25\frac{22}{27}\%$ (b) $25\frac{23}{27}\%$
(c) $25\frac{25}{27}\%$ (d) $25\frac{24}{27}\%$

239. In an election between two candidates A and B, A got 33% of total votes casted and still lost by 55522 votes. Find the total number of votes got by B.
SSC CHSL (Tier I) 01/07/2024 Shift-III

(a) 109114 (b) 109141
(c) 104911 (d) 109411

240. If 18 toys out of 75 toys are for boys and the rest are for girls, what is the percentage of girls toys?
SSC CHSL (Tier I) 01/07/2024 Shift-II

(a) 18% (b) 57%
(c) 67% (d) 76%

241. Three persons ran for office and got, 1136, 7636 and 11628 votes, respectively. What was the winning candidate's percentage of the total votes? **SSC CHSL (Tier I) 01/07/2024 Shift-II**

(a) 52% (b) 61%
(c) 59% (d) 57%

242. The price of an electric bike was ₹ 125000 last year. This year, its price got decreased by 30%. What is the price (in ₹) of the electric bike this year? **SSC CHSL (Tier I) 01/07/2024 Shift-II**

(a) 86000
(b) 87500
(c) 86500
(d) 87000

243. Mohan gets 12% increase in his sale amount in the first year and 15% increase in the second year, with that his present sale is ₹128800. What was his sale two years ago?
SSC CHSL (Tier I) 01/07/2024 Shift-I

(a) ₹125000 (b) ₹150000
(c) ₹175000 (d) ₹100000

244. A man spent 60% of his salary on household expenses, 20% of his salary on rent and out of remaining salary, he donated 80% to a trust. If he is left with ₹20000, then what is his salary?
SSC CHSL (Tier I) 01/07/2024 Shift-I

(a) ₹400000
(b) ₹500000
(c) ₹550000
(d) ₹50000

245. In an election, a candidate who gets 90% votes is elected by a margin of 800 votes. What is the total number of votes polled?

Note There are only two candidates contesting the election and assume all the votes were valid.

SSC CHSL (Tier-II) 10/01/2024 Shift-I

(a) 1050 (b) 950
(c) 1000 (d) 900

SSC CHSL 2023 (Tier I & II)

246. In an election between two candidates, 64% of the voters cast their votes, out of which 4% of the votes were declared invalid. A candidate got 12288 votes which were 64% of the total valid votes. Find the total number of votes enrolled in that election.

SSC CHSL (Tier-II) 02/11/2023 Shift-I

(a) 31250 (b) 30250
(c) 32152 (d) 20152

247. A number is increased by 25% and then decreased by 16%, the final value of the number

SSC CHSL (Tier-II) 02/11/2023 Shift-I

(a) decreases by 5%
(b) increases by 5%
(c) decreases by 13%
(d) does not change

248. The population of a certain village increase by 5 per cent annually. Its present population is 8200. After two year the population will be (approximately).

SSC CHSL (Tier-I) 14/08/2023 Shift-IV

(a) 9200 (b) 9246
(c) 9040 (d) 9161

249. A number is first increased by 16% and then increased by 20%. The number so obtained is now decreased by 40%. The net decrease percentage in the original number is

SSC CHSL (Tier-I) 14/08/2023 Shift-IV

(a) $16\frac{12}{25}\%$ (b) $15\frac{9}{25}\%$
(c) $11\frac{13}{25}\%$ (d) $13\frac{7}{25}\%$

250. The population of a city was 1250000 in the year 2010. It increased at the rate of 2% per annum during the years 2011 and 2012. In the year 2013, it decreased by 1%. Find the population of the city at the end of 2013. **SSC CHSL (Tier-I) 11/08/2023 Shift-I**

(a) 1285495
(b) 1350000
(c) 1387495
(d) 1287495

251. If four-fifths of five-sixths of one-eighth of a certain number is 4365, what is 65% of the number?

SSC CHSL (Tier-I) 11/08/2023 Shift-I

(a) 36375 (b) 53280
(c) 34047 (d) 52380

252. A number first increased by 8% and then decreased by 3% to get 2619. What is 5% of that number?

SSC CHSL (Tier-I) 10/08/2023 Shift-III

(a) 125 (b) 135
(c) 130 (d) 140

253. A spends 68% of the monthly income. If A's monthly income increases by 25% and his monthly savings increases by 150%, then the percentage increase in his monthly expenditure will be

SSC CHSL (Tier-I) 09/08/2023 Shift-I

(a) $27\frac{13}{17}\%$ (b) $29\frac{12}{17}\%$
(c) $33\frac{7}{17}\%$ (d) $31\frac{6}{17}\%$

254. Harsha's expenditure is 45% of her income. If the income from the next month is increased by 15% and the amount she saved each month remains the same, then find the percentage increase in her expenditure (rounded off to 2 decimal places). **SSC CHSL (Tier-I) 07/08/2023 Shift-IV**

(a) 33.33% (b) 15.00%
(c) 45.00% (d) 27.50%

255. Prakash spends 27% of his salary on children's education and donates 4% to a trust in a particular month. He spends ₹ 3038 on these two heads, then his total salary for that month is **SSC CHSL (Tier-I) 04/08/2023 Shift-II**

(a) ₹4402 (b) ₹9800
(c) ₹11251 (d) ₹13200

256. Bhushan's monthly income is ₹ 45000 and his monthly expenditure is ₹ 33000. If his monthly income is increased by 22% while monthly expenditure is increased by 11% then what is his new monthly savings (in ₹)?

SSC CHSL (Tier-I) 02/08/2023 Shift-I

(a) 18270 (b) 18690
(c) 18000 (d) 19000

257. If price of rice is increased by 25%, then by what percentage consumption of rice should by decreased so that the expenditure incurred on rice gets decreased by 40% ? **SSC CHSL (Tier-I) 21/03/2023 Shift-IV**

(a) 52% (b) 43.33%
(c) 42% (d) 48%

258. *P* is 20 per cent more than *Q* and *Q* is 30 per cent less than *R*. If *P* is 420, then what is the value of *R* ?

SSC CHSL (Tier-I) 21/03/2023 Shift-II

(a) 600 (b) 500 (c) 625 (d) 700

259. On decreasing the price of a fan by 30 per cent, its sales increases by 40 per cent. What will be the percentage decrease in its revenue?

SSC CHSL (Tier-I) 17/03/2023 Shift-II

(a) 2 per cent decrease
(b) 5 per cent decrease
(c) 8 per cent decrease
(d) 3 per cent decrease

260. Price of 15 chairs is 20% more than the price of 8 tables. If price of 2 tables is ₹ 2400, then what is the price of 15 chairs?

SSC CHSL (Tier-I) 16/03/2023 Shift-I

(a) ₹ 10320 (b) ₹ 12380
(c) ₹ 11520 (d) ₹ 10780

261. Rajiv scored 20% marks in an exam and failed by 25 marks. If he scores 50% marks, then he gets 20 marks more than passing marks. What is the passing marks for the exam?

SSC CHSL (Tier-I) 14/03/2023 Shift-I

(a) 40 (b) 35 (c) 55 (d) 45

262. In the Lok Sabha election, Party *A* got 30% of the total votes. Party *B* got 25% of the total votes. Party *C* got the remaining votes and they got 9000 more votes than Party *A*. Find the number of votes Party *B* got.

SSC CHSL (Tier-I) 10/03/2023 Shift-II

(a) 12000 (b) 18000
(c) 21000 (d) 15000

263. If 20% of *P* is added to 40% of *Q*, then the resultant comes as 80% of *Q*. *P* is what percentage of *Q*?

SSC CHSL (Tier-I) 09/03/2023 Shift-I

(a) 125% (b) 200%
(c) 225% (d) 150%

SSC CHSL 2022 & 2021 (Tier I)

264. The expenses of a family on wheat, vegetables and oil are in the ratio 12 : 8 : 5. The prices of these items increased by 50%, 25% and 40%, respectively. The total expenses of the family on these items increased by **SSC CHSL (Tier-I) 02/06/2022 Shift-I**

(a) 40% (b) 38% (c) 44% (d) 42%

265. A family spends 8% of its monthly income on charity. In a particular month, the family spent ₹ 1200 on charity. What is the income in that month? **SSC CHSL (Tier-I) 01/06/2022 Shift-I**

(a) ₹ 15000 (b) ₹ 16000
(c) ₹ 12000 (d) ₹ 18000

266. Bhanu spends 20% of his monthly salary on rent, 10% on stationery, 14% on transport, 18% on electricity and the balance of ₹1520 on remaining items. What is the monthly salary of Bhanu? SSC CHSL (Tier-I) 01/06/2022 Shift-I

(a) ₹10000 (b) ₹6000
(c) ₹4000 (d) ₹2000

267. The value of a machine depreciates every year by 10%. If its present value is ₹ 35000, then the value of the machine after 2 yr will be SSC CHSL (Tier-I) 30/05/2022 Shift-I

(a) ₹ 28350 (b) ₹ 27225
(c) ₹ 28000 (d) ₹ 27750

268. A number is increased by 10% and then the increased number is decreased by 20%. The net increase or decrease is SSC CHSL (Tier-I) 27/05/2022 Shift-I

(a) 18% decrease (b) 2% decrease
(c) 12% decrease (d) 12% increase

269. Admissions into a commerce course of a university increase by 5% every year. If the number of admissions presently is 2400 into that course, after three years, the number of admissions is nearest to an integer SSC CHSL (Tier-I) 27/05/2022 Shift-I

(a) 2778 (b) 2770
(c) 2775 (d) 2780

270. 24% of Reena's salary is equal to 38% of Sunita's salary. Veena's salary is two-third of the total salary of Reena and Sunita. If Veena's salary is ₹ 62000, then Sunita's salary is SSC CHSL (Tier-I) 12/08/2021 Shift-III

(a) ₹ 35000 (b) ₹ 32000
(c) ₹ 38000 (d) ₹ 36000

271. A person saves 25% of his income. If his income increases by 20% and his saving remains the same, then what will be the increased percentage of his expenditure? SSC CHSL (Tier-I) 10/08/2021 Shift-I

(a) 20 (b) 26
(c) 30 (d) $26\frac{2}{3}$

272. A is 150% of B and B is 40% of C. If $A + B + C = 20$, then the value of $2B + 3C - 4A$ is equal to SSC CHSL (Tier-I) 04/08/2021 Shift-I

(a) 16 (b) 14 (c) 20 (d) 15

273. The difference between a number and its three-fifth is 274. What is 20% of the number? SSC CHSL (Tier-I) 19/04/2021 Shift-I

(a) 137 (b) 150
(c) 165 (d) 144

274. What is the value of x, if 25% of 480 + 30% of 500 + x% of 90 = 35% of 900? SSC CHSL (Tier-I) 12/04/2021 Shift-II

(a) 45 (b) 50
(c) 55 (d) 40

SSC MTS 2024

275. If the numerator of a fraction is increased by 12% and its denominator is diminished by 8%, then the value of the fraction is $\frac{56}{69}$. Find the original fraction. SSC MTS 14/11/2024 Shift III

(a) $\frac{4}{3}$ (b) $\frac{3}{2}$ (c) $\frac{3}{4}$ (d) $\frac{2}{3}$

276. The height of Aaryan was 120 cm. After 1 yr, his height increased by 15% and in the next 1 yr, his height increased by 16%. What will be the height (in cm) of Aaryan after the second years? SSC MTS 13/11/2024 Shift III

(a) 161.08 (b) 150.56
(c) 160.08 (d) 138

277. In an election there were only two candidates, Geeta and Shyama. Geeta received 15% of the total votes and Shyama received 8700 votes. 60% of the voters did not cast their vote to either of the two candidates. Find the total percentage of votes that Shyama received, assuming that all the votes cast were valid. SSC MTS 12/11/2024 Shift III

(a) 22% (b) 23%
(c) 24% (d) 25%

278. The salary of a person was reduced by 20%. By what percentage should his reduced salary be raised so as to bring it at par with his original salary? SSC MTS 11/11/2024 Shift III

(a) 22% (b) 20%
(c) 25% (d) 30%

279. If Mohan's income is 20% less than Arvind's income, then how much per cent is Arvind's income more than Mohan's income? SSC MTS 04/11/2024 Shift III

(a) 30% (b) 20%
(c) 15% (d) 25%

280. If the price of a commodity is increased by 10% and 20% successively, what is the net percentage increase/decrease in its price, if it is further decreased by 25%? SSC MTS 30/10/2024 Shift III

(a) 1% Decrease (b) 5% Decrease
(c) 5% Increase (d) 1% Increase

281. A man's working hours per day were increased by 10% and his wages per hour were increased by 5%. By how much per cent were his daily earnings increased? SSC MTS 29/10/2024 Shift III

(a) 10.3% (b) 12.2%
(c) 5% (d) 15.5%

282. The price of an article is reduced by 40% and its sale is increased by 80%. Find the net effect on revenue. SSC MTS 23/10/2024 Shift II

(a) 8% increase (b) 10% increase
(c) 10% decrease (d) 8% decrease

283. Rajeev saves 75% of his monthly income. If his monthly expenditure is ₹ 37500, then his monthly saving (in ₹) is SSC MTS 22/10/2024 Shift II

(a) 112500 (b) 120250
(c) 110500 (d) 111500

284. The price of a commodity is increased by 20% and then again by 25%. By what per cent should the increased price be reduced to get back to the initial price? SSC MTS 21/10/2024 Shift II

(a) $33\frac{1}{3}$% (b) 45%
(c) $22\frac{1}{2}$% (d) 25%

285. In an election, 750 votes were cast for the two contestants, Bharti and Manya. Bharti defeated Manya by 16% votes. If there were no invalid vote, then how many votes did Manya get? SSC MTS 18/10/2024 Shift II

(a) 335 (b) 430 (c) 315 (d) 120

286. When the price of a laptop was reduced by 15%, its sales increased by 10%. What was the net effect on the sale? SSC MTS 17/10/2024 Shift II

(a) 6.5% increase (b) 6.5% decrease
(c) 3.5% decrease (d) 3.5% increase

287. Aniruddh invested ₹15000 in the shares of a company. The shares rose by 15% one day and fell by 10% on the other day. What is the current value (in ₹) of Aniruddh's investment? SSC MTS 16/10/2024 Shift II

(a) 15450 (b) 15525
(c) 15750 (d) 15500

288. An investment grows by 15% in the first month, 20% in the second month and then decreases by 10% in the third month. If the initial investment was ₹5000, then the final amount (in ₹) is SSC MTS 15/10/2024 Shift I

(a) 6420 (b) 6602 (c) 6340 (d) 6210

289. The ratio of the number of boys and girls in a hostel is 5 : 7. If 40% of boys and 50% of girls are getting scholarships for their studies, what is the percentage of hostel students who are not getting any scholarships? **SSC MTS 14/10/2024 Shift I**

(a) $56\frac{1}{8}\%$ (b) $54\frac{1}{6}\%$
(c) $35\frac{1}{7}\%$ (d) $45\frac{1}{5}\%$

290. If two numbers are 6.25% and 25% more than a third number, respectively, then the first number is how much per cent of the second number? **SSC MTS 14/10/2024 Shift I**

(a) 95% (b) 85%
(c) 90% (d) 80%

291. In 2016, the price of a refrigerator increased by 5%, and in 2017, it decreased by 5%. At the end of the year 2017, its price was₹ 47880. What was its price at the beginning of the year 2016? **SSC MTS 09/10/2024 Shift I**

(a) ₹48000 (b) ₹46000
(c) ₹48560 (d) ₹54050

292. The price of a computer increases by 10% in the first year, decreases by 5% in the second year and increases by 8% in the third year. If the original price was ₹50000, then the final price (in ₹) is **SSC MTS 08/10/2024 Shift I**

(a) 56430 (b) 55100
(c) 54120 (d) 55830

293. In a student council election, there were three contestants. All the voters participated in the voting and 10% of votes were declared invalid. The contestants got the votes in the ratio 8 : 7 : 5. If the second candidate in the list got 4725 votes, the total number of valid votes is **SSC MTS 07/10/2024 Shift I**

(a) 10000 (b) 11500
(c) 13500 (d) 9000

SSC MTS 2023-2021

294. A family spends 20% of its monthly income on house rent. Out of the remaining amount, the family spends 50% on household expenditure and 20% on children's education. If after doing so, its monthly savings is ₹ 6600, then what is the total monthly income of the family? **SSC MTS 13/09/2023 Shift-I**

(a) ₹25000 (b) ₹27500
(c) ₹30000 (d) ₹28000

295. The price of a bed is first increased by 32% and later on decreased by 20% due to reduction in sales. Find the net percentage change in the final price of the bed. **SSC MTS 11/09/2023 Shift-II**

(a) 5.6 % (b) 6.2 %
(c) 7.5 % (d) 4.9 %

296. If Rita's salary increases by 5% in the first year and by 2% in the next year, then what is the net percentage increase in her salary after two years? **SSC MTS 11/09/2023 Shift-I**

(a) 6.1% (b) 5.1%
(c) 8.1% (d) 7.1%

297. The income of a company increases 25% per annum. If its income is ₹ 2664000 in the year 1999, what was its income in the year 1997? **SSC MTS 08/09/2023 Shift-II**

(a) ₹ 1650000 (b) ₹ 1704960
(c) ₹ 1550000 (d) ₹ 1750000

298. A spends 20% of the daily income. If the expenditure is ₹ 250, then the daily income is **SSC MTS 06/09/2023 Shift-I**

(a) ₹ 800 (b) ₹ 1250
(c) ₹ 2500 (d) ₹ 1500

299. The strength of a school increases and decreases every alternate year by 20%. It started with an increase in the year 2015 and the initial strength was 3000. Find the strength of the school in the year 2017 and also the percentage of increase in strength, respectively. **SSC MTS 05/09/2023 Shift-II**

(a) 3456, 15.2% (b) 4456, 14.2%
(c) 4556, 17.2% (d) 3556, 16.2%

300. Vikram saves 13% of his monthly salary. If his monthly expenditure is ₹ 5220, then his monthly savings is **SSC MTS 04/09/2023 Shift-II**

(a) ₹ 680 (b) ₹ 580
(c) ₹ 349 (d) ₹ 780

301. The income of X is 12% more than that of Y. By how much per cent is Y's income less than that of X? **SSC MTS 01/09/2023 Shift-III**

(a) $10\frac{4}{7}\%$ (b) $10\frac{3}{7}\%$
(c) $10\frac{5}{7}\%$ (d) $10\frac{2}{7}\%$

302. Two numbers A and B are such that the sum of 6% of A and 4% of B is two-fifth of the sum of 7% of A and 11% of B, then the ratio $A : B$ is **SSC MTS 01/09/2023 Shift-I**

(a) 3 : 7 (b) 5 : 8
(c) 1 : 8 (d) 1 : 7

303. If the first number is 20% less than third number and the ratio of the second to the third number is 7 : 10, then the average of the first and the third number is how much per cent more than the second number? **SSC MTS 01/09/2023 Shift-I**

(a) $26\frac{4}{7}$ (b) $28\frac{2}{7}$
(c) $28\frac{4}{7}$ (d) $24\frac{2}{7}$

304. P is increased successively by 15% and 20% to get Q. If $P = 200$, then what is the value of Q? **SSC MTS 15/07/2022 Shift-I**

(a) 266 (b) 284 (c) 276 (d) 292

305. In an election between 2 candidates, the winning candidate gets 2940 valid votes, while the losing candidate gets 40% of the valid votes. If 2% of the votes polled were declared invalid, then what is the total number of votes polled ? **SSC MTS 15/07/2022 Shift-I**

(a) 4500 (b) 5000
(c) 6000 (d) 5500

306. The price of a cap is increased by 15%. If this results in a ₹ 27 increase in the price of the cap, then what is the increased price of the cap ? **SSC MTS 14/07/2022 Shift-I**

(a) ₹ 170 (b) ₹ 197 (c) ₹ 207 (d) ₹ 180

307. Ravi's monthly salary is ₹ 16000. He spends 30% of his salary on rent, 20% of his salary on education. 60% of the remaining amount is invested in mutual funds. Find the amount invested in mutual funds in a month. **SSC MTS 14/07/2022 Shift-I**

(a) ₹5000 (b) ₹4800
(c) ₹4200 (d) ₹4500

308. Anjali decided to spend 45% of her salary on shopping. On completion of her shopping, she realised that she had spent only₹ 11475, which was 60% of what she had decided to spend. How much is Anjali's salary? **SSC MTS 13/07/2022 Shift-I**

(a) ₹40800 (b) ₹29600
(c) ₹38400 (d) ₹42500

309. E% of 12.5% of 480 = 72. What is the value of E? **SSC MTS 13/07/2022 Shift-I**

(a) 95 (b) 110 (c) 105 (d) 120

310. In an office of 900 employees, on a particular day, except for 10% of the female employees, all employees were present. On the next day, except for 8% of the male employees, all employees were present. The number of employees present on each of these two days was the same. Find the total number of male employees on the payrolls of this office. SSC MTS 12/07/2022 Shift-I

(a) 550 (b) 450
(c) 800 (d) 500

311. If the population of a town is 12000 and the population increases at the rate of 10% per annum, then find the population after 3 yr. SSC MTS 12/07/2022 Shift-I

(a) 15972 (b) 12200
(c) 11200 (c) 10200

312. 600 – A = 65% of 200. What is the value of A? SSC MTS 11/07/2022 Shift-I

(a) 450 (b) 470
(c) 490 (d) 460

313. By what percentage is the percentage of the number of vowels in the word CONSONANT less than the percentage of consonants in it? SSC MTS 02/11/2021 Shift-III

(a) 33.33 (b) 200
(c) 66.67 (d) 50

314. When the price of sugar gets raised by 50%, a person increases his expenditure on sugar only by 25%. By what percentage (correct up to two decimal places) should he reduce his consumption of sugar? SSC MTS 02/11/2021 Shift-I

(a) 12.75% (b) 15.75%
(c) 16.67% (d) 11.54%

SSC GD Constable 2024

315. If A_1 is 19 times more than A_2, then A_2 is what percentage less than A_1? SSC GD Constable 26/02/2024 Shift-I

(a) 85% (b) 105%
(c) 100% (d) 95%

316. Income of L is 30 per cent more than the income of M and income of M is 20 per cent more than the income of N. The income of N is (approximately) how much percentage less than the income of L? SSC GD Constable 26/02/2024 Shift-I

(a) 36% (b) 39%
(c) 32% (d) 44%

317. If A% of A is 9604, then what is the value of A? SSC GD Constable 24/02/2024 Shift-II

(a) 920
(b) 1020
(c) 980
(d) 880

318. When a number is successively decreased by 10%, 15% and 56%, then it becomes 20196. What is that number? SSC GD Constable 24/02/2024 Shift-II

(a) 60000 (b) 80000
(c) 40000 (d) 50000

319. In a class of 40 students, 30 are girls. What is the percentage of boys in the class? SSC GD Constable 24/02/2024 Shift-I

(a) 13% (b) 18%
(c) 25% (d) 24%

320. The value of a car depreciates at the rate of 50% per annum. If its present value is ₹ 75000, then what was the value of the car 3 yr ago? SSC GD Constable 24/02/2024 Shift-I

(a) ₹ 750000 (b) ₹ 600000
(c) ₹ 300000 (d) ₹ 450000

321. A man spends 58% of his income. His income increases by 30% and his expenditure also increases by 25%. Find the percentage of increase in his savings. SSC GD Constable 23/02/2024 Shift-IV

(a) 42.5% (b) 55.7%
(c) 36.9% (d) 66.2%

322. In a class, 38% are boys and the number of girls are 31. What is the number of boys in the class? SSC GD Constable 23/02/2024 Shift-IV

(a) 17 (b) 19
(c) 16 (d) 15

323. Initial value of a car is ₹ 150000. The value of car depreciated by 20% of its initial value each year. What will be its value after 2 yr? SSC GD Constable 23/02/2024 Shift-IV

(a) ₹ 82000 (b) ₹ 84000
(c) ₹ 96000 (d) ₹ 78000

324. Monil's monthly income decreases by 18%. By what per cent approximately should his monthly income increase, so that it again becomes equal to his actual monthly income? SSC GD Constable 23/02/2024 Shift-III

(a) 22% (b) 18%
(c) 15% (d) 20%

325. If P is 15% less than Q, then Q is how much percentage more than P ? SSC GD Constable 23/02/2024 Shift-II

(a) 15.46%
(b) 18.44%
(c) 17.64%
(d) 16.64%

326. In an exam, Naveen got 21% marks and he failed by 25 marks. If he gets 46% marks, then he fails by 5 marks. What are the maximum marks of the exam? SSC GD Constable 23/02/2024 Shift-II

(a) 60 (b) 80
(c) 120 (d) 100

327. After deducting 10% from a certain sum and then deducting 70% from the remainder, 1188 is left. What was that sum? SSC GD Constable 23/02/2024 Shift-I

(a) 3300 (b) 5500
(c) 2200 (d) 4400

328. What is the value of 7.14% of 66.67% of 21.84? SSC GD Constable 22/02/2024 Shift-IV

(a) 1.07 (b) 2.02
(c) 1.09 (d) 1.04

329. The tax imposed on an article is decreased by 17% and its consumption increases by 17%. Find the percentage change in revenue. SSC GD Constable 22/02/2024 Shift-IV

(a) 2.89% increase
(b) 2.89% decrease
(c) 17% increase
(d) 17% decrease

330. In a class, 40% are boys and the number of girls are 54. What is the number of boys in the class? SSC GD Constable 22/02/2024 Shift-II

(a) 34 (b) 36 (c) 37 (d) 33

331. X, Y and Z are three students. X got 40% more marks, than Y and 20% less marks than Z. If Y got 480 marks, then what are the marks got by Z ? SSC GD Constable 22/02/2024 Shift-II

(a) 820 (b) 850
(c) 800 (d) 840

332. If P % of P is 225, then what is the value of P^2? SSC GD Constable 22/02/2024 Shift-II

(a) 22550 (b) 20500
(c) 22500 (d) 20050

333. If 35% of P = 60% of Q and Q is $(Z/3)$% of P, then what is the value of Z ? SSC GD Constable 22/02/2024 Shift-II

(a) 175 (b) 155
(c) 165 (d) 185

334. Price of 1 kg of wheat is increased by 50% and the increase is of ₹ 25. What is the new price of the wheat per kg? SSC GD Constable 22/02/2024 Shift-I

(a) ₹ 45 (b) ₹ 60
(c) ₹ 75 (d) ₹ 55

335. The population of a certain city increases by 5% in the first year and by another 8% in the second year. What is the overall percentage increase in the population?
SSC GD Constable 21/02/2024 Shift-IV
(a) 15.2% (b) 13.0%
(c) 13.4% (d) 18.3%

336. Town *A* had a population of 62500 in 2022. After one year the population of town *A* increased to 75000. What is the percentage increase in the population?
SSC GD Constable 21/02/2024 Shift-IV
(a) 15% (b) 30%
(c) 20% (d) 25%

337. If the original price of a watch is ₹ 500 and it is increased by 10%, then decreased by 15%, what is the final price?
SSC GD Constable 21/02/2024 Shift-III
(a) ₹ 476.60 (b) ₹ 467.50
(c) ₹ 405. 67 (d) ₹ 456.70

338. 27% of a number exceeds 13% of the same number by 56. What is the value of the number?
SSC GD Constable 21/02/2024 Shift-III
(a) 420 (b) 380
(c) 360 (d) 400

339. *A* is firstly increased by 20% and then it is decreased by 30%. Final value of *A* is what percentage of initial value of *A*?
SSC GD Constable 21/02/2024 Shift-II
(a) 74% (b) 156%
(c) 94% (d) 84%

340. If *U* gets 5% more marks than *V*, then by what percentage marks of *V* are less than the marks of *U* ?
SSC GD Constable 21/02/2024 Shift-II
(a) 3.7% (b) 5.7%
(c) 4.7% (d) 2.7%

341. What is the value of 64% of 512 + 46% of 215?
SSC GD Constable 21/02/2024 Shift-I
(a) 426.58 (b) 428.58
(c) 427.58 (d) 424.58

342. The price of a movie ticket was increased by 18%. The increase in ticket price reduced the number of audience by 25%. What is the effect on revenue?
SSC GD Constable 20/02/2024 Shift-III
(a) decrease by 9.5%
(b) increase by 10%
(c) decrease by 14%
(d) decrease by 11.5%

343. If the price of a dress is reduced from ₹ 800 to ₹ 720, what is the percentage decrease?
SSC GD Constable 20/02/2024 Shift-III
(a) 9% (b) 10% (c) 8% (d) 6%

344. 25% of 20% of a number is equal to 250. What is the 35% of that number? **SSC GD Constable 20/02/2024 Shift-II**
(a) 1750 (b) 1570
(c) 1650 (d) 1560

345. A student scores 75% in a test and gets 30 marks more than another student who scored 60%. What is the maximum marks in the test?
SSC GD Constable 20/02/2024 Shift-I
(a) 120 (b) 200
(c) 150 (d) 100

346. In an exam, out of total number of appeared students 93% students passed and 9275 students failed. What is the total number of students appeared in the exam?
SSC GD Constable 20/02/2024 Shift-I
(a) 135500 (b) 135550
(c) 132550 (d) 132500

SSC GD Constable 2023

347. The population of a village during the first year increases by 5% and during the second year, it diminishes by 5%. At the end of the second year, its population was 9975. What was the population at the beginning of the first year?
SSC GD Constable 13/02/2023 Shift-IV
(a) 9500 (b) 10000
(c) 9000 (d) 10500

348. In an election between two candidates, 80% of the voters cast their votes out of which 5% of votes were declared invalid. A candidate got 285000 votes which was 75% of the total valid votes. The total number of voters enrolled for that election was
SSC GD Constable 13/02/2023 Shift-II
(a) 500000 (b) 450000
(c) 400000 (d) 550000

349. The population of a village is 68000. It increases at the rate of 5% in the first year and decreases at the rate of 10% per annum for the next 2 yr. What will be the population of the village after 3 yr?
SSC GD Constable 09/02/2023 Shift-II
(a) 60832 (b) 56840
(c) 62823 (d) 57834

350. When 40 is subtracted from 40 per cent of a number the remainder is 40. Find the number.
SSC GD Constable 09/02/2023 Shift-II
(a) 200 (b) 100
(c) 300 (d) 150

351. The difference between the 110% of a number and 94.5% of the same number is 34.1. What is the original number?
SSC GD Constable 09/02/2023 Shift-II
(a) 190 (b) 110
(c) 220 (d) 134

352. If x% of y is equal to $\frac{2}{3}$ of 90, then the value of xy .... is
SSC GD Constable 09/02/2023 Shift-I
(a) 100 (b) 6000
(c) 60 (d) 90

353. The value of a motorbike depreciates by 10% per annum. What will be the value of the motorbike after 36 months, if its current value is ₹ 100000? **SSC GD Constable 08/02/2023 Shift-I**
(a) ₹ 70900 (b) ₹ 71900
(c) ₹ 72900 (d) ₹ 73900

354. A government servant spends 76% of his income. If his income is increased by 14% and his expenditure is increased by 10%, then find the percentage increase in his savings. (Correct to 2 decimal places) **SSC GD Constable 08/02/2023 Shift-I**
(a) 24.33% (b) 27.66%
(c) 26.67% (d) 28.33%

355. The present value of a house is ₹ 4640000. If its value depreciates at the rate of 5% per annum, then the value of the house after 3 yr will be
SSC GD Constable 07/02/2023 Shift-I
(a) ₹ 3978220 (b) ₹ 4408000
(c) ₹ 4070520 (d) ₹ 4187600

356. The value of a painting rises from ₹ 140000 to ₹ 182000. The percent increase in the value of the painting is **SSC GD Constable 07/02/2023 Shift-I**
(a) 50% (b) 10%
(c) 30% (d) 40%

357. If the price of tea is increased by 20%, by what percentage must the consumption of tea be diminished so as not to increase the expenditure on tea? **SSC GD Constable 07/02/2023 Shift-I**
(a) $33\frac{1}{3}$% (b) $16\frac{2}{3}$%
(c) 20% (d) 25%

358. In a city, there are 12000 voters. Out of them, 30% voted for *A*, 25% voted for *B* and 40% voted for *C*. Determine the number of voters that did not vote for any of these three participants.
SSC GD Constable 06/02/2023 Shift-I

(a) 800 (b) 600
(c) 400 (d) 500

359. In 2010, the population of a country was 256080000. By 2020, the population had increased by 10%. The population in 2020 will be
SSC GD Constable 02/02/2023 Shift-I

(a) 291475000
(b) 281688000
(c) 275040000
(d) 266050000

360. The present population of a village is 50000. Due to migration to cities, the population decreases at the rate of 5% every year. Find the population of the village after 2 yr.
SSC GD Constable 02/02/2023 Shift-I

(a) 41525 (b) 48475
(c) 45125 (d) 44875

361. The price of a mobile first successively decreases by 5%, 2% and after that the price is increased successively by 10%, 20% respectively. What is the final change in the price of the mobile?
SSC GD Constable 01/02/2023 Shift-I

(a) $17\frac{153}{250}\%$ (b) $21\frac{113}{250}\%$
(c) $22\frac{123}{250}\%$ (d) $22\frac{223}{250}\%$

362. The current birth rate per ten thousand is 450, whereas the corresponding death rate is 120 per ten thousand. Find the net growth rate in terms of the population increase in percentage.
SSC GD Constable 01/02/2023 Shift-I

(a) 2.3% (b) 2%
(c) 3% (d) 3.3%

363. The weights of two persons *A* and *B* are in ratio of 5 : 3 respectively. If the weight of *A* increases by 5% and the total weight of *A* and *B* becomes 92 kg with an increase of 15%, then find the percentage increase in the weight of *B*. (correct to 2 decimal places) **SSC GD Constable 01/02/2023 Shift-I**

(a) 31.67%
(b) 30.66%
(c) 32.66%
(d) 36.66%

364. In a college, there are two courses. In M.Com 450 students passed out of 500, while in M.A. 1500 students passed the exam out of 2000 students. What is the combined pass percentage of the college?
SSC GD Constable 01/02/2023 Shift-I

(a) 78% (b) 79%
(c) 75.5% (d) 76.75%

SSC Selection Post 2024-2022

365. Roshan owned a plot of land having an area that was 20% more than the area of the plot owned by Susan, while the area of the plot of land owned by Jacob was 30% more than the area of the plot owned by Roshan. If the area of the plot owned by Susan was 1250 square feet, what was the area (in square feet) of the plot owned by Jacob?
Matric Level 20/06/2024 Shift-IV

(a) 2050 (b) 1875
(c) 1950 (d) 2020

366. In an election between two candidates, 75% of the voters cast their votes, out of which 4% of the votes were declared invalid. A candidate got 9504 votes, which were 80% of the valid votes. Find the total number of votes enrolled in that election.
Matric Level 20/06/2024 Shift-IV

(a) 12672 (b) 13200
(c) 16500 (d) 12375

367. In an election, there were only two candidates. 12% of the voters did not cast their votes. The winner by obtaining 60% of the total votes defeated his opposite contestant by 1200 votes. Find the total number of votes. **Graduate Level 20/06/2024 Shift-III**

(a) 4000 (b) 3750
(c) 5730 (d) 3570

368. Anita saves 20% of her income. If her income is increased by 30% and she saves 25% of the new income, by what percentage will her actual savings increase?
Higher Secondary Level 20/06/2024 Shift-II

(a) 70%
(b) 83%
(c) 62.50%
(d) 65.20%

369. In an election between two candidates, the first gets 75% of the total valid votes. If 20% votes are invalid among 248000 votes, then how many votes were cast in the favour of the other candidate?
Higher Secondary Level 20/06/2024 Shift-II

(a) 53800 (b) 46800
(c) 49600 (d) 56600

370. If 20% of a number is subtracted from a second number and the second number decreases to its 70%, then what is the ratio of the first number to the second number?
Matric Level 27/06/2023 Shift-I

(a) 3:2 (b) 4:3 (c) 2:3 (d) 3:4

371. Venkat spends 65% of his income and is able to save ₹ 1100 per month. His monthly expenses (correct up to two decimals) are
Matric Level 27/06/2023 Shift-I

(a) ₹ 2024.85 (b) ₹ 2042.85
(c) ₹ 2402.8 (d) ₹ 2240.85

372. 28% of the people eligible to vote are between 20 to 25 yr. In an election 75% of those eligible to vote who were between 20 to 25 yr actually voted. In that election the number of persons between 20 to 25 who actually voted was what percentage of those eligible to vote?
Graduate Level 01/08/2022 Shift-IV

(a) 25% (b) 21%
(c) 28% (d) 22%

373. In an election there were two candidates Ram Singh and Sohan Lal. The total number of voters in the constituency was 80000 and 80% of the total votes were polled.
If 60% of the polled votes were cast in favour of Ram Singh, how many votes were received by Sohan Lal?
Higher Secondary Level 01/08/2022 Shift-II

(a) 25600 (b) 26700
(c) 38400 (d) 28000

374. By what percentage 74% of 1894 is more than 39% of the same number (correct to two decimal places).
Higher Secondary Level 01/08/2022 Shift-II

(a) 89.74% (b) 76.65%
(c) 83.53% (d) 79.65%

375. *A*'s income is 40% more than that of *B* and *B*'s income is 20% less than that of *C*. If *C*'s income is ₹2500, find *A*'s income. **Matric Level 01/08/2022 Shift-I**

(a) ₹ 2200
(b) ₹ 2500
(c) ₹ 2700
(d) ₹ 2800

376. Ramesh saves 28% of his salary, while Naresh saves 32%. If both get the same salary and Naresh saves ₹ 1736, what is the expenditure of Ramesh? **Matric Level 01/08/2022 Shift-I**

(a) ₹ 3906 (b) ₹ 4736
(c) ₹ 3736 (d) ₹ 4906

377. If a person's salary increases from ₹ 200 per day to ₹ 234 per day, what is the percent increase per day in the person's salary? **Matric Level 01/08/2022 Shift-I**

(a) 17% (b) 16%
(c) 15% (d) 14%

378. The weight of Anjali is 60 kg. After three months, her weight increased by 20% and in the next three months, it increased by 25%. What will be the weight (in kg) of Anjali after six months? **Matric Level 01/08/2022 Shift-I**

(a) 100 (b) 80 (c) 75 (d) 90

Right Answers

1 (a)	2 (d)	3 (c)	4 (a)	5 (a)	6 (d)	7 (c)	8 (a)	9 (c)	10 (c)
11 (c)	12 (a)	13 (a)	14 (a)	15 (a)	16 (c)	17 (d)	18 (c)	19 (a)	20 (d)
21 (d)	22 (b)	23 (c)	24 (b)	25 (c)	26 (d)	27 (a)	28 (a)	29 (a)	30 (c)
31 (b)	32 (b)	33 (a)	34 (c)	35 (b)	36 (b)	37 (a)	38 (c)	39 (b)	40 (d)
41 (d)	42 (d)	43 (c)	44 (d)	45 (d)	46 (a)	47 (a)	48 (a)	49 (d)	50 (b)
51 (b)	52 (d)	53 (c)	54 (b)	55 (d)	56 (a)	57 (b)	58 (c)	59 (d)	60 (d)
61 (d)	62 (d)	63 (b)	64 (c)	65 (b)	66 (d)	67 (b)	68 (d)	69 (a)	70 (d)
71 (b)	72 (b)	73 (c)	74 (b)	75 (b)	76 (c)	77 (a)	78 (b)	79 (a)	80 (d)
81 (a)	82 (c)	83 (d)	84 (b)	85 (a)	86 (b)	87 (d)	88 (d)	89 (c)	90 (a)
91 (d)	92 (a)	93 (a)	94 (b)	95 (a)	96 (b)	97 (d)	98 (c)	99 (c)	100 (d)
101 (b)	102 (c)	103 (b)	104 (c)	105 (a)	106 (a)	107 (d)	108 (c)	109 (b)	110 (d)
111 (a)	112 (c)	113 (a)	114 (a)	115 (a)	116 (b)	117 (a)	118 (c)	119 (c)	120 (a)
121 (b)	122 (b)	123 (d)	124 (c)	125 (c)	126 (d)	127 (b)	128 (b)	129 (b)	130 (a)
131 (b)	132 (b)	133 (c)	134 (b)	135 (b)	136 (c)	137 (b)	138 (a)	139 (a)	140 (c)
141 (d)	142 (b)	143 (a)	144 (c)	145 (a)	146 (d)	147 (d)	148 (b)	149 (c)	150 (c)
151 (a)	152 (b)	153 (d)	154 (b)	155 (b)	156 (a)	157 (b)	158 (b)	159 (d)	160 (a)
161 (b)	162 (d)	163 (d)	164 (b)	165 (b)	166 (c)	167 (b)	168 (d)	169 (a)	170 (a)
171 (c)	172 (b)	173 (b)	174 (c)	175 (b)	176 (a)	177 (c)	178 (a)	179 (d)	180 (a)
181 (c)	182 (a)	183 (b)	184 (d)	185 (c)	186 (b)	187 (d)	188 (c)	189 (a)	190 (d)
191 (d)	192 (b)	193 (d)	194 (a)	195 (a)	196 (a)	197 (a)	198 (c)	199 (a)	200 (b)
201 (b)	202 (c)	203 (a)	204 (d)	205 (d)	206 (a)	207 (d)	208 (d)	209 (d)	210 (c)
211 (d)	212 (c)	213 (d)	214 (b)	215 (c)	216 (c)	217 (c)	218 (d)	219 (b)	220 (c)
221 (d)	222 (c)	223 (b)	224 (c)	225 (c)	226 (d)	227 (b)	228 (c)	229 (d)	230 (a)
231 (c)	232 (b)	233 (c)	234 (b)	235 (c)	236 (b)	237 (a)	238 (c)	239 (d)	240 (d)
241 (d)	242 (b)	243 (d)	244 (b)	245 (c)	246 (a)	247 (b)	248 (c)	249 (a)	250 (d)
251 (c)	252 (a)	253 (b)	254 (a)	255 (b)	256 (a)	257 (a)	258 (b)	259 (a)	260 (c)
261 (c)	262 (d)	263 (b)	264 (a)	265 (a)	266 (c)	267 (a)	268 (c)	269 (a)	270 (d)
271 (d)	272 (b)	273 (a)	274 (b)	275 (d)	276 (c)	277 (d)	278 (c)	279 (d)	280 (a)
281 (d)	282 (a)	283 (a)	284 (a)	285 (c)	286 (b)	287 (b)	288 (d)	289 (b)	290 (b)
291 (a)	292 (a)	293 (c)	294 (b)	295 (a)	296 (d)	297 (b)	298 (b)	299 (a)	300 (d)
301 (c)	302 (c)	303 (c)	304 (c)	305 (b)	306 (c)	307 (b)	308 (d)	309 (d)	310 (d)
311 (a)	312 (b)	313 (d)	314 (c)	315 (d)	316 (a)	317 (c)	318 (a)	319 (c)	320 (b)
321 (c)	322 (b)	323 (c)	324 (a)	325 (c)	326 (b)	327 (d)	328 (d)	329 (b)	330 (b)
331 (d)	332 (c)	333 (a)	334 (c)	335 (c)	336 (c)	337 (b)	338 (d)	339 (d)	340 (c)
341 (a)	342 (d)	343 (b)	344 (a)	345 (b)	346 (d)	347 (b)	348 (a)	349 (d)	350 (a)
351 (c)	352 (b)	353 (c)	354 (c)	355 (a)	356 (c)	357 (b)	358 (b)	359 (b)	360 (c)
361 (d)	362 (d)	363 (a)	364 (a)	365 (c)	366 (c)	367 (b)	368 (c)	369 (c)	370 (a)
371 (b)	372 (b)	373 (a)	374 (a)	375 (d)	376 (a)	377 (a)	378 (d)		

Solutions

1. (a) According to the question,

Let two years ago sale = x

Present sale $= x \times \frac{106}{100} \times \frac{120}{100} = 254400$

$x = 254400 \times \frac{100}{106} \times \frac{5}{6}$

$x =$ ₹ 200000

2. (d) According to the question,

Present population of the town

$= 9487500 \times \frac{92}{100} \times \frac{92}{100}$

$= 8030220$

3. (c) According to the question,

60% of 75 – $\frac{1}{5}$ of 25

$= \frac{60}{100} \times 75 - 5 = 45 - 5 = 40$

4. (a) According to the question,

$A\left(1+\frac{6}{100}\right)^2 = 50000$

$\Rightarrow A\left(1+\frac{3}{50}\right)^2 = 50000$

$\Rightarrow A \times \frac{53}{50} \times \frac{53}{50} = 50000$

$A = \frac{50000 \times 50 \times 50}{53 \times 53} = 44500$

Again,

After 2018, the population increased by 6%.

$\therefore 50000\left(1+\frac{6}{100}\right)^2 = B$

$\Rightarrow 50000 \times \frac{53}{50} \times \frac{53}{50} = B$

$\Rightarrow B = 56180$

$\therefore$ Required value of $(B - A)$

$= 56180 - 44500 = 11680$

5. (a) Let Shyam's income be $100x$.

$\therefore$ Ram's income $= 102.5x$

$\therefore$ Required percentage $= \frac{2.5x}{102.5x} \times 100$

$= 2.43\%$

6. (d) We know that,

Income = Expenditure + Saving

$\therefore$ Original income = 3 + 1 = 4

New, income $= 4 \times \frac{125}{100} = 5$

New, savings $= 1 \times \frac{120}{100} = 1.2$

$\therefore$ New expenditure = 5 – 1.2 = 3.8

Required percentage $= \frac{0.8}{3} \times 100 = 26\frac{2}{3}\%$

7. (c) Two successive percentage decrease

Net change

$= \left(-25 + (-25) + \frac{(-25)(-25)}{100}\right)\%$

$= (-50 + 6.25)\% = 43.75\%$ (decrease)

Two successive percentage increase

New change $= \left(25 + 25 + \frac{(25)(25)}{100}\right)\%$

= 56.25% increase

$\therefore$ Required percentage $= \frac{56.25 - 43.75}{56.25} \times 100$

$= 22.22\%$

8. (a) Income of Ramesh in 2022

$= 18600 \times \frac{115}{100} = 21390$

Expenditure of Ramesh in 2022

$= 12400 \times \frac{108}{100} = 13392$

We know, Saving = Income – Expenditure

Saving in 2021 = 18600 – 12400 = 6200

Saving in 2022 = 21390 – 13392 = 7998

$\therefore$ Required percentage

$= \frac{7998 - 6200}{6200} \times 100 = 29\%$

9. (c) Initial Income : Expenditure : Saving

₹ 16500 : ₹ 12000 : ₹ 4500

↓ + 24% ↓ –10%

16500 + 3960 = 20460 : 12000 – 1200 = ₹ 10800 : ₹ 9660

Percentage increase in saving

$= \frac{9660 - 4500}{4500} \times 100$

$= \frac{5160}{4500} \times 100 = 114.66 = 115\%$

10. (c) Let total income be $100x$ spent on rent

$= \frac{30}{100} \times 100x = 30x$

Spent on groceries $= 70x \times \frac{60}{100} = 42x$

Remaining income $= 100x - 30x - 42x = 28x$

Spend on others $= 28x \times \frac{40}{100} = 11.2x$

Now, monthly saving

$= 28x - 11.2x = 16.8x = 7056$

$\Rightarrow x = \frac{7056}{16.8} = \frac{70560}{168} = 420$

$\therefore$ Amount spend on groceries $= 42x$

$= 42 \times 420 =$ ₹ 17640

11 (c) Let the total number of votes $= 100x$

Number of people cast their votes

$= 100x \times \frac{80}{100} = 80x$

Valid votes casted $= 80x \times \frac{96}{100}$

Now, $80x \times \frac{96}{100} \times \frac{80}{100} = 15360$

$x = \frac{15,360 \times 100}{96 \times 64} = 250$

$\therefore$ Total number of votes

$= 100 \times 250 = 25000$

12. (a) Income = ₹ 72000

Let his savings be x.

Expenditure $= x + x \times \frac{40}{100} = \frac{140x}{100} = \frac{7x}{5}$

$\therefore x + \frac{7x}{5} = 72000 \Rightarrow 12x = 72000 \times 5$

$x = 6000 \times 5 =$ ₹ 30,000

His savings is ₹ 30000.

13. (a) Let the total number of votes $= x$

People who cast their votes $= x \times \frac{80}{100}$

People casted valid votes $= x \times \frac{80}{100} \times \frac{90}{100}$

Votes received by $P = x \times \frac{80}{100} \times \frac{90}{100} \times \frac{42}{100}$

Votes received by $Q = x \times \frac{80}{100} \times \frac{90}{100} \times \frac{58}{100}$

Difference between votes received by P and Q

$x \times \frac{80}{100} \times \frac{90}{100} \times \frac{16}{100} = 45360$

$\Rightarrow x = \frac{45360 \times 100 \times 100}{8 \times 9 \times 16}$

$\Rightarrow x = 393750$

Total number of votes = 393750

14. (a) According to the question,

$R \times 85\% = R \times 35\% + 450$

$R \times 50\% = 450 \Rightarrow R = \frac{450}{50} \times 100$

$R = 900$

R scored marks to meet the target

$= 900 \times \frac{85}{100} = 765$

$\therefore$ Percentage increment $= \frac{765 - 450}{450} \times 100$

$= \frac{315}{450} \times 100 = 70\%$

15. (a) Let Y got $100x$ votes.

Then, Z got $125x$ votes and X got $130x$ votes.

According to the question,

$X - Z = 5000 \Rightarrow 130x - 125x = 5000$

$\Rightarrow x = 1000$

$\therefore$ Total voters voted $= 100x + 125x + 130x$

$= 355x = 355000$

71% of total voters voted = 355000

$\therefore$ Total voters votes (100%) = 500000

16. (c) Let the first increment by $x\%$.

$\therefore$ Second increment $= 2x\%$

According to the question,

$\left(x + 2x + \frac{x \times 2x}{100}\right)\% \times 1000 = 1295$

$\Rightarrow \left(3x + \frac{2x^2}{100}\right)\% \times 1000 = 1295$

$\Rightarrow \frac{300x + 2x^2}{100 \times 100} \times 1000 = 1295$

$\Rightarrow \quad 2x^2 + 300x - 12950 = 0$

$\Rightarrow \quad x^2 + 150x - 6475 = 0$

$\Rightarrow \quad x^2 + 185x - 35x - 6475 = 0$

$\Rightarrow \quad x(x + 185) - 35(x + 185) = 0$

$\Rightarrow \quad x = -185, 35$

$\therefore \quad x = 35\% \qquad [\because x \neq -185\%]$

$\therefore$ Second increment = 2 × 35% = 70%

17. (d) Expenditure = Price × Consumption

Ratio of Price = 1 : 4 $\left(300\% = \frac{3}{1}\right)$

Ratio of Consumption = 10 : 3 $\left(70\% = \frac{7}{10}\right)$

Expenditure = 10 : 12

Percentage Increase $= \frac{12-10}{10} \times 100$

$= \frac{2}{10} \times 100 = 20\%$

18. (c) Value of the investor's share after 3 days.

$= 200000 \times \frac{(100+18)}{100} \times \left(\frac{100-15}{100}\right) \times \left(\frac{100-3}{100}\right)$

$= 200000 \times \frac{97.2910}{100} = 200000 \times \left(\frac{100-2.7}{100}\right)$

$\therefore$ Value decreased by 2.7%

19. (a) Winning candidate got 88% votes and the loosing candidate got (100 – 88) = 12% votes.

The difference = 88 – 12 = 76%

According to question,

76% of total votes = 684

$\therefore$ Total votes polled $= \frac{684}{76} \times 100 = 900$

20. (d) Let total population be 100.

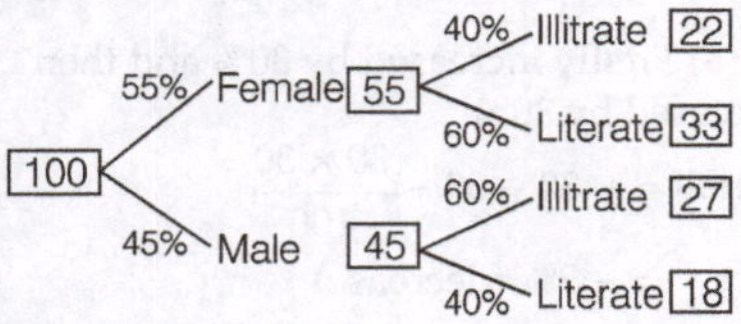

$\therefore$ Required percentage $= \frac{22-18}{18} \times 100$

$= \frac{4}{18} \times 100 = 22.22\%$

21. (d) Let the income of Ajay = ₹ 100

Expenditure $= 100 \times \frac{200}{300} = \frac{200}{3}$

Saving $= 100 - \frac{200}{3} = \frac{100}{3}$

Now, Income increased by 25%.

New Income = 100 + 25 = 125

Expenditure $= \frac{200}{3} \times \frac{120}{100} = 80$

Saving = 125 – 80 = 45

Saving difference% $= \frac{45 - \frac{100}{3}}{\frac{100}{3}} \times 100$

$= \frac{35}{100} \times 100 = 35\%$

22. (b) Let total number of votes = Z

Total casted votes = 80% of total votes

$= Z \times \frac{80}{100}$

Total valid votes = 95% of total casted votes

$= \frac{95}{100} \times \frac{80}{100} \times Z$

Winning candidate got number of votes

= 70% of total valid votes

$= \frac{70}{100} \times \frac{95}{100} \times \frac{80}{100} \times Z$

Losing candidate got = 30% of total valid votes

$= \frac{30}{100} \times \frac{95}{100} \times \frac{80}{100} \times Z$

Difference between winning and losing candidate $= \frac{40}{100} \times \frac{95}{100} \times \frac{80}{100} \times Z = 36480$

$Z = \frac{36480 \times 100 \times 100}{4 \times 95 \times 8}$

$Z = 120000$

Total number of votes = 120000

23. (c) Increase in number of employees

$a = 20\%$

Decrease in wages $b = -18\%$

$a = 20\%$ and $b = -18\%$

Net decrease $= a + b + \frac{ab}{100}$

$= 20 - 18 + \frac{(+20)(-18)}{100} = 2 - 3.60 = -1.6\%$

24. (b) Let RQ decreased by x%

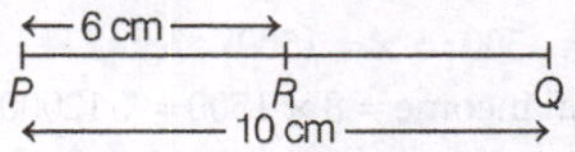

According to the question,

$6 \times \frac{105}{100} + 4 \times \frac{(100-x)}{100} = 10$

$\Rightarrow 6.3 + 4\left(\frac{100-x}{100}\right) = 10 \Rightarrow 4\frac{(100-x)}{100} = 3.7$

$\Rightarrow \quad 100 - x = 92.5 \Rightarrow x = 7.5\%$

25. (c) Let S got 100x votes

$\therefore \quad$ R got votes $= \frac{110}{100} \times 100x = 110x$

Difference = 770

$\therefore \quad 110x - 100x = 770 \Rightarrow 10x = 770 \Rightarrow x = 77$

$\therefore$ Total votes polled = 100x + 110x

$= 210x = 210 \times 77 = 16170$

26. (d) Let Suresh's spending = 3x

and Saving = x

$\therefore \quad$ Income = 4x

New income $= 4x \times \frac{125}{100} = 5x$

New saving $= x \times \frac{110}{100} = \frac{11x}{100}$

New spending $= 5x - \frac{11x}{10} = \frac{39x}{10}$

Difference in spending $= \frac{39x}{10} - 3x = \frac{9x}{10}$

Percentage change $= \frac{9x}{10 \times 3x} \times 100 = 30\%$

27. (a) Let the initial price of wheat

= ₹ 100 x / kg

and the price of rice = ₹ 20x/kg

According to the question,

$20x \times 20 + 100x \times 8 = 300$

$\Rightarrow \quad 400x + 800x = 300$

$\Rightarrow \quad 1200x = 300$

$\Rightarrow \quad x = \frac{300}{1200} = \frac{1}{4}$

$\therefore$ Initial price of wheat = ₹ 25/kg

and price of rice = ₹ 5/kg

Increased price of wheat $= 25 \times \frac{120}{100} =$ ₹ 30/kg

Let the consumption of rice is y kg, then

According to the question,

$30 \times 8 + 5 \times y = 300 \Rightarrow 5y = 60 \Rightarrow y = 12$

Reduction in rice consumption

= 20 – 12 = 8 kg

$\therefore$ Reduction percentage $= \frac{8}{20} \times 100\% = 40\%$

28. (a) Woman spends $\frac{2}{3}$ of her income.

Let her income be 3x and expense be 2x.

$\therefore \quad$ Saving = 3x – 2x = x

New income $= 3x \times \frac{118}{100} = 3.54x$

New expenditure $= 2x \times \frac{124}{100} = 2.48x$

$\therefore$ New saving = 3.54x – 2.48x = 1.06x

% increasing in saving $= \frac{1.06x - x}{x} \times 100 = 6\%$

29. (a) According to the question,

$a = +25\%, b = -12\%$

$\therefore$ Net change $= \left(a + b + \frac{ab}{100}\right)\%$

$= \left(25 + (-12) + \frac{(25)(-12)}{100}\right)\%$

$= (13 - 3)\% = 10\%$

$\therefore$ Overall change = 10% increase.

30. (c) Given, Total votes = 7560000

Votes casted $= 7560000 \times \frac{90}{100}$

Valid casted votes $= 7560000 \times \frac{90}{100} \times \frac{85}{100}$

Total number of valid votes that Q got

$= 7560000 \times \frac{90}{100} \times \frac{85}{100} \times \frac{22}{100} = 1272348$

31. (b) Let total number of voters be 100x.

$\therefore$ Total number of votes costed = 85x

Total number of valid votes

$= 85x \times \frac{98}{100} = 83.3x$

Total number of votes that Sunita got

$= 83.3x \times \frac{78}{100} = 64.974x$

$\therefore \quad 64.974x = 64974 \Rightarrow x = 1000$

$\therefore$ Total number of voters

$= 100 \times 1000 = 100000$

32. (b) Net percentage increase and decrease

$= \left(x + y - \frac{x \times y}{100}\right)\%$

$x = 12, y = 23 \Rightarrow \left(12 + 23 - \frac{12 \times 23}{100}\right)\%$

$= (35 - 2.76)\% = 32.24\%$

Now, again, $x = 32.24\%$, $y = -34\%$

$= \left(32.24 - 34 - \left(\frac{32.24 \times -34}{100}\right)\right)\%$

$= (-1.76 + 10.96)\%$

$= (9.20)\% \simeq 9\%$ decrease

33. (a) Let the total stock portfolio = 100

Portfolio represented by Stock A

$= 20\%$ of $100 = \frac{20}{100} \times 100 = 20$

Returned portfolio by Stock $A = 6\%$ of 20

$= \frac{6}{100} \times 20 = 1.2$

Portfolio represented by Stock B

$= 30\%$ of $100 = 30$

Returned portfolio by Stock $B = 8\%$ of 30

$= \frac{8}{100} \times 30 = 2.4$

Portfolio represented by Stock C

$= 20\%$ of $100 = 20$

Returned portfolio by Stock $C = 4\%$ of 20

$= \frac{4}{100} \times 20 = 0.8$

Portfolio represented by Stock $D = 30\%$ of 100

$= 30$

Returned portfolio by Stock D

$= -5\%$ of $30 = -1.5$

Average return of the portfolio

$= 1.2 + 2.4 + 0.8 - 1.5 = 2.9\%$

34. (c) Total voters = 16000

Invalid votes = 10%

and winner got 59.375%

and y% did not cast their vote.

Votes obtained by looser

$= (100 - 59.375\%) = 40.625\%$

According to the question,

$16000 \times \frac{(100-y)}{100} \times \frac{(100-10)}{100} \times \frac{(59.375 - 40.625)}{100} = 2484$

$\Rightarrow 16000 \times \frac{(100-y)}{100} \times \frac{90}{100} \times \frac{18.75}{100} = 2484$

$\Rightarrow (100 - y) = \frac{2484 \times 100}{16 \times 9 \times 18.75}$

$\Rightarrow \quad 100 - y = 92 \Rightarrow y = 8$

35. (b) Given, 20% of$(A + B) = 30\%$ of$(A - B)$

$\Rightarrow \quad \frac{20}{100}(A + B) = \frac{30}{100}(A - B)$

$\Rightarrow \quad 2A + 2B = 3A - 3B$

$\Rightarrow \quad A = 5B \Rightarrow \frac{A}{B} = \frac{5}{1}$

So, required percentage $= \frac{A}{B} \times 100$

$= \frac{5}{1} \times 100\% = 500\%$

36. (b) Monthly salary of Mrs. Deepa Devi

$= ₹ 42000$

Saving of Mrs. Deepa Devi $= 42000 \times \frac{30}{100}$

$= ₹ 12600$

Expenditure of her salary = Salary − Saving

$= 42000 - 12600 = ₹ 29400$

37. (a) Let total vote polled are $100x$.

Number of votes on first condidate got

$= 100x \times \frac{64}{100} = 64x$

Number of votes second candidate got

$= 100x - 64x = 36x$

According to the question,

$64x - 36x = 434 \Rightarrow 28x = 434$

$\Rightarrow \quad x = 15.5$

So, total number of votes $= 100x$

$= 100 \times 15.5 = 1550$

38. (c) Total number of eggs = 350

Percentage of rotten eggs = 12%

Number of good eggs

$= 350\left(\frac{100 - 12}{100}\right) = 350 \times \frac{88}{100} = 308$

39. (b) Let Soham's initial expenditure $= 5x$

and initial saving $= 3x$

Then income $= 8x$

But, $3x = 4500 \Rightarrow x = 1500$

His initial income $= 8 \times 1500 = ₹ 12000$

His income increase by 25%

$= 12000 \times \frac{125}{100} = ₹ 15000$

40. (d) Let expenditure = ₹ 100

If price of petrol increased by 81%.

Then, cost of petrol = ₹ 181

Hence, consumption of petrol decreased by

$= \frac{181 - 100}{181} \times 100\%$

$= \frac{81}{181} \times 100 = 44.75\%$

41. (d) Let the monthly income of father $= ₹ x$

Pocket money for both sons $= x \times \frac{8}{100} = ₹ \frac{8x}{100}$

Elder son gets money $= \frac{8x}{100} \times \frac{85}{100} = ₹ \frac{17x}{250}$

According to the question,

Elder son spend 90% of the given amounts.

So, he saves only 10%

Thus, $\quad \frac{17x}{250} \times \frac{10}{100} = 17 \quad$ (given)

$\Rightarrow \quad x = \frac{250 \times 100}{10} = ₹ 2500$

Monthly income of father $= ₹ 2500$

> **Speedy Method**
>
> Let father's income = ₹ 100
>
> Two sons: ₹ 8, Elder: $₹ 8 \times \frac{85}{100} = ₹ 6.8$
>
> Saving of elder son $= ₹ 6.8 \times \frac{10}{100} = ₹ 0.68$
>
> $\therefore$ Total income $= ₹ 100 = \frac{17}{0.68} \times 100 = ₹ 2500$

42. (d) Let marks of Peter $= 100x$

Marks of Sam $= 100x - 19x = 81x$

Hence, required percentage

$= \frac{19x}{81x} \times 100 = 23.46\%$

43. (c) 12% of 625 $= 625 \times \frac{12}{100} = 75$

15% of 555 $= 555 \times \frac{15}{100} = 83.25$

10% of 720 $= 720 \times \frac{10}{100} = 72$

9% of 845 $= 845 \times \frac{9}{100} = 76.05$

Thus, least value is 10% of 720.

44. (d) Let Ravi's monthly income = 100

Then, his saving = 20

If his monthly income raised by 25%, then new income = 125

and his saving raised by 5%, then

New saving $= 20 \times 5\% + 20$

$= 20 \times \frac{5}{100} + 20 = 21$

$\therefore$ Required percentage $= \frac{21}{125} \times 100$

$= \frac{84}{5} = 16.8\%$

45. (d) Firstly increased by 30% and then decreased by 30%.

Overall $= +30 - 30 - \frac{30 \times 30}{100}$

$= -9\%$ (decrease)

$\therefore$ His income decreased by 9% after two months.

46. (a) Cost price decreased by 10% and then increased by 20%.

$\therefore$ Equivalent percentage

$= -10 + 20 - \frac{20 \times 10}{100} = 10 - 2$

$= 8\%$ increased

$\because \quad 108\% \rightarrow ₹ 540$

$\therefore \quad 100\% \rightarrow ₹ \frac{540}{108} \times 100 = ₹ 500$

$\therefore$ The original cost price = ₹ 500

> **Speedy Method**
>
> Let original cost price $= ₹ x$
>
> According to question,
>
> $\frac{x \times 90 \times 120}{100 \times 100} = 540$
>
> $x = \frac{540 \times 100}{108} = ₹ 500$

47. (a) Let expenditure on food = 6 unit

Expenditure on health $= 6 + \frac{6}{2} = 9$ unit

Expenditure on entertainment $= \frac{6}{3} = 2$ unit

Expenditure on education $= 9 \times 2 = 18$ unit

Expenditure on rent $= \frac{6+9+18}{3} = 11$ unit

Total savings = 8%

Expenditure = 100 − 8 = 92%

$(6+9+2+18+11) = 46$ unit = 92%

$18 \text{ unit} = \frac{92}{46} \times 18 = 36\%$

Total income = ₹ 35000

∴ Expenditure on education

$= 35000 \times \frac{36}{100} =$ ₹ 12600

48. (a) Let total toffees = 100 unit

Wasted $= \frac{100}{10} = 10$ unit

S got $= 90 \times 35\% = 31.5$ unit

N got $= \frac{100}{8} = \frac{25}{2}$ unit

N got 10 more than wasted toffees

∴ $\frac{25}{2}$ unit = 10 tofees + 10 unit toffees

⇒ $\frac{5}{2}$ unit = 10 toffees

⇒ $31.5 \text{ unit} = \frac{20}{5} \times 31.5 = 126$

∴ S got 126 toffees.

49. (d) Let total weightage = 100

Weightage in $A = 40$

Weightage in $B = 50$

Weightage in $C = 10$

He scored in $A = 40 \times \frac{75}{100} = 30$

He scored in $B = 50 \times \frac{80}{100} = 40$

He scored in $C = 10 \times \frac{60}{100} = 6$

Total score = 30 + 40 + 6 = 76

∴ He scored $= \frac{76 \times 100}{100} = 76\%$

50. (b) Let total income be ₹ $100x$.

Total	$100x$
Goods (25%)	(−) $25x$
House Rent (18% of $75x$)	(−) $13.5x$
Travel (16% of $61.5x$)	(−) $9.84x$
Remaining income	$51.66x$

According to the question,

$51.66x = 861 \Rightarrow x = \frac{861}{51.66}$

⇒ $100x = \frac{861}{51.66} \times 100 =$ ₹ $1666\frac{2}{3}$

51. (b) Let the total number of voters = x

10% of voter not cast their vote.

Then, votes polled = 90% of x

10% of the voters polled were found invalid.

Then, valid votes = 90% of (90% of x)

According to the question,

56% of [90% of (90% of x)] −44% of [90% of (90% of x)] = 1458

⇒ $12\% \text{ of} \left[90\% \text{ of } \frac{90x}{100}\right] = 1458$

⇒ $\frac{12}{100} \times \frac{90}{100} \times \frac{90}{100} \times x = 1458$

⇒ $x = \frac{1458 \times 100 \times 100 \times 100}{12 \times 90 \times 90} \Rightarrow x = 15000$

52. (d) Let Kirti's salary in January = ₹ x

She paid EMI = 22% of $x = \frac{22}{100}x$

Remaining salary $= x - \frac{22}{100}x = \frac{78x}{100}$

He spend on shopping on cloths = ₹ 18200

Now, $\frac{5}{12} \times \frac{78x}{100} = 18200$

$x = \frac{18200 \times 100 \times 12}{5 \times 78} \Rightarrow x =$ ₹ 56000

∴ Kirti's salary in January = ₹ 56000

Then, her salary in February

$= 56000 \times \frac{116}{100} =$ ₹ 64960

53. (c) Let total marks = x

According to the question,

$\frac{x \times 20}{100} + 10 = \frac{x \times 35}{100} - 20 \Rightarrow \frac{15x}{100} = 30$

∴ $x = 200$

∴ Minimum marks required to pass

$= \frac{200 \times 20}{100} + 10 = 50$

Hence, required percentage

$= \frac{50}{200} \times 100 = 25\%$

Speedy Method

∴ Change in percentage, (35 20) = 15%

Change in marks (10 + 20) = 30

$20\% = \frac{30}{15} \times 20 = 40$

∴ Pass marks = 40 + 10 = 50

∴ 40 marks = 20%

50 marks $= \frac{20}{40} \times 50 = 25\%$

54. (b) Monthly income = ₹ 12000

Expenditure = ₹ 8000

∴ Savings = 12000 − 8000 = ₹ 4000

Next year, income $= 12000 \times \frac{110}{100} =$ ₹ 13200

and expenditure $= 8000 \times \frac{108}{100} =$ ₹ 8640

∴ Savings = 13200 − 8640 = ₹ 4560

Hence, required savings increased

$= \frac{560}{4000} \times 100 = 14\%$

55. (d) Given, pass percentage = 35%

Also, student scored 210 marks but failed by 14 marks

⇒ $35\% = 224 \Rightarrow 100\% = \frac{224}{35} \times 100 = 640$

∴ Maximum marks are 640.

56. (a) Let original price = 100 unit

After increase the price = $(100 + r)$ unit

After decrease the new price

$= (100 + r) \times \frac{(100 - r)}{100} = \frac{10000 - r^2}{100}$ unit

⇒ $\frac{10000 - r^2}{100}$ unit = ₹ 1

100 unit = ₹ $\frac{10000}{10000 - r^2}$

∴ The original price $= \frac{10000}{10000 - r^2}$

57. (b) Let male population = $100x$

and female population = $100y$

∴ $100x + 100y = 18000$ ...(i)

After increasing

$105x + 107y = 19200$ ...(ii)

Multiplying Eq. (i) by 107 and Eq. (ii) by 100, we get

$100x + 100y = 18000 \times 107$ ...(iii)

$105x + 107y = 19200 \times 100$ ...(iv)

From Eqs. (iii) and (iv), we get

⇒ $x = 30$

From Eq. (i), we get

$y = \frac{18000 - 3000}{100} = 150$

∴ Ratio of population of males to females

= 30 : 150 = 1 : 5

Speedy Method

Percentage change $= \frac{19200 - 18000}{18000} \times 100$

$= \frac{20}{3}\%$

By Alligation rules,

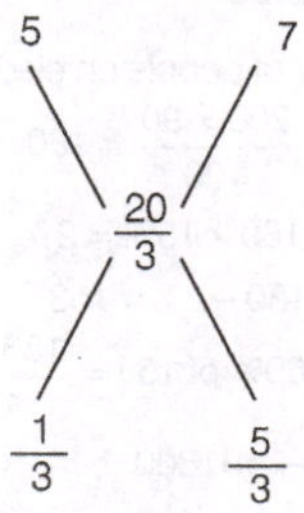

⇒ 1 : 5

58. (c) 65% of 350 − x% of 250 + 40% of 120 = 158

⇒ $350 \times \frac{65}{100} - 250 \times \frac{x}{100} + 120 \times \frac{40}{100} = 158$

⇒ $\frac{455}{2} - \frac{5x}{2} + 48 = 158$

⇒ $\frac{5x}{2} = \frac{455 + 96 - 316}{2}$

⇒ $5x = 235 \Rightarrow x = 47$

∴ Value of $x = 47$

59. (d) Let the total number of people 100%.
People who votes = 85%
and if 10% votes invalid, valid votes

$= 85\% - 8.5\% = 76.5\%$

But given total people = 300000

Then, valid votes $= 300000 \times \frac{76.5}{100} = 229500$

But Dharam received = 137700

Then, Dharam secure $= \frac{137700}{229500} \times 100 = 60\%$

60. (d) Saving = ₹ 45000 − ₹ 33000 = ₹ 12000

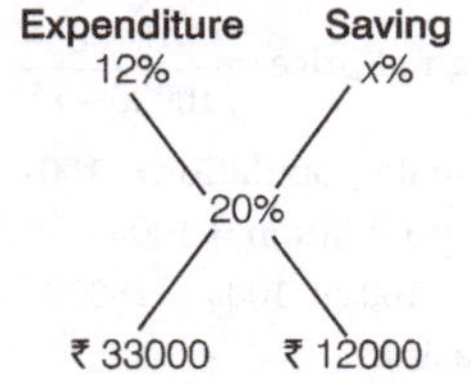

$\therefore \quad \frac{x-20}{20-12} = \frac{33000}{12000} \Rightarrow \frac{x-20}{8} = \frac{11}{4}$

$\Rightarrow 4x - 80 = 88 \Rightarrow 4x = 168 \Rightarrow x = 42\%$

61. (d) Let total number of people on the electoral roll = x.

Casted votes $= \frac{x \times 90}{100} = 0.9x$

$\because$ Invalid votes = 15%

$\therefore$ Valid votes $= \frac{0.9x \times 85}{100} = 0.765x$

According to the question,

$\frac{0.765x \times 60}{100} = 91800$

$x = \frac{91800 \times 100}{0.765 \times 60} = 200000$

Hence, total member of people on the electoral roll is 200000.

Speedy Method

Let total number of people on electoral roll = 200

Cast votes $= \frac{200 \times 90}{100} = 180$

Invalid votes $= 180 \times 15\% = 27$

Valid votes $= 180 - 27 = 153$

Jeeta secured 60% of 153 $= \frac{153 \times 6}{10}$

$\frac{153 \times 6}{10} \longrightarrow 91800$

$200 \longrightarrow \frac{918000}{153 \times 6} \times 200 = 200000$

$\therefore$ Total number of people on electoral roll = 200000

62. (d)

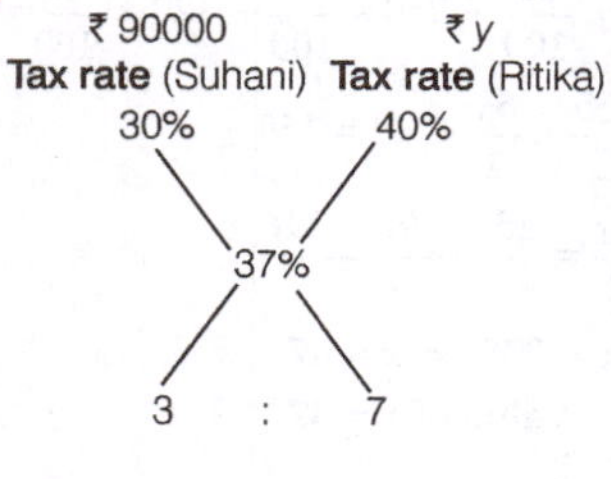

$\therefore \quad \frac{3}{7} = \frac{90000}{y}$

$y = 210000$

63. (b) Given, x% of 280 = 15% of 240 + 20% of 310

$\Rightarrow \quad \frac{x}{100} \times 280 = \frac{15}{100} \times 240 + \frac{20}{100} \times 310$

$\Rightarrow \quad \frac{28x}{10} = 36 + 62 \Rightarrow 28x = 360 + 620$

$\Rightarrow \quad x = \frac{980}{28} = 35$

64. (c) Let monthly income of Vaidic = ₹800 and his expenditure = ₹500

Then, his savings = ₹300

But, if income increase by 20%

$= 800 \times \frac{120}{100} = ₹960$

and his expenditure increase by 30%

$= 500 \times \frac{130}{100} = ₹650$

Then, his savings = 960 − 650 = ₹310

Hence, his monthly savings increase by

$= \frac{10}{300} \times 100 = 3\frac{1}{3}\%$

65. (b) Total voter = 100%

Did not participated = 2%

A got 43% of persons enrolled but 500 votes were invalid

$\therefore \quad B$ got $= (100 - 43 - 2)\% - 500$ votes

$= 55\% - 500$

$\therefore \quad 43\% - (55\% - 500) = 200$

$\Rightarrow \quad 43\% - 55\% + 500 = 200$

$\Rightarrow \quad -12\% = -300 \Rightarrow 1\% = \frac{300}{12}$

$\therefore$ Total casted votes $= 98\% = 98 \times \frac{300}{12} = 2450$

66. (d) Let Bhaskar got $100x$ votes.

$\therefore$ Saral got $98x$ votes

Also, Arjun got 50% more than Saral.

$\therefore$ Arjun's votes $= 98x \times \frac{150}{100} = 147x$

According to the question,

$100x - 98x = 1296 \Rightarrow 2x = 1296$

$\Rightarrow \quad x = \frac{1296}{2} = 648$

$\therefore$ Half of difference of Arjun and Bhaskar's votes $= \frac{147(648) - 100(648)}{2}$

$= \frac{648(47)}{2} = \frac{30456}{2} = 15228$

Speedy Method

Arjun got 50% votes more than Saral.

Then, $\frac{\text{Arjun}}{\text{Saral}} = \frac{150}{100} = \frac{3}{2} = \frac{3 \times 49}{2 \times 49} = \frac{147}{98}$

Saral got 2% votes less than Bhaskar

Then, $\frac{\text{Saral}}{\text{Bhaskar}} = \frac{98}{100}$

According to the question,

Arjun : Saral : Bhaskar
147 : 98 : 100
(difference between 147 and 100: −2)

$2 \longrightarrow 1296, \quad 1 \longrightarrow 648$

Difference of Arjun and Bhaskar = 47

Hence, $\frac{648 \times 47}{2} = \frac{30456}{2} = 15228$

67. (b) $\because A$ is 95% of B

$\Rightarrow \quad A = B \times \frac{95}{100} \Rightarrow \frac{A}{B} = \frac{95}{100} \Rightarrow \frac{B}{A} = \frac{100}{95}$

$\therefore$ Required per cent $= \frac{B}{A} \times 100$

$= \frac{100}{95} \times 100 = 105\frac{5}{19}\%$

68. (d) Given, Shiva's monthly salary = ₹75000

His expenses $= (12 + 14 + 15 + 10) \times 1000$ = ₹51000

His savings = ₹21000

$\therefore$ His expense on donation

$= (75000 - 51000) - 21000 = ₹3000$

$\therefore$ Required percentage $= \frac{3000}{75000} \times 100 = 4\%$

69. (a) Let the initial salary of the man be x.

$\therefore$ Expenditure = 60% of $x = \frac{60}{100} \times x = ₹0.6x$

$\therefore$ Initial savings $= x - 0.6x = 0.4x$

Now, increased salary $= x \times 1.3 \times 1.6 = ₹\ 2.08x$

and new savings $= 0.4x \times 3.50 = ₹1.4x$

$\therefore$ New expenditure $= (2.08 - 1.4)x = ₹0.68x$

$\therefore$ According to the question, Required %

$= \frac{0.68x}{2.08x} \times 100 = 32.69\% \approx 32.7\%$

70. (d) Let the first number $= 100x$

Then, second number $= (100 - 20)\%$ of $100x$

$= 80x$

Third number $= (100 + 200)\%$ of $80x = 240x$

Difference of the original (first) and third number $= 240x - 100x = 140x$

Difference of the second and third number

$= 240x - 80x = 160x$

$\therefore$ Required percentage $= \frac{140x - 160x}{160x} \times 100\%$

$= -\frac{25}{2}\% = -12.5\%$

Here, −ve sign = less

Speedy Method

Ist number IInd number IIIrd number

$100 \xrightarrow[-20]{-20\%} 80 \xrightarrow[+160]{+200\%} 240$

$\therefore$ Required percentage $= \frac{140 - 160}{160} \times 100$

$= -12.5\% = 12.5\%$ (less)

71. (b) Let initial strength of the school be $= x$.

Firstly, the strength is increased by 12% in first year $= x \times \frac{(100+12)}{100} = x \times \frac{112}{100}$

Then, it is decreased by 12% in second year
$= x \times \frac{112}{100} \times \frac{88}{100}$

Again, it is increased by 10% in third year
$= x \times \frac{112}{100} \times \frac{88}{100} \times \frac{110}{100}$

Given, $x \times \frac{112}{100} \times \frac{88}{100} \times \frac{110}{100} = 10842$

$\Rightarrow x = \frac{10842 \times 100 \times 100 \times 100}{112 \times 88 \times 110}$

$\Rightarrow x = 10000.3 \simeq 10000$

Speedy Method

Initial population $= \left(\frac{100+12}{100}\right) \times \left(\frac{100-12}{100}\right) \times \left(\frac{100+10}{100}\right) = 10842$

Initial population $= \frac{10842 \times 100 \times 100 \times 100}{112 \times 88 \times 110}$
$= 10000.37 \simeq 10000$

72. (b) Let the population of the town initially $= x$

After 3 yr, population of town
$= x \times \frac{95}{100} \times \frac{95}{100} \times \frac{105}{100}$

According to the question,
$\frac{x \times 19 \times 19}{20 \times 20} \times \frac{21}{20} = 947625$

$\Rightarrow x = \frac{947625 \times 20 \times 20 \times 20}{19 \times 19 \times 21}$

$\therefore \quad x = 125 \times 20 \times 20 \times 20 = 1000000$

So, town's population at the beginning of the first year, $x = 1000000$

73. (c) Let the total number of votes polled be x.

According to the question,
$\frac{76}{100} \times x = \frac{(100-76)}{100} \times x + 1480$

$\Rightarrow 0.76x = 0.24x + 1480$

$\Rightarrow 0.76x - 0.24x = 1480 \Rightarrow 0.52x = 1480$

$\Rightarrow \quad x = \frac{1480}{0.52} = 2846.154$

Considering integral part only

Total number of votes polled = 2846

Speedy Method

Vote difference = 76% − (100 − 76)%
= 76% − 24%

1480 = 52%

∴ 100% (total votes polled)
$= \frac{1480}{52} \times 100 = 2846$

74. (b) Let total votes be 100 units.

Third candidate got votes = 20 units

∴ First candidate got votes + Second candidate got votes = 80 ...(i)

∵ First candidate got votes − Second candidate got votes = 20 ...(ii)

On solving Eqs. (i) and (ii),

First candidate got votes = 50 units

Second candidate got votes = 30 units

Difference of first runner up and second runner up = 37000

10 units = 37000

∴ 50 units (winner got votes)
$= \frac{37000}{10} \times 50 = 185000$

75. (b) Let there are x number of inhabitants initially.

Now, number of inhabitants died of malaria
$= \frac{20}{100} \times x = 0.2x$

Number of inhabitants who left the village
$= (x - 0.2x) \times \frac{30}{100} = 0.8x \times 0.3 = 0.24x$

Now, population of village
$= x - (0.2x + 0.24x)$

$\Rightarrow \quad 12000 = x - 0.44x$

$\Rightarrow \quad 12000 = 0.56x$

$\Rightarrow \quad x = \frac{12000}{0.56} = 21428.57$

Hence, there are 21428 inhabitants initially.

76. (c) Number of masks manufactured in the year 2018 $= X$

Number of masks manufactured in the year 2019 $= \frac{130}{100}X$

Number of masks manufactured in the year 2020 $= \frac{115}{100} \times \frac{130}{100}X$

Number of masks manufactured in the year 2021 $= \frac{60}{100} \times \frac{115}{100} \times \frac{130}{100}X$

Given, number of masks manufactured in the year 2021 = 179400

$\Rightarrow \quad \frac{60}{100} \times \frac{115}{100} \times \frac{130}{100}X = 179400$

$\Rightarrow X = \frac{179400 \times 100 \times 100 \times 100}{60 \times 115 \times 130}$

$\Rightarrow \quad X = 200000$

77. (a) Given, population ratio of A and B in 2020 $= x \Rightarrow \frac{A}{B} = \frac{x}{1}$

After decrease in population from 2020 to 2021, ratio of population of A and B in 2021

$\frac{A}{B} = \frac{x\left(1 - \frac{p}{100}\right)}{1\left(1 - \frac{q}{100}\right)} = \frac{x(100-p)}{100-q}$

Decrease in population ratio
$= \frac{x}{1} - \frac{x(100-p)}{100-q} = \frac{x(100-q) - x(100-p)}{100-q}$

$= \frac{100x - qx - 100x + px}{100-q} = \frac{px - qx}{100-q} = \frac{x(p-q)}{100-q}$

∴ Required percentage decrease
$= \frac{\frac{x(p-q)}{100-q}}{x} \times 100\% = \frac{x(p-q)}{x(100-q)} \times 100\%$

$= \frac{100(p-q)}{100-q}\%$

78. (b) Let total number of registered voters be x.

⇒ Number of voters who are P supporters
$= \frac{70}{100} \times x = 0.7x$

⇒ Number of voters who are Q supporters
$= x - 0.7x = 0.3x$

Now, number of voters expected to vote for candidate P
$= \frac{60}{100} \times 0.7x + \frac{30}{100} \times 0.3x$
$= 0.6 \times 0.7x + 0.3 \times 0.3x$
$= 0.42x + 0.09x = 0.51x$

∴ Percentage of registered voters whom are expected to vote for candidate P
$= \frac{0.51x}{x} \times 100\% = \frac{51}{100} \times 100\% = 51\%$

79. (a) According to the question, previous savings = 26500 − 20500 = \$6000

[∵ Savings = Income − Expenditure]

Now, new savings
$= (26500 \times 1.12) - (20500 \times 1.06) = \$7950$

∴ Required % increase in savings
$= \frac{(7950 - 6000) \times 100}{6000} = 32.5\%$

80. (d) Let required percentage be x.

$\therefore \quad x\%$ of $20 = 0.5$

$\Rightarrow \quad 20 \times \frac{x}{100} = 0.5$

$\Rightarrow x = \frac{0.5 \times 100}{20} \Rightarrow x = 2.5\%$

81. (a) Let, the cost of apples be ₹ x.

⇒ Net cost of apples $= ₹x \times \frac{120}{100} \times \frac{80}{100} = ₹\frac{96x}{100}$

⇒ Net decrease in cost of apples $= x - \frac{96x}{100}$
$= \frac{4x}{100}$

Hence, percentage decrease
$= \frac{4x}{100x} \times 100\% = 4\%$

82. (c) Let initial price be ₹x.

Now, price after decrease
$= 80\%$ of $₹x = \frac{80x}{100} = ₹0.8x$

∴ Required percentage increase in consumption $= \frac{(x-0.8x)}{0.8x} \times 100\%$

$= \frac{0.2x}{0.8x} \times 100\% = \frac{200}{8}\% = 25\%$

83. (d) Given, Number p is 15% more than 150.

$\Rightarrow \quad p = 150 \times \frac{(100+15)}{100}$

$\Rightarrow \quad p = 150 \times \frac{115}{100}$ ...(i)

According to the question,

$k = p \times \left(\frac{100-15}{100}\right)$

$\Rightarrow \quad k = \frac{150 \times 115}{100} \times \frac{85}{100}$ [by Eq. (i)]

$\therefore \quad k = 146.625$

84. (b) $12\frac{1}{2}\% = \frac{1}{8}$, $75\% = \frac{3}{4}$

Let Ram have initial money = ₹ x

$\therefore \quad x \times \left(1-\frac{1}{8}\right) \times \left(1-\frac{3}{4}\right) = 630$

$\Rightarrow \quad x \times \frac{7}{8} \times \frac{1}{4} = 630 \Rightarrow x =$ ₹ 2880

85. (a) Let total number of voters = $100x$

Total number of vote casted

$= (100-12)\%$ of $100x = 88x$

First candidate votes (winner)

$= 68\%$ of $100x = 68x$

Other candidate votes $= 88x - 68x = 20x$

Given, $68x - 20x = 2880$

$\Rightarrow \quad 48x = 2880 \Rightarrow x = \frac{2880}{48} \Rightarrow x = 60$

So, total number of voters who cast their votes $= 88x = 88 \times 60 = 5280$

86. (b) Initial population (P) = 1024000

Rate of increase (r) = 2.5% p.a.

Number of inhabitants after three years

$= P\left(1+\frac{r}{100}\right)^n = 1024000\left(1+\frac{2.5}{100}\right)^3$

$= 1024000 \times \left(\frac{102.5}{100}\right)^3 = 1102736$

87. (d) Let the original price per kg of rice is ₹ x, then

New price = ₹ $0.8x$

According to the question,

$\frac{450}{0.8x} - \frac{450}{x} = 50 \Rightarrow \frac{4500-3600}{8x} = 50$

$\Rightarrow x = \frac{900}{400} \Rightarrow x = 2.25$

∴ Original price per kg is ₹ 2.25.

Speedy Method

Reduced price $= \frac{450}{50} \times 20\% =$ ₹ $\frac{9}{5}$/kg

∴ Original price $= \frac{₹\ 9/5}{80} \times 100 =$ ₹ 2.25 /kg

88. (d) Let the total number of valid voters card be x.

Then, $\frac{58}{100}x - \frac{42}{100}x = 768400$

$\Rightarrow \quad \frac{16x}{100} = 768400$

$x = \frac{768400 \times 100}{16} = 4802500$

Total invalid votes = 82560

Total number of votes cast

$= 4802500 + 82560 = 4885060$

Let total number of votes be y.

Then, $\frac{80y}{100} = 4885060 \Rightarrow y = 6106325$

Number of people who did not cast vote

$= \frac{20}{100} \times 6106325 = 1221265$

∴ Required percentage $= \frac{82560}{1221265} \times 100$

$= 6.8\%$

89. (c) Let total votes be x.

∴ Valid votes $= (100-8)\%$ of $x = \frac{92x}{100}$

Winner gets $= 48\%$ of $x = \frac{48x}{100}$

Looser get $= \frac{92x}{100} - \frac{48x}{100} = \frac{44x}{100}$

According to the question,

$\frac{48x}{100} - \frac{44x}{100} = 1100 \Rightarrow \frac{4x}{100} = 1100$

$\Rightarrow \quad x = \frac{1100 \times 100}{4} = 27500$

90. (a) Let total number of votes polled be x.

Valid votes $= 95\%$ of $x = \frac{95}{100}x$

Raju's votes $= 30\%$ of $x = \frac{30}{100}x$

Ravi's votes $= 32\%$ of $x = \frac{32}{100}x$

Winner's vote $= x\left(\frac{95}{100} - \frac{30}{100} - \frac{32}{100}\right) = \frac{33}{100}x$

Given, $\quad \frac{33}{100}x - \frac{30}{100}x = 5136$

$\Rightarrow \quad \frac{3x}{100} = 5136$

$\Rightarrow \quad x = \frac{5136 \times 100}{3} = 171200$

91. (d) Let the expenditure and savings are $5x$ and x, respectively.

Income = Expenditure + Saving

$= 5x + x = 6x$

After increase,

New income $= (100+10)\%$ of $6x$

$= \frac{110}{100} \times 6x = 6.6x$

New expenditure $= (100+20)\%$ of $5x$

$= \frac{120}{100} \times 5x = 6x$

New saving = New income − New expenditure $= 6.6x - 6x = 0.6x$

Percentage change in saving

$= \frac{x-0.6x}{x} \times 100\% = 0.4 \times 100\% = 40\%$

So, her saving is decreased by 40%.

92. (a) Let Chetan has coins = 100

Then, Gaurav has coins 40% more than Chetan $= 100 \times \frac{140}{100} = 140$

Avinash has 20% less than Gaurav

$= 140 \times \frac{80}{100} = 112$ coins

∴ Required percentage $= \frac{(112-100)}{112} \times 100$

$= \frac{12}{112} \times 100 = 10.7\%$

93. (a) Total number of students in school is 1400.

35% of student are girls $= 1400 \times \frac{35}{100}$

Number of girls = 490

Number of boys = 1400 − 490 = 910

80% of boys passed the exam

$= 910 \times \frac{80}{100} = 728$

90% of girls passed the exam

$= 490 \times \frac{90}{100} = 441$

Total number of student passed the exam

$= 728 + 441 = 1169$

Number of students who failed

$= 1400 - 1169 = 231$

∴ Per cent of student failed

$= \frac{231}{1400} \times 100 = 16.5\%$

94. (b)

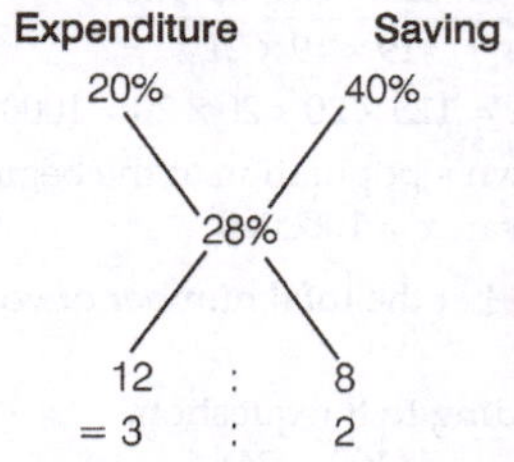

∴ Saving% $= \frac{2}{5} \times 100 = 40\%$

$\therefore \quad x\% = 40\%$

$\Rightarrow \quad x = 40$

95. (a) Let men = $100x$, women = $100y$

According to the question,

$100x + 100y = 15280$ ...(i)

Number of men increase by 25% = $125x$

Number of women increase by 15% = $115y$

Then, $125x + 115y = 18428$ ...(ii)

On solving Eqs. (i) and (ii), we get

$y = 67.2$ and $x = 85.6$

The difference between x and y

$= (85.6 - 67.2) \times 100 = 1840$

96. (b) Let weight of $C = 100$

Weight of B is 30% more than

$$C = 100 \times \frac{130}{100} = 130$$

Weight of A is 20% more than

$$B = 130 \times \frac{120}{100} = 156$$

$$\therefore \text{Required percentage} = \frac{156 - 100}{100} \times 100$$

$$= 56\%$$

97. (d) Let total number of students in class is 100.

Then, total number of boys $= 100 \times \frac{45}{100} = 45$

and total number of girls $= 100 - 45 = 55$

Now, number of boys who failed

$$= 45 \times \frac{40}{100} = 18$$

Number of girls who failed $= 55 \times \frac{30}{100} = 16.5$

Total number of students who failed

$$= 18 + 16.5 = 34.5$$

$$\therefore \text{Required percentage} = \frac{34.5}{100} \times 100 = 34.5\%$$

Speedy Method

Boys Girls

60% 70%

x%

45 55

$$\therefore \frac{70 - x}{x - 60} = \frac{45}{55} \Rightarrow 1310 = 20x \Rightarrow x = 65.5\%$$

∴ Failed student percentage $= (100 - 65.5)\%$

$= 34.5\%$

98. (c) Let red ball are $10x$.

Then, white ball $= 10x \times \frac{160}{100} = 16x$

Green ball $= \frac{16x \times 87.5}{100} = 14x$

According to the question,

$$10x + 16x + 14x = 120$$

$$\Rightarrow 40x = 120 \Rightarrow x = 3$$

∴ Total number of green ball $= 14x$

$$= 14 \times 3 = 42$$

99. (c) Let students in school $X = 100$

$$\therefore \text{Students in school } Y = 100 \times \left(\frac{100 + 130}{100}\right)$$

$$= 230$$

By Alligation rule,

80% x%

90%

100 230

$$\therefore \frac{x - 90}{90 - 80} = \frac{100}{230}$$

$$23x = 2070 + 100 \quad x = 94.35\%$$

∴ Failed students in school

$$Y = 5.65\% \simeq 5.7\%$$

100. (d) According to the question,

Let number is x, first increased by 15% then reduced by 15%.

$$\therefore x \times \frac{115}{100} \times \frac{85}{100} = 782$$

$$x = 800$$

$$\text{Now, } 800 \times \frac{75}{100} \times \frac{125}{100} \times \frac{80}{100} = 600$$

101. (b) Let the share of $A = x$

The share of B

$$= x \times \frac{100}{100 + \frac{32}{3}} = \frac{300x}{332} = \frac{75x}{83}$$

$$\text{The share of } C = x \times \frac{100}{100 - \frac{100}{3}} = \frac{300x}{200} = \frac{3x}{2}$$

According to the question,

$$\frac{x + \frac{75x}{83} + \frac{3x}{2}}{3} = 4520$$

$$\Rightarrow \frac{166x + 150x + 249x}{166} = 3 \times 4520$$

$$\Rightarrow 565x = 3 \times 4520 \times 166$$

$$\therefore x = \frac{3 \times 4520 \times 166}{565} = 3984$$

$$\therefore \text{Share of } B = \frac{75}{83} \times 3984 = ₹\,3600$$

102. (c) Let Income of $B = 100x$

$$\text{Income of } A = 100x \times \frac{145}{100} = 145x$$

$$\text{Income of } C = (100x + 145x) \times \frac{40}{100}$$

$$= 245x \times \frac{2}{5} = 98x$$

$$\text{Income of } D = 98x \times \frac{120}{100} = 117.6x$$

According to the question,

$$117.6x - 100x = 13200 \Rightarrow 17.6x = 13200$$

$$\therefore x = 750$$

Hence, income of $C = 98 \times 750 = 73500$

103. (b) Let the minimum passing marks be x, then Anita's passing marks

$$= x \times \frac{31}{100} + 16 \quad \ldots \text{(i)}$$

$$\text{Sunita's passing marks} = x \times \frac{40}{100} - 56 \quad \ldots \text{(ii)}$$

From Eqs. (i) and (ii),

$$\frac{31}{100}x + 16 = \frac{40}{100}x - 56$$

$$\Rightarrow \frac{40}{100}x - \frac{31}{100}x = 16 + 56$$

$$\Rightarrow \frac{9x}{100} = 72 \Rightarrow 9x = 72 \times 100 \Rightarrow x = 800$$

$$\therefore \text{Required passing marks} = 800 \times \frac{31}{100} + 16$$

$$= 248 + 16 = 264$$

Speedy Method

$$31\% + 16 = 40\% - 56$$

$$9\% = 72$$

$$1\% = 8$$

100% = 800 marks

$$\therefore \text{Passing marks} = 800 \times \frac{31}{100} + 16$$

$$= 248 + 16 = 264$$

104. (c) Let total number of students $= 100x$

Number of students who did not appear

$$= 100x \times \frac{4}{100} = 4x$$

Then, number of students who appear

$$= 100x - 4x = 96x$$

Number of students who could not pass

$$= 96x \times \frac{10}{100} = 9.6x$$

Remaining students who passed

$$= 96x - 9.6x = 86.4x$$

Number of students who only passed but could not get distinction marks

$$= 86.4x \times \frac{50}{100} = 43.2x$$

According to the question,

$$43.2x = 432 \Rightarrow x = 10$$

∴ Total number of students $= 100x$

$$= 100 \times 10 = 1000$$

Speedy Method

Let total students be x.

According to the question,

$$x \times \frac{(100 - 4)}{100} \times \frac{(100 - 10)}{100} \times \frac{50}{100} = 432$$

$$\Rightarrow x = 1000$$

105. (a) Let the population of city 2 yr ago was x, then

$$x \times \frac{(100 + 30)}{100} \times \frac{(100 - 15)}{100} = 11050$$

$$\Rightarrow x \times \frac{130}{100} \times \frac{85}{100} = 11050$$

$$\Rightarrow x = \frac{11050 \times 10000}{130 \times 85} \Rightarrow x = 10000$$

106. (a) Here, $a = 20\%$

$$\therefore \text{Required percentage} = \frac{a}{100 + a} \times 100$$

$$= \frac{20}{100 + 20} \times 100\% = \frac{20}{120} \times 100 = 16\frac{2}{3}\%$$

107. (d) Let the income of A be x and B be y.

Saving of A = 40% of x

Saving of B = 25% of y

According to the question,

$$(40\% \text{ of } x) = (25\% \text{ of } y) \times (120/100)$$

$$\Rightarrow x \times 40 = 25 \times y \times \frac{6}{5} \Rightarrow x : y = 3 : 4$$

Income of A is 3 and income of B is 4.

$$\therefore \text{Required per cent} = \frac{4 - 3}{4} \times 100 = 25\%$$

108. (c) Given, maximum marks = 500

A scores = 500 × (80 / 100) = 400

B scored = 400 × (100 / 125) = 320

C scored = 320 × (100 / 160) = 200

D scored = 200 × (100 / 80) = 250

Percentage of $D = \frac{250}{500} \times 100 = 50\%$

109. (b) Let the salary of A = Salary of B = ₹ x and salary of C = ₹ y

According to the question,

8% of x − 7% of x = 259

⇒ 1% of x = 259 ⇒ x = ₹ 25900

Again according to the question,

15% of x = 9% of y + 1185

⇒ $\frac{15}{100} \times 25900$ = 9% of y + 1185

⇒ 9% of y = 2700 ⇒ y = ₹ 30000

Now, Total donation of A and C = 8% of 25900 + 9% of 30000 = 2072 + 2700 = ₹ 4772

Total salaries of A, B and C

= 25900 + 25900 + 30000 = ₹ 81800

∴ Required percentage = $\frac{4772}{81800} \times 100 = 5.8\%$

110. (d) Let the total number of votes be $100x$.

Total votes cast = 95%

Winner got 75% of votes.

∴ Loser got (95 − 75) = 20% votes

Hence, [75% − 20%] × $100x$ = 5500

55% of $100x$ = 5500 ⇒ x = 100

∴ Total number of voters = $100x$

= 100 × 100 = 10000

111. (a) Population after 3rd yr

$= 15000 \times \frac{115}{100} \times \frac{125}{100} \times \frac{94}{100} = 20269$

112. (c) Given, $\frac{1}{3}$ of the sweet is sugar.

Present price of sugar = $\frac{7}{6}$ of its original price

∴ Increase in price = $\frac{7}{6} - 1 = \frac{1}{6}$

$= \frac{1}{6} \times 100 = 16.67\%$

Now, contribution of sugar to the cost = $\frac{1}{3}$

Remaining $\frac{2}{3}$ is not affected by change in price.

∴ Effective Increase = $\frac{1}{3} \times 16.67\%$

$= 5.56\% = \frac{100}{18}\%$

113. (a) Savings of Swati = $\frac{25}{100} \times$ ₹40000

= ₹ 10000

Remaining balance = 40000 − 10000 = ₹ 30000

Let the amount spent on food and education be $3x$ and $2x$, respectively.

⇒ $3x + 2x = 30000$

⇒ $5x = 30000 \Rightarrow x = 6000$

∴ Amount spent on education

= $2x$ = 2 × 6000 = ₹ 12000

Hence, required % = $\frac{12000}{40000} \times 100 = 30\%$

114. (a) Present population = 80 lakh

Let the population 3 yr ago be x.

∴ $x\left(1 + \frac{20}{100}\right)^3$ = 80 lakh

⇒ $x\left(\frac{6}{5} \times \frac{6}{5} \times \frac{6}{5}\right)$ = 80 lakh

⇒ x = 80 lakh × $\frac{125}{216}$

Let the population 2 yr ago be 'y'.

∴ $y\left(1 + \frac{20}{100}\right)^2$ = 80 lakh

⇒ $y\left(\frac{6}{5} \times \frac{6}{5}\right)$ = 80 lakh

⇒ y = 80 lakh × $\frac{25}{36}$

∴ Required difference

$= x - y$ = 80 lakh $\left[\frac{25}{36} - \frac{125}{216}\right]$

= 80 lakh $\left[\frac{150 - 125}{216}\right]$

$= 8000000 \times \frac{25}{216} = 925925.93$

115. (a) Let the value of D be 100.

Then, value of C = 100 + (20% of 100) = 120

Value of B = 120 − (30% of 120)

= 120 − 36 = 84

Value of A = 84 + (25% of 84) = 84 + 21 = 105

A is more than D by

$\frac{105 - 100}{100} \times 100 = 5\%$

116. (b) Let the weekly income of Ranita be ₹ R.

The weekly income of Bhaskar be ₹ B.

According to the question,

$R \times \frac{42}{100} = B \times \frac{56}{100}$

$\frac{R}{B} = \frac{4}{3}$ ...(i)

If Bhasker's weekly income become ₹ (B + 200).

Then, ratio of income = $\frac{R}{B + 200} = \frac{5}{4}$ ...(ii)

Solving Eqs. (i) and (ii), we get

R = ₹ 4000

117. (a) Let the number of girls be 10.

∴ Number of boys = $10 + 10 \times \frac{20}{100} = 12$

∴ Ratio of boys to that of girls = $\frac{12}{10} = \frac{6}{5} = 6 : 5$

118. (c) Number of school going children in the town at the end of 3 yr.

$= 64000 \times \frac{110}{100} \times \frac{110}{100} \times \frac{110}{100} = 85184$

119. (c) Required percentage

$= \frac{165 - 100}{165} \times 100 = \frac{6500}{165} = 39.39\%$

120. (a) Let the total votes polled be $100x$.

Invalid votes = $\frac{1}{10}$ of $100x = 10x$

∴ Valid votes = $90x$

Now, votes of $(R + S) = \frac{1}{2}(100x)$

⇒ $R + S = 50x$

∵ They get equal votes.

∴ $R = 25x$ votes and $S = 25x$ votes

Now, votes received by

$R = 25x + \frac{1}{2}(25x) + \frac{1}{2}(10x)$

$= 25x + 12.5x + 5x = 42.5x$

∴ Percentage votes secured by

$R = \frac{42.5x}{100x} \times 100 = 42.5\%$

121. (b) Let the original salary of Ramnarayan be ₹ x.

Now, according to the question,

$x - 3\frac{1}{8}\%$ of $x = x - \frac{25}{8 \times 100}x = x - \frac{1}{32}x = \frac{31}{32}x$

Now, this salary is increased by $7\frac{2}{5}\%$.

New salary, $\left(\frac{31}{32}x + 7\frac{2}{5}\% \text{ of } \frac{31}{32}x\right)$

$= \frac{31}{32}x + \frac{37}{500} \times \frac{31}{32}x$

= ₹ $(0.968x + 0.0716x)$ = ₹ $1.0404x$

∴ Percentage increase in salary

$= \frac{₹(1.0404x - x)}{x} \times 100 = 4.04\%$

122. (b) Let the annual income of shiya be ₹ $100x$.

According to the question,

30% of ₹ $100x$ = ₹153000

⇒ $100x = \frac{153000 \times 100}{30}$ ⇒ $100x$ = ₹510000

∴ Monthly income = $\frac{510000}{12}$ = ₹42500

123. (d) Population of a city after 2 yr

$= 16000\left(1 + \frac{5}{100}\right)^2 = 16000\left(\frac{105}{100}\right)^2$

$= 16000\left(\frac{21}{20}\right)^2 = 16000 \times \frac{21}{20} \times \frac{21}{20}$

$= \frac{70560}{4} = 17640$

124. (c) Given, $A - B$ = 2500 or 10% of total votes polled.

i.e. 2500 = 10% of total votes polled.

∴ Total votes polled = 25000

Now, $\frac{1}{5}$th vote polled is invalid

∴ Invalid votes = $\frac{1}{5} \times 25000 = 5000$

Hence, total valid votes = 25000 − 5000

= 20000

$\therefore \quad A + B = 20000 \quad \ldots(i)$

$A - B = 2500 \quad \ldots(ii)$

On solving Eqs. (i) and (ii), we get

$A = 11250$ And $B = 8750$

Now, 90% of invalid votes $= \frac{9}{10} \times 5000 = 4500$

According to the question, votes that B would have got

$8750 + 4500 = 13250$

$\therefore$ B would have won by

$\frac{(13250 - 11250) \times 100}{25000} = 8\%$

125. (c) According to the question,

Required net decrease percentage

$= 100 - 100 \times \frac{90}{100} \times \frac{130}{100} \times \frac{80}{100}$

$= 100 - 93.6 = 6.4\% = 6\frac{2}{5}\%$

126. (d) Let Bhavani's income be ₹ $100x$.

$\therefore$ Expenditure = 68% of $100x$ = ₹ $68x$

Hence, savings = $100x - 68x$ = ₹ $32x$

Now, Increased income

= 115% of $100x$ = ₹ $115x$

and increased expenditure

= 110% of $68x$ = ₹ $74.8x$

$\therefore$ New savings = ₹ $115x$ − ₹ $74.8x$ = ₹ $40.2x$

Hence, Percentage increase in savings

$= \frac{(40.2x - ₹\ 32x)}{₹\ 32x} \times 100 = \frac{8.2}{32} \times 100 = 25.62\%$

127. (b) Let the total number of votes be $100\ x$.

$\therefore$ Total votes costed = $81\ x$

Now, A recieved $27x$ votes

$\therefore$ B received $81x - 27x = 54x$ votes

According to the question,

$54x = 125982$

$\therefore \quad x = 2333$

$\therefore$ The number of votes received by

$A = 27x = 27 \times 2333 = 62991$

128. (b) Let the population of the village before the corona attack be x.

$x \times \left(\frac{100 - 5}{100}\right) \times \left(\frac{100 - 20}{100}\right) = 4655$

$\Rightarrow \quad x = \frac{4655 \times 100 \times 100}{95 \times 80} \Rightarrow x = 6125$

129. (b)

2012	2013	2014
+15%	−15%	+15%

Resultant increase/decrease of 2012 and 2013

$= x - y - \frac{xy}{100} = 15 - 15 - \frac{15 \times 15}{100} = -(2.25\%)$

$\therefore$ It is decrease.

Now, resultant increase/decrease of −2.25% and +15% $= 15 - 2.25 - \frac{15 \times 2.25}{100}$

$= 12.75 - 0.34 = +(12.41\%)$

$\therefore$ It is increase

Hence, net increase = 12.41%

130. (a) Let the winner get x votes and his rival get $(x - 410)$ votes.

So, total number of votes

$= x + x - 410 + 60$

$= (2x - 350) \quad \ldots(i)$

10% of voters did not cast their vote.

Hence, total number of listed voters

$= (2x - 350) \times \frac{100}{90} = \frac{20x - 3500}{9}$

Now, winner got

$x = 46\%$ of $\left(\frac{20x - 3500}{9}\right)$

$\Rightarrow \quad 9x = \frac{46x}{5} - 35 \times 46 \Rightarrow x = 8050$

Now, total listed voters $= \frac{20x - 3500}{9}$

$= \frac{(20 \times 8050) - 3500}{9} = 17500$

131. (b) Given total number of votes = 15000

$\therefore$ Total number of valid votes

$= \frac{15000 \times 75}{100} = 11250$

Hence, the number of valid votes that other candidate got $= \frac{11250 \times (100 - 60)}{100} = 4500$

132. (b) Let total number of voters = x

Total number of casted votes $= \frac{88x}{100}$

$\therefore$ Valid votes $= \frac{88x}{100} - 84$

Votes gots by Ramagya $= \frac{54x}{100}$

$\therefore$ Votes gots by Shravan $= \frac{88x}{100} - 84 - \frac{54x}{100}$

$= \frac{34x}{100} - 84$

According to the question,

$\frac{54x}{100} - \frac{34x}{100} + 84 = 1456 \Rightarrow \frac{20x}{100} = 1372$

$\therefore \quad x = 1372 \times 5 = 6860$

133. (c) From ratio method. The value of a washing machine depreciated

Old		New
40960	:	21970
4096	:	2197

{time is 3 yr}

$\sqrt[3]{4096}$	:	$\sqrt[3]{2197}$
16	:	13

Depreciation $= \frac{16 - 13}{16} \times 100$

$= \frac{3}{4} \times 25 = \frac{75}{4}\% = 18.75\%$

Hence, the correct answer is 18.75%.

134. (b) Let the total income = 100 unit

So, Ayush saved money

$= 100 - (25 + 26 + 23 + 19)$

$= (100 - 93) = 7$ unit

But, Ayush spends on food and recreation

$= 26 + 19 = 45$ unit

According to the question,

7 unit = 26600

45 unit $= \frac{26600}{7} \times 45 = 3800 \times 45 = 171000$

Hence, the correct answer is ₹ 171000.

135. (b) An investor bought the stock = ₹ 1000

According to the question,

In first year, the price of a stock increased by 30% $= 1000 \times \frac{130}{100}$ = ₹ 1300

In second year, the price of a stock decreased by 20% $= 1300 \times \frac{80}{100}$ = ₹ 1040

Hence, the final value of the investment after 2 yr at ₹ 1040.

136. (c) According to the question,

First decreased = 28% $= \frac{7}{25}$

Increased = 28% $= \frac{7}{25}$

Now,

Value	Original value	New
Decreased	⇒ 25	18
Increased	⇒ 25	32
	625 :	576

49

$\therefore \quad 49 \rightarrow 784$

Original 625 $\Rightarrow \frac{784}{49} \times 625$

$\therefore \quad 16 \times 625$ = ₹ 10000

Hence, the correct answer is 10000.

137. (b) Let his monthly salary = ₹ x per month

According to the question,

$x - 72\%$ of $x = 5740 \Rightarrow \frac{28}{100}x = 5740$

$\Rightarrow \quad x = \frac{5740 \times 100}{28}$ = ₹ 20500

Then, his annual salary

$= 20500 \times 12 = 246000$

Hence, 10% of his annual salary

= 10% of 246000 = ₹ 24600

138. (a) Let original number = 100

Then, according to the question,

New number $= 100 \times \frac{110}{100} \times \frac{120}{100} \times \frac{88}{100}$

$= 116.16$

Net increase per cent $= \frac{116.16 - 100}{100} \times 100$

= 16.16% (Increase)

Speedy Method

Assumed number

100 → (+10%) → 110 → (+ 20%) → 132 → (−12%) → 116.16

$\therefore$ Required per cent = 16.16%

139. (a) Let the man's income = ₹ 100

Expenditure = 65% of 100 = ₹ 65

Saving = ₹ (100 − 65) = ₹ 35

New income = (100 + 20)% of ₹ 100 = ₹ 120

New expenditure = (100 + 10)% of ₹ 65 = ₹ 71.5

New saving = ₹ (120 − 71.5) = ₹ 48.5

Increase in saving % = $\frac{48.5-35}{35}\times 100$ = 38.57%

140. (c) After fall in manpower, production of the company = (100 − 35)% = 65%

To restore the production *i.e.* to make 100% production, production need to be increased by 35%.

So, required percentage = $\frac{35}{65}\times 100\%$

= 53.846% = 53.85%

141. (d) According to the question,

Population after 2 yr = $P\left(1-\frac{r}{100}\right)^n$

$= 45000\left(1-\frac{2}{100}\right)^2$

$= 45000\times\frac{49}{50}\times\frac{49}{50} = 43218$

142. (b) Let Manju's income = 400 x

∴ Raju's income = (100 + 25)% of x = 500x

Rise in income of Raju = 25% of 500x = 125x

Rise in income of Manju = 40% of 400x = 160x

Required increased percentage

$= \frac{160x+125x}{500x+400x}\times 100\%$

$= \frac{285x}{900x}\times 100\% = 31.67\%$

143. (a) Let the Sohan's income = 100

According to the question,

Shyam's income = $100\times\frac{70}{100}$

Ram's income = $100\times\frac{70}{100}\times\frac{170}{100}$

Required ratio = $100\times\frac{70}{100}\times\frac{170}{100} : 100$

= 119 : 100

144. (c) Let the number of boys to that of girls is 500 and 200.

∴ Required percentage of the student who failed in the actual exam

$$= \frac{\left\{500\times\frac{(100-87)}{100} + 200\times\left(\frac{100-80}{100}\right)\right\}\times 100}{(500+200)}$$

$$= \frac{\left(500\times\frac{13}{100} + 200\times\frac{20}{100}\right)}{700}\times 100$$

$$= \left(\frac{65+40}{7}\right) = \frac{105}{7} = 15\%$$

Speedy Method

By Alligation rule,

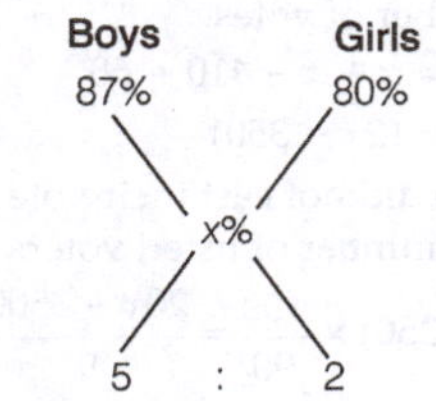

$\therefore\ \frac{87-x}{x-80} = \frac{2}{5} \Rightarrow 435 - 5x = 2x - 160$

$\Rightarrow 7x = 595 \Rightarrow x = 85\%$

∴ Failed student percentage = 100 − 85 = 15%

145. (a) Let the total number of votes = x

Defeated candidate got $\frac{42x}{100}$ votes

According to the question,

$\left[(x-1400)-\frac{42x}{100}\right]-\left[\frac{42x}{100}\right] = 3080$

$\Rightarrow\quad x-\frac{84x}{100} = 3080+1400 \Rightarrow x = \frac{4480}{16}\times 100$

$\Rightarrow\quad x = 28000$ votes

∴ Required percentage of invalid votes

$= \frac{1400}{28000}\times 100 = 5\%$

146. (d) Given,

The number of student has given at different centre are 25, 30, 40, 45, 60, 100.

And passing percentage of respective centre are 20%, 30%, 35%, 40%, 50%, 75%

Passing percentage

$$= \frac{(25\times 20\% + 30\times 30\% + 40\times 35\% + 45\times 40\% + 60\times 50\% + 100\times 75\%)}{(25+30+40+45+60+100)}\times 100$$

$$= \frac{(5+9+14+18+30+75)}{300}\times 100$$

= 50.33% ≈ 50%

147. (d) Let B's salary be ₹ 100.

A's salary is 35% more than B.

Salary of $A = \frac{100\times 135}{100}$ = ₹ 135

∴ Required percentage $= \frac{(135-100)}{135}\times 100$

$= \frac{35}{135}\times 100 = 25.92 \approx 26\%$

148. (b) Let numerator and denominator be x and y, respectively.

According to the question,

$\frac{x+\frac{60}{100}x}{y+\frac{40}{100}y} = \frac{16}{63} \Rightarrow \frac{160x}{140y} = \frac{16}{63} \Rightarrow \frac{x}{y} = \frac{2}{9}$

149. (c) Let's assume the price of diesel is ₹ 100/L and a person's consumption is 100 L.

Hence, his expenditure is 100 × 100 = 10000

Now, the price of diesel is ₹ 126 /L.

But the person want his expenditure to increase by 15% only.

∴ His new maximum expenditure is = 11500

Therefore, now the person can consume

$= \frac{11500}{126} = 91.26$ L of diesel

He should decrease his consumption by (100 − 91.26) = 8.73 ≈ 8.7%

150. (c) According to the question,

$\frac{110\times(100-x)}{100} = \frac{50\times(100+x)}{100}$

$\Rightarrow 110\times 100 - 110x = 50\times 100 + 50x$

$\Rightarrow\quad 160x = 60\times 100$

$\Rightarrow\quad x = \frac{60\times 100}{160} = 37.5$

$\therefore\ x\%$ of 650 $= \frac{37.5}{100}\times 650 = 243.75$

and $(x-10)\%$ of 780 is $= \frac{27.5}{100}\times 780 = 214.5$

Required percentage

$= \frac{243.75-214.5}{214.5}\times 100$

= 13.63 ≈ 14%

151. (a) Case-1 Monthly salary = ₹ 75000

Expenses (E) = $75000\times\frac{60}{100} = 45000$

Taxes (T) = $45000\times\frac{20}{100} = 9000$

Charity (C) = $9000\times\frac{15}{100} = 1350$

Total spending = 45000 + 9000 + 1350 = 55350

Initial saving = 75000 − 55350 = ₹ 19650

Case-2 But in 2nd case his salary increased by 40%.

New salary = $75000\times\frac{140}{100} = 105000$

New, expenses (E) = $105000\times\frac{60}{100} = 63000$

Taxes (T) = $63000\times\frac{30}{100} = 18900$

Charity (C) = $18900\times\frac{20}{100} = 3780$

∴ Total spending = 63000 + 18900 + 3780 = ₹ 85680

New saving = 105000 − 85680 = 19320

∴ Required ratio is = 19650 : 19320 = 655 : 644

152. (b) Let initial income = ₹ 100

Initial saving = Income − Expenditure = 100 − 75 = 25

Increased income = 100 + 28 = 128

Increased expenditure = $75\times\frac{120}{100} = 90$

New, savings = 128 − 90 = 38

Percentage savings increased by

$= \frac{38-25}{25}\times 100 = \frac{13}{25}\times 100 = 52\%$

153. (d) Required percentage of increase in his salary $= \frac{12000 - 7000}{7000} \times 100$

$= \frac{5000}{7000} \times 100 = 71\frac{3}{7}\%$

154. (b) Let the price of diesel per litre $= x$,

Consumption of diesel $= y$ and consumption reduced by $h\%$

The, expenditure on diesel $= xy$

Now, new price of diesel per litre $= \frac{x \times 116}{100}$

and new consumption of diesel $= y\frac{(100 - h)}{100}$

We know that,

Price $\times$ Consumption = Expenditure

According to the question,

$x \times \frac{116}{100} \times y \times \frac{(100 - h)}{100} = xy \times \frac{(110)}{100}$

$\Rightarrow 11600 - 116h = 11000$

$\Rightarrow \quad 116h = 600$

$\therefore \quad h = \frac{600}{116} = 5.1724\% \approx 5.2\%$

155. (b) Let the salary of B be ₹ 100.

A's salary = ₹ 160

$\therefore$ Required percentage $= \frac{160 - 100}{160} = 37.5\%$

156. (a) According to the question,

$(100 - x) \times \left(\frac{110}{100}\right) = (100 + x) \times \left(\frac{50}{100}\right)$

$\Rightarrow 1100 - 11x = 500 + 5x \Rightarrow 16x = 600$

$\Rightarrow \quad x = \frac{600}{16} \Rightarrow x = \frac{75}{2}$

Now, (75/2)% of 650 = 243.75

$\left(\frac{75}{2} + 20\right)\%$ of 180 = 103.5

$\therefore$ Required percentage

$= \left\{\frac{(243.75) - 103.5}{103.5}\right\} \times 100\%$

$= 135.5\% \approx 136\%$

157. (b) Price of machine after three year

$= 8000 \times \frac{95}{100} \times \frac{90}{100} \times \frac{85}{100}$

= ₹ 5814

158. (b) Let total number of votes $= x$

Total number of valid votes $= x - 58$

Number of votes got by winner

$= (x - 58)$ of 54%

Number of votes got by runner up.

$= (x - 58)$ of 46%

According to the question,

$(x - 58) \times \frac{54}{100} - (x - 58) \times \frac{46}{100} = 88$

$\Rightarrow \quad \frac{(x - 58)}{100} \times (54 - 46) = 88$

$\Rightarrow \quad (x - 58) = \frac{88 \times 100}{8} = 1100$

$\therefore \quad x = 1100 + 58 = 1158$

159. (d) Let actual salary = ₹ 100

After 20% reduction in salary, new salary

$= 100 - 100 \times \frac{20}{100} = 100 - 20 =$ ₹ 80

In order to get original salary percentage

increase $= \frac{100 - 80}{80} \times 100 = \frac{20}{80} \times 100 = 25\%$

Speedy Method

Required per cent $= \frac{20}{(100 - 20)} \times 100\%$

$= \frac{20}{80} \times 100\% = 25\%$

160. (a) Let total consumption = 1 kg

and the price per kg = ₹ 100/kg

Hence, total expenditure

= 1 kg × ₹100 /kg = ₹ 100

If price is increased by 36%.

So, new price $= 100 + 100 \times \frac{36}{100} =$ ₹136 /kg

For making total expenditure same, then

total consumption $= \frac{₹\ 100}{₹\ 136\ /\text{kg}} = \frac{100}{136}$ kg

$\therefore$ Decreased% in consumption

$= \frac{1 - \frac{100}{136}}{1} \times 100 = \frac{136 - 100}{136} \times 100$

$= \frac{36}{136} \times 100 = 26.47\% \approx 26.5\%$

Speedy Method

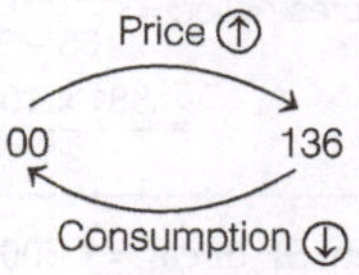

$\therefore$ Decrease % $= \frac{136 - 100}{136} \times 100$

$= \frac{36}{136} \times 100 = 26.47\% \approx 26.5\%$

161. (b) Overall percentage increase in price of product over two years

$= \left(10 + 20 + \frac{10 \times 20}{100}\right) = (30 + 2) = 32\%$

162. (d) Required percentage decrease in income

$= \frac{42800 - 37236}{42800} \times 100 = \frac{5564}{42800} \times 100 = 13\%$

163. (d) Number of employees who appeared in departmental exam in two years

$= 75 + 50 = 125$

Number of employees who passed the examination in 2 yr

$= \frac{84}{100} \times 75 + \frac{52}{100} \times 50 = 63 + 26 = 89$

$\therefore$ Average rate of pass percentage

$= \frac{89}{125} \times 100 = 71\frac{1}{5}\%$

164. (b) Let valid votes be $100x$.

Winner got 65% of valid votes $= 65x$

and loser got 35% of valid votes $= 35x$

Given, invalid votes = 200

Winner won by $1200 = 65x - 35x \Rightarrow x = 40$

$\therefore$ Total votes casted $= 100x + 200$

$= 4000 + 200 = 4200$

70% are total casted votes = 4200

$\therefore$ Total votes $= \frac{4200}{70} \times 100 = 6000$

165. (b) Let total votes be $100x$.

One of the candidate got 44% of total votes

$= 100x \times \frac{44}{100} = 44x$

Other candidate got votes $= 100x - 44x = 56x$

According to the question,

Vote difference between winner and loser

$= 1440$

$\Rightarrow \quad 56x - 44x = 1440$

$\Rightarrow \quad 12x = 1440 \Rightarrow x = 120$

$\therefore$ Total votes $= 100x = 12000$

166. (c) Let Ram's salary $= 100x$

$\therefore$ Shyam's salary $= 100x \times \left(\frac{100 - 20}{100}\right) = 80x$

Ram's salary more than Shyam's in terms of percentage

$= \frac{100x - 80x}{80x} \times 100 = \frac{20x}{80x} \times 100 = 25\%$

Speedy Method

Required per cent $= \frac{20}{(100 - 20)} \times 100\%$

$= \frac{20}{80} \times 100\% = 25\%$

167. (b) Population of village after two years.

$= 400000 \times \frac{120}{100} \times \frac{130}{100} = 624000$

168. (d) Let the third number be $100x$.

$\therefore$ First number $= 100x - \frac{61}{100} \times 100x = 39x$

Second number $= 100x - \frac{35}{100} \times 100x = 65x$

$\therefore$ Required percentage $= \frac{39x}{65x} \times 100 = 60\%$

169. (a) Given, total number of votes = 30000

Total number of valid votes

$= 30000 - 30000 \times \frac{20}{100}$

$= 30000 - 6000 = 24000$

Total number of valid votes that Ananth got

$= 24000 \times \frac{55}{100} = 13200$

$\therefore$ Total number of valid votes that Aravind got $= 24000 - 13200 = 10800$

170. (a) Given, total number of votes = 8000

Total number of valid votes

$= 8000 - \frac{15}{100} \times 8000 = 6800$

∴ Total number of votes that one candidate got $= \frac{52}{100} \times 6800 = 3536$

∴ Total number of valid votes that the other candidate got $= 6800 - 3536 = 3264$

171. (c) Let total votes $= 100x$

Loser got votes $= 100x \times \frac{40}{100} = 40x$

Winner got votes $= 100x - 40x = 60x$

∴ Difference of votes $= 60x - 40x = 298$

$x = 14.9$

Hence, total votes $= 100 \times 14.9 = 1490$

172. (b) Let the third number be $100x$.

∴ Second number $= 100x \times \left(\frac{40}{100} + 1\right) = 140x$

and first number $= 100x \times \left(\frac{30}{100} + 1\right) = 130x$

∴ $\frac{\text{Second number}}{\text{First number}} = \frac{140x}{130x} = 14 : 13$

173. (b) Let the salary be ₹ $100x$.

Salary after increment $= 100x \times \frac{109}{100} = ₹\ 109x$

Then, according to question,

$109x = 6300 \Rightarrow x = 57.79$

Thus, salary $= 100x = 57.79 \times 100$

$= ₹\ 5779$

Speedy Method

∴ $109\% \equiv 6300$

∴ $100\% \equiv \frac{6300}{109} \times 100 = ₹\ 5779$

174. (c) Let the number be x.

Then, according to question,

$x - 12 = x \times \frac{40}{100} \Rightarrow x - 12 = \frac{2}{5} \times x$

$\Rightarrow x - \frac{2}{5}x = 12 \Rightarrow \frac{3x}{5} = 12 \Rightarrow x = 20$

Thus, required number $= 20 \times \frac{2}{5} = 8$

175. (b) Total expense of Ram

$= (30 + 10 + 7 + 6)\% = 53\%$

Saving $= (100 - 53)\% = 47\%$

Monthly salary of Ram $= \frac{1880}{47} \times 100 = ₹\ 4000$

176. (a) Total votes $= 8750$.

Valid votes $= 8750 \times \frac{80}{100} = 7000$

Opponent votes $= 7000 \times \frac{(100 - 63)}{100}$

$= 7000 \times \frac{37}{100} = 2590$

177. (c) Actual cost of an article $= 3500 \times \frac{100}{70}$

$= ₹\ 5000$

178. (a) Let the number be x.

∴ $\frac{20}{100} \times \frac{35}{100} \times x = 240.8$

$\Rightarrow x = \frac{240.8 \times 100 \times 100}{20 \times 35} = 3440$

∴ Required 18% of the number

$= 3440 \times \frac{18}{100} = 619.2$

179. (d) According to the question,

Net percentage change

$= \left(a - b - \frac{ab}{100}\right)\% = \left(-25 + 50 - \frac{25 \times 50}{100}\right)\%$

$= (-25 + 50 - 12.50)\%$

$= (25 - 12.50)\% = 12.50\%$

∴ Original price $= 7650 \times \frac{100}{112.5} = ₹\ 6800$

180. (a) Given, Initial salary = ₹ 200/day

New salary = ₹ 234/day

Required percentage $= \frac{234 - 200}{200} \times 100$

$= 17\%$

181. (c) Let total number of votes polled be $100x$.

∴ Total number of votes that one of the candidates got $= \frac{35}{100} \times 100x = 35x$

∴ Total number of votes that the other candidate got $= 100x - 35x = 65x$

According to the question,

$65x - 35x = 381 \Rightarrow 30x = 381$

$\Rightarrow 100x = \frac{381}{30} \times 100 = 1270$

Speedy Method

Number of votes polled $= \frac{381 \times 100}{(65 - 35)}$

$= \frac{381 \times 100}{30} = 1270$

182. (a) Given, SP of car = ₹ 500000

As, car is sold at 20% less than its original price.

∴ Required original price of car

$= 500000 \times \frac{100}{80} = ₹\ 625000$

183. (b) Let Somu's salary be ₹ $100x$.

∴ Ramu's salary $= 100x \times \left(\frac{100 - 30}{100}\right) = ₹\ 70x$

∴ Required percentage $= \frac{100x - 70x}{70x} \times 100$

$= \frac{30x}{70x} \times 100 = 42.86\%$

Speedy Method

Required percentage $= \frac{30}{(100 - 30)} \times 100$

$= \frac{30}{70} \times 100 = 42.86\%$

184. (d) Total income of three family

= ₹ 72000

Their expenditure are 80%, 85%, 75%.

Savings ratio are 8 : 9 : 20.

Let first family savings = ₹ $8x$

Second family savings = ₹ $9x$

and third family savings = ₹ $20x$

∴ First family savings = 20% of income

$\Rightarrow 8x = 20\%$ of income

Income of first family = ₹ $40x$

Similarly, second family savings

= 15% of income

$\Rightarrow 9x = 15\%$ of income

Income of second family = ₹ $60x$

Similarly, third family savings

= 25% of income $\Rightarrow 20x = 25\%$ of income

Income of third family = ₹ $80x$

∴ Total income $= 80x + 60x + 40x$

$180x = ₹72000 \Rightarrow x = ₹\ 400$

∴ Income of second family $= 60x$

$= 60 \times 400 = ₹\ 24000$

185. (c) Let the number be $100x$.

According to the question,

$100x \times \left(\frac{100 - 18}{100}\right) \times \left(\frac{100 + 25}{100}\right) = 102.5x$

∴ Overall percentage change

$= \frac{102.5x - 100x}{100x} \times 100 = 2.5\%$

∴ Increases by 2.5%.

186. (b) Let total voters be $100x$.

Number of casted votes $= 100x \times \frac{90}{100} = 90x$

Invalid votes = 5%

Number of valid votes $= 90x \times \frac{95}{100} = 85.5x$

Number of votes got by winner

$= 85.5x \times 52.5\%$

Votes got by looser $= 85.5x \times 47.5\%$

According to the question,

$85.5x \times 52.5\% - 85.5x \times 47.5\% = 1710$

$\Rightarrow 85.5x(52.5 - 47.5)\% = 1710$

$\Rightarrow 85.5x \times 5\% = 1710$

$\Rightarrow x = \frac{1710 \times 100}{85.5 \times 5}$

$100x = \frac{1710 \times 100 \times 100}{85.5 \times 5} = 40000$

∴ Total votes = 40000

187. (d) Let his total income be ₹$100x$.

Then, initial saving $= 100x \times 45\% = ₹\ 45x$

and initial expenditure $= 100x - 45x = ₹\ 55x$

Now, new income $= 100x \times \frac{300}{100} = ₹\ 300x$

His new saving $= 45x \times 5 = ₹\ 225x$

New expenditure of person

$= 300x - 225x = ₹\ 75x$

Increase percentage in expenditure

$= \frac{75x - 55x}{55x} \times 100 = \frac{20x}{55x} \times 100$

$= 36.36 \simeq 36.40\%$

188. (c) 5% of 2% of 3 $= \frac{5}{100} \times \frac{2}{100} \times 3$

$= 0.003$

189. (a) Given,

Present value of the machine = ₹ 80000

Depreciation rate = 5% per yr

Time = 2 yr

The value of machine after n yr

$= \text{Present value of machine} \times \left(1 \pm \frac{\text{Rate}}{100}\right)^n$

∴ The value of machine after 2 yr

$= 80000\left(1 - \frac{5}{100}\right)^2 = 80000 \times \frac{19}{20} \times \frac{19}{20}$

= ₹ 72200

190. (d) Let total votes = $100x$.

One candidate got 42% of total votes

$= 100x \times \frac{42}{100} = 42x$

Other candidate got votes $= 100x - 42x = 58x$

According to question,

$58x - 42x = 800 \Rightarrow 16x = 800$

∴ $x = 50$

∴ Total vote casted $= 100x = 100 \times 50 = 5000$

Speedy Method

Difference in votes = (100 − 42)% − 42%

= 58% − 42% = 16%

Total casted votes $= \frac{800}{16} \times 100 = 5000$

191. (d) Let Ramesh pocket money was ₹ $100x$.

Then, pocket money after decrease by 25%

$= 100x \times \frac{75}{100} = 75x$

Again, pocket money after increase of 20%

$= 75x \times \frac{120}{100} = 90x$

Thus, net decrease percentage

$= \frac{100x - 90x}{100x} \times 100 = \frac{10x}{100x} \times 100 = 10\%$

192. (b) Let total number of polled votes be $100x$.

∴ Valid votes $= (100x - 68)$

According to question,

$(100x - 68) \times \frac{52}{100} - (100x - 68) \times \frac{48}{100} = 98$

$\Rightarrow (100x - 68)\left[\frac{52}{100} - \frac{48}{100}\right] = 98$

$\Rightarrow (100x - 68) \times \frac{1}{25} = 98$

$\Rightarrow 100x - 68 = 2450$

$\Rightarrow 100x = 2450 + 68 = 2518$

Hence, total number of polled votes

$= 100x = 2518$

193. (d) According to the question,

Sale of Tuesday = ₹ 1485

As, sale increased on Tuesday by 10%.

∴ Sale on Monday $= 1485 \times \frac{100}{110}$ = ₹ 1350

As, sale decreased on Monday by 10%.

∴ Sale on Sunday $= 1350 \times \frac{100}{90}$ = ₹ 1500

194. (a) Let money initially Pranav had be ₹ $100x$.

According to the question,

Money left after given to wife

$= 100x - \frac{30}{100} \times 100x = 70x$

Money given to children $= \frac{86}{100} \times 70x = 60.2x$

Money spent on other things

$= \frac{1}{2}(70x - 60.2x) = 4.9x$

∴ Remaining money $= 9.8x - 4.9x$

$\Rightarrow 4.9x = 98000$

$\Rightarrow x = \frac{98000 \times 10}{49} = 20000$

∴ Money initially Pranav had

= 100 × 20000 = ₹ 2000000

195. (a) Let income of B be ₹ $100x$.

∴ Income of A = ₹ $125x$

Also, assume savings of A = ₹ $100s$

∴ Savings of B = ₹ $120s$

∴ Expenditure of $A = 125x - 100s$

Expenditure of $B = 100x - 120s$

According to the question,

$\frac{75}{100}(125x - 100s) = 100x - 120s$

$\Rightarrow 4500s = 625x \Rightarrow \frac{x}{s} = \frac{72}{10}$

$\Rightarrow x = 72k, s = 10k$ (Assume)

∴ Income of A and B

$= (125 \times 72k)$ and $(100 \times 72k)$

$= 9000k$ and $7200k$

∴ Savings of $B = (120 \times 10k) = 1200k$

∴ Expenditure of $B = 7200k - 1200k = 6000k$

∴ Required percentage $= \frac{1200k}{6000k} \times 100 = 20\%$

196. (a) $x = -15\%$, $y = -20\%$

Total (Net) percentage decrease after two years $= x + y + \frac{xy}{100}$

$= -15 - 20 + \frac{(-15) \times (-20)}{100}$

$= -35 + \frac{300}{100} = -35 + 3 = -32\%$

197. (a) Correct time period = 2 h 25 min

= 120 + 25 = 145 min

Wrong time period = 2 h and 30.5 min

= 120 + 30.5 = 150.5

Hence, error percentage $= \frac{150.5 - 145}{145} \times 100$

$= \frac{5.5}{145} \times 100 = 3\frac{23}{29}\%$

198. (c) New price of rice $= \frac{2500}{10} \times 24\%$

$= \frac{2500}{10} \times \frac{24}{100} = \frac{5}{2} \times 24$ = ₹ 60

199. (a) Let monthly income be ₹ $100x$.

∴ Total expenses = (60 + 10 + 5) % = 75%

Savings $= 100x - 75x = 25x$

∴ Remaining salary

$= 100x - (60x + 10x + 5x)$ = ₹ $25x$

According to the question,

Remaining salary = 4000

$\Rightarrow 25x = 4000 \Rightarrow x$ = ₹ 160

∴ Monthly salary = 100 × 160 = ₹ 16000

200. (b) Given, price = $ 750

Rate of increase = 20%

Final price of motor cycle

$= 750\left(1 + \frac{20}{100}\right) = \$ 900$

201. (b) Total number of votes = 240000

Total number of valid votes

$= 240000 - \frac{3}{100} \times 240000 = 232800$

∴ Total number of votes polled in favour of candidate $= \frac{60}{100} \times 232800 = 139680$

202. (c) Percentage change

$= \frac{\text{New quantity} - \text{Old quantity}}{\text{Old quantity}} \times 100$

∴ Required percentage change

$= \frac{\frac{5}{6} - \frac{4}{5}}{\frac{4}{5}} \times 100 = \frac{25 - 24}{30} \times \frac{5}{4} \times 100$

$= \frac{1}{30} \times \frac{5}{4} \times 100 = \frac{100}{24} = \frac{25}{6} = 4.17\%$

203. (a) Net percentage change

$= \left(44 - 30 - \frac{44 \times 30}{100}\right) = (14 - 13.2)\%$

= 0.8% ≃ 1% increase

204. (d) Let total votes are 100%.

Given, one candidate gets = 72% of total votes

∴ Other person gets = [100 − 72]% = 28%

∴ Required difference

$= \frac{72 - 28}{100} \times 1000 = \frac{44}{100} \times 1000 = 440$

Hence, the winner won by 440 votes.

205. (d) According to the question,

31% − 26% = 2350

5% = 2350

∴ $7\% = \frac{2350}{5} \times 7 = 3290$

206. (a) Jitvik's salary in month of December 2020 = ₹ 24800

Increament in salary every year = 5%

Jitvik's salary in month of February 2022

$= \left[24800 \times \frac{105}{100} \times \frac{105}{100}\right]$ = ₹ 27342

207. (d) Let the income of Monica is ₹ $100x$.

∴ Income of Neha $= \left[100x \times \frac{105}{100}\right]$ = ₹ $105x$

$\therefore$ Required percentage $= \left[\frac{105x - 100x}{105x} \times 100\right]$

$= \left[\frac{5x}{105x} \times 100\right] = \left[\frac{100}{21}\right]\% = 4\frac{16}{21}\%$

Speedy Method

Required percentage $= \frac{5}{105} \times 100$

$= \frac{100}{21}\% = 4\frac{16}{21}\%$

208. (d) Let the original price of tea is ₹ 100.

Then, increased price $= 100 \times \frac{140}{100} =$ ₹ 140

$\therefore$ Reduction in consumption

$= \left[\frac{140 - 100}{140} \times 100\right] = \left[\frac{40}{140} \times 100\right] = \frac{200}{7}\%$

$= 28\frac{4}{7}\%$

209. (d) Let the income and expenditure of Ramu be $100k$ and $72k$, respectively.

$\therefore$ Savings = Income − Expenditure

$= 100k - 72k =$ ₹$28k$

$\therefore$ $y = 28k$

New income $= 100 \times \frac{112}{100} =$ ₹$112k$

New expenditure $= 72 \times \frac{105}{100} =$ ₹$75.6k$

$\therefore$ New savings $= 112k - 75.6k =$ ₹$36.4k$

$\therefore x = 36.4k$

$\left[\frac{x - y}{y} \times 100\right]\% = \left[\frac{36.4k - 28k}{28k} \times 100\right]\%$

$= \frac{8.4k}{28k} \times 100 = 30\%$

210. (c) According to the question,

$20\% = \frac{20}{100} = 0.2$

$0.5\% = \frac{0.5}{100} = 0.005$

and $0.03\% = \frac{0.03}{100} = 0.0003$

211. (d) Given, last year Geeta's monthly salary = ₹ 12000

Last year Seeta's monthly salary = ₹ 10000

This year Geeta's monthly salary = ₹ 14400

This year Seeta's monthly salary = ₹ 12500

According to the question,

$y\% = \left(\frac{14400 - 12000}{12000}\right) \times 100$

$= \frac{2400}{12000} \times 100 = 20\%$

Also, $x\% = \left(\frac{12500 - 10000}{10000}\right) \times 100$

$= \frac{250000}{10000} = 25\%$

$\therefore \left(\frac{x - y}{y} \times 100\right)\% = \left(\frac{25 - 20}{20} \times 100\right)\%$

$= 25\%$

212. (c) $x = 25\%$ increase, $y = 30\%$ decrease

$\therefore$ Required per cent $= \left(x + y + \frac{x \times y}{100}\right)$

$= \left(25 - 30 + \frac{25 \times (-30)}{100}\right) = (-5 - 7.5)\%$

$= -12.5\% = -12\frac{1}{2}\%$

Hence, there is an decrease of $12\frac{1}{2}\%$.

213. (d) Let income be ₹ 100.

$\therefore$ Expenditure = ₹ 70

Savings = ₹ 30

New income = ₹ 115

New expenditure $= 70 \times \frac{107.5}{100} =$ ₹ 75.25

$\therefore$ Savings = ₹ 39.75

$\therefore$ Increase percentage in savings

$= \frac{(39.75 - 30)}{30} \times 100 = \frac{9.75 \times 100}{30} = 32.5\%$

214. (b) Last year, Ranjan's monthly salary = ₹ 34500

This year Ranjan's monthly salary = ₹ 38640

Hence, required increase percentage

$= \frac{(38640 - 34500)}{34500} \times 100$

$= \frac{4140}{34500} \times 100 = 12\%$

215. (c) Let the total voters are 100%.

Total casted votes $= 100 \times \frac{83}{100} = 83\%$

Total valid votes $= 83 \times \frac{96}{100} = 79.68\%$

According to the question,

Total valid votes by Party

$A = 79.68 \times 83\% = 156611$

$\Rightarrow$ $66.1344\% = 156611$

$\Rightarrow$ $100\% = \frac{156611 \times 100}{66.1344} = 236807$

216. (c) Let the total income = 100%

According to the question,

Savings

$= [100\% - (10\% + 10\% + 20\% + 15\%)]$

$= (100\% - 55\%) = 45\%$

$\therefore$ Savings $= \frac{45}{100} \times 30000 =$ ₹ 13500

217. (c) $28\% = \frac{28}{100} = \frac{7}{25} = 7 : 25$

218. (d) Let the total number of registered voters $= 100x$

$\therefore$ Total casted votes $= 100x \times 90\% = 90x$

Votes of winning candidate $= 90x \times 60\% = 54x$

$\therefore$ Votes of losing candidate $= 90x - 54x = 36x$

$\therefore$ $54x - 36x = 1242$

$\Rightarrow$ $18x = 1242$

$\Rightarrow$ $100x = \frac{1242 \times 100}{18} = 6900$

$\therefore$ Total number of registered voters = 6900

219. (b) According to the question,

$12.75\% = \frac{12.75}{100} = \frac{1275}{100 \times 100} = \frac{51}{400}$

220. (c) According to the question,

Income of $P : Q = 60 : 100 = 3 : 5$

$\therefore$ Required per cent

$= \frac{(8 - 3)}{3} \times 100 = \frac{500}{3} = 166\frac{2}{3}$

221. (d) Given, fraction $= \frac{3}{5}$

After decreasing, fraction $= \frac{3}{5} - \frac{2}{5} = \frac{1}{5}$

After 20% increase in fraction

$= \frac{1}{5} \times \frac{120}{100} = \frac{6}{25}$

Hence, the required decrease in percentage

$= \frac{\frac{3}{5} - \frac{6}{25}}{3/5} \times 100 = \frac{9}{25} \times \frac{5}{3} \times 100$

$= 60\%$ decrease

222. (c) Let income of Ramana = ₹100

Expenditure of Ramana = ₹75

$\therefore$ Savings of Ramana = 100 − 75 = ₹25

New income of Ramana $= \frac{100 \times 125}{100} =$ ₹125

and new expenditure of Ramana

$= \frac{75 \times 110}{100} =$ ₹ 82.5

$\therefore$ New savings of Ramana = 125 − 82.5

= ₹42.5

Hence, percentage increase in savings

$= \frac{42.5 - 25}{25} \times 100 = \frac{17.5}{25} \times 100 = 70\%$

223. (b) Total cost price of 10 chairs = ₹ 4500

After decrease by 20% in cost price,

Cost price of 10 chairs $= \frac{4500 \times 80}{100} =$ ₹ 3600

$\therefore$ Cost price of 1 chair $= \frac{3600}{10} =$ ₹ 360

New number of chairs $= \frac{10 \times 110}{100} = 11$

Hence, cost price of 11 chairs

$= 11 \times 360 =$ ₹ 3960

224. (c) Initial expenditure = ₹ 12800

New in expenditure = ₹ 11712

Percentage decrease in his expenditure

$= \frac{12800 - 11712}{12800} \times 100$

$= \frac{1088}{12800} \times 100 = 8.5\%$

225. (c) Let the total number of vote polled be $100x$.

Winning candidate got $= 78x$

Lossing candidate got $= 22x$

$\therefore$ Difference between winning and loosing candidate $= 78x - 22x = 56x$

Now, the total number of vote polled

$$= \frac{100x \times 448}{56x} = 800$$

226. (d) Percentage of total valid votes that winning candidate secured

$= (100 - 42) = 58\%$

Difference between the winning and defeated candidate $= (58 - 42) = 16\%$

Total number of valid votes

$$= \frac{2545800}{16} \times 100 = 15911250$$

Total number of voters (both valid and invalid) $= 15911250 + 365500 = 16276750$

Total number of voters

$$= \frac{16276750 \times 100}{70} = 23252500$$

Number of people who did not cast their vote

$$= 23252500 \times 30\% = 6975750$$

Approx = 7 millions.

227. (b) Total number of votes = 7500

Invalid votes $= 7500 \times \frac{20}{100} = 1500$

$\therefore$ Valid votes $= 7500 - 1500 = 6000$

Valid votes getting by first candidate

$$= 6000 \times \frac{65}{100} = 3900$$

$\therefore$ Valid vote getting by second candidate

$$= 6000 - 3900 = 2100$$

228. (c) Let the monthly income = ₹ x

Expenses on food = 35% of x.

$\therefore$ Remaining income after food expenses

$$= x \times 65\%$$

Expenses on transport $= (x \times 65\%) \times \frac{4}{13}$

$\therefore$ Remaining income after transport expenses $= (x \times 65\%) \times \frac{9}{13}$

Now, $(x \times 65\%) \times \frac{9}{13} \times \frac{20}{100} =$ ₹ 6300

$$x = \frac{6300 \times 100 \times 100 \times 13}{65 \times 9 \times 20} = ₹\ 70000$$

229. (d) According to the question,

$$500 \times \frac{80}{100} \times \frac{(100+b)}{100} \times \frac{80}{100} \times \frac{(100+b)}{100} \times \frac{80}{100} = 1024$$

$$\Rightarrow (100+b)^2 = \frac{1024 \times 100 \times 100 \times 100 \times 100 \times 100}{500 \times 80 \times 80 \times 80}$$

$\Rightarrow (100+b)^2 = 40000$

$\therefore\ 100 + b = 200$

$\Rightarrow\ b = 100$

230. (a) Net change

$$= \left[(40-45) + \frac{40 \times (-45)}{100}\right]\%$$

$$= [-5 + (-18)]\% = -23\%$$

231. (c) Let the number added be x.

According to the question,

$$\frac{20}{100} \times 460 + x = \frac{70}{100} \times 920$$

$\Rightarrow\ 92 + x = 644 \Rightarrow x = 644 - 92$

$\therefore\ x = 552$

232. (b) Let the number be x.

According to the question,

$$x + 8 = x \times \frac{120}{100} \Rightarrow x + 8 = x \times \frac{6}{5}$$

$\Rightarrow\ 5x + 40 = 6x$

$\Rightarrow\ x = 40$

233. (c) According to the question,

$$100x \times \frac{85}{100} \times \frac{75}{100} \times \frac{75}{100} \times \frac{85}{100} = 10404$$

Total salary $(100x) \simeq$ ₹ 25600

234. (b) Population of village in first year

$$= 47880 \times \frac{100}{(100+5)} \times \frac{100}{(100-5)}$$

$$= 47880 \times \frac{100}{105} \times \frac{100}{95} = 48000$$

235. (c) Total number of persons in a group = 250

Number of males $= 250 \times \frac{40}{100} = 100$

Number of females $= 250 \times \frac{60}{100} = 150$

Now, 30 more females join the group

Number of female = 150 + 30 = 180

$\therefore$ Percentage of females in the group, now

$$= \frac{180}{(250+30)} \times 100 = \frac{180}{280} \times 100$$

$$= 64.29\%$$

236. (b) Sumit's income in 2020 = ₹ 21000

Sumit gets an increment of 10% every year.

Hence, the income of Sumit in 2022

$$= 21000 \times \frac{110}{100} \times \frac{110}{100} = ₹\ 25410$$

237. (a) Let the total number of votes = x

According to the question,

$$\frac{x \times 59}{100} - \frac{x \times 41}{100} = 97632$$

$$\Rightarrow \frac{x \times 18}{100} = 97632$$

$$\therefore x = \frac{97632 \times 100}{18} = 542400$$

Hence, the number of votes obtained by the winning candidate $= \frac{542400 \times 59}{100} = 320016$

238. (c) Let the price of an article = ₹ 100

Now, the price of article is raised by ₹ 35.

$\therefore$ New price of article $= 100 \times \frac{135}{100} =$ ₹ 135

$\therefore$ Required reduction $= \frac{(135-100)}{135} \times 100$

$$= \frac{35}{135} \times 100 = \frac{700}{27}\% = 25\frac{25}{27}\%$$

Speedy Method

Required increment percentage

$$= \frac{35}{(100+35)} \times 100\%$$

$$= \frac{35}{135} \times 100\% = 25\frac{25}{27}\%$$

239. (d) Let the total votes casted = 100%

Given, A got 33% of total votes.

$\therefore$ Votes got by $B = 100 - 33 = 67\%$

According to the question,

$67\% - 33\% = 55522 \Rightarrow 34\% = 55522$

$$\Rightarrow 100\% = \frac{55522}{34} \times 100 = 163300$$

The votes got by $B = \frac{67}{100} \times 163300 = 109411$

240. (d) Given, total toys = 75

Toys for boys = 18

$\therefore$ Toys for girls = 75 − 18 = 57

Required percentage $= \frac{57}{75} \times 100$

$$= \frac{57 \times 4}{3} = 76\%$$

241. (d) According to the question,

Winner gets = 11628 votes

Total votes = 20400

So, required percentage $= \frac{11628}{20400} \times 100 = 57\%$

242. (b) Price of electric bike this year

$$= \frac{125000 \times 70}{100} = ₹\ 87500$$

243. (d) Let the sale two years ago be ₹ x.

Then, according to the question,

$$x \times \left(\frac{100+12}{100}\right) \times \left(\frac{100+15}{100}\right) = 128800$$

$$\Rightarrow x \times \frac{112}{100} \times \frac{115}{100} = 128800$$

$$\Rightarrow x = \frac{128800 \times 100 \times 100}{112 \times 115}$$

$\therefore\ x = 100000$

244. (b) Let the salary of man be ₹ x.

Part of salary spent on household expenses = ₹ $\frac{60}{100}x$

Part of salary spent on rent = ₹ $\frac{20}{100}x$

Remaining salary $= x - \frac{60}{100}x - \frac{20}{100}x$

$$= ₹\ \frac{20}{100}x$$

Part of salary donated to trust

$$= \frac{80}{100} \times \frac{20}{100}x = ₹\ \frac{16}{100}x$$

According to the question,

$$\frac{20}{100}x - \frac{16}{100}x = 20000$$

$$\Rightarrow \frac{4}{100}x = 20000 \Rightarrow x = ₹\ 500000$$

Speedy Method

Total saving = 100% – (60 + 20)% = 20%

Now, donated amount $= 20 \times \frac{80}{100} = 16\%$

Now, left money = (20 – 16)% = 4%

Salary of man $= \frac{20000}{4} \times 100 = 500000$

245. (c) Let 100% total votes were polled between two candidates A and B

A —— 100% —— B
90% ———— 10%

(when A gets 90% votes
$\Rightarrow B$ gets (100 – 90) = 10% votes)

Given, winning candidate gets more votes

$$(90\% - 10\%) = 800$$
$$\Rightarrow \quad 80\% = 800$$
$$\Rightarrow \quad 1\% = 10 \text{ votes}$$
$$\therefore \quad 100\% = 1000 \text{ votes}$$

Hence, total number of votes polled = 1000

246. (a) Let total casted votes $= 100x$

$\because$ 4% casted votes were invalid $= 4x$

$\therefore$ Valid votes $= 100x - 4x = 96x$

Given, A got 64% of valid votes

$$\Rightarrow \quad 96x \times \frac{64}{100} = 12288 \Rightarrow x = 200$$

$\therefore$ Total casted votes (64% of total voters)

$$= 100x = 100 \times 200 = 20000$$

$\therefore$ Total number of voters enrolled,

$$100\% = \frac{20000 \times 100}{64} = 31250$$

247. (b) $x = +25\%, y = -16\%$ (decrease)

Increase/decrease % $= x + y + \frac{xy}{100}$

$$= 25 - 16 + \frac{(25)(-16)}{100} = 9 - 4$$

$\therefore$ Increase % = 5%

Hence, net increment is 5%.

248. (c) Given, present population = 8200

Percentage of population increase annually = 5%

Population after 2 yr $= 8200 \times \left(\frac{105}{100}\right)^2$

$$= 9040.5 \approx 9040$$

New population after two year = 9040

249. (a) Let original number be $100x$.

According to the question,

Now number $= 100x \times \left(\frac{100+16}{100}\right) \times \left(\frac{100+20}{100}\right) \times \left(\frac{100-40}{100}\right)$

$$= x \times 83.52$$

$\therefore$ Net percentage change

$$= \frac{100x - 83.52x}{100x} \times 100$$
$$= 16.48\% = 16\frac{12}{25}\%$$

Speedy Method

Increase 16% $= \frac{4}{25} \Rightarrow 25 : 29$

Increase 20% $= \frac{1}{5} \Rightarrow 5 : 6$

Decrease 40% $= \frac{-2}{5} \Rightarrow 5 : 3$

625 : 522

103

Net decrease $= \frac{103}{625} \times 100 = 16\frac{12}{25}\%$

250. (d) It is increased at the rate of 2% per annum during the years 2011 and 2012

$$= 1250000 \times \frac{102}{100} \times \frac{102}{100} = 1300500$$

Then, it is decreased by 1% during the year 2013 $= 1300500 \times \frac{99}{100} = 1287495$

So, the population of the city at the end of 2013 = 1287495

251. (c) Given,

Four-fifth of five-sixth of one-eighth of a certain number is 4365. So, the number is

$$= 4365 \times \frac{8}{1} \times \frac{6}{5} \times \frac{5}{4} = 52380$$

Now, 65% of 52380 is $= 52380 \times \frac{65}{100} = 34047$

252. (a) Let the original number $= x$

According to the question,

$$x \times \frac{(100+8)}{100} \times \frac{(100-3)}{100} = 2619$$
$$\Rightarrow \quad x \times \frac{108}{100} \times \frac{97}{100} = 2619$$
$$\Rightarrow \quad x = \frac{2619 \times 100 \times 100}{108 \times 97}$$
$$\therefore \quad x = 2500$$

Now, 5% of x = 5% of 2500

$$= 2500 \times \frac{5}{100} = 125$$

$\therefore$ Required number = 125

253. (b) Let A's monthly income = 500

A's monthly expenditure $= 500 \times \frac{68}{100} = 340$

A's monthly saving = 500 – 340 = 160

A's increased income $= 500 \times \frac{125}{100} = 625$

A's increased saving $= 160 \times \frac{115}{100} = 184$

A's increased expenditure = 625 – 184 = 441

$\therefore$ Required percentage $= \frac{441 - 340}{340} \times 100$

$$= \frac{101 \times 100}{340} = 29\frac{12}{17}\%$$

254. (a) Let the initial income of the Harsha = ₹ x

and the initial expenditure $= x \times \frac{45}{100} = ₹\frac{45x}{100}$

$\therefore$ Saving $= ₹\left(x - \frac{45x}{100}\right) = ₹\frac{55x}{100}$

Again, when the income is increased 15% and the amount she saved each month remains the same.

Then, $\frac{55x}{100} = \left(x + \frac{x \times 15}{100}\right)$ – New expenditure

$\Rightarrow$ New expenditure $= x \times \frac{115}{100} - x \times \frac{55}{100}$

$$= x \times \frac{60}{100} = ₹\frac{60x}{100}$$

$\therefore$ Increase expenditure %

$$= \frac{\left(\frac{60x}{100} - \frac{45x}{100}\right)}{\left(\frac{45x}{100}\right)} \times 100 = \frac{15}{45} \times 100 = 33.33\%$$

255. (b) Let total salary of Prakash be $100x$.

According to the question,

Expense on children's education + Donation = ₹3038

$$\Rightarrow \quad 27x + 4x = 3038 \Rightarrow 31x = 3038$$
$$\therefore \quad x = 98$$

$\therefore$ Total salary = ₹9800

256. (a) New income $= 45000 \times \frac{122}{100} = ₹ 54900$

New expenditure $= 33000 \times \frac{111}{100} = ₹ 36630$

$\therefore$ New savings = 54900 – 36630

Hence, new savings = ₹ 18270

257. (a) Let the price of rice = ₹ $100x$ and consumption = 100 units

As, Expenditure = Price × Consumption

$\therefore$ Expenditure $= 100x \times 100 = 10000x$

New price $= 100x \times \frac{125}{100} = ₹ 125x$

New expenditure $= 10000x \times \frac{60}{100} = 6000x$

$\therefore$ Consumption $= \frac{6000x}{125x} = 48$ units

$\therefore$ Required percentage $= \frac{100 - 48}{100} \times 100$

$$= 52\%$$

258. (b) Given, $P = 420$

Since, P is 20% more than Q.

$$\therefore \quad Q = P \times \frac{100}{120} = 420 \times \frac{100}{120} = 350$$

Again, Q is 30% less than R.

$$\therefore \quad R = 350 \times \frac{100}{70} \Rightarrow R = 500$$

Hence, required value of R is 500.

259. (a) Let the initial price of fan = ₹100

The new price of fan $= \frac{100 \times 70}{100} = 70$

Similarly, if the initial sales of fan = 100

After increasing 40%

The new sale of fan $= \frac{100 \times 140}{100} = 140$

$\therefore$ Required percentage change

$= \left(\frac{(140 \times 70) - (100 \times 100)}{100 \times 100}\right) \times 100$

$= \left(\frac{9800 - 10000}{10000}\right) \times 100 = \frac{-200}{10000} \times 100 = -2\%$

= 2% decrease (– ve sign shows decrease)

Speedy Method

Let initial revenue = ₹ 100

$\therefore$ Final revenue

$= 100 \times \left(\frac{100-30}{100}\right) \times \left(\frac{100+40}{100}\right) = ₹\,98$

Percentage decrease in revenue

$= \frac{100 - 98}{100} \times 100 = 2\%$

260. (c) Let the price of 8 tables = ₹ x

Then price of 15 chairs $= x + \frac{20}{100}x = ₹\,\frac{6x}{5}$

Price of 2 tables = ₹2400

Price of 8 tables = ₹(4 × 2400) = ₹9600

$\therefore \quad x = 9600$

$\therefore$ Price of 15 chairs $= \frac{6x}{5} = \frac{6 \times 9600}{5} = ₹\,11520$

261. (c) Let the total marks in the exam be 'x'.

So, passing marks = 20% of x + 25

Again, also, passing marks = 50% of x – 20

$\therefore$ 20% of x + 25 = 50% of x – 20

$\Rightarrow$ 30% of $x = 45 \Rightarrow \frac{30}{100} \times x = 45 \Rightarrow x = 150$

Passing marks for the exam

$= 20\% \text{ of } x + 25 = \frac{20}{100} \times 150 + 25 = 55$

Speedy Method

20% + 25 = 50% – 20

30% = 45

100% = 150

Passing marks $= 150 \times \frac{20}{100} + 25$

= 30 + 25 = 55

262. (d) Let, total number of votes be x.

Number of votes Party A got $= \frac{30}{100} \times x = 0.3x$

Number of votes Party B got $= \frac{25}{100} \times x = 0.25x$

Number of votes Party C got

$= x - (0.3x + 0.25x) = 0.45x$

According to the question,

$0.45x = 9000 + 0.3x \Rightarrow 0.15x = 9000$

$\Rightarrow \quad x = \frac{9000}{0.15} = 60000$

Hence, number of votes Party B got

$= 0.25x = 0.25 \times 60000 = 15000$

263. (b) According to the question,

$\frac{20}{100} \times P + \frac{40}{100} \times Q = \frac{80}{100} \times Q$

$\Rightarrow \quad \frac{P}{5} + \frac{2}{5}Q = \frac{4}{5}Q \Rightarrow \frac{P}{5} = \frac{2}{5}Q$

$\Rightarrow \quad P = 2Q$

$\therefore$ Required % $= \frac{P}{Q} \times 100 = \frac{2Q}{Q} \times 100 = 200\%$

264. (a) Let the expenses of the family on wheat, vegetables and oil are $12x$, $8x$ and $5x$, respectively.

Total expenses = $12x + 8x + 5x = 25x$

After increase in prices,

Total expenses = 150% of $12x$ + 125% of $8x$ + 140% of $5x$ = $18x + 10x + 7x = 35x$

$\therefore$ Required increased percentage

$= \frac{35x - 25x}{25x} \times 100 = \frac{10x}{25x} \times 100 = 40\%$

265. (a) Let the income of that month = ₹x

According to the question,

8% of x = 1200

$\therefore \quad x = \frac{1200 \times 100}{8} = 15000$

Hence, income of monthly = ₹ 15000

266. (c) Let Bhanu's monthly salary = ₹x

Then, (100 – 20 – 10 – 14 – 18)% of x = 1520

$\Rightarrow$ 38% of x = 1520

$\Rightarrow \quad x = \frac{1520 \times 100}{38} = ₹\,4000$

267. (a) The value of machine after 2 yr

$= 35000\left(1 - \frac{10}{100}\right)^2$

$= 35000 \times \frac{9}{10} \times \frac{9}{10} = ₹\,28350$

268. (c) Here, $x_1 = +10\%$, $x_2 = -20\%$

Net increase or decrease $= x_1 + x_2 + \frac{x_1 x_2}{100}$

$= 10 - 20 - \frac{200}{100} = 10 - 20 - 2 = 10 - 22$

= – 12%

$\therefore$ There is 12% decrease.

269. (a) Number of admissions after 3 yr

$= 2400 \times \frac{105}{100} \times \frac{105}{100} \times \frac{105}{100} = 2778.3 \approx 2778$

270. (d) Let the salary of Sunita be ₹ x.

$\therefore$ 24% of Reena's salary = 38% of x

$\Rightarrow$ Reena's salary $= \frac{38}{24}$ of $x = \frac{19x}{12}$

and Veena's salary $= \frac{2}{3}$ of (Reena + Sunita)'s salary

$\Rightarrow \quad 62000 = \frac{2}{3} \text{ of } \left(\frac{19x}{12} + x\right)$

$\Rightarrow \quad 62000 = \frac{2}{3} \times \frac{31x}{12}$

$\therefore \quad x = \frac{62000 \times 18}{31} = ₹\,36000$

Hence, Sunita's salary is ₹ 36000.

271. (d) Let the income of the person be ₹ x.

Then, Saving = 25% of $x = 0.25x$

$\therefore$ Expenditure $= x - 0.25x = ₹\,0.75x$

Now, new income = 120% of x = ₹ $1.2x$

and new saving = old saving = ₹ $0.25x$

$\therefore$ New expenditure $= 12x - 0.25x = ₹\,0.95x$

$\therefore$ Percentage increase in expenditure

$= \frac{(0.95x - 0.75x)}{0.75x} \times 100 = 26\frac{2}{3}\%$

Hence, increased percentage in expenditure is $26\frac{2}{3}\%$.

Speedy Method

Let income be 100.

Saving + Expenditure = Income

25 + 75 = 100

25 + 95 = 120

$\therefore$ Percentage change in expenditure

$= \frac{95 - 75}{75} \times 100 = 26\frac{2}{3}\%$

272. (b) Given, A = 150% of $B = 1.5B$,

and B = 40% of $C = 0.4C$

Now, $\quad A + B + C = 20$

$\Rightarrow 1.5 \times 0.4C + 0.4C + C = 20$

$\Rightarrow 2C = 20 \Rightarrow C = \frac{20}{2} = 10$

$\therefore \quad B = 0.4C = 0.4 \times 10 = 4$

and $A = 1.5\,B = 1.5 \times 4 = 6$

Now, the value of $2B + 3C - 4A$

$= 2 \times 4 + 3 \times 10 - 4 \times 6$

$= 8 + 30 - 24 = 14$

273. (a) Let the number be x.

According to the question,

$x - \frac{3}{5}x = 274 \Rightarrow \frac{5x - 3x}{5} = 274$

$\Rightarrow \quad 2x = 1370 \Rightarrow x = 685$

$\therefore \quad 20\% \text{ of } x = \frac{20}{100} \times 685 = 137$

274. (b) Given, 25% of 480 + 30% of 500 + x% of 90 = 35% of 900

$\Rightarrow \quad 120 + 150 + \frac{9x}{10} = 315 \Rightarrow \frac{9x}{10} = 45$

$\therefore \quad x = 50$

Hence, required value of x is 50.

275. (d) Let the fraction be $\frac{x}{y}$.

According to the question,

$\frac{x \times \frac{112}{100}}{y \times \frac{92}{100}} = \frac{56}{69}$

$\frac{x \times 112}{y \times 92} = \frac{56}{69}$

$\frac{x}{y} = \frac{56}{69} \times \frac{92}{112}$

$\frac{x}{y} = \frac{2}{3}$

276. (c) Aryan's height after 2 yr

$= 120 \times \frac{115}{100} \times \frac{116}{100} = 160.08$ cm

277. (d) Let total votes be 100 %.

$\therefore$ Shayama received votes

$= 100 - (60 + 15) = 25\ \%$

278. (c) Let his original salary be ₹ 100.

$$100 \xrightarrow[-20]{-20\%} 80 \xrightarrow[+20]{?} 100$$

$\Rightarrow$ Required percentage $= \frac{20}{80} \times 100 = 25\%$

279. (d) Let Arvind's income = 100

Mohan's income = 80

$\therefore$ Required percentage

$$= \frac{100 - 80}{80} \times 100 = \frac{20}{80} \times 100 = 25\%$$

280. (a) Let initial price be ₹ 100.

According to the question,

Final price

$$= 100 \times \left(\frac{100 + 10}{100}\right) \times \left(\frac{100 + 20}{100}\right)\left(\frac{100 - 25}{100}\right)$$

$= ₹\ 99$

Net percentage change = 1% decrease

281. (d) Let Man's working hours per day = 100

and wages per hour = ₹ 100

New working hours per day = 110

and wages per hour = ₹ 105

Required percentage increase

$$= \frac{110 \times 105 - 100 \times 100}{100 \times 100} \times 100$$

$$= \frac{11550 - 10000}{100} = 15.50\%$$

Speedy Method

Net increased in earning

$$= \left(10 + 5 + \frac{10 \times 5}{100}\right)\% = (15 + 0.5\%) = 15.5\%$$

282. (a) Net effect on revenue

$$= -40 + 80 + \frac{(-40) \times 80}{100}$$

$= 40 - 32 = 8\ \%$ increase

283. (a) Let Income be 100.

$\therefore$ Expenditure $= 100 - 75 = 25$

$25 \to ₹\ 37500$

Saving (75) $\to$ ₹ 112500

284. (a) Let Initial price be ₹ 100.

Final price $= 100 \times \frac{120}{100} \times \frac{125}{100} = ₹150$

Percentage reduction $= \frac{50}{150} \times 100 = 33\frac{1}{3}\%$

285. (c) Let Bharti got x% votes and Manya got y% votes.

According to the question,

$x + y = 100$ ...(i)

$x - y = 16$ ...(ii)

From Eq. (i) and Eq. (ii), we get

$y = 42\%$

$\because$ Total votes (100%) $\to$ 750

$\therefore$ Manya got (42%) $\to$ 315

286. (b) Net effect on sale

$$= \left(-15 + 10 + \frac{(-15) \times 10}{100}\right)\%$$

$= (-5 - 1.50)\% = 6.50\%$ decrease

287. (b) Current value of investment

$$= 15000 \times \frac{115}{100} \times \frac{90}{100} = ₹\ 15525$$

288. (d) Final amount

$$= 5000 \times \frac{115}{100} \times \frac{120}{100} \times \frac{90}{100}$$

$= ₹\ 6210$

289. (b)

	Boys	:	Girls
Total	5	:	7
Who get scholarship	$5 \times \frac{40}{100} = 2$	:	$7 \times \frac{50}{100} = 3.5$
Who didn't get scholarship	3	:	3.5

$\therefore$ Required Percentage $= \frac{3 + 3.5}{5 + 7} \times 100$

$$= \frac{6.5}{12} \times 100 = 54\frac{1}{6}\%$$

290. (b) Let the third number be 100.

First number = 106.25

Second number = 125

Now, Required Percentage

$$= \frac{106.25}{125} \times 100 = 85\%$$

291. (a) Let the price at the beginning of 2016 be ₹ x.

According to the question,

$$x \times \frac{105}{100} \times \frac{95}{100} = 47880$$

$$x = \frac{47880 \times 100 \times 100}{105 \times 95}$$

$x = ₹\ 48000$

292. (a) The final price of computer

$$= 50000 \times \frac{110}{100} \times \frac{95}{100} \times \frac{108}{100}$$

$= ₹\ 56430$

293. (c) Let the contestants got the votes are $8x$, $7x$ and $5x$ respectively.

$\therefore$ $7x = 4725$

$\Rightarrow$ $x = 675$

Thus, total valid votes $= (8x + 7x + 5x)$

$= 20 \times 675 = 13500$

294. (b) Let the monthly salary of family be $100x$.

According to the question,

20% spends on house rent $= \frac{100x \times 20}{100} = 20x$

$\therefore$ Remaining amount $= 100x - 20x = 80x$

50% remaining amount spend on household and 20% on children education

$$= \frac{80x \times 70}{100} = 56x$$

$\therefore$ Remaining amount $= 80x - 56x = 24x$

Savings of family = 6600

$\Rightarrow$ $24x = 6600 \Rightarrow x = ₹\ 275$

$\therefore$ Monthly salary of family $= 100x = 100 \times 275$

$= ₹\ 27500$

Speedy Method

Let income be $100x$ units.

Saving

$$= 100x \times \left(\frac{100 - 20}{100}\right) \times \left(\frac{100 - (20 + 50)}{100}\right)$$

$$= 100x \times \frac{80}{100} \times \frac{30}{100} = 24x$$

$\therefore$ Saving $= 24x = ₹\ 6600$

$\therefore$ $x = ₹\ 275$

$\therefore$ Income $= 100x = ₹\ 27500$

295. (a) Let original price of bed be ₹ $100x$.

So, price after increment of 32% = ₹ 132 x

and price after reduction of 20%

$$= 132x \times \frac{80}{100} = ₹\ 105.6x$$

$\therefore$ Net percentage change $= \left(\frac{105.6x - 100x}{100x}\right)$

$$= \frac{5.6x}{100x} \times 100 = 5.6\%$$

296. (d) Let the original income be $100x$.

First year increment = 105% of $100x = 105x$

Second year increment

$= 102\%$ of $105x = 107.1x$

Percentage increase in income

$$= \frac{107.1x - 100x}{100x} \times 100 = 7.1\%$$

Speedy Method

Given, 1st increment = 5%

2nd increment = 2%

$\therefore$ Net percentage increase $= 5 + 2 + \frac{5 \times 2}{100}$

$= 7 + 0.1 = 7.1\%$

297. (b) Let the income in year 1997 be $100x$.

According to the question,

$\therefore$ Income of company in year 1999

$$= 100x \times \frac{125}{100} \times \frac{125}{100} = 156.25x$$

$\Rightarrow$ $156.25x = 2664000$

$\Rightarrow$ $x = ₹\ 17049.6$

$\therefore$ Income in year 1997

$= 100x = 100\ (17049.6) = ₹\ 1704960$

298. (b) Let daily income = ₹ x

Given, 20% of $x = 250$

$\Rightarrow$ $\frac{20x}{100} = 250 \Rightarrow x = \frac{250 \times 100}{20} = ₹\ 1250$

$\therefore$ Daily income = ₹ 1250

299. (a) Strength of the school in the year 2017

$= 3000 \times \dfrac{(100+20)}{100} \times \dfrac{(100-20)}{100} \times \dfrac{(100+20)}{100}$

$= \dfrac{3000 \times 120 \times 80 \times 120}{100 \times 100 \times 100} = 3456$

The percentage of increase in strength

$= \dfrac{3456 - 3000}{3000} \times 100\% = 15.2\%$

300. (d) Let income be ₹$100x$.

$\therefore$ Saving $= 100x \times \dfrac{13}{100} = 13x$

$\therefore$ Expenditure $= 100x - 13x = 87x$

Expenditure $= 87x =$ ₹ 5220

$\Rightarrow \quad x = 60$

$\therefore$ Saving $= 13x =$ ₹ 780

301. (c) Let the income of $Y = 100x$

Income of X is 12% more than that of $Y = 112x$

So, Y's income less than that of

$= \dfrac{112x - 100x}{112} \times 100 = \dfrac{12x}{112} \times 100 = 10\dfrac{5}{7}\%$

302. (c) According to the question,

6% of A + 4% of $B = \dfrac{2}{5} \times$ (7% of A + 11% of B)

$\Rightarrow 6 \times A + 4 \times B = \dfrac{2}{5} \times (7 \times A + 11 \times B)$

$\Rightarrow 5(6A + 4B) = 2(7A + 11B)$

$\Rightarrow 30A + 20B = 14A + 22B \Rightarrow 16A = 2B$

So, $A : B = 1 : 8$

303. (c) Given, first number is 20% less than the third number and ratio of second to the third number is 7 : 10.

$[\text{I} = 10 \times \dfrac{80}{100} = 8]$

So, ratio = I : II : III

8 : 7 : 10

Average of first and third number

$= \dfrac{10 + 8}{2} = 9$

Per cent more than second number

$= \dfrac{9 - 7}{7} \times 100 = \dfrac{2}{7} \times 100 = 28\dfrac{4}{7}\%$

304. (c) According to the question,

$Q = 200 \times \dfrac{115}{100} \times \dfrac{120}{100} = 2 \times 138 = 276$

305. (b) Let the total number of votes be x.

Number of valid votes $= x \times \dfrac{98}{100}$

According to the question,

$x \times \dfrac{98}{100} \times \dfrac{60}{100} = 2940 \Rightarrow x = \dfrac{2940 \times 100 \times 100}{98 \times 60}$

$= 5000$

306. (c) Let original price be x.

According to the question,

15% of $x = 27$

$\Rightarrow \dfrac{15}{100} \times x = 27 \Rightarrow x = \dfrac{27}{15} \times 100 =$ ₹ 180

$\therefore$ Increased price = 180 + 27 = ₹ 207

307. (b) According to the question,

$\therefore$ Required amount = 60% of [16000 − (30% + 20%) of 16000]

= 60% of [16000 − 50% of 16000]

= 60% of [16000 − 8000]

= 60% of 8000 $= \dfrac{60}{100} \times 8000 =$ ₹ 4800

308. (d) Let the salary of Anjali be ₹ x.

According to the question,

60% of 45% of $x = 11475$

$\Rightarrow \quad x = 11475 \times \dfrac{100}{60} \times \dfrac{100}{45}$

$x =$ ₹ 42500

309. (d) Given, E% of 12.5% of 480 = 72

$\Rightarrow \dfrac{E}{100} \times \dfrac{12.5}{100} \times 480 = 72$

$\Rightarrow \quad E = \dfrac{72 \times 100 \times 100}{125 \times 48} = 120$

310. (d) Let the number of male and female employees are x and y, respectively.

Given, $\quad x + y = 900 \quad$ ...(i)

$x + (100 - 10)\%$ of $y = (100 - 8)\%$ of $x + y$

$\Rightarrow \quad x + 0.9y = 0.92x + y$

$\Rightarrow \quad 0.08x = 0.1y$

$\Rightarrow \quad \dfrac{x}{y} = \dfrac{5}{4} \Rightarrow x = \dfrac{900 \times 5}{9} = 500$

311. (a) Current population (P) = 12000

Rate of increase (r) = 10 % p.a.

Time (n) = 3 yr

Population after 3 yr $= P\left(1 + \dfrac{r}{100}\right)^n$

$= 12000\left(1 + \dfrac{10}{100}\right)^3$

$= 12000 \times \dfrac{11}{10} \times \dfrac{11}{10} \times \dfrac{11}{10} = 15972$

312. (b) $600 - A = \dfrac{65}{100}$ of 200

$\Rightarrow \quad 600 - A = 130$

$\Rightarrow \quad A = 600 - 130 \Rightarrow A = 470$

313. (d) Vowels O, O, A (3 letters)

Percentage of vowels $= \dfrac{3}{9} \times 100\%$

= 33.33%

Consonants C, N, S, N, N, T (6 letters)

Percentage of consonants $= \dfrac{6}{9} \times 100\%$

= 66.66%

$\therefore$ Required percentage

$= \dfrac{(66.66 - 33.33)}{66.66} \times 100\% = 50\%$

314. (c) Required percentage

$= \dfrac{(150 - 125)}{150} \times 100 = 16.67\%$

315. (d) Let the value of A_2 be x.

Then, the value of $A_1 = 20x$.

$\therefore$ Required percentage $= \left[\dfrac{20x - x}{20x}\right] \times 100$

$= \dfrac{19x}{20x} \times 100 = 95\%$

316. (a) Let income of $N =$ ₹100

According to the question,

Income of $M = 100 \times \dfrac{120}{100} =$ ₹120

and income of $L = 120 \times \dfrac{130}{100} =$ ₹156

$\therefore$ Required percentage $= \dfrac{156 - 100}{156} \times 100$

$\approx 36\%$

317. (c) According to the question,

A% of $A = 9604$

$\dfrac{A}{100} \times A = 9604 \Rightarrow A^2 = 9604 \times 100$

$\Rightarrow \quad A = 98 \times 10 \Rightarrow A = 980$

318. (a) Given that, successively decrease of number by 10%, 15% and 56%.

Let the number be n.

According to the question,

$n \times \dfrac{90}{100} \times \dfrac{85}{100} \times \dfrac{44}{100} = 20196$

$\Rightarrow \quad n \times \dfrac{18 \times 17 \times 11}{100 \times 100} = 20196$

$\Rightarrow \quad n = \dfrac{20196 \times 100 \times 100}{18 \times 17 \times 11}$

$\Rightarrow \quad n = \dfrac{20196 \times 10000}{3366} \Rightarrow n = 60000$

Speedy Method

Assumed number = 100

100 → (−10%) → 90 → (−15%) → 76.5 → (−56%) → 33.66

$\therefore$ 33.66 → 20196

1 → 600

$\therefore$ 100 → 60000

319. (c) Given that, total students = 40

$\because$ Total boys = 40 − 30 = 10

$\therefore$ Percentage of boys $= \dfrac{\text{Total boys}}{\text{Total students}} \times 100$

$= \dfrac{10}{40} \times 100 = 25\%$

320. (b) The present value of car = ₹75000

depreciates rate % = 50% per annum

So, the value of car 3 yr ago

$= 75000 \times \dfrac{100}{(100-50)} \times \dfrac{100}{(100-50)} \times \dfrac{100}{(100-50)}$

$= \dfrac{75000 \times 1000000}{50 \times 50 \times 50} =$ ₹ 600000

321. (c) Given that, man spends 58% of his income.

Let the income of man = ₹ 100

$\therefore$ Saving of man = 100 − 58 = ₹ 42

Now, according to the question,

Income increase by 30%.

$\therefore$ New income of man

$= 100 + \frac{100 \times 30}{100} = 100 + 30 = 130$

Expenditure also increased

$= 58 + \frac{58 \times 25}{100} = 58 + 14.5 = 72.5$

$\therefore$ New saving of man = 130 − 72.5 = 57.5

So, increase in saving % $= \left(\frac{57.5 - 42}{42}\right) \times 100$

$= \frac{15.5}{42} \times 100 = 36.9\%$

322. (b) Let the total students in the class = x

According to the question,

$x - \frac{x \times 38}{100} = 31 \Rightarrow x \times \left(\frac{100 - 38}{100}\right) = 31$

$\Rightarrow x \times \frac{62}{100} = 31 \Rightarrow x = \frac{100 \times 31}{62} = 50$

$\therefore$ Number of boys in the class = 50 − 31 = 19

323. (c) Initial value of car = 150000

and depreciation each year = 20%

$\therefore$ Depreciation after 2 yr

$= 150000 \times \frac{80}{100} \times \frac{80}{100} = 96000$

The depreciated value of car after 2 yr is 96000.

324. (a) According to the question,

Let Monil's salary is ₹ 100x.

And decrease by 18%

So, Monil's salary $= 100x \times \frac{82}{100} = 82x$

Now, $\frac{18x}{82x} \times 100 = 21.95\% \approx 22\%$

Hence, 22% monthly income should increase.

325. (c) Let value of Q be 100.

So, $P = 100 \times (100 - 15)\% = 100 \times 85\%$

$\therefore P = 85$

$\therefore$ Required percentage $= \frac{(100 - 85)}{85} \times 100$

$= \frac{15}{85} \times 100 = 17.64\%$

326. (b) Let maximum marks be x.

According to the question,

21% of x + 25 = 46% of x + 5

$\Rightarrow$ 46% of x − 21% of x = 25 − 5

$\Rightarrow$ 25% of x = 20 $\Rightarrow x \times \frac{25}{100} = 20$

$\Rightarrow x = \frac{20 \times 100}{25} \therefore x = 80$

$\therefore$ Maximum marks of the exam is 80.

327. (d) Let the sum be x.

$x \times (100 - 10)\% \times (100 - 70)\% = 1188$

$\Rightarrow x \times 90\% \times 30\% = 1188$

$\Rightarrow x = \frac{1188 \times 100 \times 100}{90 \times 30} \Rightarrow x = 4400$

328. (d) The value of 7.14% of 66.67% of 21.84

$= 21.84 \times \frac{2}{3} \times \frac{1}{14} = 1.04$

329. (b) Let original price of an article be 100x and original consumption be 100y units.

$\therefore$ Total revenue = (100x) (100y) = 10000xy

New revenue after change in tax and consumption = (83x) (117y) = 9711xy

$\therefore$ Required percentage $= \frac{289xy}{10000xy} \times 100$

= 2.89% decrease

> **Speedy Method**
>
> Let change in revenue
>
> $x + y + \frac{xy}{100} = 17 - 17 - \frac{17 \times 17}{100} = -2.89\%$
>
> i.e. 2.89% decrease

330. (b) Let the total number of students in the class = x

and number of girls = 54

According to the question,

$\left(\frac{100 - 40}{100}\right) \times x = 54$

$\Rightarrow \frac{60}{100} x = 54 \Rightarrow x = \frac{100 \times 54}{60}$

$\Rightarrow x = 90$

So, number of boys is the class = 90 − 54 = 36

> **Speedy Method**
>
> According to the question,
>
> 60% → 54
>
> 10% → 9
>
> ⇒ 40% → 4 × 9 = 36

331. (d) According to the question,

Marks got by Y = 480

$\therefore$ Marks got by $X = \frac{140}{100} \times 480 = 672$

Let the marks scored by Z is x. Then,

$\frac{80x}{100} = 672 \Rightarrow x = \frac{672 \times 100}{80}$

$\therefore x = 840$

332. (c) According to the question,

$P\%$ of $P = 225$

$\Rightarrow \frac{P}{100} \times P = 225 \Rightarrow P^2 = 22500$

333. (a) According to the question,

$35\% \times P = 60\% \times Q \Rightarrow \frac{P}{Q} = \frac{60}{35} = \frac{12}{7}$

And $Q = \left(\frac{Z}{3}\right)\%$ of $P \Rightarrow \frac{Q}{P} = \frac{Z}{3 \times 100}$

$\Rightarrow \frac{7}{12} = \frac{Z}{3} \times \frac{1}{100} \Rightarrow Z = \frac{7 \times 3 \times 100}{12}$

$\therefore Z = 175$

334. (c) Let the price of the 1 kg wheat = 100x

⇒ The new price of 1 kg wheat = 150x

According to the question,

$150x - 100x = 25$

$\Rightarrow 50x = 25 \Rightarrow x = \frac{25}{50} \Rightarrow x = 0.5$

$\therefore$ New price of the wheat = 150 × 0.5 = ₹ 75

> **Speedy Method**
>
> Let original price = 100%
>
> ∴ New price = 150%
>
> According to the question,
>
> 50% → 25
>
> 10% → 5
>
> 150% → 75

335. (c) Let the original population of the city = 100

Given, percentage increase in population first year = 5%

After first year = (100 + 5) = 105

and second year = 8%

In second year population of the city

$= 105 \times \frac{108}{100} = 113.4$

$\therefore$ Required increase % = 113.4 − 100 = 13.4%

> **Speedy Method**
>
> $a = +5\%, b = +8\%$
>
> ∴ The overall increase percentage
>
> $= \left[a + b + \frac{ab}{100}\right]\% = \left[5 + 8 + \left(\frac{5 \times 8}{100}\right)\right]\%$
>
> = [13 + 0.40]% = 13.40%

336. (c) Given, town A population in 2022 = 62500

After one year town A population = 75000

$\therefore$ Increase % $= \left[\frac{(75000 - 62500)}{62500}\right] \times 100 = 20\%$

337. (b) Given, original price of watch = ₹ 500

After increased of 10%

= 500 × 110 / 100 = ₹ 550

and decreased by 15%

= 550 × 85 / 100 = ₹ 467.50

Hence, final price of watch = ₹ 467.50

> **Speedy Method**
>
> Original price
>
> 500 —(+10%)→ 550 —(−15%)→ 467.50

338. (d) Let the number be x.

According to the question,

$(27/100)x - (13/100)x = 56$

$\Rightarrow \frac{14x}{100} = 56$

$\Rightarrow x = 400$

339. (d) Let the initial value of $A = x$

When value increased by 20%.

A's value $= x + \left(\frac{x \times 20}{100}\right) = \frac{120x}{100}$

After then it is decreased by 30%, then A's value

$= \left(\frac{120}{100}x\right) - \left(\frac{120x}{100} \times \frac{30}{100}\right)$

$$= \frac{120}{100}x \times \frac{70}{100} = \frac{84x}{100}$$

$\therefore$ Required % $= \frac{84x/100}{x} \times 100 = 84\%$

Speedy Method

Total increase/decrease %

$= +20 - 30 + \frac{20 \times (-30)}{100}$

$= 20 - 30 - 6 = -16\%$ (decrease)

from 100% i.e. 84% left

$\therefore$ Value of new A is 84% of initial value of A.

340. (c) Let the V's mark $= x$

U's mark $= x \times \frac{105}{100} = \frac{105}{100}x$

$$\therefore \text{Required } \% = \frac{\left(\frac{105}{100}x - x\right)}{\left(\frac{105}{100}x\right)} \times 100$$

$$= \frac{\frac{5x}{100}}{\frac{105x}{100}} \times 100 = \frac{5}{105} \times 100 = 4.7\%$$

Speedy Method

Percentage mark of V less than U

$= [(105 - 100)/105] \times 100 = 4.7\%$

341. (a) Given, 64% of 512 + 46% of 215

$= 64 \times \frac{512}{100} + 46 \times \frac{215}{100}$

$= 327.68 + 98.90 = 426.58$

342. (d) Let the price of a movie ticket = ₹100 and number of audience = 100

$\therefore$ Total revenue $= 100 \times 100 =$ ₹ 10000

Now, new price of movie ticket

$= 100 \times \frac{118}{100} =$ ₹ 118

and new number of audience

$= 100 \times \frac{75}{100} = 75$

$\therefore$ New revenue $= 118 \times 75 =$ ₹ 8850

So, required effect on revenue

$= \frac{8850 - 10000}{10000} \times 100$

$= -\frac{1150}{100} = -11.50\%$

Decreased by 11.50%

Speedy Method

Ticket price increased by 18% and audience reduce by 25%.

$\therefore$ Equivalent effect on revenue

$= x + y + \frac{xy}{100} = 18 - 25 + \frac{18 \times (-25)}{100}$

$= -7 - \frac{25 \times 18}{100} = -7 - 4.5 = -11.5$

(–ve) sign means decrease of 11.5% in revenue.

343. (b) Original price of dress = ₹ 800

Reduced price of dress = ₹ 720

Percentage is decrease $= \frac{800 - 720}{800} \times 100$

$= \frac{80}{800} \times 100 = 10\%$

344. (a) Let the number be x.

According to the question,

$x \times \frac{25}{100} \times \frac{20}{100} = 250$

$x = \frac{250 \times 100 \times 100}{25 \times 20}$

$\Rightarrow \quad x = 5000$

$\therefore \quad$ 35% of 5000 $= 5000 \times \frac{35}{100} = 1750$

345. (b) Let the maximum marks in the test be x.

$\therefore$ 75% of x = 60% of x + 30

$\Rightarrow \frac{75x}{100} = \frac{60x}{100} + 30 \Rightarrow \frac{75x}{100} - \frac{60x}{100} = 30$

$\Rightarrow \frac{75x - 60x}{100} = 30 \Rightarrow 15x = 3000$

$\therefore \quad x = \frac{3000}{15} = 200$

Speedy Method

75% – 60% = 30 marks

$\Rightarrow \quad 15\% = 30 \Rightarrow 1\% = \frac{30}{15} = 2$

$\therefore \quad$ 100% = 200 marks

Hence, maximum marks of the test is 200.

346. (d) $\because$ 93% student passed, it means 7% student failed.

But, 9275 student failed (given)

$7\% = 9275 \Rightarrow 1\% = \frac{9275}{7} = 1325$

$\therefore \quad 100\% = 1325 \times 100 = 132500$

So, total number of students = 132500.

347. (b) Let the population of village in the beginning be x, then

$x\left(1 + \frac{5}{100}\right)\left(1 - \frac{5}{100}\right) = 9975$

$\Rightarrow \quad x \times \frac{21}{20} \times \frac{19}{20} = 9975$

$\Rightarrow \quad x = \frac{9975 \times 20 \times 20}{21 \times 19} \Rightarrow x = 10000$

348. (a) Number of votes got by the candidate = 285000

$\therefore$ Total number of valid votes

$= 285000 \times \frac{100}{75} = 380000$

5% are invalid, so total number of votes casted

$= 380000 \times \frac{100}{95} = 400000$

Only 80% of voter cast their votes, total number of voters enrolled for the election

$= 400000 \times \frac{100}{80} = 500000$

349. (d) Present population of village = 68000

Population of village after 3 yr

$= 68000\left(1 + \frac{5}{10}\right)\left(1 - \frac{10}{100}\right)\left(1 - \frac{10}{100}\right)$

$= 68000 \times \frac{105}{100} \times \frac{90}{100} \times \frac{90}{100} = 57834$

350. (a) Let, number $= a$

According to the question,

$\frac{a \times 40}{100} - 40 = 40 \Rightarrow \frac{a \times 40}{100} = 80$

$\Rightarrow a = \frac{80 \times 100}{40} \Rightarrow a = 200$

Hence, required number is 200.

351. (c) Let original number $= a$

According to the question,

$\frac{110a}{100} - \frac{94.5a}{100} = 34.1 \Rightarrow 15.5a = 3410$

$\therefore \quad a = 220$

352. (b) According to the question,

$y \times \frac{x}{100} = 90 \times \frac{2}{3}$

$\Rightarrow \quad y \times \frac{x}{100} = 60 \Rightarrow xy = 6000$

353. (c) Current value of motorbike = ₹ 100000

Time = 36 months $= \frac{36}{12} = 3$ yr

Value of the motorbike after 3 yr

$= 100000 \times \frac{90}{100} \times \frac{90}{100} \times \frac{90}{100} =$ ₹72900

354. (c) Let the income of government servant = ₹ 1000

His spends $= 1000 \times \frac{76}{100} =$ ₹ 760

His saving = 1000 – 760 = ₹ 240

After increment,

His new income $= 1000 \times \frac{114}{100} =$ ₹ 1140

His new expenditure $= 760 \times \frac{110}{100} =$ ₹ 836

His new saving = ₹ (1140 – 836) = ₹ 304

Saving increase's = ₹ (304 – 240) = ₹ 64

$\therefore$ Required percentage increase

$= \frac{64}{240} \times 100 = 26.67\%$

355. (a) Value of the house after 3 yr

$= 4640000 \times \frac{95}{100} \times \frac{95}{100} \times \frac{95}{100} = 3978220$

$\therefore$ So, the value of house after 3 yr will 3978220

.

356. (c) Given, the value of painting is ₹ 140000

After rising the price the value is ₹ 182000.

Percent increase

$= \frac{\text{Final price} - \text{Initial price}}{\text{Initial price}} \times 100$

$= \frac{182000 - 140000}{140000} \times 100$

$= \frac{42000}{140000} \times 100 = 30\%$

357. (b) Let the original price of tea = ₹ 100

Price of tea increased by 20%

$= 100 \times \frac{120}{100} =$ ₹ 120

Increase in price = 120 − 100 = ₹ 20

Tea cost of ₹ 20 is to decreased out of the increased price of ₹ 120.

Percentage decrease $= \frac{20}{120} \times 100 = \frac{50}{3}\%$

∴ The consumption of tea be diminished by $16\frac{2}{3}\%$.

Speedy Method

$20\% = \frac{1}{5}$

∴ Price ⇒ 5 : 6

Consumption ⇒ 6 : 5

[∵ Expenditure remain same]

∴ Required percentage

$= \frac{6-5}{6} \times 100 = 16\frac{2}{3}\%$

358. (b) Given, total voters in city = 12000

30% voted for $A = 12000 \times \frac{30}{100} = 3600$

25% voted for $B = 12000 \times \frac{25}{100} = 3000$

40% voted for $C = 12000 \times \frac{40}{100} = 4800$

Number of voter that did not vote = Total number of voters − Number of voters who gave their vote

$= 12000 - (3600 + 3000 + 4800)$

$= 12000 - 11400 = 600$

∴ 600 voters does not vote to anyone.

Speedy Method

Voters did not vote

$= 12000 \times \frac{[100 - (25 + 30 + 40)]}{100}$

$= 12000 \times \frac{5}{100} = 600$

359. (b) Population given in the year 2010 = 256080000.

Population increased by 10% by the year 2020.

$= 256080000 \left(1 + \frac{10}{100}\right)$

$= 256080000 \times \frac{110}{100} = 281688000$

360. (c) Given, the present population of a village = 50000

Due to migration to cities, the population decreases at the rate of 5% every year.

So, after 2 yr the population

$= 50000 \times \frac{95}{100} \times \frac{95}{100} = 45125$

∴ So, population after two years = 45125

361. (d) The price of a mobile first successively decreases by 5% and 2%.

$= 100 \times \left[1 - \frac{r_1}{100}\right]\left[1 - \frac{r_2}{100}\right]$

$= 100 \times \left[1 - \frac{5}{100}\right]\left[1 - \frac{2}{100}\right]$

$= 100 \times \frac{95}{100} \times \frac{98}{100} = 93.1\%$

After that the price is increased by successively by 10% and 20%.

$= 93.1 \times \left[1 + \frac{r_1}{100}\right]\left[1 + \frac{r_2}{100}\right]$

$= 93.1 \times \left[1 + \frac{10}{100}\right]\left[1 + \frac{20}{100}\right]$

$= 93.1 \times \frac{110}{100} \times \frac{120}{100} = 122.892 = 22\frac{223}{250}\%$

Speedy Method

Let initial price = 100

∴ Final price $= 100 \times \left(\frac{100-5}{100}\right) \times \left(\frac{100-2}{100}\right) \times \left(\frac{100+10}{100}\right) \times \left(\frac{100+20}{100}\right)$

$= 100 \times \frac{95}{100} \times \frac{98}{100} \times \frac{110}{100} \times \frac{120}{100} = 122\frac{223}{250}$

∴ Change in price $= 122\frac{223}{250} - 100$

$= 22\frac{223}{250}\%$

362. (d) Given, birth rate as per ten thousand = 450

Corresponding death rate is 120 per ten thousand.

Net growth on 10000 = 450 − 120 = 330

Hence, net growth on 10000

$= \frac{330}{10000} \times 100 = 3.3\%$

363. (a) Given, ratio of weights = 5 : 3

Initial total weight $= 92 \times \frac{100}{115} = 80$ kg

Initial weight of $A = 80 \times \frac{5}{8} = 50$ kg

Initial weight of $B = 80 \times \frac{3}{8} = 30$ kg

Now, after increasing A

Weight $= 50 \times \frac{105}{100} = 52.5$ kg

∴ After increasing B's weight

$= 92 - 52.5 = 39.5$ kg

∴ Required percentage

$= \frac{(39.5 - 30)}{30} \times 100 = 31.67\%$

364. (a) Total students = 500 + 2000 = 2500

Total pass students = 1500 + 450 = 1950

∴ Required percentage $= \frac{1950}{2500} \times 100 = 78\%$

365. (c) Area of the plot owned by Susan = 1250 sq. feet

Roshan having area $= 1250 \times \frac{120}{100} = 1500$

∴ Now, Jacob having area

$= 1500 \times \frac{130}{100} = 1950$ sq. feet

366. (c) Let total votes = $100x$

Total cast votes $= 100x \times 75\% = 75x$

Total valid votes $= 75x \times 96\%$

$= 75x \times \frac{96}{100} = 3x \times \frac{96}{4} = 72x$

According to the question,

$72x \times 80\% = 9504$

⇒ $72x \times \frac{80}{100} = 9504$

⇒ $72x \times \frac{4}{5} = 9504 \Rightarrow x = \frac{9504 \times 5}{72 \times 4} = 165$

Total votes $= 100x = 16500$

367. (b) Total number of votes = x

∴ Total vote polled = 88% of x

Winner get votes = 60% of x

Looser get votes = 88% of x − 60% of x

= 28% of x

According to the question,

60% of x − 28% of x = 1200

⇒ 32% of x = 1200

⇒ $x \times \frac{32}{100} = 1200$

⇒ $x = \frac{1200 \times 100}{32} = 3750$

368. (c) Let Anita's income = ₹ 100

Anita's saving $= 100 \times \frac{20}{100} =$ ₹ 20

Anita's expense = 100 − 20 = ₹ 80

Now, new income $= 100 \times \frac{130}{100} =$ ₹ 130

New saving $= 130 \times \frac{25}{100} =$ ₹ 32.5

∴ Required percentage $= \frac{32.5 - 20}{20} \times 100$

$= 12.5 \times 5 = 62.50\%$

369. (c) Total number of votes = 248000

Valid votes $= 248000 \times \frac{80}{100} = 198400$

∴ Second candidate gets

$= 198400 \times \left(\frac{100 - 75}{100}\right) = 49600$

370. (a) Let first and second number be x and y, respectively.

According to the question,

$$y - \frac{20x}{100} = \frac{70y}{100} \Rightarrow \frac{30y}{100} = \frac{20x}{100}$$

$$\Rightarrow \quad \frac{x}{y} = \frac{3}{2}$$

$$\Rightarrow \quad x:y = 3:2$$

371. (b) Let Venkat income be ₹ x.
According to the question,
35% of x = 1100

$$\Rightarrow \quad \frac{35}{100} \times x = 1100$$

$$\Rightarrow \quad x = \frac{1100 \times 100}{35}$$

$$\therefore \text{ Venkat expenses} = \frac{1100 \times 100}{35} \times \frac{65}{100}$$

$$= ₹\ 2042.85$$

372. (b) Let the total number of people eligible to vote to be $100x$.
20 to 25 yr eligible people to vote

$$= 100x \times \frac{75}{100} = 75x$$

$$\text{Actually voted} = 75\,x \times \frac{28}{100} = 21\,x$$

$$\therefore \text{ Required percentage} = \frac{21x}{100x} \times 100\% = 21\%$$

373. (a) Total votes were polled = 80% of

$$80000 = \frac{80}{100} \times 80000 = 64000$$

∴ The votes received by Sohan Lal

$$= 64000 \times \frac{40}{100} = 25600$$

374. (a) $39\% \text{ of } 1894 = \frac{39}{100} \times 1894 = 738.66$

$$74\% \text{ of } 1894 = \frac{74}{100} \times 1894 = 1401.56$$

$$\text{Required per cent} = \frac{1401.56 - 738.66}{738.66} \times 100\%$$

$$= \frac{662.9}{738.66} \times 100\% = 89.74\%$$

375. (d) Given, C's income = ₹ 2500

$$B\text{'s income} = 2500 \times \frac{80}{100} = ₹\ 2000$$

$$\therefore A\text{'s income} = 2000 \times \frac{140}{100} = ₹\ 2800$$

376. (a) Let Naresh's salary be x.
Naresh's saving = ₹ 1736
According to the question,

$$x \times \frac{32}{100} = 1736$$

$$\therefore \quad x = \frac{1736 \times 100}{32} = ₹\ 5425$$

Ramesh's salary = Naresh's salary = 5425
Ramesh's saving [given]

$$= 5425 \times \frac{28}{100} = ₹\ 1519$$

∴ Ramesh's expenditure = 5425 − 1519
= ₹ 3906

377. (a) Percent increase in person's salary

$$= \frac{234 - 200}{200} \times 100$$

$$= \frac{34}{2} = 17\%$$

378. (d) The weight of Anjali after 6 months

$$= 60 \times \frac{120}{100} \times \frac{125}{100} = 90\text{ kg}$$

08

Profit & Loss

Profit and loss are the terms related to monetary transaction in trade and business. Whenever a purchased article is sold, other than cost price, then either profit is earned or loss is incurred.

- **Cost Price (CP)** The price at which an article is purchased is called cost price.
- **Selling Price (SP)** The price at which an article is sold is called selling price.
- **Marked Price (MP)** The list price of an item is known as its marked price.
- **Profit** When SP is more than CP (SP > CP)
- **Loss** When CP is more than SP (CP > SP)

Basic Formulae

- Profit or gain = SP – CP
- Loss = CP – SP
- $\text{Gain } \% = \dfrac{\text{Gain}}{\text{CP}} \times 100\%$
- $\text{Loss } \% = \dfrac{\text{Loss}}{\text{CP}} \times 100\%$
- $\text{SP} = \left(\dfrac{100 + \text{Gain } \%}{100}\right) \times \text{CP}$
- $\text{SP} = \left(\dfrac{100 - \text{Loss}\%}{100}\right) \times \text{CP}$
- $\text{CP} = \left(\dfrac{100}{100 + \text{Gain}\%}\right) \times \text{SP}$
- $\text{CP} = \left(\dfrac{100}{100 - \text{Loss}\%}\right) \times \text{SP}$

Note Profit and loss percentage are always calculated on cost price unless otherwise stated in the question.

Ex. 1 If an article is sold for ₹ 355, there is a loss of 29% . At what price (in ₹) should it to sold to gain 31% of profit?

Sol. SP of article = ₹ 355

Loss = 29%

$$\text{CP of article} = \frac{355}{(100 - 29)} \times 100 = ₹\, 500$$

New profit = 31%

$$\therefore \text{ New SP} = \left(\frac{100 + 31}{100}\right) \times 500 = \frac{131}{100} \times 500 = ₹\, 655$$

When Article is Sold for Multiple Times

If A sold an article to B at a profit/loss of $x\%$ and B sold this article to C at a profit or loss of $y\%$, then CP of article for C

$$= \text{Cost price for } A \times \left(1 \pm \frac{x}{100}\right)\left(1 \pm \frac{y}{100}\right)$$

Ex. 2 A sells a DVD to B at a gain of 17% and B again sells it to 'C' at a loss of 25%. If C pays ₹ 1053 to B, what is the cost price of the DVD to A?

Sol. Let CP of DVD for A be $100x$.

Then, CP of DVD for $B = 100x \times \dfrac{117}{100} = 117x$

$$\text{CP of DVD for } C = 117x \times \frac{(100 - 25)}{100} = 117x \times \frac{3}{4}$$

$$= 87.75x$$

But $87.75x = ₹\, 1053 \Rightarrow x = \dfrac{1053}{87.75} = 12$

Thus, CP of DVD for $A = 100x = 100 \times 12 = ₹\, 1200$

Alternate Method

$$\text{Cost price for } C = \text{Cost price for } A \times \left(1 + \frac{17}{100}\right)\left(1 - \frac{25}{100}\right)$$

$$1053 = \text{Cost price for } A\left(\frac{117}{100}\right) \times \frac{3}{4}$$

$$\text{Cost price of article for } A = \frac{1053 \times 4 \times 100}{117 \times 3} = ₹\, 1200$$

CP of *a* Article is Equal to SP of *b* Article

In this topic we will study the question in which CP of a article is equal to SP of b article is given and we have to find loss/gain percentage.

These question can be solved by formula also

$$\text{Profit or loss}\% = \frac{a - b}{b} \times 100 = \pm\, \% \begin{bmatrix} +\text{ ve} = \text{Profit} \\ -\text{ ve} = \text{Loss} \end{bmatrix}$$

Ex. 3 If the selling price of 12 articles is equal to cost price of 18 articles. What is the profit percentage?

Sol. SP of 12 articles = CP of 18 articles $\Rightarrow 12 \times \text{SP} = 18 \times \text{CP}$

$$\frac{\text{SP}}{\text{CP}} = \frac{3}{2}$$

$$\therefore \text{Profit percentage} = \frac{3 - 2}{2} \times 100 = 50\%$$

Alternate Method

$$\text{Profit per cent} = \frac{18 - 12}{12} \times 100 = \frac{6}{12} \times 100 = 50\%$$

When SP of Two Articles is Same

If a person sells two different article at the same selling price, one at a profit of $r\%$ and another at a loss of $r\%$, then seller always incurred a loss which is given by loss% $= \left(\frac{r^2}{100}\right)\%$

When two products are sold at same selling price, one at a loss/profit of $x\%$ and other at a loss/profit of $y\%$, then net result is equal to

$$= \left[\frac{100(x+y)+2xy}{200+x+y}\right]\%$$

Ex. 4 A shopkeeper sells two article at ₹ 594 each, in which one article earned a profit of 10% and another one incurred a loss of 10%. Find the overall profit or loss percentage.

Sol. We know, loss % $= \left(\frac{r^2}{100}\right)$

Here, $r = 10\%$

So, loss % $= \left(\frac{r^2}{100}\right) = \frac{100}{100} = 1\%$

Dishonest Shopkeeper

In this topic we will study the question in which shopkeeper pretend to sell at CP but he uses faulty weight to make some profit.

$$\text{Gain\%} = \frac{\text{Error}}{\text{True weight} - \text{Error}} \times 100\%$$

$\therefore$ [Error = True weight − False weight]

Ex. 5 A dishonest shopkeeper professes to sell his goods at cost price, but he uses a weight of 800 gm for the kilogram (kg) weight. Find out his gain percentage. [1 kg = 1000 gm]

Sol. By formula, gain % $= \frac{\text{Error}}{\text{True weight} - \text{Error}} \times 100$

$$= \frac{1000-800}{1000-(1000-800)} \times 100$$

$$= \frac{200}{800} \times 100 = 25\%$$

SSC Exam Scanner

SSC CGL 2024 (Tier I & II)

1. A man sells a mobile phone for ₹ 680 and loses something. If he had sold it for ₹ 1070, his gain would have been double the former loss. The cost price (in ₹) of the mobile phone is **SSC CGL (Tier-II) 20/01/2025 Shift-I**
   (a) 820 (b) 800
   (c) 830 (d) 810

2. A man buys 10 identical articles for a total of ₹ 15. If he sells each of them for ₹ 1.7, then his profit percentage will be ......% (rounded off to two decimal place). **SSC CGL (Tier-II) 18/01/2025 Shift-I**
   (a) 14.33 (b) 12.76
   (c) 13.33 (d) 11.76

3. A shopkeeper has a fault of 100 g in a 3 kg weight. He sold 3 kg of potatoes to Charu using the same faulty weight for ₹ 46. The cost price of the potatoes for the seller was ₹ 12 per kg. How much profit (in ₹) did he earn on the potatoes? **SSC CGL (Tier-I) 26/09/2024 Shift-III**
   (a) 11.6 (b) 10.2
   (c) 11.2 (d) 10

4. Raman fixes the sale price of his goods at 16% above the cost price. He sells his goods at 12% less than the fixed price. Find the profit percentage correct to two places of decimal. **SSC CGL (Tier-I) 26/09/2024 Shift-II**
   (a) 1.07% (b) 2.08%
   (c) 0.08% (d) 3.01%

5. If books bought at prices ranging from ₹ 200 to ₹ 260 are sold at prices ranging from ₹ 250 to ₹ 300, what is the greatest possible profit that might be made in selling 25 books? **SSC CGL (Tier-I) 26/09/2024 Shift-I**
   (a) ₹ 2300 (b) ₹ 2500
   (c) ₹ 1800 (d) ₹ 2700

6. Find the gain percentage, given that Aditi sold her scooter for ₹ 40620 gaining $\frac{1}{5}$th of the selling price. **SSC CGL (Tier-I) 25/09/2024 Shift-III**
   (a) 10% (b) 20%
   (c) 25% (d) 35%

7. A man loses 28% by selling an article for ₹ 144. If he sells it for ₹ 288, what will be his gain/loss percentage? **SSC CGL (Tier-I) 25/09/2024 Shift-II**
   (a) Gain, 41% (b) Loss, 43%
   (c) Gain, 44% (d) Loss, 46%

8. Ramesh purchased 130 books at the rate of ₹ 200 each and sold half of them at the rate of ₹ 300 each, one-fifth of them at the rate of ₹ 350 each and the rest at the cost price. Find his profit percentage. **SSC CGL (Tier-I) 25/09/2024 Shift-I**
   (a) 35% (b) 40% (c) 38% (d) 44%

9. Samreen sells a keyboard for ₹ 1260 at a profit of 25%, and another keyboard for ₹ 1,440 at a loss of 10%. What is her total gain or loss percentage? **SSC CGL (Tier-I) 24/09/2024 Shift-I**
   (a) $3\frac{86}{163}$% Loss (b) $3\frac{11}{27}$% Gain
   (c) $3\frac{11}{27}$% Loss (d) $3\frac{86}{163}$% Gain

10. The marked price of 55 items was equal to the cost price of 99 items. The selling price of 56 items was equal to the marked price of 35 items. Calculate the profit or loss percentage from the sale of each item. **SSC CGL (Tier-I) 23/09/2024 Shift-II**
   (a) 15% profit (b) 12.25% profit
   (c) 12.5% profit (d) 12.5% loss

11. A shopkeeper sells rice at the rate of ₹ 44 per kg whose cost price is ₹ 40 per kg. Not satisfied with this, he tries to increase his profit by removing 200 gm of rice from each packet. What is the shopkeeper's overall gain percentage? **SSC CGL (Tier-I) 19/09/2024 Shift-II**
   (a) 35% (b) 37.5%
   (c) 37% (d) 35.5%

12. A vendor started selling vegetables at ₹ 10 per kg, but couldn't find buyers at this rate. So he reduced the price to ₹ 7.2 per kg, but uses a faulty weight of 900 g instead of 1 kg. Find the percentage change in the actual price. **SSC CGL (Tier-I) 19/09/2024 Shift-I**
   (a) 10% (b) 15%
   (c) 20% (d) 25%

13. A seller sold 19 cookies for ₹ 95 instead of 20 cookies in one kg, cheating a customer. What is the

gain (in ₹) if the seller bought the cookies for ₹ 76?
SSC CGL (Tier-I) 18/09/2024 Shift-III

(a) 28.2 (b) 26.2
(c) 22.8 (d) 25.8

14. Find the gain percentage, given that Siddhi sold her scooter for ₹ 71785 gaining $\frac{1}{5}$th of the selling price. SSC CGL (Tier-I) 18/09/2024 Shift-II

(a) 20% (b) 25% (c) 10% (d) 15%

15. A shopkeeper sold $\frac{5}{8}$ of his articles at a gain of 20% and the remaining at the cost price. What is his gain percentage in the whole transaction?
SSC CGL (Tier-I) 18/09/2024 Shift-I

(a) $16\frac{1}{2}\%$ (b) $14\frac{1}{2}\%$
(c) $13\frac{1}{2}\%$ (d) $12\frac{1}{2}\%$

16. An article passing through two hands is sold at a total profit of 40% of the original cost price. If the first dealer makes a profit of 30%, then the profit percentage made by the second dealer is
SSC CGL (Tier-I) 17/09/2024 Shift-II

(a) $8\frac{6}{13}\%$ (b) $6\frac{3}{13}\%$
(c) $7\frac{1}{13}\%$ (d) $7\frac{9}{13}\%$

17. If a shopkeeper sells sugar at ₹ 44.8 per kg, he is able to make a 12% profit. Due to water seepage, $\frac{1}{5}$ of the sugar is damaged. What should now be the selling price per kg of the rest of the sugar to have a 5% profit? SSC CGL (Tier-I) 17/09/2024 Shift-I

(a) ₹ 49.5 (b) ₹ 52.5
(c) ₹ 48.5 (d) ₹ 51.5

18. A dishonest fruit-seller sells fruits at 20% profit but he uses 950 gm weight in place of 1 kg. What is the profit per cent?
SSC CGL (Tier-I) 13/09/2024 Shift-III

(a) $\frac{500}{17}\%$ (b) $\frac{500}{19}\%$
(c) $\frac{500}{32}\%$ (d) $\frac{700}{19}\%$

19. Ramesh sells rice at ₹ 36 per kg, which he purchased for ₹ 30 per kg. Moreover, he gives only 800 g of rice instead of 1 kg while selling. Find the actual profit percentage of Ramesh. SSC CGL (Tier-I) 13/09/2024 Shift-II

(a) 46% (b) 50%
(c) 48% (d) 52%

20. An article is sold at a profit of 250%. What is the ratio of its cost price to selling price?
SSC CGL (Tier-I) 13/09/2024 Shift-I

(a) 2 : 5 (b) 5 : 2
(c) 2 : 7 (d) 7 : 2

21. The profit gained on selling a certain product is 320% of the cost. If the cost increases by 10% but the selling price remains constant, then what percentage of the selling price is the profit (correct to one decimal place)? SSC CGL (Tier-I) 12/09/2024 Shift-III

(a) 70.2%
(b) 73.8%
(c) 75.7%
(d) 63.8%

22. A dishonest merchant sells his grocery using weights that are 12% less than the true weights and makes a profit of 10%.
Find his total gain percentage.
SSC CGL (Tier-I) 11/09/2024 Shift-I

(a) 10% (b) 20%
(c) 15% (d) 25%

23. A merchant has 1000 kg of sugar, part of which he sells at a 10% profit and the rest at a 40% profit. He gains 20% on the whole. The quantity sold at 40% profit is:
SSC CGL (Tier-I) 10/09/2024 Shift-II

(a) $543\frac{1}{3}$ kg (b) $383\frac{1}{3}$ kg
(c) $333\frac{1}{3}$ kg (d) $443\frac{1}{3}$ kg

24. Find the gain percentage, given that Priya sold her scooter for ₹ 42564 gaining $\frac{1}{6}$th of the selling price. SSC CGL (Tier-I) 10/09/2024 Shift-I

(a) 30% (b) 20%
(c) 15% (d) 40%

25. Madhav purchased an item for ₹ 42000 and sold it at a loss of 20%. With that amount, he purchased another item and sold it at a gain of 30%. What is the overall gain (in ₹)? SSC CGL (Tier-I) 09/09/2024 Shift-II

(a) 6720 (b) 4200
(c) 1680 (d) 2520

26. A grocer professes to sell rice at the cost price, but uses a fake weight of 870 g for 1 kg. Find his profit percentage (correct to two decimal places). SSC CGL (Tier-I) 09/09/2024 Shift-I

(a) 15.11%
(b) 14.94%
(c) 18.21%
(d) 11.11%

SSC CGL 2023 (Tier I & II)

27. Products pass successively through the hands of three traders and each of them sells his goods at a profit of 30% of his cost price. If the last trader sold the products for ₹ 300, then how much did the first trader pay for them?
SSC CGL (Tier-II) 03/03/2023 Shift-I

(a) ₹ 330.55 (approx)
(b) ₹ 136.55 (approx)
(c) ₹ 240.55 (approx)
(d) ₹ 137.55 (approx)

28. A man buys a machine for ₹ 5000. After one year, he sells it for ₹ 6000. After two years, again he buys the same machine at ₹ 8000 and sells it for ₹ 10000. Find the overall profit percentage for both the transactions.
SSC CGL (Tier-II) 02/03/2023 Shift-I

(a) 20.23% (b) 23.08%
(c) 18.75% (d) 15.23%

29. If the cost price of 28 oranges is equal to selling price of 24 oranges, then the profit percentage is
SSC CGL (Tier-I) 27/7/2023 Shift-III

(a) $16\frac{2}{3}\%$ (b) $16\frac{1}{3}\%$
(c) $18\frac{2}{3}\%$ (d) $18\frac{1}{3}\%$

30. A dishonest dealer sells articles at 15% loss on cost price but uses the weight of 20 g instead of 25 g. What is his profit or loss percentage?
SSC CGL (Tier-I) 27/7/2023 Shift-II

(a) 6.25% profit (b) 6.50% profit
(c) 7.55% loss (d) 5.25% loss

31. On selling a painting at ₹ 1498, the gain is 25% more than the loss incurred on selling it at ₹ 1300. In order to gain 25%, the selling price will be SSC CGL (Tier-I) 27/7/2023 Shift-I

(a) ₹ 1735 (b) ₹ 1335
(c) ₹ 1755 (d) ₹ 1388

32. A watch is purchased for ₹ 3200 and sold for ₹ 2700. Calculate the percentage loss up to two places of decimal. SSC CGL (Tier-I) 26/7/2023 Shift-IV

(a) 15.18% (b) 15.62%
(c) 16.12% (d) 16.50%

33. Ram bought a cell phone and paid 30% less than its original price. He sold it at 50% profit on the price he had paid. The percentage of profit earned by Ram on the original price was
SSC CGL (Tier-I) 26/7/2023 Shift-IV

(a) 25% (b) 50% (c) 15% (d) 5%

34. Sita sold a whiteboard marker set at 10% profit. On selling it for ₹ 20 more, she would have earned a profit of 15%. What is the cost price of the whiteboard marker set?
SSC CGL (Tier-I) 26/7/2023 Shift-III
(a) ₹ 300 (b) ₹ 350 (c) ₹ 450 (d) ₹ 400

35. *R*'s weighing machine shows 400 gm when the actual weight is 350 gm. The cost price of almonds is ₹ 880 per kg and packets of 200 gm are made using the faulty machine. What should be the selling price (in ₹) of each packet to get a profit of 25% ?
SSC CGL (Tier-I) 26/7/2023 Shift-I
(a) 197.50 (b) 175.50
(c) 182.50 (d) 192.50

36. A shopkeeper purchased 1600 mangoes at the rate of ₹ 120 per dozen. Out of these, he sold 900 mangoes at ₹ 15 per mango and the remaining mangoes at ₹ 14 per mango. His gain percentage is
SSC CGL (Tier-I) 25/7/2023 Shift-IV
(a) 45.625% (b) 38.265%
(c) 35.625% (d) 48.765%

37. Mona purchased two sets of jewellery for ₹ 4000 each. She sold these sets of jewellery, gaining 8% on one and loosing 6% on the other. Calculate her total loss or gain in this whole transaction.
SSC CGL (Tier-I) 25/7/2023 Shift-II
(a) ₹ 120 gain (b) ₹ 80 gain
(c) ₹ 80 loss (d) ₹ 120 loss

38. A shopkeeper bought certain number of apples for ₹ 3600. He sold one-fifth of them at a loss of 10%, one-fourth of the remaining apples at a loss of 5% and two-third of the rest at a profit of 15%. At what price (in ₹) should he sell the remaining apples to earn a profit of 27% overall?
SSC CGL (Tier-I) 25/7/2023 Shift-I
(a) 1548 (b) 1584 (c) 1845 (d) 1864

39. A notebook was sold for ₹ 28 with a profit of 12%, If it had been sold for ₹ 26.25, then what would have been the profit percentage?
SSC CGL (Tier-I) 24/07/2023 Shift-III
(a) 5% (b) 7% (c) 4% (d) 6%

40. A shopkeeper bought 20 chairs for ₹ 18000. On selling he had a gain equal to the selling price of four chairs. What is the selling price of each chair?
SSC CGL (Tier-I) 21/07/2023 Shift-IV
(a) ₹ 1125 (b) ₹ 1200
(c) ₹ 1250 (d) ₹ 1175

41. To earn a 12% profit, a shopkeeper sells a television for ₹ 22400. What should be the selling price (in ₹) of the television if he wants a double profit? **SSC CGL (Tier-I) 21/07/2023 Shift-II**
(a) ₹ 24000 (b) ₹ 24800
(c) ₹ 24600 (d) ₹ 25000

42. *A* sold an article to *B* at 25% profit and *B* further sold it to *C* by earning a certain profit. If the cost price of *C* is 30% more than the cost price of *A*, then find the profit percentage earned by *B*.
SSC CGL (Tier-I) 21/07/2023 Shift-I
(a) $5\frac{1}{2}\%$ (b) 4%
(c) 5% (d) $4\frac{1}{2}\%$

43. The cost price and selling price of rice are the same. Due to a faulty weighing machine, the seller earns a 15% profit. If ₹ *x* is the cost price of 1000 gm rice and the machine is changed which shows 1000 gm instead of 950 gm, what should be the selling price (in ₹) now to get the same percentage of profit?
SSC CGL (Tier-I) 20/07/2023 Shift-IV
(a) 1.0295 *x* (b) 1.0259 *x*
(c) 1.0925 *x* (d) 1.0950 *x*

44. The cost of 50 dozens of bananas is ₹ 2400 and the transport cost per banana is ₹ 0.25. The selling price is ₹ 10 for a pair of bananas. What is the profit percentage (rounded off up to one decimal place)?
SSC CGL (Tier-I) 20/07/2023 Shift-III
(a) 14.5% (b) 17.6% (c) 15.4% (d) 16.7%

45. A seller professes to sell his fruits at cost price but still gains $5\frac{5}{19}\%$. How much does he give for 1 kg?
SSC CGL (Tier-I) 20/07/2023 Shift-II
(a) 905 gm (b) 5 gm
(c) 900 gm (d) 950 gm

46. A shopkeeper sold a pair of headphones for ₹ 5520 at a gain of 20%. What would have been the gain or loss per cent, if it had been sold for ₹ 4370?
SSC CGL (Tier-I) 20/07/2023 Shift-I
(a) Gain 15% (b) Loss 5%
(c) Gain 2% (d) Loss 10%

47. A shopkeeper purchases six small cold drink bottles for ₹ 100. For how much should he sell one such bottle to get a profit of 20%?
SSC CGL (Tier-I) 18/07/2023 Shift-IV
(a) ₹ 23 (b) ₹ 22
(c) ₹ 20 (d) ₹ 21

48. By selling a watch for ₹ 2000, a shopkeeper loses 20%. How much would he gain or lose by selling it for ₹ 3000?
SSC CGL (Tier-I) 18/07/2023 Shift-III
(a) 25% loss (b) 25% gain
(c) 15% gain (d) 20% gain

49. The percentage profit earned by selling an article for ₹ 2000 is the same as the percentage loss incurred by selling the same article for ₹ 1200. At what price should that article be sold to make a profit of 20%? **SSC CGL (Tier-I) 18/07/2023 Shift-II**
(a) ₹ 2000 (b) ₹ 1800 (c) ₹ 1920 (d) ₹ 1840

50. Ram sells a suitcase to Mohan at a 20% profit. Mohan sells it to Shyam at a 40% profit. If Shyam pays ₹ 1430 for it, then the price at which Ram bought it is
SSC CGL (Tier-I) 17/07/2023 Shift-II
(a) ₹875 (b) ₹870
(c) ₹851.19 (d) ₹880

51. A shopkeeper sells an item at a profit of 15% and uses a weight which is 20% less. Find his actual profit percentage
SSC CGL (Tier-I) 17/07/2023 Shift-I
(a) 42.5% (b) 50%
(c) 40% (d) 43.75%

52. A shopkeeper gains 20% in place of 16% loss, if the selling price of an article is increased by ₹324. The cost price of the article is
SSC CGL (Tier-I) 14/07/2023 Shift-IV
(a) ₹ 900 (b) ₹ 750 (c) ₹ 1350 (d) ₹ 60

53. A dealer professing to sell his goods at cost price uses 950 gm weight for 1 kg. His gain percentage is: (rounded off to two decimal places) **SSC CGL (Tier-I) 14/07/2023 Shift-III**
(a) 5.35% (b) 5.26%
(c) 5.86% (d) 5.96%

54. A shopkeeper uses 940 gm weight in place of one kg weight. He sells it at 4% profit. What will be the actual profit percentage? (rounded off to two decimal places)
SSC CGL (Tier-I) 14/07/2023 Shift-II
(a) 9.25% (b) 10.32%
(c) 10.96% (d) 10.64%

SSC CGL 2022 (Tier I)

55. By selling an article for ₹ 33000 a man gains 10%. To get a profit of 20%, he has to sell it for
SSC CGL (Tier-I) 13/12/2022 Shift-IV
(a) ₹ 30000 (b) ₹ 35000
(c) ₹ 36000 (d) ₹ 36600

56. Ram sold an item costing ₹ 1250 at a gain of 18% to Ramesh. It was again sold by Ramesh to Shyam at a loss of 10%. Find the selling price of Ramesh.
SSC CGL (Tier-I) 13/12/2022 Shift-III
(a) ₹1328.50 (b) ₹1428.50
(c) ₹1427.50 (d) ₹1327.50

57. A girl purchases 9 mangoes for ₹ 90 and sells 10 mangoes for ₹ 95. Find the gain or loss percentage.
SSC CGL (Tier-I) 13/12/2022 Shift-II
(a) 5% gain (b) 2.5% loss
(c) 2.5% gain (d) 5% loss

58. Ramesh purchases a table and a chair for ₹ 3900. He sells the table at a profit of 8% and the chair at a profit of 16%. He earns a profit of ₹ 540. What is the difference between the original price of the table and the chair?
SSC CGL (Tier-I) 13/12/2022 Shift-I
(a) ₹ 2000 (b) ₹ 1800
(c) ₹ 1900 (d) ₹ 1700

59. A watch is sold at a profit of 25%. Had it been sold for ₹ 120 less then, there would have been loss of 15%. What is the cost price in rupees?
SSC CGL (Tier-I) 12/12/2022 Shift-III
(a) ₹ 400 (b) ₹ 350
(c) ₹ 200 (d) ₹ 300

60. A dishonest dealer professor to sell his goods at cost price but uses a false weight and thus gains 15%. For a kilogram, he uses a weight of .... (rounded off to one digit after decimal).
SSC CGL (Tier-I) 12/12/2022 Shift-II
(a) 833.3 gm (b) 876.7 gm
(c) 869.6 gm (d) 898.33 gm

61. The ratio of the cost price and selling price of an article is 10 : 11. The gain per cent is
SSC CGL (Tier-I) 12/12/2022 Shift-I
(a) 10% (b) 8%
(c) 5% (d) 15%

62. A Microwave oven is sold in Hyderabad for ₹ *M*. A retailer, Elahi from Hyderabad went to Madras and bought it for 25% less (when compared to the price in Hyderabad). He spends ₹ 1000 on transport to bring it from Madras to Hyderabad. He sold it in Hyderabad for ₹ *M* making a profit of 10%. Find the value of *M* (in ₹).
SSC CGL (Tier-I) 12/12/2022 Shift-I
(a) 6305.8 (b) 6258.8
(c) 6285.7 (d) 6527.9

63. A man sells two cows for ₹ 15640 each, gaining 15% on one and losing 15% on the other. Find his total gain or loss.
SSC CGL (Tier-I) 09/12/2022 Shift-IV
(a) ₹ 720 loss (b) ₹ 360 loss
(c) ₹ 720 gain (d) ₹ 360 gain

64. In a certain shop, the profit is 130% of the cost. If the cost increases by 28% and the selling price remains constant, then what is the profit percentage to the nearest whole number?**SSC CGL (Tier-I) 09/12/2022 Shift-III**
(a) 75% (b) 60%
(c) 59% (d) 80%

65. Sofia sold an iPhone at the cost of ₹ 46068 at a loss of 12%. At what cost will she have to sell it to get a profit of 18%?
SSC CGL (Tier-I) 09/12/2022 Shift-II
(a) ₹ 61773 (b) ₹ 65773
(c) ₹ 58350 (d) ₹ 52350

66. A dealer sells his goods at a profit of 20%, but uses a weight of 800 g in place of a kg weight. Find his real gain percentage.
SSC CGL (Tier-I) 09/12/2022 Shift-I
(a) 40% (b) 44% (c) 50% (d) 42%

67. If the cost of 20 books is equal to the selling price of 18 books, then the gain percentage is
SSC CGL (Tier-I) 08/12/2022 Shift-IV
(a) $11\frac{1}{9}\%$ (b) $11\frac{1}{3}\%$
(c) $11\frac{2}{9}\%$ (d) $10\frac{1}{9}\%$

68. Mohit purchased a table for ₹ 1260 and due to some scratches on its top, he sold it for ₹ 1197. What is his loss per cent?
SSC CGL (Tier-I) 08/12/2022 Shift-III
(a) 7% (b) 4%
(c) 6% (d) 5%

69. A shopkeeper advertises for selling cloth at 7% loss. However, by using a false scale of length 1 m he actually gains 24%. What will be the actual length he uses instead of 1 m? **SSC CGL (Tier-I) 08/12/2022 Shift-I**
(a) 75 cm (b) 31 cm
(c) 76 cm (d) 93 cm

70. Ramesh claims that he is selling onions at ₹ 36 per kg, which costs him ₹ 40 per kg, but he gives 800 gm instead of 1 kg. Find Ramesh's percentage gain or loss.
SSC CGL (Tier-I) 07/12/2022 Shift-IV
(a) Gain 13.5 % (b) Loss 13.5 %
(c) Loss 12.5 % (d) Gain 12.5 %

71. A shopkeeper bought a cycle for ₹ 1200 and sold it for ₹ 1500. Find his profit/loss percentage.
SSC CGL (Tier-II) 07/12/2022 Shift-III
(a) 3% profit (b) 15% profit
(c) 30% loss (d) 25% profit

72. A shopkeeper sells an article at $13\frac{1}{2}\%$ loss. If he sells it for ₹ 1274 more, then he gains 11%. What is the cost price of the article?
SSC CGL (Tier-I) 07/12/2022 Shift-II
(a) ₹ 4874 (b) ₹ 4800
(c) ₹ 5200 (d) ₹ 5274

73. The initial profit percentage on the sale of an item was 55%.If the cost price of the item went up by 24% but the selling price remained the same, what would be the new profit percentage?
SSC CGL (Tier-I) 07/12/2022 Shift-I
(a) 36% (b) 25% (c) 28% (d) 33%

74. The selling price of 28 items is equal to the cost price of 17 items. What is the percentage of profit or loss? **SSC CGL (Tier-I) 06/12/2022 Shift-III**
(a) $39\frac{2}{7}\%$ loss (b) $39\frac{2}{7}\%$ profit
(c) $33\frac{2}{7}\%$ profit (d) $33\frac{2}{7}\%$ loss

75. A shopkeeper has 2220 kg of rice. A part of which he sells at a 20% profit and the rest at a 12% profit. He gains 18% on the whole. The quantity (in kg) sold at a 12% profit is **SSC CGL (Tier-I) 06/12/2022 Shift-II**
(a) 555 (b) 1210
(c) 1665 (d) 425

76. Piyush sold a guitar to Anuj at 16% gain and Anuj sold it to Mayank at 32% gain. If Mayank paid ₹ 3828 for the guitar, what amount did Piyush pay for the guitar?
SSC CGL (Tier-I) 06/12/2022 Shift-II
(a) ₹ 2500 (b) ₹ 3200
(c) ₹ 1600 (d) ₹ 2800

77. Apples were purchased at 100 for ₹ 350 and sold at ₹ 48 a dozen. What is the profit or loss percentage?
SSC CGL (Tier-I) 05/12/2022 Shift-IV
(a) Profit $14\frac{2}{7}\%$ (b) Loss $18\frac{3}{5}\%$
(c) Loss 10% (d) Profit 12%

78. A dishonest dealer sells a product at 11% loss on cost price, but uses 22% less weight. What is his percentage profit or loss?
SSC CGL (Tier-I) 05/12/2022 Shift-II
(a) 14.1%% loss (b) 14.1% gain
(c) 11.4% gain (d) 11.4 % loss

79. Ram sold a plot for ₹ 400000 at a 20% loss. For what price should he sell the plot to gain a 5% profit? SSC CGL (Tier-I) 05/12/2022 Shift-I

(a) ₹ 525000 (b) ₹ 500000
(c) ₹ 505000 (d) ₹ 520000

80. A dishonest trader says to customers that he sells his goods at a cost price, but he uses a false weight and gains 12.5% as profit. How many grams does he use to weigh 1 kg? SSC CGL (Tier-I) 03/12/2022 Shift-IV

(a) 900 g (b) 880.5 g
(c) 850 g (d) 888.8 g

81. If the cost price is 72% of the selling price, then what is the percentage of profit? (Correct to 2 decimal places) SSC CGL (Tier-I) 03/12/2022 Shift-III

(a) 38.89% (b) 35.75%
(c) 32.25% (d) 28.75%

82. A trader has a weigting balance that shows 1300 g for a kg. He further marks up his cost price by 15%. The net profit percentage is SSC CGL (Tier-I) 03/12/2022 Shift-I

(a) 48.5% (b) 49.5%
(c) 50% (d) 45%

83. By selling a car for ₹ 278000, a dealer gains 25%. If the profit is reduced to 18%, then the selling price will be SSC CGL (Tier-I) 02/12/2022 Shift-IV

(a) ₹ 262432 (b) ₹ 265432
(c) ₹ 272432 (d) ₹ 260432

84. The price of some wooden furniture increases by 65%, when it passes through three hands. If the first and second sellers made a profit of 20% and 25% respectively, then find the profit percentage of the third seller. SSC CGL (Tier-I) 02/12/2022 Shift-III

(a) 10% (b) 12.5% (c) 16% (d) 8%

85. A pen was sold for ₹ 166.44 with a profit of 14%. If it were sold for ₹ 154.76, then what would have been the percentage of profit or loss? SSC CGL (Tier-I) 02/12/2022 Shift-I

(a) 5% loss (b) 6% profit
(c) 5% profit (d) 6% loss

86. Kapil sells a mobile to Sachin at a gain of 15% and Sachin again sells it to Rohit at a profit of 12%. If Rohit pays ₹ 322 what is the cost price of the mobile for Kapil? SSC CGL (Tier-I) 01/12/2022 Shift-III

(a) ₹ 350 (b) ₹ 450 (c) ₹ 250 (d) ₹ 325

87. The difference between the cost price and selling price of a pair of shoes is ₹ 1200. If the profit is 15%, the selling price is SSC CGL (Tier-I) 01/12/2022 Shift-II

(a) ₹ 8200 (b) ₹ 9200
(c) ₹ 8000 (d) ₹ 9000

88. A dishonest merchant sells goods at a 12.5% loss on the cost price, but uses 28 g weight instead of 36 g. What is his percentage profit or loss? SSC CGL (Tier-I) 01/12/2022 Shift-I

(a) 6.25 % loss (b) 12.5% gain
(c) 18.75% gain (d) 10.5% loss

SSC CGL 2021 & 2020 (Tier I)

89. A shopkeeper sold an article for ₹ 455 at a loss (in ₹). If he sells it for ₹ 490, then he would gain an amount four times the loss. At what price (in ₹) should he sell the article to gain 25%? SSC CGL (Tier-I) 24/08/2021 Shift-III

(a) 575 (b) 577.50
(c) 570.50 (d) 115.50

90. A shopkeeper sold an article at four-fifth of the marked price and suffered a loss of $3\frac{1}{3}\%$. Find the profit percent, if he sold the article at the marked price. (correct to nearest integer) SSC CGL (Tier-I) 24/08/2021 Shift-II

(a) 22 (b) 18
(c) 21 (d) 20

91. Radha bought a fridge and a washing maching together for ₹ 57300. She sold the fridge at a profit of 15% and washing machine at a loss of 24% and both are sold at the same price. The cost price of washing machine (in ₹) is SSC CGL (Tier-I) 23/08/2021 Shift-II

(a) 28650 (b) 34500
(c) 24500 (d) 22800

92. A fruit merchant bought some bananas. One fifth of them got rotten and were thrown away. He sold two fifth of the bananas with him at 15% profit and the remaining bananas at 10% profit. Find his overall loss or profit per cent? SSC CGL (Tier-I) 23/08/2021 Shift-I

(a) Loss, 10.4% (b) Profit, 10.4%
(c) Profit, 9.6% (d) Loss, 9.6%

93. *A* sold an Article to *B* at a profit of 25%. *B* sold it to *C* at a profit of 15%. The profit made by *B* is ₹ 40 less than the profit made by *A*. What is the cost price (in ₹) of the article for *A*? SSC CGL (Tier-I) 20/08/2021 Shift-I

(a) 240 (b) 640 (c) 546 (d) 400

94. If the cost price of 63 articles is equal to the selling price of 54 articles, then what is the percentage gain or loss? SSC CGL (Tier-I) 18/08/2021 Shift-III

(a) $16\frac{2}{3}\%$ loss (b) $15\frac{1}{3}\%$ loss
(c) $16\frac{2}{3}\%$ gain (d) $15\frac{1}{3}\%$ gain

95. A, TV is sold at 8% gain Had it been sold for ₹ 2553 less, there would have been loss of 15%. To gain 18%, the selling price (in ₹) of TV would be SSC CGL (Tier-I) 18/08/2021 Shift-III

(a) 13098 (b) 15000
(c) 9102 (d) 11100

96. A trader sells an article at 16% below its cost price. Had he sold it for ₹ 192.20 more, he would have gained 15%. The cost price (in ₹) of the article is SSC CGL (Tier-I) 18/08/2021 Shift-I

(a) 620 (b) 680 (c) 720 (d) 640

97. By selling an article for ₹ 640, a person loses 15% of its selling price. At what price (in ₹) should he sell it to gain 15% on its cost price? SSC CGL (Tier-I) 17/08/2021 Shift-I

(a) 832 (b) 846.40
(c) 835 (d) 836.60

98. A trader bought two articles for ₹ 490. He sold one at a loss of 20% and the other at a profit of 16%. If the selling price of both articles is same, then the cost price (in ₹) of the article sold at 20% loss is SSC CGL (Tier-I) 16/08/2021 Shift-III

(a) 310 (b) 300 (c) 290 (d) 280

99. On selling an article for ₹ 246.80, the gain is 20% more than the amount of loss incurred on selling it for ₹ 216. If the article is sold for ₹ 220.75, then what is the gain/loss per cent (correct to nearest integer)? SSC CGL (Tier-I) 16/08/2021 Shift-I

(a) Profit 7% (b) Loss 5%
(c) Loss 4% (d) Profit 3%

100. Some fruits are bought at 15 for ₹ 140 and an equal number of fruits at 10 for ₹ 120. If all the fruits are sold at ₹132 per dozen, then what is the profit per cent in the entire transaction? SSC CGL (Tier-I) 13/08/2021 Shift-I

(a) $3\frac{1}{8}$ (b) $4\frac{1}{2}$ (c) $2\frac{1}{4}$ (d) 3

101. A man buys two watches '*A*' and '*B*' at a total cost of ₹800. He sells both watches at the same selling price, and earns a profit of 18% on watch '*A*' and incurs a loss of 22% on watch '*B*'. What are the cost prices of the two watches? (two place after decimal).
SSC CGL (Tier-I) 07/03/2020 Shift-II

(a) *A* = ₹350.32 and *B* = ₹450.68
(b) *A* = ₹318.37 and *B* = ₹481.63
(c) *A* = ₹220 and *B* = ₹580
(d) *A* = ₹317 and *B* = ₹483

102. By selling 18 table fans for ₹11664 a man incurs a loss of 10%. How many fans should he sell for ₹17424 to earn 10% profit?
SSC CGL (Tier-I) 07/03/2020 Shift-I

(a) 18 (b) 22 (c) 20 (d) 23

103. An article was sold at a gain of 16%. If it had been sold for ₹ 36 more, the gain would have been 20%. The cost price of the article is
SSC CGL (Tier-I) 06/03/2020 Shift-III

(a) ₹ 862 (b) ₹ 900
(c) ₹ 720 (d) ₹ 810

104. A manufacturer sells cooking gas stoves to shopkeepers at 10% profit and in turn they sell the cooking gas stoves to customer to earn 15% profit. If a customer gets a cooking gas stove for ₹ 7590, then what is its manufacturing cost?
SSC CGL (Tier-I) 06/03/2020 Shift-II

(a) ₹5000 (b) ₹6000
(c) ₹5090 (d) ₹6500

105. Sudhir purchased a laptop for ₹ 42000 and a scanner-cum-printer for ₹ 8000. He sold the laptop for a 10% profit and the scanner-cum-printer for a 5% profit. What is his profit percentage?
SSC CGL (Tier-I) 05/03/2020 Shift-III

(a) $7\frac{1}{2}\%$ (b) $9\frac{1}{5}\%$ (c) 15% (d) $9\frac{2}{5}\%$

106. Reema sold 48 articles for ₹ 2160 and suffered a loss of 10%. How many articles should she sell for ₹ 2016 to earn a profit of 12%?
SSC CGL (Tier-I) 05/03/2020 Shift-II

(a) 36 (b) 40 (c) 28 (d) 32

107. Sudha sold an article to Renu for ₹ 576 at a loss of 20%. Renu spent a sum of ₹ 224 on its transportation and sold it to Raghu at a price which would have given Sudha, a profit of 24%. The percentage of gain for Renu is
SSC CGL (Tier-I) 05/03/2020 Shift-I

(a) 13.2% (b) 11.6%
(c) 10.5% (d) 12.9%

108. *A* sells an article to *B* at a loss of 20%, *B* sells it to *C* at a profit of 12.5% and *C* sells it to *D* at a loss of 8%. If *D* buys it for ₹ 248.40, then what is the difference between the loss incurred by *A* and *C*?
SSC CGL (Tier-I) 04/03/2020 Shift-III

(a) ₹ 36.80 (b) ₹ 38.40
(c) ₹ 42.60 (d) ₹ 39.20

SSC CPO SI 2024

109. A shopkeeper sold 3 wrist watches for ₹ 2800 each. If he has sold the watches with 40%, 25% and 12% profit, respectively, then find his overall profit percentage (correct to 2 decimal places).
SSC CPO 29/06/2024 Shift-III

(a) 24.55% (b) 24.75%
(c) 24.19% (d) 24.63%

110. A dishonest dealer claims to sell his products at 24% loss on the cost price but uses 100 g weight instead of 200g weight. His profit percentage is **SSC CPO 29/06/2024 Shift-III**

(a) 55% (b) 52% (c) 40% (d) 48%

111. A person bought two buffaloes for ₹ 11520. One is sold at a loss of 15% and the other is sold at a gain of 19%. If the selling price of both buffaloes is equal, find the cost price of the first one.
SSC CPO 29/06/2024 Shift-II

(a) ₹ 6700 (b) ₹ 6720
(c) ₹ 6710 (d) ₹ 6715

112. A trader sells an article at 16% below its cost price. Had he sold it for ₹ 192.20 more, he would have gained 15%. The new selling price (in ₹) of the article is
SSC CPO 29/06/2024 Shift-I

(a) 724 (b) 742
(c) 731 (d) 713

113. The cost price of two articles is equal. One article is sold at a profit of 12% and the other article for ₹ 3600 more than the first. If the net profit is $15\frac{27}{51}\%$, then what is the cost price of each article?
SSC CPO 29/06/2024 Shift-I

(a) ₹ 50990 (b) ₹ 50000
(c) ₹ 51000 (d) ₹ 52150

114. A trader sells pulses at a 32% profit and uses weights 20% less than the actual measure. Find his gain percentage. **SSC CPO 28/06/2024 Shift-III**

(a) 72% (b) 62%
(c) 58% (d) 65%

115. A vegetable vendor bought 100 kg of potatoes at the rate of ₹ 19 per kg and spent ₹ 100 as cartage. He sold 60 kg of potatoes with a 50% profit and half of the remaining stock with a 40% profit. He sold half of the still remaining potatoes with a 25% profit. What profit percentage should he aim for, when selling the ultimate remaining potatoes to achieve an overall profit of 42%?
SSC CPO 28/06/2024 Shift-III

(a) 10% (b) 15%
(c) 12% (d) 16%

116. A dishonest dealer professes to sell his goods at cost price but uses a false weight of 950 gm instead of 1 kg. His gain percentage is
SSC CPO 28/06/2024 Shift-II

(a) $6\frac{5}{19}\%$ (b) $7\frac{5}{19}\%$
(c) $4\frac{5}{19}\%$ (d) $5\frac{5}{19}\%$

117. A reduction of 7.5% in the cost price of a commodity enables a shopkeeper to purchase 15 kg more than what he previously purchased for a sum of ₹ 7400. In order to make a profit of 32.5% on the pre-reduction cost price of the commodity, at what price (in ₹) per kg should the commodity be sold?
SSC CPO 28/06/2024 Shift-I

(a) 54 (b) 52
(c) 51 (d) 53

118. A shopkeeper buys oranges at the rate of 10 oranges for ₹ 50 and sells them at the rate of 12 oranges for ₹ 74. Find his gain or loss percentage. **SSC CPO 28/06/2024 Shift-I**

(a) $23\frac{1}{3}\%$ gain (b) $25\frac{1}{3}\%$ loss
(c) 25% gain (d) 30% loss

119. A grocer purchased 10 kg rice for ₹ 700. He spends some amount on transportation and then sells it for ₹ 1400. If the percentage of profit made by the grocer is 30%, then what is the amount (in ₹) he spends on transportation? (round off to the nearest integer)
SSC CPO 27/06/2024 Shift-III

(a) 300 (b) 380 (c) 377 (d) 350

120. Aarav owns a watch worth ₹ 10000. He sells it to Bhavin at a profit of 15%. After some days, Bhavin sells it back to Aarav at 15% loss. Find the percentage profit or loss faced by Aarav. **SSC CPO 27/06/2024 Shift-II**

(a) 17.25% loss (b) 18.75% loss
(c) 18.25% profit (d) 17.25% profit

121. A merchant bought two watches for ₹9000 each. He sold one watch at a loss of 10%. At what price (in ₹) should he sell the other watch to earn a profit of 18% overall?
SSC CPO 27/06/2024 Shift-II
(a) 14310 (b) 14130
(c) 13410 (d) 13140

122. The cost price of 36 articles is the same as the selling price of N articles. If the profit is 20%, then the value of N is
SSC CPO 27/06/2024 Shift-I
(a) 40 (b) 30 (c) 25 (d) 42

SSC CPO SI 2023 - 2020

123. A shopkeeper sells sugar at ₹ 40 per kg, which he purchased at ₹ 36 per kg. His weighing machine is faulty and it weighs only 800 gm while selling. His percentage profit (Correct to 2 decimal places.) is
SSC CPO 05/10/2023 Shift-III
(a) 37.58% (b) 40%
(c) 39.28% (d) 38.89%

124. Ankita sold three toys. The first toy was sold for ₹1500 at a profit of 25%; the second toy was sold for ₹2800 at a loss of 50% and the third toy was sold for ₹3500 at a profit of 25%. Find her total profit or loss percentage. SSC CPO 05/10/2023 Shift-III
(a) 15.25% loss (b) 15.25% profit
(c) 18.75% profit (d) 18.75% loss

125. A vendor marked the selling price of a table at ₹ 5670 after adding 35% profit to its cost price. Since, the sale was very low at this price level, he decided to sell the table with 12% profit. Find the new selling price (in ₹).
SSC CPO 04/10/2023 Shift-II
(a) 4810 (b) 4750 (c) 4704 (d) 4608

126. The price of a land passing through three hands rises on the whole by 65%. The first and second sellers earned 20% and 25% profit, respectively. Find the profit percentage earned by the third seller. SSC CPO 04/10/2023 Shift-II
(a) 10% (b) 20% (c) 25% (d) 15%

127. The first shirt is sold at twice the selling price of the second shirt. The first shirt is sold at 8% profit and the second shirt is sold at a 3% loss. What is the overall percentage profit on the shirts (rounded off to two decimal place)?
SSC CPO 03/10/2023 Shift-I
(a) 4.86% (b) 4.07%
(c) 4.60% (d) 3.86%

128. A dishonest dealer announces selling his articles with 22% loss, but uses 35% lighter weights. What is the percentage of his profit or loss? SSC CPO 03/10/2023 Shift-I
(a) 20% loss (b) 13% profit
(c) 13% loss (d) 20% profit

129. A shopkeeper claims to sell his articles at ₹ 20 per kg which cost him ₹ 23 per kg. But while selling, he uses a false weight and gives only 800 gm instead of 1 kg. What is his profit percentage?
SSC CPO 11/11/2022
(a) $8\frac{17}{23}\%$ (b) $8\frac{16}{23}\%$
(c) $8\frac{14}{23}\%$ (d) $8\frac{15}{23}\%$

130. A man bought two bicycles for ₹ 3000 each. If he sells one bicycle at a profit of 10%, then for how much percentage profit should he sell the other bicycle so that he makes a profit of 20% on the whole? SSC CPO 10/11/2022
(a) 15% (b) 25%
(c) 30% (d) 10%

131. Swati sold a bag to Ankita at a gain of 15%. Aashi bought this bag from Ankita for ₹ 24840. Ankita earned a profit of 20%. At what price would Swati have bought the bag?
SSC CPO 10/11/2022
(a) ₹ 18500 (b) ₹ 18000
(c) ₹ 16000 (d) ₹ 20000

132. In article was sold at a loss of 13.5%. If it was sold for ₹1104 more, then there would have been a profit of 9.5%. The cost price of the article was SSC CPO 25/11/2020 Shift-II
(a) ₹ 4600 (b) ₹ 4800
(c) ₹ 4400 (d) ₹ 4200

133. A person sold an article at a loss of 16%. Had he sold if for ₹ 660 more, he would have gained 8%. What should be the selling price (in ₹) to gain a profit of 12%?
SSC CPO 23/11/2020 Shift-I
(a) 2970 (b) 3200
(c) 2750 (d) 3080

SSC CHSL 2024 (Tier I & II)

134. Sandeep made a profit of 22% when he sold an overcoat for ₹ 8540. Find the cost price of the overcoat.
SSC CHSL (Tier-II) 18/11/2024 Shift-I
(a) ₹ 6500 (b) ₹ 6000
(c) ₹ 7500 (d) ₹ 7000

135. A shopkeeper sold an article at a 26% profit. On selling it for ₹2250 more, he would get a profit of 41%. If this article is sold at 12% profit, then the selling price would be
SSC CHSL (Tier-I) 11/07/2024 Shift-III
(a) ₹16800 (b) ₹15000
(c) ₹15800 (d) ₹16120

136. The cost price of a fan is ₹ 4400. A merchant wants to make a 24% profit by selling it. At the time of sale, merchant declares a discount of 12% on the marked price. Find the marked price.
SSC CHSL (Tier-I) 11/07/2024 Shift-III
(a) ₹ 2600 (b) ₹ 2060
(c) ₹ 6200 (d) ₹ 6020

137. A shopkeeper sells his goods using weights 27% less than true weights and claims to sell his goods at the cost price. His gain per cent (rounded off to 1 decimal place) is
SSC CHSL (Tier-I) 11/07/2024 Shift-II
(a) 47.9% (b) 37.0%
(c) 39.8% (d) 40.0%

138. A costs thrice as much as B. A is sold at a loss of 10% and B is sold at $\frac{5}{4}$ of its own price. If the selling price of A is ₹ 5800 more than the selling price of B, then the cost price of A is
SSC CHSL (Tier-I) 10/07/2024 Shift-IV
(a) ₹ 4000 (b) ₹ 12000
(c) ₹ 15000 (d) ₹ 9600

139. A merchant sells 195 kg of wheat for ₹ 10,260 at a profit of ₹ 4.50 per kg of wheat. What is the cost price (in ₹, to the nearest integer) of 15 kg of wheat?
SSC CHSL (Tier-I) 10/07/2024 Shift-III
(a) 722 (b) 682
(c) 595 (d) 750

140. A vendor buys 20 dozen bananas for ₹1200 and sells 5 dozen for ₹ 350, then his gain percentage is
SSC CHSL (Tier-I) 10/07/2024 Shift-II
(a) $15\frac{1}{3}\%$ (b) $13\frac{2}{3}\%$
(c) $21\frac{1}{3}\%$ (d) $16\frac{2}{3}\%$

141. A vendor sells his goods using weights 19% less than true weights and makes a profit of 35%. His net gain percentage (rounded off to 2 decimal places) is
SSC CHSL (Tier-I) 10/07/2024 Shift-I
(a) 66.67% (b) 66.33%
(c) 81.33% (d) 81.67%

142. By selling 22 items, Rohit gains the selling price of 6 items. His gain per cent is
SSC CHSL (Tier-I) 09/07/2024 Shift-IV
(a) $37\frac{1}{2}\%$ (b) $37\frac{1}{3}\%$
(c) $33\frac{1}{2}\%$ (d) $33\frac{1}{3}\%$

143. A dishonest dealer professes to sell his goods at the cost price, but he uses a false weight of 850 gm per 1 kg weight. Find the percentage of his gain. (Correct up to two decimal places)
SSC CHSL (Tier-I) 09/07/2024 Shift-II
(a) 17.65% (b) 17.45%
(c) 17.54% (d) 17.56%

144. A trader buys 500 kg cotton for ₹ 8000. If 10% of this cotton is spoiled due to rain, at what rate (₹/kg) should he sells the rest to earn a 20% profit?
SSC CHSL (Tier-I) 09/07/2024 Shift-I
(a) $21\frac{1}{3}$ (b) $22\frac{1}{3}$
(c) $25\frac{1}{3}$ (d) $23\frac{1}{3}$

145. *A* sells an object to *B* at 10% profit, *B* sells it to *C* at 60% profit and *C* sells it to *D* at $12\frac{1}{2}\%$ profit. If *D* paid₹ 59.40, then at what price did *A* buy it? **SSC CHSL (Tier-I) 08/07/2024 Shift-IV**
(a) ₹ 30 (b) ₹ 32
(c) ₹ 28 (d) ₹ 34

146. Pradeep sells two fans at ₹ 480 each and by doing so he gains 20% on one fan and loses 20% on the other. His loss on the whole (in ₹) is
SSC CHSL (Tier-I) 08/07/2024 Shift-III
(a) 30 (b) 10
(c) 20 (d) 40

147. The profit obtained by selling an article for ₹ 86 is twice the loss obtained by selling the same article for ₹ 53. Find the cost price.
SSC CHSL (Tier-I) 08/07/2024 Shift-II
(a) ₹ 33 (b) ₹ 22
(c) ₹ 64 (d) ₹ 75

148. A shopkeeper charges his customer 14% more than the cost price. If a customer paid ₹ 18240 for a mobile phone, then the cost price of the mobile phone was
SSC CHSL (Tier-I) 08/07/2024 Shift-I
(a) ₹ 20793.60 (b) ₹ 15686.40
(c) ₹ 16600 (d) ₹ 16000

149. A shopkeeper cheats 25% in weight, while buying rice and cheats 25% while selling it. If he sells the rice at $12\frac{1}{2}\%$ profit, then find his net profit percentage.
SSC CHSL (Tier-I) 05/07/2024 Shift-IV
(a) 82.5% (b) 62.5%
(c) 87.5% (d) 92.5%

150. A mobile phone dealer buys a phone for ₹ 10000 and sells it for ₹ 12000. Later, he realizes that he could have sold it for ₹ 13000. What is the percentage loss that he incurs? **SSC CHSL (Tier-I) 05/07/2024 Shift-III**
(a) 10% (b) 20% (c) 15% (d) 25%

151. Ramendra purchased some watermelons for ₹ 1500. He sold one-fourth of them at a loss of 12%. At what gain percentage should the remaining watermelons be sold so as to gain 25% on the whole transaction (correct to two decimal places)? **SSC CHSL (Tier-I) 05/07/2024 Shift-II**
(a) 37.33% (b) 33.73%
(c) 37.65% (d) 33.43%

152. Ravath had to sell vegetables worth ₹ 4960 for ₹ 4712 due to weather conditions. What is the loss percentage that he has incurred?
SSC CHSL (Tier-I) 05/07/2024 Shift-I
(a) 20% (b) 10% (c) 5% (d) 15%

153. A shopkeeper buys 1800 kg wheat for ₹ 32400. If 20% of this wheat is spoiled due to rain, at what rate (₹/kg) should he sell the rest to earn 20%?
SSC CHSL (Tier-I) 04/07/2024 Shift-IV
(a) 29 (b) 26 (c) 25 (d) 27

154. A retailer purchased a batch of goods for ₹ 5000. Due to a manufacturing defect, 5% of the goods were damaged. If the retailer wants to make a profit of 20% on the remaining goods, at what price should the undamaged goods be sold? **SSC CHSL (Tier-I) 04/07/2024 Shift-III**
(a) ₹ 5700 (b) ₹ 5800
(c) ₹ 6000 (d) ₹ 5900

155. If 70% of the cost price of an article is equal to 40% of its selling price, what is the profit percentage?
SSC CHSL (Tier-I) 04/07/2024 Shift-I
(a) 85% (b) 80% (c) 70% (d) 75%

156. A seller decreased the selling price of each item from ₹ 5000 to ₹ 4680, by which his loss percentage increased by 4%. If he has to get 4% profit, then the selling price of the item should be
SSC CHSL (Tier-I) 03/07/2024 Shift-IV
(a) ₹ 7280 (b) ₹ 8320
(c) ₹ 8840 (d) ₹ 7800

157. By selling 30 m of cloth a shopkeeper makes a profit equivalent to the selling price of 10 m of cloth. Find the selling price of 1 m of cloth, when the cost price of 1 m of cloth is ₹ 480.
SSC CHSL (Tier-I) 03/07/2024 Shift-III
(a) ₹ 520 (b) ₹ 720 (c) ₹ 960 (d) ₹ 820

158. By selling an article at 66% of its marked price, a merchant makes a profit of 10%. If he sells the article at 80% of its marked price, then the profit percentage will be
SSC CHSL (Tier-I) 03/07/2024 Shift-II
(a) 20% (b) $33\frac{1}{3}\%$ (c) 25% (d) $33\frac{2}{3}\%$

159. *A* sells a bike to *B* at 45% profit. Then, *B*, sells it to *C* at 30% profit. If *C* pays ₹ 43355, then what is the cost price of the bike for *A*?
SSC CHSL (Tier-I) 03/07/2024 Shift-II
(a) ₹ 23000 (b) ₹ 27000
(c) ₹ 29000 (d) ₹ 21000

160. A retail fruit vendor buys a score of apples for ₹ 400 and retails them for ₹ 264 at a dozen. What was his loss/gain per cent? (a score = 20 no's) **SSC CHSL (Tier-I) 03/07/2024 Shift-I**
(a) 20% profit (b) 10% loss
(c) 10% profit (d) 5% loss

161. The difference between the cost price and the selling price of an article is ₹ 1800. If there is a profit of 20%, then the cost price of the article is
SSC CHSL (Tier-I) 02/07/2024 Shift-IV
(a) ₹ 9000 (b) ₹ 11000
(c) ₹ 8000 (d) ₹ 7000

162. A shopkeeper bought 288 oranges for ₹ 115.20. He sold 50 of them at 70 paise each and the remaining at ₹ 46.20. Find his profit or loss
SSC CHSL (Tier-I) 02/07/2024 Shift-III
(a) Profit, ₹ 25 (b) Loss, ₹ 34
(c) Profit, ₹ 37 (d) Loss, ₹ 36

163. A merchant sold two refrigerators for ₹ 10000 each. On one refrigerator, he incurred a 20% loss and on the other, he gained 20%. What was his profit/loss percentage on the whole transaction?
SSC CHSL (Tier-I) 02/07/2024 Shift-I
(a) Profit of 4% (b) Loss of 2%
(c) Loss of 4% (d) Profit of 2%

164. If the selling price of 40 articles is equal to the cost price of 50 articles, then the percentage gain is
SSC CHSL (Tier-I) 01/07/2024 Shift-IV
(a) 25% (b) 20% (c) 30% (d) 35%

165. The cost price of an item increased from ₹ 2500 to ₹ 3000. Find the increase percentage.
SSC CHSL (Tier-I) 01/07/2024 Shift-III
(a) 25% (b) 20% (c) 30% (d) 15%

166. Ravi sells his goods at a 25% loss on cost price but uses 45% less weight. What is his percentage profit or loss?
SSC CHSL (Tier-I) 01/07/2024 Shift-II
(a) Profit, $47\frac{9}{10}\%$ (b) Loss, $36\frac{4}{11}\%$
(c) Loss, $47\frac{9}{10}\%$ (d) Profit, $36\frac{4}{11}\%$

167. Sohan sells sugar at the cost price, but uses false weights thus gaining 28% profit. How many grams of sugar is he giving for 3.2 kg sugar?
SSC CHSL (Tier-II) 10/01/2024 Shift-I
(a) 1500 (b) 1900
(c) 2200 (d) 2500

SSC CHSL 2023-2021 (Tier I & II)

168. A shopkeeper sold his goods at half the list price and thus lost 17%. If he had sold on the listed price, then his gain percentage would be
SSC CHSL (Tier-II) 02/11/2023 Shift-I
(a) 41% (b) 83% (c) 17% (d) 66%

169. A seller sold a bag at a profit of 12%. If he had sold it for ₹ 900 more, he would have gained 27%. What is the CP of the bag?
SSC CHSL (Tier-I) 17/08/2023 Shift-I
(a) ₹ 6000 (b) ₹ 6500
(c) ₹ 5560 (d) ₹ 7000

170. If oranges are bought at 11 for ₹10 and sold at 10 for ₹ 11. What is the gain or loss percentage?
SSC CHSL (Tier-I) 14/08/2023 Shift-IV
(a) Gain = 11% (b) Loss = 11%
(c) Loss = 21% (d) Gain = 21%

171. A shopkeeper does a faulty weighting of an item of 930 gm instead of 1 kg and sells it at its cost price. Find his profit percentage on selling 15 kg of the item. **SSC CHSL (Tier-I) 11/08/2023 Shift-I**
(a) $8\frac{79}{83}\%$ (b) $5\frac{21}{93}\%$
(c) $7\frac{49}{93}\%$ (d) $6\frac{19}{93}\%$

172. A man sells a good at 5% profit. If he had sold it at a 10% profit, he would have received ₹ 175 more. What is selling price of the good?
SSC CHSL (Tier-I) 09/08/2023 Shift-I
(a) ₹ 3750 (b) ₹ 3850
(c) ₹ 3675 (d) ₹ 3500

173. A trader sells two. LED sets at the same price. There is a gain of 20% on one LED and 20% loss on the second LED. Which of the following statements is true?
SSC CHSL (Tier-I) 08/08/2023 Shift-II
(a) The trader makes a profit of 4%.
(b) The trader makes a profit of 2%.
(c) The trader makes no profit or no loss.
(d) The trader makes a loss of 4%.

174. A person purchased ten boxes of grapes at a cost of ₹ 2000 per box. Each box contained 20 kg of grapes. He sold each box at the rate of ₹ 2500 per box. But on the whole 10 kg of grapes were damaged. Further the paid₹ 1000 as transport charges. Find his gain or loss.
SSC CHSL (Tier-I) 07/08/2023 Shift-IV
(a) Gain ₹ 2050 (b) Loss ₹ 1000
(c) Gain ₹ 2750 (d) Loss ₹ 1500

175. A shopkeeper professes to sell sugar costing ₹ 40/kg at ₹ 42/kg but gives only 550 gm sugar in place of 600 gm using faulty weighing machine. His profit percentage (correct to 2 decimal places) is
SSC CHSL (Tier-I) 04/08/2023 Shift-II
(a) 14.54% (b) 15.54%
(c) 15.45% (d) 16.45%

176. The cost price of 44 items is the same as the selling price of x items. If the profit is 10%, then what is the value of x?
SSC CHSL (Tier-I) 21/03/2023 Shift-IV
(a) 55 (b) 40 (c) 60 (d) 50

177. A woman buys a watch for ₹ 4000 and sells it at a loss of 13%. What is the selling price of the watch?
SSC CHSL (Tier-I) 21/03/2023 Shift-II
(a) ₹ 3480 (b) ₹ 3500
(c) ₹ 3840 (d) ₹ 3620

178. Shivam purchased two watches, first for ₹ 12000 and the second for ₹ 20000. He sold both the watches, first one at the profit of 10% and the second at a loss of 20%. What is the overall profit or loss?
SSC CHSL (Tier-I) 20/03/2023 Shift-IV
(a) Profit = ₹ 2600 (b) Loss = ₹ 2800
(c) Loss = ₹ 2400 (d) Profit = ₹ 2200

179. On selling a table for ₹ 210 and ₹420 there will be loss L_1% and L_2% respectively. If $L_1 - L_2 = 7$, then what is the cost price of table?
SSC CHSL (Tier-I) 17/03/2023 Shift-II
(a) ₹ 5000 (b) ₹ 3000
(c) ₹ 7000 (d) ₹ 4000

180. Manoj bought two TV for ₹ 2280. He sold one at a loss of 20% and other at a profit of 10%. If each TV was sold for the same price, then what is the cost price of the TV which was sold at loss?
SSC CHSL (Tier-I) 16/03/2023 Shift-I
(a) ₹ 1380 (b) ₹ 1320
(c) ₹ 1050 (d) ₹ 1440

181. Selling price of a watch is ₹ 1056 and profit percentage is 10%. If selling price is ₹ 800, then what will be the loss percentage?
SSC CHSL (Tier-I) 15/03/2023 Shift-IV
(a) 16.66% (b) 25%
(c) 12.5% (d) 15%

182. On selling of 18 pens at ₹ 360. There is a loss equal to the cost of 3 pens. What is the cost price of a pen? **SSC CHSL (Tier-I) 14/03/2023 Shift-I**
(a) ₹ 10 (b) ₹ 12
(c) ₹ 24 (d) ₹ 20

183. A trader sells an article at a profit of 20%. If he buys it at half the cost price and sells it at the same selling price as before. Then, what will be the profit percentage?
SSC CHSL (Tier-I) 13/03/2023 Shift-III
(a) 60% (b) 140%
(c) 40% (d) 240%

184. Janki purchased 10 dozens of corn at the rate of ₹ 180 per dozen. She sold each corn at the rate of ₹ 22. What was her per cent profit?
SSC CHSL (Tier-I) 10/03/2023 Shift-II
(a) 46.6% (b) 18.8%
(c) 37.7% (d) 25.5%

185. A person sells wheat at a profit of 25%. If he reduces its selling price by ₹ 40, then he suffers a loss of 25%. What was the initial selling price of the wheat?
SSC CHSL (Tier-I) 09/03/2023 Shift-I
(a) ₹ 80 (b) ₹ 120
(c) ₹ 60 (d) ₹ 100

186. *A* sells an article to *B* at 10% profit. *B* sells it to *C* at 25% profit. If *C* pays ₹ 6875 for it, then the price at which *A* bought it is
SSC CHSL (Tier-I) 02/06/2022 Shift-I
(a) ₹ 4665
(b) ₹ 4850
(c) ₹ 5000
(d) ₹ 5500

187. The profit triples if the selling price is doubled. The profit percentage is
SSC CHSL (Tier-I) 01/06/2022 Shift-I
(a) 110 (b) 50
(c) 100 (d) 28

188. A pen was sold for ₹ 28.75 at a profit of 15%. If it was sold for ₹ 25.75, then what would have been the percentage of profit ?
SSC CHSL (Tier-I) 31/05/2022 Shift-I

(a) 2% (b) 3% (c) 4% (d) 1%

189. A shopkeeper normally makes a profit of 20% in a certain transaction; he weighs 900 g instead of 1 kg, due to an issue with the weighing machine. If he charges 10% less than what he normally charges, what is his actual profit or loss percentage?
SSC CHSL (Tier-I) 27/05/2022 Shift-I

(a) 20% (b) 28% (c) 25% (d) 30%

190. A shopkeeper sold an article for ₹ 3750. If he had charged 24% less, even then he would have earned a profit of 14%. What is the original cost of the article?
SSC CHSL (Tier-I) 12/08/2021 Shift-III

(a) ₹ 2850 (b) ₹ 2717
(c) ₹ 3289 (d) ₹ 2500

191. An article is sold at a certain price. If it is sold at $33\frac{1}{3}$% of this price, there is loss of $33\frac{1}{3}$%. What is the percentage profit or percentage loss when it is sold at 40% of the original selling price?
SSC CHSL (Tier-I) 10/08/2021 Shift-I

(a) Loss 12% (b) Profit 18%
(c) Loss 20% (d) Profit 15%

192. By selling an article for ₹ 1170. Elisa suffers as much loss as the would have gained by selling it at a profit of 22%. If she sells it for ₹ 1450, then her profit/loss percent (correct up to one decimal place) is
SSC CHSL (Tier-I) 04/08/2021 Shift-I

(a) Profit, 3.3% (b) Loss, 3.3%
(c) Loss, 26.2% (d) Profit, 26.2%

193. A shopkeeper bought 840 kg of rice. A part of it was sold at 25% profit and the remaining at 10% loss and on the whole, the profit was 15%. What was the quantity of rice which was sold at 10% loss?
SSC CHSL (Tier-I) 19/04/2021 Shift-I

(a) 240 kg (b) 220 kg
(c) 340 kg (d) 260 kg

194. A shopkeeper sells two refrigerator sets at the same price. He gains 40% on one refrigerator and losses 40% on the other. What in his net loss percentage in the whole transaction?
SSC CHSL (Tier-I) 12/04/2021 Shift-II

(a) 18% (b) 14% (c) 12% (d) 16%

SSC MTS 2024

195. Which of the following equations is correct? **SSC MTS 14/11/2024 Shift-III**

(a) Gain % = CP / (gain × 100)
(b) $SP = (100 - gain\%) \times \frac{CP}{100}$
(c) $SP = (100 - loss\%) \times \frac{CP}{100}$
(d) Loss = CP − SP

196. A dealer sells his goods at 5% loss on cost price but uses $12\frac{1}{2}$% less weight. Find his percentage of loss or gain. **SSC MTS 14/11/2024 Shift-III**

(a) Gain $7\frac{4}{7}$% (b) Gain $8\frac{4}{7}$%
(c) Loss $8\frac{4}{7}$% (d) Loss $7\frac{8}{7}$%

197. Find the gain percentage, given that Komal sold her scooter for ₹ 1980 gaining $\frac{1}{5}$th of the selling price. **SSC MTS 13/11/2024 Shift-III**

(a) 20% (b) 45% (c) 40% (d) 25%

198. Ramesh bought a watch for ₹ 460 and sold it for ₹ 414. Find his percentage of loss.
SSC MTS 13/11/2024 Shift-III

(a) 11% (b) 10% (c) 5% (d) 20%

199. Mihir buys a toy for ₹ 70 and sells it for ₹ 90. What is his gain percentage? **SSC MTS 12/11/2024 Shift-III**

(a) 28.57% (b) 35.62%
(c) 25.25% (d) 20%

200. Amar buys a wall clock for ₹ 300 and sells it for ₹ 200. Find his percentage loss.
SSC MTS 11/11/2024 Shift-III

(a) 32.33% gain (b) 30.33% loss
(c) 33.33% loss (d) 31.33% gain

201. A dishonest shopkeeper promises to sell his goods at cost price. However, he uses a weight that actually weights 33% less than what is written on it. Find his profit percentage. **SSC MTS 11/11/2024 Shift-III**

(a) $48\frac{17}{67}$% (b) $50\frac{18}{67}$%
(c) $49\frac{17}{67}$% (d) $51\frac{34}{67}$%

202. A dealer made some profit by selling a laptop for ₹ 88000, which is equal to the amount of loss incurred on selling the same laptop for ₹ 72000. If he had sold the laptop for ₹ 96000, then his profit percentage would have been
SSC MTS 05/11/2024 Shift-III

(a) 31.7% (b) 25% (c) 20% (d) 37.5%

203. A shopkeeper sells an article for ₹ 450.30 with a loss of 21%. What is the cost price (in ₹) of the article?
SSC MTS 05/11/2024 Shift-III

(a) 429 (b) 570 (c) 521 (d) 485

204. Mr Rao purchased a laptop for ₹ 45000. After a few months, as his office provided another laptop, he sold it at a loss of 12% to Mrs Sharma. After one year, she sold it to an engineering student for a profit of 12%. What is the amount the student had to pay?
SSC MTS 04/11/2024 Shift-III

(a) ₹ 45000 (b) ₹ 34848
(c) ₹ 44352 (d) ₹ 56448

205. 400 chickooes were bought at ₹ 1280 per hundred and were sold at a profit of ₹ 980. Find the selling price (in ₹) per dozen of chickooes.
SSC MTS 04/11/2024 Shift-III

(a) 193 (b) 173 (c) 183 (d) 198

206. By selling an article for ₹ 19.5, a dealer makes a profit of 25%. By how much should he increase his selling price (in ₹) so as to make a profit of 50%? **SSC MTS 30/10/2024 Shift-III**

(a) 6.9 (b) 5.9 (c) 4.9 (d) 3.9

207. Rahul sells an article at 8% above its cost price. If he had bought it at 5% less than what he had paid for it and sold it at ₹ 8 less, he would have gained 12%. Find the cost price of the article.
SSC MTS 30/10/2024 Shift-III

(a) ₹ 650 (b) ₹ 550
(c) ₹ 700 (d) ₹ 500

208. A vendor bought candies at ₹ 5 each. At what price must he sell to make 20% profit?
SSC MTS 29/10/2024 Shift-III

(a) ₹ 6.00 (b) ₹ 5.50
(c) ₹ 5.75 (d) ₹ 5.25

209. By selling an article for ₹ 20, a dealer makes a profit of 10%. By how much should he increase his selling price (in ₹, rounded off to two decimal place) so as to make a profit of 30%? **SSC MTS 29/10/2024 Shift-III**

(a) 6.64 (b) 3.64
(c) 5.64 (d) 4.64

210. A shopkeeper sold the Refrigerator and the Geyser set together for ₹ 30400, thereby making a profit of 25% on the Refrigerator and 10% on the Geyser. By selling them together for ₹ 30700, he would have made a 10% profit on the Refrigerator and 25% on the

Geyser. Now, if the Geyser is sold at 17% profit, then the selling price (in ₹) of the Geyser is
SSC MTS 28/10/2024 Shift-II

(a) 14380 (b) 12130
(c) 16380 (d) 17510

211. Find the percentage, given that Nidhi sold her scooter for ₹ 80442 gaining $\frac{1}{6}$th of the selling price.
SSC MTS 23/10/2024 Shift-II

(a) 20% (b) 15%
(c) 35% (d) 10%

212. Reena buys an iron for ₹ 900 and sells it at a loss of 12%. What is the selling price of the iron?
SSC MTS 23/10/2024 Shift-II

(a) ₹ 763 (b) ₹ 658
(c) ₹ 825 (d) ₹ 792

213. By selling an article for ₹ 19, a dealer makes a profit of 10%. By how much should he increase his selling price (in ₹, rounded off to two decimal place) so as to make a profit of 40%? **SSC MTS 22/10/2024 Shift-II**

(a) 7.18 (b) 8.18
(c) 6.18 (d) 5.18

214. A shopkeeper buys 15 mobiles and sells 12 mobiles at the cost price of 15 mobiles. If the shopkeeper sells all the mobiles at the same price at which he sold the 12 mobiles in the first case, what is the profit percentage? **SSC MTS 21/10/2024 Shift-II**

(a) 22.5% (b) 27.5%
(c) 20% (d) 25%

215. A dishonest dealer claims to sell groceries at cost price and still makes a profit of $2\frac{22}{39}$%. For a kg, he uses a weight of
SSC MTS 21/10/2024 Shift-II

(a) 985 gm (b) 978 gm
(c) 975 gm (d) 981 gm

216. *P* sold an article to *Q* at 11% profit and *Q* sold it to R at 11% loss. If R paid ₹ 19758 for it, then at what price (in ₹) was the article purchased by *P*?
SSC MTS 18/10/2024 Shift-II

(a) 19750 (b) 19500
(c) 22500 (d) 20000

217. *A* sold an article to *B* at 40% profit and *B* sold it to C at 15% profit. If *C* paid ₹ 4914 for the article, how much (in ₹, rounded off to the nearest integer) did *A* pay for it?
SSC MTS 18/10/2024 Shift-II

(a) 2576 (b) 3520
(c) 3250 (d) 3052

218. Find the gain percentage, given that Aditi sold her scooter for ₹ 40675 gaining $\frac{1}{5}$th of the selling price. **SSC MTS 17/10/2024 Shift-II**

(a) 5% (b) 25% (c) 15% (d) 35%

219. If the cost price of 30 books is same as the selling price of 20 books, then the gain percentage is
SSC MTS 16/10/2024 Shift-II

(a) 50% (b) 40% (c) 15% (d) 25%

220. A man bought an article for ₹ 500 and sold it for ₹ 600. Find his profit percentage. **SSC MTS 16/10/2024 Shift-II**

(a) 40% (b) 30% (c) 20% (d) 10%

221. A dishonest shopkeeper promises to sell his goods at cost price. However, he uses a weight that actually weights 19% less than what is written on it. Find his profit percentage. **SSC MTS 15/10/2024 Shift-I**

(a) $23\frac{37}{81}$% (b) $24\frac{38}{81}$%
(c) $22\frac{37}{81}$% (d) $25\frac{74}{81}$%

222. The cost price of 25 balls is the same as the selling price of 20 balls. Find the profit percentage.
SSC MTS 15/10/2024 Shift-I

(a) 18% (b) 25%
(c) 15% (d) 16.66%

223. If the cost price of an article is 75% of its selling price, then the profit percent is **SSC MTS 14/10/2024 Shift-I**

(a) 33% (b) $33\frac{1}{3}$%
(c) $25\frac{1}{3}$% (d) 25%

224. A dishonest dealer professes to sell his goods at cost price but uses a false weight and thus gains 15%. For a kilogram he uses a weight of .... grams. **SSC MTS 14/10/2024 Shift-I**

(a) 930.43 (b) 830.43
(c) 1130.43 (d) 869.57

225. Two vendors calculate their profit percentage on the cost price and selling price, respectively. What will be the difference between the profits (in ₹) if both the vendors declare a profit of 28% on the goods sold for ₹ 3200?
SSC MTS 09/10/2024 Shift-I

(a) 196 (b) 700 (c) 548 (d) 896

226. A person sold an article and got a loss of 9%. If he sold it for ₹ 51 more he would gain 8%. Find the CP. **SSC MTS 09/10/2024 Shift-I**

(a) ₹ 400 (b) ₹ 250
(c) ₹ 350 (d) ₹ 300

227. A flat worth ₹ 950000 is sold by Lakshman to Bharath at 8% profit. If Bharath sells it back to Lakshman at 3% loss, then find the gain/loss (in ₹) of Lakshman in the entire transaction?
SSC MTS 08/10/2024 Shift-I

(a) Lakshman gains ₹ 30780
(b) Lakshman gains ₹ 50200
(c) Lakshman gains ₹ 45220
(d) Lakshman loses ₹ 45220

228. Alfred buys an old scooter for ₹ 4700 and spends ₹ 800 on its repairs. If he sells the scooter for ₹ 5800, his gain percentage is
SSC MTS 08/10/2024 Shift-I

(a) 4.5% (b) $5\frac{4}{11}$%
(c) $6\frac{5}{11}$% (d) $5\frac{5}{11}$%

229. If the cash difference between the selling price of an item at a gain of 3% and 6% is ₹ 9, which of the following options is the correct ratio between the selling prices?
SSC MTS 07/10/2024 Shift-I

(a) 101 : 103 (b) 103 : 100
(c) 103 : 106 (d) 101 : 105

230. Raju sold 4 laptops at a rate of ₹ 154005 all together and incurred a loss of 25%. At what rate should he sell the laptops to gain a profit of 25%? **SSC MTS 07/10/2024 Shift-I**

(a) ₹ 225820 (b) ₹ 256675
(c) ₹ 231007.5 (d) ₹ 205340

231. Surendra bought an old bicycle for ₹ 2500 and spent ₹ 300 on its repair. He sold it for ₹ 3000. Find his profit percentage. **SSC MTS 07/10/2024 Shift-I**

(a) $7\frac{1}{7}$% (b) $11\frac{2}{3}$%
(c) $7\frac{5}{9}$% (d) $13\frac{4}{11}$%

232. By selling an article for ₹ 20, a dealer makes a profit of 10%. By how much should he increase his selling price (in ₹, rounded off to two decimal place) so as to make a profit of 20%? **SSC MTS 01/10/2024 Shift-I**

(a) 2.82 (b) 4.82
(c) 1.82 (d) 3.82

233. Atul sold two sacks of rice for ₹ 19200 each. On one, he gained 20% and on the other, he lost 20%. Find his gain or loss percentage in the whole transaction.
SSC MTS 30/09/2024 Shift-I

(a) 8% profit (b) 7% profit
(c) 4% loss (d) 5% loss

234. A man sells an article at a certain price and suffers a loss of 20%. If he sells the article at ₹100 more, he gets a profit of 30%. Find the cost price of the article (in ₹). SSC MTS 30/09/2024 Shift-I

(a) 250 (b) 300 (c) 400 (d) 200

SSC MTS 2023-2021

235. A jewel was sold passing through 3 hands and on the whole, its price is raised by 80%. The first seller earns 20% profit and the second seller earns 25% profit, respectively. Find the percentage of profit earned by the third seller. SSC MTS 14/09/2023 Shift-I

(a) 20% (b) 10% (c) 15% (d) 5%

236. Atul sells goods to a customer at a profit of P %. If the cost price of the goods for the customer is ₹ 15000 and Atul makes a profit of ₹ 3000, then what is the value of P ? SSC MTS 14/09/2023 Shift-I

(a) 22 (b) 25 (c) 20 (d) 28

237. Some oranges were purchased at ₹ 150 per hundred and sold at ₹ 24 per dozen. It gave a gain of ₹1000. How many oranges were purchased? SSC MTS 13/09/2023 Shift-I

(a) 3000 (b) 2500
(c) 1500 (d) 2000

238. By selling a calculator for ₹ 1080, there is a loss of 10%. If the article is sold for ₹ 1350, the net result in the transaction is SSC MTS 13/09/2023 Shift-I

(a) $12\frac{1}{2}$% loss (b) 12% gain
(c) $12\frac{1}{2}$% gain (d) 12% loss

239. By investing ₹ 12000 in a scheme *R* gets ₹ 15500 back in return. What is his percentage of profit? SSC MTS 11/09/2023 Shift-II

(a) 27.19% (b) 29.17%
(c) 17.92% (d) 19.17%

240. Robin purchases a fan for ₹ 2000 and later sells it at a loss of 15%. At what price did he sell the fan? SSC MTS 11/09/2023 Shift-II

(a) ₹ 1900 (b) ₹ 1800
(c) ₹ 1700 (d) ₹ 2100

241. If the manufacturer gains 10%, the wholesale dealer gains 12% and the retailer gains 15%, then find the cost production of a table, the retail price of which is ₹ 1771. SSC MTS 11/09/2023 Shift-I

(a) ₹ 1150 (b) ₹ 1050
(c) ₹ 1250 (d) ₹ 1350

242. If the selling price of 16 bulbs is equal to the cost price of 24 bulbs, what is the profit percentage? SSC MTS 11/09/2023 Shift-I

(a) 40% (b) 50%
(c) 25% (d) 20%

243. A man sold his cycle at 17% loss. If he had sold it for ₹1056 more, he would have made 5% profit. The cost price of the cycle is SSC MTS 08/09/2023 Shift-II

(a) ₹ 4700 (b) ₹ 3800
(c) ₹ 5100 (d) ₹ 4800

244. A dealer buys some goods for ₹ 3600. If the overhead expenses be 5% of the cost price, then at what price should it be sold to earn 15% ? SSC MTS 08/09/2023 Shift-II

(a) ₹ 4347 (b) ₹ 4734
(c) ₹ 4437 (d) ₹ 4743

245. By selling a book at some price, Ankita gains 10%. If the book is sold at twice the price, then what will be the gain percentage for Ankita? SSC MTS 06/09/2023 Shift-I

(a) 140% (b) 100% (c) 120% (d) 125%

246. The profit obtained by a vendor on selling goods at ₹ 3200 is equal to 7/5th of the profit obtained by selling the same goods at ₹ 3000. What is the cost price (in ₹) of the goods? SSC MTS 06/09/2023 Shift-I

(a) 2500 (b) 2700
(c) 2400 (d) 2900

247. Divya bought six candies for a rupee. How many candies for a rupee must she sell to gain 50% ? SSC MTS 05/09/2023 Shift-II

(a) Four (b) Three
(c) One (d) Two

248. Nikita made two investments she earns 10% on one investment and loss 20% on the second investment. If the investments were in the ratio 2 : 3, then she got a SSC MTS 05/09/2023 Shift-II

(a) loss of 8% (b) profit of 15%
(c) profit of 8% (d) loss of 15%

249. A grocer purchased 50 kg of sugar at ₹ 40 per kg and mixed with 70 kg of sugar at ₹ 30 per kg. At what rate should he sell the mixture (per kg) to gain 20%? SSC MTS 04/09/2023 Shift-I

(a) ₹ 60 (b) ₹ 20 (c) ₹ 35 (d) ₹ 41

250. The percentage profit earned by selling an article for ₹ 1980 is equal to the percentage loss incurred by selling the same article for ₹ 1620. At what price should the article be sold to make a 15% profit? SSC MTS 01/09/2023 Shift-III

(a) ₹ 1863 (b) ₹ 2277
(c) ₹ 2070 (d) ₹ 1800

251. Raju sold an article to Ravi at 10% gain. Ravi sold the article to Ramu at a loss of 10%. If Ramu paid ₹ 1485 to Ravi, find the selling price of Raju to Ravi. SSC MTS 01/09/2023 Shift-I

(a) ₹ 1200 (b) ₹ 1500
(c) ₹ 1650 (d) ₹ 1600

252. The cost price of an item is ₹ 4350. What is the profit percentage (rounded off to 1 decimal place), if it is sold at ₹ 5680? SSC MTS 01/09/2023 Shift-I

(a) 28.5% (b) 40.7%
(c) 36.8% (d) 30.6%

253. The selling price of a desktop is 9 times of the profit earned on selling this desktop. What is the profit percentage ? SSC MTS 15/07/2022 Shift-I

(a) 10% (b) 12.5%
(c) 11.11% (d) 8.33%

254. Vinay purchased two bottles for a total of ₹ 100 and he sells these two bottles at the rate of ₹ 100 per bottle. What is the overall profit percentage that Vinay had on selling the two bottles ? SSC MTS 15/07/2022 Shift-I

(a) 50% (b) 100%
(c) 200% (d) 80%

255. The cost prices of a pen and a notebook are ₹ 600 and ₹ 4000, respectively. If the pen and the notebook are sold at losses of 20% and 32%, respectively, what will be the approximate percentage of total loss incurred through the two sales made ? SSC MTS 14/07/2022 Shift-I

(a) 21.40% (b) 26.08%
(c) 30.43% (d) 28.42%

256. A shopkeeper sells an item at a loss of 8%. However, if he increases the selling price by ₹ 36, he could gain 12%. Find the cost price (in ₹) of the article. SSC MTS 14/07/2022 Shift-I

(a) 180 (b) 270
(c) 150 (d) 360

257. Sandeep buys a toy car for ₹ 500 and sells it for ₹ 625. What is his gain or loss percentage ? SSC MTS 13/07/2022 Shift-I

(a) 20% gain (b) 20% loss
(c) 25% gain (d) 25% loss

258. A man buys 15 identical articles for a total of ₹ 15. If he sells each of them for ₹ 1.23, then his profit percentage is **SSC MTS 13/07/2022 Shift-I**

(a) 23% (b) 32% (c) 50% (d) 8%

259. The selling prices of two articles are equal. If the first article is sold at a profit of 20% and the second article is sold at a loss of 20%, what will be the overall loss percentage? **SSC MTS 12/07/2022 Shift-I**

(a) 4% (b) 3.5% (c) 2.5% (d) 2%

260. Vishal sells a bag at a profit of 40%. If Vishal's profit is ₹880, then what is the cost price of the bag ? **SSC MTS 12/07/2022 Shift-I**

(a) ₹ 2000 (b) ₹ 2450
(c) ₹ 1900 (d) ₹ 2200

261. Prakash bought 2 items, paying the same price for each of them. He sold one item at a profit of 20% and the other item at a profit of 25%. What is the overall percentage profit he made? **SSC MTS 11/07/2022 Shift-I**

(a) 37.5% (b) 24.5%
(c) 16.5% (d) 22.5%

262. A fabric seller sells 65 m of cloth for ₹ 5850 at a profit of ₹ 11 per metre of cloth. What is the cost price of 1 m of cloth? **SSC MTS 11/07/2022 Shift-I**

(a) ₹70 (b) ₹89 (c) ₹80 (d) ₹79

263. If a shopkeeper purchases a certain number of items for a certain sum and sells a fraction of the said number for the same amount, then his profit is 300%. What is the fraction? **SSC MTS 02/11/2021 Shift-III**

(a) $\frac{1}{4}$ (b) $\frac{1}{3}$ (c) $\frac{1}{6}$ (d) $\frac{1}{2}$

264. A retailer bought 250 kg of a cereal and sold it at a profit to the extent of what he paid for 160 kg. What is his profit percentage? **SSC MTS 02/11/2021 Shift-III**

(a) 32 (b) 64 (c) 36 (d) 18

265. *A* sells an article to *B* at 12% profit. *B* sells it to C at 9% loss. If C pays ₹ 15288 for it, then at what price (in ₹) is the article sold by A? **SSC MTS 02/11/2021 Shift-II**

(a) 15000 (b) 16800
(c) 16000 (d) 14250

266. The cost price of an article is $\frac{7}{6}$ times the selling price. What is the loss/gain percentage (correct up to two decimal places)? **SSC MTS 02/11/2021 Shift-II**

(a) Loss 14.29% (b) Gain 16.67%
(c) Loss 16.67% (d) Gain 19.54%

267. A shopkeeper purchased 20 dozen pens at the rate of ₹ 190 per dozen, and spent ₹ 200 as to and for expenses to the wholesale market. He sold the pens at the rate of ₹ 22/pen. Find his profit percentage. **SSC MTS 02/11/2021 Shift-I**

(a) $38\frac{18}{19}\%$ (b) 20%
(c) 22% (d) 32%

SSC GD Constable 2024

268. If the cost price of an article is 5/8 of its selling price, then what is the profit percentage ? **SSC GD Constable 26/02/2024 Shift-I**

(a) 45% (b) 75% (c) 30% (d) 60%

269. Ramesh earns profit of ₹ 46 by selling an article for ₹ 236. What is the profit percentage? **SSC GD Constable 24/02/2024 Shift-III**

(a) 26.66% (b) 27.27%
(c) 24.21% (d) 30.03%

270. Price of 1 kg of tomato is increased by 120% and the increase is of ₹ 720. What is the new price of the tomato per kg? **SSC GD Constable 24/02/2024 Shift-III**

(a) ₹ 590 (b) ₹ 720
(c) ₹ 600 (d) ₹ 1320

271. The difference between cost price and selling price of a watch is ₹ 560. If profit percentage is 35%, then what is the selling price? **SSC GD Constable 24/02/2024 Shift-III**

(a) ₹ 2240 (b) ₹ 2200
(c) ₹ 2340 (d) ₹ 2160

272. The profit earned on selling an article for ₹ 4550 is 5 times of the loss incurred on selling the same article for ₹ 3290. What will be the selling price of the article to earn a profit of 20%? **SSC GD Constable 24/02/2024 Shift-II**

(a) ₹ 3900 (b) ₹ 4200
(c) ₹ 4000 (d) ₹ 4500

273. A person bought an article and sold it at a loss of 10%. If he had bought it for 30% less price and sold it for ₹ 20 more, then he would earn a profit of 40%. What is the cost price of the article? **SSC GD Constable 24/02/2024 Shift-I**

(a) ₹ 300 (b) ₹ 250 (c) ₹ 350 (d) ₹ 200

274. An article is sold for ₹ 4400 at a loss of 20%. What is the cost price of the article? **SSC GD Constable 24/02/2024 Shift-I**

(a) ₹ 6200 (b) ₹ 5000
(c) ₹ 5500 (d) ₹ 5200

275. *P* sells a chair to *Q* at a profit of 40% and *Q* sells it to *R* at a profit of 80%. What is the ratio of cost prices of *P* and *R* ? **SSC GD Constable 23/02/2024 Shift-IV**

(a) 12:25 (b) 25:63
(c) 13: 12 (d) 25:36

276. A shopkeeper sold a flower pot for ₹ 3500. If the cost price of the flower pot is ₹ 2800, find the profit per cent **SSC GD Constable 23/02/2024 Shift-IV**

(a) 20% (b) 30%
(c) 25% (d) 15%

277. Ratio of the cost price and the selling price of a bulb is 20 : 25. What is the profit percentage? **SSC GD Constable 23/02/2024 Shift-III**

(a) 15% (b) 20%
(c) 30% (d) 25%

278. Anil sells a table at a loss of 20%. If he sells it for ₹ 160 more, he earns a profit of 20%. What should be the selling price of the table to earn a profit of 25% ? **SSC GD Constable 23/02/2024 Shift-III**

(a) ₹ 700 (b) ₹ 800
(c) ₹ 500 (d) ₹ 750

279. Pankaj purchased two bikes, first for ₹ 24000 and the second for ₹ 20000. He sold both the bikes, first one at the profit of 20% and the second at a loss of 30%. What is the overall profit or loss? **SSC GD Constable 23/02/2024 Shift-II**

(a) Loss = ₹ 1400 (b) Profit = ₹ 1400
(c) Profit = ₹ 1200 (d) Loss = ₹ 1200

280. Riya sold a laptop for ₹ 35000, earning a profit of 25%. If she wanted to earn a profit of 30%, at what price should she have sold the laptop? **SSC GD Constable 23/02/2024 Shift-I**

(a) ₹ 34600 (b) ₹ 37200
(c) ₹ 38400 (d) ₹ 36400

281. Mohan buys an old mobile for ₹ 4000 and spends ₹ 500 on its repairs. If he sells the mobile for ₹ 5000, then what is his profit percentage? **SSC GD Constable 23/02/2024 Shift-I**

(a) 9.09% (b) 13.5%
(c) 11.11% (d) 12.5%

282. Selling price of a bag is ₹ 1056 and profit percentage is 20%. If selling price is ₹ 800, then what will be the loss percentage? **SSC GD Constable 22/02/2024 Shift-IV**

(a) 4.25% (b) 11.11%
(c) 9.09% (d) 8.08%

283. While selling a bag for ₹ 5688, a person suffered a loss of 10%. At what price he should have sold the bag to earn a profit of 20%?
SSC GD Constable 22/02/2024 Shift-III

(a) ₹ 7584 (b) ₹ 6816
(c) ₹ 7854 (d) ₹ 7216

284. If an article is sold at a loss of 20%, then what is the respective ratio of cost price and selling price of the article? **SSC GD Constable 22/02/2024 Shift-III**

(a) 4 : 5 (b) 5 : 4 (c) 7 : 4 (d) 7 : 8

285. A person bought an article and sold it at a loss of 20%. If he had bought it for 30% less price and sold in for ₹ 125 more, then he would earn profit of 50%. What is the cost price of the article
SSC GD Constable 22/02/2024 Shift-II

(a) ₹ 620 (b) ₹ 500 (c) ₹ 450 (d) ₹ 600

286. A person bought some pens at the rate of 20 for a rupee and sold them at the rate of 15 for a rupee. What is the profit percentage?
SSC GD Constable 22/02/2024 Shift-II

(a) 33.33% (b) 15%
(c) 35% (d) 40%

287. Anurag sold a refrigerator for ₹ 28000, at a loss of 30%. If he wanted to earn a profit of 25%, at what price should he have sold the refrigerator?
SSC GD Constable 22/02/2024 Shift-I

(a) ₹ 52700 (b) ₹ 52000
(c) ₹ 50000 (d) ₹ 51500

288. A watch is purchased for ₹ 6000 and sold for ₹ 5500. What is the loss percentage?
SSC GD Constable 22/02/2024 Shift-I

(a) 8.08% (b) 11.11%
(c) 8.33% (d) 7.28%

289. The difference between cost price and selling price is ₹ 132. If profit percentage is 20%, then what is the selling price?
SSC GD Constable 21/02/2024 Shift-IV

(a) ₹ 802 (b) ₹ 822 (c) ₹ 792 (d) ₹ 760

290. Suresh sells a car at the loss of 36%. What will be the ratio of cost price to selling price?
SSC GD Constable 21/02/2024 Shift-III

(a) 16 : 25 (b) 25 : 16
(c) 15 : 16 (d) 4 : 5

291. If the cost price of 5 shirts is the same as the selling price of 3 shirts, find the profit percentage.
SSC GD Constable 21/02/2024 Shift-II

(a) 55.33%, profit (b) 63.33%, profit
(c) 33.66%, profit (d) 66.66%, profit

292. A table when sold for ₹ 11480 gives a loss of 18%. Calculate the loss or gain percentage when the same table is sold ₹ 15540.
SSC GD Constable 21/02/2024 Shift-II

(a) 12% loss (b) 11% profit
(c) 12% profit (d) 10% loss

293. A man buys 35 pens for a rupee. How many pens should he sell for a rupee to earn a profit of 40%?
SSC GD Constable 21/02/2024 Shift-I

(a) 34 (b) 25
(c) 27 (d) 37

294. If 70% of total articles are sold at a profit of 20% and remaining articles are sold at a loss of 10%, then what will be the overall profit percentage?
SSC GD Constable 21/02/2024 Shift-I

(a) 15% (b) 11%
(c) 12% (d) 8%

295. If selling price of a table is 25% of its cost price, then what is the loss percentage?
SSC GD Constable 20/02/2024 Shift-IV

(a) 75% (b) 45%
(c) 55% (d) 35%

296. A man buys 35 mangoes for a rupee. How many mangoes had he sold for a rupee so that there is a loss of 30%?
SSC GD Constable 20/02/2024 Shift-III

(a) 50 (b) 27
(c) 45 (d) 33

297. Ankit sells an article at a loss of 10%. If he buys it for 30% less price and sells it for ₹ 26 less price, then his profit will be 10%. What is the cost price of the article?
SSC GD Constable 20/02/2024 Shift-III

(a) ₹ 250 (b) ₹ 200
(c) ₹ 320 (d) ₹ 300

298. If the cost price of 6 pens is the same as the selling price of 5 pens, find the profit/loss percentage.
SSC GD Constable 20/02/2024 Shift-II

(a) 20% profit
(b) 20% loss
(c) 10% loss
(d) 10% profit

299. Selling price of a table is ₹ 6875. If profit percentage is 25%, then what is the cost price of table?
SSC GD Constable 20/02/2024 Shift-II

(a) ₹ 6400 (b) ₹ 5500
(c) ₹ 5000 (d) ₹ 5200

300. Both *A* and *B* sells their watch at the rate of ₹ 5000 per watch. *A* earned a profit of 25%, while *B* incurred a loss of 10%. What is the ratio of cost price of *A* and *B* ?
SSC GD Constable 20/02/2024 Shift-I

(a) 17 : 20 (b) 18 : 25
(c) 16 : 25 (d) 9 : 10

301. Rohit buys an old bat for ₹ 2320 and spends ₹ 180 on its repairing. If he sells it for ₹ 2400, then what is the loss percentage?
SSC GD Constable 20/02/2024 Shift-I

(a) 10% (b) 5%
(c) 8% (d) 4%

SSC GD Constable 2023

302. If goods are purchased for ₹ 600 and one fifth is sold at a loss of 20%, at what gain per cent should the remainder be sold so as to gain 30% on the whole transaction?
SSC GD Constable 13/02/2023 Shift-IV

(a) 40% (b) 22%
(c) 42.5% (d) 22.5%

303. The profit on selling an item for ₹ 900 is twice the loss incurrent on selling the same item for ₹ 450. At what price should the item be add to earn 25% profit?
SSC GD Constable 13/02/2023 Shift-IV

(a) ₹ 950 (b) ₹ 650
(c) ₹ 750 (d) ₹ 850

304. A fruit merchant makes a profit of 25% by selling mangoes at a certain price. If he charges ₹ 3 more on each mango, he will gain 40%. Find the cost price of one mango
SSC GD Constable 13/02/2023 Shift-II

(a) ₹ 30 (b) ₹ 25
(c) ₹ 20 (d) ₹ 15

305. The selling price of a product is such that the seller earns a profit of 20% on the cost price. Determine the ratio of selling price to cost price. **SSC GD Constable 13/02/2023 Shift-II**

(a) $\frac{3}{4}$ (b) $\frac{5}{6}$ (c) $\frac{6}{5}$ (d) $\frac{4}{3}$

306. A dealer buys 50 chairs for ₹ 50000, but 20 of them are damaged. He decides to sell each of the damaged chairs at $\frac{3}{4}$ the price of the normal one. What should this normal price be in order that he can make a profit of 35% in the entire transaction
SSC GD Constable 09/02/2023 Shift-II

(a) ₹ 6750 (b) ₹ 5000
(c) ₹ 1125 (d) ₹ 1500

307. A milkman bought 90 litres of milk for ₹ 1630 and added 15 litres of water. If he sells it at ₹ 19.00 per litre, his profit percentage will be
SSC GD Constable 09/02/2023 Shift-I

(a) $22\frac{64}{163}\%$ (b) $22\frac{14}{163}\%$
(c) $12\frac{64}{163}\%$ (d) $20\frac{64}{163}\%$

308. What is the percentage loss when the cost price and selling price of an article are in the ratio of 5 : 3 ?
SSC GD Constable 09/02/2023 Shift-I

(a) 60% (b) 30% (c) 40% (d) 50%

309. A wholesaler has 1000 kg sugar, part of which he sells at 6% profit and the rest at 12% profit. His gain is 10% on the whole. The quantity sold at 6% profit is (consider up to two decimals)
SSC GD Constable 07/02/2023 Shift-I

(a) 666.66 kg (b) 336.33 kg
(c) 663.66 kg (d) 333.33 kg

310. A dishonest shopkeeper sells rice at the cost price but he uses a faulty weight of 925g for 1000g. Find his gain percentage.
SSC GD Constable 07/02/2023 Shift-I

(a) 6.01% (b) 7.0%
(c) 5.3% (d) 8.11%

311. The cash difference between the selling prices of an article at a profit of 5% and 10% is ₹ 5. The ratio of the two selling prices is
SSC GD Constable 06/02/2023 Shift-I

(a) 23 : 25 (b) 10 : 5
(c) 21 : 22 (d) 5 : 10

312. A grocer sells rice at a profit of 15% and uses weights that are 20% less than the market weights. The total profit earned by him will be
SSC GD Constable 02/02/2023 Shift-I

(a) 45.37% (b) 53.74%
(c) 47.35% (d) 43.75%

313. In two ways, a shopkeeper deceives his customer. He dilutes pure honey by 20% with water and raises the price of honey by 15%. He pays ₹ 30 per kg for 40 kg of pure honey. What is his total profit from selling it?
SSC GD Constable 02/02/2023 Shift-I

(a) ₹ 456 (b) ₹ 468 (c) ₹ 422 (d) ₹ 435

314. Soni sold a mobile phone to Raju at a profit of 10%. Raju sold it to Alok at a loss of 5% and Alok sold it to Sohan at a profit of 20%. If Sohan bought it for ₹ 6270, what is the cost price (in ₹) of the mobile for Soni? SSC GD Constable 01/02/2023 Shift-I

(a) ₹5000 (b) ₹5500
(c) ₹4500 (d) ₹4650

315. A dealer sold these fifths of his goods at a gain of 25% and the remaining at cost price. What is his loss or gain percent in the whole transaction?
SSC GD Constable 01/02/2023 Shift-I

(a) 15% gain (b) 18% loss
(c) 18% gain (d) 15% loss

316. *A* house worth ₹ 100000 is sold by *A* to *B* at a profit of 6%. *B* sells house back to *A* at 3% loss. What is the gain/loss of *A* in the entire transaction?
SSC GD Constable 01/02/2023 Shift-I

(a) Loss of ₹ 3280 (b) Gain of ₹ 2802
(c) Loss of ₹ 2280 (d) Gain of ₹ 2820

SSC Selection Post 2024-2022

317. A salesman purchases goods at ₹ 1250 and is forced to sell it at ₹ 1000. Find his loss percentage.
Matric Level 20/06/2024 Shift-IV

(a) 25% (b) 20% (c) 30% (d) 15%

318. A shopkeeper expects a gain of 36% on his cost price. If in a month, his sale was ₹ 614856, then what was his profit (in ₹)?
Matric Level 20/06/2024 Shift-IV

(a) 161235 (b) 163900
(c) 162756 (d) 162800

319. Rayan purchased a laptop for ₹ 56000 and a scanner-cum-printer for ₹ 22000. He sold the laptop for a 20% profit and the scanner-cum printer for a 15% profit. What is his profit percentage?
Graduate Level 20/06/2024 Shift-III

(a) $12\frac{23}{39}$ (b) $18\frac{23}{39}$ (c) $18\frac{21}{37}$ (d) $12\frac{21}{37}$

320. Sonam purchased a mobile phone for ₹ 27000 and sold it at a loss of 19%. With that money she purchased a tablet and sold it at a gain of 20%. What is her overall gain or loss?
Graduate Level 27/06/2023 Shift-IV

(a) gain of ₹ 870 (b) loss of ₹ 756
(c) loss of ₹ 856 (d) gain of ₹ 756

321. The cost price of milk is increased to ₹ 62 from ₹ 60. The milkman sold milk at 10% profit earlier. What is his profit% now if he sells milk at the same rate?
Graduate Level 27/06/2023 Shift-IV

(a) 5.46% (b) 6.54% (c) 6.45% (d) 5.64%

322. Ram sold two bags at ₹ 1260 each. On one, he gained 20% and on the other, he lost 20%. Find his gain or loss percentage in the whole transaction.
Graduate Level 27/06/2023 Shift-IV

(a) Gain 4% (b) Gain 5%
(c) Loss 4% (d) Loss 5%

323. *A* sells an article to *B* at a gain of 16%, *B* sells it to *C* at a loss of 15%, and *C* sells it to *D* at a gain of 20%. If the difference between the profits earned by *C* and *A* is ₹248, then the loss (in ₹) incurred by *B* is
Higher Secondary Level 27/06/2023 Shift-III

(a) 1250 (b) 1075 (c) 1160 (d) 1025

324. If the cost price is 94% of the selling price, then find the profit percentage. Matric Level 27/06/2023 Shift-I

(a) 6.5% (b) 4.6% (c) 6.4% (d) 5.6%

325. A grocer sells pulses at a profit of 13% and uses weights which are 24% less than the market weight. The percentage of profit (correct to 2 decimal places) earned by him will be Matric Level 27/06/2023 Shift-I

(a) 45.56% (b) 37.75%
(c) 48.68% (d) 42.35%

326. Dinesh purchased a book set at ₹1200 and sold it for ₹900 only. Find out the percentage loss incurred by him?
Graduate Level 01/08/2022 Shift-IV

(a) 30% (b) 20% (c) 25% (d) 35%

327. Sohan buys an old car for ₹ 247000 and spends ₹ 18000 on its repairs. If he sells the car for ₹ 278250, his profit percentage is
Higher Secondary 01/08/2022 Shift-II

(a) 4% (b) 6% (c) 5% (d) 3%

328. A seller sells two shirts for ₹ 3360. The cost of four such shirts for the shopkeeper was ₹ 5600. What is the profit/loss percentage on each shirt? Higher Secondary 01/08/2022 Shift-II

(a) 10% profit (b) 20% profit
(c) 25% profit (d) 5% loss

329. A notebook was sold for ₹ 23 with a profit of 15%. If it were sold for ₹ 21.25, then what would have been the percentage of profit ?
Matric Level 01/08/2022 Shift-I

(a) 7.25% (b) 6.25%
(c) 5.25% (d) 4.25%

330. By selling an article for ₹ 360, a woman incurred a loss of 10%. At what price should she sell it so that she makes a profit of 20%?
Matric Level 01/08/2022 Shift-I

(a) ₹ 520 (b) ₹ 450
(c) ₹ 480 (d) ₹ 410

Right Answers

1 (d)	2 (c)	3 (c)	4 (b)	5 (b)	6 (c)	7 (c)	8 (b)	9 (d)	10 (c)
11 (b)	12 (c)	13 (c)	14 (b)	15 (d)	16 (d)	17 (b)	18 (b)	19 (b)	20 (c)
21 (b)	22 (d)	23 (c)	24 (b)	25 (c)	26 (b)	27 (b)	28 (b)	29 (a)	30 (a)
31 (a)	32 (b)	33 (d)	34 (d)	35 (d)	36 (a)	37 (b)	38 (b)	39 (a)	40 (a)
41 (b)	42 (b)	43 (c)	44 (b)	45 (d)	46 (b)	47 (c)	48 (d)	49 (c)	50 (c)
51 (d)	52 (a)	53 (b)	54 (d)	55 (c)	56 (d)	57 (d)	58 (b)	59 (d)	60 (c)
61 (a)	62 (c)	63 (a)	64 (d)	65 (a)	66 (c)	67 (a)	68 (d)	69 (a)	70 (d)
71 (d)	72 (c)	73 (b)	74 (a)	75 (a)	76 (a)	77 (a)	78 (b)	79 (a)	80 (d)
81 (a)	82 (b)	83 (a)	84 (a)	85 (b)	86 (c)	87 (b)	88 (b)	89 (b)	90 (c)
91 (b)	92 (a)	93 (b)	94 (c)	95 (a)	96 (a)	97 (b)	98 (c)	99 (c)	100 (a)
101 (b)	102 (b)	103 (b)	104 (b)	105 (b)	106 (a)	107 (b)	108 (b)	109 (d)	110 (b)
111 (b)	112 (d)	113 (c)	114 (d)	115 (b)	116 (d)	117 (d)	118 (a)	119 (c)	120 (d)
121 (d)	122 (b)	123 (d)	124 (d)	125 (c)	126 (a)	127 (b)	128 (d)	129 (b)	130 (c)
131 (b)	132 (b)	133 (d)	134 (d)	135 (a)	136 (c)	137 (b)	138 (b)	139 (a)	140 (d)
141 (a)	142 (a)	143 (a)	144 (a)	145 (a)	146 (d)	147 (c)	148 (d)	149 (c)	150 (a)
151 (a)	152 (c)	153 (d)	154 (a)	155 (d)	156 (b)	157 (b)	158 (b)	159 (a)	160 (c)
161 (a)	162 (b)	163 (c)	164 (a)	165 (b)	166 (d)	167 (d)	168 (d)	169 (a)	170 (d)
171 (c)	172 (c)	173 (d)	174 (c)	175 (a)	176 (b)	177 (a)	178 (b)	179 (b)	180 (b)
181 (a)	182 (c)	183 (b)	184 (a)	185 (d)	186 (c)	187 (c)	188 (b)	189 (a)	190 (d)
191 (c)	192 (b)	193 (a)	194 (d)	195 (c)	196 (b)	197 (d)	198 (b)	199 (a)	200 (c)
201 (c)	202 (c)	203 (b)	204 (c)	205 (c)	206 (d)	207 (d)	208 (a)	209 (b)	210 (c)
211 (a)	212 (d)	213 (d)	214 (d)	215 (c)	216 (d)	217 (d)	218 (b)	219 (a)	220 (c)
221 (a)	222 (b)	223 (b)	224 (d)	225 (a)	226 (d)	227 (a)	228 (d)	229 (c)	230 (b)
231 (a)	232 (c)	233 (c)	234 (d)	235 (a)	236 (b)	237 (d)	238 (c)	239 (b)	240 (c)
241 (c)	242 (b)	243 (d)	244 (a)	245 (c)	246 (a)	247 (a)	248 (a)	249 (d)	250 (c)
251 (c)	252 (d)	253 (b)	254 (b)	255 (c)	256 (a)	257 (c)	258 (a)	259 (a)	260 (d)
261 (d)	262 (d)	263 (a)	264 (b)	265 (b)	266 (a)	267 (d)	268 (d)	269 (c)	270 (d)
271 (d)	272 (b)	273 (b)	274 (c)	275 (b)	276 (c)	277 (d)	278 (c)	279 (d)	280 (c)
281 (c)	282 (c)	283 (a)	284 (b)	285 (b)	286 (a)	287 (c)	288 (c)	289 (c)	290 (b)
291 (d)	292 (b)	293 (b)	294 (b)	295 (a)	296 (a)	297 (b)	298 (a)	299 (b)	300 (b)
301 (d)	302 (c)	303 (c)	304 (c)	305 (c)	306 (d)	307 (a)	308 (c)	309 (d)	310 (d)
311 (c)	312 (d)	313 (a)	314 (a)	315 (a)	316 (d)	317 (b)	318 (c)	319 (b)	320 (b)
321 (c)	322 (c)	323 (c)	324 (c)	325 (c)	326 (c)	327 (c)	328 (b)	329 (b)	330 (c)

Solutions

1. (d) We have, $SP_1 = ₹\,680$

$SP_2 = ₹\,1070$

$\because \quad CP = SP_1 + \text{loss} \quad \text{...(i)}$

and $\quad CP = SP_2 - \text{profit} \quad \text{...(ii)}$

According to the question,

Profit = 2 loss

from Eq. (ii),

$CP = SP_2 - 2\,\text{loss} \quad \text{...(iii)}$

Now, from Eqs. (i) and (iii)

$3CP = 2\,SP_1 + SP_2$

$\Rightarrow \quad 3CP = 2 \times 680 + 1070$

$\Rightarrow \quad CP = ₹\,810$

2. (c) According to the question,

CP of 10 articles = ₹ 15

and SP of 10 articles = 10 × 1.7 = ₹ 17

$\therefore$ Required profit percentage $= \dfrac{17-15}{15} \times 100$

$= \dfrac{200}{15} = 13.33\%$

3. (c) SP of faulty 3 kg (2900 gm)

Potatoes = ₹ 46

CP of 2900 gm $= \dfrac{36 \times 2900}{3000} = ₹\,34.8$

[$\because$ per kg price = ₹ 12]

$\therefore$ Profit (in ₹) = 46 − 34.8 = ₹ 11.2

4. (b) Let CP of goods be ₹ $100x$.

$\therefore$ MP of goods = ₹ $116x$

$\therefore$ SP of goods $= 116x \times \dfrac{88}{100} = 102.08\,x$

$\therefore$ Required gain%

$= \dfrac{102.08x - 100x}{100x} \times 100 = 2.08\%$

5. (b) Maximum profit

= Maximum SP − Least CP

$\therefore$ Max profit on 1 book = 300 − 200 = 100

$\therefore$ Max profit on 25 books = ₹ 25 × 100

= ₹ 2500

6. (c) Given, $\dfrac{\text{Profit}}{\text{Selling price}} = \dfrac{1}{5}$

Let profit = x and selling price = $5x$

$\therefore \quad 5x = 40620 \Rightarrow x = ₹\,8124$

$\therefore$ Cost price $= 5x - x = 4x = ₹\,32496$

$\therefore$ Profit% $= \dfrac{8124}{32496} \times 100 = 25\%$

7. (c) CP $= \frac{144}{72} \times 100 = ₹200$

SP $= ₹288$

$\therefore$ Profit % $= \frac{288-200}{200} \times 100 = 44\%$

8. (b) Total cost price of 130 books

$= 130 \times 200 = ₹26000$

Total selling price

$= \frac{130}{2} \times 300 + \frac{130}{5} \times 350 + 39 \times 200$

$= 19500 + 9100 + 7800 = ₹36400$

Profit percentage $= \frac{36400-26000}{26000} \times 100$

$= \frac{10400}{26000} \times 100 = 40\%$

9. (d) Cost price for one keyboard

$= 1260 \times \frac{100}{125} = ₹1,008$

Cost price for 2nd keyboard

$= 1440 \times \frac{100}{90} = ₹1600$

Total CP $= 1008 + 1600 = ₹2608$

Total SP $= 1260 + 1440 = ₹2,700$

$\therefore$ Gain $= 2700 - 2608 = ₹92$

Gain% $= \frac{92}{2608} \times 100 = \frac{575}{163}\% = 3\frac{86}{163}\%$

10. (c) Given, 55 MP = 99 CP ...(i)

56 SP = 35 MP ...(ii)

From Eq. (i), $\frac{MP}{CP} = \frac{99}{55} = \frac{9 \times 8}{5 \times 8} = \frac{72}{40}$

From (ii), $\frac{SP}{MP} = \frac{35}{56} = \frac{5 \times 9}{8 \times 9} = \frac{45}{72}$

Profit% $= \frac{SP - CP}{CP} \times 100 = \frac{45-40}{40} \times 100$

$= \frac{5}{40} \times 100 = 12.5\%$

11. (b) According to the question,

CP of 1000 gm rice = ₹40

New SP of 800 gm rice = ₹44

$\therefore$ New SP of 1000 gm $= \frac{44}{800} \times 1000 = ₹55$

$\therefore$ Overall profit $= \frac{55-40}{40} \times 100$

$= \frac{15}{40} \times 100 = 37.5\%$

12. (c) Actual SP of 1 kg (1000 gm) = ₹10

Actual SP of 1 gm $= \frac{10}{1000} = \frac{1}{100}$

Actual SP of 900 gm = ₹7.2

Actual SP of 1 gm $= \frac{7.2}{900} = \frac{8}{1000}$

Change in price $= \frac{1}{100} - \frac{8}{1000}$

$= \frac{10-8}{1000} = \frac{2}{1000}$

Required % $= \frac{\frac{2}{1000} \times 100}{\frac{1}{100}} = 20\%$

13. (c) Selling price of 19 cookies = ₹95 and cost price of 19 cookies

$= ₹\frac{76}{20} \times 19 = ₹72.2$

$\therefore$ Profit $= 95 - 72.2 = ₹22.8$

14. (b) Given, Profit $= \frac{1}{5} \times SP \therefore \frac{P}{SP} = \frac{1}{5}$

Let profit $= x$ and SP $= 5x$

then CP $= 5x - x = 4x$

According to the question,

$5x = 71785 \Rightarrow x = \frac{71785}{5} = 14357$

$\therefore$ Profit = ₹14357

and CP $= 4 \times 14357 = 57428$

$\therefore$ Gain% $= \frac{14357}{57428} \times 100 = 25\%$

15. (d) Let CP of each articles be ₹100 and total number of article be 8.

$\therefore$ Total SP $= 5 \times 120 + 3 \times 100$ [5 articles sold at ₹120 and 3 articles sold at ₹100] = ₹900

$\therefore$ Total CP $= 8 \times 100 = ₹800$

$\therefore$ Required gain% $= \frac{900-800}{800} \times 100$

$= 12\frac{1}{2}\%$

16. (d) Let the original cost price be ₹100.

First dealer profit = 30%

First dealer's SP $= 100 + \frac{(100 \times 30)}{100} = ₹130$

Final profit = 40%

Final SP made by dealer

$= 100 \times \frac{(100+40)}{100} = ₹140$

Profit made by second dealer

$= 140 - 130 = ₹10$

Profit% earned by second dealer

$= \frac{10}{130} \times 100 = \frac{100}{13} = 7\frac{9}{13}\%$

17. (b) Cost price per kg $= \frac{44.8}{112} \times 100$

$= ₹40$ kg

Let required selling price of rest sugar be ₹ y.

Sugar that is not damaged $= \left(1 - \frac{1}{5}\right) = \frac{4}{5}$

According to the question,

$\Rightarrow \frac{4}{5} \times y = 40 \times \frac{105}{100} \Rightarrow y = \frac{2 \times 105}{5} \times \frac{5}{4}$

$\Rightarrow y = ₹52.5$

18. (b) Here, $x = 20\%$, $y = 950$ gm and $z = 1000$ gm

$\therefore$ Profit percentage $= \left[(100 + x) \times \frac{z}{y} - 100\right]\%$

$= \left[(100 + 20) \times \frac{1000}{950} - 100\right]\%$

$= \left[120 \times \frac{1000}{950} - 100\right]\% = \left[\frac{2400}{19} - 100\right]\%$

$= \frac{500}{19}\%$

19. (b)

CP	:	SP
30	:	36
800	:	1000
30 × 800	:	36 × 1000
2	:	3

$\therefore$ Profit (%) $= \frac{3-2}{2} \times 100 = 50\%$

20. (c) Let CP be $100x$.

$\therefore$ SP $= 100x \times \left(\frac{100+250}{100}\right) = 350x$

CP : SP $= 100x : 350x = 2 : 7$

21. (b) $P = \frac{320}{100} \times CP \Rightarrow \frac{P}{CP} = \frac{16}{5}$

$\therefore$ $P = 16x$, CP $= 5x$

SP $= 21x$

Now, CP $= 5x \times \frac{110}{100} = \frac{11x}{2}$

SP $= 21x$

New profit $= 21x - \frac{11x}{2} = \frac{31x}{2}$

$\therefore$ Required % $= \frac{31x/2}{21x} \times 100$

$= \frac{31}{21} \times 50\% = \frac{1550}{21}\% = 73.8\%$

22. (d) Let the CP $= 100x$

Then, SP $= 100x \times \frac{110}{100} = 110x$

Actual CP $= 100x \times \frac{88}{100} = 88x$

$\therefore$ Actual profit $= 110x - 88x = 22x$

$\therefore$ Gain percentage $= \frac{22x}{88x} \times 100 = 25\%$

23. (c) Let the part of the sugar he sells at a 10% profit is x kg.

$\therefore$ $(1000 - x)$ kg sugar he sells at a 40% profit, the gain% on whole quantity is 20%.

According to the question,

$x \times \frac{110}{100} + (1000 - x)\frac{140}{100} = 1000 \times \frac{120}{100}$

$\Rightarrow 110x + 140000 - 140x = 120000$

$\Rightarrow 30x = 140000 - 120000$

$\Rightarrow x = \frac{20000}{30} = \frac{2000}{3}$

$\therefore$ Part of the sugar he sold at 40% profit

$= (1000 - x)$ kg $= \left(1000 - \frac{2000}{3}\right)$ kg

$= \left(\frac{1000}{3}\right)$ kg $= 333\frac{1}{3}$ kg

24. (b) Profit $= \frac{1}{6} \times$ Selling price

Selling price − Cost price $= \frac{1}{6} \times$ Selling price

$\frac{5}{6}$ Selling price = Cost price

$\frac{\text{Cost price}}{\text{Selling price}} = \frac{5}{6}$

$\therefore$ Profit% $= \frac{6-5}{5} \times 100 = 20\%$

25. (c) CP of an item = ₹42000

SP when sold at a loss

$= 42000 \times \frac{80}{100} = ₹33600$

∴ CP of new item = ₹33600

∴ SP of new item $= 33600 \times \frac{130}{100} = ₹43680$

∴ Overall gain = SP of new item – SP of old item = 43680 – 42000 = ₹1680

26. (b) Error = 1000 – 870 = 130 gm

True weight = 1000 gm

$\text{Profit} = \frac{\text{Error}}{\text{True weight} - \text{Error}} \times 100$

$= \frac{130}{1000 - 130} \times 100$

$= \frac{130}{870} \times 100 = 14.94\%$

27. (b) Let the CP of first trader be ₹ x.

Profit percentage for each trader = 30%

∴ SP of last traders

$= x \times \frac{(100+30)}{100} \times \frac{(100+30)}{100} \times \frac{(100+30)}{100}$

$\Rightarrow 300 = x \times \frac{130}{100} \times \frac{130}{100} \times \frac{130}{100}$

$\Rightarrow \quad x = 300 \times \frac{100}{130} \times \frac{100}{130} \times \frac{100}{130}$

∴ x = 136.55 (approx.)

Speedy Method

$30\% = \frac{3}{10}$

CP : SP

10 : 13

10 : 13

10 : 13

1000 : 2197

∵ 2197 = ₹ 300

∴ $1000 = \frac{300}{2197} \times 1000 = ₹ 136.55$

28. (b) Total CP of a machine

= 5000 + 8000 = ₹13000

Total SP of a machine = 6000 + 10000

= ₹16000

Profit = 16000 – 13000 = ₹3000

$\text{Profit\%} = \frac{\text{Profit}}{\text{CP}} \times 100$

$\Rightarrow \quad \text{Profit \%} = \frac{3000}{13000} \times 100 = 23.08\%$

29. (a) Let SP of 24 oranges = ₹24

(₹1 per orange)

SP of 28 oranges = ₹28

CP of 28 oranges = SP of 24 oranges = ₹24

∴ Profit per cent $= \frac{28-24}{24} \times 100$

$= \frac{50}{3}\% = 16\frac{2}{3}\%$

30. (a) Let the CP of article = ₹ 100 /gm

If, he sells on 15% loss, then

SP = ₹ 85/gm

CP of 20 gm = 100 × 20 = ₹ 2000

But he sells 25 gm, then SP of 25 gm

= 85 × 25 = ₹ 2125

$\text{Profit \%} = \frac{125}{2000} \times 100 = 6.25\%$

Speedy Method

$\frac{SP}{CP} = \frac{85}{100} \times \frac{25}{20} = \frac{17}{16}$

$\text{Profit\%} = \frac{1}{16} \times 100 = 6.25\%$

31. (a) Let CP of painting = x

When, SP is ₹ 1498, then profit = 1498 – x

When, SP is ₹ 1300, then loss = x – 1300

According to the given condition, we have

Profit = 125% of loss

$(1498 - x) = \frac{125}{100} \times (x - 1300)$

$\Rightarrow 5992 - 4x = 5x - 6500$

$\Rightarrow \quad x = ₹ 1388$

Then, SP of painting $= 1388 \times \frac{125}{100} = ₹ 1735$

32. (b) Given, CP = ₹ 3200 and SP = ₹ 2700

Then, loss% $= \frac{3200 - 2700}{3200} \times 100$

$= \frac{500}{3200} \times 100 = 15.62\%$

33. (d) Let the original price = ₹ 100

Then, Ram bought this cell phone

$= 100 - \frac{100 \times 30}{100} = ₹ 70$

and he sold it 50% profit $= 70 \times \frac{150}{100} = ₹ 105$

Then, profit percentage

$= \frac{105 - 100}{100} \times 100 = 5\%$

34. (d) Let Cost Price (CP) of white board marker = ₹x

On 10% profit,

Selling Price (SP) $= \frac{x \times 110}{100} = ₹\frac{110x}{100}$

On 15% profit,

Selling Price (SP) $= x \times \frac{115}{100} = ₹\frac{115x}{100}$

According to the question,

$\frac{115x}{100} - \frac{110x}{100} = 20$

$\Rightarrow \quad 5x = 20 \times 100$

∴ $\quad x = \frac{20 \times 100}{5} = ₹400$

Speedy Method

Let cost price be 100x.

% change in profit = Change in profit

(15% – 10%) → 20

5% → 20

∴ $100\% \to \frac{20}{5} \times 100 = ₹400$

35. (d) Given, CP of 1000 gm = ₹ 880

Given, machine shows 400 gm when actual weight 350 gm.

If packets made of 200 gm, then actual weight 175 gm

Then, CP of 1000 gm = ₹ 880

CP of 25 gm = ₹ 22

Then, cost of 175 gm = 22 × 7 = ₹ 154

Then, profit on CP is 25%

$= 154 \times \frac{125}{100} = \frac{770}{4} = ₹ 192.5$

36. (a) CP of 1 dozen mango = ₹ 120

CP of 1 mango $= \frac{120}{12} = ₹10$

Total cost price of 1600 mangoes

= 1600 × 10 = ₹ 16000

Selling price of 900 mangoes

= 900 × 15 = ₹13500

Selling price of 700 mangoes

= 700 × 14 = ₹ 9800

Total selling price of mangoes

= 13500 + 9800 = ₹ 23300

Profit = 23300 – 16000 = ₹ 7300

∴ Gain% $= \frac{7300}{16000} \times 100 = \frac{730}{16} = 45.625\%$

37. (b) Total cost price = 4000 × 2 = ₹ 8000

Selling price of first set $= 4000 \times \frac{108}{100} = ₹ 4320$

Selling price of second set

$= 4000 \times \frac{94}{100} = ₹ 3760$

Total selling price = 4320 + 3760 = ₹ 8080

∴ Gain = 8080 – 8000 = ₹80

Speedy Method

Cost price of each set = ₹ 4000

On the first set she gain = 8%

On the second set she loss = 6%

∴ Overall gain = 8 – 6 = 2%

$= 4000 \times \frac{2}{100} = ₹80$

38. (b) SP of one-fifth apples

$= 3600 \times \frac{1}{5} \times \frac{90}{100} = ₹ 648$

SP of one-fourth of remaining apples

$= 3600 \times \left(1 - \frac{1}{5}\right) \times \frac{1}{4} \times \frac{95}{100}$

$= 3600 \times \frac{4}{5} \times \frac{1}{4} \times \frac{95}{100} = ₹ 684$

SP of two-third of the rest apples

$= 3600 \times \left(\frac{4}{5} - \frac{1}{5}\right) \times \frac{2}{3} \times \frac{115}{100}$

$= 3600 \times \frac{3}{5} \times \frac{2}{3} \times \frac{115}{100} = ₹ 1656$

SP of total apples $= 3600 \times \frac{127}{100} = ₹ 4572$

$\therefore$ SP of remaining apples

$= 4572 - (648 + 684 + 1656)$

$= 4572 - 2988 = ₹ 1584$

39. (a) Given, selling price = ₹ 28

$\text{Profit} = 12\% = \frac{3}{25}$

$\text{Cost price} = \frac{28}{28} \times 25 = ₹ 25$

$\text{New selling price} = ₹ 26.25 = \frac{2625}{100}$

$\text{New profit} = \frac{2625 - 2500}{100} = \frac{125}{100}$

$\therefore \text{Profit} = \frac{\frac{125}{100} \times 100}{25} = 5\%$

Speedy Method

Old selling price ₹ 28 → 112%

New selling price

$₹ 26.25 \to \frac{26.25 \times 112}{28}\%$

₹ 26.25 → 105%

$\therefore$ Profit per cent = 5%

40. (a) Let selling price of each chair be ₹ x.

According to the question,

$20x - 18000 = 4x \Rightarrow 16x = 18000$

$\therefore \quad x = \frac{18000}{16} = ₹ 1125$

41. (b) Given, SP = ₹ 22400, Profit = 12%

$\therefore \text{CP} = 22400 \times \frac{100}{112} = ₹ 20000$

New profit = 24%

$\therefore \text{New selling price} = 20000 \times \frac{124}{100} = ₹ 24800$

Speedy Method

$\therefore \quad 112\% \to ₹ 22400, \quad 1\% \to \frac{22400}{112}$

$\therefore \quad 124\% \to \frac{22400}{112} \times 124 = ₹ 24800$

42. (b) Let cost price of article for $A = ₹ x$

$\therefore$ Selling price of article for A

$= \frac{x \times 125}{100} = ₹ 1.25x$

$\therefore$ Cost price for $B = ₹ 1.25x$

and cost price of article for $C = \frac{x \times 130}{100} = ₹ 1.3x$

$\therefore$ Selling price of article for $B = ₹ 1.3x$

Now, profit % of B

$= \frac{1.3x - 1.25x}{1.25x} \times 100 = \frac{0.05x}{1.25x} \times 100 = 4\%$

Speedy Method

$A \xrightarrow{25\% \uparrow} B \xrightarrow{x\% \uparrow} C = 30\%$ more than A

$25 + x + \frac{25x}{100} = 30$

$\Rightarrow \quad \frac{125x}{100} = 30 - 25$

$\Rightarrow \quad 5x = 20 \Rightarrow x = 4$

$\therefore$ *B* earned 4% profit.

43. (c) Cost price of 1000 gm is = ₹ x

After changing the weighting machine shows 1000 gm instead of 950 gm.

$\Rightarrow \quad \text{SP} = x \times \frac{115}{100} \times \frac{950}{1000} \Rightarrow \text{SP} = \frac{2185x}{2000}$

$\therefore \quad \text{SP} = 1.0925x$

44. (b) Total number of banana

$= 50 \times 12 = 600$

$\text{Total cost} = 2400 + 0.25 \times 12 \times 50$

$= 2400 + 150 = 2550$

$\text{Total selling price} = \frac{10}{2} \times 50 \times 12 = 3000$

$\text{Profit} = 3000 - 2550 = 450$

$\therefore \quad \text{Profit} = \frac{450}{2550} \times 100 = 17.6\%$

45. (d) His gain percent $= 5\frac{5}{19} = \frac{100}{19}\%$

Let he give x gm instead of 1 kg.

Then, by formula $\frac{100}{19} = \frac{1000 - x}{x} \times 100$

$\Rightarrow \quad 19000 - 19x = x$

$\Rightarrow \quad x = \frac{19000}{20} = 950 \text{ gm}$

46. (b) Selling price = ₹ 5520

$\text{Cost price} = 5520 \times \frac{100}{120} = ₹ 4600$

New selling price = ₹ 4370

Loss = 4600 − 4370 = ₹ 230

$\therefore \quad \text{Loss\%} = \frac{230}{4600} \times 100 = 5\%$

47. (c) Given, CP of 1 bottle = ₹ $\frac{100}{6}$

and profit = 20%

$\therefore \quad \text{SP of 1 bottle} = \frac{100}{6} \times \frac{120}{100} = ₹ 20$ per bottle

48. (d) Given, SP of watch = ₹ 2000

$\text{Then, CP} = 2000 \times \frac{100}{80} = ₹ 2500$

If he sell it for = ₹ 3000

$P\% = \frac{\text{Gain}}{\text{CP}} \times 100$

$\therefore \quad P\% = \frac{500}{2500} \times 100 = 20\%$ [gain]

Speedy Method

Selling price ₹ 2000 → 80%

New selling price ₹ 3000 → $\frac{80}{2000} \times 3000$

₹ 3000 → 120%

$\therefore$ Profit% = 20%

49. (c) Let CP of an article be ₹ $100x$.

Given profit when SP is ₹ 2000

= Loss, when SP is ₹ 1200

$\therefore 2000 - 100x = 100x - 1200$

[$\because$ Profit = SP − CP & Loss = CP − SP]

$\Rightarrow \quad 3200 = 200x \Rightarrow x = 16$

$\therefore$ CP of an article = $100x = 100(16) = ₹ 1600$

$\therefore \text{SP on 20\% Profit} = 1600 \times \frac{120}{100} = ₹ 1920$

50. (c) Let Ram bought suitcase for ₹ $100x$.

Mohan purchased suitcase for ₹ $120x$.

Also, Mohan sold suitcase at 40% profit

$\therefore$ Shyam purchased suitcase for ₹ $168x$.

According to the question,

$168x = 1430 \Rightarrow x = 8.5119$

$\therefore$ Ram bought suitcase for

$= ₹ 100 \times (8.5119) = ₹ 851.19$

Speedy Method

$\text{By formula, CP} = \frac{100}{100 + \text{Profit\%}} \times \text{SP}$

$\text{CP for Mohan} = \frac{100}{100 + 40} \times 1430 = ₹ \frac{7150}{7}$

$\therefore \quad \text{CP for Ram} = \frac{100}{100 + 20} \times \frac{7150}{7} = ₹ 851.19$

51. (d) Let the CP of 1000 g item = ₹ 100

and then SP of 1000 g = ₹ 115

But he weight 20% less, then

SP of 800 g = ₹ 115

But CP of 800 g = ₹ 80

then profit = 115 − 80 = ₹ 35

$\therefore \text{Net profit\%} = \frac{35}{80} \times 100 = 43.75\%$

Speedy Method

Here, a = 15% , b = 20%

According to the formula,

$\text{Percentage profit} = \frac{(b + a)}{100 - b} \times 100\%$

$= \frac{(20 + 15)}{(100 - 20)} \times 100 = \frac{35}{80} \times 100 = 43.75\%$

52. (a) Let CP = ₹ $100x$

If 16% loss, then SP = ₹ $84x$

If 20% profit, then SP = ₹ $120x$

Difference = $(120 - 84)x$ = ₹ $36x$

Difference is equal to ₹ 324

$36x = 324$

$\Rightarrow \quad x = \frac{324}{36} = 9$

Hence, CP = 100 × 9 = ₹ 900

53. (b) Let the CP of 1 gm = x

Given, CP of 1 kg = SP of 1 kg = $1000x$

But the CP at which he is selling = $950x$

His profit = $1000x - 950x = 50x$

Hence, required profit %

$= \frac{50x}{950x} \times 100 = 5.26\%$

54. (d) Let cost price of 1000 gm be ₹ $1000x$.

At 4% profit,

$\text{SP of 940 gm} = 1000x \times \frac{104}{100} = ₹ 1040x$

$\therefore \text{SP of 1000 gm} = \frac{1040x}{940} \times 1000 = ₹ 1106.38x$

$\therefore \quad \text{Actual profit percentage} = \frac{106.38x}{1000x} \times 100$

$= 10.638\% \approx 10.64\%$

55. (c) Given, SP = ₹ 33000

$\therefore \quad CP = \frac{33000 \times 100}{110} = ₹30000$

For 20% profit, $SP = 30000 \times \frac{120}{100} = ₹36000$

56. (d) According to the question,

Selling price of Ramesh $= \frac{1250 \times 118 \times 90}{100 \times 100}$

$= ₹1327.50$

57. (d) Cost price of 9 mangoes = ₹ 90

$\therefore$ Cost price of 1 mangoes $= ₹\frac{90}{9} = ₹10$

Selling price of 10 mangoes = ₹ 95

$\therefore$ Selling price of 1 mangoes $= ₹\frac{95}{10} = ₹9.5$

Here, SP < CP

$\therefore$ Loss per cent $= \frac{CP - SP}{CP} \times 100\%$

$= \frac{10 - 9.5}{10} \times 100\% = 5\%$

58. (b) Let the cost price of table and chair be ₹ x and ₹ y, respectively.

According to the question,

$x + y = 3900$ ...(i)

Selling price of table and chair

$= x \times \frac{108}{100} + y \times \frac{116}{100}$

$= \frac{27x}{25} + \frac{29y}{25}$

$\because$ Profit = SP – CP

$\Rightarrow \quad 540 = \frac{27x}{25} + \frac{29y}{25} - 3900$

$\Rightarrow \quad \frac{27x}{25} + \frac{29y}{25} = 4440$

$\Rightarrow \quad 27x + 29y = 111000$ ...(ii)

Solving of the Eqs. (i) and (ii),

$x = 1050, y = 2850$

$\therefore$ Required difference $= 2850 - 1050 = ₹1800$

Speedy Method

Overall profit% $= \frac{540 \times 100}{3900} = \frac{180}{13}\%$

Table 8% Chair 16%

$\frac{180}{13}$

$\frac{28}{13} : \frac{76}{13}$

7 : 19

12

$\Rightarrow$ 26 units = 3900

1 units $= \frac{3900}{26}$

$\Rightarrow$ 12 units $= \frac{300}{2} \times 12 = ₹1800$

59. (d) Let the cost price of the watch = ₹ x

At 25% profit,

Selling price $= (100 + 25)\%$ of x

$= \frac{125}{100} \times x = 1.25x$

At 15% loss,

Selling price $= (100 - 15)\%$ of x

$= \frac{85}{100} \times x = ₹0.85x$

Given, $\quad 1.25x - 0.85x = 120$

$\Rightarrow \quad 0.4x = 120$

$\Rightarrow \quad x = \frac{120}{0.4} = ₹300$

So, the cost price of the watch ₹ x = ₹300

60. (c) Let the dealer uses x gm instead of 1 kg.

Then, by the formula

$\frac{1000 - x}{x} \times 100 = 15$

$\Rightarrow \quad 20 \times 1000 - 20x = 3x$

$\therefore \quad x = \frac{20 \times 1000}{23} = 869.56$ gm

61. (a) Let cost price and selling price of an article be ₹ $10x$ and ₹ $11x$, respectively.

$\therefore$ Profit per cent $= \frac{SP - CP}{CP} \times 100$

$= \frac{11x - 10x}{10x} \times 100$

$= \frac{x}{10x} \times 100 = 10\%$

62. (c) CP of microwave in Madras

$= M \times \frac{75}{100} = ₹\frac{3M}{4}$

Total CP with transport $= \frac{3M}{4} + 1000$

According to the question,

$\left(\frac{3M}{4} + 1000\right) \times \frac{110}{100} = M$

$\Rightarrow \quad \frac{3M}{4} + 1000 = \frac{10M}{11}$

$\Rightarrow \quad \frac{10M}{11} - \frac{3M}{4} = 1000$

$\Rightarrow \quad \frac{40M - 33M}{44} = 1000$

$\Rightarrow \quad 7M = 44000$

$\Rightarrow \quad M = \frac{44000}{7}$

$\therefore \quad M = ₹6285.7$

63. (a) Selling price of each of the cows

$= ₹15640$

When one cow is sold at profit of 15%.

Cost price$_1 = 15640 \times \frac{100}{(100 + 15)}$

$= 15640 \times \frac{100}{115} = ₹13600$

When second cow is sold at loss of 15%.

Cost price$_2 = 15640 \times \frac{100}{(100 - 15)}$

$= 15640 \times \frac{100}{85} = ₹18400$

Total cost price of both the cows

$= 13600 + 18400 = ₹32000$

Total selling price of both the cows

$= 2 \times 15640 = ₹31280$

Cost price > Selling price

$\therefore$ Loss = Cost price – Selling price

$= 32000 - 31280 = ₹720$

Speedy Method

Loss percent $= \frac{(15)^2}{100} = \frac{225}{100} = 2.25\%$

Total SP $= 2 \times 15640 = ₹31280$

Total CP $= \frac{31280 \times 100}{(100 - 2.25)} = \frac{31280 \times 100}{97.75}$

$= ₹32000$

$\therefore$ Loss $= 32000 - 31280 = ₹720$

64. (d) Let cost price = $100x$

Profit $= \frac{130}{100} \times 100x = 130x$

Selling price = Cost price + Profit

$= 100x + 130x = 230x$

If cost price increases by 28%

$= 100x \times \frac{128}{100} = 128x$

Selling price remains same = $230x$

$\therefore$ Profit percentage $= \frac{SP - CP}{CP} \times 100$

$= \frac{230 - 128}{128} \times 100 = \frac{102}{128} \times 100 = 79.6\% \approx 80\%$

65. (a) Given, selling price = ₹ 46068

loss = 12%

According to the question,

Required selling price $= \frac{46068 \times 118}{(100 - 12)}$

$= \frac{46068 \times 118}{88} = ₹61773$

66. (c) Let CP of 1000 gm be ₹ 1000.

Then, SP of 1000 gm $= 1000 \times \frac{120}{100} = ₹1200$

and CP of 800 gm = ₹ 800

$\therefore$ Profit% $= \frac{1200 - 800}{800} \times 100 = \frac{400}{800} \times 100$

$= 50\%$

Speedy Method

$\frac{SP}{CP} = \frac{120}{100} \times \frac{1000}{800} = \frac{12}{8} = \frac{3}{2}$

Profit% $= \frac{1}{2} \times 100 = 50\%$

67. (a) Let CP of 20 books = ₹ 20

Then, SP of 18 books = ₹ 20

$\therefore$ SP of 20 books $= \frac{20}{18} \times 20 = ₹\frac{200}{9}$

Now, profit% $= \frac{\frac{200}{9} - 20}{20} \times 100$

$= \frac{200 - 180}{9 \times 20} \times 100 = \frac{20}{9 \times 20} \times 100$

$= 11\frac{1}{9}\%$

Speedy Method

20 CP = 18 SP

$\left.\frac{CP}{SP} = \frac{9}{10}\right] + 1$ gain

Gain% $= \frac{1}{9} \times 100 = 11\frac{1}{9}\%$

68. (d) Cost price of the table = ₹1260
Selling price of the table = ₹1197
Loss = CP − SP = ₹(1260 − 1197) = ₹63

$\therefore$ Loss per cent $= \frac{\text{Loss}}{CP} \times 100\%$

$= \frac{63}{1260} \times 100\% = 5\%$

69. (a) Let the cost price of 1 m cloth be ₹ 1.
Professed selling price of 1 m cloth

$= ₹\frac{(100-7)}{100} = ₹0.93$

Profit earned = 24 %
Actual cost price of cloth sold for ₹ 0.93

$= \frac{100}{124} \times 0.93 = ₹0.75$

$\therefore$ Actual length of scale = Length bought for ₹ 0.75 = 75 cm

70. (d) Cost of 1 kg of onions = ₹40

$\Rightarrow$ CP of 800 gm onions $= \frac{₹40}{1000} \times 800 = ₹32$

SP of 800 gm onions = ₹36 (Real value)
$\therefore$ CP = ₹32 and SP = ₹36
Here, SP > CP
Hence, gain percentage of Ramesh

$= \frac{36-32}{32} \times 100\% = \frac{4 \times 100}{32}\% = 12.5\%$ Gain

71. (d) CP of cycle = ₹1200
SP of cycle = ₹1500
$\because$ SP > CP

$\therefore$ Profit percentage $= \frac{1500-1200}{1200} \times 100\%$

$= \frac{300}{1200} \times 100\% = 25\%$

72. (c) Let CP be $100x$.

Then, SP $= \frac{100x \times (100 - 13.5)}{100} = 86.5x$

Now, new SP $= \frac{100x \times 111}{100} = 111x$

According to the question,

$\therefore \quad 111x - 86.5x = 1274$

$24.5x = 1274$

$x = 52$

Then, CP = $100x = 100 \times 52 = ₹ 5200$

73. (b) Let initially CP of the item be ₹ x.

$\therefore$ SP of the item initially $= ₹\frac{155}{100}x = ₹ 1.55x$

Now, new cost price of the item

$= ₹\frac{124}{100}x = ₹ 1.24x$

And selling price of the item = ₹ $1.55x$
Hence, new profit percentage

$= \frac{1.55x - 1.24x}{1.24x} \times 100$

$= \frac{0.31 \times 100}{1.24} = \frac{100}{4} = 25\%$

74. (a) According to the question,
CP of 17 items = SP of 28 items

$\Rightarrow \quad CP \times 17 = SP \times 28 \Rightarrow \frac{CP}{SP} = \frac{28}{17}$

Let the CP and SP are ₹ $28x$ and ₹ $17x$, respectively.
$\therefore$ Loss = $28x - 17x = 11x$

Loss per cent $= \frac{11x}{28x} \times 100 = 39\frac{2}{7}\%$

75. (a) Given, total rice = 2220 kg
By mixture and alligation method,

Profit%		Profit%
12		20
	18	
20–18 = 2	:	18–12 = 6

$\frac{\text{Rice sold at 12\% profit}}{\text{Rice sold at 20\% profit}} = \frac{2}{6}$

So, quantity of rice sold at 12% profit

$= \frac{2}{2+6} \times 2220 = \frac{2}{8} \times 2220 = 555$ kg

76. (a) Let the amount paid by Piyush for guitar be ₹ x.
Then, amount paid by Mayank

$= x \times \frac{116}{100} \times \frac{132}{100}$

$\Rightarrow \quad 3828 = x \times \frac{116}{100} \times \frac{132}{100}$

$\therefore \quad x = \frac{3828 \times 100 \times 100}{116 \times 132} = ₹ 2500$

77. (a) Cost price of 100 apples = ₹ 350

$\Rightarrow$ Cost price of 1 apple $= ₹\frac{350}{100} = ₹\frac{7}{2}$

Now, selling price of 12 apples = ₹ 48

$\Rightarrow$ Selling price of 1 apple $= ₹\frac{48}{12} = ₹ 4$

$\therefore$ Profit percentage

$= \frac{4 - \frac{7}{2}}{7/2} \times 100 = \frac{(8-7)}{7} \times 100 \quad [\because SP > CP]$

$= \frac{100}{7}\% = 14\frac{2}{7}\%$

78. (b) Let his product contains 1 kg.
Its actual weight is 22% less on 1 kg = 780 gm
Let the cost price of each gram be ₹ 1.
$\therefore$ Cost price of 780 gm = ₹780
SP of product = 89% of CP of 1 kg

$= \frac{89}{100} \times 1000 = ₹890$

$\therefore$ Profit = 890 − 780 = ₹110

$\therefore$ Profit % $= \frac{110}{780} \times 100 = 14.1\%$

79. (a) Given, SP = ₹ 400000

$\therefore \quad CP = \frac{400000 \times 100}{80} = ₹500000$

$\therefore$ SP on 5% profit $= CP \times \left(\frac{100 + \text{Profit\%}}{100}\right)$

$= 500000 \times \frac{105}{100} = ₹525000$

80. (d) Let trader use x gm instead of 1 kg by the formula,

$\frac{(1000 - x)}{x} \times 100 = 12.5$

$\Rightarrow \quad 100 \times 1000 - 100x = 12.5x$

$\Rightarrow \quad 112.5x = 100 \times 1000$

$\therefore \quad x = \frac{100 \times 1000}{112.5} = 888.8$ gm

81. (a) Let SP of the article = ₹x

$\Rightarrow$ CP of the article $= \frac{72}{100} \times x = ₹0.72x$

Hence, percentage profit $= \frac{x - 0.72x}{0.72x} \times 100$

$= \frac{0.28 \times 100}{0.72} = 38.89\%$

82. (b) According to the given data, the trader gains profit% (in weigting balance)

$= \frac{(1300 - 1000)}{1000} \times 100 = \frac{300}{1000} \times 100 = 30\%$

and when he marks up cost price 15% then he gains 30% more.

Then net profit % $= a + b + \frac{ab}{100}$

$a = 30\%, b = 15\%$

$= 30 + 15 + \frac{30 \times 15}{100}$

$= 45 + 4.50 = 49.50\%$

Hence, the next profit is 49.50%.

Speedy Method

	CP	:	SP
Marked up by 15%	20	:	23
1300 gm for 1000 gm	10	:	13
Final	200	:	299

So, profit percentage $= \frac{99}{200} \times 100 = 49.5\%$

83. (a) SP of car = ₹ 278000

$P_1 = 25\%, P_2 = 18\%$

$\therefore$ New SP $= SP \times \frac{100 + P_2}{100 + P_1}$

$= 278000 \times \frac{118}{125} = ₹ 262432$

84. (a) $\because$ Equivalent of two successive profit $x\%$ and $y\% = (x + y + \frac{xy}{100})\%$

$\therefore$ Equivalent of 20% and 25% profit made by first and second seller, respectively.

$= (20 + 25 + \frac{20 \times 25}{100})\%$

$= (45 + 5)\% = 50\%$

Let the third seller made a profit of $x\%$.

Then, $(50 + x + \frac{50 \times x}{100})\% = 65\%$

$\Rightarrow \quad 50 + x + 0.5x = 65$

$\Rightarrow 1.5x = 65 - 50 \Rightarrow x = \frac{15}{1.5} = 10$

So, profit made by third seller = 10%

85. (b) SP of pen = ₹ 166.44

Profit (P) = 14%

Then, CP of pen = $\frac{SP}{(100 + P\%)} \times 100$

$= \frac{166.44}{114} \times 100 = ₹\, 146$

New, SP = ₹ 154.76

Since SP > CP, then there is a profit percentage

$= \frac{154.76 - 146}{146} \times 100$

$= \frac{8.76}{146} \times 100 = 6\%$

86. (c) Let the cost price of the mobile for Kapil = ₹x

According to the question,

$(100 + 12)\%$ of $(100 + 15)\%$ of $x = 322$

$\Rightarrow \frac{112}{100} \times \frac{115}{100} \times x = 322$

$\Rightarrow \quad x = \frac{322 \times 100 \times 100}{112 \times 115} = ₹250$

87. (b) 15% → ₹ 1200

Then, 1% → ₹ 80

115% → 80 × 115 = ₹ 9200

88. (b) Let the cost price of 36 g of goods $= 36x$

and selling price of 28g $= 36x \times \frac{(100 - 12.5)}{100}$

$= 36x \times \frac{87.5}{100} = ₹\, \frac{63}{2}x$

Selling price of 36 g $= ₹\frac{63x}{2} \times \frac{36}{28}$

$= ₹\frac{81x}{2} = ₹40.5x$

$\therefore$ Profit percentage $= \frac{40.5x - 36x}{36x} \times 100\%$

$= \frac{4.5}{36} \times 100\% = 12.5\%$

89. (b) According to the question,

4 (CP − 455) = (490 − CP)

4 CP− 1820 = 490 − CP

5 CP = 2310

CP = ₹ 462

SP when selling at 25% profit = 125 of CP

$= 462 \times \frac{125}{100} = ₹\, 577.5$

90. (c) Let cost price = ₹ 100

Loss of $3\frac{1}{3}\%$ or $\frac{10}{3}\%$ means

Selling price $= 100 - 100 \times \frac{10}{3 \times 100}$

Selling Price = 100 − 3.33 = 96.67

According to the question,

$\frac{4}{5}$ of Marked Price = 96.67

Marked price $= 96.67 \times \frac{5}{4}$

MP = 120.8 ≈ 121

If he sold at marked price

Profit percentage $= \frac{MP - CP}{CP} \times 100$

$= \frac{121 - 100}{100} \times 100 = \frac{21}{100} \times 100 = 21\%$

91. (b) Let the price of fridge = ₹ x

Then, the price of washing machine

$= ₹\,(57300 - x)$

According to the question,

$x \times \frac{115}{100} = (57300 - x) \times \frac{76}{100}$

$\Rightarrow \quad 115x = 57300 \times 76 - 76x$

$\Rightarrow 115x + 76x = 57300 \times 76$

$\Rightarrow \quad 191x = 57300 \times 76$

$\Rightarrow \quad x = 300 \times 76 \Rightarrow x = ₹\, 22800$

$\therefore$ The cost price of washing machine is

$= 57300 - 22800 = ₹\, 34500$

92. (a) Suppose he bought ₹ 100 bananas.

One fifth got rotten in $= 100 \times \frac{1}{5} = ₹\, 20$

Remain = ₹ 80

SP of $\frac{2}{5}$ th of banana at 15% profit

$= \frac{2}{5} \times 80 \times \frac{115}{100} = 36.8$

Remaining 80 − 32 = ₹ 48 at 10% profit

SP of remaining banana $= 48 \times \frac{110}{100} = ₹\, 52.8$

Total SP = 52.8 + 36.8 = ₹ 89.6

He bought at ₹100, sold at ₹ 89.6

$\therefore$ Loss per cent $= \frac{100 - 89.6}{100} \times 100$

$\therefore \quad = 10.4\%$ Loss

Speedy Method

Let total banana be 5.

$= \frac{1 \times (-100) + 4 \times \frac{2}{5}(15) + \frac{12}{5}(10)}{5}$

$= \frac{-100 + 24 + 24}{5} = -10.4\%$

Here, – ve sign indicate the loss.

93. (b) Let CP of article is ₹ $100x$.

A sold to B at 25% profit.

$= 100x \times \frac{125}{100} = ₹\, 125x$

$\left[\because SP = CP \times \frac{(100 + P\%)}{100}\right]$

B sold to C at 15% profit $= 125x \times \frac{115}{100}$

$= ₹\, \frac{575}{4}x$

A's profit $= 125x - 100x = ₹\, 25x$

B's profit $= \frac{575}{4}x - 125x = \frac{575x - 500x}{4}$

$= ₹\, \frac{75}{4}x$

According to the question,

$25x - \frac{75}{4}x = 40$

$\Rightarrow \quad \frac{(100x - 75x)}{4} = 40 \Rightarrow x = \frac{160}{25}$

$\therefore$ The cost price of Article A

$= 100x = 100 \times \frac{160}{25} = 4 \times 160 = ₹\, 640$

94. (c) Given,

CP of 63 articles = SP of 54 articles

$\frac{CP}{SP} = \frac{54}{63} = \frac{6}{7}$) +1

$\therefore$ Profit percent $= \frac{1}{6} \times 100\% = 16\frac{2}{3}\%$

95. (a) CP of TV = ₹ x

Then, SP $= x \times \left(\frac{100 + 8}{100}\right) = ₹\, \frac{108x}{100}$

According to the question,

$\frac{108x}{100} - 2553 = x \times \left(\frac{100 - 15}{100}\right)$

$\Rightarrow \quad \frac{108x}{100} - 2553 = \frac{85x}{100}$

$\Rightarrow \quad \frac{180x}{100} - \frac{85x}{100} = 2553$

$\Rightarrow \quad x = \frac{2553 \times 100}{23} = ₹\, 11100$

$\therefore$ To gain 18%, SP $= 11100 \times \left(\frac{100 + 18}{100}\right)$

$= 111 \times 118 = ₹\, 13098$

Speedy Method

Here, (100 + 8)% − (100 − 15)% = 2553

⇒ 108% − 85% = 2553

⇒ 23% = 2553

$\therefore \quad 118\% = \frac{2553}{23} \times 118 = ₹\, 13098$

96. (a) Here, 115% − 84% = 192.20

⇒ 31% = 192.20

$\therefore$ CP (100%) $= \frac{192.20}{31} \times 100 = ₹\, 620$

97. (b) Given, SP = ₹ 640, Loss% = 15

loss $= 640 \times \frac{15}{100} = 96$

$\therefore$ CP = Loss + SP = 96 + 640 = 736

Now, to earn 15% profit on CP

$= 736 \times \frac{115}{100} = 846.40$

98. (c) Suppose, CP of first article is x and CP of second article is $(490 - x)$. Then,

$\Rightarrow \quad x \times \frac{(100 - 20)}{100} = (490 - x)\frac{(100 + 16)}{100}$

$\Rightarrow \quad x \times 80 = (490 - x)116$

$\Rightarrow \quad 80x = 490 \times 116 - 116x$

$\Rightarrow \quad 196x = 490 \times 116 \Rightarrow x = 290$

The CP of article sold at 20% loss is ₹ 290.

99. (c) Let the cost price be ₹ x.

$\therefore \quad$ loss $= x - 216$

and $\quad$ Gain $= 246.80 - x$

According to the question,

$$(246.80 - x) = (x - 216) \times \frac{120}{100}$$

$\Rightarrow 2468 - 10x = 12x - 2592$

$\Rightarrow \quad 22x = 5060$

$\Rightarrow \quad x = \frac{5060}{22} = 230$

$\therefore$ Cost Price = ₹ 230

Selling price = ₹ 220.75

$\because$ Since, SP < CP, there is a loss.

$\therefore$ Loss% $= \frac{(230 - 220.75)}{230} \times 100 \approx 4\%$

100. (a) According to the question,

15 fruits in ₹ 140, 1 fruit $= \frac{140}{15} = \frac{28}{3}$

10 fruits in ₹ 120, 1 fruit $= \frac{120}{10} = 12$

Cost price of 2 fruit $= \frac{28}{3} + 12 = \frac{64}{3}$

Sell at ₹ 132 for 1 dozen

$\therefore$ 1 fruits $= \frac{132}{12} =$ ₹11

$\Rightarrow$ 2 fruits = 22

$\therefore$ Profit per cent $= \frac{SP - CP}{CP} \times 100$

$$\Rightarrow = \frac{22 - \frac{64}{3}}{\frac{64}{3}} = \frac{2 \times 3}{3 \times 64} \times 100 = \frac{100}{32}$$

$$= \frac{25}{8} = 3\frac{1}{8}\% \text{ Profit.}$$

101. (b) Let the cost price of watch A = ₹ x

Cost price of watch B = ₹ 800 − x

According to the question,

$$x \times \frac{(100 + 18)}{100} = (800 - x) \times \frac{(100 - 22)}{100}$$

$\Rightarrow \frac{118x}{100} = (800 - x) \times \frac{78}{100}$

$\Rightarrow \quad 59x = 800 \times 39 - 39x$

$\Rightarrow \quad 98x = 800 \times 39$

$\Rightarrow \quad x = \frac{800 \times 39}{98} = 318.37$

$\therefore$ Cost price of watch A = ₹ 318.37

Cost price of watch B = 800 − 318.37

= ₹ 481.63

102. (b) Given, Selling price of 18 fans

= ₹ 11664

Cost price of 18 fans $= 11664 \times \frac{100}{90} =$ ₹ 12960

Now, CP of 1 fan $= \frac{12960}{18} =$ ₹ 720

New selling price of 1 fan

$= 720 \times \frac{11}{10} =$ ₹ 792

Let he sold x fans

Then, $792 \times x = 17424$

$\therefore \quad x = \frac{17424}{792} = 22$

Speedy Method

By formula, $\frac{n_1P_1}{R_1} = \frac{n_2P_2}{R_2}$

$$\frac{18 \times (100 - 10)}{11664} = \frac{n_2 \times (100 + 10)}{17424}$$

$$\frac{18 \times 90}{11664} = \frac{n_2 \times 110}{17424} \quad n_2 = 22$$

103. (b) Let cost price be x, then

According to the question,

$$\frac{120}{100}x - \frac{116}{100}x = 36$$

$4x = 36 \times 100 \Rightarrow \quad x = 900$

$\therefore$ The CP of article is ₹ 900.

Speedy Method

Here, $x = 16\%$, $y = 20\%$; $z =$ ₹ 36

$$\therefore \quad CP = \frac{z}{x \sim y} \times 100 = \frac{₹\ 36}{20 - 16} \times 100$$

$$= \frac{3600}{4} = ₹\ 900$$

104. (b) Let the manufacturing cost be x.

According to the question,

$$x \times \frac{110}{100} \times \frac{115}{100} = 7590 \therefore\ x = \frac{7590 \times 100 \times 100}{110 \times 115}$$

$= 3 \times 20 \times 100 =$ ₹ 6000

105. (b) Cost price of laptop = ₹ 42000

10% profit on laptop $= 42000 \times \frac{10}{100} =$ ₹4200

Cost price of scanner- cum-printer = ₹ 8000

5% profit on scanner-cum-printer

$= 8000 \times \frac{5}{100} =$ ₹ 400

$\therefore$ Total profit = 4200 + 400 = 4600

Total cost price = 42000 + 8000 = ₹50000

$\therefore$ Profit percentage $= \frac{4600}{50000} \times 100 = 9\frac{1}{5}\%$

106. (a) Given, selling price of 48 articles

= ₹ 2160

Cost price of 48 articles $= 2160 \times \left(\frac{100}{90}\right)$

= ₹ 2400

Cost price of 1article = 2400 / 48 = ₹ 50

New selling price with 12% profit

$= 50 \times \frac{112}{100} =$ ₹ 56

SP of 1 article = ₹ 56

Article sold in ₹ 1 = 1/ 56

$\therefore$ In ₹ 2016 $= \frac{2016}{56} = 36$ articles

Speedy Method

$$\frac{n_1P_1}{R_1} = \frac{n_2P_2}{R_2}$$

$$\Rightarrow \frac{48 \times (100 - 10)}{2160} = \frac{n_2 \times (100 + 12)}{2016}$$

$$\Rightarrow \frac{48 \times 90}{2160} = \frac{n_2 \times 112}{2016}$$

$\therefore \quad n_2 = 36$ article

107. (b) Sudha sold an article to Renu for ₹ 576.

CP of article for Sudha $= 576 \times \frac{100}{80} = 720$

Total CP for article for Renu

= 576 + 224 = 800

Profit 24% for Renu $= 720 \times \frac{124}{100} = 892.8$

Profit percentage on article for Renu

$$= \frac{892.8 - 800}{800} \times 100 = \frac{92.8}{800} \times 100 = 11.6\%$$

108. (b) Let the cost price of an article = ₹ x

According to the question,

$$x \times \left(\frac{100 - 20}{100}\right) = ₹\ \frac{4x}{5}$$

$$\text{SP for } B = \text{CP for } C = \frac{4x}{5}\left(\frac{100 + 12.5}{100}\right) = ₹\ \frac{9x}{10}$$

$$\text{SP for } C = \text{CP for } D = \frac{9x}{10}\left(\frac{100 - 8}{100}\right)$$

$$= ₹\left(\frac{92 \times 9x}{1000}\right)$$

Given, CP for D = 248.40

$$\Rightarrow \frac{92 \times 9x}{1000} = \frac{24840}{100}$$

$$\Rightarrow \quad x = \frac{24840 \times 10}{92 \times 9} \Rightarrow x = ₹\ 300$$

Now, SP for $A = \frac{4x}{5} = \frac{4 \times 300}{5} =$ ₹ 240

Then, loss of A = 300 − 240 = ₹ 60

CP for $C = \frac{9x}{10} = \frac{9 \times 300}{10} =$ ₹ 270

Then, loss of C = 270 − 248.40 = ₹ 21.6

Required difference = 60 − 21.6 = ₹ 38.40

109. (d) Total SP of 3 watches

= 3 × 2800 = ₹8400

Total CP of three watches

$$= \left(\frac{2800}{140} \times 100 + \frac{2800}{125} \times 100 + \frac{280}{112} \times 100\right)$$

= ₹ (2000 + 2240 + 2500) = ₹ 6740

Profit percentage $= \frac{8400 - 6740}{6740} \times 100$

$= \frac{166}{674} \times 100 = 24.63\%$

110. (b) Percentage gain by using 200g weight instead of 100g

$$= \frac{(200 - 100)}{100} \times 100 = 100\%$$

Percentage loss = 24%

Net percentage change $= x - y - \frac{xy}{100}$

Where, x = 100% gain and y = 24% loss

$\therefore$ Net percentage change

$$= 100 - 24 - \frac{24 \times 100}{100} = 76 - 24 = 52\%$$

Hence, his profit percentage is 52 %.

111. (b) Let the CP of first buffalo be ₹ x.

$\therefore$ CP of the second buffalo = ₹ (11520 − x)

According to the given question,

$\Rightarrow x \times \frac{85}{100} = (11520 - x) \times \frac{119}{100}$

$\Rightarrow \frac{11520 - x}{x} = \frac{85}{119} \Rightarrow \frac{11520 - x}{x} = \frac{5}{7}$

$\Rightarrow 80640 - 7x = 5x$

$\Rightarrow x = \frac{80640}{12} \Rightarrow x = ₹\,6720$

112. (d) Let the cost price of article be ₹ x.

Old selling price $= x - \frac{16}{100}x = \frac{84}{100}x$

According to the question,

$192.20 = \frac{115x}{100} - \frac{84x}{100}$

$19220 = 31x \Rightarrow x = ₹\,620$

$\therefore$ New selling price $= \frac{115}{100} \times 620 = ₹\,713$

113. (c) Let the cost price of each article by ₹ x.

Profit on article-I $= \frac{12x}{100}$

Profit on article-II $= \frac{12x}{100} + 3600$

Total profit $= \frac{12x}{100} + \frac{12x}{100} + 3600$

$= 15\frac{27}{51} \times \frac{1}{100} \times 2x$

According to the question,

$\frac{24x}{100} + 3600 = \frac{1584}{5100}x$

$3600 = \left(\frac{1584 - 1224}{5100}\right)x$

$x = ₹\,51000$

114. (d) Let the cost price (CP) of pulses be ₹ x.

$\therefore$ Selling price = 132% of ₹ x

$= \frac{132}{100} \times x = ₹\,1.32x$

Faulty weights are 20% less than the actual measure.

$\therefore$ Faulty weight = 1 kg − 20% of 1 kg

= (1000 − 200) gm = 800 gm

Now, SP of 800 gm pulses = ₹ $1.32x$

So, SP of 1000 gm pulse

$= \frac{1.32x \times 1000}{800} = ₹\,1.65x$

$\therefore$ Profit percentage $= \frac{(1.65x - x)}{x} \times 100$

$= 0.65 \times 100 = 65\%$

115. (b) CP of potatoes $= 19 + \frac{100}{100} = ₹\,20$/kg

Total quantity of potatoes = 100 kg

Selling price of 60 kg potatoes

$= 60 \times 20 \times \frac{150}{100} = ₹\,1800$

Selling price of 20 kg potatoes

$= 20 \times 20 \times \frac{140}{100} = ₹\,560$

Selling price of 10 kg potatoes

$= 10 \times 20 \times \frac{125}{100} = ₹\,250$

Selling price of remaining 10 kg potatoes

$= ₹\,10x$

42% profit on 100 kg of potatoes.

$\therefore$ Overall selling price $= 100 \times 20 \times \frac{142}{100}$

$= ₹\,2840$

$\therefore 2840 = 1800 + 560 + 250 + 10x$

$2840 - 2610 = 10x$

$10x = 230$

$x = 23$

$\therefore$ Profit% $= \frac{23 - 20}{20} \times 100 = 15\%$

116. (d) Gain in weight = 1000 g − 950 g = 50 g

$\therefore$ Profit % $= \frac{50}{950} \times 100 = \frac{100}{19} = 5\frac{5}{19}\%$

117. (d) Owing to reduction in cost price of the commodity, there is a saving of 7.5% on ₹ 7400.

i.e., $\frac{7.5}{100} \times 7400 = ₹\,555$

with ₹ 555, he can purchase 15 kg more.

$\therefore$ Reduced price of 15 kg = ₹ 555

So, reduced price of 1 kg $= \frac{555}{15} = ₹\,37$

Hence, original price $= \frac{100}{92.5} \times 37 = ₹\,40$

Now, to make a profit of 32.5%

Selling price of the commodity

$= 132.5\%$ of ₹ $40 = \frac{132.5}{100} \times 40 = ₹\,53$

118. (a) Cost price of 1 orange $= \frac{50}{100} = ₹\,5$

Selling price of 1 orange $= \frac{74}{12} = ₹\,\frac{37}{6}$

Gain percentage $= \frac{SP - CP}{CP} \times 100$

$= \frac{\left(\frac{37}{6} - 5\right)}{5} \times 100 = \left(\frac{37 - 30}{6 \times 5}\right) \times 100$

$= \frac{7}{6} \times 20 = \frac{70}{3} = 23\frac{1}{3}\%$ gain

119. (c) Let the amount spent on transportation be ₹ x.

Now, according to the question,

130% of cost price = Selling price

$\Rightarrow \frac{130}{100} \times (700 + x) = 1400$

$\Rightarrow (700 + x) = \frac{1400 \times 100}{130}$

$\Rightarrow (700 + x) = 1077$

$\Rightarrow x = 1077 - 700 \Rightarrow x = ₹\,377$

120. (d) Aarav sells a watch to Bhavin at 15% profit $= ₹\,10000 \times \frac{15}{100} = ₹\,1500$

$\therefore$ Aarav sells the watch to Bhavin at profit

= (10000 + 1500) = ₹11500

Now, Bhavin sells it back to Aarav at 15% loss $= ₹\,11500 \times \frac{85}{100} = ₹\,9775$

$\therefore$ Percentage profit of Aarav

$= \frac{(11500 - 9775)}{10000} \times 100 = 17.25\%$ profit

121. (d) Total cost price of both the watches

= ₹18000

Now, profit = 18% (overall)

$= 18000 \times \frac{18}{100} = ₹\,3240$

On first watch, a loss of 10% is incurred

= 10% of 9000 = ₹900

Hence, the second watch should be sold at a profit = ₹(3240 + 900) = ₹4140

$\therefore$ Selling price of second watch

= ₹(9000 + 4140) = ₹13140

122. (b) According to the question,

$CP \times 36 = SP \times N$

$\Rightarrow \frac{SP}{CP} = \frac{36}{N}$ ...(i)

Now, Profit percentage $= \frac{SP - CP}{CP} \times 100$

$\Rightarrow 20 = \left(\frac{SP}{CP} - 1\right) \times 100 \Rightarrow \frac{1}{5} = \frac{SP}{CP} - 1$

$\Rightarrow \frac{SP}{CP} = \frac{1}{5} + 1 \Rightarrow \frac{36}{N} = \frac{6}{5}$ [from Eq. (i)]

$\therefore N = 30$

123. (d) Ratio of CP and SP of Sugar

$= \frac{\text{CP of sugar} \times \text{weighs}}{\text{SP of sugar} \times \text{weighs}} = \frac{36 \times 800}{40 \times 1000}$

$\therefore \frac{CP}{SP} = \frac{36}{50}$

Then, profit% $= \frac{50 - 36}{36} \times 100$

$= \frac{14}{36} \times 100 = 38.89\%$

124. (d) For first toy, CP $= \frac{1500}{125} \times 100 = ₹\,1200$

For second toy, CP $= \frac{2800}{50} \times 100 = ₹\,5600$

For third toy, CP $= \frac{3500}{125} \times 100 = ₹\,2800$

Then, total CP = 1200 + 5600 + 2800 = ₹ 9600

And total SP = 1500 + 2800 + 3500 = ₹ 7800

CP > SP

Then, overall loss % $= \frac{9600 - 7800}{9600} \times 100$

= 18.75%

125. (c) Let cost price of a table = 100

Adding 35% profit of a table, then selling price $= 100 + 100 \times \frac{35}{100} = 135$

According to the question,

$135 = 5670 \quad 1 = \frac{5670}{135} = ₹\,42$

Now, the cost price of a table = 100

= 100 × 42 = ₹ 4200

Profit, then the new selling price of a table

$= 4200 \times \frac{112}{100} = ₹\,4704$

Hence, the correct answer is ₹ 4704.

126. (a) Equivalent profit of 20% and 25%.

$$20 + 25 + \frac{20 \times 25}{100} = 50\%$$

Let third selles gain x%.

$$\text{Then, } 50 + x + \frac{50 \times x}{100} = 65$$

$$x = 10\%$$

127. (b) Let the CP of first shirt = ₹x
then CP of second shirt = ₹y
According to the question,
SP of first shirt = 2 × SP of second shirt

$$x \times \frac{108}{100} = y \times \frac{97}{100} \times 2$$

$$\frac{x}{y} = \frac{97 \times 2}{108} = \frac{97}{54}$$

Now Let $x = 97a$ and $y = 54a$

∴ Net percentage profit

$$= \frac{97a \times \frac{8}{100} - 54a \times \frac{3}{100}}{97a + 54a} \times 100$$

$$= \frac{776 - 162}{151} = \frac{614}{151} = 4.0662 \approx 4.07\%$$

128. (d) Ratio of SP and CP of article

$$\frac{SP}{CP} = \frac{78}{100} \times \frac{100}{65}$$

$$\left.\frac{SP}{CP} = \frac{78}{65}\right] + 13$$

$$\text{Profit \%} = \frac{13}{65} \times 100 = 20\%$$

129. (b) CP of 1000 gm of article = ₹ 23
SP of 800 gm of article = ₹ 20

$$\text{SP of 1000 gm of article} = ₹\,\frac{20}{800} \times 1000 = ₹\,25$$

$$\text{Profit percentage} = \frac{25 - 23}{23} \times 100\%$$

$$= \frac{200}{23}\% = 8\frac{16}{23}\%$$

130. (c) Let the profit of other bicycle is x%
The buying price of each bicycle = ₹ 3000
According to the question,

$$3000 \times \frac{110}{100} + 3000 \times \frac{(x + 100)}{100} = 6000 \times \left(\frac{100 + 20}{100}\right)$$

$$\Rightarrow 3300 + 30x + 3000 = 7200$$

$$\Rightarrow \quad 6300 + 30x = 7200$$

$$\Rightarrow \quad 30x = 900 \Rightarrow x = 30\%$$

⇒ Other bicycle at a profit = 30%

Speedy Method

By alligation method

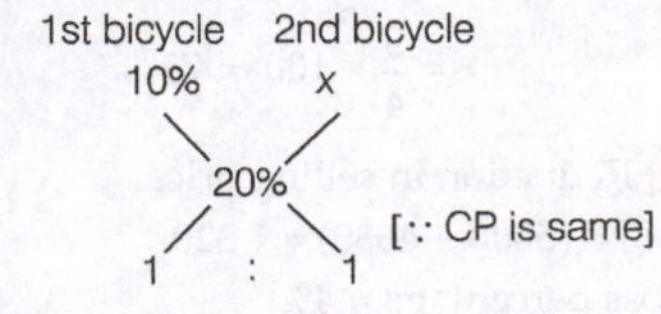

$$\frac{x - 20}{20 - 10} = \frac{1}{1} \Rightarrow x = 30\%$$

131. (b) Given,
The cost price of bag for Aashi = ₹ 24840
⇒ The cost price of bag for Ankita if she gains 20% profit $= 24840 \times \frac{100}{(100 + 20)}$ = ₹ 20700

Similarly, The cost price of bag for Swati if she gains 15% profit

$$= 20700 \times \frac{100}{(100 + 15)} = 20700 \times \frac{100}{115} = ₹\,18000$$

132. (b) Let cost price be ₹ x.

$$SP = x \times \frac{100 - 13.5}{100} = \frac{86.5x}{100}$$

According to the question,

Profit = 9.5%, then

$$\therefore \quad SP = \frac{86.5x}{100} + 1104$$

$$\Rightarrow x \times \frac{100 + 9.5}{100} = \frac{86.5x}{100} + 1104$$

$$\left[\because SP = CP \times \frac{100 + \text{Profit\%}}{100}\right]$$

$$\Rightarrow \quad \frac{109.5}{100}x - \frac{86.5x}{100} = 1104 \Rightarrow \frac{23x}{100} = 1104$$

$$\Rightarrow \quad x = \frac{1104 \times 100}{23} = ₹\,4800$$

Speedy Method

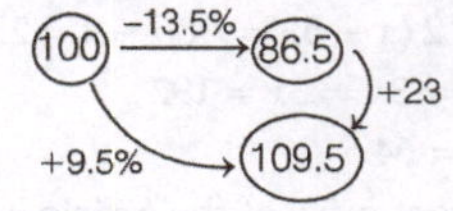

23 = ₹ 1104
1 = ₹ 48
100 = ₹ 4800

133. (d) Let CP = ₹ 100
According to the question,
With 16% loss SP = 100 – 16 = 84
With 8% profit SP = 100 + 8 = 108
Difference in two SP = 108 – 84 = 24
If the difference is ₹ 24, cost price = ₹ 100
If the difference was ₹ 660.

$$\text{Cost price} = 100 \times \frac{660}{24} = ₹\,2750$$

Therefore, for making a gain of 12% on cost price, he should have sold the item for (2750 × 112)/100
Therefore, required answer = ₹ 3080
Hence, ₹ 3080 should be the selling price to gain a profit of 12%.

134. (d) Cost price of overcoat

$$= 8540 \times \frac{100}{122} = ₹\,7000$$

135. (a) Let the cost price (CP) of article be ₹ x, then selling price (SP) of article is ₹ $\frac{126}{100}x$.

$$\text{New SP of article} = ₹\left(\frac{126}{100}x + 2250\right)$$

$$\text{Now, } \frac{\left(\frac{126}{100}x + 2250 - x\right)}{x} \times 100 = 41$$

$$\Rightarrow \quad 126x + 225000 - 100x = 41x$$

$$\Rightarrow \quad 26x + 225000 = 41x$$

$$\Rightarrow \quad 15x = 225000$$

$$x = ₹\,15000$$

∴ If the article is sold at 12% profit, then new selling price $= \frac{112}{100} \times 15000 = ₹\,16800$

Speedy Method

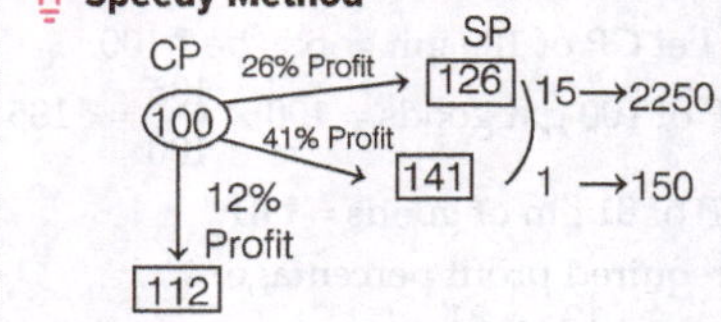

∴ Required selling price
= 112 × 150 = ₹ 16800

136. (c) Let the marked price of the article be ₹ x.
According to the question,

$$4400 \times \frac{124}{100} = x \times \left(\frac{100 - 12}{100}\right)$$

$$\Rightarrow \quad 44 \times 124 = x \times \frac{88}{100} \Rightarrow x = \frac{44 \times 124 \times 100}{88}$$

$$\therefore \quad x = 6200$$

137. (b) Let the cost price of 1000 gm be $100x$.
Weight less than 27%

$$= 1000 \times \left(\frac{100 - 27}{100}\right) = 730\text{ gm}$$

∴ Cost price of 730 gm = $73x$
We know that,

$$\text{Profit\%} = \left(\frac{\text{CP} - \text{Original cost price}}{\text{Original cost price}}\right) \times 100$$

$$= \frac{100x - 73x}{73x} \times 100 = \frac{27x}{73x} \times 100$$

Profit % = 37%

138. (b) Let cost price of B be ₹ $100x$.
∴ Cost price of $A = 3(100x) = ₹\,300x$

$$\text{SP of } A = 300x \times \frac{90}{100} = 270x$$

$$\text{SP of } B = \frac{5}{4}(100x) = ₹\,125x$$

According to the question,

$$270x - 125x = 5800$$

$$\Rightarrow \quad 145x = 5800$$

$$\Rightarrow \quad x = 40$$

∴ Cost price of A = 300 (40) = ₹ 12000

139. (a) Given, 195 kg of wheat for ₹ 10260 at a profit of ₹ 4.5 per kg of wheat.

$$\therefore \text{ Price for 1 kg of wheat} = \frac{10260}{195} = ₹\,\frac{684}{13}$$

Actual price for wheat

$$= \frac{684}{13} - 4.5 = ₹\,\frac{1251}{26} \text{ per kg}$$

$\therefore$ Cost price for 15 kg of wheat

$$= \frac{1251}{26} \times 15 = ₹722$$

140. (d) Given, CP of 20 dozen Bananas $= ₹\,1200$

and SP of 5 dozen Bananas $= ₹\,350$

$\therefore$ SP of 20 dozen Bananas $= 350 \times 4 = ₹\,1400$

Thus, gain% $= \frac{1400 - 1200}{1200} \times 100$

$$= \frac{200}{1200} \times 100 = 16\frac{2}{3}\%$$

141. (a) Let CP of 100 gm goods be ₹ 100.

Then, SP of 100 gm goods $= 100 \times \frac{135}{100} = ₹\,135$

Thus, CP of 81 gm of goods $= ₹\,81$

Hence, required profit percentage

$$= \frac{135 - 81}{81} \times 100 = 66.67\%$$

142. (a) Let selling price of 22 items be ₹ $22x$.

$\therefore$ Profit = Selling price of 6 items $= 6x$

$\therefore$ CP of 22 items $= 22x - 6x = 16x$

$\therefore$ Required gain per cent $= \frac{6x}{16x} \times 100 = 37\frac{1}{2}\%$

143. (a) Percentage of gain

$$= \left[\frac{\text{True weight} - \text{False weight}}{\text{False weight}}\right] \times 100$$

$\therefore$ Percentage gain $= \left(\frac{1000 - 850}{850}\right) \times 100$

$$= \frac{150}{850} \times 100 = 17.65\%$$

144. (a) Initial quantity of cotton $= 500$ kg

Cost price $= ₹\,8000$

Remaining cotton $= 500 \times \frac{90}{100} = 450$ kg

Buyer went to gain 20%.

Thus, selling price of 450 kg cotton

$$= 8000 \times \frac{120}{100} = ₹9600$$

Hence, rate of selling per kg

$$= \frac{9600}{450} = ₹\,21.3 = 21\frac{1}{3}\text{ kg}$$

145. (a) Let 'A' buys article at ₹ $100x$.

A sells at 10% profit

$\therefore$ Selling price to $A = 100x \times \frac{110}{100} = ₹\,110x$

Now, cost price to $B = ₹\,110x$

$\therefore$ Selling price to $B = 110x \times \frac{160}{100} = ₹\,176x$

Now, cost price to $C = ₹\,176x$

$\therefore$ Selling price to $C = 176x \times \frac{112.5}{100} = ₹\,198x$

Now, cost price to $D = ₹\,198x$

According to the question,

D paid $\Rightarrow ₹\,59.4 = 198x$

$\Rightarrow \quad x = 0.3$

$\therefore$ 'A' buys article $= ₹\,100x$

$$= 100 \times 0.3 = ₹\,30$$

Speedy Method

+10% (A→B), +60% (B→C), $+12\frac{1}{2}\%$ (C→D)

A	:	B	:	C	:	D
10	:	11	:	11	:	11
5	:	5	:	8	:	8
8	:	8	:	8	:	9
50	:	55	:	88	:	99

According to the question,

D paid $= ₹\,59.4$

So, $\quad 99 \rightarrow ₹\,59.4$

$\therefore$ 'A' buys article, $50 \rightarrow \frac{59.4}{99} \times 50 = ₹\,30$

146. (d) Given, selling price of each fan is ₹ 480.

$\therefore$ Cost price of first fan $= 480 \times \frac{100}{120} = ₹\,400$

and cost price of second fan

$$= 480 \times \frac{100}{80} = ₹\,600$$

$\therefore$ Total cost price of the fans

$$= 600 + 400 = ₹\,1000$$

Total selling price of the fans

$$= 480 + 480 = 960$$

$\therefore$ Loss = CP − SP $= 1000 - 960 = ₹\,40$

147. (c) Let the CP of an article be ₹ x.

According to the question,

$(86 - x) = 2(x - 53) \Rightarrow 86 - x = 2x - 106$

$\Rightarrow 86 + 106 = 3x \Rightarrow 3x = 192$

$\Rightarrow \quad x = 64$

Hence, the cost price of the article is ₹ 64.

148. (d) CP of mobile $= \frac{18240 \times 100}{114}$

$$= ₹\,16000$$

149. (c) Let cost price of 1000 gm $= ₹\,1000x$

Quantity of rice bought by shopkeeper

$$= 1000 \times \left(1 + \frac{25}{100}\right) = 1250\text{ gm}$$

$\therefore$ Actual price of 1000 gm

$$= \frac{1000x}{1250} \times 1000 = ₹\,800x$$

Quantity of rice sold by shopkeeper

$$= 1000 \times \left(1 - \frac{25}{100}\right) = 750\text{ gm}$$

Price of 750 gm rice

$$= 1000x \times \left(1 + \frac{12.5}{100}\right) = ₹\,1125x$$

$\therefore$ Actual price for 1000 gm

$$= \frac{1125x}{750} \times 1000 = ₹\,1500x$$

$\therefore$ Net profit % $= \frac{1500x - 800x}{800x} \times 100 = 87.5\%$

150. (a) CP of phone $= ₹\,10000$

Original SP of phone $= ₹\,12000$

New SP of phone $= ₹\,13000$

$\therefore$ Difference between original and new SP

$$= 13000 - 12000 = ₹\,1000$$

$\therefore$ Required loss per cent $= \frac{1000}{10000} \times 100$

$$= 10\%$$

151. (a) Given, total CP $= ₹\,1500$

$\therefore \quad$ Total SP $= 1500 \times \frac{125}{100} = ₹\,1875$

He sold one-fourth at 12% loss.

$\therefore \quad$ SP $= \frac{1500}{4} \times \frac{88}{100} = ₹\,330$

Remaining SP $= ₹\,[1875 - 330] = ₹\,1545$

Remaining CP $= ₹\,1500 \times \frac{3}{4} = ₹\,1125$

Required profit $= \frac{1545 - 1125}{1125} \times 100$

$$= \frac{420}{1125} \times 100 = 37.33\%$$

Speedy Method

$\frac{1}{4}(-12\%) + \frac{3}{4}(x\%) = 25\% \Rightarrow \frac{-12 + 3x}{4} = 25$

$\Rightarrow \quad 3x - 12 = 100 \quad \Rightarrow \quad 3x = 112$

$\Rightarrow x = 37.33\%$

152. (c) Loss per cent $= \left[\frac{4960 - 4712}{4960} \times 100\right]$

$$= \left[\frac{248}{4960} \times 100\right] = 5\%$$

153. (d) Total cost price $= ₹\,32400$

If 20% wheat was spoiled, remaining wheat

$$= 1800 \times \frac{80}{100} = 1440\text{ kg}$$

Cost price of 1 kg of wheat $= \left[\frac{32400}{1440}\right] = ₹\,22.5$

$\therefore$ Selling price $= \left[22.5 \times \frac{120}{100}\right] = ₹\,27$

154. (a) Let the number of goods $= 100$

Remaining goods $= 100 \times \frac{95}{100} = 95$

According to the question,

Price of remaining goods $= \frac{5000}{100} \times 95$

$$= ₹\,4750$$

Hence, the required selling price

$$= 4750 \times \frac{120}{100} = ₹\,5700$$

155. (d) According to the question,

$$\frac{70}{100} \times \text{Cost price} = \frac{40}{100} \times \text{Selling price}$$

$\therefore \quad \frac{\text{Selling price}}{\text{Cost price}} = \frac{70}{40} = \frac{7}{4}$

Gain per cent $= \frac{(7 - 4)}{4} \times 100$

$$= \frac{3}{4} \times 100 = 75\%$$

156. (b) Reduction in selling price

(SP) $= (5000 - 4680) = ₹\,320$

Now, loss percentage $= 4\%$

$$\frac{4}{100} \times \text{Cost Price (CP)} = 320$$

$$CP = \frac{320 \times 100}{4}$$

$$CP = ₹\,8000$$

Profit = 4%

$$\text{Now, SP} = CP \times \left(\frac{100 + \text{Profit\%}}{100}\right)$$

$$= 8000 \times \frac{104}{100} = ₹\,8320$$

157. (b) According to the question,

30 × (Selling price − Cost price)

= 10 × Selling price

20 × Selling price = 30 × Cost price

$$\therefore \text{ Selling price} = \text{Cost price} \times \frac{3}{2}$$

$$= 480 \times \frac{3}{2} = ₹\,720$$

158. (b) Let the cost price of article = 100 units

∴ Selling price of an article

$$= \frac{100 \times 110}{100} = 110 \text{ units}$$

Marked price of an article

$$= \frac{110 \times 100}{66} = \frac{500}{3} \text{ units}$$

$$\text{New selling price} = \frac{500 \times 80}{3 \times 100} = \frac{400}{3} \text{ units}$$

Hence, required profit per cent

$$= \frac{\frac{400}{3} - 100}{100} \times 100 = \frac{100}{3} = 33\frac{1}{3}\%$$

159. (a) Let A bought the article at ₹ x.

According to the question,

(100 + 30)% of (100 + 45)% of x = 43355

$$\frac{130}{100} \times \frac{145}{100} \times x = 43355$$

$$\Rightarrow \quad x = \frac{43355 \times 100 \times 100}{130 \times 145} = ₹\,23000$$

160. (c) Fruit vendor buys a score of apples

= ₹ 400

(a score = 20 no's)

$$\text{Price of one apple} = \frac{400}{20} = ₹\,20$$

∴ Sale dozen of apple = ₹ 264

$$\text{Selling price of one apple is} = \frac{264}{12} = ₹\,22$$

$$\therefore \text{ Profit percentage} = \frac{22 - 20}{20} \times 100$$

$$= \frac{2}{20} \times 100 = 10\% \text{ profit}$$

161. (a)

$$\text{Profit\%} = \frac{1800}{CP} \times 100$$

$$20 = \frac{1800 \times 100}{CP}$$

$$CP = \frac{1800 \times 100}{20}$$

$$CP = 1800 \times 5 = ₹\,9000$$

Speedy Method

20% = ₹ 1800

1% = 90

100% = ₹ 9000

162. (b) Cost price of 288 oranges

= 11520 paisa

Selling price of 50 oranges = 50 × 70

= 3500 paisa

Remaining 238 he sold for ₹ 46.20

= 4620 paisa

Total selling price = 3500 + 4620 = 8120 paisa

Loss = 11520 − 8120 = 3400 paisa = ₹ 34

163. (c) According to the question,

Merchant receive loss per cent in whole

$$\text{transaction} = \left(-20 + 20 - \frac{20 \times 20}{100}\right)\% = 4\%$$

Hence, loss of 4%.

164. (a) If SP of 40 articles = CP of 50 articles

So, 40 SP = 50 CP

$$\frac{CP}{SP} = \frac{40}{50}$$

Hence, the required gain percentage

$$= \frac{(50 - 40)}{40} \times 100 = 25\%$$

165. (b) Percentage increased

$$= \frac{3000 - 2500}{2500} \times 100$$

$$= \frac{500}{2500} \times 100 = 20\%$$

166. (d) Let CP of 1000 gm goods be ₹ 1000.

∴ CP of 550 gm be ₹ 550.

$$\left[\because 1000 \times \frac{(100 - 45)}{100}\right] = 550 \text{ gm}$$

$$\text{S.P of 550 gm goods} = 1000 \times \frac{75}{100} = ₹\,750$$

$$\therefore \text{ Required gain\%} = \frac{750 - 550}{550} \times 100$$

$$= \frac{200}{550} \times 100 = \frac{400}{11} = 36\frac{4}{11}\%$$

167. (d) Let Sohan is giving x kg of sugar.

∴ Profit %

$$= \frac{\text{Actual weight} - \text{False weight}}{\text{False weight}} \times 100$$

$$\Rightarrow 28 = \frac{3.2 - x}{x} \times 100$$

$$\Rightarrow \quad 28x = 320 - 100x \Rightarrow 128x = 320$$

$$\Rightarrow \quad x = \frac{320}{128} = 2.5 \text{ kg} = 2500 \text{ gm}$$

∴ Mohan is giving 2500 gm.

168. (d) According to the question,

Listed price of goods = ₹ y

and CP = ₹ 100 (Let)

$$\frac{y}{2} = 83$$

$$\left[\text{As goods is sold half of list price so, } \frac{y}{2}\right]$$

$\Rightarrow \quad y = 166$

Gain on selling at the listed price

$$= \left(\frac{166 - 100}{100}\right) \times 100 = 66\%$$

169. (a) Let the cost price of a boy = ₹ x

Profit = 12%

∴ The selling price of a boy

$$= x \times \left(1 + \frac{12}{100}\right) = ₹\, x \times \frac{112}{100}$$

According to the question,

$$\left(x \times \frac{112}{100}\right) + 900 = x \times \left(1 + \frac{27}{100}\right)$$

$$\Rightarrow \quad \frac{112}{100}x + 900 = x \times \frac{127}{100}$$

$$\Rightarrow \quad \frac{112}{100}x + 900 = \frac{127}{100}x$$

$$\Rightarrow \quad \frac{15x}{100} = 900 \Rightarrow x = \frac{900 \times 100}{15}$$

$$\therefore \quad x = ₹\,6000$$

Speedy Method

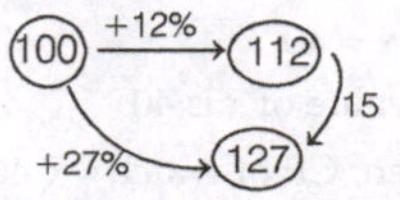

∵ 15 = ₹900

∴ 100 = ₹ 6000

170. (d) Given, CP of 11 oranges = ₹ 10

SP of 10 oranges = ₹ 11

$$\text{Then, SP of 11 oranges} = ₹\,\frac{11}{10} \times 11 = ₹\,12.1$$

$$\text{Gain \%} = \frac{12.11 - 10}{10} \times 100 = 21\%$$

Thus, required gain = 21%

171. (c) According to the question,

Faulty weight = 930 gm

True weight = 1000 gm

Error = 1000 − 930 = 70 gm

$$\text{Gain \%} = \frac{\text{Error}}{\text{True value} - \text{Error}} \times 100$$

$$= \frac{70}{1000 - 70} \times 100$$

$$= \frac{70}{930} \times 100 = \frac{7000}{930} = 7\frac{49}{93}\%$$

172. (c) Let cost price be $100x$.

Then, SP of goods = $105x$

New SP of goods = $110x$

Then, according to the question,

$110x - 105x = 175 \Rightarrow x = 37$

Then, SP = $105x$ = 105 × 35 = ₹ 3675

173. (d) By formula,

$$\text{Loss\%} = \frac{x^2}{100} = \frac{20 \times 20}{100} = 4\%$$

174. (c) According to the given information, total cost price of the box i.e., 200 kg, grapes cost price = 2000 × 10 = ₹ 20000

And total selling price of the box i.e., 190 kg grapes selling price = 2500 × 9.5 = ₹ 23750

∵ Transport charges = ₹ 1000

∴ Gain / Profit = (23750) − (20000 + 1000) = (23750) − (21000) = ₹ 2750

175. (a) Ratio of SP and CP

$$= \frac{42}{40} \times \frac{600}{550} = \frac{63}{55}$$

$$\text{Gain\%} = \frac{8}{55} \times 100 = 14.54\%$$

176. (b) According to the question,

$$44 \times CP = x \times SP$$

$$\frac{CP}{SP} = \frac{x}{44} \quad ...(i)$$

If profit is 10%,

$$CP \times \frac{110}{100} = SP \Rightarrow \frac{11}{10} = \frac{SP}{CP}$$

$$\Rightarrow \frac{11}{10} = \frac{44}{x} \quad \text{[from Eq. (i)]}$$

$$\Rightarrow x = 40$$

∴ Required value of x is 40.

177. (a) Given, CP of watch = ₹ 4000

Loss = 13%

$$\therefore \text{Selling price} = \frac{4000 \times (100 - 13)}{100} = \frac{4000 \times 87}{100} = ₹\ 3480$$

Hence, selling price is ₹ 3480.

178. (b) $(CP)_{1\text{ watch}}$ = ₹ 12000

and $(CP)_{2\text{ watch}}$ = ₹ 20000

$$\text{Now, } (SP)_{1\text{ watch}} = \frac{12000 \times 110}{100} = ₹\ 13200$$

$$\text{and } (SP)_{2\text{ watch}} = \frac{20000 \times 80}{100} = ₹\ 16000$$

Total CP = 12000 + 20000 = ₹ 32000

Total SP = 13200 + 16000 = ₹ 29200

Hence, Loss = 32000 − 29200 = ₹ 2800

179. (b) $SP_1 = 210$,

And, $SP_2 = 420$,

$$\text{Now, } CP_1 = \frac{100}{100 - L_1\%} \times 210$$

$$\text{And, } CP_2 = \frac{100}{100 - L_2\%} \times 420$$

$$\because \quad CP_1 = CP_2$$

$$\therefore \quad \frac{100}{100 - L_1} \times 210 = \frac{100}{100 - L_2} \times 420$$

$$\Rightarrow 100 - L_2 = 200 - 2L_1$$

$$\Rightarrow 2L_1 - L_2 = 100 \quad ...(i)$$

$$\text{and } L_1 - L_2 = 7 \quad (\because \text{given}) \ ...(ii)$$

By Eqs. (i) and (ii), we get

$$L_1 = 93 \text{ and } L_2 = 86$$

$$\therefore CP_1 = \frac{100}{100 - 93} \times 210 = \frac{100}{7} \times 210 = ₹\ 3000$$

180. (b) Let the CP of TV which was sold at less be ₹ x

∴ CP of TV which was sold at profit = 2280 − x

According to the question,

$$x \times \frac{80}{100} = (2280 - x) \times \frac{110}{100}$$

$$\Rightarrow 80x = 2280 \times 110 - 110x$$

$$\Rightarrow 190x = 2280 \times 110$$

$$\Rightarrow x = \frac{2280 \times 110}{190} = 1320$$

Hence, CP of TV is ₹ 1320.

181. (a) Selling price of watch (SP) = ₹ 1056

Profit percentage = 10%

$$\therefore CP = \frac{1056 \times 100}{110} = 960$$

If selling price = ₹ 800

$$\therefore \text{Loss\%} = \left(\frac{960 - 800}{960}\right) \times 100$$

$$\text{Loss\%} = \frac{160}{960} \times 100 = 16.66\%$$

182. (c) Cost price of 3 pens = Cost price of 18 pens − Selling price of 18 pens

⇒ Selling price of 18 pens = Cost price of 15 pens

$$\Rightarrow \frac{CP}{SP} = \frac{18}{15} \Rightarrow \frac{CP}{SP} = \frac{6}{5}$$

Let, CP = $6x$ and SP = $5x$

Now, $5x = 360$ (Given)

$$x = \frac{360}{5} = 72$$

$$CP = 6x = 6 \times 72 = ₹\ 432$$

$$\text{Cost price of a pen} = \frac{432}{18} = ₹\ 24$$

183. (b) Let CP of the article = ₹ 100

$$SP = 100\left[\frac{100 + 20}{100}\right] = ₹120$$

$$\text{Now, new CP} = \frac{100}{2} = ₹50$$

SP = ₹ 120

$$\text{Profit percentage} = \frac{120 - 50}{50} \times 100 = 70 \times 2 = 140\%$$

∴ Required profit% is 140%.

184. (a) Cost price of 1 dozen of corn = ₹180

$$\text{So, cost price of 1 corn} = ₹\ \frac{180}{12} = ₹\ 15$$

and Selling price of 1 corn = ₹ 22

$$\text{Hence, profit per cent} = \frac{22 - 15}{15} \times 100\% = \frac{700}{15}\% = 46.6\%$$

185. (d) Let the cost price be ₹ y.

When he had a profit of 25%.

$$SP = y + 25\% \text{ of } y = 1.25y$$

When he had a loss of 25%.

$$SP = y - 25\% \text{ of } y = y - \frac{y}{4} = 0.75y$$

According to the question,

$$1 \cdot 25y - 0 \cdot 75y = 40 \Rightarrow 0 \cdot 50y = 40$$

$$\Rightarrow y = \frac{4000}{50} = 80$$

∴ Initial selling price

$$= 1.25y = 1.25 \times 80 = ₹\ 100$$

186. (c) Let A bought the article at ₹x.

Given, (100 + 25)% of (100 + 10)% of x = 6875

$$\Rightarrow \frac{125}{100} \times \frac{110}{100} \times x = 6875$$

$$\Rightarrow x = \frac{6875 \times 4 \times 10}{5 \times 11} = ₹\ 5000$$

Hence, CP for A is ₹ 5000.

187. (c) Let Cost Price (CP) = x

and Selling Price (SP) = y

Here, $y > x$.

Profit = $y - x$

New selling price = $2y$

New profit = $2y - x$

$$\text{Given,} \quad 3(y - x) = 2y - x$$

$$3y - 2y = -x + 3x$$

$$y = 2x$$

Now, profit = $y - x = 2x - x = x$

$$\therefore \text{Profit percentage} = \frac{\text{Profit}}{CP} \times 100 = \frac{x}{x} \times 100 = 100\%$$

188. (b) Selling price of the pen = ₹ 28.75

Profit = 15%

$$\text{Cost price} = \frac{28.75}{(100 + 15)} \times 100 = ₹\ 25$$

If selling price = ₹ 25.75

$$\text{Then, profit per cent} = \frac{25.75 - 25}{25} \times 100$$

∴ Required profit per cent is = 3%

189. (a) Let CP of 100 g = ₹ x

⇒ CP of 1000 g or 1 kg = ₹ $10x$

$$\text{Now, SP of 1 kg normally} = \frac{120}{100} \times 10x = ₹12x$$

Now, when weighing machine weigh 900 g instead of 1000 g.

⇒ CP of 900 g = ₹ $9x$

$$\text{and SP} = ₹\ \frac{90}{100} \times 12x = ₹\ 10.8x$$

$$\therefore \text{Profit\%} = \frac{SP - CP}{CP} \times 100 = \frac{10.8x - 9x}{9x} \times 100 = \frac{1.8x}{9x} \times 100 = 20\%$$

190. (d) According to the question,

Original cost price of the article

$$= 3750 \times \frac{(100 - 24)}{100} \times \frac{100}{(100 + 14)} = 3750 \times \frac{76}{100} \times \frac{100}{114} = ₹\ 2500$$

191. (c) Let the cost price of the article be ₹300.

$$\text{Given, selling price} = \frac{100}{3 \times 100} \times 300 = ₹\ 100$$

According to the question,

$$33\frac{1}{3}\% = 300 - 100 \Rightarrow \frac{100}{3}\% = 200$$

$$\therefore \quad 40\% = \frac{200 \times 40 \times 3}{100} = ₹\,240$$

Since, CP (₹ 300) > SP (₹ 240),
There is a loss.

$$\text{Loss\%} = \frac{(300 - 240)}{300} \times 100 = 20\%$$

192. (b) According to the question,
Cost price of an article

$$= \frac{1170 \times 100}{(100 - 22)} = \frac{1170}{78} \times 100 = ₹\,1500$$

Given, selling price = ₹ 1450
Since, selling price < cost price.
∴ There is a loss and

$$\text{Loss\%} = \frac{(1500 - 1450)}{1500} \times 100 = 3.3\%$$

193. (a) Let the quantity sold at 10% loss be x kg.
According to the question,

$$(840 - x) \times \frac{125}{100} + x \times \frac{90}{100} = 840 \times \frac{115}{100}$$

$$\Rightarrow 1050 - 1.25x + 0.9x = 966$$

$$\Rightarrow \quad 0.35x = 84$$

$$\therefore \quad x = \frac{8400}{35} = 240 \text{ kg}$$

Speedy Method

Thus, 7 units = 840 kg
1 = 120 kg
2 units = 240 kg

194. (d) Given, $x = 40\%$, $y = -40\%$
Net per cent change in whole transaction

$$= \left(x + y + \frac{xy}{100}\right)\%$$

$$= \left(40 - 40 - \frac{40 \times 40}{100}\right)\% = -16\%$$

Where '–' sign shows the loss.

195. (c) Correct formula,

$$\text{SP} = (100 - \text{loss}\,\%) \times \frac{\text{CP}}{100}$$

196. (b)

CP	:	SP
100	:	95
87.5	:	100
87.5	:	95

∴ Required profit percentage

$$= \frac{95 - 87.5}{87.5} \times 100$$

$$= \frac{7.5}{87.5} \times 100 = 8\frac{4}{7}\%$$

197. (d) Cost price of scooter

$$= 1980 - 1980 \times \frac{1}{5}$$

$$= 1980 - 396 = ₹\,1584$$

$$\text{Gain \%} = \frac{396}{1584} \times 100 = 25\%$$

198. (b) Required loss percentage

$$= \frac{460 - 414}{460} \times 100 = 10\%$$

199. (a) $\text{Gain \%} = \frac{90 - 70}{70} \times 100 = 28.57\ \%$

200. (c) Required loss percentage

$$= \frac{300 - 200}{300} \times 100 = \frac{100}{3} = 33.33\%$$

201. (c) True weight = 1000 gm

$$\text{False weight} = 1000 \times \frac{67}{100} = 670 \text{ gm}$$

$$\text{Gain\%} = \frac{1000 - 670}{670} \times 100 = \frac{330}{670} \times 100$$

$$= 49\frac{17}{67}\%$$

202. (c)

$$\text{CP} + \text{Profit} = 88000$$

$$\underline{\text{CP} - \text{Loss} = 72000} \qquad [\because \text{Profit} = \text{Loss}]$$

$$2\text{CP} = 160000$$

$$\text{CP} = ₹\,80000$$

$$\therefore \text{Profit \%} = \frac{96000 - 80000}{80000} \times 100 = 20\%$$

203. (b) $\text{CP} = \frac{450.30}{(100 - 21)} \times 100 = ₹\,570$

204. (c) According to the question,
Amount student had to pay

$$= 45000 \times \frac{88}{100} \times \frac{112}{100} = ₹\,44352$$

205. (c) CP of chickooes per 100 = ₹ 1280

$$\text{CP of 400 chickooes} = 1280 \times \frac{400}{100} = ₹\,5120$$

Profit = ₹ 980

SP of 400 chickooes = 5120 + 980 = ₹ 6100

$$\text{SP of per dozen chickooes} = \frac{6100}{400} \times 12$$

$$= ₹\,183$$

206. (d) $\text{CP} = \frac{19.5}{125} \times 100 = ₹\,15.6$

$$\text{New, SP} = 15.6 \times \frac{150}{100} = ₹\,23.4$$

∴ Required difference = 23.4 – 19.5 = ₹ 3.9

207. (d) Let cost price be x.

$$\text{Initially selling price} = x \times \frac{108}{100} = \frac{108x}{100}$$

$$\text{New cost price} = x \times \frac{95}{100} = \frac{95}{100}x$$

According to the question,

$$\left(\frac{95}{100}x\right) \times \frac{112}{100} = \frac{108x}{100} - 8$$

$$\Rightarrow \quad \frac{108x}{100} - \frac{106.4x}{100} = 8$$

$$\Rightarrow \quad \frac{1.6x}{100} = 8$$

$$\Rightarrow \quad x = \frac{800}{1.6} = 500$$

∴ Cost price of article = ₹ 500

Speedy Method

∴ 1.6 units = 8
1 units = ₹ 5
100 units = ₹ 500

208. (a) CP of each candie = ₹ 5
∴ SP of each candie to get 20% profit

$$= 5 \times \frac{120}{100} = ₹\,6$$

209. (b) Old SP = ₹ 20

$$\text{CP} = \frac{20}{110} \times 100 = ₹\,18.18$$

$$\text{New, SP} = 18.18 \times \frac{130}{100} = ₹\,23.634$$

∴ Increases in SP = 23.634 – 20 = ₹ 3.64

210. (c) Let CP of Refrigerator and Geyser be R and G respectively.
According to the question,

$$125\% \times \text{R} + 110\% \times \text{G} = 30400$$

$$25\text{R} + 22\text{G} = 608000 \qquad \text{...(i)}$$

$$\text{and } \text{R} \times 110\% + \text{G} \times 125\% = 30700$$

$$22\text{R} + 25\text{G} = 614000 \qquad \text{...(ii)}$$

Subtracting Eq. (ii) × 25 and Eq. (i) × 22, we get

$$625\text{G} - 484\text{G} = 15350000 - 13376000$$

$$\Rightarrow \quad 141G = 1974000$$

$$\Rightarrow \quad G = 14000$$

∴ Selling price at 17% profit

$$= 14000 \times \frac{117}{100} = ₹\,16380$$

211. (a) $\text{Profit} = \frac{1}{6} \times \text{SP}$

$$\frac{\text{Profit}}{\text{SP}} = \frac{1}{6}$$

∴ CP = 6 – 1 = 5

$$\therefore \text{ Gain\%} = \frac{1}{5} \times 100 = 20\%$$

212. (d) $\text{SP} = 900 \times \frac{88}{100} = ₹\,792$

213. (d) Let CP be ₹ 100.

∴ SP = ₹ 19

110 → ₹ 19

140 → ₹ 24.18

∴ Increase in SP = 24.18 – 19 = ₹ 5.18

214. (d) Let CP of 1 mobile be ₹ 1.
CP of 15 mobile = ₹ 15
SP of 12 mobile = ₹ 15

$$\therefore \text{SP of 15 mobile} = ₹\,\frac{15 \times 15}{12} = ₹\,\frac{225}{12}$$

$$\therefore \text{Profit \%} = \frac{\text{SP} - \text{CP}}{\text{CP}} \times 100$$

$$= \frac{\frac{225}{12} - 15}{15} \times 100 = \frac{45}{12 \times 15} \times 100 = 25\%$$

215. (c) Let the error in weight be x gm.

$$\text{Profit \%} = \frac{\text{Error}}{\text{True value} - \text{Error}} \times 100$$

$\Rightarrow \quad \frac{100}{39} = \frac{x}{100-x} \times 100$

$\Rightarrow \quad 1000 - x = 39x$

$\Rightarrow \quad 40x = 1000 \Rightarrow x = 25$ gm

False weight = 1000 – 25 = 975 gm

216. (d) Overall loss percentage

$= \frac{a^2}{100} = \frac{11 \times 11}{100} = 1.21\%$

∴ Article purchased by

$P = \frac{19758}{(100-1.21)} \times 100 = ₹\,20000$

217. (d) Net % change $= 40 + 15 + \frac{40 \times 15}{100}$

$= 61\%$

Let A paid 100%

∴ C paid (161%) → ₹ 4914

∴ A paid (100%) → ₹ 3052

218. (b) Cost price of scooter

$= 40675 - 40675 \times \frac{1}{5}$

$= 40675 - 8135 = ₹\,32540$

Gain% $= \frac{8135}{32540} \times 100 = 25\%$

219. (a) Let CP of 1 book be ₹ 1.

∴ CP of 30 books = ₹ 30

SP of 20 books = ₹ 30

∴ SP of 1 book = ₹ $\frac{30}{20}$

∴ Gain percentage $= \frac{\frac{30}{20} - 1}{1} \times 100 = 50\%$

Speedy Method

CP × 30 = SP × 20

$\Rightarrow \quad \frac{CP}{SP} = \frac{20}{30}$

Gain percentage $= \frac{10}{20} \times 100 = 50\%$

220. (c) Required profit percentage

$= \frac{600-500}{500} \times 100 = \frac{100}{500} \times 100 = 20\%$

221. (a) Let True weight be 100.

∴ False weight = 81

∴ Profit %

$= \frac{\text{True weight} - \text{False weight}}{\text{False weight}} \times 100$

$= \frac{100-81}{81} \times 100 = \frac{19}{81} \times 100 = 23\frac{37}{81}\%$

222. (b) According to the question,

25 CP = 20 SP

$\Rightarrow \quad \frac{CP}{SP} = \frac{4}{5}$

∴ Profit % $= \frac{5-4}{4} \times 100 = 25\%$

223. (b) Let SP be x.

∴ $\quad CP = \frac{75x}{100}$

∴ Profit percent $= \frac{SP - CP}{CP} \times 100$

$= \frac{x - \frac{75x}{100}}{\frac{75x}{100}} \times 100 = \frac{25}{75} \times 100 = 33\frac{1}{3}\%$

Speedy Method

∵ $\quad CP = \frac{75}{100} \times SP$

$\Rightarrow \quad \frac{CP}{SP} = \frac{75}{100}$

Profit percentage $= \frac{100-75}{75} \times 100$

$= \frac{25}{75} \times 100 = 33\frac{1}{3}\%$

224. (d) Let the false weight be x g.

According to the question,

$\frac{1000-x}{x} \times 100 = 15$

$\Rightarrow \quad 100000 - 100x = 15x$

$\Rightarrow \quad 115x = 100000$

$x = \frac{100000}{115} = 869.57$ g

225. (a) Cost price for first vendor

$= 3200 \times \frac{100}{128} = ₹\,2500$

Cost price for second vendor

$= 3200 - 3200 \times \frac{28}{100} = ₹\,2304$

Profit for first vendor = 3200 – 2500 = ₹ 700

Profit for second vendor = 3200 – 2304

= ₹ 896

∴ Required difference = 896 – 700 = ₹ 196

226. (d) Let the CP be ₹ x.

∴ $\quad SP = \frac{x \times (100-9)}{100} = \frac{91x}{100}$

According to the question,

$\frac{91x}{100} + 51 = \frac{108x}{100}$

$\frac{17x}{100} = 51$

$x = \frac{5100}{17} = ₹\,300$

Speedy Method

Difference = [9 – (–8)]% → ₹ 51

17% → ₹ 51

CP (100%) → ₹ 300

227. (a) Cost of flat = ₹ 950000

SP for Lakshman and CP for Bharath

$= 950000 \times \frac{108}{100} = ₹\,1026000$

Again, Bharth sold to Lakshman SP for Bharath and CP for Lakshman

$= 1026000 \times \frac{97}{100} = ₹\,995220$

Thus, actual gain by Lakshman

= 1026000 – 995220 = ₹ 30780

228. (d) Total cost price of old scooter

= 4700 + 800 = ₹ 5500

∴ Required gain % $= \frac{5800-5500}{5500} \times 100$

$= \frac{300}{5500} \times 100 = 5\frac{5}{11}\%$

229. (c) Let SP are $103x$ and $106x$.

According to the question,

$106x - 103x = 9$

$\Rightarrow \quad 3x = 9$

$\Rightarrow \quad x = 3$

∴ Required ratio = 103 × 3 : 106 × 3

= 103 : 106

230. (b) Cost price of all 4 laptop

$= 154005 \times \frac{100}{75} = ₹\,205340$

∴ Selling price at which Raju gain (25%)

$= 205340 \times \frac{125}{100} = ₹\,256675$

231. (a) Total cost price = 2500 + 300 = ₹ 2800

and SP = ₹ 3000

∴ Profit percentage $= \frac{3000-2800}{2800} \times 100$

$= \frac{2}{28} \times 100 = 7\frac{1}{7}\%$

232. (c) SP = ₹ 20

∴ $\quad CP = \frac{20}{110} \times 100 = \frac{200}{11}$

Let selling price be increased by ₹ x.

According to the question,

$20 + x = \frac{200}{11} \times \frac{120}{100}$

$\Rightarrow \quad 20 + x = 21.818$

$\Rightarrow \quad x = ₹\,1.82$

233. (c) SP of each sack of rice = ₹19200

SP of two sacks of rice = 2 × 19200 = ₹38400

CP of 1st sack of rice $= 19200 \times \frac{100}{120} = ₹16000$

CP of 2nd sack of rice $= 19200 \times \frac{100}{80} = ₹24000$

Total CP = 16000 + 24000 = ₹40,000

∴ Required loss percentage

$= \frac{40000-38400}{40000} \times 100 = 4\%$

Speedy Method

Total loss % $= \frac{(\text{loss }\%)^2}{100} = \frac{(20)^2}{100} = 4\%$ (loss)

234. (d) Given, change in SP = ₹ 100

According to the question,

30% + 20% → ₹ 100

50% → ₹ 100

∴ $\quad$ 100% → ₹ 200

235. (a) Let the third seller gain x%.

Equivalent profit of first two seller

$= 20 + 25 + \frac{20 \times 25}{100} = 50\%$

Again, $50 + x + \frac{50 \times x}{100} = 80$

$\Rightarrow \quad \frac{150x}{100} = 30 \Rightarrow x = 20\%$

236. (b) CP for Atul = 15000 − 3000 = ₹ 12000

Profit% = $\frac{3000}{12000} \times 100 = 25\%$

237. (d) Given,

Cost of oranges = ₹ 150 per hundred

SP of oranges = ₹ 24 per dozen

Gain = ₹ 1000

Cost of 100 oranges = ₹ 150

Cost of 1 orange = ₹ 1.5

Selling price of 12 oranges = ₹ 24

Selling price of 1 orange = ₹ 2

Profit on 1 orange = 2 − 1.5 = ₹ 0.5

So, total oranges bought = $\frac{1000}{0.5} = 2000$

238. (c) Loss% = 10 = $\frac{CP - 1080}{CP} \times 100$

$\Rightarrow$ 10 CP = 100 CP − 108000

$\Rightarrow$ 90 CP = 108000 $\Rightarrow$ CP = ₹ 1200

When, SP = ₹ 1350

Profit = ₹ (1350 − 1200) = ₹ 150

$\therefore$ Profit % = $\frac{150}{1200} \times 100 = 12.5\%$

239. (b) Amount invested = ₹ 12000

Amount received back = ₹ 15500

$\therefore$ Profit = ₹ (15500 − 12000) = ₹ 3500

$\therefore$ Profit per cent = $\frac{3500}{12000} \times 100 = 29.17\%$

240. (c) Selling price of fan

$= ₹\ 2000 \times \left(\frac{100 - 15}{100}\right) = 20 \times 85 = ₹\ 1700$

241. (c) Let cost of production be ₹ $100x$.

$\therefore$ Price after manufacturer gains 10% = ₹ $110x$

Similarly,

Price after wholesale dealer gains 12% = $110x + 12\% \times 110x$ = ₹ $123.2x$

Price after retailer gains 15%

$= 123.2x + 15\%$ of $123.2x$ = ₹$141.68x$

Given, retail price = ₹ 1771

$\Rightarrow$ $141.68x = 1771 \Rightarrow x = 12.5$

$\therefore$ Cost of production

$= 100x = 100(12.5)$ = ₹ 1250

242. (b) SP of 16 bulbs = CP of 24 bulbs

$\Rightarrow$ 16 SP = 24 CP $\Rightarrow \frac{CP}{SP} = \frac{16}{24}$

Let cost price is $16x$ and selling price is $24x$.

Profit = $\frac{24x - 16x}{16x} \times 100 = 50\%$

243. (d) Let CP of cycle be ₹ $100x$.

$\therefore$ SP of cycle = CP − loss = $100x - 17x = 83x$

New SP = $105\ x$

According to the question,

$105\ x = 83\ x + 1056 \Rightarrow 22x = 1056 \Rightarrow x = 48$

$\therefore$ CP of cycle = $100\ x = 100(48)$ = ₹ 4800

244. (a) Given, Cost of goods = ₹ 3600

Overhead expenses = $\frac{3600 \times 5}{100}$ = ₹ 180

$\therefore$ Total CP = ₹ (3600 + 180) = ₹ 3780

SP to earn 15% = $\frac{115}{100} \times 3780$ = ₹ 4347

245. (c) Let cost price of the book = ₹100

At 10% profit, selling price = ₹ 110

At twice the price, selling price = ₹220

Profit % = $\frac{220 - 100}{100} \times 100 = 120\%$

246. (a) Let the cost price of the goods = ₹ x

According to the question,

$3200 - x = \frac{7}{5}(3000 - x)$

$\Rightarrow 5(3200 - x) = 7(3000 - x)$

$\Rightarrow 16000 - 5x = 21000 - 7x$

$\Rightarrow \quad 7x - 5x = 21000 - 16000$

$\therefore \quad x = \frac{5000}{2}$ = ₹ 2500

247. (a) Given, Divya bought 6 candies for ₹1.

Cost price of one candy = ₹ $\frac{1}{6}$

At 50% profit, selling price of one candy

$= (100 + 50)\%$ of $\frac{1}{6} = \frac{150}{100} \times \frac{1}{6}$ = ₹ $\frac{1}{4}$

So, Divya sells 4 candies for a rupee.

248. (a) Let the investment are $2x$ and $3x$, respectively.

Total investment = $2x + 3x = 5x$

Total return = $\frac{110}{100} \times 2x + \frac{80}{100} \times 3x = 4.6\ x$

$\therefore$ Loss % = $\frac{5x - 4.6x}{5x} \times 100\% = 8\%$

249. (d) Given, Now, cost price for 50 kg of sugar = 50 × 40 = ₹ 2000

and cost price for 70 kg of sugar

= 70 × 30 = ₹ 2100

Cost price of mixture = ₹(2000 + 2100)

= ₹ 4100

$\Rightarrow$ SP = $4100 \times \frac{120}{100}$ = ₹ 4920

Total weight of the mixture

= 50 + 70 = 120 kg

SP of 120 kg sugar = ₹ 4920

SP of 1 kg sugar = $\frac{4920}{120}$ = ₹ 41

Hence, SP of sugar is ₹ 41 per kg.

250. (c) Let the price = ₹x

According to the question,

$1980 - x = x - 1620 \Rightarrow 2x = 3600$

$\Rightarrow \quad x = 1800$

Now, price of an article for profit of 15%

$= 1800 \times \frac{115}{100}$ = ₹ 2070

251. (c) Let the price of article = ₹ 100

Raju sold an article to Ravi at 10% gain

$= 100 \times \frac{10}{100}$ = ₹ 110

Ravi sold an article to Ramu at a 10% loss

$= 110 \times \frac{90}{100}$ = ₹ 99

Ramu paid ₹ 1485 to Ravi ⇒ 99 = ₹ 1485

1 = ₹ 15

So, selling price of Raju to Ravi

= 110 × 15 = ₹ 1650

252. (d) Given, cost price of item = ₹ 4350

Selling price of item = ₹ 5680

$\therefore$ Profit percentage = $\frac{5680 - 4350}{4350} \times 100$

$= \frac{1330}{4350} \times 100 = 30.6\%$

253. (b) Let the profit earned be ₹ x.

According to the question,

Selling price = ₹ $9x$

$\therefore$ Cost price = $9x - x$ = ₹ $8x$

$\therefore$ Profit% = $\frac{x \times 100}{8x} = 12.5\%$

254. (b) CP of two bottles = ₹ 100

SP of two bottles = 2 × 100 = ₹ 200

Required profit % = $\frac{SP - CP}{CP} \times 100$

$= \frac{(200 - 100) \times 100}{100} = 100\%$

255. (c) According to the question,

$\therefore$ Total loss %

$= \frac{\left(600 \times \frac{20}{100} + 4000 \times \frac{32}{100}\right)}{(600 + 4000)} \times 100$

$= \frac{(120 + 1280)}{4600} \times 100 = \frac{1400 \times 100}{4600} = 30.43\%$

256. (a) Let the cost price of the item be ₹ x.

According to the question,

$x \times \frac{112}{100} = x \times \frac{92}{100} + 36$

$\Rightarrow \quad \frac{(112x - 92x)}{100} = 36$

$\therefore \quad x = \frac{3600}{20}$ = ₹ 180

257. (c) Since SP > CP

$\therefore$ There are the gain.

and gain% = $\frac{(625 - 500)}{500} \times 100 = 25\%$

258. (a) CP of 1 article = ₹ 1

and SP of 1 article = ₹ 1. 23

$\therefore$ Profit % = $\frac{123 - 1}{1} \times 100 = 23\%$

259. (a) Loss % = $\frac{a^2}{100}\%$

Here, $a = 20\%$

So, Loss% = $\frac{20 \times 20}{100}\% = 4\%$

260. (d) Let the cost price of the bag = ₹ x

given, 40 % of x = 880

$\therefore \quad x = \frac{880 \times 100}{40}$ = ₹ 2200

261. (d) Let the CP of each item be ₹ x then,

CP of both items = ₹ $2x$

SP of both items = $\frac{120}{100} \times x + \frac{125}{100} x$ = ₹ $\frac{245}{100} x$

$\text{Profit} = \frac{245}{100}x - 2x = ₹\ \frac{45}{100}x$

$\text{Profit percentage} = \frac{\text{Profit}}{\text{CP}} \times 100$

$= \frac{\frac{45}{100}x}{2x} \times 100 = 22.5\%$

262. (d) Total profit on 65 m cloth

$= ₹\ 11 \times 65 = ₹\ 715$

SP of 65 m cloth = ₹ 5850

CP of 65 m cloth = ₹ (5850 − 715) = ₹ 5135

CP of 1 m cloth $= \frac{5135}{65} = ₹\ 79$

263. (a) Let the total units of items = x

and CP of all the items = ₹ y

Then, CP of 1 item $= ₹\frac{y}{x}$

Now, Let the required fractions be $\frac{1}{p}$

SP of $\frac{1}{p}x$ items = ₹ y

SP of 1 such item $= ₹\ \frac{y}{\left(\frac{x}{p}\right)}$

$\text{Profit percentage} = \frac{\text{Profit}}{\text{CP}} \times 100$

$300 = \frac{\frac{y}{\left(\frac{x}{p}\right)} - \frac{y}{x}}{\frac{y}{x}} \times 100 \Rightarrow 3 = (p-1) \Rightarrow p = 4$

Hence, the required fraction is $\frac{1}{p} = \frac{1}{4}$

264. (b) Required profit percentage

$= \frac{160}{250} \times 100 = 64\%$

265. (b) Let the cost price of the article to A be ₹ x.

∴ Cost price of the article to $B = 112x$

and cost price of the article to $C = \frac{112x}{100} \times 90$

According to the question,

$\frac{112x}{100} \times 90 = 15288$

$112x = ₹\ 16986.67 \approx ₹\ 16800$

∴ Required price = ₹ 16800 (approx.)

266. (a) Given, $\text{CP} = \frac{7}{6} \times \text{SP} = \frac{7}{6}$

[Let SP be ₹ 1]

Since CP > SP, therefore there will be loss.

∴ Loss percentage

$= \frac{\left(\frac{7}{6} - 1\right)}{\left(\frac{7}{6}\right)} \times 100 = \frac{100}{7} = 14.29\ \%$

267. (d) CP of pens = (20 × 190) = ₹ 3800

Total CP including expenses

= ₹ (3800 + 200) = ₹ 4000

SP of all the pens = ₹ (20 × 12 × 22)

[∵ 1 dozen = 12 pieces]

= ₹ 5280

Therefore, profit % $= \frac{1280}{4000} \times 100 = 32\%$

268. (d) Let the SP be $8x$.

Then, $\text{CP} = 8x \times \frac{5}{8} = 5x$

$\therefore \text{Profit\%} = \frac{3x}{5x} \times 100 = 60\%$

269. (c) According to the question,

⇒ Profit = 46 = 236 − CP

⇒ CP = 236 − 46

∴ CP = 190

So, profit % $= \frac{\text{Profit}}{\text{CP}} \times 100$

$= \frac{46}{190} \times 100 = 24.21\ \%$

270. (d) Let the price of tomato (for 1 kg) be ₹ x.

According to the question,

$x \times \frac{120}{100} = 720$

$\Rightarrow \quad x = 720 \times \frac{100}{120} = ₹\ 600$

∴ The new price of the tomato (for 1 kg)

= ₹ (600 + 720) = ₹ 1320

Speedy Method

120% → 720

1% → 6

220% → ₹ 1320

271. (d) According to the question,

35% of CP = ₹ 560 [∵ 35% = profit]

$\text{CP} = \frac{560 \times 100}{35} = ₹\ 1600$

$\text{Selling price} = 1600 \times \frac{135}{100} = ₹\ 2160$

272. (b) Let its cost price be ₹ x.

According to the question,

$4550 - x = 5(x - 3290)$

$\Rightarrow 4550 - x = 5x - 16450$

$\Rightarrow \quad 6x = 21000 \Rightarrow x = \frac{21000}{6}$

$\Rightarrow \quad x = ₹\ 3500$

So, the cost price of article is ₹ 3500.

Now, {Profit = 20%}

$\therefore \text{ SP of article} = 3500 \times \frac{120}{100} = ₹\ 4200$

273. (b) Let the CP of an article = ₹ x

and loss = 10%

⇒ The SP of an article $= x - \frac{x \times 10}{100} = ₹\frac{90x}{100}$

When the price will be 30% less,

then new CP of an article $= x - \frac{x \times 30}{100} = ₹\ \frac{70x}{100}$

Now, new SP would be 40%

⇒ New SP of an article $= \frac{70x}{100} + \left(\frac{70x}{100} \times \frac{40}{100}\right)$

$= \left(\frac{70x}{100} + \frac{28x}{100}\right) = ₹\frac{98x}{100}$

According to the question,

$\frac{98x}{100} - \frac{90x}{100} = 20 \Rightarrow \frac{8x}{100} = 20$

$\Rightarrow \quad x = \frac{2000}{8} = ₹\ 250$

So, the CP of the article = ₹ 250

274. (c) Selling price of the article = ₹ 4400

and loss on the article = 20%

Then, $\text{CP} = 4440 \times \frac{100}{80} = ₹\ 5500$

Hence, CP of article = ₹ 5500

275. (b) Let the cost price of the given chair for P = 100

P sells to Q at 40% profit

⇒ Selling price for P = 140

Now, cost price of chair for

$Q = 140$ ...(i)

Q sells to R at 80% profit

$\Rightarrow \text{Selling price for } Q = 140 \times \frac{180}{100} = 252$

Now, cost price of chair for

$R = 252$ ...(ii)

By Eqs. (i) and (ii),

The ratio of cost price of P and R

= 100 : 252 = 25 : 63

276. (c) According to the question,

The selling price of a flower pot = ₹ 3500

and the cost price of a flower pot = ₹ 2800

$\text{Profit \%} = \left(\frac{3500 - 2800}{2800}\right) \times 100 = 25\%$

277. (d) Given, ratio of CP : SP = 20 : 25 = 4 : 5

Let the cost price and selling price be $4x$ and $5x$, respectively.

$\therefore \text{ Profit\%} = \frac{5x - 4x}{4x} \times 100 = 25\%$

278. (c) Let CP = ₹ x and SP = ₹ $0.8x$

According to the question,

$0.8x + 160 = 120\%$ of x

$\Rightarrow \quad 0.8x + 160 = x \times \frac{120}{100}$

$\Rightarrow \quad 0.8x + 160 = 1.2x$

$\Rightarrow \quad 0.4x = 160$

$\therefore \quad x = ₹\ 400$

So, CP will be ₹ 400 to earn a profit of 25%.

∴ SP = 400 × 125%

$= 400 \times \frac{125}{100} = ₹\ 500$

279. (d) CP of Ist bike = ₹ 24000

⇒ SP of Ist bike = 24000 × 120%

$= 24000 \times \frac{120}{100} = ₹ 28800$

and CP of IInd bike = ₹ 20000

SP of IInd bike = 20000 × 70%

$= 20000 \times \frac{70}{100} = ₹\ 14000$

Total CP = 24000 + 20000 = ₹ 44000

and Total SP = 28800 + 14000 = ₹ 42800

∴ Loss = 44000 − 42800 = ₹ 1200

280. (d) According to the question,

$CP \times (125)\% = 35000$

$\Rightarrow CP = \frac{35000}{125} \times 100$

∴ CP = ₹ 28000

To earn 30% SP will be

$SP = 28000 \times \frac{130}{100} \Rightarrow SP = ₹36400$

281. (c) According to the question,

Total Cost Price (CP) = (4000 + 500) = ₹ 4500

and Selling Price (SP) = ₹ 5000

$\because$ Profit % $= \frac{5000-4500}{4500} \times 100$

∴ Profit % = 11.11%

282. (c) According to the question,

$CP = 1056 \times \frac{100}{100+20} = 1056 \times \frac{100}{120} = ₹880$

Now, if SP = ₹ 800

$\because$ Loss % $= \left(\frac{880-800}{880}\right) \times 100$

$= \frac{80}{880} \times 100 = \frac{1}{11} \times 100$

∴ Loss % = 9.09%

283. (a) Given, SP = ₹ 5688 and Loss = 10%

$\therefore CP = \frac{5688 \times 100}{90} = ₹\ 6320$

To earn 20% profit,

$\therefore SP = 6320 \times \frac{120}{100} = ₹7584$

284. (b) According to the question,

Let CP = ₹ 100

At 20% loss,

$SP = 100 - \frac{100 \times 20}{100} = ₹\ 80$

∴ CP : SP = 100 : 80 = 5 : 4

285. (b) Let the cost price of the article = ₹x

Then, selling price of article

$= x \times \frac{(100-20)}{100} = ₹\frac{80x}{100}$

When the article bought 30% less, then new

cost price $= \frac{x \times (100-30)}{100} = ₹\frac{70x}{100}$

and then new selling price of article

$= \frac{70x}{100} \times \frac{150}{100} = ₹\frac{105}{100}x$

According to the question,

$\frac{105x}{100} - \frac{80x}{100} = 125 \Rightarrow \frac{25x}{100} = 125 \Rightarrow x = ₹\ 500$

286. (a) According to the question,

CP of 1 pen $= ₹\frac{1}{20}$

and SP of 1 pen $= ₹\frac{1}{15}$

$\therefore$ Profit % $= \left[\frac{\left(\frac{1}{15}-\frac{1}{20}\right)}{\frac{1}{20}}\right] \times 100$

$= \left[\frac{\frac{5}{15 \times 20}}{\frac{1}{20}}\right] \times 100 = \frac{1}{3} \times 100$

Profit % = 33.33

287. (c) Selling price (SP) of refrigerator = ₹ 28000

and Loss % = 30%

According to the question,

∴ New selling price

$= \frac{100}{70} \times 28000 \times \frac{125}{100} = ₹\ 50000$

288. (c) Loss% $= \left[\frac{6000-5500}{6000}\right] \times 100$

$= \frac{500}{6000} \times 100 = 8.33\%$

289. (c) ∴ 20% = ₹ 132

120% = ₹ 792

290. (b) Suresh sells a car at the loss of 36%.

∴ Ratio of CP : SP = 100 : (100 − 36)

= 100 : 64 = 25 : 16

291. (d) Cost price of 5 shirts

= Selling price of 3 shirts

$5\ CP = 3\ SP \Rightarrow \frac{SP}{CP} = \frac{5}{3}$

Profit% $= \frac{5-3}{3} \times 100 = 66.66\%$

292. (b) Selling price of a table = ₹ 11480

and loss % = 18%

Let the cost price = $100x$

According to the question,

$(100x - 18x) = 11480$

$\Rightarrow 82x = 11480 \Rightarrow x = \frac{11480}{82} \Rightarrow x = 140$

∴ CP = 140 × 100 = 14000

So, new SP = ₹ 15540

∴ Profit% $= \left(\frac{15540-14000}{14000}\right) \times 100 = 11\%$

293. (b) Cost of one pen $= \frac{1}{35}$

SP of one pen $= \frac{1}{35} \times \frac{140}{100} = \frac{1}{25}$

Thus, he sell 25 pen for one rupees.

294. (b) Let total article be 100.

Then, $\frac{70 \times 20 + 30 \times (-10)}{100} = \frac{1400-300}{100} = 11\%$

295. (a) Let the cost price of table be ₹ 100.

∴ Selling price of table $= \frac{25}{100} \times 100 = ₹\ 25$

Loss % $= \frac{100-25}{100} \times 100 = 75\%$

Hence, loss percentage = 75%

296. (a) Cost price of 35 mangoes = ₹ 1

CP of the mangoes $= ₹\frac{1}{35}$

SP of the mangoes $= \frac{1}{35} \times \frac{70}{100} = \frac{1}{5 \times 10} = \frac{1}{50}$

So, he sells 50 mangoes in one rupee.

297. (b) Suppose, the cost price of article is ₹ $100x$.

Selling price at 10% loss

$= 100x \times \frac{90}{100} = ₹90x$ ...(i)

But he buy it 30% less price.

∴ New cost price $= 100x \times \frac{70}{100} = ₹70x$

But he gain 10% on it.

New selling price

$= 70x \times \frac{110}{100} = ₹77x$ ...(ii)

From Eqs. (i) and (ii), we get

$90x - 77x = 26 \Rightarrow 13x = 26$

$\therefore x = 2$

So, required cost price of article

$= 100x = 100 \times 2 = ₹\ 200$

298. (a) According to the question,

CP of 6 pens = SP of 5 pens

$\Rightarrow \frac{CP}{SP} = \frac{5}{6} \Rightarrow \frac{SP}{CP} = \frac{6}{5}$

Profit% $= \frac{6-5}{5} = \left(\frac{1}{5} \times 100\right)$

∴ Profit% = 20%

299. (b) Given, SP = ₹ 6875

and profit = 25% ⇒ CP $= 100 \times \frac{6875}{125} = ₹\ 5500$

∴ CP = ₹ 5500

300. (b) Cost price of watch for A

$= 5000 \times \frac{100}{125} = ₹\ 4000$

Cost price of watch for B

$= 5000 \times \frac{100}{90} = 5000 \times \frac{10}{9}$

So, ratio of cost price of A and B

$= \frac{4000}{5000 \times \frac{10}{9}} = \frac{4000}{5000 \times 10} \times \frac{9}{1} = \frac{18}{25} = 18 : 25$

Hence, required ratio is 18 : 25.

301. (d) Total cost price = 2320 + 180 = ₹ 2500

Selling price of bat = ₹ 2400

Loss % $= \frac{2500-2400}{2500} \times 100 = \frac{100}{2500} \times 100 = 4\%$

302. (c) $\frac{1}{5}(-20) + \frac{4}{5}(x) = 30$

$\Rightarrow \frac{-20+4x}{5} = 30 \Rightarrow 4x = 150 + 20$

$\Rightarrow 4x = 170 \Rightarrow x = 42.5\%$

303. (c) Let the CP of the article be ₹ x.

then SP_1 = ₹ 900, SP_2 = ₹ 450

Now, profit on SP_1 = 2 × loss on SP_2

$\Rightarrow 900 - x = 2 \times (x - 450)$

$\Rightarrow \quad 900 - x = 2x - 900$

$\Rightarrow \quad 3x = 1800 \Rightarrow x = 600$

New profit = 25%

$\therefore$ Selling price (SP) $= \dfrac{125}{100} \times 600 = ₹\,750$

304. (c) Let the cost price of one mango = ₹ x

Selling price of one mango at 25% profit

$= x \times \dfrac{125}{100} = ₹\,\dfrac{5x}{4}$

According to question,

$x \times \dfrac{140}{100} = \dfrac{5x}{4} + 3 \Rightarrow \dfrac{7x}{5} - \dfrac{5x}{4} = 3$

$\Rightarrow \quad \dfrac{28x - 25x}{20} = 3 \Rightarrow x = ₹\,20$

305. (c) Let the cost price of the product = ₹ 100

Then, selling price of the product

$= 100 \times \dfrac{120}{100} = ₹\,120$

$\therefore \dfrac{\text{Selling price}}{\text{Cost price}} = \dfrac{120}{100} = \dfrac{6}{5}$

306. (d) Cost price of 50 chairs = ₹ 50,000

$\therefore$ Selling price of 50 chairs to make

35% profit $= \dfrac{50000 \times 135}{100} = ₹\,67500$

Let, normal price of 1 chair = ₹ x

According to question,

$30x + \dfrac{20x \times 3}{4} = 67500$

$\Rightarrow \quad 30x + 15x = 67500 \Rightarrow 45x = 67500$

$x = ₹\,1500$

Hence, required price of chair is ₹ 1500.

307. (a) Given, a milkman bought 90 L of milk of ₹ 1630

Per litre price of milk $= \dfrac{1630}{90} = 18.11$ per/litre

Now, after adding 15 L of water in it

Per liter price $= \dfrac{1630}{(90 + 15)} = 15.52$ per/litre

He sell it at ₹ 19 per litre.

So, his profit percentage

$= \dfrac{19 - 15.52}{15.52} \times 100 = 22\dfrac{64}{163}\%$

308. (c) Given,

Ratio of the cost price and selling price = 5 : 3

Loss% $= \dfrac{5 - 3}{5} \times 100 = \dfrac{2}{5} \times 100 = 40\%$

309. (d) Given, total sugar = 1000 kg

By alligation method,

6% 12%

10

2% 4%

1 : 2

3 unit = 1000 kg

1 unit = 333.33 kg

$\therefore$ So, he sells 333.33 kg of sugar at 6% of profit.

310. (d) Given,

Faulty weight = 925 g

Real weight = 1000 g

Error = 1000 − 925 = 75 g

$\therefore \quad$ Profit % $= \dfrac{\text{Error}}{\text{Faulty weight}} \times 100$

$= \dfrac{75}{925} \times 100 = 8.11\%$

311. (c) Let the cost price of an article is = ₹ 100

Selling price of first article $= 100 \times \dfrac{105}{100} = ₹\,105$

Selling price of first article $= 100 \times \dfrac{110}{100} = ₹\,110$

Then, the ratio of selling price of first article to second article.

= 105 : 110 = 21 : 22

312. (d) Let the CP of article be ₹ x.

$SP = x(1 + 15\%)$

$SP = x(1 + 0.15) = 1.15x$

Faulty weight are 20% less.

Actual weight 1kg

Difference = 1000 − 200 = 800 gm

Now, SP of 800 gm of article

$\Rightarrow$ SP of 1gm of rice $= \dfrac{115x}{800}$

$\Rightarrow$ SP of 1000 gm of rice $= \dfrac{1150\ x}{800} = 14375x$

Now, profit % $= \left[\dfrac{14375x - x}{x}\right] \times 100$

Profit % $= \left[\dfrac{0.4375x}{x}\right] \times 100$

Profit % $= 0.4375 \times 100 = 43.75\%$

313. (a) According to question,

Price of pure honey = 40 × 30 = ₹ 1200

Adding 20% water the value of honey

$= 40 \times \dfrac{120}{100} = 48$ kg

After increase price by 15%

$= 30 \times \dfrac{115}{100} = ₹\,34.5$ per kg

Total selling price = 48 × 34.5 = ₹ 1656

$\therefore$ Profit = 1656 − 1200 = ₹ 456

314. (a) Let the price of phone = ₹ $100x$

Soni sold a mobile phone to Raju at a profit of 10% $= 100 \times \dfrac{110}{100} = ₹\,110\,x$

Then, Raju sold it to Alok at a loss of 5%

$= 110 \times \dfrac{95}{100} = 104.5$

Then, Alok sold to Sohan at a profit of 20%

$= 104.5 \times \dfrac{120}{100} = 125.4x$

So, cost price of mobile for Soni

$= \dfrac{6270}{125.4} \times 100 = ₹\,5000$

315. (a) Let the CP of his 100 goods be ₹ 100.

He sold 60 goods at 25% gain, SP = 75

and 40 goods on CP, SP = ₹ 40 = ₹ 100

$\therefore$ Gain % $= \dfrac{75 + 40 - 100}{100} \times 100$

= 15%

316. (d) Given, house worth = ₹ 100000

Sold A to B at a profit of 6%

$= 10000 \times \dfrac{106}{100} = ₹\,106000$

After that B sells back to A at 3% loss

$= 106000 \times \dfrac{97}{100} = ₹\,102820$

A's gain in the entire transaction

= 102820 − 100000 = ₹ 2820

317. (b) Loss per cent $= \dfrac{1250 - 1000}{1250} \times 100$

$= \dfrac{250}{1250} \times 100 = 20\%$

318. (c) Let CP = x; SP $= \dfrac{136x}{100}$

According to the question,

$\dfrac{136x}{100} = 614856$

$x = \dfrac{614856}{136} \times 100 = 452100$

$\therefore$ Profit = 614856 − 452100 = 162756

319. (b) Total cost price

= 56000 + 22000 = ₹ 78000

Total selling price

$= 56000 \times \dfrac{120}{100} + 22000 \times \dfrac{115}{100}$

= 67200 + 25300 = ₹ 92500

Profit per cent $= \dfrac{92500 - 78000}{78000} \times 100\%$

$= \dfrac{14500}{780}\% = 18\dfrac{23}{39}\%$

320. (b) Cost price of mobile phone = ₹ 27000

Loss = 19%

$\therefore$ Selling price of mobile phone

$= 27000 \times \dfrac{81}{100} = ₹\,21870$

Now, cost price of tablet = ₹ 21870

Gain = 20%

$\therefore$ Selling price of tablet

$= 21870 \times \dfrac{120}{100} = ₹\,26244$

Total cost price = (27000 + 21870) = ₹ 48870

Total selling price

= (21870 + 26244) = ₹ 48114

Cost price > Selling price

$\therefore$ Total loss = (48870 − 48114) = ₹ 756

Speedy Method

Net percentage change $= a + b + \dfrac{ab}{100}$

$= 20 - 19 + \dfrac{20 \times (-19)}{100}$

$= 1 - 3.8 = -2.8\% = 2.8\%$ loss

$\therefore$ Total loss $= \dfrac{27000 \times 2.8}{100} = ₹\,756$

321. (c) The cost price of milk = ₹ 60

Profit = 10%

∴ The selling price of milk $= 60 \times \frac{110}{100} =$ ₹ 66

Now, new cost price of milk = ₹ 62

∴ New profit% $= \frac{(66-62)}{62} \times 100$

$= \frac{4}{62} \times 100 = 6.45\%$

322. (c) Selling price of 1st bag = ₹ 1260

Gain = 20%

∴ Cost price of 1st bag $= 1260 \times \frac{100}{120} =$ ₹ 1050

Now, selling price of 2nd bag = ₹ 1260

Loss = 20%

∴ Cost price of 2nd bag $= 1260 \times \frac{100}{80} =$ ₹ 1575

Total selling price = (1260 × 2) = ₹ 2520

Total cost price = (1050 + 1575) = ₹ 2625

Cost price > Selling price

∴ Total loss% $= \frac{(2625-2520)}{2625} \times 100$

$= \frac{105}{2625} \times 100 = 4\%$

Speedy Method

When 'SP' of 2 quantities is same and one is sold at '*a*%' loss and other at '*a*%' gain or *vice versa*, then there will always be a loss of $\frac{a^2}{100}\%$

∴ Loss% $= \frac{(20)^2}{100} = \frac{400}{100} = 4\%$ loss

323. (c) Let CP of article for $A = 100x$

∴ For B, CP of article $= 116x$

Profit of $A = 116x - 100x = 16x$

CP for C and SP for $B = 116x \times \frac{85}{100}$

$= 116x \times \frac{17}{20}$

Loss for $B = 116x - 116x \times \frac{17}{20}$

$= 116x\left(1 - \frac{17}{20}\right) = 116x \times \frac{3}{20}$

Profit of C $= 116x \times \frac{17}{20} \times \frac{20}{100} = 116x \times \frac{17}{100}$

According to the question,

$116x \times \frac{17}{100} - 16x = 248$

$\Rightarrow \frac{x}{100}(1972 - 1600) = 248 \Rightarrow x = \frac{248 \times 100}{372}$

∴ Loss for $B = 116 \times \frac{248 \times 100}{372} \times \frac{3}{20} =$ ₹ 1160

324. (c) Let SP be ₹ x.

∴ CP $= \frac{94x}{100} = 0.94x$

Profit per cent $= \frac{SP - CP}{CP} \times 100\%$

$= \frac{x - 0.94x}{0.94x} \times 100 = \frac{0.06x}{0.94x} \times 100$

$= \frac{600}{94} = 6.38\% \approx 6.4\%$

325. (c) Let real weight cost ₹ 100.

∴ CP $= 100 \times \frac{76}{100} = 76$;

SP $= 100 \times \frac{113}{100} = 113$

∴ Profit per cent $= \frac{113-76}{76} \times 100$

$= \frac{37 \times 100}{76} = 48.68\%$

326. (c) Loss percentage $= \frac{1200-900}{1200} \times 100\%$

$= \frac{300}{1200} \times 100\% = 25\%$

327. (c) Total CP of car = 247000 + 18000

= ₹ 265000

SP of car = ₹ 278250

∴ Profit = 278250 − 265000 = 13250

Profit per cent $= \frac{13250}{265000} \times 100\% = 5\%$

328. (b) SP of 1 shirt $= \frac{3360}{2} =$ ₹ 1680

CP of 1 shirt $= \frac{5600}{4} =$ ₹ 1400

∵ SP > CP

∴ Profit per cent $= \frac{1680-1400}{1400} \times 100$

$= \frac{280}{14} = 20\%$

329. (b) Given, SP = ₹ 23, Profit = 15%

∴ CP $= \frac{23 \times 100}{115} =$ ₹ 20

New, SP = ₹ 21.25

∴ Profit percentage $= \frac{1.25}{20} \times 100 = 6.25\%$

330. (c) SP of article = ₹ 360 and loss = 10%

∴ CP of article $= 360 \times \frac{100}{90} =$ ₹ 400

Now, SP of article at 20% profit

$= 400 \times \frac{120}{100} =$ ₹ 480

Speedy Method

New SP $= 360 \times \frac{100}{90} \times \frac{120}{100} =$ ₹ 480

09

Discount

- **Marked Price** (MP) The price on the label of an article/product is called **marked price** or **list price**.
- **Selling Price** (SP) The price at which an item is sold, is called selling price. Selling Price (SP) = Marked Price (MP) – Discount
- **Discount** When a shopkeeper reduces the marked price of an item in order to attract customers. This reduction in the marked price of an item is known as discount.

Discount = Marked price – Selling price

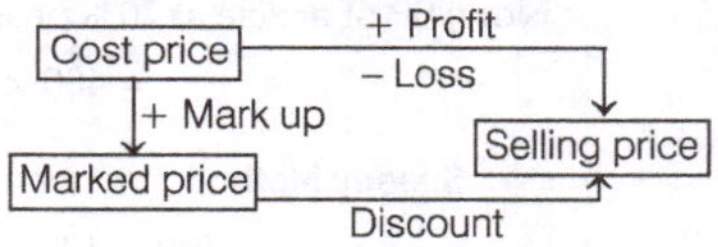

Important Formulae Related to Discount

- Selling Price $=\dfrac{\text{Marked Price} \times (100 - \text{Discount \%})}{100}$
- Marked Price $=\left(\dfrac{\text{Selling Price}}{100 - \text{Discount \%}}\right) \times 100$
- Discount Per cent $=\left(\dfrac{\text{Marked Price} - \text{Selling Price}}{\text{Marked price}}\right) \times 100$
- The discount for buying number of article a and getting number of article b free, is $=\dfrac{b}{(a+b)} \times 100.$
- Let discount $= D\%$ and profit/loss $= R\%$. Then, MP $=\dfrac{\text{CP}(100 \pm R\%)}{100 - D\%}$

Successive Discount

When two or more than two discounts allowed on the marked price, then these discounts are called successive discounts.

- Let an article is sold at successive discounts of $d_1\%$, $d_2\%$, $d_3\%$, ..., then Selling Price (SP) of the article

$$= \text{MP} \times \frac{(100 - d_1)}{100} \times \frac{(100 - d_2)}{100} \times \frac{(100 - d_3)}{100} \times \ldots$$

Ex. 1 The marked price of an article is ₹ 29500. It is sold at two successive discounts of 22% and 10%. Find the selling price of that item.

Sol. Given, the marked price of an article = ₹ 29500

After two successive discounts of 22% and 10%, the selling price of an article $= 29500 \times \left(\dfrac{100-22}{100}\right) \times \left(\dfrac{100-10}{100}\right)$

$$= 29500 \times \frac{78}{100} \times \frac{90}{100} = ₹\,20709$$

Equivalent Discount

A single discount, equivalent to two or more discounts, given by a seller on the marked price is called equivalent discount.

- If there are two discount (d_1 and d_2) offered on marked price, then single equivalent discount $=\left(d_1 + d_2 - \dfrac{d_1 \times d_2}{100}\right)\%$

Ex. 2 Suppose two discount 20% and 40% offered on MRP, then find single equivalent discount.

Sol. Single equivalent discount $=\left(20 + 40 - \dfrac{20 \times 40}{100}\right) = 60 - 8 = 52\%$

- If there are three discounts $d_1\%$, $d_2\%$ and $d_3\%$ offered on mark price, then

Single equivalent discount $=\left[1 - \left(1 - \dfrac{d_1}{100}\right)\left(1 - \dfrac{d_2}{100}\right)\left(1 - \dfrac{d_3}{100}\right)\right] \times 100$

Ex. 3 What will be an equivalent discount for three successive discount of 15%, 20% and 25%?

Sol. Single equivalent discount

$$= \left[1 - \left(1 - \frac{15}{100}\right)\left(1 - \frac{20}{100}\right)\left(1 - \frac{25}{100}\right)\right] \times 100$$

$$= \left[1 - \left(\frac{85}{100} \times \frac{80}{100} \times \frac{75}{100}\right)\right] \times 100$$

$$= \left[1 - \left(\frac{17}{20} \times \frac{4}{5} \times \frac{3}{4}\right)\right] \times 100$$

$$= \left[\frac{196}{400}\right] \times 100 = 49\%$$

SSC Exam Scanner

SSC CGL 2024 (Tier I & II)

1. Murlidhar, the owner of a grocery store, offers a discount scheme 'buy 5 water bottles get 1 for free' to his customers. What is the effective percentage discount offered by Murlidhar? (correct up to two decimal places)
SSC CGL (Tier-II) 20/01/2025 Shift-I
(a) 13.67% (b) 20.00%
(c) 13.33% (d) 16.67%

2. On the occasion of Republic Day, a retail store offers a scheme where customers can avail a discount of 26% on their total purchase. If Manish buys items worth ₹ 2050, how much money (in ₹) will he save through the scheme discount?
SSC CGL (Tier-II) 18/01/2025 Shift-I
(a) 533 (b) 544 (c) 522 (d) 511

3. An article costs ₹ 1000 for a salesman. He fixes its marked price as ₹ 1500. He sells it to a customer at a discount of 20%. He gives a further discount of 10% for each cash payment. Find the percentage of loss or gain that the salesman makes on sale. **SSC CGL (Tier I) 26/9/2024 Shift-III**
(a) gain 8% (b) gain 10%
(c) loss 8% (d) loss 10%

4. The marked price of an electronic watch in a store is ₹ 15620 and it is available at a discount of 27%. What is the price (in ₹ to the nearest tens) that a customer pays if he buys from the store? **SSC CGL (Tier I) 26/9/2024 Shift-II**
(a) 12500 (b) 11400
(c) 9880 (d) 10800

5. A person first increases the price of a commodity by 8% and then he announces a discount of 18%. The actual discount (in %) on the original price is
SSC CGL (Tier I) 26/9/2024 Shift-I
(a) 11.44 (b) 14.44
(c) 9.44 (d) 8.44

6. The single discount equivalent to the discount series of 15%, 20% and 5% is **SSC CGL (Tier I) 25/9/2024 Shift-III**
(a) 35.4% (b) 20%
(c) 32% (d) 32.5%

7. During a new-year sale, a shopkeeper offers a discount scheme to his customers, 'Buy 5 Sweaters, Get 2 Sweaters Free'. Find the effective percentage discount given by the shopkeeper.
SSC CGL (Tier I) 25/9/2024 Shift-II
(a) $28\frac{4}{7}\%$ (b) 25%
(c) $22\frac{2}{9}\%$ (d) 30%

8. Rohini buys a Bluetooth headphone set for ₹ 1700 from a wholesale shop and marks it at ₹ 2000. Later on, she allows a discount of 40% on its sale. What is her loss or gain percentage (correct up to two decimal places)?
SSC CGL (Tier I) 25/9/2024 Shift-I
(a) 25.19% loss (b) 29.41% gain
(c) 29.41% loss (d) 25.19% gain

9. If the marked price of a bag is 25% above the cost price and a discount of 18% is declared on it, then find the gain percentage.
SSC CGL (Tier I) 24/9/2024 Shift-III
(a) 1.5% (b) 2.0%
(c) 3.0% (d) 2.5%

10. An article is sold for ₹ 747 after successive discounts of 17% and x %. If the marked price of the article is ₹ 1600, what is the value of x ?
SSC CGL (Tier I) 24/9/2024 Shift-II
(a) 32.26 (b) 43.75
(c) 22.12 (d) 40.28

11. The single discount equivalent to a series discount of 60%, 70% and 80%. **SSC CGL (Tier I) 23/9/2024 Shift-III**
(a) 97.6% (b) 70%
(c) 85% (d) 95.5%

12. The marked price of a bed sheet is ₹ 500. At the time of its sale, two successive discounts of 10% and 5% are available. Find the selling price (in ₹) of the bed sheet.
SSC CGL (Tier I) 23/9/2024 Shift-II
(a) 432.50 (b) 427.50
(c) 445.00 (d) 430.00

13. Amit and Bilal buy goods for ₹ 1500 and ₹ 2000, respectively. Amit marks his goods up by y%, while Bilal marks his goods up by $2y$% and offers a discount of y%. If both make the same profit, then find the value of y. **SSC CGL (Tier I) 23/9/2024 Shift-I**
(a) 10.5 (b) 12 (c) 11.5 (d) 12.5

14. A trader offers the following discount schemes on the purchase of a refrigerator.
(i) a discount of 10% followed by a discount of 8%
(ii) successive discounts of 12% and 10%
(iii) two successive discounts of 12%
(iv) a discount of 20%
In which scheme is the selling price the lowest? **SSC CGL (Tier I) 23/9/2024 Shift-I**
(a) (iv) (b) (i)
(c) (ii) (d) (iii)

15. A cooker is marked at ₹ 12500. The dealer allows successive discounts of 6%, 6% and 4% on it. What is the net selling price of the cooker?
SSC CGL (Tier I) 19/9/2024 Shift-III
(a) ₹ 10603.20 (b) ₹ 10306
(c) ₹ 12230 (d) ₹ 12320.60

16. An article marked for ₹ 275 is sold at 5% discount. The seller still gains 4.5%. What did he pay for it?
SSC CGL (Tier I) 19/9/2024 Shift-II
(a) ₹ 250 (b) ₹ 125
(c) ₹ 200 (d) ₹ 225

17. Successive discounts of 10% and 20% are given on the purchase of a purse. If the marked price of the purse is ₹ 2250 find the selling price.
SSC CGL (Tier I) 19/9/2024 Shift-I
(a) ₹ 1320 (b) ₹ 1620
(c) ₹ 1290 (d) ₹ 1520

18. After offering two successive discounts a toy with a marked price of ₹ 150 is sold at ₹ 105. If the value of the first discount is 12.5%, what is the value of the second discount?
SSC CGL (Tier I) 18/9/2024 Shift-II
(a) 21% (b) 18%
(c) 20% (d) 22%

19. A shopkeeper offers the following discount schemes for buyers.
I. Two successive discounts of 15% and 20%
II. Successive discount of 25% and 10%
III. A discount of 33%
The selling price will be minimum under the scheme
SSC CGL (Tier I) 18/9/2024 Shift-I
(a) I (b) I or II
(c) III (d) II

20. The marked price of a TV set is ₹ 18500. If the dealer allows two successive discounts of 20% and 5%, for how much is the TV available?
SSC CGL (Tier I) 17/9/2024 Shift-III
(a) ₹ 14000 (b) ₹ 15000
(c) ₹ 15060 (d) ₹ 14060

21. A shopkeeper allows 40% discount on his goods. He further gives 20% discount. What is the single discount equivalent to these two successive discounts? SSC CGL (Tier I) 17/9/2024 Shift-II

(a) 62% (b) 52%
(c) 60% (d) 50%

22. A shopkeeper marked the price 20% more than its cost price. If he allows a discount of 30%, then find his loss per cent. SSC CGL (Tier I) 17/9/2024 Shift-I

(a) 20% (b) 16% (c) 25% (d) 15%

23. A manufacturer announces a trade discount of 30% on his products for his dealers. One of the dealers purchased 6 smart phones manufactured by the company at the rate of ₹25000 each. What is the amount of trade discount? SSC CGL (Tier I) 13/9/2024 Shift-III

(a) ₹ 50000 (b) ₹ 55000
(c) ₹ 105000 (d) ₹ 45000

24. A discount series of 10% and 16% on an invoice is the same as a single discount of SSC CGL (Tier I) 13/9/2024 Shift-II

(a) 24.4% (b) 22.4%
(c) 21.4% (d) 23.4%

25. The difference between a discount of 25% and two successive discounts of 15% and 20% on a certain bill was ₹ 28. Find the amount of the bill. SSC CGL (Tier I) 12/9/2024 Shift-III

(a) ₹ 500 (b) ₹ 400
(c) ₹ 450 (d) ₹ 550

26. The MP of an article was ₹ 180 and it was sold at a discount of 15%, the discount (in ₹) is SSC CGL (Tier I) 12/9/2024 Shift-II

(a) 12 (b) 15
(c) 27 (d) 18

27. A shopkeeper marked an article at ₹ 5000. The shopkeeper allows successive discounts of 20%, 15% and 10%. The selling price of the article is SSC CGL (Tier I) 12/9/2024 Shift-I

(a) ₹ 2750 (b) ₹ 3000
(c) ₹ 2800 (d) ₹ 3060

28. If Ram purchases a fan, he gets 8% discount, however, if he purchases three fans he gets 6% on the first, 10% on the second and 12% on the third. If the price paid by the Ram for three fans is ₹ 6800, then what will be the marked price of each fan? SSC CGL (Tier I) 11/9/2024 Shift-III

(a) ₹ 2400 (b) ₹ 2500
(c) ₹ 2450 (d) ₹ 2550

29. The cost price of a bat is 75% of the marked price. Calculate the gain percentage after allowing a discount of 15%. SSC CGL (Tier I) 11/9/2024 Shift-II

(a) 25.6% (b) 13.33%
(c) 18.16% (d) 21.33%

30. A shopkeeper allows a discount of 20% on the marked price of an item and thus gains 10%. What is the ratio of the cost price to the marked price of the item? SSC CGL (Tier I) 10/9/2024 Shift-III

(a) 8:11 (b) 7:10
(c) 9:13 (d) 11:14

31. A bronze article having a marked price of ₹ 1000 is sold during a festive season sale after three successive discounts of 20%, 30% and 10%. What will be the amount (in ₹) to be paid by a customer if she buys the article during the festival season? SSC CGL (Tier I) 10/9/2024 Shift-III

(a) 508 (b) 564 (c) 504 (d) 496

32. Two successive discounts of 40% and 30% are equal to a single discount of SSC CGL (Tier I) 10/9/2024 Shift-II

(a) 70% (b) 35% (c) 58% (d) 60%

33. If on a marked price, the difference between selling prices with a discount of 65% and with two successive discounts of 30% and 40% is ₹ 105, then the marked price is SSC CGL (Tier I) 10/9/2024 Shift-I

(a) ₹ 1650 (b) ₹ 1050
(c) ₹ 1500 (d) ₹ 1320

34. Ramesh purchased some items from a dealer on 19 November 2019. The bill generated was for ₹ 5480. He had also purchased some items on 10 November 2019 having the bill value of ₹ 9800. He cleared both the bills this time and paid the total amount in cash. If the dealer gives a scheme of 2% discount on the payments done within 10 days and 5% for the payments made in cash at the time of purchase, then find the amount paid by Ramesh on 19 November 2019. SSC CGL (Tier I) 10/9/2024 Shift-I

(a) ₹ 14850 (b) ₹ 14810
(c) ₹ 14890 (d) ₹ 14950

35. The marked price of an article is 26% more than its cost price. If a discount of 32% is given, what will be the loss percentage? SSC CGL (Tier I) 09/09/2024 Shift-II

(a) 18.64% (b) 15.25%
(c) 12.26% (d) 14.32%

36. An article is marked at ₹ 550. If it is sold at a discount of 40%, then the selling price becomes 10% more than its cost price. What is the cost price ? SSC CGL (Tier I) 09/09/2024 Shift-I

(a) ₹ 220 (b) ₹ 330
(c) ₹ 300 (d) ₹ 200

SSC CGL 2023 (Tier I & II)

37. At a clearance sale, a shopkeeper gives 45% discount. If a customer paid ₹ 330 during the sale, then what is the marked price of that shirt ? SSC CGL (Tier-II) 07/03/2023 Shift-I

(a) ₹ 600 (b) ₹ 500
(c) ₹ 650 (d) ₹ 550

38. A dishonest dealer marks up his goods by 50% and then gives a discount of 20% on the marked price. Apart from this, he uses a faulty balance which reads 1kg for 900 gm. What is his net profit percentage (rounded off to the nearest integer)? SSC CGL (Tier-II) 06/03/2023 Shift-I

(a) 24 (b) 27 (c) 36 (d) 33

39. Find the single equivalent discount for successive discounts of 12%, 18% and 25% on the marked price of a car. SSC CGL (Tier-II) 03/03/2023 Shift-I

(a) 35.28% (b) 42.65%
(c) 40.25% (d) 45.88%

40. A bike is sold for ₹ 87500 by allowing a discount of 44% on its marked price. The marked price (in ₹) of the bike is SSC CGL (Tier-II) 02/03/2023 Shift-I

(a) ₹ 156100 (b) ₹ 158225
(c) ₹ 156250 (d) ₹ 155500

41. A laptop is sold for ₹ 54000 after giving a discount of 20%. What is the list price (in ₹) of the laptop? SSC CGL (Tier-I) 27/07/2023 Shift-II

(a) 69500 (b) 67500
(c) 70000 (d) 64800

42. A shopkeeper gives a 12% additional discount on the discounted price, after giving an initial discount of 25% on the labelled price of a radio. If the final selling price of the radio is ₹ 792, then what is its labelled price (in ₹)? SC CGL (Tier-I) 27/07/2023 Shift-I

(a) 1980 (b) 2330 (c) 1320 (d) 1200

43. Which of the following will yield maximum discount on ₹ 7500? SSC CGL (Tier-I) 26/07/2023 Shift-II

1. Two successive discounts of 5% and 5%.
2. Single discount of 10%.

3. Two successive discounts of 8% and 2%.

(a) 2
(b) 1
(c) All will yield the same discount
(d) 3

44. A shopkeeper sells his goods by allowing 18% discount and still earn 30% profit. If he sells his goods by allowing 12% discount on the marked price, then what will be his profit percentage (correct to 2 decimal places)?
SSC CGL (Tier-I) 26/07/2023 Shift-I

(a) 42.62% (b) 35.45%
(c) 40.35% (d) 39.51%

45. The marked price of a microwave oven is ₹ 15990 and it is sold for ₹ 12792. What is the rate of discount offered? **SSC CGL (Tier-I) 25/07/2023 Shift-IV**

(a) 25% (b) 20%
(c) 21% (d) 24%

46. The difference between a discount of 40% and two successive discounts of 30% on a certain bill was ₹ 220. Find the amount of the bill (in ₹).
SSC CGL (Tier-I) 25/07/2023 Shift-III

(a) 2200 (b) 1100
(c) 1000 (d) 2000

47. Applied to a bill for ₹ 50000, the difference between a discount of 40% and two successive discounts of 36% and 4% is
SSC CGL (Tier-I) 25/07/2023 Shift-I

(a) ₹ 875 (b) ₹ 1440
(c) ₹ 1250 (d) ₹ 720

48. A shop provides flat 50% discount on one shirt, while another shop provides two successive discounts of 30% and 30%. If the difference in the bill is ₹ 43, then find the cost of the shirt. **SSC CGL (Tier-I) 21/07/2023 Shift-IV**

(a) ₹ 3580
(b) ₹ 3850
(c) ₹ 3260
(d) ₹ 4300

49. Ramlal marks up his goods by 40% and gives a discount of 10%. What is his net profit percentage?
SSC CGL (Tier-I) 21/07/2023 Shift-IV

(a) 24% (b) 26%
(c) 28% (d) 32%

50. What is the equivalent discount percentage corresponding to two successive discounts of 9% and 17%?
SSC CGL (Tier-I) 21/07/2023 Shift-III

(a) 27.53% (b) 26.47%
(c) 26.00% (d) 24.47%

51. A shopkeeper marks his goods in such a way that after allowing a discount of 22% he gains 20%. If the cost price of the article is ₹ 650, then its marked price is
SSC CGL (Tier-I) 21/07/2023 Shift-III

(a) ₹900 (b) ₹1000
(c) ₹850 (d) ₹950

52. Three successive discounts of 25% each on the marked price of an item are together equivalent to a single discount (correct up to 2 decimal places) of **SSC CGL (Tier-I) 21/07/2023 Shift-II**

(a) 62.35% (b) 60.25%
(c) 56.45% (d) 57.81%

53. If successive discounts of 5%, 10% and P% are equivalent to a single discount of 31.6%, then the value of P is **SSC CGL (Tier-I) 21/07/2023 Shift-I**

(a) 15 (b) 25 (c) 20 (d) 30

54. A shopkeeper offers three schemes as given below to sell a particular type of product.
Which of the following schemes offers the maximum discount percentage?
SSC CGL (Tier-I) 20/07/2023 Shift-II

A. Buy 6, get 4 free
B. Buy 5, get 5 free
C. Two successive discounts of 18% and 24%

(a) Only B (b) B and C
(c) A and C (d) Only A

55. The marked price of a frock is ₹ 4500. It is to be sold at ₹ 2400 at two successive discounts. If the first discount is 20%, then the second discount will be
SSC CGL (Tier-I) 20/07/2023 Shift-I

(a) 40% (b) 30%
(c) $66\frac{1}{3}\%$ (d) $33\frac{1}{3}\%$

56. A dealer marks an article 60% above the cost price and sells it to a customer allowing two successive discounts of 10% and 20% on the marked price. If he gains ₹ 1064 in the transaction, the cost price (in ₹) of the article is
SSC CGL (Tier-I) 19/07/2023 Shift-IV

(a) 8400 (b) 7000 (c) 6300 (d) 7200

57. The marked price of a geyser is ₹ 9400 and the shopkeeper allows a discount 4% on it. Find the selling price of the geyser.
SSC CGL (Tier-I) 19/07/2023 Shift-III

(a) ₹ 9024 (b) ₹ 9124
(c) ₹ 9324 (d) ₹ 9224

58. A shopkeeper allows a discount of 10% on the printed price of his goods and thus gains 20%. What is the ratio between the cost price and the printed price of the item?
SSC CGL (Tier-I) 19/07/2023 Shift-II

(a) 3 : 4 (b) 2 : 3
(c) 4 : 5 (d) 1 : 2

59. A saree bought for ₹ 500 is marked at 16% profit and later on sold at a sales discount of x% on the marked price. If the selling price of the saree is ₹ 493, find the value of x.
SSC CGL (Tier-I) 19/07/2023 Shift-II

(a) 18 (b) 16
(c) 17 (d) 15

60. A dealer purchased a washing machine for ₹ 9000. He allows a discount of 10% on its marked price and still gains 10%. Find the marked price of the machine.
SSC CGL (Tier-I) 19/07/2023 Shift-I

(a) ₹ 11000 (b) ₹ 12000
(c) ₹ 13000 (d) ₹ 10000

61. The marked price on a book is ₹ 1000. In a book fair, it is available for sale with a discount scheme offering two successive discounts of 12% and 8%. What is the final selling price (in ₹) of the book for a customer (rounded off to the nearest integer)? **SSC CGL (Tier-I) 18/07/2023 Shift-IV**

(a) 810 (b) 800
(c) 825 (d) 790

62. The difference (in ₹) between a discount of 35% on ₹ 3600 and two successive discounts of 30% and 5% on the same amount is
SSC CGL (Tier-I) 18/07/2023 Shift-II

(a) 54 (b) 78
(c) 82 (d) 52

63. On purchase of articles worth ₹ 10000, a shopkeeper offers a flat discount of ₹ 500 to his customers. Further, by shopping using a credit card, he gives an additional discount of 7%. If a customer purchases article worth ₹ 10000 using a credit card, then how much is he/she required to pay?
SSC CGL (Tier-I) 18/07/2023 Shift-I

(a) ₹ 8835 (b) ₹ 9000
(c) ₹ 8815 (d) ₹ 9300

64. A shopkeeper offers the following two discount schemes.
SSC CGL (Tier-I) 18/07/2023 Shift-I

A. Two successive discounts of 10% and 15%.
B. Buy 5 get 2 free.

Which scheme has the maximum discount percentage?
(a) B does not give any discount
(b) B only
(c) A and B both have the same discount percentage
(d) A only

65. After allowing a discount of 15%, the value of a washing machine is ₹ 29750. If no discount is allowed, then the shopkeeper gains 12%. The cost price of the washing machine is SSC CGL (Tier-I) 17/07/2023 Shift-III
(a) ₹ 31250 (b) ₹ 31500
(c) ₹ 31750 (d) ₹ 32000

66. A shopkeeper offers the following discount schemes for buyers on an article: SSC CGL (Tier-I) 17/07/2023 Shift-I
(i) Two successive discounts of 15% each
(ii) A discount of 25% followed by a discount of 5%
(iii) Two successive discounts of 20% and 10%
(iv) A discount of 30%
Under which scheme will the selling price be maximum?
(a) Scheme (iv) (b) Scheme (iii)
(c) Scheme (ii) (d) Scheme (i)

67. Three successive discounts of 15%, 20% and 25% are given. What will be the net discount in percentage ?
SSC CGL (Tier-I) 14/07/2023 Shift-IV
(a) 52% (b) 49% (c) 46% (d) 40%

68. A trader allows a 20% trade discount and a 30% cash discount. If the list price is ₹ 1200, then the selling price (in ₹) is SSC CGL (Tier-I) 14/07/2023 Shift-III
(a) 627 (b) 720 (c) 762 (d) 672

69. An electronic store owner allows two successive discounts of 20% and 25% on each item. The store has a reward points scheme which enables a customer to get free shopping worth ₹ 0.10 on every 1 reward point credited to the customer's account on previous purchases from the store. A customer decides to buy a laptop that is marked at ₹ 72000. What will be its net selling price if he has 2850 reward points to his credit? SSC CGL (Tier-I) 14/07/2023 Shift-II
(a) ₹ 42215 (b) ₹ 42915
(c) ₹ 42942 (d) ₹ 43200

70. A shopkeeper offers the following two discount schemes.
A. Buy 3 get 4 free
B. Buy 5 get 6 free
Which scheme has the maximum discount percentage?
SSC CGL (Tier-I) 14/07/2023 Shift-I
(a) A does not give any discount
(b) A
(c) B
(d) A and B both have the same discount percentage

71. The marked price of mustard oil is 25% more than its cost price. At what percentage less than the marked price should it be sold to have no profit and no loss?
SSC CGL (Tier-I) 14/07/2023 Shift-I
(a) 22% (b) 18%
(c) 20% (d) 15%

SSC CGL 2022 (Tier I)

72. A shopkeeper allows a discount of 12% to his customers and still gains 18%. Find the marked price of an article which costs ₹ 528 to the shopkeeper. (Answer to the nearest rupees) SSC CGL (Tier-I) 13/12/2022 Shift-IV
(a) ₹ 728 (b) ₹ 708
(c) ₹ 695 (d) ₹ 798

73. Sita gets a discount of 20% on ₹ 3000 juicer mixer machine. Since she pays cash, she gets additional 5% discount too. How much does she pay? SSC CGL (Tier-I) 13/12/2022 Shift-II
(a) ₹ 2276 (b) ₹ 2280
(c) ₹ 2278 (d) ₹ 2282

74. An article costs ₹ 4000 to a shopkeeper, who marks its price at ₹ 8400. The shopkeeper sells it to a customer at a discount of 25%. The customer gets a further discount of 15% on the discounted price if the customer redeems a coupon issued by the store previously. What is the profit percentage (to the nearest integer) earned by the shopkeeper in this transaction?
SSC CGL (Tier-I) 13/12/2022 Shift-I
(a) 34% (b) 51%
(c) 42% (d) 36%

75. Raghav went to a shopping mall to purchase clothes. He had two coupons with him, but only one can be used on a single day. Using the first coupon, a total discount of 30% could be obtained on the total amount. Using the second coupon, he will get 80% off on the price of the costliest shirt if he buys at least 3 shirts. What is the price at which Raghav can purchase 3 shirts at a minimum price if the prices of the three shirts are ₹ 1250, ₹ 1540 and ₹ 1375? SSC CGL (Tier-I) 12/12/2022 Shift-IV
(a) ₹ 2760
(b) ₹ 2915.50
(c) ₹ 2775
(d) ₹ 2933

76. The printed price of a TV set is ₹14500. It is sold for ₹10000 with two consecutive discounts. If the first discount is 10%, then what is the second discount?
SSC CGL (Tier-I) 12/12/2022 Shift-II
(a) 23.37% (b) 25.37%
(c) 20.37% (d) 27.37%

77. A grocery shop is offering 10% discount on the purchase of ₹ 500 and above. A 5% discount is given on the purchase of value above ₹ 250 but below ₹ 500. A discount of additional 1% is given if payment is made instantly in cash. how much would a customer have to pay by cash if he buys 25 packets of biscuits and one packet is priced at ₹ 30?
SSC CGL (Tier-I) 09/12/2022 Shift-IV
(a) ₹ 670.25 (b) ₹ 668.25
(c) ₹ 675 (d) ₹ 667.05

78. A megastore is offering 20% discount on all grocery items. Sakshi bought one grocery item marked at ₹ 400. What is its cost price if the store earned a profit of 25% after giving the discount?
SSC CGL (Tier-I) 09/12/2022 Shift-III
(a) ₹ 256 (b) ₹ 280
(c) ₹ 380 (d) ₹ 320

79. A shopkeeper offers a cash discount of ₹ 85 first and then two successive discounts of 10% and 2% on the marked price of a fan. If the marked price of the fan is ₹ 1285, what is its selling price (in ₹)?
SSC CGL (Tier-I) 09/12/2022 Shift-II
(a) 1058.4 (b) 1000.4
(c) 958.4 (d) 1100

80. Three successive discounts of 10% is equivalent to a single discount of
SSC CGL (Tier-I) 09/12/2022 Shift-I
(a) 27.1% (b) 19.0%
(c) 25.1% (d) 26.2%

81. A dealer offers 45% discount on a packet. She offers a further discount of 25% on the reduced price on cash payment. What does a customer has to pay for the packet of ₹ 2800 in cash, to avail both discounts?
SSC CGL (Tier-I) 08/12/2022 Shift-IV
(a) ₹ 1480 (b) ₹ 1350
(c) ₹ 1155 (d) ₹ 1230

82. A shopkeeper claims to sell his article at a discount of 10%, but marks his articles by increasing the cost of each by 20%. His gain percentage is
SSC CGL (Tier-I) 08/12/2022 Shift-III
(a) 18% (b) 12% (c) 8% (d) 16%

83. A dealer marks his goods at 15% above the cost price and allows a discount of 5% for cash payment. His profit percentage is
SSC CGL (Tier-I) 08/12/2022 Shift-I
(a) 9.25% (b) 7.25%
(c) 11.25% (d) 10.25%

84. At a Christmas sale, all the goods in a shop are on sale at 30% discount. If Jasmine buys a skirt marked at ₹ 800, how much would she need to pay? SSC CGL (Tier-I) 07/12/2022 Shift-IV
(a) ₹ 476 (b) ₹ 400
(c) ₹ 770 (d) ₹ 560

85. A discount of 20% is given for the purchase of two books by a bookseller and a discount of 25% is offered if a customer buys more than two books. A 10% discount is being offered to all the customers on purchase of one book. An additional 5% discount will be given to students. Sohan, a student of M.Com. in college, bought a book for ₹ 513. What was the marked price of the book?
SSC CGL (Tier-I) 07/12/2022 Shift-II
(a) ₹ 650 (b) ₹ 540 (c) ₹ 600 (d) ₹ 605

86. In a shop, a discount of 5 percent is provided, and if the total payable amount after discount is more than ₹ 2000, then an additional discount of 10 percent is provided. Determine the final amount to be paid (in ₹) by a customer, if he buys five products each of price ₹ 500.
SSC CGL (Tier-I) 07/12/2022 Shift-I
(a) ₹ 2500 (b) ₹ 2225.5
(c) ₹ 2375.5 (d) ₹ 2137.5

87. Rohan sold goods to Ankith worth ₹ 55000 at 15% trade discount. How much money did Ankith pay to Rohan? SSC CGL (Tier-I) 06/12/2022 Shift-IV
(a) ₹ 8250 (b) ₹ 12550
(c) ₹ 22550 (d) ₹ 46750

88. A dealer buys an article listed at ₹ 3000 and gets successive discounts of 15% and 15%. He spends ₹ 250 on transportation and sells it at a profit of 20%. Find the selling price of the article. SSC CGL (Tier-I) 06/12/2022 Shift-III
(a) ₹ 3300 (b) ₹ 2901
(c) ₹ 3250 (d) ₹ 3200

89. If 3 coconuts are offered free on purchase of 12 coconuts, priced ₹ 25 each, what is the effective discount on each coconut?
SSC CGL (Tier-I) 06/12/2022 Shift-II
(a) 20% (b) 24%
(c) 20.83% (d) 15%

90. A cap having marked price ₹ 90 is sold for ₹ 68. What is the per cent rate of discount (correct up to two decimal places)?
SSC CGL (Tier-I) 05/12/2022 Shift-IV
(a) 24.44% (b) 25.37%
(c) 22.00% (d) 23.22%

91. A shopkeeper offers three types of discount schemes for buyers. Which of them has the maximum discount percentage?
SSC CGL (Tier-I) 05/12/2022 Shift-III
I. Two successive discounts of 10% each.
II. Successive discounts of 15% and 5%.
III. 20% discount.
(a) Only discount scheme I
(b) Only discount scheme II
(c) Only discount scheme III
(d) All provide equal discount

92. A hotel is giving a discount of 12% on the booking of 2 or more rooms. Additionally, the hotel is offering a 5% discount only on payment using any card of SBI. Rakesh booked 2 rooms in the hotel for a day at the rate of ₹ 1500 per room per day. While checking out, he paid the bill using SBI Silver Card. How much amount did he have to pay?
SSC CGL (Tier-I) 05/12/2022 Shift-I
(a) ₹ 2508 (b) ₹ 2618
(c) ₹ 1254 (d) ₹ 2498

93. A man bought a watch for 12% discount. If he had bought it for 24% discount, he would have got the watch for ₹ 2400 less. The marked price of the watch is
SSC CGL (Tier-I) 03/12/2022 Shift-III
(a) ₹30000 (b) ₹22500
(c) ₹20000 (d) ₹25000

94. The marked price of an article is ₹ 10927. Due festive season, a certain percentage of discount is declared. Raju buys an article at reduced price and sells it at ₹ 10927, and makes a profit of 11.5%. What was the percentage discount offered?
SSC CGL (Tier-I) 03/12/2022 Shift-II
(a) 10.3% (b) 11.3%
(c) 11.5% (d) 10.9%

95. A shopkeeper gives two successive discounts on a watch marked ₹ 2750. The first discount given is 10%. If the customer pays ₹ 2103.75 for the watch, then what is the second discount?
SSC CGL (Tier-I) 02/12/2022 Shift-IV
(a) 15% (b) 30%
(c) 12% (d) 10%

96. Sunil purchased a fan at a 10% discount on the labelled price. If he had purchased it at a 15% discount, he would have saved ₹ 400. Find the labelled price of the fan.
SSC CGL (Tier-I) 02/12/2022 Shift-III
(a) ₹ 8400
(b) ₹ 7500
(c) ₹ 800
(d) ₹ 8000

97. A laptop is sold for ₹ 65520 after a discount of 25%. What was the marked price of the laptop?
SSC CGL (Tier-I) 02/12/2022 Shift-II
(a) ₹ 87630 (b) ₹ 87360
(c) ₹ 87370 (d) ₹ 83760

98. What is the single percentage discount equivalent to two successive discounts of 15% and 5%?
SSC CGL (Tier-I) 02/12/2022 Shift-I
(a) 19.00% (b) 19.25%
(c) 18.00% (d) 18.25%

99. A shopkeeper makes a net profit of 44% on selling an article at successive discounts of 10% and 20%. Find the net profit percentage, if the shopkeeper sells the same article at a discount of 15%.
SSC CGL (Tier-I) 01/12/2022 Shift-II
(a) 50% (b) 70%
(c) 30% (d) 40%

100. Riya could not decide between discount of 30% or two successive discounts of 25% and 5%, both given on shopping of ₹ 3840. What is the difference between both the discounts?
SSC CGL (Tier-I) 01/12/2022 Shift-I
(a) ₹ 44 (b) ₹ 48
(c) ₹ 42 (d) ₹ 46

SSC CGL 2021 (Tier I)

101. A shopkeeper marks an article at a price such that, after giving a discount of x%, he gains 20%. If the cost price and the marked price of the article are ₹ 920 and ₹ 1472 respectively, then what is the value of x? SSC CGL (Tier-I) 24/08/2021 Shift-III
(a) 18% (b) 30%
(c) 20% (d) 25%

102. Trader *A* gives a single discount of 25% and Trader *B* gives two successive discounts of 20% and 5% on an identical item. If the discount given by *A* is ₹ 320 more than the discount given by *B*, then what is the marked price (in ₹) of the item?
SSC CGL (Tier-I) 24/08/2021 Shift-II

(a) 3200 (b) 32000
(c) 30000 (d) 25000

103. A customer wanted to purchase an item marked for ₹ 10000. Shopkeeper offered two types of discounts, 25% flat discount or successive discounts of 14% and 12%. Which is the better offer for the customers and by how much?
SSC CGL (Tier-I) 24/08/2021 Shift-I

(a) first offer by ₹ 68
(b) second offer by ₹ 68
(c) first offer by ₹ 32
(d) second offer by ₹ 100

104. In festival season, a shopkeeper allows a discount of 10% on every item. Even after giving the discount, he makes a profit of 20%. If he does not give any discount, then what will be his profit percent? (correct to 2 decimal places)
SSC CGL (Tier-I) 23/08/2021 Shift-I

(a) 25
(b) 33.33
(c) 33.43
(d) 33

105. What price (in ₹) should Radha mark on a bag which costs ₹ 1680 so as to earn a profit of 25% after allowing a discount of 16% on the marked price?
SSC CGL (Tier-I) 20/08/2021 Shift-II

(a) 2800 (b) 2000
(c) 2100 (d) 2500

106. An article is marked 27% above its cost price. If x% discount is allowed on the marked price and still there is a profit of 6.68%, then what is the value of x? **SSC CGL (Tier-I) 20/08/2021 Shift-I**

(a) 15 (b) 20
(c) 16 (d) 12.5

107. A shopkeeper marked every item 25% above the cost price and allowed 10% discount. Shruti being a regular customer got 5% additional discount on the bill and paid ₹ 2394 for the item purchased. What is the cost price of the item (in ₹)?
SSC CGL (Tier-I) 18/08/2021 Shift-I

(a) 2240 (b) 2440
(c) 2220 (d) 2420

108. The marked price of an article is ₹ 1500. A shopkeeper sells it by giving 20% discount on its marked price. If the cost price of the article is ₹ 991, then his profit (in ₹) is
SSC CGL (Tier-I) 17/08/2021 Shift-I

(a) 209 (b) 319 (c) 229 (d) 189

109. A shopkeeper allows 16% discount on every item. Even after giving the discount, he makes a profit of 8%. If he gives 8% discount instead of 16% on an item marked for ₹1800, then what will be his profit per cent? (correct to 2 decimal places)
SSC CGL (Tier-I) 16/08/2021 Shift-III

(a) 19 (b) 18.31
(c) 18 (d) 18.29

110. The selling price of an article marked for ₹ 10000 after giving three discounts. 20%, 10% and k% is ₹ 6120. What will be, selling price (in ₹) of the same article if a single discount of $(k + 20)$% is allowed?
SSC CGL (Tier-I) 16/08/2021 Shift-I

(a) 8500 (b) 6800
(c) 6500 (d) 8000

111. A shopkeeper marks his goods 30% higher than the cost price and allows a discount of 10% on the marked price. In order to earn 6.5% more profit, what discount per cent should he allow on the marked price?
SSC CGL (Tier-I) 13/08/2021 Shift-III

(a) 4 (b) 5.5 (c) 6 (d) 5

SSC CGL 2020 (Tier I)

112. A shopkeeper fixes the price of an article in such a way that after allowing 32% discount, he wants a gain of 14%. If the marked price is ₹ 342, then the cost price of the article is **SSC CGL (Tier-I) 06/03/2020 Shift-III**

(a) ₹204 (b) ₹218 (c) ₹212 (d) ₹196

113. A shopkeeper marked a computer table for ₹ 7200. He allows a discount of 10% on it and yet makes profit of 8%. What will be his gain percentage, if he does not allow any discount? **SSC CGL (Tier-I) 06/03/2020 Shift-II**

(a) 2% (b) 9% (c) 20% (d) 18%

114. A shopkeeper marks the price of an article in such a way that after allowing a discount of 22%, he gets a gain of 11%. If the marked price is ₹888, then the cost price of the article is **SSC CGL (Tier-I) 06/03/2020 Shift-I**

(a) ₹ 624 (b) ₹ 782
(c) ₹ 550 (d) ₹ 895

115. A furniture shopkeeper allows a discount of 16% on the marked price on the goods to his customers and still gains 20%. What is the marked price of a dining table, which costs the shopkeeper ₹ 11900?
SSC CGL (Tier-I) 05/03/2020 Shift-III

(a) ₹ 12376 (b) ₹ 15000
(c) ₹ 17000 (d) ₹16000

116. The marked price of an item is 25% above its cost price. A shopkeeper sells it, allowing a discount of x% on the marked price. If he incurs a loss of 8%, then the value of x is
SSC CGL (Tier-I) 05/03/2020 Shift-II

(a) 25.6% (b) 26.8%
(c) 26.4% (d) 25.2%

117. A shopkeeper bought 80 kg of rice at a discount of 10%. Besides 1 kg rice was offered free to him on the purchase of every 20 kg rice. If he sells the rice at the marked price, his profit percentage will be
SSC CGL (Tier-I) 05/03/2020 Shift-I

(a) $15\frac{3}{7}$% (b) $16\frac{2}{3}$%
(c) $14\frac{2}{7}$% (d) $15\frac{1}{3}$%

118. If the selling price of an article is 8% more than the cost price and the discount offered is 10% on the marked price of the article, then what is the ratio of the cost price to the marked price?
SSC CGL (Tier-I) 04/03/2020 Shift-III

(a) 5 : 6 (b) 8 : 9 (c) 3 : 4 (d) 4 : 5

SSC CPO SI 2024

119. A seller marks an item for ₹ 500 and sells it at a discount of 25%. He also gives a gift worth ₹ 65. If he still makes 24% profit, then the cost price of the item (in ₹) is
SSC CPO 29/06/2024 Shift-III

(a) ₹ 320 (b) ₹ 270 (c) ₹ 250 (d) ₹ 280

120. A shopkeeper offers a 10% discount on dairy products and still manages to make a 20% profit. What is the actual cost (in ₹) to the shopkeeper of a dairy product marked ₹ 420 ?
SSC CPO 29/06/2024 Shift-III

(a) 325 (b) 340 (c) 350 (d) 315

121. A trader gives a 40% discount on his goods. Further, he gives 20% discount on the goods. Find the single discount equivalent to these two successive discounts.
SSC CPO 29/06/2024 Shift-II

(a) 30% (b) 60%
(c) 50% (d) 52%

122. A shopkeeper offers a discount of 24 % on the marked price. On a special sale day, he offers an extra 30% off coupon after the first discount. If the article was sold for ₹ 7700.7, what is the marked price (in ₹) of the article ? SSC CPO 29/06/2024 Shift-I

(a) 17475 (b) 14745
(c) 14475 (d) 17745

123. A shopkeeper wanted to sell ₹ 2000 worth of products. But he had two options, giving three successive discounts of 10% each or giving a single discount of 28%. What was the difference between the two options of discounts (in ₹)? SSC CPO 29/06/2024 Shift-I

(a) ₹ 16 (b) ₹ 28
(c) ₹ 18 (d) ₹ 22

124. Two successive discount of 15% and x% on the sale of an item is equivalent to a single discount of 23.5%. What is the value of x%? SSC CPO 29/06/2024 Shift-I

(a) 11% (b) 12% (c) 10% (d) 9%

125. A shopkeeper kept the marked price of an item at ₹ 500. He sold it at a scheme discount of 10% and 20% and got a profit of 25%. What was the cost price of the item? SSC CPO 28/06/2024 Shift-III

(a) ₹188 (b) ₹ 482
(c) ₹ 288 (d) ₹ 384

126. The marked price of a table is ₹ 5980. If the shopkeeper offers a discount of 18%, what is its selling price (in ₹, to the nearest rupee)? SSC CPO 28/06/2024 Shift-III

(a) ₹ 4940 (b) ₹ 4490
(c) ₹ 4094 (d) ₹ 4904

127. On the tag price, a seller offers a 10% discount and a cashback of ₹ 250. He still earns 10% profit. If the cost price is ₹ 1200, then the tag price (rounded off to 2 decimal places) is ₹ .... SSC CPO 28/06/2024 Shift-III

(a) ₹ 1774.44 (b) ₹ 1777.44
(c) ₹ 1744.44 (d) ₹ 1447.44

128. Applied to a bill for ₹ 1000, what is the difference between a discount of 40% and two successive discounts of 36% and 4%? SSC CPO 28/06/2024 Shift-II

(a) ₹ 154 (b) ₹ 144
(c) ₹ 14.40 (d) ₹ 15.40

129. A shopkeeper gives a discount of 12% on the purchase of 10 kg of sugar. The cost price of the sugar is ₹ 30/kg, and the marked price is ₹ 38/kg. The weighing machine of the shopkeeper is faulty, and it shows weight of 1 kg when the actual weight is 900 grams. Find the percentage profit of the shopkeeper (rounded off to two decimal places). SSC CPO 28/06/2024 Shift-II

(a) 23.85% (b) 22.25%
(c) 12.5% (d) 30.18%

130. A seller offers a discount of 12% if the total sale price of different products purchased by a single customer is below ₹ 3000, and discount of 15% if the total sale value of all the products exceeds ₹ 3000. A shirt costing ₹ 900 was sold to Anand after earning a margin of 9% and also a jacket costing ₹ 1900 was sold to him after a margin of 6%.How much does Anand have to pay (in ₹) for the final settlement of the bill? SSC CPO 28/06/2024 Shift-I

(a) ₹ 2645.60 (b) ₹ 2953.60
(c) ₹ 3005.40 (d) ₹ 2635.60

131. A retailer marks up his goods by 130% and offers 25% discount. What will be the selling price (in ₹) if the cost price is ₹ 1600 ? SSC CPO 28/06/2024 Shift-I

(a) ₹ 2760 (b) ₹ 1980
(c) ₹ 3680 (d) ₹ 1765

132. A product was offered at a 10% trade discount on the marked price. After a cash discount of 10%, the product was sold for ₹ 7290. The marked price (in ₹) is SSC CPO 27/06/2024 Shift-III

(a) ₹ 8510 (b) ₹ 9000
(c) ₹ 8900 (d) ₹ 8720

133. A doll is marked for ₹ 2500. A customer pays ₹ 1800 for it. If the customer got a series of two discounts and the rate of the first discount is 10%, then the rate of the second discount is SSC CPO 27/06/2024 Shift-II

(a) 15% (b) 20% (c) 25% (d) 18%

134. The marked price of an article is 35% more than its cost price. If a discount of 15% is given, what will be the profit percentage? SSC CPO 27/06/2024 Shift-II

(a) $12\frac{3}{4}\%$ (b) $10\frac{1}{4}5\%$
(c) $14\frac{3}{4}\%$ (d) $13\frac{2}{3}\%$

135. Find the single discount rate percentage equivalent to the successive discounts of 10%, 20% and 20%. SSC CPO 27/06/2024 Shift-I

(a) 40% (b) 42.4% (c) 50% (d) 54.6%

136. Ramanna purchased raw materials for a certain price to manufacture a product. However, owing to shortage of labour, 22.5% of the raw materials could not be utilised and got wasted. 80% of the cost of raw materials used was added as the cost of manufacturing. If Ramanna could sell his product at a price to earn an overall profit of 20% after offering a discount of 20%, how many times of the total cost of the raw materials purchased was the marked price of the product? SSC CPO 27/06/2024 Shift-I

(a) 2.43 times (b) 2.40 times
(c) 2.44 times (d) 4.42 times

137. A shopkeeper offers 3 schemes of discounts to his customers. Which of the following schemes will fetch the minimum discount percentage?

(A) Two successive discounts of 24% and 27%.
(B) Buy 5 get 3 free.
(C) Buy 6 and get 10.

SSC CPO 27/06/2024 Shift-I

(a) B (b) A
(c) C (d) Both A and C

SSC CPO SI 2023 - 2020

138. An article is sold at a discount of 25% and an additional discount of 28% is allowed on cash payment. If Ramendra purchased the article by paying ₹ 10800 in cash, then what was the marked price of the article? SSC CPO 05/10/2023 Shift-III

(a) ₹ 19800 (b) ₹ 20800
(c) ₹ 20000 (d) ₹ 18000

139. A shopkeeper marked the price as ₹ 15000 on an article and a successive discount of 5%, 10% and 20% was allowed on it. What is the selling price? SSC CPO 05/10/2023 Shift-III

(a) ₹ 10260 (b) ₹ 13520
(c) ₹ 11520 (d) ₹ 9850

140. If a shopkeeper allows a discount of 10% to his customers and still gains 30%, then the marked price of an article which costs ₹ 450 is SSC CPO 04/10/2023 Shift-II

(a) ₹ 700 (b) ₹ 650 (c) ₹ 500 (d) ₹ 750

141. What is the difference between a single discount of 35% on ₹ 700 and two successive discounts of 18% and 12% on the same amount (correct to two places of decimals)? SSC CPO 04/10/2023 Shift-II

(a) ₹ 51.20 (b) ₹ 50.12
(c) ₹ 52.10 (d) ₹ 49.80

142. An item with a marked price of ₹ 3800 was sold for. ₹ 3496, after a discount of y% was offered. What was the value of y? SSC CPO 03/10/2023 Shift-I
(a) 7.5% (b) 8.5% (c) 8% (d) 7%

143. If the price of an item is increased by 70% and then allows a scheme discount of 5% and 20% on this marked price. If price is paid in cash and additional discount of 20% is allowed, then what is his gain percentage? SSC CPO 03/10/2023 Shift-I
(a) 2.25% (b) 4.36%
(c) 3.25% (d) 3.36%

144. Rajkumar decides to sell his watch at a discount of 5%. However, his brother purchases it from him and receives an 8% discount. Raj loses ₹ 45 in profit as a result of this. What was the watch's marked price? SSC CPO 11/11/2022
(a) ₹ 1500 (b) ₹ 1410
(c) ₹ 1430 (d) ₹ 1560

145. A supermarket offers the following discount schemes for buyers.
I. Two successive discounts of 25% and 15%.
II. Successive discount of 35% and 5%.
III. A discount of 38%.
Which offer is better for the customer? SSC CPO 11/11/2022
(a) Either I or III (b) Only I
(c) Only II (d) Only III

146. In a showroom the price of a washing machine is ₹ 65000. The customer gets cash discount of ₹ 2000, and gets a scratch card promising percentage discount of 10% to 15%. Determine the difference between the least and the maximum selling prices of the washing machine. SSC CPO 10/11/2022
(a) ₹ 3150 (b) ₹ 3570
(c) ₹ 3200 (d) ₹ 3650

147. Find the effective discount for the scheme – Buy 5 get 3 free. SSC CPO 10/11/2022
(a) 36. 5% (b) 37. 5%
(c) 36 % (d) 37 %

148. On the marked price of ₹1250 of an article, three successive discounts of 5%, 15% and 20% were offered. The amount (in ₹) of discount received by a customer is SSC CPO 25/11/2020 Shift-II
(a) 442.50 (b) 950.25
(c) 450 (d) 807.50

149. On a marked price, the difference of selling prices with a discount of 35% and two successive discounts of 20% and 15% is ₹504. The marked price of the article (in ₹) is SSC CPO 25/11/2020 Shift-II
(a) 16000 (b) 16800
(c) 15500 (d) 18000

150. Three successive discounts of 12%, 13% and 11% are equivalent to an approximate single discount of SSC CPO 25/11/2020 Shift-I
(a) 40% (b) 32% (c) 35% (d) 42%

151. If house tax is paid before the due date, one gets a reduction of 12% on the amount of the bill. By paying the tax before the due date, a person got a reduction of ₹ 2100. The amount (in ₹) of house tax paid was SSC CPO 24/11/2020 Shift-I
(a) 21000 (b) 15400
(c) 25000 (d) 17500

152. A single discount equivalent to three successive discounts of 6%, 15% and 14% is SSC CPO 24/11/2020 Shift-I
(a) 17.5% (b) 31.286%
(c) 68.714% (d) 64.357%

153. Two successive discounts, each of x% on the marked price of an article, are equal to a single discount of ₹ 331.20. If the marked price of the article is ₹ 920, then the value of x is SSC CPO 23/11/2020 Shift-I
(a) 20 (b) 15 (c) 25 (d) 18

SSC CHSL 2024 (Tier I & II)

154. The marked price of an article is ₹ 2800. It is sold at three successive discounts of 15%, 8% and 5%. Find the selling price of the article (in ₹). SSC CHSL (Tier-II) 18/11/2024 Shift-IV
(a) 2080.12 (b) 1890.20
(c) 1997.26 (d) 1923.56

155. The marked price of a table lamp is ₹ 2165. During the festive season, it is sold for ₹ 1710.35. Find the percentage discount offered. SSC CHSL (Tier I) 11/07/2024 Shift-IV
(a) 21% (b) 20.5%
(c) 18% (d) 22.5%

156. A coat marked at ₹ 145 is offered at ₹ 127.6. The rate of retail discount offered is SSC CHSL (Tier I) 10/07/2024 Shift-III
(a) 11% (b) 12% (c) 13% (d) 10%

157. Shopkeeper A marks up his price for an item at 25% and offers a discount of 15%. The same item is marked up by at 20% by another shopkeeper B and sold at a discount of 12%. Who gets a better deal in terms of % profit and by what profit percentage he sells that item? SSC CHSL (Tier I) 10/07/2024 Shift-II
(a) B by 5.6%
(b) B by 0.65%
(c) A by 0.55%
(d) A by 6.25%

158. A shopkeeper sells an item at 20% discount on the marked price and earns a profit of 90%. If he sells the same item at 40% discount, then his new profit percentage will be SSC CHSL (Tier I) 09/07/2024 Shift-IV
(a) 48.2% (b) 45.8%
(c) 41.8% (d) 42.5%

159. Ramesh sells an article for ₹ 34440, after allowing an 18% discount on the marked price and still manages to gain 40 % profit. If Ramesh sold the article at a 12 % discount on the marked price, then what will be his profit, correct to two places of decimals? SSC CHSL (Tier I) 09/07/2024 Shift-III
(a) 50.42% (b) 48.24 %
(c) 50.24% (d) 48.42%

160. A shopkeeper allows a discount of 22% to his customers and still gains 36%. Find the marked price (in ₹) of an article, which costs ₹ 1092 to the shopkeeper. SSC CHSL (Tier I) 09/07/2024 Shift-II
(a) ₹ 1792 (b) ₹ 2024
(c) ₹ 1872 (d) ₹ 1904

161. The marked price of an item is 1.4 times the cost price. In order to earn 23.2% profit, what per cent discount can a shopkeeper allow? SSC CHSL (Tier I) 09/07/2024 Shift-I
(a) 13% (b) 17%
(c) 15% (d) 12%

162. On buying 24 bangles Meena gets 6 bangles free of cost. By what percentage does Meena get a discount? SSC CHSL (Tier I) 08/07/2024 Shift-IV
(a) 20% (b) 5%
(c) 15% (d) 10%

163. The marked price of a battery-operated rickshaw is ₹ 90000. It is available for sale at two successive discounts of 10% and 5%. What is the selling price (in ₹) of the battery-operated rickshaw? SSC CHSL (Tier I) 08/07/2024 Shift-III
(a) 78950 (b) 76950
(c) 75850 (d) 77850

164. To clear the old stock, Arshad offers a discount scheme to his customers - on buying 24 glass tumblers get 12 glass tumblers free. What is the effective percentage discount given by Arshad to his customers?
SSC CHSL (Tier I) 08/07/2024 Shift-II

(a) $30\frac{1}{3}\%$ (b) $32\frac{2}{3}\%$
(c) $33\frac{1}{3}\%$ (d) $34\frac{2}{3}\%$

165. The list price of a hand mixer at a showroom is ₹ 2000 and it is being sold at successive discounts of 15% and 10%. What is its net selling price in rupees?
SSC CHSL (Tier I) 08/07/2024 Shift-I

(a) ₹ 1600 (b) ₹ 1530
(c) ₹ 1560 (d) ₹ 1440

166. The difference (in ₹) between a discount of 37% on ₹ 2635 and two successive discounts of 23% and 7% on the same amount is (rounded off to 2 decimal places)
SSC CHSL (Tier I) 05/07/2024 Shift-IV

(a) 248.36 (b) 226.87
(c) 235.65 (d) 242.25

167. A retailer gets a discount of 40% on the printed price of an article. If the retailer sells it at the printed price, then his gain percentage is
SSC CHSL (Tier I) 05/07/2024 Shift-III

(a) $66\frac{1}{3}\%$ (b) $66\frac{2}{3}\%$
(c) $37\frac{2}{3}\%$ (d) $33\frac{1}{3}\%$

168. A shopkeeper marks up his goods 32% above the cost price and gives a discount of 21% on the marked price. Find his gain percentage on the goods.
SSC CHSL (Tier I) 05/07/2024 Shift-II

(a) 4.82% (b) 8.42%
(c) 8.24% (d) 4.28%

169. A 35% profit is made, when a discount of 35% is given on the marked price of an item. When the discount is 45%, then the profit percentage will be
SSC CHSL (Tier I) 04/07/2024 Shift-IV

(a) $17\frac{1}{13}\%$ (b) $11\frac{3}{13}\%$
(c) $14\frac{3}{13}\%$ (d) $13\frac{3}{17}\%$

170. The marked price of an article is 25% more than its cost price. If a scheme discount of 40% is given, then the loss percentage is
SSC CHSL (Tier I) 04/07/2024 Shift-III

(a) 20% (b) 25%
(c) 30% (d) 15%

171. A company sells goods at a markup of 25% above the cost price. During a sale, the company offers a 10% discount on the marked price. If the customer pays ₹ 540 after the discount, then what was the original cost price of the goods?
SSC CHSL (Tier I) 04/07/2024 Shift-II

(a) ₹ 460 (b) ₹ 470
(c) ₹ 480 (d) ₹ 450

172. Kamlesh offers the following two discount schemes to his customers on the sale of an article
(i) Two successive discounts of 25% and 5%.
(ii) Two successive discounts of 20% and 10%.
What is the difference between the selling price (in ₹) of the article under these two discount schemes if its marked price is ₹ 1000 ?
SSC CHSL (Tier I) 04/07/2024 Shift-II

(a) ₹ 7.0 (b) ₹ 7.5
(c) ₹ 6.5 (d) ₹ 8.0

173. What is the discount that Rohan should offer on the remaining ₹ 8000 of a laptop priced at ₹ 48000, given that, he has already given a 12% discount on the first ₹ 28000 and 8% discount on the next ₹ 12000 to match the discount amount of 9.5% given on the total price?
SSC CHSL (Tier I) 03/07/2024 Shift-IV

(a) ₹ 402 (b) ₹ 420
(c) ₹ 240 (d) ₹ 204

174. A dealer buys an article listed at ₹ 100 and get successive discounts of 10% and 20%. He spends 10% of the cost price on transportation. At what price should he sell the article to earn a profit of 15%?
SSC CHSL (Tier I) 03/07/2024 Shift-III

(a) ₹ 76.07 (b) ₹ 81.07
(c) ₹ 89.08 (d) ₹ 91.08

175. The marked price of an article is ₹ 600. A shopkeeper purchased it on two successive discounts of 10% and 20%. He spent ₹ 68 on transportation and sold the article for ₹ 600. Find his gain or loss percentage.
SSC CHSL (Tier I) 03/07/2024 Shift-I

(a) 25% loss (b) 15% profit
(c) 20% profit (d) 18% loss

176. Two offers were being made to Swaroop for a watch with a marked price of ₹ 1600. Either two successive discounts of 20%, or two discounts of 30% and 10% after each other is offered. If Swaroop opted for the better plan over the other, how much more must he have saved?
SSC CHSL (Tier I) 02/07/2024 Shift-IV

(a) ₹ 35 (b) ₹ 30 (c) ₹ 16 (d) ₹ 22

177. A shopkeeper marks an article at ₹150 and sells it at a discount of 25%. He also gives a gift worth ₹ 2.5. If he still makes a 10% profit, then the cost price (in ₹) of the article is
SSC CHSL (Tier I) 02/07/2024 Shift-III

(a) ₹ 100 (b) ₹ 175
(c) ₹ 112 (d) ₹ 125

178. What is the effective discount percentage, if a shopkeeper offers a scheme discount 'buy five and get one free'?
SSC CHSL (Tier I) 02/07/2024 Shift-II

(a) 15.67% (b) 16.67%
(c) 16.33% (d) 15.33%

179. A dozen pairs of gloves of ₹ 180 are available at a discount of 10%. How many pairs of gloves can be bought for ₹ 54? **SSC CHSL (Tier I) 02/07/2024 Shift-I**

(a) 2 (b) 8 (c) 4 (d) 6

180. One company is offering a 25% discount on a particular product. Anurag visited a store. He was trying to find a deal that would allow him to save at least ₹390. How many minimum items should he purchase, if each item costs ₹ 340?
SSC CHSL (Tier I) 01/07/2024 Shift-IV

(a) 7 (b) 4 (c) 6 (d) 5

181. A shopkeeper gives a 10% discount and still earns 10% profit. The marked price of the item is how many times (correct to 2 decimal places) the cost price?
SSC CHSL (Tier I) 01/07/2024 Shift-III

(a) 1.28 (b) 1.24
(c) 1.22 (d) 1.20

182. A shopkeeper decides to raise the marked price of an article by 40%. How much percentage discount should he allow to be able to sell the article at the original marked price?
SSC CHSL (Tier I) 01/07/2024 Shift-I

(a) $26\frac{3}{7}\%$ (b) $24\frac{3}{7}\%$
(c) $31\frac{2}{7}\%$ (d) $28\frac{4}{7}\%$

183. A shopkeeper marks up the price of oil by 40% and uses a faulty machine, which measures 15% less. If the shopkeeper gives a discount of 32%, the profit/loss percentage is
SSC CHSL (Tier I) 01/07/2024 Shift-I

(a) 15% Loss (b) 25% Profit
(c) 18% Loss (d) 12% Profit

184. The difference between a discount of 27% and two successive discounts of 20% and 10% on a certain bill was ₹56. Find the amount of the bill.
SSC CHSL (Tier-II) 10/01/2024 Shift-I
(a) ₹ 1866 (b) ₹ 5500
(c) ₹ 5600 (d) ₹ 1120

SSC CHSL 2023 (Tier I & II)

185. A dishonest shopkeeper sells rice at a cost price but makes a 25% profit by using faulty weights. He decides to give a discount to attract more customers. What per cent of discount should he offer to make 10% profit?
SSC CHSL (Tier-II) 02/11/2023 Shift-I
(a) 9% (b) 12% (c) 10% (d) 11%

186. For an electric bill for ₹ 50000, what is the difference between a discount of 30% and two successive discounts of 26% and 5%?
SSC CHSL (Tier-II) 02/11/2023 Shift-I
(a) ₹ 120 (b) ₹ 150
(c) ₹ 130 (d) ₹ 140

187. An article is sold for ₹ 864 after two successive equal discounts of 25% each on its marked price. What is the discount (in ₹)?
SSC CHSL (Tier I) 17/08/2023 Shift-I
(a) 698 (b) 612 (c) 584 (d) 672

188. A shopkeeper gives an additional concession of 5% on an item which is already discounted by 15% on the marked price. If the buyer pays ₹ 3068.5 for the item, then find the marked price.
SSC CHSL (Tier I) 17/08/2023 Shift-I
(a) ₹ 3500 (b) ₹ 3700
(c) ₹ 3800 (d) ₹ 3780

189. The marked price of an article is ₹ 2500 and selling price is ₹ 1800, then the discount percentage is
SSC CHSL (Tier I) 14/08/2023 Shift-IV
(a) 32% (b) 28% (c) 34% (d) 27%

190. A shopkeeper marks his goods 35% above cost price. He then allows some discount on it if he makes a profit of 14%, then the rate of discount is
SSC CHSL (Tier I) 14/08/2023 Shift-IV
(a) 17.77% (b) 15.55%
(c) 16.66% (d) 14.44%

191. The cost price of an article is 72% of the marked price. The profit percentage after allowing a discount of 6% on the marked price is (rounded off to 2 decimal places)
SSC CHSL (Tier I) 11/08/2023 Shift-I
(a) 32.50% (b) 28.23%
(c) 30.56% (d) 35.65%

192. What is a single discount equivalent to the three successive discounts of 20%, 25% and 20%?
SSC CHSL (Tier I) 10/08/2023 Shift-III
(a) 38% (b) 42%
(c) 52% (d) 58%

193. A manufacturer marked an item at ₹ 75 and sold it allowing a 14% discount. If his profit was 29%, then the cost price (in ₹) of the item was
SSC CHSL (Tier I) 10/08/2023 Shift-III
(a) 64 (b) 57 (c) 45 (d) 50

194. A tradesman marks his goods 25% above the cost price and allows his customers a discount of 12% on their bill. How much % profit tradesman realizes? SSC CHSL (Tier I) 09/08/2023 Shift-I
(a) 13% (b) 11%
(c) 12% (d) 10%

195. Shyam purchased a packet of 16 pens and got 4 pens free with it. He marked the price 20% more than the CP. If he did not allow any discount and sold all the 20 pens at this price, then what was his profit percentage?
SSC CHSL (Tier I) 08/08/2023 Shift-II
(a) $37\frac{1}{2}\%$ (b) 50%
(c) 36% (d) 48%

196. A shopkeeper sells a table at 25% discount on the marked price and earns a profit of 70%. If he sells the same table at 50% discount, then his new profit percentage will be
SSC CHSL (Tier I) 08/08/2023 Shift-II
(a) $11\frac{1}{3}\%$ (b) $12\frac{1}{2}\%$
(c) $13\frac{1}{3}\%$ (d) $13\frac{1}{2}\%$

197. A shopkeeper purchased an air conditioner for ₹ 24000. He marks it for ₹ 30000. He sells it to a customer at a discounted price and still earns a profit of 9%. What is the rate of discount given by the shopkeeper to the customer?
SSC CHSL (Tier I) 07/08/2023 Shift-IV
(a) 10.8% (b) 12.8%
(c) 13.8% (d) 14.8%

198. Etika purchased a set of wallpapers for ₹ 700 and the marked price of a set was ₹ 850. The approximate rate of discount was
SSC CHSL (Tier I) 04/08/2023 Shift-II
(a) 25.34% (b) 12.65%
(c) 22.5% (d) 17.64%

199. A retailer buys 50 pens at the marked price of 44 pens. If he sells these pens at a discount of 1% on the marked price. What is the profit per cent ? SSC CHSL (Tier I) 04/08/2023 Shift-II
(a) 10% (b) 12.5%
(c) 12% (d) 15%

200. A merchant advertise 10% off on the items bought from his store. Find the discount got by a customer who bought a bag worth ₹ 560, an exercise book worth ₹ 90 and a pen worth ₹ 45. SSC CHSL (Tier I) 04/08/2023 Shift-II
(a) ₹ 59 (b) ₹ 69.50
(c) ₹ 65 (d) ₹ 67.50

201. In a show room, the marked prices of various items are displayed in such a manner that after giving a 10% discount to the customers, the owner of the show room earns a profit of 20%. What is the ratio of the marked price and cost price of each item?
SSC CHSL (Tier I) 02/08/2023 Shift-I
(a) 3 : 4 (b) 4 : 3 (c) 5 : 2 (d) 2 : 5

202. A dishonest shopkeeper professes to sell grains at the cost price, but he uses a weight of 920 gm for 1 kg weight. Find his gain percentage (round up to two decimal places)
SSC CHSL (Tier I) 02/08/2023 Shift-I
(a) 7.90% (b) 8.70%
(c) 8.50% (d) 7.80%

203. A shopkeeper marks his goods at 80% more then their cost price and allows a discount of 48% on the marked price. His loss percentage is
SSC CHSL (Tier I) 02/08/2023 Shift-I
(a) $2\frac{1}{5}\%$ (b) $7\frac{3}{5}\%$ (c) $6\frac{2}{5}\%$ (d) $3\frac{1}{5}\%$

204. An article is sold for ₹ 1260 after giving a discount of 40%. What is the marked price of this article?
SSC CHSL (Tier I) 21/03/2023 Shift-II
(a) ₹ 2100 (b) ₹ 1800
(c) ₹ 2200 (d) ₹ 2000

205. Marked price of a computer is ₹ 80000. It is sold for ₹ 65280 after two successive discounts. If one of the discount is 15%, then what is the value of other discount?
SSC CHSL (Tier I) 20/03/2023 Shift-III
(a) 7% (b) 5% (c) 6% (d) 4%

206. Manoj sold an article on marked price for ₹ 13000. Had he offered a discount of 10% on the marked price he would have earned a profit of 30%. What is the cost price?
SSC CHSL (Tier I) 17/03/2023 Shift-II
(a) ₹ 10000 (b) ₹ 9900
(c) ₹ 9000 (d) ₹ 11000

207. The marked price of a trouser and a jacket is in the ratio of 1 : 3. The shopkeeper gives 20% discount on the trouser. If the total discount offered on both of them together is 30%, then what is the discount percentage offered on the jacket?
SSC CHSL (Tier I) 16/03/2023 Shift-I
(a) 28.56% (b) 41.25%
(c) 33.33% (d) 16.66%

208. The marked price of an article is 150% of the cost price. If 20% discount is given, then what will be the profit percentage?
SSC CHSL (Tier I) 15/03/2023 Shift-IV
(a) 20% (b) 12.5%
(c) 25% (d) 10%

209. A cycle listed at ₹ 20000 is sold to a retailer at ₹ 14000 after a discount. What is the per cent discount given to retailer?
SSC CHSL (Tier I) 14/03/2023 Shift-I
(a) 30% (b) 20%
(c) 40% (d) 10%

210. 20% of marked price is equal to 50% of the cost price. If no discount is given, then what will be the profit percentage?
SSC CHSL (Tier I) 10/03/2023 Shift-III
(a) 125% (b) 120%
(c) 150% (d) 100%

211. 2/5 of marked price is equal to 5/8 of selling price. What is the discount per cent? SSC CHSL (Tier I) 09/03/2023 Shift-I
(a) 40% (b) 42%
(c) 36% (d) 50%

SSC CHSL 2022 & 2021 (Tier I)

212. A shopkeeper gives a 35% discount on the marked price of a bottle. If the selling price of the bottle is ₹ 1755, then the marked price of the bottle will be
SSC CHSL (Tier I) 02/06/2022 Shift-I
(a) ₹2800 (b) ₹2500
(c) ₹2700 (d) ₹3500

213. The marked price of a mobile phone was ₹ 35600. The shop owner offered a 10% trade discount on the marked price but on further request by the customer, he sold the phone for ₹ 30000 after giving a cash discount. How much is this cash discount as a percentage of the price after the trade discount? (Give your answer correct to 2 decimal places.)
SSC CHSL (Tier I) 01/06/2022 Shift-I
(a) 6.37% (b) 5.75%
(c) 4.95% (d) 5.25%

214. A 37% discount was offered on an item with a marked price of ₹ 2900. What was the selling price of the item? SSC CHSL (Tier I) 01/06/2022 Shift-I
(a) ₹ 1827
(b) ₹ 1073
(c) ₹ 1823
(d) ₹ 1829

215. A 25% profit is made when a discount of 25% is given on the marked price of an item. When the discount is 35%, what will be the profit? (Give your answer correct to the nearest whole number).
SSC CHSL (Tier I) 31/05/2022 Shift-I
(a) 13% (b) 8%
(c) 9% (d) 11%

216. The marked price of a refrigerator is ₹ 60000. A shopkeeper offers a flat discount of ₹ 12000 on full cash payment. Further he offers an extra discount of 5% on the marked price to his regular customers.
How much does a regular customer have to pay for the refrigerator ?
SSC CHSL (Tier I) 31/05/2022 Shift-I
(a) ₹ 45000 (b) ₹ 48000
(c) ₹ 44000 (d) ₹ 47000

217. A shoe manufacturing company offers 3 types of discount schemes to its customers:
(i) 20% and 12%
(ii) 25% and 5%
(iii) 30% and 3% at different stages of sales. Find the best scheme for the customer.
SSC CHSL (Tier I) 30/05/2022 Shift-I
(a) Only Scheme (iii)
(b) Only Scheme (i)
(c) Only Scheme (ii)
(d) Both Schemes (i) and (ii)

218. Anil offers his customer a discount of 15% on a T-shirt and he still makes a profit of 25%. What is the actual cost of the T-shirt marked ₹ 500? SSC CHSL (Tier I) 30/05/2022 Shift-I
(a) ₹ 340 (b) ₹ 330
(c) ₹ 350 (d) ₹ 360

219. A mobile is marked at a price 25% above its cost price. At what discount percentage should it be sold to make a 10% profit?
SSC CHSL (Tier I) 27/05/2022 Shift-I
(a) 10% (b) 11%
(c) 12% (d) 13%

220. The marked price of a mobile phone is ₹ 36000. A shopkeeper gives a discount of 11% on the marked price. Further, if a customer purchases it through credit card the discount increases by 15%.Pooja purchases it through the credit card. How much does she pay?
SSC CHSL (Tier I) 27/05/2022 Shift-I
(a) ₹ 31000 (b) ₹ 32000
(c) ₹ 30880 (d) ₹ 30600

221. What will be the selling price of an article if two successive discounts of 15% and 12% are offered on its marked price of ₹ 25500?
SSC CHSL (Tier I) 27/05/2022 Shift-I
(a) ₹ 19074 (b) ₹ 25041
(c) ₹ 21165 (d) ₹ 18615

222. After allowing a discount of 15% on the marked price of an article, it was sold for ₹ 425. Had the discount not been given, the profit would have been 25%. What was the cost price (in ₹) of the article?
SSC CHSL (Tier I) 10/08/2021 Shift-I
(a) 325 (b) 450
(c) 500 (d) 400

223. One dozen notebooks quoted at ₹ 125 are available at 20% discount. How many note books can be bought for ₹ 75?
SSC CHSL (Tier I) 04/08/2021 Shift-I
(a) 10 (b) 6
(c) 9 (d) 8

224. A shopkeeper charges ₹ 1.50 to photocopy a sheet of paper and a discount of 5.5% is given on all photocopies done after 400 sheets. How much will it cost to photocopy 800 sheets of paper?
SSC CHSL (Tier I) 19/04/2021 Shift-I
(a) ₹ 1167 (b) ₹ 1160
(c) ₹ 1276 (d) ₹ 1176

SSC MTS 2024

225. A shop has two promotional offers: buy three shirts, get one shirt free, or a 25% discount on the marked price. If a customer buys five using both offers, what discount will he get all together? SSC MTS 14/11/2024 Shift-III
(a) 30% (b) 50%
(c) 25% (d) 27.5%

226. By selling a book for ₹480 at marked price, a shopkeeper gains 20%. During a clearance sale, the shopkeeper allows a discount of 10% on the marked price. What is his gain per cent during the sale?
SSC MTS 13/11/2024 Shift-III
(a) 16% (b) 8%
(c) 12% (d) 18%

227. The marked price of a mobile phone at a showroom is ₹ 25000 and is sold at successive discounts of 20%, 15% and 10%. Find its selling price. SSC MTS 12/11/2024 Shift-III

(a) ₹ 15000 (b) ₹ 15300
(c) ₹ 14960 (d) ₹ 14000

228. The marked price of a speaker is ₹ 520 and the shopkeeper offers a discount of 10% and still he gains 17%. If no discount is allowed, then find the gain percentage. SSC MTS 12/11/2024 Shift-III

(a) 27% (b) 20%
(c) 25% (d) 30%

229. The marked price of an article is ₹ 1680 and it is sold at a discount of 19%. If there is a gain of 8%, then by what percentage above the cost price was the article marked? SSC MTS 11/11/2024 Shift-III

(a) $35\frac{1}{3}\%$ (b) $31\frac{1}{3}\%$
(c) $32\frac{1}{3}\%$ (d) $33\frac{1}{3}\%$

230. A supermarket gives two successive discounts on a mobile phone marked ₹19000. The first discount given is 14%. If the customer pays ₹15048 for the phone, then what was the second discount (rounded up to two decimal points)? SSC MTS 05/11/2024 Shift-III

(a) 9.26% (b) 8.00%
(c) 7.91% (d) 7.51%

231. A clothing store announces a discount scheme 'Buy one shirt and get 40% off on another shirt of the same price'. What is the profit percentage of the store, given that each shirt has a cost price 60% below the marked price? SSC MTS 04/11/2024 Shift-III

(a) 60% (b) 120%
(c) 100% (d) 80%

232. The marked price of a washing machine is ₹ 15000. A retailer buys it at ₹ 11250, after getting two successive discount of 15% and another rate which is illegible. What is the second discount rate? SSC MTS 30/10/2024 Shift-III

(a) $8\frac{3}{7}\%$ (b) $10\frac{11}{13}\%$
(c) $12\frac{4}{9}\%$ (d) $11\frac{13}{17}\%$

233. A retailer offers the following discount schemes for buyers on an article. Which scheme will be least beneficial to the customer?
I. A discount of 30%.
II. A discount of 22% followed by a discount of 8%.
III. Successive discounts of 25% and 5%. SSC MTS 29/10/2024 Shift-III

(a) Scheme I
(b) Scheme II and Scheme III
(c) Scheme II
(d) Scheme III

234. A shopkeeper offers 38% discount on a certain item. He announces an additional 15% discount to a customer for paying cash. A customer paid a cash amount of ₹ 2108 for that item. What is the marked price (in ₹) of the item? SSC MTS 28/10/2024 Shift-II

(a) 3560 (b) 3800
(c) 4200 (d) 4000

235. A shopkeeper offered following four different discount schemes for buyers on an item.
A. Two successive discounts of 8%
B. A discount of 11% followed by a discount of 5%.
C. Successive discounts of 13% and 3%.
D. A discount of 16%.
If Rajiv wants to purchase the item from this shop at minimum price, he should opt for the discount scheme SSC MTS 23/10/2024 Shift-II

(a) C (b) B
(c) A (d) D

236. In a scheme, a shopkeeper offers 4% discount if you buy three or more products. Ritu buys three bottles of guava juice for ₹ 330. If the shopkeeper still makes a profit of 10%, find the profit he would make if had sold it without discount (rounded off to 2 decimal places). SSC MTS 22/10/2024 Shift-II

(a) 15.74% (b) 14.58%
(c) 15% (d) 15.28%

237. A tradesman marks his goods at 40% above the cost price and then allows customers a discount of 15%. What is the profit percentage for the tradesman? SSC MTS 21/10/2024 Shift-II

(a) 25% (b) 21%
(c) 19% (d) 15%

238. A shopkeeper offers buy three, get one free; what is the percentage discount being offered by the shopkeeper in this scheme? SSC MTS 18/10/2024 Shift-II

(a) 33.33% (b) 30%
(c) 20% (d) 25%

239. Ramesh purchased a piano, marked at ₹ 18000 at a successive discounts of 12% and 15%, respectively. Ramesh gave ₹ 536 as transportation charge and sold it at ₹ 21000. What is his gain percentage? SSC MTS 17/10/2024 Shift-II

(a) 35% (b) 40%
(c) 48% (d) 50%

240. The difference between discounts on a bill for ₹22500 under two schemes, a discount of 40% and two successive discounts of 36% and 4%, is SSC MTS 18/10/2024 Shift-II

(a) ₹342 (b) ₹356
(c) ₹324 (d) ₹365

241. A wholesale dealer announced during the festival season that they are offering 'buy 4 shirts, get one free', then find the net discount percentage given by the dealer. SSC MTS 15/10/2024 Shift-I

(a) 10% (b) 20%
(c) 15% (d) 5%

242. Raman paid ₹ 18656 for a mobile phone, after a single discount of 12%. If Raman is given successive discounts of 4% and 8%, then how much Raman would pay? SSC MTS 14/10/2024 Shift-I

(a) ₹17238.84 (b) ₹13728.84
(c) ₹18723.84 (d) ₹17283.84

243. If two successive discounts of 25% and 15%, respectively, are given, then what will be the net discount percent. SSC MTS 08/10/2024 Shift-I

(a) 36.20% (b) 36.25%
(c) 36.10% (d) 36.15%

244. The marked price of a folding bed is ₹ 18000. Aman bought it after two successive discount of 15% and 10%. He spent ₹ 830 on transportation and sold it for ₹ 18440. Find his profit. SSC MTS 07/10/2024 Shift-I

(a) ₹ 2869 (b) ₹ 3539
(c) ₹ 3840 (d) ₹ 3148

245. A retailer allows a trade discount of 25% and a further discount of 8% on the marked price of the products, if paid along with his shop's membership card. He makes a net profit of 15% on the cost. By what percentage are the products marked up by him? SSC MTS 01/10/2024 Shift-I

(a) $66\frac{2}{3}\%$ (b) $84\frac{1}{3}\%$
(c) $59\frac{2}{3}\%$ (d) $46\frac{1}{3}\%$

246. Riya offers 12% discount on all her goods and offers an additional discount of 6% to those customers who pay in cash. How much will a customer have to pay for a fan marked for ₹ 2400 if he pays in cash?
SSC MTS 30/09/2024 Shift-I
(a) ₹1985.28 (b) ₹1900
(c) ₹2300.50 (d) ₹2122.50

SSC MTS 2023-2021

247. The cost price of an article is ₹ 1120. After allowing a discount of ₹ 205 a gain of 15% was made, then the marked price of the article is
SSC MTS 01/09/2023 Shift-III
(a) ₹ 1760 (b) ₹ 1493
(c) ₹ 1350 (d) ₹ 1580

248. 15% of the marked price of an item is equal to 25% of its cost price. If a discount of 25% is given on the sale of the item, then what will be the profit percentage?
SSC MTS 15/07/2022 Shift-I
(a) 22.5% (b) 20%
(c) 17.5% (d) 25%

249. Find a single discount equivalent to two successive discounts of 12% and 8%.
SSC MTS 14/07/2022 Shift-I
(a) 18.8% (b) 19.04%
(c) 19.4% (d) 19.8%

250. Akshay has 30 articles, each having the same cost price. He marked the price of each article at 30% above its cost price. He sold 15 of the articles at a discount of 20% each, and the remaining 15 articles at a discount of 10% each, thereby gaining a total profit of ₹ 630. What was the cost price of each article ?
SSC MTS 12/07/2022 Shift-I
(a) ₹ 240 (b) ₹ 180
(c) ₹ 280 (d) ₹ 200

251. If 25% discount is given on an article, then there will be a loss of 15%. If the article is sold at its marked price, then what will the profit percentage be? [Give your answer correct to 2 decimal places.]
SSC MTS 11/07/2022 Shift-I
(a) 15.66% (b) 12.66%
(c) 13.33% (d) 10.22%

252. An article, whose list price was ₹ 720, was subject to two successive discounts of 20% and 10%. What is the amount (in ₹) of discount that a customer would get while purchasing the article?
SSC MTS 02/07/2021 Shift-III
(a) 198 (b) 190.8
(c) 201.6 (d) 216

253. After allowing a discount of 10% on the marked price of an article, it is sold for ₹ 450. Had the discount not been given, the profit would have been 25%. What is the 50% of the cost price (in ₹) of the article?
SSC MTS 02/11/2021 Shift-I
(a) 150 (b) 200
(c) 175 (d) 250

254. During festivals, a banner on a shop displays, 'Pay for 3 and get 5'. The discount percentage offered is
SSC MTS 02/11/2021 Shift-I
(a) $166\frac{2}{3}\%$ (b) 60%
(c) 40% (d) $66\frac{2}{3}\%$

255. A shopkeeper earns 25% profit, if he sells an article at 10% discount on the marked price ₹ 2500. Find his profit.
SSC MTS 02/11/2021 Shift-I
(a) ₹ 450 (b) ₹ 400
(c) ₹ 375 (d) ₹ 350

256. Sushant bought the goods for ₹ 8000. He get 10% discount at that goods. After discount, he paid of tax at rate 7.5%. Find the amount, that he will be paid for it goods to get at resident, it the shopkeeper take ₹ 200 for home delivery.
SSC MTS 02/11/2021 Shift-I
(a) ₹ 7940 (b) ₹ 8155
(c) ₹ 9660 (d) ₹ 6851

SSC GD Constable 2024

257. A merchant marks the price of his article 40% above the cost price. He gives some discount on it and earns a profit of 10%. What is the discount percentage ?
SSC GD 26/02/2024 Shift-I
(a) 14.28% (b) 25%
(c) 21.42% (d) 20%

258. Find a single discount equivalent to two successive discounts of 15% and 10%.
SSC GD 26/02/2024 Shift-I
(a) 21.8% (b) 23.5%
(c) 22.5% (d) 24.5%

259. What is the discount percentage offered on a book having marked price ₹ 3800 being sold at ₹ 2128?
SSC GD 24/02/2024 Shift-III
(a) 44% (b) 45% (c) 50% (d) 56%

260. The marked price of an article is 250% of the cost price. If 50% discount is given, then what will be the profit percentage?
SSC GD 24/02/2024 Shift-III
(a) 10% (b) 20%
(c) 25% (d) 15%

261. Abhishek marks the price of his laptop 80% above the cost price. He allows his customer a discount of 25% on the marked price. What is the profit percentage?
SSC GD 24/02/2024 Shift-II
(a) 35% (b) 25%
(c) 55% (d) 40%

262. If the ratio of marked price and selling price of a article is 13 : 9, then what is the discount percentage?
SSC GD 24/02/2024 Shift-II
(a) 28.76% (b) 30.77%
(c) 25% (d) 32.77%

263. An item is sold for ₹ 4964 after two successive discounts of 30% and 10%. What is the marked price of the article
SSC GD 24/02/2024 Shift-I
(a) ₹ 7200.47 (b) ₹ 7120.46
(c) ₹ 7879.36 (d) ₹ 6600

264. The marked price of a cycle is ₹ 2700. If 10% discount is given, then what will be the selling price of the cycle?
SSC GD 24/02/2024 Shift-I
(a) ₹ 2400 (b) ₹ 2560
(c) ₹ 2430 (d) ₹ 2500

265. The selling price of a car is ₹ 640. If the car is sold at a discount of 60%, then what will be the marked price of the car?
SSC GD 23/02/2024 Shift-IV
(a) ₹ 2000 (b) ₹ 2400
(c) ₹ 1600 (d) ₹ 1800

266. The marked price of an article is ₹ 1850, If 60% discount given on the article, then what will be the selling price of the article ?
SSC GD 23/02/2024 Shift-III
(a) ₹ 740 (b) ₹ 860
(c) ₹ 840 (d) ₹ 750

267. The marked price of an article was ₹ 4800, but the shopkeeper offers two discounts of 18% and 20% on that article, at what price does he finally sell the article?
SSC GD 23/02/2024 Shift-III
(a) ₹ 3258.8 (b) ₹ 3148.8
(c) ₹ 2976 (d) ₹ 3642

268. A vendor marks his goods at 40% above the cost price. If he offers a discount of 30%. What is the loss percentage?
SSC GD 23/02/2024 Shift-II
(a) 3% (b) 2.5% (c) 2% (d) 1.5%

269. 1/4 of marked price is equal to 2/3 of selling price. What is the discount per cent?
SSC GD 23/02/2024 Shift-II
(a) 62.5% (b) 65%
(c) 50% (d) 60%

270. Marked price of an article is ₹ 9600 and its selling price is ₹ 6336. What is the discount percentage? SSC GD 23/02/2024 Shift-I

(a) 25% (b) 30% (c) 34% (d) 38%

271. The marked price of an article is 25% more than its cost price. What maximum discount percentage can be offered by the shopkeeper to sell his article at no profit or no loss? SSC GD 23/02/2024 Shift-I

(a) 25% (b) 20% (c) 16.67% (d) 12.5%

272. Abhishek marks the price of his laptop 50% above the cost price. He allows his customer a discount of 30% on the marked price. What is the profit percentage? SSC GD 22/02/2024 Shift-IV

(a) 10% (b) 8% (c) 20% (d) 5%

273. A merchant marks the price of his article 50% above the cost price. If he allows 20% discount, then what is the profit or loss percentage? SSC GD 22/02/2024 Shift-III

(a) 30% profit (b) 20% profit
(c) 40% loss (d) 10% loss

274. Marked price and selling price of an article are ₹ 7600 and ₹ 6688, respectively. What is the discount percentage? SSC GD 22/02/2024 Shift-II

(a) 16% (b) 8%
(c) 12% (d) 10%

275. After giving 10% discount on an article there is still a profit of 10%. What will be the profit percentage when no discount is given ? SSC GD 22/02/2024 Shift-II

(a) 66.67% (b) 35%
(c) 33.33% (d) 22.22%

276. After giving 50% discount on an article there is still a profit of 50%. What will be the profit percentage when no discount is given? SSC GD 22/02/2024 Shift-I

(a) 300% (b) 100%
(c) 150% (d) 200%

277. A toy originally costs ₹ 25, but it's on sale with a 30% discount. What is the sale price? SSC GD 21/02/2024 Shift-IV

(a) ₹ 19.3 (b) ₹ 13.8
(c) ₹ 14.6 (d) ₹ 17.5

278. The marked price of an article is ₹ 640. If discount of 37.5% is given, then what will be the selling price of the article? SSC GD 21/02/2024 Shift-IV

(a) ₹ 600 (b) ₹ 450
(c) ₹ 550 (d) ₹ 400

279. An article is sold for ₹ 204 after two successive discounts of 40% and 50%. What is the marked price of the article? SSC GD 21/02/2024 Shift-III

(a) ₹ 840 (b) ₹ 680
(c) ₹ 720 (d) ₹ 540

280. The marked price of a chair is 10% more than its cost price. If the chair is sold for ₹ 132 after a discount of ₹ 11, then what will be the profit percentage? SSC GD 21/02/2024 Shift-III

(a) 1.53% (b) 1.78%
(c) 2% (d) 1.21%

281. Marked price and selling price of an article are ₹ 6600 and ₹ 4752, respectively. What is the discount percentage? SSC GD 21/02/2024 Shift-II

(a) 34% (b) 32% (c) 25% (d) 28%

282. On selling a book at $\frac{5}{12}$ of the marked price there is a loss of 50%. What will be the ratio of marked price and cost price of the book? SSC GD 21/02/2024 Shift-II

(a) 2 : 5 (b) 6 : 5
(c) 5 : 6 (d) 3 : 8

283. On selling a book at 16/25 of the marked price there is a loss. What will be the ratio of marked price and selling price of the book? SSC GD 21/02/2024 Shift-I

(a) 16 : 15 (b) 8 : 3
(c) 25 : 16 (d) 3 : 8

284. The selling price of an article is ₹ 1690. If discount of 35% is given, then what will be the marked price of the article? SSC GD 21/02/2024 Shift-I

(a) ₹ 2800 (b) ₹ 2600
(c) ₹ 2500 (d) ₹ 2700

285. The marked price of a chair is 20% more than its cost price. If the chair is sold for ₹ 220 after a discount of ₹ 20, then what will be the profit percentage? SSC GD 20/02/2024 Shift-IV

(a) 10% (b) 30%
(c) 20% (d) 15%

286. The marked price of an article is ₹ 11800 and its selling price is ₹ 7788. What is the discount per cent on the article? SSC GD 20/02/2024 Shift-IV

(a) 35% (b) 34% (c) 30% (d) 32%

287. Marked price of a chair is ₹ 5000. After giving two successive discount of 10% and x%, the chair is sold for ₹ 3150. What is the value of x? SSC GD 20/02/2024 Shift-III

(a) 40% (b) 25% (c) 20% (d) 30%

288. Marked price of a chair is ₹ 2000. After giving two successive discounts of 20% and x%, the chairs is sold for ₹ 1400. What is the value of x? SSC GD 20/02/2024 Shift-I

(a) 12.5% (b) 20%
(c) 25% (d) 10%

289. Selling price of an article is ₹ 5175 and discount of 25% is offered. What is the marked price of the article? SSC GD 20/02/2024 Shift-I

(a) ₹ 6600 (b) ₹ 6900
(c) ₹ 7000 (d) ₹ 8500

SSC GD Constable 2023

290. Dinesh offers his customers a discount of 15% on a raincoat and he still makes a profit of 25%. What is the actual cost of the raincoat marketed for ₹ 800? SSC GD 13/02/2023 Shift-IV

(a) ₹ 540 (b) ₹ 546
(c) ₹ 544 (d) ₹ 542

291. A single discount equivalent to 5%, 10%, 15% and 20% is SSC GD 13/02/2023 Shift-IV

(a) 42.76% (b) 41.86%
(c) 32.88% (d) 36.92%

292. Marked price of an article is ₹ 1600 but Rohan gets a discount of 20%. He sells the article for ₹ 1600. Rohan's gain per cent is SSC GD 13/02/2023 Shift-II

(a) 18% (b) 22%
(c) 25% (d) 20%

293. The cost price of an article is 64% of the marked price. Calculate the gain percentage after allowing a discount of 20%. SSC GD 13/02/2023 Shift-II

(a) 35% (b) 25%
(c) 30% (d) 20%

294. A tradesman market the price of his goods to earn a profit of 20% after giving a discount of 20%. Market price is how much percentage more than the cost price? SSC GD 09/02/2023 Shift-II

(a) 35% (b) 40%
(c) 50% (d) 20%

295. The successive discounts of 10%, 30% and 25% is equivalent to a single discount of .... (correct to a nearest whole number). SSC GD 09/02/2023 Shift-II

(a) 65%
(b) 47%
(c) 55%
(d) 53%

296. Akshit is selling a suitcase marked at ₹ 5000 by offering a 10% discount and further offers a 10% discount if the payment is made in cash. A customer bought the suitcase from Akshit and paid him in cash. How much amount (in ₹) did he pay to Akshit? SSC GD 09/02/2023 Shift-I

(a) 4150 (b) 4200
(c) 4500 (d) 4050

297. A shopkeeper announces a discount of 18% on every item in his store. What price should a customer pay for an item of ₹ 5583? (in ₹, rounded off to the nearest integer) SSC GD 09/02/2023 Shift-I

(a) 4578 (b) 3980
(c) 4275 (d) 3650

298. There was 20% discount on VIP bags. Anupam bought a bag. He also got an additional 8% discount for paying cash. If he paid ₹ 2208, then what was the price tag on the bag? SSC GD 08/02/2023 Shift-I

(a) ₹ 2300 (b) ₹ 2500
(c) ₹ 2600 (d) ₹ 3000

299. A man purchased a table marked at ₹500 at two successive discounts of 8% and 25% respectively. He spent ₹ 32 on transportation and sold the table for ₹ 500. What is the amount he gained? SSC GD 08/12/2023 Shift-I

(a) ₹130 (b) ₹120
(c) ₹123 (d) ₹124

300. A seller marked the price 25% more than its cost price. If he allows a discount of 42%, then find his loss percent. SSC GD 08/12/2023 Shift-I

(a) 33.5% (b) 27.5%
(c) 30% (d) 8.5%

301. Balvendra offers two successive discounts of 9% and 4% first and then he also provides a cash discount of ₹ 268 on the sale of a CCTV camera. If the marked price of the CCTV camera is ₹ 5000, what is the final price of the CCTV camera for a customer? SSC GD 07/02/2023 Shift-I

(a) ₹ 4000 (b) ₹ 4368
(c) ₹ 4100 (d) ₹ 4636

302. After allowing a discount of 10% on its marked price, the value of a washing machine is ₹28800. If no discount is allowed, then the shopkeeper gains 25%. The cost price of the washing machine is SSC GD 06/02/2023 Shift-I

(a) ₹26200 (b) ₹28000
(c) ₹25600 (d) ₹26600

303. A store is running a 'Buy 4 Get 1 Free' promotion scheme. What is the net discount percentage? SSC GD 06/02/2023 Shift-I

(a) 20% (b) 15%
(c) 22% (d) 18.5%

304. A dealer buys an old car listed at ₹ 85000 and gets successive discounts of 20% and 10%. He spends ₹ 3800 on its repairs and sells it at a profit of 20%. Find the selling price of the car. SSC GD 06/02/2023 Shift-I

(a) ₹ 80000
(b) ₹ 78000
(c) ₹ 75000
(d) ₹ 100000

305. The marked price of a mobile phone is ₹ 16500. A festival discount of 8% is allowed on it. Further, for cash payment a second discount of 5% is given. The cash payment, in rupees, that is to be made for buying the mobile phone is SSC GD 02/02/2023 Shift-I

(a) ₹ 14671
(b) ₹ 14872
(c) ₹ 14512
(d) ₹ 14421

306. A trader gives two successive discounts of 18% and 20%. If the marked price is ₹ 11000, then the selling price is SSC GD 02/02/2023 Shift-I

(a) ₹ 6926
(b) ₹ 6716
(c) ₹ 7926
(d) ₹ 7216

307. If you are buying one jacket at ₹ 2500 and buying two similar jackets at ₹ 4500, then find the discount percentage. (Marked price of one jacket is 2500). SSC GD 01/02/2023 Shift-I

(a) 12% (b) 15%
(c) 10% (d) 18%

308. A shopkeeper announces the following three discount schemes on the purchase of an article. Which of these schemes is the best scheme for a customer?

A. Two successive discounts of 15% and 18%
B. Buy 6 articles and get 2 free
C. A flat discount of 30%

SSC GD 01/02/2023 Shift-I

(a) Both schemes A and C give the same discount
(b) Scheme A
(c) Scheme B
(d) Scheme C

SSC Selection Post 2024-2022

309. If an electricity bill is paid before the due date, one gets a reduction of 5% on the amount of the bill. By paying the bill before the due date, a person got a reduction of ₹ 250. The original amount of his electricity bill (in ₹) was Matric Level 20/06/2024 Shift-IV

(a) ₹ 4000 (b) ₹ 4500
(c) ₹ 5000 (d) ₹ 5500

310. Which of the following schemes will yield maximum discount on purchase of ₹x?

1. 2 successive discounts of 25% and 15%
2. Single discount of 20%
3. 2 free on purchase of 3 items
4. 3 free on purchase of 7 items

Graduate Level 20/06/2024 Shift-III

(a) Scheme 4 (b) Scheme 2
(c) Scheme 1 (d) Scheme 3

311. The marked price of a grinder was ₹ 3000 and the dealer offered successive discounts of 20% and 15% on it. For how much did he sell the grinder? Higher Secondary Level 20/06/2024 Shift-II

(a) ₹ 2200 (b) ₹ 2000
(c) ₹ 2040 (d) ₹ 2400

312. A retailer buys 220 chocolates from a wholesaler for the marked price of 198 items. He then sells each chocolate at a discount of 3.7%. What is his profit percentage? Higher Secondary Level 20/06/2024 Shift-II

(a) 6.3% (b) 7%
(c) 6% (d) 7.2%

313. A trader marked a table at ₹ 37062, and sold it allowing a 33% discount. If his profit was 42%, then the cost price (in ₹) of the table was Graduate Level 27/06/2023 Shift-IV

(a) ₹ 15487 (b) ₹ 16487
(c) ₹ 17487 (d) ₹ 13487

314. What is the selling price of a calculator if a shopkeeper allows two successive discounts of 7% each on its marked price of ₹500? Higher Secondary Level 27/06/2023 Shift-III

(a) ₹430.25 (b) ₹440.85
(c) ₹435.00 (d) ₹432.45

315. Mohan purchases a table at an MRP of ₹ 800, at a discount of 10%. If he sells it at ₹ 900, then the profit percentage is Higher Secondary Level 27/06/2023 Shift-III

(a) 20% profit (b) 25% profit
(c) 15% profit (d) 30% profit

316. A silver puja thali set marked at ₹10000 is sold with two successive discounts of 10% and 5%. An additional 5% discount is offered if the payment is made in cash mode. Find the selling price of the article on cash payment. **Higher Secondary Level 27/06/2023 Shift-III**

(a) ₹8212.50 (b) ₹8122.50
(c) ₹8100.50 (d) ₹8200.50

317. Somesh is a shopkeeper who gives two successive discounts on an umbrella marked ₹ 560. The first discount given is 17%. If the customer Mahesh pays ₹ 420 for the umbrella, then find the second discount given (correct to two places of decimals). **Matric Level 27/06/2023 Shift-I**

(a) 4.69% (b) 9.64%
(c) 6.49% (d) 6.94%

318. Marked price of a TV is listed at ₹ 24500. If it's selling price is ₹ 20090, then what is the discount percentage? **Matric Level 27/06/2023 Shift-I**

(a) 22%
(b) 18%
(c) 20%
(d) 15%

319. The marked price of an air conditioner is ₹ 45000 and there are two successive discounts of 15% and 20% available on it. Find the selling price of the air conditioner. **Graduate Level 01/08/2022 Shift-IV**

(a) ₹30600
(b) ₹32000
(c) ₹30000
(d) ₹31600

320. The marked price of a TV is ₹ 50000. The difference between a discount of 30% and two successive discounts of 25% and 6% on this deal is **Higher Secondary Level 01/08/2022 Shift-II**

(a) ₹ 250 (b) ₹ 300 (c) ₹ 125 (d) ₹ 500

321. At a sale, the goods are on a sale at 45% discount. If Rama buys a skirt marked ₹ 600, how much would she need to pay? **Matric Level 01/08/2022 Shift-I**

(a) ₹ 450 (b) ₹ 330 (c) ₹ 150 (d) ₹ 270

322. The cost price of an article is 80% of its marked price. The dealer allows 15% discount on the marked price. Find the gain percentage? **Matric Level 01/08/2022 Shift-I**

(a) 9% (b) 10%
(c) 25% (d) $6\frac{1}{4}\%$

Right Answers

1	(d)	2	(a)	3	(a)	4	(b)	5	(a)	6	(a)	7	(a)	8	(c)	9	(d)	10	(b)
11	(a)	12	(b)	13	(d)	14	(d)	15	(a)	16	(a)	17	(b)	18	(c)	19	(c)	20	(d)
21	(b)	22	(b)	23	(d)	24	(a)	25	(b)	26	(c)	27	(d)	28	(b)	29	(b)	30	(a)
31	(c)	32	(c)	33	(c)	34	(b)	35	(d)	36	(c)	37	(a)	38	(d)	39	(d)	40	(c)
41	(b)	42	(d)	43	(a)	44	(d)	45	(b)	46	(d)	47	(d)	48	(d)	49	(b)	50	(d)
51	(b)	52	(d)	53	(c)	54	(a)	55	(d)	56	(b)	57	(a)	58	(a)	59	(d)	60	(a)
61	(a)	62	(a)	63	(a)	64	(b)	65	(a)	66	(d)	67	(b)	68	(d)	69	(b)	70	(b)
71	(c)	72	(b)	73	(b)	74	(a)	75	(b)	76	(a)	77	(b)	78	(a)	79	(a)	80	(a)
81	(c)	82	(c)	83	(a)	84	(d)	85	(c)	86	(d)	87	(d)	88	(b)	89	(a)	90	(a)
91	(c)	92	(a)	93	(c)	94	(a)	95	(a)	96	(d)	97	(b)	98	(b)	99	(b)	100	(b)
101	(d)	102	(b)	103	(a)	104	(b)	105	(d)	106	(c)	107	(a)	108	(a)	109	(d)	110	(c)
111	(d)	112	(a)	113	(c)	114	(a)	115	(c)	116	(c)	117	(b)	118	(a)	119	(c)	120	(d)
121	(d)	122	(c)	123	(c)	124	(c)	125	(c)	126	(d)	127	(c)	128	(c)	129	(a)	130	(d)
131	(a)	132	(b)	133	(b)	134	(c)	135	(b)	136	(a)	137	(a)	138	(c)	139	(a)	140	(b)
141	(b)	142	(c)	143	(d)	144	(a)	145	(c)	146	(a)	147	(b)	148	(a)	149	(b)	150	(b)
151	(b)	152	(b)	153	(a)	154	(a)	155	(a)	156	(b)	157	(d)	158	(d)	159	(c)	160	(d)
161	(d)	162	(a)	163	(b)	164	(c)	165	(b)	166	(b)	167	(b)	168	(d)	169	(c)	170	(b)
171	(c)	172	(b)	173	(c)	174	(d)	175	(c)	176	(c)	177	(a)	178	(b)	179	(c)	180	(d)
181	(c)	182	(d)	183	(d)	184	(c)	185	(b)	186	(b)	187	(d)	188	(c)	189	(b)	190	(b)
191	(c)	192	(c)	193	(d)	194	(d)	195	(b)	196	(c)	197	(b)	198	(d)	199	(b)	200	(b)
201	(b)	202	(b)	203	(c)	204	(a)	205	(d)	206	(c)	207	(c)	208	(a)	209	(a)	210	(c)
211	(c)	212	(c)	213	(a)	214	(a)	215	(b)	216	(a)	217	(a)	218	(a)	219	(c)	220	(d)
221	(a)	222	(d)	223	(c)	224	(a)	225	(c)	226	(b)	227	(b)	228	(d)	229	(d)	230	(c)
231	(c)	232	(d)	233	(c)	234	(d)	235	(d)	236	(b)	237	(c)	238	(d)	239	(d)	240	(c)
241	(b)	242	(c)	243	(b)	244	(c)	245	(a)	246	(a)	247	(b)	248	(d)	249	(b)	250	(d)
251	(c)	252	(c)	253	(b)	254	(c)	255	(a)	256	(a)	257	(c)	258	(b)	259	(a)	260	(c)
261	(a)	262	(b)	263	(c)	264	(c)	265	(c)	266	(a)	267	(b)	268	(c)	269	(a)	270	(c)
271	(b)	272	(d)	273	(b)	274	(c)	275	(d)	276	(d)	277	(d)	278	(d)	279	(b)	280	(a)
281	(d)	282	(b)	283	(c)	284	(b)	285	(a)	286	(b)	287	(d)	288	(a)	289	(b)	290	(c)
291	(b)	292	(c)	293	(b)	294	(c)	295	(d)	296	(d)	297	(a)	298	(d)	299	(c)	300	(b)
301	(c)	302	(c)	303	(a)	304	(b)	305	(d)	306	(d)	307	(c)	308	(b)	309	(c)	310	(d)
311	(c)	312	(b)	313	(c)	314	(d)	315	(b)	316	(b)	317	(b)	318	(b)	319	(a)	320	(a)
321	(b)	322	(d)																

Solutions

1. (d) According to the question,

$$\left.\frac{SP}{MP}=\frac{5}{6}\right]1 \text{ unit}$$

∴ Effective percentage discount

$$=\frac{1}{6}\times 100\% = 16.67\%$$

2. (a) $\text{Discount} = MP \times \dfrac{\text{Discount}\%}{100}$

$$= 2050 \times \frac{26}{100} = ₹\,533$$

3. (a) According to the question,

$$SP = 1500 \times \frac{80}{100}\times\frac{90}{100} = ₹\,1080$$

$$\therefore \quad \text{Required gain\%} = \frac{1080-1000}{1000}\times 100$$

$$= \frac{80}{1000}\times 100 = 8\%$$

4. (b) $\text{Required SP} = 15620 \times \dfrac{73}{100} \approx ₹\,11400$

5. (a) Net change in original price

$$= \left(8 + (-18) + \frac{(8)(-18)}{100}\right)\%$$

$$= (-10 - 1.44)\% = 11.44\% \text{ discount}$$

6. (a) Let MP be $100x$.

$$\therefore SP = 100x \times \left(\frac{100-15}{100}\right) \times \left(\frac{100-20}{100}\right)\times\left(\frac{100-5}{100}\right)$$

$$= 64.6x = 100x \times \left(\frac{100-35.4}{100}\right)$$

∴ Single equivalent discount = 35.4%

Speedy Method

MP	:	SP	
20	:	17	(−15%)
5	:	4	(−20%)
20	:	19	(−5%)
500	:	323	

−177

$$ED = \frac{177}{500}\times 100 = 35.4\%$$

7. (a) Let MP be $7x$.

∴ $SP = 5x$ (As 2 articles are free)

∴ $\text{Discount} = 7x - 5x = 2x$

$$\text{Discount \%} = \frac{\text{Discount}}{MP}\times 100$$

$$= \frac{2x}{7x}\times 100 = 28\frac{4}{7}\%$$

8. (c) Cost price of Bluetooth = ₹1700

Marked price of Bluetooth = ₹2000

$$\text{Selling price after discount} = 2000 \times \frac{60}{100} = ₹1200$$

$$\therefore \text{ Loss per cent} = \frac{1700-1200}{1700}\times 100$$

$$= \frac{500}{1700}\times 100 = 29.41\%$$

9. (d) Let the cost price be $100x$.

$$\text{Then mark price} = 100x \times \frac{125}{100} = 125x$$

Selling price after discount

$$= 125x \times \frac{(100-18)}{100}$$

$$= 125x \times \frac{82}{100} = 102.5x$$

$$\therefore \text{Required gain\%} = \frac{102.5x - 100x}{100x}\times 100$$

$$= \frac{2.5x}{100x}\times 100 = 2.5\%$$

10. (b) According to the question,

$$MP \times \frac{(100-17)}{100}\times\frac{(100-x)}{100} = SP$$

$$\Rightarrow \quad 1600 \times \frac{83}{100}\times\frac{(100-x)}{100} = 747$$

$$\Rightarrow \quad 16 \times 83 \times (100-x) = 747 \times 100$$

$$\Rightarrow \quad 16 \times (100 - x) = 900$$

$$\Rightarrow \quad 1600 - 16x = 900 \Rightarrow 16x = 700$$

$$\Rightarrow \quad x = \frac{700}{16} = 43.75\%$$

11. (a) Single discount equivalent to 60% and 70%

$$= \left(60 + 70 - \frac{60\times 70}{100}\right)\% = (130 - 42)\%$$

= 88%

Single discount equivalent to 88% and 80%

$$= \left(88 + 80 - \frac{88 \times 80}{100}\right)\%$$

$$= (168 - 70.4)\% = 97.6\%$$

Speedy Method

MP	:	SP	
5	:	2	(−60%)
10	:	3	(−70%)
5	:	1	(−80%)
250	:	6	

−244

$$ED = \frac{244 \times 100}{250} = 97.6\%$$

12. (b) MP of a bed sheet = ₹ 500

Two successive discounts = 10% and 5%

$$\text{Single discount} = \left(10 + 5 - \frac{5\times 10}{100}\right)\%$$

$(10 + 5 - 0.5)\% = 14.5\%$

$$\text{Selling Price} = 500\left(1 - \frac{14.5}{100}\right)$$

$$= 500 \times \frac{85.5}{100} = ₹\,427.5$$

13. (d) $\text{Amit marks MP} = 1500\left(\dfrac{100+y}{100}\right)$

$$= 1500 + 15y$$

$$\text{Bilal marks MP} = 2000 \times \left(\frac{100+2y}{100}\right)$$

Bilal selling price after y% discount

$$= 2000 \times \left(\frac{100+2y}{100}\right)\left(\frac{100-y}{100}\right)$$

Amit's profit = Bilal's profit

$$(1500 + 15y - 1500) = \frac{(100+2y)(100-y)}{5} - 2000$$

$$75y = 100y - 2y^2$$

$$2y^2 = 25y$$

$$y = 12.5\%$$

14. (d) (i) Successive discount

$$= +10 + 8 - \frac{10\times 8}{100}$$

$$= 18 - 0.8 = 17.2\%$$

(ii) $\text{Successive discount} = 12 + 10 - \dfrac{12\times 10}{100}$

$$= 22 - 1.2 = 20.8\%$$

(iii) $\text{Successive discount} = +12 + 12 - \dfrac{12\times 12}{100}$

$$= 22.56\%$$

(iv) Discount = 20%

Hence, option (iii) gives max. discount.

15. (a) MP = ₹ 12500

$$SP = 12500 \times \left(\frac{100-6}{100}\right)\times\left(\frac{100-6}{100}\right)\times\left(\frac{100-4}{100}\right)$$

$$= 12500 \times \frac{94}{100}\times\frac{94}{100}\times\frac{96}{100} = ₹\,10603.2$$

16. (a) $\text{Required CP} = 275 \times \dfrac{95}{100}\times\dfrac{100}{104.5}$

$$= ₹\,250$$

17. (b) MP of the purse = ₹2250

Successive discounts = 10% and 20%

$$\text{Single discount} = \left(10 + 20 - \frac{10 \times 20}{100}\right)$$

$$= (30 - 2) = 28\%$$

$$\text{SP of the purse} = MP\left(1 - \frac{\text{Discount\%}}{100}\right)$$

$$= 2250\left(1 - \frac{28}{100}\right)$$

$$= 2250 \times \frac{72}{100} = ₹1620$$

18. (c) The SP after first discount of 12.5%

$$= 150 \times \frac{7}{8}$$

Let x% discount given in second time

$$\therefore \quad 150 \times \frac{7}{8}\times\frac{100-x}{100} = 105$$

$$\Rightarrow \quad 100 - x = 80 \Rightarrow x = 20\%$$

19. (c) I. Net discount

$$= \left(-15 - 20 + \frac{(15)(20)}{100}\right)$$

$$= (-35 + 3)\% = 32\% \text{ discount}$$

II. Net Discount $= \left(-25 - 10 + \dfrac{(25)(10)}{100}\right)\%$

$= 32.5\%$ discount

III. Discount of 33%

$\therefore$ SP will be minimum in case III.

20. (d) MP of TV set = ₹ 18500

Two successive discounts = 20% and 5%

Single discount $= \left(20 + 5 - \dfrac{20 \times 5}{100}\right)$

$= (25 - 1)\% = 24\%$

SP of TV set $= 18500\left(1 - \dfrac{24}{100}\right)$

$= 18500 \times \dfrac{76}{100} =$ ₹ 14060

TV is available for ₹ 14060.

21. (b) Single discount by formula

$= \left(x + y - \dfrac{xy}{100}\right)\%$

$x = 40\%$ and $y = 20\%$

$= \left(40 + 20 - \dfrac{40 \times 20}{100}\right)\% = (60 - 8)\%$

$= 52\%$

22. (b) Let the cost price be 100.

Then, marked price $= 100 \times \dfrac{120}{100} = 120$

Selling price $= 120 \times \dfrac{(100 - 30)}{100}$

$= 120 \times \dfrac{70}{100} = 84$

Thus, loss% $= \dfrac{100 - 84}{100} \times 100$

$= \dfrac{16}{100} \times 100 = 16\%$

23. (d) Marked price of product = ₹25000

Discount rate = 30%

Discount for each product

$= 25000 \times \dfrac{30}{100} =$ ₹ 7500

Thus, total discount for 6 product

$= 7500 \times 6 =$ ₹ 45000

24. (a) Equivalent discount $= +a + b - \dfrac{ab}{100}$

$= 10 + 16 - \dfrac{10 \times 16}{100} = 26 - 1.6 = 24.4\%$

25. (b) Net discount on two successive discounts $= -15 - 20 + \dfrac{15 \times 20}{100} = -32\%$

$= 32\%$ discount

Difference between the discounts

$= 32 - 25 = 7\%$

According to the question,

7% is equivalent to ₹ 28.

$\therefore$ 100% is equivalent to ₹ $\dfrac{28}{7} \times 100 =$ ₹ 400

26. (c) Given, MP = ₹ 180

Discount% = 15%

$\therefore$ Discount $= 180 \times \dfrac{15}{100} =$ ₹ 27

27. (d) Required SP

$= 5000 \times \dfrac{80}{100} \times \dfrac{85}{100} \times \dfrac{90}{100} =$ ₹ 3060

28. (b) Let MP = ₹ $100x$

$\therefore$ Total SP $= 100x \times \dfrac{94}{100} + 100x \times \dfrac{90}{100} + 100x \times \dfrac{88}{100}$

$= 94x + 90x + 88x = 272x$

Now, $272x =$ ₹ 6800

$100x =$ ₹ $\dfrac{6800 \times 100}{272} =$ ₹ 2500

29. (b) According to the question,

CP = 75% of MP

$\Rightarrow \dfrac{CP}{MP} = \dfrac{75}{100} = \dfrac{3}{4} = \dfrac{15}{20}$

Also, discount $= 15\% = \dfrac{15}{100} = \dfrac{3}{20} = \dfrac{\text{Discount}}{MP}$

$\therefore$ SP = 20 − 3 = 17

$\therefore$ SP : MP = 17 : 20

$\therefore$ CP : SP : MP = 15 : 17 : 20

$\therefore$ Required profit% $= \dfrac{17 - 15}{15} \times 100$

$= \dfrac{2}{15} \times 100 = 13.33\%$

30. (a)

MP	:	SP	:	CP	
(5	:	4	:	)	× 11
(	:	11	:	10)	× 4
55	:	44	:	40	

$\therefore$ Required ratio *i.e.,*

CP : MP = 40 : 55 = 8 : 11

31. (c)

MP	:	SP	
10	:	8	$20\% = \dfrac{1}{5}$
10	:	7	$30\% = \dfrac{3}{10}$
10	:	9	$10\% = \dfrac{1}{10}$
1000	:	504	

$\therefore$ 1000 → ₹ 1000

1 → ₹ 1

$\therefore$ SP, 504 → ₹ 504

Speedy Method

SP $= 1000 \times \dfrac{70}{100} \times \dfrac{80}{100} \times \dfrac{90}{100}$

$= 1000 \times \dfrac{504000}{1000000} =$ ₹ 504

32. (c) Given, First discount = 40%

Second discount = 30%

Net discount after two successive discounts

$= 40\% + 30\% - \dfrac{40 \times 30}{100}\% = 70\% - 12\% = 58\%$

33. (c) Let MP be $100x$.

According to the question,

$100x\left(\dfrac{100 - 30}{100}\right)\left(\dfrac{100 - 40}{100}\right) - 100x \times \left(\dfrac{100 - 65}{100}\right) = 105$

$\Rightarrow 42x - 35x = 105 \Rightarrow 7x = 105$

$x = 15$

$\therefore$ MP = 100 × 15 = ₹ 1500

34. (b) Amount paid by Ramesh

$= \dfrac{9800 \times 98}{100} + \dfrac{5480 \times 95}{100} =$ ₹ 14810

35. (d) Let the CP of an article be ₹ $100x$.

$\therefore$ MP of an article = ₹ $100x + \dfrac{26}{100} \times 100x$

= ₹ $126x$

As, discount = 32%

$\therefore$ SP $= 126x - \dfrac{32}{100} \times 126x =$ ₹ $85.68x$

$\therefore$ Loss% $= \dfrac{CP - SP}{CP} \times 100$

$= \dfrac{100x - 85.68x}{100x} \times 100 = 14.32\%$

36. (c) Marked price of article is ₹ 550.

Discount $= 550 \times \dfrac{40}{100} =$ ₹ 220

Selling price of article = 550 − 220 = ₹ 330

Cost price of article $= 330\left(\dfrac{100}{100 + 10}\right)$

$= 330 \times \dfrac{100}{110} =$ ₹ 300

37. (a) Let a marked price of an article = ₹ x

According to the question,

$x \times \dfrac{(100 - 45)}{100} = 330 \Rightarrow \dfrac{55x}{100} = 330$

$\Rightarrow x = \dfrac{330 \times 100}{55} =$ ₹ 600

38. (d) Let cost price of a goods be $1000x$.

Market price of a goods

$= 1000x\left(\dfrac{100 + 50}{100}\right) = 1000x \times \dfrac{150}{100}$

$= 1500x$

SP of a goods $= 1500x\left(\dfrac{100 - 20}{100}\right)$

$= 1500x \times \dfrac{80}{100} = 1200x$

Dealer using weight = $900x$

CP = $900x$

$P = SP - CP = 1200x - 900x = 300x$

$P\% = \dfrac{P}{CP} \times 100\% = \dfrac{300x}{900x} \times 100\%$

$= 33.33\% \approx 33\%$

Speedy Method

CP	SP	MP
100	120	150
900 gm	1000 gm	
90000	120000	
90	120	

$\therefore$ Required profit percentage

$= \dfrac{120 - 90}{90} \times 100 = 33.33\% \approx 33\%$

39. (d) Required single discount

$= 100 - \left(\frac{100 \times 88 \times 82 \times 75}{100 \times 100 \times 100}\right)$

$= 100 - 54.12 = 45.88\%$

40. (c) Let the marked price of a bike ₹ x.

According to the question,

$x \times \left(\frac{100-44}{100}\right) = 87500$

$\Rightarrow \quad x \times \frac{56}{100} = 87500$

$\Rightarrow \quad x = \frac{87500 \times 100}{56} \Rightarrow x = ₹156250$

41. (b) Let the list price be ₹ x.

Then, $x - \frac{x \times 20}{100} = ₹ 54000$

$\Rightarrow \quad \frac{80x}{100} = 54000$

$\Rightarrow \quad x = \frac{54000 \times 100}{80}$

$\Rightarrow \quad x = ₹ 67500$

42. (d) Let labelled price = ₹ x

According to the question,

$x \times \frac{88}{100} \times \frac{75}{100} = 792$

$\Rightarrow \quad x = \frac{792 \times 100 \times 100}{88 \times 75}$

$\Rightarrow \quad x = ₹ 1200$

Speedy Method

Equivalent discount $= 25 + 12 - \frac{25 \times 12}{100} = 34\%$

Let labelled price of radio = 100%

∴ Selling price = 100 − 34 = 66%

∵ 66% → 792

∴ 100% → $\frac{792}{66} \times 100 = ₹1200$

43. (a) Discount in first case

$= \left[5 + 5 - \frac{5 \times 5}{100}\right]\% = [10 - 0.25]\% = 9.75\%$

Discount in second case = 10%

Discount in third case $= \left[8 + 2 - \frac{8 \times 2}{100}\right]\%$

$= [10 - 0.16]\% = 9.84\%$

∴ In second case he will get maximum discount.

44. (d) Let CP = ₹ 100

At 30% profit, SP = ₹130

At 18% discount (D),

$SP = MP \times \frac{(100 - D\%)}{100}$

$\Rightarrow MP = \frac{SP \times 100}{100 - D\%} = \frac{130 \times 100}{100 - 18} = ₹\frac{13000}{82}$

Now, at 12% discount,

$SP = \frac{13000}{82} \times \frac{(100-12)}{100} = \frac{130 \times 88}{82} = ₹139.51$

So, profit percentage

$= \frac{139.51 - 100}{100} \times 100\% = 39.51\%$

45. (b) ∴ Required discount%

$= \frac{15990 - 12792}{15990} \times 100 = 20\%$

46. (d) Let the amount of the bill = ₹ x

According to the question,

$\frac{x \times (100-40)}{100} - \frac{x \times (100-30) \times (100-30)}{100 \times 100} = 220$

$\Rightarrow \quad \frac{60x}{100} - \frac{49x}{100} = 220 \Rightarrow 11x = 22000$

$\Rightarrow \quad x = ₹2000$

Speedy Method

Equivalent discount of two successive discount of 30% each

$= 30 + 30 - \frac{30 \times 30}{100} = 51\%$

An other discount = 40%

Difference = 51 − 40 = 11%

11% = 220

$\Rightarrow \quad 100\% = \frac{220 \times 100}{11} = ₹ 2000$

47. (d) Equivalent of two successive discounts of 36% and 4%

$= 36 + 4 - \frac{36 \times 4}{100} = 40 - \frac{144}{100}$

Difference $= 40 - 40 + \frac{144}{100} = \frac{144}{100}\%$

∴ Difference $= 50000 \times \frac{144}{10000} = ₹ 720$

48. (d) Equivalent of two successive discount of 30% and 30% $= -30 - 30 + \frac{30 \times 30}{100}$

$= -60 + 9 = -51\%$

Another is 50% discount.

Difference = 51 − 50 = 1% → ₹ 43

100% → ₹ 4300

∴ The cost of the shirt = ₹ 4300

49. (b) Let CP of goods be ₹100.

∴ MP of goods = ₹140

Discount allowed = 10%

∴ SP of goods $= 140 \times \frac{90}{100} = ₹126$

∴ Profit percentage $= \frac{26}{100} \times 100 = 26\%$

50. (d) Equivalent discount%

$= \left[9 + 17 - \frac{9 \times 17}{100}\right]\%$

$= (26 - 1.53)\% = 24.47\%$

51. (b) Let marked price = 100 unit

SP = 100 − 22 = 78 unit

Gains $= 20\% = \frac{1}{5}$

Now, CP $= \frac{100}{100 + 20} \times 78$

$CP = \frac{78}{6} \times 5 = 65$ unit

∵ 65 unit → 650

∴ 100 unit → 1000

∴ Marked price of his goods = ₹ 1000

52. (d) Single discount equivalent to three successive discounts

$= \left[1 - \left(1 - \frac{r_1}{100}\right)\left(1 - \frac{r_2}{100}\right)\left(1 - \frac{r_3}{100}\right)\right] \times 100\%$

where, r_1, r_2, r_3 are successive discounts.

∴ Single discount equivalent to

$= \left[1 - \left(1 - \frac{1}{4}\right)\left(1 - \frac{1}{4}\right)\left(1 - \frac{1}{4}\right)\right] \times 100\%$

$= \frac{64 - 27}{64} \times 100\% = \frac{37}{64} \times 100\% = 57.81\%$

53. (c) Successive discount $5\% = \frac{1}{20}$,

$10\% = \frac{1}{10}$, $P\% = \frac{P}{100}$

MP	SP
20	19
10	9
100	100 − P
2000	171(100 − P)

Discount = 20000 − 17100 + 171P

= 2900 + 171P

Discount % $= \frac{2900 + 171P}{20000} \times 100$

$= \frac{2900 + 171P}{200}\%$

$\frac{2900 + 171P}{200} = 31.6 \Rightarrow \frac{2900 + 171P}{20} = 316$

$\Rightarrow \quad 171P = 6320 - 2900$

$\Rightarrow \quad P = \frac{3420}{171} = 20$

∴ Value of $P = 20$

54. (a) For Scheme A,

Total discount % $= \frac{4}{6 + 4} \times 100$

$= \frac{4}{10} \times 100 = 40\%$

For Scheme B,

Total discount % $= \frac{5}{5 + 5} \times 100$

$= \frac{5}{10} \times 100 = 50\%$

For scheme C,

Total discount % $= \left(x + y - \frac{xy}{100}\right)\%$

$= \left(18 + 24 - \frac{18 \times 24}{100}\right)\%$

$= 42 - 4.32 = 37.68\%$

Hence, Scheme B has maximum discount.

55. (d) Discount = 4500 − 2400 = ₹ 2100

Discount % $= \frac{2100}{4500} \times 100 = \frac{140}{3}\%$

One of two successive discount is 20%.

Let the other one is x%

$20 + x - \frac{20x}{100} = \frac{140}{3}$

$\Rightarrow \quad \frac{5x - x}{5} = \frac{140 - 60}{3} \Rightarrow 4x = \frac{80 \times 5}{3}$

$\Rightarrow \quad x = \frac{100}{3} = 33\frac{1}{3}\%$

∴ The second discount $= 33\frac{1}{3}\%$

56. (b) Let the CP be ₹ 100 x.
then, MP = ₹ 160 x
If he give successive discount
$= 160x \times \left(10 + 20 - \frac{200}{100}\right)\%$
$= 160x \times \frac{28}{100} = ₹\ 44.8x$
Then SP = $160x - 44.8x = ₹\ 115.2x$
According to the question,
$115.2x - 100x = 1064$
$\Rightarrow \quad 15.2x = 1064$
$\Rightarrow \quad 100x = \frac{1064}{15.2} \times 100 = ₹\ 7000$

57. (a) Selling price $= 9400 \times \frac{96}{100} = ₹\ 9024$

58. (a) Let the MP of his goods = ₹ 100x
Discount = 10%
Gain = 20%
$\therefore$ SP = $90x$
$\therefore$ CP $= 90x \times \frac{100}{120} = 75x$
$\therefore$ CP : MP = $75x : 100x = 3 : 4$

59. (d) Given, CP of saree = ₹ 500
If marked at 16% profit $= \frac{16}{100} = \frac{4}{25}$
Then, SP $= 500 \times \frac{29}{25} = ₹\ 580$
But after discount, SP = ₹ 493
Let discount = x%
Then, $580 \times \left(\frac{100 - x}{100}\right) = 493$
$\Rightarrow \quad 5800 - 58x = 4930$
$\Rightarrow \quad 58x = 5800 - 4930$
$\Rightarrow \quad x = \frac{870}{58} = 15\%$

60. (a) Marked price of the machine
$= 9000 \times \frac{110}{100} \times \frac{100}{90} = ₹\ 11000$

61. (a) Selling Price (SP) after discount
$= 1000 \times \frac{100 - 12}{100} \times \frac{100 - 8}{100}$
$= 1000 \times \frac{88}{100} \times \frac{92}{100}$
$= 809.6 \approx ₹810$ (approx.)

62. (a) Given, amount = ₹ 3600
After discount $= 3600 \times \frac{(100 - 35)}{100} = ₹\ 2340$
After successive discount
$= 3600 \times \frac{70}{100} \times \frac{95}{100} = ₹\ 2394$
Hence, required difference
$= (2394 - 2340) = ₹\ 54$

63. (a) Shopkeeper offers flat discount on ₹ 10000 is ₹ 500.
Then, price of article = ₹ 9500
Additional discount $= 9500 \times \frac{93}{100} = ₹8835$

64. (b) On scheme (A),
Discount % $= 100 - \frac{100 \times 90}{100} \times \frac{85}{100} = 100 - 76.5$
$= 23.5\%$
On scheme (B),
Discount % $= \frac{2}{2 + 5} \times 100 = 28.57\%$
Hence, scheme B has maximum discount percentage.

65. (a) Let marked price of machine = ₹ x
According to the question,
$x \times \frac{85}{100} = 29750$
$\therefore \quad x = \frac{29750 \times 100}{85} = ₹\ 35000$
If no discount is allowed.
Then, selling price of machine = ₹ 35000
Now, profit = 12%
Then, cost price of machine
$= \frac{35000 \times 100}{112} = ₹\ 31250$

66. (d) Let the CP of an article be ₹ 100.
Then, for scheme (i),
SP $= 100 \times \frac{85}{100} \times \frac{85}{100} = ₹72.25$
For scheme (ii),
SP $= 100 \times \frac{75}{100} \times \frac{95}{100} = ₹71.25$
For scheme (iii),
SP $= 100 \times \frac{80}{100} \times \frac{90}{100} = ₹72$
For scheme (iv),
SP $= 100 \times \frac{70}{100} = ₹70$
Hence, maximum SP for scheme (i).

67. (b) $\therefore$ Net discount equivalent to there successive discounts
$= \left(1 - \frac{85}{100} \times \frac{80}{100} \times \frac{75}{100}\right) \times 100\%$
$= \left(\frac{1000000 - 510000}{1000000}\right) \times 100\%$
$= \frac{490000}{1000000} \times 100\% = 49\%$

Speedy Method

MP	:	SP	
20	:	17	(–15%)
5	:	4	(–20%)
4	:	3	(–25%)
100	:	51	

–49
Net discount = 49%

68. (d) Given, a trader allows 20% trade discount and 30% cash discount
The list price = ₹ 1200
$\therefore$ Selling price (SP) $= 1200 \times \frac{80}{100} \times \frac{70}{100} = ₹\ 672$

69. (b) Equivalent of two successive discount
$= \left(20 + 25 - \frac{20 \times 25}{100}\right)\% = 40\%$
For 1 reward point customer gets ₹ 0.10.
For 2850 reward point he gets
$= 0.10 \times 2850 = ₹\ 285$
Marked price = 72000
At 40% discount,
$\therefore$ Selling price $= 72000 \times \frac{60}{100} - 285$
$= 43200 - 285 = ₹\ 42915$

70. (b) On Scheme A
Discount% $= \frac{4}{3 + 4} \times 100 = \frac{4}{7} \times 100 = 57.14\%$
On Scheme B
Discount% $= \frac{6}{6 + 5} \times 100 = \frac{6}{11} \times 100 = 54.54\%$
Hence, Scheme A has the maximum discount percentage.

71. (c) Let CP of oil be ₹ 100.
$\therefore \quad$ MP of oil $= 100 \times \frac{125}{100} = ₹\ 125$
$\because$ No profit and no loss when it be sold.
$\therefore \quad$ SP = CP = 100
Required percentage $= \frac{MP - SP}{MP} \times 100$
$= \frac{125 - 100}{125} \times 100 = 20\%$

72. (b) We know that,
SP $= MP \times \left(\frac{100 - \text{Discount\%}}{100}\right)$
$= CP \times \left(\frac{100 + \text{Profit\%}}{100}\right)$
$\Rightarrow MP \times \frac{88}{100} = 528 \times \frac{118}{100}$
$\therefore \quad MP = \frac{528 \times 118}{88} = ₹708$

73. (b) Marked price of juicer = ₹ 3000
$\therefore$ Sita pays $= 3000 \times \frac{80}{100} \times \frac{95}{100} = ₹\ 2280$

74. (a) CP of the article = ₹4000
SP $= 8400 \times \frac{75}{100} \times \frac{85}{100} = ₹5355$
$\therefore$ Profit per cent $= \frac{5355 - 4000}{4000} \times 100$
= 33.87% = 34% (in nearest integer).

75. (b) Total cost of shirts Raghav bought
$= 1250 + 1540 + 1375 = ₹4165$
When he applies first coupon, total amount paid by him $= 4165 \times \frac{(100 - 30)}{100} = ₹2915.5$
When he applies second coupon, total amount paid by him
$= (1250 + 1375 + 1540 \times \frac{20}{100})$
$= ₹\ 2933$

∴ He will apply first coupon only since he pays the minimum amount on that.

∴ Minimum price paid by him = ₹ 2915.5

76. (a) At 10% first discount,

Selling price = (100 – 10)% of ₹ 14500

$= ₹\ \frac{90}{100} \times 14500 = ₹\ 13050$

Let the second discount = x%

Then, x% of 13050 = (13050 – 10000)

$\Rightarrow \frac{x}{100} \times 13050 = 3050$

$\Rightarrow x = \frac{3050 \times 100}{13050} = 23.37\%$

77. (b) Total cost of packets of biscuits

= 25 × 30 = ₹ 750

Since, cost of biscuits is above ₹ 500, so customer will got discount of 10% and an additional 1% discount for paying cash.

∴ Customer will pay

$= 750 \times \frac{(100-10)}{100} \times \frac{(100-1)}{100}$

$= \frac{750 \times 90 \times 99}{10000} = ₹668.25$

78. (a) According to the question,

$\text{Cost price} = 400 \times \frac{80}{100} \times \frac{100}{125} = ₹256$

79. (a) Given, marked price of the fan

= ₹ 1285

According to the question,

Selling price

$= (1285 - 85) \times \frac{90}{100} \times \frac{98}{100} = ₹\ 1058.4$

80. (a) Here, $d_1 = 10\%, d_2 = 10\%, d_3 = 10\%$

∴ Single discount

$= \left[1 - \left(1 - \frac{d_1}{100}\right)\left(1 - \frac{d_2}{100}\right)\left(1 - \frac{d_3}{100}\right)\right] \times 100\%$

$= \left[1 - \left(1 - \frac{10}{100}\right)\left(1 - \frac{10}{100}\right)\left(1 - \frac{10}{100}\right)\right] \times 100\%$

$= \left[1 - \frac{90 \times 90 \times 90}{1000000}\right] \times 100\%$

= [1 – 0.729] × 100% = 0.271 × 100%

= 27.1%

81. (c) SP of the packet

$= \frac{2800 \times 55 \times 75}{100 \times 100} = 1155$

∴ Customer has to pay ₹ 1155 in cash to avail both discounts.

82. (c) Let the cost of each article = $100x$

Marked price = (100 + 20)% of $100x = 120x$

At 10% discount, selling price

= (100 – 10)% of $120x$

$= \frac{90}{100} \times 120x = 108x$

$\therefore \text{Gain percentage} = \frac{108x - 100x}{100x} \times 100\%$

= 8%

83. (a) Let the cost price be ₹ x.

According to the question, Marked price

= ₹ $1.15x$

$\text{Selling price} = 1.15x \times \frac{95}{100} = 1.0925x$

$\therefore \text{Profit percentage} = \frac{(1.0925x - x)}{x} \times 100$

= 9.25%

84. (d) $\text{SP of skirt} = \frac{70}{100} \times ₹800 = ₹560$

85. (c) Here, the student bought 1 book sc he will get discount of 10% and additional 5% discount which is given to students.

Here, SP = ₹ 513

$\therefore \text{SP} = \text{MP} \times \frac{(100 - d_1)}{100} \times \frac{(100 - d_2)}{100}$

$\Rightarrow 513 = \text{MP} \times \frac{(100-10)}{100} \times \frac{(100-5)}{100}$

$\Rightarrow \text{MP} = \frac{513 \times 100 \times 100}{90 \times 95} = ₹600$

86. (d) Price of each product = ₹ 500

⇒ Price of five such products = ₹ 500 × 5

= ₹ 2500

∴ Price customer has to pay after 5% discount

$= ₹\ 2500 \times \frac{95}{100} = ₹\ 2375$

Since, amount after discount is ₹ 2375, so customer will get additional 10% discount.

Hence, final amount customer has to pay

$= ₹\ 2375 \times \frac{90}{100} = ₹\ 2137.5$

87. (d) Money paid to Rohan by Ankith

$= 55000 \times \frac{(100-15)}{100} = 55000 \times \frac{85}{100} = ₹\ 46750$

88. (b) Price of article after successive

$\text{discounts} = 3000 \times \left(\frac{100-15}{100}\right) \times \left(\frac{100-15}{100}\right)$

$= ₹\ 3000 \times \frac{85}{100} \times \frac{85}{100} = ₹\ 2167.5$

Total price of article after adding transportation cost

= ₹(2167.5 + 250) = ₹ 2417.5

$\therefore \text{Selling price} = \left(\frac{100+20}{100}\right) \times 2417.5 = ₹\ 2901$

89. (a) Out of (12 + 3 = 15) coconuts a person has to pay only for 12 coconuts.

Discount = 3 coconuts

$\text{Discount percent} = \frac{3}{15} \times 100\% = 20\%$

90. (a) $\text{Required discount \%} = \frac{90-68}{90} \times 100$

$= \frac{2200}{90} = 24.44\%$

91. (c) I. Equivalent discount of two successive discounts of 10 % each

$= \left(10 + 10 - \frac{10 \times 10}{100}\right)\%$

= (20 – 1)% = 19%

II. Equivalent discount of 15 % and 5 %

$= \left(15 + 5 - \frac{15 \times 5}{100}\right)\% = (20 - 0.75)\% = 19.25\%$

III. 20% discount

∴ Only discount scheme III has maximum discount percentage.

92. (a) Rent on 1 day of 2 rooms

= 2 × 1500 = ₹3000

Amount to pay after discount for 2 rooms and discount to payment by SBI card

$= 3000 \times \frac{100-12}{100} \times \frac{100-5}{100}$

$= 3000 \times \frac{88}{100} \times \frac{95}{100} = ₹2508$

93. (c) Let MP of the watch be ₹x.

According to the question,

$\Rightarrow \frac{88x}{100} - \frac{76x}{100} = 2400$

$\Rightarrow \frac{12x}{100} = 2400$

$\Rightarrow x = \frac{2400 \times 100}{12} \Rightarrow x = ₹20000$

94. (a) Let the discount be x%.

According to the question,

Raju's gained the discount

$\text{Then, } 10927 \times \frac{(100-x)}{100} = \frac{10927 \times 100}{(100 + 11.5)}$

$\Rightarrow \frac{100-x}{100} = \frac{200}{223}$

$\Rightarrow 22300 - 223x = 20000$

$\Rightarrow 223x = 2300$

$\Rightarrow x = 10.3\%$

95. (a) Marked price = ₹2750

Overall discount = ₹(2750 – 2103.75)

= ₹646.25

First discount = 10 % of 2750

$= \frac{10}{100} \times 2750 = 275$

At 10% first discount,

Selling price = ₹(2750 – 275) = ₹2475

Let the second discount = x%.

Then, x% of 2475 = 646.25 – 275

$\Rightarrow \frac{x}{100} \times 2475 = 371.25$

$\Rightarrow x = \frac{371.25 \times 100}{2475} = 15\%$

96. (d) Let the labelled price = ₹ x

According to the question,

(15 – 10)% of x = 400

$\Rightarrow \frac{5}{100} \times x = 400$

$\Rightarrow x = \frac{400 \times 100}{5} = ₹\ 8000$

97. (b) Let the marked price of laptop be ₹x.

Then, $x\times\left(\frac{100-25}{100}\right)=65520$

$\Rightarrow \quad x\times\frac{75}{100}=65520$

$\Rightarrow \quad x=\frac{65520\times100}{75}\Rightarrow x=₹87360$

98. (b) Equivalent discount

$=\left(15+5-\frac{15\times5}{100}\right)\%=19.25\%$

99. (b) Let the marked price of the article be ₹ x.

According to the question,

Selling price of the article $=x\times\frac{90}{100}\times\frac{80}{100}$

$=0.72x$

Since, there is the profit of 44%.

∴ Cost price of the article

$=\frac{0.72x\times100}{144}=0.5x$

Selling price at 15% discount

$=x\times\frac{(100-15)}{100}=₹\,0.85x$

∴ Profit% $=\frac{(0.85x-0.5x)}{0.5x}\times100$

$=\frac{350}{5}\%=70\%$

100. (b) Marked price of the product = ₹ 3840

When, discount = 30%

∴ Selling price of the product

$=3840\times\frac{70}{100}=₹\,2688$

When two successive discounts of 25% and 5% given

∴ Selling price of the product

$=3840\times\frac{75}{100}\times\frac{95}{100}=₹\,2736$

∴ Required difference = 2736 − 2688 = ₹ 48

101. (d) Given, CP = ₹ 920, MP = ₹ 1472

Profit per cent = 20%

Gain always count on CP

Selling price = Cost price $\times\left[\frac{100+\text{Profit\%}}{100}\right]$

$=920\times\frac{120}{100}=₹1104$

Discount = MP − SP = 1472 − 1104 = ₹368

Discount per cent or $x\%=\frac{368}{1472}\times100=25\%.$

102. (b) According to the question,

Two successive discount of 20% and 5%.

$=20+5-\frac{20\times5}{100}=25-1=24\%$

Discount given by A is 320 more then B

$\Rightarrow$ 25% − 24% → 320

$\Rightarrow$ 1% → 320

100% → 32000

Marked price of item is ₹ 32000.

103. (a) According to the question,

25% discount $=10000\times\frac{25}{100}=₹\,2500$

Now, 14% and 12% succesive discount

$=14+12-\frac{14\times12}{100}$

$=26-1.68=24.32\%$

Now, 24.32 discount $=10000\times\frac{24.32}{100}=₹\,2432$

∴ 25% discount is better offer by

= ₹ (2500 − 2432) = ₹ 68.

104. (b) Suppose MP of item = ₹100.

Discount = 10%

$\text{SP}=100\times\frac{90}{100}=₹\,90$

According to the question,

120% of CP = SP $\Rightarrow\frac{120}{100}\times\text{CP}=90$

CP = ₹ 75

If discount is not given then selling price will be ₹100.

∴ Profit per cent $=\frac{100-75}{75}\times100=\frac{25}{75}\times100$

$=33.33\%$

105. (d) Let marked price = ₹ x

According to the question,

$1680\times\frac{125}{100}=x\times\frac{84}{100}$

∴ $=₹\,2500$

106. (c) Let CP is ₹ 100.

$\text{MP}=100\times\frac{127}{100}=₹\,127$

According to the question,

$100\times\left(\frac{100+6.68}{100}\right)=127\times\left(\frac{100-x}{100}\right)$

$\Rightarrow \quad 106.68=\frac{127}{100}\times(100-x)$

$\Rightarrow \quad 84=100-x\Rightarrow x=16\%$

107. (a) According to the question,

MP of the item $=2394\times\frac{100}{90}\times\frac{100}{95}=₹\,2800$

∴ CP of the item $=2800\times\frac{100}{125}=₹\,2240$

108. (a) $\text{SP}=1500\times\frac{80}{100}=₹1200$

CP = ₹991 (given)

∴ Profit = (SP − CP) = 1200 − 991 = ₹ 209

109. (d) Marked price = ₹ 1800

At 16% discount, SP $=\frac{1800\times84}{100}=₹1512$

He get 8% profit of CP,

Let CP = ₹ $x\Rightarrow x\times\frac{108}{100}=1512$

$\Rightarrow \quad x=\frac{1512\times100}{108}=1400$

CP = ₹ 1400

If discount is 8% instead of 16%.

Then, SP $=\frac{1800\times92}{100}=1656$

Profit per cent $=\frac{(1656-1400)}{1400}\times100$

$=18.29\%$

110. (c) Given, MP = ₹ 10000, $d_1=20\%$, $d_2=10\%$, $d_3=k\%$

∴ $\text{MP}\times\frac{(100-d_1)}{100}\times\frac{(100-d_2)}{100}\times\frac{(100-d_3)}{100}=6120$

$\Rightarrow 10000\times\frac{(100-20)}{100}\times\frac{(100-10)}{100}\times\frac{(100-k)}{100}=6120$

$\Rightarrow \quad 80\times90\times\frac{(100-k)}{100}=6120$

$\Rightarrow \quad 100-k=\frac{6120}{72}=85$

∴ $\quad k=100-85=15\%$

Now, discount

$=(k+20)\%=(15+20)\%=35\%$

∴ Required SP $=10000\times\frac{(100-35)}{100}=100\times65$

$=₹\,6500$

111. (d) Let CP = 100

$\text{MP}=100\times\frac{130}{100}=130$

$\text{SP}=130\times\frac{90}{100}=117$

If he want 6.5% more profit that means new profit %

$=\frac{117-100}{100}\times100+6.5=17\%+6.5\%=23.5\%$

$\text{SP}=100\times\frac{123.5}{100}=123.5$

∴ Discount per cent $=\frac{130-123.5}{130}\times100$

$=\frac{6.5}{130}\times100=5\%$

112. (a) Let x is cost price.

$\Rightarrow x\times\frac{(100+\%\text{ gain})}{100}=342\times\frac{(100-\%\text{ discount})}{100}$

$\Rightarrow x\times\frac{100+14}{100}=342\times\frac{(100-32)}{100}$

$\Rightarrow \quad x\times114=342\times68$

$\Rightarrow \quad x=3\times68=₹\,204$

The value of cost price is ₹ 204.

113. (c) Let the cost price of table be ₹ x.

According to the question,

$x\times\frac{108}{100}=7200\times\frac{90}{100}\Rightarrow x=7200\times\frac{90}{108}$

$\Rightarrow \quad x=₹\,6000$

The gain percent, if he does not allow any discount.

CP = ₹ 6000, SP = ₹ 7200

∴ Profit per cent $=\frac{(7200-6000)}{6000}\times100$

$=\frac{1200}{6000}\times100=20\%$

114. (a) Market price of article is ₹ 888.

$\text{SP}=888\times\left(\frac{100-22}{100}\right)=888\times\frac{78}{100}$

Now, $CP = SP\left[\frac{100}{100+P\%}\right]$

$= 888 \times \frac{78}{100} \times \left[\frac{100}{100+11}\right]$

$= 888 \times \frac{78}{100} \times \frac{100}{111} = ₹624$

115. (c) Cost price of dining table = ₹11900

Selling price $= 11900 \times \frac{120}{100} = ₹\ 14280$

∴ Marked price of dining table

$= 14280 \times \frac{100}{84} = ₹\ 17000$

116. (c) Let CP of article be ₹ 100.

Then, Marked price of article

$= 100 \times \frac{125}{100} = ₹125$

Selling price $= 100 \times \frac{92}{100} = ₹\ 92$

∴ Discount % $= \frac{125-92}{125} \times 100 = 26.4\%$

117. (b) Let SP of 1 kg rice = ₹ 1

⇒ SP of 80 kg rice = 80

CP of 80 kg rice = 80 × 90 / 100

= 72 (∵ 10% discount)

Rice got free on 80 kg = 4 kg

Total rice = 80 + 4 = 84 kg

Total SP of rice = ₹84

∴ Profit % $= \frac{(84-72)}{72} \times 100 = 16\frac{2}{3}\%$

118. (a) Let the cost price of the article is ₹ 100 and the marked price of the article is ₹ x.

We know the formula,

$\frac{\text{Marked price}}{\text{Cost price}} = \frac{100 \pm r}{100 - D}$

[r = rate of profit or loss, D = rate of discount]

According to the question,

$r = 8\%, D = 10\%$

$\Rightarrow \frac{x}{100} = \frac{100+8}{100-10}$

$\Rightarrow \frac{x}{100} = \frac{108}{90}$

$\Rightarrow x = \frac{108 \times 100}{90} = ₹\ 120$

∴The ratio of the cost price to marked price

= 100 : 120 = 5 : 6

119. (c) Let the cost price (CP) be ₹x.

Given, marked price (MP) of item = ₹500

According to the question,

Selling price (SP) $= \left[500 - \left(\frac{25}{100} \times 500\right) - 65\right]$

= (500 – 125 – 65) = ₹ 310

Also, cost price = SP $- \frac{24}{100}$ (CP)

$\Rightarrow x = 310 - \frac{24}{100}x$

$\Rightarrow x\left(1 + \frac{24}{100}\right) = 310$

$\Rightarrow x = \frac{310 \times 100}{124} = ₹\ 250$

120. (d) Let the cost price be ₹x.

Given, marked price = ₹420

Selling price $= 420 - 420 \times \frac{10}{100} = ₹378$

According to the question,

$378 = x + \frac{20x}{100}$

$\Rightarrow 378 = \frac{120}{100}x \Rightarrow x = \frac{378 \times 100}{120}$

∴ $x = ₹315$

∴ Cost price of dairy products = ₹315

121. (d) Successive discount are 40% and 20%.

Equivalent discount

$=(-40)+(-20)+\frac{(-40)(-20)}{100}$

$= -60 + \frac{800}{100} = -60 + 8 = -52\%$

∴The single equivalent discount = 52%

122. (c) Let the MP be ₹ 100.

Now, SP $= 100 \times \frac{76}{100} \times \frac{70}{100} = ₹\ 53.2$

When the final SP is ₹ 53.2, then MP is ₹ 100.

When the final SP is ₹ 7700.7, then MP

$= \frac{100}{53.2} \times 7700.7 = ₹\ 14475$

123. (c) Marked price of product = ₹ 2000

Selling price of product after three successive discounts of 10% each

$= 2000 \times \frac{90}{100} \times \frac{90}{100} \times \frac{90}{100} = ₹\ 1458$

Selling price of product after a single discount of 28% is $= ₹\ 2000 - 2000 \times \frac{28}{100}$

= ₹ 1440

∴Difference = ₹ 1458 – 1440 = ₹ 18

124. (c) Equivalent discount of d_1% and d_2%

$= \left(d_1 + d_2 - \frac{d_1 d_2}{100}\right)\%$

$\Rightarrow 23.5\% = \left(15 + x - \frac{15x}{100}\right)\%$

$\Rightarrow 23.5 = 15 + \frac{100x - 15x}{100}$

$\Rightarrow (23.5 - 15) \times 100 = 85x$

$\Rightarrow x = \frac{8.5 \times 100}{85} = 10\%$

125. (c) According to the question,

Cost price of the item

$= 500 \times \frac{90}{100} \times \frac{80}{100} \times \frac{100}{125} = ₹\ 288$

126. (d) Selling price = (100 – 18)% × 5980

= 82% × 5980 = ₹ 4904

127. (c) Selling price = 110% of ₹1200

$= \frac{110}{100} \times 1200 = ₹1320$

Now, Marked price × 90%

= Selling price + Cashback

$\Rightarrow$ Marked price $\times \frac{90}{100} = 1320 + 250$

⇒ Marked price (tag price)

$= ₹1570 \times \frac{100}{90} = ₹1744.44$

128. (c) Discount of 40% on ₹ 1000

$= 1000 \times \frac{60}{100}$

= ₹600 will be the selling price.

Now, net discount after two successive discounts of 36% and 4%

$= \left(x + y - \frac{xy}{100}\right)\% = \left(36 + 4 - \frac{36 \times 4}{100}\right)\%$

= 40 – 1.44 = 38.56 %

∴ Selling price = 61.44% of ₹ 1000 = ₹ 614.4

Hence, the required difference

= (614.4 – 600) = ₹ 14.40

129. (a) Marked price = ₹ 38/kg

Discount = 12% on 10 kg sugar

∴ Selling price of 1 kg $= \frac{MP \times 88\%}{\frac{900}{1000}}$

$= \frac{38 \times \frac{88}{100}}{0.9} = \frac{38 \times \frac{22}{25}}{0.9} = ₹\ 37.15$

Now, cost price = ₹ 30/kg

∴ Profit per cent $= \frac{(37.15 - 30)}{30} \times 100$

$= \frac{7.15 \times 100}{30} = 23.85\%$

130. (d) Total bill = Cost of shirt + Cost of jacket

= (₹ 900 + 9% of 900) + (₹ 1900 + 6% of ₹ 1900)

= ₹ 981 + ₹ 2014 = ₹ 2995 i.e., below ₹ 3000

Hence, a discount of 12% will be given.

∴ Amount that Anand had to pay

$= 88\%$ of ₹ 2995 $= \frac{88}{100} \times 2995$

= ₹ 2635.60

131. (a) Marked price = 1600 + 130% of 1600

= 1600 + 2080 = ₹ 3680

∴Selling price = 75% of 3680

$= \frac{3}{4} \times 3680 = ₹\ 2760$

132. (b) ∴Net discount percentage

$= 10 + 10 - \frac{10 \times 10}{100}$

= 20 – 1 = 19%

Now, selling price = (100 – 19)% of marked price

⇒ Marked price $= \frac{7290 \times 100}{81} = ₹\ 9000$

133. (b) Given, Marked price of doll = ₹2500

First discount = 10%

Let the second discount = x%

Now, according to the question,

2500 × 90% × (100 – x)% = ₹1800

$\Rightarrow 2500 \times \frac{90}{100} \times \frac{(100-x)}{100} = 1800$

$\Rightarrow 2500 \times \frac{9}{10} \times \frac{(100-x)}{100} = 1800$

$\Rightarrow (100-x) = 80 \Rightarrow x = 20\%$

134. (c) Let the cost price (CP) be ₹100.

∴ Marked price (MP) = ₹135

Now, discount = 15%

∴ $MP \times 85\% = SP \Rightarrow 135 \times \frac{85}{100} = SP$

SP = ₹114.75

∴ $\text{Profit }\% = \frac{114.75 - 100}{100} \times 100$

$= 14.75\% = 14\frac{3}{4}\%$

Speedy Method

$35\% = \frac{7}{20}$ and $15\% = \frac{3}{20}$

CP		SP
20	:	27
20	:	17
400	:	459

$\text{Profit}\% = \frac{459-400}{400} \times 100 = \frac{59}{400} \times 100$

$= 14\frac{3}{4}\%$

135. (b) Successive discount for 10% and 20%

$= 10 + 20 - \frac{10 \times 20}{100}$

$= 30 - 2 = 28\%$

Now, successive discount for 28% and 20%

$= 28 + 20 - \frac{28 \times 20}{100}$

$= 48 - 5.6 = 42.4\%$

Speedy Method

MP		SP
10	:	9
10	:	8
10	:	8
1000	:	576

$\text{Single Discount}\% = \frac{1000-576}{1000} \times 100 = 42.4\%$

136. (a) Let Remanna purchased 100 kg of raw materials for ₹ 100.

Now, 22.5% of it got wasted.

∴ Remaining raw material

$= 100 - 22.5 = 77.5$ kg

Now, According to the question,

$80\% \text{ of } 77.5 = \frac{80}{100} \times 77.5 = 62$

So, ₹ 62 was added as the cost of manufacturing.

Total cost = 100 + 62 = ₹ 162

Now, 120% of 162 = 80% of marked price (MP)

$\Rightarrow \frac{6}{5} \times 162 = \frac{4}{5} \times MP \Rightarrow$ M.P = ₹ 243

Now, 243 = 2.43 times of 100.

137. (a) (A) Successive discounts

$= 24 + 27 - \frac{24 \times 27}{100} = 44.52\%$

(B) Buy 5 get 3 free

$\text{Discount percentage} = \frac{\text{Free}}{\text{Total}} \times 100$

$= \frac{3}{(5+3)} \times 100 = \frac{3}{8} \times 100 = 37.5\%$

(C) Buy 6 and get 10 which means buy 6 get 4 free.

Discount Percentage

$= \frac{4}{(6+4)} \times 100 = \frac{4}{10} \times 100 = 40\%$

∴ Scheme 'B' will give minimum discount percentage.

138. (c) Let the marked price of the article = x

According to the question,

$10800 = x \times \frac{100-25}{100} \times \frac{100-28}{100}$

$\Rightarrow x = \frac{10800 \times 100 \times 100}{75 \times 72}$

$\Rightarrow x =$ ₹ 20000

139. (a) Using formula,

$MP \times \frac{(100 - D_1\%)}{100} \times \frac{(100 - D_2\%)}{100} \times \frac{(100 - D_3\%)}{100} = SP$

$SP = 15000 \times \frac{(100-5)}{100} \times \frac{(100-10)}{100} \times \frac{(100-20)}{100}$

$SP = 15000 \times \frac{95}{100} \times \frac{90}{100} \times \frac{80}{100} =$ ₹ 10260

140. (b) $\frac{CP}{MP} = \frac{100 - D\%}{100 + P\%}$

$\frac{450}{\text{Marked price}} = \frac{(100-10)}{(100+30)} = \frac{90}{130}$

$\text{Marked price} = \frac{13}{9} \times 450 =$ ₹650

141. (b) Single discount $= 700 \times \frac{35}{100} =$ ₹ 245

Now, successive discounts

$= 18 + 12 - \frac{18 \times 12}{100}\%$

$= 30 - 2.16 = 27.84\%$

So, discount $= 700 \times \frac{27.84}{100} =$ ₹194.88

Difference = 245 − 194.88 = ₹ 50.12

142. (c) Discount% = $y\%$

$= \frac{MP - SP}{MP} \times 100 = \frac{3800 - 3496}{3800} \times 100$

$MP = \frac{304}{3800} \times 100 = 8\%$

143. (d) Let CP of article = ₹ 100

$MP = 100 + 100 \times \frac{70}{100} =$ ₹ 170

$\text{Net discount} = x + y - \frac{xy}{100}$

$= 20 + 5 - \frac{20 \times 5}{100} = 24\%$

And again 20% additional discount on cash payment then net discount

$= 24 + 20 - \frac{24 \times 20}{100} = 44 - 4.8 = 39.2\%$

Now, SP of article $= 170 \times \left(\frac{100 - 39.2}{100}\right)$

= ₹ 103.36

Then, profit $= \frac{103.36 - 100}{100} \times 100 = 3.36\%$

144. (a) Let watch's marked price = ₹ x

Given, (8 − 5)% of x = ₹ 45

$\Rightarrow \frac{3}{100} \times x = 45$

$\Rightarrow x = 15 \times 100 =$ ₹ 1500

145. (c) I. $x = 25$, $y = 15$

$\text{Equivalent discount} = \left(25 + 15 - \frac{25 \times 15}{100}\right)\%$

$= 36.25\%$

II. $x = 35\%$, $y = 5\%$

$\text{Equivalent discount} = \left(35 + 5 - \frac{35 \times 5}{100}\right)\%$

$= 38.25\%$

III. Discount = 38%

So, offer II is best for customer as it offer best discount out of given options.

146. (a) Given,

The price of washing machine = ₹ 65000

Discount = ₹ 2000

The price of washing machine after giving a discount = ₹ (65000 − 2000) = ₹ 63000

∴ Required difference price after giving a scratch card offer $= 63000 \times \left(\frac{15-10}{100}\right)$

$= 63000 \times \frac{5}{100} =$ ₹ 3150

147. (b) $\text{Effective discount} = \frac{3}{5+3} \times 100\%$

$= \frac{3}{8} \times 100\% = 37.5\%$

148. (a) $SP = 1250 \times \frac{95}{100} \times \frac{85}{100} \times \frac{80}{100} =$ ₹ 807.5

Discount = MP − SP = 1250 − 807.5 = ₹ 442.5

149. (b) Let the marked price of the article be x.

Then, SP at discount of 35%

$= x \times \frac{100-35}{100} = \frac{65}{100}x$

Equivalent discounts of two successive discounts of 20% and 15%

$= 20 + 15 - \frac{20 \times 15}{100}$

$= 35 - 3 = 32\%$

$\therefore$ SP at discount of 32% $= x \times \frac{100-32}{100} = \frac{68}{100}x$

According to the question,

$\frac{68x}{100} - \frac{65x}{100} = 504 \Rightarrow \frac{3x}{100} = 504$

$\Rightarrow \quad x = \frac{504 \times 100}{3} = ₹\ 16800$

150. (b) We know that, formula of successive discount is $\left(x + y - \frac{xy}{100}\right)\%$

According to the question,

$12 + 13 - \frac{12 \times 13}{100} = 25 - 1.56 = 23.44$

Then, $23.44 + 11 - \frac{23.44 \times 11}{100}$

$= 34.44 - \frac{23.44 \times 11}{100} = 31.87 \approx 32\%$

(approximate single discount)

Speedy Method

Single discount

$= 100 - \left[100 \times \frac{88}{100} \times \frac{87}{100} \times \frac{89}{100}\right]$

$= 100 - 68.13 = 31.86 \approx 32\%$

151. (b) Let, amount of house tax $= ₹\ x$

$\therefore \quad x \times \frac{12}{100} = 2100$

$x = \frac{2100 \times 100}{12} = ₹\ 17500$

$\therefore$ Paid amount $= 17500 - 2100 = ₹\ 15400$

152. (b) For 6% and 15% successive discount the actual percentage of discount will be

$= 6 + 15 - \frac{6 \times 15}{100} = 21 - 0.9 = 20.1$

Again for 20.1% and 14% successive discount the actual percentage of discount will be

$= 20.1 + 14 - \frac{20.1 \times 14}{100}$

$= 34.1 - 2.814 = 31.286\%$

153. (a) 1st discount $= x\%$ of $920 = ₹\ 9.2x$

Amount to be paid ₹ $(920 - 9.2x)$

2nd discount $x\%$ of ₹ $(920 - 9.2x)$

$= \frac{(920 - 9.2x)}{100}x$

According to the question,

$9.2x + x(920 - 9.2x)/100 = 33120$

$\Rightarrow \quad 920x + 920x - 9.2x^2 = 33120$

$\Rightarrow 9.2x^2 - 1840x + 33120 = 0$

$\Rightarrow \quad x^2 - 200x + 3600 = 0$

$\Rightarrow \quad (x - 180)(x - 20) = 0$

$\therefore \quad x = 20 \quad [\because x \neq 180]$

$\therefore$ The value of x is 20.

154. (a) Selling Price of article

$= 2800 \times \frac{85}{100} \times \frac{92}{100} \times \frac{95}{100} = ₹\ 2080.12$

155. (a) Percentage discount

$= \frac{2165 - 1710.35}{2165} \times 100$

$= \frac{454.65}{2165} \times 100 = 21\%$

156. (b) Discount per cent

$= \frac{145 - 127.6}{145} \times 100 = 12\%$

157. (d) Let cost price of item be $100x$.

For shopkeeper A, Selling price of item

$= 100x \times \frac{125}{100} \times \frac{85}{100} = ₹\ 106.25x$

$\therefore$ Profit percentage $= \frac{6.25x}{100x} \times 100 = 6.25\%$

For shopkeeper B,

Selling price $= 100x \times \frac{120}{100} \times \frac{88}{100}$

Gain % $= ₹\ 105.6x$

$\therefore \quad$ Gain % $= \frac{5.6x}{100x} \times 100 = 5.6\%$

Hence, for shopkeeper A the deal is better and he gains 6.25% profit.

158. (d) Let the marked price of an item be ₹ 100 x.

$\therefore$ SP of an item after 20% discount

$= 100x - 20x = 80x$

As, shopkeeper earns a profit of 90%,

$\therefore$ CP of an item $= 80x \times \frac{100}{190} = ₹ 42.10x$

If discount is 40%, then

SP of an item $= 100x - 40x = 60x$

$\therefore$ Required profit percentage

$= \frac{60x - 42.10x}{42.10x} \times 100 = 42.5\%$

159. (c) Given,

SP after allowing discount of 18% = ₹ 34440

$\therefore$ MP of an article $= 34440 \times \frac{100}{82} = ₹\ 42000$

As, Ramesh manages to earn a gain of 40%.

$\therefore$ CP of an article $= 34440 \times \frac{100}{140} = ₹\ 24600$

Now, if discount of 12% is allowed on the marked price, then

SP of an article $= 42000 - \frac{12}{100} \times 42000$

$= ₹\ 36960$

$\therefore$ Actual profit % $= \frac{12360}{24600} \times 100 = 50.24\%$

160. (d) $\frac{CP}{MP} = \frac{100 - \text{Discount}\%}{100 + \text{Profit}\%} = \frac{100 - 22\%}{100 + 36\%}$

$\Rightarrow \quad \frac{CP}{MP} = \frac{78}{136} = \frac{39}{68}$

But 39 unit = ₹ 1092

$\Rightarrow \quad$ 1 unit $= \frac{1092}{39} = ₹\ 28$

$\therefore \quad$ 68 unit $= 28 \times 68 = ₹\ 1904$

161. (d) Ratio of marked price and cost price

$= \frac{14}{10}$

$\frac{MP}{CP} = \frac{7}{5}$

Let MP be ₹ $70x$ and CP be ₹ $50x$ to gain 23.2% profit, he has to sell item at

$= \frac{50x \times 123.2}{100} = 61.6x$

Hence, required discount

$= \frac{70x - 61.6x}{70x} \times 100 = \frac{8.4x}{70x} \times 100 = 12\ \%$

162. (a) We know that,

Discount percentage

$= \frac{\text{Number of free items}}{\text{Total number of items}} \times 100$

$= \frac{6}{24+6} \times 100 = 20\%$

163. (b) Selling price of battery- rickshaw after two successive discounts

$= 90000 \times \frac{(100-10)}{100} \times \frac{(100-5)}{100}$

$= 90000 \times \frac{90}{100} \times \frac{95}{100}$

$= 9 \times 90 \times 95 = ₹\ 76950$

$\therefore$ Required selling price = ₹ 76950

164. (c) Required effective percentage

discount $= \frac{12}{36} \times 100 = 33\frac{1}{3}\%$

165. (b) Net discount $= \left(-15 - 10 + \frac{150}{100}\right)\%$

$= (-25 + 1.5)\% = -23.5\%$

$= 23.5\%$ discount

$\therefore$ Net selling price $= 2000 \times \frac{76.5}{100} = ₹ 1530$

166. (b) Case I,

$\therefore$ Discount $= 2635 \times \frac{37}{100} = ₹\ 974.95$

Case II,

$\therefore$ Effective discount %

$= -23 - 7 + \frac{(-23) \times (-7)}{100}$

$= -30 + 1.61 = -28.39\%$

$\therefore$ Discount $= 2635 \times \frac{28.39}{100} = 748.0765$

$\therefore$ Required difference $= 974.95 - 748.0765$

$\approx ₹\ 226.87$

167. (b) Let the printed price be ₹ $100x$.

Cost price to retailer $= 100x - \frac{40}{100} \times 100x$

$= ₹\ 60x$

Retailer sells an article at printed price

$= ₹\ 100x$

$\therefore$ Required gain percentage

$= \frac{100x - 60x}{60x} \times 100$

$= \frac{40x}{60x} \times 100 = \frac{200}{3}\% = 66\frac{2}{3}\%$

168. (d) Let the cost price be $100x$.

Then, marked price $= 100x \times \frac{132}{100} = 132x$

Thus, selling price after discount

$= 132x \times \frac{(100-21)}{100} = 104.28x$

$\therefore$ Gain% $= \frac{104.28x - 100x}{100x} \times 100 = 4.28\%$

169. (c) Let the marked price = ₹ 100

$\therefore$ Selling price $= \left[100 \times \frac{65}{100}\right] = ₹\ 65$

Cost price $= \left[65 \times \frac{100}{135}\right] = ₹\ \frac{1300}{27}$

When 45% discount is given on marked price.

$\therefore$ New selling price $= \left[100 \times \frac{55}{100}\right] = ₹\ 55$

$\therefore$ Required profit $= \frac{55 - \frac{1300}{27}}{\frac{1300}{27}} \times 100$

$= \frac{185}{13} = 14\frac{3}{13}\%$

170. (b) Let the cost price of an article = ₹ 100

Marked price of an article = ₹ 125

$\therefore$ Selling price of an article

$= 125 \times \frac{60}{100} = ₹\ 75$

Hence, the loss per cent

$= \frac{(100 - 75)}{100} \times 100 = 25\%$

171. (c) Let cost price = ₹ x

According to the question,

$x \times \frac{(100 + 25)}{100} \times \frac{(100 - 10)}{100} = 540$

$\Rightarrow x \times \frac{125}{100} \times \frac{90}{100} = 540$

$\Rightarrow x = \frac{540 \times 100 \times 100}{125 \times 90} = 480$

$\therefore$ Cost price = ₹ 480

172. (b) According to the question,

(i) Successive discount

$= 25 + 5 - \frac{25 \times 5}{100} = 28.75\%$

(ii) successive discount

$= 20 + 10 - \frac{20 \times 10}{100} = 28\%$

Difference = 28.75% – 28% = 0.75%

$\therefore$ Required difference $= 1000 \times \frac{0.75}{100} = ₹\ 7.5$

173. (c) Total discount to be given on total price $= \frac{9.5}{100} \times 48000 = ₹\ 4560$

Discount of first ₹ 28000 $= \frac{12}{100} \times 28000$

$= ₹\ 3360$

Discount on next ₹ 12000

$= \frac{8}{100} \times 12000 = ₹\ 960$

Remaining discount

$= [4560 - (3360 + 960)]$

$= 4560 - 4320 = ₹\ 240$

$\therefore$ Rohan should offer a discount of ₹ 240 on remaining ₹ 8000.

174. (d) According to the question,

Let marked price = ₹ 100

Cost price $= 100 \times \frac{90}{100} \times \frac{80}{100} \times \frac{110}{100} = ₹\ 79.2$

$\because$ The article should be sold in order to earn a profit of 15%.

Selling price $= 79.2 \times \frac{115}{100} = ₹\ 91.08$

175. (c) Equivalent discount

$= 10 + 20 - \frac{(10 \times 20)}{100} = 28\%$

Cost price of the article

$= 600 \times \frac{(100 - 28)}{100} = ₹\ 432$

Spent on the transportation

$= 432 + 68 = ₹\ 500$

Then, they sold again at the rate = ₹ 600

$\therefore$ Gain percentage $= \frac{600 - 500}{500} \times 100$

$= \frac{100}{500} \times 100 = 20\%$ profit

176. (c) From Scheme 1, two successive discount of 20% $= \left(20 + 20 - \frac{20 \times 20}{100}\right)\% = 36\%$

From Scheme 2, two discount 30% and 10% $= \left(30 + 10 - \frac{30 \times 10}{100}\right)\% = 37\%$

If Swaroop choose the second offer, then he saved, $= 1600 \times (37\% - 36\%)$

$= 1600 \times 1\% = ₹\ 16$

177. (a) $\therefore$ Discount $= \left(150 \times \frac{25}{100}\right) + 2.5$

$= (37.5 + 2.5) = ₹\ 40$

$\therefore$ Selling price $= 150 - 40 = ₹\ 110$

Cost price $= 110 \times \frac{100}{110} = ₹\ 100$

178. (b) The effective discount percentage

$= \frac{1}{1+5} \times 100 = \frac{1}{6} \times 100 = 16.67\%$

179. (c) According to the question,

Price of 1 dozen pairs of gloves

$= 180 \times \left(\frac{100 - 10}{100}\right)$

$= 180 \times \frac{90}{100} = ₹\ 162$

$\therefore$ 1 dozen of gloves can be buy in ₹ 162, then number of gloves which can buy in ₹ 54

$= \frac{54 \times 12}{162} = 4$

180. (d) Let the minimum cost on minimum number of items = ₹ x

According to the question,

$x \times \frac{25}{100} \geq 390 \Rightarrow x \geq 390 \times 4$

$x \geq ₹\ 1560$

Given, cost of one product = ₹ 340

Hence, the number of minimum items

$\geq \frac{1560}{340}$ i.e., 5

181. (c) $\frac{CP}{MP} = \frac{100 - 10}{100 + 10} = \frac{90}{110}$

$\left[\frac{CP}{MP} = \frac{100 - \text{Discount}\%}{100 + \text{Profit}\%}\right]$

$\therefore \frac{MP}{CP} = \frac{11}{9} = 1.22$

$MP = 1.22 \times CP$

Thus, MP is 1.22 times the CP.

182. (d) Let the marked price (MP) of an article be ₹ 100.

New marked price (MP) of an article

$= 100 \times \left(\frac{140}{100}\right) = ₹\ 140$

To sell the article at same price, the discount required = (140 – 100) = ₹ 40

$\therefore$ Required discount percentage

$= \frac{40}{140} \times 100 = 28\frac{4}{7}\%$

Speedy Method

100 (MP$_1$) —+40%→ 140 (MP$_2$); –40

Discount% $= \frac{40}{140} \times 100 = 28\frac{4}{7}\%$

183. (d) Let the cost price (CP) of oil be ₹ 100.

$\therefore$ Marked price (MP) of oil

$= \frac{100 \times 140}{100} = ₹\ 140$

Selling price (SP) of oil $= \frac{140 \times 68}{100} = ₹\ 95.2$

CP after using faulty machine

$= 100 \times \left(\frac{100 - 15}{100}\right) = ₹\ 85$

$\therefore$ Required profit percentage

$= \frac{95.2 - 85}{85} \times 100 = 12\%$

184. (c) Equivalent discount of 20% and 10%

$= 20 + 10 - \frac{20 \times 10}{100} = 28\%$

Given that, difference of two discounts (28% – 27%) of bill = ₹ 56

$\therefore$ 1% = ₹ 56

$\therefore$ 100% = ₹ 5600

Hence, total bill amount = ₹ 5600

185. (b) Let the actual weight of rice

= 1000 gm

and let the false weight of rice = x gm

According to the question,

$25 = \frac{1000 - x}{x} \times 100$

$\Rightarrow 25x = 100000 - 100x$

$\Rightarrow x = \frac{100000}{125} = 800$ gm

$\therefore$ For 10% profit false weight

$= \frac{800 \times 110}{100} = 880$ gm

$\therefore$ Discount to be offered

$= \frac{1000 - 880}{1000} \times 100 = 12\%$

186. (b) Equivalent discount

$= 26 + 5 - \frac{26 \times 5}{100} = 31 - 1.3 = 29.7\%$

Other discount = 30%

$\therefore$ Difference = (30 – 29.7)% = 0.3%

$\therefore$ Difference in bill after discounts

$= 50000 \times \frac{0.3}{100} = ₹\ 150$

187. (d) $\therefore$ Marked price

$= 864 \times \frac{100}{(100-25)} \times \frac{100}{(100-25)}$

$= 864 \times \frac{100}{75} \times \frac{100}{75} = ₹1536$

Discount = 1536 – 864 = ₹ 672

188. (c) The marked price of shopkeeper

$= 3068 \times \frac{100}{(100-5)} \times \frac{100}{(100-15)}$

$= ₹\ 3068 \times \frac{100}{95} \times \frac{100}{85}$

= ₹ 3799.38 ~ ₹ 3800

189. (b) Given, MP = ₹ 2500, SP = ₹ 1800

Discount percentage

$= \frac{2500-1800}{2500} \times 100 = 28\%$

190. (b) Let CP be ₹ 100 x.

$\therefore \quad SP = \frac{100x \times 114}{100} = 114x$

and $MP = 100x + \frac{35}{100} \times 100x = 135x$

$\therefore$ Discount rate $= \frac{135x - 114x}{135x} \times 100 = 15.55\%$

191. (c) Let, the marked price of article = ₹ 100x

So, the cost price of article $= 100x \times \frac{72}{100} = 72x$

and $\quad SP = 94x$

$\therefore$ Profit% $= \frac{SP - CP}{CP} \times 100$

$= \frac{94x - 72x}{72x} \times 100 = \frac{22}{72} \times 100 = 30.56\%$

192. (c) Single discount of 20% and 25%

$= 20 + 25 - \frac{20 \times 25}{100} = 45 - 5 = 40\%$

Now, equivalent discount of 40% and 20%

$= 40 + 20 - \frac{40 \times 20}{100} = (60 - 8)\% = 52\%$

193. (d) Selling price $= 75 \times \frac{(100-14)}{100}$

$= 75 \times \frac{86}{100} = ₹\ \frac{129}{2}$

$\therefore$ Cost price $= \frac{129}{2} \times \frac{100}{129} = ₹\ 50$

194. (d) Let CP be 100x.

$MP = 100x \times \frac{125}{100} = 125x$

Discount $= \frac{12}{100} \times 125x = 15x$

$SP = 125x - 15x = 110x$

Profit% $= \frac{110x - 100x}{100x} \times 100 = 10\%$

195. (b) Let CP of 16 pens be 160x.

$\therefore$ CP of 1 pen = ₹ 10x

MP of 1 pen = 12x

$\therefore$ MP of 20 pens = ₹ 240x

$\therefore$ Profit $= \frac{240x - 160x}{160x} \times 100 = 50\%$

196. (c) Let marked price of table = 100

Selling price at 25% discount

$= 100 \times \frac{(100-25)}{100} = 75$

Now, Cost price $= 75 \times \frac{100}{100+70} = \frac{750}{17}$

Selling price at 50% discount $= 100 \times \frac{50}{100} = 50$

New profit $= 50 - \frac{750}{17} = \frac{850-750}{17} = \frac{100}{17}$

New profit percentage

$= \frac{\frac{100}{17}}{\frac{750}{17}} \times 100 = \frac{100 \times 100}{750} = \frac{40}{3} = 13\frac{1}{3}\%$

197. (b) $SP = 24000\left(\frac{100+9}{100}\right)$

= 240 × 109 = ₹ 26160

$\therefore$ Discount % $= \frac{(30000 - 26160)}{30000} \times 100$

$= \frac{3840}{300} = 12.8\%$

198. (d) $\therefore$ Discount per cent $= \frac{MP - SP}{MP} \times 100$

$= \frac{150}{850} \times 100 = 17.64\%$

199. (b) Let CP of 1 pen = ₹1

CP for retailer = ₹44

MP for retailer = ₹50

After allowing a discount of 1%,

SP = 50 – 1% of 50 = 49.5

$\therefore$ Profit percentage $= \frac{5.5}{44} \times 100 = 12.5\%$

200. (b) Total amount of items bought

= 560 + 90 + 45 = ₹695

$\therefore$ Amount of discount $= 695 \times \frac{10}{100} = ₹69.5$

$\therefore$ Required discount is ₹ 69.5.

201. (b) Let MP of items be ₹ 100x.

$\therefore \quad SP = MP - Discount = 100x - 10x = 90x$

$\therefore CP = SP \times \frac{100}{120} = 90x \times \frac{100}{120} = 75x$

$\therefore$ Required ratio = 100x : 75x = 4 : 3

202. (b) Let CP of 1 kg grains be ₹ 100x.

$\therefore$ SP of 920 gm = 100x

$\therefore$ SP of 1 kg (1000 gm) $= \frac{100x}{920} \times 1000$

= ₹ 108.69 = 108.70x

$\therefore$ Profit % $= \frac{8.70x}{100x} \times 100 = 8.70\%$

203. (c) Let CP of goods be ₹ 100x

$\therefore$ MP of goods = 180x

$\therefore$ Discount allowed = 48% of 180x = 86.4x

$\therefore$ SP = MP – Discount = 180x – 86.4x = 93.6x

$\therefore$ Loss % $= \frac{CP - SP}{CP} \times 100 = \frac{100x - 93.6x}{100x} \times 100$

$= \frac{6.4x}{100x} \times 100 = 6\frac{2}{5}\%$

204. (a) Discount % $= \frac{MP - SP}{MP} \times 100$

$\Rightarrow \quad 40 = \frac{MP - 1260}{MP} \times 100$

$\Rightarrow \quad 2 = \frac{(MP - 1260)}{MP} \times 5$

$\Rightarrow \quad 2MP = 5\ MP - 6300$

$\Rightarrow \quad 3MP = 6300 \Rightarrow MP = ₹\ 2100$

> **Speedy Method**
>
> Marked price of article $= \frac{1260}{60} \times 100 = ₹\ 2100$

205. (d) Discount% $= \frac{80000 - 65280}{80000} \times 100$

= 18.4%

Single equivalent discount $= r_1 + r_2 - \frac{r_1 \cdot r_2}{100}$

$\Rightarrow \quad 18.4 = 15 + r_2 - \frac{15r_2}{100} \qquad \{r_1 = 15\%\}$

$\Rightarrow \quad 3.4 = \frac{85r_2}{100} \Rightarrow r_2 = \frac{3.4 \times 100}{85}$

$\therefore \quad r_2 = 4\%$

206. (c) $\because \frac{CP}{MP} = \frac{100 - 10\%}{100 + 30\%} \Rightarrow \frac{CP}{13000} = \frac{90}{130}$

$\Rightarrow \quad CP = ₹\ 9000$

207. (c) MP of trouser and jacket be x and 3x, respectively.

Let the discount on the jacket be y%.

According to the question,

$\frac{x \times 80}{100} + \frac{3x \times (100-y)}{100} = \frac{(x+3x) \times 70}{100}$

$\Rightarrow \quad 80 + 3(100 - y) = 280$

$\Rightarrow \quad 80 + 300 - 3y = 280$

$\Rightarrow \quad 3y = 100 \Rightarrow y = 33.33\%$

> **Speedy Method**
>
> Let discount on the jacket = x%
>
> By alligation rule,
>
> 20 x
>
>   30
>
> 1   :   3
>
> $\therefore \frac{x - 30}{30 - 20} = \frac{1}{3} \Rightarrow 3x - 90 = 10$
>
> $x = \frac{100}{3} = 33.33\%$

208. (a) Let CP = 100

$MP = \frac{100 \times 150}{100} = 150$

$SP = \frac{150 \times 80}{100} = 120$

$\therefore$ Profit% $= \frac{120 - 100}{100} \times 100 = 20\%$

209. (a) Discount% $= \frac{MP - SP}{MP} \times 100$

$= \left(\frac{20000 - 14000}{20000}\right) \times 100 = \frac{6000}{20000} \times 100$

= 30%

210. (c) According to the question,

20% of MP = 50% of CP

$\Rightarrow \quad MP \times \frac{20}{100} = CP \times \frac{50}{100}$

$\Rightarrow \quad \frac{MP}{CP} = \frac{5}{2}$

If no discount is given,

$\therefore$ Profit percentage $= \frac{5-2}{2} \times 100 = 3 \times 50$

$= 150\%$

211. (c) According to the question,

$\frac{2}{5} \times MP = \frac{5}{8} \times SP \Rightarrow \frac{MP}{SP} = \frac{25}{16}$

$\therefore$ Discount% $= \frac{MP - SP}{MP} \times 100$

$= \frac{25-16}{25} \times 100 = \frac{9}{25} \times 100 = 36\%$

212. (c) $\therefore$ Marked price $= \frac{1755}{(100-35)} \times 100$

$= \frac{175500}{65} = ₹2700$

213. (a) Given, marked price of the mobile phone = ₹ 35600

Trade discount = 10% of 35600 = ₹ 3560

Cash discount = (35600 – 3560) – 30000

= 32040 – 30000 = ₹ 2040

$\therefore$ Required cash discount percentage

$= \frac{2040}{32040} \times 100 = 6.367\% \approx 6.37\%$

214. (a) Selling price of the item

= (100 – 37)% of 2900 = 63% of 2900

$= \frac{63}{100} \times 2900 = ₹1827$

215. (b) Let marked price = ₹ 100

Selling price after 25% discount

= (100 – 25)% of 100 = ₹ 75

Cost price of the item $= \frac{75}{100+25} \times 100 =$ ₹ 60

Selling price at 35% discount = 65

$\therefore$ Required profit per cent $= \frac{65-60}{60} \times 100$

$= \frac{500}{60} = 8.33\% \approx 8\%$

216. (a) Marked price of the refrigerator

= ₹ 60000

Discount on full cash payment = ₹ 12000

Extra discount for regular customers

= 5% of ₹ 60000 = ₹ 3000

$\therefore$ Refrigerator price for regular customer

= ₹ (60000 – 12000 – 3000) = ₹ 45000

217. (a) (i) 20% and 12%

Net discount $= \left(20 + 12 - \frac{20 \times 12}{100}\right)\% = 29.6\%$

(ii) 25% and 5%

Net discount $= \left(25 + 5 - \frac{25 \times 5}{100}\right)\% = 28.75\%$

(iii) 30% and 3%

Net discount $= \left(30 + 3 - \frac{30 \times 3}{100}\right)\% = 32.1\%$

Clearly, scheme (iii) gives the maximum net discount out of given scheme.

218. (a) Market price of the T-shirt = ₹ 500

Selling price of the T-shirt

= (100 – 15)% of ₹ 500 = ₹ 425

$\therefore$ Cost price of the T-shirt

$= ₹ \frac{100}{(100+25)} \times 425 = ₹ 340$

219. (c) Let CP of an article be ₹ 100.

Then, MP = ₹ 125

$SP = \frac{110}{100} \times 100 = ₹ 110$

$\therefore$ Required discount per cent

$= \frac{125-110}{125} \times 100 = \frac{15}{125} \times 100 = 12\%$

220. (d) MP of an article = ₹ 36000

Total discount = 15%

Pooja pays $= ₹ \frac{(100-15)}{100} \times 36000$

($\because$ Pooja purchased it by credit card)

$= ₹ \frac{85}{100} \times 36000 = ₹ 30600$

221. (a) Selling price after two successive discounts

$= MP \times \left(\frac{100 - d_1}{100}\right) \times \left(\frac{100 - d_2}{100}\right)$

$= 25500 \times \frac{85}{100} \times \frac{88}{100} = ₹ 19074$

222. (d) Marked price $= \frac{\text{Selling price} \times 100}{(100 - \text{Discount})}$

$= \frac{425 \times 100}{(100-15)} = \frac{425 \times 100}{85} = ₹ 500$

$\therefore$ Cost price $= \frac{\text{Marked / Selling price} \times 100}{(100 + \text{Profit})}$

$= \frac{500 \times 100}{(100+25)} = \frac{50000}{125} = ₹ 400$

223. (c) After discount, cost of one dozen (i.e. 12) note books $= 125 \times \frac{80}{100} = ₹ 100$

$\therefore$ Number of note book bought for ₹ 75

$= \frac{12}{100} \times 75 = 9$

224. (a) According to the question,

Cost to photocopy after 400 sheets

$= (400 \times 1.50) \times \frac{94.5}{100} = ₹ 567$

and cost to photocopy first 400 sheets

$= 400 \times 1.50 = ₹ 600$

$\therefore$ Cost of photocopy total 800 sheets

= 600 + 567 = ₹ 1167

225. (c) Let MP of each shirt be ₹ 100.

Buy 3 shirts get on free

$\therefore \frac{1}{4} \times 100 = 25\%$ discount

But when he buy five shirt,

From first offer, he got 4 shirts, having

MRP of four shirt = 4 × 100 = ₹ 400

and SP of four shirt = 3 × 100 = ₹300

From second offer he buy one more shirt

MRP = ₹ 100

and SP of one shirt $= 100 \times \frac{75}{100} = ₹ 75$

$\therefore$ Total MRP for five shirt = ₹ 500

Total SP for five shirt = 300 + 75 = 375

Net discount $= \frac{500-375}{500} \times 100 = \frac{125}{5} = 25\%$

226. (b) Cost Price of book

$= 480 \times \frac{100}{120} = ₹ 400$

Selling Price of book after discount

$= 480 \times \frac{90}{100} = ₹ 432$

Gain % $= \frac{432-400}{400} \times 100 = \frac{32}{4} = 8\%$

227. (b) $SP = 25000 \times \frac{80}{100} \times \frac{85}{100} \times \frac{90}{100}$

= ₹ 15300

228. (d) $MP \times \frac{90}{100} = CP \times \frac{117}{100}$

$\frac{MP}{CP} = \frac{117}{90} = \frac{13}{10}$

$\therefore \quad SP = MP$

$\frac{SP}{CP} = \frac{13}{10}$

Gain % = 30%

229. (d) MP of an article = ₹ 1680

SP of the article $= 1680 \times \frac{81}{100} = ₹ 1360.8$

CP of the article $= 1360.8 \times \frac{100}{108} = ₹ 1260$

Required percentage $= \frac{1680-1260}{1260} \times 100$

$= \frac{420}{1260} \times 100 = \frac{100}{3} = 33\frac{1}{3}\%$

230. (c) MP = ₹ 19000

Let second discount be $x\%$.

According to the question,

$19000 \times \left(\frac{100-14}{100}\right) \times \left(\frac{100-x}{100}\right) = 15048$

$\left(1 - \frac{x}{100}\right) = 0.92093$

$\Rightarrow \quad \frac{x}{100} = 0.0791$

$\Rightarrow \quad x = 7.91\%$

231. (c) Let MRP of each shirt is ₹ 100.

$\therefore$ Cost price of each shirt is $= 100 \times \frac{40}{100} = ₹ 40$

According to scheme,

Shopkeeper sold first shirt at MRP and offered 40% discount on second shirt.

SP of two shirt $= ₹ 100 + \frac{60}{100} \times 100 = ₹ 160$

CP of two shirt = 40 × 2 = ₹ 80

$\therefore$ Profit precentage $= \frac{160-80}{80} \times 100$

$= \frac{80}{80} \times 100 = 100\%$

232. (d) Let second discount be $x\%$.
According to the question,
$$15000 \times \left(\frac{100-15}{100}\right) \times \left(\frac{100-x}{100}\right) = ₹\ 11250$$
$$\Rightarrow 1 - \frac{x}{100} = \frac{11250}{12750} \Rightarrow \frac{x}{100} = \frac{1500}{12750}$$
$$\Rightarrow \quad x = 11\frac{13}{17}\%$$

233. (c) First offer → 30% discount
Net discount of second scheme
$$= 22 + 8 - \frac{22 \times 8}{100} = 30 - 1.76 = 28.24\%$$
Net discount of third scheme
$$= 25 + 5 - \frac{25 \times 5}{100}$$
$$= 30 - 1.25 = 28.75\%$$
For customer least beneficial scheme is Scheme II which given the least discount.

234. (d) Marked price of item
$$= 2108 \times \frac{100}{62} \times \frac{100}{85} = ₹\ 4000$$

235. (d) (A) Successive discount
$$= 8 + 8 - \frac{8 \times 8}{100} = 15.36\ \%$$
(B) Successive discount $= 11 + 5 - \frac{11 \times 5}{100}$
$$= 16 - 0.55 = 15.45\ \%$$
(C) Successive discount $= 13 + 3 - \frac{13 \times 3}{100}$
$$= 16 - 0.39 = 15.61\ \%$$
(D) Discount = 16 %
Max. discount will give minimum price.
Therefore, scheme (D) will give minimum price.

236. (b) $MP \times \frac{96}{100} = CP \times \frac{110}{100}$
$$\frac{MP}{CP} = \frac{110}{96}$$
$$\frac{MP}{CP} = \frac{114.58}{100}$$
Now, MP = SP
$$\frac{SP}{CP} = \frac{114.58}{100}$$
∴ Profit % = 14.58%

237. (c) $CP \times \frac{140}{100} \times \frac{85}{100} = SP$
$$\frac{SP}{CP} = \frac{119}{100}$$
$$\therefore \text{Profit }\% = \frac{119-100}{100} \times 100 = 19\%$$

238. (d) Discount % $= \frac{\text{Free article}}{\text{Total articles}} \times 100$
$$= \frac{1}{3+1} \times 100 = 25\%$$

239. (d) Price after successive discount
$$= 18000 \times \frac{88}{100} \times \frac{85}{100} = ₹\ 13464$$
Total cost = 13464 + 536 = 14000
$$\text{Gain}\% = \frac{21000 - 14000}{14000} \times 100 = 50\%$$

240. (c) First scheme offer 40% discount.
Net discount of 2nd scheme
$$= 36 + 4 - \frac{36 \times 4}{100}$$
$$= 40 - 1.44 = 38.56\%$$
Difference between discounts
$$= 22500 \times \frac{(40 - 38.56)}{100} = ₹\ 324$$

241. (b) Discount % $= \frac{\text{Free article}}{\text{Total article}} \times 100$
$$= \frac{1}{5} \times 100 = 20\%$$

242. (c) MP of mobile phone
$$= \frac{18656 \times 100}{88} = ₹\ 21200$$
Now, after two successive discount of 4% and 8% Raman would pay
$$= 21200 \times \frac{96}{100} \times \frac{92}{100}$$
$$= ₹\ 18723.84$$

243. (b) Net discount $= 25 + 15 - \frac{25 \times 15}{100}$
$$= 40 - 3.75 = 36.25\%$$

244. (c) Selling price of folding bed
$$= 18000 \times \frac{85}{100} \times \frac{90}{100}$$
$$= 18 \times 85 \times 9 = ₹\ 13770$$
∴ Total cost for Aman = 13770 + 830 = ₹ 14600
Hence, required profit = 18440 − 14600
= ₹3840

245. (a) According to the question,
$$CP \times \left(\frac{100+15}{100}\right) = MP \times \left(\frac{100-25}{100}\right) \times \left(\frac{100-8}{100}\right)$$
$$\frac{CP}{MP} = \frac{69}{115}$$
$$\text{Mark up }\% = \frac{115-69}{69} \times 100 = 66\frac{2}{3}\%$$

246. (a) Customer will have to pay
$$= 2400 \times \left(\frac{100-12}{100}\right) \times \left(\frac{100-6}{100}\right)$$
$$= ₹2400 \times \frac{88}{100} \times \frac{94}{100} = ₹1985.28$$

247. (b) Let marked price = ₹ x
$$x - 205 = 1120 \times \frac{115}{100}$$
$$\Rightarrow \quad x - 205 = 1288$$
$$\therefore \quad x = ₹1493$$

248. (d) 15% of MP = 25% of CP
$$\frac{MP}{CP} = \frac{25}{15}$$
$$\therefore \quad SP = \frac{25 \times 75}{100} = \frac{75}{4}$$
$$\text{Profit}\% = \frac{\frac{75}{4} - 15}{15} \times 100$$
$$= \frac{15}{15 \times 4} \times 100 = 25\%$$

249. (b) ∴ Required single discount
$$= \left(12 + 8 - \frac{12 \times 8}{100}\right)\%$$
$$= (20 - 0.96)\ \% = 19.04\ \%$$

250. (d) Let the cost of each article = ₹ x
Cost price of 30 articles = ₹ 30 x
Marked price of each article.
$$= (100 + 30)\ \%\text{ of } x = ₹\ 1.3x$$
Selling price of 15 articles at 20% discount each
$$= ₹\ [(100-20)\%\text{ of } 1.3x] \times 15$$
$$= ₹\ 1.04x \times 15 = ₹\ 15.6x$$
Selling price of remaining 15 articles 10 % discount each.
$$= ₹\ [(100-10)\%\text{ of } 1.3x] \times 15 = ₹\ 1.17x \times 15$$
$$= ₹\ 17.55x$$
Total selling price of 30 articles
$$= ₹(15.6x + 17.55x) = ₹\ 33.15x$$
Profit = SP − CP
$$\Rightarrow \quad 630 = 33.15x - 30x$$
$$\Rightarrow \quad 630 = 3.15x$$
$$\therefore \quad x = \frac{630}{3.15} = ₹\ 200$$

251. (c) Let the marked price (MP) of article be ₹ x, then
$$SP = ₹\ \frac{75}{100}x, \quad \text{Loss} = 15\%$$
$$\text{Then CP} = \frac{\left(\frac{75}{100}\right)x}{(100-15)} \times 100 = ₹\ \frac{75}{85}x$$
Now, when article is sold at MP i.e, ₹ x
$$\text{Then, Profit} = x - \frac{75}{85}x = ₹\ \frac{10}{85}x$$
$$\therefore \quad \text{Profit per cent} = \frac{\left(\frac{10}{85}\right)x}{\left(\frac{75}{85}\right)x} \times 100 = 13.33\%$$

252. (c) Equivalent discount %
$$= 20 + 10 - \frac{20 \times 10}{100} = 30 - 2 = 28\%$$
$$\text{Amount of discount} = \frac{28}{100} \times 720 = ₹\ 201.6$$

253. (b) Marked price $= \frac{450}{90} \times 100 = ₹\ 500$
∵ Discount is not given,
$$\therefore 50\%\text{ of cost price} = \frac{50}{100} \times \frac{500}{125} \times 100 = ₹\ 200$$

254. (c) Required discount percentage
$$= \frac{5-3}{5} \times 100 = \frac{2}{5} \times 100 = 40\%$$

255. (a) $SP = \left(\frac{100-10}{100}\right) \times 2500 = ₹\ 2250$
$$CP = \frac{2250}{(100+25)} \times 100 = \frac{2250}{125} \times 100 = ₹\ 1800$$
∴ Profit = SP − CP = ₹ (2250 − 1800) = ₹ 450

256. (a) SP of article = ₹ 8000
Discount (x) = 10%
Tax (y) = 7.5%

Cost of delivery = ₹ 200

$\therefore$ Amount paid $= 8000 \times \frac{90}{100} \times \frac{107.5}{100} + 200$

$= 7740 + 200 =$ ₹ 7940

257. (c) Let CP = ₹100

MP of article $= 100 \times \frac{140}{100} =$ ₹140

and SP of article $= 100 \times \frac{110}{100} =$ ₹110

$\therefore$ Discount % $= \frac{140 - 110}{140} \times 100$

$= \frac{30}{140} \times 100 = 21.42\%$

258. (b) Let marked price = ₹ 100

According to the question,

Selling Price $= 100 \times \left(\frac{100-15}{100}\right) \times \left(\frac{100-10}{100}\right)$

$= 100 \times \frac{85}{100} \times \frac{90}{100} =$ ₹ 76.50

$\therefore$ Overall equivalent discount

$= \frac{100 - 76.5}{100} \times 100 = \frac{23.5}{100} \times 100 = 23.5\%$

Speedy Method

Single equivalent discount $= 15 + 10 - \frac{15 \times 10}{100}$

$= 25 - 1.5 = 23.5\%$

259. (a) $\therefore$ Discount % $= \frac{MP - SP}{MP} \times 100$

$= \left(\frac{3800 - 2128}{3800}\right) \times 100 = \frac{1672}{3800} \times 100 = 44\%$

260. (c) Let the cost price of article = ₹ 100

So, the marked price $= 100 \times \frac{250}{100} =$ ₹ 250

SP $= 250 \times \frac{50}{100} =$ ₹ 125

$\because$ Profit % $= \frac{125 - 100}{100} \times 100$

$= \frac{25}{100} \times 100 = 25\%$

261. (a) Let the cost price of laptop = ₹100

So, marked price of laptop

= 100 + 80% of 100 = 100 + 80 = ₹180

$\because$ Selling price $= \frac{180 \times 75}{100} =$ ₹ 135

$\because$ Profit % $= \frac{SP - CP}{CP} \times 100$

$= \frac{135 - 100}{100} \times 100 = 35\%$

262. (b) Let the marked price and selling price of the article is $13x$ and $9x$, respectively.

Discount $= 13x - 9x =$ ₹ $4x$

$\therefore$ Discount % $= \frac{4x}{13x} \times 100 = 30.77\%$

263. (c) Let the marked price of the article be x.

According to the question,

$x \times \frac{70}{100} \times \frac{90}{100} = 4964$

$\Rightarrow \quad x = \frac{496400}{63}$

$\therefore \quad x =$ ₹ 7879.36

Speedy Method

Assumed MP

100 → (−30%) → 70 → (−10%) → 63

$\because$ 63 → 4964

$\therefore$ 100 → $\frac{4964}{63} \times 100 =$ ₹7879.36

264. (c) Selling price of a cycle

$= MP \times \left(\frac{100 - \text{Discount }\%}{100}\right)$

$= 2700 \times \left(\frac{100 - 10}{100}\right) = 2700 \times \frac{90}{100} =$ ₹ 2430

265. (c) The marked price of a car

$= \frac{SP}{(100 - \text{Discount}\%)} \times 100$

$= \frac{640}{(100 - 60)} \times 100$

$= \frac{640}{40} \times 100 =$ ₹ 1600

266. (a) According to the question,

Selling price $= 1850 \times (100 - 60)\%$

$= 1850 \times \frac{40}{100} =$ ₹740

267. (b) Selling price of the article

$= 4800 \times \frac{(100 - 18)}{100} \times \frac{(100 - 20)}{100}$

$= 4800 \times \frac{82}{100} \times \frac{80}{100}$

$= 48 \times 82 \times \frac{8}{10} =$ ₹ 3148.8

268. (c) Let the cost price be 100.

Marked price = 100 × 140% = 140

Now, Selling price = 140 × (100 − 30)%

= 140 × 70% = 98

$\because$ Loss % $= \frac{CP - SP}{CP} \times 100$

$= \frac{100 - 98}{100} \times 100 = 2\%$

269. (a) According to the question,

$\frac{1}{4}$ of MP $= \frac{2}{3}$ of SP $\Rightarrow \frac{MP}{SP} = \frac{2}{3} \times \frac{4}{1} = \frac{8}{3}$

Let MP $= 8k$ and SP $= 3k$

$\therefore$ Discount % $= \frac{(8-3)k}{8k} \times 100$

$= \frac{5}{8} \times 100 = 62.5\%$

270. (c) Discount % $= \frac{(9600 - 6336)}{9600} \times 100$

$= \frac{3264}{9600} \times 100 = 34\%$

271. (b) Let CP = ₹100

So, MP = 100 × 125% = ₹ 125

$\therefore$ Maximum discount $= \frac{(125 - 100)}{125} \times 100$

$= \frac{25}{125} \times 100 = 20\%$

If we give 20% discount, then no profit no loss will be incurred.

272. (d) Let CP be ₹ 100.

Then, marked price = 100 × 150% = ₹ 150

So, SP $= 150 \times \frac{70}{100} \Rightarrow$ SP = ₹ 105

$\because$ Profit% $= \left(\frac{SP - CP}{CP}\right) \times 100$

$\therefore$ Profit % $= \frac{105 - 100}{100} \times 100 = 5\%$

273. (b) Let CP = ₹100

$\therefore$ MP $= 100 + \frac{100 \times 50}{100} =$ ₹150

$\therefore$ SP $= 150 \times \frac{80}{100} =$ ₹ 120

Profit% $= \frac{SP - CP}{CP} \times 100$

$= \frac{120 - 100}{100} \times 100 = 20\%$

274. (c) Discount $= \left[\frac{MP - SP}{MP}\right] \times 100$

$= \left[\frac{(7600 - 6688)}{7600}\right] \times 100 = 12\%$

275. (d) Let the marked price (MP) of an article be ₹ 100.

Selling Price (SP) $= 100\left(\frac{100-10}{100}\right) =$ ₹ 90

So, Cost Price (CP) $= 90 \times \left(\frac{100}{100 + 10}\right)$

= ₹ $\frac{900}{11} =$ ₹ 81.81

$\therefore$ Required profit percentage

$= \frac{100 - 81.81}{81.81} \times 100 = 22.22\%$

276. (d) Let CP be x.

$\therefore \quad MP \times \left(\frac{100-50}{100}\right) = CP \times \left(\frac{100+50}{100}\right)$

$SP = CP \times \frac{150}{50} = 3\,CP \qquad [\because MP = SP]$

$\therefore \quad SP = 3x$

$\therefore$ Profit% $= \frac{3x - x}{x} \times 100 = 200\%$

277. (d) Sale price or selling price

$= 25 - \frac{30}{100} \times 25 =$ ₹ 17.5

278. (d) $\therefore$ Selling price $= 640 - \left(640 \times \frac{37.5}{100}\right)$

= 640 − 240 = ₹ 400

279. (b) Given, Selling Price (SP) of an article = 204

According to the question,

$204 = \frac{60}{100} \times \frac{50}{100} \times MP$

$MP = 204 \times \frac{100}{60} \times \frac{100}{50}$

$\therefore$ Marked price = ₹ 680

Speedy Method

Successive discount of 40% and 50%

$= 40 + 50 - \frac{40 \times 50}{100} = 90 - 20 = 70\%$

$\therefore$ MP of the article $= 204 \times \frac{100}{(100-70)}$

$= 204 \times \frac{100}{30} = ₹ 680$

280. (a) Let the Cost Price (CP) = $100x$

Then, the Marked Price (MP) = $110x$

According to the question,

$110x - 11 = 132$

$\Rightarrow 110x = 132 + 11 = 143 \Rightarrow x = 1.3$

Now, CP = ₹ 130 and MP = ₹ 143

$\therefore$ Profit percentage

$= [(132 - 130) / 130] \times 100 = 1.53\%$

281. (d) Discount

$= [(6600 - 4752) / 6600] \times 100 = 28\%$

282. (b) Let the marked price be ₹ x.

So, the selling price of a book

$= x \times \frac{5}{12} = ₹ \frac{5}{12}x$

$\therefore$ The cost price of a book

$= \frac{\text{SP}}{(100 - \text{loss }\%)} \times 100$

$= \frac{\frac{5}{12}x}{(100-50)} \times 100 = \frac{5}{12}x \times \frac{100}{50} = ₹ \frac{5}{6}x$

Now, required ratio = MP : CP

$= x : \frac{5}{6}x = 1 : \frac{5}{6} = 6 : 5$

283. (c) According to the question,

$\text{SP} = \frac{16}{25}\text{MP} \Rightarrow \frac{\text{MP}}{\text{SP}} = \frac{25}{16}$

$\Rightarrow$ MP : SP = 25 : 16

284. (b) $\text{MP} = \frac{1690 \times 100}{(100-35)} = \frac{1690 \times 100}{65}$

$= ₹ 2600$

285. (a) Let cost price of chair = ₹ $100x$

Then, marked price $= 100x \times \frac{120}{100} = ₹ 120x$

According to the question,

$120x - 20 = 220 \Rightarrow 120x = 240$

$\Rightarrow x = \frac{240}{120} = 2$

$\therefore$ Cost price $= 100x = 100 \times 2 = ₹ 200$

$\therefore$ Profit % $= \frac{\text{SP} - \text{CP}}{\text{CP}} \times 100 = \frac{220-200}{200} \times 100$

$= \frac{20}{200} \times 100 = 10\%$

286. (b) Discount percentage

$= \frac{\text{MP} - \text{SP}}{\text{MP}} \times 100\%$

$= \frac{11800 - 7788}{11800} \times 100\% = \frac{4012}{11800} \times 100\%$

$= 34\ \%$

287. (d) Marked price of a chair = ₹ 5000

Selling price after first discount

$= 5000 \times \frac{90}{100} = ₹ 4500$

$\therefore$ Second discount % $= \frac{4500 - 3150}{4500} \times 100$

$= \frac{1350}{4500} \times 100 = \frac{90}{3} = 30\%$

288. (a) $\because$ Marked price = ₹ 2000

Selling price after 20% (first discount)

$= 2000 \times \frac{(100-20)}{100} = 2000 \times \frac{80}{100} = ₹ 1600$

Again, discount offered and sold at ₹ 1400.

$\therefore\ x\% = \frac{1600 - 1400}{1600} \times 100 = \frac{200}{1600} \times 100$

$x = 12.5\%$

289. (b) $\because$ Marked price $= \text{SP} \times \frac{100}{(100-d)}$

$= 5175 \times \frac{100}{75} = ₹ 6900$

290. (c) Selling price (SP) $= 800 \times \left(\frac{100-15}{100}\right)$

$= 800 \times \frac{85}{100} = ₹ 680$

Then, Cost Price (CP) $= \frac{\text{SP}}{(100+25)} \times 100$

$= \frac{680}{125} \times 100 = ₹ 544$

291. (b) Let the marked price be ₹ 100

Then, selling price

$= 100 \times \left(\frac{100-5}{100}\right)\left(\frac{100-10}{10}\right)\left(\frac{100-15}{100}\right)\left(\frac{100-20}{100}\right)$

$= 100 \times \frac{95}{100} \times \frac{90}{100} \times \frac{85}{100} \times \frac{80}{100} = ₹ 58.14$

$\therefore$ Single equivalent discount

$= 100 - 58.14 = 41.86\%$

292. (c) Cost price of article for Rohan

$= 1600 \times \frac{80}{100} = ₹ 1280$

Selling price of article for Rohan = ₹ 1600

Rohan's gain = (1600 – 1280) = ₹ 320

Rohan's gain percentage $= \frac{320}{1280} \times 100 = 25\%$

293. (b) Let the marked price of the article

= ₹ 100

Then, cost price of the article

$= 100 \times \frac{64}{100} = ₹ 64$

Selling price of the article $= 100 \times \frac{80}{100} = ₹ 80$

Gain = ₹ (80 – 64) = ₹ 16

$\therefore$ Gain percentage $= \frac{16}{64} \times 100 = 25\%$

294. (c) Let CP of goods = 100 unit

$\therefore$ SP of goods $= \frac{100 \times 120}{100} = 120$ unit

Marked price of goods $= \frac{120}{80} \times 100 = 150$ unit

Hence, required percentage

$= \frac{150 - 100}{100} \times 100 = 50\%$

295. (d) Let marked price = 100 unit

SP after discount $= \frac{100 \times 90 \times 70 \times 75}{100 \times 100 \times 100} \approx 47\%$

Hence, required successive discount

$= 100 - 47 = 53\%$

296. (d) SP after first discount

$= 5000 \times \frac{(100-10)}{100} = 5000 \times \frac{90}{100} = ₹ 4500$

SP after second discount $= 4500 \times \frac{(100-10)}{100}$

$= 4500 \times \frac{90}{100} = ₹ 4050$

$\therefore$ ₹ 4050 is paid by customer to Akshit.

297. (a) Amount paid by customer

$= 5583 \times \frac{(100-18)}{100} = 5583 \times \frac{82}{100}$

= ₹ 4578.06 (rounded off)

$\therefore$ = ₹ 4578

298. (d) Selling price of bag = ₹ 2208

Marked price of the bag

$= ₹ \left(2208 \times \frac{100}{92} \times \frac{100}{80}\right) = ₹ 3000$

299. (c) Cost price of table for man

$= \left(500 \times \frac{92}{100} \times \frac{75}{100} + 32\right) = (345 + 32) = ₹ 377$

Selling price of the table for man = ₹ 500

$\therefore$ Profit = ₹ (500 – 377) = ₹ 123

300. (b) Let the cost price of the object = ₹ 100

Marked price of the object

$= \frac{100 \times 125}{100} = ₹ 125$

Selling price of the object $= \frac{125 \times 58}{100} = ₹ 72.5$

Loss = ₹ (100 – 72.5) = ₹ 27.5

$\therefore$ Loss percentage $= \frac{27.5}{100} \times 100 = 27.5\%$

301. (c) Marked price of CCTV camera

= ₹ 5000

Given, two successive discount = 9% and 4%

Successive discount

$= 5000 \times \left(1 - \frac{r_1}{100}\right) \times \left(1 - \frac{r_2}{100}\right)$

$= 5000 \times \left(1 - \frac{9}{100}\right) \times \left(1 - \frac{4}{100}\right)$

$= 5000 \times \frac{91}{100} \times \frac{96}{100} = ₹ 4368$

Then given cash discount of ₹ 268

= 4368 – 268 = ₹ 4100

$\therefore$ So, the final price of CCTV camera for customer is ₹ 4100.

302. (c) Value of washing machine before discount $= \frac{28800 \times 100}{90} = ₹32000$

$\therefore$ Cost price $= \frac{\text{Marked price} \times 100}{(\text{Gain}\,\% + 100)}$

$= \frac{32000 \times 100}{(25\% + 100)} = \frac{32000 \times 100}{125} = ₹25600$

303. (a) Let MP of 1 good be ₹x.
Let MP of 5 articles = ₹ $5x$

$\therefore$ Net discount $= \frac{x}{5x} \times 100 = 20\%$

304. (b) Successive discount of 20% and 10%.
Price of car after discount

$= 85000 \times \frac{80}{100} \times \frac{90}{100} = ₹61200$

Total CP = 61200 + 3800 = ₹65000

$\therefore$ Required SP $= \frac{65000 \times 120}{100} = ₹\,78000$

305. (d) Cost price = Marked price

$\times \left(1 - \frac{r_1}{100}\right) \times \left(1 - \frac{r_2}{100}\right)$

$= 16500 \times \left(1 - \frac{8}{100}\right) \times \left(1 - \frac{5}{100}\right)$

$= 16500 \times \frac{92}{100} \times \frac{95}{100} = ₹\,14421$

306. (d) Given, marked price = ₹ 11000
Selling price = Marked price

$\times \left(1 - \frac{r_1}{100}\right)\left(1 - \frac{r_2}{100}\right)$

$= 11000 \times \left(1 - \frac{18}{100}\right)\left(1 - \frac{20}{100}\right)$

$= 11000 \times \frac{82}{100} \times \frac{80}{100} = ₹\,7216$

307. (c) Cost of two similar jackets = ₹ 4500
$\therefore$ Marked price of two jacket

$= 2500 \times 2 = ₹\,5000$

Discount % $= \frac{5000 - 4500}{5000} \times 100$

$= \frac{500}{5000} \times 100 = 10\%$

308. (b) A. Successive discount

$= X + Y - \frac{XY}{100} = 15 + 18 - \frac{(15 \times 18)}{100}$

$= 33 - \frac{270}{100} = 30.3\%$

B. Let MP of 1 good be ₹ x.

MP of 8 goods = $8x$

Net discount $= \frac{2x}{8x} \times 100 = 25\%$

C. A flat discount of 30%.
Hence, the scheme A is the best scheme for a customer.

309. (c) Let total electrical bill = ₹ $100x$
According to the question,

$5x = 250$

$x = 50$

$\therefore \quad 100x = 50 \times 100 = ₹\,5000$

310. (d) From option (a), discount

$= \left(25 + 15 - \frac{25 \times 15}{100}\right)\%$

$= (40 - 3.75)\% = 36.25\%$

From option (b), discount = 20%

From option (c), discount $= \frac{2}{5} \times 100\% = 40\%$

From option (d), discount $= \frac{3}{10} \times 100\% = 30\%$

Hence, scheme 3 will yield maximum discount.

311. (c) Here, $d_1 = 20\%$, $d_2 = 15\%$
Marked price = ₹ 3000
$\therefore$ Selling price = Marked price

$\times \left(\frac{100 - d_1}{100}\right) \times \left(\frac{100 - d_2}{100}\right)$

$= 3000 \times \left(\frac{100 - 20}{100}\right) \times \left(\frac{100 - 15}{100}\right)$

$= 3000 \times \frac{80}{100} \times \frac{85}{100} = ₹\,2040$

312. (b) 198 MP = 220 CP

$\frac{\text{MP}}{\text{CP}} = \frac{220}{198}$

Let CP of 220 chocolates = ₹ 198
and MP of 220 chocolates = ₹ 220

SP of 220 chocolates $= 220 \times \left(\frac{100 - 3.7}{100}\right)$

$= 211.86$

$\therefore$ Required percentage

$= \frac{211.86 - 198}{198} \times 100 = 7\%$

313. (c) Selling price of table

$= 37062 \times \frac{(100 - 33)}{100}$

$= 37062 \times \frac{67}{100} = ₹\,24831.54$

$\therefore$ Cost price of table $= 24831.54 \times \frac{100}{142}$

$= ₹\,17487$

314. (d) SP of calculator

$= 500 \times \frac{93}{100} \times \frac{93}{100} = ₹\,432.45$

315. (b) CP $= 800 \times \frac{90}{100} = ₹\,720$

$\therefore$ Profit per cent $= \frac{\text{SP} - \text{CP}}{\text{CP}} \times 100\%$

$= \frac{900 - 720}{720} \times 100\% = \frac{180}{720} \times 100\% = 25\%$

316. (b) SP of the article

$= 10000 \times \frac{90}{100} \times \frac{95}{100} \times \frac{95}{100} = ₹\,8122.50$

317. (b) SP $= \text{MP} \times \frac{100 - d_1\%}{100} \times \frac{100 - d_2\%}{100}$

$\Rightarrow \quad 420 = 560 \times \frac{100 - 17}{100} \times \frac{100 - d_2}{100}$

$\Rightarrow \quad 100 - d_2 = \frac{420 \times 10000}{83 \times 560}$

$\Rightarrow \quad 100 - d_2 = 90.36$

$\Rightarrow \quad d_2 = 100 - 90.36 \Rightarrow d_2 = 9.64\%$

318. (b) Discount% $= \frac{\text{MP} - \text{SP}}{\text{MP}} \times 100$

$= \frac{24500 - 20090}{24500} \times 100 = 18\%$

319. (a) Selling price of an air conditioner

$= 45000 \times \frac{85}{100} \times \frac{80}{100} = ₹\,30600$

320. (a) Single discount of two successive discount 25% and 6%

$= \left(25 + 6 - \frac{25 \times 6}{100}\right)\% = 31 - 1.5 = 29.5\%$

$\therefore$ Required difference

$= 50000 \times \frac{30}{100} - 50000 \times \frac{29.5}{100}$

$= 50000 \times \frac{0.5}{100} = ₹\,250$

321. (b) Selling price $= 600 \times \left(\frac{100 - 45}{100}\right)$

$= 6 \times 55 = ₹\,330$

322. (d) Let the marked price = ₹ 100

Cost price $= 100 \times \frac{80}{100} = ₹\,80$

Selling price $= 100 \times \left(\frac{100 - 15}{100}\right) = ₹\,85$

$\therefore$ Required gain percentage

$= \frac{85 - 80}{80} \times 100 = \frac{25}{4} = 6\frac{1}{4}\%$

10

Partnership

When two or more persons make an association for a business to earn profits is called partnership. The persons who make such associations are called partners.

Simple Partnership

If all the partners invest their different capitals for the same time period or same capital for different time periods, then their profit or loss is divided in the ratio of their investments or time periods of investment. Such a partnership is called simple partnership.

Case 1 Ratio of profit in case of simple partnership

(i) $P_1 : P_2 : P_3 .... = I_1 : I_2 : I_3$ (ii) $P_1 : P_2 : P_3 .... = t_1 : t_2 : t_3$

Ex. 1 *A* and *B* start a business by investing ₹ 4000 and ₹ 12000, respectively. What is the ratio of their profits after 1 yr?

Sol. The gain will be distributed amongst *A* and *B* in the ratio of their investments.

i.e. $\dfrac{\text{Investment of } A}{\text{Investment of } B} = \dfrac{\text{Profit of } A}{\text{Profit of } B}$

Hence, ratio of their profits $= \dfrac{4000}{12000} = \dfrac{1}{3} = 1:3$

Compound Partnership

If all partners invest their different capitals (money) for different time periods, then their profit not only depends on their investment but also on the time period of their investment then such a partnership is called compound partnership.

Case 2 Ratio of profit in case of compound partnership.

When capital investment $X_1, X_2, X_3 ...$ is invested for different time period $T_1, T_2, T_3, ...$ then, $P_1 : P_2 : P_3 : .... = X_1T_1 : X_2T_2 : X_3T_3 ...$

Ex. 2 *A* starts a business with ₹ 2000 and *B* joins him after 3 months with ₹ 8000. What is the ratio of their profits at the end of the year?

Sol. Here, *A* invested for 1 yr (12 months) and *B* invested 3 months later. It means *B* invested for $(12 - 3)$ months.

$\because$ Ratio of profit of *A* and *B* = Capital invested × Time period of investment

$\therefore$ *A*'s share: *B*'s share $= 2000 \times 12 : 8000 \times (12 - 3)$

$= 2 \times 12 : 8 \times 9 = 24 : 72 = 1 : 3$

Based on Joining and Withdrawl of Partner

In this topic, we will study the question in which one partner join or withdrawl some part of investment for some time.

Ex. 3 Two persons *A* and *B* started a business by investing ₹ 6000 and ₹ 8000, respectively. After 4 months, *B* withdraw the whole amount but *C* entered into a partnership by investing 40% less than the initial investment of *B*. Find the total profit at the end of the year, if the share of *A* is ₹ 6750?

Sol. Ratio of profit of *A*, *B* and *C* = Ratio of the share of *A*, *B* and *C*

$= (6000 \times 12) : (8000 \times 4) : \left(8000 \times \dfrac{60}{100} \times 8\right)$

$= 720 : 320 : 384 = 45 : 20 : 24$

Share of $A = \dfrac{45}{45 + 20 + 24} \times$ Total profit

$\Rightarrow \quad 6750 = \dfrac{45}{89} \times$ Total profit

$\therefore \quad$ Total profit $= \dfrac{6750 \times 89}{45} =$ ₹ 13350

Ex. 4 *A* and *B* enter into a partnership with capital in the ratio 5 : 6. After 4 months, *A* withdraws $\dfrac{1}{5}$ of his capital, while *B* increases his capital by $33\dfrac{1}{3}$%. What is the share (in ₹ lakhs) of *B* in the annual profit of ₹ 6.3 lakhs?

Sol. *A* and *B* enter into partnership with capital 5 : 6.

According to the question,

$A : B = 5x \times 4 + 5x \times \dfrac{4}{5} \times 8 : 6x \times 4 + 6x \times \dfrac{4}{3} \times 8$

$= 20x + 32x : 24x + 64x = 52x : 88x = 13 : 22$

$\therefore$ *B*'s profit $= \dfrac{22}{35} \times 630000 =$ ₹ 396000

$\therefore$ Profit of *B* is 3.96 lakh.

SSC Exam Scanner

SSC CGL 2024-2022 (Tier I & II)

1. Three people, *A*, *B* and *C*, invest in a business in the ratio 2 : 3 : 5. It was decided that 9% of the profits will go to charity. If the total profit was ₹ 250000, then find the share of *C* in the profit (in ₹).
SSC CGL (Tier-I) 26/09/2024 Shift-I
(a) 126950 (b) 111650
(c) 121850 (d) 113750

2. *A*, *B* and *C* invested money in a business such that 2 times *A*'s share, 4 times B's share and 6 times *C*'s share are all equal. If they earned ₹ 44000, find the share of *A*.
SSC CGL (Tier-I) 24/09/2024 Shift-I
(a) ₹ 22000 (b) ₹ 12000
(c) ₹ 24000 (d) ₹ 20000

3. Two friends *A* and *B* started a business by investing ₹ 150000 and ₹ 250000 respectively. They agreed to distribute their earnings in the same ratio of their investments. After an year, the profit earned was ₹ 600000. Each of them added ₹ 50000 to their respective profits and invested in a different project. If this project gave an yield of ₹ 420000 then *A*'s share in the profit is?
SSC CGL (Tier-II) 26/10/2023 Shift-I
(a) ₹ 235000 (b) ₹ 165000
(c) ₹ 197000 (d) ₹ 184000

4. *A* starts a business with ₹ 75000 and *B* joins the business 5 months later with an investment of ₹ 80000. After 1 yr, they earn a profit of ₹ 408800. Find the share of *A* and *B* (in ₹).
SSC CGL (Tier-II) 7/3/2023 Shift-II
(a) 252000 and 156800
(b) 250000 and 158800
(c) 248000 and 160800
(d) 249500 and 159300

5. *A*, *B* and *C* invested capital in the ratio of 3 : 4 : 8. At the end of the business term, they received the profit in the ratio of 2 : 3 : 5. What is the ratio of their invested time?
SSC CGL (Tier-II) 6/3/2023 Shift-II
(a) 15 : 16 : 13
(b) 13 : 18 : 15
(c) 16 : 18 : 15
(d) 16 : 21 : 18

6. Suresh, Dinesh and Ramesh became partners in a business by investing money in the ratio of 3 : 6 : 8. If their investments is increased by 5%, 15% and 20%, respectively, then what will be the ratio of their profits for one year? **SSC CGL (Tier-II) 3/3/2023 Shift-I**
(a) 7 : 46 : 64 (b) 19 : 46 : 64
(c) 21 : 46 : 64 (d) 35 : 46 : 64

7. *A*, *B* and *C* did certain investments and the ratio of their time periods is 3 : 2 : 7 respectively. Ratio of the profits of *A*, *B* and *C* is 4 : 3 : 14, respectively. What is the ratio of the investments of *A*, *B* and *C*?
SSC CGL (Tier-II) 2/3/2023 Shift-I
(a) 1 : 3 : 4 (b) 7 : 9 : 11
(c) 8 : 9 : 12 (d) 2 : 3 : 11

8. *A* and *B* invested money in a business in the ratio of 7 : 5. If 15% of the total profit goes for charity, and *A*'s share in the profit is ₹ 5950, then what is the total profit?
SSC CGL (Tier-I) 18/7/2023 Shift-IV
(a) ₹ 10500 (b) ₹ 11750
(c) ₹ 12000 (d) ₹ 12500

9. Nihit starts a business with ₹ 700. After 5 months Amit and Patel joined him with ₹ 300 and ₹ 400, respectively. At the end of the year, the business gave a profit of ₹ 627. Find the share of Patel in the profit.
SSC CGL (Tier-I) 08/12/2022 Shift-IV
(a) ₹ 127 (b) ₹ 145
(c) ₹ 132 (d) ₹ 156

10. *A* and *B* invested their money in a business in the ratio of 9 : 5. If 10% of the total profit goes for charity and *A*'s share is ₹ 29840, what is the total profit (in ₹, to the nearest integer)?
SSC CGL (Tier-I) 08/12/2022 Shift-II
(a) ₹ 51745 (b) ₹ 55715
(c) ₹ 57545 (d) ₹ 51575

SSC CPO SI 2020

11. *A*, *B*, *C* subscribe a sum of ₹ 75500 for a business. *A* subscribes ₹ 3500 more than *B*, and *B* subscribes ₹ 4500 more than *C*. Out of a total profit of ₹ 45300, how much (in ₹) does *A* receive? **SSC CPO 25/11/2020 Shift-II**
(a) 17400 (b) 14700
(c) 12600 (d) 15000

12. A sum of ₹ 8200 was divided among *A*, *B* and *C* in such a way that *A* had ₹ 500 more than *B* and *C* had ₹ 300 more than *A*. How much was *C*'s share (in ₹)? **SSC CPO 24/11/2020 Shift-I**
(a) 3100 (b) 2000
(c) 2300 (d) 2800

13. *A* and *B* started a business investing amounts of ₹ 92500 and ₹ 112500, respectively. If *B*'s share in the profit earned by them is ₹ 9000. What is the profit (in ₹) earned by *A*?
SSC CPO 24/11/2020 Shift-I
(a) 9000 (b) 10000
(c) 7400 (d) 11240

14. *A*, *B* and *C* started a business by investing ₹ 13750, ₹ 16250 and ₹ 18750, respectively. If *B*'s share in the profit earned by them is ₹ 5200, what is the total profit (in ₹) earned by them together?
SSC CPO 23/11/2020 Shift-I
(a) 18200 (b) 17500
(c) 15600 (d) 16600

SSC CHSL 2024 & 2023 (Tier I & II)

15. *A*, *B* and *C* jointly started a business in which *A* invested ₹ 7000 for 12 months, *B* invested ₹ 8000 for 10 months and *C* invested ₹ 12000 for 6 months. *A* was the working member for which he received 20% of the profits as his remuneration. The total profit earned at the end of one year was ₹ 14750. What is *C*'s share (in ₹) in the profit?
SSC CHSL (Tier II) 18/11/2024 Shift I
(a) 4000 (b) 4200
(c) 2950 (d) 3600

16. ₹ 7786 is divided among *A*, *B* and *C* in such a manner that the ratio of the amount of *A* to that of *B* is 3 : 4 and the ratio of the amount of *B* to that of *C* is 12 : 13. The amount of money received by *B* is
SSC CHSL (Tier II) 10/1/2024 Shift-I
(a) ₹ 7138
(b) ₹ 2977
(c) ₹ 2748
(d) ₹ 5038

17. *A* and *B* enter into a partnership with ₹ 25000 and ₹ 50000 respectively, in a company for a year. After 7 months, *C* gets into a partnership with them with ₹ 30000 and *A* withdraws his contribution after 9 months. What would be *C*'s share in the profit, assuming a total profit of ₹ 3900 at the end of the year? **SSC CHSL (Tier II) 02/11/2023 Shift-I**
(a) ₹ 1000 (b) ₹ 600
(c) ₹ 800 (d) ₹ 1200

18. *A* sum of money is divided among *A*, *B* and *C* in the ratio 4 : 3 : 6. If the share of *C* is ₹ 600 more than *B*, then how much amount will *A* get more than *B*? **SSC CHSL (Tier II) 02/11/2023 Shift-I**

(a) ₹ 200 (b) ₹ 250
(c) ₹ 100 (d) ₹ 150

19. *A*, *B* and *C* started a business by investing ₹ 9000, ₹ 18000 and ₹ 21000, respectively. If *B*'s share in the profit earned by them is ₹ 759, then the total profit earned by them together is **SSC CHSL (Tier I) 10/08/2023 Shift-III**

(a) ₹ 2808
(b) ₹ 2024
(c) ₹ 2504
(d) ₹ 2208

20. Anam and Bikash invest in a business in the ratio 3:2. If in a particular month, Anam gets ₹ 3840 as profit, the total profit is **SSC CHSL (Tier I) 04/08/2023 Shift-II**

(a) ₹ 5800 (b) ₹ 6300
(c) ₹ 6550 (d) ₹ 6400

21. An amount of ₹ 12029 is divided among *P*, *Q* and *R* such that *P*'s share is 5 times *Q'S* share and *R*'s share is one-third of P's share. What is the share of *R*? **SSC CHSL (Tier I) 15/03/2023 Shift-IV**

(a) ₹ 2718
(b) ₹ 2312
(c) ₹ 2615
(d) ₹ 2518

22. *P* invested ₹ 4000 for one year. *Q* joined him with an investment of ₹ 6000 after few months. If at the end of one year the ratio of profits of *P* and *Q* is 4 : 3, then *Q* joined after how many months? **SSC CHSL (Tier I) 14/03/2023 Shift-I**

(a) 4 months (b) 3 months
(c) 8 months (d) 6 months

SSC MTS 2023 & 2022

23. Arvind, Bilal, Carmen invest ₹ 49000 towards a business. Arvind invests ₹ 5000 more than Bilal and Bilal invests ₹ 4000 more than Carmen. Out of a total profit of ₹ 98000, how much does Bilal receive? **SSC MTS 11/09/2023 Shift-I**

(a) ₹ 34400 (b) ₹ 33200
(c) ₹ 30500 (d) ₹ 32000

24. Profit of ₹ 29120 is divided among *A*, *B* and *C* so that *A*'s share is $2\frac{1}{2}$ times *B*'s and *B*'s share is $1\frac{1}{5}$ times *C*. Find *B*'s share. **SSC MTS 05/09/2023 Shift-II**

(a) ₹ 6940 (b) ₹ 7820
(c) ₹ 6720 (d) ₹ 7140

25. Swati starts a business with₹ 4200, and after 5 months, Bani joins Swati as her partner. After a year, the profit is divided among Swati and Bani in the ratio 2 : 5. What is Bani's contribution ? **SSC MTS 1/09/2023 Shift-III**

(a) ₹ 18000 (b) ₹ 17050
(c) ₹ 19000 (d) ₹ 16500

26. In a partnership business, *A* and *B* invested in the ratio of 5 : 6. At the end of 8 months *A* withdrew his capital. If they shared the eventual profit in the ratio of 5 : 9, then what is the number of months for which *B* invested his capital ? **SSC MTS 13/07/2022 Shift-I**

(a) 6 months
(b) 10 months
(c) 12 months
(d) 11 months

SSC GD Constable 2023

27. Mohan and Sohan invested ₹ 6000 and ₹ 8000 respectively in a property simultaneously and after 6 months Sohan withdraws his invested amount. What is the ratio of money received by Mohan and Sohan respectively at the end of one year? **SSC GD 13/02/2023 Shift-IV**

(a) 4 : 3
(b) 2 : 3
(c) 3 : 4
(d) 3 : 2

28. *A*, *B* and *C* invested ₹ 10000, ₹ 15000 and ₹ 20000, respectively. After one year each of *A* and *B* invested ₹ 5000 more, while *C* withdrew ₹ 10000. What will be the ratio of profit of *A*, *B* and *C* after three years from starting? **SSC GD 06/02/2023 Shift-I**

(a) 8 : 11 : 8 (b) 2 : 2 : 4
(c) 2 : 3 : 4 (d) 8 : 8 : 11

Right Answers

1	(d)	2	(c)	3	(b)	4	(a)	5	(c)	6	(c)	7	(c)	8	(c)	9	(c)	10	(d)
11	(a)	12	(a)	13	(c)	14	(c)	15	(d)	16	(c)	17	(b)	18	(a)	19	(b)	20	(d)
21	(c)	22	(d)	23	(d)	24	(c)	25	(a)	26	(c)	27	(d)	28	(a)				

Solutions

1. (d) Total Profit = ₹ 250000

$\therefore$ Charity = 9%

$\therefore$ Profit after charity

$= 250000 - \dfrac{9}{100} \times 250000 = 227500$

$\therefore$ Required share of $C = 227500 \times \dfrac{5}{10}$

$= ₹\ 113750$

2. (c) Given, $2 \times A$'s share $= 4 \times B$'s share $= 6 \times C$'s share

Divide by 12, $\dfrac{A}{6} = \dfrac{B}{3} = \dfrac{C}{2}$ [$\because$ LCM of 2, 4, 6 = 12]

$\therefore$ $A : B : C = 6 : 3 : 2$

Let, A's share $= 6x$

B's share $= 3x$

C's share $= 2x$

$\therefore$ Total $= 6x + 3x + 2x = 11x$

According to the question,

$11x = 44000 \Rightarrow x = 4000$

$\therefore$ A's share $= 6 \times 4000 = ₹\ 24000$

3. (b) Ratio of profit of A and B

$= 150000 : 250000 = 3 : 5$

$\therefore$ Share of A in the profit

$= \dfrac{3}{3+5} \times 600000 = ₹\ 225000$

Share of B in the profit

$= 600000 - 225000 = ₹\ 375000$

New investment of $A = 225000 + 50000$

$= ₹\ 275000$

and new investment of

$B = 375000 + 50000 = ₹\ 425000$

Now, ratio of new profit of A and B

$= 275000 : 425000 = 11 : 17$

Hence, required profit of A

$= \dfrac{11}{11+17} \times 420000 = ₹\ 165000$

4. (a) Ratio of profit of A and B

[$\because$ Profit = Investment × Time period]

$A : B = 75000 \times 12 : 80000 \times 7 = 45 : 28$

Total profit = 408800

$\therefore$ Share of $A = \dfrac{45}{73} \times 408800 = 252000$

and share of $B = \dfrac{28}{73} \times 408800 = 156800$

5. (c) Ratio of A, B and C investment $= 3 : 4 : 8$

Ratio of their profit $= 2 : 3 : 5$

So, ratio of their time period

$= \dfrac{2}{3} : \dfrac{3}{4} : \dfrac{5}{8} = \dfrac{2}{3} \times 24 : \dfrac{3}{4} \times 24 : \dfrac{5}{8} \times 24$

$= 16 : 18 : 15$

6. (c) Ratio of investment (Suresh, Dinesh and Ramesh) $= 3 : 6 : 8$

According to the question,

Suresh : Dinesh : Ramesh

$= 3 \times \dfrac{105}{100} : 6 \times \dfrac{115}{100} : 8 \times \dfrac{120}{100}$

$= 315 : 690 : 960 = 21 : 46 : 64$

7. (c) Given,

Ratio of their time period$(A : B : C) = 3 : 2 : 7$

Ratio of their profit $(A : B : C) = 4 : 3 : 14$

According to the question,

Total Profit = Investment × Time

$\Rightarrow$ Investment $= \dfrac{\text{Profit}}{\text{Time}}$

So, ratio of their investment

$A : B : C = \dfrac{4}{3} : \dfrac{3}{2} : \dfrac{14}{7} = \dfrac{4}{3} : \dfrac{3}{2} : 2$

Multiply by 6, $A : B : C = 8 : 9 : 12$

So, required ratio of their investment

$= 8 : 9 : 12$

8. (c) If A and B two person invested in a business in the ratio of $a : b$ and k % of total profit goes for any other, then

Profit of $A = \dfrac{a}{a+b} \times \dfrac{100-k}{100} \times$ total profit

Profit of $B = \dfrac{b}{a+b} \times \dfrac{100-k}{100} \times$ total profit

Let the total profit be 'x'.

Profit earned by A

$= \dfrac{7}{12} \times \dfrac{85}{100} \times x = 5950$

$\Rightarrow$ $x = \dfrac{5950 \times 12 \times 100}{7 \times 85}$

$\Rightarrow$ $x = ₹12000$

Hence, total profit is ₹ 12000.

9. (c) Ratio of profit of Nihit, Amit and Patel

$= 700 \times 12 : 300 \times 7 : 400 \times 7$

$= 84 : 21 : 28$

$\therefore$ Share of Patel in the profit

$= ₹\ \dfrac{28}{84 + 21 + 28} \times 627$

$= ₹\ \dfrac{28 \times 627}{133} = ₹\ 132$

10. (d) Let the total profit = ₹ x

Now, $(100 - 10)\%$ of $x = \dfrac{9+5}{9} \times 29840$

$\Rightarrow$ $\dfrac{90}{100} \times x = \dfrac{14 \times 29840}{9}$

$\Rightarrow$ $x = \dfrac{14 \times 29840 \times 10}{9 \times 9} = 51575.3$

So, the total profit = ₹ $x \approx$ ₹ 51575.

11. (a) Let C's investment be x.

According to the question, B is $x + 4500$.

and, $A = x + 4500 + 3500 = x + 8000$

Total investment $= A + B + C = 75500$

$x + x + 4500 + x + 8000 = 75500$

$\Rightarrow$ $3x = 75500 - 12500$

$\Rightarrow$ $3x = 63000$

$\Rightarrow$ $x = ₹21000$

Investment of $A = x + 8000 = 21000 + 8000$

$= ₹\ 29000$

Investment of B

$= x + 4500 = 21000 + 4500 = ₹\ 25500$

Investment of $C = x = ₹\ 21000$

$\therefore$ Ratio of profit $A : B : C$

$= 29000 : 25500 : 21000 = 58 : 51 : 42$

$\therefore$ A's share $= \dfrac{58}{(58 + 51 + 42)} \times 45300$

$= \dfrac{58}{151} \times 45300$

$= 58 \times 300 = ₹17400$

12. (a) Let, share of $B = x$

So, A's share $= x + 500$

and C's share $= (x + 500) + 300 = x + 800$

According to the question,

$(x + 500) + x + (x + 800) = 8200$

$\Rightarrow$ $3x = 8200 - 1300$

$\Rightarrow$ $3x = 6900 \Rightarrow x = 2300$

So, C's share $= 2300 + 800 = 3100$

13. (c) Ratio of profit = Ratio of investment

$A : B = 92500 : 112500 = 37 : 45$

B's share = ₹ 9000

Total profit $= ₹\ 9000 \times \dfrac{37 + 45}{45} = ₹\ 16400$

So, profit earned by A is

$= ₹\ (16400 - 9000) = ₹\ 7400$

14. (c) Given,

$A : B : C = 13750 : 16250 : 18750$

$\Rightarrow$ $A : B : C = 11 : 13 : 15$

Let profit of A, B and C be $11x$, $13x$ and $15x$, respectively.

As, B's share = 5200

$\Rightarrow$ $13x = 5200$

$\Rightarrow$ $x = 400$

$\therefore$ Total profit $= 11x + 13x + 15x = 39x$

Total profit $= ₹\ (39 \times 400) = ₹\ 15600$

15. (d) Ratio of Profit of A, B and C

A	:	B	:	C
7000 × 12		8000 × 10		12000 × 6
84	:	80	:	72
21	:	20	:	18

Now, $(21 + 20 + 18)$ units $= 14750 \times \dfrac{80}{100}$

1 unit $= \dfrac{1475 \times 8}{59} = ₹\ 200$

$\therefore$ 18 units $= 200 \times 18 = ₹\ 3600$

Thus, C is share ₹ 3600.

16. (c) Given, $A + B + C = ₹\ 7786$

$A : B = 3 : 4$

$\Rightarrow$ $A : B = 9 : 12$ (multiply by 3 to equal B)

$B : C = 12 : 13$

$\therefore \quad A : B : C = 9 : 12 : 13$

Or $\quad 9x : 12x : 13x$

$\therefore A + B + C = 9x + 12x + 13x = 7786$

$\Rightarrow \quad 34x = 7786$

$\Rightarrow \quad x = 229$

$\therefore$ B's share $= 12 \times 229 = ₹\ 2748$

Hence, B received = ₹ 2748

17. (b) As given in question, A, B and C invest their amount for the time 9 months, 12 months, 5 months, respectively.

$\therefore$ Ratio of profit share of A, B, C

$= 25000 \times 9 : 50000 \times 12 : 30000 \times 5$

[$\because$ Share = Invested amount × Time]

$= 15 : 40 : 10$

Let profit be 15x, 40x and 10x.

$\therefore$ Total profit $= 15x + 40x + 10x$

$\Rightarrow \quad 65x = 3900$

$\therefore \quad x = 60$

$\therefore$ C's profit $= 10x = 10 \times 60 = ₹\ 600$

18. (a) Ratio of money divided among A, B and C = 4 : 3 : 6

Let the money be 4x, 3x and 6x.

Given that,

C's share – B's share = ₹ 600

$\Rightarrow \quad 6x - 3x = 600 \Rightarrow x = 200$

$\therefore$ A's share more than

$B = 4x - 3x = x = ₹\ 200$

Hence, A's share is ₹200 more than B.

19. (b) Given,

A, B and C started a business by investing ₹ 9000, ₹ 18000 and ₹ 21000, respectively.

A	B	C
9000	18000	21000

$\therefore A : B : C = 3 : 6 : 7$

Let the investment are 3x, 6x and 7x.

As given, Share of profit of B = ₹759

$\therefore$ Share of profit of all A, B and

$$\text{C together} = \frac{759}{6x} \times 16x = ₹2024$$

20. (d) Given, Investment made by Anam and Bikash in the ratio = 3:2

$\therefore \quad \text{Total profit} = 3840 \times \frac{5}{3}$

$\Rightarrow \quad$ Total profit = ₹6400

21. (c) Let P's share be = ₹ x

According to the question,

$Q\text{'s share} = \frac{x}{5}$

$R\text{'s share} = \frac{x}{3}$

$\therefore P : Q : R = x : \frac{x}{5} : \frac{x}{3} = 15x : 3x : 5x = 15 : 3 : 5$

$\therefore \text{Share of } R = \frac{5}{(5 + 3 + 15)} \times 12029$

$= \frac{5}{23} \times 12029 = 5 \times 523 = ₹\ 2615$

22. (d) Let Q joined for t months.

Ratio of their profit = Ratio of their investments

$\Rightarrow \quad \frac{4000 \times 12}{6000 \times t} = \frac{4}{3}$

$\Rightarrow \quad \frac{2}{3} \times \frac{12}{t} = \frac{4}{3}$

$\therefore \quad t = 6$ months

Hence, number of months after which Q joined = 12 – 6 = 6 months

23. (d) Let Carmen invested = ₹ x

$\therefore$ Bilal invested $= x + 4000$

Arvind invested $= x + 4000 + 5000$

$= x + 9000$

Also, together three invested = ₹ 49000

$\Rightarrow x + x + 4000 + x + 9000 = ₹49000$

$\Rightarrow 3x + 13000 = 49000$

$\Rightarrow \quad 3x = 36000$

$\Rightarrow \quad x = 12000$

$\therefore$ Capitals invested by

Arvind = 12000 + 9000 = ₹21000

Bilal = 12000 + 4000 = ₹16000

Carmen = ₹12000

$\therefore$ Profit sharing ratio of Arvind, Bilal and Carmen respectively

= 21000 : 16000 : 12000 = 21 : 16 : 12

$\therefore \text{Bilal's profit share} = \frac{16}{49} \times 98000$

= ₹ 32000

24. (c) Let C's share = ₹ x

$B\text{'s share} = ₹\ \frac{6x}{5},$

$A\text{'s share} = ₹\frac{5}{2} \times \frac{6x}{5} = ₹\ 3x$

$\text{Share of } A : B : C = 3x : \frac{6x}{5} : x = 15 : 6 : 5$

$\therefore B\text{'s Share} = ₹\ \frac{6}{15 + 6 + 5} \times 29120 = ₹\ 6720$

25. (a) Swati starts a business with amount = ₹ 4200

Given, Bani joins Swati as her partner after 5 months.

Let share of Bani = ₹ x

According to the question,

$4200 \times 12 : x \times 7 = 2 : 5$

$\Rightarrow \quad \frac{4200 \times 12}{7x} = \frac{2}{5} \Rightarrow 14x = 4200 \times 12 \times 5$

$\Rightarrow \quad x = 300 \times 60 \Rightarrow x = ₹\ 18000$

$\therefore$ Bani's contribution of amount = ₹ 18000

26. (c) Let B invested the sum for x months.

According to the question,

$5 \times 8 : 6 \times x = 5 : 9$

$\therefore \quad x = \frac{8 \times 5 \times 9}{6 \times 5} = 12$ months

27. (d) Ratio of investment by Mohan and Sohan

M : S

6000 : 8000

3 : 4

Profit ratio of Mohan and Sohan

$= (3 \times 12) : (4 \times 6) = 6 : 4 = 3 : 2$

Hence, required ratio is 3 : 2.

28. (a) Investment of A, B and C is ₹10000, ₹15000, and ₹20000.

A's investment

$= 10000 \times 3 + 2 \times 5000 = ₹40000$

B's investment

$= 15000 \times 3 + 2 \times 5000 = ₹55000$

C's investment

$= 20000 \times 1 + 10000 \times 2 = ₹40000$

Now, the ratio of the profit

= 40000 : 55000 : 40000 = 8 : 11 : 8

11

Mixture & Alligation

Mixture

When two or more than two substances are mixed in a certain ratio, then the resultant is called mixture.

Alligation Rule

If a substance of dearer price (₹ d per unit) is mixed with another substance of cheaper price (₹ c per unit) to form a mixture, whose mean price is ₹ m per unit, then

$$\frac{\text{Quantity of cheaper substance } (n_1)}{\text{Quantity of dearer substance } (n_2)} = \frac{\text{Dearer Price } (d) - \text{Mean Price } (m)}{\text{Mean Price } (m) - \text{Cheaper Price } (c)}$$

Where, n_1/n_2 is the ratio in which the quantities of the given substance must be mixed.

The Alligation rule is represented as,

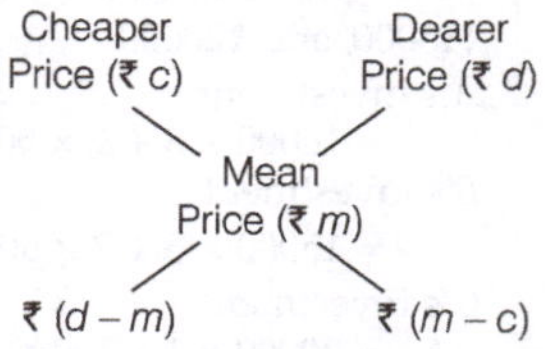

Hence, Quantity of cheaper : Quantity of dearer

$$= (d - m) : (m - c) = \frac{d - m}{m - c}$$

Ex. 1 In what ratio must water be mixed with milk, costing ₹ 35 per litre, in order to get a mixture costing ₹ 28 per litre.

Sol. By Alligation rule,

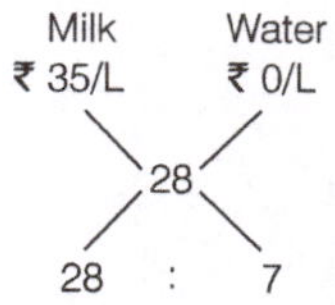

∴ Water : Milk $= 7 : 28 = 1 : 4$

Diluting Mixture

If a container contains 'x' units of liquid, from which 'y' units is taken out and replaced with another liquid, then after n number of such operations, the final quantity of the original liquid in the container $= \left[x\left(1 - \frac{y}{x}\right)^n\right]$ units.

Ex. 2 A jar has 100 L, from the jar 20L of wine was taken out and replaced by equal quantity of water. If 20L of the newly formed mixture is taken out of the jar, what is the final quantity of wine left in the jar?

Sol. Here, $x = 100\text{L}, y = 20\text{L}$ and $n = 2$

$$\therefore \text{ Quantity of wine} = x\left(1 - \frac{y}{x}\right)^n = 100\left(1 - \frac{20}{100}\right)^2 = 100 \times \frac{16}{25} = 64 \text{ L}$$

Creating New Mixture

If two vessels of equal capacity contain mixture of liquid x and y in ratio of $a : b$ and $c : d$, respectively, emptied into a new vessel, then the ratio of

$$\text{liquid } x \text{ and } y \text{ in new vessel} = \left[\frac{a}{a+b} + \frac{c}{c+d}\right] : \left[\frac{b}{a+b} + \frac{d}{c+d}\right]$$

Ex. 3 Two containers have milk and water in the ratio 1 : 2 and 3 : 4, respectively. If both containers are emptied into a bigger container, then find the ratio of milk to water in bigger container?

Sol. Here, $a = 1, b = 2, c = 3$ and $d = 4$

∴ Ratio of milk to water in bigger container

$$= \left(\frac{a}{a+b} + \frac{c}{c+d}\right) : \left(\frac{b}{a+b} + \frac{d}{c+d}\right) = \left(\frac{1}{1+2} + \frac{3}{3+4}\right) : \left(\frac{2}{1+2} + \frac{4}{3+4}\right)$$

$$= \left(\frac{1}{3} + \frac{3}{7}\right) : \left(\frac{2}{3} + \frac{4}{7}\right) = \frac{16}{21} : \frac{26}{21} = 8 : 13$$

Ex. 4 Two varities of tea costing ₹ 8/kg and ₹ 10/kg respectively are mixed in the ratio 5 : 3. Find the cost price per kg of resultant mixture.

Sol. Here, $x = 8,\ y = 10,\ a = 5,\ b = 3$

$$\text{Average price per kg} = \frac{ax + by}{a + b} = \frac{5 \times 8 + 3 \times 10}{5 + 3} = \frac{70}{8} = ₹\ 8.7/\text{kg}$$

SSC Exam Scanner

SSC CGL 2024 (Tier I & II)

1. 8 kg of maize costing ₹ 51 per kg, is mixed with 9 kg of maize costing ₹ 68 per kg. The average per kg price of mixed maize is:
SSC CGL (Tier-II) 20/01/2025 Shift-I
(a) ₹ 60 (b) ₹ 58
(c) ₹ 59 (d) ₹ 61

2. Vessel A contains milk and water in the ratio 4 : 5. Vessel B contains milk and water in the ratio 2 : 1. If x L mixture of A is mixed with y L mixture of B, then the ratio of milk to water in the mixture becomes 8 : 5. Find the ratio $x : y$.
SSC CGL (Tier-II) 18/01/2025 Shift-I
(a) 3 : 10 (b) 5 : 6
(c) 2 : 5 (d) 3 : 4

3. How much rice of ₹ 4 per kg should be mixed to 15 kg of rice of ₹ 10 per kg, so as to make a mixture worth ₹ 6.50 per kg?
SSC CGL (Tier-I) 26/09/2024 Shift-III
(a) 15 kg (b) 21 kg
(c) 30 kg (d) 40 kg

4. Half litre of a solution contains 15% of alcohol. To change the alcohol concentration to 50%, find the quantity of alcohol to be mixed.
SSC CGL (Tier-I) 26/09/2024 Shift-II
(a) 250 ml (b) 350 ml
(c) 175 ml (d) 400 ml

5. A man buys 10 kg of wheat at a rate of ₹ 26/kg. The wheat is mixed with 6 kg of other good quality of wheat to get a mixture at a price of ₹ 35/kg. The price of good quality wheat per kg (in ₹) is
SSC CGL (Tier-I) 24/09/2024 Shift-II
(a) 38 (b) 42
(c) 50 (d) 46

6. The ratio of milk to water in 10 L of a mixture is 3 : 2. If this ratio is to be made 2 : 3, then the quantity of water to be added to the mixture is
SSC CGL (Tier-I) 24/09/2024 Shift-II
(a) 10 L (b) 8 L
(c) 5 L (d) 12 L

7. In what ratio, sugar costing ₹ 78 per kg be mixed with sugar costing ₹ 46 per kg such that by selling the mixture at ₹ 75 per kg there is a gain of 20%? SSC CGL (Tier-I) 24/09/2024 Shift-I
(a) 33 : 37 (b) 31 : 29
(c) 37 : 31 (d) 33 : 31

8. A mango juice is made by mixing water and mango concentrate in the ratio 9 : 7. If x L of water and $3x$ L of mango concentrate is mixed in 160 L of mango juice, then the new ratio becomes 13 : 14. What is the quantity of the new mango juice (in litres) ?
SSC CGL (Tier-I) 23/09/2024 Shift-II
(a) 197 (b) 212 (c) 206 (d) 216

9. There is a 32 L mixture of milk and water. The ratio of milk and water in this mixture is 5 : 3. How many litres of water should be added to this mixture so that the resultant mixture has 50% water in it?
SSC CGL (Tier-I) 23/09/2024 Shift-I
(a) 8 (b) 6 (c) 5 (d) 4

10. 15 kg of ₹ 10 per kg wheat is mixed with 5 kg of another type of wheat to get a mixture costing ₹ 30 per kg. Find the price (per kg) of the costlier wheat. SSC CGL (Tier-I) 19/09/2024 Shift-I
(a) ₹ 70 (b) ₹ 80
(c) ₹ 60 (d) ₹ 90

11. 42 L of milk at ₹ 25 per L is mixed with 28 litres of milk at ₹ 40 per L. Find the average price of the mixture. SSC CGL (Tier-I) 17/09/2024 Shift-III
(a) ₹ 31.5 (b) ₹ 32.5
(c) ₹ 32 (d) ₹ 31

12. Two different quantities of the same solution having ingredients A and B are stored in two different containers. In the first container, there are 252 L of A and 441 litre of B. In the second container, the total quantity of the solution was 1188 L. How much of the solution in the second container was made up of ingredient B?
SSC CGL (Tier-I) 13/09/2024 Shift-II
(a) 765 L (b) 756 L
(c) 752 L (d) 760 L

13. 2 varieties of tea powders worth ₹ 250/kg and ₹ 300/kg are mixed with a third variety of tea powder in the ratio 1 : 1 : 2. If the mixture is worth ₹ 350/kg, find the price of the third variety tea powder.
SSC CGL (Tier-I) 13/09/2024 Shift-II
(a) ₹ 450/kg (b) ₹ 400/kg
(c) ₹ 425/kg (d) ₹ 500/kg

14. A shopkeeper mixes two types of rice costing ₹ 250/5 kg and ₹ 280/5 kg in the ratio 7 : 8. Find the net cost of the resultant mixture (per kg).
SSC CGL (Tier-I) 13/09/2024 Shift-I
(a) ₹ 32.50 (b) ₹ 53.20
(c) ₹ 52.30 (d) ₹ 25.30

15. A merchant mixes two varieties of sugar of 5 kg and 3 kg, which costs him ₹ 4 and ₹ 6 per kg, respectively. What is the cost price (in ₹) of the mixture per kg?
SSC CGL (Tier-I) 12/09/2024 Shift-III
(a) ₹ 4.35 (b) ₹ 4.45
(c) ₹ 4.75 (d) ₹ 4.21

16. If one man adds 6 L of water to 10 L of milk and another man adds 4 L of water to 8 L of milk. Find the ratio of milk in the two mixtures.
SSC CGL (Tier-I) 10/09/2024 Shift-III
(a) 16 : 15 (b) 12 : 11
(c) 16 : 17 (d) 15 : 16

17. The concentrations of three acids, A, B and C, are specified as 20%, 30% and 40%, respectively. They are blended in a ratio of 3 : 5 : a, yielding a solution with a concentration of 30%. What is the value of 'a'?
SSC CGL (Tier-I) 10/09/2024 Shift-II
(a) 3 (b) 1 (c) 2 (d) 4

SSC CGL 2023-2020 (Tier I & II)

18. How many kilogram of rice costing ₹ 60 per kg must be mixed with 24 kg of rice costing ₹ 42 per kg so that there may be a gain of 12% by selling the mixture at ₹ 56 per kg?
SSC CGL (Tier-II) 07/03/2023 Shift-II
(a) 22 kg (b) 19.2 kg
(c) 20 kg (d) 21.2 kg

19. If 80 L of milk solution has 60% milk in it, then how much milk should be added to make milk 80% in the solution?
SSC CGL (Tier-II) 06/03/2023 Shift-II
(a) 70 L (b) 50 L (c) 60 L (d) 80 L

20. 40 L of milk are kept in a container. 4 L of milk were removed from this container and replaced with water. This procedure was performed two more times. How much milk does the container now hold?
SSC CGL (Tier-II) 02/03/2023 Shift-I
(a) 30 L (b) 34.23 L
(c) 29.16 L (d) 32 L

21. Rini has mixed two colours 'C_1' and 'C_2', in the ratio 2 : 3. If the rate of the colour 'C_1' is 500 per unit and she is selling the mixture of the two colours at ₹ 650 per unit at

breakeven price, then what is the rate (in ₹) per unit of the second colour, that is, 'C_2'?
SSC CGL (Tier-I) 27/07/2023 Shift-I

(a) 750 (b) 725
(c) 760 (d) 765

22. A vessel is filled with liquid, 5 parts of which are water and 11 parts syrup. what part of the mixture must be drawn off and replaced with water, so that the mixture may be syrup and water in the ratio 3 : 2?
SSC CGL (Tier-I) 26/07/2023 Shift-I

(a) $\frac{14}{45}$ (b) $\frac{27}{35}$
(c) $\frac{36}{65}$ (d) $\frac{7}{55}$

23. A 40 L mixture contains 25% alcohol and 75% water. If 10 L of water are added to the mixture, then the percentage of alcohol in the new mixture is
SSC CGL (Tier-I) 25/07/2023 Shift-IV

(a) 27% (b) 18% (c) 20% (d) 25%

24. Rice worth ₹ 35 per kg and ₹ 38 per kg are mixed with a third variety in the ratio 2 : 1 : 2. If the mixture is worth ₹ 42 per kg, the price of the third variety per kg is
SSC CGL (Tier-I) 25/07/2023 Shift-III

(a) ₹ 52 (b) ₹ 53
(c) ₹ 54 (d) ₹ 51

25. If two qualities of pulses 'X' and 'Y' of prices ₹ 100 and ₹ 150 per kg are mixed in the ratio 7 : 20, then what is the price (in ₹) of this mixture of pulses (correct to the nearest ₹?)
SSC CGL (Tier-I) 18/07/2023 Shift-II

(a) 137 (b) 135
(c) 134 (d) 136

26. One quality of rice at ₹ 45 per kg is mixed with another quality at a certain rate in the ratio of 3 : 2. If the mixture so formed is worth ₹ 50 per kg, what is the rate per kg of the second quality of rice?
SSC CGL (Tier-I) 17/07/2023 Shift-III

(a) ₹ 57 (b) ₹ 57.5
(c) ₹ 58 (d) ₹ 58.5

27. In what ratio must water be mixed with milk, costing ₹ 32 per L, in order to get a mixture costing ₹ 28 per L ? SSC CGL (Tier-I) 14/07/2023 Shift-II

(a) 8 : 1 (b) 7 : 1
(c) 1 : 7 (d) 1 : 8

28. *P* and *Q* are two alloys of aluminium and copper. The ratios of aluminium and copper in *P* and *Q* are 5 : 11 and 3 : 5, respectively. If a third alloy is formed by mixing alloys *P* and *Q* in the ratio of 1 : 3, then aluminium is what percentage (rounded off to the nearest integer) of the copper in the third alloy?
SSC CGL (Tier-I) 13/12/2022 Shift-IV

(a) 63% (b) 52% (c) 48% (d) 56%

29. A can of water and milk mixture contains 60% milk. A part of this mixture is replaced by another mixture containing 50% milk and the percentage of milk was found to be 52%. The quantity of mixture replaced is
SSC CGL (Tier-I) 13/12/2022 Shift-II

(a) $\frac{1}{5}$ (b) $\frac{4}{5}$ (c) $\frac{2}{5}$ (d) $\frac{3}{5}$

30. A 100 mL solution of H_2SO_4 having concentration of 20% is mixed with a 50% concentrated *x* ml mixture such that the net mixture is 30% concentrated. Determine *x*.
SSC CGL (Tier-I) 08/12/2022 Shift-I

(a) 70 mL (b) 80 mL
(c) 60 mL (d) 50 mL

31. A mixture contains milk and water in the ratio of 5 : 3, respectively. On adding 7 L of water, the ratio of milk to water becomes 1 : 2. Find the quantity of milk in the mixture.
SSC CGL (Tier-I) 08/12/2022 Shift-I

(a) 7 L (b) 10 L (c) 5 L (d) 3 L

32. Wheat worth ₹ 80 per kg and ₹ 50 per kg is mixed with a third variety in the ratio 1 : 2 : 3 . If the mixture is worth ₹ 75 per kg, then the price of the third variety per kg will be equal to
SSC CGL (Tier-I) 07/12/2022 Shift-I

(a) ₹95 (b) ₹85 (c) ₹80 (d) ₹90

33. A mixture of milk and water measures 60 L. It contains 10% water. How much water should be added to it, so that the water may be 25%? SSC CGL (Tier-I) 02/12/2022 Shift-I

(a) 18 L (b) 14 L
(c) 16 L (d) 12 L

34. A container contains 25 L of milk, From this container, 5 L of milk is taken out and replaced by water. This process is further repeated two times. How much milk is there in the container now?
SSC CGL (Tier-I) 01/12/2022 Shift-III

(a) 11.5 L (b) 14.8 L
(c) 13.5 L (d) 12.8 L

35. Alloy A contains metals x and y in the ratio 5 : 2 and Alloy B contains these metals in the ratio 3 : 4. Alloy C is prepared by mixing A and B in the ratio 4 : 5. The percentage of *y* in Alloy *C* is SSC CGL (Tier-I) 18/08/2021 Shift-III

(a) $55\frac{5}{9}$% (b) $33\frac{4}{9}$%
(c) $44\frac{4}{9}$% (d) $66\frac{4}{9}$%

36. 25 L of a mixture contains 30% of spirit and rest water. If 5 L of water be mixed in it, the percentage of spirit in the new mixture is
SSC CGL (Tier-I) 06/03/2020 Shift-III

(a) $12\frac{1}{2}$% (b) $33\frac{1}{3}$%
(c) 45% (d) 25%

SSC CPO SI 2024

37. The quantity of a milk in a mixture of milk and water is $\frac{4}{5}$ of the volume of the mixture. After adding 1 L of milk to 5 L of the mixture, the percentage of water in the mixture is
SSC CPO 29/06/2024 Shift-III

(a) $\frac{200}{6}$% (b) 15%
(c) $\frac{100}{6}$% (d) 17.5%

38. An alloy contains the metals *A*, *B* and C in the ratio 2 : 3 : 1 and another contains the metals *B*, *C* and *D* in the ratio 5 : 4 : 3. If equal weights of both alloys are mixed together to form a third alloy, then how much part of the Metal *B* is in new alloy? SSC CPO 29/06/2024 Shift-III

(a) $\frac{1}{8}$ (b) $\frac{1}{6}$ (c) $\frac{3}{24}$ (d) $\frac{11}{24}$

39. A drink is made by mixing water and juice in the ratio 9 : 7. If *x* L of water and 2*x* L of juice are mixed in 160 L of drink, then the new ratio becomes 13 : 15. The quantity of drink (in litres) is
SSC CPO 29/06/2024 Shift-II

(a) 240 (b) 280
(c) 300 (d) 260

40. If two kinds of rice which cost ₹ 25 a kg and ₹ 40 a kg are mixed in the ratio of 3 : 2, then find the cost of the mixture per kg. SSC CPO 29/06/2024 Shift-I

(a) ₹ 31 (b) ₹ 30
(c) ₹ 32 (d) ₹ 33

41. A vessel contains 18 L mixture of milk and water in the ratio 5 : 1. If 3 L of milk is added to the vessel, then how much water (in L) should be added to the vessel to have milk and water in the ratio 9 : 2?
SSC CPO 28/06/2024 Shift-III

(a) 2 (b) 1.5 (c) 1 (d) 0.5

42. In alloys A and B, the ratio of lead to tin is 5 : 3 and 3 : 1, respectively. 80 kg of alloy A and 100 kg of alloy B are mixed together to form a new alloy. What is the amount of tin (in kg) in the new alloy?
SSC CPO 27/06/2024 Shift-III
(a) 90 (b) 55 (c) 81.3 (d) 68

43. A mixture of 750 kg of alloy of copper and tin contains 25% tin. How much tin must be added, so that it becomes 70% of the mixture?
SSC CPO 27/06/2024 Shift-II
(a) 956 kg (b) 1125 kg
(c) 1097 kg (d) 895 kg

44. A 12 L solution of acid and water contains 30% acid. How much water (in litres) must be added to get a solution having 20% acid?
SSC CPO 27/06/2024 Shift-I
(a) 3 (b) 6 (c) 5 (d) 4

SSC CHSL 2024 - 2022 (Tier I & II)

45. Pomegranate juice contains 10% sugar solution and orange juice contains 30% sugar solution. What is the percentage of sugar solution in a mixture of two litres of pomegranate juice and three litres of orange juice?
SSC CHSL (Tier-I) 11/07/2024 Shift-II
(a) 22% (b) 25% (c) 20% (d) 40%

46. A bucket contains a mixture of milk and water in the proportion of 7: 5. If 9 L of milk is replaced by water, then the ratio becomes 7 : 9. How much milk was there in the bucket initially?
SSC CHSL (Tier-I) 10/07/2024 Shift-IV
(a) 36 L (b) 35 L (c) 30 L (d) 25 L

47. Ratna buys 10 kg of rice for ₹ 88 per kg and another 20 kg of rice for ₹187 per kg. What is the per kg cost (in ₹) of the total mixture of rice for her?
SSC CHSL (Tier-I) 10/07/2024 Shift-II
(a) 148 (b) 150 (c) 158 (d) 154

48. In what proportion must tea worth ₹ 27 and ₹ 31 per kg be mixed, so as to gain 25% by selling the mixture at ₹ 36 per kg?
SSC CHSL (Tier-I) 09/07/2024 Shift-I
(a) 3 : 7 (b) 2 : 11
(c) 11 : 9 (d) 9 : 11

49. A mixture contains alcohol and water in the ratio of 12 : 5. On adding 14 L of water, the ratio of alcohol to water becomes 4 : 3. The quantity of alcohol in mixture is
SSC CHSL (Tier-I) 04/07/2024 Shift-IV
(a) 18 L (b) 28 L (c) 30 L (d) 42 L

50. How much water should be added to 60 L of milk at $1\frac{1}{2}$ L a rupee, so as to have a mixture worth $1\frac{7}{8}$ L a rupee? **SSC CHSL (Tier-I) 02/07/2024 Shift-I**
(a) 15 L (b) 12 L
(c) 27 L (d) 20 L

51. In what ratio must a grocer mix two varieties of pulses costing ₹ 60 and ₹ 75 per kg, respectively, so as to get a mixture worth ₹ 65 per kg?
SSC CHSL (Tier-I) 01/07/2024 Shift-III
(a) 3 : 4 (b) 2 : 1
(c) 2 : 3 (d) 1 : 2

52. The concentration of three wines A, B and C are 10%, 20% and 30%, respectively. They are mixed in the ratio 2 : 3 : x resulting in a 23% concentration solution. Find the value of x.
SSC CHSL (Tier-II) 02/11/2023 Shift-I
(a) 5 (b) 8 (c) 6 (d) 7

53. A mixture of 70 L of wine and water contains 10% of water. How much water must be added to make the water $12\frac{1}{2}$% of the resulting mixture?
SSC CHSL (Tier-I) 14/08/2023 Shift-IV
(a) 5 L (b) 3 L
(c) 2 L (d) 4 L

54. A blended tea in a barrel contains Assam, Darjeeling and Nilgiri Hills in the ratio 2 : 3 : 1. Another barrel contains Darjeeling, Nilgiri Hills and Kangra Valley in the ratio 5 : 4 : 3. If equal weights of both blended tea mix together to make a new brand, then the weight of Kangra Valley per kilogram in the new brand is
SSC CHSL (Tier-I) 10/08/2023 Shift-III
(a) 500 gm (b) 100 gm
(c) 250 gm (d) 125 gm

55. A grocer mixes two varieties of tea priced at ₹ 80/kg and ₹ 85/kg in a certain ratio to produce a new variety priced at ₹ 82/kg. What is the ratio in which the two varieties were mixed to obtain the new variety?
SSC CHSL (Tier-I) 10/08/2023 Shift-III
(a) 1 : 3 (b) 2 : 5
(c) 4 : 4 (d) 3 : 2

56. In what ratio, wheat at ₹ 23 per kg should be mixed with wheat at ₹ 14 per kg, so that on selling the mixture at ₹ 20 per kg there is a profit of 25%?
SSC CHSL (Tier-I) 09/08/2023 Shift-I
(a) 5 : 7 (b) 3 : 5 (c) 2 : 3 (d) 2 : 7

57. In what ratio does a grocer mix tea at ₹ 26 per kg and ₹ 32 per kg so that by selling the mixture at ₹ 30 per kg they may gain 10%?
SSC CHSL (Tier-I) 08/08/2023 Shift-II
(a) 7 : 26 (b) 16 :7
(c) 26 : 7 (d) 7 :16

58. In two alloys, the ratio of Aluminium to Zinc are 5 : 6 and 3 : 5. If 242 kg of the first alloy and 144 kg of the second alloy are mixed, then the ratio of Aluminium and Zinc in the new alloy will be
SSC CHSL (Tier-I) 07/08/2023 Shift-IV
(a) 76 : 117 (b) 82 : 111
(c) 93 : 100 (d) 68 : 125

59. Two vessels of equal capacity contain juice and water in the ratio of 3 : 5 and 3 : 1, respectively. The mixture of both the vessels are mixed and transferred into a bigger vessel. What is the ratio of juice and water in the new mixture?
SSC CHSL (Tier-I) 21/03/2023 Shift-IV
(a) 13 : 9 (b) 9 : 7
(c) 8 : 9 (d) 7 : 3

60. A beaker is filled with a liquid, 3 parts of which are water and 7 parts some medicine. What part of the mixture should be replaced with water so that the resultant mixture has water and medicine in a ratio 1 : 1? **SSC CHSL (Tier-I) 02/06/2022 Shift-I**
(a) $\frac{2}{7}$ (b) $\frac{1}{7}$ (c) $\frac{2}{5}$ (d) $\frac{1}{5}$

61. Find the ratio in which a grocer should mix two varieties of pulses costing ₹ 75 and ₹ 90 per kg, respectively, so as to get a mixture costing ₹ 80 per kg.
SSC CHSL (Tier-I) 02/06/2022 Shift-I
(a) 2 : 3 (b) 3 : 2
(c) 1 : 2 (d) 2 : 1

62. In what ratio must a grocer mix two varieties of pulses costing ₹ 15 and ₹ 20 per kg, respectively, so as to get a mixture worth ₹ 18 per kg.
SSC CHSL (Tier-I) 31/05/2022 Shift-I
(a) 3 : 2 (b) 3 : 4 (c) 2 : 3 (d) 2 : 5

63. A beaker contains a mixture of two liquids X and Y in the ratio 5 : 3. When 6 L of the mixture is drawn off and then replaced with Y, the ratio of X and Y becomes 5 : 7. How many litres of liquid X was contained in the beaker initially? **SSC CHSL (Tier-I) 30/05/2022 Shift-I**
(a) 18.25 (b) 22.5
(c) 11.25 (d) 15.5

SSC MTS 2024

64. Arjun mixed three different oils to form a mixture costing ₹ 25 per litre. The ratio of the three varieties of oil was 1 : 5 : 2. What is the cost (per litre in ₹) of the second variety, if the cost per litre of the first and third varieties was ₹ 20 and ₹ 30, respectively?
SSC MTS 29/10/2024 Shift-III

(a) 25 (b) 28
(c) 26 (d) 24

65. A grocer wishes to sell a mixture of two varieties of rice worth ₹ 48 per kg. In what ratio must he mix the rice to reach this selling price, when the cost of one variety of rice is ₹ 42 per kg and the other is ₹ 60 per kg?
SSC MTS 29/10/2024 Shift-III

(a) 1 : 2 (b) 2 : 1
(c) 3 : 2 (d) 2 : 3

66. In what ratio must a shopkeeper mix sugar at ₹ 30/kg and ₹ 32.5/kg so that by selling the mixture at ₹ 34.1/kg, he may get 10% profit?
SSC MTS 28/10/2024 Shift-II

(a) 3 : 2 (b) 5 : 4
(c) 4 : 3 (d) 2 : 1

67. Find the ratio in which tomatoes worth ₹ 45/kg can be mixed with tomatoes worth ₹ 60/kg, so that the mixture will be worth ₹ 54/kg.
SSC MTS 28/10/2024 Shift-II

(a) 3 : 7 (b) 3 : 5
(c) 2 : 3 (d) 2 : 5

68. A jar contains a mixture with 45% syrup. A portion of this mixture is replaced by another mixture containing 30% syrup. The new mixture is found to have 34% syrup. What is the ratio in which these mixtures should be mixed to obtain the new mixture?
SSC MTS 23/10/2024 Shift-II

(a) 7 : 10 (b) 5 : 13
(c) 3 : 14 (d) 4 : 11

69. Raj prepares a 60 gm mixture by combining two ingredients X and Y. The cost of ingredient X is ₹ 80 per 5 gm, and the cost of ingredient Y is ₹ 80 per 10 gm. Ingredients X and Y are mixed in a manner that the cost of the resulting mixture is ₹ 14 per gm. What is the quantity of ingredient X (in gm) in the mixture?
SSC MTS 22/10/2024 Shift-II

(a) 30 (b) 45
(c) 15 (d) 60

70. A can contains a mixture of two liquids, grape juice and pineapple juice in the ratio 13 : 11. When 8 litres of the mixture is drawn off, and the can is filled with pineapple juice, the ratio becomes 13 : 14. How many litres of pineapple juice was initially contained in the can?
SSC MTS 21/10/2024 Shift-II

(a) 14 L (b) 28 L
(c) 11 L (d) 33 L

71. A chef has two cans of acids and water mixture. He combines the contents of both cans in a beaker. The resulting mixture has half water and half acid. What is the quantity in which he mixed the contents of can 1 and can 2, given that can 2 has an acid-to-water ratio of 2 : 3 and can 1 has an acid-to-water ratio of 5 : 3?
SSC MTS 18/10/2024 Shift-II

(a) 2 : 3 (b) 4 : 5 (c) 4 : 7 (d) 3 : 7

72. In what proportion must a man mix milk worth ₹ 3.3/litre with milk worth ₹ 1.8/litre so that the mixture may be worth ₹ 2.4/litre?
SSC MTS 17/10/2024 Shift-II

(a) 2 : 3 (b) 4 : 5 (c) 3 : 2 (d) 1 : 3

73. In what ratio must a shopkeeper mix 2 types of rice worth ₹ 80/kg and ₹ 100/kg, so that the average cost of the mixture is ₹ 95/kg?
SSC MTS 16/10/2024 Shift-II

(a) 1 : 4 (b) 1 : 3 (c) 1 : 2 (d) 2 : 3

74. A mixture contains 8 kg of tea costing ₹ 295 per kilogram and 10 kg of tea costing ₹ 250 per kilogram. The average price per kilogram (in ₹) of the mixture is
SSC MTS 14/10/2024 Shift-I

(a) 270 (b) 259.60
(c) 250.70 (d) 273

75. A chemist prepares 100 grams of medicine by mixing two ingredients X and Y. The rate of X is ₹ 1500 per 100 grams and that of Y is ₹ 50 per 10 grams. X and Y are mixed in such a way that the cost of the resulting medicine is ₹ 13 per gram. What is the quantity of X (in grams) in the medicine?
SSC MTS 09/10/2024 Shift-I

(a) 10 (b) 30 (c) 80 (d) 20

76. A commodity is made of two metals, A and B, which cost ₹ 35 per kg and ₹ 40 per kg, respectively, in the ratio of 2 : 3. What is the cost (in ₹) of 12 kilograms of this commodity?
SSC MTS 09/10/2024 Shift-I

(a) 228 (b) 152 (c) 456 (d) 38

77. There is a 21 litres mixture of milk and water. The ratio of milk and water in the mixture is 4 : 3. Find the amount of water (in litres) that should be added to this mixture so that the resulting mixture has 50% of water in it.
SSC MTS 08/10/2024 Shift-I

(a) 4 (b) 1
(c) 3 (d) 2

78. Two vessels A and B, contain spirit and water in the ratio 3 : 4 and 5 : 3, respectively. Find the ratio in which these two mixtures be mixed to obtain a new mixture in vessel C containing spirit and water in the ratio 4 : 3.
SSC MTS 07/10/2024 Shift-I

(a) 3 : 8 (b) 3 : 7
(c) 5 : 8 (d) 4 : 7

79. A vendor wants to gain 25% by adding water to milk and selling the mixture at the cost price. Find the ratio of water and milk in the mixture.
SSC MTS 07/10/2024 Shift-I

(a) 2 : 5 (b) 1 : 4
(c) 2 : 7 (d) 1 : 5

80. A grocer mixes two varieties of tea worth ₹120/kg and ₹125/kg in a ratio to produce a new variety worth ₹122/kg. What is the ratio of the varieties to be mixed to obtain the new variety?
SSC MTS 01/10/2024 Shift-I

(a) 2 : 5 (b) 4 : 4
(c) 1 : 3 (d) 3 : 2

81. Rice worth ₹43/kg and ₹67/kg are mixed with a third variety in the ratio 2 : 1 : 5. If the mixture is worth ₹96/kg, the price (in ₹) of the third variety of rice per kg will be
SSC MTS 30/09/2024 Shift-I

(a) 131 (b) 159
(c) 123 (d) 142

SSC MTS 2023-2021

82. Mixture I with a volume of 8 L has 80% milk and mixture II with a volume of 6 L has 60% milk. Both the mixtures are mixed. Find the percentage of milk in the final mixture.
SSC MTS 14/09/2023 Shift-I

(a) $\frac{600}{7}$ (b) $\frac{500}{9}$
(c) $\frac{500}{7}$ (d) $\frac{800}{9}$

83. A milk vendor has 2 vessels of milk and water. The first contains 80% milk and the rest is water. The second contains 50% milk. How much mixture (in L) should he mix from each of the vessels so as to get 9 L of mixture such that the ratio of water to milk is 1 : 2 ? (Write your answer in the order of vessel 1st and vessel 2nd) SSC MTS 13/09/2023 Shift-I

(a) 6, 3 (b) 4, 5
(c) 3, 6 (d) 5, 4

84. A milk vendor mixes water with milk and by selling the mixture at the cost price, he gains $16\frac{1}{4}\%$. Find the ratio of milk to water in the mixture. SSC MTS 11/09/2023 Shift-II

(a) 7 : 40 (b) 80 : 13
(c) 13 : 80 (d) 40 : 7

85. In some quantity of water, four times the quantity of milk is added and the quantity of the mixture is now 7.5 L. How much more milk is to be added to the mixture to have 90% milk in the mixture? SSC MTS 11/09/2023 Shift-I

(a) 9 L (b) 9.5 L
(c) 6 L (d) 7.5 L

86. In what ratio, rice costing ₹ 185 per kg be mixed with rice costing ₹ 95 per kg such that by selling the mixture at ₹ 140 per kg, there is a gain of 40% ? SSC MTS 08/09/2023 Shift-II

(a) 2 : 19 (b) 3 : 23
(c) 2 : 13 (d) 1 : 17

87. A vessel contains liquid *A* and liquid *B* in the ratio 4 : 9. If 8 L of liquid *A* is added to the vessel, then the new ratio becomes 8 : 9. Find the quantity of liquid *A* (in litres) in the original mixture. SSC MTS 04/09/2023 Shift-II

(a) 12 (b) 9
(c) 8 (d) 6

88. A grocery seller mixes two varieties of tea costing ₹ 300 per kg and ₹ 160 per kg in such a ratio that by selling this mixture at the rate of ₹ 187 per kg the shopkeeper earns 10% profit. In what respective, ratio does the grocery seller mix the two varieties of tea? SSC MTS 04/09/2023 Shift-II

(a) 2 : 13
(b) 13 : 3
(c) 13 : 2
(d) 1 : 13

89. In what ratio must a grocer mix two varieties of pulses costing ₹ 18 per kg and ₹ 22 per kg, respectively. So, as to get a mixture worth ₹ 19.50 per kg ? SSC MTS 01/09/2023 Shift-III

(a) 5 : 3 (b) 5 : 1
(c) 1 : 5 (d) 5 : 2

90. From a container having pure milk, 35% is replaced by water and the process is repeated thrice. At the end of the third operation the purity of the milk is SSC MTS 01/09/2023 Shift-III

(a) $21\frac{23}{80}\%$ (b) $37\frac{21}{80}\%$
(c) $23\frac{37}{80}\%$ (d) $27\frac{37}{80}\%$

91. In what ratio must a grocer mix two varieties of rice costing ₹ 128 and ₹ 143 per kg, respectively, to get a mixture of rice worth ₹ 137.75 per kg? SSC MTS 01/09/2023 Shift-I

(a) 12:5 (b) 7:13 (c) 5:4 (d) 6:7

92. Two beakers contain acid and water in the ratio 2 : 3 and 3 : 4, respectively. If equal volumes of the mixtures from these two beakers are poured into a common beaker, find the resultant ratio of acid to water in the mixture in the common beaker ? SSC MTS 12/07/2022 Shift-I

(a) 7 : 5 (b) 21 : 29
(c) 5 : 7 (d) 29 : 41

93. 80 L of a mixture of alcohol and water contains 60% alcohol. If 'X' L of water is added to this mixture, then the percentage of alcohol in the new mixture becomes 40%. What is the value of 'X' ? SSC MTS 12/07/2022 Shift-I

(a) 20 (b) 80 (c) 40 (d) 60

94. Two kinds of rice, the first costing ₹ 65 per kg and the second ₹ 95 per kg are mixed together. Find the ratio in which the 2 types are mixed, so that the mixture costs ₹ 83 per kg. SSC MTS 02/11/2021 Shift-I

(a) 19 : 13 (b) 13 : 19
(c) 2 : 3 (d) 3 : 2

95. A container has 30 L of milk from which 3 L of milk is taken out and replaced with water. The process is done three times. What is the final ratio of the water and the milk in the container? SSC MTS 02/11/2021 Shift-I

(a) 729 : 271 (b) 19 : 81
(c) 81 : 19 (d) 271 : 729

SSC GD Constable 2024

96. In a mixture, milk and water are in ratio of 7 : 9. Some milk is added to the mixture because of which ratio of milk and water becomes 11 : 9. How much milk was added as a percentage of initial mixture? SSC GD 24/02/2024 Shift-II

(a) 60% (b) 30% (c) 25% (d) 10%

97. In a mixture of 220L the ratio of water and milk is 6 : 5, respectively. How much water must be added to make the ratio of water and milk as 5:4, respectively? SSC GD 23/02/2024 Shift-IV

(a) 2 L (b) 5 L (c) 10 L (d) 3 L

98. The ratio of water and milk in a mixture is 8 : 21. If milk is 26 L more than water in this mixture, then what is the quantity of milk in the mixture? SSC GD 23/02/2024 Shift-III

(a) 46 L (b) 26 L (c) 42 L (d) 16 L

99. In a mixture of 120 L the ratio of water and milk is 5 : 7 respectively. How much water must be added to make the ratio of water and milk as 1 : 1 respectively? SSC GD 23/02/2024 Shift-II

(a) 20 L (b) 15 L (c) 10 L (d) 25 L

100. In a mixture of 110 L the ratio of water and milk is 4 : 7 respectively. How much water must be added to make the ratio of water and milk as 8 : 7 respectively? SSC GD 22/02/2024 Shift-III

(a) 30 L (b) 10 L (c) 40 L (d) 20 L

101. A mixture contains acid and water in the ratio of 7 : 4. If 2 L of water is added to it, then the ratio of acid and water becomes 7 : 5. What is the quantity of acid in the mixture? SSC GD 21/02/2024 Shift-III

(a) 14 L (b) 7 L (c) 20 L (d) 21 L

102. In a mixture, milk and water are in ratio of 2 : 3. Some milk is added to the mixture because of which ratio of milk and water becomes 10 : 3. How much milk was added as a percentage of initial mixture? SSC GD 21/02/2024 Shift-I

(a) 160% (b) 140%
(c) 100% (d) 120%

SSC Selection Post 2023

103. 20 kg of rice costing ₹ 80 per kg is mixed with *y* kg of rice costing ₹100 per kg. If the cost of this mixed rice is ₹ 84 per kg, what is the value of *y*? Graduate Level 27/06/2023 Shift-IV

(a) 6 (b) 3 (c) 4 (d) 5

104. If 36 L of 20% milk solution is mixed with 48 L of 10% milk solution, then what will be the percentage concentration of milk in the final solution? Higher Secondary Level 27/06/2023 Shift-III

(a) 14.28% (b) 15.48%
(c) 12.38% (d) 13.36%

Right Answers

1 (a)	2 (a)	3 (b)	4 (b)	5 (c)	6 (c)	7 (d)	8 (d)	9 (a)	10 (d)
11 (d)	12 (b)	13 (c)	14 (b)	15 (c)	16 (d)	17 (a)	18 (b)	19 (d)	20 (c)
21 (a)	22 (d)	23 (c)	24 (d)	25 (a)	26 (b)	27 (b)	28 (d)	29 (b)	30 (d)
31 (c)	32 (d)	33 (d)	34 (d)	35 (c)	36 (d)	37 (c)	38 (d)	39 (b)	40 (a)
41 (c)	42 (b)	43 (b)	44 (b)	45 (a)	46 (a)	47 (d)	48 (c)	49 (d)	50 (a)
51 (b)	52 (a)	53 (c)	54 (d)	55 (d)	56 (d)	57 (c)	58 (b)	59 (b)	60 (a)
61 (d)	62 (c)	63 (c)	64 (d)	65 (b)	66 (a)	67 (c)	68 (d)	69 (b)	70 (d)
71 (b)	72 (a)	73 (b)	74 (a)	75 (c)	76 (c)	77 (c)	78 (a)	79 (b)	80 (d)
81 (c)	82 (c)	83 (d)	84 (b)	85 (d)	86 (d)	87 (c)	88 (d)	89 (a)	90 (d)
91 (b)	92 (d)	93 (c)	94 (c)	95 (d)	96 (c)	97 (b)	98 (c)	99 (a)	100 (c)
101 (a)	102 (a)	103 (d)	104 (a)						

Solutions

1. (a) According to the question,

8 kg of maize → ₹ 51 per kg

9 kg of maize → ₹ 68 per kg

∴ Average per kg price of mixed maize

$$= \frac{8 \times 51 + 9 \times 68}{17} = \frac{408 + 612}{17}$$

$$= \frac{1020}{17} = ₹\,60$$

2. (a) Milk : Water

A 4 : 5

B 2 : 1

By Alligation Method

Milk in Vessel A Milk in Vessel B

$\frac{4}{9}$ $\frac{2}{3}$

$\frac{8}{13}$

$\frac{6}{117}$: $\frac{20}{117}$

$\Rightarrow$ $x : y = 3 : 10$

3. (b) According to the question,

₹ 4/kg ₹ 10/kg

₹ 6.50/kg

3.50 2.50

2.5 → 15 kg

∴ $3.5 \rightarrow \frac{15}{2.5} \times 3.5 = 21$ kg

∴ Required quantity = 21 kg

4. (b) Let quantity to be added by x ml.

According to the question,

$$\frac{500 \times \frac{15}{100} + x}{500 + x} \times 100 = 50$$

$$\Rightarrow \frac{75 + x}{500 + x} = \frac{1}{2}$$

$\Rightarrow$ $150 + 2x = 500 + x$

$\Rightarrow$ $x = 350$ ml

5. (c) By Alligation Method,

First variety (good) other variety

₹ 26/kg ₹ x/kg

₹ 35/kg

10 6

$$\Rightarrow \frac{x - 35}{35 - 26} = \frac{10}{6} \Rightarrow \frac{x - 35}{9} = \frac{5}{3}$$

$\Rightarrow$ $x = 15 + 35 = ₹\,50$/kg

Thus, price of other good quality wheat is ₹ 50/kg.

6. (c) Here, Milk = 6 L and Water = 4 L

Let x L water to be added in the mixture.

Then, $\frac{6}{4 + x} = \frac{2}{3} \Rightarrow 18 = 8 + 2x$

$\Rightarrow$ $2x = 10 \Rightarrow x = 5$ L

7. (d) Selling price = ₹ 75/ kg

Gain% = 20%

∴ Net cost price $= 75 \times \frac{100}{120} = ₹\,62.5$/kg

78 46

62.5

16.5 15.5

∴ The required ratio = 16.5:15.5 = 33 : 31

8. (d) Ratio of water and mango concentrate = 9 : 7

Quantity of water in 160 L of mixture

$= \frac{9}{16} \times 160 = 90$ L

Quantity of mango concrete in 160 L of mixture $= \frac{7}{16} \times 160 = 70$ L

When x L of water and $3x$ L of mango concrete is mixed with minute.

Quantity of water in new mixture = $90 + x$

Quantity of mango concrete mixture = $70 + 3x$

According to the question,

Ratio = 13 : 14

$$\frac{(90 + x)}{(70 + 3x)} = \frac{13}{14} \Rightarrow 1260 + 14x = 910 + 39x$$

$\Rightarrow$ $25x = 350 \Rightarrow x = \frac{350}{25} = 14$

Quantity of new mango juice

$= 90 + x + 70 + 3x$

$= 90 + 14 + 70 + 42 = 160 + 56 = 216$ L

9. (a) m w

5 : 3 ⇒ 8 → 32 ⇒ 1 → 4

20 : 12

+ x) +8

1 : 1

20 : 20

∴ $x = 8$ L

10. (d) Cost of 15 kg of wheat = 15 × 10 = ₹ 150

Cost of mixture (15 + 5) kg of wheat

= 20 × 30 = ₹ 600

Price of costlier wheat = 600 − 150 = ₹ 450

∴ Price of costlier wheat per kg $= \frac{450}{5}$

= ₹ 90 /kg

11. (d) Total quantity of milk = 42 + 28 = 70

Total quantity of mixture = 42 × 25 + 28 × 40

= 1050 + 1120 = ₹ 2170

∴ Average price of mixture $= \frac{2170}{70} = ₹\,31$

12. (b) $A : B$ in first container = 252 : 441

∴ Quantity of B is second container

$$= \frac{441}{252 + 441} \times 1188 = 756 \text{ L}$$

13. (c) Let worth of third variety be ₹ x /kg

$$\text{Average} = \frac{250 \times 1 + 300 \times 1 + 2 \times x}{4} = 350$$

$\Rightarrow$ $250 + 300 + 2x = 1400$

$\Rightarrow$ $2x = 850$

$\Rightarrow$ $x = ₹\,425$/ kg

14. (b) Net cost of resultant mixture

$$= \frac{7\times\left(\frac{250}{5}\right)+8\times\left(\frac{280}{5}\right)}{7+8}$$

$$= \frac{350+448}{15} = ₹\,53.2$$

15. (c) Cost price of mixture $= \frac{5\times4+6\times3}{5+3}$

$$= \frac{20+18}{8} = \frac{38}{8}$$

$$= ₹\,4.75\,/\,\text{kg}$$

16. (d) Part of milk in Mixture-I $= \frac{10}{16} = \frac{5}{8}$

Part of milk in Mixture-II $= \frac{8}{12} = \frac{2}{3}$

$$\therefore \text{Required ratio} = \frac{5}{8} : \frac{2}{3} = \frac{\frac{5}{8}}{\frac{2}{3}} = \frac{5}{8}\times\frac{3}{2}$$

$$= 15:16$$

17. (a) The concentrations of acids A, B and C are 20%, 30% and 40%, respectively.

And their blended ratio

$A:B:C$

$3:5:a$

$\therefore$ According to the question,

$0.2\times3+0.3\times5+0.4\times a = 0.3(3+5+a)$

$\Rightarrow 0.6+1.5+0.4a = 0.3(8+a)$

$\Rightarrow 2.1+0.4a = 2.4+0.3a$

$\Rightarrow 0.4a-0.3a = 2.4-2.1$

$\Rightarrow 0.1a = 0.3$

$\Rightarrow a = \frac{0.3}{0.1} = 3$

$\Rightarrow a = 3$

18. (b) Cost price of mixture

$$= \frac{56\times100}{112} = ₹\,50\,/\,\text{kg}$$

By mixture Alligation method,

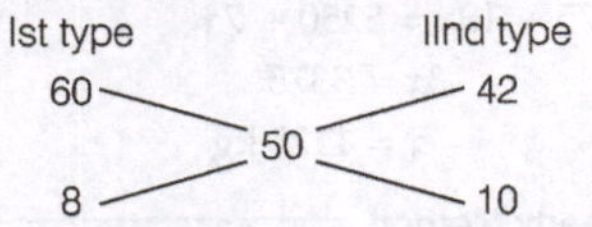

Ist type : IInd type = 8:10 = 4 : 5

$\because$ 5 units = 24 kg

$\therefore$ 4 units $= \frac{24\times4}{5} = 19.2$ kg

19. (d) Milk $= 80\times\frac{60}{100} = 48$

Water $= \frac{80\times40}{100} = 32$

Let the quantity of milk added in mixture be A.

According to the question,

$$\frac{48+A}{32} = \frac{80}{20} = \frac{4}{1}$$

$\Rightarrow 48+A = 128$

$\Rightarrow A = 80$ L

20. (c) Initial quantity of milk $(T) = 40$ L

Replaced quantity $(r) = 4$ L

Total number of times $(n) = 3$

$$\text{Milk} = T\left(1-\frac{r}{T}\right)^n = 40\left(1-\frac{4}{40}\right)^3$$

$$= 40\times\frac{9}{10}\times\frac{9}{10}\times\frac{9}{10}$$

$\therefore$ Milk = 29.16 L

21. (a) C_1 and C_2 in the ratio = 2 : 3

and cost of C_1 per unit = ₹ 500

and cost of (C_1+C_2) per unit = ₹ 650

Let cost of C_2 = ₹ x

Then, $2\times500+3\times x = 650\times5$

$\Rightarrow 3x = 3250-1000 \Rightarrow x = ₹\,750$

Hence, cost of C_2 per unit = ₹ 750

22. (d) Let initial quantity of mixture is 16 L and x L mixture is replaced with water.

After replacement,

$$\text{Water} = 16\times\frac{5}{16}-\frac{5}{16}\times x+x = \frac{80+11x}{16}$$

$$\text{Syrup} = 16\times\frac{11}{16}-\frac{11}{16}\times x = \frac{176-11x}{16}$$

Given, $\frac{80+11x}{16} : \frac{176-11x}{16} = 2:3$

$\Rightarrow 80+11x : 176-11x = 2:3$

$\Rightarrow 240+33x = 352-22x$

$\Rightarrow x = \frac{112}{55}$

So, part of the mixture replaced

$$= \frac{x}{16} = \frac{112}{55}\times\frac{1}{16} = \frac{7}{55}$$

Speedy Method

Initially in mixture, let water = $5x$ L And syrup = $11x$ L and 16 y L of mixture is replaced with water.

Given, $\frac{5x-5y+16y}{11x-11y} = \frac{2}{3}$

$\Rightarrow 15x+33y = 22x-22y$

$\Rightarrow 33y+22y = 22x-15x \Rightarrow \frac{y}{x} = \frac{7}{55}$

$\therefore$ Part of the mixture replaced

$$= \frac{16y}{5x+11x} = \frac{y}{x} = \frac{7}{55}$$

23. (c) Alcohol : Water = 25 : 75 = 1 : 3

Alcohol $= \frac{40}{4}\times1 = 10$ L

After adding 10 L water,

Total mixture = 40 + 10 = 50 L

$\therefore$ Alcohol $= \frac{10}{50}\times100 = 20\%$

24. (d) Let worth of third variety = ₹ p per kg.

Quantities are $2x$ kg, x kg and $2x$ kg, respectively.

Total price $= 35\times2x+38\times x+2xp$

$= 70x+38x+2xp$

Worth of the mixture = ₹ 42 per kg

$70x+38x+2xp = 42(2x+x+2x)$

$\Rightarrow 108x+2xp = 210x \Rightarrow 2xp = 102x$

$\Rightarrow p = \frac{102x}{2x} \Rightarrow p = ₹\,51$/kg

25. (a) Total cost $= 100\times7+150\times20$

$= 700+3000 = ₹\,3700$

So, cost of mix pulses $= \frac{3700}{20+7} = \frac{3700}{27}$

$\approx ₹\,137$ per kg

Speedy Method

Let the price of mixture be ₹ x

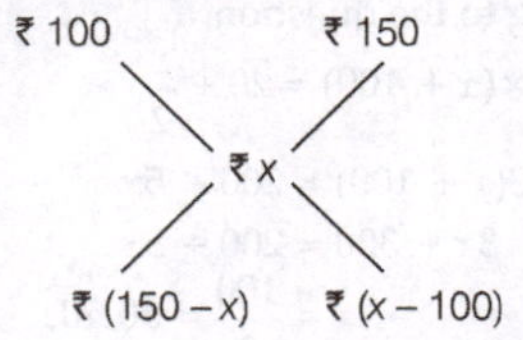

$\therefore \frac{150-x}{x-100} = \frac{7}{20} \Rightarrow 3000-20x = 7x-700$

$\Rightarrow 27x = 3700 \Rightarrow x = ₹137$ per kg

26. (b) Let another quality of rice = ₹ x / kg

By Alligation rule,

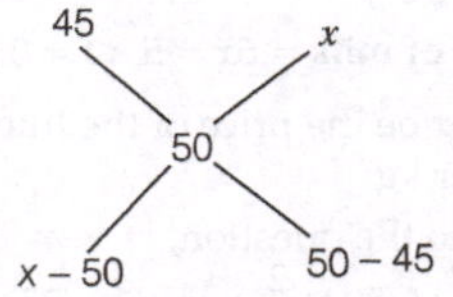

So, $\frac{x-50}{50-45} = \frac{3}{2} \Rightarrow 2x-100 = 5\times3$

$\therefore x = \frac{15+100}{2} = 57.5$

27. (b) By Alligation rule,

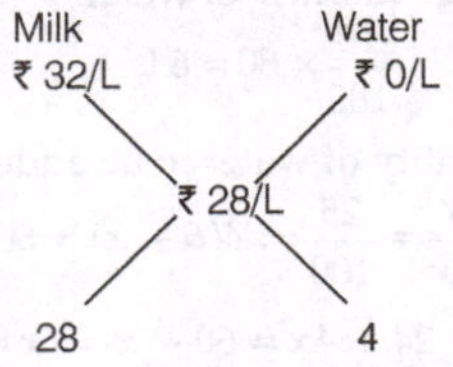

$\therefore$ Milk : Water = 28 : 4 = 7 : 1

28. (d) Let the quantity of alloy P and Q mixing be x and $3x$, respectively.

Quantity of aluminium in third alloy

$$= x\times\frac{5}{16}+3x\times\frac{3}{8} = \frac{5x+18x}{16} = \frac{23x}{16}$$

Quantity of copper in third alloy

$$= x\times\frac{11}{16}+3x\times\frac{5}{8} = \frac{11x+30x}{16} = \frac{41x}{16}$$

$$\therefore \text{Required per cent} = \frac{\frac{23x}{16}}{\frac{41x}{16}}\times100$$

$$= \frac{23}{41}\times100 = 56.09\%$$

= 56% (in nearest integer)

29. (b)

Initially milk		Replaced milk
60		50
	52	
2	:	8 ⇒ 1:4

Hence, required part $= \frac{4}{1+4} = \frac{4}{5}$

30. (d) Given, 20% of 100 mL = 20 mL

and 50% of x mL $= \frac{x}{2}$ mL

According to the question,

$\frac{30}{100} \times (x+100) = 20 + \frac{x}{2}$

$\Rightarrow \quad 3(x+100) = 200 + 5x$

$\Rightarrow \quad 3x + 300 = 200 + 5x$

$\therefore \quad x = \frac{100}{2} = 50$ mL

31. (c) Let the quantity of milk and water be $5x$ L and $3x$ L, respectively.

According to the question,

$\frac{5x}{3x+7} = \frac{1}{2} \Rightarrow 10x = 3x + 7 \Rightarrow 7x = 7$

$\Rightarrow \quad x = 1$

$\therefore$ Quantity of milk $= 5x = 5 \times 1 = 5$ L

32. (d) Let, x be the price of the third variety of wheat per kg

According to the question,

$80 \times \frac{1}{6} + 50 \times \frac{2}{6} + x \times \frac{3}{6} = 75 \times 1$

$\Rightarrow \quad 80 + 100 + 3x = 75 \times 6 \Rightarrow 180 + 3x = 450$

$\Rightarrow \quad 3x = 450 - 180 \Rightarrow 3x = 270$

$\therefore \quad x = \frac{270}{3} = ₹90$

33. (d) Initial quantity of water

$= \frac{10}{100} \times 60 = 6$ L

Let the quantity of water to be added be x L,

Then, $\frac{6+x}{60+x} = \frac{25}{100} \Rightarrow 4(6+x) = 60 + x$

$\Rightarrow \quad 24 + 4x = 60 + x \Rightarrow x = 12$ L

34. (d) Amount of milk left $= x\left(1 - \frac{y}{x}\right)^n$

$= 25\left(1 - \frac{5}{25}\right)^3 = 25\left(1 - \frac{1}{5}\right)^3$

$= 25 \times \frac{4}{5} \times \frac{4}{5} \times \frac{4}{5} = \frac{64}{5} = 12.8$ L

35. (c) Quantity of metal x in Alloy $A = \frac{5}{7}$

Quantity of metal y in Alloy $A = \frac{2}{7}$

Quantity of metal x in Alloy $B = \frac{3}{7}$

Quantity of metal y in Alloy $B = \frac{4}{7}$

The ratio of x and y in Alloy C

$$= \frac{\left(\frac{5}{7}\right) \times 4 + \left(\frac{3}{7}\right) \times 5}{\left(\frac{2}{7}\right) \times 4 + \left(\frac{4}{7}\right) \times 5} = \frac{\frac{20}{7} + \frac{15}{7}}{\frac{8}{7} + \frac{20}{7}} = \frac{\frac{35}{7}}{\frac{28}{7}} = \frac{35}{28} = \frac{5}{4}$$

Quantity of y in Alloy $C = \frac{4}{9}$

$\therefore$ Percentage of y in Alloy $C = \frac{4}{9} \times 100$

$= 44\frac{4}{9}\%$

Speedy Method

$\quad\quad x \quad y$

$A \rightarrow \quad (5:2) \times 4 = 20:8$

$B \rightarrow \quad (3:4) \times 5 = 15:20$

$C \rightarrow \quad 35:28 = 5:4$

Hence, required % $= \frac{4}{5+4} \times 100$

$= \frac{400}{9} = 44\frac{4}{9}\%$

36. (d) Quantity of spirit in 25 L mixture

$= 25 \times \left(\frac{30}{100}\right) = 7.5$

New quantity of mixture if 5 L water add

$= 25 + 5 = 30$ L

$\therefore$ New percentage of spirit in new mixture

$= \frac{7.5}{30} \times 100 = 25\%$

37. (c) Given, Volume of mixture = 5 L

$\therefore \quad \frac{\text{Milk}}{\text{Mixture}} = \frac{4}{5} \Rightarrow$ Milk : Water = 4 : 1

Now, 1 L of milk is added, so total quantity of milk becomes 5 L and that of mixture becomes 6 L. Quantity of water remains same i.e. 1 L.

$\therefore$ Percentage of water in the mixture

$= \frac{1}{6} \times 100 = \frac{100}{6}\%$

Speedy Method

Initial mixture $\frac{MW}{4L\ 1L} = 5$ L

$\quad\quad +1$

Final mixture = 5L 1L

$\therefore$ Water percentage in mixture

$= \frac{1}{6} \times 100 = \frac{100}{6}\%$

38. (d) In the first alloy,

ratio of $A : B : C = 2 : 3 : 1$

Now, let the weight of first alloy be 12 kg

$\therefore$ Weight of $A = 4$ kg, Weight of $B = 6$ kg

Weight of $C = 2$ kg

Now, In second alloy,

ratio of $B : C : D = 5 : 4 : 3$

Let the weight of second alloy be 12 kg.

$\therefore$ Weight of $B = 5$ kg

Weight of $C = 4$ k

Weight of $D = 3$ kg

Weight of new alloy = 12 + 12 = 24 kg

$\therefore$ Amount of Metal B in new alloy

$= \frac{6+5}{24} = \frac{11}{24}$

39. (b) In 160 L of drink, water = 90 L and juice = 70 L

According to the question,

$\frac{90+x}{70+2x} = \frac{13}{15} \Rightarrow 1350 + 15x = 910 + 26x$

$\Rightarrow \quad 440 = 11x \Rightarrow x = 40$

Total addition of extra water and juice in the drink $= x + 2x = 3x = 120$ L

$\therefore$ The new quantity of drink

$= 160 + 120 = 280$ L

40. (a) Cost of 1 kg mixture

$= \frac{25 \times 3 + 40 \times 2}{3+2} = \frac{155}{5} = ₹31$

41. (c) Amount of mixture in vessel = 18 L

$\therefore$ Amount of milk $= \frac{5}{6} \times 18 = 15$ L

Amount of water $= \frac{1}{6} \times 18 = 3$ L

Now, let 'w' L of water be added.

$\therefore$ According to the given condition,

$\frac{15+3}{3+w} = \frac{9}{2} \Rightarrow 3 + w = 4 \Rightarrow w = 1$

Hence, 1 L of water should be added to the vessel.

42. (b) Tin in Alloy $A = \frac{3}{8} \times 80 = 30$ kg

Tin in Alloy $B = \frac{1}{4} \times 100 = 25$ kg

$\therefore$ Amount of tin in new alloy

$= 30 + 25 = 55$ kg

43. (b) 750 kg of mixture contains 25% tin.

$\therefore$ Amount of tin $= \frac{25}{100} \times 750 = 187.5$ kg

Now, let the amount of tin added be x kg.

$\therefore$ According to the question,

$\frac{187.5 + x}{750 + x} = \frac{70}{100}$

$\Rightarrow \quad 1875 + 10x = 5250 + 7x$

$\Rightarrow \quad 3x = 3375$

$\Rightarrow \quad x = 1125$ kg

Speedy Method

$25\% \rightarrow \frac{1}{4}$ and $70\% \rightarrow \frac{7}{10}$

T : C

Initial mixture = 1 : 3 = 750 kg

$\quad +6 \ (+x$

Final mixture = 7 : 3

$x = 6$

$\because \quad 4 \rightarrow 750$ kg

$\therefore \quad x = 6 \rightarrow 1125$ kg

44. (b) Given, A 12 L solution has 30% acid.

$\therefore$ Amount of acid $= \frac{30}{100} \times 12 = 3.6$ L

Now, according to the question,

$\Rightarrow \quad 20\%$ of (12 + water) = 3.6

$\Rightarrow 12 + \text{Water} = \dfrac{3.6 \times 100}{20}$

$\therefore$ Water = 18 − 12 = 6 L

45. (a) Let x be the percentage of sugar in mixture.

Pomegranate juice to orange juice = 2 : 3

According to the rule of Alligation,

10% 30%
x
2 : 3

$\therefore \dfrac{30 - x}{x - 10} = \dfrac{2}{3} \Rightarrow 90 - 3x = 2x - 20$

$\Rightarrow 5x = 110$

$\therefore x = 22\%$

46. (a) Let the milk and water in the bucket be $7x$ and $5x$ L.

According to the question,

$\dfrac{7x - 9}{5x + 9} = \dfrac{7}{9} \Rightarrow 63x - 81 = 35x + 63$

$\Rightarrow 28x = 144 \Rightarrow x = \dfrac{144}{28} = \dfrac{36}{7}$

$\therefore$ Original quantity of milk $= 7x = 7 \times \dfrac{36}{7}$

= 36 L

47. (d) By Alligation rule,

Let the cost of mixture be ₹ x.

₹88 ₹187
x
10 : 20
1 : 2

$\therefore \dfrac{187 - x}{x - 88} = \dfrac{1}{2} \Rightarrow x - 88 = 374 - 2x$

$\Rightarrow x =$ ₹ 154

48. (c) Cost price of mixture $= 36 \times \dfrac{100}{125}$

= ₹28.8/kg

Thus, by Alligation rule,

27 31
28.8
2.2 : 1.8
11 : 9

$\therefore$ Required ratio = 11 : 9

49. (d) Let the amount of alcohol be $12x$ and amount of water be $5x$.

According to the question,

$\dfrac{12x}{5x + 14} = \dfrac{4}{3}$

$\Rightarrow 36x = 20x + 56$

$\Rightarrow 36x - 20x = 56$

$\Rightarrow 16x = 56 \Rightarrow x = \dfrac{56}{16} = 3.5$ L

$\therefore$ Quantity of alcohol = 12 × 3.5 = 42 L

50. (a) In ₹ 1 value $1\frac{1}{2}$ L of milk.

$\Rightarrow$ 60 L milk $= \dfrac{60}{3/2} =$ ₹ 40

In a mixture, value of $1\frac{7}{8}$ L milk in ₹ 1.

$\therefore$ Value of milk and water in ₹ 40

$= 40 \times \dfrac{15}{8} = 75$ L

$\therefore$ Value of water = (75 − 60) L = 15 L

51. (b) According to the rule of alligation,

60 75
65
10 5

$\therefore$ Required ratio = 2 : 1

52. (a) Ratio of concentration of wine in percentage

A		B		C	Total
2	:	3	:	x	(2+3+x)
10	:	20	:	30	23% (given)

$\therefore$ Total concentrated wine,

$\dfrac{2 \times 10}{100} + \dfrac{3 \times 20}{100} + \dfrac{x \times 30}{100} = (2 + 3 + x) \times \dfrac{23}{100}$

$\Rightarrow 20 + 60 + 30x = (5 + x) \times 23$

$\Rightarrow 80 + 30x = 115 + 23x \Rightarrow 7x = 35$

$\therefore x = 5$

53. (c) Amount of water in 70 L mixture

= 10% of 70 = 7 L

Let, x L of water is added to mixture.

According to the question,

$7 + x = \dfrac{12.5}{100} \times (70 + x)$

$\Rightarrow 700 + 100x = 875 + 12.5x$

$\Rightarrow 87.5x = 175 \Rightarrow x = 2$ L

54. (d) Let the equal weight of both blended tea is 60 gm.

Kangara tea $= \dfrac{3}{12} \times 60 = 15$ gm

Fraction of Kangara valley tea in mixture

$= \dfrac{15}{60 + 60} = \dfrac{15}{120}$

Weight per kg of Kangara valley tea

$= \dfrac{15}{120} \times 1000 = 125$ gm

55. (d) By the rule of Alligation,

I II
80 85
82
(85–82) =3 (82–80) =2

$\therefore$ Required ratio = 3 : 2

56. (d) Cost price of mixture

$= 20 \times \left(\dfrac{100}{100 + 25}\right) =$ ₹ 16 per kg

By alligation rule,

I II
23 14
16
2 7

$\therefore$ Required ratio = 2 : 7

57. (c) CP of mixture $= \dfrac{100}{110} \times 30 =$ ₹ $\dfrac{300}{11}$

By Alligation rule,

26 32
$\dfrac{300}{11}$
$\dfrac{52}{11}$ $\dfrac{14}{11}$

$\therefore$ Required ratio $= \dfrac{52}{11} : \dfrac{14}{11} = 26 : 7$

58. (b) In first alloy,

The quantity of Aluminium

$= \dfrac{242}{(5 + 6)} \times 5 = 110$ kg

and the quantity of Zinc = 242 − 110 = 132 kg

In second alloy,

The quantity of Aluminium

$= \dfrac{144}{(3 + 5)} \times 3 = 18 \times 3 = 54$ kg

and the quantity of Zinc

$= \dfrac{144}{(3 + 5)} \times 5 = 18 \times 5 = 90$ kg

Now, the ratio of Aluminium and Zinc in the new alloy = (110 + 54) : (132 + 90)

= 164 : 222 = 82 : 111

59. (b) Quantity of juice in bigger vessel

$= \dfrac{3}{8} + \dfrac{3}{4} = \dfrac{3 + 6}{8} = \dfrac{9}{8}$

and quantity of water in bigger vessel

$= \dfrac{5}{8} + \dfrac{1}{4} = \dfrac{5 + 2}{8} = \dfrac{7}{8}$

$\therefore$ Required ratio $= \dfrac{9}{8} : \dfrac{7}{8} = 9 : 7$

Speedy Method

	Juice		Water
I →	(3	:	5) × 1 = 3 : 5
II →	(3 : 1) × 2 = 6 : 2		
III. →			= 9 : 7

60. (a) In a beaker, water = 3 parts and medicine = 7 parts

So, water $= \dfrac{3}{3 + 7} = \dfrac{3}{10}$

and medicine $= \dfrac{7}{3 + 7} = \dfrac{7}{10}$

Let x amount of mixture is replaced with water.

Water in x amount of mixture $= \frac{3x}{10}$

Medicine in x amount of mixture $= \frac{7x}{10}$

After replacement,

Water $= \frac{3}{10} - \frac{3x}{10} + x = \frac{3+7x}{10}$

Medicine $= \frac{7}{10} - \frac{7x}{10} = \frac{7-7x}{10}$

Given, after replacement, $\frac{\text{Water}}{\text{Medicine}} = \frac{1}{1}$

$\Rightarrow$ Water = Medicine $\Rightarrow \frac{3+7x}{10} = \frac{7-7x}{10}$

$\Rightarrow \quad 3+7x = 7-7x$

$\Rightarrow \quad 7x+7x = 7-3$

$\Rightarrow \quad 14x = 4 \Rightarrow x = \frac{4}{14} = \frac{2}{7}$

61. (d) By Alligation rule,

75   90

80

90 − 80 = 10   80 − 75 = 5

$\therefore$ Required ratio $= \frac{10}{5} = 2:1$

62. (c) By Alligation rule,

15   20

18

20 − 18 = 2   18 − 15 = 3

$\therefore$ Required ratio = 2 : 3

63. (c) Let the beaker initially contained $5K$ L and $3K$ L of X and Y liquids, respectively.

In 6L of drawn mixture,

Liquid $X = 6 \times \frac{5}{5+3}$ L $= \frac{15}{4}$ L

Liquid $Y = 6 \times \frac{3}{5+3}$ L $= \frac{9}{4}$ L

Given, $\frac{5K - \frac{15}{4}}{3K - \frac{9}{4} + 6} = \frac{5}{7}$

$\Rightarrow \quad 35K - \frac{105}{4} = 15K - \frac{45}{4} + 30$

$\Rightarrow \quad 35K - 15K = \frac{105}{4} - \frac{45}{4} + 30$

$\Rightarrow \quad 20K = \frac{105 - 45 + 120}{4} = 45$

$\therefore \quad K = \frac{45}{20} = \frac{9}{4}$

Liquid X in the beaker initially $= 5K$ L

$= 5 \times \frac{9}{4}$ L $= 11.25$ L

64. (d) Let the cost of second variety be ₹ y.

According to the question,

$(x + 5x + 2x) \times 25$

$= x \times 20 + 5x \times y + 2x \times 30$

$\Rightarrow \quad 200x = 20x + 5xy + 60x$

$\Rightarrow \quad 200x - 80x = 5xy$

$\Rightarrow \quad \frac{120x}{5x} = y \Rightarrow y =$ ₹ 24

65. (b) By Alligation Method

One Variety   Other Variety

42   60

48

12 : 6

$\therefore$ Required ratio = 2 : 1

66. (a) Cost price of mixture $= 34.1 \times \frac{100}{110}$

= 31/kg

Now, **By Alligation Method**

I type   IInd type

30/kg   32.5/kg

31/kg

1.5   1

$\therefore$ Required ratio = 3 : 2

67. (c) By Alligation Method

I type   II type

3.3 /liter   1.8 /liter

2.4 liter

0.6   0.9

$\therefore$ Required ratio = 2 : 3

68. (d) Ist mix 45%   IInd mix 30%

34%

4 : 11

$\therefore$ Required ratio = 4 : 11

69. (b) X Y

$\frac{80}{5} = 16$ $\frac{80}{10} = 8$

14

6 : 2

3 : 1

$\therefore$ Quantity of Ingredient $X = \frac{3}{4} \times 60 = 45$ gm

70. (d) Let the quantity of grape juice and pine apple juice be $13x$ and $11x$ respectively.

$\therefore$ Total liquid $= 13x + 11x = 24x$

When 8L of the mixture is drawn off, the quantity of grape juice drawn

$= 8 \times \frac{13x}{24x} = \frac{13}{3}$ L and the quantity of pine apple juice drawn $= 8 \times \frac{11x}{24x} = \frac{11}{3}$ L

According to the question,

$\frac{13x - \frac{13}{3}}{11x - \frac{11}{3} + 8} = \frac{13}{14}$

$\Rightarrow \quad 13(x - \frac{1}{3}) \times 14 = 13 \times (11x + \frac{13}{3})$

$\Rightarrow \quad 14x - \frac{14}{3} = 11x + \frac{13}{3} \Rightarrow 3x = \frac{27}{3} = 9$

Hence, initial quantity of pineapple juice

$= 11 \times 3 = 33$ L

Speedy Method

GJ   PJ

13 : 11 = 24

−8

13 : 11 = 24

+8   +3

13 : 14

$\because$ 3 Unit $\rightarrow$ 8

$\therefore$ Initial mixture (24 unit) $\rightarrow 64 + 8 = 72$ L

$\therefore$ Pineapple juice $= \frac{11}{24} \times 72 = 33$ L

71. (b) Can 1   Can 2

$\frac{5}{8}$ $\frac{2}{5}$

$\frac{1}{2}$

$\frac{1}{10}$ $\frac{1}{8}$

$\therefore$ Required ratio = 4 : 5

72. (a) By Alligation Method

I type   II type

3.3 /L   1.8 /L

2.4 L

0.6   0.9

$\therefore$ Required ratio $\longrightarrow 2:3$

73. (b) By Alligation Method

1 type   2 type

80 /kg   100 /kg

95 kg

5 : 15

$\therefore$ Required ratio = 1 : 3

74. (a) Average price of mixture

$= \frac{8 \times 295 + 10 \times 250}{8 + 10} = \frac{2360 + 2500}{18}$

$= \frac{4860}{18} =$ ₹ 270

75. (c) Rate of X per g = ₹ 15

Rate of Y per g = ₹ 5

By Alligation Method

X Y

15   5

13

8 : 2

4 : 1

$\because \quad 4 + 1 \rightarrow 100 \quad \therefore \quad 1 \rightarrow 20$

$\therefore \quad 4 \rightarrow 80$ g

76. (c) Cost of commodity

$= \frac{35 \times 2 + 40 \times 3}{5}$

$= \frac{70 + 120}{5} = \frac{190}{5} = ₹38$ kg

$\therefore$ Total cost $= 38 \times 12 = ₹456$

77. (c) Initial quality of milk

$= \frac{4}{7} \times 21 = 12$ L

Initial quality of water $= \frac{3}{7} \times 21 = 9$ L

Let x litre water is added.

According to the question,

$\frac{12}{9 + x} = \frac{1}{1}$

$\Rightarrow \quad 12 = 9 + x \Rightarrow x = 3$ L

78. (a) By Alligation Method

Quantity of spirit in A: $\frac{3}{7}$ Quantity of spirit in B: $\frac{5}{8}$

Quantity of spirit in mixture: $\frac{4}{7}$

$\frac{3}{56} : \frac{1}{7}$

$3 : 8$

79. (b) In this type of question, where water is added to gain P% and sell the mixture at cost price then ratio of water and milk

$= P:100 = 25:100 = 1:4$

80. (d) Ist Variety

IInd Variety

120   125

122

3 : 2

$\therefore$ Required ratio $= 3:2$

81. (c) Let cost of third quantity be ₹ x / kg.

Average cost of mixture

$= \frac{\text{Total cost}}{\text{Total quantity}}$

$\Rightarrow 96 = \frac{43 \times 2 + 67 \times 1 + x \times 5}{(2 + 1 + 5)}$

$\Rightarrow 768 = 86 + 67 + 5x \Rightarrow 615 = 5x$

$\Rightarrow \quad x = ₹123$ / kg

82. (c) Mixture I

Volume = 8 L

Quantity of milk $= \frac{8 \times 80}{100} = 6.4$ L

Mixture II

Volume = 6 L

Quantity of milk $= \frac{6 \times 60}{100} = 3.6$ L

Total milk in mixed mixture = 6.4 + 3.6 = 10 L

Total volume of mixed mixture

= 8 + 6 = 14 L

$\therefore$ Percentage of milk in final mixture

$= \frac{10}{14} \times 100 = \frac{500}{7}$ %

83. (d) Ratio of milk and water in vessel first

= 4 : 1

Ratio of milk and water in vessel second = 1 : 1

Ratio of water to milk in new vessel = 1 : 2

$\frac{4}{5}$ $\frac{1}{2}$

$\frac{2}{3}$

$\frac{1}{6}$ $\frac{2}{15}$

Required ratio $= \frac{1}{6} : \frac{2}{15} = 5:4$

$\therefore$ Hence, required quantity = (5, 4)

84. (b) Let CP of 1L milk be ₹ 1.

$\therefore$ SP of 1L mixture = ₹ 1

Gain $= 16\frac{1}{4}\% = \frac{65}{4}\% = \frac{65}{400}$

$\therefore$ CP of 1L mixture $= \frac{400}{465} \times 1 = ₹\frac{80}{93}$

By rule of alligation,

Water $= 1 - \frac{80}{93} = ₹\frac{13}{93}$

$\therefore$ Required ratio $= \frac{80}{93} : \frac{13}{93} = 80:13$

85. (d) Let the quantity of water be $100x$ L.

Quantity of milk = $400x$ L

$\therefore$ Total quantity of mixture = 7.5 L

$\Rightarrow \quad 500x = 7.5 \Rightarrow x = 0.015$

$\therefore$ Quantity of water $= 100 \times 0.015 = 1.5$ L

Quantity of milk $= 400 \times 0.015 = 6$ L

Let P L of milk to be added to make it 90% of milk in the solution.

$\therefore \quad \left(\frac{6 + P}{7.5 + P}\right) \times 100 = 90$

$\Rightarrow \quad 600 + 100P = 675 + 90P$

$\Rightarrow \quad 10P = 75 \Rightarrow P = 7.5$ L

86. (d) CP of mixture $= \frac{140}{140} \times 100 = ₹100$

By Alligation rule,

185   95

100

5   85

$\therefore$ Required ratio = 5 : 85 = 1 : 17

87. (c) Let quantity of liquid A be $4x$ and liquid B be $9x$.

According to the question,

$\frac{4x + 8}{9x} = \frac{8}{9}$

$\Rightarrow \quad 36x + 72 = 72x$

$\Rightarrow \quad 36x = 72$

$\therefore \quad x = 2$

Hence, Quantity of liquid A in original mixture $= 4x = 8$ L

88. (d) CP of mixture $= \frac{187}{110} \times 100 = ₹170$

By Alligation rule,

300   160

170

10 : 130 $\Rightarrow$ 1 : 13

Hence, required ratio = 1 : 13

89. (a) By Alligation rule,

18   22

19.50

2.5   1.5

$\therefore$ Required ratio = 5 : 3

90. (d) Let the quantity of milk = 100 L

$\therefore$ Purity of the milk $= 100 \times \frac{65}{100} \times \frac{65}{100} \times \frac{65}{100}$

$= 27\frac{37}{80}\%$

91. (b) By Alligation rule,

128   143

137.75

5.25   9.75

So, the ratio = 7 : 13

92. (d) According to the question,

$\therefore$ Required ratio $= \left(\frac{2}{5} + \frac{3}{7}\right) : \left(\frac{3}{5} + \frac{4}{7}\right)$

$= \left(\frac{14 + 15}{35}\right) : \left(\frac{21 + 20}{35}\right)$

$= \frac{29}{35} : \frac{41}{35} = 29:41$

93. (c) Given, mixture = 80L,

Alcohol = 60 % of mixture

Alcohol = 60 % of 80L = 48L

Also, given, $\frac{48}{(80 + X)} \times 100 = 40$

$\Rightarrow \quad (80 + X) = \frac{48 \times 100}{40} = 120$

$\therefore \quad X = 120 - 80 = 40$ L

94. (c) First variety   Second variety

65   95

83

12   18

$\therefore$ Required ratio = 12 : 18 = 2 : 3

95. (d) Final volume of milk in the mixture

$= 30\left(1 - \frac{3}{30}\right)^3 = 30\left(\frac{9}{10}\right)^3$

$$= 30 \times \frac{9 \times 9 \times 9}{10 \times 10 \times 10} = \frac{21870}{1000} = 21.87 \text{ L}$$

Final volume of water = 30 − 21.87 = 8.13 L

$\therefore$ Required ratio $= \frac{8.13}{21.87} = \frac{271}{729} = 271 : 729$

96. (c) Let the quantity of milk and water be $7x$ and $9x$ respectively and the added quantity of milk be k L According to the question,

$$\frac{7x + k}{9x} = \frac{11}{9}$$

$\Rightarrow 63x + 9k = 99x \Rightarrow 9k = 99x - 63x$

$\therefore \quad k = \frac{36x}{9} = 4x$

$\therefore$ Required % $= \left(\frac{4x}{7x + 9x}\right) \times 100$

$$= \frac{4}{16} \times 100 = 25\%$$

97. (b) Let the quantity of water and milk be $6x$ and $5x$ L, respectively.

$\therefore \quad 6x + 5x = 220 \Rightarrow x = \frac{220}{11} = 20$

$\therefore$ Milk present in mixture = 20 × 5 = 100 L

$\therefore$ Water present in mixture = 20 × 6 = 120 L

Let the added water be y.

$\therefore \quad \frac{120 + y}{100} = \frac{5}{4} \Rightarrow 480 + 4y = 500$

$\Rightarrow \quad 4y = 500 - 480 \Rightarrow y = \frac{20}{4}$

$\therefore \quad y = 5$

So, the added water is 5 L .

98. (c) Let quantity of water is x L.

$\therefore$ Quantity of milk will be $(x + 26)$ L.

According to the question,

$$\frac{x}{x + 26} = \frac{8}{21} \Rightarrow 21x = 8x + 208$$

$\Rightarrow \quad 13x = 208 \Rightarrow x = \frac{208}{13}$

$\therefore \quad x = 16$

Hence, quantity of milk in the mixture

$= (x + 26) = (16 + 26) = 42$ L

99. (a) The quantity of water

$$= \frac{120}{(5 + 7)} \times 5 = 50 \text{ L}$$

and the quantity of milk = 120 − 50 = 70 L

Let the added quantity of water = k

$\therefore \quad \frac{50 + k}{70} = \frac{1}{1} \Rightarrow 50 + k = 70$

$\Rightarrow \quad k = 70 - 50 = 20 \Rightarrow k = 20$ L

So, the added quantity of water = 20 L

Speedy Method

Water : Milk

(5 : 7) × 1 = 5 : 7

(1 : 1) × 7 = 7 : 7

$\because \quad (5 + 7) \rightarrow 120$

$\therefore \quad (7 - 5) \rightarrow \frac{120}{12} \times 2 = 20$ L

Hence, required water = 20 L

100. (c) According to the question,

Quantity of water in 110 L $= \frac{4}{11} \times 110 = 40$ L

and quantity of milk in 110 L

$$= \frac{7}{11} \times 110 = 70 \text{ L}$$

Let the added water be x L.

Now, $\frac{(40 + x)}{70} = \frac{8}{7} \Rightarrow 280 + 7x = 560$

$\Rightarrow \quad 7x = 280$

$\therefore \quad x = 40$

So, 40 L of water will be added.

101. (a) Let the quantity of acid and water be $7x$ and $4x$ respectively.

According to the question,

$$\frac{7x}{4x + 2} = \frac{7}{5} \Rightarrow 35x = 28x + 14$$

$\Rightarrow \quad 7x = 14 \Rightarrow x = 2$

$\therefore$ Quantity of acid in mixture = 7 × 2 = 14 L

102. (a) Let the milk and water be $2x$L and $3x$L respectively and added some milk be k L,

As per question,

$$\frac{2x + k}{3x} = \frac{10}{3} \Rightarrow 6x + 3k = 30x$$

$\Rightarrow \quad 3k = 24x \Rightarrow k = 8x$

$\therefore$ Required percentage $= \left(\frac{8x}{2x + 3x}\right) \times 100$

$$= \frac{8}{5} \times 100 = 160\%$$

103. (d)

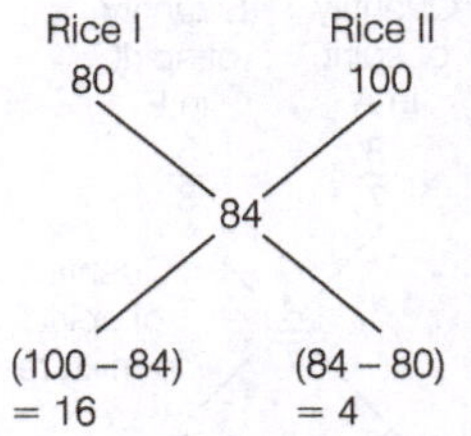

Ratio of Rice I and Rice II $= \frac{16}{4} = 4 : 1$

$\therefore$ Quantity of Rice II $= \frac{20}{4} \times 1 = 5$ kg

104. (a) Required per cent of milk

$$= \frac{36 \times \frac{20}{100} + 48 \times \frac{10}{100}}{36 + 48} \times 100\%$$

$$= \frac{720 + 480}{84}\% = \frac{1200}{84}\% = 14.28\%$$

12

Simple Interest

When a person borrows some amount of money from another person or organisation (bank), then the person borrowing money (borrower) pays some extra money during repayment, that extra money during repayment is called **Interest**.

Important Terms Related to Simple Interest

- **Principal** (*P*) Principal is the money borrowed or deposited for a certain time.
- **Amount** (*A*) The sum of principal and interest is called amount.
- **Rate of Interest** (*R*) It is the rate at which the interest is charged on principal. It is always specified in percentage terms.
- **Time** (*T*) The period, for which the money is borrowed or deposited, is called time.
- **Simple Interest** (SI) If the interest is calculated only on the original principal for any duration of time, then it is called simple interest.

Important Formulae Related to Simple Interest

- Simple Interest (SI) $= \dfrac{\text{Principal }(P)\times \text{Rate }(R)\times \text{Time }(T)}{100}$

$\Rightarrow \quad \text{SI} = \dfrac{PRT}{100}$ or $R = \dfrac{\text{SI}\times 100}{P\times T}$ or $T = \dfrac{\text{SI}\times 100}{P\times R}$

- Amount = Principal + Simple Interest $\Rightarrow A = P + \text{SI} \Rightarrow A = P\left(1+\dfrac{RT}{100}\right)$
- If the simple interest received on the principal amount is x/y of principal amount and rate of interest and time are equal, then

$$\text{Time} = \text{Rate} = \sqrt{\frac{x}{y}\times 100}$$

When Amount Becomes *n* Times

- If a certain sum of money becomes *n* times itself in *T* yr at simple interest, then rate of interest per annum is $R = \dfrac{100(n-1)}{T}\%$
- If a certain sum of money becomes *n* times itself in T_1 yr at a simple interest, then the time in which it will become *m* times itself is given by,

$$T_2 = \frac{(m-1)}{(n-1)}\times T_1$$

Note If *R* given in the question, then we interchange *T* and *R*.

Ex. 1 A certain sum becomes 3 times in 5 yr at simple interest. In how many years will the same sum becomes 6 times at the same rate of simple interest?

Sol. Given, $n = 3$, $T_1 = 5$ yr and $m = 6$

Using formula, $T_2 = \dfrac{(m-1)}{(n-1)}T_1 = \dfrac{(6-1)\times 5}{(3-1)} = \dfrac{25}{2} = 12.5$ yr

Question Based on Installment

The annual installment that will discharge a debt of ₹ '*A*' due in *t* yr at *R*% per annum is $= \dfrac{100\times A}{100\times t + \dfrac{R\times t(t-1)}{2}}$

Ex. 2 Find out the annual installment that will discharge a debt of ₹ 12900 due in 4 yr at 5% per annum simple interest.

Sol. Here, $A =$ ₹ 12900, $T = 4$ yr, $R = 5\%$

$\therefore$ Annual installment $= \dfrac{100\times A}{100\times T + \dfrac{RT(T-1)}{2}} = \dfrac{100\times 12900}{(100\times 4)+\dfrac{5\times 4(4-1)}{2}}$

$= \dfrac{100\times 12900}{400+30} = \dfrac{100\times 12900}{430} =$ ₹ 3000

When Principal is Divided and Lent at Two or More Different Rates of Interest

Ex. 3 Reena had ₹ 10000 with her. Out of this money, she lent some money to Akshay for 2 yr at 15% simple interest. She lent remaining money to Brijesh for an equal number of years at the rate of 18%. After 2 yr, Reena found that Akshay had given her ₹ 360 more as interest as compared to Brijesh. The amount of money which Reena had lent to Brijesh must be

Sol. Let the money lent to Akshay = ₹ *x*

Then, money lent to Brijesh = ₹ $(10000 - x)$

SI for Akshay $= \dfrac{x\times 15\times 2}{100} =$ ₹ $\dfrac{3x}{10}$

SI for Brijesh $= \dfrac{(10000-x)\times 18\times 2}{100} =$ ₹ $\dfrac{9}{25}(10000-x)$

According to the given condition,

$\dfrac{3x}{10} - \dfrac{9}{25}(10000-x) = 360$ [as SI (Akshay) − SI (Brijesh) = 360]

$\Rightarrow \dfrac{3x}{10} - 3600 + \dfrac{9x}{25} = 360 \Rightarrow \dfrac{3x}{10}+\dfrac{9x}{25} = 360+3600 = 3960$

$\Rightarrow \quad x =$ ₹ 6000

$\therefore$ Amount of money lent to Brijesh = 10000 − 6000 = ₹ 4000.

SSC Exam Scanner

SSC CGL 2024 (Tier I & II)

1. Find the simple interest (in ₹) on ₹ 2000 at 6.5% per annum rate of interest for the period from 13 February, 2023 to 27 April, 2023.
SSC CGL (Tier-II) 20/01/2025 Shift-I
(a) 27 (b) 25
(c) 26 (d) 24

2. Find the simple interest (in ₹) on ₹ 2000 at 6.5% per annum rate of interest for the period from 14 February, 2023 to 28 April, 2023.
SSC CGL (Tier-II) 18/01/2025 Shift-I
(a) 24 (b) 27
(c) 26 (d) 25

3. In how much time will ₹ 5000 at 4% per annum simple interest produce the same interest as ₹ 8000 in $2\frac{1}{2}$ yr at 8% per annum simple interest?
SSC CGL (Tier-I) 26/09/2024 Shift-III
(a) 8 yr (b) 5 yr
(c) 4 yr (d) 2 yr

4. What principal would amount to ₹ 21420 in 2 yr at the rate of 9.5% p.a. simple interest?
SSC CGL (Tier-I) 26/09/2024 Shift-II
(a) ₹ 11273 (b) ₹ 12000
(c) ₹ 18000 (d) ₹ 16000

5. If ₹1875 becomes ₹2625 in 4 yr, what will ₹24000 become at the end of 9 yr at the same rate of interest, under simple interest?
SSC CGL (Tier-I) 26/09/2024 Shift-I
(a) ₹45600 (b) ₹21600
(c) ₹34800 (d) ₹43200

6. Pranav borrows a sum of ₹ 335180 at the rate of 13% per annum simple interest. At the end of the first year, he repays ₹ 23060 towards return of principal amount borrowed. If Pranav clears all pending dues at the end of the second year, including interest payment that accrued during the first year, how much does he pay (in ₹) at the end of the second year? SSC CGL (Tier-I) 25/09/2024 Shift-III
(a) 398876 (b) 393949
(c) 396269 (d) 388076

7. Naman borrows a sum of ₹ 348020 at the rate of 8% per annum simple interest. At the end of the first year, he repays ₹ 15090 towards return of principal amount borrowed. If Naman clears all pending dues at the end of the second year, including interest payment that accrued during the first year, how much does he pay (in ₹) at the end of the second year?
SSC CGL (Tier-I) 25/09/2024 Shift-II
(a) 379386 (b) 387406
(c) 388931 (d) 392733

8. The simple interest on a sum for 6 yr is three-fifth of the sum. The rate of interest per annum is:
SSC CGL (Tier-I) 25/09/2024 Shift-I
(a) 3% (b) 7%
(c) 10% (d) 5%

9. Ramu lent ₹ 3000 to Raju and a certain sum to Ravi at the same time and at the same rate of simple interest of 8% p.a. After 5 yr, he received a sum of ₹1600 from Raju and Ravi together as interest. Find the sum lent to Ravi.
SSC CGL (Tier-I) 24/09/2024 Shift-III
(a) ₹1000 (b) ₹1250
(c) ₹1200 (d) ₹1500

10. A cell phone is available for ₹ 600 or for ₹ 300 cash down payment together with ₹ 360 to be paid after two months. Find the rate of interest charged under this scheme. SSC CGL (Tier-I) 24/09/2024 Shift-II
(a) 60% (b) 120%
(c) 20% (d) 50%

11. In how much time (in years, rounded off to 2 decimal places) will ₹ 10800 amount to ₹ 24800 if invested at simple interest at the rate of 15.5% per annum?
SSC CGL (Tier-I) 24/09/2024 Shift-I
(a) 7.72 (b) 8.36
(c) 9.54 (d) 6.89

12. The simple interest on a sum for 8 yr is three-fifth of the sum. The rate of interest per annum is
SSC CGL (Tier-I) 23/09/2024 Shift-II
(a) $5\frac{1}{2}$% (b) $7\frac{1}{2}$%
(c) 6% (d) 9%

13. The difference between the simple interests on the principal of ₹ 500 at an interest rate of 5% per annum for 3 yr and 4% per annum for 4 yr is
SSC CGL (Tier-I) 23/09/2024 Shift-I
(a) ₹ 7.5 (b) ₹ 5
(c) ₹ 15 (d) ₹ 10

14. Pranav borrows a sum of ₹ 598397 at the rate of 20% per annum simple interest. At the end of the first year, he repays ₹ 24284 towards return of principal amount borrowed. If Pranav clears all pending dues at the end of the second year, including interest payment that accrued during the first year, how much does he pay (in ₹) at the end of the second year? SSC CGL (Tier-I) 19/09/2024 Shift-III
(a) 812514 (b) 808615
(c) 818513 (d) 817567

15. A sum of ₹1456, when invested for ten years, amounts to ₹ 2366 on maturity. Find the rate of simple interest per annum that was to be paid on the sum invested.
SSC CGL (Tier-I) 19/09/2024 Shift-II
(a) 5.75% (b) 6.5%
(c) 6.25% (d) 6.15%

16. Aman invested a sum of money in scheme *A* at the rate of 8% p.a. for a period of 5 yr on simple interest. He invested four times of the sum of scheme *A* in scheme *B* at the rate of 5% p.a. for 7 yr on simple interest. He received a total interest amount of ₹ 1620. How much (in ₹) did he invest in scheme *B*?
SSC CGL (Tier-I) 19/09/2024 Shift-I
(a) 2400 (b) 900
(c) 3200 (d) 3600

17. Aman borrows a sum of ₹ 192208 at the rate of 15% per annum simple interest. At the end of the first year, he repays ₹ 20196 towards return of principal amount borrowed. If Aman clears all pending dues at the end of the second year, including interest payment that accrued during the first year, how much does he pay (in ₹) at the end of the second year?
SSC CGL (Tier-I) 18/09/2024 Shift-III
(a) ₹ 226645 (b) ₹ 221777
(c) ₹ 221757 (d) ₹ 230028

18. A total of ₹ 200000 is divided into two parts for investing in different banks on simple interest. One yields 4% p.a. while the other yields 6% p.a. If the total interest at the end of one year is equivalent to 4.7% p.a. on the whole amount, the amount (in ₹) invested in each bank is ...., respectively.
SSC CGL (Tier-I) 18/09/2024 Shift-II
(a) 130000 and 70000
(b) 145000 and 55000
(c) 120000 and 80000
(d) 160000 and 40000

19. A certain sum of money is given at a certain rate of simple interest for 6 yr. Had it been given at 7% higher rate, it would have fetched ₹ 1512 more. Find the sum (in ₹).
SSC CGL (Tier-I) 18/09/2024 Shift-I
(a) 3200 (b) 3600
(c) 3100 (d) 4200

20. In a bank, 6% interest is given on the deposited amount. The bank then invests the money in the stock market and is able to earn ₹ 30000 for every ₹ 300000. How much money is the bank earning finally if the total amount deposited in the bank is ₹ 6000000?
SSC CGL (Tier-I) 17/09/2024 Shift-III
(a) ₹ 300000 (b) ₹ 640000
(c) ₹ 240000 (d) ₹ 360000

21. In how many years will ₹ 7200 amount to ₹ 8928 at a simple interest rate of 8% per annum?
SSC CGL (Tier-I) 17/09/2024 Shift-III
(a) Four (b) Three
(c) Two (d) Five

22. What is the rate of interest per annum for simple interest at which ₹ 1040 amounts to ₹ 1230 in $1\frac{1}{2}$ yr?
SSC CGL (Tier-I) 17/09/2024 Shift-II
(a) $11\frac{7}{39}$ % (b) $10\frac{7}{39}$ %
(c) $12\frac{7}{39}$ % (d) $13\frac{7}{39}$ %

23. If the simple interest on ₹ 7200 in 3 yr at the rate of 16% per annum equals the simple interest on ₹ 9600 at the rate of x% per annum in 4 yr. The value of x is equal to
SSC CGL (Tier-I) 17/09/2024 Shift-I
(a) 9 (b) 11
(c) 8 (d) 10

24. A sum of ₹ 10000 is taken as a loan by Rajesh at a rate of 15% p.a. simple interest for 2 yr. But Rajesh could not repay it at the agreed time and asked for an extension of two more years. So, the lender included the interest amount for the period as principal for the next two years at the same rate of interest. The total amount paid by Rajesh at the end of 4 yr is **SSC CGL (Tier-I) 13/09/2024 Shift-III**
(a) ₹ 18590 (b) ₹ 16900
(c) ₹ 17650 (d) ₹ 15630

25. A trader owes a merchant ₹ 9810 due in 1 yr, but the trader wants to settle the account after 6 months. If the rate of simple interest is 9% per annum, how much cash (in ₹) should he pay?
SSC CGL (Tier-I) 13/09/2024 Shift-I
(a) 9550 (b) 9450
(c) 9540 (d) 9405

26. Pranav borrows a sum of ₹ 623305 at the rate of 10% per annum simple interest. At the end of the first year, he repays ₹ 16390 towards return of principal amount borrowed. If Pranav clears all pending dues at the end of the second year, including interest payment that accrued during the first year, how much does he pay (in ₹) at the end of the second year? **SSC CGL (Tier-I) 13/09/2024 Shift-I**
(a) 725903 (b) 729025
(c) 738700 (d) 729937

27. How much simple interest will ₹ 6700 earn in 13 months at a 12% interest rate per annum?
SSC CGL (Tier-I) 12/09/2024 Shift-III
(a) ₹ 871 (b) ₹ 889 (c) ₹ 821 (d) ₹ 813

28. A person borrowed some money on simple interest. After 4 yr, he returned $\frac{9}{5}$ of the money to lender. What was the rate of interest?
SSC CGL (Tier-I) 12/09/2024 Shift-II
(a) 20% p.a. (b) 18% p.a.
(c) 17% p.a. (d) 19% p.a.

29. A certain sum of money becomes seven times itself when invested at a certain rate of simple interest, in 14 yr. How much time(in yr, rounded off to 2 decimal places) will it take to become 18 times itself at the same rate?
SSC CGL (Tier-I) 12/09/2024 Shift-I
(a) 27.33 (b) 39.67
(c) 42.78 (d) 35.5

30. Sohan borrows a sum of ₹ 141545 at the rate of 11% per annum simple interest. At the end of the first year, he repays ₹ 25490 towards return of principal amount borrowed. If Sohan clears all pending dues at the end of the second year, including interest payment that accrued during the first year, how much does he pay (in ₹) at the end of the second year? **SSC CGL (Tier-I) 11/09/2024 Shift-III**
(a) 140391 (b) 136453
(c) 141222 (d) 137407

31. How many years will it take for ₹ 8400 to amount to ₹ 11928 at a simple interest rate of 7% per annum?
SSC CGL (Tier-I) 11/09/2024 Shift-II
(a) 8 (b) 5 (c) 2 (d) 6

32. S borrowed some amount from R and promised to pay him 8% interest. Then, S invested the borrowed amount in a scheme, upon which he earned a profit of 5% after paying R, the principal amount with interest. How much percentage R would have gained, if he would have invested in the scheme directly? **SSC CGL (Tier-I) 11/09/2024 Shift-II**
(a) 13.4% (b) 13%
(c) 14.4% (d) 14%

33. The interest accrued on a sum of ₹16000 lent at a simple interest rate of 14% p.a. for the time in those many yr, which gives a simple interest of three-fifths of a certain sum at 10% p.a., is
SSC CGL (Tier-I) 11/09/2024 Shift-I
(a) ₹ 13440 (b) ₹ 12970
(c) ₹ 15360 (d) ₹ 14280

34. Simple interest on a certain sum is one-fifth of the sum and the interest rate per cent per annum is 5 times the number of yr. If the rate of interest increases by 3%, then how much will the simple interest (in ₹) be on ₹ 5600 for 6 yr?
SSC CGL (Tier-I) 10/09/2024 Shift-III
(a) 4668 (b) 4168
(c) 4268 (d) 4368

35. What annual instalment will discharge a debt of ₹ 26160 due in 4 yr at 6% simple interest p.a.?
SSC CGL (Tier-I) 10/09/2024 Shift-II
(a) ₹ 4500 (b) ₹ 5500
(c) ₹ 6000 (d) ₹ 5800

36. Kiran lent ₹ 4,000 to two persons such that one part of it at the rate of 8% per annum and the remaining part at the rate of 10% per annum. He got an annual simple interest of ₹ 352. Then the sum lent at 10% is
SSC CGL (Tier-I) 10/09/2024 Shift-I
(a) ₹ 1800 (b) ₹ 2200
(c) ₹ 2400 (d) ₹ 1600

37. Ramesh has ₹ 18000. He deposited ₹ 7000 in a bank at the rate of 5% per annum and ₹ 6000 in other bank at the rate of 6% per annum simple interest. If he received ₹ 1160 as simple interest at the end of one year, then the rate of interest per annum on rest of the capital is equal to **SSC CGL (Tier-I) 09/09/2024 Shift-III**
(a) 10% (b) 11%
(c) 9% (d) 8%

38. If a sum of ₹ 5000 is taken at a simple rate of interest of 15% per annum for 3 yr and another sum of

₹ 8000 is taken at a simple interest of 12% per annum for 4 yr, the positive difference of the interests paid is SSC CGL (Tier-I) 09/09/2024 Shift-II

(a) ₹ 1643 (b) ₹ 1590
(c) ₹ 1286 (d) ₹ 1378

39. Mohan borrows a sum of ₹ 422092 at the rate of 20% per annum simple interest. At the end of the first year, he repays ₹ 21679 towards return of principal amount borrowed. If Mohan clears all pending dues at the end of the second year, including interest payment that accrued during the first year, how much does he pay (in ₹) at the end of the second year? SSC CGL (Tier-I) 09/09/2024 Shift-I

(a) 556367 (b) 558380
(c) 561347 (d) 564914

SSC CGL 2023 (Tier I & II)

40. A sum triples itself in 9 yr at simple interest. Find the rate of interest per annum is SSC CGL (Tier-II) 07/03/2023 Shift-I

(a) $33\frac{1}{3}\%$ (b) $22\frac{2}{9}\%$
(c) $27\frac{1}{9}\%$ (d) $38\frac{2}{9}\%$

41. In 5 yr, the simple interest on an amount of ₹ X is $\frac{2th}{5}$ of the principal. The rate of interest per annum is SSC CGL (Tier-II) 06/03/2023 Shift-I

(a) 12% (b) 8% (c) 10% (d) 5%

42. What is the ratio of the simple interest earned on a certain amount at the rate of 21% per annum for 8 yr to that earned on the same sum at the same rate for 21 yr? SSC CGL (Tier-II) 03/03/2023 Shift-I

(a) 8 : 21 (b) 21 : 5
(c) 5 : 21 (d) 21 : 8

43. The difference of simple interest from two banks on ₹ 8000 in 3 yr is ₹ 800. If the rate of interest per annum in two banks are R_1 and R_2, then what is the value of $R_1 - R_2$? (where $R_1 > R_2$) SSC CGL (Tier-II) 02/03/2023 Shift-I

(a) $5\frac{1}{3}\%$ (b) $3\frac{1}{3}\%$
(c) $1\frac{1}{3}\%$ (d) $2\frac{1}{3}\%$

44. In what time will ₹ 3720 amount to ₹ 5282.4 at 12% simple interest per annum? SSC CGL (Tier-I) 27/07/2023 Shift-III

(a) 3 yr (b) $3\frac{1}{2}$ yr
(c) $5\frac{1}{2}$ yr (d) 5 yr

45. The simple interest on an amount for 6 yr at 4% p.a. is ₹ 7500 less than the simple interest on the same amount for 11 yr. Find the amount. SSC CGL (Tier-I) 27/07/2023 Shift-II

(a) ₹ 38000 (b) ₹ 37500
(c) ₹ 37000 (d) ₹ 38500

46. Find the simple interest on ₹ 27000 at $14\frac{2}{3}\%$ per annum for 8 months. SSC CGL (Tier-I) 27/07/2023 Shift-I

(a) ₹ 2600 (b) ₹ 2630
(c) ₹ 2610 (d) ₹ 2640

47. A sum of money at simple interest amounts to ₹ 1200 in 3 yr and to ₹ 1350 in 4 yr. The sum is SSC CGL (Tier-I) 26/07/2023 Shift-IV

(a) ₹ 650 (b) ₹ 850
(c) ₹ 450 (d) ₹ 750

48. What is the present worth of ₹ 1100 due in 2 yr at 5% simple interest per annum? SSC CGL (Tier-I) 26/07/2023 Shift-III

(a) ₹ 3000 (b) ₹ 2000
(c) ₹ 1000 (d) ₹ 1500

49. The interest earned on ₹ 21000 in 3 yr at simple interest is ₹ 6400. What is the rate of interest per annum? SSC CGL (Tier-I) 26/07/2023 Shift-II

(a) $10\frac{5}{63}\%$ (b) $10\frac{2}{63}\%$
(c) $10\frac{13}{63}\%$ (d) $10\frac{10}{63}\%$

50. At what rate per cent per annum simple interest, a sum of money triples itself in 16 yr? SSC CGL (Tier-I) 26/07/2023 Shift-I

(a) 11.5% (b) 11%
(c) 12% (d) 12.5%

51. *S* deposits a total of ₹ 50000 in two accounts which give 8% and 12% simple interest annually, respectively. After, one year, he gets a total ₹ 5200. How much money does he deposit in the account with a 12% interest rate? SSC CGL (Tier-I) 25/07/2023 Shift-IV

(a) ₹ 30000 (b) ₹ 32000
(c) ₹ 20000 (d) ₹ 25000

52. The rate of simple interest for which ₹ 9000 will amount to ₹ 10200 in 4 yr is SSC CGL (Tier-I) 25/07/2023 Shift-III

(a) $4\frac{2}{3}\%$ (b) $7\frac{1}{3}\%$
(c) $5\frac{1}{2}\%$ (d) $3\frac{1}{3}\%$

53. ₹ 8500 becomes ₹ 11050 in 6 yr at a certain rate of simple interest. If the rate becomes 1.8 times of itself, the amount of the same principal in 5 yr will be SSC CGL (Tier-I) 25/07/2023 Shift-II

(a) ₹ 15625 (b) ₹ 14350
(c) ₹ 13550 (d) ₹ 12325

54. The simple interest on a certain sum at the rate of 12.5% per annum for 6 yr is ₹ 13500 less than the principal. Find the simple interest. SSC CGL (Tier-I) 25/07/2023 Shift-I

(a) ₹ 13500 (b) ₹ 54000
(c) ₹ 40000 (d) ₹ 40500

55. The time required for a sum of money to amount to three times itself at 8% simple interest p.a. will be SSC CGL (Tier-I) 24/07/2023 Shift-IV

(a) 35 yr (b) 25 yr
(c) 30 yr (d) 20 yr

56. The interest on a certain deposit at 4.5% p.a. is ₹ 135 in one year. How much will the additional interest in one year be on the same deposit at 5% p.a.? SSC CGL (Tier-I) 24/07/2023 Shift-III

(a) ₹ 16 (b) ₹ 15
(c) ₹ 14 (d) ₹ 18

57. The simple interest on ₹ 800 for 6 yr at 5.5% per annum is equal to the simple interest on ₹ 600 at 4% per annum for a certain period of time. The period of time is SSC CGL (Tier-I) 24/07/2023 Shift-II

(a) 11 yr (b) 9 yr
(c) 12 yr (d) 10 yr

58. The rate at which a sum becomes four times of itself in 12 yr at simple interest will be SSC CGL (Tier-I) 24/07/2023 Shift-I

(a) 20% (b) 25% (c) 35% (d) 30%

59. *R* wants to deposit ₹ 80000 in the bank for a year. In his account, the bank gives 12% simple annual interest but charges ₹ 3000 as a processing fee for the account. What would be his percentage earnings in the account? SSC CGL (Tier-I) 21/07/2023 Shift-IV

(a) 8.75% (b) 9%
(c) 8.5% (d) 8.25%

60. A certain amount is lent at $x\%$ p.a. simple interest for 3 yr. Instead, if the amount was lent at $3x\%$ p.a. simple interest for 'y' more years, then the simple interest would have been seven times the earlier interest. What is the value of y? SSC CGL (Tier-I) 21/07/2023 Shift-III

(a) 3 (b) 4
(c) 5 (d) 6

61. A person borrowed some money on simple interest. After 4 yr, he returned $\frac{9}{5}$ of the money to the lender. What was the rate of interest? SSC CGL (Tier-I) 21/07/2023 Shift-II

(a) 25% p.a. (b) 10% p.a.
(c) 15% p.a. (d) 20% p.a.

62. At simple interest a sum of ₹ 6400 becomes ₹ 8320 in 3 yr. What will ₹ 7200 become in 5 yr at the same rate? SSC CGL (Tier-I) 21/07/2023 Shift-I

(a) ₹ 10200 (b) ₹ 10600
(c) ₹ 10800 (d) ₹ 10400

63. A sum of ₹ 30000 becomes ₹ 38400 after being invested at a simple interest of 8% per annum in how many years? SSC CGL (Tier-I) 20/07/2023 Shift-IV

(a) 3.5 (b) 4
(c) 2.5 (d) 3

64. A person invests ₹ 9840 at 5% per annum simple interest to obtain a total amount of ₹ 12300. For how many years did he invest the sum? SSC CGL (Tier-I) 20/07/2023 Shift-III

(a) 5 yr (b) 4.5 yr
(c) 3.5 yr (d) 3 yr

65. A sum of money earns a simple interest at 7.25% per annum for the first eight years, at 8.5% for the next 6 yr, and at 6.5% for the final 4 yr. If the total interest earned during these 18 yr was ₹ 35100, what was the original sum invested (in ₹)? SSC CGL (Tier-I) 20/07/2023 Shift-II

(a) 25800 (b) 25500
(c) 26400 (d) 26000

66. A sum of money becomes $\frac{8}{7}$ of itself in 2 yr at a certain rate of simple interest. The rate per annum is SSC CGL (Tier-I) 20/07/2023 Shift-I

(a) $6\frac{3}{7}\%$ (b) $8\frac{1}{7}\%$
(c) $7\frac{1}{7}\%$ (d) $7\frac{3}{7}\%$

67. A sum of money at a fixed rate of simple interest amounts to ₹ 1630 in 3 yr and to ₹ 1708 in 4 yr. Find the sum (in ₹). SSC CGL (Tier-I) 19/07/2023 Shift-IV

(a) 1132 (b) 1296
(c) 1396 (d) 1448

68. Archana took a loan of ₹ 78000 from a bank on 24th January, 2012 at $8\frac{3}{4}\%$ per annum simple interest and paid it back on 18th June, 2012. Find the total amount paid by Archana(Approximated to nearest integer) SSC CGL (Tier-I) 19/07/2023 Shift-III

(a) ₹ 80723 (b) ₹ 90730
(c) ₹ 85733 (d) ₹ 88730

69. A man took a loan of ₹ 32400 at a certain rate of simple interest per annum. The rate of interest is one-fourth of the number of years for which the loan is taken. If he paid ₹ 11664 as interest at the end of the loan period, the rate of interest was SSC CGL (Tier-I) 19/07/2023 Shift-II

(a) 3% (b) 8%
(c) 5% (d) 12%

70. How much simple interest will ₹ 6000 earn in 21 months at 8% per annum? SSC CGL (Tier-I) 19/07/2023 Shift-I

(a) ₹ 750 (b) ₹880
(c) ₹ 620 (d) ₹ 840

71. An amount becomes double in 8 yr on simple interest. In how many years would ₹ 25000 become ₹ 100000 with the same rate of interest? SSC CGL (Tier-I) 18/07/2023 Shift-IV

(a) 32 (b) 28 (c) 16 (d) 24

72. In how many years will a sum of ₹ 9500 amount to ₹ 11780 at the rate of 8% per annum at simple interest? SSC CGL (Tier-I) 18/07/2023 Shift-III

(a) 5 (b) 2
(c) 3 (d) 4

73. If the simple interest for 5 yr is equal to 25% of the principal, then the interest will be equal to the principal after........... years. SSC CGL (Tier-I) 18/07/2023 Shift-I

(a) 20 (b) 30
(c) 25 (d) 22

74. Money was lent on simple interest. After 12 yr, its simple interest becomes $\frac{3}{5}$ of the money. Find the rate of interest. SSC CGL (Tier-I) 17/7/2023 Shift-IV

(a) 5% p.a. (b) 4% p.a.
(c) 2% p.a. (d) 3% p.a..

75. A person took a loan at 5% per annum simple interest during the first year and with an increase of 0.5% simple interest every year from the second year onwards. After 4 yr, he paid ₹ 4600 as a total interest to settle the loan completely. How much was the loan? SSC CGL (Tier-I) 17/07/2023 Shift-III

(a) ₹ 20000 (b) ₹ 19000
(c) ₹ 18000 (d) ₹ 21000

76. A sum of money invested at a certain rate of simple interest per annum amounts to ₹ 14522 in 7 yr and to ₹ 18906 in 11 yr. Find the sum invested (in ₹). SSC CGL (Tier-I) 17/07/2023 Shift-II

(a) 6850 (b) 6900
(c) 6800 (d) 6750

77. A person deposited ₹ 500 for 3 yr, ₹ 650 for 5 yr and ₹ 1250 for 7 yr at the same rate of interest. He received a total simple interest of ₹ 1620. The rate of interest per annum is SSC CGL (Tier-I) 17/07/2023 Shift-I

(a) 12% (b) 13%
(c) 10.8% (d) 11%

78. If ₹ 72 amounts to ₹ 104.4 in 3 yr, what will ₹ 120 amount to in 5 yr at the same rate per cent per annum? SSC CGL (Tier-I) 14/07/2023 Shift-IV

(a) ₹ 450 (b) ₹ 330
(c) ₹ 210 (d) ₹ 215

79. A man invests a total sum of ₹ 10000 in a company. A part of the sum was invested at 10% simple interest per annum and the remaining part at 15% simple interest per annum. If the total interest accrued to him in two years equals ₹ 2400, the sum invested at 15% simple interest per annum is SSC CGL (Tier-I) 14/07/2023 Shift-III

(a) ₹ 8000 (b) ₹ 4000
(c) ₹ 6000 (d) ₹ 5000

80. If the simple interest at the same interest rate on ₹ 500 for 4 yr and ₹ 700 for 2 yr, combined together, is ₹ 280, then what is the rate of interest? SSC CGL (Tier-I) 14/07/2023 Shift-II

(a) $8\frac{4}{17}\%$ (b) $6\frac{5}{17}\%$
(c) $9\frac{3}{17}\%$ (d) $7\frac{3}{17}\%$

81. In what time will ₹ 10000 at 4% per annum, produce the same interest as ₹ 8000 does in 4 yr at 5% simple interest? SSC CGL (Tier-I) 14/07/2023 Shift-I

(a) 3 yr (b) 5 yr
(c) 6 yr (d) 4 yr

SSC CGL 2022 (Tier I)

82. A certain sum of money lent at simple interest amounts to ₹ 1200 in 2 yr and ₹ 1600 in 4 yr. The rate per cent per annum is SSC CGL (Tier-I) 13/12/2022 Shift-IV

(a) 20% (b) 30%
(c) 25% (d) 16%

83. A person borrowed ₹ 2000 at 5% annual simple interest repayable in 3 equal annual installments. What will be the annual installment? SSC CGL (Tier-I) 13/12/2022 Shift-III

(a) ₹$730\frac{10}{63}$ (b) ₹$840\frac{9}{61}$
(c) ₹$640\frac{11}{63}$ (d) ₹$250\frac{10}{63}$

84. The monthly income of Mr. Roy is ₹ 18000. He took a loan of ₹ 30000 on simple interest for 3 yr at the rate of 5% per annum. The amount that he will be paying as simple interest in 3 yr is what per cent of his monthly salary? SSC CGL (Tier-I) 13/12/2022 Shift-I

(a) 30% (b) 35% (c) 20% (d) 25%

85. A sum of money doubles itself in 7 yr at simple interest. In how much time will it become 5 times of itself? SSC CGL (Tier-I) 12/12/2022 Shift-IV

(a) 25 yr (b) 28 yr
(c) 23 yr (d) 21 yr

86. A person deposited ₹ 15600 in a fixed deposit at 10% per annum simple interest. After every second year he adds his interest earned to the principal. The interest at the end of 4 yr is SSC CGL (Tier-I) 12/12/2022 Shift-III

(a) ₹ 6655 (b) ₹ 6864
(c) ₹ 3975 (d) ₹ 3744

87. What is the rate of interest per annum for simple interest at which ₹ 880 amount to ₹ 913 in $1\frac{1}{2}$ yr? SSC CGL (Tier-I) 12/12/2022 Shift-II

(a) $2\frac{2}{3}$% (b) $2\frac{1}{4}$%
(c) $2\frac{1}{2}$% (d) $2\frac{1}{3}$%

88. A person borrows ₹ 100000 from a bank at 10% per annum simple interest and clears the debt in five years. If the installment paid at the end of the first, second, third and fourth years to clear the debt are ₹ 10000, ₹ 20000, ₹ 30000 and ₹ 40000, respectively, what amount should be paid at the end of the fifth year to clear the debt? SSC CGL (Tier-I) 12/12/2022 Shift-I

(a) ₹ 38250
(b) ₹ 39490
(c) ₹ 40450
(d) ₹ 36450

89. In how many least number of complete years a sum of money become more than four times of itself at the rate of 50 per cent per annum on simple interest? SSC CGL (Tier-I) 09/12/2022 Shift-IV

(a) 9 yr (b) 7 yr
(c) 6 yr (d) 5 yr

90. Monty paid a simple interest of ₹ 480 on a particular sum after 2 yr. The rate was 8% per annum. Find the sum. SSC CGL (Tier-I) 09/12/2022 Shift-III

(a) ₹ 2200 (b) ₹ 2000
(c) ₹ 3000 (d) ₹ 2500

91. In how much time will a sum of ₹ 10200 amounts to ₹ 19125 at the rate of 12.5 per cent per annum at simple interest? SSC CGL (Tier-I) 09/12/2022 Shift-I

(a) 6 yr (b) 5 yr
(c) 8 yr (d) 7 yr

92. A certain sum of money is given at a certain rate for 3 yr. Had it been given at 5% higher rate, it would have fetched ₹ 600 more. Find the sum. SSC CGL (Tier-I) 08/12/2022 Shift-IV

(a) ₹ 8000 (b) ₹ 5000
(c) ₹ 6000 (d) ₹ 4000

93. A certain amount will become 6 times in 20 yr. How long does it take for the same amount to become 5 times? Assume the same rate of simple interest in each case. SSC CGL (Tier-I) 08/12/2022 Shift-III

(a) 16 yr 8 months (b) 15 yr 8 months
(c) 15 yr (d) 16 yr

94. Anuradha invests her money in a firm where the principal amount becomes 3 times in 10 yr. What is the yearly rate of simple interest offered by the firm? SSC CGL (Tier-I) 08/12/2022 Shift-II

(a) 25% (b) 20%
(c) 22% (d) 18%

95. In a certain duration of time, a sum become 2 times itself at the rate of 5% per annum simple interest. What will be the rate of interest if the same sum becomes 5 times itself in the same duration? SSC CGL (Tier-I) 08/12/2022 Shift-I

(a) 20% (b) 16%
(c) 10% (d) 18%

96. Find the simple interest on ₹ 2700 for 8 months at 5 paisa per rupee per month? SSC CGL (Tier-I) 07/12/2022 Shift-IV

(a) ₹ 950 (b) ₹ 720
(c) ₹ 540 (d) ₹ 1080

97. What annual installment will discharge a debt of ₹ 9600 due in 5 yr at 10% simple interest? SSC CGL (Tier-I) 07/12/2022 Shift-III

(a) ₹ 1450 (b) ₹ 1550
(c) ₹ 1500 (d) ₹ 1600

98. A sum is deposited in a bank which gives simple interest. The sum becomes 1.25 times in 3 yr. If there is a requirement of ₹ 760000 after 7 yr, how much amount (in ₹) should one deposit to fulfil the requirement? SSC CGL (Tier-I) 07/12/2022 Shift-II

(a) 520000 (b) 570000
(c) 480000 (d) 600000

99. A person lent certain sum of money at the annual rate of 7 per cent on simple interest and the interest received in 11 yr is ₹ 920 less than the sum lent. What is the sum lent? SSC CGL (Tier-I) 07/12/2022 Shift-I

(a) ₹ 41200 (b) ₹ 4000
(c) ₹ 52000 (d) ₹ 2400

100. A person lent ₹ 23000 to B for 3 yr and ₹ 19000 to C for 4 yr on simple interest at the same rate of interest and received ₹ 3625 in all from both of them as interest. What is the annual rate of interest? SSC CGL (Tier-I) 06/12/2022 Shift-IV

(a) 1.5% (b) 3%
(c) 2.5% (d) 4%

101. A sum of money amounts to ₹ 767 in 3 yr, and to ₹ 806 in 4 yr on simple interest at 6% annum. What is the sum? SSC CGL (Tier-I) 06/12/2022 Shift-III

(a) ₹ 600 (b) ₹ 560
(c) ₹ 675 (d) ₹ 650

102. A car with a price of ₹ 650000 is bought by making some down payment. On the balance, a simple interest of 10% is charged in lump sum and the money is to be paid in 20 equal annual installments of ₹ 25000. How much is the down payment? SSC CGL (Tier-I) 06/12/2022 Shift-II

(a) ₹ 155945 (b) ₹ 195455
(c) ₹ 194555 (d) ₹ 145955

103. The simple interest received on a sum is $\frac{25}{36}$ of the sum. The number of years is equal to the annual rate of interest. What is the annual rate of interest? SSC CGL (Tier-I) 06/12/2022 Shift-I

(a) 9.25% (b) 10.25%
(c) 6.62% (d) 8.33%

104. A certain sum amounts to ₹ 3640 in 2 yr and ₹ 4060 in 8 yr at simple interest. Find the approximate rate percentage per annum? SSC CGL (Tier-I) 05/12/2022 Shift-IV

(a) 4% (b) 2%
(c) 1% (d) 3%

105. A sum of money invested at simple interest becomes $\frac{17}{10}$ of itself in 2 yr and 6 months. What is the rate of interest per annum? SSC CGL (Tier-I) 05/12/2022 Shift-III

(a) 22% (b) 16%
(c) 28% (d) 34%

106. A sum becomes ₹15500 in 7 yr on simple interest at the rate of 30 per cent per annum. What is the total interest for the 7 yr? **SSC CGL (Tier-I) 03/12/2022 Shift-IV**
(a) ₹12200 (b) ₹147000
(c) ₹10500 (d) ₹11500

107. A certain sum of money becomes triple of itself in 26 yr at simple interest. In how many years it will becomes five times of itself? **SSC CGL (Tier-I) 05/12/2022 Shift-II**
(a) 64 yr (b) 52 yr (c) 56 yr (d) 60 yr

108. In how much time will a sum of ₹ 5250 amounts to ₹ 9870 at the rate of 11 per cent per annum at simple interest? **SSC CGL (Tier-I) 05/12/2022 Shift-I**
(a) 8 yr (b) 12 yr
(c) 15 yr (d) 14 yr

109. Suman paid ₹ 9600 in interest on a loan she obtained 5 yr ago with a simple interest rate of 16%. What was the amount of the loan she had taken? **SSC CGL (Tier-I) 03/12/2022 Shift-II**
(a) ₹ 13250 (b) ₹ 12500
(c) ₹ 12000 (d) ₹ 11750

110. ₹5000 is divided into two parts such that if one part is invested at 4% and the other at 5%, then the whole annual interest from both the sums is ₹ 223. How much was invested at 4%? **SSC CGL (Tier-I) 03/12/2022 Shift-I**
(a) ₹ 2600 (b) ₹ 2700
(c) ₹ 2400 (d) ₹ 2300

111. On simple interest a sum of ₹640 becomes ₹832 in 2 yr. What will ₹860 become in 4 yr at the same rate of simple interest? **SSC CGL (Tier-I) 02/12/2022 Shift-IV**
(a) ₹ 1250 (b) ₹ 1376
(c) ₹ 1426 (d) ₹ 1150

112. Damani purchased an item costing ₹ 7500 and paid ₹ 3500 as a down payment for the same. If the simple interest charged for the remaining amount is 9% per annum and Damani cleared all dues after 4 months of the purchase, how much did Damani pay after 4 months as interest? **SSC CGL (Tier-I) 01/12/2022 Shift-IV**
(a) ₹ 120 (b) ₹ 100
(c) ₹ 132 (d) ₹ 125

113. The simple interest on a certain sum for 3 yr at 14% per annum is ₹ 4200 less than the simple interest on the same sum for 5 yr at the same rate. Find the sum. **SSC CGL (Tier-I) 01/12/2022 Shift-III**
(a) ₹ 16000 (b) ₹10000
(c) ₹ 15000 (d) ₹ 12000

114. A person lent certain sum of money at the annual rate of 25 per cent on simple interest in 6 yr. The interest amounted to ₹ 360 more than the sum lent. What is the sum lent? **SSC CGL (Tier-I) 01/12/2022 Shift-II**
(a) ₹ 600 (b) ₹ 360 (c) ₹ 720 (d) ₹ 540

115. ₹ 2500, when invested for 8 yr at a given rate of simple interest per year, amounted to ₹ 3725 on maturity. What was the rate of simple interest that was paid per annum? **SSC CGL (Tier-I) 01/12/2022 Shift-I**
(a) 6% (b) 6.125%
(c) 6.25% (d) 5.875%

SSC CGL 2021 & 2020 (Tier I)

116. A sum of ₹25600 is invested on simple interest partly at 7% per annum and the remaining at 9% per annum. The total interest at the end of 3 yr is ₹ 5832. How much money (in ₹) was invested at 9% per annum? **SSC CGL (Tier-I) 23/08/2021 Shift-I**
(a) 16000 (b) 7600
(c) 9600 (d) 18000

117. A certain sum amounts to ₹ 81840 in 3 yr and to ₹ 92400 in 5 yr at x% p.a under simple interest. If the rate of interest is becomes $(x + 2)$%, then in how many years will the sum double itself? **SSC CGL (Tier-I) 20/08/2021 Shift-I**
(a) 8 (b) 10 (c) 20 (d) $12\frac{1}{2}$

118. A sum of money was lent in two parts in the ratio 4 : 5 for 4 yr and 5 yr respectively, both at the rate of 8% p.a. simple interest. If the difference between the interests earned from the two parts is ₹ 4680, then what was the total sum lent (in ₹)? **SSC CGL (Tier-I) 18/08/2021 Shift-III**
(a) 58500 (b) 42120
(c) 46800 (d) 65000

119. Two equal sums were lent on simple interest at 6% and 10% p.a., respectively. The first sum was recovered 2 yr later, than the second sum and the amount in each case was ₹ 1105. What was the sum (in ₹) lent in each scheme? **SSC CGL (Tier-I) 13/08/2021 Shift-III**
(a) 850 (b) 936
(c) 891 (d) 900

120. If in 13 yr a fixed sum doubles at simple interest, what will be the interest rate per year? (Correct to two decimal places) **SSC CGL (Tier-I) 07/03/2020 Shift-II**
(a) 7.69% (b) 7.92%
(c) 8.69% (d) 7.29%

121. The rate of simple interest on a sum of money is 5% p.a. for the first 4 yr, 8% p.a. for the next 3 yr and 10% p.a. for the period beyond 7 yr. If the interest accrued by the sum over a period of 10 yr is ₹ 1850, then the sum is **SSC CGL (Tier-I) 06/03/2020 Shift-III**
(a) ₹1500 (b) ₹2750
(c) ₹1650 (d) ₹2500

SSC CPO SI 2024 - 2020

122. A man borrowed ₹ 29000 for 3 yr and ₹ 45000 for 5 yr at the same rate of simple interest. If he paid a total interest of ₹ 62400, then what was the rate of interest? **SSC CPO 29/06/2024 Shift-III**
(a) 18% (b) 20%
(c) 27% (d) 25%

123. If the simple interest on a certain sum of money for 20 months at the rate of 19.2% per annum exceeds the simple interest on the same sum for 15 months at the rate of 11.2% per annun by ₹ 2920, then what is the sum (in ₹ , to the nearest hundreds)? **SSC CPO 29/06/2024 Shift-II**
(a) 16620 (b) 12660
(c) 16660 (d) 16200

124. A part of ₹ 48500 is invested at a simple interest of 15% per annum. The rest of the money is invested at the rate of 10% simple interest per annum after 2 yr of the first investment. The ratio of interest after 5 yr from the time when the first amount was invested is 5 : 3. How much is the second part that was invested (in ₹) at the rate of 10% simple interest? **SSC CPO 29/06/2024 Shift-I**
(a) 29100 (b) 20940
(c) 19400 (d) 24900

125. The simple interest on a certain sum for 4 yr at 14% per annum is ₹ 6160 less than the simple interest on the same sum at the same rate for 8 yr. Find the sum. **SSC CPO 28/06/2024 Shift-III**
(a) ₹ 9000
(b) ₹ 12000
(c) ₹ 11000
(d) ₹ 10000

126. A certain sum of money is given at a certain rate of simple interest for 4 yr. Had it been given at 11% higher rate for the same time, it would have fetched ₹ 1320 more. Find the sum (in ₹). **SSC CPO 28/06/2024 Shift-II**
(a) 4580 (b) 3000
(c) 2500 (d) 3240

127. In how many year will ₹ 2500 be invested at the rate of 12% per annum simple interest, which amounts to ₹ 4900 ?
SSC CPO 28/06/2024 Shift-I

(a) 4 (b) 6 (c) 8 (d) 2

128. A person deposited some amount of money in the bank at simple interest. After 20 yr, the amount became nine times the amount deposited. In how many yr will the amount become 13 times the amount if the interest rate remains the same?
SSC CPO 27/06/2024 Shift-III

(a) 28 (b) 30
(c) 25 (d) 23

129. What annual instalment will discharge a debt of ₹ 10192 due in 3 yr at 10% simple interest?
SSC CPO 27/06/2024 Shift-II

(a) ₹ 3044.48 (b) ₹ 3088.48
(c) ₹ 3144.48 (d) ₹ 3188.48

130. A person borrowed ₹ 1760 at 6% p.a. and ₹ 2240 at 9% p.a. at simple interest for the same period. He had to pay ₹ 1536 in all as interest. Find the time (in yr). SSC CPO 27/06/2024 Shift-I

(a) 2 (b) 3 (c) 4 (d) 5

131. In a store, Arun has two options to buy a mobile phone, either he can pay the full amount of ₹ 2500 or he may buy at an installment scheme, i.e., ₹ 520 in down payment and four equal installments, rate of interest being charged at 25% p.a. simple interest. Arun buys a mobile phone on the installment scheme. What is the monthly installment for Arun?
SSC CPO 05/10/2023 Shift-III

(a) ₹ 510 (b) ₹ 530
(c) ₹ 550 (d) ₹ 520

132. Ramesh borrowed ₹15000 at a certain rate of simple interest from a bank. He repaid (the principal but not interest) ₹ 6000 after 5 yr, and after 5 more years he paid ₹ 18600 and settled his account. Find the rate of simple interest per annum.
SSC CPO 04/10/2023 Shift-II

(a) 12% (b) 10%
(c) 8% (d) 6%

133. Rajesh invested ₹ 10000 by dividing it into two different investment schemes, A and B, at simple interest rates of 8% and 10%, respectively. If the total interest earned in 2 yr is ₹ 1680, the amount invested in scheme A is SSC CPO 03/10/2023 Shift-I

(a) ₹ 8000 (b) ₹ 2000
(c) ₹ 6000 (d) ₹ 4000

134. A sum of ₹ 36000 is divided into two parts A and B, such that the simple interest at the rate of 15% p.a. on A and B after 2 yr and 4 yr, respectively, is equal. The total interest (in ₹) received from A is
SSC CPO 25/11/2020 Shift-II

(a) 1800 (b) 3600
(c) 7200 (d) 5400

135. A person invested ₹ 12000 on simple interest for 7 yr to obtain a total amount of ₹ 20400 on a certain annual rate of interest. What was the rate of interest to obtain the above amount? SSC CPO 25/11/2020 Shift-I

(a) 7% (b) 9%
(c) 8% (d) 10%

136. If the annual rate of simple interest increase from 11% to $17\frac{1}{2}$%, then a person's yearly income increases by ₹ 1071.20. The simple interest (in ₹) on the same sum at 10% for 5 yr is
SSC CPO 24/11/2020 Shift-I

(a) 16480 (b) 9120
(c) 8240 (d) 7250

137. Sunita invested ₹ 12000 on simple interest at the rate of 10% p.a. to obtain a total amount of ₹ 20400 after a certain period. For how many years did she invest to obtain the above amount? SSC CPO 23/11/2020 Shift-I

(a) 8 (b) 9
(c) 6 (d) 7

SSC CHSL 2024 (Tier I & II)

138. A sum on simple interest at the rate of 5% per annum amounts to ₹ 4160 in 6 yr. Find the sum.
SSC CHSL (Tier-II) 18/11/2024

(a) ₹ 2900 (b) ₹ 2800
(c) ₹ 3200 (d) ₹ 3100

139. How much simple interest will ₹5000 earn in 14 months at a 12% interest rate per annum?
SSC CHSL (Tier-I) 11/07/2024 Shift-IV

(a) ₹ 600 (b) ₹ 800
(c) ₹ 700 (d) ₹ 500

140. In how many yr will a sum of ₹4250 yield a simple interest of ₹510 at a rate of 6% per annum?
SSC CHSL (Tier-I) 11/07/2024 Shift-III

(a) $3\frac{1}{2}$ yr (b) $2\frac{1}{2}$ yr
(c) 3 yr (d) 2 yr

141. A sum of ₹ 5000 was lent to two people, one at the rate of 16% and the other at the rate of 24%. If the simple interest after one year is ₹ 960, what is the sum lent at the higher rate ?
SSC CHSL (Tier-I) 11/07/2024 Shift-II

(a) ₹ 1500 (b) ₹ 3000
(c) ₹ 2500 (d) ₹ 2000

142. A laptop charger is sold for ₹ 2540 in cash or for a down payment of ₹ 1340 in cash together with ₹ 1205 to be paid after one month. Find the rate of interest charged in the instalment scheme.
SSC CHSL (Tier-I) 11/07/2024 Shift-I

(a) 20% p.a. (b) 10% p.a.
(c) 5% p.a. (d) 15% p.a.

143. Ramu invested some money at 8% simple interest per annum, and it was grown up to ₹ 820 in 8 yr. If the same sum was invested at 20% simple interest per annum for a period of 10 yr, find the amount.
SSC CHSL (Tier-I) 10/07/2024 Shift-IV

(a) ₹ 1000 (b) ₹ 1200
(c) ₹ 1320 (d) ₹ 1500

144. A certain sum of money amounts to ₹ 1860 in 2 yr and to ₹ 2130 in $3\frac{1}{2}$ yr at simple interest. Find the sum and the rate of interest, respectively.
SSC CHSL (Tier-I) 10/07/2024 Shift-III

(a) ₹ 1500, 12% (b) ₹ 1200, 10%
(c) ₹ 1500, 15% (d) ₹ 1200, 12%

145. A certain sum of money is lent out at simple interest. If that money becomes ₹24000 in 2 yr and ₹32000 in 4 yr, the annual rate of interest is
SSC CHSL (Tier-I) 10/07/2024 Shift-II

(a) 30% (b) 16%
(c) 25% (d) 20%

146. A sum of ₹ 2430 gives a simple interest of ₹ 1093.50 in 3 yr. The rate of interest per annum is
SSC CHSL (Tier-I) 10/07/2024 Shift-I

(a) 20% (b) 10%
(c) 15% (d) 25%

147. What will be the amount due on ₹ 36000 in 2 yr when the rate of simple interest for successive yr is 8% and 6%, respectively?
SSC CHSL (Tier-I) 09/07/2024 Shift-IV

(a) ₹ 38880 (b) ₹ 40320
(c) ₹ 41760 (d) ₹ 41040

148. An amount invested fetched a total simple interest of ₹ 4050 at the rate of 9% per annum in 5 yr. What is the amount invested (in ₹)?
SSC CHSL (Tier-I) 09/07/2024 Shift-III

(a) 9000 (b) 8300
(c) 7500 (d) 9050

149. If a sum of ₹ 3260 on simple interest amounts to ₹ 5420 in 6 yr, then what will this sum amount to in 4 yr at the same rate of interest?
SSC CHSL (Tier-I) 09/07/2024 Shift-II
(a) ₹ 4700 (b) ₹ 3700
(c) ₹ 3900 (d) ₹ 4500

150. In how much time (in yr) will ₹ 7200 amount to ₹ 8928 at simple interest at the rate of 8% per annum?
SSC CHSL (Tier-I) 09/07/2024 Shift-I
(a) 3 (b) 2 (c) 5 (d) 4

151. Ram invested a certain sum of money at simple interest. It amounted to $\frac{5}{4}$ of itself in 3 yr. What will be its rate per cent per annum?
SSC CHSL (Tier-I) 08/07/2024 Shift-IV
(a) 9.12 % (b) 8.33%
(c) 8.20% (d) 7.25%

152. A sum of money becomes five times its original value in 15 yr, when invested at a certain simple interest rate. If the sum was invested twice the time at the same rate of interest, what would be the final amount?
SSC CHSL (Tier-I) 08/07/2024 Shift-III
(a) The money becomes 7 times its original value
(b) The money becomes 9 times its original value
(c) The money becomes 6 times its original value
(d) The money becomes 8 times its original value

153. What will be the amount due on ₹ 12000 in 2 yr, when the rate of simple interest on successive yr is 9% and 10%, respectively?
SSC CHSL (Tier-I) 08/07/2024 Shift-II
(a) ₹ 14250 (b) ₹ 14280
(c) ₹ 14350 (d) ₹ 14150

154. A person borrowed some money at the rate of 8% per annum for the first two yr, at the rate of 11% per annum for the next three yr, and at the rate of 16% per annum for the period beyond five yr. If he pays a total interest of ₹ 21400 at the end of nine yr, how much money did he borrow (round to the nearest unit) ?
SSC CHSL (Tier-I) 08/07/2024 Shift-I
(a) ₹ 11938 (b) ₹ 18738
(c) ₹ 15938 (d) ₹ 18938

155. Find the amount to be paid at the end if ₹ 4500 is invested for a period of 4 yr at the rate of 8% simple interest per annum.
SSC CHSL (Tier-I) 05/07/2024 Shift-IV
(a) ₹ 5490 (b) ₹ 6080
(c) ₹ 5940 (d) ₹ 6300

156. If the ratio of principal and simple interest for 5 yr is 10 : 7, then the rate of interest per annum is
SSC CHSL (Tier-I) 05/07/2024 Shift-III
(a) 10% (b) 15% (c) 14% (d) 11%

157. An equal sum of money was lent to P and Q at 8.6% per annum for a period of 7 yr and 8 yr, respectively. If the difference in interest paid by them was ₹172, then the sum lent to each was
SSC CHSL (Tier-I) 05/07/2024 Shift-II
(a) ₹ 3000 (b) ₹ 2150
(c) ₹ 185 (d) ₹ 2000

158. A sum of ₹ 18000 gives a simple interest of ₹ 3240 in 2 yr and 3 months. The rate of interest per annum is **SSC CHSL (Tier-I) 05/07/2024 Shift-I**
(a) 10% (b) 12%
(c) 8% (d) 7%

159. An amount of ₹ 8000 was invested for 2 yr, partly in scheme 1 at the rate of 5% simple interest per annum and the rest in scheme 2 at the rate of 4% simple interest per annum. The total interest received at the end was ₹ 720. The amount of money invested in scheme 1 is
SSC CHSL (Tier-I) 04/07/2024 Shift-IV
(a) ₹ 3640 (b) ₹ 7200
(c) ₹ 4400 (d) ₹ 4000

160. Rahna decided to buy a scooty that costs ₹ 40000. The shopkeeper agreed to sell the scooty under the condition of ₹ 25000 cash down payment and ₹ 4000 each month for four months. Find the rate of interest at which the shopkeeper sold the scooty under the instalment scheme.
SSC CHSL (Tier-I) 04/07/2024 Shift-III
(a) 33% (b) $10\frac{1}{3}$%
(c) $18\frac{1}{2}$% (d) $16\frac{1}{2}$%

161. How much time (in yr) will it take for an amount of ₹ 450000 to yield ₹ 45000 as simple interest at a 5% per annum rate of interest?
SSC CHSL (Tier-I) 04/07/2024 Shift-II
(a) 5 (b) 4
(c) 2 (d) 3

162. A clock is sold for ₹ 550 cash or in the instalment scheme, for ₹ 250 cash down payment and ₹ 310 after one month. Find the rate of interest charged in the instalment scheme.
SSC CHSL (Tier-I) 04/07/2024 Shift-I
(a) 40% (b) 20%
(c) 35% (d) 45%

163. The simple interest on a sum for 8 yr is $\frac{4}{5}$ of the sum. The rate of interest per annum is
SSC CHSL (Tier-I) 03/07/2024 Shift-IV
(a) 5% (b) 15%
(c) 10% (d) 20%

164. An amount of ₹ 50000 becomes ₹ 72000 in 4 yr on a simple rate of interest. The rate of interest is .... per annum.
SSC CHSL (Tier-I) 03/07/2024 Shift-III
(a) 9% (b) 10%
(c) 11% (d) 12%

165. A man invested a sum of ₹ 5000 on simple interest for 5 yr such that the rate of interest for the first 2 yr is 10% per annum, for the next 3 yr it is 12% per annum. How much interest (in ₹), will he earn at the end of 5 yr? **SSC CHSL (Tier-I) 03/07/2024 Shift-II**
(a) 3180 (b) 2800
(c) 3000 (d) 2450

166. What is the present worth of ₹ 2400 due in 4 yr at a rate of 5% simple interest per annum?
SSC CHSL (Tier-I) 03/07/2024 Shift-I
(a) ₹ 2240 (b) ₹ 2000
(c) ₹ 2456 (d) ₹ 2200

167. A sum becomes ₹ 6600 in 4 yr at simple interest at a yearly interest rate of 5% per annum. What is the sum? **SSC CHSL (Tier-I) 02/07/2024 Shift-IV**
(a) ₹ 4400 (b) ₹ 3300
(c) ₹ 5500 (d) ₹ 6000

168. Find the total amount of debt that will be discharged by 5 equal instalments of ₹ 200 each, if the debt is due in 5 yr at 5% p.a. at simple interest.
SSC CHSL (Tier-I) 02/07/2024 Shift-III
(a) ₹ 1400
(b) ₹ 1100
(c) ₹ 1200
(d) ₹ 1255

169. The simple interest on a sum of money for $1\frac{1}{2}$ yr at 10% per annum is ₹30 more than the simple interest on the same sum for 1 yr at 12% per annum. Find the sum.
SSC CHSL (Tier-I) 02/07/2024 Shift-II
(a) ₹ 1000 (b) ₹ 1050
(c) ₹ 1250 (d) ₹ 1200

170. A bank charges simple interest for ₹ K at the rate of $r^{\frac{1}{2}}$ for n^2 yr. Another bank charges simple interest for ₹ L at the rate of $r^{\frac{3}{2}}$ for

n^3 yr and gives the same interest. The ratio between K and L is
SSC CHSL (Tier-I) 02/07/2024 Shift-I

(a) $\frac{1}{r}:\frac{1}{n}$ (b) $r\,n:1$
(c) $r^2:n^2$ (d) $r^{\frac{1}{2}}:n^{\frac{1}{2}}$

171. The simple interest on the sum for 12 yr is three-fifth of the sum. The rate of interest per annum is
SSC CHSL (Tier-I) 01/07/2024 Shift-IV

(a) 4% (b) 6%
(c) 5% (d) 3%

172. An amount becomes double in 7 yr on simple interest. The amount would be four times in .... yr on the same rate of simple interest.
SSC CHSL (Tier-I) 01/07/2024 Shift-III

(a) 14 (b) 28
(c) 21 (d) 18

173. Reshma took a loan of ₹1200000 with simple interest for as many yr as the rate of interest. If she paid ₹ 972000 as interest at the end of the loan period, what was the rate of interest per annum ?
SSC CHSL (Tier-I) 01/07/2024 Shift-III

(a) 7.5% (b) 8%
(c) 8.7% (d) 9%

174. In how many yr will the simple interest on a sum of money be equal to the principle at the rate of $2\frac{6}{7}$% per annum?
SSC CHSL (Tier-I) 01/07/2024 Shift-I

(a) 35 yr (b) 34 yr
(c) 33 yr (d) 37 yr

175. In how many years will ₹ 2500 invested at the rate of 16% p.a. simple interest, amount to ₹ 4100?
SSC CHSL (Tier-II) 10/01/2024 Shift-I

(a) 4 (b) 3 (c) 5 (d) 6

SSC CHSL 2023-2021 (Tier I & II)

176. A person borrowed some money on simple interest. After 3 yr, he returned $\frac{4}{3}$ of the money to the lender. What was the rate of interest? SSC CHSL (Tier-II) 02/11/2023 Shift-I

(a) $11\frac{4}{9}$% p.a. (b) $11\frac{1}{9}$% p.a.
(c) $11\frac{2}{9}$% p.a. (d) $11\frac{3}{9}$% p.a.

177. The sum of money at simple interest amounts to ₹ 750 in 3 yr and to ₹ 825 in 4 yr. The sum is
SSC CHSL (Tier-I) 17/08/2023 Shift-I

(a) ₹ 475 (b) ₹ 500
(c) ₹ 550 (d) ₹ 525

178. In 't' yr, the simple interest earned on a certain amount at the rate of 10% per annum is $\frac{5}{8}$th of the principal amount. If the rate of interest is made three-fourth of 10% and the simple interest remains the same, which of the following statements is true about the changed value of time?
SSC CHSL (Tier-I) 14/08/2023 Shift-IV

(a) It remains the same as 't'
(b) It becomes three-fourth of the time 't'
(c) It increases to $8\frac{1}{3}$ yr
(d) It decreases to $5\frac{1}{2}$ yr

179. A man invested ₹ 4400 at 10% and ₹ 7500 at 8% simple interest. What amount (in ₹) will he get from his investments after 12 yr?
SSC CHSL (Tier-I) 11/08/2023 Shift-I

(a) 24830 (b) 24380
(c) 28380 (d) 28840

180. At what annual rate (rounded off to the nearest integer) of simple interest will a sum of money become five times its initial value in 18 yr?
SSC CHSL (Tier-I) 10/08/2023 Shift-III

(a) 18% (b) 20%
(c) 22% (d) 24%

181. Simple interest on a certain sum is $\frac{1}{4}$ of the sum and the interest rate per annum is 4 times the number of years. If the rate of interest increases by 2%. Then, how much will the simple interest (in ₹) be on ₹ 3600 for 6 yr? SSC CHSL (Tier-I) 09/08/2023 Shift-I

(a) 2562 (b) 2514
(c) 2642 (d) 2592

182. If a sum of money becomes ₹ 6000 in 3 yr and ₹ 10500 in $7\frac{1}{2}$ yr at same rate of simple interest, then what is rate of interest.
SSC CHSL (Tier-I) 07/08/2023 Shift-IV

(a) $33\frac{1}{3}$% (b) $25\frac{1}{2}$%
(c) $45\frac{2}{3}$% (d) $66\frac{1}{3}$%

183. How long (in years) will a sum of money invested at 6% per annum simple interest to increase its value by 40%? SSC CHSL (Tier-I) 02/08/2023 Shift-I

(a) $6\frac{2}{3}$ (b) $5\frac{2}{3}$
(c) $6\frac{1}{3}$ (d) $4\frac{1}{3}$

184. A person borrows ₹ 20000 at the rate of 6% per annum on simple interest for 3 yr. He immediately lends it to another person at the rate of 8.5% per annum on simple interest for 3 yr. What is the value of gain per year ? SSC CHSL (Tier-I) 21/03/2023 Shift-IV

(a) ₹ 1500 (b) ₹ 500
(c) ₹ 800 (d) ₹ 200

185. In how much time will a sum of ₹ 12500 amounts to ₹ 20000 at the rate of 8% per cent per annum at simple interest?
SSC CHSL (Tier-I) 21/03/2023 Shift-II

(a) 10 yr (b) 7.5 yr
(c) 8 yr (d) 12.5 yr

186. What amount a man would have received on a principal of ₹ 7500 afer 2 yr at simple interest at the rate of 7% per annum?
SSC CHSL (Tier-I) 16/03/2023 Shift-I

(a) ₹ 8400 (b) ₹ 8550
(c) ₹ 7600 (d) ₹ 7400

187. A person lent ₹ 12000 to B for 3 yr and ₹ 10000 to C for 4 yr on simple interest at the same rate of interest and received ₹ 6080 in all from both of them as interest. What is the annual rate of interest?
SSC CHSL (Tier-I) 14/03/2023 Shift-I

(a) 15% (b) 8%
(c) 11% (d) 5%

188. A sum of ₹ 2000 amounts to ₹ 3120 in 2 yr at a certain rate of simple interest. What is the annual interest rate?
SSC CHSL (Tier-I) 13/03/2023 Shift-III

(a) 33% per year
(b) 34% per year
(c) 30% per year
(d) 28% per year

189. A man invests an amount of ₹ 105750 at simple interest in the name of his son, daughter and his wife in such a way that they get the same interest after 3, 4 and 5 yr, respectively. If the rate of interest is 5% per annum, then the amount invested for the wife is
SSC CHSL (Tier-I) 12/08/2021 Shift-III

(a) ₹ 27000 (b) ₹ 28000
(c) ₹ 25000 (d) ₹ 30000

SSC MTS 2024

190. Find the simple interest (in ₹) on ₹ 3500 as a sum borrowed at 7% per year rate of interest for 4 years.
SSC MTS 14/11/2024 Shift-III

(a) 1020 (b) 920
(c) 980 (d) 940

191. What sum (in ₹) will earn a simple interest of ₹ 360 in 3 years at 12% per year rate of interest? **SSC MTS 14/11/2024 Shift-III**

(a) 1000 (b) 2000
(c) 500 (d)1500

192. For a sum of ₹ 15000 the rate of interest of 8.5% per annum simple interest, find the interest earned (in ₹) in 5 years 3 months. **SSC MTS 14/11/2024 Shift-III**

(a) 21693.75 (b) 21375
(c) 6375 (d) 6693.75

193. What sum (in ₹) will earn a simple interest of ₹ 240 in 3 years at 20% per year rate of interest? **SSC MTS 13/11/2024 Shift-III**

(a) 200 (b) 400
(c) 800 (d) 600

194. The difference between simple interests on a certain sum at the annual rate of 6% for 6 years and 8% for 8 years is ₹ 1176. What is the sum? **SSC MTS 13/11/2024 Shift-III**

(a) ₹ 3800 (b) ₹ 4000
(c) ₹ 4400 (d) ₹ 4200

195. What sum (in ₹) will earn a simple interest of ₹ 360 in 2 yr at 20% per year rate of interest? **SSC MTS 13/11/2024 Shift-III**

(a) 450 (b) 1200
(c) 900 (d) 1800

196. Find the simple interest (in ₹) on ₹ 2500 as a sum borrowed at 3% per year rate of interest for 3 yr. **SSC MTS 12/11/2024 Shift-III**

(a) 185 (b) 225 (c) 265 (d) 165

197. Find the simple interest (in ₹) on ₹3500 as a sum borrowed at 6% per year rate of interest for 6 yr. **SSC MTS 12/11/2024 Shift-III**

(a) 1220 (b) 1260
(c) 1200 (d) 1300

198. A sum of money at simple interest amounts to ₹2500 in three years and ₹3000 in five years. What is the rate of interest (Correct up to two decimal places)? **SSC MTS 12/11/2024 Shift-III**

(a) 15% (b) 13.56%
(c) 14.29% (d) 14.25%

199. Find the simple interest (in ₹) on ₹ 2000 as a sum borrowed at 8% per year rate of interest for 5 yr. **SSC MTS 11/11/2024 Shift-III**

(a) 760 (b) 800
(c) 840 (d) 740

200. A sum was deposited at a certain rate of simple interest for 4 years. If it had been a 5% higher rate of interest, then it would have amounted to ₹5200 more. The sum deposited is **SSC MTS 11/11/2024 Shift-III**

(a) ₹10400 (b) ₹13000
(c) ₹ 26000 (d) ₹25000

201. How long (in years) will it take for a sum of money invested at 4% per annum on simple interest to increase its value by 30%? **SSC MTS 11/11/2024 Shift-III**

(a) $7\frac{1}{2}$ (b) $4\frac{1}{2}$
(c) $8\frac{1}{2}$ (d) $5\frac{1}{2}$

202. Find the simple interest (in ₹) on ₹2500 as a sum borrowed at 9% per year rate of interest for 5 yr. **SSC MTS 05/11/2024 Shift-III**

(a) 1085 (b) 1165
(c) 1065 (d) 1125

203. Find the simple interest (in ₹) on ₹3500 as a sum borrowed at 4% per year rate of interest for 5 yr. **SSC MTS 05/11/2024 Shift-III**

(a) 640 (b) 740
(c) 660 (d) 700

204. At what rate of simple interest will a sum of money double itself in 12 yr? **SSC MTS 05/11/2024 Shift-III**

(a) $16\frac{2}{3}\%$ (b) $8\frac{1}{3}\%$
(c) 12% (d) 18%

205. Find the simple interest (in ₹) on ₹ 2500 as a sum borrowed at 8% per year rate of interest for 3 years. **SSC MTS 04/11/2024 Shift-III**

(a) 640 (b) 540
(c) 600 (d) 560

206. Ram borrowed ₹ 20000 at 6% per annum and ₹ 25000 at 8% per annum, for the same duration. He had to pay ₹ 9600 in all as interest. What is the time period? **SSC MTS 04/11/2024 Shift-III**

(a) 5 yr (b) 3 yr (c) 4 yr (d) 2 yr

207. Find the simple interest (in ₹) on ₹ 2500 as a sum borrowed at 6% per year rate of interest for 2 years. **SSC MTS 04/11/2024 Shift-III**

(a) 340 (b) 260 (c) 240 (d) 300

208. What sum (in ₹) will earn a simple interest of ₹ 240 in 2 yr at 4% per year rate of interest? **SSC MTS 30/10/2024 Shift-III**

(a) 3000 (b) 1500
(c) 4000 (d) 6000

209. A money lender lent out ₹ 40000 in two parts, one at 7% p.a. and the other at 6% p.a.. If the total annual simple interest on the amount is ₹ 2550, what is the amount of money lent at 7%? **SSC MTS 30/10/2024 Shift-III**

(a) ₹ 21000 (b) ₹ 18000
(c) ₹ 15000 (d) ₹ 26000

210. Find the simple interest (in ₹) on ₹ 2000 as a sum borrowed at 8% per year rate of interest for 6 yr. **SSC MTS 30/10/2024 Shift-III**

(a) 1000 (b) 960
(c) 900 (d) 920

211. Find the simple interest (in ₹) on ₹ 2500 as a sum borrowed at 4% per year rate of interest for 2 yr. **SSC MTS 29/10/2024 Shift-III**

(a) 240 (b) 200
(c) 160 (d) 140

212. What sum (in ₹) will earn a simple interest of ₹ 240 in 4 yr at 16% per year rate of interest? **SSC MTS 29/10/2024 Shift-III**

(a) 375 (b) 500
(c) 800 (d) 750

213. The money invested by Gopal at simple interest amounts to ₹ 16150 in 3 yr and to ₹ 16540 in 4 yr. What was the principal amount invested by him? **SSC MTS 29/10/2024 Shift-III**

(a) ₹ 11150 (b) ₹ 16150
(c) ₹ 18150 (d) ₹ 14980

214. Arun has taken some money as loan on simple interest for 6 yr. The money lender levied interest at 4% per annum for the first 2 yr, at 8% per annum for the next 3 years and at 12% per annum for the period beyond 5 yr. If Arun clears his loan by paying ₹5472, then what was the sum (in ₹) he had taken as loan? **SSC MTS 28/10/2024 Shift-II**

(a) 3800 (b) 6840
(c) 3040 (d) 12436

215. Find the simple interest (in ₹) on ₹ 3000 as a sum borrowed at 8% per year rate of interest for 4 years. **SSC MTS 28/10/2024 Shift-II**

(a) 920 (b) 1000
(c) 960 (d) 900

216. What sum (in ₹) will earn a simple interest of ₹ 360 in 2 years at 4% per year rate of interest? **SSC MTS 28/10/2024 Shift-II**

(a) 2250 (b) 6000
(c) 4500 (d) 9000

217. What will be the ratio of simple interest earned by a certain amount at the same rate of interest for 12 yr and that for 15 yr? **SSC MTS 23/10/2024 Shift-II**

(a) 4 : 5 (b) 2 : 5
(c) 3 : 4 (d) 2 : 3

218. Find the simple interest (in ₹) on ₹ 3000 as a sum borrowed at 8% per year rate of interest for 2 years.
SSC MTS 23/10/2024 Shift-II

(a) 420 (b) 480
(c) 520 (d) 440

219. Find the simple interest (in ₹) on ₹ 2000 as a sum borrowed at 9% per year rate of interest for 4 yr.
SSC MTS 23/10/2024 Shift-II

(a) 660 (b) 680
(c) 760 (d) 720

220. Find the simple interest (in ₹) on ₹ 3500 as a sum borrowed at 3% per year rate of interest for 5 years.
SSC MTS 22/10/2024 Shift-II

(a) 465 (b) 485
(c) 565 (d) 525

221. Find the simple interest (in ₹) on ₹ 3500 as a sum borrowed at 5% per year rate of interest for 3 years.
SSC MTS 22/10/2024 Shift-II

(a) 565 (b) 525
(c) 465 (d) 485

222. A person borrow some money on simple interest. After 15 years, the simple interest will be $\frac{19}{15}$ of the borrowed amount. What is the rate of interest per annum?
SSC MTS 22/10/2024 Shift-II

(a) $5\frac{4}{9}\%$ (b) $6\frac{4}{9}\%$
(c) $7\frac{4}{9}\%$ (d) $8\frac{4}{9}\%$

223. Find the simple interest (in ₹) on ₹ 3500 as a sum borrowed at 3% per year rate of interest for 6 yr.
SSC MTS 21/10/2024 Shift-II

(a) 670 (b) 630
(c) 590 (d) 570

224. A sum of money amounts to ₹ 7436 after 6 years and ₹ 9460 after 10 years at the same rate of simple interest. Find the rate of interest per annum.
SSC MTS 21/10/2024 Shift-II

(a) 12.5% (b) 13%
(c) 11.5% (d) 12%

225. Find the simple interest (in ₹) on ₹ 2500 as a sum borrowed at 5% per year rate of interest for 6 years.
SSC MTS 21/10/2024 Shift-II

(a) 710 (b) 690
(c) 790 (d) 750

226. Find the simple interest (in ₹) on ₹4000 as a sum borrowed at 4% per year rate of interest for 6 years.
SSC MTS 18/10/2024 Shift-II

(a) 920 (b) 900
(c) 960 (d) 1000

227. Find the simple interest (in ₹) on ₹ 3000 as a sum borrowed at 3% per year rate of interest for 6 years.
SSC MTS 18/10/2024 Shift-II

(a) 480 (b) 500
(c) 580 (d) 540

228. The simple interest on a sum of ₹ 4200 at the end of 3 years is ₹ 756. What will be the simple interest (in ₹) on ₹ 5400 at the same rate and for the same time period?
SSC MTS 18/10/2024 Shift-II

(a) 972 (b) 987 (c) 998 (d) 980

229. Rakesh obtained a simple interest of ₹ 3195 on a certain principal in 6 yr at the rate of 15% per annum. What amount of simple interest would he get if he invested ₹ 1250 more than the previous principal for 3 yr at the same rate of interest?
SSC MTS 17/10/2024 Shift-II

(a) ₹ 2255 (b) ₹ 2160
(c) ₹ 2050 (d) ₹ 2400

230. Find the simple interest (in ₹) on ₹ 2000 as a sum borrowed at 7% per year rate of interest for 6 yr.
SSC MTS 17/10/2024 Shift-II

(a) 880 (b) 780 (c) 800 (d) 840

231. Find the simple interest (in ₹) on ₹ 2500 as a sum borrowed at 5% per year rate of interest for 3 yr.
SSC MTS 17/10/2024 Shift-II

(a) 415 (b) 375 (c) 315 (d) 335

232. Find the simple interest (in ₹) on ₹ 940 for 3 years at 5% per annum.
SSC MTS 16/10/2024 Shift-II

(a) ₹142 (b) ₹143
(c) ₹140 (d) ₹141

233. Find the simple interest (in ₹) on ₹3500 as a sum borrowed at 6% per year rate of interest for 4 years.
SSC MTS 16/10/2024 Shift-II

(a) 800 (b) 880 (c) 780 (d) 840

234. Find the simple interest (in ₹) on ₹2000 as a sum borrowed at 7% per year rate of interest for 3 yr.
SSC MTS 15/10/2024 Shift-I

(a) 460 (b) 380
(c) 360 (d) 420

235. Vipul, Ashima and Priya invested a total of ₹ 21000 at 3%, 6% and 5% per annum, respectively, on simple interest. If at the end of the year, all three persons received an equal amount of interest, then the amount (in ₹) invested by Ashima is
SSC MTS 15/10/2024 Shift-I

(a) 5000 (b) 3000
(c) 2000 (d) 4000

236. Find the simple interest (in ₹) on ₹3000 as a sum borrowed at 8% per year rate of interest for 6 yr.
SSC MTS 15/10/2024 Shift-I

(a) 1400 (b) 1480
(c) 1440 (d) 1380

237. The simple interest on a certain sum for 4 years at 23% per annum is ₹ 11960 less than the simple interest on the same sum for 8 years. Find the sum.
SSC MTS 14/10/2024 Shift-I

(a) ₹ 12000 (b) ₹ 12500
(c) ₹ 13500 (d) ₹ 13000

238. Find the simple interest (in ₹) on ₹ 3500 as a sum borrowed at 6% per year rate of interest for 3 years.
SSC MTS 14/10/2024 Shift-I

(a) 630 (b) 670
(c) 590 (d) 570

239. Find the simple interest (in ₹) on ₹ 2500 as a sum borrowed at 6% per year rate of interest for 5 yr.
SSC MTS 14/10/2024 Shift-I

(a) 750 (b) 710
(c) 790 (d) 690

240. Find the simple interest (in ₹) on ₹ 2500 as a sum borrowed at 7% per year rate of interest for 3 yr.
SSC MTS 09/10/2024 Shift-I

(a) 465 (b) 485
(c) 565 (d) 525

241. Find the simple interest (in ₹) on ₹ 2500 as a sum borrowed at 9% per year rate of interest for 4 years.
SSC MTS 09/10/2024 Shift-I

(a) 900 (b) 860
(c) 840 (d) 940

242. At a certain rate of simple interest, a sum becomes ₹ 9430 in 3 yr and ₹ 11070 in 7 yr. Find the sum.
SSC MTS 09/10/2024 Shift-I

(a) ₹ 8200 (b) ₹ 8000
(c) ₹ 8350 (d) ₹ 7800

243. Rakesh rented out an amount to Samarth for 6 yr at simple interest rate. At the end of the 6th year, Samarth paid $\frac{8}{7}$ of the amount to Rakesh to clear out the amount. The rate of simple interest per annum was
SSC MTS 08/10/2024 Shift-I

(a) $2\frac{7}{21}\%$ (b) $2\frac{3}{20}\%$
(c) $2\frac{1}{12}\%$ (d) $2\frac{8}{21}\%$

244. Find the simple interest (in ₹) on ₹ 3000 as a sum borrowed at 3% per year rate of interest for 4 yr.
SSC MTS 08/10/2024 Shift-I

(a) 400 (b) 360
(c) 300 (d) 320

245. Find the simple interest (in ₹) on ₹ 2500 as a sum borrowed at 3% per year rate of interest for 6 yr. **SSC MTS 08/10/2024 Shift-I**

(a) 410 (b) 390
(c) 490 (d) 450

246. Find the simple interest (in ₹) on ₹ 3000 as a sum borrowed at 6% per year rate of interest for 4 yr. **SSC MTS 07/10/2024 Shift-I**

(a) 660 (b) 680
(c) 760 (d) 720

247. Find the simple interest (in ₹) on ₹ 2500 as a sum borrowed at 9% per year rate of interest for 6 yr. **SSC MTS 07/10/2024 Shift-I**

(a) 1390 (b) 1310
(c) 1350 (d) 1290

248. A sum of ₹ 2380 is lent out into two parts, one at 25% p.a. and another at 20% p.a. . If the total annual income is ₹ 500, find the money (in ₹) lent at 25% rate. **SSC MTS 07/10/2024 Shift-I**

(a) 320 (b) 240
(c) 480 (d) 560

249. What sum (in ₹) will earn a simple interest of ₹240 in 4 yr at 12% per year rate of interest? **SSC MTS 01/10/2024 Shift-I**

(a) 250 (b) 1000
(c) 500 (d) 750

250. Find the simple interest (in ₹) on ₹ 2500 as a sum borrowed at 7% per year rate of interest for 5 yr. **SSC MTS 01/10/2024 Shift-I**

(a) 815 (b) 875 (c) 915 (d) 835

251. A borrows ₹89500 for 3 yr at 7% p.a. simple interest. B borrows the same amount at simple interest of 9% for the first year, 8% for the second year, and 7% for the third year. What is the total simple interest (in ₹) paid by A and B? **SSC MTS 01/10/2024 Shift-I**

(a) 45027 (b) 47025
(c) 42075 (d) 40275

252. A sum invested at 5% simple interest per annum grows to ₹806 in 6 yr. If the amount remains the same, how much will it grow at a 12% simple interest rate in 5 yr ? **SSC MTS 30/09/2024 Shift-I**

(a) ₹ 992 (b) ₹ 985
(c) ₹ 1000 (d) ₹ 1120

253. Find the simple interest (in ₹) on ₹3500 as a sum borrowed at 7% per year rate of interest for 6 yr. **SSC MTS 30/09/2024 Shift-I**

(a) 1430 (b) 1470
(c) 1510 (d) 1410

254. Find the simple interest (in ₹) on ₹3000 as a sum borrowed at 7% per year rate of interest for 5 yr. **SSC MTS 30/09/2024 Shift-I**

(a) 1050 (b) 990
(c) 1010 (d) 1090

SSC MTS 2023

255. A certain sum is invested at a simple interest rate of 12% per annum for a certain period of time. If the sum becomes four times the principal at the end of the period, what is the duration of the investment? **SSC MTS 14/09/2023 Shift-I**

(a) 22 yr (b) 24 yr
(c) 25 yr (d) 20 yr

256. In how many years will ₹ 2000 invested at the rate of 11% p.a. simple interest, amount to ₹ 3100? **SSC MTS 13/09/2023 Shift-I**

(a) 3 (b) 4
(c) 2 (d) 5

257. ₹ 8000 becomes ₹ 9800 in 3 yr at simple interest rate. If the rate of interest becomes 2 times of itself, then what will be the amount of the same principal in 4 yr? **SSC MTS 11/09/2023 Shift-II**

(a) ₹ 10800 (b) ₹ 11800
(c) ₹ 12800 (d) ₹ 13500

258. What sum of money (in ₹) will earn an interest of ₹ 1800 at the rate of 6% per annum simple interest in 5 yr? **SSC MTS 11/09/2023 Shift-I**

(a) ₹ 18000 (b) ₹ 6000
(c) ₹ 8000 (d) ₹ 5000

259. In a certain time, a sum becomes 5 times at the rate of 6% per annum on simple interest. At what rate of interest, the same sum becomes 8 times in the same duration? **SSC MTS 08/09/2023 Shift-II**

(a) 8.5% (b) 10.5%
(c) 5.5% (d) 12.5%

260. Find the simple interest (in ₹) on ₹ 5400 for 7 yr at 4% per annum. **SSC MTS 06/09/2023 Shift-I**

(a) 1512 (b) 1230
(c) 1380 (d) 1172

261. How much simple interest will ₹ 6000 earn in 15 months at the rate of 12% per annum ? **SSC MTS 05/09/2023 Shift-II**

(a) ₹ 900 (b) ₹ 600
(c) ₹ 750 (d) ₹ 800

262. A sum invested at the rate of 6% simple interest per annum grows to ₹ 113880 in 5 yr. What is the simple interest, if the same amount is invested for 8 yr at the rate of 9% per annum? **SSC MTS 04/09/2023 Shift-II**

(a) ₹ 63072 (b) ₹ 60565
(c) ₹ 65392 (d) ₹ 58050

263. If ₹3650 amounts to ₹ 4526 in 3 yr at simple interest, what is the rate of interest per annum? **SSC MTS 01/09/2023 Shift-III**

(a) 8% (b) 10%
(c) 12% (d) 6%

264. Disha invested an amount of ₹ 20000 for 9 yr at a simple interest per annum and obtain the total amount of ₹ 33500. What is the rate of interest? **SSC MTS 01/09/2023 Shift-I**

(a) 8% (b) 8.5%
(c) 7.5% (d) 9%

SSC MTS 2022 & 2021

265. If on a certain sum, the simple interest for 4 yr is ₹ 2000, then what is the simple interest for 6 yr on the same sum? **SSC MTS 15/07/2022 Shift-I**

(a) ₹ 3500 (b) ₹ 3000
(c) ₹ 4000 (d) ₹ 2800

266. The amount received after 8 yr on a certain sum of money invested at the rate of 18% simple interest per annum is ₹ 1220. What was the initial sum invested? **SSC MTS 14/07/2022 Shift-I**

(a) ₹ 500 (b) ₹ 480
(c) ₹ 420 (d) ₹ 450

267. Sashi took a loan of ₹ 700 on simple interest for as many years as the rate of interest per annum. If he paid ₹ 343 as interest at the end of the loan period, what was the rate of interest? **SSC MTS 14/07/2022 Shift-I**

(a) 6% (b) 4%
(c) 10% (d) 7%

268. At what rate of simple interest per annum will a sum triple itself in 30 yr? [Give your answer correct to 2 decimal places] **SSC MTS 11/07/2022 Shift-I**

(a) 6.67% (b) 4.75%
(c) 8.33% (d) 3.33%

269. A certain sum was invested on simple interest for a period of seven years. During the period of the sixth and the seventh years combined, the interest earned was ₹ 292. If the maturity amount is ₹ 3942, then what is the rate percentage of the interest? **SSC MTS 02/11/2021 Shift-III**

(a) 5 (b) 2
(c) 6.25 (d) 2.5

270. 6 copies of a book can be bought for a certain sum payable at the end of a year,and 7 copies of the same book can be bought for the same sum in cash money.What is the rate per annum of simple interest (correct to one decimal place)? SSC MTS 02/11/2021 Shift-II
(a) 10.9% (b) 15.5%
(c) 16.7% (d) 30.4%

271. The simple interest accrued on a sum of ₹ 15000 at the end of 5 yr is ₹ 9750. If the rate of interest is 3% lesser, then the interest would be SSC MTS 02/11/2021 Shift-I
(a) ₹ 7950 (b) ₹ 5850
(c) ₹ 3250 (d) ₹ 7500

SSC GD Constable 2024

272. A sum becomes ₹ 1320 in 2 yr and ₹ 1380 in 3 yr at simple interest. What is the annual rate of interest ? SSC GD 26/02/2024 Shift-I
(a) 4% (b) 5%
(c) 10% (d) 8%

273. What is that rate of simple interest at which a sum of money becomes three time of itself in 24 yr? SSC GD 24/02/2024 Shift-III
(a) 10.28% (b) 8.68%
(c) 8.33% (d) 9.28%

274. The difference between simple interest on a certain sum at the annual rate of 10% for 7 yr and 8 yr is ₹ 57. What is the sum? SSC GD 24/02/2024 Shift-II
(a) ₹ 550 (b) ₹ 610
(c) ₹ 570 (d) ₹ 590

275. The difference between simple interest on a certain sum at the annual rate of 11% for 8 yr and 9 yr is ₹ 132. What is the sum? SSC GD 24/02/2024 Shift-I
(a) ₹ 1450
(b) ₹ 1300
(c) ₹ 1100
(d) ₹ 1200

276. What is that rate of simple interest at which a sum of money becomes three times of itself in 34 yr? SSC GD 23/02/2024 Shift-IV
(a) 5.29% (b) 5.88%
(c) 5.68% (d) 6.82%

277. A person lent a certain sum of money at 3% per annum on simple interest. The interest received in 25 yr is ₹ 600 less than the amount lent. What is the amount lent? SSC GD 23/02/2024 Shift-III
(a) ₹ 1200 (b) ₹ 800
(c) ₹ 1600 (d) ₹ 2400

278. A certain sum of money amounts to ₹ 1060 in 2.5 yr and ₹ 1000 in 1 yr at simple interest. What is the annual rate of interest? SSC GD 23/02/2024 Shift-II
(a) 6.28% (b) 4.17%
(c) 5.28% (d) 5.45%

279. John deposited ₹ 1200 in a bank account. After 4 yr, the total amount in the account is ₹ 1400. Find the rate of simple interest per annum. SSC GD 23/02/2024 Shift-I
(a) 5.13% (b) 4.17%
(c) 5.83% (d) 6.23%

280. A person lent certain sum of money at the annual rate of 24% on simple interest. In 5 yr the interest amounted to ₹ 1200 more than the sum lent. What is the sum lent? SSC GD 22/02/2024 Shift-IV
(a) ₹ 3600 (b) ₹ 3000
(c) ₹ 6000 (d) ₹ 2400

281. A certain sum of money becomes 3.5 times of itself in 14 yr at a rate of simple interest. In 28 yr, that amount it will become how many times of itself at the same rate of simple interest? SSC GD 22/02/2024 Shift-III
(a) 6 (b) 10 (c) 4 (d) 8

282. Simple interest on a sum for 5 yr is equal to 20% of the principal. In how many years interest will be equal to the principal? SSC GD 22/02/2024 Shift-II
(a) 35 yr (b) 30 yr
(c) 25 yr (d) 40 yr

283. The simple interest received on a certain sum is ₹ 1782 for 3 yr. What will be the simple interest on the same sum at the same rate of interest for 10 yr? SSC GD 22/02/2024 Shift-I
(a) ₹ 6940 (b) ₹ 6800
(c) ₹ 5940 (d) ₹ 6840

284. Find the sum required to earn a monthly interest of ₹ 350 at 7% per annum at simple interest. SSC GD 21/02/2024 Shift-IV
(a) ₹ 60000 (b) ₹ 65000
(c) ₹ 50000 (d) ₹ 55000

285. The simple interest on a certain sum of money is ₹ 2275 at 13% per annum in 5 yr. Find the sum of money? SSC GD 21/02/2024 Shift-III
(a) ₹ 5600 (b) ₹ 3500
(c) ₹ 4200 (d) ₹ 4000

286. John deposited ₹ 1000 in a bank account that offers a simple interest rate of 5% per annum. How much interest will be earn after 2 yr? SSC GD 21/02/2024 Shift-II
(a) ₹ 115 (b) ₹ 100 (c) ₹ 110 (d) ₹ 120

287. The simple interest received on a sum for 20 yr is $\frac{2}{5}$ of the sum. What is the annual rate of interest? SSC GD 21/02/2024 Shift-I
(a) 2.5% (b) 4%
(c) 3% (d) 2%

288. A certain sum becomes 7 times of itself in 10 yr at a rate of simple interest. In 20 yr, it will become how many times of itself at the same rate of simple interest? SSC GD 20/02/2024 Shift-IV
(a) 14 (b) 10
(c) 12 (d) 13

289. If a certain sum of money becomes thrice of itself in 8 yr 6 months at simple interest, then what will be the annual rate of interest? SSC GD 20/02/2024 Shift-III
(a) 21.28% (b) 24.78%
(c) 23.52% (d) 24.48%.

290. The simple interest received on a sum for 5 yr is $\frac{2}{5}$ of the sum. What is the annual rate of interest? SSC GD 20/02/2024 Shift-II
(a) 9% (b) 12%
(c) 10% (d) 8%

291. The simple interest received on a sum for 40 yr is $\frac{2}{5}$ of the sum. What is the annual rate of interest ? SSC GD 20/02/2024 Shift-I
(a) 1.5% (b) 2%
(c) 1% (d) 3%

SSC Selection Post 2024-2022

292. ₹ 1380 has to be paid after 4 yr. If four equal instalments are required with a simple interest of 10% on each instalment, then what is the value of each instalment? Matric Level 20/06/2024 Shift-IV
(a) ₹ 200 (b) ₹ 500
(c) ₹ 300 (d) ₹ 400

293. Sanjana borrows ₹ 16000 at 24% per annum simple interest and Savithri borrows ₹ 18200 at 20% per annum simple interest. In how many yr will their amounts of debts be equal? Matric Level 20/06/2024 Shift-IV
(a) 10 (b) 11
(c) 15 (d) 12

294. A sum of ₹ 2400 gives a simple interest of ₹ 378 in 2 yr 4 months. What is the rate of interest per annum? Matric Level 20/06/2024 Shift-IV
(a) 6.95% (b) 6.75%
(c) 6.85% (d) 7.05%

295. A sum of ₹1250 is lent on simple interest at a rate of $5\frac{1}{2}\%$ per annum for three yr. Find the interest (in ₹). **Graduate Level 20/06/2024 Shift-III**

(a) 210.25 (b) 215.75
(c) 206.25 (d) 200.00

296. What annual installment will discharge a debt of ₹ 3658 due in four yr at 12% simple interest per annum? **Higher Secondary Level 20/06/2024 Shift-II**

(a) ₹ 825 (b) ₹ 725
(c) ₹ 750 (d) ₹ 775

297. What would be the simple interest (in ₹) on principal amount of ₹ 1 lakh for 2 yr at the rate of 12% per annum? **Graduate Level 27/06/2023 Shift-IV**

(a) ₹ 25000 (b) ₹ 30000
(c) ₹ 12000 (d) ₹ 24000

298. A sum of ₹ 16875 was lent out at simple interest, and at the end of 1 yr 8 months, the total amount was ₹ 18000. Find the rate of interest per annum. **Graduate Level 27/06/2023 Shift-IV**

(a) 3.7% (b) 4%
(c) 5% (d) 6.66%

299. A sum of ₹84000 is deposited in a bank on simple interest at the rate of 15% for the period of 3 yr. How much simple interest (in ₹) will be received? **Higher Secondary Level 27/06/2023 Shift-III**

(a) ₹ 37800 (b) ₹ 38700
(c) ₹ 37200 (d) ₹ 39800

300. What would be the simple interest on principle amount of ₹2 lakh for 3 yr at a rate of 8% per annum? **Higher Secondary Level 27/06/2023 Shift-III**

(a) ₹32000 (b) ₹48000
(c) ₹40000 (d) ₹ 36000

301. Aravind deposited ₹ 18500 for 5 yr at simple interest. After 5 yr, he received ₹ 4625 as interest. The annual rate of interest was **Matric Level 27/06/2023 Shift-I**

(a) 6% (b) 6.5%
(c) 5% (d) 7%

302. The simple interest earned on ₹7000 in 2 yr at the rate of R% per annum equals to the simple interest earned on ₹ 5000 at the rate of 5% per annum in 14 yr. The value of R (in percentage) is **Matric Level 27/06/2023 Shift-I**

(a) 28% (b) 15%
(c) 25% (d) 20%

303. A person borrowed some money on simple interest. After 5 yr he returned $\frac{7}{5}$ of the money to the lender. What was the rate of interest? **Higher Secondary Level 01/08/2022 Shift-III**

(a) 8% p.a. (b) 4% p.a.
(c) 9% p.a. (d) 6% p.a.

304. On a certain sum, the simple interest at the end of 15 yr becomes $\frac{3}{10}$ of the sum. What is the rate of interest per annum? **Matric Level 01/08/2022 Shift-I**

(a) 15% (b) 10%
(c) 2% (d) 3%

Right Answers

1	(c)	2	(c)	3	(a)	4	(c)	5	(a)	6	(c)	7	(b)	8	(c)	9	(a)	10	(b)
11	(b)	12	(b)	13	(b)	14	(b)	15	(c)	16	(d)	17	(a)	18	(a)	19	(b)	20	(c)
21	(b)	22	(c)	23	(a)	24	(b)	25	(d)	26	(d)	27	(a)	28	(a)	29	(b)	30	(a)
31	(d)	32	(b)	33	(a)	34	(d)	35	(c)	36	(d)	37	(c)	38	(b)	39	(d)	40	(b)
41	(b)	42	(a)	43	(b)	44	(b)	45	(b)	46	(d)	47	(d)	48	(c)	49	(d)	50	(d)
51	(a)	52	(d)	53	(d)	54	(d)	55	(b)	56	(b)	57	(a)	58	(b)	59	(d)	60	(b)
61	(d)	62	(c)	63	(a)	64	(a)	65	(d)	66	(c)	67	(c)	68	(a)	69	(a)	70	(d)
71	(d)	72	(c)	73	(a)	74	(a)	75	(a)	76	(a)	77	(a)	78	(c)	79	(b)	80	(a)
81	(d)	82	(c)	83	(a)	84	(d)	85	(b)	86	(b)	87	(c)	88	(b)	89	(b)	90	(c)
91	(d)	92	(d)	93	(d)	94	(b)	95	(a)	96	(d)	97	(d)	98	(c)	99	(b)	100	(c)
101	(d)	102	(b)	103	(d)	104	(b)	105	(c)	106	(c)	107	(b)	108	(a)	109	(c)	110	(b)
111	(b)	112	(a)	113	(c)	114	(c)	115	(b)	116	(b)	117	(b)	118	(a)	119	(a)	120	(a)
121	(d)	122	(b)	123	(d)	124	(a)	125	(c)	126	(b)	127	(c)	128	(b)	129	(b)	130	(d)
131	(d)	132	(c)	133	(a)	134	(c)	135	(d)	136	(c)	137	(d)	138	(c)	139	(c)	140	(d)
141	(d)	142	(c)	143	(d)	144	(a)	145	(c)	146	(c)	147	(d)	148	(a)	149	(a)	150	(a)
151	(b)	152	(b)	153	(b)	154	(d)	155	(c)	156	(c)	157	(d)	158	(c)	159	(d)	160	(a)
161	(c)	162	(a)	163	(c)	164	(c)	165	(b)	166	(b)	167	(c)	168	(b)	169	(a)	170	(b)
171	(c)	172	(c)	173	(d)	174	(a)	175	(a)	176	(b)	177	(d)	178	(c)	179	(b)	180	(c)
181	(d)	182	(a)	183	(a)	184	(b)	185	(b)	186	(b)	187	(b)	188	(d)	189	(a)	190	(c)
191	(a)	192	(d)	193	(b)	194	(d)	195	(c)	196	(b)	197	(b)	198	(c)	199	(b)	200	(c)
201	(a)	202	(d)	203	(d)	204	(b)	205	(c)	206	(b)	207	(d)	208	(a)	209	(c)	210	(b)
211	(b)	212	(a)	213	(d)	214	(a)	215	(c)	216	(c)	217	(a)	218	(b)	219	(d)	220	(d)
221	(b)	222	(d)	223	(b)	224	(c)	225	(d)	226	(c)	227	(d)	228	(a)	229	(b)	230	(d)
231	(b)	232	(d)	233	(d)	234	(d)	235	(a)	236	(c)	237	(d)	238	(a)	239	(a)	240	(d)
241	(a)	242	(a)	243	(d)	244	(b)	245	(d)	246	(d)	247	(c)	248	(c)	249	(c)	250	(b)
251	(d)	252	(a)	253	(b)	254	(a)	255	(c)	256	(d)	257	(c)	258	(b)	259	(b)	260	(a)
261	(a)	262	(a)	263	(a)	264	(c)	265	(b)	266	(a)	267	(d)	268	(a)	269	(a)	270	(c)
271	(d)	272	(b)	273	(c)	274	(c)	275	(d)	276	(b)	277	(d)	278	(b)	279	(b)	280	(c)
281	(a)	282	(c)	283	(c)	284	(a)	285	(b)	286	(b)	287	(d)	288	(d)	289	(c)	290	(d)
291	(c)	292	(c)	293	(b)	294	(b)	295	(c)	296	(d)	297	(d)	298	(b)	299	(a)	300	(b)
301	(c)	302	(c)	303	(a)	304	(c)												

Solutions

1. (c) Given, $P = ₹ 2000$

$R = 6.5\%$ per annum

$T = \frac{73}{365}$ yr

$\because \text{SI} = \frac{P \times R \times T}{100} = \frac{2000 \times 6.5 \times 73}{100 \times 365} = ₹ 26$

2. (c) $P = ₹ 2000$, $R = 6.5\%$, $T = 73$ days

$\text{SI} = \frac{2000 \times 6.5 \times 73}{100 \times 365} = ₹ 26$

3. (a) According to the question,

$\frac{5000 \times 4 \times T}{100} = \frac{8000 \times 5 \times 8}{2 \times 100}$

$\Rightarrow T = \frac{8000 \times 20}{5000 \times 4} = 8$ yr

4. (c) Let principal be ₹ P.

According to the question,

Amount $= P + \text{SI}$

$21420 = P + \frac{P \times R \times T}{100}$

$\Rightarrow 21420 = P\left(1 + \frac{9.5 \times 2}{100}\right)$

$P = \frac{21420 \times 100}{100 + 19} = ₹ 18000$

5. (a) We know, SI = Amount − Principal

$\text{SI} = 2625 - 1875 = 750$

$\text{SI} = \frac{P \times R \times T}{100} \Rightarrow 750 = \frac{1875 \times R \times 4}{100}$

$\Rightarrow R = \frac{750 \times 100}{1875 \times 4} = 10\%$

Now, if $P = ₹ 24000$

$\therefore \text{SI} = \frac{24000 \times 10 \times 9}{100} = ₹ 21600$

$\therefore$ Required amount $= 24000 + 21600$

$= ₹ 45600$

Speedy Method

SI for 4 yr $= \frac{2625 - 1875}{1875} \times 100 = 40\%$

SI for 9 yr = 90 %

$\therefore$ Amount $= 24000 \times 190\% = ₹ 45600$

6. (c) Simple interest for Ist year

$= \frac{335180 \times 13 \times 1}{100} = ₹ 43573.4$

Amount paid in first year = ₹ 23060

$\therefore$ Remaining amount

$= 335180 - 23060 = ₹ 312120$

Simple interest on remaining amount for second year $= \frac{312120 \times 13 \times 1}{100} = ₹ 40575.6$

$\therefore$ Amount paid at the end of second year

$= 312120 + 43573.4 + 40575.6 = ₹ 396269$

7. (b) Simple interest for Ist year

$= \frac{348020 \times 1 \times 8}{100} = ₹ 27841.6$

Amount paid in first year = ₹ 15090

$\therefore$ Remaining amount

$= 348020 - 15090 = 332930$

Simple interest on remaining amount for second year $= \frac{332930 \times 8 \times 1}{100} = ₹ 26634.4$

$\therefore$ Amount paid at the end of second year

$= 332930 + 27841.6 + 26634.4 = ₹ 387406$

8. (c) As we know, $\text{SI} = \frac{P \times R \times T}{100}$

$\Rightarrow \frac{3}{5}P = \frac{P \times R \times 6}{100} \Rightarrow R = \frac{3}{5}P \times \frac{100}{6 \times P}$

$\Rightarrow R = 10\%$

$\therefore$ Required rate of interest = 10%

9. (a) Let the sum lent to Ravi be ₹ x.

According to the question,

$3000 \times \frac{8 \times 5}{100} + \frac{x \times 8 \times 5}{100} = ₹ 1600$

$\Rightarrow \frac{120000}{100} + \frac{40x}{100} = 1600$

$\Rightarrow 120000 + 40x = 160000$

$\Rightarrow 40x = 40000 \Rightarrow x = ₹ 1000$

Hence, amount lent to Ravi $x = ₹ 1000$

10. (b) Price of cell phone is ₹ 600.

On 300 cash down payment

Remaining amount $= 600 - 300 = ₹ 300$

But he paid ₹ 360 in two month

Thus, monthly rate of interest

$= \frac{30}{300} \times 100 = 10\%$

Hence, rate of interest annually

$= 12 \times 10 = 120\%$

11. (b) Given, $P = ₹ 10800$, $R = 15.5\%$

$A = ₹ 24800$

$\therefore \text{SI} = (24800 - 10800) = ₹ 14000$

$\therefore \text{SI} = \frac{P \times R \times T}{100} \Rightarrow 14000 = \frac{10800 \times 15.5 \times t}{100}$

$\Rightarrow t = \frac{14000 \times 100}{10800 \times 15.5} \Rightarrow t = 8.36$ yr

12. (b) Let the principal be ₹ x.

$\text{SI} = ₹ \frac{3}{5}x$; $T = 8$ yr

$\Rightarrow \text{SI} = \frac{x \times 8 \times R}{100} \Rightarrow \frac{3}{5}x = \frac{x \times 8 \times R}{100}$

$\Rightarrow R = \frac{3 \times 100}{5 \times 8} \Rightarrow R = 7\frac{1}{2}\%$

13. (b) $\text{SI} = \frac{P \times R \times T}{100}$

According to the question,

$\therefore$ Required difference

$= \frac{500 \times 4 \times 4}{100} - \frac{500 \times 3 \times 5}{100} = ₹ 5$

14. (b) Principal = ₹ 598397, Rate = 20%

Interest after 1st year $= 598397 \times \frac{20}{100}$

$= ₹ 119679.4$

But, he repaid ₹ 24284 at the end of first year.

New principal for 2nd year $= 598397 - 24284$

$= ₹ 574113$

Interest for 2nd year

$= 574113 \times \frac{20}{100} = ₹ 114822.6$

Thus, total amount he paid at the end of 2nd year $= ₹ 119679.4 + 574113 + 114822.6$

$= ₹ 808615$

15. (c) We know,

SI = Amount − P

$\text{SI} = 2366 - 1456 = 910$

As, $\text{SI} = \frac{P \times R \times T}{100}$

$\Rightarrow 910 = \frac{1456 \times R \times 10}{100}$

$\Rightarrow R = \frac{910 \times 100}{1456 \times 10} = 6.25\%$

16. (d) Let the sum of money invested in

$A = ₹ x$; $R = 8\%$; $T = 5$ yr

Sum of money invested in $B = ₹ 4x$

$R = 5\%$; $T = 7$ yr

According to the question,

$\Rightarrow \frac{x \times 8 \times 5}{100} + \frac{4x \times 5 \times 7}{100} = 1620$

$\Rightarrow \frac{40x}{100} + \frac{140x}{100} = 1620$

$\Rightarrow 180x = 1620 \times 100 \Rightarrow x = ₹ 900$

$\therefore$ Sum of money invested in scheme $B = 4x$

$= 4 \times 900 = ₹ 3600$

17. (a) We know, $\text{SI} = \frac{P \times R \times T}{100}$

According to the question,

Simple interest

$= \frac{192208 \times 1 \times 15}{100} + \frac{172012 \times 1 \times 15}{100}$

$= 28831.2 + 25801.8 = ₹ 54633$

$\therefore$ He pay at the end of second year

$= 172012 + 54633 = ₹ 226645$

18. (a) Let the amount invested in 4% p.a

SI = ₹ x

and the amount invested in 6% p.a. SI

$= ₹ (200000 - x)$

According to the question,

$\frac{x \times 4 \times 1}{100} + \frac{(200000 - x) \times 6 \times 1}{100}$

$= \frac{(200000) \times 4.7 \times 1}{100}$

$\Rightarrow 4x + 1200000 - 6x = 940000$

$\Rightarrow 2x = 260000 \Rightarrow x = 130000$

Two amounts are ₹ 130000 and ₹ 70000.

Speedy Method

One		Other
4%		6%
	4.7%	
1.3%		0.7%

One amount invested $= 20000 \times \frac{13}{20} = ₹\ 13000$

and other amount invested $= 20000 \times \frac{7}{20}$

$= ₹\ 7000$

19. (b) According to the question,

$$SI = \frac{P \times R \times 6}{100} \quad \ldots(i)$$

$$\text{Also, } SI + 1572 = \frac{P \times (R+7) \times 6}{100} \quad \ldots(ii)$$

From Eqs. (i) and (ii),

$$\frac{6PR}{100} + 1512 = \frac{6PR + 42P}{100}$$

$$\Rightarrow \frac{6PR + 42P - 6PR}{100} = 1512$$

$$\Rightarrow \frac{42P}{100} = 1512 \Rightarrow P = \frac{151200}{42} = ₹\ 3600$$

20. (c) Total deposited amount = ₹ 6000000

Bank is paying 6% interest to customer

$$= 6000000 \times \frac{6}{100} = ₹\ 360000$$

But bank deposited this amount in stock where he get 10% return.

$$\text{Return from stock} = 6000000 \times \frac{10}{100} = ₹\ 600000$$

$$\left[\frac{30000}{300000} \times 100 = 10\%\right]$$

Thus, bank's profit = 600000 − 360000 = ₹ 240000

21. (b) Given, $P = ₹\ 7200$, $R = 8\%$

$A = ₹\ 8928$, $T = t$

$SI = A - P$

$SI = 8928 - 7200$

$SI = ₹\ 1728$

$$\text{Now, } 1728 = \frac{7200 \times 8 \times t}{100} \Rightarrow \frac{1728}{72 \times 8} = t$$

$\Rightarrow t = 3$ yr

22. (c) Given, $P = ₹\ 1040$, $T = 1\frac{1}{2}$ yr

$A = ₹\ 1230$

$SI = A - P$

$SI = 1230 - 1040 = ₹\ 190$

Thus,

$$190 = \frac{1040 \times R \times 3}{100 \times 2} \Rightarrow R = \frac{190 \times 100 \times 2}{1040 \times 3}$$

$$R = \frac{475}{39} \Rightarrow R = 12\frac{7}{39}\%$$

23. (a) Given, Principal $(P) = ₹\ 7200$

Time $(t) = 3$ yr, Rate $(r) = 16\%$ per annum

$$\text{We know, } SI = \frac{P \times r \times t}{100}$$

According to the question,

$$\frac{7200 \times 16 \times 3}{100} = \frac{9600 \times x \times 4}{100}$$

$$\Rightarrow 72 \times 48 = 96 \times 4x \Rightarrow x = \frac{72 \times 48}{96 \times 4} = 9$$

$\therefore x = 9\%$

24. (b) Principal sum = ₹10000, Rate = 15%

$$SI \text{ for 2 yr} = 10000 \times \frac{15 \times 2}{100} = ₹\ 3000$$

Amount after 2 yr = 10000 + 3000 = ₹ 13000

Now, new principal = ₹ 13000

$r = 15\%$

$$SI \text{ for next two yr} = 13000 \times \frac{15 \times 2}{100} = 3900$$

$\therefore$ Amount after 4 yr = ₹13000 + 3900 = ₹16900

25. (d) Given, amount = ₹ 9810

$$\therefore \text{Principal} = \frac{9810 \times 100}{100 + 9} = 9000$$

$$\therefore \text{Interest of 6 month} = \frac{9000 \times 9}{100 \times 2} = 405$$

$\therefore$ Required amount to pay = 9000 + 405 = ₹ 9405

26. (d) Simple interest after 1 yr

$$= \frac{623305 \times 10 \times 1}{100} = ₹\ 62330.5$$

Remaining amount after 1 yr

= 623305 − 16390 = ₹ 606915

Interest on remaining amount

$$= \frac{606915 \times 10 \times 1}{100} = ₹\ 60691.5$$

The amount he pays at the end of 2 yr

= 606915 + 60691.5 + 62330.5 = ₹ 729937

27. (a) Given, $P = ₹\ 6700$,

$$t = 13 \text{ months} = \frac{13}{12} \text{ yr}$$

$r = 12\%$ p.a.

$$\therefore SI = \frac{P \times r \times t}{100} = \frac{6700 \times 12 \times 13}{12 \times 100} = ₹\ 871$$

28. (a) Let borrowed money = ₹ P

$$\text{Time } (t) = 4 \text{ yr, Amount } (A) = \frac{9}{5}P$$

$$\therefore SI = A - P = \frac{9}{5}P - P = \frac{4}{5}P$$

$$\therefore SI = \frac{P \times R \times T}{100} \Rightarrow \frac{4}{5}P = \frac{P \times r \times 4}{100}$$

$$\Rightarrow r = \frac{100}{5} = 20\% \text{ p.a} \Rightarrow r = 20\% \text{ p.a}$$

Speedy Method

$$SI \text{ for 4 yr} \rightarrow \frac{9}{5} - 1 = \frac{4}{5}$$

$$SI \text{ for 1 yr} \rightarrow \frac{1}{5}$$

$$\text{Rate} = \frac{1}{5} \times 100 = 20\%$$

29. (b) Let the principal be ₹ P.

We know, Amount $(A) = P + SI$

$$7P = P + \frac{P \times R \times T}{100} \Rightarrow 6P = \frac{P \times R \times 14}{100}$$

$$\Rightarrow R = \frac{600}{14} = 42.85\%$$

$$\text{Now, } 18P = P + \frac{P \times 42.85 \times T}{100}$$

$$17 = \frac{42.85 \times T}{100}$$

$$\Rightarrow T = \frac{1700}{42.85} = 39.67 \text{ yr}$$

30. (a) Total principal amount = ₹ 141545

$$\text{Interest for Ist year} = 141545 \times \frac{11}{100} = ₹\ 15569.95$$

But he repaid ₹ 25490 at the end of first year.

Principal amount for 2nd year

= 141545 − 25490 = ₹ 116055

$$\text{Interest for 2nd year} = 116055 \times \frac{11}{100} = ₹\ 12766.05$$

Thus, total amount he paid at the end of 2nd year = 11569.95 + 116055 + 12766.05 = ₹ 140391

31. (d) According to the question,

$$SI = \frac{P \times R \times T}{100}$$

$$3528 = \frac{8400 \times 7 \times T}{100} \quad \left[\because SI = A - P = 11928 - 8400 = 3528\right]$$

$$T = \frac{3528}{84 \times 7} = 6 \text{ yr}$$

32. (b) Let the borrowed amount be ₹ 100.

$\therefore$ Amount payable = 100 + 8% of 100 = ₹ 108

$\therefore$ *S* invested the borrowed money in a scheme on which he earned 5% profit.

$\therefore$ *S* must have invested in a scheme of rate = 13%

$\therefore$ Amount *S* earned = ₹ 100 + 13% of 100 = ₹ 113

$\therefore$ Net profit after paying $R = 5\%$

$\therefore$ *S* should have earned 13% by investing directly.

33. (a) Let *P* is a certain sum then,

$$\frac{3}{5} \times P = \frac{P \times 10 \times t}{100} \Rightarrow t = 6 \text{ yr}$$

$$\text{The required SI} = \frac{16000 \times 14 \times 6}{100} = ₹\ 13440$$

34. (d) Let the principal be ₹*P* and time be *t* yr.

According to the question,

$$\Rightarrow \frac{P}{5} = \frac{P \times 5t \times t}{100} \quad \left[\because SI = \frac{P \times R \times T}{100}\right]$$

$$R = 5t \Rightarrow t^2 = \frac{100}{25} = 4$$

$\Rightarrow t = 2$

$\therefore$ Rate of interest $(R) = 5t = 5(2) = 10\%$

New rate of interest = (10 + 3)% = 13%

$$\therefore \text{Required SI} = \frac{5600 \times 13 \times 6}{100} = ₹\ 4368$$

35. (c) Given, $A = ₹\,21160$, $t = 4$ yr, $r = 6\%$ p.a

$\therefore$ Annual installment

$$= \frac{100 \times A}{100 \times t + \frac{rt(t-1)}{2}} = \frac{100 \times 26160}{100 \times 4 + \frac{24 \times 3}{2}}$$

$$= \frac{100 \times 26160}{400 + 36} = \frac{100 \times 26160}{436} = ₹\,6000$$

36. (d) Let one part be ₹ x and other part be ₹ $(4000 - x)$.

According to the question,

$$\frac{x \times 8 \times 1}{100} + \frac{(4000 - x) \times 10 \times 1}{100} = ₹\,352$$

$$\Rightarrow \frac{8x}{100} + 400 - \frac{10x}{100} = ₹\,352$$

$$\Rightarrow \frac{2x}{100} = ₹\,48$$

$$\Rightarrow x = ₹\,2400$$

$\therefore$ Other part $(4000 - x)$

$$= 4000 - 2400 = ₹\,1600$$

Speedy Method

Net rate $= \frac{352}{4000} \times 100 = 8.8\%$

One part 8% | Other part 10%

8.8%

1.2% | 0.8%

$\Rightarrow$ 3 : 2

Other part $= \frac{2}{5} \times 4000 = ₹\,1600$

37. (c) Total Principal $(P) = ₹\,18000$

For one bank $P = ₹\,7000$; $R = 5\%$; $T = 1$ yr

For other bank $P = ₹\,6000$; $R = 6\%$; $T = 1$ yr

Rest principal $= 18000 - (7000 + 6000)$

$= ₹\,5000$

$R = ?$; $T = 1$ yr

According to the question,

$$\Rightarrow \frac{7000 \times 5 \times 1}{100} + \frac{6000 \times 6 \times 1}{100} + \frac{5000 \times R \times 1}{100} = 1160$$

$\Rightarrow$ $350 + 360 + 50R = 1160$

$\Rightarrow$ $50R = 1160 - 710$

$\Rightarrow$ $50R = 450 \Rightarrow R = 9\%$

$\therefore$ Rate for rest of the capital $= 9\%$ p.a.

38. (b) According to the question,

$$SI = \frac{P \times R \times T}{100}$$

For 3 yr, Here, Principal $(P) = ₹\,5000$,

Rate $(R) = 15\%$

$$\therefore \text{ SI for 3 yr} = \frac{5000 \times 15 \times 3}{100} = ₹\,2250$$

Principal $(P) = ₹\,8000$; Rate (R) $= 12\%$

Time $= 4$ yr

$$\text{Now, SI for 4 yr} = \frac{8000 \times 12 \times 4}{100} = ₹\,3840$$

$\therefore$ Required difference

$= 3840 - 2250 = ₹\,1590$

39. (d) Principal amount $= ₹\,422092$

Rate $= 20\%$

Interest for first year

$$= 422092 \times \frac{20}{100} = ₹\,84418.4$$

But he repaid ₹ 21679 at the end of first year.

Reamining principal

$= 422092 - 21679 = ₹\,400413$

and interest for 2nd year

$$= 400413 \times \frac{20}{100} = ₹\,80082.6$$

Thus, total amount he repays at the end of 2nd year $= 400413 + 84418.4 + 80082.6$

$= ₹\,564914$

40. (b) Let principal (P) be ₹ x.

Simple Interest (SI) $= ₹(3x - x) = ₹\,2x$ and $t = 9$ yr

$$\because \quad SI = \frac{Prt}{100}$$

$$\therefore 2x = \frac{x \times r \times 9}{100} \Rightarrow r = \frac{200}{9}\% \Rightarrow r = 22\frac{2}{9}\%$$

41. (b) Let the principal be ₹ P.

$$\therefore \quad \frac{2P}{5} = \frac{P \times r \times 5}{100} \Rightarrow r = \frac{2 \times 100}{5 \times 5} = 8\%$$

42. (a) $SI_1 = \frac{P \times 21 \times 8}{100}$; $SI_2 = \frac{P \times 21 \times 21}{100}$

According to the question,

$$\frac{SI_1}{SI_2} = \frac{P \times 21 \times 8 \times 100}{100 \times P \times 21 \times 21}$$

$$\Rightarrow \frac{SI_1}{SI_2} = \frac{8}{21} \Rightarrow SI_1 : SI_2 = 8 : 21$$

43. (b) According to the question,

$$\frac{8000 \times R_1 \times 3}{100} - \frac{8000 \times R_2 \times 3}{100} = 800$$

$$\Rightarrow \frac{8000 \times 3}{100}(R_1 - R_2) = 800$$

$$\Rightarrow R_1 - R_2 = \frac{800}{80 \times 3} = \frac{10}{3}$$

$$\Rightarrow R_1 - R_2 = 3\frac{1}{3}\%$$

44. (b) Let time $= t$

According to the question,

$$5282.4 - 3720 = \frac{3720 \times 12 \times t}{100}$$

$$\Rightarrow t = \frac{1562.4 \times 100}{3720 \times 12}$$

$$\Rightarrow t = \frac{7}{2} = 3\frac{1}{2} \text{ yr}$$

45. (b) Let the amount be ₹ x.

According to the question,

$$\frac{x \times 4 \times 11}{100} - \frac{x \times 4 \times 6}{100} = 7500$$

$$\Rightarrow \frac{20x}{100} = 7500 \Rightarrow x = ₹\,37500$$

46. (d) Given, $T = 8$ months $= \frac{8}{12}$ yr

$$\text{Then, } SI = \frac{P \times R \times T}{100} = \frac{27000 \times 44 \times 8}{100 \times 3 \times 12}$$

$$= ₹\,2640 \qquad \left[\because R = 14\frac{2}{3}\%\right]$$

47. (d) SI for 1 yr $= 1350 - 1200 = ₹\,150$

$\therefore$ SI for 3 yr $= 3 \times 150 = ₹\,450$

$\because$ Amount after 3 yr $= ₹\,1200$

$\therefore$ Required sum $= 1200 - 450 = ₹\,750$

48. (c) Let principal $= ₹\,P$

$\therefore$ $A = P + SI$

$$P + \frac{P \times 5 \times 2}{100} = 1100 \Rightarrow \frac{11P}{10} = 1100$$

$\Rightarrow$ $P = ₹\,1000$

$\therefore$ The sum is ₹ 1000.

49. (d) Rate of interest,

$$r = \frac{6400 \times 100}{21000 \times 3} \Rightarrow r = \frac{640}{21 \times 3} = 10\frac{10}{63}\%$$

50. (d) Let the sum $= ₹\,x$

Then, SI $= 3x - x = ₹\,2x$

$$\because \quad SI = \frac{P \times R \times T}{100}$$

$$\therefore \quad R = \frac{2x \times 100}{x \times 16} \Rightarrow R = 12.5\%$$

51. (a) Let S deposits ₹ x at 12% p.a.

According to the question,

$$\frac{[50000 - x] \times 8}{100} + \frac{12x}{100} = 5200$$

$\Rightarrow$ $400000 - 8x + 12x = 520000$

$\Rightarrow$ $4x = 120000 \Rightarrow x = ₹\,30000$

52. (d) Let the rate of interest $= r\%$

Simple interest $= 10200 - 9000 = ₹\,1200$

$$\text{Now,} \quad \frac{9000 \times 4 \times r}{100} = 1200$$

$$\therefore \quad r = \frac{1200}{4 \times 90} = \frac{10}{3} = 3\frac{1}{3}\%$$

53. (d) Let rate of interest $= r\%$

Simple interest $= 11050 - 8500 = ₹\,2550$

According to the question,

$$\frac{8500 \times 6 \times r}{100} = 2550 \Rightarrow r = \frac{2550}{510} = 5\%$$

$$\text{New rate of interest} = 5 \times \frac{18}{10} = 9\%$$

$$\text{Interest} = \frac{8500 \times 9 \times 5}{100} = ₹\,3825$$

$\therefore$ Total amount $= 8500 + 3825 = ₹\,12325$

54. (d) Let the sum $= ₹\,P$

Interest $= P - 13500$

According to the question,

$$\frac{P \times 12.5 \times 6}{100} = P - 13500$$

$\Rightarrow$ $75P = 100P - 1350000$

$\Rightarrow$ $25P = 1350 \times 1000$

$\Rightarrow$ $P = 1350 \times 40 = 54000$

$\therefore$ Simple interest $= 54000 - 13500 = ₹\,40500$

55. (b) Let the sum = ₹P and time = t yr
Simple interest = $3P - P$ = ₹$2P$

$\Rightarrow \quad \frac{P \times 8 \times t}{100} = 2P \Rightarrow t = \frac{200}{8} = 25$ yr

56. (b) Let the sum = ₹ P

$\frac{P \times 4.5 \times 1}{100} = 135 \Rightarrow P =$ ₹ 3000

For 5% p.a. on same sum interest will be

$= \frac{3000 \times 5 \times 1}{100} =$ ₹ 150

∴ Additional interest = 150 − 135 = ₹ 15

57. (a) According to the question,

$\frac{800 \times 6 \times 5.5}{100} = \frac{600 \times 4 \times T}{100}$

$T = \frac{5.5 \times 8}{4} \Rightarrow T = 11$ yr

58. (b) Let the principal = ₹P
and the amount in 12 yr = ₹ $4P$
Then, SI = $4P - P$ = ₹$3P$

$\therefore \quad \frac{P \times 12 \times R}{100} = 3P \Rightarrow R = \frac{100 \times 3P}{12 \times P}$

Hence, R = 25%

59. (d) According to the question,

$SI = \frac{80000 \times 12 \times 1}{100} =$ ₹9600

∴ Amount = P + SI = 80000 + 9600 = ₹89600
Processing fee = ₹3000
∴ Total amount to be credited
= 89600 − 3000 = ₹86600

∴ Total earning = $\frac{86600 - 80000}{80000} \times 100 = 8.25\%$

60. (b) Let sum = ₹ P
Rate of interest = x% p.a., Time = 3 yr

Simple interest = ₹ $\frac{3Px}{100}$

Now, rate of interest = $3x$% p.a.
Time = $(y + 3)$ yr

$\therefore \quad$ Simple interest = ₹ $\frac{3Px(y+3)}{100}$

Now, according to the question,

$\frac{7 \times 3Px}{100} = \frac{3Px(y+3)}{100} \Rightarrow y + 3 = 7 \Rightarrow y = 4$

61. (d) Let the principal = ₹P and rate of interest = r% p.a.

Simple interest = $\frac{9P}{5} - P$ = ₹ $\frac{4P}{5}$

$\therefore \quad \frac{P \times 4 \times r}{100} = \frac{4P}{5} \Rightarrow r = 20\%$

62. (c) Interest = 8320 − 6400 = ₹1920

$\therefore \quad \frac{6400 \times 3 \times r}{100} = 1920 \Rightarrow r = \frac{192000}{3 \times 6400} = 10\%$

∴ Required amount = $\frac{7200 \times 5 \times 10}{100} + 7200$
= ₹10800

63. (a) Interest = 38400 − 30000 = ₹8400

$\therefore \quad SI = \frac{P \times R \times T}{100} = \frac{30000 \times 8 \times T}{100} = 8400$

$\therefore \quad T = \frac{84}{24} = 3.5$ yr

64. (a) Let time = t yr,
Simple interest = 12300 − 9840 = ₹2460

$\Rightarrow \quad \frac{9840 \times t \times 5}{100} = 2460$

$\Rightarrow \quad t = \frac{246 \times 20}{984} = 5$ yr

65. (d) Let the principal = ₹x
Then, according to the question,

$x \times \frac{1}{100}(7.25 \times 8 + 8.5 \times 6 + 6.5 \times 4) =$ ₹ 35100

$\Rightarrow \quad x \times \frac{1}{100}(58 + 51 + 26) =$ ₹35100

$\Rightarrow \quad x = \frac{35100 \times 100}{135} \Rightarrow x =$ ₹ 26000

Hence, principal = ₹ 26000

66. (c) Let the sum = ₹ P and

Simple interest = $\frac{8P}{7} - P = \frac{P}{7}$

$\therefore \quad \frac{P \times 2 \times r}{100} =$ ₹$\frac{P}{7} \Rightarrow r = \frac{50}{7} = 7\frac{1}{7}\%$

67. (c) SI for 1 yr = 1708 − 1630 = ₹ 78
∴ SI for 3 yr = 3 × 78 = ₹ 234
∵ Amount after 3 yr = ₹ 1630
∴ Required sum = 1630 − 234 = ₹1396

68. (a) Principal, (P) = ₹ 78000

Time (T) = 146 days = $\frac{146}{366}$ yr

Rate of Interest (R) = $8\frac{3}{4}$% p.a. = $\frac{35}{4}$% p.a.

∴ Simple interest = $78000 \times \frac{35}{4} \times \frac{1}{100} \times \frac{146}{366}$
= ₹ 2723

∴ Total amount paid by Archana
= 78000 + 2723 = ₹ 80723

69. (a) According to the question,
Rate of interest = r%
Then, time = $4r$

$SI = \frac{P \times R \times T}{100} \Rightarrow 11664 = \frac{32400 \times r \times 4r}{100}$

$\Rightarrow r^2 = 9 \Rightarrow r = 3\%$

70. (d) Given, time = 21 months = $\frac{21}{12}$ yr

$\therefore \quad SI = \frac{6000 \times 21 \times 8}{1200} =$ ₹ 840

71. (d) Let principal = ₹ 100
Then, it will double in 8 yr.

$\therefore \quad 200 - 100 = \frac{100 \times R \times 8}{100}$

$\Rightarrow \quad \frac{100}{8} = R \Rightarrow R = \frac{25}{2}\%$

Then, for 2nd condition
SI = 100000 − 25000 = ₹ 75000

$\therefore \quad 75000 = \frac{25000 \times 25 \times T}{100 \times 2}$

$\Rightarrow \quad T = \frac{75 \times 100 \times 2}{25 \times 25} \Rightarrow T = 24$ yr

72. (c) Simple interest = 11780 − 9500
= ₹ 2280

We know that,

Time $(T) = \frac{100 \times SI}{\text{Principal} \times \text{Rate}}$

$\Rightarrow \quad T = \frac{100 \times 2280}{9500 \times 8}$

$\therefore \quad T = 3$ yr

73. (a) $SI = \frac{P \times R \times T}{100}$

$\Rightarrow \frac{25}{100} \times P = \frac{P \times R \times 5}{100} \Rightarrow R = 5\%$

For SI = $P \Rightarrow P = \frac{5PT}{100} \Rightarrow T = 20$ yr

74. (a) Let principal = ₹ 100

Interest in 12 yr = $100 \times \frac{3}{5}$ = ₹ 60

∴ Rate = $\frac{60 \times 100}{100 \times 12}$ = 5% p.a.

75. (a) Let the principal = ₹ P

Interest on first year = $\frac{P \times 5}{100}$ = ₹ $\frac{P}{20}$

Interest on second year = $\frac{P \times 5.5}{100}$ = ₹ $\frac{11P}{200}$

Interest on third year = $\frac{P \times 6}{100}$ = ₹ $\frac{3P}{50}$

Interest on fourth year = $\frac{P \times 6.5}{100}$ = ₹ $\frac{13P}{200}$

∴ Total interest $\frac{P}{20} + \frac{11P}{200} + \frac{3P}{50} + \frac{13P}{200} = 4600$

$\Rightarrow \quad \frac{10P + 11P + 12P + 13P}{200} = 4600$

$\Rightarrow \quad \frac{46P}{200} = 4600$

$\therefore \quad P = 100 \times 200 =$ ₹20000

∴ The loan was ₹ 20000.

Speedy Method

Let the principal = ₹ P
∴ According to the question,

$\frac{P \times T}{100}(R_1 + R_2 + R_3 + R_4) = 4600$

$\Rightarrow \quad \frac{P \times 1}{100}[5 + 5.5 + 6 + 6.5] = 4600$

$\therefore \quad P = \frac{4600 \times 100}{23} =$ ₹ 20000

76. (a) SI for 4 yr = 18906 − 14522 = ₹4384

SI for 7 yr = $\frac{4384}{4} \times 7$ = ₹7672

∴ Required sum = 14522 − 7672 = ₹6850

77. (a) Let the rate of interest = r% p.a.

Then, $SI = \frac{P \times r \times t}{100}$

$1620 = \frac{r}{100}(500 \times 3 + 650 \times 5 + 1250 \times 7)$

$\Rightarrow 1620 = \frac{r}{100}(1500 + 3250 + 8750)$

$\Rightarrow 1620 = \frac{r}{100} \times 13500 \Rightarrow r = \frac{1620}{135} = 12\%$

78. (c) SI for 3 yr = 104.4 − 72 = ₹ 32.4

$\therefore \quad r = \frac{32.4 \times 100}{72 \times 3} = 15\%$

Now, the required amount

$= 120 + \frac{120 \times 15 \times 5}{100} = 120 + 90 = ₹\ 210$

79. (b) Let the money invest at 15% be ₹ x.
Then, according to the question,

$2400 = \left(\frac{x \times 15 \times 2}{100}\right) + \left(\frac{(10000 - x) \times 10 \times 2}{100}\right)$

$\Rightarrow \quad 2400 = \frac{3x}{10} + \frac{(10000 - x)}{5}$

$\Rightarrow \quad 2400 = \frac{3x + 20000 - 2x}{10}$

$\Rightarrow \quad 24000 = x + 20000 \Rightarrow x = 4000$

80. (a) Let the rate of interest = r%
According to the question,

$\frac{500 \times r \times 4}{100} + \frac{700 \times r \times 2}{100} = 280$

$\Rightarrow \quad 20r + 14r = 280 \Rightarrow 34r = 280$

$\therefore \quad r = \frac{140}{17} = 8\frac{4}{17}\%$

81. (d) Let, time = t yr
According to the question,

$\frac{10000 \times 4 \times t}{100} = \frac{8000 \times 4 \times 5}{100}$

$\Rightarrow \quad t = \frac{8 \times 5}{10} \Rightarrow t = 4$ yr

82. (c) ∴ SI of 2 yr = 1600 − 1200 = ₹400
∴ Principle (P) = 1200 − 400 = ₹800

$\therefore \quad 400 = \frac{800 \times r \times 2}{100} \Rightarrow r = \frac{200}{8} = 25\%$

83. (a) We know, if total amount of ₹ A is paid at R % per annum in n equal yearly installments, then

$A = \left[x + \left(x + \frac{x \times R \times 1}{100}\right) + \left(x + \frac{x \times R \times 2}{100}\right) + \ldots + \left(x + \frac{x \times R \times (n-1)}{100}\right)\right]$

Where, $A = P + \frac{P \times n \times R}{100}$

and n = each installment.
According to the question,

$\left(2000 + \frac{2000 \times 3 \times 5}{100}\right) = \left[x + \left(x + \frac{x \times 5 \times 1}{100}\right) + \left(x + \frac{x \times 5 \times 2}{100}\right)\right]$

$\Rightarrow \quad (2000 + 300) = x \times \left[1 + \frac{21}{20} + \frac{11}{10}\right]$

$\Rightarrow \quad x \times \frac{63}{20} = 2300$

$\Rightarrow \quad x = \frac{2300 \times 20}{63} = \frac{46000}{63} = ₹730\frac{10}{63}$

84. (d) $SI = \frac{30000 \times 5 \times 3}{100} = ₹\ 4500$

∴ Required per cent $= \frac{4500}{18000} \times 100 = 25\%$

85. (b) We know, if a sum of money at a certain interest becomes n times in T_1 yr and m times in T_2 yr, then $T_2 = \left(\frac{m-1}{n-1}\right) \times T_1$

According to the question,

∴ Required time $= \frac{(5-1)}{(2-1)} \times 7 = \frac{4}{1} \times 7 = 28$ yr

86. (b) Interest earned at the end of 2 yr

$= \frac{15600 \times 10 \times 2}{100} = ₹\ 3120 \quad \left[\because SI = \frac{PRT}{100}\right]$

Now, for 2 yr

$P = 15600 + 3120 = ₹\ 18720$

Interest for the last 2 yr

$= \frac{18720 \times 10 \times 2}{100} = ₹\ 3744$

∴ Total interest earned at the end of 4 yr

$= 3120 + 3744 = ₹\ 6864$

87. (c) Time (T) $= 1\frac{1}{2} = \frac{3}{2}$ yr

Now, SI = 913 − 880 = ₹ 33

Also, $SI = \frac{PRT}{100} \Rightarrow 33 = \frac{880 \times R \times 3}{2 \times 100}$

$\Rightarrow \quad R = \frac{33 \times 2 \times 100}{880 \times 3} \Rightarrow R = \frac{5}{2} = 2\frac{1}{2}\%$

88. (b) Amount payable after 1 yr

$= 100000 + \frac{100000 \times 10 \times 1}{100} = ₹\ 110000$

Balance amount after 1 yr

$= 110000 - 10000 = ₹\ 100000$

Amount payable after 2 yr

$= 100000 + \frac{100000 \times 10 \times 1}{100} = ₹110000$

Balance amount after 2 yr

$= 110000 - 20000 = ₹\ 90000$

Amount payable after 3 yr

$= 90000 + \frac{90000 \times 10 \times 1}{100} = ₹99000$

Balance amount after 3 yr

$= 99000 - 30000 = ₹\ 69000$

Amount payable after 4 yr

$= 69000 + \frac{69000 \times 10 \times 1}{100} = ₹75900$

Balance amount after 4 yr

$= 75900 - 40000 = ₹35900$

∴ Amount payable at the end of 5th year

$= 35900 + \frac{35900 \times 10 \times 1}{100} = 35900 + 3590$

$= ₹39490$

89. (b) Let the principal = ₹x
∴ Amount = ₹$4x$; r = 50%

$\therefore \quad (4x - x) = \frac{x \times 50 \times t}{100}$

$\Rightarrow \quad 3x = \frac{x \times 50 \times t}{100} \Rightarrow t = 6$ yr

After 6 yr money become four times of itself. For more than four times of itself money must have completed 7 yr.
So, required years = 7 yr

90. (c) According to the question,

$480 = \frac{P \times 8 \times 2}{100} \Rightarrow P = \frac{480 \times 100}{8 \times 2}$

∴ P = ₹ 3000

Hence, the required sum = ₹ 3000

91. (d) Here, $A = P +$ SI

$A = P + \frac{P \times R \times T}{100}$

$\Rightarrow \quad 19125 = 10200 + \frac{10200 \times 12.5 \times T}{100}$

$\Rightarrow \quad 8925 = 102 \times 12.5 \times T$

$\Rightarrow \quad 8925 = 1275 \times T$

$\therefore \quad T = \frac{8925}{1275} = 7$ yr

92. (d) Let the sum of money be ₹ P. T = 3 yr and let the rate of interest = r%

$\therefore \quad SI = \frac{P \times r \times 3}{100} \Rightarrow SI = \frac{3Pr}{100}$

Now, when rate of interest is 5% more,

$SI = \frac{P \times (r + 5) \times 3}{100}$

According to the question,

$SI + 600 = \frac{3P(r + 5)}{100}$

$\Rightarrow \quad \frac{3Pr}{100} + 600 = \frac{3Pr}{100} + \frac{15P}{100}$

$\Rightarrow \quad 600 = \frac{15P}{100} \Rightarrow P = \frac{600 \times 100}{15}$

$\Rightarrow \quad P = ₹\ 4000$

Speedy Method

$\frac{\text{Principal} \times \text{Change in rate} \times \text{Time}}{100} = \text{Change in SI}$

$\therefore \quad \frac{\text{Principal} \times 5 \times 3}{100} = 600$

Principal = ₹ 4000

93. (d) We know that, $T_2 = \frac{m-1}{n-1} \times T_1$

Here, m = 5, n = 6 and T_1 = 20 yr
∴ The required time,

$T_2 = \frac{5-1}{6-1} \times 20 = \frac{4}{5} \times 20 = 16$ yr

94. (b) Let principal amount = ₹P
Time = 10 yr; Rate of interest = R%
Amount = A = 3P

Now, $A - P = \frac{P \times R \times 10}{100}$

$\Rightarrow \quad 3P - P = \frac{PR}{10} \Rightarrow 2P = \frac{PR}{10}$

$\therefore \quad R = 2 \times 10 = 20\%$

So, rate of interest = R% = 20%

95. (a) Let the sum be ₹ x and it becomes 2 times in t yr

$\therefore \quad (2x - x) = \frac{x \times 5 \times t}{100}$

$\Rightarrow \quad t = \frac{100}{5} = 20$ yr

Now, according to the question,
Let the required rate of interest be R % per annum $(5x - x) = \frac{x \times R \times 20}{100}$

$$R = \frac{4 \times 100}{20} = 20\% \text{ per annum.}$$

96. (d) Here, $P = ₹2700$; $T = 8$ months
$R = 5$ paise per rupee per month
$= 5\%$ per month

$$\therefore \quad SI = \frac{2700 \times 5 \times 8}{100}$$

Hence, SI = ₹1080

97. (d) According to the question,
∴ Annual installment

$$= \frac{100 \times A}{100 \times t + \frac{rt(t-1)}{2}} = \frac{100 \times 9600}{100 \times 5 + \frac{5 \times 10(5-1)}{2}}$$

$$= \frac{100 \times 9600}{500 + 100} = \frac{100 \times 9600}{600} = ₹1600$$

98. (c) Let principal = ₹ P

$$\therefore 1.25P - P = \frac{P \times R \times 3}{100} \Rightarrow 0.25 = \frac{3R}{100}$$

$$\Rightarrow R = \frac{0.25 \times 100}{3} = \frac{25}{3}\%$$

Now, $T' = 7$ yr, $A' = ₹ 760000$

$$\text{Then, } 760000 = \frac{P' \times 25 \times 7}{3 \times 100} + P'$$

$$\Rightarrow 760000 = \frac{175P' + 300P'}{300} \Rightarrow 760000 = \frac{475P'}{300}$$

$$\therefore \quad P' = ₹ 480000$$

99. (b) According to the question,

$$P - 920 = \frac{P \times 7 \times 11}{100}$$

$$\Rightarrow P - \frac{77P}{100} = 920 \Rightarrow \frac{23P}{100} = 920 \Rightarrow P = ₹4000$$

100. (c) According to the question,

$$\frac{23000 \times 3 \times r}{100} + \frac{19000 \times 4 \times r}{100} = 3625$$

$$\Rightarrow \quad 1450r = 3625 \Rightarrow r = 2.5\%$$

101. (d) Let the principal (sum) be ₹ x, then SI (Simple Interest for 1 yr)
= ₹ (806 − 767) = ₹ 39
Now, the sum = 767 − 3 × 39
= 767 − 117 = ₹ 650

102. (b) Let the down payment = ₹ x
Given, $R = 10\%$, $T = 1$ yr
So, total amount to be paid in installment

$$= (650000 - x) + \frac{(650000 - x) \times 10 \times 1}{100}$$

$$= \frac{110}{100} \times (650000 - x)$$

According to the question,

$$\frac{110}{100} \times (650000 - x) = 20 \times 25000$$

$$\Rightarrow \quad 11 \times (650000 - x) = 500000 \times 10$$

$$\Rightarrow \quad 7150000 - 11x = 5000000$$

$$\Rightarrow \quad 11x = 7150000 - 5000000 = 2150000$$

$$\Rightarrow \quad x = \frac{2150000}{11} = ₹ 195454.54$$

$$\therefore \quad x \approx ₹ 195455$$

103. (d) Let the principal amount = ₹ P

$$\therefore \quad SI = \frac{25P}{36} \text{ and } T = R = x$$

$$\therefore \quad \frac{25P}{36} = \frac{P \times x \times x}{100} \Rightarrow x^2 = \frac{25 \times 100}{36}$$

$$\therefore x = \frac{5 \times 10}{6} = \frac{50}{6} = 8.33\%$$

104. (b) SI in 6 yr = 4060 − 3640 = ₹ 420

$$\text{SI in 2 yr} = \frac{420}{3} = ₹ 140$$

Sum = 3640 − 140 [∵ $A = P +$ SI]
= ₹ 3500
According to the question,

$$140 = \frac{3500 \times R \times 2}{100} \Rightarrow R = \frac{140}{35 \times 2} = 2\%$$

105. (c) Let the sum invested be ₹ x.

$$\text{Amount } (A) = \frac{17}{10} \times x$$

$$\text{Time } (T) = 2 \text{ yr } 6 \text{ months} = \frac{5}{2} \text{ yr}$$

According to the question,

$$\frac{17}{10}x - x = \frac{x \times R \times \frac{5}{2}}{100} \Rightarrow \frac{7x}{10} = \frac{x \times R \times 5}{200}$$

$$\therefore \quad R = \frac{7 \times 200}{5 \times 10} = 28\%$$

106. (c) According to the question,

$$15500 = P + \frac{P \times R \times T}{100}$$

$$\Rightarrow 15500 = P + \frac{P \times 30 \times 7}{100}$$

$$\Rightarrow \quad 310P = 1550000 \Rightarrow P = ₹5000$$

$$\therefore \quad SI = 15500 - 5000 = ₹ 10500$$

107. (b) According to the question,

$$\text{Required time} = \left(\frac{5-1}{3-1}\right) \times 26 = \frac{4}{2} \times 26$$

= 52 yr

108. (a) Let time be t yr.

$$\therefore \quad SI = A - P \Rightarrow \frac{Prt}{100} = 9870 - 5250$$

$$\Rightarrow \quad \frac{5250 \times 11 \times t}{100} = 4620 \Rightarrow t = \frac{4620 \times 100}{5250 \times 11} = 8 \text{ yr}$$

109. (c) Let the loan amount = ₹ P
According to the question,

$$\therefore \quad P = \frac{100 \times 9600}{16 \times 5} = ₹ 12000$$

110. (b) Let the ₹ x invested at 4% per annum rate.
According to the question,

$$\frac{x \times 4 \times 1}{100} + \frac{(5000 - x) \times 5 \times 1}{100} = 223$$

$$\Rightarrow \quad 4x + (5000 - x) \times 5 = 223 \times 100$$

$$\Rightarrow \quad -x + 25000 = 22300$$

$$\therefore \quad x = ₹ 2700$$

Speedy Method

$$\text{Combined rate} = \frac{223}{5000} \times 100 = 4.46\%$$

By using Alligation rule,

4%   5%
4.46%
0.54 : 0.46
27 : 23

$$\therefore \text{ Money invested at } 4\% = \frac{27}{(23 + 27)} \times 5000$$

= ₹ 2700

111. (b) SI for 2 yr = 832 − 640 = ₹192
According to the question,

$$\Rightarrow \quad 192 = \frac{640 \times R \times 2}{100}$$

$$\Rightarrow \quad R = \frac{192 \times 100}{640 \times 2} = 15\%$$

$$\text{Now, } SI = \frac{860 \times 15 \times 4}{100} = ₹516$$

∴ Amount $(A) = 860 + 516 = ₹1376$

112. (a) Remaining amount
$(P) = 7500 - 3500 = ₹ 4000$
$R = 9\%$ per annum
$T = 4 \text{ month} = \frac{4}{12}$ yr

$$\therefore \text{ Required interest} = \frac{4000 \times 9 \times 4}{100 \times 12} = ₹ 120$$

113. (c) Let sum = ₹ P
According to the question,

$$4200 = \frac{P \times 14 \times 5}{100} - \frac{P \times 14 \times 3}{100}$$

$$\Rightarrow \quad 4200 \times 100 = P \times 14(5 - 3)$$

$$\Rightarrow \quad 420000 = P \times 14 \times 2$$

$$\therefore \quad P = ₹ 15000$$

114. (c) Let the sum lent be ₹ x.
∴ Simple interest = ₹ $(x + 360)$
According to the question,

$$\Rightarrow \quad (x + 360) = \frac{x \times 25 \times 6}{100}$$

$$\Rightarrow \quad 4x + 4 \times 360 = 6x$$

$$\Rightarrow \quad 2x = 4 \times 360$$

$$\therefore \quad x = ₹ 720$$

115. (b) Let the rate of interest be R% per annum.
According to the question,

$$3725 = 2500 + \frac{2500 \times R \times 8}{100}$$

$$\therefore \quad R = \frac{1225 \times 100}{2500 \times 8} = 6.125\%$$

116. (b) Let money invested at the rate of 9% = ₹ x
∴ According to the question,

$$\frac{3}{100}[9x + (25600 - x)7] = 5832$$

$\Rightarrow \quad 2x + 179200 = 194400$

$\therefore \quad x = \dfrac{15200}{2} = ₹\,7600$

117. (b) According to the question,

$\therefore \quad 81840 = P + \dfrac{3PR}{100}$ ...(i)

Also, $92400 = P + \dfrac{P \times R \times 5}{100}$ ...(ii)

On dividing Eqs. (i) and (ii), we get

$$\frac{81840}{92400} = \frac{P + \frac{3PR}{100}}{P + \frac{5PR}{100}}$$

$$\Rightarrow \frac{1023}{1155} = \frac{1 + \frac{3R}{100}}{1 + \frac{5R}{100}}$$

$\Rightarrow \quad 1023 + \dfrac{5115R}{100} = 1155 + \dfrac{3465R}{100}$

$\Rightarrow \quad 132 = \dfrac{1650R}{100} \Rightarrow R = 8\%$

$\Rightarrow \quad R = 8\%$ or $x = 8\%$

Now, if rate increase by $(x+2)\%$

$= 8 + 2 = 10\%$

$\therefore \quad P = \dfrac{P \times 10 \times T}{100}$

$\therefore$ Time = 10 yr

118. (a) Let principal (P) = ₹ $4x$ and ₹ $5x$

According to the question,

$\Rightarrow \quad \dfrac{5x \times 8 \times 5}{100} - \dfrac{4x \times 8 \times 4}{100} = 4680$

$\Rightarrow \quad 2x - \dfrac{32x}{25} = 4680$

$\Rightarrow \quad \dfrac{18x}{25} = 4680 \Rightarrow x = 4680 \times \dfrac{25}{18}$

$\Rightarrow \quad x = 6500$

$\therefore$ Total principal $= 4x + 5x$

$= 9x = 9 \times 6500 = ₹\,58500$

119. (a) Let sum = ₹ P

and time for second sum = t yr

Time for first sum = $(t+2)$ yr

According to the question,

$P + \dfrac{P \times 6 \times (t+2)}{100} = P + \dfrac{P \times 10 \times t}{100}$

$\Rightarrow \quad \dfrac{P \times 6 \times (t+2)}{100} = \dfrac{P \times 10 \times t}{100}$

$\Rightarrow \quad 3t + 6 = 5t \Rightarrow t = 3$ yr

$\therefore$ Time for first sum = 3 + 2 = 5 yr

Now, $P + \dfrac{P \times 6 \times 5}{100} = 1105$

$\Rightarrow \dfrac{130P}{100} = 1105 \Rightarrow P = \dfrac{1105 \times 100}{130} = ₹\,850$

120. (a) Let P = ₹ x, then A = ₹ $2x$ (given)

SI $= A - P = 2x - x = ₹\,x$

According to the question,

$x = \dfrac{x \times r \times 13}{100} \Rightarrow r = \dfrac{100}{13} \Rightarrow r = 7.69\%$

121. (d) According to the question,

$\dfrac{P \times 5 \times 4}{100} + \dfrac{P \times 8 \times 3}{100} + \dfrac{P \times 10 \times 3}{100} = 1850$

$\Rightarrow \quad 74P = 1850 \times 100$

$\therefore \quad P = ₹\,2500$

122. (b) Let the rate of interest be $R\%$.

$\therefore$ Interest on ₹ 29000 for 3 yr

$= I_1 = \dfrac{29000 \times R \times 3}{100} = ₹\,870\,R$

Interest on ₹ 45000 for 5 yr

$= I_2 = \dfrac{45000 \times R \times 5}{100} = ₹\,2250\,R$

$\therefore$ Total interest paid $= I_1 + I_2$

$= (870 + 2250)\,R$

$62400 = 3120\,R \Rightarrow R = \dfrac{62400}{3120} = 20\%$

123. (d) Let the original sum be ₹ P.

According to the question,

$P \times \dfrac{20}{12} \times \dfrac{19.2}{100} = P \times \dfrac{15}{12} \times \dfrac{112}{100} + ₹\,2920$

$\Rightarrow \quad 0.32P = 2920 + 0.14P$

$\Rightarrow 0.32P - 0.14P = 2920$

$\Rightarrow \quad 0.18P = 2920 \Rightarrow P = \dfrac{2920}{0.18}$

$\therefore \quad P = ₹\,16222.22 \approx ₹\,16200$

124. (a) Let ₹ A is invested at 15% for 5 yr.

$\therefore$ Interest of ₹ A = ₹ $\dfrac{A \times 15 \times 5}{100}$

Let ₹ B is invested at 10% for 3 yr.

$\therefore$ Interest of ₹ B = ₹ $\dfrac{B \times 10 \times 3}{100}$

$\dfrac{\text{Interest of } A}{\text{Interest of } B} = \dfrac{A \times 15 \times 5 \times 100}{B \times 10 \times 3 \times 100} = \dfrac{5}{3}$

$\dfrac{A}{B} = \dfrac{2}{3} \Rightarrow B = \dfrac{3}{5} \times 48500 = ₹\,29100$

125. (c) According to the question,

$\dfrac{P \times 14 \times 8}{100} - \dfrac{P \times 14 \times 4}{100} = 6160$

$\Rightarrow \quad \dfrac{14P}{100}(8-4) = 6160$

$\Rightarrow \quad \dfrac{14P}{100} \times 4 = 6160 \Rightarrow P = \dfrac{6160 \times 100}{14 \times 4}$

$\therefore \quad P = ₹\,11000$

126. (b) According to the question,

$\dfrac{4P(R+11)}{100} - \dfrac{4PR}{100} = 1320$

$\Rightarrow \quad \dfrac{4P}{100}(R + 11 - R) = 1320$

$\Rightarrow P \times 11 = \dfrac{1320 \times 100}{4} \Rightarrow P = ₹\,3000$

Speedy Method

Let principal be ₹100.

11% × 4 → ₹ 1320

44% → ₹ 1320

Principal (100%) → ₹ 3000

127. (c) SI = ₹ 4900 − ₹ 2500 = ₹ 2400

Now, $\text{SI} = \dfrac{P \times R \times T}{100}$ [Rate $= R = 12\%$ p.a.]

$\Rightarrow \quad 2400 = \dfrac{2500 \times 12 \times T}{100}$

$\Rightarrow \quad T = \dfrac{2400 \times 100}{2500 \times 12} \Rightarrow T = 8$ yr

128. (b) Let the principal be P.

Amount $= 9P$

$\therefore$ Simple Interest (SI) $= 9P - P = 8P$

So, $R = \dfrac{\text{SI} \times 100}{P \times T} = \dfrac{8P \times 100}{P \times 20} = 40\%$

Now, time taken to become 13 times the amount will be

$T = \dfrac{\text{SI} \times 100}{\text{P} \times \text{R}} \Rightarrow T = \dfrac{(13P - P) \times 100}{P \times 40}$

$\Rightarrow \quad T = \dfrac{12P \times 100}{P \times 40} \Rightarrow T = 30$ yr

Speedy Method

$n_1 = 9, t_1 = 20, n_2 = 13, t_2 = ?$

We know, $\dfrac{n_1 - 1}{t_1} = \dfrac{n_2 - 1}{t_2}$

$\dfrac{9-1}{20} = \dfrac{13-1}{t_2}$

$\dfrac{8}{20} = \dfrac{12}{t_2}$

$t_2 = 30$ yr

129. (b) $\because$ Annual installment

$= \dfrac{100 \times A}{100 \times t + \dfrac{r \times t(t-1)}{2}} = \dfrac{100 \times 10192}{100 \times 3 + \dfrac{3 \times 10(3-1)}{2}}$

$= \dfrac{100 \times 10192}{300 + 30} = \dfrac{100 \times 10192}{330}$

$= ₹\,3088.48$

Speedy Method

Let installment be ₹ 100.

$100 + \dfrac{100 \times 10 \times 2}{100}$

$100 + \dfrac{100 \times 10 \times 1}{100}$

$\dfrac{100}{300 + 30}$

330 → ₹ 10192

$\therefore$ Installment (100) → ₹ 3088.48

130. (d) Interest at 6% p.a. for 1 yr

$= \dfrac{1760 \times 6 \times 1}{100} = ₹\,105.6$

Interest at 9% p.a. for 1 yr

$= \dfrac{2240 \times 9 \times 1}{100} = ₹\,201.6$

Now, total interest in 1 yr

$= 105.6 + 201.6 = ₹\,307.2$

$\therefore$ Required time $= \dfrac{1536}{307.2} = 5$ yr

131. (d) Remaining amount = 2500 − 520 = ₹ 1980

Then, SI on ₹ 1980 at 25% per annum

$$SI = \frac{1980 \times 25 \times 4}{100 \times 12} = ₹\ 165$$

Amount due = 1980 + 165 = ₹ 2145

Let monthly installment be ₹ x.

$$\therefore\ 2145 = x + \left(x + \frac{x \times \frac{1}{12} \times 25}{100}\right) + \left(x + \frac{x \times \frac{2}{12} \times 25}{100}\right) + \left(x + \frac{x \times \frac{3}{12} \times 25}{100}\right)$$

$$\Rightarrow\ x + x + \frac{x}{48} + x + \frac{x}{24} + x + \frac{x}{16} = 2145$$

$$\Rightarrow\ 4x + \frac{x + 2x + 3x}{48} = 2145$$

$$\Rightarrow\ \frac{32x + x}{8} = 2145 \Rightarrow x = \frac{2145 \times 8}{33} = ₹\ 520$$

132. (c) According to the question,

SI = (6000 + 18600 − 15000)

SI = ₹ 9600

Total interest

$$= \left[\left(\frac{15000 \times 5 \times R}{100}\right) + \left(\frac{9000 \times 5 \times R}{100}\right)\right]$$

$$\Rightarrow\ 750R + 450R = 9600 \Rightarrow R = 8\%$$

133. (a) Let amount invested in scheme A = ₹ x

According to the question,

$$1680 = \frac{x \times 8 \times 2}{100} + \frac{(10000 - x) \times 10 \times 2}{100}$$

$$\Rightarrow\ 1680 \times 100 = 16x + 200000 - 20x$$

$$\Rightarrow\ 4x = 200000 - 168000 \Rightarrow 4x = 32000$$

$$\therefore\ x = ₹\ 8000$$

Hence, Rajesh invested in scheme A = ₹ 8000.

134. (c) Let principal of A be ₹ x.

∴ Principal of B is ₹ (36000 − x).

According to the question,

$$\text{SI of } A = \frac{x \times 15 \times 2}{100} = \frac{3x}{10}$$

$$\text{SI of } B = \frac{(36000 - x) \times 15 \times 4}{100} = 21600 - \frac{3}{5}x$$

According to the question,

SI of A = SI of B

$$\frac{3x}{10} = 21600 - \frac{3}{5}x \Rightarrow \frac{9}{10}x = 21600$$

$$\Rightarrow\ x = ₹ 24000$$

$$\therefore\ \text{SI of } A = \frac{3}{10} \times 24000 = ₹\ 7200$$

135. (d) Let's take the rate of interest is x%.

According to the question,

$$12000 \times \frac{x}{100} \times 7 + 12000 = 20400$$

$$\Rightarrow 840x = 20400 - 12000 = 8400$$

$$\therefore\ x = \frac{8400}{840} = 10\%$$

136. (c) Let the sum be ₹ P.

According to the question,

$$\frac{P \times 1 \times 17\frac{1}{2}}{100} - \frac{P \times 1 \times 11}{100} = 1071.20$$

$$\Rightarrow\ P\left(17\frac{1}{2} - 11\right) = 107120$$

$$\Rightarrow\ P = \frac{107120}{\frac{13}{2}} = \frac{107120 \times 2}{13}$$

$$= ₹\ 16480$$

So, simple interest on the amount ₹ 16480 for 5 yr at 10% rate $= \frac{16480 \times 5 \times 10}{100} = ₹\ 8240$

137. (d) Here, SI = 20400 − 12000 = ₹ 8400

$$\because\ 8400 = \frac{12000 \times 10 \times T}{100}$$

$$\Rightarrow\ 8400 = 1200 \times T$$

$$\therefore\ T = 7 \text{ yr}$$

138. (c) Let the sum be ₹ P.

$$4160 - P = \frac{P \times 5 \times 6}{100}$$

$$\Rightarrow\ 416000 - 100P = 30P$$

$$\Rightarrow\ 130P = 416000$$

$$\Rightarrow\ P = ₹\ 3200$$

139. (c) $SI = \frac{5000 \times 12 \times 14}{100 \times 12} = ₹\ 700$

140. (d) We know that,

$$SI = \frac{P \times r \times t}{100}$$

$$\Rightarrow\ 510 = \frac{4250 \times 6 \times t}{100} \Rightarrow t = \frac{510 \times 100}{4250 \times 6}$$

$$\therefore\ t = 2 \text{ yr}$$

141. (d) Let one part be ₹ x.

∴ Other part be ₹ (5000 − x).

According to the question,

$$\frac{x \times 16 \times 1}{100} + \frac{(5000 - x) \times 24 \times 1}{100} = 960$$

$$\Rightarrow\ 16x + 24 \times 5000 - 24x = 96000$$

$$\Rightarrow\ 8x = 24000$$

$$\therefore\ x = ₹\ 3000$$

Hence, sum lent at higher rate

$$= 5000 - 3000 = ₹\ 2000$$

142. (c) Selling price of charger

= ₹ 2540 in cash

Down payment = ₹ 1340

Amount after down payment

= 2540 − 1340 = ₹ 1200

But, he paid ₹ 1205 after one month.

Let rate of interest be r%.

$$\text{Then, } 1205 - 1200 = 1200 \times \frac{R \times 1}{12 \times 100}$$

$$R = 5\%$$

Thus, rate of interest is 5%.

143. (d) Let the sum initially invested be P.

According to the question,

$$\text{Amount} = P + \frac{P \times 8 \times 8}{100}$$

[∵ Amount = ₹ 820, R = 8%, T = 8 yr]

$$\Rightarrow 820 = P + \frac{64P}{100} \Rightarrow 820 = \frac{164P}{100}$$

$$\Rightarrow\ P = 500$$

If the same amount invested for 10 yr.

$$A = 500 + \frac{500 \times 20 \times 10}{100}$$

$$= 500 + 1000 = ₹\ 1500$$

144. (a) Let principal be ₹ P and rate be r%.

According to the question,

$$1860 = P + \frac{P \times r \times 2}{100}$$

$$1860 = P + \frac{2Pr}{100} \quad \text{...(i)}$$

$$\text{Again,}\quad 2130 = P + \frac{7 \times P \times r}{2 \times 100}$$

$$2130 = P + \frac{7Pr}{200} \quad \text{...(ii)}$$

Multiplying Eq. (i) with $\frac{7}{4}$ and subtracting from Eq. (ii),

$$P = ₹ 1500$$

Putting value of P in Eq. (i),

$$\therefore\ r = 12\%$$

> **Speedy Method**
>
> SI for 1.5 yr = 2130 − 1860 = ₹ 270
>
> 1 yr = ₹ 180
>
> 2 yr = ₹ 360
>
> Principal = 1860 − 360 = ₹ 1500
>
> $R\% = \frac{180}{1500} \times 100 = 12\%$

145. (c) SI for 2 yr = 32000 − 24000 = ₹ 8000

Principal sum = 24000 − 8000 = ₹ 16000

$$\text{SI for 2 yr} = \frac{16000 \times R \times 2}{100}$$

(Here R = rate of interest p.a.)

$$\Rightarrow\ 8000 = \frac{16000 \times R \times 2}{100}$$

$$\therefore\ R = 25\% \text{ p.a.}$$

146. (c) According to the question,

$$1093.50 = \frac{2430 \times R \times 3}{100}$$

$$\Rightarrow\ R = \frac{1093.5 \times 100}{2430 \times 3} \Rightarrow R = 15\%$$

Hence, rate of interest = 15%

147. (d) SI in 2 yr

$$= \frac{36000 \times 1 \times 8}{100} + \frac{36000 \times 1 \times 6}{100}$$

$$= 2880 + 2160 = 5040$$

∴ Amount due after 2 yr

$$= 36000 + 5040 = ₹\ 41040$$

148. **(a)** Let the amount invested be ₹ P.
According to the question,

$$4050 = \frac{P \times 9 \times 5}{100}$$

$$\Rightarrow \quad P = \frac{4050 \times 100}{45} = ₹\,9000$$

149. **(a)** SI for 6 yr = 5420 − 3260 = ₹ 2160

SI for 1 yr = $\frac{2160}{6}$ = ₹ 360

SI for 4 yr = 360 × 4 = ₹ 1440

Thus, amount after 4 yr

= 3260 + 1440 = ₹ 4700

150. **(a)** SI = 8928 − 7200 = ₹ 1728
and rate of interest (R) = 8%
Let time = t yr

$$\Rightarrow \quad 1728 = \frac{7200 \times 8 \times t}{100} \Rightarrow t = 3 \text{ yr}$$

∴ Required time = 3 yr

151. **(b)** According to the question,

$$\frac{5}{4}\text{Principal} - \text{Principal} = \frac{\text{Principal} \times 3 \times \text{Rate}}{100}$$

$$\Rightarrow \frac{1}{4}\text{Principal} = \frac{\text{Principal} \times 3 \times \text{Rate}}{100}$$

$$\therefore \quad \text{Rate} = \frac{100}{12} = 8.33\%$$

152. **(b)** Let the principal sum be ₹ P.
It becomes $5P$ in 15 yr at certain rate.

$$5P - P = \frac{P \times R \times 15}{100}$$

$$\Rightarrow \quad 4P = \frac{P \times R \times 15}{100} \Rightarrow R = \frac{80}{3}\%$$

Again, if time period be double, then
time = 30 yr

$$\therefore \quad \text{SI} = P \times \frac{80}{3} \times \frac{30}{100} \Rightarrow \text{SI} = ₹\,8P$$

∴ Amount = SI + Principal = $8P + P$ = ₹ $9P$
Thus, final amount become 9 times its original value.

153. **(b)** According to the question,

$$\text{SI} = \frac{12000 \times 9 \times 1}{100} + \frac{12000 \times 10 \times 1}{100}$$

= 1080 + 1200

∴ SI = ₹ 2280

∴ Required amount = P + SI

= 12000 + 2280 = ₹ 14280

154. **(d)** Let the money initially borrowed be ₹ P.
According to the question,

$$21400 = \frac{P \times 8 \times 2}{100} + \frac{P \times 11 \times 3}{100} + \frac{P \times 16 \times 4}{100}$$

⇒ $16P + 33P + 64P = 21400 \times 100$

⇒ $113P = 21400 \times 100$

$$\therefore \quad P = \frac{21400 \times 100}{113} = ₹\,18938$$

155. **(c)** We know that,
Amount = Principal

$$+ \frac{\text{Principal} \times \text{Time} \times \text{Rate}}{100}$$

$$= 4500 + \frac{4500 \times 4 \times 8}{100}$$

= 4500 + 1440 = ₹ 5940

156. **(c)** Given, $\frac{\text{Principal } (P)}{\text{SI}} = \frac{10}{7}$

$$\frac{P \times 100}{P \times R \times T} = \frac{10}{7} \left[\because \text{SI} = \frac{P \times R \times T}{100}\right]$$

$$\frac{100}{5 \times R} = \frac{10}{7}$$

$$\Rightarrow \quad \frac{2}{R} = \frac{1}{7} \Rightarrow R = 14\%$$

157. **(d)** Let the money lent was P.
According to the question,

$$\frac{P \times 8.6 \times 8}{100} - \frac{P \times 8.6 \times 7}{100} = ₹\,172$$

⇒ $P \times 8.6$ = ₹ 172 × 100

$$\Rightarrow \quad P = ₹\,\frac{172 \times 100}{8.6} \Rightarrow P = ₹\,2000$$

Hence, the sum lent to each was ₹ 2000.

158. **(c)** Given, Principal (P) = ₹ 18000
Simple interest (SI) = ₹ 3240,

Time (T) = 2 yr 3 months = $2\frac{3}{12} = \frac{9}{4}$ months

According to the question,

$$\text{SI} = 3240 = \frac{18000 \times \text{Rate} \times 9}{100 \times 4}$$

$$\Rightarrow \quad \text{Rate} = \left[\frac{3240 \times 100 \times 4}{18000 \times 9}\right]$$

∴ Rate = 8%

159. **(d)** Let the amount invested at rate of 5% is x and amount invested at 4% is $(8000 - x)$.
According to the question,

$$\frac{x \times 5 \times 2}{100} + \frac{(8000 - x) \times 4 \times 2}{100} = 720$$

$$\Rightarrow \quad \frac{x \times 10}{100} + 640 - \frac{x \times 8}{100} = 720$$

$$\Rightarrow \quad \frac{x \times 10}{100} - \frac{x \times 8}{100} = 720 - 640$$

$$\Rightarrow \quad \frac{x \times 2}{100} = 80 \Rightarrow x = 4000$$

∴ Amount invested at Scheme 1
= Amount invested at 5% per annum
= ₹ 4000

160. **(a)** Given, cost price of scooty = ₹ 40000
Cash down payment = ₹ 25000,
Left amount = 40000 − 25000 = ₹ 15000
Total interest = 4 × 4000 − 15000
= ₹ 1000
According to the question,

$$1000 = \frac{15000 \times R \times 1}{12 \times 100} + \frac{11000 \times R \times 1}{12 \times 100} + \frac{7000 \times R \times 1}{12 \times 100} + \frac{3000 \times R \times 1}{12 \times 100}$$

$$\Rightarrow \quad 1000 = \frac{R}{12 \times 100}[36000]$$

$$\Rightarrow \quad R = \frac{1000 \times 12 \times 100}{36000}$$

∴ $R = 33.33\% \approx 33\%$

161. **(c)** According to the question,

$$\therefore \quad \text{Time} = \frac{\text{SI} \times 100}{P \times R} = \frac{45000 \times 100}{450000 \times 5} = 2 \text{ yr}$$

162. **(a)** Given, total amount = ₹ 550
Down payment = ₹ 250
Amount paid = ₹ 310
Time = 1 month

∴ The remaining amount after down payment = 550 − 250 = ₹ 300

Interest = 310 − 300 = ₹ 10

$$\text{Now,} \quad \text{SI} = \frac{P \times R \times T}{100}$$

$$\therefore \quad 10 = \frac{300 \times R}{100} \times \frac{1}{12} \Rightarrow R = 40\%$$

163. **(c)** Let the principal be ₹ P.
According to the question,

$$\frac{4}{5}P = \frac{P \times r \times 8}{100} \Rightarrow r = \frac{4 \times 100}{5 \times 8}$$

∴ $r = 10\%$ p.a.

164. **(c)** According to the question,

$$\therefore \text{ Rate of interest} = \frac{\text{Simple interest} \times 100}{\text{Principal} \times \text{Time}}$$

$$= \frac{22000 \times 100}{50000 \times 4} = 11$$

∴ Rate of interest = 11%

165. **(b)** Given, Principal = ₹ 5000
Rate of interest for first 2 yr = 10%
Rate of interest for next 3 yr = 12%

We know that, $\text{SI} = \frac{PRT}{100}$

∵ Interest for first 2 yr = $5000 \times \frac{10}{100} \times 2$

= ₹ 1000

Interest for next 3 yr

$= 5000 \times \frac{12}{100} \times 3$ = ₹ 1800

Hence, total interest earned at the end of 5 yr

= (1000 + 1800) = ₹ 2800

166. **(b)** Given, amount = ₹ 2400
Present value = ₹ x
∴ SI = ₹ $(2400 - x)$
According to the question

$$\Rightarrow \quad 2400 - x = \frac{x \times 5 \times 4}{100}$$

⇒ $240000 - 100x = 20x$

$$\Rightarrow \quad x = \frac{240000}{120} = ₹\,2000$$

Hence, the present value is ₹ 2000.

167. **(c)** Let the principal = ₹ P

$$\therefore \quad P + \frac{P \times 5 \times 4}{100} = 6600$$

$$\frac{P(100 + 20)}{100} = 6600$$

$P = \frac{6600 \times 100}{120} = ₹\,5500$

168. (b) Let principal = ₹ P

According to the question,

$P = (200 \times 5) + \left(200 \times \frac{5}{100} \times 4\right) + \left(200 \times \frac{5}{100} \times 3\right) + \left(200 \times \frac{5}{100} \times 2\right) + \left(200 \times \frac{5}{100} \times 1\right)$

$\Rightarrow \quad P = [1000 + 40 + 30 + 20 + 10]$

$\therefore \quad P = ₹\,1100$

Speedy Method

Let each installment be ₹ 100.

100 100 100 100 100 → × 2 = ₹ 200

→ 100

→ 105

→ 110

→ 115

→ 120

Total debt = 550 × 2 = ₹ 1100

169. (a) Let principal = ₹ P

According to the question,

$\frac{P \times 3 \times 10}{2 \times 100} - \frac{P \times 1 \times 12}{100} = 30$

$\frac{15P}{100} - \frac{12P}{100} = 30 \Rightarrow \frac{3P}{100} = 30$

$\therefore \quad P = ₹\,1000$

170. (b) Given, the simple interest in both the bank is same.

$\frac{K \times n^2 \times r^{1/2}}{100} = \frac{L \times n^3 \times r^{3/2}}{100}$

$\Rightarrow \quad \frac{K}{L} = \frac{r^{3/2} \times n^3}{r^{1/2} \times n^2} = \frac{r \times n}{1}$

So, ratio between K and L is $rn : 1$.

171. (c) Let the principal be ₹ P.

$\therefore$ Simple interest = ₹ $\frac{3P}{5}$

According to the question,

$\frac{3P}{5} = \frac{P \times R \times 12}{100} \Rightarrow R = \frac{3 \times 100}{5 \times 12} = 5\%$

Hence, the rate of interest = 5%

172. (c) Given, time (T) = 7 yr

Let sum = ₹ P

An amount becomes double *i.e.*, $2P$ in 7 yr,

$SI = 2P - P = P$

$\therefore \; SI = \frac{P \times R \times T}{100} \Rightarrow P = \frac{P \times R \times 7}{100}$

$R = \frac{100}{7}\%$

Again, amount becomes 4 times in T yr.

$SI = 4P - P = 3P$

$\therefore \; SI = \frac{P \times R \times T}{100} \Rightarrow 3P = \frac{P \times 100 \times T}{7 \times 100}$

$\therefore \quad T = 21$ yr

Speedy Method

We know, $\frac{t_1}{t_2} = \frac{(n_1 - 1)}{n_2 - 1}$

$\frac{7}{t_2} = \frac{(2-1)}{(4-1)} \Rightarrow \frac{7}{t_2} = \frac{1}{3} \Rightarrow t = 21$ yr

173. (d) Loan amount = ₹ 1200000

Interest = ₹ 972000

According to the question,

$\Rightarrow \quad 972000 = \frac{1200000 \times x \times x}{100}$

[$\because$ Time and rate are same]

$\Rightarrow \quad x^2 = 81 \Rightarrow x = 9$

Hence, rate (R) = 9%

174. (a) Let the principle be ₹ P.

then, simple interest (SI) = ₹ P

Rate of interest $(r) = 2\frac{6}{7}\%$ p.a. $= \frac{20}{7}\%$ p.a.

Let the required time be 't' yr.

According to the question,

$\Rightarrow \quad P = \frac{P \times \frac{20}{7} \times t}{100} \Rightarrow t = 35$ yr

175. (a) Here, SI = 4100 − 2500 = ₹1600

Let, Time = t yr

According to the question,

$\Rightarrow \quad 1600 = \frac{2500 \times 16 \times t}{100} \quad \therefore \quad t = 4$ yr

176. (b) Let principal = ₹x

According to the question,

$\frac{4}{3}x - x = \frac{x \times r \times 3}{100}$

$\Rightarrow \quad \frac{1}{3} = \frac{3r}{100} \Rightarrow r = \frac{100}{9} = 11\frac{1}{9}\%$

177. (d) SI for 1 yr = 825 − 750 = ₹ 75

and SI for 3 yr = 3 × 75 = ₹ 225

$\therefore$ Required sum = 750 − 225 = ₹ 525

178. (c) Given, R = 10%, $T = t$ yr

$SI = \frac{5}{8}P$

According to the question,

$\frac{5}{8}P = \frac{P \times 10 \times t}{100} \Rightarrow t = \frac{50}{8} = 6\frac{1}{4}$ yr

When, $R = \frac{3}{4}$th of 10% $= \frac{15}{2}\%$ and SI = ₹ $\frac{5}{8}P$

and let $T = t' \Rightarrow \frac{5}{8}P = \frac{P \times 15 \times t'}{100 \times 2}$

$\Rightarrow \quad t' = \frac{5}{8} \times \frac{100 \times 2}{15} \Rightarrow t' = 8\frac{1}{3}$ yr

179. (b) According to the question,

$\therefore$ Total amount $= 4400 + \frac{4400 \times 10 \times 12}{100} + 7500 + \frac{7500 \times 8 \times 12}{100}$

= 4400 + 5280 + 7500 + 7200 = ₹ 24380

180. (c) Let principal = ₹ P

Amount, A = ₹ $5P$

Simple Interest (SI) = $5P - P$ = ₹ $4P$

$\therefore$ Rate $(r) = \frac{SI \times 100}{\text{Principal} \times \text{Time}} = \frac{4P \times 100}{P \times 18}$

$= \frac{200}{9} = 22.22\% \approx 22\%$

181. (d) Given, SI = ₹$\frac{P}{4}$ and $T = \frac{R}{4}$

$\therefore \quad \frac{P}{4} = \frac{P \times R \times \frac{R}{4}}{100} \Rightarrow R^2 = 100 \Rightarrow R = 10\%$

New rate of interest = 10 + 2 = 12%

$\therefore \quad SI = \frac{3600 \times 12 \times 6}{100} = ₹\,2592$

182. (a) Simple interest for $\left(\frac{15}{2} - 3\right)$ yr

= 10500 − 6000 = ₹4500

Simple interest for 1 yr $= \frac{4500}{\frac{9}{2}} = 1000$

$\therefore$ Principal = 6000 − 1000 × 3 = ₹3000

Now, rate of interest $= \frac{1000}{3000} \times 100 = 33\frac{1}{3}\%$

183. (a) Let principal be ₹ P and amount be ₹ A.

According to the question,

$SI = \frac{140}{100} - P = \frac{40P}{100}$

$\because \quad SI = \frac{2}{5}P \Rightarrow \frac{2}{5}P = \frac{P \times 6 \times T}{100}$

$\therefore \quad T = \frac{100}{5 \times 3} = \frac{20}{3} = 6\frac{2}{3}$ yr

184. (b) Total gain he get

$= \frac{20000 \times 3}{100}[8.5 - 6]$

= 600 × 2.5 = ₹ 1500

$\therefore$ Value of gain per year $= \frac{1500}{3} = ₹500$

185. (b) According to the question,

$20000 - 12500 = \frac{12500 \times 8 \times T}{100}$

$\therefore \quad 7500 = 125 \times 8 \times T \Rightarrow T = 7.5$ yr

186. (b) $SI = \frac{7500 \times 7 \times 2}{100}$

SI = ₹ 1050

$\therefore$ Amount = 7500 + 1050 = ₹ 8550

187. (b) According to the question,

$\frac{12000 \times 3 \times r}{100} + \frac{10000 \times r \times 4}{100} = 6080$

$\Rightarrow \quad 360r + 400r = 6080 \Rightarrow 760r = 6080$

$\therefore \quad r = \frac{6080}{760} = 8\%$ p.a.

188. (d) SI = 3120 − 2000 = ₹ 1120

$\therefore$ Rate of interest, $R = \frac{SI \times 100}{P \times T}$

$= \frac{1120 \times 100}{2000 \times 2} = 28\%$

189. (a) Let the amount invested for son, daughter and wife are ₹ x, ₹ y and ₹ z, respectively.

According to the question,

$$\frac{x \times 5 \times 3}{100} = \frac{y \times 5 \times 4}{100} = \frac{z \times 5 \times 5}{100}$$

$$3x = 4y = 5z$$

$$\frac{3x}{60} : \frac{4y}{60} : \frac{5z}{60} \text{ or } \frac{x}{20} : \frac{y}{15} : \frac{z}{12}$$

Then, $x : y : z = 20 : 15 : 12$

Hence, amount invested for his wife

$$= \frac{105750 \times 12}{47} = ₹\ 27000$$

190. (c) Required Simple Interest

$$= \frac{3500 \times 7 \times 4}{100} = 35 \times 28 = ₹\ 980$$

191. (a) Simple Interest $= \frac{P \times 3 \times 12}{100}$

$$360 = \frac{P \times 3 \times 12}{100}$$

$$P = ₹\ 1000$$

192. (d) Simple Interest $= \frac{15000 \times 8.5 \times 5\frac{3}{12}}{100}$

$$= \frac{15000 \times 8.5 \times 21}{100 \times 4} = ₹\ 6693.75$$

193. (b) $SI = \frac{P \times R \times T}{100}$

$$240 = \frac{P \times 20 \times 3}{100}$$

$$P = \frac{24000}{60} = ₹\ 400$$

194. (d) Let the sum be ₹ P.

According to the question

$$\Rightarrow P \times \frac{8 \times 8}{100} - P \times \frac{6 \times 6}{100} = 1176$$

$$\Rightarrow \frac{28}{100} \times P = 1176 \Rightarrow P = ₹4200$$

195. (c) $SI = \frac{P \times R \times T}{100}$

$$\Rightarrow 360 = \frac{P \times 20 \times 2}{100}$$

$$\Rightarrow P = \frac{36000}{40} = ₹\ 900$$

196. (b) $SI = \frac{2500 \times 3 \times 3}{100} = ₹\ 225$

197. (b) $SI = \frac{3500 \times 6 \times 6}{100} = ₹\ 1260$

198. (c) SI for 2 yr = 3000 − 2500 = ₹ 500

SI for 1 yr = ₹ 250

According to the question,

$$P + 3 \times 250 = 2500$$

$$P = 1750$$

$$\text{Rate of Interest} = \frac{250}{1750} \times 100$$

$$= 14.29\%$$

199. (b) Simple Interest $= \frac{2000 \times 8 \times 5}{100} = ₹\ 800$

200. (c) Let the sum deposited be ₹ P.

Then, let the rate be R%.

$$SI = \frac{P \times R \times 4}{100}$$

$$\text{Amount} = P + \frac{P \times R \times 4}{100}$$

Now, Interest is increased by 5%

$$SI = \frac{P \times (R+5) \times 4}{100}$$

$$\text{Amount} = P + \frac{P \times (R+5) \times 4}{100} = 5200 + A$$

$$\Rightarrow P + \frac{P \times R \times 4}{100} + \frac{P \times 5 \times 4}{100} = 5200 + A$$

$$\Rightarrow A + \frac{P}{5} = 5200 + A$$

$$\Rightarrow P = 5200 \times 5$$

$$\Rightarrow P = ₹\ 26000$$

Speedy Method

$4 \times 5\% = ₹\ 5200 \Rightarrow 20\% = 5200$

$\Rightarrow 1\% = 260 \Rightarrow 100\% = ₹\ 26000$

201. (a) Let the time taken be t yr.

Let the sum invested be ₹ 100.

According to the question,

$$30 = \frac{100 \times 4 \times t}{100}$$

$$t = \frac{15}{2} = 7\frac{1}{2} \text{ yr}$$

202. (d) $SI = \frac{2500 \times 9 \times 5}{100} = ₹\ 1125$

203. (d) Required SI $= \frac{3500 \times 4 \times 5}{100}$

$$= ₹\ 700$$

204. (b) Let principal be ₹ P.

Amount = $2P$

$$SI = 2P - P = P$$

$$\text{We know, } SI = \frac{P \times R \times T}{100}$$

$$P = \frac{P \times R \times 12}{100} \quad R = 8\frac{1}{3}\%$$

205. (c) Simple Interest

$$= \frac{2500 \times 8 \times 3}{100} = 25 \times 24 = ₹\ 600$$

206. (b) According to the question,

$$\frac{20000 \times 6 \times t}{100} + \frac{25000 \times 8 \times t}{100} = 9600$$

$$\Rightarrow 1200t + 2000t = 9600$$

$$\Rightarrow 3200t = 9600 \Rightarrow t = 3 \text{ yr}$$

207. (d) Required simple interest

$$= \frac{2500 \times 6 \times 2}{100} = 25 \times 12 = ₹\ 300$$

208. (a) Let the principal be ₹ P.

According to the question,

$$240 = \frac{P \times 2 \times 4}{100}$$

$$P = ₹\ 3000$$

209. (c) Let the amount of money at 7% be ₹ x.

According to the question,

$$\frac{x \times 7 \times 1}{100} + \frac{(40000 - x) \times 6 \times 1}{100} = ₹\ 2550$$

$$\Rightarrow \frac{7x}{100} + 2400 - \frac{6x}{100} = ₹\ 2550$$

$$\Rightarrow \frac{x}{100} = ₹\ 150$$

$$\Rightarrow x = ₹\ 15000$$

210. (b) $SI = \frac{2000 \times 8 \times 6}{100} = ₹\ 960$

211. (b) Required SI $= \frac{2500 \times 4 \times 2}{100} = ₹\ 200$

212. (a) Let the sum be ₹ P.

$$240 = \frac{P \times 16 \times 4}{100}$$

$$P = \frac{24000}{64} = ₹\ 375$$

213. (d) Amount for 3 yr = ₹ 16150

Amount for 4 yr = ₹ 16540

$\Rightarrow$ SI for (4 − 3) yr

= (16540 − 16150) = ₹ 390

$\Rightarrow$ SI for 3 yr = 3 × 390 = ₹1170

= 16150 − 1170 = ₹ 14980

214. (a) Let the loan sum be P.

According to the question,

$$\Rightarrow P + \left(P \times \frac{4 \times 2}{100} + P \times \frac{8 \times 3}{100} + P \times \frac{12 \times 1}{100}\right) = 5472$$

$$\Rightarrow P + \frac{44}{100}P = 5472$$

$$\Rightarrow \frac{144P}{100} = 5472$$

$$\Rightarrow P = \frac{5472 \times 100}{144} = ₹\ 3800$$

215. (c) Required SI $= \frac{3000 \times 8 \times 4}{100} = ₹\ 960$

216. (c) $SI = \frac{PRT}{100}$

$$\Rightarrow 360 = \frac{P \times 4 \times 2}{100} \Rightarrow P = \frac{36000}{8} = ₹\ 4500$$

217. (a) Required ratio $= \dfrac{\frac{P \times R \times 12}{100}}{\frac{P \times R \times 15}{100}} = \frac{4}{5} = 4 : 5$

218. (b) $SI = \frac{3000 \times 8 \times 2}{100} = ₹\ 480$

219. (d) $SI = \frac{2000 \times 9 \times 4}{100} = ₹\ 720$

220. (d) $SI = \frac{3500 \times 3 \times 5}{100} = ₹\ 525$

221. (b) Required SI $= \frac{3500 \times 3 \times 5}{100} = ₹\ 525$

222. (d) Let Principal be ₹ P.

According to the question,

$$\frac{19}{15}P = \frac{P \times R \times 15}{100}$$

$$\Rightarrow R = \frac{1900}{225} = 8\frac{4}{9}\%$$

223. (b) Required SI $= 3500 \times \frac{3 \times 6}{100} = ₹ 630$

224. (c) Amount = Principal $+ \frac{\text{Principal} \times \text{Time} \times \text{Rate}}{100}$

$$\Rightarrow P + \frac{P \times 6 \times R}{100} = ₹ 7436 \quad \ldots(i)$$

$$\Rightarrow P + \frac{P \times 10 \times R}{100} = ₹ 9460 \quad \ldots(ii)$$

Dividing both Eqs. (i) and (ii), we get

$$\Rightarrow \frac{1 + \frac{6R}{100}}{1 + \frac{10R}{100}} = \frac{7436}{9460}$$

Using C and D rule,

$$\Rightarrow \frac{2 + \left(\frac{16R}{100}\right)}{\frac{4R}{100}} = \frac{16896}{2024}$$

$$\Rightarrow \frac{50}{R} + 4 = \frac{16896}{2024} \Rightarrow \frac{50}{R} = \frac{8800}{2024}$$

$$\Rightarrow R = 11.5\%$$

225. (d) Simple Interest $= \frac{2500 \times 5 \times 6}{100} = ₹ 750$

226. (c) Simple Interest $= \frac{4000 \times 4 \times 6}{100} = ₹ 960$

227. (d) Simple interest $= \frac{3000 \times 3 \times 6}{100} = 540$

228. (a) Let New Simple Interest be SI.

We know, $\frac{P \times R \times T}{100} = \text{SI}$

$$R = \frac{\text{SI} \times 100}{P \times T}$$

According to the question,

$$\frac{756 \times 100}{4200 \times 3} = \frac{\text{SI} \times 100}{5400 \times 3}$$

$$\therefore \quad \text{SI} = ₹ 972$$

229. (b) SI $= \frac{P \times 6 \times 15}{100}$ $\left[\because \text{SI} = \frac{PRT}{100}\right]$

$$3195 = \frac{P \times 90}{100} \Rightarrow P = ₹ 3550$$

New, Principal = 3550 + 1250 = ₹4800

Now, SI $= 4800 \times 3 \times \frac{15}{100} = ₹ 2160$

230. (d) Required SI $= 2000 \times 7 \times \frac{6}{100} = ₹ 840$

231. (b) Required SI $= 2500 \times 5 \times \frac{3}{100} = ₹ 375$

232. (d) Required SI

$$= \frac{940 \times 3 \times 5}{100} = \frac{14100}{100} = ₹ 141$$

233. (d) SI $= \frac{3500 \times 6 \times 4}{100} = ₹ 840$

234. (d) Simple Interest $= \frac{2000 \times 7 \times 3}{100} = ₹ 420$

235. (a) Let Vipul, Ashima and Priya invested amount P_1, P_2 and P_3 respectively.

According to the question,

$$P_1 \times \frac{3}{100} = P_2 \times \frac{6}{100} = P_3 \times \frac{5}{100}$$

$$\frac{P_1}{10} = \frac{P_2}{5} = \frac{P_3}{6}$$

$$\therefore \quad P_1 : P_2 : P_3 = 10 : 5 : 6$$

Amount invested by Ashima

$$= \frac{P_2}{P_1 + P_2 + P_3} \times 21000$$

$$= \frac{5}{21} \times 21000 = ₹ 5000$$

236. (c) SI $= \frac{3000 \times 8 \times 6}{100} = ₹ 1440$

237. (d) SI of (8 – 4) yr = ₹ 11960

$\Rightarrow$ SI of 4 yr = 11960 $\Rightarrow$ SI of 1 yr = 2990

Now, $2990 = \frac{P \times 23 \times 1}{100} \Rightarrow P = ₹ 13000$

238. (a) Required Simple Interest

$$= \frac{3500 \times 6 \times 3}{100} = ₹ 630$$

239. (a) Simple Interest $= \frac{2500 \times 6 \times 5}{100}$

$$= ₹ 750$$

240. (d) SI $= \frac{2500 \times 7 \times 3}{100} = 21 \times 25 = ₹ 525$

241. (a) Required SI $= \frac{2500 \times 9 \times 4}{100}$

$$= 25 \times 36 = ₹ 900$$

242. (a) $\because$ Amount for 3 yr = ₹ 9430

Amount for 7 yr = ₹ 11070

$\therefore$ SI for (7 – 3) yr = 11070 – 9430

$\Rightarrow$ SI for 4 yr = ₹ 1640

$\Rightarrow$ SI for 1 yr = ₹ 410

$\Rightarrow$ SI for 3 yrs = 410 × 3 = ₹ 1230

Now, P = 9430 – 1230 = ₹ 8200

243. (d) According to the question,

$$\frac{8}{7}P - P = \frac{P \times R \times 6}{100}$$

$$\Rightarrow R = \frac{1}{7} \times \frac{100}{6} = \frac{50}{21} = 2\frac{8}{21}\%$$

244. (b) SI $= 3000 \times \frac{3 \times 4}{100}$ $\left[\because \text{SI} = \frac{PRT}{100}\right]$

$$= ₹ 360$$

245. (d) Simple Interest $= \frac{2500 \times 3 \times 6}{100}$

$\left[\because \text{SI} = \frac{PRT}{100}\right]$

$$= 25 \times 18 = ₹ 450$$

246. (d) Simple Interest,

$$\text{SI} = \frac{P \times R \times T}{100} = 3000 \times \frac{6 \times 4}{100} = ₹ 720$$

247. (c) SI $= 2500 \times \frac{9 \times 6}{100} = ₹ 1350$

248. (c) Total annual rate % $= \frac{500}{2380} \times 100$

$$= \frac{2500}{119}\%$$

By Alligation Method,

Ist Part 25%   2nd Part 20%

$\frac{2500}{119}$

$\frac{120}{119}$: $\frac{475}{119}$

$\Rightarrow$ 24 : 95

Thus, money lent on 25%

$$= \frac{24}{24 + 95} \times 2380$$

$$= \frac{24}{119} \times 2380 = ₹ 480$$

249. (c) Simple Interest $= \frac{P \times R \times T}{100}$

$$240 = \frac{P \times 12 \times 4}{100} \Rightarrow P = ₹ 500$$

250. (b) Simple Interest $= \frac{2500 \times 7 \times 5}{100}$

$$= ₹ 875$$

251. (d) Total simple Interest $= \text{SI}_A + \text{SI}_B$

$$= \frac{89500 \times 3 \times 7}{100} + \frac{89500 \times 9}{100} + \frac{89500 \times 8}{100} + \frac{89500 \times 7}{100}$$

$$= \frac{89500 \times 21}{100} + \frac{89500 \times 24}{100}$$

$$= \frac{89500 \times 45}{100} = ₹ 40275$$

252. (a) We know,

Amount = Principal $+ \frac{\text{Principal} \times \text{Rate} \times \text{time}}{100}$

$$\Rightarrow \text{Principal} + \frac{\text{Principal} \times 5 \times 6}{100} = 806$$

$$\Rightarrow \text{Principal} \times \frac{130}{100} = 806$$

Principal = ₹620

$\therefore$ New amount $= \frac{620 \times 12 \times 5}{100} + 620$

$$= ₹992$$

253. (b) We know, SI $= \frac{P \times R \times T}{100}$

$$\Rightarrow \text{SI} = \frac{3500 \times 7 \times 6}{100} \Rightarrow \text{SI} = ₹1470$$

254. (a) We know,

Simple Interest $= \frac{\text{Principal} \times \text{Rate} \times \text{Time}}{100}$

$$= \frac{3000 \times 7 \times 5}{100} = ₹1050$$

255. (c) Let the principal be ₹ P.

Amount = ₹ 4 P

Simple interest = 4P − P = ₹3P

According to the question,

$$3P = \frac{P \times R \times T}{100} \Rightarrow 3P = \frac{P \times 12 \times T}{100}$$

∴ $T = 25$ yr

256. (d) According to the question,

$$3100 - 2000 = \frac{2000 \times 11 \times T}{100}$$

$$\Rightarrow 1100 = \frac{2000 \times 11 \times T}{100} \Rightarrow T = 5 \text{ yr}$$

257. (c) SI = 9800 − 8000 = ₹ 1800

$$1800 = \frac{8000 \times R \times 3}{100}$$

$$\Rightarrow R = \frac{1800}{80 \times 3} = \frac{15}{2}\%$$

Now, according to the question,

$$SI = \frac{8000 \times 2 \times 15 \times 4}{2 \times 100} = ₹4800$$

∴ Amount = P + SI = 8000 + 4800 = ₹ 12800

258. (b) Let principal be ₹ P.

$$P = \frac{1800 \times 100}{5 \times 6} = ₹ 6000$$

259. (b) We know that,

If a sum of money in a certain time becomes n times at R_1 rate of interest and m times at R_2 rate of interest,

$$R_2 = R_1 \times \left(\frac{m-1}{n-1}\right)$$

According to the question,

$$\text{Required rate of interest} = \frac{(8-1) \times 6}{(5-1)} = \frac{42}{4} = 10.5\%$$

260. (a) $SI = \frac{5400 \times 4 \times 7}{100} = ₹ 1512$

261. (a) Time (T) = 15 months = $\frac{15}{12}$ yr

$$\therefore SI = \frac{6000 \times 12 \times 15}{100 \times 12} = ₹ 900$$

262. (a) Let the principal be ₹ x.

∴ SI = ₹(113880) − x

For R = 6% and T = 5 yr

$$SI = \frac{x \times 6 \times 5}{100} \Rightarrow 113880 - x = ₹ \frac{30x}{100}$$

⇒ 11388000 − 100x = 30x

⇒ x = ₹ 87600

For P = ₹ 87600, r = 9% and T = 8 yr

$$\Rightarrow SI = \frac{87600 \times 9 \times 8}{100}$$

∴ SI = ₹ 63072

263. (a) Interest received in 3 yr

= 4526 − 3650 = ₹ 876

$$\therefore \text{Rate of interest} = \frac{876 \times 100}{3650 \times 3} = 8\%$$

264. (c) Amount gain in 9 yr

= 33500 − 20000 = ₹ 13500

$$\text{Interest earn in 1 yr} = \frac{13500}{9} = ₹1500$$

$$\text{Now, the rate of interest} = \frac{1500}{20000} \times 100 = 7.5\%$$

Speedy Method

$$r = \frac{SI \times 100}{P \times t} = \frac{(33500 - 20000) \times 100}{20000 \times 9} = \frac{13500 \times 100}{20000 \times 9} = 7.5\%$$

265. (b) Given, principal is same.

Simple interest for 4 yr = ₹ 2000

$$\text{Simple interest for 1 yr} = \frac{2000}{4} = ₹ 500$$

∴ Simple interest for 6 yr = 6 × 500 = ₹3000

266. (a) Let the initial sum be ₹ P.

According to the question,

$$1220 - P = \frac{P \times 18 \times 8}{100}$$

⇒ 122000 − 100P = 144P

⇒ 244P = 122000

$$\therefore P = \frac{122000}{244} = ₹ 500$$

267. (d) Let the rate of interest be R% per annum.

According to the question,

Time = Rate = R yr

$$\therefore 343 = \frac{700 \times R \times R}{100} \Rightarrow R^2 = 49$$

$$\therefore R = \sqrt{49} = 7\%$$

268. (a) Let the principal (P) be ₹ x.

Then, Simple Interest (SI) = 3x − x = ₹ 2x

According to the question,

$$2x = \frac{x \times r \times 30}{100} \Rightarrow r = \frac{200}{30} \Rightarrow r = 6.67\%$$

269. (a) Let r% be the rate of interest per annum and ₹ P be the principal.

Interest for 2 yr = ₹ 292

$$\frac{P \times r \times 2}{100} = 292 \Rightarrow P \times r = 14600$$

$$\Rightarrow P = \frac{14600}{r}$$

Amount for first 5 yr = 3942 − 292 = ₹ 3650

$$\therefore 3650 - P = \frac{P \times r \times 5}{100}$$

$$\Rightarrow 3650 - P = \frac{\frac{14600}{r} \times r \times 5}{100}$$

⇒ 3650 − P = 730

$$\Rightarrow P = ₹ 2920 \Rightarrow r = \frac{14600}{p} = \frac{14600}{2920} = 5\%$$

270. (c) Let the cost price of each of 6 copies be ₹ 1.

Total money for 6 copies = 6 × 1 = ₹ 6

∴ According to the question,

∴ Required rate of interest

$$= \frac{(7-6)}{6} \times 100 = \frac{100}{6} = 16.7\%$$

271. (d) Let the rate of interest is r per cent per annum.

According to the question,

$$r = \frac{9750 \times 100}{15000 \times 5} = 13\%$$

New rate of interest = 13 − 3 = 10%

$$\text{New simple interest} = \frac{15000 \times 10 \times 5}{100} = ₹ 7500$$

272. (b) Here, SI for 1 yr = 1380 − 1320 = ₹60

Now, SI for 2 yr = 60 × 2 = ₹120

Principal (P) = 1320 − 120 = ₹1200

$$\therefore \text{Rate of interest} = \frac{SI \times 100}{P \times T} = \frac{120 \times 100}{1200 \times 2} = 5\%$$

273. (c) According to the question,

Let the principal = ₹ 100

After 24 yr amount = ₹ 300

⇒ Interest = 300 − 100 = ₹ 200

$$\therefore \text{Rate of interest} = \frac{200 \times 100}{100 \times 24} = 8.33\%$$

274. (c) Let us assume the sum is ₹ x.

According to the question,

$$57 = \left(\frac{x \times 10 \times 8}{100}\right) - \left(\frac{x \times 10 \times 7}{100}\right)$$

$$\Rightarrow \frac{x}{10}(8-7) = 57 \Rightarrow x = ₹570$$

275. (d) Let us assume the sum is x.

According to the question,

$$132 = \frac{(x \times 11 \times 9)}{100} - \frac{(x \times 11 \times 8)}{100}$$

$$\Rightarrow 132 = \left(\frac{11x}{100}\right) \times (9-8) \Rightarrow x = \frac{132 \times 100}{11}$$

∴ x = ₹ 1200

276. (b) Let principal = ₹ P, Amount = ₹3P,

∴ SI = 3P − P = ₹2P

According to the question,

$$2P = \frac{P \times R \times 34}{100} \Rightarrow R = \frac{100}{17}$$

⇒ R = 5.88%

277. (d) Let the amount lent = ₹ P

∵ SI = ₹ (P − 600) (Given)

According to the question,

$$\frac{P \times 3 \times 25}{100} = P - 600$$

$$\Rightarrow P\left[1 - \frac{25 \times 3}{100}\right] = 600 \Rightarrow P\left[\frac{25}{100}\right] = 600$$

∴ P = ₹ 2400

278. (b) According to the question,

SI for (2.5 − 1) yr = 1060 − 1000

⇒ SI for 1.5 yr = ₹ 60

$$\Rightarrow \text{SI for 1 yr} = \frac{60}{1.5} = ₹ 40$$

∵ Principal = 1000 − 40 = ₹ 960

$$\therefore \frac{960 \times R \times 1}{100} = 40 \Rightarrow R = \frac{40 \times 100}{960}$$

∴ R = 4.17%

279. (b) SI for 4 yr = 1400 − 1200 = ₹200

$\Rightarrow$ SI = ₹ 200

$\therefore$ Rate of interest $= \frac{200 \times 100}{1200 \times 4} = 4.17\%$

280. (c) Let the sum be ₹ P.

SI = ₹$(P + 1200)$

According to the question,

$\frac{PRT}{100} = P + 1200 \Rightarrow \frac{P \times 24 \times 5}{100} - P = 1200$

$\Rightarrow \frac{20P}{100} = 1200 \Rightarrow P = \frac{1200 \times 100}{20}$

$\Rightarrow P = 60 \times 100 \Rightarrow P =$ ₹ 6000

281. (a) Here, $m = 3.5$, $n = ?$, $T = 14$ yr, $t = 28$ yr.

According to the question,

$T = \frac{(m-1)}{(n-1)} \times t \Rightarrow 14 = \frac{(3.5-1)}{(n-1)} \times 28$

$\Rightarrow n - 1 = 5 \Rightarrow n = 6$ times

282. (c) Let principal be ₹ P

According to the question,

$\frac{20P}{100} = \frac{P \times R \times 5}{100}$ ...(i)

$P = \frac{P \times R \times T}{100}$ ...(ii)

On dividing Eqs. (i) by (ii), we get

$\frac{20}{100} = \frac{5}{T} \Rightarrow T = 25$ yr

283. (c) Let the rate of interest = R%

According to the question,

$\text{SI} = 1782 = \frac{P \times R \times 3}{100}$

$\Rightarrow PR = 59400$ ... (i)

Now, $T = 10$ yr

Again, $\text{SI} = \frac{P \times R \times 10}{100}$

$\Rightarrow \text{SI} = \frac{59400 \times 10}{100}$

$\therefore$ SI = ₹ 5940

284. (a) Given, SI = ₹ 350, $R = 7\%$

and $T = 1$ month $= \frac{1}{12}$ yr

According to the question,

$350 = \frac{(P \times 7 \times 1)}{100 \times 12}$

$\Rightarrow P = \frac{350 \times 1200}{7} =$ ₹ 60000

$\therefore$ Sum is ₹ 60000.

285. (b) $\because \text{SI} = \frac{P \times R \times T}{100}$

$\Rightarrow P = \frac{2275 \times 100}{13 \times 5} \Rightarrow P =$ ₹ 3500

286. (b) $\text{SI} = \frac{1000 \times 5 \times 2}{100} =$ ₹100

287. (d) Let the principle be ₹ P

According to the question,

$\frac{2}{5}P = \frac{P \times R \times 20}{100} \Rightarrow R = 2\%$

288. (d) Here, $T_1 = 10$ yr, $T_2 = 20$ yr

$n = 7$ and $m = ?$

$\because T_2 = \frac{m-1}{n-1} \times T_1$

$\Rightarrow 20 = \frac{m-1}{7-1} \times 10$

$m = 12 + 1 = 13$ times

289. (c) Let sum be ₹ P.

According to the question,

$\Rightarrow 3P - P = \frac{P \times R \times 17}{100 \times 2}$

$\left[\because T = 8 \text{ yr} + \frac{1}{2} \text{ yr} = \frac{17}{2} \text{ yr}\right]$

$\therefore R = \frac{400}{17} = 23.52\%$

290. (d) Let P = Principal, R = Rate of interest

According to the question,

$\frac{2}{5} \times P = \frac{P \times R \times 5}{100} \Rightarrow R = \frac{200}{25} \Rightarrow R = 8\%$

291. (c) Let the sum = ₹ P

$\therefore$ According to the question,

$\frac{2}{5}P = \frac{P \times R \times 40}{100} \Rightarrow R = \frac{200}{200} = 1\%$

292. (c) Each installment

$= \frac{\text{Paid money} \times 100}{100 \times t + \frac{t \times r \times (t-1)}{2}} = \frac{1380 \times 100}{100 \times 4 + \frac{4 \times 10 \times 3}{2}}$

$= \frac{1380 \times 100}{400 + 60} = \frac{1380 \times 100}{460} = 3 \times 100 =$ ₹300

293. (b) Let the required time be x yr.

Amount borrow by Sanjana = ₹ 16000

$\text{SI} = \frac{16000 \times 24 \times x}{100} =$ ₹ $3840x$

Amount borrow by Savithri = ₹ 18200

$\text{SI} = \frac{18200 \times 20 \times x}{100} =$ ₹ $3640x$

According to the question,

$16000 + 3840x = 18200 + 3640x$

$\Rightarrow 200x = 2200 \Rightarrow x = 11$ yr

294. (b) $\text{SI} = \frac{P \times r \times t}{100}$

$\Rightarrow 378 = \frac{2400 \times r \times 2\frac{1}{3}}{100}$

$r = \frac{378 \times 100 \times 3}{2400 \times 7} = 6.75\%$

295. (c) $\text{SI} = \frac{Prt}{100} = \frac{1250 \times 11 \times 3}{2 \times 100}$

$= \frac{41250}{200} =$ ₹ 206.25

296. (d) Annual installment

$= \frac{100A}{100t + \frac{Rt}{2}(t-1)}$

$= \frac{100 \times 3658}{100 \times 4 + \frac{12 \times 4}{2} \times (4-1)}$

$= \frac{365800}{400 + 72} = \frac{365800}{472} =$ ₹ 775

297. (d) Simple interest $= \frac{100000 \times 2 \times 12}{100}$

= ₹ 24000

298. (b) Time = 1 yr 8 month $= 1\frac{2}{3} = \frac{5}{3}$ yr

Simple interest = (18000 − 16875) = ₹ 1125

$\therefore \text{Rate} = \frac{\text{SI} \times 100}{P \times t} = \frac{1125 \times 100}{16875 \times \frac{5}{3}} = 4\%$

299. (a) $\text{SI} = \frac{84000 \times 15 \times 3}{100} =$ ₹ 37800

300. (b) $\text{SI} = \frac{200000 \times 8 \times 3}{100} =$ ₹ 48000

301. (c) Let the annual rate be r% per annum

$\text{SI} = \frac{Prt}{100} \Rightarrow 4625 = \frac{18500 \times r \times 5}{100}$

$\Rightarrow r = \frac{4625 \times 100}{18500 \times 5} = 5\%$

302. (c) According to the question,

$\frac{7000 \times R \times 2}{100} = \frac{5000 \times 5 \times 14}{100}$

$\Rightarrow R = \frac{5000 \times 5 \times 14}{7000 \times 2} = 25\%$

303. (a) Let sum be x and rate of interest be r% per annum.

$\therefore P = x$, $A = \frac{7}{5}x$, $t = 5$yr $\Rightarrow \text{SI} = \frac{prt}{100}$

$\frac{7}{5}x - x = \frac{x \times r \times 5}{100} \Rightarrow \frac{2}{5} = \frac{r}{20}$

$\Rightarrow r = \frac{20 \times 2}{5} = 8\%$ per annum

304. (c) Let the sum $= P$

Then, $\text{SI} = \frac{3P}{10}$ and time = 15 yr

$\because \text{SI} = \frac{P \times R \times T}{100} \Rightarrow \frac{3P}{10} = \frac{P \times R \times 15}{100}$

$\Rightarrow R = \frac{3 \times 100}{10 \times 15} = \frac{300}{150} \Rightarrow R = 2\%$

13

Compound Interest

When interest is calculated on the principal as well as on the interest due on the principal is called compound interest.

- **Amount** Sum of principal and compound interest is known as amount. It is denoted by A.

Important Formulae Related to CI

- When principal (P) is given on compound interest at the rate R% per annum, for t time, then $A = P\left(1+\frac{R}{100}\right)^t$ and $CI = A - P$

$$CI = P\left[\left(1+\frac{R}{100}\right)^t - 1\right]$$

- If the principal (P) is given on compound interest half-yearly at rate of R%, for time 't', then Amount (A) $= P\left(1+\frac{R}{2\times 100}\right)^{2t}$
- If the principal (P) is given on compound interest annually at rate R% for time $\left(t = c\frac{a}{b}\text{ yr}\right)$, then Amount (A) $= P\left(1+\frac{R}{100}\right)^c \times \left(1+\frac{\frac{a}{b}\times R}{100}\right)$
- When principal (P) is given for different compound interest rate for different years. Suppose interest rate are R_1%, R_2% and R_3% for 1st year, 2nd year and for 3rd year, then

$$A = P\left(1+\frac{R_1}{100}\right)\times\left(1+\frac{R_2}{100}\right)\times\left(1+\frac{R_3}{100}\right)$$

- If a certain principal at compound interest becomes x times in t_1 yr and y times in t_2 yr, then $(x)^{\frac{1}{t_1}} = (y)^{\frac{1}{t_2}}$

Ex. 1 The compound interest (in ₹, to the nearest integer) on ₹ 8950 for 2 yr at the rate of 9% per annum compounded annually is

Sol. Compound interest $= P\left[\left(1+\frac{r}{100}\right)^t - 1\right] = 8950\left[\left(1+\frac{9}{100}\right)^2 - 1\right]$

$$= 8950\left[\left(\frac{109}{100}\right)^2 - 1\right] = 8950\left[\frac{11881-10000}{10000}\right]$$

$$= 8950\times\frac{1881}{10000} = ₹\ 1683.495 \approx ₹\ 1683$$

Difference Between SI and CI

- When difference between simple interest and compound interest is given for rate R% on principal (P) for time 2 year, then

Difference between SI and CI (D) $= P\times\frac{R^2}{(100)^2}$

- When difference between SI and CI is given for rate R% on principal (P) for time 3 yr, then

Difference between SI and CI (D) $= \frac{P\times R^2\times(300+R)}{(100)^3}$

Ex. 2 The difference between the compound interest and simple interest on a certain sum for 2 yr at 10% per annum is ₹ 300. Find the sum.

Sol. Let the principal be ₹ P.

Rate of interest (r) = 10% per annum

$\therefore$ Difference (D) $= \frac{PR^2}{(100)^2}$ [$\because$ given for 2 yr]

$$\Rightarrow 300 = \frac{P(10)^2}{(100)^2} \Rightarrow P = 300\times 100 \Rightarrow P = ₹\ 30000$$

Installment

When a borrower pays the sum P in n installments, then

$$P = \left[\frac{x}{\left(1+\frac{R}{100}\right)} + \frac{x}{\left(1+\frac{R}{100}\right)^2} + \ldots.. \frac{x}{\left(1+\frac{R}{100}\right)^n}\right]$$

Where x is value of each installment and, n = Number of installments

Ex. 3 A loan of ₹ 9930 is to be returned in three equal installments where the rate of interest is 10% compounded annually. The value of each installment is

Sol. Let each installment be ₹ x.

$$\therefore\quad A = x\left(\frac{100}{100+R}\right) + x\left(\frac{100}{100+R}\right)^2 + x\left(\frac{100}{100+R}\right)^3$$

$$\Rightarrow 9930 = x\left(\frac{10}{11}\right) + x\left(\frac{10}{11}\right)^2 + x\left(\frac{10}{11}\right)^3 \quad [\because R = 10\%]$$

$$\Rightarrow 9930 = \frac{x\times 10}{11}\left\{1+\frac{10}{11}+\frac{100}{121}\right\} = \frac{x\times 10}{11}\left\{\frac{121+110+100}{121}\right\}$$

$$\Rightarrow x = \frac{9930\times 11\times 121}{10\times 331} \Rightarrow x = ₹\ 3993$$

SSC Exam Scanner

SSC CGL 2023-2020 (Tier I & II)

1. Rajnish borrowed ₹ 1500 from a bank and repaid the entire amount with interest in two equal annual installments, the first installment being paid a year after Rajnish borrowed from the bank. If the rate of interest was 40% p.a., compounded annually, then what was the value (in ₹) of each installment paid by Rajnish? **SSC CGL (Tier-II) 07/03/2023 Shift-I**

(a) 1125 (b) 1470
(c) 1350 (d) 1225

2. Find the amount (integral value only) if a sum of ₹ 6500 is being borrowed at 10% interest per annum for 2 yr if interest is compounded half-yearly. **SSC CGL (Tier-II) 06/03/2023 Shift-I**

(a) ₹ 8150 (b) ₹ 7900
(c) ₹ 7650 (d) ₹ 8250

3. What is the compound interest on a sum of ₹ 25000 after 3 yr at a rate of 12% p.a. interest compounded yearly? **SSC CGL (Tier-II) 03/03/2023 Shift-I**

(a) ₹ 10123.20 (b) ₹ 9624.00
(c) ₹ 10520.00 (d) ₹ 9956.86

4. If interest be compounded half-yearly, then find the compound interest on ₹ 8000 at the rate of 20% p.a. for 1 yr. **SSC CGL (Tier-II) 02/03/2023 Shift-I**

(a) ₹ 1675 (b) ₹ 1690
(c) ₹ 1685 (d) ₹ 1680

5. What is the present value of ₹ 10000 received in 2 yr, if the interest rate is 12% per year discounted semi-annually? **SSC CGL (Tier-I) 09/12/2022 Shift-II**

(a) ₹ 7020.94 (b) ₹ 7920.90
(c) ₹ 7920.94 (d) ₹ 7900.94

6. What would be the compound interest on ₹ 15750 at 20% p.a., in two year, if the interest is compounded half yearly? **SSC CGL (Tier-I) 03/12/2022 Shift-III**

(a) ₹ 5213.25 (b) ₹ 3307.5
(c) ₹ 7305.975 (d) ₹ 7309.575

7. A sum of ₹ 6000 is to be paid back in two equal annual installments, each installment is to be paid at the end of every year. How much is each installment if the interest is compounded annually at 2% p. a..? (Rounded-off up to two decimal places) **SSC CGL (Tier-I) 02/12/2022 Shift-I**

(a) ₹ 2092.29 (b) ₹ 3090.30
(c) ₹ 2291.29 (d) ₹ 3589.30

8. What is the difference between the compound interest (in ₹) compounded yearly and compounded half-yearly for 18 months at 20% p.a. on a sum of ₹ 12000? **SSC CGL (Tier-II) 24/08/2021 Shift-III**

(a) 121 (b) 132 (c) 145 (d) 165

9. Atul borrowed a sum of ₹ 12000 and agreed to repay it by paying ₹ 4800 at the end of first year and ₹9240 at the end of second year. What is the rate of compound interest compounded annually? **SSC CGL (Tier-II) 24/08/2021 Shift-II**

(a) 10% (b) 8% (c) 12% (d) $\frac{8}{5}$%

10. A sum of ₹ 9500 amounts to ₹ 11495 in 2 yr at a certain rate per cent per annum, interest compounded yearly. What is the simple interest (in ₹) on the same sum for the same time and double the rate? **SSC CGL (Tier-I) 24/08/2021 Shift-I**

(a) 3990 (b) 3420
(c) 4560 (d) 3800

11. At what rate per cent per annum will ₹ 7200 amount to ₹ 7938 in one year, if interest is compounded half yearly? **SSC CGL (Tier-I) 23/08/2021 Shift-I**

(a) 5% (b) 8% (c) 12% (d) 10%

12. The interest (in ₹) to be paid on a sum of ₹ 30000 at 15% p.a. after $2\frac{2}{3}$ yr. If interest compounded yearly, is **SSC CGL (Tier-I) 20/08/2021 Shift-II**

(a) 14362.50 (b) 12364.50
(c) 16342.50 (d) 13642.50

13. What is the difference (in ₹) between the simple interest and the compound interest on a sum of ₹ 8000 for $2\frac{2}{5}$ yr at the rate of 10% p.a., when the interest is compounded yearly? **SSC CGL (Tier-I) 18/08/2021 Shift-I**

(a) 147.20 (b) 152.80
(c) 155 (d) 150

14. A man borrowed a certain sum and agrees to repay it by paying ₹4000 at the end of first year and ₹7700 at the end of second year. If the rate of compound interest compounded annually is 10% p.a., then find the sum (in ₹) borrowed. **SSC CGL (Tier-I) 17/08/2021 Shift-III**

(a) 11000 (b) 10000
(c) 9000 (d) 11500

15. A certain sum becomes ₹ 13650 at 15% p.a. simple interest after 2 yr. What will be the amount (in ₹) of the same sum after 1 yr at the same rate of interest, if the interest is compounded half yearly? (nearest to a ₹) **SSC CGL (Tier-I) 17/08/2021 Shift-I**

(a) 12134 (b) 10500
(c) 13625 (d) 11000

16. A certain sum amounts to ₹ 291600 in 2 yr and to ₹ 314928 in 3 yr on compound interest compounded annually. How much will be the simple interest (in ₹) on ₹ 40000 at the same rate for 2 yr? **SSC CGL (Tier-I) 16/08/2021 Shift-III**

(a) 6400 (b) 8000
(c) 7500 (d) 9600

17. A sum of ₹ 7500 amounts to ₹ 9075 at 10% p.a., interest being compounded yearly in a certain time. The simple interest (in ₹) on the same sum for the same time and the same rate is **SSC CGL (Tier-I) 16/08/2021 Shift-I**

(a) 1500 (b) 1520
(c) 1480 (d) 1530

18. What is the compound interest (in ₹) on a sum of ₹8192 for $1\frac{1}{4}$ yr at 15% p.a. if interest is compounded 5-monthly? **SSC CGL (Tier-I) 13/08/2021 Shift-I**

(a) 1634 (b) 1740 (c) 1735 (d) 1640

19. A sum lent out at compound interest amounts to ₹ 1250 in 1 yr and to ₹ 1458 in 3 yr at a certain rate percentage per annum. What is the simple interest on the same sum for $5\frac{2}{5}$ yr at the same rate of interest? **SSC CGL (Tier-I) 07/03/2020 Shift-II**

(a) ₹520 (b) ₹600 (c) ₹500 (d) ₹480

20. The simple interest on a sum of ₹50000 at the end of 2 yr is ₹ 4000. What would be the compound interest on the same sum at the same rate for the same period? **SSC CGL (Tier-I) 07/03/2020 Shift-I**

(a) ₹ 4040 (b) ₹ 4080
(c) ₹ 4008 (d) ₹ 8000

21. Amit borrowed a sum of ₹ 25000 on simple interest. Bhola borrowed the same amount on compound interest (interest compounded yearly). At the end of 2 yr, Bhola had to pay ₹ 160 more interest than Amit. The rate of interest charged per annum is
SSC CGL (Tier-I) 06/03/2020 Shift-II
(a) $\frac{16}{25}$% (b) 8%
(c) $\frac{8}{25}$% (d) $3\frac{1}{8}$%

22. What will be the difference in compound interest on a sum of ₹ 7800 at 8% for 1 yr, when the interest is paid yearly and half yearly? SSC CGL (Tier-I) 06/03/2020 Shift-I
(a) ₹ 29.18 (b) ₹ 12.48
(c) ₹ 24.72 (d) ₹ 19.46

23. A certain amount of money at compound interest grows to ₹ 66550 in 3 yr and ₹ 73205 in 4 yr. The rate per cent per annum is
SSC CGL (Tier-I) 05/03/2020 Shift-III
(a) 10% (b) 5%
(c) 9% (d) 11%

24. *A* and *B* together borrowed a sum of ₹ 51750 at an interest rate of 7% p.a. compound interest in such a way that to settle the loan, *A* paid as much amount after 3 yr as paid by *B* after 4 yr from the day of borrowing. The sum (in ₹) borrowed by *A* was
SSC CGL (Tier-I) 05/03/2020 Shift-II
(a) 25650 (b) 26750
(c) 25000 (d) 24860

25. The compound interest on a certain sum at $16\frac{2}{3}$% p.a. for 3 yr is ₹ 6350. What will be the simple interest on the same sum at the same rate for $5\frac{2}{3}$ yr?
SSC CGL (Tier-I) 05/03/2020 Shift-I
(a) ₹ 10200 (b) ₹ 7620
(c) ₹ 11400 (d) ₹ 9600

26. A sum of ₹ 8000 invested at 10% p.a. amounts to ₹ 9261 in a certain time, interest compounded half-yearly. What will be the compound interest (in ₹) on the same sum for the same time at double the earlier rate of interest, when interest is compounded annually?
SSC CGL (Tier-I) 04/03/2020 Shift-III
(a) ₹ 2520 (b) ₹ 2480
(c) ₹ 2560 (d) ₹ 2500

SSC CPO SI 2024-2020

27. Sita takes a loan of ₹ 35000 at an interest rate of 10% compound interest, compounded annually. She agrees to pay two equal installments in 2 years, one installment at the end of each year. Find the value of each installment. (Round off to the nearest integer)
SSC CPO 29/06/2024 Shift-I
(a) ₹ 10167 (b) ₹ 30167
(c) ₹ 20167 (d) ₹ 40167

28. A certain amount of money becomes thrice in 5 yr at compound interest. How many years it will take to become 9 times ? SSC CPO 28/06/2024 Shift-I
(a) 15 yr (b) 10 yr
(c) 8 yr (d) 25 yr

29. A sum of money at compound interest doubles itself in 4 yr. In how many years does the sum become 8 times of itself at the same rate of interest? SSC CPO 27/06/2024 Shift-I
(a) 10 (b) 15 (c) 12 (d) 8

30. Peter invested a certain sum of money in a scheme paying 10% simple interest per annum, while Rachel invested half of the sum that Peter invested in a scheme paying 10% interest per annum compounded annually. Also, while Peter invested for 2 yr, Rachel invested for 3 yr. If the difference in the interest earned by Peter and Rachel was ₹ 897, what was the sum that Rachel had invested?
SSC CPO 04/10/2023 Shift-II
(a) ₹ 13000 (b) ₹ 12900
(c) ₹ 13100 (d) ₹ 12960

31. Jonathan had borrowed a sum of money 3 yr ago at 10% interest per annum compounded annually for a 5yr period, with the amount to be paid at the end of the period being ₹161051. However, there is no pre-payment penalty and Jonathan has received some bonus payment now, with which he has decided to clear his debt. How much does Jonathan have to pay now to clear his debt? SSC CPO 03/10/2023 Shift-I
(a) ₹ 133000 (b) ₹ 132900
(c) ₹ 133100 (d) ₹ 133200

32. A man borrowed ₹ 50000 from a bank at 10% p.a., compounded annually. At the end of every year, he pays ₹ 15000 as part payment of the loan and interest. How much does he still owe to the bank after three such installments?
SSC CPO 10/11/2022 Shift-II
(a) ₹ 16900 (b) ₹ 15800
(c) ₹ 15200 (d) ₹ 16200

33. The simple interest on a sum of money at 10% p.a. for 2 yr is ₹ 8100. What would be the compound interest (in ₹) on the same sum for the same period at 15% p.a. when the interest is compounded yearly? (nearest to ₹ 1) SSC CPO 25/11/2020 Shift-II
(a) ₹ 8100 (b) ₹ 12751
(c) ₹ 14671 (d) ₹ 13061

34. A sum amounts to ₹ 7562 in 4 yr and to ₹8469.44 in 5 yr, at a certain rate per cent per annum when the interest is compounded yearly. If ₹ 10000 at the same rate of interest is borrowed for 2yr, then what will be the compound interest (in ₹) ?
SSC CPO 25/11/2020 Shift-I
(a) 2544 (b) 1736
(c) 2764 (d) 1965

35. If the difference between the compound interest and simple interest at 17% on a sum of money for 2 yr (compound annually) is ₹ 433.50, then the compound interest (in ₹) is
SSC CPO 24/11/2020 Shift-I
(a) 2735.50 (b) 2500
(c) 5100 (d) 5533.50

36. A sum amounts to ₹ 7562 in 4 yr and to ₹ 8469.44 in 5 yr at a certain rate per cent per annum, when the interest is compounded yearly. The rate of interest is
SSC CPO 23/11/2020 Shift-I
(a) 12% (b) 15%
(c) 20% (d) 8%

SSC CHSL 2024-2021 (Tier I & II)

37. If an increase of 40% is observed on an amount in 4 yr at simple interest, what will be the compound interest on ₹ 80000 after 4 yr at the same rate of interest?
SSC CHSL (Tier-II) 18/11/2024
(a) ₹ 39724 (b) ₹ 29728
(c) ₹ 17128 (d) ₹ 37128

38. The compound interest of ₹ 6000 in 2 yr, if the rate of interest is 2.5% p.a. for the first year and 2% p.a. for the second year, will be
SSC CHSL (Tier-II) 10/01/2024 Shift-I
(a) ₹ 273 (b) ₹ 135
(c) ₹ 270 (d) ₹ 240

39. Compound interest on a certain sum of money invested for 1.5 yr at the rate of 10% p.a., compounded half-yearly is ₹ 5044. What is the sum? SSC CHSL (Tier-I) 17/08/2023 Shift-I

(a) ₹ 32000 (b) ₹ 37044
(c) ₹ 33000 (d) ₹ 22000

40. What is the difference between the compound interest on ₹ 6400 for 1 yr at 5% p. a. compounded yearly and half-yearly? SSC CHSL (Tier-I) 10/08/2023 Shift-III

(a) ₹ 8 (b) ₹ 9 (c) ₹ 4 (d) ₹ 7

41. The difference between the simple interest and the compound interest on a certain amount at 9% p.a for 2 yr is ₹ 162, what is the principal? SSC CHSL (Tier-I) 09/08/2023 Shift-I

(a) ₹ 19700 (b) ₹ 19000
(c) ₹ 20000 (d) ₹ 19500

42. Radha deposited ₹ 160000 at a 10% rate of compound interest per annum for 2 yr. If the interest is compounded semi-annually, then what is the compound interest (in ₹)? SSC CHSL (Tier-I) 07/08/2023 Shift-IV

(a) 16400 (b) 34481
(c) 74256 (d) 33600

43. What is the compound interest on ₹ 25000 for 3 yr at 10% p.a. compounded yearly ? SSC CHSL (Tier-I) 04/08/2023 Shift-II

(a) ₹ 8125 (b) ₹ 8000
(c) ₹ 8200 (d) ₹ 8275

44. A certain amount of money was lent for a period of 1 yr 9 months at a rate of 10% p.a. compounded annually. If the compound interests ₹ 1460, then find the amount of money lent. SSC CHSL (Tier-I) 02/08/2023 Shift-I

(a) ₹ 8200 (b) ₹ 7500
(c) ₹ 6000 (d) ₹ 8000

45. The difference between the compound interest (compounding half yearly) for 1 yr and the simple interest for 1 yr on a certain sum lent out at the annual rate of 10% is ₹ 25. What is the sum? SSC CHSL (Tier-I) 20/03/2023 Shift-III

(a) ₹ 12000 (b) ₹ 6000
(c) ₹ 8000 (d) ₹ 10000

46. What is the compound interest for 1 yr on a sum of ₹ 18000 at the annual rate of 20% p.a. compounding half-yearly? SSC CHSL (Tier-I) 17/03/2023 Shift-II

(a) ₹ 3780 (b) ₹ 2450
(c) ₹ 4500 (d) ₹ 3650

47. Rajeev invested ₹ 3000 for 2 yr at compound interest (compounded annually) in a company, which paid him interest of ₹ 1320. What will be the annual rate of interest at which Rajeev invested his money? SSC CHSL (Tier-I) 15/03/2023 Shift-IV

(a) 30% (b) 24%
(c) 16% (d) 20%

48. ₹ 6000 is lent at the annual rate of 10% for 2 yr. Which of the following is statement(s) is/are correct? SSC CHSL (Tier-I) 10/03/2023 Shift-II

I. Simple interest to be received on this sum is ₹ 1200.
II. Compound interest (compounding annually) to be received on this sum is ₹ 1260.

(a) Statement I is correct
(b) Both Statements I and II are correct
(c) Statement II is correct
(d) None of them are correct

49. What will be the compound interest on ₹ 14000 for 2 yr at the rate of 10% p.a. compounded annually? SSC CHSL (Tier-I) 09/03/2023 Shift-I

(a) ₹ 1490 (b) ₹ 6940
(c) ₹ 3490 (d) ₹ 2940

50. What will be the present value of ₹ 90774 due 2 yr hence, when the interest is compounded at 23% p.a.? SSC CHSL (Tier-I) 02/06/2022 Shift-I

(a) ₹ 65000 (b) ₹ 62950
(c) ₹ 60850 (d) ₹ 60000

51. A certain sum is invested at 26% p.a. interest compounded annually. In how many years (approx) will it double? SSC CHSL (Tier-I) 01/06/2022 Shift-I

(a) 4 (b) 3 (c) 2 (d) 5

52. Find the compound interest on ₹ 40000 after 2 yr 6 months at 20% p.a., if the interest is compounded half-yearly. SSC CHSL (Tier-I) 30/05/2022 Shift-I

(a) ₹ 24820.40 (b) ₹ 25520
(c) ₹ 24420.40 (d) ₹ 24920.40

53. A loan is to be repaid in two equal yearly installments. If the rate of interest is 10% p.a., compounded annually and each installment is ₹ 6897, then find the total interest charged. SSC CHSL (Tier-I) 27/05/2022 Shift-I

(a) ₹ 1644 (b) ₹ 1824
(c) ₹ 1914 (d) ₹ 1734

54. The simple interest on a sum of ₹ 12000 at the end of 5 yr is ₹ 6000. What would have been the compound interest on the same sum at the same rate for 3 yr when compounded annually? SSC CHSL (Tier-I) 10/08/2021 Shift-I

(a) ₹ 3970 (b) ₹ 3972
(c) ₹ 3600 (d) ₹ 2520

55. A man invests ₹ 7000 at 8% p.a. simple interest for 2 yr and ₹ 10000 at compound interest at the same rate for the same period, compounded annually. What will be the total interest and the total amount (in ₹) respectively, on maturity? SSC CHSL (Tier-I) 04/08/2021 Shift-I

(a) 19748 and 2874 (b) 2748 and 19784
(c) 19784 and 2784 (d) 2784 and 19784

56. In how many years, the compound interest, if compounded annually on a sum of ₹ 60000 at rate of 8% p.a. is ₹ 9984? SSC CHSL (Tier-I) 19/04/2021 Shift-I

(a) 3 (b) 1 (c) 4 (d) 2

57. The compound interest (in ₹, to the nearest integer) on ₹ 8950 for 2 yr at the rate of 9% p.a., compounded annually is SSC CHSL (Tier-I) 12/04/2021 Shift-II

(a) 1523 (b) 1683 (c) 1685 (d) 1468

SSC MTS 2023-2021

58. Mr. Kalra borrowed ₹ 135000 to meet the expenses of his son's education. If the rate of interest is 12% p.a. compounded annually, then how much amount will he have to make after 2 yr and 3 months to settle the account? SSC MTS 14/09/2023 Shift-I

(a) ₹ 174424.32 (b) ₹ 150640.40
(c) ₹ 149920.32 (d) ₹ 174760

59. On what sum of money will the difference between the simple interest and compound interest (Compounded annually) for 3 yr at 5% p.a. be ₹ 15.25 ? SSC MTS 13/09/2023 Shift-I

(a) ₹ 2500 (b) ₹ 1000
(c) ₹ 4000 (d) ₹ 2000

60. What is the compound interest (in ₹) on ₹ 20500 for 2 yr at 10% p.a., if the interest is compounded annually? SSC MTS 11/09/2023 Shift-II

(a) 5403 (b) 4305
(c) 4530 (d) 4350

61. An amount of ₹ 2000 amounts to ₹ 2880 in 2 yr. What will be the rate of interest, if compounded annually? SSC MTS 11/09/2023 Shift-I

(a) 12% (b) 28% (c) 10% (d) 20%

62. Find the amount, if ₹ 10200 is invested at the rate of 8% p.a. compound interest for $1\frac{1}{2}$ yr, when interest is compounded half-yearly (upto two decimal places).
SSC MTS 08/09/2023 Shift-II
(a) ₹ 11743.61 (b) ₹ 11473.61
(c) ₹ 11764.28 (d) ₹ 11347.28

63. What is the difference between the compound interest, interest compounded half-yearly on ₹ 72000 for 1.5 yr at 10% p.a. and its simple interest for 3 yr at 5% p.a.?
SSC MTS 06/09/2023 Shift-I
(a) ₹ 559 (b) ₹ 549
(c) ₹ 540 (d) ₹ 449

64. Find the amount of ₹ 75000 for 1 yr at the rate of 16% p.a., if the interest is compounded quarterly. (rounded off to two decimal places)
SSC MTS 05/09/2023 Shift-II
(a) ₹ 87379.40
(b) ₹ 89773.40
(c) ₹ 87937.40
(d) ₹ 87739.40

65. Find the compound interest (Compounded annually) on ₹ 2000 for $2\frac{1}{2}$ yr at 10% p.a.
SSC MTS 04/09/2023 Shift-II
(a) ₹ 561 (b) ₹ 500
(c) ₹ 521 (d) ₹ 541

66. The difference in interests earned on ₹150000 at an 8% rate of interest per annum in a year when the interest in compounded semi-annually and annually respectively is ₹ .... .
SSC MTS 01/09/2023 Shift-III
(a) 360 (b) 120
(c) 240 (d) 420

67. Geeta deposited a certain sum of money in her bank account which amounted to ₹ 27783 in 3 yr at 5% p.a. the interest being compounded annually. What amount did she deposit? SSC MTS 01/09/2023 Shift-I
(a) ₹ 25500 (b) ₹ 25000
(c) ₹ 26000 (d) ₹ 24000

68. The difference between the compound interest and the simple interest on a certain sum of money at 10% p.a. for 2 yr is ₹ 200. What is the sum of money, if in the case of compound interest, interest is compounded annually?
SSC MTS 15/07/2022 Shift-II
(a) ₹ 25000 (b) ₹ 15000
(c) ₹ 12000 (d) ₹ 20000

69. If the rate of interest is 4% for the first year, 5% for the second year and 6% for the third year, then find the compound interest on ₹ 10000 for 3 yr, if interest is compounded annually ? SSC MTS 13/07/2022 Shift-I
(a) ₹ 1580.25 (b) ₹ 1575.20
(c) ₹ 1500.00 (d) ₹ 1570.50

70. The compound interest on ₹ 20000 at 5% p.a., compounded annually, is ₹ 2050. What is the time period? SSC MTS 13/07/2022 Shift-I
(a) 2.5 yr (b) 2 yr
(c) 4 yr (d) 3 yr

71. Rachit invests ₹ 12000 for a 2 yr period at a certain rate of simple interest p.a.. Prasad invests ₹ 12000 for a 2 yr period at the same rate of interest p.a. as Rachit, but in Prasad's case the interest is compounded annually. Find the rate of interest p.a. in Prasad receives ₹ 172.80 more as interest than Rachit at the end of the 2 yr period. SSC MTS 12/07/2022 Shift-I
(a) 10% (b) 8% (c) 12% (d) 5 %

72. ₹ 12000 is lent for one year at the rate of 15% p.a., the interest being compounded annually. If the compounding of the interest is done half-yearly, then how much more interest will be obtained at the end of the 1 yr period on the same initial sum ?
SSC MTS 12/07/2022 Shift-I
(a) ₹ 72.5 (b) ₹ 82.8
(c) ₹ 60.5 (d) ₹ 67.5

73. The difference between the simple interest and the compound interest at the same rate for ₹ 32000 for 2 yr is ₹ 80. What is the rate of interest, if in the case of compound interest interest is compounded annually?
SSC MTS 11/07/2022 Shift-I
(a) 8% p.a. (b) 2% p.a.
(c) 5% p.a. (d) 12% p.a.

74. The interest compounded annually, on a sum of ₹ 3240 after 2 yr is ₹ 370. What is the rate of interest, correct up to two decimal places? SSC MTS 02/11/2021 Shift-III
(a) 5.26% (b) 4.67%
(c) 5.56% (d) 4.05%

75. A farmer borrowed ₹ 132000 from a money lender to do cultivation in his field. The rate of interest is 12.5% p.a. compounded annually. At the end of 2 yr, he cleared his loan by paying ₹ 107062.50 and his scooter. The cost (in ₹) of the scooter is SSC MTS 02/11/2021 Shift-II
(a) 75000 (b) 45000
(c) 60000 (d) 50000

76. If a sum increases by 21% after 2 yr, then the rate of compound interest p.a., when compounded annually must be
SSC MTS 02/11/2021 Shift-I
(a) 10.5% (b) 11.5%
(c) 10% (d) 11%

SSC GD Constable 2024 & 2023

77. A principal is lent at a certain rate of compound interest (compounding annually). The amount at the end of 1 yr is ₹ 1150 and at the end of 2 yr is ₹ 1322.5. What is the principal ?
SSC GD 26/02/2024 Shift-I
(a) ₹ 1450 (b) ₹ 1600
(c) ₹ 1750 (d) ₹ 1000

78. A principal is lent at a certain rate of compound interest (compounding annually). The amount at the end of 3 yr is ₹ 13310 and at the end of 4 yr is ₹ 14641. What is the principal?
SSC GD 24/02/2024 Shift-III
(a) ₹ 10700 (b) ₹ 12200
(c) ₹ 14500 (d) ₹ 10000

79. What will be the compound interest (compounding annually) on a sum of ₹ 9000 at the rate of 32% p.a. for 2 yr?
SSC GD 24/02/2024 Shift-II
(a) ₹ 6681.6
(b) ₹ 6400.4
(c) ₹ 6790.7
(d) ₹ 6908.3

80. The compound interest (compounding half-yearly) received on ₹ 2200 for 1.5 yr is ₹ 3836.8 What is the rate of interest p.a.? SSC GD 24/02/2024 Shift-I
(a) 75% (b) 65%
(c) 80% (d) 60%

81. The principal amount of ₹ 30000 is borrowed at compound interest (compounded annually) at the rate of 7% p.a.. What will be the amount after 2 yr?
SSC GD 23/02/2024 Shift-III
(a) ₹ 31247
(b) ₹ 33248
(c) ₹ 34347
(d) ₹ 35687

82. What will be the compound interest (compounding annually) on a principal sum of ₹ 72000 for 3 yr at the rate of 16% p.a.? SSC GD 23/02/2024 Shift-III

(a) ₹ 38245.22 (b) ₹ 42248.64
(c) ₹ 40384.51 (d) ₹ 36574.31

83. A person borrowed ₹ 15000 on compound interest at the rate of 30% p.a.. If the interest is compounded half-yearly, then what will be the amount to be paid after 1 yr? SSC GD 23/02/2024 Shift-I

(a) ₹ 19837.5 (b) ₹ 20428.5
(c) ₹ 18282.5 (d) ₹ 17482.5

84. Compound interest (compounding annually) on a sum for 2 yr is ₹ 967.5. If rate of interest is 15% p.a., then what is the sum? SSC GD 22/02/2024 Shift-IV

(a) ₹ 2800 (b) ₹ 2700
(c) ₹ 3000 (d) ₹ 2400

85. On a sum, simple interest at the annual rate of 10% for 8 yr is ₹ 8000. What will be the compound interest on the same sum at the annual rate of per cent (compounding annually) for 3 yr? SSC GD 22/02/2024 Shift-II

(a) ₹ 3220 (b) ₹ 3310
(c) ₹ 3750 (d) ₹ 3450

86. A sum of ₹ 15000 invested at compound interest (compounding annually) at the rate of 12% p.a. for 2 yr. Find the compound interest. SSC GD 22/02/2024 Shift-III

(a) ₹ 4124 (b) ₹ 4024
(c) ₹ 3668 (d) ₹ 3816

87. The simple interest on a certain sum of money at rate of interest 6% p.a. for 2 yr is ₹ 960. What is the compound interest (compounding annually) on the same sum for the same period and at the same rate of interest? SSC GD 22/02/2024 Shift-I

(a) ₹ 985.4 (b) ₹ 988.8
(c) ₹ 1122.2 (d) ₹ 1025.1

88. The difference between the compound interest (compounding half-yearly) for 1 yr and the simple interest for 1 yr on a certain sum lent out at the annual rate of 30% is ₹ 337.5. What is the sum? SSC GD 21/02/2024 Shift-IV

(a) ₹ 17700
(b) ₹ 15000
(c) ₹ 17000
(d) ₹ 18500

89. The compound interest (compounding half-yearly) received on ₹ 1000 for 2 yr is ₹ 464.1. What is the rate of interest p.a.? SSC GD 21/02/2024 Shift-III

(a) 35% (b) 30%
(c) 25% (d) 20%

90. The compound interest (compounding half-yearly) received on ₹ 22000 for 2 yr is ₹ 10210.2. What is the rate of interest p.a.? SSC GD 21/02/2024 Shift-III

(a) 20% (b) 40%
(c) 25% (d) 30%

91. Simple interest and compound interest (compounding annually) on a principal at a certain rate of interest for 2 yr is ₹ 12000 and ₹ 14400, respectively. What is the principal? SSC GD 21/02/2024 Shift-I

(a) ₹ 18000 (b) ₹ 15000
(c) ₹ 17000 (d) ₹ 22000

92. If interest is being compounded annually, then what sum will amount to ₹ 9464 in 2 yr at the rate of 30% p.a. at compound interest? SSC GD 20/02/2024 Shift-III

(a) ₹ 6800 (b) ₹ 5750
(c) ₹ 5600 (d) ₹ 5400

93. Simple interest and compound interest on a principal at a certain rate of interest for 2 yr is ₹ 12800 and ₹ 14400, respectively. What is the principal? SSC GD 20/02/2024 Shift-IV

(a) ₹ 27800 (b) ₹ 25600
(c) ₹ 24400 (d) ₹ 29900

94. ₹ 9000 is lent at the rate of 80% p.a. on compound interest (compounded half yearly). What will be the compound interest of 12 months? SSC GD 20/02/2024 Shift-II

(a) ₹ 8700 (b) ₹ 9000
(c) ₹ 8640 (d) ₹ 8760

95. A sum of money placed at compound interest (compounding annually) doubles itself in 10 yr. Find the time in which it will amount to 4 times itself. SSC GD 20/02/2024 Shift-I

(a) 10 yr (b) 15 yr
(c) 14 yr (d) 20 yr

96. A principal becomes ₹ 19683 in 3 yr at 8% p.a. compound interest. compounding annually. What is the principal? SSC GD 13/02/2023 Shift-IV

(a) ₹ 16825 (b) ₹ 14825
(c) ₹ 15625 (d) ₹ 13526

97. Vidhi gave Radha ₹ 8000 on compound interest for 2 yr at 5% p.a., compounding annually. How much loss would Vidhi have suffered had she given it to Radha for 2 yr at 5% p.a. on simple interest? SSC GD 13/02/2023 Shift-IV

(a) ₹ 12 (b) ₹ 18
(c) ₹ 20 (d) ₹ 15

98. Divide ₹ 5309 between A and B, so that the amount of A after 4 yr is equal to the amount of B after 6 yr, the interest being compounded at 6% p.a.. compounding annually. SSC GD 13/02/2023 Shift-II

(a) ₹ 2809, ₹ 2500
(b) ₹ 2759, ₹ 2550
(c) ₹ 2659, ₹ 2650
(d) ₹ 2709, ₹ 2600

99. If the difference between the simple interest and the compound interest, compounding annually on a certain sum borrowed for 2 yr at 8% p.a. is ₹ 512, then find the sum borrowed (in ₹). SSC GD 09/02/2023 Shift-II

(a) ₹ 62100 (b) ₹ 2100
(c) ₹ 1200 (d) ₹ 80000

100. Find the principal if the interest compounded at the rate of 12% p.a., compounding annually for 2 yr is ₹ 1908. SSC GD 09/02/2023 Shift-I

(a) ₹ 6500 (b) ₹ 5400
(c) ₹ 7500 (d) ₹ 4500

101. What is the rate of compound interest p.a., if a sum becomes $\frac{64}{27}$ times in 3 yr? SSC GD 08/02/2023 Shift-I

(a) $21\frac{1}{3}\%$

(b) $16\frac{1}{3}\%$

(c) $25\frac{1}{4}\%$

(d) $33\frac{1}{3}\%$

102. A certain sum amounts to ₹ 7200 in 2 yr at 6% p.a. compound interest, compounded annually. Find the sum (in ₹ to the nearest integer). SSC GD 08/02/2023 Shift-I

(a) ₹ 6400 (b) ₹ 6449
(c) ₹ 6408 (d) ₹ 6507

103. At what rate of compound interest does a sum of money become 3.375 fold in 3 yr, compounding annually? SSC GD 07/02/2023 Shift-I

(a) 50% (b) 200%
(c) 100% (d) 150%

104. Compound interest is charged on a certain sum for 2 yr at 10% rate p.a., compounding annually. If the amount becomes ₹605, then the principal (in ₹) is
SSC GD 06/02/2023 Shift-I

(a) 600 (b) 550 (c) 500 (d) 650

105. The compound interest on ₹1000000 at 3% p.a., compounding annually is ₹ 92727. The number of years required for this is
SSC GD 06/02/2023 Shift-I

(a) 4 (b) 2 (c) 5 (d) 3

106. If the rate of interest be 16% p.a. for the first year, 20% p.a. for the second year and 15% p.a. for the third year, then find the compound interest on ₹15000 for 3 yr.
SSC GD 02/02/2023 Shift-I

(a) ₹ 8012 (b) ₹ 9012
(c) ₹ 8015 (d) ₹ 9015

107. A sum of money amounts of ₹ 14112 at the rate of 20% p.a. compounded annually for 3 yr. Find the sum of money.
SSC GD 01/02/2023 Shift-I

(a) ₹ 8099.60
(b) ₹ 7167.70
(c) ₹ 9160.67
(d) ₹ 8166.67

SSC Selection Post 2023-2022

108. An item is bought on a condition that three equal installments of ₹ 3993 are to be paid at a rate of 10% compound interest, compounded annually. The cost of the item is **Matric Level 27/06/2023 Shift-I**

(a) ₹ 10000
(b) ₹ 9050
(c) ₹ 9590
(d) ₹ 9930

109. Arif repaid a loan by paying ₹15625 after 3 yr at a rate of 25% p.a. compounded annually. What was the amount of the loan?
Graduate Level 01/08/2022 Shift-IV

(a) ₹10000 (b) ₹ 8000
(c) ₹ 9500 (d) ₹ 9000

110. The compound interest on ₹ 50000 at the rate of 7% per annum compounded annually, for a certain period of time, is ₹ 7245. Find the time period (in years).
Matric Level 01/08/2022 Shift-I

(a) 1 (b) 2 (c) 2.5 (d) 1.5

111. A sum of money doubles itself in 5 yr at a certain rate of compound interest. In how many years will it be sixteen times at the same rate?
Matric Level 01/08/2022 Shift-I

(a) 15 (b) 10 (c) 25 (d) 20

Right Answers

1	(d)	2	(b)	3	(a)	4	(d)	5	(c)	6	(d)	7	(b)	8	(b)	9	(a)	10	(d)
11	(d)	12	(d)	13	(a)	14	(b)	15	(a)	16	(a)	17	(a)	18	(a)	19	(c)	20	(b)
21	(b)	22	(b)	23	(a)	24	(b)	25	(a)	26	(c)	27	(c)	28	(b)	29	(c)	30	(a)
31	(c)	32	(a)	33	(d)	34	(a)	35	(d)	36	(a)	37	(d)	38	(a)	39	(a)	40	(c)
41	(c)	42	(b)	43	(d)	44	(d)	45	(d)	46	(a)	47	(d)	48	(b)	49	(d)	50	(d)
51	(b)	52	(c)	53	(b)	54	(b)	55	(c)	56	(d)	57	(b)	58	(a)	59	(d)	60	(b)
61	(d)	62	(b)	63	(b)	64	(d)	65	(d)	66	(c)	67	(d)	68	(d)	69	(b)	70	(b)
71	(c)	72	(d)	73	(c)	74	(c)	75	(c)	76	(c)	77	(d)	78	(d)	79	(a)	80	(c)
81	(c)	82	(c)	83	(a)	84	(c)	85	(b)	86	(d)	87	(b)	88	(b)	89	(d)	90	(a)
91	(b)	92	(c)	93	(b)	94	(c)	95	(d)	96	(c)	97	(c)	98	(a)	99	(d)	100	(c)
101	(d)	102	(c)	103	(a)	104	(c)	105	(d)	106	(b)	107	(d)	108	(d)	109	(b)	110	(b)
111	(d)																		

Solutions

1. (d) Given, $A = ₹\,1500$ and $r = 40\%$ p.a.

Number of installments = 2

Let the value of each installment = ₹ x

$$\text{Borrowed amount} = \frac{x}{\left(1+\frac{r}{100}\right)^1} + \frac{x}{\left(1+\frac{r}{100}\right)^2}$$

$$\Rightarrow 1500 = \frac{x}{\left(1+\frac{40}{100}\right)^1} + \frac{x}{\left(1+\frac{40}{100}\right)^2}$$

$$\Rightarrow 1500 = \frac{x}{\left(1+\frac{2}{5}\right)^1} + \frac{x}{\left(1+\frac{2}{5}\right)^2}$$

$$\Rightarrow 1500 = \frac{5x}{7} + \frac{25x}{49}$$

$$\Rightarrow 1500 = \frac{35x+25x}{49} \Rightarrow 1500 = \frac{60x}{49}$$

$$\Rightarrow \quad x = \frac{1500 \times 49}{60} \Rightarrow x = 25 \times 49$$

Each installment = ₹ 1225

Speedy Method

$R = 40\% = \frac{2}{5}$

Principal	:	Installment
(5	:	7) × 7
$(5)^2$	:	$(7)^2$

(∵ Installment is same)

Total borrowed amount = (35 + 25) → ₹ 1500

60 → ₹ 1500

∴ Each installment (49) → ₹ 1225

2. (b) Given, $P = ₹\,6500$, $r = 10\%$ p.a.

$$\therefore A = P\left(1+\frac{r}{2\times 100}\right)^{2t} \text{ (Half yearly)}$$

$$= 6500\left(1+\frac{10}{200}\right)^{2\times 2}$$

$$= 6500 \times \frac{21}{20} \times \frac{21}{20} \times \frac{21}{20} \times \frac{21}{20} = 7900.79$$

$A = ₹\,7900$

3. (a) $A = 25000\left(1+\frac{12}{100}\right)^3$

$$= 25000 \times \frac{28}{25} \times \frac{28}{25} \times \frac{28}{25}$$

$A = 35123.20$

∵ CI = $A - P$ = 35123.20 − 25000

∴ CI = ₹ 10123.20

4. (d) $(P) = ₹\,8000$

$(r) = 20\%, (t) = 1$ yr

For half-yearly,

$$A = P\left(1+\frac{r}{2\times 100}\right)^{2\times t}$$

$$A = 8000\left(1+\frac{20}{2\times 100}\right)^{2\times 1}$$

$$= 8000 \times \frac{11}{10} \times \frac{11}{10} = 80 \times 121$$

$A = ₹\,9680$

Compound Interest (CI)

$= A - P = 9680 - 8000$

$CI = ₹\ 1680$

5. (c) Here, $r = \frac{12}{2} = 6\%$ per half year

and $t = 2 \times 2 = 4$

According to the question,

Required present value $(P) = A \div \left(1 + \frac{R}{100}\right)^t$

$= 10000 \div \left(1 + \frac{6}{100}\right)^4$

$= 10^4 \times \left(\frac{50}{53}\right)^4 = \left(\frac{10 \times 50}{53}\right)^4$

$= (9.43396)^4 = ₹\ 7920.94$

6. (d) Here, $P = ₹\ 15750$

$R = 20\%, T\ 2$ yr

$\because$ Compounded half yearly,

$\therefore \quad A = 15750\left(1 + \frac{10}{100}\right)^4$

$\Rightarrow \quad A = \frac{15750 \times 11 \times 11 \times 11 \times 11}{10 \times 10 \times 10 \times 10}$

$= ₹\ 23059.575$

Hence, $CI = ₹\ (23059.575 - 15750) = ₹\ 7309.575$

7. (b) $R = 2\% = \frac{1}{50}$

$P : I$

$2550\ (50 : 51)_{\times 51} = 2601$

$2500 : 2601$

Total sum $= ₹\ 6000$

$2550 + 2500 = ₹\ 6000$

$5050 = ₹\ 6000$

$1 = ₹\ \frac{6000}{5050}$

$\therefore \quad 2601 = ₹\ \frac{6000}{5050} \times 2601 = ₹\ 3090.30$

8. (b) For compound interest yearly.

$P = ₹\ 12000, R = 20\%$ p.a.

$T = 18 \text{ months} = 1 + \frac{6}{12} = 1\frac{1}{2}$ yr

$$CI = 12000\left[\left(1 + \frac{20}{100}\right)^1\left(1 + \frac{20 \times \frac{1}{2}}{100}\right) - 1\right]$$

$$= 12000\left[\frac{6}{5} \times \frac{11}{10} - 1\right] = 12000\left[\frac{33 - 25}{25}\right]$$

$= 480 \times 8 = ₹\ 3840$

For compound interest half yearly

$P = ₹\ 12000, R = \frac{20}{2} = 10\%, T = 3$ yr

$$\therefore\ CI = P\left[\left(1 + \frac{R}{100}\right)^T - 1\right]$$

$$= 12000\left[\left(1 + \frac{10}{100}\right)^3 - 1\right]$$

$$= 12000\left[\frac{1331 - 1000}{1000}\right] = 12 \times 331$$

$= ₹\ 3972$

$\therefore$ Required difference $= 3972 - 3840 = ₹\ 132$

Speedy Method

For $1\frac{1}{2}$ yr	For 3 yr
Rate $= 20\% = \frac{20}{100}$	$R = 10\% = \frac{1}{10}$
$P : A$	$P : A$
$100 : 120$	$10 : 11$
$100 : 110$	$10 : 11$
$1000 : 13200$	$10 : 11$
	$1000 : 1331$
	$10000 : 13310$

$\because 10000 \rightarrow ₹\ 12000$

$\therefore$ CI difference $= 13310 - 13200 = 110$

$\therefore$ CI difference $= 110 \times \frac{12000}{10000} = ₹\ 132$

9. (a) Principal for the second year

= Amount of 1st year − 4800

Principal $= 12000\left(1 + \frac{R}{100}\right)^1 - 4800$

Now, put this principal value in

$A = P\left(1 + \frac{R}{100}\right)^t$, where

P is given above, and $A = ₹\ 9240$, t = 1 yr

$\therefore \quad A = P\left(1 + \frac{r}{100}\right)^t$

$\Rightarrow 9240 = \left[12000\left(1 + \frac{r}{100}\right)^1 - 4800\right]\left(1 + \frac{r}{100}\right)$

$\Rightarrow 9240 = (12000 + 120r - 4800)\left(1 + \frac{r}{100}\right)$

$\Rightarrow 9240 = (120r + 7200)\left(1 + \frac{r}{100}\right)$

$\Rightarrow 9240 = 120r + 1 \cdot 2r^2 + 7200 + 72r$

$\Rightarrow \quad 1.2r^2 + 192r - 2040 = 0 \quad$ [Divide by 1.2]

$\Rightarrow \quad r^2 + 160r - 1700 = 0$

$\Rightarrow (r + 170)(r - 10) = 0 \Rightarrow r = 10\%$

Hence, required rate% = 10%

10. (d) We know that, $A = P\left(1 + \frac{r}{100}\right)^t$

$\Rightarrow \quad \frac{11495}{9500} = \left(1 + \frac{r}{100}\right)^2$

$\Rightarrow \quad \sqrt{\frac{11495}{9500}} = \left(1 + \frac{r}{100}\right)$

$\Rightarrow \quad 1.1 = 1 + \frac{r}{100} \Rightarrow 1.1 - 1 = \frac{r}{100}$

$\Rightarrow \quad 0.1 = \frac{r}{100} \quad \Rightarrow r = 10\%$

Hence, $SI = \frac{9500 \times 20 \times 2}{100} = ₹\ 3800$

11. (d) Principal : Amount

$7200 : 7938$

$\sqrt{400} : \sqrt{441}$

$20 : 21$

+1

Rate% $= \frac{(21 - 20)}{20} \times 100\% = 5\%$

As interest is compounded half yearly.

So, $r = 2 \times 5\% = 10\%$

12. (d) We know that,

$A = P\left(1 + \frac{r}{100}\right)^t \times \left(1 + \frac{x}{y}\frac{r}{100}\right)$

$= 30000\left(1 + \frac{15}{100}\right)^2 \times \left(1 + \frac{2}{3} \times \frac{15}{100}\right)$

$= 30000 \times \frac{115}{100} \times \frac{115}{100} \times \frac{330}{300} = ₹\ 43642.5$

$\therefore CI = A - P = 43642.5 - 30000$

$= ₹\ 13642.5$

13. (a) We know that,

$SI = \frac{Prt}{100} = \frac{8000 \times 12 \times 10}{5 \times 100} = ₹\ 1920$

and $A = P\left(1 + \frac{r}{100}\right)^t\left(1 + \frac{x}{y}\frac{r}{100}\right)$

$= 8000\left(1 + \frac{10}{100}\right)^2\left(1 + \frac{2}{5} \times \frac{10}{100}\right)$

$= 8000 \times \frac{11}{10} \times \frac{11}{10} \times \frac{26}{25} = ₹\ 10067.2$

Now, $CI = A - P$

$= 10067.2 - 8000 = ₹\ 2067.2$

$\therefore$ Required difference

$= 2067.2 - 1920 = ₹\ 147.20$

14. (b) $\because \quad A_1 = P_1\left(1 + \frac{r}{100}\right)^n$

$\therefore \quad 4000 = P_1\left(1 + \frac{10}{100}\right)$

$\Rightarrow \quad P_1 = \frac{4000 \times 100}{110} = ₹\ \frac{40000}{11}$

Again, $A_2 = P_2\left(1 + \frac{r}{100}\right)^n$

$\Rightarrow \ 7700 = P_2\left(1 + \frac{10}{100}\right)^2$

$\Rightarrow P_2 = \frac{7700 \times 100 \times 100}{110 \times 110} = ₹\ \frac{70000}{11}$

$\therefore$ Total sum $= \frac{40000}{11} + \frac{70000}{11}$

$= \frac{110000}{11} = ₹\ 10000$

15. (a) $A = P + \frac{P \times 15 \times 2}{100}$

$\Rightarrow 13650 = 1.3P$

$\therefore \quad P = ₹\ 10500$

Same principal,

By using CI method,

Amount (A) $= P\left(1 + \frac{R}{100}\right)^T$

For half-yearly time let 2 cycle

Rate $= \frac{15}{2}\%$

$\therefore \quad A = 10500\left(1 + \frac{15}{2 \times 100}\right)^2 = 10500 \times \left(\frac{43}{40}\right)^2$

Amount $= 10500 \times 1.15$

$= 12134.06 \approx 12134$

16. (a) *A* certain sum amounts to 291600 in 2 yr and 314928 in 3 yr.

Rate per cent $= \left[\dfrac{A_2 - A_1}{A_1}\right] \times 100$

$= \dfrac{(314928 - 291600)}{291600} \times 100$

$= \dfrac{23328}{291600} \times 100 = 8\%$

$R = 8\%,\ T = 2$ yr, $P = ₹\ 40000$

$\therefore\ \text{SI} = \dfrac{40000 \times 8 \times 2}{100}$

$\Rightarrow\ \text{SI} = ₹\ 6400$

17. (a) We know that, $A = P\left(1 + \dfrac{R}{100}\right)^t$

$\therefore\ 9075 = 7500\left(1 + \dfrac{10}{100}\right)^t$

$\Rightarrow\ \dfrac{9075}{7500} = \left(1 + \dfrac{1}{10}\right)^t \Rightarrow \left(\dfrac{121}{100}\right) = \left(\dfrac{11}{10}\right)^t$

$\Rightarrow\ \left(\dfrac{11}{10}\right)^2 = \left(\dfrac{11}{10}\right)^t\ \therefore\ t = 2$ yr

Hence, $\text{SI} = \dfrac{7500 \times 10 \times 2}{100} = ₹\ 1500$

18. (a) Time = 15 months

Rate = 15% p.a.

Rate for 12 months = 15%

Rate for 5 months $= \dfrac{15}{12} \times 5 = \dfrac{75}{12} = \dfrac{25}{4}\%$

By Formula, $A = P\left(1 + \dfrac{R}{100}\right)^t$

$\Rightarrow\ A = 8192\left(1 + \dfrac{25}{4 \times 100}\right)^3$

$\Rightarrow\ A = 8192 \times \left(1 + \dfrac{1}{16}\right)^3$

$\Rightarrow\ A = 8192\left(\dfrac{17}{16}\right)^3$

$\Rightarrow\ A = 8192 \times \dfrac{17 \times 17 \times 17}{16 \times 16 \times 16} = ₹\ 9826$

Hence, CI = 9826 − 8192 = ₹ 1634

19. (c) $1250 = P\left(1 + \dfrac{r}{100}\right)^1$ ...(i)

$1458 = P\left(1 + \dfrac{r}{100}\right)^3$ ...(ii)

From Eqs. (i) and (ii), we get

$\dfrac{1458}{1250} = \dfrac{\left(1 + \dfrac{r}{100}\right)^3}{\left(1 + \dfrac{r}{100}\right)^1}$

$\Rightarrow\ \left(1 + \dfrac{r}{100}\right)^2 = \dfrac{729}{625}$

$\Rightarrow\ \left(1 + \dfrac{r}{100}\right) = \sqrt{\dfrac{729}{625}} = \dfrac{27}{25}$

$\Rightarrow\ \dfrac{r}{100} = \dfrac{27}{25} - 1 = \dfrac{2}{25}$

$\Rightarrow\ r = \dfrac{2 \times 100}{25} = 8\%$

From Eq. (i), $1250 = P\left(1 + \dfrac{8}{100}\right)$

$\Rightarrow\ P = \dfrac{1250 \times 25}{27}$

For simple interest same sum,

$t = 5\dfrac{2}{5}\text{yr} = \dfrac{27}{5}\text{ yr},\ r = 8\%$

$\text{SI} = \dfrac{P \times r \times t}{100} = \dfrac{1250 \times 8 \times 27 \times 25}{27 \times 5 \times 100}$

$\therefore$ SI = 125 × 4 = ₹ 500

20. (b) $\text{SI} = 4000 = \dfrac{50000 \times r \times 2}{100}$

$\Rightarrow\ r = 8/2 = 4\%$

$\therefore$ Amount $(A) = 50000\left(1 + \dfrac{4}{100}\right)^2$

$= 50000 \times \dfrac{26}{25} \times \dfrac{26}{25}$

Amount $(A) = ₹\ 54080$

$\therefore$ CI = 54080 − 50000 = ₹ 4080

21. (b) Given, $P = ₹\ 25000$, time = 2 yr,

Difference = ₹ 160

We know, the difference between CI and SI for 2 yr $= P\left(\dfrac{r}{100}\right)^2$

$\therefore\ 160 = \dfrac{25000 \times r^2}{100 \times 100} \Rightarrow r^2 = 64 \Rightarrow r = 8\%$

22. (b) Interest rate for 1 yr, when interest compounded half-yearly $= \dfrac{8}{2} = 4\%$

Total interest rate for, at the end of the year when interest compounded half-yearly

$= \left[4 + 4 + \dfrac{4 \times 4}{100}\right] = [8 + 0.16]\% = 8.16\%$

Difference of rate = 8.16 − 8 = 0.16%

Now, 0.16% of ₹ 7800 $= \dfrac{7800 \times 16}{100 \times 100} = ₹\ 12.48$

23. (a) Interest of 1 yr = 73205 − 66550

= ₹ 6655

$\therefore\ R\% = \dfrac{6655}{66550} \times 100 = 10\%$

24. (b) Let amount borrowed by $A = ₹\ x$

Then, amount borrowed by $B = ₹\ (51750 - x)$

We know that, $A = P\left(1 + \dfrac{r}{100}\right)^t$

According to the question,

$x\left(1 + \dfrac{7}{100}\right)^3 = (51750 - x)\left(1 + \dfrac{7}{100}\right)^4$

$\Rightarrow\ x = (51750 - x)\left(\dfrac{107}{100}\right)$

$\Rightarrow\ 100x + 107x = 51750 \times 107$

$\therefore\ x = \dfrac{51750 \times 107}{207} = ₹\ 26750$

25. (a) $\text{CI} = 6350 = P\left[\left(1 + \dfrac{50}{300}\right)^3 - 1\right]$

$\Rightarrow\ 6350 = P\left[\left(\dfrac{7}{6}\right)^3 - 1\right]$

$\Rightarrow\ 6350 = P\left[\dfrac{343 - 216}{216}\right]$

$\Rightarrow\ P = \dfrac{6350 \times 216}{127}$

$\therefore\ P = ₹\ 10800$

$\therefore\ \text{SI} = \dfrac{10800 \times \dfrac{50}{3} \times \dfrac{17}{3}}{100}$

$= \dfrac{1200 \times 50 \times 17}{100} = ₹\ 10200$

26. (c) As we know,

$P : A$ for 1 yr $= \sqrt[3]{8000} : \sqrt[3]{9261} = 20 : 21$

$\therefore$ Percentage $= \dfrac{1}{20} \times 100 = 5\%$ (satisfied)

Time = 1 yr 6 months [three half yearly cycle]

Now rate = 20%

Rate for 1 yr 6 months $= 20 + 10 + \dfrac{(20 \times 10)}{100}$

= 30 + 2 = 32%

$\therefore$ 32% of 8000 = ₹ 2560

27. (c) Let the value of each installment be ₹ X.

Total amount is ₹ P.

$\therefore\ P = X(K + K^2 + K^3 + \dots)$

Where, $K = \dfrac{100}{100 + R}$

In this question, there are only two years and $R = 10\%$, then,

$P = X(K + K^2)$

$\Rightarrow\ 35000 = X\left\{\left(\dfrac{10}{11}\right) + \left(\dfrac{10}{11}\right)^2\right\}$

$\Rightarrow\ 35000 = X\left\{\dfrac{10}{11} + \dfrac{100}{121}\right\}$

$\Rightarrow\ 35000 = X\left\{\dfrac{210}{121}\right\}$

$\therefore\ X = ₹\ 20167$

Speedy Method

$R\% = 10\%,\ t = 2$ yr

P	:	Installment
(110) 10 × 11	:	11 × 11 (121)
(100) 10 × 10	:	11 × 11 (121)
210		

Now, 210 = 35000

$\therefore\ 121 = \dfrac{121 \times 35000}{210} = 20167$

28. (b) Let the sum be P.

It becomes $3P$ in 5 yr.

i.e., $P\left(1 + \dfrac{r}{100}\right)^5 = 3P$ [$t = 5$ yr]

$\Rightarrow\ \left(1 + \dfrac{r}{100}\right)^5 = 3$

Now, when it becomes 9 times i.e. $(3)^2$,

$\Rightarrow\ \left[\left(1 + \dfrac{r}{100}\right)^5\right]^2 = (3)^2$

$\Rightarrow\ \left(1 + \dfrac{r}{100}\right)^{10} = 9 \Rightarrow t = 10$ yr

Speedy Method

If a certain principle at compound interest becomes x times in t_1 yr and y times in t_2 yr then,

$(x)^{1/t_1} = (y)^{1/t_2}$

Now, $(3)^{1/5} = (9)^{1/t_2}$

$(3)^{1/5} = (3^2)^{1/t_2}$

$\therefore \frac{1}{5} = \frac{2}{t_2} \Rightarrow t_2 = 10$ yr

29. (c) Given, A sum of money 'P' becomes '$2P$' in 4 yr.

i.e. $P\left(1+\frac{r}{100}\right)^4 = 2P$

$\Rightarrow \left(1+\frac{r}{100}\right)^4 = 2$

Now, To become 8 times *i.e*, 2^3, we have

$\left[\left(1+\frac{r}{100}\right)^4\right]^t = (2)^3 \Rightarrow t = 4\times 3 = 12$ yr

Speedy Method

$x^{1/t_1} = y^{1/t_2}$

$(2)^{1/4} = (8)^{1/t_2}$

$(2)^{1/4} = (2^3)^{1/t_2}$

$\therefore \frac{1}{4} = \frac{3}{t_2} \Rightarrow t_2 = 12$ yr

30. (a) Let Peter invest = ₹ 100

Then, Rachel invest $= \frac{100}{2} =$ ₹ 50

Peter's simple interest $= \frac{100\times 10\times 2}{100} =$ ₹ 20

Rachel's compound interest

$= 50\left[\left(1+\frac{10}{100}\right)^3 - 1\right] = 50\left[\left(\frac{110}{100}\right)^3 - 1\right]$

$= 50\left[\frac{1331}{1000} - 1\right] = 50\times\frac{331}{1000} = 16.55$

Difference = SI − CI = ₹ (20 − 16.55) = ₹ 3.45

According to the question,

$3.45 \to 897$

$1 \to \frac{897}{3.45}$

Rachels invested money $= \frac{897}{3.45}\times 50$

= ₹ 13000

Hence, the correct answer is ₹ 13000.

31. (c) Let the amount borrowed be ₹ P.

Amount (A) = ₹16105

Then, $P\left(1+\frac{10}{100}\right)^5 = 161051$

$\Rightarrow P\left(1+\frac{10}{100}\right)^3 \times \left(\frac{11}{10}\right)^2 = 161051$

$\therefore$ Amount paid after 3 yr, $P\left(1+\frac{10}{100}\right)^3$

$= \frac{161051\times 100}{121} =$ ₹133100

32. (a) Borrowed amount = ₹ 50000.

Rate = 10%

According to the question,

The first year, $50000\times\frac{110}{100} =$ ₹55000

Remaining amount = 55000 − 15000 = ₹40000

The second year, $40000\times\frac{110}{100} =$ ₹ 44000

$\therefore$ Remaining amount = 44000 − 15000

= ₹ 29000

The third year, $29000\times\frac{110}{100} =$ ₹ 31900

$\therefore$ Remaining amount = 31900 − 15000

= ₹ 16900

33. (d) According to the question,

$8100 = \frac{P\times 10\times 2}{100}$

$\therefore P =$ ₹ 40500

Compound interest, $A = 40500\left(1+\frac{15}{100}\right)^2$

$\Rightarrow A = 40500\times\frac{23}{20}\times\frac{23}{20}$

$\Rightarrow A = 53561.25$

$\therefore CI = A - P$

$= 53561.25 - 40500$

= ₹13061.25 ≈ ₹13061

34. (a) For interest rate

$(R) = \frac{8469.44 - 7562}{7562}\times 100$

$= \frac{907.44\times 100}{7562} = 12\%$

If ₹ 10000 at 12% interest rate borrowed for 2 yr, then the compound interest will be

$CI = 10000\left(1+\frac{12}{100}\right)^2 - 10000$

CI = ₹ 12544 − ₹ 10000

CI = ₹ 2544

35. (d) Let principal = ₹ P,

Rate of interest = 17%

Time = 2 yr

Then difference between compound interest and simple interest $= \frac{Pr^2}{100^2}$

According to the question,

$\frac{Pr^2}{100^2} = 433.50 \Rightarrow P = \frac{433.50\times 100^2}{r^2}$

$\Rightarrow P = \frac{433.50\times 100\times 100}{17^2} =$ ₹15000

$\therefore$ Required compound interest

$= P\left(1+\frac{r}{100}\right)^2 - P$

$=$ ₹$15000\left(1+\frac{17}{100}\right)^2 - 15000$

= 20533.5 − 15000 = ₹ 5533.5

36. (a) We know that,

$\Rightarrow 8469.44 = 7562\left(1+\frac{R}{100}\right)^1$

$\Rightarrow \frac{8469.44}{7562} - 1 = \frac{R}{100}$

$\Rightarrow \left[\frac{8469.44 - 7562}{7562}\right] = \frac{R}{100}$

$\Rightarrow R = \frac{907.44}{7562}\times 100 \therefore R = 12\%$

37. (d) According to the question,

$SI = \frac{P\times R\times T}{100}$

$40\%\ P = \frac{P\times R\times 4}{100}$

$\Rightarrow R = \frac{40}{100}\times\frac{100}{4} = 10\%$

Principal = 80000

$CI = 80000\left[\left(1+\frac{10}{100}\right)^4 - 1\right]$

$CI = 80{,}000\left[\left(\frac{11}{10}\right)^4 - 1\right]$

$CI = 80000\left[\frac{14641 - 10000}{10000}\right]$

CI = ₹ 37128

Speedy Method

Rate $(r) = \frac{40\%}{4} = 10\%$

$CI = 8000\times\left[\left(\frac{11}{10}\right)^4 - 1\right] =$ ₹37128

38. (a) Amount after two year

$= 6000\times\frac{102.5}{100}\times\frac{102}{100} =$ ₹ 6273

Compound interest = 6273 − 6000 = ₹ 273

39. (a) Rate (R) = 10% p.a.

$= \frac{10}{2}\%$ (half yearly)

$T = (2\times 1.5) = 3$

and CI = ₹ 5044

$\Rightarrow 5044 = P\left[\left(1+\frac{10}{200}\right)^3 - 1\right]$

$\Rightarrow 5044 = P\left[\frac{9261}{8000} - 1\right]$

$\Rightarrow P = \frac{5044}{1261}\times 8000 =$ ₹ 32000

So, the invested sum of money ₹ 32000.

40. (c) For yearly,

$A = 6400\times\left(1+\frac{5}{100}\right) = \frac{6400\times 105}{100} =$ ₹ 6720

$(CI)_1 = 6720 - 6400 =$ ₹ 320

For half-yearly,

$A = 6400\times\left(1+\frac{5}{200}\right)^2 = 6400\times\frac{205}{200}\times\frac{205}{200}$

= ₹ 6724

$(CI)_2 = 6724 - 6400 =$ ₹ 324

$\therefore$ Required difference

$= (CI)_2 - (CI)_1 = 324 - 320 =$ ₹ 4

41. (c) $D = CI - SI = ₹\,162$, $R = 9\%$ p.a., $P = ?$

$$\therefore \quad D = CI - SI = \frac{PR^2}{(100)^2} \Rightarrow 162 = \frac{P \times 9^2}{10000}$$

$$\therefore \quad P = \frac{162 \times 10000}{81} = ₹\,20000$$

Hence, required principle = ₹ 20000

42. (b) $\frac{10\%}{2} = 5\%$ (For half yearly)

$$5\% = \frac{1}{20}$$

$P : A$

$(20)^4 : (21)^4$ [∵ tenure is 4 yr]

160000 : 194481

∴ Compound interest = ₹ 34481

43. (d) $CI = P\left[\left(1+\frac{r}{100}\right)^n - 1\right]$

$$= 25000\left[\left(1+\frac{10}{100}\right)^3 - 1\right]$$

$$= 25000\left[\left(\frac{11}{10}\right)^3 - 1\right] = 25000\left[\frac{1331-1000}{1000}\right]$$

$$= 25000 \times \frac{331}{1000} = 25 \times 331$$

$= ₹\,8275$

44. (d) According to the question,

$$1460 = P\left[\left(1+\frac{10}{100}\right)\left(1+\frac{3}{4}\times\frac{10}{100}\right) - 1\right]$$

$$\Rightarrow \quad 1460 = P\left[\left(\frac{11}{10}\times\frac{43}{40}\right) - 1\right]$$

$$\Rightarrow \quad 1460 = P\left[\frac{473-400}{400}\right]$$

$$\therefore \quad P = \frac{1460 \times 400}{73} = ₹\,8000$$

45. (d) $R = 10\%$

For half yearly 5% equivalent rate

$$= 5 + 5 + \frac{25}{100} = 10.25\%$$

⇒ 10.25 − 10 = ₹ 25

⇒ 0.25% = 25

⇒ 1% = 100

100% = ₹ 10000

46. (a) $CI = 18000\left[\left(1+\frac{10}{100}\right)^2 - 1\right]$

[For half yearly $\frac{R}{2} = 10\%$]

$$= 18000\left[\frac{11}{10}\times\frac{11}{10} - 1\right] = 18000\left[\frac{121}{100} - 1\right]$$

$$= 18000 \times \frac{21}{100} = 180 \times 21 = ₹\,3780$$

47. (d) Amount = 3000 + 1320 = ₹ 4320

According to the question,

$$4320 = 3000\left(1+\frac{R}{100}\right)^2$$

$$\Rightarrow \quad \frac{36}{25} = \left(1+\frac{R}{100}\right)^2$$

$$\Rightarrow \quad \frac{6}{5} - 1 = \frac{R}{100} \Rightarrow R = 20\%$$

48. (b) For Statement I,

$$SI = \frac{6000 \times 10 \times 2}{100} = ₹\,1200$$

Hence, Statement I is correct.

For Statement II,

$$CI = 6000\left[\left(1+\frac{10}{100}\right)^2 - 1\right] = 6000\left[\frac{121}{100} - 1\right]$$

$$= 6000 \times \frac{21}{100} = ₹\,1260$$

Hence, both Statements I and II are correct.

49. (d) Amount $= 14000\left[1+\frac{10}{100}\right]^2$

$$= 14000 \times \frac{11}{10} \times \frac{11}{10} = ₹\,16940$$

Compound Interest (CI)

= 16940 − 14000 = ₹ 2940

50. (d) $A = 90774 = P\left(1+\frac{23}{100}\right)^2$

$$\Rightarrow \quad 90774 = P \times \frac{123}{100} \times \frac{123}{100}$$

$$\Rightarrow \quad P = \frac{90774 \times 100 \times 100}{123 \times 123}$$

$\therefore \quad P = ₹\,60000$

Hence, present value = ₹ 60000

51. (b) Here, $A = ₹\,2P$, $t = ?$

By formula, $A = P\left(1+\frac{r}{100}\right)^t$

$$\Rightarrow \quad 2P = P\left(1+\frac{26}{100}\right)^t \Rightarrow 2 = (1.26)^t$$

By hit and trial method,

Let $t = 2$ then, $(1.26)^2 = 1.5876 \neq 2$

Let $t = 3$ then, $(1.26)^3 = 2.000376 \approx 2$

Hence, $t = 3$

52. (c) Given, $P = ₹\,40000$

$n = 2$ yr 6 months $= 2\frac{1}{2}$ yr $= \frac{5}{2}$ yr

$r = 20\%$ p.a.

If the interest is compounded half-yearly.

Then, $n = \frac{5}{2} \times 2 = 5$ and $r = \frac{20}{2}\% = 10\%$

Now, by formula

$$CI = P\left[\left(1+\frac{r}{100}\right)^n - 1\right]$$

$$= 40000\left[\left(1+\frac{10}{100}\right)^5 - 1\right]$$

$$= 40000 \times \left[\left(\frac{11}{10}\right)^5 - 1\right]$$

$$= 40000\left[\frac{161051-100000}{100000}\right]$$

$$= 40000 \times \frac{61051}{100000} = ₹\,24420.40$$

53. (b) $10\% = \frac{1}{10}$

Principal : Installment

110 $(10:11)_{\times 11}$ 121

100 : 121

Total loan = 110 + 100 = 210

and total installment = 121 × 2 = 242

Interest = 242 − 210 = 32

Each installment 121 = ₹ 6897 ⇒ 1 = ₹ 57

32 = ₹ 1824

54. (b) Rate of interest $= \frac{6000 \times 100}{12000 \times 5} = 10\%$

Now, compound interest for 3 yr

$$CI = 12000 \times \left(1+\frac{10}{100}\right)^3 - 12000$$

$$= 12000 \times \frac{11 \times 11 \times 11}{1000} - 12000$$

$= 15972 - 12000 = ₹\,3972$

55. (c) Amount getting on SI for 2 yr,

$$A = 7000 + \frac{7000 \times 8 \times 2}{100} = 7000 + 1120$$

$\therefore \quad A = ₹\,8120$

$\therefore \quad SI = A - P = 8120 - 7000 = ₹\,1120$

Amount getting on CI for 2 yr,

$$A = 10000 \times \left(1+\frac{8}{100}\right)^2 = ₹\,11664$$

$\therefore \quad CI = A - P = 11664 - 10000 = ₹\,1664$

and total amount = 11664 + 8120 = ₹ 19784

Now, total interest = 1664 + 1120 = ₹ 2784

56. (d) Let time for interest be x yr.

∵ Compound interest

$$CI = 9984 = 60000 \times \left[\left(1+\frac{8}{100}\right)^x - 1\right]$$

$$\Rightarrow \quad \frac{9984}{60000} + 1 = \left(1+\frac{8}{100}\right)^x$$

$$\Rightarrow \quad \left(\frac{108}{100}\right)^x = \frac{69984}{60000} = \frac{11664}{10000} = \left(\frac{108}{100}\right)^2$$

On comparison, $x = 2$ yr.

57. (b) According to the question,

Compound interest

$$CI = 8950\left[\left(1+\frac{9}{100}\right)^2 - 1\right]$$

$$= 8950\left[\left(\frac{109}{100}\right)^2 - 1\right]$$

$$= 8950\left[\frac{11881-10000}{10000}\right] = 8950 \times \frac{1881}{10000}$$

$= ₹\,1683.495 \approx ₹\,1683$

58. (a) Given, principal = ₹ 135000

Rate of interest = 12% p.a.

Rate of interest for next 3 months $= \frac{12}{4} = 3\%$

$\left[\because 3 \text{ months} = \frac{3}{12} \text{ yr} = \frac{1}{4} \text{ yr}\right]$

Amount $(A) = 135000\left(1+\frac{12}{100}\right)^2 \times \left(1+\frac{3}{100}\right)$

$= 135000 \times \frac{28}{25} \times \frac{28}{25} \times \frac{103}{100}$

$= ₹\ 174424.32$

59. (d) $T = 3$ yr, $r = 5\%$

Difference = ₹ 15.25

For 3 yr, this difference is equal to

$= \frac{Pr^2(300 + r)}{(100)^3}$

$15.25 = \frac{P(5)^2 \times (305)}{100 \times 100 \times 100}$

$\Rightarrow P = \frac{15.25 \times 100 \times 100 \times 100}{7625} \Rightarrow P = ₹\ 2000$

60. (b) Given, principal $(P) = ₹\ 20500$

Time, $n = 2$ yr

Rate of interest $(r) = 10\%$

$CI = 20500\left[\left(1+\frac{10}{100}\right)^2 - 1\right]$

$= 20500\left(\frac{121}{100} - 1\right) = 20500\left(\frac{21}{100}\right)$

$\therefore$ CI $= 205 \times 21 = ₹\ 4305$

61. (d) $P : A$

$\sqrt{2000} : \sqrt{2880}$

$\sqrt{25} : \sqrt{36}$

$\underbrace{5 : 6}_{+1}$ for 2 yr

we take square root of both sides

$\therefore\ R = \frac{1}{5} \times 100 = 20\%$

62. (b) Since, it is compounded half yearly,

$\therefore$ Rate of interest, $r = \frac{8}{2} = 4\%$

$n = 3$ cycles

$\Rightarrow\ A = 10200\left(1+\frac{4}{100}\right)^3$

$\Rightarrow\ A = 10200 \times \left(\frac{104}{100}\right)^3 = ₹\ 11473.61$

63. (b) Given, in case of compound Interest

Principal = ₹ 72000

Rate of interest = 10%

[compounded half-yearly] $= R = \frac{10}{2} = 5\%$

Time = 1.5 yr

Half yearly = 3 half yearly

In case of simple interest

Principal = ₹ 72000

Rate of interest = 5 %

Time = 3 yr

Difference CI and SI for 3 yr

$= P \times \frac{R^2}{(100)^3} \times (300 + R)$

$= 72000 \times \frac{5 \times 5}{1000000} \times 305 = ₹\ 549$

64. (d) Here, the interest is compounded quarterly.

So, Rate of Interest $(R) = \frac{16}{4}\ \% = 4\%$,

$n = 1 \times 4 = 4$

[$\because A$ = Amount, P = Principal]

$A = P\left(1+\frac{R}{100}\right)^n = 75000\left(1+\frac{4}{100}\right)^4$

$= ₹\ 87739.40$

65. (d) Time $= 2\frac{1}{2}$ yr

Rate of interest, $(R) = 10\%$

$\therefore\ CI = P\left(1+\frac{r}{100}\right)^n - P$

$= 2000\left[\left(1+\frac{10}{100}\right)^2\left(1+\frac{10}{2 \times 100}\right)\right] - 2000$

$= \left[2000 \times \left(\frac{11}{10}\right)^2 \times \frac{21}{20}\right] - 2000$

$= 2541 - 2000$

$\therefore$ CI = ₹ 541

66. (c) $A = 150000 \times \left(1+\frac{8}{100}\right)^1$

$\Rightarrow\ A = 150000 \times \frac{108}{100}$

$\therefore\ A = ₹ 162000$

CI = (₹ 162000 − 150000) = ₹ 12000

Now, same principal invested for half-yearly.

$= 150000 \times \frac{104}{100} \times \frac{104}{100}$

$= ₹\ 162240$

CI = ₹(162240 − 150000) = ₹ 12240

So, the difference between interest

= ₹(12240 − 12000) = ₹ 240

67. (d) $5\% = \frac{1}{20}$

$P : A$

$(20)^3 : (21)^3$ [$\because$ Time is 3 yr]

[8000 : 9261] × 3

₹ 24000 : ₹ 27783

Hence, the deposited amount is ₹ 24000.

68. (d) Given,

Difference of CI and SI for 2 yr = ₹ 200

Rate of Interest (R) = 10% p.a.

Let the principal be ₹ P.

$\therefore$ Difference $(D) = \frac{P \times (R)^2}{(100)^2}$

$\Rightarrow\ 200 = \frac{P \times (10)^2}{(100)^2} = \frac{P \times 100}{10000}$

$\therefore\ P = 200 \times 100 = ₹\ 20000$

69. (b) According to the question,

Amount for 3 yr

$= 10000 \times \left(1+\frac{4}{100}\right)\left(1+\frac{5}{100}\right)\left(1+\frac{6}{100}\right)$

$= ₹\ 11575.2$

$\therefore$ Required Compound Interest (CI)

= 11575.2 − 10000 = ₹ 1575.20

70. (b) Let the time period be t yr.

According to the question,

$2050 = 20000 \times \left[\left(1+\frac{5}{100}\right)^t - 1\right]$

$\Rightarrow \frac{2050}{20000} = \left[\left(1+\frac{5}{100}\right)^t - 1\right]$

$\Rightarrow \frac{2050}{20000} + 1 = \left(1+\frac{5}{100}\right)^t$

$\Rightarrow \frac{22050}{20000} = \left(1+\frac{5}{100}\right)^t \Rightarrow \frac{441}{400} = \left(\frac{21}{20}\right)^t$

$\Rightarrow \left(\frac{21}{20}\right)^2 = \left(\frac{21}{20}\right)^t$

On comparison, $t = 2$ yr

71. (c) For 2 yr,

Difference between SI and CI, $D = P\left(\frac{R}{100}\right)^2$

$\Rightarrow 172.80 = 12000\left(\frac{R}{100}\right)^2$

$\Rightarrow\ R^2 = \frac{172.80 \times 100 \times 100}{12000} = 144$

$\therefore\ R = \sqrt{144} = 12\ \%$

72. (d) When interest compounded annually,

P = ₹ 12000, $r = 15\ \%$, $n = 1$ yr

$CI = P\left[\left(1+\frac{r}{100}\right)^n - 1\right] = 12000\left[\left(1+\frac{15}{100}\right) - 1\right]$

$= 12000 \times \frac{15}{100} = ₹ 1800$

When interest compounded half - yearly,

$CI = 12000\left[\left(1+\frac{15}{200}\right)^2 - 1\right]$

$= 12000 \times \frac{43}{40} \times \frac{43}{40} - 12000$

= 13867.5 − 12000 = ₹ 1867.5

$\therefore$ Required difference = ₹ (1867.5 - 1800)

= ₹ 67.5

73. (c) Let the rate of interest be 'r'% p.a., then,

Difference between CI and SI $= P\left(\frac{r}{100}\right)^2$

$\Rightarrow\ 80 = 32000\left(\frac{r}{100}\right)^2 \Rightarrow \frac{80}{32000} = \left(\frac{r}{100}\right)^2$

$\Rightarrow\ \frac{1}{400} = \left(\frac{r}{100}\right)^2 \Rightarrow \frac{1}{20} = \frac{r}{100}$

$\therefore\ r = 5\%$ p.a.

74. (c) Let the rate of interest be r% p.a..

$370 = 3240\left[\left(1+\frac{r}{100}\right)^2 - 1\right]$

$\Rightarrow \frac{370}{3240} = \left(1+\frac{r}{100}\right)^2 - 1$

$\Rightarrow \frac{37}{324} + 1 = \left(1+\frac{r}{100}\right)^2$

$\Rightarrow \quad \dfrac{361}{324} = \left(1 + \dfrac{r}{100}\right)^2 \Rightarrow \dfrac{r}{100} = \dfrac{1}{18}$

$\therefore \quad r = \dfrac{100}{18} = 5.56\%$ p.a.

75. (c) Let the cost of the scooter be ₹ x.
According to the question,

$\Rightarrow 107062.50 + x = 132000 \times \left(1 + \dfrac{12.5}{100}\right)^2$

$\Rightarrow \quad 107062.50 + x = 132000 \times 1.265625$

$\Rightarrow \quad 107062.50 + x = 167062.5$

$\Rightarrow \quad x = 167062.5 - 107062.5$

$\therefore \quad x =$ ₹ 60000

76. (c) Let the principal be ₹ P.

Then, amount $(A) =$ ₹ $\left(P + \dfrac{21}{100}P\right) =$ ₹ $\dfrac{121}{100}P$

According to the question,

$\Rightarrow \quad \dfrac{121}{100}P = P\left(1 + \dfrac{r}{100}\right)^2$

[$\because r =$ Rate of interest p.a.]

$\Rightarrow \quad \dfrac{121}{100} = \left(1 + \dfrac{r}{100}\right)^2 \Rightarrow \dfrac{11}{10} = 1 + \dfrac{r}{100}$

$\Rightarrow \quad \dfrac{r}{100} = \dfrac{1}{10}$

$\therefore \quad r = 10\%$ p.a.

77. (d) According to the question,

1 yr 2 yr

$P \rightarrow 1150 \rightarrow 1322.5$

Thus, $\rightarrow \dfrac{1322.5}{1150} = \dfrac{1150}{P}$

$(1150)^2 = P \times 1322.5$

$\therefore \quad P = \dfrac{1150 \times 1150}{1322.5} =$ ₹ 1000

78. (d) Amount after 3 yr = 13310

Amount after 4 yr = ₹ 14641

Rate% $= \dfrac{14641 - 13310}{13310} \times 100 = 10\%$

Now, $13310 = P\left(1 + \dfrac{10}{100}\right)^3$

$13310 = \left(\dfrac{1331}{1000}\right) \times P$

$\therefore \quad P =$ ₹ 10000

79. (a) Given, Principal $(P) =$ ₹ 9000

Rate of interest $(R) = 32\%$

and Time = 2 yr

$\therefore \quad CI = P\left[\left(1 + \dfrac{R}{100}\right)^T - 1\right]$

$= 9000\left[\left(1 + \dfrac{32}{100}\right)^2 - 1\right]$

$= 9000\left[\left(\dfrac{132}{100}\right)^2 - 1\right]$

$= 9000\left[\left(\dfrac{17424}{10000} - 1\right)\right] = 9000 \times 0.7424$

$=$ ₹ 6681.6

80. (c) Here, Compound Interest (CI) = 3836.8

Principal (P) = ₹ 2200 and time = 1.5 yr

$\therefore$ Amount $(A) = 2200 + 3836.8 =$ ₹ 6036.8

Amount when interest is compounded half-yearly $= P\left[\left(1 + \dfrac{R}{200}\right)\right]^{2t}$

$\Rightarrow \quad 6036.8 = 2200\left[\left(1 + \dfrac{R}{200}\right)\right]^{2 \times 1.5}$

$\Rightarrow \quad 6036.8 = 2200\left[\left(1 + \dfrac{R}{200}\right)\right]^3$

$\Rightarrow \quad \dfrac{6036.8}{2200} = \left(1 + \dfrac{R}{200}\right)^3$

$\Rightarrow \quad \dfrac{2744}{1000} = \left(1 + \dfrac{R}{200}\right)^3 \Rightarrow \dfrac{R}{200} = \dfrac{4}{10}$

$\therefore \quad R = 80\%$

Hence, the rate of interest is 80% p.a..

81. (c) $7\% = \dfrac{7}{100}$

$P : A$

$(100)^2 : (107)^2$

$10000 : 11449$

$\downarrow \times 3 \quad \downarrow \times 3$

₹ 30000 ₹ 34347

$\therefore$ Amount after two year will be ₹ 34347.

82. (c) Here, $P =$ ₹ 72000, Time = 3 yr and Rate = 16% p.a.

$\because \quad CI = P\left[\left(1 + \dfrac{R}{100}\right)^t - 1\right]$

$= 72000\left[\left(1 + \dfrac{16}{100}\right)^3 - 1\right]$

$= 72000\,[1.560896 - 1]$

$= 72000 \times 0.560896 =$ ₹ 40384.51

83. (a) According to the question,

Interest for half-year = 15% half-yearly

Time = 2 half-year

and Principal $(P) =$ ₹ 15000

Now, Amount $(A) = P\left(1 + \dfrac{R}{100}\right)^t$

$= 15000\left(1 + \dfrac{15}{100}\right)^2 = 15000 \times \dfrac{115}{100} \times \dfrac{115}{100}$

$\therefore \quad$ Amount $(A) =$ ₹ 19837.5

84. (c) $R = 15\% = \dfrac{3}{20}$

$P : A$

$20 : 23$

$(20)^2 : (23)^2$

$400 : 529$

$129 \rightarrow 967.5$

$1 \rightarrow 7.5$

$400 \rightarrow$ ₹ 3000

Thus, sum = ₹ 3000

85. (b) Let the principal be ₹ P.

$SI = 8000 = \dfrac{(P \times 10 \times 8)}{100} \Rightarrow P = \dfrac{8000 \times 100}{10 \times 8}$

$\therefore \quad P =$ ₹ 10000

$\Rightarrow \quad CI = 10000\left[\left(1 + \dfrac{10}{100}\right)^3 - 1\right]$

$\Rightarrow \quad CI = 10000 \times \dfrac{331}{1000} \Rightarrow CI =$ ₹ 3310

86. (d) $12\% = \dfrac{3}{25}$ at time = 2 yr

$P : A$

$(25)^2 : (28)^2$

$625 : 784$

$+159$

$\because \quad 625 \rightarrow$ ₹ 1500

$\therefore \quad 159 \rightarrow$ ₹ 3816

87. (b) $SI = 960 = \dfrac{P \times 6 \times 2}{100}$

$\Rightarrow \quad P = \dfrac{960 \times 100}{6 \times 2}, P =$ ₹ 8000

$\therefore CI = 8000\left(1 + \dfrac{6}{100}\right)^2 - 8000$

$\Rightarrow CI = 8000\left(\dfrac{106}{100}\right)^2 - 8000$

$\Rightarrow \quad CI = 8000\,[0.1236] \Rightarrow CI =$ ₹ 988.8

88. (b) $R = \dfrac{30}{2} = 15\%$ [for half yearly]

By formula, Difference $= P \times \dfrac{R^2}{10000}$

$\Rightarrow 337.5 = P \times \dfrac{15 \times 15}{10000} \Rightarrow P = \dfrac{3375000}{225}$

$=$ ₹ 15000

89. (d) $P : A$ [$A = 1000 + 464.1 =$ ₹ 1464.1 and rate is half yearly]

$1000 : 1464.1$

$\sqrt[4]{10000} : \sqrt[4]{14641}$

[four half yearly cycle in 2 yr]

$10 : 11$

$+1$

$R\% = \dfrac{1}{10} \times 100 = 10\%$

But for annually = 2 × 10 = 20%

90. (a) $\therefore$ Amount (A) = 22000 + 10210.2 = ₹ 32210.2

$\Rightarrow \quad 32210.2 = 22000\left(1 + \dfrac{R}{200}\right)^4$

$\Rightarrow \quad 1.4641 = \left(1 + \dfrac{R}{200}\right)^4$

$\Rightarrow \quad (1.1)^4 = \left(1 + \dfrac{R}{200}\right)^4 \Rightarrow 1.1 = 1 + \dfrac{R}{200}$

$\Rightarrow \quad 0.1 \times 200 = R \;\therefore\; R = 20\%$ p.a.

91. (b) $SI = \dfrac{PRT}{100}$,

$CI = P\left\{\left[1 + \dfrac{R}{100}\right]^n - 1\right\}$

∴ Let the principal be P.

$\Rightarrow 12000 = P \times R \times \dfrac{2}{100}$ ...(i)

Also, $14400 = P\left(1 + \dfrac{R^2}{10000} + \dfrac{2R}{100} - 1\right)$

$\Rightarrow 14400 = PR\left(\dfrac{R}{10000} + \dfrac{1}{50}\right)$ ...(ii)

Dividing Eq. (ii) by Eq. (i), we get,

$\dfrac{6}{5} = \left(\dfrac{R}{10000} + \dfrac{1}{50}\right) \times 50$

$\Rightarrow \dfrac{6}{5} = \dfrac{R}{200} + 1 \Rightarrow \dfrac{1}{5} = \dfrac{R}{200}$

$\Rightarrow R = 40\%$ p.a.

Thus, $\Rightarrow 12000 = \dfrac{P \times 40 \times 2}{100}$

$\therefore P = ₹\,15000$

92. (c) $(A) = 9464 = P \times \left(1 + \dfrac{30}{100}\right)^2$

$\Rightarrow 9464 = P \times \dfrac{13}{10} \times \dfrac{13}{10}$

$\therefore P = \dfrac{9464 \times 10 \times 10}{13 \times 13} = ₹\,5600$

Hence, sum will be ₹ 5600.

93. (b) Simple interest for 2 yr is ₹ 12800 and compound interest for 2 yr is ₹ 14400.

SI for 1 yr $= \dfrac{12800}{2} = ₹\,6400$

CI for 1 yr = ₹ 6400

CI for 2nd yr = 14400 − 6400 = ₹ 8000

Then, rate of interest

$= \dfrac{8000 - 6400}{6400} \times 100 = \dfrac{1600}{6400} \times 100 = 25\%$

Now, let principal amount be ₹ P.

SI for 2 yr $= \dfrac{P \times R \times T}{100}$

$12800 = \dfrac{P \times 25 \times 2}{100}$

$\therefore P = ₹\,25600$

So, required principal amount = ₹ 25600

94. (c) $A = 9000\left(1 + \dfrac{80}{200}\right)^2 = 9000 \times \left(\dfrac{7}{5}\right)^2$

$= ₹\,17640$

$\therefore$ CI $= A - P = ₹(17640 - 9000) = ₹\,8640$

95. (d) By formula $(x)^{\frac{1}{t_1}} = (y)^{\frac{1}{t_2}}$

$\Rightarrow (2)^{\frac{1}{10}} = (4)^{\frac{1}{t_2}} \Rightarrow (2)^{\frac{1}{10}} = (2)^{\frac{2}{t_2}}$

$\Rightarrow \dfrac{1}{10} = \dfrac{2}{t_2} \Rightarrow t_2 = 20$ yr

96. (c) Given, Amount (A) = ₹ 19683

Rate of Interest (R) = 8% p.a.

Time (T) = 3 yr

$\because A = P\left(1 + \dfrac{r}{100}\right)^n$

$\Rightarrow 19683 = P\left(1 + \dfrac{8}{100}\right)^3 \Rightarrow 19683 = P(1.08)^3$

$\Rightarrow P(1.259712) = 19683$

$\Rightarrow P = ₹\,15625$

Hence, the sum is ₹ 15625.

97. (c) CI $= 8000\left[\left(1 + \dfrac{5}{100}\right)^2 - 1\right]$

$= 8000(1.1025 - 1)$

$\therefore$ CI = ₹ 820 $\Rightarrow$ SI $= \dfrac{8000 \times 5 \times 2}{100}$

$\therefore$ SI = ₹800

Difference in CI and SI = CI − SI = ₹ 20

Hence, Vidhi would have suffered a loss of ₹ 20, if she had given money at simple interest.

Speedy Method

$\text{CI} - \text{SI} = P\left(\dfrac{R}{100}\right)^2 = 8000 \times \left(\dfrac{5}{100}\right)^2$

$= 8000 \times \dfrac{25}{10000} = ₹\,20$

98. (a) Let the amount given to A = ₹ x

Then the amount given to B = ₹ $(5309 - x)$

According to the question,

$x\left(1 + \dfrac{6}{100}\right)^4 = (5309 - x)\left(1 + \dfrac{6}{100}\right)^6$

$\Rightarrow x = (5309 - x)\left(\dfrac{100 + 6}{100}\right)^2$

$\Rightarrow x = (5309 - x)\dfrac{53 \times 53}{2500}$

$\Rightarrow 2500x = 5309 \times 53 \times 53 - 2809x$

$\Rightarrow 5309x = 5309 \times 2809$

$\therefore x = ₹\,2809$

∴ Amount given to A = ₹ 2809

Amount given to B = ₹(5309 − 2809)

= ₹ 2500

99. (d) We know that,

$(\text{CI} - \text{SI})$ for 2 yr $= P\left(\dfrac{r}{100}\right)^2$

$\therefore 512 = P\left(\dfrac{8}{100}\right)^2 \Rightarrow 512 = \dfrac{P \times 2 \times 2}{25 \times 25}$

$\Rightarrow P = \dfrac{512 \times 25 \times 25}{2 \times 2}$

$\therefore P = ₹\,80000$

Hence, required sum is ₹ 80000.

100. (c) According to the question,

$\text{CI} = 1908 = P\left[\left(1 + \dfrac{12}{100}\right)^t - 1\right]$

$\Rightarrow 1908 = P\left[\dfrac{784}{625} - 1\right] \Rightarrow 1908 = P\left[\dfrac{159}{625}\right]$

$\therefore P = \dfrac{1908 \times 625}{159} = ₹\,7500$

101. (d) According to the question,

$P\left(1 + \dfrac{r}{100}\right)^3 = \dfrac{64P}{27}$

$\Rightarrow \left(1 + \dfrac{r}{100}\right)^3 = \dfrac{64}{27} = \left(\dfrac{4}{3}\right)^3$

$\Rightarrow \left(1 + \dfrac{r}{100}\right) = \dfrac{4}{3} \Rightarrow \dfrac{100 + r}{100} = \dfrac{4}{3}$

$\Rightarrow 300 + 3r = 400$

$\therefore r = \dfrac{100}{3} = 33\dfrac{1}{3}\%$

102. (c) Let the sum = ₹ P

According to the question,

$P\left(1 + \dfrac{6}{100}\right)^2 = 7200 \Rightarrow P \times \left(\dfrac{53}{50}\right)^2 = 7200$

$\Rightarrow P \times 53 \times 53 = 7200 \times 50 \times 50 = 6407.97$

= ₹ 6408 (approx)

103. (a) Let the sum of money = ₹ P

Amount $(A) = 3.375\,P$

$\because A = P\left(1 + \dfrac{R}{100}\right)^n$

$\Rightarrow 3.375\,P = P\left(1 + \dfrac{R}{100}\right)^3$

$\Rightarrow \sqrt[3]{3.375} = 1 + \dfrac{R}{100} \Rightarrow 1.5 - 1 = \dfrac{R}{100}$

$\therefore R = 0.5 \times 100 = 50\%$

104. (c) $\because A = P\left[1 + \left(\dfrac{R}{100}\right)^n\right]$

$\therefore 605 = P\left[1 + \left(\dfrac{10}{100}\right)^2\right]$

$\therefore 605 = P\left(\dfrac{110}{100}\right)^2 \Rightarrow P = \left(605 \times \dfrac{100}{121}\right)$

$\therefore P = ₹\,500$

∴ Principal is ₹ 500.

105. (d) $\because \text{CI} = P\left[\left(1 + \dfrac{R}{100}\right)^n - 1\right]$

$\therefore 92727 = 1000000\left[\left(1 + \dfrac{3}{100}\right)^n - 1\right]$

$\Rightarrow 92727 = 1000000\left[\left(\dfrac{103}{100}\right)^n - 1\right]$

$\Rightarrow \left[\dfrac{103}{100}\right]^n = \dfrac{92727}{1000000} + 1$

$\Rightarrow \left(\dfrac{103}{100}\right)^n = \dfrac{1092727}{1000000} \Rightarrow \left(\dfrac{103}{100}\right)^n = \left(\dfrac{103}{100}\right)^3$

On comparing, $n = 3$ yr

106. (b) Amount after 3 yr

$= ₹\,15000 \times \dfrac{116}{100} \times \dfrac{120}{100} \times \dfrac{115}{100} = ₹\,24012$

Thus, required interest

= 24012 − 15000 = ₹ 9012

107. (d) $\therefore A = P\left(1 + \dfrac{20}{100}\right)^n$

$\Rightarrow 14112 = P\left(1 + \dfrac{20}{100}\right)^3$

$\Rightarrow 14112 = P \times \dfrac{6}{5} \times \dfrac{6}{5} \times \dfrac{6}{5}$

$\Rightarrow P = 14112 \times \dfrac{5}{6} \times \dfrac{5}{6} \times \dfrac{5}{6} \therefore P = ₹\,8166.67$

108. (d) Required cost of item

$$= \frac{3993}{\left(1+\frac{10}{100}\right)^1} + \frac{3993}{\left(1+\frac{10}{100}\right)^2} + \frac{3993}{\left(1+\frac{10}{100}\right)^3}$$

$$= 3993\left[\frac{10}{11} + \frac{100}{121} + \frac{1000}{1331}\right]$$

$$= 3993 \times \frac{10}{11} \times \left[1 + \frac{10}{11} + \frac{100}{121}\right]$$

$$= 3993 \times \frac{10}{11} \times \frac{121+110+100}{121}$$

$$= 3993 \times \frac{10}{11} \times \frac{331}{121} = ₹\,9930$$

Speedy Method

$R = 10\%$

P	:	Installment
$(1210)\ 11^2 \times 10$	:	$11 \times 11^2 (1331)$
$(1100)\ 11 \times 10^2$	:	$11^2 \times 11 (1331)$
$(1000)\ 10^3$	:	$11^3 (1331)$
3310		

Now, each installment 1331 = 3993

$\therefore$ Total cost $3310 = \frac{3993 \times 3310}{1331} = 9930$

109. (b) Let amount of loan be ₹ P.

$A = ₹\,15625$, $r = 25\%$, $n = 3$ yr

$$\therefore \quad A = P\left(1+\frac{r}{100}\right)^n$$

$$\Rightarrow 15625 = P\left(1+\frac{25}{100}\right)^3 \Rightarrow 15625 = P \times \left(\frac{5}{4}\right)^3$$

$$\Rightarrow P = \frac{15625 \times 64}{125} = ₹\,8000$$

Speedy Method

Given, $A = 15625$, $t = 3$yr, $r = 25\%$

Now, $P : A\left(+25\% = \frac{5}{4}\right)$

$(4)^3 : (5)^3$ $[t = 3\text{ yr}]$

64 : 125

$\because$ 125 = 15625

Principle $64 = \frac{15625 \times 64}{125} = ₹8000$

110. (b) $\because$ $CI = P\left[\left(1+\frac{R}{100}\right)^T - 1\right]$

$$\therefore \quad 7245 = 50000\left[\left(1+\frac{7}{100}\right)^T - 1\right]$$

$$\Rightarrow \frac{7245}{50000} = \left(\frac{107}{100}\right)^T - 1 \Rightarrow \left(\frac{107}{100}\right)^T = \frac{7245}{50000} + 1$$

$$\Rightarrow \left(\frac{107}{100}\right)^T = \frac{57245}{50000} = \frac{11449}{10000}$$

$$\Rightarrow \left(\frac{107}{100}\right)^T = \left(\frac{107}{100}\right)^2 \Rightarrow T = 2\text{ yr}$$

111. (d) According to the question,

$$2P = P\left(1+\frac{R}{100}\right)^5 \Rightarrow 2 = \left(1+\frac{R}{100}\right)^5$$

and $16P = P\left(1+\frac{R}{100}\right)^T$

$$\Rightarrow 16 = \left(1+\frac{R}{100}\right)^T \Rightarrow 2^4 = \left(1+\frac{R}{100}\right)^T$$

$$\Rightarrow \left[\left(1+\frac{R}{100}\right)^5\right]^4 = \left(1+\frac{R}{100}\right)^T$$

$$\Rightarrow \left(1+\frac{R}{100}\right)^{20} = \left(1+\frac{R}{100}\right)^T$$

On comparing both sides,

$T = 20$ yr

Speedy Method

We know, $(x)^{1/t_1} = (y)^{1/t_2}$

$(2)^{1/5} = (16)^{1/t_2}$

$(2)^{1/5} = (2^4)^{1/t_2}$

$(2)^{1/5} = 2^{4/t_2}$

On comparing, $\frac{1}{5} = \frac{4}{t_2} \Rightarrow t_2 = 20$ yr

14

Speed, Time and Distance

- **Distance** The length of the path travelled by any object or a person between two places is known as distance.
- **Speed** Speed is the distance covered by an object in unit time. It is calculated by dividing the distance travelled by the time taken.

i.e. $$\text{Speed} = \frac{\text{Distance}}{\text{Time}}$$

Conversion of Units

- $x \text{ km/h} = \frac{x \times 1000\text{m}}{3600\text{s}} = \frac{5x}{18} \text{ m/s}$
- $x \text{ m/s} = \frac{x \times \frac{1}{1000 \text{ km}}}{\frac{1}{3600 \text{ h}}} = \frac{18x}{5} \text{ km/h}$

Ex. 1 A motorcycle travelled 1000m at 36 km/h. Find the time (in seconds) taken by the motorcycle to cover this distance.

Sol. Speed of motorcycle $= 36 \text{ km/h} = 36 \times \frac{5}{18} \text{ m/s} = 10 \text{ m/s}$

Distance travelled = 1000 m

$\therefore$ $$\text{Required time} = \frac{1000}{10} = 100 \text{ sec}$$

Average Speed

$$\text{Average speed} = \frac{\text{Total distance covered by a body}}{\text{Total time taken by the body}}$$

If a body covers a distance D_1 at S_1 km/h, D_2 at S_2 km/h, D_3 at S_3 km/h and so on upto D_n at S_n, then

$$\text{Average speed} = \frac{D_1 + D_2 + D_3 + D_4 + \ldots + D_n}{\frac{D_1}{S_1} + \frac{D_2}{S_2} + \frac{D_3}{S_3} + \frac{D_4}{S_4} + \ldots + \frac{D_n}{S_n}}$$

Ex. 2 A person covers 9 km with a speed of 3 km/h, 25 km with a speed of 5 km/h and 30 km with a speed of 10 km/h. Find out the average speed of person.

Sol. Here, $D_1 = 9$ km, $D_2 = 25$ km, $D_3 = 30$ km, $S_1 = 3$ km/h, $S_2 = 5$ km/h and $S_3 = 10$ km/h

$$\therefore \text{Required average speed} = \frac{D_1 + D_2 + D_3}{\frac{D_1}{S_1} + \frac{D_2}{S_2} + \frac{D_3}{S_3}} = \frac{9 + 25 + 30}{\frac{9}{3} + \frac{25}{5} + \frac{30}{10}} = \frac{64}{3+5+3}$$

$$= \frac{64}{11} = 5\frac{9}{11} \text{ km/h}$$

Relative Speed

When two bodies A and B are moving with speeds x km/h and y km/h, respectively, then the relative speed of two bodies is

(i) $(x + y)$ km/h (if they are moving in opposite direction)

(ii) $(x - y)$ km/h (if they are moving in same direction)

Ex. 3 A and B are 15 km apart and when travelling towards each other, meet after half an hour, whereas they meet two and a half hours later, if they travel in the same direction. The faster of the two travels at the speed of

Sol. Let speed of $A = x$ km/h and speed of $B = y$ km/h

When both are in same direction, then

$$\text{Relative speed} = \frac{\text{Distance}}{\text{Time}} \Rightarrow x - y = \frac{15}{\frac{5}{2}}$$

$$\Rightarrow \quad x - y = 6 \quad \ldots\text{(i)}$$

When both are in opposite direction, then

$$x + y = \frac{15}{\frac{1}{2}} \Rightarrow x + y = 30 \quad \ldots\text{(ii)}$$

From Eqs. (i) and (ii), we get $x = 18$ km/h and $y = 12$ km/h

Hence, speed of faster man = 18 km/h

Some Important Formulae

- When a certain distance is covered at speed x and the same distance is covered at speed y, then the average speed during the whole journey is given by $\frac{2xy}{x+y}$.
- When a person covers a distance without stoppage with speed x km/h and with stoppage it covers the same distance with speed y km/h, $x > y$ then number of minutes per hour does he stop $= \frac{x-y}{x} \times 60$
- When a person covers a certain distance between two places with speed 'S_1' but he reaches his destination late be time t_1 but when he covers the same distance with speed 'S_2' he reaches his destination t_2 time earlier. In this case, the distance between two places is given by

$$D = \frac{S_1 S_2 (t_1 \sim t_2)}{S_1 \sim S_2}$$

- Two persons A and B start running at the same time in opposite directions from two points and after passing each other, they complete their journeys in 't_1', h and 't_2' h respectively.

Then, A's speed : B's speed $= \sqrt{t_2} : \sqrt{t_1}$ and if they meet after t h, then $t = \sqrt{t_1 \times t_2}$.

- If a man changes his speed to $\left(\frac{x}{y}\right)$ of his usual speed and gets late by t min or reaches early by t min, then usual time taken by him $= \frac{tx}{y-x}$, if $(y > x)$ and $\frac{tx}{(x-y)}$, if $(x > y)$.
- Total distance travelled when a man covers a certain distance at speed x km/h and comes back at speed of y km/h. Then total 't' h to complete the whole journey is Distance $(d) = \left(\frac{xy}{x+y}\right) t$ km
- Total distance travelled when a man covers a certain distance at speed x km/h and comes back at speed of y km/h. If he takes 't' h more to come back than go is Distance $(d) = \left(\frac{xy}{x-y}\right) t$ km

Circular Track

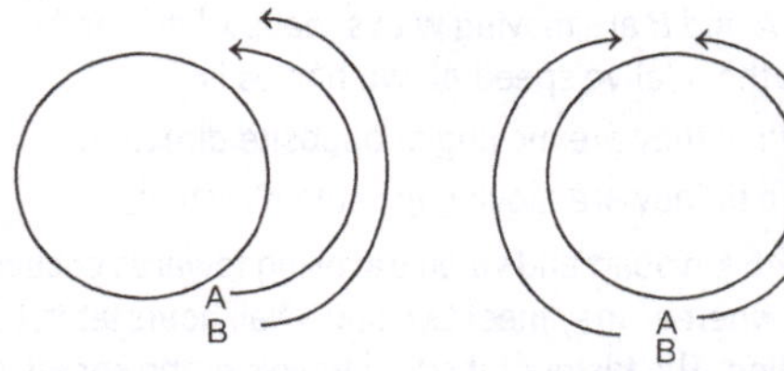

Same direction Opposite direction

- Meet first time each other at any point on the track in opposite direction $= \frac{L}{x+y}$ sec
- Meet first time each other at any point on the track in same direction $= \frac{L}{x-y}$ sec
- Meet each other exactly at starting point in same or opposite direction $= \text{LCM of} \left(\frac{L}{x}, \frac{L}{y}\right)$ sec
- When three persons A, B and C are running around a circular track of length of L m with speed x, y and z m/s in the same direction, then meet each other at any point on the track $= \text{LCM of} \left(\frac{L}{x-y}, \frac{L}{y-z}\right)$ sec.

(Where L is the length of the track in meters and x m/s and y m/s are speeds of A and B respectively).

Number of Meeting Points (In Circular Race)

If the ratio of speeds of two persons be $a : b$ then

- Number of meeting points when both are in same direction $= a \sim b$
- Number of meeting points when both are in opposite direction $= a + b$

Ex. 4 Two people A and B started running from the same point on a circular track of length 800 m in opposite directions with initial speeds 10 m/s and 40 m/s, respectively. Whenever they meet, A's speed doubles and B's speed halves. After what time from the start will they meet for the third time?

Sol. Time taken when they meet for Ist time $= \frac{800}{10+40} = 16$ sec.

Time taken when they meet for 2nd time $= \frac{800}{20+20} = 20$ sec.

Time taken when they meet for 3rd time $= \frac{800}{40+10} = 16$ sec.

$\therefore$ Total time $= 16 + 20 + 16 = 52$ sec.

Race

- **Linear race** It is a straight path such that the starting and finishing point don't coincide with each other.
- **Circular race** It is a circular path such that the starting and finishing point coincide with each other.
- **Start** If two persons A and B are contesting a race and before the start of the race, A is at the starting point and B is ahead of A by x m (say), then it is said that A gives B a start of x m.
  e.g. If A and B are contestants for a 100 m race and A has to cover 100 m, while B has to cover $(100-20) = 80$ m, then A gives B a start of 20m.
- **Dead Heat Race** A race is said to be a dead heat race, if all the contestants reach the finishing point exactly at the same time.
- **Game of 100** A game of 100 means that the contestant who scores 100 points first, is declared as the winner.
  e.g. If in a 100 points game, A scores 100 points, while B scores 85 points. Then, it is said that A can give $(100-85) = 15$ points to B.

Some Important Facts about Race

Let the length of the race be L m.

- If A beats B by x m, then

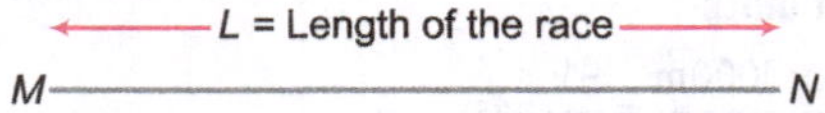

Distance covered by A (winner) $= L$ m.
Distance covered by B (loser) $= (L - x)$ m
If B starts x m ahead of A (or A gives B a start of x m), then

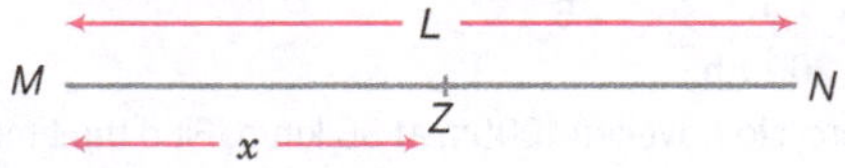

A starts from M and B starts from Z.
$\therefore$ Distance covered by $B = (L - x)$ m

- If A beat B by T s, then

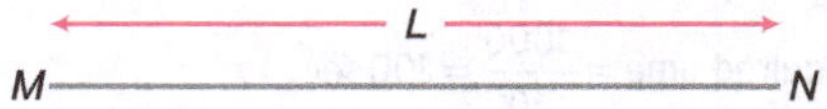

A and B both start from point M.
$\therefore$ Time taken by A (winner) = Time taken by B (loser) $- T$
It means that A completes the race in T s less time than that of B.

- If B starts the race T s before A starts (or if A gives B a start of T s), then we say that A starts T s after B starts

Ex. 5 A can run 1 km in 5 min and B can run the same distance in 6 min. How many metres start can A give to B in 1 km race, so that the race may end in a dead heat?

Sol. Time taken by A to run 1 km = 300 s.
Time taken by B to run 1 km = 360 s.
A can give B a start of $(360 - 300)$s $= 60$s
$\because$ In 360 s, B runs 1000 m.
$\therefore$ In 60 s B runs $\frac{1000}{360} \times 60 = \frac{1000}{6} = \frac{500}{3} = 166\frac{2}{3}$ m

Hence, A can give a start of $166\frac{2}{3}$ m.

SSC Exam Scanner

SSC CGL 2024 (Tier I & II)

1. P and Q take part in 400 m race. P runs at 12 km/h. P gives Q a start of 20 m and still beats him by 13 sec. The speed of Q is
SSC CGL (Tier-II) 20/01/2025 Shift-I
(a) 11.38 km/h (b) 10.29 km/h
(c) 11.61 km/h (d) 10.87 km/h

2. On a 2200 m long circular track, Sarita and Kavita drove their cycles from the same point but in opposite direction with the speeds 20 km/h and 16 km/h respectively. After how much time will they meet again for the first time?
SSC CGL (Tier-II) 18/01/2025 Shift-I
(a) 2 min 20 sec
(b) 3 min 20 sec
(c) 2 min 50 sec
(d) 3 min 40 sec

3. In a circular race of 1600 m in length, Bhaskar and Vinay start with speeds of 27 km/h and 45 km/h starting at the same time from the same point. When will they meet for the first time on the track, when running in the opposite directions and the same direction, respectively?
SSC CGL (Tier I) 26/9/2024 Shift-III
(a) 1min 20 sec and 5 min 20 sec
(b) 1 min 40 sec and 5 min 20 sec
(c) 2 min 40 sec and 5 min 40 sec
(d) 1 min 20 sec and 4 min 20 sec

4. A thief takes off on his bike at a certain speed, after seeing a police car at a distance of 250 m. The police car starts chasing the thief and catches him. If the thief runs 1.5 km before being caught and the speed of the police car is 70 km/h, then what is the speed of thief's bike (in km/h)?
SSC CGL (Tier I) 26/9/2024 Shift-II
(a) 65 km/h (b) 60 km/h
(c) 55 km/h (d) 50 km/h

5. Two athletes are participating in a race on a circular track of 220 m. Ravi runs at the speed of 22 m/s, while Kapil runs at the speed of 11 m/s. They start from the same point, at the same time and in the same direction. After how many seconds will they meet for the first time? **SSC CGL (Tier I) 26/9/2024 Shift-I**
(a) 15 sec (b) 16 sec
(c) 20 sec (d) 24 sec

6. Seema walks around a circular field at the rate of 3 rounds per hour, while Priya runs around it at the rate of 8 rounds per hour. They start in the same direction from the same point at 11:54 P.M. They shall first cross each other at
SSC CGL (Tier I) 25/9/2024 Shift-III
(a) 12:06 pm (b) 12:00 am
(c) 12:06 am (d) 11:59 pm

7. A policeman noticed a thief at some distance. The policeman started running to catch the thief and the thief also started running at the same time. The speed of both policeman and the thief was 12 km/h and 10 km/h, respectively. It took 30 min for the policeman to catch the thief. Find the initial distance (in metres) between them.
SSC CGL (Tier I) 25/9/2024 Shift-II
(a) 500 m (b) 600 m
(c) 1000 m (d) 100 m

8. Suppose A starts walking at a speed of 8 km/h. After 8 h B started travelling on a bicycle at a speed of 24 km/h. The distance from the starting B can catch A is
SSC CGL (Tier I) 25/9/2024 Shift-I
(a) 64 km (b) 96 km
(c) 72 km (d) 88 km

9. A policeman is chasing a thief at a speed of 82 km/h. The thief is 1300 m away and is running at a speed of 64 km/h. In how much time will the policeman catch the thief, if both are riding on bikes?
SSC CGL (Tier I) 24/9/2024 Shift-III
(a) 350 sec (b) 260 sec
(c) 250 sec (d) 300 sec

10. A thief is spotted by a policeman from a distance of 100 m. The thief starts running and the policeman chases him. If the speed of thief and policeman are 21 km/h and 23 km/h, respectively, then how far will the thief have to run before he is over taken?
SSC CGL (Tier I) 24/9/2024 Shift-I
(a) 1020 m (b) 1050 m
(c) 1090 m (d) 1080 m

11. A thief is noticed by a policeman from a distance of 92 m. The thief starts running and the policeman chases him. The thief and the policeman run at the speed of 90 km/h and 104.4 km/h, respectively. In how much time will the policeman catch the thief ?
SSC CGL (Tier I) 23/9/2024 Shift-I
(a) 21 sec (b) 26 sec
(c) 23 sec (d) 22 sec

12. A thief is spotted by a policeman from a distance of 195 m. When the policeman starts the chase, the thief also starts running. If the speed of the thief is 22 km/h and that of the policeman is 27 km/h, then how far would the thief have run (in m) before he is overtaken?
SSC CGL (Tier I) 19/9/2024 Shift-III
(a) 825 m (b) 951 m
(c) 858 m (d) 958 m

13. Arvind and Chetan started running simultaneously from the same point in the same direction on a circular track of length 210 m. If Arvind takes 180 sec to complete one round and Chetan takes 420 sec to complete one round, after how much time will they meet for the first time at the starting point on the track?
SSC CGL (Tier I) 17/9/2024 Shift-III
(a) 10 min (b) 15 min
(c) 21 min (d) 28 min

14. Akshara and Siddharth travel from point P to Q, a distance of 72 km at a rate of 8 km/h and 10 km/h, respectively. Siddharth reaches Q first and returns immediately and meets Akshara at R. Find the distance from P to R.
SSC CGL (Tier I) 17/9/2024 Shift-I
(a) 65 km (b) 63 km
(c) 64 km (d) 66 km

15. P and Q start running in opposite directions on a circular track from the same point. If their speeds are 10 m/s and 8 m/s, respectively, then after what time will they meet if the length of the track is 1620 m?
SSC CGL (Tier I) 13/9/2024 Shift-II
(a) 110 sec (b) 70 sec
(c) 120 sec (d) 90 sec

16. A thief pursued by a policeman was 150 m ahead at the start. If the ratio of the speed of the policeman to that of the thief was 5 : 4, then how far (distance in metres) could the thief go before he is caught by the policeman?
SSC CGL (Tier I) 12/9/2024 Shift-II
(a) 350 m (b) 20 m
(c) 600 m (d) 400 m

17. *M* and *N* walk along a circular track. They start at 5:00 a.m. from the same point in the opposite directions. *M* and *N* walk at a speed of 5 rounds per hour and 2 rounds per hour, respectively. How many times will they cross each other before 6.30 am on the same day?
SSC CGL (Tier I) 12/9/2024 Shift-II
(a) 10 (b) 3 (c) 5 (d) 7

18. A thief is noticed by a policeman from a distance of 200 m. The thief starts running and the policeman chases him. The thief and the policeman run at the rate of 10 km/h and 11 km/h, respectively. What is the distance (in metres) between them after 9 min?
SSC CGL (Tier I) 11/9/2024 Shift-II
(a) 40 m (b) 50 m
(c) 30 m (d) 60 m

19. Atul gives Vishu a head-start of 20 sec in a 900 m race and beats him by 135 m. While running the same race again Atul gives a start of 189 m and beats him by 8 sec. In how much time can Vishu complete the full race of 900 m?
SSC CGL (Tier I) 11/9/2024 Shift-I
(a) 3 min 30 sec (b) 2 min 50 sec
(c) 3 min 20 sec (d) 3 min 10 sec

20. Places *A* and *B* are 20 km apart on the highway. *A* car starts from *A* and another from *B* at the same time. If the cars travel in the same direction at different speeds, they meet in one hour. If they travelled towards each other, they met in 12 min. What are the speeds (in km/h) of two cars?
SSC CGL (Tier I) 10/9/2024 Shift-II
(a) 60, 40 (b) 52, 48
(c) 51, 49 (d) 55, 45

21. A policeman noticed a thief at a distance of 500 m. The policeman started running and the thief also started running at the same time. The thief is running at a speed of 15 km/h. It took 15 min for the policeman to catch the thief. Find the speed of the policeman (in km/h).
SSC CGL (Tier I) 10/9/2024 Shift-II
(a) 11 km/h (b) 17 km/h
(c) 12 km/h (d) 10 km/h

22. In a circular race of 750 m, *X* and *Y* start from the same point and at the same time with speeds of 9 km/h and 13.5 km/h, respectively. If they are running in the same direction then, when will they meet again for the first time on the track?
SSC CGL (Tier I) 10/9/2024 Shift-I
(a) 750 sec (b) 900 sec
(c) 500 sec (d) 600 sec

23. A bus travels $\frac{1}{3}$ of the distance initially at a speed of 40 km/h, the next $\frac{1}{3}$ of the distance 50 km/h, and the final $\frac{1}{3}$ of the distance at 60 km/h. Find the average speed of the bus for the entire journey. (Rounded off to two decimal places)
SSC CGL (Tier I) 10/9/2024 Shift-I
(a) 48.65 km/h (b) 51.43 km/h
(c) 54.13 km/h (d) 46.85 km/h

24. A thief noticed a policeman at a distance of 600 metres. The thief started running and the policeman chased him. The thief and policeman are running at speeds of 12 km/h and 15 km/h, respectively. Find the time (in minutes) required for the policeman to catch the thief.
SSC CGL (Tier I) 09/9/2024 Shift-III
(a) 8 min (b) 10 min
(c) 12 min (d) 15 min

25. Varun and Sandeep started for a car race from the same point, in the same direction and at the same time on a circular track of length 1635 m with the speeds of 90 km/h and 108 km/h, respectively. After how much time (in s) will they meet again for the first time?
SSC CGL (Tier I) 09/9/2024 Shift-II
(a) 324 sec (b) 325 sec
(c) 327 sec (d) 326 sec

26. In a circular race of 840 m, *A* and *B* start running in the same direction at the same time from the same point at the speeds of 6 m/s and 12 m/s, respectively. After how much time will they meet next?
SSC CGL (Tier I) 09/9/2024 Shift-I
(a) 140 sec (b) 20 sec
(c) 40 sec (d) 70 sec

SSC CGL 2023 (Tier I & II)

27. Vipin travels one-third of the distance of a journey at a speed of 30 km/h and the remaining distance at a speed of 40 km/h. If he took a total of 12 h to complete the journey, what was the total distance (in km) of the journey?
SSC CGL (Tier-II) 26/10/2023 Shift-IV
(a) 432 (b) 450
(c) 445 (d) 412

28. Reshma covers 45 km at a speed of 15 km/h by bicycle, 80 km at a speed of 40 km/h by car, and another 6 km at a speed of 2 km/h on foot. Find her average speed for the whole journey (correct to 2 decimal places).
SSC CGL (Tier-II) 06/03/2023 Shift-I
(a) 16.38 km/h (b) 43.50 km/h
(c) 18.36 km/h (d) 15.25 km/h

29. In a circular path of 600 m, Pankaj and Rohit start walking in opposite directions from the same point at the speeds of 2.85 m/s and 5.4 km/h, respectively. After how many minutes will they meet for the first time? (Rounded off to one decimal point.)
SSC CGL (Tier-I) 27/07/2023 Shift-III
(a) 3.2 (b) 2.3 (c) 2.7 (d) 4.7

30. A certain distance is covered by a person at a certain speed. If another person covers 25% of the distance in triple the time, the ratio of the speed of the first person to that of the second person is
SSC CGL (Tier-I) 27/07/2023 Shift-II
(a) 1 : 6 (b) 1 : 12
(c) 6 : 1 (d) 12 : 1

31. A thief robs precious metals from a store which is 1150 m away from the police. The thief starts running at 6 km/h and the police starts catching at 11 km/h at the same time. How much distance (in m) will the thief run before being caught?
SSC CGL (Tier-I) 27/07/2023 Shift-II
(a) 1485 (b) 1380
(c) 1125 (d) 1280

32. Two motorists start together to travel to a certain destination, one at the speed of 4 km/h and the other at the speed of 6 km/h. Find the distance travelled by them (in km) if the motorist travelling at 4 km/h arrives half an hour after the other motorist.
SSC CGL (Tier-I) 27/07/2023 Shift-I
(a) 8 (b) 5 (c) 6 (d) 4

33. Sohan and Amit started a car race from the same point in the same direction and at the same time on a circular track of length 1125 m with speeds of 36 km/h and 54 km/h, respectively. After how much time (in seconds) will they meet for the first time since the start of the race?
SSC CGL (Tier-I) 27/07/2023 Shift-I
(a) 220 (b) 215 (c) 210 (d) 225

34. In 1 km linear race, P beats Q by 120 m in 30 sec. What is the time taken by P to cover the race?
SSC CGL (Tier-I) 26/07/2023 Shift-IV
(a) 220 sec (b) 250 sec
(c) 235 sec (d) 240 sec

35. A cyclist rides 20 km in 120 min and rides another 25 km in 150 min. What is the average speed of the cyclist, in km/h?
SSC CGL (Tier-I) 26/07/2023 Shift-III
(a) 15 (b) 11
(c) 10 (d) 12.5

36. Ram and Shyam are racing along a circular track. The speed of Ram is thrice the speed of Shyam. The length of the circular track is 1440 m. After the start of the race from the same point simultaneously. Ram meets Shyam for the first time at the end of the 8th minute. If Ram and Shyam start the race again from the same starting point simultaneously, then the time taken by Shyam to finish the race is: (Given that the length of the race is same as the length of the track)
SSC CGL (Tier-I) 26/07/2023 Shift-II
(a) 7.5 min
(b) 16 min
(c) 30 min
(d) 22.5 min

37. A policeman saw a thief at a distance of 400 m. The thief started running at a speed of 10 km/h and the policeman chased him at a speed of 12 km/h in the same direction. At what distance from the starting point will the policeman catch the thief?
SSC CGL (Tier-I) 26/07/2023 Shift-I
(a) 2.4 km (b) 3 km
(c) 2 km (d) 2.8 km

38. A thief steals an item and escapes, running at a speed of 15 km/h. A policeman arrives at the spot of the crime after 4 min and immediately starts chasing the thief. 16 min after the policeman started to chase the thief; there is still a gap of 200 m between the two. At what distance from the spot of the crime will the policeman catch up the thief and what is the speed (in km/h) of the policeman?
SSC CGL (Tier-I) 25/07/2023 Shift-IV
(a) 5.5 km, 16.5 (b) 6 km, 18
(c) 6.5 km, 19.5 (d) 5 km, 15

39. Having started from the same point and at the same time, two runners P and Q are running around a circular track of length 500 m in opposite directions with the speeds of 6 m/s and 10 m/s, respectively. If they exchange their speeds after meeting for the first time, who will reach the starting point first?
SSC CGL (Tier-I) 25/07/2023 Shift-IV
(a) Q
(b) P
(c) Both P and Q will reach at the same time
(d) No one of the P and Q

40. Ramesh, on his way to his hometown, travelled the first 250 km at a speed of 75km/h and the next 250 km at a speed of 85 km/h. Find the average speed for the whole journey(correct to 2 decimal places). SSC CGL (Tier-I) 25/07/2023 Shift-II
(a) 80.55 km/h (b) 79.69 km/h
(c) 79.20 km/h (d) 80.69 km/h

41. A policeman starts chasing a thief when he was already 600 m ahead. If the policeman is running at a speed of 9 km/h and the thief at 8 km/h, then the thief would be caught at a distance of
SSC CGL (Tier-I) 25/07/2023 Shift-I
(a) 6.5 km (b) 6 km
(c) 5 km (d) 5.4 km

42. A car covers a distance of 350 km in 5 h and covers another 450 km at a speed of 90 km/h. What is the average speed (in km/h) of the car?
SSC CGL (Tier-I) 24/07/2023 Shift-III
(a) 72 (b) 82
(c) 80 (d) 85

43. In a 200 m linear race, if A gives B a start of 25 m, then A wins the race by 10 sec. Alternatively, if A gives B a start of 45 m. the race ends in a dead heat. How long does A take to run 200 m?
SSC CGL (Tier-I) 24/07/2023 Shift-III
(a) 78 sec (b) 77 sec
(c) 78.5 sec (d) 77.5 sec

44. An airplane travels five times as fast as a bus. If the bus covers 60 km in 80 min, then what distance (in km) will the airplane cover in 25 min?
SSC CGL (Tier-I) 24/07/2023 Shift-III
(a) 95.35 (b) 93.75
(c) 65.35 (d) 18.75

45. In a circular race of 4225 m, X and Y start from the same point and at the same time at speeds of 54 km/h and 63 km/h. When they will meet again for the first time on the track when they are running in the opposite direction?
SSC CGL (Tier-I) 24/07/2023 Shift-II
(a) 140 sec (b) 150 sec
(c) 130 sec (d) 120 sec

46. Two men walk from a place at speeds of 9 km/h and 12 km/h, respectively. The first man takes 20 min more than the second one to cover the journey. Find the distance of the journey.
SSC CGL (Tier-I) 24/07/2023 Shift-II
(a) 10 km (b) 13 km
(c) 15 km (d) 12 km

47. A thief is noticed by a policeman from a distance of 500 m. The thief starts running and the policeman chases him. The thief and the policeman run at the rate of 17 km/h and 20 km/h, respectively. What is the distance between them after 8 min?
SSC CGL (Tier-I) 24/07/2023 Shift-I
(a) 100 m (b) 180 m
(c) 200 m (d) 150 m

48. A policeman chases a thief. The speeds of the policeman and the thief are 8 km/h and 6 km/h, respectively. If the policeman started 10 min late, at what distance he will catch the thief?
SSC CGL (Tier-I) 24/07/2023 Shift-I
(a) 6 km (b) 8 km
(c) 4 km (d) 2 km

49. Anil and Tirath drove between two points A and B 192 km apart. Anil started the journey from point A at 8:20 am; drove at a speed of 64 km/h; reached point B and immediately returned to A at the same speed. Tirath started the journey from point A at 9:50 am; drove at a speed of 96 km/h; reached point B and immediately returned to A at the same speed. At what time did Anil and Tirath first meet each other?
SSC CGL (Tier-I) 21/07/2023 Shift-IV
(a) 11:38 am (b) 11:28 am
(c) 11:43 am (d) 11:33 am

50. In a circular race of 1600 m, A and B start from the same point and at the same time with speeds of 27 km/h and 45 km/h, respectively. After how long will they meet again for the first time on the track when they are running in the same direction?
SSC CGL (Tier-I) 21/07/2023 Shift-III
(a) 90 sec (b) 320 sec
(c) 240 sec (d) 180 sec

51. A policeman chasing a thief is 0.5 km behind the thief. The speed of thief is 80% of the speed of the policeman and policeman catches him in 12 min. What is the speed of the thief (in km/h)?
SSC CGL (Tier-I) 21/07/2023 Shift-II
(a) 10 (b) 12.5 (c) 15 (d) 7.5

52. The distance between two towns is covered in 7 h and 30 min at the speed of 72 km/h. The time saved if the speed is increased by 25% is
SSC CGL (Tier-I) 21/07/2023 Shift-II
(a) 1 h 36 min (b) 1 h 50 min
(c) 1 h 30 min (d) 1 h 20 min

53. Anuj and Anup have to travel from a place *A* to a place *B* in their respective cars. Anuj is driving at 70 km/h and takes 3 halts of 10 min each, while Anup is driving at 80 km/h and takes 4 halts of 15 min each. The time taken by Anup to reach place *B*, if Anuj takes 8.5 h, is
SSC CGL (Tier-I) 21/07/2023 Shift-I
(a) 8 h (b) 7 h (c) 4 h (d) 6 h

54. Anand covers a certain distance in the first lag of 5 h at the speed of 50 km/h. In the second lag, he increased the speed by 20% due to which he covered 20% extra distance than that of the first lag. He covered the third lag at the average speed of the first two lags and covered 10% extra distance than that of the second lag distance. How much total time (in hours) did he take to complete all three lags?
SSC CGL (Tier-I) 21/07/2023 Shift-I
(a) 16 (b) 15 (c) 18 (d) 14

55. Raghav covers a distance of 3300 m in 45 min. What is his speed (in km/h)? SSC CGL (Tier-I) 21/07/2023 Shift-I
(a) 5 (b) 4.4 (c) 2.25 (d) 3.75

56. Ram rides at the rate of 36 km/h but stops for five minutes to take a drink at the end of every 10 km. Find the time that Ram will take to cover a distance of 84 km.
SSC CGL (Tier-I) 20/07/2023 Shift-IV
(a) 180 min (b) 60 min
(c) 220 min (d) 120 min

57. *P* gives *Q* a head-start of 2 sec in a 400 m race, but both finish the race at the same time. Find the time taken by *P* to finish the race if the speed of *Q* is 2 m/s.
SSC CGL (Tier-I) 20/07/2023 Shift-III
(a) 198 sec (b) 199 sec
(c) 200 sec (d) 195 sec

58. A thief is chased by a policeman and distance between them is 3 km. The speed of policeman is 75 km/h and the speed of the thief is 60 km/h. The policeman will be able to catch the thief when the thief would have covered the distance of .... km.
SSC CGL (Tier-I) 20/07/2023 Shift-II
(a) 18 (b) 12 (c) 15 (d) 10

59. Ashok runs $2\frac{2}{3}$ times as fast as Bharat. If Ashok gives Bharat a head start of 160 m, then how far must the winning post be so that Ashok and Bharat can reach it at the same time?
SSC CGL (Tier-I) 19/07/2023 Shift-IV
(a) 225 m (b) 256 m
(c) 240 m (d) 200 m

60. A thief seeing a policeman from a distance of 300 m starts running at a speed of 10 km/h. The policeman gives chase immediately at a speed of 12 km/h and the thief is caught. What is the distance run by the thief? SSC CGL (Tier-I) 19/07/2023 Shift-IV
(a) 2 km (b) 2.5 km
(c) 3.2 km (d) 1.5 km

61. A thief committed a crime and escaped from the spot at a speed of 12 m/h. A security guard started chasing him 20 min after the thief started running and caught him in the next 20 min. What is the speed (in m/h) of the security guard?
SSC CGL (Tier-I) 19/07/2023 Shift-II
(a) 24 (b) 30 (c) 32 (d) 36

62. Two persons started running on a circular track simultaneously with speeds of 20 m/s and 30 m/s in opposite directions. If the circumference of the circular track is 100 m, then find at how many distinct points they will cross each other? SSC CGL (Tier-I) 19/07/2023 Shift-II
(a) 3 (b) 2 (c) 10 (d) 5

63. On day one, with speed v, R covers a distance x, in t time. On the next day, he covers a distance $2.5x$ in $0.75t$ time. What is his speed the next day?
SSC CGL (Tier-I) 19/07/2023 Shift-I
(a) $3.5\,v$ (b) $\frac{10}{3}v$ (c) $4.5\,v$ (d) $\frac{5}{3}v$

64. In an 1170 m race, Raman reaches the final point in 65 sec and Mohan reaches the final point in 90 sec. By how much distance does Raman beat Mohan?
SSC CGL (Tier-I) 19/07/2023 Shift-I
(a) 325 m (b) 300 m
(c) 375 m (d) 350 m

65. A man drives his car for 24 km at a speed of 48 km/h and for the next 1.5 h he drives at a speed of 80 km/h. Find his average speed (in km/h) for the entire journey.
SSC CGL (Tier-I) 19/07/2023 Shift-I
(a) 64 (b) 72 (c) 68 (d) 75

66. A thief is a spotted by a policeman from a distance of 210 m. When the policeman starts the chase, the thief also starts running. If the speed of the thief is 25 km/h and that of the policeman is 32 km/h, then how far would the thief have run (in m) before he is overtaken?
SSC CGL (Tier-I) 18/07/2023 Shift-IV
(a) 920 (b) 1200 (c) 750 (d) 480

67. Sudhin cycled at 8.5 km/h for 4 h then took an auto and travelled at 20 km/h for 1.5 h and then walked at 4 km/h for y h. If Sudhin's overall average speed for the entire journey was 10 km/h, what is the value of y?
SSC CGL (Tier-I) 18/07/2023 Shift-IV
(a) 1.75 (b) 2 (c) 1.5 (d) 1.25

68. In a 1500 m race, *X* beats *Y* by 100 m and *X* beats *Z* by 240 m. By what distance does *Y* beat *Z* in the same race?
SSC CGL (Tier-I) 18/07/2023 Shift-III
(a) 150 m (b) 140 m
(c) 200 m (d) 160 m

69. A policeman follows a thief who is 600 m ahead of the policeman. If the policeman and the thief run at speeds of 10 km/h and 8 km/h, respectively, in how much time (in minutes), will the policeman catch the thief?
SSC CGL (Tier-I) 18/07/2023 Shift-II
(a) 16 (b) 14 (c) 18 (d) 12

70. A thief is spotted by a policeman from a distance of 400m. When the policeman starts chasing, the thief also starts running. If the speed of the thief is 32 km/h and that of the policeman is 40 km/h, then how far would the thief have run before he is overtaken?
SSC CGL (Tier-I) 18/07/2023 Shift-I
(a) 1500 m (b) 1000 m
(c) 1200 m (d) 1600 m

71. Racer *A* and racer *B* run a race of 18 km on a circular track of length 800 m. Both complete one round in 200 sec and 250 sec, respectively. After how much time from the

start will the faster person meet the slower person for the last time?
SSC CGL (Tier-I) 17/07/2023 Shift-IV

(a) 2700 sec (b) 4000 sec
(c) 1800 sec (d) 2250 sec

72. A part of a journey is covered in 37.5 min at 90 km/h and the remaining part in 14 min at 80 km/h. The total distance (in km) of the journey is
SSC CGL (Tier-I) 17/07/2023 Shift-IV

(a) $76\frac{5}{12}$ (b) $62\frac{11}{12}$
(c) $78\frac{5}{12}$ (d) $74\frac{11}{12}$

73. A constable Ram is 225 m behind a thief Somesh. Ram runs 50 m and Somesh runs 30 m in a minute. At what time will the constable Ram catch the thief Somesh?
SSC CGL (Tier-I) 17/07/2023 Shift-III

(a) 10 min 16 sec (b) 15 min 11 sec
(c) 16 min 10 sec (d) 11 min 15 sec

74. A man is walking at a speed of 14 km/h. After every kilometer, he takes rest for 7 min. How much time will he take to cover a distance of 7 km?
SSC CGL (Tier-I) 17/07/2023 Shift-III

(a) $1\frac{1}{5}$ h (b) $2\frac{1}{3}$ h (c) $1\frac{1}{3}$ h (d) $\frac{1}{5}$ h

75. A thief is spotted by a constable from 200 m. When the constable starts the chase, the thief also starts running. If the speed of the constable is 8 km/h and thief runs at the speed of 6 km/h, then how far (in m) will the thief be able to run before he is overtaken?
SSC CGL (Tier-I) 17/07/2023 Shift-II

(a) 600 (b) 400 (c) 550 (d) 500

76. *A*, *B* and *C* run simultaneously, starting from a point, around a circular track of length 1200 m, at respective speeds of 2 m/s, 4 m/s and 6 m/s. *A* and *B* run in the same direction, while *C* runs in the opposite direction to the other two. After how much time will they meet for the first time?
SSC CGL (Tier-I) 17/07/2023 Shift-II

(a) 11 min (b) 10 min
(c) 9 min (d) 12 min

77. On a circular path of 693 m, Sujata and Anjali start walking from the same point but in the opposite directions at the speed of 2.85 km/h and 1.5 m/sec, respectively. When they will meet for the first time?
SSC CGL (Tier-I) 17/07/2023 Shift-I

(a) After 6.75 min (b) After 6.05 min
(c) After 5.04 min (d) After 4.56 min

78. A policeman noticed a thief from 300 m. The thief started running and the policeman was chasing him. The thief and the policeman ran at the speeds of 8 km/h and 9 km/h, respectively. What was the distance between them after 3 min?
SSC CGL (Tier-I) 17/07/2023 Shift-I

(a) 225 m (b) 250 m
(c) 300 m (d) 200 m

79. A policeman follows a thief, who is 1250 m ahead of him. The policeman and the thief run at the speed of 10 km/h and 8 km/h, respectively. The distance (in km) run by the thief before he is nabbed by the policeman is
SSC CGL (Tier-I) 14/07/2023 Shift-IV

(a) 7 (b) 4 (c) 5 (d) 6

80. Jehangir had to cover a distance of 90 km in an hour. During the first 25 min he travelled at a speed of 15.2 m/s. How many metres did Jehangir cover per second during the remaining period to reach his destination just on time?
SSC CGL (Tier-I) 14/07/2023 Shift-III

(a) 30.8 (b) 32. 5
(c) 32 (d) 31.2

81. Two friends *P* and *Q* simultaneously start running from same point around a circular track. They run in the same direction. *P* runs at 6 m/s and *Q* runs at *b* m/s. If they cross each other at exactly two points on the circular track and *b* is a natural number less than 6, then how many values can *b* take?
SSC CGL (Tier-I) 14/07/2023 Shift-III

(a) 2 (b) 1 (c) 4 (d) 3

82. In a race around a circular cycling track of 75 km, two cyclists are riding at a speed of 30 km/h and 25 km/h. After what time (in hours) will they meet at the point from where they started their journey?
SSC CGL (Tier-I) 14/07/2023 Shift-II

(a) 16 (b) 7 (c) 15 (d) 14

83. A thief steals a van at 3:00 am and drives it at a speed of 57 km/h. The thief is discovered at 4:00 am and the owner starts the chase with another van at a speed of 76 km/h. At what time will he catch the thief ? **SSC CGL (Tier-I) 14/07/2023 Shift-II**

(a) 7:30 am (b) 7:00 am
(c) 6:00 am (d) 7:00 pm

84. Two runners, Sony and Mony, start running on a circular track of length 200 m at speeds of 18 km/h and 24 km/h respectively, in the same direction. After how much time from the start will they meet again at the starting point?
SSC CGL (Tier-I) 14/07/2023 Shift-I

(a) 110 sec (b) 90 sec
(c) 100 sec (d) 120 sec

85. As part of his journey, a person travels 120 km at 80 km/h, the next 100 km at 40 km/h and comes back to the starting point at 75 km/h. The average speed of the person throughout the journey (approximately) is
SSC CGL (Tier-I) 14/07/2023 Shift-I

(a) 68.15 km/h (b) 58.74 km/h
(c) 63.46 km/h (d) 49.58 km/h

SSC CGL 2022 (Tier I)

86. In a 1000 m race, Arjun, Balaji and Charan are running. Arjun beats Balaji by 100 m and Balaji beats Charan by 100 m. In the next 1000 m race (the speeds are the same as in the previous), Balaji gives Charan a head start of 100 m and Arjun gives Balaji a head start of 100 m. Find the distance by which the winner is ahead of the person just behind him.
SSC CGL (Tier-I) 13/12/2022 Shift-I

(a) 100 m (b) 40 m
(c) 30 m (d) 20 m

87. A policeman spotted a thief 40 m ahead of him. The moment they both saw each other they started running in the same direction on the same track. The thief was running at 10 m/sec and the policeman was chasing him at the speed of 12 m/sec. How much distance (in metres) the policeman needed to cover to catch the thief?
SSC CGL (Tier-I) 12/12/2022 Shift-IV

(a) 180 (b) 240
(c) 200 (d) 225

88. Some students went on a field trip. At a speed of 6 km/h, they travelled by bikes for 2 hours, then at a speed of 2 km/h, they walked for another hour, then they took rest for an hour and had lunch for half an hour; then at a speed of 1 m/s, they walked for an hour to visit a garden and finally at a speed 4 km/h, they returned home in 3 h. Their average speed, in

km/h (rounded off to two places of decimal) is
SSC CGL (Tier-I) 12/12/2022 Shift-III

(a) 3.48 (b) 129.23 (c) 0.28 (d) 251.62

89. Ram starts from point A at 8 am and reaches point B at 2 pm on the same day. On the same day, Raju starts from point B at 8 am and reaches point A at 6 pm on the same day. Both points A and B are separated by only a straight line track. At what time they both meet? SSC CGL (Tier-I) 12/12/2022 Shift-III

(a) 11 : 45 am
(b) 9 : 42 am
(c) 10 : 42 am
(d) 12 : 42 pm

90. A thief running at speed of 'x' km/h is chased by a policeman running at a speed of 10 km/h. If the thief is ahead by 100 m, the policeman catches the thief after 3 min. At what speed is the thief running ('x' being the unknown speed)? SSC CGL (Tier-I) 9/12/2022 Shift-III

(a) 4 km/h (b) 8 km/h
(c) 10 km/h (d) 6 km/h

91. A person covers a certain distance by bus at 45 km/h and immediately returns to the starting point by car at a speed of 80 km/h. What is his average speed during the whole journey?
SSC CGL (Tier-I) 9/12/2022 Shift-III

(a) 57.6 km/h (b) 63.2 km/h
(c) 73.5 km/h (d) 45.5 km/h

92. Menu and Daya travel from point *A* to *B*, a distance of 105 km, at speeds of 10 km/h and 25 km/h, respectively. Daya reaches point *B* first and returns immediately and meets Menu at point *C*. Find the distance from point *A* to point *C*.
SSC CGL (Tier-I) 9/12/2022 Shift-II

(a) 35 km (b) 60 km
(c) 45 km (d) 62 km

93. Two cities *A* and *B* are 135 km apart on a straight track. One car starts from *A* at 8 am and travels towards *B* at 25 km/h. Another car starts from *B* at 9 am and travels towards *A* at a speed of 30 km/h. At what time will they meet?
SSC CGL (Tier-I) 9/12/2022 Shift-I

(a) 11 am (b) 10 am
(c) 10.45 am (d) 11.30 am

94. A thief stole jewellery from a shop at 8:15 pm and left on a bike at a speed of 60 km/h. The police were informed at 8:30 pm. If the police want to arrest the thief at 9:00 pm, what should be the minimum speed of the police jeep?
SSC CGL (Tier-I) 8/12/2022 Shift-IV

(a) 60 km/h (b) 75 km/h
(c) 80 km/h (d) 90 km/h

95. In a linear race of 500 m, *A* can beat *B* by 50 m and in a race of 600 m, *B* can beat *C* by 60 m. By how many metres will *A* beat *C* in a race of 400 m? SSC CGL (Tier-I) 8/12/2022 Shift-III

(a) 70 (b) 68 (c) 76 (d) 72

96. John drives 250 km at 50 km/h and then he drives 350 km at 70 km/h. Find his average speed for the whole journey in km/h.
SSC CGL (Tier-I) 8/12/2022 Shift-II

(a) 55 km/h (b) 60 km/h
(c) 58 km/h (d) 65 km/h

97. *A* starts from a point at a speed of 34 m/s. After 5 seconds, *B* starts chasing *A* from the same point at a speed of 44 m/s. What will be the distance travelled by *B* before *A* is caught by *B*?
SSC CGL (Tier-I) 7/12/2022 Shift-III

(a) 748 m (b) 862 m (c) 675 m (d) 549 m

98. In a 1500 m race, if vehicle *P* gives vehicle *Q* a start of 200 m, then vehicle *P* wins the race by 8 sec. Alternatively, if vehicle *P* gives vehicle *Q* a start of 400 m, the race ends in a dead heat. How long does vehicle *P* take to run 1500 m?
SSC CGL (Tier-I) 7/12/2022 Shift-I

(a) 44 sec (b) 45 sec
(c) 40 sec (d) 60 sec

99. In a race, there are 4 members in a team. Each member has to cover 5 km one after another. If the total time taken is 30 min, then what would have been the average speed? SSC CGL (Tier-I) 6/12/2022 Shift-IV

(a) 50 km/h (b) 40 km/h
(c) 50 m/s (d) 40 m/s

100. In a linear race of 1000 m, *A* beats *B* by 50 m or 5 sec. What is the difference between the speeds (in m/s) of *A* and *B* ?
SSC CGL (Tier-I) 6/12/2022 Shift-III

(a) $1\frac{10}{19}$ (b) $\frac{10}{19}$ (c) $\frac{9}{19}$ (d) $\frac{9}{10}$

101. A dog saw a cat at a distance of 280 m. The cat started running at the speed of 10 km/h and the dog also ran to catch it with the speed of 24 km/h. How much time will the dog take to catch the cat?
SSC CGL (Tier-I) 6/12/2022 Shift-II

(a) 1.4 min (b) 1.5 min
(c) 1.2 min (d) 1.3 min

102. Prasad goes 96 km on a bike at a speed of 16 km/h, 124 km at 31 km/h in a car, and 105 km at 7 km/h in a horse cart. Find his average speed for the entire distance travelled.
SSC CGL (Tier-I) 5/12/2022 Shift-IV

(a) 16 km/h (b) 13 km/h
(c) 17 km/h (d) 11 km/h

103. Two tourist buses start from the same point and move along two roads at right angles at speeds of 48 km/h and 36 km/h, respectively. The distance between the buses after 15 seconds is ________.
SSC CGL (Tier-I) 5/12/2022 Shift-IV

(a) 175m (b) 350m
(c) 250m (d) 150m

104. Which of the following is not a correct statement?
SSC CGL (Tier-I) 5/12/2022 Shift-III

(a) The speed of 20 m/s is less than the speed of 85 km/h.
(b) Time may be calculated by dividing the distance by the speed.
(c) Covering the same distance in lesser time implies a higher speed.
(d) The speed of 99 km/h is less than the speed of 24 m/s.

105. A policeman saw a thief from a distance of 450 m. When the policeman started chasing him, the thief also started running. The ratio of speeds of the thief to the policeman is 7 : 8. After running how much distance (in km) can the policeman catch the thief ? SSC CGL (Tier-I) 5/12/2022 Shift-I

(a) 3.6 (b) 3.4 (c) 3.15 (d) 3.75

106. *R* jogs at twice the speed of walking and runs at twice the speed of jogging. From his home to office, he covers half of the distance by walking and the rest by jogging. From his office to home, he covers half the distance jogging and the rest by running. What is his average speed (in km/h) in a complete round from his home to office and back home if the distance between his office and home is 10 km and he walks at the speed of 5 km/h?
SSC CGL (Tier-I) 5/12/2022 Shift-I

(a) $\frac{80}{9}$ (b) $\frac{90}{8}$ (c) $\frac{60}{9}$ (d) $\frac{60}{8}$

107. In a 1200 m race, bike *A* beats bike *B* by 100 m. Bike *B* beats bike *C* by 100 m in a 600 m race. If bike *A* beats bike *C* by 30 sec in a 720 m

race, then what is the speed of bike C? SSC CGL (Tier-I) 03/12/2022 Shift-IV

(a) $\frac{17}{3}$ m/sec (b) $\frac{26}{9}$ m/sec
(c) $\frac{17}{9}$ m/sec (d) $\frac{26}{3}$ m/sec

108. With an average speed of 45 km/h, a train reaches its destination on time. If it goes with an average speed of 30 km/h, it is late by 15 min. The total journey is
SSC CGL (Tier-I) 03/12/2022 Shift-IV

(a) 20.5 km (b) 40.5 km
(c) 22.5 km (d) 30.5 km

109. A thief steals a bike at 12:30 pm and drives it at 48km/h. But the theft is discovered after half an hour. The bike owner starts to chase him on another bike at 58km/h. The thief will be caught at ______ SSC CGL (Tier-I) 03/12/2022 Shift-II

(a) 3 : 40 pm (b) 3 : 54 pm
(c) 3 : 10 pm (d) 3 : 24 pm

110. Vikas covered a certain distance by bike. If he covers 40% of the distance at 40 km/h, 50% of the distance at 25 km/h and the remaining 10% distance at 10 km/h. Find his average speed over the whole distance.
SSC CGL (Tier-I) 03/12/2022 Shift-II

(a) 25 km/h (b) 28 km/h
(c) 26 km/h (d) 30 km/h

111. A car starts from point A toward point B, travelling at the speed of 20 km/h, $1\frac{1}{2}$ h later, another car from point A and travelling at the speed of 30 km/h and reaches $2\frac{1}{2}$ h before the first car. Find the distance between A and B.
SSC CGL (Tier-I) 03/12/2022 Shift-I

(a) 300 km (b) 240 km
(c) 260 km (d) 280 km

112. If a man travels at $\frac{1}{x}$ km/h on a journey and returns at $\frac{1}{x^2}$ km/h, then his average speed for the journey is
SSC CGL (Tier-I) 02/12/2022 Shift-III

(a) $\frac{x+1}{x^2}$ (b) $\frac{2}{x+x^2}$ (c) $\frac{1}{x+x^2}$ (d) $\frac{2x^2}{x+1}$

113. In a 400 m race, A runs at a speed of 16 m/s. If A gives B a start of 15 m and still beats him by 10 sec, then what is the speed of B?
SSC CGL (Tier-I) 2/12/2022 Shift-II

(a) 11 m/s (b) 10 m/s
(c) 13 m/s (d) 9 m/s

114. A thief is noticed by a policeman from a distance of 97 m. The thief starts running and the policeman chases him. The thief and the policeman run at a speed of 21 m/s and 23 m/s, respectively. What is the time taken by the policeman to catch the thief ?
SSC CGL (Tier-I) 02/12/2022 Shift-I

(a) 40 sec (b) 45 sec
(c) 62.5 sec (d) 48.5 sec

115. If Ram covers a certain journey at 60% of his usual speed, he reaches the destination late by 36 min. His usual time (in min) to reach the destination is
SSC CGL (Tier-I) 1/12/2022 Shift-IV

(a) 60 (b) 72 (c) 50 (d) 54

116. Two-thirds of a certain distance was covered at the speed of 45 km/h, one-fourth at the speed of 60 km/h and the rest at the speed of 75 km/h. Find the average speed per hour for the whole journey. (correct to 2 decimal places)
SSC CGL (Tier-I) 1/12/2022 Shift-IV

(a) 51.25 km/h (b) 45.75 km/h
(c) 58.25 km/h (d) 49.77 km/h

117. In a 1500 m race, Anil beats Bakul by 150 m and in the same race Bakul beats Charles by 75 m. By what distance does Anil beat Charles? SSC CGL (Tier-I) 1/12/2022 Shift-I

(a) 217.50 m (b) 200.15 m
(c) 293.50 m (d) 313.75 m

SSC CGL 2021 & 2020 (Tier I)

118. A car can cover a distance of 144 km in 1.8 h. In what time (in hours) will it cover double the distance when its speed is increased by 20%?
SSC CGL (Tier-I) 23/08/2021 Shift-II

(a) 3 (b) 2.5 (c) 2 (d) 3.2

119. A takes 2 h more than B to cover a distance of 40 km. If A doubles his speed, he takes $1\frac{1}{2}$ h more than B to cover 80 km. To cover a distance of 120 km, how much time (in hours) will B take travelling at his same speed?
SSC CGL (Tier-I) 23/08/2021 Shift-I

(a) $1\frac{2}{3}$ (b) $1\frac{1}{4}$ (c) $1\frac{1}{3}$ (d) $1\frac{1}{2}$

120. Akhil takes 30 min extra to cover a distance of 150 km. If he drive 10 km slower than his usual speed. How much time will be take to drive 90 km if he drives 15 km per hour slower than his usually speed? SSC CGL (Tier-I) 18/08/2021 Shift-I

(a) 2 h 45 m (b) 2 h 30 m
(c) 2h (d) 2 h 15 m

121. Two cars A and B leave Delhi at 8:30 am and at 9 am for Shimla, respectively. They travel at the speeds of 40 km/h and 50 km/h, respectively.
How many kilometers away from Delhi will the two cars be together?
SSC CGL (Tier-I) 07/03/2020 Shift-I

(a) 45 km (b) 100 km
(c) 200 km (d) 5 km

122. Two cyclists X and Y start at the same time from place A and go towards place B at a speed of 6 km/h and 8 km/h, respectively. Despite stopping for 15 min during the journey, Y reaches 10 min earlier than X. The distance between the places A and B is
SSC CGL (Tier-I) 06/03/2020 Shift-II

(a) 6 km (b) 16.5 km
(c) 10 km (d) 8 km

123. A student takes 1.25 h to travel from home to school at a speed of 4 km/h. By what percentage should he increase his speed to reduce the time by 25% to cover the same distance from school to home?
SSC CGL (Tier-I) 06/03/2020 Shift-I

(a) $33\frac{1}{3}$% (b) 50% (c) 45% (d) 25%

124. Places A and B are 144 km apart. Two cars start simultaneously, one from A and the other from B. If they move in the same direction, they meet after 12 h, but if they move towards each other they meet after $\frac{9}{8}$ h. The speed (in km/h) of the car moving at a faster speed, is
SSC CGL (Tier-I) 04/03/2020 Shift-III

(a) 70 (b) 72
(c) 60 (d) 64

SSC CPO SI 2024

125. If a car runs at a speed of 60 km/h and takes 180 min to cover a certain distance,then what time will it take to cover the same distance at a speed of 40 km/h?
SSC CPO 29/06/2024 Shift-III

(a) 4 h 30 min (b) 3 h
(c) 3 h 15 min (d) 3 h 45 min

126. A student goes to his school by cycle. The distance from his house to school is 5 km and he covers this distance in 1 h. While going he

stops twice for 5 min each. Find his average speed (in km/h).
SSC CPO 29/06/2024 Shift-III

(a) 5.5 km/h (b) 6 km/h
(c) 6.5 km/h (d) 4.5 km/h

127. A man travels some distance from his house to the exhibition ground by an auto at a speed of 30 km/h and returns by a cab at a speed of 50 km/h. What is his average speed (in km/h)? **SSC CPO 29/06/2024 Shift-III**

(a) 37.5 km/h (b) 40 km/h
(c) 28 km/h (d) 38 km/h

128. In a 100 km journey, the average speed of *S* is 40 km/h. He covers the first 60 km in 40 min and the next 20 km in 50 min. What is his speed in the last 20 km (in km/h)?
SSC CPO 29/06/2024 Shift-I

(a) 30 km/h (b) 40 km/h
(c) 25 km/h (d) 20 km/h

129. Ashish covers 72 km at a speed of 45 km/h by bike, 28 km at a speed of 4 km/h by bicycle and another 160 km at a speed of 20 km/h by car. Find his average speed (in km/h) for the whole journey. (Rounded off to two decimal places) **SSC CPO 28/06/2024 Shift-III**

(a) 15.66 (b) 28.33
(c) 25.25 (d) 27.65

130. *A* travels for 8 h at the rate of 4 km/h and for 4 h at the rate of 8 km/h. The average speed of the journey (in km/h) is
SSC CPO 28/06/2024 Shift-III

(a) $4\frac{2}{3}$ km/h (b) $5\frac{1}{3}$ km/h
(c) $4\frac{1}{3}$ km/h (d) $5\frac{2}{3}$ km/h

131. A man travels 1200 km by train at 80 km/h, 1600 km by ship at 40 km/h, 1000 km by plane at 400 km/h, and 200 km by car at 50 km/h. What is the average speed for the entire distance? (rounded off to 2 decimal places)
SSC CPO 28/06/2024 Shift-II

(a) 65.04 km/h
(b) 72.40 km/h
(c) 68.14 km/h
(d) 75.40 km/h

132. Two towns *P* and *Q* are 275 km apart. A motorcycle rider starts from *P* towards *Q* at 10:00 am at the speed of 25 km/h. Another rider starts from *Q* towards *P* at 12 noon on the same day at the speed of 20 km/h. At what time will they cross each other?
SSC CPO 28/06/2024 Shift-II

(a) 1:15 pm (b) 3:00 pm
(c) 4:30 pm (d) 5:00 pm

133. The distance (*d*) a moving body travels, varies directly with the time (*t*) when it moves. A train travels 72 km in 2 h. Find the equation that relates *d* and *t*.
SSC CPO 28/06/2024 Shift-II

(a) $d = \frac{t}{36}$ (b) $d = t - 36$
(c) $d = t + 36$ (d) $d = 36t$

134. *S* drives his car and covers 37 km and 500 m in 90 min. What is his average speed(in km/h)?
SSC CPO 28/06/2024 Shift-I

(a) 25 km/h (b) 20 km/h
(c) 40 km/h (d) 22.5 km/h

135. *R* reaches office from home in 30 min and comes back in 20 min. The distance to his office from home is 12.5 km. What is his average speed (in km/h) from home to office and then back home? **SSC CPO 27/06/2024 Shift-III**

(a) 30 km/h (b) 60 km/h
(c) 25 km/h (d) 20 km/h

136. A man travels some distance at a speed of 12 km/h and returns at a speed of 8 km/h. If the total time taken by him is 3 h and 45 min, then the total distance (in km) travelled is **SSC CPO 27/06/2024 Shift-III**

(a) 42 (b) 24 (c) 32 (d) 36

137. Two cars run to a place at the speeds of 45 km/h and 55 km/h, respectively. If the second car takes 40 min less than the first for the journey, then what is the length of the journey (in km)?
SSC CPO 27/06/2024 Shift-II

(a) 180 (b) 165 (c) 99 (d) 145

138. A bus covers the first 50 km of its journey in 40 min and covers the remaining 75km in 40 min. What is the average speed (in km/h) of the bus? **SSC CPO 27/06/2024 Shift-II**

(a) $101\frac{1}{4}$ (b) $105\frac{3}{4}$
(c) $93\frac{3}{4}$ (d) $95\frac{1}{4}$

139. A thief running at 7 km/h is chased by a policeman, whose speed is 12 km/h. If the thief is 280 m ahead of the policeman, then the time required for the policeman to catch the thief will be **SSC CPO 27/06/2024 Shift-I**

(a) $3\frac{1}{25}$ min (b) $3\frac{9}{25}$ min
(c) $4\frac{9}{25}$ min (d) $3\frac{2}{25}$ min

140. A car covers 20 km in the first quarter of an hour, 25 km in the second quarter of that hour and 15 km in the third quarter. The average speed of the car (in km/h) over the entire journey is
SSC CPO 27/06/2024 Shift-I

(a) 80 (b) 70 (c) 65 (d) 75

SSC CPO SI 2023

141. A man covers a certain distance by bike. If he covers 25% of the distance at the speed of 25 km/h, 50% of the distance at the speed of 50 km/h and the remaining distance at the speed of 12.5 km/h, find his average speed over the whole journey.
SSC CPO 05/10/2023 Shift-III

(a) 20 km/h (b) 30 km/h
(c) 25 km/h (d) 35 km/h

142. In a 1200 m race, Rakesh reaches the final point in 36 sec and Rajesh reaches in 40 sec. By how much distance does Rakesh beat Rajesh?
SSC CPO 05/10/2023 Shift-III

(a) 130 m (b) 120 m
(c) 140 m (d) 150 m

143. The time taken to travel the same distance by three cars are in the ratio of 12:15:10. What is the ratio of the speeds of the three cars?
SSC CPO 04/10/2023 Shift-II

(a) 4 : 5 : 6 (b) 4 : 6 : 5
(c) 5 : 4 : 6 (d) 5 : 6 : 4

144. A car, during its entire journey of 5 h, travels the first 45 min at a certain speed, the next 75 min at a speed of 85 km/h, and the last 3 h at a speed of 70 km/h. During its entire journey, the average speed of the car is found to be 73 km/h. What is the speed (in km/h) of the car during the first 45 min?
SSC CPO 04/10/2023 Shift-II

(a) 65 (b) 68 (c) 62 (d) 72

145. A man runs for 40 km. The time taken by him in the first 10 km is twice the time taken by him in the second 10 km. The time taken in the third 10 km is half of the time taken in the fourth 10 km, and the time taken in the fourth 10 km is equal to the time taken in the first 10 km. If his speed in the first 10 km is 40 km/h, then what is the average speed for 40 km?
SSC CPO 03/10/2023 Shift-I

(a) 50 km/h (b) $\frac{70}{3}$ km/h
(c) $\frac{160}{3}$ km/h (d) 40 km/h

146. A tourist van travels the distance of 35 km from Dehradun to Mussoorie at an average speed of 36 km/h and returns at 60 km/h. What is the approximate average speed (in km/h) of the tourist van for the entire journey? **SSC CPO 03/10/2023 Shift-I**
(a) 48 (b) 42
(c) 45 (d) 50

147. A person crosses a 900 m long street in 6 min. The speed of the person, in km/h, is **SSC CPO 03/10/2023 Shift-I**
(a) 10 (b) 9
(c) 5 (d) 8

SSC CPO SI 2022-2020

148. In a race of 1200 m, Ram can beat Shyam by 200 m or by 20 sec. What must be the speed of Ram? **SSC CPO 11/11/2022 Shift-I**
(a) 14 m/s (b) 12 m/s
(c) 10 m/s (d) 16 m/s

149. The speeds of *A* and *B* are in the ratio 3 : 5. *A* takes 30 min more than *B* to reach the destination. In how much time does *A* reach the destination? **SSC CPO 11/11/2022 Shift-I**
(a) 1 h 15 min (b) 1 h 10 min
(c) 1 h (d) 1 h 5 min

150. If a man goes from place *A* to *B* at a speed of 12 km/h and return at a speed of 18 km/h, then the average speed for the whole journey is **SSC CPO 11/11/2022 Shift-I**
(a) 6 km/h (b) 30 km/h
(c) $14\frac{2}{5}$ km/h (d) 15 km/h

151. A car travels with a speed of 21 m/s in the first 10 min, 9.0 km in the next 10 min and 10 km in the last 10 min of its journey. What is the average speed of the car in km/h during its entire journey? **SSC CPO 10/11/2022 Shift-I**
(a) 60.0 km/h (b) 63.2 km/h
(c) 62.0 km/h (d) 65.3 km/h

152. A car covered the first 100 km at a speed of 50 km/h. It covered next 140 km at a speed of 70 km/h. What is its average speed? **SSC CPO 10/11/2022 Shift-I**
(a) 60 km/ h (b) 62 km/h
(c) 58 km/h (d) 64 km/h

153. Geeta runs 5/2 times as fast as Babita. In a race, if Geeta gives a lead of 40 m to Babita, find the distance from the starting point where both of them will meet (correct up to two decimal places). **SSC CPO 10/11/2022 Shift-I**
(a) 66.67 m (b) 65 m
(c) 65.33 m (d) 66 m

154. *A* takes 2 h 30 min more than *B* to walk 40 km. If *A* doubles his speed, then he can make it in 1 h less than *B*. What is the average time taken by *A* and *B* to walk a 40 km distance? **SSC CPO 25/11/2020 Shift-I**
(a) 7 h 15 min (b) 5 h 45 min
(c) 6 h (d) 5 h 15 min

155. A bus covers a 60 km distance in 1 h 30 min, where as the same distance is covered by a car in 45 min. What is the ratio of the speed of the car to the speed of the bus? **SSC CPO 24/11/2020 Shift-I**
(a) 5 : 3 (b) 3 : 5
(c) 1 : 2 (d) 2 : 1

156. A person covers a distance of 300 km and then returns to the starting point. The time taken by him for the outward journey is 5 h more than the time taken for the return journey. If he returned at a speed of 10 km/h more than the speed of going, what was the speed (in km/h) for the onward journey? **SSC CPO 24/11/2020 Shift-I**
(a) 15 (b) 20 (c) 30 (d) 25

157. *A* takes 2 h 30 min more than *B* to walk 40 km. If *A* doubles his speed, then he can make it in 1 h less than *B*. How much time (in hours) does *A* require for walking a 40 km distance? **SSC CPO 23/11/2020 Shift-I**
(a) 6 (b) 7 (c) 9 (d) 5

SSC CHSL 2024 (Tier I & II)

158. Tarun gives Hari a head-start of 60 sec in a 2400 m race and still beats him by 40 sec. If the speed of Hari is 6 m/s, find the speed of Tarun. **SSC CHSL (Tier-II) 18/11/2024 Shift-I**
(a) 8.5 m/s (b) 7.5 m/s
(c) 8 m/s (d) 7 m/s

159. Tom travelled 285 km in 6 h. In his total travelling, he travelled the first part by bus at 40 km/h and the remaining part by train at 55 km/h. How much distance has he travelled by train? **SSC CHSL (Tier-I) 11/07/2024 Shift-IV**
(a) 155 km (b) 120 km
(c) 165 km (d) 135 km

160. By what percentage should a racer increase the speed to reduce the time by 25% to cover a fixed distance? **SSC CHSL (Tier-I) 11/07/2024 Shift-I**
(a) 31% (b) 41%
(c) $37\frac{1}{3}$% (d) $33\frac{1}{3}$%

161. A police travelling at 65 km/h is chasing a thief who is 1200 m away from him and is travelling at 41 km/h. Find the time taken by the policeman to catch the thief. **SSC CHSL (Tier-I) 11/07/2024 Shift-I**
(a) 1 min (b) 3 min
(c) 2 min (d) 4 min

162. A man walking at the speed of 4 km/h covers a certain distance in 6 h and 15 min. If he covers the same distance by cycle in 5 h and 10 min, then the speed of the cycle (in km/h) is **SSC CHSL (Tier-I) 10/07/2024 Shift-IV**
(a) $2\frac{9}{31}$ km/h (b) $3\frac{11}{31}$ km/h
(c) $4\frac{26}{31}$ km/h (d) $3\frac{21}{31}$ km/h

163. With a uniform speed, a car covers a distance in 16 h. Had the speed been increased by 20 km/h, the same distance would have been covered in 12 h. The total distance covered by the car is **SSC CHSL (Tier-I) 10/07/2024 Shift-III**
(a) 720 km (b) 1080 km
(c) 960 km (d) 480 km

164. A policeman was asked to chase a thief. Before the policeman started the chase, he realised that the thief was 200 m ahead of him and was running at a speed of 16 km/h. The policeman started the chase at a speed of 20 km/h. How far will the thief run before he is overtaken by the policeman? **SSC CHSL (Tier-I) 10/07/2024 Shift-II**
(a) 1000 m (b) 700 m
(c) 800 m (d) 600 m

165. A cyclist rides 10 km at an average speed of 15 km/h and then the next 15 km at an average speed of 10 km/h. The average speed of the entire ride is **SSC CHSL (Tier-I) 10/07/2024 Shift-I**
(a) 20 km/h (b) 12.5 km/h
(c) 10 km/h (d) 11.54 km/h

166. The speed of a thief is $\frac{4}{5}$ times the speed of a policeman. The thief covers a distance of 6 km before he was caught by the policeman in 30 min. Initially, what was the

distance between the policeman and the thief (in km)?
SSC CHSL (Tier-I) 09/07/2024 Shift-IV

(a) 0.8 (b) 1.0 (c) 1.5 (d) 1.2

167. A part of the journey is covered in 22.5 min at a speed of 68 km/h and the remaining part in 12 min at a speed of 72 km/h. The total distance of the journey is (to the nearest integer)
SSC CHSL (Tier-I) 09/07/2024 Shift-II

(a) 40 km (b) 38 km
(c) 42 km (d) 35 km

168. In a 2 km linear race, if P completes the race in 200 sec and Q in 220 sec, then the distance by which P beats Q is
SSC CHSL (Tier-I) 09/07/2024 Shift-I

(a) $167\frac{6}{11}$ m (b) $173\frac{7}{11}$ m
(c) $191\frac{7}{11}$ m (d) $181\frac{9}{11}$ m

169. A policeman is chasing a thief at a speed of 12 km/h, and the thief is running at a speed of 8 km/h. If the policeman started 30 min late, find the time taken by the policeman to catch the thief.
SSC CHSL (Tier-I) 08/07/2024 Shift-I

(a) 120 min (b) 60 min
(c) 90 min (d) 100 min

170. A person divides his total route of journey into three equal parts and decides to travel the three parts at the speeds of 80 km/h, 60 km/h and 30 km/h, respectively. What is the average speed during the journey?
SSC CHSL (Tier-I) 05/07/2024 Shift-IV

(a) 45 km/h (b) 40 km/h
(c) 49 km/h (d) 48 km/h

171. A motorcyclist rides his motorcycle at a speed of 90 km/h in the first one hour and the next two hours at a speed of 120 km/h. Find the average speed of the rider.
SSC CHSL (Tier-I) 05/07/2024 Shift-III

(a) 110 km/h (b) 120 km/h
(c) 105 km/h (d) 115 km/h

172. To reach at a destination, D takes 45 min, if he drives at a speed of 60 km/h. Due to some urgency, he is to reach the destination in 30 min. What should be his speed in km/h?
SSC CHSL (Tier-I) 05/07/2024 Shift-II

(a) 90 km/h (b) 60 km/h
(c) 80 km/h (d) 75 km/h

173. A girl walking at a speed of 9 km/h crosses a bridge in 45 min. Find the length of the bridge in metres.
SSC CHSL (Tier-I) 05/07/2024 Shift-I

(a) 6349 (b) 6398 (c) 6750 (d) 7532

174. In a 100 m race, A beats B by 20 m and B beats C by 5 m. In the same race, find the distance by which A beats C.
SSC CHSL (Tier-I) 04/07/2024 Shift-IV

(a) 22 m (b) 24 m (c) 26 m (d) 25 m

175. A car covers a certain distance in 85 min, if it runs at a speed of 36 km/h. The speed at which the car must run to reduce the time of journey to 51 min will be
SSC CHSL (Tier-I) 04/07/2024 Shift-III

(a) 70 km/h (b) 80 km/h
(c) 60 km/h (d) 50 km/h

176. Arun and Bhaskar run a race of 3 km. First, Arun gives Bhaskar a head start of 400 m and beats him by 30 sec. While coming back, Arun gives Bhaskar a lead of 2.5 min and gets beaten by 500 m. What is the difference between the times in minutes in which Arun and Bhaskar can run the race for one side separately?
SSC CHSL (Tier-I) 04/07/2024 Shift-II

(a) 3 min (b) 1.5 min
(c) 2.5 min (d) 2 min

177. Shankar covers a certain distance by a car driving at 40 km/h and he returns to the starting point riding on a scooter with a speed of 20 km/h. Find the average speed of the whole journey.
SSC CHSL (Tier-I) 04/07/2024 Shift-I

(a) $22\frac{2}{3}$ km/h (b) $29\frac{2}{3}$ km/h
(c) $24\frac{2}{3}$ km/h (d) $26\frac{2}{3}$ km/h

178. Ram and Shyam start walking from the same place in the opposite direction. If Shyam walks at a speed of $5\frac{1}{4}$ km/h and Ram at a speed of 3 km/h, then after how much time will they be 44 km apart?
SSC CHSL (Tier-I) 03/07/2024 Shift-IV

(a) 3 h 20 min (b) 5 h 20 min
(c) 6 h 20 min (d) 4 h 20 min

179. In 800 m race, the ratio of the speeds of two contestants Ankur and Neha is 5 : 6. If Ankur has a head-start of 200 m, then Ankur will win by ……… .
SSC CHSL (Tier-I) 03/07/2024 Shift-III

(a) 89 m (b) 80 m (c) 76 m (d) 69 m

180. A policeman starts chasing a thief, who is 500 m ahead of him. The speed of the thief is 18 km/h and the speed of the policeman is 36 km/h. Find the time taken by the policeman to catch the thief.
SSC CHSL (Tier-I) 03/07/2024 Shift-II

(a) 300 sec (b) 100 sec
(c) 150 sec (d) 250 sec

181. A bus driver must complete a 240 km trip in 4 h. If his average speed 70 km/h for the first 3 h of his trip. How fast must he travel (in km/h) in the last/final hour?
SSC CHSL (Tier-I) 03/07/2024 Shift-I

(a) 60 km/h (b) 50 km/h
(c) 30 km/h (d) 35 km/h

182. Two stations T_1 and T_2 300 km apart. A car starts from station T_1 at 8 am and moves towards station T_2 at a speed of 45 km/h and at 10 am another car starts from station T_2 towards T_1 at a speed of 60 km/h. Then the cars will meet at
SSC CHSL (Tier-I) 03/07/2024 Shift-I

(a) 11 : 00 am (b) 1 : 00 pm
(c) 12 : 00 pm (d) 10 : 00 am

183. Mithila covers 50 km by bus in 90 min. After deboarding the bus, she takes rest for 15 min and covers another 30 km by a taxi in 35 min. Find the average speed (in km/h) for the whole journey.
SSC CHSL (Tier-I) 02/07/2024 Shift-III

(a) $31\frac{2}{7}$ (b) $32\frac{2}{7}$
(c) $34\frac{2}{7}$ (d) $33\frac{2}{7}$

184. A policeman received information that a thief is at a distance of 1.5 km from him. The thief starts moving by car and the policeman chases him by car. The thief and the policeman are moving at the speeds of 90 km/h and 120 km/h, respectively. At what distance (in km) will the police catch the thief?
SSC CHSL (Tier-I) 02/07/2024 Shift-III

(a) 45 km (b) 5 km
(c) 6 km (d) 4.5 km

185. Moving at $\frac{6}{7}$ of its usual speed, a bus is 20 min late. What is its usual time to cover the journey?
SSC CHSL (Tier-I) 02/07/2024 Shift-II

(a) 2 h (b) 4 h
(c) 1.5 h (d) 3 h

186. A robber steals a bag from a man at 5 pm and starts running at 10 km/h. A policeman is informed about the robber at 5 : 12 pm and he chases him on a cycle at 15 km/h. At what time is the robber caught by the policeman?
SSC CHSL (Tier-I) 01/07/2024 Shift-IV

(a) 5:48 pm (b) 5:36 pm
(c) 5:12 pm (d) 5:40 pm

187. Ram travelled an equal distance with the speed of 40 km/h, 45 km/h and 60 km/h. What is the average speed of Ram during the whole journey? Correct to two decimal places. **SSC CHSL (Tier-I) 01/07/2024 Shift-II**

(a) 66.94 km/h (b) 94.66 km/h
(c) 64.96 km/h (d) 46.96 km/h

188. A man walking at the speed of 5 km/h covers a certain distance in 3 h 45 min. If he covers the same distance by a cycle in 2 h 10 min, then the speed of the cycle (in km/h) is **SSC CHSL (Tier-I) 01/07/2024 Shift-I**

(a) $7\frac{16}{26}$ (b) $9\frac{11}{26}$ (c) $8\frac{17}{26}$ (d) $5\frac{11}{26}$

SSC CHSL 2023 (Tier I & II)

189. A person covers $\frac{1}{4}$ of his journey at the speed of 25 km/h, $\frac{1}{2}$ of the journey at 40km/h and the remaining at the speed of 50 km/h. Find his average speed per hour for the whole journey (in km/h).
SSC CHSL (Tier-II) 2/11/2023 Shift-I

(a) $36\frac{4}{11}$ (b) $34\frac{4}{11}$
(c) $34\frac{6}{11}$ (d) $36\frac{6}{11}$

190. By driving the car at an average speed of 40 km/h, I reach my destination in 7 h. With what speed I can reach the same destination in 5 h? **SSC CHSL (Tier-I) 17/08/2023 Shift-I**

(a) 50 km/h (b) 56 km/h
(c) 55 km/h (d) 65 km/h

191. *A* and *B* are running on a circular track of length 1400 m. The speed of *A* is 33 m/sec and the speed of *B* is 47 m/sec. They start from the same point at the same time in the opposite direction. After how much time will they meet for the second time? **SSC CHSL (Tier-I) 17/08/2023 Shift-I**

(a) 33 sec (b) 38 sec
(c) 35 sec (d) 32 sec

192. Anil and Arun started for car race from the same point in the same direction and at the same time on a circular track of length 2575 m with speeds 72 km/h and 90 km/h, respectively. After how much time (in seconds) will they meet again for the first time?
SSC CHSL (Tier-I) 14/08/2023 Shift-IV

(a) 520 (b) 525
(c) 510 (d) 515

193. Two cities *P* and *Q* are 181 km apart on a straight road. One man starts from *P* at 8 : 30 am and travels toward *Q* at 30 km/h. If another man starts from *Q* at 8 : 54 am and travels towards *P* at a speed of 35 km/h, then at what time will they meet?
SSC CHSL (Tier-I) 11/08/2023 Shift-I

(a) 11 : 30 am (b) 10 : 00 am
(c) 10 : 30 am (d) 11 : 00 am

194. *A* rides his bicycle at 15 km/h, while *B* starts his ride after 6 h to catch *A* with a speed of 25 km/h. Time taken by *B* to catch *A* (in hours) is
SSC CHSL (Tier-I) 10/08/2023 Shift-III

(a) 9 (b) 8 (c) 10 (d) 6

195. Anil completed a certain journey by a car. If he covered 35% of the distance at 70 km/h, 40% of the distance at 80 km/h and the remaining distance at 50 km/h, his average speed (in km/h) for the entire journey is
SSC CHSL (Tier-I) 09/08/2023 Shift-I

(a) $66\frac{3}{3}$ km/h (b) $66\frac{2}{3}$ km/h
(c) $66\frac{1}{3}$ km/h (d) $66\frac{4}{3}$ km/h

196. The speed of a car is 63 km/h. What is the distance travelled by it in 10 sec?
SSC CHSL (Tier-I) 08/08/2023 Shift-II

(a) 175 m (b) 1.75 km
(c) 185 m (d) 17.5 m

197. Zeenat and Nasreen participate in a circular race of 1.2 km. They start the race at a speed of 18 km/h and 27 km/h respectively, from the same point at the same time. After how much time (in minutes) will they meet at the starting point for the first time, if they are running in the same direction?
SSC CHSL (Tier-I) 21/08/2023 Shift-I

(a) 9 (b) 7 (c) 10 (d) 8

198. A person goes to his office by scooter at the speed of 80 km/h and reaches 60 min earlier. If he goes at the speed 50 km/h, then he reaches 48 min late. What will be the speed of the scooter to reach on the usual time?
SSC CHSL (Tier-I) 21/03/2023 Shift-II

(a) 64 km/h (b) 66 km/h
(c) 60 km/h (d) 62 km/h

199. Excluding stoppages, the speed of a bus is 60 km/h and including stoppages, it is 54 km/h. For how many minutes does the bus stop per hour?
SSC CHSL (Tier-I) 20/03/2023 Shift-III

(a) 4 min (b) 6 min
(c) 7 min (d) 5 min

200. One third part of a certain journey is covered at the speed of 10 km/h, one fourth part at the speed of 15 km/h and the rest part at the speed of 20 km/h. What will be the average speed for the whole journey?
SSC CHSL (Tier-I) 16/03/2023 Shift-I

(a) 15 km/h (b) 200/17 km/h
(c) 240/17 km/h (d) 280/17 km/h

201. A bus starts from a bus stand after every 50 min in the same direction. Mohit is walking in opposite direction with a speed of 50 km/h. If Mohit meets each bus in 10 min, then what is the speed of bus?
SSC CHSL (Tier-I) 15/03/2023 Shift-IV

(a) 14.5 km/h (b) 15 km/h
(c) 12.5 km/h (d) 10.5 km/h

202. Ram needs to reach the examination center in 6 h, the journey itself in 250 km. If Ram has covered (3/5)th of the distance in 3.5 h then what is the speed required to reach the destination 30 min early than the required time? **SSC CHSL (Tier-I) 10/03/2023 Shift-II**

(a) 50 km/h (b) 90 km/h
(c) 40 km/h (d) 60 km/h

203. A car travels a distance of 60 km at uniform speed. If the speed of car is increased by 8 km/h, then it takes 2 h less to cover the same distance. What is the original speed of the car?
SSC CHSL (Tier-I) 09/03/2023 Shift-I

(a) 12 km/h (b) 16 km/h
(c) 10 km/h (d) 15 km/h

SSC CHSL 2022 & 2021 (Tier I & II)

204. In a circular race of 2500 m, a man and a woman start from a point towards opposite directions with speeds of 37 km/h and 35 km/h, respectively. After how much time from the start of the race will they meet for the first time?
SSC CHSL (Tier-I) 02/06/2022 Shift-I

(a) 2 min 40 sec (b) 2 min 30 sec
(c) 2 min 5 sec (d) 2 min 20 sec

205. A man rides his bicycle for 10 km at a speed of 12 km/h, then for another 12 km at a speed of 10 km/h. What is his average speed for the entire trip approximately?
SSC CHSL (Tier-I) 01/06/2022 Shift-I

(a) 10.8 km/h (b) 11.8 km/h
(c) 11.4 km/h (d) 10 km/h

206. Roshni travelled at the speed of 66 km/h while going from point A to point B and returned via the same route at the speed of 92.4 km/h. What was Roshni's overall average speed during the two-way journey?
SSC CHSL (Tier-I) 01/06/2022 Shift-I
(a) 77 km/h (b) 79.2 km/h
(c) 79 km/h (d) 78 km/h

207. Sunita drive her car at an average speed of 45 km/h for the first 75 km of a trip and then at an average speed of 70 km/h for the remaining 45 km of the trip. If she made no stops during the trip, what was Sunita's average speed (in km/h) for the entire trip ?
SSC CHSL (Tier-I) 31/05/2022 Shift-I
(a) 52 (b) $51\frac{3}{7}$
(c) 51 (d) $51\frac{93}{97}$

208. A car takes 50 min to cover a certain distance at a speed of 54 km/h. If the speed is increased by 25%, then how long will it take to cover three-fourth of the same distance?
SSC CHSL (Tier-I) 12/08/2021 Shift-III
(a) 35 min (b) 40 min
(c) 30 min (d) 25 min

209. One-fifth of a journey is covered at a speed of 30 km/h, one-fourth of the journey at a speed of 25 km/h and the rest at 60 km/h. What is the average speed (in km/h, correct to one decimal place) for the whole journey?
SSC CHSL (Tier-I) 04/08/2021 Shift-I
(a) 38.7 (b) 30.6
(c) 40.5 (d) 25.4

210. A man walking at a rate of 4 km/h crossed a tunnel in 18 min. What is the length of the tunnel in meters?
SSC CHSL (Tier-I) 09/04/2021 Shift-III
(a) 1800 (b) 1400
(c) 1200 (d) 1600

SSC MTS 2024

211. A person can complete a journey in 21 h. He covers the first one-third of the journey at the speed of 40 km/h and the remaining distance at the speed of 60 km/h. What is the total distance of his journey? **SSC MTS 13/11/2024 Shift-III**
(a) 720 km (b) 1080 km
(c) 360 km (d) 1140 km

212. A man covers 30 km by car at a speed of 60 km/h and another 20 km by cycle. His whole journey is completed in 3 h. What is the speed (in km/h) of the cycle?
SSC MTS 13/11/2024 Shift-III
(a) 10 (b) 12 (c) 8 (d) 6

213. A policeman travelling at a speed of 120 km/h chases a thief 5000 m away from him, and travelling at a speed of 100 km/h.
What is the time taken by the policeman to catch the thief?
SSC MTS 12/11/2024 Shift-III
(a) 20 min (b) 10 min
(c) 15 min (d) 13.5 min

214. A man travels a certain distance at 10 km/h and returns to the starting point at 8 km/h. The total time taken by him for the entire journey is one and a half hours. The total distance (in km) covered by him is
SSC MTS 11/11/2024 Shift-III
(a) $11\frac{1}{3}$ (b) $14\frac{2}{5}$
(c) $13\frac{1}{3}$ (d) $12\frac{2}{3}$

215. A thief is 150 m away from a policeman. If the speed of the thief is 93 km/h and the speed of the policeman is 108 km/h, then the time taken by the policeman to catch the thief is
SSC MTS 05/11/2024 Shift-III
(a) 32 sec (b) 40 sec
(c) 38 sec (d) 36 sec

216. A thief seeing a policemen from a distance of 525 m started running at a speed of 18 km/h. The policeman chased him immediately at a speed of 21 km/h and the thief was caught. How far did the thief run before he was caught by the policeman? **SSC MTS 30/10/2024 Shift-III**
(a) 3175 m (b) 3125 m
(c) 3100 m (d) 3150 m

217. A thief is noticed by a policeman from a distance of 400 m. The thief starts running at a speed of 8 km/h and the policeman chases him at a speed of 9 km/h. What is the distance between them after 18 min? **SSC MTS 30/10/2024 Shift-III**
(a) 200 m (b) 300 m
(c) 150 m (d) 100 m

218. Two athletes X and Y are jogging on a circular path, whose circumference is 500 m. Athlete X jogs at a speed of 18 km/h and Y jogs at 9 km/h, jogging in opposite directions. The time at which they will meet for the first time is
SSC MTS 29/10/2024 Shift-III
(a) 66.66 sec (b) 50 sec
(c) 200 sec (d) 27.77 sec

219. In a circular race of 1 km, two persons X and Y start with the speed of 9 km/h and 18 km/h, respectively, at the same time from the same point. When will they meet for the first time at the starting point, when running in the same direction?
SSC MTS 29/10/2024 Shift-III
(a) 400 sec (b) 360 sec
(c) 180 sec (d) 240 sec

220. A car covers the first 12 km distance at a speed of 30 km per hour, the next 15 km distance at a speed of 45 km/h and the next 20 km distance at a speed of 60 km/h. Find the average speed of the car. **SSC MTS 28/10/2024 Shift-II**
(a) $33\frac{1}{17}$ km/h (b) $47\frac{3}{26}$ km/h
(c) $44\frac{1}{16}$ km/h (d) $39\frac{2}{19}$ km/h

221. The speed of a car is 81 km/h. The distance covered by the car in 24 seconds is **SSC MTS 23/10/2024 Shift-II**
(a) 540 m (b) 560 m
(c) 270 m (d) 280 m

222. Walking at a speed of 5.4 km/h, Rohit takes 40 min to reach his school from his home. What time will he take if he walks 8 km/h?
SSC MTS 22/10/2024 Shift-II
(a) 25 min (b) 24 min
(c) 23 min (d) 27 min

223. A person has to cover a distance of 8 km in 1 hour. If he covers one-fourth of the distance in one-third of the total time, then what should his speed (in km/h) be to cover the remaining distance in the remaining time so that the person reaches the destination exactly on time?
SSC MTS 22/10/2024 Shift-II
(a) 8 (b) 7 (c) 9 (d) 6

224. Raghav covers a distance of 45 km in 1 hour 40 minutes. Assuming he maintains a constant speed throughout his journey, what is Raghav's speed (in m/s)?
SSC MTS 21/10/2024 Shift-II
(a) 9 (b) 6
(c) 7.5 (d) 7.2

225. Distance between A and B is 1200 km. If they start moving towards each other at same time, they will meet in 24 h. If A starts 10 h after B, then they will meet after

another 20 h. What are their respective speeds? SSC MTS 21/10/2024 Shift-II

(a) 30 km/h, 20 km/h
(b) 25 km/h, 35 km/h
(c) 35 km/h, 25 km/h
(d) 40 km/h, 25km/h

226. *A* and *B* start running simultaneously, around a circular track of 1200 m, in the same direction, at a speed of 8 m/s and 12 m/s, respectively. A and B will meet at the starting point for the first time after SSC MTS 18/10/2024 Shift-II

(a) 80 sec (b) 150 sec
(c) 300 sec (d) 100 sec

227. A thief is running away on a straight road on a bike moving at the speed of 28 m/s. A policeman chases him in a car moving at the speed of 30 m/s. If the instantaneous separation of the bike from the car is 400 m, how long will it take for the policeman to catch the thief? SSC MTS 18/10/2024 Shift-II

(a) 200 sec (b) 100 sec
(c) 150 sec (d) 300 sec

228. A thief steels a bike at 10:30 am and drives it at 50 km/h. But the thief is found after half an hour. The bike owner started to chase him by another bike at 60 km/h. The time at which the thief is caught is SSC MTS 17/10/2024 Shift-II

(a) 1: 30 pm (b) 2: 30 pm
(c) 12: 30 pm (d) 1: 00 pm

229. A car driver covers a total distance of 120 km. He covers the first 80 km at a uniform speed of 50 km/h and the next 40 km at a uniform speed of 40 km/h. The average speed of the car is: SSC MTS 16/10/2024 Shift-II

(a) $46\frac{1}{13}$ km/h (b) $46\frac{5}{13}$ km/h
(c) $46\frac{3}{13}$ km/h (d) $46\frac{2}{13}$ km/h

230. *A* and *B* are running in the same direction at the speeds of 9 km/h and 3 km/h, respectively, on a circular track of length 27 km. They will meet again after: SSC MTS 16/10/2024 Shift-II

(a) 4.5 h (b) 4 h
(c) 3.5 h (d) 3 h

231. A runner runs 300 m race in 36 sec. The runner's speed in km/h is SSC MTS 15/10/2024 Shift-I

(a) 48 (b) 24 (c) 30 (d) 36

232. A person sees another person snatching a chain from a lady, at a distance of 300 metres. He starts running and catches the thief by running at 10 km/h after running a total distance of 1.5 km. The speed at which the thief was running was SSC MTS 15/10/2024 Shift-I

(a) 8.5 km/h (b) 9 km/h
(c) 9.5 km/h (d) 8 km/h

233. A cyclist covers a distance of 2.5 km in 4 min 10 sec. How long will he take to cover a distance of 6 km at the same speed? SSC MTS 09/10/2024 Shift-I

(a) 11 min (b) 12 min
(c) 9 min (d) 10 min

234. A car can cover 275 km in 5 hours. If its speed is reduced by 5 km/h, then how much time will the car take to cover a distance of 300 km? SSC MTS 09/10/2024 Shift-I

(a) 5 h 30 min (b) 6 h
(c) 5 h (d) 4 h 30 min

235. A man riding his bicycle covers 75 m in 12.5 sec. What is his speed (in km/h)? SSC MTS 08/10/2024 Shift-I

(a) 21.6 (b) 15.5 (c) 11.1 (d) 6

236. A thief saw a policeman and he started running at a speed of 12 m/s. After a certain time, the policeman starts running behind the thief at a speed of 18 m/s. If the policeman covered a 540 m distance to catch the thief, the time (in sec) after which the policeman started running is SSC MTS 08/10/2024 Shift-I

(a) 10 (b) 12 (c) 15 (d) 18

237. The speeds of three cars are in the ratio 5 : 3 : 4. The ratio between the time taken by these cars to cover the same distance is SSC MTS 08/10/2024 Shift-I

(a) 12:20:15 (b) 10:13:15
(c) 16:13:15 (d) 12:13:15

238. A person travels equal distances with speeds of 3 km/h, 4 km/h and 8 km/h, respectively and takes a total of 425 min. What is the total distance (in km) travelled? SSC MTS 07/10/2024 Shift-I

(a) 32 (b) 28 (c) 27 (d) 30

239. Ravi goes to college from his village at the speed of 5 km/h and returns at the speed of 4km/h. If he takes 9 h in all, find the distance (in km) between the village and the college. SSC MTS 01/10/2024 Shift-I

(a) 20 (b) 40 (c) 18 (d) 9

240. A thief saw a policeman and he started running at a speed of 18 m/s. After 12 sec, the policeman starts running behind the thief at a certain speed. If the policeman covered 864 m distance to reach the thief, then the speed (in m/s) of the policeman is SSC MTS 30/09/2024 Shift-I

(a) 28 (b) 15 (c) 30 (d) 24

SSC MTS 2023

241. A man decided to cover 7.5 km in 72 min. He decided to cover two thirds of the distance at 5 km/h and the remaining at some different speed. Find the speed after two third distance has been covered. SSC MTS 14/9/2023 Shift-I

(a) 14.3 km/h (b) 15.5 km/h
(c) 12.5 km/h (d) 10 km/h

242. The distance between two towns is covered in 9 h at speed of 60 km/h. By how much should the speed (in km/h) be increased, so that 1 h of the travelling time is saved? SSC MTS 14/9/2023 Shift-I

(a) 7.5 (b) 10 (c) 15 (d) 12.5

243. Amit drive for 6 h at a speed of 60 miles per h and for 6 h at 40 miles per h. What was his average speed (in miles per h) for the whole journey? SSC MTS 14/9/2023 Shift-I

(a) 48 (b) 44 (c) 46 (d) 50

244. A thief is spotted by a policeman from a distance of 250 m. When the policeman starts chase, the thief also starts running. Assuming that the speed of the thief is 10 km/h and that of the policeman is 12.5 km/h. How far will have the thief run before he is caught? SSC MTS 14/9/2023 Shift-I

(a) 3 km (b) 1 km (c) 4 km (d) 2 km

245. Neha walks at the rate of 8 km/h and crosses a bridge in 27 min. What is the length of the bridge (in m)? SSC MTS 11/9/2023 Shift-II

(a) 4850 (b) 3600 (c) 3000 (d) 2400

246. If the ratio among the time taken by three cars to travel a certain distance is 2 : 3 : 5, then the ratio of speeds of these cars will be SSC MTS 11/9/2023 Shift-I

(a) 10 : 6 : 15 (b) 15 : 9 : 8
(c) 10 : 15 : 8 (d) 15 : 10 : 6

247. Two cyclists start at the same time from opposite ends of a 200 km long straight road. One cyclist travels at a speed of 20 km/h and

the other at a speed of 30 km/h. How long will it take them to meet? SSC MTS 11/9/2023 Shift-I

(a) 5 h (b) 4 h
(c) 5.5 h (d) 4.5 h

248. A man runs across an 1800 m long street in 6 min. calculate his speed (in m/s). SSC MTS 8/9/2023 Shift-II

(a) 5 (b) 4 (c) 6 (d) 8

249. A thief is spotted by a policeman from a distance of 108 m. The thief starts running and the policeman chases him. If the speed of the thief and policeman are 21 km/h and 23km/h respectively, then how far will the thief have to run (in m) before he is overtaken by the policeman? SSC MTS 8/9/2023 Shift-I

(a) 2534 (b) 3121 (c) 1216 (d) 1134

250. A policeman sees a thief from a distance of 185 m. The thief starts running away and the policeman chases him. The thief and the policeman move at speeds of 8 m/s and 9 m/s, respectively. What is the distance between them after 2 min? SSC MTS 5/9/2023 Shift-II

(a) 65 m (b) 92 m
(c) 120 m (d) 130 m

251. A man takes 8 h 30 min to go to a place by bicyle and return from there by scooter. If he travels both ways by bicycle, it takes 10 h. How much time (in hours) will it take for him to travel both ways by scooter? SSC MTS 5/9/2023 Shift-II

(a) $4\frac{1}{2}$ (b) 7 (c) $3\frac{1}{2}$ (d) 4

252. The total journey is of 800 km. A car travels the first 320 km of the journey at the speed of 64 km/h. What should be the speed of the next 480 km so that, average speed will become 80 km/h? SSC MTS 5/9/2023 Shift-II

(a) 96 km/h (b) 69 km/h
(c) 86 km/h (d) 89 km/h

253. Yug covers a certain distance with a speed of 56 km/h in $\frac{3}{2}$ h. If he wants to cover the same distance in 7 h, what would be his speed (in km/h)? SSC MTS 4/9/2023 Shift-II

(a) 16 (b) 20 (c) 14 (d) 12

254. A man travels from point A to point B at a speed of 40 km/h and returns to point A at a speed of 60 km/ h. If the total time taken for the journey is 5 h, what is the distance between point A and point B? SSC MTS 1/9/2023 Shift-III

(a) 135 km (b) 120 km
(c) 125 km (d) 130 km

255. A truck driver drove 60 km/h for three hours. Then, he stopped for one hour and did not go anywhere. Then, he drove four more hours at 60 km/h. What was the driver's average speed (in km/h)? SSC MTS 1/9/2023 Shift-I

(a) 52.5 (b) 62.4 (c) 50.4 (d) 42.8

SSC MTS 2022 & 2021

256. A leaves station P at 8 : 00 am and reaches station Q at 11 : 00 am. B leaves station Q at 9 : 00 am and reaches station P at 11: 00 am. At what time will they cross each other ? SSC MTS 15/7/2022 Shift-I

(a) 10 : 00 am (b) 10 : 05 am
(c) 9 : 48 am (d) 9 : 52 am

257. A bus can travel 20% faster than a scooter. Both start from point P at the same time and reach point Q, 60 km away from point P, at the same time. On the way, however, the bus lost about 10 min while stopping at bus stations, while the scooter did not stop anywhere. What is the speed of the bus? SSC MTS 15/7/2022 Shift-I

(a) 68 km/h (b) 80 km/h
(c) 60 km/h (d) 72 km/h

258. Piu and Titu start from the same place at the same time and walk in opposite directions. If Piu walks at 5 km/h and Titu walks at 2 km/h, after what time will they be 10.5 km apart? SSC MTS 14/7/2022 Shift-I

(a) 3.5 h (b) 1.5 h
(c) 2.5 h (d) 2 h

259. A person goes from P to Q at a speed of 20 km/h. Then he goes from Q to R at a speed of q km/h. Finally the person goes from R to S at a speed of r km/h. The distances from P to Q, Q to R and R to S are equal. If the average speed from P to R is $\frac{280}{11}$ km/h and the average speed from Q to S is $\frac{112}{3}$ km/h, then what is the value of r? SSC MTS 14/7/2022 Shift-I

(a) 40 (b) 37.5 (c) 42.5 (d) 45

260. During a journey a person travels half of the distance at a speed of 18 km/h and the remaining half of the journey at a speed of 22 km/h. What is his average speed for the entire journey? SSC MTS 13/7/2022 Shift-I

(a) 21.4 km/h (b) 20.2 km/h
(c) 19.2 km/h (d) 19.8 km/h

261. The speed of Ashu is 15 km/h more than the speed of Vishu. They start moving in the same direction at the same time, but initially Vishu is ahead of Ashu by a certain distance. If Ashu crosses Vishu 6 h after they start moving. What is the initial distance between them ? SSC MTS 11/7/2022 Shift-I

(a) 45 km (b) 60 km
(c) 90 km (d) 80 km

262. The speed of light is very nearly equal to 3×10^{17} nanometre per second. How much time (in seconds) approximately, does it take light to travel from the moon to the Earth, the average distance between them being 384000 km? (1 nanometer = 10^{-9} metre) SSC MTS 2/11/2021 Shift-III

(a) 38.4 (b) 12.8
(c) 3.84 (d) 1.28

263. Two cyclists start simultaneously from two points A and B, their destinations being B and A, respectively. After crossing each other, they precisely take 2 h 33 min 36 s and 1 h 26 min 24 s respectively to reach their destinations. What is the ratio of the speed of the first to that of the second cyclist? SSC MTS 2/11/2021 Shift-III

(a) 2 : 3
(b) 3 : 2
(c) 4 : 3
(d) 3 : 4

264. An aeroplane covers a certain distance at a speed of 280 km/h in $4\frac{3}{4}$ h. To cover the same distance in 7 h, it must travel at a speed (in km/h) of SSC MTS 2/11/2021 Shift-II

(a) 140 (b) 190
(c) 175 (d) 180

265. A truck driver has to cover a total distance of 260 km in 4 h. He drives at a speed of 56 km/h for the first 75 min, and the next 90 km at a speed of 60 km/h. At what speed (in km/h) must he drive the remaining distance in order to complete the journey in 4 h? SSC MTS 2/11/2021 Shift-I

(a) 65 (b) 58
(c) 80 (d) 75

SSC GD Constable 2024 & 2023

266. A man covers half part of certain distance at 45 km/h. He covers 40% of remaining distance at the speed of 8 km/h and covers rest of the distance at the speed of 24 km/h. What is his average speed for the entire journey? **SSC GD 26/02/2024 Shift-I**
(a) 164/7 km/h (b) 144/7 km/h
(c) 156/7 km/h (d) 128/7 km/h

267. A bus left 60 min later than the scheduled time but in order to reach its destination 150 km away in time, it had to increase its usual speed by 5 km/h. What is the usual speed of the bus? **SSC GD 24/02/2024 Shift-III**
(a) 15 km/h (b) 30 km/h
(c) 25 km/h (d) 20 km/h

268. A thief steals a car at 2:00 pm and drives it at 70 km/h. The theft is discovered at 3:00 pm and the owner sets off in another car at 105 km/h. At what time owner will overtake the thief? **SSC GD 24/02/2024 Shift-II**
(a) 5:00 pm (b) 4:30 pm
(c) 3:30 pm (d) 3:45 pm

269. Aman goes to his office by car at the speed of 80 km/h and reaches 10 min earlier. If he goes at the speed 30 km/h, then he reaches 10 min late. What will be the speed of the car to reach on time? **SSC GD 24/02/2024 Shift-I**
(a) 480/11 km/h (b) 240/6 km/h
(c) 450/7 km/h (d) 480/13 km/h

270. Rohit travels four journeys of equal distance. In the first journey, his speed was 400 km/h and in each subsequent journey, his speed was half of the speed of the previous journey, what is the average speed of Rohit in all the four journeys? **SSC GD 23/02/2024 Shift-III**
(a) 400/3 km/h (b) 440/3 km/h
(c) 320/3 km/h (d) 100 km/h

271. A certain distance is covered at a certain speed. If double of this distance is covered in six times the time, then find the ratio of the two speeds. **SSC GD 23/02/2024 Shift-II**
(a) 3 : 1 (b) 3 : 4 (c) 2 : 1 (d) 4 : 5

272. A person walks at a speed of 6 km/h and covers a certain distance in 4 h. If the person increases the speed to 8 km/h, how long will it take to cover the same distance? **SSC GD 22/02/2024 Shift-IV**
(a) 5 h (b) 2 h (c) 4.5 h (d) 3 h

273. A car left 42 min early than the scheduled time but in order to reach its destination 210 km away in time, it had to slow its usual speed by 10 km/h. What is the usual speed of the car? **SSC GD 22/02/2024 Shift-III**
(a) 40 km/h (b) 60 km/h
(c) 50 km/h (d) 30 km/h

274. If a car travels 150 km at a speed of 50 km/h, how long does it take to complete the journey? **SSC GD 22/02/2024 Shift-I**
(a) 3 h (b) 3.5 h
(c) 4.5 h (d) 4 h

275. Two cars start from the same point and travel in opposite directions. If one car travels at 40 km/h and the other at 50 km/h, after 5 h, how far apart are they? **SSC GD 21/02/2024 Shift-IV**
(a) 480 km (b) 410 km
(c) 450 km (d) 460 km

276. Two boys are standing on the opposite ends of a 900 m long bridge. If they walk towards each other at the speed of 10 m/min and 8 m/min respectively, then in how much time will they meet each other? **SSC GD 21/02/2024 Shift-III**
(a) 38 min (b) 62 min
(c) 50 min (d) 25 min

277. From point *P*, *X* walks at a speed of 12 km/h and 6 h after his start, *Y* also starts walking from same point *P* on his cycle after him at the speed of 16 km/h. How far from the starting point *P* will *Y* catch *X* ? **SSC GD 21/02/2024 Shift-II**
(a) 224 km (b) 288 km
(c) 256 km (d) 324 km

278. A person covers first 11 km in 60 min and next 22 km in 30 min. What is his average speed for the whole journey? **SSC GD 21/02/2024 Shift-I**
(a) 18 km/h
(b) 25 km/h
(c) 22 km/h
(d) 27 km/h

279. A car is travelling at a uniform speed of 51 km/h. The distance travelled by the car from 10 : 40 am to 1 : 00 pm is **SSC GD 13/02/2023 Shift-IV**
(a) 125 km (b) 119 km
(c) 100 km (d) 115 km

280. Shlok drives the first 140 km in 3 h and the next 180 km in 5 h. What is his average speed (in km/h) for the entire trip? **SSC GD 13/02/2023 Shift-II**
(a) 50 (b) 45 (c) 30 (d) 40

281. A car takes 5 h to cover a distance, if its speed is 30 km/h. What should be its speed to cover the same distance in 2.5 h? **SSC GD 09/02/2023 Shift-I**
(a) 40 km/h (b) 60 km/h
(c) 70 km/h (d) 50 km/h

282. Amisha walks 3 km at a speed of 2 km/h, runs 7 km at a speed of 4 km/h and goes another 32 km by bus. If the speed of the bus is 28 km/h, then find Amisha's average speed for the whole journey. **SSC GD 08/02/2023 Shift-I**
(a) $\frac{392}{41}$ km/h (b) $\frac{394}{41}$ km/h
(c) $\frac{391}{41}$ km/h (d) $\frac{393}{41}$ km/h

283. Ram and Ramesh run two kilometres and Ram wins by 40 sec. Ram and Naresh run two kilometres and Ram wins by 650 m. When Ramesh and Naresh run the same distance, Ramesh wins by 25 sec. Find the time taken by Ram to run two kilometres. **SSC GD 07/02/2023 Shift-I**
(a) 3 min, 15 sec
(b) 2 min, 15 sec
(c) 3 min, 35 sec
(d) 2 min, 35 sec

284. A person travels three equal distances at the speeds of 2 km/h, 3 km/h and 4 km/h and takes a total time of 52 min. The total distance is **SSC GD 07/02/2023 Shift-I**
(a) 2.8 km (b) 2.7 km
(c) 2.4 km (d) 2.5 km

285. *A*, *B* and *C* runs at speeds 5 m/s, 3 m/s and 8 m/s, respectively. They start the race at the same time from the same point. After some time, it was found that the distance between *A* and *C* is 6 m. Determine the distance between *A* and *B*. **SSC GD 07/02/2023 Shift-I**
(a) 3 m (b) 2 m (c) 5 m (d) 4 m

286. An object moves 15 m in 2.6 min and the next 26 km at a speed of 30 km/h. Find its average speed (in m/sec) for the whole movement. **SSC GD 07/02/2023 Shift-I**
(a) 8.59 (b) 3.76
(c) 7.94 (d) 2.92

287. In a race of 1000 m, John beats Khan by 120 m. If the speed of John is 40 km/h, then the speed of Khan is **SSC GD 02/02/2023 Shift-I**
(a) 28.5 km/h (b) 38.7 km/h
(c) 27 km/h (d) 35.2 km/h

288. In a trip, Kiran travelled 50 miles per hour for 3 h on bike. Further he travelled by car for 2 h at 65 miles per hour. He stopped for 2 h for rest. After rest he travelled on bike for 4 h at 80 miles per hour to reach his destination. Find Kiran's average speed for the entire journey. (in miles per hour) (Rounded off to two places of decimals) **SSC GD 02/02/2023 Shift-I**

(a) 54.54 (b) 65.68
(c) 60.06 (d) 50.44

289. A police officer follows a thief who is at a distance of 800 m from him. If they run at a speed of 8 km/h and 7 km/h, respectively, how long does the police officer have to run to catch up with the thief? **SSC GD 01/02/2023 Shift-I**

(a) 4000 m (b) 4800 m
(c) 5600 m (d) 6400 m

290. A thief started running at a speed of 15 m/s, after running for 12 sec a policeman started running to catch the thief in the same direction at a speed of 20 m/s. How many metre will the policeman run to catch the thief? **SSC GD 01/02/2023 Shift-I**

(a) 740 m (b) 754 m
(c) 720 m (d) 744 m

SSC Selection Post 2024-2022

291. If Tanmay covers three equal distances at the speeds of 2 km/h, 3 km/h and 4 km/h,respectively. Then, find his average speed (in km/h) during the whole journey. (Rounded off to 2 decimal places) **Matric Level 20/06/2024 Shift-IV**

(a) 3.25 (b) 5.75
(c) 4.35 (d) 2.77

292. A thief is noticed by a policeman from a distance of 500 m. The thief starts running and the policeman chases him. The thief and the policeman run at the speed of 12 km/h and 13 km/h, respectively. What is the distance between them after 12 min? **Matric Level 20/06/2024 Shift-IV**

(a) 150 m (b) 100 m
(c) 300 m (d) 200 m

293. A teacher travelled a distance of 22 km in 7 h. He travelled partly on foot at the speed of 2 km/h and partly on bicycle at the rate of 4 km/h. The distance travelled on foot is **Matric Level 20/06/2024 Shift-IV**

(a) 10 km (b) 3 km
(c) 6 km (d) 8 km

294. A truck travels 75 km in the first hour and 33 km in the second hour. Find the average speed of the truck (in km/h). **Graduate Level 20/06/2024 Shift-III**

(a) 42 km/h (b) 108 km/h
(c) 54 km/h (d) 60 km/h

295. In a 150-m race, if *R* gets a 5 m head start, then he would beats *S* by 35 m. If *S* gets a 25 m head start in a 100 m race, then...would win the race by ....m. **Graduate Level 20/06/2024 Shift-III**

(a) S, 4.44 (b) R, 4.44
(c) R, 5.44 (d) S, 5.44

296. Sahil covers a distance of 96 km at the speed of 16 km/h and covers another distance at the speed of 21 km/h in 5 h. What is his average speed (in km/h)? (Rounded off to 2 decimal places) **Higher Secondary Level 20/06/2024 Shift-II**

(a) 18.50 (b) 18.27
(c) 17.47 (d) 19.45

297. A bus covers 1200 km in 30 h. What is its average speed in m/s? **Higher Secondary Level 20/06/2024 Shift-II**

(a) $12\frac{1}{9}$ (b) $12\frac{1}{3}$ (c) $11\frac{1}{9}$ (d) $13\frac{1}{9}$

298. The distance between two places is 1200 km. To cover this distance, a person *X* takes 5 h lesser than another person *Y*, whose average speed is 40 km/h lesser than that of *X*. The time taken by *Y* to complete the travel is **Higher Secondary Level 27/06/2023 Shift-III**

(a) 16 h (b) 14 h (c) 18 h (d) 15 h

299. A person covers 48 km at the speed of 8 km/h, 36 km at the speed of 18 km/h and 16 km at the speed of 8 km/h. What is his average speed in covering the whole distance? **Matric Level 27/06/2023 Shift-I**

(a) 9 km/h (b) 11 km/h
(c) 10.5 km/h (d) 10 km/h

300. In a circular race along a track of length 3600 m, *X* and *Y* run at speeds of 27 km/h and 45 km/h, respectively. Suppose they start at the same time and in the same direction, when will they meet again at the starting point? **Matric Level 27/06/2023 Shift-I**

(a) 1440 sec (b) 720 sec
(c) 2200 sec (d) 1200 sec

301. A thief was noticed by a policeman from a distance of 80 m. The speed of the thief is 21 km/h and the policeman is 20 km/h. What is the distance between them after 18 sec? **Graduate Level 01/08/2022 Shift-IV**

(a) 70 m (b) 95 m
(c) 90 m (d) 85 m

302. Rahul runs at a speed of 6 km/h in a 100 m race. Rahul gives Bharat a start of 4 m and still beats him by 4 sec. Find Bharat's speed. **Higher Secondary Level 01/08/2022 Shift-II**

(a) 5.8 km/h (b) 4.5 km/h
(c) 4.9 km/h (d) 5.4 km/h

303. Atul walks 4 km at a speed of 2 km/h, runs 10 km at a speed of 6 km/h and goes by bus for another 45 km. The speed of the bus is 30 km/h. Find the average speed of Atul **Higher Secondary Level 01/08/2022 Shift-II**

(a) $11\frac{13}{31}$ km/h (b) $12\frac{41}{14}$ km/h
(c) $11\frac{31}{13}$ km/h (d) $12\frac{14}{41}$ km/h

304. A plane in flight from Mumbai to Delhi covers a distance of 1728 km in 180 min. What is the speed of the plane (in m/sec)? **Matric Level 01/08/2022 Shift-I**

(a) 185 (b) 140
(c) 160 (d) 175

305. Tejasvi drove at an average speed of 35 miles/h for the first 35 miles of a trip and then at an average speed of 65 miles/h for the remaining 35 miles of the trip. If she made no stops during the trip, what was her average speed (in miles/h) for the entire trip? **Matric Level 01/08/2022 Shift-I**

(a) 43.5 (b) 46.5
(c) 45.5 (d) 44.5

Right Answers

1	(b)	2	(d)	3	(a)	4	(b)	5	(c)	6	(c)	7	(c)	8	(b)	9	(b)	10	(b)
11	(c)	12	(c)	13	(c)	14	(c)	15	(d)	16	(c)	17	(a)	18	(b)	19	(c)	20	(a)
21	(b)	22	(d)	23	(a)	24	(c)	25	(c)	26	(a)	27	(a)	28	(a)	29	(b)	30	(d)
31	(b)	32	(c)	33	(d)	34	(a)	35	(c)	36	(b)	37	(a)	38	(b)	39	(c)	40	(b)
41	(d)	42	(c)	43	(d)	44	(b)	45	(c)	46	(d)	47	(a)	48	(c)	49	(a)	50	(b)
51	(a)	52	(c)	53	(a)	54	(a)	55	(b)	56	(a)	57	(a)	58	(b)	59	(b)	60	(d)
61	(a)	62	(d)	63	(b)	64	(a)	65	(b)	66	(c)	67	(c)	68	(a)	69	(c)	70	(d)
71	(b)	72	(d)	73	(d)	74	(a)	75	(a)	76	(b)	77	(c)	78	(b)	79	(c)	80	(c)
81	(b)	82	(c)	83	(b)	84	(d)	85	(c)	86	(d)	87	(b)	88	(a)	89	(a)	90	(b)
91	(a)	92	(b)	93	(a)	94	(d)	95	(c)	96	(b)	97	(a)	98	(a)	99	(b)	100	(b)
101	(c)	102	(b)	103	(c)	104	(d)	105	(a)	106	(a)	107	(a)	108	(c)	109	(d)	110	(a)
111	(b)	112	(b)	113	(a)	114	(d)	115	(d)	116	(d)	117	(a)	118	(a)	119	(d)	120	(c)
121	(b)	122	(c)	123	(a)	124	(a)	125	(a)	126	(b)	127	(a)	128	(d)	129	(a)	130	(b)
131	(a)	132	(d)	133	(d)	134	(a)	135	(a)	136	(d)	137	(b)	138	(c)	139	(b)	140	(a)
141	(c)	142	(b)	143	(c)	144	(a)	145	(c)	146	(c)	147	(b)	148	(b)	149	(a)	150	(c)
151	(b)	152	(a)	153	(a)	154	(b)	155	(d)	156	(b)	157	(b)	158	(c)	159	(c)	160	(d)
161	(b)	162	(c)	163	(c)	164	(c)	165	(d)	166	(c)	167	(a)	168	(d)	169	(b)	170	(d)
171	(a)	172	(a)	173	(c)	174	(b)	175	(c)	176	(b)	177	(d)	178	(b)	179	(b)	180	(b)
181	(c)	182	(c)	183	(c)	184	(c)	185	(a)	186	(b)	187	(d)	188	(c)	189	(a)	190	(b)
191	(c)	192	(d)	193	(a)	194	(a)	195	(b)	196	(a)	197	(d)	198	(c)	199	(b)	200	(c)
201	(c)	202	(a)	203	(a)	204	(c)	205	(a)	206	(a)	207	(d)	208	(c)	209	(a)	210	(c)
211	(b)	212	(c)	213	(c)	214	(c)	215	(d)	216	(d)	217	(d)	218	(a)	219	(a)	220	(c)
221	(a)	222	(d)	223	(c)	224	(c)	225	(a)	226	(c)	227	(a)	228	(a)	229	(d)	230	(a)
231	(c)	232	(d)	233	(d)	234	(b)	235	(a)	236	(c)	237	(a)	238	(d)	239	(a)	240	(d)
241	(c)	242	(a)	243	(d)	244	(b)	245	(b)	246	(d)	247	(b)	248	(a)	249	(d)	250	(a)
251	(b)	252	(a)	253	(d)	254	(b)	255	(a)	256	(c)	257	(d)	258	(b)	259	(a)	260	(d)
261	(c)	262	(d)	263	(d)	264	(b)	265	(c)	266	(b)	267	(c)	268	(a)	269	(a)	270	(c)
271	(a)	272	(d)	273	(b)	274	(a)	275	(c)	276	(c)	277	(b)	278	(c)	279	(b)	280	(d)
281	(b)	282	(a)	283	(b)	284	(c)	285	(d)	286	(c)	287	(d)	288	(a)	289	(d)	290	(c)
291	(d)	292	(c)	293	(c)	294	(c)	295	(d)	296	(b)	297	(c)	298	(d)	299	(d)	300	(b)
301	(d)	302	(d)	303	(a)	304	(c)	305	(c)										

Solutions

1. (b) Time taken by P to complete the race

$$= \frac{\text{Distance}}{\text{Speed}} \Rightarrow t = \frac{400}{12 \times \frac{5}{18}} = 120 \text{ sec}$$

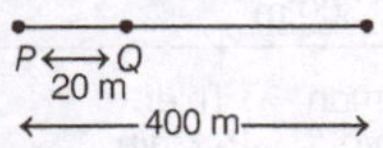

According to the question,

	P	Q
Distance	400	380
Time	t	$t + 13$

$$\therefore \text{ Speed of } Q = \frac{380}{t+13} \times \frac{18}{5}$$

$$= \frac{380}{120+13} \times \frac{18}{5}$$

$$= 10.29 \text{ km/h}$$

2. (d) Relative speed $= 20 + 16 = 36$ km/h

$$= 36 \times \frac{5}{18} = 10 \text{ m/s}$$

They will meet first time $= \frac{2200}{10}$

$$= 220 \text{ sec} = 3 \text{ min } 40 \text{ sec}$$

3. (a) Length of circular track = 1600 m

Relative speed (opposite direction)

$$= 27 + 45 = 72 \text{ km/h} = 72 \times \frac{5}{18} = 20 \text{ m/sec}$$

Relative speed (Same direction)

$$= 45 - 27 = 18 \text{ km/h } = 18 \times \frac{5}{18} = 5 \text{ m/sec}$$

$\therefore$ Required time (first meet – opposite direction) $= \frac{1600}{20} = 80 \text{ sec} = 1 \text{ min } 20 \text{ sec}$

$\therefore$ Required time (first meet – same direction)

$$= \frac{1600}{5} = 320 \text{ sec} = 5 \text{ min } 20 \text{ sec}$$

4. (b) Let the speed of thief be 'a' km/h.

According to the question,

Distance covered by thief

$$= \text{Initial distance} \left(\frac{\text{Speed of thief}}{\text{Reletive speed}} \right)$$

$$1.5 = 0.25 \left(\frac{a}{70 - a} \right) \Rightarrow 6 = \frac{a}{70 - a}$$

$$\Rightarrow \quad 420 - 6a = a \Rightarrow 7a = 420$$

$$\Rightarrow \quad a = 60 \text{ km/h}$$

5. (c) Total length of track = 220 m

Relative speed = 22 – 11 = 11 m/s

$\therefore$ Required time (first meet)

$$= \frac{\text{Length of circular track}}{\text{Relative speed}} = \frac{220}{11} = 20 \text{ sec}$$

6. (c) Relative speed = 8 – 3 = 5 rounds/h

Time taken to complete one round

$$= \frac{1}{5} \times 60 = 12 \text{ min}$$

They first cross each other at

11 : 54 + 12 = 12 : 06 am

7. (c) Time × Relative Speed = Distance

$$\therefore \text{ Distance} = \frac{30}{60} \times 2 = 1 \text{ km} = 1000 \text{ m}$$

[$\because$ relative speed = 12 – 10 = 2 km/h]

8. (b) Distance travelled by A in 8 h

$= 8 \times 8 = 64$ km

Time to catch A by $B = \frac{64}{24-8} = \frac{64}{16} = 4$ h

Thus distance travelled by A before catch by $B = 64 + 8 \times 4 = 64 + 32 = 96$ km

9. (b) Speed of thief is 64 km/h

Speed of policeman is 82 km/h

Distance between policeman and thief is 1300 m.

Time taken to catch thief by policeman

$= \frac{1.300 \text{ km}}{82-64} = \frac{1.3}{18} = \frac{13}{180}$ h

$= \frac{13}{180} \times 60 \times 60 \text{sec} = 260$ sec

10. (b) Let after t h. the policeman catches the thief.

Relative distance = 100 m

$= \frac{100}{1000}$ km = 0.1 km

Relative speed = (23 − 21) = 2 km/hr

∴ Time (t)= $\frac{0.1}{2} = 0.05$ hr

∴ Distance travelled by thief

$= 21 \times 0.05$ km = 1.05 km

$= 1.05 \times 1000$ m = 1050 m

11. (c) Relative speed = 104.4 − 90 = 14.4 km/h

$= 14.4 \times \frac{5}{18} = 4$ m/sec

∴ Time to catch the thief $= \frac{\text{Distance}}{\text{Relative speed}}$

$= \frac{92}{4} = 23$ sec

12. (c) Relative speed = 27 − 22 = 5 km/h

Time taken by policeman to catch the thief

$= \frac{195}{5 \times \frac{5}{18}} = 140.4$sec

∴ Thief would have run

$= \left(27 \times \frac{5}{18} \times 140.4\right) - 195$

= 1053 − 195 = 858 m

13. (c) Time taken by Arvind = 180 sec

Time take by Chetan = 420 sec

Arvind and Chetan will meet at LCM

= (180, 420) = 1260 sec

$= \frac{1260}{60}$ min = 21 min

They will meet after 21 min.

14. (c) Let the distance from P to R is x km.

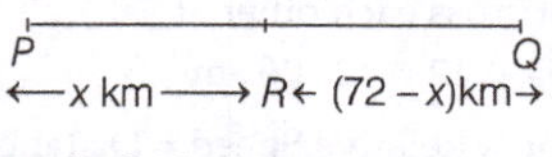

Given, speed of Akshara = 8 km/h

Speed of Siddharth = 10 km/h

Then, According to the question,

The time to travel distance x by Akshara

= Time to travel distance $(72 + 72 - x)$ by Siddharth

$\Rightarrow \quad \frac{x}{8} = \frac{72 + 72 - x}{10}$

$\Rightarrow \quad 10x = 144 \times 8 - 8x$

$\Rightarrow \quad 18x = 144 \times 8$

$\Rightarrow \quad x = \frac{144 \times 8}{18} = 64$ km

So, the required distance PR = 64 km

15. (d) Required time (they meet after)

$= \frac{\text{Distance}}{\text{Relative speed}} = \frac{1620}{10+8} = 90$sec

16. (c) Let the speed of the policeman = $5x$ m/s and the speed of the thief = $4x$ m/s

Relative speed = $(5x - 4x)$ m/s = x m/s and relative distance = 150 m

∴ Time taken to cover this relative distance

$= \frac{150}{x}$ sec.

Now, distance covered by the thief in $\frac{150}{x}$ sec

$= 4x \times \frac{150}{x} = 600$ m

17. (a) According to the question,

M's speed = 5 rounds/h

N's speed = 2 rounds/h

Since, M and N move in opposite direction.

∴ Relative speed of M and N = (5 + 2)

= 7 rounds/h

Time duration between 5 a.m. and 6:30 am

$= 1\frac{1}{2}$ h $= \frac{3}{2}$ h

∴ Required number of rounds in $\frac{3}{2}$ h

$= \frac{3}{2} \times 7 = \frac{21}{2} = 10.5$ rounds

∴ They will cross each other 10 times.

18. (b) According to the question,

Total time taken to catch thief

$= \frac{200}{(11-10) \times \frac{1000}{60}} = \frac{200 \times 3}{50} = 12$ min

∴ Distance covered in 12 min= 200 m

∴ Distance covered in 9 min

$= \frac{200 \times 9}{12} = 150$ m

∴ Required distance between policeman and thief = 200 − 150 = 50 m

19. (c) Let speed of Vishu = x m/s and the speed of Atul = y m/s

∴ According to the question,

$x = \frac{765}{t_1}$ and $y = \frac{900}{t_1 - 20}$

Where t_1 is time taken by Vishu to cover 765 m.

Again, $x = \frac{711}{t_2}$ and $y = \frac{900}{t_2 - 8}$

Where t_2 is time taken by Vishu to cover 711 m.

∴ $\frac{765}{t_1} = \frac{711}{t_2}$

$\Rightarrow \quad t_1 = \frac{85}{79} t_2$ (On comparing x) ...(i)

and $\frac{900}{t_1 - 20} = \frac{900}{t_2 - 8}$ (on comparing y)

$\Rightarrow \quad t_1 - t_2 = 12$ ...(ii)

Solving Eqs. (i) and (ii)

$t_1 = 170$ sec, $t_2 = 158$ sec and $x = \frac{765}{170}$ m/s

∴ Required time $= \frac{900 \times 170}{765}$ sec

= 200sec = 3 min, 20 sec

20. (a) Let the speed of first car = x km/h and the speed of second car = y km/h

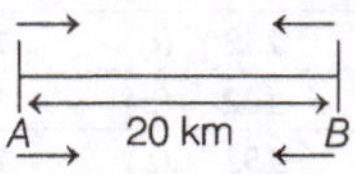

Case I If they travel in same direction relative speed = $(x - y)$ km/h

Distance = 20 km, Time = 1 h

∴ $\quad x - y = \frac{20}{1}$

$\Rightarrow \quad x - y = 20$ ...(i)

Case II If they travel in opposite direction relative speed = $(x + y)$ km/h

Distance = 20 km

Time = 12 min $= \frac{12}{60}$ h $= \frac{1}{5}$ h

∴ $\quad x + y = \frac{20}{\frac{1}{5}} = 20 \times 5 = 100$

$\Rightarrow \quad x + y = 100$ ...(ii)

Now, Eq. (i) + Eqs. (ii),

$2x = 120$

$\Rightarrow \quad x = 60$

Put $x = 60$ in Eq. (i),

$y = 60 - 20 = 40$

∴ Speed of cars = 60, 40 in (km/h)

21. (b) Let the speed of the policeman

$= x$ km/h

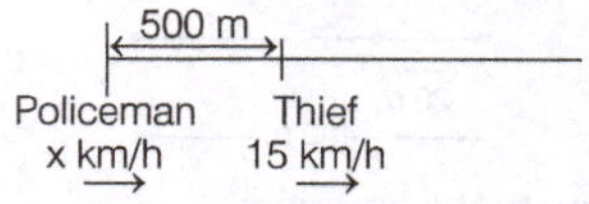

Given, the speed of thief = 15 km/h

Time taken by policeman to catch the thief

= 15 min $= \frac{15}{60}$ h

Distance to covered by policeman

= 500 m $= \frac{500}{1000} = \frac{1}{2}$ km

∴ Relative speed = $(x - 15)$ km/h

We know,

Speed $= \frac{\text{Distance}}{\text{Time}} \Rightarrow x - 15 = \frac{\frac{1}{2}}{\frac{15}{60}} = \frac{\frac{1}{2}}{\frac{1}{4}}$

$\Rightarrow x - 15 = \frac{1}{2} \times \frac{4}{1} = 2 \Rightarrow x = 2 + 15 = 17$

Hence, speed of the policeman = 17 km/h

22. (d) They meet first time = $\frac{\text{Distance}}{\text{Relative speed}}$

$= \frac{750 \times 18}{(13.5 - 9) \times 5} = \frac{750 \times 18}{4.5 \times 5} = 600$ sec

23. (a) Average speed = $\frac{\text{Total distance}}{\text{Total time}}$

$= \frac{\frac{1}{3} + \frac{1}{3} + \frac{1}{3}}{\frac{\frac{1}{3}}{40} + \frac{\frac{1}{3}}{50} + \frac{\frac{1}{3}}{60}} = \frac{1}{\frac{1}{3}\left(\frac{15 + 12 + 10}{600}\right)}$

$= \frac{1}{\frac{1}{3}\left(\frac{37}{600}\right)} = \frac{1800}{37} = 48.65$ km/h

24. (c) Distance between the thief and policeman = 600 m

Policeman's speed = 15 km/h

Thief's speed = 12 km/h

Relative speed = (15 − 12) km/h = 3 km/h

$= 3 \times \frac{5}{18}$ m/s

$\therefore$ Time $= \frac{\text{Distance}}{\text{Speed}} = \frac{600}{3 \times \frac{5}{18}} = \frac{600 \times 18}{15}$

= 720 sec = 12 min

25. (c) Required time $= \frac{1635}{(108 - 90) \times \frac{5}{18}}$

$= \frac{1635}{18 \times \frac{5}{18}} = 327$ sec

26. (a) Circulr race length = 840 m

Speed of A and B are 6 m/sec and 12 m/s

They will meet next after $= \frac{840}{12 - 6}$

[$\because$ Running in same direction]

$= \frac{840}{6} = 140$ sec

27. (a) Let total distance of journey = d km

According to the question,

$\frac{d}{3 \times 30} + \frac{2d}{3 \times 40} = 12 \Rightarrow \frac{d}{90} + \frac{2d}{120} = 12$

$\Rightarrow \frac{4d + 6d}{360} = 12 \Rightarrow d = 12 \times 36 = 432$ km

28. (a) Average speed = $\frac{\text{Total distance}}{\text{Total time}}$

$= \frac{45 + 80 + 6}{\frac{45}{15} + \frac{80}{40} + \frac{6}{2}} = \frac{131}{3 + 2 + 3} = \frac{131}{8}$

= 16.38 km/h

29. (b) Total length of circular path = 600 m

Speed of Pankaj = 2.85 m/s

Speed of Rohit = 5.4 km/h $= 5.4 \times \frac{5}{18} = 1.5$ m/s

$\therefore$ They meet first time at $= 600 \times \frac{1}{2.85 + 1.5}$

$= \frac{600}{4.35} = 137.93$ sec $= \frac{137.9}{60} = 2.3$ min

Speedy Method

$\therefore$ Required time $= \frac{600}{2.85 + 5.4 \times \frac{5}{18}}$

$= \frac{600}{2.85 + 1.5} = \frac{600}{4.35} = 137.9 \approx 138$ sec.

$= \frac{138}{60} = 2.3$ min.

30. (d) Let the first person cover 100 m distance in 100 min.

Then the second person cover 25 m distance in 300 min.

Then, ratio of their speed

$= \frac{100}{100} : \frac{25}{300} = 1 : \frac{1}{12} = 12 : 1$

31. (b) Police caught the thief at $= d \times \frac{a}{b - a}$

$= 1150 \times \frac{6}{11 - 6} = 1150 \times \frac{6}{5} = 1380$ m

[where a = 6 km/h and b = 11 km/h]

32. (c) Let distance = d km

According to the question,

$\frac{d}{4} - \frac{d}{6} = \frac{1}{2} \Rightarrow \frac{6d - 4d}{24} = \frac{1}{2}$

$\Rightarrow 2d = \frac{24}{2} \Rightarrow d = 6$ km

33. (d) Required time for first time meet

$= \frac{1125}{(54 - 36) \times \frac{5}{18}} = \frac{1125}{18 \times 5} \times 18 = 225$ sec.

34. (a) Clearly, Q covers 120 m in 30 sec.

$\therefore$ Time to cover the entire race by Q

$= \frac{30}{120} \times 1000 = 250$ sec

$\therefore$ Time taken by P to cover the entire race

= (250 − 30) = 220 sec

35. (c) Average speed of the cyclist

$= \frac{\text{Total distance}}{\text{Total time}} \left[(120 + 150)\text{min} = \frac{9}{2}\text{h}\right]$

$= \frac{45}{\left(\frac{9}{2}\right)} = \frac{45 \times 2}{9} = 10$ km/h

36. (b) Let speed of Shyam = x m/min

Speed of Ram = $3x$ m/min

Length of circular track = 1440 m

Time taken by Shyam $= \frac{1440}{x}$ min

Time taken by Ram $= \frac{1440}{3x} = \frac{480}{x}$ min

According to the question,

Meeting time = LCM of $\frac{1440}{x}$ and $\frac{480}{x}$

$= \frac{1440}{x}$

$\Rightarrow \frac{1440}{x} = 8 \Rightarrow x = \frac{1440}{8} = 180$

They meet when Shyam covers distance

= 180 × 8 = 1440 m

The next 1440 m will be covered in 8 min.

$\therefore$Total time taken by Shyam = 8 + 8 = 16 min

37. (a) Required distance

$= 400 \times \frac{12}{12 - 10} = 400 \times \frac{12}{2}$

= 2400 m = 2.4 km

38. (b) Speed of the thief = 15 km/h

$= \frac{15000}{60}$ m/min = 250 m/min

In 20 min, distance covered by the thief

= 250 × 20 = 5000 m

In (20 − 4) min the police covers distance

= 5000 − 200 = 4800 m

Speed of the police $= \frac{4800}{20 - 4} = \frac{4800}{16}$

= 300 m/min

Let the thief will be caught after t min from 20 min of starting running

$(300 - 250)t = 200 \Rightarrow t = 4$

$\therefore$ Distance = 300 × (16 + 4)

= 6000 m = 6 km

Speed of the policeman

$= \frac{300 \times 60}{1000}$ km/h = 18 km/h

39. (c) Total length of the circular path

= 500 m

Relative speed = 10 + 6 = 16 m/s

Let meeting time = t sec

$\Rightarrow t = \frac{500}{16} = \frac{125}{4}$

Speed of them exchanged.

Now, P has to cover $= \frac{125}{4} \times 10$ m

$\therefore$ Time taken by $P = \frac{1250}{4 \times 10} = \frac{125}{4}$ sec

Q has to cover $= \frac{125}{4} \times 6$ m

$\therefore$Time taken by $Q = \frac{125 \times 6}{4 \times 6} = \frac{125}{4}$ sec

Hence, P and Q will reach at the same time.

40. (b) Average speed $= \frac{250 + 250}{\frac{250}{75} + \frac{250}{85}}$

$= \frac{500}{\frac{4250 + 3750}{1275}}$

$= \frac{500 \times 1275}{8000} = 79.69$ km/h

Speedy Method

Average speed $= \frac{2 \times 75 \times 85}{75 + 85}$

$= \frac{12750}{160} = 79.69$ km/h

41. (d) Let the police will catch the thief after t h.

$9t - 8t = 0.6 \Rightarrow t = 0.6$

$\therefore$ The thief would be caught at

$9 \times 0.6 = 5.4$ km

42. (c) Time taken by another car $= \frac{450}{90} = 5\text{ h}$

Total distance $= 350 + 450 = 800$ km

Total time taken $= 5 + 5 = 10$ h

$\therefore$ Average speed $= \frac{800}{10} = 80$ km/h

43. (d) When A gives B a start of 25 m then A wins by 10 sec.

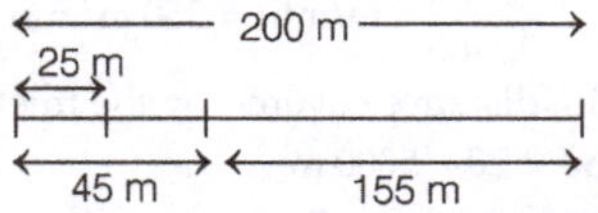

When A gives B a start of 45 m then the race ends in a dead heat.

$\therefore$ Speed of $B = \frac{45-25}{10} = 2$ m/s

$\therefore$ Time taken by A to run 200 m

= that of B's 155 m $= \frac{155}{2} = 77.5$ sec

44. (b) Speed of a bus $= \frac{60 \times 3}{4} = 45$ km/h

Speed of airplane $= 45 \times 5 = 225$ km/h

In 60 min airplane covers = 225 km/h

$\therefore$ In 25 min airplane covers

$= \frac{225}{60} \times 25 = 93.75$ km

45. (c) Given, length of circular track

= 4225 m

Relative speed $= (54 + 63) = \left(117 \times \frac{5}{18}\right)$ m/s

Then, they meet on first time

$= \frac{\text{Distance}}{\text{Speed}} = \frac{4225}{117 \times 5} \times 18$

$= 65 \times 2 = 130$ sec

46. (d) Let, distance $= x$ km.

According to question,

$\frac{x}{9} - \frac{x}{12} = \frac{20}{60} \Rightarrow \frac{3x}{108} = \frac{1}{3} \Rightarrow x = 12$ km

47. (a) Thief covers distance in 8 min

$= 17 \times 8 \times \frac{1000}{60} = \frac{6800}{3}$ m

But thief is infront of policeman at

500 m then $= \frac{6800}{3} + 500 = \frac{8300}{3}$

Policeman covers distance in 8 min

$= 20 \times 8 \times \frac{1000}{60} = \frac{8000}{3}$ m

$\therefore$ Distance between them

$= \frac{8300}{3} - \frac{8000}{3} = 100$ m

Speedy Method

Required distance between them

$= 500 - \left[(20-17) \times \frac{5}{18} \times 8 \times 60\right]$

$= 500 - \left[3 \times \frac{5}{18} \times 8 \times 60\right]$

$= 500 - 400 = 100$ m

48. (c) Distance covered by the thief in 10 min $= \frac{6 \times 10}{60} = 1$ km

Relative speed in same direction

$= (8-6)$ km/h $= 2$ km/h

Time taken by police to catch thief

$= \frac{\text{Distance}}{\text{Relative speed}} = \frac{1}{2}$ h

Hence, the police will cover a distance

$= 8 \times \frac{1}{2}$ h $= 4$ km

49. (a) Total distance = 192 km

Speed of Anil = 64 km/h

Time $= \frac{192}{64} = 3$ h

$\Rightarrow$ Time = 8 : 20 + 3 h = 11:20 am

Speed of Tirath = 96 km/h

Tirath started 9:50 − 8:20 = 1 h 30 min late

In 3h − 1 h 30 min

= 1 h 30 min Tirath covers

$96 \times 1.5 = 144$ km at 11:20 am

Let they will meet after 't' h from 11:20 am

$\therefore$ $192 - 144 = (96 + 64)t$

$\Rightarrow$ $t = \frac{48}{160}$ h $= \frac{48 \times 60}{160}$ min = 18 min

$\therefore$ They will meet at

= 11:20 + 18 min = 11:38 am

50. (b) Total circular distance = 1600 m

Speed of $A = 27$ km/h $= \frac{27 \times 5}{18} = \frac{15}{2}$ m/s

Speed of $B = 45$ km/h $= 45 \times \frac{5}{18} = \frac{25}{2}$ m/s

Relative speed for same direction

$= \frac{25}{2} - \frac{15}{2} = 5$ m/s

$\therefore$ They will meet for first time

$= \frac{1600}{5} = 320$ sec

51. (a) Let speed of the police $= 5x$ km/h

Then, speed of the thief $= 4x$ km/h

According to the question,

$(5x - 4x) \times \frac{12}{60} = 0.5$

$\Rightarrow$ $\frac{x}{5} = \frac{1}{2} \Rightarrow x = \frac{5}{2}$

$\therefore$ Speed of the thief $= 4 \times \frac{5}{2} = 10$ km/h

52. (c) Speed = 72 km/h

Time taken = 7 h 30 min $= \frac{15}{2}$ h

Distance $= 72 \times \frac{15}{2} = 540$ km

New speed = 72 + 72 × 25% = 72 + 18

= 90 km/h

Time taken $= \frac{540}{90} = 6$ h

$\therefore$ Time saved $= \frac{15}{2} - 6 = 1$h 30 min

53. (a) Anuj's 3 halts of 10 min

= 30 min = 0.5 h

Total time = 8.5 h

$\therefore$ Travel time = 8.5 − 0.5 = 8 h

Speed of Anuj = 70 km/h

$\therefore$ Distance from A to $B = 70 \times 8 = 560$ km

Anup's speed = 80 km/h

4 halts of 15 min takes = 4 × 15 = 60 min

= 1 h

$\therefore$ Total time taken by Anup $= \frac{560}{80} + 1 = 8$ h

54. (a) First lag

Distance = 50 × 5 = 250 km

Second lag

Distance $= 250 \times \frac{120}{100} = 300$ km

Speed $= 50 \times \frac{120}{100} = 60$ km/h

$\therefore$ Time taken to cover the distance

$= \frac{300}{60} = 5$ h

Third lag

Speed $= \frac{50 + 60}{2} = 55$ km/h

Distance $= 300 \times \frac{110}{100} = 330$ km

Time taken $= \frac{330}{55} = \frac{30}{5} = 6$ h

$\therefore$ Total time taken to total distance

= 5 + 5 + 6 = 16 h

55. (b) Distance = 3300 m = 3.3 km

Time taken = 45 min $= \frac{45}{60}$ h $= \frac{3}{4}$ h

$\therefore$ Speed $= \frac{3.3}{3/4} = \frac{33}{30} \times 4 = \frac{44}{10} = 4.4$ km/h

56. (a) In every 10 km he takes 5 min break.

In 84 km he takes $= \frac{5}{10} \times 80 = 40$ min break

Time $= \frac{84}{36} = \frac{7}{3} = \frac{6+1}{3} = \left(2 + \frac{1}{3}\right)$h

$= 120 + \frac{60}{3}$ min = 140 min

$\therefore$ Total time taken = 140 + 40 = 180 min

57. (a) P gives Q head of 2 sec.

Distance = 400 m

Speed of Q = 2 m/s

Time taken by $Q = \frac{400}{2} = 200$ sec

$\therefore$ Time taken by $P = 200 - 2 = 198$ sec

58. (b) Required distance $= d \times \frac{b}{a-b}$

$= 3 \times \frac{60}{75-60} = 3 \times \frac{60}{15} = 12$ km

59. (b) Ashok run faster than Bharat

$= 2\frac{2}{3} = \frac{8}{3}$ times

Ratio of speed = 8 : 3

Difference in speed = 5

If Ashok gives Bharat a head start = 160 m

Then, 1 units $= \frac{160}{5} = 32$

Hence, winning post must be = 32 × 8 = 256 m

60. (d) Given, distance $(d) = 300$ m

Speed of thief $(a) = 10$ km/h

Speed of policeman $(b) = 12$ km/h

$\therefore$ Distance run by the thief

$$= d \times \frac{a}{b-a} = 300 \times \frac{10}{12-10}$$

$$= 1500 \text{ m} = 1.5 \text{ km}$$

61. (a) Distance covered by thief in 40 min

$$= 12 \times \frac{40}{60} = 8 \text{ m}$$

$\therefore$ Security guard's speed $= \frac{8}{20} \times 60 = 24$ m/h

62. (d) Given, length of circular track= 100 m

$\therefore$ Time taken by first person to cover 100 m

$$= \frac{100}{20} = 5 \text{ sec}$$

Time taken by second person to cover 100 m

$$= \frac{100}{30} = \frac{10}{3} \text{ sec}$$

$\therefore$ They meet at starting point

$$= \text{LCM } (5, \frac{10}{3}) = 10 \text{ sec}$$

Also, time taken by both persons to cover 100 m together

$$= \frac{\text{Distance}}{\text{Relative speed}} = \frac{100}{20+30} = \frac{100}{50} = 2 \text{ sec}$$

$\therefore$ Number of times, they meet each other

$$= \frac{10}{2} = 5$$

63. (b) First day speed $= v$, distance $= x$, time $= t \Rightarrow v = \frac{x}{t}$

Next day he covers $2.5x$ distance in $0.75\,t$

$$\therefore \text{Speed} = \frac{2.5x}{0.75t} = \frac{250}{75} \times \frac{x}{t} = \frac{10}{3} \times \frac{x}{t} = \frac{10}{3} v$$

64. (a) Time difference $= 90 - 65 = 25$ sec

Speed of Mohan $= \frac{1170}{90} = 13$ m/s

$\therefore$ Raman beat Mohan by $13 \times 25 = 325$ m

65. (b) The man drives his car for 24 km at 48 km/h speed.

$\therefore$ Time taken $= \frac{24}{48} = \frac{1}{2}$ h

For the next 1.5 h he drives at 80 km/h,

$\therefore$ Distance covered

$$= 1.5 \times 80 = 120 \text{ km}$$

Total distance $= 120 + 24 = 144$ km

and total time $= \frac{1}{2} + \frac{3}{2} = 2$h

$\therefore$ Average speed $= \frac{144}{2} = 72$ km/h

66. (c) Given,

Distance of thief spotted (d) = 210 m

and speed of thief (a) = 25 km/h

and speed of policeman $(b) = 32$ km/h

$\therefore$ Required distance $= d \times \frac{a}{b-a}$

$$= 210 \times \frac{25}{7} = 750 \text{ m}$$

67. (c) $\because$ Average speed $= \frac{\text{Total distance}}{\text{Total time}}$

$$\Rightarrow \quad 10 = \frac{8.5 \times 4 + 20 \times 1.5 + 4 \times y}{4 + 1.5 + y}$$

$$\Rightarrow \quad 10 = \frac{34 + 30 + 4y}{5.5 + y}$$

$$\Rightarrow \quad 55 + 10y = 64 + 4y$$

$$\Rightarrow \quad y = \frac{9}{6} = \frac{3}{2} = 1.5 \text{ h}$$

68. (a) Total distance of race = 1500 m

Then, $X : Y : Z$

1500 : 1400 : 1260

When Y goes 1500, Z goes

$$= \frac{1260}{1400} \times 1500 = 1350$$

$\therefore$ Y beat Z by $1500 - 1350 = 150$ m

69. (c) Relative speed in same direction

$$= 10 - 8 = 2 = \frac{2 \times 5}{18} = \frac{5}{9} \text{ m/s}$$

Time taken to catch the thief

$$= \frac{\text{Distance}}{\text{Relative speed}}$$

$$= \frac{600 \times 9}{5} = 1080 \text{ sec}$$

$$= \frac{1080}{60} = 18 \text{ min}$$

70. (d) Relative speed $= (40 - 32)$ km/h

$$= 8 \text{ km/h} = \left(8 \times \frac{5}{18}\right) \text{m/s} = \frac{20}{9} \text{ m/s}$$

$\therefore$ Time taken by policeman to overtake the thief $= \frac{400}{\frac{20}{9}} = 400 \times \frac{9}{20} = 180$sec

$\therefore$ Distance covered by the thief

$$= 180 \times 32 \times \frac{5}{18} = 1600 \text{ m}$$

71. (b) Number of round to complete the race $= \frac{18000}{800} = \frac{45}{2}$ round.

Total time taken by $A = 200 \times \frac{45}{2} = 4500$ sec

Now, when A and B both start running,

First meet will take place in

LCM (200, 250) sec = 1000 sec

Next meet will take place

$$= 1000 \times 2 = 2000 \text{ sec}$$

For next meet,

Time would be 3000 sec.

Similarly, next meet at 4000 sec. and next meet at 5000 sec which is not possible as A completes the race in 4500 sec.

So, faster person will meet the slower person last time at 4000 sec.

72. (d) Total distance $= 90 \times \frac{37.5}{60} + 80 \times \frac{14}{60}$

$$= \frac{225}{4} + \frac{56}{3} = \frac{899}{12} = 74\frac{11}{12} \text{ km}$$

73. (d) Let at 't' min Somesh will be caught.

According to the question,

$$50t - 30t = 225$$

$$\Rightarrow \quad t = \frac{225}{20} = \frac{220}{20} + \frac{5}{20}$$

$$= 11\text{min} + \frac{5}{20} \times 60 \text{ sec} = 11 \text{min } 15\text{sec}$$

$\therefore$ Ram will catch the thief after11min 15 sec.

74. (a) To go 7 km the man take 6 breaks of 7 min.

$\therefore$ Time taken to rest $= 6 \times 7 = 42$ min

$$= \frac{42}{60} \text{h} = \frac{7}{10} \text{h}$$

Time $= \frac{7}{14} = \frac{1}{2}$ h

$\therefore$ Total time taken $= \frac{1}{2} + \frac{7}{10} = \frac{12}{10}$

$$= \frac{6}{5} \text{h} = 1\frac{1}{5} \text{h}$$

75. (a) Required distance $= d \times \frac{a}{(b-a)}$

$$= 200 \times \frac{6}{(8-6)} = 200 \times \frac{6}{2} = 600 \text{ m}$$

76. (b) A, B and C takes time to finish race

$$= \frac{1200}{2}, \frac{1200}{4}, \frac{1200}{6} \text{ respectively}$$

$$= (600, 300, 200) \text{ sec}$$

$\therefore$ They meet for the first time

= LCM (600, 300, 200) = 600 sec = 10 min

77. (c) Given, speed of Sujata = 2.85 km/h

$$= \frac{2.85 \times 1000}{60} = 47.5 \text{ m/min}$$

Speed of Anjali = 1.5 m/s

$$= 1.5 \times 60 \text{ min} = 90 \text{ m/min}$$

Length of circular path = 693 m

$\therefore$ They will meet first time $= \frac{693}{90 + 47.5}$

$$= \frac{693}{137.5} = 5.04 \text{ min}$$

78. (b) Thief covered distance in 3 min

$$= 3 \times 8 \times \frac{5}{18} \times 60 = 400 \text{ m}$$

Policeman covered distance in 3 min

$$= 3 \times 9 \times \frac{5}{18} \times 60 = 450 \text{ m}$$

Then distance between them after 3 min

$$= (400 + 300) - 450 = 700 - 450 = 250 \text{ m}$$

79. (c) Distance run to catch the thief by policeman $= d \times \frac{b}{a-b} = 1.25 \times \frac{8}{10-8}$

$$= 1.25 \times \frac{8}{2} = 5 \text{ km}$$

80. (c) Given, Jehangir had to cover 90 km in 1 h i.e 90000 m in 3600 sec.

Distance covered = 15.2 × 1500 = 22800 m

$\therefore$ Speed for remaining distance

$$= \frac{\text{Remaining distances}}{\text{Remaining time}}$$

$$= \frac{90000 - 22800}{3600 - 1500} = \frac{67200}{2100} = 32 \text{ m/s}$$

81. (b) Let length of track = T

Time to meet first time = $\frac{T}{6-b}$ [$\because b < 6$]

Time for A to complete one round = $\frac{T}{6}$

Time for B to complete one round = $\frac{T}{b}$

So, time taken to meet for first time at starting point = LCM of $\left(\frac{T}{6}, \frac{T}{b}\right) = \frac{T}{\text{HCF}(6, b)}$

So, number of meeting point

Time to meet for first

$= \frac{\text{Time to meet at starting point}}{\text{Time to meet first time}}$

$2 = \frac{T/\text{HCF}(6, b)}{T/(6-b)} = \frac{6-b}{\text{HCF}(6, b)}$

$2 = \frac{6-b}{\text{HCF}(6, b)}$

So, $b = 2$

Hence, we can take only 1 value of b.

82. (c) Time taken by first cyclist = $\frac{75}{30} = \frac{5}{2}$ h

Time taken by second cyclist = $\frac{75}{25} = 3$ h

LCM of (5/2 and 3) = 15

$\therefore$ They will meet after 15 h.

83. (b) Speed of owner = 76 km/h

Speed of the thief = 57 km/h

Distance covered by thief in 1h = 57 km

Let owner will catch the thief in 't' h.

$\therefore \quad (76-57)t = 57 \Rightarrow 19t = 57 \Rightarrow t = 3\text{h}$

$\therefore$ Required time = 4 : 00 am + 3h = 7 : 00 am

84. (d) Total length of track = 200 m

HCF of two runner's speed

= HCF (18, 24) = 6 km/h

$= \frac{6 \times 5}{18} = \frac{5}{3}$ m/s

Then time will they meet again

$= \frac{200 \times 3}{5} = 120$ s

85. (c) Total distance

= (120 + 100) × 2 = 440 km

Time taken by covered total distance

$= \frac{120}{80} + \frac{100}{40} + \frac{220}{75} = \frac{3}{2} + \frac{5}{2} + \frac{44}{15}$

$= \frac{45 + 75 + 88}{30} = \frac{208}{30}$

$\therefore$ Average speed = $\frac{\text{Total distance}}{\text{Total time}}$

$= \frac{440 \times 30}{208} = 63.46$ km/h (approx)

86. (d) In first race, in same time;

Distance cover by Arjun = 1000 m

Distance cover by Balaji = 900 m

Distance cover by Charan = 800 m

$\therefore$ The ratio of their speed = 1000 : 900 : 800

= 10 : 9 : 8

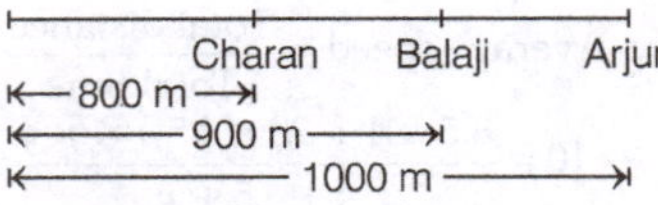

In second race

$\therefore$ Required distance = (10 − 8) × 10

= 2 × 10 = 20 m

87. (b) Time taken by policeman to catch the thief = $\frac{40}{(12-10)} = \frac{40}{2} = 20$ sec

$\therefore$ Distance covered by policeman in 20 sec

= 12 × 20 = 240 m

88. (a) Total distance covered

$= (6 \times 2 + 2 \times 1 + \frac{18}{5} \times 1 + 4 \times 3)$ km

[$\because 1$ m/s $= \frac{18}{5}$ km/h]

= (12 + 2 + 3.6 + 12) = 29.6 km

Total time taken = $(2 + 1 + 1 + \frac{1}{2} + 1 + 3) = 8.5$ h

$\therefore$ Average speed = $\frac{\text{Total distance}}{\text{Total time}}$

$= \frac{29.6}{8.5} = 3.48$ km/h

89. (a) Let the distance between the points A and $B = x$ km.

Time taken by Ram = 6 h

Speed of the Ram = $\frac{x}{6}$ km/h

Time taken by Raju = 10 h

Speed of the Raju = $\frac{x}{10}$ km/h

Let they meet after t h.

Then, $\frac{x}{6} \times t + \frac{x}{10} \times t = x$

$\Rightarrow \quad \frac{t}{6} + \frac{t}{10} = 1 \Rightarrow \frac{5t + 3t}{30} = 1$

$\Rightarrow \quad 8t = 30 \Rightarrow t = \frac{30}{8} = \frac{15}{4} = 3\frac{3}{4}$

$= 3h\frac{3}{4} \times 60$ min = 3 h 45 min.

So they meet after 8 am + 3 h 45 min

= 11:45 am.

Speedy Method

Ratio of time = 6 : 10

$\therefore$ Ratio of speed = 10 : 6

Let total distance = 6 × 10 = 60 units

$\therefore$ Meeting time = $\frac{60}{6 + 10} = \frac{60}{16} = 3$ h 45 min

Hence, required time = 8 : 00 am + 3 h 45 min

= 11 : 45 am

90. (b) Time taken to catch the thief

$= \frac{\text{Distance}}{\text{Relative speed}}$

$3 \times 60 = \frac{100 \times 18}{(10 - x) \times 5}$

$10 - x = 2 \Rightarrow x = 8$ km/h

91. (a) Average speed = $\frac{2 \times x_1 \times x_2}{x_1 + x_2}$

$= \frac{2 \times 45 \times 80}{45 + 80} = \frac{2 \times 45 \times 80}{125} = 57.6$ km/h

92. (b) Time taken by Daya to cover 105 km.

$= \frac{105}{25} = 4.2$ h

In 4.2 h, distance covered by menu

= 10 × 4.2 = 42 km

$\therefore$ Remaining distance between them

= 105 − 42 = 63 km

Now, time duration when they meet

$= \frac{63}{(25 + 10)} = 1.8$ h

$\therefore$ Distance between A to C = 42 + 10 × 1.8

= 42 + 18 = 60 km

93. (a) Car A covers 25 km till 9 am.

Now, distance between Car A and B

= (135 − 25) km = 110 km

Time they meet from 9 am

$= \frac{110}{(25 + 30)} = \frac{110}{55}$ h = 2 h

Hence, required time = 9 am + 2 h = 11 am

94. (d) Time of police from 8 : 30 pm.to 9 : 00 pm = 30 min

Now, distance travelled by thief till 9:00 pm

= Speed × Time

$= 60 \times \frac{45}{60} = 45$ km

$\therefore$ Minimum speed of the police jeep

$= \frac{45}{\frac{30}{60}} = \frac{45 \times 60}{30} = 45 \times 2 = 90$ km/h

95. (c) If A runs 500 m, then B runs 450 m.

So, it A runs 400 m, then B runs

$= \frac{450}{500} \times 400 = 360$ m

Also, if B runs 600 m, then C runs 540 m.

So, it B runs 360 m, then C runs

$= \frac{540}{600} \times 360$ m = 54 × 6 = 324 m

Hence, in 400 m race, A will beat C by (400 − 324) m = 76 m

Speedy Method

Distance ratio

A : B : C

10 9

10 9

100 : 90 : 81

$A \Rightarrow 100 \xrightarrow{\times 4} 400$m

A beat $C \Rightarrow 19 \xrightarrow{\times 4} 76$m

96. (b) Total distance = 250 + 350 = 600 km

Total time = $\left(\frac{250}{50} + \frac{350}{70}\right)$ h = (5 + 5) h = 10 h

$\therefore$ Average speed = $\frac{600}{10}$ km/h = 60 km/h

97. (a) Distance travelled by A in $(t+5)$ seconds = Distance travelled by B in t sec

$\Rightarrow \quad 34\times(t+5) = 44\times t$

$\Rightarrow \quad 34\times t + 170 = 44t \Rightarrow 10t = 170$

$\Rightarrow \quad t = 17$ sec

Total distance travelled by B

$= 44t = 44\times 17 = 748$ m

> **Speedy Method**
>
> Distance travelled by A in 5 sec $= 34\times 5$ m
>
> Hence, required distance $= d\times\dfrac{b}{b-a}$
>
> $= 34\times 5\times\dfrac{44}{44-34} = 748$ m

98. (a) Case I. Let P finish the race in t sec.

Speed of $P = \dfrac{1500}{t}$ m/s

$\Rightarrow$ Speed of $Q = \dfrac{1300}{t+8}$ m/s

Case II. Time taken by P to complete the race = time taken by Q to complete the race.

$\Rightarrow \dfrac{1500}{\frac{1500}{t}} = \dfrac{1100}{\frac{1300}{t+8}} \Rightarrow t = \dfrac{11}{13}\times(t+8)$

$\Rightarrow 13t = 11t + 88 \Rightarrow 2t = 88$

$\Rightarrow \quad t = 44$ sec

99. (b) Distance covered by 4 members

$= 5\times 4 = 20$ km

Total time taken = 30 min

$= \dfrac{30}{60} = \dfrac{1}{2}$ h (1 h = 60 min)

$\therefore$ Average speed $= \dfrac{20}{\frac{1}{2}} = 20\times 2 = 40$ km/h

100. (b) A beats B by 50 m or 5 sec means, B covers 50 m in 5 sec.

Speed of $B = \dfrac{50}{5} = 10$ m/s

Time taken by B to cover 1000 m

$= \dfrac{1000}{10} = 100$ sec

Time taken by A to cover 1000 m

$= 100 - 5 = 95$ sec

$\therefore$ Difference between their speed

$= \dfrac{1000}{95} - 10 = \dfrac{200}{19} - 10$

$= \dfrac{200-190}{19} = \dfrac{10}{19}$ m/s

101. (c) Relative speed of the dog

$= 24 - 10 = 14$ km/h

Distance to cover = 280 m = 0.28 km

$\therefore$ Time $= \dfrac{\text{Distance}}{\text{Speed}} = \dfrac{0.28}{14}$ h

$= \dfrac{28}{100\times 14}\times 60$ min

$= \dfrac{120}{100}$ min $= 1.2$ min

102. (b) Average speed

$= \dfrac{\text{Total distance travelled}}{\text{Total time taken}}$

$= \dfrac{96+124+105}{\frac{96}{16}+\frac{124}{31}+\frac{105}{7}}$

$= \dfrac{325}{6+4+15} = \dfrac{325}{25}$

$= 13$ km/h

103. (c) Speed of bus $A = 48\times\dfrac{5}{18} = \dfrac{40}{3}$ m/s

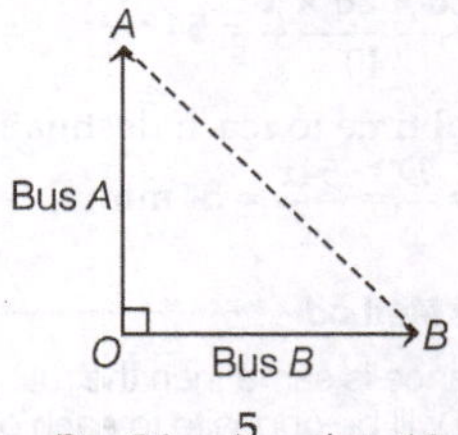

Speed of bus $B = 36\times\dfrac{5}{18}$ m/s $= 10$ m/s

$\Rightarrow OA = \dfrac{40}{3}\times 15$ m $= 200$ m

$\Rightarrow OB = 10\times 15$ m $= 150$ m

Now, in ΔAOB,

$AB = \sqrt{40000 + 22500}$

$\Rightarrow \quad AB = \sqrt{62500} = 250$ m

Hence, distance between the buses after 15 sec $= 250$ m

104. (d) From option (a),

First speed = 20 m/s

Second speed = 85 km/h $= 85\times\dfrac{5}{18} = 23.6$ m/s

Since, $20 < 23.6$

$\therefore$ First option's statement is correct.

From option (b),

Since, Time $= \dfrac{\text{Distance}}{\text{Speed}}$

$\therefore$ Second option's statement is correct.

From option (c), Third option's statement is correct because $t \propto \dfrac{1}{S}$.

From option (d),

First speed = 99 km/h $= 99\times\dfrac{5}{18} = 27.5$ m/s

Second speed = 24 m/s

Since $27.5 > 24$

$\therefore$ Fourth option's statement is not correct.

105. (a) Let the speeds of theif and policeman be $7x$ km/h and $8x$ km/h respectively and the policeman will catch the theif after t h.

According to the question,

$\dfrac{450}{1000} + 7xt = 8xt$

$\Rightarrow \quad xt = 0.45$

$\therefore$ Required distance $= 8\times 0.45$

$= 3.6$ km

> **Speedy Method**
>
> Required distance $= d\times\dfrac{b}{b-a}$
>
> $= 450\times\dfrac{8}{8-7} = 3600$ m $= 3.6$ km

106. (a) R's speed of walking = 5 km/h

R's speed of jogging $= 2\times 5 = 10$ km/h

R's speed of running $= 2\times 10 = 20$ km/h

Time taken by R, go to office from home

$= \dfrac{5}{5} + \dfrac{5}{10} = 1 + \dfrac{1}{2} = \dfrac{3}{2}$ h.

Time taken by R, to come back home from office $= \dfrac{5}{10} + \dfrac{5}{20} = \dfrac{1}{2} + \dfrac{1}{4} = \dfrac{2+1}{4} = \dfrac{3}{4}$.

$\therefore$ Required average speed $= \dfrac{\text{Total distance}}{\text{Total time}}$

$= \dfrac{10+10}{\frac{3}{2}+\frac{3}{4}} = \dfrac{20}{\frac{6+3}{4}} = \dfrac{80}{9}$ km/h

107. (a) Let the speed of bike A, bike B and bike C be a, b and c m/s, respectively.

In Case I,

Time taken by bike A to cover 1200 m = Time taken by bike B to cover 1100 m.

$\Rightarrow \quad \dfrac{1200}{a} = \dfrac{1100}{b} \Rightarrow \dfrac{a}{b} = \dfrac{12}{11}$

In Case II,

Time taken by bike B to cover 600 m = Time taken by bike C to cover 500 m.

$\Rightarrow \quad \dfrac{600}{b} = \dfrac{500}{c} \Rightarrow \dfrac{b}{c} = \dfrac{6}{5}$

$\therefore \quad a:b:c = 72:66:55$

Now, let a, b and c be $72x$, $66x$ and $55x$, respectively.

In case III,

Let A covers 720 m distance in time t.

$\Rightarrow \quad t = \dfrac{720}{a} = \dfrac{720}{72x} = \dfrac{10}{x} \Rightarrow xt = 10$

and, C covers 720 m distance in time $t + 30$ sec.

$\Rightarrow t + 30 = \dfrac{720}{C} = \dfrac{720}{55x} = \dfrac{144}{11x} \Rightarrow t + 30 = \dfrac{144}{11x}$

$\Rightarrow \quad 11xt + 330x = 144$

$\Rightarrow 11\times 10 + 330x = 144 \quad (\because xt = 10)$

$\Rightarrow \quad 110 + 330x = 144 \Rightarrow x = \dfrac{34}{330}$

Now, hence, speed of bike $C = c$ m/s

$= 55x = \dfrac{55\times 34}{330}$ m/s $= \dfrac{17}{3}$ m/s

> **Speedy Method**
>
> Distance ratio
>
> | | A | | B | | C |
> |---|---|---|---|---|---|
> | | 12 | : | 11 | : | |
> | | | : | 6 | : | 5 |
> | | 72 | | 66 | | 55 |
> | ×10 | 720 m | | | | 550 m |
>
> Speed$_C = \dfrac{170}{30} = \dfrac{17}{3}$ m/s

108. (c) Average speed $= \dfrac{\text{Total distance}}{\text{Time}}$

Let, d km be the total distance and t h be the time.

$\Rightarrow \quad 45 = \dfrac{d}{t} \Rightarrow t = \dfrac{d}{45}$ ...(i)

Also, $\quad 30 = \dfrac{d}{t + \dfrac{15}{60}}$

$\Rightarrow \quad 30 = \dfrac{d}{\dfrac{d}{45} + \dfrac{15}{60}}$ [From Eq. (i)]

$\Rightarrow \quad 30\left(\dfrac{d}{45} + \dfrac{15}{60}\right) = d$

$\Rightarrow \quad 30 \times \dfrac{d}{45} + \dfrac{30 \times 15}{60} = d$

$\Rightarrow \quad \dfrac{2d}{3} + \dfrac{15}{2} = d \Rightarrow d - \dfrac{2d}{3} = \dfrac{15}{2}$

$\Rightarrow \quad \dfrac{d}{3} = \dfrac{15}{2} \Rightarrow d = \dfrac{15 \times 3}{2} = \dfrac{45}{2} = 22.5$

> **Speedy Method**
>
> Required distance $= \dfrac{S_1 S_2}{S_1 - S_2} \times \Delta t$
>
> $= \dfrac{45 \times 30}{(45 - 30)} \times \dfrac{15}{60} = 22.5$ km

109. (d) Distance travelled by thief in half on hour $= \dfrac{1}{2} \times 48 = 24$ km

Time taken to catch the thief by owner

$= \dfrac{24}{58 - 48} = \dfrac{24}{10} = 2.4\text{ h} = 2\text{ h }24\text{ min}$

Hence, required time

$= 01:00\text{ pm} + 2\text{ h }24\text{ min} = 3:24\text{ pm}$

110. (a) Let total distance = 100 km

$\therefore$ Average speed

$= \dfrac{100}{\dfrac{40}{40} + \dfrac{50}{25} + \dfrac{10}{10}} = \dfrac{100}{4} = 25$ km/h

111. (b) Distance between A and B

$= \dfrac{S_1 S_2}{S_2 - S_1} \times (t_1 + t_2) = \dfrac{20 \times 30}{30 - 20} \times \left(1\dfrac{1}{2} + 2\dfrac{1}{2}\right)$

$= \dfrac{20 \times 30}{10} \times 4 = 240$ km

112. (b) Average speed $= \dfrac{2xy}{x + y}$

$= \dfrac{2 \times \dfrac{1}{x} \times \dfrac{1}{x^2}}{\dfrac{1}{x} + \dfrac{1}{x^2}} = \dfrac{2}{x^3} \times \dfrac{x^2}{(x+1)} = \dfrac{2}{x + x^2}$

113. (a) Time taken by A to cover 400 m

$= \dfrac{400}{16} = 25$ sec

B covers $(400 - 15) = 385$ m in $(25 + 10)$

$= 35$ sec

$\therefore$ Speed of $B = \dfrac{385}{35} = 11$ m/s

114. (d) Relative speed of thief and police

$= (23 - 21) = 2$ m/s

Time taken by police to catch thief

$= \dfrac{97}{2} = 48.5$ sec

115. (d) Let total distance = D km

and Ram's usual speed = x km/min

According to the question,

$\dfrac{D}{60\% \text{ of } x} - \dfrac{D}{x} = 36$

$\Rightarrow \dfrac{100D}{60x} - \dfrac{D}{x} = 36 \Rightarrow \dfrac{D(100 - 60)}{60x} = 36$

$\Rightarrow \; 40D = 60 \times 36 \times x$

$\therefore \quad D = \dfrac{60 \times 36 \times x}{40} = 54x$

So, his usual time to reach destination

$= \dfrac{D}{x} = \dfrac{54x}{x} = 54$ min

> **Speedy Method**
>
> When distance is same then the ratio of time and speed will be opposite to each other
>
> Normal new
>
> So, $2 \xrightarrow{\times 18} 36$
>
> $3 \xrightarrow{\times 18} 54$
>
> Speed → 5 : 3
>
> Time → 3 : 5

116. (d) Let total distance = 120 km

Average speed $= \dfrac{120}{\dfrac{80}{45} + \dfrac{30}{60} + \dfrac{10}{75}}$

$= \dfrac{120}{\dfrac{16}{9} + \dfrac{1}{2} + \dfrac{2}{15}} = \dfrac{120 \times 90}{217} \approx 49.77$ km/h

117. (a) Ratio of speeds of Anil and Bakul

$= \dfrac{1500}{(1500 - 150)} = \dfrac{1500}{1350} = 10:9$

Ratio of speeds of Bakul and Charles

$= \dfrac{1500}{(1500 - 75)} = \dfrac{1500}{1425} = 20:19$

$\therefore$ Ratio of speeds of Anil and Charles

$= \dfrac{10 \times 20}{9 \times 19} = 200:171$

$\therefore$ Required distance $= \dfrac{1500 \times (200 - 171)}{200}$

$= 217.50$ m

118. (a) Speed $= \dfrac{\text{Distance}}{\text{Time}} = \dfrac{144}{1.8} = 80$ km/h

Now, new speed $= 80 \times \dfrac{120}{100} = 96$ km/h

and new distance $= 2 \times 144 = 288$ km

$\therefore$ Time $= \dfrac{\text{Distance}}{\text{New speed}} = \dfrac{288}{96} = 3$ h

119. (d) Let speed of A is x km/h.

Speed of B is y km/h.

According to the question,

$\dfrac{40}{x} - \dfrac{40}{y} = 2$ ...(i)

and $\dfrac{80}{2x} - \dfrac{80}{y} = \dfrac{3}{2}$ ...(ii)

From Eqs. (i) and (ii), we get

$x = 16$ km/h and $y = 80$ km/h

Hence, required time $= \dfrac{120}{80} = \dfrac{3}{2} = 1\dfrac{1}{2}$ h

120. (c) Let usual speed is S km/h.

According to the question,

$\dfrac{150}{S - 10} - \dfrac{150}{S} = \dfrac{1}{2} \Rightarrow \dfrac{150S - 150(S - 10)}{(S - 10)S} = \dfrac{1}{2}$

$\Rightarrow \; S^2 - 10S - 3000 = 0$

$\Rightarrow \; (S + 50)(S - 60) = 0$

$S = -50, S = 60$

$\therefore \quad$ Time $= \dfrac{90}{45} = 2$ h

121. (b) Relative speed = 50 − 40 = 10 km/h

Distance cover by Car A in $\dfrac{1}{2}$ h

$= 40 \times \dfrac{1}{2} = 20$ km

Now, Time = Distance/Speed = 20/10 = 2 h

$\therefore$ Distance cover by Car B in next 2 h to meet first car = 50 × 2 = 100 km.

122. (c) Given, speed of X = 6 km/h and speed of Y = 8 km/h

Ratio of speed of $X : Y = 6 : 8 = 3 : 4$

We know, time is inversely proportional to speed only when the distance travelled by them is equal

Time ratio of $X : Y = 4 : 3$

Time difference between X and Y

= 15 min + 10 min = 25 min

$\Rightarrow (4 - 3)$ unit = 1 unit = 25 min

Time taken by $X = 4 \times 25 = 100$ min

$= \dfrac{100}{60}\text{ h} = \dfrac{5}{3}$ h

$\therefore$ Distance between A and $B = 6 \times \dfrac{5}{3} = 10$ km

123. (a) $D = 4 \times 1.25 = 5$ km

New time $= 1.25 \times \dfrac{(100 - 25\%)}{100}$

$= 1.25 \times \dfrac{75}{100} = 1.25 \times \dfrac{3}{4} = \dfrac{15}{16}$ h

New speed $= \dfrac{\text{Distance}}{\text{New time}} = \dfrac{5}{\dfrac{15}{16}} = \dfrac{5 \times 16}{15} = \dfrac{16}{3}$

$\therefore$ Required percentage $= \dfrac{\dfrac{16}{3} - 4}{4} \times 100$

$= \dfrac{16 - 12}{3 \times 4} \times 100$

$= \dfrac{100}{3} = 33\dfrac{1}{3}\%$

> **Speedy Method**
>
> Before After
>
> Time → 4 : 3
>
> Speed → 3 : 4
>
> +1
>
> $\therefore$ Reduced speed $= \dfrac{1}{3} \times 100\% = 33\dfrac{1}{3}\%$

124. (a) According to the question,

$$\frac{144}{x-y} = 12 \Rightarrow x - y = 12 \quad \ldots\text{(i)}$$

and $$\frac{144}{x+y} = \frac{9}{8}$$

$$\Rightarrow \quad x + y = 128 \quad \ldots\text{(ii)}$$

From Eqs. (i) and (ii), we get

$x = 70$ km/h, $y = 58$ km/h

Hence, the speed of faster car = 70 km/h

125. (a) Speed of car = 60 km/h

Distance covered by car in 180 min

(3 h) = 60 × 3 = 180 km

$\therefore$ Time taken $= \frac{180}{40} = 4.5\text{ h} = 4\text{ h } 30\text{ min}$

126. (b) Since, student stops twice for 5 min each.

$\therefore$ Actual time taken to cover 5 km by student $= 1\text{h} - 10\text{ min} = 50\text{ min} = \frac{50}{60}\text{ h}$

Average speed $= \frac{\text{Total distance}}{\text{Total time taken}}$

$$= \frac{5\text{ km}}{\left(\frac{50}{60}\right)\text{h}} = \frac{5 \times 60}{50}\text{ km/h} = 6\text{ km/h}$$

127. (a) Let the distance between his house to exhibition ground = 150 km

Now, average speed $= \frac{\text{Total distance}}{\text{Total time taken}}$

$$= \frac{150+150}{\frac{150}{30}+\frac{150}{50}} = \frac{300}{5+3} = \frac{300}{8} = 37.5\text{ km/h}$$

128. (d) Total distance = 100 km.

Average speed $= \frac{\text{Total distance}}{\text{Total time}}$

$$40 = \frac{100}{\text{Total time}}$$

Total time $= \frac{100}{40} = 2.5\text{ h} = 150\text{ min}$

$\therefore$ Time taken for last 20 km

$= 150 - (40 + 50) = 60\text{ min}$

$\therefore$ Speed in last 20 km

$= \frac{20}{60} \times 60\text{ km/h} = 20\text{ km/h}$

129. (a) Average speed $= \frac{\text{Total distance}}{\text{Total time taken}}$

$$= \frac{(72+28+160)}{\left(\frac{72}{45}+\frac{28}{4}+\frac{160}{20}\right)}\text{ km/h}$$

$$= \left(\frac{260}{1.6+7+8}\right)\text{km/h}$$

$$= \left(\frac{260}{16.6}\right) = 15.66\text{ km/h}$$

130. (b) Total distance travelled by *A*

$= (8 \times 4)\text{ km} + (4 \times 8)\text{ km}$

$= (32 + 32) = 64\text{ km}$

Total time = (8 + 4) h = 12 h

$\therefore$ Average speed $= \left(\frac{64}{12}\right)\text{km/h} = \left(5\frac{1}{3}\right)\text{km/h}$

Speedy Method

$\because$ Distance is equal.

So, average speed $= \frac{2 \times 4 \times 8}{4+8}$

$$= \frac{64}{12} = 5\frac{1}{3}\text{ km/h}$$

131. (a) Average speed $= \frac{\text{Total distance}}{\text{Total time taken}}$

$$= \frac{1200+1600+1000+200}{\frac{1200}{80}+\frac{1600}{40}+\frac{1000}{400}+\frac{200}{50}}$$

$$= \left(\frac{4000}{15+40+2.5+4}\right) = \left(\frac{4000}{61.5}\right)$$

$= 65.04$ km/h

132. (d)

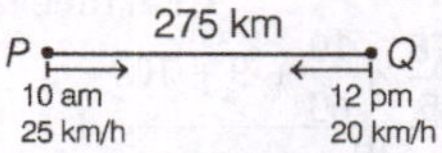

In 2 h distance covered by first rider

$= 25 \times 2 = 50$ km

$\therefore$ Remaining distance $= 275 - 50 = 225$ km

Relative speed = (25 + 20) = 45 km/h

(opposite direction)

Time after they meet each other $= \frac{225}{45} = 5$ h

$\therefore$ Required time of meeting each other

= 12 pm + 5 h = 5.00 pm

133. (d) We know that, distance (*d*) is directly proportional to time (*t*)

i.e., $d \alpha t$

or $d = kt$ where 'k' is a proportionality constant

Now, given $d = 72$ km and $t = 2$ h

$$\therefore \quad k = \frac{d}{t} = \frac{72}{2} = 36$$

Hence, $d = 36t$ will be correct equation.

134. (a) Average speed $= \frac{37.5\text{ km}}{\frac{90}{60}\text{ h}}$

$$= \left(\frac{37.5 \times 60}{90}\right)\text{km/h}$$

= 25 km/h

135. (a) Average speed $= \frac{\text{Total distance}}{\text{Total time taken}}$

$$= \frac{(12.5+12.5)\text{ km}}{(30+20)\text{ min}} = \frac{25}{\frac{50}{60}}\text{ km/h}$$

$$= \frac{25 \times 60}{50}\text{ km/h} = 30\text{ km/h}$$

136. (d) Let the total distance be $2x$ km.

According to the question,

$$\frac{x}{12} + \frac{x}{8} = 3\text{ h } 45\text{ min}$$

$$\Rightarrow \quad \frac{x}{12} + \frac{x}{8} = 3\frac{3}{4} \Rightarrow \frac{3x+2x}{24} = \frac{15}{4}$$

$5x = 90 \Rightarrow x = 18$ km

$\therefore$ Total distance $= 2x = 2 \times 18 = 36$ km

Speedy Method

Average speed $= \frac{2 \times 12 \times 8}{12+8} = \frac{192}{20}$ km/h

$\therefore$ Total distance $= \frac{192}{20} \times \left(3\frac{3}{4}\right)$

$$= \frac{192}{20} \times \frac{15}{4} = 36\text{ km}$$

137. (b) Let the total distance be x km.

Now, according to the question,

$$\frac{x}{45} - \frac{x}{55} = \frac{40}{60} \Rightarrow \frac{55x - 45x}{45 \times 55} = \frac{40}{60}$$

$$\Rightarrow \quad \frac{10x}{45 \times 55} = \frac{4}{6} \Rightarrow x = 165\text{ km}$$

Speedy Method

Distance $= \frac{S_1 . S_2}{S_1 \sim S_2} \times \Delta t$

$$= \frac{45 \times 55}{10} \times \frac{40}{60} = 165\text{ km}$$

138. (c) Here, total distance

= 50 km + 75 km = 125 km

Total time taken = (40 + 40) min

$= 80\text{ min} = \frac{80}{60}\text{ h}$

$\therefore$ Average speed $= \frac{\text{Total distance}}{\text{Total time taken}}$

$$= \frac{125}{\frac{80}{60}} = \frac{125 \times 3}{4} = 93\frac{3}{4}\text{ km/h}$$

139. (b) Relative speed = (12 − 7) = 5 km/h

$$= \left(5 \times \frac{5}{18}\right)\text{m/s}$$

$\therefore$ Required time

$$= \left(\frac{280}{5 \times \frac{5}{18}}\right)\text{sec} = \left(\frac{280 \times 18}{25 \times 60}\right)\text{min}$$

$$= \left(\frac{84}{25}\right)\text{min} = 3\frac{9}{25}\text{ min}$$

140. (a) Quarter of an hour = 15 min

$\therefore$ Average speed $= \frac{(20+25+15)\text{ km}}{(15+15+15)\text{ min}}$

$$= \left(\frac{60}{\frac{45}{60}}\right)\text{km/h} = \left(\frac{60 \times 60}{45}\right)\text{km/h}$$

= 80 km/h

141. (c) Let total distance = 100 km

$\therefore$ Average speed $= \frac{100}{\frac{25}{25}+\frac{50}{50}+\frac{25}{12.5}}$

$$= \frac{100}{4} = 25\text{ km/h}$$

142. (b) Distance by which Rakesh beat Rajesh

$$= \frac{1200}{40} \times 4 = 120\text{ m}$$

143. (c) Here, distance = constant

$\because \quad \text{Time} \propto \frac{1}{\text{Speed}}$

Ratio of time = 12 : 15 : 10

Then, ratio of speeds

$= (15 \times 10):(12 \times 10):(12 \times 15)$

$= 150 : 120 : 180 = 5 : 4 : 6$

144. (a) Let distance of first 45 min = x km

$\therefore$ Total distance $= x + 85 \times \frac{75}{60} + 70 \times 3$

$= (x + 316.25)$ km

$$\text{Average speed} = \frac{\text{Total distance}}{\text{Total time}}$$

$$73 = \frac{x + 316.25}{5}$$

$x = 365 - 316.25 = 48.75$ km

Hence, required speed $= \frac{48.75}{45} \times 60$

$= 65$ km/h

145. (c) Time for first 10 km

$= \frac{\text{Distance}}{\text{Speed}} = \frac{10}{40} = \frac{1}{4}$ h

$\therefore$ Time for second 10 km $= \frac{1}{8}$ km

Time for fourth 10 km $= \frac{1}{4}$ h

Time for third 10 km $= \frac{1}{8}$ h

Total time $= \frac{1}{4} + \frac{1}{8} + \frac{1}{4} + \frac{1}{8} = \frac{6}{8}$ h

$\therefore$ Average speed $= \frac{40}{\frac{6}{8}} = \frac{40 \times 8}{6} = \frac{160}{3}$ km/h

146. (c) Average speed for the entire journey

$= \frac{2xy}{x + y} = \frac{2 \times 36 \times 60}{36 + 60} = 45$ km/h

147. (b) Speed $= \frac{\text{Distance}}{\text{Time}} = \frac{900}{6} \frac{\text{m}}{\text{min}}$

$= \frac{900}{6} \times \frac{60}{1000}$ km/h $= 9$ km/h

148. (b) Shyam covers 200 m in 20 sec.

Shyam's speed $= \frac{200}{20}$ m/s $= 10$ m/s

Given, Ram beats Shyam by 200 m in 1200 m race when Ram covers 1200 m, Shyam covers 1000 m.

Time taken by Shyam to cover 1000 m.

$= \frac{1000}{10}$ sec $= 100$ sec

$\therefore$ Ram's speed $= \frac{1200}{100} = 12$ m/s

149. (a) Given, speed ratio of A and $B = 3 : 5$

$\therefore$ Ratio of time taken by $A : B = 5 : 3$

$\therefore \quad 5x - 3x = 30 \Rightarrow x = 15$ min

Time taken by A to reach destination $= 5x$

$= 5 \times 15$ min $= 75$ min

$= 1$ h 15 min

150. (c) Let the distance between A and B $= x$ km

$$\text{Average speed} = \frac{\text{Total distance}}{\text{Total time taken}}$$

$$= \frac{x + x}{\frac{x}{12} + \frac{x}{18}} \text{ km/h} = \frac{2 \times 36}{3 + 2} \text{ km/h}$$

$= 14\frac{2}{5}$ km/h

Speedy Method

$$\text{Average speed} = \frac{2xy}{x + y} = \frac{2 \times 12 \times 18}{12 + 18}$$

$= 14\frac{2}{5}$ km/h

151. (b) According to the question,

$\therefore$ Average speed of car $= \frac{\text{Total distance}}{\text{Total time taken}}$

$$= \frac{21 \times \frac{18}{5} \times \frac{10}{60} + 9 + 10}{\frac{10}{60} \times 3}$$

$$= \frac{\frac{21 \times 18}{5} \times \frac{1}{6} + 9 + 10}{3 \times \frac{10}{60}}$$

$$= \frac{\frac{75.6}{6} + 19}{3 \times \frac{10}{60}} = \frac{12.6 + 19}{1/2} = 63.2 \text{ km/h}$$

152. (a) Required average speed

$$= \frac{100 + 140}{\frac{100}{50} + \frac{140}{70}} = \frac{(100 + 140)}{(2 + 2)} = \frac{240}{4} = 60 \text{ km/h}$$

153. (a) Let they will be covered x km distance. So time of Babita = Time of Geeta

$$\frac{x - 40}{1} = \frac{x}{5/2} \Rightarrow \frac{5}{2}(x - 40) = x$$

$$\Rightarrow \quad 3x = 200 \Rightarrow x = \frac{200}{3} = 66.67 \text{ m}$$

154. (b) Let's take the original speed of A is x km/h.

According to the question,

$$\frac{40}{x} - \frac{40}{2x} = 2.5 + 1$$

$$\Rightarrow \quad \frac{80 - 40}{2x} = 3.5 \Rightarrow \frac{40}{2x} = \frac{7}{2}$$

$$\Rightarrow \quad x = \frac{40 \times 2}{7 \times 2} = \frac{40}{7} \text{ km/h}$$

$\therefore$ Time taken by A to walk 40 km is

$$= \frac{40}{\frac{40}{7}} = 7 \text{ h}$$

So, time taken by B to walk 40 km

$= 7 - 2.5 = 4.5$ h

$\therefore$ Average time taken by A and B to walk 40 km distances

$$= \frac{7 + 4.5}{2} = \frac{11.5}{2} = 5.75 \text{ h}$$

$= 5 \text{ h} + \frac{75}{100} \times 60$ min $= 5$ h 45 min

Speedy Method

	Before		After
$\text{Speed}_A \rightarrow$	1	:	2
$\text{Time}_A \rightarrow$	2	:	1

1 unit = 2.5 + 1 = 3.5

Real time of $A \rightarrow 2$ unit = 7 h

Time of $B \rightarrow 7 - 2.5 = 4.5$

$\therefore$ Average $= \frac{7 + 4.5}{2} = 5$ h 45 min

155. (d) Speed of bus $= \frac{60}{3} \times 2 = 40$ km/h

Speed of car $= \frac{60}{45} \times 60 = 80$ km/h

$\therefore$ Required ratio $= 80 : 40 = 2 : 1$

156. (b) Let the speed of outward journey $= x$ km/h

So, speed of return journey $= (x + 10)$ km/h

According to the question,

$$\Rightarrow \quad \frac{300}{x} - \frac{300}{x + 10} = 5 \Rightarrow 300\left[\frac{1}{x} - \frac{1}{x + 10}\right] = 5$$

$$\Rightarrow x^2 + 10x - 600 = 0 \Rightarrow (x + 30)(x - 20) = 0$$

$\Rightarrow \quad (x + 30) = 0 \mid (x - 20) = 0$

$\quad\quad x = -30 \mid x = 20$

As, speed can never be negative. So, the speed of the outward journey is 20 km/h.

157. (b) Let speed of A is x km/h.

Time taken by $B = \left(\frac{40}{x} - 2.5\right)$ h

When A doubled his speed, time taken by $A = \frac{40}{2x}$ h

Now, $\left[\left(\frac{40}{x}\right) - 2.5\right] - \left(\frac{40}{2x}\right) = 1$

$$\Rightarrow \quad \left(\frac{40}{x}\right) - \left(\frac{40}{2x}\right) = 3.5$$

$$\Rightarrow \quad \frac{40}{2x} = \frac{7}{2} \Rightarrow x = \frac{40}{7} \text{ km/h}$$

Time taken by A to cover the distance

$$= 40 \div \left(\frac{40}{7}\right) = 7 \text{ h}$$

A need 7 h to walk a 40 km distance.

Speedy Method

	Before		After
$\text{Speed}_A \rightarrow$	1	:	2
$\text{Time}_A \rightarrow$	2	:	1

1 unit $\rightarrow 2.5 + 1 = 3.5$ h

Time_A, 2 unit $\rightarrow 7$ h

158. (c) Time taken by Hari to complete race

$= \frac{2400}{6} = 400$ sec

$\therefore$ Time taken by Tarun $= 400 - 40 - 60$

$= 300$ sec

Speed of Tarun $= \frac{2400}{300} = 8$ m/s

159. (c) Let first part travel by bus for t h.

$\therefore$ Remaining part travel by train = $(6 - t)$ h

According to the question,

$$t \times 40 + (6 - t) \times 55 = 285$$

$$\Rightarrow 40t + 330 - 55t = 285$$

$$\Rightarrow -15t = 285 - 330 \Rightarrow -15t = -45$$

$$\therefore t = \frac{45}{15} = 3\text{ h}$$

Hence, distance travelled by train

$$= 55\text{ km/h} \times 3\text{ h} = 165\text{ km}$$

160. (d) Let the distance be d km and speed be s km/h and time is 't' h.

Initial speed $= \frac{d}{t}$, $s = \frac{d}{t}$ km/h

Again, after time reduce by 25%.

$$\text{New time} = t \times \frac{75}{100} = \frac{3}{4}t$$

$$\text{New speed } (s') = \frac{d}{\frac{3}{4}t} = \frac{4d}{3t}$$

$\therefore$ Required percentage increase in speed

$$= \frac{\frac{4}{3}\frac{d}{t} - \frac{d}{t}}{\frac{d}{t}} \times 100 = \frac{\frac{1}{3}\frac{d}{t}}{\frac{d}{t}} \times 100$$

$$= \frac{1}{3} \times 100 = 33\frac{1}{3}\%$$

Speedy Method

Time ratio	4 : 3	[Distance is constant]
Speed ratio	3 : 4 (difference 1)	

$\therefore$ Required % $= \frac{1}{3} \times 100 = 33\frac{1}{3}\%$

161. (b) Speed of policeman = 65 km/h

Speed of thief = 41 km/h

Distance between police and thief = 1200 m

Relative speed of policeman and thief

$$= 65 - 41 = 24\text{ km/h}$$

$\therefore$ Required time to catch thief by police

$$= \frac{12}{24} \quad [1200\text{ m} = 1.2\text{ km}]$$

$$= \frac{1}{20}\text{ h} = \frac{1}{20} \times 60\text{ min} = 3\text{ min}$$

162. (c) Given, original speed (s) = 4 km/h

Original time taken (T) = 6 h 15 min

$$= 6\frac{15}{60}\text{ h} = 6\frac{1}{4}\text{ h} = \frac{25}{4}\text{ h}$$

$$\therefore \text{Distance} = 4 \times \frac{25}{4} = 25\text{ km}$$

Now, if a man takes 5 h 10 min for the same distance, then

$\therefore$ Required speed

$$\text{Time} = 5\text{ h } 10\text{ min} = 5\frac{1}{6} = \frac{31}{6}\text{ h}$$

$$= \frac{25 \times 6}{31} = 4\frac{26}{31}\text{ km/h}$$

163. (c) Let the speed of car be x km/h.

$\therefore$ Distance = $16x$

New speed = $(x + 20)$ km/h

According to the question,

$$\frac{16x}{x + 20} = 12 \Rightarrow 16x = 12x + 240$$

$$\Rightarrow x = 60\text{ km/h}$$

Distance travelled by car = $16x = 16 \times 60$

$$= 960\text{ km}$$

164. (c) Given, speed of police = 20 km/h

Speed of thief = 16 km/h

Distance between thief and police = 200 m

Thus, relative speed = $(20 - 16)$ = 4 km/h

$$= 4 \times \frac{5}{18} = \frac{20}{18}\text{ m/s}$$

According to the question,

$$\text{Time} = \frac{200}{\frac{20}{18}} = \frac{200 \times 18}{20} = 180\text{ sec.}$$

Thus, police captured thief after 180 sec.

Distance travelled by thief

$$= 180 \times 16 \times \frac{5}{18} = 800\text{ m}$$

165. (d) Average speed of entire ride

$$= \frac{10 + 15}{\frac{10}{15} + \frac{15}{10}} = \frac{25}{\frac{2}{3} + \frac{3}{2}} = \frac{25 \times 6}{13} = 11.54\text{ km/h}$$

166. (c) According to the question,

Thief covers 6 km in 30 min i.e. $\left(\frac{1}{2}\right)$ h.

$\therefore$ Distance covered by thief in 1 h = 12 km

$\therefore$ Actual speed of thief = 12 km/h

$\therefore$ Actual speed of policeman

$$= 12 \times \frac{5}{4} = 15\text{ km/h}$$

$\therefore$ Distance between policeman and thief

$$= \frac{1}{2}(15 - 12) = \frac{1}{2} \times 3 = 1.5\text{ km}$$

$[\because 30\text{ min} = 1/2\text{ h}]$

167. (a) According to the question,

$$\therefore \text{Distance} = s_1t_1 + s_2t_2 = 68 \times 0.375 + 72 \times 0.2$$

$$= 25.5 + 14.4 = 39.9\text{ km} \cong 40\text{ km}$$

$[\because 22.5\text{ min} = 0.375\text{ h}, 12\text{ min} = 0.2\text{ h}]$

168. (d) According to the question,

Time taken by P = 200 sec

Time taken by Q = 220 sec

P defeat Q by 20 sec.

Now, distance travelled by Q in 220 sec

= 2000 m

$\therefore$ Distance travelled by Q in 20 sec

$$= \frac{2000 \times 20}{220} = \frac{2000}{11}\text{ m} = 181\frac{9}{11}\text{ m}$$

169. (b) Let the distance be D km.

According to the question,

$$\frac{D}{8} - \frac{D}{12} = \frac{30}{60} \Rightarrow \frac{D}{24} = \frac{1}{2}$$

$$\therefore D = 12\text{ km}$$

$$\text{Time taken by police} = \frac{\text{Distance}}{\text{Speed}} = \frac{12}{12}$$

$$= 1\text{ h} = 60\text{ min}$$

Speedy Method

Distance travelled by thief in 30 min = 4 km

$$\text{Thus, time taken by police} = \frac{4}{12 - 8} = \frac{4}{4} = 1\text{ h}$$

$$= 60\text{ min}$$

170. (d) Let the distance of equal part = 1 unit

$$\therefore \text{Average speed} = \frac{1 + 1 + 1}{\frac{1}{80} + \frac{1}{60} + \frac{1}{30}} = \frac{240 \times 3}{15}$$

$$= 16 \times 3 = 48\text{ km/h}$$

171. (a) According to the question,

Distance covered in first hour

$$= 90 \times 1 = 90\text{ km}$$

Distance covered in next two hour

$$= 120 \times 2 = 240\text{ km}$$

$$\text{Average speed} = \frac{240 + 90}{2 + 1} = \frac{330}{3} = 110\text{ km/h}$$

172. (a) Total distance $= 60 \times \frac{45}{60} = 45$ km

To reach destination in 30 min,

$$\text{Speed} = \frac{45}{30} \times 60 = 90\text{ km/h}$$

173. (c) Speed of girl = 9 km/h

Time to cross a bridge = 45 min

$$\text{Length of bridge} = 9 \times \frac{45}{60} \times 1000\text{ m}$$

$[\because 1\text{ km} = 1000\text{ m}]$

$$= 6750\text{ m}$$

174. (b) According to the question,

When A covers 100 m, B covers

$(100 - 20)$ m = 80 m

$\therefore$ $A : B = 100 : 80 = 5 : 4$

When B covers 100 m, C covers

$(100 - 5)$ m = 95 m

$\therefore$ $B : C = 100 : 95 = 20 : 19$

Now, $A : B$ and $B : C$ are 5 : 4 and 20 : 19

$\Rightarrow$ $A : B : C = 25 : 20 : 19$

$= 100 : 80 : 76$ [multiply with 4]

So, A beats C by $(100 - 76)$ m = 24 m

175. (c) According to the question,

Distance travelled by car in 85 min

$$= 36 \times \frac{85}{60} = 51\text{ km} \quad [\because 1\text{ h} = 60\text{ min}]$$

$$\therefore \text{Required speed} = \frac{51}{\frac{51}{60}} = \frac{51}{51} \times 60$$

$$= 60\text{ km/h}$$

176. (b) Let the speed of Arun = S_A

Speed of Bhaskar = S_B

According to the question,

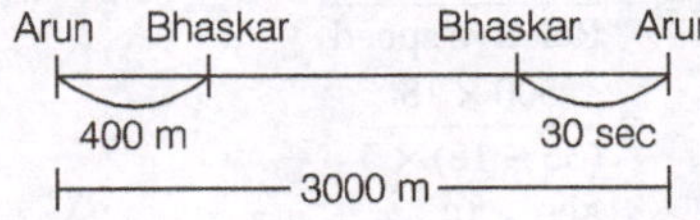

By first condition,

$$\frac{3000}{S_A} = \frac{2600}{S_B} - 30$$

$$\frac{3000}{S_A} = \frac{2600 - 30S_B}{S_B} \quad \text{...(i)}$$

By second condition,

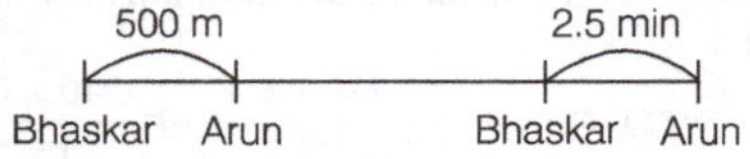

$$\frac{2500}{S_A} = \frac{3000 - S_B \times 2.5 \times 60}{S_B} \quad \text{...(ii)}$$

By Eqs. (i) and (ii),

$$\frac{6}{5} = \frac{2600 - 30S_B}{3000 - 150S_B} = \frac{260 - 3S_B}{300 - 15S_B}$$

$$\Rightarrow \quad 1800 - 90S_B = 1300 - 15S_B$$

$$\Rightarrow \quad S_B = \frac{500}{75} = \frac{20}{3}$$

By Eq. (i), $S_A = \frac{25}{3}$

$$\therefore \quad t_A = \frac{3000}{\frac{25}{3}} = \frac{3000 \times 3}{25} = 360 \text{ sec}$$

$$t_B = \frac{3000}{\frac{20}{3}} = \frac{3000 \times 3}{20} = 450 \text{ sec}$$

∴ Required difference = 450 − 360

= 90 sec = 1.5 min

177. (d) Average speed= $\frac{2 \times 40 \times 20}{40 + 20}$

$= \frac{1600}{60} = 26\frac{2}{3}$ km / h

178. (b) Relative speed of Ram and Shyam

$= \left(3 + 5\frac{1}{4}\right) = 3 + \frac{21}{4} = \frac{33}{4}$ km/h

∴ Required time $= \frac{44}{\left(\frac{33}{4}\right)} = \frac{16}{3}$ h = 5 h 20 min

179. (b) According to the question,

Speed of Ankur : Speed of Neha = 5 : 6

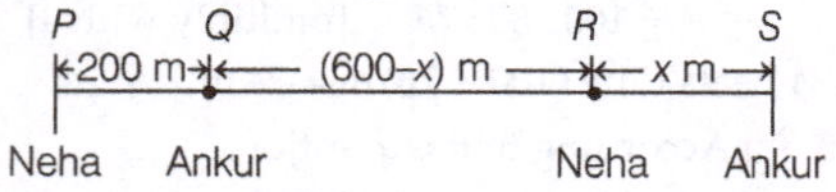

Let Ankur will win by x m.

∴ Time taken by Neha from P to R and time taken by Ankur from Q to S is same.

∴ Time of Neha = Time of Ankur

$$\frac{800 - x}{6} = \frac{600}{5} \Rightarrow 4000 - 5x = 3600$$

$$\Rightarrow \quad 5x = 400 \therefore \quad x = 80 \text{ m}$$

∴ Ankur will win by 80 m.

180. (b) Time taken by policeman to catch the thief $= \frac{\text{Distance}}{\text{Relative speed}}$

$= \frac{500 \times 18}{(36 - 18) \times 5}$

$= \frac{500 \times 18}{18 \times 5} = 100$ sec

181. (c) According to the question,

If his average speed for first 3 h at 70 km/h then distance = 210 km

∴ He travel fast in the last hour.

∴ Required speed = (240 − 210) ÷ 1

= 30 km/h

182. (c) Distance covered by T_1 till 10 am

= 45 × 2 = 90 km

Remaining distance = 300 − 90 = 210 km

Relative speed = 45 + 60 = 105 km/h

Time to cover 210 km $= \frac{210}{105} = 2$ h

So, they meet 2 h after 10 am *i.e.*, 12 : 00 pm.

183. (c) Total distance covered by Mithila

= 50 + 30 = 80 km

Total time taken by Mithila

= (90 + 15 + 35) min = 140 min

∴ Average speed $= \frac{80}{\frac{140}{60}} = 34.28 \sim 34\frac{2}{7}$ km/h

184. (c) Given,

Speed of police = 120 km/h

Speed of thief = 90 km/h

Distance between them = 1.5 km

Time when police catch the thief

$= \frac{3}{2(120 - 90)} \quad \left[\because \text{Time} = \frac{\text{Distance}}{\text{Speed}}\right]$

$= \frac{3}{2 \times 30} = \frac{1}{20}$

Distance covered by police in $\frac{1}{20}$ h

$= \frac{1}{20} \times 120 \quad [\because \text{Distance} = \text{Speed} \times \text{Time}]$

= 6 km

185. (a) New speed $= \frac{6}{7}$ of usual speed

$\left[\because \text{Speed} \propto \frac{1}{\text{Time}}\right]$

Now, time taken $\frac{7}{6}$ of usual speed time taken

with $\left[\frac{7}{6}\text{of usual speed} - \text{usual speed}\right]$

= 20 min

$\Rightarrow \frac{1}{6}$ of the usual speed = 20 min

Time taken with usual speed = 120 min = 2 h

Speedy Method

	Usual		New
Speed →	7	:	6
Time →	6	:	7

1 unit → 20 m

Usual time 6 unit → 120 min

186. (b) Distance travelled by robber in 12 min = Speed × Time $= 10 \times \frac{12}{60} = 2$ km

∴ Time taken to chase a robber

$= \frac{2}{15 - 10} = \frac{2}{5}$ h $= \frac{2}{5} \times 60$ min = 24 min

Hence, required time = 5 : 12 pm + 24 min

= 5 : 36 pm

187. (d) Let distance = d

∴ Average speed $= \frac{d + d + d}{\frac{d}{40} + \frac{d}{45} + \frac{d}{60}}$

$= \frac{3d}{\frac{90d + 80d + 60d}{3600}} = \frac{3d \times 3600}{230d} = \frac{1080}{23}$

= 46.96 km/h

188. (c) Speed of man = 5 km/h

Time taken = 3 h 45 min $= 3\frac{3}{4}$ h

Distance covered $= 5 \times 3\frac{3}{4} = \frac{75}{4}$ km

Now, time taken by cycle = 2 h 10 min

$= 2\frac{1}{6}$ h $= \frac{13}{6}$ h

∴ Speed of the cycle $= \frac{\left(\frac{75}{4}\right)}{\left(\frac{13}{6}\right)}$

$= \frac{450}{52} = 8\frac{17}{26}$ km/h

189. (a) Let total distance = D

∵ Average speed $= \frac{\text{Total distance}}{\text{Total time}}$,

$= \frac{D}{\left(\frac{\frac{1}{4}D}{25} + \frac{\frac{1}{2}D}{40} + \frac{\frac{1}{4}D}{50}\right)} = \frac{D}{D\left[\frac{1}{100} + \frac{1}{80} + \frac{1}{200}\right]}$

$= \frac{1}{\left[\frac{4 + 5 + 2}{400}\right]} = 36\frac{4}{11}$ km/h

190. (b) ∵ Distance = 40 × 7 = 280 km

So, new speed $= \frac{280}{5} = 56$ km/h

191. (c) When they start from the same point at the same time in the opposite direction. Then first time they meet

$= \frac{1400}{(33 + 47)} = \frac{1400}{80} = \frac{35}{2}$ sec

So, the second time they meet

$= 2 \times \frac{35}{2} = 35$ sec

192. (d) Given, Length of track = 2575 m

Speed of Anil = 72 km/h

$= 72 \times \frac{5}{18}$ m/s = 20 m/s

Speed of Arun = 90 km/h

$= 90 \times \frac{5}{18}$ m/s = 25 m/s

Relative speed of Anil and Arun

= 25 − 20 = 5 m/s

∴ Time taken to meet first time

$= \frac{2575}{5} = 515$ sec.

193. (a) Total distance covered by Ist car upto 8 : 54 am $= 30 \times \frac{24}{60} = 12$ km

$\therefore$ Remaining distance between both the cars

$= 181 - 12 = 169$ km

Now, meeting time of both cars

$= \frac{\text{Distance between both cars}}{\text{Relative speed of cars}}$

$= \frac{169}{30+35} = \frac{169}{65}\text{ h} = \frac{169}{65} \times 60 = 156$ min

Hence, both cars will meet at

$= 8:54\text{ am} + 156\text{ min} = 11:30$ am

194. (a) Distance travelled by A in 6 h

$= 15 \times 6 = 90$ km

Relative speed $= 25 - 15 = 10$ km/h

Hence, required time to catch A by B

$= \frac{90}{10} = 9$ h.

195. (b) Let the total distance be 100 km.

$\therefore$ Average speed $= \frac{100}{\frac{35}{70} + \frac{40}{80} + \frac{25}{50}}$

$= \frac{100}{\frac{1}{2} + \frac{1}{2} + \frac{1}{2}} = \frac{100}{\frac{3}{2}}$

$= \frac{200}{3} = 66\frac{2}{3}$ km/h

196. (a) Speed of the car $= 63$ km/h

$= 63 \times \frac{5}{18} = 17.5$ m/s

Distance travelled by it in 10 sec

$= 17.5 \times 10 = 175$ m

197. (d) Given, distance $= 1.2$ km

Relative speed $= 27 - 18 = 9$ km/h

$\therefore$ Time $= \frac{12}{9 \times 10} \times 60 = 8$ min

198. (c) Let the usual time of the person to reach the office $= t$ h

According to the question,

$80 \times (t - 1) = 50\left(t + \frac{48}{60}\right)$

[$\because$ Distance = Speed × Time]

$\Rightarrow$ $80t - 80 = 50t + 40$

$\Rightarrow$ $30t = 80 + 40 \Rightarrow t = \frac{120}{30} = 4$ h

$\therefore$ Required speed $= \left(\frac{D}{t}\right) = \frac{80(4-1)}{4}$

$= \frac{80 \times 3}{4} = 60$ km/h

199. (b) The bus stops for per hour

$= \frac{(60 - 54)}{60} \times 60$ min

$= 6$ min

200. (c) Let total distance $= 120$ km

$\therefore$ Average speed $= \frac{120}{\frac{40}{10} + \frac{30}{15} + \frac{50}{20}}$

$= \frac{120}{8.5} = \frac{1200}{85} = \frac{240}{17}$ km/h

201. (c) Given, speed of Mohit $= 50$ km/h

Let, the speed of the bus be x km/h

According to the question,

The distance travelled by bus in

$(50 - 10) = 40$ min

The distance travelled by Mohit in 10 min

$\therefore$ Distance covered by bus in $\frac{40}{60}h$

$=$ Distance covered by Mohit in $\frac{10}{60}$ h

$\Rightarrow$ $\frac{40}{60} \times x = 50 \times \frac{10}{60}$

[$\because$ Distance = Speed × Time]

$\Rightarrow$ $x = \frac{25}{2} \Rightarrow x = 12.5$ km/h

Hence, required speed of bus $= 12.5$ km/h

202. (a) Remaining distance $= 250 - 250 \times \frac{3}{5}$

Remaining time $= 6 - 3.5 - 0.5 = 2$ h

Hence, required speed $= \frac{100}{2} = 50$ km/h

203. (a) Let the original speed of car is x km/h.

According to the question,

$\frac{60}{x} - \frac{60}{x+8} = 2$

$\Rightarrow$ $60x + 480 - 60x = 2x(x + 8)$

$\Rightarrow$ $x^2 + 8x - 240 = 0$

$(x + 20)(x - 12) = 0$

$\therefore$ $x = 12$ km/h

Hence, original speed of car $= 12$ km/h

204. (c) Required time $= \frac{\text{Distance}}{\text{Relative speed}}$

$= \frac{2500 \times 18}{(37 + 35) \times 5} = \frac{2500 \times 18}{72 \times 5} = 125$ sec

$= 2$ min 5 sec

205. (a) Average speed $= \frac{\text{Total distance}}{\text{Total time}}$

$= \frac{10 + 12}{\frac{10}{12} + \frac{12}{10}} = \frac{22 \times 60}{50 + 72} = \frac{22 \times 60}{122} = 10.819$

≈ 10.8 km/h

206. (a) Average speed $= \frac{2 \times 66 \times 92.4}{66 + 92.4}$

$= \frac{2 \times 66 \times 92.4}{158.4} = 77$ km/h

207. (d) Average speed $= \frac{\text{Total distance}}{\text{Total time}}$

$= \frac{75 + 45}{\frac{75}{45} + \frac{45}{70}} = \frac{120}{\frac{1050 + 405}{630}}$

$= \frac{5040}{97} = 51\frac{93}{97}$ km/h

208. (c) Given, speed $= 54$ km/h

$= \frac{54}{60}$ km/min $= \frac{9}{10}$ km/min

Time $= 50$ min

$\therefore$ Distance = speed × time

$= \frac{9}{10} \times 50 = 45$ km

If speed is increased by 25%

Then, new speed $= \frac{9}{10} \times \frac{125}{100} = \frac{9}{10} \times \frac{5}{4}$

$= \frac{9}{8}$ km/min

and new distance $= 45 \times \frac{3}{4} = \frac{135}{4}$ km

$\therefore$ Required time $= \frac{\frac{135}{4}}{\frac{9}{8}} = \frac{135 \times 8}{4 \times 9} = 30$ min

209. (a) Let the total distance to cover be d km.

$\therefore$ Average speed $= \frac{d}{\frac{\frac{d}{5}}{30} + \frac{\frac{d}{4}}{25} + \frac{d - \frac{d}{5} - \frac{d}{4}}{60}}$

$= \frac{1}{\frac{1}{150} + \frac{1}{100} + \frac{11}{1200}} = \frac{1}{\frac{8 + 12 + 11}{1200}}$

$= \frac{1200}{31} = 38.7$ km/h

210. (c) Given, man's speed $= 4$ km/h.

$= 4 \times \frac{5}{18}$ m/s

$\therefore$ Distance covered in 18 min or in

$18 \times 60\text{ sec} = 4 \times \frac{5}{18} \times 18 \times 60 = 1200$ m.

211. (b) Let the total distance be 3d.

According to the question,

$\frac{d}{40} + \frac{2d}{60} = 21$

$\Rightarrow$ $\frac{3d + 4d}{120} = 21$

$\Rightarrow$ $7d = 21 \times 120$

$\Rightarrow$ $d = 360$ km

$\therefore$ Total distance $= 3 \times d = 3 \times 360 = 1080$ km

212. (c) Let speed of cycle be x km/h.

$\frac{30}{60} + \frac{20}{x} = 3 \Rightarrow \frac{20}{x} = \frac{5}{2} \Rightarrow x = 8$ km/h

213. (c) Time taken to catch the thief

$= \frac{5000}{(120 - 100) \times \frac{5}{18}}$

$= 900$ sec $= 15$ min

214. (c) Let the total distance covered be $2D$.

According to the question,

$\frac{D}{10} + \frac{D}{8} = \frac{3}{2}$

$\Rightarrow$ $\frac{D(4+5)}{40} = \frac{3}{2}$

$\Rightarrow$ $D = \frac{3}{2} \times \frac{40}{9}$

$\Rightarrow$ $D = \frac{20}{3}$ km

Total distance covered $= 2 \times \frac{20}{3}$

$= \frac{40}{3} = 13\frac{1}{3}$ km

215. (d) Time taken to catch the theif

$= \frac{\text{Distance}}{\text{Relative speed}}$

$= \frac{150}{(108-93)\times\frac{5}{18}} = 36 \text{ sec}$

216. (d) Time taken to catch the thief

$= \frac{525}{(21-18)\times\frac{5}{18}} = \frac{525\times 18}{15} = 630 \text{ sec}$

Distance covered by thief $= 18\times\frac{5}{18}\times 630$

$= 3150 \text{ m}$

217. (d) Distance between them after 18 min

$= 400-(9-8)\times\frac{18}{60}\times 1000$

$= 400-300 = 100 \text{ m}$

218. (a) They will meet first time at

$= \frac{500}{(18+9)\times\frac{5}{18}} = \frac{500}{\frac{15}{2}} = \frac{1000}{15} = 66.66 \text{ sec}$

219. (a) They meet first time at

$= \frac{1}{18-9} = \frac{1}{9} \text{h} = 400 \text{ sec}$

220. (c) Average speed of car

$= \frac{12+15+20}{\frac{12}{30}+\frac{15}{45}+\frac{20}{60}} = \frac{47}{\frac{16}{15}} = \frac{47\times 15}{16}$

$= 44\frac{1}{16} \text{ km/h}$

221. (a) Distance = Speed × Time

$= 81\times\frac{5}{18}\times 24 = 540 \text{ m}$

222. (d) Distance = Speed × Time

$= 5.4\times\frac{40}{60} = 8\times\text{time}$

Time = 0.45 h = 27 min

223. (c) Let speed of the person be x km/h.

Speed $= \frac{\text{Remaining distance}}{\text{Remaining time}}$

$= \frac{\left(8-\frac{8}{4}\right)}{1-\frac{1}{3}} = \frac{6}{\frac{2}{3}} = 9 \text{ km/h}$

224. (c) Speed $= \frac{\text{Distance}}{\text{Time}} = \frac{45}{1+\frac{40}{60}}$

$= \frac{45}{1+\frac{2}{3}} = \frac{45}{5}\times 3 = 27 \text{ km/h}$

$= 27\times\frac{5}{18} = 7.5 \text{ m/s}$

225. (a) Let speed be A km/h and B km/h.

$\frac{1200}{A+B} = 24 \Rightarrow A+B = 50$ ...(i)

Distance = 10B + 20(A + B) = 1200

3B + 2A = 120 ...(ii)

From Eqs. (i) and (ii), we get

B = 20 km/h and A = 30 km/h

226. (c) They will meet first time

$= \frac{\text{Distance}}{\text{Relative speed}}$

$= \frac{1200}{12-8} = 300 \text{ sec}$

227. (a) Time $= \frac{\text{Distance}}{\text{Relative speed}}$

$= \frac{400}{(30-28)} = 200 \text{ sec}$

228. (a) Distance covered by thief in half hour

$= 50\times\frac{1}{2} = 25 \text{ km}$

Time taken by owner to catch the thief

$= \frac{25}{60-50} = 2\frac{1}{2} \text{h}$

The time at which thief caught

$= 11:00 + 2:30 = 1:30 \text{ pm}$

229. (d) Average speed of car

$= \frac{120}{\frac{80}{50}+\frac{40}{40}} = \frac{120}{\frac{8}{5}+1}$

$= 120\times\frac{5}{13} = 46\frac{2}{13} \text{ Km/h}$

230. (a) They will meet after $= \frac{27}{9-3}$

$= \frac{27}{6} = 4.5 \text{h.}$

231. (c) Speed $= \frac{\text{Distance}}{\text{Time}}$

$= \frac{300}{36} = \frac{150}{18} \text{ m/s}$

$= \frac{150}{18}\times\frac{18}{5} = 30 \text{ km/h}$

232. (d) Let speed of thief be x km/h.

As, Time $= \frac{\text{Distance}}{\text{Speed}}$

$\frac{300/1000}{10-x} = \frac{1.5}{10}$

$\Rightarrow 30 = 150-15x$

$\Rightarrow 15x = 120$

$\Rightarrow x = 8 \text{ km/h}$

233. (d) Speed of cyclist $= \frac{2.5}{\frac{5}{72}}$

$\left[4 \text{ min } 10 \text{ sec} = 4\frac{1}{6}\times\frac{1}{60} = \frac{25}{6}\times\frac{1}{60} = \frac{5}{72} \text{h}\right]$

$= \frac{2.5\times 72}{5} = 36 \text{ km/h}$

Time to cover 6 km of distance $= \frac{6}{36}$

$= \frac{1}{6} \text{h} = \frac{60}{6} = 10 \text{ min}$

234. (b) Required Speed $= \frac{275}{5} = 55 \text{ km/h}$

Now, Speed is reduced by 5 km/h Distance

$= 300 \text{ km}$

$\therefore T = \frac{300}{(55-5)} = \frac{300}{50} = 6 \text{h}$

235. (a) Speed of Bicycle $= \frac{75}{12.5} = 6 \text{ m/s}$

$= 6\times\frac{18}{5} = 21.6 \text{ km/h}$

236. (c) Time taken to catch the thief

$= \frac{540}{18} = 30 \text{ sec}$

As, $\frac{\text{Distance between thief and police}}{18-12} = 30$

$\therefore$ Distance between thief and police = 180 m

Thus, policeman start after $= \frac{180}{12} = 15 \text{ sec}$

237. (a) Ratio of speeds of three car = 5 : 3 : 4

Ratio of time of three car $= \frac{1}{5}:\frac{1}{3}:\frac{1}{4}$

$= 12:20:15$

238. (d) Let the distance be x km.

Total time = 425 min $= \frac{85}{12}$ h

According to the question,

$\frac{x}{3}+\frac{x}{4}+\frac{x}{8} = \frac{85}{12}$

$\Rightarrow \frac{8x+6x+3x}{24} = \frac{85}{12}$

$\Rightarrow \frac{17x}{24} = \frac{85}{12} \Rightarrow \frac{x}{24} = \frac{5}{12}$

$\Rightarrow x = 10 \text{ km}$

$\therefore$ Total distance $= 3\times 10 = 30$ km

239. (a) Let total distance be x km.

According to the question,

$\frac{x}{5}+\frac{x}{4} = 9 \Rightarrow \frac{9x}{20} = 9$

$x = 20 \text{ km}$

240. (d) Let speed of police be x m/s.

Time $= \frac{\text{Distance}}{\text{Speed}}$

$\therefore \frac{864-12\times 18}{18} = \frac{864}{x}$

$\Rightarrow x = 24 \text{ m/s}$

241. (c) Remaining distance

$= 7.5-\frac{2\times 7.5}{3} = 2.5 \text{ km}$

Remaining time $= \frac{72}{60}-\frac{5}{5} = \frac{12}{60} \text{h}$

Hence, required speed $= \frac{2.5}{12}\times 60 = 12.5 \text{ km/h}$

242. (a) Distance between two towns

$= 9\times 60 = 540 \text{ km}$

Travel same distance in 8 h, then,

Speed $= \frac{540}{8} = 67.5 \text{ km/h}$

$\therefore$ Increment in speed $= 67.5-60 = 7.5$ km/h

243. (d) Total distance covered in whole journey $= 60\times 6+40\times 6$

$= 360+240 = 600 \text{ miles}$

Total time taken to cover whole journey

$= 6+6 = 12 \text{h}$

$\therefore$ Average speed $= \frac{600}{12} = 50 \text{ miles/h}$

244. (b) Relative speed between policeman and thief = (12.5 − 10) = 2.5 km/h

$= 2.5 \times \frac{5}{18}$ m/s $= \frac{12.5}{18}$ m/s

Time taken to caught the thief

$= \frac{250}{12.5} \times 18 = 360$ sec

$= \frac{360}{60 \times 60} = \frac{1}{10}$ h

Distance covered by thief after spotted

$= \frac{1}{10} \times 10 = 1$ km

245. (b) Given,

Speed = 8 km/h = 8 × 1000 m/h = 8000 m/h

Time = 27 min $= \frac{27}{60}$ h

∴ Length of bridge = Speed × Time

$= 8000 \times \frac{27}{60} = 3600$ m

246. (d) Ratio of time = 2 : 3 : 5

∴ Ratio of speeds $= \frac{1}{2} : \frac{1}{3} : \frac{1}{5}$

$= \frac{1}{2} \times 30 : \frac{1}{3} \times 30 : \frac{1}{5} \times 30$

= 15 : 10 : 6

247. (b) Relative speed = (20 + 30)

= 50 km/h

∴ Time $= \frac{\text{Distance}}{\text{Relative speed}} = \frac{200}{50} = 4$ h

248. (a) Given, Distance = 1800 m

Time = 6 min = 6 × 60 s = 360 s

∴ Speed $= \frac{\text{Distance}}{\text{Time}} = \frac{1800}{360} = 5$ m/s

249. (d) Relative speed of the policeman with respect to thief = (23 − 21) km/h = 2 km/h

Time taken to cover 108 m $= \frac{108}{2 \times 1000}$ h

Distance covered by the thief before overtaken by the policeman $= \frac{21 \times 108}{2 \times 1000}$ km

$= \frac{21 \times 108 \times 1000}{2 \times 1000} = 1134$ m

250. (a) Relative speed of policeman with respect to thief = (9 − 8) m/s = 1 m/s

Distance covered in 2 min i.e.,

120 sec = 120 m

∴ Required distance = (185 − 120) = 65 m

251. (b) Time taken to cover one way by bicycle $= \frac{10}{2} = 5$ h

Time taken to cover both ways by scooter

= (8 h 30 min − 5 h) × 2 = 7 h

252. (a) Total time to cover 800 km at 80 km/h $= \frac{800}{80} = 10$ h

Time taken to cover 320 km $= \frac{320}{64} = 5$ h

∴ Required speed $= \frac{480}{10 - 5} = 96$ km/h

253. (d) Distance = Speed × Time

$= 56 \times \frac{3}{2} = 84$ km

∴ Required speed $= \frac{84}{7} = 12$ km/h

254. (b) Average speed $= \frac{2AB}{A + B}$

$= \frac{40 \times 60 \times 2}{40 + 60} = 48$ km/h

Average time from one side $= \frac{5}{2} = 2.5$ h

∴ Required distance = 48 × 2.5 = 120 km

255. (a) Distance travelled in 3 h

= 60 × 3 = 180 km.

Then, he stopped for one hour.

Distance travelled four more hours

= 60 × 4 = 240 km

∵ Average speed $= \frac{\text{Total distance}}{\text{Total time}}$

$= \frac{180 + 240}{3 + 1 + 4} = \frac{420}{8} = 52.5$ km/h

256. (c) Time taken by A from P to Q

= 11 : 00 − 8 : 00 = 3 h

Time taken by B from Q to P

= 11 : 00 − 9 : 00 = 2 h

Ratio of time taken by A and B = 3 : 2

∴ Ratio of speed of A and B = 2 : 3

Let total distance = 6 km

Distance covered by A in one hour = 2 km

Remaining distance = 6 − 2 = 4 km

They meet after 9 : 00 am

$= \frac{4}{3 + 2} \times 60 = 48$ min

∴ They cross each other at 9 : 48 am.

257. (d) Let the speed of the scooter be x km/h.

∴ Speed of the bus = $1.2x$ km/h

According to the question,

$\frac{60}{x} - \frac{60}{1.2x} = \frac{10}{60}$

$\Rightarrow \frac{72 - 60}{1.2x} = \frac{1}{6} \Rightarrow \frac{12}{1.2x} = \frac{1}{6}$

$\Rightarrow 1.2x = 72$

∴ Speed of the bus = 72 km/h

258. (b) Given, speed of Piu = 5 km/h

Speed of Titu = 2 km/h

According to the question,

∴ Required time $= \frac{10.5}{7} = 1.5$ h

259. (a) According to the question,

$\frac{2 \times 20 \times q}{(20 + q)} = \frac{280}{11}$

$\Rightarrow 40q \times 11 = 280 \times 20 + 280q$

$\Rightarrow 440q = 5600 + 280q \Rightarrow 160q = 5600$

$\Rightarrow q = \frac{5600}{160} = 35$ km/h

and $\frac{2qr}{q + r} = \frac{112}{3} \Rightarrow \frac{2 \times 35 \times r}{35 + r} = \frac{112}{3}$

$\Rightarrow 210r = 3920 + 112r$

$\Rightarrow 210r - 112r = 3920 \Rightarrow 98r = 3920$

$\therefore r = \frac{3920}{98} = 40$ km/h

260. (d) Average speed $= \frac{2 \times 18 \times 22}{(18 + 22)} = \frac{792}{40}$

= 19.8 km/h

261. (c) Relative speed of Vishu and Ashu = 15 km/h

Let the distance between Vishu and Ashu be x km, then

$\frac{x}{6} = 15 \Rightarrow x = 90$ km

262. (d) Speed of light $= 3 \times 10^{17}$ nm/s

$= 3 \times 10^{17} \times 10^{-9}$ m/s $= 3 \times 10^8$ m/s

Distance between Moon and Earth

= 384000 km = 384000 × 1000 m

∴ Required time $= \frac{\text{Distance}}{\text{Speed}}$

$= \frac{384000 \times 1000}{3 \times 10^8} = 128$ s

263. (d) Time taken by cyclist from point A to point $B(T_1)$ = 2 h 33 min 36 s

= (2 × 3600) + (33 × 60) + 36 = 9216 s

Time taken by cyclist from point B to point $A(T_2)$ = 1 h 26 min 24 s

= (1 × 3600) + (26 × 60) + 24 = 5184 s

We know that,

Ratio of speeds of first to that of the second cyclist $= \sqrt{\frac{T_2}{T_1}} = \sqrt{\frac{5184}{9216}} = \sqrt{\frac{9}{16}} = 3 : 4$

264. (b) Distance covered by aeroplane

$= 280 \times \frac{19}{4} = 1330$ km

∴ To cover the same distance in 7 h

Speed $= \frac{1330}{7} = 190$ km/h

265. (c) Distance covered at the speed of 56 km/h $= 56 \times \frac{75}{60} = 70$ km

Distance covered at the speed of 60 km/h

= 90 km

Time taken $= \frac{90}{60} = 1.5$ h

Remaining distance = 260 − (90 + 70)

= 260 − 160 = 100 km

∴ Remaining time $= 4 - \left(1.5 + \frac{75}{60}\right)$

= 4 − (1.5 + 1.25)

= 4 − 2.75 = 1.25 h

∴ Required speed $= \frac{100}{1.25} = 80$ km/h

266. (b) Let the total distance be 360 km (LCM of 45, 8, 24).

Time taken to cover half distance $= \frac{180}{45} = 4$ h

$\therefore$ Remaining distance = 360 − 180 = 180 km

40% of remaining distance time

$= 180 \times \frac{40}{100} = 72$ km

Time taken to cover 72 km $= \frac{72}{8} = 9$ h

Now, rest distance = 360 − (180 + 72) = 108 km

Now, Time taken to cover rest of distance

$= \frac{108}{24} = \frac{9}{2}$ h

$\because$ Average speed $= \frac{\text{Total distance}}{\text{Total time taken}}$

$= \frac{360}{9 + 4 + \frac{9}{2}} = \frac{720}{35} = \frac{144}{7}$ km/h

267. (c) Let the actual speed of bus be $= x$ km/h

and the actual time taken by bus be $= y$ h

So, distance $= xy$ km

According to the question,

New speed $= (x + 5)$ km/h

and time taken $= (y - 1)$ h

So, distance $= (x + 5)(y - 1)$

$\because$ The total distance of the journey remains the same $(x + 5)(y - 1) = xy$

$\Rightarrow xy - x + 5y - 5 = xy$

$5y - x = 5$ ...(i)

$\because$ Actual distance $xy = 150$

$\Rightarrow y = \frac{150}{x}$

$5\left(\frac{150}{x}\right) - x = 5$ [from Eq. (i)]

$\Rightarrow x^2 + 5x - 750 = 0$

$\Rightarrow (x - 25)(x + 30) = 0$

$\therefore x = 25$ km/h

So, the actual speed = 25 km/h

268. (a) Speed of car of thief = 70 km/h

Distance travelled by theif in 1 h

$= 70 \times 1 = 70$ km

So, relative speed = 105 − 70 = 35 km/h

$\therefore$ Time taken to cover the distance

$= \frac{70}{35} = 2$ h

So, owner will over take the thief at (3pm +2) 5:00 pm.

269. (a) Distance between home and office

$= \frac{s_1 s_2}{s_1 - s_2} \times (t_1 + t_2)$

$= \frac{80 \times 30}{80 - 30}\left(\frac{10 + 10}{60}\right)$

$= \frac{2400 \times 20}{50 \times 60} = 16$ km

Actual time $= \frac{16}{80} + 10$ min $= \frac{16}{80} \times 60 + 10$

$= 12 + 10 = 22$ min

$\therefore$ Required speed $= \frac{16}{22} \times 60 = \frac{480}{11}$ km/h

270. (c) Let each distance be x km.

$\therefore$ Total distance $= 4x$ km

According to the question,

$\therefore$ Average speed $= \frac{4x}{\frac{x}{400} + \frac{x}{200} + \frac{x}{100} + \frac{x}{50}}$

$= \frac{4x}{\frac{x + 2x + 4x + 8x}{400}}$

$= \frac{4x \times 400}{15x} = \frac{320}{3}$ km/h

271. (a) According to the question,

Let distance = x unit and time = y unit

Speed (1) $= \frac{x}{y}$ and Speed (2) $= \frac{2x}{6y}$

So, Ratio of $\frac{\text{Speed (1)}}{\text{Speed (2)}} = \frac{\left(\frac{x}{y}\right)}{\left(\frac{2x}{6y}\right)} = \frac{6}{2} = \frac{3}{1}$

$\therefore$ Speed (1) : Speed (2) = 3 : 1

272. (d) Distance = Time × Speed

$= 4 \times 6 = 24$ km

Hence, required time $= \frac{24}{8} = 3$ h

273. (b) Let x be the usual speed of car.

The decreased speed $= (x - 10)$ km/h

According to the question,

$\Rightarrow \frac{210}{(x - 10)} - \frac{210}{x} = \frac{42}{60}$

$\Rightarrow \frac{210x - 210x + 2100}{x^2 - 10x} = \frac{7}{10}$

$\Rightarrow x^2 - 10x - 3000 = 0$

$\Rightarrow (x + 50)(x - 60) = 0$

$x = -50, 60$

$\because -50$ (impossible)

So, usual speed of car is 60 km/h.

274. (a) Speed of the car (S) = 50 km/h

and Distance (D) = 150 km

$\because$ Time $(T) = \frac{D}{S} = \frac{150}{50} = 3$ h

275. (c) Given,

Speed of first car = 40 km/h

Speed of the second car = 50 km/h

After 5 h the distance between them

$= (40 + 50) \times 5 = 450$ km

276. (c) Relative speed = 10 + 8 = 18 m/min

$\because$ Time = Distance / Relative speed

$\therefore$ Time = 900 / 18 = 50 min

277. (b) As per the given information,

Speed of y = 16 km/h and speed of x = 12 km/h

The distance covered by x in 6 h

$= 12 \times 6 = 72$ km

Now, y will catch the x in $= \frac{72}{16 - 12} = 18$ h

$\therefore$ The required covered distance by y

$= 18 \times 16 = 288$ km

278. (c) $\because$ Average speed $= \frac{\text{Total distance}}{\text{Total time}}$

$= \frac{11 + 22}{1 + \frac{1}{2}} = \frac{\frac{33}{3}}{\frac{3}{2}} = \frac{33 \times 2}{3}$

[$\because$ 60 min = 1h; 30 min $= \frac{1}{2}$ h]

$\therefore$ Average speed $= 11 \times 2 = 22$ km/h

279. (b) Given, speed of car = 51 km/h

Time between 10 : 40 am to

1 : 00 pm = 2h 20 min $= 2\frac{1}{3}$ h

$\therefore$ Distance = Speed × Time

$= 51 \times \frac{7}{3} = 119$ km

280. (d) $\because$ Average speed $= \frac{\text{Total distance}}{\text{Total time}}$

$= \frac{140 + 180}{3 + 5} = \frac{320}{8} = 40$ km/h

281. (b) Total distance covered by car

$= 30 \times 5 = 150$ km

$\therefore$ Required speed $= \frac{150}{2.5} = 60$ km/h

282. (a) Total time $= \frac{3}{2} + \frac{7}{4} + \frac{32}{28}$

$= \frac{84 + 98 + 64}{56}$

$= \frac{246}{56} = \frac{123}{28}$ h

Total distance = (3 + 7 + 32) km = 42km

$\therefore$ Average speed $= \frac{\text{Total distance}}{\text{Total time}}$

$= \frac{42}{123} \times 28 = \frac{392}{41}$ km/h

283. (b) Let Ram run 2 km in t sec.

Time taken by Ramesh and Naresh to run 2 km are $(t + 40)$ sec and $(t + 40 + 25)$ sec.

Speed of Naresh $= \frac{2000}{t + 65}$ m/sec

Given, in 2 km run, Ram beats Naresh by 650 m.

$\therefore$ Time taken by Ram to run 2000 m

= Time taken by Naresh to Run 1350 m

$\Rightarrow t = \frac{1350}{2000} \times (t + 65)$

$\Rightarrow 40t = 27t + 27 \times 65$

$\Rightarrow 40t - 27t = 27 \times 65$

$\Rightarrow t = \frac{27 \times 65}{13} = 135$ sec = 2 min 15sec

284. (c) $\because$ Time $= \frac{\text{Distance}}{\text{Speed}}$

Let total distance $= 3D$

$\frac{D}{2} + \frac{D}{3} + \frac{D}{4} = \frac{52}{60}$

$\Rightarrow \frac{30D + 20D + 15D}{60} = \frac{52}{60}$

$\Rightarrow \frac{65D}{60} = \frac{52}{60}$

$\Rightarrow D = 0.8$

$\therefore$ Total distance $= 0.8 \times 3 = 2.4$ km

285. (d) Given,
Speeds of A, B and C are 5 m/s, 3m/s and 8m/s respectively.
Distance between A and C = 6 m
Difference between speed of A and
$C = 8 - 5 = 3$ m/s
Time taken to cover 6m distance $= \frac{6}{3} = 2$ sec
Now, difference between speeds of
A and $B = 5 - 3 = 2$ m/s
Distance between A and B in 2 sec.
$= 2 \times 2 = 4$ m
$\therefore$ Required answer = 4 m

286. (c) Given, object moves 26 km at a speed of 30 km/h.
$\therefore$ Total time $= \frac{26}{30} \times 60 = 52$ min
An object moves 15 m in 2.6 min.
$\therefore$ Average speed $= \frac{\text{Total distance}}{\text{Total time}}$
$= \frac{26000 + 15}{54.6} = \frac{26000 + 15}{54.6 \times 60} = 7.94$ m/sec.

287. (d) Given, total distance = 1000 m
John beats Khan by distance = 120 m
So, Khan travelled only
$= 1000 \text{ m} - 120 \text{ m} = 880$ m
If John run 1000 m in 40 km/h
$\Rightarrow$ 1000 m = 40 km / h
$\Rightarrow$ 25 m = 1 km / h
And, Khan travelled only 880 m
$\therefore$ Speed of Khan $= \frac{880 \text{ m}}{25} = 35.2$ km/h

288. (a) Total distance travelled
$= (50 \times 3 + 65 \times 2 + 80 \times 4)$
= 600 miles
Total time = 2h + 3h + 2h + 4h = 11h
$\therefore$ Average speed $= \frac{600}{11} = 54.54$ mile/h

289. (d) $\because$ Distance = Distance $\times \left[\frac{\text{Police speed}}{\text{Thief speed} \sim \text{Police speed}}\right]$
$\therefore$ Distance $= 800 \times \left[\frac{8}{8-7}\right] = 6400$ m

290. (c) Distance travelled by theif in 12 sec
$= 15 \times 12 = 180$ m
$\therefore$ Required distance $= \frac{180 \times 20}{(20-15)} = 720$ m

291. (d) Let the distance be 12 km.
$\because$ (LCM of 2, 3, 4) = 12
Time taken to cover 12 km by 2 km/h
$= \frac{12}{2} = 6$ h
Time taken to cover 12 km by 3 km/h
$= \frac{12}{3} = 4$ h
Time taken to cover 12 km by 4 km/h
$= \frac{12}{4} = 3$ h
$\therefore$ Average speed $= \frac{3 \times \text{Distance}}{\text{Total time}}$
$= \frac{3 \times 12}{6 + 4 + 3} = \frac{36}{13} = 2.77$ km/h

292. (c) Distance = Relative speed × Time
$= (13 - 12) \times \frac{12}{60} = \frac{1}{5}$ km = 200 m
Hence, distance between policeman and thief in 12 min = 500 − 200 = 300 m

293. (c) Let the time in which he travelled on foot = x h
Then, the time in which he travelled on bicycle = $(7 - x)$ h
According to the question,
$2x + 4(7 - x) = 22$
$\Rightarrow 2x + 28 - 4x = 22$
$\Rightarrow 2x = 6$
$\Rightarrow x = 3$
Distance travelled on foot
$= 2x = 2 \times 3 = 6$ km

294. (c) Average speed
$= \frac{75 + 33}{2} = \frac{108}{2} = 54$ km/h

295. (d) Distance covered by
$R = 150 - 5 = 145$ m
Distance covered by $S = 150 - 35 = 115$ m
$\therefore$ Ratio of speeds of R and S
$= 145 : 115 = 29 : 23$
Time taken by $S = \frac{75}{23}$
Distance covered by $R = 29 \times \frac{75}{23}$
Difference in distance to win for S
$= 100 - 29 \times \frac{75}{23} = \frac{2300 - 2175}{23}$
$= \frac{125}{23} \approx 5.44$ m

296. (b) Time taken to cover 96 km
$= \frac{\text{Distance}}{\text{Speed}} = \frac{96}{16} = 6$ h
Distance covered at 21 km/h = 21 × 5 = 105
Total distance = 96 + 105 = 201 km
Total time = 6 + 5 = 11 h
$\therefore$ Average speed $= \frac{\text{Total distance}}{\text{Total time}}$
$= \frac{201}{11} = 18.27$ km/h

297. (c) Average speed $= \frac{1200}{30} = 40$ km/h
$= 40 \times \frac{5}{18} = 11\frac{1}{9}$ m/s

298. (d) Let speed of $X = a$ km/h
$\therefore$ Speed of $Y = (a - 40)$ km/h
According to the question,
$\frac{1200}{a - 40} - \frac{1200}{a} = 5$
$\Rightarrow \frac{1200(a - a + 40)}{a^2 - 40a} = \frac{5}{1}$
$\Rightarrow a^2 - 40a = 9600 \Rightarrow a^2 - 40a - 9600 = 0$
$\Rightarrow (a - 120)(a + 80) = 0$
$\therefore a = 120$ $[\because a \neq -80]$
$\therefore$ Time taken by Y in complete to travel
$= \frac{1200}{a - 40} = \frac{1200}{120 - 40} = \frac{1200}{80} = 15$ h

299. (d) Arrange speed $= \frac{\text{Total distance}}{\text{Total time}}$
$= \frac{48 + 36 + 16}{\frac{48}{8} + \frac{36}{18} + \frac{16}{8}} = \frac{100}{6 + 2 + 2} = \frac{100}{10} = 10$ km/h

300. (b) They run in the same direction, then relative speed = 45 − 27 = 18 km/h
$= 18 \times \frac{5}{18}$ m/sec = 5 m/sec
$\therefore$ Required time $= \frac{3600}{5} = 720$ sec

301. (d) Relative speed of thief and policeman
$= 21 - 20 = 1 \text{ km/h} = \frac{5}{18}$ m/s
Difference of distance after 18 sec
$= 80 + 18 \times \frac{5}{18} = 80 + 5 = 85$ m

302. (d) Time taken by Rahul for race
$= \frac{100 \times 18}{6 \times 5} = 60$sec
Cover distance by Bharat = 100 − 4 = 96 m
Time taken by Bharat = 60 + 4 = 64 sec
$\therefore$ Speed of Bharat $= \frac{96}{64}$ m/sec
$= \frac{96}{64} \times \frac{18}{5} = 5.4$ km/h

303. (a) Average speed $= \frac{\text{Total distance}}{\text{Total time}}$
$= \frac{4 + 10 + 45}{\frac{4}{2} + \frac{10}{6} + \frac{45}{30}} = \frac{59}{2 + \frac{5}{3} + \frac{3}{2}}$
$= \frac{59 \times 6}{12 + 10 + 9} = \frac{354}{31} = 11\frac{13}{31}$ km/h

304. (c) Speed of plane $= \frac{1728}{180} = \frac{1728}{\frac{180}{60}}$
$[\because 1 \text{ h} = 60 \text{ min}]$
$= \frac{1728 \times 60}{180} = 576$ km/h
$= 576 \times \frac{5}{18} = 160$ m/sec

305. (c) Average speed $= \frac{2xy}{x + y}$
(when distances are same)
$= \frac{2 \times 35 \times 65}{35 + 65} = \frac{2 \times 35 \times 65}{100}$
= 45.5 miles/h

15

Problems Based on Train

Problems based on trains are an application of the 'Speed, Time and Distance'.

Speed of train $(s) = \dfrac{\text{Distance covered } (d)}{\text{Time taken } (t)}$ or $s = \dfrac{d}{t}$

Based on Relative Speed

- If two trains or a train and a man are moving in opposite directions with speeds of S_1 and S_2, then their

  Relative speed = Sum of their speeds $= (S_1 + S_2)$
- If two trains or a train and a man are moving in same direction with speeds of S_1 and S_2, then their

  Relative speed = Difference of speeds $= (S_1 - S_2)$

Ex. 1 Two trains are moving in opposite directions with speed of 4 m/s and 8 m/s respectively. Find their relative speed.

Sol. Relative speed of trains when they are moving in opposite directions

$$= u + v = 4 + 8 = 12 \text{ m/s}$$

When Train Crosses a Pole/Signal Post/Tree/Standing Man

The distance covered by train in passing Pole/Signal post/Tree/Standing man is equal to the length of train.

Ex. 2 A train covers 85 m in passing a signal post. What is the length of the train?

Sol. We know that the distance covered by a train in passing a pole or a standing man or a signal post or any other object (of negligible length) is equal to the length of the train.

$\therefore$ Length of the train = 85 m

When Train Crosses a Platform/Tunnel/Bridge

The distance covered by train in passing platform/Tunnel/Bridge is equal to the sum of length of train and that particular stationary object.

Ex. 3 A 29 m long train passes a platform which is 100 m long. Find the distance covered by the train in passing the platform.

Sol. The distance covered by train is equal to the sum of the length of train and that particular stationary object.

$\therefore$ Required distance = Length of train + Length of platform
$= (29 + 100)\text{ m} = 129\text{ m}.$

When Train Passes a Walking/Running Man or Man Sitting in a Moving Train

The distance covered by train in passing a walking man is equal to the length of train.

$\therefore$ Time taken by train to pass man $= \dfrac{\text{Length of train}}{\text{Relative speed of train and man}}$

Ex. 4 A train with speed of 20 m/s passes a walking man in opposite direction at the rate of 4 m/s in 10 sec. What is the length of train?

Sol. Time taken by train to pass walking man $= \dfrac{\text{Length of train}}{(20+4)}$

$$10 = \frac{\text{Length of train}}{24} \Rightarrow \text{Length of train} = 240 \text{ m}$$

When Train Passes any Moving Objects

Let two trains of length x and y are moving with speeds u km/h and v km/h respectively.

(i) If they are moving in the opposite direction, then time taken to cross each other $= \dfrac{x+y}{u+v}$

(ii) If they are moving in the same direction, then time taken to cross each other $= \dfrac{x+y}{u-v}, u > v$

Ex. 5 Two trains of lengths 80 m and 90 m are moving in opposite directions at 10 m/s and 7 m/s, respectively. Find the time taken by the trains to cross each other.

Sol. Here, $x = 80$ m, $y = 90$ m, $u = 10$ m/s and $v = 7$ m/s

$\because$ Both trains are moving in opposite directions.

According to the formula, required time

$$= \frac{x+y}{u+v} = \frac{80+90}{10+7} = \frac{170}{17} = 10 \text{ s}$$

SSC Exam Scanner

SSC CGL 2024-2020 (Tier I & II)

1. Two goods trains 132 m and 108 m in length are running towards each other on parallel tracks. The first train is running at a speed of 32 km/h and the second at a speed of 40 km/h. How much time will they take to cross each other after meeting? **SSC CGL (Tier I) 24/09/2024 Shift-II**

(a) 12 sec (b) 10 sec
(c) 13 sec (d) 15 sec

2. Two trains of lengths 150 m and 250 m run on parallel lines. When they run in the same direction, they take 20 sec to cross each other and, when they run in the opposite direction, they take 5 sec to cross each other. What is the speed of the two trains?
SSC CGL (Tier I) 19/09/2024 Shift-I

(a) 150 km/h and 105 km/h
(b) 150 km/h and 250 km/h
(c) 180 km/h and 108 km/h
(d) 160 km/h and 106 km/h

3. A goods train 350 m long passes through a tunnel of length 1250 m in 80 sec.What is the speed of the train?
SSC CGL (Tier-II) 07/03/2023 Shift-I

(a) 56 km/h (b) 64 km/h
(c) 72 km/h (d) 78 km/h

4. A 252 m long train is running at a speed of 125 km/h. What is the time (in seconds) in which it will pass a man who starts from the engine running at the speed of 17 km/h in the same direction as that of the train? **SSC CGL (Tier-I) 27/07/2023 Shift-III**

(a) 7.6 (b) 8 (c) 8.4 (d) 6.4

5. Rajdhani Express train of length 108 m is running at the speed of 128 km/h. Another train of length 148 m is standing at the station. In what time will the Rajdhani Express cross the other train?
SSC CGL (Tier-I) 26/07/2023 Shift-III

(a) 8 sec (b) 7.5 sec
(c) 9 sec (d) 7.2 sec

6. S_1 and S_2 are two stations which are 195 km apart. A train starts from S_1 at 4:00 pm and moves towards S_2 at the speed of 65 km/h. Another train starts from S_2 at 5:00 pm and moves towards S_1 at the speed of 35 km/h. At what time will the two trains meet? **SSC CGL (Tier-I) 21/07/2023 Shift-III**

(a) 6:06 pm (b) 6:30 pm
(c) 6:15 pm (d) 6:18 pm

7. Two trains of length 130 m and 120 m are running on parallel lines in the same direction at a speed of 40 km/h and 50 km/h, respectively. In how much time will they pass each other?
SSC CGL (Tier-I) 20/07/2023 Shift-I

(a) 85 sec (b) 62 sec
(c) 63 sec (d) 90 sec

8. Two trains P and Q of lengths 320 m and 540 m, respectively, are running in the same direction on parallel tracks at 108 km/h and 144 km/h, respectively. How much time will the trains take to cross each other completely?
SSC CGL (Tier-I) 18/07/2023 Shift-I

(a) 86 sec (b) 54 sec
(c) 32 sec (d) 68 sec

9. Two stations R and S are 400 km apart from each other. A train leaves from R to S and simultaneously another train leaves from S to R. Both trains meet after 10 h. If the speed of the first train is 4 km/h more than the second train, then what is the speed of the slower train? **SSC CGL (Tier-I) 13/12/2022 Shift-IV**

(a) 18 km/h (b) 26 km/h
(c) 16 km/h (d) 22 km/h

10. Train A running at 81 km/h takes 72 sec to overtake train B, when both the trains are running in the same direction, but it takes 36 sec to cross each other if the trains are running in the opposite direction. If the length of train B is 600 m, then find the length of train A. (in m)
SSC CGL (Tier-I) 13/12/2022 Shift-III

(a) 600 (b) 480 (c) 590 (d) 900

11. A train travels at a speed of 18 m/s in the first 5 min, covers 7.5 km in the next 10 min and covers 12 km in another 10 min. What is its average speed (in km/h, rounded off to one decimal place) for the entire journey? **SSC CGL (Tier-I) 13/12/2022 Shift-III**

(a) 59.8 (b) 71.2
(c) 45.7 (d) 64.6

12. A person travels in a car at 40 km/h for 3 h, on a bike at 30 km/h for 2 h, and in a train at 80 km/h for 5 h. What is the average speed at which he travelled?
SSC CGL (Tier-I) 09/12/2022 Shift-I

(a) 56 km/h (b) 60 km/h
(c) 62 km/h (d) 58 km/h

13. Two trains are moving in the opposite direction at the speed of 48 km/h and 60 km/h respectively. The time taken by the slower train to cross a man sitting in the faster train is 12 seconds. What is the length of the slower train?
SSC CGL (Tier-I) 08/12/2022 Shift-II

(a) 480 m (b) 720 m
(c) 180 m (d) 360 m

14. Two trains are moving in the same direction at the speed of 36 km/h and 48 km/h. The time taken by faster train to cross a man sitting in the slower train is 33 sec. What will be the length of the faster train?
SSC CGL (Tier-I) 07/12/2022 Shift-IV

(a) 770 m (b) 90 m
(c) 110 m (d) 180 m

15. From point H, at 6 : 30 pm, a train starts moving towards point K at the speed of 90 km/h. Another train starts moving from point K at 7:30 pm towards point H at the speed of 72 km/h. Both the train meet at 11:30 pm at point J. What is the ratio of the distance HJ and KJ ?
SSC CGL (Tier-I) 06/12/2022 Shift-IV

(a) 25 : 16 (b) 5 : 16
(c) 36 : 25 (d) 31 : 19

16. Two trains P and Q start from stations S and T towards each other. Train P takes 4 h 48 min and train Q takes 3 h 20 min to reach T and S respectively, after they meet. If the speed of train P is 45 km/h, what is the speed of train Q?
SSC CGL (Tier-I) 02/12/2022 Shift-IV

(a) 48 km/h (b) 50 km/h
(c) 54 km/h (d) 55 km/h

17. The distance covered by a train in $(5y-1)$ hours is $(125y^3-1)$ km. The speed of the train is
SSC CGL (Tier-I) 02/12/2022 Shift-II

(a) $(5y^3-1)$ km/h
(b) $(25y^2-5y+1)$ km/h
(c) $(5y+1)$ km/h
(d) $(25y^2+5y+1)$ km/h

18. A train covers 450 km at a uniform speed. If the speed had been 5 km/h more, it would have taken 1 h less to cover the same distance. How much time will it take to cover 315 km at its usual speed?
SSC CGL (Tier-I) 24/08/2021 Shift-I

(a) 7 h 52 min (b) 6 h 30 min
(c) 6 h 18 min (d) 7 h

19. If a train runs with the speed of 72 km/h, it reaches its destination late by 15 min. However, if its speed is 90 km/h it is late by only 5 min. The correct time to cover its journey (in minutes) is
SSC CGL (Tier-I) 18/08/2021 Shift-III
(a) 45 (b) 40
(c) 35 (d) 32

20. A train runs first 75 km at a certain uniform speed and next 90 km at an average speed of 10 km/h more than the normal speed. If it takes 3 h to complete the journey, then how much time will the train take to cover 300 km with normal speed?
SSC CGL (Tier-I) 16/08/2021 Shift-I
(a) 5 h 15 min (b) 5 h 25 min
(c) 5 h (d) 6 h

21. A train is to cover 370 km at a uniform speed. After running 100 km, the train could run at a speed of 5 km/h less than its normal speed due to some technical fault. The train got delayed by 36 min. What is the normal speed of the train (in km/h)?
SSC CGL (Tier-I) 13/08/2021 Shift-III
(a) 45 (b) 50 (c) 40 (d) 48

22. The two trains leave Varanasi for Lucknow at 11:00 a.m. and at 11:30 a.m. respectively and travel at a speed of 110 km/h and 140 km/h, respectively. How many kilometers from Varanasi will both trains meet?
SSC CGL (Tier-I) 07/03/2020 Shift-II
(a) $246\frac{1}{3}$ km (b) $238\frac{2}{3}$ km
(c) $255\frac{1}{3}$ km (d) $256\frac{2}{3}$ km

23. A train crosses platform 180 m long in 60 sec at a speed of 72 km/h. The time taken by the train to cross an electric pole is
SSC CGL (Tier-I) 06/03/2020 Shift-III
(a) 5.1 sec (b) 51 sec
(c) 5.1 min (d) 0.51 min

24. The distance between two stations A and B is 428 km. A train starts from station A at 6:00 am, and moves towards station B at an average speed of 48 km/h. Another train starts from station B at 6:20 am, and moves towards station A at an average speed of 55 km/h. At what time will the trains meet?
SSC CGL (Tier-I) 05/03/2020 Shift-III
(a) 10:00 am (b) 10:40 am
(c) 9:40 am (d) 10:20 am

25. A train takes $2\frac{1}{2}$ h less for a journey of 300 km, if its speed is increased by 20 km/h from its usual speed. How much time will it take to cover a distance of 192 km at its usual speed? SSC CGL (Tier-I) 05/03/2020 Shift-I
(a) 6 h (b) 4.8 h
(c) 3 h (d) 2.4 h

SSC CPO SI 2024-2020

26. Two Trains, P and Q are running on parallel tracks in opposite directions with lengths of 110 m and 140 m, respectively. Train P is running at a speed of 70 km/h and took 5 sec to cross Train Q. The speed of Train Q is SSC CPO 29/06/2024 Shift-III
(a) 110 km/h (b) 120 km/h
(c) 110 km/h (d) 90 km/h

27. A 234 m long train passes a person running at 9 km/h in the opposite direction, in 6 sec. In how much time (in sec) will it pass another person, who is moving at 23.4 km/h, in the same direction?
SSC CPO 29/06/2024 Shift-II
(a) 7.8 (b) 7.2
(c) 8 (d) 8.4

28. The distance between two stations A and B is 800 km. A train covers the journey from A to B at a speed of 90 km/h and returns to A with a uniform speed of 65 km/h. Find the average speed of train during the whole journey (in km/h)?
SSC CPO 29/06/2024 Shift-II
(a) 75.48 (b) 70.45
(c) 82.36 (d) 80.50

29. A 320 m long train completely crosses a 240 m long train, coming from the opposite direction, in y seconds. If the first train is travelling at the speed of 44 km/h and the second train is travelling at 56.8 km/h, then what is the value of y?
SSC CPO 29/06/2024 Shift-I
(a) 18 (b) 22
(c) 21 (d) 20

30. Two trains, 140 m and 120 m in length, are running in the same direction at the speed of 60 km/h and 78 km/h, respectively. In how much time will they completely cross each other?
SSC CPO 29/06/2024 Shift-I
(a) 58 sec (b) 65 sec
(c) 48 sec (d) 52 sec

31. Two trains are moving in the same direction at 60 km/h and 42 km/h. The faster train crosses a man in the slower train in 36 sec. Find the length of the faster train.
SSC CPO 28/06/2024 Shift-III
(a) 185 m (b) 195 m
(c) 180 m (d) 175 m

32. A train covers a distance of 72 km in 40 min. Travelling at the same speed, how many metres will the train cover in 6 sec?
SSC CPO 28/06/2024 Shift-III
(a) 210 (b) 174
(c) 192 (d) 180

33. A train covers a distance of 850 m in 45 sec. Travelling at the same speed, how many kilometres will the train cover in an hour?
SSC CPO 28/06/2024 Shift-II
(a) 69 (b) 67.2 (c) 67.5 (d) 68

34. Two trains 230 m and 270 m long are running in opposite directions at speeds of 42km/h and 48 km/h, respectively. They cross each other in SSC CPO 28/06/2024 Shift-I
(a) 22 sec (b) 20 sec
(c) 25 sec (d) 30 sec

35. A train covers a distance of 56 km in 35 min. Travelling at the same speed, in how many seconds will the train cover a distance of 720 m ?
SSC CPO 27/06/2024 Shift-III
(a) 32 (b) 27 (c) 30 (d) 24

36. A 255 m long train is running at a speed of 72 km/h. It crosses a platform of length 745m in
SSC CPO 27/06/2024 Shift-III
(a) 50 sec (b) 53 sec
(c) 51 sec (d) 40 sec

37. A fast local of Mumbai takes 45 min less than a slow local for a journey of 150 km. If the speed of the fast local is 10 km/h more than that of the slow local, find the speed (in km/h) of the slow local train.
SSC CPO 05/10/2023 Shift-III
(a) 30 (b) 35
(c) 45 (d) 40

38. Travelling a distance of 1000 km, a train slowed down due to repairs of the tracks. Its average speed for the trip reduced by 75 km/h and the time of travel increased by 3 h. The original duration of the travel is
SSC CPO 04/10/2023 Shift-II
(a) 6 h (b) 5 h
(c) 5.5 h (d) 6.5 h

39. A train covers a distance of 540 km between two stations in 240 min. It travels at a speed of 90 km/h to another station in 5 h. What is the average speed of the train (in km/h)?
SSC CPO 04/10/2023 Shift-II

(a) 112 (b) 110
(c) 100 (d) 120

40. Two trains of lengths 200 m and 250 m are running on parallel rail tracks at speeds of 68 km/h and 50 km/h, respectively. In how much time (in seconds) will they cross each other if they are running in the same direction?
SSC CPO 04/10/2023 Shift-II

(a) 90 (b) 85
(c) 80 (d) 75

41. Two trains with a speed of 80 km/h and 120 km/h, respectively, are 500 km apart and face each other. Find the distance between them 10 min before crossing.
SSC CPO 11/11/2022 Shift-II

(a) 72.33 km (b) 33.33 km
(c) 63.33 km (d) 52.74 km

42. Two trains, running between Bangalore and Chennai, start at the same time from their respective locations and proceed towards each other at the speed of 80km/h and 95km/h. When they meet, it is found that one train has travelled 180 km more than the other.The distance between Bangalore and Chennai is ....
SSC CPO 10/11/2022 Shift-II

(a) 1200 km
(b) 2100 km
(c) 345km
(d) 400 km

43. Two stations are 120 km apart on a straight line. A train starts from station *A* at 8 a.m. and moves towards station *B* at 20 km/h, and another train starts from station *B* at 9 am and travels towards station *A* at a speed of 30 km/h. At what time will they meet?
SSC CPO 10/11/2022 Shift-II

(a) 10:30 am (b) 10:00 am
(c) 11:00 am (d) 11:30 am

44. A train covers 400 km at a uniform speed. If the speed had been 10 km/h more, it would have taken 2 h less for the same journey. What is the usual time taken (in hours) by it to complete the journey?
SSC CPO 25/11/2020 Shift-II

(a) 12 (b) 15
(c) 8 (d) 10

45. A train *x* running at 74 km/h crosses another Train *y* running at 52 km/h in the opposite direction in 12 sec. If the length of *y* is two-third that of *x*, then what is the length of *y* (in m)?
SSC CPO 25/11/2020 Shift-I

(a) 252 (b) 168
(c) 210 (d) 200

46. A train *x* running at 74 km/h crosses another train *y* running at 52 km/h in the opposite direction in 12 sec. If the length of *y* is two-thirds that of *x*, then what is the length of *x* (in m)?
SSC CPO 23/11/2020 Shift-I

(a) 210 (b) 200
(c) 252 (d) 168

SSC CHSL 2024-2021 (Tier I & II)

47. *A* and *B* are two stations 420 km apart. *A* train starts from *A* at 11 am and travels towards *B* at the speed of 70 km/h. Another train starts from *B* at 12 noon and travels towards *A* at the speed of 30 km/h. At what time do they meet?
SSC CHSL (Tier I) 11/07/2024 Shift-II

(a) 2 pm
(b) 1 : 30 pm
(c) 3 : 30 pm
(d) 3 pm

48. If Tanya walks at the speed of 6 km/h, she misses a train by 2 min. However, if she walks at the speed of 8 km/h, she reaches the station 3 min before the arrival of the train. The distance covered by Tanya to reach the station is
SSC CHSL (Tier I) 09/07/2024 Shift-III

(a) 3 km (b) 2.5 km
(c) 2.75 km (d) 2 km

49. A train 550 m long is running at a speed of 78 km/h. How many seconds will it take to cross a 350 m long train running in the opposite direction at a speed of 30 km/h?
SSC CHSL (Tier I) 05/07/2024 Shift-III

(a) 40 sec (b) 20 sec
(c) 50 sec (d) 30 sec

50. Two trains of lengths 310 m and 330 m, respectively, are 160 m apart. They start moving towards each other on parallel tracks, at speeds 130 km/h and 158 km/h, respectively. In how much time (in sec) will the trains cross each other?
SSC CHSL (Tier I) 02/07/2024 Shift-IV

(a) 10 (b) 8
(c) 12 (d) 18

51. If a train 130 m long takes $6\frac{1}{2}$ sec to cross a man who is walking at 12 km/h in the same direction in which the train going, then the speed of the train (in km/h) is
SSC CHSL (Tier-I) 04/08/2023 Shift-II

(a) 84 (b) 64 (c) 48 (d) 74

52. A train starts from a place *S* at 10 : 00 am and arrives at another place *T* at 2:30 pm on the same day. If the speed of the train is 40 m/s, then what will be the distance covered by the train ?
SSC CHSL (Tier-I) 21/03/2023 Shift-IV

(a) 706 km (b) 648 km
(c) 726 km (d) 616 km

53. The distance between *P* and *Q* is 720 km. *A* train leaves *P* at 6 am and runs at a speed of 20 m/s. The train stops on the way for 1 h 30 min. At what time train will reach at *Q*?
SSC CHSL (Tier-I) 17/03/2023 Shift-II

(a) 5 : 00 pm (b) 4 : 45 pm
(c) 5 : 15 pm (d) 5 : 30 pm

54. Speed of a train is 30% more than the speed of a car. Both start from point *P* at the same time and reach point *Q* at the same time. *P* and *Q* are 130 km apart from each other. On the way train stops for 30 min at a station. What is the speed of the train? **SSC CHSL (Tier-I) 14/03/2023 Shift-I**

(a) 78 km/h (b) 72 km/h
(c) 60 km/h (d) 70 km/h

55. The speed of a train with stoppage is 75 km/h and without stoppage, it is 90 km/h. For how many minutes does the train stop per hour?
SSC CHSL (Tier-I) 13/03/2023 Shift-III

(a) 11 min (b) 10 min
(c) 20 min (d) 15 min

56. A train crosses a 400 m long platform in 50 sec. It crosses another 600 m long platform in 60 sec. What are the length and the speed of the train ? **SSC CHSL (Tier-I) 31/05/2022 Shift-I**

(a) 600 m, 72 km/h (b) 550 m, 75 km/h
(c) 500 m, 70 km/h (d) 650 m, 74 km/h

57. A train covers the distance between two stations *X* and *Y* in 6 h. If the speed of the train is reduced by13 km/h, then it travels the same distance in 9 h. Find the distance between the two stations.
SSC CHSL (Tier-I) 30/05/2022 Shift-I

(a) 220 km (b) 234 km
(c) 185 km (d) 215 km

58. Two trains start at the same time from two stations and proceed towards each other at speeds of 90 km/h and 70 km/h, respectively. When they meet, it is found that one train has travelled 140 km more than the other. What is the distance (in km) between the two stations?
SSC CHSL (Tier-I) 12/04/2021 Shift-II
(a) 1100 (b) 1120
(c) 980 (d) 1200

SSC MTS 2024-2021

59. A train increases its regular speed by 12.5% and reaches its destination 20 minutes earlier. What is the actual time taken by the train on the journey? SSC MTS 14/11/2024 Shift-III
(a) 110 min (b) 120 min
(c) 150 min (d) 180 min

60. Two trains of lengths 110 m and 100 m are running towards each other on parallel lines at the speed of 50 km/h and 58 km/h, respectively. How long will they take to cross each other after they meet? SSC MTS 14/11/2024 Shift-III
(a) 4 sec (b) 5 sec
(c) 6 sec (d) 7 sec

61. Two trains start at the same time from two stations and proceed towards each other at speeds of 120 km/h and 80 km/h, respectively. When they meet, it is found that one train has travelled 60 km more than the other. What is the distance (in km) between the two stations?
SSC MTS 12/11/2024 Shift-III
(a) 387 (b) 300
(c) 268 (d) 452

62. Two trains start at the same time from two stations and travel towards each other with speeds of 72 km/h and 84 km/h, respectively. When they cross each other, it is found that one train has covered 108 km more than the other. What is the distance (in km) between the two stations, and after how many hours will they meet, respectively?
SSC MTS 11/11/2024 Shift-III
(a) 1440; 10 (b) 1244; 8
(c) 1404; 9 (d) 1084; 7

63. A 296-m long train is running at a speed of 72 km/h. In how much time will it pass a 144 m long bridge?
SSC MTS 05/11/2024 Shift-III
(a) 30 sec (b) 25 sec
(c) 22 sec (d) 27.5 sec

64. Two trains are running in opposite directions at the same speed. If the length of each train is 150 m and they cross each other in 15 sec, find the speed of each train (in km/h).
SSC MTS 04/11/2024 Shift-III
(a) 18 (b) 24
(c) 36 (d) 42

65. A train travelling at a speed of 36 km/h crosses a pole in 24 sec. What is the length of the train?
SSC MTS 04/11/2024 Shift-III
(a) 1.5 m (b) 300 m
(c) 240 m (d) 30 m

66. A 735 m long train passes through a 225 m long tunnel in 48 sec. Find the speed of the train.
SSC MTS 28/10/2024 Shift-II
(a) 54 km/h (b) 66 km/h
(c) 72 km/h (d) 82 km/h

67. A 375 m long train takes 15 sec to cross a pole. How much time will it take to cross a 975 m long platform.
SSC MTS 17/10/2024 Shift-II
(a) 54 sec (b) 90 sec
(c) 72 sec (d) 60 sec

68. Two trains of lengths 125 m and 175 m respectively are running in the same direction at 40 km/h and 22 km/h respectively.
How much time will they take to pass each other completely?
SSC MTS 14/10/2024 Shift-I
(a) 55 sec (b) 1 min
(c) 50 sec (d) $12\frac{4}{5}$ sec

69. Two trains running towards each other on parallel tracks, at speeds of 45 km/h and 51 km/h, take 21 sec to cross each other. If the length of one train is 290 m, then the length (in m) of the other train is
SSC MTS 01/10/2024 Shift-I
(a) 250 (b) 290
(c) 230 (d) 270

70. Two trains, 148 m and 152 m long, are running towards each other on parallel lines at 62 km/h and 46km/h, respectively. In what time will they be clear of each other from the moment they meet ?
SSC MTS 30/09/2024 Shift-I
(a) 5 sec (b) 20 sec
(c) 10 sec (d) 15 sec

71. Two trains are travelling in the same direction on parallel tracks. Train *A* is travelling at 30 km/h and Train *B* is travelling at 60 km/h. If Train *A* is 400 m long and it takes Train *B* two minutes to pass Train *A*, what is the length of Train *B* ?
SSC MTS 13/09/2023 Shift-I
(a) 700 m (b) 500 m
(c) 400 m (d) 600 m

72. Two trains of equal length are running on parallel lines in the same direction at 36 km/h and 54 km/h. The faster train passes the slower train in 48 s. The length of each train (in m) is SSC MTS 06/09/2023 Shift-I
(a) 80 (b) 160
(c) 240 (d) 120

73. Two trains started from a station, at the same time in the same direction, at speeds of 90 km/h and 80 km/h. What will be the distance between the two trains after 5 h?
SSC MTS 04/09/2023 Shift-II
(a) 55 km (b) 50 km
(c) 45 km (d) 40 km

74. Two trains of length 110 m and 85 m are moving in the same directions at 12 m/s and 7 m/s, respectively. Find the time (in second) taken by the faster train to cross the slower train.
SSC MTS 01/09/2023 Shift-I
(a) 39 (b) 35 (c) 19 (d) 29

75. A train moves at a speed of 35 km/h for the first 2 h and at a speed of 50 km/h for the next 4 h. Find the average speed of the train during the entire journey. SSC MTS 12/07/2022 Shift-I
(a) 47 km/h (b) 50 km/h
(c) 45 km/h (d) 35 km/h

76. A 480 m long train takes 16 sec to pass a pole. How long will it take to pass a platform that is 900 m long ?
SSC MTS 12/07/2022 Shift-I
(a) 47 sec (b) 45 sec
(c) 46 sec (d) 48 sec

77. A 900 m long train crosses a 1200 m long platform completely in 70 sec. What is the speed of the train ?
SSC MTS 12/07/2022 Shift-I
(a) 117 km/h (b) 108 km/h
(c) 99 km/h (d) 90 km/h

78. Two trains of the same length are running on parallel tracks in the same direction at 44 km/h and 32 km/h. The faster train passed the other train in 72 s. What is the sum of the lengths (in m) of both trains?
SSC MTS 02/11/2021 Shift-II
(a) 240 (b) 200
(c) 190 (d) 250

SSC GD Constable 2024 & 2023

79. Two trains are running in opposite direction with the same speed. If the length of each train is 160 m and they cross each other in 32 sec, then what is the speed of each train? **SSC GD 23/02/2024 Shift-IV**

(a) 18 km/h (b) 45 km/h
(c) 72 km/h (d) 36 km/h

80. Two trains, one 390 m and the other 250 m long are running in opposite directions on parallel tracks, at the speed of 78 km/h and 66 km/h, respectively. How much time will they take to cross each other? **SSC GD 23/02/2024 Shift-I**

(a) 24 sec (b) 30 sec
(c) 36 sec (d) 16 sec

81. A 600 m long train crosses a man walking in opposite direction in 20 sec. If the speed of train is 5 times to the speed of man, then what is the speed of train? **SSC GD 21/02/2024 Shift-I**

(a) 54 km/h (b) 108 km/h
(c) 90 km/h (d) 72 km/h

82. A train of length 384 m crosses an electric pole in 12 sec and crosses another train of the same length travelling in opposite direction in 12 sec. What is the speed of the second train? **SSC GD 20/02/2024 Shift-II**

(a) 45 m/s (b) 39 m/s
(c) 32 m/s (d) 25 m/s

83. Two trains are running in opposite direction with the same speed. If the length of each train is 320 m and they cross each other in 18 sec, then what is the speed of each train? **SSC GD 20/02/2024 Shift-I**

(a) 64 km/h (b) 56 km/h
(c) 72 km/h (d) 48 km/h

84. At 46 km/h and 36 km/h, two trains of equal length are travelling in the same direction on parallel lines. What is the length of each train, if the quicker train passes the slower train in 36 sec? **SSC GD 13/02/2023 Shift-IV**

(a) 47 m (b) 50 m
(c) 44 m (d) 41 m

85. Two trains of lengths 257.5 m and 272.5 m, travelling in opposite directions crossed each other in 15.9 sec. What is their approximate combined speed per hour? **SSC GD 08/02/2023 Shift-I**

(a) 150 km/h (b) 136 km/h
(c) 145 km/h (d) 120 km/h

86. A train is moving at a uniform speed of 80 km/h. How much distance is covered by the train in 30 min? **SSC GD 08/02/2023 Shift-I**

(a) 40 km (b) 50 km
(c) 70 km (d) 60 km

87. The length of a train is 150 m. In 3 sec, it passes a man travelling at 2 km/h in the same direction as the train. Determine the train's speed. **SSC GD 08/02/2023 Shift-I**

(a) 176 km/h (b) 191 km/h
(c) 168 km/h (d) 182 km/h

88. Two trains start at the same time from two stations and proceed towards each other at the speed of 40 km/h and 45 km/h, respectively. When they meet, it is found that one train has travelled 20 km more than the other. Find the distance between the two stations. **SSC GD 06/02/2023 Shift-I**

(a) 390 km
(b) 400 km
(c) 395 km
(d) 340 km

89. A train crosses another train running at the same speed in the opposite direction in 5 sec. If the speed of the first train is doubled and the speed of the second train is halved, then the time taken by the trains to cross is .... sec. **SSC GD 06/02/2023 Shift-I**

(a) 6 (b) 4 (c) 3 (d) 5

90. A train starts from station P, runs through stations Q, R, S, T and reaches station U. It stops at stations Q, R, S and T for 2 min, 4 min, 6 min, and 8 min, respectively. The distance between P and U is 50 km. What is the average speed of the train between stations P and U (in km/h), if it runs for 70 min between the stations, with uniform speed? **SSC GD 06/02/2023 Shift-I**

(a) $\frac{100}{6}$ (b) $\frac{110}{3}$ (c) $\frac{110}{4}$ (d) $\frac{100}{3}$

SSC Selection Post 2024

91. A train passes a 500 m long platform in 12 sec and a man standing on the platform in 4 sec. Find the speed of the train. **Matric Level 20/06/2024 Shift-IV**

(a) 252.5 km/h (b) 125 km/h
(c) 225 km/h (d) 152.5 km/h

92. A goods train, travelling at constant speed, crossed two persons walking in the same direction (as that of the train) in 11.6 sec and 11.8 sec, respectively. The first person was walking at 5.85 km/h, while the second was walking at 6.3 km/h. What was the speed of the train (in km/h)? **Higher Secondary Level 20/06/2024 Shift-IV**

(a) 32.5 (b) 32.6
(c) 32.4 (d) 32.2

Right Answers

1 (a)	2 (c)	3 (c)	4 (c)	5 (d)	6 (d)	7 (d)	8 (a)	9 (a)	10 (b)
11 (a)	12 (d)	13 (d)	14 (c)	15 (a)	16 (c)	17 (d)	18 (d)	19 (c)	20 (d)
21 (b)	22 (d)	23 (b)	24 (d)	25 (b)	26 (a)	27 (a)	28 (a)	29 (d)	30 (d)
31 (c)	32 (d)	33 (d)	34 (b)	35 (b)	36 (a)	37 (d)	38 (b)	39 (b)	40 (a)
41 (b)	42 (b)	43 (c)	44 (d)	45 (b)	46 (c)	47 (c)	48 (d)	49 (d)	50 (a)
51 (a)	52 (b)	53 (d)	54 (a)	55 (b)	56 (a)	57 (b)	58 (b)	59 (d)	60 (d)
61 (b)	62 (c)	63 (c)	64 (c)	65 (c)	66 (c)	67 (a)	68 (b)	69 (d)	70 (c)
71 (d)	72 (d)	73 (b)	74 (a)	75 (c)	76 (c)	77 (b)	78 (a)	79 (a)	80 (d)
81 (c)	82 (c)	83 (a)	84 (b)	85 (d)	86 (a)	87 (d)	88 (d)	89 (b)	90 (d)
91 (c)	92 (c)								

Solutions

1. (a) Length of trains are 132 m and 108 m and speed of trains are 32 km/h and 40 km/h.

Time required to cross each other

$= \frac{132 + 108}{(32 + 40) \times \frac{5}{18}} = \frac{240}{20} = 12 \text{sec}$

2. (c) Let the speed of two trains

$= x$ m/s and y m/s

When trains run in the same direction,

Time Taken $= \frac{150 + 250}{x - y} = \frac{400}{x - y} = 20$

$x - y = 20$ ...(i)

When trains run in the opposite direction,

Time taken $= \frac{400}{x + y} \Rightarrow 5 = \frac{400}{x + y}$

$x + y = 80$ ...(ii)

From Eqs. (i) and (ii),

$2x = 100, \ x = 50$ m/s

$x = 50 \times \frac{18}{5} = 180$ km/h

and $x + y = 80, \ 50 + y = 80$

$y = 30 \text{ m/s} \Rightarrow y = 30 \times \frac{18}{5}$

$y = 108$ km/h

$\therefore$ Speed of two trains = 180 km/h and 108 km/h

3. (c) Time $(t) = 80$ sec

$\because S = \frac{L_1 + L_2}{t} = \frac{350 + 1250}{80}$ m/s

$= \frac{1600}{80} \times \frac{18}{5} \text{ km/h} = 4 \times 18 \Rightarrow S = 72 \text{ km/h}$

4. (c) Relative speed $= (125 - 17)$ km/h

$= 108 \times \frac{5}{18}$ m/s $= 30$ m/s

$\therefore$ Required time $= \frac{\text{Length of the train}}{\text{Relative speed}}$

$= \frac{252}{30} = 8.4$ sec

5. (d) Speed of Rajdhani Express

$= 128 \text{ km/h} = 128 \times \frac{5}{18} \text{ m/s} = \frac{320}{9} \text{ m/s}$

Total distance $= 108 + 148 = 256$ m

$\therefore$ Required time $= \frac{256}{\left(\frac{320}{9}\right)}$

$= \frac{256 \times 9}{320} = 7.2$ sec

6. (d) Total distance between S_1 and S_2 = 195 km

Speed of first train = 65 km/h

In 1 h first train covers = 65 km

Remaining distance between two trains

$= 195 - 65 = 130$ km

Relative speed of the trains

$= 65 + 35 = 100$ km/h

Let they will meet after t h.

$100t = 130$ [$\because$ Speed $\times$ Time = Distance]

$\Rightarrow t = \frac{130}{100} = 1.3 = 1 \text{ h } \frac{3}{10} \times 60 \text{ min}$

$= 1$ h 18 min

$\therefore$ The two trains will meet at 6:18 pm.

7. (d) Relative speed $= (50 - 40) = 10$ km/h

$= 10 \times \frac{5}{18} = \frac{50}{18}$ m/s

Time required to cross each other

$= \frac{130 + 120}{\frac{50}{18}} = \frac{250}{50} \times 18 = 90$ sec

8. (a) Distance covered by two trains

$= 320 + 540 = 860$ m

If trains are parallel, then $S_1 - S_2$

Relative speed $= (144 - 108)$ km/h

$= 36 \times \frac{5}{18}$ m/s $= 10$ m/s

Hence, time taken to cross each other

completely $= \frac{860}{10} = 86$ sec

9. (a) Let the speed of the slower train (or second train) be x km/h.

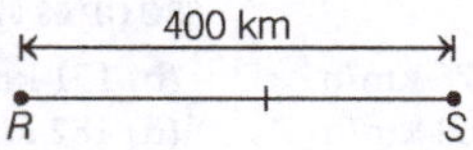

$\therefore$ The speed of the faster train (or first train)

$= (x + 4)$ km/h.

According to the question,

$10(x + 4) + 10x = 400$

$\Rightarrow 10x + 40 + 10x = 400$

$\Rightarrow 20x = 360 \Rightarrow x = 18$

Hence, the speed of the slower train is 18 km/h.

10. (b) Let the speed of train B be x m/s.

And let the length of train A be L m.

Speed of train $A = 81 \text{ km/h} = \frac{81 \times 5}{18} = 22.5$ m/s

According to the question,

$(22.5 - x) = \frac{(L + 600)}{72}$ ...(i)

and $(22.5 + x) = \frac{(L + 600)}{36}$ ...(ii)

On adding Eqs. (i) and (ii),

$\frac{(L + 600)}{72} + \frac{(L + 600)}{36} = 45$

$\Rightarrow L + 600 + 2L + 1200 = 45 \times 72$

$\Rightarrow 3L = 1440$

$\Rightarrow L = \frac{1440}{3} = 480$ m

11. (a) According to the question

Total distance covered by train

$= (18 \times 300) + (7500) + (12000) = 24900$ m

Total time taken

$= 300 + 600 + 600 = 1500$ sec

$\therefore$ Average speed $= \frac{24900}{1500}$ m/s

$= \frac{24900}{1500} \times \frac{18}{5} \text{ km/h} = 59.76 \approx 59.8 \text{ km/h}$

12. (d) Required average speed

$= \frac{[(40 \times 3) + (30 \times 2) + (80 \times 5)]}{(3 + 2 + 5)}$

$= \frac{580}{10} = 58$ km/h

13. (d) Relative speed of trains

$= (48 + 60)$ km/h

$= 108 \text{ km/h} = 108 \times \frac{5}{18} \text{ m/s} = 30$ m/s

Length of the slower train

= Relative speed $\times$ Time

$= 30 \text{ m/s} \times 12 \text{ sec} = 360$ m

14. (c) According to the question,

$(48 - 36) \times \frac{5}{18} = \frac{l}{33}$

$\Rightarrow$ Length of faster train

$(l) = \frac{12 \times 5 \times 33}{18} = 110$ m

Hence, length of the faster train = 110 m

15. (a)

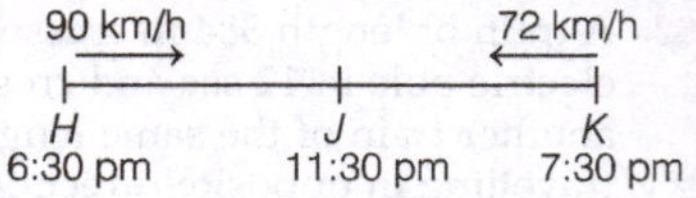

Time taken by H to reach the point J

$= 11:30 \text{ pm} - 6:30 \text{ pm} = 5$ h

Speed of $H = 90$ km/h

Distance covered by H to reach J (HJ)

$= 90 \times 5 = 450$ km

Time taken by K to reach the point J

$= 11:30 \text{ pm} - 7:30 \text{ pm} = 4$ h

Speed of $K = 72$ km/h

Distance covered by K to reach J (KJ)

$= 72 \times 4 = 288$ km

Ratio of the distance HJ and KJ

$= \frac{\text{Distance of } HJ}{\text{Distance of } KJ} = \frac{450}{288} = \frac{25}{16} = 25:16$

16. (c) Let train meet after t h at R and speed of the train Q is x km/h.

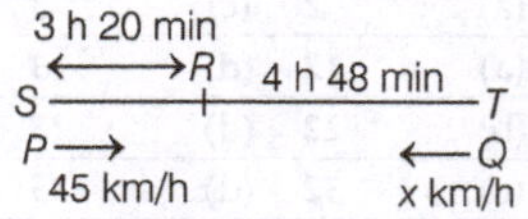

Now, Distance between R and T

$= \text{Speed} \times \text{Time} = 45 \times (4 + \frac{48}{60})$ km

$= 45 \times (4 + \frac{4}{5}) \text{ km} = 45 \times \frac{24}{5} \text{ km} = 216$ km

Now, $x \times t = 216$ ...(i)

Also, distance between S and R

$= x \times (3 + \frac{20}{60}) \text{ km} = x \times (3 + \frac{1}{3})$ km

$= \frac{10x}{3}$ km

Now, $45 \times t = \frac{10x}{3}$

$\Rightarrow \quad t = \frac{10x}{3} \times \frac{1}{45} = \frac{2x}{27}$ ...(ii)

From Eqs. (i) and (ii),

$x \times t = 216 \Rightarrow x \times \frac{2x}{27} = 216$

$\Rightarrow x^2 = \frac{216 \times 27}{2} = 108 \times 27 = 4 \times 27 \times 27$

$\Rightarrow x = 2 \times 27 = 54$

So, speed of the train $Q = 54$ km/h

Speedy Method

$\because \frac{\text{Speed of train } P}{\text{Speed of train } Q} = \sqrt{\frac{\text{Time taken by } Q \text{ after meet}}{\text{Time taken by } P \text{ after meet}}}$

$\therefore \frac{S_P}{S_Q} = \sqrt{\frac{t_Q}{t_P}} \Rightarrow \frac{S_P}{S_Q} = \sqrt{\frac{t_Q}{t_P}}$

$= \sqrt{\frac{\frac{10}{3}}{\frac{24}{5}}} = \sqrt{\frac{10}{3} \times \frac{5}{24}}$

$\Rightarrow \frac{45}{S_Q} = \sqrt{\frac{5 \times 5}{3 \times 12}} = \frac{5}{6}$

$\Rightarrow S_Q = \frac{45 \times 6}{5}$ km/h = 54 km/h

17. (d) Speed of train $= \frac{125y^3 - 1}{5y - 1} = \frac{(5y)^3 - 1^3}{5y - 1}$

$[\because a^3 - b^3 = (a - b)(a^2 + ab + b^2]$

$= \frac{(5y - 1)[(5y)^2 + 1^2 + 5y]}{(5y - 1)}$

$= (5y)^2 + 1^2 + 5y = 25y^2 + 5y + 1$

18. (d) Let speed of train x km/h.

$\therefore \quad T = \frac{450}{x}$ ...(i)

and $\quad (T - 1) = \frac{450}{x + 5}$ ...(ii)

From Eq. (i) – Eq. (ii),

$\frac{450}{x} - \frac{450}{(x + 5)} = (T - T + 1)$

$\Rightarrow \frac{450x + 2250 - 450x}{x(x + 5)} = 1$

$\Rightarrow \quad 2250 = x(x + 5) \Rightarrow x^2 + 5x - 2250 = 0$

$\Rightarrow (x - 45)(x + 50) = 0 \Rightarrow x = 45$

and $x = -50$ (Not taken)

We have, speed of train $x = 45$ km/h

Time taken to cover 315 km is

$\text{Time} = \frac{315}{45} = 7$ h

19. (c) Speed ratio $= 72 : 90 = 4 : 5$

$\therefore$ Time ratio $= 5 : 4$

1 unit $= (15 - 5)$ min

1 unit = 10 min

5 units = 50 min

So actual time to reach destination

$= 50 - 15 = 35$ min

20. (d) Let train normal speed $= x$ km/h.

According to the question,

$\frac{75}{x} + \frac{90}{(10 + x)} = 3$ h

$\Rightarrow \quad 75(10 + x) + 90(x) = 3x(x + 10)$

$\Rightarrow \quad 3x^2 + 30x - 90x - 75x - 750 = 0$

$\Rightarrow \quad 3x^2 - 135x - 750 = 0$

$\Rightarrow \quad x^2 - 45x - 250 = 0$

$\Rightarrow \quad x(x - 50) + 5(x - 50) = 0$

$\Rightarrow \quad x = 50$ km/h

$x = -5$ (not taken)

$\therefore$ Required time $= \frac{300}{50} = 6$ h

21. (b) Let the normal speed of the train $= x$

According to the question,

$-\frac{270}{x} + \frac{270}{(x - 5)} = \frac{36}{60}$

$\Rightarrow \quad -\frac{270(x - 5) + 270x}{x(x - 5)} = \frac{3}{5}$

$\Rightarrow \quad \frac{-270 \times x + 270 \times 5 + 270x}{x^2 - 5x} = \frac{3}{5}$

$\Rightarrow \quad 270 \times 5 \times 5 = 3x^2 - 15x$ (divided by 3)

$\Rightarrow \quad x^2 - 5x - 2250 = 0$

$\Rightarrow \quad (x - 50)(x + 45) = 0 \Rightarrow x = 50$ km/h,

$x = -45$ km/h (can't be taken)

Take $x = 50$ km/h

$\therefore$ The speed of train is 50 km/h.

22. (d) Let both trains meet t h after 11 : 00 a.m.

According to the question,

$110 \times t = 140\left(t - \frac{1}{2}\right)$

$\Rightarrow \quad 30t = 70 \Rightarrow t = \frac{7}{3}$ h

$\therefore$ Trains meet at $= 110 \times \frac{7}{3} = \frac{770}{3} = 256\frac{2}{3}$ km

23. (b) Given, $72 \times \frac{5}{18} = 20$ m/s

Let length of train $= x$ m

Length of platform = 180 m

Time given 60 sec.

So, $\quad 20 = \frac{(180 + x)}{60} = 180 + x = 1200$

$\Rightarrow \quad x = 1020$ m

Time taken to cross pole $= \frac{1020}{20} = 51$ sec

24. (d) Distance between A and B = 428 km

Distance covered by the first train in 20 min

$= \text{Speed} \times \text{Time} = \frac{48}{60} \times 20 = 16$ km

Remaining distance $= 428 - 16 = 412$ km

Speed of second train = 55 km/h

Relative speed $= 48 + 55 = 103$ km/h

Time $= 412 / 103 = 4$ h

Train meet each other

6 : 20 am + 4 h = 10 : 20 am

25. (b) Let speed of train be x km/h.

According to the question,

$\frac{300}{x} - \frac{300}{(x + 20)} = \frac{5}{2}$

$\Rightarrow \frac{300x + 6000 - 300x}{(x^2 + 20x)} = \frac{5}{2}$

$\Rightarrow x^2 + 20x - 2400 = 0$

$\Rightarrow x(x + 60) - 40(x + 60) = 0$

$x = -60, 40$

Speed of train = 40 km/h

$\because \quad 40 = \frac{192}{\text{Time}}$

Time $= 192 / 40 = 4.8$ h

26. (a) Let the speed of train $Q = x$ km/h

Now, relative speed $= (70 + x)$ km/h

According to the given condition,

Time taken $= \frac{\text{Total length of trains}}{\text{Relative speed}}$

$\Rightarrow 5 = \frac{(110 + 140)}{(70 + x) \times \frac{5}{18}} \Rightarrow 5 = \frac{250 \times 18}{(70 + x)\, 5}$

$\Rightarrow \quad \frac{250 \times 18}{25} = 70 + x \Rightarrow 70 + x = 180$

$\Rightarrow \quad x = 110$ km/h

$\therefore$ Speed of train $Q = 110$ km/h

27. (a) Let speed of train $= x$ m/s

Relative speed of train and person running in opposite direction

$= \left(x + 9 \times \frac{5}{18}\right) = \left(x + \frac{5}{2}\right)$ m/s

According to the question,

$\left(x + \frac{5}{2}\right) = \frac{234}{6} \Rightarrow x = \frac{78}{2} - \frac{5}{2}$

$x = \frac{73}{2}$ m/s

Relative speed of train and person running in same direction $= \frac{73}{2} - 23.4 \times \frac{5}{18} = 30$ m/s

$\therefore$ Time taken $= \frac{\text{Length of train}}{\text{Relative speed}}$

$= \frac{234}{30} = 7.8$ sec

28. (a) Average speed $= \frac{2S_1 S_2}{S_1 + S_2} = \frac{2 \times 90 \times 65}{90 + 65}$

$= \frac{11700}{155} = 75.48$ km/h

29. (d) Total distance $= 320 + 240 = 560$ m

$\because$ Both trains are moving in opposite direction.

$\therefore$ Relative speed of trains

$= 56.8 + 44 = 100.8$ km/h

Time taken to completely cross each other $= y$ sec

$\because \quad y = \frac{560 \times 18}{100.8 \times 5} = 20$ sec

30. (d) Total distance $= (140 + 120)$ m $= 260$ m

Relative speed of trains $= (78 - 60)$

$= 18 \times \frac{5}{18} = 5$ m/s

Time taken = $\frac{\text{Distance}}{\text{Speed}}$

$\therefore$ Time taken = $\frac{260}{5} = 52$ sec

31. (c) Relative speed of trains

$= (60 - 42) = 18$ km/h $= 18 \times \frac{5}{18} = 5$ m/s

Now, length of the faster train

= Speed × Time = 5 × 36 = 180 m

32. (d) Speed of the train = $\frac{72 \text{ km}}{\frac{40}{60} \text{ h}}$

$= \frac{72 \times 60}{40} = 108$ km/h

$= 108 \times \frac{5}{18} = 30$ m/s

$\therefore$ Distance covered by the train in 6 sec = 30 × 6 = 180 m

33. (d) Speed of the train = $\frac{\text{Distance covered}}{\text{Time taken}}$

$= \frac{850}{45}$ m/s $= \frac{850}{45} \times \frac{18}{5}$ km/h

= 68 km/h

Hence, the train will cover 68 km in one hour.

34. (b) Total distance to be covered

= (230 + 270) m = 500 m

Relative speed = (42 + 48) km/h = 90 km/h

$= \left(90 \times \frac{5}{18}\right)$ m/s = 25 m/s

$\therefore$ Time taken by the trains to cross each other = $\frac{500 \text{ m}}{25 \text{ m/s}} = 20$ sec

35. (b) Speed of the train = $\frac{\text{Distance}}{\text{Time}}$

$= \frac{56 \text{ km}}{35 \text{ min}} = \left(\frac{56}{\frac{35}{60}}\right)$ km/h $= \frac{56 \times 60}{35} = 96$ km/h

Now, time taken to cover 720 m

$= \left(\frac{720}{96 \times \frac{5}{18}}\right) = \frac{720 \times 18}{96 \times 5} = 27$ sec

36. (a) Given, length of the train = 255 m

Speed of train = 72 km/h

$= \left(72 \times \frac{5}{18}\right)$ m/s = 20 m/s

Time taken to cross the platform of length 745 m = $\frac{255 + 745}{20} = \frac{1000}{20} = 50$ sec

37. (d) According to the question,

$D = 150 = \frac{S(S+10)}{10} \times \frac{45}{60}$

Using formula,

$D = \frac{S_1 \times S_2}{S_1 \sim S_2} \times (t_1 \sim t_2)$ [$\because$ 1h = 60 min]

$\Rightarrow \frac{150 \times 10 \times 60}{45} = S(S+10)$

$\Rightarrow S(S+10) = 2000$

$\Rightarrow S^2 + 10S - 2000 = 0$

$\Rightarrow (S+50)(S-40) = 0$

$\Rightarrow S = -50, S = 40$

$\because$ Speed can't be –ve,

$\therefore S = -50$ is neglected

$\therefore S = 40$ km/h

Hence, the correct answer is 40 km/h.

38. (b) $\frac{1000}{s-75} - \frac{1000}{s} = 3$

$\Rightarrow \frac{1000s - 1000s + 1000 \times 75}{s(s-75)} = 3$

$\Rightarrow s^2 - 75s - 25000 = 0$

$s = 200$ km/h

Thus original time = $\frac{1000}{200} = 5$ h

39. (b) $D = 90 \times 5$ [240 min = 4 h]

$D = 450$ km

($\because$ Distance between another stations)

$\therefore$ Average speed = $\frac{450 + 540}{5 + 4} = \frac{990}{9}$

= 110 km/h

40. (a) Required time

$= \frac{200 + 250}{(68 - 50) \times \frac{5}{18}} = \frac{450}{5} = 90$ sec

41. (b) Required distance between the trains

$= \left(80 \times \frac{10}{60} + 120 \times \frac{10}{60}\right)$ km [$D = S \times T$]

= (13.33 + 20) km = 33.33 km

42. (b) Given, the speed of first and second train is 80 km/h and 95 km/h respectively.

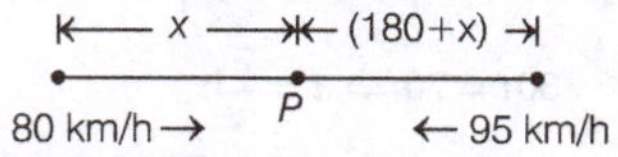

Let the slower train travelled = x km

$\Rightarrow$ the faster train travelled = 180 + x

So, $\frac{x}{80} = \frac{180 + x}{95} \Rightarrow 95x = 14400 + 80x$

$\Rightarrow 15x = 14400 \Rightarrow x = 960$ km

The distance between Bangalore and Chennai is = 960 + (960 + 180) = 2100 km

43. (c) Required hours when the trains will meet each other = $\frac{(120 - 20)}{(20 + 30)} = \frac{100}{50} = 2$ h

actual time for meeting

= 9:00 am + 2 h = 11:00 am

44. (d) Distance = 400 = $\frac{s(s+10)}{10} \times 2$

$\left[\because D = \frac{S_1 \times S_2}{S_1 \sim S_2} \times t_1 \sim t_2\right]$

$\Rightarrow s^2 + 10s - 2000 = 0$

$\Rightarrow (s+50)(s-40) = 0$

$s = 40$ km/h

$\therefore$ Actual time = $\frac{400}{40} = 10$ h

45. (b) According to question,

Let, length of train $x = 3L$

Length of train $y = 2L$

$\Rightarrow \frac{3L + 2L}{126 \times \frac{5}{18}} = 12 \Rightarrow 5L = 12 \times 35 \Rightarrow L = 84$ m

Length of train $y = 2L = 2 \times 84 = 168$ m

46. (c) According to the question,

$(74 + 52) = 126$ km/h $= 126 \times \left(\frac{5}{18}\right) = 35$ m/s

Time taken to cross each other = 12 sec

Total distance covered = (12 × 35) = 420 m

The length of y is two-third that of x

Let, the length of train x is a meter.

$a + \left(\frac{2a}{3}\right) = 420 \Rightarrow a = 420 \times \left(\frac{3}{5}\right)$

$\Rightarrow a = 252$

$\therefore$ The length of train x is 252 m.

47. (c)

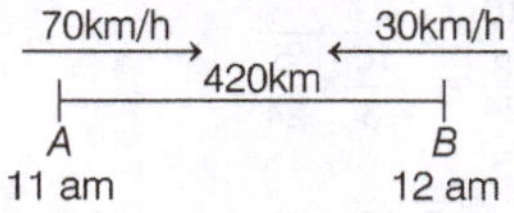

Let they meet after x h.

According to the question,

$70 \times x + 30 \times (x - 1) = 420$

$\Rightarrow 70x + 30x - 30 = 420$

$\Rightarrow 100x = 450 \Rightarrow x = 4.5$ h

$\therefore$ Meeting time = 11 am + 4.5 h = 3 : 30 pm

48. (d) Let the total distance be x km and time taken to cover this distance be t h.

According to the question,

Case I Tanya's speed = 6 km/h

$\therefore t + \frac{2}{60} = \frac{x}{6}$

$\Rightarrow t = \frac{x}{6} - \frac{2}{60}$ ...(i)

Case II Tanya's speed = 8 km/h

$t - \frac{3}{60} = \frac{x}{8}$

$\Rightarrow t = \frac{x}{8} + \frac{3}{60}$ ...(ii)

From Eqs. (i) and (ii),

$\frac{x}{6} - \frac{2}{60} = \frac{x}{8} + \frac{3}{60} \Rightarrow \frac{x}{6} - \frac{x}{8} = \frac{5}{60}$

$\Rightarrow \frac{4x - 3x}{24} = \frac{5}{60} \Rightarrow \frac{x}{24} = \frac{5}{60}$

$\Rightarrow x = 2$ km

Speedy Method

Distance = $\frac{S_1 \times S_2}{\text{Difference of speed}} \times$ Time difference

$= \frac{6 \times 8}{2} \times \frac{5}{60} = 2$ km

49. (d) According to the question,

Total length of two trains = 550 + 350 = 900 m

Relative speeds of two trains = 78 + 30

= 108 km/h

$= 108 \times \frac{5}{18}$ m/s $= 30$ m/s

$\therefore$ Required time $= \frac{900}{30} = 30$ sec

50. (a) Time taken by both the trains to cross each other $= \frac{\text{Length of both trains + Distance between both trains}}{\text{Relative speed of trains}}$

$= \frac{(310 + 330 + 160)}{(130 + 158) \times \frac{5}{18}} = \frac{800 \times 18}{288 \times 5} = 10$ sec

Hence, train will cross each other in 10 sec.

Let the speed of the train be x km/h.

51. (a) According to the question,

$\frac{\frac{130}{1000}}{(x - 12)} = \frac{13}{2} \times \frac{1}{60} \times \frac{1}{60}$

$\Rightarrow \frac{130 \times 60 \times 60 \times 2}{1000} = 13 \times (x - 12)$

$\Rightarrow x - 12 = 72 \Rightarrow x = 84$ km/h

52. (b) Time taken by train to reach place T from S

$= 2:30 \text{ pm} - 10:00 \text{ am} = 4:30 = 4\frac{1}{2} = \frac{9}{2}$ h

$\therefore$ Distance covered by the train

$= \text{Speed} \times \text{Time} = 144 \times \frac{9}{2} = 648$ km

$\left[\because 40 \times \frac{18}{5} = 144 \text{ km/h}\right]$

53. (d) Speed $= 20$ m/s $= 20 \times \frac{18}{5} = 72$ km/h

Time $= \frac{720}{72} = 10$ h

Total time $= 10 + 1$ h 30 min $= 11$ h 30 min

$\therefore$ Required time $= 6:00$ am $+ 11$ h 30 min $= 5:30$ pm

54. (a) Let the speed of the car $= y$ km/h

$\therefore$ Speed of the train $= y \times \frac{130}{100} = \frac{13y}{10}$ km/h

According to the question,

$\frac{130}{y} = \frac{1300}{13y} + \frac{1}{2}$

$\Rightarrow \frac{130}{y} = \frac{100}{y} + \frac{1}{2} \Rightarrow \frac{130}{y} = \frac{200 + y}{2y}$

$\Rightarrow y = 60$ km/h

$\therefore$ Speed of train $= \frac{13y}{10} = \frac{13 \times 60}{10} = 78$ km/h

55. (b) The train stops per hour $T = \frac{W.S - S}{W.S}$

$= \frac{90 - 75}{90} \times 60 = 10$ min

56. (a) Let length of the train $= x$ m

Given, $\frac{x + 400}{50} = \frac{x + 600}{60}$

[$\because$ Speed will be equal in both conditions]

$\Rightarrow 6x + 2400 = 5x + 3000 \Rightarrow x = 600$ m

$\therefore$ Speed of the train $= \frac{x + 400}{50} = \frac{600 + 400}{50}$

$= 20$ m/s $= 20 \times \frac{18}{5}$ km/h $= 72$ km/h

Hence, length of the train $= x = 600$ m

Speed of the train $= 72$ km/h

57. (b) Let the distance between stations X and Y is D km.

Speed of the train $= \frac{D}{6}$ km/h

$9\left(\frac{D}{6} - 13\right) = D \Rightarrow \frac{3D}{2} - 117 = D$

$\Rightarrow \frac{3D}{2} - D = 117 \Rightarrow \frac{D}{2} = 117$

$\Rightarrow D = 2 \times 117 = 234$

So, the distance between two stations $= D$ km $= 234$ km

58. (b)

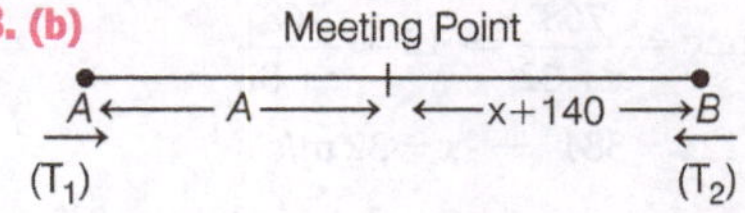

Let the distance travelled by train $T_1 = x$ km

$\therefore$ The distance travelled by Train $T_2 = (x + 140)$ km

According to the question,

$\frac{x + 140}{90} = \frac{x}{70} \Rightarrow 90x - 70x = 140 \times 70$

$\Rightarrow 20x = 140 \times 70 \Rightarrow x = 490$ km

$\therefore$ Distance between two stations

$= x + x + 140 = 2x + 140 = 2 \times 490 + 140$

$= 1120$ km

59. (d) Let the distance covered be d km.

Let the normal speed of train be x km/h.

new speed $= x \times \frac{112.5}{100} = \frac{9x}{8}$ km/h

According to the question, $\frac{d}{x} - \frac{d}{\frac{9x}{8}} = \frac{20}{60}$

$\Rightarrow \frac{d}{x} - \frac{8d}{9x} = \frac{1}{3} \Rightarrow \frac{d}{9x} = \frac{1}{3} \Rightarrow d = 3x$

$\therefore$ Actual time taken $= \frac{d}{x} = \frac{3x}{x} = 3$ h

$= 180$ min

Speedy Method

Speed	8	:	9
Time	9	:	8

+1

$\therefore 1 \rightarrow 20$ min $\therefore 9 \rightarrow 20 \times 9 = 180$ min

60. (d) Time taken by trains to cross each other $= \frac{110 + 100}{(50 + 58) \times \frac{5}{18}} = \frac{210 \times 18}{108 \times 5} = 7$ sec

61. (b) According to the question,

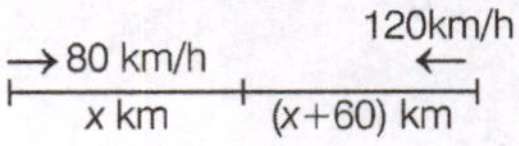

Time $= \frac{\text{Distance}}{\text{Speed}}$

$\frac{x}{80} = \frac{x + 60}{120} \Rightarrow x = 120$ km

Distance $= 2x + 60 = 240 + 60 = 300$ km

62. (c) Let distance covered by first train be d km and distance covered by the other train be $(d + 108)$ km.

According to the question,

$\frac{d}{72} = \frac{d + 108}{84} \Rightarrow 7d = 6d + 648$

$\Rightarrow d = 648$ km

Total distance between stations

$= 648 + 648 + 108 = 1404$ km

Time taken to meet each other $= \frac{648}{72} = 9$ h

63. (c) Time $= \frac{\text{Total length}}{\text{Speed}}$

$= \frac{144 + 296}{72 \times \frac{5}{18}} = \frac{440}{20} = 22$ sec

64. (c) Speed of each train $= \frac{150}{15} = 10$ m/s

$= 10 \times \frac{18}{5} = 36$ km/h

65. (c) Speed $= 36$ km/h $= 36 \times \frac{5}{18} = 10$m/s

Length of the train

$= \text{Speed} \times \text{Time} = 10 \times 24 = 240$ m

66. (c) Speed of train $= \frac{735 + 225}{48} = 20$ m/sec

$= 20 \times \frac{18}{5} = 72$ km/h

67. (a) Speed of train $= \frac{375}{15} = 25$ m/sec

Taken to pass 975m Platform

$= \frac{975 + 375}{25} = \frac{1350}{25} = 54$ sec

68. (b) Time taken by trains to cross each other

$= \frac{125 + 175}{(40 - 22) \times \frac{5}{18}} = \frac{300}{5} = 60$sec $= 1$ min

69. (d) Let length of other train be x m.

We know,

$\because$ Time $= \frac{\text{Total distance}}{\text{Total speed}}$

$\Rightarrow 21 = \frac{290 + x}{(45 + 51) \times \frac{5}{18}}$

$\Rightarrow 290 + x = 560 \Rightarrow x = 270$ m

70. (c) They will meet $= \frac{\text{Total distance}}{\text{Relative speed}}$

$= \frac{148 + 152}{(62 + 46) \times \frac{5}{18}} = \frac{300}{30} = 10$ sec

71. (d) Let length of train B be x.

Total distance $= (400 + x)$ m

Relative speed $= (60 - 30)$ km/h

$= 30$ km/h $= 30 \times \frac{5}{18} = \frac{75}{9}$ m/s

Time taken = 2 min = 120 sec

$\Rightarrow \dfrac{400+x}{\frac{75}{9}} = 120 \Rightarrow 400 + x = 1000$

$\Rightarrow \quad x = 600$ m

Hence, length of Train B is 600 m.

72. (d) Relative speed of the faster train

$= (54-36) = 18 \times \dfrac{5}{18} = 5$ m/s

Let the length of each train $= x$

According to the question,

$\dfrac{x+x}{5} = 48 \Rightarrow x = \dfrac{48 \times 5}{2} = 120$ m

73. (b) Relative speed of train in same direction $= 90 - 80 = 10$ km/h

Distance between trains after

5 h $= 10 \times 5 = 50$ km

74. (a) Given, total length of both trains

$= 110 + 85 = 195$ m

Relative speed of both trains $= 12 - 7 = 5$ m/s

Time $= \dfrac{195}{5} = 39$ sec

75. (c) Average speed $= \dfrac{\text{Total distance}}{\text{Total time}}$

$= \dfrac{35 \times 2 + 50 \times 4}{2+4} = \dfrac{70 + 200}{6}$

$= 45$ km/h

76. (c) Speed of the train $= \dfrac{480}{16}$ m/s $= 30$ m/s

$\therefore$ Time to pass platform

$= \dfrac{480 + 900}{30}$ sec $= 46$ sec

77. (b) Total distance covered

$= (900 + 1200)$ m $= 2100$ m

Speed $= \dfrac{2100}{70} = 30$ m/s

$= 30 \times \dfrac{18}{5} \quad \left[\because 1 \text{ m/s} = \dfrac{18}{5} \text{ km/h}\right]$

$= 108$ km/h

78. (a) Sum of the lengths of both trains

$=$ Relative speed $\times$ Time

$= (44-32) \times \dfrac{5}{18} \times 72 = 240$ m

79. (a) Let speed of each train be x m/s.

According to the question,

$\dfrac{160 + 160}{x + x} = 32$

$\Rightarrow x = 5 \text{ m/s} = 5 \times \dfrac{18}{5} = 18$ km/h

80. (d) According to the question,

$(78 + 66) = \dfrac{(390 + 250)}{\text{Time}}$

$\Rightarrow \quad \text{Time} = \dfrac{640}{144 \times \frac{5}{18}} = 16$ sec

81. (c) Let the speed of man $= x$ m/s

Then, speed of train $= 5x$ m/s

According to the question,

$\dfrac{600}{x + 5x} = 20 \Rightarrow \dfrac{600}{6x} = 20$

$\Rightarrow \quad x = 5$

$\therefore$ Speed of train $= 5x$ m/s

$= 5 \times 5 \times \dfrac{18}{5}$ km/h $= 90$ km/h

82. (c) Length of train $= 384$ m

Time to cross an electric pole $= 12$ sec

$\therefore$ Speed of 1st train $= \dfrac{384}{12} = 32$ m/s

Let the speed of the 2nd train $= x$ m/s

Relative speed $= x + 32$

Total length of the train $= 384 + 384 = 768$ m

$\because$ Time $= \dfrac{768}{x + 32} \Rightarrow 12 = \dfrac{768}{x + 32}$

$\Rightarrow \quad 12x = 384 \quad \Rightarrow \quad x = 32$ m/s

83. (a) Let speed of each train be x m/s.

Time $= 18 = \dfrac{320 + 320}{x + x \text{ (Opposite direction)}}$

$\Rightarrow \quad 18 = \dfrac{640}{2x} \Rightarrow 18 = \dfrac{320}{x}$

$\Rightarrow \quad x = \dfrac{320}{18}$ m/s $= \dfrac{320}{18} \times \dfrac{18}{5}$ km/h

$= 64$ km/h

84. (b) Let the length of each train be x m.

Relative speed of trains $= 46 - 36$

$= 10 \text{ km/h} \times \dfrac{5}{18} = \dfrac{50}{18}$ m/s

According to the question,

$36 = \dfrac{x + x}{10 \times \frac{5}{18}}$

$\Rightarrow 36 \times 10 \times \dfrac{5}{18} = 2x \Rightarrow x = 50$ m

Hence, length of each train is 50 m.

85. (d) Total distance travelled by both trains to cross each other

$= (257.5 + 272.5)$ m $= 530$ m

Combined speed $= \dfrac{530}{15.9} \times \dfrac{18}{5}$ km/h

$= 120$ km/h (approx)

86. (a) According to the question,

Distance covered by train in 30 min

$= 80 \times \dfrac{1}{2} = 40$ km

87. (d) Speed of man $= 2 \times \dfrac{5}{18} = \dfrac{5}{9}$ m/s

Let the speed of train $= x$ m/s

According to the question,

$\dfrac{150}{x - \frac{5}{9}} = 3 \Rightarrow \dfrac{150 \times 9}{9x - 5} = 3$

$\Rightarrow \quad 9x = 450 + 5$

$\Rightarrow \quad x = \dfrac{455}{9}$ m/s

Speed of train in km/h $= \dfrac{455}{9} \times \dfrac{18}{5} = 182$ km/h

88. (d) Let first train meet after x km.

Then, according to the question,

$\dfrac{x}{40} = \dfrac{x + 20}{45}$

$\Rightarrow \quad 9x = 8x + 160 \Rightarrow x = 160$ km

Then total distance between station

$= 160 + 160 + 20 = 340$ km

89. (b) Let the speed of the first train $= x$ m/s

So, speed of the second train $= x$ m/s

Relative speed $= 2x$ m/s

Distance $= 5 \times 2x = 10x$

First train speed is doubled and second is halved $= \dfrac{x}{2} + 2x = \dfrac{5x}{2}$

$\therefore$ Required time $= \dfrac{10x}{\frac{5x}{2}} = \dfrac{10x \times 2}{5x} = 4$ sec

90. (d) Average speed $= \dfrac{\text{Total distance}}{\text{Total time}}$

Total time $= 2 + 4 + 6 + 8 + 70$

$= 90 \text{ min} = \dfrac{3}{2}$ h

Given, distance $= 50$ km

$\therefore$ Average speed of the train between stations P and $U = 50 \times \dfrac{2}{3} = \dfrac{100}{3}$ km/h

91. (c) Let length of train be T and speed of train be S.

$T + 500 = S \times 12 \quad \ldots$(i)

$T = S \times 4 \quad \ldots$(ii)

From Eqs. (i) and (ii),

$500 \text{ m} = S \times (12 - 4) \Rightarrow 500 \text{ m} = S \times 8$

$\Rightarrow \quad S = 62.5$ m/s

Speed of train in km/h $= 62.5 \times \dfrac{18}{5}$

$= 225$ km/h

92. (c) Let speed of train be x km/h and length of train be y km.

For first person, $\dfrac{11.6}{3600} = \dfrac{y}{x - 5.85}$

$\Rightarrow \quad y = \dfrac{11.6}{3600}(x - 5.85) \quad \ldots$(i)

For second person, $\dfrac{11.8}{3600} = \dfrac{y}{x - 6.3}$

$\Rightarrow \quad y = \dfrac{11.8}{3600}(x - 6.3) \quad \ldots$(ii)

From Eqs. (i) and (ii),

$11.6(x - 5.85) = 11.8(x - 6.3)$

$\Rightarrow \quad 11.6x - 67.86 = 11.8x - 74.34$

$\Rightarrow \quad 0.2x = 6.48 \Rightarrow x = \dfrac{648}{20} = 32.4$ km/h

16

Boat and Stream

Boats and streams is an application of concepts of speed, time and distance.

- **Still water** Water is considered to be stationary and speed of the water is zero
- **Stream** The moving water in a river is called a stream.
- **Downstream speed** If the boat is flowing along the direction of the stream, it is called downstream speed.
- **Upstream speed** If the boat is flowing in the opposite direction to the stream, it is called upstream speed.

Basic Formulae

If the speed of a boat in still water is x km/h and speed of the stream is y km/h, then

- Speed downstream $= (x + y)$ km/h
- Speed upstream $= (x - y)$ km/h.
- Speed of a boat in still water, $x = \frac{1}{2}$ (Speed downstream + Speed upstream)
- Speed of stream, $y = \frac{1}{2}$ (Speed downstream − Speed upstream)
- If it takes time T to row to a place and back, then distance between two places $(D) = \dfrac{T(x^2 - y^2)}{2x}$

Simple Concept of Upstream and Downstream

Ex. 1 Speed of a boat is 5 km/h in still water and the speed of the stream is 3 km/h. If the boat takes 3h to go to a place and come back, the distance of the place is

Sol. Let the required distance be x km, then

Speed upstream $= (5 - 3)$ km/h

Speed downstream $= (5 + 3)$ km/h

According to the question,

$$\frac{x}{5+3} + \frac{x}{5-3} = 3 \Rightarrow \frac{x}{8} + \frac{x}{2} = 3 \Rightarrow \frac{x + 4x}{8} = 3$$

$$\Rightarrow \quad 5x = 24 \Rightarrow x = \frac{24}{5} = 4.8 \text{ km}$$

Mixed Concept of Upstream and Downstream

Ex. 2 A man can row 52 km upstream and 42 km downstream in 10 h. It is also known that he can row 66 km downstream and 60 km upstream in 13 h. Find the speed of the man in still water.

Sol. Let speed of man $= x$ km/h and speed of current $= y$ km/h

According to the question,

$$\frac{52}{x-y} + \frac{42}{x+y} = 10 \quad \text{...(i)}$$

$$\frac{66}{x+y} + \frac{60}{x-y} = 13 \quad \text{...(ii)}$$

On solving Eqs. (i) and (ii)

$$x + y = 12 \quad \text{...(iii)}$$

$$x - y = 8 \quad \text{...(iv)}$$

On solving Eqs. (iii) and (iv), we get

$x = 10$ km/h and $y = 2$ km/h

Hence, speed of man in still water = 10 km/h

Ex. 3 A man can row a boat in still water at a speed of 5 m/s. He covers a stretch of 200 m in a river downstream during high and low tides in 10 sec and 25 sec, respectively.

What is the ratio of the speed (in m/s) of the water flowing in the river during high and low tides?

Sol. Speed of a boat in still water = 5 m/s

Let the speed of the water flowing in the river during high and low be x and y, respectively.

According to the question,

$$10 = \frac{200}{5 + x} \quad \left[\because \text{Time} = \frac{\text{Distance}}{\text{Speed}}\right]$$

$$\Rightarrow \quad 5 + x = 20 \Rightarrow x = 15 \text{ m/s}$$

and $$25 = \frac{200}{5 + y}$$

$$\Rightarrow \quad 5 + y = 8 \Rightarrow y = 3 \text{ m/s}$$

$\therefore$ Required ratio $= x : y$

$= 15 : 3 = 5 : 1$

SSC Exam Scanner

SSC CGL 2024 & 2023 (Tier I & II)

1. A boat covers a distance of 55 km downstream in 5 h while it takes 11 h to cover the same distance upstream. What is the speed of the boat?
SSC CGL (Tier I) 23/09/2024 Shift-IV
(a) 8 km/h (b) 9 km/h
(c) 11 km/h (d) 7 km/h

2. A motorboat, whose speed in 15 km/h in still water goes 50 km downstream and comes back in a total of 7 h 30 min. The speed of the stream (in km/h) is
SSC CGL (Tier I) 23/09/2024 Shift-II
(a) 9 (b) 5 (c) 11 (d) 7

3. A man can row a distance of 6 km in 1 h in still water. He can row the same distance in 45 min with the current. Find the total time taken by him to row a distance of 16 km with the current and to return to the starting point.
SSC CGL (Tier I) 18/09/2024 Shift-III
(a) 4 h and 40 min
(b) 6 h
(c) 4 h
(d) 6 h and 40 min

4. A motorboat travelling at some speed can cover 24 km upstream and 40 km downstream in 17 h. At the same speed it can travel 32 km downstream and 12 km upstream in 10 h. The speed of the stream is
SSC CGL (Tier I) 18/09/2024 Shift-I
(a) 5 km/h (b) 4 km/h
(c) 2 km/h (d) 3 km/h

5. A motorboat takes 18 h to go downstream, and it takes 36 h to return the same distance. Find the ratio of the speed of the boat in still water to the speed of the stream.
SSC CGL (Tier I) 17/09/2024 Shift-II
(a) 3 : 1 (b) 2 : 3 (c) 2 : 1 (d) 3 : 2

6. A boatman rows to a place 30 km distance and back in 14 h. He finds that he can row 10 km with the stream at the same time as 4 km against the stream. Find the speed (in km/h) of the stream.
SSC CGL (Tier I) 13/09/2024 Shift-III
(a) $\frac{9}{2}$ (b) $\frac{9}{4}$ (c) $\frac{2}{9}$ (d) $\frac{4}{9}$

7. A boat can travel 78 km upstream and back in a total of 32 h. It can travel 15 km upstream and 52 km downstream in a total of 9 h. How much distance will the boat cover in 12 h in still water?
SSC CGL (Tier I) 13/09/2024 Shift-I
(a) 92 km (b) 96 km
(c) 104 km (d) 100 km

8. A boatman goes 2 km against the current of the stream in 1 h and goes 1 km along with the current in 10 min. How long will it take to go 6 km in stationary water?
SSC CGL (Tier I) 12/09/2024 Shift-III
(a) 1 h 30 min (b) 1 h 15 min
(c) 2 h 30 min (d) 1 h 45 min

9. A boat can go 54 km upstream in 6 h. If the speed of the stream is 4.8 km/h, then how much time (in hours) will the boat take to cover a distance of 279 km downstream?
SSC CGL (Tier I) 11/09/2024 Shift-III
(a) 20 (b) 15
(c) 18 (d) 16

10. The speed of a boat in still water is 18 km/h and the speed of the stream is 3 km/h. How much time (in hours) will it take to cover a distance of 105 km in downstream and in coming back?
SSC CGL (Tier I) 10/09/2024 Shift-III
(a) 12 (b) 10 (c) 15 (d) 9

11. A boat covers 35 km downstream in 2 h and covers the same distance upstream in 7 h. Find the speed (in km/h) of the boat in still water.
SSC CGL (Tier-II) 03/03/2023 Shift-I
(a) 11.25 (b) 28.75
(c) 18.25 (d) 10.55

12. A man can row 10 km/h in still water. When the river is running at a speed of 4.5 km/h, then it takes him 2 h to row to a place and comes back to the initial point. How far is the place (in km) (rounded off to two decimal places)?
SSC CGL (Tier-II) 02/03/2023 Shift-I
(a) 5.50 (b) 8.98
(c) 7.98 (d) 6.25

13. A boat running upstream takes 10 h to cover a certain distance, while it takes 7 h to cover the same distance running downstream. What is the ratio between the speed of the boat and that of the water current, respectively?
SSC CGL (Tier-I) 25/07/2023 Shift-III
(a) 17 : 5 (b) 3 : 17
(c) 2 : 17 (d) 17 : 3

14. The effective speed of a boat is 15.2 km/h against the stream and 20.8 km/h along the stream. Find the speed of the stream.
SSC CGL (Tier-I) 25/07/2023 Shift-III
(a) 18 km/h (b) 1.8 km/h
(c) 2.8 km/h (d) 3 km/h

15. A boat covers a distance of 12 km in 1 h upstream and in 45 min downstream. Find the speed of the boat and the stream (in km/h).
SSC CGL (Tier-I) 25/07/2023 Shift-II
(a) 16 ; 4 (b) 16 ; 2
(c) 14 ; 2 (d) 12 ; 4

16. A boat covers a distance of 80 km downstream in 8 h while it takes 10 h to cover the same distance upstream, what is the speed (in km/h) of the boat in still water?
SSC CGL (Tier-I) 24/07/2023 Shift-IV
(a) 18 (b) 12 (c) 9 (d) 16

17. Dharmendra can row 80 km upstream and 110 km downstream in 13 h, Also, he can row 60 km upstream and 88 km downstream in 10 h. What is the speed (in km/h) of the current?
SSC CGL (Tier-I) 24/07/2023 Shift-IV
(a) 6 (b) 16 (c) 10 (d) 12

18. A boat can cover 120 km upstream and back in a total of 30 h and 25 km upstream and 40 km downstream in a total of 7 h. How much distance will the boat cover in 16 h in still water?
SSC CGL (Tier-I) 24/07/2023 Shift-I
(a) 200 km (b) 180 km
(c) 175 km (d) 225 km

19. A boat's speed in still water is 45 km/h, while the river is flowing at a speed of 15 km/h. The time taken to cover a certain distance upstream is 9 h more than the time taken to cover the same distance downstream. Find the distance (in km). **SSC CGL (Tier-I) 20/07/2023 Shift-IV**
(a) 540 (b) 320 (c) 480 (d) 450

20. The ratio of the speed of a motorboat to that of the current of water is 31 : 6. The motorboat starts from a point and covers a certain distance along the current in 4 h 10 min. Find the time taken by the motorboat to come back to its initial point. **SSC CGL (Tier-I) 20/07/2023 Shift-IV**
(a) 4 h 10 min (b) 5 h 10 min
(c) 5 h 50 min (d) 6 h 10 min

21. A boat can go 60 km downstream and 40 km upstream in 12 h 30 min. It can go 84 km downstream and 63 km upstream in 18 h 54 min. What is the speed (in km/h, to the nearest integer) of the boat in still water ? SSC CGL (Tier-I) 20/07/2023 Shift-I

(a) 7 (b) 8 (c) 9 (d) 10

22. The speed of a boat down the stream is 125% of the speed in still water If the boat takes 30 min to cover 20 km in still water, then how much time (in hours) will it take to cover 15 km upstream?

SSC CGL (Tier-I) 19/07/2023 Shift-III

(a) $\frac{3}{4}$ (b) $\frac{1}{2}$ (c) $\frac{1}{4}$ (d) 1

23. To go a distance of 144 km upstream, a rower takes 12 h while it takes her only 9 h to row the same distance downstream. What is the speed of the stream?

SSC CGL (Tier-I) 18/07/2023 Shift-II

(a) 3 km/h (b) 1 km/h
(c) 1.5 km/h (d) 2 km/h

24. A man takes 15 min to row 16 km downstream, which is 25% less than the time he takes to row the same distance upstream. How many kilometres can the man row in an hour in still water? (Rounded off to nearest whole number)

SSC CGL (Tier-I) 14/07/2023 Shift-IV

(a) 56 (b) 60 (c) 58 (d) 54

SSC CGL 2022-2020 (Tier I)

25. A boat covers a certain distance against the stream in 9 h 36 min and it covers the same distance along the stream in 6 h. What is the ratio of the speed of the boat in still water to that of the stream?

SSC CGL (Tier-I) 12/12/2022 Shift-II

(a) 13 : 3 (b) 9 : 2
(c) 11 : 6 (d) 8 : 5

26. A boat moves 25 km upstream and 39 km downstream in 8 h. It travels 35 km upstream and 52 km downstream in 11 h. What is the speed of the stream if it travels at a uniform speed?

SSC CGL (Tier-I) 12/12/2022 Shift-I

(a) 4 km/h (b) 5 km/h
(c) 6 km/h (d) 3 km/h

27. A man rows to a place 48 km distance and comes back in 14 h. He finds that he can row 4 km with the stream in the same time as 3 km against the stream. The speed of the stream is

SSC CGL (Tier-I) 07/12/2022 Shift-I

(a) 1.5 km/h (b) 3.5 km/h
(c) 1.8 km/h (d) 1 km/h

28. A boat racer can row $21\frac{3}{2}$ km/h in still water. If the speed of river is 12.5 km/h, it takes him 40 min to row to a place and back, how far off is the place (consider up to two decimals)?

SSC CGL (Tier-I) 06/12/2022 Shift-I

(a) $5\frac{5}{27}$ km (b) $5\frac{2}{5}$ km
(c) $4\frac{5}{27}$ km (d) $3\frac{5}{27}$ km

29. The speed of a boat in still water is $5\frac{1}{3}$ km/h. It is found the boat takes thrice as much time to row up than it does to row down the same distance in the river stream. Find the speed of the river stream.

SSC CGL (Tier-I) 05/12/2022 Shift-II

(a) $\frac{23}{27}$ m/s (b) $\frac{22}{27}$ m/s
(c) $\frac{20}{27}$ m/s (d) $\frac{19}{27}$ m/s

30. A swimmer swims from a point P against the current for 6 min and then swims back along the current for next 6 min and reaches at a point Q. If the distance between P and Q is 120 m, then the speed of the current (in km/h) is

SSC CGL (Tier-I) 01/12/2022 Shift-III

(a) 0.4 (b) 0.2 (c) 1 (d) 0.6

31. A man rows a boat a certain distance downstream in 9 h, while it takes 18 h to row the same distance upstream. How many hours will it take him to row three-fifth of the same distance in still water?

SSC CGL (Tier-I) 01/12/2022 Shift-II

(a) 9.5 (b) 7.2
(c) 10 (d) 12

32. The speed of a motorboat in still water is 20 km/h. It travels 150 km downstream and then returns to the starting point. If the round trip takes a total of 16 h, what is the speed (in km/h) of the flow of river? SSC CGL (Tier-I) 24/08/2021 Shift-III

(a) 8 (b) 6
(c) 5 (d) 4

33. A boat covers a round trip journey between two Points A and B in a river in T h. If its speed in still water becomes 2 times, it would take $\frac{80}{161}T$ h for the same journey. Find the ratio of its speed in still water the speed of the river

SSC CGL (Tier-I) 23/08/2021 Shift-I

(a) 1 : 11 (b) 2 : 1
(c) 161 : 40 (d) 11 : 1

34. A boat can go 5 km upstream and $7\frac{1}{2}$ km downstream in 45 min. It can also go 5 km downstream and 2.5 km upstream in 25 min. How much time (in minutes) will it take to go 6 km downstream?

SSC CGL (Tier-I) 20/08/2021 Shift-II

(a) 10 (b) 12
(c) 15 (d) 20

35. A man can row a distance of 8 km downstream in a certain time and can row 6 km upstream in the same time. If he rows 24km upstream and the same distance downstream in $1\frac{3}{4}$ h, then the speed (in km/h) of the current is

SSC CGL (Tier-I) 17/08/2021 Shift-III

(a) $4\frac{1}{2}$ (b) 4
(c) 3 (d) $2\frac{1}{2}$

36. A boat goes 27 km upstream and 33 km downstream is 6 h. In the same time it can go 36 km upstream and 22 km downstream. How much time will it take to go 36 km upstream and 44 km downstream?

SSC CGL (Tier-I) 16/08/2021 Shift-III

(a) 8 h 30 m
(b) 8 h 10 m
(c) 8 h
(d) 7 h 50 m

37. X, Y are two points in a river. Points P and Q divide the straight line XY into three equal parts. The river flows along XY and the time taken by a boat to row from X to Q and from Y to Q are in the ratio 4 : 5. The ratio of the speed of the boat downstream to that of the river current is equal to

SSC CGL (Tier-I) 13/08/2021 Shift-I

(a) 3:10 (b) 10:3
(c) 3:4 (d) 4:3

38. A boat can go 3.6 km upstream and 5.4 km downstream in 54 min, while it can go 5.4 km upstream and 3.6 km downstream in 58.5 min. The time (in min) taken by the boat in going 10 km downstream is

SSC CGL (Tier-I) 05/03/2020 Shift-II

(a) 48 (b) 50
(c) 45 (d) 54

SSC CPO SI 2024-2020

39. The ratio of the speed of a boat to that of the current water is 35 : 8. The boat goes along with the current in 5 h 10 min. What will be the time taken by the boat to come back? **SSC CPO 29/06/2024 Shift-III**

(a) 5 h 15 min 58 sec
(b) 9 h 30 min 49 sec
(c) 6 h 45 min 10 sec
(d) 8 h 13 min 48 sec

40. A man rows 48 km and back in 48 h. He can row 4 km with the stream in the same time as 3 km against the stream. The speed of the stream (in km/h) is **SSC CPO 29/06/2024 Shift-II**

(a) $\frac{7}{21}$ (b) $\frac{3}{29}$ (c) $\frac{5}{21}$ (d) $\frac{7}{24}$

41. The speed of a boat, when travelling downstream is 33 km/h, whereas when travelling upstream it is 27 km/h. What is the speed of the boat in still water? **SSC CPO 29/06/2024 Shift-II**

(a) 30 km/h (b) 60 km/h
(c) 12 km/h (d) 6 km/h

42. A boat can travel 16.9 km downstream in 52 min. If the speed of the current is 3 km/h, then how much time (in hours) will the boat take to travel 84 km upstream? **SSC CPO 29/06/2024 Shift-I**

(a) 6.22 (b) 6 (c) 13.5 (d) 7.5

43. A boat covers 24 km upstream and 36 km downstream in 10 h, and 36 km upstream and 24 km downstream in 12 h. The speed of the current is **SSC CPO 28/06/2024 Shift-I**

(a) $\frac{33}{13}$ km/h (b) $\frac{26}{9}$ km/h
(c) $\frac{24}{7}$ km/h (d) $\frac{25}{8}$ km/h

44. A boatman rows 2 km in 10 min, along the stream and 12 km in 2 h against the stream. What is the speed of the stream? **SSC CPO 28/06/2024 Shift-I**

(a) 4 km/h (b) 35 km/h
(c) 3 km/h (d) 2.5 km/h

45. A man's speed in still water is 4 km/h more than the speed of the current. If the man takes a total of 10 h to cover 45 km downstream and 35 km upstream, then the speed of the man in still water is **SSC CPO 27/06/2024 Shift-III**

(a) 15 km/h (b) 22 km/h
(c) 18 km/h (d) 20 km/h

46. Ashu can row 7.5 km an hour in still water. He finds that it takes four times as much time to row upstream, as it takes to row downstream. The speed of the stream is **SSC CPO 27/06/2024 Shift-II**

(a) 2.5 km/h (b) 4.5 km/h
(c) 3.5 km/h (d) 1.5 km/h

47. A man wishes to cover 1 km distance in river water. In still water he takes 12 min to cover it, but in the flowing river he takes 13 min. The speed of the flowing water of the river is **SSC CPO 27/06/2024 Shift-I**

(a) 22 km/h (b) $\frac{7}{12}$ km/h
(c) 25km/h (d) $\frac{5}{13}$ km/h

48. The upstream speed of a boat is 8 km/h and the downstream is 15 km/h. What is the speed of the boat in still water and the speed of the stream (in km/h), respectively? **SSC CPO 04/10/2023 Shift-II**

(a) 11 and 3 (b) 3 and 11
(c) 11.5 and 3.5 (d) 3.5 and 11.5

49. Let the speed of the boat in still water be 17 km/h and let the speed of the stream be 5 km/h. What is the time taken by the boat to go 110 km downstream? **SSC CPO 03/10/2023 Shift-II**

(a) 4.5 h (b) 6 h (c) 5.5 h (d) 5 h

50. The speed of a boat in still water is 15 km/h and the speed of the current is 5 km/h. In how much time (in hours) will the boat travel a distance of 60 km upstream and the same distance downstream? **SSC CPO 25/11/2020 Shift-II**

(a) 20 (b) 12
(c) 9 (d) 10

SSC CHSL 2024-2021 (Tier I & II)

51. If the speed of a boat in still water is 3 km/h and if its speed upstream is 1 km/h, find the speed of the stream. **SSC CHSL (Tier I) 11/07/2024 Shift-III**

(a) 2 km/h (b) 1 km/h
(c) 0.25 km/h (d) 0.5 km/h

52. A man can row a boat at speed 8 km/h in still water. It takes thrice as long to row upstream as it does to row downstream. Find the speed of the stream (in km/h). **SSC CHSL (Tier I) 08/07/2024 Shift-IV**

(a) 5 (b) 4
(c) 6 (d) 3

53. The speed of a boat in still water is 12 km/h and the speed of the stream is 3 km/h. A man goes to a place by boat, 45 km and comes back to the starting point. Find the total time taken by him. **SSC CHSL (Tier I) 08/07/2024 Shift-III**

(a) 9 h (b) 6 h (c) 8 h (d) 7 h

54. The ratio of the speeds of a boat, while going upstream and going downstream is 2 : 3 and the sum of these two speeds is 15 km/h. What is the speed of the stream? **SSC CHSL (Tier I) 08/07/2024 Shift-II**

(a) 3.5 km/h (b) 1.5 km/h
(c) 3 km/h (d) 2.5 km/h

55. A boat can travel 60 km downstream in 4 h. If the speed of the boat in still water is 13 km/h, then in what time will it cover 30 km upstream? **SSC CHSL (Tier I) 02/07/2024 Shift-I**

(a) $2\frac{8}{11}$ h (b) $3\frac{4}{7}$ h
(c) $2\frac{4}{7}$ h (d) $3\frac{5}{7}$ h

56. A man can row 18 km/h in still water. It takes him two times as long to row up as to row down the river. Find the rate of the stream. **SSC CHSL (Tier I) 01/07/2024 Shift-III**

(a) 12 km/h (b) 6 km/h
(c) 24 km/h (d) 9 km/h

57. A boat is moving 3 km against the current of the stream in 1 h and moves 1 km in the direction of the current in 12 min. How long will it take the boat to go 6 km in stationary water? **SSC CHSL (Tier-II) 10/01/2024 Shift-I**

(a) 1 h and 25 min
(b) 1 h and 15 min
(c) 1 h and 30 min
(d) 1 h and 20 min

58. A ship goes at 18 km/h downstream and at 16 km/h upstream. What will be the speed of the ship in still water? **SSC CHSL (Tier-I) 07/08/2023 Shift-IV**

(a) 14 km/h (b) 17 km/h
(c) 16 km/h (d) 15 km/h

59. A watercraft is rowed down 32 km along a river in 4 h and 10 km against the river in 5 h. Find the speed of the watercraft and that of the river. **SSC CHSL (Tier-I) 01/06/2022 Shift-I**

(a) 4.5 km/h and 2.5 km/h
(b) 4 km/h and 3 km/h
(c) 5 km/h and 3 km/h
(d) 3.5 km/h and 1.5 km/h

60. Sunil can row a boat 20 km upstream in 1 h 15 min. If the speed of the current of the river is 2 km/h, then how much time will he take to row the boat 30 km downstream?
SSC CHSL (Tier-I) 10/08/2021 Shift-I
(a) 1 h 10 min (b) 1 h 45 min
(c) 1 h 30 min (d) 1 h 20 min

61. A boat can travel with a speed of 19 km/h in still water. If the speed of the stream is 3 km/h, then what will be the total time (in hours) taken by the boat to go 88 km downstream and 24 km upstream?
SSC CHSL (Tier-I) 04/08/2021 Shift-I
(a) 4.5 (b) 5 (c) 4 (d) 5.5

SSC MTS 2024-2022

62. The speed of a boat in still water is 12 km/h and the stream flows at a speed of 3 km/h. The distance travelled in the boat downstream in 24 minutes is
SSC MTS 23/10/2024 Shift-II
(a) 6 km (b) 4 km
(c) 5 km (d) 7 km

63. A boat can travel at a speed of 28 km/h in still water. If the speed of the stream is 4 km/h, what is the average speed (in km/h) of the boat if it travels 192 km downstream, stops there for one hour and then returns to the starting point?
SSC MTS 14/10/2024 Shift-I
(a) 25.6 (b) 24.8
(c) 36.5 (d) 28.5

64. The speed of a boat in still water is 15 km/h and the speed of the current is 3 km/h. How much distance (in km) can be covered going down stream in 12 min?
SSC MTS 07/10/2024 Shift-I
(a) 3.5 (b) 3.7 (c) 3.4 (d) 3.6

65. A boat travels upstream from B to A and downstream from A to B in 3 h. If the speed of the boat in still water is 9 km/h and the speed of the current is 3.5 km/h, the distance between A and B is (correct upto two decimal places)
SSC MTS 13/09/2023 Shift-I
(a) 14.46 km (b) 13.46 km
(c) 12.46 km (d) 11.46 km

66. A man rows to a place at a distance of 72 km and comes back in 36 h. He finds that he can row 12 km with the stream in the same time as 4 km against the stream. The speed (in km/h, rounded off to 2 decimal places) of the stream is
SSC MTS 11/09/2023 Shift-II
(a) 3.75 (b) 2.45 (c) 2.67 (d) 2.33

67. A boat covers a certain distance downstream in 5 h but takes 8 h to return upstream to the starting point. If the speed of the stream is 6 km/h, then find the speed of the boat in still water.
SSC MTS 08/09/2023 Shift-II
(a) 26 km/h (b) 13 km/h
(c) 78 km/h (d) 39 km/h

68. A sailor rows a boat 36 km downstream and 24 km upstream in 6 h. When, it rows 24 km downstream and 36 km upstream the sailor takes 6 and half-hours, Then the speed of the current is
SSC MTS 01/09/2023 Shift-III
(a) 1.5 km/h (b) 4 km/h
(c) 3 km/h (d) 2 km/h

69. A boat takes 20 h for travelling downstream from point A to point B and comes back to a mid-point C between A and B. The speed of the stream is 5 km/h and the speed of the boat in still water is 10 km/h. Find the distance between A and B (in km).
SSC MTS 01/09/2023 Shift-I
(a) 100 (b) 120 (c) 150 (d) 75

70. A boat can travel 5 km upstream in 15 min. If the ratio of the speed of the boat in still water to the speed of the stream is 6 : 1, then how much time will the boat take to cover 19.6 km downstream?
SSC MTS 13/07/2022 Shift-I
(a) 54 min (b) 26 min
(c) 42 min (d) 31 min

SSC GD Constable 2024 & 2023

71. A boat travels a distance of 54 km at uniform speed. If the speed of boat is increased by 3 km/h, then it takes 3 h less to cover the same distance. What is the original speed of the boat? **SSC GD 22/02/2024 Shift-II**
(a) 3 km/h (b) 9 km/h
(c) 12 km/h (d) 6 km/h

72. A boat is moving in still water at a speed of 15 km/h. The speed of the stream in 3 km/h. How much time will the boat take to cover 6 km upstream ? **SSC GD 13/02/2023 Shift-II**
(a) 30 min (b) 15 min
(c) 20 min (d) 45 min

73. A boat can travel at a speed of 30 km/h in still water. If the flow of the stream is 2 km/h. How long will it take by the boat to travel 56 km upstream?
SSC GD 09/02/2023 Shift-II
(a) 28 h (b) 3 h (c) 2 h (d) $\frac{28}{15}$ h

74. Speed of a boat in still water is 8 km/h and the speed of the stream is 2 km/h. A man rows to a place at 90 km and comes back to the starting point. What is the total time taken by him in the given two-way movement?
SSC GD 09/02/2023 Shift-II
(a) 30 h (b) 24 h (c) 21 h (d) 20 h

75. A river is running at 2 km/h. A boat goes 40 km upstream from A to B and also returns back from B to A in total 10 h. The speed of the boat in still water is **SSC GD 02/02/2023 Shift-I**
(a) 6.23 km/h (b) 7.97 km/h
(c) 7.32 km/h (d) 8.47 km/h

Right Answers

1 (a)	2 (b)	3 (b)	4 (d)	5 (a)	6 (b)	7 (b)	8 (a)	9 (b)	10 (a)
11 (a)	12 (c)	13 (d)	14 (c)	15 (c)	16 (c)	17 (a)	18 (a)	19 (a)	20 (d)
21 (c)	22 (b)	23 (d)	24 (a)	25 (a)	26 (a)	27 (d)	28 (a)	29 (c)	30 (d)
31 (b)	32 (c)	33 (d)	34 (b)	35 (b)	36 (c)	37 (b)	38 (b)	39 (d)	40 (d)
41 (a)	42 (a)	43 (d)	44 (c)	45 (d)	46 (b)	47 (d)	48 (c)	49 (d)	50 (c)
51 (a)	52 (b)	53 (c)	54 (b)	55 (a)	56 (b)	57 (c)	58 (b)	59 (c)	60 (c)
61 (d)	62 (a)	63 (a)	64 (d)	65 (d)	66 (c)	67 (a)	68 (d)	69 (b)	70 (c)
71 (d)	72 (a)	73 (c)	74 (b)	75 (d)					

Solutions

1. (a) Let the speed of boat in still water $= x$ km/h

and speed of stream $= y$ km/h

When boat goes downstream,

We know, Speed $= \frac{\text{Distance}}{\text{Time}}$

$$x + y = \frac{55}{5} = 11 \quad \ldots(i)$$

When boat goes upstream,

Similarly,

$$x - y = \frac{55}{11} = 5 \quad \ldots(ii)$$

From Eq. (i) and (ii),

$x = 8$ km/h and $y = 3$ km/h

$\therefore$ Speed of boat $= 8$ km/h

2. (b) Speed of boat in still water $= 15$ km/h

Let speed of the stream be x km/h.

Distance $(d) = 50$ km

According to the question,

$$\frac{d}{15+x} + \frac{d}{15-x} = 7\frac{30}{60}$$

$$\Rightarrow d\left[\frac{1}{15+x} + \frac{1}{15-x}\right] = 7\frac{1}{2}$$

$$\Rightarrow d\left[\frac{15-x+15+x}{225-x^2}\right] = \frac{15}{2}$$

$$\Rightarrow d\left[\frac{30}{225-x^2}\right] = \frac{15}{2}$$

$$\Rightarrow 50\left[\frac{30}{225-x^2}\right] = \frac{15}{2}$$

$$\Rightarrow 15[225 - x^2] = 2 \times 30 \times 50$$

$$\Rightarrow 225 - x^2 = 200 \Rightarrow x^2 = 25$$

Speed of stream $x = 5$ km/h

3. (b) Speed of man in still water

$$= \frac{\text{Distance}}{\text{Time}} = \frac{6}{1} = 6 \text{ km/h}$$

Let speed of current be x km/h.

According to the question,

$$\text{Time} = \frac{\text{Distance}}{\text{Speed}} \Rightarrow \frac{45}{60} = \frac{6}{x+6}$$

$$\Rightarrow \frac{3}{4} = \frac{6}{x+6} \Rightarrow x = 2 \text{ km/h}$$

Again, $\frac{16}{2+6} + \frac{16}{6-2} = \frac{16}{8} + \frac{16}{4} = 2 + 4 = 6$ h

4. (d) Let the speed of boat in still water be x km/h and speed of stream be y km/h.

According to the question,

$$\frac{24}{x-y} + \frac{40}{x+y} = 17 \quad \ldots(i)$$

$$\frac{12}{x-y} + \frac{32}{x+y} = 10 \quad \ldots(ii)$$

Multiply Eq. (ii) by 2

$$\frac{24}{x-y} + \frac{64}{x+y} = 20 \quad \ldots(iii)$$

From Eqs. (i) and (iii),

$$\frac{24}{x-y} + \frac{40}{x+y} = 17$$

$$\frac{24}{x-y} + \frac{64}{x+y} = 20$$

$$\underline{- \quad - \quad -}$$

$$-\frac{24}{x+y} = -3$$

$\Rightarrow$ $x + y = 8$ ...(iv)

and $x - y = 2$ ...(v)

From Eqs. (iv) and (v),

$2x = 10 \Rightarrow x = 5$ and $y = 3$

5. (a) Let the speed of boat in still water be x km/h and speed of the stream be y km/h.

Distance $= d$

Downstream speed $= (x + y)$ km/h

Upstream speed $= (x - y)$ km/h

Now,
$$\frac{d}{x+y} = 18 \quad \ldots(i)$$

$$\frac{d}{x-y} = 36 \quad \ldots(ii)$$

By Eqs. (i) and (ii),

$$18(x + y) = 36(x - y)$$

$$18x + 18y = 36x - 36y$$

$$18x = 54y$$

$$\frac{x}{y} = \frac{3}{1}$$

$$x : y = 3 : 1$$

Speed of boat in still water : Speed of stream $= 3 : 1$

6. (b) Let the speed of boat in still water be B km/h and speed of stream by S km/h.

According to the question,

$$\frac{30}{B+S} + \frac{30}{B-S} = 14 \quad \ldots(i)$$

According to the question,

$$\frac{10}{B+S} = \frac{4}{B-S} \quad \ldots(ii)$$

Multiply by 3 both sides,

$$\frac{30}{B+S} = \frac{12}{B-S}$$

$$\frac{12}{B-S} + \frac{30}{B-S} = 14$$

$$\Rightarrow \frac{42}{B-S} = 14 \quad \text{[from Eq. (i)]}$$

$$B - S = 3 \quad \ldots(iii)$$

From Eq. (ii), $\frac{10}{B+S} = \frac{4}{3}$

$$B + S = \frac{15}{2} \quad \ldots(iv)$$

From Eqs. (iii) and (iv),

$$2S = \frac{9}{2} \Rightarrow S = \frac{9}{4}$$

$\therefore$ Speed of stream $= \frac{9}{4}$ km/h

7. (b) Let upstream speed of boat $= u$

and downstream speed of boat $= v$

According to the question,

$$\frac{78}{u} + \frac{78}{v} = 32 \quad \ldots(i)$$

and
$$\frac{15}{u} + \frac{52}{v} = 9 \quad \ldots(ii)$$

From Eqs. (i) and (ii),

$u = 3$ and $v = 13$

$\therefore$ Speed of boat $= \frac{13+3}{2} = 8$ km/h

$\therefore$ Distance $= 12 \times 8 = 96$ km

8. (a) Let the speed of the man in still water $= x$ km/h

and the speed of water $= y$ km/h

In upstream,

Distance $(x - y) \times 1 = 2$

$$x - y = 2 \quad \ldots(i)$$

In downstream, $(x + y) \times \frac{10}{60} = 1$

$$x + y = 6 \quad \ldots(ii)$$

Eq (i) + Eq. (ii),

$2x = 8$ (Speed of man in still water)

$\Rightarrow$ $x = 4$

Put $x = 4$ in Eq. (i),

$4 - y = 2$

$\Rightarrow$ $y = 2$

Time required to go 6 km in stationary water

$$= \frac{6}{4} = \frac{3}{2} \text{ h} = 1 \text{ h } 30 \text{ min}$$

9. (b) Upstream speed $= \frac{54}{6} = 9$ km/h

Speed of stream $= 4.8$ km/h

Upstream speed = Speed of boat − Speed of stream

$9 =$ Speed of boat $- 4.8$

Speed of boat $= 13.8$ km/h

$\therefore$ Time taken $= \frac{\text{Distance}}{\text{Downstream speed}}$

$$= \frac{279}{13.8 + 4.8} = 15 \text{ h}$$

10. (a) Moving downstream,

Time taken $= \frac{105}{(18+3)}$

$\left[\because \text{Time} = \frac{\text{Distance}}{\text{Speed}}\right]$

$$= \frac{105}{21} = 5 \text{ h}$$

Moving upstream,

Time taken $= \frac{105}{(18-3)} = \frac{105}{15} = 7$ h

$\therefore$ Total time taken $= 5 + 7 = 12$ h

11. (a) Let speed of a boat in still water be x and speed of stream be y.

In downstream, $x + y = \frac{35}{2} = 17.5$ km/h ...(i)

In upstream, $x - y = \frac{35}{7} = 5$ km/h ...(ii)

Adding Eqs. (i) and (ii),

$x + y + x - y = 17.5 + 5$

$\Rightarrow 2x = 22.5$

$\Rightarrow x = \frac{22.5}{2}$

$\Rightarrow x = 11.25$ km/h

12. (c) Speed of man in still water (x) = 10 km/h

Speed of river (y) = 4.5 km/h

Let the distance be 'd' km.

Speed of upstream $= x - y = 10 - 4.5 = 5.5$ km/h

Speed of downstream $= x + y = 10 + 4.5 = 14.5$ km/h

According to the question,

$\frac{d}{5.5} + \frac{d}{14.5} = 2 \Rightarrow \frac{10d}{55} + \frac{10d}{145} = 2$

$\Rightarrow \frac{2d}{11} + \frac{2d}{29} = 2 \Rightarrow 2\left[\frac{29d + 11d}{319}\right] = 2$

$\Rightarrow 40d = 319 \Rightarrow d = 7.975$

$\therefore d \approx 7.98$ km (approx.)

Speedy Method

$\because D = \frac{T(x^2 - y^2)}{2x} \Rightarrow D = \frac{2[(10)^2 - (4.5)^2]}{2 \times 10}$

$\Rightarrow D = \frac{2 \times 79.75}{2 \times 10} \Rightarrow D = 7.975 \text{ km} \approx 7.98 \text{ km}$

13. (d) Time in upstream : Time in downstream = 10 : 7

$\therefore$ Upstream speed : Downstream speed = 7 : 10 ($\because S \propto \frac{1}{T}$, when D is constant)

Speed of boat $= \frac{7 + 10}{2} = \frac{17}{2}$ unit

Speed of stream $= \frac{10 - 7}{2} = \frac{3}{2}$ unit

$\therefore$ Ratio between speed of boat and speed of stream $= \frac{17}{2} : \frac{3}{2} = 17 : 3$

14. (c) Upstream speed = 15.2 km/h

Downstream speed = 20.8 km/h

$\therefore$ Speed of stream $= \frac{20.8 - 15.2}{2} = \frac{5.6}{2} = 2.8$ km/h

15. (c) Distance = 12 km

Upstream speed $= \frac{12}{1} = 12$ km/h

Downstream speed $= \frac{12 \times 60}{45} = 16$ km/h

$\therefore$ Speed of the boat $= \frac{16 + 12}{2} = 14$ km/h

and speed of stream $= \frac{16 - 12}{2} = \frac{4}{2} = 2$ km/h

16. (c) Upstream speed $= \frac{80}{10} = 8$ km/h

Downstream speed $= \frac{80}{8} = 10$ km/h

$\therefore$ Speed of the boat $= \frac{8 + 10}{2} = 9$ km/h

17. (a) Let the speed of boat = x km/h

Also, let the speed of current = y km/h

According to the question,

$\frac{80}{x - y} + \frac{110}{x + y} = 13$ ...(i)

$\frac{60}{x - y} + \frac{88}{x + y} = 10$ ...(ii)

Solving Eqs. (i) and (ii), we get

$\Rightarrow x + y = 22$ ...(iii)

Similarly, $x - y = 10$ ...(iv)

Further solving Eqs. (iii) and (iv), we get

$x = 16$ km/h and $y = 6$ km/h

$\therefore$ Speed of current = 6 km/h

18. (a) Let the speed of boat in downstream = D km/h

and the speed of boat in upstream = U km/h

According to the question,

$\frac{120}{D} + \frac{120}{U} = 30$ h ...(i)

and $\frac{40}{D} + \frac{25}{U} = 7$ h ...(ii)

Then solving these equations, we get

$D = 20$ km and $U = 5$ km/h

$\therefore$ Speed of boat in still water

$= \frac{D + U}{2} = \frac{20 + 5}{2} = 12.5$ km/h

Then, total distance covers in 16 h in still water $= 12.5 \times 16 = 200$ km

19. (a) Let distance be D km.

According to the question,

$\frac{D}{45 - 15} - \frac{D}{45 + 15} = 9$

$\Rightarrow \frac{D}{30} - \frac{D}{60} = 9 \Rightarrow \frac{D}{60} = 9$

$\therefore D = 540$ km

20. (d) Boat speed : Current speed = 31 : 6

Let distance = D,

time = 4 h 10 min = 250 min

Time $= \frac{D}{31 + 6} = 250$

$\Rightarrow D = 250 \times 37$ min

$\therefore$ Upstream time $= \frac{250 \times 37}{31 - 6} = 370$ min = 6 h 10 min

21. (c) Let upstream speed be U km/h. and downstream speed be V km/h

$\therefore \frac{40}{U} + \frac{60}{V} = \frac{25}{2}$ ...(i)

and $\frac{63}{U} + \frac{84}{V} = 18\frac{9}{10} \Rightarrow 21\left(\frac{3}{U} + \frac{4}{V}\right) = \frac{21 \times 9}{10}$

$\Rightarrow \frac{30}{U} + \frac{40}{V} = 9$ ...(ii)

From Eqs. (i) and (ii), we get

$V = \frac{40}{3}$ km/h and $U = 5$ km/h

$\therefore$ Speed of the boat $= \frac{\frac{40}{3} + 5}{2} = \frac{55}{6}$ = 9 (approx) = 9 km/h

22. (b) Speed of the boat in still water

$= \frac{20}{\frac{1}{2}} = 40$ km/h

Speed of the boat in downstream

$= 40 \times 125\% = 50$ km/h

Speed of stream = 50 − 40 = 10 km/h

Speed of the boat in up stream

= 40 − 10 = 30 km/h

$\therefore$ To cover 15 km upstream, the boat will take $= \frac{15}{30} = \frac{1}{2}$ h

23. (d) Let the speed of stream be y km/h and the speed of rower be x km/h.

According to the question,

$x - y = \frac{144}{12} = 12$ ... (i)

and $x + y = \frac{144}{9} = 16$ ... (ii)

From Eqs. (i) and (ii),

$y = 2$ km/h

$\therefore$ Speed of stream is 2 km/h.

24. (a) Downstream speed (x)

$= \frac{16}{15/60} = 64$ km/h

If he takes 25% less time for downstream.

$\therefore$ Upstream speed $(y) = 64 \times \frac{75}{100} = 48$ km/h

Hence, speed in still water $= \frac{x + y}{2}$

$= \frac{64 + 48}{2} = 56$ km

25. (a) Let speed of boat = x km/h and speed of stream = y km/h $(x > y)$.

Now, $(x - y) \times 9$ h 36 min $= (x + y) \times 6$ h

$\Rightarrow (x - y) \times \left(9 + \frac{36}{60}\right)\text{h} = (x + y) \times 6$

$\Rightarrow (x - y) \times \frac{48}{5} = 6x + 6y$

$48x - 48y = 30x + 30y$

$\Rightarrow 48x - 30x = 30y + 48y \Rightarrow 18x = 78y$

$\therefore \frac{x}{y} = \frac{13}{3} = 13 : 3$

26. (a) Let speed of boat and current be x km/h and y km/h, respectively.

According to the question,

$\frac{25}{x - y} + \frac{39}{x + y} = 8$ ...(i)

and $\dfrac{35}{x-y}+\dfrac{52}{x+y}=11$ ...(ii)

Solving Eqs. (i) and (ii), we get

$x+y=13$ ...(iii)

and $x-y=5$ ...(iv)

To solve of Eqs. (iii) and (iv),

$x=9,\ y=4$

Hence, the speed of current is 4 km/h.

27. (d) Let the speed of boat be x km/h, and speed of stream be y km/h.

According to the question,

$$\frac{4}{x+y}=\frac{3}{x-y}$$

$\Rightarrow\ 4x-4y=3x+3y$

$\Rightarrow\ x=7y$

Now, time to row 48 km upstream + Time to row 48 km downstream = 14 h

$$\frac{48}{x-y}+\frac{48}{x+y}=14$$

$\Rightarrow\ 48(x+y)+48(x-y)=14(x+y)(x-y)$

$\Rightarrow\ 48x+48y+48x-48y=14(x^2-y^2)$

$\Rightarrow\ 96x=14((7y)^2-y^2)\ [\because x=7y]$

$\Rightarrow\ 96\times 7y=14\times 48y^2$

$\Rightarrow\ \dfrac{96\times 7}{14\times 48}=y\Rightarrow\ y=1$ km/h

28. (a) Given, speed of boat in still water

$=21\frac{3}{2}$ km/h $=22.5$ km/h

Speed of river = 12.5 km/h

$\therefore$ Speed of boat in upstream

$=(22.5-12.5)=10$ km/h

$\Rightarrow$ speed of boat in downstream

$=(22.5+12.5)=35$ km/h

Let, the place be x km far off.

Now, time to travel upstream + time to travel downstream = 40 min

$\Rightarrow \dfrac{x}{10}+\dfrac{x}{35}=\dfrac{40}{60}\ \Rightarrow\ \dfrac{35x+10x}{350}=\dfrac{4}{6}$

$\Rightarrow\ 45x=\dfrac{4\times 350}{6}\ \Rightarrow x=\dfrac{140}{27}$ km

$\therefore\ x=5\frac{5}{27}$ km

29. (c) Given, speed of boat in still water

$=5\frac{1}{3}$ km/h $=\dfrac{16}{3}$ km/h

$=\dfrac{16}{3}\times\dfrac{5}{18}=\dfrac{40}{27}$ m/s

Let the speed of the river stream be x m/s and the distance be d m.

According to the question,

$$3\times\frac{d}{\left(x+\frac{40}{27}\right)}=\frac{d}{\left(\frac{40}{27}-x\right)}$$

$\Rightarrow\ 3x+x=\dfrac{40}{9}-\dfrac{40}{27}\Rightarrow 4x=\dfrac{80}{27}$

$\therefore\ x=\dfrac{20}{27}$ m/s

30. (d) Let the swimmer's speed = x m/min.

and current's speed = y m/min

Given, $6(x+y)-6(x-y)=120$

$\Rightarrow\ 6x+6y-6x+6y=120$

$\Rightarrow\ 12y=120\Rightarrow y=\dfrac{120}{12}=10$

So, speed of the current = 10 m/min.

$=10\times\dfrac{60}{1000}$ km/h = 0.6 km/h

31. (b) Let the distance be d km.

Let the speed of boat in still water be x km/h and speed of the current be y km/h.

According to the question,

$x+y=\dfrac{d}{9}$ ...(i)

and $x-y=\dfrac{d}{18}$ ...(ii)

Added Eqs. (i) and (ii),

$2x=\dfrac{d}{9}+\dfrac{d}{18}=\dfrac{d}{6}$

$\therefore\ x=\dfrac{d}{12}$

Now, time taken to cover $\frac{3}{5}$th of the same distance in still water,

$t=\dfrac{(3/5)d}{x}=\dfrac{3\times d\times 12}{5\times d}=\dfrac{36}{5}$

$\therefore\ t=7.2$ h.

32. (c) Let speed of flow of river = y

When boat move downstream = $20+y$

When boat move upstream = $20-y$

Time = $\dfrac{\text{Distance}}{\text{Speed}}$

$\Rightarrow\ 16=\dfrac{150}{(20+y)}+\dfrac{150}{(20-y)}$

$\Rightarrow\ 16=\dfrac{150(20-y)+150(20+y)}{(20)^2-y^2}$

$[\because a^2-b^2=(a+b)(a-b)]$

$\Rightarrow 16\times 20^2-16y^2$

$=150\times 20-150y+150\times 20+150y$

$\Rightarrow\ 16\times 400-16y^2=3000+3000$

$\Rightarrow\ 16y^2=6400-6000$

$\Rightarrow\ y^2=25\ \Rightarrow\ y=5$ km/h

Speedy Method

Given, $D=150$ km, $x=20$ km/h, $T=16$ h,

$\therefore\ 150=\dfrac{16[(20)^2-y^2]}{2\times 20}$

$\dfrac{150\times 40}{16}=(20)^2-y^2$

$y^2=25\Rightarrow y=5$ km/h

33. (d) Let distance be a.

According to the question,

Speed of boat is x and stream = y

Speed = $\dfrac{\text{Distance}}{\text{Time}}$

So, $\dfrac{a}{x+y}+\dfrac{a}{x-y}=T$ ...(i)

If speed is 2 times, time will be $\dfrac{80}{161}T$

$\dfrac{a}{2x+y}+\dfrac{a}{2x-y}=\dfrac{80}{161}T$ ...(ii)

From Eqs. (i) and (ii),

$$\frac{\dfrac{a}{(x+y)}+\dfrac{a}{(x-y)}}{\dfrac{a}{(2x+y)}+\dfrac{a}{(2x-y)}}=\frac{T}{\frac{80}{161}T}$$

$$\Rightarrow\ \frac{\dfrac{(x-y+x+y)}{(x+y)(x-y)}}{\dfrac{(2x-y+2x+y)}{(2x+y)(2x-y)}}=\frac{161}{80}$$

$\Rightarrow\ \dfrac{2x}{(x+y)(x-y)}\times\dfrac{(2x-y)(2x-y)}{4x}=\dfrac{161}{80}$

$\Rightarrow\ 40(4x^2-y^2)=161(x^2-y^2)$

$\Rightarrow\ 160x^2-40y^2=161x^2-161y^2$

$\Rightarrow\ x^2=121y^2\Rightarrow \dfrac{x^2}{y^2}=\dfrac{121}{1}$

$\Rightarrow\ \dfrac{x}{y}=\sqrt{\dfrac{121}{1}}=\dfrac{11}{1}=11:1$

Speedy Method

According to the question,

We know that, $D=\dfrac{T(x^2-y^2)}{2x}$

$D=T\left(\dfrac{x^2-y^2}{2x}\right)$ ...(i)

$D=\dfrac{80T}{161}\dfrac{[(2x)^2-y^2]}{2(2x)}$

$D=\dfrac{80T}{161}\dfrac{(4x^2-y^2)}{4x}$ ...(ii)

On dividing Eqs. (i) and (ii), we get

$\dfrac{x^2-y^2}{4x^2-y^2}\times 2=\dfrac{80}{161}$

$161x^2-161y^2=160x^2-40y^2$

$x^2=121y^2\Rightarrow\left(\dfrac{x}{y}\right)^2=\left(\dfrac{11}{1}\right)^2$

$\therefore\ x:y=11:1$

34. (b) Let upstream speed = U km/h

Downstream speed = D km/h

According to the question,

$\dfrac{5}{U}+\dfrac{\frac{15}{2}}{D}=\dfrac{45}{60}$ ...(i)

and $\dfrac{2.5}{U}+\dfrac{5}{D}=\dfrac{25}{60}$ ...(ii)

Eq. (ii) multiply by 2 – Eq. (i),

$\dfrac{5}{U}+\dfrac{10}{D}-\dfrac{5}{U}-\dfrac{7.5}{D}=\dfrac{50}{60}-\dfrac{45}{60}$

$\Rightarrow\ \dfrac{2.5}{D}=\dfrac{5}{60}\Rightarrow D=30$ km/h

Time will take to cover 6 km downstream.

Time = $\dfrac{\text{Distance}}{\text{Speed}}=\dfrac{6}{30}$

$=\dfrac{1}{5}$ h $=12$ min

35. (b) Let the speed of boat = x km/h and the speed of current = y km/h

We know that, Speed = $\frac{\text{Distance}}{\text{Time}}$

According to the question,

$$\frac{8}{x+y} = \frac{6}{x-y} \Rightarrow 8x - 8y = 6x + 6y$$

$$\Rightarrow 2x = 14y \Rightarrow x = 7y$$

Now, $\frac{24}{(x-y)} + \frac{24}{(x+y)} = \frac{7}{4}$

$$\Rightarrow \frac{24(x+y+x-y)}{(x^2-y^2)} = \frac{7}{4} \Rightarrow \frac{24(2x)}{(x^2-y^2)} = \frac{7}{4}$$

$$\Rightarrow \frac{24 \times 2 \times 7y}{(7y)^2 - y^2} = \frac{7}{4} \Rightarrow \frac{48 \times 7y}{48y^2} = \frac{7}{4}$$

$$\therefore \quad y = 4 \text{ km/h}$$

36. (c) Let downstream speed = x

Upstream speed = y

According to the question,

$$\frac{33}{x} + \frac{27}{y} = 6 \quad \text{...(i)}$$

and $$\frac{22}{x} + \frac{36}{y} = 6 \quad \text{...(ii)}$$

From Eqs. (i) and (ii),

$y = 9$ and $x = 11$

$\therefore$ Required time $= \frac{36}{y} + \frac{44}{x}$

$$= \frac{36}{9} + \frac{44}{11} = 4 + 4 = 8 \text{ h}$$

37. (b) Let the speed of boat in still water and speed of current are B and S respectively.

According to the question,

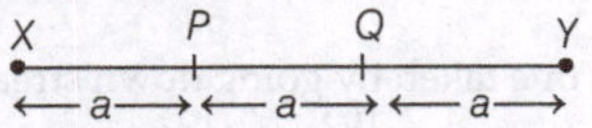

Speed = $\frac{\text{Distance}}{\text{Time}}$

Boat row from X to Q that means distance $= 2a$

$$\Rightarrow \quad \text{Time} = \frac{2a}{B+S}$$

Boat row from Y to Q opposite the stream.

$$\Rightarrow \quad \text{Time} = \frac{a}{B-S}$$

Time ratio of X to Q and Y to $Q = 4:5$

$$\Rightarrow \frac{\frac{2a}{B+S}}{\frac{a}{B-S}} = \frac{4}{5} \Rightarrow \frac{2\times(B-S)}{(B+S)} = \frac{4}{5}$$

$$\Rightarrow 5(B-S) = 2(B+S) \Rightarrow 5B - 5S = 2B + 2S$$

$$\Rightarrow 3B = 7S \Rightarrow \frac{B}{S} = \frac{7}{3}$$

$\therefore$ $\frac{\text{Speed of boat in downstream}}{\text{River current}}$

$$= \frac{B+S}{S} = \frac{7+3}{3} = \frac{10}{3} = 10:3$$

38. (b) Let upstream = U km/h and

Downstream = D km/h

We know that, Speed = $\frac{\text{Distance}}{\text{Time}}$

$$\frac{3.6}{U} + \frac{5.4}{D} = 54 \text{ min} \quad \text{..(i)}$$

$$\frac{5.4}{U} + \frac{3.6}{D} = 58.5 \text{ min} \quad \text{...(ii)}$$

Both equation divide by 1.8

$$\frac{2}{U} + \frac{3}{D} = \frac{30}{60} = \frac{1}{2} \text{ h} \quad \text{...(iii)}$$

$$\frac{3}{U} + \frac{2}{D} = 32.5 \text{ min}$$

$$= \frac{32.5}{60} = \frac{13}{24} \text{ h} \quad \text{...(iv)}$$

Multiply Eq. (iii) by 3 and Eq. (iv) by 2 and subtract, we get $D = 12$ km/h

Thus time taken to cover 10 km in downstream $= \frac{10}{12} \times 60 = 50$ min

39. (d) Let the speed of boat be $35x$ and that of water current $= 8x$

Upstream speed $= 35x - 8x = 27x$

Downstream speed $= 35x + 8x = 43x$

Time = 5 h 10 min = 310 min

Now, according to the question,

$$D = 310 \times 43x \quad \text{...(i)}$$

Now, let the time taken to go upstream $= T$

$$D = 27x \times T \quad \text{...(ii)}$$

From Eqs. (i) and (ii),

$$27x \times T = 310 \times 43x$$

$$T = 493.7 \text{ min} \Rightarrow T = 8.228 \text{ h}$$

$\therefore$ $T = 8$ h 13 min 48 sec

40. (d) Let the speed of boat be 'a' km/h and the speed of stream be 'b' km/h.

Upstream speed $=(a-b)$ km/h

Downstream speed $= (a+b)$ km/h

According to the question,

$$\frac{4}{a+b} = \frac{3}{a-b}$$

$$\Rightarrow \quad a = 7b \quad \text{...(i)}$$

and $$\frac{48}{a+b} + \frac{48}{a-b} = 48 \text{ h}$$

$$\Rightarrow \quad \frac{1}{8b} + \frac{1}{6b} = 1 \quad \text{[From Eq. (i)]}$$

$$\Rightarrow \quad \frac{3+4}{24b} = 1 \Rightarrow b = \frac{7}{24}$$

$\therefore$ Speed of the stream $= \frac{7}{24}$ km/h

41. (a) Given, upstream speed (U) = 27 km/h and downstream speed (D) = 33 km/h

$\therefore$ Speed of boat in still water

$$= \frac{U+D}{2} = \frac{27+33}{2} = 30 \text{ km/h}$$

42. (a) Let the speed of boat be x km/h.

The speed of stream $= y = 3$ km/h

According to the question,

$$x + y = \frac{16.9}{52} \times 60$$

$$x = 19.5 - 3 \Rightarrow x = 16.5 \text{ km/h}$$

Let the time taken by boat to travel 84 km upstream be t h.

$$x - y = \frac{84}{t}$$

$$16.5 - 3 = \frac{84}{t} \Rightarrow t = \frac{84}{13.5} \Rightarrow t = 6.22 \text{ h}$$

43. (d) Let the speed of boat $= B$ km/h and speed of current/stream $= S$ km/h

According to the question,

$$\frac{24}{B-S} + \frac{36}{B+S} = 10$$

Let $\frac{1}{B-S} = a$ and $\frac{1}{B+S} = b$

So, $$24a + 36b = 10$$

$$\Rightarrow \quad 12a + 18b = 5 \quad \text{...(i)}$$

Now, $\frac{36}{B-S} + \frac{24}{B+S} = 12$

$$\Rightarrow \quad 36a + 24b = 12$$

$$\Rightarrow \quad 9a + 6b = 3 \quad \text{...(ii)}$$

On solving Eqs. (i) and (ii), we get

$$a = \frac{4}{15} \text{ and } b = \frac{1}{10}$$

$$\Rightarrow \quad B - S = \frac{15}{4}$$

...(iii)

And $B + S = 10$ ...(iv)

On solving Eqs. (iii) and (iv),

$$2B = \frac{15}{4} + 10 \Rightarrow 2B = \frac{55}{4} \Rightarrow B = \frac{55}{8} \text{ km/h}$$

$$\therefore \quad S = 10 - \frac{55}{8} = \frac{80-55}{8} = \frac{25}{8} \text{ km/h}$$

(speed of current)

44. (c) Let the speed of boat be 'B' km/h and that of stream be 'S' km/h.

Now, according to the question,

$$\frac{2}{\frac{10}{60}} = B + S$$

$$\Rightarrow \quad B + S = 12 \text{ km/h} \quad \text{...(i)}$$

and $$\frac{12}{2} = B - S$$

$$\Rightarrow \quad B - S = 6 \text{ km/h} \quad \text{...(ii)}$$

Adding Eqs. (i) and (ii), we get

$$B = 9 \text{ km/h}$$

$\therefore$ Speed of stream $= S = 12 - B$

$$= 12 - 9 = 3 \text{ km/h}$$

45. (d) Let the speed of stream/current be x km/h.

$\therefore$ Speed of boat $= (x + 4)$ km/h

Now, according to the question,

$$\frac{45}{x + (x+4)} + \frac{35}{4} = 10$$

$$\Rightarrow \quad \frac{45}{2x+4} = 10 - \frac{35}{4} \Rightarrow \frac{45}{2x+4} = \frac{5}{4}$$

$$\Rightarrow \quad 2x + 4 = 36 \Rightarrow 2x = 32 \Rightarrow x = 16$$

Hence, speed of man in still water

$$= x + 4 = 16 + 4 = 20 \text{ km/h}$$

46. (b) Let the speed of stream = S

Speed of boat (B) $= \frac{7.5 \text{ km}}{1 \text{ h}} = 7.5$ km/h

According to the question,

$$\frac{\text{Distance}}{B-S} = 4 \times \frac{(\text{Distance})}{B+S}$$

$\Rightarrow$ $(B+S) = 4(B-S) \Rightarrow 3B = 5S$

$\therefore$ $S = \frac{3B}{5} \Rightarrow S = \frac{3 \times 7.5}{5} = 4.5$ km/h

$\therefore$ Speed of stream = 4.5 km/h.

47. (d) Speed of man in still water

$= \frac{1}{12} \times 60 = 5$ km/h

Let speed of water = x km/h

Now, $\frac{1}{5-x} = \frac{13}{60}$

$\Rightarrow$ $65 - 13x = 60 \Rightarrow x = \frac{5}{13}$ km/ h

48. (c) Let the speed of the boat in still water = x km/h

and the speed of the stream = y km/h

According to the question,

$x - y = 8$ ....(i)

and $x + y = 15$ ...(ii)

Adding Eqs. (i) and (ii),

$2x = 23$

$\Rightarrow$ $x = \frac{23}{2} = 11.5$ km/h

Subtract Eqs. (i) and (ii),

$2y = 7 \Rightarrow y = \frac{7}{2} = 3.5$ km/h

49. (d) We know, Time = $\frac{\text{Distance}}{\text{Speed}}$

Then, time taken by the boat to go 110 km

downstream = $\frac{110}{17+5} = \frac{110}{22} = 5$ h

50. (c) We knowt that,

$$\text{Time} = \frac{\text{Distance}}{\text{Time}}$$

Given, d = 60 km downward and 60 km upwards speed of boat in still water

= 15 km/h

and speed of current = 5 km/h

So, time = $\frac{60}{15+5} + \frac{60}{15-5}$

$= \frac{60}{20} + \frac{60}{10} = 3 + 6 = 9$ h

51. (a) Speed of stream = Speed of boat in still water − Speed upstream = 3 − 1= 2 km/h

52. (b) Given, speed of boat in still water

= 8 km/h

Let the speed of stream be x km/h.

According to the question,

$$\frac{\text{Distance}}{8-x} = 3\left(\frac{\text{Distance}}{8+x}\right)$$

$\Rightarrow$ $\frac{1}{8-x} = \frac{3}{8+x}$

$\Rightarrow$ $8 + x = 24 - 3x \Rightarrow 4x = 16$

$\therefore$ $x = 4$ km/h

53. (c) According to the question,

Speed of boat in downstream

= (12 + 3) = 15 km/h

Speed of boat in upstream

= (12 − 3) = 9 km/h

Required time to travel 45 km

$= \frac{45}{15} + \frac{45}{9} = 3 + 5 = 8$ h

$\therefore$ Required time taken = 8 h

54. (b) Let the upstream and downstream speeds be $2x$ and $3x$, respectively.

According to the question,

$2x + 3x = 15 \Rightarrow 5x = 15 \Rightarrow x = 3$

$\therefore$ Upstream speed = 2 × 3 = 6 km/h

Downstream speed = 3 × 3 = 9 km/h

$\therefore$ Required speed of streams

$= \frac{1}{2}$(Downstream speed − Upstream speed)

$= \frac{1}{2}(9-6) = \frac{1}{2} \times 3 = 1.5$ km/h

55. (a) Speed of the boat in still water

= 13 km/h

Let the speed of water is y km/h.

According to the question,

$\frac{60}{13+y} = 4 \Rightarrow 15 = 13 + y$

$\Rightarrow$ $y = 2$ km/h

$\therefore$ Time taken to cover 30 km upstream

$= \frac{30}{(13-2)} = \frac{30}{11} = 2\frac{8}{11}$ h

56. (b) Let rate of stream = a km/h

$\therefore$ Rate of downstream = $(18 + a)$ km/h

Rate of upstream = $(18 - a)$ km/h

According to the question,

$\frac{18+a}{y} = 2\frac{(18-a)}{y}$

$\Rightarrow$ $18 + a = 36 - 2a$

$\Rightarrow$ $3a = 18 \Rightarrow a = 6$ km/h

Hence, the rate of stream is 6 km/h.

57. (c) Let speed of boat be x km/h and speed of current (water) be y km/h.

$\therefore$ Upstream speed = $\frac{3}{1} = 3$

$x - y = 3$ ... (i)

Downstream speed = $\frac{1}{12/60} = 5$

$x + y = 5$ ... (ii)

Solving both Eqs. (i) and (ii), we get

$x = 4$ km/h and $y = 1$ km/h

$\therefore$ Time taken by boat in stationary water to go 6 km = $\frac{6}{4} = 1.5$ h = 1 h 30 min

58. (b) Let the speed of the ship in still water

= x km/h

and the speed of the water flow = y km/h

According to the question,

$x + y = 18$ ...(i) (Downstream)

and $x - y = 16$ ...(ii) (Upstream)

By Eqs. (i) and (ii),

$x = \frac{18+16}{2} = 17$ km/h

So, the speed of the ship 17 km/h.

59. (c) Watercraft's downstream speed

$= \frac{32}{4} = 8$ km/h

Watercraft's upstream speed = $\frac{10}{5} = 2$ km/h

Watercraft's speed = $\frac{1}{2}(8+2) = 5$ km/h

River's speed = $\frac{1}{2}(8-2) = 3$ km/h

60. (c) Let the speed of boat in Still water be x km/h.

According to the question,

$(x-2) = \frac{20}{\frac{5}{4}} = 16 \Rightarrow x = 16 + 2$

$\therefore$ $x = 18$ km/h

$\therefore$ Time taken to row the boat 30 km

downstream = $\frac{30}{18+2} = \frac{30}{20} = 1.5$ h

= 1 h 30 min

61. (d) Downstream speed

= 19 + 3 = 22 km/h

Upstream speed = 19 − 3 = 16 km/h

$\therefore$ Required time = $\frac{24}{16} + \frac{88}{22} = 1.5 + 4 = 5.5$ h

62. (a) Distance in downstream

$= (12 + 3) \times \frac{24}{60} = 6$ km

63. (a) Time taken by going down stream

$= \frac{192}{(28+4)} = \frac{192}{32}$ h = 6 h

Time taken by going upstream

$= \frac{192}{28-4} = \frac{192}{24}$ h = 8 h

Average speed of boat

$= \frac{\text{Total distance covered}}{\text{Total time taken}}$

$= \frac{384}{6+1+8} = \frac{384}{15} = 25.6$

64. (d) Speed of boat in down stream

= (15 + 3) km/h = 18 km/h

$\therefore$ Distance covered in downstream in

12 min = $18 \times \frac{12}{60} = 3.6$ km

65. (d) Given, time taken to travel B to A and A to B = 3 h

Speed of boat in still water = 9 km/h

Speed of current = 3.5 km/h

Let distance between A and B be x km.

According to the question,

$\frac{x}{9+3.5} + \frac{x}{9-3.5} = 3$

$\Rightarrow$ $\frac{x}{12.5} + \frac{x}{5.5} = 3$

$\Rightarrow \quad 110x + 250x = 4125$

$\therefore \quad x = 11.46$ km

Speedy Method

$$D = \frac{[(9)^2 - (3.5)^2] \times 3}{2 \times 9} = \frac{68.75 \times 3}{18}$$

$D = 11.46$ km

66. (c) Given, A man rows to a place at a distance of 72 km and comes back in 36 h.

Let man rows 12 km downstream in x h.

$\therefore$ Downstream speed $= \frac{12}{x}$ km/h

Upstream speed $= \frac{4}{x}$ km/h

According to the question,

$$36 = \frac{72}{\frac{12}{x}} + \frac{72}{\frac{4}{x}}$$

$$\Rightarrow \quad 36 = \frac{72x}{12} + \frac{72x}{4}$$

$\Rightarrow 36 = 6x + 18x \Rightarrow 24x = 36 \Rightarrow x = 1.5$

Downstream speed $= \frac{12}{1.5} = 8$ km/h

Upstream speed $= \frac{4}{1.5} = 2.66$ km/h

$\therefore$ Speed of stream $= \frac{1}{2}[8 - 2.66] = \frac{1}{2}(5.34)$

$= 2.67$ km/h

67. (a) Let speed of boat in still water be x km/h and distance travelled be 'D'.

$\therefore$ Upstream speed $= (x - 6)$ km/h

Downstream speed $= (x + 6)$ km/h

According to the question,

$$5 = \frac{D}{x+6}$$

$\Rightarrow \quad D = 5x + 30 \quad$ ...(i)

Also, $\quad 8 = \frac{D}{x-6}$

$\Rightarrow \quad D = 8x - 48 \quad$ ...(ii)

From Eqs. (i) and (ii),

$5x + 30 = 8x - 48$

$\Rightarrow \quad 3x = 78 \Rightarrow x = 26$ km/h

68. (d) Let speed of boat and current be x km/h and y km/h, respectively.

According to the question,

$$\frac{36}{x+y} + \frac{24}{x-y} = 6 \quad \text{...(i)}$$

and $$\frac{24}{x+y} + \frac{36}{x-y} = \frac{13}{2} \quad \text{...(ii)}$$

Solving Eqs. (i) and (ii), we get

$x + y = 12 \quad$ ...(iii)

and $\quad x - y = 8 \quad$ ...(iv)

Solving Eqs. (iii) and (iv) we get,

$x = 10, \ y = 2$

$\therefore$ Speed of current is 2 km/h.

69. (b) Given, speed of stream $(y) = 5$ km/h

Speed of boat in still water $(x) = 10$ km/h

Let the distance from A to B be 'M'.

As C, the mid-point between A and B, then distance from B to $C = \frac{M}{2}$

According to the question,

$$\frac{M}{x+y} + \frac{M}{2(x-y)} = 20$$

Putting, $x = 10$ and $y = 5$

$$\frac{M}{10+5} + \frac{M}{2(10-5)} = 20$$

$$\Rightarrow \quad \frac{M}{15} + \frac{M}{2(5)} = 20 \Rightarrow \frac{25M}{150} = 20$$

$\therefore \quad M = 120$ km

70. (c) Upstream speed $= \frac{5}{15}$ km/min

$= 5 \times \frac{60}{15} = 20$ km/h

Let the speed of the boat in still water and speed of stream be $6x$ km/h and x km/h, respectively.

$\therefore \quad 6x - x = 20 \Rightarrow x = \frac{20}{5} = 4$ km/h

$\therefore$ Downstream speed $= 6x + x = 7x$

$= 7 \times 4 = 28$ km/h

$\therefore$ Required time taken $= \frac{19.6}{28} \times 60 = 42$ min

71. (d) $\because$ Distance $(D) = 54$ km

Let the old speed $= x$ km/h

Now, new speed $= (x + 3)$ km/h

According to the question,

$$\frac{54}{x} - \frac{54}{x+3} = 3 \Rightarrow \frac{54(x+3-x)}{x(x+3)} = 3$$

$\Rightarrow \quad x(x+3) = 54 \Rightarrow x^2 + 3x - 54 = 0$

$\Rightarrow \quad x^2 + 9x - 6x - 54 = 0$

$\Rightarrow \quad (x+9)(x-6) = 0$

$\Rightarrow \quad x = -9 \quad$ (not possible)

So, $\quad x = 6$

$\therefore$ Speed of boat is 6 km/h.

72. (a) Given, speed of boat in still water $= 15$ km/h

and speed of the stream $= 3$ km/h

$\therefore$ Speed of boat in upstream

$= 15 - 3 = 12$ km/h

Time taken by boat to cover 6 km upstream

$= \frac{6}{12} = \frac{1}{2}$ h $= 30$ min

73. (c) Upstream speed $= 30 - 2 = 28$ km/h

Hence, required time $= \frac{56}{28} = 2$ h

74. (b) Time taken in upstream $= \frac{90}{8-2} = 15$ h

Time taken in downstream $= \frac{90}{8+2} = 9$ h

Hence, total time $= 15 + 9 = 24$ h

75. (d) Let the speed of boat be x km/h.

According to the question,

$$\frac{40}{(x+2)} + \frac{40}{(x-2)} = 10$$

$$\Rightarrow \quad \frac{(x-2)\,40 + (x+2) \times 40}{x^2 - 4} = 10$$

$\Rightarrow \quad 40x - 80 + 40x + 80 = 10x^2 - 40$

$\Rightarrow \quad 80x = 10x^2 - 40 \Rightarrow 10x^2 - 80x - 40 = 0$

$\Rightarrow \quad x^2 - 8x - 4 = 0$

Using formula

$$x = \frac{-b \pm \sqrt{b^2 - 4ac}}{2a}$$

$$\Rightarrow \quad x = \frac{(8 \pm \sqrt{80})}{2} \Rightarrow x = \frac{(8 \pm 4\sqrt{5})}{2}$$

$\Rightarrow \quad x = 4 \pm 2\sqrt{5}$

So, speed of the boat in still water

$= 4 + 2\sqrt{5} = 8.47$ km/h

[As, $x = 4 - 2\sqrt{5}$ is negative quantity]

17

Work and Time

Time Time is the duration in which any activity or work can be completed.

Work It is a task to achieve a certain result.

> **Important Facts and Formulae**
>
> - If a person can do a work in n days then, that person's 1 day's work $= \frac{1}{n}$
> - If A can do a piece of work in x days and B can do the same work in y days then, $(A+B)$'s 1 day's work $= \frac{1}{x} + \frac{1}{y} = \frac{x+y}{xy}$
>
>   Time taken by $(A+B)$ to complete the work $= \frac{xy}{x+y}$
> - If A and B can complete a work in x days and A alone can complete that work in y days, then the number of days required to complete the work by $B = \frac{xy}{y-x}$ days

Ex. 1 *A* can finish a piece of work by working alone in 6 days; while working alone *B*, can finish the same work in 12 days. If both of them work together, then in how many days, the work will be completed?

Sol. Here, $X = 6, Y = 12$

$\therefore$ Time taken by $(A+B)$ to complete the task $= \left(\frac{6 \times 12}{6+12}\right) = 4$ days

Based on Efficiency

Efficiency of work means how much work one person can do in one day. Efficiency is inversely proportional to time when work is constant.

$$\text{Efficiency} \propto \frac{1}{\text{Time}}$$

- If a person is n times efficient than the second person, then work done by first person : second person $= n:1$

  and time to complete the work by first person : second person $= 1:n$
- If x takes a days more to complete a work than the time taken by $(x+y)$ to do same work and y takes b days more than the time taken by $(x+y)$ to do the same work, then $(x+y)$ do the work in $\sqrt{ab}$ days.

Ex. 2 *A* and *B* together can do a piece of work in 3 days. If *A* does thrice as much work as *B* in a given time, then find how long *A* alone would take to do the work?

Sol. Let *A* and *B* takes x and $3x$ days, respectively.

According to the question,

$$\frac{1}{x} + \frac{1}{3x} = \frac{1}{3} \Rightarrow \frac{3+1}{3x} = \frac{1}{3} \Rightarrow x = 4$$

$\therefore$ *A* will complete the entire work in 4 days.

Based on MDH Formula

If M_1 persons can do W_1 work in D_1 days working H_1 hours in a day and earns a sum R_1 and M_2 persons can do W_2 work in D_2 days working H_2 hours in a day and earns a sum R_2, then the relationship between them is $\frac{M_1D_1H_1}{W_1 \times R_1} = \frac{M_2D_2H_2}{W_2 \times R_2}$

Ex. 3 If 10 persons can complete $\frac{2}{5}$ of a work in 8 days, then find out the number of persons required to complete the remaining work in 12 days.

Sol. Using MDH formula,

$$\frac{M_1D_1}{W_1} = \frac{M_2D_2}{W_2} \Rightarrow \frac{10 \times 8}{\frac{2}{5}} = \frac{M_2 \times 12}{\frac{3}{5}}$$

$$\Rightarrow M_2 = \frac{10 \times 8 \times 3}{2 \times 12} = 10$$

Based on Salary/Wages

Wages/Salary of a person is divided in the ratio of their efficiencies.

Ex. 4 *A* and *B* together finished the work in 12 days and earned ₹ 24000. *A* is 3 times as efficient as *B*. *A*'s share is

Sol. According to the question,

$$\text{eff}_A : \text{eff}_B = 3:1$$

$\therefore$ *A*'s share $= \frac{3}{4} \times 24000 =$ ₹ 18000

SSC Exam Scanner

SSC CGL 2024 & 2023 (Tier I & II)

1. Rani and Adya, working separately, can finish a task in 12 days and 16 days, respectively. They work in stretches of one day alternately. If Rani starts working first, then the task will be completed in **SSC CGL (Tier II) 18/01/2025 Shift-I**

(a) $12\frac{1}{3}$ days (b) $13\frac{2}{3}$ days
(c) $13\frac{1}{3}$ days (d) $12\frac{2}{3}$ days

2. Varun and Raju, working together, can complete a job in 40 h, whereas Varun alone can complete the same job in 50 h. The number of hours required by Raju to complete the job alone is **SSC CGL (Tier I) 26/9/2024 Shift-II**

(a) 200 (b) 150 (c) 170 (d) 190

3. A and B can do a work in 12 days and 16 days, respectively. If they work together for 6 days, then the fraction of the work left is......... . **SSC CGL (Tier I) 19/9/2024 Shift-II**

(a) $\frac{5}{7}$ (b) $\frac{7}{8}$ (c) $\frac{1}{8}$ (d) $\frac{1}{7}$

4. Rajesh, in his printing press, got an order to print some books, out of which he completed $\frac{17}{27}$ of the order in 34 days. In how many days did he complete the entire order of printing? **SSC CGL (Tier I) 09/09/2024 Shift-I**

(a) 60 (b) 20 (c) 54 (d) 56

5. Working for 10 h per day, 6 men can build a wall in a certain number of days. By working for how many hours/minutes per day can 12 men build the wall in the same days? **SSC CGL (Tier-II) 07/03/2023 Shift-I**

(a) 10 h (b) 7 h 30 min
(c) 20 h (d) 5 h

6. P, Q and R can finish a work in 5 days, 10 days, and 15 days, respectively, working alone. P and Q works on first day, P and R works on second day and P and Q works on third day and so on till the work is completed. In how many days the work will be completed? **SSC CGL (Tier-II) 07/03/2023 Shift-I**

(a) $\frac{5}{2}$ (b) $\frac{13}{2}$ (c) $\frac{7}{2}$ (d) $\frac{9}{2}$

7. A and B can complete a work together in 48 days. A is 4 times as work efficient as B. In how many days can B alone complete the work? **SSC CGL (Tier-II) 06/03/2023 Shift-I**

(a) 220 days (b) 320 days
(c) 240 days (d) 120 days

8. A can finish a job in 8 h and B can finish the same job in 12 h independently. If they work simultaneously, in how many hours can they do the same job? **SSC CGL (Tier-I) 27/07/2023 Shift-III**

(a) 4.8 (b) 3.7 (c) 4.5 (d) 3.2

9. Ram can complete a piece work in 15 days, Rohan in 25 days and Rohit in 30 days. Rohan and Rohit worked together for 2 days and then Rohit was replaced by Ram. In how many days altogether was the work completed? **SSC CGL (Tier-I) 27/07/2023 Shift-III**

(a) 10 days (b) 8 days
(c) 12 days (d) 7 days

10. Sara can finish a work in 18 days and Tara can complete the same work in 15 days. Tara worked for 10 days and left the job. In how many days can Sara finish the remaining work alone? **SSC CGL (Tier-I) 27/07/2023 Shift-III**

(a) 6 (b) 7 (c) 8 (d) 5

11. 40 men can complete a work in 30 days. However, if 10 men leave the group, how many days will the group take to complete the work? **SSC CGL (Tier-I) 27/07/2023 Shift-III**

(a) 40 (b) 35 (c) 45 (d) 50

12. Benny can do a piece of work in 24 days. Chethan and David can do the same work individually in 36 and 48 days, respectively. All of them begin the work together. However, Benny leaves the work 4 days before the completion of work and Chethan leaves the work 10 days before the completion of the work. David worked till the end and completed the work. Find the number of days in which the work was completed. **SSC CGL (Tier-I) 27/07/2023 Shift-II**

(a) 16 (b) 20 (c) 18 (d) 15

13. A, B and C can do a piece of work in 20, 30 and 60 days, respectively. In how many days can A do the work if he is assisted by both B and C on every third day? **SSC CGL (Tier-I) 27/07/2023 Shift-II**

(a) 10 (b) 15 (c) 12 (d) 18

14. Ram and Ramesh can do a work in 12 days, Ramesh and Somesh in 15 days and Somesh and Ram in 10 days. If Ram, Ramesh and Somesh work together, in how many days will they complete the work? **SSC CGL (Tier-I) 27/07/2023 Shift-II**

(a) 10 (b) 8 (c) 12 (d) 6

15. P, Q and R can complete a piece of work in 9, 12 and 18 days, respectively. Working together, how much work can they complete in one day? **SSC CGL (Tier-I) 27/07/2023 Shift-II**

(a) $\frac{2}{3}$ (b) $\frac{1}{2}$ (c) $\frac{1}{3}$ (d) $\frac{1}{4}$

16. Ashok and Anil undertake to do a piece of work for ₹ 4500. Ashok alone could do the work in the 8 days and Anil in 12 days. With the assistance of Amar, they finished the work in 4 days. What is the share of Amar? **SSC CGL (Tier-I) 27/07/2023 Shift-I**

(a) ₹ 1500 (b) ₹ 750
(c) ₹ 2250 (d) ₹ 2500

17. A man, a woman and a boy can complete a job in 3, 5 and 15 days. respectively. How many boys must assist 1 man and 1 woman to complete the job in $\frac{1}{5}$ of a day? **SSC CGL (Tier-I) 27/07/2023 Shift-I**

(a) 67 (b) 35 (c) 56 (d) 47

18. Ramesh alone can complete a work in 24 days. Ramesh and Somesh can complete it in 8 days. How long will Somesh alone take to complete the work? **SSC CGL (Tier-I) 26/07/2023 Shift-IV**

(a) 10 days (b) 15 days
(c) 14 days (d) 12 days

19. 15 men complete a work in 10 days. 15 women complete the same work in 12 days. If all these men and women work together, then the number of days required to complete that work is **SSC CGL (Tier-I) 26/07/2023 Shift-IV**

(a) $5\frac{5}{11}$ (b) $4\frac{3}{11}$
(c) $7\frac{2}{11}$ (d) $6\frac{4}{11}$

20. 10 women take 16 days to complete a work which can be completed by 6 men in 8 days. 12 men started working and after 2 days 6 men left and 5 women joined them. In how many days will the work be completed?
SSC CGL (Tier-I) 26/07/2023 Shift-III
(a) $\frac{3}{2}$ (b) $\frac{16}{5}$ (c) $\frac{5}{2}$ (d) $\frac{26}{5}$

21. A, B and C can finish a work in 15 days working alternately in the same order. The efficiency of A is the same as that of B and the efficiency of C is equal to that of A. In how many days will the work be finished if they work alternately in the order C, A and B?
SSC CGL (Tier-I) 26/07/2023 Shift-III
(a) 12 (b) 14 (c) 15 (d) 16

22. X, Y and Z can complete a work in 5 days, 15 days and 30 days, respectively. In how many days can the work be completed if X is assisted by Y and Z together, on every second day?
SSC CGL (Tier-I) 26/07/2023 Shift-III
(a) 5 days (b) 4 days
(c) 7 days (d) 6 days

23. A group of men decided to do a job in 11 days but 16 men left the work after each day. The work, as a result, got completed in 15 days. How many men were there initially in the group?
SSC CGL (Tier-I) 26/07/2023 Shift-I
(a) 400 (b) 480
(c) 420 (d) 450

24. 4 men's work is equal to 6 women's work and 4 women's work is equal to 6 boy's work. A boy can finish the work in 60 days. In how many days can the work be finished by a man and a woman together?
SSC CGL (Tier-I) 26/07/2023 Shift-I
(a) 16 (b) 24
(c) 20 (d) 12

25. 20 women and 15 men together can complete a work in 6 days. It takes 150 days for a single woman to complete the work. In how many days can a single man complete the work?
SSC CGL (Tier-I) 25/07/2023 Shift-IV
(a) 450 (b) 225 (c) 350 (d) 210

26. A group of college students had decided to complete a project in 10 days. As 2 students dropped out every day, the project got completed at the end of the 15th day. The number of students at the beginning of the project was
SSC CGL (Tier-I) 25/07/2023 Shift-IV
(a) 42 (b) 40 (c) 35 (d) 45

27. A is 50% more efficient than B. B worked to finish the same work in 20 days, If A and B worked together, then how much time will they take to finish the same work?
SSC CGL (Tier-I) 25/07/2023 Shift-III
(a) 10 days (b) 7 days
(c) 8 days (d) 9 days

28. A can complete a piece of work in 14 days, while A and B together can complete it in $3\frac{1}{2}$ days. How long will B alone take to complete it?
SSC CGL (Tier-I) 25/07/2023 Shift-III
(a) 4 days (b) 5 days
(c) $\frac{3}{14}$ days (d) $\frac{14}{3}$ days

29. 2 men can finish a work in 6 days and 3 women can finish the same work in 4 days. In how many days will the work be finished by 1 man and 3 women, working together every day?
SSC CGL (Tier-I) 25/07/2023 Shift-III
(a) 4 (b) 6 (c) 8 (d) 9

30. P and Q together complete a job in $4\frac{2}{5}$ days. R and S complete the same job in $4\frac{8}{9}$ days. If P, Q, R and S work together. How many days do they need to complete the same job? **SSC CGL (Tier-I) 25/07/2023 Shift-II**
(a) $2\frac{7}{18}$ (b) $1\frac{7}{18}$
(c) $1\frac{6}{19}$ (d) $2\frac{6}{19}$

31. A can complete $\frac{1}{3}$ of a work in 7 days and B can complete $\frac{2}{7}$ of the same work in 10 days. In how many days can both A and B together complete the work?
SSC CGL (Tier-I) 25/07/2023 Shift-II
(a) $12\frac{3}{8}$ (b) $11\frac{7}{8}$ (c) $13\frac{1}{8}$ (d) $15\frac{1}{7}$

32. A can do $\frac{1}{3}$ of a piece of work in 32 days. B can do $37\frac{1}{2}$% of the same work in 24 days, while C can do 60% of the same work in 48 days. B and C together started and worked for x days. After x days, B left the work and A joined C and both completed the remaining work in $(x + 8)$ days. If the ratio of the work done by $(B + C)$ together to the work done by $(A + C)$ together is $9 : 11$, then what fraction of the same work can be completed by C alone in $3.5x$ days?
SSC CGL (Tier-I) 25/07/2023 Shift-II
(a) $\frac{18}{25}$ (b) $\frac{4}{5}$ (c) $\frac{7}{10}$ (d) $\frac{3}{4}$

33. A can finish a work in 60 days. He works at it for 15 days and then B alone finishes the remaining work in 48 days. In how much time can A and B working together finish the work?
SSC CGL (Tier-I) 25/07/2023 Shift-II
(a) $\frac{960}{31}$ days (b) $\frac{171}{37}$ days
(c) 51 days (d) 45 days

34. A group of men decided to do a job in 13 days but 9 men left the work after each day. The work, as a result, got completed in 16 days. How many men were initially in the group?
SSC CGL (Tier-I) 25/07/2023 Shift-I
(a) 378 (b) 360
(c) 330 (d) 380

35. Raju and Rajat working together take 5 days to complete a piece of work. If Raju alone can do this work in 7 days, how long would Rajat take to complete the same work? **SSC CGL (Tier-I) 25/07/2023 Shift-I**
(a) 18 days (b) 16.5 days
(c) 17 days (d) 17.5 days

36. 4 men and 6 women can complete a work in 8 days, while 3 men and 7 women can complete it in 10 days. In how many days will 25 women complete it?
SSC CGL (Tier-I) 25/07/2023 Shift-I
(a) 20 (b) 16 (c) 25 (d) 18

37. R, S and T can finish a work in 20, 15 and 10 days, respectively. R works on all days and S and T work on alternate days with T starting the work on the first day. In how many days is the work finished?
SSC CGL (Tier-I) 24/07/2023 Shift-IV
(a) 61 / 7 (b) 50 / 7
(c) 52 / 7 (d) 57 / 8

38. 6 labourers can finish a work in 16 days. 10 labourers are available, but the work is to be finished by 8 days. How many more labourers are to be called to finish the work in time? **SSC CGL (Tier-I) 24/07/2023 Shift-IV**
(a) 2 (b) 0 (c) 4 (d) 1

39. A can complete a work in 9 days and B in 12 days. If they work together on it for 5 days, then the fraction of the work left is
SSC CGL (Tier-I) 24/07/2023 Shift-III
(a) $\frac{1}{35}$ (b) $\frac{1}{36}$ (c) $\frac{5}{36}$ (d) $\frac{35}{36}$

40. 4 women and 7 men earn a total of ₹ 11480 in 7 days, while 10 women and 17 men earn a total of ₹ 36360 in 9 days. How much will 11 women and 9 men together earn (in ₹) in 13 days?
SSC CGL (Tier-I) 24/07/2023 Shift-III
(a) 42770 (b) 42640
(c) 42510 (d) 42900

41. Ram can copy 60 pages in 15 h. If Ram and Riya together can copy 180 pages in 30 h, then in how many hours can Riya copy 20 pages? **SSC CGL (Tier-I) 24/07/2023 Shift-III**
(a) 29 h (b) 12 h
(c) 20 h (d) 10 h

42. P and Q together can complete a piece of work in 6 days. If P can alone complete the work in 18 days, then the number of days required for Q to finish the work is
SSC CGL (Tier-I) 24/07/2023 Shift-II
(a) 10 days (b) 8 days
(c) 11 days (d) 9 days

43. A can do a certain piece of work in 1.5 times the number of days in which B and C together can do it. If A and B together can do the said piece of work in 30 days and C alone can do it in 120 days, then how many days will B take to do this piece of work alone?
SSC CGL (Tier-I) 24/07/2023 Shift-II
(a) 75 (b) 45 (c) 60 (d) 50

44. P takes twice as long as Q or three times as long as R to complete a task. If they work together, they can complete the task in two days. How long will it take Q to complete the task on his own?
SSC CGL (Tier-I) 24/07/2023 Shift-I
(a) 8 days (b) 6 days
(c) 5 days (d) 7 days

45. A is 40% more efficient than B. How much time will they take to work together to complete a job, which A alone could have done in 31 days? **SSC CGL (Tier-I) 21/07/2023 Shift-IV**
(a) $\frac{217}{12}$ days (b) $\frac{515}{32}$ days
(c) $\frac{215}{12}$ days (d) $\frac{517}{32}$ days

46. A can do a piece of work in 8 days, while B can do it in 18 days. In how many days will the work be completed if they both work on alternate days starting with B?
SSC CGL (Tier-I) 21/07/2023 Shift-IV
(a) $11\frac{1}{3}$ (b) $12\frac{1}{3}$
(c) 10 (d) $10\frac{1}{3}$

47. Richa, Rita and Reena can independently complete a work in 8 h, 12 h and 24 h, respectively. If they work together, how much time will they take to complete that work? **SSC CGL (Tier-I) 21/07/2023 Shift-III**
(a) 4 h (b) 5 h (c) 2 h (d) 3 h

48. Rekha alone can complete a work in 16 days, and Bina alone can complete the same work in 12 days. Starting with Rekha, they work on alternate days.The total work will be complete in
SSC CGL (Tier-I) 21/07/2023 Shift-III
(a) $12\frac{3}{4}$ days (b) 12 days
(c) 13 days (d) $13\frac{3}{4}$ days

49. A can do 20% of a work in 4 days and B can do $33\frac{1}{3}$% of the same work in 10 days. They worked together for 9 days and then C completed the remaining work in 6 days. B and C together will complete 75% of the same work in
SSC CGL (Tier-I) 21/07/2023 Shift-III
(a) 12 days (b) 9 days
(c) 11 days (d) 10 days

50. A works 5.4 times as fast as B, and A takes 22 days less than B to complete the job when each works alone. Calculate the number of days taken to complete the same job if A and B work together.
SSC CGL (Tier-I) 21/07/2023 Shift-II
(a) $4\frac{1}{4}$ (b) $4\frac{3}{16}$
(c) $4\frac{7}{32}$ (d) $4\frac{5}{32}$

51. Amit can complete a piece of work in 5 h. Jeevan and Paul together can complete it in 4 h, while Amit and Paul together can complete it in 3 h. Approximately, how many hours will Jeevan alone take to complete the work (rounded off to the nearest integer)?
SSC CGL (Tier-I) 21/07/2023 Shift-II
(a) 5 (b) 6 (c) 9 (d) 8

52. A works 3.5 times as fast as B and A takes 45 days, less than B to complete a job when each works alone. Calculate the number of days taken to complete the same job, if A and B work together.
SSC CGL (Tier-I) 21/07/2023 Shift-I
(a) 10.5 (b) 17.5 (c) 21 (d) 14

53. A worker completes $\frac{3}{5}$ of a work in 12 days. In how many days will he complete $\frac{3}{4}$ of the work?
SSC CGL (Tier-I) 21/07/2023 Shift-I
(a) 18 (b) 20 (c) 16 (d) 15

54. P and Q can do a job in 24 days, Q and R can do it in 30 days, while P and R can do it in 40 days. X is four times as efficient as P, Y is half as efficient as Q, and Z is 2.5 times as efficient as R. Determine the number of days required to complete the same job if X, Y and Z work together.
SSC CGL (Tier-I) 20/07/2023 Shift-III
(a) 9 (b) 12 (c) 8 (d) 10

55. A and B working together can finish a piece of work in 8 days while B alone can do it in 24 days. In how many days can A alone finish the work?
SSC CGL (Tier-I) 20/07/2023 Shift-III
(a) 10 (b) 16 (c) 12 (d) 14

56. Supraja and Kausalya can complete a work in 30 days and 20 days, respectively. If Supraja starts the work and they work on alternate days, in how many days will 75% of the work be completed?
SSC CGL (Tier-I) 20/07/2023 Shift-III
(a) 28 (b) 24
(c) 20 (d) 18

57. A and B can complete a piece of work in 12 days and 18 days, respectively. If they work at it alternatively, A beginning, in how many days will the work be finished? **SSC CGL (Tier-I) 20/07/2023 Shift-II**
(a) $14\frac{2}{3}$ (b) $14\frac{1}{3}$ (c) $15\frac{1}{3}$ (d) $15\frac{2}{3}$

58. A, B and C can do a work in 10 days, 15 days and 20 days, respectively. They finished that work together and got ₹ 2600 as wages. Find C's wage.
SSC CGL (Tier-I) 20/07/2023 Shift-II
(a) ₹ 550 (b) ₹ 600
(c) ₹ 575 (d) ₹ 625

59. *A* and *B* can individually complete a piece of work in 18 days and 30 days, respectively. *A* and *B* started working together, but *A* left $16\frac{2}{3}$ days before the work is completed and *B* alone completed the rest of the work. For how many days did *A* work? **SSC CGL (Tier-I) 20/07/2023 Shift-I**

(a) 4 (b) 5 (c) 6 (d) 3

60. 14 persons can build a house in 60 days. How long will it take 30 persons to build the same house, provided that they all work at the same rate?
SSC CGL (Tier-I) 19/07/2023 Shift-IV

(a) 28 days (b) 30 days
(c) 32 days (d) 56 days

61. $(N + 15)$ persons, each working for 9 h a day, can complete 36% of a work 8 days. $(N + 9)$ persons can complete the remaining work in 20 days, if each of them works for 7 h per day. Determine the value of *N*.
SSC CGL (Tier-I) 19/07/2023 Shift-IV

(a) 55 (b) 52 (c) 64 (d) 50

62. 12 men can complete a work in 10 days. How many more men are required to complete the work in 6 days? **SSC CGL (Tier-I) 19/07/2023 Shift-IV**

(a) 24 (b) 10 (c) 8 (d) 20

63. Susan can type 12 pages in 6 min, Mary can type 6 pages in 12 min working together, how many pages can they type in 32 min?
SSC CGL (Tier-I) 19/07/2023 Shift-III

(a) 80 (b) 65 (c) 70 (d) 75

64. 10 women can do a work in 6 days and 6 men can do the same work in 5 days. If all these men and women work together, then how many days will they take to finish this work? **SSC CGL (Tier-I) 19/07/2023 Shift-III**

(a) $2\frac{8}{11}$ (b) $4\frac{6}{11}$ (c) $1\frac{2}{11}$ (d) $3\frac{4}{11}$

65. Anil and Bipin together can complete a work in 15 days, while Bipin alone can finish it 20 days. In how many days can Anil alone finish the work?
SSC CGL (Tier-I) 19/07/2023 Shift-II

(a) 40 (b) 60 (c) 65 (d) 30

66. *A* can do a work in 4 days and *B* in 12 days. If they work on it together for 2 days, then the fraction of the work that will be left is
SSC CGL (Tier-I) 19/07/2023 Shift-II

(a) $\frac{2}{3}$ (b) $\frac{2}{5}$ (c) $\frac{1}{3}$ (d) $\frac{1}{5}$

67. If Mohit can complete $\frac{2}{3}$ rd of a work in 24 days, then in how many days can $\frac{1}{9}$th of the work be completed by him?
SSC CGL (Tier-I) 19/07/2023 Shift-I

(a) 8 (b) 4 (c) 6 (d) 5

68. $(N + 18)$ persons, each working for 7.5 h a day, can complete 48% of a work in 20 days. $(N + 12)$ persons can complete the remaining work in 30 days, if each of them works for 6.5 h per day. Determine the value of *N*.
SSC CGL (Tier-I) 19/07/2023 Shift-I

(a) 18 (b) 16 (c) 20 (d) 22

69. A man and a woman can finish a work together in half the time taken by a woman and a boy together. A boy can finish the work alone in 20 days and 2 women together can finish it in 30 days. In how many days will the work be finished by 4 men?
SSC CGL (Tier-I) 18/07/2023 Shift-IV

(a) 2.5 (b) 2 (c) 2.14 (d) 3

70. Suresh and Anil are working on a special project. Suresh takes 5 h to type 40 pages and Anil needs 6 h to type 32 pages on a computer. How much time will it take them to type a 110-pages assignment if the work on the different computers?
SSC CGL (Tier-I) 18/07/2023 Shift-IV

(a) 8 h 15 min (b) 8 h 40 min
(c) 7 h 35 min (d) 8 h

71. In a company, a piece of work can be completed in 4, 6 and 18 days alone by *R*, *S* and *T*, respectively. In how many days will the work be completed if they work together? (Rounded off to 2 decimal places)
SSC CGL (Tier-I) 18/07/2023 Shift-IV

(a) 3.21 (b) 2.12 (c) 3.32 (d) 2.42

72. *A* and *B* are equally efficient and each could individually complete a piece of work in 30 days, if none took any holiday. *A* and *B* started working together on this piece of work, but *A* took a day off after every four days of work, while *B* took a day off after every five days of work. If the duo had started work on 01 August, 2022, on which date was the work completed?
SSC CGL (Tier-I) 18/07/2023 Shift-III

(a) 16 August, 2022
(b) 18 August, 2022
(c) 19 August, 2022
(d) 17 August, 2022

73. *A* alone can finish a work in 15 days. *A* works only for the first two days and last two days. The rest work is done by *B* and the work is completed in 20 days. In how many days *A* and *B* together can finish the work?
SSC CGL (Tier-I) 18/07/2023 Shift-III

(a) $\frac{80}{9}$ (b) $\frac{90}{8}$
(c) $\frac{70}{8}$ (d) $\frac{80}{7}$

74. *A* and *B* can finish a work in 10 days, *B* and *C* can finish it in 12 days and *C* and *A* can finish in 6 days. In how many days *A* alone can finish the work?
SSC CGL (Tier-I) 18/07/2023 Shift-III

(a) $\frac{120}{9}$ (b) $\frac{121}{12}$
(c) $\frac{120}{11}$ (d) 12

75. *A* and *B* can do a piece of work in 5 days and 10 days, respectively. They began the work together but *A* left after some days and *B* finished the remaining work in 8 days. After how many days did *A* leave? **SSC CGL (Tier-I) 18/07/2023 Shift-II**

(a) $3\frac{1}{8}$ (b) $5\frac{1}{8}$
(c) $6\frac{1}{8}$ (d) $\frac{2}{3}$

76. Raja and Rocky together can complete painting work in 5 days. Together they both start painting, but after 2 days, Rocky falls sick and leaves the work. If Raja completes the remaining painting in 4 days, find the number of days in which Rocky alone can do the work. **SSC CGL (Tier-I) 18/07/2023 Shift-II**

(a) 12 days (b) 15 days
(c) 20 days (d) 10 days

77. *A* and *B* alone can do a piece of work in 4 and 9 days, respectively. In how many days will the work be completed, if they both work on alternate days, starting with *B*?
SSC CGL (Tier-I) 18/07/2023 Shift-II

(a) $5\frac{1}{3}$ (b) $5\frac{2}{3}$
(c) 5 (d) $5\frac{1}{4}$

78. *A* can finish a work in 20 days and *B* can complete the same work in 15 days. *B* worked for 9 days and left the job. In how many days can *A* alone finish the remaining work?
SSC CGL (Tier-I) 18/07/2023 Shift-I

(a) 10 days (b) 8 days
(c) 9 days (d) 7 days

79. 10 men can do a work in 25 days. After 12 days of work, 3 more men were engaged to finish the work. The number of days required to complete the remaining work is SSC CGL (Tier-I) 18/07/2023 Shift-I

(a) 10 (b) 8
(c) 6 (d) 12

80. 30 men can complete a work in 12 days. After 6 days, 24 more men joined them. How many days will they now take to complete the remaining work? SSC CGL (Tier-I) 18/07/2023 Shift-I

(a) $3\frac{1}{3}$ days (b) $3\frac{2}{3}$ days
(c) $3\frac{1}{2}$ days (d) $2\frac{1}{3}$ days
(c) 52% (d) 45%

81. 15 men and 21 women, working together, can do a job in 56 days, while 12 men and 24 women, working together, can do the same job in 64 days. In how many days can the same job be done by 18 men and 24 women, working together? SSC CGL (Tier-I) 17/07/2023 Shift-IV

(a) $47\frac{6}{19}$ (b) $47\frac{9}{19}$
(c) $47\frac{5}{19}$ (d) $47\frac{3}{19}$

82. Pratima and Diksha can complete a typing work separately in 10 h and 15h respectively. After typing for 4 h alone, Pratima leaves the work. In how many hours will Diksha complete the remaining typing work? SSC CGL (Tier-I) 17/07/2023 Shift-III

(a) 8 (b) 10
(c) 9 (d) 7

83. Sarthak and Mohan have been assigned a work to design a room for a ceremony, Sarthak can design the entire room in 12 days, while Mohan can design the room in 15 days. In how many days will the work be completed if they work together? (Rounded off to 2 decimal places) SSC CGL (Tier-I) 17/07/2023 Shift-III

(a) 5.67 (b) 6.67
(c) 7.33 (d) 6.00

84. 12 men and 16 boys can do a piece of work in 5 days, while 13 men and 24 boys can do it in 4 days. In how many days can 29 men and 22 boys complete the work? SSC CGL (Tier-I) 17/07/2023 Shift-III

(a) 2.5 (b) 2.45
(c) 2.6 (d) 2.4

85. Ravi can do a piece of work in 40 days and Sudha can do the same piece of work in 60 days. If they work on alternative days starting with Sudha on the first day, then in how many days will the work be completed? SSC CGL (Tier-I) 17/07/2023 Shift-II

(a) 48 (b) 60
(c) 40 (d) 45

86. Working 5 h a day, *A* can complete a task in 8 days and working 6 h a day, *B* can finish the same task in 10 days. Working 8 h a day, they can jointly complete the task in........ SSC CGL (Tier-I) 17/07/2023 Shift-II

(a) 6 days (b) 5 days
(c) 3 days (d) 4.5 days

87. 15 men can complete a work in 25 days and 25 women can complete the same work in 40 days. If all the 15 men and 25 women work together, in how many days will the work get completed? SSC CGL (Tier-I) 17/07/2023 Shift-II

(a) $15\frac{4}{13}$ days (b) $15\frac{5}{13}$ days
(c) $10\frac{5}{13}$ days (d) $15\frac{5}{12}$ days

88. *A*, *B* and *C*, working alone, can complete a job in 16, 24 and 36 days, respectively. In how many days can they complete the job if they work together? SSC CGL (Tier-I) 17/07/2023 Shift-I

(a) $7\frac{11}{19}$ (b) $5\frac{17}{19}$
(c) $4\frac{13}{19}$ (d) $6\frac{7}{19}$

89. Rakshit, Ajay and Satish are sanitation workers in a Municipal Corporation. Rakshit alone takes 20 h to clean a drain while Ajay takes 12 h when working alone to do the same. All three together take only 5 h to clean the drain. In how many hours, can Satish complete the work alone? SSC CGL (Tier-I) 17/07/2023 Shift-I

(a) 12 (b) 10
(c) 15 (d) 18

90. 15 men and 25 women can complete a piece of work in 9.6 days. If 16 women can complete the same work in 27 days, find the number of days in which 16 men can complete the same work. SSC CGL (Tier-I) 17/07/2023 Shift-I

(a) 22.50 (b) 20.25
(c) 19.20 (d) 21.60

91. *A*, *B* and *C* can separately complete a work in 12, 15 and 20 days, respectively. They worked together 4 days. What will be the remaining work? SSC CGL (Tier-I) 14/07/2023 Shift-IV

(a) $\frac{1}{2}$ (b) $\frac{1}{5}$ (c) $\frac{1}{6}$ (d) $\frac{1}{8}$

92. To do a certain work, Ajay and Bharat work on alternate days, with Bharat starting the work on the first day. Ajay can finish the work alone in 32 days. If the work gets completed in exactly 8 days, then Bharat alone can finish 7 times the same work in .... days. SSC CGL (Tier-I) 14/07/2023 Shift-IV

(a) $\frac{28}{8}$ (b) 4 (c) $\frac{32}{7}$ (d) 32

93. Virat can complete a work in 30 days and Daniel is 60% more efficient than Virat to complete the same work. Find the total time taken by Daniel to complete the work. SSC CGL (Tier-I) 14/07/2023 Shift-III

(a) $16\frac{3}{5}$ days (b) $18\frac{3}{4}$ days
(c) $19\frac{5}{3}$ days (d) $17\frac{5}{3}$ days

94. *A*'s efficiency is twice that of *B*'s. *A* can work only for 8 h a day while *B* can work for 12 h a day. If *A* can finish a work in 12 days, in how many days can *B* finish the same work? SSC CGL (Tier-I) 14/07/2023 Shift-III

(a) 8 (b) 10
(c) 16 (d) 12

95. *X* and *Y* can complete a work in 9 days and 36 days, respectively. *X* begin to do the work and they work alternately one at a time for one day each. The whole work will be complete in SSC CGL (Tier-I) 14/07/2023 Shift-II

(a) $15\frac{1}{5}$ days (b) $12\frac{1}{2}$ days
(c) $13\frac{1}{3}$ days (d) $14\frac{1}{4}$ days

96. 4 women or 6 boys can finish a work in the same number of days. A boy can finish it in 60 days. In how many days can 5 women finish the work, working together every day? SSC CGL (Tier-I) 14/07/2023 Shift-II

(a) 4 (b) 8
(c) 10 (d) 6

97. *P* is two times more efficient than *Q*. *P* is able to complete a piece of work in 40 days less than *Q*. Working together, the whole

number of days taken by them to complete the work is
(Round off to the nearest integer)
SSC CGL (Tier-I) 14/07/2023 Shift-II

(a) 26 (b) 27 (c) 28 (d) 25

98. 5 women and 9 girls earn a total of ₹ 18720 in 9 days, while 9 women and 16 girls earn a total of ₹ 52080 in 14 days. How much will 12 women and 7 together earn (in ₹) in 13 days ?
SSC CGL (Tier-I) 14/07/2023 Shift-II

(a) 42120 (b) 42510
(c) 41990 (d) 42380

99. 8 men can complete a work in 45 days. 8 women can complete the same work in 18 days. In how many days will 5 men and 8 women, together, complete the same work?
SSC CGL (Tier-I) 14/07/2023 Shift-I

(a) $14\frac{2}{5}$ (b) $12\frac{4}{5}$
(c) $15\frac{3}{5}$ (d) $13\frac{1}{5}$

100. A man, a boy and a woman can finish a work in 10 days, 15 days and 30 days, respectively. In how many days can the work be finished by a man, a woman and a boy when all of them work together? SSC CGL (Tier-I) 14/07/2023 Shift-I

(a) 10 (b) 8
(c) 5 (d) 6

101. A can complete a piece of work in 25 days while B can complete the same work in 30 days. They work on alternate basis, starting with A. Both A and B follow this pattern for 5 days and then A leaves the work. In how many days will B finish the remaining work?
SSC CGL (Tier-I) 14/07/2023 Shift-I

(a) $24\frac{2}{5}$ (b) $5\frac{3}{5}$
(c) $24\frac{3}{5}$ (d) $5\frac{2}{5}$

SSC CGL 2022 (Tier I)

102. Two persons A and B working separately can sanitise a building in 6 and 10 h, respectively. They work in stretches of one hour alternately. If A begins at 8 am, then when will the work be finished?
SSC CGL (Tier-I) 13/12/2022 Shift-III

(a) $9\frac{1}{3}$ h (b) $7\frac{1}{3}$ h
(c) $6\frac{1}{3}$ h (d) $8\frac{1}{3}$ h

103. A, B and C can all together do a piece of work in 10 days, in which B takes 3 times as long as A and C together to do the work. In how many days can B alone do the work? SSC CGL (Tier-I) 13/12/2022 Shift-II

(a) 40 days (b) 50 days
(c) 10 days (d) 15 days

104. A is 20% more efficient than B. How much time will they working together take to complete a job which A alone could have done in 29 days? SSC CGL (Tier-I) 13/12/2022 Shift-I

(a) $\frac{145}{11}$ (b) $\frac{116}{11}$
(c) $\frac{203}{11}$ (d) $\frac{174}{11}$

105. Aarif, Arun and Abraham can do a work in 12, 20 and 24 days, respectively. They all begin together. Aarif leaves the work 1 day, Arun 3 days and Abraham 4 days before its completion. In how many days is the work finished?
SSC CGL (Tier-I) 12/12/2022 Shift-IV

(a) 8 (b) 10
(c) 11 (d) 9

106. A is 40% more efficient than B. How much time will both, working together, take to finish the work, which B alone can finish in 36 days? SSC CGL (Tier-I) 12/12/2022 Shift-III

(a) 18 days (b) $9\frac{1}{3}$ days
(c) 15 days (d) $11\frac{2}{3}$ days

107. Raju, Shobha and Mohan can do a work in 15 days, 20 days and 25 days respectively. In how many days, will the work be finished, if they do it on alternate days?
SSC CGL (Tier-I) 12/12/2022 Shift-II

(a) $15\frac{9}{10}$ days (b) $18\frac{7}{10}$ days
(c) $21\frac{7}{10}$ days (d) $18\frac{9}{10}$ days

108. A machine takes 10 h to cut 240 tools. How many tools will it cut in 25 h? SSC CGL (Tier-I) 12/12/2022 Shift-I

(a) 600 (b) 480
(c) 550 (d) 360

109. A, B and C can separately do a work in 6, 10 and 15 days, respectively. They started to work together but C left after 2 days. In how many days will the remaining work be finished?
SSC CGL (Tier-I) 9/12/2022 Shift-IV

(a) $1\frac{2}{4}$ (b) $1\frac{1}{4}$ (c) $1\frac{5}{8}$ (d) $2\frac{7}{4}$

110. Two persons P and Q can do a job together in 36 days. P is 3 times as efficient as Q. In how many days can Q alone complete the work?
SSC CGL (Tier-I) 9/12/2022 Shift-IV

(a) 148 (b) 140
(c) 144 (d) 146

111. Abha and Anuj working together completed a job in $\frac{40}{9}$ days. If Abha had worked twice as efficiently as she actually did and Anuj had worked $\frac{1}{3}$ of his actual efficiency, then the work would have been completed $\frac{60}{17}$ in days. Find the time Abha would take to complete the work alone.
SSC CGL (Tier-I) 9/12/2022 Shift-III

(a) 10 days (b) 8 days
(c) 12 days (d) 6 days

112. 20 men can finish a work in 220 days, but at the end of 90 days, 20 additional men are employed. In how many more days will the work be completed?
SSC CGL (Tier-I) 9/12/2022 Shift-II

(a) 50 (b) 60
(c) 65 (d) 55

113. A and B can complete a piece of work in 13 and 17 days, respectively. A begins to do the work, and they work alternatively one at a time for one day each. The whole work will be completed in
SSC CGL (Tier-I) 8/12/2022 Shift-IV

(a) $17\frac{11}{17}$ days (b) $17\frac{17}{19}$ days
(c) $14\frac{11}{17}$ days (d) $11\frac{11}{17}$ days

114. Raju, Sunil and Vishal can separately finish a work in 20, 30 and 40 days, respectively. In how many days Raju can finish the work, if he is assisted by Sunil and Vishal on alternate days, starting with Sunil?
SSC CGL (Tier-I) 8/12/2022 Shift-III

(a) $12\frac{3}{5}$ (b) $12\frac{1}{20}$
(c) $11\frac{1}{20}$ (d) $11\frac{3}{5}$

115. In a factory, Ajay and Vijay work on the same machine to cut diamonds but on alternate hour basis. Ajay works for the first hour and then Vijay works for the second hour and so on. Ajay can complete the work in 6 h while Vijay completes it in 16 h if they

work individually. In how much time can they complete the work if they are using the machine on alternate basis?
SSC CGL (Tier-I) 8/12/2022 Shift-II

(a) 8 h 30 min (b) 8 h
(c) 9 h (d) 9 h 30 min

116. Ten men begin to do a work. But after some days, four of them left the job. As a result, the job that could have been completed in 40 days is completed in 50 days. How many days after the commencement of the work did the four men leave?
SSC CGL (Tier-I) 8/12/2022 Shift-I

(a)30 (b) 20
(c) 35 (d) 25

117. 12 men and 12 women can complete a piece of work in 9 days. 6 men and 15 women can complete the same work in 12 days. How long (in days) would it take 9 women to complete half the work?
SSC CGL (Tier-I) 7/12/2022 Shift-IV

(a) 36 (b) 12
(c) 18 (d) 24

118. A civil contractor planned to build an over bridge of 3 km distance in 600 days. For this purpose, he employed 90 workers. After 200 days of work, it was observed that only 0.5 km of the bridge was completed. What is the number of extra workers required to complete the work in time?
SSC CGL (Tier-I) 7/12/2022 Shift-III

(a) 100 (b) 140
(c) 125 (d) 135

119. In a partnership firm two partners, Vijay and Praveen are working on an assignment. It will take 12 weeks for Vijay to complete the entire assignment alone, while Praveen will take 8 weeks to complete it alone. Due to work pressure, they decided to work on that assignment on the alternate week basis. In the first week Praveen will work and in the second week Vijay will work and so on. In how many weeks the work will be completed if they work on alternate week basis?
SSC CGL (Tier-I) 7/12/2022 Shift-II

(a) 8 (b) 8.5
(c) 9.5 (d) 9

120. 25 men and 45 women can complete a piece of work in 15 days, while 15 men and 60 women can complete it in 20 days. In how many days can 69 men and 67 women complete the work?
SSC CGL (Tier-I) 7/12/2022 Shift-I

(a) 10 (b) 5 (c) 8 (d) 6

121. 1 man and 4 women can complete a work in $\frac{65}{4}$ days, while 3 men and 4 women can complete it in $\frac{13}{2}$ days. In how many days will 13 women complete the same?
SSC CGL (Tier-I) 6/12/2022 Shift-IV

(a) 20 (b) 16 (c) 14 (d) 18

122. A group of men decided to do a job in 6 days, but 18 men dropped out every day. If the job was completed in 8 days, then how many men initially decided to do the job.
SSC CGL (Tier-I) 6/12/2022 Shift-II

(a) 300 (b) 252 (c) 188 (d) 150

123. 40 men can complete a work in 15 days. Three days after they started working, 20 more men joined them. In how many days the total work will be completed?
SSC CGL (Tier-I) 5/12/2022 Shift-III

(a) 12 (b) 13 (c) 11 (d) 10

124. A contractor decided to complete a work in 80 days and employed 60 men at the beginning and 20 men additionally after 20 days and got the work completed as per schedule. If he had not employed the additional men, how many extra days would he have needed to complete the work (round off to the nearest integer)?
SSC CGL (Tier-I) 5/12/2022 Shift-II

(a) 32 days (b) 20 days
(c) 30 days (d) 26 days

125. Numan does half as much work as Gagan in four-fifth of the time. If together they take 16 days to complete to work, how much time shall Gagan take to do it?
SSC CGL (Tier-I) 5/12/2022 Shift-I

(a) 24 days (b) 25 days
(c) 26 days (d) 23 days

126. 5 men and 8 women can complete a work in 12 days working together, while 3 men and 7 women together can complete the same work in 15 days. In how many days will 11 women complete the same work?
SSC CGL (Tier-I) 3/12/2022 Shift-III

(a) 12 (b) 8
(c) 6 (d) 16

127. *A* and *B* can do a certain work in 6h, and *A*, *B* and *C* together take 4 h to do the same. How long will it take for *C* alone to accomplish the task?
SSC CGL (Tier-I) 3/12/2022 Shift-II

(a) 12 h (b) 4 h
(c) 2 h (d) 6 h

128. Ruchi, Khushi and Teju can do a piece of work in 30, 40 and 60 days respectively. In how many days can Ruchi do the work, if she is assisted by both Khushi and Teju on every third day?
SSC CGL (Tier-I) 3/12/2022 Shift-I

(a) $\frac{550}{12}$ days (b) $\frac{85}{4}$ days
(c) $\frac{71}{2}$ days (d) $\frac{360}{17}$ days

129. *A* and *B* together can do a piece of work in 50 days. If *A* is 40% less efficient than *B*, in how many days can *A* working alone complete 60% of the work?
SSC CGL (Tier-I) 2/12/2022 Shift-IV

(a) 70 (b) 110
(c) 80 (d) 105

130. If one man or two women or four boys or five girls can finish a work in 39 days, then how many days will one man, one woman, one boy and one girl together take to finish the same work?
SSC CGL (Tier-I) 2/12/2022 Shift-III

(a) 40 (b) 10
(c) 30 (d) 20

131. If 6 women can complete a work in 3 days and 9 girls can complete the same work in 2 days, then find the time taken to complete the same work by 8 women and 6 girls?
SSC CGL (Tier-I) 2/12/2022 Shift-I

(a) 3 days (b) 4 days
(c) 6 days (d) 9/7 days

132. 6 men and 8 women can do a piece of work in 10 days, whereas 26 men and 48 women can do the same work in 2 days. What will be the time taken by 15 men and 20 women to do the same work?
SSC CGL (Tier-I) 1/12/2022 Shift-IV

(a) 6 days (b) 10 days
(c) 4 days (d) 8 days

133. *A* takes 4 times as much time as *B* or 5 times as much time as *C* to finish a piece of work. Working together, they can finish the work in 4 days. *B* can do the work alone in
SSC CGL (Tier-I) 1/12/2022 Shift-III

(a) 10 days (b) 15 days
(c) 12 days (d) 20 days

134. If 450 men can finish construction of an apartment in 20 days, then how many men are needed to complete the same work in 30 days? **SSC CGL (Tier-I) 1/12/2022 Shift-III**

(a) 150 (b) 300 (c) 400 (d) 250

135. *A*, *B* and *C* can complete a piece of work separately in 10, 20 and 40 days, respectively. In how many days will the work be completed if *A* is assisted by both *B* and *C* every third day? **SSC CGL (Tier-I) 1/12/2022 Shift-II**

(a) $8\frac{2}{7}$ (b) 9 (c) $10\frac{2}{3}$ (d) 6

136. *P* and *Q* can complete a project in 15 days and 10 days, respectively. They started doing the work together, but after 2 days, *Q* had to leave and *P* alone completed the remaining work. In how many days was the whole work completed? **SSC CGL (Tier-I) 1/12/2022 Shift-I**

(a) 11 (b) 12 (c) 13 (d) 10

SSC CGL 2021 & 2020 (Tier I)

137. Eighteen men can complete a work in 14 days. Three women do as much work as two men. Five men and six women started the work and continued for 4 days. Subsequently 3 more men joined the group. In how many total days was the work completed? **SSC CGL (Tier-I) 24/08/2021 Shift-II**

(a) $21\frac{1}{3}$ (b) $17\frac{1}{3}$ (c) 18 (d) 22

138. *A* can complete a work in $11\frac{1}{2}$ days. *B* is 25% more efficient than *A* and *C* is 50% efficient than *B*. Working together *A*, *B* and *C* will complete the same work. **SSC CGL (Tier-I) 24/08/2021 Shift-I**

(a) 5 days (b) 4 days
(c) 3 days (d) 8 days

139. To do a certain work, efficiencies of *A* and *B* are in the ratio 7 : 5. Working together, they can complete the work in $17\frac{1}{2}$ days. In how many days, will *B* alone complete, 50% of the same work? **SSC CGL (Tier-I) 23/08/2021 Shift-II**

(a) 42 (b) 21 (c) 15 (d) 30

140. 5 men can complete a work in 20 days. 10 women can complete the same work in 15 days. 2 men and 6 women started working together. After 5 days, 3 women left the work and a new men joined the work. The group continued working together till the end of the work. In how many days will they be able to do the remaining work? **SSC CGL (Tier-I) 18/08/2021 Shift-III**

(a) $16\frac{2}{3}$ (b) 14 (c) $18\frac{1}{3}$ (d) 19

141. *A* and *B* together can complete a certain work in 20 days whereas *B* and *C* together can complete it in 24 days. If *A* is twice as good a workman as *C*, then in what time will *B* alone do 40% of the same work? **SSC CGL (Tier-I) 18/08/2021 Shift-I**

(a) 12 days (b) 15 days
(c) 18 days (d) 10 days

142. Each one of the five men independently can complete a work in 20 days. The work is started by one person. Next day one more person joins the work and every next day one more person joins. From the fifth day, five persons continued working as a team. In how many days, will the work be completed? **SSC CGL (Tier-I) 17/08/2021 Shift-III**

(a) 6 (b) 2 (c) 5 (d) 3

143. Samir and Puneet can complete the same work in 10 days and 15 days respectively. The work was assigned for ₹ 4500. After working together for 3 days Samir and Puneet involved Ashok. The work was completed in total 5 days. What amount (in ₹) was paid to Ashok? **SSC CGL (Tier-I) 16/08/2021 Shift-III**

(a) 800 (b) 1500
(c) 750 (d) 1071

144. *A* can do a certain work in 15 days. *B* is 25% more efficient than *A*. Both worked together for 4 days. *C* alone completed the remaining work in 8 days. *A*, *B* and *C* together will complete the same work in? **SSC CGL (Tier-I) 16/08/2021 Shift-I**

(a) $4\frac{1}{2}$ days (b) 5 days
(c) $6\frac{1}{2}$ days (d) 4 days

145. A man and a woman, working together can do a work in 66 days. The ratio of their working efficiencies is 3 : 2. In how many days 6 men and 2 women working together can do the same work? **SSC CGL (Tier-I) 13/08/2021 Shift-III**

(a) 14 (b) 12
(c) 15 (d) 18

146. To do a certain work, *A* and *B* work on alternate days with *B* beginning the work on the first day. *A* alone can complete the same work in 24 days. If the work gets completed in $11\frac{1}{3}$ days, then *B* alone can complete $\frac{7}{9}$ th part of the original work in **SSC CGL (Tier-I) 13/08/2021 Shift-I**

(a) $4\frac{1}{2}$ days (b) 6 days
(c) $5\frac{1}{2}$ days (d) 4 days

147. If 18 men can cut a field in 35 days, then in how many days can 21 men cut the same field? **SSC CGL (Tier-I) 07/03/2020 Shift-II**

(a) 32 (b) 30 (c) 27 (d) 28

148. A contract is to be completed in 75 days and 187 men are to work 15 h per day. After 65 days, $\frac{3}{5}$ of the work is completed. How many additional men may be employed, so that the work may be completed in time, each man now working 17 h per day? **SSC CGL (Tier-I) 07/03/2020 Shift-II**

(a) 514 (b) 532 (c) 528 (d) 495

149. Ten men or twelve women can finish the same work in 10 days. If 5 men and 2 women undertake the work together, how many days will they take to complete the work? **SSC CGL (Tier-I) 07/03/2020 Shift-I**

(a) 15 (b) 40 (c) 20 (d) 60

150. *A*, *B* and *C* can individually complete a task in 20 days, 16 day and 30 days, respectively. If *A* and *B* started working on the task and they worked for 4 days and left, then the number of days required by *C* to finish remaining task is **SSC CGL (Tier-I) 06/3/2020 Shift-III**

(a) $16\frac{1}{2}$ days (b) $12\frac{1}{2}$ days
(c) 13 days (d) 10 days

151. Sixteen men can finish a work in 8 days. Eight men and nine women working together can finish the same work in 10 days. In how many days will twenty women finish the same work? **SSC CGL (Tier-I) 05/3/2020 Shift-III**

(a) 12 (b) 9 (c) 11 (d) 13

152. To complete a certain task, *X* is 40% more efficient than *Y* and *Z* is 40% less efficient than *Y*. Working together, they can complete the task in 21 days. *Y* and *Z* together worked for 35 days. The remaining work will be completed by X alone in SSC CGL (Tier-I) 05/3/2020 Shift-II

(a) 8 days (b) 4 days
(c) 6 days (d) 5 days

153. 4 men and 6 women can complete a certain piece of work in 5 days, whereas 3 men and 4 women can complete it in 7 days. How many men should assist 25 women to complete $2\frac{1}{2}$ times the same work in 5 days?
SSC CGL (Tier-I) 04/3/2020 Shift-III

(a) 8 (b) 10 (c) 4 (d) 5

SSC CPO SI 2024

154. Sumit and Rajiv, working together, can do a job in 20 h whereas Sumit alone can do the same job in 25 h. In how many hours can Rajiv alone do the job? SSC CPO 29/06/2024 Shift-III

(a) 90 (b) 100 (c) 70 (d) 80

155. If 12 people can print 540 identical books in 10 days, then how many more people will be required to print 720 such books in 8 days?
SSC CPO 29/06/2024 Shift-III

(a) 8 (b) 6 (c) 12 (d) 4

156. Sapna is double efficient as compared to Rakesh. If they both work together on a project and complete it in 48 days, then the number of days in which Sapna alone can complete the project is
SSC CPO 29/06/2024 Shift-II

(a) 68 (b) 72 (c) 52 (d) $69\frac{1}{2}$

157. A hostel had food provision for 300 students for a month. After 20 days, 50 students left the hostel. How long would the remaining food last? (1 month = 30 days)
SSC CPO 29/06/2024 Shift-II

(a) 14 days (b) 12 days
(c) 10 days (d) 16 days

158. Rajan and Rajat can do a work in 64 days and 48 days, respectively. Starting with Rajat, they work on alternate days. In how many days will the work be completed?
SSC CPO 29/06/2024 Shift-II

(a) 55 (b) $54\frac{3}{4}$
(c) 54 (d) $55\frac{3}{4}$

159. Amita can build a room in the same amount of time that Bina and Sita working together can build. If Amita and Bina together could do it in 25 days and Sita alone in 35 days, then how many days are required for Bina alone to do the same work? SSC CPO 29/06/2024 Shift-I

(a) 180 days (b) 165 days
(c) 152 days (d) 175 days

160. P can do a piece of work in 30 days and Q in 40 days. They work together for 4 days and then Q leaves. The number of days taken by P to finish the remaining work is SSC CPO 28/06/2024 Shift-III

(a) 28 days (b) 23 days
(c) 30 days (d) 7 days

161. Manish, Nakul and Pintoo alone can complete a certain work in 21days, 28 days and 15days, respectively. Manish and Pintoo started the work together while Nakul joined them after 5 days and worked with them till the completion of the work. For how many days did Nakul work?
SSC CPO 28/06/2024 Shift-II

(a) $5\frac{1}{2}$ (b) $2\frac{6}{7}$
(c) $2\frac{1}{2}$ (d) $3\frac{1}{2}$

162. Ronak and Riya can do a work in 12 and 18 days, respectively. They worked together for six days and then Ronak left. Find the time taken by Riya to complete the work. SSC CPO 28/06/2024 Shift-II

(a) 3 days (b) 5 days
(c) 6 days (d) 7 days

163. Ravi and Sanju together can do a job in 2 days, Sanju and Mahesh can do it in 4 days,while Ravi and Mahesh can do it in 2 days. What is the number of days required for Ravi to do the same job alone?
SSC CPO 28/06/2024 Shift-I

(a) 4 days (b) $\frac{8}{3}$ days
(c) $\frac{5}{3}$ days (d) 9 days

164. A and B together can complete a piece of work in 25 days, B and C together can complete the same piece of work in 36 days, while C and A together can complete it in 30 days. If A, B, C, and D together can complete this piece of work in 18 days, then in how many days can D alone complete this piece of work? SSC CPO 28/06/2024 Shift-I

(a) 210 (b) 180
(c) 200 (d) 225

165. 18 workers can complete a piece of work in 96 days. They start working together and after 26 days 10 more workers join them. In how many days in all will the work be completed? SSC CPO 27/06/2024 Shift-III

(a) 72 (b) 69
(c) 71 (d) 70

166. If 24 people can build 90 identical walls in 25 days, then how many more days will 27 people require to build 162 such walls?
SSC CPO 27/06/2024 Shift-III

(a) 14 (b) 13
(c) 15 (d) 16

167. A and B can do a work in 13 days and 26 days, respectively. If they work for a day alternately, starting with A, then in how many days will the work be completed?
SSC CPO 27/06/2024 Shift-II

(a) 16 (b) 17 (c) 14 (d) 13

168. Arvind works 4 times as fast as Suresh. If Suresh can complete a work in 20 days indpendently, then find the number of days in which Arvind and Suresh can together finish the workSSC CPO 27/06/2024 Shift-II

(a) 6 (b) 5 (c) 3 (d) 4

169. A can do a work in 20 days and B in 30 days. If they work on it together for 2 days,then what is the fraction of the work that is left?
SSC CPO 27/06/2024 Shift-I

(a) $\frac{5}{8}$ (b) $\frac{3}{5}$ (c) $\frac{5}{7}$ (d) $\frac{5}{6}$

170. A can complete a piece of work alone in 200 days, while B can complete the same piece of work alone in 100 days. In every three-day cycle, both A and B work on day 1,only A works on day 2 and only B works on day 3. This cycle continues till the work is completed. How many days in all does it take the duo to complete the work? SSC CPO 27/06/2024 Shift-I

(a) 100 (b) $99\frac{2}{3}$
(c) $100\frac{1}{2}$ (d) $100\frac{1}{3}$

SSC CPO SI 2023-2020

171. A and B are equally efficient, and each can individually complete a piece of work in 36 days, if none takes any holiday. A and B started working together on this piece of work, but A took a day off after every five days of work, while B

took a day off after every seven days of work. If the duo had started work on 1 July, 2021, on which date was the work completed? SSC CPO 05/10/2023 Shift-III

(a) 22nd July, 2021 (b) 19th July, 2021
(c) 21st July, 2021 (d) 20th July, 2021

172. If Arun can complete $\frac{2}{3}$ rd of a work in 12 days, then in how many days can be complete $\frac{1}{6}$ th of the same work? SSC CPO 05/10/2023 Shift-III

(a) 3 (b) 4 (c) 5 (d) 2

173. *A*, *B* and *C* can do a piece of work in 11 days, 20 days and 55 days respectively. How soon can the work be done if *A* works with *B* on first day, *A* works with *C* on second day and so on? SSC CPO 05/10/2023 Shift-III

(a) $8\frac{1}{2}$ days (b) $9\frac{1}{2}$ days
(c) 8 days (d) 9 days

174. Akshita and Raina are typing a book, but have only one laptop to work upon. They decided that they will work on alternate basis such that Akshita works for the first day, Raina works for the second day, Akshita for the third day and so on. Akshita alone can finish the typing work in 16 days, while Raina will take 24 days if they work alone on the entire book. How many days will they take to finish the typing work if they work on alternate basis? SSC CPO 04/10/2023 Shift-II

(a) 15 (b) 18 (c) 19 (d) 17

175. In an office, 75 employees can finish a project in 60 days. After few days, 15 employees left the job and the project was completed in 65 days. After how many days did the 15 employees leave? SSC CPO 04/10/2023 Shift-II

(a) 50 (b) 4 (c) 30 (d) 40

176. *P*, *Q* and *R*, when working individually, can complete a job in, respectively, 36 days, 48 days and 144 days. *P*, *Q* and *R* start working together. *P* leaves the job 12 days before completion and *Q* leaves the job 8 days before completion. *R* works from the beginning till the end of the job. Determine the total number of days taken to complete the job. SSC CPO 03/10/2023 Shift-I

(a) 24 (b) 27 (c) 30 (d) 25

177. *A*, *B* and *C* can do a piece of work in 20 days, 30 days and 60 days, respectively. If *A* works daily and on every third day *B* and *C* also work with *A*, then in how many days, will the work be completed? SSC CPO 03/10/2023 Shift-I

(a) 21 (b) 18 (c) 12 (d) 15

178. If 3 goats or 5 sheeps can graze a field in 54 days, then in how many days can 6 goats and 8 sheep graze the same field? SSC CPO 03/10/2023 Shift-I

(a) 15 (b) 12 (c) 10 (d) 8

179. A group of men committed to completing a task in 20 days. The work was completed in 40 days because 5 workers did not come for work. Determine the number of men who originally agreed to do the work. SSC CPO 11/11/2022 Shift-II

(a) 15 (b) 10 (c) 12 (d) 18

180. *P* and *Q* can do a piece of work in 14 days. *Q* and R together can do it in 21 days. If *P* is twice as good a workman as *R*, then in how many days *Q* alone can do the work? SSC CPO 11/11/2022 Shift-II

(a) 42 days (b) 40 days
(c) 35 days (d) 38 days

181. At a construction site, Raju can paint a wall in 36 h, while Angad can do the same work in 18 h. Sumit can paint the same wall in 24 h. In how much time can they paint the wall if they all work together? SSC CPO 10/11/2022 Shift-II

(a) 9 h (b) 12 h (c) 6 h (d) 8 h

182. Aarush and Maahi together can do a piece of work in 10 days. If Aarush alone can do the same work in 15 days, then how many days Maahi alone will take to do the same work? SSC CPO 10/11/2022 Shift-II

(a) 25 (b) 15 (c) 30 (d) 20

183. *A* can complete a certain work in 35 days and *B* can complete the same work in 15 days. They worked together for 7 days then *B* left the work. In how many days will *A* alone complete 60% of the remaining work? SSC CPO 25/11/2020 Shift-II

(a) 10 (b) 15 (c) 8 (d) 7

184. *A* and *B* can do a job in 10 days and 5 days, respectively. They worked together for two days, after which *B* was replaced by *C* and the work was finished in the next three days. How long will *C* alone take to finish 40% of the job? SSC CPO 25/11/2020 Shift-I

(a) 18 days (b) 12 days
(c) 15 days (d) 10 days

185. *A* is twice as good a workman as *B* and together they finish a piece of work in 13 days. In how many days will A alone finish the work? SSC CPO 25/11/2020 Shift-I

(a) 41 (b) 39
(c) $19\frac{1}{2}$ (d) $9\frac{1}{4}$

186. *A* and *B* can do a piece of work in 25 days. *B* alone can do $66\frac{2}{3}$% of the same work in 30 days. In how many days can *A* alone do $\frac{4}{15}$ part of the same work? SSC CPO 24/11/2020 Shift-I

(a) 18 (b) 15 (c) 12 (d) 20

187. *A* and *B* can do a piece of work in 36 days. *B* and *C* can do the same work in 60 days. *A* and *C* can do the same work in 45 days. In how many days can *B* alone complete the same work? SSC CPO 24/11/2020 Shift-I

(a) 45 (b) 60
(c) 90 (d) 120

188. *A* is twice as good a workman as *B* and together they finish a piece of work in 13 days. In how many days will *B* alone finish the work? SSC CPO 23/11/2020 Shift-I

(a) 39 (b) 42
(c) 21 (d) 18.5

189. *A* and *B* can do a job in 10 days and 5 days, respectively. They worked together for two days, after which *B* was replaced by *C* and the work was finished in the next three days. How long will *C* alone take to finish 60%, of the job? SSC CPO 23/11/2020 Shift-I

(a) 18 days (b) 30 days
(c) 25 days (d) 24 days

SSC CHSL 2024 (Tier I & II)

190. Ratnesh and Vineet worked on alternate days, starting with Ratnesh. The entire work got completed in $54\frac{3}{4}$ days. If Ratnesh alone can finish the work in 48 days, then in how many days can Vineet alone do the work? SSC CHSL (Tier II) 18/11/2024

(a) 60 (b) 64
(c) 66 (d) 62

191. X, Y and Z can do a work in 24 days, 5 days and 12 days, respectively. In how many days can they do the same work, if they work together?
SSC CHSL (Tier I) 11/7/2024 Shift-IV
(a) 4 days (b) $3\frac{1}{13}$ days
(c) $\frac{1}{24}$ days (d) $\frac{7}{24}$ days

192. Teena does half of a task in 6 days. Later, with Shyam's help, she completes the remaining work in 4 days. Shyam alone can finish the entire work in
SSC CHSL (Tier I) 11/7/2024 Shift-III
(a) 21 days (b) 24 days
(c) 18 days (d) 12 days

193. Mira can complete a piece of work in 20 days, Nina in 30 days and Sima in 40 days. Mira and Sima worked together for 4 days and then Mira was replaced by Nina. In how many days, altogether, was the work completed?
SSC CHSL (Tier I) 11/7/2024 Shift-II
(a) 14 (b) 18 (c) 16 (d) 20

194. Nirmal completed the school project in 45 days. How many days will Amit take to complete the same work, if he is 25% more efficient than Nirmal?
SSC CHSL (Tier I) 11/7/2024 Shift-I
(a) 36 (b) 25 (c) 38 (d) 30

195. P completes a work in 12 days and Q in 24 days. In how many days P and Q working together can complete the same work?
SSC CHSL (Tier I) 10/7/2024 Shift-IV
(a) 12 days (b) 8 days
(c) 6 days (d) 16 days

196. Reena and Riya together can complete a piece of work in 36 days. Riya and Geeta together can complete it in 54 days. Reena and Geeta together can complete it in 81 days. In how many days can Reena alone complete the work?
SSC CHSL (Tier I) 10/7/2024 Shift-III
(a) $82\frac{4}{7}$ days (b) $87\frac{4}{7}$ days
(c) $97\frac{4}{7}$ days (d) $92\frac{4}{7}$ days

197. P and Q can do a work in 12 days and 9 days, respectively. They both worked together and earned ₹63000. The share of P (in ₹) is
SSC CHSL (Tier I) 10/7/2024 Shift-II
(a) 21000 (b) 36000
(c) 9000 (d) 27000

198. To finish a work, P takes half of the number of days required by Q to finish it. If they together can finish the work in 36 days, then in how many days Q alone can finish the work?
SSC CHSL (Tier I) 10/7/2024 Shift-I
(a) 108 (b) 84 (c) 60 (d) 24

199. A can finish a piece of work by working alone in 4 days. B, while working alone, can finish the same work in 12 days. If both of them work together, then in how many days will the work be completed?
SSC CHSL (Tier I) 09/7/2024 Shift-IV
(a) 8 (b) 6 (c) 3 (d) 4

200. If 6 engineers can complete a work in 5 days and 5 skilled workers can complete the same work in 7 days, then the time taken (in days) to complete the same work by 7 engineers and 4 skilled workers will be **SSC CHSL (Tier I) 09/7/2024 Shift-III**
(a) $2\frac{64}{70}$ (b) $3\frac{64}{73}$ (c) $2\frac{64}{73}$ (d) $2\frac{65}{73}$

201. 30 men working 5 h a day can do work in 18 days. In how many days will 20 men working 7 h a day do the same work?
SSC CHSL (Tier I) 09/7/2024 Shift-II
(a) $11\frac{3}{7}$ (b) $16\frac{5}{7}$
(c) $19\frac{2}{7}$ (d) $13\frac{1}{7}$

202. Tanvi can do a work in 25 days, and Tai can complete the same work in 30 days. They started the work together for 5 days. How much work is left?
SSC CHSL (Tier I) 08/7/2024 Shift-IV
(a) $\frac{11}{30}$ (b) $\frac{19}{30}$ (c) $\frac{11}{12}$ (d) $\frac{1}{12}$

203. R can finish a work in 6 days if he works 10 h a day. S can finish it in 5 days, if he works 8 h a day. If both start a work and work daily for 6 h, the work will be finished in ..... days. **SSC CHSL (Tier I) 08/7/2024 Shift-III**
(a) 3 (b) 4 (c) 5 (d) 6

204. Rohan takes 10 h to mow a large lawn. Rohan and Mohan together can mow it in 4 h. How long will Mohan take to mow the lawn, if he works alone?
SSC CHSL (Tier I) 08/7/2024 Shift-II
(a) $\frac{16}{3}$ h (b) $\frac{20}{3}$ h (c) $\frac{40}{3}$ h (d) $\frac{10}{3}$ h

205. Antony and Julie can simultaneously complete a work of floor decoration in 15 days and Julie alone in 20 days. In how many days can Antony alone complete the work of floor decoration?
SSC CHSL (Tier I) 08/7/2024 Shift-I
(a) 55 (b) 45 (c) 50 (d) 60

206. A's marks in Mathematics are directly proportional to practice time. In 6 h of practice, A gets 70 marks. What should be the practice time (approximately) to get 90 marks? **SSC CHSL (Tier I) 08/7/2024 Shift-I**
(a) 8 h (b) 8.3 h
(c) 7 h (d) 7.7 h

207. X and Y can do a job in 18 days. Y and Z can do the same in 24 days. If all the three can finish the job in 12 days, in how many days can X and Z complete the job?
SSC CHSL (Tier I) 05/7/2024 Shift-IV
(a) 5 days (b) $12\frac{3}{5}$ days
(c) 7 days (d) $14\frac{2}{5}$ days

208. A work can be done by a man and a woman in 12 days and 8 days, respectively. In how many days will the work be done by 6 men and 4 women?
SSC CHSL (Tier I) 05/7/2024 Shift-III
(a) 1 (b) $\frac{1}{2}$
(c) 2 (d) $\frac{3}{4}$

209. Shobhita can complete a painting work in 20 h while Saroj can complete the same work in 15 h. In how much time (in hours) can the entire work of painting be completed, if both Shobhita and Saroj work simultaneously?
SSC CHSL (Tier I) 05/7/2024 Shift-II
(a) 7 (b) $8\frac{4}{7}$ (c) $7\frac{4}{7}$ (d) 8

210. Sapna finishes a job in 12 h working alone. If Sapna and Riya finish the same job in 8 h working together at their respective constant rates, then, in how many hours can Riya do the job working alone?
SSC CHSL (Tier I) 05/7/2024 Shift-I
(a) 18 (b) 24 (c) 16 (d) 20

211. Akhil can complete a piece of work in 24 days. Shyam can complete the same piece of work in 12 days. If both of them work together, in how many days can they complete the same piece of work?
SSC CHSL (Tier I) 04/7/2024 Shift-IV
(a) 12 days (b) 6 days
(c) 10 days (d) 8 days

212. To finish a work in 12 days, 8 workers are engaged. After 2 days, due to some urgency, the work is to be finished in next 2 days. How many more workers are to be engaged now to finish it on time?
SSC CHSL (Tier I) 04/7/2024 Shift-III
(a) 30 (b) 32 (c) 36 (d) 40

213. *A* can complete a piece of work in 20 days and *B* can complete the same work in 10 days. With the help of *C*, working together they completed the work in 5 days. The number of days in which *C* alone can complete the work is
SSC CHSL (Tier I) 04/7/2024 Shift-II
(a) 25 (b) 10 (c) 15 (d) 20

214. *A* and *B* can complete a piece of work in 15 days, *B* and *C* in 30 days and *C* and *A* in 45 days. In how many days will they complete the work, if they start working together? **SSC CHSL (Tier I) 04/7/2024 Shift-I**
(a) $8\frac{3}{11}$ (b) $11\frac{1}{3}$ (c) $11\frac{2}{3}$ (d) $16\frac{4}{11}$

215. Riya and Sangeeta can finish a work in 6 days and 8 days, respectively. Riya started the work alone and then after 3 days, Sangeeta joined Riya. They both finish the remaining work. How long did the total work last?
SSC CHSL (Tier I) 03/7/2024 Shift-IV
(a) $4\frac{3}{7}$ days (b) $4\frac{5}{7}$ days
(c) $4\frac{2}{7}$ days (d) $4\frac{4}{7}$ days

216. 18 men can complete $\frac{1}{5}$ of a work in 10 days. How many people are required to complete $\frac{2}{5}$ of the same work in 5 days ?
SSC CHSL (Tier I) 03/7/2024 Shift-II
(a) 36 (b) 90 (c) 72 (d) 54

217. *A*, *B* and *C* can complete a work in 12, 15 and 20 days, respectively. How many days are required to finish the work if they work together?
SSC CHSL (Tier I) 02/7/2024 Shift-IV
(a) 5 days (b) 3 days
(c) 6 days (d) 4 days

218. *A* and *B*, working together, take 15 days to complete a piece of work. If *A* alone can do this work in 18 days, then how long would *B* take to complete the same work?
SSC CHSL (Tier I) 02/7/2024 Shift-III
(a) 33 days (b) 90 days
(c) 8 days (d) 15 days

219. 47 masons can dig a 35 m long trench in one day. How many masons should be employed for digging a 105 m long trench of the same type in one day?
SSC CHSL (Tier I) 02/7/2024 Shift-II
(a) 94 (b) 141 (c) 128 (d) 70

220. Twelve men working for 9 h a day complete a piece of work in 24 days. In how many days can 8 men working for 12 h a day complete the same piece of work?
SSC CHSL (Tier I) 02/7/2024 Shift-I
(a) 27 days (b) 28 days
(c) 21 days (d) 24 days

221. Fifteen persons working 12 h a day earn ₹18000 per week. How many rupees will 18 persons working 9 h a day earn per week?
SSC CHSL (Tier I) 01/7/2024 Shift-IV
(a) ₹16020 (b) ₹12600
(c) ₹12060 (d) ₹16200

222. *A* and *B* can do a piece of work in 9 days and 15 days, respectively. If they work together, then the work will be completed in
SSC CHSL (Tier I) 01/7/2024 Shift-III
(a) $3\frac{3}{8}$ days (b) $2\frac{1}{8}$ days
(c) $5\frac{5}{8}$ days (d) $4\frac{5}{8}$ days

223. *A* and *B* can do a piece of work in eight days and *B* alone can do it in 16 days. In how many days, can *A* do it alone?
SSC CHSL (Tier I) 01/7/2024 Shift-II
(a) 24 days (b) 10 days
(c) 18 days (d) 16 days

SSC CHSL 2023 (Tier I & II)

224. *A* and *B* can complete a work in 9 days, while *B* and *C* can complete the same work in 18 days. When working together *A*, *B* and *C*, can finish the same work in 8 days. How many days will it take for *A* and *C* to complete the work together?
SSC CHSL (Tier II) 02/11/2023 Shift-I
(a) 13 (b) 14 (c) 12 (d) 11

225. Raju and Akbar take 4 h and 6 h to type 32 pages and 48 pages, respectively, on a computer. They are given an assignment of typing 256 pages. If they work together, typing on two different computers, starting at the same time, how much time will they take to complete the assignment (in hours)?
SSC CHSL (Tier I) 17/08/2023 Shift-I
(a) 16 (b) 14 (c) 18 (d) 12

226. Ram can complete a piece of work in 18 days. Reena can complete the same work in 12 days and with the help of Shyam. they finish the same work in six days. In how many days can Shyam alone complete the same work?
SSC CHSL (Tier-I) 14/8/2023 Shift-IV
(a) 42 days (b) 36 days
(c) 30 days (d) 24 days

227. 30 women working 5 h a day can complete a work in 18 days. In how many days will 21 women working 8 h a day complete the same work?
SSC CHSL (Tier-I) 11/8/2023 Shift-I
(a) $18\frac{7}{13}$ days (b) $17\frac{11}{13}$ days
(c) $16\frac{1}{14}$ days (d) $13\frac{3}{14}$ days

228. George can do 35% of the total work in 6 days. Jim and George together completed a piece of work in 12 days. In how many days could Jim, working alone, complete the entire task?
SSC CHSL (Tier-I) 10/8/2023 Shift-III
(a) 36 (b) 40
(c) 42 (d) 45

229. *X* can do a piece of work in 14 days, *Y* can complete the same work in 28 days and *Z* can do it in 42 days. In how many days can *X*, *Y* and *Z*, together complete the work? **SSC CHSL (Tier-I) 09/08/2023 Shift-I**
(a) $7\frac{9}{11}$ (b) $7\frac{7}{11}$ (c) $7\frac{5}{11}$ (d) $7\frac{3}{11}$

230. In a camp of 70 boys, there are food provisions for 36 days. If 50 more boys join the camp, then how many days will the provisions last?
SSC CHSL (Tier-I) 08/08/2023 Shift-II
(a) 25 days (b) 24 days
(c) 21 days (d) 18 days

231. *A* and *B* together can complete a piece of work in 15 days and *B* alone can complete it in 21 days. In how many days can *A* complete if alone? **SSC CHSL (Tier-I) 08/08/2023 Shift-II**
(a) $41\frac{1}{2}$ days (b) $52\frac{1}{2}$ days
(c) $31\frac{1}{2}$ days (d) $57\frac{1}{2}$ days

232. If 7 people working 4h a day can complete a task in 14 days. The number of days taken by 12 people working 8h a day will be
SSC CHSL (Tier-I) 04/08/2023 Shift-II
(a) $5\frac{1}{8}$ days (b) 8 days
(c) $4\frac{1}{12}$ days (d) $7\frac{1}{4}$ days

233. To complete a wall, X takes 50% more time than Y. If together they complete the wall in 15 days, then how much time will X alone take to complete it?
SSC CHSL (Tier-I) 21/03/2023 Shift-IV
(a) 36.5 days (b) 42.5 days
(c) 37.5 days (d) 40 days

234. A and B together can complete a work in 20 days. B and C together can complete the same work in 15 days. If A, B and C all work together, then the same work gets completed in 10 days. How many days will A and C together take to complete the same work?
SSC CHSL (Tier-I) 20/03/2023 Shift-III
(a) 8 days (b) 10 days
(c) 15 days (d) 12 days

235. Rani can do a work in 10 days. Priya can do the same work in 15 days and Guddu can do the same work in 12 days. If they do that work together and they are paid ₹ 9000, then what is the share of Priya?
SSC CHSL (Tier-I) 17/03/2023 Shift-II
(a) ₹ 2400 (b) ₹ 3000
(c) ₹ 3500 (d) ₹ 3600

236. 4 men and 7 women can do a work in 8 days. 7 men and 4 women can do the same work in 5 days. Find the number of days in which 8 women can finish the work.
SSC CHSL (Tier-I) 16/03/2023 Shift-I
(a) 60 days (b) 55 days
(c) 40 days (d) 45 days

237. P, Q and R can complete a work alone in 12, 15 and 20 days respectively. They started the work together. P left the work 8 days before the work was completed and Q left the work 5 days after P had left. R completed the remaining work alone. How many days will be required to complete the whole work?
SSC CHSL (Tier-I) 15/03/2023 Shift-IV
(a) 32/3 days
(b) 10 days
(c) 28/3 days
(d) 25/3 days

238. 10 women do half of the total work in 20 days. How many more women will be required to complete the remaining work in 10 days? **SSC CHSL (Tier-I) 14/03/2023 Shift-I**
(a) 30 (b) 40
(c) 20 (d) 10

239. A can do a work in 9 days. B is 80% more efficient than A. In how many days B and A together will complete the same work?
SSC CHSL (Tier-I) 13/03/2023 Shift-III
(a) 54/13 days (b) 44/13 days
(c) 47/14 days (d) 45/14 days

240. If A alone can complete a work in 20 days and B alone can complete the same work in 30 days, then which of the following statement(s) is/are correct?
SSC CHSL (Tier-I) 10/03/2023 Shift-II
I. Ratio of efficiency of A and B is 3 : 2.
II. Working together A and B can complete the same work in 12 days.
(a) Neither I nor II (b) Both I and II
(c) Only II (d) Only I

241. Tina alone can do a piece of work in 12 days and Meena alone can do the same work in 15 days. If Tina and Meena undertook to do this work for ₹ 18000, then how much amount will Meena get, if they work together?
SSC CHSL (Tier-I) 09/03/2023 Shift-I
(a) ₹ 10000 (b) ₹ 6000
(c) ₹ 12000 (d) ₹ 8000

242. A is 3 times as fast as B and is, therefore, able to complete a work in 32 days lesser than B. A and B, working together, can complete the work in ______.
SSC CHSL (Tier-I) 02/06/2023 Shift-I
(a) 10 days (b) 12 days
(c) 16 days (d) 14 days

SSC CHSL 2022 & 2021 (Tier I)

243. A man can complete a work in 20 days and a woman can complete the same work in 10 days. If they work on it together for 5 days, then how many days will the woman take to complete the rest of the work? **SSC CHSL (Tier-I) 01/06/2022 Shift-II**
(a) $2\frac{1}{2}$ (b) $1\frac{1}{4}$
(c) $3\frac{1}{2}$ (d) $1\frac{1}{2}$

244. A man and a boy together can do a certain amount of digging in 24 days. Their speeds in digging are in the ratio of 4 : 3. How many days will the boy take to complete the work if engaged alone?
SSC CHSL (Tier-I) 27/05/2022 Shift-I
(a) 52 days (b) 26 days
(c) 60 days (d) 56 days

245. Anu can complete a piece of work in 22 days. Shama is 60% more efficient than Anu. How many days does Shama alone take to complete the same piece of work?
SSC CHSL (Tier-I) 02/08/2021 Shift-III
(a) $36\frac{2}{3}$ (b) $35\frac{1}{3}$
(c) $13\frac{1}{5}$ (d) $13\frac{3}{4}$

246. 10 men or 15 women can complete a work in 30 days. In how many days can 15 men and 27 women complete the work?
SSC CHSL (Tier-I) 10/08/2021 Shift-I
(a) $6\frac{1}{11}$ (b) $5\frac{1}{11}$
(c) $11\frac{1}{11}$ (d) $9\frac{1}{11}$

247. P and Q can complete a work in 9 days and 15 days, respectively. If they work together for three days, then in how many days will the remaining work be completed by Q alone? **SSC CHSL (Tier-I) 19/04/2021 Shift-I**
(a) 8 (b) 9
(c) 7 (d) 12

248. Varun and Syan can do a work in 3 days, Syan and Anil can do it in 4 days, and Anil and Varun can do it in 6 days. How many days will Anil alone take to do the work?
SSC CHSL (Tier-I) 12/04/2021 Shift-II
(a) 22 (b) 18
(c) 20 (d) 24

SSC MTS 2024-2021

249. If 80 workers took 25 days to finish a task, how many days will it take to finish the same task if 20 more workers join? **SSC MTS 04/11/2024 Shift-III**
(a) 12 (b) 16
(c) 8 (d) 20

250. A earns ₹ 88 per hour and works for 10 h. B earns ₹ 95 per hour and works for 8 h. The ratio of per day wages of A to B is
SSC MTS 22/10/2024 Shift-II
(a) 19 : 21 (b) 19 : 22
(c) 21 : 19 (d) 22 : 19

251. A total of 24 men working 7 h a day can complete a task in 10 days. In how many days will 21 men working 9 h a day complete the same task? **SSC MTS 21/10/2024 Shift-II**
(a) $7\frac{7}{8}$ days (b) $9\frac{9}{10}$ days
(c) $6\frac{6}{7}$ days (d) $8\frac{8}{9}$ days

252. In a school sports camp, there is food provision for 200 students for 30 days. If 50 more persons join the sports camp on the then for how many days will the provision last?
SSC MTS 18/10/2024 Shift-II

(a) 24 (b) 26
(c) 22 (d) 20

253. In a company, if 40 workers can make 50 bags in 4 days, then how many bags will 24 workers will make in 8 days?
SSC MTS 09/10/2024 Shift-I

(a) 60 (b) 40 (c) 54 (d) 45

254. 6 skilled workers can complete a work in 4 days. After three days 3 more skilled workers joined them. How many days will they now take to complete the remaining work? SSC MTS 14/09/2023 Shift-I

(a) $\frac{2}{3}$ (b) $\frac{1}{2}$ (c) $\frac{1}{3}$ (d) $\frac{3}{4}$

255. A and B can do a piece of work in 30 days and 40 days, respectively. They began the work together but after a certain time, A leaves off and B complete the remaining work in 25 days. After how many days did A leave?
SSC MTS 14/09/2023 Shift-I

(a) $6\frac{3}{7}$ (b) $5\frac{3}{7}$ (c) $5\frac{2}{7}$ (d) $6\frac{1}{7}$

256. A and B can do a piece of work in 5 days, while C and D can do the same work in 20 days. In how many days will A, B, C and D do it together? SSC MTS 13/09/2023 Shift-I

(a) 3 (b) 4 (c) 5 (d) 6

257. A and B working separately can do a piece of work in 16 days and 28 days, respectively. If they work on alternate days beginning with B, in how many days will the work be completed? SSC MTS 11/09/2023 Shift-II

(a) $18\frac{1}{2}$ (b) $20\frac{1}{2}$ (c) $21\frac{1}{2}$ (d) $19\frac{1}{2}$

258. In a fort, 160 men had food for 94 days. After 10 days, 20 men left the fort. How long (in days) would the food last at the same rate?
SSC MTS 11/09/2023 Shift-I

(a) 84 (b) 90
(c) 96 (d) 100

259. Mohan can complete a piece of work in 24 days. He worked for 6 days and left the work. Thereafter, Sohan finished the remaining work in 21 days. In how many days, can Mohan and Sohan together complete it? SSC MTS 11/09/2023 Shift-I

(a) $12\frac{12}{13}$ days (b) $12\frac{9}{13}$ days
(c) $12\frac{11}{13}$ days (d) $12\frac{10}{13}$ days

260. Aisha and Razia can complete a work in 50 days, and 75 days, respectively. In how many days will the entire work be completed, if both of them work together?
SSC MTS 08/09/2023 Shift-II

(a) 32 (b) 25 (c) 30 (d) 28

261. Surjeet alone can finish an assignment in 8 days and Manjeet alone can finish the same assignment in 6 days. Surjeet and Manjeet decided to do this assignment by working on alternate days, starting with Surjeet. In how many days will the assignment be finished?
SSC MTS 06/09/2023 Shift-I

(a) 7 days (b) 8.5 days
(c) 8 days (d) 7.5 days

262. X can type 8 pages in 3 min. Y can type 3 pages in 5 min. Working together, how many pages can they type in 15 min?
SSC MTS 06/09/2023 Shift-I

(a) 42 (b) 40
(c) 46 (d) 49

263. Reena, Ritu and Sita can independently complete a piece of work in 6 h, 9h and 18 h, respectively. If they work together, then how much time (in h) will they take to complete that piece of work ? SSC MTS 05/09/2023 Shift-II

(a) 3 (b) 5 (c) 4 (d) 2

264. A, B and C can complete a work in 10, 15 and 20 days, respectively. They work on alternate days such that 1st day A, 2nd day B and 3rd day C. Again 4th day A, 5th day B and so on. If they work in the same way, in how many days will the work be completed?
SSC MTS 04/09/2023 Shift-II

(a) $13\frac{1}{4}$ (b) 15
(c) 14 (d) $13\frac{1}{2}$

265. 20 men can complete a piece of work in 40 days, and 40 women can do the same work in 60 days. If 10 men and 20 women work together, then in how many days will the work be completed?
SSC MTS 04/09/2023 Shift-II

(a) 60 (b) 50
(c) 48 (d) 40

266. 12 days are taken by one man and one women together to complete the work. A man alone can complete the work in 15 days. In how many days can one woman alone complete the work?
SSC MTS 01/09/2023 Shift-III

(a) 45 days (b) 30 days
(c) 60 days (d) 12 days

267. A and B can do a piece of work in 9 and 18 days, respectively. They started working together. After some days A left the work and B finished the remaining work in 15 days. After how many days did A leave? SSC MTS 01/09/2023 Shift-III

(a) 1 (b) 2 (c) 4 (d) 3

268. A, B and C can do a piece of work in 10, 15, 12 days, respectively. A and B worked alternately for 5 days each and left. Then C joined and completed the work. In how many days did C complete the remaining work?
SSC MTS 01/09/2023 Shift-I

(a) 3 (b) 1
(c) 4 (d) 2

269. A, B and C together can do a piece of work in 6 days. A and B together can do the same work in 12 days. B alone can do the same work in 18 days. In how many days can A and C together do the same work ?
SSC MTS 15/07/2022 Shift-I

(a) 9 (b) 10.5 (c) 8 (d) 7.5

270. A can do a piece of work alone in 40 days. A and B together can do the same work in 10 days. C is 50% less efficient than B. In how many days can A and C together complete the same work ?
SSC MTS 15/07/2022 Shift-I

(a) 20 (b) 24 (c) 16 (d) 12

271. X alone can complete a piece of work in 16 days, while Y alone can complete the same work in 24 days. They work on alternate days starting with Y. In how many days will 50% of the total work be completed ? SSC MTS 14/07/2022 Shift-I

(a) $\frac{24}{3}$ (b) $\frac{29}{3}$ (c) $\frac{32}{3}$ (d) 9

272. Zee and Gee can complete a task together in 24 days. If the efficiencies of Zee and Gee are in the ratio 3 : 8, respectively, then in how many days can Gee complete the task alone ? SSC MTS 14/07/2022 Shift-I

(a) 33 (b) 55 (c) 88 (d) 44

273. In a job Z_1, Z_2 and Z_3 work for 8, 10 and 15 days, respectively. The ratio of the daily wages of Z_1, Z_2 and Z_3 is 3 : 4 : 4, respectively. If they receive ₹ 4960 as total wages for the work done, then what is the combined share of Z_2 and Z_3 in the total wages received?
SSC MTS 13/07/2022 Shift-I

(a) ₹ 4800 (b) ₹ 4000
(c) ₹ 4400 (d) ₹ 4200

274. D_1 and D_2 can do a piece of work together in 16 days, D_2 and D_3 can do the same work together in 24 days, while D_3 and D_1 can do it together in 48 days. In how many days can all three, working together, do $\frac{5}{6}$ of the work ?
SSC MTS 13/07/2022 Shift-I

(a) $\frac{31}{3}$ days (b) $\frac{40}{3}$ days
(c) $\frac{35}{3}$ days (d) $\frac{38}{3}$ days

275. Ishita can read a newspaper in 'n' min. What part of the newspaper can she read in 7 min ? ($n > 7$)
SSC MTS 12/07/2022 Shift-I

(a) $\frac{n}{7}$ (b) $7n^2$ (c) $7n$ (d) $\frac{7}{n}$

276. 24 women and 9 men can complete a certain piece of work in 18 days. Each women takes twice the amount of time taken by a man to finish the work. In how many days can only 9 men finish the same work ? **SSC MTS 11/07/2022 Shift-I**

(a) 42 (b) 35 (c) 39 (d) 48

277. Y takes five days more than X to finish a work. Working together, they finish the work in six days. In how many days can Y finish it working alone?
SSC MTS 02/11/2021 Shift-III

(a) 16 (b) 12 (c) 15 (d) 10

278. A alone can do a piece of work in 10 days and B alone in 15 days. A and B undertook to do it for ₹ 42000, with the help of C, they completed the work in 5 days. How much (in ₹) is to be paid to B?
SSC MTS 02/11/2021 Shift-II

(a) 14000 (b) 15000
(c) 21000 (d) 7000

279. Twenty persons take 15 days to complete a certain work, working 8 h a day. To complete the same work in 4 days, working 10 h a day, the number of persons required is
SSC MTS 02/11/2021 Shift-II

(a) 75 (b) 60 (c) 80 (d) 55

280. 6 men and 10 boys, as well as 2 men and 20 boys can finish the same work in 12 days. In how many days will 10 boys finish the same work? **SSC MTS 02/11/2021 Shift-I**

(a) 24 (b) 26 (c) 16 (d) 30

281. If a man completes $\frac{3}{7}$ work in 6 days, then how many more days will he require for completing the remaining work?
SSC MTS 02/11/2021 Shift-I

(a) 8 (b) 14 (c) 9 (d) 7

SSC GD Constable 2024

282. C alone can complete a work in 50 days and D alone can complete the same work in half of the time taken by C. In how many days will both together complete 3/10 part of the total work ? **SSC GD 26/02/2024 Shift-I**

(a) 6.5 days (b) 5 days
(c) 6 days (d) 4 days

283. Mohan and Rohan undertook a work for ₹ 3300. Mohan alone can do that work in 10 days and Rohan alone can do the same work in 12 days. If they work together, then what will be the difference in the amount they receive ?
SSC GD 26/02/2024 Shift-I

(a) ₹ 300 (b) ₹ 370
(c) ₹ 350 (d) ₹ 400

284. After working for 8 days, Payal finds that only 10% of the work is completed. She employs Pinky who is 50% more efficient than Payal. How many more days will they together take to complete the remaining work?
SSC GD 24/02/2024 Shift-III

(a) 28.8 days (b) 27 days
(c) 25 days (d) 30 days

285. B_1 and B_2 together can complete a work in 20 days. B_2 alone can complete the same work in 60 days. In how many days B_1 alone can complete the same work?
SSC GD 24/02/2024 Shift-III

(a) 25 days (b) 10 days
(c) 30 days (d) 35 days

286. A is four times as good a workman as B and together they finish a piece of work in $\frac{84}{15}$ days. In how many days can A alone finish the work? **SSC GD 24/02/2024 Shift-II**

(a) 10 days (b) 15 days
(c) 9 days (d) 7 days

287. If 25 workers can build a wall in 10 days, how many days will it take for 20 workers to build a similar wall? **SSC GD 24/02/2024 Shift-II**

(a) $\frac{25}{2}$ days (b) $\frac{23}{3}$ days
(c) $\frac{25}{4}$ days (d) $\frac{21}{2}$ days

288. T alone can complete a work in 90 days. 20% of the same work will be completed by T in how many days?
SSC GD 24/02/2024 Shift-I

(a) 20 days (b) 7 days
(c) 21 days (d) 18 days

289. Anil and Karan together can do a work in 20 days. Karan and Himanshu together can do the same work in 25 days, Himanshu and Anil together can do the same work in 50 days. In how many days can Himanshu alone do the same work? **SSC GD 24/02/2024 Shift-I**

(a) 250 days (b) 240 days
(c) 180 days (d) 200 days

290. A is 40% less efficient than B. If B can make a helmet in 16 days, then in how many days can A make the same helmet? **SSC GD 23/02/2024 Shift-IV**

(a) 80/3 days (b) 80/7 days
(c) 90/7 days (d) 75/4 days

291. A can do a piece of work in 55 days. He works for 20 days and then B alone finishes the remaining work in 49 days. How many days will both take together to complete the work? **SSC GD 23/02/2024 Shift-IV**

(a) $\frac{385}{12}$ days (b) $\frac{514}{55}$ days
(c) $\frac{124}{5}$ days (d) $\frac{445}{14}$ days

292. If 15 men can build a house in 18 days, then in how many days will 12 men build the same house?
SSC GD 23/02/2024 Shift-II

(a) 19 days (b) 22.5 days
(c) 18 days (d) 20 days

293. Gaurav is four times as efficient as Shambu. Gaurav takes 67.5 days less than Shambu to complete a work. If both of them work together, then in how many days will the same work be completed?
SSC GD 23/02/2024 Shift-II

(a) 90 days (b) 18 days
(c) 55 days (d) 25 days

294. P can do a work in 14 days. What part of the total work can be done by P in 4 days? **SSC GD 23/02/2024 Shift-I**

(a) 3/8 (b) 4/9 (c) 2/7 (d) 6/7

295. M_1 alone can do a work in 14 days and M_2 alone can do the same work in 70 days. With help of M_3, they finish the same work in 7 days In how many days M_3 alone can do the same work? **SSC GD 23/02/2024 Shift-I**

(a) 20 days (b) 19 days
(c) 17.5 days (d) 21 days

296. Anil can do a work in 80 days. What per cent work of the total work can be done by Anil in 30 days? **SSC GD 22/02/2024 Shift-IV**

(a) 38% (b) 40% (c) 42% (d) 37.5%

297. 22 men can make a wall in 2 days. How many men are required to complete the same work in half a day? **SSC GD 22/02/2024 Shift-III**

(a) 90 (b) 88 (c) 80 (d) 72

298. Dinesh alone can do a work in 96 h. Dinesh and Rahul together can do the same work in 48 h. Rahul and Tarun together can do the same work in 16 h. In how many hours can Tarun alone do the same work? **SSC GD 22/02/2024 Shift-III**

(a) 19.2 h (b) 30 h (c) 28 h (d) 20 h

299. Rakesh, Mahesh and Puneesh together can make a chair in 20 min. Rakesh and Mahesh together can make it in 25 min. How much time will Puneesh alone take to that chair? **SSC GD 22/02/2024 Shift-II**

(a) 80 min (b) 95 min
(c) 100 min (d) 110 min

300. Amar is 10% more efficient than Sachin. If Sachin alone can finish a work in 44 days, then in how many days will Amar alone finish the same work? **SSC GD 22/02/2024 Shift-I**

(a) 40 days (b) 52 days
(c) 47 days (d) 45 days

301. Z_1, Z_2 and Z_3 can do a work in 100, 50 and 75 days, respectively. All three of them began the work together but Z_2 left 15 days before the completion of the work. In how many days was the work completed? **SSC GD 21/02/2024 Shift-IV**

(a) 40 days (b) 45 days
(c) 30 days (d) 35 days

302. Seema can do a work in 120 days, Anjali can do the same work in 144 days and Soniya can do the same work in 180 days. If they do that work together and they are paid ₹ 3300, then what is the share of Anjali? **SSC GD 21/02/2024 Shift-III**

(a) ₹ 1100 (b) ₹ 2000
(c) ₹ 1700 (d) ₹ 2500

303. S_1 alone can do a work in 16 days and S_2 alone can do the same work in 80 days. With help of S_3, they finish the same work in 6 days. In how many days S_3 alone can do the same work? **SSC GD 21/02/2024 Shift-III**

(a) $\frac{120}{11}$ days (b) 9 days
(c) 12 days (d) 7 days

304. A can do a piece of work in 7 h, B and C can do it in $\frac{21}{4}$ h and C and A can do it in $\frac{7}{2}$ h. How long will B alone take to do it? **SSC GD 21/02/2024 Shift-II**

(a) 24 h (b) 21 h
(c) 20 h (d) 22 h

305. A and B can do a piece of work in $\frac{14}{3}$ days while B and C can do the same work in $\frac{12}{5}$ days and C and A in $\frac{16}{3}$ days. By working together what part of the same work all three can finish in 2 days? **SSC GD 21/02/2024 Shift-II**

(a) $\frac{275}{336}$ (b) $\frac{225}{336}$
(c) $\frac{127}{336}$ (d) $\frac{277}{336}$

306. Arvind can do a work in 20 days and Bakshi in 22 days. If they work on it together for 5 days, then the fraction of the work that is left is **SSC GD 21/02/2024 Shift-I**

(a) 28/15 (b) 17/7
(c) 23/44 (d) 63/20

307. X_1, X_2 and X_3 can do a work in 90, 45 and 67.5 days, respectively. All three of them began the work together, but X_2 left 13.5 days before the completion of the work. In how many days was the work completed? **SSC GD 20/02/2024 Shift-IV**

(a) 25 days (b) 18 days
(c) 24 days (d) 27 days

308. Sonu alone can make a table in 125 days, while Monu alone can make it in 250 days. Monu started the work and worked for 75 days. In how many days, Sonu can finish the remaining work? **SSC GD 20/02/2024 Shift-IV**

(a) 135 days (b) 87.5 days
(c) 100 days (d) 120 days

309. A and B can complete a work alone in 20 days and 60 days, respectively. They began the work together but A left the work after some days and B completed the remaining work in 12 days. After how many days from the beginning A left the work ? **SSC GD 20/02/2024 Shift-III**

(a) 12 days (b) 9 days
(c) 15 days (d) 10 days

310. Swapnil can build a sofa in 16 days. Working together with Revathi he can finish the work in 128/17 days. Find the number of days taken by Revathi to complete the work, if she works alone. **SSC GD 20/02/2024 Shift-II**

(a) 128/17 days (b) 128/16 days
(c) 6 days (d) 128/9 days

311. If 72 binders can bind 720 books in 22 days, how many binders will be required to bind 660 books in 12 days? **SSC GD 20/02/2024 Shift-II**

(a) 124 (b) 120 (c) 121 (d) 123

312. After working for 8 days. Rakhi finds that only 10% of the work is completed. She employs Poonam who is 20% more efficient than Rakhi. How many more days will they together take to complete the remaining work? **SSC GD 20/02/2024 Shift-I**

(a) 340/11 days (b) 340/7 days
(c) 360/7 days (d) 360/11 days

313. R can do a work in 90 days. What per cent work of the total work can be done by R in 45 days? **SSC GD 20/02/2024 Shift-I**

(a) 70% (b) 65% (c) 50% (d) 56%

SSC GD Constable 2023

314. Anit can do a piece of work in 77 days. Ram can do the same work in 11 days. Ram and Anit start working together but Ram left the work 3 days before the completion of the work. Find the approximate number of days in which the work is completed. **SSC GD 13/02/2023 Shift-IV**

(a) 17 days (b) 11 days
(c) 14 days (d) 12 days

315. Atul alone can complete a work in 114 days. How many persons were required with the same efficiency as Atul to complete the same work in 19 days? **SSC GD 13/02/2023 Shift-II**

(a) 7 (b) 6 (c) 5 (d) 8

316. Two persons P and Q working together can do a piece of work in 36 days. Q alone can do it in 45 days. Q alone start the work and

left the work after 5 days. How many days will *P* take to complete the remaining work?
SSC GD 13/02/2023 Shift-II

(a) 180 (b) 120 (c) 140 (d) 160

317. *R* can complete a painting task in 12 days. With the help of two helpers, he can complete it in 8 days. In how many days the task will be completed by a helper alone? **SSC GD 9/02/2023 Shift-II**

(a) 24 (b) 48 (c) 42 (d) 36

318. *P*, *Q* and *R* working separately can do a piece of work in 50,100, and 300 days, respectively. If they work on alternate days, *P* works on the first day, Q works on the second day, *R* works on the third day and then again *P* work on the fourth day and so on, then in how many days, the work be completed?
SSC GD 9/02/2023 Shift-II

(a) 40 days (b) 50 days
(c) 90 days (d) 60 days

319. Ranu can finish a piece of work in 10 days while Ruby can finish the same work in 15 days. In how many days the whole work will be finished. If they work on alternate days, starting with Ranu?
SSC GD 09/02/2023 Shift-I

(a) 13 (b) 12 (c) 11 (d) 14

320. Pramod, Akhil and Raman can do a piece of work in 14 days. Akhil and Raman can do the same work in 77 days. Find the number of days in which Pramod can complete the same work.
SSC GD 09/02/2023 Shift-I

(a) $\frac{154}{9}$ days (b) $\frac{177}{9}$ days
(c) $\frac{164}{9}$ days (d) $\frac{144}{9}$ days

321. Pooja, Neha and Manoj can do a piece of work in 16, 22, and 20 days respectively. On which day will the work get finished if Pooja is assisted by both Neha and Manoj on every second day?
SSC GD 08/02/2023 Shift-I

(a) 10th day (b) 8th day
(c) 9th day (d) 7th day

322. *P* can do a piece of work in 20 days and *Q* can do it in 25 days. If they work on it together for 4 days, then what percentage of work will be left? **SSC GD 08/02/2023 Shift-I**

(a) 68% (b) 52%
(c) 64% (d) 36%

323. 24 men complete a work in 9 days. 3 days after they started working, 8 more men joined them. How many days will all of them take to complete the remaining work?
SSC GD 07/02/2023 Shift-I

(a) 9 (b) 4
(c) 5.5 (d) 4.5

324. *P* and *Q* can complete a work in 8 days, *Q* and *R* in 12 days, and *R* and *P* in 15 days. How many days will *R* alone take to complete the work? **SSC GD 06/02/2023 Shift-I**

(a) 90 (b) 50
(c) 80 (d) 70

325. Anish can do a piece of work in 88 days. Yug can do this work in 66 days. Anish started the work alone. After how many days should Yug join him, so that the work is finished in 44 days?
SSC GD 06/02/2023 Shift-I

(a) 13 days (b) 11 days
(c) 15 days (d) 12 days

326. *A* can repair 11 benches in an hour and *B* can repair 5 benches in an hour. Determine how much time they will require to repair 64 benches when they work together?
SSC GD 02/02/2023 Shift-I

(a) 3 h (b) 4 h
(c) 5 h (d) 6 h

327. Akash can do a piece of work in 21 days and Diya can do the same work in 63 days. Find the time required to complete the same work if they work on alternate days and Akash starts the work.
SSC GD 02/02/2023 Shift-I

(a) 31 days
(b) 28 days
(c) 29 days
(d) 27 days

328. *A* can paint 5 chairs in an hour and *B* can paint 3 chairs in an hour. Determine how much time they will require to paint 40 chairs when they work together.
SSC GD 01/02/2023 Shift-I

(a) 12 h (b) 10 h
(c) 8 h (d) 5 h

329. If 12 men or 9 women can do a piece of work in 36 days, then how many days will 16 men and 18 women take to finish the same work? **SSC GD 01/02/2023 Shift-I**

(a) $13\frac{1}{5}$ (b) $12\frac{4}{5}$
(c) $14\frac{3}{5}$ (d) $10\frac{4}{5}$

SSC Selection Post 2024-2022

330. A garrison of 140 men has provisions for 35 days. At the end of 10 days, 35 more men joined them. How many days can they sustain on the remaining provisions? **Matric Level 20/06/2024 Shift-IV**

(a) 10 (b) 20
(c) 25 (d) 35

331. At a construction site, 15 men or 10 machines can construct a room in 66 days. In how many days can 5 men and 4 machines together complete the work?
Matric Level 20/06/2024 Shift-IV

(a) 80 (b) 75
(c) 85 (d) 90

332. Eight labourers working 10 h a day completed a work in 18 days. If only 5 labourers are working, then in how many hours a day should they work to finish the work in 24 days? **Graduate Level 20/06/2024 Shift-III**

(a) 9 h (b) 8 h
(c) 10 h (d) 12 h

333. *P* and *Q* can complete a job in 4 days and 12 days, respectively. They work on alternate days with *P* starting the job. In how many days will the job be completed?
Higher Secondary Level 20/06/2024 Shift-II

(a) 6 days (b) 3 days
(c) 8 days (d) 4 days

334. If 8 men or 16 women or 32 boys can do a piece of work in 8 months, then in how many months can 4 men, 4 women and 4 boys together complete the work?
Higher Secondary Level 20/06/2024 Shift-II

(a) $6\frac{3}{7}$ (b) $10\frac{5}{7}$ (c) $9\frac{1}{7}$ (d) $8\frac{2}{7}$

335. Anita and Anand can complete a work in 12 days and 18 days, respectively. They undertook to complete that work for ₹ 48000. With the help of Arun, they completed the work in 6 days. Find the sum of the shares of Anita and Anand (in ₹).
Graduate Level 17/06/2023 Shift-IV

(a) 40000 (b) 8000
(c) 16000 (d) 24000

336. Abhay can do a work in 22 days. Nidhi is 28% more efficient than Abhay. The number of days Nidhi will take to do the same piece of work is
Higher Secondary Level 27/06/2023 Shift-III

(a) $17\frac{3}{16}$ (b) $16\frac{3}{17}$
(c) $17\frac{1}{16}$ (d) $16\frac{1}{17}$

337. Food is available for 27 days for 35 students in a hostel. For how many days will this food be sufficient for 45 students? **Matric Level 27/06/2023 Shift-I**

(a) 25 (b) 22
(c) 23 (d) 21

338. *A*, *B* and *C* can separately complete a work in 20, 25 and 30 days, respectively. If *A* works on the first day alone, *B* on second day alone and *C* on the third day alone, and this sequence goes on further, in how many days will the entire work be finished?

Matric Level 27/06/2023 Shift-I

(a) $25\frac{4}{15}$ (b) $24\frac{1}{75}$
(c) $25\frac{1}{75}$ (d) $24\frac{4}{15}$

339. Mahesh and Suresh can complete a work in 16 days and 12 days, respectively. Starting with Mahesh, they work on alternate basis. How many days will take to finalise the complete work?

Graduate Level 01/08/2022 Shift-IV

(a) 14 days (b) $13\frac{1}{4}$ days
(c) $13\frac{3}{4}$ days (d) 13 days

340. *A*, *B* and *C* can complete a piece of work in 3 days, 4 days and 6 days, respectively. They get ₹ 432 for completing the job. If *A*, *B* and *C* work together to complete the job, *A*'s share is

Higher Secondary Level 01/08/2022 Shift-II

(a) ₹ 108 (b) ₹ 144
(c) ₹ 72 (d) ₹ 192

341. 20 men can complete a work in 10 days. Five days after they started working, 5 more men joined them. In how many days will the total work be completed?

Matric Level 01/08/2022 Shift-I

(a) 10 (b) 12 (c) 9 (d) 11

342. If the salary of 16 men for 30 days is ₹ 20736, then what is the salary of 1 man for 15 days?

Matric Level 01/08/2022 Shift-I

(a) ₹ 520 (b) ₹ 812
(c) ₹ 648 (d) ₹ 742

Right Answers

1 (b)	2 (a)	3 (c)	4 (c)	5 (d)	6 (c)	7 (c)	8 (a)	9 (a)	10 (a)
11 (a)	12 (a)	13 (b)	14 (b)	15 (d)	16 (b)	17 (a)	18 (d)	19 (a)	20 (d)
21 (c)	22 (b)	23 (c)	24 (a)	25 (a)	26 (a)	27 (c)	28 (d)	29 (a)	30 (d)
31 (c)	32 (c)	33 (a)	34 (b)	35 (d)	36 (b)	37 (c)	38 (a)	39 (b)	40 (b)
41 (d)	42 (d)	43 (c)	44 (b)	45 (d)	46 (a)	47 (a)	48 (d)	49 (d)	50 (c)
51 (c)	52 (d)	53 (d)	54 (d)	55 (c)	56 (d)	57 (b)	58 (b)	59 (b)	60 (a)
61 (a)	62 (c)	63 (a)	64 (a)	65 (b)	66 (c)	67 (b)	68 (a)	69 (c)	70 (a)
71 (b)	72 (b)	73 (a)	74 (c)	75 (d)	76 (c)	77 (b)	78 (b)	79 (a)	80 (a)
81 (d)	82 (c)	83 (b)	84 (a)	85 (a)	86 (c)	87 (b)	88 (a)	89 (c)	90 (b)
91 (b)	92 (d)	93 (b)	94 (c)	95 (d)	96 (b)	97 (b)	98 (a)	99 (a)	100 (c)
101 (a)	102 (b)	103 (a)	104 (d)	105 (a)	106 (c)	107 (d)	108 (a)	109 (b)	110 (c)
111 (b)	112 (c)	113 (c)	114 (a)	115 (a)	116 (d)	117 (c)	118 (d)	119 (c)	120 (d)
121 (a)	122 (b)	123 (c)	124 (b)	125 (a)	126 (a)	127 (a)	128 (b)	129 (c)	130 (d)
131 (d)	132 (c)	133 (a)	134 (b)	135 (a)	136 (b)	137 (d)	138 (b)	139 (b)	140 (b)
141 (a)	142 (a)	143 (c)	144 (b)	145 (c)	146 (b)	147 (b)	148 (c)	149 (a)	150 (a)
151 (a)	152 (d)	153 (d)	154 (b)	155 (a)	156 (b)	157 (b)	158 (b)	159 (d)	160 (b)
161 (b)	162 (a)	163 (b)	164 (c)	165 (c)	166 (c)	167 (b)	168 (d)	169 (d)	170 (b)
171 (c)	172 (a)	173 (c)	174 (c)	175 (d)	176 (b)	177 (d)	178 (a)	179 (b)	180 (a)
181 (d)	182 (c)	183 (d)	184 (b)	185 (c)	186 (b)	187 (c)	188 (a)	189 (a)	190 (b)
191 (b)	192 (b)	193 (c)	194 (a)	195 (b)	196 (d)	197 (d)	198 (a)	199 (c)	200 (c)
201 (c)	202 (b)	203 (b)	204 (b)	205 (d)	206 (d)	207 (d)	208 (a)	209 (b)	210 (b)
211 (d)	212 (b)	213 (d)	214 (d)	215 (b)	216 (c)	217 (a)	218 (b)	219 (b)	220 (a)
221 (d)	222 (c)	223 (d)	224 (c)	225 (a)	226 (b)	227 (c)	228 (b)	229 (b)	230 (c)
231 (b)	232 (c)	233 (c)	234 (d)	235 (a)	236 (b)	237 (c)	238 (d)	239 (d)	240 (b)
241 (d)	242 (b)	243 (a)	244 (d)	245 (d)	246 (d)	247 (c)	248 (d)	249 (d)	250 (d)
251 (d)	252 (a)	253 (a)	254 (a)	255 (a)	256 (b)	257 (b)	258 (c)	259 (a)	260 (c)
261 (a)	262 (d)	263 (a)	264 (d)	265 (c)	266 (c)	267 (a)	268 (d)	269 (a)	270 (c)
271 (b)	272 (a)	273 (b)	274 (b)	275 (d)	276 (a)	277 (c)	278 (a)	279 (b)	280 (d)
281 (a)	282 (b)	283 (a)	284 (a)	285 (c)	286 (d)	287 (a)	288 (d)	289 (d)	290 (a)
291 (a)	292 (b)	293 (b)	294 (c)	295 (c)	296 (d)	297 (b)	298 (a)	299 (c)	300 (a)
301 (c)	302 (a)	303 (a)	304 (b)	305 (a)	306 (c)	307 (d)	308 (b)	309 (a)	310 (d)
311 (c)	312 (d)	313 (c)	314 (d)	315 (b)	316 (d)	317 (b)	318 (c)	319 (b)	320 (a)
321 (a)	322 (c)	323 (d)	324 (c)	325 (b)	326 (b)	327 (a)	328 (d)	329 (d)	330 (b)
331 (d)	332 (d)	333 (a)	334 (c)	335 (a)	336 (a)	337 (d)	338 (d)	339 (c)	340 (d)
341 (c)	342 (c)								

Solutions

1. (b)

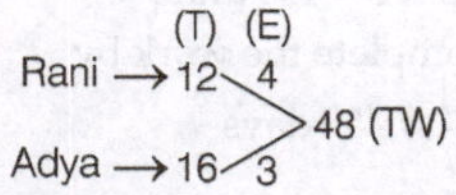

Rani and Adya's 2 days work = 7 unit

Rani and Adya's 12 days work
$= 42$ unit

Rani and Adya's 13 days work
$= 42 + 4 = 46$ unit

Remaining work done by Adya
$= \frac{48 - 46}{3} = \frac{2}{3}$

$\therefore$ Task will be completed in $13\frac{2}{3}$ days.

2. (a) According to the question,

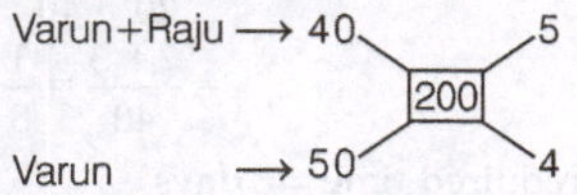

$\therefore$ Efficiency of Raju $= 5 - 4 = 1$

$\therefore$ Required number of hours taken by Raju

$= \frac{\text{Total work}}{\text{Efficiency of Raju}} = \frac{200}{1} = 200$ h

3. (c)

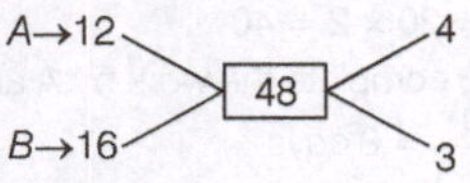

Total work done in 6 days
$= 6(4 + 3) = 42$ unit

$\therefore$ Remaining work $= 48 - 42 = 6$ unit

$\therefore$ Fraction of work left $= \frac{6}{48} = \frac{1}{8}$

4. (c) $\frac{17}{27}$ of order print in 34 days.

Thus, entire order print in
$= 34 \times \frac{27}{17} = 54$ days

5. (d) Let the required time taken be x h.

According to the question,

$\therefore \quad M_1D_1H_1 = M_2D_2H_2$

$\Rightarrow \quad 6 \times D \times 10 = 12 \times D \times x$

$\Rightarrow \quad x = \frac{60}{12} \Rightarrow x = 5$ h

6. (c) According to the question,

First day (P and Q)'s work $= \frac{1}{5} + \frac{1}{10} = \frac{3}{10}$

Second day (P and R)'s work $= \frac{1}{5} + \frac{1}{15} = \frac{4}{15}$

Third day (P and Q)'s work $= \frac{1}{5} + \frac{1}{10} = \frac{3}{10}$

Remaining work $= 1 - \left(\frac{3}{10} + \frac{4}{15} + \frac{3}{10}\right)$

$= 1 - \left(\frac{9 + 8 + 9}{30}\right) = \frac{30 - 26}{30} = \frac{4}{30} = \frac{2}{15}$

Required time taken $= \frac{\frac{2}{15}}{\frac{4}{15}} = \frac{1}{2}$

So, total time $= 1 + 1 + 1 + \frac{1}{2} = 3 + \frac{1}{2}$

$= \frac{7}{2}$ days

7. (c) Let A take x days to complete the work and B take $4x$ days to complete the work.

According to the question,

$\frac{1}{x} + \frac{1}{4x} = \frac{1}{48} \Rightarrow \frac{4 + 1}{4x} = \frac{1}{48} \Rightarrow x = 60$

B alone can complete the work in
$4 \times 60 = 240$ days

8. (a) Let total work = 24 unit

($\because$ LCM of 8 and 12 = 24)

Efficiency of A = 3 unit/h

Efficiency of B = 2 unit/h

Then $(A + B)$ = 5 unit/h

Time taken by A and B together $= \frac{24}{5} = 4.8$ h

9. (a) Let total work = 150 unit

($\because$ LCM of 15, 25 and 30 = 150)

Efficiency of Ram = 10 unit/day

Efficiency of Rohan = 6 unit/day

Efficiency of Rohit = 5 unit/day

Work done by (Rohan + Rohit) in 2 days
$= (6 + 5) \times 2 = 22$ units

Remaining work $= 150 - 22 = 128$ units

(Ram + Rohan)'s 1 day work = 16 units

Then, remaining work finished in
$= \frac{128}{16} = 8$ days

Hence, total work finished in
$= (8 + 2)$ days $= 10$ days

10. (a) Let total work = 90 units

($\because$ LCM of 18 and 15 = 90)

Efficiency of Sara = 5 units/day

Efficiency of Tara = 6 units / day

Work done by Tara in 10 days
$= 6 \times 10 = 60$ units

$\therefore$ Remaining work $= 90 - 60 = 30$ units

30 units work finished by Sara in
$= \frac{30}{5} = 6$ days

> **Speedy Method**
>
> Tara's 10 days work $= \frac{10}{15} = \frac{2}{3}$
>
> Let Sara complete the remaining work in x days.
>
> So, $\frac{x}{18} = 1 - \frac{2}{3} \Rightarrow x = \frac{1 \times 18}{3} = 6$ days

11. (a) If 40 men can complete a work in
$= 30$ days

1 man can complete a work in
$= 30 \times 40 = 1200$ days

$\therefore$ 30 men can complete the work in
$= \frac{1200}{30} = 40$ days

12. (a) Let number of days required to complete the work be 'x'.

According to the question,

$\frac{(x - 4)}{24} + \frac{(x - 10)}{36} + \frac{x}{48} = 1$

$\Rightarrow \quad \frac{6(x - 4) + 4(x - 10) + 3x}{144} = 1$

$\Rightarrow \quad 6x - 24 + 4x - 40 + 3x = 144$

$\Rightarrow \quad 13x - 64 = 144 \Rightarrow 13x = 208$

$\therefore \quad x = \frac{208}{13} = 16$ days

13. (b) Let total work = 60 units

One day's work of

$A = \frac{60}{20} = 3$ units

$B = \frac{60}{30} = 2$ units

$C = \frac{60}{60} = 1$ unit

If B and C assist A on every third day then,

Total work in three days
$= 3 + 3 + (3 + 2 + 1) = 12$ units

Then, total work can be completed in
$= \frac{60 \times 3}{12} = 15$ days.

14. (b) Let total work = 60 units

($\therefore$ LCM of 12, 15 and 10 = 60)

(Ram + Ramesh)'s one day's work
$= \frac{60}{12} = 5$ units/day

(Ramesh + Somesh)'s one day's work
$= \frac{60}{15} = 4$ units/day

(Somesh + Ram)'s one day's work
$= \frac{60}{10} = 6$ units/day

Then, 2(Ram + Ramesh + Somesh)'s 1 day's work $= 5 + 4 + 6 = 15$

(Ram + Ramesh + Somesh)'s 1 day's work
$= \frac{15}{2}$ units/day

Then, time taken to complete the work
$= \frac{60}{\frac{15}{2}} = 60 \times \frac{2}{15} = 8$ days

15. (d) One day work of P, Q and R
$= \frac{1}{9} + \frac{1}{12} + \frac{1}{18} = \frac{4 + 3 + 2}{36} = \frac{9}{36} = \frac{1}{4}$

16. (b) Total work = LCM of 8, 12 and 4 = 24

$\therefore$ Efficiency of Ashok and Anil
$= \frac{24}{8} + \frac{24}{12} = 3 + 2 = 5$ unit/day

and efficiency of Ashok, Anil and Amar
$= \frac{24}{4} = 6$

Then, efficiency of Amar = 6 − 5 = 1 unit/day

Now, share of Amar $= 4500 \times \dfrac{1}{(3+2+1)}$

$= 4500 \times \dfrac{1}{6} = ₹\,750$

17. (a) 1 day's work of man $= \dfrac{1}{3}$

$\therefore \quad \dfrac{1}{5}$ day's work of man $= \dfrac{1}{15}$

1 day's work of woman $= \dfrac{1}{5}$

$\therefore \quad \dfrac{1}{5}$ day's work of woman $= \dfrac{1}{25}$

Let required number of boys be x.

1 day's work of x boys $= \dfrac{x}{15}$

$\therefore \quad \dfrac{1}{5}$ day's work of x boys $= \dfrac{x}{75}$

Now, $\dfrac{1}{15} + \dfrac{1}{25} + \dfrac{x}{75} = 1$

$\Rightarrow \quad \dfrac{5+3+x}{75} = 1$

$\therefore \quad x = 75 - 8 = 67$

Hence, number of boys is 67.

18. (d) One day's work of Ramesh $= \dfrac{1}{24}$

One day's work of Ramesh and Somesh $= \dfrac{1}{8}$

$\therefore$ One day's work of Somesh

$= \dfrac{1}{8} - \dfrac{1}{24} = \dfrac{3-1}{24} = \dfrac{2}{24} = \dfrac{1}{12}$

$\therefore$ Time taken by Somesh = 12 days

Speedy Method

	Total work	
Ramesh ⟶ 24	24	1
Ramesh+Somesh ⟶ 8		3

Efficiency of Somesh = 3 − 1 = 2

Hence, time taken by Somesh $= \dfrac{24}{2} = 12$ days

19. (a) One day's work of 15 men $= \dfrac{1}{10}$

One day's work of 15 women $= \dfrac{1}{12}$

$\therefore$ One day's work of (15 men + 15 women)

$= \dfrac{1}{10} + \dfrac{1}{12} = \dfrac{6+5}{60} = \dfrac{11}{60}$

$\therefore$ Time taken by 15 men and 15 women

$= \dfrac{60}{11} = 5\dfrac{5}{11}$ days

20. (d) Let total work = 320 unit

Efficiency of 10 women $= \dfrac{320}{16} = 20$

Efficiency of 5 women $= \dfrac{20}{10} \times 5 = 10$

Efficiency of 6 men $= \dfrac{320}{8} = 40$

Efficiency of 12 men = 40 × 2 = 80

Part of work completed by 12 men in 2 days

= 80 × 2 = 160 units

$\therefore$ Remaining work = 320 − 160 = 160 units

$\therefore$ Remaining work completed by 6 men and 5 women $= \dfrac{160}{10+40} = \dfrac{160}{50} = \dfrac{16}{5}$ days.

$\therefore$ Total time taken $= 2 + \dfrac{16}{5} = \dfrac{26}{5}$ days

21. (c) According to the question,

Efficiency of A = Efficiency of B = Efficiency of C = 1 unit work (Let)

$\because$ A, B and C can finish a work in 15 days working alternately

3 days ⟶ (1 + 1 + 1) = 3 units of work

(3 × 5) = 15 days ⟶ 3 × 5 = 15 units of work

Now, C, A and B can do the work alternately then, (1 + 1 + 1) = 3 units of work ⟶ 3 days

$\therefore$ 15 units of work $\to 3 \times \dfrac{15}{3} = 15$ days

22. (b) Let total work = 30

Efficiency of X $= \dfrac{30}{5} = 6$

Efficiency of $Y = \dfrac{30}{15} = 2$

Efficiency of $Z = \dfrac{30}{30} = 1$

X is assisted by Y and Z together on every second day.

The work done by them in 2 days

= 6 + (6 + 2 + 1) = 15 units

$\therefore$ The whole work will be completed in

$\dfrac{30}{15} \times 2 = 4$ days.

23. (c) Let total people in group = x

Then, $x + x - 16 + x - (16 \times 2) + x - (16 \times 3) + \ldots\ldots\ldots + x - (16 \times 14) = 11x$

$\Rightarrow 15x - 16(1+2+3+ \ldots + 14) = 11x$

$\left[\because 1+2+3+\ldots n = \dfrac{n(n+1)}{2}\right]$

$\Rightarrow \quad 15x - 16 \times 7 \times 15 = 11x$

$\Rightarrow \quad 15x - 11x = 16 \times 7 \times 15$

$\Rightarrow \quad x = \dfrac{16 \times 7 \times 15}{4} \Rightarrow x = 420$

24. (a) Work done of

$4M = 6W \Rightarrow 8M = 12W$ ...(i)

and $4W = 6B \Rightarrow 12W = 18B$ ...(ii)

From Eqs. (i) and (ii),

$8M = 12W = 18B$

$\Rightarrow \quad M:W:B = \dfrac{1}{8} : \dfrac{1}{12} : \dfrac{1}{18}$

$\Rightarrow \quad M:W:B = 9:6:4$

1 boy complete the work in 60 days.

So, total work = 60 × 4 = 240 unit

Time taken by 1 man and 1 woman to finish the work $= \dfrac{240}{9+6} = 16$ days.

25. (a) According to the question,

$(20W + 15M) \times 6 = 150\,W$

$\Rightarrow \quad 20W + 15M = 25W$

$\Rightarrow \quad 15M = 5W \Rightarrow \dfrac{M}{W} = \dfrac{1}{3}$

Total work = 150 × 3 = 450 units

Time taken to complete the work by single man $= \dfrac{450}{1} = 450$ days

26. (a) Let initial number of students be x.

Total work $= x \times 10 = 10x$

If 2 students dropped out everyday the project got completed in 15 days.

$x + x - 2 + x - 4 + \ldots + x - 28 = 10x$

$\Rightarrow \quad 15x - 2(1 + 2 + \ldots + 14) = 10x$

$\Rightarrow \quad 5x = 210 \Rightarrow x = 42$

27. (c) As, A is 50% more efficient than B.

$\therefore$ 1 day's work of $A = \dfrac{1}{20} \times \dfrac{150}{100} = \dfrac{3}{40}$

$\therefore$ 1 day's work of A and $B = \dfrac{1}{20} + \dfrac{3}{40}$

$= \dfrac{2+3}{40} = \dfrac{1}{8}$

Hence, required time = 8 days

Speedy Method

Let efficiency of B = 2

Efficiency of A = 2 + 1 = 3

$\because$ B finish the work in 20 days.

$\therefore$ Total works = 20 × 2 = 40

$\therefore$ Time taken to complete the work by A and B together $= \dfrac{40}{2+3} = 8$ days

28. (d) Let total work = 14 units

Efficiency of $A = \dfrac{14}{14} = 1$ unit/day

Efficiency of $(A + B) = \dfrac{14 \times 2}{7} = 4$ unit/day

Efficiency of B = 4 − 1 = 3 unit/day

$\therefore$ B can finish the whole work in $\dfrac{14}{3}$ days.

29. (a) According to the question,

$2M \times 6 = 3W \times 4$

$\Rightarrow \quad \dfrac{M}{W} = \dfrac{12}{12} \Rightarrow \dfrac{M}{W} = \dfrac{1}{1}$

Total work = 2 × 1 × 6 = 12 units

$\therefore$ 1 man and 2 women can finish it by working together $= \dfrac{12}{1 + 2 \times 1} = 4$ days.

30. (d) Let total work = 44 units

Efficiency of $(P + Q) = \dfrac{44}{\frac{22}{5}} = \dfrac{44 \times 5}{22} = 10$

Efficiency of $(R + S) = \dfrac{44}{\frac{44}{9}} = \dfrac{44 \times 9}{44} = 9$

$\therefore$ P, Q, R and S together can complete the work in $\dfrac{44}{10+9} = \dfrac{44}{19} = 2\dfrac{6}{19}$ days.

31. (c) Let total work = 21

A can do $\dfrac{21}{3} = 7$ units of work in 7 days.

Efficiency of $A = \frac{7}{7} = 1$

B can do $\frac{21 \times 2}{7} = 6$ units of work in 10 days.

Efficiency of $B = \frac{6}{10} = \frac{3}{5}$

$\therefore$ A and B together can complete the work in

$$\frac{21}{1+\frac{3}{5}} = \frac{21 \times 5}{8} = \frac{105}{8} = 13\frac{1}{8} \text{ days}$$

32. (c) Let total work = 960

A can do $\frac{1}{3}$ of 960 = 320 units of work in 32 days.

Efficiency of $A = \frac{320}{32} = 10$ units/day

In $(x + 8)$ days A can do $= 10(x + 8)$ work

B can do $37\frac{1}{2}\%$ of $960 = \frac{960 \times 3}{8} = 360$ units of work in 24 days.

Efficiency of $B = \frac{360}{24} = 15$ units/day

In x days B can do $15x$ work.

C can do 60% of 960 = 576 units of work in 48 days.

Efficiency of $C = \frac{576}{48} = 12$ units/day

In $(x + x + 8)$ days C can do $= 12(2x + 8)$ work

Total work $= 10x + 80 + 15x + 24x + 96$

$= 49x + 176$

So, $49x + 176 = 960$

$\Rightarrow \quad x = \frac{960 - 176}{49} \Rightarrow x = \frac{784}{49} \Rightarrow x = 16$

$\therefore$ C can do $= 12 \times 3.5x$

$= 672$ work in $3.5x$ days.

$\therefore$ The work done by C in $3.5x$ days is

$= \frac{672}{960} = \frac{7}{10}$ part of the total work.

33. (a) Let the total work = 240 units

Efficiency of $A = \frac{240}{60} = 4$ units/day

A works for 15 days and completed

$= 4 \times 15 = 60$ units

Remaining work = 240 − 60 = 180 units

$\therefore$ Efficiency of $B = \frac{180}{48} = \frac{15}{4}$

$\therefore$ A and B together can finish the work

in $\frac{240}{4+\frac{15}{4}} = \frac{240 \times 4}{31} = \frac{960}{31}$ days.

34. (b) Let there were x men initially,

Total work = $13x$

$x + (x - 9) + (x - 18) + \ldots = 13x$

$\Rightarrow \quad 16x - 9(1 + 2 + \ldots + 15) = 13x$

$\Rightarrow \quad 3x = 9 \times 15 \times 8$

$\Rightarrow \quad x = \frac{9 \times 120}{3}$

$\Rightarrow \quad x = 360$

$\therefore$ There were 360 men initially.

35. (d) Let total work = 35

Efficiency of Raju $= \frac{35}{7} = 5$

Efficiency of Raju and Rajat $= \frac{35}{5} = 7$

Efficiency of Rajat = 7 − 5 = 2

$\therefore$ Rajat can complete the work in

$\frac{35}{2} = 17.5$ days.

36. (b) $(4M + 6W)\,8 = (3M + 7W)10$

$\Rightarrow \quad 32M + 48W = 30M + 70W$

$\Rightarrow \quad 2M = 22W$

$\Rightarrow \quad \frac{M}{W} = \frac{11}{1}$

$\therefore$ Total work $= (4 \times 11 + 6 \times 1) \times 8$

$= 400$ units

$\therefore$ 25 women can complete in $\frac{400}{25} = 16$ days

37. (c) Let total work = LCM (20, 15, 10)

= 60 units

$\therefore$ Efficiency of $R = \frac{60}{20} = 3$ units/day

$\therefore$ Efficiency of $S = \frac{60}{15} = 4$ units/day

$\therefore$ Efficiency of $T = \frac{60}{10} = 6$ units/day

According to the question,

Total work in 2 days

$= (3 + 6) + (3 + 4) = 16$ units

$\because$ Total work 60 units $= 16 \times 3 + 12$

$= 16 \times 3 + 9 \times 1 + 3$

$\therefore$ Total time taken $= 3 \times 2 + 1 + \frac{3}{7}$

$= \frac{49 + 3}{7} = \frac{52}{7}$ days

38. (a) Given, $M_1 = 6$, $M_2 = ?$

$D_1 = 16$, $D_2 = 8$

$\therefore$ $M_1D_1 = M_2D_2$

$16 \times 6 = M_2 \times 8$

$\Rightarrow \quad M_2 = 12$

Hence, required labourers = 12 − 10 = 2

Speedy Method

Total work = 6 × 16 = 96 units

Labourers need $= \frac{96}{8} = 12$ labourers are required to finish the work in 8 days.

$\therefore$ 12 − 10 = 2 more labourers need to join.

39. (b) Let total work = 36

Efficiency of $A = \frac{36}{9} = 4$

Efficiency of $B = \frac{36}{12} = 3$

In 5 days they together can complete

$= (4 + 3)\,5 = 35$ units

Remaining work = 36 − 35 = 1

$\therefore$ The work left is $\frac{1}{36}$.

40. (b) 1 day's earnings of 4 women and 7 men i.e., $(4W + 7M) = \frac{11{,}480}{7} = ₹\,1640$ ...(i)

Also, 1 day's earnings of 10 women and 17 men i.e.,

$(10W + 17M) = \frac{36360}{9} = ₹\,4040$ ...(ii)

Multiply Eq. (i) by 10 and Eq. (ii) by 4,

$\therefore \quad 40W + 70M = 16400$

$40W + 68M = 16160$

$-\quad\; -\quad\; -$

$2M = 240 \Rightarrow M = 120$

From Eq. (i),

$4W = 1640 - 7(120) = 800 \Rightarrow W = 200$

$\therefore$ 1 day's earnings of 11 women and 9 men

$= 11 \times 200 + 9 \times 120 = ₹\,3280$

$\therefore$ 13 day's earnings of 11 women and 9 men

$= 3280 \times 13 = ₹\,42640$

41. (d) Efficiency of Ram $= \frac{60}{15} = 4$

Efficiency of (Ram + Riya) $= \frac{180}{30} = 6$

Efficiency of Riya = 6 − 4 = 2

$\therefore$ Riya can copy 20 pages in $= \frac{20}{2} = 10$ h

42. (d) P and Q together can do work in 6 days.

P can do work in 18 days.

Q's 1 day's work $= \frac{1}{6} - \frac{1}{18} = \frac{2}{18} = \frac{1}{9}$

Then, Q finish the work in 9 days.

43. (c) $(A + B)$'s 1 day work $= \frac{1}{30}$

C's 1 day work $= \frac{1}{120}$

(A+B+C)'s one day work $= \frac{1}{30} + \frac{1}{120}$

Let B and C together complete the work in x days.

Then, A can complete the same work in $1.5x$ days.

So, $\frac{1}{x} + \frac{1}{1.5x} = \frac{1}{30} + \frac{1}{120}$

$\Rightarrow \quad \frac{1.5 + 1}{1.5x} = \frac{4 + 1}{120}$

$\Rightarrow \quad x = \frac{2.5 \times 120}{5 \times 1.5} = 40$

B's one day's work $= \frac{1}{x} - \frac{1}{120} = \frac{1}{40} - \frac{1}{120}$

$= \frac{2}{120} = \frac{1}{60}$

So, time taken by B to complete the work

= 60 days

44. (b) Let P completes the work in x days.

Q completes the work $= \frac{x}{2}$ days

R completes the work $= \frac{x}{3}$ days

P's 1 day's work $= \frac{1}{x}$

Q's 1 day day's work $= \frac{2}{x}$

R's 1 day's work $= \frac{3}{x}$

$(P + Q + R)$'s 1 day's work $= \frac{1}{x} + \frac{2}{x} + \frac{3}{x} = \frac{6}{x}$

$\because$ They finish all work in two days

then, $x = 6 \times 2 = 12$

Hence, Q takes to complete the work

$= \frac{12}{2} = 6$ days

45. (a) Let efficiency of B be 100 units/day.

$\therefore$ Efficiency of $A = 140$ units/day

As, A alone can complete the work = 31 days

$\therefore$ Total work = $31 \times 140 = 4340$ units

$\therefore$ Required time $= \frac{4340}{100 + 140}$

$= \frac{4340}{240} = \frac{217}{12}$ days

46. (a) Let total work = 72

Efficiency of $A = \frac{72}{8} = 9$ units/day

$\therefore$ Efficiency of $B = \frac{72}{18} = 4$ units/day

Starting with B,

13 units of work is done in 2 days.

$\therefore$ 65 units of work is done in 10 days.

On 11th day, B will complete his 4 units of work.

$\therefore$ Remaining 3 units of work will be done by A in $\frac{3}{9} = \frac{1}{3}$ day

$\therefore$ Total time taken by A and B together working alternately $= 11\frac{1}{3}$ days

47. (a) (Richa + Rita + Reena)'s 1 day's work

$= \frac{1}{8} + \frac{1}{12} + \frac{1}{24} = \frac{3+2+1}{24}$

$= \frac{6}{24} = \frac{1}{4}$

Hence, time taken to complete the work by all is 4 h.

Speedy Method

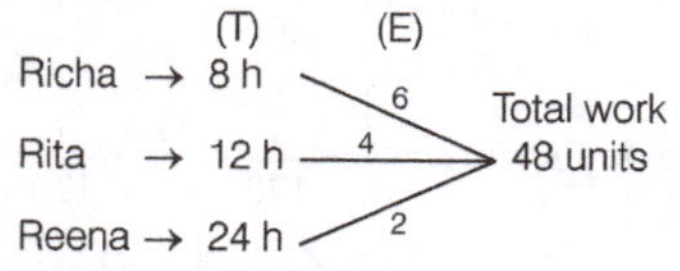

$\therefore$ Time taken to complete the work by all of three $= \frac{48}{6+4+2} = \frac{48}{12} = 4$ h

48. (d) Let the total work = 48

($\because$ LCM of 16 and 12 = 48)

Efficiency of Rekha $= \frac{48}{16} = 3$

Efficiency of Bina $= \frac{48}{12} = 4$

Work done in 2 days = 4 + 3 = 7

Work done in 12 days = $7 \times 6 = 42$

On 13th day, Rekha will complete 3 units of work

$\therefore$ Remaining work = 48 − 42 − 3 = 3 units

Time taken to complete remaining work by Bina $= \frac{3}{4}$ days

So, total time $= 13 + \frac{3}{4} = 13\frac{3}{4}$ days

49. (d) Let total work = 300 unit

Part of work completed by A in 4 days = 20% of 300 = 60 units

$\therefore$ Efficiency of $A = \frac{60}{4} = 15$ units/day

Part of work completed by B in 10 days

$= 33\frac{1}{3}\%$ of 300 = 100 units

$\therefore$ Efficiency of $B = \frac{100}{10} = 10$ units/day

$(A + B)$'s 9 day's work

$= (15 + 10) \times 9 = 225$ units

$\therefore$ Remaining work = 300 − 225 = 75 units

$\therefore$ Efficiency of $C = \frac{75}{6} = \frac{25}{2}$

Time taken to complete 75% of the same work by B and $C = \frac{75 \times 3}{10 + \frac{25}{2}}$

$= \frac{75 \times 3 \times 2}{45} = 10$ days

50. (c) Let B's efficiency $= \frac{1}{x}$

$\therefore$ A's efficiency $= \frac{1}{x - 22}$

According to the question,

$\frac{1}{x-22} = 5.4 \times \frac{1}{x} \Rightarrow x = 27$ days

Time taken to complete the work by A and B

$= \frac{27 \times 5}{27 + 5} = \frac{135}{32} = 4\frac{7}{32}$ days

51. (c) According to the question,

Paul's 1 h work $= \frac{1}{3} - \frac{1}{5} = \frac{5-3}{15} = \frac{2}{15}$

Jeevan's 1 h work $= \frac{1}{4} - \frac{2}{15} = \frac{15-8}{60} = \frac{7}{60}$

$\therefore$ Jeevan can alone complete the work

$= \frac{60}{7}$ h ≈ 9 h

52. (d) According to the question,

A is 3.5 times as efficient as B.

$\therefore$ $A = 3.5\,B \Rightarrow A : B = 7 : 2$

$\therefore$ Ratio of time taken by A and B i.e.,

$A : B = 2 : 7$.

Let time taken by A and B be $7x$ and $2x$, respectively.

As, A takes 45 days less than B

$\therefore$ $7x - 2x = 45 \Rightarrow 5x = 45 \Rightarrow x = 9$

$\therefore$ Time taken by $A = 7(9) = 63$ days

Time taken by $B = 2(9) = 18$ days

Now, $(A + B)$'s 1 day's work

$= \frac{1}{63} + \frac{1}{18} = \frac{2+7}{126}$

$= \frac{9}{126} = \frac{1}{14}$

$\therefore$ $(A + B)$ will complete the work in 14 days.

53. (d) According to the question,

A complete $\frac{3}{5}$th of work in 12 days

$\therefore$ A can complete the entire work

$= 12 \times \frac{5}{3} = 20$ days

$\therefore$ A can complete $\left(\frac{3}{4}\right)$th of work in

$= 20 \times \frac{3}{4} = 15$ days

54. (d) Let total work = 120

($\because$ LCM of 24, 30 and 40 = 120)

Efficiency of $(P + Q) = \frac{120}{24} = 5$ units/day

Efficiency of $(Q + R) = \frac{120}{30} = 4$ units/day

Efficiency of $(P + R) = \frac{120}{40} = 3$ units/day

Efficiency of $(P + Q + R)$

$= \frac{5+4+3}{2} = 6$ units/day

$P = 6 - (Q + R) = 6 - 4 = 2$

$Q = 6 - (P + R) = 6 - 3 = 3$

$R = 6 - (P + Q) = 6 - 5 = 1$

Efficiency of $X = 4P$

Efficiency of $Y = \frac{Q}{2}$

Efficiency of $Z = \frac{5R}{2}$

Efficiency of $(X + Y + Z) = 4P + \frac{Q}{2} + \frac{5R}{2}$

$= \frac{8P + Q + 5R}{2}$

$= \frac{8 \times 2 + 3 + 5}{2} = 12$ units/day

$\therefore$ X, Y and Z can complete the work in 120/12

= 10 days

55. (c) Let total work = 24

($\because$ LCM of 8 and 24 = 24)

Efficiency of $B = \frac{24}{24} = 1$

Efficiency of $(A + B) = \frac{24}{8} = 3$

Efficiency of $A = 3 - 1 = 2$

$\therefore$ A can finish the whole work in

$\frac{24}{2} = 12$ days

Speedy Method

A's 1 day's work $= \frac{1}{8} - \frac{1}{24} = \frac{3-1}{24} = \frac{2}{24} = \frac{1}{12}$

$\therefore$ A can complete the work in 12 days.

56. (d) Supraja and Kausalya's 2 day's work

$= \frac{1}{30} + \frac{1}{20} = \frac{2+3}{60} = \frac{1}{12}$

So, together they complete the work in

$12 \times 2 = 24$ days

Work to be done $= 75\% = \frac{75}{100} = \frac{3}{4}$

$\therefore$ Time taken to complete 75% of the work

$= \frac{3}{4} \times 24 = 18$ days

Speedy Method

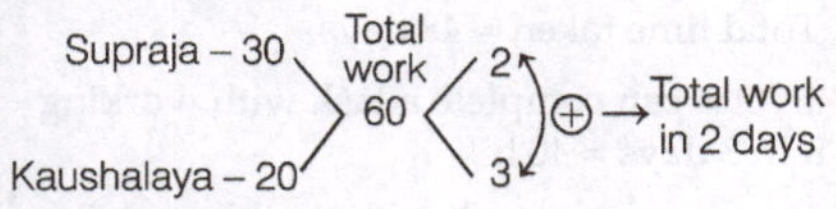

$\therefore$ 5 units of work is done in 2 days

$\Rightarrow \frac{75}{100}(12 \times 5)$ of work will be done in

$\frac{75}{100} \times (12 \times 2) = 18$ days.

$\Rightarrow$ 45 units of work will be done in 18 days.

57. (b) According to the question,

$(A+B)$'s one day work $= \frac{1}{12} + \frac{1}{18} = \frac{5}{36}$

$\therefore$ 5 units of work is done in 2 days.

$\Rightarrow$ 35 units of work is done in 14 days.

$\therefore$ Remaining work can be done by A in

$\frac{\frac{1}{36}}{\frac{1}{12}} = \frac{12}{36} = \frac{1}{3}$ days

$\therefore$ Total time $= 14\frac{1}{3}$ days.

58. (b) Let total work = LCM (10, 15, 20) = 60

$\therefore$ Ratio of efficiencies i.e.,

$A : B : C = 6:4:3$

$\therefore$ Share of $C = \frac{3}{13} \times 2600 =$ ₹600

59. (b) Let total work = 90

Efficiency of $A = \frac{90}{18} = 5$

Efficiency of $B = \frac{90}{30} = 3$

B can do in $16\frac{2}{3}$ days $= 3 \times \frac{50}{3} = 50$ units

Remaining work = 90 – 50 = 40 units

$\therefore$ Time taken to complete remaining work

$= \frac{40}{5+3} = 5$ days

$\therefore$ A worked for 5 days.

60. (a) $\because$ 1 person build a house $= 60 \times 14$ days

Then 30 person build a house

$= \frac{60 \times 14}{30} = 28$ days

61. (a) According to the question,

$\frac{(N+15) \times 9 \times 8}{36} = \frac{(N+9) \times 20 \times 7}{64}$

$\Rightarrow 32N + 480 = 35N + 315$

$\Rightarrow 3N = 165$

Hence, $N = 55$

62. (c) We know that,

$M_1D_1 = M_2D_2$

$\Rightarrow 12 \times 10 = M_2 \times 6$

$\Rightarrow M_2 = \frac{12 \times 10}{6} = 20$

$\therefore$ Extra men required = 20 – 12 = 8 men

63. (a) Efficiency of Susan $= \frac{12}{6} = 2$ pages/min

Efficiency of Mary $= \frac{6}{12} = \frac{1}{2}$ pages/min

Efficiency of both together

$= 2 + \frac{1}{2} = \frac{5}{2}$ pages/min

$\therefore$ In 32 min they can type $\frac{5}{2} \times 32 = 80$

64. (a) $10W \times 6 = 6M \times 5$

$\Rightarrow \frac{M}{W} = \frac{10}{5} \Rightarrow \frac{M}{W} = \frac{2}{1}$

Total work $= 10 \times 1 \times 6 = 60$ units

Efficiency of 10 women and 6 men together

$= 10 \times 1 + 6 \times 2 = 22$

$\therefore$ Time taken by them to finish the work

$= \frac{60}{22} = 2\frac{8}{11}$ days

65. (b) Anil's one day's work

$= \frac{1}{15} - \frac{1}{20} = \frac{4-3}{60} = \frac{1}{60}$

$\therefore$ Anil can complete the work in 60 days.

66. (c) $(A+B)$'s 2 day's work

$= 2\left(\frac{1}{4} + \frac{1}{12}\right) = 2\left(\frac{4}{12}\right) = \frac{2}{3}$

$\therefore$ Remaining work $= 1 - \frac{2}{3} = \frac{1}{3}$

67. (b) According to the question,

$\left(\frac{2}{3}\right)$rd of work is done in 24 days.

$\therefore \left(\frac{1}{9}\right)$th of work will be done in

$= \frac{1}{9} \times \left(24 \times \frac{3}{2}\right) = 4$ days

68. (a) Here, $M_1 = (N+18)$, $t_1 = 7.5$, $D_1 = 20$, $W_1 = 48\%$, $M_2 = (N+12)$, $t_2 = 6.5$, $D_2 = 30$, $W_2 = (100-48) = 52\%$

$\frac{(N+18) \times 7.5 \times 20}{(N+12) \times 6.5 \times 30} = \frac{48}{52}$

$\Rightarrow \frac{(N+18) \times 15 \times 2}{(N+12) \times 13 \times 3} = \frac{12}{13}$

$\Rightarrow 5N + 90 = 6N + 72 \Rightarrow N = 18$

69. (c) $(1B + 1W)$'s 1 day's work

$= \frac{1}{20} + \frac{1}{2 \times 30} = \frac{4}{60} = \frac{1}{15}$

Time taken by one boy and a woman to complete the work = 15 days

According to the question,

1 man and 1 woman's 1 day work $= \frac{2}{15}$

One man one day work

$= \frac{2}{15} - \frac{1}{2 \times 30} = \frac{8-1}{60} = \frac{7}{60}$

4 mens one day work $= \frac{7 \times 4}{60} = \frac{7}{15}$

$\therefore$ Time taken by 4 men to complete the work

$= \frac{15}{7} = 2.14$ days

70. (a) Efficiency of Suresh $= \frac{40}{5}$ pages/h

Efficiency of Anil $= \frac{32}{6}$ pages/h

Number of pages typed by both in 1 h

$= \frac{40}{5} + \frac{32}{6} = \frac{40}{3}$

Time taken by both to type 110 pages

$= 110 \times \frac{3}{40} = \frac{33}{4} = 8$ h 15 min.

71. (b) $(R+S+T)$'s one day work

$= \frac{1}{4} + \frac{1}{6} + \frac{1}{18} = \frac{9+6+2}{36} = \frac{17}{36}$

So, time taken to complete the work

together $= \frac{36}{17} = 2.117$ days $= 2.12$ days

72. (b) Let total work = 30 unit

A's one day work = 1 unit

B's one day work = 1 unit

$(A+B)$'s work in 6 days $= 4 \times 2 + 1 + 1$

= 10 unit

Total work completed in $= 6 \times 3 = 18$ days

$\therefore$ Work finished on = 1 August 2022

+ 18 days

= 18 August 2022

[Day of 01 August, 2022 is included]

73. (a) A's complete work = 15 days

If A works only first two days and last Two days, then A's work $= \frac{4}{15}$

and B complete remaining work

$= 1 - \frac{4}{15} = \frac{11}{15}$

B's 16 days work $= \frac{11}{15}$

B's one day's work $= \frac{11}{15 \times 16}$

$(A+B)$'s one day work

$= \frac{1}{15} + \frac{11}{15 \times 16} = \frac{16+11}{15 \times 16} = \frac{27}{15 \times 16} = \frac{9}{80}$

So, A and B together finish the work in $\frac{80}{9}$ days.

74. (c) $(A+B+C)$'s one day work

$= \left(\frac{6+5+10}{60}\right) \times \frac{1}{2} = \frac{7}{40}$

A's one day work $= \frac{7}{40} - \frac{1}{12} = \frac{21-10}{120} = \frac{11}{120}$

So, time taken to complete the work by A alone $= \frac{120}{11}$ days

75. (d) Let A leave work after x days.

x days work of A and B

$$= x\left(\frac{1}{5}+\frac{1}{10}\right) = \frac{(2+1)x}{10} = \frac{3x}{10}$$

Remaining work $= 1 - \frac{3x}{10}$

According to the question,

$$8 = \frac{1-\frac{3x}{10}}{\frac{1}{10}} \Rightarrow 8 = 10 - 3x$$

$\therefore$ $x = \frac{2}{3}$

76. (c) Let total work = LCM (5, 4) = 20 unit

Efficiency of Raja and Rocky

$$= \frac{20}{5} = 4 \text{ unit/day}$$

Work completed in 2 days = 8 unit

Remaining work = 20 − 8 = 12 unit

Remaining work completed by Raja in 4 days.

Then, efficiency of Raja $= \frac{12}{4} = 3$ unit/day

Then, efficiency of Rocky = 4 − 3 = 1 unit/day

$\therefore$ Rocky alone do this work

$$= \frac{20}{1} \text{ days} = 20 \text{ days}$$

77. (b) A's one day work $= \frac{1}{4}$

B's one day work $= \frac{1}{9}$

$\therefore$ 2 day's work of B and A

$$= \frac{1}{4}+\frac{1}{9} = \frac{9+4}{36} = \frac{13}{36}$$

$\therefore$ 4 day's work by B and $A = \frac{13\times 2}{36} = \frac{26}{36}$

Remaining work $= 1 - \frac{26}{36} = \frac{10}{36}$

5th day's work by $B = \frac{1}{9}$

Now, remaining work $= \frac{10}{36} - \frac{1}{9} = \frac{1}{6}$

$\therefore$ Time taken to complete remaining work by $A = \frac{1}{6}\times\frac{36}{9} = \frac{2}{3}$ day

Hence, required time $= 5 + \frac{2}{3} = 5\frac{2}{3}$ days

78. (b) 9 day's work of $B = \frac{9}{15} = \frac{3}{5}$

$\therefore$ Remaining work $= 1 - \frac{3}{5} = \frac{2}{5}$

$\therefore$ Time taken by A to complete the work

$$= \frac{\frac{2}{5}}{\frac{1}{20}} = \frac{2}{5}\times\frac{20}{1} = 8 \text{ days}$$

79. (a) Total work = 25 × 10 = 250 units

10 men do work in 12 days

$\therefore$ Work done by 10 men = 10 × 12 = 120 units

$\therefore$ Remaining work = 250 − 120 = 130 units

After 12 days, 3 more men joined

Then total men = 10 + 3 = 13

$\therefore$ Required time $= \frac{130}{13} = 10$ days

80. (a) Total work = 30 × 12 = 360 units

In 6 days half of the work done by 30 men then,

Remaining work $= \frac{360}{2} = 180$ unit

6 days later 24 more men joined them.

Then total number of men = 30 + 24 = 54 men

$\therefore$ Time taken to complete remaining work by 54 men $= \frac{180}{54} = 3\frac{1}{3}$ days

81. (d) According to the question,

$(15M + 21W)\times 56 = (12M + 24W)\times 64$

$\Rightarrow$ $105M + 147W = 96M + 192W$

$\Rightarrow$ $9M = 45W \Rightarrow 1M = 5W$

$\Rightarrow$ $\frac{M}{W} = \frac{5}{1}$

Total work done in 56 days

$= (15\times 5 + 21)\times 56$

$= 5376$ units

Then, work done by 18 men and 24 women in 1 day is = 18 × 5 + 24 = 90 + 24 = 114 units

$\therefore$ Work completed in $= \frac{5376}{114} = 47\frac{3}{19}$ days

82. (c) Let total work = 30 units

Efficiency of Pratima $= \frac{30}{10} = 3$

Efficiency of Diksha $= \frac{30}{15} = 2$

Pratima do 3 × 4 = 12 units work in 4 h

$\therefore$ Remaining work = 30 − 12 = 18 units

$\therefore$ Diksha will complete the remaining work in $\frac{18}{2} = 9$ h

83. (b) Let total work = LCM of 12 and 15 = 60 units

$\therefore$ Efficiency of Sarthak $= \frac{60}{12} = 5$

$\therefore$ Efficiency of Mohan $= \frac{60}{15} = 4$

Time taken to complete the work together

$$= \frac{60}{5+4} = \frac{60}{9} = 6.67 \text{ days.}$$

84. (a) According to the question,

$(12M + 16B)\times 5 = (13M + 24B)\times 4$

$\Rightarrow$ $60M + 80B = 52M + 96B$

$\Rightarrow$ $8M = 16B$

$\Rightarrow$ $\frac{M}{B} = \frac{2}{1}$

$\therefore$ Total work = (12 × 2 + 16 × 1) × 5

= 40 × 5 = 200 units

Time taken to complete the work by 29 men and 22 boys

$$= \frac{200}{(29\times 2 + 22)} = \frac{200}{(58+22)}$$

$$= \frac{200}{80} = 2.5 \text{ days}$$

85. (a) According to the question,

(Ravi + Sudha)'s 2 day's work

$$= \frac{1}{40} + \frac{1}{60} = \frac{10}{240}$$

$\Rightarrow$ 10 units of work is done in 2 days.

$\therefore$ 240 units of work is done in 48 days.

$\therefore$ Total time taken = 48 days

86. (c) A can complete a task with working 5 h in 8 days = 40 h

B can complete a task with working 6 h in 10 days = 60 h

Then, total work = 120 units

Efficiency of $A = \frac{120}{40} = 3$ units/h

Efficiency of $B = \frac{120}{60} = 2$ units/h

Then $(A + B)$'s work can complete in

$$= \frac{120}{5} = 24 \text{ h}$$

If they work only 8 h a day, then

$$= \frac{24}{8} = 3 \text{ days}$$

87. (b) According to the question,

$15\,M\times 25 = 25\,W\times 40 \Rightarrow 3M = 8W \Rightarrow \frac{M}{W} = \frac{8}{3}$

Let $M = 8k$, $W = 3k$

$\therefore$ Total work = 15(8k) × 25 = 3000k units.

$\therefore$ Required time $= \frac{3000k}{15(8k) + 25(3k)}$

$$= \frac{3000k}{195k} = \frac{200}{13} = 15\frac{5}{13} \text{ days}$$

88. (a) $(A + B + C)$'s 1 day's work

$$= \frac{1}{16} + \frac{1}{24} + \frac{1}{36} = \frac{9+6+4}{144} = \frac{19}{144}$$

$\therefore$ A, B and C together will complete work in

$$\frac{144}{19} = 7\frac{11}{19} \text{ days}$$

89. (c) Satish's one hour work

$$= \frac{1}{5} - \frac{1}{20} - \frac{1}{12} = \frac{4}{60} = \frac{1}{15}$$

$\therefore$ Satish can complete the work in 15 h.

90. (b) Given that,

$(15\,m + 25\,w)\times 9.6 = 16\,w\times 27$

$\Rightarrow$ $30\,m + 50\,w = 90\,w$

$\Rightarrow$ $40\,w = 30\,m$

$\Rightarrow$ $\frac{w_{Eff}}{m_{Eff}} = \frac{3}{4}$

Then, total work = 16 × 3 × 27

Total work done by 16 men

$$= \frac{16\times 3\times 27}{16\times 4} = \frac{81}{4} = 20.25 \text{ days}$$

91. (b) $(A+B+C)$'s 4 day's work

$= 4\left(\frac{1}{12}+\frac{1}{15}+\frac{1}{20}\right) = 4\times\frac{1}{5} = \frac{4}{5}$

$\therefore$ Remaining work $= 1-\frac{4}{5} = \frac{1}{5}$

92. (d) Ajay and Bharat work on alternate, days then the work finish in 8 days.

So, Ajay and Bharat together finish a work in 4 days.

Then, Ajay's one day work $= \frac{1}{32}$

Ajay and Bharat's one day work $= \frac{1}{4}$

$\therefore$ Bharat's one day work $= \frac{1}{4}-\frac{1}{32} = \frac{7}{32}$

$\therefore$ Bharat can complete work in $\frac{32}{7}$ days.

Then, Bharat finish 7 times the same work in $= \frac{32\times 7}{7} = 32$ days

93. (b) Let efficiency of Virat = 100% and efficiency of Daniel 60% more than Virat

	Virat	Daniel
	100%	160%
Efficiency →	5	8
Time taken	8	5

(Time is opposite of efficiency)

Let Virat and Daniel can do a work in $8x$ and $5x$ days, respectively.

Given, Virat can do the work in 30 days then

$8x = 30 \Rightarrow x = \frac{15}{4}$

Then, Daniel can do the work in

$5x = 5\times\frac{15}{4} = 18\frac{3}{4}$ days

94. (c) Given, A's efficiency is twice that of B's.

Total work done by A in 12 days

$= 12\times 8\text{ h} = 96$ units

$\therefore$ B can finish the same work

$= \frac{96\times 2}{12} = 16$ days

95. (d) Let total work = 36 units

[$\because$ LCM of 9 and 36 = 36]

Efficiency of $X = \frac{36}{9} = 4$ unit/day

Efficiency of $Y = \frac{36}{36} = 1$ unit/day

X and Y together can do $4+1 = 5$ unit in 2 days

$\therefore$ They can do 35 unit in $= \frac{2}{5}\times 35 = 14$ days

Remaining work $= 36-35 = 1$

So, X can complete 1 unit in $\frac{1}{4}$ days

$\therefore$ Total time taken $= 14\frac{1}{4}$ days

96. (b) A boy can finish the work in 60 days.

6 boy can finish the work in $\frac{60}{6}\times 1 = 10$ days

4 women can finish it in 10 days.

$\therefore$ 5 women can finish it in $= \frac{10}{5}\times 4 = 8$ days

97. (b) Let P complete a work in x days,

$\therefore Q$ will complete the same work in $2x$ days.

$\therefore \quad 2x - x = 40 \Rightarrow x = 40$

$\therefore$ $(P+Q)$'s one day's work $= \frac{1}{x}+\frac{1}{2x}$

$= \frac{1}{40}+\frac{1}{2\times 40} = \frac{2+1}{80} = \frac{3}{80}$

So, P and Q together can complete the work

$= \frac{80}{3} = 26.667 \approx 27$ days

98. (a) 5 women and 9 girls earn

₹$\frac{18720}{9}$ = ₹2080 in 1 day

9 women and 16 girls earn ₹$\frac{52080}{14}$ = ₹3720 in 1 day

$5w + 9g = 2080 \quad \ldots\text{(i)}\times 9$

$9w + 16g = 3720 \quad \ldots\text{(ii)}\times 5$

$45w + 81g = 18720$

$\underline{45w + 80g = 18600}$ (−, −, −)

$1g =$ ₹ 120

From Eq. (i), we get,

$5w = 2080 - 1080$

$\Rightarrow \quad 1w =$ ₹ 200

$\therefore$ 12 women and 7 girls together earn in 13 days $= 3240\times 13 =$ ₹ 42120

99. (a) According to the question,

$8M\times 45 = 8W\times 18$

$\Rightarrow \quad \frac{M}{W} = \frac{2}{5} \Rightarrow M = \frac{2}{5}W$

$\therefore \quad (5M+8W)\times d = 8W\times 18$

$\Rightarrow \quad \left(5\times\frac{2}{5}+8\right)\times d = 8\times 18$

$\Rightarrow \quad d = \frac{8\times 18}{10} = \frac{72}{5} = 14\frac{2}{5}$ days

100. (c) Let, total work = LCM of 10, 15 and 30 = 30 unit

$\therefore$ Efficiency of a man $= \frac{30}{10} = 3$ units/day

Efficiency of a women $= \frac{30}{15} = 2$ units/day

And efficiency of a boy $= \frac{30}{30} = 1$ unit/day

Hence, required time $= \frac{30}{3+2+1} = 5$ days

101. (a) According to the question,

5 day's work $= \frac{3}{25}+\frac{2}{30} = \frac{18+10}{150}$

$= \frac{28}{150} = \frac{14}{75}$

Remaining work $= 1-\frac{14}{75} = \frac{61}{75}$

$\therefore$ B finish the remaining work in

$= \frac{\frac{61}{75}}{\frac{1}{30}} = \frac{61\times 30}{75}$

$= \frac{122}{5} = 24\frac{2}{5}$ days

Speedy Method

Total work = 150 (LCM of 25 and 30)

Efficiency of $A = \frac{150}{25} = 6$ unit

Efficiency of $B = \frac{150}{30} = 5$ unit

When they work on alternate basis, then

5 day's work $= 3\times 6+2\times 5 = 28$

Remaining work $= 150-28 = 122$

B finish the remaining work in

$= \frac{122}{5} = 24\frac{2}{5}$ days

102. (b) According to the question,

$(A+B)$'s 2 h work $= \frac{1}{6}+\frac{1}{10} = \frac{5+3}{30} = \frac{8}{30}$

$\therefore$ 6 h work of A and $B = \frac{24}{30}$

$\therefore$ 24 units of work is done in 6 h.

Now, in 7th h, A will complete his 5 units of work.

$\therefore$ Remaining $= 30-(24+5) = 1$ unit

$\therefore$ B will complete 1 unit of work in $= \frac{1}{3}$ h

$\therefore$ Total time $= 7\frac{1}{3}$ h

103. (a) Let A and C together can do the work in x days.

$\therefore$ B alone can do the work in $3x$ days.

$(A+B+C)$'s 1 day's work $= \frac{1}{10}$

$\therefore \quad \frac{1}{x}+\frac{1}{3x} = \frac{1}{10}$

$\Rightarrow \quad \frac{3+1}{3x} = \frac{1}{10} \Rightarrow 3x = 40$

Hence, B alone will complete the work in 40 days.

104. (d) Let 1 day's work of $B = \frac{1}{x}$

$\therefore$ 1 day's work of $A = \frac{1}{x}\times\frac{120}{100}$

According to the question,

$\frac{120}{100x} = \frac{1}{29} \Rightarrow x = \frac{6\times 29}{5} = \frac{174}{5}$

$\therefore$ 1 day's work of A and B together

$= \frac{1}{29}+\frac{5}{174} = \frac{6+5}{174} = \frac{11}{174}$

$\therefore$ A and B together will complete the work in

$= \frac{1}{\frac{11}{174}} = \frac{174}{11}$ days.

105. (a) Let number of days required to complete the work be x.

$\therefore$ According to the question,

$$\frac{(x-1)}{12}+\frac{(x-3)}{20}+\frac{(x-4)}{24}=1$$

$$\Rightarrow \frac{10x-10+6x-18+5x-20}{120}=1$$

$$\Rightarrow 21x=120+48=168$$

$$\Rightarrow x=\frac{168}{21}=8 \text{ days}$$

106. (c) Let the efficiency of $B = 100$ units/day

Efficiency of $A = (100 + 40)\%$ of 100 units/day

$= 140$ units/day

$\because$ B alone complete the work in 36 days

Total work = efficiency × days = 100×36 units

Total efficiency of A and B together

$= (100 + 140) = 240$ units/day

Time taken by A and B together to finish the work $=\frac{\text{Total work}}{\text{Total efficiency}}=\frac{100\times 36}{240}=15$ days

107. (d) (Raju + Shobha + Mohan)'s 3 days work $=\frac{1}{15}+\frac{1}{20}+\frac{1}{25}=\frac{20+15+12}{300}=\frac{47}{300}$

(Raju + Shubh + Mohan)'s 18 days work

$=6\times\frac{47}{300}=\frac{47}{50}$

Remaining work $=1-\frac{47}{50}=\frac{3}{50}$

The remaining work $\frac{3}{50}$ is done by Raju as they work on alternate days.

Time taken by Raju to complete the remaining work $=\frac{3}{50}\div\frac{1}{15}$

$=\frac{3}{50}\times\frac{15}{1}=\frac{9}{10}$ days

Number of days required to complete the work $=\left(18+\frac{9}{10}\right)$ days $=18\frac{9}{10}$ days

108. (a) A machine cuts in 10 h = 240 tools

A machine cuts in 1 h $=\frac{240}{10}$ tools

$\therefore$ A machine cuts in 25 h

$=\frac{240}{10}\times 25$ tools = 600 tools

109. (b) According to the question,

$(A+B+C)$'s 2 days work $=2\left(\frac{1}{6}+\frac{1}{10}+\frac{1}{15}\right)$

$=2\left(\frac{10+6+4}{60}\right)=2\left(\frac{20}{60}\right)=\frac{2}{3}$

$\therefore$ Remaining work $=1-\frac{2}{3}=\frac{1}{3}$

and $(A+B)$'s 1 day's work

$=\frac{1}{6}+\frac{1}{10}=\frac{5+3}{30}=\frac{8}{30}=\frac{4}{15}$

$\therefore$ $\frac{1}{3}$ work done by A and B in

$=\frac{1}{3}\times\frac{15}{4}=\frac{5}{4}=1\frac{1}{4}$ days

110. (c) Let Q can complete the work in x days alone then P can complete the work in $\frac{x}{3}$ days alone.

According to the question,

$\frac{1}{x}+\frac{3}{x}=\frac{1}{36} \Rightarrow \frac{4}{x}=\frac{1}{36} \Rightarrow x=36\times 4$

$\Rightarrow x = 144$ days

111. (b) Let the efficiency of Abha $= x$

Efficiency of Anuj $= y$

If both together completed a job in $\frac{40}{9}$ days,

then work done $=(x+y)\times\frac{40}{9}$ ...(i)

If efficiency of Abha is doubled and efficiency of Anuj is $\frac{1}{3}$rd, then both have completed the work in $\frac{60}{17}$ days.

So, work done $=\left(2x+\frac{y}{3}\right)\times\frac{60}{17}$ ...(ii)

Total work must remain same in both Eqs. (i) and (ii),

$$(x+y)\frac{40}{9}=\left(2x+\frac{y}{3}\right)\frac{60}{17}$$

$$\Rightarrow (x+y)\frac{2}{9}=\left(2x+\frac{y}{3}\right)\frac{3}{17}$$

$$\Rightarrow (x+y)\,34=\left(2x+\frac{y}{3}\right)27$$

$$\Rightarrow 34x+34y=54x+9y$$

$$\Rightarrow 20x=25y$$

$$\Rightarrow \frac{x}{y}=\frac{5}{4}$$

Work done $=(5+4)\times\frac{40}{9}$ [from Eq. (i)]

$=9\times\frac{40}{9}=40$

$\therefore$ Abha would complete the work alone in

$=\frac{40}{5}=8$ days

112. (c) Let the number of more days be x.

According to the question,

$20\times 220=20\times 90+40\times x$

$\therefore$ $x=\frac{4400-1800}{40}=\frac{2600}{40}=65$ days

113. (c) $(A+B)$'s 2 day's work

$=\frac{1}{13}+\frac{1}{17}=\frac{17+13}{13\times 17}=\frac{30}{221}$

$\therefore$ Work done in 14 days $=\frac{30}{221}\times 7=\frac{210}{221}$

$\therefore$ Remaining work $=1-\frac{210}{221}=\frac{11}{221}$

Now, A will complete the remaining work in

$\frac{11}{221}\times 13$ days $=\frac{11}{17}$ days

Hence, whole work will be completed in

$14+\frac{11}{17}=14\frac{11}{17}$ days.

114. (a) According to the question,

2 day's work of Raju when assisted by Sunil and Vishal

$=\left(\frac{1}{20}+\frac{1}{30}\right)+\left(\frac{1}{20}+\frac{1}{40}\right)=\left(\frac{3+2}{60}\right)+\left(\frac{2+1}{40}\right)$

$=\frac{10+9}{120}=\frac{19}{120}$

$\therefore$ $(6\times 19) = 114$ units of work is done in $(6\times 2) = 12$ days

$\therefore$ (Raju + Sunil) will complete the remaining work $=\frac{6}{10}=\frac{3}{5}$ days

$\therefore$ Total time taken $=12\frac{3}{5}$ days

115. (a) (Ajay + Vijay)'s 2 h work

$=\frac{1}{6}+\frac{1}{16}=\frac{8+3}{48}=\frac{11}{48}$

(Ajay + Vijay)'s 8 h work $=4\times\frac{11}{48}=\frac{11}{12}$

Remaining work $=1-\frac{11}{12}=\frac{12-11}{12}=\frac{1}{12}$

Remaining work $\frac{1}{12}$, will be done by Ajay.

Ajay complete the remaining work in

$=\frac{1}{12}\div\frac{1}{6}=\frac{1}{12}\times\frac{6}{1}=\frac{1}{2}$ h

Total time taken to complete the work $=8$ h $+\frac{1}{2}$ h $= 8$ h 30 min

$\left[\because \frac{1}{2}\text{h} = 30 \text{ min}\right]$

116. (d) 10 men 40 days work $= 10\times 40$

Let 10 men working x days together.

Then 10 men's x days work $= 10x$

After 4 men left,

6 men complete the work in $= (50 - x)$ days

According to the question,

$$10x+6(50-x)=10\times 40$$

$$\Rightarrow 10x+300-6x=400$$

$$\Rightarrow 4x=100$$

$$\Rightarrow x=\frac{100}{4}=25 \text{ days}$$

117. (c) 1 day of work $12\,M$ and $12\,W=\frac{1}{9}$

$\Rightarrow 12M+12W=\frac{1}{9}$ ...(i)

1 day work of $6\,M$ and $15\,W=\frac{1}{12}$

$\Rightarrow 2\times(6M+15W)=2\times\frac{1}{12}$

$\Rightarrow 12M+30W=\frac{1}{6}$ ...(ii)

Now, Eqs. (ii) − (i)

$12M+30W-12M-12W=\frac{1}{6}-\frac{1}{9}$

$\Rightarrow 18W=\frac{3-2}{18}\Rightarrow 18W=\frac{1}{18}\Rightarrow 1W=\frac{1}{324}$

$\therefore$ 9 women will complete the same work in

$324\times\frac{1}{9}=36$ days

Hence, 9 women will complete the half work in $\frac{36}{2} = 18$ days.

118. (d) Let, x be the extra workers required to complete the work in time.

By the formula, $\frac{M_1D_1}{W_1} = \frac{M_2D_2}{W_2}$

$$\Rightarrow \frac{90 \times 200}{0.5} = \frac{(90+x) \times 400}{2.5}$$

$$\Rightarrow 90 + x = \frac{90 \times 2.5 \times 200}{0.5 \times 400}$$

$$\Rightarrow 90 + x = 225 \Rightarrow x = 225 - 90 \Rightarrow x = 135$$

Hence, 135 extra workers required to complete the work in time.

119. (c) (Praveen + Vijay)'s 2 week's work

$$= \frac{1}{8} + \frac{1}{12} = \frac{3+2}{24} = \frac{5}{24}$$

∴ 5 units of work is done in 2 weeks

∴ $(5 \times 4) = 20$ units of work is done in $(4 \times 2) = 8$ weeks

∴ In the 9th week, Parveen will complete his 3 units of work.

∴ Remaining 1 unit can be done by Vijay in $\frac{1}{2}$ week.

∴ Total time taken $= 9\frac{1}{2} = 9.5$ weeks

120. (d) 1 day work of 25 M and 45 $W = \frac{1}{15}$

and 1 day work of 15 M and 60 $W = \frac{1}{20}$

$$3 \times \left(25M + 45W = \frac{1}{15}\right)$$

$$\Rightarrow 75M + 135W = \frac{1}{5} \quad \ldots(i)$$

$$5 \times \left(15M + 60W = \frac{1}{20}\right)$$

$$\Rightarrow 75M + 300W = \frac{1}{4} \quad \ldots(ii)$$

Eq. (ii) – Eq. (i),

$$165W = \frac{1}{4} - \frac{1}{5} \Rightarrow 165W = \frac{1}{20}$$

$$\Rightarrow 1 \text{ day work of } 1W = \frac{1}{3300}$$

$$\therefore 75M + 300W = \frac{1}{4} \Rightarrow$$

$$75M + 300 \times \frac{1}{3300} = \frac{1}{4}$$

$$\Rightarrow 75M = \frac{1}{4} - \frac{1}{11} \Rightarrow 75M = \frac{7}{44}$$

$$\Rightarrow 1M = \frac{7}{44 \times 75} = \frac{7}{3300}$$

$$\Rightarrow 1 \text{ day work of } 1M = \frac{7}{3300}$$

Hence, 1 day's work of 69 M and 67 W

$$= 69 \times \frac{7}{3300} + \frac{67 \times 1}{3300} = \frac{483+67}{3300}$$

$$= \frac{550}{3300} = \frac{1}{6}$$

Hence, 69 men and 67 women can complete the work in 6 days.

121. (a) We know, $M_1D_1 = M_2D_2$

$$(1M + 4W) \times \frac{65}{4} = (3M + 4W) \times \frac{13}{2}$$

$$\Rightarrow (1M + 4W) \times \frac{5}{2} = 3M + 4W$$

$$\Rightarrow 5M + 20W = 6M + 8W$$

$$\Rightarrow M = 12W \Rightarrow \frac{M}{W} = \frac{12}{1}$$

Total work $= (1M + 4W) \times \frac{65}{4}$

$$= (1 \times 12 + 4 \times 1) \times \frac{65}{4} = 16 \times \frac{65}{4} = 65 \times 4$$

∴ Number of days required to complete the same work by 13 women $= \frac{65 \times 4}{13 \times 1} = 20$ days

122. (b) Let the number of men initially decided to do the job $= x$

By formula, $M_1D_1 = M_2D_2$

$$6x = x \times 1 + (x - 18) \times 1 + (x - 36) \times 1 + (x - 54) \times 1 + \ldots + (x - 126) \times 1$$

$$\Rightarrow 6x = x + x - 18 + x - 36 + \ldots + x - 126$$

$$\Rightarrow 6x = 8x - 18 - 36 - 54 - \ldots - 126$$

$$\Rightarrow 8x - 6x = 18 + 36 + 54 + \ldots + 126$$

$$\Rightarrow 2x = 18(1 + 2 + 3 + \ldots + 7)$$

$$\Rightarrow 2x = 18 \times \frac{7 \times (7+1)}{2} \quad \left[\because S_n = \frac{n(n+1)}{2}\right]$$

$$\Rightarrow 2x = 18 \times 7 \times 4$$

$$\Rightarrow x = \frac{18 \times 7 \times 4}{2} = 18 \times 7 \times 2 = 252$$

123. (c) Total work $= 40 \times 15 = 600$ units

Since 40 men worked for 3 days, so the work done in 3 days by 40 men

$$= 40 \times 3 = 120 \text{ units.}$$

Now, 20 men joined so the total men

$$= 40 + 20 = 60$$

∴ The remaining work

$$= 600 - 120 = 480 \text{ units}$$

∴ Time taken by 60 men to complete the remaining work

$$= \frac{480}{60} = 8 \text{ days}$$

∴ Total time taken $= 8 + 3 = 11$ days

124. (b) According to the question,

So men do the remaining work in 60 days.

∴ 60 men do the remaining work

$$= \frac{60 \times 80}{60} = 80 \text{ days} \quad \left[\because D_1 = \frac{M_2D_2}{M_1}\right]$$

∴ 60 men do the total work in $(80 + 20) = 100$ days

∴ Required extra days needed = 20 days

125. (a) Let Gagan do x work in $\frac{4}{5}$ days.

∴ Numan do $\frac{x}{2}$ work in $\frac{4}{5}$ days.

1 day's work of Gagan $= \frac{5x}{4}$

1 day's work of Numan $= \frac{5x}{8}$

According to the question,

$$\frac{5x}{4} + \frac{5x}{8} = \frac{1}{16} \Rightarrow \frac{10x + 5x}{8} = \frac{1}{16}$$

$$\Rightarrow 15x = \frac{1}{2} \Rightarrow x = \frac{1}{30}$$

∴ 1 day's work of Gagan $= \frac{5}{4} \times \frac{1}{30} = \frac{1}{24}$

∴ Time taken by Gagan, to complete the work $= \frac{1}{\frac{1}{24}} = 24$ days

126. (a) According to the question,

$$(5M + 8W) \times 12 = (3M + 7W) \times 15$$

$$\Rightarrow 60M + 96W = 45M + 105W$$

$$\Rightarrow 15M = 9W$$

$$\Rightarrow 5M = 3W \quad \ldots(i)$$

One day work of $5M + 8W = \frac{1}{12}$

$$\Rightarrow 3W + 8W = \frac{1}{12} \quad \text{[from Eq. (i)]}$$

$$\Rightarrow 11W = \frac{1}{12}$$

Hence, 11 women will complete the same work in 12 days.

127. (a) A and B can do a certain work in 6 h.

1 h work of A and B is $\frac{1}{6}$ unit.

A, B and C do the complete work in 4 h.

1 h work of A, B and C is $\frac{1}{4}$ unit.

So, 1 h work of $C = \frac{1}{4} - \frac{1}{6} = \frac{2}{24} = \frac{1}{12}$ unit

∴ C alone can accomplish the task in 12 h.

128. (b) According to the question,

3 day's work of Ruchi when assisted by Khushi and Teju on every third day

$$= \frac{1}{30} + \frac{1}{30} + \left(\frac{1}{40} + \frac{1}{60} + \frac{1}{30}\right)$$

$$= \frac{2}{30} + \left(\frac{3+2+4}{120}\right)$$

$$= \frac{8}{120} + \frac{9}{120} = \frac{17}{120}$$

3 days work will be $\frac{17}{120}$ unit

So, (3×7) days work will be $\frac{119}{120}$ unit.

21 days work will be $\frac{119}{120}$ unit.

Remaining work $= 1 - \frac{119}{120} = \frac{1}{120}$

Now, Ruchi's turn, it will be completed in

$$\frac{\frac{1}{120}}{\frac{1}{30}} = \frac{1}{4} \text{ days}$$

So, total work will be completed in

$$\left(21 + \frac{1}{4}\right) \text{days} = \frac{85}{4} \text{ days}$$

129. (c) Let the efficiency of $B = 100$

A's efficiency $= (100 - 40)\%$ of $B = \frac{60}{100} \times 100$

$= 60$

Total work = Time × Efficiency

$= 50 \times (100 + 60) = 50 \times 160 = 8000$

60% of total work $= \frac{60}{100} \times 8000 = 4800$

Time taken by A alone to complete 60% of the work $= \frac{\text{Work}}{\text{Efficiency}} = \frac{4800}{60} = 80$ days.

130. (d) Given, 1 man = 2 women

= 4 boys = 5 girls

$\Rightarrow \quad 1\,M = 2\,W = 4\,B = 5\,G$

So, $1\,M + 1\,W + 1\,B + 1\,G = 5\,G + \frac{5}{2}G + \frac{5}{4}G + G$

$= \frac{20G + 10G + 5G + 4G}{4} = \frac{39G}{4}$

Also, 5 G's one day work $= \frac{1}{39}$

1 G's one day work $= \frac{1}{39 \times 5}$

$\frac{39}{4}$ G's one day work $= \frac{1}{39 \times 5} \times \frac{39}{4} = \frac{1}{20}$

So, together they will finish the work in 20 days.

131. (d) Total work $= 6 \times 3 = 18$ units

One day work of 8 women and 6 girls

$= \frac{8}{18} + \frac{6}{18} = \frac{14}{18} = \frac{7}{9}$

Time taken by 8 women and 6 girls to complete the work $= \frac{9}{7}$ days

132. (c) According to the question,

$10(6M + 8\,W) = 2(26M + 48W)$

$\Rightarrow \quad 60M + 80W = 52M + 96W$

$\Rightarrow \quad 60M - 52M = 96W - 80W$

$\Rightarrow \quad 8M = 16W$

$\Rightarrow \quad 1M = 2W$

6 men and 8 women $= 6 \times 2W + 8W = 20W$

Now, 15 men and 20 women $= 15M + 20W$

$= 30W + 20W = 50W$

∴ Required number of days

$= \frac{20 \times 10}{50} \quad [\because M_1D_1 = M_2D_2]$

$= \frac{200}{50} = 4$ days.

133. (a) Let A takes x days to finish a work. Then, time taken by B and C to finish the same work are $\frac{x}{4}$ and $\frac{x}{5}$ days, respectively.

Now, $(A + B + C)$'s one day work $= \frac{1}{x} + \frac{4}{x} + \frac{5}{x}$

According to the question,

$\frac{1}{4} = \frac{1 + 4 + 5}{x}$

$\Rightarrow \quad x = 4 \times 10 = 40$

Time taken by B to do the work alone $= \frac{x}{4}$ days $= \frac{40}{4} = 10$ days

134. (b) According to the question,

$M_1D_1 = M_2D_2$

$\Rightarrow \quad 450 \times 20 = M_2 \times 30$

$\Rightarrow \quad M_2 = \frac{450 \times 20}{30} = 300$

135. (a) Total work done by A, B and C in 3 days $= \frac{3}{10} + \frac{1}{20} + \frac{1}{40} = \frac{15}{40}$

∴ 15 units of work is done in 3 days

⇒$(2 \times 15) = 30$ units of work is done in $(2 \times 3) = 6$ days

∴ In next two days, A will complete has $(4 + 4) = 8$ units of work

Required time to complete the remaining

work $= \frac{\text{Remaining work}}{(A + B + C)\text{'s 1 day's work}} = \frac{\frac{2}{40}}{\frac{7}{40}} = \frac{2}{7}$

∴ Total time $= 8\frac{2}{7}$ days.

136. (b) Let the total number of days to complete the work be x.

According to the question,

$\frac{x}{15} + \frac{2}{10} = 1 \Rightarrow \frac{x}{15} = 1 - \frac{1}{5} = \frac{4}{5}$

$\therefore \quad x = 15 \times \frac{4}{5} = 12$ days.

137. (d) 18 men completed a work in 14 days.

3 women = 2 men (given)

$\frac{\text{Men}}{\text{Women}} = \frac{3}{2}$

Total work = 18 men × 14 days

$= 18 \times 3 \times 14 = 756$

According to the question,

∴ 3 more men added after 4 days

$756 = (5 \text{ men} + 6 \text{ women})\, 4 + x$

(8 men + 6 women)

$\Rightarrow \quad 756 = (5 \times 3 + 6 \times 2)4 + (8 \times 3 + 6 \times 2)x$

$\Rightarrow 756 = 27 \times 4 + 36 \times x$

$\Rightarrow \quad 756 - 108 = 36x \Rightarrow 648 = 36x$

$\Rightarrow \quad x = 18$ days

∴ Total number of days to complete work is = 18 days + 4 day = 22 days.

138. (b) Time taken by $A = \frac{23}{2}$ days

Efficiency ratio of A, B and C

$= 100 : 100 \times \frac{125}{100} : 100 \times \frac{125}{100} \times \frac{1}{2} = 1 : \frac{5}{4} : \frac{5}{8}$

$= 8 : 10 : 5 = (23)$ units

Total work $= 8 \times \frac{23}{2} = 4 \times 23 = 92$ units

Time taken by A, B and C together

$= \frac{92}{23} = 4$ days

139. (b) Given, efficiency of $A : B = 7 : 5$,

Working together they can complete the work in $\frac{35}{2}$ days

Then, total work $= 12 \times \frac{35}{2} = 210$ units

∴ Number of days B take to complete

50% of work $= \frac{210}{5} \times \frac{50}{100} = \frac{210}{10} = 21$ days

140. (b) According to the question,

5 men × 20 days = 10 women × 15 days

⇒ 2 men = 3 women ⇒ $\frac{\text{men}}{\text{women}} = \frac{3}{2}$

Now, total work = 5 men × 20 days

$= 5 \times 3 \times 20 = 300$ unit

First start work by = (2 men + 6 women) × 5 days $= (2 \times 3 + 6 \times 2) \times 5 = (6 + 12) \times 5$

$= 18 \times 5 = 90$ unit

Remaining work to complete

$= 300 - 90 = 210$ unit

After that, 3 women left the work and 1 men join

So, now the work done by the $(2m + 3w + 1m)$

∴ Total days to complete the remaining work,

$(3m + 3w) \times x \text{ days} = 210$

$\Rightarrow \quad (3 \times 3 + 3 \times 2) \times x \text{ days} = 210$

$\Rightarrow \quad 15 \times x \text{ days} = 210 \Rightarrow x \text{ days} = 14$ days

So, remaining work will complete in 14 days.

141. (a) Given, $(A + B)$'s 1 day work

$= \frac{1}{20}$ ...(i)

$(B + C)$'s 1 day work $= \frac{1}{24}$ ...(ii)

By Eqs. (i) and (ii),

$(A - C)$'s 1 day work $= \frac{1}{20} - \frac{1}{24} = \frac{6 - 5}{120} = \frac{1}{120}$

Let C's 1 day work $= \frac{1}{2x}$

The, A's 1 day work $= \frac{1}{x}$

According to the question,

$\frac{1}{x} - \frac{1}{2x} = \frac{1}{120} \Rightarrow \frac{2 - 1}{2x} = \frac{1}{120}$

$\Rightarrow \quad x = 60$

Then, A's 1 day work $= \frac{1}{60}$

and C's 1 day work $= \frac{1}{120}$

Put the value of A in Eq. (i), we get

B's 1 day work $= \frac{1}{20} - \frac{1}{60} = \frac{3 - 1}{60} = \frac{2}{60} = \frac{1}{30}$

Now, 100% of work completed by B

= 30 days

∴ 40% of work completed by B

$= \frac{40}{100} \times 30 = 12$ days.

142. (a) According to the question,
Let efficiency of each person is 1.
Total work = 20 units
On first day 1 units done,
2 nd day = 2 units,
3rd day = 3 units,
4th day = 4 units,
5th day = 5 units
Total work completed = $1+2+3+4+5 = 15$ units
Remaining work to complete $= 20 - 15 = 5$ units
After that next day all 5 person jointly work 5 units.
So, total 6 days will required to complete a work.

143. (c) Samir and Puneet 1 day work
$$= \frac{1}{10} + \frac{1}{15} = \frac{3+2}{30} = \frac{5}{30} = \frac{1}{6}$$
Samir and Puneet 5 days work $= \frac{5}{6}$
Remaining work $= 1 - \frac{5}{6} = \frac{1}{6}$
∴ Amount was paid to Ashok
$$= \frac{1}{6} \times 4500 = ₹\ 750$$

144. (b) *A* can do a work in 15 days.
B is 25% more efficient than *A*.
$$\frac{B}{A} = \frac{125}{100} \Rightarrow \frac{5}{4} = \frac{B}{A}$$
Total work ⇒ $15 \times 4 = 60$ units
A and *B* together work for 4 days
$(4+5) \times 4 = 9 \times 4 = 36$ units
Remaining units $= 60 - 36 = 24$ units
Now, 24 units completed by *C* in 8 days
⇒ *C* efficiency $= \frac{24}{8} = 3$ units
∴ Required number of days
$$= \frac{60}{(4+5+3)} = 5 \text{ days}$$
Hence, *A*, *B*, *C* together can complete the same work in 5 days.

145. (c) A man and a woman can complete a work in 66 days.
Total work $= 66 \times (3+2) = 66 \times 5 = 330$
[∵ Men : Women, efficiency = 3 : 2]
$6M + 2W$ can complete a work in
$(6M + 2W)d = 330$
$$\text{days} = \frac{330}{(6 \times 3 + 2 \times 2)}$$
$$\Rightarrow \text{days} = \frac{330}{22} = 15 \text{ days.}$$

146. (b) According to the question, *A* and *B* work on alternate days. Starting from *B* and complete a work in $11\frac{1}{3}$ days. On first day *B* work and second day *A* work.
So, $B + A + B + A + B + A + B + A + B + A + B$
B works for 6 days
A works for $5\frac{1}{3}$ days
A alone can complete a work in 24 days.
A one day work $= \frac{1}{24}$ units
$$A \text{ work for } 5\frac{1}{3} \text{ days} = \frac{1}{24} \times \frac{16}{3} = \frac{2}{9}$$
$$\text{Remaining work} = 1 - \frac{2}{9} = \frac{7}{9}$$
∴ $\frac{7}{9}$th part of work complete by *B* in 6 days.

147. (b) Here, $M_1 = 18, D_1 = 35$
$M_2 = 21, D_2 = ?$
$18 \times 35 = 21 \times D_2$
$$\Rightarrow D_2 = \frac{18 \times 35}{21} = 6 \times 5$$
$$\Rightarrow D_2 = 30 \text{ days}$$

148. (c) Here, $M_1 = 187, D_1 = 65,$
$H_1 = 15, \quad W_1 = \frac{3}{5}$
$M_2 = ?, \quad D_2 = 10$
$H_2 = 17, \quad W_2 = 1 - \frac{3}{5} = \frac{2}{5}$
$$\frac{187 \times 65 \times 15}{3/5} = \frac{M_2 \times 10 \times 17}{2/5}$$
$$\Rightarrow M_2 = \frac{187 \times 65 \times 15 \times 2 \times 5}{3 \times 10 \times 17 \times 5}$$
$$\Rightarrow M_2 = 11 \times 13 \times 5 = 715$$
Thus, number of additional men needed
$= 715 - 187 = 528$

149. (a) According to the question,
10 Men = 12 women ⇒ 5 Men = 6 women
We know that, $M_1 D_1 = M_2 D_2$
⇒ 12 women × 10 = (5 men + 2 Women) × D
⇒ 12 women × 10 = (6 women + 2 Women) × D
⇒ 12 women × 10 = 8 women × D
$$\therefore \quad D = \frac{12 \times 10}{8} = 15 \text{ days}$$

150. (a) Let *C* can finish the remaining task in *x* days.
According to the question,
$$\frac{4}{20} + \frac{4}{16} + \frac{x}{30} = 1 \Rightarrow \frac{x}{30} = 1 - \frac{1}{5} - \frac{1}{4}$$
$$\Rightarrow \frac{x}{30} = \frac{20-4-5}{20} \Rightarrow x = \frac{11 \times 3}{2} = 16\frac{1}{2} \text{ days}$$
Hence, *C* can complete the remaining task in $16\frac{1}{2}$ days.

151. (a) Here, Man = *M*, Woman = *W*
We know that, $M_1D_1 = M_2D_2$
$$\Rightarrow 16M \times 8 = (8M + 9W) \times 10$$
$$\Rightarrow 16M \times 4 = (8M + 9W) \times 5$$
$$\Rightarrow 64M = 40M + 45W$$
$$\Rightarrow 24M = 45W$$
$$\Rightarrow 8M = 15W \quad \text{...(i)}$$
$$\Rightarrow \frac{M}{W} = \frac{15}{8}$$
Let 20 women will finish the work = *d* once again,
$$M_1D_1 = M_2D_2$$
$$\Rightarrow 16M \times 8 = 20W \times d$$
$$\Rightarrow 16 \times \frac{15}{8}W \times 8 = 20W \times d$$
$$\therefore d = \frac{16 \times 15 \times 8}{20 \times 8} = 12 \text{ days}$$

152. (d) Let efficiency of *Y* be 5 units.
$$\text{Efficiency of X} = 5 \times \frac{140}{100} = 5 \times \frac{7}{5} = 7$$
$$\text{Efficiency of Z} = 5 \times \frac{60}{100} = 5 \times \frac{3}{5} = 3$$
According to the question,
$(Y + Z)$ together work $= (5 + 3) \times 35 = 8 \times 35 = 280$
Total work $= (5 + 7 + 3) \times 21 = 315$
Remaining work $= 315 - 280 = 35$
Remaining work will be completed by *X* alone in $\frac{35}{7} = 5$ days

153. (d) According to the question,
$$5(4M + 6W) = 7(3M + 4W)$$
$$\Rightarrow 20M + 30W = 21M + 28W$$
$$\Rightarrow M = 2W \Rightarrow \frac{M}{W} = \frac{2}{1}$$
Let *x* men should assist the women
Then, 25 women $= \frac{25}{2}$ men
$$\text{Again} \Rightarrow \frac{(4M + 3M) \times 5}{1} = \frac{\left(x + \frac{25}{2}\right) M \times 5}{\frac{5}{2}}$$
[∵ 2*W* = *M*]
$$\Rightarrow 7M \times 5 = \frac{(2x + 25)\ M \times 2}{2}$$
$$\Rightarrow 35 = 2x + 25 \Rightarrow x = \frac{35 - 25}{2} = 5 \text{ Men}$$
Hence, 5 men should assist 25 women.

154. (b) Work done by Sumit and Rajiv together in 1 h $= \frac{1}{20}$
Work done by Sumit alone in 1 h $= \frac{1}{25}$
$$\text{Work done by Rajiv alone in 1 h} = \frac{1}{20} - \frac{1}{25} = \frac{5-4}{100} = \frac{1}{100}$$
∴ Time taken by Rajiv to do the complete Job = 100 h

155. (a) We know that, $\frac{M_1 \times D_1}{W_1} = \frac{M_2 D_2}{W_2}$
Here, $M_1 = 12, D_1 = 10$ and $W_1 = 540$ and $D_2 = 8, W_2 = 720$
Let the extra people needed be *x*.
∴ $M_2 = 12 + x$
$$\text{Hence,} \quad \frac{12 \times 10}{540} = \frac{(12 + x) \times 8}{720}$$
$$\Rightarrow \quad 12 + x = 20$$

$\Rightarrow \quad x = 8$

So, 8 more people will be required.

156. (b) Ratio of efficiency of Sapna and Rakesh = 2 : 1

$\therefore$ Total work = (2 + 1) × 48 = 144 unit

Hence, time taken to complete the project by Sapna $= \frac{144}{2} = 72$ days

157. (b) Here, $M_1 = 300$,

$T_1 = 30 - 20 = 10$ days

and $M_2 = 300 - 50 = 250$, $T_2 = ?$

$\therefore \quad M_1 \times T_1 = M_2 \times T_2$

$\Rightarrow \quad 300 \times 10 = 250 \times T_2$

$\Rightarrow \quad T_2 = \frac{300 \times 10}{250} = 12$ days

158. (b) (Rajan + Rajat)'s 2 days work

$= \frac{1}{64} + \frac{1}{48} = \frac{7}{192}$

In 54 days, work of (Rajan + Rajat)

$= \frac{54}{2} \times \frac{7}{192} = \frac{189}{192}$

Remaining work $= 1 - \frac{189}{192} = \frac{3}{192}$

Time takan to completed remaining work by Rajat $= \frac{3}{192} \times 48 = \frac{3}{4}$ day

Hence, required time $= 54 + \frac{3}{4} = 54\frac{3}{4}$ days

159. (d) Given, efficiency of Amit = Efficiency of (Bina + Sita)

According to the question,

	Days	Total work	Efficiency
Amit + Bina ⟶	25	175	7
Sita ⟶	35		5

Now, Amit = Bina + Sita

Amit − Bina = 5 ...(i)

[$\because$ Efficiency of Sita = 5]

and Amit + Bina = 7 ...(ii)

From Eqs. (i) and (ii),

Efficiency of Bina = 1

Hence, Bina alone can complete the work

$= \frac{175}{1} = 175$ days

160. (b) According to the question,

		Total work	Efficiency
P ⟶	30	120	4
Q ⟶	40		3

Work done by P and Q in 4 days

$= (4 + 3) \times 4 = 28$ units

$\therefore$ Remaining work = 120 − 28 = 92 units.

So, time taken by P to finish the remaining work $= \frac{92}{4} = 23$ days.

161. (b) Let the total work be 420 units.

$\therefore$ Efficiency of Manish = 420 / 21 = 20

Efficiency of Nakul = 420 / 28 = 15

Efficiency of Pintoo = 420 / 15 = 28

Now, work done by (Manish + Pintoo) in 5 days = (20 + 28) × 5 = 240

$\therefore$ Remaining work = 420 − 240 = 180 units

$\therefore$ Time taken to finish the remaining work by all

$= \frac{180}{20 + 15 + 28} = \frac{180}{63} = \frac{20}{7}$ days

$= 2\frac{6}{7}$ days.

162. (a) 1 day's work of Ronak $= \frac{1}{12}$

1 day's work of Riya $= \frac{1}{18}$

1 day's work by both $= \frac{1}{12} + \frac{1}{18}$

$= \frac{3 + 2}{36} = \frac{5}{36}$

6 day's work together $= \frac{6 \times 5}{36} = \frac{30}{36}$

Remaining work $= 1 - \frac{30}{36} = \frac{6}{36} = \frac{1}{6}$

This remaining work done by Riya in

$= \frac{1}{6} \times 18 = 3$ days.

163. (b) According to the question,

		Total work	Efficiency
Ravi + Sanju ⟶	2		2
Sanju + Mahesh ⟶	4	4	1
Ravi + Mahesh ⟶	2		2

Efficiency of (Ravi + Sanju + Mahesh)

$= \frac{2 + 1 + 2}{2} = \frac{5}{2}$

$\therefore$ Efficiency of Ravi $= \frac{5}{2} - 1 = \frac{3}{2}$

Hence, total time taken by Ravi to do work done $= \frac{4}{\frac{3}{2}} = \frac{8}{3}$ days.

164. (c) According to the question,

	Time	Total work	Eff.
A + B ⟶	25		36
B + C ⟶	36	900	25
C + A ⟶	30		30
A + B + C + D ⟶	18		50

$\therefore \; (A + B + C) = \frac{36 + 25 + 30}{2} = \frac{91}{2} = 45.5$

And $A + B + C + D = 50$

Efficiency of $D = 50 - 45.5 = 4.5$

Hence, D can do the entire work alone in

$= \frac{900}{4.5} = 200$ days

165. (c) Total work = Number of workers × Number of days

$18 \times 96 = (18 \times 26) + \{(18 + 10) \times x\}$

$\Rightarrow (18 \times 96) - (18 \times 26) = 28 \times x$

$\Rightarrow \quad 18 \times 70 = 28 \times x \Rightarrow x = 45$ days

$\therefore$ Total time taken to finish the work

= (26 + 45) days = 71 days

166. (c) We know that,

$\frac{M_1 \times D_1}{W_1} = \frac{M_2 \times D_2}{W_2} \Rightarrow \frac{24 \times 25}{90} = \frac{27 \times D_2}{162}$

$\Rightarrow \quad D_2 = 40$ days

Hence, 15 = (40 − 25) more days will be required to complete the given work.

167. (b) Let the total work be 26 units (LCM of 13, 26)

$\therefore$ Efficiency of $A = \frac{26}{13} = 2$

Efficiency of $B = \frac{26}{26} = 1$

$\therefore$ 2 days work, if they work alternately = 3 units

$\therefore$ In 16 days (2 × 8), 24 units (3 × 8) work is completed.

Remaining work = 26 − 24 = 2 units

Now, A will work on 17th day to complete the remaining work.

$\therefore$ Total days required to complete the work = 17

168. (d) Let the efficientcy of Suresh be 1.

$\therefore$ Efficiency of Arvind = 4

Now, total work = 20

$\therefore$ Time taken by Arvind and Suresh to finish the work together $= \frac{20}{(4 + 1)} = \frac{20}{5} = 4$ days

169. (d) Let total work be 60 units (LCM of 20, 30).

$\therefore$ Efficiency of $A = \frac{60}{20} = 3$

Efficiency of $B = \frac{60}{30} = 2$

$\therefore$ Total work done by ($A + B$) in 2 days

= (3 + 2) × 2 = 10 units

Remaining work = 60 − 10 = 50 units.

$\therefore$ Fraction of work that is left $= \frac{50}{60} = \frac{5}{6}$

170. (b) Let the total work be 200 units (LCM of 100 and 200).

$\therefore$ Efficiency of $A = \frac{200}{200} = 1$

Efficiency of $B = \frac{200}{100} = 2$

3 days of work = 1 + 2 + 1 + 2 = 6 units

Now, 99 days of work $= \frac{99}{3} \times 6 = 198$ units

Remaining work = 200 − 198 = 2 units

Time taken to complete remaining work by $(A + B) = \frac{2}{3}$.

$\therefore$ Total time required $= 99\frac{2}{3}$ days

171. (c) Let the total work = 36 unit

So, Efficiency of A and B = 1 unit/day

According to the question,

A and B started working together but A took a day off after every five days of work. While B took a day off after every seven days of work.

So, per day work A and $B = 1 + 1 = 2$ unit

So, work done on each day

$= 2+2+2+2+2+1+2+1+2+2+2+$
$+2+2+2+1+2+1+2+2+1 = 36$ units

So, the work will be completed on 21st July, 2021.

172. (a) If Arun can complete $\frac{2}{3}$rd of a work in 12 days.

Then, they can complete total work in

$= \frac{3}{2} \times 12 = 18$ days

Hence, he can complete $\frac{1}{6}$th of the same work in $= \frac{1}{6} \times 18$ days $= 3$ days

173. (c) Given,

Time		Efficiency
$A = 11$ days	20	20 Unit/day
$B = 20$ days	11	LCM (11, 20, 55)
$C = 55$ days	4	Total work = 220 Units

According to the question,

In Ist day A and B together complete 31 unit work.

In 2nd day A and C together complete 24 unit work.

Total units of work in 2 days

$= (31 + 24)$ units $= 55$ units

$\therefore$ 220 units of work is done in $= \frac{220}{55} = 4$

$\therefore$ Total time $= 4 \times 2$ days $= 8$ days

174. (c) Given, Akshita alone can finish the typing work in 16 days.

Raina alone can finish the typing work in 24 days.

Akshita	16	3	48 (LCM –16,24)
Raina	24	2	

Let, total work = 48 units

They work on alternate basis, i.e. day 1 Akshita and on day 2 Raina

So, in 2 days they finished = 5 unit work

2 days $\longrightarrow$ 5 units

$2 \times 9 \longrightarrow 5 \times 9 = 45$ units work

In 18 days they finished 45 unit work and day 19th Akshita works and entire work will be finished.

175. (d) Given, number of employees = 75

Number of days to complete the work = 60

$\therefore$ Total work $= 75 \times 60 = 4500$

But 15 employees left the job, so now number of employees = 60

Work done in 65 days

$60 \times 65 = 3900$

Let after x days 15 employees left so 15 employees' work for x days

$\because \quad 15x = 4500 - 3900$

$\Rightarrow \quad 15x = 600 \Rightarrow x = 40$ days

176. (b)

$P \longrightarrow$ 36d	4	
$Q \longrightarrow$ 48d	3	144 (Total unit)
$R \longrightarrow$ 144d	1	

If P, Q and R work together then work of 1 day $= 4 + 3 + 1 = 8$ units

If P works 12 days before work completed

$= 4 \times 12 = 48$ units

And Q works 8 days before work completed

$= 3 \times 8 = 24$ units

Then, total work will be

$= 144 + 48 + 24 = 216$ units

Hence, time will be taken to do complete work $= \frac{216}{4 + 3 + 1}$ days $= 27$ days

177. (d)

$A \longrightarrow$ 20	3	
$B \longrightarrow$ 30	2	60 (Total unit)
$C \longrightarrow$ 60	1	

Let A works in 1 day = 3 units

B works in 1 day = 2 units

C works in 1 day = 1 units

A works daily and third day B and C also work with A, then work completed in 3 days

$= 3 + 3 + (2 + 1 + 3) = 6 + 6 = 12$ units

If total work = 60 units

And 12 units work done in 3 days.

Then, 60 units work done in

$= \frac{3}{12} \times 60 = 15$ days

178. (a) According to the question,

3 goats = 5 sheeps

$\because \quad$ 6 goats = 10 sheeps

6 goats and 8 sheeps $= 10 + 8 = 18$ sheeps.

Time taken by 5 sheeps to graze the field

= 54 days

$\therefore$ Time taken by 18 sheeps to graze the field

$= \frac{54}{18} \times 5 = 15$ days

$\therefore$ 6 goats and 18 sheeps will graze the field in 15 days.

179. (b) Let the number of men originally working be x.

According to the question,

$x \times 20 = (x - 5) \times 40 \Rightarrow x = (x - 5) \times 2$

$x = 2x - 10 \Rightarrow x = 10$

Thus, earlier 10 men are working.

180. (a) Let P alone can do the piece of work in x days. Then, R alone can do the same piece of work in $2x$ days.

Now, $(P - R)$'s one day work

$= [(P + Q)'s - (Q + R)'s]$ one day work

$\Rightarrow \quad \frac{1}{x} - \frac{1}{2x} = \frac{1}{14} - \frac{1}{21} \Rightarrow \frac{1}{2x} = \frac{3 - 2}{42}$

$\Rightarrow \quad \frac{1}{2x} = \frac{1}{42} \Rightarrow x = 21$ days

Also, $\frac{1}{P} + \frac{1}{Q} = \frac{1}{14} \Rightarrow \frac{1}{x} + \frac{1}{Q} = \frac{1}{14}$

$\Rightarrow \quad \frac{1}{Q} = \frac{1}{14} - \frac{1}{x} = \frac{1}{14} - \frac{1}{21} = \frac{1}{42}$

So, Q alone can do the same piece of work in 42 days.

181. (d) One day efficiency of Raju, Angad and Sumit is $\frac{1}{36}$ unit, $\frac{1}{18}$ unit, $\frac{1}{24}$ unit respectively.

$\Rightarrow$ One day efficiency of all if they all work together $= \frac{1}{36} + \frac{1}{18} + \frac{1}{24} = \frac{2 + 4 + 3}{72}$

$= \frac{9}{72} = \frac{1}{8}$ unit

$\Rightarrow$ Total work will be completed in 8 h, if they are doing all work together.

182. (c) 1 day's work of Aarush and Maahi $= \frac{1}{10}$

1 day's work of Aarush $= \frac{1}{15}$

$\therefore$ 1 day's work of Maahi alone

$= \frac{1}{10} - \frac{1}{15} = \frac{3 - 2}{30} = \frac{1}{30}$

$\therefore$ Maahi alone will do the same work in

$= \frac{1}{\frac{1}{30}} = 30$ days

Speedy Method

$A + M \rightarrow 10$	3	30
$A \rightarrow 15$	2	

Efficiency of $M = 3 - 2 = 1$

Required time $= \frac{30}{1} = 30$ days

183. (d) A can complete work in 35 days.

B can complete in 15 days.

Let total work is 105 units.

A done 3 units per day.

B done 7 units per day.

$(A$ and $B)$'s 7 days work $= (3 + 7) \times 7$

$\Rightarrow \quad 10 \times 7 = 70$ units

Remaining units $(105 - 70) = 35$ units

60% of remaining units $= \frac{35 \times 6}{10} = 21$ units

A alone complete 60% of remaining work in $\frac{21}{3} = 7$ days

184. (b) According to the question,

A – 10	1	10 units
B – 5	2	

Work done in two days $2 \times (1 + 2) = 6$ units

and $\frac{10 - 6}{A + C} = 3 \Rightarrow \frac{4}{1 + C} = 3 \Rightarrow C = \frac{1}{3}$

$\therefore$ Required time $= 10 \times \frac{\frac{40}{100}}{1/3} = \frac{4}{\frac{1}{3}} = 12$ days

185. (c) Ratio efficiency of A and B = $A:B$

$= 2:1$

Total work = $(2+1) \times 13 = 39$ unit

$\therefore$ Time taken by $A = \frac{39}{2} = 19\frac{1}{2}$ days

186. (b) $(A+B)$'s 1 day work = $\frac{1}{25}$ part of total work

B alone can do 100% = $\frac{30}{\frac{200}{3}} \times 100 = 45$ days

So, B's 1 day work = $\frac{1}{45}$ part of the total work

So, A's 1 day work = $\frac{1}{25} - \frac{1}{45}$

$= \frac{9-5}{45 \times 5} = \frac{4}{45 \times 5}$

Now, to complete $\frac{4}{15}$ part of the same work

A required = $\frac{\frac{4}{15}}{\frac{4}{45 \times 5}} = \frac{4 \times 45 \times 5}{15 \times 4} = 15$ days

187. (c) According to the question,

$2(A+B+C)$'s 1 day work = $\frac{1}{36} + \frac{1}{60} + \frac{1}{45}$

$= \frac{5+3+4}{180} = \frac{12}{180} = \frac{1}{15}$

$(A+B+C)$'s 1 day work = $\frac{1}{2} \times \frac{1}{15} = \frac{1}{30}$

B's 1 day work = $(A+B+C) - (C+A)$

$= \frac{1}{30} - \frac{1}{45} = \frac{3-2}{90} = \frac{1}{90}$

So, B alone can complete the same work in $\frac{1}{\frac{1}{90}} = 90$ days.

188. (a) The efficiency ratio of A and B is 2 : 1.

Total work = $(2+1) \times 13 = 39$ units

Time taken $B = \frac{39}{1} = 39$ days

189. (a) A can do a job in 10 days.

B can do a job in 5 days.

LCM = 10 = Total work

Efficiency of $A = \frac{10}{10} = 1$ units/day

Efficiency of $B = \frac{10}{5} = 2$ units/day

A and B work for 2 days

$= (1+2) \times 2$ units = 6 units

Remaining work = $(10-6)$ units = 4 units

A and C can complete the remaining work in 3 days.

(A and C) is one day work = $\frac{4}{3}$

C's one day work $\left(\frac{4}{3}\right) - 1 = \frac{1}{3}$

$\because$ 60% of total work = $10 \times \frac{60}{100} = 6$ units

$\therefore$ C can complete 60% of work in = $\frac{6}{\left(\frac{1}{3}\right)}$

= 18 days

190. (b) According to the question,

Let efficiency Ratnesh and Vineet are R and V respectively equating work

$\therefore \quad 27\frac{3}{4} \times R + 27 \times V = R \times 48$

$\Rightarrow \quad \frac{111}{4}R + 27V = 48R$

$\Rightarrow \quad 111R + 108V = 192R$

$\Rightarrow \quad 81R = 108V$

$\Rightarrow \quad \frac{R}{V} = \frac{108}{81} = \frac{12}{9} = \frac{4}{3}$

Total work = $4 \times 48 = 192$ units

Time taken by Vineet to finish work

$= \frac{192}{3} = 64$ days

191. (b)

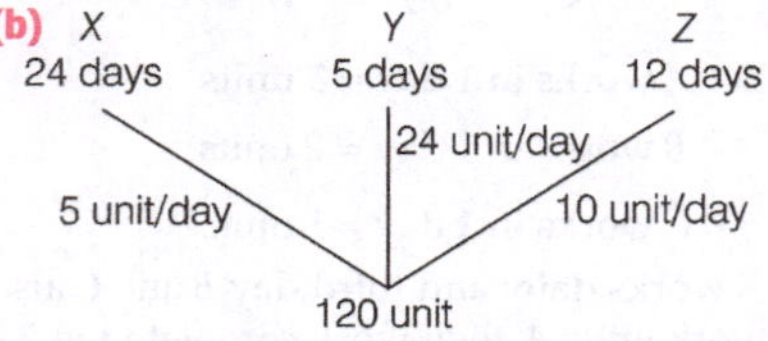

Total number of days if X, Y and Z work together = $\frac{120}{(5+24+10)}$ unit/day

$= \frac{120}{39} = \frac{40}{13} = 3\frac{1}{13}$ days

192. (b) According to the question,

$\frac{\text{Teena} \times 6}{1/2} = \frac{(\text{Teena} + \text{Shyam}) \times 4}{1/2}$

$\Rightarrow \quad \frac{\text{Teena}}{\text{Shyam}} = \frac{2}{1}$

Now, Shyam alone can complete the work in

(Teena)'s efficiency × Days

= (Shyam)'s efficiency × Days

$\Rightarrow \quad 2 \times 12 = 1 \times \text{Days}$

$\therefore$ Shyam alone can complete the work in

= 24 days

193. (c) Mira's one day work = $\frac{1}{20}$

Nina's one day work = $\frac{1}{30}$

and Sima's one day work = $\frac{1}{40}$

According to the question,

$4\left(\frac{1}{20} + \frac{1}{40}\right) + x\left(\frac{1}{30} + \frac{1}{40}\right) = 1$

$\Rightarrow \quad \frac{12}{40} + x\left(\frac{7}{120}\right) = 1$

$\Rightarrow \quad \frac{7x}{120} = \frac{28}{40}$

$\Rightarrow \quad x = 4 \times 3 = 12$ days

The work was completed in $(12+4) = 16$ days in total.

194. (a) Ratio of efficiency of Nirmal and Amit

$N : A$

$100 : 100 \times \frac{125}{100}$

Efficiency = 4 : 5

Thus, total work done by Nirmal

= 45 days × 4 = 180 units

$\therefore$ Time taken by Amit to do complete work

$= \frac{180}{5} = 36$ days

195. (b) P's 1 day's work = $\frac{1}{12}$

Q's 1 day's work = $\frac{1}{24}$

$\therefore$ $(P+Q)$'s 1 day's work = $\frac{1}{12} + \frac{1}{24} = \frac{2+1}{24}$

$= \frac{3}{24} = \frac{1}{8}$

$\therefore$ $(P+Q)$ can complete the work in = 8 days

196. (d) (Reena and Riya)'s one day's work

$= \frac{1}{36}$

(Riya and Geeta)'s one day's work = $\frac{1}{54}$

(Reena and Geeta)'s one day's work = $\frac{1}{81}$

$\therefore$ (Reena + Riya + Geeta)'s one day's work

$= \frac{1}{2}\left(\frac{1}{36} + \frac{1}{54} + \frac{1}{81}\right) = \frac{1}{2} \times \frac{19}{324} = \frac{19}{648}$

$\therefore$ Reena's one day's work = $\frac{19}{648} - \frac{1}{54} = \frac{7}{648}$

Hence, Reena alone can do complete the work in $\frac{648}{7} = 92\frac{4}{7}$ days

197. (d) Total work = LCM of 12 and 9

= 72 unit

Efficiency of $P = \frac{72}{12} = 6$ unit/day

Efficiency of $Q = \frac{72}{9} = 8$ unit/day

The share of $P = \frac{6}{6+8} \times 63000$

$= \frac{6}{14} \times 63000 =$ ₹ 27000

198. (a) Ratio of time taken by P and Q

$= P : Q$

Time ratio = $\frac{x}{2} : x = 1 : 2$

Efficiency ratio = 2 : 1

Thus, total work done

$= (2+1) \times 36 = 108$ units

$\therefore$ Time taken by Q alone to finish the work

$= \frac{108}{1} = 108$ days

199. (c) A's 1 day's work = $\frac{1}{4}$

B's 1 day's work = $\frac{1}{12}$

$\therefore$ $(A+B)$'s 1 day's work

$= \frac{1}{4} + \frac{1}{12} = \frac{3+1}{12} = \frac{4}{12} = \frac{1}{3}$

$\therefore$ A and B can complete the work in = 3 days

200. (c) Let efficiency of engineers and skilled workers be denoted by E and W, respectively.

According to the question,

$6E \times 5 = 5W \times 7 \Rightarrow \frac{E}{W} = \frac{7}{6}$

Let $E = 7k$, $W = 6k$

$\therefore$ Total work = $6(7k) \times 5 = 210k$ units.

$\therefore$ Time taken by 7 engineers and 4 skilled workers $= \frac{210k}{7(7k) + 4(6k)} = \frac{210k}{73k} = 2\frac{64}{73}$ days

201. (c) According to the question,

$\frac{30 \times 5 \times 18}{W_1} = \frac{20 \times 7 \times D_2}{W_1}$

$\therefore \quad D_2 = 19\frac{2}{7}$ days

202. (b) Let the total work be 1 unit.

$\therefore$ Tanvi's one day work $= \frac{1}{25}$

Tai's one day work $= \frac{1}{30}$

$\therefore$ Work done in 5 days by both of them

$= 5 \times \left(\frac{1}{25} + \frac{1}{30}\right) = 5 \times \frac{11}{150} = \frac{55}{150}$

$\therefore \quad$ Left work $= 1 - \frac{55}{150} = \frac{95}{150} = \frac{19}{30}$

203. (b) R can complete the work

$= 6 \times 10 = 60$ h

S can complete the work $= 5 \times 8 = 40$ h

R's 1 h work $= \frac{1}{60}$; S's 1 h work $= \frac{1}{40}$

$\therefore$ (R + S)'s 1 h work $= \frac{1}{40} + \frac{1}{60} = \frac{5}{120}$

$\therefore$ Both can finish the work in $\frac{120}{5}$ h.

Both work for 6h daily i.e.,

Work will be finished in $= \frac{120}{5} \times \frac{1}{6}$ days

$\therefore$ The work will be finished in 4 days.

204. (b) Given, Rohan's 1 hour's work $= \frac{1}{10}$

(Rohan + Mohan)'s 1 hour's work $= \frac{1}{4}$

According to the question,

Mohan's 1 hour's work

$= \frac{1}{4} - \frac{1}{10} = \frac{5-2}{20} = \frac{3}{20}$

$\therefore$ Mohan can complete the work $= \frac{20}{3}$ h

205. (d) Antony and Julie's one day work $= \frac{1}{15}$

Julie's one day work $= \frac{1}{20}$

$\therefore$ Antony's one day work $= \frac{1}{15} - \frac{1}{20} = \frac{1}{60}$

$\therefore$ Antony complete the work in 60 days.

206. (d) Marks $\propto$ Practice time

He got 70 marks by practicing 6 h.

Then, he got 1 mark by practicing $= \frac{6}{70}$ h

Then, he got 90 marks by practicing

$= \frac{6}{70} \times 90 = \frac{54}{7} = 7.7$ h

207. (d) According to the question,

X + Y ⟶ 18 days — 4
Y + Z ⟶ 24 days — 3 ⟹ Total work 72 units
X + Y + Z ⟶ 12 days — 6

[LCM of 18, 24 and 12 is 72]

Efficiency of X = 6 − 3 = 3 units/day

Efficiency of Z = 6 − 4 = 2 units/day

Time taken by X and Z together

$= \frac{72}{3+2} = 14\frac{2}{5}$ days.

208. (a) According to the question,

$1M \times 12 = 1W \times 8$

$\Rightarrow \quad \frac{M}{W} = \frac{8}{12} = \frac{2}{3}$

Let $M = 2K$, $W = 3K$

$\therefore$ Total work $= 2K \times 12 = 24K$ units

$\therefore$ Required time to complete the work by 6 men and 4 women

$= \frac{24K}{6 \times 2K + 4 \times 3K} = \frac{24K}{12K + 12K} = \frac{24K}{24K} = 1$ day

209. (b) Given, Shobita's 1 h work $= \frac{1}{20}$

Saroj's 1 h work $= \frac{1}{15}$

(Shobita's + Saroj's) 1h work

$= \frac{1}{20} + \frac{1}{15} = \frac{3+4}{60} = \frac{7}{60}$

$\therefore$ Both can complete the entire work in

$= \frac{60}{7} = 8\frac{4}{7}$ h

210. (b) 1 h work of Sapna $= \frac{1}{12}$

1 h work of Sapna and Riya $= \frac{1}{8}$

1 h work of Riya $= \left(\frac{1}{8} - \frac{1}{12}\right) = \frac{3-2}{24} = \frac{1}{24}$

$\therefore$ Riya can do the job working alone in 24 h.

211. (d) Akhil's 1 day's work $= \frac{1}{24}$

Shyam's 1 day's work $= \frac{1}{12}$

(Akhil + Shyam)'s 1 day's work

$= \frac{1}{24} + \frac{1}{12} = \frac{1+2}{24} = \frac{3}{24} = \frac{1}{8}$

$\therefore$ Akhil and Shyam complete the work together in 8 days.

212. (b) Let required number of workers = x

According to the question,

$12 \times 8 = 8 \times 2 + (8 + x)2$

$\Rightarrow \quad 96 = 16 + 16 + 2x$

$\Rightarrow 96 - 32 = 2x \Rightarrow x = \frac{64}{2} = 32$

213. (d) According to the question,

A ⟶ 20 days — 1
B ⟶ 10 days — 2 ⟹ Total work 20 units
A + B + C ⟶ 5 days — 4

[LCM of 20, 10 and 5 is 20]

Efficiency of C = 4 − (2 + 1) = 1 unit/day

$\therefore$ Time taken by C $= \frac{20}{1} = 20$ days

214. (d) Here, (A + B)'s 1 day's work $= \frac{1}{15}$

(B + C)'s 1 day's work $= \frac{1}{30}$

(C + A)'s 1 day's work $= \frac{1}{45}$

Now, 2 (A + B + C)'s 1 day's work

$= \frac{1}{15} + \frac{1}{30} + \frac{1}{45} = \frac{6+3+2}{90} = \frac{11}{90}$

$\therefore$ (A + B + C)'s 1 day work $= \frac{11}{90 \times 2} = \frac{11}{180}$

Hence, (A + B + C) complete the work in $\frac{180}{11}$ days $= 16\frac{4}{11}$ days

215. (b) Riya's one day's work $= \frac{1}{6}$ units

Sangeeta's one day's work $= \frac{1}{8}$ units

Part of work completed by Riya in 3 days

$= 3 \times \frac{1}{6} = \frac{1}{2}$ units

Remaining work $= 1 - \frac{1}{2} = \frac{1}{2}$ units

Number of days taken by Riya and Sangeeta to complete the remaining work

$= \frac{\left(\frac{1}{2}\right)}{\left(\frac{1}{6} + \frac{1}{8}\right)} = \frac{\left(\frac{1}{2}\right)}{\left(\frac{4+3}{24}\right)} = \frac{12}{7}$ days

$\therefore$ Time taken to complete the total work

$= 3 + \frac{12}{7} = \frac{21+12}{7} = \frac{33}{7} = 4\frac{5}{7}$ days

216. (c) According to the question,

$\frac{18 \times 10 \times 5}{1} = \frac{M_2 \times 5 \times 5}{2}$

$\Rightarrow M_2 = 18 \times 2 \times 2 = 72$ people are required.

217. (a) A's one day's work $= \frac{1}{12}$

B's one day's work $= \frac{1}{15}$

C's one day's work $= \frac{1}{20}$

Together A, B and C can complete the work in 1 day $= \frac{1}{12} + \frac{1}{15} + \frac{1}{20} = \frac{5+4+3}{60} = \frac{12}{60} = \frac{1}{5}$

$\therefore$ They all together can complete the work in 5 days.

218. (b) $(A+B)$'s 1 day's work $= \frac{1}{15}$

A's 1 day's work $= \frac{1}{18}$

$\therefore$ B's 1 day's work $= \left[\frac{1}{15} - \frac{1}{18}\right] = \frac{3}{18 \times 15} = \frac{1}{90}$

Hence, total days taken by B to complete the work is 90 days.

219. (b) According to the question,

$M_1 = 47, W_1 = 35, M_2 = ?, W_2 = 105$

$\therefore \quad \frac{M_1}{W_1} = \frac{M_2}{W_2} \Rightarrow \frac{47}{35} = \frac{M_2}{105} \Rightarrow M_2 = 141$

$\therefore$ The 141 masons on should be employed for digging 105 m long trench.

220. (a) According to the question,

$M_1 \times D_1 \times H_1 = M_2 \times D_2 \times H_2$

$\Rightarrow \quad 12 \times 24 \times 9 = 8 \times x \times 12$

$\Rightarrow \quad x = \frac{12 \times 24 \times 9}{8 \times 12} = 27$ days

221. (d) According to the question,

$\frac{M_1 T_1}{W_1} = \frac{M_2 T_2}{W_2}$

$\Rightarrow \quad \frac{15 \times 12}{18000} = \frac{18 \times 9}{W_2}$

$\Rightarrow \quad W_2 = \frac{18 \times 9 \times 18000}{15 \times 12} =$ ₹ 16200

Hence, 18 persons working 9 h a day earn ₹ 16200 per week.

222. (c) A's 1 day's work $= \frac{1}{9}$

B's 1 day's work $= \frac{1}{15}$

$(A+B)$'s 1 day's work $= \frac{1}{9} + \frac{1}{15} = \frac{5+3}{45} = \frac{8}{45}$

$\therefore$ $(A+B)$ complete the whole work in

$= \frac{45}{8} = 5\frac{5}{8}$ days

223. (d) According to the question,

A +B — 8 days — 2
B — 16 days — 1
LCM → 16

Let total work = 16

So, A alone can do it in $= \frac{16}{2-1} = 16$ days

224. (c) According to the question,

$(A+B+C)$'s 1 day work $= \frac{1}{8}$ ...(i)

$(A+B)$'s 1 day work $= \frac{1}{9}$ ...(ii)

$(B+C)$'s 1 day work $= \frac{1}{18}$ ...(iii)

From Eqs. (i) and (iii)

A's 1 day work $= \frac{1}{8} - \frac{1}{18} = \frac{5}{72}$

$(A+C)$'s 1 day work $= \frac{1}{72} + \frac{5}{72} = \frac{6}{72} = \frac{1}{12}$

$\therefore$ A and C can complete the whole work in

$= \frac{1}{\frac{1}{12}} = 12$ days

Speedy Method

A+B → 9 (8)
A+B+C → 8 (9) → (72)
B+C → 18 (4)

$\therefore$ Efficiency of $C = 9 - 8 = 1$

Efficiency of $A = 9 - 4 = 5$

Time to complete work by A and C together

$= \frac{72}{1+5} = \frac{72}{6} = 12$ days.

225. (a) According to the question,

Raju's one hour work $= \frac{32}{4} = 8$ page/h

And, Ahbar's are hour work $= \frac{48}{6} = 8$ page/h

When they work together, then onehour work of Raju and Akbar = 8 + 8 = 16 page/h

Now, For 256 Pages typing taken time is

$= \frac{256}{16} = 16$ h.

226. (b) Let, Shyam alone can complete work in $= x$ days.

According to the question,

Efficiency of Ram, Reena, and Shyam together in 1 day $= \frac{1}{18} + \frac{1}{12} + \frac{1}{x}$

$\Rightarrow \quad \frac{1}{6} = \frac{1}{18} + \frac{1}{12} + \frac{1}{x} \Rightarrow \frac{1}{x} = \frac{1}{6} - \frac{1}{18} - \frac{1}{12}$

$\Rightarrow \quad \frac{1}{x} = \frac{1}{36}$

Hence, Shyam alone can complete work in 36 days.

227. (c) According to the question,

$30 \times 5 \times 18 = 21 \times 8 \times D_2$

$\Rightarrow \quad \frac{30 \times 5 \times 18}{21 \times 8} = D_2$

$\Rightarrow \quad D = \frac{2700}{168} = 16\frac{1}{14}$ days

228. (b) George complete the work in

$= 6 \times \frac{100}{35} = \frac{120}{7}$ days

George and Jim complete the task = 12 days.

Total work = LCM of $\frac{120}{7}$, and 12 days

= 120 units

Efficiency of George $= \frac{120}{\frac{120}{7}} = 7$ units/day

Efficiency of Jim and George

$= \frac{120}{12} = 10$ units/day

$\therefore$ Efficiency of Jim = 10 − 7 = 3 units/day

$\therefore$ Required time $= \frac{120}{3} = 40$ days

229. (b) Given, X can complete work in 14 days.

Y can complete work in 28 days.

Z can complete work in 42 days.

Efficiency of X, Y and Z together in 1 day

$= \frac{1}{14} + \frac{1}{28} + \frac{1}{42} = \frac{11}{84}$

Hence, X, Y and Z together can complete work in $\frac{84}{11}$ days $= 7\frac{7}{11}$ days

230. (c) Given, $M_1 = 70, D_1 = 36$ days

$M_2 = 70 + 50 = 120, D_2 = ?$

$\Rightarrow \quad 70 \times 36 = 120 \times D_2$

$\therefore \quad D_2 = \frac{70 \times 36}{120} = 21$ days

231. (b) According to the question,

One day's work of $(A+B) = \frac{1}{15}$

One day's work of $B = \frac{1}{21}$

Now, one day's work of $A = \frac{1}{15} - \frac{1}{21} = \frac{2}{105}$

Hence, A can complete the work alone

$= \frac{1}{\frac{2}{105}} = \frac{105}{2} = 52\frac{1}{2}$ days

232. (c) Given, $M_1 = 7, D_1 = 14, T_1 = 4$ h

$M_2 = 12, T_2 = 8$ h, $D_2 = ?$

Since,

$\therefore \quad 7 \times 14 \times 4 = 12 \times D_2 \times 8$

$\therefore \quad D_2 = \frac{7 \times 14 \times 4}{12 \times 8} = \frac{49}{12} = 4\frac{1}{12}$ days

233. (c) Let Y take 'n' days to complete the wall alone.

Time taken by $X = \frac{3}{2}n$ days

When they work together they complete the wall in 15 days,

$\therefore$ X's 1 day work + Y's 1 day work $= \frac{1}{15}$

$\Rightarrow \quad \frac{2}{3n} + \frac{1}{n} = \frac{1}{15} \Rightarrow \frac{2+3}{3n} = \frac{1}{15} \Rightarrow \frac{5}{3n} = \frac{1}{15}$

$\Rightarrow \quad n = 25$ days

$\therefore$ Time taken by X to complete the wall

$= \frac{3}{2} \times 25 = 37.5$ days

234. (d) According to the question,

One day's work of $(A+B) = \frac{1}{20}$

One day's work of $(B+C) = \frac{1}{15}$

One day's work of $(A+B+C) = \frac{1}{10}$

Now, one day work of A

$= \frac{1}{10} - \frac{1}{15} = \frac{3-2}{30} = \frac{1}{30}$

Similarly, one day work of C

$= \frac{1}{10} - \frac{1}{20} = \frac{2-1}{20} = \frac{1}{20}$

$\therefore$ One day work of $(A+C)$

$= \frac{1}{30} + \frac{1}{20} = \frac{5}{60} = \frac{1}{12}$

Hence, A and C can complete the whole work in 12 days.

235. (a) According to the question,

Rani's 1 day work $= \frac{1}{10}$

Priya's 1 day work $= \frac{1}{15}$

and Guddu's 1 day work $= \frac{1}{12}$

Ratio of the work of Rani, Priya and Guddu

$= \frac{1}{10} : \frac{1}{15} : \frac{1}{12} = 6:4:5$

Total paid = ₹ 9000

$\therefore$ Share of Priya $= \frac{4}{15} \times 9000$

$= 4 \times 600 =$ ₹ 2400

236. (b) We know that,
According to the question,

$(4M + 7W)8 = (7M + 4W)5$

$\Rightarrow 32M + 56W = 35M + 20W$

$\Rightarrow 3M = 36W \Rightarrow \frac{M}{W} = \frac{36}{3} = \frac{12}{1}$

Total work $= (4M + 7W) \times 8$

$= (4 \times 12 + 7 \times 1)8 = 55 \times 8 = 440$

Number of days in which 8 women can finish the work $= \frac{440}{8 \times 1} = 55$ days

237. (c) Let the work be completed in x days.

P's one day work $= \frac{1}{12}$

P's $(x-8)$ day's work $= \frac{(x-8)}{12}$

Q's one day work $= \frac{1}{15}$

Q's $(x-3)$ days' work $= \frac{(x-3)}{15}$

R's one day work $= \frac{1}{20}$

R's x day's work $= \frac{x}{20}$

$\Rightarrow \frac{x-8}{12} + \frac{x-3}{15} + \frac{x}{20} = 1$

$\Rightarrow \frac{5(x-8) + 4(x-3) + 3x}{60} = 1$

$\Rightarrow 5x - 40 + 4x - 12 + 3x = 60$

$\Rightarrow 12x - 52 = 60 \Rightarrow 12x = 60 + 52$

$\Rightarrow x = \frac{112}{12} \Rightarrow x = \frac{28}{3}$

$\therefore$ The work has completed in $\frac{28}{3}$ days.

Speedy Method

Total work = LCM of 12, 15 and 20= 60 units

Efficiency of $P = \frac{60}{12} = 5$ units/day

Efficiency of $Q = \frac{60}{15} = 4$ units/day

Efficiency of $R = \frac{60}{20} = 3$ units/day

According to the question,

$\therefore$ Work done by P in 8 days $= 5 \times 8 = 40$ units

Work done by Q in 3 days $= 3 \times 4 = 12$ units

$\therefore$ Time taken to complete work

$= \frac{60 + 40 + 12}{5 + 4 + 3} = \frac{112}{12} = \frac{28}{3}$ days

238. (d) Here, $M_1 = 10, W_1 = \frac{1}{2}, D_1 = 20$

Let be x more women.

Then, $M_2 = (10 + x), W_2 = \frac{1}{2}, D_2 = 10$

$\therefore \frac{10 \times 20}{\frac{1}{2}} = \frac{(10 + x) \times 10}{\frac{1}{2}}$

$\Rightarrow 20 = 10 + x \Rightarrow x = 10$

239. (d) A's 1 day work $= \frac{1}{9}$

B's 1 day work $= \frac{1}{9} \times \frac{180}{100} = \frac{1}{5}$

$(A+B)$'s 1 day work $= \frac{1}{9} + \frac{1}{5} = \frac{5+9}{45} = \frac{14}{45}$

So, B and A together will complete the same work in $\frac{45}{14}$ days.

240. (b) For Statement I,

Ratio of efficiency of A and $B = \frac{\frac{1}{20}}{\frac{1}{30}} = \frac{30}{20} = 3:2$

Hence, Statement I is correct.

For Statement II,

Part of work done by A alone in 1 day $= \frac{1}{20}$

Part of work done by B alone in 1 day $= \frac{1}{30}$

$\therefore$ Part of work done by A and B together in 1 day $= \frac{1}{20} + \frac{1}{30} = \frac{3+2}{60} = \frac{5}{60} = \frac{1}{12}$

$\therefore$ Number of days required by A and B together to complete the work 12 days

Hence, both Statement I and II are correct.

241. (d) Tina's 1 day work $= \frac{1}{12}$

Meena's 1 day work $= \frac{1}{15}$

Ratio of one day work of Tina and Meena

$= \frac{1}{12} : \frac{1}{15} = 5:4$

$\therefore$ Meena get amount $= \frac{4}{5+4} \times 18000$

$=$ ₹ 8000

242. (b) Let A able to complete the work in x days.

As A is 3 times as fast as B. So, time taken by B to complete same work $= 3x$ days

Given, $3x - x = 32 \Rightarrow x = 16$ days

Now, $(A + B)$'s one day work

$= \frac{1}{x} + \frac{1}{3x} = \frac{1}{16} + \frac{1}{48} = \frac{3+1}{48} = \frac{1}{12}$

Thus, A and B, working together complete the work in 12 days.

243. (a) A man and a woman 5 days work

$= 5\left(\frac{1}{20} + \frac{1}{10}\right) = \frac{3}{4}$

Remaining work $= 1 - \frac{3}{4} = \frac{1}{4}$

$\therefore$ Time taken by the woman to complete remaining work $= \frac{1}{4} \times 10 = 2\frac{1}{2}$ days

244. (d) Efficiency of man and boys = 4 : 3

Total work $= 24 \times (3 + 4) = 24 \times 7$ units

Time taken to complete work by boys

$= \frac{24 \times 7}{3} = 56$ days

245. (d) Given, time taken by Anu to complete the work = 22 days

Since, Shama is 60% more efficient than Anu.

$\therefore$ Time taken by Shama to complete the work

$= \frac{22}{160} \times 100 = \frac{220}{16} = 13\frac{3}{4}$ days.

246. (d) Given, $15W = 10M$ can complete the work in 30 days.

$\therefore 27W = \frac{10 \times 27}{15} M = 18M$

Now, $15M + 27W = 15M + 18M = 33M$

Since, $10M$ can complete the work in 30 days.

$33M$ can complete the work in

$= \frac{30 \times 10}{33}$ days $= \frac{300}{33} = 9\frac{1}{11}$ days

247. (c) Work done by P and Q together in 3 days,

$= \frac{3}{9} + \frac{3}{15} = \frac{1}{3} + \frac{1}{5} = \frac{5+3}{15} = \frac{8}{15}$

$\therefore$ Remaining work $= 1 - \frac{8}{15} = \frac{15-8}{15} = \frac{7}{15}$

$\therefore$ Time taken by Q alone to complete the remaining work $= 15 \times \frac{7}{15} = 7$ days

248. (d) One day work of all three

$= \frac{1}{2}\left[\frac{1}{3} + \frac{1}{4} + \frac{1}{6}\right] = \frac{1}{2}\left[\frac{4+3+2}{12}\right] = \frac{1}{2}\left[\frac{9}{12}\right] = \frac{3}{8}$

Anil's 1 day work $= \frac{3}{8} - \frac{1}{3} = \frac{9-8}{24} = \frac{1}{24}$

$\therefore$ Anil alone can do the total work in 24 days.

249. (d) By using the formula,

$M_1D_1 = M_2D_2 \Rightarrow 80 \times 25 = 100 \times D_2$

$D_2 = 20$ days

250. (d) Wages of A for one day

$= 88 \times 10 =$ ₹ 880

Wages of B for one day $= 95 \times 8 =$ ₹ 760

$\therefore$ Required ratio $= \frac{880}{760} = \frac{22}{19}$

251. (d) By formula,

$M_1D_1H_1 = M_2D_2H_2$

$24 \times 10 \times 7 = 21 \times D_2 \times 9$

$\Rightarrow D_2 = \frac{24 \times 10 \times 7}{21 \times 9}$

$\Rightarrow D_2 = \frac{80}{9} = 8\frac{8}{9}$ days

252. (a) We know,

$M_1D_1 = M_2D_2$

$200 \times 30 = (200 + 50) \times D_2$

$\Rightarrow D_2 = 24$ days

253. (a) Using the formula,

$\frac{M_1D_1}{W_1} = \frac{M_2D_2}{W_2}$

$$\frac{40\times4}{50}=\frac{24\times8}{W_2}$$

$\therefore \quad W_2 = 6\times10 = 60$ bags

254. (a) Let the work done by 1 worker in one day = W

Time taken to complete the remaining work = x days

According to the question,

$$4\times6W=(6W\times3)+(6W+3W)\times x$$

$$\Rightarrow 24W = 18W + 9Wx$$

$$\Rightarrow x=\frac{24-18}{9}=\frac{6}{9}=\frac{2}{3}$$

Thus, the remaining work will complete in $\frac{2}{3}$ day.

255. (a) One day's work of $A=\frac{1}{30}$

One day's work of $B=\frac{1}{40}$

Let the work will be completed in x days.

$$\frac{1}{30}\times(x-25)+\frac{1}{40}\times x=1$$

$$\Rightarrow \frac{x}{30}-\frac{5}{6}+\frac{x}{40}=1$$

$$\Rightarrow \frac{4x+3x}{120}=1+\frac{5}{6}=\frac{11}{6}$$

$$\Rightarrow \frac{7x}{120}=\frac{11}{6}$$

$$\Rightarrow x=\frac{11\times120}{7\times6}=\frac{220}{7}\text{ days}$$

Total number of days, A works

$$=x-25=\frac{220}{7}-25$$

$$=\frac{220-175}{7}=\frac{45}{7}=6\frac{3}{7}\text{ days}$$

256. (b) One day work of A and $B=\frac{1}{5}$

One day work of C and $D=\frac{1}{20}$

One day work of A, B, C and D

$$=\frac{1}{5}+\frac{1}{20}=\frac{5}{20}=\frac{1}{4}$$

Hence, A, B, C and D together can complete work in 4 days.

257. (b) Time taken by A to complete the work = 16 days

Time taken by B to complete the work = 28 days

$\therefore$ A's one day work $=\frac{1}{16}$

and B's one day work $=\frac{1}{28}$

$$(A+B)\text{'s one day work}=\frac{1}{16}+\frac{1}{28}$$

$$=\frac{7+4}{112}=\frac{11}{112}$$

Given, they work alternatively, starting with B.

$\therefore$ 11 units of work will be done in 2 days.

$\therefore$ 110 units of work will be done in 20 days.

$\therefore$ On 21st day, B will complete remaining 2 units of work in 1/2 day.

$\therefore$ Time taken to complete the whole work

$$=20\frac{1}{2}\text{ days}$$

258. (c) Remaining number of men

$$=(160-20)=140$$

Remaining number of days = $(94-10)=84$

$\therefore$ 160 men had provision for 84 days.

$\therefore$ 1 man had provision for (160×84) days

$\Rightarrow$ 140 men had provision for

$$\frac{160\times84}{140}=96\text{ days}$$

259. (a) Mohan's one day work $=\frac{1}{24}$

Mohan's 6 days work $=\frac{6}{24}$

$\therefore$ Remaining work $=1-\frac{6}{24}=\frac{18}{24}$

Remaining work completed by Sohan in 21 days.

$\therefore$ Sohan's 21 days work $=\frac{18}{24}$

Sohan's one day work $=\frac{18}{24}\times\frac{1}{21}=\frac{6}{168}$

If both Mohan and Sohan work together,

$\therefore$ (Mohan and Sohan)'s one day work

$$=\frac{1}{24}+\frac{6}{168}=\frac{13}{168}$$

$\therefore$ (Mohan + Sohan) can complete work in

$$=\frac{168}{13}=12\frac{12}{13}\text{ days}$$

260. (c) Aisha's one day work $=\frac{1}{50}$

Razia's one day work $=\frac{1}{75}$

$\therefore$ If Aisha and Razia together can complete the work in $=\frac{1}{50}+\frac{1}{75}=\frac{1}{30}$

$\therefore$ Aisha and Razia together can complete work in 30 days.

261. (a) Surjeet's one day work $=\frac{1}{8}$

Manjeet's one day work $=\frac{1}{6}$

Together 2 days work (alternate)

$$=\frac{1}{8}+\frac{1}{6}=\frac{3+4}{24}=\frac{7}{24}$$

Together 6 days work $=\frac{7}{24}\times3=\frac{7}{8}$

Remaining work $=1-\frac{7}{8}=\frac{1}{8}$

$\because$ Remaining work $\frac{1}{8}$ is done by Surjeet in 1 day.

$\therefore$ Total number of days $6+1=7$ days

262. (d) In 3 min, X can type 8 pages.

So, in 15 min, X can type $8\times5=40$ pages

In 5 min, Y can type 3 pages.

So, in 15 min, Y can type $=3\times3=9$ pages

Thus, together they can type

$$=40+9=49\text{ pages in 15 min.}$$

263. (a) Given, Reena, Ritu and Sita can independently complete a piece of work in 6h, 9h and 18 h, respectively.

So, (Reena + Ritu + Sita)'s one hour work

$$=\frac{1}{6}+\frac{1}{9}+\frac{1}{18}=\frac{3+2+1}{18}=\frac{1}{3}$$

So, together they will complete the work in 3 h.

264. (d) Total work done by A, B, C in 3 days

$$=\frac{1}{10}+\frac{1}{15}+\frac{1}{20}=\frac{13}{60}$$

They work on alternative days.

So, $\frac{13}{60}$ work is done in 3 days.

Work done in 12 $(=3\times4)$ days $=\frac{13}{60}\times4=\frac{52}{60}$

$\therefore$ Remaining work $=1-\frac{52}{60}=\frac{8}{60}$

Then, 'A' do work on next day $=\frac{1}{10}$

$\therefore$ Remaining work $=\frac{8}{60}-\frac{1}{10}=\frac{8-6}{60}=\frac{2}{60}$

Now, B do the remaining work in $\dfrac{\frac{2}{60}}{\frac{1}{15}}=\frac{1}{2}$ day

$\therefore$ Total day $=12+1+\frac{1}{2}=13\frac{1}{2}$ days

265. (c) According to the question,

$$20M\times40=40W\times60\Rightarrow\frac{M}{W}=\frac{3}{1}$$

Again, $20\times3\times40=(10M+20W)\times x$

$$\Rightarrow 800\times3=(10\times3+20\times1)\times x$$

$$\Rightarrow 800\times3=50\times x\Rightarrow 48=x$$

266. (c) According to the question,

$$12(M+W)=15M$$

$$\Rightarrow 12M+12W=15M$$

$$\Rightarrow 12W=3M\Rightarrow W:M=1:4$$

Total work $=5\times12=60$ unit

One woman completes the work in

$$=\frac{60}{1}=60\text{ days}$$

267. (a) Given, A can do a work = 9 days

B can do a work = 18 days

A – 9 ↘ 2
　　　> 18 (Total work)
B – 18 ↗ 1

Efficiency of $A=2$

Efficiency of $B=1$

B finished the remaining work in 15 days

$$=15\times1=15\text{ units}$$

So, $(18-15)=3$ units of work A and B do together in $=\frac{3}{2+1}=\frac{3}{3}=1$ day

Hence, A leave the work after 1day.

268. (d) Given,

A can do a piece of work = 10 days

B can do a piece of work = 15 days

C can do a piece of work = 12 days

Take LCM: $A \longrightarrow 10$ (6), $B \longrightarrow 15$ (4), $C \longrightarrow 12$ (5); 60 Total work

One day work of A, B and C = 6, 4, 5

A and B work alternatively for 5 days

A's work = 6 × 5 = 30 unit

and B's work = 4 × 5 = 20 unit

Remaining work = 60 − 50 = 10 unit

$\therefore$ Work done by C in $= \frac{10}{5} = 2$ days

269. (a) According to the question,

$$(A+B+C)\text{'s 1 day work} = \frac{1}{6} \quad \text{...(i)}$$

$$(A+B)\text{'s 1 day work} = \frac{1}{12} \quad \text{...(ii)}$$

From Eqs. (i) and (ii),

$$C\text{'s 1 day work} = \frac{1}{6} - \frac{1}{12} = \frac{1}{12} \quad \text{...(iii)}$$

$$B\text{'s 1 day work} = \frac{1}{18} \quad \text{...(iv)}$$

From Eqs. (ii) and (iv),

$$A\text{'s 1day work} = \frac{1}{36}$$

$$\text{1 day's work or } A \text{ and } C = \frac{1}{36} + \frac{1}{12} = \frac{1}{9}$$

$\therefore$ A and C will do the whole work in 9 days.

270. (c) Given, 1 day work of A, $= \frac{1}{40}$ ...(i)

1 day's work of A and B,

$$(A+B) = \frac{1}{10} \quad \text{...(ii)}$$

From Eqs. (i) and (ii),

$$B = \frac{1}{10} - \frac{1}{40} = \frac{4-1}{40} = \frac{3}{40}$$

According to the question,

C is 50% less efficient than B.

$$\therefore \quad C = \frac{3}{80} \quad \text{...(iii)}$$

Now, from Eqs. (i) and (iii),

$$(A+C) = \frac{1}{40} + \frac{3}{80} = \frac{2+3}{80} = \frac{5}{80}$$

$\therefore$ Time taken by A and C together to complete the whole work $= \frac{80}{5} = 16$ days

271. (b) Let the total work be 48 units.

According to the question,

Efficiency of $X = \frac{48}{16} = 3$ units/day

Efficiency of $Y = \frac{48}{24} = 2$ units/day

Alternate and starting with Y, work done in 9 days = (2 + 3) × 4 + 2 = 22 units

Now, to complete 50% of work i.e. 24 units of work, remaining 2 units of work will be completed by X.

Time taken by X to complete 2 units of work $= \frac{2}{3}$ days

$\therefore$ Total time taken by X and Y to complete 50% of the work $= \left(9 + \frac{2}{3}\right)$ days

$$= \left(\frac{27+2}{3}\right) = \frac{29}{3} \text{ days}$$

272. (a) According to the question,

Total time taken by Gee to complete the task alone $= \frac{24 \times (3+8)}{8}$

$= 3 \times 11 = 33$ days

273. (b) Ratio of wages of Z_1, Z_2 and Z_3

$= (8 \times 3) : (10 \times 4) : (15 \times 4)$

$= 24 : 40 : 60 = 6 : 10 : 15$

Given, total wages = ₹ 4960

$\therefore$ Total wages received by Z_2 and Z_3

$$= \frac{4960 \times (10+15)}{(6+10+15)} = \frac{4960 \times 25}{31} = ₹\,4000$$

274. (b) According to the question,

$$2 \times (D_1 + D_2 + D_3) = \frac{1}{16} + \frac{1}{24} + \frac{1}{48}$$

$$= \frac{3+2+1}{48}$$

$$\Rightarrow \quad D_1 + D_2 + D_3 = \frac{6}{48} \times \frac{1}{2} = \frac{1}{16}$$

$\therefore$ Required number of days

$$= 16 \times \frac{5}{6} = \frac{40}{3} \text{ days}$$

275. (d) n min is taken to read one newspaper.

In one minute, she will read $\frac{1}{n}$ part

So, in 7 min, she will read $\frac{7}{n}$ part.

276. (a) Let each man take x days to complete the work, then a woman will take $2x$ days to complete the work.

According to the question,

$$\frac{9}{x} + \frac{24}{2x} = \frac{1}{18} \Rightarrow \frac{18+24}{2x} = \frac{1}{18}$$

$$\Rightarrow \quad \frac{42}{2x} = \frac{1}{18} \Rightarrow x = 42 \times 9 = 378$$

Now, 9 men will complete the work in

$$\frac{378}{9} = 42 \text{ days}$$

277. (c) Let Y can complete the work in y days.

$\therefore$ x alone can complete the work in $(y-5)$ days.

According to the question,

$$\Rightarrow \quad \frac{1}{y} + \frac{1}{y-5} = \frac{1}{6} \Rightarrow \frac{2y-5}{y^2-5y} = \frac{1}{6}$$

$$\Rightarrow \quad y^2 - 17y + 30 = 0$$

$$\Rightarrow \quad (y-15)(y-2) = 0$$

$$\Rightarrow \quad y = 15$$

$$\because \quad y = 2 \text{ (not possible)}$$

Hence, y can alone complete that work in 15 days.

278. (a) Let C completes the work in x days.

$\therefore$ According to the question,

$$\frac{1}{10} + \frac{1}{15} + \frac{1}{x} = \frac{1}{5}$$

$$\Rightarrow \quad \frac{1}{x} = \frac{1}{5} - \frac{1}{6} = \frac{6-5}{30} = \frac{1}{30}$$

$\therefore$ Ratio of efficiencies of A, B and C

$$= \frac{1}{10} : \frac{1}{15} : \frac{1}{30} = 3 : 2 : 1$$

Since, total wages = ₹ 42000

$$\therefore \text{Share of } B = \frac{42000}{(3+2+1)} \times 2 = ₹\,14000$$

279. (b) Let the number of persons required be x.

$\therefore$ According to the question,

$$x \times 10 \times 4 = 20 \times 8 \times 15$$

$$\Rightarrow \quad x = \frac{20 \times 8 \times 15}{10 \times 4} = 60$$

280. (d) According to the question,

$$12(6M + 10B) = 12(2M + 20B)$$

$$\Rightarrow \quad 6M + 10B = 2M + 20B$$

$$\Rightarrow \quad 2M = 5B$$

Therefore, Total work $= 12 \times (2M + 20B)$

$= 12 \times (5B + 20B) = 12 \times 25B$

Hence, 10 boys will complete the work in

$$= \frac{12 \times 25B}{10B} = 30 \text{ days}$$

281. (a) Man will complete total work in

$$= \frac{6}{\left(\frac{3}{7}\right)} = 14 \text{ days}$$

So, he will require = 14 − 6 = 8 days

282. (b) Time taken by C = 50 days

Time taken by $D = \frac{50}{2}$ days = 25 days

Total work = LCM of of 50, 25 = 50 units

Efficiency of $C = \frac{50}{50} = 1$ unit/day

Efficiency of $D = \frac{50}{25} = 2$ units/day

$$\therefore \text{Required time} = \frac{50}{(2+1)} \times \frac{3}{10} = 5 \text{ days}$$

283. (a) Given, Mohan and Rohan undertook a work for = ₹ 3300

According to the question,

When they work together, then one day work of (Mohan + Rohan) $= \frac{1}{10} + \frac{1}{12}$

$$= \left(\frac{6+5}{60}\right) = \frac{11}{60}$$

So, the difference in amount they receive

$$= \frac{3300 \times \left(\frac{1}{10} - \frac{1}{12}\right)}{\frac{11}{60}} = \frac{3300}{\frac{11}{60}} \times \frac{1}{60} = ₹\,300$$

284. (a) Let the total work be = 100 units
Efficiency of Pinky and Payal are 3 : 2.
According to the question,
Payal will took 80 days to complete 100 units.

Per day work by Payal $= \frac{100}{80} = \frac{5}{4}$ units.

and per day work by Pinky $= \frac{5}{4} \times \frac{150}{100} = \frac{15}{8}$ units

If they work together for the remaining work. Then,

90 units $= \left(\frac{5}{4} + \frac{15}{8}\right) \times$ Time

$\Rightarrow \quad 90 = \left(\frac{25}{8}\right) \times T \Rightarrow T = \frac{90 \times 8}{25} = 28.8$ days

285. (c) According to the question,

One day's work of $(B_1 + B_2) = \frac{1}{20}$

One day's work of $B_2 = \frac{1}{60}$

Now, one day's work of $B_1 = \frac{1}{20} - \frac{1}{60} = \frac{1}{30}$

Thus, B_1 can complete work in 30 days.

286. (d) Let A's one day work $= \frac{1}{x}$

$\Rightarrow \quad B$'s one day work $= \frac{1}{4x}$

Now $(A + B)$'s one day work

$= \frac{1}{x} + \frac{1}{4x} = \left(\frac{4+1}{4x}\right) = \frac{5}{4x}$

Since, they finish the work $= \frac{84}{15}$ days

$\Rightarrow \quad \frac{4x}{5} = \frac{84}{15} \Rightarrow x = \frac{84}{15} \times \frac{5}{4} = 7$ days

So, A can alone finish the work in $= 7$ days

287. (a) By formula $M_1D_1 = M_2D_2$

$25 \times 10 = 20 \times x$

$\Rightarrow \quad 250 = 20x$

$\Rightarrow \quad \frac{250}{20} = x \Rightarrow x = \frac{25}{2}$

288. (d) 100% of work completed in 90 days.

$\therefore$ 20% of work completed is $\frac{90}{100} \times 20$

$= 18$ days

289. (d) According to the question,
(when they done work together then one day work of all) $= \frac{1}{2}\left(\frac{1}{20} + \frac{1}{25} + \frac{1}{50}\right)$

$= \frac{1}{2} \times \left(\frac{5+4+2}{100}\right) = \frac{11}{200}$

Now, work done by Himanshu alone

$= \frac{11}{200} - \frac{1}{20} = \frac{1}{200}$

$\therefore$ Time taken by Himanshu = 200 days

290. (a) If A is 40% less efficient.
Then, time taken by A to make same helmet

$= 16 \times \frac{100}{60} = \frac{80}{3}$ days

291. (a) As per the given information,

One day work of $A = \frac{1}{55}$

$\Rightarrow$ 20 days work of $A = \frac{20}{55}$

$\therefore$ Remaining work $= 1 - \frac{20}{55} = \frac{55 - 20}{55} = \frac{35}{55}$

This work done by B in 49 days, so one day work of $B = \frac{\frac{35}{55}}{49} = \frac{35}{55} \times \frac{1}{49} = \frac{1}{77}$

Now, when they do together to complete the work, $= \frac{1}{55} + \frac{1}{77} = \left(\frac{7+5}{5 \times 11 \times 7}\right) = \frac{12}{385}$

Then, required days $= \frac{385}{12}$ days

292. (b) According to the question,

$15 \times 18 = 12 \times D_2$

$\Rightarrow \quad D_2 = \frac{15 \times 18}{12}$

$\Rightarrow \quad D_2 = 22.5$ days

293. (b) Let Shambu complete the work $= x$ days

So, Gaurav complete the work $= \frac{x}{4}$ days

According to the question,

$x - \frac{x}{4} = 67.5 \Rightarrow \frac{4x - x}{4} = 67.5$

$\Rightarrow \quad \frac{3x}{4} = 67.5$

$\Rightarrow \quad x = 90$

1 day work of Shambu and Gaurav

$= \frac{1}{90} + \frac{1}{\left(\frac{90}{4}\right)} = \frac{1}{90} + \frac{4}{90} = \frac{1}{18}$

$\therefore$ Required days = 18

Speedy Method

Ratio of efficiency of Gaurav and Shambhu

G : S

$E \rightarrow 4 : 1$

Time – 1 : 4

$3 \rightarrow 67.5$ days

$1 \rightarrow 22.5$ days

And $4 \rightarrow 90.0$ days

Total work = LCM of $\frac{45}{2}$ and 90 = 90 units

$\therefore$ Required days $= \frac{90}{4+1} = 18$ days

294. (c) According to the given information,

One day work of $P = \frac{1}{14}$

Now, total work of 4 days $= \frac{4}{14} = \frac{2}{7}$

i.e., $\frac{2}{7}$ part of the work done in 4 days.

295. (c) One day work of $M_1 = \frac{1}{14}$

One day work of $M_2 = \frac{1}{70}$

and one day work of $(M_1 + M_2 + M_3) = \frac{1}{7}$

According to the question,

$M_1 + M_2 + M_3 = \frac{1}{7} \Rightarrow \frac{1}{14} + \frac{1}{70} + M_3 = \frac{1}{7}$

$\Rightarrow M_3 = \frac{1}{7} - \frac{1}{14} - \frac{1}{70} \Rightarrow M_3 = \frac{4}{70}$

$\therefore \quad M_3$ alone can do the same work in $\frac{70}{4} = 17.5$ days.

Speedy Method

Total work = LCM of 14, 70, 7 = 70 units

$M_1 \rightarrow 14$ — 5
$M_2 \rightarrow 70$ — 1 — (70) units
$M_1 + M_2 + M_3 \rightarrow 7$ — 10

Efficiency of $M_3 = 10 - 5 - 1 = 4$ units/day

Time taken by $M_3 = \frac{70}{4} = 17.5$ days

296. (d) According to the question,

One day work of Anil $= \frac{1}{80}$

30 days work of Anil $= \frac{30}{80}$

$\therefore$ Required percentage $= \frac{30}{80} \times 100 = 37.5\%$

Speedy Method

According to the question,

$= \frac{30}{80} \times 100 = \frac{3}{8} \times 100 = \frac{75}{2} = 37.5\%$

297. (b) According to the question,

$M_1D_1 = M_2D_2$

$\Rightarrow \quad 22 \times 2 = M_2 \times \left(\frac{1}{2}\right) \Rightarrow 22 \times 2 \times 2 = M_2$

$\therefore \quad M_2 = 88$ men

298. (a) According to the question,

Dinesh's 1 h work $= \frac{1}{96}$

(Dinesh and Rahul)'s 1 h work $= \frac{1}{48}$

(Rahul and Tarun)'s 1 h work $= \frac{1}{16}$

$\therefore \quad$ Rahul's 1 h work $= \frac{1}{48} - \frac{1}{96} = \frac{2-1}{96} = \frac{1}{96}$

Hence, Tarun's 1 h work

$= \frac{1}{16} - \frac{1}{96} = \frac{6-1}{96} = \frac{5}{96}$

So, Tarun can complete the work in

$= \frac{96}{5} = 19.2$ h

299. (c) As per the given information,
One minute work of Rakesh, Mahesh and Puneesh $= \frac{1}{20}$ and one minute work of Rakesh and Mahesh $= \frac{1}{25}$

One minute work of Puneesh

$= \frac{1}{20} - \frac{1}{25} = \left(\frac{5-4}{100}\right) = \frac{1}{100}$

Hence, Puneesh will complete the work in 100 min.

Speedy Method

	Time (in min)	Per unit work
Rakesh + Mahesh + Puneesh	20	5
	100	
Rakesh + Mahesh	25	4

∴ Puneesh will complete the work

$= \frac{100}{(5-4)} = 100$ min

300. (a) Sachin can finish the work in $= 44$ days

Amar is 10% more efficient than Sachin, then

Amar can finish the work $= \frac{44}{110} \times 100$

$= 40$ days

301. (c) Total work = LCM of 100, 50, 75 days = 300 units

Efficiency of $Z_1 = \frac{300}{100} = 3$ units/day

Efficiency of $Z_2 = \frac{300}{50} = 6$ units/day

Efficiency of $Z_3 = \frac{300}{75} = 4$ units/day

Work done by Z_2 in 15 days

$= 6 \times 15 = 90$ units

∴ Time taken to complete work

$= \frac{300 + 90}{(3+6+4)} = 30$ days

302. (a) According to the question,

Work done by Seema in 1 day $= \frac{1}{120}$

Work done by Anjali in 1 day $= \frac{1}{144}$

and work done by Soniya in 1 day $= \frac{1}{180}$

∵ Total work done in 1 day

$= \frac{1}{120} + \frac{1}{144} + \frac{1}{180}$

$= \left(\frac{12+10+8}{1440}\right) = \frac{30}{1440} = \frac{1}{48}$

∴ Share of Anjali $= \frac{1}{144} \times \frac{48}{1} \times 3300 =$ ₹ 1100

303. (a) According to the given information,

Work done by S_1 in 1 day $= \frac{1}{16}$

Work done by S_2 in 1 day $= \frac{1}{80}$

and work done by S_1, S_2 and S_3 is 1 day $= \frac{1}{6}$

$\frac{1}{16} + \frac{1}{80} + \frac{1}{S_3} = \frac{1}{6}$

$\Rightarrow \frac{5+1}{80} + \frac{1}{S_3} = \frac{1}{6} \Rightarrow \frac{1}{S_3} = \frac{1}{6} - \frac{3}{40}$

$\Rightarrow \frac{1}{S_3} = \frac{11}{120}$

Hence, S_3 alone can do the same works in $\frac{120}{11}$ days.

304. (b) As per the given information,

Work done by A in 1 h $= \frac{1}{7}$

Work done by $B + C$ in 1 h $= \frac{4}{21}$

Work done by $C + A$ in 1 h $= \frac{2}{7}$

Now, work done by B in 1 h $= \frac{4}{21} - \frac{2}{7} + \frac{1}{7}$

$= \frac{4-6+3}{21} = \frac{1}{21}$

∴ B can do a piece of work in 21 h.

305. (a) As per the given information,

One day work of A and $B = \frac{3}{14}$

One day work of B and $C = \frac{5}{12}$

and one day work of C and $A = \frac{3}{16}$

One day work of $(A + B + C)$ together

$= \frac{1}{2}\left(\frac{3}{14} + \frac{5}{12} + \frac{3}{16}\right)$

$= \frac{1}{2}\left(\frac{72+140+63}{336}\right) = \frac{1}{2}\left(\frac{275}{336}\right)$

∴ Two days work of $(A + B + C)$ together

$= \frac{2}{2}\left(\frac{275}{336}\right) = \frac{275}{336}$

306. (c) According to the question,

They work on it together for 5 days

$= \frac{5}{20} + \frac{5}{22} = \frac{55+50}{220} = \frac{105}{220} = \frac{21}{44}$

∴ Remaining work $= 1 - \frac{21}{44} = \frac{23}{44}$

307. (d) X_1 can do the work in 90 days.

X_2 can do the work in 45 days.

X_3 can do the work in 67.5 days.

Total work = LCM of 90, 45, and 67.5 = 1350.

Efficiency of $X_1 = \frac{1350}{90} = 15$ units /day

Efficiency of $X_2 = \frac{1350}{45} = 30$ units /day

Efficiency of $X_3 = \frac{1350}{67.5} = 20$ units /day

As, we know X_1, X_2 and X_3 together do the work.

But X_2 left in work 13.5 days before completion of work.

Work done by X_2 in $13.5 = 13.5 \times 30$

$= 405$ units

So, number of days required to complete the work $= \frac{1350 + 405}{15 + 30 + 20} = \frac{1755}{65} = 27$ days

∴ Total required days = 27 days

308. (b) Sonu alone can make a table in 125 days.

Monu alone can make a table in 250 days.

LCM of 125 and 250 = 250 (total work).

Efficiency of Sonu $= \frac{250}{125} = 2$ units /day

Efficiency of Monu $= \frac{250}{250} = 1$ unit /day

Monu worked for 75 days $= 75 \times 1 = 75$ units

Remaining work $= 250 - 75 = 175$ units

∴ Remaining work done by Sonu

$= \frac{175}{2} = 87.5$ days

309. (a) According to the given information,

One day work of $A = \frac{1}{20}$

and one day work of $B = \frac{1}{60}$

Let A left the work after the x days.

According to the question,

$x\left(\frac{1}{20} + \frac{1}{60}\right) + \frac{12}{60} = 1 \Rightarrow x\left(\frac{3+1}{60}\right) + \frac{1}{5} = 1$

$\Rightarrow x\left(\frac{4}{60}\right) = 1 - \frac{1}{5} \Rightarrow x\left(\frac{1}{15}\right) = \frac{4}{5}$

$\Rightarrow \quad x = 4 \times 3 = 12$ days

310. (d) According to the given information,

Number of days taken by Swapnil = 16 days

Number of days taken by both (Swapnil and Revathi) $= \frac{128}{17}$ days

∴ Part of work done by Revathi

$= \frac{17}{128} - \frac{1}{16} = \frac{17-8}{128} = \frac{9}{128}$

∴ Number of days taken by Revathi

$= \frac{128}{9}$ days

311. (c) Let the binders be x.

$\frac{M_1D_1}{W_1} = \frac{M_2D_2}{W_2} \Rightarrow \frac{72 \times 22}{720} = \frac{12 \times x}{660}$

$\Rightarrow \quad x = \frac{72 \times 22}{720} \times \frac{660}{12} = 121$

312. (d) Ratio of efficiency of Rakhi and Poonam is $R : P = 5 : 6 \Rightarrow 11$ units

Work done by Rakhi in 8 days $= 8 \times 5 = 40$ units (which is 10% of total work)

∴ Total work $= 40 \times 10 = 400$ unit

Remaining work $= 400 - 40 = 360$ units

∴ Time required $= \frac{360}{11}$ days

313. (c) ∵ R can do a work in 90 days.

So, in 45 days R can do half of the work means he will do 50% of work.

314. (d) 1 day's work of Anit $= \frac{1}{77}$

1 day's work of Ram $= \frac{1}{11}$

1 day's work of (Anit + Ram) $= \frac{1}{77} + \frac{1}{11} = \frac{8}{77}$

$\therefore$ 3 day's work of Anit $= \frac{3}{77}$

Remaining work $= 1 - \frac{3}{77} = \frac{74}{77}$

Time taken to complete the remaining work by Anit and Ram $= \frac{74}{77} \times \frac{77}{8} = 9.25$ day

$\therefore$ Required time $= 9.25 + 3 = 12.25 \approx 12$ days

315. (b) Let the one day work of Atul $= x$ and the number of persons required $= y$

Atul's one day work = Each person's one day work

According to the question,

$$x \times 114 = xy \times 19$$

$$\Rightarrow \quad y = \frac{x \times 114}{19x} = 6$$

Thus, 6 persons were required.

316. (d) Work done by P and Q in one day $= \frac{1}{36}$

Work done by Q in one day $= \frac{1}{45}$

Work done by P in one day $= \frac{1}{36} - \frac{1}{45}$

$$= \frac{5-4}{180} = \frac{1}{180}$$

Work done by Q in 5 days $= \frac{1}{45} \times 5 = \frac{1}{9}$

Remaining work $= 1 - \frac{1}{9} = \frac{8}{9}$

$\therefore$ Time taken to complete the remaining work $= 180 \times \frac{8}{9} = 160$ days

317. (b) Total work = LCM of 12 and 8

$= 24$ units

1 day's work of $R = \frac{24}{12} = 2$ units

1 day's work of R with two helper

$= \frac{24}{8} = 3$ units

$\therefore$ 1 day's work of two helper $= 3 - 2 = 1$ units

$\therefore$ 1 day's work of one helper $= \frac{1}{2} = 0.5$ units

Hence, time taken to complete the work by one helper $= \frac{24}{0.5} = 48$ days

318. (c) Total work = LCM of 50, 100 and 300 = 300 units

1 day's work of $P = \frac{300}{50} = 6$ units

1 day's work of $Q = \frac{300}{100} = 3$ units

1 day's work of $R = \frac{300}{300} = 1$ units

$\therefore$ 3 day's work of all $= 6 + 3 + 1 = 10$ units

Hence, required time $= \frac{300}{10} \times 3 = 90$ days.

Speedy Method

		Efficiency
$P \to 50$	Total work 300	6
$Q \to 100$		3
$R \to 300$		1

$\therefore$ 3 days work of P, Q and $R = 6 + 3 + 1 = 10$ units

Hence, required time $= \frac{300}{10} \times 3 = 90$ days.

319. (b) According to the question,

Ranu $\longrightarrow$ 10, 3
Ruby $\longrightarrow$ 15, 2
30 (Total work)

They start work on alternate days.

Starting with Ranu

$\Rightarrow$ Ranu does 3 units in one day.

$\Rightarrow$ Next day Ruby does 2 units in one day.

$\Rightarrow$ It means 5 units of work is done in 2 days.

So, 30 units of work will be done in

$= \frac{30 \times 2}{5} = 12$ days

320. (a) According to the question,

Pramod + Akhil + Raman $\longrightarrow$ 14, 11
Akhil + Raman $\longrightarrow$ 77, 2
154

Total work = 154 units

Efficiency of Pramod $= 11 - 2 = 9$ units/day

$\therefore$ Pramod complete the work alone

$= \frac{154}{9}$ days

321. (a) One day work of Pooja $= \frac{1}{16}$

One day work of Neha and Manoj

$= \frac{1}{20} + \frac{1}{22} = \frac{11+10}{220} = \frac{21}{220}$

2 days work of Pooja $= \frac{1}{16} \times 2 = \frac{1}{8}$

2 days work of all three

$= \frac{21}{220} + \frac{1}{8} = \frac{42+55}{440} = \frac{97}{440}$

$\because \frac{97}{440}$ work can be done in 2 days.

$\therefore$ 1 work can be done in $\frac{440 \times 2}{97} = 9.07$ days

≈ 10 th day

Speedy Method

Pooja 16, 55
Neha 22, 40
Manoj 20, 44
(880 units)

Work done on first day = 55 units

Work done on 2nd day = 55 + 40 + 44 = 139 units

Total work done in 2 days = 194 units

Work done in 8 days = 776 units

Work done on 9th day = 776 + 55 = 831 units.

Remaining work will be completed on 10th day.

So, the work get finished in 10th day.

322. (c) 1 day work of $P = \frac{1}{20}$

1 day work of $Q = \frac{1}{25}$

4 day work of P and $Q = 4\left(\frac{1}{20} + \frac{1}{25}\right)$

$$= 4\left(\frac{5+4}{100}\right) = \frac{9}{25}$$

Remaining work $= 1 - \frac{9}{25} = \frac{16}{25}$

$\therefore$ Required remaining work percentage

$= \frac{16}{25} \times 100 = 64\%$

323. (d) By formula, $M_1D_1 = M_2D_2$

Let remaining work will complete in x days.

$$24 \times 9 = 24 \times 3 + (24 + 8) \times x$$

$\Rightarrow 216 = 72 + 32x \Rightarrow x = \frac{144}{32} \Rightarrow x = 4.5$ days.

324. (c) According to the question,

$P + Q = 8$ days

$Q + R = 12$ days

$R + P = 15$ days

Take the LCM of (8, 12, 15)

Total work = 120 units

$P + Q = \frac{120}{8} = 15$

$Q + R = \frac{120}{12} = 10$

$R + P = \frac{120}{15} = 8$

$\frac{\text{Total efficiency}}{2} = \frac{33}{2} = 16.5$

Since, P and Q together complete 15 units of work.

$\therefore$ R will do $(16.5 - 15 = 1.5)$ units of work alone.

Now, time taken by R to complete the work $= \frac{120}{1.5} = 80$ days.

$\therefore$ In 80 days R can complete the work.

325. (b) LCM of (88 and 66) = 264 (total work)

One day work of Anish $= \frac{264}{88} = 3$ units

One day work of Yug $= \frac{264}{66} = 4$ units

We have to find that after how many days Yug join.

Complete work done by Anish alone

$= 44 \times 3 = 132$ units

Remaining work done by Yug alone in days

$= \frac{132}{4} = 33$ days

$\therefore$ Yug should join Anish after $(44 - 33) = 11$ days.

326. (b) A can repair benches in one hour = 11

B can repair benches in one hour = 5

When A and B work together, then they can repair benches in one hour

$= 11 + 5 = 16$

∴ Required time to repair 64 benches

$= \frac{64}{16} = 4\,h$

327. (a) Work done by (Akash + Diya) in 2 days $= \left(\frac{1}{21} + \frac{1}{63}\right) = \frac{4}{63}$ th part of work

Work done by (Akash + Diya) in 15 pairs of day

i.e., Work done by (Akash + Diya) in 30 days

$= \frac{4 \times 15}{63} = \frac{60}{63}$ th part of work

Remaining work $= 1 - \frac{60}{63} = \frac{3}{63}$ part of work.

On the 31st day, again Akash will work separately.

So, time taken by Akash to complete the $\frac{3}{63}$th part of work = 1 day

∴ Total time taken = 30 + 1 = 31 days

328. (d) If they work together, then

Number of chair paint in one hour

$= (5 + 3)$ chair = 8 chair

Then, time required to paint 40 chair

$= \frac{40}{8} = 5\,h$

329. (d) According to the question,

$M \times 12 \times 36 = 9 \times 36 \times W$

$\Rightarrow \frac{M}{W} = \frac{3}{4}$

Total work $= 12 \times 3 \times 36 = 1296$ units

Work done by men in one day $= 16 \times 3 = 48$

and work done by women in one day

$= 18 \times 4 = 72$

Time takey by 16 men and 18 women

$= \frac{1296}{(48 + 72)} = \frac{1296}{120} = 10\frac{4}{5}$ days

330. (b) Here, $M_1 = 140$

$D_1 = (35 - 10) = 25$

$M_2 = (140 + 35) = 175$

$D_2 = ?$

$\therefore \quad M_1D_1 = M_2D_2$

$\Rightarrow \quad 140 \times 25 = 175 \times D_2$

$\Rightarrow \quad D_2 = \frac{140 \times 25}{175} = 20$ days

331. (d) 15 men = 10 machines

$\Rightarrow$ 3 men = 2 machines

Hence, 5 men + 4 machines = 5 men + 6 men = 11 men

$M_1D_1 = M_2D_2$

$15 \times 66 = 11 \times D_2$

$\Rightarrow \quad D_2 = \frac{15 \times 66}{11} = 15 \times 6 = 90$ days

332. (d) $M_1 = 8, H_1 = 10, D_1 = 18$

$M_2 = 5, H_2 = ?, D_2 = 24$

$\therefore \quad M_1D_1H_1 = M_2D_2H_2$

$\Rightarrow 8 \times 18 \times 10 = 5 \times 24 \times H_2$

$\Rightarrow \quad H_2 = \frac{8 \times 18 \times 10}{5 \times 24} = 12\,h$

333. (a) Let total work is = 12 units

Efficiency of *P*'s work = 3

Efficiency of *Q*'s work = 1

∵ *P* and *Q* work on alternate days.

∴ $(P + Q)$'s 2 day's work = 3 + 1 = 4

$(P + Q)$'s 6 day's work = 4 × 3 = 12

∴ Required number of days = 6

334. (c) Given, $8\,M = 16\,W = 32\,B$

$M = 2\,W = 4\,B$

From $M_1D_1 = M_2D_2$

$32B \times 8 = (4M + 4W + 4B) \times D_2$

$\Rightarrow 32B \times 8 = (4 \times 4B + 4 \times 2B + 4B) \times D_2$

$\Rightarrow 32 \times 8 = (16 + 8 + 4) \times D_2$

$\therefore D_2 = \frac{32 \times 8}{28} = \frac{64}{7} = 9\frac{1}{7}$ days

335. (a) According to the question,

	Day	E	
Anita →	12	3	Total work
Anand →	18	2	36 (LCM of 12, 18 and 6)
(Anita+Anand+Aruna) →	6	6	

∴ Total sum of the shares of Anita and Anand $= 48000 \times \frac{(3 + 2)}{6}$

$= 8000 \times 5 =$ ₹ 40000

336. (a) 1 day work of Abhay $= \frac{1}{22}$

1 day work of Nidhi $= \frac{1}{22} \times \frac{128}{100} = \frac{16}{275}$

∴ Nidhi will take to complete the work

$= \frac{275}{16} = 17\frac{3}{16}$ days

337. (d) $D_1 = 27, M_1 = 35,$

$M_2 = 45, D_2 = ?$

$\therefore \quad M_1D_1 = M_2D_2$

$\Rightarrow \quad 27 \times 35 = 45 \times D_2$

$\Rightarrow \quad D_2 = \frac{27 \times 35}{45} = 21$ days

338. (d) According to the question,

20 days A	15	Total work
25 days B	12	= 300 units
30 days C	10	(LCM of 20, 25, 30)

Total work done by *A*, *B* and *C* in 3 days

$= 15 + 12 + 10 = 37$ units

Total work done by *A*, *B* and *C* in 24 days

$= 8 \times 37 = 296$ units

Remaining work = 300 − 296 = 4 units

Remaining work done by *A* in $= \frac{4}{15}$ days.

∴ Total time $= 24 + \frac{4}{15} = 24\frac{4}{15}$ days

339. (c) According to the question,

They work on alternate day starting with Mahesh,

2 day's work of Mahesh and Suresh

$= \frac{1}{16} + \frac{1}{12} = \frac{3 + 4}{48} = \frac{7}{48}$

∴ 12 day's work of Mahesh and Suresh

$= \frac{7}{48} \times \frac{12}{2} = \frac{42}{48}$

Remaining work $= 1 - \frac{42}{48} = \frac{6}{48} = \frac{1}{8}$

Now, Mahesh turn,

∴ Mahesh work done in 13th day $= \frac{1}{16}$

Remaining work $= \frac{1}{8} - \frac{1}{16} = \frac{1}{16}$

Remaining work done by Suresh in

$= \frac{\frac{1}{16}}{\frac{1}{12}} = \frac{12}{16} = \frac{3}{4}$ days

∴ Total time to complete the work

$= 12 + 1 + \frac{3}{4} = 13\frac{3}{4}$ days

Speedy Method

	E	
$M \rightarrow$ 16 days	3	Total work
$S \rightarrow$ 20 days	4	48

∴ (M + S)'s 2 days's work = 3 + 4 = 7

M's 1 day's work = 3

(M + S)'s 12 day's work = 42

Remaining work done by *S*

$= \frac{48 - (42 + 3)}{4} = \frac{3}{4}$

∴ Time taken $= 12 + 1 + \frac{3}{4} = 13\frac{3}{4}$ days.

340. (d) Ratio of work of *A*, *B* and *C*

$= \frac{1}{3} : \frac{1}{4} : \frac{1}{6} = 4 : 3 : 2$

∴ *A*'s share $= \frac{4}{4 + 3 + 2} \times 432 =$ ₹ 192

341. (c) Let the remaining work will be completed in *x* days.

$\therefore \quad 20 \times 10 = 20 \times 5 + (20 + 5) \times x$

$\Rightarrow \quad 200 = 100 + 25x$

$\Rightarrow \quad 25x = 100$

$\therefore \quad x = \frac{100}{25} = 4$ days

Hence, total work will be completed

$= 5 + 4 = 9$ days

342. (c) Given, $M_1 = 16, D_1 = 30$ days,

$W_1 =$ ₹ 20736

$M_2 = 1, D_2 = 15$ days, $W_2 = ?$

$\because \quad \frac{M_1D_1}{W_1} = \frac{M_2D_2}{W_2} \Rightarrow \frac{16 \times 30}{20736} = \frac{1 \times 15}{W_2}$

$\Rightarrow \quad W_2 = \frac{15 \times 20736}{16 \times 30}$

$\therefore \quad W_2 =$ ₹ 648

18

Pipe and Cistern

Problems on Pipe and Cistern are based on the basic concept of time and work. Pipes are connected to a tank or cistern and are used to fill or empty the tank or cistern. In pipe and cistern, the work is done in form of filling or emptying a cistern/tank.

- **Inlet Pipe** It fills a tank/cistern/reservoir.
- **Outlet Pipe** It empties a tank/cistern/reservoir.

Important Facts Related to Pipe and Cisterns

- If a pipe can fill/empty a tank in 'm' h, then the part of tank filled/empited in 1h $= \frac{1}{m}$.
- If a pipe can fill/empty '$\frac{1}{m}$' part of a tank in t h, then it can fill/empty the whole tank in mt h.
- If a pipe fills a tank in x h and another pipe can fill the same tank in y h, then time taken to fill the tank when both pipes are opened together $= \frac{xy}{x+y}$ h.
- If a pipe fills a tank in x h and another pipe can empty it in y h. Then, time taken to fill the tank by both pipes working together

$$= \frac{1}{\frac{1}{x}-\frac{1}{y}} = \frac{xy}{y-x} \text{ h} \qquad [\text{when } y > x]$$

Ex. 1 Two pipes A and B can fill a tank in 12 h and 18 h, respectively. Both pipes are opened simultaneously. In how much time will the empty tank be filled completely?

Sol. Part of tank filled by $(A+B)$ in 1 h $= \frac{1}{12}+\frac{1}{18}=\frac{3+2}{36}=\frac{5}{36}$

Hence, both the pipes together will fill the tank in $\frac{36}{5}$ h or 7 h and 12 min.

Efficiency and Capacity of Pipe/tank

- Efficiency and time taken are inversely proportional.
- Efficiency or capacity of a pipe = Part filled/emptied by the pipe in unit time
- Capacity of a cistern/tank = Rate of filling × Time

Ex. 2 Pipe A can fill the tank 3 times faster in comparison to pipe B. It takes 36 min for pipe A and B to fill the tank together. How much time will pipe B alone take to fill the tank?

Sol. Let the time taken by pipe B be x min.

So, the time taken by pipe $A = \frac{x}{3}$ min

According to the question,

$$\frac{1}{x}+\frac{3}{x}=\frac{1}{36} \Rightarrow \frac{4}{x}=\frac{1}{36}$$

$$\Rightarrow \quad x = 36 \times 4 = 144 \text{ min}$$

Based on any Pipe is Closed/Opened in between Work Period

Ex. 3 Two taps A and B fill a tank in 24 min and 32 min, respectively. If both the taps are opened simultaneously, after how many minutes tap B should be closed so that the tank fills up in 18 min.

Sol. Tap A fills $\frac{1}{24}$ of the tank in 1 min. Tap B fills $\frac{1}{32}$ of the tank in 1 min.

Let after x min tap B should be closed, then

$$\frac{18}{24}+\frac{x}{32}=1$$

$$\Rightarrow \quad \frac{x}{32}=1-\frac{18}{24}$$

$$\Rightarrow \quad \frac{x}{32}=\frac{6}{24} \Rightarrow x = 8 \text{ min}$$

SSC Exam Scanner

SSC CGL 2024 (Tier I & II)

1. A tank when full can be emptied by an outlet pipe A in 5.6 h, while an inlet pipe B can fill the same empty tank in 7 h. If pipes A and B are turned on alternatively for 1 h each starting with pipe A when the tank is full, how long will it take to empty the tank? **SSC CGL (Tier-II) 20/01/2025 Shift-I**

(a) 48 h (b) 47 h
(c) 56 h (d) 55 h

2. A tank is filled in 45 min by two pipes, A and B. Pipe B fills the tank twice as fast as A. How much time (in minutes) will pipe A alone take to fill the tank? **SSC CGL (Tier-I) 26/09/2024 Shift-III**

(a) 135 (b) 140
(c) 125 (d) 115

3. One pipe can fill a tank four times as fast as another pipe. If together the two pipes can fill the tank in 48 min, the slower pipe alone will be able to fill the tank in: **SSC CGL (Tier-I) 26/09/2024 Shift-I**

(a) 192 min (b) 288 min
(c) 240 min (d) 144 min

4. A tap can fill a cistern in 10 min and another tap can empty it in 12 min. If both the taps are open, the time (in hours) taken to fill the tank will be: **SSC CGL (Tier-I) 25/09/2024 Shift-III**

(a) 1.5 h (b) 2.5 h
(c) 2 h (d) 1 h

5. Two pipes X and Y can fill a tank in 14 h and 21 h, respectively. Both pipes are opened simultaneously to fill the tank. In how many hours will the empty tank be filled? **SSC CGL(Tier-I) 25/09/2024 Shift-II**

(a) $8\frac{2}{5}$ h (b) $6\frac{2}{5}$ h
(c) $7\frac{2}{5}$ h (d) $5\frac{2}{5}$ h

6. An inlet pipe can fill a water storage tank in 11 h and an outlet pipe can empty the completely filled tank in 15 h .If both pipes opened simultaneously. The time taken to fill the empty tank (in hrs) is **SSC CGL (Tier-I) 25/09/2024 Shift-I**

(a) $45\frac{1}{2}$ (b) $41\frac{1}{4}$
(c) $49\frac{3}{4}$ (d) 40

7. Pipe A can fill a cistern in 4 h and Pipe B can fill the same cistern in 5 h. Pipe C can empty a full cistern in 3 h. If all three pipes are opened together, then the time (in minutes) taken to fill the tank is (round to the nearest minute) **SSC CGL (Tier-I) 24/09/2024 Shift-III**

(a) 625 (b) 445 (c) 800 (d) 514

8. Pipe A takes $\frac{4}{5}$ of the time required by pipe B to fill an empty tank individually. When an outlet pipe C is also opened simultaneously with pipes A and B, it takes $\frac{4}{5}$ more time to fill the empty tank than it takes when only pipe A and pipe B are opened together. If it takes 40 h to fill the tank when all the three pipes are opened simultaneously, in what time (in hours) will pipe C empty the full tank, operating alone? **SSC CGL (Tier-I) 24/09/2024 Shift-II**

(a) 50 (b) 45 (c) 65 (d) 75

9. One pipe can fill a tank 6 times faster than another pipe. If both the pipes together can fill the tank in 40 min, then in how many minutes will the slower pipe alone be able to fill the tank? **SSC CGL 24/09/2024 Shift-I**

(a) 275 (b) 285
(c) 290 (d) 280

10. Two pipes A and B can fill a tank in 20 and 30 h, respectively. Both pipes are opened to fill the tank, but when the tank is one-third full, a leak develops through which one-fourth of the water supplied by both pipes goes out. Find the total time (in hours) taken to fill the tank. **SSC CGL 23/09/2024 Shift-III**

(a) $14\frac{2}{3}$ (b) 14 (c) $11\frac{2}{5}$ (d) $12\frac{1}{3}$

11. Three pipes, P, Q and R, together take four hours to fill a tank. All the three pipes were opened at the same time. After three hours, P was closed, and Q and R filled the remaining tank in two hours. How many hours will P alone take to fill the tank? **SSC CGL (Tier-I) 23/09/2024 Shift-II**

(a) 8 (b) 10
(c) 12 (d) 9

12. A tank can be filled by pipe A in 4 h and pipe B in 6 h. At 8:00 am, pipe A was opened. At what time will the tank be filled if pipe B is opened at 9:00 am? **SSC CGL (Tier-I) 23/09/2024 Shift-I**

(a) 10:16 am (b) 10:22 am
(c) 10:48 am (d) 10:18 am

13. Two inlet pipes, P_1 and P_2 can fill a cistern in 20 h and 30 h, respectively. They were opened at the same time, but pipe P_1 had to be closed 5 h before the cistern was full. How many hours in total did it take for the two pipes to fill the cistern? **SSC CGL (Tier-I) 19/09/2024 Shift-III**

(a) 15 h (b) 9 h
(c) 12 h (d) 10 h

14. Pipe X can fill a tank in 9 h and Pipe Y can fill it in 21 h. If they are opened on alternate hours and Pipe X is opened first, in how many hours shall the tank be full? **SSC CGL (Tier-I) 19/09/2024 Shift-I**

(a) $10\frac{3}{7}$ (b) $12\frac{3}{7}$ (c) $9\frac{3}{7}$ (d) $11\frac{3}{7}$

15. Pipe Q can fill the tank in 60 h while pipe R may fill in 45 h. Q and R pipes are opened together for 6 h after which pipe W is also opened to empty the tank. All three pipes are opened simultaneously for 24 h to reach the half level mark. How much time (in hours) will pipe W alone take to empty the entire tank? **SSC CGL (Tier-I) 18/09/2024 Shift-III**

(a) 48 (b) 42 (c) 36 (d) 30

16. Pipes A and B can fill a tank in 6 h and 8 h, respectively. Both pipes are opened together for 3 h. After that pipe A is closed and B continues to fill the tank. In how many hours will the tank be filled? **SSC CGL (Tier-I) 18/09/2024 Shift-II**

(a) 2 (b) 4 (c) 3 (d) 6

17. Pipe X can fill a tank in 60 h while pipe Y can fill the tank in 72 h. Both pipes are opened together for 20 h. How much of the tank is left empty ? **SSC CGL (Tier-I) 18/09/2024 Shift-I**

(a) $\frac{1}{8}$ (b) $\frac{243}{360}$ (c) $\frac{7}{18}$ (d) $\frac{3}{8}$

18. Two pipes can fill a tank in 12 h and 18 h, respectively, while a third pipe can empty it in 8 h. How long (in hours) will it take to fill the empty tank if all three pipes are opened simultaneously? **SSC CGL (Tier-I) 17/09/2024 Shift-III**

(a) 48 (b) 24 (c) 36 (d) 72

19. A cistern can be filled by two pipes in 8 min and 10 min, separately. Both the pipes are opened together for a certain time, but due to an obstruction, only $\frac{5}{8}$ of the full quantity of water flowed through the former pipe and $\frac{3}{5}$ through the latter pipe. However, the obstruction was suddenly removed, and the cistern was filled in 3 min from that moment. How long did it take before the full flow began?
SSC CGL (Tier-I) 17/09/2024 Shift-II
(a) $3\frac{1}{16}$ min (b) $2\frac{6}{17}$ min
(c) $9\frac{6}{7}$ min (d) $2\frac{30}{37}$ min

20. Pipes A and B can fill a tank in 15 h and 25 h, respectively, whereas pipe C can empty the full tank in 40 h. All three pipes are opened together, but pipe A is closed after 5 h. After how many hours will the remaining part of the tank be filled?
SSC CGL (Tier-I) 17/09/2024 Shift-I
(a) $41\frac{4}{9}$ (b) $43\frac{4}{9}$
(c) $44\frac{4}{9}$ (d) $39\frac{4}{9}$

21. Two pipes P and Q can fill a tank in 36 min and 45 min, respectively. If both pipes are opened together, the time taken to fill the tank is **SSC CGL (Tier-I) 13/09/2024 Shift-III**
(a) 81 min (b) 20 min
(c) 40.5 min (d) 10 min

22. A pipe can fill an empty tank in 5 min and another pipe can empty in 6 min. If both pipes are opened simultaneously, how much time will be taken to fill the tank?
SSC CGL (Tier-I) 13/09/2024 Shift-II
(a) 33 min (b) 30 min
(c) 35 min (d) 25 min

23. There are two pipes used to fill a tank and when opened together, they can fill the tank in 20 min. If one pipe can fill the tank two and a half times as quickly as the other, then the faster pipe alone can fill the tank in **SSC CGL (Tier-I) 13/09/2024 Shift-I**
(a) 30 min (b) 32 min
(c) 34 min (d) 28 min

24. Two pipes A and B can fill a tank in $1\frac{1}{3}$ h and 2 h, respectively. If both the pipes are opened simultaneous, then, in how much time will the empty tank be filled?
SSC CGL (Tier-I) 12/09/2024 Shift-III
(a) $1\frac{1}{4}$ h (b) 55 min
(c) 48 min (d) $1\frac{2}{3}$ h

25. Two pipes A and B can fill a tank in 48 min and 66 min, respectively. If both the pipes are opened simultaneously, then after how many minutes should pipe B be closed so that the tank gets filled in 32 min? **SSC CGL (Tier-I) 12/09/2024 Shift-II**
(a) 18 (b) 16
(c) 22 (d) 20

26. Two pipes, A and B, can fill a tank in 10 min and 20 min, respectively. The pipe C can empty the tank in 30 min. All the three pipes are opened at a time in the beginning. However, pipe C is closed 2 min before the tank is filled. In what time, will the tank be full (in minutes)?
SSC CGL (Tier-I) 12/09/2024 Shift-I
(a) 12 (b) 10 (c) 8 (d) 6

27. The tank is filled by three pipes with different uniform flow rates. While the first two pipes are operating simultaneously, they fill the tank in the same duration that the third pipe takes to fill it alone. The second pipe can fill the tank 5 h quicker than the first pipe, yet 4 h slower than the third pipe. What is the time (in hours) needed for the first pipe to fill the tank?
SSC CGL (Tier-I) 11/09/2024 Shift-III
(a) 18 (b) 12
(c) 9 (d) 15

28. Pipe A usually fills a tank in 6 h. But due to a leak at the bottom of the tank, it takes extra 2 h to fill the tank. If the tank is full, then how much time will it take to get emptied due to the leak?
SSC CGL (Tier-I) 11/09/2024 Shift-II
(a) 16 h (b) 20 h
(c) 12 h (d) 24 h

29. There are two pipes to fill a tank. Together, they can fill the tank in 15 min. If one pipe can fill the tank in one and a half times as fast as the other, the faster pipe alone can fill the tank in
SSC CGL (Tier-I) 11/09/2024 Shift-I
(a) 10 min (b) 25 min
(c) 20 min (d) $32\frac{1}{2}$ min

30. Pipes P and Q can completely fill a water tank in 10 h and 15 h, respectively. A pipe R can empty a tank filled completely with water in 12 h. Initially, the tank is empty and only pipes P and Q are opened at 6 am and pipe R is also opened at 9 am By what time will the tank be completely filled?
SSC CGL (Tier-I) 10/09/2024 Shift-III
(a) 1 pm (b) 2 pm
(c) 11 am (d) 3 pm

31. Pipe L can fill a pool in 30 h and pipe M in 45 h. If both the pipes are opened in an empty pool, how much time will they take to fill it?
SSC CGL (Tier-I) 10/09/2024 Shift-II
(a) 24 h (b) 17 h
(c) 18 h (d) 20 h

32. Three pipes P, Q and R can fill a cistern in 40 min, 80 min and 120 min, respectively. Initially, all the pipes are opened. After how much time (in minutes) should the pipes Q and R be turned off so that the cistern will be completely filled in just half an hour?
SSC CGL (Tier-I) 10/09/2024 Shift-I
(a) 14 (b) 10
(c) 16 (d) 12

33. A pipe can fill an overhead tank in 12 h. But due to a leak at the bottom, it is filled in 18 h. If the tank is full, how much time will the leak take to empty it?
SSC CGL (Tier-I) 09/09/2024 Shift-III
(a) 3.6 h (b) 63 h
(c) 7.2 h (d) 36 h

34. Pipes M, N and S can fill a tank in 25, 50 and 100 min, respectively. Initially, pipes N and S are kept open for 10 min, and then pipe N is shut while pipe M is opened. Pipe S is closed 15 min before the tank overflows. How much time (in minutes) will it take to fill the tank if the three pipes work in this pattern?
SSC CGL (Tier-I) 09/09/2024 Shift-III
(a) 30 (b) 33
(c) 42 (d) 27

35. Pipe P is 21 times faster than pipe Q. If Q can fill a cistern in 110 min, find the time it takes to fill the cistern when both pipes are opened together. **SSC CGL (Tier-I) 09/09/2024 Shift-I**
(a) 5 min (b) 4 min
(c) 3 min (d) 6 min

SSC CGL 2023-2020 (Tier I & II)

36. There are two inlets A and B connected to a tank. A and B can fill the tank in 32 h and 28 h, respectively. If both the pipes are opened alternately for 1 h, starting with A, then in how much time (in hours, to nearest integer) will the tank be filled?
SSC CGL (Tier-II) 03/03/2023 Shift-I

(a) 22 (b) 30 (c) 36 (d) 24

37. There are three taps of diameter 2 cm, 3 cm and 4 cm, respectively. The ratio of the water flowing through them is equal to the ratio of the square of their diameters. The biggest tap can fill an empty tank alone in 81 min. If all the taps are opened simultaneously, then how long will the tank take (in min) to be filled? **SSC CGL (Tier-II) 02/03/2023 Shift-I**

(a) $34\frac{20}{29}$ (b) $64\frac{20}{29}$
(c) $54\frac{20}{29}$ (d) $44\frac{20}{29}$

38. Pipe A can fill 50% of the tank is 6 h and pipe B can completely fill the same tank in 18 h. If both the pipes are opened at the same time, in how much time (in min) will the empty tank be completely filled?
SSC CGL (Tier-I) 26/07/2023 Shift-II

(a) 420 (b) 425
(c) 432 (d) 435

39. Pipe A and pipe B running together can fill a cistern in 6 min. If B takes 5 min more than A to fill it, then the time in which A and B will fill that cistern separately will be, respectively, ...
SSC CGL (Tier-I) 26/07/2023 Shift-II

(a) 15 min and 10 min
(b) 15 min and 20 min
(c) 25 min and 20 min
(d) 10 min and 15 min

40. Each inlet pipe can fill an empty cistern in 84 h while each drain pipe can empty the same cistern from a filled condition in 105 h. When the cistern is empty, 9 inlet pipes and 10 outlet pipes are simultaneously opened. After how many hours will the cistern be completely filled?
SSC CGL (Tier-I) 26/07/2023 Shift-II

(a) 84 (b) 88
(c) 80 (d) 90

41. A pipe can fill a tank in 30 h. Due to a leakage at the bottom, it is filled in 50 h. How much time will the leakage take to empty the completely filled tank?
SSC CGL (Tier-I) 24/07/2023 Shift-II

(a) 60 h (b) 85 h
(c) 70 h (d) 75 h

42. Two pipes S_1 and S_2 alone can fill an empty tank in 15 h and 20 h, respectively. Pipe S_3 alone can empty that completely filled tank in 40 h. Firstly both pipe S_1 and S_2 are opened and after 2 h pipe S_3 is also opened. In how much time tank will be completely filled after S_3 is opened?
SSC CGL (Tier-I) 21/07/2023 Shift-II

(a) $\frac{90}{17}$ h (b) $\frac{89}{12}$ h
(c) $\frac{90}{13}$ h (d) $\frac{92}{11}$ h

43. An inlet pipe can fill an empty tank in $4\frac{1}{2}$ h while an outlet pipe drains a completely filled tank in $7\frac{1}{5}$ h. The tank is initially empty, and the two pipes are alternately opened for an hour each, till the tank is completely filled, starting with the inlet pipe. In how many hours will the tank be completely filled?
SSC CGL (Tier-I) 21/07/2023 Shift-II

(a) 24 (b) $20\frac{1}{4}$
(c) $20\frac{3}{4}$ (d) $22\frac{3}{8}$

44. Pipe A can fill a tank in 12 min, pipe B can fill it in 18 min, while pipe C can empty the full tank in 36 min. If all the pipes are opened simultaneously, how much time will it take to fill the empty tank completely?
SSC CGL (Tier-I) 20/07/2023 Shift-IV

(a) 7 min 30 sec (b) 10 min
(c) 9 min (d) 6 min

45. An inlet pipe can fill an empty tank in 120 h while an outlet pipe drains a completely-filled tank in 54 h. If 8 inlet pipes and 3 outlet pipes are opened simultaneously, when the tank is empty, then in how may hours will the tank get completely filled? **SSC CGL (Tier-I) 20/07/2023 Shift-I**

(a) 81 (b) 96
(c) 72 (d) 90

46. Inlet Pipes A and B can together fill an empty tank in 1.5 h. Outlet Pipe C, when opened alone, can empty the completely filled tank, in 4.5 h. When only Pipes A and C are opened together, the empty tank is filled in 6 h. Find the time taken by Pipe B, when opened alone, to fill the empty tank.
SSC CGL (Tier-I) 19/07/2023 Shift-II

(a) 3 h 30 min (b) 2 h 36 min
(c) 3 h 32 min (d) 3 h 40 min

47. Pipe A can fill an empty tank in 18 h and pipe B can fill the same empty tank in 24 h. If both the pipes are opened simultaneously, how much time (in hours) will they take to fill the empty tank?
SSC CGL (Tier-I) 14/07/2023 Shift-IV

(a) $11\frac{3}{7}$ (b) $10\frac{1}{7}$
(c) $10\frac{2}{7}$ (d) $11\frac{2}{7}$

48. An inlet pipe can fill an empty tank in 140 h while an outlet pipe drains a completely-filled tank in 63 h. If 8 inlet pipes and y outlet pipes are opened simultaneously, when the tank is empty, then the tank gets completely filled in 105 h. Find the value of y.
SSC CGL (Tier-I) 14/07/2023 Shift-III

(a) 1 (b) 4
(c) 2 (d) 3

49. There are 3 taps A, B, and C in a tank. These can fill the tank in 10 h, 20 h and 25 h, respectively. At first, all three taps are opened simultaneously. After 2 h, tap C is closed and A and B keep running. After 4 h from the beginning, tap B is also closed. The remaining tank is filled by tap A alone. Find the percentage of work done by tap A itself. **SSC CGL (Tier-I) 5/12/2022 Shift-IV**

(a) 32% (b) 75%
(c) 52% (d) 72%

50. A tank is filled in 4 h by three pipes A, B and C. The pipe C is $1\frac{1}{2}$ times as fast as B and B is 3 times as fast as A. How many hours will pipe A alone take to fill the tank?
SSC CGL (Tier-I) 24/8/2021 Shift-III

(a) 17 (b) 30
(c) 34 (d) 15

51. Pipes A and B can fill a tank in 12 h and 16 h respectively, and pipe C can empty the full tank in 24 h. All three pipes are opened together, but after 4 h pipe B is closed. In how many hours, the empty tank will be completely filled?
SSC CGL (Tier-I) 23/8/2021 Shift-I

(a) 32 (b) 28 (c) 18 (d) 14

52. Two pipes A and B can fill an empty tank in 10 h and 16 h, respectively. They are opened alternately for 1 h each, opening pipe B first. In how many hours, will the empty tank be filled? **SSC CGL (Tier-I) 20/8/2021 Shift-II**

(a) $14\frac{2}{5}$ (b) $16\frac{2}{5}$ (c) $10\frac{2}{5}$ (d) $12\frac{2}{5}$

53. Pipes A and B can fill a tank in 10 h and 40 h, respectively. C is an outlet pipe attached to the tank. If all the three pipes are opened simultaneously, it takes 80 min more time than A and B together take to fill the tank. A and B are kept opened for 7 h and then closed and C was opened. C will now empty the tank in **SSC CGL (Tier-I) 05/03/2020 Shift-I**

(a) 42 h (b) 45.5 h
(c) 49 h (d) 38.5 h

SSC CPO SI 2020

54. A pump can fill a tank with water in 1 h. Because of a leak, it took $1\frac{1}{3}$ h to fill the tank. In how many hours can the leak alone drain all the water of the tank when it is full? **SSC CPO 25/11/2020 Shift-II**

(a) 5 (b) 1 (c) 2 (d) 4

55. Two pipes A and B can fill a cistern in $12\frac{1}{2}$ h and 25 h, respectively. The pipes are opened simultaneously and it is found that due to a leakage in the bottom, it took 1 h 40 min more to fill the cistern. When the cistern is full, in how much time will the leak empty the cistern? **SSC CPO 25/11/2020 Shift-II**

(a) 45 h (b) 42 h
(c) 48 h (d) 50 h

56. Pipes A and B can fill a tank in 16 h and 24 h, respectively, whereas Pipe C can empty the full tank in 40 h. All three pipes are opened together, but Pipe C is closed after 10 h. After how many hours will the remaining part of the tank be filled? **SSC CPO 25/11/2020 Shift-I**

(a) $2\frac{1}{2}$ (b) 2 (c) $5\frac{1}{2}$ (d) 5

57. Two pipes A and B can fill a tank in 12 h and 18 h, respectively. Both pipes are opened simultaneously. In how much time will the empty tank be filled completely? **SSC CPO 25/11/2020 Shift-I**

(a) 9 h 30 min (b) 8 h
(c) 7 h 12 min (d) 10 h 24 min

58. Pipes A, B and C can fill an empty tank in $\frac{30}{7}$ h, if all the three pipes are opened simultaneously, A and B are filling pipes and C is an emptying pipe. Pipe A can fill the tank in 15 h and pipe C can empty it in 12 h. In how long (in hours) can pipe B alone fill the empty tank? **SSC CPO 24/11/2020 Shift-I**

(a) 3 (b) 5 (c) 6 (d) 4

59. When operated separately, pipe A takes 5 h less than pipe B to fill a cistern and when operated together, the cistern gets filled in 6 h. In how much time (in hours) will pipe A fill the cistern, if operated separately? **SSC CPO 24/11/2020 Shift-I**

(a) 15 (b) 18
(c) 10 (d) 9

60. Pipes A and B can fill a tank in 16 h and 24 h, respectively, whereas Pipe C can empty the full tank in 40 h. All three pipes are opened together, but Pipe A is closed after 10 h. After how many hours will the remaining part of the tank be filled? **SSC CPO 23/11/2020 Shift-I**

(a) $12\frac{1}{2}$ (b) 10 (c) 20 (d) $15\frac{1}{2}$

61. Two Pipes A and B can fill a tank in 15 h and 18 h, respectively. Both pipes are opened simultaneously to fill the tank. In how many hours will the empty tank be filled? **SSC CPO 23/11/2020 Shift-I**

(a) $8\frac{2}{11}$ (b) $9\frac{2}{11}$
(c) $7\frac{2}{11}$ (d) $10\frac{2}{11}$

SSC CHSL 2024-2021 (Tier I & II)

62. Two pipes can fill a cistern separately in 36 min and 45 min, respectively. A waste pipe can drain off 40 L per min. If all the three pipes are opened, the cistern fills in 1 h. The capacity (in litres) of the cistern is **SSC CHSL (Tier-II) 10/01/2024 Shift-I**

(a) 600 (b) 1200
(c) 300 (d) 400

63. A container is normally filled in 5 h. However, it takes 6 h when there is a leak at the bottom. If the container is full, in what time would the leak empty it, if no water is allowed into the container during that period? **SSC CHSL (Tier-I) 30/05/2022 Shift-I**

(a) 5 h (b) 6 h (c) 15 h (d) 30 h

64. Tap P can fill a cistern in 6 h and tap Q can empty the full cistern in 10 h. If both taps P and Q are kept open simultaneously, then in how many hours will the empty cistern be completely full? **SSC CHSL (Tier-I) 04/08/2021 Shift-I**

(a) 15 (b) 18 (c) 16 (d) 12

SSC MTS 2023-2021

65. 5 pipes are required to fill a tank in 1 h and 40 min. How long (in min) will it take to fill the same tank, if 4 pipes of the same type are used? **SSC MTS 11/09/2023 Shift-II**

(a) 115 (b) 150 (c) 125 (d) 140

66. Two inlet pipes can separately fill a cistern completely in 8 h and 10 h, respectively. They are operated for 2 h, after which the second pipe is closed and an outlet pipe which can drain out water from the full cistern in 20 h is opened.
How much time will it take to fill the cistern completely from the instant of opening to outlet pipe? **SSC MTS 02/11/2021 Shift-III**

(a) 7 h (b) 8 h
(c) 7 h 20 min (d) 8 h 40 min

Right Answers

1 (b)	2 (a)	3 (c)	4 (d)	5 (a)	6 (b)	7 (d)	8 (a)	9 (d)	10 (a)
11 (a)	12 (c)	13 (a)	14 (b)	15 (c)	16 (b)	17 (c)	18 (d)	19 (b)	20 (d)
21 (b)	22 (b)	23 (d)	24 (c)	25 (c)	26 (c)	27 (d)	28 (d)	29 (b)	30 (d)
31 (c)	32 (d)	33 (d)	34 (d)	35 (a)	36 (b)	37 (d)	38 (c)	39 (d)	40 (a)
41 (d)	42 (d)	43 (c)	44 (c)	45 (d)	46 (a)	47 (c)	48 (d)	49 (d)	50 (c)
51 (c)	52 (d)	53 (c)	54 (d)	55 (d)	56 (b)	57 (c)	58 (d)	59 (c)	60 (a)
61 (a)	62 (b)	63 (d)	64 (a)	65 (c)	66 (c)				

Solutions

1. (b) Let the capacity of tank be 28 units. (by taking LCM of 5.6 and 7)

Efficiency of pipe $A = \frac{28}{-5.6} = -5$

Efficiency of pipe $B = \frac{28}{7} = 4$

Workdone by both pipes in 2 h
$= -5 + 4 = -1$ unit

At the last hour, pipe A will work alone.
Hence, 5 units will be done by pipe A.

$\therefore$ Remaining work $= 28 - 5 = 23$ units

Time taken $= 23 \times 2 = 46$ h

$\therefore$ It will take $(46 + 1 = 47)$ h to empty the tank.

2. (a) Let the time taken by pipe A to fill the tank be $2x$ min.

$\therefore$ Time taken by pipe B be x min.

$A \rightarrow 2x$ — 1
[$2x$]
$B \rightarrow x$ — 2

$\therefore$ Total time taken by $(A + B) = 45$ min

$\therefore \quad \frac{2x}{1+2} = 45$

$\Rightarrow \quad \frac{2x}{3} = 45 \Rightarrow 2x = 135$ min

$\therefore$ A will fill the tank in 135 min.

3. (c) Let one pipe can fill a tank in $4x$ min.

$\therefore$ Another pipe will fill a tank in x min.

A — $4x$ — 1
[$4x$]
B — x — 4

$\therefore$ Total time taken by $(A + B)$ to fill a tank $= 48$ min

$\therefore \quad \frac{4x}{1+4} = 48$

$\Rightarrow \quad \frac{4x}{5} = 48 \Rightarrow x = 60$

$\therefore$ Time taken by slower pipe $= 4(60)$
$= 240$ min

4. (d)

	(T)	(E)	Tank capacity
$P_1 \rightarrow$	10 min	6	60
$P_2 \rightarrow$	12 min	–5	

$\therefore$ Required time $= \frac{60}{6-5} = 60$ min $= 1$ h

5. (a)

	(T)	(E)	Tank capacity
$X \rightarrow$	14h	3	42
$Y \rightarrow$	21h	2	

$\therefore$ Time taken to fill the tank $= \frac{42}{3+2} = 8\frac{2}{5}$ h

6. (b) Inlet pipe 11 h — +15 — (165) Capacity of tank
Outlet pipe 15 h — –11

[$\because$ LCM of 11 and 15 is 165]

Thus, time taken to fill tank when both are opened $= \frac{165}{15-11} = \frac{165}{4} = 41\frac{1}{4}$ h

7. (d) Pipe A 4 — 15 units/h
Pipe B 5 — 12 units/h — (60) units
Pipe C 3 — –20 units/h
(Empty pipe)

[$\because$ LCM of 4, 5, 3 = 60]

Time taken to fill the tank when all pipes are opened $= \frac{60}{15+12-20} = \frac{60}{7}$ h

$= \frac{60}{7} \times 60$ min

$= 514$ min

8. (a) Let pipe A takes $4x$ h

Then pipe B takes $5x$ h

work done in 1 h by A and $B = \frac{1}{4x} + \frac{1}{5x} = \frac{9}{20x}$

Time taken when A and B accompanied by C

$= \frac{20x}{9} + \frac{20x}{9} \times \frac{4}{5}$

$= \frac{100x + 80x}{45} = \frac{180x}{45} = 4x$

But $4x = 40$ (Given)

$x = 10$ h

Thus, $\frac{1}{40} + \frac{1}{50} - \frac{1}{C} = \frac{1}{40}$

$\Rightarrow \quad \frac{1}{C} = \frac{1}{50} \Rightarrow C = 50$ h

9. (d) Efficiency ratio of first pipe and second pipe

I : II

6 : 1 = 7 units

Total capacity of tank $= 7 \times 40 = 280$ units

Thus, time required to fill by slower pipe

$= \frac{280}{1} = 280$ min

10. (a) Pipe A (20h) — 3 — 60 units
Pipe B (30h) — 2

Time required to fill tank one-third

$= \frac{60 \times \frac{1}{3}}{3+2} = \frac{20}{5} = 4$ h

Now, Leakage developed,

Time required to fill remaining part of tank by $\frac{3}{4}$ th of water supply $= \frac{40}{5 \times \frac{3}{4}} = \frac{32}{3}$ h

Thus, total time to fill tank

$= 4 + \frac{32}{3} = \frac{44}{3} = 14\frac{2}{3}$ h

11. (a) Part filled in 3 h $= \frac{3}{4}$

Remaining part $= 1 - \frac{3}{4} = \frac{1}{4}$

$(Q + R)$'s 1 h work $= \frac{1}{4} \times \frac{1}{2} = \frac{1}{8}$

P's 1 h work $= (P + Q + R)$'s 1 h work $- (P + Q)$'s 1 h work $= \frac{1}{4} - \frac{1}{8} = \frac{2-1}{8} = \frac{1}{8}$

P alone will take 8 h to fill the tank.

12. (c)

	(T)	(E)	Total capacity of tank
$A \rightarrow$	4	3	12
$B \rightarrow$	6	2	

Let pipe B opened for x h.

According to the question,

$A(x + 1) + Bx = 12$

$\Rightarrow \quad 3(x + 1) + 2x = 12$

$\Rightarrow \quad 5x + 3 = 12$

$\Rightarrow \quad x = \frac{9}{5}$ h

$= 108$ min $= 1$ h 48 min

$\therefore$ Required time $= 9:00$ am $+ 1$ h 48 min
$= 10:48$ am

13. (a) Let total time taken by both pipes together be x h.

	(T)	(E)	Total capacity of tank
$P_1 \rightarrow$	20h	3	60
$P_2 \rightarrow$	30h	2	

According to the question,

$(x - 5)(P_1 + P_2) + 5P_2 = 60$

$\Rightarrow (x - 5) \times (3 + 2) + 5 \times 2 = 60$

$\Rightarrow \quad (x - 5) = 10$

$\Rightarrow \quad x = 15$ h

14. (b) Total capacity of tank
$=$ LCM of $(21, 9) = 63$

Tank filled by X in 1 h $= \frac{63}{9} = 7$ unit

Tank filled by Y in 1 h $= \frac{63}{21} = 3$ unit

Tank filled by both pipes in 2 h
$= 7 + 3 = 10$ unit

Tank filled by both pipes in 12 h
$= 10 \times \frac{12}{2} = 60$

Remaining part $= 63 - 60 = 3$

Tank taken by pipe X to fill the remaining part $= \frac{3}{7}$

$\therefore$ Total time $= 12\frac{3}{7}$ h

15. (c)

	(T)	(E)	(T.W.)
$Q \rightarrow$	60 h	3	180 units
$R \rightarrow$	45 h	4	

According to the question,

$$6(Q+R)+24(Q+R+W)=\frac{180}{2}$$
$$6\times(3+4)+24(4+3+W)=90$$
$$24(7+W)=48$$
$$7+W=2$$
$$W=-5 \text{ (outlet pipe)}$$

$\therefore$ W will empty the tank in $\frac{180}{5}=36$ h

16. (b)

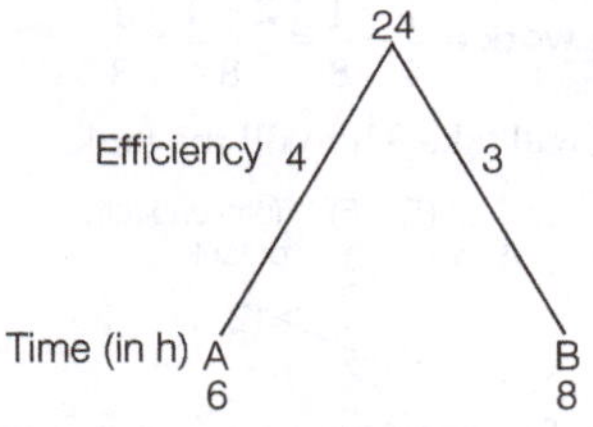

Let total work = 24 unit.

$\therefore$ Efficiency of A and B is 4 and 3 respectively.

$(A+B)$ will work in 3 hr $=(4+3)\times 3$
$= 21$ units

Work left $= 24-21 = 3$ unit.

Left work will be completed by B in $\frac{3}{3}=1$ h.

$\therefore$ Total work done in $(3+1)$ h $= 4$ h.

17. (c)

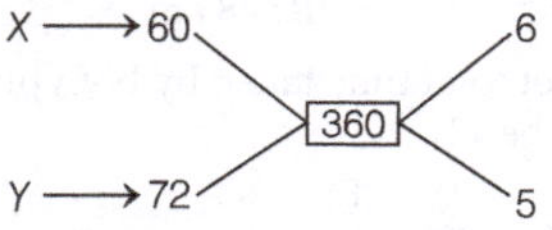

Part of tank filled in 1 h = 6 + 5 = 11 units.

$\therefore$ Part of tank filled in 20 h
$= 20\times 11 = 220$ units

$\therefore$ Remaining part $= 360-220 = 140$ units

$\therefore$ Remaining portion of tank $=\frac{140}{360}=\frac{7}{18}$

18. (d) Time pipe A takes $=\frac{1}{12}$

Time pipe B takes $=\frac{1}{18}$

Time pipe C takes $=\frac{1}{8}$

According to the question,

$$\frac{1}{12}+\frac{1}{18}-\frac{1}{8}=\frac{6+4-9}{72}=\frac{1}{72}$$

Total time taken = 72 h.

19. (b)

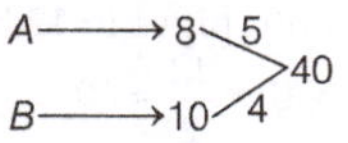

{$\because$ LCM of (8, 10) = 40}

The efficiency of pipe $P_1 = 5\times\frac{5}{8}=\frac{25}{8}$

and efficiency of pipe $P_2 = 4\times\frac{3}{5}=\frac{12}{5}$

Cistern filled by both P_1 and P_2 without obstruction in last 3 min $=(5+4)\times 3 = 27$ L.

Then remaining volume of cistern
$= 40-27 = 13$ L.

The time taken by P_1 and P_2 to fill 13 liter water with obstruction $=\frac{13}{\frac{25}{8}+\frac{12}{5}}$

$$=\frac{13}{\frac{25\times 5+12\times 8}{40}}=\frac{13\times 40}{221}$$

$$=\frac{13\times 40}{13\times 17}=\frac{40}{17}=2\frac{6}{17}\text{ min}$$

20. (d) Total capacity of tank = LCM of 15, 25 and 40 = 600 unit

Efficiency of pipe $A=\frac{600}{15}=40$ unit/h

Efficiency of pipe $B=\frac{600}{25}=24$ unit/h

Efficiency of pipe C $=\frac{600}{40}=-15$ unit/h

Tank filled in 5 h by all $(40+24-15)\times 5$
$= 245$ unit

Remaining part $= 600-245 = 355$ unit

Required time $=\frac{355}{24-15}=\frac{355}{9}=39\frac{4}{9}$ h

21. (b) Total capacity of tank
= LCM of 36 and 45 = 180

Efficiency of Pipe $P=\frac{180}{36}=5$

Efficiency of Pipe $Q=\frac{180}{45}=4$

Time required to fill the tank when both pipes are opened $=\frac{180}{5+4}=20$ min

22. (b)

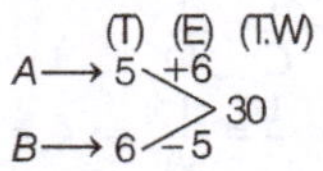

$\therefore$ Required time $=\frac{30}{6-5}=30$ min

23. (d) Slower Faster

Effeciency $= 1 : \frac{5}{2}$

$2 : 5$

Time $5 : 2$

$\therefore$ Total work $=(2+5)\times 20 = 140$ unit

$\therefore$ Time taken by faster pipe $=\frac{140}{5}=28$ min

24. (c) A can fill the tank in $\frac{4}{3}$ h.

B can fill the tank in 2 h.

Time taken by A and B to fill part of tank

$\Rightarrow$ $$\frac{3}{4}+\frac{1}{2}=\frac{5}{4}$$

Both can fill the complete tank in $\frac{4}{5}$ h

$$=\frac{4}{5}\times 60 = 48\text{ min}$$

25. (c) In 48 min, A can fill 1 part of tank.

$\therefore$ In 1 min, A can fill $\frac{1}{48}$ part of tank.

In 66 min, B can fill 1 part of tank.

$\therefore$ In 1 min, B can fill $\frac{1}{66}$ part of tank.

Let after x min, pipe B is closed.

$\therefore$ A work for whole 32 min.

$\therefore$ According to the question,

$$\frac{32}{48}+\frac{x}{66}=1$$

$\Rightarrow$ $$\frac{32\times 11+8x}{528}=1$$

$\Rightarrow$ $352+8x=528$

$\Rightarrow$ $8x=176$

$\Rightarrow$ $x=22$

$\therefore$ After 22 min pipe B is closed.

26. (c)

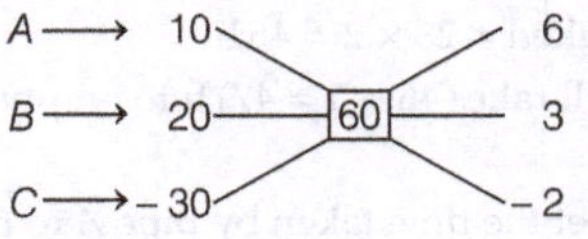

Let tank is filled in x min.

$\therefore$ $x(A+B)+(x-2)(C)=60$

$x(6+3)+(x-2)(-2)=60$

$\Rightarrow$ $9x-2x+4=60$

$\Rightarrow$ $7x=56$

$\Rightarrow$ $x=8$ min

27. (d) Let third pipe fill the tank in t h.

Then, second pipe fill the tank in $(t+4)$ h and first pipe fill the tank in $(t+9)$ h.

According to the question,

$$\frac{1}{t+9}+\frac{1}{t+4}=\frac{1}{t}\Rightarrow\frac{2t+13}{t^2+13t+36}=\frac{1}{t}$$

$\Rightarrow$ $2t^2+13t=t^2+13t+36$

$\Rightarrow$ $t^2=36\Rightarrow t=6$ h

$\therefore$ Time taken by first pipe $=6+9=15$ h

28. (d)

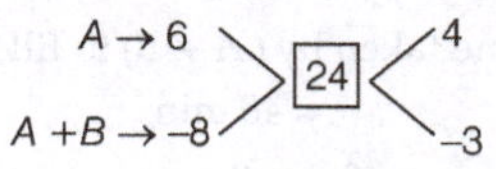

$\therefore$ Required time taken $=\frac{24}{4-3}=\frac{24}{1}=24$ h

29. (b) Ratio of efficiency of A and B

A	:	B
1.5	:	1
3	:	2

Thus, total capacity of tank $=5\times 15 = 75$ L

$\therefore$ Required time $=\frac{75}{3}=25$ min

30. (d)

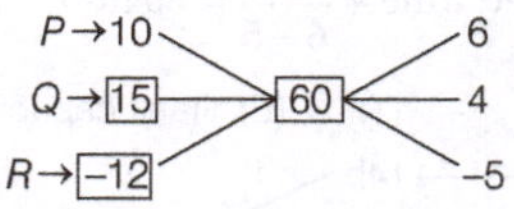

Part of tank filled in 3 h (*i.e.*, 6 am – 9 am)
$=3(P+Q)=3(6+4)=30$ units

$\therefore$ Remaining part $= 60-30 = 30$ units

$\therefore$ Time taken to fill the remaining part

$$=\frac{30}{(6+4-5)}=\frac{30}{5}=6\text{ h}$$

$\therefore$ Total time taken = 9 am + 6 h = 3 pm

$\therefore$ Tank will be filled by 3 pm.

31. (c) For pipe L,
In 30 h pipe L can fill 1 part.
$\therefore$ In 1 h pipe L can fill $\frac{1}{30}$ part.
For pipe M,
In 45 h pipe M can fill 1 part.
$\therefore$ In 1 h pipe M can fill $\frac{1}{45}$ part.
$\therefore$ In 1 h pipe $(L+M)$ can fill
$$\left(\frac{1}{30}+\frac{1}{45}\right)\text{part}$$
$$=\frac{3+2}{90}=\frac{5}{90}\text{ part}=\frac{1}{18}\text{ part}$$
$\therefore$ Pipe $(L+M)$ will take 18 h to fill the pool.

32. (d) P's efficiency $=\frac{1}{40}$
Q's efficiency $=\frac{1}{80}$
R's efficiency $=\frac{1}{120}$
Let pipes Q and R turned off after x min.
According to the question,
$$x\left(\frac{1}{80}+\frac{1}{120}\right)+\frac{1}{40}\times 30=1$$
$$\Rightarrow \quad x\left(\frac{5}{240}\right)+\frac{3}{4}=1$$
$$\Rightarrow \quad x\left(\frac{5}{240}\right)=\frac{1}{4}$$
$$\therefore \quad x = 12\text{ min}$$

33. (d) Part of tank filled by pipe in 1 h $=\frac{1}{12}$
Part of tank filled by pipe and leak in 1 h
$$=\frac{1}{18}$$
Part of tank empty by leak in 1 h
$$=\frac{1}{12}-\frac{1}{18}=\frac{3-2}{36}=\frac{1}{36}$$
Total time taken to empty full tank = 36 h

34. (d) According to the question,

$M \longrightarrow 25$ — 4
$N \longrightarrow 50$ — 100 — 2
$S \longrightarrow 100$ — 1

Let tank is filled in x min.
$$10(N+S)+x(M)+(x-15)(S)=100$$
$$\Rightarrow \quad 10(3)+x(4)+(x-15)(1)=100$$
$$\Rightarrow \quad 4x+x-15=70$$
$$\Rightarrow \quad x=\frac{85}{5}=17$$
$\therefore$ Total time = 10 + 17 = 27 min

35. (a) Ratio of Efficiency of P and Q = $P:Q$
21 : 1
Total capacity of cistern = 1 × 110 = 110 litre
Time required to fill cistern when both pipes are opened $=\frac{110}{(21+1)}=\frac{110}{22}=5$ min

36. (b) Pipe A fills the tank in 1 h $=\frac{1}{32}$
Pipe B fills the tank in 1 h $=\frac{1}{28}$
$$\text{Work of 2 h}=\frac{1}{32}+\frac{1}{28}=\frac{7+8}{224}=\frac{15}{224}=\frac{1}{15}$$
So, complete tank will fill in 30 h.

37. (d) $\because$ The ratio of the water flowing through them is equal to the ratio of the square of their diameter.
$$\therefore \quad A:B:C=2^2:3^2:4^2=4:9:16$$
$\therefore$ Efficiency of $A:B:C=4:9:16$
Total work = 16 × 81 = 1296 units
$$\therefore \text{ Required time}=\frac{\text{Total work}}{\text{Total efficiency}}$$
$$=\frac{1296}{4+9+16}=44\frac{20}{29}\text{ min}$$

38. (c) Let total work = 36
$$\therefore \text{ Efficiency of } A=\frac{36\times 50\%}{6}=3$$
$$\therefore \text{ Efficiency of } B=\frac{36}{18}=2$$
Time taken to fill the tank by A and B together
$$=\frac{36}{3+2}=\frac{36}{5}\times 60\text{ min}=432\text{ min}$$

39. (d) Let A can fill the tank in x min and B can fill the tank in $(x+5)$ min.
According to the question,
$$\frac{1}{x}+\frac{1}{x+5}=\frac{1}{6}$$
$$\Rightarrow \quad \frac{2x+5}{x^2+5x}=\frac{1}{6}$$
$$\Rightarrow \quad x^2 \;\; 7x-30=0$$
$$\Rightarrow \quad (x-10)(x+3)=0$$
$$\therefore \quad x=10\text{ min}$$
$\therefore$ A can fill the tank = 10 min
and B can fill the tank = 10 + 5 = 15 min

40. (a) Let total work = LCM of 84 and 105
= 420 units
$$\text{Efficiency of each inlet pipe}=\frac{420}{84}=5\text{ units}$$
Efficiency of each draining pipe
$$=\frac{420}{105}=4\text{ units}$$
Efficiency of 9 inlet pipe and 10 draining pipe opened simultaneously
$$=9\times 5-4\times 10=5\text{ units}$$
$$\text{Hence, required time}=\frac{420}{5}=84\text{ h}$$

41. (d) Let the time taken by the leak to empty the whole tank be t h.
$$\text{Then,} \quad \frac{1}{30}-\frac{1}{50}=\frac{1}{t}$$
$$\Rightarrow \quad \frac{1}{t}=\frac{5-3}{150}$$
$$\Rightarrow \quad t=\frac{150}{2} \Rightarrow t=75\text{ h}$$

42. (d) Part filled in 2 h by S_1 and S_2
$$=2\left(\frac{1}{15}+\frac{1}{20}\right)=2\left(\frac{4+3}{60}\right)=\frac{7}{30}$$
$$\therefore \text{ Remaining part}=1-\frac{7}{30}=\frac{23}{30}$$
Let tank will be filled in x min after third pipe is opened.
$$\therefore \quad x\left(\frac{1}{15}+\frac{1}{20}-\frac{1}{40}\right)=\frac{23}{30}$$
$$\Rightarrow \quad x\left(\frac{8+6-3}{120}\right)=\frac{23}{30}$$
$$\Rightarrow \quad x=\frac{92}{11}\text{ h}$$

Speedy Method

$S_1 \longrightarrow 15$ (+8)
$S_2 \longrightarrow 20$ (+6) → 120 (Total work)
$S_3 \longrightarrow 40$ (−3)

Work of S_1 and S_2 in 2h = 2(8 + 6) = 28
Remaining work = 120 − 28 = 92
$$\text{Hence, required time}=\frac{92}{8+6-3}=\frac{92}{11}\text{ h}$$

43. (c)

$\frac{9}{2}$ — 8
→ 36
$\frac{36}{5}$ — −5

$$\left[\because \text{ LCM of } \frac{9}{2} \text{ and } \frac{36}{5} \text{ is } 36\right]$$

Part of tank fill in 2 h while working alternate
2 h → (8 − 5)
2 h → 3 L
↓ ×10 ↓×10
20 h → 30 L
Now, remaining part filled by inlet pipe is
$$\frac{6}{8}=\frac{3}{4}\text{ h}$$
$$\text{Thus, total time}=20+\frac{3}{4}=20\frac{3}{4}\text{ h}$$

44. (c) If all three pipes are opened together then, $(A+B+C)$'s one min work
$$=\frac{1}{12}+\frac{1}{18}-\frac{1}{36}=\frac{1}{9}$$
$\therefore$ Tank will be filled completely in 9 min.

45. (d) Let total capacity of tank = 1080 L
$$\text{Efficiency of inlet pipe}=\frac{1080}{120}=9$$
$$\text{Efficiency of outlet pipe}=\frac{1080}{54}=20$$
8 inlet and 3 outlet pipes are opened simultaneously.
$\therefore$ The tank will get completely filled in
$$=\frac{1080}{9\times 8-3\times 20}=\frac{1080}{12(6-5)}=90\text{ h}$$

46. (a) Let total capacity be 18 L.
$$\therefore \text{ Efficiency of } (A+B)=\frac{18}{1.5}=12$$

Efficiency of Pipe $C = \frac{18}{4.5} = -4$

Efficiency of pipe $(A + C) = \frac{18}{6} = 3$

Then, efficiency of $A = 3 - (-4) = 7$

Efficiency of $B = 12 - 7 = 5$

Then, time taken by $B = \frac{18}{5}$ h $= 3$ h 30 min

47. (c) (Pipe A + Pipe B)'s 1 h work

$$= \frac{1}{18} + \frac{1}{24} = \frac{4+3}{72} = \frac{7}{72}$$

$\therefore$ Pipe A and Pipe B together can fill the tank in $= \frac{72}{7}$ h $= 10\frac{2}{7}$ h

48. (d) Let total work = LCM of 140 and 63

$= 1260$ unit

$\therefore$ Efficiency of 1 inlet $= \frac{1260}{140} = 9$ unit

and efficiency of 1 drain $= \frac{1260}{63} = 20$ unit

According to the question,

$$9 \times 8 - 20 \times y = \frac{1260}{105} \Rightarrow 20y = 72 - 12$$

$\therefore \quad y = 3$

49. (d) Part of tank filled in first 2 h

$$= \left(\frac{1}{10} + \frac{1}{20} + \frac{1}{25}\right) \times 2$$

$$= \left(\frac{10+5+4}{100}\right) \times 2 = \frac{19}{50}$$

Now, part of tank filled in next 2 h when tap C is closed $= \left(\frac{1}{10} + \frac{1}{20}\right) \times 2 = \frac{3}{10}$

Now, part of tank filled in 4 h

$$= \frac{19}{50} + \frac{3}{10} = \frac{34}{50}$$

$\therefore$ Remaining part of tank to be filled

$$= 1 - \frac{34}{50} = \frac{16}{50}$$

Hence, $\frac{16}{50}$ part of tank is to be filled by tap A alone.

$\therefore$ Total part of tank filled by tap A

$$= \frac{1}{10} \times 4 + \frac{16}{50} = \frac{4}{10} + \frac{16}{50} = \frac{36}{50}$$

Required % $= \dfrac{\frac{36}{50}}{1} \times 100\% = 72\%$

Speedy Method

$A \longrightarrow 10$ (10)
$B \longrightarrow 20$ (5) $\longrightarrow 100$ (Total work)
$C \longrightarrow 25$ (4)

4 h's work $= 10 \times 4 + 5 \times 4 + 4 \times 2 = 68$

$\therefore$ Remaining work $= 100 - 68 = 32$

$\therefore$ Total work of $A = 10 \times 4 + 32 = 72$

Hence, required% $= \frac{72}{100} \times 100 = 72\%$

50. (c) Let efficiency of $A = x$

Efficiency of $B = 3x$

Efficiency of $C = \frac{3}{2} \times 3x = \frac{9x}{2}$

$\therefore$ Ratio of efficiencies of A, B and C

$$= x : 3x : \frac{9x}{2} = 2 : 6 : 9$$

Total work $= (2 + 6 + 9) \times 4 = 68$

Hence, required time $= \frac{68}{2} = 34$ h

51. (c) Let the empty tank will be filled in x h.

According to the question,

$$\frac{x}{12} + \frac{4}{16} - \frac{x}{24} = 1 \Rightarrow \frac{2x - x}{24} = 1 - \frac{1}{4}$$

$$\Rightarrow \quad \frac{x}{24} = \frac{3}{4} \Rightarrow x = 3 \times 6$$

$\therefore \quad x = 18$ h

52. (d) In 1 h, part filled by pipe $A = \frac{1}{10}$

In 1 h, part filled by pipe $B = \frac{1}{16}$

Now, In 2 h, part filled $= \frac{1}{10} + \frac{1}{16} = \frac{13}{80}$

In 12 h, part filled $= \frac{13 \times 6}{80} = \frac{78}{80}$

Remaining part $= 1 - \frac{78}{80} = \frac{2}{80} = \frac{1}{40}$

$\therefore$ $\frac{1}{40}$ part filled by pipe $B = \dfrac{\frac{1}{40}}{\frac{1}{16}} = \frac{2}{5}$ h

Hence, total time taken by pipe A and B

$$= \left(12 + \frac{2}{5}\right) \text{h} = 12\frac{2}{5} \text{ h}$$

53. (c) Part filled by pipe A and B in 1 h

$$= \frac{1}{10} + \frac{1}{40} = \frac{4+1}{40} = \frac{5}{40} = \frac{1}{8}$$

Pipe A and B will fill the tank = 8 h

All three pipes fill the tank

= 8 h + 80 min

$$= 8 + 1 + \frac{20}{60} = 9\frac{1}{3} = \frac{28}{3} \text{ h}$$

According to the question,

$$\frac{1}{A} + \frac{1}{B} - \frac{1}{C} = \frac{3}{28} \Rightarrow \frac{1}{8} - \frac{1}{C} = \frac{3}{28}$$

$$\Rightarrow \quad \frac{1}{C} = \frac{1}{8} - \frac{3}{28} \Rightarrow \frac{1}{C} = \frac{28 - 24}{28 \times 8} = \frac{4}{28 \times 8}$$

C can empty the tank in 56 h.

Now, part filled by pipe A and B in 7 h $= \frac{7}{8}$

$\therefore$ C will empty $\frac{7}{8}$ part of the tank

$$= \frac{7}{8} \times 56 = 7 \times 7 = 49 \text{ h}$$

54. (d) Work done by the leak in 1 h

$$= 1 - \frac{3}{4} = \frac{1}{4}$$

$\therefore$ Leak will empty the tank in 4 h.

55. (d) Pipe A can fill a cistern in $\frac{25}{2}$ h.

$\therefore$ Part of tank filled by pipe $A = \frac{2}{25}$

Pipe B can fill in 25 h.

Part of tank filled by pipe B in 1 h $= \frac{1}{25}$

Work done by both pipes in 1 h

$$= \frac{2}{25} + \frac{1}{25} = \frac{3}{25}$$

Time taken together by both pipes is $\frac{25}{3}$ h

1 h = 60 min

$$\frac{25}{3} \text{ h} = 60 \times \frac{25}{3} = 8 \text{ h } 20 \text{ min}$$

Due to leak 8 h 20 min + 1 h 40 min = 10 h

Part of tank empty by leak in 1 h

$$= \frac{3}{25} - \frac{1}{10} = \frac{5}{250} = \frac{1}{50}$$

$\therefore$ Time taken to empty the tank by leak is 50 h.

56. (b)
$A \longrightarrow 16$ (15)
$B \longrightarrow 24$ (10) $\longrightarrow 240$
$C \longrightarrow 40$ (−6)

$\therefore$ Work of $(A + B + C)$ in 10 h

$= 10 \times (15 + 10 - 6) = 190$

Remaining work $= 240 - 190 = 50$

Hence, required time $= \frac{50}{15 + 10} = 2$ h

57. (c) Part of tank fill in 1 h

$$= \frac{1}{12} + \frac{1}{18} = \frac{3+2}{36} = \frac{5}{36}$$

Hence, both the pipes together will fill the tank in $\frac{36}{5}$ h or 7 h 12 min.

58. (d)
$A + B + C \longrightarrow \frac{30}{7}$ (14)
$A \longrightarrow 15$ (4) $\longrightarrow 60$ (Total work)
$C \longrightarrow 12$ (−5)

$\therefore$ Efficiency of $B = 14 - (4 - 5) = 15$

Hence, required time $= \frac{60}{15} = 4$ h

59. (c) Let if pipe A separately can fill the cistern in x h.

So, pipe B separately can fill the cistern in $(x + 5)$ h.

According to the question,

$$\frac{1}{x} + \frac{1}{x+5} = \frac{1}{6}$$

$$\Rightarrow \quad 12x + 30 = x^2 + 5x$$

$$\Rightarrow \quad x^2 - 7x - 30 = 0$$

$$\Rightarrow \quad (x - 10)(x + 3) = 0$$

$\therefore \quad x = 10$

So, pipe A alone can fill the cistern in 10 h.

60. (a)
$A \longrightarrow 16$ (15)
$B \longrightarrow 24$ (10) $\longrightarrow 240$
$C \longrightarrow 40$ (−6)

10 h work of $(A+B+C)$

$$= 10 \times (15 + 10 - 6) = 190$$

Remaining work = 240 − 190 = 50

Hence, required time $= \frac{50}{10-6} = \frac{25}{2} = 12\frac{1}{2}$ h

61. (a) Part of tank filled by both pipes in 1 h

$$= \frac{1}{15} + \frac{1}{18} = \frac{6+5}{90} = \frac{11}{90}$$

Time taken by both pipes to fill the tank

$$= \frac{90}{11} \text{ h} = 8\frac{2}{11} \text{ h}$$

62. (b) Let the waste pipe empty the cistern in x min.

According to the question,

$$\frac{1}{36} + \frac{1}{45} - \frac{1}{x} = \frac{1}{60} \quad [\because 1 \text{ h} = 60 \text{ min}]$$

$$\Rightarrow \frac{1}{x} = \frac{1}{36} + \frac{1}{45} - \frac{1}{60} \Rightarrow \frac{1}{x} = \frac{5+4-3}{180}$$

$$\Rightarrow \frac{1}{x} = \frac{6}{180} \Rightarrow x = 30 \text{ min}$$

Therefore, capacity of cistern

$$= 30 \times 40 = 1200 \text{ L}$$

Speedy Method

First pipe 36 min → 5
Second pipe 45 min → 4 → (180)
All three pipe 60 min → 3

Thus, efficiency of drainage pipe

$$= 5 + 4 - 3 = 6$$

Time taken to empty the cistern

$$= \frac{180}{6} = 30 \text{ min}$$

Thus, capacity of cistern is

$$= 40 \times 30 = 1200 \text{ L.}$$

63. (d) Part emptied by leak in an hour

$$= \frac{1}{5} - \frac{1}{6} = \frac{1}{30}$$

So, leak would take 30 h to empty the full container.

64. (a) Part filled by both Tap P and Q in 1 h

$$= \frac{1}{6} - \frac{1}{10} = \frac{10-6}{60} = \frac{1}{15}$$

Hence, both taps together will fill the empty cistern in $\frac{1}{\frac{1}{15}} = 15$ h

65. (c) Given, 5 pipes can fill a tank in 100 min.

$\therefore$ 1 pipe can fill a tank in 100 × 5 = 500 min

4 pipe can fill a tank in $= \frac{500}{4} = 125$ min

66. (c) Part of tank filled in 2 h by inlet pipe

$$= 2\left(\frac{1}{8} + \frac{1}{10}\right) = \frac{9}{20}$$

Remaining part of tank $= 1 - \frac{9}{20} = \frac{11}{20}$

Now, second inlet pipe is closed and outlet pipe is opened then,

Part of tank filled in 1 h $= \frac{1}{8} - \frac{1}{20} = \frac{3}{40}$

$\therefore$ Time required to fill the tank

$$= \frac{\frac{11}{20}}{\frac{3}{40}} = \frac{22}{3} = 7 \text{ h } 20 \text{ min}$$

19

Algebra

An algebraic expression consists of variables, coefficients, constants and mathematical operations like addition, subtraction, multiplication, and division.

For example, $2x^2 - 3yz + 6z^2 + 7$ is an algebraic expression where x, y and z are variables and 2, –3 and 6 are coefficients and 7 is constant.

Degree or Order of a Polynomial

The highest exponent of a variable in an algebraic polynomial is known as its degree.

For example, in the polynomial $x^2 + 2x + 3$, the highest power of variable x is 2.

Hence, the degree of polynomial is 2.

Algebraic Formulae

- $(a+b)^2 = a^2 + b^2 + 2ab$
- $(a-b)^2 = a^2 + b^2 - 2ab$
- $(a+b)^2 - 4ab = (a-b)^2$
- $a^2 - b^2 = (a+b)(a-b)$
- $a^4 - b^4 = (a^2+b^2)(a+b)(a-b)$
- $a^2 + \frac{1}{a^2} = \left(a + \frac{1}{a}\right)^2 - 2 = \left(a - \frac{1}{a}\right)^2 + 2$
- $a^2 + b^2 + c^2 - ab - bc - ca = \frac{1}{2}\{(a-b)^2 + (b-c)^2 + (c-a)^2\}$
- $(a+b)^3 = a^3 + b^3 + 3ab(a+b)$
- $(a-b)^3 = a^3 - b^3 - 3ab(a-b)$
- $a^3 + b^3 = (a+b)(a^2 + b^2 - ab)$
- $a^3 - b^3 = (a-b)(a^2 + b^2 + ab)$
- $a^3 + b^3 + c^3 - 3abc = (a+b+c)(a^2 + b^2 + c^2 - ab - bc - ca)$

$$= \frac{1}{2}(a+b+c)\{(a-b)^2 + (b-c)^2 + (c-a)^2\}$$
$$= (a+b+c)[(a+b+c)^2 - 3(ab+bc+ca)]$$
$$= \frac{1}{2}(a+b+c)[3(a^2+b^2+c^2) - (a+b+c)^2]$$

- If $a^3 + b^3 + c^3 = 3abc$, then either $a = b = c$ or $a + b + c = 0$
- $(a+b+c)^2 = a^2 + b^2 + c^2 + 2(ab + bc + ac)$
- $a^4 + a^2b^2 + b^4 = (a^2 + ab + b^2)(a^2 - ab + b^2)$
- If $(x^2 + y^2 + z^2) = 0$, then $x = 0, y = 0, z = 0$
- If $x + \frac{1}{x} = a$, then $x^2 + \frac{1}{x^2} = a^2 - 2$
- If $x + \frac{1}{x} = a$, then $x^3 + \frac{1}{x^3} = a^3 - 3a$
- If $x - \frac{1}{x} = a$, then $x^3 - \frac{1}{x^3} = a^3 + 3a$
- If $x - \frac{1}{x} = a$, then $x^2 + \frac{1}{x^2} = a^2 + 2$
- If $x + \frac{1}{x} = a$, then $x - \frac{1}{x} = \sqrt{a^2 - 4}$
- If $x - \frac{1}{x} = a$, then $x + \frac{1}{x} = \sqrt{a^2 + 4}$
- If $x + \frac{1}{x} = a$, then $x^2 - \frac{1}{x^2} = a\sqrt{a^2 - 4}$
- If $x - \frac{1}{x} = a$, then $x^2 - \frac{1}{x^2} = a\sqrt{a^2 + 4}$
- If $x + \frac{1}{x} = \pm\sqrt{3}$, then $x^6 = -1$
- If $x + \frac{1}{x} = 1$, then $x^3 = -1$
- If $x + \frac{1}{x} = -1$, then $x^3 = 1$
- If $x + \frac{1}{x} = 2$, then $x = 1$,
- Similarly, if $x + \frac{1}{x} = -2$, then $x = -1$

Ex. 1 If $x + \frac{1}{x} = 3$, then find the value of $x^2 + \frac{1}{x^2}$.

Sol. Given, $x + \frac{1}{x} = 3 \Rightarrow x^2 + \frac{1}{x^2} = (3)^2 - 2 = 9 - 2 = 7$

Remainder Theorem

- Let $f(x)$ be a polynomial of degree m, greater than or equal 1 (i.e. $m \geq 1$) and a be any real number. If $f(x)$ is divided by $(x - a)$, then the remainder is $f(a)$.

Ex. 2 Find remainder when we divide $3x^4 - 2x^2 + 4x - 1$ by $2x - 1$

Sol. Let $f(x) = 3x^4 - 2x^2 + 4x - 1$

and $f(x)$ is divided by $2x - 1$

$\therefore \quad 2x - 1 = 0,\ 2x = 1,\ x = \frac{1}{2}$

$\therefore$ Remainder $= f\left(\frac{1}{2}\right) = 3\times\left(\frac{1}{2}\right)^4 - 2\times\left(\frac{1}{2}\right)^2 + 4\times\frac{1}{2} - 1$

$= \frac{3}{16} - \frac{1}{2} + 2 - 1 = \frac{3-8+32-16}{16} = \frac{11}{16}$

Linear Equation

An equation with one or more than one variable of degree 1 is called a linear equation. It is written as $ax + by + c = 0$

e.g., $2x + 5 = 0$

Consistency of Linear Equation

- Let us consider two linear equation $a_1x + b_1y + c_1 = 0$ and $a_2x + b_2y + c_2 = 0$
- If $\frac{a_1}{a_2} \neq \frac{b_1}{b_2}$, then equations are consistent and has unique solution.
- If $\frac{a_1}{a_2} = \frac{b_1}{b_2} = \frac{c_1}{c_2}$, then equations are consistent and have infinite solution.
- If $\frac{a_1}{a_2} = \frac{b_1}{b_2} \neq \frac{c_1}{c_2}$, then equations are inconsistent and have no solution.

Ex. 3 The value of k for which equation $2x + 3y - 7 = 0$ and $4x - ky - 14$ has infinite solution

Sol. We know, for infinite solution

$$\frac{a_1}{a_2} = \frac{b_1}{b_2} = \frac{c_1}{c_2}$$

Here, $a_1 = 2, b_1 = 3, c_1 = -7$ and $a_2 = 4, b_2 = -k, c_2 = -14$

$$\frac{2}{4} = \frac{3}{-k} = \frac{-7}{-14}$$

$\Rightarrow \quad -k = 6 \Rightarrow k = -6$

Quadratic Equations

An equation in which the highest power of the variable is two. It is written as $ax^2 + bx + c = 0$

e.g. $3x^2 + 2x + 5 = 0$

Formation of Quadratic Equations

If $ax^2 + bx + c = 0$, then Sum of roots $(\alpha + \beta) = -\frac{b}{a}$

Product of roots $(\alpha\beta) = \frac{c}{a}$

Where, α and β are roots of the given quadratic equation.

Nature of Roots of Quadratic Equation

The nature of roots of quadratic depend on the value of discriminant (D) $(D = b^2 - 4ac)$

- If $D > 0$, then roots are real and distinct
- If $D = 0$, then roots are real and equal
- If $D < 0$, then roots are imaginary

Cubic Equation

An equation in which highest power of the variable is three. It is written as $ax^3 + bx^2 + cx + d = 0$

Then, Sum of roots $(\alpha + \beta + \gamma) = \frac{-b}{a}$

Sum of its roots taken two at a time $(\alpha\beta + \beta\gamma + \gamma\alpha) = \frac{c}{a}$

Product of roots $(\alpha\beta\gamma) = \frac{-d}{a}$

Law of Indices

- $a^m \times a^n = a^{m+n}$
- $\frac{a^m}{a^n} = a^{m-n}$
- $(a^m)^n = a^{mn}$
- $\left(\frac{a}{b}\right)^n = \frac{a^n}{b^n}$
- $a^0 = 1$
- $a^{\frac{1}{n}} = \sqrt[n]{a}$

If a is negative number and n is an odd number then $(-a)^n = -a^n$

Laws of Surds

- $\sqrt[n]{a} = a^{\frac{1}{n}}$
- $\sqrt[n]{a} \times \sqrt[n]{b} = \sqrt[n]{ab}$
- $\frac{\sqrt[n]{a}}{\sqrt[n]{b}} = \sqrt[n]{\frac{a}{b}}$
- $\sqrt[m]{\sqrt[n]{a}} = \sqrt[mn]{a}$
- $(\sqrt[n]{a})^m = \sqrt[n]{a^m}$

Ex. 4 If $2x - \frac{2}{x} + 3 = 0$, then $x^3 - \frac{1}{x^3}$ is

Sol. Given, $2x - \frac{2}{x} + 3 = 0 \Rightarrow 2x - \frac{2}{x} = -3$

$\Rightarrow \quad 2\left(x - \frac{1}{x}\right) = -3 \Rightarrow x - \frac{1}{x} = \frac{-3}{2}$

Cube on both sides $x^3 - \frac{1}{x^3} - 3\left(x - \frac{1}{x}\right) = \left(\frac{-3}{2}\right)^3$

$\Rightarrow x^3 - \frac{1}{x^3} - 3\times\left(\frac{-3}{2}\right) = -\frac{27}{8} \Rightarrow x^3 - \frac{1}{x^3} = \frac{-27}{8} - \frac{9}{2}$

$\therefore \quad x^3 - \frac{1}{x^3} = \frac{-63}{8}$

SSC Exam Scanner

SSC CGL 2024 (Tier I & II)

1. $\dfrac{(a^5 \times b^3 \times c^7)}{(a^4 \times b^8 \times c^9)}$ in simplified form is
SSC CGL (Tier-II) 20/01/2025 Shift-I
(a) $(a^1) \times (b^{-5}) \times (c^{-2})$
(b) $(a^{-3}) \times (b^{-10}) \times (c^{-4})$
(c) $(a^{-1}) \times (b^4) \times (c^{-5})$
(d) $(a^6) \times (b^6) \times (c^{-4})$

2. If $x = 4 + \sqrt{6}$ and $y = 4 - \sqrt{6}$, then the value of $x^2 + y^2$ is
SSC CGL (Tier-II) 20/01/2025 Shift-I
(a) 43 (b) 42 (c) 51 (d) 44

3. Simplify
$(5z - 7y)^2 + (7z + 5y)^2 - 49z^2$
SSC CGL (Tier-II) 20/01/2025 Shift-I
(a) $25z^2 + 74y^2$ (b) $35z^2 + 70y^2$
(c) $26z^2 + 82y^2$ (d) $30z^2 + 83y^2$

4. Simplify
$(5z - 12y)^2 + (12z + 5y)^2 - 144z^2$
SSC CGL (Tier-II) 18/01/2025 Shift-I
(a) $25z^2 + 169y^2$ (b) $23z^2 + 174y^2$
(c) $30z^2 + 170y^2$ (d) $23z^2 + 177y^2$

5. If $x = 8 + \sqrt{5}$ and $y = 8 - \sqrt{5}$, then the value of $x^2 + y^2$ is:
SSC CGL (Tier-II) 18/01/2025 Shift-I
(a) 138 (b) 143
(c) 140 (d) 124

6. $\dfrac{(a^7 \times b^8 \times c^7)}{(a^9 \times b^5 \times c^4)}$ in simplified form is
SSC CGL (Tier-II) 18/01/2025 Shift-I
(a) $(a^0) \times (b^2) \times (c^1)$
(b) $(a^{-7}) \times (b^2) \times (c^{-4})$
(c) $(a^{-2}) \times (b^3) \times (c^3)$
(d) $(a^{-5}) \times (b^{-8}) \times (c^0)$

7. Find the value of y, if
$x - 2y + 2z = 16$, $x - y + z = 9$ and $2x - 3y - z = 9$.
SSC CGL (Tier-II) 18/01/2025 Shift-I
(a) 2 (b) −3 (c) −4 (d) 4

8. Find the value of the unknowns
$x + 1.5y + 2z = 5.5$
$x + 5y + 7z = 15$
$3x + 11y + 13z = 25$
SSC CGL (Tier-I) 26/09/2024 Shift-III
(a) $x = 2, y = -3, z = 4$
(b) $x = -3, y = 2, z = 4$
(c) $x = 4, y = -3, z = 2$
(d) $x = 2, y = 4, z = -3$

9. If $\dfrac{x}{x^2 - 2x + 1} = \dfrac{1}{3}$, then the value of $x^3 + \dfrac{1}{x^3}$ is
SSC CGL (Tier-I) 26/09/2024 Shift-III
(a) 110 (b) 130
(c) 160 (d) 180

10. Simplify $\dfrac{4x^2 - 49y^2}{2x + 7y} + 7y - 2x$
SSC CGL (Tier-I) 26/09/2024 Shift-III
(a) $4x - 14y$ (b) $7y$
(c) $4x$ (d) 0

11. If $2a - b = 3$ and $8a^3 - b^3 = 999$, then find the value of $4a^2 - b^2$.
SSC CGL (Tier-I) 26/09/2024 Shift-II
(a) 63 (b) 65 (c) 61 (d) 67

12. If $x = \sqrt{6} + 2$ and $y = \sqrt{6} - 2$, then what is the value of $\left(\dfrac{x}{y} + \dfrac{y}{x}\right)^2 - 3$?
SSC CGL (Tier-I) 26/09/2024 Shift-II
(a) 42 (b) 97 (c) 35 (d) 22

13. Given a linear equation in two variables: $5x + 7y - 8 = 0$, which of the following linear equations, along with the given equation, forms a system of linear equations having no solution?
SSC CGL (Tier-I) 26/09/2024 Shift-I
(a) $5x + 7y - 16 = 0$
(b) $7x + 5y - 8 = 0$
(c) $5x - 7y - 8 = 0$
(d) $10x + 14y - 16 = 0$

14. 'x' varies directly with the cube of 'y', and inversely with the sqaure of 'z'. If $x = \dfrac{1}{36}$ when $y = 2$ and $z = 3$, then what is the value of 800x when $y = 3$ and $z = 5$?
SSC CGL (Tier-I) 25/09/2024 Shift-III
(a) $\dfrac{9}{800}$ (b) 27 (c) $\dfrac{800}{9}$ (d) 9

15. Cindy bought 15 apples and 12 oranges and paid a sum of ₹ 447 for the purchase. Which of the statements given below is inconsistent with the information given in the previous statement, leading to no possible prices of the two fruits?
SSC CGL (Tier-I) 25/09/2024 Shift-III
(a) Purchased 25 apples and 20 oranges and paid a sum of ₹ 745
(b) Purchased 10 apples and 13 oranges and paid a sum of ₹ 353
(c) Purchased 12 apples and 8 oranges and paid a sum of ₹ 340
(d) Purchased 35 apples and 28 oranges and paid a sum of ₹ 1029

16. If $a^2 + b^2 = 148$ and $ab = 54$, then find the value of $\dfrac{a + b}{a - b}$.
SSC CGL (Tier-I) 25/09/2024 Shift-III
(a) $\dfrac{8}{\sqrt{10}}$ (b) $\dfrac{2}{\sqrt{10}}$ (c) $8\sqrt{7}$ (d) $5\sqrt{3}$

17. Find the value of 'k' for which the system of equations $4x + 6y = 7$ and $6x + (k + 4)y - 21 = 0$ has a unique solution. **SSC CGL (Tier-I) 25/09/2024 Shift-II**
(a) $k = 5$ (b) $k \neq 5$
(c) $k = 7$ (d) $k \neq 7$

18. The relation between K_1 and K_2 for which the system of linear equations $K_1x + 3y = 8$ and $4x + K_2y = 16$ represents coincident lines, is
SSC CGL (Tier-I) 25/09/2024 Shift-II
(a) $K_2 = 3K_1$ (b) $K_2 + 3K_1 = 0$
(c) $K_2 = K_1$ (d) $K_1 + K_2 = 0$

19. Find the values of 'a' and 'b' for which the system of equations $3x + y = 3$ and $(a - b)x + (a + b)y = 3a + b - 3$ has infinite solutions.
SSC CGL (Tier-I) 25/09/2024 Shift-I
(a) $a = 3, b = -\dfrac{2}{3}$ (b) $a = -\dfrac{3}{2}, b = 2$
(c) $a = 3, b = -\dfrac{3}{2}$ (d) $a = 2, b = -\dfrac{3}{2}$

20. If $x^2 + 7x + 8 = 0$, then find the value of $\dfrac{4x}{x^2 - 5x + 8}$.
SSC CGL (Tier-I) 25/09/2024 Shift-I
(a) $\dfrac{1}{2}$ (b) $\dfrac{-1}{4}$ (c) $\dfrac{-1}{3}$ (d) $\dfrac{1}{6}$

21. If $a^3 + \dfrac{1}{a^3} = 2(1(a > 0)$, then the value of $a + \dfrac{1}{a}$ is **SSC CGL (Tier-I) 25/09/2024 Shift-I**
(a) 1 (b) 3 (c) 2 (d) 4

22. If $a + b = c$, then the expression $a^3 + b^3 - c^3 + 3abc$ will be equal to
SSC CGL (Tier-I) 24/09/2024 Shift-III
(a) 0 (b) 3 (c) 2 (d) 1

23. Simplify the following expression.
$(3x + 17 - 2y)(3x - 17 - 2y)$
SSC CGL (Tier-I) 24/09/2024 Shift-I
(a) $9x^2 + 12xy + 4y^2 + 289$
(b) $9x^2 + 12xy + 4y^2 - 289$
(c) $9x^2 - 12xy + 4y^2 - 289$
(d) $9x^2 - 6xy + 4y^2 - 289$

24. What conclusion can be drawn about the solution of the following system of linear equations in two variables.
$3x + 2y = 7$
$2x + 3y = 7$
SSC CGL (Tier-I) 24/09/2024 Shift-I
(a) No solution
(b) Unique solution
(c) Infinite solutions
(d) More than two solutions

25. Let $3t - \frac{1}{3t} = 3$, then which of the following expressions has the value equal to 12?
SSC CGL (Tier-I) 23/09/2024 Shift-III
(a) $9t^2 + \frac{1}{9t^2} + 2$ (b) $9t^2 + \frac{1}{9t^2} - 2$
(c) $9t^2 + \frac{1}{9t^2} + 1$ (d) $9t^2 + \frac{1}{9t^2}$

26. If $3x + 2y = 10$ and $2xy = 7$, then find the value of $3x - 2y$ (if $3x - 2y > 0$).
SSC CGL (Tier-I) 23/09/2024 Shift-III
(a) 4 (b) 10 (c) 8 (d) 6

27. Ten chairs and six tables together cost ₹ 5140 three chairs and two tables together cost ₹ 1635. The cost of 1 chair and 1 table is
SSC CGL (Tier-I) 23/09/2024 Shift-II
(a) ₹ 900 (b) ₹ 600
(c) ₹ 800 (d) ₹ 700

28. If $a + b + c = 0$, then the value of $(a^2 + b^2 + 2ab)$ is equal to
SSC CGL (Tier-I) 23/09/2024 Shift-II
(a) c^2 (b) $-c^2$ (c) c (d) $-c$

29. Aman has certain number of notes of denomination ₹ 20 and ₹ 10 which amount to ₹ 390. If the numbers of notes of each kind are interchanged, then the new amount is ₹ 90 less than before. Find the number of notes of ₹ 20 denomination.
SSC CGL (Tier-I) 23/09/2024 Shift-I
(a) 16 (b) 12 (c) 15 (d) 14

30. For the equations $ax + (a^2 + 1)y = 4$ and $4x + ay = a^2$, which of the following statements is true?
SSC CGL (Tier-I) 19/09/2024 Shift-III
(a) If $a = 6$, then $x = \frac{325}{28}$, $y = \frac{25}{28}$ are the solutions.
(b) If $a = 6$, then $x = 48$, $y = 4$ are the solutions.
(c) If $a = -12$, then $x = \frac{325}{28}$, $y = -\frac{25}{28}$ are the solutions.
(d) If $a = -12$, then $x = 48$, $y = 4$ are the solutions.

31. If $\left(x + \frac{1}{x}\right) = 7$, $x > 0$. The positive value of $\left(x - \frac{1}{x}\right)$ is
SSC CGL (Tier-I) 19/09/2024 Shift-II
(a) $5\sqrt{4}$ (b) $5\sqrt{5}$
(c) $3\sqrt{5}$ (d) $4\sqrt{5}$

32. If $\left(a + \frac{1}{a}\right) = 7\sqrt{3}$, then what is the value of $\left(a^6 + \frac{1}{a^6}\right)$?
SSC CGL (Tier-I) 19/09/2024 Shift-I
(a) 3048190 (b) 3048542
(c) 3048132 (d) 3048625

33. Each of Ravi and Kavita had some marbles. Kavita had 12 more marbles than Ravi had. If each of them had one more marble, then three times the number of marbles Kavita would then have had would have been equal to four times the number of marbles Ravi would then have had. How many marbles did Kavita actually have?
SSC CGL (Tier-I) 19/09/2024 Shift-I
(a) 43 (b) 47 (c) 51 (d) 48

34. What number should be subtracted from $x^3 - 4x^2 - 8x + 11$ to make the number divisible by $(x + 2)$?
SSC CGL (Tier-I) 19/09/2024 Shift-I
(a) 9 (b) 5 (c) 3 (d) 7

35. If $3a + 2b = 27$ and $27a^3 + 8b^3 = 1458$, then find $2ab$.
SSC CGL (Tier-I) 18/09/2024 Shift-III
(a) 72 (b) 70 (c) 77 (d) 75

36. If $x + \frac{1}{x} = 2$, then find the value of $\left(x^{2733} + \frac{1}{x^{3356}}\right)$.
SSC CGL (Tier-I) 18/09/2024 Shift-II
(a) 1 (b) 2 (c) 0 (d) – 1

37. If $x = 7 - 4\sqrt{3}$, then find the value of $\left(x^2 + \frac{1}{x^2}\right)$.
SSC CGL (Tier-I) 18/09/2024 Shift-I
(a) 188 (b) 194
(c) 186 (d) 196

38. If the system of the following equations has the value of the variables as three consecutive integers, then the value of a is ....
$x\ y + z = 2a$
$x + 4y - 2z = 3(4 - a)$
$2x - 3y + 4z = 6 - 2a$
SSC CGL (Tier-I) 18/09/2024 Shift-I
(a) 2 (b) 4
(c) 1 (d) 3

39. There are y yellow marbles and b blue marbles in a box. 18% of the yellow marbles were added to 24% of the blue marbles and the total was 30. Three times the number of yellow marbles exceeds two times the number of blue marbles by 200. What is the ratio of y^2 to b^2?
SSC CGL (Tier-I) 17/09/2024 Shift-III
(a) 6 : 5 (b) 4 : 1
(c) 2 : 1 (d) 5 : 2

40. If $a^3 + 3a^2 + 3a = 7$, then the value of $a^2 + 2a$ is
SSC CGL (Tier-I) 17/09/2024 Shift-II
(a) 3 (b) 1 (c) 2 (d) 4

41. If $8a^3 + b^3 + 27c^3 = 18abc$, then the relation among a, b and c is
SSC CGL (Tier-I) 17/09/2024 Shift-II
(a) $b + 3c = 2a$ (b) $2a + b = 3c$
(c) $2a + 3c = b$ (d) $b + 3c = -2a$

42. For what value of k, the system of equations $4x + 12y + 36 = 0$ and $5x + ky + 45 = 0$ has an infinite number of solutions?
SSC CGL (Tier-I) 17/09/2024 Shift-II
(a) 20 (b) 25 (c) 22 (d) 15

43. If $x > 1$ and $x^2 + \frac{1}{x^2} = 83$, then $x^3 - \frac{1}{x^3}$ is
SSC CGL (Tier-I) 17/09/2024 Shift-I
(a) 884 (b) 876 (c) 754 (d) 756

44. For what value of k, the system of equations $kx - 15y + 7 = 0$ and $7x - 21y - 19 = 0$ has no solution?
SSC CGL (Tier-I) 17/09/2024 Shift-I
(a) 5 (b) 12 (c) 25 (d) 6

45. Simplify the following expression. $(g - h)^2 - (g + h)^2 + 4gh$
SSC CGL (Tier-I) 13/09/2024 Shift-III
(a) $4gh$ (b) $-4gh$
(c) 4 (d) 0

46. For which of the following values of a and b do the given equations, have no solution?
SSC CGL (Tier-I) 13/09/2024 Shift-III
$x - ay = 2 - a$
$(1 - a)x + 6y = a + b$
(a) $a = -3, b \neq 1$ (b) $a = 3, b \neq -1$
(c) $a = -3, b \neq -1$ (d) $a = 3, b \neq 1$

47. Simplify
$$\frac{25a^2 - 10ab - 48b^2}{5a + 6b} \times (5a + 8b)$$
SSC CGL (Tier-I) 13/09/2024 Shift-II
(a) $25a^2 - 64b^2$
(b) $(5a - 8b)^2$
(c) $(5a + 8b)^2$
(d) $25a^2 - 36b^2$

48. Let $a + b = 1$, then the value of $\left(\frac{1}{a^2} + \frac{1}{b^2} + \frac{2}{ab}\right)$ is:
SSC CGL (Tier-I) 13/09/2024 Shift-II
(a) $\frac{1}{a^2b^2}$ (b) $\frac{1}{ab}$
(c) $\frac{1}{a^2b}$ (d) $\frac{1}{ab^2}$

49. At a cafe, Rama bought drinks for her 7 friends at ₹ 240. Some of them wanted coffee, while others wanted black tea. A regular cup of coffee cost ₹ 40 and a regular cup of black tea cost ₹ 30. How many cups of tea did she purchase?
SSC CGL (Tier-I) 13/09/2024 Shift-I
(a) 5 (b) 4 (c) 3 (d) 6

50. Simplify the following expression.
$$\frac{(x-y)^3+(y-z)^3+(z-x)^3}{(x-y)(y-z)(z-x)}$$
SSC CGL (Tier-I) 13/09/2024 Shift-I

(a) 3 (b) 1 (c) 0 (d) 2

51. Find the values of x, y and z, so as to satisfy the equations given below:
$5x-3y+7z=22$; $3x-5y-2z=-46$; $2x-2y+5z=24$
SSC CGL (Tier-I) 12/09/2024 Shift-III

(a) $x=-5, y=3, z=-8$
(b) $x=5, y=-8, z=3$
(c) $x=-5, y=3, z=8$
(d) $x=-5, y=-3, z=8$

52. If $a^2+b^2+c^2=2(a+c-1)$, then the value of $a^3+b^3+c^3=?$
SSC CGL (Tier-I) 12/09/2024 Shift-III

(a) 0 (b) 2 (c) 4 (d) 1

53. Which of the following is the sum of the values of a and b if the equations $2x+y=a$, $8x+by=12$ have infinite solutions?
SSC CGL (Tier-I) 12/09/2024 Shift-III

(a) 16 (b) 9
(c) 7 (d) 18

54. If $m+n=24$, then $(m-16)^3+(n-8)^3$ is: **SSC CGL (Tier-I) 12/09/2024 Shift-II**

(a) 0 (b) 40
(c) 576 (d) 320

55. Let $t=\frac{2}{5}$, then the value of the expression $t^3+\left(\frac{3}{5}\right)^3+\frac{9}{5}t$ is:
SSC CGL (Tier-I) 12/09/2024 Shift-I

(a) $\frac{1}{5}$ (b) 1 (c) 2 (d) $\frac{1}{2}$

56. If $x+\frac{1}{9x}=3$, then the value of $9x^2+\frac{1}{9x^2}$ is
SSC CGL (Tier-I) 11/09/2024 Shift-III

(a) 87 (b) 81 (c) 77 (d) 79

57. Simplify the following expression.
$\left(\frac{3}{a}+3a\right)\left(\frac{9}{a^2}-9+9a^2\right)$ if $a=1$
SSC CGL (Tier-I) 11/09/2024 Shift-III

(a) 27 (b) 63 (c) 81 (d) 54

58. If $0.4x+0.16y=1.7$ and $0.3x+0.12y=3.4$, then which of the following is correct?
SSC CGL (Tier-I) 11/09/2024 Shift-II

(a) The system has finitely many solutions but not unique.
(b) The system has infinitely many solutions.
(c) The system has no solution.
(d) The system has unique solution.

59. Mrudula starts her job with a certain monthly salary and earns a fixed increment every year. If her salary was ₹ 28400 after six years of service and ₹ 52997 after fifteen years, find her annual increment.
SSC CGL (Tier-I) 11/09/2024 Shift-I

(a) ₹ 12002 (b) ₹ 1200
(c) ₹ 2733 (d) ₹ 1824

60. Solve the given set of three equations to get the value of the unknowns
$$x+2z=3$$
$$x+2y+3z=5$$
$$3x-5z=-13$$
SSC CGL (Tier-I) 11/09/2024 Shift-I

(a) $x=0, y=-1, z=2$
(b) $x=-1, y=0, z=2$
(c) $x=-1, y=2, z=0$
(d) $x=2, y=0, z=-1$

61. If $x+\frac{1}{x}=2\sqrt{10}$, where $x>1$, then the value of $\left(x^3-\frac{1}{x^3}\right)$ is
SSC CGL (Tier-I) 11/09/2024 Shift-I

(a) 221 (b) 234
(c) 198 (d) 216

62. If $x^2+y^2=280$ and $xy=120$, then find the value of $\frac{x-y}{x+y}$.
SSC CGL (Tier-I) 10/09/2024 Shift-III

(a) $\frac{1}{\sqrt{13}}$ (b) $\sqrt{15}$ (c) $\sqrt{13}$ (d) $\frac{1}{\sqrt{15}}$

63. If $\sqrt{x}+\frac{1}{\sqrt{x}}=7$, then the value of $x+\frac{1}{x}$ is equal to **SSC CGL (Tier-I) 10/09/2024 Shift-II**

(a) 47 (b) 49
(c) 51 (d) 45

64. If $a+\frac{1}{a}=12$, then find the value of $a^2+\frac{1}{a^2}$. **SSC CGL (Tier-I) 10/09/2024 Shift-I**

(a) 144 (b) 146
(c) 142 (d) 140

65. If the sum of three numbers is 18 and the sum of their squares is 36, then find the difference between the sum of their cubes and three times of their product.
SSC CGL (Tier-I) 10/09/2024 Shift-I

(a) 1449 (b) – 1944
(c) – 1494 (d) 4149

66. If x, y and z are positive number and $x+y+z=1$, then the least value of $\frac{1}{x}+\frac{1}{y}+\frac{1}{z}$ is
SSC CGL (Tier-I) 09/09/2024 Shift-III

(a) 7 (b) 5 (c) 9 (d) 11

67. If the equations $4x+(k-2)y+3=0$ and $(k-2)x+9y-5=0$ $(k>0)$ are parallel, then find the value of k^2+6. **SSC CGL (Tier-I) 09/09/2024 Shift-III**

(a) 68 (b) 70 (c) 72 (d) 64

68. Let $a+b=2c$, then which of the following expressions is true?
SSC CGL (Tier-I) 09/09/2024 Shift-III

(a) $a^2+2ac=b^2+2bc$
(b) $a^2-2bc=b^2-2ac$
(c) $a^2+2bc=b^2+2ac$
(d) $a^2-ac=b^2-bc$

69. R pays ₹ 100 to P with ₹ 5, ₹ 2 and ₹ 1 coins. The total number of coins used for paying are 40. What is the number of coins of denomination ₹ 5 in the payment?
SSC CGL (Tier-I) 09/09/2024 Shift-I

(a) 16 (b) 17 (c) 18 (d) 13

70. Simplify
$$\frac{x^3+15x^2+75x+125}{x^2-25}(x-5).$$
SSC CGL (Tier-I) 09/09/2024 Shift-I

(a) x^2+25 (b) $x^2+5x+25$
(c) $x^2+10x+25$ (d) x^2-25

SSC CGL 2023 (Tier I & II)

71. If two LED TVs and one mobile phone cost ₹ 31000, while two mobile phones and one LED TV cost ₹ 35000, then the value of one mobile phone is
SSC CGL (Tier-II) 07/03/2023 Shift-I

(a) ₹ 12000 (b) ₹ 13500
(c) ₹ 12500 (d) ₹ 13000

72. If $2^x+3^y=17$ and $2^{x+2}-3^{y+1}=5$, then **SSC CGL (Tier-II) 07/03/2023 Shift-I**

(a) $x=1, y=3$ (b) $x=1, y=2$
(c) $x=3, y=3$ (d) $x=3, y=2$

73. If $4x^2+y^2=40$ and $xy=6$, then find the value of $2x+y$.
SSC CGL (Tier-II) 06/03/2023 Shift-I

(a) 6 (b) 8 (c) 5 (d) 4

74. If the highest common factor (HCF) of x and y is 15, then the HCF of $36x^2-81y^2$ and $81x^2-9y^2$ is divisible by ....
SSC CGL (Tier-II) 06/03/2023 Shift-I

(a) 135 (b) 120
(c) 180 (d) 90

75. Rewa has some hens and some goats. If the total number of animal heads is 100 and the total number of animal feet is 348, then what is the total number of goats with Rewa?
SSC CGL (Tier-II) 03/03/2023 Shift-I

(a) 76 (b) 74
(c) 55 (d) 80

76. The LCM of $x^2 - 8x + 15$ and $x^2 - 5x + 6$ is

SSC CGL (Tier-II) 03/03/2023 Shift-I

(a) $(x-2)(x-3)(x-5)$
(b) $(x-6)^2(x+1)(x-3)$
(c) $(x-6)(x+1)(x-3)$
(d) $(x+6)(x+1)(x-3)$

77. What is the simplified form of the expression $(1+x)(1+x^2)(1+x^4)(1+x^8)(1-x)$?

SSC CGL (Tier-II) 03/03/2023 Shift-I

(a) $1-x^{40}$ (b) $1-x^{32}$
(c) $1-x^{16}$ (d) $1-x^{42}$

78. For what value of m will the system of equations $17x + my + 102 = 0$ and $23x + 299y + 138 = 0$ have infinite number of solutions?

SSC CGL (Tier-II) 02/03/2023 Shift-I

(a) 221 (b) 223 (c) 220 (d) 219

79. If $\left(x+\frac{1}{x}\right)=6$ and $x>1$, find the value of $\left(x^2-\frac{1}{x^2}\right)$.

SSC CGL (Tier-I) 27/07/2023 Shift-III

(a) $18\sqrt{2}$ (b) $30\sqrt{2}$
(c) $24\sqrt{2}$ (d) $12\sqrt{10}$

80. If $(a+b+c)=14$ and $(a^3+b^3+c^3-3abc)=98$, find the value of $(a^2+b^2+c^2)$.

SSC CGL (Tier-I) 27/07/2023 Shift-II

(a) 70 (b) 64
(c) 68 (d) 72

81. If $x^2-\frac{1}{x^2}=4\sqrt{2}$, what is the value of $x^4-\frac{1}{x^4}$?

SSC CGL (Tier-I) 27/07/2023 Shift-II

(a) $16\sqrt{2}$ (b) $8\sqrt{2}$
(c) $24\sqrt{2}$ (d) $32\sqrt{2}$

82. If $2x+3y=16$ and $xy=9$, then find $8x^3+27y^3$.

SSC CGL (Tier-I) 27/07/2023 Shift-I

(a) 1980 (b) 2980
(c) 1504 (d) 2189

83. Expand and simplify the algebraic expression $(x-5)^2+(x+3)^2+4x$

SSC CGL (Tier-I) 26/07/2023 Shift-IV

(a) $2(x^2-17)$
(b) $2(x^2+17)$
(c) (x^2+17)
(d) $2(x^2-5x+17)$

84. If $\left(x-\frac{1}{x}\right)=10$, what is the value of $\left(x^4+\frac{1}{x^4}\right)$?

SSC CGL (Tier-I) 26/07/2023 Shift-III

(a) 10404 (b) 10402
(c) 10406 (d) 10400

85. If $b=5$, determine the value of an expression $\left(\frac{5}{b}+5b\right)\left(\frac{25}{b^2}-25+25b^2\right)$ using an identity.

SSC CGL (Tier-I) 26/07/2023 Shift-III

(a) 25726 (b) 15626
(c) 15438 (d) 25636

86. If $(a^3+b^3+c^3-3abc)=405$ and $(a-b)^2+(b-c)^2+(c-a)^2=54$, find the value of $(a+b+c)$.

SSC CGL (Tier-I) 26/07/2023 Shift-II

(a) 15 (b) 45 (c) 9 (d) 27

87. If $(a+b+c)=13$ and $(ab+bc+ca)=54$, find the value of $(a^2+b^2+c^2)$.

SSC CGL (Tier-I) 26/07/2023 Shift-II

(a) 63 (b) 65 (c) 61 (d) 59

88. If $\left(x^2+\frac{1}{x^2}\right)=6$ and $0<x<1$, then what is the value of $x^4-\frac{1}{x^4}$?

SSC CGL (Tier-I) 26/07/2023 Shift-I

(a) $24\sqrt{2}$ (b) $-24\sqrt{2}$
(c) $-12\sqrt{10}$ (d) $12\sqrt{10}$

89. If $x=\frac{1}{x-3}$, $(x>0)$, then the value of $x+\frac{1}{x}$ is

SSC CGL (Tier-I) 26/07/2023 Shift-I

(a) $\sqrt{11}$ (b) $\sqrt{17}$ (c) $\sqrt{15}$ (d) $\sqrt{13}$

90. Simplify the expression $\frac{s^2+t^2+2st-u^2}{s^2-t^2-2tu-u^2}$, provided $(s+t+u)\neq 0$.

SSC CGL (Tier-I) 25/07/2023 Shift-IV

(a) $\frac{s+t-u}{s-t-u}$ (b) $\frac{s+t+u}{s-t+u}$
(c) $\frac{s-t-u}{s+t-u}$ (d) $\frac{s-t+u}{s+t+u}$

91. Simplify the expression $\frac{\sqrt{x}-\sqrt{y}}{\sqrt{x}+\sqrt{y}}$, where $x=2$ and $y=3$.

SSC CGL (Tier-I) 25/07/2023 Shift-IV

(a) $2\sqrt{6}-6$ (b) $\sqrt{6}-5$
(c) $5-2\sqrt{6}$ (d) $2\sqrt{6}-5$

92. If $(a+b-c)=20$, and $a^2+b^2+c^2=152$, then find the value of $a^3+b^3-c^3+3abc$.

SSC CGL (Tier-I) 25/07/2023 Shift-IV

(a) 480 (b) 720
(c) 640 (d) 560

93. If $\left(y+\frac{1}{y}\right)=4$, find the value of $\left(y^6+\frac{1}{y^6}\right)$.

SSC CGL (Tier-I) 25/07/2023 Shift-III

(a) 2702 (b) 2704
(c) 4096 (d) 2706

94. The cube of the sum of two given numbers is 1728, while the product of the two given numbers is 32. Find the positive difference between the cubes of the two given numbers.

SSC CGL (Tier-I) 25/07/2023 Shift-III

(a) 448 (b) 576
(c) 480 (d) 512

95. Simplify the following expression.
$\frac{x^2-2x-63}{x^2+14x+49}$

SSC CGL (Tier-I) 25/07/2023 Shift-III

(a) $\frac{x+9}{x+7}$ (b) $\frac{x-7}{x+7}$
(c) $\frac{x+7}{x-7}$ (d) $\frac{x-9}{x+7}$

96. If $7a-\frac{7}{a}+4=0$, then find $a^3-\frac{1}{a^3}-1$.

SSC CGL (Tier-I) 25/07/2023 Shift-II

(a) $\frac{-995}{343}$ (b) $\frac{-875}{248}$
(c) $\frac{-694}{315}$ (d) $\frac{-765}{262}$

97. If $p+q+r=pqr=\frac{1}{p}+\frac{1}{q}+\frac{1}{r}=1$, then find $p^3+q^3+r^3$.

SSC CGL (Tier-I) 25/07/2023 Shift-II

(a) 1 (b) −1 (c) 5 (d) −5

98. Simplify $\frac{256x^4-16y^4}{(80x^2-20y^2)(16x^2+4y^2)}$

SSC CGL (Tier-I) 25/07/2023 Shift-II

(a) 5 (b) $\frac{1}{20}$ (c) $\frac{1}{5}$ (d) $\frac{2}{5}$

99. If $x^2-15x+1=0$, what is the value of x^4-223x^2+6?

SSC CGL (Tier-I) 25/07/2023 Shift-I

(a) 9 (b) 5
(c) 6 (d) 0

100. Simplify $\frac{1}{2+2p}+\frac{1}{2+2q}+\frac{1}{2+2r}$, where $p=\frac{x}{y+z}$, if $q=\frac{y}{z+x}$ and $r=\frac{z}{x+y}$.

SSC CGL (Tier-I) 24/07/2023 Shift-IV

(a) 1 (b) $x+y+z$
(c) 2 (d) $\frac{1}{2}$

101. If $x+\frac{1}{x}=9$, then find $x^4+\frac{1}{x^4}$.

SSC CGL (Tier-I) 24/07/2023 Shift-IV

(a) 5431 (b) 6561
(c) 6156 (d) 6239

102. Simplify the following expression $(4x+1)^2-(4x+3)(4x-1)$

SSC CGL (Tier-I) 24/07/2023 Shift-II

(a) $(4x+1)$ (b) 4
(c) $(4x-3)$ (d) $4x$

103. The value of $\frac{p^2-(q-r)^2}{(p+r)^2-q^2}+\frac{q^2-(p-r)^2}{(p+q)^2-r^2}+\frac{r^2-(p-q)^2}{(q+r)^2-p^2}$ is

SSC CGL (Tier-I) 24/07/2023 Shift-I

(a) 1 (b) 2 (c) 0 (d) 3

104. If $a = 101$, $b = 102$ and $c = 103$, then $a^2 + b^2 + c^2 - ab - bc - ca =$ ....

SSC CGL (Tier-I) 24/07/2023 Shift-I

(a) 2 (b) 4 (c) 3 (d) 6

105. If $(a - b) = 1$, then what is the value of $(a^3 - b^3)$?

SSC CGL (Tier-I) 21/07/2023 Shift-IV

(a) $a^2 + ab + b^2$ (b) $(a + b)^2 + 3ab$
(c) $a^2 - ab + b^2$ (d) $a^2 + 2ab + b^2$

106. If $\left(x^2+\frac{1}{x^2}\right) = 18$, and $x > 0$, what is the value of $\left(x^3+\frac{1}{x^3}\right)$?

SSC CGL (Tier-I) 21/07/2023 Shift-IV

(a) $36\sqrt{5}$ (b) $40\sqrt{5}$
(c) $46\sqrt{5}$ (d) $34\sqrt{5}$

107. What is the value of $64x^3 + 36x^2y + 24xy^2 + 2y^3$, when $x = 3$ and $y = -4$?

SSC CGL (Tier-I) 21/07/2023 Shift-IV

(a) 304 (b) 1456
(c) 1584 (d) 432

108. Simplify the following expression. $[(1+p)(1+p^2)(1+p^4)(1+p^8)(1+p^{16})(1-p)-1]$

SSC CGL (Tier-I) 21/07/2023 Shift-III

(a) $-p^{32}$ (b) p^{32}
(c) $(1+p^{32})$ (d) $(1-p^{32})$

109. If x and y are positive numbers such that $x - y = 5$ and $xy = 150$, then the value of $(x + y)$ is

SSC CGL (Tier-I) 21/07/2023 Shift-III

(a) 45 (b) 25
(c) 35 (d) 15

110. If $\left(x^2-\frac{1}{x^2}\right) = 4\sqrt{6}$, and $x > 1$, what is the value of $\left(x^3-\frac{1}{x^3}\right)$?

SSC CGL (Tier-I) 21/07/2023 Shift-III

(a) $20\sqrt{2}$ (b) $24\sqrt{2}$
(c) $18\sqrt{2}$ (d) $22\sqrt{2}$

111. What is the value of $\left(\frac{1}{a}-\frac{1}{b}-\frac{1}{c}\right)$ if, $\frac{2a-5}{a}-\frac{4b-5}{b}+\frac{6c+5}{c}=0$?

SSC CGL (Tier-I) 21/07/2023 Shift-II

(a) $\frac{4}{5}$ (b) $-\frac{8}{5}$ (c) $\frac{2}{5}$ (d) $-\frac{12}{5}$

112. If $\left(x-\frac{1}{x}\right) = 2\sqrt{2}$, what is the value of $\left(x^6+\frac{1}{x^6}\right)$?

SSC CGL (Tier-I) 21/07/2023 Shift-II

(a) 1030 (b) 960
(c) 1000 (d) 970

113. What is the value of $(27x^3 + 58x^2y + 31xy^2 + 8y^3)$, when $x = 5$ and $y = -7$? SSC CGL (Tier-I) 21/07/2023 Shift-II

(a) 1924 (b) –1926
(c) –1924 (d) 1926

114. Simplify the given expression, $(a - 2b)(b - 3a) + (a + b)(a - 3b) - (b - 3a)(4a - 5b)$

SSC CGL (Tier-I) 21/07/2023 Shift-I

(a) $8a^2 + 10ab$
(b) $8a^2 + 10ab$
(c) $10a^2 - 14ab$
(d) $10a^2 - 4ab$

115. If $x + y = 7$ and $xy = 19$, then calculate the value of $x^2 + y^2$.

SSC CGL (Tier-I) 21/07/2023 Shift-I

(a) 17 (b) 12 (c) 11 (d) 19

116. If $(a + b + c) = 12$ and $(ab + bc + ca) = 47$, find the value of $(a^3 + b^3 + c^3 - 3abc)$.

SSC CGL (Tier-I) 21/07/2023 Shift-I

(a) 24 (b) 36 (c) 48 (d) 42

117. If $\left(x+\frac{1}{x}\right) = 3\sqrt{2}$, and $x > 1$, what is the value of $\left(x^8-\frac{1}{x^8}\right)$?

SSC CGL (Tier-I) 20/07/2023 Shift-IV

(a) $24364\sqrt{7}$ (b) $24384\sqrt{11}$
(c) $24384\sqrt{7}$ (d) $12192\sqrt{7}$

118. If $a + b + c = 7$, $ab + bc + ca = 11$ and $abc = -1$, then $a^3 + b^3 + c^3$ is equal to

SSC CGL (Tier-I) 20/07/2023 Shift-III

(a) 101 (b) 107 (c) 109 (d) 111

119. If $\left(x-\frac{1}{x}\right) = 2\sqrt{2}$, and $x > 1$, what is the value of $\left(x^6-\frac{1}{x^6}\right)$?

SSC CGL (Tier-I) 20/07/2023 Shift-III

(a) $372\sqrt{6}$ (b) $384\sqrt{6}$
(c) $396\sqrt{6}$ (d) $420\sqrt{6}$

120. If $x + y + z = 4$ and $x^2 + y^2 + z^2 = 12$, then find $xy + yz + xz$.

SSC CGL (Tier-I) 20/07/2023 Shift-II

(a) 4 (b) 6 (c) 7 (d) 2

121. If $x > 0$ and $x^4+\frac{1}{x^4} = 142$, what is the value of $x^7+\frac{1}{x^7}$?

SSC CGL (Tier-I) 20/07/2023 Shift-II

(a) $1561\sqrt{14}$ (b) $1563\sqrt{14}$
(c) $1560\sqrt{14}$ (d) $1562\sqrt{14}$

122. If $(a^3 + b^3 + c^3 - 3abc) = 405$ and $(a + b + c) = 15$, find the value of $(a-b)^2 + (b-c)^2 + (c-a)^2$.

SSC CGL (Tier-I) 20/07/2023 Shift-I

(a) 27 (b) 54 (c) 18 (d) 45

123. If $x+\frac{1}{x} = 2$, then find the value of $x^7+\frac{1}{x^{117}}$ is

SSC CGL (Tier-I) 19/07/2023 Shift-IV

(a) 1 (b) 4
(c) 3 (d) 2

124. If $x^2 - 7x + 1 = 0$ and $0 < x < 1$, what is the value of $x^2-\frac{1}{x^2}$?

SSC CGL (Tier-I) 19/07/2023 Shift-III

(a) $21\sqrt{5}$ (b) $-21\sqrt{5}$
(c) $28\sqrt{5}$ (d) $-28\sqrt{5}$

125. If $(a + b + c) = 12$ and $(a^2 + b^2 + c^2) = 50$, find the value of $(a^3 + b^3 + c^3 - 3abc)$.

SSC CGL (Tier-I) 19/07/2023 Shift-II

(a) 36 (b) 24 (c) 42 (d) 48

126. If $\left(3y-\frac{3}{y}\right) = 5$, find the value of $\left(y^2+\frac{1}{y^2}\right)$.

SSC CGL (Tier-I) 19/07/2023 Shift-II

(a) $\frac{47}{9}$ (b) $\frac{49}{9}$ (c) $\frac{41}{9}$ (d) $\frac{43}{9}$

127. Simplify the following. $\frac{3a+b}{2}-\frac{a-3b}{3}+2b$

SSC CGL (Tier-I) 19/07/2023 Shift-I

(a) $\frac{5(a+3b)}{6}$ (b) $\frac{7a+3b}{6}$
(c) $\frac{7(a+3b)}{6}$ (d) $\frac{a+3b}{6}$

128. If $\left(x+\frac{1}{x}\right) = 2\sqrt{2}$ and $x > 1$, what is the value of $\left(x^6-\frac{1}{x^6}\right)$?

SSC CGL (Tier-I) 19/07/2023 Shift-I

(a) $140\sqrt{2}$ (b) $116\sqrt{2}$
(c) $144\sqrt{2}$ (d) $128\sqrt{2}$

129. If $p=\frac{\sqrt{2}+1}{\sqrt{2}-1}$ and $q=\frac{\sqrt{2}-1}{\sqrt{2}+1}$, then find the value of $\frac{p^2}{q}+\frac{q^2}{p}$

SSC CGL (Tier-I) 18/07/2023 Shift-IV

(a) 188 (b) 196
(c) 200 (d) 198

130. If $a^2 + b^2 + c^2 = ab + bc + ac$, then the value of $\frac{11a^4+13b^4+17c^4}{17a^2b^2+9b^2c^2+15c^2a^2}$ is

SSC CGL (Tier-I) 18/07/2023 Shift-III

(a) 4 (b) 11 (c) 2 (d) 1

131. If $\left(x+\frac{1}{x}\right)=5$ and $x>1$, what is the value of $\left(x^8-\frac{1}{x^8}\right)$?
SSC CGL (Tier-I) 18/07/2023 Shift-III
(a) $60705\sqrt{21}$ (b) $60615\sqrt{21}$
(c) $60725\sqrt{21}$ (d) $60605\sqrt{21}$

132. If $x-\frac{1}{x}=-6$, what will be the value of $x^5-\frac{1}{x^5}$?
SSC CGL (Tier-I) 18/07/2023 Shift-II
(a) – 8898 (b) – 8896
(c) – 8886 (d) – 8892

133. If $(a+b+c)=19$ and $(a^2+b^2+c^2)=155$, find the value of $(a-b)^2+(b-c)^2+(c-a)^2$.
SSC CGL (Tier-I) 18/07/2023 Shift-II
(a) 104 (b) 108
(c) 100 (d) 98

134. What is the value of $\frac{x}{y}$, if $\frac{x-5y}{x+5y}=\frac{7}{13}$?
SSC CGL (Tier-I) 17/07/2023 Shift-IV
(a) $\frac{100}{7}$ (b) $\frac{50}{3}$ (c) $\frac{23}{7}$ (d) $\frac{24}{9}$

135. What is the value of $(27x^3-58x^2y+31xy^2-8y^3)$, when $x=-5$ and $y=-7$?
SSC CGL (Tier-I) 17/07/2023 Shift-IV
(a) –1926 (b) 1926
(c) 1924 (d) –1924

136. If $x+\frac{1}{x}=-6$, what will be the value of $x^5+\frac{1}{x^5}$?
SSC CGL (Tier-I) 17/07/2023 Shift-III
(a) – 7776 (b) – 6726
(c) – 6738 (d) – 6732

137. What is the value of the given expression?
$(a+b+c)^2-a^2-b^2-c^2$
SSC CGL (Tier-I) 17/07/2023 Shift-III
(a) $2abc$ (b) $2(ab+bc+ca)$
(c) $2(a+b+c)$ (d) $2ab+bc-2ca$

138. If $\left(x-\frac{1}{x}\right)=\sqrt{6}$, and $x>1$, what is the value of $\left(x^8-\frac{1}{x^8}\right)$?
SSC CGL (Tier-I) 17/07/2023 Shift-II
(a) $992\sqrt{15}$ (b) $1024\sqrt{15}$
(c) $1012\sqrt{15}$ (d) $998\sqrt{15}$

139. Simplify, $\frac{x^4-2x^2+1}{x^2-2x+1}$.
SSC CGL (Tier-I) 17/07/2023 Shift-II
(a) x^2+2x+2 (b) x^2+x+1
(c) x^2+2x+1 (d) x^2-2x+1

140. If $\left(x^2+\frac{1}{x^2}\right)=7$, and $0<x<1$ find the value of $x^2-\frac{1}{x^2}$.
SSC CGL (Tier-I) 17/07/2023 Shift-I
(a) $3\sqrt{5}$ (b) $4\sqrt{3}$ (c) $-4\sqrt{3}$ (d) $-3\sqrt{5}$

141. Simplify the following expression.
$(3x+5)^2+(3x-5)^2$
SSC CGL (Tier-I) 17/07/2023 Shift-I
(a) $500x$ (b) $450x$
(c) $9x^2+50$ (d) $2(9x^2+25)$

142. Simplify the given expression.
$y+2x-[y-(y-x+y)-\overline{(x+y)+y}]-2y$
SSC CGL (Tier-I) 17/07/2023 Shift-I
(a) $-y$ (b) $-2x$ (c) y (d) $2x$

143. If $x>0$, and $x^4+\frac{1}{x^4}=254$, what is the value of $x^5+\frac{1}{x^5}$?
SSC CGL (Tier-I) 14/07/2023 Shift-IV
(a) $717\sqrt{2}$ (b) $723\sqrt{2}$
(c) $720\sqrt{2}$ (d) $726\sqrt{2}$

144. If $x+\frac{1}{x}=7$, then the value of $x^6+\frac{1}{x^6}$ is
SSC CGL (Tier-I) 14/07/2023 Shift-III
(a) 113682 (b) 103682
(c) 103882 (d) 103862

145. What is the value of $64x^3+38x^2y+20xy^2+y^3$, when $x=3$ and $y=-4$?
SSC CGL (Tier-I) 14/07/2023 Shift-II
(a) 536 (b) 488 (c) 1236 (d) 1256

146. What is the value of $a^3+b^3+c^3$, if $(a+b+c)=0$?
SSC CGL (Tier-I) 14/07/2023 Shift-II
(a) $a^2+b^2+c^2-3abc$
(b) 0
(c) $3abc$
(d) $a^2+b^2+c^2-ab-bc-ca$

147. If $7b-\frac{1}{4b}=7$, then what is the value of $16b^2+\frac{1}{49b^2}$?
SSC CGL (Tier-I) 14/07/2023 Shift-I
(a) $\frac{120}{7}$ (b) $\frac{104}{7}$ (c) $\frac{80}{49}$ (d) $\frac{7}{2}$

148. What is the value of $(3x^3+5x^2y+12xy^2+7y^3)$, when $x=-4$ and $y=-1$?
SSC CGL (Tier-I) 14/07/2023 Shift-I
(a) – 329 (b) – 359
(c) – 361 (d) – 327

SSC CGL 2022 (Tier I)

149. If $a=-12$, $b=-6$ and $c=18$, then what is the value of $(2abc)/9$
SSC CGL (Tier-I) 13/12/2022 Shift-IV
(a) 554 (b) 288 (c) –288 (d) 144

150. If $a+b+c=5$, $a^3+b^3+c^3=85$ and $abc=25$, then find the value of $a^2+b^2+c^2-ab-bc-ca$.
SSC CGL (Tier-I) 13/12/2022 Shift-IV
(a) 2 (b) 4 (c) 6 (d) 8

151. If $x=2-2^{\frac{1}{3}}+2^{\frac{2}{3}}$, then find the value of x^3-6x^2+18x.
SSC CGL (Tier-I) 13/12/2022 Shift-IV
(a) 40 (b) 33 (c) 45 (d) 22

152. If $\frac{a}{b}+\frac{b}{a}=-1$ and $a-b=2$, then the value of a^3-b^3 is
SSC CGL (Tier-I) 13/12/2022 Shift-III
(a) 0 (b) $\frac{1}{2}$ (c) 1 (d) –1

153. If $\frac{r}{13}+\frac{13}{r}=1$, then the value of r^3 is SSC CGL (Tier-I) 13/12/2022 Shift-III
(a) –2157 (b) 2197
(c) 2157 (d) –2197

154. Which of the following statement is correct? SSC CGL (Tier-I) 13/12/2022 Shift-III
I. The value of $100^2-99^2+98^2-97^2+96^2-95^2+94^2-93^2+.....+22^2-21^2$ is 4840.
II. The value of $\left(k^2+\frac{1}{k^2}\right)\left(k-\frac{1}{k}\right)\left(k^4+\frac{1}{k^4}\right)\left(k+\frac{1}{k}\right)\left(k^4-\frac{1}{k^4}\right)$ is $k^{16}-\frac{1}{k^{16}}$.
(a) Neither I nor II
(b) Both I and II
(c) Only II
(d) Only I

155. Which of the following statement is correct? SSC CGL (Tier-I) 13/12/2022 Shift-II
I. If $x=12$, $y=-2$ and $z=-10$, then $x^3+y^3+z^3=720$
II. If $x+y=48$ and $4xy=128$, then the value of $4x^2+4y^2$ is 8960
(a) Both I and II (b) Neither I nor II
(c) Only I (d) Only II

156. If $2p+q=19$ and $8p^3+q^3=361$, then find the value of pq.
SSC CGL (Tier-I) 13/12/2022 Shift-II
(a) 57 (b) 59 (c) 58 (d) 56

157. If $k+\frac{1}{k}+2=0$ and $k<0$, then what is the value of $k^{11}+\frac{1}{k^4}$?
SSC CGL (Tier-I) 13/12/2022 Shift-I
(a) 0 (b) –2 (c) –1 (d) –170

158. If $x+\frac{1}{x}=6$, then find the value of $\frac{3x}{2x^2-5x+2}$.
SSC CGL (Tier-I) 13/12/2022 Shift-I
(a) 1 (b) $\frac{3}{7}$ (c) $\frac{2}{3}$ (d) 0

159. If the roots of $6x^2 + 13x + 7 = 0$ are α, β, then find the equation where roots are α^2, β^2.
SSC CGL (Tier-I) 13/12/2022 Shift-I

(a) $36x^2 - 87x + 49 = 0$
(b) $36x^2 - 85x - 49 = 0$
(c) $36x^2 - 85x + 49 = 0$
(d) $36x^2 + 87x - 49 = 0$

160. If $x + y + z = 0$ and $x^2 + y^2 + z^2 = 40$, then what is the value of $xy + yz + zx$?
SSC CGL (Tier-I) 12/12/2022 Shift-IV

(a) –20 (b) 5 (c) –5 (d) –10

161. If $x^4 + \frac{16}{x^4} = 15617$, $x > 0$, then find the value of $x + \frac{2}{x}$.
SSC CGL (Tier-I) 12/12/2022 Shift-III

(a) $\sqrt{121}$ (b) $\sqrt{129}$ (c) $\sqrt{123}$ (d) $\sqrt{127}$

162. If $p = 8.15$, $q = 9.06$ and $r = -17.21$, then the value of $p^3 + q^3 + r^3 - 3pqr$ is **SSC CGL (Tier-I) 12/12/2022 Shift-III**

(a) –3.81 (b) –5.62
(c) 4.75 (d) 0

163. If $\frac{x}{8} + \frac{8}{x} = 1$, then the value of x^3 is **SSC CGL (Tier-I) 12/12/2022 Shift-II**

(a) –256 (b) –512 (c) 256 (d) 512

164. What is the value of $a^2 + b^2 + c^2 - 2ab - 2bc + 2ca$?
SSC CGL (Tier-I) 12/12/2022 Shift-II

(a) $(2a + b + c)^2$ (b) $(a - b + c)^2$
(c) $(a - b - 2c)^2$ (d) $(a + 2b - c)^2$

165. If $5x - \frac{5}{x} + 6 = 0$, then $x^2 + \frac{1}{x^2}$ is
SSC CGL (Tier-I) 12/12/2022 Shift-I

(a) $\frac{86}{25}$ (b) $\frac{43}{12}$ (c) $\frac{81}{10}$ (d) $\frac{86}{11}$

166. If $a = 26$ and $b = 22$, then the value of $\frac{a^3 - b^3}{a^2 - b^2} - \frac{3ab}{a + b}$ is ....
SSC CGL (Tier-I) 12/12/2022 Shift-I

(a) $\frac{5}{3}$ (b) $\frac{13}{11}$ (c) $\frac{1}{3}$ (d) $\frac{11}{13}$

167. If $m + \frac{1}{m-2} = 4$, then find the value of $(m-2)^2 + \frac{1}{(m-2)^2}$.
SSC CGL (Tier-I) 12/12/2022 Shift-I

(a) –2 (b) 4 (c) 0 (d) 2

168. $a^3 + b^3 + c^3 = 3abc$, if.......... .
SSC CGL (Tier-I) 09/12/2022 Shift-IV

(a) $a = b = c$ (b) $a + b + c = 0$
(c) $a + b + c = 1$ (d) $a + b + c = -1$

169. If $y + \frac{1}{y} = 11$, then the value of $y^3 - \frac{1}{y^3}$ is **SSC CGL (Tier-I) 09/12/2022 Shift-IV**

(a) $345\sqrt{13}$ (b) $360\sqrt{13}$
(c) $352\sqrt{13}$ (d) $368\sqrt{13}$

170. If $\left(x - \frac{1}{x}\right)^2 = 12$, what is the value of $\left(x^2 - \frac{1}{x^2}\right)$, given that $x > 0$?
SSC CGL (Tier-I) 09/12/2022 Shift-IV

(a) $6\sqrt{2}$ (b) $8\sqrt{3}$
(c) $6\sqrt{3}$ (d) $8\sqrt{2}$

171. If $k + \frac{1}{k} = 4$, then what is the value of $k^4 + \frac{1}{k^4}$?
SSC CGL (Tier-I) 09/12/2022 Shift-II

(a) 410 (b) 192 (c) 212 (d) 194

172. If $x^2 + \frac{1}{x^2} = 66$, the value of $x - \frac{1}{x}$ is ...... **SSC CGL (Tier-I) 09/12/2022 Shift-II**

(a) 10 (b) 8 (c) 9 (d) 6

173. If $x + y + z = 0$, then the value of $\frac{x^2}{yz} + \frac{y^2}{zx} + \frac{z^2}{xy}$ is
SSC CGL (Tier-I) 09/12/2022 Shift-I

(a) 3 (b) 1 (c) 0 (d) 2

174. The value of $\frac{(p-q)^3 + (q-r)^3 + (r-p)^3}{12(p-q)(q-r)(r-p)}$, where $p \neq q \neq r$ is equal to
SSC CGL (Tier-I) 09/12/2022 Shift-I

(a) $\frac{1}{9}$ (b) $\frac{1}{3}$ (c) $\frac{1}{4}$ (d) $\frac{1}{2}$

175. What is the value of $(a + b)^3 - a^3 + b^3$?
SSC CGL (Tier-I) 09/12/2022 Shift-I

(a) $-3ab(a - b) + 2b^3$
(b) $3ab(a + b) + 2b^3$
(c) $3ab(a - b)b^3$
(d) $-3ab(a + b) + b^3$

176. If $x + \frac{1}{x} = 2\sqrt{5}$ where $x > 1$, then the value of $x^3 - \frac{1}{x^3}$ is
SSC CGL (Tier-I) 08/12/2022 Shift-IV

(a) 82 (b) 76 (c) 86 (d) 78

177. What is the value of $a^2 + b^2 + c^2$, if $a + b + c = 9$ and $ab + bc + ca = 23$?
SSC CGL (Tier-I) 08/12/2022 Shift-IV

(a) 22 (b) 32 (c) 49 (d) 35

178. If $4(z + 7)(2z - 1) = Az^2 + Bz + C$, then the value of $A + B + C$ is
SSC CGL (Tier-I) 08/12/2022 Shift-III

(a) 28 (b) 32 (c) 74 (d) 81

179. If $abc = 5$, what is the value of

$$\left(\frac{1}{1 + a + b^{-1}} + \frac{1}{1 + b + 5c^{-1}} + \frac{1}{1 + \frac{c}{5} + a^{-1}}\right)?$$

SSC CGL (Tier-I) 08/12/2022 Shift-III

(a) 5 (b) 1
(c) $\frac{1}{5}$ (d) $(a + b + c)$

180. If $y = 1 + \sqrt{3} + \sqrt{4}$, then the value of $2y^4 - 8y^3 - 6y^2 + 28y - 84$ is
SSC CGL (Tier-I) 08/12/2022 Shift-II

(a) $40\sqrt{3}$ (b) $80\sqrt{3}$
(c) $20\sqrt{3}$ (d) $60\sqrt{3}$

181. If $x = \frac{\sqrt{5} - \sqrt{4}}{\sqrt{5} + \sqrt{4}}$ and $y = \frac{\sqrt{5} + \sqrt{4}}{\sqrt{5} - \sqrt{4}}$, then the value of $\frac{x^2 - xy + y^2}{x^2 + xy + y^2} = ?$

SSC CGL (Tier-I) 08/12/2022 Shift-II

(a) $\frac{361}{363}$ (b) $\frac{341}{343}$ (c) $\frac{384}{387}$ (d) $\frac{321}{323}$

182. If $\frac{2p}{p^2 - 5p + 1} = \frac{1}{10}$, $p \neq 0$, then the value of $\left(p + \frac{1}{p}\right)$ is

SSC CGL (Tier-I) 08/12/2022 Shift-II

(a) 10 (b) 25 (c) 1 (d) 15

183. If m and n are two positive real numbers such that $9m^2 + n^2 - 40$ and $mn = 4$, then the value of $3m + n$ is **SSC CGL (Tier-I) 08/12/2022 Shift-I**

(a) 160 (b) 64 (c) 10 (d) 8

184. What is the value of $(a + b)^2 - (a - b)^2$?
SSC CGL (Tier-I) 08/12/2022 Shift-I

(a) $2(a^2 + b^2)$ (b) $4(a^2 + b^2)$
(c) $8ab$ (d) $4ab$

185. The factors of $x^2 + 4y^2 + 4y - 4xy - 2x - 8$ are
SSC CGL (Tier-I) 08/12/2022 Shift-I

(a) $(x - 2y - 4)(x - 2y + 2)$
(b) $(x^2 - 2y - 4)(x^2 - 2y + 2)$
(c) $(x + 2y - 4)(x + 2y + 2)$
(d) $(x^2 - 2y - 4)(x^2 + 2y + 2)$

186. Find the remainder, when we divide $3x^4 - 2x^2 + 4x - 1$ by $2x - 1$.
SSC CGL (Tier-I) 07/12/2022 Shift-IV

(a) 2 (b) 3 (c) $\frac{11}{16}$ (d) $\frac{15}{16}$

187. If $(a + 1)^2 + (a + 2)^2 = 16$, then what is the value of $40 + 12a + 4a^2$?
SSC CGL (Tier-I) 07/12/2022 Shift-IV

(a) 56 (b) 62 (c) 74 (d) 52

188. Which of the following statement is correct ? **SSC CGL (Tier-I) 07/12/2022 Shift-IV**

I. If $k + \frac{1}{k} = 12$, then $k^2 + \frac{1}{k^2} = 142$

II. The value of $\left(k^2 + \frac{1}{k^2}\right)\left(k - \frac{1}{k}\right)\left(k^4 + \frac{1}{k^4}\right)\left(k + \frac{1}{k}\right)$ is $k^{16} - \frac{1}{k^{16}}$.

(a) Only I (b) Neither I nor II
(c) Both I and II (d) Only II

189. If $x+\frac{1}{x}=7$, find the value of $x^3+\frac{1}{x^3}$. SSC CGL (Tier-I) 07/12/2022 Shift-IV

(a) 343 (b) 322 (c) 340 (d) 332

190. Simplify $\sqrt{36x^2-108x+81}$
SSC CGL (Tier-I) 07/12/2022 Shift-III

(a) $6x-9$ (b) $2x-9$
(c) $5x-9$ (d) $3x-3$

191. Simplify the given expression.
$(5x+8y)(25x^2+64y^2-40xy)$
SSC CGL (Tier-I) 07/12/2022 Shift-III

(a) $125x^3-512y^3$
(b) $25x^3+64y^3$
(c) $125x^3+512y^3$
(d) $25x^3-64y^3$

192. If $x^4+\frac{1}{x^4}=194$ and $x^3+\frac{1}{x^3}=?$
SSC CGL (Tier-I) 07/12/2022 Shift-III

(a) 52 (b) 58 (c) 76 (d) 67

193. If $k+\frac{1}{k}+2=0$ and $k<0$, then what is the value of $k^{10}+\frac{1}{k^{11}}$?
SSC CGL (Tier-I) 07/12/2022 Shift-II

(a) 1 (b) 0
(c) – 1 (d) 2

194. $3\left[a-\frac{1}{a}\right]+\left[a-\frac{1}{a}\right]^3=?$
SSC CGL (Tier-I) 07/12/2022 Shift-II

(a) $a^2-\frac{1}{a^3}$ (b) $a^3-\frac{1}{a^3}$
(c) $a^3+\frac{1}{a^3}$ (d) $a^2-\frac{1}{a^2}$

195. If $x^2+y^2+2y+4x+5=0$, then $\frac{x+y}{x-y}=$ ________.
SSC CGL (Tier-I) 07/12/2022 Shift-I

(a) 3 (b) $\frac{1}{3}$
(c) – 1 (d) 3

196. The value of $\frac{(x-y)^3+(y-z)^3+(z-x)^3}{6(x-y)(y-z)(z-x)}$, where $x\neq y\neq z$, is equal to
SSC CGL (Tier-I) 07/12/2022 Shift-I

(a) $\frac{1}{4}$ (b) $\frac{1}{2}$ (c) $\frac{1}{3}$ (d) $\frac{1}{9}$

197. If, for a non-zero x, $5x^2+7x+5=0$, then the value of $x^3+\frac{1}{x^3}$ is SSC CGL (Tier-I) 06/12/2022 Shift-IV

(a) $\frac{496}{125}$ (b) $\frac{532}{343}$
(c) $\frac{125}{532}$ (d) $\frac{182}{125}$

198. If $mx^m-nx^n=0$, then what is the value of $\frac{1}{x^m+x^n}+\frac{1}{x^m-x^n}$ terms of x^n is where x, m, n are >0
SSC CGL (Tier-I) 06/12/2022 Shift-IV

(a) $2mn/(x^n(n^2+m^2)$
(b) $2mn/(x^n(m^2-n^2)$
(c) $2mn/(x^n(m^2+n^2)$
(d) $2mn/(x^n(n^2-m^2)$

199. If $(4x-7y)=11$ and $xy=8$. What is the value of $16x^2+49y^2$, given that x and y are positive numbers?
SSC CGL (Tier-I) 06/12/2022 Shift-III

(a) 596 (b) 484
(c) 569 (d) 448

200. If $\frac{a}{b}+\frac{b}{a}=1$ and $a+b=2$, then the value of a^3+b^3 is
SSC CGL (Tier-I) 06/12/2022 Shift-II

(a) 0 (b) 3 (c) 1 (d) 2

201. $8m^3-n^3$ is equal to
SSC CGL (Tier-I) 06/12/2022 Shift-II

(a) $(2m-n)(4m^2+4mn+n^2)$
(b) $(2m-n)(4m^2+2mn+n^2)$
(c) $(2m-n)(4m^2-2mn+n^2)$
(d) $(2m-n)(4m^2-4mn+n^2)$

202. If $p=7+4\sqrt{3}$, then what is the value of $\frac{p^6+p^4+p^2+1}{p^3}$?
SSC CGL (Tier-I) 06/12/2022 Shift-II

(a) 2617 (b) 2167
(c) 2716 (d) 2176

203. If $x^2+y^2+z^2=xy+yz+zx$ and $x=1$, then find the value of $\frac{10x^4+5y^4+7z^4}{13x^2y^2+6y^2z^2+3z^2x^2}$
SSC CGL (Tier-I) 05/12/2022 Shift-IV

(a) 2 (b) 0 (c) – 1 (d) 1

204. If $x+\frac{1}{2x}=3$, then evaluate $8x^3+\frac{1}{x^3}$.
SSC CGL (Tier-I) 05/12/2022 Shift-IV

(a) 212 (b) 216
(c) 180 (d) 196

205. If $x^2-2xy=84$ and $x-y=-10$, then the value of y is
SSC CGL (Tier-I) 05/12/2022 Shift-IV

(a) 2 (b) 1 (c) 4 (d) 3

206. Select the correct algebraic expression.
SSC CGL (Tier-I) 05/12/2022 Shift-III

(a) $ab-a-b+1=(a-1)(b-1)$
(b) $ab+a-b+1=(1-a)(1-b)(1-a)(1+b)$
(c) $ab-a-b+1=(1-a)(b-1)$
(d) $ab-a-b+1=(a-1)(1-b)$

207. If $x^2=y+z$, $y^2=z+x$ and $z^2=x+y$, then value of $\frac{1}{x+1}\times\frac{1}{y+1}\times\frac{1}{z+1}$ is
SSC CGL (Tier-I) 05/12/2022 Shift-II

(a) 4 (b) –1 (c) 2 (d) 1

208. If $\frac{1}{x^2+a^2}=x^2-a^2$, then the value of x is SSC CGL (Tier-I) 05/12/2022 Shift-II

(a) $(1-a^4)^{1/4}$ (b) a
(c) $(a^4-1)^{1/4}$ (d) $(a^4+1)^{1/4}$

209. If $x+\frac{1}{x}=-14$, and $x<-1$, what will be the value of $x^2-\frac{1}{x^2}$?
SSC CGL (Tier-I) 05/12/2022 Shift-I

(a) $112\sqrt{3}$ (b) $140\sqrt{2}$
(c) $-140\sqrt{2}$ (d) $-112\sqrt{3}$

210. If $k^4+\frac{1}{k^4}=47$, then what is the value of $k^3+\frac{1}{k^3}$?
SSC CGL (Tier-I) 05/12/2022 Shift-I

(a) 4.5 (b) 9
(c) 18 (d) 54

211. The simplified form of $(x+2y)^3+(x-2y)^3$ is
SSC CGL (Tier-I) 05/12/2022 Shift-I

(a) x^3-8y^3 (b) x^3+8y^3
(c) $2x^3-24xy^2$ (d) $2x^3+24xy^2$

212. What is the possible value of $(a+b+c)-3$, if $a^2+b^2+c^2=9$ and $ab+bc+ca=8$?
SSC CGL (Tier-I) 03/12/2022 Shift-IV

(a) 5 (b) 3
(c) 9 (d) 2

213. If $\frac{\sqrt{5}+\sqrt{3}}{\sqrt{5}-\sqrt{3}}=a+b\sqrt{15}$, then the value of a is
SSC CGL (Tier-I) 03/12/2022 Shift-IV

(a) 5 (b) 4 (c) 8 (d) 3

214. $(mx+n)$ is a factor of
SSC CGL (Tier-I) 03/12/2022 Shift-IV

(a) $m^2x^2+2nx+n^2$
(b) $m^2x^2+2mnx+n^2$
(c) $m^2x^2+2mn+n^2$
(d) $m^2x^2-2mn+n^2$

215. Find the value of the following expression. $12^3+(-8)^3+(-4)^3$
SSC CGL (Tier-I) 03/12/2022 Shift-III

(a) 952 (b) 1152
(c) 1052 (d) 852

216. If $8a^3+27b^3=16$ and $2a+3b=4$, then find the value of $16a^4+81b^4$.
SSC CGL (Tier-I) 03/12/2022 Shift-III

(a) 26 (b) 30
(c) 28 (d) 32

217. If $x = 3 + 2\sqrt{2}$, $x > 0$, then the value of $\sqrt{x} - \frac{1}{\sqrt{x}}$ is

SSC CGL (Tier-I) 03/12/2022 Shift-II

(a) 1 (b) $\sqrt{2}$
(c) 2 (d) $2\sqrt{2}$

218. If $x + \frac{1}{x} = -2$, then what is the value of $x^{17} + x^{-17} + x^{12} + x^{-12}$

SSC CGL (Tier-I) 03/12/2022 Shift-II

(a) – 2 (b) – 1
(c) 1 (d) 0

219. If $x - y = 1$ and $x^2 + y^2 = 41$ where $x, y \geq 0$, then the value of $x + y$ will be SSC CGL (Tier-I) 03/12/2022 Shift-II

(a) 9 (b) 8 (c) 6 (d) 7

220. If $\left(4a + \frac{5}{a} + 5\right) = 14$, what is the value of $\left(16a^2 + \frac{25}{a^2}\right)$?

SSC CGL (Tier-I) 03/12/2022 Shift-I

(a) 25 (b) 36
(c) 41 (d) 40

221. The factors of $x^4 + x^2 + 25$ are

SSC CGL (Tier-I) 03/12/2022 Shift-I

(a) $(x^2 + 3x - 5)(x^2 - 3x + 5)$
(b) $(x^2 + 3x + 5)(x^2 - 3x + 5)$
(c) $(x^2 - 3x + 5)(x^2 - 3x + 5)$
(d) $(x^2 + 3x + 5)(x^2 + 3x + 5)$

222. If $x - \frac{1}{x} = 13$, what will be the value of $x^4 + \frac{1}{x^4}$?

SSC CGL (Tier-I) 03/12/2022 Shift-I

(a) 28561 (b) 29243
(c) 27887 (d) 29239

223. If $x + \frac{1}{x} = 8$, then find the value of $\frac{5x}{x^2 - 8x + 2}$.

SSC CGL (Tier-I) 02/12/2022 Shift-IV

(a) 3 (b) 4 (c) 0 (d) 5

224. Which of the following statement is correct? SSC CGL (Tier-I) 02/12/2022 Shift-IV

I. The value of $100^2 - 99^2 + 98^2 - 97^2 + 96^2 - 95^2 + 94^2 - 93^2 + ...+ 2^2 - 1^2$ is 5050.

II. If $8x + \frac{8}{x} = -16$ and $x < 0$, then the value of $x^{197} + x^{-197}$ is 2.

(a) Only I (b) Only II
(c) Both I and II (d) Neither I nor II

225. If $K + \frac{1}{K} = 3$, then what is the value of $\frac{1}{K^3} + K^3$?

SSC CGL (Tier-I) 02/12/2022 Shift-IV

(a) 36 (b) 10
(c) 18 (d) 54

226. If $x = \frac{\sqrt{5} - 2}{\sqrt{5} + 2}$, then the value of $x^2 + x^{-2}$ is

SSC CGL (Tier-I) 02/12/2022 Shift-I

(a) 350 (b) 345
(c) 284 (d) 322

227. Simplify $x + 3(y + x - 2) - (x + y)$.

SSC CGL (Tier-I) 02/12/2022 Shift-I

(a) $x + 2y - 6$ (b) $2x + y - 6$
(c) $2x + 3y - 6$ (d) $3x + 2y - 6$

228. If $x > 0$, and $x^4 + \frac{1}{x^4} = 2207$, what is the value of $x^7 + \frac{1}{x^7}$?

SSC CGL (Tier-I) 02/12/2022 Shift-I

(a) 710649 (b) 710647
(c) 710654 (d) 710661

229. If $y + \frac{1}{y} = 3$, then what is the value of $\frac{1}{y^3} + y^3 + 2$?

SSC CGL (Tier-I) 01/12/2022 Shift-III

(a) 24 (b) 18 (c) 20 (d) 29

230. If $x + y = 36$, then find $(x - 27)^3 + (y - 9)^3$.

SSC CGL (Tier-I) 01/12/2022 Shift-III

(a) 1 (b) 81 (c) $2y$ (d) 0

231. If $a + b = 11$ and $ab = 35$, then what is the value of $(a^4 + b^4)$?

SSC CGL (Tier-I) 01/12/2022 Shift-III

(a) 151 (b) 261
(c) 124 (d) 102

232. k is a negative number such that $k + k^{-1} = -2$, then what is the value of $\frac{k^2 + 4k - 2}{k^2 + k - 5}$?

SSC CGL (Tier-I) 01/12/2022 Shift-II

(a) 7 (b) 1 (c) – 7 (d) – 1

233. If $x^2 - 5x + 1 = 0$, then the value of $\frac{x^6 + x^4 + x^2 + 1}{5x^3} = ?$

SSC CGL (Tier-I) 01/12/2022 Shift-I

(a) 30 (b) 25 (c) 23 (d) 28

SSC CGL 2021 & 2020 (Tier I)

234. What is the coefficient of x^2 in the expansion of $\left(5 - \frac{x^2}{3}\right)^3$?

SSC CGL (Tier-I) 24/08/2021 Shift-III

(a) –25 (b) $-\frac{25}{3}$
(c) 25 (d) $-\frac{5}{3}$

235. Given that, $x^8 - 34x^4 + 1 = 0$, $x > 0$. What is the value of $(x^3 - x^{-3})$?

SSC CGL (Tier-I) 24/08/2021 Shift-III

(a) 14 (b) 12 (c) 18 (d) 16

236. If $y = 2x + 1$, then what is the value of $(8x^3 - y^3 + 6xy)$?

SSC CGL (Tier-I) 24/08/2021 Shift-II

(a) 1 (b) – 1 (c) 15 (d) –15

237. Simplify the following expression.

$$\frac{5(a^6 - b^6)^3 + 5(b^6 - c^6)^3 + 5(c^6 - a^6)^3}{2(a^3 - b^3)^3 + 2(b^3 - c^3)^3 + 2(c^3 - a^3)^3}$$

SSC CGL (Tier-I) 24/08/2021 Shift-II

(a) $\frac{5}{2}(a^3 + b^3)(b^3 - c^3)(c^3 - a^3)$
(b) $\frac{5}{2}(a^3 - b^3)(b^3 + c^3)(c^3 + a^3)$
(c) $\frac{5}{2}(a^3 - b^3)(b^3 - c^3)(c^3 + a^3)$
(d) $\frac{5}{2}(a^3 + b^3)(b^3 + c^3)(c^3 + a^3)$

238. If $x - \frac{2}{x} = 15$, then what is the value of $\left(x^2 + \frac{4}{x^2}\right)$?

SSC CGL (Tier-I) 24/08/2021 Shift-II

(a) 229 (b) 227 (c) 221 (d) 223

239. If $2x + 3y + 1 = 0$, then what is the value of $(8x^3 + 8 + 27y^3 - 18xy)$?

SSC CGL (Tier-I) 24/08/2021 Shift-I

(a) –7 (b) 7 (c) –9 (d) 9

240. If $a^4 + b^4 + a^2b^2 = 273$ and $a^2 + b^2 - ab = 21$, then one of the values of $\left(\frac{1}{a} + \frac{1}{b}\right)$ is

SSC CGL (Tier-I) 24/08/2021 Shift-I

(a) $-\frac{9}{4}$ (b) $-\frac{3}{4}$ (c) $\frac{9}{8}$ (d) $\frac{3}{2}$

241. If $(x + 6)^3 + (2x + 3)^3 + (3x + 5)^3 = (3x + 18)(2x + 3)(3x + 5)$, then what is the value of x ?

SSC CGL (Tier-I) 23/08/2021 Shift-II

(a) $-\frac{5}{3}$ (b) $\frac{5}{3}$ (c) $-\frac{7}{3}$ (d) $\frac{7}{3}$

242. If $x + \frac{1}{x} = \frac{17}{4}$, $x > 1$, then what is the value of $x - \frac{1}{x}$?

SSC CGL (Tier-I) 23/08/2021 Shift-I

(a) $\frac{8}{3}$ (b) $\frac{15}{4}$ (c) $\frac{3}{2}$ (d) $\frac{9}{4}$

243. If $2x^2 - 7x + 5 = 0$, then what is the value of $x^3 + \frac{125}{8x^3}$?

SSC CGL (Tier-I) 23/08/2021 Shift-I

(a) $12\frac{5}{8}$ (b) $16\frac{5}{8}$ (c) $18\frac{5}{8}$ (d) $10\frac{5}{8}$

244. If $8 + 2px^2 - 36x - 27x^3 = (2 - 3x)^3$, then what is the value of p?

SSC CGL (Tier-I) 23/08/2021 Shift-I

(a) 27 (b) 9 (c) –27 (d) 54

245. If $\sqrt{x} - \frac{1}{\sqrt{x}} = \sqrt{7}$, then the value of $x^2 + \frac{1}{x^2}$ is SSC CGL (Tier-I) 20/08/2021 Shift-II

(a) 81 (b) 60 (c) 79 (d) 75

246. If $\frac{x}{y} + \frac{y}{x} = 2, (x, y \neq 0)$, then the value of $(x - y)$ is
SSC CGL (Tier-I) 20/08/2021 Shift-II
(a) 1 (b) 0 (c) 2 (d) – 2

247. Simplify $(x - y + z)^2 - (x - y - z)^2$.
SSC CGL (Tier-I) 20/08/2021 Shift-I
(a) $4xz - 4yz$ (b) $2xz + 2yz$
(c) $4yz - 4xz$ (d) $4xz + 4yz$

248. If $\left(2a + \frac{3}{a} - 1\right) = 11$, what is the value of $\left(4a^2 + \frac{9}{a^2}\right)$?
SSC CGL (Tier-I) 20/08/2021 Shift-I
(a) 121 (b) 148 (c) 132 (d) 110

249. If $a^2 + b^2 + c^2 + 216 = 12(a + b - 2c)$, then $\sqrt{ab - bc - ca}$ is
SSC CGL (Tier-I) 20/08/2021 Shift-I
(a) $3\sqrt{5}$ (b) $8\sqrt{5}$
(c) $6\sqrt{5}$ (d) $4\sqrt{5}$

250. If $a^3 - b^3 = 2349$ and $(a - b) = 9$, then $(a + b)^2 - ab$ is equal to
SSC CGL (Tier-I) 18/08/2021 Shift-III
(a) 280 (b) 244
(c) 261 (d) 229

251. If $x - \frac{1}{x} = \sqrt{77}$, then one of the values of $x^3 + \frac{1}{x^3}$ is
SSC CGL (Tier-I) 18/08/2021 Shift-III
(a) $80\sqrt{77}$ (b) 702
(c) $77\sqrt{77}$ (d) $3\sqrt{77}$

252. If $a + b + c = 0$, then what is the value of $\frac{(b+c)^2}{bc} + \frac{(c+a)^2}{ca} + \frac{(a+b)^2}{ab}$?
SSC CGL (Tier-I) 18/08/2021 Shift-III
(a) 1 (b) – 3
(c) – 1 (d) 3

253. If $x + y = 3$ and $\frac{1}{x} + \frac{1}{y} = -\frac{3}{10}$, then the value of $(x^2 + y^2)$ is
SSC CGL (Tier-I) 18/08/2021 Shift-I
(a) 29 (b) 28
(c) 26 (d) 34

254. If $x^2 + 9y^2 + 4z^2 = 12(x - 2y + 2z) - 88$, then the value of $(x - 3y + z)$ is
SSC CGL (Tier-I) 17/08/2021 Shift-III
(a) 11 (b) 13 (c) 10 (d) 5

255. If $4x^4 = 5x^2 - 1, x > \frac{1}{\sqrt{2}}$, then what is the value of $(2x^2 - x - 1)$?
SSC CGL (Tier-I) 17/08/2021 Shift-III
(a) 1 (b) –2 (c) 0 (d) 2

256. If $(54\sqrt{2}x^3 + 24\sqrt{3}y^3) \div (\sqrt{18}x + \sqrt{12}y) = Ax^2 + By^2 + Cxy$, then what is the value of $A^2 - (B^2 + C^2)$?
SSC CGL (Tier-I) 17/08/2021 Shift-I
(a) 12 (b) – 36
(c) – 24 (d) 24

257. If $x + y + z = 7, x^2 + y^2 + z^2 = 85$ and $x^3 + y^3 + z^3 = 913$, then the value of $\sqrt[3]{xyz}$ is
SSC CGL (Tier-I) 17/08/2021 Shift-I
(a) 1 (b) 2 (c) 4 (d) 8

258. If $x^2 + 4y^2 = 53$ and $x - 2y = 5$, then what is the value of $x^3 - 8y^3$?
SSC CGL (Tier-I) 16/08/2021 Shift-III
(a) 155 (b) 335
(c) –85 (d) 85

259. If $x + y = 2$ and $\frac{1}{x} + \frac{1}{y} = \frac{18}{5}$, then the value of $(x^3 + y^3)$ is
SSC CGL (Tier-I) 16/08/2021 Shift-III
(a) $4\frac{2}{3}$ (b) $4\frac{3}{5}$
(c) $3\frac{1}{5}$ (d) $3\frac{1}{3}$

260. If $x + y + z = 2$ and $xy + yz + zx = -11$, then the value of $x^3 + y^3 + z^3 - 3xyz$ is
SSC CGL (Tier-I) 16/08/2021 Shift-I
(a) 78 (b) 71 (c) 74 (d) 69

261. If $2x^2 - 8x - 1 = 0$, then what is the value of $8x^3 - \frac{1}{x^3}$?
SSC CGL (Tier-I) 13/08/2021 Shift-III
(a) 560 (b) 524 (c) 464 (d) 540

262. If $x^4 + \frac{1}{x^4} = 727, x > 1$, then what is the value of $\left(x - \frac{1}{x}\right)$?
SSC CGL (Tier-I) 13/08/2021 Shift-III
(a) 6 (b) 5 (c) – 5 (d) – 6

263. If $x - \frac{1}{x} = 1$, then what is the value of $x^8 + \frac{1}{x^8}$?
SSC CGL (Tier-I) 13/08/2021 Shift-III
(a) 119 (b) – 1
(c) 3 (d) 47

264. If $x + y = 4$ and $\frac{1}{x} + \frac{1}{y} = \frac{16}{15}$, then what is the value of $(x^3 + y^3)$?
SSC CGL (Tier-I) 13/08/2021 Shift-I
(a) 18 (b) 16 (c) 19 (d) 21

265. If $x + y + z = 10$ and $xy + yz + zx = 15$, then find the value of $x^3 + y^3 + z^3 - 3xyz$.
SSC CGL (Tier-I) 07/03/2020 Shift-II
(a) 525 (b) 575
(c) 550 (d) 660

266. If $a^2 + b^2 + c^2 = 300$ and $ab + bc + ca = 50$, then what is the value of $a + b + c$? (given that a, b and c are all positive).
SSC CGL (Tier-I) 07/03/2020 Shift-II
(a) 25 (b) 22 (c) 20 (d) 15

267. Expand $\left(\frac{x}{3} + \frac{y}{5}\right)^3$
SSC CGL (Tier-I) 07/03/2020 Shift-II
(a) $\frac{x^3}{27} + \frac{x^2y}{25} + \frac{xy^2}{25} + \frac{y^3}{125}$
(b) $\frac{x^3}{27} + \frac{x^2y}{15} + \frac{xy^2}{25} + \frac{y^3}{125}$
(c) $\frac{x^3}{25} + \frac{x^2y}{15} + \frac{xy^2}{25} + \frac{y^3}{125}$
(d) $\frac{x^3}{27} + \frac{xy}{15} + \frac{xy^2}{25} + \frac{y^3}{125}$

268. If $1 - 64x^3 - 12x + px^2 = (1 - 4x)^3$, then the value of p is
SSC CGL (Tier-I) 07/03/2020 Shift-I
(a) 48 (b) – 12 (c) – 48 (d) 16

269. If $b + c = ax, c + a = by, a + b = cz$, then the value of $\frac{1}{9}\left[\frac{1}{x+1} + \frac{1}{y+1} + \frac{1}{z+1}\right]$ is
SSC CGL (Tier-I) 06/03/2020 Shift-III
(a) 0 (b) 1 (c) $\frac{1}{9}$ (d) $\frac{1}{3}$

270. If $x^2 - 4x + 4 = 0$, then the value of $16\left(x^4 - \frac{1}{x^4}\right)$ is
SSC CGL (Tier-I) 06/03/2020 Shift-III
(a) $\frac{127}{16}$ (b) 127 (c) $\frac{255}{16}$ (d) 255

271. If $a^3 + \frac{1}{a^3} = 52$, then the value of $2\left(a + \frac{1}{a}\right)$ is
SSC CGL (Tier-I) 06/03/2020 Shift-III
(a) 4 (b) 8 (c) 6 (d) 2

272. The coefficient of x in $(x - 3y)^3$ is
SSC CGL (Tier-I) 06/03/2020 Shift-II
(a) $-3y^2$ (b) $27y^2$
(c) $-27y^2$ (d) $3y^2$

273. If the value of $(a + b - 2)^2 + (b + c - 5)^2 + (c + a - 5)^2 = 0$, then the value of $\sqrt{(b+c)^a + (c+a)^b - 1}$ is
SSC CGL (Tier-I) 06/03/2020 Shift-I
(a) 1 (b) 2 (c) 3 (d) 0

274. If $3^a = 27^b = 81^c$ and $abc = 144$, then the value of $12\left(\frac{1}{a} + \frac{1}{2b} + \frac{1}{5c}\right)$ is
SSC CGL (Tier-I) 06/03/2020 Shift-I
(a) $\frac{18}{120}$ (b) $\frac{18}{10}$ (c) $\frac{33}{10}$ (d) $\frac{17}{120}$

275. The coefficient of x^2 in $(2x + y)^3$ is
SSC CGL (Tier-I) 05/03/2020 Shift-III
(a) $12y^2$ (b) $12y$
(c) 8 (d) 12

276. $(a+b+c-d)^2 - (a-b-c+d)^2 = ?$
SSC CGL (Tier-I) 05/03/2020 Shift-III
(a) $2a(b + c + d)$ (b) $4a(b + c - d)$
(c) $2a(b + c - d)$ (d) $4a(b + c + d)$

277. $\dfrac{x^2(x-4)^2}{(x+4)^2-4x} \div \dfrac{(x^2-4x)^3}{(x+4)^2} \times \dfrac{64-x^3}{16-x^2}$ is equal to

SSC CGL (Tier-I) 05/03/2020 Shift-II

(a) $\dfrac{x-4}{x+4}$ (b) $\dfrac{x+4}{x(4-x)}$

(c) $\dfrac{x+4}{x(x-4)}$ (d) $\dfrac{x+4}{x-4}$

278. If $x^2 - 2\sqrt{5}x + 1 = 0$, then what is the value of $x^5 + \dfrac{1}{x^5}$?

SSC CGL (Tier-I) 05/03/2020 Shift-I

(a) $408\sqrt{5}$ (b) $610\sqrt{5}$

(c) $406\sqrt{5}$ (d) $612\sqrt{5}$

279. If $P = \dfrac{x^3+y^3}{(x-y)^2+3xy}$,

$Q = \dfrac{(x+y)^2-3xy}{x^3-y^3}$

and $R = \dfrac{(x+y)^2+(x-y)^2}{x^2-y^2}$, then what is the value of $(P \div Q) \times R$?

SSC CGL (Tier-I) 05/03/2020 Shift-I

(a) $2xy$ (b) $2(x^2+y^2)$

(c) x^2+y^2 (d) $4xy$

280. If $16a^4 + 36a^2b^2 + 81b^4 = 91$ and $4a^2 + 9b^2 - 6ab = 13$, then what is the value of $3ab$?

SSC CGL (Tier-I) 05/03/2020 Shift-I

(a) -3 (b) 5

(c) $\dfrac{3}{2}$ (d) $-\dfrac{3}{2}$

281. If $2x^2 + y^2 + 8z^2 - 2\sqrt{2}xy + 4\sqrt{2}yz - 8zx = (Ax + y + Bz)^2$, then the value of $(A^2 + B^2 - AB)$ is

SSC CGL (Tier-I) 04/03/2020 Shift-III

(a) 16 (b) 14

(c) 6 (d) 18

282. If $x + y + z = 3$ and $x^2 + y^2 + z^2 = 101$, then what is the value of $\sqrt{x^3 + y^3 + z^3 - 3xyz}$?

SSC CGL (Tier-I) 04/03/2020 Shift-III

(a) 19 (b) 21

(c) 24 (d) 28

SSC CPO SI 2024-2020

283. If $2a + 2b + c = 0$, then find the value of $\dfrac{4a^2+4b^2+4c^2}{5c^2-8ab}$.

SSC CPO 29/06/2024 Shift-III

(a) -1 (b) 1

(c) $-2\sqrt{3}$ (d) $2\sqrt{3}$

284. If $a = (\sqrt{2}-1)^{\frac{1}{3}}$, then the value of $\left(a - \dfrac{1}{a}\right)^3 + 3\left(a - \dfrac{1}{a}\right)$ is

SSC CPO 29/06/2024 Shift-III

(a) $\sqrt{2}$ (b) 2 (c) -2 (d) $-\sqrt{2}$

285. If $x^2 - 6x - 1 = 0$, then find the value of $x^2 + \dfrac{1}{x^2} - 8$.

SSC CPO 29/06/2024 Shift-III

(a) 34 (b) 32

(c) 28 (d) 30

286. 18 students of a class took part in a quiz. If the number of girls is 8 more than the number of boys, find the product of the number of boys and girls. **SSC CPO 29/06/2024 Shift-II**

(a) 63 (b) 36 (c) 56 (d) 65

287. If $a + b + c = 13$ and $ab + bc + ca = 22$, then the value of $a^3 + b^3 + c^3 - 3abc$ is .... **SSC CPO 29/06/2024 Shift-II**

(a) 1225 (b) 1625

(c) 1339 (d) 1911

288. If $x^2 + 4y^2 + 2x + 1 = 0$, then find the value of $x^{39} + y^{36}$.

SSC CPO 29/06/2024 Shift-II

(a) 1 (b) -1 (c) 2 (d) -2

289. Determine the value of the product $(4a + 3b)(16a^2 - 12ab + 9b^2)$ for $a = 2$ and $b = 3$. **SSC CPO 29/06/2024 Shift-I**

(a) 1141 (b) 1231

(c) 1241 (d) 1131

290. If $x = 11$, then the value of $(x^5 - 12x^4 + 12x^3 - 12x^2 + 12x - 1)$ is **SSC CPO 28/06/2024 Shift-III**

(a) 14 (b) 9 (c) 8 (d) 10

291. If $\dfrac{a}{b} + \dfrac{b}{a} = 1, a \neq 0, b \neq 0$, then find the value of $\dfrac{a^3+b^3}{3ab}$.

SSC CPO 28/06/2024 Shift-III

(a) 3 (b) 2 (c) -3 (d) 0

292. If the polynomial $(2x^3 + ax^2 + 3x - 5)$ and $(x^3 + x^2 - 2x + a)$ leave the same remainder, when divided by $(x-2)$, find the remainder

SSC CPO 28/06/2024 Shift-III.

(a) 4 (b) 2 (c) 3 (d) 5

293. If $(a-18)^2 + (b-12)^2 + (c-6)^2 = 0$, then find the value of $(a+b+c)^{\frac{1}{2}}$.

SSC CPO 28/06/2024 Shift-II

(a) ± 3 (b) ± 2

(c) ± 4 (d) ± 6

294. If $x = 110$, $y = 111$, $z = 112$, then find the value of $x^3 + y^3 + z^3 - 3xyz$.

SSC CPO 28/06/2024 Shift-I

(a) 999 (b) 995

(c) 997 (d) 991

295. If $a + 2b + 3c = 0$, then what is the value of $(a^3 + 8b^3 + 27c^3)$?

SSC CPO 28/06/2024 Shift-I

(a) $18\,abc$ (b) $12\,abc$

(c) $6\,abc$ (d) 0

296. If $x + \dfrac{1}{x} = 2$, then find the value of $\left(x^4 + \dfrac{4}{x^4}\right)\left(x^3 - \dfrac{4}{x^3}\right)$

SSC CPO 27/06/2024 Shift-III

(a) -10 (b) 10 (c) -15 (d) 15

297. If $x = 3y + 4$, then what is the value of $(x^3 - 27y^3 - 36xy)$?

SSC CPO 27/06/2024 Shift-II

(a) 8 (b) 1 (c) 64 (d) 27

298. If $\alpha + \beta + \gamma = 0$, then $\dfrac{3\beta^2 + \alpha^2 + \gamma^2}{2\beta^2 - \alpha\gamma} = ?$ **SSC CPO 27/06/2024 Shift-II**

(a) $\dfrac{1}{4}$ (b) 1 (c) $\dfrac{1}{2}$ (d) 2

299. The possible value of x satisfying $\dfrac{(143 \div 13 \times x - 3 \times 3)}{(6^2 - 7 \times 5 + x^2)} = 1$ is

SSC CPO 27/06/2024 Shift-I

(a) 4 (b) 1 (c) 3 (d) 2

300. The sum of two numbers x and y (where x is greater than y) is equal to four times of their difference. Find the value of $\dfrac{5xy}{3(x^2-y^2)}$.

SSC CPO 27/06/2024 Shift-I

(a) $\dfrac{25}{16}$ (b) 16 (c) $2\dfrac{3}{16}$ (d) 25

301. Simplify the given expression. $(x-2y)(y-3x) + (x+y)(x-y) + (x-3y)(2x+y)$

SSC CPO 05/10/2023 Shift-III

(a) $2y(x-3y)$

(b) $2y(x+3y)$

(c) $2x(x-3y)$

(d) $2x(x+3y)$

302. Simplify the given expression. $b + 2a - [(3b+a) - (2a+b) + 2a] - a$

SSC CPO 05/10/2023 Shift-III

(a) $-a$ (b) b (c) $-b$ (d) a

303. If $a + b = 10$ and $ab = 6$, then the value of $a^3 + b^3$ is

SSC CPO 03/10/2023 Shift-I

(a) 800 (b) 820 (c) 860 (d) 840

304. If $\dfrac{x}{y} + \dfrac{y}{x} = 1$ and $x + y = 2$, then the value of $x^3 + y^3$ is

SSC CPO 03/10/2023 Shift-I

(a) 1 (b) 3 (c) 0 (d) 2

305. If $r = 55$, then the value of $r(r^2 + r + 3)$ is: **SSC CPO 03/10/2023 Shift-I**

(a) 105000 (b) 176615

(c) 175616 (d) 175615

306. If a, b and c are positive integers such that $a^2 + b^2 = 82$ and $b^2 + c^2 = 65$, then the value of $2a + 7b - 3c$ is **SSC CPO 11/11/2022 Shift-I**

(a) 2 (b) 5 (c) 49 (d) 1

307. If $x(x-5)=-1$, then the value of $x^3(x^3-110)=?$ SSC CPO 11/11/2022 Shift-I
(a) 0 (b) −1 (c) 1 (d) 2

308. If $x+y=10$, $2xy=48$ and $x>y$, then find $2x-y$. SSC CPO 10/11/2022 Shift-I
(a) 6 (b) 8 (c) 4 (d) 3

309. What are the values of x and y, respectively, from the following equations? SSC CPO 10/11/2022 Shift-I
$6x+7y=5xy$, $10y-4x=4xy$
(a) 3 and 4 (b) 4 and 5
(c) 2 and 4 (d) 2 and 5

310. If $a+b+c=0$, then the value of $\frac{a^2}{bc}+\frac{b^2}{ca}+\frac{c^2}{ab}$ is SSC CPO 25/11/2020 Shift-II
(a) 1 (b) 3 (c) −1 (d) 0

311. If $a^2+b^2=82$ and $ab=9$, then a possible value of a^3+b^3 is SSC CPO 25/11/2020 Shift-II
(a) 720 (b) 750 (c) 830 (d) 730

312. If $(5\sqrt{5}x^3-3\sqrt{3}y^3)\div(\sqrt{5}x-\sqrt{3}y)=(Ax^2+By^2+Cxy)$, then what is the value of $(3A-B-\sqrt{15}C)$? SSC CPO 25/11/2020 Shift-I
(a) − 3 (b) − 5 (c) 8 (d) 12

313. If $x^4+x^{-4}=194$, $x>0$, then what is the value of $x+\frac{1}{x}+2$? SSC CPO 25/11/2020 Shift-I
(a) 8 (b) 14 (c) 6 (d) 4

314. If $x+y+z=17$, $xyz=171$ and $xy+yz+zx=111$, then the value of $\sqrt[3]{x^3+y^3+z^3+xyz}$ is SSC CPO 24/11/2020 Shift-I
(a) − 64 (b) 4 (c) 0 (d) − 4

315. If $x^2-3x+1=0$, then the value of $\left(x^4+\frac{1}{x^2}\right)\div(x^2+1)$ is SSC CPO 24/11/2020 Shift-I
(a) 5 (b) 6 (c) 9 (d) 7

316. If $x^2+8y^2+12y-4xy+9=0$, then the value of $(7x+8y)$ is SSC CPO 24/11/2020 Shift-I
(a) − 33 (b) 9 (c) 33 (d) − 9

317. If $a^2+b^2+c^2+216=12(a+b-2c)$, then $\sqrt{ab-bc+ca}$ is SSC CPO 23/11/2020 Shift-I
(a) 8 (b) 3 (c) 6 (d) 4

SSC CHSL 2024 & 2023 (Tier I & II)

318. Simplify:
$(2z-5y)^2+(5z+2y)^2-25z^2$. SSC CHSL (Tier-II) 18/11/2024 Shift-I
(a) $19y^2-4z^2$ (b) $29y^2-4z^2$
(c) $29y^2+4z^2$ (d) $19y^2+4z^2$

319. For what value of k ($k>0$) will the lines $5x+ky-2=0$ and $(k+1)x+4y+7=0$ be parallel? SSC CHSL (Tier-I) 10/07/2024 Shift-IV
(a) 4 (b) 3 (c) 2 (d) 5

320. The cost of 21 pencils and 9 pens is ₹ 276 and the cost of 6 pencils and 3 pens is ₹ 84 The cost of 1 pencil and 1 pen is SSC CHSL (Tier-I) 10/07/2024 Shift-III
(a) ₹ 20 (b) ₹ 10 (c) ₹ 40 (d) ₹ 30

321. In an election, a voter has choices to vote for one candidate out of three candidates. There is also an option 'None Of The Above' (NOTA) to reject all candidates. The three candidates get votes that are 6 times NOTA. The winner gets votes that are twice the second runner-up's votes. The first runner-up gets 900 votes more than NOTA and defeats the second runner-up by 150 votes. What is the total number of votes polled? SSC CHSL (Tier-I) 05/07/2024 Shift-IV
(a) 17715 (b) 15177
(c) 11025 (d) 11577

322. If the average of a number and its reciprocal is 2, then the average of its cube and its reciprocal is equal to SSC CHSL (Tier-I) 04/07/2024 Shift-III
(a) 28 (b) 26 (c) 48 (d) 36

323. Find the remainder, when we divide $2x^3-3x^2+6x-4$ by $2x-3$. SSC CHSL (Tier-I) 04/07/2024 Shift-III
(a) 5 (b) 6 (c) −5 (d) −6

324. There are 160 multiple choice questions in a test. 4 marks are allotted for a correct answer and 1 mark is deducted for a wrong answer or un-attempted question from the total score of correct answers. If a candidate scored 400 marks in the test, how many questions did he answer correctly? SSC CHSL (Tier-I) 03/07/2024 Shift-IV
(a) 110 (b) 115 (c) 112 (d) 120

325. Solve the following system of linear equations.
$x+y+z=15$, $2x-y+z=12$ and $x-y-z=-1$ SSC CHSL (Tier-I) 03/07/2024 Shift-III
(a) $x=7, y=5, z=3$
(b) $x=2, y=5, z=3$
(c) $x=7, y=2, z=3$
(d) $x=7, y=5, z=1$

326. If the point of intersection of lines $x+y=2$ and $2x-y=1$ lies on $y=Kx+5$, what is the value of K? SSC CHSL (Tier-I) 02/07/2024 Shift-IV
(a) 3 (b) −4 (c) 4 (d) −3

327. The simplified form of the expression $\frac{(x^2-9)\times(9x^2-1)}{\left(x-\frac{1}{3}\right)\times\left(1-\frac{x}{3}\right)}\times\frac{9}{\left(x+\frac{1}{3}\right)\left(1+\frac{x}{3}\right)}$ is SSC CHSL (Tier-II) 10/01/2024 Shift-I
(a) −729 (b) −81 (c) 729 (d) 81

328. If $(a-2b)=8$ and $2ab=9$, then find the value of $(a+2b)$. SSC CHSL (Tier-II) 02/11/2023 Shift-I
(a) 6 (b) 8 (c) 10 (d) 12

329. If $\sqrt[3]{0.08\times0.8\times p}=0.008\times0.8\times\sqrt[3]{q}$, then find the value of $\frac{p}{q}$. SSC CHSL (Tier-II) 02/11/2023 Shift-I
(a) $8^3\times10^{-9}$ (b) $8^3\times10^{-8}$
(c) $8^4\times10^{-8}$ (d) $8^4\times10^{-9}$

330. A and B each have a certain number of oranges. A says to B, "If you give me 10 of your oranges, I will have twice the number of oranges left with you." B replies, "If you give me 10 of your oranges, I will have the same number of oranges left with you." Find the number of oranges that A has. SSC CHSL (Tier-II) 02/11/2023 Shift-I
(a) 70 (b) 50 (c) 55 (d) 65

331. The cost of 4 chairs and 3 tables is ₹ 2100 and the cost of 5 chairs and 2 tables is ₹ 1750.
Find the cost (in ₹) of a chair. SSC CHSL (Tier-II) 02/11/2023 Shift-I
(a) 130 (b) 140
(c) 150 (d) 125

332. If $p^2-4p-1=0$, then the value of $p^2+3p+\frac{1}{p^2}-\frac{3}{p}$ is SSC CHSL (Tier-I) 17/08/2023 Shift-I
(a) 40 (b) 50
(c) 65 (d) 30

333. If $a^2+b^2+c^2=160$ and $a+b+c=16$, then find $ab+bc+ca$. SSC CHSL (Tier-I) 17/08/2023 Shift-I
(a) 96 (b) 84
(c) 48 (d) 42

334. Simplify the expression $\frac{1}{8}\left[\frac{1}{b-1}-\frac{1}{b+1}-\frac{2}{b^2+1}-\frac{4}{b^4+1}\right]$ SSC CHSL (Tier-I) 14/08/2023 Shift-IV
(a) $\frac{1}{b^8-1}$ (b) $\frac{8}{b^8+1}$
(c) $\frac{8}{b^8-1}$ (d) $\frac{1}{b^8+1}$

335. The sum of the cubes of two given numbers is 10234, while the sum of the two given numbers is 34. What

is the positive difference between the cubes of the two given numbers?

SSC CHSL (Tier-I) 11/08/2023 Shift-I

(a) 3484 (b) 3488 (c) 3356 (d) 8602

336. If $\left(3y+\frac{3}{y}\right)=8$, find the value of $\left(y^2+\frac{1}{y^2}\right)$.

SSC CHSL (Tier-I) 11/08/2023 Shift-I

(a) $5\frac{1}{9}$ (b) $4\frac{5}{6}$ (c) $7\frac{1}{9}$ (d) $9\frac{1}{9}$

337. If $x^2-\sqrt{9.76}\,x+1=0$ and $x>1$, the value of $\left(x^3-\frac{1}{x^3}\right)$ is

SSC CHSL (Tier-I) 10/08/2023 Shift-III

(a) 21.042 (b) 24.024
(c) 21.024 (d) 24.024

338. If $2x+5y=15$ and $xy=6$, then the value of $4x^2+25y^2$ is ....

SSC CHSL (Tier-I) 10/08/2023 Shift-III

(a) 105 (b) 95 (c) 100 (d) 90

339. If $x=(\sqrt{6}-1)^{\frac{1}{3}}$, then the value of $\left(x-\frac{1}{x}\right)^3+3\left(x-\frac{1}{x}\right)$ is

SSC CHSL (Tier-I) 09/08/2023 Shift-I

(a) $\frac{2\sqrt{6}-6}{5}$ (b) $\frac{4\sqrt{6}-6}{5}$
(c) $\frac{4\sqrt{6}-6}{3}$ (d) $\frac{4\sqrt{3}-6}{5}$

340. The algebraic expression $4x^2-y^2+6y-9$ is equal to

SSC CHSL (Tier-I) 09/08/2023 Shift-I

(a) $(2x+y-3)(2x-y+3)$
(b) $(2x-y-3)(2x-y+3)$
(c) $(2x+y-3)^2$
(d) $(2x+y+3)^2$

341. If $\left(x-\frac{1}{x-2}\right)=7$, then the value of $(x-2)^3-\frac{1}{(x-2)^3}$ is

SSC CHSL (Tier-I) 07/08/2023 Shift-IV

(a) 130 (b) 115 (c) 140 (d) 125

342. Simplify the given expression $\frac{x^3+y^3+z^3-3xyz}{(x-y)^2+(y-z)^2+(z-x)^2}$

SSC CHSL (Tier-I) 07/08/2023 Shift-IV

(a) $\frac{1}{3}(x+y+z)$ (b) $(x+y+z)$
(c) $\frac{1}{4}(x+y+z)$ (d) $\frac{1}{2}(x+y+z)$

343. If $x+\frac{2}{x}=1$, then the value of $\frac{x^2+7x+2}{x^2+13x+2}$ is

SSC CHSL (Tier-I) 04/08/2023 Shift-II

(a) $\frac{5}{7}$ (b) $\frac{3}{7}$ (c) $\frac{4}{7}$ (d) $\frac{2}{7}$

344. Which of the following is an identity ?

SSC CHSL (Tier-I) 04/08/2023 Shift-II

(a) $(a-b)^2=a^2-b^2$
(b) $(a+b)^2=a^2+b^2+2ab$
(c) $(a+b)^2=a^2+b^2$
(d) $(a-b)^2=a^2-b^2-2ab$

345. If $\sqrt{\frac{a}{b}}=\frac{8}{3}-\sqrt{\frac{b}{a}}$ and $a-b=10$, then the value of ab is

SSC CHSL (Tier-I) 04/08/2023 Shift-II

(a) $32\frac{1}{7}$ (b) $32\frac{3}{7}$
(c) $32\frac{4}{7}$ (d) $32\frac{2}{7}3$

346. If $5x+3y=15$ and $2xy=6$, then the value of $5x-3y$ is

SSC CHSL (Tier-I) 02/08/2023 Shift-I

(a) $3\sqrt{3}$ (b) $3\sqrt{5}$
(c) $3\sqrt{2}$ (d) $3\sqrt{4}$

347. If $x+\frac{1}{x}=7$, then the value of $x^2+\frac{1}{x^2}$ is

SSC CHSL (Tier-I) 02/08/2023 Shift-I

(a) 49 (b) 51
(c) 47 (d) 5

348. If $2x+\frac{2}{x}=5$, then the value of $\left(x^3+\frac{1}{x^3}+2\right)$ will be

SSC CHSL (Tier-I) 02/08/2023 Shift-I

(a) $\frac{81}{11}$ (b) $\frac{81}{7}$ (c) $\frac{71}{8}$ (d) $\frac{81}{8}$

349. What is the value of $\left(k+\frac{1}{k}\right)\left(k-\frac{1}{k}\right)\left(k^2+\frac{1}{k^2}\right)\left(k^4+\frac{1}{k^4}\right)$?

SSC CHSL (Tier-I) 21/03/2023 Shift-IV

(a) $k^{16}+\frac{1}{k^{16}}$ (b) $k^{16}-\frac{1}{k^{16}}$
(c) $k^8-\frac{1}{k^8}$ (d) $k^8+\frac{1}{k^8}$

350. If $x-\frac{1}{x}=4$, then what is the value of $\left(x^6+\frac{1}{x^6}\right)$?

SSC CHSL (Tier-I) 21/03/2023 Shift-IV

(a) 4689 (b) 4786
(c) 5832 (d) 5778

351. If $(a+b)=16$ and $a^3+b^3=1456$, then what is the value of ab?

SSC CHSL (Tier-I) 21/03/2023 Shift-II

(a) 50 (b) 48
(c) 64 (d) 55

352. If $\frac{k}{k^2-2k+1}=\frac{1}{6}$, then what is the value of $\frac{1}{k^3}+k^3$?

SSC CHSL (Tier-I) 21/03/2023 Shift-II

(a) 472 (b) 492
(c) 512 (d) 488

353. If $m-\frac{1}{m}=7$, then what is the value of $m^2+\frac{1}{m^2}$?

SSC CHSL (Tier-I) 20/03/2023 Shift-III

(a) 0 (b) 51 (c) 53 (d) 49

354. What is the value of $\frac{1+x}{1-x^2}\div\frac{1+x}{1-x^4}-\frac{1-x^4}{1-x}\times\frac{(1+x)}{1-x^2}$?

SSC CHSL (Tier-I) 20/03/2023 Shift-III

(a) $\frac{2x(1+x^2)}{(1-x)}$ (b) $\frac{2x(1+x^2)}{(x-1)}$
(c) $(1-x)^2$ (d) $(1+x^2)$

355. If $a=12, b=-7$ and $c=-5$, then what is the value of $a^3+b^3+c^3$?

SSC CHSL (Tier-I) 17/03/2023 Shift-II

(a) 1260 (b) 1125
(c) 1200 (d) 1380

356. If the sum of a number and its reciprocal is 4, find the sum of their squares.

SSC CHSL (Tier-I) 17/03/2023 Shift-II

(a) 12 (b) 16 (c) 14 (d) 18

357. If $a+b+c=0$ and $a^2+b^2+c^2=40$, then what is the value of $ab+bc+ca$?

SSC CHSL (Tier-I) 17/03/2023 Shift-II

(a) −30 (b) −20
(c) −25 (d) −40

358. If $x+\frac{1}{x}=\frac{k}{2}$, then what is the value of $\frac{x^8+1}{x^4}$?

SSC CHSL (Tier-I) 16/03/2023 Shift-I

(a) $\frac{k^4-16k^2+32}{16}$ (b) $\frac{k^4-8k^2+36}{32}$
(c) $\frac{k^4-8k^2-32}{16}$ (d) $\frac{k^4-8k^2+32}{16}$

359. If $a^2+b^2+c^2=62$ and $a+b+c=12$, then what is the value of $4ab+4bc+4ca$?

SSC CHSL (Tier-I) 16/03/2023 Shift-I

(a) 164 (b) 148
(c) 152 (d) 160

360. If $K+\frac{1}{K}=-3$, then what is the value of $\left(\frac{K^6+1}{K^3}\right)+\left(\frac{K^4+1}{K^2}\right)$?

SSC CHSL (Tier-I) 15/03/2023 Shift-IV

(a) 27 (b) − 11
(c) 11 (d) − 27

361. If $P+\frac{1}{P}=5$, then what is the value of $P^3+\frac{1}{P^3}$?

SSC CHSL (Tier-I) 15/03/2023 Shift-IV

(a) 110 (b) 95
(c) 125 (d) 120

362. If $a^3 = b^3 + 988$ and $a - b = 4$, then what is the value of $2a^2 + 2ab + 2b^2$?
SSC CHSL (Tier-I) 14/03/2023 Shift-I
(a) 516 (b) 494
(c) 500 (d) 247

363. What is the value of $a^2 + b^2 + c^2 - 2ab - 2bc + 2ca$?
SSC CHSL (Tier-I) 14/03/2023 Shift-I
(a) $(a-b-c)^2$ (b) $(a+b-c)^2$
(c) $(a+b+c)^2$ (d) $(a-b+c)^2$

364. If $a + \frac{1}{a} = 2$ and $b + \frac{1}{b} = -2$, then what is the value of $a^2 + \frac{1}{a^2} + b^2 + \frac{1}{b^2}$?
SSC CHSL (Tier-I) 13/03/2023 Shift-III
(a) 8 (b) 4 (c) 2 (d) 0

365. What is the value of $x^2 + 4y^2 + z^2 - 4xy + 4yz - 2xz$?
SSC CHSL (Tier-I) 13/03/2023 Shift-II
(a) $(x+2y-z)^2$ (b) $(x-2y+z)^2$
(c) $(2y-x+z)^2$ (d) $(2x-y+z)^2$

366. If $2p + 5q = 12$ and $pq = 3$, find the value of $4p^2 + 25q^2$.
SSC CHSL (Tier-I) 10/03/2023 Shift-II
(a) 64 (b) 24 (c) 84 (d) 44

367. If $(a - b) = 5$ and $ab = 150$, then what is the value of $(a^3 - b^3)$?
SSC CHSL (Tier-I) 10/03/2023 Shift-II
(a) 2640 (b) 1125
(c) 2375 (d) 2250

368. What is the value of $\frac{1+x^2}{1-x} + \frac{1-x^4}{x-1} \times \frac{x(1-x)}{(1+x)}$?
SSC CHSL (Tier-I) 09/03/2023 Shift-I
(a) $\frac{-x}{1+2x^2}$ (b) $\frac{-x}{1+x}$
(c) $\frac{-x}{(1+x)^2}$ (d) $\frac{-x}{1+x^2}$

SSC CHSL 2022 & 2021 (Tier I)

369. If $8x^2 + 9x + 8 = 0$, then the value of $x^3 + \frac{1}{x^3}$ is
SSC CHSL (Tier-I) 01/06/2022 Shift-I
(a) $\frac{999}{212}$ (b) $\frac{199}{212}$ (c) $\frac{999}{512}$ (d) $\frac{199}{512}$

370. If $x + y = 14$, then the value of $x^3 + y^3 + 42xy$ is
SSC CHSL (Tier-I) 31/05/2022 Shift-I
(a) 2744 (b) 2644
(c) 2742 (d) 2714

371. If $p^4 = 4354 - \frac{1}{p^4}$, then the value of $p^3 - \frac{1}{p^3}$ can be
SSC CHSL (Tier-I) 31/05/2022 Shift-I
(a) 536 (b) 436
(c) 416 (d) 516

372. If $\frac{a}{b} + \frac{b}{a} = -1, a \neq 0, b \neq 0$, then the value of $6(a^3 - b^3)$ is
SSC CHSL (Tier-I) 31/05/2022 Shift-I
(a) 6 (b) 3 (c) 0 (d) 1

373. If $8x^3 + 27y^3 + 64z^3 = 72xyz$, then the relation between x, y and z can be
SSC CHSL (Tier-I) 30/05/2022 Shift-I
(a) $2x + 3y = -4z$
(b) $2x + y + z = 0$
(c) $2x - 3y + 4z = 0$
(d) $2x + 3y = 4z$

374. If $x^2 + 4y^2 = 40, xy = 6$, and $x > 2y$, then the value of $x - 2y$ is :
SSC CHSL (Tier-I) 27/05/2022 Shift-I
(a) 1 (b) 3 (c) 2 (d) 4

375. If $x^2 + \frac{1}{x^2} = 83, x > 0$, then the value of $x^3 - \frac{1}{x^3}$ is
SSC CHSL (Tier-I) 12/08/2021 Shift-III
(a) 756 (b) 675
(c) 576 (d) 746

376. If $x^2 + (4 - \sqrt{3})x - 1 = 0$, then what is the value of $x^2 + \frac{1}{x^2}$?
SSC CHSL (Tier-I) 12/08/2021 Shift-III
(a) $9 - 8\sqrt{3}$ (b) $21 - 12\sqrt{3}$
(c) $21 - 8\sqrt{3}$ (d) $17 - 8\sqrt{3}$

377. If $x^6 - 6\sqrt{6}y^6 = (x^2 + Ay^2)(x^4 + Bx^2y^2 + Cy^4)$, then what will be the value of $(A^2 - B^2 + C^2)$?
SSC CHSL (Tier-I) 10/08/2021 Shift-I
(a) 27 (b) 42 (c) 36 (d) 18

378. Simplify the given expression.
$\left(x - \frac{2}{x}\right)^3 - \left(x + \frac{2}{x}\right)^3$
SSC CHSL (Tier-I) 10/08/2021 Shift-I
(a) $-4\left(3x + \frac{4}{x^3}\right)$ (b) $4\left(3x - \frac{4}{x^3}\right)$
(c) $-4\left(x + \frac{4}{x^3}\right)$ (d) $2\left(x - \frac{4}{x^3}\right)$

379. If $a + b = p$, $ab = q$, then $(a^4 + b^4)$ is equal to
SSC CHSL (Tier-I) 04/08/2021 Shift-I
(a) $p^4 - 2p^2q^2 + q^2$
(b) $p^4 - 4p^2q^2 + 2q^2$
(c) $p^4 - 4p^2q + q^2$
(d) $p^4 - 4p^2q + 2q^2$

380. Using algebraic identities, simplify the following expression.
$\frac{(x^4 + x^2 + 1)}{(x^2 + x + 1)}$
SSC CHSL (Tier-I) 04/08/2021 Shift-I
(a) $(x^2 - 2x + 1)$
(b) $(x^2 + x + 1)$
(c) $(x^2 + 2x + 1)$
(d) $(x^2 - x + 1)$

381. If $a^2 + 49b^2 + c^2 + 18 = 2(28b - c - a)$, then the value of $(a + 7b - c)$ is
SSC CHSL (Tier-I) 19/04/2021 Shift-I
(a) 2 (b) 4 (c) 6 (d) –1

382. If $a + b + c = 4$, $ab + bc + ca = -14$ and $abc = -18$, then the value of $\sqrt{4a^3 + 4b^3 + 4c^3 - 36}$ will be
SSC CHSL (Tier-I) 19/04/2021 Shift-I
(a) 26 (b) 24 (c) 25 (d) 18

383. If $x^8 - 2599x^4 + 1 = 0$, then the positive value of $x - \frac{1}{x}$ will be
SSC CHSL (Tier-I) 19/04/2021 Shift-I
(a) 7 (b) 12 (c) 6 (d) 8

384. If the difference between two numbers is 5 and the difference between their cubes is 1850, then the difference between their squares is
SSC CHSL (Tier-I) 12/04/2021 Shift-II
(a) $5\sqrt{484}$ (b) $5\sqrt{482}$
(c) $5\sqrt{485}$ (d) $5\sqrt{483}$

SSC MTS 2024-2021

385. In an amusement park, all rides are equally priced and the entry ticket for the park costs an additional ₹180. Rohan had 15 rides and paid a total of ₹ 1380 for his visit to the park. How much (in ₹) in all would Rohan have to pay for his visit to the amusement park if he had opted for 20 rides?
SSC MTS 15/10/2024 Shift-I
(a) 1840 (b) 1760
(c) 1800 (d) 1780

386. If the $\frac{5}{6}$ of a number is 10 less than the number itself, then $\frac{7}{5}$ of the number is ....
SSC MTS 13/09/2023 Shift-I
(a) 72 (b) 96 (c) 60 (d) 84

387. When 8 is added to the numerator and 12 is added to its denominator, the fraction becomes $\frac{1}{2}$. When 2 is subtracted from its numerator and denominator, the fraction becomes $\frac{1}{8}$. Find the original fraction.
SSC MTS 15/07/2022 Shift-I
(a) $\frac{9}{19}$ (b) $\frac{3}{10}$ (c) $\frac{4}{7}$ (d) $\frac{5}{11}$

388. If $x : y : z = 1 : 2 : 3$, then what is the value of $\left(\frac{3x^2 - 2y^2 + 4z^2}{x^2 + 2y^2 + z^2}\right)$?
SSC MTS 02/11/2021 Shift-II
(a) $\frac{31}{21}$ (b) $\frac{31}{16}$ (c) $\frac{31}{18}$ (d) $\frac{31}{19}$

SSC GD Constable 2024 & 2023

389. If $p - q = 9$ and $p^2 + q^2 = 127$. Find the value of pq.
SSC GD 02/11/2024 Shift-III

(a) 23 (b) 27 (c) 12 (d) 15

390. If y varies directly with x and $y = 16$ when $x = 24$, then find the value of y when $x = 45$. **SSC GD 08/2/2023 Shift-I**

(a) 24 (b) 40 (c) 30 (d) 45

SSC Selection Post 2024-2022

391. If $x^2 + \frac{1}{x^2} = 119 \, (x > 0)$, then the value of $\left(x^3 + \frac{1}{x^3}\right)$ is
Higher Secondary Level 20/06/2024 Shift-II

(a) 1331 (b) 1298
(c) 1125 (d) 1920

392. In an examination, a student scores 4 marks for every correct answer and losses 1 mark for every wrong answer. A student attempted all 200 questions and scored 500 marks. What is the number of questions, he answered correctly?
Graduate Level 27/06/2023 Shift-IV

(a) 140 (b) 130 (c) 180 (d) 160

393. If $\frac{2x}{x+2} + \frac{1}{2x+4} - \frac{12-x}{2x^2+4x} = a + \frac{b}{x}$, where a and b are integers, then the value of ab = …………
Graduate Level 27/06/2023 Shift-IV

(a) 3 (b) −6 (c) 6 (d) −3

394. If $(a + b) = \sqrt{11}$ and $(a - b) = \sqrt{7}$, then find the value of $a^2b^2(a^2 + b^2)$.
Graduate Level 01/08/2022 Shift-IV

(a) 9 (b) 11 (c) 7 (d) 5

395. If $2^x = 3^y = 6^z$, then $\frac{1}{x} + \frac{1}{y} - \frac{1}{z}$ is equal to. **Graduate Level 01/08/2022 Shift-IV**

(a) 1 (b) $\frac{3}{2}$
(c) 0 (d) $\frac{-1}{2}$

396. A farmer counted the heads of the animals and birds on the farm and found it to be 40. When, he counted the legs, he found it to be 120. If the farm had either pigeons or horses and nothing else, how many horses were there on the farm? On the farm, each horse had four legs and each pigeon had two legs.
Matric Level 01/08/2022 Shift-I

(a) 26 (b) 22
(c) 24 (d) 20

Right Answers

1	(a)	2	(d)	3	(a)	4	(a)	5	(a)	6	(c)	7	(b)	8	(a)	9	(a)	10	(d)
11	(a)	12	(b)	13	(a)	14	(b)	15	(d)	16	(a)	17	(b)	18	(a)	19	(c)	20	(c)
21	(c)	22	(a)	23	(c)	24	(b)	25	(c)	26	(a)	27	(d)	28	(a)	29	(a)	30	(d)
31	(c)	32	(a)	33	(b)	34	(c)	35	(d)	36	(b)	37	(b)	38	(c)	39	(b)	40	(a)
41	(d)	42	(d)	43	(d)	44	(a)	45	(d)	46	(b)	47	(a)	48	(a)	49	(b)	50	(a)
51	(c)	52	(b)	53	(c)	54	(a)	55	(b)	56	(d)	57	(d)	58	(c)	59	(c)	60	(b)
61	(b)	62	(a)	63	(a)	64	(c)	65	(b)	66	(c)	67	(b)	68	(c)	69	(d)	70	(c)
71	(d)	72	(d)	73	(b)	74	(a)	75	(b)	76	(a)	77	(c)	78	(a)	79	(c)	80	(a)
81	(c)	82	(c)	83	(b)	84	(b)	85	(b)	86	(a)	87	(c)	88	(b)	89	(d)	90	(a)
91	(d)	92	(d)	93	(a)	94	(a)	95	(d)	96	(a)	97	(a)	98	(c)	99	(b)	100	(a)
101	(d)	102	(b)	103	(a)	104	(c)	105	(a)	106	(d)	107	(b)	108	(a)	109	(b)	110	(d)
111	(a)	112	(d)	113	(c)	114	(c)	115	(c)	116	(b)	117	(c)	118	(c)	119	(c)	120	(d)
121	(a)	122	(b)	123	(d)	124	(b)	125	(a)	126	(d)	127	(c)	128	(a)	129	(d)	130	(d)
131	(d)	132	(c)	133	(a)	134	(b)	135	(c)	136	(b)	137	(b)	138	(a)	139	(c)	140	(d)
141	(d)	142	(d)	143	(a)	144	(b)	145	(d)	146	(c)	147	(a)	148	(d)	149	(b)	150	(a)
151	(d)	152	(a)	153	(d)	154	(d)	155	(a)	156	(a)	157	(a)	158	(b)	159	(c)	160	(a)
161	(b)	162	(d)	163	(b)	164	(b)	165	(a)	166	(c)	167	(d)	168	(b)	169	(b)	170	(b)
171	(d)	172	(b)	173	(a)	174	(c)	175	(b)	176	(b)	177	(d)	178	(b)	179	(b)	180	(a)
181	(d)	182	(b)	183	(d)	184	(d)	185	(a)	186	(c)	187	(b)	188	(a)	189	(b)	190	(a)
191	(c)	192	(a)	193	(b)	194	(b)	195	(d)	196	(b)	197	(d)	198	(d)	199	(c)	200	(a)
201	(b)	202	(c)	203	(d)	204	(c)	205	(c)	206	(a)	207	(d)	208	(d)	209	(a)	210	(c)
211	(d)	212	(d)	213	(b)	214	(b)	215	(b)	216	(d)	217	(c)	218	(d)	219	(a)	220	(c)
221	(b)	222	(d)	223	(d)	224	(a)	225	(c)	226	(d)	227	(d)	228	(b)	229	(c)	230	(d)
231	(a)	232	(b)	233	(c)	234	(a)	235	(a)	236	(b)	237	(d)	238	(a)	239	(b)	240	(b)
241	(c)	242	(b)	243	(b)	244	(a)	245	(c)	246	(b)	247	(a)	248	(c)	249	(c)	250	(c)
251	(b)	252	(d)	253	(a)	254	(b)	255	(c)	256	(b)	257	(c)	258	(b)	259	(a)	260	(c)
261	(a)	262	(b)	263	(d)	264	(c)	265	(c)	266	(c)	267	(b)	268	(a)	269	(c)	270	(d)
271	(b)	272	(b)	273	(c)	274	(c)	275	(b)	276	(b)	277	(c)	278	(b)	279	(b)	280	(d)
281	(b)	282	(b)	283	(b)	284	(c)	285	(d)	286	(d)	287	(c)	288	(b)	289	(c)	290	(d)
291	(d)	292	(d)	293	(d)	294	(a)	295	(a)	296	(c)	297	(c)	298	(d)	299	(b)	300	(a)
301	(a)	302	(c)	303	(b)	304	(c)	305	(d)	306	(d)	307	(b)	308	(b)	309	(c)	310	(b)
311	(d)	312	(a)	313	(c)	314	(d)	315	(b)	316	(a)	317	(c)	318	(c)	319	(a)	320	(a)
321	(c)	322	(b)	323	(a)	324	(c)	325	(a)	326	(b)	327	(a)	328	(c)	329	(d)	330	(a)
331	(c)	332	(d)	333	(c)	334	(a)	335	(a)	336	(a)	337	(c)	338	(a)	339	(b)	340	(a)
341	(c)	342	(d)	343	(c)	344	(b)	345	(a)	346	(b)	347	(c)	348	(d)	349	(c)	350	(d)
351	(d)	352	(d)	353	(b)	354	(b)	355	(a)	356	(c)	357	(b)	358	(a)	359	(a)	360	(b)
361	(a)	362	(b)	363	(d)	364	(b)	365	(c)	366	(c)	367	(c)	368	(c)	369	(c)	370	(a)
371	(a)	372	(c)	373	(a)	374	(d)	375	(a)	376	(c)	377	(c)	378	(a)	379	(d)	380	(d)
381	(b)	382	(a)	383	(a)	384	(c)	385	(d)	386	(d)	387	(b)	388	(c)	389	(a)	390	(c)
391	(b)	392	(a)	393	(b)	394	(a)	395	(c)	396	(d)								

Solutions

1. (a) $\frac{a^5 \times b^3 \times c^7}{a^4 \times b^8 \times c^9}$

$= a^{(5-4)} \times b^{(3-8)} \times c^{(7-9)} \quad \left[\because \frac{a^m}{a^n} = a^{m-n}\right]$

$= a^1 \times b^{(-5)} \times c^{(-2)}$

2. (d) We have, $x = 4 + \sqrt{6}$ and $y = 4 - \sqrt{6}$

$x^2 + y^2 = (4+\sqrt{6})^2 + (4-\sqrt{6})^2$

$= 2[(4)^2 + (\sqrt{6})^2]$

$[\because (a+b)^2 + (a-b)^2 = 2(a^2+b^2)]$

$= 2(16+6) = 44$

3. (a) $(5z - 7y)^2 + (7z + 5y)^2 - 49z^2$

$= 25z^2 + 49y^2 - 70yz + 49z^2 + 25y^2 + 70yz - 49z^2$

$= 25z^2 + 74y^2 \quad \left[\begin{array}{l}\because (a+b)^2 = a^2 + b^2 + 2ab \\ (a-b)^2 = a^2 + b^2 - 2ab\end{array}\right]$

4. (a) $(5z - 12y)^2 + (12z + 5y)^2 - 144z^2$

$= 25z^2 + 144y^2 - 120zy + 144z^2 + 25y^2 + 120yz - 144z^2$

$= 25z^2 + 169y^2$

5. (a) $x = 8 + \sqrt{5}$ and $y = 8 - \sqrt{5}$

$\therefore x^2 + y^2 = (8+\sqrt{5})^2 + (8-\sqrt{5})^2$

$[\because (a+b)^2 + (a-b)^2 = 2(a^2+b^2)]$

$= 2(8^2 + (\sqrt{5})^2)$

$= 2(64+5) = 2 \times 69 = 138$

6. (c) $\frac{a^7 \times b^8 \times c^7}{a^9 \times b^5 \times c^4} = a^{(7-9)} \times b^{(8-5)} \times c^{(7-4)}$

$= a^{(-2)} \times b^3 \times c^3$

7. (b) Given equations,

$x - 2y + 2z = 16$ ...(i)

$x - y + z = 9$ ...(ii)

$2x - 3y - z = 9$ ...(iii)

From Eqs. (i) and (ii) × 2

$x - 2y + 2z = 16$

$2x - 2y + 2z = 18$

$-\quad +\quad -\quad -$

$-x = -2$

$\Rightarrow x = 2$

Again from Eqs. (ii) and (iii),

$x - y + z = 9$

$2x - 3y - z = 9$

$3x - 4y = 18$

$\Rightarrow 4y = 3x - 18$

$\Rightarrow 4y = 3 \times 2 - 18$

$\Rightarrow y = \frac{-12}{4} = -3$

8. (a) Given equations

$x + 1.5y + 2z = 5.5$ ...(i)

$x + 5y + 7z = 15$ ...(ii)

$3x + 11y + 13z = 25$ ...(iii)

Subtracting Eqs. (i) from (ii), we get

$x + 5y + 7z - x - 1.5y - 2z = 15 - 5.5$

$3.5y + 5z = 9.5$

$35y + 50z = 95$

$\Rightarrow 7y + 10z = 19$ ...(iv)

Now, subtract Eq. (iii) from 3 × Eq. (ii)

$3x + 15y + 21z - 3x - 11y - 13z = 45 - 25$

$4y + 8z = 20$

$\Rightarrow y + 2z = 5$ ...(v)

Subtract Eq. (iv) from 5 × Eq. (v)

$5y + 10z - 7y - 10z = 25 - 19$

$\Rightarrow -2y = 6 \Rightarrow y = -3$

From Eqs. (iv) $z = \frac{19 - 7(-3)}{10} = \frac{40}{10} = 4$

Substitute $y = -3$ and $z = 4$ in Eq. (i), we get

$x = 5.5 - 1.5(-3) - 2(4) \Rightarrow x = 2$

9. (a) Given, $\frac{x}{x^2 - 2x + 1} = \frac{1}{3}$

$\Rightarrow \frac{x^2 - 2x + 1}{x} = \frac{3}{1} \Rightarrow \frac{x^2}{x} - \frac{2x}{x} + \frac{1}{x} = \frac{3}{1}$

$\Rightarrow x - 2 + \frac{1}{x} = 3 \Rightarrow x + \frac{1}{x} = 5$

We know, $\left(x^2 + \frac{1}{x^2}\right) = \left(x + \frac{1}{x}\right)^2 - 2$

$\Rightarrow x^2 + \frac{1}{x^2} = (5)^2 - 2 = 23$

$\therefore x^3 + \frac{1}{x^3} = \left(x + \frac{1}{x}\right)\left(x^2 + \frac{1}{x^2} - 1\right)$

$= (5)(23 - 1) = 110$

10. (d) We have,

$\frac{4x^2 - 49y^2}{2x + 7y} + 7y - 2x$

$= \frac{(2x)^2 - (7y)^2}{(2x+7y)} + 7y - 2x$

$= \frac{(2x - 7y)(2x + 7y)}{(2x + 7y)} + 7y - 2x$

$= 2x - 7y + 7y - 2x = 0$

11. (a) We know,

$(a - b)^3 = a^3 - b^3 - 3(ab)(a - b)$

$\therefore (2a - b)^3 = (2a)^3 - (b)^3 - 3(2ab)(2a - b)$

$\Rightarrow (3)^3 = 8a^3 - b^3 - 3(2ab)(3)$

$\Rightarrow 27 = 999 - 18ab$

$\Rightarrow 18ab = 972 \Rightarrow ab = 54$

Now, $(2a - b)^2 = 4a^2 + b^2 - 4ab$

$\Rightarrow 9 = 4a^2 + b^2 - 4(54)$

$\Rightarrow 4a^2 + b^2 = 225$

Also, $(2a + b)^2 = 4a^2 + b^2 + 4ab = 225 + 4(54)$

$= 225 + 216 = 441$

$\therefore (2a + b) = 21$

As, $4a^2 - b^2 = (2a - b)(2a + b)$

$= (3)(21) = 63$

12. (b) We have,

$\left(\frac{x}{y} + \frac{y}{x}\right)^2 - 3 = \left(\frac{x^2 + y^2}{xy}\right)^2 - 3$

$= \left[\frac{(\sqrt{6}-2)^2 + (\sqrt{6}-2)^2}{(\sqrt{6}+2)(\sqrt{6}-2)}\right]^2 - 3$

$= \left[\frac{6 + 4 + 4\sqrt{6} + 6 + 4 - 4\sqrt{6}}{6 - 4}\right]^2 - 3$

$= \left[\frac{20}{2}\right]^2 - 3 = 100 - 3 = 97$

13. (a) From the given equation and options

$5x + 7y - 8 = 0$

$5x + 7y - 16 = 0$

$\therefore a_1 = 5, b_1 = 7, c_1 = -8;$

$a_2 = 5, b_2 = 7, c_2 = -16$

$\therefore \frac{a_1}{a_2} = \frac{5}{5} = 1, \frac{b_1}{b_2} = \frac{7}{7} = 1,$

$\frac{c_1}{c_2} = \frac{-8}{-16} = \frac{1}{2}$

$\therefore \frac{a_1}{a_2} = \frac{b_1}{b_2} \neq \frac{c_1}{c_2} \Rightarrow$ No solution

14. (b) $x \propto \frac{y^3}{z^2} \therefore x = \frac{ky^3}{z^2}$

We can write it as,

$\frac{x_1}{x_2} = \frac{y_1^3 / z_1^2}{y_2^3 / z_2^2} = \frac{y_1^3}{y_2^3} \times \frac{z_2^2}{z_1^2}$

$x_1 = \frac{1}{36}, y_1 = 2, z_1 = 3$ and $x_2 = ?, y_2 = 3, z_2 = 5$

$\frac{1}{36x_2} = \frac{8}{27} \times \frac{25}{9} \Rightarrow x_2 = \frac{27}{800}$

$\therefore 800x_2 = \frac{27}{800} \times 800 = 27$

15. (d) According to the question,

15 apple + 12 orange = 447

$\Rightarrow$ 5 apple + 4 orange −149 = 0 ...(i)

From option (b),

15 apple + 13 orange −353 = 0 ...(ii)

From Eqs. (i) and (ii),

$\frac{5}{15} \neq \frac{4}{13}$

[using solution consistent]

From option (c),

12 apple + 8 orange − 340 = 0 ...(iii)

$\Rightarrow$ From Eqs. (i) and (ii),

$\frac{5}{15} \neq \frac{4}{8}$

[$\because$ using solution consistent]

From option (a),

25 apple + 20 orange − 745 = 0

5 apple + 4 orange − 149 = 0 ...(iv)

From (i) and (iv),

$\frac{5}{5} = \frac{4}{4} = \frac{-149}{-149}$

[Infinite solution consistent]

From option (d),

35 apple + 28 apple −1029 = 0

5 apple + 4 orange −147 = 0 ...(v)

From Eqs. (i) aand (v),

$$\frac{5}{5}=\frac{4}{4}=\frac{-149}{-147}$$

∴ Inconsistent (no solution)

Hence, option (d) is the correct answer.

16. (a) Given, $a^2+b^2=148$ and $ab=54$

We know, $(a+b)=\sqrt{a^2+b^2+2ab}$

$=\sqrt{148+2\times 54}=16$

$(a-b)=\sqrt{a^2+b^2-2ab}$

$=\sqrt{148-2\times 54}=\sqrt{40}=2\sqrt{10}$

We have, $\frac{a+b}{a-b}=\frac{16}{2\sqrt{10}}=\frac{8}{\sqrt{10}}$

17. (b) Given, $4x+6y=7$ and

$6x+(k+4)y-21=0$

$a_1=4, a_2=6, b_1=6, b_2=(k+4)$

∵ Unique solution

∴ $a_1/a_2\neq b_1/b_2$

$4/6\neq 6/(k+4)$

$36\neq 4(k+4)\quad (4+k)\neq 9$

$k\neq 5$

18. (a) Given, $K_1x+3y=8$ and $4x+K_2y=16$

when two lines coinciden,

then, $\frac{K_1}{4}=\frac{3}{K_2}=\frac{8}{16}$

$\frac{K_1}{4}=\frac{8}{16}\Rightarrow K_1=2$

$\frac{3}{K_2}=\frac{8}{16}\Rightarrow K_2=6$

∴ $K_2=3K_1$

19. (c) As we know for infinite solution

$\frac{a_1}{a_2}=\frac{b_1}{b_2}=\frac{c_1}{c_2}\Rightarrow 3x+y=3$

and $(a-b)x+(a+b)y=3a+b-3$

∴ $\frac{3}{a-b}=\frac{1}{a+b}=\frac{3}{3a+b-3}$

$\frac{1}{a+b}=\frac{3}{3a+b-3}$

$\Rightarrow 3a+b-3=3a+3b\Rightarrow 2b=-3$

$\Rightarrow b=\frac{-3}{2}$

Again, $\frac{3}{a+\left(\frac{3}{2}\right)}=\frac{1}{a-\frac{3}{2}}\Rightarrow 3a-\frac{9}{2}=a+\frac{3}{2}$

$\Rightarrow 2a=\frac{12}{2}\Rightarrow a=3$

Thus, $a=3$ and $b=\frac{-3}{2}$

20. (c) $x^2+7x+8=0\Rightarrow x\left(x+7+\frac{8}{x}\right)=0$

$\Rightarrow x+\frac{8}{x}=-7$ ...(i)

Now, $\frac{4x}{x^2-5x+8}=\frac{4x}{x\left(x-5+\frac{8}{x}\right)}$

From Eq (i), $\left(\frac{4}{-7-5}\right)=\frac{4}{-12}=\frac{-1}{3}$

21. (c) $a^3+\frac{1}{a^3}=2$

By option (c), put $a=1$

Then, $1^3+\frac{1}{1^3}=1+\frac{1}{1}=2$

Thus, $a+\frac{1}{a}=1+\frac{1}{1}=2$

22. (a) $a+b=c$

Cubing both sides, $(a+b)^3=c^3$

$\Rightarrow a^3+b^3+3ab(a+b)=c^3\ [a+b=c]$

$\Rightarrow a^3+b^3-c^3+3abc=0$

23. (c) $(3x+17-2y)(3x-17-2y)$

$=[(3x-2y)+17][(3x-2y)-17]$

$=[(3x-2y)^2-(17)^2]$

$[\because a^2-b^2=(a+b)(a-b)]$

$=9x^2+4y^2-12xy-289$

$=9x^2-12xy+4y^2-289$

24. (b) Here, $3x+2y=7$

$2x+3y=7$

$a_1=3, b_1=2, c_1=-7$

$a_2=2, b_2=3, c_2=-7$

∴ $\frac{a_1}{a_2}=\frac{3}{2}$ and $\frac{b_1}{b_2}=\frac{2}{3}\Rightarrow\frac{a_1}{a_2}\neq\frac{b_1}{b_2}$

⇒ following system of linear equation has unique solution.

25. (c) $3t-\frac{1}{3t}=3$

Squaring both sides, $\left(3t-\frac{1}{3t}\right)^2=(3)^2$

$\Rightarrow 9t^2+\frac{1}{9t^2}-2=9\Rightarrow 9t^2+\frac{1}{9t^2}=11$

$\Rightarrow 9t^2+\frac{1}{9t^2}+1=1+11$

$\Rightarrow 9t^2+\frac{1}{9t^2}+1=12$

26. (a) $3x+2y=10$ ...(i)

$2xy=7$

Squaring Eqs. (i) from both sides,

$(3x+2y)^2=(10)^2$

$\Rightarrow 9x^2+4y^2+2xy\times 6=100$

$\Rightarrow 9x^2+4y^2+6\times 7=100$

$\Rightarrow 9x^2+4y^2=100-42$

$\Rightarrow 9x^2+4y^2=58$

Now, $(3x-2y)^2=9x^2+4y^2-2\times 3x\times 2y$

$=58-7\times 6$

$\Rightarrow (3x-2y)^2=16$

$\Rightarrow 3x-2y=4$

27. (d) $10C+6T=$ ₹ 5140 ...(i)

$3C+2T=$ ₹ 1635 × 3

$9C+6T=$ ₹ 4905 ...(ii)

From Eq. (i) and (ii), $C=$ ₹ 235

Put this value in Eq. (i),

$10\times 235+6T=5140\Rightarrow 6T=5140-2350$

$\Rightarrow 6T=2790\Rightarrow T=\frac{2790}{6}$

$\Rightarrow T=465$

Cost of 1 chair + 1 table = 235 + 465 = ₹ 700

28. (a) $a+b+c=0$

$a+b=-c$

Squaring both sides,

$(a+b)^2=(-c)^2$

$a^2+b^2+2ab=c^2$

29. (a) Let number of notes of denomination ₹ 20 be x and number of notes of denomination ₹ 10 be y

According to the question,

$20x+10y=390$ ...(i)

$20y+10x=390-90$

$20y+10x=300$ ...(ii)

From Eqs. (i) and (ii), we get

$x=16, y=7$

Hence, number of notes of ₹ 20 denomination is 16.

30. (d) From option (d), $a=-12, x=48, y=4$

Given, $ax+(a^2+1)y=4$ ...(i)

LHS $=ax+(a^2+1)y$

$=-12\times 48+((-12)^2+1)\times 4$

$=-576+580=4$

LHS = RHS

Hence, option satisfies the given Eq. (i).

Again, $4x+ay=a^2$ ...(ii)

LHS $=4x+ay=4\times 48+(-12)(4)$

$=192-48=144$

RHS $=a^2=(-12)^2=144$

LHS = RHS

Hence, option satisfies the given Eq. (ii).

Hence, option (d) is true.

31. (c) As, $x+\frac{1}{x}=7$

Squaring both sides, we get

$\left(x+\frac{1}{x}\right)^2=(7)^2$

$\Rightarrow x^2+\frac{1}{x^2}+2=49\Rightarrow x^2+\frac{1}{x^2}=47$

We know, $\left(x-\frac{1}{x}\right)^2=x^2+\frac{1}{x^2}-2$

$\Rightarrow \left(x-\frac{1}{x}\right)^2=47-2\Rightarrow\left(x-\frac{1}{x}\right)^2=45$

∴ $x-\frac{1}{x}=3\sqrt{5}$

32. (a) $a+\frac{1}{a}=7\sqrt{3}$ ...(i)

Cubing both sides,

$a^3+\frac{1}{a^3}+3\times 1\times 7\sqrt{3}=1029\sqrt{3}$

$a^3+\frac{1}{a^3}=1008\sqrt{3}$ ...(ii)

Squaring both sides of Eq. (ii),

$\left(a^3+\frac{1}{a^3}\right)^2=(1008\sqrt{3})^2$

$\Rightarrow a^6+\frac{1}{a^6}=3048192-2$

$\Rightarrow a^6+\frac{1}{a^6}=3048190$

33. (b) Let the number of marbles Kavita have be = x

Let the number of marbles Ravi have $= x - 12$

According to the question,

$$3(x+1) = 4(x-12+1)$$
$$\Rightarrow \quad 3x + 3 = 4x - 44$$
$$\Rightarrow \quad x = 47$$

34. (c) Number $= x^3 - 4x^2 - 8x + 11$ ...(i)

One factor $(x+2) = 0$, $x = -2$

Put this value in Eq. (i),

$$(-2)^3 - 4(-2)^2 - 8(-2) + 11$$
$$= -8 - 16 + 16 + 11 = 3$$

$\therefore$ 3 should be subtracted from the number.

35. (d) Given, $3a + 2b = 27$ and

$$27a^3 + 8b^3 = 1458 \quad \text{...(i)}$$
$$(3a+2b)^3 = (27)^3$$
$$[\because (a+b)^3 = a^3 + b^3 + 3ab(a+b)]$$
$$(3a)^3 + (2a)^3 + 3 \times 3a \times 2b(3a+2b) = 19683$$
$$1458 + 18ab \times 27 = 19683 \text{ [From Eq. (i)]}$$
$$2ab = 75$$

36. (b) $x + \dfrac{1}{x} = 2$ ...(i)

Squaring on both sides, $x^2 + \dfrac{1}{x^2} + 2 = 4$

$$x^2 + \frac{1}{x^2} = 2 \quad \left(x - \frac{1}{x}\right)^2 = 2 - 2 = 0$$
$$\Rightarrow \quad x - \frac{1}{x} = 0 \quad \text{...(ii)}$$

From Eq. (i) and Eq. (ii),

$$2x = 2 \Rightarrow x = 1$$
$$\therefore \quad x^{2723} + \frac{1}{x^{3356}} = (1)^{2723} + \frac{1}{(1)^{3356}} = 1 + 1 = 2$$

37. (b) If $x = 7 - 4\sqrt{3}$

$$\therefore \quad \frac{1}{x} = \frac{1}{7-4\sqrt{3}} \times \frac{(7+4\sqrt{3})}{(7+4\sqrt{3})} = \frac{(7+4\sqrt{3})}{1}$$
$$= 7 + 4\sqrt{3}$$
$$\therefore \quad \left(x + \frac{1}{x}\right)^2 = x^2 + \frac{1}{x^2} + 2$$
$$\Rightarrow \quad x^2 + \frac{1}{x^2} = \left(x + \frac{1}{x}\right)^2 - 2$$
$$\therefore \quad x^2 + \frac{1}{x^2} = (7 - 4\sqrt{3} + 7 - 4\sqrt{3})^2 - 2$$
$$= (14)^2 - 2 = 194$$

38. (c) We have, $x - y + z = 2a$

$$\Rightarrow \quad z = 2a - x + y \quad \text{...(i)}$$
$$x + 4y - 2z = 3(4-a) \quad \text{...(ii)}$$
$$2x - 3y + 4z = 6 - 2a \quad \text{...(iii)}$$

From Eqs. (i) and (ii), we get

$$x + 4y - 2(2a - x + y) = 3(4-a)$$
$$\Rightarrow \quad 3x + 2y = 12 + a \quad \text{...(iv)}$$

From Eqs. (i) and (iii)

$$2x - 3y + 4(2a - x + y) = 6 - 2a$$
$$\Rightarrow \quad -2x + y = 6 - 10a \quad \text{...(v)}$$

From Eqs. (iv) and (v)

$$x = 3a \text{ and } y = 6 - 4a$$

From Eq. (i), $z = 2a - 3a + 6 - 4a$

$$z = 6 - 5a$$

As, values of the variables are consecutive number,

$\therefore$ their difference = 1

$$\therefore \quad x - y = 1 \Rightarrow 3a - 6 + 4a = 1$$
$$\Rightarrow \quad 7a = 7 \Rightarrow a = 1$$

39. (b) Yellow marbles = y

Blue marbles = b

$$\because \quad 3y = 2b + 200$$
$$3y - 2b = 200 \quad \text{...(i)}$$

Now, 18% of y + 24% of b = 30

6 (3% of y + 4% of b) = 30

$$\frac{3y}{100} + \frac{4b}{100} = 5$$
$$3y + 4b = 500 \quad \text{...(ii)}$$

From Eqs. (i) and (ii),

$$9y = 900$$
$$y = 100$$

Put this in Eq. (i),

$$3 \times 100 - 2b = 200$$
$$b = 50$$
$$\text{Ratio} = y^2 : b^2 = \frac{100 \times 100}{50 \times 50} = 4 : 1$$

40. (a) $a^3 + 3a^2 + 3a = 7$

$$a^3 + 3a^2 + 3a - 7 = 0$$
$$\Rightarrow \quad (a+1)^3 - 8 = 0$$
$$\Rightarrow \quad (a+1)^3 = 8$$
$$\Rightarrow \quad (a+1)^3 = (2)^3$$
$$\Rightarrow \quad (a+1) = 2$$
$$\Rightarrow \quad a = 2 - 1 = 1$$

Now, $a^2 + 2a$

$$(1)^2 + 2 \times 1 = 1 + 2 = 3$$

41. (d) $8a^3 + b^3 + 27c^3 = 18abc$

$$(2a)^3 + b^3 + (3c)^3 = 3 \times 2a \times b \times 3c$$

(If $x + y + z = 0$, Then $x^3 + y^3 + z^3 = 3xyz$)

So, $2a + b + 3c = 0$

$$b + 3c = -2a$$

42. (d) Given equations,

$$4x + 12y + 36 = 0$$
$$5x + ky + 45 = 0$$

If equations have infinite number of solutions.

$$\text{Then, } \frac{a_1}{a_2} = \frac{b_1}{b_2} = \frac{c_1}{c_2} \Rightarrow \frac{4}{5} = \frac{12}{k} = \frac{36}{45}$$
$$\Rightarrow \quad \frac{4}{5} = \frac{12}{k} \Rightarrow k = \frac{12 \times 5}{4} \Rightarrow k = 15$$

43. (d) Given, $x^2 + \dfrac{1}{x^2} = 83$

$$\Rightarrow \quad x^2 + \frac{1}{x^2} - 2 = 83 - 2$$
$$\Rightarrow \quad \left(x - \frac{1}{x}\right)^2 = 81 \Rightarrow x - \frac{1}{x} = 9$$
$$\text{Then, } x^3 - \frac{1}{x^3} = (9)^3 + 3 \times 9 \quad [\because A^2 + 3A]$$
$$= 729 + 27 = 756$$

44. (a) $kx - 15y + 7 = 0$ and $7x - 21y - 19 = 0$ has no solution

$$\text{Then, } \frac{a_1}{a_2} = \frac{b_1}{b_2} \neq \frac{7}{19} \Rightarrow \frac{k}{7} = \frac{-15}{-21}$$
$$\Rightarrow \quad \frac{k}{7} = \frac{5}{7} \Rightarrow k = 5$$

45. (d) $(g-h)^2 - (g+h)^2 + 4gh$

$$\left[\begin{array}{l}\therefore (a+b)^2 = a^2 + b^2 + 2ab \\ (a-b)^2 = a^2 + b^2 - 2ab\end{array}\right]$$
$$= g^2 + h^2 - 2gh - (g^2 + h^2 + 2gh) + 4gh$$
$$= g^2 + h^2 - 2gh - g^2 - h^2 - 2gh + 4gh = 0$$

46. (b) $x - ay = 2 - a$

$$x - ay + (a - 2) = 0$$
$$\text{and} \quad (1-a)x + 6y = a + b$$
$$(1-a)x + 6y - (a+b) = 0$$

If no solution

$$\text{Then } \frac{a_1}{a_2} = \frac{b_1}{b_2} \neq \frac{c_1}{c_2}$$
$$\frac{1}{1-a} = \frac{-a}{6} \neq \frac{a-2}{-(a+b)}$$
$$6 = a(a-1)$$
$$a^2 - a - 6 = 0$$
$$\Rightarrow \quad (a-3)(a+2) = 0$$
$$\therefore \quad a = 3$$
$$\text{and} \quad -(a+b) \neq (1-a)(a-2)$$
$$-3 - b \neq (1-3)(3-2)$$
$$-3 - b \neq (-2) \times 1$$
$$-3 - b \neq -2$$
$$-b \neq 1$$
$$\therefore \quad b \neq -1$$

Hence, $a = 3$ and $b \neq -1$

47. (a) $\dfrac{25a^2 - 10ab - 48b^2}{5a + 6b} \times (5a + 8b)$

$$= \frac{(5a)^2 - 2 \times 5a \times b + b^2 - (7b)^2}{(5a + 6b)} \times (5a + 8b)$$
$$= \frac{(5a - b)^2 - (7b)^2}{(5a + 6b)} \times (5a + 8b)$$
$$= \frac{(5a - b + 7b) \times (5a - b - 7b)}{(5a + 6b)} \times (5a + 8b)$$
$$= \frac{(5a + 6b)(5a - 8b)}{(5a + 6b)} \times (5a + 8b)$$
$$= (5a - 8b)(5a + 8b) = 25a^2 - 64b^2$$

48. (a) Given, $a + b = 1$

$$a^2 + b^2 + 2ab = 1 \quad \text{...(i)}$$
$$\therefore \quad \frac{1}{a^2} + \frac{1}{b^2} + \frac{2}{ab} = \frac{b^2 + a^2 + 2ab}{a^2b^2}$$
$$= \frac{1}{a^2b^2} \quad \text{[from Eq. (i)]}$$

49. (b) Let cups of tea be x

$\therefore$ Cup of coffee $= (7 - x)$

According to the question,

$$40(7-x) + 30x = 240$$
$$\Rightarrow \quad 280 - 40x + 30x = 240$$
$$\Rightarrow \quad 40 = 10x$$

Coffee $(x) = 4$

50. (a) $\frac{(x-y)^3+(y-z)^3+(z-x)^3}{(x-y)(y-z)(z-x)}$
$= \frac{3(x-y)(y-z)(z-x)}{(x-y)(y-z)(z-x)}$
[If $A+B+C=0$ then $A^3+B^3+C^3=3ABC$]
$= 3$

51. (c) $5x-3y+7z=22$ ...(i)
$3x-5y-2z=-46$ ...(ii)
$2x-2y+5z=24$ ...(iii)
2 × Eq. (i) + 7 × Eq. (ii),
$31x-41y=-278$ ...(iv)
5 × Eq. (ii) + 2 Eq. (iii),
$19x-29y=-182$ ...(v)
On solving Eqs. (iv) and (v), $x=-5$, $y=3$
From Eq. (i), we get $z=8$
Hence, $x=-5$, $y=3$ and $z=8$

52. (b) Given, $a^2+b^2+c^2=2(a+c-1)$
$a^2-2a+1+b^2+c^2-2c+1=0$
$(a-1)^2+(b-0)^2+(c-1)^2=0$
$\therefore \quad a=1, b=0, c=1$
$\therefore \quad a^3+b^3+c^3=1+1+0=2$

53. (c) $2x+y=a$
$8x+by=12$
For infinite solution,
$\frac{a_1}{a_2}=\frac{b_1}{b_2}=\frac{c_1}{c_2} \Rightarrow \frac{2}{8}=\frac{1}{b}=\frac{a}{12}$
$\Rightarrow \quad a=3, b=4$
$\therefore \quad a+b=3+4=7$

54. (a) Given, $m+n=24$
$m+n=16+8$
$\Rightarrow \quad (m-16)=(8-n)$
$\Rightarrow \quad (m-16)=-(n-8)$
Cubing on both sides,
$(m-16)^3=(-(n-8))^3$
$\Rightarrow \quad (m-16)^3=-(n-8)^3$
$\Rightarrow \quad (m-16)^3+(n-8)^3=0$

55. (b) According to the question,
$t^3+\left(\frac{3}{5}\right)^3+\frac{9}{5}t=\left(\frac{2}{5}\right)^3+\left(\frac{3}{5}\right)^3+\frac{9}{5}\left(\frac{2}{5}\right)$
$=\frac{8}{125}+\frac{27}{125}+\frac{18}{25}$
$=\frac{8+27+90}{125}=\frac{125}{125}=1$

56. (d) Given, $x+\frac{1}{9x}=3 \Rightarrow 3x+\frac{1}{3x}=9$
Squaring both side,
$9x^2+\frac{1}{9x^2}+2=81 \Rightarrow 9x^2+\frac{1}{9x^2}=79$

57. (d) $\left(\frac{3}{a}+3a\right)\left(\frac{9}{a^2}-9+9a^2\right)$
$=\left(\frac{3}{a}+3a\right)\left[\left(\frac{3}{a}\right)^2-3a\times\frac{3}{a}+(3a)^2\right]$
$=\left(\frac{3}{a}\right)^3+(3a)^3$
[$\because a^3+b^3=(a+b)(a^2+b^2-ab)$]
At $a=1=27+27=54$

58. (c) We have,
$0.4x+0.16y=1.7$
$\Rightarrow 0.4x+0.16y-1.7=0$
$0.3x+0.12y=3.4$
$\Rightarrow 0.3x+0.12y-3.4=0$
Here, $a_1=0.4, b_1=0.16$, $c_1=-1.7$
$a_2=0.3, b_2=0.12, c_2=-3.4$
$\therefore \quad \frac{a_1}{a_2}=\frac{0.4}{0.3}=\frac{4}{3}, \frac{b_1}{b_2}=\frac{0.16}{0.12}=\frac{16}{12}=\frac{4}{3},$
$\frac{c_1}{c_2}=\frac{-1.7}{-3.4}=\frac{1}{2}$
$\therefore \quad \frac{a_1}{a_2}=\frac{b_1}{b_2}\neq\frac{c_1}{c_2}$
$\therefore$ System of equation has no solution.

59. (c) Let a is her first salary and d is the increment of every year.
$\therefore$ According to the question,
$[a+(6-1)d]=a+5d=28400$ ...(i)
and $[a+(15-1)d]=a+14d=52997$ ...(ii)
$\therefore$ Eqs. (ii) – Eq. (i),
$9d=24597 \Rightarrow d=\frac{24597}{9} \Rightarrow d=2733$
$\therefore$ Annual increment = ₹ 2733

60. (b) $x+2z=3$ ...(i)
$x+2y+3z=5$ ...(ii)
$3x-5z=-13$ ...(iii)
$5\times$ Eq. (i) + $2\times$ Eq. (iii),
$5x+10z+6x-10z=15+(-26)$
$11x=-11 \Rightarrow x=-1$
Put, $x=-1$ in Eq. (i),
$2z=3+1=4 \Rightarrow z=2$
Put, the value of x and z in Eq. (ii),
$-1+2y+3\times 2=5$
$\Rightarrow \quad 2y=5-6+1=0$
$\Rightarrow \quad y=0$
$\therefore \quad x=-1, y=0, z=2$

61. (b) $x+\frac{1}{x}=2\sqrt{10}$ where, $x>1$
Squaring on both sides,
$\left(x+\frac{1}{x}\right)^2=(2\sqrt{10})^2 \Rightarrow x^2+\frac{1}{x^2}+2=40$
$\Rightarrow \quad x^2+\frac{1}{x^2}+2-4=40-4$
$\Rightarrow \quad x^2+\frac{1}{x^2}-2=36 \Rightarrow \left(x-\frac{1}{x}\right)^2=36$
$\Rightarrow \quad x-\frac{1}{x}=6$ ($\because x>1$ is given)
Now, cubing on both sides,
$\left(x-\frac{1}{x}\right)^3=(6)^3$
$\Rightarrow \quad x^3-\frac{1}{x^3}-3\times x\times\frac{1}{x}\left(x-\frac{1}{x}\right)=216$
$\Rightarrow \quad x^3-\frac{1}{x^3}-3\times 6=216$
$\Rightarrow \quad x^3-\frac{1}{x^3}=216+18=234$
$\therefore \quad x^3-\frac{1}{x^3}=234$

62. (a) According to the question,
$(x-y)^2=x^2+y^2-2xy=280-2(120)$
$\Rightarrow \quad (x-y)^2=280-240=40$
$\Rightarrow \quad x-y=\sqrt{40}=2\sqrt{10}$
Also, $(x+y)^2=x^2+y^2+2xy$
$=280+2(120)$
$=280+240=520$
$\Rightarrow \quad x+y=\sqrt{520}=2\sqrt{130}$
$\therefore$ Required value
i.e., $\frac{x-y}{x+y}=\frac{2\sqrt{10}}{2\sqrt{130}}=\frac{2\sqrt{10}}{2\sqrt{13}\times\sqrt{10}}$
$\therefore \quad \frac{x-y}{x+y}=\frac{1}{\sqrt{13}}$

63. (a) Given, $\sqrt{x}+\frac{1}{\sqrt{x}}=7$
Squaring on both sides,
$\left(\sqrt{x}+\frac{1}{\sqrt{x}}\right)^2=7^2$
$\Rightarrow x+\frac{1}{x}+2\times\sqrt{x}\times\frac{1}{\sqrt{x}}=49$
$\Rightarrow x+\frac{1}{x}=49-2=47 \Rightarrow x+\frac{1}{x}=47$

64. (c) Given, $a+\frac{1}{a}=12$
We know that, $a^2+\frac{1}{a^2}=\left(a+\frac{1}{a}\right)^2-2$
$=(12)^2-2=142$

65. (b) Let numbers be x, y and z.
$x+y+z=18$ ...(i)
$x^2+y^2+z^2=36$ ...(ii)
We know that,
$(x+y+z)^2=x^2+y^2+z^2+2(xy+yz+zx)$
$(18)^2=36+2(xy+yz+zx)$
[From Eqs. (i) and (ii)]
$144=xy+yz+zx$ ...(iii)
We know that,
$x^3+y^3+z^3-3xyz=(x+y+z)$
$(x^2+y^2+z^2-(xy+yz+zx))$
$x^3+y^3+z^3-3xyz=(18)(36-144)=-1944$
[From Eqs. (i), (ii) and (iii)]

66. (c) Given that, $x+y+z=1$
Let assume, $x=y=z=\frac{1}{3}$
Now, $\frac{1}{x}+\frac{1}{y}+\frac{1}{z}=\frac{1}{\frac{1}{3}}+\frac{1}{\frac{1}{3}}+\frac{1}{\frac{1}{3}}=3+3+3=9$

67. (b) Given equations,
$4x+(k-2)y+3=0$
$(k-2)x+9y-5=0$
Where, $(k>0)$
If two equations are parallel,
Then, $\frac{a_1}{a_2}=\frac{b_1}{b_2}\neq\frac{c_1}{c_2} \Rightarrow \frac{4}{k-2}=\frac{k-2}{9}\neq\frac{3}{-5}$
$\Rightarrow \quad \frac{4}{k-2}=\frac{k-2}{9}$ [By Eqs. I and II]
$\Rightarrow (k-2)^2=36 \Rightarrow (k-2)^2=(6)^2 \Rightarrow k-2=6$

$\Rightarrow \quad k = 6 + 2 = 8$

Value of $k^2 + 6 = (8)^2 + 6 = 64 + 6 = 70$

68. (c) Given, $a + b = 2c$

$$a + b = c + c$$
$$a - c = c - b$$

By squaring both sides, we get

$$(a - c)^2 = (c - b)^2$$
$$a^2 - 2ac + c^2 = c^2 - 2bc + b^2$$
$$a^2 - 2ac = b^2 - 2bc$$
$$a^2 + 2bc = b^2 + 2ac$$

69. (d) By option (a),

Let there are 13 coin of ₹5, then

Amount collected by ₹5 = 13 × 5 = 65

Now, remaining coin = 40 − 13 = 27

and suppose 8 coin are of ₹2 and 19 coin are of ₹1.

Thus, 8 × 2 + 19 × 1 = ₹35

Thus, total amount = 65 + 35 = ₹100 (satisfied)

Thus, it is true that there are 13 coin of ₹5.

70. (c) $\dfrac{x^3 + 15x^2 + 75x + 125}{x^2 - 25} \times (x - 5)$

$$= \frac{x^3 + 15x^2 + 75x + 125}{(x - 5)(x + 5)} \times (x - 5)$$
$$= \frac{x^3 + 15x^2 + 75x + 125}{(x + 5)}$$
$$= \frac{(x + 5)(x^2 + 10x + 25)}{x + 5}$$

$= x^2 + 10x + 25$

71. (d) Let cost of one LED is x and one mobile is y.

According to the question,

$$2x + y = 31000 \quad \ldots(i)$$
$$x + 2y = 35000 \quad \ldots(ii)$$

Multiply by 2 in Eq. (ii) and subtract from Eq. (i),

$$2x + y = 31000$$
$$2x + 4y = 70000$$
$$- \quad - \quad -$$
$$-3y = -39000$$
$$y = 13000$$

72. (d) $2^x + 3^y = 17 \quad \ldots(i)$

$$2^{x+2} - 3^{y+1} = 5$$
$$2^x \cdot 2^2 - 3^y \cdot 3^1 = 5$$
$$4 \cdot 2^x - 3 \cdot 3^y = 5 \quad \ldots(ii)$$

From Eq. (i) multiply by 3 and adding in Eq. (ii),

$$3 \cdot 2^x + 3 \cdot 3^y = 51$$
$$4 \cdot 2^x - 3 \cdot 3^y = 5$$
$$7 \cdot 2^x = 56$$

$\Rightarrow \quad 2^x = \dfrac{56}{7} = 8$

$\Rightarrow \quad 2^x = 2^3 \Rightarrow x = 3$

Value of x putting in Eq. (i),

$$2^3 + 3^y = 17$$

$\Rightarrow \quad 3^y = 17 - 8 \Rightarrow 3^y = 9 \Rightarrow y = 2$

73. (b) Given, $4x^2 + y^2 = 40$

$$xy = 6$$
$$(2x + y)^2 = 4x^2 + y^2 + 4xy$$
$$= 40 + 4 \times 6 = 40 + 24$$
$$(2x + y)^2 = 64$$
$$2x + y = 8$$

74. (a) HCF of x and y = 15

$$36x^2 - 81y^2 = 9(4x^2 - 9y^2)$$
$$= 9[(2x)^2 - (3y)^2]$$
$$= 9(2x - 3y)(2x + 3y)$$
$$81x^2 - 9y^2 = 9(9x^2 - y^2) = 9[(3x)^2 - y^2]$$
$$= 9(3x - y)(3x + y)$$

So, required HCF = 9 × 15 = 135

75. (b) Let the number of hens be x and number of goats be y.

According to the question,

$$x + y = 100 \quad \ldots(i)$$

As, goat has 4 feet and hen has 2 feet

$\therefore \quad 2x + 4y = 348 \quad \ldots(ii)$

Multiply by 2 in Eq. (i) and subtract by Eq. (ii),

$$2x + 2y - 2x - 4y = 200 - 348$$

$\Rightarrow \quad -2y = -148 \Rightarrow y = 74$

76. (a) $f(x)_1 = x^2 - 8x + 15$

$$= x^2 - 5x - 3x + 15$$
$$f(x)_1 = (x - 5)(x - 3)$$
$$f(x)_2 = x^2 - 5x + 6 = x^2 - 3x - 2x + 6$$
$$f(x)_2 = (x - 3)(x - 2)$$

LCM of $f(x)_1$ and $f(x)_2$

$= (x - 2)(x - 3)(x - 5)$

77. (c) $(1 + x)(1 + x^2)(1 + x^4)(1 + x^8)(1 - x)$

$$= (1 + x)(1 - x)(1 + x^2)(1 + x^4)(1 + x^8)$$
$$[\because (a + b)(a - b) = a^2 - b^2]$$
$$= (1 - x^2)(1 + x^2)(1 + x^4)(1 + x^8)$$
$$= (1 - x^4)(1 + x^4)(1 + x^8)$$
$$= (1 - x^8)(1 + x^8) = 1 - x^{16}$$

78. (a) Given equation,

$$17x + my + 102 = 0$$
$$23x + 299y + 138 = 0$$

For infinite number of solution,

$$\frac{17}{23} = \frac{m}{299} = \frac{102}{138} \Rightarrow \frac{17}{23} = \frac{m}{299}$$

$\therefore \quad m = 221$

79. (c) Given, $x + \dfrac{1}{x} = 6 \Rightarrow x^2 + \dfrac{1}{x^2} = 36 - 2$

$$[\because a^2 + b^2 = (a + b)^2 - 2ab]$$

$\Rightarrow \quad x^2 + \dfrac{1}{x^2} = 34 \Rightarrow x^2 + \dfrac{1}{x^2} - 2 = 34 - 2$

$\Rightarrow \quad \left(x - \dfrac{1}{x}\right)^2 = 32$

Then, $x - \dfrac{1}{x} = \sqrt{32} = 4\sqrt{2}$

Hence, $x^2 - \dfrac{1}{x^2} = \left(x - \dfrac{1}{x}\right)\left(x + \dfrac{1}{x}\right)$

$$= 6 \times 4\sqrt{2} = 24\sqrt{2}$$

Speedy Method

If $x + \dfrac{1}{x} = a$, then $x^2 - \dfrac{1}{x^2} = a\sqrt{a^2 - 4}$

Here, $a = 6$

$$x^2 - \frac{1}{x} = 6\sqrt{6^2 - 4}$$
$$= 6\sqrt{32} = 6 \times 4\sqrt{2} = 24\sqrt{2}$$

80. (a) Given, $(a + b + c) = 14 \quad \ldots(i)$

and $a^3 + b^3 + c^3 - 3abc = 98 \quad \ldots(ii)$

On squaring Eq. (i),

$$(a + b + c)^2 = (14)^2$$
$$a^2 + b^2 + c^2 + 2(ab + bc + ca) = 196 \quad \ldots(iii)$$

From Eq. (ii),

$a^3 + b^3 + c^3 - 3abc$

$$= (a + b + c)[(a^2 + b^2 + c^2 - (ab + bc + ca)]$$
$$98 = 14 \times [a^2 + b^2 + c^2 - (ab + bc + ca)]$$

$\Rightarrow \quad 7 = a^2 + b^2 + c^2 - (ab + bc + ca)$

$$a^2 + b^2 + c^2 - 7 = ab + bc + ca \quad \ldots(iv)$$

From Eqs. (iii) and (iv),

$$a^2 + b^2 + c^2 + 2(a^2 + b^2 + c^2 - 7) = 196$$
$$a^2 + b^2 + c^2 = \frac{210}{3} = 70$$

81. (c) Given, $x^2 - \dfrac{1}{x^2} = 4\sqrt{2}$

On squaring both sides,

$$x^4 + \frac{1}{x^4} = 32 + 2 \quad [\because (a - b)^2 = a^2 + b^2 - 2ab]$$

Again squaring both sides,

$$\left(x^4 + \frac{1}{x^4}\right)^2 = (34)^2$$

$\Rightarrow \quad (x^4)^2 + \left(\dfrac{1}{x^4}\right)^2 = 1156 - 2$

$\Rightarrow \quad (x^4)^2 + \left(\dfrac{1}{x^4}\right)^2 - 2 = 1154 - 2$

$\Rightarrow \quad \left(x^4 - \dfrac{1}{x^4}\right)^2 = 1152$

$\therefore \quad x^4 - \dfrac{1}{x^4} = 24\sqrt{2}$

82. (c) Given, $2x + 3y = 16$ and $xy = 9$

Now, $(2x + 3y)^3 = (16)^3$

$\Rightarrow 8x^3 + 27y^3 + 3 \times 2x \times 3y(2x + 3y) = 4096$

$\Rightarrow \quad 8x^3 + 27y^3 + 18 \times 9(16) = 4096$

$\therefore \quad 8x^3 + 27y^3 = 4096 - 2592 = 1504$

83. (b) Given, $(x - 5)^2 + (x + 3)^2 + 4x$

$$= x^2 + 25 - 10x + x^2 + 9 + 6x + 4x$$
$$= 2x^2 + 34 = 2(x^2 + 17)$$

84. (b) $x - \dfrac{1}{x} = 10$

$\Rightarrow x + \dfrac{1}{x} = \sqrt{10^2 + 4} = \sqrt{104}$

$\Rightarrow \quad x^2 + \dfrac{1}{x^2} = (\sqrt{104})^2 - 2 = 102$

$\Rightarrow \quad x^4 + \dfrac{1}{x^4} = (102)^2 - 2 = 10404 - 2$

$= 10402$

Speedy Method

If $x - \frac{1}{x} = a$, then $x^4 + \frac{1}{x^4} = (a^2 + 2)^2 - 2$

Here, $a = 10$

$$x^4 + \frac{1}{x^4} = (10^2 + 2)^2 - 2$$
$$= (102)^2 - 2 = 10402$$

85. (b) Given, $b = 5$

$\therefore \left(\frac{5}{b} + 5b\right)\left(\frac{25}{b^2} - 25 + 25b^2\right)$

$= \left(\frac{5}{b} + 5b\right)\left[\left(\frac{5}{b}\right)^2 - \frac{5}{b} \times 5b + (5b)^2\right]$

$= \left(\frac{5}{b}\right)^3 + (5b)^3$

$[\therefore a^3 + b^3 = (a + b)(a^2 - ab + b^2)]$

$= \left(\frac{5}{5}\right)^3 + (5 \times 5)^3 = 15626 \quad [\because b = 5]$

86. (a) Given,

$(a^3 + b^3 + c^3 - 3abc) = 405;$

$(a - b)^2 + (b - c)^2 + (c - a)^2 = 54$

$\because \frac{1}{2}(a + b + c)\{(b - c)^2 + (c - a)^2 + (a - b)^2\}$

$= a^3 + b^3 + c^3 - 3abc$

$\therefore \quad a + b + c = \frac{405 \times 2}{54} = 15$

$\therefore \quad (a + b + c) = 15$

87. (c) Given, $(a + b + c) = 13;$

$(ab + bc + ca) = 54$

$\because (a + b + c)^2 = a^2 + b^2 + c^2 + 2(ab + bc + ca)$

$\Rightarrow \quad 169 - 108 = a^2 + b^2 + c^2$

$\therefore \quad a^2 + b^2 + c^2 = 61$

88. (b) Given, $x^2 + \frac{1}{x^2} = 6 \quad \ldots(i)$

$\Rightarrow \quad x^2 + \frac{1}{x^2} - 2 = 6 - 2$

$\Rightarrow \quad \left(x - \frac{1}{x}\right)^2 = 4 \Rightarrow x - \frac{1}{x} = \pm 2$

$x - \frac{1}{x} = -2 \quad \ldots(ii)$

$[\therefore 0 < x < 1]$

From Eq. (i), $x^2 + \frac{1}{x^2} + 2 = 6 + 2$

$x + \frac{1}{x} = 2\sqrt{2} \quad \ldots(iii)$

$x^4 - \frac{1}{x^4} = \left(x^2 - \frac{1}{x^2}\right)\left(x^2 + \frac{1}{x^2}\right)$

$= \left(x - \frac{1}{x}\right)\left(x + \frac{1}{x}\right)\left(x^2 + \frac{1}{x^2}\right)$

$= -2 \times 2\sqrt{2} \times 6$

$= -24\sqrt{2}$ (for $0 < x < 1$)

Hence, $x^4 - \frac{1}{x^4} = -24\sqrt{2}.$

89. (d) Given, $x = \frac{1}{x - 3}$

Then, $x^2 - 3x = 1 \Rightarrow x - \frac{1}{x} = 3$

$\therefore \quad x + \frac{1}{x} = \sqrt{(3)^3 + 4}$

Hence, $x + \frac{1}{x} = \sqrt{13}$

90. (a) $\frac{s^2 + t^2 + 2st - u^2}{s^2 - t^2 - 2tu - u^2} \quad [\because (s + t + u) \neq 0]$

$= \frac{(s + t)^2 - u^2}{s^2 - (t + u)^2} = \frac{(s + t + u)(s + t - u)}{(s + t + u)(s - t - u)}$

$= \frac{s + t - u}{s - t - u}$

91. (d) $\frac{\sqrt{x} - \sqrt{y}}{\sqrt{x} + \sqrt{y}} = \frac{(\sqrt{x} - \sqrt{y})^2}{(\sqrt{x} + \sqrt{y})(\sqrt{x} - \sqrt{y})}$

$= \frac{(\sqrt{x})^2 - 2\sqrt{xy} + (\sqrt{y})^2}{(\sqrt{x})^2 - (\sqrt{y})^2}$

$= \frac{x + y - 2\sqrt{xy}}{x - y} = \frac{2 + 3 - 2\sqrt{6}}{2 - 3}$

$[\because x = 2, y = 3]$

$= 2\sqrt{6} - 5$

92. (d) $(a + b - c) = 20$ and $a^2 + b^2 + c^2 = 152$

$(a + b - c)^2 = a^2 + b^2 + c^2 + 2(ab - bc - ca)$

$\Rightarrow \quad ab - bc - ca = \frac{400 - 152}{2} = 124$

$\therefore \quad a^3 + b^3 - c^3 + 3abc$

$= (a + b - c)\{a^2 + b^2 + c^2 - (ab - bc - ca)\}$

$= 20\{152 - 124\} = 20 \times 28 = 560$

93. (a) Given, $y + \frac{1}{y} = 4$

$\Rightarrow \quad y^2 + \frac{1}{y^2} = 4^2 - 2 = 14$

$\therefore \quad y^6 + \frac{1}{y^6} = \left(y^2 + \frac{1}{y^2}\right)^3 - 3\left(y^2 + \frac{1}{y^2}\right)$

$= 14^3 - 3 \times 14$

$= 14(196 - 3) = 14 \times 193 = 2702$

94. (a) Let two numbers are a and b

$\therefore \quad (a + b)^3 = 1728 \quad \ldots(i)$

and $\quad ab = 32$

From Eq. (i), we get

$a + b = 12$

$\therefore \quad (a - b) = \sqrt{(a + b)^2 - 4ab} = \sqrt{12^2 - 4 \times 32}$

$= \sqrt{16} = 4$

$\therefore \quad a^3 - b^3 = (a - b)^3 + 3ab(a - b)$

$= 4^3 + 3 \times 32 \times 4 = 64 + 384 = 448$

$\therefore$ The difference between the cubes of two given numbers is 448.

95. (d) $\frac{x^2 - 2x - 63}{x^2 + 14x + 49} = \frac{(x - 9)(x + 7)}{(x + 7)(x + 7)}$

$= \frac{x - 9}{x + 7}$

96. (a) $7a - \frac{7}{a} + 4 = 0 \Rightarrow a - \frac{1}{a} = -\frac{4}{7}$

$[\because a^3 - b^3 = (a - b)^3 + 3ab(a - b)]$

$\Rightarrow \quad a^3 - \frac{1}{a^3} = \left(-\frac{4}{7}\right)^3 + 3\left(-\frac{4}{7}\right) = -\frac{64}{343} - \frac{12}{7}$

$= \frac{-64 - 588}{343} = \frac{-652}{343}$

$\therefore \quad a^3 - \frac{1}{a^3} - 1 = -\frac{652}{343} - 1$

$= \frac{-652 - 343}{343} = \frac{-995}{343}$

97. (a) $p + q + r = pqr = \frac{1}{p} + \frac{1}{q} + \frac{1}{r}$

$= \frac{pq + qr + rp}{pqr} = 1$

$p^2 + q^2 + r^2 = 1 - 2 = -1$

$\therefore \quad p^3 + q^3 + r^3 = (p^2 + q^2 + r^2) - (pq + qr + rp) + 3pqr$

$= -1 - 1 + 3 = 1$

98. (c) $\frac{256x^4 - 16y^4}{(80x^2 - 20y^2)(16x^2 + 4y^2)}$

$= \frac{256x^4 - 16y^4}{5(16x^2 - 4y^2)(16x^2 + 4y^2)}$

$= \frac{1}{5} \times \frac{(256x^4 - 16y^4)}{(256x^4 - 16y^4)} = \frac{1}{5}$

$[\because a^2 - b^2 = (a + b)(a - b)]$

99. (b) $x^2 - 15x + 1 = 0 \Rightarrow x - 15 + \frac{1}{x} = 0$

$\Rightarrow x + \frac{1}{x} = 15 \Rightarrow x^2 + \frac{1}{x^2} = 225 - 2$

$[\because a^2 + b^2 = (a - b)^2 + 2ab]$

$\therefore \quad x^2 + \frac{1}{x^2} = 223$

$\Rightarrow x^4 - 223x^2 + 1 = 0 \Rightarrow x^4 - 223x^2 + 6 = 5$

$\therefore$ Value of $x^4 - 223x^2 + 6 = 5$

100. (a) $p = \frac{x}{y + z} \Rightarrow 1 + p = \frac{x + y + z}{y + z}$

$\Rightarrow \quad \frac{1}{1 + p} = \frac{y + z}{x + y + z} \Rightarrow q = \frac{y}{z + x}$

$\Rightarrow 1 + q = \frac{x + y + z}{z + x} \Rightarrow \frac{1}{1 + q} = \frac{z + x}{x + y + z}$

$\Rightarrow r = \frac{z}{x + y} \Rightarrow 1 + r = \frac{x + y + z}{x + y}$

$\Rightarrow \frac{1}{1 + r} = \frac{x + y}{x + y + z}$

$\therefore \quad \frac{1}{2 + 2p} + \frac{1}{2 + 2q} + \frac{1}{2 + 2r}$

$= \frac{1}{2}\left(\frac{1}{1 + p} + \frac{1}{1 + q} + \frac{1}{1 + r}\right)$

$= \frac{1}{2}\left(\frac{y + z}{x + y + z} + \frac{z + x}{x + y + z} + \frac{x + y}{x + y + z}\right)$

$= \frac{1}{2} \times \frac{2(x + y + z)}{(x + y + z)} = 1$

101. (d) $x + \frac{1}{x} = 9 \Rightarrow x^2 + \frac{1}{x^2} = \left(x + \frac{1}{x}\right)^2 - 2$

$= 9^2 - 2 = 79$

$\therefore \quad x^4 + \frac{1}{x^4} = \left(x^2 + \frac{1}{x^2}\right)^2 - 2 = 79^2 - 2$

$= 6241 - 2 = 6239$

Speedy Method

If $x + \frac{1}{x} = a$, then $x^4 + \frac{1}{x^4} = (a^2 - 2)^2 - 2$

Here, $a = 9$, then $x^4 + \frac{1}{x^4} = (a^2 - 2)^2 - 2$

$= (9^2 - 2)^2 - 2 = 6241 - 2 = 6239$

102. (b) Given, $(4x+1)^2 - (4x+3)(4x-1)$

$= 16x^2 + 1 + 8x - [16x^2 + 12x - 4x - 3]$

$= 16x^2 + 1 + 8x - 16x^2 - 12x + 4x + 3 = 4$

103. (a) Given,

$$\frac{p^2-(q-r)^2}{(p+r)^2-q^2} + \frac{q^2-(p-r)^2}{(p+q)^2-r^2} + \frac{r^2-(p-q)^2}{(q+r)^2-p^2}$$

$$= \frac{[p-(q-r)](p+q-r)}{(p+r-q)(p+r+q)} + \frac{[q-(p-r)](q+p-r)}{(p+q-r)(p+q+r)} + \frac{[r-(p-q)](r+p-q)}{(q+r-p)(q+r+p)}$$

$$= \frac{p+q-r}{(p+r+q)} + \frac{q-p+r}{(p+q+r)} + \frac{r+p-q}{(p+q+r)}$$

$$= \frac{p+q-r+q-p+r+r+p-q}{(p+q+r)} = \frac{p+q+r}{p+q+r} = 1$$

104. (c) Let $a^2 + b^2 + c^2 - ab - bc - ca = x$

On multiply by 2 both sides.

$2a^2 + 2b^2 + 2c^2 - 2ab - 2bc - 2ca = 2x$

$\Rightarrow (a^2 + b^2 - 2ab) + (a^2 + c^2 - 2ca) + (b^2 + c^2 - 2bc) = 2x$

$\Rightarrow (a-b)^2 + (a-c)^2 + (b-c)^2 = 2x$

$\Rightarrow (101-102)^2 + (101-103)^2 + (102-103)^2 = 2x$

$\Rightarrow 1 + 4 + 1 = 2x \Rightarrow 6 = 2x$

Then, $x = 3$

105. (a) We know,

$\therefore a^3 - b^3 = (a-b)(a^2 + ab + b^2)$

$= (a^2 + ab + b^2)$

106. (d) As,

$\therefore \left(x + \frac{1}{x}\right)^2 = x^2 + \frac{1}{x^2} + 2 = 18 + 2 = 20$

$\Rightarrow x + \frac{1}{x} = \sqrt{20}$

$\Rightarrow x^3 + \frac{1}{x^3} = \left(x + \frac{1}{x}\right)^3 - 3\left(x + \frac{1}{x}\right)$

$\Rightarrow x^3 + \frac{1}{x^3} = (\sqrt{20})^3 - (\sqrt{20}) \times 3$

$= 17\sqrt{20} = 34\sqrt{5}$

107. (b) $64x^3 + 36x^2y + 24xy^2 + 2y^3$

$= (4x)^3 + 3\cdot(4x)^2\cdot y + 3\cdot 4x\cdot y^2 + y^3 + y^3 + 12xy^2 - 12x^2y$

$= (4x+y)^3 + y(y^2 + 12xy - 12x^2)$

$= \{(4\times 3 + (-4)\}^3 + (-4)\{(-4)^2 + 12\times 3(-4) - 12\cdot 3^2\}$

$= 512 + (-4)\{16 + 36(-4) - 108\}$

$= 512 + (-4)\{-236\} = 512 + 944 = 1456$

108. (a) $[(1+p)(1+p^2)(1+p^4)(1+p^8)(1+p^{16})(1-p) - 1]$

$= [(1-p^2)(1+p^2)(1+p^4)(1+p^8)(1+p^{16}) - 1]$

$[\because (a+b)(a-b) = a^2 - b^2]$

$= [(1-p^4)(1+p^4)(1+p^8)(1+p^{16}) - 1]$

$= [(1-p^8)(1+p^8)(1+p^{16}) - 1]$

$= [(1-p^{16})(1+p^{16}) - 1]$

$= [1 - p^{32} - 1] = -p^{32}$

109. (b) $x - y = 5, xy = 150$

$(x+y)^2 = (x-y)^2 + 4xy$

$= 5^2 + 4\times 150 = 625$

$\therefore x + y = \sqrt{625} = 25$

110. (d) $x^2 - \frac{1}{x^2} = 4\sqrt{6}$

$\Rightarrow x^4 + \frac{1}{x^4} = \left(x^2 - \frac{1}{x^2}\right)^2 + 2$

$= (4\sqrt{6})^2 + 2 = 98$

$\Rightarrow x^2 + \frac{1}{x^2} = \sqrt{x^4 + \frac{1}{x^4} + 2} = \sqrt{98 + 2} = 10$

$\Rightarrow x - \frac{1}{x} = \sqrt{x^2 + \frac{1}{x^2} - 2} = \sqrt{10 - 2} = \sqrt{8}$

$\therefore x^3 - \frac{1}{x^3} = \left(x - \frac{1}{x}\right)^3 + 3\left(x - \frac{1}{x}\right)$

$= (\sqrt{8})^3 + 3\sqrt{8} = 8\sqrt{8} + 3\sqrt{8}$

$= 11\times 2\sqrt{2} = 22\sqrt{2}$

111. (a) Given, $\frac{2a-5}{a} - \frac{4b-5}{b} + \frac{6c+5}{c} = 0$

$\Rightarrow \frac{2a}{a} - \frac{5}{a} - \frac{4b}{b} + \frac{5}{b} + \frac{6c}{c} + \frac{5}{c} = 0$

$\Rightarrow 2 - \frac{5}{a} - 4 + \frac{5}{b} + 6 + \frac{5}{c} = 0$

$\Rightarrow (2 - 4 + 6) - 5\left(\frac{1}{a} - \frac{1}{b} - \frac{1}{c}\right) = 0$

$\Rightarrow 4 - 5\left(\frac{1}{a} - \frac{1}{b} - \frac{1}{c}\right) = 0 \Rightarrow \frac{1}{a} - \frac{1}{b} - \frac{1}{c} = \frac{4}{5}$

112. (d) Given, $x - \frac{1}{x} = 2\sqrt{2}$

$x + \frac{1}{x} = \sqrt{(2(2)^2) + 4} = \sqrt{12} = 2\sqrt{3}$

and $\left(x + \frac{1}{x}\right)^3 = x^3 + \frac{1}{x^3} + 3\left(x + \frac{1}{x}\right)$

$\Rightarrow (2\sqrt{3})^3 - 3(2\sqrt{3}) = x^3 + \frac{1}{x^3}$

$\Rightarrow x^3 + \frac{1}{x^3} = 24\sqrt{3} - 6\sqrt{3} = 18\sqrt{3}$

Now, $\left(x^3 + \frac{1}{x^3}\right)^2 = x^6 + \frac{1}{x^6} + 2$

$\Rightarrow x^6 + \frac{1}{x^6} = (18\sqrt{3})^2 - 2 = 972 - 2 = 970$

113. (c) $27x^3 + 58x^2y + 31xy^2 + 8y^3$

$= (3x)^3 + 54x^2y + 36xy^2 + 8y^3 + 4x^2y - 5xy^2$

$= (3x)^3 + 3\cdot(3x)^2\cdot 2y + 3\cdot 3x\cdot(2y)^2 + (2y)^3 + xy(4x - 5y)$

$= (3x + 2y)^3 + xy(4x - 5y)$

$= \{3\times 5 + 2(-7)\}^3 + 5(-7)\{4\times 5 - 5(-7)\}$

$= 1 + (-35)\times 55 = 1 - 1925 = -1924$

114. (c) $(a - 2b)(b - 3a) + (a + b)(a - 3b) - (b - 3a)(4a - 5b)$

$= ab - 3a^2 - 2b^2 + 6ab + a^2 - 3ab + ab - 3b^2 - 4ab + 5b^2 + 12a^2 - 15ab$

$= 10a^2 - 14ab$

115. (c) $x + y = 7$ and $xy = 19$

$\therefore x^2 + y^2 = (x+y)^2 - 2xy$

$= 7^2 - 2\times 19 = 49 - 38 = 11$

116. (b) We know that,

$(a + b + c)^2 = a^2 + b^2 + c^2 + 2(ab + bc + ca)$

$\Rightarrow a^2 + b^2 + c^2 = 144 - 94 = 50$

$\therefore a^3 + b^3 + c^3 - 3abc$

$= \{a^2 + b^2 + c^2 - (ab + bc + ca)\}(a + b + c)$

$= \{50 - 47\}\times 12 = 3\times 12 = 36$

117. (c) Given, $x + \frac{1}{x} = 3\sqrt{2}, x > 1$

$\therefore \left(x + \frac{1}{x}\right)^2 = x^2 + \frac{1}{x^2} + 2$

$\Rightarrow x^2 + \frac{1}{x^2} = (3\sqrt{2})^2 - 2 = 16$

Also, $\left(x - \frac{1}{x}\right)^2 = x^2 + \frac{1}{x^2} - 2$

$\Rightarrow \left(x - \frac{1}{x}\right)^2 = 16 - 2 = 14 \Rightarrow x - \frac{1}{x} = \sqrt{14}$

and $\left(x^2 + \frac{1}{x^2}\right)^2 = x^4 + \frac{1}{x^4} + 2$

$\Rightarrow x^4 + \frac{1}{x^4} = (16)^2 - 2 = 256 - 2 = 254$

$\therefore \left(x^8 - \frac{1}{x^8}\right) = \left(x^4 + \frac{1}{x^4}\right)\left(x^2 + \frac{1}{x^2}\right)\left(x + \frac{1}{x}\right)\left(x - \frac{1}{x}\right) = (254)(16)(3\sqrt{2})(\sqrt{14})$

$\therefore \left(x^8 - \frac{1}{x^8}\right) = 24384\sqrt{7}$

118. (c) We know that,

$(a + b + c)^2 = (a^2 + b^2 + c^2) + 2(ab + bc + ca)$

$\Rightarrow 49 = 2(ab + bc + ca) + (a^2 + b^2 + c^2)$

$\Rightarrow a^2 + b^2 + c^2 = 49 - 2\times 11 = 27$

$\therefore a^3 + b^3 + c^3 = (a + b + c)\{(a^2 + b^2 + c^2) - (ab + bc + ca)\} + 3abc$

$= 7\{27 - 11\} + 3(-1)$

$= 7\times 16 - 3 = 112 - 3 = 109$

119. (c) $x - \frac{1}{x} = 2\sqrt{2}$

$\left(x + \frac{1}{x}\right)^2 = \left(x - \frac{1}{x}\right)^2 + 4$

$x + \frac{1}{x} = \sqrt{(2\sqrt{2})^2 + 4} = \sqrt{12}$

$x^2 - \frac{1}{x^2} = 2\sqrt{2}\times\sqrt{12} = 4\sqrt{6}$

$[\because (a^2 - b^2) = (a - b)(a + b)]$

$= 2\sqrt{4\times 6} = 4\sqrt{6}$

$\left(x^2 - \frac{1}{x^2}\right)^3 = x^6 - \frac{1}{x^6} - 3\left(x^2 - \frac{1}{x^2}\right)$

$\therefore \quad x^6 - \frac{1}{x^6} = (4\sqrt{6})^3 + 3 \times 4\sqrt{6}$

$= 384\sqrt{6} + 12\sqrt{6} = 396\sqrt{6}$

120. (d) As, $(x+y+z)^2 = (4)^2$

$x^2 + y^2 + z^2 + 2(xy + yz + xz) = 16$

$12 + 2(xy + yz + xz) = 16$

$\therefore \quad xy + yz + xz = \frac{16-12}{2} = \frac{4}{2} = 2$

121. (a) Given, $x^4 + \frac{1}{x^4} = 142$ and $x > 0$

$x^7 + \frac{1}{x^7} = \left(x^4 + \frac{1}{x^4}\right)\left(x^3 + \frac{1}{x^3}\right) - \left(x + \frac{1}{x}\right) \quad \ldots(i)$

$\Rightarrow \quad (x^2)^2 + \left(\frac{1}{x^2}\right)^2 + 2 = 142 + 2$

$\Rightarrow \left(x^2 + \frac{1}{x^2}\right)^2 = 144 \Rightarrow x^2 + \frac{1}{x^2} = 12$

Similarly, $\quad x + \frac{1}{x} = \sqrt{14}$

On cubic both sides, $\left(x + \frac{1}{x}\right)^3 = (\sqrt{14})^3$

$\Rightarrow \quad x^3 + \frac{1}{x^3} + 3\left(x + \frac{1}{x}\right) = 14\sqrt{14}$

$\Rightarrow \quad x^3 + \frac{1}{x^3} = 14\sqrt{14} - 3\sqrt{14} = 11\sqrt{14}$

Then, from Eq. (i),

$x^7 + \frac{1}{x^7} = 142 \times 11\sqrt{14} - \sqrt{14} = 1561\sqrt{14}$

122. (b) We know,

$a^3 + b^3 + c^3 - 3abc = \frac{1}{2}(a+b+c)$
$\{(a-b)^2 + (b-c)^2 + (c-a)^2\}$

$\Rightarrow \quad 405 \times 2 = 15\{(a-b)^2 + (b-c)^2 + (c-a)^2\}$

$\Rightarrow (a-b)^2 + (b-c)^2 + (c-a)^2 = \frac{810}{15} = 54$

123. (d) Given, $x + \frac{1}{x} = 2$

$\Rightarrow x^2 + 1 = 2x \Rightarrow x^2 + 1 - 2x = 0$

$\Rightarrow (x-1)^2 = 0 \Rightarrow x = 1$

$\therefore x^7 + \frac{1}{x^{117}} = (1)^7 + \frac{1}{(1)^{117}} = 1 + 1 = 2$

124. (b) $x^2 - 7x + 1 = 0$

On dividing by x we get,

$x - 7 + \frac{1}{x} = 0 \Rightarrow x + \frac{1}{x} = 7$

$\left(x - \frac{1}{x}\right)^2 = \left(x + \frac{1}{x}\right)^2 - 4$

$x - \frac{1}{x} = \pm\sqrt{7^2 - 4} = \pm\sqrt{45} = \pm 3\sqrt{5}$

Given, $0 < x < 1$

So, $\quad x - \frac{1}{x} = -3\sqrt{5}$

$\therefore \quad x^2 - \frac{1}{x^2} = \left(x + \frac{1}{x}\right)\left(x - \frac{1}{x}\right)$

$= 7 \times -3\sqrt{5} = -21\sqrt{5}$

125. (a) According to question,

$(a+b+c)^2 = (12)^2$

$\Rightarrow a^2 + b^2 + c^2 + 2(ab + bc + ca) = 144$

$\Rightarrow ab + bc + ca = \frac{144 - 50}{2} = 47$

$\therefore a^3 + b^3 + c^3 - 3abc = (a+b+c)$
$(a^2 + b^2 + c^2 - (ab + bc + ca))$

$= (12)[50 - 47] = 36$

126. (d) As, $\quad y - \frac{1}{y} = \frac{5}{3}$

$\left(y - \frac{1}{y}\right)^2 = y^2 + \frac{1}{y^2} - 2$

Then, $\quad y^2 + \frac{1}{y^2} = \left(\frac{5}{3}\right)^2 + 2 = \frac{43}{9}$

127. (c) $\frac{3a+b}{2} - \frac{a-3b}{3} + 2b$

$= \frac{9a + 3b - 2a + 6b + 12b}{6}$

$= \frac{7a + 21b}{6} = \frac{7(a+3b)}{6}$

128. (a) Given, $x + \frac{1}{x} = 2\sqrt{2}$

$\therefore \quad x^2 + \frac{1}{x^2} = \left(x + \frac{1}{x}\right)^2 - 2 = (2\sqrt{2})^2 - 2 = 6$

$\therefore \quad \left(x - \frac{1}{x}\right)^2 = x^2 + \frac{1}{x^2} - 2 = 6 - 2 = 4$

$\therefore \quad x - \frac{1}{x} = 2 \quad (\because x > 1)$

As, $x^6 - \frac{1}{x^6} = \left(x^3 + \frac{1}{x^3}\right)\left(x^3 - \frac{1}{x^3}\right) \quad \ldots(i)$

$\therefore \quad x^3 + \frac{1}{x^3} = \left(x + \frac{1}{x}\right)^3 - 3\left(x + \frac{1}{x}\right)$

$= (2\sqrt{2})^3 - 3(2\sqrt{2}) = 10\sqrt{2} \quad \ldots(ii)$

Also, $x^3 - \frac{1}{x^3} = \left(x - \frac{1}{x}\right)^3 + 3\left(x - \frac{1}{x}\right)$

$= (8) + 6 = 14 \quad \ldots(iii)$

$\therefore$ From Eqs. (i), (ii) and (iii),

$x^6 - \frac{1}{x^6} = (14)(10\sqrt{2}) = 140\sqrt{2}$

129. (d) Given, $p = \frac{\sqrt{2}+1}{\sqrt{2}-1}$ and $q = \frac{\sqrt{2}-1}{\sqrt{2}+1}$

On rationalising the denominator, we get

$p = \frac{\sqrt{2}+1}{\sqrt{2}-1} \times \frac{\sqrt{2}+1}{\sqrt{2}+1} = 3 + 2\sqrt{2}$

Similarly, $q = 3 - 2\sqrt{2}$

Now, $\frac{p^2}{q} + \frac{q^2}{p} = \frac{(3+2\sqrt{2})^2}{3-2\sqrt{2}} + \frac{(3-2\sqrt{2})^2}{3+2\sqrt{2}}$

$= \frac{(3+2\sqrt{2})^3 + (3-2\sqrt{2})^3}{(3-2\sqrt{2})(3+2\sqrt{2})}$

$= \frac{(3+2\sqrt{2}+3-2\sqrt{2})[(3+2\sqrt{2})^2 + (3-2\sqrt{2})^2 - (3+2\sqrt{2})(3-2\sqrt{2})]}{(3)^2 - (2\sqrt{2})^2}$

$= \frac{6 \times [(9+8) \times 2 - (9-8)]}{9-8} = 198$

130. (d) Given, $a^2 + b^2 + c^2 = ab + bc + ac$

$2(a^2 + b^2 + c^2) = 2(ab + bc + ca)$

$\Rightarrow 2a^2 + 2b^2 + 2c^2 - 2ab - 2bc - 2ca = 0$

$\Rightarrow (a^2 + b^2 - 2ab) + (b^2 + c^2 - 2bc) + (c^2 + a^2 - 2ac) = 0$

$\Rightarrow \quad (a-b)^2 + (b-c)^2 + (c-a)^2 = 0$

$\Rightarrow \quad a - b = 0, b - c = 0, c - a = 0$

$\Rightarrow \quad a = b = c \quad \ldots(i)$

Now, $\frac{11a^4 + 13b^4 + 17c^4}{17a^2b^2 + 9b^2c^2 + 15c^2a^2}$

$= \frac{11a^4 + 13a^4 + 17a^4}{17a^4 + 9a^4 + 15a^4}$ [from Eq. (i)]

$= \frac{41a^4}{41a^4} = 1$

131. (d) Given, $x + \frac{1}{x} = 5$

$x^8 - \frac{1}{x^8} = \left(x^4 + \frac{1}{x^4}\right)\left(x^2 + \frac{1}{x^2}\right)\left(x^2 - \frac{1}{x^2}\right)$

So, $x^2 + \frac{1}{x^2} = 25 - 2 = 23$

$x^4 + \frac{1}{x^4} = (23)^2 - 2 = 527$

$\because \quad \left(x - \frac{1}{x}\right)^2 = \left(x + \frac{1}{x}\right)^2 - 4$

$\Rightarrow \quad x - \frac{1}{x} = \sqrt{25 - 4} = \sqrt{21}$

$\Rightarrow \quad x^2 - \frac{1}{x^2} = \left(x + \frac{1}{x}\right)\left(x - \frac{1}{x}\right)$

$\therefore \quad x^2 - \frac{1}{x^2} = 5 \times \sqrt{21} = 5\sqrt{21}$

So, $x^8 - \frac{1}{x^8} = 527 \times 23 \times 5\sqrt{21} = 60605\sqrt{21}$

132. (c) Given, $x - \frac{1}{x} = -6$

$x^2 + \frac{1}{x^2} = (-6)^2 + 2 = 38$

and $\quad x^3 - \frac{1}{x^3} = (-6)^3 - 18 = -234$

$\therefore \quad x^5 - \frac{1}{x^5} = \left(x^2 + \frac{1}{x^2}\right)\left(x^3 - \frac{1}{x^3}\right) - \left(x - \frac{1}{x}\right)$

$= 38(-234) + 6 = -8886$

133. (a) According to the question,

$a + b + c = 19$

$\Rightarrow \quad (a+b+c)^2 = (19)^2$

$\Rightarrow a^2 + b^2 + c^2 + 2(ab + bc + ca) = 361$

$\Rightarrow \quad 2(ab + bc + ca) = 361 - 155$

$\Rightarrow \quad 2(ab + bc + ca) = 206$

$(a-b)^2 + (b-c)^2 + (c-a)^2$

$= a^2 + b^2 - 2ab + b^2 + c^2 - 2bc + c^2 + a^2 - 2ac$

$= 2(a^2 + b^2 + c^2) - 2(ab + bc + ca)$

$= 2 \times 155 - 2(ab + bc + ca)$

$= 310 - 206 = 104$

134. (b) Given, $\frac{x - 5y}{x + 5y} = \frac{7}{13}$

$\Rightarrow \quad 13x - 65y = 7x + 35y \Rightarrow 6x = 100y$

$\therefore \quad \frac{x}{y} = \frac{100}{6} \Rightarrow \frac{x}{y} = \frac{50}{3}$

135. (c) $27x^3 - 58x^2y + 31xy^2 - 8y^3$

$= (3x)^3 - 54x^2y - 4x^2y + 36xy^2 - 5xy^2 - (2y)^3$

$= (3x)^3 - (2y)^3 - 3 \times 3x \times 2y(3x + 2y) - 4x^2y - 5xy^2$

$= (3x - 2y)^3 - 4x^2y - 5xy^2$

$= [3\times(-5) - 2\times(-7)]^3$
$-4(-5)^2(-7) - 5(-5)(-7)^2$
$[\because x = -5, y = -7]$
$= (-15+14)^3 + 4\times 25\times 7 + 25\times 49$
$= -1 + 700 + 1225 = 1924$

136. (b) $x + \frac{1}{x} = -6$

$\Rightarrow x^2 + \frac{1}{x^2} = (-6)^2 - 2 = 34$

$[\because (a+b)^2 = a^2 + b^2 + 2ab]$

$x^3 + \frac{1}{x^3} = \left(x+\frac{1}{x}\right)^3 - 3\left(x+\frac{1}{x}\right)$
$= (-6)^3 - 3(-6)$
$= -216 + 18 = -198$

$\therefore \left(x^5 + \frac{1}{x^5}\right) = \left(x^2 + \frac{1}{x^2}\right)\left(x^3 + \frac{1}{x^3}\right) - \left(x + \frac{1}{x}\right)$
$= (34)(-198) - (-6)$
$= -6732 + 6 = -6726$

137. (b) $\because a^2 + b^2 + c^2 + 2(ab + bc + ca) = (a+b+c)^2$

$\therefore (a+b+c)^2 - a^2 - b^2 - c^2 = 2(ab + bc + ca)$

138. (a) Given, $\left(x - \frac{1}{x}\right) = \sqrt{6}$

Squaring on both sides,

$x^2 + \frac{1}{x^2} - 2 = 6 \Rightarrow x^2 + \frac{1}{x^2} = 6 + 2 = 8$

We know, $\left(x + \frac{1}{x}\right)^2 = x^2 + \frac{1}{x^2} + 2 = 8 + 2 = 10$

$\Rightarrow \left(x^2 + \frac{1}{x^2}\right)^2 = x^4 + \frac{1}{x^4} + 2$

$\Rightarrow x^4 + \frac{1}{x^4} = (8)^2 - 2 = 62$

Then, $\left(x + \frac{1}{x}\right) = \sqrt{\left(x - \frac{1}{x}\right)^2 + 4} = \sqrt{10}$

Now, $x^8 - \frac{1}{x^8} = \left(x^4 - \frac{1}{x^4}\right)\left(x^4 + \frac{1}{x^4}\right)$

$[\because (a^2 - b^2) = (a-b)(a+b)]$

$= \left(x^2 - \frac{1}{x^2}\right)\left(x^2 + \frac{1}{x^2}\right)\left(x^4 + \frac{1}{x^4}\right)$

$= \left(x - \frac{1}{x}\right)\left(x + \frac{1}{x}\right)\left(x^2 + \frac{1}{x^2}\right)\left(x^4 + \frac{1}{x^4}\right)$

$= \sqrt{6}\times\sqrt{10}\times 8\times 62 = 992\sqrt{15}$

139. (c) Given, $\frac{x^4 - 2x^2 + 1}{x^2 - 2x + 1} = \frac{(x^2)^2 - 2x^2 + 1}{x^2 - 2x + 1}$

$[\because a^2 - 2ab + b^2 = (a-b)^2]$

$= \frac{(x^2-1)^2}{(x-1)^2}$

$= \frac{(x-1)(x+1)\times(x-1)(x+1)}{(x-1)(x-1)}$

$= (x+1)(x+1) = x^2 + 2x + 1$

140. (d) Given, $x^2 + \frac{1}{x^2} = 7$

We know that,

$\left(x + \frac{1}{x}\right)^2 = x^2 + \frac{1}{x^2} + 2\times x\times\frac{1}{x}$

$\Rightarrow \left(x + \frac{1}{x}\right)^2 = 7 + 2$

$\Rightarrow x + \frac{1}{x} = \sqrt{9} = \pm 3$ ...(i)

Also, $\left(x - \frac{1}{x}\right)^2 = x^2 + \frac{1}{x^2} - 2\times x\times\frac{1}{x}$

$\Rightarrow \left(x - \frac{1}{x}\right)^2 = 7 - 2$

$\Rightarrow x - \frac{1}{x} = \pm\sqrt{5}$ ...(ii)

But given that, $0 < x < 1$, so, we take positive value of Eq. (i) and negative value of Eq. (ii)

$x^2 - \frac{1}{x^2} = \left(x - \frac{1}{x}\right)\left(x + \frac{1}{x}\right) = 3\times(-\sqrt{5})$
$= -3\sqrt{5}$

141. (d) $(3x+5)^2 + (3x-5)^2 = 2[(3x)^2 + (5)^2]$

$[\because (a+b)^2 + (a-b)^2 = 2(a^2 + b^2)]$

$= 2(9x^2 + 25)$

142. (d) According to the question,

$(y + 2x) - [y - y + x - y - x - y + y] - 2y$
$= y + 2x - [-y] - 2y = y + 2x + y - 2y$
$= 2x$

143. (a) Given, $x^4 + \frac{1}{x^4} = 254$

$\left(x^2 + \frac{1}{x^2}\right)^2 = x^4 + \frac{1}{x^4} + 2$

$\Rightarrow \left(x^2 + \frac{1}{x^2}\right)^2 = 256 \Rightarrow x^2 + \frac{1}{x^2} = 16$

Similarly, $x + \frac{1}{x} = \sqrt{18} = 3\sqrt{2}$

$\therefore x^3 + \frac{1}{x^3} = (3\sqrt{2})^3 - 3\times 3\sqrt{2}$

$\Rightarrow x^3 + \frac{1}{x^3} = 54\sqrt{2} - 9\sqrt{2} = 45\sqrt{2}$

Now, $\left(x^3 + \frac{1}{x^3}\right)\left(x^2 + \frac{1}{x^2}\right) = x^5 + \frac{1}{x^5} + \left(x + \frac{1}{x}\right)$

$\Rightarrow 45\sqrt{2}(16) = x^5 + \frac{1}{x^5} + 3\sqrt{2}$

$\Rightarrow x^5 + \frac{1}{x^5} = 720\sqrt{2} - 3\sqrt{2}$

$\Rightarrow x^5 + \frac{1}{x^5} = 717\sqrt{2}$

144. (b) Given, $x + \frac{1}{x} = 7$

$x^3 + \frac{1}{x^3} = \left(x + \frac{1}{x}\right)^3 - 3\left(x + \frac{1}{x}\right)$

Then, $x^3 + \frac{1}{x^3} = (7)^3 - 3\times 7$

$\Rightarrow x^3 + \frac{1}{x^3} = 343 - 21 = 322$

Now, $\left(x^3 + \frac{1}{x^3}\right)^2 = (322)^2$

$\Rightarrow x^6 + \frac{1}{x^6} + 2\times x^3\times\frac{1}{x^3} = 103684$

$\Rightarrow x^6 + \frac{1}{x^6} = 103684 - 2 = 103682$

145. (d) $64x^3 + 38x^2y + 20xy^2 + y^3$
$= (4x)^3 + 3(4x)^2\cdot y + 3\cdot 4x\cdot (y)^2 + (y)^3 - 10x^2y + 8xy^2$
$= (4x+y)^3 - 2xy(5x - 4y)$
$= \{4\times 3 - 4\}^3 - 2\times 3(-4)\{5\times 3 - 4(-4)\}$

$[\because x = 3, y = -4]$

$= 8^3 + 24\{15 + 16\} = 512 + 24\times 31$
$= 512 + 744 = 1256$

146. (c) We know that,

$a^3 + b^3 + c^3 - 3abc = (a+b+c)(a^2 + b^2 + c^2 - ab - bc - ca)$

$\Rightarrow a^3 + b^3 + c^3 - 3abc = 0$ $[\because (a+b+c) = 0]$

$\Rightarrow a^3 + b^3 + c^3 = 3abc$

147. (a) Given, $7b - \frac{1}{4b} = 7$

Then, $\frac{4}{7}\times 7b - \frac{1}{4b}\times\frac{4}{7} = 7\times\frac{4}{7}$

$\Rightarrow 4b - \frac{1}{7b} = 4$

On squaring both side,

$16b^2 + \frac{1}{49b^2} - 2(4b)\left(\frac{1}{7b}\right) = 16$

$\Rightarrow 16b^2 + \frac{1}{49b^2} = 16 + 2\left(4\times\frac{1}{7}\right)$

$\Rightarrow 16b^2 + \frac{1}{49b^2} = 16 + \frac{8}{7} = \frac{120}{7}$

148. (d) Given, $x = -4$ and $y = -1$

Then, $3x^3 + 5x^2y + 12xy^2 + 7y^3$
$= 3\times(-4)^3 + 5\times(-4)^2\times(-1) + 12\times(-4)\times(-1)^2 + 7\times(-1)^3$
$= -192 - 80 - 48 - 7 = -327$

149. (b) Given, $a = -12, b = -6$ and $c = 18$

$\therefore \frac{2abc}{9} = \frac{2(-12)(-6)(18)}{9} = 288$

150. (a) Given, $a + b + c = 5$ ...(i)

$a^3 + b^3 + c^3 = 85$ ...(ii)

$abc = 25$ ...(iii)

$\because a^3 + b^3 + c^3 - 3abc = (a+b+c)(a^2 + b^2 + c^2 - ab - bc - ca)$

$\Rightarrow 85 - 3(25) = 5(a^2 + b^2 + c^2 - ab - bc - ca)$

$\therefore a^2 + b^2 + c^2 - ab - bc - ca = \frac{85 - 75}{5} = \frac{10}{5} = 2$

151. (d) Given, $x = 2 - 2^{\frac{1}{3}} + 2^{\frac{2}{3}}$

$\Rightarrow x - 2 = 2^{\frac{2}{3}} - 2^{\frac{1}{3}}$

Cubing both sides,

$x^3 - 3x^2(2) + 3x(4) - 8 = 2^2 - 2 - 3\cdot 2^{\frac{2}{3}}\cdot 2^{\frac{1}{3}}(2^{\frac{2}{3}} - 2^{\frac{1}{3}})$

$\Rightarrow x^3 - 6x^2 + 12x - 8 = 4 - 2 - 6(x - 2)$

$\Rightarrow x^3 - 6x^2 + 12x - 8 = 2 - 6x + 12$

$\therefore x^3 - 6x^2 + 18x = 22$

152. (a) Given, $\frac{a}{b} + \frac{b}{a} = -1$

$\Rightarrow a^2 + b^2 = -ab$ ...(i)

and $a-b=2$ ...(ii)

Now, $a^3-b^3=(a-b)(a^2+b^2+ab)$

$\Rightarrow a^3-b^3=2(-ab+ab)$ [from Eqs. (i) and (ii)]

$\therefore a^3-b^3=2\times0=0$

153. (d) Given, $\frac{r}{13}+\frac{13}{r}=1$

$\Rightarrow r^2+(13)^2=13r$ ...(i)

Now, we know that

$a^3+b^3=(a+b)(a^2+b^2-ab)$

$\therefore r^3+(13)^3=(r+13)\ (r^2+13^2-13r)$

$\Rightarrow r^3+(13)^3=(r+13)(13r-13r)$ [From Eq. (i)]

$\Rightarrow r^3+(13)^3=0 \Rightarrow r^3=-(13)^3=-2197$

154. (d) From Statement I,

$100^2-99^2+98^2-97^2+96^2-95^2+.......+22^2-21^2$

$=(100-99)(100+99)+(98-97)(98+97)+(96-95)(96+95)+.....+(22-21)(22+21)$

$[\because a^2-b^2=(a+b)(a-b)]$

$=199+195+191+.....+43$

$\because$ Difference of the series

$=199-195=195-191=4$

$\therefore$ This is an arithmetic progression.

Let the number of terms in the series be n.

Then, $l=a+(n-1)d$

$\Rightarrow 199=43+(n-1)4 \Rightarrow n=40$

$\therefore$ Sum of n terms

$\Rightarrow S_{40}=\frac{n}{2}(a+l)$

$\Rightarrow S_{40}=\frac{40}{2}\times(43+199)=4840$

So, Statement I is correct.

From the Statement II,

$\left(k^2+\frac{1}{k^2}\right)\left(k-\frac{1}{k}\right)\left(k^4+\frac{1}{k^4}\right)\left(k+\frac{1}{k}\right)\left(k^4-\frac{1}{k^4}\right)$

$=\left(k^2+\frac{1}{k^2}\right)\left(k^2-\frac{1}{k^2}\right)\left(k^4+\frac{1}{k^4}\right)\left(k^4-\frac{1}{k^4}\right)$

$[\because (a+b)(a-b)=a^2-b^2]$

$=\left(k^4-\frac{1}{k^4}\right)\left(k^8-\frac{1}{k^8}\right)=k^{12}-\frac{1}{k^4}-k^4+\frac{1}{k^{12}}$

$=\left(k^{12}+\frac{1}{k^{12}}\right)-\left(k^4+\frac{1}{k^4}\right)\neq k^{16}-\frac{1}{k^{16}}$

So, Statement II is not correct.

$\therefore$ Only Statement I is correct.

155. (a) I. $x=12, y=-2, z=-10$

$\because x+y+z=12-2-10=0$

$\therefore x^3+y^3+z^3=3xyz$

$\Rightarrow x^3+y^3+z^3=3(12)(-2)(-10)=720$

So, Statement I is correct.

II. $x+y=48$ and $4xy=128$

$\therefore (x+y)^2=(48)^2$

$\Rightarrow x^2+y^2=2304-2xy$

$\Rightarrow 2x^2+2y^2=4608-4xy$

[multiplying by 2 of both sides]

$\Rightarrow 2x^2+2y^2=4608-128$

$\Rightarrow 2x^2+2y^2=4480 \Rightarrow 4x^2+4y^2=8960$

[again multiplying by 2 of both sides]

$\therefore$ Statement II is correct.

Hence, Statements I and II both are correct.

156. (a) As, $2p+q=19$

On cubing both sides, we get

$8p^3+q^3+3(2p)(q)(2p+q)=(19)^3$

$\Rightarrow 8p^3+q^3+6pq(2p+q)=6859$

$\Rightarrow 361+6pq(19)=6859$

$\Rightarrow 114pq=6859-361$

$\Rightarrow pq=\frac{6498}{114}=57$

157. (a) Given, $k+\frac{1}{k}+2=0$

$\Rightarrow k^2+1+2k=0$

$\Rightarrow (k+1)^2=0$

$\Rightarrow k=-1$

$\therefore k^{11}+\frac{1}{k^4}=(-1)^{11}+\frac{1}{(-1)^4}=-1+1=0$

158. (b) Given, $x+\frac{1}{x}=6$

$\Rightarrow x^2+1=6x$ ...(i)

$\therefore \frac{3x}{2x^2-5x+2}=\frac{3x}{2(x^2+1)-5x}$

$=\frac{3x}{2(6x)-5x}=\frac{3x}{7x}=\frac{3}{7}$ [From Eq. (i)]

159. (c) Given, $6x^2+13x+7=0$

$(6x+7)(x+1)=0 \Rightarrow x=-1,-\frac{7}{6}$

Let $\alpha=-1, \beta=-\frac{7}{6}\ \therefore \alpha^2=1, \beta^2=\frac{49}{36}$

Hence, an equation whose roots are α^2, β^2.

$\Rightarrow x^2-(\alpha^2+\beta^2)x+\alpha^2\beta^2=0$

$\Rightarrow x^2-\left(1+\frac{49}{36}\right)x+\frac{49}{36}=0$

$\Rightarrow x^2-\frac{85}{36}x+\frac{49}{36}=0 \Rightarrow 36x^2-85x+49=0$

160. (a) As, $(x+y+z)^2=x^2+y^2+z^2+2\times(xy+yz+zx)$

$\Rightarrow (0)^2=40+2\times(xy+yz+zx)$

$\therefore (xy+yz+zx)=\frac{-40}{2}=-20$

161. (b) Given, $x^4+\frac{16}{x^4}=15617$

$\Rightarrow \left(x^2+\frac{4}{x^2}\right)^2-8=15617$

$[\because (a+b)^2-2ab=a^2+b^2]$

$\Rightarrow x^2+\frac{4}{x^2}=\sqrt{15625}=125$

$\Rightarrow \left(x+\frac{2}{x}\right)^2-4=125$

$\Rightarrow \left(x+\frac{2}{x}\right)^2=125+4=129$

$\therefore x+\frac{2}{x}=\sqrt{129}$

162. (d) As, $p+q+r=8.15+9.06-17.21$

$=17.21-17.21=0$

$\therefore p^3+q^3+r^3-3pqr$

$=0\times(p^2+q^2+r^2-pq-qr-rp)=0$

163. (b) Given, $\frac{x}{8}+\frac{8}{x}=1 \Rightarrow \frac{x^2+64}{8x}=1$

$\Rightarrow x^2+64-8x=0$ ...(i)

Now, $x^3+8^3=(x+8)(x^2+8^2-8x)$

$=(x+8)\times0$ [from Eq. (i)]

$\Rightarrow x^3+8^3=0 \Rightarrow x^3=-8^3=-512$

164. (b) $a^2+b^2+c^2-2ab-2bc+2ca$

$=a^2-ab+ac-ab+b^2-bc+ca-bc+c^2$

$=a(a-b+c)-b(a-b+c)+c(a-b+c)$

$=(a-b+c)(a-b+c)=(a-b+c)^2$

165. (a) As, $x-\frac{1}{x}=-\frac{6}{5}$

Squaring both sides,

$x^2+\frac{1}{x^2}-2=\frac{36}{25} \Rightarrow x^2+\frac{1}{x^2}=\frac{36}{25}+2$

$\therefore x^2+\frac{1}{x^2}=\frac{86}{25}$

166. (c) Given, $a=26, b=22$

$\therefore \frac{a^3-b^3}{a^2-b^2}-\frac{3ab}{a+b}$

$=\frac{(a-b)(a^2+b^2+ab)}{(a-b)(a+b)}-\frac{3ab}{a+b}$

$=\frac{a^2+b^2+ab}{a+b}-\frac{3ab}{a+b}=\frac{a^2+b^2-2ab}{a+b}$

$=\frac{(a-b)^2}{a+b}=\frac{(26-22)^2}{26+22}$

[Putting the value of a and b]

$=\frac{16}{48}=\frac{1}{3}$

167. (d) Given, $m+\frac{1}{m-2}=4$

Subtracting 2 from both sides,

$(m-2)+\frac{1}{(m-2)}=2$

Squaring both sides,

$(m-2)^2+\frac{1}{(m-2)^2}+2=4$

$\therefore (m-2)^2+\frac{1}{(m-2)^2}=2$

168. (b) $\because a^3+b^3+c^3-3abc=(a+b+c)(a^2+b^2+c^2-ab-bc-ca)$

If $a+b+c=0$

Then, $a^3+b^3+c^3=3abc$

169. (b) As, $\left(y+\frac{1}{y}\right)^2=y^2+\frac{1}{y^2}+2\times y+\frac{1}{y}$

$[\because (a+b)^2=a^2+b^2+2ab]$

$\Rightarrow (11)^2=y^2+\frac{1}{y^2}+2$

$\Rightarrow y^2+\frac{1}{y^2}=119$ ...(i)

and $\left(y-\frac{1}{y}\right)^2=y^2+\frac{1}{y^2}-2\times y\times\frac{1}{y}$

$[\because (a-b)^2=a^2+b^2-2ab]$

$\Rightarrow \quad \left(y-\frac{1}{y}\right)^2 = 119-2$

$\Rightarrow \quad y-\frac{1}{y} = \sqrt{117} = 3\sqrt{13}$ ...(ii)

Now, $y^3 - \frac{1}{y^3} = \left(y-\frac{1}{y}\right)\left(y^2+\frac{1}{y^2}+y\times\frac{1}{y}\right)$

$[\because a^3 - b^3 = (a-b)(a^2+b^2+ab)]$

From Eqs. (i) and (ii),

$y^3 - \frac{1}{y^3} = 120\times 3\sqrt{13} = 360\sqrt{13}$

170. (b) As, $\left(x-\frac{1}{x}\right) = \sqrt{12} = 2\sqrt{3}$

We know that, $(a+b)^2 = (a-b)^2 + 4ab$

$\left(x+\frac{1}{x}\right)^2 = \left(x-\frac{1}{x}\right)^2 + 4\cdot x\cdot\frac{1}{x}$

$\Rightarrow \left(x+\frac{1}{x}\right)^2 = 12+4 \Rightarrow \left(x+\frac{1}{x}\right) = \sqrt{16} = 4$

Now, $x^2 - \frac{1}{x^2} = \left(x+\frac{1}{x}\right)\left(x-\frac{1}{x}\right)$

$= 4\times 2\sqrt{3} = 8\sqrt{3}$

171. (d) As, $\left(k+\frac{1}{k}\right)^2 = (4)^2$

$\Rightarrow k^2 + \frac{1}{k^2} + 2 = 16 \Rightarrow k^2 + \frac{1}{k^2} = 16-2 = 14$

Squaring again on both sides,

$\left(k^2+\frac{1}{k^2}\right)^2 = (14)^2$

$\therefore \quad k^4 + \frac{1}{k^4} = 196 - 2 = 194$

172. (b) Given, $x^2 + \frac{1}{x^2} = 66$

$\therefore \left(x-\frac{1}{x}\right)^2 = x^2 + \frac{1}{x^2} - 2\times x\times\frac{1}{x}$

$= x^2 + \frac{1}{x^2} - 2$

$\Rightarrow \left(x-\frac{1}{x}\right)^2 = 66-2 = 64 \therefore x - \frac{1}{x} = \sqrt{64} = 8$

173. (a) Given, $x+y+z=0$

Now, $\frac{x^2}{yz} + \frac{y^2}{zx} + \frac{z^2}{xy} = \frac{x^3+y^3+z^3}{xyz} = \frac{3xyz}{xyz}$

$[\because$ When, $x+y+z=0,\ x^3+y^3+z^3 = 3xyz]$

$= 3$

174. (c) Given, $\frac{(p-q)^3+(q-r)^3+(r-p)^3}{12(p-q)(q-r)(r-p)}$

Let $p-q=a,\ q-r=b,\ r-p=c$

Then, $\frac{a^3+b^3+c^3}{12abc}$

We know that if $a+b+c=0$, then

$a^3+b^3+c^3 = 3abc$

$\Rightarrow \quad a+b+c = p-q+q-r+r-p$

$a+b+c=0$

$\therefore \quad \frac{a^3+b^3+c^3}{12abc} = \frac{3abc}{12abc} = \frac{1}{4}$

175. (b) $(a+b)^3 - a^3 + b^3$

$= a^3 + b^3 + 3ab(a+b) - a^3 + b^3$

$= 3ab(a+b) + b^3 + b^3 = 3ab(a+b) + 2b^3$

176. (b) Given, $x + \frac{1}{x} = 2\sqrt{5}$

Squaring both sides, $\left(x+\frac{1}{x}\right)^2 = (2\sqrt{5})^2$

$\Rightarrow \quad x^2 + \frac{1}{x^2} + 2 = 4\times 5$

$[\because (a+b)^2 = a^2+b^2+2ab]$

$\Rightarrow \quad x^2 + \frac{1}{x^2} = 18$ ...(i)

Now, $\left(x-\frac{1}{x}\right)^2 = x^2 + \frac{1}{x^2} - 2$

$[\because (a-b)^2 = a^2+b^2-2ab]$

$\Rightarrow \quad \left(x-\frac{1}{x}\right)^2 = 18-2$ [From Eq. (i)]

$\Rightarrow \quad \left(x-\frac{1}{x}\right)^2 = 16 \Rightarrow x - \frac{1}{x} = \sqrt{16} = 4$

Now, $\quad x - \frac{1}{x} = 4$ ...(ii)

Taking cube on both sides, $\left(x-\frac{1}{x}\right)^3 = (4)^3$

$\Rightarrow x^3 - \frac{1}{x^3} - 3\times x\times\frac{1}{x}\times\left(x-\frac{1}{x}\right) = 64$

$[\because (a-b)^3 = a^3 - b^3 - 3ab(a-b)]$

$\Rightarrow \quad x^3 - \frac{1}{x^3} - 3\times 4 = 64$ [From Eq. (ii)]

$\Rightarrow \quad x^3 - \frac{1}{x^3} = 64 + 12 \Rightarrow x^3 - \frac{1}{x^3} = 76$

Speedy Method

$x + \frac{1}{x} = 2\sqrt{5}$

If $x + \frac{1}{x} = k$, then $x - \frac{1}{x} = \sqrt{k^2-4}$

$x - \frac{1}{x} = \sqrt{(2\sqrt{5})^2 - 4} = \sqrt{20-4} = 4$

If $x - \frac{1}{x} = A$, then $x^3 - \frac{1}{x^3} = A^3 - 3A$

$\therefore\ x^3 - \frac{1}{x^3} = (4)^3 + 3\times 4 = 64 + 12 = 76$

177. (d) We know that,

$a^2+b^2+c^2 = (a+b+c)^2 - 2(ab+bc+ca)$

$\Rightarrow \quad a^2+b^2+c^2 = (9)^2 - 2\times 23$

$\Rightarrow \quad a^2+b^2+c^2 = 81-46$

$\therefore \quad a^2+b^2+c^2 = 35$

178. (b) Given,

$4(z+7)(2z-1) = Az^2+Bz+C$

$\Rightarrow \quad Az^2+Bz+C = 4(z+7)(2z-1)$

$= 4\,[2z^2+14z-z-7]$

$= 4\,[2z^2+13z-7]$

$= 8z^2+52z-28$

On comparing,

$A = 8,\ B = 52$ and $C = -28$

$\therefore \quad A+B+C = 8+52-28 = 60-28 = 32$

179. (b) $\frac{1}{1+a+b^{-1}} + \frac{1}{1+b+5c^{-1}} + \frac{1}{1+\frac{c}{5}+a^{-1}}$

$= \frac{1}{1+a+\frac{1}{b}} + \frac{1}{1+b+\frac{5}{c}} + \frac{1}{1+\frac{c}{5}+\frac{1}{a}}$

$= \frac{b}{b+ab+1} + \frac{c}{c+bc+5} + \frac{5a}{5a+ac+5}$

$= \frac{b}{b+ab+1} + \frac{c}{c+bc+abc} + \frac{5a}{5a+ac+abc}$

$[\because abc = 5]$

$= \frac{b}{b+ab+1} + \frac{c}{c(1+b+ab)} + \frac{5a}{a(5+c+bc)}$

$= \frac{b}{b+ab+1} + \frac{1}{1+b+ab} + \frac{5}{5+c+bc}$

$= \frac{b}{1+b+ab} + \frac{1}{1+b+ab} + \frac{abc}{abc+c+bc}$

$= \frac{b}{1+b+ab} + \frac{1}{1+b+ab} + \frac{abc}{c(ab+1+b)}$

$= \frac{b}{1+b+ab} + \frac{1}{1+b+ab} + \frac{ab}{1+b+ab}$

$= \frac{b+1+ab}{1+b+ab} = 1$

180. (a) Given, $y = 1+\sqrt{3}+\sqrt{4}$

$= 1+\sqrt{3}+2 = 3+\sqrt{3}$

$y^2 = (3+\sqrt{3})^2 = 12+6\sqrt{3}$

Now, $2y^4 - 8y^3 - 6y^2 + 28y - 84$

$= 2y^2(y^2-4y) - 6y^2 + 28y - 84$

$= 2(12+6\sqrt{3})(12+6\sqrt{3} - 4(3+\sqrt{3}))$

$- 6(12+6\sqrt{3}) + 28(3+\sqrt{3}) - 84$

$= 2(12+6\sqrt{3})(12+6\sqrt{3} - 12 - 4\sqrt{3})$

$- 72 - 36\sqrt{3} + 84 + 28\sqrt{3} - 84$

$= 2(12+6\sqrt{3})(2\sqrt{3}) - 72 - 8\sqrt{3}$

$= 48\sqrt{3} + 24\times 3 - 72 - 8\sqrt{3}$

$= 48\sqrt{3} + 72 - 72 - 8\sqrt{3}$

$= 48\sqrt{3} - 8\sqrt{3} = 40\sqrt{3}$

181. (d) As, $x+y = \frac{\sqrt{5}-\sqrt{4}}{\sqrt{5}+\sqrt{4}} + \frac{\sqrt{5}+\sqrt{4}}{\sqrt{5}-\sqrt{4}}$

$= \frac{[(\sqrt{5}-\sqrt{4})(\sqrt{5}-\sqrt{4}) + (\sqrt{5}+\sqrt{4})(\sqrt{5}+\sqrt{4})]}{(\sqrt{5}+\sqrt{4})(\sqrt{5}-\sqrt{4})}$

$= \frac{[5+4-2\times\sqrt{5}\times\sqrt{4} + 5+4+2\times\sqrt{5}\times\sqrt{4}]}{(\sqrt{5})^2 - (\sqrt{4})^2}$

$x+y = \frac{9+9}{5-4} = 18$ ...(i)

$xy = \frac{\sqrt{5}-\sqrt{4}}{\sqrt{5}+\sqrt{4}} \times \frac{\sqrt{5}+\sqrt{4}}{\sqrt{5}-\sqrt{4}} = 1$ ...(ii)

$\therefore \quad \frac{x^2-xy+y^2}{x^2+xy+y^2} = \frac{x^2+y^2+2xy-2xy-xy}{x^2+y^2+2xy-xy}$

$= \frac{(x+y)^2 - 3xy}{(x+y)^2 - xy} = \frac{(18)^2 - 3\times 1}{(18)^2 - 1}$

[from Eqs. (i) and (ii)]

$= \frac{324-3}{324-1} = \frac{321}{323}$

182. (b) Given, $\frac{2p}{p^2-5p+1} = \frac{1}{10}$

$\Rightarrow \quad p^2 - 5p + 1 = 10\times 2p$

$\Rightarrow \quad p^2 + 1 = 20p + 5p$

$\Rightarrow \quad p\left(p+\frac{1}{p}\right) = 25p \Rightarrow p + \frac{1}{p} = 25$

183. (d) Given, $9m^2 + n^2 = 40$ ...(i)

and $\quad mn = 4$ ...(ii)

Taking square of $3m+n$

$(3m+n)^2 = 9m^2 + n^2 + 2\times 3mn$

$\Rightarrow \quad (3m+n)^2 = 40 + 6\times 4$ [From Eq. (i) and Eq. (ii)]

$\Rightarrow \quad (3m+n)^2 = 64$

$\therefore \quad 3m + n = \sqrt{64} = 8$

184. (d) $(a+b)^2 - (a-b)^2$
$= (a^2+b^2+2ab) - (a^2+b^2-2ab)$
$= a^2 + b^2 + 2ab - a^2 - b^2 + 2ab = 4ab$

185. (a) Given, $x^2 + 4y^2 + 4y - 4xy - 2x - 8$

$\Rightarrow x^2 + 4y^2 - 4xy + 4y - 2x - 8$

$\Rightarrow \quad (x-2y)^2 + 2(2y - x) - 8$

$\Rightarrow \quad (x-2y)^2 - 2(x-2y) - 8$

Let $A = x - 2y$

$\therefore$ The equation becomes

$A^2 - 2A - 8 = (A-4)(A+2)$

Resubstitute the value of A,

$x^2 + 4y^2 + 4y - 4xy - 2x - 8$
$= (x - 2y - 4)(x - 2y + 2)$

186. (c) Here, $2x - 1 = 0 \Rightarrow 2x = 1 \Rightarrow x = \frac{1}{2}$

By remainder theorem,

Remainder $= 3x^4 - 2x^2 + 4x - 1$

$= 3\times\left(\frac{1}{2}\right)^4 - 2\times\left(\frac{1}{2}\right)^2 + 4\times\frac{1}{2} - 1$

$= \frac{3}{16} - \frac{2}{4} + \frac{4}{2} - 1 = \frac{3 - 8 + 32 - 16}{16} = \frac{11}{16}$

187. (b) Given, $(a+1)^2 + (a+2)^2 = 16$

$\Rightarrow a^2 + 1 + 2a + a^2 + 4 + 4a = 16$

$\Rightarrow 2a^2 + 6a + 5 = 16 \Rightarrow 2a^2 + 6a = 11$

$\Rightarrow 2\times(2a^2 + 6a) = 2\times 11 \Rightarrow 4a^2 + 12a = 22$

Adding 40 in both sides,

Hence, $40 + 12a + 4a^2 = 40 + 22 = 62$

188. (a) Statement I, $k + \frac{1}{k} = 12$

Squaring both sides, $\left(k + \frac{1}{k}\right)^2 = (12)^2$

$\Rightarrow \quad k^2 + \frac{1}{k^2} + 2\times k\times\frac{1}{k} = 144$

$[\because (a+b)^2 = a^2 + b^2 + 2ab]$

$\Rightarrow \quad k^2 + \frac{1}{k^2} + 2 = 144 \Rightarrow k^2 + \frac{1}{k^2} = 142$

$\therefore$ Statement I is correct.

Statement II, $\left(k^2 + \frac{1}{k^2}\right)\left(k - \frac{1}{k}\right)$

$\left(k^4 + \frac{1}{k^4}\right)\left(k + \frac{1}{k}\right) = \left(k^2 + \frac{1}{k^2}\right)\left(k^2 - \frac{1}{k^2}\right)\left(k^4 + \frac{1}{k^4}\right)$

$[\because (a-b)(a+b) = a^2 - b^2]$

$= \left((k^2)^2 - \frac{1}{(k^2)^2}\right)\left(k^4 + \frac{1}{k^4}\right)$

$[\because (a+b)(a-b) = a^2 - b^2]$

$= \left(k^4 - \frac{1}{k^4}\right)\left(k^4 + \frac{1}{k^4}\right)$

$[\because (a-b)(a+b) = a^2 - b^2]$

$= k^8 - \frac{1}{k^8}$

$\therefore$ Statement II is incorrect

Hence, only I is correct.

189. (b) Given, $x + \frac{1}{x} = 7$ ...(i)

Taking cube on both sides,

$\left(x + \frac{1}{x}\right)^3 = (7)^3$

$\Rightarrow x^3 + \frac{1}{x^3} + 3\times x\times\frac{1}{x}\left(x + \frac{1}{x}\right) = 343$

$[\because (a+b)^3 = a^3 + b^3 + 3ab(a+b)]$

$\Rightarrow \quad x^3 + \frac{1}{x^3} + 3\times 7 = 343$ [From Eq. (i)]

$\Rightarrow \quad x^3 + \frac{1}{x^3} + 21 = 343$

Hence, $\quad x^3 + \frac{1}{x^3} = 322$

> **Speedy Method**
>
> If $x + \frac{1}{x} = a$, then $x^3 + \frac{1}{x^3} = a^3 - 3a$
>
> Here, $a = 7$
>
> $x^3 + \frac{1}{x^3} = (7)^3 - 3\times 7 = 322$

190. (a) $\sqrt{36x^2 - 108x + 81}$

$= \sqrt{(6x)^2 - 2\times 6x\times 9 + (9)^2}$

$= \sqrt{(6x-9)^2}$

$[\because a^2 - 2ab + b^2 = (a-b)^2]$

$= 6x - 9$

191. (c) $(5x + 8y)(25x^2 + 64y^2 - 40xy)$

$= (5x+8y)((5x)^2 + (8y)^2 - 5x\times 8y)$

$= (5x)^3 + (8y)^3$

$[\because (a+b)(a^2 + b^2 - ab) = a^3 + b^3]$

$= 125x^3 + 512y^3$

192. (a) Given, $x^4 + \frac{1}{x^4} = 194$

$\Rightarrow (x^2)^2 + \left(\frac{1}{x^2}\right)^2 = 194 \Rightarrow \left(x^2 + \frac{1}{x^2}\right)^2 - 2 = 194$

$[\because a^2 + b^2 = (a+b)^2 - 2ab]$

$\Rightarrow \left(x^2 + \frac{1}{x^2}\right)^2 = 196 \Rightarrow x^2 + \frac{1}{x^2} = \sqrt{196} = 14$

Now, $\quad x^2 + \left(\frac{1}{x}\right)^2 = 14 \Rightarrow \left(x + \frac{1}{x}\right)^2 - 2 = 14$

$[\because a^2 + b^2 = (a+b)^2 - 2ab]$

$\Rightarrow \quad \left(x + \frac{1}{x}\right)^2 = 16 \Rightarrow x + \frac{1}{x} = \sqrt{16} = 4$

Now, $x^3 + \frac{1}{x^3} = \left(x + \frac{1}{x}\right)\left(x^2 + \frac{1}{x^2} - x\times\frac{1}{x}\right)$

$[\because a^3 + b^3 = (a+b)(a^2 + b^2 - ab)]$

$= (4)(14 - 1) = 4\times 13 = 52$

193. (b) Given, $k + \frac{1}{k} + 2 = 0$

$\Rightarrow \quad k^2 + 1 + 2k = 0 \Rightarrow (k+1)^2 = 0$

$[\because a^2 + b^2 + 2ab = (a+b)^2]$

$\Rightarrow \quad k = -1$

$\therefore \quad k^{10} + \frac{1}{k^{11}} = (-1)^{10} + \frac{1}{(-1)^{11}}$

$= 1 + \frac{1}{-1} = 1 - 1 = 0$

194. (b) $3\left[a - \frac{1}{a}\right] + \left[a - \frac{1}{a}\right]^3$

$= 3\left[a - \frac{1}{a}\right] + a^3 - \frac{1}{a^3} - 3\times a\times\frac{1}{a}\left[a - \frac{1}{a}\right]$

$[\because (x-y)^3 = x^3 - y^3 - 3xy(x-y)]$

$= 3\left[a - \frac{1}{a}\right] + a^3 - \frac{1}{a^3} - 3\left[a - \frac{1}{a}\right] = a^3 - \frac{1}{a^3}$

195. (d) $x^2 + y^2 + 2y + 4x + 5 = 0$

$\Rightarrow x^2 + 4x + 4 + y^2 + 2y + 1 = 0$

$\Rightarrow \quad (x+2)^2 + (y+1)^2 = 0$

$\Rightarrow \quad x + 2 = 0;\ y + 1 = 0$

$\Rightarrow \quad x = -2;\ y = -1$

$\therefore \quad \frac{x+y}{x-y} = \frac{-2-1}{-2+1} = \frac{-3}{-1} = 3$

196. (b) $\frac{(x-y)^3 + (y-z)^3 + (z-x)^3}{6(x-y)(y-z)(z-x)}$

$= \frac{3(x-y)(y-z)(z-x)}{6(x-y)(y-z)(z-x)}$

$[\because$ If $a + b + c = 0$, then $a^3 + b^3 + c^3 = 3abc]$

$= \frac{1}{2}$

197. (d) Given, $5x^2 + 7x + 5 = 0$

Divide it by x,

$\frac{5x^2}{x} + \frac{7x}{x} + \frac{5}{x} = 0 \Rightarrow 5x + 7 + \frac{5}{x} = 0$

$\Rightarrow \quad 5x + \frac{5}{x} = -7 \Rightarrow x + \frac{1}{x} = -\frac{7}{5}$

Now, $\left(x + \frac{1}{x}\right)^3 = x^3 + \frac{1}{x^3} + 3\times x\times\frac{1}{x}\left(x + \frac{1}{x}\right)$

$\Rightarrow \quad \left(-\frac{7}{5}\right)^3 = x^3 + \frac{1}{x^3} + 3\left(-\frac{7}{5}\right)$

$\Rightarrow \quad \frac{-343}{125} = x^3 + \frac{1}{x^3} - \frac{21}{5}$

$\Rightarrow \quad x^3 + \frac{1}{x^3} = \frac{-343}{125} + \frac{21}{5} \Rightarrow x^3 + \frac{1}{x^3} = \frac{182}{125}$

198. (d) If, $mx^m - nx^n = 0 \Rightarrow mx^m = nx^n$

$\Rightarrow \quad x^m = \frac{n\times x^n}{m}$

Now, $\frac{1}{x^m + x^n} + \frac{1}{x^m - x^n} = \frac{2x^m}{(x^m)^2 - (x^n)^2}$

$= \frac{2\times n\times x^n}{m\times\left[\left(\frac{n\times x^n}{m}\right)^2 - (x^n)^2\right]}$

$= \frac{2\times n\times x^n}{m\times\left(\frac{n^2x^{2n}}{m^2} - x^{2n}\right)}$ $\left[\because x^m = \frac{nx^n}{m}\right]$

$= \frac{2\times n\times x^n\times m}{x^{2n}(n^2 - m^2)} = \frac{2mn}{x^n(n^2 - m^2)}$

199. (c) $4x - 7y = 11$

Squaring both sides,

$(4x - 7y)^2 = (11)^2$

$\Rightarrow \quad 16x^2 + 49y^2 - 56xy = 121$

$\Rightarrow \quad 16x^2 + 49y^2 - 56\times 8 = 121 \quad (\because xy = 8)$

$\therefore \quad 16x^2 + 49y^2 = 569$

200. (a) Given, $\frac{a}{b}+\frac{b}{a}=1$

$\Rightarrow \frac{a^2+b^2}{ab}=1$

$\Rightarrow a^2+b^2=ab$

$\Rightarrow a^2+b^2-ab=0$ ...(i)

and $a+b=2$ ...(ii)

Now, $a^3+b^3=(a+b)(a^2-ab+b^2)$

$=2\times 0$ [from Eqs. (i) and (ii)]

$=0$

201. (b) Given, $8m^3-n^3$

We know, $a^3-b^3=(a-b)(a^2+ab+b^2)$

$\therefore (2m)^3-(n)^3$

$=(2m-n)[(2m)^2+(2m)(n)+(n)^2]$

$=(2m-n)(4m^2+2mn+n^2)$

202. (c) Given, $p=7+4\sqrt{3}$ ...(i)

$\frac{1}{p}=\frac{1}{7+4\sqrt{3}}=\frac{7-4\sqrt{3}}{(7+4\sqrt{3})(7-4\sqrt{3})}$

$[\because a^2-b^2=(a+b)(a-b)]$

$=\frac{7-4\sqrt{3}}{7^2-(4\sqrt{3})^2}=7-4\sqrt{3}$ ...(ii)

Now, $\frac{p^6+p^4+p^2+1}{p^3}=p^3+p+\frac{1}{p}+\frac{1}{p^3}$

$=p^3+\frac{1}{p^3}+p+\frac{1}{p}$

$=p^3+\frac{1}{p^3}+7+4\sqrt{3}+7-4\sqrt{3}$

[from Eqs. (i) and (ii)]

$=p^3+\frac{1}{p^3}+14$

$[\because a^3+b^3=(a+b)^3-3ab(a+b)]$

$=\left(p+\frac{1}{p}\right)^3-3\times p\times\frac{1}{p}\left(p+\frac{1}{p}\right)+14$

$=(7+4\sqrt{3}+7-4\sqrt{3})^3$

$-3(7+4\sqrt{3}+7-4\sqrt{3})+14$

$=(14)^3-3(14)+14$

$=2744-42+14=2716$

203. (d) Given,

$x^2+y^2+z^2=xy+yz+zx$

$\Rightarrow x^2+y^2+z^2-xy-yz-zx=0$

$\Rightarrow 2x^2+2y^2+2z^2-2xy-2yz-2zx=0$

$\Rightarrow (x^2-2xy+y^2)+(y^2-2yz+z^2)$

$+(z^2-2zx+x^2)=0$

$\Rightarrow (x-y)^2+(y-z)^2+(z-x)^2=0$

$\Rightarrow x-y=0 \Rightarrow y-z=0 \Rightarrow z-x=0$

$\because x-y=0$

$\Rightarrow 1-y=0\Rightarrow y=1$ $(\because x=1)$

Also, $y-z=0\Rightarrow 1-z=0\Rightarrow z=1$

Now, $\frac{10x^4+5y^4+7z^4}{13x^2y^2+6y^2z^2+3z^2x^2}$

$=\frac{10\times(1)^4+5\times(1)^4+7(1)^4}{13\times(1)^2\times(1)^2+6\times(1)^2\times(1)^2+3\times(1)^2\times(1)^2}$

$=\frac{10+5+7}{13+6+3}=\frac{22}{22}=1$

204. (c) $x+\frac{1}{2x}=3$

Multiplying by 2 on both sides, $2x+\frac{1}{x}=6$

Now, taking cube on both sides,

$\left(2x+\frac{1}{x}\right)^3=(6)^3$

$\Rightarrow (2x)^3+\left(\frac{1}{x}\right)^3+3\times 2x\times\frac{1}{x}\times\left(2x+\frac{1}{x}\right)=216$

$[\because (a+b)^3=a^3+b^3+3ab(a+b)]$

$\Rightarrow 8x^3+\frac{1}{x^3}+6\times 6=216$

$\Rightarrow 8x^3+\frac{1}{x^3}=216-36$

$\Rightarrow 8x^3+\frac{1}{x^3}=180$

205. (c) Given, $x-y=-10$

$\Rightarrow x=-10+y=y-10$

Now, $x^2-2xy=84$

$\Rightarrow (y-10)^2-2\times(y-10)\times y=84$

$\Rightarrow y^2+100-20y-2y^2+20y=84$

$\Rightarrow -y^2+100=84$

$\Rightarrow y=\sqrt{16}=4$

206. (a) Expression given in option (a).

$ab-a-b+1=(a-1)(b-1)$

$\Rightarrow a(b-1)-1(b-1)=(a-1)(b-1)$

$(a-1)(b-1)=(a-1)(b-1)$

RHS = LHS

$\therefore$ This algebraic expression is correct.

207. (d) Given, $x^2=y+z$ ...(i)

$y^2=z+x$ ...(ii)

$z^2=x+y$ ...(iii)

From Eq. (i) adding x on both sides

$x^2+x=x+y+z$

$\Rightarrow x(x+1)=(x+y+z)$

$\Rightarrow (x+1)=\frac{1}{x}(x+y+z)$

Similarly, from the Eqs. (ii) and (iii),

$(y+1)=\frac{1}{y}(x+y+z)$

and $(z+1)=\frac{1}{z}(x+y+z)$

$\therefore \frac{1}{x+1}+\frac{1}{y+1}+\frac{1}{z+1}$

$=\frac{x}{(x+y+z)}+\frac{y}{(x+y+z)}+\frac{z}{(x+y+z)}$

$=\frac{(x+y+z)}{(x+y+z)}=1$

208. (d) Given, $\frac{1}{x^2+a^2}=x^2-a^2$

$\Rightarrow (x^2-a^2)(x^2+a^2)=1$

$\Rightarrow (x^4-a^4)=1$

$[\because (a+b)(a-b)=(a^2-b^2)]$

$\Rightarrow x^4=1+a^4$

$\Rightarrow x=(a^4+1)^{1/4}$

209. (a) Given, $x+\frac{1}{x}=-14$ and $x<-1$.

$\therefore x-\frac{1}{x}=\sqrt{\left(x+\frac{1}{x}\right)^2-4}$

$[\because (a-b)=\sqrt{(a+b)^2-4ab}]$

$\Rightarrow x-\frac{1}{x}=\sqrt{196-4}\Rightarrow x-\frac{1}{x}=\pm 8\sqrt{3}$

$\Rightarrow x-\frac{1}{x}=-8\sqrt{3}$ $[\because x<-1]$

$\therefore x^2-\frac{1}{x^2}=\left(x+\frac{1}{x}\right)\left(x-\frac{1}{x}\right)$

$=(-14)(-8\sqrt{3})=112\sqrt{3}$

210. (c) Given, $k^4+\frac{1}{k^4}=47$

$\Rightarrow (k^2)^2+\left(\frac{1}{k^2}\right)^2+2=47+2$

$\Rightarrow k^2+\frac{1}{k^2}=7\Rightarrow k^2+\frac{1}{k^2}+2=9$

$\Rightarrow k+\frac{1}{k}=3$ ...(i)

Cubing both sides,

$k^3+\frac{1}{k^3}+3\cdot k\cdot\frac{1}{k}\left(k+\frac{1}{k}\right)=27$

$\Rightarrow k^3+\frac{1}{k^3}+3\times 3=27$ [From Eq. (i)]

$\therefore k^3+\frac{1}{k^3}=27-9=18$

211. (d) $(x+2y)^3+(x-2y)^3$

$=x^3+8y^3+6xy(x+2y)$

$+x^3-8y^3-6xy(x-2y)$

$[\because (a+b)^3=a^3+b^3+3ab(a+b)$

and $(a-b)^3=a^3-b^3-3ab(a-b)]$

$=2x^3+6x^2y+12xy^2-6x^2y+12xy^2$

$=2x^3+24xy^2$

212. (d) We know,

$(a+b+c)^2=a^2+b^2+c^2+2(ab+bc+ca)$

$\Rightarrow (a+b+c)^2=9+(2\times 8)$

$(\because a^2+b^2+c^2=9$ and $ab+bc+ca=8)$

$\Rightarrow (a+b+c)^2=9+16=25$

$\Rightarrow a+b+c=\sqrt{25}=5$

Hence, $(a+b+c)-3=5-3=2$

213. (b) $\frac{\sqrt{5}+\sqrt{3}}{\sqrt{5}-\sqrt{3}}=a+b\sqrt{15}$

$\Rightarrow \frac{\sqrt{5}+\sqrt{3}}{\sqrt{5}-\sqrt{3}}\times\frac{\sqrt{5}+\sqrt{3}}{\sqrt{5}+\sqrt{3}}=a+b\sqrt{15}$

$\Rightarrow \frac{5+3+2\sqrt{5}}{5-3}=a+b\sqrt{15}$

$\Rightarrow \frac{8+2\sqrt{15}}{2}=a+b\sqrt{15}$

$\Rightarrow 4+\sqrt{15}=a+b\sqrt{15}$

On comparing, we get

$a=4$ and $b=1$

214. (b) $(mx+n)$ is a factor of a quadratic expression.

Here, in option (b) $m^2x^2+2mnx+n^2$ is a quadratic expression.

$m^2x^2+2mnx+n^2$

$= m^2x^2 + mnx + mnx + n^2$
$= mx(mx+n) + n(mx+n)$
$= (mx+n)(mx+n)$
Hence, $mx+n$ is a factor of $m^2x^2 + 2mnx + n^2$

215. (b) Here, $a = 12, b = -8, c = -4$
$\Rightarrow a+b+c = 12+(-8)+(-4) = 0$
When $a+b+c=0$
Then, $a^3+b^3+c^3 = 3abc$
$\therefore (12)^3 + (-8)^3 + (-4)^3$
$= 3\times 12\times(-8)\times(-4) = 36\times 32 = 1152$

216. (d) Given,
$8a^3 + 27b^3 = 16$ ...(i)
$2a + 3b = 4$ ...(ii)
Taking cube on both sides of Eq. (ii)
$(2a+3b)^3 = (4)^3$
$\Rightarrow (2a)^3 + (3b)^3 + 3\times 2a\times 3b\times(2a+3b) = 64$
$[\because (x+y)^3 = x^3 + y^3 + 3xy(x+y)]$
$\Rightarrow 8a^3 + 27b^3 + 18ab(2a+3b) = 64$
$\Rightarrow 16 + 18ab\times 4 = 64$
$\Rightarrow 72ab = 64 - 16$
$\Rightarrow ab = \frac{48}{72} = \frac{2}{3} \Rightarrow a = \frac{2}{3b}$
Now, $2a+3b = 4 \Rightarrow 2\times\frac{2}{3b} + 3b = 4$
$\Rightarrow 4 + 9b^2 = 4\times 3b$
$\Rightarrow 9b^2 - 12b + 4 = 0 \Rightarrow (3b-2)(3b-2) = 0$
$\Rightarrow b = \frac{2}{3} \Rightarrow a = \frac{2}{3b} = \frac{2\times 3}{3\times 2} = 1$
Hence, $16a^4 + 81b^4 = 16\times(1)^2 + 81\times\left(\frac{2}{3}\right)^4$
$= 16 + 16 = 32$

217. (c) Given, $x = 3 + 2\sqrt{2}, x > 0$
$\Rightarrow x = 2 + 1 + 2\sqrt{2}$
$\Rightarrow (\sqrt{x})^2 = (\sqrt{2}+1)^2$
$\Rightarrow \sqrt{x} = \sqrt{2} + 1$
$\Rightarrow \frac{1}{\sqrt{x}} = \frac{\sqrt{2}-1}{(2-1)} = \sqrt{2} - 1$
Then, $\sqrt{x} - \frac{1}{\sqrt{x}} = (\sqrt{2}+1) - (\sqrt{2}-1) = 2$

218. (d) Given, $x + \frac{1}{x} = -2$
$\Rightarrow x^2 + 1 = -2x \Rightarrow (x+1)^2 = 0$
$\Rightarrow x = -1$
$\therefore x^{17} + x^{-17} + x^{12} + x^{-12}$
$= (-1)^{17} + (-1)^{-17} + (-1)^{12} + (-1)^{-12}$
$= (-1)^{17} + \frac{1}{(-1)^{17}} + (-1)^{12} + \frac{1}{(-1)^{12}}$
$= -1 - 1 + 1 + 1 = 0$

219. (a) Given, $x - y = 1$
and $x^2 + y^2 = 41$ where $x, y \geq 0$
Since, $(x-y)^2 = x^2 + y^2 - 2xy$
$\Rightarrow (1)^2 = 41 - 2xy$
$\Rightarrow 2xy = 41 - 1 = 40 \Rightarrow xy = 20$
Now, $(x+y)^2 = x^2 + y^2 + 2xy$
$\Rightarrow (x+y)^2 = 41 + 2(20)$
$= 41 + 40 = 81$
$\Rightarrow (x+y) = \pm 9$ (– ve impossible)
$\Rightarrow (x+y) = 9$

220. (c) Given, $\left(4a + \frac{5}{a} + 5\right) = 14$
$\Rightarrow 4a + \frac{5}{a} = 14 - 5 = 9$
Squaring both sides,
$16a^2 + \frac{25}{a^2} + 2(4a)\left(\frac{5}{a}\right) = 81$
$\Rightarrow 16a^2 + \frac{25}{a^2} + 40 = 81$
$\Rightarrow 16a^2 + \frac{25}{a^2} = 41$

221. (b) Given expression,
$= x^4 + x^2 + 25 = x^4 + 25 + x^2$
$= (x^2)^2 + (5)^2 + x^2$
$= (x^2)^2 + (5)^2 + 10x^2 - 10x^2 + x^2$
$= (x^2+5)^2 - 9x^2 = (x^2+5)^2 - (3x)^2$
$= (x^2 + 5 - 3x)(x^2 + 5 + 3x)$
$= (x^2 - 3x + 5)(x^2 + 3x + 5)$
Hence, option (b) is correct.

222. (d) Given, $x - \frac{1}{x} = 13$
Squaring both sides,
$\left(x^2 + \frac{1}{x^2} - 2\right) = 169$
$\Rightarrow \left(x^2 + \frac{1}{x^2}\right) = 169 + 2 = 171$
Again squaring both sides,
$\left(x^2 + \frac{1}{x^2}\right)^2 = (171)^2$
$\Rightarrow \left(x^4 + \frac{1}{x^4} + 2\right) = (171)^2 = 29241$
$\Rightarrow \left(x^4 + \frac{1}{x^4}\right) = 29239$

Speedy Method
If $x - \frac{1}{x} = a$, then $x^4 + \frac{1}{x^4} = (a^2+2)^2 - 2$
Here, $a = 13$
Then, $x^4 + \frac{1}{x^4} = (13^2 + 2)^2 - 2$
$= 29241 - 2 = 29239$

223. (d) Given, $x + \frac{1}{x} = 8$
$\Rightarrow x^2 + 1 = 8x$
$\Rightarrow x^2 - 8x + 1 = 0$ ...(i)
Now, $\frac{5}{x^2 - 8x + 2} = \frac{5}{(x^2 - 8x + 1) + 1}$
$= \frac{5}{0+1} = 5$ [from Eq. (i)]

224. (a) I. $100^2 - 99^2 + 98^2 - 97^2 + 96^2 - 95^2 + ... + 2^2 - 1^2$
$= (100+99)(100-99) + (98+97)(98-97) + (96+95)(96-95) + ... + (2+1)(2-1)$
$= 100 + 99 + 98 + 97 + 96 + 95 + ... + 2 + 1$
$\left[\because S_n = \frac{n(n+1)}{2}\right]$
$= \frac{100(100+1)}{2} = 50\times 101 = 5050$
II. $8x + \frac{8}{x} = -16 \Rightarrow 8\left(x + \frac{1}{x}\right) = -16$
$\Rightarrow x + \frac{1}{x} = \frac{-16}{8} = -2$
Let $x = -1$ as $x < 0$
$x^{197} + x^{-197} = x^{197} + \frac{1}{x^{197}} = (-1)^{197} + \frac{1}{(-1)^{197}}$
$= -1 - 1$ $[\because (-1)^{odd} = -1]$
$= -2 \neq 2$
So, only Statement I is correct.

225. (c) Given, $K + \frac{1}{K} = 3$
$\Rightarrow \left(K + \frac{1}{K}\right)^3 = (3)^3$
$\Rightarrow K^3 + \frac{1}{K^3} + 3\times K\times\frac{1}{K}\left(K + \frac{1}{K}\right) = 27$
$[\because (a+b)^3 = a^3 + b^3 + 3ab(a+b)]$
$\Rightarrow K^3 + \frac{1}{K^3} + 3\times(3) = 27$
$\Rightarrow K^3 + \frac{1}{K^3} = 27 - 9 = 18$

226. (d) $x = \frac{\sqrt{5}-2}{\sqrt{5}+2}$
$x = \frac{\sqrt{5}-2}{\sqrt{5}+2}\times\frac{\sqrt{5}-2}{\sqrt{5}-2}$
(on rationalizing the denominator)
$\Rightarrow x = \frac{5 + 4 - 4\sqrt{5}}{1} = 9 - 4\sqrt{5}$
$\Rightarrow \frac{1}{x} = \frac{1}{9 - 4\sqrt{5}} \Rightarrow \frac{1}{x} = \frac{9 + 4\sqrt{5}}{9^2 - (4\sqrt{5})^2}$
(On rationalizing the denominator)
$\frac{1}{x} = 9 + 4\sqrt{5}$
Now, $x^2 + x^{-2} = x^2 + \frac{1}{x^2}$
$= \left(x + \frac{1}{x}\right)^2 - 2 = (9 - 4\sqrt{5} + 9 + 4\sqrt{5})^2 - 2$
$= (18)^2 - 2 = 324 - 2 = 322$

227. (d) $x + 3(y + x - 2) - (x + y)$
$= x + 3y + 3x - 6 - x - y$
$= 3x + 2y - 6$

228. (b) $x^4 + \frac{1}{x^4} = 2207$
$\Rightarrow \left(x^2 + \frac{1}{x^2}\right)^2 - 2 = 2207$
$\Rightarrow x^2 + \frac{1}{x^2} = \sqrt{2209} = 47$
Now $\left(x + \frac{1}{x}\right)^2 - 2 = 47 \Rightarrow \left(x + \frac{1}{x}\right) = 7$
and $x^3 + \frac{1}{x^3} = \left(x + \frac{1}{x}\right)^3 - 3\times\left(x + \frac{1}{x}\right)$
$= (7)^3 - 3\times 7 = 322$

$\therefore\ x^7+\frac{1}{x^7}=\left(x^4+\frac{1}{x^4}\right)\left(x^3+\frac{1}{x^3}\right)-\left(x+\frac{1}{x}\right)$

$=2207\times 322-7=710654-7=710647$

229. (c) Given, $y+\frac{1}{y}=3\Rightarrow\left(y+\frac{1}{y}\right)^3=(3)^3$

$[\because (a+b)^3=a^3+b^3+3ab(a+b)]$

$\Rightarrow\ y^3+\frac{1}{y^3}+3\left(y+\frac{1}{y}\right)=27$

$\Rightarrow\ y^3+\frac{1}{y^3}=27-3\left(y+\frac{1}{y}\right)=27-3\times 3$ $\left[\because y+\frac{1}{y}=3\right]$

$\therefore\ y^3+\frac{1}{y^3}+2=27-9+2=20$

Speedy Method

If $x+\frac{1}{x}=a$, then $x^3+\frac{1}{x^3}=a^3-3a$

Here, $a=3$

Then, $x^3+\frac{1}{x^3}=a^3-3a=(3)^3-3\times 3=18$

$\therefore\ x^3+\frac{1}{x^3}+2=18+2=20$

230. (d) $(x-27)^3+(y-9)^3$

$=(x-27+y-9)[(x-27)^2-(x-27)(y-9)+(y-9)^2]$

$[a^3+b^3=(a+b)(a^2-ab+b^2)]$

$=(x+y-27-9)[(x-27)^2-(x-27)(y-9)+(y-9)^2]$

$=(36-27-9)[(x-27)^2-(x-27)(y-9)+(y-9)^2]$

$=0\times[(x-27)^2-(x-27)(y-9)+(y-9)^2]$ $[\because x+y=36]$

$=0$

231. (a) Given, $a+b=11$ and $ab=35$

Now, $(a+b)^2=(11)^2$

$\Rightarrow a^2+b^2+2ab=121$

$\Rightarrow\ a^2+b^2=121-2\times 35$

$\Rightarrow a^2+b^2=121-70=51$

$\Rightarrow\ (a^2+b^2)^2=(51)^2$

$\Rightarrow\ a^4+b^4+2a^2b^2=2601$

$\Rightarrow\ a^4+b^4=2601-2a^2b^2=2601-2(ab)^2$

$\Rightarrow\ a^4+b^4=2601-2\times 35\times 35$

$=2601-2450=151$

232. (b) Given, k is a negative number and $k+k^{-1}=-2$

$\Rightarrow\ k+\frac{1}{k}=-2\Rightarrow k^2+2k+1=0$

$\Rightarrow\ (k+1)(k+1)=0\Rightarrow k=-1$

$\therefore$ The value of $\frac{k^2+4k-2}{k^2+k-5}$

$=\frac{(-1)^2+4\times -1-2}{(-1)^2+(-1)-5}=\frac{1-4-2}{1-1-5}=\frac{-5}{-5}=1$

233. (c) Given, $x^2-5x+1=0$

$\Rightarrow\ x^2+1=5x$

$\Rightarrow\ x+\frac{1}{x}=5$ ...(i)

Squaring both sides, we get

$x^2+\frac{1}{x^2}+2=25$

$\Rightarrow\ x^2+\frac{1}{x^2}=25-2=23$

$\therefore\ x^3+\frac{1}{x^3}=\left(x+\frac{1}{x}\right)\left(x^2+\frac{1}{x^2}-1\right)$

$=5\times(23-1)=5\times 22=110$ ...(ii)

Now, $\frac{x^6+x^4+x^2+1}{5x^3}$

$=\frac{1}{5}\times\left(x^3+x+\frac{1}{x}+\frac{1}{x^3}\right)$

$=\frac{1}{5}\times\left(x^3+\frac{1}{x^3}+x+\frac{1}{x}\right)$

$=\frac{1}{5}\times(110+5)$ [$\because$ from Eqs. (i) and (ii)]

$=\frac{1}{5}\times 115=23$

234. (a) $\left(5-\frac{x^2}{3}\right)^3$

$=125-\frac{x^6}{27}-3\times 5\times\frac{x^2}{3}\left(5-\frac{x^2}{3}\right)$

$[\because (a-b)^3=a^3-b^3-3ab(a-b)]$

$=125-\frac{x^6}{27}-3\times 5\times\frac{x^2}{3}\times 5-3\times 5\times\frac{x^2}{3}\times\frac{x^2}{3}$

$=125-\frac{x^6}{27}-25x^2-\frac{5}{3}x^4$

The coefficient of x^2 is -25.

235. (a) Given,

$x^8-34x^4+1=0$

$x^8+1=34x^4$

Divided by x^4 on both sides,

$x^4+\frac{1}{x^4}=34$

$\Rightarrow x^4+\frac{1}{x^4}+2=34+2$

$\Rightarrow\left(x^2+\frac{1}{x^2}\right)^2=36\Rightarrow\left(x^2+\frac{1}{x^2}\right)=6$

Now, $\left(x-\frac{1}{x}\right)^2=x^2+\frac{1}{x^2}-2\times x\times\frac{1}{x}$

$[\because (a-b)^2=a^2+b^2-2ab]$

$\left(x-\frac{1}{x}\right)=\sqrt{4}=2$

Take cube on both sides, $\left(x-\frac{1}{x}\right)^3=(2)^3$

$\because\ x^3-\frac{1}{x^3}-3\times x\times\frac{1}{x}\left(x-\frac{1}{x}\right)=8$

$[\because (a-b)^3=a^3-b^3-3ab(a-b)]$

$\Rightarrow\ x^3-\frac{1}{x^3}=8+3\times 2=8+6$

$\Rightarrow\ x^3-\frac{1}{x^3}=14$ or $x^3-x^{-3}=14$

236. (b) Given, $y=2x+1$ or $2x-y=-1$

Cube on both sides, $(2x-y)^3=(-1)^3$

$\Rightarrow 8x^3-y^3-3\times 2x\times y(2x-y)=-1$

$\Rightarrow\ 8x^3-y^3-6xy(-1)=-1$

$\because\ [(a-b)^3=a^3-b^3-3ab(a-b)]$

$\therefore\ 8x^3-y^3+6xy=-1$

237. (d) We know that, if $a+b+c=0$ then $a^3+b^3+c^3=3abc$

So, here $a^6-b^6+b^6-c^6+c^6-a^6=0$

Put $3(a^6-b^6)(b^6-c^6)(c^6-a^6)$ in place of numerator similar in denominator.

$=\frac{5}{2}\left[\frac{3(a^6-b^6)(b^6-c^6)(c^6-a^6)}{3(a^3-b^3)(b^3-c^3)(c^3-a^3)}\right]$

$=\frac{5}{2}\left[\frac{(a^3-b^3)(a^3+b^3)\times(b^3+c^3)(b^3-c^3)\times(c^3+a^3)(c^3-a^3)}{(a^3-b^3)(b^3-c^3)(c^3-a^3)}\right]$

$[\because (a+b)(a-b)=a^2-b^2]$

$=\frac{5}{2}(a^3+b^3)(b^3+c^3)(c^3+a^3)$

238. (a) Given, $x-\frac{2}{x}=15$

Square on both sides we get,

$\Rightarrow\ \left(x-\frac{2}{x}\right)^2=(15)^2$

$\Rightarrow\ x^2+\frac{4}{x^2}-2\times x\times\frac{2}{x}=225$

$[\because (a-b)^2=a^2+b^2-2ab]$

$\therefore\ x^2+\frac{4}{x^2}=229$

239. (b) As, $2x+3y=-1$

Take cube both sides, $(2x+3y)^3=(-1)^3$

$[\because (a+b)^3=a^3+b^3+3ab(a+b)]$

$\Rightarrow\ 8x^3+27y^3+3\times 2x\times 3y(2x+3y)=-1$

$\Rightarrow\ 8x^3+27y^3+18xy(-1)=-1$

$[\because 2x+3y=-1]$

$\Rightarrow\ 8x^3+27y^3-18xy=-1$

$\Rightarrow\ 8x^3+27y^3-18xy+8=-1+8$

$\therefore\ 8x^3+27y^3-18xy+8=7$

240. (b) Given, $a^4+b^4+a^2b^2=273$ ...(i)

and $a^2+b^2-ab=21$ ...(ii)

Dividing Eq. (i) by Eq. (ii),

$\frac{a^4+b^4+a^2b^2}{a^2+b^2-ab}=\frac{273}{21}$

$\Rightarrow\ \frac{(a^2+b^2)^2-a^2b^2}{(a^2+b^2-ab)}=\frac{273}{21}$

$\Rightarrow\ \frac{(a^2+b^2)^2-(ab)^2}{(a^2+b^2-ab)}=13$

$\Rightarrow\frac{(a^2+b^2-ab)(a^2+b^2+ab)}{(a^2+b^2-ab)}=13$

$[\because x^2-y^2=(x+y)(x+y)]$

$\Rightarrow\ (a^2+b^2+ab)=13$

$\Rightarrow\ (a+b)^2-ab=13$ ...(iii)

Now, from Eq. (ii),

$21+2ab=13$

$\Rightarrow \quad 2ab = 13 - 21$

$\Rightarrow \quad ab = -4$

Similarly, $a + b = 3$ [from Eq. (iii)]

$\therefore \quad \frac{1}{a} + \frac{1}{b} = \frac{a+b}{ab} = \frac{-3}{4}$

241. (c) $(x+6)^3 + (2x+3)^3 + (3x+5)^3$
$= (3x+18)(2x+3)(3x+5)$

We know that $a^3 + b^3 + c^3 = 3abc$

Then, $a + b + c = 0$

$\Rightarrow \quad (x+6) + (2x+3) + (3x+5) = 0$

$\Rightarrow \quad 6x + 14 = 0 \Rightarrow 6x = -14$

$\Rightarrow \quad x = -\frac{14}{6} = -\frac{7}{3}$

242. (b) Given, $\left(x + \frac{1}{x}\right) = \frac{17}{4}$

Square on both sides, $\left(x + \frac{1}{x}\right)^2 = \left(\frac{17}{4}\right)^2$

$\Rightarrow \quad x^2 + \frac{1}{x^2} + 2 \times x \times \frac{1}{x} = \frac{289}{16}$

$\Rightarrow \quad x^2 + \frac{1}{x^2} = \frac{289}{16} - 2$

$= \frac{289 - 32}{16} = \frac{257}{16}$ ...(i)

Now, $\left(x - \frac{1}{x}\right)^2 = x^2 + \frac{1}{x^2} - 2 \times x \times \frac{1}{x}$

$\Rightarrow \quad \left(x - \frac{1}{x}\right)^2 = \frac{257}{16} - 2 \quad \left\{\because x^2 + \frac{1}{x^2} = \frac{257}{16}\right\}$

$\Rightarrow \quad \left(x - \frac{1}{x}\right)^2 = \frac{225}{16} \Rightarrow \left(x - \frac{1}{x}\right) = \frac{15}{4}$

Speedy Method

If $x + \frac{1}{x} = a$, then $x - \frac{1}{x} = \sqrt{a^2 - 4}$

Here, $a = \frac{17}{4}$

Then, $x - \frac{1}{x} = \sqrt{\left(\frac{17}{4}\right)^2 - 4}$

$= \sqrt{\frac{289 - 64}{16}} = \sqrt{\frac{225}{16}} = \frac{15}{4}$

243. (b) Given, $2x^2 - 7x + 5 = 0$

Divided by $2x$ on both sides, $x + \frac{5}{2x} = \frac{7x}{2x}$

Cube on both sides, $\left(x + \frac{5}{2x}\right)^3 = \left(\frac{7}{2}\right)^3$

$\Rightarrow \quad x^3 + \frac{125}{8x^3} + 3 \times x \times \frac{5}{2x}\left(x + \frac{5}{2x}\right) = \frac{343}{8}$

$\Rightarrow \quad x^3 + \frac{125}{8x^3} = \frac{343}{8} - \frac{15}{2}\left(x + \frac{5}{2x}\right)$

$\Rightarrow \quad x^3 + \frac{125}{8x^3} = \frac{343}{8} - \frac{15}{2} \times \frac{7}{2}$

$\left(x^3 + \frac{125}{8x^3}\right) = \frac{133}{8} = 16\frac{5}{8}$

244. (a) Given,

$8 + 2px^2 - 36x - 27x^3 = (2 - 3x)^3$

We know that, $(a - b)^3 = a^3 - b^3 - 3ab(a - b)$

$\Rightarrow \quad (2 - 3x)^3 = (2)^3 - (3x)^3 - 3 \times 2 \times 3x(2 - 3x)$

$= 8 - 27x^3 - 36x + 54x^2$

Compare with $8 - 27x^3 - 36x + 2px^2$

We get, $54x^2 = 2px^2$

$\Rightarrow \quad 2p = 54 \Rightarrow p = 27$

245. (c) Given, $\sqrt{x} - \frac{1}{\sqrt{x}} = \sqrt{7}$

Square on both sides, $\left(\sqrt{x} - \frac{1}{\sqrt{x}}\right)^2 = (\sqrt{7})^2$

$\Rightarrow (\sqrt{x})^2 + \left(\frac{1}{\sqrt{x}}\right)^2 - 2 \times \sqrt{x} \times \frac{1}{\sqrt{x}} = 7$

$\Rightarrow \quad x + \frac{1}{x} = 7 + 2 = 9$

Again, square both side,

$\left(x + \frac{1}{x}\right)^2 = (9)^2 \Rightarrow x^2 + \frac{1}{x^2} + 2 \times x \times \frac{1}{x} = 81$

$\therefore \quad x^2 + \frac{1}{x^2} = 79$

246. (b) Given, $\frac{x}{y} + \frac{y}{x} = 2 \Rightarrow \frac{x^2 + y^2}{xy} = \frac{2}{1}$

Now, The value of $x^2 + y^2 = 2$, $xy = 1$

We know that,

$(x - y)^2 = x^2 + y^2 - 2xy$

$\Rightarrow \quad (x - y)^2 = 2 - 2 \times 1 \Rightarrow (x - y)^2 = 0$

$\therefore \quad (x - y) = 0$

247. (a) $(x - y + z)^2 - (x - y - z)^2$

By formula, $a^2 - b^2 = (a + b)(a - b)$

$= (x - y + z + x - y - z)(x - y + z - x + y + z)$

$= (2x - 2y)(2z) = 4xz - 4yz$

248. (c) As, $2a + \frac{3}{a} = 12$

Squaring on both sides,

$\left(2a + \frac{3}{a}\right)^2 = (12)^2$

$\Rightarrow \quad 4a^2 + \frac{9}{a^2} + 2 \times 2a \times \frac{3}{a} = 144$

$\Rightarrow 4a^2 + \frac{9}{a^2} = 144 - 12 \Rightarrow 4a^2 + \frac{9}{a^2} = 132$

249. (c) As, $a^2 + b^2 + c^2 + 216$
$= 12a + 12b - 24c$

$\Rightarrow a^2 - 12a + b^2 - 12b$
$+ c^2 + 24c + 36 + 36 + 144 = 0$

$\Rightarrow (a^2 + (6)^2 - 2 \times 6 \times a) + (b^2 + 6^2$
$- 2 \times 6 \times b) + (c^2 + (12)^2 + 2 \times 12 \times c) = 0$

$\Rightarrow (a - 6)^2 + (b - 6)^2 + (c + 12)^2 = 0$

$\Rightarrow a = 6, b = 6, c = -12$

$\therefore \sqrt{ab - bc - ca}$

$= \sqrt{[6 \times 6 - 6 \times (-12) - (-12 \times 6)]}$

$= \sqrt{180} = 6\sqrt{5}$

250. (c) We know that,

$a^3 - b^3 = (a - b)(a^2 + b^2 + ab)$

$\Rightarrow \quad 2349 = 9(a^2 + b^2 + ab)$

$\Rightarrow \quad (a^2 + b^2 + ab) = 261$

Then, $(a + b)^2 - ab = a^2 + b^2 + 2ab - ab$

$[\because (a + b)^2 = a^2 + b^2 + 2ab]$

$\therefore (a + b)^2 - ab = a^2 + b^2 + ab = 261$

251. (b) Given, $x - \frac{1}{x} = \sqrt{77}$

Take square on both sides,

$\left(x - \frac{1}{x}\right)^2 = (\sqrt{77})^2 \Rightarrow x^2 + \frac{1}{x^2} - 2 = (\sqrt{77})^2$

$\Rightarrow x^2 + \frac{1}{x^2} + 2 - 2 - 2 = (\sqrt{77})^2$

$\Rightarrow (\sqrt{77})^2 = \left(x + \frac{1}{x}\right)^2 - 4 \Rightarrow \left(x + \frac{1}{x}\right) = \sqrt{81} = 9$

Take cube on both sides,

$x^3 + \frac{1}{x^3} + 3x \times \frac{1}{x}\left(x + \frac{1}{x}\right) = 9 \times 9 \times 9$

$[\because (a + b)^3 = a^3 + b^3 + 3ab(a + b)]$

$\Rightarrow x^3 + \frac{1}{x^3} = 729 - 3 \times 9 = 729 - 27$

$\therefore \quad x^3 + \frac{1}{x^3} = 702$

252. (d) Given, $a + b + c = 0$

If we put $a = 2$, $b = -1$, $c = -1$ then

$2 - 1 - 1 = 0$, It will satisfy the equation.

$\therefore \quad \frac{(b + c)^2}{bc} + \frac{(c + a)^2}{ca} + \frac{(a + b)^2}{ab}$

$= \frac{(-1 - 1)^2}{-1 \times (-1)} + \frac{(-1 + 2)^2}{-1 \times 2} + \frac{(2 - 1)^2}{2 \times (-1)}$

$= 4 - \frac{1}{2} - \frac{1}{2} = 4 - 1 = 3$

253. (a) Given, $x + y = 3$ and $\frac{1}{x} + \frac{1}{y} = -\frac{3}{10}$

$\Rightarrow \quad \frac{(x + y)}{xy} = -\frac{3}{10}$

We know that,

$(x + y)^2 = x^2 + y^2 + 2xy$

Here, $\quad x + y = 3, xy = -10$

So, $\quad (3)^2 = x^2 + y^2 + 2(-10)$

$\Rightarrow \quad 9 = x^2 + y^2 - 20$

$\therefore \quad x^2 + y^2 = 29$

254. (b) Given,

$x^2 + 9y^2 + 4z^2 = 12(x - 2y + 2z) - 88$

$\Rightarrow (x^2 - 12x + 36) + [(3y)^2 + 24y + 16]$
$+ [(2z)^2 - 24z + 36] = 0$

$\Rightarrow \quad (x - 6)^2 + (3y + 4)^2 + (2z - 6)^2 = 0$

$\Rightarrow \quad x = 6, y = \frac{-4}{3}, z = 3$

$\therefore \quad (x - 3y + z) = 6 - 3 \times \left(-\frac{4}{3}\right) + 3$

$= 6 + 4 + 3 = 13$

255. (c) Given, $4x^4 = 5x^2 - 1$,

$\Rightarrow \quad 4x^4 - 5x^2 + 1 = 0$

$\Rightarrow \quad 4x^4 - 4x^2 - x^2 + 1 = 0$

$\Rightarrow \quad (4x^2 - 1)(x^2 - 1) = 0$

$\Rightarrow \quad x^2 = \frac{1}{4}$ and $x^2 = 1$

$\Rightarrow \quad x = \frac{1}{2}$ and $x = 1$

We can't take $x = \frac{1}{2}$ because the value of x is more then $\frac{1}{\sqrt{2}}$.

Now, we will take $x = 1$

$\therefore \quad 2x^2 - 1 - x = 2(1)^2 - 1 - 1 = 2 - 2 = 0$

256. (b) Given, $(54\sqrt{2}x^3 + 24\sqrt{3}y^3) \div (\sqrt{18}x + \sqrt{12}y)$

$= Ax^2 + By^2 + Cxy$

We know that,

$a^3 + b^3 = (a+b)(a^2 + b^2 - ab)$

Then, $[(3\sqrt{2}x)^3 + (2\sqrt{3}y)^3]$

$= [3\sqrt{2}x + 2\sqrt{3}y]$

$[18x^2 + 12y^2 - 6\sqrt{6}xy]$

So, compare the equations

$$\frac{(3\sqrt{2}x + 2\sqrt{3}y)(18x^2 + 12y^2 - 6\sqrt{6}xy)}{(3\sqrt{2}x + 2\sqrt{3}y)} = Ax^2 + By^2 + Cxy$$

$\Rightarrow (18x^2 + 12y^2 - 6\sqrt{6}xy) = Ax^2 + By^2 + Cxy$

Comparing, we get

$A = 18, B = 12$ and $C = -6\sqrt{6}$

So, $A^2 - (B^2 + C^2)$

$= (18)^2 - [12^2 + (-6\sqrt{6})^2]$

$= 324 - 360 = -36$

257. (c) We know that,

$(x+y+z)^2 = x^2 + y^2 + z^2 + 2(xy + yz + zx)$

$\Rightarrow (7)^2 = 85 + 2(xy + yz + zx)$

$\Rightarrow 2(xy + yz + zx) = 49 - 85 = -36$

$\Rightarrow xy + yz + zx = -18$

Now, $x^3 + y^3 + z^3 - 3xyz = (x+y+z)(x^2 + y^2 + z^2 - xy - yz - zx)$

$\Rightarrow 913 - 3xyz = 7(85 + 18)$

$\Rightarrow 3xyz = 913 - 7 \times 103 = 913 - 721$

$\Rightarrow xyz = \frac{192}{3} = 64$

$\therefore \sqrt[3]{xyz} = \sqrt[3]{64} = 4$

258. (b) Given, $x^2 + 4y^2 = 53$, $x - 2y = 5$,

$(x - 2y) = 5$ Take cube on both sides,

$\Rightarrow x^3 - 8y^3 - 3 \times x \times 2y(x - 2y) = 125$

$\Rightarrow x^3 - 8y^3 = 125 + 6xy(5)$

$\Rightarrow x^3 - 8y^3 = 125 + 30xy$ ...(i)

Now, $(x - 2y)^2 = (5)^2$

$\Rightarrow x^2 + 4y^2 - 2 \times x \times 2y = 25$

$\Rightarrow x^2 + 4y^2 - 25 = 4xy$

$\Rightarrow 53 - 25 = 4xy$

$\Rightarrow 4xy = 28$

$\Rightarrow xy = 7$

Put in Eq. (i),

$x^3 - 8y^3 = 125 + 30 \times 7$

$= 125 + 210 = 335$

259. (a) Given,

$\frac{1}{x} + \frac{1}{y} = \frac{18}{5} = \frac{x+y}{xy} = \frac{18}{5}$

and $x + y = 2$ given

$\frac{(2)}{xy} = \frac{18}{5} \Rightarrow xy = \frac{5}{9}$

$\Rightarrow (x+y)^3 = x^3 + y^3 + 3xy(x+y)$

$\Rightarrow (2)^3 = x^3 + y^3 + 3 \times \frac{5}{9}(2)$

$\Rightarrow x^3 + y^3 = 8 - \frac{10}{3} = \frac{14}{3}$

$\Rightarrow x^3 + y^3 = 4\frac{2}{3}$

260. (c) We know that,

$x^3 + y^3 + z^3 - 3xyz$

$= (x+y+z) \times [(x+y+z)^2 - 3(xy + yz + zx)]$

$= 2 \times [(2)^2 - 3(-11)] = 2 \times [4 + 33] = 74$

261. (a) Given, $2x^2 - 8x - 1 = 0$

$\Rightarrow 2x^2 - 1 = 8x$ [divided by x]

$\Rightarrow 2x - \frac{1}{x} = 8$

Take cube on both sides,

$$\left(2x - \frac{1}{x}\right)^3 = (8)^3$$

$\Rightarrow 8x^3 - \frac{1}{x^3} - 3 \times 2x \times \frac{1}{x}\left(2x - \frac{1}{x}\right) = 512$

$\Rightarrow 8x^3 - \frac{1}{x^3} = 512 + 6 \times 8 = 512 + 48$

$\Rightarrow 8x^3 - \frac{1}{x^3} = 512 + 48$

$\therefore 8x^3 - \frac{1}{x^3} = 560$

262. (b) Given, $x^4 + \frac{1}{x^4} = 727$

$\Rightarrow x^4 + \frac{1}{x^4} + 2 = 727 + 2$

{add 2 on both sides}

$\Rightarrow \left(x^2 + \frac{1}{x^2}\right)^2 = 729 \Rightarrow x^2 + \frac{1}{x^2} = 27$

Now, $\left(x - \frac{1}{x}\right)^2 = x^2 + \frac{1}{x^2} - 2 \times x \times \frac{1}{x}$

$\Rightarrow \left(x - \frac{1}{x}\right)^2 = 27 - 2 = 25$

$\therefore x - \frac{1}{x} = \sqrt{25} = 5$

Speedy Method

If $x - \frac{1}{x} = a$, then $x^4 + \frac{1}{x^4} = (a^2 + 2)^2 - 2$

According to question,

$x^4 + \frac{1}{x^4} = (a^2 + 2)^2 - 2$

$\Rightarrow 727 = (a^2 + 2)^2 - 2$

$\Rightarrow 27 = a^2 + 2 \Rightarrow a = 5$

$\therefore x - \frac{1}{x} = 5$

263. (d) Given, $\left(x - \frac{1}{x}\right) = 1$

Squaring on both sides,

$x^2 + \frac{1}{x^2} - 2 = 1 \Rightarrow x^2 + \frac{1}{x^2} = 3$

Again, squaring on both sides,

$x^4 + \frac{1}{x^4} + 2 \times x^2 \times \frac{1}{x^2} = 9$

$\Rightarrow x^4 + \frac{1}{x^4} = 7$

Again, taking square on both sides,

$x^8 + \frac{1}{x^8} + 2 \times x^4 \times \frac{1}{x^4} = 49$

$\Rightarrow x^8 + \frac{1}{x^8} = 49 - 2 = 47$

$\therefore$ The value of $x^8 + \frac{1}{x^8} = 47$

264. (c) Given, $x + y = 4$ and $\frac{1}{x} + \frac{1}{y} = \frac{16}{15}$

$\Rightarrow \frac{x+y}{xy} = \frac{16}{15} \Rightarrow \frac{4}{xy} = \frac{16}{15} \Rightarrow xy = \frac{15}{4}$

We know that,

$(a+b)^3 = a^3 + b^3 + 3ab(a+b)$

Now, $x^3 + y^3 = (x+y)^3 - 3xy(x+y)$

$= (4)^3 - 3 \times \frac{15}{4} \times (4)$

$= 64 - 45 = 19$

265. (c) We know that,

$(x+y+z)^2 = x^2 + y^2 + z^2 + 2(xy + yz + zx)$

$\Rightarrow x^2 + y^2 + z^2 = (x+y+z)^2 - 2(xy + yz + zx)$

$\Rightarrow x^2 + y^2 + z^2 = (10)^2 - 2 \times 15 = 100 - 30$

$\therefore x^2 + y^2 + z^2 = 70$

We know that,

$x^3 + y^3 + z^3 - 3xyz = (x+y+z)[x^2 + y^2 + z^2 - xy - yz - zx]$

$= 10[70 - 15] = 10 \times 55 = 550$

266. (c) We know that,

$(a+b+c)^2 = a^2 + b^2 + c^2 + 2(ab + bc + ca)$

$\therefore (a+b+c)^2 = 300 + 2 \times 50$

$= 300 + 100 = 400$

$a + b + c = \sqrt{400} = 20$

The value of $a + b + c$ is 20.

267. (b) We know that,

$(a+b)^3 = a^3 + b^3 + 3ab(a+b)$

$\therefore \left(\frac{x}{3} + \frac{y}{5}\right)^3 = \frac{x^3}{27} + \frac{y^3}{125} + 3 \times \frac{x}{3} \times \frac{y}{5}\left(\frac{x}{3} + \frac{y}{5}\right)$

$= \frac{x^3}{27} + \frac{y^3}{125} + \frac{x^2y}{15} + \frac{xy^2}{25}$

268. (a) Given,

$1 - 64x^3 - 12x + px^2 = (1 - 4x)^3$

$\Rightarrow 1 - 64x^3 - 12x + px^2 = 1 - 64x^3 - 12x(1 - 4x)$

$[\because (a-b)^3 = a^3 - b^3 - 3ab(a-b)]$

$\Rightarrow 1 - 64x^3 - 12x + px^2 = 1 - 64x^3 - 12x + 48x^2$

On comparing both sides, we get $p = 48$

269. (c) Given, $b + c = ax$, $c + a = by$, $a + b = cz$

$x = \frac{b+c}{a}, y = \frac{c+a}{b}, z = \frac{a+b}{c}$

Put these in above given expression

$$= \frac{1}{9}\left[\frac{1}{x+1} + \frac{1}{y+1} + \frac{1}{z+1}\right]$$

$$= \frac{1}{9}\left[\frac{1}{\frac{b+c}{a}+1} + \frac{1}{\frac{c+a}{b}+1} + \frac{1}{\frac{a+b}{c}+1}\right]$$

$$= \frac{1}{9}\left[\frac{a}{a+b+c} + \frac{b}{a+b+c} + \frac{c}{a+b+c}\right]$$

$$= \frac{1}{9}\left[\frac{a+b+c}{a+b+c}\right] = \frac{1}{9}$$

270. (d) Given, $x^2 - 4x + 4 = 0$

$\Rightarrow \quad (x-2)(x-2) = 0$

$\Rightarrow \quad x = 2$

The value of x, put in given expression

$= 16\left(x^4 - \frac{1}{x^4}\right) = 16\left((2)^4 - \frac{1}{(2)^4}\right)$

$= 16\left[16 - \frac{1}{16}\right] = 16\left[\frac{256-1}{16}\right]$

$= 16 \times \frac{255}{16} = 255$

271. (b) We know, $a^3 + \frac{1}{a^3} = 52$

As we know

$\left(a + \frac{1}{a}\right)^3 = a^3 + \frac{1}{a^3} + 3\left(a + \frac{1}{a}\right) \quad \ldots(i)$

From the option,

$2\left(a + \frac{1}{a}\right) = 8 \Rightarrow \left(a + \frac{1}{a}\right) = 4$

From Eq. (i),

$4^3 = a^3 + \frac{1}{a^3} + 3 \times 4$

$\Rightarrow \quad a^3 + \frac{1}{a^3} = 64 - 12 = 52$ (satisfied)

272. (b) We know,

$(a-b)^3 = a^3 - b^3 - 3ab(a-b)$

$\therefore (x-3y)^3 = x^3 - (3y)^3 - 3x(3y)(x-3y)$

$= x^3 - 27y^3 - 9xy(x-3y)$

$= x^3 - 27y^3 - 9x^2y + 27xy^2$

$\therefore$ The coefficient of $x = 27y^2$

273. (c) If $(a-b)^2 + (x-y)^2 = 0$, then $a - b = 0$ and $x - y = 0$

$(a+b-2)^2 + (b+c-5)^2 + (c+a-5)^2 = 0$

So, $a + b - 2 = 0$

$\Rightarrow \quad a + b = 2 \quad \ldots(i)$

$b + c - 5 = 0$

$\Rightarrow \quad b + c = 5 \quad \ldots(ii)$

$c + a - 5 = 0$

$\Rightarrow \quad c + a = 5 \quad \ldots(iii)$

Solving Eqs. (i), (ii) and (iii), we get

$a = 1, b = 1, c = 4$

Now, $\sqrt{(b+c)^a + (c+a)^b - 1}$

$= \sqrt{(1+4)^1 + (4+1)^1 - 1}$

$= \sqrt{(5)^1 + (5)^1 - 1} = \sqrt{9} = 3$

274. (c) $3^a = 27^b = 81^c$ also written as $3^a = 3^{3b} = 3^{4c}$

Let $a = 3b = 4c = k, a = k,$

$b = \frac{k}{3}, c = k/4 \Rightarrow abc = 144$

$\Rightarrow \quad k \times (k/3)(k/4) = 144$

$\Rightarrow k^3 = 144 \times 12 \Rightarrow k = 12$

The value of $a = 12$, $b = \frac{12}{3} = 4$, $c = \frac{12}{4} = 3$

Now, $12\left(\frac{1}{a} + \frac{1}{2b} + \frac{1}{5c}\right) = 12\left(\frac{1}{12} + \frac{1}{8} + \frac{1}{15}\right)$

$= 12 \times \frac{(10+15+8)}{120} = \frac{33}{10}$

275. (b) Given, $(2x+y)^3$

We know that,

$(a+b)^3 = a^3 + b^3 + 3ab(a+b)$

$\therefore (2x+y)^3 = (2x)^3 + y^3 + 3(2x)(y)(2x+y)$

$= 8x^3 + y^3 + 6xy(2x+y)$

$= 8x^3 + y^3 + 12x^2y + 6xy^2$

The coefficient of x^2 is $12y$.

276. (b) Given, $(a+b+c-d)^2 - (a-b-c+d)^2$

We know that, $a^2 - b^2 = (a-b)(a+b)$

$(a+b+c-d)^2 - (a-b-c+d)^2$

$= (a+b+c-d-a+b+c-d)$

$(a+b+c-d+a-b-c+d)$

$= (2b+2c-2d)(2a) = 4a(b+c-d)$

277. (c) $\frac{x^2(x-4)^2}{(x+4)^2 - 4x} \div \frac{(x^2-4x)^3}{(x+4)^2} \times \frac{64-x^3}{16-x^2}$

$= \frac{x^2(x-4)^2}{(x^2+16+8x-4x)} \times \frac{(x+4)^2}{(x^2-4x)^3} \times \frac{4^3-x^3}{4^2-x^2}$

$= \frac{x^2(x-4)^2}{(x^2+4x+16)} \times \frac{(x+4)^2}{x^3(x-4)^3} \times \frac{(4-x)(16+x^2+4x)}{(4-x)(4+x)}$

$= \frac{(x+4)}{x(x-4)}$

278. (b) $x^2 - 2\sqrt{5}x + 1 = 0$

$\Rightarrow \quad x^2 + 1 = 2\sqrt{5}x$ (divide by x both sides)

$\Rightarrow \quad x + \frac{1}{x} = 2\sqrt{5} \quad \ldots(i)$

On squaring Eq. (i),

$x^2 + \frac{1}{x^2} + 2 = 4 \times 5$

$\Rightarrow \quad x^2 + 1/x^2 = 18 \quad \ldots(ii)$

On Cubing Eq. (i),

$x^3 + \frac{1}{x^3} + 3x \times \frac{1}{x}(x + 1/x) = (2\sqrt{5})^3$

$\Rightarrow \quad x^3 + 1/x^3 = 40\sqrt{5} - 3(2\sqrt{5})$

$= 34\sqrt{5} \quad \ldots(iii)$

Multiply Eq. (ii) and Eq. (iii),

$\left(x^2 + \frac{1}{x^2}\right)\left(x^3 + \frac{1}{x^3}\right) = 18 \times 34\sqrt{5}$

$\Rightarrow \quad \left(x^5 + \frac{1}{x} + x + \frac{1}{x^5}\right) = 18 \times 34\sqrt{5}$

$\Rightarrow \quad x^5 + \frac{1}{x^5} = 612\sqrt{5} - (x + 1/x)$

$\Rightarrow \quad x^5 + \frac{1}{x^5} = 612\sqrt{5} - 2\sqrt{5} = 610\sqrt{5}$

279. (b) As, $(P \div Q) \times R$

$= \frac{x^3+y^3}{(x^2+y^2-2xy)+3xy} \times \frac{(x^3-y^3)}{(x^2+y^2+2xy)-3xy} \times \frac{x^2+y^2+2xy+x^2+y^2-2xy}{(x+y)(x-y)}$

$= \frac{x^3+y^3}{(x-y)(x^2+y^2+2xy)} \times \frac{x^3-y^3}{(x+y)(x^2+y^2-xy)} \times 2(x^2+y^2)$

$= \frac{x^3+y^3}{(x^3-y^3)} \times \frac{(x^3-y^3)}{x^3+y^3} \times 2(x^2+y^2)$

$= 2(x^2+y^2)$

280. (d) We can write, $(x^4 + y^4 - x^2y^2)$ as $(x^2+y^2+xy)(x^2+y^2-xy)$

Given,

$(4a^2 + 9b^2 - 6ab) = 13 \quad \ldots(i)$

$16a^4 + 36a^2b^2 + 81b^4 = 91$ (apply here the above formula)

$\Rightarrow \quad (4a^2+9b^2+6ab)(4a^2+9b^2-6ab) = 91$

Put the value from Eq. (i) to here, we get

$(4a^2+9b^2+6ab)(13) = 91$

$\Rightarrow \quad 4a^2 + 9b^2 + 6ab = \frac{91}{13}$

$\Rightarrow \quad 4a^2 + 9b^2 + 6ab = 7 \quad \ldots(ii)$

Subtracting Eq. (i) from Eq. (ii), we get

$4a^2 + 9b^2 + 6ab - 4a^2 - 9b^2 + 6ab = 7 - 13$

$\Rightarrow \quad 12ab = -6$

$\Rightarrow \quad ab = -\frac{6}{12} \Rightarrow ab = -\frac{1}{2}$

$\therefore \quad 3ab = -\frac{3}{2}$

281. (b) Given,

$2x^2 + y^2 + 8z^2 - 2\sqrt{2}xy + 4\sqrt{2}yz - 8zx = (Ax + y + Bz)^2$

$\Rightarrow (\sqrt{2}x)^2 + (y)^2 + (-2\sqrt{2}z)^2 + [2(\sqrt{2}x)(-y) + 2(-y)(2\sqrt{2}z) + 2(-2\sqrt{2}z)(\sqrt{2}x)] = (Ax + y + Bz)^2$

$\Rightarrow \quad (\sqrt{2}x + y - 2\sqrt{2}z)^2 = (Ax + y + Bz)^2$

$\therefore A = \sqrt{2}, B = -2\sqrt{2}$

$\therefore (A^2 + B^2 - AB)$

$= (\sqrt{2})^2 + (-2\sqrt{2})^2 - [(\sqrt{2})(-2\sqrt{2})]$

$= 2 + 8 + 4 = 14$

282. (b) Given, $x + y + z = 3$ and

$x^2 + y^2 + z^2 = 101$

We know that,

$(x+y+z)^2 = x^2 + y^2 + z^2 + 2(xy + yz + zx)$

$\Rightarrow \quad 2(xy + yz + zx) = (x+y+z)^2 - (x^2+y^2+z^2)$

$\Rightarrow \quad 2(xy + yz + zx) = (3)^2 - (101)$

$\Rightarrow \quad xy + yz + zx = \frac{9-101}{2} = \frac{-92}{2} = -46$

$\therefore \sqrt{x^3 + y^3 + z^3 - 3xyz}$

$= \sqrt{(x+y+z)[(x^2+y^2+z^2) - (xy+yz+zx)]}$

$= \sqrt{(3)[(101) - (-46)]}$

$= \sqrt{3(101+46)}$

$= \sqrt{3 \times 147} = \sqrt{441} = 21$

Speedy Method

$x^3 + y^3 + z^3 - 3xyz = \frac{(x+y+z)}{2}[3(x^2+y^2+z^2)-(x+y+z)^2]$

$= \frac{3}{2}[3 \times 101 - 9] = 441$

Thus, $\sqrt{x^3+y^3+z^3-3xyz} = \sqrt{441} = 21$

283. (b) Given, $2a + 2b + c = 0$

$\Rightarrow 2a + 2b = -c$

$\Rightarrow (2a+2b)^2 = (-c)^2$

$\Rightarrow (2a)^2 + (2b)^2 + 8ab = c^2$

$\Rightarrow 4a^2 + 4b^2 - c^2 = -8ab$

$\Rightarrow 4a^2 + 4b^2 - c^2 + 5c^2 = 5c^2 - 8ab$

$\therefore \frac{4a^2+4b^2+4c^2}{5c^2-8ab} = 1$

284. (c) $\left(a - \frac{1}{a}\right)^3 + 3\left(a - \frac{1}{a}\right)$

We know that,

$(a-b)^3 = a^3 - b^3 - 3ab(a-b)$

$\Rightarrow (a-b)^3 + 3ab(a-b) = a^3 - b^3$

$\therefore \left(a - \frac{1}{a}\right)^3 + 3\left(a - \frac{1}{a}\right) = a^3 - \frac{1}{a^3}$

Putting $a = (\sqrt{2}-1)^{\frac{1}{3}}$

$\therefore \left(a - \frac{1}{a}\right)^3 + 3\left(a - \frac{1}{a}\right)$

$= [(\sqrt{2}-1)^{\frac{1}{3}}]^3 - \left[\frac{1}{(\sqrt{2}-1)^{\frac{1}{3}}}\right]^3$

$= (\sqrt{2}-1) - \frac{1}{\sqrt{2}-1}$

$= \sqrt{2} - 1 - \frac{1 \times (\sqrt{2}+1)}{(\sqrt{2}-1)(\sqrt{2}+1)}$

$= \sqrt{2} - 1 - \sqrt{2} - 1 = -2$

285. (d) Given, $x^2 - 6x - 1 = 0$

Dividing it by x, we get

$x - 6 - \frac{1}{x} = 0 \Rightarrow x - \frac{1}{x} = 6$

Squaring it on both the sides, we get

$\left(x - \frac{1}{x}\right)^2 = (6)^2$

$\Rightarrow x^2 + \frac{1}{x^2} - 2 \times x \times \frac{1}{x} = 36$

$\Rightarrow x^2 + \frac{1}{x^2} = 36 + 2 \Rightarrow x^2 + \frac{1}{x^2} = 38$

Now, the value of $x^2 + \frac{1}{x^2} - 8$

$\therefore x^2 + \frac{1}{x^2} - 8 = 38 - 8 = 30$

286. (d) Let the number of boys be x.

$\therefore$ Number of girls $= 8 + x$

$\therefore x + (x+8) = 18 \Rightarrow 2x = 18 - 8 \Rightarrow x = 5$

Number of boys $\times$ Number of girls

$= x \times (x+8) = 5 \times (5+8) = 65$

287. (c) $(a+b+c)^2 = a^2 + b^2 + c^2 + 2(ab + bc + ca)$

$\Rightarrow (13)^2 = (a^2+b^2+c^2) + 2(22)$

$\Rightarrow a^2 + b^2 + c^2 = 169 - 44$

$\Rightarrow a^2 + b^2 + c^2 = 125$

$a^3 + b^3 + c^3 - 3abc$

$= (a+b+c)[a^2+b^2+c^2 - (ab+bc+ca)]$

$= 13[125 - 22] = 13 \times 103 = 1339$

288. (b) $x^2 + 4y^2 + 2x + 1 = 0$

$\Rightarrow (x^2 + 2x + 1) + (4y^2) = 0$

$\Rightarrow (x+1)^2 + (2y)^2 = 0$

Thus, $x + 1 = 0 \Rightarrow x = -1$

and $2y = 0 \Rightarrow y = 0$

$\therefore x^{39} + y^{36} = (-1)^{39} + (0)^{36} = -1$

$[\because (-1)^{\text{odd}} = -1]$

289. (c) $(4a + 3b)(16a^2 - 12ab + 9b^2)$

$= (4a+3b)[(4a)^2 - (4a)(3b) + (3b)^2]$

$= (4a)^3 + (3b)^3$

Put, $a = 2$ and $b = 3$

$= (4 \times 2)^3 + (3 \times 3)^3 = (8)^3 + (9)^3$

$= 512 + 729 = 1241$

290. (d) $x^5 - 12x^4 + 12x^3 - 12x^2 + 12x - 1$

$= x^5 - 11x^4 - x^4 + 11x^3 + x^3 - 11x^2 - x^2 + 11x + x - 1$

$= x^4(x-11) - x^3(x-11) + x^2(x-11) - x(x-11) + x - 1$

When $x = 11 = 11 - 1 = 10$

291. (d) Given, $\frac{a}{b} + \frac{b}{a} = 1$

$\Rightarrow \frac{a^2+b^2}{ab} = 1 \Rightarrow a^2 + b^2 = ab$

$\Rightarrow a^2 + b^2 - ab = 0$ ...(i)

Now, the value of $\frac{a^3+b^3}{3ab}$

$= \frac{(a+b)(a^2+b^2-ab)}{3ab}$

$= \frac{(a+b) \times 0}{3ab} = 0$ [using Eq. (i)]

292. (d) Here, $(x-2) = 0 \Rightarrow x = 2$

Putting the value of x in $2x^3 + ax^2 + 3x - 5$

$= 2(2)^3 + a(2)^2 \times 3(2) - 5$

$= 2 \times 8 + a \times 4 + 6 - 5 = 16 + 4a + 1$

$= 17 + 4a$ ...(i)

Now, using $x = 2$ in $(x^3 + x^2 - 2x + a)$

$= (2)^3 + (2)^2 - 2(2) + a = 8 + 4 - 4 + a$

$= 8 + a$ ...(ii)

Now, $17 + 4a = 8 + a \Rightarrow a = -3$

Using it in Eq. (i),

$17 + 4(-3) = 17 - 12 = 5$

$\therefore$ Remainder $= 5$

293. (d) Given,

$(a-18)^2 + (b-12)^2 + (c-6)^2 = 0$

$\Rightarrow (a-18)^2 = 0$ $[\because a = 18]$

$\Rightarrow (b-12)^2 = 0$ $[\because b = 12]$

$\Rightarrow (c-6)^2 = 0$ $[\because c = 6]$

Now, $(a+b+c)^{\frac{1}{2}} = \sqrt{(a+b+c)}$

$= \sqrt{(18+12+6)} = \sqrt{36} = \pm 6$

294. (a) Given, $x = 110$, $y = 111$, $z = 112$

We know that,

$x^3 + y^3 + z^3 - 3xyz = \frac{1}{2}(x+y+z)[(x-y)^2 + (y-z)^2 + (z-x)^2]$

$= \frac{1}{2}(110 + 111 + 112)[(110-111)^2 + (111-112)^2 + (112-110)^2]$

$= \frac{1}{2} \times 333 \times [(-1)^2 + (-1)^2 + (2)^2]$

$= \frac{1}{2} \times 333 \times [1 + 1 + 4] = \frac{1}{2} \times 333 \times 6$

$= 999$

295. (a) We know that,

$a^3 + b^3 + c^3 - 3abc = (a+b+c)(a^2 + b^2 + c^2 - ac - bc - ab)$

If $a + b + c = 0$

Then, $a^3 + b^3 + c^3 = 3abc$

$\because a + 2b + 3c = 0$ (given)

$\therefore a^3 + 8b^3 + 27c^3 = 3a \times 2b \times 3c = 18abc$

296. (c) Let the value of $x = 1$

$x + \frac{1}{x} = 2$ holds true for $x = 1$

Now, the value of $\left(x^4 + \frac{4}{x^4}\right)\left(x^3 - \frac{4}{x^3}\right)$

$= \left\{1^4 + \frac{4}{1^4}\right\}\left\{1^3 - \frac{4}{1^3}\right\}$

$= (1+4)(1-4) = 5 \times (-3) = -15$

297. (c) Given, $x = 3y + 4$

$\Rightarrow x - 3y = 4$

Cubing on both the sides,

$(x - 3y)^3 = (4)^3$

$\Rightarrow x^3 - 27y^3 - 3(x)(3y)(x - 3y) = 64$

$\Rightarrow x^3 - 27y^3 - 9xy \times 4 = 64$

$\Rightarrow x^3 - 27y^3 - 36xy = 64$

298. (d) Let $\alpha = 1, \beta = -1$ and $\gamma = 0$

then, $\frac{3\beta^2 + \alpha^2 + \gamma^2}{2\beta^2 - \alpha\gamma} = \frac{3(-1)^2 + (1)^2 + 0}{2(-1)^2 - 1 \times 0}$

$= \frac{3+1}{2} = \frac{4}{2} = 2$

299. (b) $\frac{(143 \div 13 \times x - 3 \times 3)}{(6^2 - 7 \times 5 + x^2)} = 1$

$\Rightarrow \frac{(11 \times x - 9)}{(36 - 35 + x^2)} = 1$

$\Rightarrow 11x - 9 = 1 + x^2$

$\Rightarrow x^2 - 11x + 10 = 0$

$\Rightarrow (x-1)(x-10) = 0$

$\Rightarrow x = 1, x = 10$

Now, according to the given option, (b) $x = 1$.

300. (a) According to the question,

$x + y = 4(x - y) \Rightarrow x + y = 4x - 4y$

$\Rightarrow 3x = 5y$

Now, The value of $\frac{5xy}{3(x^2-y^2)}$

$$=\frac{5\times\frac{5y}{3}\times y}{3\left[\left(\frac{5}{3}y\right)^2-y^2\right]}=\frac{\frac{25y^2}{3}}{3\left[\frac{25}{9}y^2-y^2\right]}$$

$$=\frac{25y^2}{9\left[\frac{25y^2-9y^2}{9}\right]}=\frac{25y^2\times 9}{9\times 16y^2}=\frac{25}{16}$$

301. **(a)** $(x-2y)(y-3x)$
$+(x+y)(x-y)+(x-3y)(2x+y)$
$=xy-3x^2-2y^2+6xy+x^2-y^2$
$+2x^2+xy-6xy-3y^2$
$=3x^2-3x^2-2y^2-y^2-3y^2$
$+xy+6xy+xy-6xy$
$=-6y^2+2xy=2y(x-3y)$

302. **(c)** $b+2a-[(3b+a)-(2a+b)+2a]-a$
$b+2a-[3b+a-2a-b+2a]-a$
$=b+2a-(2b+a)-a$
$=b+2a-2b-a-a=2a-2a-b=-b$

303. **(b)** Given, $a+b=10$ ...(i)
And $ab=6$ ...(ii)
On squaring both sides of Eq. (i),
$(a+b)^2=(10)^2$
$\Rightarrow\ a^2+b^2+2ab=100$
$\Rightarrow\ a^2+b^2=100-2\times 6=88$ ...(iii)
Now, $a^3+b^3=(a+b)(a^2+b^2-ab)$
From Eqs. (i), (ii) and (iii), we get,
$a^3+b^3=10\times(88-6)=10\times 82=820$

304. **(c)** Given, $x+y=2$ ...(i)
and $\frac{x}{y}+\frac{y}{x}=1$
$\Rightarrow\ x^2+y^2=xy$ ...(ii)
Now, $x^3+y^3=(x+y)(x^2+y^2-xy)$
$=2(xy-xy)$ [$\because$ from Eq. (ii)]
$=2\times 0$
Hence, $x^3+y^3=0$

305. **(d)** The value of $r(r^2+3r+3)$ for $r=55$ is
$=55(55^2+3\times 55+3)$
$=55(50+5)^2+165+3]$
$=55[2500+25+500+168]=55\times 3195$
$=175615$

306. **(d)** Given, $a^2+b^2=82$ and $b^2+c^2=65$
By hit and trial method $a=9$, $b=1$ and $c=8$
Now, $2a+7b-3c=2\times 9+7\times 1-3\times 8$
$=25-24=1$

307. **(b)** Given, $x(x-5)=-1$
$\Rightarrow\ x-5=-\frac{1}{x}\Rightarrow x+\frac{1}{x}=5$
$\Rightarrow\ \left(x+\frac{1}{x}\right)^3=(5)^3$
$\Rightarrow\ x^3+\frac{1}{x^3}+3\left(x+\frac{1}{x}\right)=125$
$\Rightarrow\ x^3+\frac{1}{x^3}+3\times 5=125$ $\left[\because x+\frac{1}{x}=5\right]$
$\Rightarrow\ x^3+\frac{1}{x^3}=125-15$
$\Rightarrow\ x^6+1=110x^3$
$\Rightarrow\ x^6-110x^3=-1$
$\Rightarrow\ x^3(x^3-110)=-1$

308. **(b)** We know,
$(x+y)^2-2xy=100-48=52$
$\Rightarrow\ x^2+y^2=52$
If $x^2+y^2-2xy=52-48=4$
$(x-y)^2=4$
$\Rightarrow\ (x-y)=2$ ...(i)
($\because x>y$)
Also, $x+y=10$ ...(ii)
From Eqs. (i) and (ii),
$x=6, y=4$
Then, $2x-y=2\times 6-4=8$

309. **(c)** Given, $6x+7y=5xy$
$\Rightarrow\ \frac{6x}{xy}+\frac{7y}{xy}=5$
$\Rightarrow\ \frac{6}{y}+\frac{7}{x}=5$ ...(i)
Similarly, $10y-4x=4xy$
$\Rightarrow\ \frac{10}{x}-\frac{4}{y}=4$ ...(ii)
Let $\frac{1}{x}=u,\ \frac{1}{y}=v$
$\therefore\ 7u+6v=5$ ...(iii)
$10u-4v=4$ ...(iv)
Solving Eqs. (iii) and (iv) we get,
$u=\frac{1}{2},\frac{1}{v}=\frac{1}{4}\ \Rightarrow\ x=2, y=4$

310. **(b)** If $a+b+c=0$, then
$a^3+b^3+c^3=3abc$
$\therefore\ \frac{a^3+b^3+c^3}{abc}=3$
$\Rightarrow\ \frac{a^2}{bc}+\frac{b^2}{ac}+\frac{c^2}{ab}=3$

311. **(d)** We know, $(a+b)^2=a^2+b^2+2ab$
$\Rightarrow(a+b)^2=82+2\times 9=82+18$
$\Rightarrow(a+b)^2=100\Rightarrow\ a+b=10$
$(a+b)^3=a^3+b^3+3ab(a+b)$
$\Rightarrow\ (10)^3=a^3+b^3+3\times 9\times 10$
$\Rightarrow\ 1000=a^3+b^3+270$
$\therefore\ a^3+b^3=730$

312. **(a)** $(5\sqrt{5}x^3-3\sqrt{3}y^3)\div(\sqrt{5}x-\sqrt{3}y)$
$=(Ax^2+By^2+Cxy)$
$\frac{(\sqrt{5}x)^3-(\sqrt{3}y)^3}{\sqrt{5}x-\sqrt{3}y}=Ax^2+By^2+Cxy$
$\frac{(\sqrt{5}x-\sqrt{3}y)[(\sqrt{5}x)^2+\sqrt{5}x\cdot\sqrt{3}y+(\sqrt{3}y)^2]}{(\sqrt{5}x-\sqrt{3}y)}$
$=Ax^2+By^2+Cxy$
$\Rightarrow\ 5x^2+\sqrt{15}xy+3y^2=Ax^2+By^2+Cxy$
$\therefore\ A=5, B=3, C=\sqrt{15}$
$\therefore\ 3A-B-\sqrt{15}\,C$
$=3(5)-3-\sqrt{15}(\sqrt{15})=15-3-15=-3$

313. **(c)** $x^4+\frac{1}{x^4}=194$
$\Rightarrow\left(x^2+\frac{1}{x^2}\right)^2-2\times x^2\times\frac{1}{x^2}=194$
$\Rightarrow\ \left(x^2+\frac{1}{x^2}\right)^2-2=194$
$\Rightarrow\ \left(x^2+\frac{1}{x^2}\right)^2=196$
$\Rightarrow\ x^2+\frac{1}{x^2}=\sqrt{196}=14$
$\Rightarrow\ \left(x+\frac{1}{x}\right)^2-2\times x\times\frac{1}{x}=14$
$\Rightarrow\ \left(x+\frac{1}{x}\right)^2=14+2=16$
$\Rightarrow\ x+\frac{1}{x}=\sqrt{16}=4$
Then, the value of
$x+\frac{1}{x}+2=4+2=6$

314. **(d)** We know, $x^3+y^3+z^3+xyz$
$=x^3+y^3+z^3-3xyz+4xyz$
$=(x+y+z)(x^2+y^2+z^2-xy$
$-yz-zx)+4xyz$
$=(x+y+z)\{x^2+y^2+z^2+2xy$
$+2yz+2zx-3(xy+yz+zx)\}+4xyz$
$=(x+y+z)\{(x+y+z)^2$
$-3(xy+yz+zx)\}+4xyz$
$=17\{17^2-3\times 111\}+4\times 171$
$=-748+684=-64$
So, $\sqrt[3]{x^3+y^3+z^3+xyz}=\sqrt[3]{-64}=-4$

315. **(b)** $x^2-3x+1=0$
$\Rightarrow\ x^2+1=3x$
$\Rightarrow\ \frac{x^2+1}{x}=3\Rightarrow\frac{x^2}{x}+\frac{1}{x}=3\Rightarrow\ x+\frac{1}{x}=3$
$\therefore\left(x^4+\frac{1}{x^2}\right)\div(x^2+1)=\frac{x\left(x^3+\frac{1}{x^3}\right)}{x\left(x+\frac{1}{x}\right)}$
[$\because a^3+b^3=(a+b)^3-3ab(a+b)$]
$=\frac{\left(x+\frac{1}{x}\right)^3-3x\cdot\frac{1}{x}\left(x+\frac{1}{x}\right)}{\left(x+\frac{1}{x}\right)}=\frac{3^3-3\cdot 3}{3}$
$=\frac{3[3^2-3]}{3}=9-3=6$

316. **(a)** $x^2+8y^2+12y-4xy+9=0$
$\Rightarrow\ x^2-4xy+8y^2+12y+9=0$
$\Rightarrow x^2-2\cdot x\cdot 2y+4y^2+4y^2+2\cdot 2y\cdot 3+9=0$
$\Rightarrow\ (x-2y)^2+(2y+3)^2=0$
If sum of two square term is zero, then they each must be equal to zero.
$(2y+3)^2=0;\ (x-2y)^2=0$
$\Rightarrow\ 2y+3=0\ \Rightarrow\ x-2y=0$
$\Rightarrow\ 2y=-3\ \Rightarrow\ x=2y$
$\Rightarrow y=-\frac{3}{2}\ \Rightarrow\ x=-\frac{3}{2}\times 2=-3$

So, $7x + 8y$

$= 7 \times (-3) + 8 \times \left(-\frac{3}{2}\right) = -21 - 12 = -33$

317. (c) $a^2 + b^2 + c^2 + 216 = 12(a + b - 2c)$

$\Rightarrow a^2 + b^2 + c^2 + 216 = 12a + 12b - 24c$

$\Rightarrow a^2 - 12a + b^2 - 12b + c^2 + 24c + 216 = 0$

$\Rightarrow a^2 + 36 - 2 \times 6 \times a + b^2 + 36 - 2 \times 6 \times b + c^2 + 144 + 2 \times 12 \times c = 0$

$\Rightarrow (a-6)^2 + (b-6)^2 + (c+12)^2 = 0$

So, $a - 6 = 0 \Rightarrow a = 6$

$b - 6 = 0 \Rightarrow b = 6$

$c - 12 = 0 \Rightarrow c = 12$

Hence, $\sqrt{ab - bc + ca}$

$= \sqrt{6 \times 6 + 6 \times 12 - 12 \times 6}$

$= \sqrt{36 + 72 - 72} = \sqrt{36} = 6$

318. (c) $(2z - 5y)^2 + (5z + 2y)^2 - 25z^2$

$= (2z - 5y)^2 + (5z + 2y)^2 - (5z)^2$

$= (2z - 5y)^2 + [(10z + 2y)2y]$

$= 4z^2 + 25y^2 - 20zy + 20zy + 4y^2$

$= 29y^2 + 4z^2$

319. (a) Given equations,

$5x + ky - 2 = 0$ and $(k+1)x + 4y + 7 = 0$

We know, condition for parallel lines is

$$\frac{a_1}{a_2} = \frac{b_1}{b_2} = \frac{c_1}{c_2}$$

Here, $a_1 = 5, b_1 = k, c_1 = -2$

$a_2 = (k+1), b_2 = 4, c_2 = 7$

$\therefore \frac{5}{k+1} = \frac{k}{4} = \frac{-2}{7} \Rightarrow \frac{5}{k+1} = \frac{k}{4}$

$\Rightarrow k^2 + k = 20$

$\Rightarrow k^2 + k - 20 = 0 \Rightarrow (k+5)(k-4) = 0$

$\Rightarrow k = 4, -5$

As, $k > 0 \therefore k = 4$

320. (a) Let the cost price of pencil = ₹x and the cost price of pen = ₹y

According to the question,

$21x + 9y = ₹276$

$\Rightarrow 7x + 3y = ₹92$ ...(i)

$6x + 3y = ₹84$ ...(ii)

On solving Eq. (i) and Eq. (ii),

$x = ₹8$ and $y = ₹12$

$\therefore$ Cost of (1 pencil + 1 pen) $= x + y$

$= 8 + 12 = ₹20$

321. (c) Let NOTA got x votes.

$\therefore$ First runner up got votes $= x + 900$

$\therefore$ Second runner up got votes

$= x + 900 - 150 = x + 750$

$\therefore$ Winner got votes $= 2(x + 750) = 2x + 1500$

According to the question,

The three candidates got votes that are 6 times NOTA.

$\therefore x + 900 + x + 750 + 2x + 1500 = 6x$

$\Rightarrow 2x = 3150 \Rightarrow x = \frac{3150}{2} = 1575$

$\therefore$ Total votes polled $= x + 6x$

$= 7x = 7 \times 1575 = 11025$

322. (b) Let number = x

According to the question,

$$\frac{x + \frac{1}{x}}{2} = 2 \Rightarrow x + \frac{1}{x} = 4$$

On cubing both the sides,

$x^3 + \frac{1}{x^3} + 3x \times \frac{1}{x}\left(x + \frac{1}{x}\right) = 64$

$\Rightarrow x^3 + \frac{1}{x^3} + 3 \times 4 = 64$

$\Rightarrow x^3 + \frac{1}{x^3} = 52$

Hence, required average $= \frac{52}{2} = 26$

323. (a) $f(x) = 2x^3 - 3x^2 + 6x - 4$

To find the remainder,

$2x - 3 = 0, x = \frac{3}{2}$

$\therefore f\left(\frac{3}{2}\right) = 2 \times \left(\frac{3}{2}\right)^3 - 3\left(\frac{3}{2}\right)^2 + 6 \times \frac{3}{2} - 4$

$= 2 \times \frac{27}{8} - 3 \times \frac{9}{4} + 9 - 4$

$= \frac{27}{4} - \frac{27}{4} + 9 - 4 = 5$

Hence, required remainder = 5

324. (c) Let the candidates answered x number of questions correctly, then, number of questions, which are either incorrect or unattempted are $(160 - x)$.

According to the question,

$4x - 1(160 - x) = 400$

$\Rightarrow 4x - 160 + x = 400$

$\Rightarrow 5x = 560$

$x = \frac{560}{5} = 112$

$\therefore$ He attempted 112 questions correctly.

325. (a) According to the question,

$x + y + z = 15$ ...(i)

$2x - y + z = 12$ ...(ii)

and $x - y - z = -1$ ...(iii)

On adding Eqs. (i) and (iii), we get

$\Rightarrow 2x = 14 \Rightarrow x = 7$ ...(iv)

From Eq. (i), $7 + y + z = 15$

$\Rightarrow y + z = 8$ ...(v)

From Eq. (ii), $2x - y + z = 12$

$\Rightarrow 2 \times 7 - y + z = 12$

$\Rightarrow z - y = -2$ ...(vi)

On adding Eqs. (v) and (vi), we get

$\Rightarrow 2z = 6 \Rightarrow z = 3$

From Eq. (v), $y + 3 = 8 \Rightarrow y = 5$

$\therefore x = 7, y = 5$ and $z = 3$

326. (b) According to the question,

$x + y = 2$ ...(i)

$2x - y = 1$ ...(ii)

From Eqs. (i) and (ii),

$x = 1$

$\therefore y = 1$ [From Eq. (i)]

$\because$ Point $(x, y) = (1, 1), y = kx + 5$

This is satisfied the situation,

$\therefore 1 = k \times 1 + 5 \Rightarrow k = -4$

327. (a) $\frac{(x^2 - 9) \times (9x^2 - 1)}{\left(x - \frac{1}{3}\right) \times \left(1 - \frac{x}{3}\right)} \times \frac{9}{\left(x + \frac{1}{3}\right)\left(1 + \frac{x}{3}\right)}$

$[\because a^2 - b^2 = (a+b)(a-b)]$

$= \frac{(x+3)(x-3)(3x+1)(3x-1)}{-\frac{(3x-1)}{3} \times \frac{(x-3)}{3}} \times \frac{9}{\frac{(3x+1)}{3} \times \frac{(x+3)}{3}}$

$= -9 \times 9 \times 9 = -729$

328. (c) Let $x = a$ and $y = 2b$

$\because (x + y)^2 = (x - y)^2 + 4xy$

$\therefore (a + 2b)^2 = (a - 2b)^2 + 4(a \cdot 2b)$

$\Rightarrow (a + 2b)^2 = (8)^2 + 4(9)$ [given in question]

$\Rightarrow (a + 2b)^2 = 64 + 36$

$\therefore (a + 2b)^2 = 100 \therefore a + 2b = 10$

329. (d) $\sqrt[3]{0.08 \times 0.8 \times p} = 0.008 \times 0.8 \times \sqrt[3]{q}$

$\Rightarrow \sqrt[3]{\frac{64}{1000} \times p} = \frac{8 \times 8}{1000 \times 10} \times \sqrt[3]{q}$

$\Rightarrow \frac{4}{10}\sqrt[3]{p} = \frac{64}{1000 \times 10} \times \sqrt[3]{q} \Rightarrow \sqrt[3]{\frac{p}{q}} = \frac{2^3 \times 2}{10^3}$

Cubing on both sides, we get

$\frac{p}{q} = (8 \times 2 \times 10^{-3})^3 = 8^3 \times 8 \times 10^{-9}$

$\therefore \frac{p}{q} = 8^4 \times 10^{-9}$

330. (a) Let the oranges with A and B is x and y respectively.

Then, according to the question,

$x + 10 = 2(y - 10)$

$\Rightarrow x - 2y = -30$ ...(i)

and $x - 10 = y + 10$

$\Rightarrow x - y = 20$ ...(ii)

Solving Eqs. (i) and (ii), we get

$x - 2y = -30$

$x - y = 20$

$- \quad + \quad -$

$y = 50$

$\therefore x - 50 = 20 \Rightarrow x = 70$

$\therefore$ Number of oranges with A has = 70

331. (c) Let the cost of 1 chair and 1 table be ₹C and ₹T respectively.

According to the question,

$4C + 3T = 2100$ ...(i)

$5C + 2T = 1750$ ...(ii)

Multiplying the Eq. (i) with 2 and Eq. (ii) with 3, we get

$8C + 6T = 4200$ ...(iii)

$15C + 6T = 5250$ ...(iv)

Subtracting Eq. (iii) from Eq. (iv), we get

$-7C = -1050$

$\Rightarrow C = \frac{1050}{7} = 150$

$\therefore$ Cost of 1 chair = ₹ 150

332. (d) Given equations,

$$P^2 - 4P - 1 = 0 \Rightarrow \frac{P^2 - 4P - 1}{P} = 0$$

$$\Rightarrow \quad P - 4 - \frac{1}{P} = 0$$

$$\Rightarrow \quad \left(P - \frac{1}{P}\right) = 4 \quad \ldots\text{(i)}$$

Now, the value of

$$P^2 + 3P + \frac{1}{P^2} - \frac{3}{P}$$

$$= \left(P^2 + \frac{1}{P^2}\right) + \left(3P - \frac{3}{P}\right)$$

$$= \left(P - \frac{1}{P}\right)^2 + 2 + 3\left(P - \frac{1}{P}\right)$$

From Eq. (i),

$$= (4)^2 + 2 + 3(4) = 16 + 2 + 12 = 30$$

333. (c) As, $a + b + c = 16$

Squaring both sides, we get

$$(a + b + c)^2 = 256$$

$$\Rightarrow \quad a^2 + b^2 + c^2 + 2(ab + bc + ca) = 256$$

$$\Rightarrow \quad 160 + 2(ab + bc + ca) = 256$$

$$\Rightarrow \quad ab + bc + ca = 48$$

334. (a) According to the question,

$$\frac{1}{8}\left[\frac{1}{b-1} - \frac{1}{b+1} - \frac{2}{b^2+1} - \frac{4}{b^4+1}\right]$$

$$= \frac{1}{8}\left[\frac{b+1-b+1}{(b-1)(b+1)} - \frac{2}{b^2+1} - \frac{4}{b^4+1}\right]$$

$$= \frac{1}{8}\left[\frac{2}{b^2-1} - \frac{2}{b^2+1} - \frac{4}{b^4+1}\right]$$

$$= \frac{1}{8}\left[\frac{2b^2 + 2 - 2b^2 + 2}{(b^2-1)(b^2+1)} - \frac{4}{b^4+1}\right]$$

$$= \frac{1}{8}\left[\frac{4}{b^4-1} - \frac{4}{b^4+1}\right]$$

$$= \frac{1}{8}\left[\frac{4b^4 + 4 - 4b^4 + 4}{(b^4-1)(b^4+1)}\right]$$

$$= \frac{1}{8} \times \frac{8}{b^8 - 1} = \frac{1}{b^8 - 1}$$

335. (a) Let the two number are x and y respectively

$$x^3 + y^3 = 10234$$

and $\quad x + y = 34$

$$(x + y)^3 = x^3 + y^3 + 3xy(x + y)$$

$$\Rightarrow \quad (34)^3 = 10234 + 3xy(34)$$

$$\Rightarrow \quad 39304 = 10234 + 102xy$$

$$\Rightarrow \quad 102xy = 39304 - 10234$$

$$\Rightarrow \quad 102xy = 29070$$

$$\Rightarrow \quad xy = \frac{29070}{102} = 285$$

$$\therefore \quad (x - y)^2 = (x + y)^2 - 4xy$$

$$\Rightarrow \quad (x - y)^2 = (34)^2 - 4 \times 285$$

$$\Rightarrow \quad (x - y)^2 = 1156 - 1140$$

$$\Rightarrow \quad (x - y)^2 = 16 \Rightarrow x - y = 4$$

So, the number, $x = 19$ and $y = 15$.

Difference between their cubes

$$= (19)^3 - (15)^3 = 6859 - 3375 = 3484$$

336. (a) Given, $\left(3y + \dfrac{3}{y}\right) = 8$

$$\Rightarrow y + \frac{1}{y} = \frac{8}{3} \Rightarrow \left(y^2 + \frac{1}{y^2}\right) = \left(\frac{64}{9}\right) - 2$$

$$\Rightarrow \quad \left(y^2 + \frac{1}{y^2}\right) = \frac{64 - 18}{9} = \frac{46}{9} = 5\frac{1}{9}$$

337. (c) As given, $x^2 - \sqrt{9.76}\,x + 1 = 0$

$$\Rightarrow \quad x^2 + 1 = \sqrt{9.76}\,x$$

On dividing both sides by x, we have

$$x + \frac{1}{x} = \sqrt{9.76}$$

$$\left(x - \frac{1}{x}\right)^2 = \left(x + \frac{1}{x}\right)^2 - 4$$

$$= 9.76 - 4 = 5.76$$

$$\therefore \quad x - \frac{1}{x} = \sqrt{5.76} = 2.4 \quad \ldots\text{(i)}$$

$$\left(x - \frac{1}{x}\right)^3 = x^3 - \frac{1}{x^3} - 3\left(x - \frac{1}{x}\right)$$

$$\Rightarrow x^3 - \frac{1}{x^3} = \left(x - \frac{1}{x}\right)^3 + 3\left(x - \frac{1}{x}\right)$$

$$\Rightarrow \quad x^3 - \frac{1}{x^3} = (2.4)^3 + 3 \times 2.4$$

$$\Rightarrow \quad x^3 - \frac{1}{x^3} = 13.824 + 7.2$$

$$\therefore \quad x^3 - \frac{1}{x^3} = 21.024$$

338. (a) Given,

$$2x + 5y = 15 \quad \ldots\text{(i)}$$

and $\quad xy = 6$

Squaring both sides of Eq. (i), we have

$$(2x + 5y)^2 = (15)^2$$

$$\Rightarrow \quad 4x^2 + 25y^2 + 20xy = 225$$

$$\Rightarrow \quad 4x^2 + 25y^2 + 20 \times 6 = 225$$

$$\Rightarrow \quad 4x^2 + 25y^2 = 225 - 120$$

$$\therefore \quad 4x^2 + 25y^2 = 105$$

339. (b) Given, $x = (\sqrt{6} - 1)^{1/3}$

$$\Rightarrow \quad x^3 = \sqrt{6} - 1 \text{ and } \frac{1}{x^3} = \frac{1}{\sqrt{6} - 1}$$

$$\Rightarrow \frac{1}{x^3} = \frac{1}{\sqrt{6} - 1} \times \frac{\sqrt{6} + 1}{\sqrt{6} + 1} \Rightarrow \frac{1}{x^3} = \frac{\sqrt{6} + 1}{5}$$

Now, $\left(x - \dfrac{1}{x}\right)^3 + 3\left(x - \dfrac{1}{x}\right)$

$$\Rightarrow \quad x^3 - \frac{1}{x^3} - 3\left(x - \frac{1}{x}\right) + 3\left(x - \frac{1}{x}\right)$$

$$= x^3 - \frac{1}{x^3} = \sqrt{6} - 1 - \frac{\sqrt{6} + 1}{5}$$

$$= \frac{5\sqrt{6} - 5 - \sqrt{6} - 1}{5} = \frac{4\sqrt{6} - 6}{5}$$

340. (a) $4x^2 - y^2 + 6y - 9$

$$= 4x^2 - (y^2 - 2 \times 3y + 3^2)$$

$$= (2x)^2 - (y - 3)^2 = (2x + y - 3)(2x - y + 3)$$

341. (c) According to the questions

$$\left(x - \frac{1}{x - 2}\right) = 7$$

$$\Rightarrow (x - 2) - \left(\frac{1}{x - 2}\right) = 7 - 2 = 5$$

We know, if $x - \dfrac{1}{x} = a$

$$\Rightarrow \quad x^3 - \frac{1}{x^3} = a^3 + 3a$$

$$\therefore \quad (x - 2) - \frac{1}{(x - 2)} = 5$$

$$\Rightarrow \quad (x - 2)^3 - \frac{1}{(x - 2)^3} = (5)^3 + 3(5)$$

$$\Rightarrow \quad (x - 2)^3 - \frac{1}{(x - 2)^3} = 125 + 15 = 140$$

342. (d) According to the question,

$$\frac{x^3 + y^3 + z^3 - 3xyz}{(x - y)^2 + (y - z)^2 + (z - x)^2}$$

$$= \frac{\frac{1}{2}(x + y + z)\{(x - y)^2 + (y - z)^2 + (z - x)^2\}}{\{(x - y)^2 + (y - z)^2 + (z - x)^2\}}$$

$$= \frac{1}{2}(x + y + z)$$

343. (c) As, $\dfrac{x^2 + 7x + 2}{x^2 + 13x + 2} = \dfrac{\frac{x^2}{x} + \frac{2}{x} + \frac{7x}{x}}{\frac{x^2}{x} + \frac{2}{x} + \frac{13x}{x}}$

$$= \frac{x + \frac{2}{x} + 7}{x + \frac{2}{x} + 13} = \frac{1 + 7}{1 + 13} = \frac{8}{14} = \frac{4}{7}$$

344. (b) This can be answered by checking the options.

Option (b) is the only correct identity given.

345. (a) As, $\quad a - b = 10 \therefore (a - b)^2 = (10)^2$

$$\Rightarrow \quad 100 = a^2 + b^2 - 2ab$$

$$\Rightarrow \quad a^2 + b^2 = 100 + 2ab \quad \ldots\text{(i)}$$

and $\quad \sqrt{\dfrac{a}{b}} = \dfrac{8}{3} - \sqrt{\dfrac{b}{a}} \Rightarrow \sqrt{\dfrac{a}{b}} + \sqrt{\dfrac{b}{a}} = \dfrac{8}{3}$

Squaring both sides,

$$\frac{a}{b} + \frac{b}{a} + 2(1) = \frac{64}{9}$$

$$\Rightarrow \quad \frac{a^2 + b^2}{ab} = \frac{64}{9} - 2 \Rightarrow \frac{a^2 + b^2}{ab} = \frac{46}{9}$$

$$\Rightarrow \quad \frac{100 + 2ab}{ab} = \frac{46}{9} \quad \text{[From Eq. (i)]}$$

$$\Rightarrow \quad 900 + 18ab = 46ab$$

$$\Rightarrow \quad 28ab = 900$$

$$\therefore \quad ab = \frac{900}{28} = 32\frac{1}{7}$$

346. (b) Given, $5x + 3y = 15$ and $2xy = 6$

$$\therefore (5x + 3y)^2 = 25x^2 + 9y^2 + 2(5x)(3y)$$

$$\Rightarrow \quad (15)^2 = 25x^2 + 9y^2 + 15(2xy)$$

$$\Rightarrow \quad 225 = 25x^2 + 9y^2 + 15(6)$$

$$\Rightarrow \quad 25x^2 + 9y^2 = 225 - 90 = 135$$

Now, $(5x - 3y)^2 = 25x^2 + 9y^2 - 15(2xy)$

$$= 135 - 90 = 45$$

$$\therefore 5x - 3y = \sqrt{45} = 3\sqrt{5}$$

347. (c) Given, $x + \dfrac{1}{x} = 7$

$$\therefore \left(x + \frac{1}{x}\right)^2 = x^2 + \frac{1}{x^2} + 2$$

$$\Rightarrow \quad (7)^2 - 2 = x^2 + \frac{1}{x^2} \Rightarrow x^2 + \frac{1}{x^2} = 47$$

348. (d) Given, $2x+\frac{2}{x}=5 \Rightarrow x+\frac{1}{x}=\frac{5}{2}$

$$x^3+\frac{1}{x^3}=\left(\frac{5}{2}\right)^3-3\left(\frac{5}{2}\right)=\frac{65}{8}$$

$\because x^3+\frac{1}{x^3}+2=\frac{65}{8}+2=\frac{81}{8}$

349. (c) According to the question,

$\left(k+\frac{1}{k}\right)\left(k-\frac{1}{k}\right)\left(k^2+\frac{1}{k^2}\right)\left(k^4+\frac{1}{k^4}\right)$

$[\because a^2-b^2=(a+b)(a-b)]$

$=\left(k^2-\frac{1}{k^2}\right)\left(k^2+\frac{1}{k^2}\right)\left(k^4+\frac{1}{k^4}\right)$

$=\left(k^4-\frac{1}{k^4}\right)\left(k^4+\frac{1}{k^4}\right)=k^8-\frac{1}{k^8}$

350. (d) If $x-\frac{1}{x}=a \Rightarrow x^3-\frac{1}{x^3}=a^3+3a$

$\therefore \quad x-\frac{1}{x}=4$

$\Rightarrow \quad x^3-\frac{1}{x^3}=(4)^3+3(4)=64+12$

$\Rightarrow \quad x^3-\frac{1}{x^3}=76$

Squaring on both sides,

$$\left(x^3-\frac{1}{x^3}\right)^2=(76)^2$$

$\Rightarrow \quad x^6+\frac{1}{x^6}=5776+2=5778$

351. (d) Given, $(a+b)=16$

Cubing both sides, we get

$a^3+b^3+3ab(a+b)=4096$

$\Rightarrow \quad 1456+48ab=4096 \Rightarrow ab=55$

352. (d) $\frac{k}{k^2-2k+1}=\frac{1}{6}$

$\Rightarrow \quad \frac{k^2-2k+1}{k}=\frac{6}{1} \Rightarrow k+\frac{1}{k}-2=6$

$\Rightarrow \quad k+\frac{1}{k}=8 \quad$ ...(i)

$\Rightarrow \quad k^3+\frac{1}{k^3}=(8)^3-3(8)=488$

353. (b) We know,

$x-\frac{1}{x}=a \Rightarrow x^2+\frac{1}{x^2}=a^2+2$

$\therefore \quad m-\frac{1}{m}=7 \Rightarrow m^2+\frac{1}{m^2}=(7)^2+2=51$

354. (b) $\frac{1+x}{1-x^2}\div\frac{1+x}{1-x^4}-\frac{1-x^4}{1-x}\times\frac{(1+x)}{1-x^2}$

$=\frac{1+x}{1-x^2}\times\frac{(1-x^2)(1+x^2)}{1+x}-\frac{(1-x^2)(1+x^2)}{1-x}\times\frac{(1+x)}{(1-x^2)}$

$=(1+x^2)-\frac{(1+x^2)(1+x)}{(1-x)}$

$=\frac{(1+x^2)(1-x)-(1+x^2)(1+x)}{(1-x)}$

$=\frac{(1+x^2)(1-x-1-x)}{(1-x)}$

$=\frac{-2x(x^2+1)}{(1-x)}=\frac{2x(1+x^2)}{(x-1)}$

355. (a) Given, $a=12, b=-7, c=-5$

$\because \quad a+b+c=12-7-5=0$

$\therefore \quad a^3+b^3+c^3=3abc=3(12)(-7)(-5)=1260$

356. (c) Let the number be a.

According to the question, $a+\frac{1}{a}=4$

Squaring on both sides, $\left(a+\frac{1}{a}\right)^2=(4)^2$

$\Rightarrow \quad a^2+\frac{1}{a^2}+2\cdot a\cdot\frac{1}{a}=16$

$\Rightarrow a^2+\frac{1}{a^2}+2=16 \Rightarrow a^2+\frac{1}{a^2}=14$

357. (b) We know,

$(a+b+c)^2=a^2+b^2+c^2+2(ab+bc+ac)$

$\Rightarrow \quad 0=40+2(ab+bc+ca)$

$\Rightarrow \quad 2(ab+bc+ca)=-40$

$\Rightarrow \quad ab+bc+ca=-20$

358. (a) $x+\frac{1}{x}=\frac{k}{2}$

$\therefore$ Squaring both sides, $x^2+\frac{1}{x^2}+2=\frac{k^2}{4}$

$\Rightarrow \quad x^2+\frac{1}{x^2}=\frac{k^2}{4}-2$

Again squaring both sides,

$x^4+\frac{1}{x^4}+2\cdot x^2\cdot\frac{1}{x^2}=\frac{k^4}{16}+4-2\cdot 2\cdot\frac{k^2}{4}$

$\Rightarrow \quad x^4+\frac{1}{x^4}+2=\frac{k^4}{16}+4-k^2$

$\Rightarrow \quad x^4+\frac{1}{x^4}=\frac{k^4}{16}+2-k^2$

$\Rightarrow \quad \frac{x^8+1}{x^4}=\frac{k^4-16k^2+32}{16}$

359. (a) Given, $a^2+b^2+c^2=62$

and $a+b+c=12$

$\therefore (a+b+c)^2=a^2+b^2+c^2+2ab+2bc+2ac$

$\Rightarrow \quad (12)^2=62+2ab+2bc+2ac$

$\Rightarrow \quad 144=62+2ab+2bc+2ac$

$\Rightarrow \quad 82=2ab+2bc+2ac$

Now, $4ab+4bc+4ac=2(2ab+2bc+2ac)$

$=2\times 82=164$

360. (b) Given, $\quad K+\frac{1}{K}=-3 \quad$ ...(i)

Squaring both sides of Eq. (i),

$K^2+\frac{1}{K^2}+2=9 \Rightarrow K^2+\frac{1}{K^2}=7$

$\Rightarrow \quad \frac{K^4+1}{K^2}=7 \quad$ ...(ii)

Again cubing both sides of Eq. (i),

$K^3+\frac{1}{K^3}+3\left(K+\frac{1}{K}\right)=-27$

$\Rightarrow \quad K^3+\frac{1}{K^3}=-27+9$

$\Rightarrow \quad \frac{K^6+1}{K^3}=-18 \quad$ ...(iii)

Now, adding Eq. (ii) and Eq. (iii)

$\frac{K^6+1}{K^3}+\frac{K^4+1}{K^2}=-18+7=-11$

361. (a) Given, $P+\frac{1}{P}=5 \quad$ ...(i)

Cubing both sides,

$P^3+\frac{1}{P^3}+3\times P\times\frac{1}{P}\left(P+\frac{1}{P}\right)=125$

$\Rightarrow \quad P^3+\frac{1}{P^3}+3(5)=125 \quad$ {from Eq. (i)}

$\therefore \quad P^3+\frac{1}{P^3}=125-15=110$

362. (b) We know that,

$a^3-b^3=(a-b)(a^2+b^2+ab)$

$\Rightarrow \quad 988=(4)(a^2+b^2+ab)$

$\Rightarrow \quad a^2+b^2+ab=\frac{988}{4}$

$\Rightarrow \quad a^2+b^2+ab=247$

So, $2a^2+2b^2+2ab=2(a^2+b^2+ab)$

$=2\times 247=494$

363. (d) According to the question,

$a^2+b^2+c^2-2ab-2bc+2ca$

$=(a)^2+(-b)^2+(c)^2+2(a)(-b)+2(-b)(c)+2(c)(a)$

$=(a-b+c)^2$

364 (b) Given, $a+\frac{1}{a}=2$

$\Rightarrow \quad \left(a+\frac{1}{a}\right)^2=(2)^2 \Rightarrow a^2+\frac{1}{a^2}+2=4$

$\Rightarrow \quad a^2+\frac{1}{a^2}=2 \quad$ ...(i)

Similarly, $\quad b+\frac{1}{b}=-2 \Rightarrow \left(b+\frac{1}{b}\right)^2=(-2)^2$

$\Rightarrow \quad b^2+\frac{1}{b^2}+2=4$

$\Rightarrow \quad b^2+\frac{1}{b^2}=2 \quad$ ...(ii)

Adding Eqs. (i) and (ii), we get

$a^2+\frac{1}{a^2}+b^2+\frac{1}{b^2}=2+2=4$

365. (c) $x^2+4y^2+z^2-4xy+4yz-2xz$

$=(-x)^2+(2y)^2+z^2+2(-x)(2y)+2(2y)(z)+2(-x)(z)$

$=(-x+2y+z)^2=(2y-x+z)^2$

366. (c) Given, $2p+5q=12 \quad$ ...(i)

and $\quad pq=3 \quad$ ...(ii)

On squaring Eq. (i), we get,

$(2p+5q)^2=(12)^2$

$\Rightarrow \quad (2p)^2+(5q)^2+2\times 2p\times 5q=144$

$\Rightarrow \quad 4p^2+25q^2+20pq=144$

$\Rightarrow \quad 4p^2+25q^2+20\times 3=144$

$\Rightarrow \quad 4p^2+25q^2=144-60$

$\Rightarrow \quad 4p^2+25q^2=84$

367. (c) Given, $a-b=5 \quad$ ...(i)

$ab=150 \quad$ ...(ii)

On squaring Eq. (i), we get,

$(a-b)^2=(5)^2 \Rightarrow a^2+b^2-2ab=25$

$\Rightarrow \quad a^2+b^2-2\times 150=25 \quad$ [From Eq. (i)]

$\Rightarrow \quad a^2+b^2=325$

Now, $\quad a^3-b^3=(a-b)(a^2+ab+b^2)$

$=(5)(325+150)=5\times 475=2375$

368. (c) $\frac{1+x^2}{1-x} \div \frac{1-x^4}{x-1} \times \frac{x(1-x)}{(1+x)}$

$= -\frac{1+x^2}{1-x} \times \frac{(1-x)}{(1)^2-(x^2)^2} \times \frac{x(1-x)}{(1+x)}$

$= -\frac{1+x^2}{(1-x)} \times \frac{(1-x)}{(1-x^2)(1+x^2)} \times \frac{x(1-x)}{(1+x)}$

$= -\frac{1}{(1-x)(1+x)} \times \frac{x(1-x)}{(1+x)} = -\frac{x}{(1+x)^2}$

369. (c) Given, $8x^2+9x+8=0$

$\Rightarrow \quad 8x^2+8=-9x \Rightarrow 8(x^2+1)=-9x$

$\Rightarrow \quad 8x\left(x+\frac{1}{x}\right)=-9x \Rightarrow x+\frac{1}{x}=\frac{-9}{8}$

On cubing both sides,

$\left(x+\frac{1}{x}\right)^3=\left(\frac{-9}{8}\right)^3$

$\Rightarrow x^3+\frac{1}{x^3}+3\times x\times\frac{1}{x}\left(x+\frac{1}{x}\right)=\frac{-729}{512}$

$\Rightarrow x^3+\frac{1}{x^3}+3\left(\frac{-9}{8}\right)=\frac{-729}{512} \quad \left(\because x+\frac{1}{x}=\frac{-9}{8}\right)$

$\Rightarrow x^3+\frac{1}{x^3}=\frac{-729}{512}+\frac{27}{8}=\frac{-729+1728}{512}=\frac{999}{512}$

370. (a) Given, $x+y=14$

$\Rightarrow \quad (x+y)^3=(14)^3$

$\Rightarrow x^3+y^3+3xy(x+y)=2744$

$\Rightarrow \quad x^3+y^3+3xy\times 14=2744$

$\therefore \quad x^3+y^3+42xy=2744$

371. (a) $\because \quad p^4+\frac{1}{p^4}=4354$

$\Rightarrow \quad p^4+\frac{1}{p^4}+2=4354+2$

$\Rightarrow \left(p^2+\frac{1}{p^2}\right)^2=4356 \Rightarrow p^2+\frac{1}{p^2}=66$

$\Rightarrow \quad p^2+\frac{1}{p^2}-2=66-2 \Rightarrow \left(p-\frac{1}{p}\right)^2=64$

$\therefore \quad p-\frac{1}{p}=8$

Now, $p^3-\frac{1}{p^3}=\left(p-\frac{1}{p}\right)^3+3\times p\times\frac{1}{p}\left(p-\frac{1}{p}\right)$

$=8^3+3(8)=536$

372. (c) Given, $\frac{a}{b}+\frac{b}{a}=-1$

$\Rightarrow \quad \frac{a^2+b^2}{ab}=-1$

$\Rightarrow \quad a^2+b^2=-ab$

$\Rightarrow \quad a^2+b^2+ab=0 \quad \ldots$(i)

Now, $6(a^3-b^3)=6(a-b)(a^2+ab+b^2)$

$=6(a-b)\times 0$ [From Eq. (i)]

$=0$

373. (a) Given,

$8x^3+27y^3+64z^3=72xyz$

$\Rightarrow \quad (2x)^3+(3y)^3+(4z)^3=3(2x)(3y)(4z)$

By formula,

$a^3+b^3+c^3=3abc$ only if $a+b+c=0$

Here, $a=2x$, $b=3y$ and $c=4z$

So, $2x+3y+4z=0 \Rightarrow 2x+3y=-4z$

374. (d) $(x-2y)^2=x^2+4y^2-4xy$

$\because \quad (a-b)^2=a^2+b^2-2ab$

$\Rightarrow \quad (x-2y)^2=40-4(6)$

$\Rightarrow \quad (x-2y)^2=16 \Rightarrow ?x-2y=4$

375. (a) Given, $x^2+\frac{1}{x^2}=83$

$\Rightarrow x^2+\frac{1}{x^2}-2+2=83 \Rightarrow \left(x-\frac{1}{x}\right)^2+2=83$

$\Rightarrow \quad \left(x-\frac{1}{x}\right)^2=83-2=81$

$\Rightarrow \quad x-\frac{1}{x}=\sqrt{81}=9$

$\therefore x^3-\frac{1}{x^3}=\left(x-\frac{1}{x}\right)^3+3\times x\times\frac{1}{x}\times\left(x-\frac{1}{x}\right)$

$=(9)^3+3\times 9=729+27=756$

376. (c) $x^2+(4-\sqrt{3})x-1=0$

$\Rightarrow \quad x^2-1=(-4+\sqrt{3})x$

$\Rightarrow \quad \frac{x^2-1}{x}=\sqrt{3}-4 \Rightarrow x-\frac{1}{x}=\sqrt{3}-4$

Squaring on both sides,

$x^2+\frac{1}{x^2}-2=3+16-8\sqrt{3}$

$\Rightarrow \quad x^2+\frac{1}{x^2}=21-8\sqrt{3}$

377. (c) According to the question,

$x^6-6\sqrt{6}y^6=(x^2+Ay^2)(x^4+Bx^2y^2+Cy^4)$

$\Rightarrow (x^2)^3-(\sqrt{6}y^2)^3$

$=(x^2+Ay^2)(x^4+Bx^2y^2+Cy^4)$

Since, $a^3-b^3=(a-b)(a^2+ab+b^2)$

$(x^2-\sqrt{6}y^2)(x^4+\sqrt{6}x^2y^2+6y^4)$

$=(x^2+Ay^2)(x^4+Bx^2y^2+Cy^4)$

On comparison of both sides,

$A=-\sqrt{6}, B=\sqrt{6}$ and $C=6$

$\therefore \ (A^2-B^2+C^2)=(-\sqrt{6})^2-(\sqrt{6})^2+(6)^2$

$=6-6+36=36$

378. (a) We know,

$(a^3-b^3)=(a-b)(a^2+b^2+ab)$

$\therefore \left(x-\frac{2}{x}\right)^3-\left(x+\frac{2}{x}\right)^3=\left(x-\frac{2}{x}-x-\frac{2}{x}\right)$

$\left[\left(x-\frac{2}{x}\right)^2+\left(x+\frac{2}{x}\right)^2+\left(x-\frac{2}{x}\right)\left(x+\frac{2}{x}\right)\right]$

$=\frac{-4}{x}\left[x^2+\frac{4}{x^2}-4+x^2+\frac{4}{x^2}+4+x^2-\frac{4}{x^2}\right]$

$=\frac{-4}{x}\left[3x^2+\frac{4}{x^2}\right]=-4\left(3x+\frac{4}{x^3}\right)$

379. (d) Given, $(a+b)=p$ and $ab=q$

$\because (a+b)^2=a^2+b^2+2ab$

$\therefore \quad p^2=a^2+b^2+2q$

$\Rightarrow \quad a^2+b^2=p^2-2q$

Squaring on both sides,

$a^4+b^4+2a^2b^2=p^4+4q^2-4p^2q$

$\Rightarrow a^4+b^4+2q^2=p^4+4q^2-4p^2q \quad [\because ab=q]$

$\Rightarrow a^4+b^4=p^4+4q^2-4p^2q-2q^2$

$\Rightarrow a^4+b^4=p^4-4p^2q+2q^2$

380. (d) Given, $\frac{(x^4+x^2+1)}{(x^2+x+1)}$

$=\frac{x^4+x^2+1+x^2-x^2}{(x^2+x+1)}$

$=\frac{(x^4+1+2x^2)-x^2}{(x^2+x+1)}=\frac{(x^2+1)^2-x^2}{(x^2+x+1)}$

$=\frac{(x^2+1+x)(x^2+1-x)}{(x^2+x+1)}=(x^2-x+1)$

381. (b) Given,

$a^2+49b^2+c^2+18=2(28b-c-a)$

$\Rightarrow a^2+49b^2+c^2+18=56b-2c-2a$

$\Rightarrow a^2+1+2a+(7b)^2+16-56b$

$+c^2+1+2c=0$

$\Rightarrow (a+1)^2+(7b-4)^2+(c+1)^2=0$

Now, $a+1=0 \Rightarrow a=-1$

$7b-4=0 \Rightarrow b=\frac{4}{7}$ and $c+1=0 \Rightarrow c=-1$

$\therefore$ The value of $(a+7b-c)$

$=\left[-1+7\times\frac{4}{7}-(-1)\right]$

$=-1+4+1=4$

382. (a) Given, $a+b+c=4$, $ab+bc+ca=-14$ and $abc=-18$

$\therefore (a+b+c)^2=a^2+b^2+c^2+2(ab+bc+ca)$

$\Rightarrow a^2+b^2+c^2=(4)^2-2\times(-14)=44$

$\therefore$ The value of

$\sqrt{4a^3+4b^3+4c^3-36}=\sqrt{4(a^3+b^3+c^3)-36}$

$=\sqrt{4[(a+b+c)(a^2+b^2+c^2-ab-bc-ca)+3abc]-36}$

$=\sqrt{4\times[4\times(44+14)+3\times-18]-36}$

$=\sqrt{676}=26$

383. (a) Given, $x^8-2599x^4+1=0$

$\Rightarrow \quad x^8+1=2599x^4 \Rightarrow x^4+\frac{1}{x^4}=2599$

We know, $\left(x^2+\frac{1}{x^2}\right)^2=x^4+\frac{1}{x^4}+2$

So, $\left(x^2+\frac{1}{x^2}\right)^2=2599+2=2601$

$\Rightarrow \quad x^2+\frac{1}{x^2}=\sqrt{2601}=51$

$\because \quad \left(x-\frac{1}{x}\right)^2=x^2+\frac{1}{x^2}-2=51-2=49$

$\therefore$ The positive value of $x-\frac{1}{x}=\sqrt{49}=7$

384. (c) Let the two numbers be x and y and $x>y$.

According to the question,

$x-y=5 \quad \ldots$(i)

and $\quad x^3-y^3=1850 \quad \ldots$(ii)

$\because x^3-y^3=(x-y)^3+3xy(x-y)$

$\Rightarrow \quad 1850=(5)^3+3xy\times 5$

[$\because$ from Eqs. (i) and (ii)]

$\Rightarrow \quad xy=115$

Now, we know, $(x-y)^2=x^2+y^2-2xy$

$\therefore \quad (5)^2=x^2+y^2-2\times 115$

$\Rightarrow \quad x^2+y^2=255$

$\therefore \quad (x+y)^2 = x^2 + y^2 + 2xy = 255 + 2 \times 115$

$x + y = \sqrt{485}$ ...(iii)

From Eqs. (i) and (iii),

$(x-y)(x+y) = 5 \times \sqrt{485}$

$\Rightarrow \quad (x^2 - y^2) = 5\sqrt{485}$

385. (d) Let per ride fare be ₹ x.

Expense of Rohan = number of side × per ride fare + Entry free

$15 \times x + 180 = 1380$

$15x = 1200$

$x = ₹\,80$

New expense of Rohan

$= 20 \times 80 + 180 = ₹\,1780$

386. (d) Let required number be x.

According to the question,

$\frac{5}{6} \times x = x - 10 \Rightarrow 5x = 6x - 60 \Rightarrow x = 60$

Hence, $\frac{7}{5}$ of number $= \frac{7}{5} \times 60 = 84$

387. (b) Let the original fraction be $\frac{x}{y}$

According to the question,

$\frac{x+8}{y+12} = \frac{1}{2} \Rightarrow 2x + 16 = y + 12$

$\Rightarrow \quad 2x - y = -4$ ...(i)

and $\quad \frac{x-2}{y-2} = \frac{1}{8}$

$\Rightarrow \quad 8x - 16 = y - 2$

$\Rightarrow \quad 8x - y = 14$ ...(ii)

On subtracting Eqs. (i) and (ii),

$6x = 18 \Rightarrow x = \frac{18}{6} = 3$

Put the value of x in Eq. (ii),

$2 \times 3 - y = -4 \Rightarrow y = 6 + 4 = 10$

$\therefore$ Fraction $= \frac{x}{y} = \frac{3}{10}$

388. (c) Given, $x : y : z = 1 : 2 : 3$

$$\therefore \left(\frac{3x^2 - 2y^2 + 4z^2}{x^2 + 2y^2 + z^2}\right)$$

$$= \left(\frac{3 \times 1^2 - 2 \times 2^2 + 4 \times 3^2}{1^2 + 2 \times 2^2 + 3^2}\right)$$

$$= \left(\frac{3 \times 1 - 2 \times 4 + 4 \times 9}{1 + 2 \times 4 + 9}\right)$$

$$= \frac{3 - 8 + 36}{1 + 8 + 9} = \frac{39 - 8}{18} = \frac{31}{18}$$

389. (a) $p - q = 9$ ...(i)

and $\quad p^2 + q^2 = 127$

Squaring Eq. (i) in both sides,

$(p-q)^2 = 9^2$

$\Rightarrow \quad p^2 + q^2 - 2pq = 81$

$\Rightarrow \quad 127 - 2pq = 81$

$\Rightarrow \quad 2pq = 127 - 81 = 46$

$\Rightarrow \quad pq = 23$

390. (c) y varies directly with x.

$\frac{x}{y} = \frac{24}{16} = \frac{3}{2}$

When $x = 45$

$\frac{45}{y} = \frac{3}{2} \Rightarrow y = \frac{45 \times 2}{3} = 30$

391. (b) Given, $x^2 + \frac{1}{x^2} = 119$

$x^2 + \frac{1}{x^2} + 2 = 119 + 2$

$\Rightarrow \quad \left(x + \frac{1}{x}\right)^2 = 121 \Rightarrow x + \frac{1}{x} = 11$

$\therefore \quad x^3 + \frac{1}{x^3} = \left(x + \frac{1}{x}\right)\left(x^2 + \frac{1}{x^2} - 1\right)$

$= 11 \times (119 - 1) = 11 \times 118 = 1298$

392. (a) Let the number of questions correctly answered by students be x.

Total number of questions = 200

Total number of questions answered incorrectly $= (200 - x)$

According to the question,

$x \times 4 - 1(200 - x) = 500$

$\Rightarrow \quad 4x - 200 + x = 500 \Rightarrow 5x = 700$

$\therefore \quad x = \frac{700}{5} = 140$

393. (b) $\frac{2x}{x+2} + \frac{1}{2x+4} - \frac{12-x}{2x^2+4x} = a + \frac{b}{x}$

$\Rightarrow \quad \frac{4x^2 + x - 12 + x}{2x^2 + 4x} = a + \frac{b}{x}$

$\Rightarrow \quad \frac{4x^2 + 2x - 12}{2x(x+2)} = a + \frac{b}{x}$

$\Rightarrow \quad \frac{2x^2 + x - 6}{x(x+2)} = a + \frac{b}{x}$

$\Rightarrow \quad \frac{2x^2 + 4x - 3x - 6}{x(x+2)} = a + \frac{b}{x}$

$\Rightarrow \quad \frac{2x(x+2) - 3(x+2)}{x(x+2)} = a + \frac{b}{x}$

$\Rightarrow \quad \frac{(2x-3)(x+2)}{x(x+2)} = \frac{ax + b}{x}$

$\Rightarrow \quad (2x - 3) = ax + b$

Comparing on both sides, we get

$a = 2$ and $b = -3$

$\therefore$ The value of $ab = 2 \times (-3) = -6$

Speedy Method

On putting $x = 1$

$\frac{2}{3} + \frac{1}{6} - \frac{11}{6} = a + b \Rightarrow a + b = \frac{4 + 1 - 11}{6}$

$\Rightarrow \quad a + b = -1$

On putting $x = -1$

$-2 + \frac{1}{2} + \frac{13}{2} = a - b$

$\Rightarrow \quad a - b = \frac{-4 + 1 + 13}{2} \Rightarrow a - b = 5$

Now, $(a+b)^2 = (a-b)^2 + 4ab$

$\Rightarrow \quad 1 = 25 + 4ab$

$\Rightarrow \quad 4ab = -24 \Rightarrow ab = -6$

394. (a) $a + b = \sqrt{11} \Rightarrow (a+b)^2 = 11$

and $\quad a - b = \sqrt{7} \Rightarrow (a-b)^2 = 7$

We know that, $(a+b)^2 = (a-b)^2 + 4ab$

$\Rightarrow \quad 11 = 7 + 4ab \quad \Rightarrow \quad ab = 1$

Now, $a^2b^2(a^2 + b^2) = (ab)^2$

$[\because (a^2 + b^2) = (a+b)^2 - 2(ab)]$

$= 1[11 - 2 \times 1] = 9$

395. (c) $2^x = 3^y = 6^z = k$ (Let)

$\therefore \quad 2 = (k)^{\frac{1}{x}}, 3 = (k)^{\frac{1}{y}}$ and $6 = (k)^{\frac{1}{z}}$

$\Rightarrow \quad 2 \times 3 = (k)^{\frac{1}{z}} \Rightarrow (k)^{\frac{1}{x}} \times (k)^{\frac{1}{y}} = (k)^{\frac{1}{z}}$

$\Rightarrow \quad (k)^{\frac{1}{x} + \frac{1}{y}} = (k)^{\frac{1}{z}}$

Comparing on both sides;

$\frac{1}{x} + \frac{1}{y} = \frac{1}{z} \Rightarrow \frac{1}{x} + \frac{1}{y} - \frac{1}{z} = 0$

396. (d) Let the number of horses $= x$ and the number of pigeon $= y$

According to the question,

$x + y = 40$ ...(i)

and $\quad 4x + 2y = 120$ ...(ii)

On solving Eqs. (i) and (ii), we get

$x = 20, y = 20$

Hence, the number of horses = 20

20

Geometry

An introduction to geometry typically covers the fundamental concepts of lines, angles, shapes and their interrelationships.

Point A directionless figure i.e. a figure whose length, breadth and height cannot be measured is called a point.

Line A figure made up of infinite numbers of points and has only one dimension. i.e. Only length but has no width is called a line.

i.e. It is endless and thus can be extended infinitely in both directions.

Types of Lines

(i) Parallel Lines Two lines which lie in the same plane, having no common intersection point, when produced on either sides are called parallel lines.

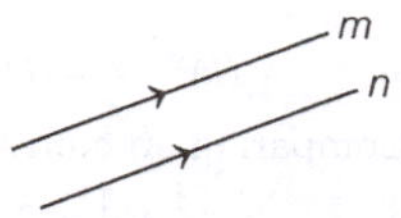

Here, m and n are parallel lines and thus denoted as $m \| n$.

(ii) Perpendicular Lines Two lines, lying in the same plane and intersect each other at right angle, are called perpendicular lines.

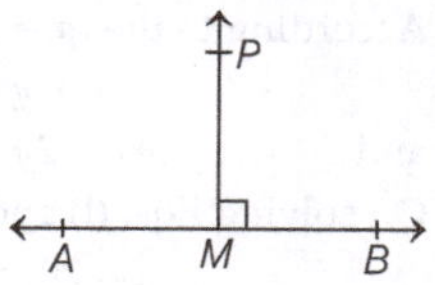

Here, $PM \perp AB$

Transversal Lines

If a straight lines intersect two or more parallel lines at different points, known as a transversal line.

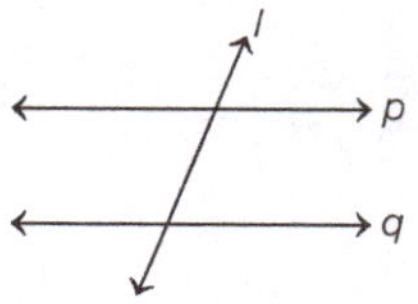

Here, 'p' and 'q' are parallel lines and 'l' is a transversal line.

Angle

An angle is formed when two rays meet at a common initial point.

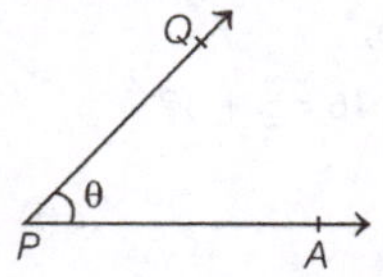

e.g. Let P be the common point, then P is said to be a vertex of the angle. In general, angles are measured in degree i.e. $\angle APQ = \theta°$

Types of Angles

(i) **Acute Angle** The angle whose value lies between 0° and 90°, is called an acute angle.

(ii) **Right Angle** The angle whose value is 90°, is called a right angle.

(iii) **Obtuse Angle** The angle whose value lies between 90° and 180°, is called an obtuse angle.

(iv) **Straight Angle** The angle whose value is 180°, is called a straight angle.

(v) **Reflex Angle** The angle whose value lies between 180° and 360°, is called reflex angle.

(vi) **Complete Angle** The angle whose value is 360°, is called a complete angle.

(vii) **Complementary Angles** If the sum of two angles is 90°, then they are called complementary angles.

(viii) **Supplementary Angles** If the sum of two angles is 180°, then they are called supplementary angles.

Linear Pair of Angles

If non-common arms of two adjacent angles form a line, then these angles are called linear pair of angles.

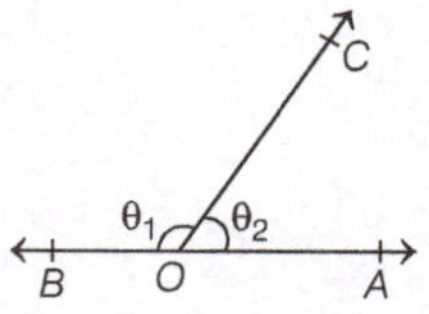

Thus, $\angle\theta_1 + \angle\theta_2 = 180°$

Angles made by a Transversal Let P and Q be parallel lines and l be the transversal which cuts these parallel lines.

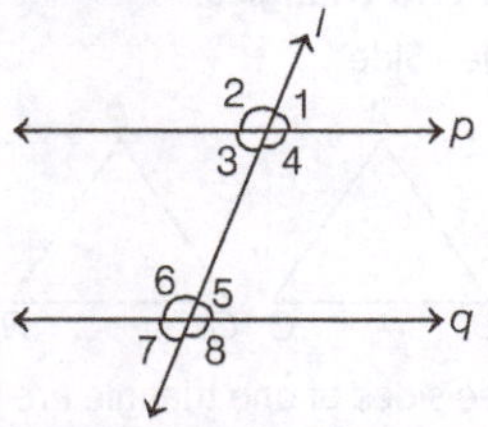

(i) **Vertically Opposite Angles** Pairs of vertically opposite angles are $\angle 1$ and $\angle 3$, $\angle 4$ and $\angle 2$, $\angle 8$ and $\angle 6$, $\angle 5$ and $\angle 7$. All pairs of vertically opposite angles are always equal.

i.e. $\angle 1 = \angle 3$, $\angle 4 = \angle 2$, $\angle 8 = \angle 6$, $\angle 5 = \angle 7$

(ii) **Corresponding Angles** Pairs of corresponding angles are $\angle 1$ and $\angle 5$, $\angle 2$ and $\angle 6$, $\angle 4$ and $\angle 8$, $\angle 3$ and $\angle 7$. All pairs of corresponding angles are always equal.

i.e. $\angle 1 = \angle 5$, $\angle 2 = \angle 6$, $\angle 4 = \angle 8$ and $\angle 3 = \angle 7$

(iii) **Alternate Interior Angles** Pairs of alternate interior angles are always equal.

Here, $\angle 3$ and $\angle 5$, $\angle 4$ and $\angle 6$ are pairs of alternate interior angles and are equal i.e. $\angle 3 = \angle 5$ and $\angle 4 = \angle 6$

(iv) **Alternate Exterior Angles** Pairs of alternate exterior angles are $\angle 2$ and $\angle 8$, $\angle 1$ and $\angle 7$.

Pairs of alternate exterior angles are equal i.e. $\angle 2 = \angle 8$ and $\angle 1 = \angle 7$

Note

(i) The sum of interior angles on the same side of transveral is equal to 180°. i.e. $\angle 3 + \angle 6 = 180°$ and $\angle 4 + \angle 5 = 180°$

(ii) The sum of exterior angles on the same side of transversal is equal to 180°. i.e. $\angle 2 + \angle 7 = 180°$ and $\angle 1 + \angle 8 = 180°$.

Types of Triangles

1. Based on Angles

(i) **Acute Angle Triangle** A triangle in which every angle is less than 90°, but greater than 0°.

(ii) **Right Angled Triangle** A triangle in which one of the angle is equal to 90°.

(iii) **Obtuse Angle Triangle** A triangle in which one of the angle is greater than 90°.

Based on Sides

(i) **Scalene Triangle** A triangle in which all the sides are of different measures.

(ii) **Isosceles Triangle** A triangle in which two sides are equal.

(iii) **Equilateral Triangle** A triangle in which all the sides are equal.

Note
- Sum of two sides of triangle is always greater than third side.
- Difference of two sides of a triangle is always less than third side.

Important Terms Related to Triangle

Altitude (Height) The perpendicular drawn from the opposite vertex of a side in triangle is called an altitude of triangle.

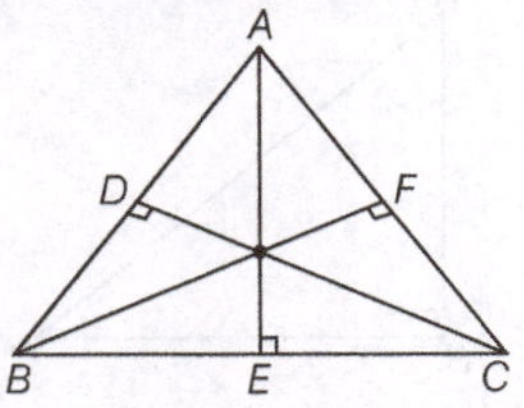

Note In any triangle, there are three altitudes.

Median A line segment joining the mid-point of a side to the opposite vertex is called median.

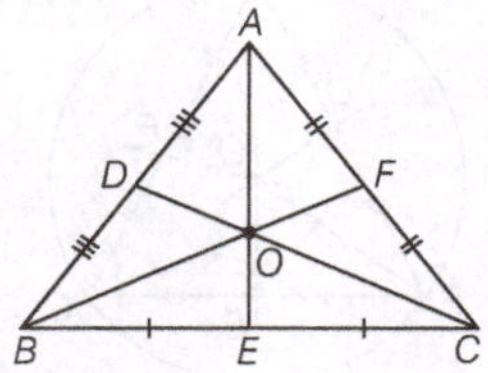

Note In ΔABC,

(i) There are three medians namely, AE, CD, BF.

(ii) The medians of a triangles are concurrent.

(iii) A median bisect the area of the triangle i.e,

$$\text{ar}\Delta ABE = \text{ar}\Delta AEC .... = \frac{1}{2}\text{ar}\Delta ABC ....$$

$$\text{ar}\Delta BOE = \text{ar}\Delta EOC .... = \frac{1}{6}\text{ar}\Delta ABC$$

Centroid The point at which all three medians intersect is called the centroid.

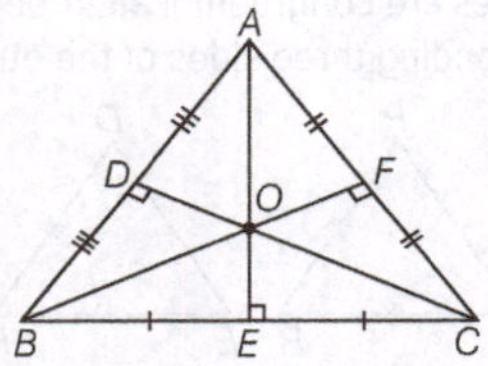

$$AO : OE = CO : OD = BO : OF = 2 : 1$$

$$AB^2 + AC^2 = 2(AE^2 + BE^2)$$

Incentre The intersection point of the angle bisectors of a triangles is called its incentre.

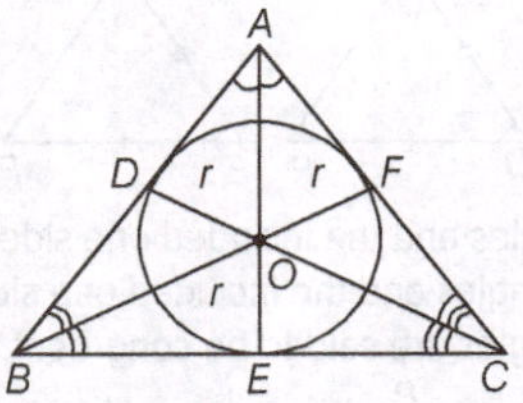

Note (i) Incentre O is always equidistant from all three sides.

(ii) Inradius of an equilateral triangle $= \frac{1}{3} \times \text{Height} = \frac{\text{Side}}{2\sqrt{3}}$

(iii) Inradius $(r) = \frac{\text{Area of triangle}}{\text{Semi - perimeter of triangle}} = \frac{\Delta}{S}$

(iv) $AO : OE = AB + AC : BC$

$BO : OF = AB + BC : AC$

$CO : OD = AC + BC : AB$

Orthocentre The intersection point of three altitudes of triangles is called the orthocentre.

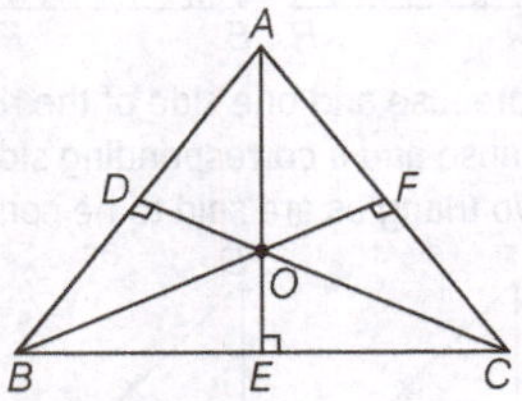

Here, point O is the orthocentre.

Note $\angle BOC = 180° - \angle A$

Circumcentre The intersection point of perpendicular bisector of sides of a triangle is called its circumcentre.

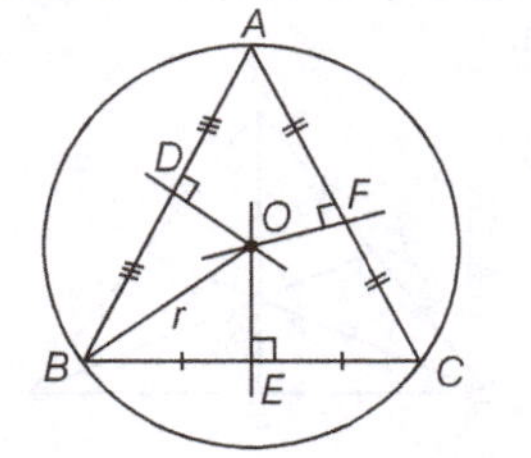

Note

(i) Circumcentre O is always equidistant from all the three vertices A, B and C.

(ii) Radius of circumcircle is called circumradius.

(iii) Circumradius of an equilateral triangle $= \frac{2}{3} \times \text{Height} = \frac{1}{\sqrt{3}} \times \text{Side}$

(iv) $\angle BOC = 2\angle A$

Congruent Triangles

Criteria for Congruence of Triangles

SSS Criteria Two triangles are congruent if all three sides of one triangle are equal to the corresponding three sides of the other triangles.

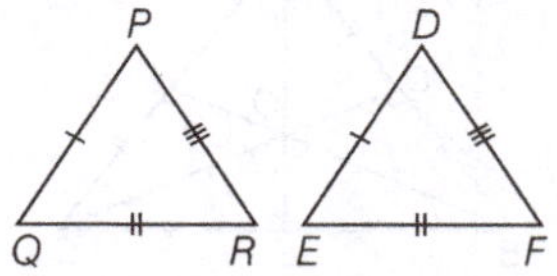

SAS Criteria If two sides and the angle included between them are equal to the corresponding sides and the angle included between them, then two triangles are said to be congruent.

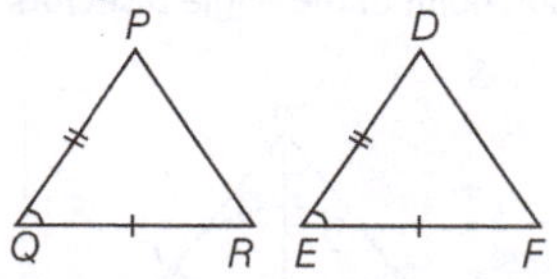

ASA Criteria If two angles and the included one side of a triangle are equal to the corresponding angles and the included one side of the other triangle, then two triangles are said to be congruent.

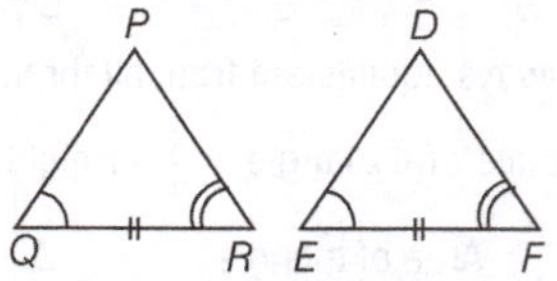

AAS Criteria If two angles and a side other than the included side of one triangle are equal to the corresponding angles and a side other than the included side of the other triangle, then two triangles are said to be congruent.

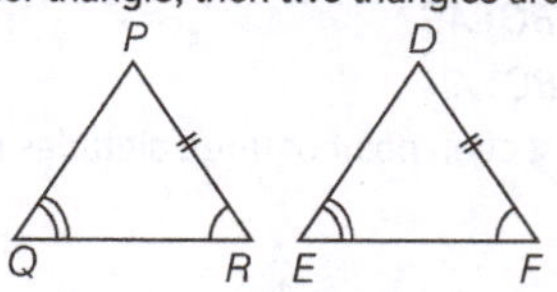

RHS Criteria If the hypotenuse and one side of the right angled triangle are equal to the hypotenuse and a corresponding side of the other right angled triangle, then two triangles are said to be congruent.

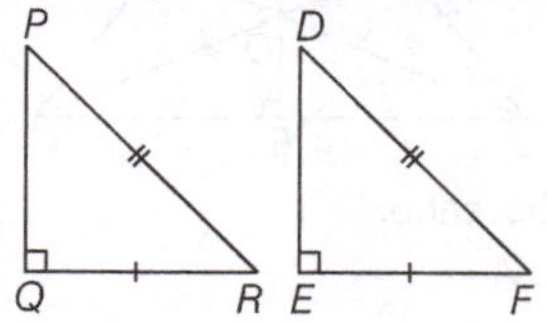

Similar Triangles

Criteria for Similarity of Two Triangles

SSS Similarity Side - Side - Side

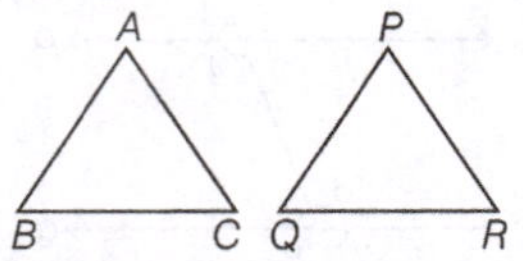

If the corresponding three sides of one triangle are proportional to the corresponding three sides of the other triangle, then the two triangles are said to be similar.

SAS Similarity Side - Angle - Side

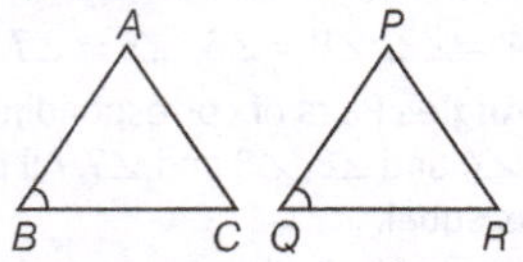

If the corresponding two sides of one triangle are proportional to the corresponding two sides of the other triangle and the included angles are equal, then two triangles are similar.

AAA Similarity Angle - Angle - Angle

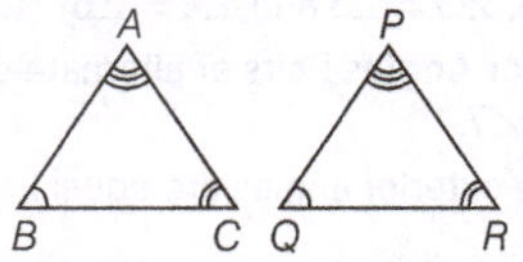

If the corresponding angles of one triangle are equal to corresponding angles of the other triangle, then triangles are said to be similar.

Corollary (AA - Similarity) If two angles of one triangle are equal to the corresponding two angles of the other triangle, then triangles are said to be similar.

Some Important Results of a Triangle

- In a triangle, sum of two sides is always greater than third side and difference of two sides is always less than third side.

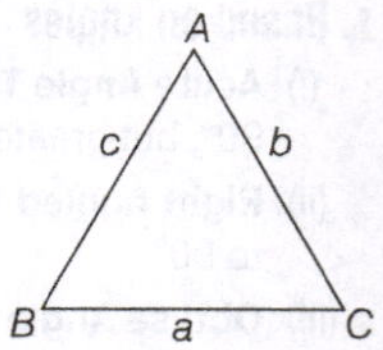

i.e. $a + b > c$

$b + c > a$

$c + a > b$

and $a - b < c$, $b - c < a$, $c - a < b$

- An exterior angle is equal to the sum of two opposite interior angles.

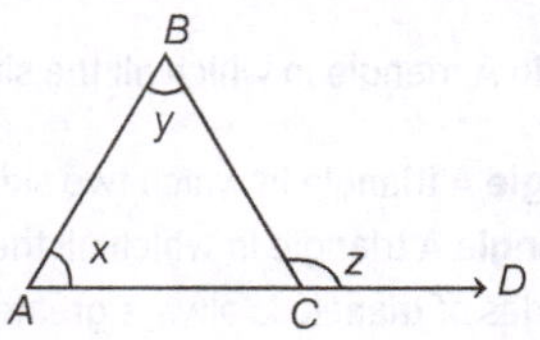

$$\angle z = \angle x + \angle y$$

- **Pythagoras Theorem** The square of the hypotenuse of a right angled triangle is equal to the sum of the squares of the other two sides i.e.,

$$(AC)^2 = (AB)^2 + (BC)^2$$

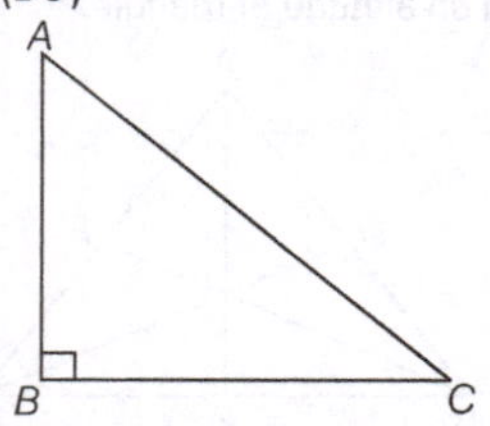

Note Converse of this theorem is also true.

- **Interior Angle Bisector Theorem** In a triangle, the angle bisector of an angle divides the opposite side to the angle in the ratio of the remaining two sides i.e., $\frac{AB}{AC} = \frac{BD}{DC}$

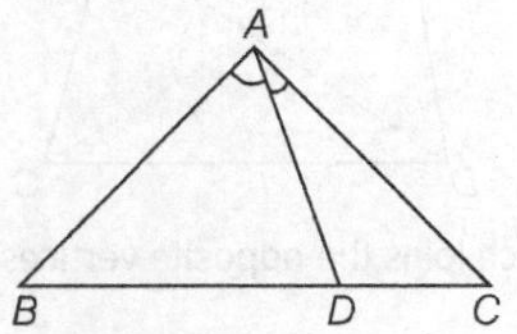

- **Exterior Angle Bisector Theorem** In a triangle, the angle bisector of any exterior angle of a triangle divides the side opposite to the external angle in the ratio of remaining two sides i.e., $\frac{BE}{AE} = \frac{BC}{AC}$

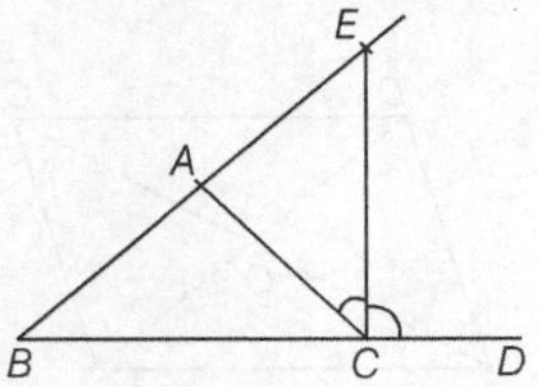

- In right triangle PQR, $\angle Q = 90°$ and PR is hypotenuse. If the perpendicular QT falls on hypotenuse PR from vertex Q, then

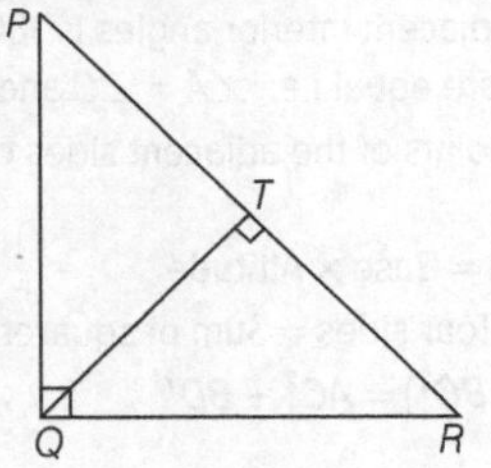

- $QT = \frac{PQ \times QR}{PR}$
- $PT = \frac{PQ^2}{PR}$
- $RT = \frac{QR^2}{PR}$
- $\frac{1}{QT^2} = \frac{1}{PQ^2} + \frac{1}{QR^2}$

- When the bisector of one internal base angle and the bisector of other external base angle meet at a point, then the angle formed is equal to half of the vertical angle. Here, $\angle BEC = \frac{1}{2}\angle BAC$.

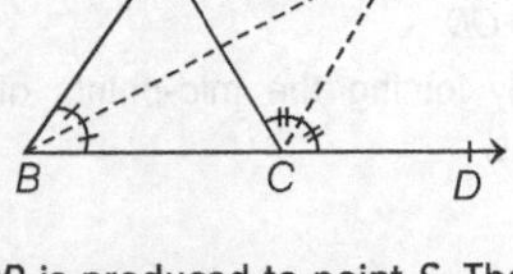

- The side QR of ΔPQR is produced to point S. The bisector of $\angle P$ meets QR at T. Then, $\angle PQR + \angle PRS = 2\angle PTR$.

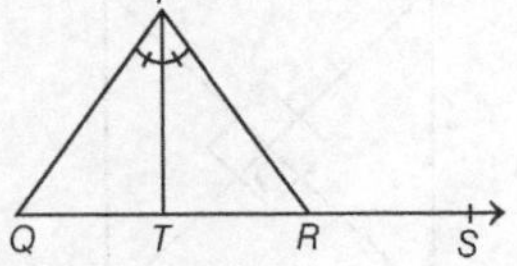

- In an equilateral ΔABC, if the side BC is trisected at D, then $9AD^2 = 7AC^2$.

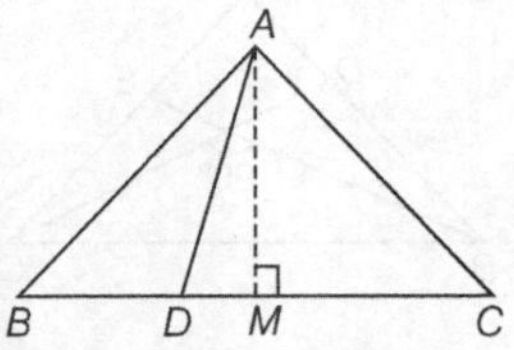

- In a ΔABC the bisector of $\angle B$ and $\angle C$ intersect each other at a point O. Then, $\angle BOC = 90° + \frac{1}{2}\angle A$

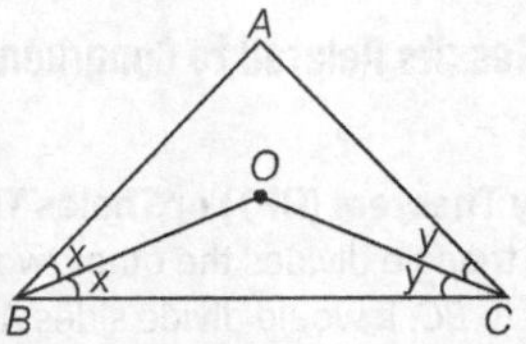

- In a ΔABC, the side AB and AC are produced to P and Q, respectively. The bisectors of $\angle PBC$ and $\angle QCB$ intersect at a point O.

Then, $\angle BOC = 90° - \frac{1}{2}\angle A$

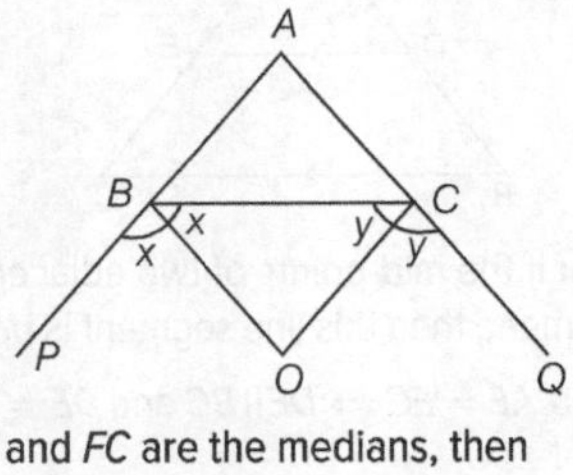

- In ΔABC, if AD, BE and FC are the medians, then

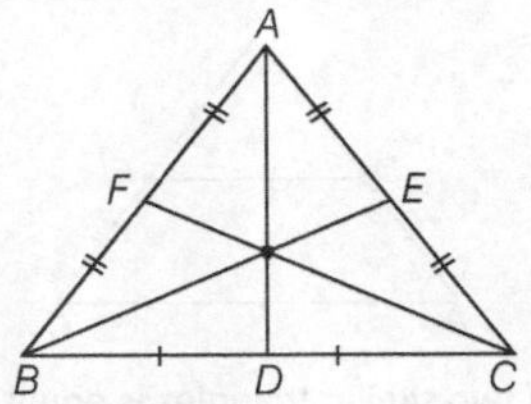

Then, $3(AB^2 + BC^2 + AC^2) = 4(AD^2 + BE^2 + CF^2)$

- In $\Delta ABC, \angle B > \angle C$, if AM is the bisector of $\angle BAC$ and $AN \perp BC$, then $\angle MAN = \frac{1}{2}(\angle B - \angle C)$

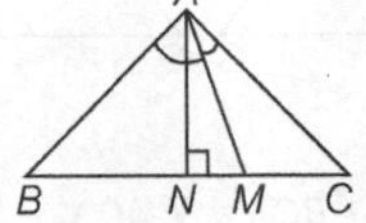

- If ΔABC is right angle triangle and AD, CE are medians, then

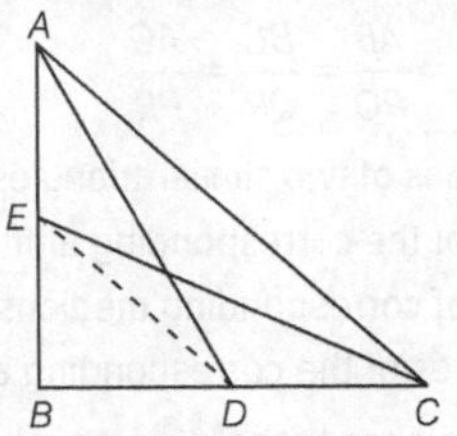

$4(AD^2 + CE^2) = 5AC^2$ and $AD^2 + CE^2 = AC^2 + DE^2$

- If two medians are perpendicular to each other, then

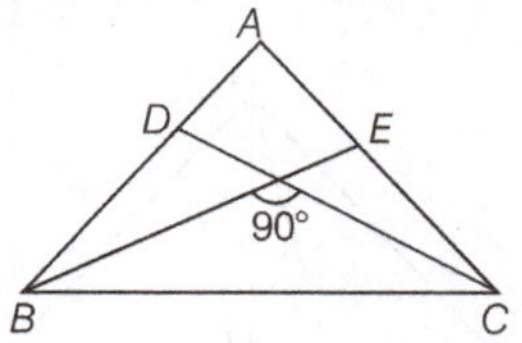

$AB^2 + AC^2 = 5BC^2$

- If all three median of triangle given, then

Area of triangle $= \frac{4}{3}$ (Area of triangle formed by medians)

Important Theorems/Results Related to Congruency and Similarity of Triangles

1. Basic Proportionality Theorem (BPT) or Thales Theorem Any line parallel to one side of a triangle divides the other two sides proportionally. So, DE is drawn parallel to BC, it would divide sides AB and AC proportionally i.e., $\frac{AD}{DB} = \frac{AE}{EC}$ or $\frac{AD}{AB} = \frac{AE}{AC}$

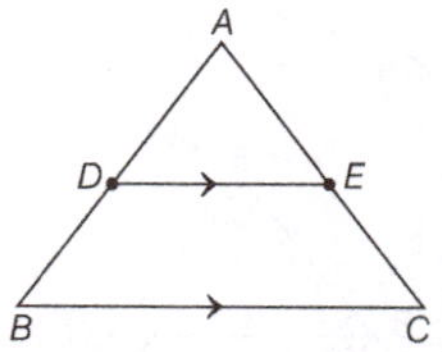

2. Mid- Point Theorem If the mid-points of two adjacent sides of triangle are joined by a line segment, then this line segment is parallel to the third side, i.e., if $AD = BD$ and $AE = EC \Rightarrow DE \parallel BC$ and $DE = \frac{1}{2}BC$

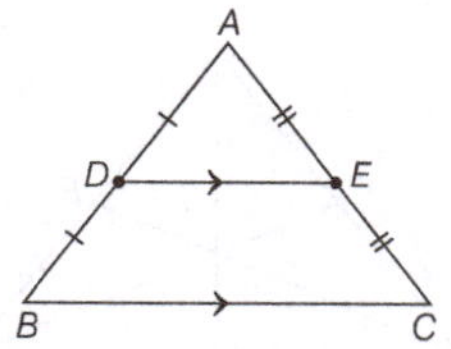

3. The ratio of areas of two similar triangles is equal to the square of the ratio of their corresponding sides.

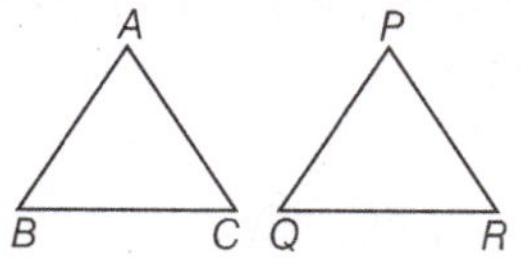

Here, $\Delta ABC \sim \Delta PQR$, then

(i) $\frac{ar(\Delta ABC)}{ar(\Delta PQR)} = \left(\frac{AB}{PQ}\right)^2 = \left(\frac{BC}{QR}\right)^2 = \left(\frac{AC}{PR}\right)^2$

(ii) $\frac{\text{Perimeter of } ABC}{\text{Perimeter of } PQR} = \frac{AB}{PQ} = \frac{BC}{QR} = \frac{AC}{PR}$

Note The ratio of the areas of two similar triangles is equal to the

(i) Ratio of squares of the corresponding altitudes.

(ii) Ratio of squares of corresponding medians.

(iii) Ratio of the squares of the corresponding angle bisector segments.

4. The area of two congruence triangle are equal.

5. Area of the triangle formed by joining the mid-points of the sides of the given triangles is $\frac{1}{4}$ of the area of the given triangle.

Quadrilaterals

A plane figure enclosed by four straight lines is called as quadrilateral.

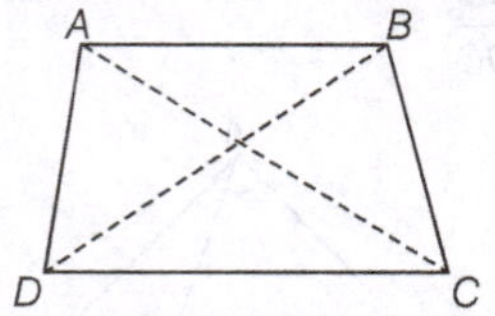

The line segments which joins the opposite vertices of quadrilateral are called diagonals.

Note Sum of all four angles of a quadrilateral is 360°.

There are following types of quadrilateral given below

Parallelogram

A quadrilateral in which the opposite sides are equal and parallel, is called a parallelogram.

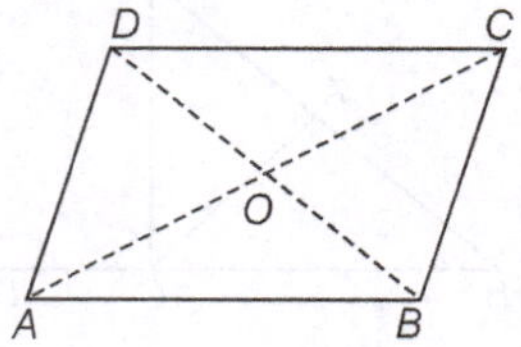

Properties

- The diagonals bisect each other.
- The sum of any two adjacent interior angles is 180°.
- The opposite angles are equal i.e., $\angle A = \angle C$ and $\angle B = \angle D$.
- Line joining the mid-points of the adjacent sides of a quadrilateral form of a parallelogram.
- Area of parallelogram = Base × Altitude
- Sum of squares of all four sides = Sum of squares of diagonals. i.e.

$$2(AB^2 + BC^2) = AC^2 + BD^2$$

Rectangle

A parallelogram whose opposite sides are equal and each interior angle is 90°, then it is called a rectangle.

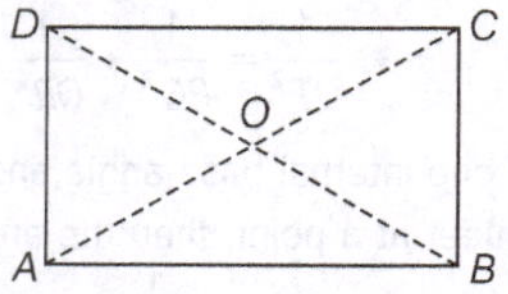

Properties

- The diagonals of rectangle are equal i.e., $AC = BD$.
- The diagonals of rectangle bisect each other.
  i.e, $OA = OC$ and $OB = OD$
- The figure formed by joining the mid-points of adjacent sides of a rectangle is a rhombus.

Square

A parallelogram in which all the sides are equal and each interior angle is 90°, is called a square.

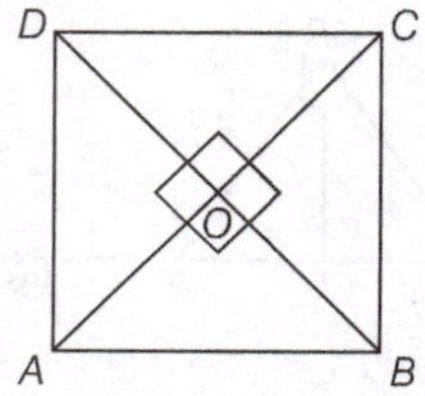

Properties

- The diagonals of square are equal i.e., $AC = BD$
- The diagonals bisect each other at 90° i.e., $OA = OC$ and $OB = OD$
  Also, $\angle AOB = \angle BOC = \angle COD = \angle AOD = 90°$
- The figure formed by joining the mid-points of adjacent sides of square is a square.

Rhombus

A parallelogram in which all the sides are equal, is called a rhombus,

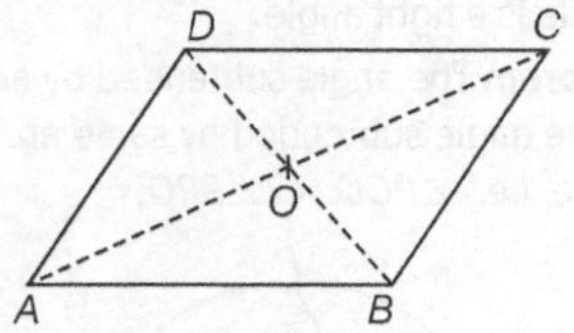

Properties

- The opposite sides are equal and parallel.
- The sum of any two adjacent interior angles is 180°.
- The diagonals bisect each other at 90°.
- The opposite angles are equal.
- Figure formed by joining the mid-points of the adjacent sides of rhombus is a rectangle.

Trapezium

A quadrilateral in which one pair of sides are parallel and the other pair of sides are non-parallel, is called a trapezium.

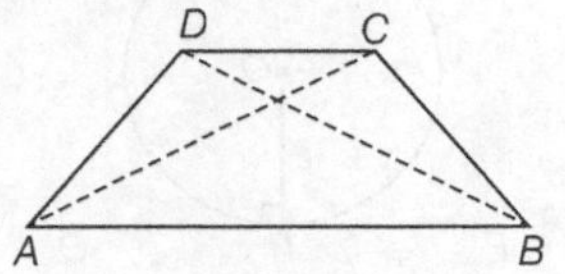

Properties

- If the non-parallel sides are equal, then diagonals will also be equal to each other.
- Area of trapezium, $ABCD = \frac{1}{2} \times$ (Sum of parallel side) $\times$ Height

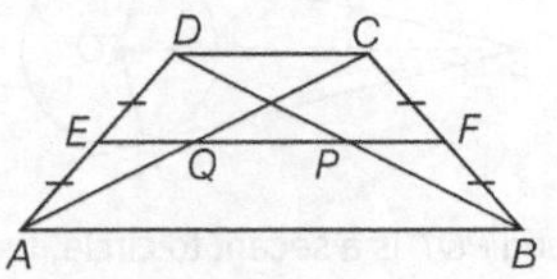

- If E is the mid-point of AD and F is the mid-point of BC, then, $EF = \frac{AB + CD}{2}$
- If P is the mid-point of diagonal BD and Q is the mid-point of diagonal AC, then $PQ = \frac{AB - CD}{2}$

Polygons

Polygons are closed plane figures formed by line segments. For examples triangle, rectangle, square, etc. The different types of polygon are

(i) **Regular Polygon** A polygon in which all the sides and angles are equal.

(ii) **Irregular Polygon** A polygon in which all the sides and angles are of different measure, is called an irregular polygon.

Important Formulae

Let n be the number of sides of a regular polygon, then

- Sum of all interior angles $= (n - 2) \times 180°$
- Each interior angle of regular polygon $= \frac{(n-2) \times 180}{n}$
- Sum of all exterior angles $= 360°$
- Each exterior angle of regular polygon $= \frac{360°}{n}$
- Sum of each interior and exterior angle $= 180°$
- Number of diagonals of polygon of n sides $= \frac{n(n-3)}{2}$

Circles

A set of all points in a plane which are at a fixed distance from a fixed point is called a circle. This fixed point is called centre of circle.

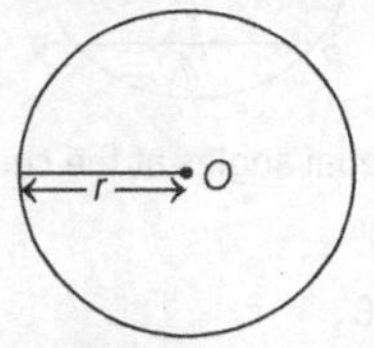

In this figure, O is the centre of circle and r is the radius of circle.
Diameter $= 2 \times$ radius, Area $= \pi r^2$, Circumference $= 2\pi r$

Semi-circle

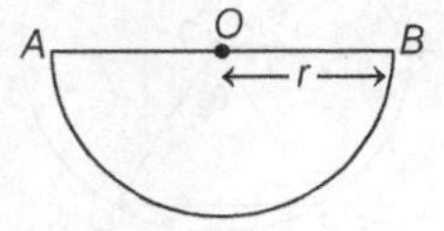

Perimeter $= \pi r + 2r$ or $\frac{36}{7} r$, Area $= \frac{\pi r^2}{2}$

Some Important Terms of Circles

Chord A line segment whose end points lie on the circle.

Sector The region bounded by an arc and two radii is called a sector of the circle. In figure, $OPQO$ is the sector of circle.

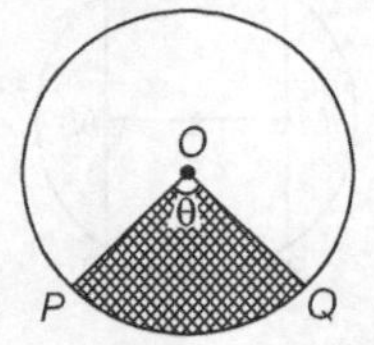

Segment A chord of a circle divides it into two regions. These regions are called the segments of a circle. In the figure, $ABCA$ is the major segment and $ABDA$ is the minor segment.

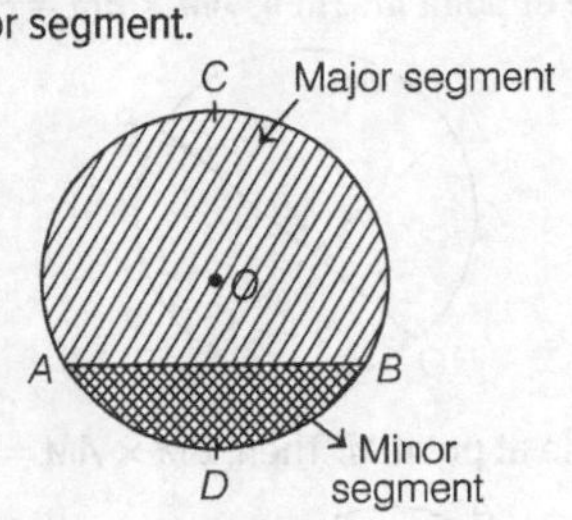

Secant A secant is a line which intersects the circle in two distinct points. In the figure, PQ is a secant which intersect the circle at two distinct points A and B.

Tangent A tangent is defined as a straight line that touches a curve at exactly one point. Here, RS is a tangent.

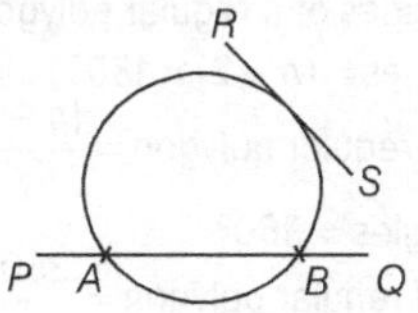

Some Important Theorems of Circles

1. The perpendicular from the centre of circle to a chord bisects the chord.

$\because$ $OM \perp PQ$ $\therefore$ $PM = QM$

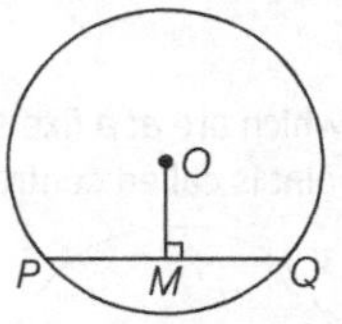

2. Equal chords subtends equal angles at the centre.

$\because$ $AB = PQ$

$\therefore$ $\angle\theta_1 = \angle\theta_2$

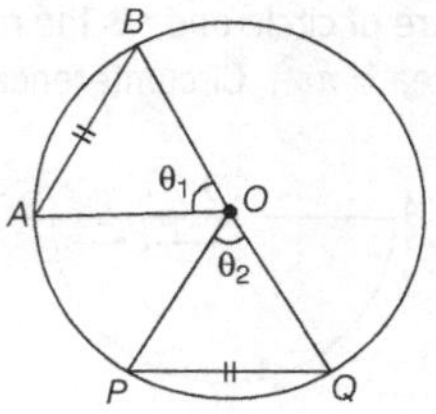

Note Converse of the above theorem is also true.

3. Equal chords are equidistant from the centre.

$\because$ $AB = PQ$

$\therefore$ $OM = ON$

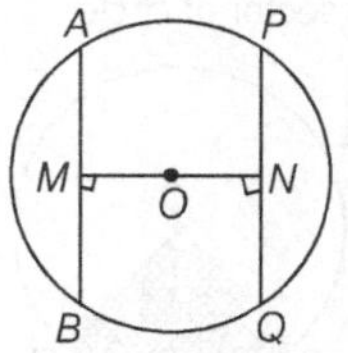

Note Converse of the above theorem is also true.

4. Intersecting Chord Theorem When two chords of a circle intersect.

(i) Within the circle at point M. Then, $AM \times BM = PM \times QM$

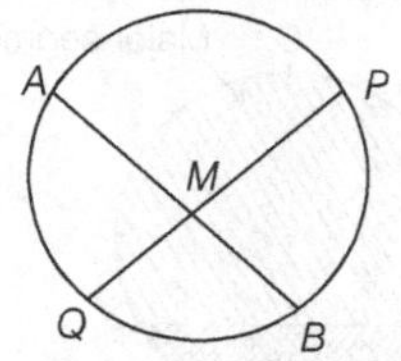

(ii) Outside the circle at point M. Then, $BM \times AM = QM \times PM$

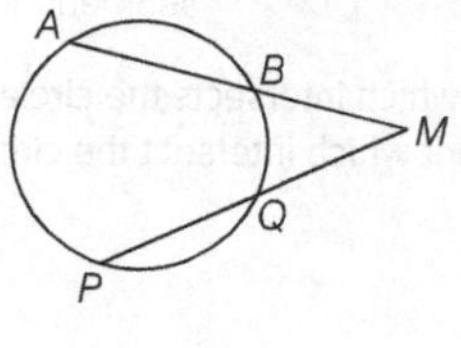

5. Same Segment Theorem Angles in the same segment of a circle are equal. i.e., $\angle PSQ = \angle PRQ$

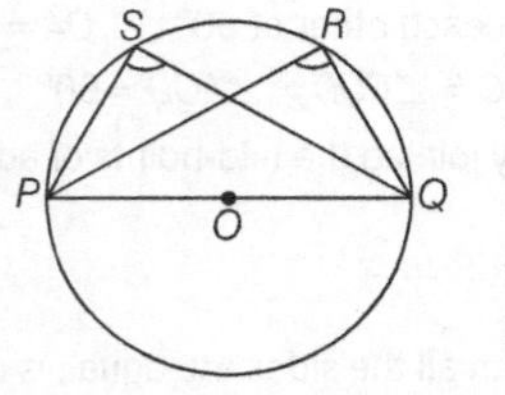

6. Angle in a semi-circle is a right angle.

7. Central Angle Theorem The angle subtended by and arc at the centre of the circle is twice the angle subtended by same arc at any point on the remaining part of circle. i.e., $\angle POQ = 2\angle PRQ$.

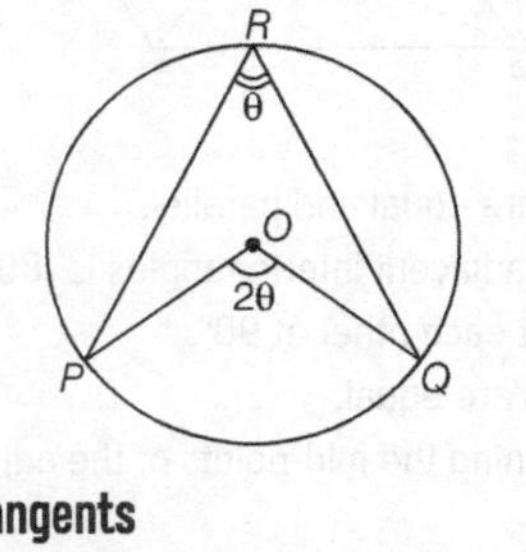

Theorems Based on Tangents

8. A tangent at any point of a circle is perpendicular to the radius through the point of contact.

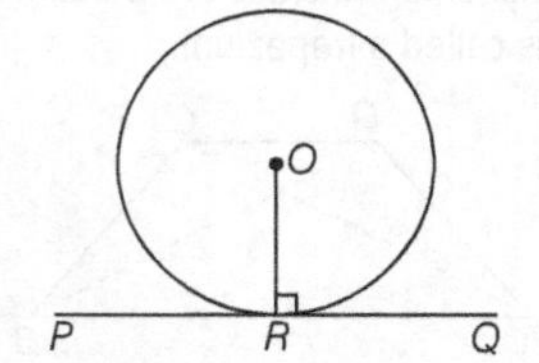

Note Converse of this theorem is also true.

9. The length of two tangents drawn from an external point to a circle are equal. i.e., $PQ = PR$

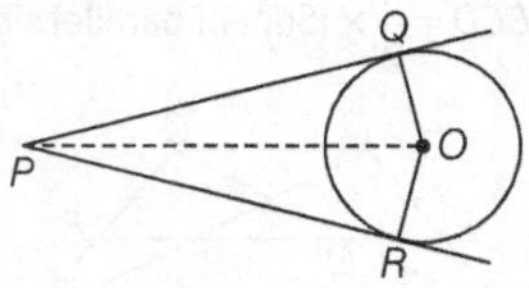

10. If RT is a tangent and PQT is a secant to circle, then $(RT)^2 = TQ \times TP$

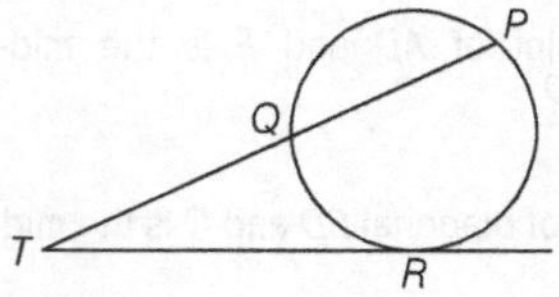

11. Alternate Segment Theorem The angle which is formed by a chord and a tangent at its point of contact is equal to the angle made by the chord in the alternate segment.

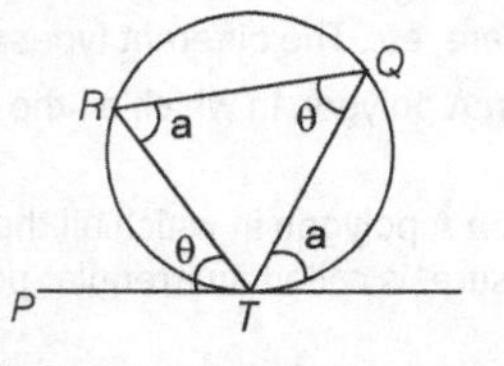

$\angle PTR = \angle RQT$, where RT is a chord and PT is a tangent to the circle.

12. In a given pair of circles, there are two types of tangents. The direct tangents and the transverse (or cross) tangents. In figure below, AB and CD are the direct tangents. EH and GF are two cross (or transverse) tangents.

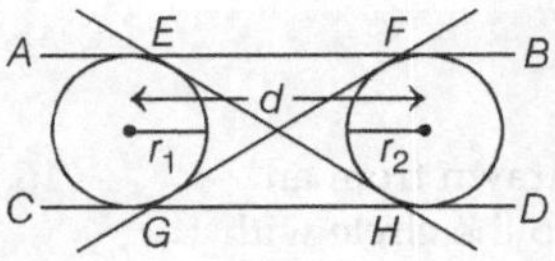

Length of the direct common tangent $= \sqrt{d^2 - (r_1 - r_2)^2}$

Length of transverse common tangent $= \sqrt{d^2 - (r_1 + r_2)^2}$

13. If a circle touches all four sides of a quadrilateral internally, then

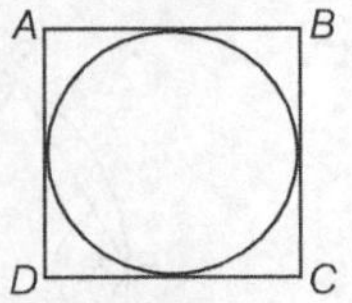

$AB + DC = BC + AD$

Cyclic Quadrilateral

A quadrilateral whose all vertices lie on a circle is called cyclic quadrilateral.

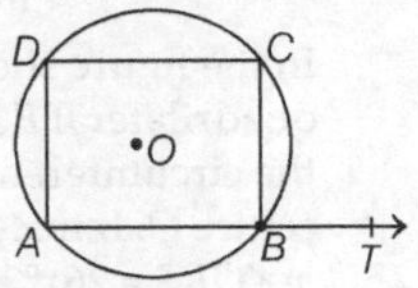

Properties of Cyclic Quadrilateral

- The sum of pair of opposite angles of a cyclic quadrilateral is 180°.
- The exterior angle, formed by producing a side of a cyclic quadrilateral is equal to the interior opposite angle.

i.e., $\angle CBT = \angle ADC$

Ex. 1 In the given figure, lines AB and CD are parallel to line FG. E is a point on the line FG. It is given that $\angle ABE = 110°$, $\angle ECD = 95°$ and $\angle BEC = x°$. Then value of x is

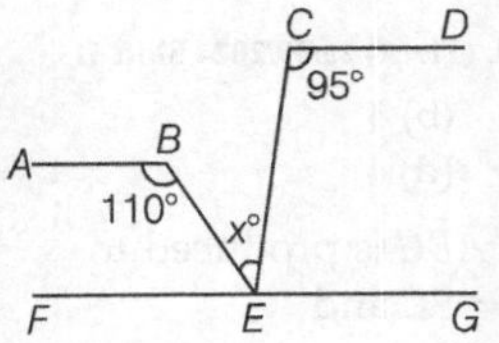

Sol. Given, $AB \| FG$ and $CD \| FG$.

Also, $\angle ABE = 110°$ and $\angle DCE = 95°$

As, $AB \| FG \quad \therefore \angle ABE + \angle BEF = 180°$

[∵ Angles on the same side of transversal are supplementary]

$\Rightarrow \quad \angle BEF = 180° - 110° = 70°$

Similarly, $\angle CEG = 85°$

Now, $\angle BEF + \angle BEC + \angle CEG = 180°$ [∵ Linear pair]

$\Rightarrow \quad x = 180° - 70° - 85° = 25°$

Ex. 2 If $\dfrac{AB}{AC} = \dfrac{BD}{DC}$, then $\angle ABC$ is

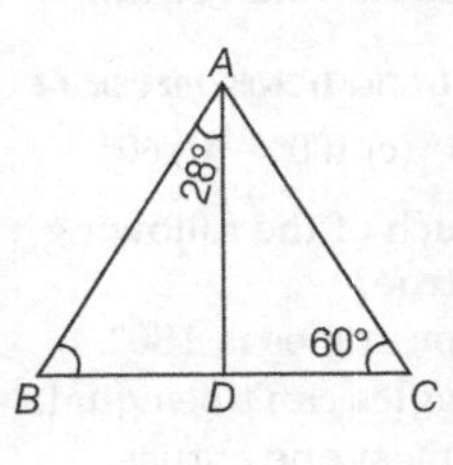

Sol. Since, $\dfrac{AB}{AC} = \dfrac{BD}{DC}$

Then, AD is the angle bisector of $\angle BAC$.

$\therefore \quad \angle BAC = 2\angle BAD$

$= 2 \times 28° = 56°$

In ΔABC, $\angle ABC + \angle BAC + \angle ACB = 180°$ [∵ Sum of interior angles is 180°]

$\Rightarrow \angle ABC = 180° - 56° - 60° = 64°$

Ex. 3 In a ΔABC, D and E are two points on sides AB and AC such that DE is parallel to BC and $AD : DB = 2 : 1$. If area of $\Delta ADE = 34 \text{ cm}^2$, then find the area of $\square DECB$.

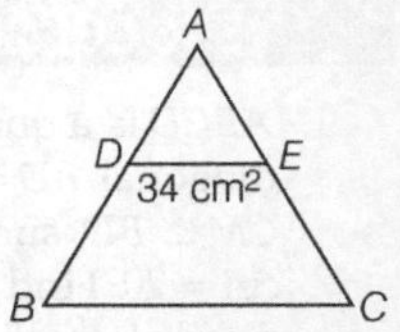

Sol. $\Delta ADE \sim \Delta ABC$

$\therefore \quad \dfrac{AD}{AB} = \dfrac{\text{Area of } \Delta ADE}{\text{Area of } \Delta ABC}$

$\dfrac{2}{2+1} = \dfrac{34}{\text{Area of } \Delta ABC}$

Area of $\Delta ABC = 51 \text{ cm}^2$

Area of $\square DECB$ = Area of ΔABC − Area of $\Delta ADE = 51 - 34 = 17 \text{ cm}^2$

Ex. 4 Find x, if $ABCD$ a parallelogram as given in figure below, with two diagonals AC and BD intersecting at O and $OA = x + 3$, $OB = y + 2$, $OC = 2x + y$, $OD = 3y$

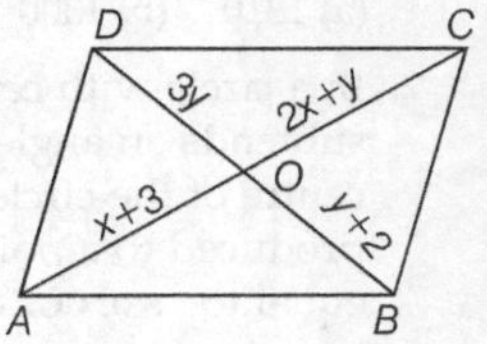

Sol. We know that, diagonals of parallelogram bisect each other

$\therefore \quad OA = OC$ and $OB = OD$

$\Rightarrow \quad x + 3 = 2x + y$ ...(i)

and $\quad 3y = y + 2 \Rightarrow 2y = 2 \Rightarrow y = 1$

From Eq. (i) $\quad x + 3 = 2x + 1 \Rightarrow \quad x = 2$

Ex. 5 Find the number of sides of a regular polygon whose sum of all interior angles is 2700°.

Sol. Let the number of sides be n.

$\because \quad$ Sum of interior angles $= (n - 2) \times 180°$

$\Rightarrow (n-2) \times 180° = 2700° \Rightarrow (n-2) = \dfrac{2700°}{180°}$

$\Rightarrow \quad n - 2 = 15 \Rightarrow n = 17$

Ex. 6 In the following figure, AD is tangent of the circle and ABC is secant. If $AB = 4$ cm and $BC = 5$ cm, then the length of tangent AD is

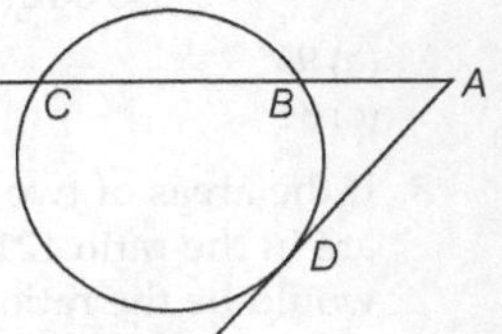

Sol. We know that,

$AD^2 = AC \times AB$

$\Rightarrow \quad AD = \sqrt{(5+4) \times 4}$

$= \sqrt{9 \times 4} = 6$ cm

Ex. 7 If $ABCD$ is a cyclic quadrilateral, find the value of x and y.

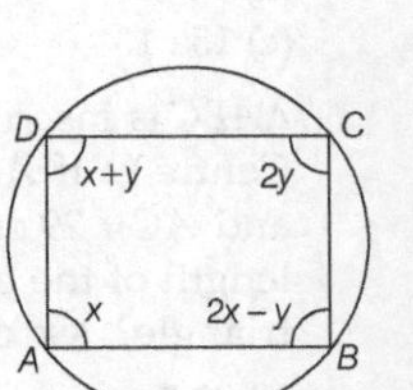

Sol. We know, sum of opposite angles of a cyclic quadrilateral is 180°.

$\therefore \quad \angle BAD + \angle BCD = 180°$

$x + 2y = 180°$ ...(i)

and similarly, $\angle ADC + \angle ABC = 180°$

$x + y + 2x - y = 180°$

$\Rightarrow \quad 3x = 180° \Rightarrow x = 60°$

Put the value of x in Eq. (i), $60° + 2y = 180°$

$\Rightarrow \quad 2y = 120°$

$\Rightarrow \quad x = y = 60°$

SSC Exam Scanner

SSC CGL 2024 (Tier I & II)

1. $ABCD$ is a quadrilateral in which diagonal $BD = 70$ cm, $AL \perp BD$ and $CM \perp BD$ such that $AL = 18$ cm and cm = 20. Find the area (in cm^2) of the quadrilateral $ABCD$.
SSC CGL (Tier II) 20/01/2025 Shift-I

(a) 1310 (b) 1300 (c) 1330 (d) 1320

2. In a circle with centre O, an arc ABC subtends an angle of 134° at the centre of the circle. The chord AB is produced to a point P. $\angle CBP$ is equal to **SSC CGL (Tier II) 20/01/2025 Shift-I**

(a) 67° (b) 113° (c) 45° (d) 89°

3. In a circle centered at O, a diameter AB is extended to a point C outside the circle. CD is a tangent at point D on the circle. If $CD = 7\sqrt{3}$ cm and $\angle DBC = 120°$, then the length of the diameter of the circle is equal to
SSC CGL (Tier II) 20/01/2025 Shift-I

(a) 16 cm (b) 14 cm (c) 18 cm (d) 20 cm

4. In a triangle HJK, $HJ = HK$. G is a point on HJ such that $HG = GK = JK$. What is the degree measure of two-third of $(\angle HGK + \angle GKJ)$?
SSC CGL (Tier II) 18/01/2025 Shift-I

(a) 96° (b) 136°
(c) 84° (d) 90°

5. If the areas of two similar triangles are in the ratio 121 : 225, what would be the ratio of the corresponding sides?
SSC CGL (Tier II) 18/01/2025 Shift-I

(a) 9 : 11 (b) 11 : 15
(c) 15 : 13 (d) 11 : 13

6. ΔABC is inscribed in a circle with Centre O. If $AB = 21$ cm, $BC = 20$ cm and $AC = 29$ cm, then what is the length of the circumradius of the triangle? **SSC CGL (Tier II) 18/01/2025 Shift-I**

(a) 32.5 cm (b) 13.5 cm
(c) 21.5 cm (d) 14.5 cm

7. In triangle XYZ, A is a point on YZ such that $XA = YA$. If $\angle XYA = 50°$ and $\angle AXZ = 19°$, what is the degree measure of Z?
SSC CGL (Tier I) 26/09/2024 Shift-III

(a) 61° (b) 53°
(c) 49° (d) 41°

8. In a triangle PQR, $\angle P + \angle Q = 84°$. Find the value of $\angle R$.
SSC CGL (Tier I) 26/09/2024 Shift-III

(a) 74° (b) 96°
(c) 60° (d) 102°

9. A secant PAB is drawn from an external point P to the circle with the center at O, intersecting it at A and B. If $OP = 17$ cm, $PA = 12$ cm and $PB = 22.5$ cm, then the radius of the circle is
SSC CGL (Tier I) 26/09/2024 Shift-III

(a) $\sqrt{23}$ cm (b) $\sqrt{21}$ cm
(c) $\sqrt{17}$ cm (d) $\sqrt{19}$ cm

10. If the altitude from two vertices of a triangle to the opposite sides are equal, then the triangle will be
SSC CGL (Tier I) 26/09/2024 Shift-III

(a) isosceles triangle
(b) equilateral triangle
(c) scalene triangle
(d) obtuse angle triangle

11. In a circle with center O, an arc ABC subtends an angle of 138° at the centre of the circle. The chord AB is produced to a point P. Then, the measure of $\angle CBP$ is
SSC CGL (Tier I) 26/09/2024 Shift-II

(a) 108° (b) 42°
(c) 111° (d) 69°

12. In ΔABC, $DE \parallel BC$ and $5AE = 3EC$. If $AB = 6.4$ units, then the value of DB (in units) is
SSC CGL (Tier I) 26/09/2024 Shift-II

(a) 2.4 (b) 5
(c) 3.2 (d) 4

13. The side BC of ΔABC is produced to a point D. If $AC = BC$ and $\angle BAC = 70°$, then find the value of $2.5\angle ACD - 1.5\angle ABC$.
SSC CGL (Tier I) 26/09/2024 Shift-II

(a) 245° (b) 235°
(c) 225° (d) 230°

14. If the angles of a triangle are in the ratio 7 : 8 : 3, then the value of the largest angle is:
SSC CGL (Tier I) 26/09/2024 Shift-I

(a) 120° (b) 80° (c) 100° (d) 60°

15. For triangles, which of the following statement(s) are true?
A. Sum of interior angles is 180°.
B. All interior angles can't be equal.
C. Can have at most one obtuse angle.
D. Sum of two sides may or may not be equal to the third side.
SSC CGL (Tier I) 26/09/2024 Shift-I

(a) (A) and (B)
(b) (B), (C) and (D)
(c) (A), (B) and (D)
(d) (A) and (C)

16. ΔABC is a right-angled with $\angle ABC = 90°$. If $m(\overline{AB}) = 28$ cm and $m(\overline{BC}) = 96$ cm, find the area (in cm^2) of the circumcircle of ΔABC. (Use $\pi = 3.14$).
SSC CGL (Tier I) 26/09/2024 Shift-I

(a) 7850 (b) 8164
(c) 7693 (d) 7536

17.

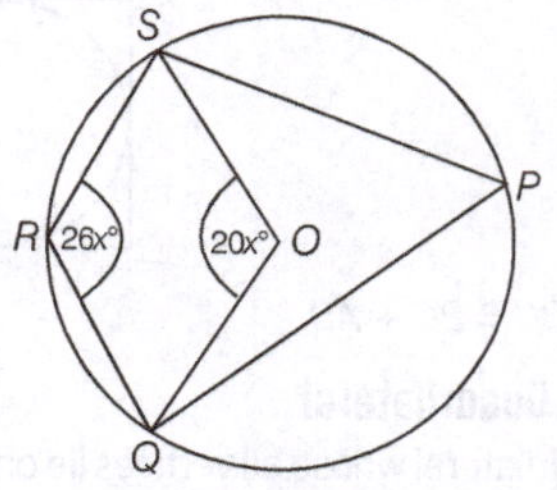

(Not to Scale)

In the figure shown above, quadrilateral $PQRS$ has its vertices on the circumference of the circle with centre O. If $m\angle QOS = 20x°$ and $m\angle QRS = 26x°$, then what is the value of 'x'? **SSC CGL (Tier I) 25/09/2024 Shift-III**

(a) 6 (b) 5 (c) 4 (d) 3

18. From a point T, a tangent TP at point P, is drawn to a circle with centre O. A secant TQR (point Q is near to point T) is drawn from the point T. ΔPQR is inscribed into the circle by joining the points P, Q and R. Draw lines OQ and OR. If $\angle PTQ$ is 27° and $\angle TPQ = 55°$, what is the degree measure of $\angle ROQ$?
SSC CGL (Tier I) 25/09/2024 Shift-III

(a) 86 (b) 82
(c) 98 (d) 94

19. In ΔPQR, S and T are the midpoints of the sides PQ and PR, respectively. The length of the side QR is 12 cm. If ST is parallel to QR, then find the length (in cm) of ST.
SSC CGL (Tier I) 25/09/2024 Shift-III

(a) 4 (b) 10 (c) 6 (d) 8

20. The two circles intersect at two points P and Q. PR and PS are diameters of the two circles. What is $\angle PQR$? **SSC CGL (Tier I) 25/09/2024 Shift-II**

(a) 90° (b) 0° (c) 45° (d) 60°

21. In a quadrilateral $ABCD$, $AB = BC$, $AD = DC$. $\angle ABD = 68°$, $\angle ADB = (2y - 7)°$, $\angle BDC = 33°$, $\angle DBC = (3x + 2)°$. Then the value of $2x + 3y$ is
SSC CGL (Tier I) 25/09/2024 Shift-II

(a) 108 (b) 144
(c) 104 (d) 118

22. The side BC of ΔABC is produced to a point D. If $AC = BC$ and $\angle BAC = 70°$, then find the value of $\angle ACD - \angle ABC$.
SSC CGL (Tier I) 25/09/2024 Shift-I

(a) 70° (b) 60°
(c) 75° (d) 45°

23. If the lengths of two sides of an isosceles triangle are 6 cm and 12 cm, then find the length of the third side. **SSC CGL (Tier I) 25/09/2024 Shift-I**

(a) 8 cm (b) 6 cm
(c) 12 cm (d) 14 cm

24. It is always possible to draw a circle passing through .... non-collinear points in a plane.
SSC CGL (Tier I) 25/09/2024 Shift-I

(a) 3 (b) 6
(c) 5 (d) 4

25. A line cuts two concentric circles. The length of chords formed by this line on the circles is 6 cm and 18 cm. Find the difference in the squares of the radii of two circles.
SSC CGL (Tier I) 24/09/2024 Shift-III

(a) 90 (b) 120
(c) 60 (d) 72

26. In ΔABC, $AB = 6$ cm, $BC = 9$ cm and $AC = 12$ cm. If AD is the angle bisector of $\angle BAC$, where D is a point on BC, then DC is
SSC CGL (Tier I) 24/09/2024 Shift-III

(a) 9 (b) 6
(c) 3 (d) 7

27. Let ABC be a triangle. If the mid-points of AB, BC and AC are D, E and F, respectively, then ΔDEF is not congruent to ....
SSC CGL (Tier I) 24/09/2024 Shift-III

(a) ΔBDE (b) ΔECF
(c) ΔADF (d) ΔABC

28. If two straight lines are coinciding with each other, then the number of points of intersection is/are
SSC CGL (Tier I) 24/09/2024 Shift-III

(a) infinitely many points of intersection
(b) finite number of point of intersection
(c) no points of intersection
(d) unique point of intersection

29. In ΔDEF, $DE = 12$ cm, $EF = 15$ cm and $\angle DEF = 90°$. ΔDEF is congruent to ΔXYZ. If $YZ = 15$ cm, then what is the length of XZ?
SSC CGL (Tier I) 24/09/2024 Shift-II

(a) $3\sqrt{41}$ cm
(b) $2\sqrt{41}$ cm
(c) $5\sqrt{41}$ cm
(d) $4\sqrt{41}$ cm

30. Let C be a circle with centre O and PQ be a minor arc on C. Let R and S be two points on the major arc of PQ on C. If PQ subtends an angle 80° at O, find $\angle PRQ$ and $\angle PSQ$, respectively.
SSC CGL (Tier I) 24/09/2024 Shift-II

(a) 40° and 60° (b) 50° and 80°
(c) 40° and 40° (d) 40° and 50°

31. PQ is the diameter of a circle with centre A. M is a point on the circumference of the circle. If $m\angle MAP = 110°$, then find the value of $m\angle MQA$.
SSC CGL (Tier I) 24/09/2024 Shift-I

(a) 55° (b) 35° (c) 65° (d) 70°

32. The radius of a circle is 12.5 cm and the length of one its chords is 11 cm. What is the distance of the chord from the centre?
(correct to one decimal place)
SSC CGL (Tier I) 24/09/2024 Shift-I

(a) 11.2 cm (b) 13.2 cm
(c) 10 cm (d) 12 cm

33. Triangle XYZ is an isosceles triangle with sides $XY = XZ$. If the measure of angle Y is 80°, what is the measure of angle X?
SSC CGL (Tier I) 24/09/2024 Shift-I

(a) 30° (b) 40°
(c) 20° (d) 50°

34. In ΔPQR, if $4\angle P = 5\angle Q = 20\angle R$, then the value of $\angle Q$ is
SSC CGL (Tier I) 23/09/2024 Shift-III

(a) 72° (b) 36°
(c) 90° (d) 45°

35. The length of the tangent drawn from a point 10 cm away from the centre of a circle with radius 4 cm, is
SSC CGL (Tier I) 23/09/2024 Shift-III

(a) $3\sqrt{14}$ (b) $3\sqrt{21}$
(c) $2\sqrt{21}$ (d) $2\sqrt{14}$

36. If the medians of a triangle are equal, then the triangle will be
SSC CGL (Tier I) 23/09/2024 Shift-II

(a) equilateral triangle
(b) obtuse angle triangle
(c) scalene triangle
(d) right angled triangle

37. XAB and XCD are two secants to a circle. If $XA = 18$ cm, $AB = 22$ cm and $XC = 24$ cm, then find the value of XD (in cm).
SSC CGL (Tier I) 23/09/2024 Shift-II

(a) 28 (b) 21
(c) 30 (d) 34

38. AB is the chord of the circle with centre O. A line segment DOC originating from a point D on the circumference of the circle in major segment meets AB produced at C such that $BC = OD$. If angle $BCO = 30°$, then angle AOD is
SSC CGL (Tier I) 23/09/2024 Shift-II

(a) 30° (b) 90°
(c) 60° (d) 80°

39. A triangle ABC is made on a circle, where AB is diameter of the circle. If BC is equal to the radius of the circle and $\angle ABC = x\,\angle BAC$, then x is :
SSC CGL (Tier I) 23/09/2024 Shift-I

(a) 2.5 (b) 2
(c) 1 (d) 1.5

40. For two circles of radius 7 units and $\frac{7}{2}$ units, whose centres are 15 units apart, what is the length of the direct common tangent in units? (Correct to 3 decimal places)
SSC CGL (Tier I) 23/09/2024 Shift-I

(a) 14.586 (b) 18.654
(c) 15.486 (d) 16.584

41. From a point A, a tangent line is drawn to the circle of radius 7 unit. From the same point, a secant is drawn to the circle which cuts the circle at B and C and the point B is near A than C. What is the length of BC in units if the length of the tangent to the circle from point A is 21 unit and the length of AB is 14 unit? **SSC CGL (Tier I) 19/09/2024 Shift-III**

(a) 18.5 (b) 16.5
(c) 15.5 (d) 17.5

42. In a kite $ABCD$, longer diagonal BD is drawn. If $\angle ABD = 54°$ and $\angle ADB = 50°$, then what is the measure (in degrees) of the $\angle DCB$?
SSC CGL (Tier I) 19/09/2024 Shift-III

(a) 108° (b) 76°
(c) 100° (d) 54°

43. A quadrilateral $PQRS$ is inscribed in a circle of centre O, such that PQ is a diameter and $\angle PSR = 120°$. Find the value of $\angle QPR$.
SSC CGL (Tier I) 19/09/2024 Shift-II

(a) 30° (b) 60°
(c) 40° (d) 50°

44. PQ and RS are common tangents to two circles intersecting at A and B. A and B, when produced on both the sides, meet the tangents PQ and RS at X and Y, respectively. If $AB = 3$ cm and $XY = 5$ cm, then PQ is .... **SSC CGL (Tier I) 19/09/2024 Shift-II**

(a) 5 cm (b) 3 cm
(c) 6 cm (d) 4 cm

45. P, Q and R are the three angles of a triangle. If $P - Q = 20°$ and $Q - R = 26°$, then $\angle P$ is equal to **SSC CGL (Tier I) 19/09/2024 Shift-I**

(a) 52° (b) 46°
(c) 92° (d) 82°

46. R is a point outside a circle and is 18 cm away from its centre. A secant drawn from the point R intersects the circle at points A and B in such a way that $RA = 7$ cm and $AB = 5$ cm. The radius of the circle (in cm) is **SSC CGL (Tier I) 19/09/2024 Shift-I**

(a) $4\sqrt{15}$ (b) $5\sqrt{15}$
(c) $7\sqrt{15}$ (d) $3\sqrt{15}$

47. $WXYZ$ is a quadrilateral in which XQ and ZP are perpendicular to WY such that $XQ = ZP$. Diagonals ZX and WY intersect each other at point O. If $OX = 12$ cm, then find the value of ZX (in cm). **SSC CGL (Tier I) 19/09/2024 Shift-I**

(a) 12 (b) 24
(c) 36 (d) 18

48. If we extend a chord infinitely on both sides, then the chord becomes a ……… . **SSC CGL (Tier I) 18/09/2024 Shift-III**

(a) diameter (b) tangent
(c) secant (d) normal

49. The side MN of a parallelogram $MNOP$ is produced to Q such that $MN = NQ$. PQ intersects ON at R. The point R divides ON in the ratio **SSC CGL (Tier I) 18/09/2024 Shift-III**

(a) 3 : 1 (b) 2 : 1
(c) 1 : 2 (d) 1 : 1

50. Two equal circles pass through each other's centre. If the radius of each of the circle is 13 cm, then what is the length of the common chord? **SSC CGL (Tier I) 18/09/2024 Shift-III**

(a) $13\sqrt{6}$ cm (b) $7\sqrt{3}$ cm
(c) $13\sqrt{2}$ cm (d) $13\sqrt{3}$ cm

51. If arcs PAQ and RBS of a circle are congruent, then find the ratio of PQ and RS. **SSC CGL (Tier I) 18/09/2024 Shift-II**

(a) 2 : 3 (b) 1 : 3
(c) 1 : 1 (d) 1 : 2

52. On a circle of radius 7 units, PQ and QR are chords of length 7 units each. What is the length of the chord PR in units? **SSC CGL (Tier I) 18/09/2024 Shift-I**

(a) $\frac{28}{\sqrt{3}}$ (b) $\frac{7}{\sqrt{3}}$ (c) $\frac{14}{\sqrt{3}}$ (d) $\frac{21}{\sqrt{3}}$

53. If ΔABC and ΔQPR are congruent triangles such that $AB = 7$ cm, $AC = 8$ cm, $\angle B = 65°$ and $\angle C = 75°$, then which of the following is true? **SSC CGL (Tier I) 18/09/2024 Shift-I**

(a) $\angle R = 75°$ and $PQ = 8$ cm
(b) $PQ = 7$ cm and $\angle R = 75°$
(c) $\angle Q = 40°$ and $RQ = 7$ cm
(d) $AC = PR$ and $\angle P = 65°$

54. In a circle with centre O, AOC is the diameter. B is a point on the circumference of the circle such that arc AB is $\frac{1}{5}$ of the arc BC. What is the degree measure of $\angle BOC$? **SSC CGL (Tier I) 18/09/2024 Shift-I**

(a) 120° (b) 150°
(c) 80° (d) 30°

55. If a triangle has a perimeter of 52 units, then all its sides have length ________ units. **SSC CGL (Tier I) 17/09/2024 Shift-III**

(a) < 26 (b) < 20
(c) < 24 (d) < 18

56. In triangle ABC, D is the mid-point of BC. If DL perpendicular to AB and DM perpendicular to AC such that $DL = DM$, then the triangle will be **SSC CGL (Tier I) 17/09/2024 Shift-III**

(a) isosceles triangle
(b) right angled triangle
(c) obtuse angle triangle
(d) equilateral triangle

57. In a triangle, the lengths of sides are 6 units, 12 units and x units. How many possible integer values are there for x? **SSC CGL (Tier I) 17/09/2024 Shift-III**

(a) 9 (b) 12
(c) 11 (d) 10

58. In a rhombus $PQRS$, O is any interior point such that $OP = OR$. What is the degree measure of $\angle SOQ$? **SSC CGL (Tier I) 17/09/2024 Shift-II**

(a) 120° (b) 180°
(c) 240° (d) 200°

59. AB and CD are two parallel chords drawn in a circle with centre O. The distance between the two chords is 21 cm. If the lengths of AB and CD are 24 cm and 18 cm, respectively, then the radius of the circle is equal to: **SSC CGL (Tier I) 17/09/2024 Shift-II**

(a) 15 cm (b) 20 cm
(c) 18 cm (d) 24 cm

60. M and N are, respectively, the centres of two circles of radii 12 cm and 8 cm. QR is the common tangent to the circles. If $MN = 16$ cm, then what will be the length of QR? **SSC CGL (Tier I) 17/09/2024 Shift-II**

(a) $5\sqrt{17}$ cm
(b) $4\sqrt{15}$ cm
(c) $3\sqrt{19}$ cm
(d) $6\sqrt{8}$ cm

61. AP and AQ are two tangents drawn to a circle with center O from an external point A. If $\angle PAQ = 40°$, then $\angle POQ$ is **SSC CGL (Tier I) 17/09/2024 Shift-I**

(a) 120° (b) 130°
(c) 150° (d) 140°

62. The perimeters of two similar triangles ΔRST and ΔABC are 26 cm and 39 cm, respectively. If $AB = 24$ cm, then RS is ……… . **SSC CGL (Tier I) 13/09/2024 Shift-III**

(a) 16 cm (b) 36 cm
(c) 18 cm (d) 24 cm

63. The angle turned by minutes hand in 25 min in a clock is **SSC CGL (Tier I) 13/09/2024 Shift-III**

(a) π (b) $\frac{\pi}{2}$
(c) $\frac{5\pi}{3}$ (d) $\frac{5\pi}{6}$

64. Two circles, centred at P and Q intersect at two points C and D. AB is tangent to the two circles at A and B. If $\angle ADB = 68°$, then $\angle ACB =$ ……… . **SSC CGL (Tier I) 13/09/2024 Shift-III**

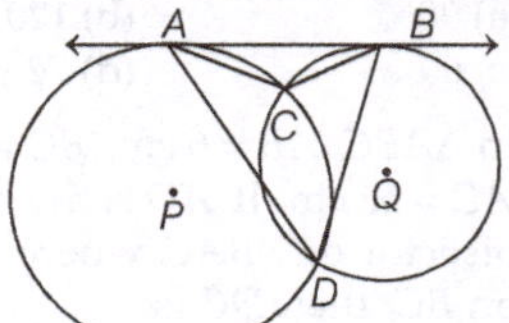

(a) 132° (b) 112°
(c) 124° (d) 102°

65. ABC is an equilateral triangle. P, Q and R are the mid-points of sides AB, BC and CA, respectively. If the length of the side of the triangle ABC is 11 cm, then the area (in cm^2) of ΔPQR is **SSC CGL (Tier I) 13/09/2024 Shift-II**

(a) $\frac{21\sqrt{3}}{16}$ (b) $\frac{11\sqrt{3}}{16}$
(c) $\frac{121\sqrt{3}}{16}$ (d) $\frac{111\sqrt{3}}{16}$

66. If $\Delta PQR \cong \Delta ABC$, $AB = 6$ cm, $\angle B = 50°$ and $\angle A = 70°$, then which of the following is true? **SSC CGL (Tier I) 13/09/2024 Shift-II**

(a) $QR = 6$ cm, $\angle Q = 60°$
(b) $QR = 6$ cm, $\angle R = 60°$
(c) $QP = 6$ cm, $\angle P = 60°$
(d) $QP = 6$ cm, $\angle R = 60°$

67. From a circle of radius 7 units, an arc length is cut by a chord of length 7 units. What is the arc length of the smaller portion (in units)? **SSC CGL (Tier I) 13/09/2024 Shift-I**

(a) $\frac{8}{3}\pi$ (b) $\frac{7}{6}\pi$ (c) $\frac{7}{3}\pi$ (d) $\frac{7}{4}\pi$

68. A and B are centres of two circles with radii 2 cm and 1 cm respectively, where $AB = 5$ cm. C is the centre of another circle of radius r cm, which touches each of the above two circles externally. If $\angle ACB = 90°$, then the value of r is: **SSC CGL (Tier I) 13/09/2024 Shift-I**

(a) 5 cm (b) 2 cm (c) 3 cm (d) 4 cm

69. In ΔABD and ΔFEC, $\angle BAD = 60°$, $l(BD) = l(EC)$, $\angle ABD = \angle FEC = 90°$ and $l(AB) = l(FE)$. Find the ratio of $\frac{\angle BAD}{\angle FCE}$. **SSC CGL (Tier I) 12/09/2024 Shift-III**

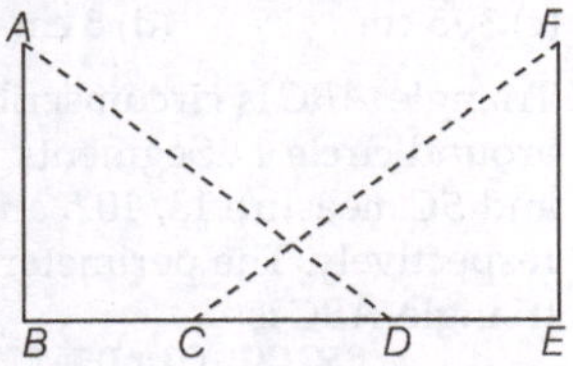

(a) 2 : 3 (b) 1 : 2
(c) 2 : 5 (d) 2 : 1

70. A pair of straight lines from an external point F intersects a circle at A and B ($FA < FB$) and touches the circle at C. O is the centre of the circle. Given that $\angle ACF = 50°$ and $\angle AFC = 30°$, find $\angle AOB$. **SSC CGL (Tier I) 12/09/2024 Shift-III**

(a) 80° (b) 90°
(c) 100° (d) 40°

71. In ΔDEF, the bisector of $\angle D$ intersects side EF at point N. If $DE = 36$ cm, $DF = 40$ cm and $EF = 38$ cm, then the length (in cm) of NF is .... **SSC CGL (Tier I) 12/09/2024 Shift-II**

(a) 16 (b) 20 (c) 18 (d) 12

72. The measures of the three angles of a triangle are in the ratio 17 : 13 : 15. Find the positive difference between the greatest and the smallest of these three angles. **SSC CGL (Tier I) 12/09/2024 Shift-I**

(a) 16° (b) 24°
(c) 20° (d) 12°

73. Two circles C_1 and C_2 touch each other externally. The radius of $C_1 = 16$ cm and the radius of $C_2 = 8$ cm. Find the length (in cm) of their common tangent. **SSC CGL (Tier I) 12/09/2024 Shift-I**

(a) $8\sqrt{3}$ (b) $16\sqrt{3}$
(c) $8\sqrt{2}$ (d) $16\sqrt{2}$

74. In a triangle PQR, S is a point on the side QR such that $PS \perp QR$, then which of the following options is true? **SSC CGL (Tier I) 12/09/2024 Shift-I**

(a) $PS^2 + PR^2 = PQ^2 + QR^2$
(b) $PR^2 + QS^2 = PQ^2 + SR^2$
(c) $PQ^2 + PR^2 = QS^2 + SR^2$
(d) $PS^2 + QS^2 = PQ^2 + PR^2$

75. In ΔABC, two medians AD and BE intersect at O at right angles. If $AD = 12$ cm and $BE = 9$ cm, then the length of AB is equal to: **SSC CGL (Tier I) 11/09/2024 Shift-III**

(a) 14 cm (b) 16 cm
(c) 12 cm (d) 10 cm

76. In a ΔLMN, $\angle L = 118°$ and $LM = LN$. Find $\angle N$. **SSC CGL (Tier I) 11/09/2024 Shift-III**

(a) 42° (b) 31°
(c) 65° (d) 62°

77. P and Q are centres of two circles whose radii are 7 cm and 3 cm, respectively. If the direct common tangents to the circles meet PQ extended at A, then A divides PQ .... **SSC CGL (Tier I) 11/09/2024 Shift-III**

(a) externally in the ratio 3 : 7
(b) internally in the ratio 3 : 7
(c) externally in the ratio 7 : 3
(d) internally in the ratio 7 : 3

78. In ΔPQR, M, N, and S are the mid-points of sides PQ, PR and QR, respectively. If the area of the ΔPQR is 46 cm^2, what is the area (in cm^2) of the quadrilateral $MNRQ$? **SSC CGL (Tier I) 11/09/2024 Shift-II**

(a) 39 (b) 27.6
(c) 23 (d) 34.5

79. In a rhombus $ABCD$, O is any interior point such that $OA = OC$. What is five-ninths of the degree measure of $\angle DOB$? **SSC CGL (Tier I) 11/09/2024 Shift-I**

(a) 120° (b) 150°
(c) 100° (d) 90°

80. In a circle, two chords MN and PQ intersect at O. If $MO = 9$ cm, $ON = 5$ cm and $OQ = 6$ cm, then the value of OP (in cm) is **SSC CGL (Tier I) 11/09/2024 Shift-I**

(a) 7.5 (b) 6.5 (c) 6 (d) 7

81. The radii of two circle are 5 cm and 10 cm and the distance between their centres is 17 cm. Find the length of the transverse common tangent. **SSC CGL (Tier I) 10/09/2024 Shift-III**

(a) 9 cm (b) 8 cm
(c) 6 cm (d) 7.5 cm

82. If $\Delta PQR \cong \Delta MON$ such that $\angle PQR = 82°$, $\angle QRP = 47°$, $\angle RPQ = 51°$, $\angle MON = (5y - 8)°$, $QR = 24$ and $ON = 3x + y$, then find $(x + y)$. **SSC CGL (Tier I) 10/09/2024 Shift-III**

(a) 14 (b) 18
(c) 16 (d) 20

83. X, Y, and Z are three points on a plane with $XY = 11$ cm, $YZ = 13$ cm, and $XZ = 24$ cm. The number of circles that travel through points X, Y and Z is **SSC CGL (Tier I) 10/09/2024 Shift-I**

(a) 0 (b) 2
(c) 1 (d) 3

84. By applying which of the following criteria can two triangles not be proved congruent? **SSC CGL (Tier I) 10/09/2024 Shift-I**

(a) angle-side-angle
(b) angle-angle-angle
(c) side-side-side
(d) side-angle-side

85. Two circles of radii 18 cm and 12 cm touch each other externally. Find the length (in cm) of their direct common tangent. **SSC CGL (Tier I) 10/09/2024 Shift-I**

(a) $15\sqrt{6}$ (b) $10\sqrt{6}$
(c) $12\sqrt{6}$ (d) $18\sqrt{6}$

86. Two triangles EFG and HIJ are congruent. If the area of ΔEFG is 124 cm^2, then the area of ΔHIJ will be **SSC CGL (Tier I) 09/09/2024 Shift-II**

(a) 124 cm^2 (b) 248 cm^2
(c) 62 cm^2 (d) 31 cm^2

87. In a ΔPQR, the bisectors of $\angle Q$ and $\angle R$ meet at point O, inside the triangle. If $\angle QOR = 107°$, then the measure of $\angle P$ is **SSC CGL (Tier I) 09/09/2024 Shift-III**

(a) 40° (b) 23°
(c) 17° (d) 34°

88. The angles of triangle are such that one is average of other two, then the angles are:

1. $\frac{\pi}{6}, \frac{\pi}{3}, \frac{\pi}{2}$ 2. $\frac{\pi}{3}, \frac{\pi}{3}, \frac{\pi}{2}$
3. $\frac{\pi}{6}, \frac{\pi}{3}, \frac{\pi}{4}$ 4. $\frac{\pi}{2}, \frac{\pi}{2}, \frac{\pi}{3}$

SSC CGL (Tier I) 09/09/2024 Shift-II

(a) 4 (b) 3
(c) 2 (d) 1

89. The points P and S are on the same side of the line segment QR, such that $\angle PQR = 90°$, $\angle SRQ = 90°$ and $PQ = SR$. Select the correct statement. **SSC CGL (Tier I) 09/09/2024 Shift-II**

(a) $\Delta PQR \cong \Delta SRQ$ by RHS
(b) $\Delta PQR \cong \Delta SQR$ by SAS
(c) $\Delta PQR \cong \Delta SQRQ$ by RHS
(d) $\Delta PQR \cong \Delta SRQ$ by SAS

90. The distance between the centres of two circles of radii 22 cm and 10 cm is 37 cm. If the points of contact of a direct common tangent to these

circles are M and Q, then find the length of the line segment MQ.
SSC CGL (Tier I) 09/09/2024 Shift-I

(a) 35 cm (b) 39 cm
(c) 29 cm (d) 25 cm

91. Let O be the centre of the circle and AB and CD are two parallel chords on the same side of the centre. OP is perpendicular to AB and OQ is perpendicular to CD. If $AB = 10$ cm, $CD = 24$ cm and $PQ = 7$ cm, then the diameter (in cm) of the circle is equal to **SSC CGL (Tier I) 09/09/2024 Shift-I**

(a) 26 (b) 13
(c) 12 (d) 24

92. If the sum of two sides of an equilateral triangle is 16 cm, then find the third side.
SSC CGL (Tier I) 09/09/2024 Shift-I

(a) 4 cm
(b) 16 cm
(c) Cannot be found
(d) 8 cm

SSC CGL 2023 (Tier I & II)

93. An equilateral triangle ABC surmounts a square $BCDE$. The value of $\angle EAB + 3\angle AEB$ is
SSC CGL (Tier II) 26/10/2023 Shift I

(a) 60° (b) 80°
(c) 280° (d) 240°

94. One chord of a circle is given as 20.5 cm. Then, the radius (r) of the circle must be.
SSC CGL (Tier II) 26/10/2023 Shift I

(a) $r = 10$ cm (b) $r < 10.25$
(c) $r > 10.25$ (d) $r \geq 10.25$

95. If one of the interior angles of a regular polygon is $\frac{15}{16}$ times of one of the interior angles of a regular decagon, then find the number of diagonals of the polygon.
SSC CGL (Tier II) 07/03/2023 Shift I

(a) 14 (b) 2 (c) 20 (d) 35

96. It is given that $\Delta ABC \cong \Delta PQR$, $AB = 5$ cm, $\angle B = 40°$, and $\angle A = 80°$. Which of the following options is true?
SSC CGL (Tier II) 07/03/2023 Shift I

(a) $PQ = 5$ cm and $\angle R = 60°$
(b) $QR = 5$ cm and $\angle Q = 60°$
(c) $QR = 5$ cm and $\angle R = 60°$
(d) $PQ = 5$ cm and $\angle P = 60°$

97. $PQRS$ is a cyclic quadrilateral. If $\angle P$ is three times of $\angle R$ and $\angle S$ is four times of $\angle Q$, then the sum of $\angle S + \angle R$ will be **SSC CGL (Tier II) 07/03/2023 Shift I**

(a) 189° (b) 171° (c) 187° (d) 169°

98. The centroid of an equilateral triangle PQR is L. If $PQ = 6$ cm, the length of PL is
SSC CGL (Tier II) 06/03/2023 Shift I

(a) $4\sqrt{3}$ cm (b) $3\sqrt{3}$ cm
(c) $2\sqrt{3}$ cm (d) $5\sqrt{3}$ cm

99. Two chords AB and CD of a circle intersect at point F inside the circle. If $AF = 4$ cm, $BF = 6$ cm, and $CF = 3$ cm then find the length of CD?
SSC CGL (Tier II) 06/03/2023 Shift I

(a) 8 cm (b) 11 cm
(c) 16 cm (d) 12 cm

100. $ABCD$ is a cyclic quadrilateral and BC is a diameter of the related circle on which A and D also lie. $\angle BCA = 19°$ and angle $\angle CAD = 32°$. What is the measure of angle $\angle ACD$?
SSC CGL (Tier II) 03/03/2023 Shift I

(a) 41° (b) 38°
(c) 40° (d) 39°

101. If the external angle of a regular polygon is 18°, then the number of diagonals in this polygon is
SSC CGL (Tier II) 03/03/2023 Shift I

(a) 180 (b) 150
(c) 170 (d) 140

102. In ΔPQR, $PQ = QR$ and O is an interior point of ΔPQR such that $\angle OPR = \angle ORP$.
SSC CGL (Tier II) 02/03/2023 Shift I

Consider the following statements
(i) ΔPOR is an isosceles triangle.
(ii) O is the centroid of ΔPQR.
(iii) ΔPQO is congruent to ΔRQO.
Which of the above statements are correct?
(a) (i) and (ii) (b) (i) and (iii)
(c) (ii) and (iii) (d) Only (ii)

103. A circle touches all four sides of a quadrilateral $ABCD$. If $AB = 18$ cm, $BC = 21$ cm and $AD = 15$ cm, then length CD is
SSC CGL (Tier II) 02/03/2023 Shift I

(a) 16 cm (b) 14 cm
(c) 12 cm (d) 18 cm

104. A, B, C are three points such that $AB = 9$ cm, $BC = 11$ cm and $AC = 20$ cm. The number of circles passing through points A, B, C is
SSC CGL (Tier II) 02/03/2023 Shift I

(a) 2 (b) 0 (c) 1 (d) 3

105. If the measure of one angle of a right triangle is 30° more than the measure of the smallest angle, then the measure of the smallest angle is
SSC CGL (Tier I) 27/07/2023 Shift III

(a) 90° (b) 60°
(c) 30° (d) 75°

106. The distance between the centres of two circles having radii 22 cm and 18 cm, is 32 cm. The length (in cm) of the direct common tangent of the two circles is
SSC CGL (Tier I) 27/07/2023 Shift II

(a) $2\sqrt{252}$ cm (b) $2\sqrt{152}$ cm
(c) $3\sqrt{242}$ cm (d) $3\sqrt{252}$ cm

107. ABC is a triangle and D is a point on the side BC. If $BC = 16$ cm, $BD = 11$ cm and $\angle ADC = \angle BAC$, then the length of AC is equal to
SSC CGL (Tier I) 27/07/2023 Shift II

(a) $4\sqrt{5}$ cm (b) 4 cm
(c) $3\sqrt{5}$ cm (d) 5 cm

108. Triangle ABC is circumscribed around circle D. Segments AQ, BR and SC measure 13, 10.5 and 6 cm, respectively. The perimeter of triangle ABC is
SSC CGL (Tier I) 26/07/2023 Shift-IV

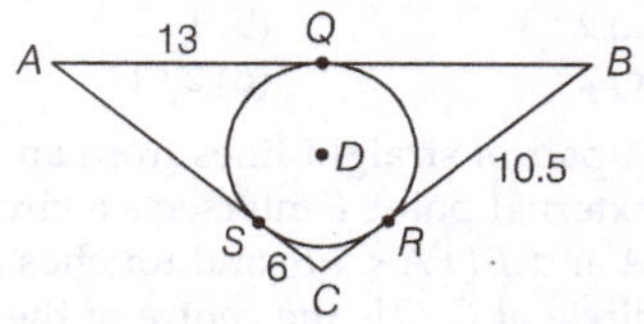

(a) 29.5 cm (b) 59 cm
(c) 108 cm (d) 15 cm

109. In the figure PT is a tangent. If $TP = 12$ cm, $PB = x + 7$ cm and $PA = x$ cm, then find the value of x.
SSC CGL (Tier I) 26/07/2023 Shift-IV

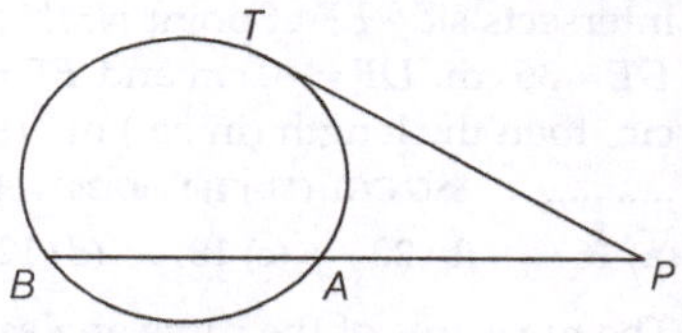

(a) 9 (b) 6 (c) 7 (d) 5

110. In a triangle ABC, the three angles are x, y and $y + 10$.
Also, $2x - 4y = 20°$. Which type of triangle is ABC?
SSC CGL (Tier I) 26/07/2023 Shift III

(a) Equilateral (b) Obtuse
(c) Acute (d) Right-angled

111. For congruent triangles ΔABC and ΔDEF, which of the following statements is correct?
SSC CGL (Tier I) 26/07/2023 Shift II

(a) Perimeter of $\Delta ABC = \frac{1}{2}$ Perimeter of ΔDEF
(b) Perimeter of ΔABC = Perimeter of ΔDEF
(c) Perimeter of $\Delta ABC <$ Perimeter of ΔDEF
(d) Perimeter of $\Delta ABC >$ Perimeter of ΔDEF

112. In the given figure, O is the centre of the circle and $\angle AOB = 130°$. Find $\angle APB$. **SSC CGL (Tier I) 26/07/2023 Shift I**

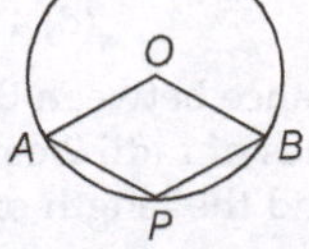

(a) 110° (b) 115° (c) 100° (d) 95°

113. There are two circles that touch each other externally. Radius of the first circle with centre O is 12 cm. Radius of the second circle with centre A is 8 cm. Find the length of their common tangent BC. **SSC CGL (Tier I) 26/07/2023 Shift I**

(a) $6\sqrt{6}$ cm (b) $8\sqrt{3}$ cm
(c) $8\sqrt{2}$ cm (d) $8\sqrt{6}$ cm

114. Which of the following sets of lengths (in cm) will give three sides of an obtuse angled triangle? **SSC CGL (Tier I) 26/07/2023 Shift I**

(a) 15, 62, 64 (b) 17, 64, 66
(c) 16, 63, 65 (d) 18, 65, 67

115. In ΔABC, $DE \parallel BC$ and $\frac{AD}{DB} = \frac{4}{5}$. If $DE = 12$ cm, then find the length of BC. **SSC CGL (Tier I) 26/07/2023 Shift I**

(a) 48 cm (b) 12 cm
(c) 30 cm (d) 27 cm

116. In the figure given below, PQ is the diameter of the circle with centre O. If $\angle QOR = 100°$, then the measure of $\angle PSR$ is **SSC CGL (Tier I) 25/07/2023 Shift IV**

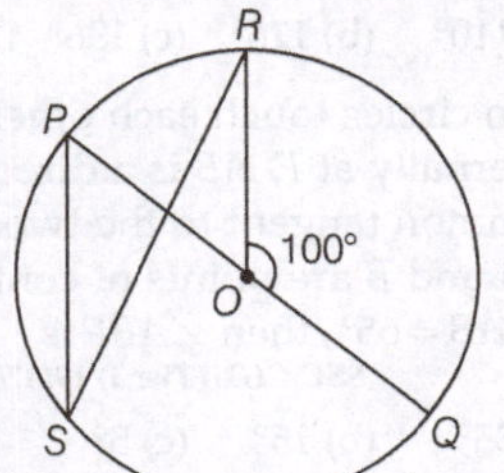

(a) 160° (b) 80° (c) 40° (d) 100°

117. A circle of radius 4 cm is drawn inscribed in a right angle triangle ABC, right angled at C. If $AC = 12$ cm, then the value of CB is **SSC CGL (Tier I) 25/07/2023 Shift IV**

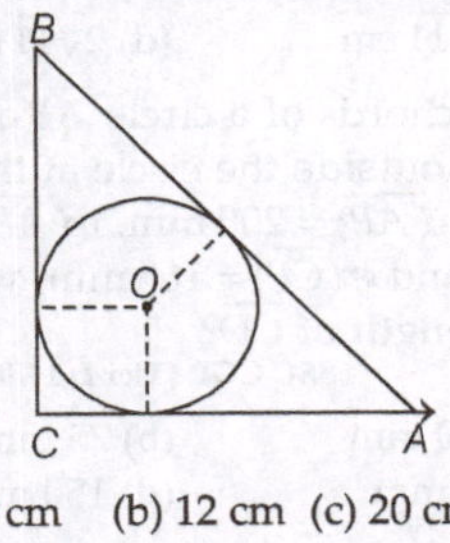

(a) 8 cm (b) 12 cm (c) 20 cm (d) 16 cm

118. Two circles touch each other externally. The radius of the first circle with centre O is 6 cm. The radius of the second circle with centre P is 3 cm. Find the length of their common tangent AB. **SSC CGL (Tier I) 25/07/2023 Shift III**

(a) $3\sqrt{2}$ cm (b) $4\sqrt{2}$ cm
(c) $6\sqrt{3}$ cm (d) $6\sqrt{2}$ cm

119. If RP and RQ are two tangents to a circle with centre O such that $\angle POQ = 120°$, where P and Q are the points on the circle and R is a point outside the circle then $\angle PRQ$ is equal to **SSC CGL (Tier I) 25/07/2023 Shift II**

(a) 90° (b) 75°
(c) 60° (d) 45°

120. In the following figure, there are two circles that touch each other externally. The radius of the first circle with centre P is 25 cm. The radius of the second circle with centre Q is 4 cm. Find the length of their direct common tangent AB. **SSC CGL (Tier I) 25/07/2023 Shift I**

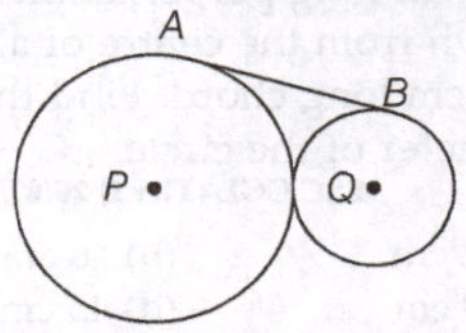

(Figure is not to scale and is only for representational purpose.)

(a) 21 cm (b) 18 cm
(c) 20 cm (d) 22 cm

121. In the given figure, chord XY and PQ intersect each other at point L. Find the length of XY (in cm). **SSC CGL (Tier I) 24/07/2023 Shift IV**

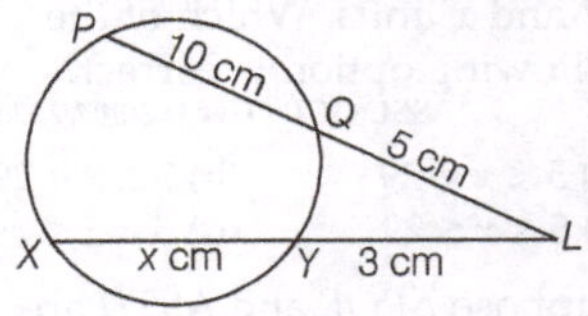

(a) 21 (b) 20 (c) 22 (d) 23

122. Two equal circles of radius 18 cm intersect each other, such that each passes through the centre of the other. The length of the common chord is ________. **SSC CGL (Tier I) 24/07/2023 Shift IV**

(a) $6\sqrt{27}$ cm (b) $9\sqrt{27}$ cm
(c) $\sqrt{3}$ cm (d) $3\sqrt{3}$ cm

123. If $\Delta ABC \cong \Delta PQR$, which of the following need not be necessarily true? **SSC CGL (Tier-I) 24/07/2023 Shift-III**

(a) $m(\overline{AB}) = m(\overline{PQ})$; $m(\overline{BC}) = m(\overline{RP})$; $\angle A = \angle P$
(b) $m(\overline{AB}) = m(\overline{PQ})$; $m(\overline{BC}) = m(\overline{QR})$; $m(\overline{CA}) = m(\overline{PR})$
(c) $m(\overline{AB}) = m(\overline{PQ})$; $m(\overline{BC}) = m(\overline{QR})$; $\angle A = \angle P$
(d) $\angle A = \angle P$; $\angle B = \angle Q$; $\angle C = \angle R$

124. Two circles with radii 22 cm and 16 cm touch each other externally. The length of the direct common tangent is **SSC CGL (Tier I) 24/07/2023 Shift III**

(a) $4\sqrt{22}$ cm (b) $8\sqrt{11}$ cm
(c) $4\sqrt{11}$ cm (d) $8\sqrt{22}$ cm

125. If ΔABC and ΔDEF are congruent triangles, then which of the following is false? **SSC CGL (Tier I) 24/07/2023 Shift III**

(a) The ratio of AC to DF is 2:1.
(b) The perimeter of both the triangles is equal.
(c) $AB = DE$ and $BC = EF$.
(d) The ratio of the angles in both the triangles is the same.

126. In ΔABC, D is the mid-point of BC and G is the centroid. If $GD = 10$ cm, then the length of AD is **SSC CGL (Tier I) 24/07/2023 Shift II**

(a) 20 cm (b) 30 cm (c) 15 cm (d) 10 cm

127. The length of the common chord of two circles of radii 15 cm and 13 cm whose centres are 14 cm apart, is **SSC CGL (Tier I) 24/07/2023 Shift II**

(a) 14 cm (b) 12 cm (c) 15 cm (d) 24 cm

128. DE is a chord and KDE is a secant of a circle. If $KD = 9$ cm, $DE = 7$ cm and KH is a tangent to the circle at point H, then find KH. **SSC CGL (Tier I) 24/07/2023 Shift I**

(a) 12 cm (b) 25 cm
(c) 16 cm (d) 144 cm

129. If the length of a chord, drawn at a distance of 21 cm from the centre of circle, is 40 cm, then the radius (in cm) of the circle is **SSC CGL (Tier I) 24/07/2023 Shift I**

(a) 29 (b) 21 (c) 25 (d) 20

130. In the given figure, PQ is a chord passing through the centre 'O' of the circle. Calculate $\angle PQS$. **SSC CGL (Tier I) 21/07/2023 Shift IV**

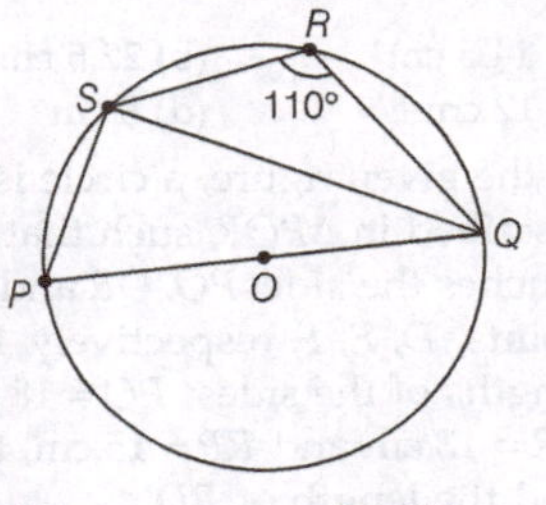

(a) 40° (b) 60°
(c) 20° (d) 80°

131. Which of the following statements is false? **SSC CGL (Tier I) 21/07/2023 Shift IV**

(a) Two triangles are congruent if the size and shape of the triangles may or may not be equal.
(b) SAS an SSS are both conditions of congruency of triangles.
(c) If two angles and the included side of one triangle is equal to two angles and the included side of other triangle, then the triangles are congruent.
(d) If two triangles are congruent, then one of them can be superimposed on the other triangle.

132. Two chords AB and CD of a circle meet inside the circle at point P. If $AP = 12$ cm, $AB = 20$ cm and $CP = 16$cm, then $CD = ?$
SSC CGL (Tier I) 21/07/2023 Shift III

(a) 22 cm (b) 15 cm
(c) 21 cm (d) 24 cm

133. The sides of two similar triangles are in the ratio 5 : 7. The areas of these triangles are in the ratio
SSC CGL (Tier I) 21/07/2023 Shift II

(a) 35 : 49 (b) 15 : 49
(c) 25 : 49 (d) 36 : 49

134. $AB = 28$ cm and $CD = 22$ cm are two parallel chords on the same side of the centre of a circle. The distance between them is 4 cm. The radius of the circle is ....
(Consider up to two decimals)
SSC CGL (Tier I) 21/07/2023 Shift II

(a) 15.20 cm
(b) 14.82 cm
(c) 15.82 cm
(d) 13.20 cm

135. In the given figure, diameter AB and chord CD of a circle meet at P. PT is a tangent to the circle at T. If $CD = 8$ cm, $PD = 10$ cm and $PB = 8$ cm, find AB. **SSC CGL (Tier I) 21/07/2023 Shift I**

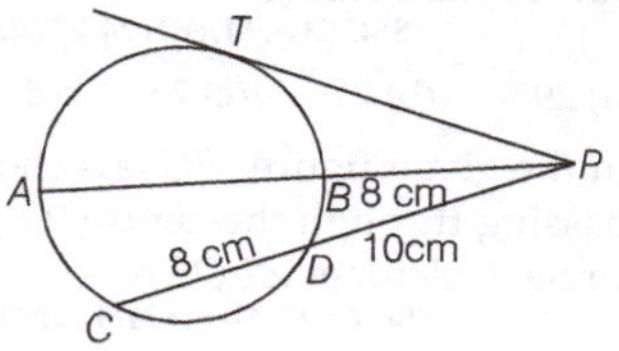

(a) 14.5 cm (b) 22.5 cm
(c) 12 cm (d) 8 cm

136. In the given figure, a circle is inscribed in ΔPQR, such that it touches the sides PQ, QR and RP at points, D, E, F, respectively. If the lengths of the sides, $PQ = 18$ cm, $QR = 13$ cm and $RP = 15$ cm, then find the length of PD.
SSC CGL (Tier I) 21/07/2023 Shift I

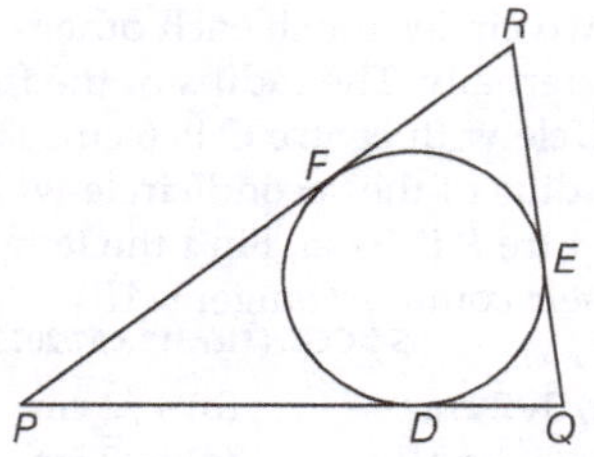

(a) 10 cm (b) 8 cm
(c) 15 cm (d) 12 cm

137. In the given figure $\Delta QPS \cong \Delta SRQ$. Find the measure of $\angle PSR$.
SSC CGL (Tier I) 21/07/2023 Shift I

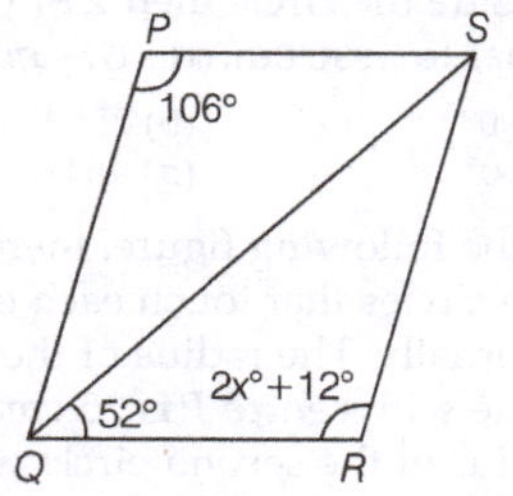

(a) 64° (b) 74° (c) 52° (d) 82°

138. A 15 cm long perpendicular is drawn from the centre of a circle to a 40 cm long chord. Find the diameter of the circle.
SSC CGL (Tier I) 20/07/2023 Shift IV

(a) 52 cm (b) 48 cm
(c) 50 cm (d) 45 cm

139. In a circle with centre O, PA and PB are the tangents at A and B, respectively, from an external point P. If $\angle APB = 24°$, then find $\angle AOB$.
SSC CGL (Tier I) 20/07/2023 Shift III

(a) 158° (b) 48°
(c) 156° (d) 180°

140. The three sides of a triangle are 12, 17 and x units. Which of the following option is correct?
SSC CGL (Tier I) 20/07/2023 Shift III

(a) $5 < x < 29$ (b) $5 \le x < 29$
(c) $5 \le x \le 29$ (d) $5 < x \le 29$

141. Suppose ΔPQR and ΔSTU are congruent triangles under ASA. If $\angle PQR = 60°$, $\angle PRQ = 30°$ and $\angle STU = 60°$, find $\angle TSU$.
SSC CGL (Tier I) 20/07/2023 Shift II

(a) 90° (b) 75°
(c) 60° (d) 45°

142. PT is a tangent to a circle whose centre is O and where T is a point on the circle. If $PT = 12$ cm and $PO = 13$ cm, then find the radius of the circle.
SSC CGL (Tier I) 20/07/2023 Shift I

(a) 4 cm (b) 6 cm
(c) 4.5 cm (d) 5 cm

143. The mid-points of AB and AC of a ΔABC are X and Y, respectively. If $BC + XY = 18$ units, then the value of $BC - XY$ is
SSC CGL (Tier I) 19/07/2023 Shift IV

(a) 12 cm (b) 6 cm
(c) 8 cm (d) 4 cm

144. The distance between the centres of two circles of radii 2 cm and 6 cm is 5 cm. Find the length of the direct common tangent.
SSC CGL (Tier I) 19/07/2023 Shift IV

(a) 6 cm (b) 3 cm
(c) 9 cm (d) 5/2 cm

145. In the shown figure, BC is a chord and CD is a tangent through the point C. If $\angle AOC = 112°$, then find $\angle ACD$. **SSC CGL (Tier I) 19/07/2023 Shift IV**

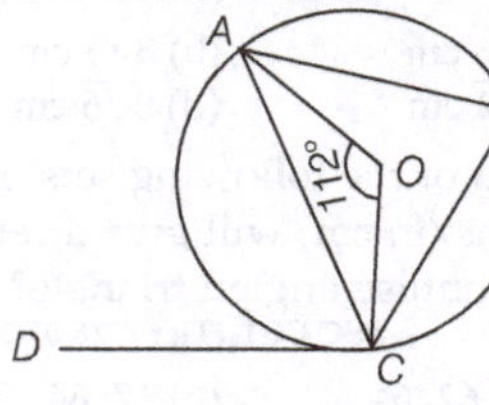

(a) 63° (b) 59° (c) 65° (d) 56°

146. What is the number of common tangents that can be drawn to two circles that touch each other externally?
SSC CGL (Tier I) 19/07/2023 Shift III

(a) 2 (b) 4 (c) 3 (d) 1

147. In a ΔABC, the angle bisectors of $\angle B$ and $\angle C$ meet at O. If $\angle BAC = 72°$, then the value of $\angle BOC$ is
SSC CGL (Tier I) 19/07/2023 Shift II

(a) 110° (b) 126° (c) 136° (d) 146°

148. Two circles touch each other externally at P. AB is a direct common tangent to the two circles. If A and B are points of contact and $\angle PAB = 65°$, then $\angle ABP$ is
SSC CGL (Tier I) 19/07/2023 Shift II

(a) 35° (b) 15° (c) 5° (d) 25°

149. Two circles of same radius 6 cm, intersect each other at P and Q. If $PQ = 10$ cm, then what is the distance between the centres of the two circles?
SSC CGL (Tier I) 19/07/2023 Shift I

(a) 10 cm (b) 8 cm
(c) $6\sqrt{11}$ cm (d) $2\sqrt{11}$ cm

150. Two chords of a circle $\overline{AB}$ and $\overline{CD}$, meet outside the circle at the point P. If $m(\overline{AP}) = 200$ mm, $m(\overline{AB}) = 120$ mm and $m(\overline{CP}) = 160$ mm, what is the length of $\overline{CD}$?
SSC CGL (Tier I) 19/07/2023 Shift I

(a) 100 mm (b) 75 mm
(c) 60 mm (d) 150 mm

151. Observe the given figure. The distance between the two centers AB is **SSC CGL (Tier I) 18/07/2023 Shift IV**

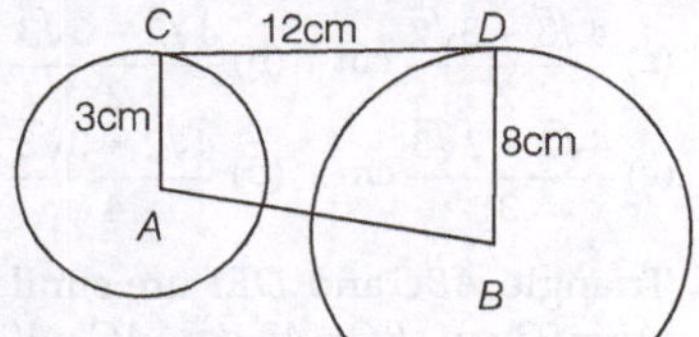

(a) 10 cm (b) 13 cm
(c) 12 cm (d) 11 cm

152. D and E are points on the sides AB and AC, respectively, of ΔABC such that DE is parallel to BC and $AD : DB = 7 : 9$. If CD and BE intersect each other at F, then find the ratio of areas of ΔDEF and ΔCBF. **SSC CGL (Tier I) 18/07/2023 Shift III**

(a) 256 : 49 (b) 49 : 144
(c) 49 : 81 (d) 49 : 256

153. ΔPQR is an equilateral triangle inscribed in a circle. S is any point on the arc QR. Find the measure of $\angle PSQ$. **SSC CGL (Tier I) 18/07/2023 Shift III**

(a) 60° (b) 30° (c) 90° (d) 45°

154. Let A, B, C can be the mid-points of sides PQ, QR PR, respectively, of ΔPQR. If the area of ΔPQR is 32 cm^2, then find the area of ΔABC. **SSC CGL (Tier I) 18/07/2023 Shift I**

(a) 24 cm^2 (b) 16 cm^2
(c) 32 cm^2 (d) 8 cm^2

155. Which of the following statements is incorrect? **SSC CGL (Tier I) 17/07/2023 Shift IV**

(a) The ratio of circumference of two circles is equal to the ratio of their radii.
(b) Radius is the longest chord of a circle.
(c) Circles are congruent to each other if they have equal radii.
(d) The perpendicular drawn from the centre of the circle on the chord of the circle bisects the chord.

156. The distance between the centres of two circles having radii 16 cm and 8 cm, is 26 cm. The length (in cm) of the direct common tangent of the two circles is **SSC CGL (Tier I) 17/07/2023 Shift III**

(a) $2\sqrt{132}$ (b) $\sqrt{153}$
(c) $2\sqrt{153}$ (d) $\sqrt{132}$

157. The length of the three sides of a triangle are 30 cm, 42 cm and x cm. Which of the following is correct ? **SSC CGL (Tier I) 17/07/2023 Shift II**

(a) $12 < x < 72$ (b) $12 \le x < 72$
(c) $12 \le x \le 72$ (d) $12 > x > 72$

158. $\Delta ABC \sim \Delta DEF$ and the perimeters of ΔABC and ΔDEF are 40 cm and 12 cm, respectively. If $DE = 6$ cm, then AB is **SSC CGL (Tier I) 17/07/2023 Shift I**

(a) 12.6 cm (b) 24 cm
(c) 20 cm (d) 10 cm

159. If $\Delta XYZ \cong \Delta LMR$, then $m + x + p =$ .... **SSC CGL (Tier I) 14/07/2023 Shift IV**

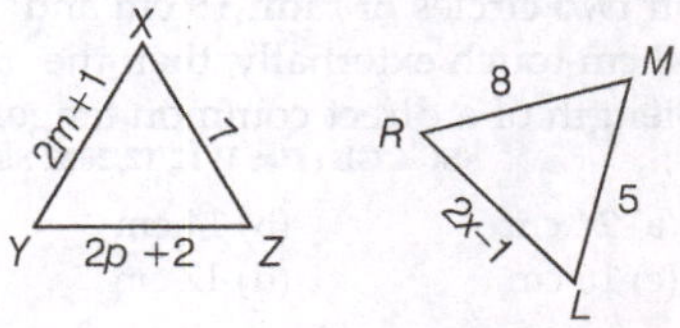

(a) 7 (b) 6 (c) 9 (d) 13

160. In the given figure 'G' is the centre of the circle. Find the $\angle ACB$, when $\angle AGB = 132°$. **SSC CGL (Tier I) 14/07/2023 Shift IV**

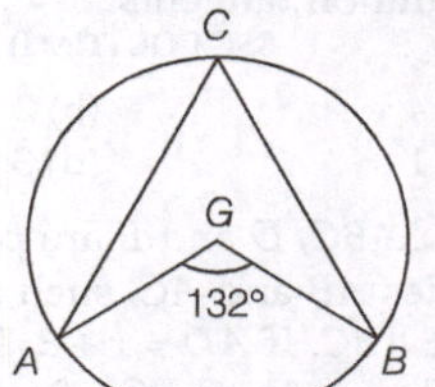

(a) 62° (b) 66°
(c) 64° (d) 60°

161. Which of the following statements is incorrect? **SSC CGL (Tier I) 14/07/2023 Shift III**

(a) If a chord is extended outside the circle on both ends then it is called secant.
(b) Tangent is perpendicular to the radius of the circle at the point of contact.
(c) A line which intersects two distinct points of a circle is called tangent.
(d) Tangent is a line touching only one point of the circle.

162. AB is the diameter of a circle with centre O. P be a point on it. If $\angle AOP = 95°$, then $\angle OBP =$ ..... **SSC CGL (Tier I) 14/07/2023 Shift III**

(a) 57.5° (b) 45.5°
(c) 47.5° (d) 55.5°

163. If D is the mid-point of BC in ΔABC and $\angle A = 90°$, then $AD =$ .... **SSC CGL (Tier I) 14/07/2023 Shift II**

(a) $\frac{BC}{4}$ (b) $\frac{BC}{2}$
(c) BC (d) 2 BC

164. Two concentric circles are of radii 10 cm and 6 cm. Find the length of the chord of the larger circle which touches the smaller circle. **SSC CGL (Tier I) 14/07/2023 Shift I**

(a) 9 cm (b) 8 cm
(c) 12 cm (d) 16 cm

165. In the given figure, PAB is a secant and PT is a tangent to the circle from P. If $PT = 8$ cm, $PA = 6$ cm and $AB = x$ cm, then the value of x is **SSC CGL (Tier I) 14/07/2023 Shift I**

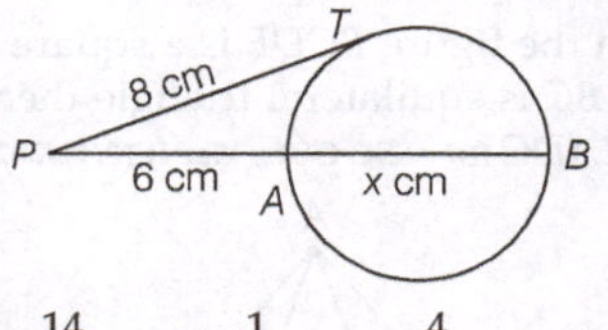

(a) $\frac{14}{3}$ (b) $\frac{1}{3}$ (c) $\frac{4}{3}$ (d) $\frac{14}{9}$

SSC CGL 2022 (Tier I)

166. In the given figure, if $KI = IT$ and $EK = ET$, then $\angle TEI =$ .... **SSC CGL (Tier I) 13/12/2022 Shift IV**

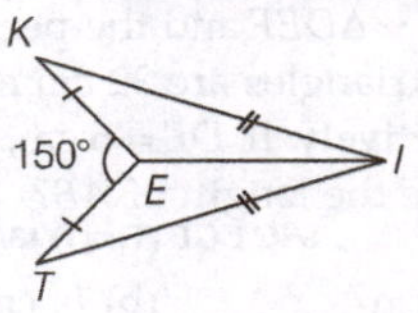

(a) 75° (b) 125°
(c) 105° (d) 150°

167. In the given figure, $\angle ABC = 81°$ and $\angle ACB = 9°$. What is the value of $\angle BDC$? **SSC CGL (Tier I) 13/12/2022 Shift IV**

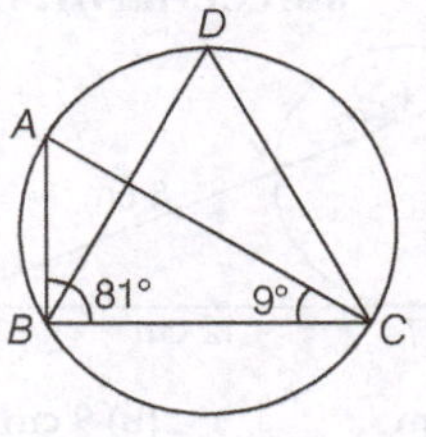

(a) 80° (b) 90°
(c) 70° (d) 60°

168. If $\Delta ABC \cong \Delta PQR$ and $\angle ABC = (x + 60°)$, $\angle PQR = (85 - 4x)°$, and $\angle RPQ = (3x + 65)°$, then the value of $\angle ABC$ in degree is **SSC CGL (Tier I) 13/12/2022 Shift III**

(a) 15 (b) 5 (c) 45 (d) 65

169. The length of the chord of a circle is 24 cm, and the perpendicular distance between the centre and the chord is 5 cm. The radius of the circle is **SSC CGL (Tier I) 13/12/2022 Shift III**

(a) 24 cm (b) 10 cm
(c) 12 cm (d) 13 cm

170. Select the incorrect statement with respect to the properties of a circle. **SSC CGL (Tier I) 13/12/2022 Shift II**

(a) The diameter of a circle is the longest chord of a circle.
(b) Two tangents drawn at the end of the diameter of a circle are parallel.

(c) The radius drawn perpendicular to a chord bisects the chord.
(d) The perpendicular distance from the centre of a circle increases when the length of a chord increases.

171. In the figure $BCDE$ is a square and ABC is equilateral triangle then $\angle ADC$ is **SSC CGL (Tier I) 13/12/2022 Shift I**

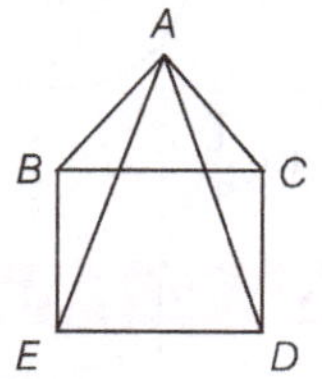

(a) 45° (b) 30°
(c) 60° (d) 15°

172. $\Delta ABC \sim \Delta DEF$ and the perimeters of these triangles are 32 cm and 12 cm, respectively. If $DE = 6$ cm, then what will be the length of AB?
SSC CGL (Tier I) 13/12/2022 Shift I

(a) 16 cm (b) 14 cm
(c) 12 cm (d) 18 cm

173. In the figure, XYZ is a secant and ZT is a tangent to the circle at T. If $TZ = 12$ cm and $YZ = 8$ cm, then find the length of XY.
SSC CGL (Tier I) 12/12/2022 Shift IV

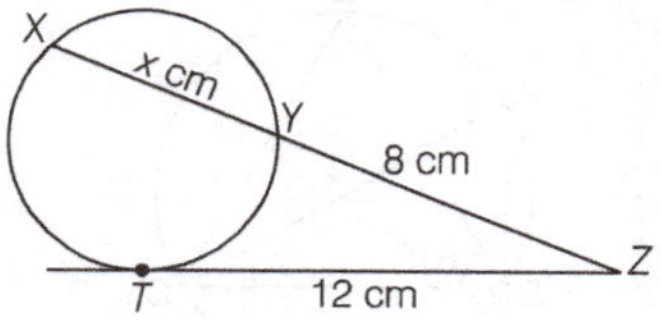

(a) 8 cm (b) 9 cm
(c) 6 cm (d) 10 cm

174. What is the ASA congruence rule of triangles, where A and S represents angle and side of triangle respectively?
SSC CGL (Tier I) 12/12/2022 Shift III

(a) Two triangles are said to be congruent if all three sides of both the triangles are equal
(b) Two triangles are said to be congruent if 2 angles and the included side of one triangle are equal to 2 angles and the included side of the other triangle
(c) Two triangles are said to be congruent if 2 sides and the included angle of one triangle are equal to 2 sides and the included angle of the other triangle
(d) Two triangles are said to be congruent if any pair of 2 angles and any 1 pair of sides of both the triangles are equal

175. The diameters of two circles are 12 cm and 20 cm, respectively and the distance between their centres is 16 cm. Find the number of common tangents to the circles.
SSC CGL (Tier I) 12/12/2022 Shift III

(a) 2 (b) 3
(c) 1 (d) 4

176. If two circles of radii 18 cm and 8 cm touch externally, then the length of a direct common tangent is
SSC CGL (Tier I) 12/12/2022 Shift III

(a) 24 cm (b) 14 cm
(c) 16 cm (d) 12 cm

177. If C_1, C_2 be the centres of two circles and r_1, r_2 be the respective radii such that the distance between the centres is equal to the sum of the radii of the two circles, find the number of common tangents.
SSC CGL (Tier I) 12/12/2022 Shift II

(a) 4 (b) 2
(c) 1 (d) 3

178. In ΔABC, D and E are points on sides AB and AC, such that $DE \parallel BC$. If $AD = x + 3$, $DB = 2x - 3$, $AE = x + 1$ and $EC = 2x - 2$, then the value of x is
SSC CGL (Tier I) 12/12/2022 Shift I

(a) $\frac{4}{5}$ (b) $\frac{1}{2}$
(c) $\frac{3}{5}$ (d) $\frac{1}{5}$

179. Radius of a circle is 5 cm. Length of chord AB in this circle is 6 cm. What is the distance of this chord from the centre of the circle?
SSC CGL (Tier I) 12/12/2022 Shift I

(a) 4 cm (b) 5 cm
(c) 6 cm (d) 8 cm

180. If $\Delta ABC \cong \Delta PQR$, $BC = 6$ cm, and $\angle A = 75°$, then which one of the following is true?
SSC CGL (Tier I) 09/12/2022 Shift III

(a) $QR = 6$ cm, $\angle R = 75°$
(b) $QR = 6$ cm, $\angle Q = 75°$
(c) $QR = 6$ cm, $\angle P = 75°$
(d) $PR = 6$ cm, $\angle P = 75°$

181. If it is given that for two right angled triangles ABC and DFE, $\angle A = 25°$, $\angle E = 25°$, $\angle B = \angle F = 90°$ and $AC = ED$, then which one of the following is true?
SSC CGL (Tier I) 09/12/2022 Shift III

(a) $\Delta ABC \cong \Delta FED$ (b) $\Delta ABC \cong \Delta DFE$
(c) $\Delta ABC \cong \Delta EFD$ (d) $\Delta ABC \cong \Delta DEF$

182. In a circle of radius 3 cm, two chords of length 2 cm and 3 cm lie on the same side of a diameter. What is the perpendicular distance between the two chords?
SSC CGL (Tier I) 09/12/2022 Shift II

(a) $\frac{4\sqrt{3} - 3\sqrt{2}}{2}$ cm (b) $\frac{4\sqrt{2} - 3\sqrt{3}}{2}$ cm
(c) $\frac{4\sqrt{2} - 3\sqrt{3}}{3}$ cm (d) $\frac{4\sqrt{2} - 3\sqrt{3}}{4}$ cm

183. Triangle ABC and DEF are similar. If $AB = 92$ cm, $BC = 48$ cm, $AC = 120$ cm and the length of the smallest side of DEF is 200 cm, then find the length of the longest side of triangle DEF? **SSC CGL (Tier I) 09/12/2022 Shift II**

(a) 400 cm (b) 225 cm
(c) 350 cm (d) 500 cm

184. If PT is a tangent at T to a circle whose centre is O and $OP = 17$ cm and $OT = 8$ cm, find the length of the tangent segment PT.
SSC CGL (Tier I) 09/12/2022 Shift I

(a) 13 cm (b) 14 cm
(c) 16 cm (d) 15 cm

185. There are two circles which touch each other externally. The radius of the first circle with centre O is 17 cm and radius of the second circle with centre A is 7 cm. BC is a direct common tangent to these two circles, where B and C are points on the circles with centres O and A, respectively. The length of BC is
SSC CGL (Tier I) 08/12/2022 Shift IV

(a) $2\sqrt{118}$ cm (b) $2\sqrt{119}$ cm
(c) $2\sqrt{113}$ cm (d) $2\sqrt{117}$ cm

186. In the following figure, if $l \parallel m$, then find the measures of angles marked by a and b.
SSC CGL (Tier I) 08/12/2022 Shift IV

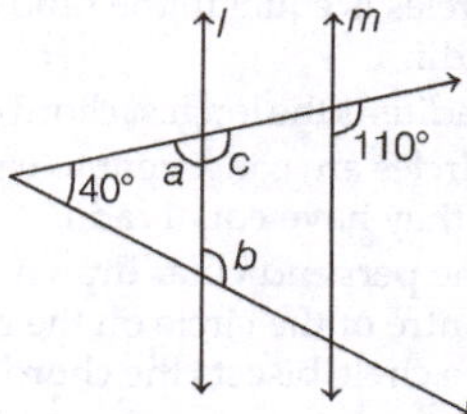

(a) $a = 90°$ and $b = 90°$
(b) $a = 55°$ and $b = 125°$
(c) $a = 70°$ and $b = 110°$
(d) $a = 60°$ and $b = 120°$

187. The radius of a circle is 5 cm. Calculate the length of a tangent drawn to this circle from a point at a distance of 10 cm from its centre.
SSC CGL (Tier I) 08/12/2022 Shift III

(a) $5\sqrt{5}$ cm (b) $5\sqrt{2}$ cm
(c) 5 cm (d) $5\sqrt{3}$ cm

188. In a ΔABC, AD, BE and CF are the medians from vertices A, B and C, respectively. The point of intersection of AD, BE and CF is called ....

SSC CGL (Tier I) 08/12/2022 Shift III

(a) median point (b) orthocentre
(c) centroid (d) incentre

189. If two circles do not touch or intersect each other and one does not lie inside the other, then find the number of common tangents.

SSC CGL (Tier I) 08/12/2022 Shift II

(a) 5 (b) 4 (c) 2 (d) 3

190. In ΔABC and ΔDEF, $\angle A = 55°$, $AB = DE$, $AC = DF$ $\angle E = 85°$ and $\angle F = 40°$. By which property are ΔABC and ΔDEF congruent?

SSC CGL (Tier I) 08/12/2022 Shift II

(a) SAS property (b) ASA property
(c) RHS property (d) SSS property

191. In ΔABC, P and Q are points on AB and BC respectively, such that $PQ \parallel AC$. Given that $AB = 26$, $PQ = 7$ and $AC = 10$ find the value of AP.

SSC CGL (Tier I) 08/12/2022 Shift I

(a) 7.1 (b) 7.8 (c) 18.2 (d) 16.4

192. $ABCD$ is a square and ΔMAB is an equilateral triangle. MC and MD are joined. What is the degree measure of $\angle MDC$? **SSC CGL (Tier I) 08/12/2022 Shift I**

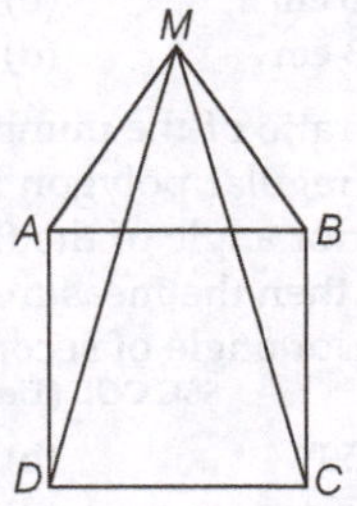

(a) 78° (b) 60° (c) 65° (d) 75°

193. In the given figure, O is the centre of the circle and $\angle AOC = 140°$. Find $\angle ABC$. **SSC CGL (Tier I) 07/12/2022 Shift IV**

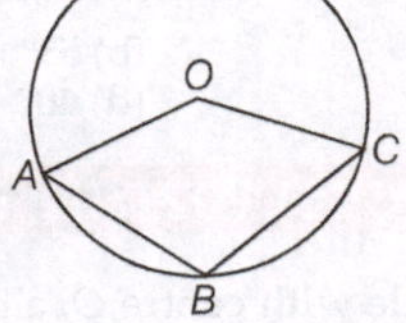

(a) 95° (b) 110° (c) 120° (d) 103°

194. In a ΔXYZ, XO is the median and $XO = \frac{1}{2}YZ$. If $\angle YXO = 30°$, then what is the value of $\angle XYZ$?

SSC CGL (Tier I) 07/12/2022 Shift III

(a) 15° (b) 90° (c) 30° (d) 60°

195. In triangle XYZ, P is the incentre of the triangle XYZ. If angle $XYZ = 50°$, then what is the value of angle XPZ?

SSC CGL (Tier I) 07/12/2022 Shift II

(a) 100° (b) 115°
(c) 140° (d) 130°

196. If $\Delta ABC \sim \Delta DEF$ such that $2AB = DE$ and $BC = 8$ cm, then the length of EF is **SSC CGL (Tier I) 07/12/2022 Shift II**

(a) 16 cm (b) 18 cm
(c) 22 cm (d) 20 cm

197. A circle is inscribed in a ΔABC having sides $AB = 16$ cm, $BC = 20$ cm and $AC = 24$ cm, and side AB, BC and AC touches circle at D, E and F, respectively. The measure of AD is

SSC CGL (Tier I) 07/12/2022 Shift II

(a) 10 cm (b) 20 cm
(c) 6 cm (d) 14 cm

198. Two concentric circles are drawn with radii 20 cm and 16 cm. What will be the length of a chord of the larger circle which is tangent to the smaller circle? **SSC CGL (Tier I) 07/12/2022 Shift II**

(a) 34 cm (b) 24 cm
(c) 48 cm (d) 12 cm

199. The number of parallel tangents of a circle with a given tangent is

SSC CGL (Tier I) 06/12/2022 Shift IV

(a) 1 (b) 2 (c) 3 (d) 4

200. ΔPQR is an isosceles triangle and $PQ = PR = 2a$ unit, $QR = a$ unit. Draw $PX \perp QR$, and find the length of PX.

SSC CGL (Tier I) 06/12/2022 Shift IV

(a) $\sqrt{5}a$ (b) $\frac{\sqrt{5}a}{2}$

(c) $\frac{\sqrt{10}a}{2}$ (d) $\frac{\sqrt{15}a}{2}$

201. In the figure, O is the centre of the circle. Its two chords AB and CD intersect each other at the point P within the circle. If $AB = 20$ cm, $PB = 12$ cm and $CP = 8$ cm, then find the measure of PD.

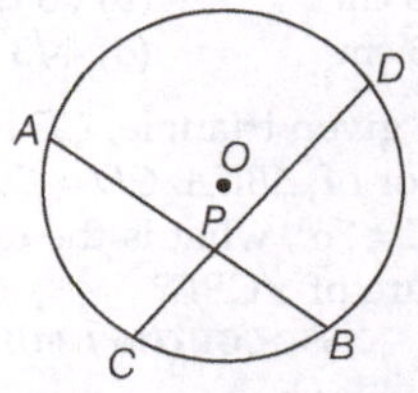

SSC CGL (Tier I) 06/12/2022 Shift III

(a) 12 cm (b) 11 cm
(c) 22 cm (d) 14 cm

202. A tangent is drawn from a point M to a circle, which meets the circle at T such that $MT = 12$ cm. A secant MAB intersects the circle at points A and B. If $MA = 8$ cm, what is the length (in cm) of the chord AB?

SSC CGL (Tier I) 06/12/2022 Shift II

(a) 16 (b) 10
(c) 12 (d) 9

203. How many circles can be drawn that passes through two fixed points?

SSC CGL (Tier I) 06/12/2022 Shift II

(a) Infinite (b) Only two
(c) One or two (d) Only one

204. A chord of length 40 cm is drawn in a circle having diameter 50 cm. What is the minimum distance of other parallel chord of length 30 cm in the same circle from 40 cm long chord? **SSC CGL (Tier I) 06/12/2022 Shift II**

(a) 10 cm (b) 15 cm
(c) 5 cm (d) 20 cm

205. The mid points of AB and AC of a ΔABC are X and Y, respectively. If $BC + XY = 24$ cm, then the value of $BC - XY$ is

SSC CGL (Tier I) 06/12/2022 Shift I

(a) 5 cm (b) 4 cm
(c) 6 cm (d) 8 cm

206. AD is the median of triangle ABC. P is the centroid of triangle ABC. If $AP = 14$ cm, then what is the length of PD? **SSC CGL (Tier I) 06/12/2022 Shift I**

(a) 14 cm (b) 28 cm
(c) 21 cm (d) 7 cm

207. The lengths (in cm) of three sides of a triangle are, respectively, 48, 55 and 73. What is the length (in cm) of the median joining the mid-point of the longest side to its opposite vertex? **SSC CGL (Tier I) 05/12/2022 Shift III**

(a) 27.5 (b) 73
(c) 24 (d) 36.5

208. In a ΔABC, the angle bisectors of the angle B and the angle C intersect at an angle of 105. What is the value of the angle A?

SSC CGL (Tier I) 05/12/2022 Shift III

(a) 52.5° (b) 75°
(c) 15° (d) 30°

209. ΔABC and ΔDEF are congruent respectively. If $AB = 6 = DE$, $BC = 8 = EF$ and $m\angle B = 30°$, then $m\angle D + m\angle C = $ ....

SSC CGL (Tier I) 05/12/2022 Shift II

(a) 160° (b) 120° (c) 130° (d) 150°

210. Find the number of common tangents, if $r_1 + r_2 = C_1C_2$. (With usual notations, r_1 and r_2 and C_1 and C_2 are the radii and centres of the two circles). **SSC CGL (Tier I) 05/12/2022 Shift I**

(a) 4 (b) 1 (c) 3 (d) 0

211. In a ΔABC, the median BE intersects AC at E. If $BG = 12$ cm, where G is the centroid, then BE is equal to **SSC CGL (Tier I) 03/12/2022 Shift IV**

(a) 16 cm (b) 18 cm
(c) 15 cm (d) 13 cm

212. Two identical circles each of radius 30 cm intersect each other such that the circumference of each one passes through the centre of the other. What is the area of the intersecting region? **SSC CGL (Tier I) 03/12/2022 Shift IV**

(a) $400\pi - 250\sqrt{3}$ cm^2
(b) $300\pi - 150\sqrt{3}$ cm^2
(c) $500\pi - 350\sqrt{3}$ cm^2
(d) $600\pi - 450\sqrt{3}$ cm^2

213. Suppose ΔABC be a right angled triangle where $\angle A = 90°$ and $AD \perp BC$. If area $(\Delta ABC) = 80$ cm^2 and $BC = 16$ cm, then the length of AD is **SSC CGL (Tier I) 03/12/2022 Shift III**

(a) 10 cm (b) 24 cm
(c) 18 cm (d) 12 cm

214. Let O be the centre of circle and P be a point in the exterior of circle. If PAB is the secant of the circle cutting circle at points A and B and T is the tangent of the circle, then calculate the length of PT. Given, $PA = 3$ cm and $AB = 9$ cm. **SSC CGL (Tier I) 03/12/2022 Shift III**

(a) $3\sqrt{3}$ cm (b) $4\sqrt{3}$ cm
(c) 6 cm (d) 8 cm

215. In an equilateral triangle ABC, D is the mid-point of side BC. If the length of BC is 8 cm, then the height of the triangle is **SSC CGL (Tier I) 03/12/2022 Shift II**

(a) 5.5 cm (b) 4.5 cm
(c) $6\sqrt{3}$ cm (d) $4\sqrt{3}$ cm

216. Select the correct option with respect to the given statement. Two tangents are drawn at the end of the diameter of a circle. **SSC CGL (Tier I) 03/12/2022 Shift I**

(a) They intersect each other
(b) They pass through origin
(c) They are parallel to each other
(d) They are perpendicular to each other.

217. O is the incentre of the triangle PQR. If angle $POR = 140°$, then what is the angle PQR ? **SSC CGL (Tier I) 02/12/2022 Shift IV**

(a) 40° (b) 140° (c) 100° (d) 70°

218. From the circumcentre L of ΔXYZ, perpendicular LM is drawn on side YZ. If $\angle YXZ = 60°$, then the measure of $\angle YLM$ is **SSC CGL (Tier I) 02/12/2022 Shift IV**

(a) 60° (b) 120° (c) 180° (d) 90°

219. The length of the tangent to a circle from a point P is 15 cm. Point P is 17 cm away from the centre. What is the radius of the circle? **SSC CGL (Tier I) 02/12/2022 Shift III**

(a) 7 cm (b) 9 cm
(c) 8 cm (d) 4 cm

220. In ΔABC, $AB = AC$, O is a point on BC such that $BO = CO$ and OD is perpendicular to AB and OE is perpendicular to AC. If $\angle BOD = 60°$, then measure of $\angle AOE$ is **SSC CGL (Tier I) 02/12/2022 Shift II**

(a) 120° (b) 60° (c) 30° (d) 90°

221. In the given figure, a circle is inscribed in ΔPQR, such that it touches the sides PQ, QR and RP at points D, E, F, respectively. If the lengths of the sides $PQ = 15$ cm, $QR = 11$ cm and $RP = 13$ cm, then find the length of PD. **SSC CGL (Tier I) 02/12/2022 Shift I**

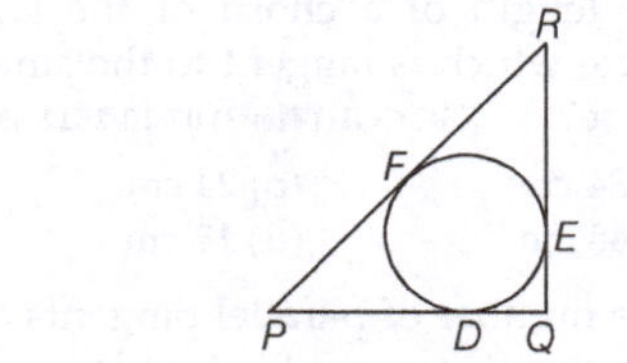

(a) 9 cm (b) 8 cm
(c) 7.5 cm (d) 8.5 cm

222. A chord of length 42 cm is drawn in a circle having diameter 58 cm. What is the minimum distance of other parallel chord of length 40 cm in the same circle from 42 cm long chord? **SSC CGL (Tier I) 01/12/2022 Shift IV**

(a) 4 cm (b) 1 cm
(c) 3 cm (d) 2 cm

223. Two equal circles of radius 8 cm intersect each other in such a way that each passes through the centre of the other. The length of the common chord is **SSC CGL (Tier I) 01/12/2022 Shift IV**

(a) $8\sqrt{3}$ cm (b) $\sqrt{3}$ cm
(c) $2\sqrt{3}$ cm (d) $4\sqrt{3}$ cm

224. In the given triangle, CD is the bisector of $\angle BCA$. $CD = DA$. If $\angle BDC = 76°$, what is the degree measure of $\angle CBD$? **SSC CGL (Tier I) 01/12/2022 Shift IV**

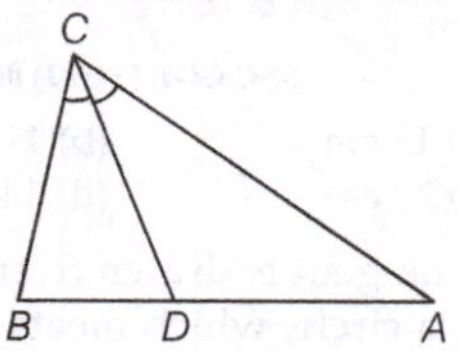

(a) 32° (b) 76°
(c) 80° (d) 66°

225. In triangle ABC, the bisector of angle BAC cuts the line BC at D. If $BD = 6$ and $BC = 14$ then what is the value of $AB : AC$? **SSC CGL (Tier I) 01/12/2022 Shift III**

(a) 3 : 4 (b) 7 : 3
(c) 3 : 10 (d) 3 : 7

226. From the following figure find $x + y + z$. **SSC CGL (Tier I) 01/12/2022 Shift III**

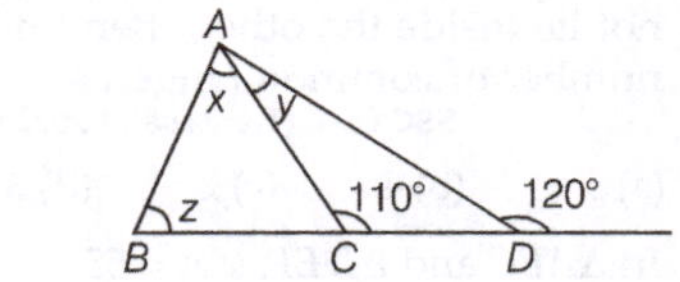

(a) 100° (b) 130°
(c) 120° (d) 110°

227. If areas of similar triangles ΔABC and ΔDEF are x^2cm^2 and y^2cm^2 respectively, and $EF = a$ cm, then BC (in cm) is **SSC CGL (Tier I) 01/12/2022 Shift II**

(a) $\frac{y^2}{a^2x^2}$ (b) $\frac{y}{ax}$
(c) $\frac{ax}{y}$ (d) $\frac{a^2x^2}{y^2}$

228. O is the centre of this circle. Tangent drawn from a point P, touches the circle at Q. If $PQ = 24$ cm and $OQ = 10$ cm, then what is the value of OP? **SSC CGL (Tier I) 01/12/2022 Shift II**

(a) 26 cm (b) 52 cm
(c) 13 cm (d) 15 cm

229. The ratio of the number of sides of two regular polygon is 1 : 2. If each interior angle of the first polygon is 140, then the measure of each interior angle of second polygon is **SSC CGL (Tier I) 01/12/2022 Shift I**

(a) 150° (b) 140°
(c) 170° (d) 160°

230. Two circles touch each other externally at P. AB is a direct common tangent to the two circles, A and B are points of contact and $\angle PAB = 40°$. The measure of $\angle ABP$ is **SSC CGL (Tier I) 01/12/2022 Shift I**

(a) 45° (b) 55°
(c) 50° (d) 40°

SSC CGL 2021 (Tier I)

231. In circle with centre O, a diameter AB is produced to a point P lying outside the circle and PT is a tangent to the circle at a point C on it. If $\angle BPT = 28°$, then what is the measure of $\angle BCP$? **SSC CGL (Tier I) 24/08/2021 Shift III**

(a) 62° (b) 45°
(c) 28° (d) 31°

232. ΔABC is right angled at B. BD is an altitude intersecting AC at D. If $AC = 9$ cm and $CD = 3$ cm, then find the measure of AB (in cm).
SSC CGL (Tier I) 24/08/2021 Shift III
(a) $3\sqrt{6}$ (b) 3
(c) $6\sqrt{3}$ (d) 6

233. ΔABC is right angled at B and D is a point of BC such that $BD = 5$ cm, $AD = 13$ cm and $AC = 37$ cm, then find the length of DC (in cm).
SSC CGL (Tier I) 24/08/2021 Shift III
(a) 25 (b) 30 (c) 5 (d) 35

234. In a circle with centre O, points A, B, C and D in this order are concyclic such that BD is a diameter of the circle. If $\angle BAC = 22°$, then find the measure (in degrees) of $\angle COD$.
SSC CGL (Tier I) 24/08/2021 Shift III
(a) 79 (b) 136
(c) 158 (d) 68

235. Points A, B and C are on a circle with centre O such that $\angle BOC = 84°$. If AC is produced to a point D such that $\angle BDC = 40°$, then find the measure of $\angle ABD$ (in degrees).
SSC CGL (Tier I) 24/08/2021 Shift II
(a) 98 (b) 92 (c) 56 (d) 102

236. In a circle with centre O, AB is a chord of length 10 cm. Tangents at points A and B intersect outside the circle at P. If $OP = 2\ OA$, then find the length (in cm) of AP.
SSC CGL (Tier I) 24/08/2021 Shift II
(a) 12.5 (b) 10
(c) 12 (d) 15

237. In ΔABC and ΔDEF, we have $\frac{AB}{DF} = \frac{BC}{DE} = \frac{AC}{EF}$, then which of the following is true?
SSC CGL (Tier I) 24/08/2021 Shift II
(a) $\Delta BCA \sim \Delta DEF$ (b) $\Delta DEF \sim \Delta ABC$
(c) $\Delta DEF \sim \Delta BAC$ (d) $\Delta CAB \sim \Delta DEF$

238. The vertices of a ΔABC lie on a circle with centre O. AO is produced to meet the circle at the point P. D is a point on BC such that, $AD \perp BC$. If $\angle B = 68°$ and $\angle C = 52°$, then the measure of $\angle DAP$ is
SSC CGL (Tier I) 24/08/2021 Shift I
(a) 18° (b) 16° (c) 12° (d) 28°

239. $ABCD$ is a cyclic quadrilateral such that when sides AB and DC are produced, they meet at E and sides AD and BC meet at F, when produced. If $\angle ADE = 80°$ and $\angle AED = 50°$, then what is the measure of $\angle AFB$?
SSC CGL (Tier I) 24/08/2021 Shift I
(a) 40° (b) 20° (c) 50° (d) 30°

240. Let $\Delta ABC \sim \Delta RPQ$ and $\frac{ar(\Delta ABC)}{ar(\Delta RPQ)} = \frac{16}{25}$. If $PQ = 4$ cm, $QR = 6$ cm and $PR = 7$ cm, then AC is equal to
SSC CGL (Tier I) 24/08/2021 Shift I
(a) 6 cm (b) 4.8 cm
(c) 3.6 cm (d) 7.2 cm

241. In ΔABC, D is a point on BC such that $\angle BAD = \frac{1}{2}\angle ADC$, $\angle BAC = 77°$ and $\angle C = 45°$. What is the measure of $\angle ADB$?
SSC CGL (Tier I) 23/08/2021 Shift II
(a) 77° (b) 64°
(c) 58° (d) 45°

242. In triangle ABC, D and E are the mid-points of AB and BC, respectively. If area $(\Delta BED) = 8\text{ cm}^2$, then what is the area $(ADEC)$ (in cm^2)?
SSC CGL (Tier I) 23/08/2021 Shift II
(a) 24 (b) 21
(c) 32 (d) 16

243. A tangent is drawn from a point P to a circle, which meets the circle at T such that $PT = 8$ cm. A secant PAB intersects the circle in points A and B. If $PA = 5$ cm, what is the length (in cm) of the chord AB?
SSC CGL (Tier I) 23/08/2021 Shift II
(a) 8.0 (b) 8.4
(c) 6.4 (d) 7.8

244. In triangle ABC, AD is the bisector of $\angle A$. If $AB = 5$ cm, $AC = 7.5$ cm and $BC = 10$ cm, then what is the distance of D from the mid-point of BC (in cm)?
SSC CGL (Tier I) 23/08/2021 Shift II
(a) 1.5 (b) 1
(c) 2.2 (d) 2

245. A circle is incribed in quadrilateral $ABCD$, touching sides AB, BC, CD and DA at P, Q, R and S, respectively. If $AS = 6$ cm, $BC = 12$ cm and $CR = 5$ cm, then the length of AB (in cm) is
SSC CGL (Tier I) 23/08/2021 Shift I
(a) 15 (b) 11
(c) 12 (d) 13

246. Vertices A, B, C and D of a quadrilateral $ABCD$ lie on a circle, $\angle A$ is three times $\angle C$ and $\angle D$ is two times $\angle B$. What is the difference between the measures of $\angle D$ and $\angle C$?
SSC CGL (Tier I) 23/08/2021 Shift I
(a) 65° (b) 45°
(c) 75° (d) 55°

247. Two circles of radii 18 cm and 16 cm intersect each other and the length of their common chord is 20 cm. What is the distance (in cm) between their centres?
SSC CGL (Tier I) 20/08/2021 Shift II
(a) $4\sqrt{14} - 2\sqrt{39}$ (b) $4\sqrt{10} - 2\sqrt{39}$
(c) $4\sqrt{10} + 2\sqrt{39}$ (d) $4\sqrt{14} + 2\sqrt{39}$

248. The angles of a triangle are in AP (arithmetic progression). If measure of the smallest angle is 50° less than that of the largest angle, then find the largest angle
SSC CGL (Tier I) 20/08/2021 Shift II
(a) 90° (b) 85°
(c) 80° (d) 75°

249. Points A, D, C, B and E are concyclic. If $\angle AEC = 50°$ and $\angle ABD = 30°$, then what is the measure (in degrees) of $\angle CBD$?
SSC CGL (Tier I) 20/08/2021 Shift II
(a) 20 (b) 10
(c) 15 (d) 30

250. Points P and Q are on the sides AB and BC, respectively of a triangle ABC, right angled at B. If $AQ = 11$ cm, $PC = 8$ cm, and $AC = 13$ cm, then find the length (in cm) of PQ.
SSC CGL (Tier I) 20/08/2021 Shift II
(a) $\sqrt{15}$ (b) 4.5
(c) 4 (d) $4\sqrt{7}$

251. ΔABC is an equilateral triangle. D and E are points on AB and AC respectively such that DE is parallel to BC and is equal to half the length of BC. If $AD + CE + BC = 30$ cm, then find the perimeter (in cm) of the quadrilateral $BCED$.
SSC CGL (Tier I) 20/08/2021 Shift I
(a) 37.5 (b) 25
(c) 45 (d) 35

252. In ΔABC, D is a point on side AB such that $BD = 3$ cm and $DA = 4$ cm. E is a point on BC such that $DE \parallel AC$. Then, area of a ΔBDE : Area of trapezium $ACED$ is
SSC CGL (Tier I) 20/08/2021 Shift I
(a) 40 : 9 (b) 33 : 16
(c) 16 : 33 (d) 9 : 40

253. In a circle with centre O and radius 13 cm, a chord AB is drawn. Tangents at A and B intersect at P such that $\angle APB = 60°$. If distance of AB from the centre O is 5 cm, then what is the length (in cm) of AP?
SSC CGL (Tier I) 20/08/2021 Shift I
(a) 12 (b) 11
(c) 22 (d) 24

254. In a circle, chords AB and CD intersect internally at E. If $CD = 16$ cm, $DE = 6$ cm, $AE = 12$ cm and $BE = x$ cm, then the value of x is
SSC CGL (Tier I) 20/08/2021 Shift I
(a) 6 (b) 17 (c) 5 (d) 9

255. In a circle with centre O, AB and CD are parallel chords on the opposite sides of a diameter. If $AB = 12$ cm, $CD = 18$ cm and the distance between the chords AB and CD is 15 cm, then find the radius of the circle (in cm).
SSC CGL (Tier I) 18/08/2021 Shift III

(a) $9\sqrt{13}$ (b) 9
(c) $3\sqrt{13}$ (d) 12

256. In a right angled ΔABC, the lengths of the sides containing the right angle are 5 cm and 12 cm respectively. A circle is inscribed in the ΔABC. What is the radius of the circle (in cm)?
SSC CGL (Tier I) 18/08/2021 Shift III

(a) 2 (b) 2.8
(c) 2.5 (d) 3

257. In ΔABC, AB and AC are produced to points D and E respectively. If the bisectors of $\angle CBD$ and $\angle BCE$ meet at point O, such that $\angle BOC = 63°$, then $\angle A = ?$ **SSC CGL (Tier I) 18/08/2021 Shift III**

(a) 36° (b) 27°
(c) 54° (d) 63°

258. Points A and B are on a circle with centre O. Point C is on the major arc AB. If $\angle OAC = 35°$ and $\angle OBC = 45°$, then what is the measure (in degrees) of the angle subtended by the minor arc AB at the centre?
SSC CGL (Tier I) 18/08/2021 Shift III

(a) 70 (b) 160
(c) 80 (d) 100

259. $\Delta ABC \sim \Delta DEF$. If the areas of ΔABC and ΔDEF are 100 cm^2 and 81 cm^2, respectively and the altitude of ΔDEF is 6.3 cm, then the corresponding altitude of ΔABC is
SSC CGL (Tier I) 18/08/2021 Shift I

(a) 9 cm (b) 5.6 cm
(c) 7 cm (d) 8.4 cm

260. AB is a chord of a circle in minor segment with centre O. C is a point on the minor arc of the circle between the points A and B. The tangents to the circle at A and B meet at the point P. If $\angle ACB = 102°$, then what is the measure of $\angle APB$?
SSC CGL (Tier I) 18/08/2021 Shift I

(a) 29° (b) 27° (c) 23° (d) 24°

261. Chord AB of a circle of radius 10 cm is at a distance 8 cm from the centre O. If tangents drawn at A and B intersect at P, then the length of the tangent AP (in cm) is
SSC CGL (Tier I) 18/08/2021 Shift I

(a) 7.5 cm (b) 4 cm
(c) 3.75 cm (d) 15 cm

262. Point P lies outside a circle with centre O. Tangents PA and PB are drawn to meet the circle at A and B respectively. If $\angle APB = 80°$, then $\angle OAB$ is equal to
SSC CGL (Tier I) 18/08/2021 Shift I

(a) 70° (b) 40° (c) 140° (d) 35°

263. In a circle, a 10 cm long chord is at a distance of 12 cm from the centre of the circle. Length of the diameter of the circle (in cm) is
SSC CGL (Tier I) 17/08/2021 Shift III

(a) 20 (b) 22 (c) 26 (d) 13

264. In ΔABC, D is a point on BC such that $BD : DC = 3:4$. E is a point on AD such that $AE : ED = 2:3$. Find the ratio ar (ΔECD) : ar (ΔAEB).
SSC CGL (Tier I) 17/08/2021 Shift III

(a) 9 : 8 (b) 2 : 1
(c) 1 : 2 (d) 8 : 9

265. Points A and B are on a circle with centre O. PAM and PBN are tangents to the circle at A and B respectively from a point P outside the circle. Point Q is on the major arc AB such that, $\angle QAM = 58°$ and $\angle QBN = 50°$, then find the measure (in degrees) of $\angle APB$.
SSC CGL (Tier I) 17/08/2021 Shift III

(a) 36 (b) 40
(c) 30 (d) 32

266. In a ΔABC, a point D lies on AB and points E and F lies on BC, such that DF is parallel to AC and DE is parallel to AF. If $BE = 4$ cm, $EF = 6$ cm, then find the length (in cm) of BC. **SSC CGL (Tier I) 17/08/2021 Shift I**

(a) 30 (b) 20
(c) 25 (d) 15

267. A ΔABC has sides 5 cm, 6 cm and 7 cm. AB extended touches a circle at P and AC extended touches the same circle at Q. Find the length (in cm) of AQ.
SSC CGL (Tier I) 17/08/2021 Shift I

(a) 13 (b) 9 (c) 11 (d) 12

268. In ΔABC, D and E are the points on the sides AB and AC, respectively and $DE \parallel BC$. $BC = 8$ cm and $DE = 5$ cm. If the area of $\Delta ADE = 45$ cm^2, then what is the area (in cm^2) of ΔABC? **SSC CGL (Tier I) 17/08/2021 Shift I**

(a) 115.2 (b) 105.2
(c) 125 (d) 64

269. ΔABC is inscribed in a circle with centre O, such that $\angle ACB = 115°$. O is joined to A. What is the measure of $\angle OAB$? **SSC CGL (Tier I) 16/08/2021 Shift III**

(a) 25° (b) 20° (c) 35° (d) 30°

270. In ΔABC, D is the mid-point of side AC and E is a point on side AB such that EC bisects BD at F. If $AE = 30$ cm, then the length of EB is
SSC CGL (Tier I) 16/08/2021 Shift III

(a) 20 cm (b) 10 cm
(c) 18 cm (d) 15 cm

271. In a circle with centre O, AB and CD are two parallel chords on the same side of the diameter. If $AB = 12$ cm, $CD = 18$ cm and distance between the chords AB and CD is 3 cm, then find the radius of the circle (in cm).
SSC CGL (Tier I) 16/08/2021 Shift III

(a) 12 (b) $3\sqrt{13}$
(c) 15 (d) 9

272. In ΔABC, $DE \parallel AB$, where D and E are the points on sides AC and BC, respectively. If $AD = x - 3$, $AC = 2x$, $BE = x - 2$ and $BC = 2x + 3$, then what is the value of x?
SSC CGL (Tier I) 16/08/2021 Shift III

(a) 10 (b) 9 (c) 12 (d) 8

273. In a circle with centre O and radius 5 cm. AB and CD are two parallel chords of lengths 6 cm and x cm, respectively and the chords are on the opposite side of the centre O. The distance between the chords is 7 cm. What is the value of x?
SSC CGL (Tier I) 16/08/2021 Shift I

(a) 9 (b) 12
(c) 8 (d) 10

274. In a circle with centre O, AB is a diameter and CD is a chord such that $\angle ABC = 34°$ and $CD = BD$. What is the measure of $\angle DBC$?
SSC CGL (Tier I) 16/08/2021 Shift I

(a) 24° (b) 28°
(c) 32° (d) 30°

275. Angle between the angle bisectors of two angles $\angle B$ and $\angle C$ of a ΔABC is 132°, then the value of $\angle A$ is
SSC CGL (Tier I) 16/08/2021 Shift I

(a) 62° (b) 72° (c) 84° (d) 48°

276. In ΔABC, $\angle A = 90°$, $AD \perp BC$ at D. If $AB = 12$ cm and $AC = 16$ cm, then what is the length (in cm) of BD?
SSC CGL (Tier I) 16/08/2021 Shift I

(a) 7.8 (b) 6.4 (c) 7.2 (d) 8.4

277. The radii of two concentric circles are 12 cm and 13 cm. AB is a diameter of the bigger circle. BD is a tangent to a smaller circle touching it at D. Find the length (in cm) of AD? (correct to one decimal place)
SSC CGL (Tier I) 13/08/2021 Shift III

(a) 23.5 (b) 25.5
(c) 24.5 (d) 17.6

278. A circle touches all the four sides of a quadrilateral $ABCD$ whose sides are $AB = 8.4$ cm, $BC = 9.8$ cm and $CD = 5.6$ cm. The length of side AD, (in cm), is **SSC CGL (Tier I) 13/08/2021 Shift III**

(a) 2.8 (b) 4.2 (c) 3.8 (d) 4.9

279. In ΔABC, $\angle C = 90°$ and Q is the mid-point of BC. If $AB = 10$ cm and $AC = 2\sqrt{10}$ cm, then the length of AQ is **SSC CGL (Tier I) 13/08/2021 Shift III**

(a) $5\sqrt{2}$ cm (b) $3\sqrt{5}$ cm
(c) $\sqrt{55}$ cm (d) $5\sqrt{3}$ cm

280. Sides AB and DC of a cyclic quadrilateral $ABCD$ are produced to meet at E and sides AD and BC are produced to meet at F. If $\angle ADC = 78°$ and $\angle BEC = 52°$, then the measure of $\angle AFB$ is **SSC CGL (Tier I) 13/08/2021 Shift I**

(a) 28° (b) 26° (c) 32° (d) 30°

281. A chord 21 cm long is drawn in a circle of diameter 25 cm. The perpendicular distance of the chord from the centre is **SSC CGL (Tier I) 13/08/2021 Shift I**

(a) $\sqrt{41}$ (b) $\sqrt{23}$ (c) $\sqrt{56}$ (d) $\sqrt{46}$

282. $\Delta ABC \sim \Delta PQR$. The areas of ΔABC and ΔPQR are 64 cm^2 and 81 cm^2, respectively and AD and PT are the medians of ΔABC and ΔPQR, respectively. If $PT = 10.8$ cm, then $AD = ?$ **SSC CGL (Tier I) 13/08/2021 Shift I**

(a) 8.4 cm (b) 9 cm
(c) 9.6 cm (d) 12 cm

283. Let $\Delta ABC \sim \Delta PQR$ and $\frac{ar(\Delta ABC)}{ar(\Delta PQR)} = \frac{144}{49}$, If $AB = 12$ cm, $BC = 7$ cm and $AC = 9$ cm, then PR (in cm) is equal to **SSC CGL (Tier I) 13/08/2021 Shift I**

(a) $\frac{49}{12}$ (b) $\frac{108}{7}$ (c) $\frac{21}{4}$ (d) 12

SSC CGL 2020 (Tier I)

284. AB is a diameter of a circle with centre O. The tangent at a point C on the circle meets AB produced at Q. If $\angle CAB = 42°$, then what is the measure of $\angle CQA$? **SSC CGL (Tier I) 07/03/2020 Shift II**

(a) 17° (b) 6° (c) 5° (d) 7°

285. In ΔABC, D, E and F are the mid-points of sides AB, BC and CA, respectively. If $AB = 12$ cm, $BC = 20$ cm and $CA = 15$ cm, then the value of $\frac{1}{2}(DE + EF + DF)$ is **SSC CGL (Tier I) 07/03/2020 Shift II**

(a) 23.5 cm (b) 11.75 cm
(c) 5.88 cm (d) 15.67 cm

286. In quadrilateral $PQRS$, $RM \perp QS$, $PN \perp QS$ and $QS = 6$ cm. If $RM = 3$ cm and $PN = 2$ cm, then the area of $PQRS$ is **SSC CGL (Tier I) 07/03/2020 Shift II**

(a) 15 cm^2 (b) 13 cm^2
(c) 14 cm^2 (d) 11 cm^2

287. In the given figure, ΔABC is an isosceles triangle, in which $AB = AC$, $AD \perp BC$, $BC = 6$ cm and $AD = 4$ cm. The length of AB is **SSC CGL (Tier I) 07/03/2020 Shift I**

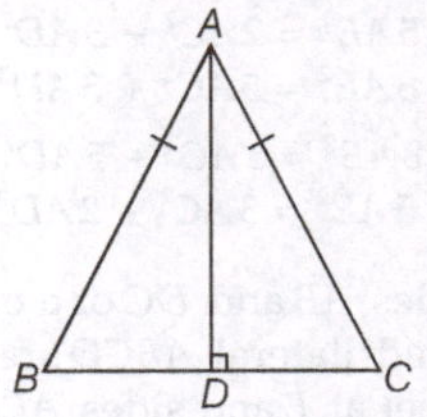

(a) 7 cm (b) 6 cm
(c) 5 cm (d) 4 cm

288. In the figure, if $\angle A = 100°$, then $\angle C = ?$ **SSC CGL (Tier I) 07/03/2020 Shift I**

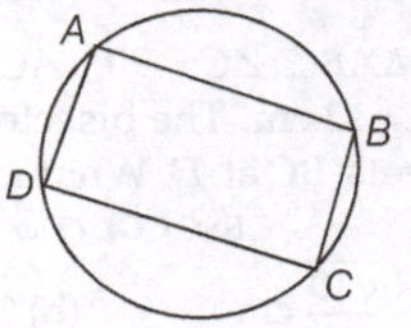

(a) 50° (b) 90° (c) 80° (d) 100°

289. In the given figure, the measure of $\angle BAC$ is **SSC CGL (Tier I) 07/03/2020 Shift I**

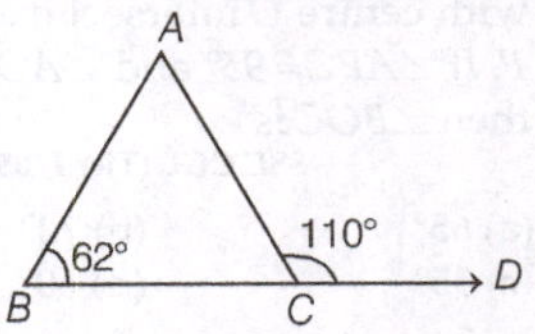

(a) 56° (b) 62°
(c) 58° (d) 48°

290. In the given figure, MP is tangent to a circle with centre A and NQ is a tangent to a circle with centre B. If $MP = 15$ cm, $NQ = 8$ cm, $PA = 17$ cm and $BQ = 10$ cm, then AB is **SSC CGL (Tier I) 07/03/2020 Shift I**

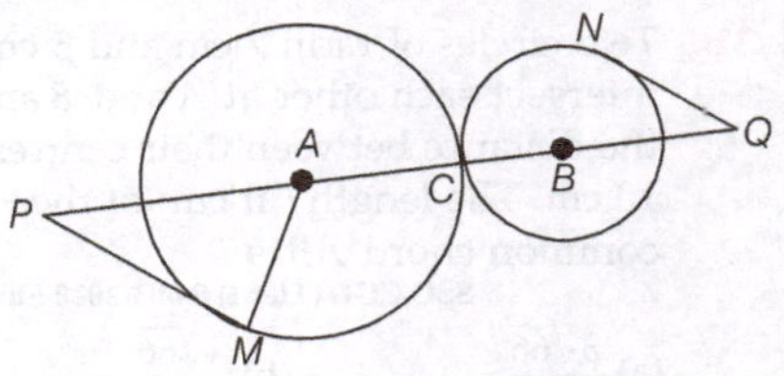

(a) 28 cm (b) 14 cm
(c) 13.5 cm (d) 23 cm

291. A, B and C are three points on a circle such that the angles subtended by the chords AB and AC at the centre O are 80° and 120°, respectively. The value of $\angle BAC$ is **SSC CGL (Tier I) 06/03/2020 Shift III**

(a) 75° (b) 85°
(c) 70° (d) 80°

292. In ΔABC, if the ratio of angles is in the proportion 3 : 5 : 4, then the difference between the biggest and the smallest angles (in degrees)is **SSC CGL (Tier I) 06/03/2020 Shift III**

(a) 35° (b) 25°
(c) 30° (d) 20°

293. Two circles of radii 8 cm and 6 cm touch each other externally. The length of the direct common tangent is **SSC CGL (Tier I) 06/03/2020 Shift III**

(a) 13.86 (b) 20
(c) 24 (d) 10.12

294. In a ΔABC, DE is parallel to BC, $AD = a$, $DB = a + 4$, $AE = 2a + 3$, $EC = 7a$. What is the value of 'a', if $a > 0$? **SSC CGL (Tier I) 06/03/2020 Shift III**

(a) 3 (b) 5
(c) 6 (d) 4

295. In the given figure, if $AB = 8$ cm, $AC = 10$ cm, $\angle ABD = 90°$ and $AD = 17$ cm, then the measure of CD is **SSC CGL (Tier I) 06/03/2020 Shift II**

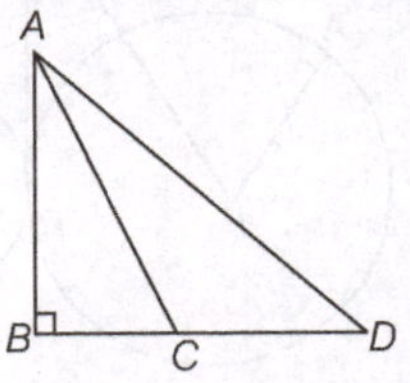

(a) 10 cm (b) 11 cm
(c) 9 cm (d) 8 cm

296. In the given figure, if $AB = 10$ cm, $CD = 7$ cm, $SD = 4$ cm and $AS = 5$ cm, then $BC = ?$ **SSC CGL (Tier I) 06/03/2020 Shift II**

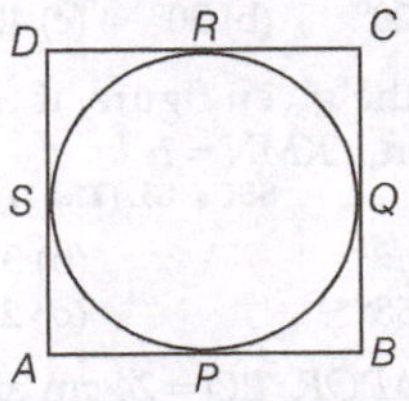

(a) 8 cm (b) 7.5 cm
(c) 9 cm (d) 6 cm

297. In the given figure, if $\angle APO = 35°$, then which of the following options is correct? **SSC CGL (Tier I) 06/03/2020 Shift II**

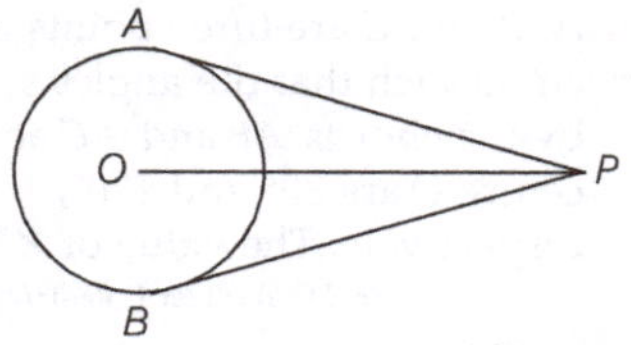

(a) $\angle BPO = 55°$ (b) $\angle APB = 60°$
(c) $\angle BPO = 35°$ (d) $\angle APB = 80°$

298. ABC is an equilateral triangle. P, Q and R are the mid-points of sides AB, BC and CA, respectively. If the length of the sides of the ΔABC is 8 cm, then the area of ΔPQR is
SSC CGL (Tier I) 06/03/2020 Shift I

(a) $\frac{\sqrt{3}}{3}\text{cm}^2$ (b) $\frac{\sqrt{3}}{4}\text{cm}^2$
(c) $4\sqrt{3}\text{ cm}^2$ (d) $8\sqrt{3}\text{ cm}^2$

299. Two tangents PA and PB are drawn to a circle with centre O from an external point P. If $\angle OAB = 30°$, then $\angle APB$ is
SSC CGL (Tier I) 06/03/2020 Shift I

(a) 120° (b) 30° (c) 15° (d) 60°

300. In the figure, two circles with centres P and Q touch externally at R. Tangents AT and BT meet the common tangent TR at T. If $AP = 6$ cm and $PT = 10$ cm, then $BT = ?$
SSC CGL (Tier I) 05/03/2020 Shift III

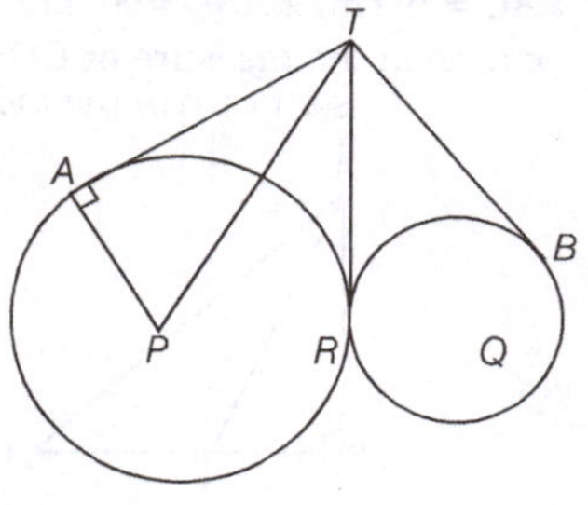

(a) 8 cm (b) 10 cm
(c) 6 cm (d) 12 cm

301. If angles of a triangle are in the ratio of 2 : 3 : 4, then the measure of the smallest angle is
SSC CGL (Tier I) 05/03/2020 Shift III

(a) 20° (b) 30° (c) 40° (d) 50°

302. In the given figure, if $\angle KLN = 58°$, then $\angle KMN = ?$
SSC CGL (Tier I) 05/03/2020 Shift III

(a) 42° (b) 32°
(c) 58° (d) 26°

303. In ΔPQR, $PQ = 24$ cm and $\angle Q = 58°$. S and T are the points on side PQ and PR respectively, such that $\angle STR = 122°$. If $PS = 14$ cm and $PT = 12$ cm, then the length of RT is
SSC CGL (Tier I) 05/03/2020 Shift II

(a) 14.8 cm (b) 16 cm
(c) 15 cm (d) 16.4 cm

304. Diameter AB of a circle with centre O is produced to a point P such that $PO = 16.8$ cm. PQR is a secant which intersects the circle at Q and R such that $PQ = 12$ cm and $PR = 19.2$ cm. The length of AB (in cm) is
SSC CGL (Tier I) 05/03/2020 Shift II

(a) 14.2 (b) 15.2
(c) 15.8 (d) 14.4

305. In ΔABC, $\angle B = 90°$. If points D and E are on side BC such that $BD = DE = EC$, then which of the following is true?
SSC CGL (Tier I) 05/03/2020 Shift II

(a) $5AE^2 = 2AC^2 + 3AD^2$
(b) $8AE^2 = 5AC^2 + 3AD^2$
(c) $8AE^2 = 3AC^2 + 5AD^2$
(d) $5AE^2 = 3AC^2 + 2AD^2$

306. Sides AB and DC of a cyclic quadrilateral $ABCD$ are produced to meet at E and sides AD and BC are produced to meet at F. If $\angle ADC = 75°$ and $\angle BEC = 52°$, then the difference between $\angle BAD$ and $\angle AFB$ is **SSC CGL (Tier I) 05/03/2020 Shift I**

(a) 31 (b) 22 (c) 21 (d) 23

307. In ΔABC, $\angle C = 90°$, $AC = 5$ cm and $BC = 12$ cm. The bisector of $\angle A$ meets BC at D. What is the length of AD? **SSC CGL (Tier I) 05/03/2020 Shift I**

(a) $\frac{5\sqrt{13}}{3}$ cm (b) $2\sqrt{13}$ cm
(c) $\frac{4}{3}\sqrt{13}$ cm (d) $\frac{2}{3}\sqrt{13}$ cm

308. Two chords AB and CD of a circle with centre O intersect each other at P. If $\angle APC = 95°$ and $\angle AOD = 110°$, then $\angle BOC$ is
SSC CGL (Tier I) 05/03/2020 Shift I

(a) 65° (b) 70°
(c) 55° (d) 60°

309. D is the mid-point of side BC of ΔABC. Point E lies on AC such that $CE = \frac{1}{3}AC$. BE and AD intersect at G. What is $\frac{AG}{GD}$?
SSC CGL (Tier I) 05/03/2020 Shift I

(a) 4 : 1 (b) 8 : 3
(c) 3 : 1 (d) 5 : 2

310. Two circles of radii 7 cm and 5 cm intersect each other at A and B and the distance between their centres is 10 cm. The length (in cm) of the common chord AB is
SSC CGL (Tier I) 04/03/2020 Shift III

(a) $\frac{3\sqrt{66}}{5}$ (b) $\frac{4\sqrt{66}}{5}$
(c) $\frac{2\sqrt{74}}{5}$ (d) $\frac{3\sqrt{74}}{5}$

311. In ΔABC, $AC = 8.4$ cm and $BC = 14$ cm. P is a point on AB such that $CP = 11.2$ cm and $\angle ACP = \angle B$. What is the length (in cm) of BP?
SSC CGL (Tier I) 04/03/2020 Shift III

(a) 4.12 (b) 2.8
(c) 3.78 (d) 3.6

312. In ΔABC, $\angle B = 72°$ and $\angle C = 44°$. Side BC is produced to D. The bisectors of $\angle B$ and $\angle ACD$ meet at E. What is the measure of $\angle BEC$?
SSC CGL (Tier I) 04/03/2020 Shift III

(a) 58° (b) 46°
(c) 32° (d) 36°

SSC CPO SI 2024

313. A scalene triangle ABC has two sides whose measures are 3.8 cm and 6 cm, respectively. Which of the following cannot be the measure (in cm) of its third side?
SSC CPO 29/06/2024 Shift-III

(a) 3.0 (b) 2.4
(c) 2.7 (d) 2.2

314. In a circle, the chords AB and CD intersect each other at point L (internally). If $AL = 8$ cm, $LB = 6$ cm and $LD = 5$ cm, then find the CL.
SSC CPO 29/06/2024 Shift-III

(a) 10.6 cm (b) 8.6 cm
(c) 7.6 cm (d) 9.6 cm

315. The side PR of a ΔPQR is extended to S such that $QR = RS$. If $\angle PRQ = 86°$, then find the value of $\angle PSQ$. **SSC CPO 29/06/2024 Shift-III**

(a) 43° (b) 86° (c) 54° (d) 94°

316. Taking any three of the line segments out of segments of length 2 cm, 5 cm, 7 cm and 8 cm, the number of triangles that can be formed is **SSC CPO 29/06/2024 Shift-II**

(a) 1 (b) 3 (c) 4 (d) 2

317. The secant CD intersects the circle at E and CF is tangent to the circle at F. If the length of the secant CD is equal to 20 cm and the length of tangent CF is 15 cm, find the length of the chord DE.
SSC CPO 29/06/2024 Shift-II

(a) 8.75 cm (b) 11.25 cm
(c) 9.25 cm (d) 3.75 cm

318. The distance between the centres of the two circles, with radii 3 cm and 2 cm, respectively, is 13 cm. The length (in cm) of a transverse common tangent is:
SSC CPO 29/06/2024 Shift-I

(a) 18 cm (b) 9 cm
(c) 16 cm (d) 12 cm

319. If one angle of triangle PQR is greater than the sum of the other two, the triangle PQR will be **SSC CPO 29/06/2024 Shift-I**

(a) equilateral
(b) acute angle
(c) obtuse angle
(d) right angle

320. The sum of any two sides of a triangle is **SSC CPO 28/06/2024 Shift-III**

(a) less than the third side
(b) greater than the third side
(c) equal to third side
(d) less than or equal to third side

321. If the sides of a triangle are 7, 12 and x, and x is an integer, then find the number of possible values of x. **SSC CPO 28/06/2024 Shift-II**

(a) 13 (b) 14 (c) 12 (d) 15

322. What is the length (in cm) of chord PQ in a circle with a radius of 7 cm, where a diameter AB and non-diameter chord PQ intersect perpendicularly at point C, and the ratio of AC to BC is 4 : 3? **SSC CPO 28/06/2024 Shift-II**

(a) $6\sqrt{3}$ (b) $2\sqrt{3}$
(c) $4\sqrt{3}$ (d) $8\sqrt{3}$

323. If the three sides of a triangle are 12, 22 and m units, then which of the following is correct? **SSC CPO 28/06/2024 Shift-II**

(a) $10 \leq m < 34$
(b) $10 \leq m \leq 34$
(c) $10 < m < 34$
(d) $10 < m \leq 34$

324. The angles of a triangle are in the ratio 1 : 2 : 3, then find the ratio of the corresponding sides. **SSC CPO 28/06/2024 Shift-I**

(a) $1 : \sqrt{3} : 2$ (b) $1 : 2 : \sqrt{3}$
(c) $1 : \sqrt{2} : 3$ (d) 1 : 2 : 3

325. Which of the following statements is/are correct?

A. A triangle can have all angles less than 60°.
B. A triangle can have one obtuse angle.
C. A triangle can have two right angles.
D. A triangle can have two acute angles. **SSC CPO 28/06/2024 Shift-I**

(a) A (b) B and D
(c) B (d) A and C

326. Two similar triangles of ΔXYZ and ΔLMN. If area of $(\Delta XYZ) = 16$ cm^2, area of $(\Delta LMN) = 25$ cm^2 and $YZ = 2.4$ cm, then the measure of MN is. **SSC CPO 27/06/2024 Shift-III**

(a) 3 cm (b) 1 cm
(c) 4 cm (d) 2 cm

327. Triangle DEF is an equilateral triangle with a side length of 12 cm. If Point G is the mid-point of side DE, what is the length (in cm) of side FG? **SSC CPO 27/06/2024 Shift-III**

(a) 12 (b) $6\sqrt{3}$ (c) 6 (d) $3\sqrt{6}$

328. If two circles of radii 35 cm and 25 cm touch each other externally, then the length (in cm) of a common tangent is (rounded off to 2 decimal places) **SSC CPO 27/06/2024 Shift-III**

(a) 60.00 (b) 59.16
(c) 45.29 (d) 52.25

329. If L is the mid-point of the side YZ of XYZ, and the area of XYL is 13 cm^2, then the area (in cm^2) of XYZ is **SSC CPO 27/06/2024 Shift-II**

(a) 24 (b) 22
(c) 20 (d) 26

330. Two circles with centers B and D have radii $DA = 8$ cm and $BC = x$ cm, respectively. AC is tangent to both circles. If DB and AC intersect the Point E, $AE = 12$ cm and $EC = 18$cm, then find the value of x (in cm). **SSC CPO 27/06/2024 Shift-II**

(a) 12 (b) 11 (c) 10 (d) 13

331. From external point A, tangents AP and AQ are drawn to a circle with centre O. If $\angle APQ = 40°$, then find $\angle POQ$. **SSC CPO 27/06/2024 Shift-I**

(a) 60° (b) 100°
(c) 110° (d) 80°

332. In ΔABC, AD is the angle bisector of $\angle A$, meeting the side BC at D. If $BD = 5$ cm, $BC = 7.5$ cm, then $AB : AC$ is **SSC CPO 27/06/2024 Shift-I**

(a) 2 : 1 (b) 1 : 3
(c) 1 : 2 (d) 3 : 1

333. In ΔABC, P is a point on AB such that $PB : AP = 3 : 4$ and PQ is parallel to AC. If AR and QS are perpendicular to PC and $QS = 9$ cm, what is the length (in cm) of AR? **SSC CPO 27/06/2024 Shift-I**

(a) 35 (b) 28
(c) 21 (d) 14

SSC CPO SI 2023

334. In ΔABC with sides 8 cm, 9 cm and 12 cm, the angle bisector of the largest angle divides the opposite sides into two segments. What is the length of the shorter segment? **SSC CPO 05/10/2023 Shift III**

(a) $5\frac{11}{17}$ cm (b) $4\frac{11}{17}$ cm
(c) $6\frac{13}{17}$ cm (d) $3\frac{9}{17}$ cm

335. PQR is right angled at Q such that $PQ = (x - y), QR = x$ and $PR = (x + y)$. S is a point on QR such that $QS = PQ$. The ratio $QS : SR$ for any values of x and y is **SSC CPO 05/10/2023 Shift III**

(a) 3 : 1 (b) 2 : 1
(c) 1 : 2 (d) 1 : 3

336. The chord of a circle is equal to its radius. Find the difference between the angle subtended by this chord at the minor arc and major arc of the circle. **SSC CPO 05/10/2023 Shift III**

(a) 30° (b) 120° (c) 60° (d) 150°

337. The length of the common chord of two intersecting circles is 24 cm. If the diameter of the circles are 30 cm and 26 cm, then the distance between the centres (in cm) is **SSC CPO 05/10/2023 Shift III**

(a) 16 cm (b) 14 cm
(c) 18 cm (d) 12 cm

338. Let ABC, PQR be two congruent triangle such that $\angle A = \angle P = 90°$. If $BC = 17$ cm, $PR = 8$ cm, find AB (in cm). **SSC CPO 04/10/2023 Shift II**

(a) 12 (b) 15 (c) 14 (d) 9

339. In a ΔPQR, $\angle P : \angle Q : \angle R = 3 : 4 : 8$. The shortest side and the longest side of the triangle, respectively, are **SSC CPO 04/10/2023 Shift II**

(a) PQ and PR (b) QR and PR
(c) PQ and QR (d) QR and PQ

340. In a circle centred at O, PQ is a tangent at P. Furthermore, AB is the chord of the circle and is extended to Q. If $PQ = 12$ cm and $QB = 8$ cm, then the length of AB is equal to **SSC CPO 04/10/2023 Shift II**

(a) 20 cm (b) 4 cm
(c) 10 cm (d) 8 cm

341. In a triangle ABC, if $\angle B = 90°$, $\angle C = 45°$ and $AC = 4$ cm, then the value of BC is **SSC CPO 04/10/2023 Shift II**

(a) $\sqrt{2}$ cm (b) 4 cm
(c) $2\sqrt{2}$ cm (d) $4\sqrt{2}$ cm

342. ΔPQR is an equilateral triangle inscribed in a circle. S is any point on the arc QR. Measure of $\frac{1}{2}\angle PSQ$ is **SSC CPO 03/10/2023 Shift I**

(a) 20° (b) 15° (c) 30° (d) 60°

343. If the hypotenuse of a right-angled triangle is 29 cm and the sum of the other two sides is 41 cm, then the difference between the other two sides is **SSC CPO 03/10/2023 Shift I**

(a) 5 cm (b) 1 cm
(c) 2 cm (d) 10 cm

SSC CPO SI 2022-2020

344. Two circles touch each other externally. The radius of the first circle with centre A is 18cm. The radius of the second circle with centre B is 8cm. Find the length of their common tangent CD. **SSC CPO 11/11/2022**

(a) 23 cm (b) 26 cm
(c) 24 cm (d) 25 cm

345. If in ΔABC, $AB = AC$ and $\angle ACD = 125°$, then $\angle BAC$ is **SSC CPO 11/11/2022**

(a) 75° (b) 55°
(c) 60° (d) 70°

346. AB is a common tangent to both the circles in the given figure. Find the distance (correct to two decimal places) between the centres of the two circles. **SSC CPO 10/11/2022**

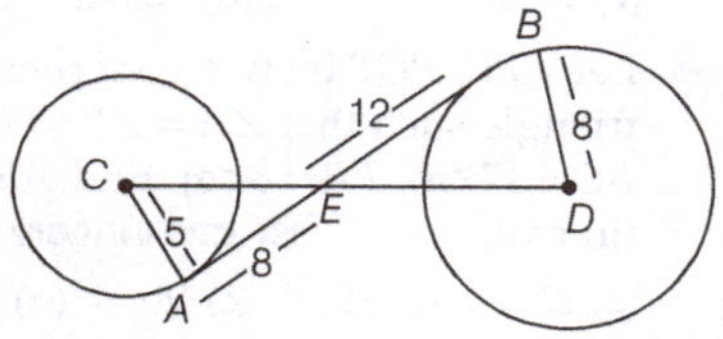

(a) 18.98 units (b) 23.85 units
(c) 26.59 units (d) 21.62 units

347. The sides PQ and PR of ΔPQR are produced to points S and T, respectively. The bisectors of $\angle SQR$ and $\angle TRQ$ meet at U. If $\angle QUR = 59°$, then the measure of $\angle P$ is **SSC CPO 25/11/2020 Shift II**

(a) 31° (b) 62°
(c) 41° (d) 49°

348. In a circle with centre O, AD is a diameter and AC is a chord. Point B is on AC such that, $OB = 7$ cm and $\angle OBA = 60°$. If $\angle DOC = 60°$, then what is the length of BC? **SSC CPO 25/11/2020 Shift II**

(a) $3\sqrt{7}$ cm (b) 3.5 cm
(c) 7 cm (d) $5\sqrt{7}$ cm

349. In ΔABC, $\angle A = 54°$. If I is the incentre of the triangle, then the measure of $\angle BIC$ is **SSC CPO 25/11/2020 Shift II**

(a) 68° (b) 54°
(c) 148° (d) 117°

350. PA and PB are two tangents from a point P outside the circle with centre O. If A and B are points on the circle such that $\angle APB = 142°$, then $\angle OAB$ is equal to **SSC CPO 25/11/2020 Shift I**

(a) 31° (b) 58°
(c) 71° (d) 64°

351. In ΔABC, $BD \perp AC$ at D. E is a point on BC such that $\angle BEA = x°$. If $\angle EAC = 62°$ and $\angle EBD = 60°$, then the value of x is **SSC CPO 25/11/2020 Shift I**

(a) 92° (b) 78° (c) 76° (d) 68°

352. In a ΔABC, the bisector of $\angle B$ and $\angle C$ meet at O in the triangle. If $\angle BOC = 134°$, then the measure of $\angle A$ is **SSC CPO 25/11/2020 Shift I**

(a) 116° (b) 104°
(c) 52° (d) 88°

353. $ABCD$ is a cyclic quadrilateral such that AB is a diameter of the circle circumscribing it and $\angle ADC = 118°$. What is the measure of $\angle BAC$? **SSC CPO 24/11/2020 Shift I**

(a) 28° (b) 45°
(c) 32° (d) 30°

354. In ΔABC, AB and AC are produced to points D and E, respectively. If the bisectors of $\angle CBD$ and $\angle BCE$ meet at the point O, and $\angle BOC = 57°$, then $\angle A$ is equal to **SSC CPO 24/11/2020 Shift I**

(a) 93° (b) 66°
(c) 114° (d) 57°

355. Let $\Delta ABC \sim \Delta RPQ$ and $\frac{ar(\Delta ABC)}{ar(\Delta PQR)} = \frac{4}{9}$.

If $AB = 3$ cm, $BC = 4$ cm and $AC = 5$ cm, then RP (in cm) is equal to **SSC CPO 24/11/2020 Shift I**

(a) 6 (b) 5 (c) 4.5 (d) 12

356. In a ΔABC, the bisectors of $\angle B$ and $\angle C$ meet at O. If $\angle BOC = 142°$, then the measure of $\angle A$ is **SSC CPO 23/11/2020 Shift I**

(a) 52° (b) 68°
(c) 104° (d) 116°

357. A circle is inscribed in a ΔABC. It touches sides AB, BC and AC at points R, P and Q, respectively. If $AQ = 3.5$ cm, $PC = 4.5$ cm and $BR = 7$ cm, then the perimeter (in cm) of the ΔABC is **SSC CPO 23/11/2020 Shift I**

(a) 30 (b) 15 (c) 28 (d) 45

358. In ΔABC, $BD \perp AC$ at D, E is a point on BC such that $\angle BEA = x°$. If $\angle EAC = 46°$ and $\angle EBD = 60°$, then the value of x is **SSC CPO 23/11/2020 Shift I**

(a) 72° (b) 78°
(c) 68° (d) 76°

359. PA and PB are two tangents from a point P outside the circle with centre O. If A and B are points on the circle such that $\angle APB = 128°$, then $\angle OAB$ is equal to **SSC CPO 23/11/2020 Shift I**

(a) 72° (b) 52°
(c) 38° (d) 64°

SSC CHSL 2024 (Tier I & II)

360. A quadrilateral having equal diagonals and equal opposite sides is always a .... **SSC CHSL (Tier II) 18/11/2024 Shift-I**

(a) trapezium (b) kite
(c) rhombus (d) rectangle

361. $ABCD$ is a trapezium in which AB is parallel to CD and E and F are the mid-points of non-parallel sides AD and BC. If EF is parallel to AB, $AB = 28$ cm and $CD = 18$ cm, then find EF (in cm). **SSC CHSL (Tier II) 18/11/2024 Shift-I**

(a) 23 (b) 46 (c) 5 (d) 10

362. In a triangle PQR, incentre is A and $\angle QAR = 116°$. Find the measure of $\angle QPR$. **SSC CHSL (Tier II) 18/11/2024 Shift-I**

(a) 54° (b) 27°
(c) 26° (d) 52°

363. In an obtuse-angled triangle ABC, the length of its longest side AB is 50 cm and one of the other two sides is 42 cm. If the area of the triangle is 294 cm^2, what is the length (in cm) of its third side? **SSC CHSL (Tier I) 11/07/2024 Shift-IV**

(a) $8\sqrt{35}$ (b) $15\sqrt{21}$
(c) $2\sqrt{58}$ (d) $12\sqrt{43}$

364. If L is the mid-point of side BC of ΔABC and the area of ΔABL is 15 cm^2 then the area (in sq cm) of ΔABC is **SSC CHSL (Tier I) 11/07/2024 Shift-IV**

(a) 32 (b) 30 (c) 27 (d) 25

365. In ΔABC, D and E are points on sides AB and AC, such that $DE \parallel BC$. If $AD = x$, $DB = x - 3$, $AE = x + 3$ and $EC = x - 2$, then the value of x is **SSC CHSL (Tier I) 11/07/2024 Shift-IV**

(a) 5.2 (b) 4.0
(c) 4.5 (d) 4.2

366. There are two circles touching each other externally. The radius of the first circle with centre O is 12 cm. The radius of the second circle with centre A is 5 cm. Find the length of their common tangent touching the two circles at points P and Q. **SSC CHSL (Tier I) 11/07/2024 Shift-III**

(a) $4\sqrt{15}$ cm (b) $14\sqrt{5}$ cm
(c) $5\sqrt{41}$ cm (d) $5\sqrt{14}$ cm

367. $\Delta ABC \sim \Delta EDF$ and area (ΔABC) : area $(\Delta EDF) = 1 : 4$. If $AB = 7$ cm, $BC = 8$ cm and $CA = 9$ cm, then DF is equal to **SSC CHSL (Tier I) 11/07/2024 Shift-III**

(a) 16 cm (b) 18 cm
(c) 14 cm (d) 12 cm

368. Let C be a circle with centre O and PQ be the diameter of C. Let AB be a chord on C. If $\angle QOB = 40°$, $\angle AOP = 80°$, then find $\angle AOB$.
SSC CHSL (Tier I) 11/07/2024 Shift-III

(a) 100° (b) 60°
(c) 90° (d) 70°

369. ΔABC and ΔDEF are similar triangles and their areas are 81 cm^2 and 144 cm^2, respectively. If $EF = 20$ cm, then what is the value of BC?
SSC CHSL (Tier I) 11/07/2024 Shift-III

(a) 9 cm (b) 13 cm
(c) 15 cm (d) 12 cm

370. O is the centre of the circle. Its two chord AB and CD intersect each other at the point P (internally) within the circle. If $AB = 22$ cm, $PB = 14$ cm, $CP = 8$ cm, then find the value of PD.
SSC CHSL (Tier I) 11/07/2024 Shift-II

(a) 14 cm (b) 11 cm
(c) 22 cm (d) 12 cm

371. In $\Delta DEW, AB \parallel EW$. If $AD = 4$ cm, $DE = 12$ cm and $DW = 24$ cm, then find the length of DB.
SSC CHSL (Tier I) 11/07/2024 Shift-II

(a) 7 cm (b) 6 cm
(c) 9 cm (d) 8 cm

372. Which of the following is not true regarding a circle?
SSC CHSL (Tier I) 11/07/2024 Shift-II

(a) The largest chord in a circle has a length twice its radius
(b) Given any three points in a plane, there is always a circle passing through these points
(c) The ratio of the perimeter and radius of a circle is always constant
(d) A triangle with vertices on a circle and one side as its diameter is a right-angled triangle

373. From a circle of radius r units, the largest equilateral triangle is cut out. What is the length (in units) of the side of the triangle?
SSC CHSL (Tier I) 11/07/2024 Shift-I

(a) $\sqrt{2}r$ (b) $\frac{r}{\sqrt{3}}$
(c) $\sqrt{3}r$ (d) $\frac{r}{\sqrt{2}}$

374. PQR is a triangle. MN is a line segment intersecting PQ in M and PR in N such that $MN \parallel QR$ and divides ΔPQR into two parts, which are equal in area. What is the ratio of MQ to PQ?
SSC CHSL (Tier I) 11/07/2024 Shift-I

(a) $\sqrt{2} : (\sqrt{2} - 1)$ (b) $\sqrt{2} : 1$
(c) $(\sqrt{2} - 1) : \sqrt{2}$ (d) $1 : \sqrt{2}$

375. Find the altitude (in cm) from the vertex Q to side PR of triangle PQR with side lengths $PQ = 40$ cm, $PR = 40$ cm and $QR = 60$ cm.
SSC CHSL (Tier I) 11/07/2024 Shift-I

(a) $25\sqrt{7}$ (b) $15\sqrt{7}$
(c) $30\sqrt{7}$ (d) $20\sqrt{7}$

376. PBA and PDC are two secants. AD is the diameter of the circle with the centre at O. $\angle A = 30°$, $\angle P = 20°$. Find the measure of $\angle DBC$.
SSC CHSL (Tier I) 11/07/2024 Shift-I

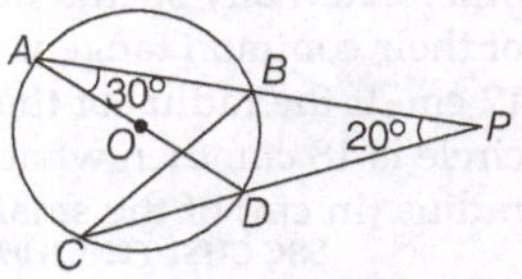

(a) 50° (b) 30°
(c) 45° (d) 40°

377. ΔABC and ΔPQR are similar. The areas of these two triangles are 289 sq.cm and 576 sq.cm, respectively. If $PR = 12$ cm, then $AC = ?$ **SSC CHSL (Tier I) 10/07/2024 Shift-IV**

(a) 7.25 cm (b) 8.5 cm
(c) 12 cm (d) 6 cm

378. In an isosceles triangle, the vertex angle is four times the sum of the base angles. The measure of the square root of the vertex angle is
SSC CHSL (Tier I) 10/07/2024 Shift-IV

(a) 16° (b) 18° (c) 10° (d) 12°

379. Two chords AB and CD of a circle are produced to intersect each other at a point P outside the circle. If $AB = 7$ cm, $BP = 4.2$ cm and $PD = 2.8$ cm, then the length of CD is
SSC CHSL (Tier I) 10/07/2024 Shift-IV

(a) 11 cm (b) 18 cm
(c) 16 cm (d) 14 cm

380. In ΔABC, if $AB = \sqrt{3}$ units, $BC = 1$ unit and $AC = 2$ units, then $\angle ACB$ is equal to **SSC CHSL (Tier I) 10/07/2024 Shift-IV**

(a) 60° (b) 90° (c) 30° (d) 45°

381. The sides AB and AC of ΔABC are produced to points D and E, respectively. The bisectors of $\angle CBD$ and $\angle BCE$ meet at P. If $\angle A = 72°$, then the measure of $\angle P$ is
SSC CHSL (Tier I) 10/07/2024 Shift-III

(a) 55° (b) 65°
(c) 54° (d) 35°

382. The centres of two circles of radii 20 cm and 32 cm are 60 cm apart. What is the ratio of the length of the direct common tangent to the length of the transverse common tangent to these circles?
SSC CHSL (Tier I) 10/07/2024 Shift-III

(a) $3\sqrt{3} : \sqrt{7}$ (b) $3\sqrt{2} : \sqrt{7}$
(c) $3\sqrt{7} : \sqrt{3}$ (d) $7\sqrt{3} : 3$

383. In a triangle PQR, RS intersects PQ at point S. The sides of the triangle $QR = 36$ cm, $SQ = 27$ cm, $RS = 18$ cm and $\angle QRS = \angle QPR$. What is the ratio of the perimeter ΔPRS to that of ΔQSR? **SSC CHSL (Tier I) 10/07/2024 Shift-III**

(a) $\frac{8}{6}$ (b) $\frac{9}{12}$ (c) $\frac{7}{9}$ (d) $\frac{5}{8}$

384. The length (in cm) of a direct common tangent to two circles of radii 14 cm and 5 cm whose centres are separated by a distance of 40 cm is
SSC CHSL (Tier I) 10/07/2024 Shift-II

(a) 40 cm (b) 41 cm
(c) $\sqrt{1539}$ cm (d) $\sqrt{1519}$ cm

385. In an isosceles triangle ABC, $AB = AC$. D is a point inside the triangle such that $\angle BAD = 20° = \angle DCB$, $\angle CAD = 80°$. The value of $\angle ABC$ is **SSC CHSL (Tier I) 10/07/2024 Shift-II**

(a) 25° (b) 15° (c) 20° (d) 40°

386. R wishes to use a stick of length 6 units as common internal tangent to two circles of radius two units and three units. What can be the maximum distance (in units) between the centres of the circle?
SSC CHSL (Tier I) 10/07/2024 Shift-I

(a) $\sqrt{67}$ (b) $\sqrt{61}$
(c) $\sqrt{33}$ (d) $\sqrt{37}$

387. By decreasing 17° from each angle of a triangle, the ratio of their angles is 3 : 4 : 7. The radian measure of the greatest angle is
SSC CHSL (Tier I) 09/07/2024 Shift-IV

(a) $\frac{153\pi}{360}$ (b) $\frac{167\pi}{180}$ (c) $\frac{163\pi}{360}$ (d) $\frac{163\pi}{180}$

388. In the diagram, if $\overline{AB} \parallel \overline{CE}$, $AG = GD = DH = HB$, then which of the following is correct?
I. $\Delta ACG \cong \Delta BEH$
II. $\Delta CDE \cong \Delta DEB \cong \Delta DCA$
III. $\Delta HFB \cong \Delta AFG$
SSC CHSL (Tier I) 09/07/2024 Shift-IV

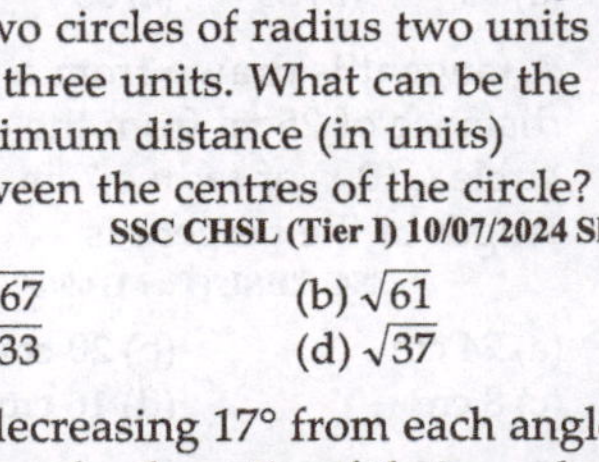

(a) I and III (b) I and II
(c) I, II and III (d) Only I

389. In a circle with center O, the diameter AB extended to the point C, outside the circle. CD is a tangent at the point D on the circle. If the radius of circle is 6 cm and $\angle DBC = 120°$, then the length of CD is equal to
SSC CHSL (Tier I) 09/07/2024 Shift-IV
(a) $5\sqrt{3}$ cm (b) $3\sqrt{3}$ cm
(c) $6\sqrt{3}$ cm (d) $4\sqrt{3}$ cm

390. In a right-angled triangle with sides 12 cm and 16 cm and hypotenuse 20 cm, the length of altitude drawn on the hypotenuse from the opposite vertex is K. Find the value of K.
SSC CHSL (Tier I) 09/07/2024 Shift-III
(a) 6.9 cm (b) 9.6 cm
(c) 6.8 cm (d) 8.6 cm

391. The sides ST and TR and the median SU of the ΔSTR are equal to the sides MN and NJ and the median MV of the ΔMNJ respectively. If $\angle TSU = 46°$, $\angle NMJ = 79°$ and $\angle MVN = 88°$, what is the degree measure of $\frac{7}{11}\angle SRT$?
SSC CHSL (Tier I) 09/07/2024 Shift-III
(a) 35° (b) 55° (c) 56° (d) 47°

392. A tangent is drawn from a point at a distance of 25cm from the centre of a circle $C(0,r)$ of radius 7cm. The length of the tangent is
SSC CHSL (Tier I) 09/07/2024 Shift-III
(a) 24 cm (b) 20 cm
(c) 8 cm (d) 16 cm

393. Consider AD is a tangent to a circle of radius 6 cm. AC is a secant meeting the circle at B and CD is a diameter. If AB is 7 cm, then the value of AC (in cm) is
SSC CHSL (Tier I) 09/07/2024 Shift-II
(a) 9 (b) 18
(c) 20 (d) 16

394. PQ is the diameter of a circle with centre O. PT is a tangent touching the circle at P. The secant QT intersects the circle at S. O and S are joined. If $\angle SOP = 104°$, what is the measure (in degrees) of $\angle PTQ$?
SSC CHSL (Tier I) 09/07/2024 Shift-II
(a) 45 (b) 62
(c) 76 (d) 38

395. PQ and RS are two chords of a circle such that $PQ = 12$ cm and $RS = 20$ cm and PQ is parallel to RS. If the distance between PQ and RS is 4 cm, find the diameter of the circle.
SSC CHSL (Tier I) 09/07/2024 Shift-II
(a) $2\sqrt{34}$ cm (b) $3\sqrt{34}$ cm
(c) $6\sqrt{34}$ cm (d) $4\sqrt{34}$ cm

396. ΔXYZ is similar to ΔPQR. If the ratio of the perimeter of ΔXYZ to the perimeter of ΔPQR is 16 : 9 and $PQ = 3.6$ cm, then what is the length (in cm) of XY?
SSC CHSL (Tier I) 09/07/2024 Shift-II
(a) $2\frac{3}{5}$ (b) $4\frac{3}{5}$
(c) $6\frac{2}{5}$ (d) $3\frac{4}{5}$

397. A bigger circle centre at O and a smaller circle centre at P touch each other externally such that the length of their common tangent LM is 12 cm. If the radius of the bigger circle is 18 cm, then what will be the radius (in cm) of the smaller circle ?
SSC CHSL (Tier I) 09/07/2024 Shift-I
(a) 4 (b) 3
(c) 2 (d) 1

398. Find the length of the sides of a triangle, if its angles are in the ratio 2 : 4 : 6 and its circumradius is 12 cm.
SSC CHSL (Tier I) 09/07/2024 Shift-I
(a) 5 cm, 6 cm, 10 cm
(b) 15 cm, $15\sqrt{3}$ cm, 30 cm
(c) 12 cm, $12\sqrt{3}$ cm, 24 cm
(d) 6 cm, $6\sqrt{3}$ cm, 12 cm

399. In a circle, the chords AB and CD intersect each other at point L (internally). If $AL = 9$ cm, $LB = 7$ cm and $LD = 3$ cm, then find CL (in cm).
SSC CHSL (Tier I) 09/07/2024 Shift-I
(a) 20 (b) 21
(c) 18 (d) 19

400. Side BC of a ΔABC is extended upto D such that $CD = AC$. If $\angle BAD = 118°$ and $\angle ACB = 80°$, then the value of $\angle ABC$ is equal to
SSC CHSL (Tier I) 08/07/2024 Shift-IV
(a) 36° (b) 32°
(c) 22° (d) 27°

401. Two triangles ABC and DEF are similar. The smallest side of ABC is equal to 15 units. If the sides of ABC are in the ratio 3 : 4 : 5, and the area of DEF is half of the area of ABC, then what is the largest side of DEF (in units)?
SSC CHSL (Tier I) 08/07/2024 Shift-IV
(a) $25\sqrt{2}$ (b) $25\sqrt{3}$
(c) $\frac{25}{\sqrt{3}}$ (d) $\frac{25}{\sqrt{2}}$

402. The distance between the centres of two circles is 81 cm, and their radii are 42 cm and 51 cm. What is the length (in cm) of the direct common tangent to the circles?
SSC CHSL (Tier I) 08/07/2024 Shift-IV
(a) $51\sqrt{6}$ (b) $36\sqrt{5}$
(c) $31\sqrt{3}$ (d) $40\sqrt{2}$

403. Find the altitude (in cm) of side MT of triangle MNT with side $MN = 36$ cm, $MT = 36$ cm and $NT = 48$ cm.
SSC CHSL (Tier I) 08/07/2024 Shift-III
(a) $16\sqrt{5}$ (b) $18\sqrt{3}$
(c) $12\sqrt{5}$ (d) $24\sqrt{3}$

404. In a triangle ABC, P and Q are two points on AB and AC, respectively, such that PQ parallel to BC. If $AC = 5QC$, then the ratio $PQ : BC$ is equal to
SSC CHSL (Tier I) 08/07/2024 Shift-III
(a) 3 : 4 (b) 5 : 4
(c) 4 : 5 (d) 4 : 3

405. The length of a common external tangent to two circles of an equal radius of 5 units is equal to the diameter of the circle. Which of the following can be the distance between the centres of the circles in units?
SSC CHSL (Tier I) 08/07/2024 Shift-II
(a) 10 (b) 12
(c) 9 (d) 8

406. ABC is a right-angled triangle, at A in such a way that $AB = AC$ and the bisector of angle B intersects the side AC at D. DM is perpendicular to BC, intersecting BC at M. If $AB = 12$ cm and $BC = 12\sqrt{2}$ cm, then find the length of side AD.
SSC CHSL (Tier I) 08/07/2024 Shift-II
(a) $12(\sqrt{2} + 2)$ cm
(b) $12(\sqrt{2} - 2)$ cm
(c) $12(\sqrt{2} - 1)$ cm
(d) $12(\sqrt{2} + 1)$ cm

407. Two circles have radii of 27 cm and 36 cm. The distance between their centres is 45 cm. What is the length (in cm) of their common chord?
SSC CHSL (Tier I) 08/07/2024 Shift-II
(a) 37.2 cm (b) 40.5 cm
(c) 43.2 cm (d) 47.5 cm

408. In a triangle ABC, D and E are two points on sides AB and AC, respectively, such that DE is parallel to BC and $AD : DB = 3 : 5$. If $AC = 5.6$ cm, then find the value (in cm) of AE.
SSC CHSL (Tier I) 08/07/2024 Shift-I
(a) 2.3 (b) 2.1
(c) 1.9 (d) 2.5

409. Two circles of radii 16 cm and 4 cm, respectively, touch each other externally at point A. PQ is the direct common tangent of these circles with centres C_1 and C_2, respectively. What is the length of PQ?
SSC CHSL (Tier I) 08/07/2024 Shift-I
(a) 15 cm (b) 20 cm
(c) 16 cm (d) 18 cm

410. In ΔABC, O is the point of intersection of the bisectors of $\angle B$ and angle $\angle A$. If the $\angle BOC = 108°$, then $\angle BAO$ is **SSC CHSL (Tier I) 05/07/2024 Shift-IV**

(a) 26° (b) 16° (c) 22° (d) 18°

411. Let ABC be a triangle such that $\angle ABC = 70°$ and $\angle ACB = 50°$. Let O be the incentre of the triangle. Find $\angle BOC$. **SSC CHSL (Tier I) 05/07/2024 Shift-IV**

(a) 120° (b) 100° (c) 60° (d) 130°

412. Two similar triangles have area 490 sq cm. and 640 sq cm. If the length of the one side of the first triangle is 21 cm, then what is the length of the corresponding side of the second triangle? **SSC CHSL (Tier I) 05/07/2024 Shift-IV**

(a) 24 cm (b) 21 cm
(c) 16 cm (d) 14 cm

413. Two parallel chords are drawn in a circle of radius 25 cm. The distance between the two chords is 27 cm. If the length of one chord is 48 cm, then length of the other chord is equal to **SSC CHSL (Tier I) 05/07/2024 Shift-III**

(a) 42 cm (b) 36 cm
(c) 48 cm (d) 30 cm

414. In a triangle ABC, BD is perpendicular to AC. E is a point on BC such that angle $BEA = x°$. If angle $EAC = 38°$ and angle $EBD = 40°$, then the value of x is **SSC CHSL (Tier I) 05/07/2024 Shift-III**

(a) 82 (b) 88 (c) 96 (d) 48

415. PQ is a chord of a circle. The tangent XR at point X on the circle intersects the extension of PQ at point R. Given that $XR = 12$ cm, $PQ = x$ cm, and $QR = (x - 2)$ cm, find the value of x. **SSC CHSL (Tier I) 05/07/2024 Shift-II**

(a) 11 cm (b) 9 cm
(c) 8 cm (d) 10 cm

416. The radii of two concentric circles are 35 cm and 21 cm. If the chord of the greater circle is a tangent to the smaller circle, then the length of that chord is **SSC CHSL (Tier I) 05/07/2024 Shift-II**

(a) 70 cm (b) 42 cm
(c) 56 cm (d) 28 cm

417. A chord of length 12 units in a circle of radius 10 units is ……… units away from its centre. **SSC CHSL (Tier I) 05/07/2024 Shift-II**

(a) 8 (b) 9
(c) 10 (d) 6

418. ΔABC and ΔDEF are similar and their areas are respectively 0.64 m^2 and 0.0121 m^2. If $EF = 0.154$ m, then BC is **SSC CHSL (Tier I) 05/07/2024 Shift-II**

(a) 1.15 m (b) 11.2 m
(c) 1.12 m (d) 2.12 m

419. In triangle XYZ, $XY = YZ$ and $m\angle X = 78°$. Find the value of $m\angle Y$. **SSC CHSL (Tier I) 05/07/2024 Shift-I**

(a) 28° (b) 24°
(c) 34° (d) 39°

420. AB is parallel to DC in a trapezium $ABCD$. It is given that $AB > DC$ and the diagonals AC and BD intersect at O. If $AO = 3x - 15$, $OB = x + 9$, $OC = x - 5$ and $OD = 5$ and x has two values x_1 and x_2, then the value of $(x_1^2 + x_2^2)$ is **SSC CHSL (Tier I) 05/07/2024 Shift-I**

(a) 45 (b) 61 (c) 73 (d) 56

421. ΔABC is similar to ΔDEF and the ratio of the area of triangle ABC to triangle DEF is 25 : 144. If $AB = p$ cm, $AC = q$ cm and $BC = r$ cm, then $DE = ?$ **SSC CHSL (Tier I) 05/07/2024 Shift-I**

(a) $\frac{5}{12}q$ (b) $\frac{12}{5}q$ (c) $\frac{5}{12}p$ (d) $\frac{12}{5}p$

422. In a triangle ABC, $AB = AC$. BC is extended to D such that $CD = AB$ and the angle ADC is 30°. What are the angles of triangle ABC? **SSC CHSL (Tier I) 04/07/2024 Shift-IV**

(a) 30°, 60°, 90° (b) 50°, 60°, 70°
(c) 60°, 60°, 60° (d) 45°, 60°, 75°

423. Two parallel chords of length 5 units and 8 units are on opposite sides of the centre of a circle of radius 7 units. What is the distance between the chords? (round your answer to two decimal places) **SSC CHSL (Tier I) 04/07/2024 Shift-IV**

(a) 11.82 units (b) 12.28 units
(c) 11.28 units (d) 12.82 units

424. In a circle, O is the centre and AOB is the diameter. AT is a tangent to the circle. Line TB intersects the circle at Q. Given that $\angle AOQ = 94°$, find $\angle ATQ$. **SSC CHSL (Tier I) 04/07/2024 Shift-IV**

(a) 86° (b) 43° (c) 47° (d) 133°

425. A circle of diameter 26 cm has two equal chords of length 10 cm each, separated by a distance h cm. What is the value of h? **SSC CHSL (Tier I) 04/07/2024 Shift-III**

(a) 18 cm (b) 12 cm
(c) 24 cm (d) 16 cm

426. ΔDEF and ΔGHI are two similar triangles. If $DE = 64$ cm, $GH = 24$ cm and the perimeter of ΔGHI is 72 cm, then what is the sum of the lengths (in cm) of the sides EF and FD of the ΔDEF? **SSC CHSL (Tier I) 04/07/2024 Shift-III**

(a) 192 (b) 96 (c) 128 (d) 82

427. Two circles with centres M and N have radii 5 cm and 8 cm, respectively. The circles touch each other externally at point T. A line PR is drawn such that the points M, T and N lie on PR, P being closer to M. From P, a tangent $PQ = 12$ cm is drawn to the circle with centre M touching at Q and from R, another tangent $RS = 15$ cm is drawn to the circle with centre N touching at S. What is the length (in cm) of PR? **SSC CHSL (Tier I) 04/07/2024 Shift-III**

(a) 37 (b) 43 (c) 53 (d) 26

428. In right triangle ABC with right angle at C, M is the mid-point of hypotenuse AB. C is joined to M and produced to a point D, such that $DM = CM$. Point D is joined to B. If $CD = 10$ cm and $BD = 6$ cm, find the value of CM. **SSC CHSL (Tier I) 04/07/2024 Shift-II**

(a) 8 cm (b) 5 cm
(c) 9.5 cm (d) 11.4 cm

429. The centers of two circles of radii 25 cm and 35 cm are 80 cm apart. What is the ratio of the lengths of the transverse common tangent to the direct common tangent to these circles? **SSC CHSL (Tier I) 04/07/2024 Shift-II**

(a) 2 : 3 (b) $\sqrt{7}$: 3
(c) $3\sqrt{7}$: 2 (d) 2 : $\sqrt{7}$

430. In ΔABC, P and Q are the middle points of the sides AB and AC, respectively. R is a point on the segment PQ such that $PR : RQ = 1 : 5$. If $PR = 6$ cm, then $BC = ……$. **SSC CHSL (Tier I) 04/07/2024 Shift-II**

(a) 70 cm (b) 66 cm
(c) 68 cm (d) 72 cm

431. In the given figure, O is the centre of the circle, AE is the diameter and $\angle AOC = 100°$. The value of $\angle CDE + \angle CEA$ is **SSC CHSL (Tier I) 04/07/2024 Shift-I**

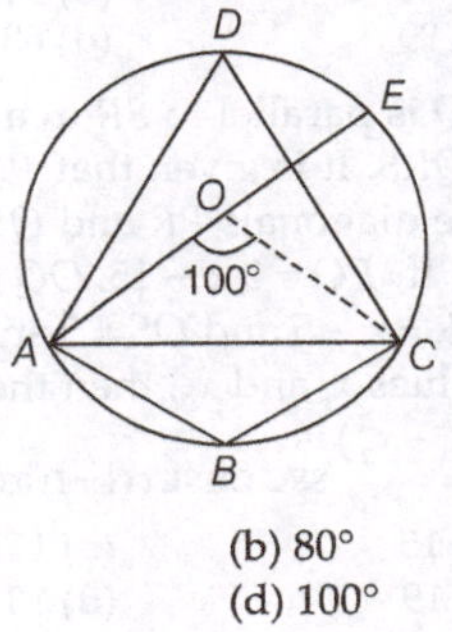

(a) 90° (b) 80°
(c) 60° (d) 100°

432. There is a circle with a centre T and a radius of 8 cm. Two tangents KE and KI are drawn from point K, which is 17 cm from the centre. The area of the quadrilateral $TEKI$ is
SSC CHSL (Tier I) 04/07/2024 Shift-I
(a) 130 sq.cm (b) 136 sq.cm
(c) 120 sq.cm (d) 127.5 sq.cm

433. ΔABC is a right-angles triangle where $m\angle ABC = 90°$. If $m(\overline{AB}) = 15$ cm, $m(\overline{BC}) = 20$ cm, and $\overline{BD} \perp \overline{AC}$, intersecting $\overline{AC}$ at the point D, find $m(\overline{BD})$ (in cm).
SSC CHSL (Tier I) 04/07/2024 Shift-I
(a) 12.5 (b) 12
(c) 10 (d) 9

434. Two parallel chords of length 8 units each are 6 units away from each other in a circle. What is the radius of the circle in units?
SSC CHSL (Tier I) 03/07/2024 Shift-IV
(a) 3 (b) 6
(c) 5 (d) 4

435. Two circles with centre O and A touch each other externally. The radius of the first circle with centre O is 6 cm. The radius of the second circle with centre A is 3 cm. Find the length of their common tangent CB (in cm). **SSC CHSL (Tier I) 03/07/2024 Shift-IV**
(a) $3\sqrt{2}$ (b) $4\sqrt{3}$
(c) $4\sqrt{2}$ (d) $6\sqrt{2}$

436. $\Delta ABC \sim \Delta EDF$ and area (ΔABC) : area $(\Delta EDF) = 9:4$. If $AB = 5$ cm, $BC = 8$ cm and $CA = 10$ cm, then DF is equal to
SSC CHSL (Tier I) 03/07/2024 Shift-IV
(a) $3\frac{2}{3}$ cm (b) $3\frac{1}{4}$ cm
(c) $5\frac{1}{3}$ cm (d) $4\frac{2}{3}$ cm

437. If the perimeters of two similar triangles are in the ratio of 4 : 7 and the sum of the areas is 195 cm^2, then what is $\frac{1}{3}$rd of the difference between the areas (in cm^2) of the two triangles?
SSC CHSL (Tier I) 03/07/2024 Shift-IV
(a) 33 (b) 54
(c) 99 (d) 63

438. PQ is parallel to SR in a trapezium $PQRS$. It is given that $PQ > SR$ and the diagonals PR and QS intersect at O. If $PO = 3x - 15$, $OQ = x + 9$, $OR = x - 5$ and $OS = 5$ and x has two values x_1 and x_2, then the value of $(x_1^2 - x_2^2)$ is
SSC CHSL (Tier I) 03/07/2024 Shift-III
(a) 15 (b) 11
(c) 19 (d) 13

439. AB and AC are two tangents to a circle having centres at the point X. What will be the measure of $\angle BAC$, if $\angle BXC = 125°$?
SSC CHSL (Tier I) 03/07/2024 Shift-III
(a) 50° (b) 48°
(c) 55° (d) 52°

440. If 6,18, x are sides of a triangle and x is an integer, then the number of possible values of x is
SSC CHSL (Tier I) 03/07/2024 Shift-III
(a) 11 (b) 15
(c) 13 (d) 14

441. A, B, C are three points such that $AB = 11$ cm, $BC = 13$ cm and $AC = 24$ cm. Number of circles passing through the points A, B, C is
SSC CHSL (Tier I) 03/07/2024 Shift-II
(a) 0 (b) 3 (c) 1 (d) 2

442. Two circles touch each other externally at M. PQ is a direct common tangent to the two circles, P and Q are points of contact and $\angle MPQ = 38°$. $\angle MQP$ is
SSC CHSL (Tier I) 03/07/2024 Shift-II
(a) 38° (b) 52°
(c) 42° (d) 48°

443. In a right-angled triangle ABC such that $\angle BAC = 90°$ and AD is perpendicular to BC. If the area of ΔABC is 63 cm^2, area of $\Delta ACD = 7$ cm^2 and $AC = 5$ cm, then the length of BC is equal to
SSC CHSL (Tier I) 03/07/2024 Shift-II
(a) 10 cm (b) 15 cm
(c) 18 cm (d) 12 cm

444. A and B are centres of two circles of radii 32 cm and 8 cm, respectively. CD is a direct common tangent to the circles. If the length of $AB = 30$ cm, then the length of CD will be
SSC CHSL (Tier I) 03/07/2024 Shift-I
(a) 10 cm (b) 20 cm
(c) 9 cm (d) 18 cm

445. In ΔPQR, S and T are points on PQ and PR, respectively, such that $ST \parallel QR$ and ST divides the ΔPQR into two parts of equal areas. Then the ratio of PS and QS is
SSC CHSL (Tier I) 03/07/2024 Shift-I
(a) $1:\sqrt{2}-1$ (b) $1:1$
(c) $1:\sqrt{2}+1$ (d) $1:\sqrt{2}$

446. In a circle with centre O, ABC is a secant intersecting the circle at A and B and DC is a tangent to the circle at D. If $DC = 12$ cm and $BC = 6$ cm, then the length of AB is equal to **SSC CHSL (Tier I) 03/07/2024 Shift-I**
(a) 20 cm (b) 18 cm
(c) 22 cm (d) 16 cm

447. The triangle has sides 3 cm, 4 cm and 5 cm. What is the length of the perpendicular from the opposite vertex to the side whose length is 5 cm? **SSC CHSL (Tier I) 02/07/2024 Shift-IV**
(a) 2.4 cm (b) 3.5 cm
(c) 1.4 cm (d) 2.2 cm

448. In ΔPQR, $PR = 10$ cm. Find the length of PT, where $ST \parallel QR$. Given that $PS = 6$ cm and $QS = 14$ cm.
SSC CHSL (Tier I) 02/07/2024 Shift-IV
(a) 2 cm (b) 4 cm
(c) 1.5 cm (d) 3 cm

449. In ΔABC the straight line parallel to the side BC meets AB and AC at the points P and Q, respectively. If $AP = QC$, the length of AB is 12 cm and the length of AQ is 2 cm, then the length (in cm) of CQ is
SSC CHSL (Tier I) 02/07/2024 Shift-IV
(a) 6 (b) 4 (c) 3 (d) 2

450. In ΔEFG, $XY \parallel FG$, area of the quadrilateral $XFGY = 44$ m^2. If $EX : XF = 2:3$, then find the area of ΔEXY (in m^2).
SSC CHSL (Tier I) 02/07/2024 Shift-IV
(a) 8.38 (b) 9.46
(c) 7.28 (d) 8.10

451. Let C be a circle with Centre O and P be an external point to C. Let PQ and PR be the tangents to C, such that Q and R be the points of tangency, respectively.
If $\angle ROQ = 110°$, find $\angle RPQ$.
SSC CHSL (Tier I) 02/07/2024 Shift-III
(a) 90° (b) 70°
(c) 80° (d) 110°

452. If $\Delta ABC \sim \Delta QRP$, area of ΔABC : area of $\Delta PQR = 9:4$; $AB = 18$ cm and $BC = 15$ cm, then find the length of PR. **SSC CHSL (Tier I) 02/07/2024 Shift-III**
(a) 15 cm (b) 10 cm
(c) 12 cm (d) 14 cm

453. If ΔABC and ΔPQR are similar. $AB = 8$ cm, $PQ = 12$ cm, $QR = 18$ cm and $RP = 24$ cm, then the perimeter of ΔABC is
SSC CHSL (Tier I) 02/07/2024 Shift-II
(a) 27 cm (b) 36 cm
(c) 42 cm (d) 54 cm

454. Two equal circles are drawn on a square in such a way that opposite side of the square forms the diameter of each circle. If the remaining area of the square is 42 cm^2, what is the measurement (in cm) of the diameter of each circle?
SSC CHSL (Tier I) 02/07/2024 Shift-II
(a) 3.5 (b) 2.5 (c) 14 (d) 7

455. The distance between the centres of two circles of radii 4 cm and 2 cm is 10 cm. The length (in cm) of a transverse common tangent is
SSC CHSL (Tier I) 02/07/2024 Shift-II
(a) 13 (b) 11 (c) 6 (d) 8

456. Consider two concentric circles having radii 17 cm and 15 cm. What is the length (in cm) of the chord, of the bigger circle, which is a tangent to the smaller circle?
SSC CHSL (Tier I) 02/07/2024 Shift-II
(a) 16 (b) 10 (c) 12 (d) 8

457.
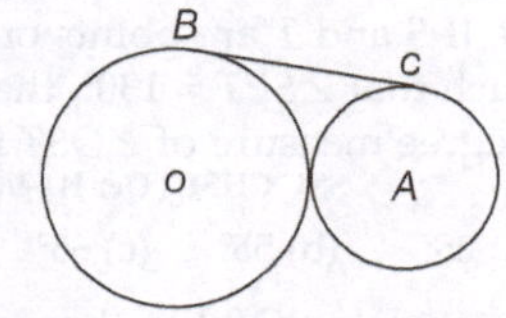

Two circles touch each other externally as shown in the figure above. The radius of the circle with centre O is 49 cm. The radius of the circle with centre A is 16 cm. Find the length (in cm) of their common tangent BC.
SSC CHSL (Tier I) 02/07/2024 Shift-I
(a) 56 (b) 55
(c) 58 (d) 57

458. The areas of two similar triangles ΔPQR and ΔXYZ are 12.96 cm^2 and 635.04 cm^2, respectively. If $QR = 2.9$ cm, then the length (in cm) of YZ equals SSC CHSL (Tier I) 02/07/2024 Shift-I
(a) 30.4 (b) 20.3
(c) 23.2 (d) 25.2

459. In $\Delta ABC, XY$ is drawn parallel to BC, cutting sides at X and Y, where $AB = 5.4$ cm, $BC = 7.2$ cm and $BX = 3$ cm. What is the length of XY (in cm)? SSC CHSL (Tier I) 02/07/2024 Shift-I
(a) 4.3 (b) 3.0
(c) 3.2 (d) 2.8

460. Which of the following are the sides of a right-angled triangle?
SSC CHSL (Tier I) 01/07/2024 Shift-IV
(a) 6 cm, 7 cm, 10 cm
(b) 5 cm, 11 cm, 13 cm
(c) 12 cm, 16 cm, 20 cm
(d) 16 cm, 31 cm, 34 cm

461. Diagonals of a trapezium $ABCD$ with $AB \parallel DC$, intersect each other at the point 'O'. If $AB = 2.5CD$, find the ratio of the area of triangle AOB to the area of triangle COD.
SSC CHSL (Tier I) 01/07/2024 Shift-IV
(a) 25:4 (b) 16:1
(c) 5:2 (d) 9:2

462. Given is a circle with centre at C. A, B and D are the points on the circumference. Find $\angle ABC$.
SSC CHSL (Tier I) 01/07/2024 Shift-IV
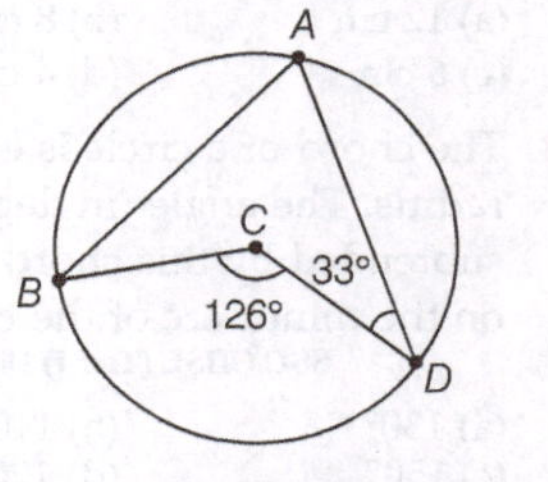

(a) 30° (b) 37°
(c) 35° (d) 33°

463. In an isosceles triangle, the angle between equal sides is 40°. The bisectors of the other two angles will intersect each other at an angle of
SSC CHSL (Tier I) 01/07/2024 Shift-III
(a) 100° (b) 105°
(c) 120° (d) 110°

464. If the radii of two circles are 6 cm and 3 cm and the length of the transverse common tangent is 8 cm, then the distance between the two circles is SSC CHSL (Tier I) 01/07/2024 Shift-III
(a) $\sqrt{145}$ cm (b) $\sqrt{141}$ cm
(c) $\sqrt{147}$ cm (d) $\sqrt{143}$ cm

465. In a ΔABC, $AB = 6$ units, $BC = 8$ units and $AC = 10$ units. Let M be a point on AC such that $BM = 5$ units. With a point D, a ΔBMD is formed and the ΔBMD is similar to the triangle ABC with $\frac{BM}{AB} = \frac{BD}{AC}$. What is the length of BD in units?
SSC CHSL (Tier I) 01/07/2024 Shift-III
(a) $\frac{35}{3}$ (b) $\frac{40}{3}$ (c) $\frac{25}{3}$ (d) $\frac{10}{3}$

466. CD is a tangent to a circle of circumference of 88 cm with its centre at O. OC cuts the circle at P, while OD cuts circle at V such that $\angle COD = 90°$. Length of PC is 6 cm. What is half of CD (in cm), if OD exceeds OC by 1 cm?
SSC CHSL (Tier I) 01/07/2024 Shift-III
(a) 15.5 (b) 14.5
(c) 31 (d) 16.5

467. Two circles touch each other at a point O. AB is a simple common tangent to both the circles touching at point A and point B. If radii of the circles are 9 cm and 4 cm, then find AB. SSC CHSL (Tier I) 01/07/2024 Shift-II
(a) 72 cm (b) 144 cm
(c) 12 cm (d) 24 cm

468. PQ is a diameter of a circle with centre O. The tangents at R meets PQ produced at A. If $\angle RPQ = 27°$, then measure of $\angle RQP$ is
SSC CHSL (Tier I) 01/07/2024 Shift-II
(a) 63° (b) 54°
(c) 153° (d) 27°

469. In a ΔABC, two medians AD and BE intersect at G at right angles. If $AD = 18$ cm and $BE = 12$ cm, then the length of BD is equal to
SSC CHSL (Tier I) 01/07/2024 Shift-II
(a) 10 cm (b) 15 cm
(c) 8 cm (d) 20 cm

470. In a circle, $ABCD$ is a cyclic quadrilateral in which AE is drawn parallel to CD, and BA is produced to F. If $\angle ABC = 85°$ and $\angle FAE = 24°$, find the value of $\angle BCD$.
SSC CHSL (Tier I) 01/07/2024 Shift-II
(a) 125° (b) 115°
(c) 124° (d) 119°

471. Two parallel chords on the same side of the centre of a circle are 12 cm and 20 cm long and the radius of the circle is $5\sqrt{13}$ cm. What is the distance between the chords? SSC CHSL (Tier I) 01/07/2024 Shift-I
(a) 3 cm (b) 5 cm
(c) 2 cm (d) 4 cm

472. If PQ and PR are the two tangents to a circle with centre O, and $\angle QOR = 150°$, then $\angle QPR$ is equal to
SSC CHSL (Tier I) 01/07/2024 Shift-I
(a) 60° (b) 30°
(c) 90° (d) 45°

473. Given that the perimeters of two similar triangles, ΔABC and ΔDEF, are 24 cm and 9 cm, respectively, and $DE = 3$ cm, what is the ratio between the area of ΔABC and that of ΔDEF ?
SSC CHSL (Tier I) 01/07/2024 Shift-I
(a) 64 : 9 (b) 54 : 9
(c) 64 : 7 (d) 54 : 7

474. Which of the following is a correct statement?
SSC CHSL (Tier I) 01/07/2024 Shift-I
(a) The sum of the angles of a cyclic quadrilateral is always 180°
(b) Equal chords are equidistant from the centre of the circle but not always subtend equal angle at centre of the circle
(c) If two circles touch each other, the point of contact lies on the line joining the two centres
(d) Angles subtended by the arc in the same segment of the circle are in ratio of 2 : 1

475. In ΔXYZ, if $XY = 5$ cm, $XZ = 7$ cm and Q is a point on YZ, such that XQ bisects $\angle X$, then $YQ : QZ$ is
SSC CHSL (Tier II) 10/01/2024 Shift I

(a) 5 : 7 (b) 7 : 12
(c) 7 : 5 (d) 5 : 12

476. The measures of two angles of a triangle are in the ratio 3 : 7. If the sum of these two measures is equal to the measure of the third angle, then find the smallest angle.
SSC CHSL (Tier II) 10/01/2024 Shift I

(a) 27° (b) 3°
(c) 9° (d) 36°

SSC CHSL 2023 (Tier I & II)

477. Which of the following statements is not true?
SSC CHSL (Tier II) 02/11/2023 Shift I

(a) The area of the triangle with the largest side l always has an area less than $\frac{l^2}{2}$
(b) If the sides of a triangle are in the ratio 13 : 5 : 12, then two of its angles are acute angles
(c) The triangle formed by connecting the mid-points of the sides of a triangle has one-fourth area of the bigger triangle
(d) The area of an isosceles triangle with sides $2a$, $2a$ and $3a$ is $\frac{3\sqrt{3}a^2}{2}$

478. Triangle ABC is an isosceles triangle with $AB = AC$. If angle $BAC = 50°$, then the degree measure of angle ABC is equal to
SSC CHSL (Tier I) 17/08/2023 Shift I

(a) 70° (b) 55°
(c) 60° (d) 65°

479. Three angles of a triangle are $(x - 15)°$, $(x + 45)°$ and $(x + 60)°$. Identify the type of triangle.
SSC CHSL (Tier I) 17/08/2023 Shift I

(a) Obtuse angle triangle
(b) Right angle triangle
(c) Isosceles triangle
(d) Equilateral triangle

480. The area of two similar triangles TUV and PQR are 18 cm² and 32 cm², respectively. It $TU = 6$ cm, then PQ is equal to
SSC CHSL (Tier I) 14/08/2023 Shift IV

(a) 4 cm (b) 8 cm
(c) 2 cm (d) 64 cm

481. If $\Delta ABC \cong \Delta PQR$ and $\angle Q = 35°$ $\angle R = 90°$, then the value of $\angle A$ is
SSC CHSL (Tier I) 11/08/2023 Shift I

(a) 55° (b) 90°
(c) 35° (d) 45°

482. The distance between two parallel chords of length 6 cm each, in a circle of diameter 10 cm is
SSC CHSL (Tier I) 11/08/2023 Shift I

(a) 12 cm (b) 8 cm
(c) 6 cm (d) 4 cm

483. The chord of a circle is equal to its radius. The angle (in degrees) subtended by this chord at any point on the minor arc of the circle is
SSC CHSL (Tier I) 10/08/2023 Shift III

(a) 130° (b) 140°
(c) 150° (d) 120°

484. Chords $\overline{AB}$ and $\overline{CD}$ of a circle intersect inside the circle at point F. If $m(\overline{AF}) = 2.4$ cm $m(\overline{BF}) = 1.8$ cm and $m(\overline{CD}) = 5.7$ cm, what is the length (in cm) of the longer of the 2 line segments. $\overline{CF}$ and $\overline{DF}$?
SSC CHSL (Tier I) 09/08/2023 Shift I

(a) 4.5 (b) 4.8
(c) 5.4 (d) 3.6

485. 2 circles touch each other externally at any point C. PQ is the direct common tangent to both the circles touching the circles at points P and Q. If the radii of the circles are 36 cm and 16 cm, respectively, then the length of PQ is
SSC CHSL (Tier I) 09/08/2023 Shift I

(a) 42 cm (b) 24 cm
(c) 48 cm (d) 36 cm

486. The largest chord of the circle is
SSC CHSL (Tier I) 09/08/2023 Shift I

(a) point (b) tangent
(c) diameter (d) radius

487. Two triangles XYZ and UVW are congruent. If the area of ΔXYZ is 58 cm², then the area of ΔUVW will be
SSC CHSL (Tier I) 08/08/2023 Shift II

(a) 58 cm² (b) 116 cm²
(c) 29 cm² (d) 15 cm²

488. The diameter PQ of a circle with centre O is perpendicular to the chord RS, PQ intersects RS at T. If $RS = 16$ cm and $QT = 4$ cm, what is the length (in cm) of the diameter of the circle?
SSC CHSL (Tier I) 07/08/2023 Shift IV

(a) 20 (b) 48 (c) 24 (d) 10

489. The perpendicular distance from the centre of a circle to the chord is 20 cm. Calculate the chord's length in centimetres, if the circle's diameter is 58 cm.
SSC CHSL (Tier I) 07/08/2023 Shift IV

(a) 42 (b) 21 (c) 56 (d) 28

490. If TM and TN are the two tangents to a circle with centre O so that $\angle MON = 105°$, then $\angle MTN$ will be equal to
SSC CHSL (Tier I) 07/08/2023 Shift IV

(a) 70° (b) 60° (c) 75° (d) 85°

491. In a rhombus $STUV$, S and U are joined $\angle SUV = 44°$, $\angle STU = 92°$, what is the degree measure of $4\angle SVU - 3\angle TSU$?
SSC CHSL (Tier I) 04/08/2023 Shift II

(a) 451° (b) 360°
(c) 169° (d) 236°

492. PS and PT are two tangents from a point P outside the circle with centre O. If S and T are points on the circle such that $\angle SPT = 130°$, then the degree measure of $\angle OST$ is equal to
SSC CHSL (Tier I) 04/08/2023 Shift II

(a) 25° (b) 55° (c) 65° (d) 35°

493. A triangle PQR has three sides equal in measurement and if PM is perpendicular to QR, then which of following equality holds ?
SSC CHSL (Tier I) 04/08/2023 Shift II

(a) $3PM^2 = 2PQ^2$ (b) $3PQ^2 = 4PM^2$
(c) $3PM^2 = 4PQ^2$ (d) $3PQ^2 = 2PM^2$

494. A tangent AB at point A of a circle of radius 6 cm meets a line through the center O at point B. If $OB = 10$ cm, then the length of AB (in cm) is equal to
SSC CHSL (Tier I) 02/08/2023 Shift I

(a) 5 (b) 6 (c) 4 (d) 8

495. Two circles of radii 12 cm and 13 cm are concentric. The length of the chord of the larger circle which touches the smaller circle is
SSC CHSL (Tier I) 02/08/2023 Shift I

(a) 8 cm (b) 18 cm (c) 10 cm (d) 12 cm

496. Sum of the angles made by a chord at the centre and on the major arc of circle is 180°. What will be the angle made at the centre of the circle ?
SSC CHSL (Tier I) 21/03/2023 Shift II

(a) 60° (b) 90° (c) 75° (d) 120°

497. The medians JX and KY of ΔJKL intersect each other at Z at right angles. If $KL = 22$ cm and $KY = 12$ cm, then what is the length of JX ?
SSC CHSL (Tier I) 21/03/2023 Shift IV

(a) $6\sqrt{19}$ cm (b) $3\sqrt{57}$ cm
(c) $2\sqrt{57}$ cm (d) $4\sqrt{19}$ cm

498. Tangent drawn from a point X, touches the circle at U. O is the centre of this circle. If $XU = 15$ cm and $OU = 8$ cm, then what is the value of OX ?
SSC CHSL (Tier I) 21/03/2023 Shift IV

(a) 12 cm (b) 19 cm
(c) 21 cm (d) 17 cm

499. Angle subtended by a chord at the centre of a circle is 180°. What will be the angle subtended by the same chord on the circumference of this circle? **SSC CHSL (Tier I) 21/03/2023 Shift II**

(a) 120° (b) 95° (c) 90° (d) 45°

500. Angle subtended by a chord AB on the centre of the circle is 140°. What will be the angle subtended by the chord AB on the major arc of the circle? **SSC CHSL (Tier I) 21/03/2023 Shift II**

(a) 80° (b) 60° (c) 35° (d) 70°

501. ΔABC is similar to ΔPQR, $AB = 4$ cm, $BC = 8$ cm and $AC = 10$ cm. If $QR = 16$ cm, then what is the area of ΔPQR? **SSC CHSL (Tier I) 21/03/2023 Shift II**

(a) $2\sqrt{231}$ cm^2 (b) $4\sqrt{231}$ cm^2
(c) $4\sqrt{462}$ cm^2 (d) $8\sqrt{462}$ cm^2

502. Tangent drawn from a point P, touches the circle at Q. O is the centre of this circle. If $PQ = 12$ cm and $OQ = 5$ cm, then what is the value of OP? **SSC CHSL (Tier I) 21/03/2023 Shift II**

(a) 15 cm (b) $\sqrt{119}$ cm
(c) $\sqrt{179}$ cm (d) 13 cm

503. PM is the median of ΔPQR. O is the centroid of ΔPQR. If $PO = 27$ cm, then what is the length of PM? **SSC CHSL (Tier I) 21/03/2023 Shift II**

(a) 18 cm (b) 54 cm
(c) 40.5 cm (d) 12 cm

504. In a cyclic quadrilateral $EFGH$, $\angle E$ is opposite to G. If $\angle E = 95°$, then what is the value of $\angle G$? **SSC CHSL (Tier I) 20/03/2023 Shift III**

(a) 80° (b) 75°
(c) 85° (d) 105°

505. The intersection point of the medians of a triangle is called **SSC CHSL (Tier I) 20/03/2023 Shift III**

(a) Orthocentre (b) Incentre
(c) Circumcentre (d) Centroid

506. Ratio of the angles of a triangle are 2 : 2 : 5. What is the largest angle? **SSC CHSL (Tier I) 17/03/2023 Shift II**

(a) 120° (b) 80°
(c) 110° (d) 100°

507. L is the incentre of ΔONP. If $\angle OLP + \angle ONP = 195°$, then what will be the value of $\angle OLP$? **SSC CHSL (Tier I) 17/03/2023 Shift II**

(a) 115° (b) 140°
(c) 135° (d) 125°

508. In ΔPQR, PN is the median on QR. If $PN = QN$, then what is the value of $\angle QPR$? **SSC CHSL (Tier I) 17/03/2023 Shift II**

(a) 90° (b) 80° (c) 60° (d) 75°

509. Radii of two circles are 20 cm and 4 cm. Length of direct common tangent is 30 cm. What is the distance between their centres? **SSC CHSL (Tier I) 17/03/2023 Shift II**

(a) 36 cm (b) 38 cm
(c) 34 cm (d) 32 cm

510. In ΔXYZ, points P, Q and R are points on the sides XY, YZ and XZ respectively, $\angle YXZ = 50°$, $XR = PR$, $ZR = QR$ and $\angle RQZ = 80°$. What is the value of $\angle PRQ$? **SSC CHSL (Tier I) 16/03/2023 Shift I**

(a) 80° (b) 90°
(c) 75° (d) 60°

511. Distance of a chord JK from the centre is 7 cm. If diameter of this circle is 50 cm, then what will be length of this chord? **SSC CHSL (Tier I) 16/03/2023 Shift I**

(a) 74 cm (b) 96 cm
(c) 48 cm (d) 24 cm

512. Angle subtended by a chord OP on the circumference of a circle is 90°. If diameter of the circle is 44 cm, then what will be the length of chord OP? **SSC CHSL (Tier I) 16/03/2023 Shift I**

(a) 44 cm (b) 88 cm
(c) 66 cm (d) 22 cm

513. Sum of the angles made by a chord at the centre and on the major arc of a circle is 225°. What will be the angle made at the major at of this circle? **SSC CHSL (Tier I) 15/03/2023 Shift IV**

(a) 125° (b) 150° (c) 90° (d) 75°

514. Two circles having equal radius intersect each other such that each passes through the centre of the other. Length of the common chord is 24 cm, then what will be the diameter of each circle? **SSC CHSL (Tier I) 15/03/2023 Shift IV**

(a) $16\sqrt{3}$ cm (b) $8\sqrt{3}$ cm
(c) $12\sqrt{3}$ cm (d) $10\sqrt{3}$ cm

515. In ΔXYZ, $\angle YXZ = 90°$. P is a point on side YZ such that XP is perpendicular to YZ. If $XP = YP = 10$ cm, then what will be value of PZ? **SSC CHSL (Tier I) 15/03/2023 Shift IV**

(a) 8 cm (b) 9 cm (c) 12 cm (d) 10 cm

516. In a cyclic quadrilateral $ABCD$, $\angle A$ is opposite to $\angle C$. If $\angle A = 110°$, then what is the value of $\angle C$? **SSC CHSL (Tier I) 15/03/2023 Shift IV**

(a) 60° (b) 50° (c) 70° (d) 55°

517. AB is the chord of a circle and O is the center of a circle. $\angle AOB = 130°$. What is the angle subtended by the same chord in the major segment of the circle? **SSC CHSL (Tier I) 14/03/2023 Shift I**

(a) 80° (b) 55° (c) 65° (d) 60°

518. In $\Delta PQR, \angle P = 46°$ and $\angle R = 64°$. If ΔPQR is similar and congruent to ΔABC, then what is the value of $\angle B$? **SSC CHSL (Tier I) 13/03/2023 Shift III**

(a) 90° (b) 110° (c) 100° (d) 70°

519. ΔMNO is similar to ΔSTU. The perimeters of ΔMNO and ΔSTU are 80 cm and 200 cm, respectively. If $ON = 25$ cm, then what is the length of TU? **SSC CHSL (Tier I) 13/03/2023 Shift III**

(a) 62.5 cm (b) 60.5 cm
(c) 59 cm (d) 61 cm

520. All points D, E and F lie on the circumference of a circle with centre O. If $\angle DEF = 48°$, then what is the possible value of $\angle DOF$? **SSC CHSL (Tier I) 13/03/2023 Shift III**

(a) 84° (b) 96° (c) 90° (d) 48°

521. In a triangle ABC, $AB = 6$ cm, $BC = 11$ cm. How many integral values of AC can be possible? **SSC CHSL (Tier I) 10/03/2023 Shift II**

(a) 10 (b) 8 (c) 12 (d) 11

522. Length of chord MN is 40 cm. Distance of chord MN from the centre is 15 cm. What will be the radius of this circle? **SSC CHSL (Tier I) 10/03/2023 Shift II**

(a) 42 cm (b) 32 cm
(c) 30 cm (d) 25 cm

523. Radii of two circles are 12 cm and 5 cm. Distance between their centres is 25 cm. What is the length of the direct common tangent? **SSC CHSL (Tier I) 09/03/2023 Shift I**

(a) 21 cm (b) 24 cm
(c) 22 cm (d) 23 cm

SSC CHSL 2022 & 2021 (Tier I)

524. In the given figure, chords AB and CD intersect each other at point L. Find CL. **SSC CHSL (Tier I) 02/06/2022 Shift I**

(a) 6 cm (b) 4 cm (c) 7 cm (d) 5 cm

525. The ratio of measures of the angles of a triangle is given as 3 : 4 : 8. What is the measure of the smallest of the three angles? **SSC CHSL (Tier I) 31/05/2022 Shift I**

(a) 33° (b) 39° (c) 30° (d) 36°

526. If $AB = QR$, $BC = PR$ and $CA = PQ$, then **SSC CHSL (Tier I) 30/05/2022 Shift I**

(a) $\Delta PQR . \cong \Delta BCA$
(b) $\Delta ABC . \cong \Delta PQR$
(c) $\Delta CBA . \cong \Delta PRQ$
(d) $\Delta BAC . \cong \Delta RPQ$

527. Two circles with centres O and P and radii 17 cm and 10 cm, respectively. Intersect each other at A and B. The length of the common chord AB is 16 cm. What is the perimeter of the ΔOAP (in cm)? **SSC CHSL (Tier I) 12/08/2021 Shift III**

(a) 33 (b) 25
(c) 48 (d) 40

528. Two equal circles of radius 8 cm intersect each other such that each passes through the centre of the other. The length of the common chord is **SSC CHSL (Tier I) 12/08/2021 Shift III**

(a) 8 cm (b) $4\sqrt{3}$ cm
(c) $8\sqrt{3}$ cm (d) $8\sqrt{2}$ cm

529. In ΔABC, $AC = BC$ and the length of the base AB is 10 cm. If $CG = 8$ cm, where G is the centroid, then what is the length of AC? **SSC CHSL (Tier I) 12/08/2021 Shift III**

(a) 13 cm (b) 15 cm
(c) $\sqrt{91}$ cm (d) 12 cm

530. In ΔABC, points D and E are on AB and AC, respectively, such that DE is parallel to BC. If $AD = 3$ cm, $BD = 6$ cm and $AE = 2$ cm, then find the length of CE. **SSC CHSL (Tier I) 10/08/2021 Shift I**

(a) 6 cm (b) 16 cm
(c) 8 cm (d) 4 cm

531. In ΔABC, AD is the internal bisector of $\angle A$ meeting BC at D. If $BD = 3.6$ cm and $BC = 8$ cm, then the ratio of AB to AC will be **SSC CHSL (Tier I) 10/08/2021 Shift I**

(a) 11 : 9 (b) 7 : 13
(c) 13 : 7 (d) 9 : 11

532. Let O be the centre of a circle and AC be the diameter. BD is a chord intersecting AC at E. AD and AB are joined. If $\angle BOC = 40°$ and $\angle AOD = 120°$, then $\angle BEC$ is equal to **SSC CHSL (Tier I) 10/08/2021 Shift I**

(a) 55° (b) 80°
(c) 90° (d) 70°

533. ABC is a triangle inscribed in a circle and $\angle ACB$ is equal to 35°. P is a point on the circle on the side AB, opposite to C. $\angle APB$ is **SSC CHSL (Tier I) 10/08/2021 Shift I**

(a) 72.5 (b) 145 (c) 175 (d) 70

534. In a ΔABC, $\angle BAC = 90°$ and AD is perpendicular to BC. If $AD = 8.4$ cm and $BD = 4.8$ cm, then the length of BC is **SSC CHSL (Tier I) 04/08/2021 Shift I**

(a) 19.5 cm (b) 15 cm
(c) 18 cm (d) 18.5 cm

535. From a point P that is at a distance of 15 cm from centre O of a circle of radius 9 cm, in the same plane, a pair of tangents PQ and PR is drawn to the circle. The area of quadrilateral $PQOR$ is **SSC CHSL (Tier I) 19/04/2021 Shift I**

(a) 114 cm^2 (b) 108 cm^2
(c) 118 cm^2 (d) 106 cm^2

536. In a right angled triangle ABC, if $\angle ABC = 90°$, $AB = 6$ cm, $BC = 8$ cm and BD is perpendicular to AC, then $AD : DC$ is **SSC CHSL (Tier I) 19/04/2021 Shift I**

(a) 7 : 16 (b) 8 : 15 (c) 9 : 14 (d) 9 : 16

537. The centroid of an equilateral ΔABC is O. If $AB = 27$ cm, then the length of AO is **SSC CHSL (Tier I) 12/04/2021 Shift II**

(a) $9\sqrt{3}$ cm (b) $6\sqrt{3}$ cm
(c) $7\sqrt{3}$ cm (d) $8\sqrt{3}$ cm

538. AB and AC are tangents to a circle with centre O from an external point A. The tangents AB and AC touch the circle at B and C, respectively, such that $\angle BAC = 118°$. Find the measure of $\angle OCB$. **SSC CHSL (Tier I) 12/04/2021 Shift II**

(a) 59° (b) 62° (c) 60° (d) 54°

SSC MTS 2021

539. Two circles of radii 14 cm and 10 cm intersect each other and the length of their common chord is 16 cm. What is the distance (in cm) between their centres? **SSC MTS 02/11/2021 Shift II**

(a) $6 + 4\sqrt{33}$ (b) $6 + 2\sqrt{33}$
(c) $6 + 5\sqrt{33}$ (d) $6 + 3\sqrt{33}$

SSC Selection Post 2024-2022

540. If $x^2 - 1, 2x$ and $x^2 + 1$ are the three sides of a right angled triangle, then which of the following can be its hypotenuses? **Graduate Level 20/06/2024 Shift-III**

(a) $x^2 + 1$ (b) x^2
(c) $2x$ (d) $x^2 - 1$

541. The median AD of a triangle ABC is produced and a perpendicular CF is dropped on it. BE is perpendicular to AD. If $BC = 34$ cm and $DF = 8$ cm, what is the length (in cm) of BE? **Graduate Level 20/06/2024 Shift-III**

(a) 17 (b) 9
(c) 15 (d) 19

542. PQ is a diameter of a circle and PS is a chord. If PQ is 82 cm and PS is 80 cm, the distance (in cm) of PS from the center of the circle is **Graduate Level 20/06/2024 Shift-III**

(a) 18 (b) 9
(c) 39 (d) 24

543. If the vertical angle of an isosceles triangle is 42°, then the measure of the other two angles will be **Higher Secondary Level 20/06/2024 Shift-II**

(a) 59° and 59° (b) 79° and 79°
(c) 89°and 89° (d) 69° and 69°

544. In ΔABC, D and F are the middle points of the sides AB and AC, respectively. E is a point on the segment DF such that $DE : EF = 1 : 2$. If $DE = 4$ cm, then BC is equal to **Graduate Level 27/06/2023 Shift-IV**

(a) 20 cm (b) 26 cm
(c) 22 cm (d) 24 cm

545. In ΔABC, P and Q are the middle points of the sides AB and AC, respectively. R is a point on the segment PQ such that $PR : RQ = 1 : 4$. If $PR = 5$ cm, then $BC = ?$ **Higher Secondary Level 27/06/2023 Shift-III**

(a) 46 cm (b) 50 cm
(c) 48 cm (d) 44 cm

546. In ΔTAP, $\angle TAP = 60°$, $TA = 6$cm, $AP = 8$cm. K is the midpoint of AP. A line from K is produced to meet TP at O such that $\angle AKO = 120°$. Find the length of OK. **Graduate Level 01/08/22 Shift-IV**

(a) 5 cm (b) 4 cm
(c) 3 cm (d) 6 cm

547. If a tangent PQ at a point P of a circle of radius 5 cm meets a line through the centre O at the point Q so that OQ =13 cm, then the length of the tangent is **Graduate Level 01/08/22 Shift-IV**

(a) 14 cm (b) 13 cm
(c) 12 cm (d)11 cm

Right Answers

1	(c)	2	(a)	3	(b)	4	(a)	5	(b)	6	(d)	7	(a)	8	(b)	9	(d)	10	(a)
11	(d)	12	(d)	13	(a)	14	(b)	15	(d)	16	(a)	17	(b)	18	(a)	19	(c)	20	(a)
21	(c)	22	(a)	23	(c)	24	(a)	25	(d)	26	(b)	27	(d)	28	(a)	29	(a)	30	(c)
31	(a)	32	(a)	33	(c)	34	(a)	35	(c)	36	(a)	37	(c)	38	(b)	39	(b)	40	(a)
41	(d)	42	(b)	43	(a)	44	(d)	45	(d)	46	(a)	47	(b)	48	(c)	49	(d)	50	(d)
51	(c)	52	(d)	53	(b)	54	(b)	55	(a)	56	(a)	57	(c)	58	(b)	59	(a)	60	(b)
61	(d)	62	(a)	63	(d)	64	(b)	65	(c)	66	(d)	67	(c)	68	(b)	69	(d)	70	(c)
71	(b)	72	(a)	73	(d)	74	(b)	75	(d)	76	(b)	77	(c)	78	(d)	79	(c)	80	(a)
81	(b)	82	(d)	83	(a)	84	(b)	85	(c)	86	(a)	87	(d)	88	(d)	89	(d)	90	(a)
91	(a)	92	(d)	93	(a)	94	(d)	95	(c)	96	(a)	97	(a)	98	(c)	99	(b)	100	(d)
101	(c)	102	(b)	103	(d)	104	(b)	105	(c)	106	(a)	107	(a)	108	(b)	109	(a)	110	(d)
111	(b)	112	(b)	113	(d)	114	(a)	115	(d)	116	(c)	117	(d)	118	(d)	119	(c)	120	(c)
121	(c)	122	(a)	123	(a)	124	(d)	125	(a)	126	(b)	127	(d)	128	(a)	129	(a)	130	(c)
131	(a)	132	(a)	133	(c)	134	(c)	135	(a)	136	(a)	137	(b)	138	(c)	139	(c)	140	(a)
141	(a)	142	(d)	143	(b)	144	(b)	145	(d)	146	(c)	147	(b)	148	(d)	149	(d)	150	(c)
151	(b)	152	(d)	153	(a)	154	(d)	155	(b)	156	(c)	157	(a)	158	(c)	159	(c)	160	(b)
161	(c)	162	(c)	163	(b)	164	(d)	165	(a)	166	(c)	167	(b)	168	(d)	169	(d)	170	(d)
171	(d)	172	(a)	173	(d)	174	(b)	175	(b)	176	(a)	177	(d)	178	(c)	179	(a)	180	(c)
181	(c)	182	(b)	183	(d)	184	(d)	185	(b)	186	(c)	187	(d)	188	(c)	189	(b)	190	(a)
191	(b)	192	(d)	193	(b)	194	(c)	195	(b)	196	(a)	197	(a)	198	(b)	199	(a)	200	(d)
201	(a)	202	(b)	203	(a)	204	(c)	205	(d)	206	(d)	207	(d)	208	(d)	209	(d)	210	(c)
211	(b)	212	(d)	213	(a)	214	(c)	215	(d)	216	(c)	217	(c)	218	(a)	219	(c)	220	(c)
221	(d)	222	(b)	223	(a)	224	(d)	225	(a)	226	(c)	227	(c)	228	(a)	229	(d)	230	(c)
231	(d)	232	(a)	233	(b)	234	(b)	235	(a)	236	(b)	237	(a)	238	(b)	239	(d)	240	(b)
241	(b)	242	(a)	243	(d)	244	(b)	245	(d)	246	(c)	247	(d)	248	(b)	249	(a)	250	(c)
251	(a)	252	(d)	253	(d)	254	(c)	255	(c)	256	(a)	257	(c)	258	(b)	259	(c)	260	(d)
261	(a)	262	(b)	263	(c)	264	(b)	265	(a)	266	(c)	267	(b)	268	(a)	269	(a)	270	(d)
271	(b)	272	(b)	273	(c)	274	(b)	275	(c)	276	(c)	277	(c)	278	(b)	279	(c)	280	(a)
281	(d)	282	(c)	283	(c)	284	(b)	285	(b)	286	(a)	287	(c)	288	(c)	289	(d)	290	(b)
291	(d)	292	(c)	293	(a)	294	(a)	295	(c)	296	(a)	297	(c)	298	(c)	299	(d)	300	(a)
301	(c)	302	(c)	303	(b)	304	(d)	305	(c)	306	(a)	307	(a)	308	(d)	309	(a)	310	(b)
311	(c)	312	(c)	313	(d)	314	(d)	315	(a)	316	(d)	317	(a)	318	(d)	319	(c)	320	(b)
321	(a)	322	(d)	323	(c)	324	(a)	325	(b)	326	(a)	327	(b)	328	(b)	329	(d)	330	(a)
331	(d)	332	(a)	333	(c)	334	(a)	335	(a)	336	(b)	337	(b)	338	(b)	339	(d)	340	(c)
341	(c)	342	(c)	343	(b)	344	(c)	345	(d)	346	(b)	347	(b)	348	(c)	349	(d)	350	(c)
351	(a)	352	(d)	353	(a)	354	(b)	355	(c)	356	(c)	357	(a)	358	(d)	359	(d)	360	(d)
361	(a)	362	(d)	363	(c)	364	(b)	365	(c)	366	(a)	367	(a)	368	(b)	369	(c)	370	(a)
371	(d)	372	(b)	373	(c)	374	(c)	375	(b)	376	(d)	377	(b)	378	(d)	379	(d)	380	(a)
381	(c)	382	(a)	383	(c)	384	(d)	385	(d)	386	(b)	387	(c)	388	(b)	389	(c)	390	(b)
391	(a)	392	(a)	393	(d)	394	(d)	395	(d)	396	(c)	397	(c)	398	(c)	399	(b)	400	(c)
401	(d)	402	(b)	403	(a)	404	(c)	405	(a)	406	(c)	407	(c)	408	(b)	409	(c)	410	(d)
411	(a)	412	(a)	413	(d)	414	(b)	415	(d)	416	(c)	417	(a)	418	(c)	419	(b)	420	(b)
421	(d)	422	(c)	423	(b)	424	(b)	425	(c)	426	(c)	427	(b)	428	(b)	429	(a)	430	(d)
431	(a)	432	(c)	433	(b)	434	(c)	435	(d)	436	(c)	437	(a)	438	(b)	439	(c)	440	(a)
441	(a)	442	(b)	443	(b)	444	(d)	445	(a)	446	(b)	447	(a)	448	(d)	449	(b)	450	(a)
451	(b)	452	(b)	453	(b)	454	(c)	455	(d)	456	(a)	457	(a)	458	(b)	459	(c)	460	(c)
461	(a)	462	(a)	463	(d)	464	(a)	465	(c)	466	(b)	467	(c)	468	(a)	469	(a)	470	(d)
471	(c)	472	(b)	473	(a)	474	(c)	475	(a)	476	(a)	477	(d)	478	(d)	479	(b)	480	(b)
481	(a)	482	(b)	483	(c)	484	(b)	485	(c)	486	(c)	487	(a)	488	(a)	489	(a)	490	(c)
491	(d)	492	(c)	493	(b)	494	(d)	495	(c)	496	(d)	497	(b)	498	(d)	499	(c)	500	(d)
501	(b)	502	(d)	503	(c)	504	(c)	505	(d)	506	(d)	507	(d)	508	(a)	509	(c)	510	(a)
511	(c)	512	(a)	513	(d)	514	(a)	515	(d)	516	(c)	517	(c)	518	(d)	519	(a)	520	(b)
521	(d)	522	(d)	523	(b)	524	(b)	525	(d)	526	(c)	527	(c)	528	(c)	529	(a)	530	(d)
531	(d)	532	(b)	533	(b)	534	(a)	535	(b)	536	(d)	537	(a)	538	(a)	539	(b)	540	(a)
541	(c)	542	(b)	543	(d)	544	(d)	545	(b)	546	(c)	547	(c)						

Solutions

1. (c) Given, diagonal $BD = 70$ cm.

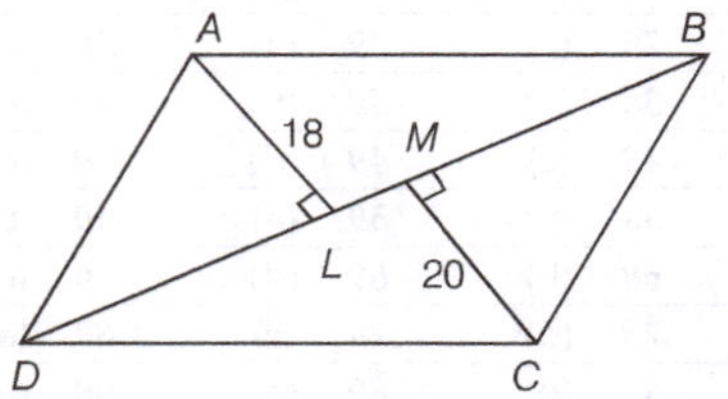

$\because$ Area of quadrilateral $= \frac{1}{2}(18 + 20) \times 70$

$= 35 \times 38 = 1330 \text{ cm}^2$

2. (a)

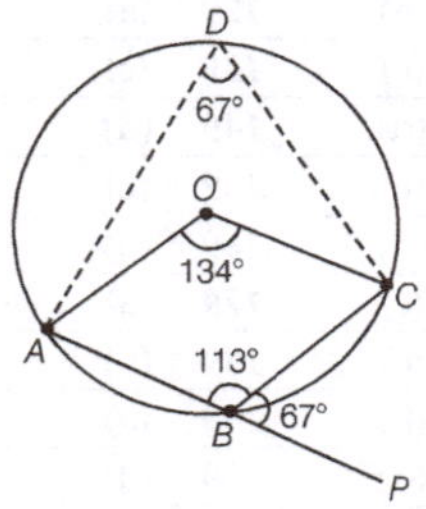

Given, angle subtended by arc ABC at the centre O = 134°

Since, when two angles are subtended by the same arc, the angle at the circumference is half of the angle at the centre.

$\therefore \quad \angle ADC = \frac{1}{2} \times 134° = 67°$

In cyclic quadrilateral $ABCD$.

$\angle ABC + \angle ADC = 180°$

$\Rightarrow \angle ABC = 180° - 67° = 113°$

Now, $\angle CBP = 180° - \angle ABC$

$= 180° - 113° = 67°$ [linear pair]

3. (b)

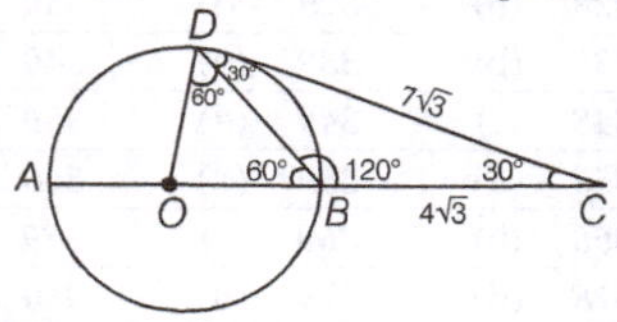

In ΔBCD,

Ratio of angles, 30° : 30° : 120°

$\therefore$ Ratio of sides, $1 : 1 : \sqrt{3}$

Here, $\sqrt{3} \rightarrow 7\sqrt{3} \Rightarrow 1 \rightarrow 7$

So, radius = 7 cm

$\therefore$ Diameter of circle $(AB) = 2 \times 7 = 14$ cm

4. (a)

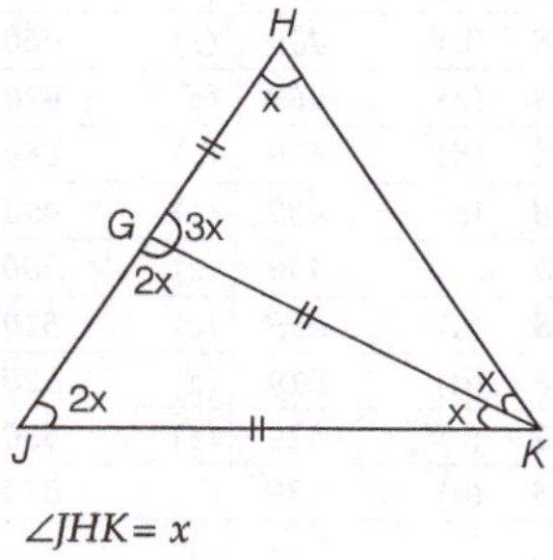

Let $\angle JHK = x$

Given, $HG = GK = JK$

$\therefore \quad \angle GHK = \angle HKG = x$

and $HJ = HK$

$\because \quad \angle JGK = 2x$ (external angle)

$\therefore \quad \angle HJK = \angle HKJ = 2x$

Now, $\angle HGK = \angle HJK + \angle JKG$

$= x + 2x = 3x$ (external angle)

In ΔHGK,

$x + x + 3x = 180°$

$5x = 180° \Rightarrow x = 36°$

$\therefore \quad \frac{2}{3}(\angle HGK + \angle GKJ) = \frac{2}{3}(3x + x)$

$= \frac{2}{3} \times 4x = \frac{8}{3} \times 36 = 96°$

5. (b) Ratio of corresponding sides of triangles

$= \sqrt{\text{Ratio of areas of triangles}}$

$\Rightarrow \frac{a}{b} = \sqrt{\frac{121}{225}} \Rightarrow \frac{a}{b} = \frac{11}{15}$

6. (d)

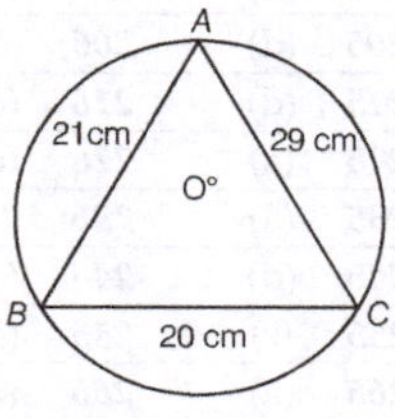

Length of circumradius

$= \frac{abc}{\sqrt{(a+b+c)(b+c-a)(c+a-b)(a+b-c)}}$

$= \frac{20 \times 29 \times 21}{\sqrt{(20+29+21)(29+21-20)(21+20-29)(20+29-21)}}$

$= \frac{20 \times 29 \times 21}{\sqrt{70 \times 30 \times 12 \times 28}} = \frac{20 \times 29 \times 21}{840}$

$= 14.5$ cm

7. (a) According to the question,

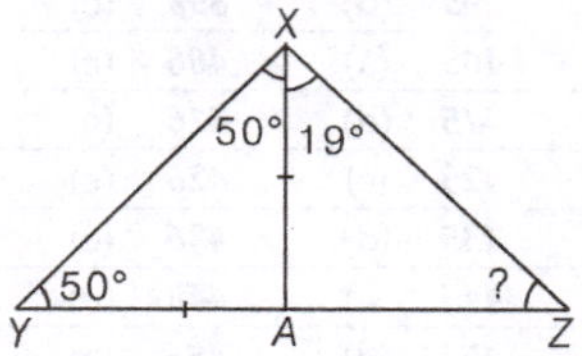

$XA = YA \Rightarrow \angle XYA = \angle AXY = 50°$

$\therefore \quad \angle ZXY = 50° + 19° = 69°$

In ΔXYZ, $\angle Z = 180° - \angle YXZ - \angle Y$

$\angle Z = 180° - 69° - 50° = 61°$

8. (b) We know, sum of all the interior angle of a triangle is 180°.

$\therefore \quad \angle P + \angle Q + \angle R = 180°$

$\angle R = 180° - (\angle P + \angle Q)$

$= 180° - 84° = 96°$

9. (d) As, PAB is a secant and PT is a tangent.

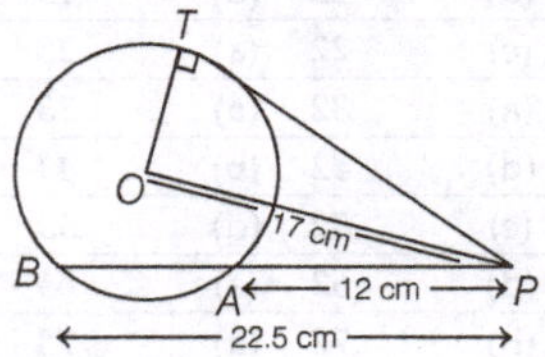

$\therefore \quad PT^2 = PA \times PB$

$PT^2 = 12 \times 22.5 = 270$

Also, OT is a radius and $OT \perp PT$

$\therefore \Delta OTP$ is a right tirangle.

$\therefore$ In ΔOTP, Using Pythagoras theorem, we get

$OT^2 + PT^2 = OP^2 \Rightarrow OT^2 + 270 = (17)^2$

$\Rightarrow OT^2 = 289 - 270 = 19$

$\therefore$ Radius $(OT) = \sqrt{19}$ cm

10. (a) From the properties of a triangle. We know, if the altitude from two vertices of a triangle to the opposite sides are equal, then the triangle will be an isosceles triangle.

11. (d) According to the question,

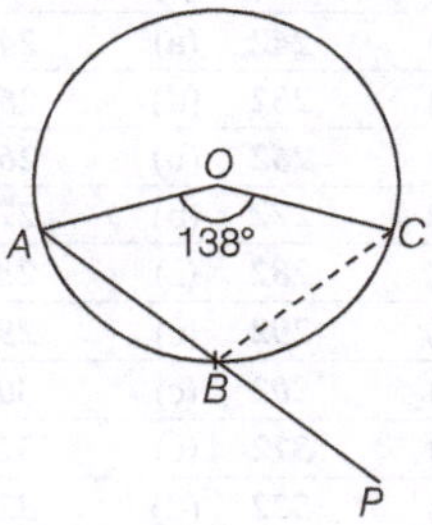

Reflex $\angle AOC = 360° - \angle AOC$

$= 360° - 138° = 222°$

We know, angle subtended at the centre is double the angle subtended at any other remaining part of circle.

$\therefore \quad \angle ABC = \frac{1}{2}$ Reflex $\angle AOC = \frac{1}{2} \times 222° = 111°$

$\therefore \quad \angle CBP = 180° - \angle ABC$ [$\because$ linear pair]

$= 180° - 111° = 69°$

12. (d) As, $DE \parallel BC$ and DE intersects AB and AC at distinct points D and E.

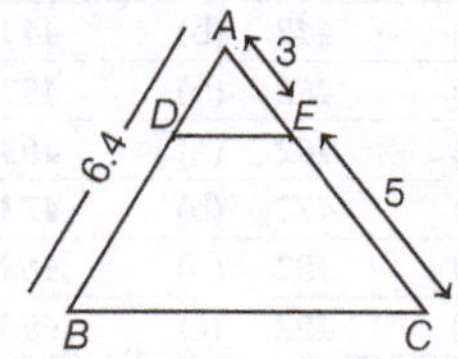

Also, $\frac{AE}{EC} = \frac{3}{5}$

$\therefore$ By Basic proportionality theorem,

$\frac{EC}{AC} = \frac{DB}{AB} \Rightarrow \frac{5}{8} = \frac{DB}{6.4} \Rightarrow DB = 4$ units

13. (a) According to the question,

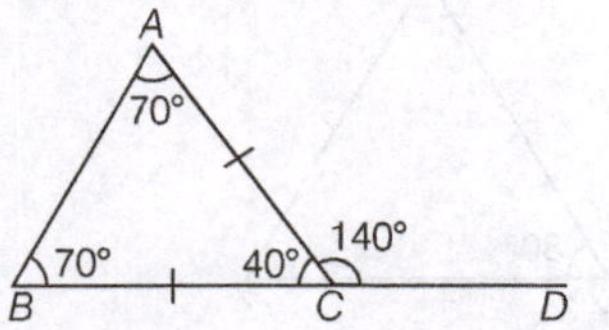

As, $AC = BC \Rightarrow \angle ABC = \angle BAC = 70°$

$\therefore$ In ΔABC, $\angle ACB = 180° - \angle ABC - \angle BAC$

$= 180° - 70° - 70° = 40°$

Also, $\angle ACD = \angle BAC + \angle ABC$

$= 70° + 70° = 140°$

[$\because$ by exterior angle property]

$\therefore$ Required value $= 2.5\angle ACD - 1.5\angle ABC$

$= 2.5\,(140) + 1.5\,(70)$

$= 350 - 105 = 245$

14. (b) According to the question,

$7 + 8 + 3 \rightarrow 180$

$18 \rightarrow 180$

$1 \rightarrow 10$

$\therefore$ Largest angle, $8 \rightarrow 80°$

15. (d) We know,

(i) Sum of interior angle of a triangle is 180°.

(ii) A triangle can have atmost one obtuse angle.

$\therefore$ Only statement (A) and (C) are correct.

16. (a) We know, ΔABC is a right triangle and AC is a diameter.

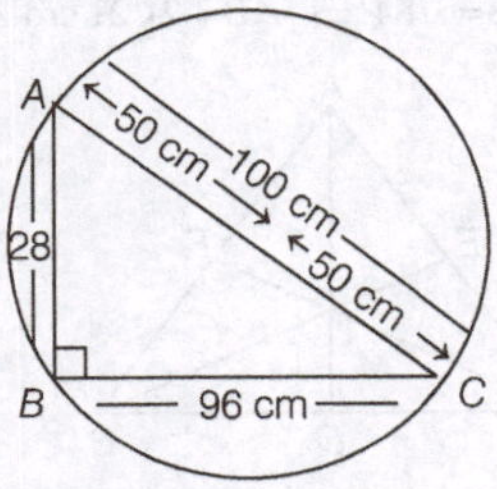

Using Pythagoras theorem,

$(AC)^2 = (AB)^2 + (BC)^2$

$\Rightarrow \quad (AC)^2 = (28)^2 + (96)^2$

$= 784 + 9216 = 10000$

$\Rightarrow \quad AC = 100$ cm

$\therefore$ Required area of circle $= \pi r^2$

$= 3.14 \times (50)^2 = 7850 \text{ cm}^2$

17. (b) We know,

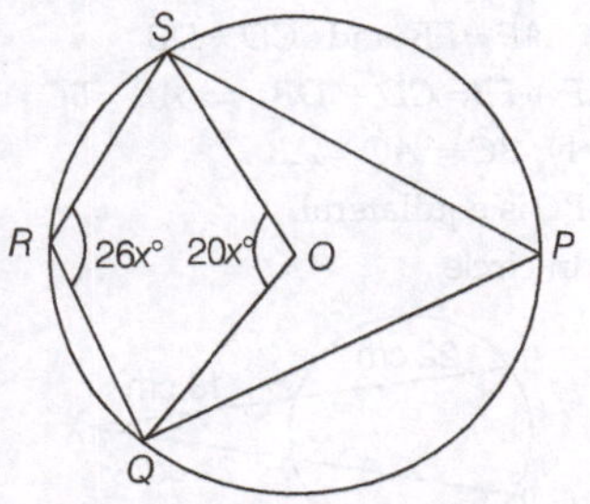

The angle made at the centre is twice the angle made at the circumference

$\therefore \quad \angle SPQ = \dfrac{20x}{2} = 10x \quad \ldots$(i)

The sum of each pair of opposite angle in a cyclic quadrilateral is 180°.

$\therefore \quad 26x + 10x = 180°$

$36x = 180$ [from Eq. (i)]

$x = 5°$

18. (a) We know,

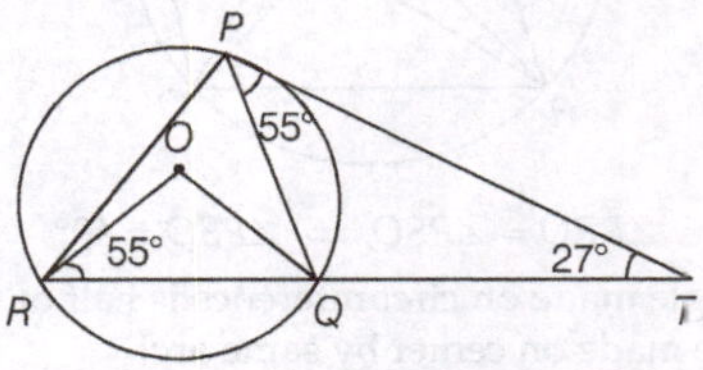

Chord made angle of 55° with tangent.

$\therefore \quad \angle PRQ = \angle QPT = 55°$

$\angle PQR = 55° + 27° = 82°$ [Ext. angle]

In ΔPQR, $\angle P + \angle Q + \angle R = 180°$

$\angle P + 55° + 82° = 180° \quad \angle P = 43°$

$\angle ROQ = 2\angle P$ [The angle made at the centre is twice the angle made at circumference]

$\angle ROQ = 2 \times 43° = 86°$

19. (c) $\because ST \parallel QR$

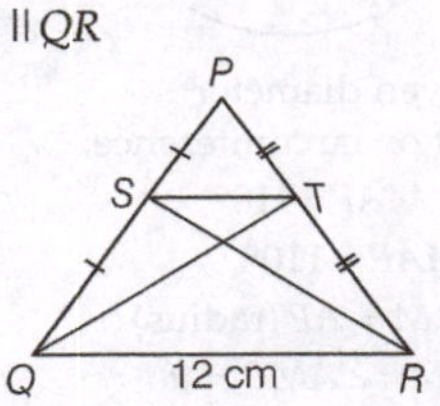

$\therefore \quad \Delta PST \sim \Delta PQR$

Let $\quad PS = x$ cm

We know, $\dfrac{PS}{PQ} = \dfrac{ST}{QR}$

$\Rightarrow \quad \dfrac{x}{2x} = \dfrac{ST}{12} \Rightarrow ST = 6$ cm

20. (a) In circle O,

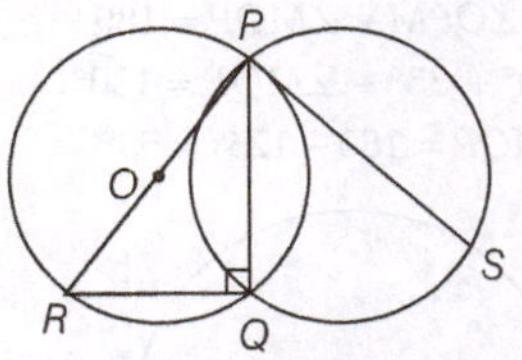

We know, angle formed in a semicircle is always 90°.

$\therefore \quad \angle PQR = 90°$

21. (c)

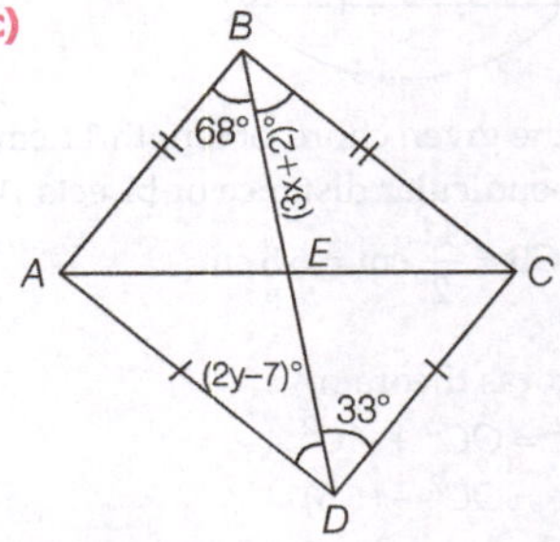

$\Delta DAB \cong \Delta DCB$

$\because \quad AB = BC, AD = CD,$

BD is common $\therefore \angle EBC = \angle EBA$

$68° = (3x + 2)° \Rightarrow 3x = 66$

$\Rightarrow \quad x = 22°$

$\therefore \quad \angle EDC = \angle EDA$

$33° = (2y - 7)° \Rightarrow 40° = 2y$

$\Rightarrow \quad y = 20°$

$\therefore 2x + 3y = 2 \times 22 + 3 \times 20 = 44 + 60$

$= 104°$

22. (a)

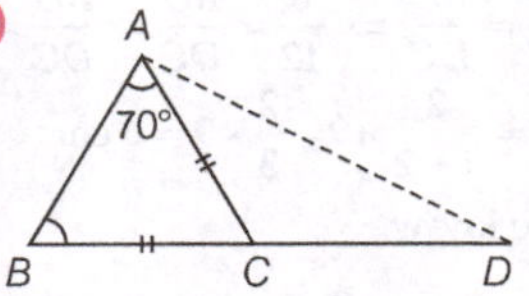

In ΔABC, $AC = BC$

Thus $\quad \angle ABC = \angle BAC \quad \therefore \angle ABC = 70°$

and $\quad \angle ACD = \angle ABC + \angle BAC$

[By external angle property]

$\angle ACD = 70 + 70 = 140°$

$\therefore$ Required angle $= \angle ACD - \angle ABC$

$= 140° - 70° = 70°$

23. (c)

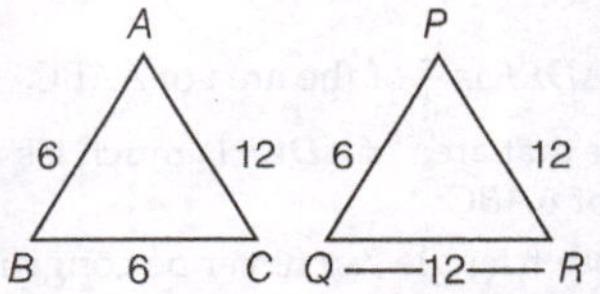

We draw two sides of triangle supporting third side be 6 cm and 12 cm.

[$\because$ triangle is isosceles Δ]

In ΔABC, $6 + 6 = 12$ [$\because a + b > c$]

$12 = 12$

Thus triangle is not possible.

Thus only triangle PQR is possible.

Hence, third side will be 12 cm.

24. (a) As we know, we need minimum three non-collinear points to draw a circle in a plane. Thus it is possible to draw a circle through 3 non-collinear points.

25. (d) Here, $AB = 18$ cm, $CD = 6$ cm

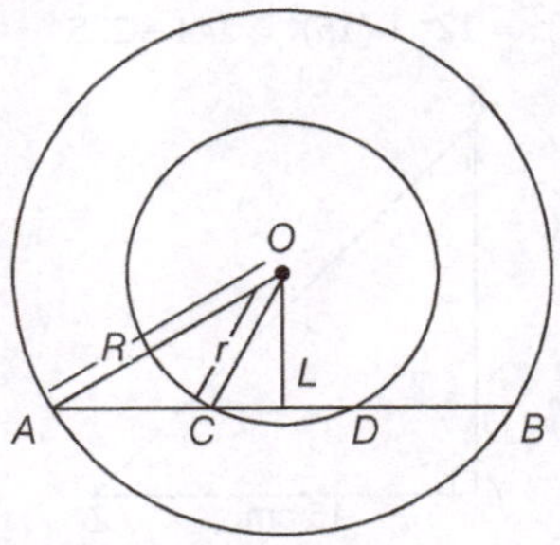

In ΔAOL, $(AO)^2 = (OL)^2 + (AL)^2$

$(R)^2 = (OL)^2 + \left(\dfrac{18}{2}\right)^2$

$(AO)^2 = (R)^2 = (OL)^2 + 9^2$

In ΔOLC, $(OC)^2 = r^2 = (OL)^2 + (3)^2$

$\therefore \quad (R)^2 - (r)^2 = (OL)^2 + 9^2 - (OL)^2 - (3)^2$

$= 81 - 9 \Rightarrow R^2 - r^2 = 72$ cm

26. (b)

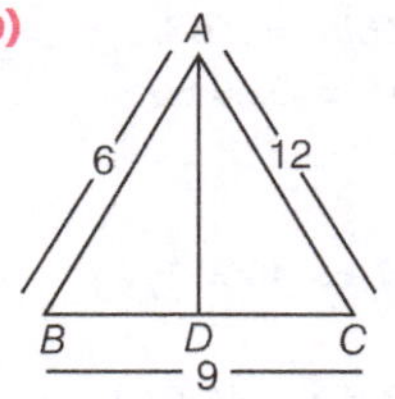

By Angle Bisector theorem,

$$\frac{AB}{AC}=\frac{BD}{DC}\Rightarrow\frac{6}{12}=\frac{BD}{DC}\Rightarrow\frac{BD}{DC}=\frac{1}{2}$$

Thus, $DC=\frac{2}{1+2}\times 9=\frac{2}{3}\times 9=6$ cm

27. (d) As we know,

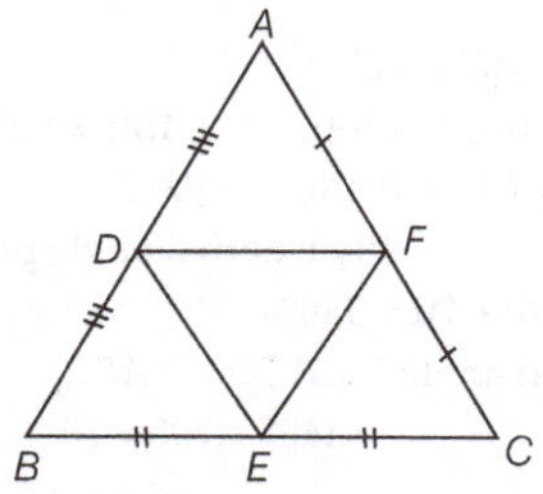

Area of ΔDEF is $\frac{1}{4}$ of the area of ΔABC.

It is clear that area of ΔDEF is much lesser than or of ΔABC.

Thus, both triangle can never be congruent.

28. (a) If two lines are coinciding with each other then number of intersection points are infinite. Thus, option (a) is correct.

29. (a) In ΔDEF,

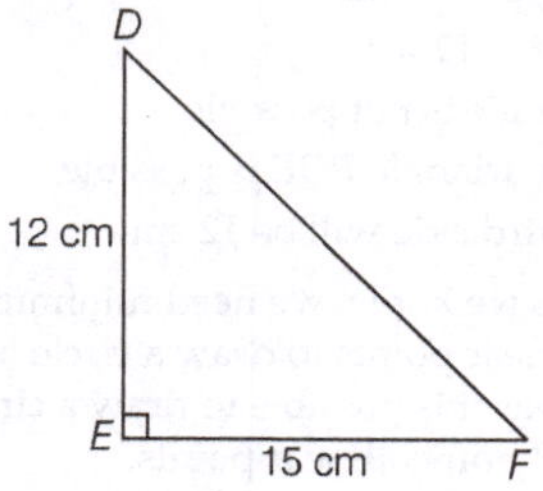

By Pythagoras theorem,

$$(DF)^2=12^2+(15)^2=144+225$$

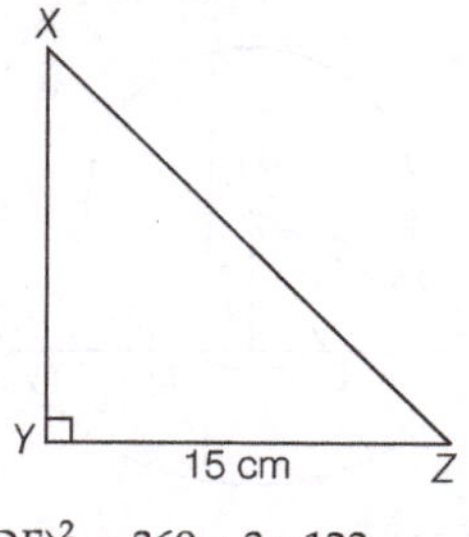

$$(DF)^2=369=3\times 123$$
$$(DF)^2=3\times 3\times 41$$
$$\Rightarrow DF=\sqrt{9\times 41}$$
$$DF=3\sqrt{41}\text{ cm}$$

As we know, if two triangles are congruent then their corresponding sides are equal.

Thus. $DF=XZ \Rightarrow XZ=3\sqrt{41}$ cm

30. (c) $\angle PRQ=\frac{\angle POQ}{2}\Rightarrow\angle PRQ=\frac{80°}{2}=40°$

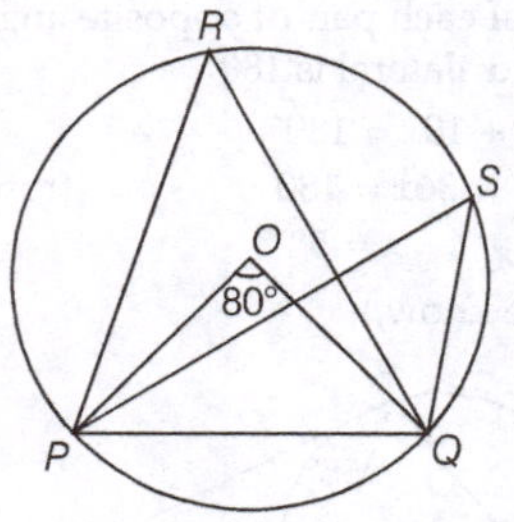

and $\angle PRQ=\angle PSQ,\Rightarrow\angle PSQ=40°$

∵ Angle made on circumference is half of the angle made on center by same arc]

[∵ angle made by same arc area equal]

31. (a)

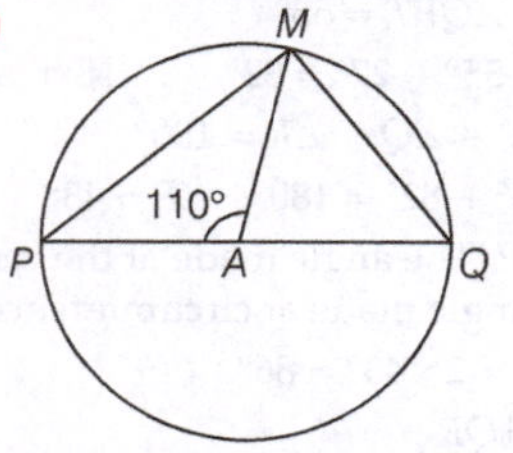

PQ is the given diameter.

M is a point on circumference.

Such that, $\angle MAP=110°$

In $\Delta MAP=110°$

In ΔMAP, $AM=AP$ (radius)

$\therefore\ \angle APM=\angle AMP=\theta$

$\therefore\ 110°+\theta+\theta=180°$

$\Rightarrow\ 2\theta=70°$

$\Rightarrow\ \theta=35°$

$\therefore\ \angle APM=35°$ and $\angle PMQ=90°$

(∵ Diameter makes a right angle on its circumference)

∴ In ΔMPQ, (Angle sum property)

$\angle PMQ+\angle QPM+\angle MQP=180°$

$90°+35°+\angle MQP=180°$

$\therefore\ \angle MQP=180-125°=55°$

32. (a)

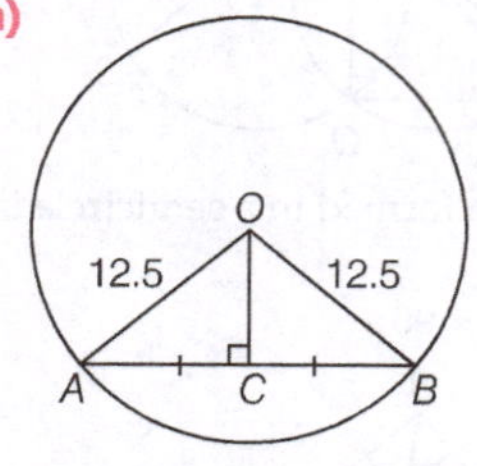

Let AB is the given chord of length 11 cm.

Since perpendicular distance or bisects AB.

$\therefore\ AC=CB=\frac{11}{2}$ cm $=5.5$ cm

In ΔOCA,

By Pythagoras theorem,

$$OA^2=OC^2+AC^2$$
$$(12.5)^2=OC^2+(5.5)^2$$
$$\Rightarrow OC^2=(12.5)^2-(5.5)^2=18\times 7=126$$
$$\Rightarrow OC=\sqrt{126}=11.2\text{ cm}$$

33. (c)

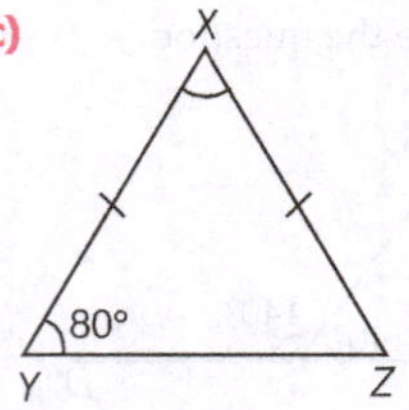

In ΔXYZ, $XY=XZ\Rightarrow\angle Y=\angle Z=80°$

(By angle sum property)

$\therefore\ \angle X=180°-(80+80°)=180-160°$

$\therefore\ \angle X=20°$

34. (a) In ΔPQR, $4\angle P=5\angle Q=20\angle R$

$$\frac{\angle P}{\angle Q}=\frac{5}{4},\frac{\angle Q}{\angle R}=\frac{20}{5}=\frac{4}{1}$$

$\angle P:\angle Q:\angle R\Rightarrow 5:4:1$

Let the angles be $5x, 4x$ and $1x$

Perimeter $=5x+4x+1x=180°$

$10x=180°\ \ x=18°$

Value of $\angle Q=4\times 18°=72°$

35. (c)

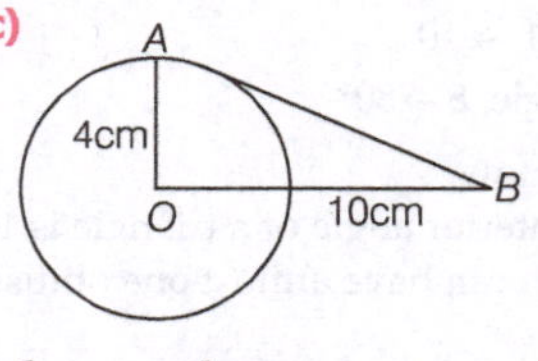

By Pythagoras theorem,

$\Rightarrow\ (10)^2=(4)^2+(AB)^2\Rightarrow$

$100-16=(AB)^2$

$\Rightarrow\ AB=\sqrt{84}\Rightarrow AB=2\sqrt{21}$ cm

36. (a)

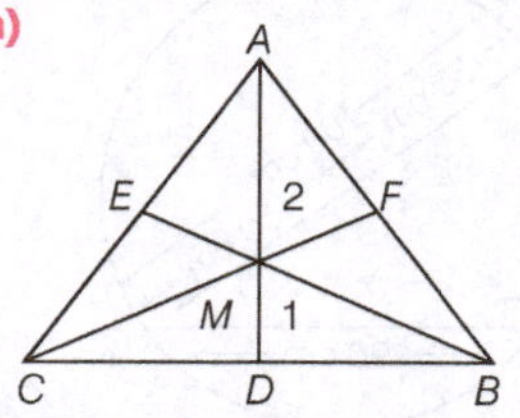

If the medians of a triangle are equal,

Then, $\frac{AM}{MD}=\frac{BM}{ME}=\frac{CM}{ME}=\frac{2}{1}$

$AM=BM=CM=2$ and $MD=ME=MF=1$

In ΔCDM and ΔAFM,

$CM=AM\Rightarrow MD=MF$

$\Rightarrow\ \angle AMF=\angle CMD$

$\Delta CDM\cong\Delta AFM$ (By SAS)

$CD=AF$ (By CPCT)

Now, $AF=FB$ and $CD=DB$

$\Rightarrow\ AF+FB=CD+DB\Rightarrow AB=BC$

Similarly, $BC=AC=AB$

So, ΔABC is equilateral.

37. (c) In circle,

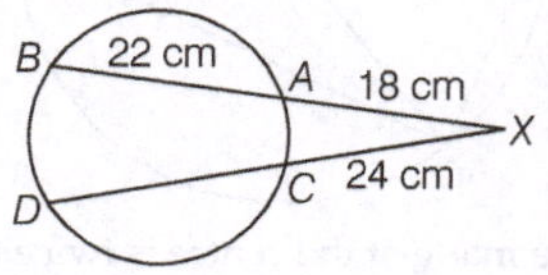

$XA=18$ cm, $AB=22$ cm,

$XC = 24$ cm $\Rightarrow XA \times XB = XC \times XD$

$\Rightarrow 18 \times (18 + 22) = 24 \times XD$

$\Rightarrow \dfrac{18 \times 40}{24} = XD \Rightarrow XD = 30$ cm

38. (b)

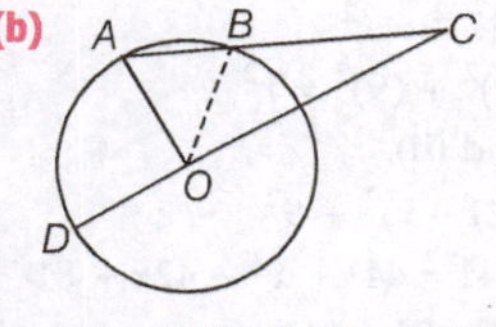

Given, $BC = OD$ = Radius of circle

$\Rightarrow BC = OB$

Angle opposite to equal sides are equal.

$\angle BOC = \angle BCO = 30°$

An exterior angle is equal to the sum of two opposite interior angles.

$\angle ABO = \angle BCO + \angle BOC = 30° + 30°$

$\angle ABO = 60°$ ...(1)

Now In ΔOAB, $OA = OB$ (radii of circle)

$\angle OAB = \angle ABO = 60°$

By angle sum property,

$\Rightarrow \angle AOB + \angle OAB + \angle OBA = 180°$

$\Rightarrow \angle AOB + 60° + 60° = 180° \Rightarrow \angle AOB = 60°$

As DOC is a straight line.

$\Rightarrow \angle AOD + \angle AOB + \angle BOC = 180°$ (Linear pair)

$\Rightarrow \angle AOD + 60° + 30° = 180° \Rightarrow \angle AOD = 90°$

39. (b) Let $\angle BAC = \theta \Rightarrow \angle ABC = x\theta$

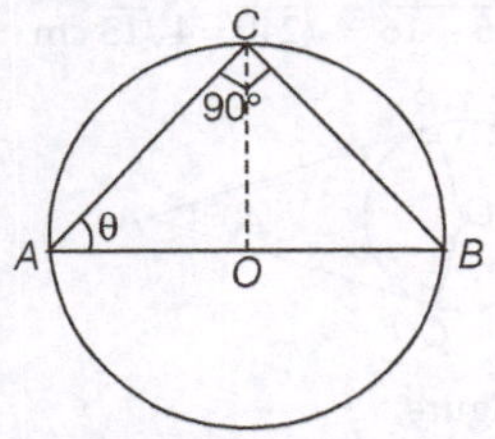

$OA = OB = OC = r$ (radius)

$\therefore$ ΔOCB is a equilateral triangle.

$\angle OBC = 60° = x\theta$ ...(i)

$\angle ACB = 90°$, [Angle in semicircle]

In ΔABC $\theta + 90° + x\theta = 180°$

$\theta + 90° + 60° = 180° \Rightarrow \theta = 30°$

From Eq. (i), $x \times 30° = 60° \Rightarrow x = 2°$

40. (a) Length of direct common tangent

$= \sqrt{\text{(Distance between centres)}^2 - \text{(Difference between radius)}^2}$

$= \sqrt{(15)^2 - \left(7 - \dfrac{7}{2}\right)^2} = \sqrt{225 - \dfrac{49}{4}}$

$= \sqrt{\dfrac{851}{4}} = 14.586$ unit

41. (d) We know,

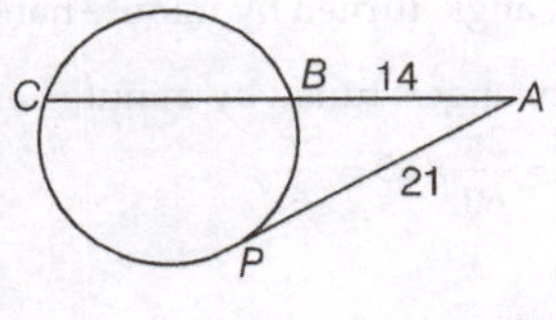

$\Rightarrow AP^2 = AB \times AC \Rightarrow (21)^2 = 14 \times AC$

$\Rightarrow AC = 31.5$

$\therefore BC = 31.5 - 14 = 17.5$ unit

42. (b) In a kite, $AD = DC$, $AB = BC$

Diagonal intersect each other at 90°.

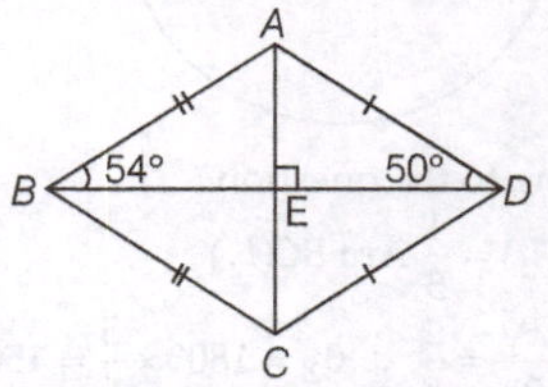

In ΔAED, $\angle EAD = 180° - (50° + 90°) = 40°$

In ΔAEB, $\angle BAE = 180° - (54° + 90°) = 36°$

$\because AD = CD$

$\angle DAE = \angle DCE = 40°$

$\because AB = BC \quad \therefore \angle BAE = \angle BCE = 36°$

$\therefore \angle BCD = \angle BCE + \angle CDE = 36° + 40° = 76°$

43. (a)

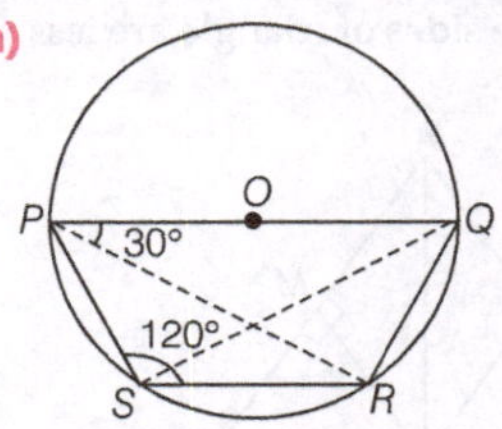

As, PQ is a diameter.

$\therefore \angle PSQ = \angle PRQ = 90°$

[$\because$ Triangle in a semi-circle is a right triangle]

$\therefore \angle QSR = \angle PSR - \angle PSQ$

$\Rightarrow \angle QSR = 120° - 90° = 30°$

As, $\angle QSR = \angle QPR = 30°$

[$\because$ Angle in same segment are equal]

44. (d)

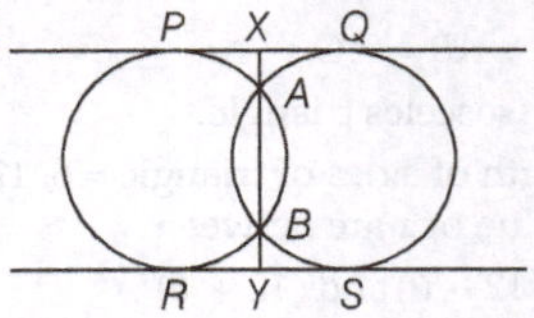

We have, $XY = 5$ cm and $AB = 3$ cm

As, $XA = YB$

And, $XY = XA + AB + YB$

$5 = 2\,XA + 3$

$\Rightarrow XA = 1 \Rightarrow XA = YB = 1$

$\because XB = XA + AB = 1 + 3 = 4$

As, PX is a tangent and XB is a chord from a common point X.

$\therefore PX^2 = XA \times XB \Rightarrow PX^2 = 1 \times 4$

$\Rightarrow PX = 2$ cm $\therefore PQ = 2PX$

$\therefore PQ = 2\,(2) = 4$ cm

45. (d) Given, $P - Q = 20°$

$Q - R = 26°$

$\Rightarrow P = Q + 20°$ ...(i)

$\Rightarrow R = Q - 26°$ ...(ii)

Sum of three angles of Δ is 180°

$\angle P + \angle Q + \angle R = 180°$

(By angle sum property)

$\angle Q + 20° + \angle Q + \angle Q - 26° = 180°$

$3\angle Q - 6° = 180° \Rightarrow 3\angle Q = 180° + 6°$

$\Rightarrow \angle Q = \dfrac{186°}{3} \Rightarrow \angle Q = 62°$

Put this value in Eq. (i),

$\angle P = 62° + 20° \Rightarrow \angle P = 82°$

46. (a)

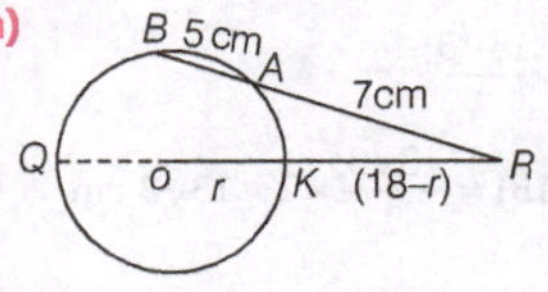

Let given, $OK = OQ = r$ cm (radius)

$RA = 7$ cm, $AB = 5$ cm, $OR = 18$ cm

By intersecting secant theorem,

$\Rightarrow RA \times RB = RK \times RQ$

$\Rightarrow 7 \times (7 + 5) = (18 - r)(18 + r)$

$\Rightarrow 12 \times 7 = 324 - r^2 \Rightarrow r^2 = 324 - 84$

$\Rightarrow r^2 = 240 \Rightarrow r = 4\sqrt{15}$ cm

47. (b)

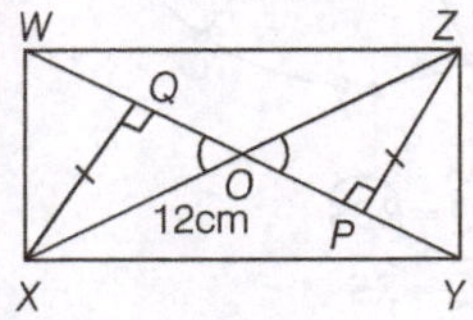

In ΔOQX and ΔOPZ,

$\Rightarrow \angle Q = \angle P$ (each 90°)

$\Rightarrow XQ = PZ$ (given)

$\Rightarrow \angle XOQ = \angle POZ$

(vertically opposite angle)

$\Rightarrow \Delta OQX \cong \Delta OPZ$

$\Rightarrow OX = OZ$ (by CPCT)

So, $OX = OZ = 12$ cm $\Rightarrow ZX = 2 \times (OX)$

$\Rightarrow ZX = 2 \times 12 \Rightarrow ZX = 24$ cm

48. (c) If we extend a chord infinitely on both sides, then the chord becomes a secant.

49. (d)

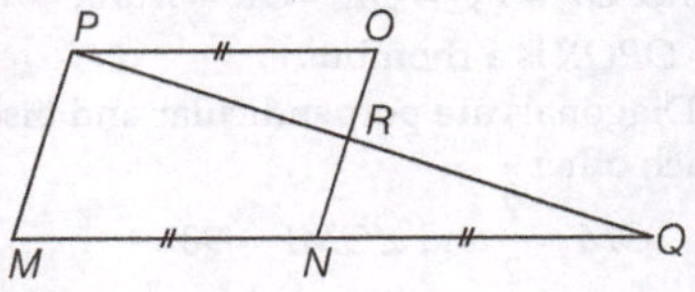

In ΔPOR and ΔRNQ,

$\angle NRQ = \angle PRO$ [vertically opposite angle]

$\angle RQN = \angle RPO$ [Alternate angle]

$\therefore \Delta POR \sim \Delta QNR$ [By angle rule]

$\therefore \dfrac{OR}{RN} = \dfrac{PO}{QN} = \dfrac{QN}{QN}$ [$\because MN = NQ = PO$]

$= 1$

Hence, $OR : RN = 1 : 1$

50. (d) $PQ = 13$ cm

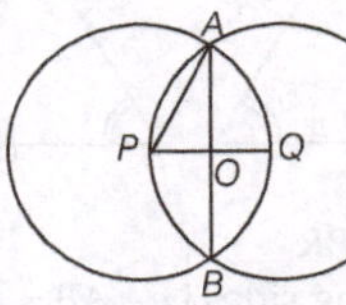

$\because$ Chord AB intersect PQ at mid-point O.

$\therefore OQ = \dfrac{PQ}{2} = 6.5$ cm and $AQ = 13$ cm

In ΔAOQ, Using Pythagoras theorem,

$$(AO)^2 + (OQ)^2 = (AQ)^2$$
$$(6.5)^2 + (AO)^2 = (13)^2$$
$$(AO)^2 = \frac{(13)^2 \times 3}{4}$$
$$AO = \frac{13\sqrt{3}}{2}$$

$\therefore$ Chord $(AB) = \frac{13\sqrt{3}}{2} \times 2 = 13\sqrt{3}$ cm

51. (c)

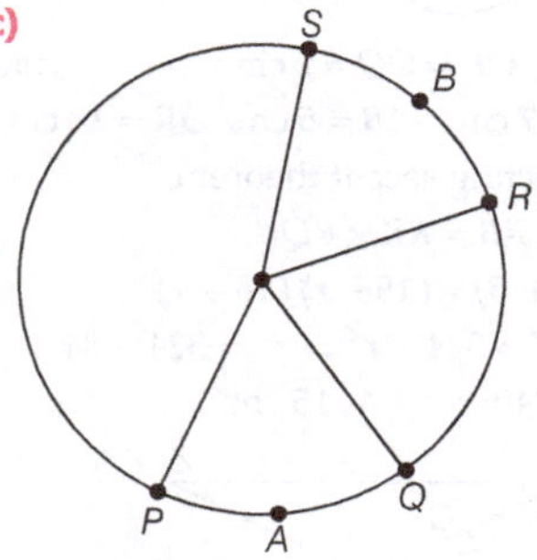

Given, $\widehat{PAQ} = \widehat{RBS}$

$\therefore$ $\widehat{PQ} = \widehat{RS}$

$\therefore$ $\frac{\widehat{PQ}}{\widehat{RS}} = \frac{1}{1} = 1:1$

52. (d)

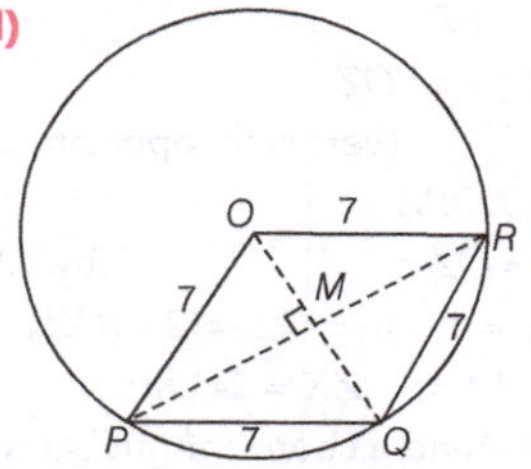

Since $OP = PQ = QR = OR = 7$ unit

$\therefore$ $OPQR$ is a rhombus

$\therefore$ Diagonals are perpendicular and bisect each other

$\therefore$ $OM = \frac{7}{2}$ and $\angle OMP = 90°$

and $PR = 2 \times PM$

In ΔOMP, $PM = \sqrt{OP^2 - OM^2} = \sqrt{7^2 - \left(\frac{7}{2}\right)^2}$

$$= 7\sqrt{1 - \frac{1}{4}} \Rightarrow = 7 \times \frac{\sqrt{3}}{2}$$

$\therefore$ $PR = 7 \times \frac{\sqrt{3}}{2} \times 2 = 7\sqrt{3} \times \frac{\sqrt{3}}{\sqrt{3}} = \frac{21}{\sqrt{3}}$ units

53. (b)

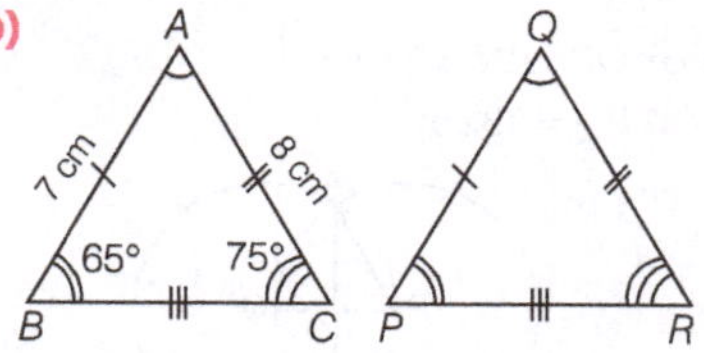

As, $\Delta ABC \cong \Delta QPR$

$\therefore$ Corresponding sides i.e., $AB = PQ = 7$ cm and corresponding angle i.e.,

$$\angle C = \angle R = 75°$$

54. (b)

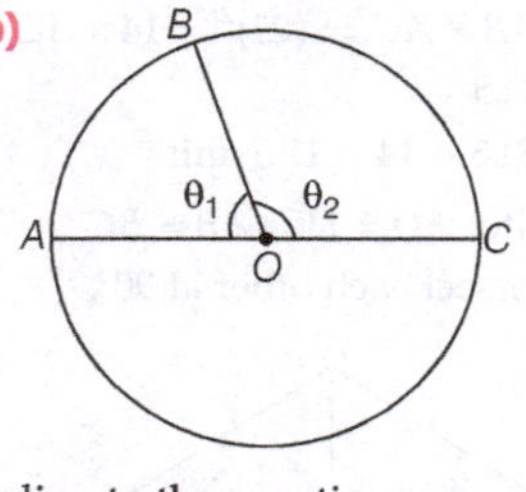

According to the question,

Arc $AB\,(l_1) = \frac{1}{5}$ Arc $BC(l_2)$

$\Rightarrow$ $\frac{l_1}{l_2} = \frac{\theta_1}{\theta_2} = \frac{1}{5}$ $\therefore$ $\theta_2 = 180° \times \frac{5}{6} = 150°$

55. (a) $a + b + c =$ Perimeter $= 52$ unit

As we know,

$a + b > c$ [$\because$ adding c both side]

$a + b + c > c + c$

$2c < 52$

$c < 26$ unit

$\therefore$ Thus, all the sides of triangle are less than 26.

56. (a)

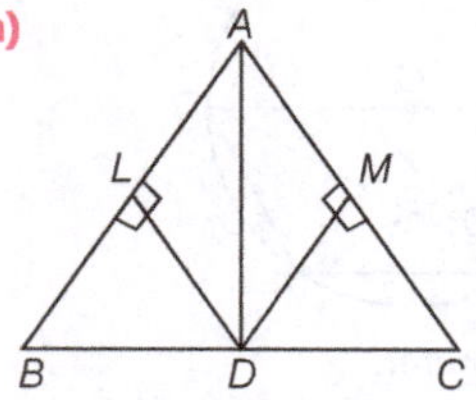

Given, D is the mid point of BC

$DL = DM$

$\because$ Area of $\Delta ABD =$ Area of ΔACD

$\therefore$ $\frac{1}{2} \times AB \times DL = \frac{1}{2} \times AC \times DM$

$\frac{1}{2} \times AB \times DL = \frac{1}{2} \times AC \times DL$

$AB = AC$

So, the Δ is isosceles triangle.

57. (c) Length of sides of triangle $= 6, 12, x$

Possible value of x are between

$= (12 - 6)$ and $(12 + 6)$

i.e. possible values are between 6 to 18

$= 7, 8, 9, 10, 11, 12, 13, 14, 15, 16, 17$

Possible value of $x = 11$

58. (b)

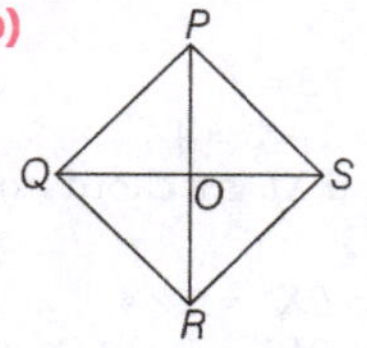

In rhombus $PQRS$, $OP = OR$

Then, $\angle POR = 180°$ and $\angle SOQ = 180°$

(SOQ is a straight line)

59. (a)

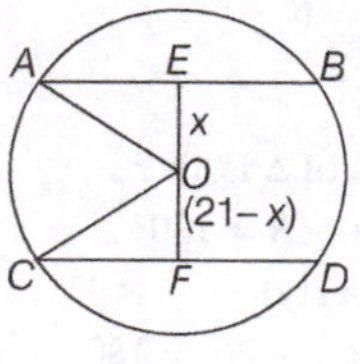

Given, $AB = 24$ cm, $CD = 18$ cm

Distance between the chords $= 21$ cm

Let $OE = x$ and radius $= r$

Then, $OE = x$, $OF = (21 - x)$

$$x^2 + (12)^2 = r^2 \quad \text{...(i)}$$
$$(21 - x)^2 + (9)^2 = r^2 \quad \text{...(ii)}$$

From Eqs. (i) and (ii),

$$x^2 + (12)^2 = (21 - x)^2 + 9^2$$

$\Rightarrow$ $x^2 + 144 = 441 + x^2 - 42x + 81$

$\Rightarrow$ $42x = 441 + 81 - 144$

$\Rightarrow$ $42x = 522 - 144$

$\Rightarrow$ $42x = 378$

$\Rightarrow$ $x = 9$

Put the value of x in Eq. (i),

$r^2 = (9)^2 + (12)^2$ $r^2 = 81 + 144$

$r^2 = 225 \Rightarrow r = 15$ cm

Radius of the circle is 15 cm.

60. (b)

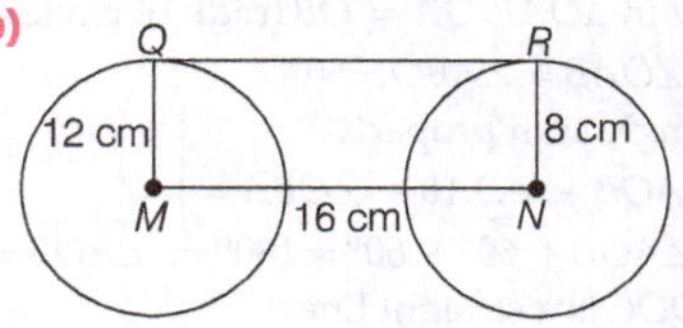

By using formula,

Tangent $QR = \sqrt{d^2 - (R - r)^2}$

$= \sqrt{(16)^2 - (12 - 8)^2} = \sqrt{(16)^2 - (4)^2}$

$= \sqrt{256 - 16} = \sqrt{240} = 4\sqrt{15}$ cm

61. (d)

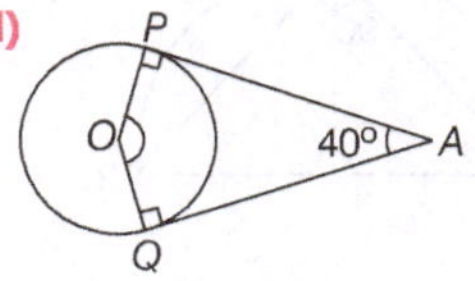

In given figure,

$\because$ We know meeting point of radius and tangent is perpendicular.

$\therefore$ $\angle OPA = \angle OQA = 90°$

Now, in Quadrilateral $POQA$

$\angle OPA + \angle PAQ + \angle AQO + \angle QOP = 360°$

$90° + 40° + 90° + \angle POQ = 360°$

$\angle POQ = 140°$

62. (a) If two triangles are similar then ratio of their corresponding side are equal,

Here, ΔRST and ΔABC

$$\frac{\text{Perimeter of } \Delta RST}{\text{Perimeter of } \Delta ABC} = \frac{\text{Side of } \Delta RST}{\text{Side of } \Delta ABC}$$

$$\frac{26}{39} = \frac{RS}{AB} \Rightarrow \frac{2}{3} = \frac{RS}{24}$$

$RS = 16$ cm

63. (d) In 60 min, angle turned by minute hand $= 2\pi$

In 1 min, angle turned by minute hand $= \frac{2\pi}{60}$

In 25 min, angels tuned by minute hand

$$= \frac{2\pi}{60} \times 25 = \frac{5\pi}{6}$$

64. (b)

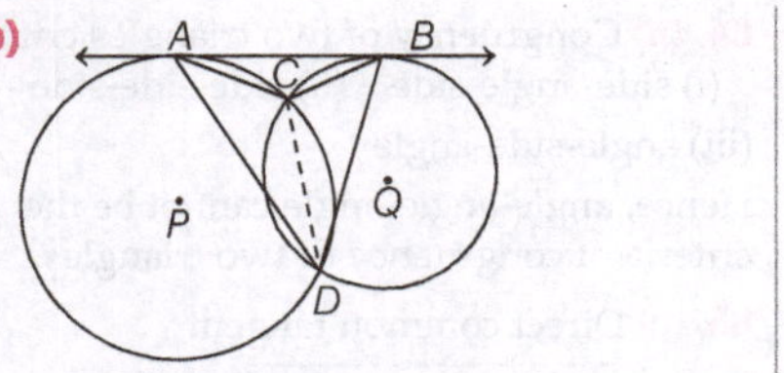

Let $\angle BAC = x°$

$\therefore$ By alternate-segment theorem

$\angle ADC = x°$

Similarly, $\angle ABC = y°$ then $\angle BDC = y°$

$\therefore \quad \angle ADB = \angle ADC + \angle BDC$

$\Rightarrow \quad x + y = 68°$

In ΔABC,

$\angle ACB = 180° - (x + y) = 180° - 68° = 112°$

$\therefore \quad \angle ACB = 112°$

65. (c) We know,

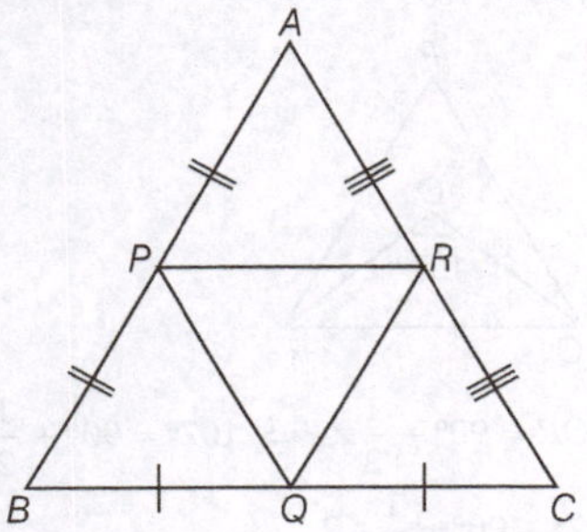

Area of $\Delta PQR = \frac{1}{4}$ Area of ΔABC

$$= \frac{1}{4}\left[\frac{\sqrt{3}}{4} \times (11)^2\right] = \frac{121\sqrt{3}}{16}$$

66. (d) Given, $\Delta ABC \cong \Delta PQR$, $AB = 6$ cm, $\angle B = 50°$ and $\angle A = 70°$

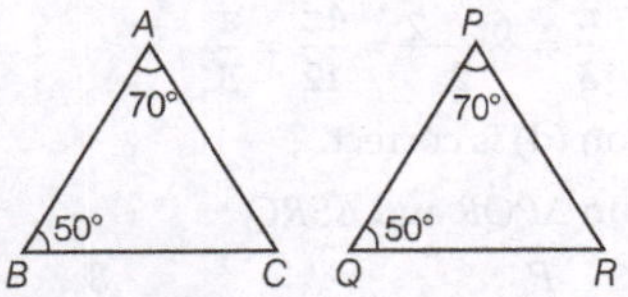

$\angle BCA = 180° - (70° + 50°) = 60°$

By using side angle side congruency

$\therefore \quad AB = PQ = 6$ cm

$\angle R = \angle C = 60°$

67. (c) $\because$ ABC is a equilateral triangle

$\therefore \quad \angle A = 60°$

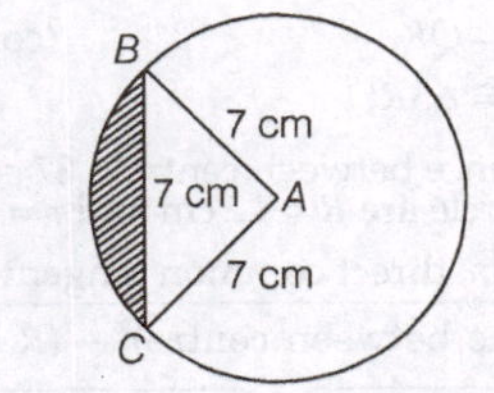

$\therefore$ Length of arc $BC = 2\pi r \times \frac{60°}{360°}$

$$= 2 \times \pi \times 7 \times \frac{1}{6} = \frac{7\pi}{3}$$

68. (b) Let radius of circle(c) $= r$

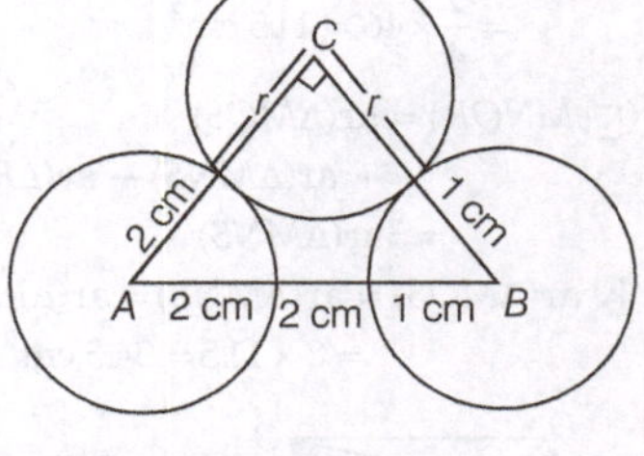

Using Pythagoras theorem,

$BC^2 + AC^2 = AB^2$

$\Rightarrow \quad (r+1)^2 + (r+2)^2 = 5^2$

$\Rightarrow \quad r^2 + 1 + 2r + r^2 + 4 + 4r = 25$

$\Rightarrow \quad 2r^2 + 6r - 20 = 0$

$\Rightarrow \quad r^2 + 3r - 10 = 0$

$\Rightarrow \quad (r+5)(r-2) = 0$

$\therefore \quad r = 2$ cm

69. (d)

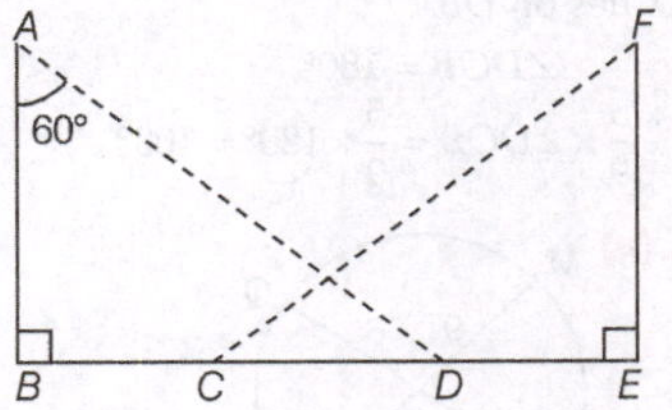

In ΔABD and ΔFEC,

$\angle BAD = 60°$

$BD = EC$ (Given)

$\angle ABD = \angle FEC = 90°$

$AB = FE$ (Given)

$\therefore \quad \Delta ABD \cong \Delta FEC$ (by SAS)

$\therefore$ By CPCT, $\angle BAD = \angle EFC = 60°$

$\therefore \quad$ In ΔFEC, $\angle FCE = 180° - (90° + 60°)$

$= 180° - 150° = 30°$

$\therefore \quad \frac{\angle BAD}{\angle FCE} = \frac{60}{30} = \frac{2}{1} = 2:1$

70. (c)

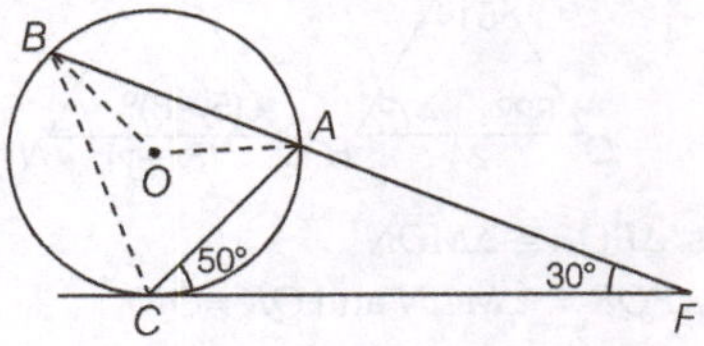

$\because \quad \angle ACF = 50°, \angle AFC = 30°$

$\therefore \quad \angle ABC = 50°$

(by alternate segment theorem)

In ΔBCF,

$\angle B = 50°, \angle F = 30°$

$\therefore \quad \angle BCF = 180° - (50° + 30°) = 100°$

$\therefore \quad \angle BCA = 100° - \angle ACF = 100° - 50° = 50°$

$\therefore \quad \angle BOA = 2 \times \angle BCA = 2 \times 50° = 100°$

($\because$ Angle made by a chord on centre is double the angle made on the circumference)

71. (b) Given,

$DE = 36$ cm, $DF = 40$ cm, $EF = 38$ cm

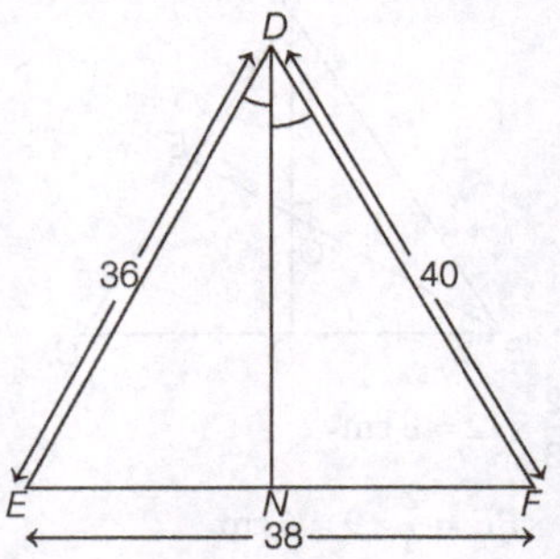

$\therefore$ By angle bisector theorem,

$$\frac{EN}{NF} = \frac{DE}{DF} = \frac{36}{40} = \frac{9}{10}$$

$\therefore \quad EN = 9x, NF = 10x$

$\therefore \quad EF = EN + NF = 9x + 10x = 19x$

$\therefore \quad 19x = 38 \Rightarrow x = 2$

$\therefore \quad NF = 10x = 10 \times 2 = 20$ cm

72. (a) Let the three, internal angles of triangle be $17x$, $13x$ and $15x$.

According to the question,

$17x + 13x + 15x = 180°$

$\Rightarrow \quad 45x = 180°$

$\Rightarrow \quad x = 4$

$\therefore$ Required difference $= 17x - 13x$

$= 4x = 4(4) = 16°$

73. (d)

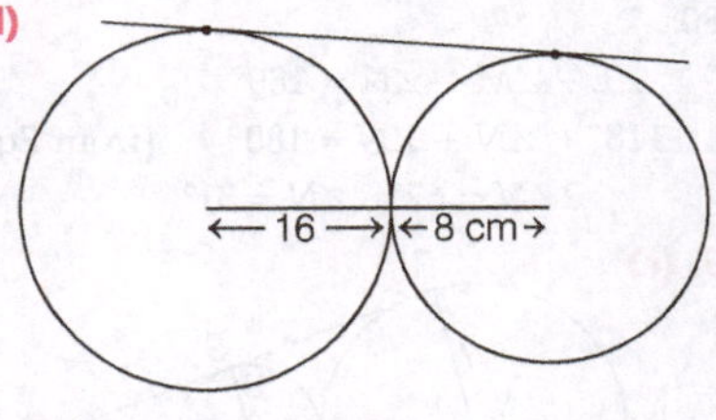

Length of direct common tangent

$= \sqrt{d^2 - (r_1 - r_2)^2} = \sqrt{(24)^2 - (16-8)^2}$

$= \sqrt{576 - 64} = \sqrt{512}$

$= 16\sqrt{2}$ cm

74. (b)

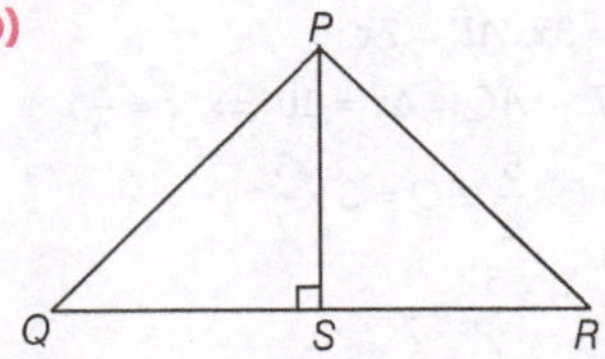

According to the question, $PS \perp QR$

In ΔPQS, $PQ^2 = PS^2 + QS^2$

$\Rightarrow \quad PS^2 = PQ^2 - QS^2 \quad$ ...(i)

In ΔPSR, $PS^2 + SR^2 = PR^2$

$PS^2 = PR^2 - SR^2 \quad$ ...(ii)

From Eqs. (i) and (ii)

$PQ^2 - QS^2 = PR^2 - SR^2$

$PQ^2 + SR^2 = PR^2 + QS^2$

75. (d) $AO = \frac{2}{3} \times AD$

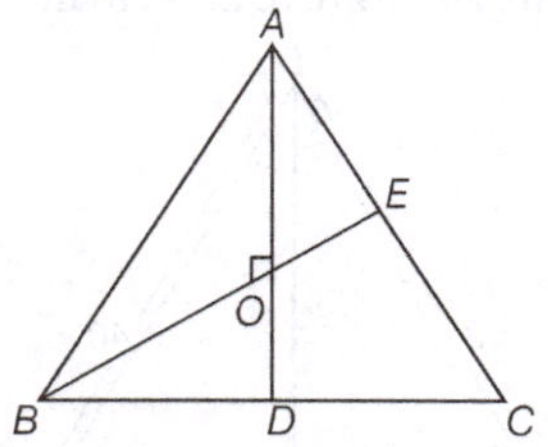

$= \frac{2}{3} \times 12 = 8$ cm

$BO = \frac{2}{3} \times BE = \frac{2}{3} \times 9 = 6$ cm

Now, in ΔABC, $(AB)^2 = 6^2 + 8^2 = (10)^2$

$AB = 10$ cm

76. (b) $\because$ $LM = LM$

$\therefore \Delta LMN$ is an isosceles triangle.

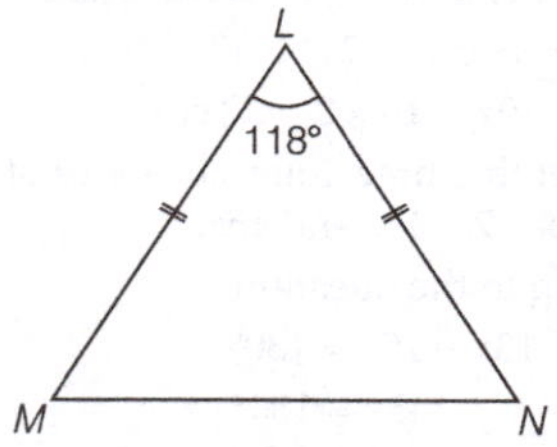

$\therefore \quad \angle N = \angle M \quad$ ...(i)

We know,

Sum of internal angle of a triangle is always 180°.

$\angle L + \angle M + \angle N = 180°$

$118° + \angle N + \angle N = 180° \quad$ [from Eq. (i)]

$2\angle N = 62° \quad \angle N = 31°$

77. (c)

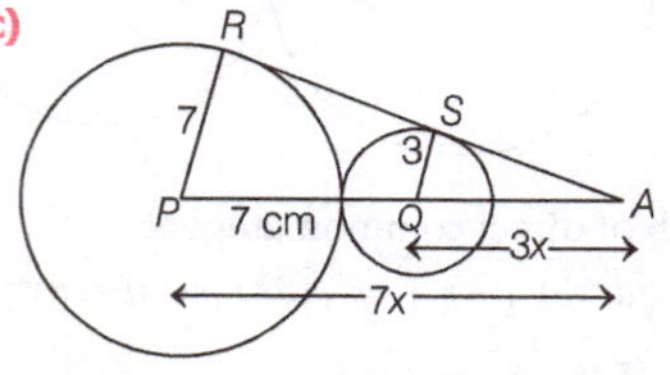

$\because \quad \Delta AQS \sim \Delta APR \Rightarrow \frac{AQ}{AP} = \frac{QS}{PR} = \frac{3}{7}$

Let $AQ = 3x$, $AP = 7x$

$PQ = AP - AQ = 4x = 10 \Rightarrow x = \frac{5}{2}$

$\Rightarrow \quad AP = 7 \times \frac{5}{2}$, $AQ = 3 \times \frac{5}{2}$

$\Rightarrow \quad \frac{AP}{AQ} = \frac{7 \times \frac{5}{2}}{3 \times \frac{5}{2}} = \frac{7}{3}$

78. (d) As, M, N, S are the mid-points of ΔPQR.

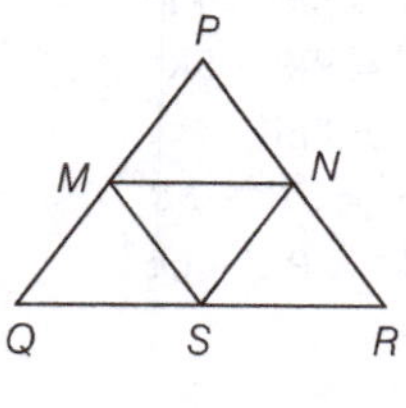

$\therefore \quad \text{ar } \Delta MNS = \frac{1}{4} \text{ ar } (\Delta PQR)$

$= \frac{1}{4} \times 46 = 11.5 \text{ cm}^2$

As, ar(□ $MNQR$) = ar(ΔMQS) + ar(ΔMNS) + ar(ΔRSN)

= 3ar(ΔMNS)

[$\because$ ar(ΔMQS) = ar(ΔMNS) = ar(ΔRSN)]

$= 3 \times 11.5 = 34.5 \text{ cm}^2$

79. (c)

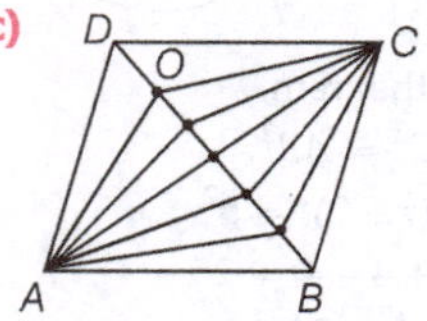

Given, $ABCD$ is a rhombus and O is any point in the interior of rhombus, $AO = OC$

$\therefore$ 'O' must lies on the perpendicular bisector of AC which is line DB.

$\therefore$ 'O' lies on DB.

$\therefore \quad \angle DOB = 180°$

$\therefore \quad \frac{5}{9} \times \angle DOB = \frac{5}{9} \times 180° = 100°$

80. (a)

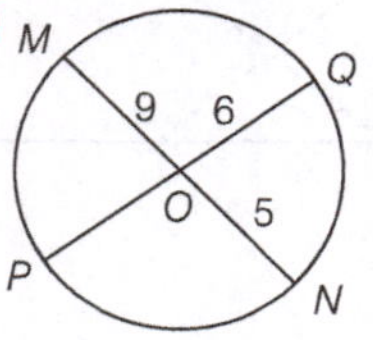

We know, $MO \times ON = OP \times OQ$

$\Rightarrow \quad OP = \frac{9 \times 5}{6} = 7.5$

81. (b) We know,

Length of transverse common tangent

$= \sqrt{d^2 - (r_1 + r_2)^2} = \sqrt{(17)^2 - (5 + 10)^2}$

$= \sqrt{289 - 225} = \sqrt{64} = 8$ cm

82. (d)

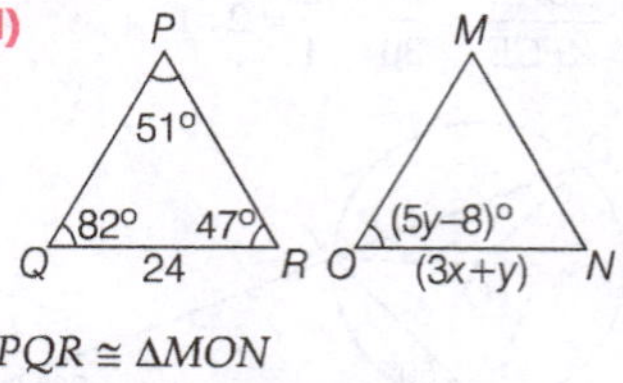

As, $\Delta PQR \cong \Delta MON$

$\therefore \angle PQR = \angle MON$ and $QR = ON$

$\Rightarrow \quad 82 = (5y - 8)$ and $24 = 3x + y$

$\Rightarrow \quad y = 18$ and $x = \frac{24 - y}{3}$

$\Rightarrow \quad x = \frac{24 - 18}{3} = \frac{6}{3} = 2 \Rightarrow x = 2$

$\therefore$ Required value, $(x + y) = (18 + 2) = 20$

83. (a) Here, $xz = xy + yz$

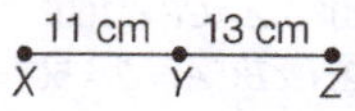

$24 = 11 + 13$

$\therefore$ All the points are on a line.

Hence, the number of circle that travel through points x, y and z is 0.

84. (b) Congruency of two triangles criteria.

(i) side-angle-side (ii) side-side-side

(iii) angle-side-angle

Hence, angle-angle-angle cannot be the criteria of congruency of two triangles.

85. (c) Direct common tangent

$= \sqrt{(r_1 + r_2)^2 - (r_1 - r_2)^2}$

$= \sqrt{(18 + 12)^2 - (18 - 12)^2}$

$= \sqrt{900 - 36} = \sqrt{864} = 12\sqrt{6}$ cm

86. (a) Given, ΔEFG and ΔHIJ are congruent.

Area of $\Delta EFG = 124 \text{ cm}^2$

($\because$ If two triangles are congruent, they superimpose on each other, there area will be equal)

Area of ΔEFG = Area of $\Delta HIJ = 124 \text{ cm}^2$

Hence, option (a) is correct.

87. (d)

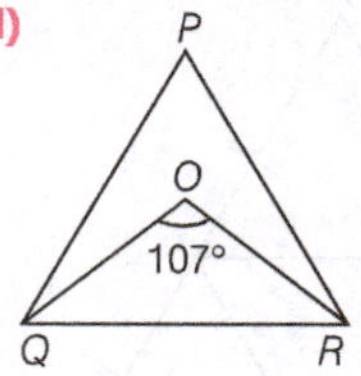

$\Rightarrow \angle QOR = 90° + \frac{1}{2}\angle P \Rightarrow 107° = 90° + \frac{1}{2}\angle P$

$\Rightarrow \quad 107° - 90° = \frac{1}{2}\angle P$

$\Rightarrow \quad 17° = \frac{1}{2}\angle P$

$\therefore \quad \angle P = 34°$

88. (d) From Statement I,

One angle = Average of the other two angles

$\therefore \quad \frac{\pi}{3} = \frac{\frac{\pi}{6} + \frac{\pi}{2}}{2} = \frac{4\pi}{12} = \frac{\pi}{3}$

$\therefore$ Option (d) is correct.

89. (d) In ΔPQR and ΔSRQ,

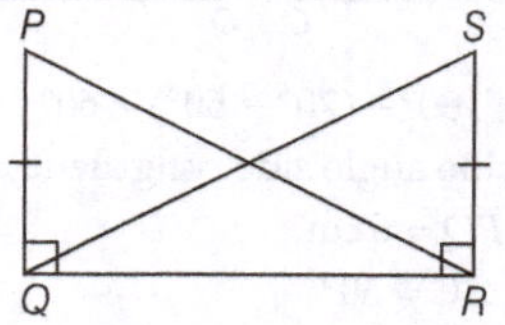

$PQ = SR$ (given)

$\angle PQR = \angle SRQ$ (each 90°)

$QR = QR$ (common)

$\therefore \quad \Delta PQR \cong \Delta SRQ$ (SAS)

90. (a) Distance between centre = 37 cm

Radius of circle are $R = 22$ cm and $r = 10$ cm

$\therefore$ By formula, direct common tangent

$= \sqrt{(\text{Distance between centre})^2 - (R - r)^2}$

$= \sqrt{(37)^2 - (22 - 10)^2} = \sqrt{(37)^2 - (12)^2}$

$= \sqrt{(37 + 12)(37 - 12)} = \sqrt{49 \times 25}$

$= 7 \times 5 = 35$ cm

Thus, length of direct common tangent (MQ) = 35 cm

91. (a)

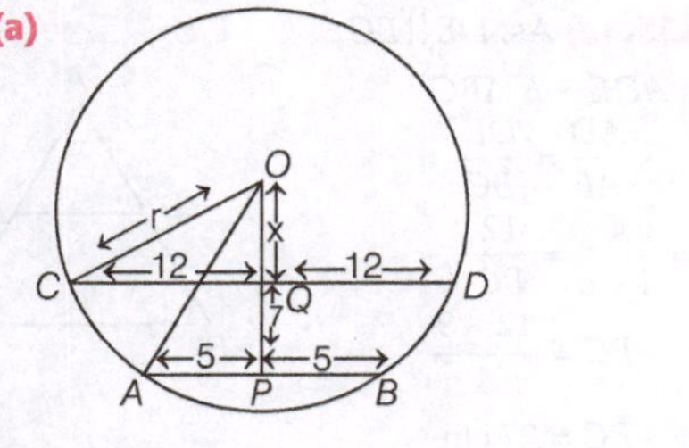

In ΔOQC,

$$r^2 = (12)^2 + x^2 \quad \ldots\text{(i)}$$

Again in ΔOAP,

$$r^2 = (5)^2 + (x+7)^2 \quad \ldots\text{(ii)}$$

From Eqs. (i) and (ii),

$$(12)^2 + x^2 = 25 + x^2 + 49 + 14x$$

$$\Rightarrow 144 + x^2 = 25 + x^2 + 49 + 14x$$

$$\Rightarrow \quad 14x = 144 - 25 - 49$$

$$\Rightarrow \quad 14x = 70 \Rightarrow x = \frac{70}{14} = 5$$

Thus radius, $r^2 = 144 + 25 \Rightarrow r = 13$

$\therefore$ Diameter $= 13 \times 2 = 26$ cm

92. (d) As, we know all sides of equilateral triangle are equal.

Then, sum of two sides = 16 cm

Each side of equilateral triangle = 8 cm

93. (a)

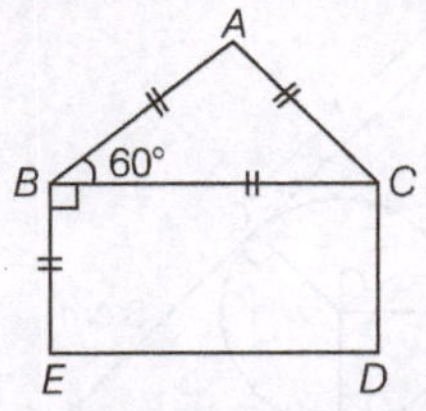

We know that the angles of opposite to equal sides are equal.

$\therefore \quad \angle EAB = \angle AEB = x°$

Now, in ΔABE, $90° + 60° + x° + x° = 180$

$\therefore \quad x = 15°$

Hence, value of $\angle EAB + 3\angle AEB$

$$= x + 3x = 4x = 4 \times 15 = 60°$$

94. (d) We know that the longest chord of a circle is its diameter

$\therefore \quad 2r \geq 20.5 \quad r \geq 10.25$

Hence, radius of the circle must be ≥ 10.25

95. (c) Interior angle of a regular decagon

$$= \frac{(n-2) \times 180}{n} = \frac{10-2}{10} \times 180$$

$$= 8 \times 18 = 144°$$

According to the question,

Interior angle of a regular polygon

$$= \frac{15}{16} \times 144 = 15 \times 9 = 135$$

$$\therefore \quad \frac{(n-2) \times 180°}{n} = 135°$$

$$(n-2) \times 4 = 3n \Rightarrow 4n - 8 = 3n \Rightarrow n = 8$$

$\because$ Number of diagonals $= \dfrac{n(n-3)}{2}$

$$= \frac{8(8-3)}{2} = 4 \times 5 = 20$$

96. (a) Given, $\Delta ABC \cong PQR$

$AB = 5$ cm $\angle B = 40°$ and $\angle A = 80°$

$\therefore \quad \angle C = 60°$

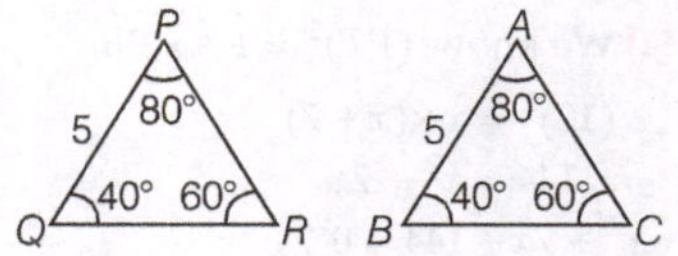

If two triangles are congruent,

$AB = PQ = 5$ cm $\Rightarrow \angle C = \angle R = 60°$

Hence, option (a) is true.

97. (a)

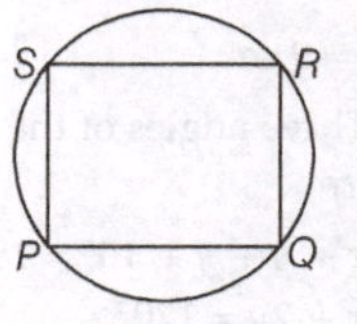

Let $\angle R = x$ and $\angle P = 3x$

$\therefore \quad \angle Q = y$ and $\angle S = 4y$

We know that, in a cycle quadrilateral sum of opposite angle is equal to 180°.

$\because \quad \angle P + \angle R = 180°$

$\Rightarrow \quad x + 3x = 180° \Rightarrow 4x = 180 \Rightarrow x = 45°$

$\because \quad \angle S + \angle Q = 180°$

$$y + 4y = 180°$$

$\Rightarrow \quad 5y = 180° \Rightarrow y = 36°$

$\Rightarrow \quad \angle S + \angle R = 4y + x = 4 \times 36° + 45°$

$$= 144° + 45°$$

$\Rightarrow \quad \angle S + \angle R = 189°$

98. (c) $PQ = 6$ cm $= a$ and $PD \perp QR$

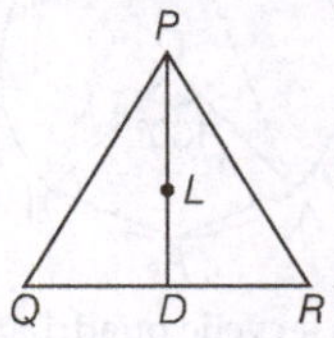

$$PD = \frac{\sqrt{3}}{2}a = \frac{\sqrt{3}}{2} \times 6 = 3\sqrt{3} \text{ cm}$$

If L is centroid of a triangle,

$\because \quad PL : LD = 2 : 1$

$\Rightarrow \quad PL = \dfrac{2}{3}PD$

Then, $\quad PL = \dfrac{2}{3}PD = \dfrac{2}{3} \times 3\sqrt{3} = 2\sqrt{3}$ cm

99. (b) We know,

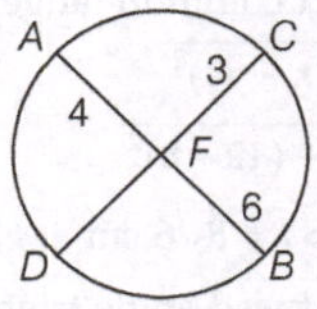

$$AF \times FB = CF \times FD$$

$$4 \times 6 = 3 \times DF$$

$$DF = 8 \text{ cm}$$

Therefore, $CD = 3 + 8 = 11$ cm

100. (d) $\angle BAC = 90°$

(Angle in semi-circle is always 90°)

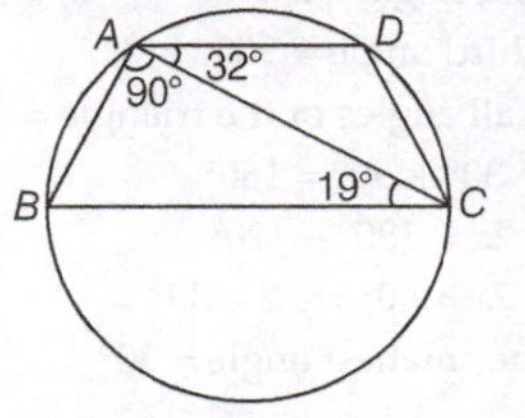

$$\angle A + \angle C = 180°$$

(Opposite angles in cyclic quadrilateral)

$$32° + 90° + 19° + \angle ACD = 180°$$

$\Rightarrow \quad \angle ACD = 180° - 141° \Rightarrow \angle ACD = 39°$

101. (c) Number of sides of a regular polygon $(n) = \dfrac{360°}{18°} \Rightarrow n = 20$

Number of diagonals $= \dfrac{n(n-3)}{2}$

$$= \frac{20(20-3)}{2} = \frac{20 \times 17}{2} = 170$$

102. (b) (i) In ΔOPR, $\angle OPR = \angle ORP$

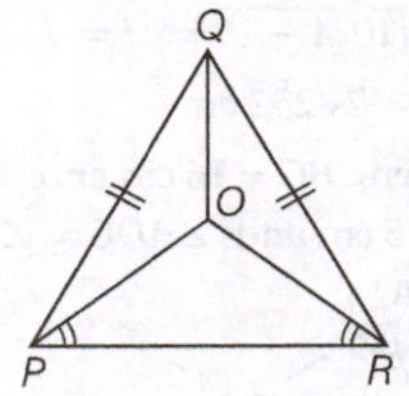

So, $OP = OR$

$\therefore$ ΔOPR is an isosceles triangle.

(ii) O is the centroid of ΔPQR.

No, because O is not a intersection point of their medians.

(iii) In ΔPQO and ΔRQO

$PQ = QR$ (given)

$PO = OR$ (proved above)

$OQ = OQ$ (common)

So, $\Delta PQO \cong \Delta RQO$ [by SSS criteria]

Therefore, statements (i) and (iii) are correct.

103. (d)

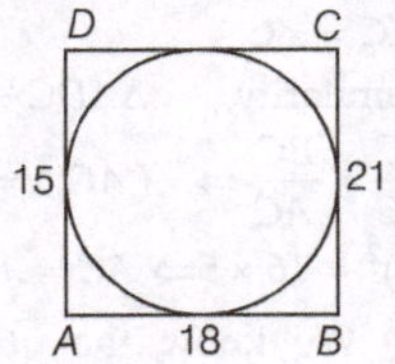

We know that,

Sum of opposite sides are equal,

$$AB + DC = BC + AD$$

$\Rightarrow \quad 18 + DC = 21 + 15 \Rightarrow 18 + DC = 36$

$\Rightarrow \quad DC = 18$ cm

104. (b) Sum of two sides is always greater than third side,

$$AB + BC > AC$$

$\Rightarrow \quad 9 + 11 > 20 \Rightarrow 20 \not> 20$

So, we have 0 circle passing through these points.

105. (c) Let the smallest angle = $x°$

The second angle = $x + 30°$

and the third angle = $90°$

$\therefore$ Sum of all angles of the triangle = $180°$

$\therefore x + x + 30° + 90° = 180°$

$\Rightarrow \quad 2x = 180° - 120°$

$\Rightarrow \quad 2x = 60° \Rightarrow x = 30°$

Hence, the smallest angle = $30°$

106. (a)

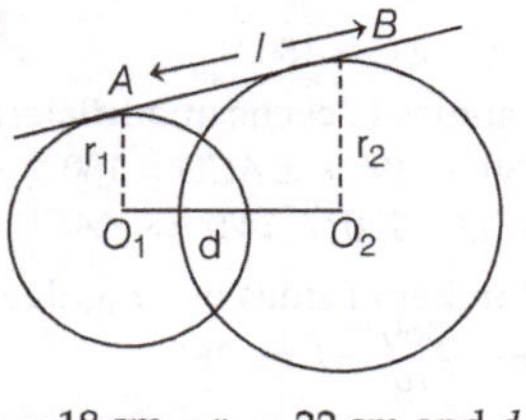

Given, $r_1 = 18$ cm, $r_2 = 22$ cm and $d = 32$ cm

Length of common tangent

$$l = \sqrt{d^2 - (r_2 - r_1)^2}$$

$\therefore$ Length = $\sqrt{(32)^2 - (22 - 18)^2}$

$\Rightarrow \quad l = \sqrt{1024 - 16} \Rightarrow l = \sqrt{1008}$

$\therefore \quad AB = l = 2\sqrt{252}$ cm

107. (a) Given, $BC = 16$ cm and $BD = 11$ cm

Then, $DC = 5$ cm and $\angle ADC = \angle BAC$

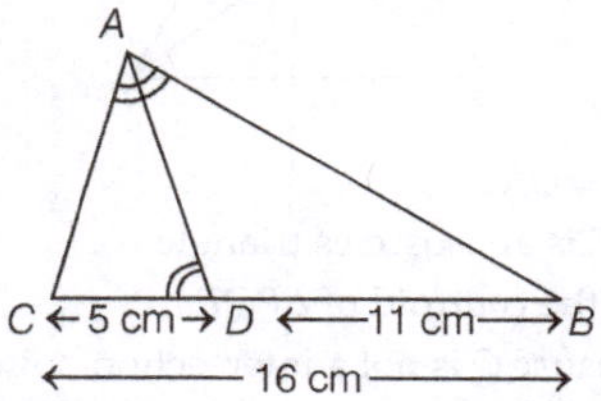

In ΔADC and ΔBAC,

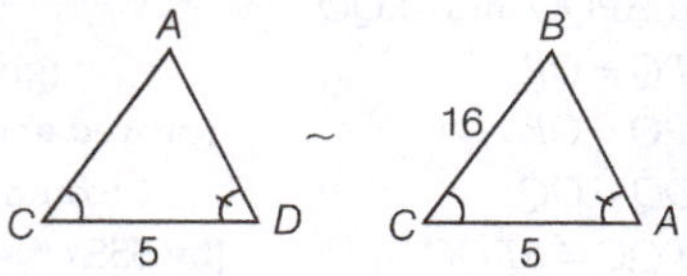

$\angle ADC = \angle BAC$ [given]

$\angle C = \angle C$ [common]

By AA similarity, $\quad \Delta ADC \sim \Delta BAC$

$$\frac{AC}{DC} = \frac{BC}{AC} \Rightarrow (AC)^2 = BC \times CD$$

$\Rightarrow (AC)^2 = 16 \times 5 \Rightarrow AC = \sqrt{16 \times 5} = 4\sqrt{5}$ cm

108. (b) We know that, tangents from a common point to a circle are equal in length.

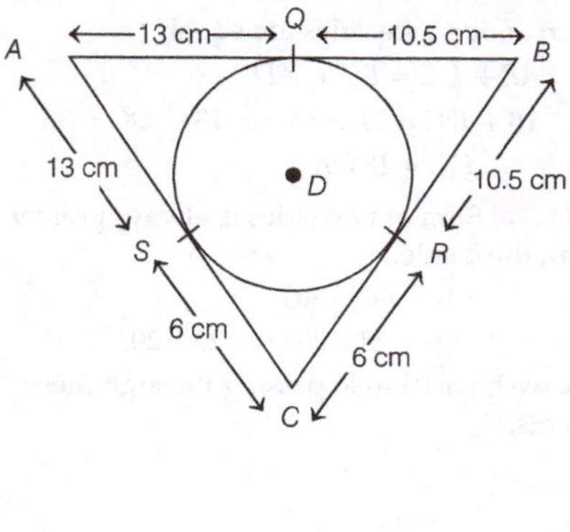

$\therefore$ Perimeter of $\Delta ABC = AB + BC + AC$

$= 13 + 10.5 + 10.5 + 6 + 13 + 6$

$= 23.5 + 16.5 + 19 = 59$ cm

109. (a) We know, $(PT)^2 = PA \times PB$

$\Rightarrow \quad (12)^2 = x \times (x + 7)$

$\Rightarrow \quad 144 = x^2 + 7x$

$\Rightarrow \quad x^2 + 7x - 144 = 0$

$\Rightarrow \quad (x + 16)(x - 9) = 0$

$x = -16$ and $x = 9$ cm

Length is never negative, then value of $x = 9$ cm

Thus, $PA = 9$ cm

110. (d) Three angles of the triangle are x, y and $y + 10°$.

$x + y + y + 10° = 180°$

$\Rightarrow \quad x + 2y = 170°$

$\Rightarrow \quad 2x + 4y = 340° \quad$ ...(i)

$\Rightarrow \quad 2x - 4y = 20°$ (given) $\quad$ ...(ii)

From Eqs. (i) and (ii), we get

$x = 90°$

$\therefore$ The triangle is a right angled triangle.

111. (b) Triangle ΔABC is congruent to triangles ΔDEF.

$\therefore$ Perimeter of ΔABC = Perimeter of ΔDEF.

112. (b) By central angle theorem,

$$\angle AQB = \frac{1}{2}\angle AOB = \frac{1}{2} \times 130° = 65°$$

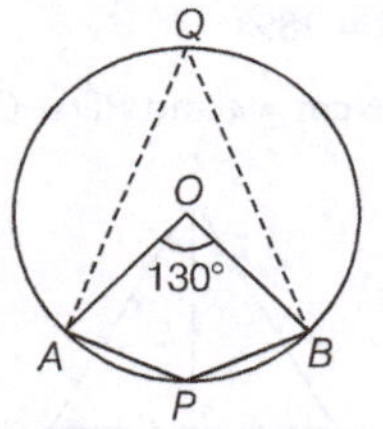

Now, $APBQ$ is a cyclic quadrilateral

So, $\quad \angle AQB + \angle APB = 180°$

$\Rightarrow \quad \angle APB = 180° - \angle AQB$

$= 180° - 65° = 115°$

113. (d)

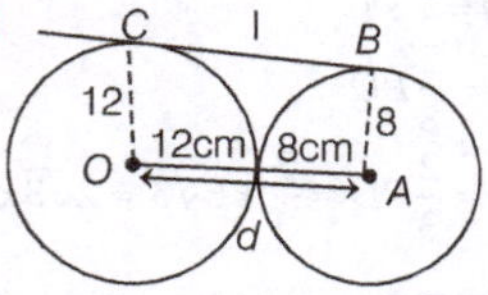

Length of direct common tangents

$$l = \sqrt{d^2 - (r_1 - r_2)^2}$$

$\Rightarrow \quad l = \sqrt{(20)^2 - (12 - 8)^2}$

$\Rightarrow \quad l = \sqrt{384} \Rightarrow l = 8\sqrt{6}$ cm

114. (a) For obtused angle triangle if, a, b and c are sides and c is largest side

Then, $a^2 + b^2 < c^2$

From option (a), $15^2 + 62^2 < 64^2$

15, 62, 64 satisfies this condition.

115. (d) As, $DE \parallel BC$

$\Delta ADE \sim \Delta ABC$

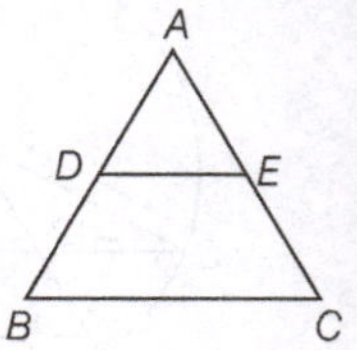

$$\therefore \quad \frac{AD}{AB} = \frac{DE}{BC}$$

$$\Rightarrow \frac{4}{4+5} = \frac{12}{BC}$$

$$\Rightarrow \quad BC = \frac{12 \times 9}{4}$$

$\Rightarrow \quad BC = 27$ cm

116. (c) Given, $\angle QOR = 100°$

$\angle POR = 180° - 100° = 80°$

$\because$ Angle made on circum ference is half of the angle made on center by same arc

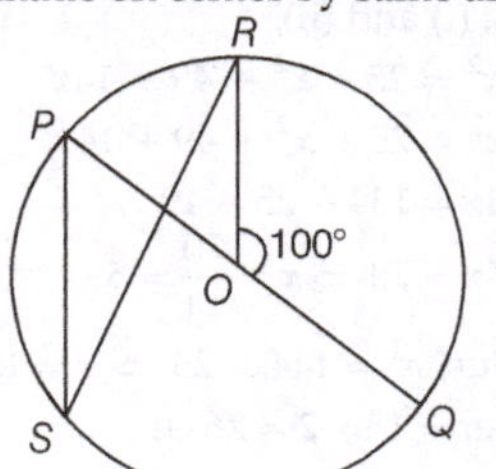

$$\therefore \quad \angle PSR = \frac{1}{2}\angle POR = \frac{1}{2} \times 80° = 40°$$

117. (d) In triangle ABC,

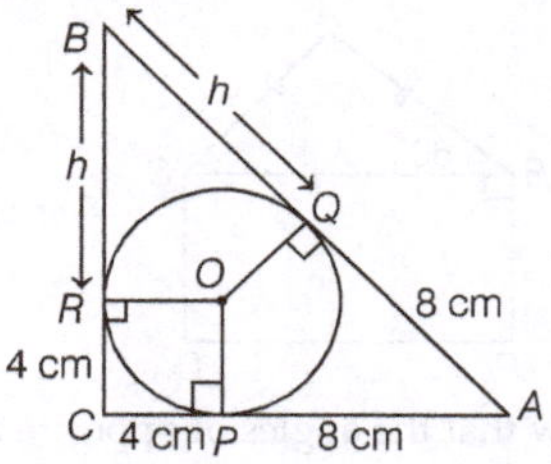

Let $BR = BQ = h$ cm

In ΔABC, By Pythagoras theorem,

$(h + 8)^2 = (h + 4)^2 + 12^2$

$\Rightarrow \quad (h + 8)^2 - (h + 4)^2 = 12 \times 12$

$\Rightarrow \quad (2h + 12) \times 4 = 12 \times 12$

$\Rightarrow \quad 2h = 36 - 12$

$\Rightarrow \quad h = \frac{24}{2} \Rightarrow h = 12$

$\therefore \quad BC = 12 + 4 = 16$ cm

118. (d) $\because$ Two circle touch each other extremely

$\therefore \quad d = 6 + 3 = 9$ cm

Now, length of common tangent

$$= \sqrt{d^2 - (r_1 - r_2)^2} = \sqrt{9^2 - 3^2} = 6\sqrt{2} \text{ cm}$$

119. (c) RP and RQ are two tangents of circle with centre O.

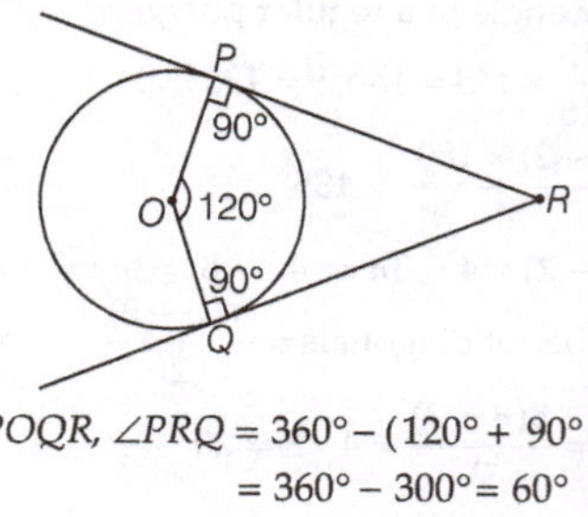

In $\square POQR$, $\angle PRQ = 360° - (120° + 90° + 90°)$

$= 360° - 300° = 60°$

120. (c) Radii of circles with centre P and Q are 25 cm and 4 cm, respectively.

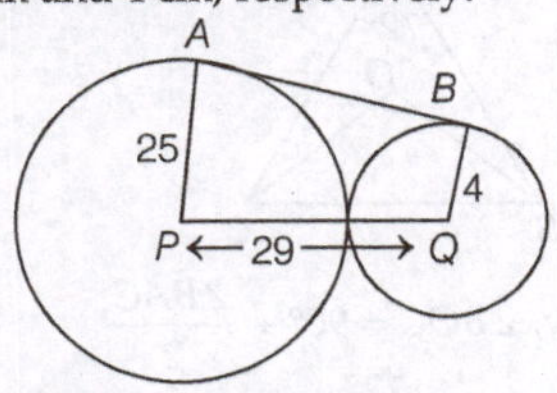

$\therefore$ Their common tangent

$= \sqrt{29^2 - 21^2} = \sqrt{400} = 20$ cm

121. (c) XY and PQ intersect each other at L.

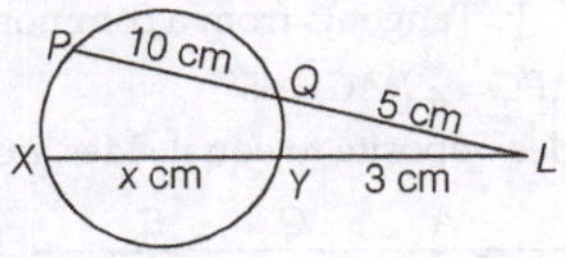

$LQ \times LP = LY \times LX$

$\Rightarrow \quad 5 \times 15 = 3 \times (x + 3)$

$\Rightarrow \quad x + 3 = 25 \Rightarrow x = 22$

122. (a) Radius of each circle is 18 cm.

$AC = 18$ cm

$AB = \frac{18}{2} = 9$ cm

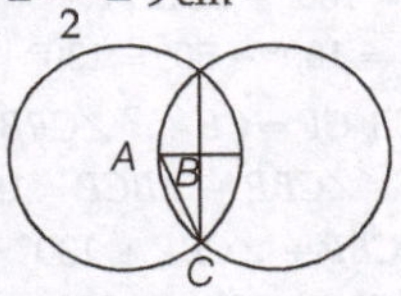

$BC = \sqrt{18^2 - 9^2} = \sqrt{(18+9)(18-9)}$

$= \sqrt{27 \times 9} = 3\sqrt{27}$ cm

$\therefore$ Length of the common chord

$= 2 \times 3\sqrt{27} = 6\sqrt{27}$ cm

123. (a) We know, two triangles are said to be congruent if, pairs of corresponding sides and corresponding angles are equal.

Given, $\Delta ABC \cong \Delta PQR$

However, $BC \neq RP$ because these are not corresponding sides.

124. (d) Length of the common tangent

$= \sqrt{d^2 - (r_1 - r_2)^2}$

$= \sqrt{(22+16)^2 - (22-16)^2}$

$= \sqrt{38^2 - 6^2} = 8\sqrt{22}$ cm

125. (a) Given, ΔABC and ΔDEF are congruent triangles.

So, $\Delta ABC \cong \Delta DEF$

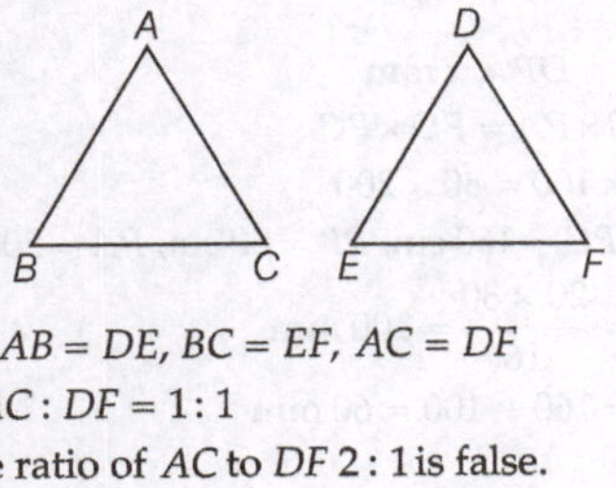

Here $AB = DE$, $BC = EF$, $AC = DF$

$\therefore \quad AC : DF = 1 : 1$

$\therefore$ The ratio of AC to DF 2 : 1 is false.

126. (b)

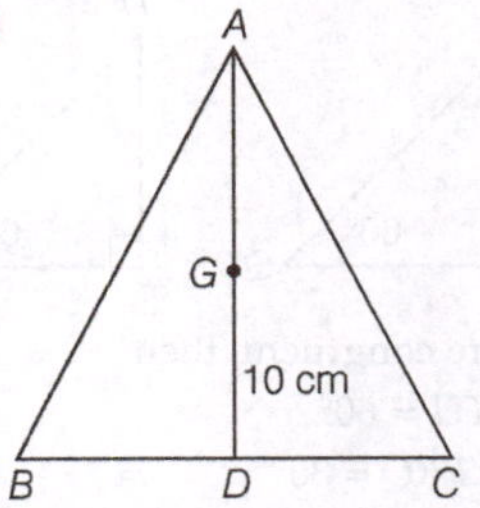

$AD = 3 \times GD = 3 \times 10 = 30$ cm

127. (d) According to the question,

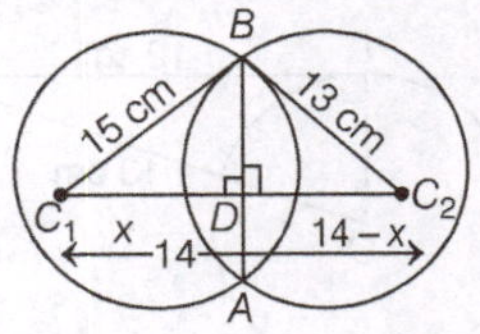

By Pythagoras theorem,

$BD^2 = 15^2 - x^2$

Also, $BD^2 = 13^2 - (14 - x)^2$

$\Rightarrow 15^2 - x^2 = 13^2 - (14 - x)^2$

$\Rightarrow 225 - x^2 = 169 - 196 - x^2 + 28x$

$\Rightarrow \quad x = \frac{225 + 27}{28} = 9$

Now, $BD = \sqrt{15^2 - x^2} = \sqrt{225 - 81}$

$= 12$ cm

Length of the common chord

$= AB = 2BD = 24$ cm

128. (a)

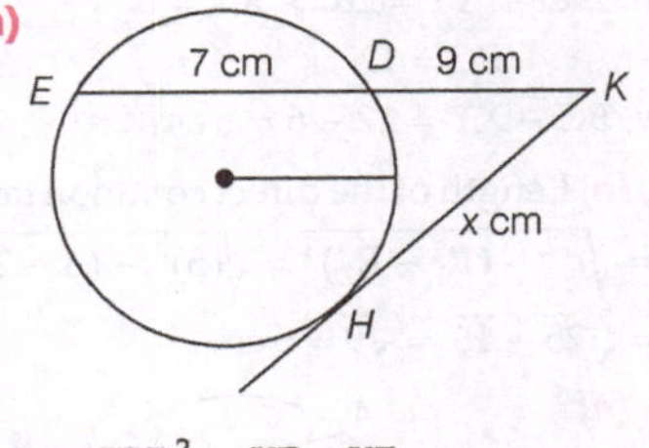

We know, $(KH)^2 = KD \times KE$

$KH^2 = 9 \text{ cm} \times 16 \text{ cm}$

$(KH)^2 = 144 \text{ cm}^2$

Hence, $\quad KH = \sqrt{144} = 12$ cm

129. (a)

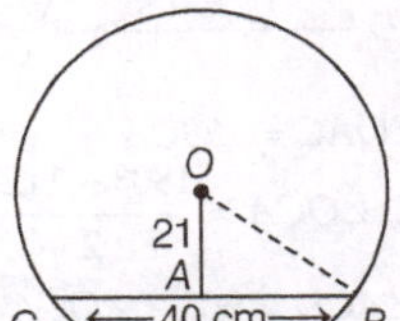

$AB = \frac{40}{2} = 20$ cm

In ΔAOB,

$(OB)^2 = (OA)^2 + (AB)^2$

$\Rightarrow \quad (OB)^2 = (21)^2 + (20)^2$

$\Rightarrow \quad (OB)^2 = 841$

$\Rightarrow \quad (OB) = \sqrt{841} = 29$ cm

130. (c)

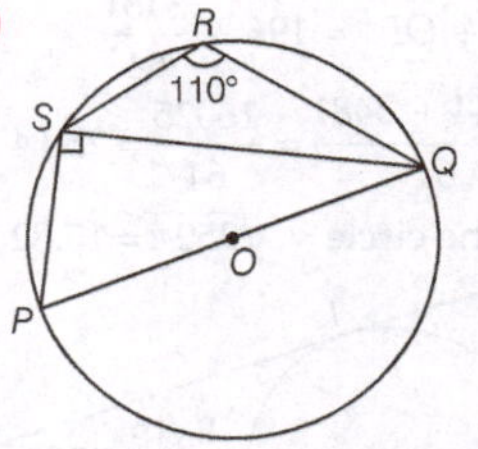

$PQRS$ is a cyclic quadrilateral

$\therefore \quad \angle QPS = 180° - 110° = 70°$

$\angle PSQ = 90°$ (Angle in semi circle)

$\therefore \quad \angle PQS = 180° - (90° + 70°) = 20°$

131. (a) Statement in option (a) is false.

Correction Two triangles are congruent if the size and shape of the triangles are equal.

132. (a)

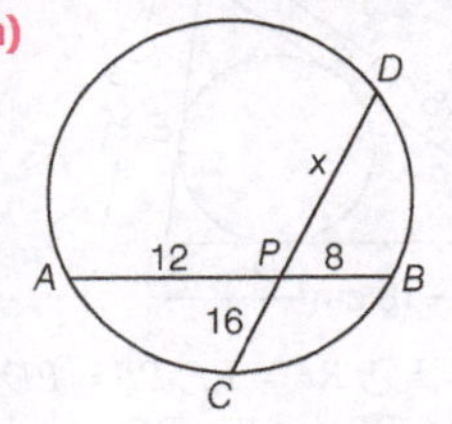

Let $\quad PD = x$, $AP \times PB = CP \times PD$

$\Rightarrow \quad 8 \times 12 = 16x \Rightarrow x = 6$

$\therefore \quad CD = 16 + 6 = 22$ cm

133. (c) We know, if two triangles are similar, then ratio of areas is equal to the ratio of square of correspondingsides.

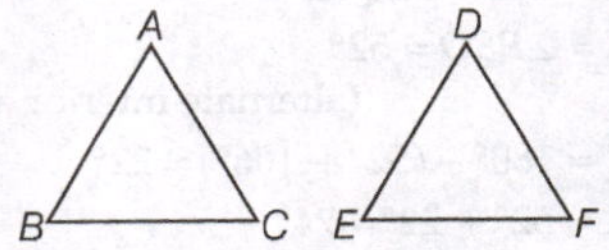

i.e., $\frac{\text{Area}(\Delta ABC)}{\text{Area}(\Delta DEF)} = \frac{AB^2}{DE^2} = \frac{AC^2}{DF^2} = \frac{BC^2}{BF^2}$

$\therefore$ Required ratio $= \left(\frac{5}{7}\right)^2 = \frac{25}{49} = 25 : 49$

134. (c) AB and CD are two chords on the same side of the centre O of a circle with

$AB = 28$ cm, $CD = 22$ cm, $AP = 14$ cm, $CQ = 11$ cm, $PQ = 4$ cm

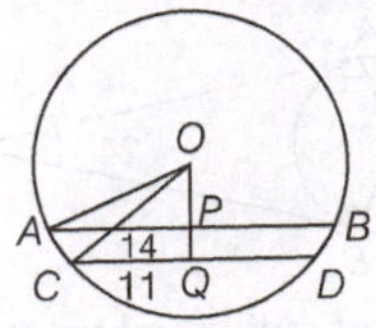

Let radius $= r$ cm $= AO = CO$

According to the question,

$11^2 + OQ^2 = 14^2 + OP^2$

$\Rightarrow -OP^2 + OQ^2 = 14^2 - 11^2$

$\Rightarrow -OP^2 + (OP + 4)^2 = 196 - 121$

$\Rightarrow -OP^2 + OP^2 + 8OP + 16 = 75$

$\Rightarrow 8OP = 75 - 16 \Rightarrow OP = \frac{59}{8}$

$$r^2 = 14^2 + OP^2 = 196 + \frac{3481}{64}$$

$$= \frac{12544 + 3481}{64} = \frac{16025}{64} = 250.4$$

$\therefore$ Radius of the circle $= \sqrt{250.4} = 15.82$ cm

135. (a)

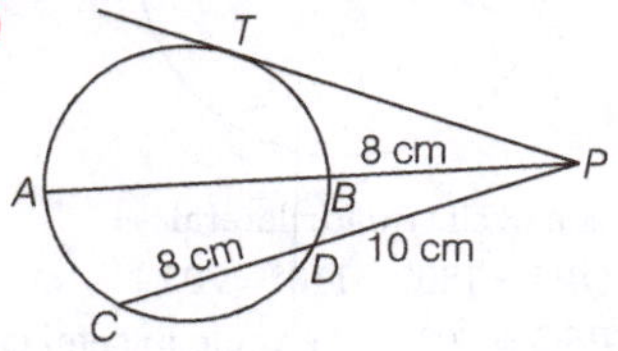

We know, $\because PD \times PC = PB \times PA$

$10 \times 18 = 8 \times (8 + AB)$

$\Rightarrow \quad 45 = 16 + 2AB \Rightarrow AB = 14.5$ cm

136. (a)

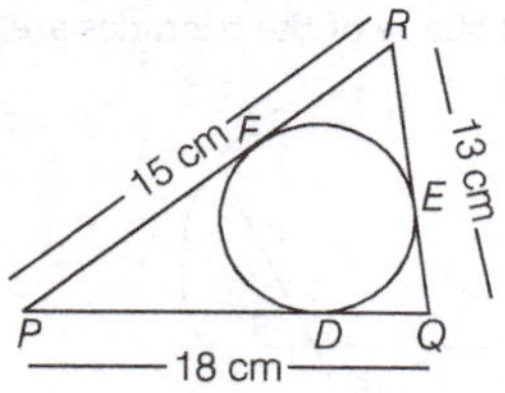

We know, $DQ = EQ$, $RE = RF$, $PF = PD$

$PD + DQ + EQ + RE + RF + PF$

$= 18 + 13 + 15 = 46$

$\Rightarrow \quad 2PD + 2EQ + 2RE = 46$

$\Rightarrow \quad 2PD + 2(EQ + RE) = 46$

$\Rightarrow \quad 2PD = 46 - 2 \times 13 \Rightarrow PD = \frac{20}{2} = 10$ cm

137. (b) $\because \Delta QPS \cong \Delta SRQ$

$\therefore \angle QPS = 106° = \angle QRS$

$\angle RQS = \angle PSQ = 52°$

(alternate interior angle)

$\angle QSR = 180° - (52° + 106°) = 22°$

$\therefore \angle PSR = 52° + 22° = 74°$

138. (c) $OA = \sqrt{20^2 + 15^2} = 25$

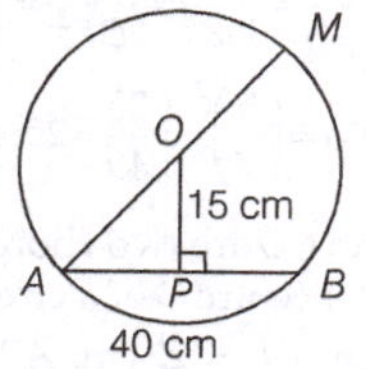

$\therefore$ Diameter of the circle, $AM = 25 \times 2 = 50$ cm

139. (c)

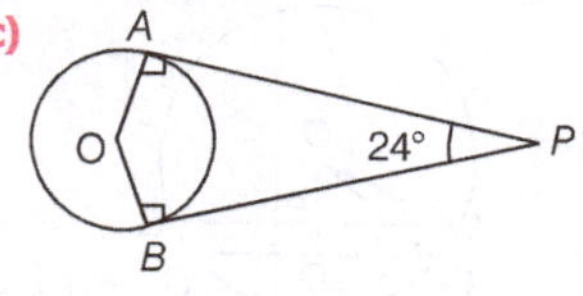

Contact point of radius and tangent is always perpendicular (90°).

Sum of interior angle of a quadrilateral is 360°.

$\therefore \angle AOB = 360° - (90° + 90° + 24°)$

$= 360° - 204° = 156°$

140. (a) Three sides of a triangle are 12, 17 and x units.

For a ΔABC of sides a, b and c $(a > b)$

$(a - b) < c < (a + b) \Rightarrow (17 - 12) < x < (17 + 12)$

$\therefore 5 < x < 29$ is correct.

141. (a)

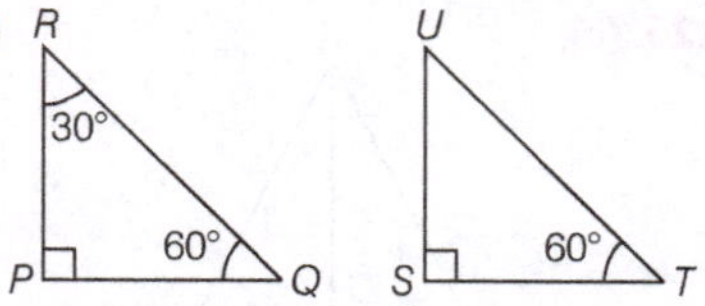

If triangles are congruent, then

$\angle PQR = \angle STU = 60°$

$\Rightarrow \angle SUT = \angle PRQ = 30°$

Sum of all angles of triangle = 180°

$60° + 30° + \angle TSU = 180°$

$\angle TSU = 180° - 90° \Rightarrow \angle TSU = 90°$

142. (d)

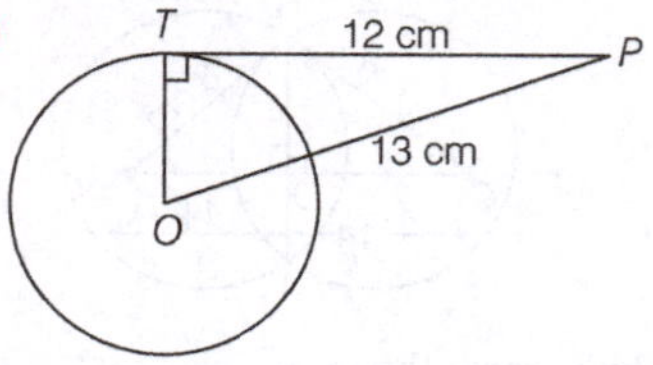

Using Pythagoras theorem,

$OT = \sqrt{13^2 - 12^2} = 5$ cm

143. (b) Given, $BC + XY = 18$

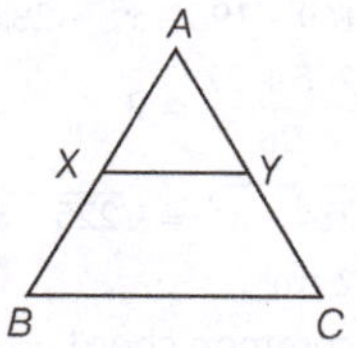

We know, $BC = 2\,XY$

Then, $2XY + XY = 18 \Rightarrow XY = 6$

So, $BC = 12$

Now, $BC - XY = 12 - 6 = 6$ cm

144. (b) Length of the direct common tangent

$= \sqrt{d^2 - (R_1 - R_2)^2} = \sqrt{(5)^2 - (6-2)^2}$

$= \sqrt{25 - 16} = \sqrt{9} = 3$ cm

145. (d)

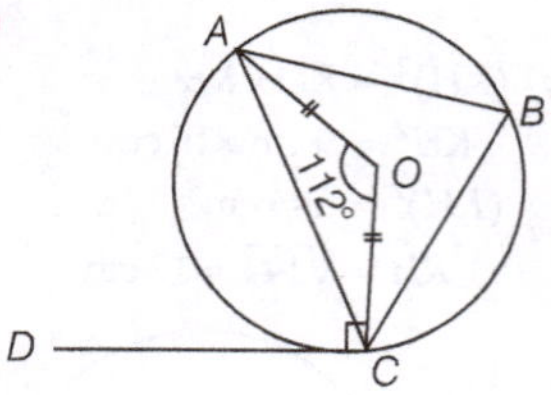

$\angle OAC = \angle OCA$

In ΔAOC, $\angle OCA = \frac{180° - 112°}{2} = 34°$

Then, $\angle ACD = 90° - \angle OCA = 90° - 34°$

$\therefore \quad \angle ACD = 56°$

146. (c) If two circles touch each other externally then number of common tangents that can be drawn is 3.

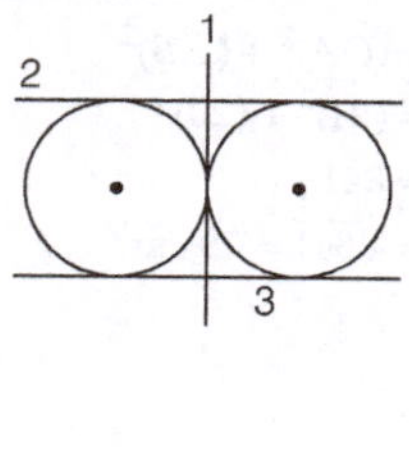

147. (b)

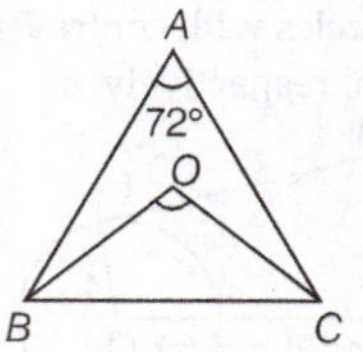

We know, $\angle BOC = 90° + \frac{\angle BAC}{2}$

$= 90° + \frac{72°}{2} = 90° + 36° = 126°$

148. (d) Given, $\angle PAB = 65°$

$CA = CP$

[$\because$ Tangents from a common point]

$\angle APC = \angle PAC = 65°$

[Angles opposite to equal sides are equal]

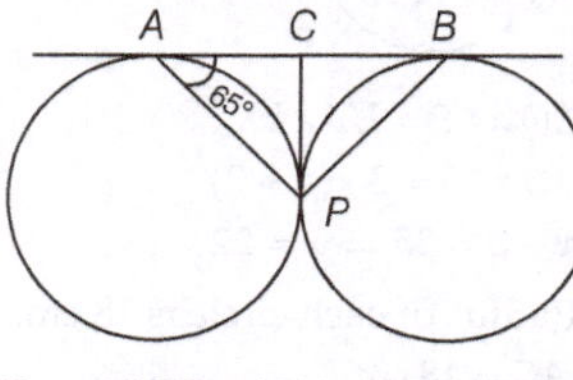

In ΔACP, $\quad \angle ACP = 180° - 65° - 65° = 50°$

Then, $\angle BCP = 180° - \angle ACP$

$= 180° - 50° = 130°$

Now, in ΔPCB, $CP = CB \;\therefore\; \angle CPB = \angle CBP$

Then, $\angle CPB + \angle CBP + \angle BCP = 180°$

$\Rightarrow \quad \angle CBP + \angle CBP + 130° = 180°$

$\Rightarrow \quad 2\angle CBP = 180° - 130°$

$\Rightarrow \quad \angle ABP = \angle CBP = \frac{50°}{2} = 25°$

149. (d)

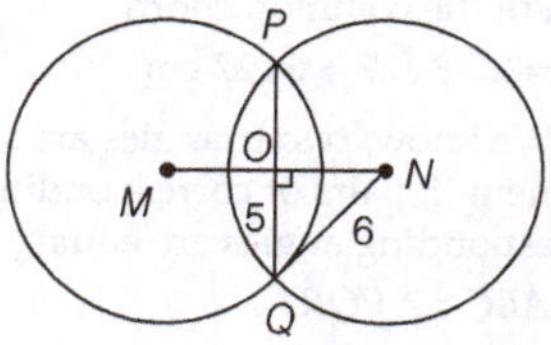

$PO = OQ = 5$ cm

Using Pythagoras theorem,

$OM = ON = \sqrt{6^2 - 5^2} = \sqrt{11}$

$\therefore$ Distance between their centres $= 2\sqrt{11}$ cm

150. (c)

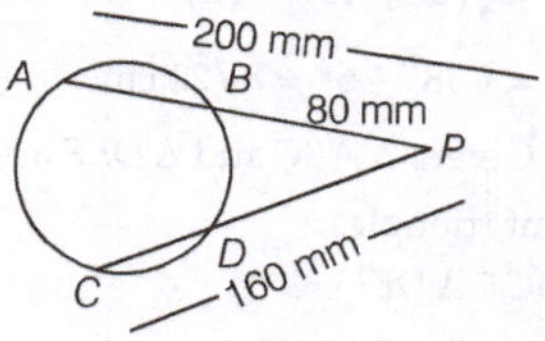

Let $\quad DP = x$ mm

$\because \quad PB \times PA = PD \times PC$

$\Rightarrow \quad x \times 160 = 80 \times 200$

{$\because PC = 160$ cm, $PB = 80$ cm, $PA = 200$ cm}

$\Rightarrow \quad x = \frac{20 \times 80}{16} = 100$ mm

$\therefore CD = 160 - 100 = 60$ mm

151. (b) Given,

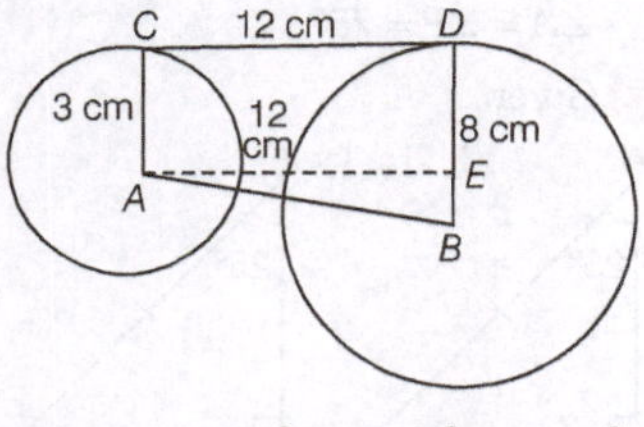

Then, in $\Delta AEB, (AB)^2 = (AE)^2 + (BE)^2$

$= (12)^2 + (5)^2 = 144 + 25$

$\therefore \quad AB = \sqrt{169} = 13$ cm

152. (d) Given, $AD : DB = 7 : 9$

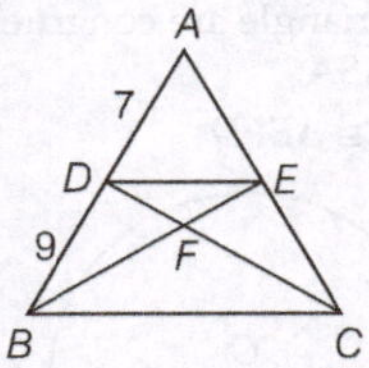

Apply Thales theorem,

$\frac{AD}{AB} = \frac{DE}{BC} \Rightarrow \frac{DE}{BC} = \frac{7}{16}$

In ΔDEF and ΔCBF, $DE \| BC$

$\angle DEB = \angle CBE$

$\angle EDC = \angle BCD$

$\angle DFE = \angle BFC$

So, $\Delta DEF \sim \Delta CBF$

$\therefore$ Ratio of their area $= \frac{(\text{Side of } \Delta DEF)^2}{(\text{Side of } \Delta CBF)^2}$

$= \left(\frac{7}{16}\right)^2 = \frac{49}{256} = 49 : 256$

153. (a) If ΔPQR is an equilateral triangle.

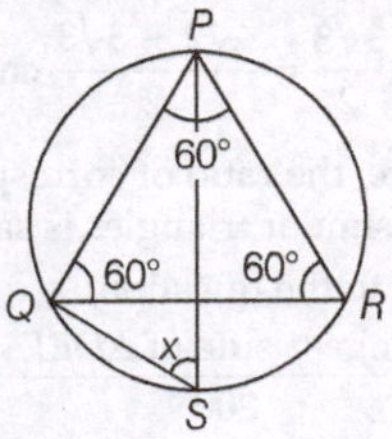

Then, $\angle PRQ = 60°$

By same segment theorem,

$\angle PRQ = \angle PSQ = 60°$

154. (d)

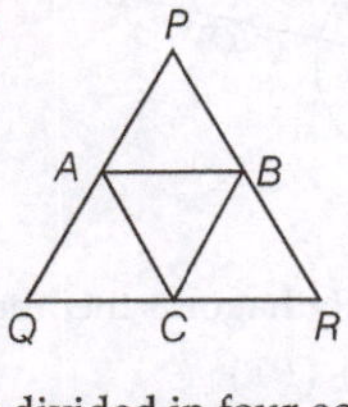

ΔPQR is divided in four equal parts

$\therefore$ Area $(\Delta ABC) = \frac{\text{Area}(\Delta PQR)}{4} = \frac{32}{4}$ cm^2

$= 8$ cm^2

155. (b) We know, diameter is the longest chord of a circle.

156. (c) We know,

Length of direct common tangent

$= \sqrt{d^2 - (r_1 - r_2)^2} = \sqrt{26^2 - 8^2}$

$= \sqrt{(26+8)(26-8)}$

$= \sqrt{2 \times 17 \times 2 \times 9} = 2\sqrt{153}$ cm

157. (a) If a, b, c are sides of triangle $(b > a)$

then, $\quad (b-a) < c < (b+a)$

$\Rightarrow \quad (42-30) < x < (42+30)$

$\therefore \quad 12 < x < 72$

158. (c) If $\Delta ABC \sim \Delta DEF$, then

$\frac{\text{Perimeter of } \Delta ABC}{\text{Perimeter of } \Delta DEF} = \frac{AB}{DE}$

Then, $\quad \frac{40}{12} = \frac{AB}{6}$

Hence, $AB = 20$ cm

159. (c) Given, $\Delta XYZ \cong \Delta LMR$

Then, $\quad XY = LM$

and $\quad YZ = RM,\ XZ = LR$

So, $\quad 2m + 1 = 5 \Rightarrow m = 2$

and $2p + 2 = 8 \Rightarrow p = 3$ and $2x - 1 = 7$

$\Rightarrow \quad x = 4$

Hence, $m + x + p = 2 + 4 + 3 = 9$

160. (b) Given, $\angle AGB = 132°$

We know, $\quad \angle AGB = 2 \times \angle ACB$

$\therefore \quad \angle ACB = \frac{132°}{2} = 66°$

161. (c) We know, a line which intersects two distinct points of a circle is called secant of circle.

Hence, statement in option (c) is incorrect.

162. (c)

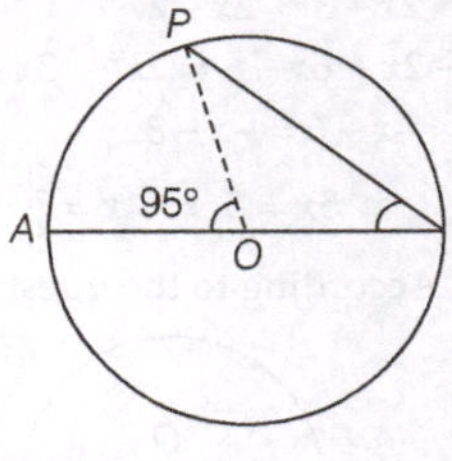

$2\angle PBA = \angle POA$

$\therefore \quad \angle OBP = \angle PBA = \frac{95°}{2} = 47.5°$

163. (b)

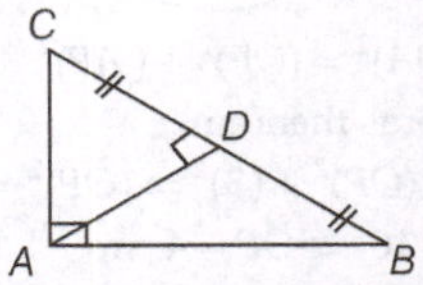

We know that, if D is a mid-point of hypotenuse BC, then $AD = \frac{1}{2} BC$

$\therefore \quad AD = \frac{BC}{2}$

164. (d)

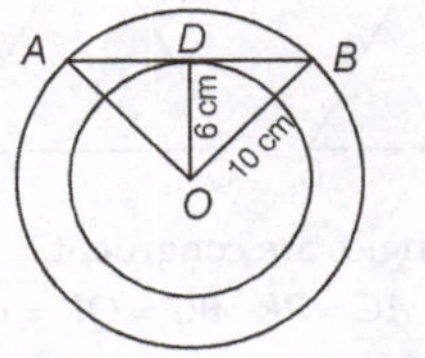

By Pythagoras theorem, in ΔODB

$\Rightarrow 6^2 + (BD)^2 = 10^2 \Rightarrow (BD)^2 = 100 - 36$

$\Rightarrow \quad (BD)^2 = 64 \Rightarrow BD = 8$ cm

$\therefore$ Length of the chord of the larger circle

$= AB = 2 \times 8 = 16$ cm

165. (a) From properties of circle

$PT^2 = PA \times PB$

$\Rightarrow \quad (8)^2 = 6(x+6) \Rightarrow x + 6 = \frac{64}{6}$

$\Rightarrow \quad x = \frac{32}{3} - 6 = \frac{14}{3}$ cm

166. (c) In the given figure,

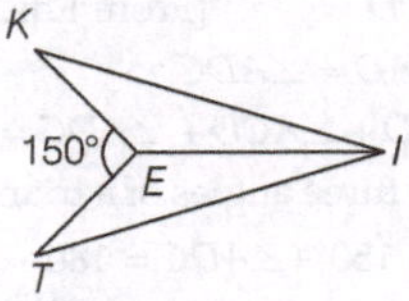

$\angle KET = 150°$

$\therefore$ Reflex angle $KET = 360° - 150° = 210°$

In ΔKEI and ΔTEI, $KI = IT$

$\therefore \quad \angle TEI = \angle KEI = \frac{\text{Reflex } \angle KET}{2}$

$\therefore \quad \angle TEI = \frac{210°}{2} = 105°$

167. (b) In ΔABC,

$\angle ABC + \angle ACB + \angle BAC = 180°$

[$\because$ The sum of three angles of a triangle be 180°]

$\Rightarrow \quad 81° + 9° + \angle BAC = 180°$

$\Rightarrow \angle BAC = 180° - 90° = 90°$

$\because$ The angles of same segment be equal.

$\therefore \quad \angle BDC = \angle BAC = 90°$

168. (d) Given, $\Delta ABC \cong \Delta PQR$

and $\quad \angle ABC = (x + 60°)$,

$\angle PQR = (85 - 4x)°$ and

$\angle RPQ = (3x + 65)°$

Since, they are congruent triangles.

$\therefore$ Angle of B = Angle of Q

$\therefore \quad x + 60 = 85 - 4x$

$\Rightarrow \quad 4x + x = 85 - 60$

$\Rightarrow \quad 5x = 25 \Rightarrow x = \frac{25}{5} = 5°$

$\therefore$ The value of $\angle ABC = (x + 60)°$

$= (5 + 60)° = 65°$

169. (d) According to the question,

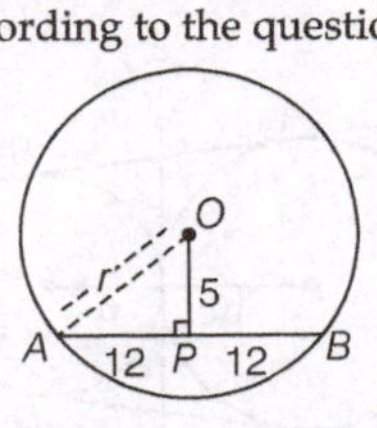

In ΔOAP, $OA^2 = OP^2 + AP^2$

[By Pythagoras theorem]

$\Rightarrow \quad r^2 = 25 + 144 \Rightarrow r^2 = 169 \Rightarrow r = 13$ cm

170. (d) Option (d), the perpendicular distance from the centre of a circle increases, when the length of a chord increase is incorrect, because the perpendicular distance from the centre of a circle decrease, when the length of a chord increase.

171. (d) In the given figure, $BCDE$ is a square.

$\therefore \quad BC = CD = DE = BE \quad$ ...(i)

and $\quad \angle BCD = 90°$

$\because \Delta ABC$ is an equilateral triangle.

$\therefore \quad AB = BC = AC \quad$ ...(ii)

and $\quad \angle BAC = \angle ABC = \angle ACB = 60°$

In ΔADC, $\angle ACD = \angle BCD + \angle ACB$

$= 90° + 60° = 150°$

and $\quad AC = CD \quad$ [From Eqs. (i) and (ii)]

$\therefore \quad \angle CAD = \angle ADC \quad$ ...(iii)

Now, $\angle CAD + \angle ACD + \angle ADC = 180°$

[Sum of three angles of a triangle be 180°]

$\Rightarrow \quad \angle ADC + 150° + \angle ADC = 180°$

[From Eq. (iii)]

$\Rightarrow \quad 2\angle ADC = 30° \Rightarrow \angle ADC = 15°$

172. (a) Given, $\Delta ABC \sim \Delta DEF$

$\therefore \quad \dfrac{\text{Perimeter of } \Delta ABC}{\text{Perimeter of } \Delta DEF} = \dfrac{AB}{DE}$

$\Rightarrow \quad \dfrac{32}{12} = \dfrac{AB}{6} \Rightarrow AB = \dfrac{32 \times 6}{12} = 16$ cm

173. (d) According to the question,

by the formula,

$ZT^2 = ZY \times ZX \Rightarrow (12)^2 = 8 \times (8 + x)$

$\Rightarrow \quad (8 + x) = \dfrac{144}{8} = 18$

$\therefore \quad x = 18 - 8 = 10$ cm

174. (b) ASA congruence rule : Two triangles are said to be congruent if 2 angles and the included side of one triangle are equal to 2 angles and the included side of the other triangle.

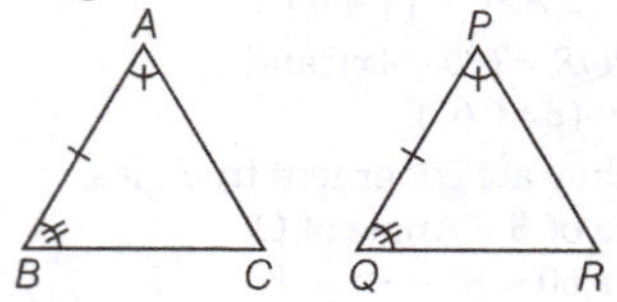

Here, $\Delta ABC \cong \Delta PQR$

by ASA rule, if $\angle A = \angle P, \angle B = \angle Q$ and $AB = PQ$.

175. (b) Radii of the given circles are 6 cm and 10 cm.

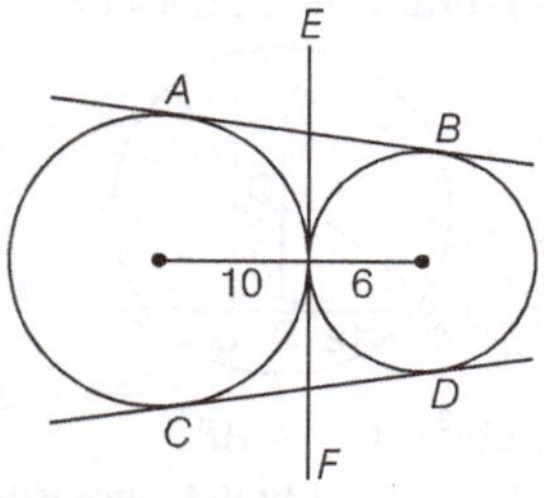

Here, distance between their centres

= Sum of the radii of the circles

$\Rightarrow$ 16 cm = (6 + 10) cm

i.e. given circles touch externally.

So, the number of common tangents

$= 3(AB, CD, EF)$.

176. (a) The length of direct common tangent

$= \sqrt{(\text{Distance between centres})^2 - (r_1 - r_2)^2}$

$= \sqrt{(18+8)^2 - (18-8)^2} = \sqrt{26^2 - 10^2}$

$= \sqrt{676 - 1000} = \sqrt{576} = 24$ cm

177. (d) Total number of tangents = 3

$(AB, CD$ and $EF)$

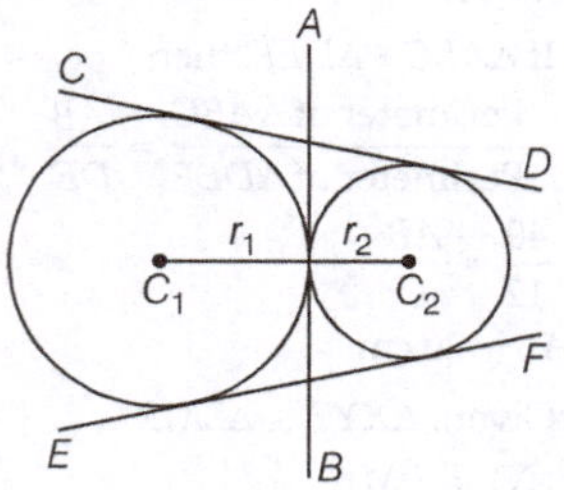

178. (c) Given, $AD = x + 3$, $DB = 2x - 3$, $AE = x + 1$ and $EC = 2x - 2$

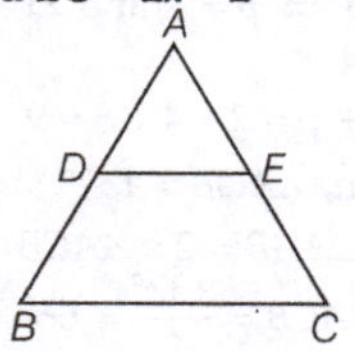

$\because \quad DE \parallel BC \therefore \dfrac{AD}{DB} = \dfrac{AE}{EC}$

(By Thales's theorem)

$\Rightarrow \quad \dfrac{x+3}{2x-3} = \dfrac{x+1}{2x-2}$

$\Rightarrow \quad 2x^2 - 2x + 6x - 6 = 2x^2 - 3x + 2x - 3$

$\Rightarrow \quad 4x - 6 = -x - 3$

$\Rightarrow \quad 5x = 3 \Rightarrow x = \dfrac{3}{5}$

179. (a) According to the question,

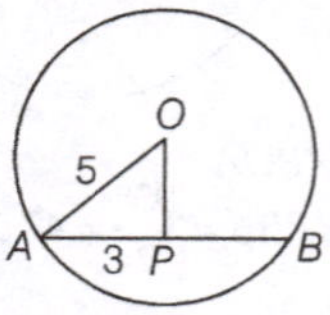

In $\Delta OAP, (OA)^2 = (OP)^2 + (AP)^2$

(By Pythagoras theorem)

$\Rightarrow \quad (5)^2 = (OP)^2 + (3)^2 \Rightarrow (OP)^2 = 25 - 9$

$\Rightarrow \quad (OP)^2 = 16 \Rightarrow OP = 4$ cm

Hence, the distance of chord from centre of circle is 4 cm.

180. (c) Given, $\Delta ABC \cong \Delta PQR$

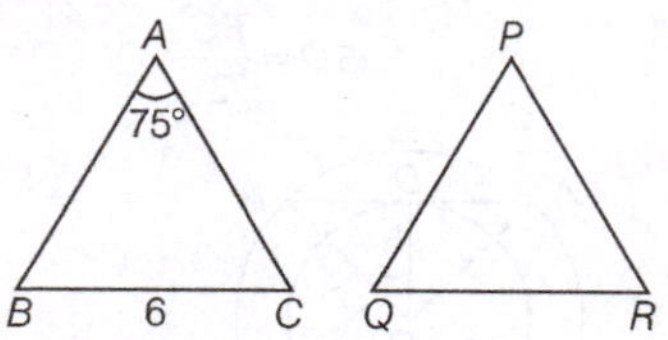

If both the triangles are congruent,

$\therefore \quad AB = PQ \quad AC = PR \quad BC = QR = 6$ cm

Corresponding angles are equal

$\angle A = \angle P = 75°$

181. (c) Given,

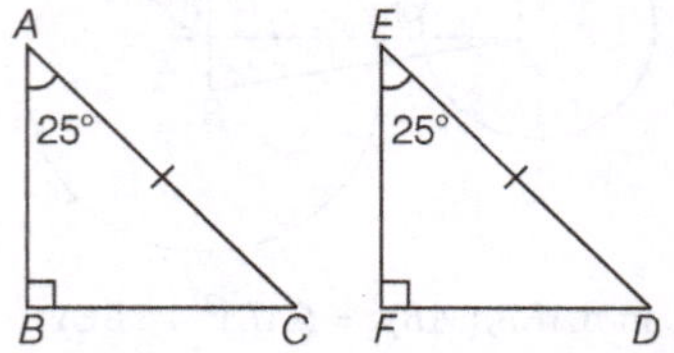

As, $\angle A = \angle E = 25°$

$\angle B = \angle F = 90° \therefore \angle C = \angle D$

And $AC = ED$

So, both the triangle are congruent by the property of ASA,

Hence, $\Delta ABC \cong \Delta EFD$

182. (b)

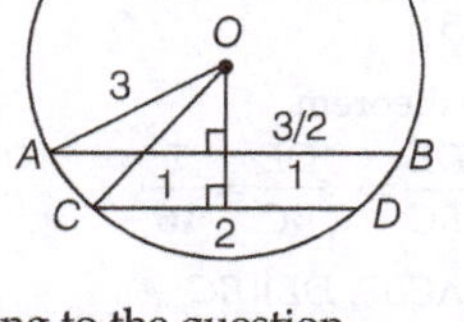

According to the question,

Perpendicular distance on smaller chord

$= \sqrt{(3)^2 - (1)^2} = \sqrt{9 - 1} = \sqrt{8} = 2\sqrt{2}$ cm

and perpendicular distance on larger chord

$= \sqrt{(3)^2 - \left(\dfrac{3}{2}\right)^2} = \sqrt{\left(9 - \dfrac{9}{4}\right)} = \sqrt{\dfrac{36 - 9}{4}}$

$= \sqrt{\dfrac{27}{4}} = \dfrac{3\sqrt{3}}{2}$ cm

$\therefore$ Perpendicular distance between two chords

$= 2\sqrt{2} - \dfrac{3\sqrt{3}}{2} = \dfrac{4\sqrt{2} - 3\sqrt{3}}{2}$ cm

183. (d) Since, the ratio of corresponding sides of two similar triangles is same/equal.

$\therefore$ According to the question,

$\dfrac{120}{48} = \dfrac{\text{longest side of } \Delta DEF}{200}$

$\therefore$ Longest side of $\Delta DEF = \dfrac{120 \times 200}{48} = 500$ cm

184. (d)

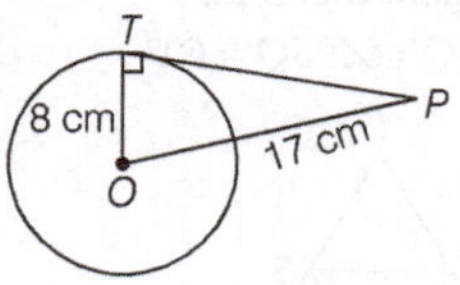

Here, $\angle OTP = 90°$

Now, in ΔOTP, By Pythagoras theorem,

$(OP)^2 = (OT)^2 + (PT)^2$

$\Rightarrow \quad (17)^2 = (8)^2 + (PT)^2$

$\Rightarrow \quad 289 - 64 = (PT)^2$

$\Rightarrow \quad PT = \sqrt{225} = 15$

Hence, $\quad PT = 15$ cm

185. (b) Length of direct common tangent

$(BC) = \sqrt{d^2 - (r_1 - r_2)^2} = \sqrt{(17+7)^2 - (17-7)^2}$

$= \sqrt{576 - 100} = 2\sqrt{119}$ cm

186. (c) Given,

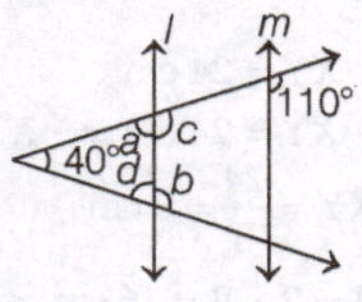

$\because$ $l \parallel m \Rightarrow c = 110°$

($\because$ Corresponding angles of parallel lines are equal.)

$a + c = 180°$ ($\because$ linear pair)

$\Rightarrow a + 110° = 180° \Rightarrow a = 180° - 110°$

$\Rightarrow a = 70°$

Now, $40° + a + d = 180°$

($\because$ Angle sum property of triangle)

$\Rightarrow 40° + 70° + d = 180° \Rightarrow 110° + d = 180°$

$\Rightarrow d = 70°$

Now, $d + b = 180°$ ($\because$ linear pair)

$\Rightarrow 70° + b = 180° \Rightarrow b = 180° - 70°$

$\Rightarrow b = 110°$

Hence, $a = 70°$ and $b = 110°$

187. (d) Let PQ is the tangent and OQ is the radius.

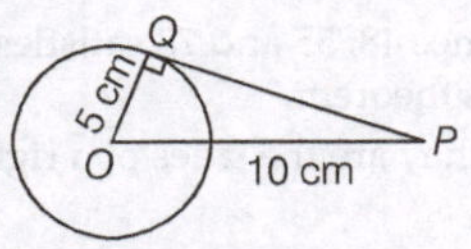

$\angle OQP = 90° \Rightarrow OQ = 5$ cm (radius)

$\Rightarrow OP = 10$ cm

In ΔOQP, $PQ^2 = OP^2 - OQ^2 = 10^2 - 5^2$

$= 100 - 25 = 75\text{ cm}^2$

$\Rightarrow PQ = \sqrt{75}$ cm $= 5\sqrt{3}$ cm

188. (c) The point of intersection of the three medians of a triangle is called centroid of the triangle.

189. (b) For any two circles who do not touch each other and one does not lie inside the other, then number of common tangents = 4

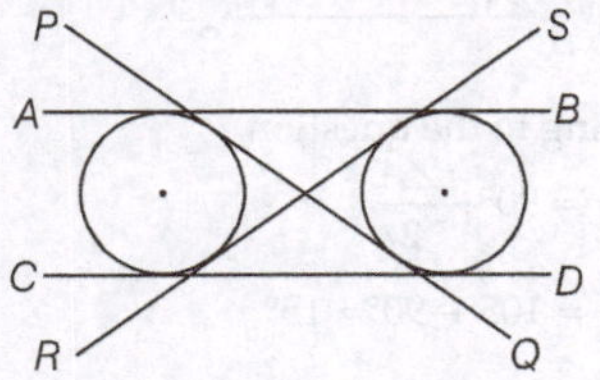

Here, AB and CD are direct common tangent. PQ and RS are transverse common tangent.

190. (a)

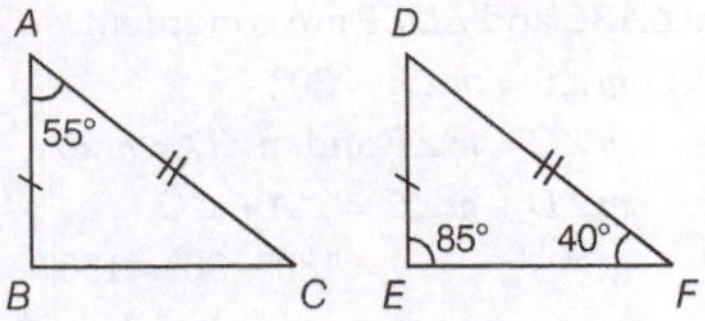

Here, $\angle D = 180° - (85° + 40°)$

(By triangle's property)

$= 180° - 125° = 55° = \angle A$

$\therefore$ By SAS property,

ΔABC and ΔDEF are congruent.

191. (b) Given,

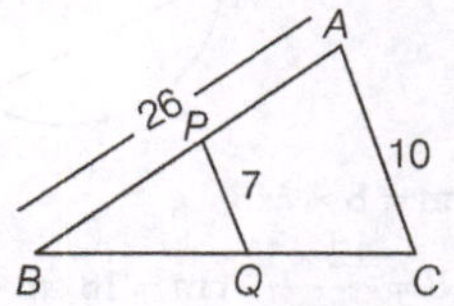

As, $PQ \parallel AC$, $\Delta BPQ \sim \Delta BAC$

We know that, $\frac{PB}{AB} = \frac{PQ}{AC}$

[$\because$ Similar triangles properties]

$\therefore \frac{PB}{26} = \frac{7}{10} \Rightarrow PB = \frac{26 \times 7}{10} = 18.2$

$\therefore AP = 26 - 18.2 = 7.8$

192. (d) Since ΔMAB is an equilateral triangle.

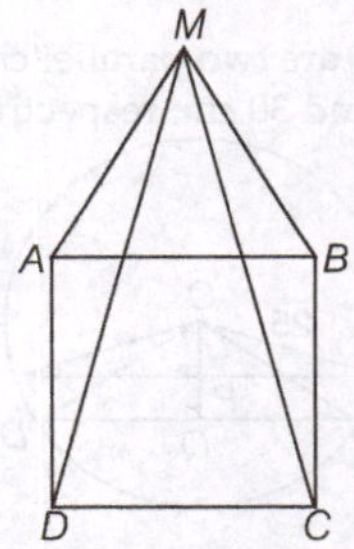

$\therefore \angle M = \angle A = \angle B = 60°$

Since $ABCD$ is a square,

Therefore $\angle DAB = \angle CBA = \angle D = \angle C = 90°$

Therefore $\angle DAM = 90° + 60° = 150°$

$\therefore$ In ΔDAM,

$\angle ADM = \angle AMD = \frac{(180° - 150°)}{2} = 15°$

$\therefore \angle MDC = 90° - 15° = 75°$

193. (b) According to the question,

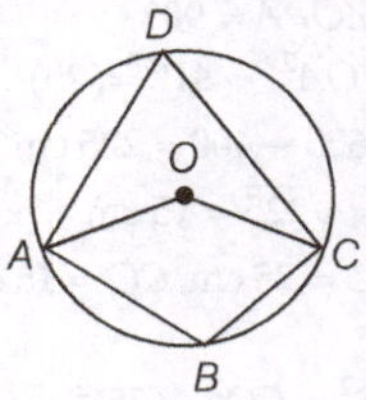

$\therefore \angle ADC = \frac{1}{2}\angle AOC = \frac{1}{2} \times 140° = 70°$

Since, $ABCD$ is a cyclic quadrilateral.

$\therefore \angle ADC + \angle ABC = 180° \Rightarrow 70° + \angle ABC = 180°$

Hence, $\angle ABC = 110°$

194. (c) According to the question,

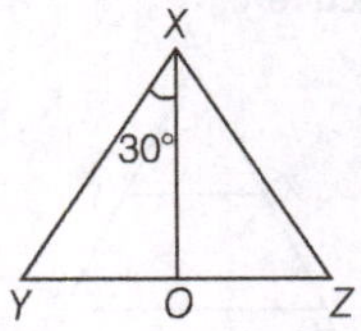

Given, $XO = \frac{1}{2}YZ$ and $\angle YXO = 30°$

Since, XO is the median.

$\Rightarrow OY = OZ = \frac{1}{2}YZ$

also, $XO = \frac{1}{2}YZ \therefore OY = XO$

$\Rightarrow \angle YXO = \angle XYZ = 30°$

($\because$ In a triangle, opposite angles of equal sides are equal.)

195. (b) According to the question,

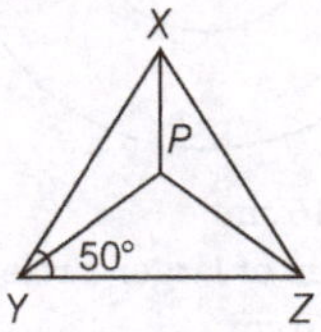

Given, $\angle XYZ = 50°$

$\angle XPZ = 90° + \frac{1}{2} \times (\angle XYZ)$

[$\because$ Angle formed at the incentre is $90° + \frac{1}{2}$ of vertex angle opposite to it]

$\Rightarrow \angle XPZ = 90° + \frac{1}{2} \times 50°$

$\Rightarrow \angle XPZ = 90° + 25°$

$\therefore \angle XPZ = 115°$

196. (a) Given, $\Delta ABC \sim \Delta DEF$

$\therefore \frac{AB}{DE} = \frac{BC}{EF} = \frac{AC}{DF}$

Given, $2AB = DE$

$BC = 8$ cm

Taking, $\frac{AB}{DE} = \frac{BC}{EF} \Rightarrow \frac{AB}{2AB} = \frac{8}{EF}$

$\Rightarrow \frac{1}{2} = \frac{8}{EF}$

$\Rightarrow EF = 8 \times 2 = 16$ cm

Hence, length of $EF = 16$ cm

197. (a) Given, $AB = 16$ cm, $AC = 24$ cm, $BC = 20$ cm

Let, $AD = x$ cm $\Rightarrow BD = 16 - x$ cm

and $AF = y$ cm $\Rightarrow CF = 24 - y$ cm

and $BE = z$ cm $\Rightarrow CE = 20 - z$ cm

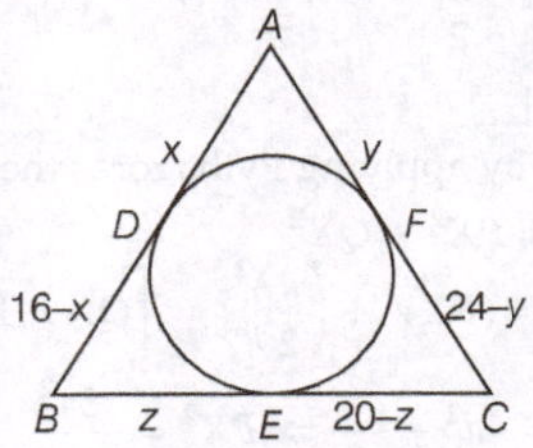

Now, we know, the length of two tangents drawn from the external point to the circle are equal

$AD = AF$ and $BD = BE$

and $CE = CF$

$\therefore x = y$ ...(i)

$16 - x = z$ ...(ii)

and $20 - z = 24 - y$ ... (iii)

Now, put the value of z in Eq. (ii),

$\Rightarrow \quad 16 - x = x - 4 \Rightarrow 16 + 4 = x + x$

$\Rightarrow \quad 2x = 20 \Rightarrow x = \frac{20}{2} = 10$

Hence, $AD = 10$ cm

198. (b)

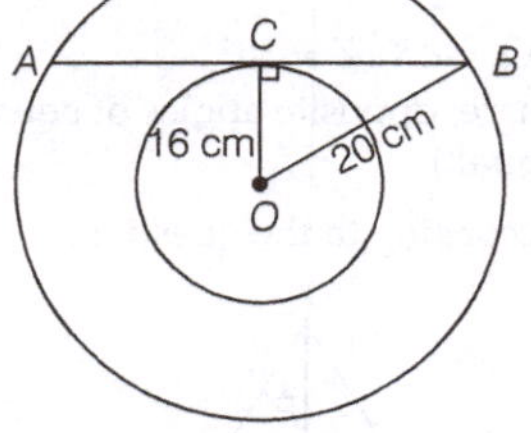

$\Rightarrow \quad OC = 16$ cm

and OB = Radius of larger circle

$\Rightarrow \quad OB = 20$ cm

$\because OC \perp AB$ (every tangent is $\perp$ to the corresponding radius)

Now, in ΔOCB,

By Pythagoras theorem,

$(OC)^2 + (BC)^2 = (OB)^2$

$\Rightarrow \quad (16)^2 + (BC)^2 = (20)^2$

$\Rightarrow \quad 256 + (BC)^2 = 400$

$\Rightarrow \quad (BC)^2 = 400 - 256$

$\Rightarrow \quad BC = \sqrt{144}$

$\Rightarrow \quad BC = 12$ cm

Similarly, $AC = 12$ cm

Hence, required length $= AC + BC$

$= (12 + 12)$ cm $= 24$ cm

199. (a)

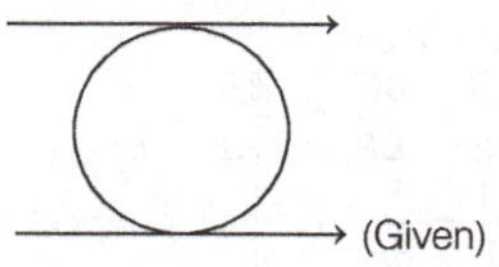

Only 1 tangent is possible to be parallel to a given tangent.

200. (d)

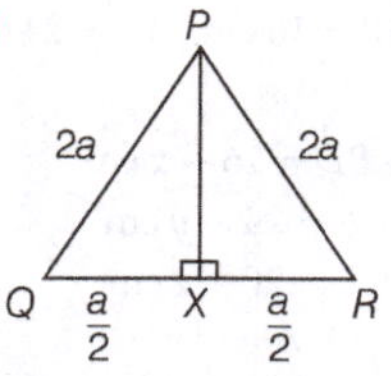

$[PX \perp QR]$

In ΔPQX, by applying Pythagoras theorem

$PQ^2 = PX^2 + QX^2$

$\Rightarrow \quad (2a)^2 = (PX)^2 + \left(\frac{a}{2}\right)^2 \quad \left[QX = XR = \frac{a}{2}\right]$

$\Rightarrow \quad PX^2 = 4a^2 - \frac{a^2}{4} \Rightarrow PX^2 = \frac{15a^2}{4}$

$\Rightarrow \quad PX = \sqrt{\frac{15a^2}{4}} \Rightarrow PX = \frac{\sqrt{15}\,a}{2}$

201. (a) We know that,

$AP \times PB = PD \times CP$ (Here, $AP = AB - PB$,

$\Rightarrow \quad AP = 20 - 12 = 8$ cm

$\Rightarrow \quad 8 \times 12 = PD \times 8$

$\Rightarrow \quad PD = 12$ cm

202. (b) By the formula,

$(MT)^2 = MA \times MB$

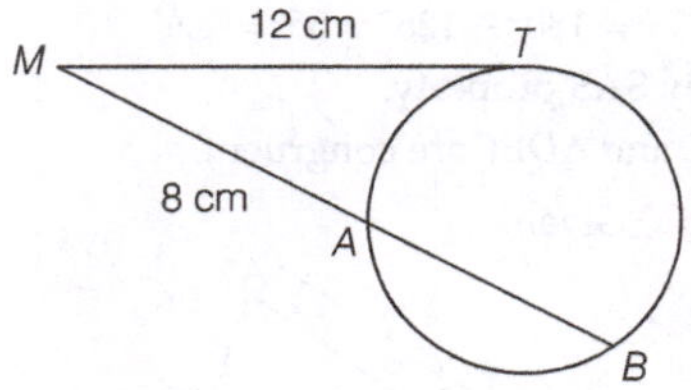

$\Rightarrow \quad 12 \times 12$ cm $= 8 \times MB$

$\Rightarrow \quad MB = \frac{12 \times 12}{8}$ cm $= 18$ cm

Now, chord $AB = MB - MA$

$= (18 - 8)$ cm $= 10$ cm

203. (a) For any two fixed points, there are infinite number of circles can be drawn that passes through the two fixed points.

204. (c) For minimum distance parallel chords should be on the same side of the centre.

Let AB and CD are two parallel chord having length 40 cm and 30 cm, respectively.

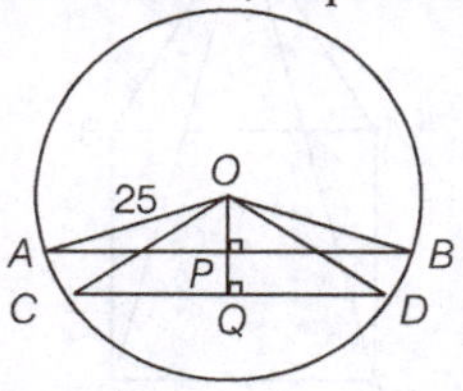

'O' is the centre of the circle.

$OA = OC = 25$ cm (radius)

$\because$ Perpendicular drawn from the centre bisect the chord.

$\therefore \quad AP = PB = \frac{40}{2}$ cm $= 20$ cm

$CQ = QD = \frac{30}{2} = 15$ cm

In ΔOAP, $OA = 25$ cm,

$AP = 20$ cm, $\angle OPA = 90°$

$OP^2 = OA^2 - AP^2 = (25)^2 - (20)^2$

$= 625 - 400 = 225 \text{ cm}^2$

$OP = \sqrt{225} = 15$ cm

In ΔOCQ, $OC = 25$ cm, $CQ = 15$ cm,

$\angle OQC = 90°$

$OQ^2 = OC^2 - CQ^2 = (25)^2 - (15)^2$

$= 625 - 225 = 400 \text{ cm}^2$

$OQ = \sqrt{400}$ cm $= 20$ cm

Distance between the two chords

$= OQ - OP = 20$ cm $- 15$ cm $= 5$ cm

205. (d) Here, X and Y are mid points of AB and AC, respectively.

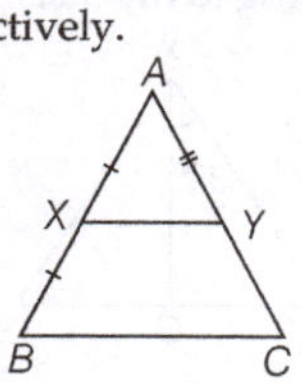

$\therefore XY = \frac{1}{2} \times BC$ ($\because$ line joining the mid-points of two sides of a triangle is half of the third side)

$\Rightarrow BC = 2XY$

Given, $BC + XY = 24$ cm

$\Rightarrow \quad 2XY + XY = 24 \text{ cm} \Rightarrow 3XY = 24$ cm

$\Rightarrow \quad XY = \frac{24}{3} = 8$ cm

$\therefore BC = 2 \times 4 = 2 \times 8 = 16$ cm

Hence, $BC - XY = (16 - 8)$ cm $= 8$ cm

206. (d) Given,

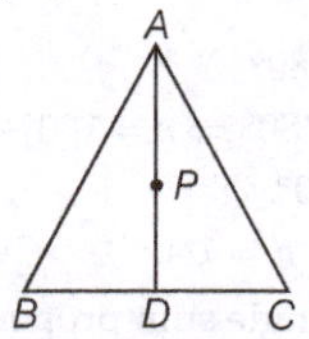

Here, P is the centroid of ΔABC.

Centroid divides the median in the ratio of 2 : 1

$\Rightarrow \quad \frac{AP}{PD} = \frac{2}{1}$

Given, $\quad AP = 14 \text{ cm} \Rightarrow \frac{14}{PD} = \frac{2}{1}$

$\Rightarrow \quad PD = \frac{14}{2} = 7$ cm

207. (d) Since 48, 55 and 73 satisfies pythagoras theorem.

Therefore they are the sides of a right-angled triangle.

Since, the longest side of a right-angled triangle is its hypotenuse and the length of median joining the mid-point of the

$\text{Hypotenuse} = \frac{\text{Hypotenuse}}{2}$

$\therefore$ Required length $= \frac{73}{2} = 36.5$ cm

208. (d)

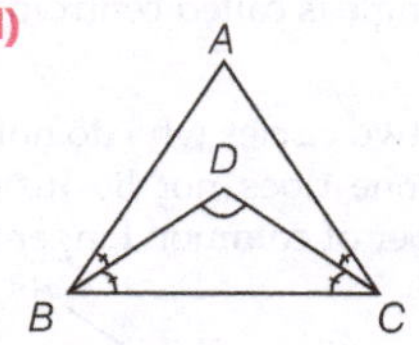

According to the question,

$105° = 90° + \frac{\angle A}{2}$

$\frac{\angle A}{2} = 105° - 90° = 15°$

$\angle A = 15 \times 2 = 30°$

209. (d) We know that, all the sides and angles of two congruent triangles are equal.

$\because \Delta ABC$ and ΔDEF are congruent

$\therefore \quad m\angle B = m\angle E = 30°$,

$m\angle C = m\angle F$ and $m\angle D = m\angle A$

$\therefore \quad m\angle D + m\angle C = \angle A + \angle C$

$= 180° - 30° = 150°$

210. (c) Given, $r_1 + r_2 = C_1C_2$, then the tangent can draw of the following,

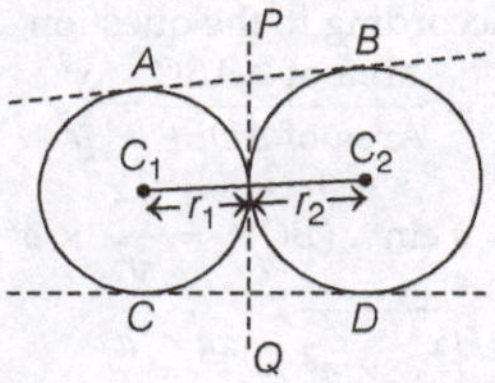

Hence, the number of common tangents = 3 (AB, CD and PQ).

211. (b) Given, $BG = 12$ cm

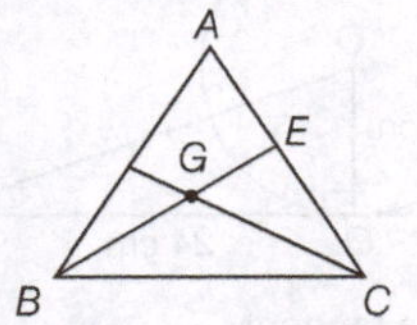

Centroid of a triangle divides the median in the ratio 2 : 1.

$$\frac{BG}{GE} = \frac{2}{1} \Rightarrow \frac{12}{GE} = \frac{2}{1}$$

$$\Rightarrow \quad GE = \frac{12}{2} = 6 \text{ cm}$$

Hence, $BE = BG + GE = 12 + 6 = 18$ cm

212. (d) Let O and O' be the centre of both circle.

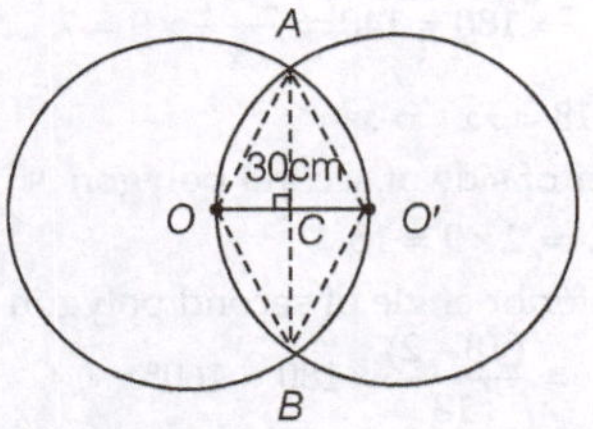

In triangle AOO',

$OA = O'A = OO' = 30$ cm (radius)

$\Rightarrow AOO'$ is an equilateral triangle.

$\Rightarrow \angle AOO' = 60° \Rightarrow \angle AOB = 60° + 60° = 120°$

In triangle, ACO,

$$AC^2 = OA^2 - OC^2$$

$$AC^2 = (30)^2 - (15)^2$$

$$AC^2 = 900 - 225$$

$$AC = \sqrt{675} = 15\sqrt{3} \text{ cm}$$

$$\Rightarrow \quad AB = 2 \times 15\sqrt{3} = 30\sqrt{3} \text{ cm}$$

Now, area of $AO'BA$ = area of sector $AO'BO$ – area of ΔAOB

$$= \frac{120°}{360°} \times \pi \times (30)^2 - \frac{1}{2} \times 30\sqrt{3} \times 15$$

$$= 300\pi - 225\sqrt{3} \text{ cm}^2$$

$\therefore$ Required area $= 2 \times (300\pi - 225\sqrt{3}) \text{ cm}^2$

$$= 600\pi - 450\sqrt{3} \text{ cm}^2$$

213. (a) Given, area $(\Delta ABC) = 80 \text{ cm}^2$

$BC = 16$ cm

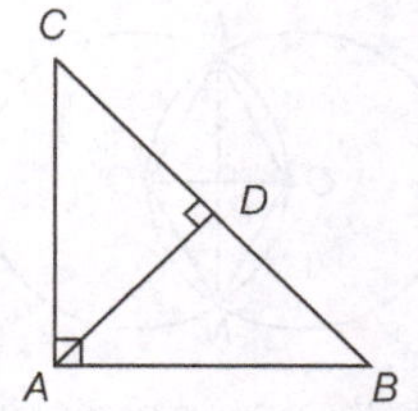

Now, area of triangle $= \frac{1}{2} \times \text{base} \times \text{height}$

$$\Rightarrow \quad \text{area}(\Delta ABC) = \frac{1}{2} \times BC \times AD$$

$$\Rightarrow \quad 80 = \frac{1}{2} \times 16 \times AD$$

$$\Rightarrow \quad AD = \frac{80 \times 2}{16} = 5 \times 2 = 10 \text{ cm}$$

214. (c) Given, $PA = 3$ cm, $AB = 9$ cm

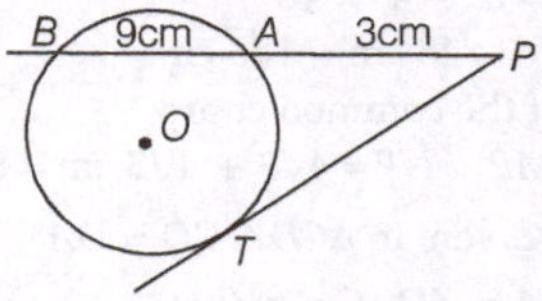

We know that, $PT^2 = PA \times PB$

$$PT = \sqrt{3 \times 12}$$

$$PT = \sqrt{36} = 6 \text{ cm}$$

Hence, $PT = 6$ cm

215. (d)

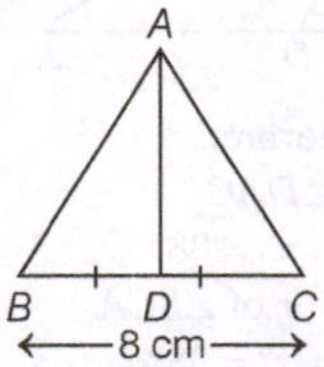

Height $AD = \frac{\sqrt{3}}{2} \times \text{side} = \frac{\sqrt{3}}{2} \times 8 = 4\sqrt{3}$ cm

216. (c) According to the question,

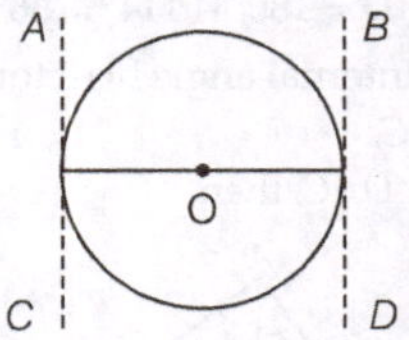

Hence, they are parallel to each other.

217. (c) As we know,

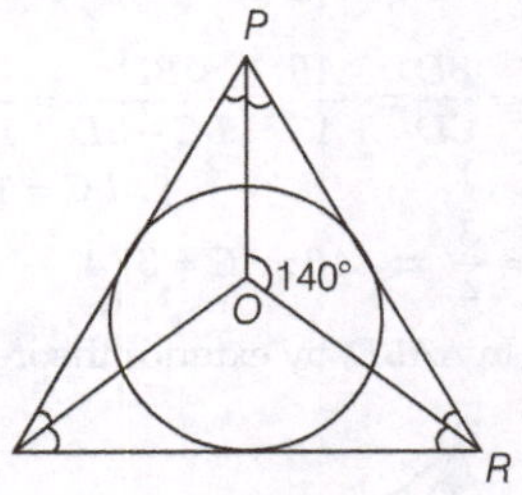

$$\angle POR = 90° + \frac{\angle PQR}{2} \Rightarrow 140° = 90° + \frac{\angle PQR}{2}$$

$$\frac{\angle PQR}{2} = 50° \Rightarrow \angle PQR = 100°$$

218. (a) Given, $\angle YXZ = 60°$, $LM \perp YZ$

L is the circumcentre of the ΔXYZ.

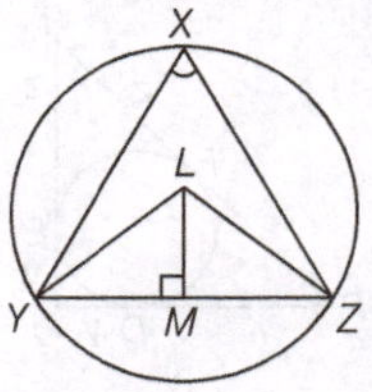

So, $\angle YLZ = 2 \times \angle YXZ = 2 \times 60° = 120°$

(central angle theorem)

Now, in ΔYLZ, $YL = LZ$ = radius

i.e. $\angle LYZ = \angle LZY$

In ΔLYZ,

$$\Rightarrow \quad 120° + \angle LYZ + \angle LYZ = 180°$$

$$\Rightarrow 2\angle LYZ = 180° - 120° = 60°$$

$$\Rightarrow \quad \angle LYZ = \frac{60°}{2} = 30°$$

Now, $\angle LYM = \angle LYZ = 30°$

$\angle LMY = 90°$

In ΔLYM,

$$\Rightarrow \quad 30° + \angle YLM + 90° = 180$$

$$\Rightarrow \angle YLM = 180° - 30° - 90° = 60°$$

219. (c) Let the tangent touch the circle of centre O at point Q.

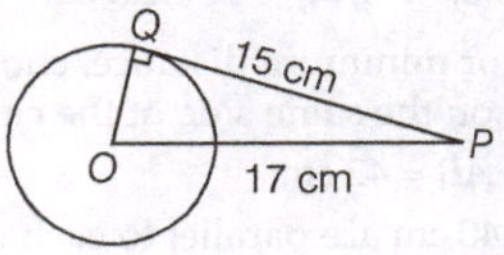

So, $OQ \perp PQ$ *i.e.* $\angle OQP = 90°$

By Pythagoras theorem,

$$OQ^2 = OP^2 - PQ^2 = (17)^2 - (15)^2 \text{ cm}^2$$

$$= 289 - 225 \text{ cm}^2 = 64 \text{ cm}^2$$

$$OQ = \sqrt{64} \text{ cm} = 8 \text{ cm}$$

Radius of the circle $= OQ = 8$ cm

220. (c) In ΔBOD and ΔCOE,

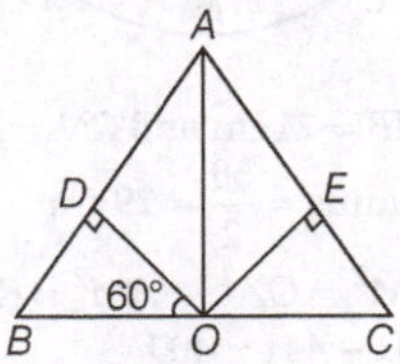

$\angle BDO = \angle CEO = 90°$

$\angle B = \angle C$ $\quad (\because AB = AC)$

$\therefore$ By AA similarity $\Delta BOD \sim \Delta COE$

$\therefore \angle COE = 60°$

(angles of similar triangles are equal)

Now, $\angle DOB + \angle DOE + \angle EOC = 180°$

$$\Rightarrow \quad 60° + \angle DOE + 60° = 180°$$

$$\Rightarrow \quad \angle DOE = 180° - 120° = 60°$$

Now, $\angle AOE = \frac{1}{2}\angle DOE = \frac{1}{2} \times 60° = 30°$

221. (d) We know that, tangent from same external point are equal in lengths,

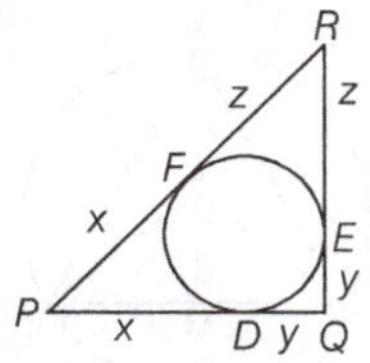

$\therefore \quad PD = PF = x$ (let) ; $QD = QE = y$ (let)

and $RF = RE = z$ (let)

Now, $\quad PQ = 15$ cm

$\Rightarrow \quad x + y = 15$ cm ...(i)

and $\quad QR = 11$ cm

$\Rightarrow \quad z + y = 11$ cm ...(ii)

and $\quad RP = 13$ cm

$x + z = 13$ cm ...(iii)

Adding Eqs. (i), (ii) and (iii), we get

$2(x + y + z) = 39$

$x + y + z = \frac{39}{2}$ ...(iv)

Subtracting Eqs. (ii) from (iv), we get

$x = \frac{39}{2} - 11$

$\Rightarrow \quad x = \frac{39 - 22}{2} \Rightarrow x = \frac{17}{2}$

$x = 8.5$ cm $\Rightarrow \quad PD = 8.5$ cm

222. (b) For minimum distance, chords should be on the same side of the circle.

Let chord $AB = 42$ cm

and $CD = 40$ cm are parallel to each other.

$\because$ Perpendicular from centre bisect the chord.

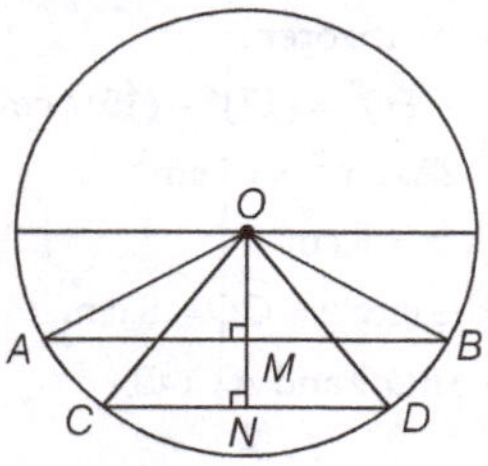

$\therefore \quad AM = MB = 21$ cm and $CN = ND = 20$ cm

$OA = OC = \text{radius} = \frac{58}{2} = 29$ cm

In ΔOAM, $OM^2 = OA^2 - AM^2 = (29)^2 - (21)^2$

$= 841 - 441 = 400$

$OM = \sqrt{400}$ cm $= 20$ cm

Now, ΔOCN,

$ON^2 = OC^2 - CN^2 = (29)^2 - (20)^2$

$= 841 - 400 = 441$

$ON = \sqrt{441} = 21$ cm

$\therefore$ Required distance

$= ON - OM = (21 - 20)$ cm $= 1$ cm

223. (a) Let two circles of radii 8 cm and centre O and O'.

Here, $OM = ON = O'M = O'N = 8$ cm (radius)

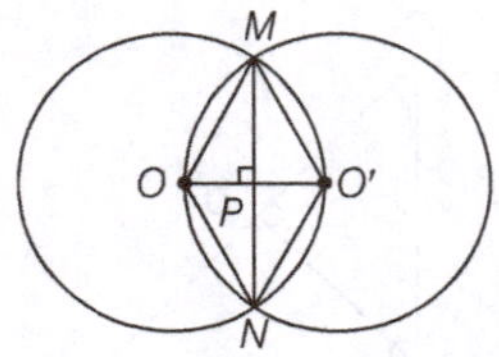

$\because$ Line joining the centres of the circles will be perpendicular to the common chord and bisect the chord.

$\therefore \quad OP \perp MN$ and $MP = NP$

Also, $OP = O'P = \frac{8}{2}$ cm $= 4$ cm

In ΔOMP, $\angle P = 90°$, $OM = 8$ cm, $OP = 4$ cm

$MP^2 = OM^2 - OP^2$

[$\because$ By Pythagoras theorem]

$= 8^2 - 4^2 = 48$

$MP = \sqrt{48}$ cm $= 4\sqrt{3}$ cm

Length of the common chord,

$MN = MP + NP = 4\sqrt{3} + 4\sqrt{3}$ cm $= 8\sqrt{3}$ cm

224. (d) Given, In ΔCDA, $CD = DA$

i.e., $\angle DCA = \angle DAC = x°$ (Let)

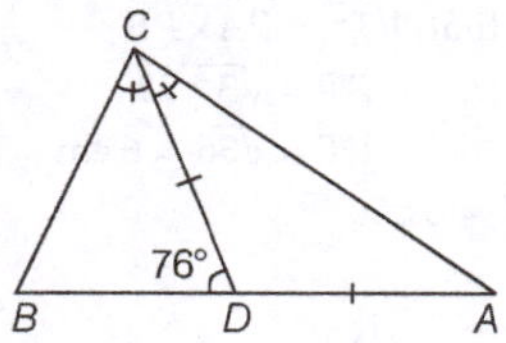

By exterior angle theorem,

$\angle CDB = \angle DCA + \angle DAC$

$76° = x° + x° \Rightarrow \quad x° = 38°$

Also, CD is the bisector of $\angle BCA$

i.e., $\angle BCD = \angle DCA = x° = 38°$

In ΔBCD, $\angle BCD + \angle BDC + \angle CBD = 180°$

($\because$ triangle's angle sum)

$\Rightarrow \quad 38° + 76° + \angle CBD = 180°$

$\Rightarrow \quad \angle CBD = 180° - 114° = 66°$

225. (a) By internal angle bisector theorem, for any ΔABC,

If $\angle BAD = \angle DAC$, then

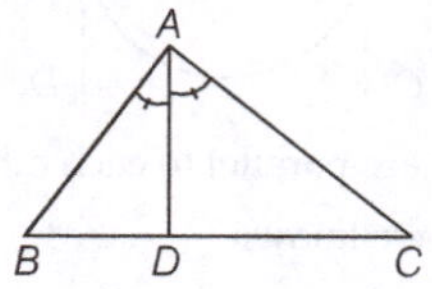

$\frac{AB}{AC} = \frac{BD}{CD} \Rightarrow \frac{AB}{AC} = \frac{BD}{BC - BD} = \frac{6}{14 - 6}$

[$\because BC = 14, BD = 6$]

$= \frac{6}{8} = \frac{3}{4} \Rightarrow \quad AB : AC = 3 : 4$

226. (c) In ΔABD, by exterior theorem,

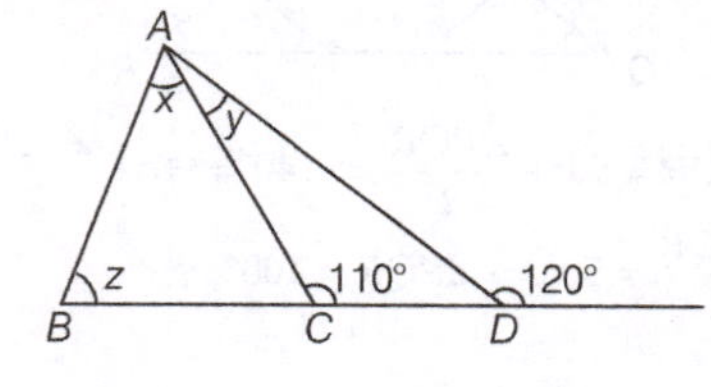

$\angle BAD + \angle ABD = 120°$

$\Rightarrow \quad x + y + z = 120°$

227. (c) According to the question,

$$\frac{(BC)^2}{(EF)^2} = \frac{\text{Area of } \Delta ABC}{\text{Area of } \Delta DEF} = \frac{x^2}{y^2}$$

Since $EF = a$ cm $\therefore (BC)^2 = \frac{x^2}{y^2} \times a^2$

$\therefore \quad BC = \sqrt{\frac{x^2}{y^2} \times a^2} = \frac{xa}{y} = \frac{ax}{y}$

228. (a) Given,

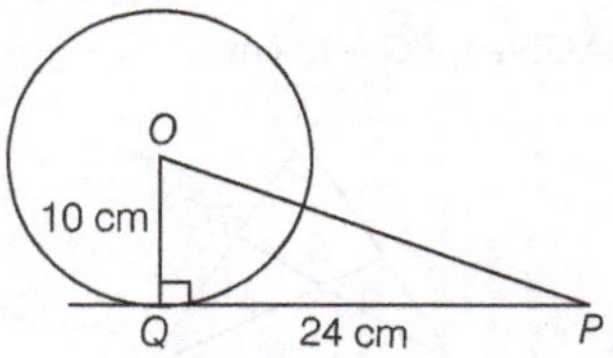

Since PQ is a tangent,

$\therefore \quad \angle OQP = 90°$

Now, by Pythagoras theorem,

$(OP)^2 = (OQ)^2 + (PQ)^2$

$OP = \sqrt{(24)^2 + (10)^2}$

$= \sqrt{576 + 100} = \sqrt{676} = 26$ cm

229. (d) Let side of two regular polygon be x and $2x$. Given each interior of first polygon angle is 140.

$\Rightarrow \quad \frac{x - 2}{x} \times 180 = 140 \Rightarrow \frac{x - 2}{x} \times 9 = 7$

$\Rightarrow 9x - 18 = 7x \quad \Rightarrow x = 9$

Number of side of second polygon is

$= 2 \times 9 = 18$

Each interior angle of second polygon is

$= \frac{(18 - 2)}{18} \times 180 = 160°$

230. (c) Given,

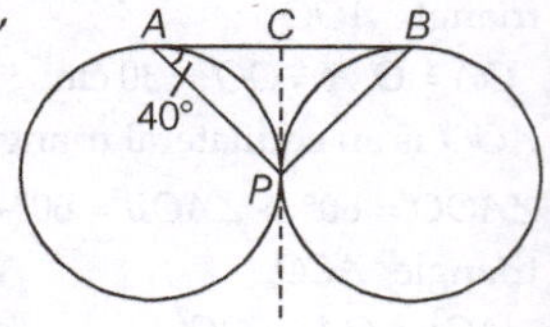

$\angle PAB = 40°$

tangent at P be PC.

Since $AC = PC \therefore \quad \angle PAC = \angle APC = 40°$

and $\angle ACP = 180° - 2 \times 40° = 100°$

$\therefore \quad \angle PCB = 180° - 100° = 80°$

Now, $\angle ABP = \frac{180° - 80°}{2} = \frac{100°}{2} = 50°$

231. (d)

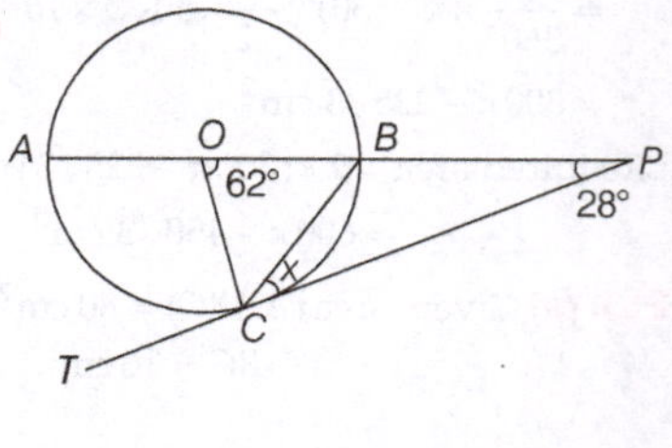

Given, $\angle BPT = 28°$, PT = tangent,

AB = Diameter

In ΔOCP, $\angle OCP + \angle CPO + \angle COP = 180°$

$90° + 28° + \angle COP = 180°$

$[\because \angle OCP = 90°]$

$\Rightarrow \angle COP = 180°-90°-28° \Rightarrow \angle COP = 62°$

where OC is perpendicular to tangent PT.

In ΔOCB, $OC = OB$ = radius

so, $\angle OCB = \angle OBC$

$\Rightarrow \angle OCB + \angle CBO + \angle BOC = 180°$

$\Rightarrow 2\angle OCB = 180° - \angle BOC = 180° - 62°$

$\Rightarrow 2\angle OCB = 118°$

$\Rightarrow \angle OCB = 59°$

In ΔOCP, $\angle OCB + \angle BCP = \angle OCP$

$\Rightarrow 59° + x° = 90° \Rightarrow x° = 90° - 59°$

$x° = 31° = \angle BCP$

232. (a) Given, $AC = 9$ cm, $CD = 3$ cm

then, $AD = AC - CD = 9 - 3 = 6$ cm

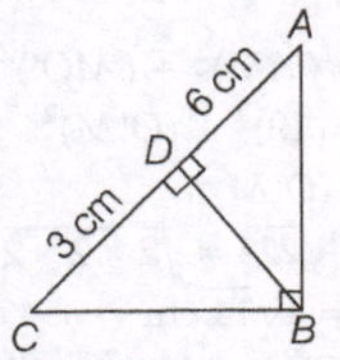

In ΔABC and ΔADB,

$\angle ABC = \angle ADB = 90°$

$\angle BAC = \angle DAB$ (common angles)

$\therefore \Delta ABC \sim \Delta ADB$

$\therefore \frac{AC}{AB} = \frac{AB}{AD} \Rightarrow \frac{9}{AB} = \frac{AB}{6}$

$\Rightarrow AB^2 = 9 \times 6 \Rightarrow AB = 3\sqrt{6}$ cm

233. (b) Given, $AC = 37$ cm, $BD = 5$ cm, $AD = 13$ cm

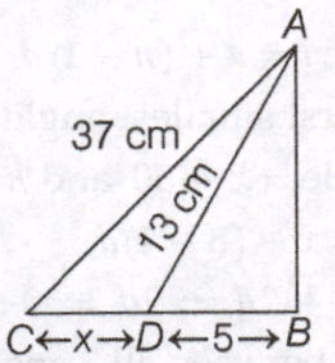

Applying Pythagoras theorem,

In ΔABD, $(AD)^2 = (AB)^2 + (BD)^2$

$(13)^2 = (AB)^2 + (5)^2 \Rightarrow (AB)^2 = 169 - 25$

$(AB)^2 = 144 \Rightarrow AB = 12$

Again applying Pythagoras theorem in ΔABC

$\Rightarrow (AC)^2 = (AB)^2 + (BC)^2$

$\Rightarrow (37)^2 = (12)^2 + (BC)^2$

$\Rightarrow 1369 - 144 = (BC)^2 \Rightarrow 1225 = (BC)^2$

$\Rightarrow BC = \sqrt{1225} = 35$ cm

$\Rightarrow BD + DC = 35 \Rightarrow 5 + x = 35$

$\Rightarrow DC = x = 35 - 5 = 30$ cm

234. (b) Given, BD = Diameter $\angle BAC = 22°$

Angles subtended by the same arc at the circumference are equal.

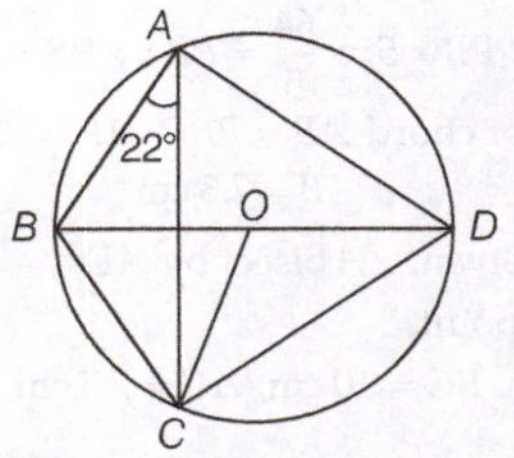

So, $\angle BAC = \angle BDC = 22°$

In ΔBCD, $\angle BCD + \angle CDB + \angle DBC = 180°$

$\Rightarrow 90° + 22° + \angle DBC = 180°$

$\Rightarrow \angle DBC = 180° - 90° - 22° = 68°$

We know that, $\angle COD = 2\angle DBC$

$\Rightarrow \angle COD = 2 \times 68° = 136°$

$\Rightarrow \angle COD = 136°$

235. (a) We know that, $\angle BAC = \frac{BOC}{2}$

$\Rightarrow \angle BAC = \frac{84}{2} = 42°$

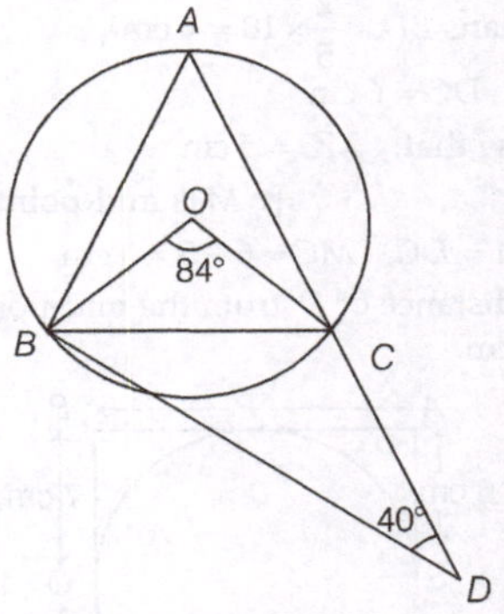

In ΔABD, $\angle ABD + \angle BDA + \angle DAB = 180°$

$\Rightarrow \angle ABD + 40° + 42° = 180°$

$\Rightarrow \angle ABD = 180° - 82° \Rightarrow \angle ABD = 98°$

236. (b)

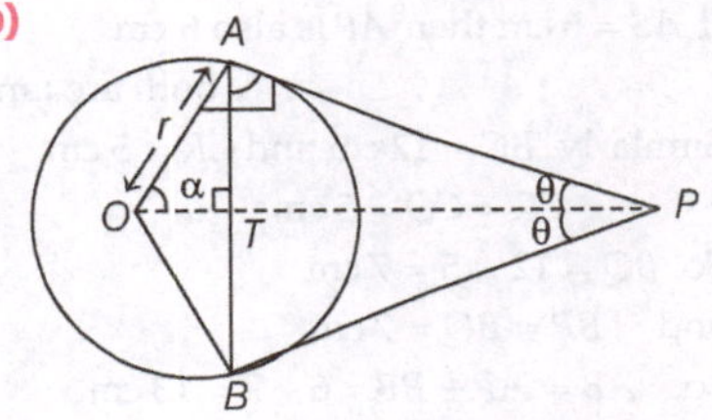

In ΔOAT and ΔOPA, $AT = \frac{AB}{2} = \frac{10}{2} = 5$ cm

By applying similarity,

$\frac{AT}{AP} = \frac{OA}{OP} = \frac{OT}{AO} \Rightarrow \frac{5}{AP} = \frac{r}{2r}$

$\Rightarrow \frac{5}{AP} = \frac{1}{2} \Rightarrow AP = 10$ cm

237. (a) Given, $\frac{AB}{DF} = \frac{BC}{DE} = \frac{AC}{EF}$

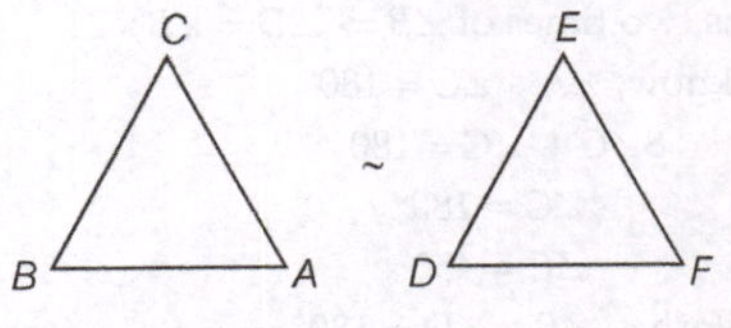

So, $\Delta BCA \sim \Delta DEF$

238. (b) Given, $AD \perp BC$, $\angle C = 52°$, $\angle B = 68°$

Since, AD is altitude.

Then, $\angle ADB = \angle ADC = 90°$

In ΔADC

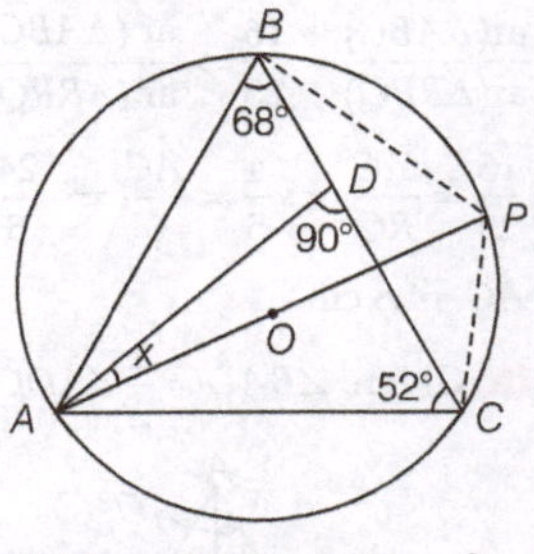

$\Rightarrow \angle ADC + \angle DCA + \angle CAD = 180°$

$\Rightarrow 90° + 52° + \angle CAD = 180°$

$\Rightarrow \angle CAD = 180° - 142°$

$\Rightarrow \angle CAD = 38°$ ....(i)

Similarly, in ΔADB.

$\Rightarrow \angle ADB + \angle DBA + \angle DAB = 180°$

$\Rightarrow 90° + 68° + \angle DAB = 180°$

$\Rightarrow \angle DAB = 180° - 158°$

$\Rightarrow \angle BAD = 22°$ ....(ii)

Given, AP is diameter which means AP divide the circle into 2 semi-circle and we know that, arc of semi circular length always subtends the right angle 90° at any point on circle. So,

$\angle ABP = \angle ACP = 90°$

We have, $\angle BCP = \angle ACP - \angle ACB$

$\Rightarrow \angle BCP = 90° - 52° = 38°$

We know that, angle substended by same arc have equal measure.

So, $\angle BAP = \angle BCP = 38°$

$\angle BAP = 38°$ and we know, $\angle DAB = 22°$

From Eq. (ii),

$\angle DAP = \angle BAP - \angle DAB = 38° - 22°$

$\therefore \angle DAP = 16°$

239. (d) Given, $\angle ADE = 80°$, $\angle AED = 50°$

We know that, in ΔAED

$\angle AED + \angle EDA + \angle DAE = 180°$

$\Rightarrow 50° + 80° + \angle DAE = 180°$

$\Rightarrow \angle DAE = 180° - 130° \Rightarrow \angle DAE = 50°$

Now, $\angle ADC + \angle ABC = 180°$

$\Rightarrow \angle ABC = 180° - 80° = 100°$

Now, in ΔAFB

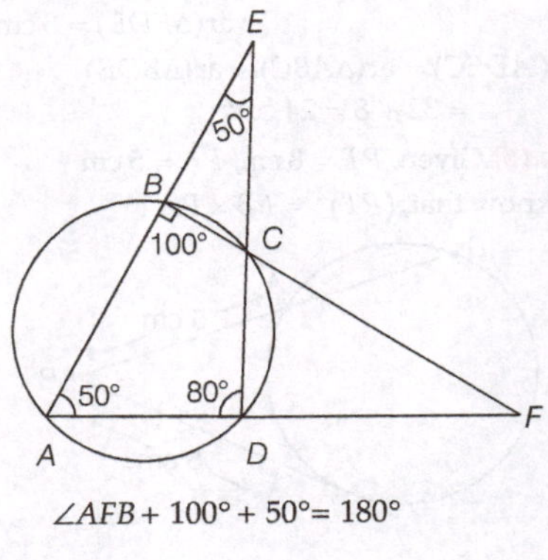

$\Rightarrow \angle AFB + 100° + 50° = 180°$

$\Rightarrow \angle AFB = 180°-100°-50° = 180°-150°$

$\therefore \angle AFB = 30°$

240. (b) Given, $\Delta ABC \sim \Delta RPQ$

and $\frac{ar(\Delta ABC)}{ar(\Delta RPQ)} = \frac{16}{25} \Rightarrow \frac{ar(\Delta ABC)}{ar(\Delta RPQ)} = \left(\frac{AC}{RQ}\right)^2$

$\Rightarrow \sqrt{\frac{16}{25}} = \frac{AC}{RQ} \Rightarrow \frac{4}{5} = \frac{AC}{6} \Rightarrow \frac{24}{5} = AC$

$\therefore \quad AC = 4.8$ cm

241. (b) Given, $\angle BAD = \frac{1}{2}\angle ADC,$

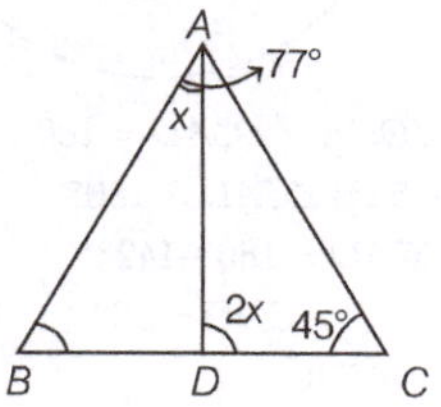

$\angle BAC = 77°, \angle C = 45°$

$\angle ADB = ?$

We know that, $\angle BAD + \angle B = \angle ADC$

[Exterior angle property]

$\Rightarrow \quad x + \angle B = 2x \Rightarrow \angle B = x$

In ΔABC, $\angle A + \angle B + \angle C = 180°$

$\Rightarrow \quad 77° + \angle B + 45° = 180°$

$\Rightarrow \angle B = 180° - (77° + 45°)$

$= (180° - 122)° = 58°$

$\Rightarrow \angle B = 58° = x$

Now, $\quad \angle BDC = \angle ADB + \angle ADC$

[$\because$ Linear angle]

$\Rightarrow \quad 180° = \angle ADB + 2 \times 58°$

$\Rightarrow \angle ADB = 180° - 116° = 64° \Rightarrow \angle ADB = 64°$

242. (a) Given, $ar(\Delta BED) = 8\ cm^2$

ar $(ADEC) = ?$

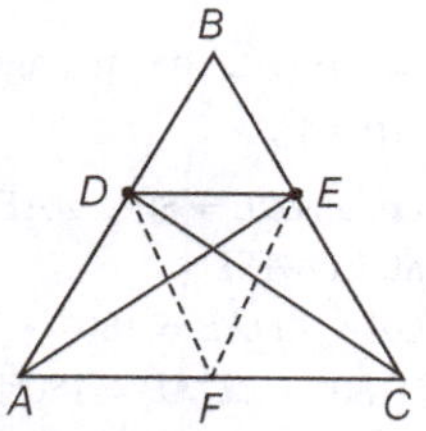

We know that, mid-point cut the line in 1 : 2.

So, $\quad \frac{ar\ \Delta BDE}{ar\ \Delta BAC} = \left(\frac{1}{2}\right)^2 = \frac{1}{4}$

$\Rightarrow$ ar $(\Delta BAC) = 4 \times 8 = 32\ cm^2$

[$\because ar(\Delta BDE) = 8\ cm^2$]

$\therefore$ ar$(ADEC)$ = ar(ΔABC) − ar(ΔBDE)

$= 32 - 8 = 24\ cm^2$

243. (d) Given, $PT = 8$ cm, $PA = 5$ cm

We know that, $(PT)^2 = PB \times PA$

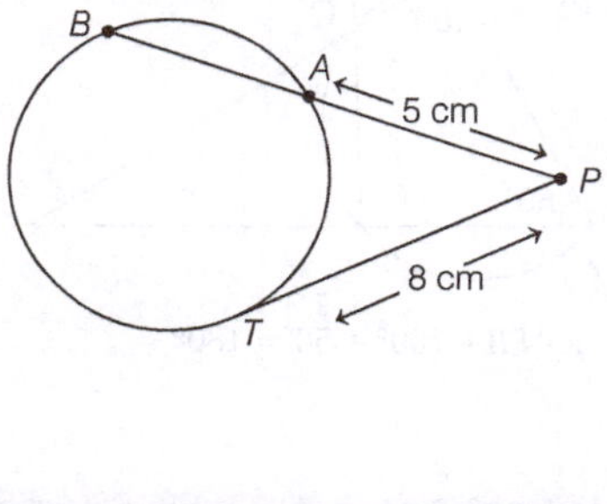

$\Rightarrow \quad (8)^2 = PB \times 5 \Rightarrow \frac{64}{5} = PB \Rightarrow PB = 12.8$ cm

$\therefore$ Length of chord $AB = PB - AP = 12.8 - 5$

$B = 7.8$ cm

244. (b) Given, $\angle A$ bisect by AD

M = mid-point

$AB = 5$ cm, $BC = 10$ cm, $AC = 7.5$ cm

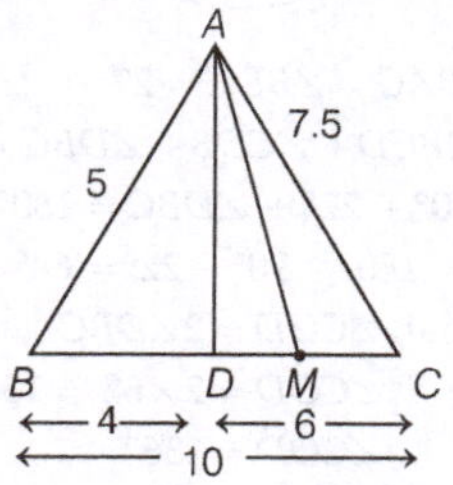

We know that, $\frac{BD}{DC} = \frac{AB}{AC} \Rightarrow \frac{BD}{DC} = \frac{5}{7.5} = \frac{2}{3}$

$BD : DC = 2:3$

That means $BD = \frac{2}{5} \times 10 = 4$ cm

$DC = 6$ cm

We know that, $\quad MC = 5$ cm

{$\because$ M is mid-point of BC}

So, $\quad DM = DC - MC = 6 - 5 = 1$ cm

So, the distance of D from the mid-point of BC is 1 cm.

245. (d)

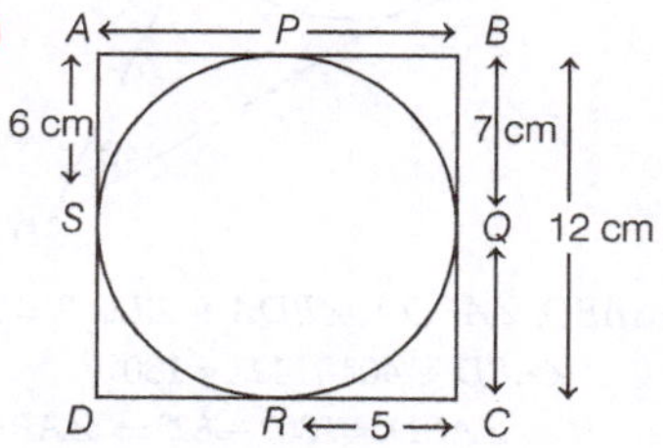

If $AS = 6$ cm then AP is also 6 cm

{$\because$ both are tangents}

Similarly, $BC = 12$ cm and $CR = 5$ cm

$CR = CQ = 5$ cm

So, $BQ = 12 - 5 = 7$ cm

and $\quad BP = BQ = 7$ cm

So, $\quad AB = AP + PB = 6 + 7 = 13$ cm

246. (c) According to the question,

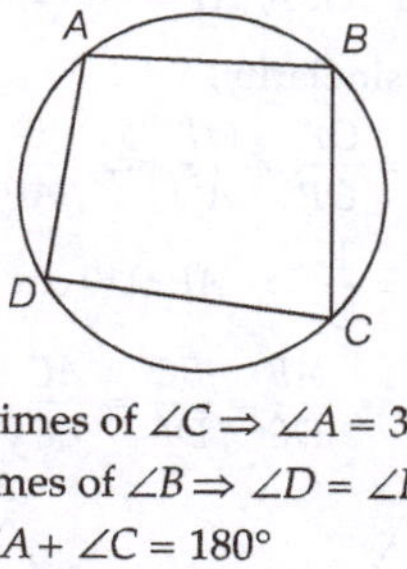

$\angle A$ is three times of $\angle C \Rightarrow \angle A = 3\angle C$

$\angle D$ is two times of $\angle B \Rightarrow \angle D = \angle B \times 2$

We know, $\angle A + \angle C = 180°$

So, $\quad 3\angle C + \angle C = 180$

$4\angle C = 180°$

$\angle C = 45°$

Similarly, $\quad \angle B + \angle D = 180°$

So, $\quad \frac{\angle D}{2} + \angle D = 180$

$\frac{3\angle D}{2} = 180° \quad$ [$\because \angle D = 2\angle B$]

$\angle D = 120°$

Difference between $\angle D$ and $\angle C$

$= 120° - 45° = 75°$

247. (d) Given, $AO' = 18$ cm, $AO = 16$ cm

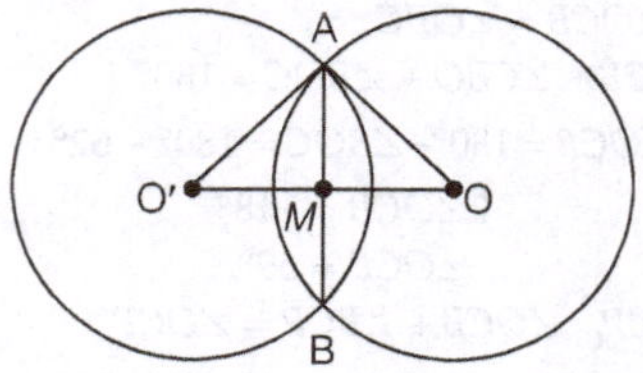

Common chord $AB = 20$ cm

Then, $AM + MB = 20$ cm

$AM = MB = 10$ cm

In $\Delta AO'M$,

$(AO')^2 = (AM)^2 + (MO')^2$

$\Rightarrow \quad (18)^2 = (10)^2 + (O'M)^2$

$\Rightarrow 324 - 100 = (O'M)^2$

$\Rightarrow \quad MO' = \sqrt{224} = \sqrt{2 \times 2 \times 2 \times 14 \times 2}$

$\Rightarrow \quad MO' = 4\sqrt{14}$ cm

In ΔAOM, $(AO)^2 = (AM)^2 + (MO)^2$

$\Rightarrow \quad (16)^2 = (10)^2 + (MO)^2$

$\Rightarrow \quad 256 - 100 = (MO)^2$

$\Rightarrow \quad MO = \sqrt{156} = \sqrt{2 \times 2 \times 3 \times 13}$

$\Rightarrow \quad MO = 2\sqrt{39}$ cm

$\therefore$ Distance between the centre

$OO' = O'M + MO = 4\sqrt{14} + 2\sqrt{39}$ cm

248. (b) The angles of triangle are in AP.

Given, smallest angle is 50° less than largest angle.

We know that, $l = a + (n-1)d$

Here, let a = first smallest angle is x.

l = largest angle = $x + 50$ and $n = 3$ (angle)

$\Rightarrow \quad 50 + x = x + (3-1)d$

$\Rightarrow \quad 50 + x = x + 2d \Rightarrow 2d = 50 \Rightarrow d = 25$

The difference between all 3 angle is 25.

Sum of all 3 triangle is 180°.

Then, $\quad a$ + 2nd angle + $l = 180°$

$\Rightarrow x + x + 25 + x + 50 = 180°$

$\Rightarrow \quad 3x + 75 = 180°$

$\Rightarrow \quad 3x = 105° \Rightarrow x = 35°$

$\therefore$ Largest angle $l = x + 50° = 35° + 50° = 85°$

Speedy Method

Let angle are $a - d$, a and $a + d$.

As we know, $a - d + a + a + d = 180°$

$3a = 180°, a = 60°$

Again, according to the question

$a + d - (a - d) = 50, \quad a + d - a + d = 50$

$d = 25$

Hence, largest angle

$a + d = 60 + 25 = 85°$

249. (a) Given, $\angle AEC = 50°$, $\angle ABD = 30°$

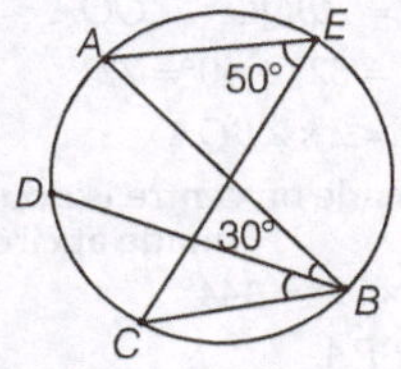

We know that, $\angle AEC = \angle ABC = 50°$

[angle made by same arc]

$\Rightarrow \quad 50° = \angle ABD + \angle DBC$

$\Rightarrow \quad 50° = 30° + \angle CBD \Rightarrow \angle CBD = 20°$

250. (c)

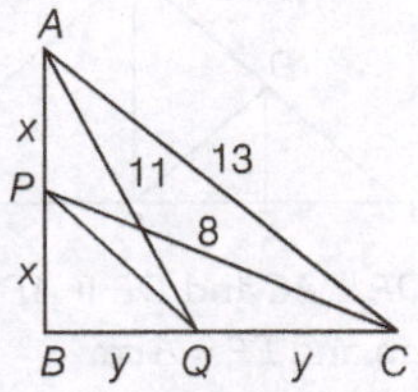

We know that, $AC^2 + PQ^2 = AQ^2 + PC^2$

$\Rightarrow \quad (13)^2 + PQ^2 = (11)^2 + (8)^2$

$\Rightarrow \quad PQ^2 = 121 + 64 - 169 \Rightarrow PQ^2 = 16$

$\therefore \quad PQ = 4$ cm

251. (a) Given, $DE = \dfrac{BC}{2}$

and $AD + CE + BC = 30$

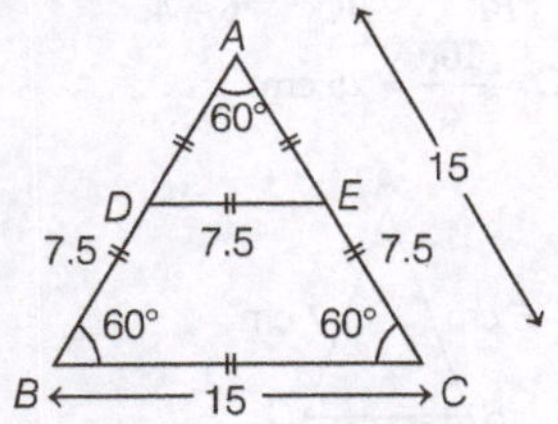

$AD = AE, AB = BC = AC$

$\Rightarrow \quad AE + EC + BC = 30$

$\Rightarrow \quad AC + BC = 30$

$\Rightarrow \quad AC = BC = 15 = AB$

and $\quad DE = \dfrac{BC}{2} = \dfrac{15}{2} = 7.5$ cm

Perimeter of $BCED = BC + CE + ED + DB$

$= 15 + 7.5 + 7.5 + 7.5 = 37.5$ cm

252. (d) Given, $AD = 4$ cm, $DB = 3$ cm

DE parallel to AC.

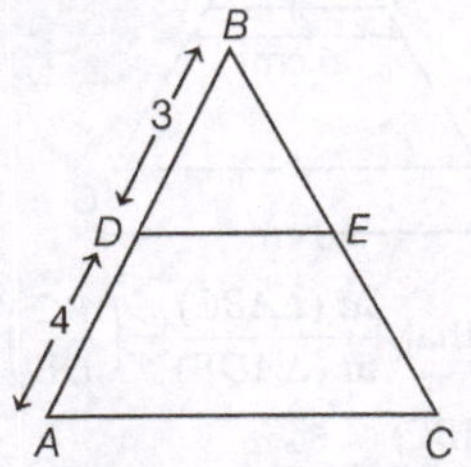

$$\frac{\Delta BDE}{\Delta BAC} = \left(\frac{\text{Side of } \Delta BDE}{\text{Side of } \Delta BAC}\right)^2$$

$$\Rightarrow \frac{\Delta BDE}{\Delta BAC} = \frac{3^2}{(4+3)^2} = \frac{9}{7^2} = \frac{9}{49}$$

$$\therefore \frac{\text{Area of } \Delta BDE}{\text{Area of trapezium } ACED}$$

$$= \frac{9}{\text{Area}(\Delta BAC - \Delta BDE)} = \frac{9}{49-9}$$

$$= \frac{9}{40} = 9:40$$

253. (d) In ΔAOM,

$\Rightarrow \quad (AO)^2 = (OM)^2 + (MA)^2$

$\Rightarrow \quad (13)^2 = (5)^2 + (MA)^2$

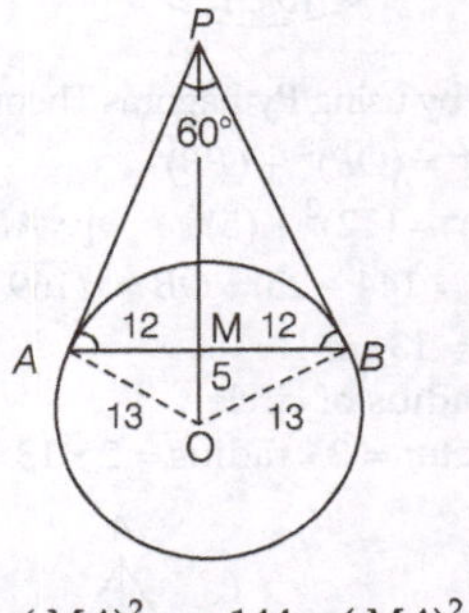

$\Rightarrow 169 - 25 = (MA)^2 \Rightarrow 144 = (MA)^2$

$\Rightarrow \quad MA = 12$ cm $= MB = AB = 24$ cm

In ΔAPB, $\angle APB + \angle PAB + \angle ABP = 180°$

[$\because AP = PB \therefore \angle PAB = \angle PBA$]

$\Rightarrow \quad 2\angle PAB = 180° - 60°$

$\Rightarrow \quad 2\angle PAB = 120° \Rightarrow \angle PAB = 60°$

Now, ΔPAB is equilateral triangle

Thus, all sides are equal

$AP = AB = PB = 24$ cm

254. (c) Given, $CD = 16$ cm, $DE = 6$ cm

$AE = 12$ cm, $EB = x$ cm

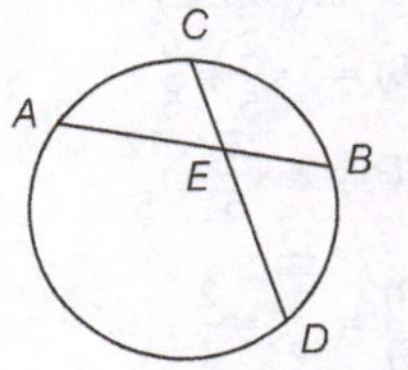

Then, $EC = CD - DE = 16 - 6 = 10$ cm

we know that,

$\Rightarrow \quad AE \times EB = CE \times ED \Rightarrow 12 \times x = 10 \times 6$

$\therefore \quad x = EB = 5$ cm

255. (c)

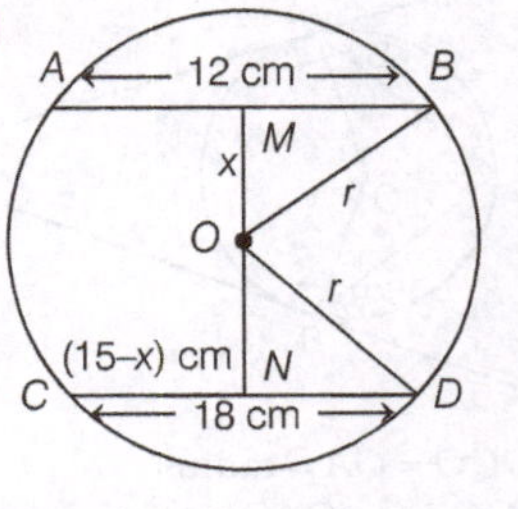

$\therefore$ In ΔOBM, $r^2 = x^2 + (6)^2$

$\Rightarrow \quad r^2 = x^2 + 36 \quad \ldots$ (i)

In ΔODN, $\quad r^2 = (15 - x)^2 + (9)^2$

$\Rightarrow \quad r^2 = (15 - x)^2 + 81 \quad \ldots$ (ii)

Equating Eqs. (i) and (ii),

$x^2 + 36 = (15 - x)^2 + 81$

$\Rightarrow x^2 + 36 = 225 + x^2 - 30x + 81$

$\Rightarrow \quad 30x = 225 - 36 + 81 = 270$

$\Rightarrow \quad x = \dfrac{270}{30} \Rightarrow x = 9$

Value of x put in Eq. (i)

$r^2 = (9)^2 + 36 \Rightarrow r^2 = 81 + 36 = 117$

$\Rightarrow \quad r = \sqrt{117} = \sqrt{13 \times 9}$

$\therefore$ Radius of circle $= 3\sqrt{13}$ cm

256. (a) Given, perpendicular = 12 cm

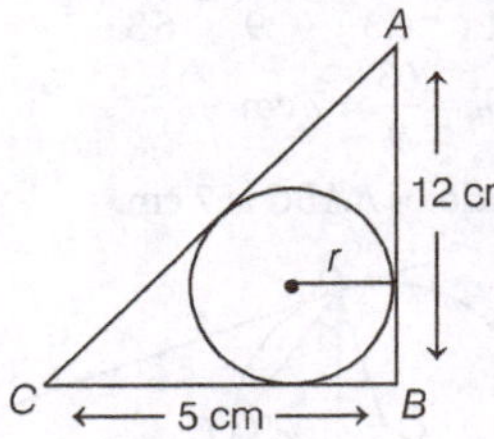

Base = 5 cm

By Pythagoras theorem,

$(\text{Hypotenuse})^2 = (P)^2 + (B)^2$

$\Rightarrow \quad (H)^2 = (12)^2 + (5)^2 = 144 + 25$

$\Rightarrow \quad (H)^2 = 169 \Rightarrow H = 13$ cm

Formula of in radius of circle inscribed in ΔABC

$$= \frac{(\text{Perpendicular} + \text{Base} - \text{Hypotenuse})}{2}$$

$$= \frac{12 + 5 - 13}{2} = \frac{4}{2}$$

$\therefore$ Radius = 2 cm

257. (c)

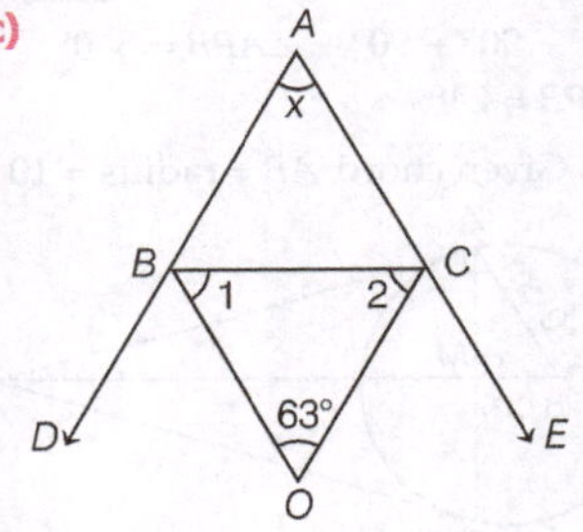

As we know,

$$\angle BOC = 90 - \frac{\angle A}{2} \Rightarrow 63 = 90 - \frac{\angle A}{2}$$

$$\Rightarrow \quad \frac{\angle A}{2} = 27 \Rightarrow \angle A = 54°$$

258. (b) Given,

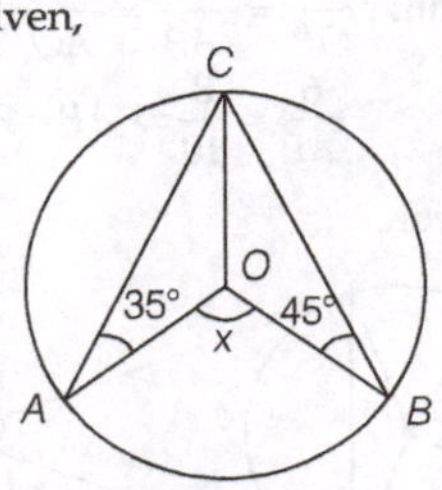

$\angle OAC = 35°$, and $\angle OBC = 45°$

$OC = OA = OB =$ radius

Then, $\quad \angle OAC = \angle OCA = 35°$

And $\quad \angle OBC = \angle OCB = 45°$

So, $\quad \angle ACB = \angle OCA + \angle OCB$

$\Rightarrow \quad \angle ACB = 35° + 45° = 80°$

$\therefore \quad \angle AOB = 2 \times \angle ACB$

[$\because$ Central angle is twice of circumference angle made by same arc]

$= 2 \times 80° = 160°$

259. (c) Given, $\Delta ABC \sim \Delta DEF$

We know that,

$$\frac{\text{Area of } \Delta ABC}{\text{Area of } \Delta DEF} = \left(\frac{\text{Side of } \Delta ABC}{\text{Side of } \Delta DEF}\right)^2$$

$\Rightarrow \sqrt{\frac{100}{81}} = \frac{h}{6.3} \Rightarrow \frac{10}{9} = \frac{h}{6.3}$

$\therefore \quad h = \frac{63}{9} = 7$ cm

Then, altitude of ΔABC is 7 cm.

260. (d)

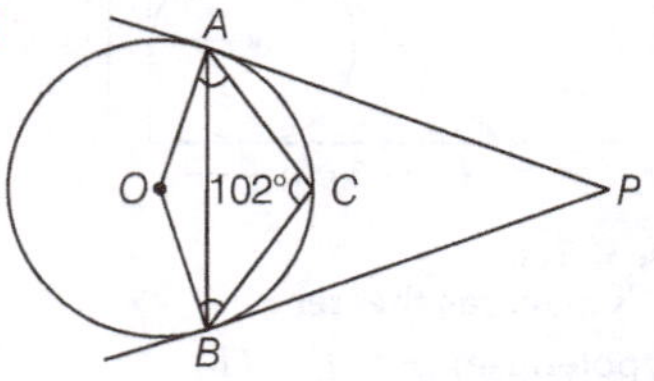

We know that, $\angle AOB = 2 \times \angle ACB$

[angle made on centre is double the angle made by same arc on circumference]

$\angle AOB = 204$ [major arc]

$\therefore \angle AOB$ (minor arc) $= 360 - 204 = 156°$

Now, In quadrilateral $AOBP$,

Sum of all angles is 360°

$\angle AOB$ (minor arc) $+ \angle OBP + \angle OAP$

$\angle APB = 360°$

$\Rightarrow \quad 156° + 90° + 90° + \angle APB = 360°$

$\Rightarrow \quad \angle APB = 24°$

261. (a) Given chord AB = radius = 10 cm

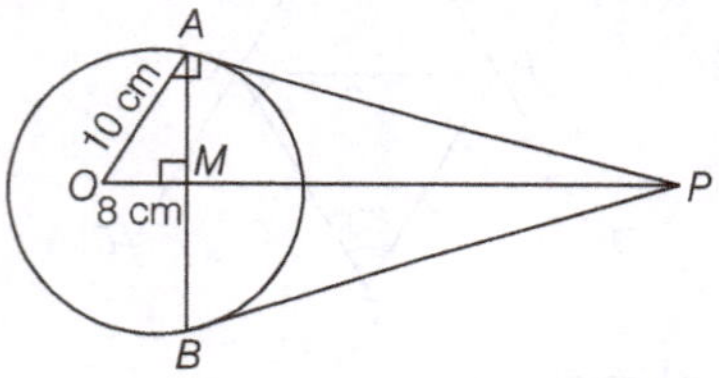

In ΔAOM, $(AO)^2 = (AM)^2 + (MO)^2$

$\Rightarrow (10)^2 - (8)^2 = (AM)^2 \Rightarrow AM = \sqrt{36} = 6$ cm

In ΔAOM and ΔPOA,

Both are similar $\frac{OA}{OP} = \frac{AM}{AP} = \frac{OM}{AO}$

$\Rightarrow \quad \frac{6}{AP} = \frac{8}{10} \Rightarrow AP = 7.5$ cm

262. (b) Given,

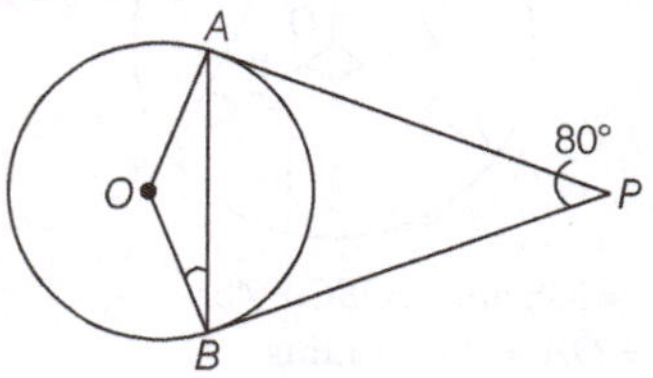

In quadrilateral $APBO$.

$\angle O + \angle A + \angle P + \angle B = 360°$

$\Rightarrow \quad \angle O = 360° - 90° - 90° - 80° \Rightarrow \angle O = 100°$

In ΔAOB, $\angle OAB = \angle OBA = x$

[$\because OA = OB$ = Radius]

Now, $\angle OAB + \angle OBA + AOB = 180°$

$\Rightarrow \quad x + x + 100° = 180° \Rightarrow 2x = 80° \Rightarrow x = 40°$

$\therefore \quad \angle OAB = 40°$

263. (c)

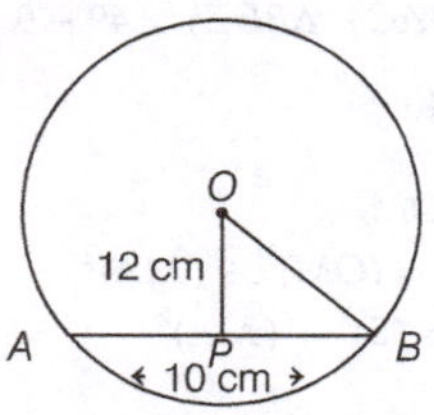

In ΔOPB, by using Pythagoras Theorem,

$\Rightarrow \quad (OB)^2 = (OP)^2 + (PB)^2$

$\Rightarrow \quad ((OB)^2 = (12)^2 + (5)^2 \quad [\because AP + PB = 10]$

$\Rightarrow (OB)^2 = 144 + 25 \Rightarrow OB = \sqrt{169}$

$\Rightarrow \quad OB = 13$ cm

$\because OB$ is radius of circle

So, diameter $= 2 \times$ radius $= 2 \times 13 = 26$ cm

264. (b)

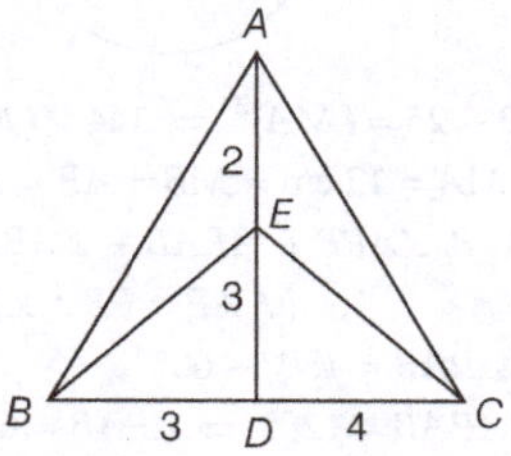

We know that,

If a line from vertex cuts the opposite side in a certain ratio, then the area of two new triangles is also divided in that ratio.

Ratio of $\frac{BD}{DC} = \frac{\text{ar}(\Delta ADB)}{\text{ar}(\Delta ADC)}$

So, $\text{ar}(\Delta AEB) = 3 \times \frac{2}{5} = \frac{6}{5}$

and $\text{ar}(\Delta ECD) = 4 \times \frac{3}{5} = \frac{12}{5}$

$\Rightarrow \frac{\text{ar}(\Delta ECD)}{\text{ar}(\Delta AEB)} = \frac{\frac{12}{5}}{\frac{6}{5}} = \frac{2}{1}$

$\therefore \quad \text{ar}(\Delta ECD) : \text{ar}(\Delta AEB) = 2 : 1$

265. (a)

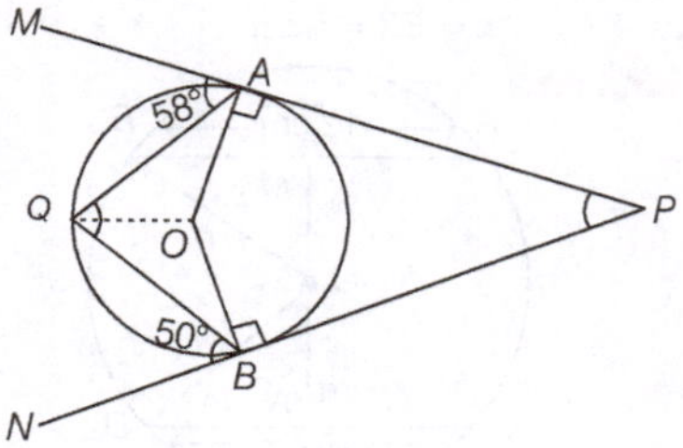

In ΔQOA, $QO = OA$ = radius

Then, $\angle OQA = \angle OAQ = x°$

In ΔOQB, $QO = OB$ = radius

Then, $\angle OQB = \angle OBQ = y°$

Now, $\angle MAP = \angle MAQ + \angle QAO + \angle OAP$

[linear angle]

$\Rightarrow 58° + x + 90° = 180° \Rightarrow x = 32°$

Now, $\angle NBP = \angle NBQ + \angle QBO + \angle OBP$

[linear angle]

$\Rightarrow 50° + y + 90° = 180° \Rightarrow y = 40°$

Now, $\angle BQA = \angle BQO + \angle OQA$

$= 32° + 40° = 72°$

Then, $\angle BOA = 2 \times \angle BQA$

[$\because$ Angle made on centre is double of angle made at circumference]

$= 2 \times 72° = 144°$

Now, In $\square OBPA$,

$\angle O + \angle A + \angle P + \angle B = 360°$

$\Rightarrow \quad \angle APB = 360° - 144° - 90° - 90° = 36°$

266. (c) According to the question,

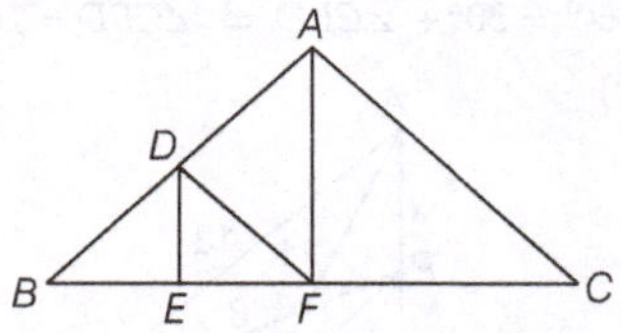

Given, $DF \parallel AC$ and $DE \parallel AF$

$BE = 4$ cm and $EF = 6$ cm

In ΔABC, $DF \parallel AC$

then $\frac{BD}{BA} = \frac{BF}{BC}$ ...(i)

In ΔBAF, $DE \parallel AF$

$\frac{BE}{BF} = \frac{BD}{AB}$ ...(ii)

From Eqs. (i) and (ii),

$\frac{BF}{BC} = \frac{BE}{BF} \Rightarrow \frac{6+4}{BC} = \frac{4}{6+4}$

$\Rightarrow \quad BC = \frac{100}{4} = 25$ cm

267. (b)

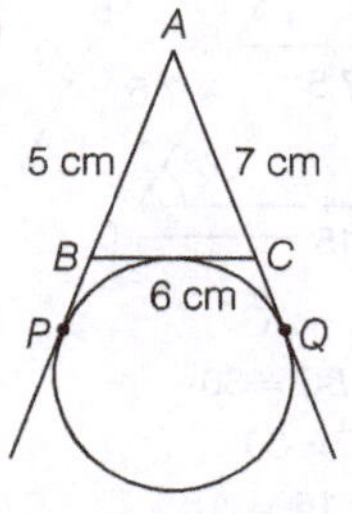

We know that, $AB + BC + CA = 2AP = 2AQ$

$\Rightarrow \quad 5 + 6 + 7 = 2AQ$

$\Rightarrow \quad 18 = 2AQ \Rightarrow AQ = 9$ cm

268. (a)

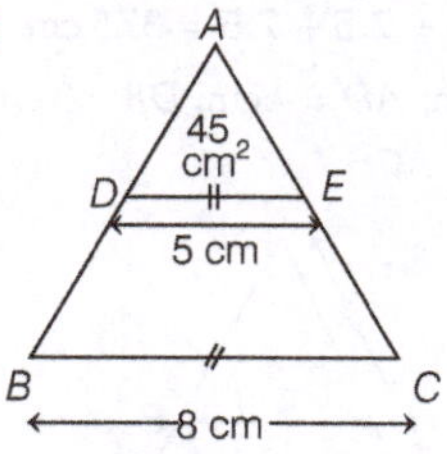

We know that, $\frac{\text{ar}(\Delta ABC)}{\text{ar}(\Delta ADE)} = \left(\frac{BC}{DE}\right)^2$

$\Rightarrow \quad \frac{\text{ar}(\Delta ABC)}{\text{ar}(\Delta ADE)} = \frac{64}{25}$

$\Rightarrow \quad \text{ar}(\Delta ABC) = 64 \times \frac{45}{25} = 64 \times \frac{9}{5}$

[$\because \text{ar}(\Delta ADE) = 45$]

$\Rightarrow \quad \text{ar}(\Delta ABC) = 115.2 \text{ cm}^2$.

269. (a)

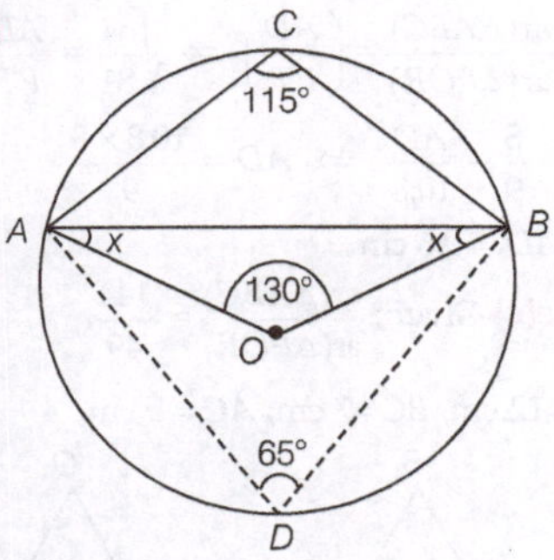

We know that, the sum of opposite angles of a cyclic quadrilateral is 180°.

$\Rightarrow \quad 115° + \angle ADB = 180°$

$\Rightarrow \quad \angle ADB = 65°$

$\therefore \quad \angle AOB = 2\angle ADB = 2 \times 65° = 130°$

{$\because$ Angle at centre is twice the angle at circumference}

Let $\angle OAB = \angle ABO = x$ {$\because OA = OB$ = radius}

$\therefore \angle OAB + \angle ABO + \angle AOB = 180°$

$\Rightarrow \quad x + x + 130° = 180° \Rightarrow 2x = 50°$

$\Rightarrow \quad x = 25°$

The value of $\angle OAB = 25°$

270. (d) Given, $AE = 30$ cm

$AD = DC$ and $BF = DF$

Now, we draw a line DH from point D parallel to line CE

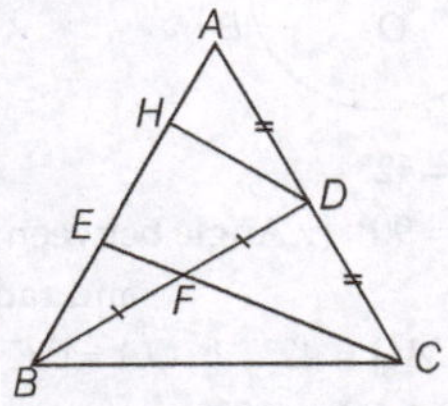

$\therefore \quad DH \parallel CE \ \therefore \ \Delta AHD \sim \Delta AEC$

$\therefore \quad \dfrac{AD}{AC} = \dfrac{AH}{AE} \Rightarrow \dfrac{\frac{AC}{2}}{AC} = \dfrac{AH}{30} \Rightarrow AH = 15$ cm

$\Rightarrow \quad HE = AE - AH = 30 - 15 = 15$ cm

Now, $\Delta BEF \sim \Delta BHD$ {$\because EF \parallel HD$}

$\therefore \quad \dfrac{BE}{BH} = \dfrac{BF}{BD} \Rightarrow \dfrac{BE}{BE + EH} = \dfrac{\frac{BD}{2}}{BD}$

$\Rightarrow \quad \dfrac{BE}{BE + 15} = \dfrac{1}{2}$

$\Rightarrow 2BE = BE + 15$

$\therefore \quad BE = 15$ cm

271. (b) Given, $AB = 12$, cm $CD = 18$ cm

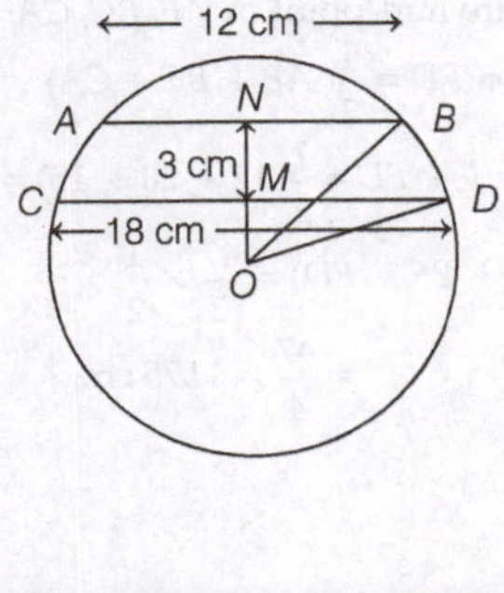

Distance between chords = 3 cm

Let distance between O and $M = x$ cm

$OD = OB$ = Radius of circle

In ΔOBN, $(OB)^2 = (ON)^2 + (NB)^2$

$\Rightarrow \quad (OB)^2 = (x+3)^2 + (6)^2 \quad$ ...(i)

In ΔODM, $(OD)^2 = (OM)^2 + (MD)^2$

$\Rightarrow \quad (OD)^2 = (x)^2 + (9)^2 \quad$ ...(ii)

Eq. (i) = Eq. (ii)

$\Rightarrow \quad (x+3)^2 + 36 = x^2 + 81$

$\Rightarrow \quad x^2 + 9 + 6x + 36 = x^2 + 81$

$\Rightarrow \quad 6x = 81 - 45 = 36$

$x = 6$

$\therefore \ (OD)^2 = (OM)^2 + (MD)^2 = (6)^2 + (9)^2$

$(OD)^2 = 36 + 81 = 117 \Rightarrow OD = \sqrt{117}$

$OD = 3\sqrt{13}$ cm

272. (b) Given, $AD = x - 3$, $AC = 2x$,

$BE = x - 2$, $BC = 2x + 3$, $x = ?$

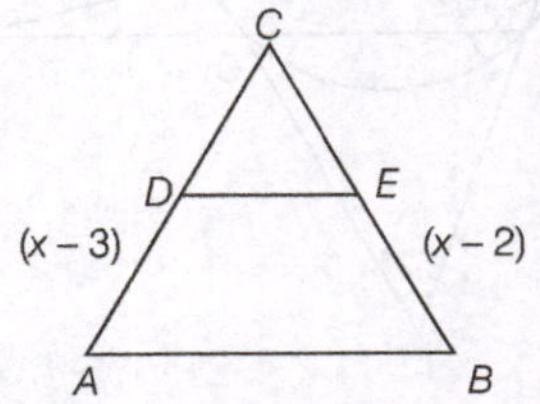

$\Rightarrow \quad \dfrac{BE}{BC} = \dfrac{AD}{AC} \Rightarrow \dfrac{(x-2)}{(2x+3)} = \dfrac{(x-3)}{2x}$

$\Rightarrow \ 2x^2 - 4x = (x-3)(2x+3)$

$\Rightarrow \ 2x^2 - 4x = 2x^2 + 3x - 6x - 9$

$\Rightarrow -4x - 3x + 6x = -9 \Rightarrow \quad x = 9$

$\therefore$ Required value of x is 9.

273. (c) Given, $AB = 6$ cm, $CD = x$ cm

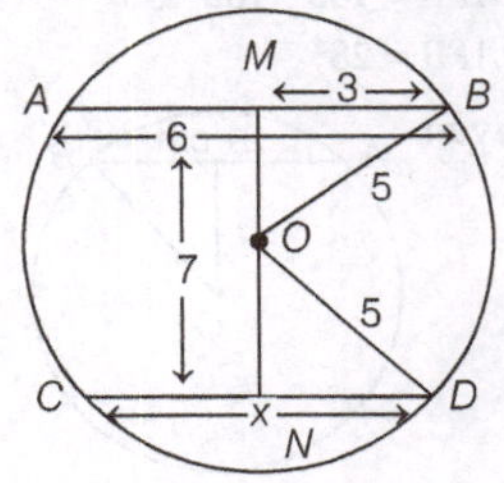

and radius = 5 cm.

In ΔOMB using Pythagoras theorem,

$(OB)^2 = (OM)^2 + (MB)^2$

$\Rightarrow \quad (5)^2 = (OM)^2 + (3)^2$

$\Rightarrow \quad 25 - 9 = (OM)^2 \Rightarrow 16 = (OM)^2$

$\Rightarrow \quad OM = 4$ cm

Given, $OM + ON = MN = 7$ cm

$\Rightarrow \quad ON = 7 - 4 = 3$ cm

In ΔODN, $(OD)^2 = (ON)^2 + (ND)^2$

$\Rightarrow \quad (5)^2 = (3)^2 + (ND)^2$

$\Rightarrow \quad 25 - 9 = (ND)^2 \Rightarrow 16 = (ND)^2$

$\Rightarrow \quad ND = 4$ cm

If $ND = 4$, then NC is also 4.

So, total length of chord

$CD = 4 + 4 = 8$ cm

274. (b) Given, $\angle ABC = 34°$

Now, $\angle ABC = \angle ADC = 34°$

(angle makes on circumference by a same chord is equal)

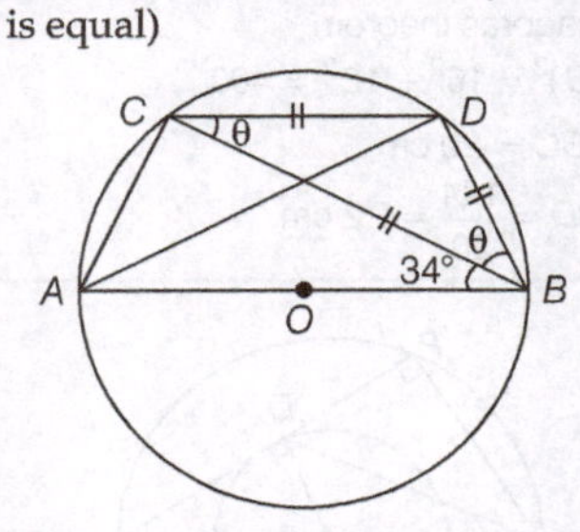

$\angle ADB = 90°$ [$\because$ Angle in semi-circle]

Now, $\quad \angle CDB = 90° + 34° = 124°$

$\Rightarrow \angle CBD + \angle BDC + \angle DCB = 180°$

$\Rightarrow \quad \theta + 124° + \theta = 180°$

[$\because CD = DB$ and $\angle DCB = \angle DBC = \theta$]

$\Rightarrow \quad 2\theta = 56° \Rightarrow \theta = 28° \therefore \ \angle DBC = \theta = 28°$

275. (c)

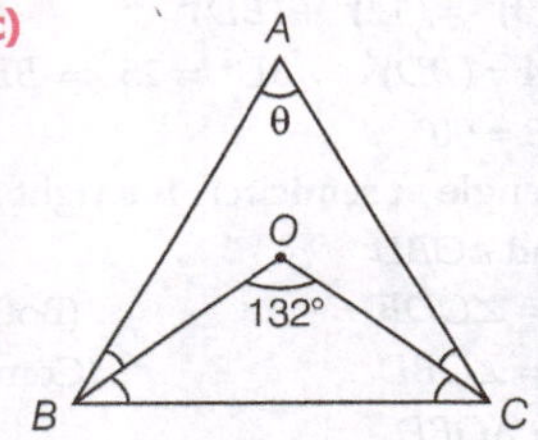

We know that, $\angle BOC = 90° + \dfrac{\angle A}{2}$

$132 = 90° + \dfrac{\angle A}{2} \Rightarrow \dfrac{\angle A}{2} = 132° - 90° = 42°$

$\therefore \quad \angle A = 42° \times 2° = 84°$

276. (c)

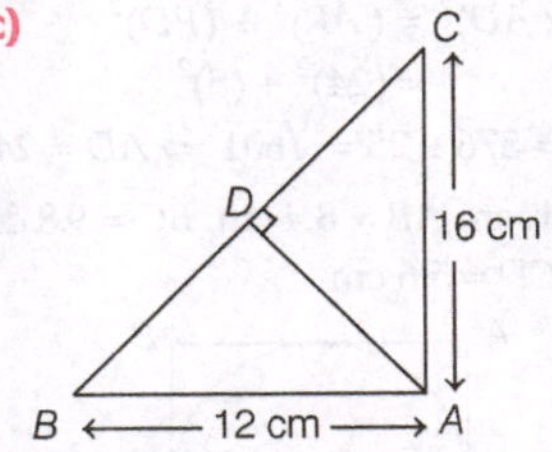

In ΔABC, by Pythagoras theorem,

$(BC)^2 = (AB)^2 + (CA)^2$

$\Rightarrow \quad (BC)^2 = (12)^2 + (16)^2 = 144 + 256$

$\Rightarrow \quad (BC)^2 = 400 \Rightarrow BC = 20$ cm

Let $\quad BD = x$, then $DC = 20 - x$

By Pythagoras theorem in ΔABD and ΔDAC

$AD^2 = BA^2 - BD^2 = (12)^2 - x^2$

$AD^2 = 144 - x^2 \quad$ ...(i)

and $\quad AD^2 = AC^2 - DC^2$

$= (16)^2 - (20 - x)^2$

$\Rightarrow \quad AD^2 = 256 - (20 - x)^2 \quad$ ...(ii)

From Eq. (i) and (ii),

$144 - x^2 = 256 - 400 - x^2 + 40x$

$\Rightarrow \quad 40x = 144 + 144 = 288$

$\Rightarrow \quad x = \dfrac{288}{40} = 7.2$ cm

Speedy Method

As we know, $BD = \frac{AB^2}{BC}$

By Pythagoras theorem

$(BC)^2 = 16^2 + 12^2 = 400$

$\Rightarrow \quad BC = 20$ cm

Thus, $BD = \frac{144}{20} = 7.2$ cm

277. (c)

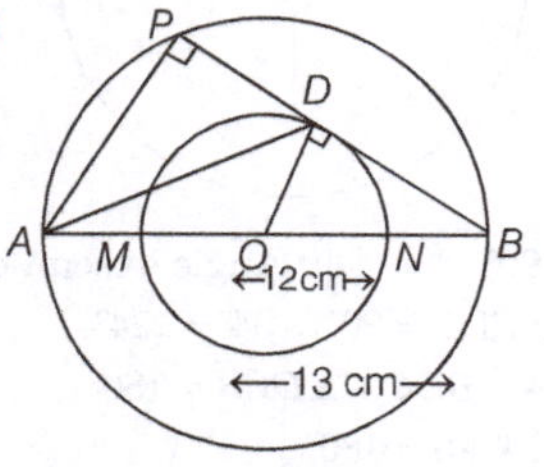

In ΔOBD, by Pythagoras theorem,

$(OB)^2 = (OD)^2 + (BD)^2$

$\Rightarrow \quad (13)^2 = (12)^2 + (BD)^2$

$\Rightarrow 169 - 144 = (BD)^2 \Rightarrow BD^2 = 25 \Rightarrow BD = 5$

$\angle APB = 90°$

($\because$ angle in semicircle is *a* right angle)

In ΔAPB and ΔOBD

$\angle APB = \angle ODB$ (Both 90°)

$\angle ABP = \angle OBD$ (Common)

$\therefore \quad \Delta ABP \sim \Delta OBD$

(AA similarety)

$AO = OB = 13$ cm, $BD = DP = 5$ cm

$OD = 12$ cm,

$AP = 2 \times 12 = 24$ cm

[By Pythagoras theorem]

In ΔAPD, $(AD)^2 = (AP)^2 + (PD)^2$

$= (24)^2 + (5)^2$

$\Rightarrow (AD)^2 = 576 + 25 = \sqrt{601} \Rightarrow AD = 24.5$ cm

278. (b) Given, $AB = 8.4$ cm, $BC = 9.8$ cm

$CD = 5.6$ cm

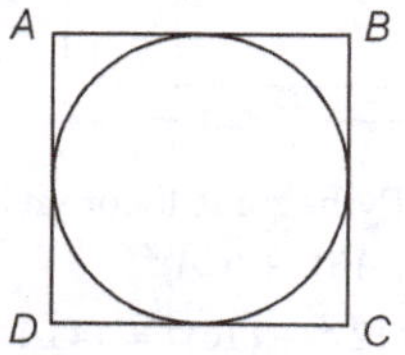

We know that, $AB + CD = AD + BC$

$\Rightarrow \quad 8.4 + 5.6 = AD + 9.8$

$\Rightarrow \quad AD = 8.4 + 5.6 - 9.8 \Rightarrow AD = 4.2$ cm.

279. (c) In ΔABC,

By Pythagoras theorem

$(AB)^2 = (AC)^2 + (BC)^2$

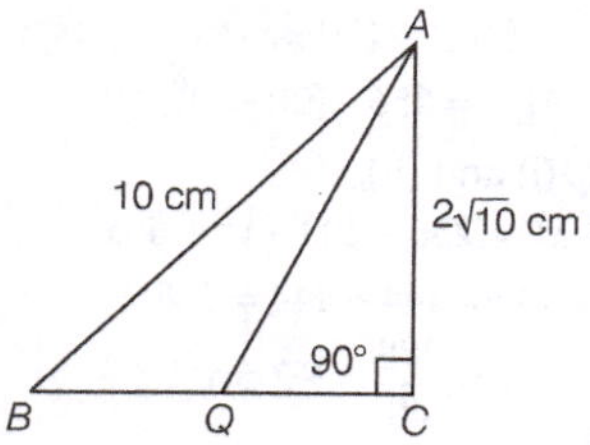

$\Rightarrow \quad (10)^2 = (2\sqrt{10})^2 + (BC)^2$

$\Rightarrow 100 - 4 \times 10 = (BC)^2$

$\Rightarrow \quad 60 = (BC)^2 \Rightarrow BC = \sqrt{60}$

$\Rightarrow \quad BC = 2\sqrt{15}$

If $BC = 2\sqrt{15}$ that means

$BQ = QC = \frac{BC}{2} \Rightarrow BQ = \sqrt{15}, QC = \sqrt{15}$

Now, $(AQ)^2 = (AC)^2 + (CQ)^2$

$(AQ)^2 = (2\sqrt{10})^2 + (\sqrt{15})^2$

$= 4 \times 10 + 15 = 40 + 15 = 55$

$\Rightarrow \quad AQ = \sqrt{55}$ cm

280. (a) Given, $\angle ADC = 78°$ and $\angle BEC = 52°$

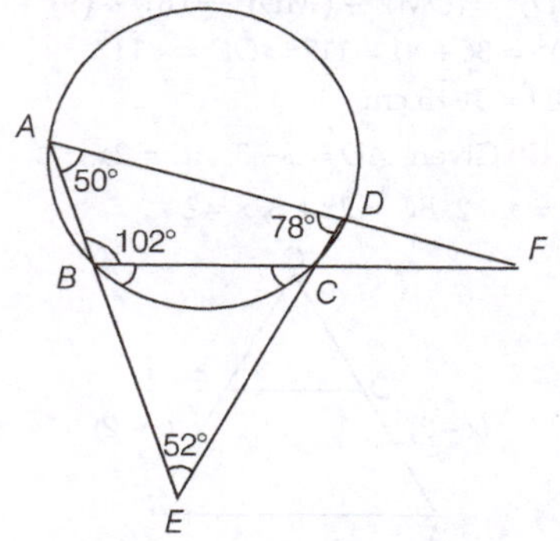

In cyclic quadrilateral $ABCD$

$\angle ABC + \angle ADC = 180°$

$\angle ABC = 180° - 78° = 102°$

In ΔADE, $\angle BAD + 78° + 52° = 180°$

$\Rightarrow \quad \angle BAD = 50°$

Again in ΔABF,

$\angle BAF + \angle AFB + \angle ABF = 180°$

$\Rightarrow \quad \angle AFB = 180° - 102° - 50°$

$\therefore \quad \angle AFB = 28°$

281. (d) Given,

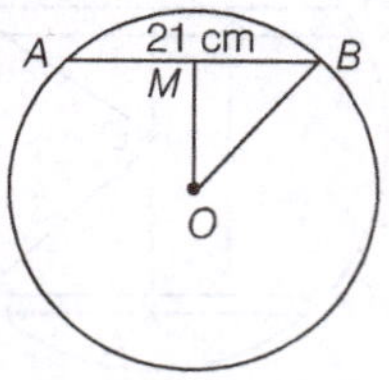

Let AB = Chord = 21 cm, $MB = \frac{21}{2}$

Diameter = 25 cm $\Rightarrow$ radius $= \frac{25}{2}$

In ΔOBM, by Pythagoras theorem,

$\Rightarrow \quad \left(\frac{25}{2}\right)^2 = (OM)^2 + \left(\frac{21}{2}\right)^2$

$\Rightarrow \quad \frac{625}{4} - \frac{441}{4} = (OM)^2 \Rightarrow \frac{184}{4} = (OM)^2$

$\Rightarrow \quad 46 = (OM)^2 \Rightarrow OM = \sqrt{46}$

282. (c) Given, $\Delta ABC \sim \Delta PQR$

ar(ΔABC) = 64 cm^2, ar(ΔPQR) = 81 cm^2

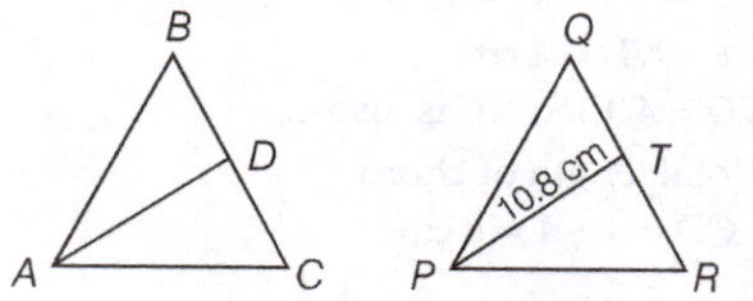

$\Rightarrow \quad \frac{ar(\Delta ABC)}{ar(\Delta PQR)} = \left(\frac{AD}{PT}\right)^2 \Rightarrow \sqrt{\frac{64}{81}} = \frac{AD}{PT}$

$\Rightarrow \quad \frac{8}{9} = \frac{AD}{10.8} \Rightarrow AD = \frac{10.8 \times 8}{9}$

$\therefore \quad AD = 9.6$ cm

283. (c) Given, $\frac{ar(\Delta ABC)}{ar(\Delta PQR)} = \frac{144}{49}$,

$AB = 12$ cm, $BC = 7$ cm, $AC = 9$ cm

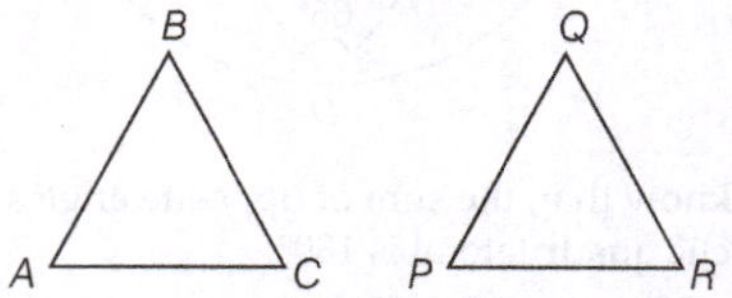

We know that, if two triangle are similar then,

$\frac{ar(\Delta ABC)}{ar(\Delta PQR)} = \left(\frac{\text{side of } ABC}{\text{side of } PQR}\right)^2$

$\{\because \Delta ABC \sim \Delta PQR\}$

$\Rightarrow \quad \frac{ar(\Delta ABC)}{ar(\Delta PQR)} = \left(\frac{AC}{PR}\right)^2 \Rightarrow \sqrt{\frac{144}{49}} = \left(\frac{AC}{PR}\right)$

$\Rightarrow \quad \frac{12}{7} = \frac{9}{PR} \Rightarrow PR = \frac{63}{12} \Rightarrow PR = \frac{21}{4}$ cm

284. (b) From the figure,

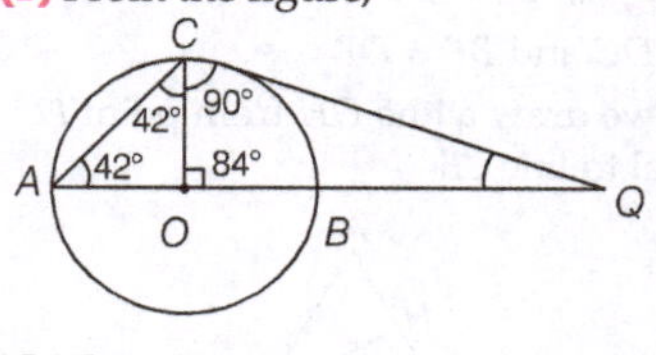

$\angle CAQ = 42°$

$\angle OCQ = 90°$ {$\because$ Angle between tangent and radius is 90°}

$\angle ACO = \angle CAQ = 42°$ {$\because OA = OC$ = Radius}

$\angle ACQ = 42° + 90° = 132°$

In ΔCAQ, $\angle CAQ + \angle ACQ + \angle CQA = 180°$

$\Rightarrow \quad 42° + 132° + \angle CQA = 180°$

$\Rightarrow \angle CQA = 180° - 42° - 132°$

$= 180° - 174° = 6°$

$\Rightarrow \quad \angle CQA = 6°$

285. (b) We know that,

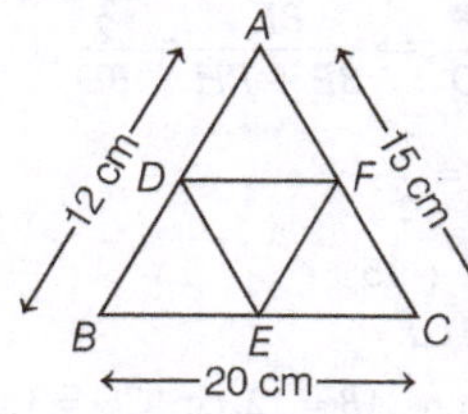

If D, E, F are mid-point of AB, BC, CA, then

$DE + EF + FD = \frac{1}{2}(AB + BC + CA)$

$\Rightarrow DE + EF + FD = \frac{1}{2}(12 + 20 + 15) = \frac{47}{2}$

So, $\frac{1}{2}(DE + EF + FD) = \frac{47}{2} \times \frac{1}{2}$

$= \frac{47}{4} = 11.75$ cm

286. (a)

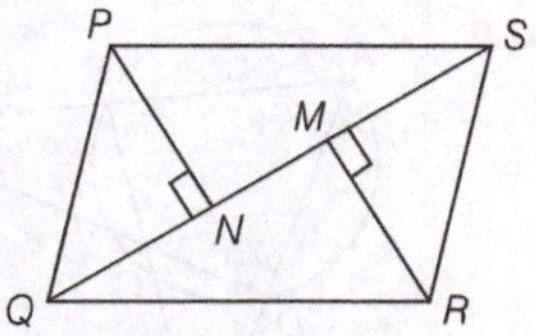

Area of □PQRS = Area of ΔPQS + Area of ΔRQS

$= \frac{1}{2} \times QS \times PN + \frac{1}{2} \times QS \times RM$

$= \frac{1}{2} \times QS[PN + RM] = \frac{1}{2} \times 6 \times [2 + 3]$

$= 3 \times 5 = 15\ cm^2$

287. (c) Given, $BC = 6$ cm

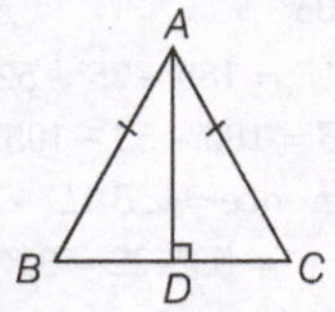

Then, BD $= \frac{BC}{2} = \frac{6}{2} = 3$ cm and $AD = 4$ cm

In right angle ΔADB,

Apply Pythagoras theorem,

$\Rightarrow \quad (AB)^2 = (4)^2 + (3)^2 = 16 + 9$

$\Rightarrow \quad (AB)^2 = 25 \therefore AB = \sqrt{25} = 5$ cm

288. (c) Given, $\angle A = 100°$ we know that, sum of the opposite angle of a cyclic quadrilateral is 180°.

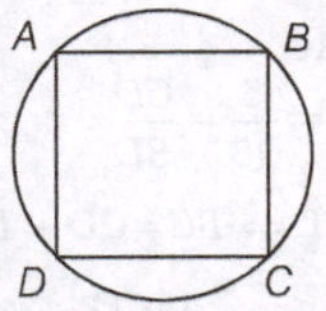

Now, $\angle A + \angle C = 180° \Rightarrow 100° + \angle C = 180°$

$\therefore \quad \angle C = 180° - 100° = 80°$

289. (d) Given $\angle ABC = 62°$, $\angle ACD = 110°$

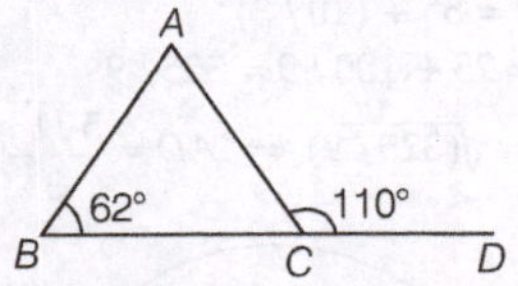

We know that, $\angle ACD = \angle CAB + \angle CBA$

[exterior angle property]

$\Rightarrow \quad 110° = \angle BAC + 62°$

$\therefore \quad \angle BAC = 110° - 62° = 48°$

290. (b) From given figure,

$MP = 15$ cm, $NQ = 8$ cm,

$PA = 17$ cm, $BQ = 10$ cm

In right angle ΔPMA,

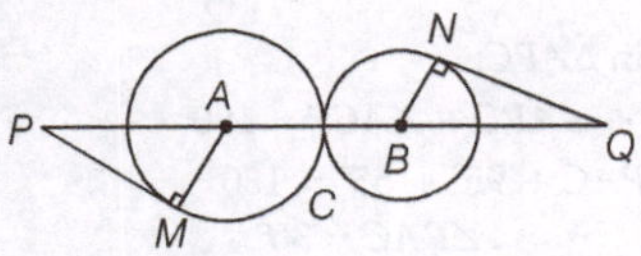

By Pythagoras theorem,

$\Rightarrow \quad 17^2 = 15^2 + AM^2$

$\Rightarrow \quad AM^2 = 289 - 225 = 64$

$\Rightarrow \quad AM = \sqrt{64} = 8$

Now, In right angle ΔBNQ,

$\Rightarrow 10^2 = BN^2 + 8^2$

$\Rightarrow \quad BN^2 = 100 - 64 = 36$

$\Rightarrow \quad BN = \sqrt{36} = 6$

We know, $AM = AC = 8$ and

$BN = BC = 6$ cm

$\therefore \quad AB = AC + BC$

$\Rightarrow \quad AB = 8 + 6 = 14$ cm

291. (d)

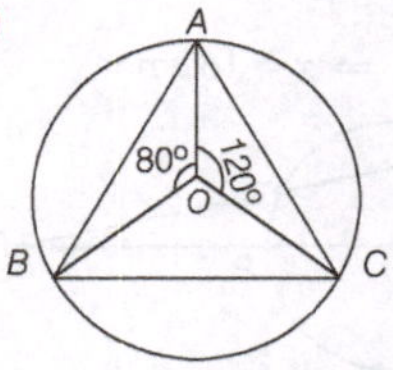

$\angle BOC + \angle AOB + \angle AOC = 360°$

$\Rightarrow \quad \angle BOC = 360° - 80° - 120°$

$\Rightarrow \quad \angle BOC = 160°$

Now, $\angle BAC = \frac{\angle BOC}{2} = \frac{160°}{2} = 80°$

292. (c) We know that,

Sum of all three angles of triangle = 180°

Ratio of all three angles of triangle is 3 : 5 : 4.

So, $3x + 5x + 4x = 180° \Rightarrow 12x = 180°$

$\Rightarrow \quad x = 15°$

Difference between biggest and smallest angle

$= 5x - 3x = 5 \times 15 - 3 \times 15$

$= 75 - 45 = 30°$

293. (a) $OO' = BC = 8 + 6 = 14$ cm

$OC = O'B = 6$ cm

and $AC = OA - OC = 8 - 6 = 2$

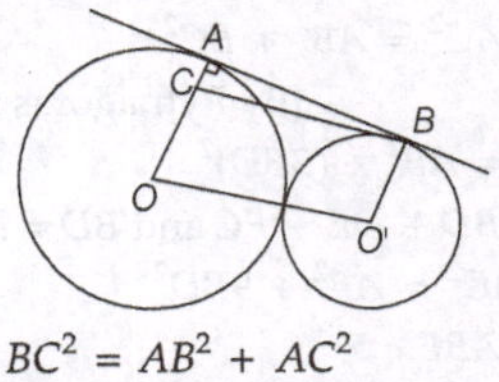

In ΔABC, $BC^2 = AB^2 + AC^2$

$\Rightarrow \quad 14^2 = AB^2 + 2^2$

$\Rightarrow \quad AB^2 = 196 - 4$

$\Rightarrow \quad AB = \sqrt{192} = 13.86$

> **Speedy Method**
>
> When two circle touch externally then
>
> Length of common tangent $= 2\sqrt{r_1 r_2}$
>
> $= 2\sqrt{8 \times 6} = 2 \times \sqrt{2 \times 4 \times 2 \times 3}$
>
> $= 8 \times \sqrt{3} = 8 \times 1.732 = 13.86$ cm

294. (a)

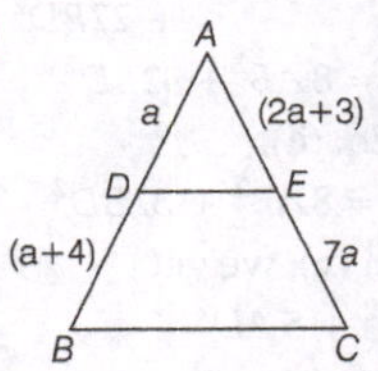

$\because \quad DE \parallel BC \therefore \Delta ADE \sim \Delta ABC$

We know that, $\frac{AD}{DB} = \frac{AE}{EC}$

$\Rightarrow \quad \frac{a}{(a+4)} = \frac{(2a+3)}{7a}$

$\Rightarrow a \times 7a = (a + 4)(2a + 3)$

$\Rightarrow \quad 7a^2 = 2a^2 + 3a + 8a + 12$

$\Rightarrow \quad 5a^2 - 11a - 12 = 0$

$\Rightarrow \quad 5a^2 - 15a + 4a - 12 = 0$

$\Rightarrow \quad 5a(a - 3) + 4(a - 3) = 0$

$\Rightarrow \quad (5a + 4)(a - 3) = 0 \Rightarrow a = -\frac{4}{5}, a = 3$

$\therefore$ Required value of a is 3.

295. (c)

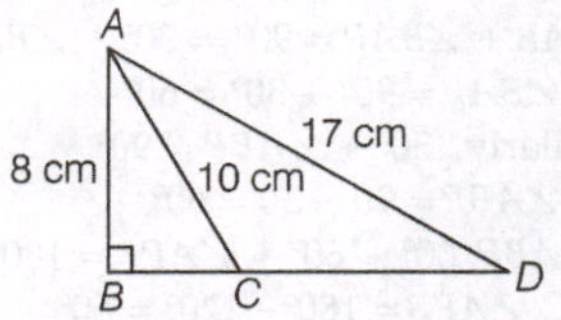

In ΔABD by Pythagoras theorem,

$(AD)^2 = (BD)^2 + (AB)^2$

$\Rightarrow \quad (17)^2 = (BD)^2 + (8)^2$

$\Rightarrow \quad 289 - 64 = (BD)^2$

$\Rightarrow \quad 225 = (BD)^2 \Rightarrow BD = 15$ cm

Now, apply Pythagoras theorem in ΔABC,

$(AC)^2 = (AB)^2 + (BC)^2$

$\Rightarrow (10)^2 = (8)^2 + (BC)^2 \Rightarrow 100 - 64 = (BC)^2$

$\Rightarrow \quad (BC)^2 = 36 \Rightarrow BC = 6$ cm

We know, from figure $BD = BC + CD$

$\Rightarrow \quad 15 = 6 + CD \Rightarrow CD = 9$ cm

296. (a)

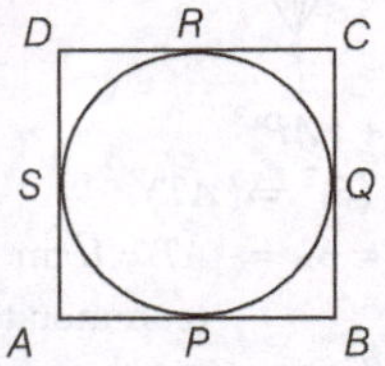

We know, $AB + CD = AD + BC$

$\Rightarrow \quad 10 + 7 = (AS + SD) + BC$

$\Rightarrow \quad 10 + 7 - 9 = BC \Rightarrow BC = 8$ cm

297. (c)

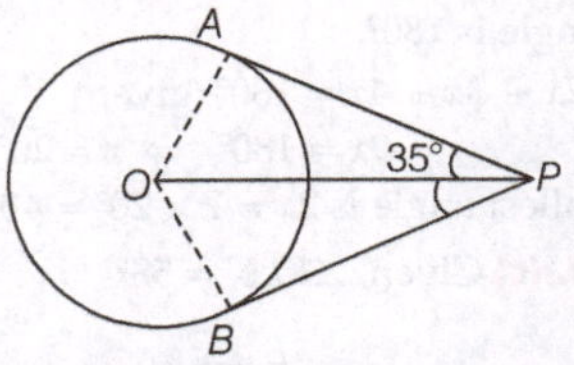

Here, AP and BP are the tangent of the circle.

Then, OP bisects the $\angle ABP$.

$\therefore \quad \angle APO = \angle BPO = 35°$

298. (c) Side of triangle, $a = 8$ cm

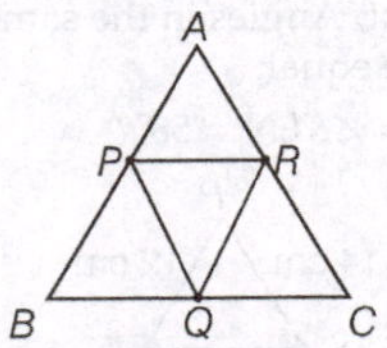

Area of equilateral triangle

$\Rightarrow \quad \frac{\sqrt{3}}{4} a^2 \Rightarrow \frac{\sqrt{3}}{4} \times (8)^2 = 16\sqrt{3}$

If P, Q, R are mid-point of side AB, BC, AC then Area of $\Delta PQR = \frac{1}{4} \times$ Area of ΔABC

$$= \frac{1}{4} \times 16\sqrt{3} = 4\sqrt{3}$$

Area of $\Delta PQR = 4\sqrt{3}$ cm^2

299. (d)

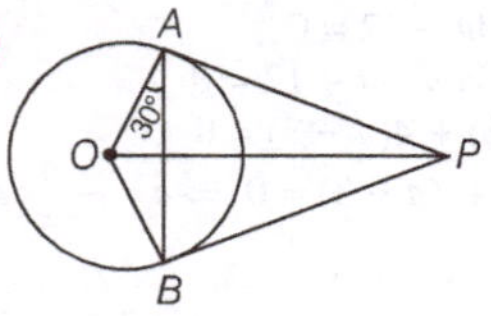

$\angle OAB + \angle BAP = 90° \Rightarrow 30° + \angle BAP = 90°$

$\Rightarrow \angle BAP = 90° - 30° = 60°$

Similarly, $30° + \angle ABP = 90°$

$\Rightarrow \angle ABP = 90 - 30 = 60°$

In ΔABP, $60° + 60° + \angle APB = 180°$

$\Rightarrow \angle APB = 180° - 120° = 60°$

300. (a) In right angle ΔPAT, $\angle A = 90°$

By Pythagoras theorem,

$(\text{Hypotenuse})^2 = (\text{Perpendicular})^2 + (\text{Base})^2$

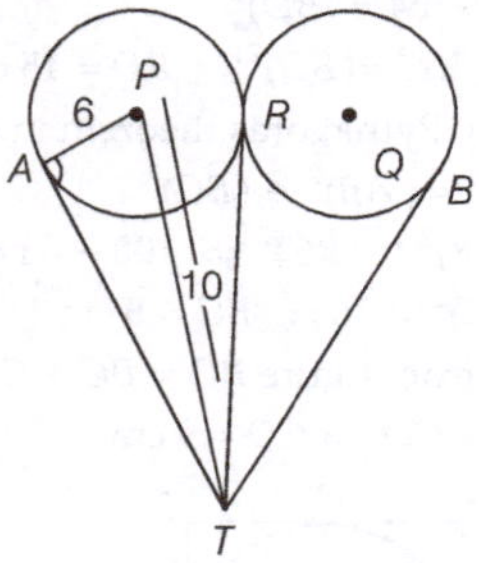

$\Rightarrow (10)^2 = (AT)^2 + (AP)^2$

$\Rightarrow 100 = (AT)^2 + (6)^2 \Rightarrow (AT)^2$

$= 100 - 36 = 64 \Rightarrow AT = 8$ cm

and $AT = TR$ (common tangent)

Similarly, $TR = TB$ is common tangent.

$\therefore AT = TR = TB = 8$ cm

Hence, the value of BT is 8 cm.

301. (c) We know that, sum of all angles in triangle is 180º.

$\therefore 2x + 3x + 4x = 180°$ (given)

$\Rightarrow 9x = 180° \Rightarrow x = 20°$

Smallest angle is $2x = 2 \times 20° = 40°$

302. (c) Given, $\angle KLN = 58º$

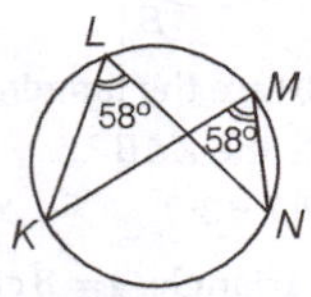

We know that, Angles in the same segment of a circle are equal.

$\therefore \angle KMN = \angle KLN = 58°$

303. (b)

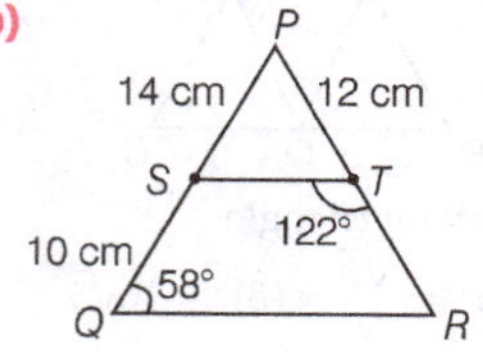

Let $RT = x$ cm and $180° = 122° + \angle STP$

$\Rightarrow \angle STP = 58°$

Now, in ΔPST and ΔPQR

$\angle P = \angle P$ [common angle]

and $\angle PQR = \angle PTS = 58º$

Then, by 'AA' property of triangle,

$\Delta PTS \sim \Delta PQR$

We know that, $\frac{PT}{PQ} = \frac{PS}{PR}$

$\Rightarrow \frac{12}{24} = \frac{14}{12 + x}$ [$\because PR = PT + TR$]

$\Rightarrow 12 + x = 28 \Rightarrow x = 16$ cm

304. (d)

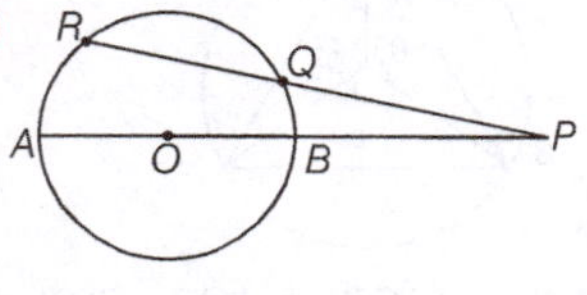

Let, radius $AO = OB = r$

$PA = (16.8 + r)$ and $PB = (16.8 - r)$

We know that, $PA \times PB = PR \times PQ$

$\Rightarrow (16.8 + r) \times (16.8 - r) = 19.2 \times 12$

$\Rightarrow (16.8)^2 - r^2 = 230.4$

$\Rightarrow 282.24 - 230.4 = r^2$

$\Rightarrow r^2 = 51.84$

$\Rightarrow r = \sqrt{51.84} = 7.2$

$\therefore$ Diameter, $D = 2 \times 7.2 = 14.4$

Hence, the length of AB is 14.4 cm.

305. (c)

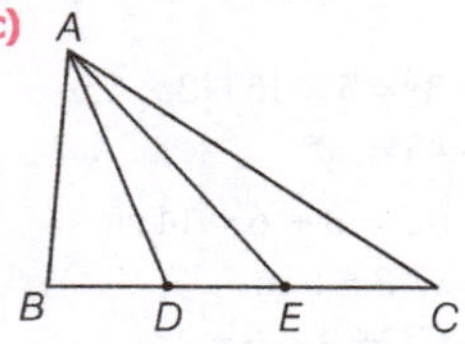

In ΔABC, $AC^2 = AB^2 + BC^2$

[By Pythagoras theorem]

$\Rightarrow AC^2 = AB^2 + (3BD)^2$

[$\because BC = BD + DE + EC$ and $BD = DE = EC$]

$\Rightarrow AC^2 = AB^2 + 9BD^2$ ... (i)

Now, in ΔABE,

$AE^2 = AB^2 + BE^2$

$\Rightarrow AE^2 = AB^2 + (2BD)^2$

$\Rightarrow AE^2 = AB^2 + 4BD^2$ ... (ii)

and in ΔABD,

$AD^2 = AB^2 + BD^2$ ... (iii)

Add equations after multiplying by 3 in Eq. (i) and multiplying by 5 in Eq. (iii), we get

$3AC^2 + 5AD^2 = 3AB^2 + 5AB^2 + 27BD^2 + 5BD^2$

$\Rightarrow 3AC^2 + 5AD^2 = 8AB^2 + 32BD^2$ ...(iv)

Multiply by 8 in Eq. (ii),

$8AE^2 = 8AB^2 + 32BD^2$ ... (v)

From Eqs. (iv) and (v), we get

$8AE^2 = 3AC^2 + 5AD^2$

306. (a)

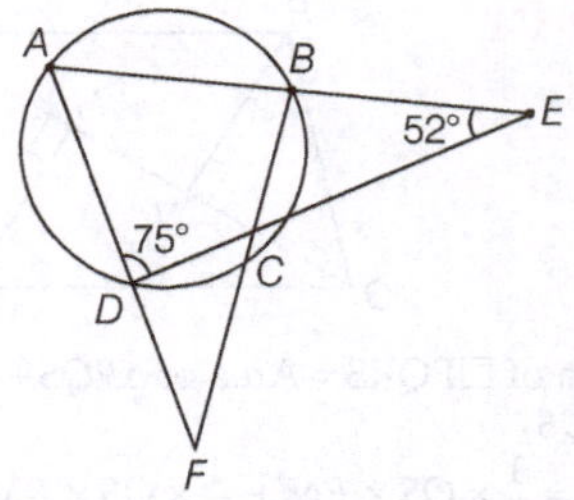

We know, in cyclic quadrilateral

Sum of opposite angle = 180°

$\angle ADC + \angle ABC = 180°$

$\angle ABC = 180º - 75°$

$\angle ABC = 105°$

In ΔADE, $\angle DAE = 180° - 75° - 52° = 53°$

In ΔABF, $\angle AFB = 180° - 53° - 105° = 22°$

Required difference $= \angle BAD - \angle AFB$

$= 53° - 22 = 31°$

307. (a) $AB^2 = 5^2 + 12^2$

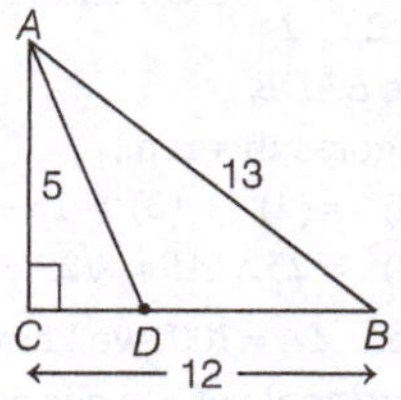

$AB^2 = 169 \Rightarrow AB = 13$

AD bisect $\angle BAC$,

$\frac{AC}{AB} = \frac{CD}{BD} \Rightarrow \frac{5}{13} = \frac{CD}{BD}$

$BD = \frac{13}{5} CD \Rightarrow BC = CD + DB$

$= CD + \frac{13}{5} CD = \frac{18CD}{5} \Rightarrow \frac{18}{5} CD = 12$

$\Rightarrow CD = 10/3$

In ΔACD, $AD^2 = AC^2 + CD^2$

$\Rightarrow AD^2 = 5^2 + (10/3)^2$

$= 25 + 100/9 = 325/9$

$\Rightarrow AD = \sqrt{(325/9)} \Rightarrow AD = \frac{5\sqrt{13}}{3}$ cm

308. (d)

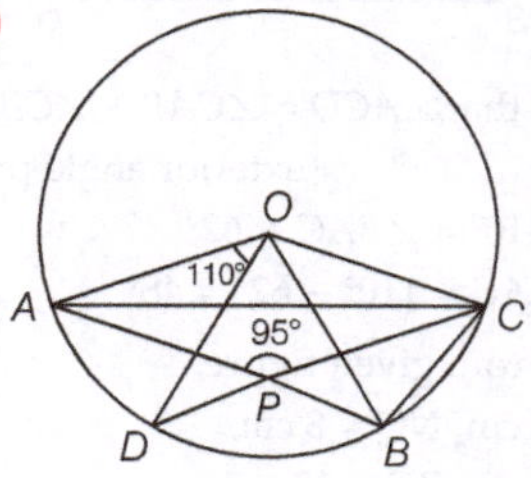

$\angle AOD = 110° \therefore \angle ACD = \frac{110°}{2} = 55°$

Now, in ΔAPC,

$\angle PAC + \angle APC + \angle ACP = 180°$

$\angle PAC + 95° + 55° = 180°$

$\Rightarrow \angle PAC = 30°$

Now, $\angle BOC = 2 \times \angle PAC = 2 \times 30° = 60°$

$\therefore \angle BOC = 60°$

309. (a)

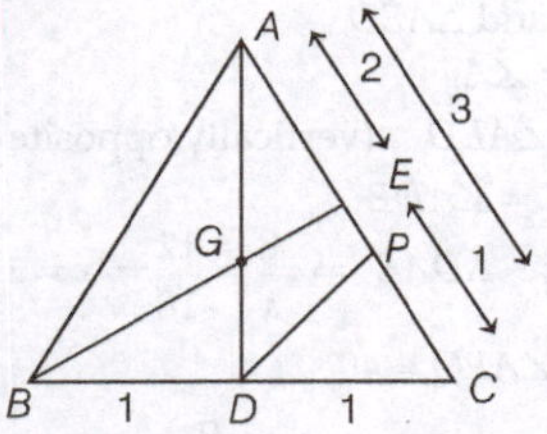

Draw line DP which is parallel to BE.

$\angle CEB = \angle CPD$ (corresponding angle between two parallel lines)

$\angle CBE = \angle CDP, \Delta BCE \sim \Delta DCP$ (rule of similarity)

$\Rightarrow BC / DC = CE / CP$

$\Rightarrow (BD + DC) / DC = (CP + PE) / CP$

$\Rightarrow BD / DC + 1 = 1 + PE / CP$

$\Rightarrow PE / CP = 1/1$ ... (i)

ΔADP and ΔAGE (rule of similarity)

$\angle ADP = \angle AGE,$

$\angle APD = \angle AEG$

$$\frac{AD}{AG} = \frac{AP}{AE} \Rightarrow \frac{(AG + GD)}{AG} = \frac{(AE + EP)}{AE}$$

$$\Rightarrow \left(\frac{AG}{AG} + \frac{GD}{AG}\right) = \left(\frac{AE}{AE} + \frac{PE}{AE}\right)$$

$$\Rightarrow 1 + \frac{GD}{AG} = 1 + \frac{PE}{AE}$$

$$\Rightarrow \frac{AG}{GD} = \frac{AE}{PE} \quad \text{... (ii)}$$

From Eq. (i), $\frac{PE}{CP} = \frac{1}{1} \Rightarrow PE = CP = CE / 2$

$$\frac{PE}{CE} = \frac{1}{2}$$

$$\Rightarrow PE = \frac{CE}{2} \quad \text{...(iii)}$$

Put Eq. (iii) in Eq. (ii), we get

$$\frac{AG}{GD} = \frac{AE}{(CE/2)} \Rightarrow \frac{AG}{GD} = 2\left(\frac{AE}{CE}\right)$$

We know that, the value of

$$\frac{AG}{GD} = 2 \times \left(\frac{2}{1}\right) = \frac{4}{1} = 4:1$$

310. (b) Given,

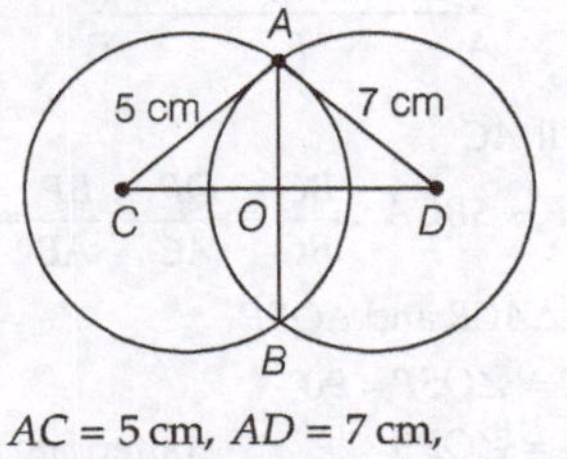

$AC = 5$ cm, $AD = 7$ cm,

$CD = 10$ cm

$\because \ CD \perp AB$ and $AO = OB = \frac{1}{2} AB$

Let $CO = x$ cm,

Then, $OD = (10 - x)$ cm

In ΔAOC, $AC^2 = AO^2 + CO^2$

$\Rightarrow AO^2 = 5^2 - x^2$ ... (i)

In ΔAOD, $AD^2 = AO^2 + DO^2$

$\Rightarrow AO^2 = 7^2 - (10 - x)^2$ ... (ii)

From Eqs. (i) and (ii),

$$5^2 - x^2 = 7^2 - (10 - x)^2$$

$$\Rightarrow 25 - x^2 = 49 - 100 + 20x - x^2$$

$$\Rightarrow 20x = 76 \Rightarrow x = \frac{19}{5} \text{ cm}$$

Substitute value of x in Eq. (i), we get

$$AO^2 = 5^2 - \left(\frac{19}{5}\right)^2 = 25 - \frac{361}{25} = \frac{264}{25}$$

$$\Rightarrow AO = \frac{\sqrt{264}}{5} \text{ cm}$$

As, $AO = \frac{1}{2} AB$

$$\therefore \quad AB = 2AO = \frac{2\sqrt{264}}{5} = \frac{4\sqrt{66}}{5} \text{ cm}$$

Speedy Method

In ΔACD, $AC = 5$ cm, $AD = 7$ cm, $CD = 10$ cm

Area of $ADC = \sqrt{s(s-a)(s-b)(s-c)}$

$$s = \frac{a+b+c}{2} = \frac{5+7+10}{2} = 11\text{cm}$$

Area $\Delta ADC = \sqrt{11 \times 6 \times 1 \times 4} = 2\sqrt{66}$ cm^2 [From Eq. (i)]

Again, Area of $ACD = \frac{1}{2} CD \times AO$

$$2\sqrt{66} = \frac{1}{2} \times 10 \times AO \Rightarrow AO = \frac{2\sqrt{66}}{5}$$

Now, $AB = 2 \times AO = 2 \times \frac{2\sqrt{66}}{5} = \frac{4\sqrt{66}}{5}$ cm

311. (c) Given,

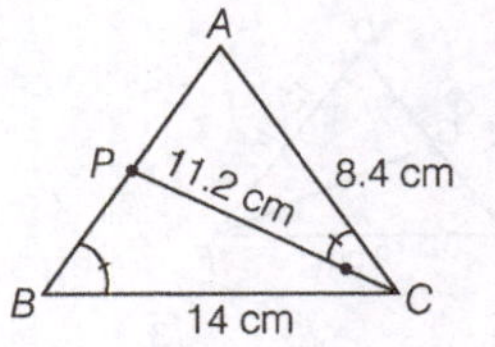

$\angle B = \angle ACP$ (given)

and $\angle A = \angle A$ (common angle)

By 'AA' property of triangle $\Delta ABC \sim \Delta ACP$

We know that, $\frac{AC}{AP} = \frac{BC}{CP} \Rightarrow \frac{8.4}{AP} = \frac{14}{11.2}$

$\Rightarrow AP = 6.72$ cm

Again, $\frac{AB}{AC} = \frac{BC}{CP} \Rightarrow \frac{AB}{8.4} = \frac{14}{11.2}$

$\Rightarrow AB = 10.5$

$\therefore \ BP = AB - AP = 10.5 - 6.72 = 3.78$ cm

312. (c) Given, that $\angle B = 72°$ and $\angle C = 44°$ in ΔABC. It is also given that bisectors of $\angle B$ and $\angle ACD$ meet at E, side BC is produced to D.

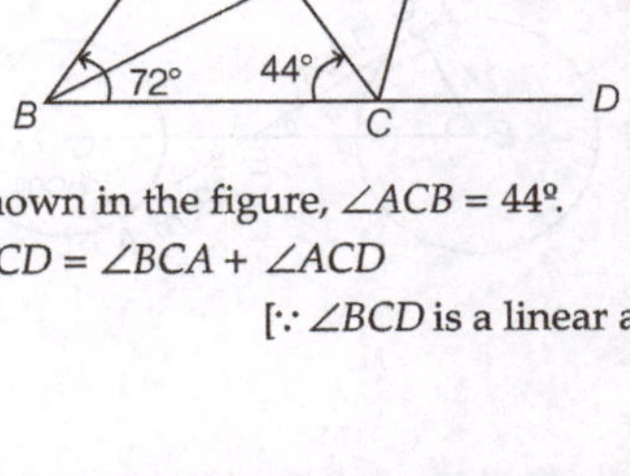

As shown in the figure, $\angle ACB = 44°$.

$\angle BCD = \angle BCA + \angle ACD$

[$\because \angle BCD$ is a linear angle]

$\therefore \ \angle ACD = 180° - 44° = 136°$

As, $\angle ACD$ is bisectored, so

$$\frac{\angle ACD}{2} = \angle ACE = \angle ECD$$

$$\therefore \ \frac{136°}{2} = 68° = \angle ACE = \angle ECD$$

$\therefore \ \angle BCE = \angle BCA + \angle ACE$

$= 44° + 68° = 112°$

As, in ΔABC, $\angle B$ is bisectored,

So, $\frac{\angle ABC}{2} = \angle EBC = \frac{72°}{2} = 36°$

$\therefore \angle BEC = 180° - (\angle BCE + \angle EBC)$

$= 180° - (112° + 36°) = 32°$

Speedy Method

In ΔABC, $\angle A + \angle B + \angle C = 180°$

$\Rightarrow \angle A = 180° - 72° - 44°$

$\Rightarrow \angle A = 64°$

As we know, $\angle BEC = \frac{\angle A}{2} = \frac{64}{2} = 32°$

313. (d) We know that in a triangle, the measure of any one side is always greater than the sum of other two sides and always greater than difference of these two sides.

Given sides = 3.8 cm and 6 cm

Now, let third side = x cm

$(6 - 3.8) < x < (6 + 3.8)$

$2.2 < x < 9.8$

Hence, it cannot be equal to 2.2 cm.

314. (d) Given,

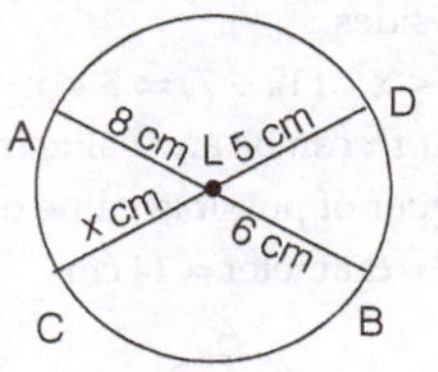

Let $CL = x$ cm

Now, we know that when two chords intersect internally,

$AL \times LB = CL \times LD \Rightarrow 8 \times 6 = x \times 5$

$$\Rightarrow x = \frac{8 \times 6}{5} \Rightarrow x = \frac{48}{5}$$

$\therefore \ CL(x) = 9.6$ cm

315. (a)

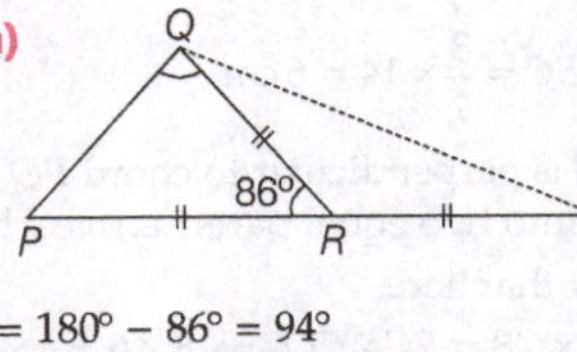

$\angle QRS = 180° - 86° = 94°$

Now, in triangle QRS, $QR = RS$

$\therefore \ \angle RQS = \angle RSQ = x°$ (let)

$\therefore \ 94° + x° + x° = 180°$

$\Rightarrow 2x° = 86° \Rightarrow x = 43°$

$\therefore \ \angle PSQ = 43°$

316. (d) Out of 2 cm, 5 cm, 7 cm and 8 cm, only two triangle can be made by (5 cm, 7 cm, 8 cm) and (2 cm, 7 cm, 8 cm).

317. (a)

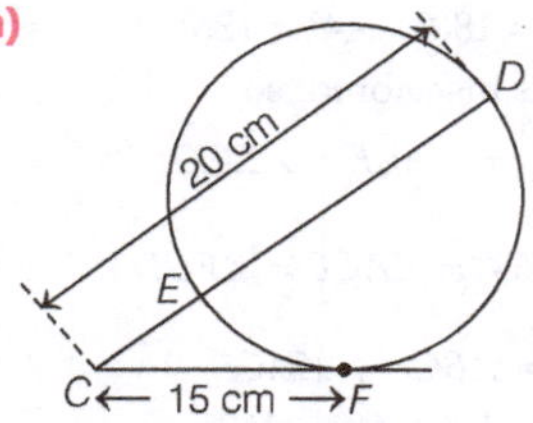

Using the tangent-secant theorem,

$CF^2 = CE \times CD \Rightarrow 15 \times 15 = CE \times 20$

$\Rightarrow \quad CE = \frac{225}{20} \Rightarrow CE = 11.25$ cm

$\therefore$ Length of chord $DE = CD - CE$

$= 20 - 11.25 = 8.75$ cm

318. (d) Length of transverse common tangent $= \sqrt{d^2 - (R_1 + R_2)^2}$

$= \sqrt{(13)^2 - (3+2)^2} = \sqrt{169 - 25}$

$= \sqrt{144} = 12$ cm

319. (c) Let PQR be a triangle.

$\angle R > \angle P + \angle Q$

Adding $\angle R$ to both sides,

$2\angle R > \angle P + \angle Q + \angle R$

$2\angle R > 180° \Rightarrow \angle R > 90°$

$\therefore$ ΔPQR is an obtuse angled triangle.

320. (b) The sum of any two sides of a triangle is always greater than its third side.

321. (a) We know that, the third side of any triangle is always greater than the difference of the other two sides and less than the sum of the other sides.

So, $(12 - 7) < x < (12 + 7) \Rightarrow 5 < x < 19$

$\therefore$ The value of x can be any value from 6 to 18.

Hence, number of possible value of $x = 13$.

322. (d) AB = diameter = 14 cm

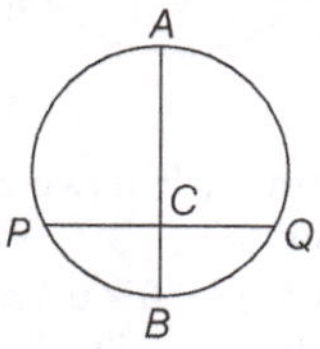

$AC : BC :: 4 : 3$

$\Rightarrow \quad AC = \frac{4}{7} \times 14 = 8$ cm

and $\quad BC = \frac{3}{7} \times 14 = 6$ cm

Now, AB is perpendicular to chord PQ and divide it into two equal parts i.e., a each

We know that here,

$AC \times CB = PC \times CQ \Rightarrow 8 \times 6 = a \times a$

$\Rightarrow \quad 48 = a^2 \Rightarrow a = 4\sqrt{3}$ cm

$\therefore \quad PQ = 2 \times 4\sqrt{3} = 8\sqrt{3}$ cm

323. (c) We know, the length of any one side is greater than the difference of other two sides and less than the sum of other two sides.

If three sides of the triangle are 12,22 and m units, $(22 - 12) < m < (12 + 22) \Rightarrow 10 < m < 34$

324. (a) For a triangle ABC,

$A : B : C = 1 : 2 : 3$

Now, $\angle A + \angle B + \angle C = 180°$

$\Rightarrow \quad x + 2x + 3x = 180°$

$\Rightarrow \quad x = 30°$

$\therefore$ $\angle A = 30°, \angle B = 60°, \angle C = 90°$

Using sine rule,

$\frac{a}{\sin A} = \frac{b}{\sin B} = \frac{c}{\sin C}$

$\Rightarrow \frac{a}{c} = \frac{\sin A}{\sin C} = \frac{1}{2}$ and $\frac{a}{b} = \frac{\sin A}{\sin B} = \frac{1}{\sqrt{3}}$

$\therefore$ Ratio of corresponding sides $= 1 : \sqrt{3} : 2$

325. (b) The sum of all the angles of a triangle is 180°.

Hence, all the angles cannot be less than 60°.

A triangle can have one obtuse angle i.e., more than 90°. A triangle cannot have two right angles, because then the third angle will be zero which is not possible.

A triangle can have two acute angles.

326. (a) If ΔXYZ and ΔLMN are similar, then,

$\frac{\text{Area}(\Delta XYZ)}{\text{Area}(\Delta LMN)} = \left(\frac{XY}{LM}\right)^2 = \left(\frac{YZ}{MN}\right)^2 = \left(\frac{XZ}{LN}\right)^2$

$\Rightarrow \quad \frac{16}{25} = \left(\frac{YZ}{MN}\right)^2 \Rightarrow \frac{16}{25} = \left(\frac{2.4}{MN}\right)^2$

$\Rightarrow \quad \frac{4}{5} = \frac{2.4}{MN} \Rightarrow MN = 3$ cm

327. (b)

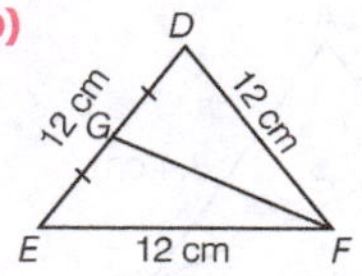

$FG = \text{Median} = \frac{\sqrt{3}}{2}a = \frac{\sqrt{3}}{2} \times 12 = 6\sqrt{3}$

328. (b) Length of $DCT = \sqrt{d^2 - (r_1 - r_2)^2}$

$= \sqrt{(35 + 25)^2 - (35 - 25)^2}$

$= \sqrt{(60)^2 - (10)^2}$

$= \sqrt{3600 - 100}$

$= \sqrt{3500} = 59.16$ cm

329. (d)

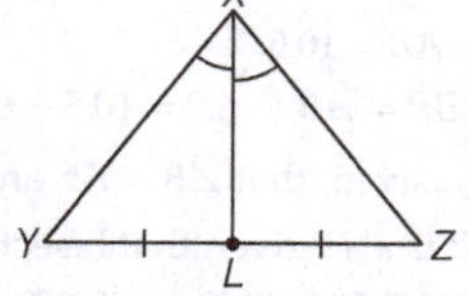

We know that, median divides a triangle into two equal parts.

$\therefore$ Area of $XYZ = (2 \times 13)$ cm^2 = 26 cm^2

330. (a)

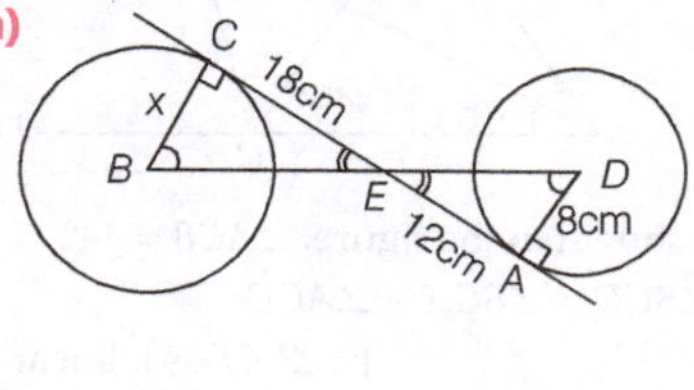

In ΔBCE and ΔAED,

$\angle C = \angle A$ (90°)

$\angle BEC = \angle AED$ (vertically opposite angles)

$\therefore$ $\angle CBE = \angle ADE$

So, $\Delta BCE \sim \Delta DAE \Rightarrow \frac{8}{x} = \frac{12}{18} \Rightarrow x = 12$ cm

331. (d) $\angle APQ = 40°$

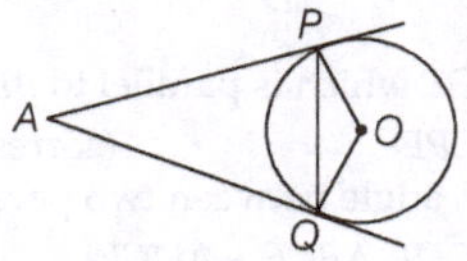

$\therefore \quad \angle AQP = 40° \quad (\because AP = AQ)$

$\therefore \quad \angle PAQ = 180° - 80° = 100°$

Now, $\angle APO = 90°$ and $\angle APQ = 40°$

[angle made by radius, to the tangent = 90°]

$\therefore$ $\angle QPO = 50°$

Similarly, $\angle PQO = 50°$

$\therefore$ In ΔPOQ, $\angle QPO + \angle PQO + \angle POQ = 180°$

$50° + 50° + \angle POQ = 180° \Rightarrow \angle POQ = 80°$

332. (a)

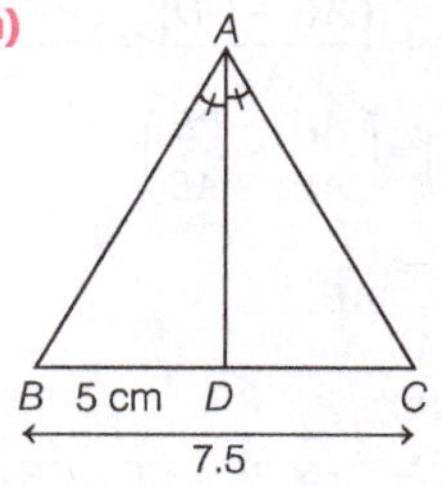

$\therefore \quad DC = (7.5 - 5)$ cm = 2.5 cm

Now, according to angle bisector theorem,

$\Rightarrow \quad \frac{BD}{DC} = \frac{AB}{AC} \Rightarrow \frac{AB}{AC} = \frac{5}{2.5} = \frac{2}{1} = 2 : 1$

333. (c) Given, $\frac{PB}{AP} = \frac{3}{4}$

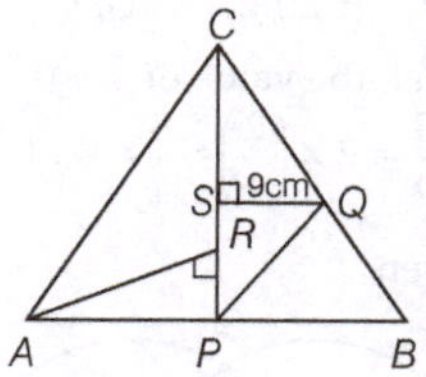

And $PQ \parallel AC$

So, $\Delta BQP \sim \Delta BCA \therefore \frac{BQ}{BC} = \frac{QP}{AC} = \frac{BP}{AB} = \frac{3}{7}$

Now, in ΔACR and ΔQSP

$\angle ARC = \angle QSP = 90°$

$\angle ACR = \angle QPS$ (alternate angles)

$\therefore$ $\angle CAR = \angle SQP$

$\therefore$ $\Delta ARC \sim \Delta QSP$ (*AAA* similarity)

$\therefore \quad \frac{AR}{QS} = \frac{RC}{SP} = \frac{AC}{QP}$

$\Rightarrow \quad \frac{AR}{QS} = \frac{AC}{QP} = \frac{7}{3}$

$\therefore \quad AR = \frac{7}{3} \times QS = \frac{7}{3} \times 9 = 21$ cm

334. (a)

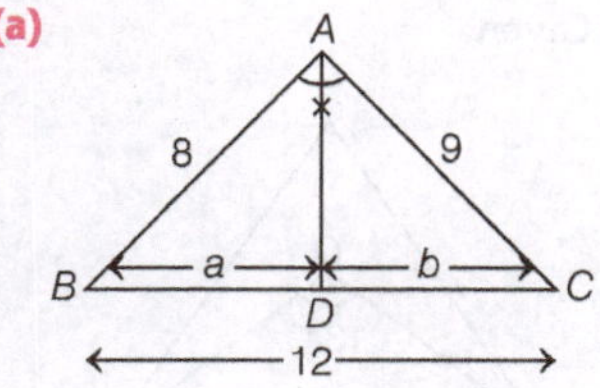

$$\frac{a}{b} = \frac{8}{9}$$

Where, $a = 8$ (shorter segment)

$b = 9$ (larger segment)

Shorter segment $= \frac{12}{17} \times 8 = \frac{96}{17} = 5\frac{11}{17}$ cm

335. (a) According to the question,

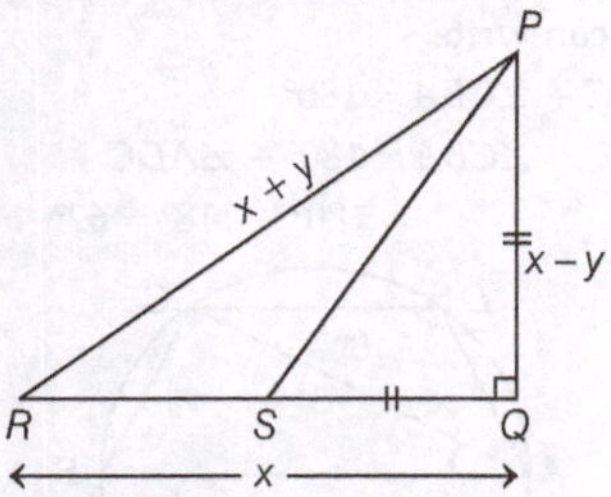

In ΔPQR, $(x+y)^2 = (x-y)^2 + x^2$

$\Rightarrow x^2 + y^2 + 2xy = x^2 + y^2 - 2xy + x^2$

$\Rightarrow x^2 = 4xy \Rightarrow x = 4y$

Now, $\frac{QS}{SR} = \frac{x-y}{x-(x-y)} = \frac{x-y}{y} = \frac{4y-y}{y} = \frac{3}{1}$

$\therefore$ $QS : SR = 3 : 1$

Speedy Method

Given, $PQ = SQ$

Let $PQ = 3$ $QR = 4$ $PR = 5$

All are triplets

Then, $QS : SR = 3 : (RQ - SQ)$

$= 3 : (4 - 3) = 3 : 1$

336. (b) If chord of a circle = Radius of circle, then ΔAOB is an equilateral triangle.

So, all angles are 60°.

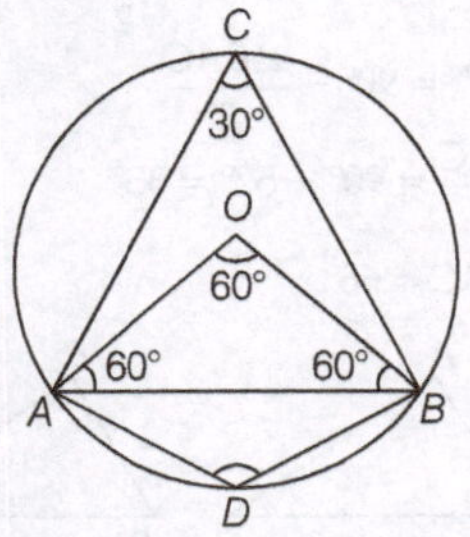

According to the theorem,

$$\angle ACB = \frac{\angle AOB}{2} = \frac{60°}{2} = 30°$$

And, in quadrilateral sum of opposite angles are 180°.

Then, $\angle ADB = 180° - 30° = 150°$

Required difference $= \angle ADB - \angle ACB$

$= 150° - 30° = 120°$

337. (b) Given, $AB = 24$ cm

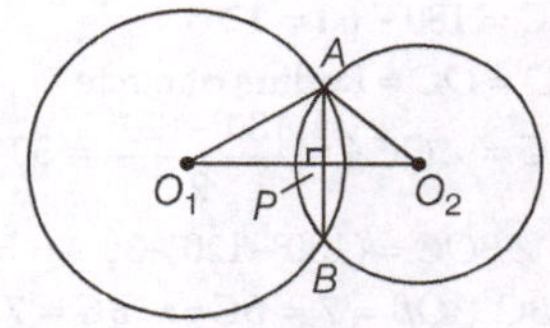

Then, $AP = \frac{AB}{2} = \frac{24}{2} = 12$ cm

And $O_1A = \frac{30}{2}$ cm $= 15$ cm

and $O_2A = \frac{26}{2}$ cm $= 13$ cm

So, in ΔAO_1P,

$(O_1P)^2 = (15)^2 - (12)^2 = 225 - 144$

$O_1P = \sqrt{81} = 9$ cm

Similarly, in ΔAO_2P,

$(O_2P)^2 = (13)^2 - (12)^2 = 169 - 144$

$O_2P = \sqrt{25} = 5$ cm

Then, distance between two centres

$= O_1P + PO_2 = 9 + 5 = 14$ cm

338. (b) Given,

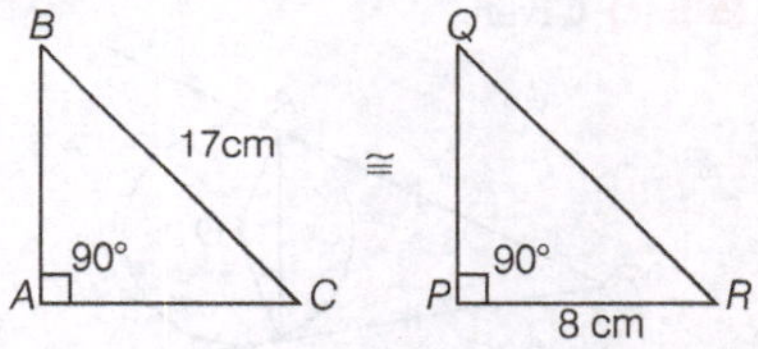

As both are congruent triangles

$\therefore AC = PR$, $AB = PQ$ and $BC = QR$

So, $AC = PR = 8$ cm

$AB = PQ = ?$ $BC = QR = 17$cm

By Pythagoras theorem,

$(BC)^2 = (AB)^2 + (AC)^2 \Rightarrow (17)^2 = AB^2 + (8)^2$

$\Rightarrow (AB)^2 = 289 - 64$

$\Rightarrow (AB)^2 = 225 \Rightarrow AB = 15$ cm

339. (d)

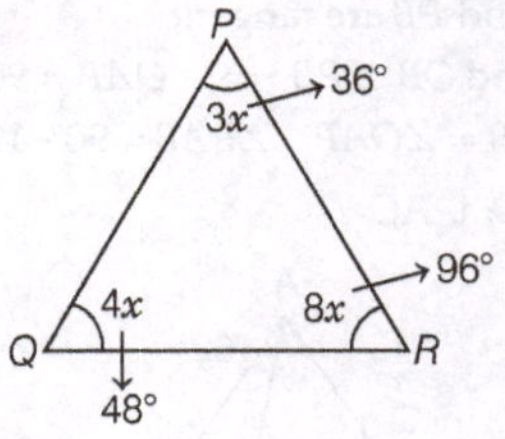

Let $\angle P = 3x$, $\angle Q = 4x$, $\angle R = 8x$

We know that, $\angle P + \angle Q + \angle R = 180°$

According to the question,

$3x + 4x + 8x = 180° \Rightarrow 15x = 180°$

$\Rightarrow x = 12°$

$\angle P = 3x = 3 \times 12 = 36°$, $\angle Q = 4 \times 12 = 48°$,

$\angle R = 8x = 8 \times 12 = 96°$

We can see that, PQ is the longest side and QR is the shortest side.

340. (c) According to the question,

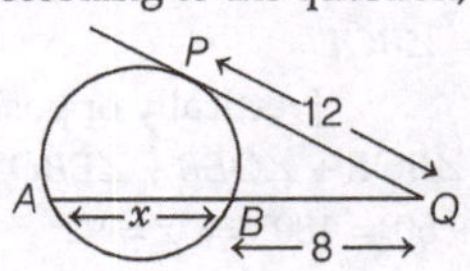

Let $AB = x$

$PQ^2 = AQ \times QB \Rightarrow (12)^2 = (8 + x)\,8$

$\Rightarrow \frac{144}{8} = 8 + x \Rightarrow x = 18 - 8$

$\therefore$ $x = 10$ cm

341. (c)

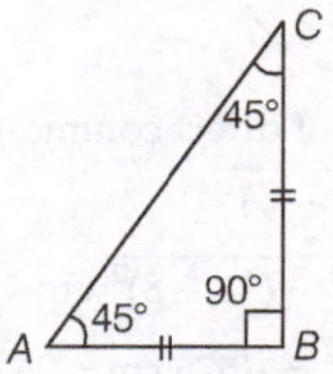

Here, $AB = BC$

$\because AB^2 + BC^2 = AC^2$

$\Rightarrow 2BC^2 = 4^2 = 16$

$\therefore BC = \sqrt{8} = 2\sqrt{2}$ cm

342. (c) According to the question,

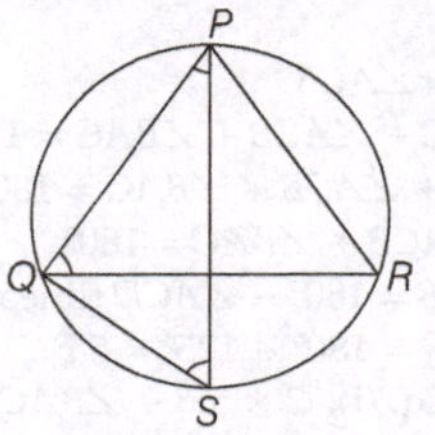

We know, In equilateral triangle all angles are 60°.

Then, $\angle PSQ = \angle PRQ = 60°$

(angle in the same segment)

So, $\frac{1}{2}\angle PSQ = \frac{60°}{2} = 30°$

343. (b)

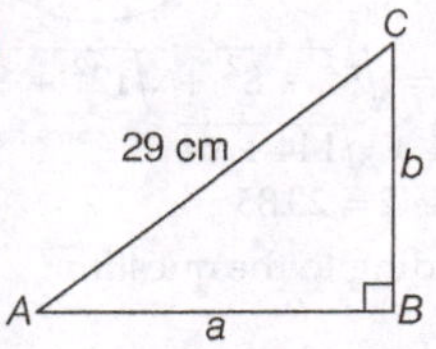

Then, according to question,

$a + b = 41$ cm ...(i)

And by Pythagoras theorem,

$a^2 + b^2 = (29)^2 = 841$ ...(ii)

Squaring on both sides Eq. (i), we get

$(a + b)^2 = (41)^2$

$\Rightarrow a^2 + b^2 + 2ab = 1681$

$\Rightarrow 841 + 2ab = 1681$ [$\because$ from Eq. (i)]

$\Rightarrow 2ab = 1681 - 841 = 840$

$\Rightarrow ab = 420$ ...(iii)

Now, $(a - b)^2 = a^2 + b^2 - 2ab$

$= 841 - 2 \times 420 = 841 - 840$

$(a - b)^2 = 1 \Rightarrow a - b = 1$

Hence, difference between two sides

$= a - b = 1$

344. (c) Given, $AC = 18$ cm and $BD = 8$ cm (radius of circle)

$AC \perp CD$ and $BD \perp CD$ as CD is the common tangent.

Drawing $DE \parallel AB$

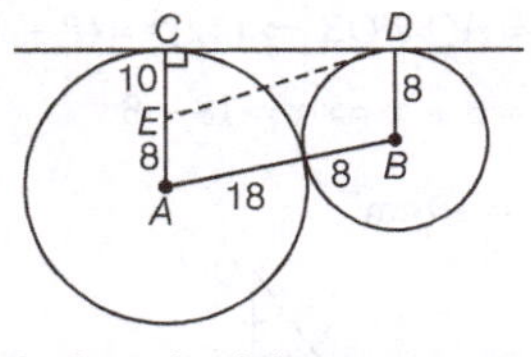

By formula, length of direct common tangent

$$= \sqrt{d^2 - (r_1 - r_2)^2}$$

So, $CD = \sqrt{(18+8)^2 - (18-8)^2}$ cm

$$= \sqrt{26^2 - 10^2} = \sqrt{576} \text{ cm} = 24 \text{ cm}$$

345. (d) Given, in ΔABC, $AB = AC$

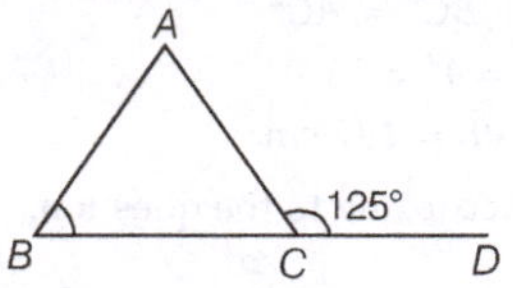

So, $\angle ABC = \angle ACB$

Also, $\angle ABC + \angle ACB + \angle BAC = 180°$

$\Rightarrow \angle ACB + \angle ACB + \angle BAC = 180°$

$\Rightarrow 2\angle ACB + \angle BAC = 180°$ ...(i)

Here, $\angle ACB = 180° - \angle ACD$ (linear angle)

$= 180° - 125° = 55°$

Putting in Eq. (i), $2 \times 55° + \angle BAC = 180°$

$\angle BAC = 180° - 110° = 70°$

346. (b) $\therefore$ Required distance

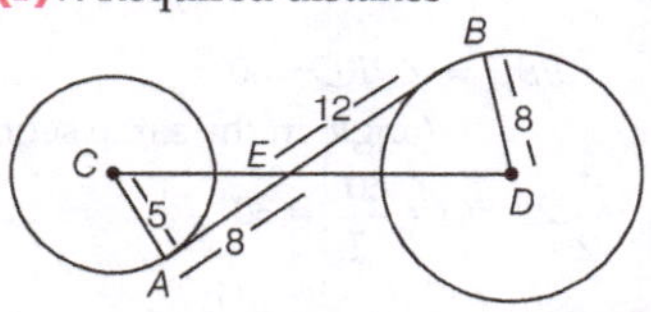

$CD = CE + ED = \sqrt{5^2 + 8^2} + \sqrt{12^2 + 8^2}$

$= \sqrt{25+64} + \sqrt{144+64}$

$= 9.43 + 14.42 = 23.85$

347. (b) According to the question,

We know,

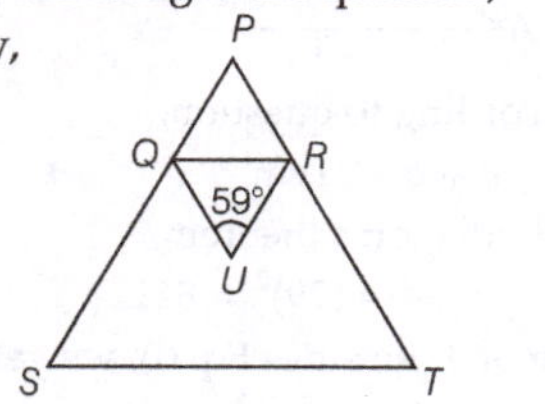

$\angle QUR = 90° - \frac{\angle P}{2} \Rightarrow 59° = 90° - \frac{\angle P}{2}$

$\Rightarrow \frac{\angle P}{2} = 90° - 59° = 31° \Rightarrow \angle P = 62°$

348. (c) AD is diameter and AC is chord.

$\angle DOC = 60°$

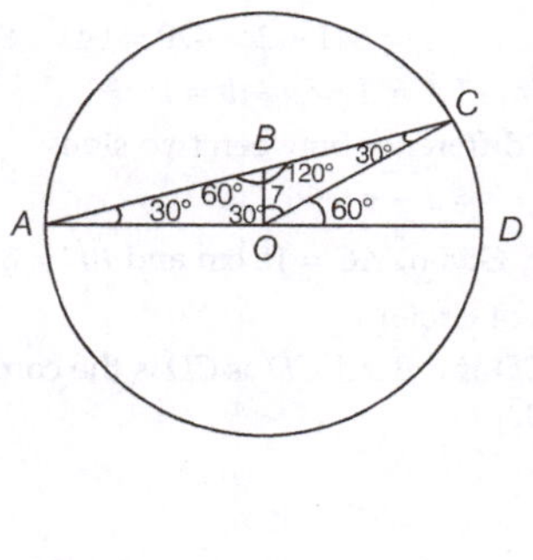

We know that, $\angle AOC + \angle DOC = 180°$

$\Rightarrow \angle AOC = 180 - 60 = 120°$

$AO = OC$ = Radius of circle

$\Rightarrow \angle OAC = \angle OCA = \frac{180° - 120°}{2} = 30°$

In ΔBOC, $\angle BOC = (180° - 120° - 30°) = 30°$

$OB = BC$, $OB = 7 = BC \Rightarrow BC = 7$ cm

349. (d) In is the incentre of ΔABC.

$\therefore$ BI and CI are the bisectors of $\angle A$ and $\angle B$.

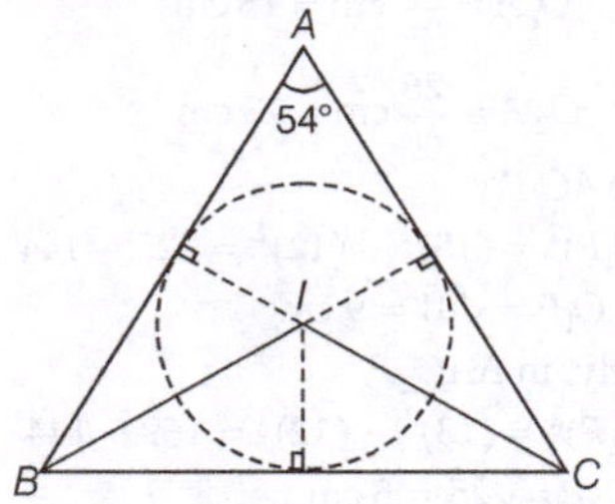

$\angle BIC = 90° + \frac{\angle A}{2} \Rightarrow \angle BIC = 90° + \frac{54}{2}$

$\Rightarrow \angle BIC = 90° + 27° = 117°$

350. (c) Given,

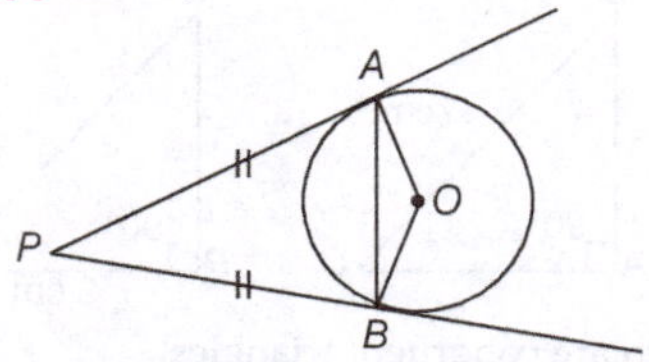

PA and PB are tangent from a point P outside the circle.

Hence, $PA = PB$

In ΔABP, $\angle APB + \angle PAB + \angle PBA = 180°$

$\Rightarrow \angle PAB + \angle PBA = 180° - 142 = 38°$

$\Rightarrow 2\angle PAB = 38°$ [as, $PA = PB$]

$\Rightarrow \angle PAB = 19°$

Since, PA and PB are tangent

$OA \perp PA$ and $OB \perp PB \Rightarrow \angle OAP = 90°$

$\Rightarrow \angle OAB = \angle OAP - \angle PAB = 90° - 19° = 71°$

351. (a) $BD \perp AC$

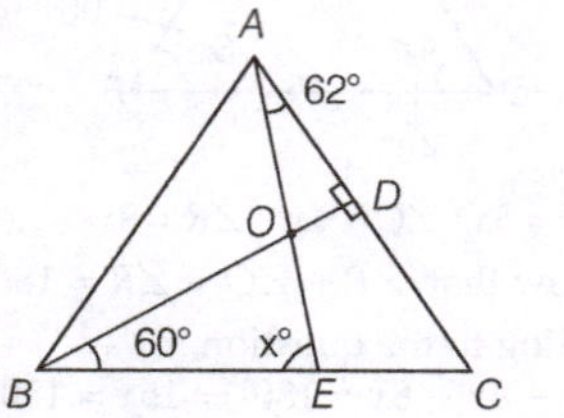

$\angle BDC = \angle BDA = 90°$

In ΔAOD, $\angle OAD + \angle ODA + \angle AOD = 180°$

$\Rightarrow 62° + 90° + \angle AOD = 180°$

[$\because \angle ODA = \angle BDA$]

$\Rightarrow \angle AOD = 28°$

$\angle AOD = \angle BOE$

[vertically opposite angles]

In ΔBOE, $\angle BOE + \angle OEB + \angle EBO = 180°$

$\Rightarrow 28° + x + 60° = 180° \Rightarrow x = 92°$

352. (d) Given,

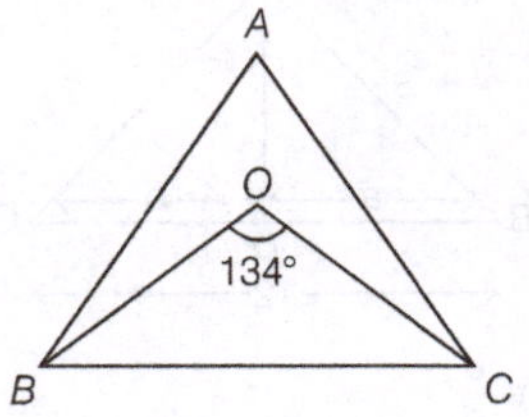

As we know, $\angle BOC = 90° + \frac{\angle A}{2}$

$134° = 90° + \frac{\angle A}{2} \Rightarrow \frac{\angle A}{2} = 44°$

$\angle A = 88°$

353. (a) According to the question,

So, we can write,

$\angle ADC + \angle CBA = 180°$

$\Rightarrow \angle CBA = 180° - \angle ADC$

$= 180° - 118° = 62°$

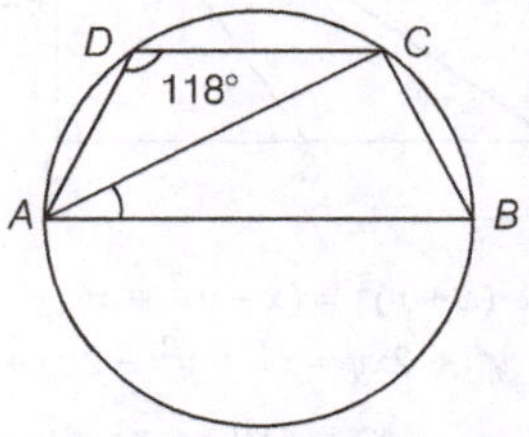

For ΔABC, $\angle CBA = 62°$, $\angle ACB = 90°$

And, $\angle ACB + \angle CBA + \angle BAC = 180°$

$\Rightarrow \angle BAC = 180° - (\angle ACB + \angle CBA)$

$= 180° - (90° + 62°)$

$= 90° - 62° = 28°$

354. (b)

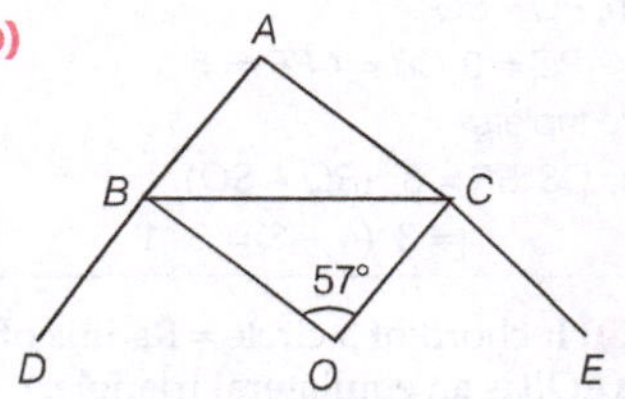

We know, $\angle BOC = 90° - \frac{\angle BAC}{2}$

$\Rightarrow 57° = 90° - \frac{\angle BAC}{2}$

$\Rightarrow \frac{\angle BAC}{2} = 90° - 57° = 33°$

$\Rightarrow \angle BAC = 66°$

355. (c)

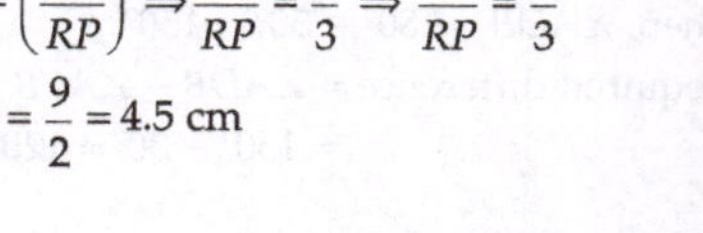

As, $\Delta ABC \sim \Delta RPQ$ we can write,

$$\frac{AB}{RP} = \frac{BC}{PQ} \quad \frac{\text{ar}\Delta ABC}{\text{ar}\Delta RPQ} = \frac{(AB)^2}{(RP)^2}$$

$\Rightarrow \frac{4}{9} = \left(\frac{AB}{RP}\right)^2 \Rightarrow \frac{AB}{RP} = \frac{2}{3} \Rightarrow \frac{3}{RP} = \frac{2}{3}$

$\Rightarrow RP = \frac{9}{2} = 4.5$ cm

356. (c)

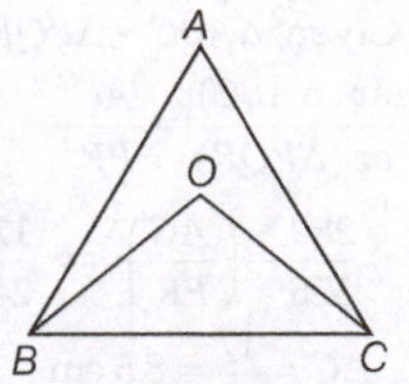

$\therefore \quad \angle BOC = 90° + \frac{\angle A}{2} \Rightarrow 142° = 90° + \frac{\angle A}{2}$

$\frac{\angle A}{2} = 52° \Rightarrow \angle A = 104°$

357. (a) As,

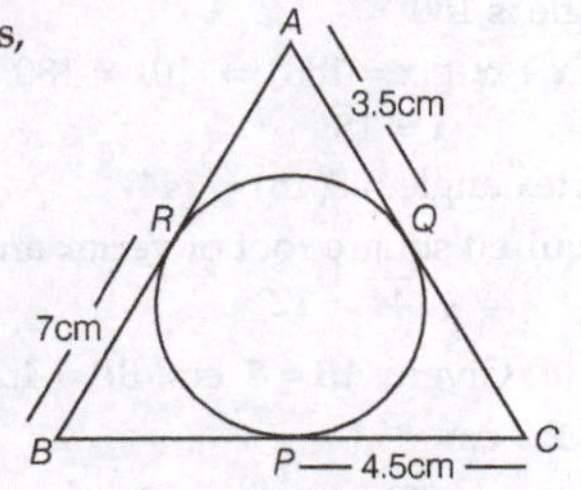

Perimeter = $AB + BC + CA$

Perimeter = $AQ + CQ + CP + BP + BR + AR$

Perimeter = $3.5 + 4.5 + 4.5 + 7 + 7 + 3.5$

$\therefore$ Perimeter = 30 cm

358. (d) Given, in ΔABC,

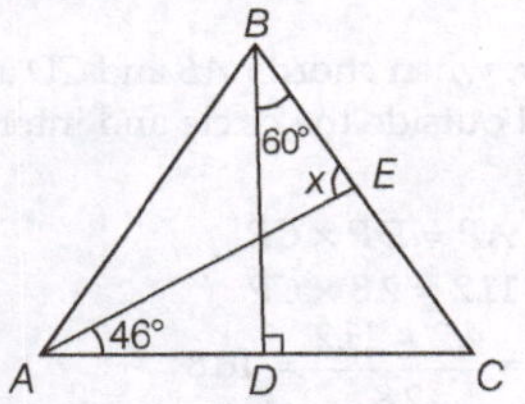

$\angle EBD = 60°$ and $\angle BDC = 90°$

$\angle DCB = 180° - (60° + 90°)$

$\Rightarrow \quad \angle DCB = 30°$

In ΔAEC, $\angle AEB = \angle EAC + \angle ACE$

$x = 46 + 30$ [exterior angle property]

$\Rightarrow \quad x = 76$

359. (d)

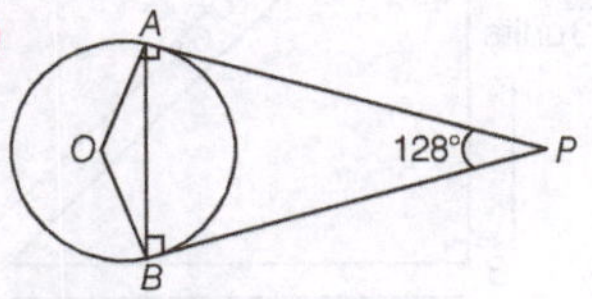

As, $OAPB$ is a quadrilateral,

$\angle OAP + \angle APB + \angle PBO + \angle BOA = 360°$

$\Rightarrow \; 90° + 128° + 90° + \angle BOA = 360°$

$\Rightarrow \; \angle BOA = 360° - 308° = 52°$

As, $(OA = OB$ Radii)

In OAB, $\angle OAB = \angle OBA$ (in a triangle, angles opposite to equal sides are equal)

$\angle OAB + \angle OBA + \angle BOA = 180°$

$\Rightarrow \quad 2 \times \angle OAB + 52° = 180°$

$\Rightarrow \; \angle OAB = \frac{(180° - 52°)}{2} \Rightarrow \angle OAB$ is 64°.

360. (d) A quadrilateral having equal diagonals and equal opposite side is always a "rectangle".

361. (a)

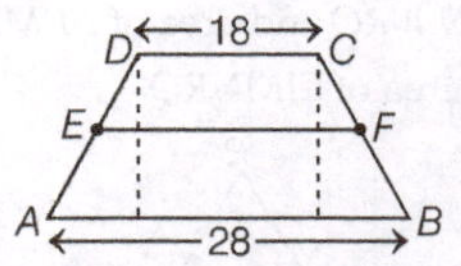

Here, $EF = \frac{AB + CD}{2} \Rightarrow EF = \frac{28 + 18}{2}$

$\therefore \quad EF = 23$ cm

362. (d)

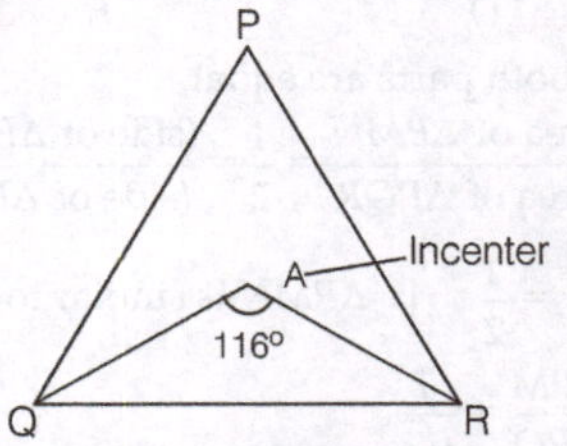

$\angle QAR = 90° + \frac{\angle QPR}{2}$

$\Rightarrow \quad 116° = 90° + \frac{\angle QPR}{2}$

$\Rightarrow \quad \angle QPR = (116 - 90) \times 2 = 52°$

363. (c) According to the question,

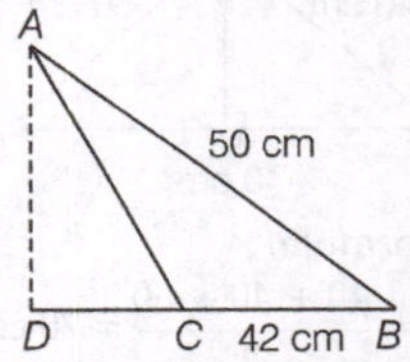

$AB = 50$ cm $\; BC = 42$ cm

Draw AD perpendicular to extended part of BC.

Area of $\Delta ABC = \frac{1}{2} \times BC \times AD$

$\Rightarrow 294 = \frac{1}{2} \times 42 \times AD \Rightarrow AD = \frac{294}{21} = 14$ cm

In ΔABD, $AB^2 = AD^2 + BD^2$

$\Rightarrow \quad (50)^2 = (14)^2 + (BD)^2$

$\Rightarrow 2500 - 196 = (BD)^2$

$\therefore \quad BD = \sqrt{2304} = 48$ cm

Hence, $CD = BD - BC = 48 - 42 = 6$ cm

In ΔADC, $AC^2 = (AD)^2 + (CD)^2$

$= (14)^2 + (6)^2 = 196 + 36 = 232$

$\therefore AC = \sqrt{232} = \sqrt{4 \times 58} = 2\sqrt{58}$

364. (b) According to the question,

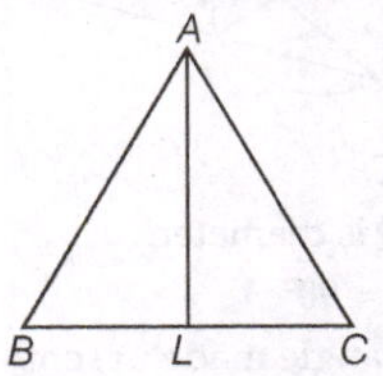

Since, L is mid-point of BC,

$\therefore$ AL is the median of ΔABC.

We know that median of a triangle divides it into two triangles of equal area.

$\Rightarrow$ ar (ΔABL) = ar (ΔACL)

$\therefore$ ar $(\Delta ACL) = 15 \text{ cm}^2$

[$\because$ given ar $(\Delta ABL) = 15 \text{ cm}^2$]

$\therefore$ ar (ΔABC) = ar (ΔABL) + ar (ΔACL)

$= 15 \text{ cm}^2 + 15 \text{ cm}^2 = 30 \text{ cm}^2$

365. (c) According to the question,

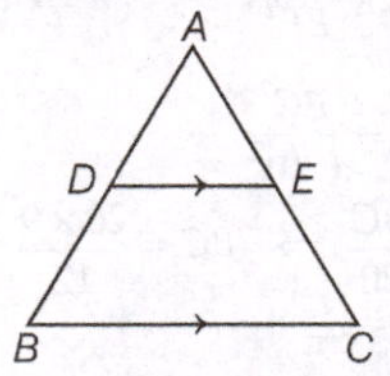

$\because \quad DE \parallel BC \Rightarrow \frac{AD}{BD} = \frac{AE}{EC}$ [Thales theorem]

$\Rightarrow \quad \frac{x}{x-3} = \frac{x+3}{x-2}$

$\Rightarrow \quad x(x-2) = (x-3)(x+3)$

$\Rightarrow \quad x^2 - 2x = x^2 + 3x - 3x - 9$

$\Rightarrow \quad -2x = -9 \Rightarrow x = \frac{9}{2} = 4.5$

366. (a) According to the question,

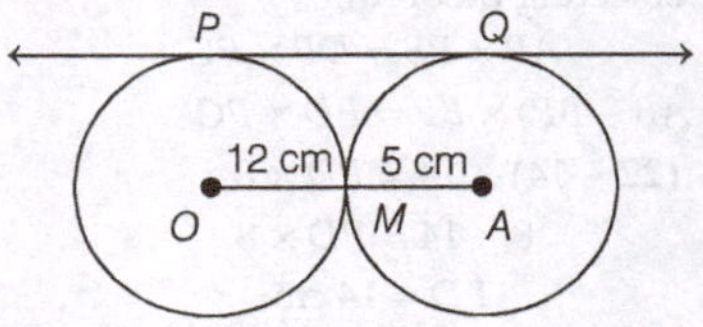

Length of common tangent

$= \sqrt{\text{(Distance between centers)}^2 - \text{(Difference between radius of two circles)}^2}$

$PQ = \sqrt{(OA)^2 - (OM - AM)^2}$

$\Rightarrow \quad PQ = \sqrt{(17)^2 - (12-5)^2}$

$\Rightarrow \quad PQ = \sqrt{289 - 49}$

$\Rightarrow \quad PQ = \sqrt{240}$

$\Rightarrow \quad PQ = 4\sqrt{15}$ cm

367. (a) $\Delta ABC \sim \Delta EDF$

By Area Similarity theorem

$\frac{\text{ar } \Delta ABC}{\text{ar } \Delta EDF} = \frac{BC^2}{DF^2} \Rightarrow \frac{1}{4} = \frac{8^2}{DF^2}$

$\Rightarrow \quad \frac{1}{4} = \frac{64}{DF^2} \Rightarrow DF = \sqrt{256}$

$\therefore \quad DF = 16$ cm

368. (b) C is the circle with centre 'O'.

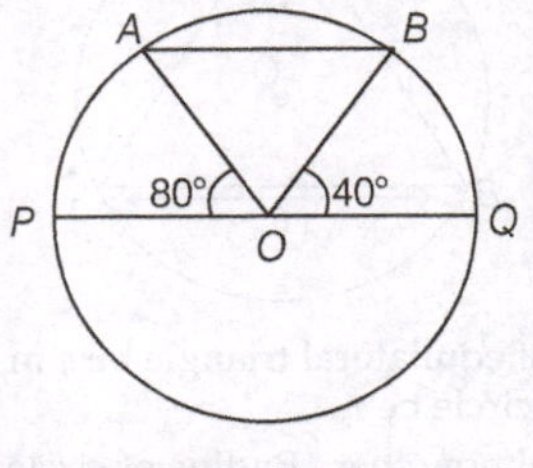

AB is chord and PQ is the diameter.

In ΔAOB,

$\angle AOP + \angle AOB + \angle BOQ = 180°$

$\Rightarrow \quad 80° + \angle AOB + 40° = 180°$

$\therefore \quad \angle AOB = 60°$

369. (c) Given, $\Delta ABC \sim \Delta DEF$

By Area Similarity theorem,

$$\frac{\text{ar } \Delta ABC}{\text{ar } \Delta DEF} = \frac{BC^2}{EF^2}$$

$$\Rightarrow \quad \frac{81}{144} = \frac{BC^2}{(20)^2} \qquad (\because EF = 20)$$

$$\Rightarrow \quad \frac{9}{12} = \frac{BC}{20} \Rightarrow BC = \frac{20 \times 9}{12}$$

$$\therefore \quad BC = 15 \text{ cm}$$

370. (a) Given,

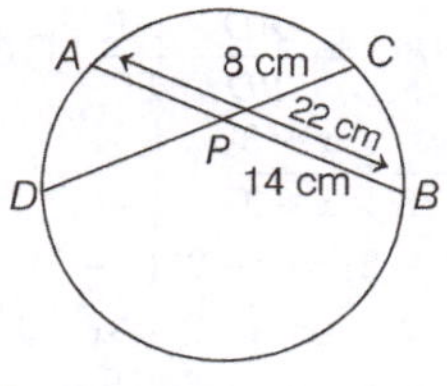

$AB = 22$ cm, $PB = 14$ cm, $CP = 8$ cm

Let the length of $PD = x$ cm

By intersecting theorem,

$$AP \times PB = DP \times PC$$

$$\Rightarrow \quad (AB - BP) \times BP = PD \times PC$$

$$\Rightarrow \quad (22 - 14) \times 14 = PD \times 8$$

$$\Rightarrow \quad 8 \times 14 = PD \times 8$$

$$\therefore \quad PD = 14 \text{ cm}$$

371. (d) Given,

$AD = 4$ cm, $DE = 12$ cm, $DW = 24$ cm

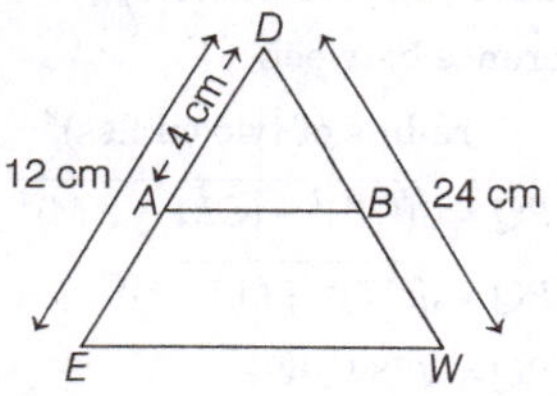

We know that,

Line drawn parallel to one side of a triangle, then $\dfrac{AD}{DE} = \dfrac{DB}{DW} \Rightarrow \dfrac{4}{12} = \dfrac{DB}{24} \Rightarrow DB = 8$ cm

372. (b) Option (b) is false regarding a circle because three points can not always make a circle.

373. (c) Let ΔABC be an equilateral triangle.

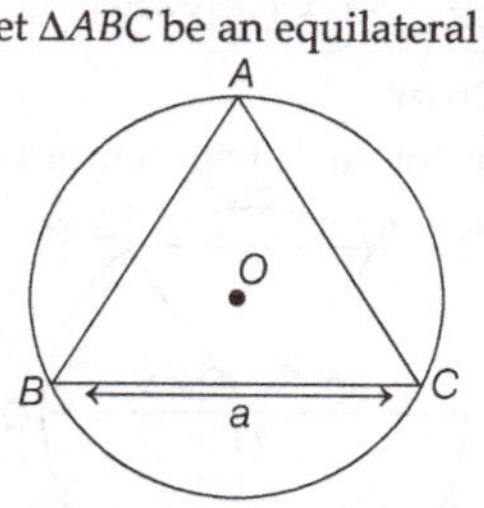

Let side of equilateral triangle be a m and radius of circle be r.

Then, we know that, Radius of circle circumscribing an equilateral triangle,

$$r = \frac{a}{\sqrt{3}}$$

Thus, $\quad a = \sqrt{3} \times$ radius of circle

$$a = \sqrt{3} \times r$$

374. (c) $MN \parallel RQ$ and area of ΔPMN

$= $ area of $\square MNRQ$

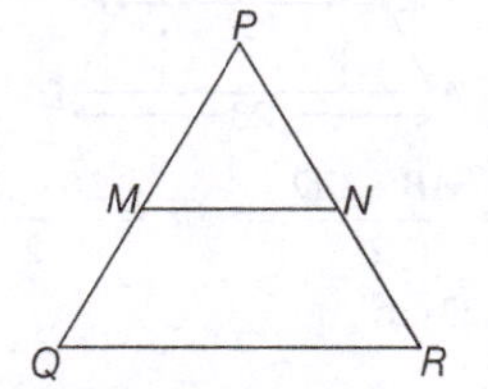

Area of both parts are equal.

Thus, $\dfrac{\text{area of } \Delta PMN}{\text{area of } \Delta PQR} = \dfrac{1}{2} = \dfrac{(\text{side of } \Delta PMN)^2}{(\text{side of } \Delta PQR)^2}$

$$\left(\frac{PM}{PQ}\right)^2 = \frac{1}{2} \qquad [\because \Delta PMN \text{ is similar to } \Delta PQR]$$

$$\Rightarrow \quad \frac{PM}{PQ} = \frac{1}{\sqrt{2}}$$

Thus, $MQ = \sqrt{2} - 1$ and $PQ = \sqrt{2}$

$$\therefore \text{ Required ratio} = \frac{MQ}{PQ} = \frac{\sqrt{2} - 1}{\sqrt{2}}$$

375. (b) In ΔPQR,

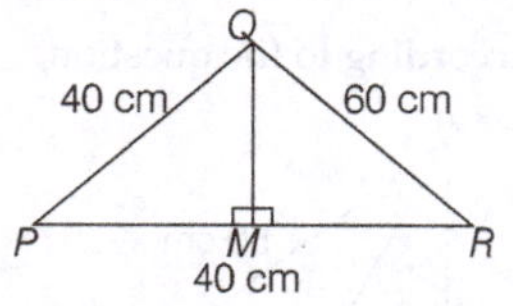

By Heron's formula,

$$s = \frac{a + b + c}{2} = \frac{40 + 40 + 60}{2} = 70 \text{ cm}$$

$$\text{Area of } \Delta PQR = \sqrt{s(s-a)(s-b)(s-c)}$$

$$= \sqrt{70 \times 30 \times 30 \times 10}$$

Area of $\Delta PQR = 30 \times 10 \times \sqrt{7} = 300\sqrt{7}$

Again,

Area of ΔPQR taking PR as base.

Then, $\quad \dfrac{1}{2} \times PR \times QM = 300\sqrt{7}$

$$\Rightarrow \frac{1}{2} \times 40 \times QM = 300\sqrt{7} \Rightarrow QM = \frac{300\sqrt{7}}{40} \times 2$$

$$\therefore \quad QM = 15\sqrt{7} \text{ cm}$$

Hence, required altitude $= 15\sqrt{7}$ cm

376. (d) Given,

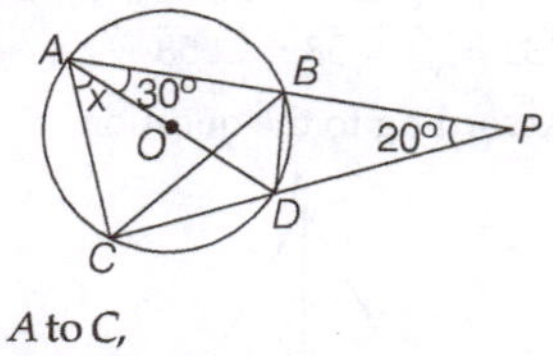

Joining A to C,

As, given AD is diameter.

Then, $\angle ACD = 90°$

[angle made in semi-circle is 90°]

Now, in ΔACP,

$$\angle PAC + \angle ACP + \angle CPA = 180°$$

$$\Rightarrow \quad 30 + x + 90° + 20° = 180° \Rightarrow x = 40°$$

Here, $\angle DAC = x = 40°$

$$\angle DAC = \angle DBC = 40°$$

[angle in same segment are equal]

377. (b) Given, $\Delta ABC \sim \Delta PQR$

$$\therefore \quad \frac{\text{ar}(\Delta ABC)}{\text{ar}(\Delta PQR)} = \frac{AC^2}{PR^2}$$

$$\Rightarrow \quad \frac{289}{576} = \left(\frac{AC}{PR}\right)^2 \Rightarrow \frac{17}{24} = \frac{AC}{12}$$

$$\Rightarrow \quad AC = \frac{17}{2} = 8.5 \text{ cm}$$

378. (d) Let the base angle be x.

$\therefore$ Vertex angle $= 4(x + x) = 8x$

We know, sum of the interior angle of a triangle is 180°.

$$\therefore \quad 8x + x + x = 180° \Rightarrow 10x = 180°$$

$$\Rightarrow \quad x = 18°$$

$\therefore$ Vertex angle $= 8(18) = 144°$

$\therefore$ Required square root of vertex angle

$$= \sqrt{144} = 12°$$

379. (d) Given, $AB = 7$ cm, $BP = 4.2$ cm, $PD = 2.8$ cm

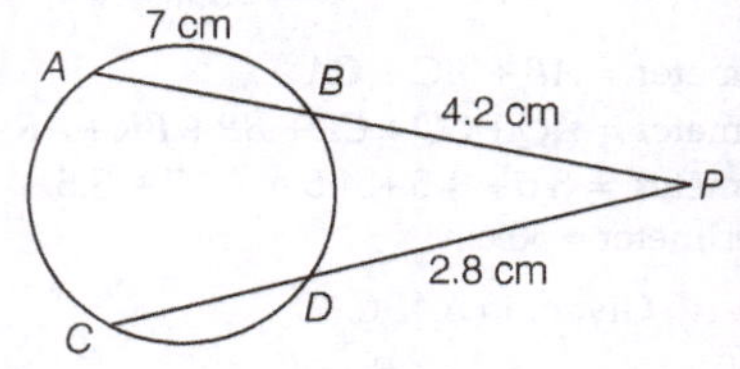

We know, when chords AB and CD are produced outside the circle and intersect at P, then

$$BP \times AP = DP \times CP$$

$$4.2 \times 11.2 = 2.8 \times CP$$

$$\Rightarrow \quad CP = \frac{4.2 \times 11.2}{2.8} = 16.8$$

$$\therefore \quad CD = CP - DP = 16.8 - 2.8 = 14 \text{ cm}$$

380. (a) Given,

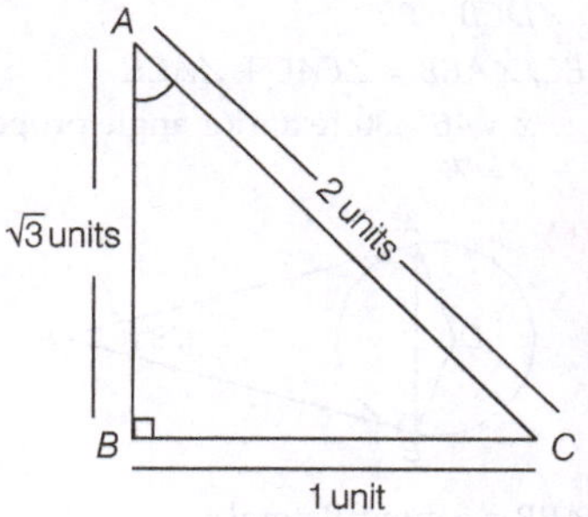

By Cosine rule, $\cos C = \dfrac{b^2 + a^2 - c^2}{2ba}$

$$\Rightarrow \cos C = \frac{2^2 + 1^2 - (\sqrt{3})^2}{2 \times 2 \times 1} = \frac{5 - 3}{4} = \frac{1}{2}$$

$$\Rightarrow \cos C = \cos 60° \Rightarrow \angle ACB = 60°$$

381. (c) Given,

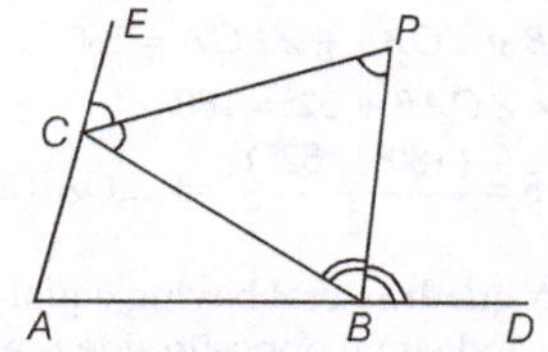

Using Angle Bisector theorem,

$$\angle BPC = 90° - \frac{\angle A}{2}$$
$$= 90° - \frac{72°}{2} = 90° - 36° = 54°$$

382. (a) Given, $r_1 = 20$ cm, $r_2 = 32$ cm

Distance between centres $(d) = 60$ cm

Length of direct common tangent

$$= \sqrt{d^2 - (r_1 - r_2)^2}$$
$$= \sqrt{(60)^2 - (20 - 32)^2}$$
$$= \sqrt{3600 - 144} = \sqrt{3456} = 24\sqrt{6}$$

Length of transversal common tangent

$$= \sqrt{d^2 - (r_1 + r_2)^2}$$
$$= \sqrt{(60)^2 - (20 + 32)^2} = 8\sqrt{14}$$

$\therefore$ Required ratio $= 24\sqrt{6} : 8\sqrt{14} = 3\sqrt{3} : \sqrt{7}$

383. (c) Given,

$QR = 36$ cm, $SQ = 27$ cm, $RS = 18$ cm

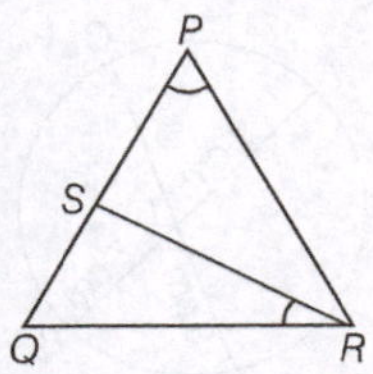

In ΔPQR and ΔRQS,

$\therefore \quad \angle RPQ = \angle SRQ \Rightarrow \Delta PQR \sim \Delta RQS$

$$\frac{PQ}{RQ} = \frac{QR}{QS} = \frac{PR}{RS}$$
$$\Rightarrow \quad \frac{27 + PS}{36} = \frac{36}{27} = \frac{PR}{18}$$
$$\Rightarrow \quad \frac{27 + PS}{36} = \frac{36}{27} \Rightarrow 27 + PS = 48$$

$\therefore \quad PS = 21$ cm

$\therefore \quad PQ = PS + SQ = 21 + 27 = 48$ cm

Now, $\dfrac{PR}{18} = \dfrac{36}{27} \therefore PR = 24$ cm

Perimeter of $\Delta PRS = 24 + 18 + 21 = 63$ cm

Perimeter of $\Delta QSR = 27 + 18 + 36 = 81$ cm

$\therefore$ Required ratio $= 63 : 81 = 7 : 9$

384. (d) Direct common tangent

$$= \sqrt{d^2 - (r_2 - r_1)^2} = \sqrt{(40)^2 - (14 - 5)^2}$$
$$= \sqrt{1600 - 81} = \sqrt{1519} \text{ cm}$$

385. (d) In ΔABC,

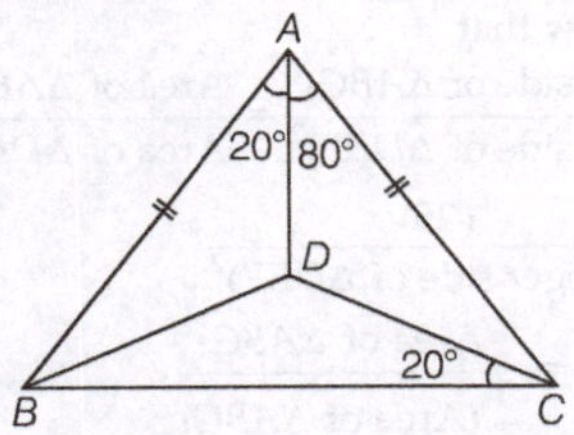

$AB = AC$ [$\because \Delta ABC$ is an isosceles triangle]

$\angle B = \angle C$

Thus, $\angle BAC = \angle BAD + \angle DAC$

$= 20 + 80 = 100°$

$$\therefore \quad \angle ABC = \angle ACB = \frac{180° - 100°}{2}$$
$$= \frac{80°}{2} = 40° \qquad [\because AB = AC]$$

386. (b) Here, $AC = 3$ units, $BD = 2$ units

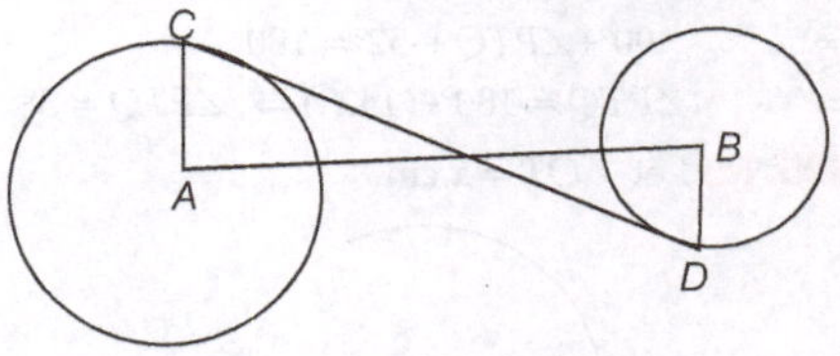

Length of transverse tangent

$$= \sqrt{(AB)^2 - (AC + BD)^2}$$
$$6 = \sqrt{(AB)^2 - 5^2} \Rightarrow 36 = (AB)^2 - 5^2$$
$$\Rightarrow AB^2 = 36 + 25 = 61$$
$$\Rightarrow AB = \sqrt{61}$$

Thus, length of internal tangent is $\sqrt{61}$.

387. (c) Let the angles after decrement be $3x$, $4x$ and $7x$, respectively.

According to the question,

$(3x + 17°) + (4x + 17°) + (7x + 17°) = 180°$

$\therefore \quad 14x + 51 = 180°$

$\Rightarrow \quad 14x = 129 \Rightarrow x = \dfrac{129}{14}$

$\therefore \quad$ Greatest angle $= 7 \times \dfrac{129}{14} + 17$

$$= \frac{129°}{2} + 17 = \frac{163°}{2}$$

$\therefore$ Required radian measure

$$= \frac{163}{2} \times \frac{\pi}{180} = \frac{163\pi}{360}$$

388. (b)

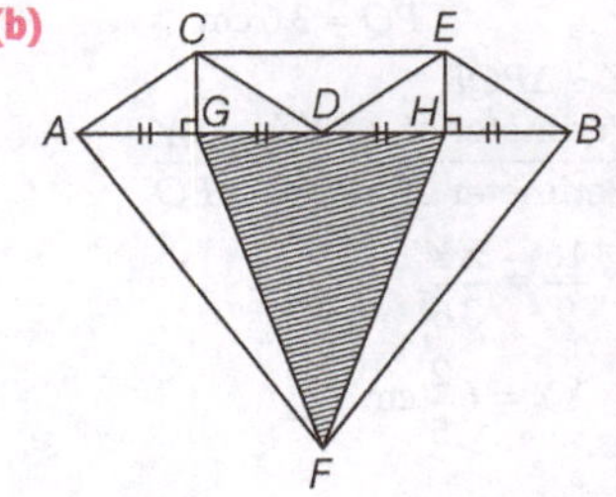

Given, $AB \parallel CE$,

$AG = GD = DH = HB$

In ΔACG and ΔBEH, $AG = BH$ (given)

$\angle AGC = \angle BHE$ (each 90°)

$CG = EH$

(distance between parallel sides)

$\therefore \quad \Delta ACG \cong \Delta BEH$ (SAS)

In ΔCDE and ΔDEB,

$DE = DE$ (common)

$\angle CED = \angle BDE$

(alternate Interior Angles as $AB \parallel CE$)

$CE = BD \quad [\because CE = GH \Rightarrow CE = BD]$

$\therefore \quad \Delta CDE \cong \Delta DEB$ (SAS)

Similarly, $\Delta CDE \cong \Delta ACD$

$\therefore \quad \Delta CDE \cong \Delta DEB \cong \Delta ACD$

Now, in ΔHFB and ΔAFG

$AG = HB$ (given)

and no more corresponding sides and angle are equal

Thus, $\Delta HFB \not\cong \Delta AFG$

Thus, only I and II are correct.

389. (c)

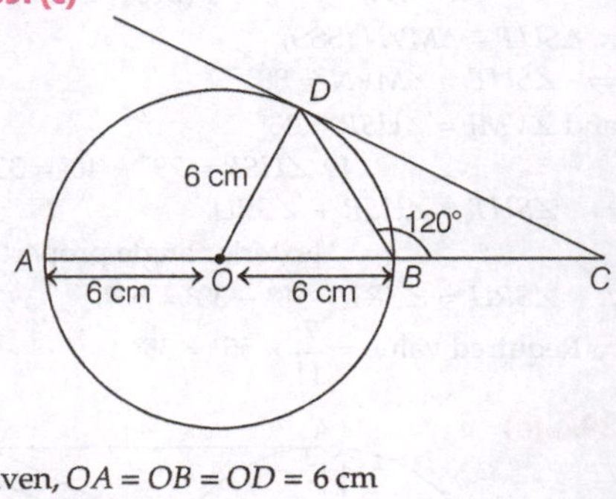

Given, $OA = OB = OD = 6$ cm

and $\angle ODC = 90°$

Also, given, $\angle DBC = 120°$

$\therefore \angle DBO = 180° - 120° = 60°$ [linear pair]

$\Rightarrow \quad \angle ODB = \angle DBO = 60°$

$\therefore \quad \angle BOD = 180° - \angle ODB - \angle DBO$

$= 180° - 60° - 60° = 60°$

$\therefore \Delta OBD$ is an equilateral triangle.

$\therefore \quad \angle BDC = 90° - 60° = 30°$

$\Rightarrow \quad \angle BCD = 180° - 120° - 30° = 30°$

$\therefore \Delta BCD$ is an isosceles triangle

$\therefore \quad CB = DB = 6$ cm

In ΔOCD, $CD^2 = OC^2 - OD^2 = (6 + 6)^2 - (6)^2$

$= 144 - 36 = 108 \Rightarrow CD = 6\sqrt{3}$ cm

390. (b)

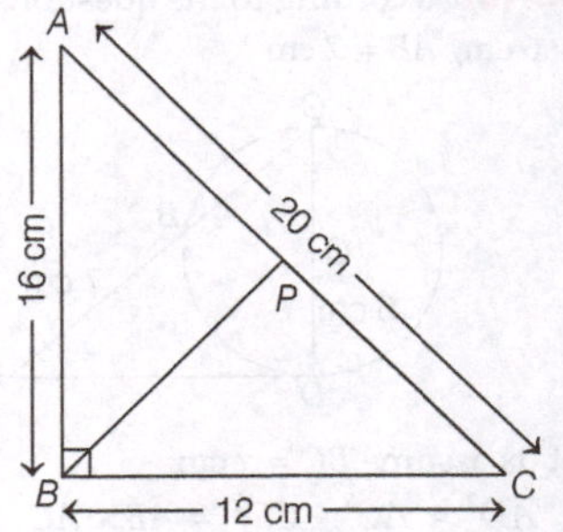

Given, sides $= 12$ cm and 16 cm

Hypotenuse $= 20$ cm

According to the question,

$$BP = \frac{AB \times BC}{AC},$$
$$BP = \frac{16 \times 12}{20} = 9.6 \text{ cm}$$

391. (a)

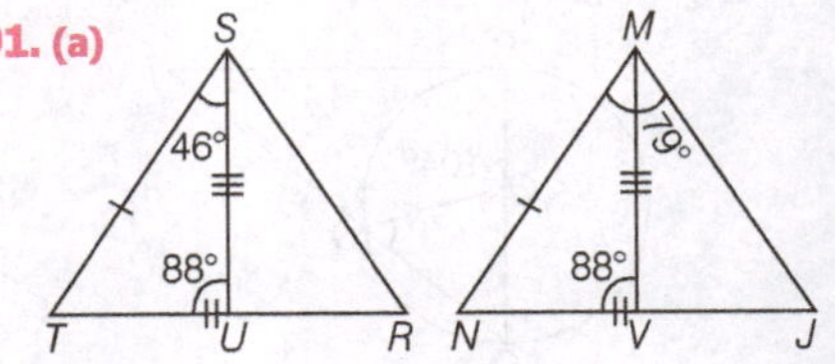

Given, $ST = MN$

$SU = MV$ and $TR = NJ$

$\Rightarrow \quad \frac{1}{2}TR = \frac{1}{2}NJ \Rightarrow TU = NV$

[$\because$ SU and MV are medians]

In ΔSUT and ΔMVN,

$ST = MN$ (given)

$SU = MV$ (given)

$TU = NV$ (proved above)

$\therefore \; \Delta SUT \cong \Delta MVN$ (SSS)

$\Rightarrow \; \angle SUT = \angle MVN = 88°$

and $\angle VMJ = \angle USR = 33°$

[$\because \angle USR = 79° - 46° = 33°$]

$\therefore \quad \angle SUT = \angle USR + \angle SRU$

[exterior angle property]

$\therefore \quad \angle SRU = \angle SRT = 88° - 33° = 55°$

$\therefore$ Required value $= \frac{7}{11} \times 55° = 35°$

392. (a)

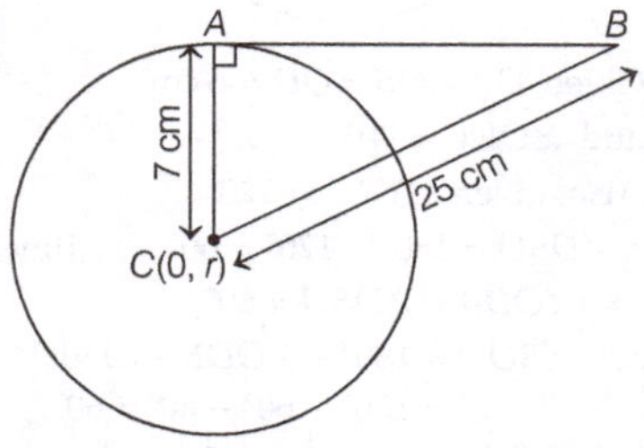

Let AB represents the tangent of a circle.

$\therefore$ ΔABC is a right-angled triangle.

In ΔABC,

$$(AB)^2 = (BC)^2 - (AC)^2 = (25)^2 - (7)^2$$
$$= 625 - 49 = 576$$

$\therefore \quad AB = 24$ cm

393. (d) According to the question,

$r = 6$ cm, $AB = 7$ cm

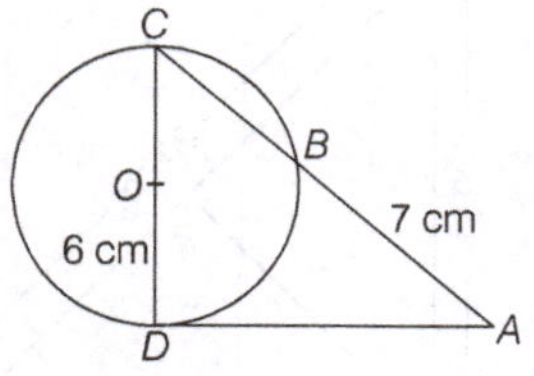

Let us assume $BC = x$ cm

$\therefore \quad AD^2 = AC^2 - CD^2 = AB \times AC$

$\Rightarrow \quad (7 + x)^2 - (12)^2 = 7(7 + x)$

$\Rightarrow \quad 49 + x^2 + 14x - 144 = 49 + 7x$

$\Rightarrow \quad x^2 + 7x - 144 = 0$

$\Rightarrow \quad (x + 16)(x - 9) = 0 \Rightarrow x = 9$

$\therefore \quad AC = x + 7 = 9 + 7 = 16$ cm

394. (d) According to the question,

$OQ = OS = r$

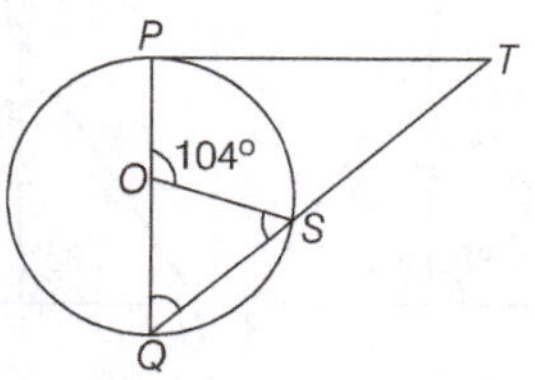

Let $\angle OSQ = \angle OQS = x$

(angle opposite to equal sides are equal)

$\therefore \quad x + x = 104°$ (exterior angle theorem)

$\Rightarrow \quad x = 52°$

Now, in ΔPQT, $\angle QPT = 90°$

(angle made on tangent)

$\therefore \angle QPT + \angle PTQ + \angle PQT = 180°$

$\Rightarrow \quad 90° + \angle PTQ + 52° = 180°$

$\Rightarrow \quad \angle PTQ = 180° - (142°) \Rightarrow \angle PTQ = 38°$

395. (d) Let $OT = x$ cm

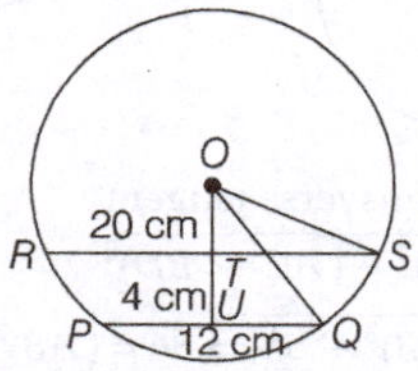

In ΔOQU, by using Pythagoras theorem,

$OU^2 + UQ^2 = OQ^2 = (\text{Radius})^2$ ...(i)

In ΔOST, by using Pythagoras theorem,

$OT^2 + TS^2 = OS^2 = (\text{Radius})^2$ ...(ii)

Equating both equations,

$OU^2 + UQ^2 = OT^2 + TS^2$

$\Rightarrow (x + 4)^2 + (6)^2 = x^2 + (10)^2$

$\Rightarrow \quad 8x + 52 = 100 \Rightarrow 8x = 48$

$\therefore \quad x = 6$ cm

$\therefore$ Radius $= \sqrt{x^2 + (10)^2} = \sqrt{36 + 100}$

[from Eq. (ii)]

$= 2\sqrt{34}$

$\therefore$ Diameter $= 2 \times 2\sqrt{34} = 4\sqrt{34}$ cm

396. (c) Given, $\Delta XYZ \sim \Delta PQR$

$$\frac{\text{Perimeter of } \Delta XYZ}{\text{Perimeter of } \Delta PQR} = \frac{16}{9}$$

$PQ = 3.6$ cm

If $\Delta XYZ \sim \Delta PQR$

Then, $\frac{\text{Perimeter of } \Delta XYZ}{\text{Perimeter of } \Delta PQR} = \frac{XY}{PQ}$

$\Rightarrow \quad \frac{16}{9} = \frac{XY}{3.6}$

$\Rightarrow \quad XY = 6\frac{2}{5}$ cm

397. (c) According to the question,

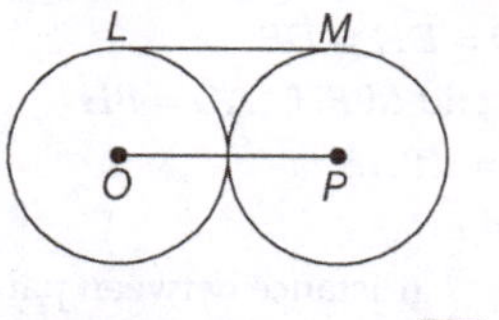

Length of common tangent $= 2\sqrt{r_1 r_2}$

$12 = 2\sqrt{18 \times r_2} \Rightarrow \sqrt{18 \times r_2} = 6$

$\Rightarrow \quad 18 \times r_2 = 6^2 = 36 \Rightarrow r_2 = 2$ cm

Thus, radius of smaller circle = 2 cm

398. (c) Let the angles of triangle are $2x$, $4x$ and $6x$.

$2x + 4x + 6x = 180° \Rightarrow 12x = 180° \Rightarrow x = 15°$

Then, angles are $2x = 30°$, $4x = 60°$, $6x = 90°$

Circumradius of circle = 12 cm

As, we know in right-angled triangle.

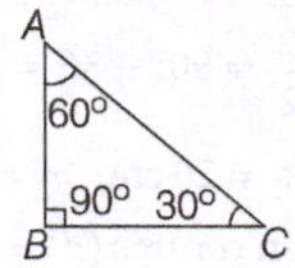

$\frac{AC}{2} = 12 \text{ cm} \Rightarrow AC = 24$ cm

Then, $\sin 30° = \frac{AB}{AC}$ and $\cos 30° = \frac{BC}{AC}$

$\frac{1}{2} = \frac{AB}{AC} \Rightarrow \frac{\sqrt{3}}{2} = \frac{BC}{24}$

$\Rightarrow \quad \frac{1}{2} = \frac{AB}{24} \Rightarrow BC = 12\sqrt{3}$

$AB = 12$ cm

Hence, all sides are 12 cm, $12\sqrt{3}$ cm and 24 cm.

399. (b) AB and CD are two chords of circle, which intersect at point L.

As, we know that,

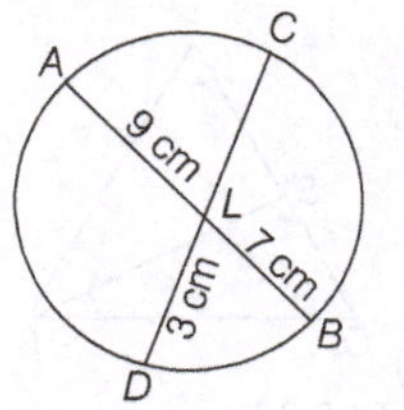

$AL \times LB = LC \times LD \Rightarrow 9 \times 7 = LC \times 3$

$\Rightarrow \quad LC = 21$ cm

400. (c)

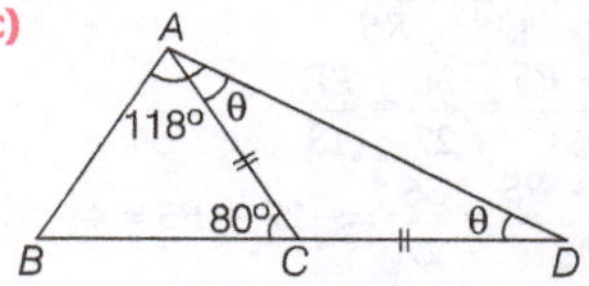

In ΔACD, (exterior angle)

$\angle\theta + \angle\theta = 80° \Rightarrow 2\angle\theta = 80° \Rightarrow \angle\theta = 40°$

Now, in ΔBAD

$\angle ABD + \angle BAD + \angle ADB = 180°$

$\Rightarrow \angle ABC + 118° + 40° = 180°$

$\Rightarrow \angle ABC = 180° - 118° - 40°$

$\Rightarrow \angle ABD = \angle ABC = 22°$

401. (d) Given, $\Delta ABC \sim \Delta DEF$

Ratio of sides of $\Delta ABC = 3 : 4 : 5$

Smaller side of $\Delta ABC = 15$ units

$\therefore$ Larger side $= \frac{15}{3} \times 5 = 25$ units

We know that,

$$\frac{(\text{Larger side of } \Delta ABC)^2}{(\text{Larger side of } \Delta DEF)^2} = \frac{\text{Area of } \Delta ABC}{\text{Area of } \Delta DEF}$$

$$\Rightarrow \frac{(25)^2}{(\text{Larger side of } \Delta DEF)^2} = \frac{\text{Area of } \Delta ABC}{\frac{1}{2}(\text{Area of } \Delta ABC)}$$

$$\Rightarrow \frac{(25)^2}{(\text{Larger side of } \Delta DEF)^2} = 2$$

$\therefore$ Larger side of $\Delta DEF = \frac{25}{\sqrt{2}}$

402. (b) Length of direct common tangent

$$= \sqrt{\{(\text{Distance between centres})^2 - (\text{Difference between radius of circles})^2\}}$$

$$= \sqrt{(81)^2 - (51-42)^2} = \sqrt{(81)^2 - (9)^2}$$

$$= \sqrt{(81+9)(81-9)} = \sqrt{72 \times 90}$$

$$= 9 \times 4\sqrt{5} = 36\sqrt{5} \text{ cm}$$

403. (a) In ΔMNT,

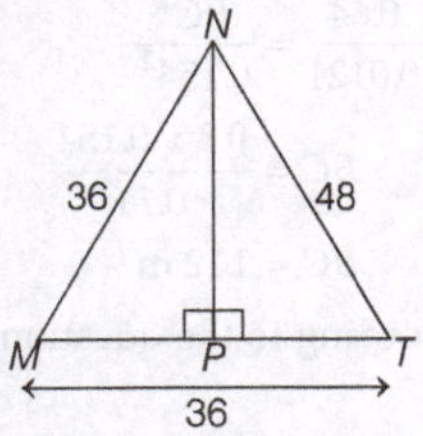

$MN = 36$ cm, $MT = 36$ cm and $NT = 48$ cm

$$s = \frac{a+b+c}{2} = \frac{36+36+48}{2} = 60$$

Area of $\Delta MNT = \sqrt{s(s-a)(s-b)(s-c)}$

$$= \sqrt{60 \times 24 \times 24 \times 12}$$

$$= \sqrt{12 \times 5 \times 24 \times 24 \times 12}$$

$$= 12 \times 24 \times \sqrt{5} \text{ cm}^2$$

Again, area of ΔMNT having MT as base.

Then, $\frac{1}{2} \times MT \times NP = 12 \times 24 \times \sqrt{5}$

$\Rightarrow \frac{1}{2} \times 36 \times NP = 12 \times 24 \times \sqrt{5}$

$\therefore NP = 16\sqrt{5}$ cm

404. (c) In ΔABC,

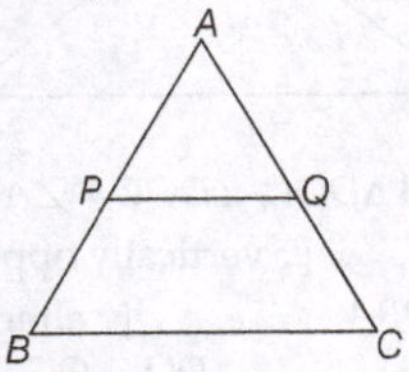

$PQ \parallel BC$ and $AC = 5\,QC$

$\therefore \frac{AC}{QC} = \frac{5}{1}$

Then, ratio of $\frac{AQ}{AC} = \frac{(5-1)}{5} = \frac{4}{5}$

As we know,

ΔAPQ and ΔABC are similar because all angles are equal.

Then, ratio of all sides of triangles are equal.

Hence, $\frac{PQ}{BC} = \frac{4}{5}$

405. (a) According to the question,

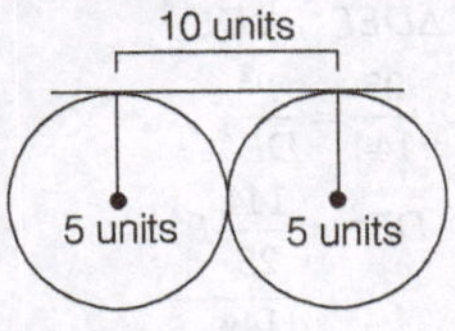

Given, length of direct common tangent $= 10$ units

Radius of both circles $= 5$ units

We know, length of direct common tangent

$$= \sqrt{d^2 - (r_1 - r_2)^2}$$

$$10 = \sqrt{d^2 - (5-5)^2}$$

Squaring of both sides, we get

$$100 = d^2 \Rightarrow d = 10 \text{ units}$$

406. (c) Let $AD = x$ and $CD = (12 - x)$ cm

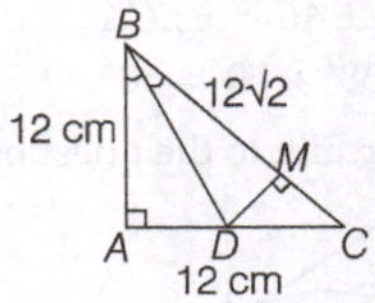

We know, by Angle Bisector theorem,

$$\frac{AB}{AC} = \frac{AD}{CD} \Rightarrow \frac{12}{12\sqrt{2}} = \frac{x}{12-x}$$

$$\Rightarrow \frac{1}{\sqrt{2}} = \frac{x}{12-x} \Rightarrow 12 - x = x\sqrt{2}$$

$$\Rightarrow x(\sqrt{2}+1) = 12 \Rightarrow x = \frac{12}{\sqrt{2}+1} \times \frac{\sqrt{2}-1}{\sqrt{2}-1}$$

$$\therefore x = 12(\sqrt{2}-1)$$

407. (c) Given, radii of circles are 27 cm and 36 cm.

Distance between centres $= 45$ cm

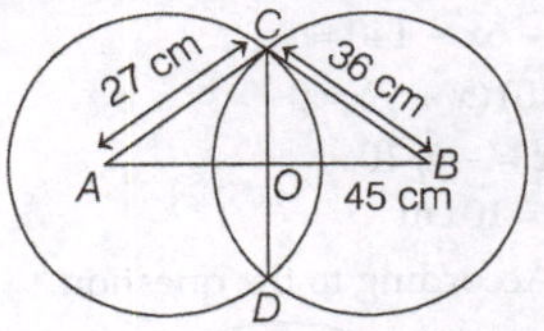

In ΔABC semi-perimeter,

$$s = \frac{27+36+45}{2} = \frac{108}{2} = 54$$

$\therefore$ ar (ΔABC)

$$= \sqrt{54(54-27)(54-36)(54-45)}$$

$$= \sqrt{27 \times 2 \times 27 \times 9 \times 2 \times 9} = 9 \times 2 \times 27$$

Also, ar $(\Delta ABC) = \frac{1}{2} \times AB \times OC$

$$= \frac{1}{2} \times 45 \times OC$$

$$\therefore \frac{1}{2} \times 45 \times OC = 9 \times 2 \times 27$$

$$\Rightarrow OC = \frac{108}{5} = 21.6$$

$\therefore CD = 2 \times OC = 2 \times 21.6 = 43.2$ cm

408. (b) Here, ABC is a triangle.

$DE \parallel BC$ and $AD : DB = 3 : 5$

and $AC = 5.6$ cm,

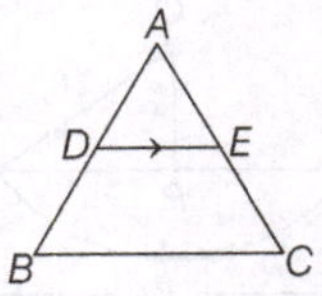

As we know,

ΔADE is similar to ΔABC.

Thus, by BPT theorem

$$\frac{AD}{AB} = \frac{3}{3+5} = \frac{3}{8} = \frac{AE}{AC}$$

Here, $AC = 5.6$ cm

$$\Rightarrow \frac{AE}{AC} = \frac{3}{8} \Rightarrow \frac{AE}{5.6} = \frac{3}{8}$$

$$\Rightarrow AE = \frac{5.6 \times 3}{8}$$

$$\Rightarrow AE = 0.7 \times 3 = 2.1 \text{ cm}$$

409. (c) Radii of circles are 16 cm and 4 cm.

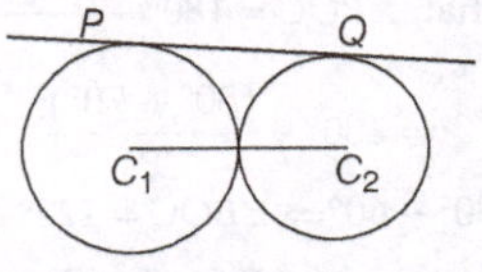

Distance between C_1 and $C_2 = 16 + 4 = 20$ cm

Length of common tangent

$$= \sqrt{d^2 - (r_2 - r_1)^2} = \sqrt{(20)^2 - (16-4)^2}$$

$$= \sqrt{(20)^2 - (12)^2} = \sqrt{400 - 144}$$

$$= \sqrt{256} = 16 \text{ cm}$$

$\therefore$ Hence, required length of common tangent is 16 cm.

410. (d)

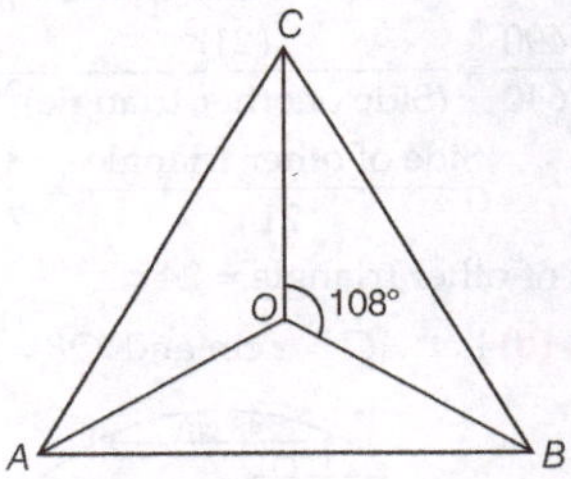

In ΔBOC, $\frac{\angle B}{2} + \frac{\angle C}{2} + \angle BOC = 180°$

$$\Rightarrow \frac{\angle B + \angle C}{2} + 108° = 180°$$

$$\Rightarrow \frac{\angle B + \angle C}{2} = 72°$$

$$\Rightarrow \angle B + \angle C = 144°$$

Now, in ΔABC, $\angle A + \angle B + \angle C = 180°$

$$\angle A = 180° - 144° = 36°$$

Now, $\angle BAO = \frac{36°}{2} = 18°$

Speedy Method

Here O is the in centre.

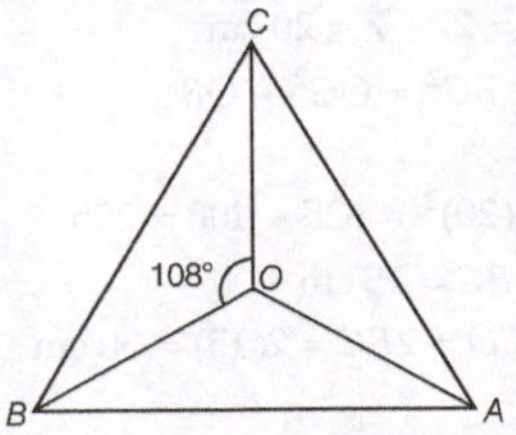

[bisector of $\angle C$ is also passed through O]

$\therefore 90 + \frac{\angle A}{2} = 108° \Rightarrow \frac{\angle A}{2} = 18°$

$\Rightarrow \angle BAO = 18°$

411. (a) Given, $\angle ABC = 70°$ and $\angle ACB = 50°$

Incentre of triangle,

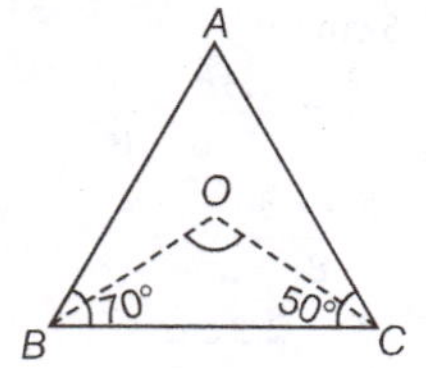

We know that, $\angle BOC = 180° - \left(\frac{\angle B + \angle C}{2}\right)$

$= 180° - \frac{(50° + 70°)}{2}$

$\angle BOC = 180° - 60° \Rightarrow \angle BOC = 120°$

412. (a) Given, area of first triangle $= 490$ sq cm

Area of other triangle = 640 sq cm

Length of side of first triangle = 21 cm

In similar triangle,

We know that, $\frac{\text{Area of first triangle}}{\text{Area of other triangle}} = \left(\frac{\text{Side of first triangle}}{\text{Side of other triangle}}\right)^2$

$\frac{490}{640} = \frac{(21)^2}{(\text{Side of other triangle})^2}$

$\Rightarrow \frac{\text{Side of other triangle}}{21} = \frac{8}{7}$

Side of other triangle = 24 cm

413. (d) Let $AO = x$ cm and $OB = (27 - x)$ cm

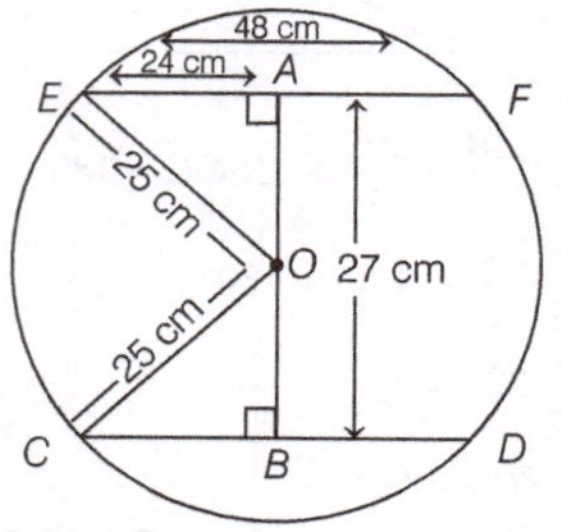

As, perpendicular from the centre of a circle bisects the chord.

$\therefore \quad AE = AF = 24$ cm

In ΔAOE, $EO^2 = AO^2 + AE^2$

$(25)^2 = (x)^2 + (24)^2$

$\Rightarrow \quad x^2 = 625 - 576 = 49 \Rightarrow x = 7$ cm

$\therefore \quad OB = 27 - 7 = 20$ cm

In ΔOBC, $BC^2 = OC^2 - OB^2$

$= (25)^2 - (20)^2 = 625 - 400 = 225$

$\therefore \quad BC = 15$ cm

$\therefore \quad CD = 2BC = 2(15) = 30$ cm

414. (b)

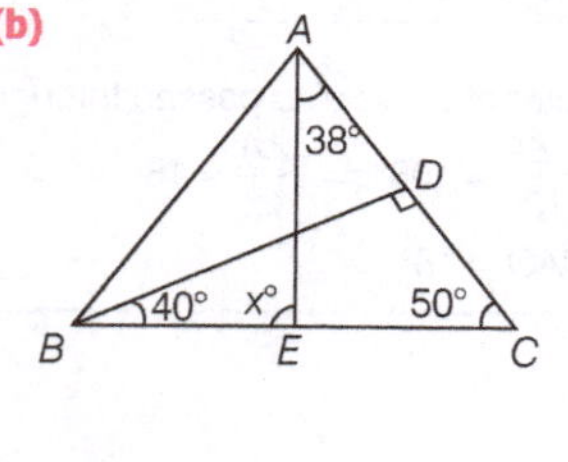

Given, $\angle BEA = x°$, $\angle EAC = 38°$

$\angle EBD = 40°$ and $\angle BDC = 90°$

In ΔBDC, $\angle BCD = 180° - \angle BDC - \angle CBD$

[$\because$ Sum of all the interior angles of a triangle is 180°]

$\Rightarrow \quad \angle BCD = 180° - 90° - 40° = 50°$

As, $\angle BEA$ is an exterior angle of ΔAEC.

$\therefore \quad \angle BEA = \angle EAC + \angle ECA$

$x° = 38° + 50° = 88°$

415. (d) According to the question,

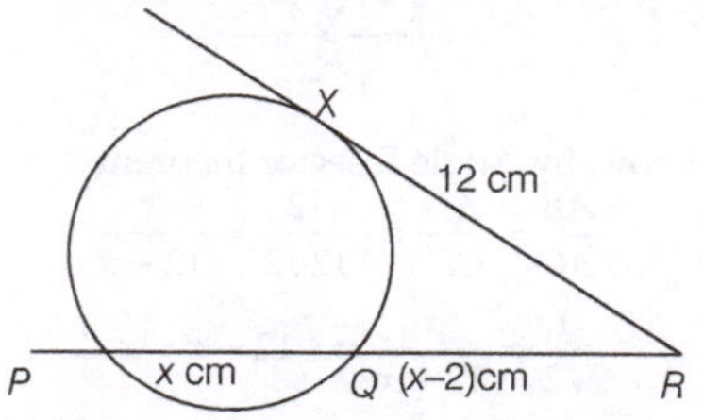

Now, when RX is a tangent and PQ is a chord in circle.

So, $RX^2 = QR \times PR$

$(12)^2 = (x - 2) \times (x + x - 2)$

$\Rightarrow \quad 144 = (x - 2)(2x - 2)$

$\Rightarrow \quad 144 = 2x^2 - 2x - 4x + 4$

$\Rightarrow \quad 2x^2 - 6x - 140 = 0$

$\Rightarrow \quad (x - 10)(x + 7) = 0$

$\Rightarrow \quad x = -7, 10$

Hence, $x = 10$ cm

416. (c) According to the question,

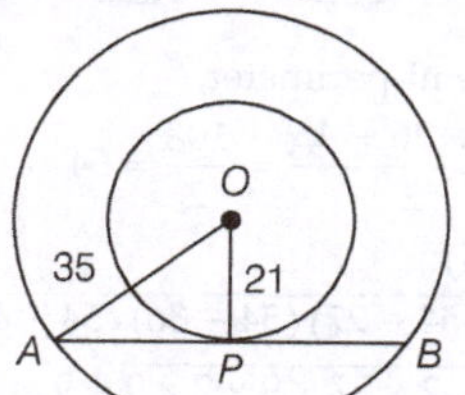

In ΔAOP, $AO^2 = AP^2 + PO^2$

$35^2 = AP^2 + 21^2$

$\Rightarrow \quad AP^2 = 35^2 - 21^2$

$\Rightarrow \quad AP^2 = 1225 - 441$

$\Rightarrow \quad AP^2 = 784$

$\Rightarrow \quad AP = 28$ cm

Length of chord $= 28 \times 2 = 56$ cm

417. (a) According to the question,

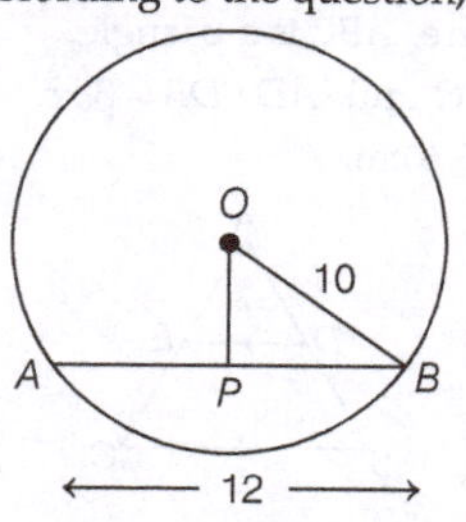

We know that, in a circle a perpendicular divides a chord into 2 equal sides.

So, $AP = PB = \frac{AB}{2} = \frac{12}{2} = 6$ units

In ΔPOB, $OP^2 = (10)^2 - (6)^2$

$\Rightarrow \quad OP^2 = 100 - 36 \Rightarrow OP^2 = 64$

$\Rightarrow \quad OP = 8$ units

Hence, the chord is 8 units away from its centre.

418. (c) Given, $\Delta ABC \sim \Delta DEF$

So, $\frac{\text{Area of } \Delta ABC}{\text{Area of } \Delta DEF} = \frac{BC^2}{EF^2}$

$\frac{0.64}{0.0121} = \frac{BC^2}{0.154^2}$

$\Rightarrow \quad BC = \frac{0.8 \times 0.154}{0.11}$

$\therefore \quad BC = 1.12$ m

419. (b) According to the question,

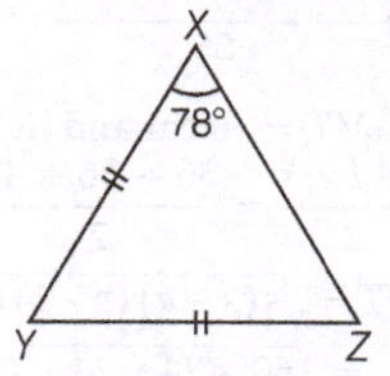

As, $XY = YZ$, therefore, $\angle X = \angle Z = 78°$

$\therefore \quad \angle Y = [180° - (78 + 78)°]$

$\angle Y = (180° - 156°) = 24°$

420. (b) According to the question,

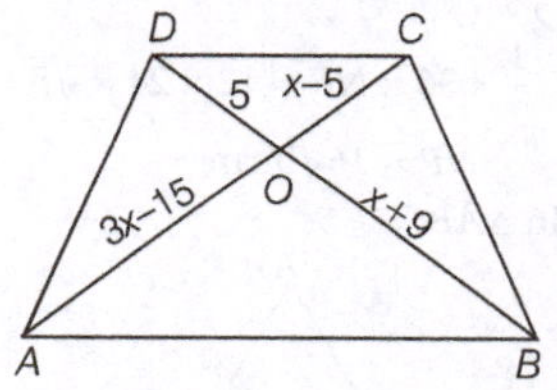

In ΔAOB and ΔDOC, $\angle DOC = \angle AOB$

[$\because$ vertically opposite angle]

$\angle ODC = \angle OBA$ [$\because$ alternate angle]

$\therefore \quad \Delta DOC \sim \Delta BOA \Rightarrow \frac{DO}{BO} = \frac{OC}{OA}$

$\frac{5}{x + 9} = \frac{x - 5}{3x - 15}$

$\Rightarrow \quad 5(3x - 15) = (x - 5)(x + 9)$

$\Rightarrow \quad 15x - 75 = x^2 - 5x + 9x - 45$

$\Rightarrow \quad x^2 - 11x + 30 = 0$

$\Rightarrow \quad (x - 6)(x - 5) = 0 \Rightarrow x = 6, 5$

$\therefore \quad x_1 = 6, x_2 = 5$

Now, $x_1^2 + x_2^2 = 6^2 + 5^2 = 36 + 25 = 61$

421. (d) Given, $\Delta ABC \sim \Delta DEF$,

So, $\frac{\text{Area of } \Delta ABC}{\text{Area of } \Delta DEF} = \left(\frac{AB}{DE}\right)^2$

$\Rightarrow \quad \frac{25}{144} = \frac{P^2}{DE^2}$

$\Rightarrow \quad DE^2 = \frac{144}{25} P^2$

$\Rightarrow \quad DE = \sqrt{\frac{144}{25} P^2}$

$\Rightarrow \quad DE = \frac{12}{5} P$

422. (c) According to the question,

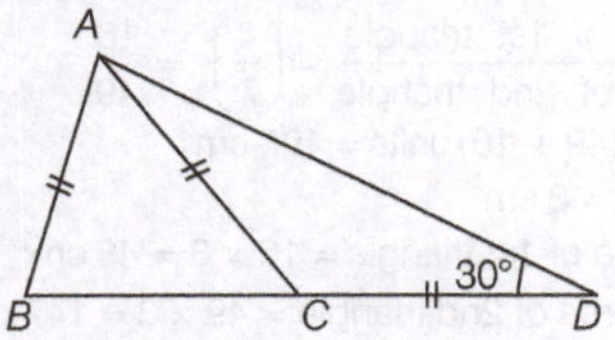

Here, $\angle ADC = \angle DAC = 30°$

$[\because AC = AB = CD]$

$\therefore \quad \angle ACD = 180° - (\angle ADC + \angle DAC)$

$\Rightarrow \quad \angle ACD = 180° - (30° + 30°)$

$\therefore \quad \angle ACD = 120°$

Now, $\quad \angle ACB = 180° - \angle ACD = 180° - 120°$

$= 60°$

$\therefore \quad \angle ACB = \angle ABC = 60° \quad [\because AB = AC]$

Now, $\angle BAC = 180° - (\angle ACB + \angle ABC)$

$= 180° - (60 + 60)°$

$\angle BAC = 60° \quad$ [∵ angles sum property]

Hence, all angles of triangle are $\angle ACB$, $\angle ABC$ and $\angle BAC = 60°, 60°$ and $60°$.

423. (b) According to the question,

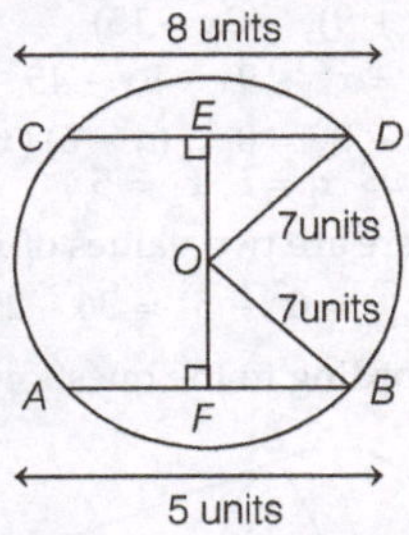

In ΔFOB, $OB^2 = OF^2 + FB^2$

$\Rightarrow \quad OB^2 = OF^2 + \left(\frac{AB}{2}\right)^2$

[∵ perpendicular from centre to chord bisect the chord]

$(7)^2 = OF^2 + \left(\frac{5}{2}\right)^2 \Rightarrow OF^2 = 49 - 6.25 = 42.75$

$\Rightarrow \quad OF = 6.53$ units

In ΔEOD, $OD^2 = OE^2 + ED^2$

$\Rightarrow \quad OD^2 = OE^2 + \left(\frac{CD}{2}\right)^2$

$\Rightarrow \quad 7^2 = OE^2 + \left(\frac{8}{2}\right)^2$

$\Rightarrow OE^2 = 49 - 16 = 33 \Rightarrow OE = 5.74$ units

Distance between the chords

$= OF + OE = 6.53 + 5.74$

$= 12.27 \sim 12.28$ units

424. (b) According to the question,

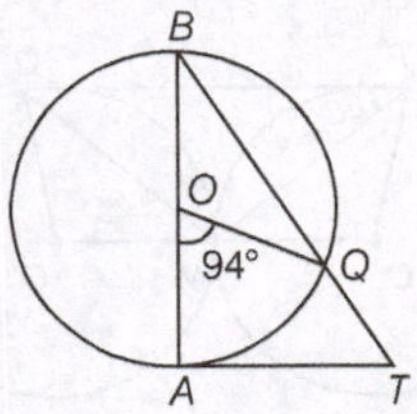

As, AT is a tangent, therefore $\angle BAT = 90°$

Now, $\angle ABQ = \frac{1}{2}\angle AOQ = \frac{1}{2} \times 94° = 47°$

In $\Delta ABT, \Rightarrow \quad 90° + 47° + \angle ATQ = 180°$

$[\because \angle ATB = \angle ATQ]$

$\Rightarrow \quad \angle ATQ = 180° - 137° \Rightarrow \angle ATQ = 43°$

425. (c) $\because d = 26$ cm, $r = \frac{26}{2} = 13$ cm

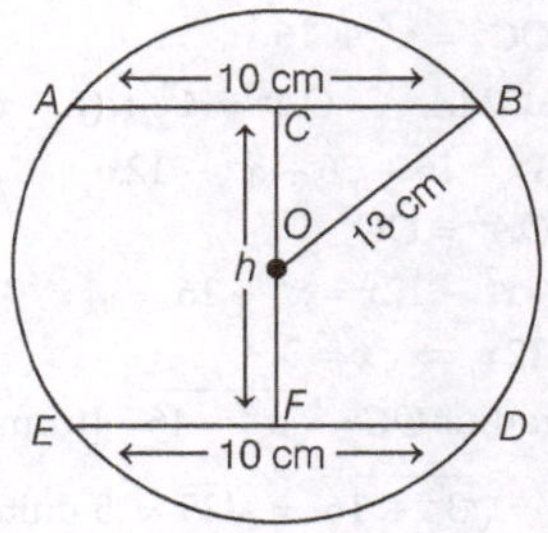

In ΔOCB, by Pythagoras theorem,

$OB^2 = OC^2 + BC^2$

$\Rightarrow \quad 13^2 = OC^2 + 5^2$

$\Rightarrow \quad OC^2 = 169 - 25$

$\Rightarrow \quad OC = \sqrt{144}$

$\therefore \quad OC = 12$ cm

Hence, $h = OC + OF = 12 + 12 \quad [\because OC = OF]$

$= 24$ cm

426. (c) Given, $\Delta DEF \sim \Delta GHI$

$DE = 64$ cm, $GH = 24$ cm

Also, perimeter of $\Delta GHI = 72$ cm

$\because \quad \Delta DEF \sim \Delta GHI$

$\therefore \quad \frac{DE}{GH} = \frac{\text{Perimeter of } \Delta DEF}{\text{Perimeter of } \Delta GHI}$

$\frac{64}{24} = \frac{\text{Perimeter of } \Delta DEF}{72}$

Perimeter of $\Delta DEF = 192$ cm

Hence, $EF + FD = 192 - 64$

$= 128$ cm

427. (b) Given, $MQ = 5$ cm, $NS = 8$ cm

$PQ = 12$ cm and $RS = 15$ cm

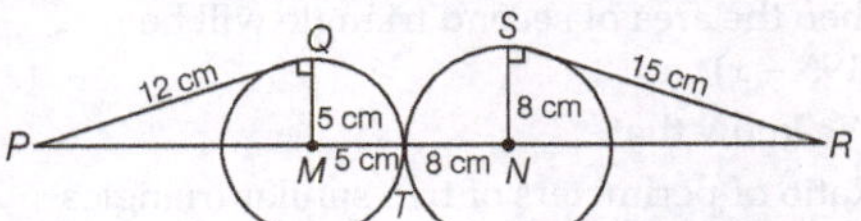

$\therefore$ In ΔPMQ, by Pythagoras theorem,

$PM^2 = PQ^2 + MQ^2$

$\Rightarrow \quad PM^2 = 12^2 + 5^2$

$\Rightarrow \quad PM = \sqrt{144 + 25}$

$\Rightarrow \quad PM = \sqrt{169} = 13$ cm

In ΔRNS, by Pythagoras theorem,

$RN^2 = NS^2 + SR^2$

$\Rightarrow \quad RN^2 = 8^2 + 15^2$

$\Rightarrow \quad RN = \sqrt{64 + 225}$

$\therefore \quad RN = \sqrt{289} = 17$ cm

$\therefore \quad PR = PM + MT + TN + RN$

$= 13 + 5 + 8 + 17 = 43$ cm

428. (b) According to the question,

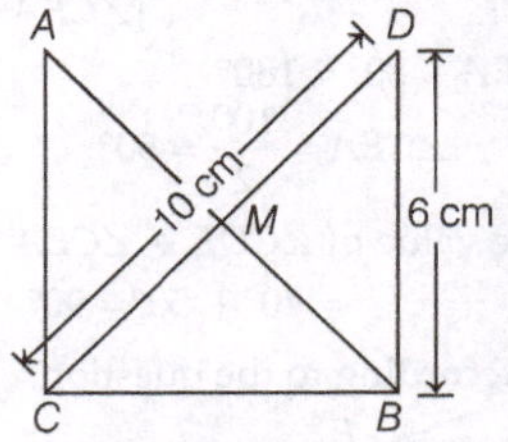

$\because \quad CD = 10$ cm

$\therefore \quad CM + MD = 10$ cm

$CM + CM = 10$ cm $\quad [\because CM = MD]$

$\Rightarrow \quad 2CM = 10 \text{ cm} \Rightarrow CM = 5$ cm

429. (a) According to the question,

Length of direct common tangent

$= \sqrt{d^2 - (r_1 - r_2)^2} = \sqrt{(80)^2 - (35 - 25)^2}$

$= \sqrt{6400 - 100} = \sqrt{6300}$ cm $\quad$ ...(i)

Length of transverse common tangent

$= \sqrt{d^2 - (r_1 + r_2)^2} = \sqrt{(80)^2 - (35 + 25)^2}$

$= \sqrt{6400 - 3600} = \sqrt{2800}$

Now, required ratio $= \frac{\sqrt{2800}}{\sqrt{6300}} = \frac{10 \times 2\sqrt{7}}{10 \times 3\sqrt{7}} = \frac{2}{3}$

$= 2 : 3$

430. (d) According to the question,

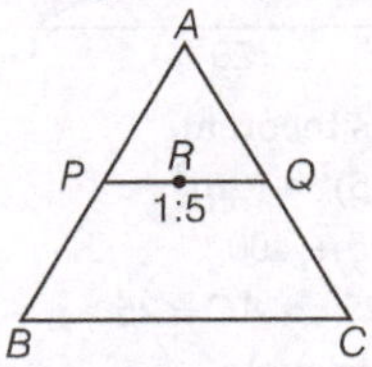

$PR : RQ = 1 : 5 = x : 5x$ and $x = 6$ cm

$\therefore \quad 6x = 6 \times 6 = 36 \text{ cm} \Rightarrow PQ = 36$ cm

Now, $\quad BC = 2 \times PQ = 2 \times 36 = 72$ cm

$\left[\because PQ = \frac{BC}{2}\right]$

431. (a) According to the question,

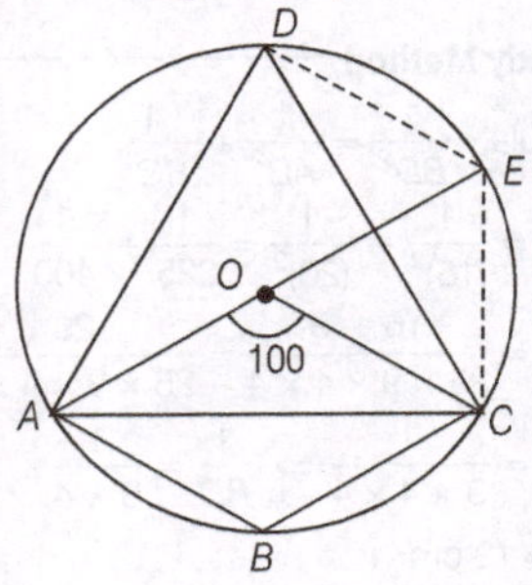

In ΔADC,

$\angle ADC = \frac{1}{2} \times \angle AOC = \frac{1}{2} \times 100° = 50°$

$[\because AC$ is a chord$]$

Now, $\angle ADE = \angle ADC + \angle CDE$

$\Rightarrow \quad 90° = 50° + \angle CDE$

$[\because AE$ is a diameter$]$

$\Rightarrow \quad \angle CDE = 90° - 50° = 40°$

Again, in ΔOEC,

$\angle CEO + \angle ECO + \angle COE = 180°$

$\Rightarrow\ 2\angle CEA + \angle COE = 180°$ $[\angle CEA = \angle ECO]$

$\Rightarrow\ 2\angle CEA + 80° = 180°$

$\Rightarrow\ \angle CEA = \frac{100}{2} = 50°$

Hence, the value of $\angle CDE + \angle CEA$ $= 40° + 50° = 90°$

432. (c) According to the question,

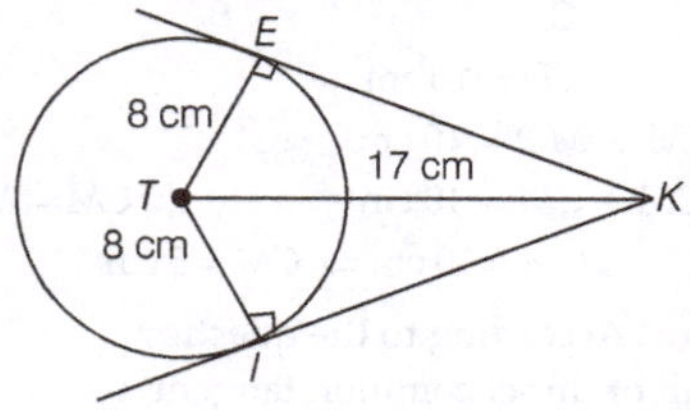

In ΔETK, $TK^2 = ET^2 + EK^2$

$\Rightarrow\ (17)^2 = (8)^2 + EK^2$

$\Rightarrow\ EK^2 = 289 - 64 = 225 \Rightarrow EK = 15$

Now, area of quadrilateral $TEKI$

$= \frac{1}{2} \times 15 \times 8 \times 2 = 120$ sq. cm

433. (b)

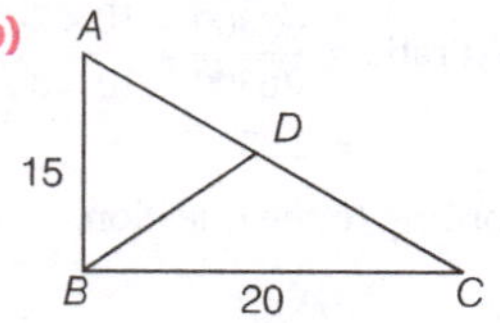

By Pythagoras theorem,

$AC^2 = (15)^2 + (20)^2$

$\Rightarrow\ AC^2 = 225 + 400$

$\Rightarrow\ AC^2 = 625 \Rightarrow AC = 25$

Now, area of triangle

$= \frac{1}{2} \times AB \times BC = \frac{1}{2} \times AC \times BD$

$\Rightarrow\ \frac{1}{2} \times 15 \times 20 = \frac{1}{2} \times 25 \times BD$

$\Rightarrow\ BD = \frac{15 \times 20}{25} \Rightarrow BD = 12$

Speedy Method

By formula, $\frac{1}{BD^2} = \frac{1}{AB^2} + \frac{1}{BC^2}$

$\Rightarrow\ \frac{1}{BD^2} = \frac{1}{(15)^2} + \frac{1}{(20)^2} = \frac{1}{225} + \frac{1}{400}$

$\Rightarrow\ \frac{1}{BD^2} = \frac{16+9}{25 \times 9 \times 4 \times 4} = \frac{25}{25 \times 9 \times 4 \times 4}$

$\Rightarrow\ \frac{1}{BD^2} = \frac{1}{9 \times 4 \times 4} \Rightarrow \frac{1}{BD} = \frac{1}{3 \times 4}$

$\therefore\ BD = 12$ cm

434. (c) Given, two parallel chords AB and CD.

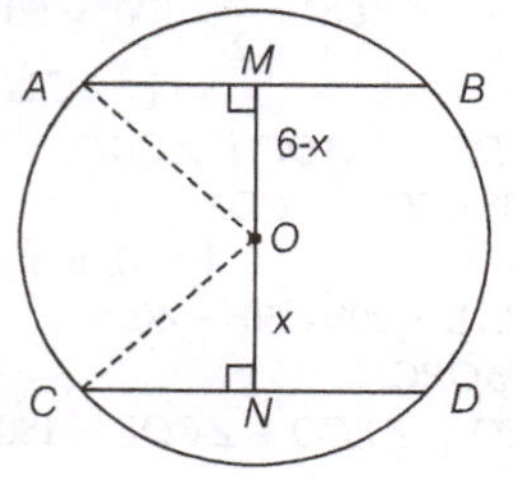

$AB = CD = 8$ units,

Let $ON = x$ units,

Then, $OM = (6 - x)$ units

Now, $AM = \frac{1}{2} \times 8 = 4$ units

$CN = \frac{1}{2} \times 8 = 4$ units

In right ΔONC,

$OC^2 = ON^2 + CN^2 \Rightarrow OC^2 = x^2 + 4^2$

$\Rightarrow\ OC^2 = x^2 + 16$

In right ΔOMA, $OA^2 = 4^2 + (6 - x)^2$

$\Rightarrow\ OA^2 = 16 + 36 + x^2 - 12x$

Now, $OA^2 = OC^2$

$16 + 36 + x^2 - 12x = x^2 + 16$

$\Rightarrow\ 36 = 12x \Rightarrow x = 3$

Now, radius $OC = \sqrt{x^2 + 16}$ [from Eq. (i)]

$= \sqrt{3^2 + 16} = \sqrt{25} = 5$ units

435. (d) Given,

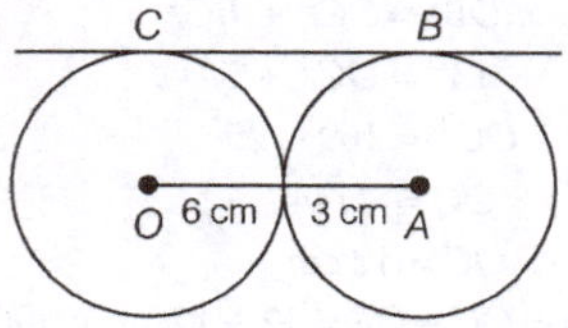

Radius of first circle $(R) = 6$ cm

Radius of second circle $(r) = 3$ cm

Length of their common tangent

$(CB) = 2 \times \sqrt{R \times r} = 2 \times \sqrt{6 \times 3}$

$= 2 \times \sqrt{18} = 6\sqrt{2}$ cm

436. (c) Given, $\Delta ABC \sim \Delta DEF$

By Area similarity theorem,

$\frac{\text{ar}(\Delta ABC)}{\text{ar}(\Delta EDF)} = \frac{BC^2}{DF^2}$

$\frac{9}{4} = \frac{8^2}{DF^2} \Rightarrow \frac{9}{4} = \frac{64}{DF^2} \Rightarrow DF^2 = \frac{64 \times 4}{9}$

$\Rightarrow\ DF = \sqrt{\frac{64 \times 4}{9}} = \frac{16}{3} = 5\frac{1}{3}$

437. (a) Let the area of first triangle be x cm^2, then the area of second triangle will be $(195 - x)$ cm^2.

We know that,

Ratio of perimeters of two similar triangles

= Ratio of their corresponding sides

$\Rightarrow$ Ratio of their corresponding sides $= \frac{4}{7}$

By similarity, $\frac{x}{195 - x} = \left(\frac{4}{7}\right)^2$

$49x = 3120 - 16x \Rightarrow 65x = 3120$

$\Rightarrow\ x = \frac{3120}{65} \Rightarrow x = 48$ cm^2

Area of second triangle $= 195 - x$

$= 195 - 48 = 147$ cm^2

$\frac{1}{3}$ rd of the difference between areas

$= \frac{1}{3}(147 - 48) = \frac{99}{3} = 33$ cm^2

Speedy Method

$\frac{\text{area of 1st triangle}}{\text{area of 2nd triangle}} = \left(\frac{4}{7}\right)^2 = \frac{16}{49}$

Here $(49 + 16)$ units $= 195$ cm^2

1 unit $= 3$ cm^2

$\therefore$ Area of 1st triangle $= 16 \times 3 = 48$ cm^2

and area of 2nd triangle $= 49 \times 3 = 147$ cm^2

$\therefore$ Required value $= (147 - 48) \times \frac{1}{3} = \frac{99}{3}$

$= 33$ cm^2

438. (b) According to the question,

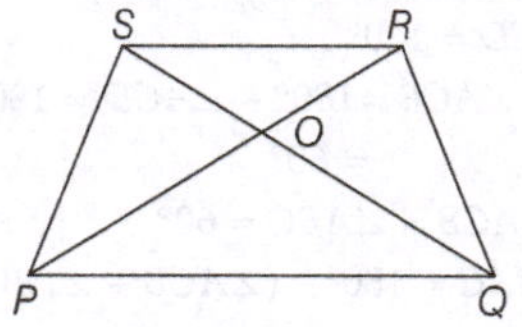

In equilateral trapezium $PQRS$,

$PO = 3x - 15 \Rightarrow OQ = x + 9 \Rightarrow OR = x - 5$

$OS = 5$

Now, $\Delta SRO \sim \Delta QPO \therefore \frac{SO}{QO} = \frac{RO}{PO}$

$\Rightarrow\ \frac{5}{(x+9)} = \frac{(x-5)}{(3x-15)}$

$\Rightarrow\ 15x - 75 = x^2 + 9x - 5x - 45$

$\Rightarrow\ x^2 - 11x + 30 = 0 \Rightarrow (x-6)(x-5) = 0$

$\Rightarrow\ x = 6, 5 \Rightarrow x_1 = 6, x_2 = 5$

[$\because$ there are two values of x, x_1 and x_2]

Now, $(x_1^2 - x_2^2) = 6^2 - 5^2 = 36 - 25 = 11$

439. (c) According to the question,

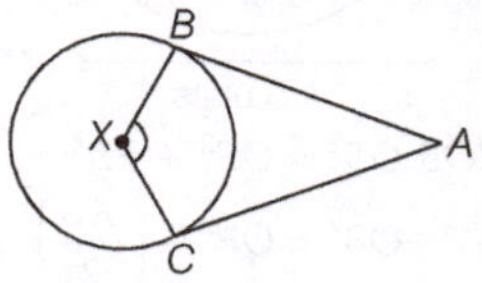

$\angle BXC = 125°$

$\therefore\ \angle BXC + \angle BAC = 180°$

$\therefore \angle BAC = 180° - \angle BXC$ $\quad \because \angle B + \angle C = \sqrt{80}]$

$= 180° - 125° = 55°$

440. (a) According to the question,

Let the third side $= x$

$\therefore\ (18 + 6) > x > (18 - 6) \Rightarrow 24 > x > 12$

$\therefore$ Possible value of $x = 13, 14, 15, 16, 17, 18, 19, 20, 21, 22, 23$

$\therefore$ Total possible value of $x = 11$

441. (a) $\because AC = AB + BC$

$\Rightarrow\ 24 = 11 + 13 \Rightarrow 24 = 24$

$\therefore A, B, C$ are collinear.

So, there do not exist any circle, which is passed to the colinear points.

442. (b) Given,

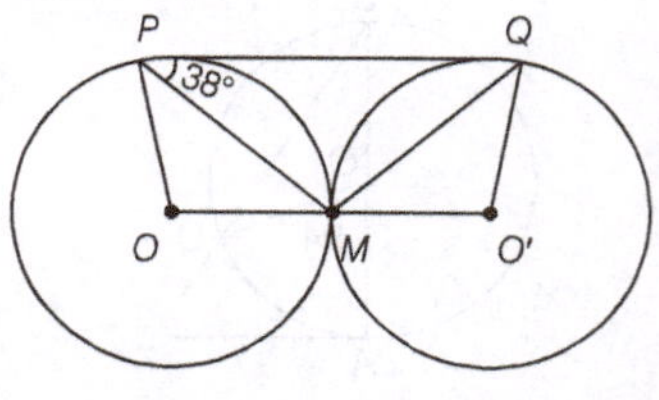

$\because \quad \angle OPQ = 90°$ and $\angle O'QP = 90°$

$\therefore \quad \angle OPM = 90° - 38° = 52° = \angle PMO$

[$OP = OM$]

In ΔOPM, $\angle POM = 180° - (52° + 52°) = 76°$

In quadrilateral $POO'Q$,

$90° + 76° + 90° + \angle QO'O = 360°$

$\Rightarrow \quad \angle QO'O = 360° - 256°$

$\angle QO'O = \angle QO'M = 104°$

In $\Delta MQO'$,

$\angle O'MQ = \angle MQO' = \dfrac{180° - 104°}{2} = 38°$

$\therefore \quad \angle MQP = 90 - 38° = 52°$

443. (b) According to the question,

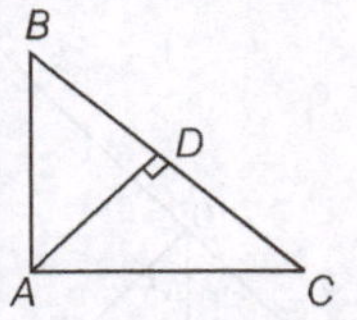

In ΔACB and ΔACD, $\angle BAC = \angle ADC = 90°$

$\angle ACB = \angle ACD$

$\therefore \quad \Delta BAC \sim \Delta ADC$ [from AA rule]

$\dfrac{\Delta BAC}{\Delta CDA} = \dfrac{BC^2}{CA^2} \Rightarrow \dfrac{63}{7} = \dfrac{BC^2}{5^2}$

$BC^2 = 9 \times 25 = 225 \Rightarrow BC = 15$ cm

444. (d) Given,

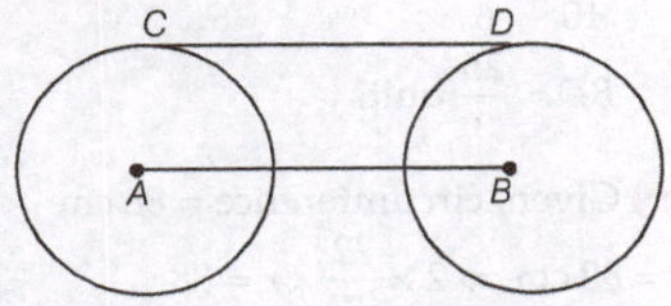

Distance between the centres $(d) = 30$ cm

and $r_1 = 32$ cm, $r_2 = 8$ cm

$\therefore \quad CD = \sqrt{d^2 - (r_1 - r_2)^2}$

$= \sqrt{(30)^2 - (32-8)^2}$

$= \sqrt{30^2 - 24^2} = \sqrt{(30+24)(30-24)}$

$= \sqrt{54 \times 6} = \sqrt{3 \times 18 \times 6} = \sqrt{18 \times 18} = 18$

$\therefore \quad CD = 18$ cm

445. (a) Given,

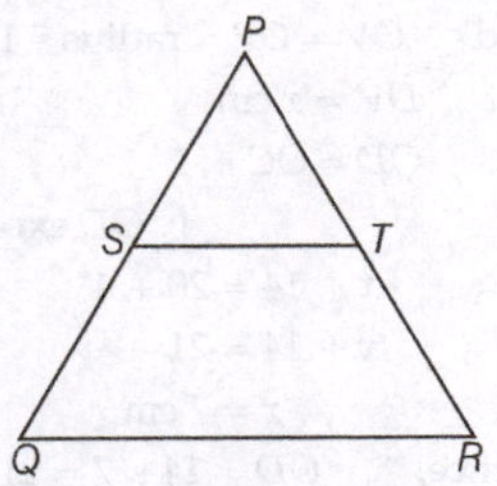

In ΔPQR and ΔPST,

$\angle QPR = \angle SPT$

$\angle PQR = \angle PST$ [$\because ST \parallel QR$]

$\therefore \quad \Delta PQR \sim \Delta PST$

Let the area of ΔPQR and ΔPST be 2 : 1

[$\because ST$, ΔPQR is divided into two equal area]

$= \dfrac{\text{area of } \Delta PQR}{\text{area of } \Delta PST} = \dfrac{PQ^2}{PS^2}$

$\therefore \quad \dfrac{PQ^2}{PS^2} = \dfrac{2}{1} \Rightarrow \dfrac{PQ}{PS} = \dfrac{\sqrt{2}}{1}$

$QS = PQ - PS = \sqrt{2} - 1$

Hence, $PS : QS = (1 : \sqrt{2} - 1)$

446. (b) Given,

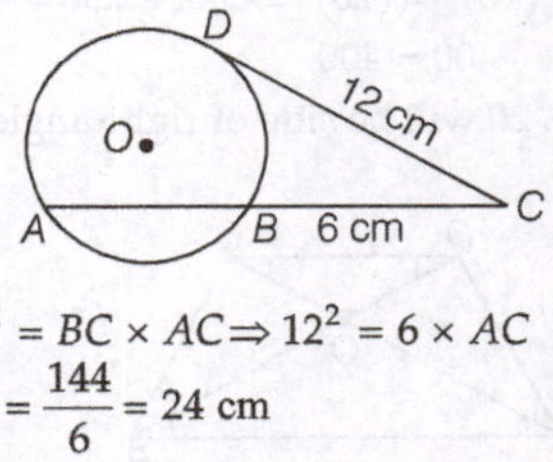

$CD^2 = BC \times AC \Rightarrow 12^2 = 6 \times AC$

$\Rightarrow \quad AC = \dfrac{144}{6} = 24$ cm

$\therefore \quad AB = AC - BC = 24 - 6 = 18$ cm

447. (a) Given, let BE is the height of ΔABC.

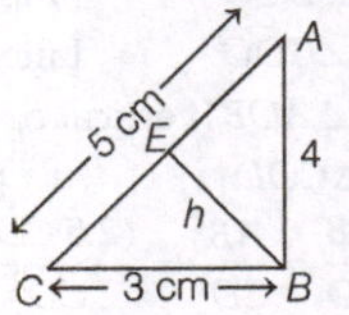

$\therefore$ Area of $\Delta ABC = \dfrac{1}{2} \times$ Base $\times$ Height

$\Rightarrow \quad \dfrac{1}{2} \times 5 \times h = \dfrac{1}{2} \times 3 \times 4$

$\Rightarrow \quad h = \dfrac{12}{5} = 2.4$ cm

$\therefore$ Length of perpendicular vertex = 2.4 cm

Speedy Method

$\therefore BE = \dfrac{AB \times BC}{AC} = \dfrac{4 \times 3}{5} = 2.4$ cm

448. (d) According to the question,

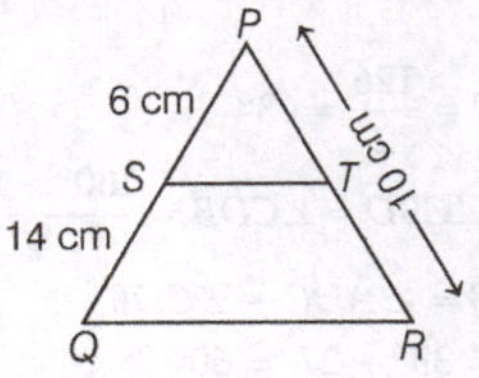

Given, $PR = 10$ cm, $PS = 6$ cm

and $QS = 14$ cm

$\because \quad \Delta PST \sim \Delta PQR$

$\therefore \quad \dfrac{PT}{PR} = \dfrac{PS}{PQ} = \dfrac{6}{(6+14)} = \dfrac{PT}{10}$

$\therefore \quad PT = 3$ cm

449. (b) $AP = QC = x$ cm (let)

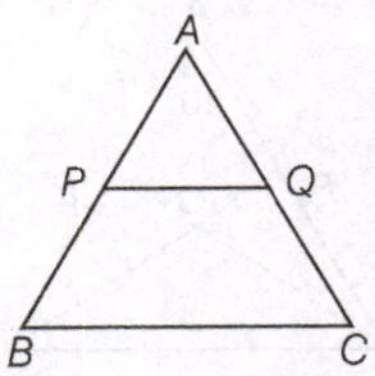

Given, $AB = 12$ cm $\Rightarrow AQ = 2$ cm

$\therefore \quad \Delta APQ \sim \Delta ABC$

$\therefore \quad \dfrac{AP}{AB} = \dfrac{AQ}{AC} \Rightarrow \dfrac{x}{12} = \dfrac{2}{x+2}$

$\Rightarrow \quad x(x+2) = 4 \times 6$

On comparing, $x = 4$ cm

$\therefore$ Length of $CQ = 4$ cm

450. (a) According to the question,

$XY \parallel FG$ and $EX : XF = 2 : 3$

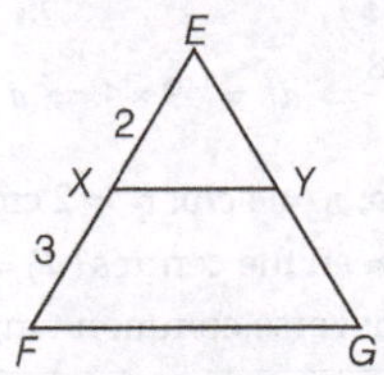

Area of $(XYGF) = 44$ cm^2

Let the area of $\Delta EXY = x$ cm^2

Then, $\quad \Delta EXY \sim \Delta EFG$

$\therefore \dfrac{\text{Area of } (\Delta EXY)}{\text{Area of } (\Delta EFG)} = \dfrac{(EX)^2}{(EF)^2} = \dfrac{x}{(x+44)}$

$\Rightarrow \quad \dfrac{(2)^2}{(5)^2} = \dfrac{x}{x+44} \Rightarrow 25x = 4x + 176$

$\Rightarrow \quad x = \dfrac{176}{21} = 8.38$

$\therefore$ Area of $\Delta EXY = 8.38$ cm^2

451. (b) According to the question,

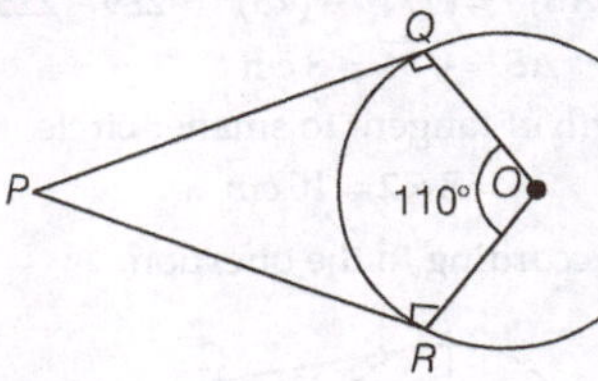

$\angle P + \angle Q + \angle C + \angle R = 360°$

$\Rightarrow \angle P + 90° + 110° + 90° = 360°$

$\Rightarrow \quad \angle P = 360° - 290° = 70°$

452. (b) Given, $\Delta ABC \sim \Delta QRP$, $AB = 18$ cm

$BC = 15$ cm

We know that,

$\dfrac{\text{Area } \Delta ABC}{\text{Area } \Delta QRP} = \dfrac{AB^2}{QR^2} = \dfrac{BC^2}{PR^2}$

$\Rightarrow \quad \dfrac{9}{4} = \dfrac{15^2}{PR^2} \Rightarrow PR^2 = \dfrac{225 \times 4}{9}$

$\Rightarrow \quad PR^2 = 100 \Rightarrow PR = 10$ cm

453. (b) Given, $\Delta ABC \sim \Delta PQR$

$\therefore \quad \dfrac{AB}{PQ} = \dfrac{BC}{QR} = \dfrac{AC}{PR} = \dfrac{\text{Perimeter of } \Delta ABC}{\text{Perimeter of } \Delta PQR}$

Now, $\dfrac{AB}{PQ} = \dfrac{BC}{QR} \Rightarrow \dfrac{8}{12} = \dfrac{BC}{18} \Rightarrow BC = 12$ cm

and $\dfrac{AB}{PQ} = \dfrac{AC}{PR} \Rightarrow \dfrac{8}{12} = \dfrac{AC}{24} \Rightarrow AC = 16$ cm

Perimeter of $\Delta ABC = AB + BC + AC$

$= 8 + 12 + 16 = 36$ cm

454. (c) Let diameter of circle = a cm

According to the question,

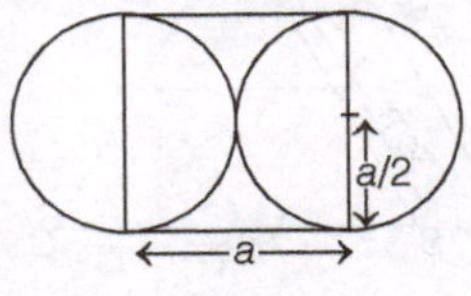

$$\pi r^2 + 42 = a^2 \Rightarrow \pi\left(\frac{a}{2}\right)^2 + 42 = a^2$$

$$\Rightarrow \frac{\pi a^2}{4} + 42 = a^2 \Rightarrow a^2\left(1 - \frac{\pi}{4}\right) = 42$$

$$\Rightarrow a^2\left(1 - \frac{22}{7 \times 4}\right) = 42 \Rightarrow a^2 \times \frac{6}{28} = 42$$

$$\Rightarrow a^2 = \frac{42 \times 28}{6} \Rightarrow a^2 = 49 \times 4 \Rightarrow a = 14 \text{ cm}$$

455. (d) Given, $r_1 = 4$ cm, $r_2 = 2$ cm,

Distance between the centres $(d) = 10$ cm

Length of transverse common tangent

$$= \sqrt{(d)^2 - (r_1 + r_2)^2} = \sqrt{(10)^2 - (4 + 2)^2}$$

$$= \sqrt{100 - 36} = \sqrt{64} = 8 \text{ cm}$$

456. (a) Given, $r = 15$ cm, $R = 17$ cm

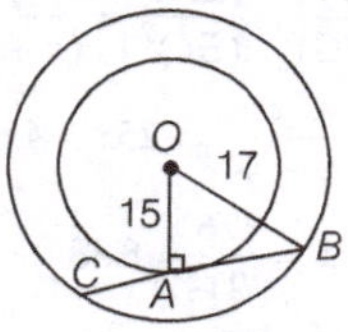

In ΔAOB, $(AB)^2 = (OB)^2 - (OA)^2$

$$\Rightarrow (AB)^2 = (17)^2 - (15)^2 = 289 - 225$$

$$\Rightarrow AB = \sqrt{64} = 8 \text{ cm}$$

$\therefore$ The length of tangent to smaller circle $= 8 \times 2 = 16$ cm

457. (a) According to the question,

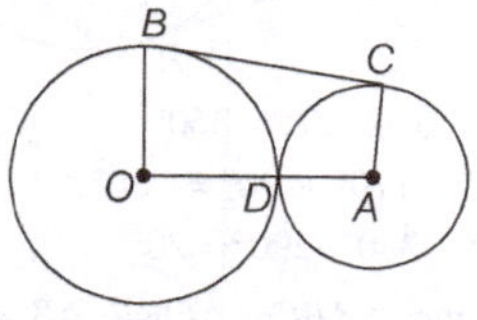

Length of the common tangent (BC)

$$= \sqrt{(OA)^2 - (OB - AC)^2}$$

$$= \sqrt{(49 + 16)^2 - (49 - 16)^2}$$

$$= \sqrt{(65)^2 - (33)^2} = \sqrt{4225 - 1089} = 56$$

458. (b) Given, area of two triangles ΔPQR and ΔXYZ are 12.96 cm^2 and 635.04 cm^2.

If $QR = 2.9$ cm

$$\therefore \left(\frac{PQ}{XY}\right)^2 = \left(\frac{QR}{YZ}\right)^2 = \frac{\text{Area of } \Delta PQR}{\text{Area of } \Delta XYZ}$$

$$\Rightarrow \left(\frac{2.9}{YZ}\right)^2 = \frac{12.96}{635.04} \Rightarrow \frac{8.41}{(YZ)^2} = \frac{12.96}{635.04}$$

$$\Rightarrow (YZ)^2 = \frac{8.41 \times 635.04}{12.96} = 412.09$$

$$\Rightarrow YZ = \sqrt{412.09} = 20.3 \text{ cm}$$

459. (c) According to the question,

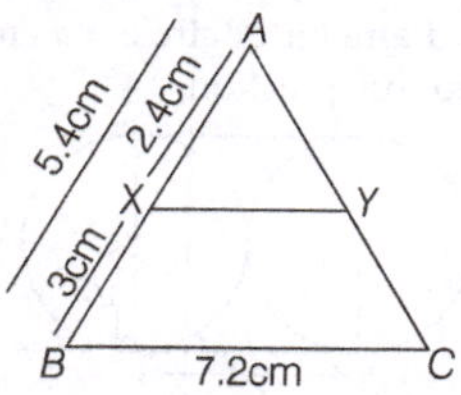

$$\frac{AX}{AB} = \frac{XY}{BC} \Rightarrow \frac{2.4}{5.4} = \frac{XY}{7.2}$$

$$\Rightarrow XY = \frac{2.4 \times 7.2}{5.4} = 3.2 \text{ cm}$$

460. (c) From option (d),

$$(12)^2 + (16)^2 = (20)^2 \Rightarrow 144 + 256 = 400$$

$$\Rightarrow 400 = 400$$

So, 12, 16, 20 will be side of right-angled triangle.

461. (a)

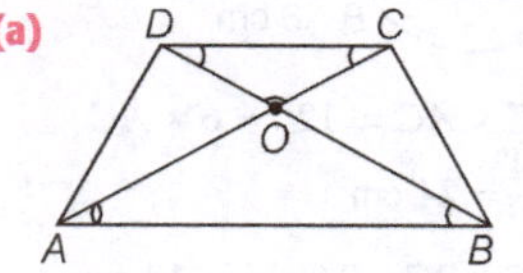

In ΔOCD and ΔOAB,

$\angle BAO = \angle DCO$ [alternate angles]

$\angle ABO = \angle CDO$ [alternate angles]

and $\angle COD = \angle AOB$ [vertical opposite angle]

$\therefore \Delta AOB \sim \Delta COD$ [rule of AAA]

$$\frac{\text{Area of } \Delta AOB}{\text{Area of } \Delta COD} = \frac{AB^2}{CD^2} = \frac{(2.5\,CD)^2}{CD^2}$$

$$= \frac{6.25}{1} = \frac{625}{100} = \frac{25}{4} = 25:4$$

462. (a)

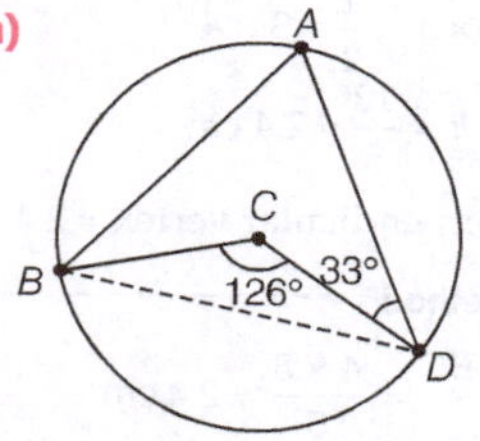

$\because$ The angle formed at the circumference of circle is the half of that of the centre of the circle.

$$\therefore \angle BAD = \frac{126}{2} = 63°$$

In ΔBCD, $\angle CBD = \angle CDB = \dfrac{180° - 126°}{2} = 27°$

$$\therefore \angle ADB = \angle ADC + \angle CDB = 33° + 27° = 60°$$

In ΔABD, $\angle ABD + \angle BAD + \angle ADB = 180°$

$$\angle ABD + 63° + 60° = 180°$$

$$\therefore \angle ABD = 180° - 123° = 57°$$

Hence, $\angle ABC = \angle ABD - \angle CBD$

$$= 57° - 27° = 30°$$

463. (d) Let isosceles triangle is ABC, where $AB = AC$

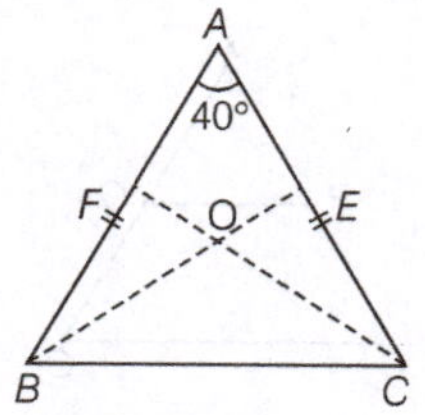

According to the question,

$$\angle BAC = 40° \text{ and } \angle BOC = 90° + \frac{\angle A}{2}$$

[from angle bisector theorem]

$$\Rightarrow \angle BOC = 90° + \frac{40°}{2}$$

$$\Rightarrow \angle BOC = 110°$$

464. (a) Given, $r_1 = 6$ cm, $r_2 = 3$ cm,

Transverse common tangent = 8 cm

Let the distance between the two circles $= d$ cm

$\therefore$ (Transverse common tangent)^2

$$= (d)^2 - (r_1 + r_2)^2 \Rightarrow 8^2 = d^2 - (6 + 3)^2$$

$$\Rightarrow 64 = d^2 - 81 \therefore d^2 = 81 + 64$$

$$d = \sqrt{145}$$

$\therefore$ Distance betweeen two circles $= \sqrt{145}$ cm

465. (c) According to the question,

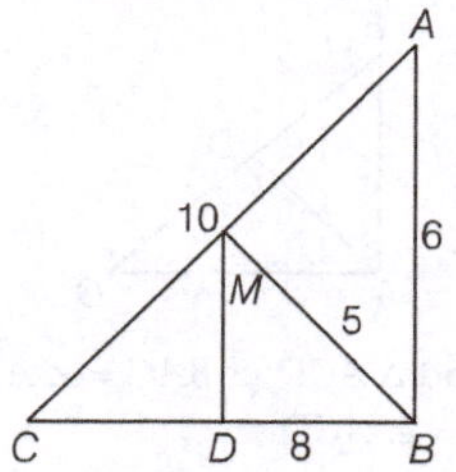

$AB = 6$ units, $BC = 8$ units

$AC = 10$ units, $BM = 5$ units.

$$\Delta BMD \sim \Delta ABC \therefore \frac{BD}{AC} = \frac{BM}{AB}$$

$$\Rightarrow \frac{BD}{10} = \frac{5}{6} \Rightarrow BD = \frac{5 \times 10}{6}$$

$$\Rightarrow BD = \frac{25}{3} \text{ units}$$

466. (b) Given, circumference = 88 cm

$$\Rightarrow 2\pi r = 88 \text{ cm} \Rightarrow 2 \times \frac{22}{7} \times r = 88$$

$$\therefore r = 14 \text{ cm}$$

According to the question,

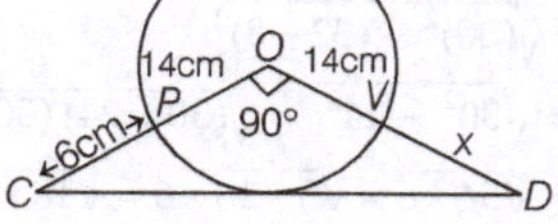

$PC = 6$ cm (given)

and $OV = OP =$ radius $= 14$ cm

Let $DV = x$ cm

As, $OD = OC + 1$

[$\because OD$ exceeds OC by 1 cm]

$$\therefore x + 14 = 20 + 1$$

$$\Rightarrow x + 14 = 21$$

$$\therefore x = 7 \text{ cm}$$

Hence, $OD = 14 + 7 = 21$ cm

In ΔCOD, by Pythagoras, we get

$$CD = \sqrt{(OC)^2 + (OD)^2}$$

$$\Rightarrow CD = \sqrt{(20)^2 + (21)^2}$$

$$\Rightarrow CD = \sqrt{400 + 441} = \sqrt{841}$$

$$\therefore CD = 29 \text{ cm}$$

Now, half of $CD = \dfrac{29}{2} = 14.5$ cm

467. (c) According to the question,

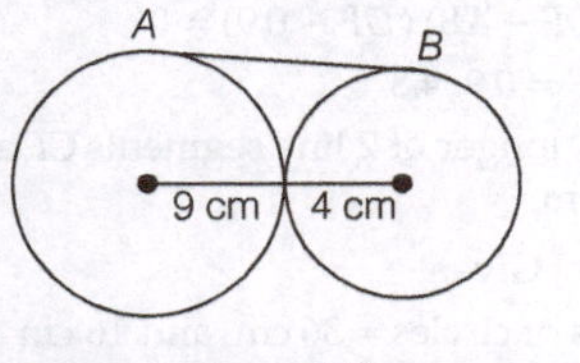

By using tangent-segment theorem,

$AB = \sqrt{d^2 - (r_1 - r_2)^2}$

$AB = \sqrt{13^2 - (9-4)^2}$ [$\because r_1 = 9$ cm, $r_2 = 4$ cm]

$= \sqrt{169 - 25} = \sqrt{144}$

$\therefore \quad AB = 12$

Hence, length of $AB = 12$ cm

468. (a) Given, $\angle RPQ = 27°$

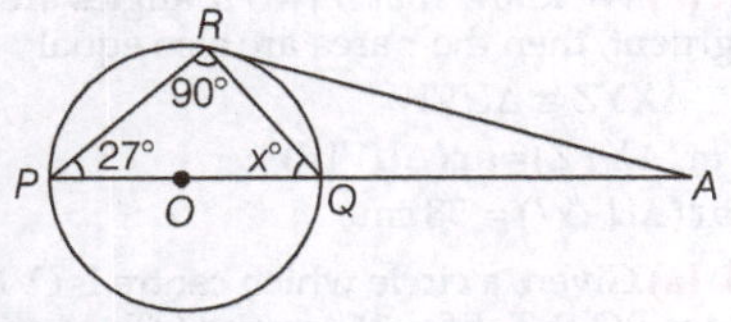

Since, PQ is a diameter.

$\therefore \angle PRQ$ is 90° because it is subtended by a diameter in semi-circle.

By applying angle sum property,

$\angle PRQ + \angle RPQ + \angle RQP = 180°$

$\Rightarrow \quad 90° + 27° + \angle RQP = 180°$

$\Rightarrow \quad \angle RQP = 180° - 117° = 63°$

469. (a) Given, AD and BE are medians of ΔABC and they intersect at G at right angles.

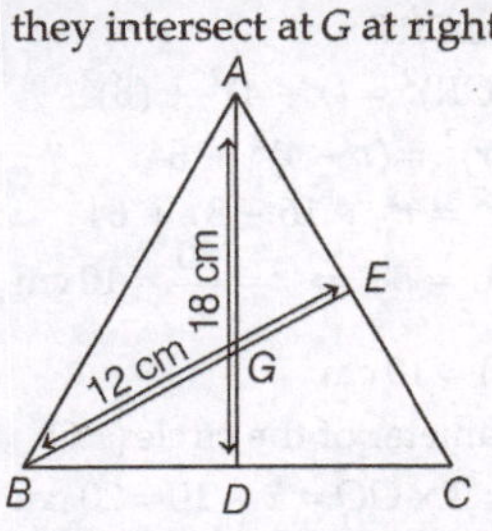

$\because$ In any triangle, the centroid divides each median into a ratio of 2 : 1 with the longer segment being closer to the vertex.

$GD = \frac{1}{3} \times 18 = 6$ cm

$BG = \frac{2}{3} \times 12 = 8$ cm

By using Pythagoras theorem,

$BD^2 = BG^2 + GD^2$

$\Rightarrow \quad BD^2 = 8^2 + 6^2$

$\therefore \quad BD = 10$ cm

Hence, length of $BD = 10$ cm

470. (d) $\because$ $ABCD$ is a cyclic quadrilateral.

$\therefore \angle ABC + \angle ADC = 180°$

$\Rightarrow \quad 85° + \angle ADC = 180°$

$\Rightarrow \quad \angle ADC = 95°$

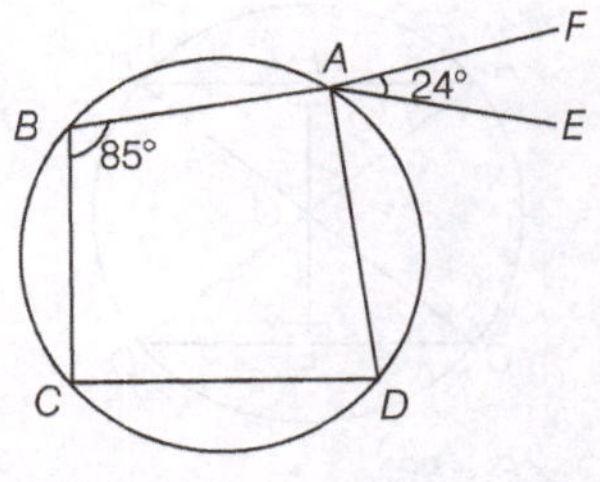

According to the question,

$AE \parallel CD$

$\therefore \angle EAD = \angle ADC = 95°$ ($\because$ alternate angles)

We know that, the exterior angle of a cyclic quadrilateral is equal to the interior opposite angle.

$\therefore \quad \angle BCD = \angle DAF$

$\angle BCD = \angle EAD + \angle EAF$

$\Rightarrow \angle BCD = 95° + 24°$

$\Rightarrow \angle BCD = 119°$

Hence, $\angle BCD = 119°$

471. (c) Chord, $AB = 20$ cm and $CD = 12$ cm,

Radius, $\quad OA = OC = 5\sqrt{13}$ cm

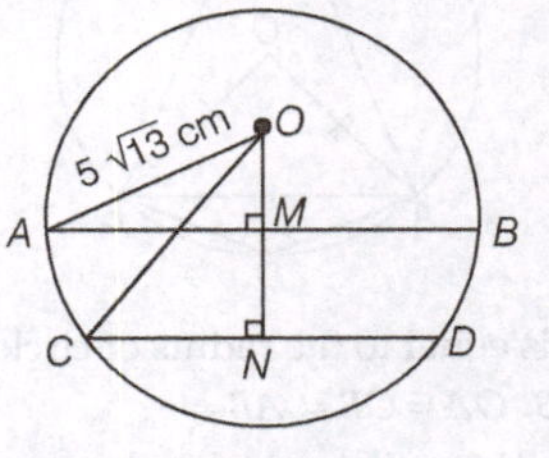

$\therefore AM = MB$ and $CN = ND$

In right ΔOMA,

$(5\sqrt{13})^2 = OM^2 + \left(\frac{20}{2}\right)^2 \quad \left(\because AM = \frac{1}{2} AB\right)$

$\Rightarrow \quad 325 = OM^2 + 100 \Rightarrow OM^2 = 225$

$\therefore \quad OM = \sqrt{225} = 15$ cm

Similarly, in right ΔONC,

$OC^2 = ON^2 + CN^2$

$(5\sqrt{13})^2 = ON^2 + \left(\frac{12}{2}\right)^2 \quad \left(\because CN = \frac{1}{2} \times CD\right)$

$\Rightarrow \quad 325 = ON^2 + 36 \Rightarrow ON^2 = 289$

$\Rightarrow \quad ON = \sqrt{289} = 17$ cm

$\therefore$ Distance between two chords $= MN$

$= ON - OM = 17 - 15 = 2$ cm

472. (b) Given,

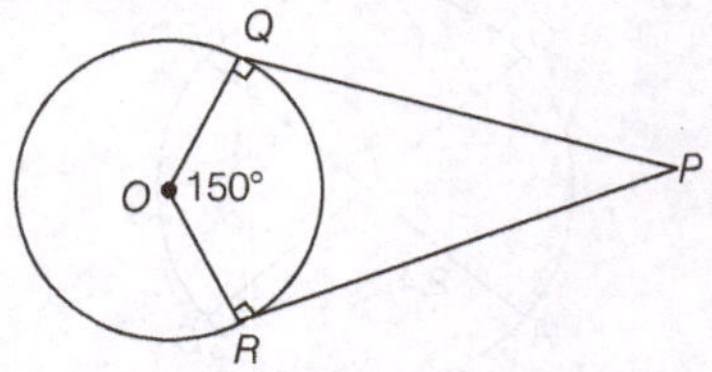

$\angle QOR = 150°, \angle OQP = 90°$

and $\quad \angle ORP = 90°$

In quadrilateral $OQPR$

$\angle QOR + \angle OQP + \angle ORP + \angle QPR = 360°$

($\because$ angles sum property of quadrilateral)

$\Rightarrow \quad 150° + 90° + 90° + \angle QPR = 360°$

$\Rightarrow \quad 330° + \angle QPR = 360°$

$\therefore \quad \angle QPR = 360° - 330° = 30°$

473. (a) We know that, $\Delta ABC \sim \Delta DEF$

We know that, the ratio of perimeters of two similar triangles is equal to the ratio of their corresponding sides.

$\frac{\text{Perimeter of } \Delta ABC}{\text{Perimeter of } \Delta DEF} = \frac{AB}{DE}$

$\Rightarrow \quad \frac{24}{9} = \frac{AB}{3} \Rightarrow AB = 8$ cm

Now, by Area similarity theorem,

$\frac{\text{Area } (\Delta ABC)}{\text{Area } (\Delta DEF)} = \frac{AB^2}{DE^2} = \frac{8^2}{3^2} = \frac{64}{9}$

$\therefore$ Required ratio $= 64 : 9$

474. (c) According to the question,

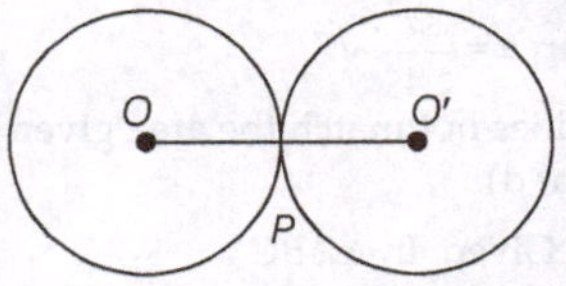

Statement given in option (c) is true, that if two circles touch each other, the point of contact (P) lies on the line joining the two centres O and O'.

475. (a) $\because$ XQ bisects $\angle X$,

$\therefore \quad \frac{XY}{XZ} = \frac{YQ}{QZ}$

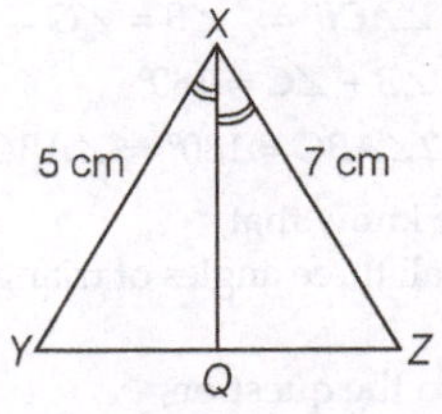

$\Rightarrow \quad \frac{5}{7} = \frac{YQ}{QZ}$ Hence, $\frac{YQ}{QZ} = \frac{5}{7} = 5:7$

476. (a) Let the three angles of triangle are $\angle A, \angle B, \angle C$.

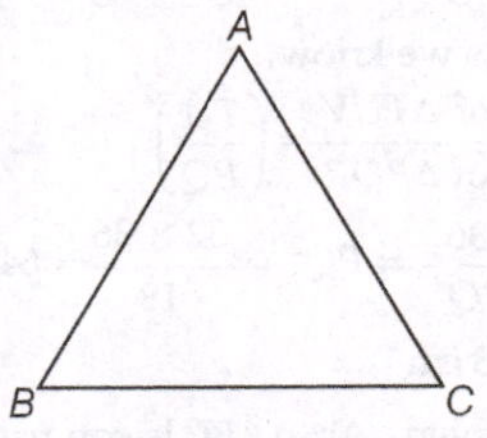

Given, ratio of two angles $\angle A : \angle B = 3:7$

Let angles are $3x$ and $7x$.

$\therefore \quad \angle A + \angle B + \angle C = 180°$

$3x + 7x + \angle C = 180°$

$\therefore \quad \angle C = 180 - 10x$

According to the question,

$\angle A + \angle B = \angle C$

$\Rightarrow \quad 3x + 7x = 180° - 10x \therefore 20x = 180°$

$\Rightarrow \quad x = 9$

Smallest angle, $3x = 9 \times 3 = 27$

Hence, the smallest angle $= 27°$

477. (d) Except option (d), all are true. Only statement (d) is not true because area of isosceles triangle $= \frac{y}{4}\sqrt{4x^2 - y^2}$

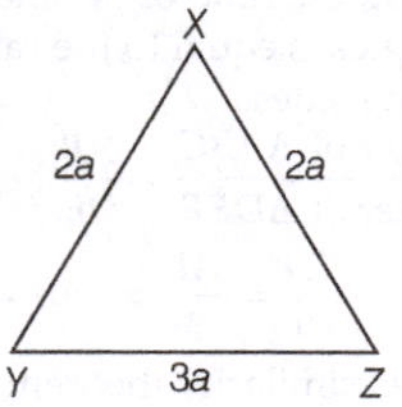

Here, $x = 2a$, $y = 3a$

$\therefore$ Area $= \frac{3a}{4}\sqrt{4(2a)^2 - (3a)^2}$

$= \frac{3a}{4}\sqrt{16a^2 - 9a^2} = \frac{3a}{4}\sqrt{7a^2}$

Hence, area $= \frac{3a^2}{4}\sqrt{7}$

(which does not match the area given in statement d).

478. (d) Given, In ΔABC

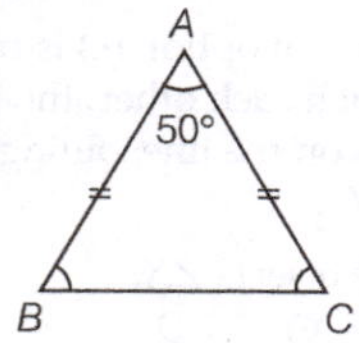

As given, $AB = AC$

$\therefore\ \angle ABC = \angle ACB \Rightarrow \angle B = \angle C$

Then, $\angle A + \angle B + \angle C = 180°$

$\Rightarrow\ 50 + 2\angle ABC = 180° \Rightarrow \angle ABC = 65°$

479. (b) We know that,

The sum of all three angles of triangle are 180°.

According to the question,

$(x - 15)° + (x + 45)° + (x + 60)° = 180°$

$\Rightarrow (3x + 90)° = 180°$

$\Rightarrow 3x = 180° - 90° = 90° \Rightarrow x = \frac{90°}{3} = 30°$

$\therefore$ The triangle will be right angled triangle.

480. (b) As we know,

$\therefore\ \frac{\text{Area of } \Delta TUV}{\text{Area of } \Delta PQR} = \left(\frac{TU}{PQ}\right)^2$

$\Rightarrow \frac{18}{32} = \frac{36}{PQ^2} \Rightarrow PQ^2 = \frac{32 \times 36}{18} = 64$

$\Rightarrow PQ = 8$ cm

481. (a) Given, As, ΔABC is congruent to ΔPQR, Then $\angle A = \angle P$

In ΔPQR, from the angle sum property of a triangle, we can write

$\angle P + \angle Q + \angle R = 180°$

$\Rightarrow \angle P + 35° + 90° = 180°$

$\Rightarrow \angle P = 180° - (35° + 90°)$

$\Rightarrow \angle P = 180° - 125° \Rightarrow \angle P = 55°$

So, $\angle A = \angle P = 55°$

482. (b) According to the question,

$AB = CD = 6$ cm, $R = \frac{10}{2} = 5$ cm

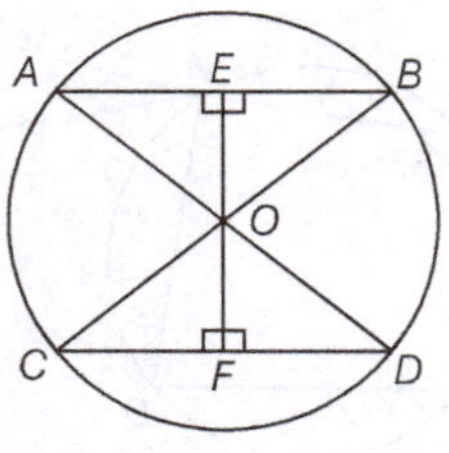

In ΔBEO, $\angle E = 90°$,

$OB = 5$ cm, $BE = \frac{6}{2} = 3$ cm,

By Pythagoras theorem,

$EO = \sqrt{(OB^2 - BE^2)} = \sqrt{(5^2 - 3^2)} = \sqrt{(25 - 9)}$

$= \sqrt{(16)} = 4$ cm

Now, the length of $EF = 2 \times OE$

$= 2 \times 4 = 8$ cm

Required distance between chord is 8 cm.

483. (c) According to the question,

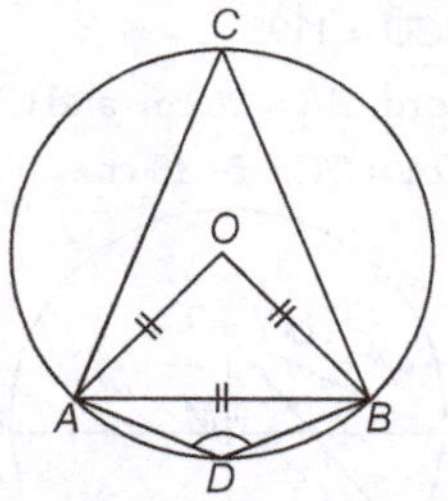

Let, AB is equal to the radius of circle.

In ΔAOB, $OA = OB = AB = r$

So, ΔOAB is equilateral triangle.

$\therefore\ \angle AOB = 60°$

$\therefore\ \angle ACB = \frac{1}{2} \times \angle AOB = \frac{1}{2} \times 60° = 30°$

Now, $\square ABCD$ is cyclic quadrilateral,

$\therefore\ \angle ACB + \angle ADB = 180°$

$\Rightarrow\ 30° + \angle ADB = 180°$

$\therefore\ \angle ADB = 180° - 30° = 150°$

Hence, angle subtended by the chord at any point on the minor arc of the circle is 150°.

484. (b) Given, $m(\overline{AF}) = 2.4$ cm

$m(\overline{BF}) = 1.8$ cm

$m(\overline{CD}) = 5.7$ cm

If AB and CD are are 2 chords that intersect at point F, then $AF \times BF = CF \times DF$

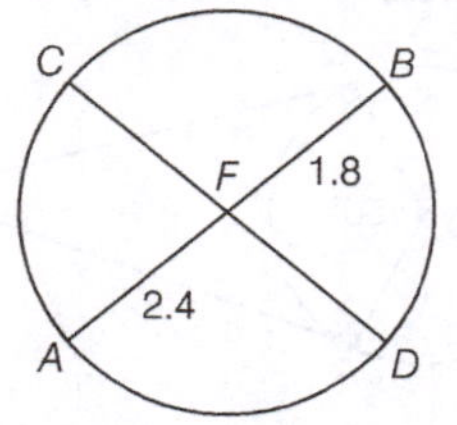

We can say,

$CF = CD - DF$ ...(i)

$\Rightarrow 2.4 \times 1.8 = (CD - DF)\, DF$

$\Rightarrow 4.32 = 5.7DF - DF^2$

$\Rightarrow DF^2 - 5.7DF + 4.32 = 0$

$\Rightarrow DF^2 - 4.8DF - 0.9DF + 4.32 = 0$

$\Rightarrow DF(DF - 4.8) - 0.9(DF - 4.8) = 0$

$\Rightarrow (DF - 4.8)(DF - 0.9) = 0$

$\therefore\ DF = 0.9, 4.8$

Hence, longer of 2 line segments $\overline{CF}$ and $\overline{DF}$ is 4.8 cm.

485. (c) Given,

Radius of circles = 36 cm and 16 cm

Length of direct common tangent

$= \sqrt{(\text{Distance between centre of circles})^2 - (\text{Difference in radius})^2}$

$PQ = \sqrt{(36 + 16)^2 - (36 - 16)^2}$

$= \sqrt{2704 - 400} = \sqrt{2304} = 48$ cm

486. (c) A diameter is a chord that passes through the center of the circle and it is the longest possible chord in a circle.

487. (a) We know that if two triangles are congruent, then their area are also equal

As, $\Delta XYZ \cong \Delta UVW$

$\Rightarrow ar(\Delta XYZ) = ar(\Delta UVW)$

$\therefore\ ar(\Delta UVW) = 58\ cm^2$

488. (a) Given, a circle which centre is O. RS divides PQ at T, $RS = 16$ cm and $QT = 4$ cm

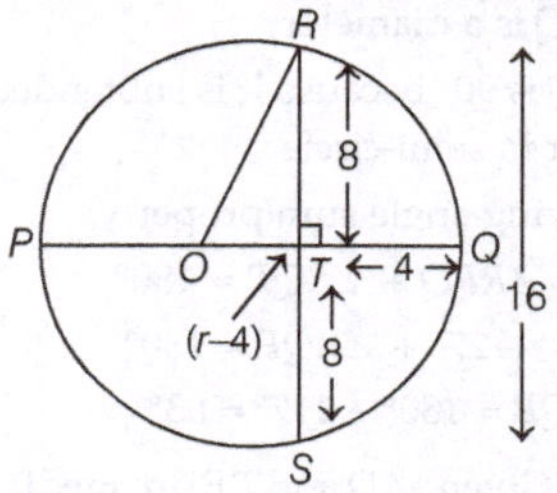

Now, the ΔORT

$\Rightarrow\ (OR)^2 = (r - 4)^2 + (8)^2$

$\Rightarrow\ (r)^2 = (r - 4)^2 + 64$

$\Rightarrow\ r^2 = r^2 + 16 - 8r + 64$

$\Rightarrow\ 8r = 80 \Rightarrow r = \frac{80}{8} = 10$ cm

$\therefore\ OR(r) = 10$ cm

So, the diameter of the circle (PQ)

$= 2 \times OQ = 2 \times 10 = 20$ cm

489. (a) Given, A circle which has O centre, $OP = 20$ cm and $AD = 58$ cm

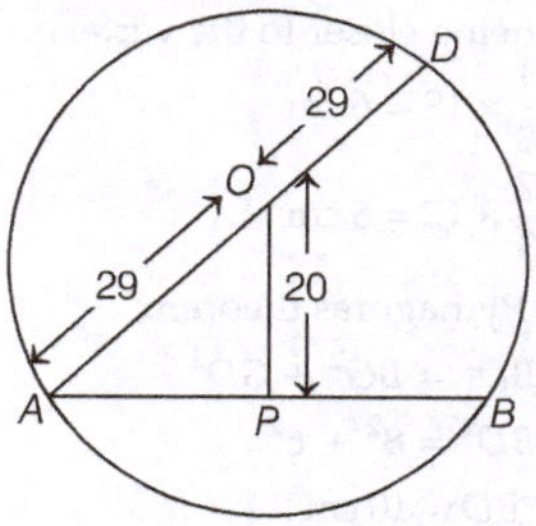

In ΔOAP, by Pythagoras theorem,

$(OA)^2 = (AP)^2 + (OP)^2$

$\left[\because AP = \frac{AB}{2}, \text{because } OP \perp AB\right]$

$\Rightarrow\ (29)^2 = (AP)^2 + (20)^2$

$\Rightarrow\ 841 = (AP)^2 + 400$

$\Rightarrow \quad (AP)^2 = 841 - 400 = 441$

$\Rightarrow \quad AP = \sqrt{441} = 21\text{ cm}$

$\therefore \quad AB = 2 \times AP = 2 \times 21 = 42\text{ cm}$

490. (c) Given, In a circle which has O centre, MT and NT are two tangents $\angle MON = 105°$

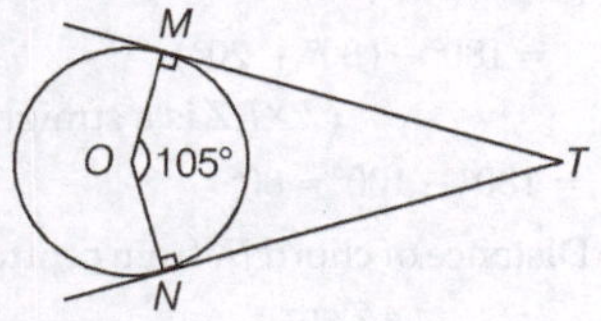

Now, in $\square MONT$,

$\angle M + \angle T + \angle N + \angle O = 360°$

$\Rightarrow \quad 90° + \angle T + 90° + 105° = 360°$

$\Rightarrow \quad \angle T = 360° - (90° + 90° + 105°)$

$\therefore \quad \angle T = 360° - (285°) = 75°$

So, $\angle T = \angle MTN = 75°$

491. (d) Given, $\angle SUV = 44°$, $\angle STU = 92°$

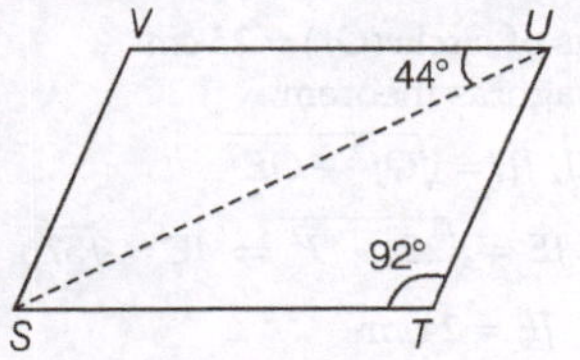

Since, $\angle STU = \angle SVU = 92°$

[$\because$ opposite angles are equal in magnitude]

Also, $\angle SUV = \angle TSU = 44°$

[$\because$ Alternate interior angles]

$\therefore \; 4\angle SVU - 3\angle TSU = 4(92°) - 3(44°)$

$= 368° - 132° = 236°$

492. (c)

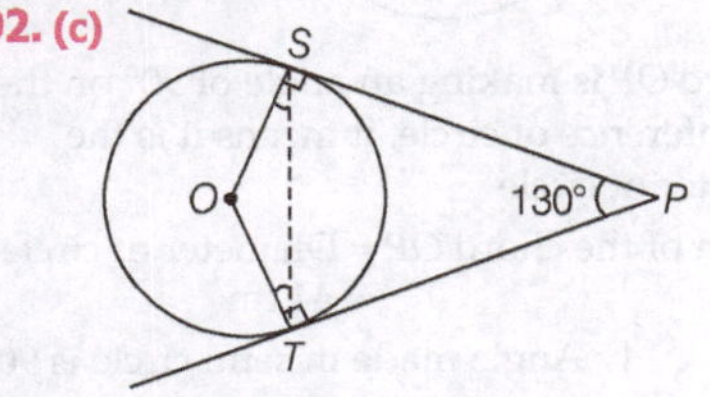

Given, $\angle SPT = 130°$

Also, $\quad OS = OT \quad$ [Radii of same circle]

$\Rightarrow \quad \angle OSP = \angle OTP = 90°$

[$\because$ Radii of circle is perpendicular to tangent]

$\therefore$ In quadrilateral $OSPT$,

$\angle SPT + \angle OSP + \angle OTP + \angle SOT = 360°$

$\Rightarrow \quad 130° + 90° + 90° + \angle SOT = 360°$

$\Rightarrow \quad \angle SOT = 50°$

In ΔOST, $\angle SOT + \angle OST + \angle OTS = 180°$

$\Rightarrow \quad 2\angle OST + 50° = 180°$

[$\because$ As, $OS = OT \Rightarrow \angle OST = \angle OTS$]

$\Rightarrow 2\angle OST = 130° \Rightarrow \angle OST = 65°$

493. (b)

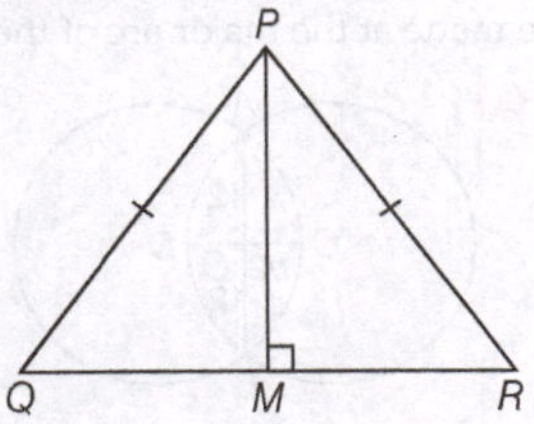

We know, $PM = \dfrac{\sqrt{3}}{2} \times (\text{side})$

$\Rightarrow \quad PM = \dfrac{\sqrt{3}}{2}(PQ) \Rightarrow 2PM = \sqrt{3}PQ$

Squaring both sides,

$\therefore \quad 3PQ^2 = 4PM^2$

494. (d) Given, AB is a tangent and OA is radius.

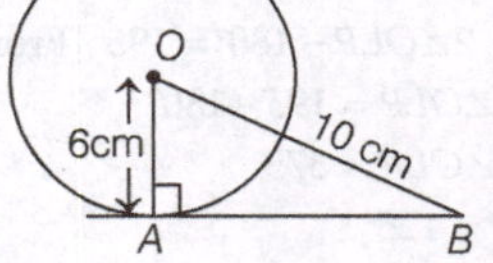

$\therefore \quad OA \perp AB$

$\therefore$ In ΔAOB, $AB^2 = OB^2 - OA^2$

$= (10)^2 - (6)^2 = 100 - 36 = 64$

$\therefore \quad AB = 8\text{ cm}$

495. (c) Given, $OA = 13$ cm, $OC = 12$ cm

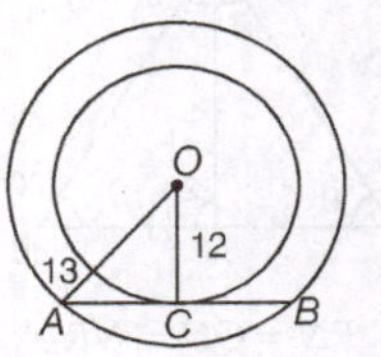

$\therefore$ In ΔAOC, AC^2

$= (13)^2 - (12)^2 = 169 - 144 = 25$

$\therefore \quad AC = 5\text{ cm}$

$\therefore \quad AB = 2 \times 5 = 10\text{ cm}$

496. (d)

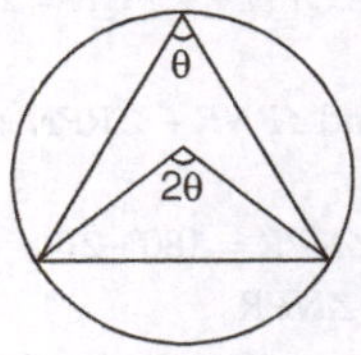

According to the question,

$\theta + 2\theta = 180° \Rightarrow 3\theta = 180° \Rightarrow \theta = 60°$

$\therefore$ Angle made at the centre of circle

$= 2\theta = 2 \times 60° = 120°$

497. (b)

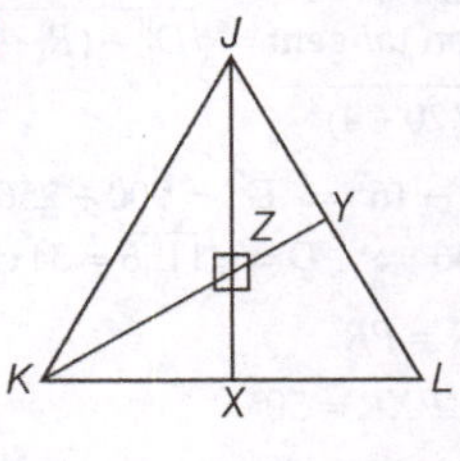

Given, $\quad KL = 22$ cm, $KY = 12$ cm

$\because$ JX is a median.

$\therefore \quad KX = \dfrac{KL}{2} = 11$

$\because$ Z is the centroid.

$\therefore \quad KZ = \dfrac{2}{3} \times KY = \dfrac{2}{3} \times 12 = 8\text{ cm}$

By applying Pythagoras theorem in ΔKZX.

$KX^2 = KZ^2 + ZX^2 \Rightarrow (11)^2 = (8)^2 + (ZX)^2$

$\Rightarrow \quad 121 = 64 + (ZX)^2 \Rightarrow (ZX)^2 = 121 - 64$

$\Rightarrow \quad ZX = \sqrt{57}\text{ cm}$

Centroid Z divides the median in the ratio of 2 : 1.

$\therefore \quad JX = 3ZX = 3\sqrt{57}\text{ cm}$

498. (d)

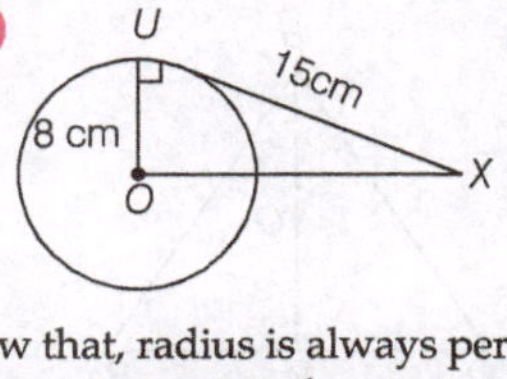

We know that, radius is always perpendicular to the tangent at point of contact.

In ΔOUX, by applying Pythagoras theorem,

$\Rightarrow \quad (OX)^2 = (8)^2 + (15)^2 \Rightarrow (OX)^2 = 64 + 225$

$\Rightarrow \quad (OX)^2 = 289 \Rightarrow OX = 17\text{ cm}$

499. (c)

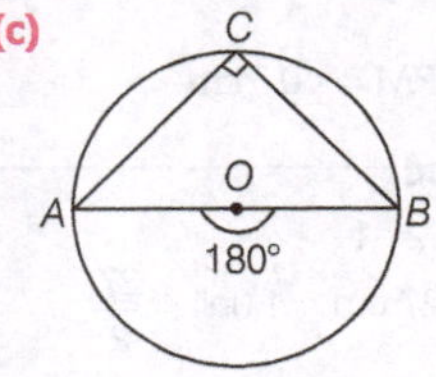

Given, $\quad \angle AOB = 180°$

$\therefore \quad \angle ACB = \dfrac{1}{2} \times \angle AOB = \dfrac{1}{2} \times 180° = 90°$

500. (d)

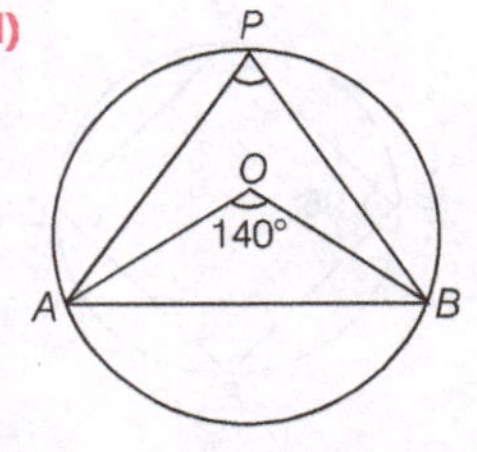

$\therefore$ Required angle $= \dfrac{140°}{2} = 70°$

501. (b) Given, in ΔABC

$AB = 4$ cm, $BC = 8$ cm

and $AC = 10$ cm

$\therefore \quad s = \dfrac{4 + 8 + 10}{2} = 11$

Area of $\Delta ABC = \sqrt{s(s-a)(s-b)(s-c)}$

$= \sqrt{11(11-4)(11-8)(11-10)}$

$= \sqrt{11 \times 7 \times 3 \times 1} = \sqrt{231}\text{ cm}^2$

According to the property of similar triangle

$\Rightarrow \quad \dfrac{\text{Area of } \Delta ABC}{\text{Area of } \Delta PQR} = \dfrac{BC^2}{QR^2}$

$\Rightarrow \quad \dfrac{\sqrt{231}}{\text{Area of } \Delta PQR} = \dfrac{64}{256}$

$\Rightarrow \quad \text{Area of } \Delta PQR = 4\sqrt{231}\text{ cm}^2$

502. (d) Given, $PQ = 12$ cm, $OQ = 5$ cm

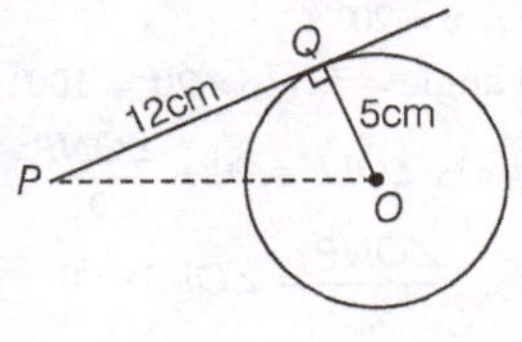

Since, $OQ \perp PQ$

$\Rightarrow \quad PO^2 = 5^2 + 12^2 = 25 + 144 = 169$

Hence, $PO = 13$ cm

503. (c) In ΔPQR, PM is the median.

O is centroid and $PO = 27$ cm

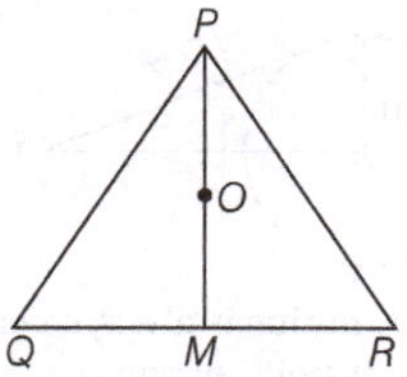

Since, $\dfrac{PO}{OM} = \dfrac{2}{1} \Rightarrow \dfrac{PO}{PM - PO} = \dfrac{2}{1}$

$\Rightarrow \quad \dfrac{27}{PM - 27} = \dfrac{2}{1} \Rightarrow \quad 27 = 2PM - 54$

$\Rightarrow \quad 2PM = 81 \Rightarrow PM = 40.5$ cm

Speedy Method

Since, $PO : OM = 2 : 1$

$\therefore$ PO (2 units) = 27 cm $\therefore$ 1 unit = $\dfrac{27}{2}$

$\Rightarrow$ 3 units = $\dfrac{27}{2} \times 3 \Rightarrow PM$ (3 units)

= 40.5 cm

504. (c)

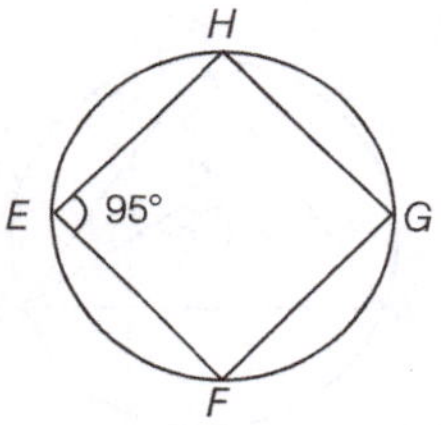

In a cyclic quadrilateral the sum of opposite angles should be 180°.

$\therefore \quad \angle E + \angle G = 180° \Rightarrow 95° + \angle G = 180°$

$\therefore \qquad \angle G = 85°$

505. (d) The intersection point of the medians of a triangle is called centroid.

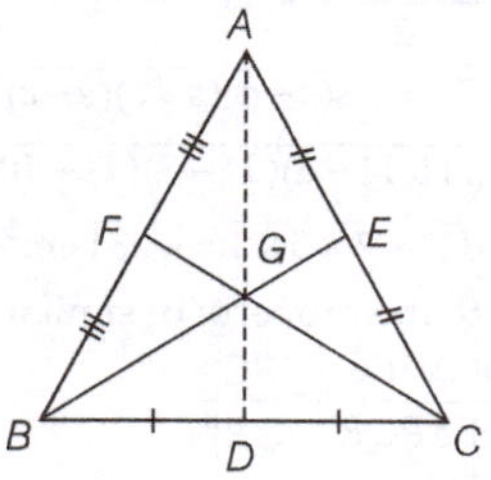

506. (d) Let angles of a triangle be $2x$, $2x$ and $5x$.

Sum of all angles of triangle = 180°

$\therefore \quad 2x + 2x + 5x = 180° \Rightarrow 9x = 180°$

$\Rightarrow \qquad x = 20°$

So, largest angle = $5x = 5 \times 20° = 100°$

507. (d) Since, $\angle OLP = 90° + \dfrac{\angle ONP}{2}$

$\Rightarrow \qquad \dfrac{\angle ONP}{2} = \angle OLP - 90°$

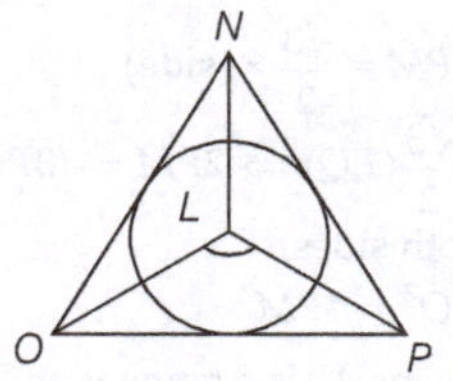

$\Rightarrow \quad \angle ONP = 2\angle OLP - 180° \qquad$ ...(i)

Given, $\angle OLP + \angle ONP = 195°$

$\Rightarrow \angle OLP + 2\angle OLP - 180° = 195°$ [From Eq. (i)]

$\Rightarrow \qquad 3\angle OLP = 195° + 180°$

$\Rightarrow \qquad 3\angle OLP = 375°$

$\Rightarrow \quad \angle OLP = 125°$

508. (a) Given, $PN = QN$

PN is median so it divides the QR also in two equal parts.

i.e., $QN = NR$

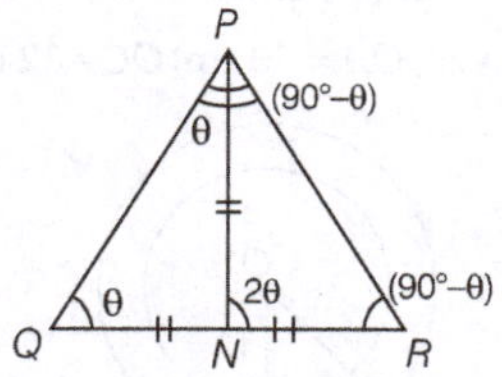

$\therefore \qquad PN = QN = NR$

In ΔPQN, $\angle QPN = \angle PQN$

($\because$ opposite sides are equal)

Let $\angle QPN = \angle PQN = \theta°$

So external angle

$\angle PNR = \angle QPN + \angle PQN = 2\theta$

In ΔPNR,

$\angle PNR = 2\theta$ and $\angle PNR + \angle RPN + \angle PRN = 180°$

So, $\angle PRN + \angle NPR = 180° - 2\theta$

and $\angle PRN = \angle NPR$

($\because$ opposite sides are equal)

$\therefore \angle PRN = \angle NPR = 90° - \theta$

Now, $\angle QPR = \angle NPR + \angle QPN$

$= 90° - \theta° + \theta° = 90°$

509. (c) Using formula

Direct common tangent = $\sqrt{D^2 - (R_1 - R_2)^2}$

$30 = \sqrt{D^2 - (20-4)^2}$

$\Rightarrow (30)^2 = D^2 - 16^2 \Rightarrow D^2 = 900 + 256$

$\Rightarrow \quad D^2 = 1156 \Rightarrow \quad D = \sqrt{1156} = 34$ cm

510. (a) $\because XR = PR$

So, $\angle XPR = \angle PXR = 50°$

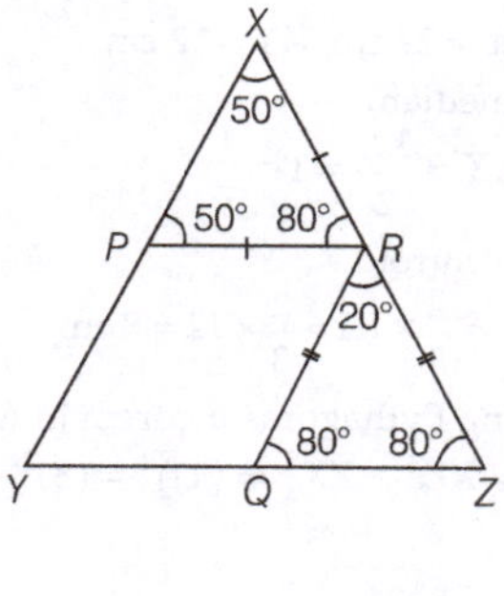

In ΔXPR, $\angle XRP = 180° - (50° + 50°) = 80°$

$\because \qquad ZR = QR$

$\therefore \qquad \angle RQZ = \angle RZQ = 80°$

In ΔRQZ, $\angle QRZ = 180° - (80° + 80°) = 20°$

So, $\angle PRQ = 180° - (\angle XRP + \angle QRZ)$

$= 180° - (80° + 20°)$

($\because$ XRZ is a straight line)

$= 180° - 100° = 80°$

511. (c) Distance of chord JK from centre (OE) = 7 cm

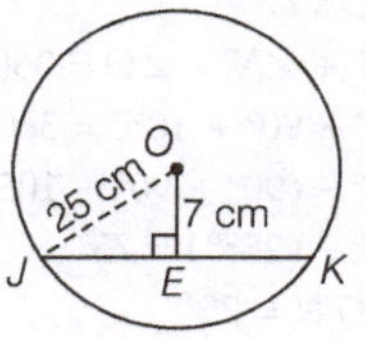

Diameter of circle = 50 cm

$\therefore$ Radius of circle (OJ) = 25 cm

By Pythagoras theorem

In, ΔOEJ, $JE = \sqrt{OJ^2 - OE^2}$

$JE = \sqrt{25^2 - 7^2} \Rightarrow JE = \sqrt{576}$

$\Rightarrow \qquad JE = 24$ cm

So, $JK = 2JE = 2 \times 24 = 48$ cm

512. (a)

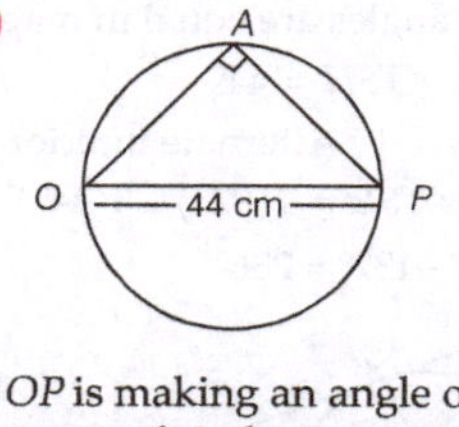

If chord OP is making an angle of 90° on the circumference of circle, it means it is the diameter of circle

Length of the chord OP = Diameter of circle = 44 cm

[$\because$ Angle made in semi circle is 90°]

513. (d)

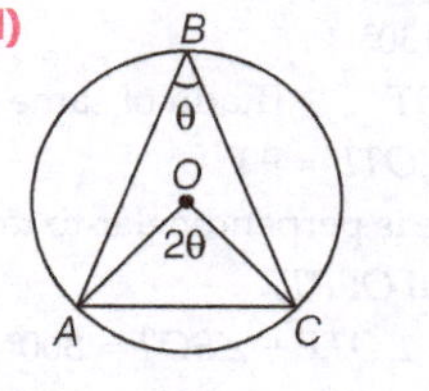

If $\qquad \angle ABC = \theta$

Then, $\quad \angle AOC = 2\theta$

According to the question,

$\theta + 2\theta = 225°$

$\Rightarrow \quad 3\theta = 225° \Rightarrow \quad \theta = \dfrac{225}{3} \Rightarrow \quad \theta = 75°$

Angle made at the major arc of the circle is 75°.

514. (a)

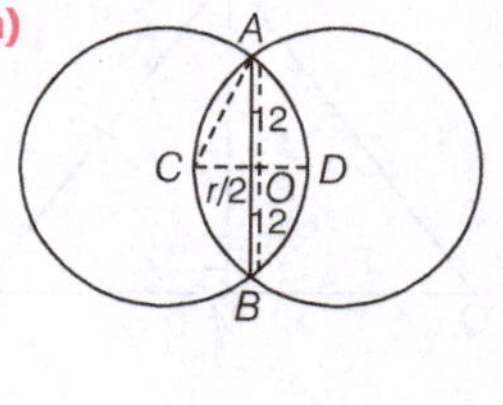

AB and *CD* intersect each other at 90°, so they bisect each other,

$$AO = OB = 12\text{ cm},\ CO = OD = \frac{r}{2}$$

In ΔAOC, by applying Pythagoras theorem,

$$AC^2 = AO^2 + OC^2$$

$$\Rightarrow r^2 = (12)^2 + \left(\frac{r}{2}\right)^2 \Rightarrow r^2 = 144 + \frac{r^2}{4}$$

$$\Rightarrow r^2 - \frac{r^2}{4} = 144 \Rightarrow \frac{3r^2}{4} = 144$$

$$\Rightarrow r^2 = \frac{144 \times 4}{3} \Rightarrow r = \frac{12 \times 2}{\sqrt{3}} \times \frac{\sqrt{3}}{\sqrt{3}} = 8\sqrt{3}$$

So, diameter of each circle = 2 × radius of circle = $2 \times 8\sqrt{3} = 16\sqrt{3}$

515. (d)

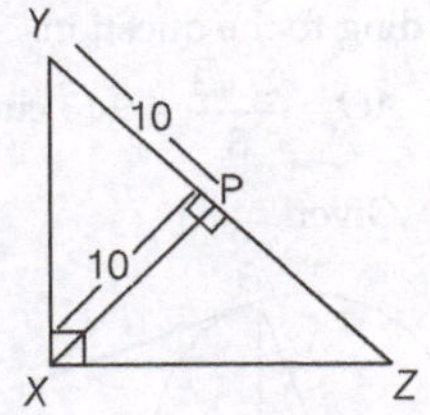

For right angle triangle,

$$XP^2 = YP \times PZ$$

$$\Rightarrow (10)^2 = 10 \times PZ \Rightarrow 100 = 10 \times PZ$$

$$\therefore\ PZ = \frac{100}{10} = 10\text{ cm}$$

516. (c) Given, $\angle A = 110°$

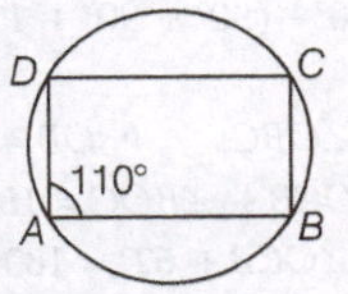

In a cyclic quadrilateral, sum of opposite angles is 180°.

$$\therefore\ \angle A + \angle C = 180° \Rightarrow 110° + \angle C = 180°$$

$$\Rightarrow\ \angle C = 180° - 110° \Rightarrow \angle C = 70°$$

517. (c)

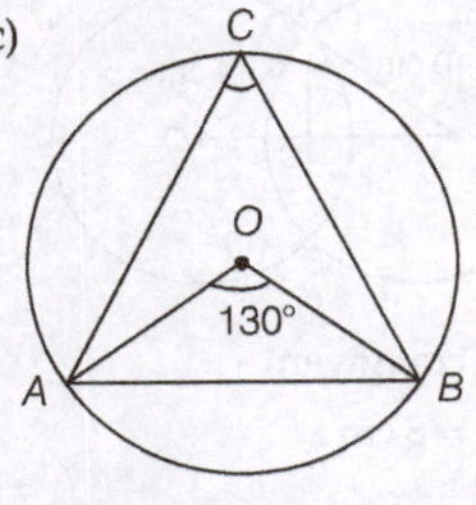

Angle subtended by chord *AB* at the centre of a circle = 2 × Angle subtended by chord *AB* at the major segment of the circle.

∴ Angle subtended by chord in the major segment of circle $= \frac{1}{2} \times 130° = 65°$

518. (d) Given, $\angle P = 46°, \angle R = 64°$

We know that, $\angle P + \angle Q + \angle R = 180°$

$$\Rightarrow\ 46° + \angle Q + 64° = 180°$$

$$\Rightarrow\ \angle Q = 180° - 110° = 70°$$

$\because \Delta PQR$ is similar and congruent to ΔABC

$$\therefore\ \angle B = \angle Q = 70°$$

519. (a) Given,

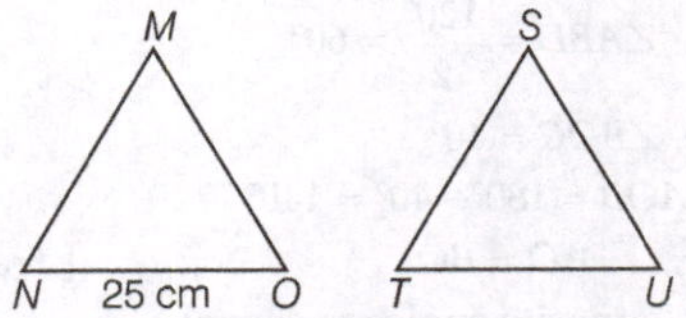

Perimeter of ΔMNO = 80 cm

Perimeter of ΔSTU = 200 cm

and ON = 25 cm

We know that, $\dfrac{\text{Perimeter of } \Delta MNO}{\text{Perimeter of } \Delta STU} = \dfrac{ON}{TU}$

$$\Rightarrow \frac{80}{200} = \frac{25}{TU} \Rightarrow TU = \frac{25 \times 200}{80}$$

$$\therefore\ TU = 62.5\text{ cm}$$

520. (b) Given, *D*, *E* and *F* lie on the circumference of circle and $\angle DEF = 48°$

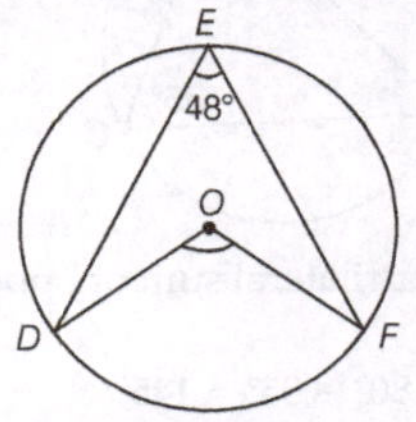

$$\therefore\ \angle DOF = 2\angle DEF = 2 \times 48° = 96°$$

521. (d)

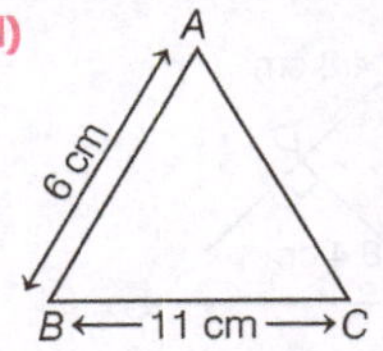

Let, length of *AC* be *x*

For a triangle to be possible, sum of two sides should be greater than third side and difference of two sides should be less than third side.

∴ $11 + 6 > x$ and $11 - 6 < x \Rightarrow 17 > x$ and $5 < x$

So, $5 < x < 17$

So, integral values of *x* can be

6,7,8,9,10,11,12,13,14,15,16.

Hence, there are 11 integral values of *AC* that can be possible.

522. (d)

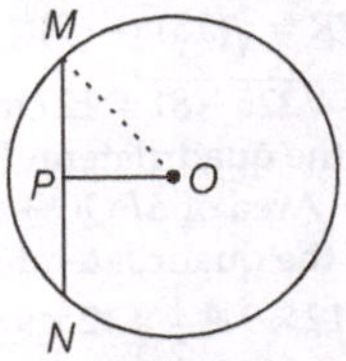

In ΔOMP, $(OM)^2 = (PM)^2 + (OP)^2$

$$\Rightarrow\ (r)^2 = (20)^2 + (15)^2 \quad \left[\because PM = \frac{MN}{2}\right]$$

$$\Rightarrow\ r^2 = 400 + 225$$

$$\Rightarrow\ r^2 = 625$$

$$\Rightarrow\ r = \sqrt{625} = 25\text{ cm}$$

Hence, radius of the circle is 25 cm.

523. (b) ∴ Length of direct common tangent

$$= \sqrt{(\text{Distance between centres})^2 - (R_1 - R_2)^2}$$

$$= \sqrt{(25)^2 - (12-5)^2} = \sqrt{625 - 49}$$

$$= \sqrt{576} = 24\text{ cm}$$

524. (b) From intersecting chord theorem,

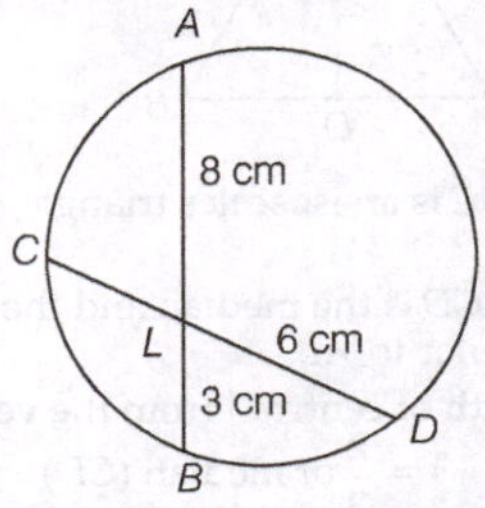

$$AL \times LB = CL \times LD \Rightarrow 8 \times 3 = CL \times 6$$

$$\therefore\ CL = 4\text{ cm}$$

525. (d) Sum of the angles of a triangle = 180°

∴ Smallest angle of the given triangle

$$= \frac{3}{3+4+8} \times 180° = 36°$$

526. (c) Given, $AB = QR$, $BC = PR$ and $CA = PQ$

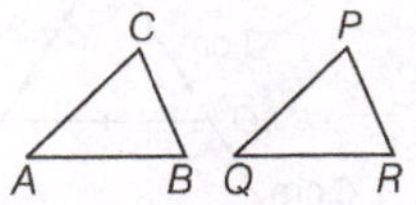

By SSS congruence theorem, $\Delta CBA \cong \Delta PRQ$.

527. (c)

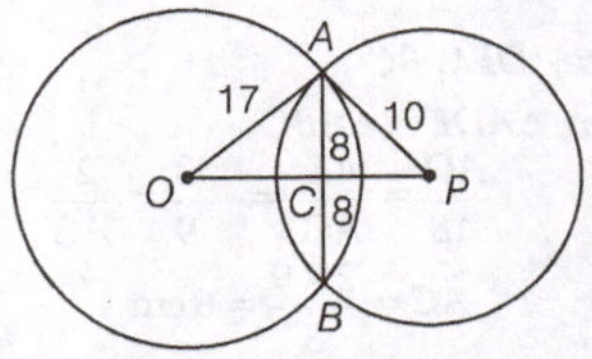

In ΔOAC, $OC = \sqrt{(17)^2 - (8)^2}$

[∵ Perpendicular on chord from centre is divided the chord in two equal parts]

$$= \sqrt{289 - 64} = \sqrt{225} = 15\text{ cm}$$

In ΔPAC, $CP = \sqrt{(10)^2 - (8)^2} = \sqrt{100 - 64}$

$$= \sqrt{36} = 6\text{ cm}$$

$$\therefore\ OP = OC + CP = 15 + 6 = 21\text{ cm}$$

Now, the perimeter of

$$\Delta OAP = OA + AP + OP$$

$$= 17 + 10 + 21 = 48\text{ cm}$$

528. (c) Given, $OO' = 8$ cm

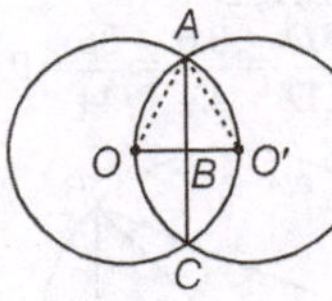

In ΔAOB,

$$AB^2 = AO^2 - OB^2 = (8)^2 - (4)^2$$

$$= 64 - 16 = 48$$

$$AB = 4\sqrt{3}\text{ cm}$$

$\therefore$ Length of common chord, AC

$= 2 \times 4\sqrt{3} = 8\sqrt{3}$ cm

529. (a)

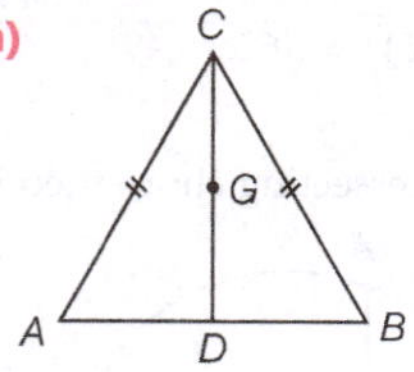

Since, ΔABC is an isosceles triangle, where $AC = BC$.

Therefore, CD is the median and the perpendicular to AB.

Since, length of centroid from the vertex (CG)

$= \frac{2}{3}$ of median (CD)

$\therefore$ Median (CD) $= \frac{8 \times 3}{2} = 12$ cm

and $AD = \frac{AB}{2} = \frac{10}{2} = 5$ cm

Now, in right angle triangle ADC,

$\Rightarrow AC^2 = (5)^2 + (12)^2 = 25 + 144 = 169$

$\therefore AC = \sqrt{169} = 13$ cm

530. (d) Given,

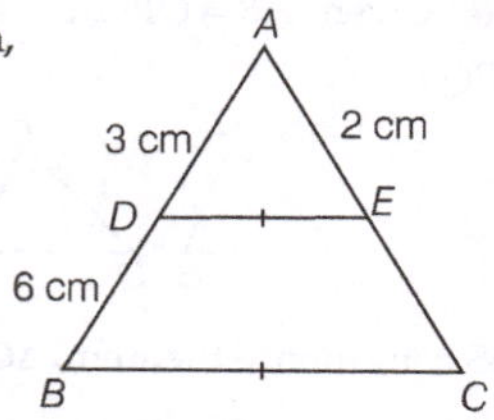

Since, $DE \parallel BC$

Then, $\Delta ADE \sim \Delta ABC$

$\therefore \frac{AD}{AB} = \frac{AE}{AC} \Rightarrow \frac{3}{9} = \frac{2}{AC}$

$\Rightarrow AC = \frac{2 \times 9}{3} = 6$ cm

$\therefore CE = AC - AE = 6 - 2 = 4$ cm

531. (d)

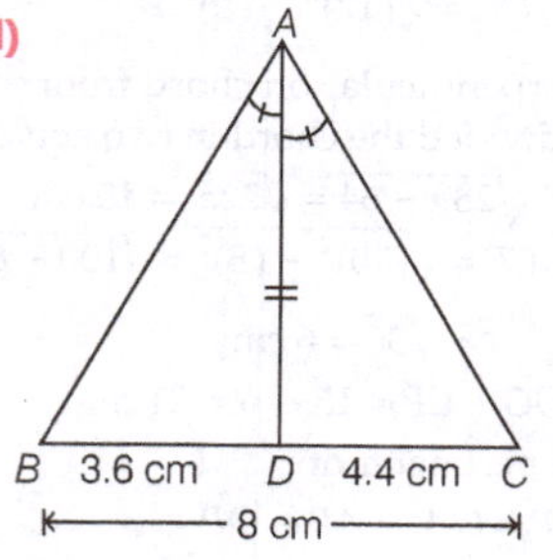

$CD = BC - BD = 8 - 3.6 = 4.4$ cm

Angle bisector theorem,

Since, $\Delta ABD \sim \Delta ACD$

$\therefore \frac{AB}{AC} = \frac{BD}{CD} = \frac{3.6}{4.4} = \frac{36}{44} = 9 : 11$

532. (b)

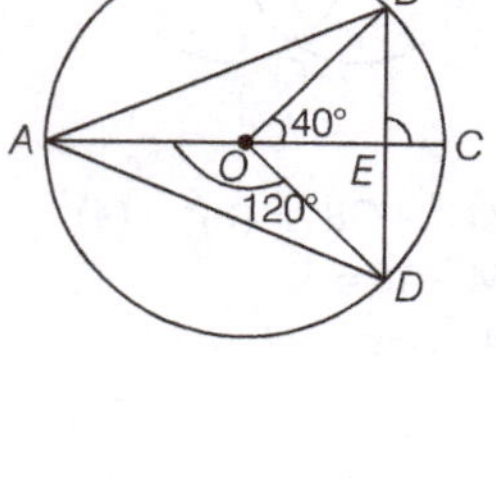

Since, $\angle AOD = 120°$

$\therefore \angle ABD = \frac{120°}{2} = 60°$

Since, $\angle BOC = 40°$

$\therefore \angle AOB = 180° - 40° = 140°$

Since, $AO = BO$ [$\because$ radii]

Then, opposite angles are equal

$\therefore \angle ABO = \frac{180° - 140°}{2} = 20°$

[$\because \angle ABD - \angle ABO$]

Now, $\angle OBE = 60° - 20° = 40°$

In ΔBOE, $\angle BEC = \angle BOE + \angle OBE$

[$\because$ external angle sum of two opposite internal angles]

$= 40° + 40° = 80°$

533. (b)

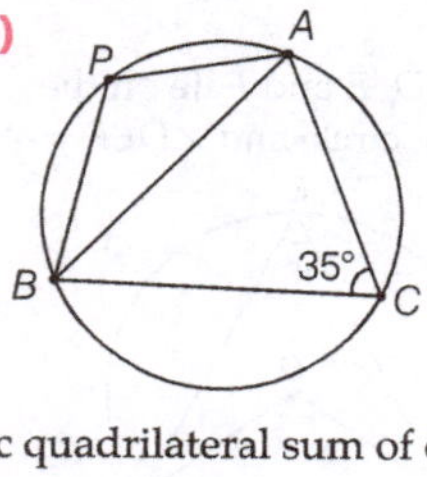

In cyclic quadrilateral sum of opposite angles is 180°.

$\therefore \angle APB = 180° - 35° = 145°$

534. (a) In ΔABC, $AD^2 = BD \times DC$

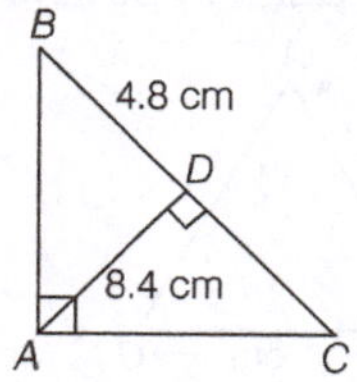

$\Rightarrow DC = \frac{8.4 \times 8.4}{4.8} = 14.7$ cm

$\therefore BC = BD + DC = 4.8 + 14.7 = 19.5$ cm

535. (b)

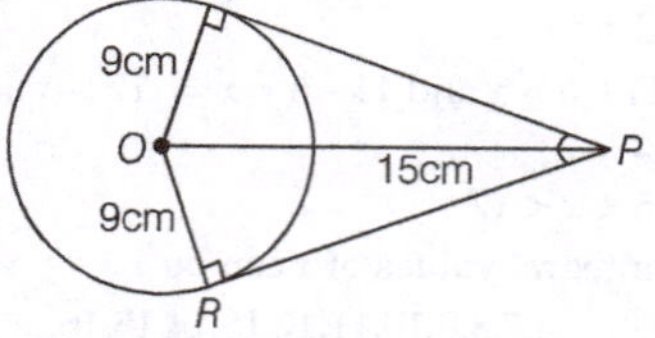

$\therefore \angle PQO = \angle PRO = 90°$

Since, ΔPQO and ΔPRO are right angle triangle

$\therefore PQ = PR = \sqrt{(15)^2 - (9)^2}$

$= \sqrt{225 - 81} = 12$ cm

$\therefore$ Area of the quadrilateral $PQOR$

$=$ Area of ΔPQO + Area of ΔPRO

$\therefore$ Area of the quadrilateral $PQOR$

$= \frac{1}{2} \times 12 \times 9 + \frac{1}{2} \times 12 \times 9 = 108 \text{ cm}^2$

536. (d) Given,

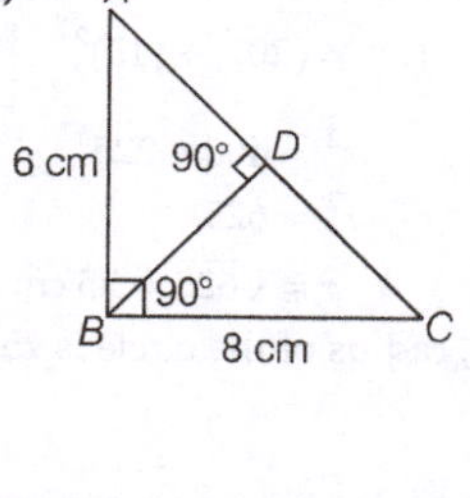

As we know, $AD = \frac{AB^2}{AC}$ and $CD = \frac{BC^2}{AC}$

Thus, required ratio

$= \frac{AD}{CD} = \frac{\frac{AB^2}{AC}}{\frac{BC^2}{AC}} = \frac{AB^2}{AC} \times \frac{AC}{BC^2}$

$\frac{AD}{CD} = \frac{AB^2}{BC^2} = \frac{6^2}{8^2} = \frac{9}{16} = 9 : 16$

537. (a) We know that, in an equilateral triangle of side a unit, distance of the centroid (centre of mass) from any vertex is $\frac{a\sqrt{3}}{3}$.

$\therefore$ According to the question,

$AO = \frac{27\sqrt{3}}{3} = 9\sqrt{3}$ cm

538. (a) Given,

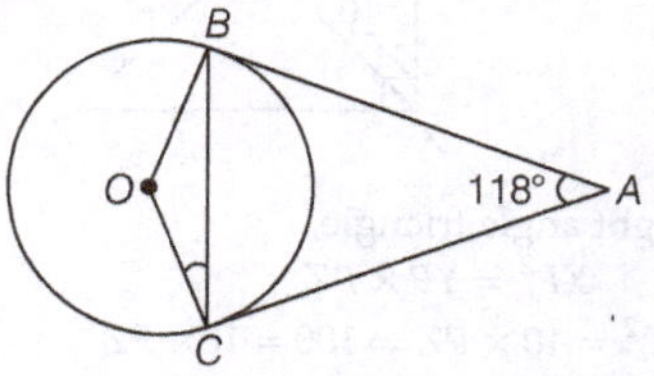

Since, AB and AC are tangent on radii point B and C on the circle.

$\angle OBA = \angle OCA = 90°$

$\therefore \angle BOC = 360° - (90° + 90° + 118°) = 62°$

In ΔOBC,

$\angle OCB = \angle OBC$ ($\because OB = OC$ = radius)

$\therefore \angle OBC + \angle OCB + \angle BOC = 180°$

$\angle OCB + \angle OCB + 62° = 180°$

$2\angle OCB = 180° - 62° = 118°$

$\therefore \angle OCB = \frac{118°}{2} = 59°$

539. (b) Given,

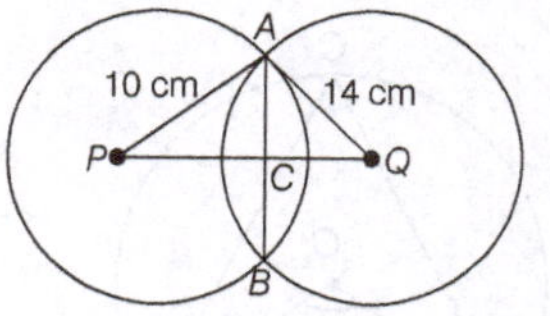

Since, AB = 16 cm (given)

$\therefore AC = \frac{16}{2} = 8$ cm

$\therefore$ Distance between their centres

$= (\sqrt{(14)^2 - (8)^2}) + (\sqrt{(10)^2 - (8)^2})$

$= \sqrt{132} + \sqrt{36} = 2\sqrt{33} + 6$

$= (6 + 2\sqrt{33})$ cm

540. (a) Sides of triangle, $x^2 - 1, 2x$ and $x^2 + 1$.

The longest side = Hypotenuse = $x^2 + 1$

Speedy Method

$H^2 = B^2 + P^2$

Here, $(x^2 + 1)^2 = (x^2 - 1)^2 + (2x)^2$

541. (c) $BC = 34$ cm, $DF = 8$ cm

$\therefore$ AD is median.

$\therefore BD = CD = \frac{34}{2} = 17$ cm

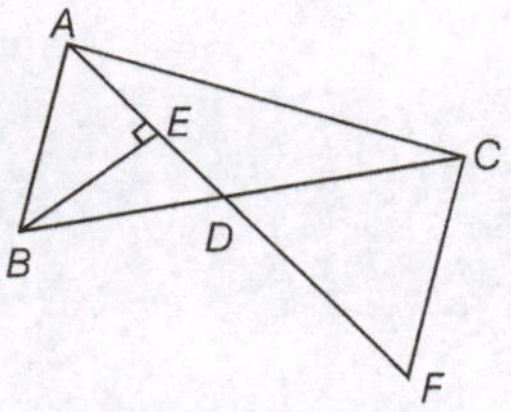

In $\Delta CFD, CF = \sqrt{(CD)^2 - (DF)^2)}$

$= \sqrt{(17)^2 - (8)^2} = \sqrt{289 - 64}$

$= \sqrt{225} = 15$ cm

In ΔCDF and ΔBED, $\angle F = \angle E$ (each 90°)

$\angle D = \angle D$ (vertically opposite angle)

$CD = BD$ (given)

$\therefore \Delta CDF \cong \Delta BDE \Rightarrow BE = CF = 15$ cm

542. (b) $PQ = 82$ cm, $PS = 80$ cm

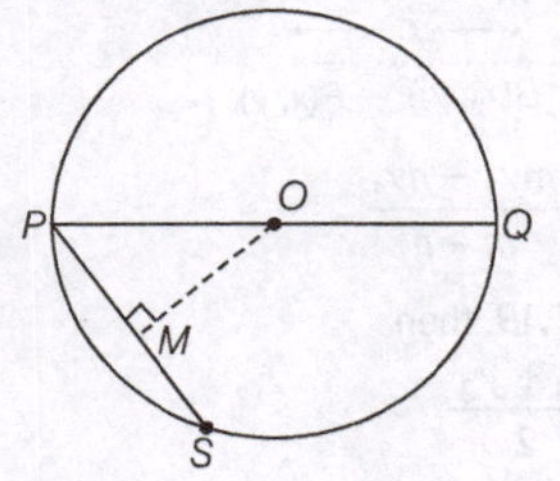

$\therefore OP = \frac{PQ}{2} = \frac{82}{2} = 41$ cm

$PM = \frac{PS}{2} = \frac{80}{2} = 40$ cm $(\because OM \perp PS)$

In $\Delta OMP, OM = \sqrt{OP^2 - PM^2}$

$= \sqrt{(41)^2 - (40)^2} = \sqrt{1681 - 1600} = \sqrt{81} = 9$ cm

543. (d) Let the other two angles are x and x.

$\because$ Sum of angles = 180°

$\Rightarrow \quad 42° + x + x = 180°$

$\Rightarrow \quad 2x = 180° - 42° \Rightarrow 2x = 138°$

$\therefore \quad x = 69°$

Hence, other two angles are 69° and 69°.

544. (d) Given, $DE = 4$ cm

$\frac{DE}{EF} = \frac{1}{2} \Rightarrow \frac{4}{EF} = \frac{1}{2}$

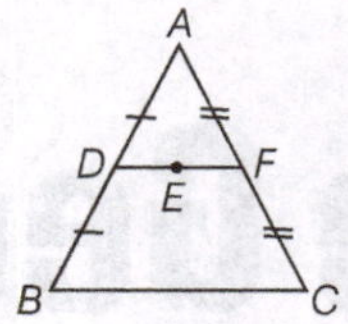

$\therefore \; EF = 8$ cm

$DF = DE + EF = 4 + 8 = 12$ cm

$DF \parallel BC$

[D and F is the mid-point of AB and AC, respectively]

$\therefore DF = \frac{1}{2} BC$ (mid-point theorem)

$\therefore BC = 2DF = 2 \times 12 = 24$ cm

545. (b) Given, $PR = 5$ cm

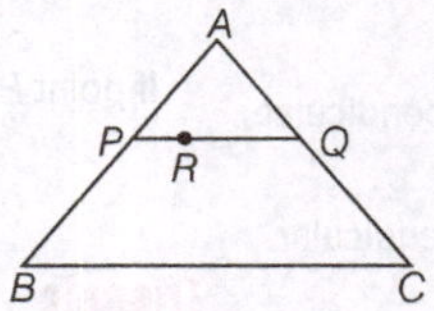

$\because$ P and Q are mid-points of sides AB and AC

$\therefore \; \frac{AP}{AB} = \frac{PQ}{BC} = \frac{AQ}{AC} = \frac{1}{2}$

$\Rightarrow \; BC = 2PQ$ ...(i)

and $\frac{PR}{RQ} = \frac{1}{4} \Rightarrow \frac{5}{RQ} = \frac{1}{4}$

$\Rightarrow \; RQ = 20$

$\therefore \; PQ = PR + RQ = 5 + 20 = 25$ cm

From Eq. (i), $BC = 2 \times 25 = 50$ cm

546. (c) $\angle TAP = 60°, TA = 6$ cm, $AP = 8$ cm

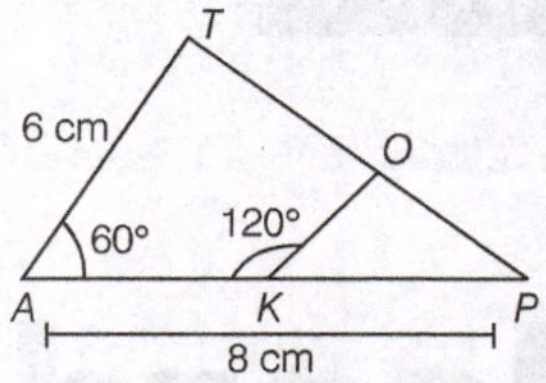

$\because \angle AKO = 120°$

$\therefore \angle PKO = 180° - 120° = 60°$

K is the mid point of AP and

$\angle TAP = \angle PKO = 60°$

$\therefore \quad OK \parallel AT$,

$\therefore \quad OK = \frac{1}{2} AT$

(converse of the mid-point theorem)

$= \frac{1}{2} \times 6 = 3$ cm

547. (c) $OQ = 13$ cm; $OP = 5$ cm

Here, $\angle OPQ = 90°$

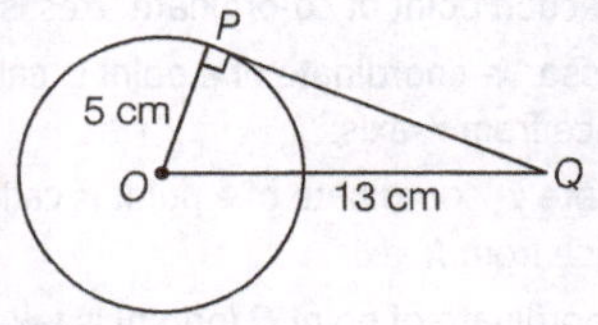

$\therefore$ Length of tangent,

$PQ = \sqrt{(OQ)^2 - OP^2} = \sqrt{(13)^2 - (5)^2}$

$= \sqrt{169 - 25} = \sqrt{144} = 12$ cm

21

Coordinate Geometry

Coordinate geometry is the branch of geometry, in which we study the position of any point on a plane with the help of its coordinates (i.e. an ordered pair of numbers).

- A cartesian system in two dimensions is defined by an ordered pairs of perpendicular lines called axes. The two lines taken together are called the coordinate axes.
- Intersection point of co-ordinate axes is called origin.
- **Abscissa** x–coordinate of a point is called abscissa, it is a perpendicular distance from Y-axis.
- **Ordinate** y–coordinate of a point is called ordinate, it is a perpendicular distance from X-axis.
- The coordinate of point O (origin) is taken as (0, 0).
- The coordinates of any point on X-axis are of the form $(x, 0)$.
- The coordinates of any point on Y-axis are of the form $(0, y)$.

Distance Between Two Points

If $A(x_1, y_1)$ and $B(x_2, y_2)$ are two points separated by a distance d, then

$$AB = d = \sqrt{(x_2 - x_1)^2 + (y_2 - y_1)^2}$$

Ex. 1. If the distance between the points $(x, 0)$ and $(-7, 0)$ is 10 units, then the possible values of x are

Sol. Given, distance between the points $(x, 0)$ and $(-7, 0) = 10$ units

Here, $x_1 = x$, $y_1 = 0$, $x_2 = -7$ and $y_2 = 0$

$\therefore$ Required distance $= \sqrt{(x_2 - x_1)^2 + (y_2 - y_1)^2}$

$\Rightarrow \sqrt{(-7 - x)^2 + (0 - 0)^2} = 10 \quad \Rightarrow \pm(x + 7) = 10$

If $\quad x + 7 = 10$, then $x = 3$

If $\ -(x + 7) = 10$, then $x = -17$

Section Formulae

Let $A(x_1, y_1)$ and $B(x_2, y_2)$ be two points on the cartesian plane.

- If point $P(x, y)$ divides the line AB in the ratio of $m : n$ internally. Then,

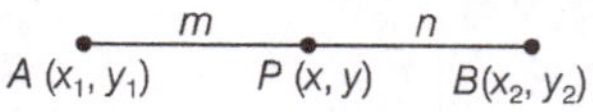

$$AP : PB = m : n$$

$$x = \frac{mx_2 + nx_1}{m + n}, y = \frac{my_2 + ny_1}{m + n}$$

- If point $P(x, y)$ divides AB externally, then

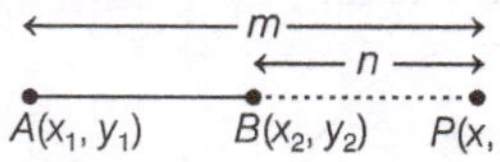

$$x = \frac{mx_2 - nx_1}{m - n}, y = \frac{my_2 - ny_1}{m - n}$$

- If point $P(x, y)$ is the mid-point of AB, then

$$x = \frac{x_1 + x_2}{2}, y = \frac{y_1 + y_2}{2}$$

Triangle

If $A(x_1, y_1)$, $B(x_2, y_2)$ and $C(x_3, y_3)$ are three vertices of a ΔABC, then

(i) Area of $\Delta ABC = \frac{1}{2}|x_1(y_2 - y_3) + x_2(y_3 - y_1) + x_3(y_1 - y_2)|$

(ii) Centroid of $\Delta ABC = \left(\frac{x_1 + x_2 + x_3}{3}, \frac{y_1 + y_2 + y_3}{3}\right)$

(iii) Incentre of $\Delta ABC = \left(\frac{ax_1 + bx_2 + cx_3}{a + b + c}, \frac{ay_1 + by_2 + cy_3}{a + b + c}\right)$

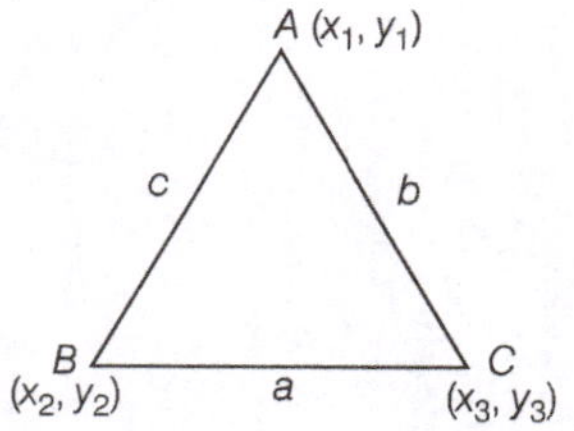

Ex. 2. If the coordinate of the mid-points of the sides of a triangle are (1, 1), (2, – 3) and (3, 4) then find the coordinates of the centroid.

Sol. Let $P(1, 1)$, $Q(2, -3)$ and $R(3, 4)$ be the mid-points of sides AB, BC and CA, respectively of ΔABC.

Now, let $A(x_1, y_1)$ $B(x_2, y_2)$ and $C(x_3, y_3)$ be the vertices of ΔABC.

Since, P is mid-point of AB.

$\therefore \quad \frac{x_1 + x_2}{2} = 1, \frac{y_1 + y_2}{2} = 1$

$\Rightarrow \quad x_1 + x_2 = 2, y_1 + y_2 = 2 \quad$ ...(i)

Since, Q is mid-point of BC.

$\therefore \quad \frac{x_2+x_3}{2}=2, \frac{y_2+y_3}{2}=-3$

$\Rightarrow \quad x_2+x_3=4, y_2+y_3=-6$ ...(ii)

Since, R is mid-point of AC.

$\therefore \quad \frac{x_1+x_3}{2}=3, \frac{y_1+y_3}{2}=4$

$\Rightarrow \quad x_1+x_3=6, y_1+y_3=8$ ...(iii)

From Eqs. (i), (ii) and (iii), we get

$$x_1+x_2+x_3=6, y_1+y_2+y_3=2$$

Then, coordinates of the centroid $=\left(\frac{x_1+x_2+x_3}{3}, \frac{y_1+y_2+y_3}{3}\right)$

$$=\left(\frac{6}{3}, \frac{2}{3}\right)=\left(2, \frac{2}{3}\right)$$

Collinearity of Three Points

Three points $A(x_1, y_1), B(x_2, y_2)$ and $C(x_3, y_3)$ are collinear, if

(i) Area of $\Delta ABC=0$

(ii) Distance AB + Distance BC = Distance AC

(iii) Slope of AB = Slope of BC = Slope of AC

Quadrilateral

If $(x_1, y_1), (x_2, y_2), (x_3, y_3), (x_4, y_4)$ are the vertices of a quadrilateral then,

Area of Quadrilateral

$$=\frac{1}{2}[(x_1y_2+x_2y_3+x_3y_4+x_4y_1)-(x_2y_1+x_3y_2+x_4y_3+x_1y_4)]$$

Slope of a Line Passing Through Two Points

If a line passes through two points $A(x_1, y_1)$ and $B(x_2, y_2)$, then the slope of line m is given by, $m=\tan\theta=\frac{y_2-y_1}{x_2-x_1}$

Slope or Gradient of a Line

The equation of a line with slope m making an intercept c on Y-axis is $y=mx+c$.

This is also called slope intercept form of a line.

Equations of a Straight Line in Different Forms

Following are the different forms of equations of a straight line.

(i) Point-Slope Form The equation of a line which passes through a point $P(x_1, y_1)$ and has the slope m is $y-y_1=m(x-x_1)$.

(ii) Two Points Form The equation of a line passing through two points $A(x_1, y_1)$ and $B(x_2, y_2)$ is given by, $(y-y_1)=\frac{(y_2-y_1)}{(x_2-x_1)}(x-x_1)$

(iii) Intercept Form If a line makes intercepts a and b on X and Y-axes respectively, then the equation of line is $\frac{x}{a}+\frac{y}{b}=1$

EX. 3. What is the equation of line having slope $\frac{2}{3}$ and passing through point (3, 5)?

Sol. As we know, $y-y_1=m(x-x_1)$

Here, $m=\frac{2}{3}$ and $(x_1, y_1)=(3,5)$

$$y-5=\frac{2}{3}(x-3) \Rightarrow 3y-15=2x-6$$

$$\Rightarrow \quad 3y-2x-9=0 \Rightarrow 2x-3y+9=0$$

Angle Between Two Straight Lines

If there are two lines i.e., $y=m_1x+c_1$ and $y=m_2x+c_2$, then the angle between the lines is given by

$$\theta=\tan^{-1}\left(\frac{m_2-m_1}{1+m_1m_2}\right)$$

$m_1=m_2$, if lines are parallel

$m_1 \times m_2=-1$, if lines are perpendicular

- **Distance of a Point from a Line** Perpendicular distance (D) of a point $P(x_1, y_1)$ from a line $ax+by+c=0$ is

$$D=\left|\frac{ax_1+by_1+c}{\sqrt{a^2+b^2}}\right|$$

- **Distance Between Parallel Lines** Distance (D) between two parallel lines $ax+by+c=0$ and $ax+by+d=0$ is

$$D=\left|\frac{d-c}{\sqrt{a^2+b^2}}\right|$$

Ex. 4. The distance of point (2, 3) from line $6x+8y+13=0$ is

Sol. Required distance $=\left|\frac{ax_1+by_1+c}{\sqrt{a^2+b^2}}\right|=\left|\frac{6\times2+8\times3+13}{\sqrt{6^2+8^2}}\right|$

$$=\left|\frac{12+24+13}{10}\right|=\frac{49}{10}=4.9 \text{ unit}$$

Equation of Circle and Sphere

- **General Equation of Circle** $x^2+y^2+2gx+2fy+c=0$
  where, center is $(-g,-f)$ and radius $=\sqrt{g^2+f^2-c}$
- **Equation of Circle** $(x-h)^2+(y-k)^2=r^2$
  where, (h,k) is the coordinate of centre and r is radius of circle
- **Equation of Sphere** $(x-a)^2+(y-b)^2+(z-c)^2=r^2$
  where, (a, b, c) are coordinate of centre of sphere and r is radius of sphere.

SSC Exam Scanner

SSC CGL 2023 (Tier II)

1. Find the coordinates of the points where the graph $57x - 19y = 399$ cuts the coordinate axes.
SSC CGL (Tier-II) 07/03/2023 Shift-I
(a) X-axis at (7, 0) and Y-axis at (0, – 21)
(b) X-axis at (7, 0) and Y-axis at (0, 21)
(c) X-axis at (– 7, 0) and Y-axis at (0, 21)
(d) X-axis at (– 7, 0) and Y-axis at (0, – 21)

SSC CHSL 2024-2022 (Tier I & II)

2. Find the equation of the sphere having centre (–1, 2, –3) and the radius of 3 units.
SSC CHSL (Tier-I) 09/07/2024 Shift-III
(a) $x^2 + y^2 + z^2 - 2x + 4y - 6z + 5 = 0$
(b) $x^2 + y^2 + z^2 + x - 2y + 3z + 5 = 0$
(c) $x^2 + y^2 + z^2 + 2x - 4y + 6z + 5 = 0$
(d) $x^2 + y^2 + z^2 - x + 2y - 3z + 5 = 0$

3. The lines $x + y = 10$ and $-3x + y = 2$ have a unique solution. What is the distance (in units) between the unique solution and the point of intersection of the line $x + y = 10$ and the X-axis?
SSC CHSL (Tier-I) 09/07/2024 Shift-III
(a) $8\sqrt{2}$ (b) 8
(c) 10 (d) $10\sqrt{2}$

4. If the intersection point of the equations $3p - 2q + 23 = 0$ and $-2p + q - 13 = 0$ on the graph is (p, q), then the value of $(3p + q)$ is equal to
SSC CHSL (Tier-I) 09/07/2024 Shift-II
(a) 2 (b) 1
(c) – 2 (d) – 1

5. If the graph of the equation $20x + 21y = 420$ cuts the co-ordinate axis at P and Q, then what is the measure of the length (in units) of PQ? **SSC CHSL (Tier-I) 05/07/2024 Shift-IV**
(a) 25 (b) 29 (c) 40 (d) 35

6. The perpendicular length from the origin to the line $6x + 8y - 48 = 0$ is
SSC CHSL (Tier-I) 05/07/2024 Shift-III
(a) 2.6 units (b) 4.8 units
(c) 8.3 units (d) 5.2 units

7. What is the area of the region created by the two linear equations $2x + y = 6$ and $2x - y = -2$ bounded by these lines and the X-axis?
SSC CHSL (Tier-I) 03/07/2024 Shift-II
(a) 5 sq. units (b) 8 sq. units
(c) 3 sq. units (d) 6 sq. units

8. The length of the portion of the straight line $5x + 12y = 60$ intercepted between the axis is
SSC CHSL (Tier-I) 03/07/2024 Shift-I
(a) 5 (b) 13 (c) 17 (d) 12

9. If a circle whose centre is (2, 3) touches the line $4x + 3y - 7 = 0$, then the radius of the circle is
SSC CHSL (Tier-I) 03/07/2024 Shift-I
(a) 4 units (b) 1 unit
(c) 2 units (d) 3 units

10. The shortest length of the intercept between the X-axis and Y-axis of the equation $6x + 8y - 48 = 0$ is
SSC CHSL (Tier-I) 02/07/2024 Shift-III
(a) 10 units (b) 6 units
(c) 14 units (d) 12 units

11. If equation of line p is $x + y = 5$ and that of line q is $x - y = 3$, what are the co-ordinates of the point common to both the lines?
SSC CHSL (Tier-I) 01/07/2024 Shift-I
(a) (2, 1) (b) (2, 3)
(c) (4, 1) (d) (1, 4)

12. Calculate the area of the quadrilateral formed with the vertices (–3, 2),(5, 4),(7,–6) and (–5, –4). **SSC CHSL (Tier-I) 27/05/2022 Shift-I**
(a) 80 square units
(b) 160 square units
(c) 0 square units
(d) 150 square units

SSC MTS 2024

13. Find the area of the quadrilateral $ABCD$, the coordinates of whose vertices are A(6, – 3), B(–4,–2), C(3, 1) and D(5, 0)?
SSC MTS (Tier-I) 01/04/2024 Shift-I
(a) 21 unit^2 (b) 30 unit^2
(c) 25 unit^2 (d) 16 unit^2

Right Answers

1	(a)	2	(c)	3	(a)	4	(c)	5	(b)	6	(b)	7	(b)	8	(b)	9	(c)	10	(a)
11	(c)	12	(a)	13	(a)														

Solutions

1. (a) $57x - 19y = 399$

At Y-axis, $x = 0$

$57 \times 0 - 19y = 399$

$\Rightarrow \quad 0 - 19y = 399$

$\Rightarrow \quad -19y = 399$

$\Rightarrow \quad y = \dfrac{399}{-19} = -21$

$\therefore \quad y = -21$

At X-axis, $y = 0$

$57x - 13 \times 0 = 399 \Rightarrow 57x = 399$

$\Rightarrow \quad x = \dfrac{399}{57} \Rightarrow x = 7$

X-axis at (7, 0) and Y-axis at (0, – 21).

2. (c) Given, Centre point = (–1, 2, – 3)

Radius = 3 units

We know,

General form of equation of sphere is

$$(x - a)^2 + (y - b)^2 + (z - c)^2 = (r)^2$$

Here, $a = -1, b = 2, c = -3, r = 3$

$\therefore$ Required equation of sphere is

$[x - (-1)]^2 + (y - 2)^2 + [z - (-3)]^2 = (3)^2$

$\Rightarrow (x + 1)^2 + (y - 2)^2 + (z + 3)^2 = 9$

$\Rightarrow x^2 + 1 + 2x + y^2 + 4 - 4y + z^2 + 9 + 6z = 9$

$\Rightarrow x^2 + y^2 + z^2 + 2x - 4y + 6z + 14 - 9 = 0$

$\Rightarrow \quad x^2 + y^2 + z^2 + 2x - 4y + 6z + 5 = 0$

3. (a) Given equations,

$x + y = 10 \Rightarrow y = 10 - x$ ...(i)

$-3x + y = 2$ ...(ii)

Substitute Eq. (i) in Eq. (ii),

$-3x + (10 - x) = 2 \Rightarrow -3x + 10 - x = 2$

$\Rightarrow \quad -4x + 10 = 2$

$\Rightarrow \quad 4x = 8 \Rightarrow x = 2$

From Eq. (i), $\quad y = 10 - 2 = 8$

Now, point of intersection of the line

$x + y = 10$ and X-axis i.e., $(x, 0)$

$\Rightarrow \quad x + 0 = 10 \Rightarrow x = 10$

$\therefore$ Point of intersection = (10, 0)

Hence, required distance between (2, 8) and (10, 0) $= \sqrt{(10-2)^2 + (0-8)^2}$

$= \sqrt{(8)^2 + (8)^2} = \sqrt{64+64}$

$= \sqrt{64 \times 2} = 8\sqrt{2}$

4. (c) Given equations,

$3p - 2q + 23 = 0$ ...(i)

$-2p + q - 13 = 0$ ...(ii)

On solving Eqs. (i) and (ii),

2 × Eq. (ii) + Eq. (i)

$3p - 2q + 23 = 0$

$-4p + 2q - 26 = 0$

$-p - 3 = 0$

$\therefore \quad p = -3$

Put $p = -3$ in Eq. (ii), we get

$-2 \times (-3) + q - 13 = 0 \Rightarrow +6 + q - 13 = 0$

$\Rightarrow \quad q = 7$

$\therefore \quad (p, q) = (-3, 7)$

$\therefore$ The value of $(3p + q) = 3 \times (-3) + 7 = -2$

5. (b) Given, $20x + 21y = 420$ ...(i)

At P, $y = 0$ put in Eq. (i),

$20x = 420 \Rightarrow x = 21$

$\therefore$ Coordinate at $P = (21, 0)$

At Q, $x = 0$ put in Eq. (i)

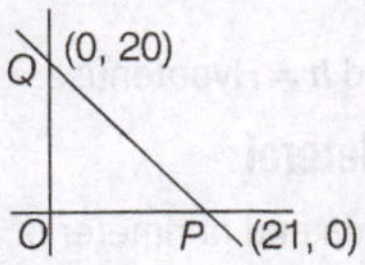

$21y = 420 \Rightarrow y = 20$

$\therefore$ Coordinate at $Q = (0, 20)$

$\therefore$ Length of $PQ = \sqrt{(y_2 - y_1)^2 + (x_2 - x_1)^2}$

$= \sqrt{(0-20)^2 + (21-0)^2}$

$= \sqrt{400 + 441} = \sqrt{841}$

$\Rightarrow \quad PQ = 29$ units

6. (b) Given, Point $P(0, 0)$

Line : $6x + 8y - 48 = 0$

We know, Distance of a point from a line (D)

$= \left| \dfrac{ax_1 + by_1 + c}{\sqrt{a^2 + b^2}} \right|$

Here, $a = 6$, $b = 8$, $c = -48$,

$x_1 = 0, y_1 = 0$

$\therefore \quad D = \left| \dfrac{6(0) + 8(0) - 48}{\sqrt{(6)^2 + (8)^2}} \right|$

$\Rightarrow \quad D = \left| \dfrac{-48}{10} \right| = 4.8$ units

7. (b) Given equation,

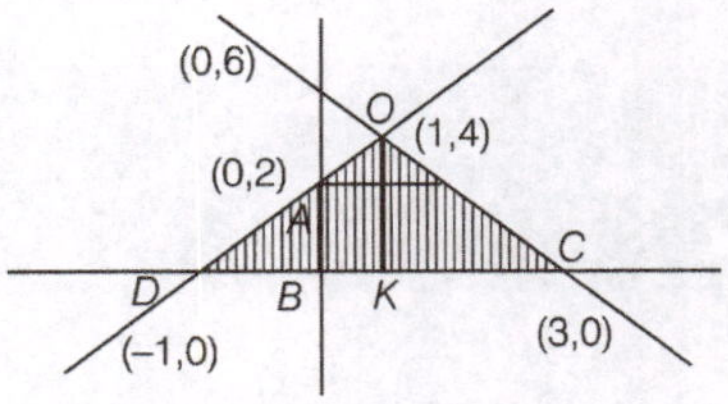

$2x + y = 6 \Rightarrow \dfrac{x}{3} + \dfrac{y}{6} = 1$ ...(i)

and $\quad 2x - y = -2 \Rightarrow \dfrac{x}{-1} + \dfrac{y}{2} = 1$ ...(ii)

From Eqs. (i) and (ii),

$4x = 4 \Rightarrow x = 1$ and $y = 4$

Area of $\Delta DOC = \dfrac{1}{2} DC \times OK$

$= \dfrac{1}{2} \times 4 \times 4 = 8$ sq. units

8. (b) Given, $5x + 12y = 60$

$\therefore \quad \dfrac{5x}{60} + \dfrac{12y}{60} = \dfrac{60}{60} \Rightarrow \dfrac{x}{12} + \dfrac{y}{5} = 1$

So, the length of portion straight line

$= \sqrt{12^2 + 5^2} = \sqrt{144 + 25} = \sqrt{169} = 13$

9. (c) We need to determine the perpendicular distance from the centre of the circle to the line. The distance will be equal to the radius of the circle.

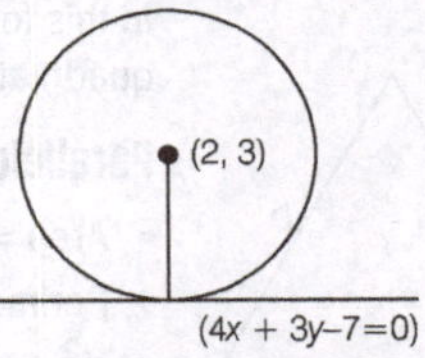

$\therefore$ Perpendicular distance d from a point (x_1, y_1) to line $Ax + By + C = 0$

$\Rightarrow d = \dfrac{|Ax_1 + By_1 + C|}{\sqrt{A^2 + B^2}} \quad [\because (x_1, y_1) = (2, 3)]$

$A = 4$, $B = 3$ and $C = -7$

$d = \dfrac{|4(2) + 3(3) - 7|}{\sqrt{4^2 + 3^2}} = \dfrac{|8 + 9 - 7|}{\sqrt{16 + 9}}$

$= \dfrac{10}{\sqrt{25}} = \dfrac{10}{5} = 2$ units

$\therefore$ Radius of the circle is 2 units.

10. (a) Given equation, $6x + 8y - 48 = 0$

Length of intercept at X-axis, when $y = 0$

$6x + 0 = 48$

$\Rightarrow \quad 6x = 48 \Rightarrow x = 8$

$\Rightarrow \quad x = (8, 0)$

Length of intercept at Y-axis, when $x = 0$

$0 + 8y = 48$

$\Rightarrow \quad 8y = 48 \Rightarrow y = 6 \Rightarrow y = (0, 6)$

$\therefore$ Shortest length $= \sqrt{8^2 + 6^2} = \sqrt{100}$

$= 10$ units

11. (c) Equation of line p is $x + y = 5$ ...(i)

Equation of line q is $x - y = 3$ ...(ii)

Adding Eqs. (i) and (ii), we get

$2x = 8 \quad x = 4$

Putting $x = 4$ in Eq. (i), we get

$4 + y = 5 \quad y = 1$

$\therefore$ Co-ordinates of points common to both are is (4, 1).

12. (a) Area of ΔABC

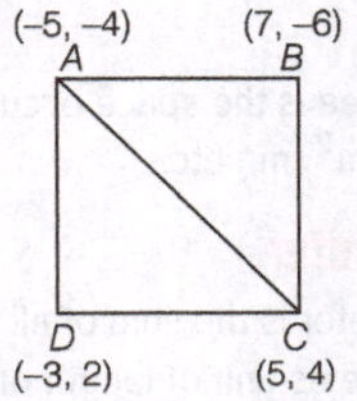

$= \dfrac{1}{2} | -5(-6-4) + 7(4+4) + 5(-4+6) |$

$= \dfrac{1}{2} | 50 + 56 + 10 | = \dfrac{1}{2} | 116 | = 58$ sq unit

Area of $\Delta ACD = \dfrac{1}{2} | -5(4-2) + 5(2+4) - 3(-4-4) |$

$= \dfrac{1}{2} | -10 + 30 + 24 | = \dfrac{1}{2} \times 44 = 22$ sq unit

$\therefore$ Area of quadrilateral $ABCD$

$= \Delta ABC + \Delta ACD$

$= 58 + 22 = 80$ sq units

13. (a) Here, $(x_1, y_1) = (6, -3)$, $(x_2, y_2) = (-4, -2)$, $(x_3, y_3) = (3, 1)$ and $(x_4, y_4) = (5, 0)$

Area of quadrilateral

$= \dfrac{1}{2} \left| \begin{matrix} (x_1 y_2 + x_2 y_3 + x_3 y_4 + x_4 y_1) \\ -(x_2 y_1 + x_3 y_2 + x_4 y_3 + x_1 y_4) \end{matrix} \right|$

$= \dfrac{1}{2} \left| \begin{matrix} (6 \times -2) + (-4) \times 1 + 3 \times 0 + 5(-3) \\ -(-4 \times -3) + 3 \times (-2) + 5 \times 1 + 6 \times 0 \end{matrix} \right|$

$= \dfrac{1}{2} |(-12 - 4 - 15) - (12 - 6 + 5)|$

$= \dfrac{1}{2} |-31 - 11| = 21 \text{ unit}^2$

22

Area and Perimeter

Area

The area is the space occupied by plane figure. The unit of area is sq. units like, cm^2, m^2 etc.

Perimeter

Perimeter is the sum of all the sides of a plane figure. The unit of perimeter is same as unit of length of the sides of a plane figure.

Based on Area and Perimeter of Triangle

In this topic we will see how to find the area and perimeter of all types of triangle.

Scalene Triangle

- Area $= \sqrt{s(s-a)(s-b)(s-c)}$ [Heron's formula] where, $s = \dfrac{a+b+c}{2}$ and a, b and c are the sides of the triangle and s is the semi-perimeter.
- Perimeter $= a + b + c$
- Inradius $= \dfrac{\Delta}{s}$
- Circumradius $= \dfrac{abc}{4\Delta}$

where, Δ = Area of scalene triangle

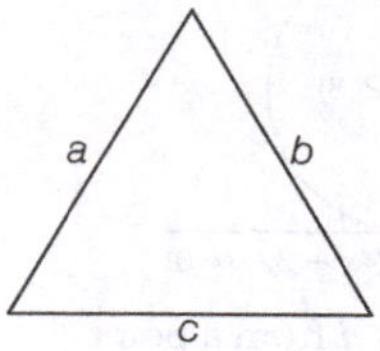

Isosceles Triangle

- Area $= \dfrac{b}{4}\sqrt{4a^2 - b^2}$
- Height $= \sqrt{a^2 - \left(\dfrac{b}{2}\right)^2} = \dfrac{1}{2}\sqrt{4a^2 - b^2}$
- Perimeter $= 2a + b$ Where, a = Each of two equal sides; b = Third side

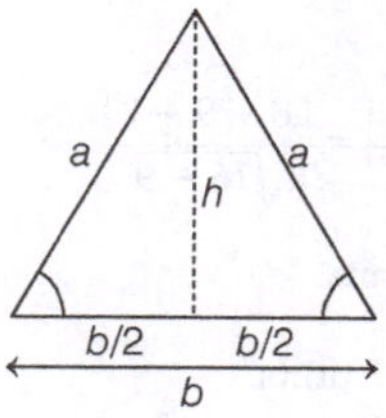

Equilateral Triangle

- Area $= \dfrac{\sqrt{3}}{4}a^2$
- Perimeter $= 3a$
- Height $= \dfrac{\sqrt{3}a}{2}$
- Inradius $= \dfrac{a}{2\sqrt{3}}$
- Circumradius $= \dfrac{a}{\sqrt{3}}$

Where, a = Side of the triangle

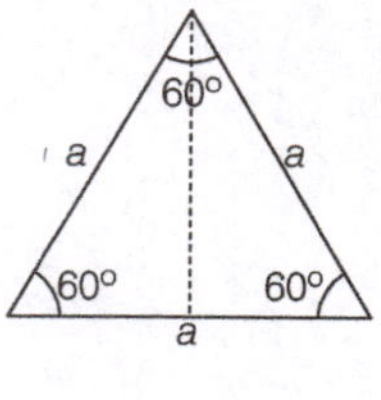

Right angled Triangle

- Area $= \dfrac{1}{2} \times b \times p$
- Perimeter $= p + b + h$
- Pythagoras theorem : $h^2 = p^2 + b^2$
- Inradius $(r) = \dfrac{p+b-h}{2}$
- Circumradius $(R) = \dfrac{h}{2}$

Where, p = Perpendicular, b = Base and h = Hypotenuse

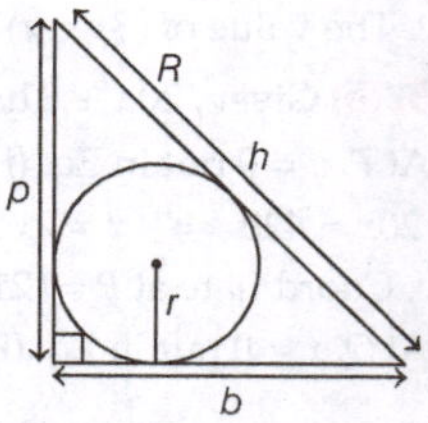

Based on Area and Perimeter of Quadrilateral

In this topic we will see how to find the area and perimeter of all type quadrilateral.

Parallelogram

- Area $= b \times h$
- Perimeter $= 2(a + b)$
- $d_1^2 + d_2^2 = 2(a^2 + b^2)$

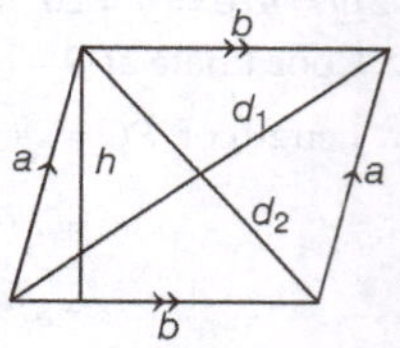

Square

- Area $= a^2 = \dfrac{1}{2}d^2$
- Perimeter $= 4a$
- Diagonal $(d) = a\sqrt{2}$

Where a = Side, d = Diagonal

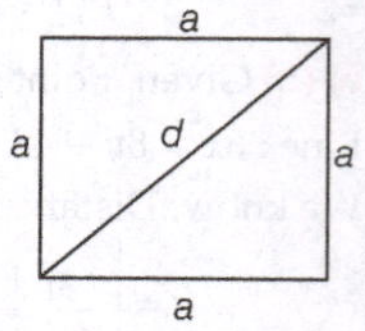

Rhombus

- Area $= \dfrac{1}{2} \times d_1 \times d_2$
- Perimeter $= 4a$
- Side $(a) = \dfrac{1}{2}\sqrt{d_1^2 + d_2^2}$
- $4a^2 = d_1^2 + d_2^2$

Where, a = Side, d_1 and d_2 are diagonals.

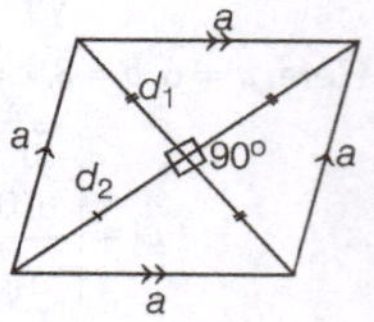

Rectangle

- Area = Length × Breadth $= L \times B$
- Perimeter $= 2(L + B)$
- Diagonal $(d) = \sqrt{L^2 + B^2}$

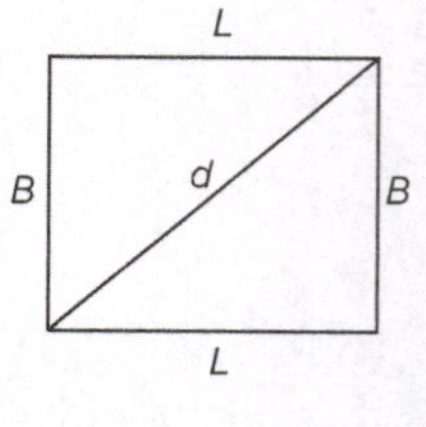

Trapezium

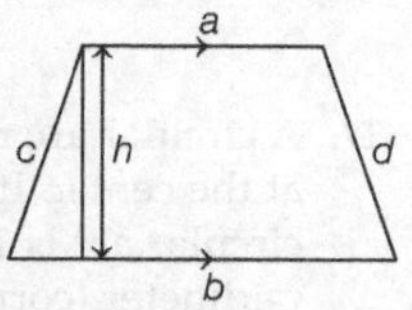

- Area $= \frac{1}{2}$ (Sum of the parallel sides) × Height $= \frac{1}{2}(a+b)h$
- Perimeter $= a+b+c+d$

Where, a and b are parallel sides and h is the height or perpendicular distance between a and b.

Based on Area and Circumference of Circle

In this topic we will see how to find the area and perimeter of sector, semicircle and circular path.

Circle

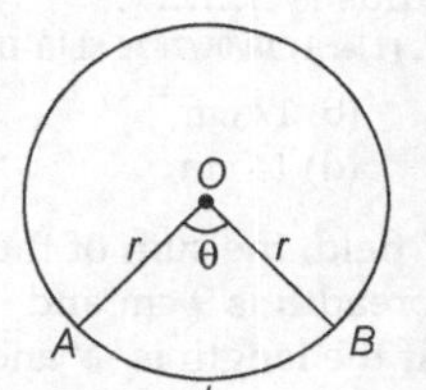

- Area $= \pi r^2$
- Circumference (Perimeter) $= 2\pi r$
- Diameter $= 2r$
- Length of the arc $(l) = \frac{\pi r \theta}{180°}$
- Area of sector $AOB = \frac{\pi r^2 \theta}{360°}$

Where, θ = Angle enclosed between two radii (in degree), r = radius and $\pi = \frac{22}{7} = 3.14$

Semi-circle

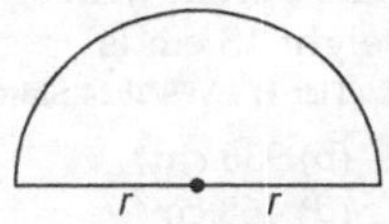

- Area $= \frac{1}{2}\pi r^2$
- Perimeter $= \pi r + 2r = \frac{36}{7}r$

Where, r = Radius of semi-circle

Circular Ring

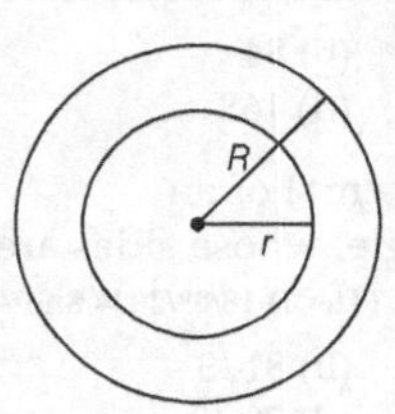

- Area $= \pi(R^2 - r^2)$
- Difference in circumference of both the rings $= (2\pi R - 2\pi r) = 2\pi(R - r)$

Where, R = Radius of bigger ring,
r = Radius of smaller ring

Important Formulae Related to Area and Perimeter

1. If the **length** and **breadth** of a **rectangle** are **increased** by a% and b% respectively, then area will be **increased** by $\left(a+b+\frac{ab}{100}\right)$%
2. If **all the sides** of any two-dimensional figure are changed by a%, then its area will be changed by $\left(2a+\frac{a^2}{100}\right)$%. In case of circle, radius (or diameter) is increased in place of sides.
3. If all the measuring sides of any two-dimensional figure are changed (increased or decreased) by a%, then its perimeter also changes by a%. In case of circle, such change takes place because of the change in radius (or diameter).
4. If a pathway of width x is made inside or outside a rectangular plot of length l and breadth b, then area of pathway is
   (i) $2x(l+b+2x)$, if path is made outside the plot.
   (ii) $2x(l+b-2x)$, if path is made inside the plot.
5. If the two paths, each of width x are made parallel to length (l) and breadth (b) of the rectangular plot in the middle of the plot, then area of the paths is $x(l+b-x)$.

Ex. 1 Find the area of triangle whose sides are 26 cm, 28 cm and 30 cm.

Sol. By Heron's formula, $s = \frac{a+b+c}{2} = \frac{26+28+30}{2} = \frac{84}{2} = 42$

Area of triangle $= \sqrt{s(s-a)(s-b)(s-c)}$

$= \sqrt{42 \times (42-26)(42-28) \times (42-30)}$

$= \sqrt{42 \times 16 \times 14 \times 12} = 336$ sq. cm

Ex. 2 If area of a square is 44 cm, find the area of circle formed by the same perimeter.

Sol. As we know, Area of square = (side)^2; 44 = (side)^2; side $= 2\sqrt{11}$ cm

∴ Perimeter of square $= 4 \times$ side $= 4 \times 2\sqrt{11} = 8\sqrt{11}$ cm

According to the question,

Circumference of circle = Perimeter of square $\Rightarrow 2\pi r = 8\sqrt{11} \Rightarrow r = \frac{4\sqrt{11}}{\pi}$

∴ Area of circle $= \pi r^2 = \pi \times \left(\frac{4\sqrt{11}}{\pi}\right)^2$

$= \pi \times 4 \times \frac{4 \times 11}{\pi^2} = \frac{16 \times 11 \times 7}{22} = 56$ sq. cm

SSC Exam Scanner

SSC CGL 2024 (Tier I & II)

1. Akshay places three identical rings of diameter 21 cm in such a manner that each one touches the other two rings. He observes that there is a space enclosed by circles. What is the area (in cm^2) of this portion? $\left(\text{Take } \pi = \dfrac{22}{7}\right)$

Note Rounded off to nearest 2 decimal places and $\sqrt{3} = 1.732$

SSC CGL (Tier-II) 20/01/2025 Shift-I

(a) 18.25 (b) 24.12
(c) 17.70 (d) 20.65

2. The ratio between the length and the breadth of a rectangular park is 3 : 2, and the perimeter of the park is 120 m. Find the area (in m^2) of the park. **SSC CGL (Tier-II) 20/01/2025 Shift-I**

(a) 864 (b) 968
(c) 144 (d) 454

3. The central angle of a sector is 80° and whose arc length is 96π. What is the radius of the circle?

SSC CGL (Tier-I) 26/09/2024 Shift-II

(a) 196 units (b) 204 units
(c) 116 units (d) 216 units

4. The ratio of circumference and diameter of a circle is 3 : 5. If the circumference is 6 cm, then the radius of the circle is

SSC CGL (Tier I) 25/09/2024 Shift-III

(a) 10 cm (b) 15 cm
(c) 5 cm (d) 18 cm

5. A circular arc; whose radius is 14 cm, makes an angle of 45° at the centre. Find the perimeter (in cm) of the sector. $\left(\text{Use } \pi = \dfrac{22}{7}\right)$

SSC CGL (Tier I) 25/09/2024 Shift-II

(a) 38 (b) 28
(c) 39 (d) 34

6. Find the diameter (in cm) of a circle, whose circumference is equal to the sum of the circumferences of two circles of radii 12 cm and 16 cm.

SSC CGL (Tier I) 25/09/2024 Shift-II

(a) 32 (b) 56 (c) 64 (d) 28

7. The radii of two circles are 8 cm and 15 cm. The perimeter of the circle having area equal to the sum of the areas of the two circles (in cm) is

SSC CGL (Tier I) 24/09/2024 Shift-II

(a) 32π (b) 30π (c) 28π (d) 34π

8. If each side of an equilateral triangle is $37\sqrt{3}$ cm,then its altitude (in cm) is equal to

SSC CGL (Tier I) 23/09/2024 Shift-III

(a) 37.5 (b) 18.5
(c) 60.5 (d) 55.5

9. Find the area of a rectangle whose length is 52 m and breadth is 9 m.

SSC CGL (Tier I) 23/09/2024 Shift-III

(a) 468 m^2 (b) 253 m^2
(c) 625 m^2 (d) 552 m^2

10. If the area of a sector of a circle is 462 cm^2 and the central angle is 120°, then its radius is ....

SSC CGL (Tier I) 19/09/2024 Shift-III

(a) 18 cm (b) 17 cm
(c) 21 cm (d) 14 cm

11. In a rectangular field, the sum of the length and the breadth is 9 cm and area is 18 cm^2. If the length is 'a' and breadth is 'b', then find the value of $(a^2 - ab + b^2)$.

SSC CGL (Tier I) 19/09/2024 Shift-III

(a) 36 (b) 24 (c) 18 (d) 27

12. The area of a parallelogram with base 26 cm and height 18 cm is

SSC CGL (Tier I) 19/09/2024 Shift-I

(a) 234 cm^2 (b) 936 cm^2
(c) 932 cm^2 (d) 468 cm^2

13. Find the area (in cm^2) of the sector, where the radius of the circle is 24 cm and length of the arc is 7 cm.

SSC CGL (Tier I) 18/09/2024 Shift-III

(a) 72 (b) 84
(c) 48 (d) 168

14. Find the area (in cm^2) of an equilateral triangle, whose sides are 18 cm. **SSC CGL (Tier I) 18/09/2024 Shift-II**

(a) $75\sqrt{3}$ (b) $81\sqrt{3}$
(c) $77\sqrt{3}$ (d) $79\sqrt{3}$

15. A circular arc, whose radius is 24 cm makes an angle of 60° at the centre. The perimeter of the sector formed is (use $\pi = 3.14$)

SSC CGL (Tier I) 18/09/2024 Shift-I

(a) 73.22 cm (b) 63.12 cm
(c) 74.32 cm (d) 73.12 cm

16. The perimeter of a rectangular garden is 48 m. If the length is 6 m more than the breadth, the area (in m^2) of the garden is

SSC CGL (Tier I) 18/09/2024 Shift-I

(a) 135 (b) 96
(c) 84 (d) 112

17. A circular arc makes an angle of 15° at the center. If the radius of the circular arc is 14 cm, what is the perimeter (correct up to two decimal places) of the sector so formed? ($\pi = 3.14$)?

SSC CGL (Tier I) 17/09/2024 Shift-III

(a) 17.66 cm (b) 21.32 cm
(c) 35.32 cm (d) 31.66 cm

18. At what angle is the arc length half the perimeter of the circle?

SSC CGL (Tier I) 17/09/2024 Shift-I

(a) 120° (b) 180°
(c) 90° (d) 270°

19. What is the difference in area (in cm²) of ΔABC having sides of 10 cm, 20 cm and 20 cm, and a right angled triangle ΔPQR with hypotenuse of 13 cm and one of the perpendicular of 12 cm?

Note $\sqrt{2} = 1.41$, $\sqrt{3} = 1.73$, $\sqrt{7} = 2.65$, $\sqrt{13} = 3.61$, $\sqrt{15} = 3.87$, $\sqrt{21} = 4.58$

SSC CGL (Tier I) 17/09/2024 Shift-I

(a) 70.05 (b) 36.57
(c) 66.75 (d) 53.58

20. Find the measure of the central angle of a sector if its area is 16π and the radius is 8.

SSC CGL (Tier I) 17/09/2024 Shift-I

(a) 75° (b) 60° (c) 108° (d) 90°

21. The area of a sector of a circle of radius 12 cm, formed by an arc of length 7 cm is

SSC CGL (Tier I) 13/09/2024 Shift-III

(a) 42 cm^2 (b) 84 cm^2
(c) 21 cm^2 (d) 28 cm^2

22. One-quarter of a circular pizza of radius 21 cm was removed from the whole pizza. What is the perimeter (in cm) of the remaining pizza? (Use $\pi = \dfrac{22}{7}$)

SSC CGL (Tier I) 13/09/2024 Shift-I

(a) 99 (b) 141
(c) 128 (d) 131

23. If the sectorial angle with radius 9.6 units is 75°, what is the length of the arc? **SSC CGL (Tier I) 12/09/2024 Shift-III**

(a) 2π (b) 4π (c) π (d) 3π

24. A circular arc whose radius is 12 cm makes an angle of 30° at the centre. Find the perimeter (in cm) of the sector formed. (Use $\pi = 3.14$)

SSC CGL (Tier I) 12/09/2024 Shift-III

(a) 32.38 (b) 30.28
(c) 28.64 (d) 26.24

25. In triangle ABC, the length of side BC is 2 cm less than twice the length of side AB. The length of side AC exceeds the length of side AB by 10 cm. The perimeter of the triangle is 40 cm. Determine the length (in cm) of the smallest side of the triangle. **SSC CGL (Tier I) 12/09/2024 Shift-II**

(a) 12 (b) 14
(c) 10 (d) 8

26. Find the area of a sector with an arc length of 44 cm, which subtends a central angle of 30°.
SSC CGL (Tier I) 12/09/2024 Shift-II

(a) 1488 cm^2 (b) 1584 cm^2
(c) 1848 cm^2 (d) 1884 cm^2

27. Find the area of a square, one of whose diagonals is 4.8 m long.
SSC CGL (Tier I) 11/09/2024 Shift-II

(a) 12.5m^2 (b) 10.5 m^2
(c) 9.5 m^2 (d) 11.52 m^2

28. If the perimeter of an equilateral triangle is 36 units, then its area is (in square units)
SSC CGL (Tier I) 11/09/2024 Shift-I

(a) $144\sqrt{2}$ (b) $36\sqrt{2}$
(c) $144\sqrt{3}$ (d) $36\sqrt{3}$

29. A rectangular courtyard is 4 m 95 cm long and 16 m 65 cm broad. It is to be paved with the square tiles of the same size. Find the least number of such square tiles required to pave the rectangular courtyard.
SSC CGL (Tier I) 11/09/2024 Shift-I

(a) 877 (b) 944 (c) 388 (d) 407

30. The inner and outer radii of a circular track are 28 m and 25 m, respectively. The cost (in ₹) of levelling the track at ₹28 per m^2 is $\left[\text{Use } \pi = \frac{22}{7}\right]$
SSC CGL (Tier I) 11/09/2024 Shift-I

(a) ₹ 15421 (b) ₹ 13992
(c) ₹ 11229 (d) ₹ 17355

31. What is the central angle of a sector of a circle whose area and perimeter are respectively, equal to 209 cm^2 and 63 cm if it is given that its radius is a non-negative integer (roundup to one decimal place)?
SSC CGL (Tier I) 10/09/2024 Shift-III

(a) 55.5° (b) 53.5°
(c) 49.5° (d) 51.5°

32. The area of a square is $16x^2 + 40x + 25$ square units. Find the perimeter of the square.
SSC CGL (Tier I) 10/09/2024 Shift-III

(a) $3(10x + 8)$ (b) $3(8x + 10)$
(c) $2(10x + 8)$ (d) $2(8x + 10)$

33. The side of an equilateral triangle is 28 cm. Taking each vertex as the centre, a circle is described with a radius equal to half the length of the side of the triangle. Find the area of that part of the triangle which is not included in the circles (Use $\pi = \frac{22}{7}$ and $\sqrt{3} = 1.73$).
SSC CGL (Tier I) 10/09/2024 Shift-I

(a) 30.89 cm^2 (b) 38.08 cm^2
(c) 31.08 cm^2 (d) 39.08 cm^2

34. What is the perimeter (in cm, rounded off to one decimal place) of the sector of a circle with a radius of 10 cm and of angle 30°? (use $\pi = 3.14$)
SSC CGL (Tier I) 09/09/2024 Shift-III

(a) 20.4 (b) 35.7
(c) 82.8 (d) 25.2

35. Find the area (in cm^2) of the sector whose perimeter is $\frac{64}{3}$ cm and central angle is 60°. $\left(\text{use } \pi = \frac{22}{7}\right)$
SSC CGL (Tier I) 09/09/2024 Shift-III

(a) $\frac{47}{3}$ (b) $\frac{77}{3}$
(c) $\frac{68}{3}$ (d) $\frac{85}{3}$

36. A right-angled isosceles triangle has an area of 50 square units. Its hypotenuse is (in units):
SSC CGL (Tier I) 09/09/2024 Shift-II

(a) $10\sqrt{3}$ (b) $5\sqrt{5}$
(c) $10\sqrt{2}$ (d) $5\sqrt{2}$

37. From a circle with the radius of 15.75 cm, a sector with the arc length of 11 cm is cut off. Find the area (in cm^2) of this sector.
SSC CGL (Tier I) 09/09/2024 Shift-II

(a) 86.525 cm^2 (b) 86.625 cm^2
(c) 86.875 cm^2 (d) 86.125 cm^2

SSC CGL 2023 (Tier I & II)

38. In a trapezium $ABCD$, AB and DC are parallel to each other with a perpendicular distance of 8 m between them. Also, $(AD) = (BC) = 10$ m, and $(AB) = 15$ m $< (DC)$. What is the perimeter (in m) of the trapezium $ABCD$? **SSC CGL (Tier II) 07/03/2023 Shift-I**

(a) 66 (b) 62
(c) 58 (d) 50

39. What is the perimeter of a square inscribed in a circle of radius 5 cm? **SSC CGL (Tier II) 06/03/2023 Shift-I**

(a) $20\sqrt{2}$ cm (b) $40\sqrt{2}$ cm
(c) $30\sqrt{2}$ cm (d) $10\sqrt{2}$ cm

40. The difference between the length of two parallel sides of a trapezium is 12 cm. The perpendicular distance between these two parallel sides is 60 cm. If the area of the trapezium is 1380 cm^2, then find the length of each of the parallel sides (in cm).
SSC CGL (Tier II) 06/03/2023 Shift-I

(a) 27, 15 (b) 31, 19
(c) 29, 17 (d) 24, 12

41. A rhombus has one of its diagonal 65% of the other. A square is drawn using the longer diagonal as side. What will be the ratio of the area of the rhombus as that of the square?
SSC CGL (Tier I) 03/03/2023 Shift-I

(a) 18 : 15 (b) 15 : 18
(c) 40 : 13 (d) 13 : 40

42. A rectangular park is 120 m long and 104 m wide. A 1 m wide path runs along the boundary of the park, remaining completely inside the park area. Thus, the outside edges of the path run along the boundary wall of the park. The inside edges of the path are marked with a white line of negligible thickness. If it costs ₹ 2.50 to mark each metre with the white line, then how much would it cost (in ₹) to fully mark the inside edges of the path?
SSC CGL (Tier II) 02/03/2023 Shift-I

(a) 1090 (b) 1080
(c) 1120 (d) 1100

43. A circular arc whose radius is 4 cm makes an angle 45° at the centre. Find the perimeter of the sector formed. $\left(\text{Take}, \pi = \frac{22}{7}\right)$
SSC CGL (Tier I) 27/07/2023 Shift-III

(a) $\frac{78}{7}$ cm (b) $\frac{72}{7}$ cm
(c) $\frac{74}{7}$ cm (d) $\frac{76}{7}$ cm

44. In the following figure, the length of arc AB is equal to five times of the radius r of the circle. Find the area of sector AOB.
SSC CGL (Tier I) 27/07/2023 Shift-I

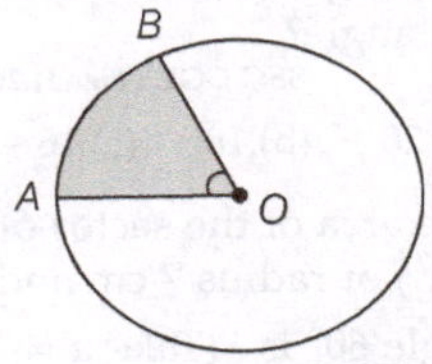

(a) $2.5r^2$ (b) $\frac{1}{2}r^2$
(c) $3r^2$ (d) $2r^2$

45. Find the area of an equilateral triangle whose sides are 16 cm each.
SSC CGL (Tier I) 26/07/2023 Shift-III
(a) $60\sqrt{3}$ cm^2 (b) $62\sqrt{3}$ cm^2
(c) $64\sqrt{3}$ cm^2 (d) $66\sqrt{3}$ cm^2

46. What is the area of the sector of a circle of radius 8 cm and formed by an arc of length 12 cm?
SSC CGL (Tier I) 25/07/2023 Shift-III
(a) 45 cm^2 (b) 47 cm^2
(c) 48 cm^2 (d) 84 cm^2

47. A field is 150 m long and 80 m wide. How many times (rounded off to 1 decimal place) is its perimeter to the length of its diagonal?
SSC CGL (Tier I) 25/07/2023 Shift-I
(a) 2.3 (b) 2.5
(c) 2.7 (d) 3.1

48. The following formula is used to calculate which of the following?
$$\frac{\text{Angle of arc at centre}}{360^\circ} \times \pi \times \text{diameter}$$
SSC CGL (Tier I) 25/07/2023 Shift-I
(a) Length of a sector
(b) Area of an arc
(c) Radius of a circle
(d) Length of an arc

49. The side of an equilateral triangle is 12 cm. What is the area (in cm^2, rounded off to 2 decimal places) of the triangle? Given, $\sqrt{3} = 1.732$
SSC CGL (Tier I) 24/07/2023 Shift-IV
(a) 68.07 (b) 63.89
(c) 62.35 (d) 65.23

50. The ratio of the length and width of a certain rectangle is 3 : 2 and the area is 150 cm^2. The perimeter of the rectangle (in cm) is
SSC CGL (Tier I) 24/07/2023 Shift-I
(a) 20 (b) 30 (c) 50 (d) 40

51. The perimeter of an isosceles triangle is 100 cm. If the base is 36 cm, then find its semi perimeter (in cm). **SSC CGL (Tier I) 21/07/2023 Shift-II**
(a) 64 (b) 60 (c) 45 (d) 50

52. The width of a rectangle is 2 m less than its length. If the perimeter of the rectangle is 68 m, then what is the length (in metres) of the rectangle?
SSC CGL (Tier I) 20/07/2023 Shift-IV
(a) 20 (b) 18 (c) 16 (d) 17

53. The area of the sector of a circle (in cm^2) of radius 7 cm and central angle 60° is (Take $\pi = \frac{22}{7}$)
SSC CGL (Tier I) 18/07/2023 Shift-III
(a) $\frac{77}{2}$ (b) 77 (c) $\frac{77}{3}$ (d) $\frac{77}{4}$

54. Find the length of the arc of the sector of a circle of diameter 7 cm with a central angle of 108°. [Use $\pi = 22/7$]
SSC CGL (Tier I) 19/07/2023 Shift-I
(a) 6.6 cm (b) 5.6 cm
(c) 13.2 cm (d) 11.2 cm

55. Area of a sector is 1848 m^2 and the central angle of the sector is 270°. Find the radius of the circle. (Take, $\pi = 22/7$)
SSC CGL (Tier I) 18/07/2023 Shift-IV
(a) 28 m (b) 784 m (c) 22 m (d) 28 m

56. The perimeter of an equilateral triangle is 48 cm. Find its area (in cm^2). **SSC CGL (Tier I) 18/07/2023 Shift-II**
(a) $81\sqrt{3}$ (b) $8\sqrt{3}$
(c) $25\sqrt{3}$ (d) $64\sqrt{3}$

57. The ratio of the length of each equal side and the third side of an isosceles triangle is 3 : 5. If the area of the triangle is $30\sqrt{11}$ cm^2, then the length of the third side (in cm) is
SSC CGL (Tier I) 18//07/2023 Shift-II
(a) $10\sqrt{6}$ (b) $5\sqrt{6}$
(c) $13\sqrt{6}$ (d) $11\sqrt{6}$

58. The area of the sector of a circle of radius 12 cm is 32 π cm^2. Find the length of the corresponding arc of the sector.
SSC CGL (Tier I) 17/07/2023 Shift-IV
(a) $\frac{8}{3}\pi$ cm (b) $\frac{13}{3}\pi$ cm
(c) $\frac{10}{3}\pi$ cm (d) $\frac{16}{3}\pi$ cm

59. A sector of a circle of radius 10 cm is formed at 60° angle at the centre. What will be its area (take $\pi = 3.14$)?
SSC CGL (Tier I) 17/07/2023 Shift-IV
(a) 75.28 cm^2 (b) 60.67 cm^2
(c) 55.00 cm^2 (d) 52.33 cm^2

60. Find the area of the sector of a circle with radius 5 cm and angle 60° (rounded off to one decimal).
SSC CGL (Tier I) 17/07/2023 Shift-III
(a) 12.8 cm^2 (b) 14.1 cm^2
(c) 13.1 cm^2 (d) 15.1 cm^2

61. An arc of length 23.1 cm subtends an 18° angle at the centre. What is the area of the circle ? [Use $\pi = \frac{22}{7}$]
SSC CGL (Tier I) 17/07/2023 Shift-II
(a) 16878.50 cm^2 (b) 16978.50 cm^2
(c) 16988.50 cm^2 (d) 16798.50 cm^2

62. If the side of an equilateral triangle is increased by 34%, then by what percentage will its area increase?
SSC CGL (Tier I) 17/07/2023 Shift-II
(a) 68.25% (b) 75.15%
(c) 79. 56% (d) 70.65%

SSC CGL 2022 (Tier I)

63. Find the area of the shaded portion of an equilateral triangle with sides 6 units shown in the following figure. A circle of radius 1 unit is centred at midpoint of a side of the triangle.

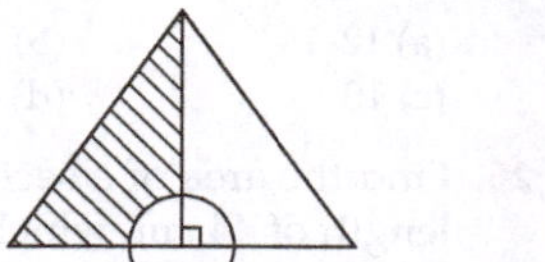

SSC CGL (Tier I) 13/12/2022 Shift-IV
(a) $\frac{1}{2}\left(9\sqrt{3} - \frac{11}{7}\right)$unit^2
(b) $\frac{1}{4}\left(9\sqrt{3} - \frac{11}{7}\right)$unit^2
(c) $\frac{1}{2}\left(6\sqrt{3} - \frac{11}{7}\right)$unit^2
(d) $\frac{1}{2}\left(9\sqrt{3} - \frac{22}{7}\right)$unit^2

64. A triangle and a parallelogram have the same base 28 cm and the same area. If the height of the parallelogram is 12 cm, then find the length of the altitude of the triangle.
SSC CGL (Tier I) 13/12/2022 Shift-II
(a) 28 cm (b) 21 cm
(c) 24 cm (d) 23 cm

65. A horse is grazing in a field. It is tied to a pole with a rope of length 6 m. The horse moves from point A to point B making an arch with an angle of 70°. Find the area of the sector grazed by the horse.
SSC CGL (Tier I) 13/12/2022 Shift-II
(a) 22 m^2 (b) 21 m^2
(c) 20 m^2 (d) 23 m^2

66. The hour hand moves through 4 h and has a length of 6 cm. Find the area (in cm^2, rounded off to two decimal places) of the sector covered by the hour hand.
SSC CGL (Tier I) 13/12/2022 Shift-I
(a) 32.69 (b) 30.67
(c) 37.71 (d) 35.75

67. The circumference of the two circles is 110 cm and 330 cm, respectively. What is the difference between their radii? **SSC CGL (Tier I) 13/12/2022 Shift-I**
(a) 70 cm (b) 15 cm
(c) 46 cm (d) 35 cm

68. The area of a triangle is 96 cm^2 and the ratio of its sides is 6 : 8 : 10. What is the perimeter of the triangle? **SSC CGL (Tier I) 12/12/2022 Shift-II**
(a) 48 cm (b) 56 cm
(c) 64 cm (d) 44 cm

69. A coconut tree swings with the wind in such a manner that the angle covered by its trunk is 18°. If the topmost portion of the tree covers a distance of 44 meters, find the length of the tree.
SSC CGL (Tier I) 12/12/2022 Shift-II
(a) 120 m (b) 210 m
(c) 140 m (d) 70 m

70. The minute hand of a clock is 20 cm long. Find the area on the face of the clock swept by the minute hand between 8 am and 8:45 am.
SSC CGL (Tier I) 12/12/2022 Shift-I
(a) $\frac{6600}{7}$ cm^2 (b) $\frac{6600}{9}$ cm^2
(c) $\frac{6600}{18}$ cm^2 (d) $\frac{6600}{14}$ cm^2

71. The circumference of the two circles is 264 cm and 396 cm, respectively. What is the difference between their radii? SSC CGL (Tier I) 09/12/2022 Shift-I
(a) 25 cm (b) 32 cm
(c) 16 cm (d) 21 cm

72. Three circles of radius 7 cm are kept touching each other. The string is tightly tied around these three circles. What is the length of the string? SSC CGL (Tier I) 08/12/2022 Shift-I
(a) $42 + 7\pi$ cm (b) $21\pi + 14$ cm
(c) $42 + 14\pi$ cm (d) $7 + 14\pi$ cm

73. If the side of an equilateral triangle is 8 cm, then find the area of the triangle (correct to two decimal places). SSC CGL (Tier I) 07/12/2022 Shift-IV
(a) 27.17 cm^2 (b) 27.27 cm^2
(c) 27.71 cm^2 (d) 27.72 cm^2

74. The length of the altitude of an equilateral triangle is $6\sqrt{3}$ m. The perimeter of the equilateral triangle (in m) is, SSC CGL (Tier I) 07/12/2022 Shift-III
(a) $12\sqrt{2}$ (b) $36\sqrt{2}$
(c) 36 (d) $24\sqrt{3}$

75. The perimeter of a square is 124 m. What is its area?
SSC CGL (Tier I) 07/12/2022 Shift-II
(a) 448 m^2 (b) 884 m^2
(c) 764 m^2 (d) 961 m^2

76. The height of an equilateral triangle is $9\sqrt{3}$ cm. What is the area of this equilateral triangle?
SSC CGL (Tier I) 07/12/2022 Shift-I
(a) $92\sqrt{3}$ cm^2 (b) $67\sqrt{3}$ cm^2
(c) $49\sqrt{3}$ cm^2 (d) $81\sqrt{3}$ cm^2

77. If the circumference of a circle is 220 cm, then what is its radius?
SSC CGL (Tier I) 07/12/2022 Shift-I
(a) 26 cm (b) 25 cm
(c) 35 cm (d) 40 cm

78. The diagonal of the square is $8\sqrt{2}$ cm. Find the diagonal of another square whose area is triple that of the first square.
SSC CGL (Tier I) 06/12/2022 Shift-IV
(a) $8\sqrt{5}$ cm (b) $8\sqrt{3}$ cm
(c) $8\sqrt{2}$ cm (d) $8\sqrt{6}$ cm

79. The diagonal of a square is $\sqrt{200}$ cm. If the sides of a rectangle are in the ratio 5 : 2, which has the same as the area of square, then what is the length of the rectangle?
SSC CGL (Tier I) 06/12/2022 Shift-IV
(a) $2\sqrt{10}$ cm (b) $\sqrt{250}$ cm
(c) $\sqrt{200}$ cm (d) $\sqrt{20}$ cm

80. The ratio of the outer and the inner circumference of a circular path is 5 : 4. If path is 50 m wide, then what is the radius of the inner circle?
SSC CGL (Tier I) 06/12/2022 Shift-III
(a) 2500 m (b) 300 m
(c) 200 m (d) 210 m

81. Calculate the area of a sector of a circle with radius 10 m and angle of 90° at the centre.
SSC CGL (Tier I) 06/12/2022 Shift-III
(a) 79.3 m^2 (b) 79.5 m^2
(c) 78.5 m^2 (d) 75 m^2

82. The sides of a triangle are in the ratio $\frac{1}{3}:\frac{1}{5}:\frac{1}{6}$. If the perimeter is 147 cm, then the length of the smallest side is SSC CGL (Tier I) 06/12/2022 Shift-III
(a) 12 cm (b) 25 cm
(c) 30 cm (d) 35 cm

83. The height of an equilateral triangle is $7\sqrt{3}$ cm. What is the area of this equilateral triangle?
SSC CGL (Tier I) 06/12/2022 Shift-II
(a) $36\sqrt{3}$ cm^2 (b) $25\sqrt{3}$ cm^2
(c) $49\sqrt{3}$ cm^2 (d) $32\sqrt{3}$ cm^2

84. A wire is in the form of square with side 11 cm. It is bent to form a circle. What is the radius of the circle?
SSC CGL (Tier I) 06/12/2022 Shift-I
(a) 11 cm (b) 5 cm
(c) 9 cm (d) 7 cm

85. Find the area of the sector of a circle with radius 4 cm and angle 30°.
SSC CGL (Tier I) 06/12/2022 Shift-I
(a) 7.186 cm^2 (b) 6.186 cm^2
(c) 4.186 cm^2 (d) 5.186 cm^2

86. Three circles of radius 4 cm are kept touching each other. The string is tightly tied around these three circles. What is the length of the string? SSC CGL (Tier I) 05/12/2022 Shift-IV
(a) $24 + 8\pi$ cm (b) $24\pi + 16$ cm
(c) $32 + 16\pi$ cm (d) $24 + 18\pi$ cm

87. The area of a sector of a circle is 308 cm^2, with the central angle measuring 45°. The radius of the circle is SSC CGL (Tier I) 03/12/2022 Shift-IV
(a) 14 cm (b) 21 cm
(c) 7 cm (d) 28 cm

88. Three circles of radius 6 cm are kept touching each other. The string is tightly tied around these three circles. What is the length of the string? SSC CGL (Tier I) 03/12/2022 Shift-II
(a) $36 + 12\pi$ cm (b) $36 + 18\pi$ cm
(c) $24 + 36\pi$ cm (d) $36 + 20\pi$ cm

89. The area of a sector of a circle is 66 cm^2 and the angle of the sector is 60°. Find the radius of the circle.
SSC CGL (Tier I) 31/12/2022 Shift-I
(a) $5\sqrt{15}$ cm (b) $6\sqrt{14}$ cm
(c) $7\sqrt{19}$ cm (d) $3\sqrt{14}$ cm

90. In the given figure, a square *ABCD* is inscribed in a quadrant *APCQ*. If *AB* = 16 cm, find the area of the shaded region. (take π = 3.14) correct to two places of decimal.
SSC CGL (Tier I) 02/12/2022 Shift-II

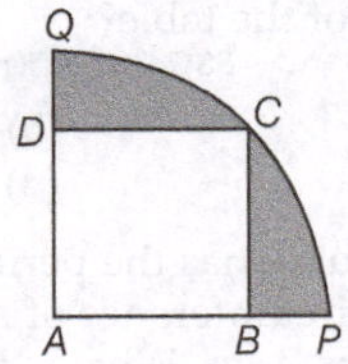

(a) 155.98 cm^2 (b) 179.68 cm^2
(c) 163.85 cm^2 (d) 145.92 cm^2

91. If the side of an equilateral triangle is 20 cm, then what is its area?
SSC CGL (Tier I) 02/12/2022 Shift-II
(a) $110\sqrt{3}$ cm^2 (b) $125\sqrt{3}$ cm^2
(c) $200\sqrt{3}$ cm^2 (d) $100\sqrt{3}$ cm^2

92. A circular clock has the hour hand of length 6 inch. Find the length of the distance it covers by it's tip from 9 pm to 3 am
SSC CGL (Tier I) 02/12/2022 Shift-I
(a) 4π inch (b) 2π inch
(c) 6π inch (d) 8π inch

93. The area of a triangle is 480 cm^2 and the ratio of its sides is 10 : 24 : 26. What is the perimeter of the triangle? SSC CGL (Tier I) 01/12/2022 Shift-IV
(a) 120 cm (b) 30 cm
(c) 150 cm (d) 60 cm

94. The side of an equilateral triangle is 12 cm. What is the radius of the circle circumscribing this equilateral triangle? SSC CGL (Tier I) 01/12/2022 Shift-II
(a) $6\sqrt{3}$ cm (b) $4\sqrt{3}$ cm
(c) $9\sqrt{3}$ cm (d) $5\sqrt{3}$ cm

95. The circumference of the two circles is 198 cm and 352 cm, respectively. What is the difference between their radii? SSC CGL (Tier I) 01/12/2022 Shift-I

(a) 45 cm (b) 16.5 cm
(c) 49.5 cm (d) 24.5 cm

96. The length and breadth of a rectangle are increased by 8% and 5%, respectively. By how much percentage will the area of the rectangle increase?
SSC CGL (Tier I) 01/12/2022 Shift-I

(a) 13.4% (b) 15.4%
(c) 12.4% (d) 16.4%

SSC CGL 2021 & 2020 (Tier I)

97. A man walking at a speed of 3 km/h crosses a square field diagonally in 5 min. What is the area of the field (in m^2)? SSC CGL (Tier I) 24/08/2021 Shift-II

(a) 31250 (b) 3125
(c) 312.5 (d) 3.125

98. The area of a table top in the shape of an equilateral triangle is $9\sqrt{3}$ cm^2. What is the length (in cm) of each side of the table?
SSC CGL (Tier I) 24/08/2021 Shift-I

(a) 6 (b) 2
(c) 4 (d) 3

99. A square has the perimeter equal to the circumference of a circle having radius 7 cm. What is the ratio of the area of the circle to area of the square? $\left(\text{Use } \pi = \frac{22}{7}\right)$
SSC CGL (Tier I) 23/08/2021 Shift-II

(a) 121 : 44 (b) 7 : 2
(c) 14 : 11 (d) 7 : 11

100. The area of a circular path enclosed by two concentric circles is 3080 m^2. If the difference between the radius of the outer edge and that of inner edge of the circular path is 10 m, what is the sum (in m) of the two raddi? $\left(\text{Take } \pi = \frac{22}{7}\right)$
SSC CGL (Tier I) 23/08/2021 Shift-II

(a) 112 (b) 70
(c) 84 (d) 98

101. The area of a square shaped field is 1764m^2. The breadth of a rectangular park is $\frac{1}{6}$th of the side of the square field and the length is four times its breadth. What is the cost (in ₹) of levelling the park at ₹ 30 per m^2?
SSC CGL (Tier I) 23/08/2021 Shift-I

(a) 6342 (b) 4768
(c) 5880 (d) 2940

102. The area of a quadrant of a circle is $\frac{\pi}{9}m^2$. Its radius (in m) is equal to
SSC CGL (Tier I) 23/08/2021 Shift-I

(a) $\frac{2}{3}$ (b) $\frac{1}{3}$ (c) $\frac{1}{2}$ (d) $\frac{3}{2}$

103. What is the length (in cm) of the smallest altitude of the triangle whose sides are 5 cm, 12 cm, 13 cm? (correct to one decimal place)
SSC CGL (Tier I) 18/08/2021 Shift-III

(a) 12.0 (b) 5.1 (c) 2.6 (d) 4.6

104. The perimeter of a semi-circle is 25.7 cm. What is its diameter (in cm)? (π = 3.14)
SSC CGL (Tier I) 18/08/2021 Shift-I

(a) 10 (b) 9 (c) 12 (d) 8

105. The area of a square shaped field is 1764 m^2. The breadth of a rectangular park is $\frac{1}{3}$ rd the side of the square field and its length is two times its breadth. What is the cost (in ₹) of levelling the park at ₹15 per/m^2? SSC CGL (Tier I) 16/08/2021 Shift-III

(a) 4290 (b) 4200
(c) 5880 (d) 4320

106. The area of a circular park is 12474 m^2. There is 3.5 m wide path around the park. What is the area (in m^2) of the path? (Take $\pi = \frac{22}{7}$)
SSC CGL (Tier I) 13/08/2021 Shift-III

(a) 1424.5 (b) 1435.5
(c) 1440.5 (d) 1380.5

107. Length of each side of a rhombus is 13 cm and one of the diagonal is 24 cm. What is the area (in cm^2) of the rhombus?
SSC CGL (Tier I) 13/08/2021 Shift-I

(a) 120 (b) 300 (c) 60 (d) 240

108. If the perimeter of a certain rectangle is 50 units and its area is 150 sq units, then how many units is the length of its shorter side?
SSC CGL (Tier I) 07/03/2020 Shift-II

(a) 15 (b) 12 (c) 10 (d) 9

109. The perimeter of an isosceles triangle is 50 cm. If the base is 18 cm, then find the length of the equal sides. SSC CGL (Tier I) 07/03/2020 Shift-II

(a) 25 cm (b) 32 cm
(c) 18 cm (d) 16 cm

110. If radius of a circle is decreased by 11%,then the total decrease in the area of the circle is given as
SSC CGL (Tier I) 07/03/2020 Shift-II

(a) 20.79% (b) 19.50%
(c) 20.50% (d) 21%

111. The diagonal and one side of a rectangular plot are 65 m and 63 m respectively. What is the perimeter (m) of the rectangular plot?
SSC CGL (Tier I) 07/03/2020 Shift-I

(a) 158 (b) 256
(c) 225 (d) 196

112. The inner and outer radius of a circular track are, respectively, 29 m and 23 m. The cost of levelling the track at ₹ 7/m^2 is
SSC CGL (Tier I) 06/03/2020 Shift-III

(a) ₹3284 (b) ₹5300
(c) ₹7215 (d) ₹6864

113. The length of the diagonals of a rhombus are 16 cm and 12 cm. Its area is SSC CGL (Tier I) 06/03/2020 Shift-II

(a) 28 cm^2 (b) 69 cm^2
(c) 48 cm^2 (d) 96 cm^2

114. If the area of an equilateral triangle is $36\sqrt{3}$ cm^2, then the perimeter of the triangle is
SSC CGL (Tier I) 06/03/2020 Shift-I

(a) $36\sqrt{3}$ cm (b) 36 cm
(c) $18\sqrt{3}$ cm (d) 12 cm

115. A circular disc of area 0.64 πm^2 rolls down a length of 1.408 km. The number of revolutions it makes is (Take $\pi = \frac{22}{7}$)
SSC CGL (Tier I) 06/03/2020 Shift-I

(a) 280 (b) 360 (c) 140 (d) 180

116. The perimeter of a square is 64 cm. Its area will be
SSC CGL (Tier I) 05/03/2020 Shift-III

(a) 128 cm^2 (b) 256 cm^2
(c) 32 cm^2 (d) 8 cm^2

117. The diagonal of a square A is $(a + b)$ units. What is the area (in square units) of the square drawn on the diagonal of square B whose area is twice the area of A?
SSC CGL (Tier I) 05/03/2020 Shift-I

(a) $4(a + b)^2$ (b) $(a + b)^2$
(c) $8(a + b)^2$ (d) $2(a + b)^2$

118. The area of a field in the shape of a regular hexagon is $2400\sqrt{3}$ m^2. The cost of fencing the field at ₹ 16.80/m is SSC CGL (Tier I) 04/03/2020 Shift-III

(a) ₹ 4536 (b) ₹ 3024
(c) ₹ 4032 (d) ₹ 3528

SSC CPO SI 2024 & 2023

119. The area of a circle is 256π cm^2. The length of its longest chord (in cm) is
SSC CPO 29/06/2024 Shift-III

(a) 32 (b) 36 (c) 34 (d) 16

120. The length of a side of an equilateral triangle is 18 cm. The area (in cm^2) of the region lying between the circumcircle and the incircle of the triangle is $\left[\text{use } \pi = \frac{22}{7}\right]$

SSC CPO 29/06/2024 Shift-III

(a) $254\frac{4}{7}$ (b) $254\frac{3}{7}$
(c) $254\frac{2}{7}$ (d) $254\frac{1}{7}$

121. What is the area of the sector of a circle, whose radius is 35 cm and whose arc subtends an angle of 72° at the centre of the circle? $\left(\text{use } \pi = \frac{22}{7}\right)$

SSC CPO 29/06/2024 Shift-II

(a) 770 cm^2 (b) 610 cm^2
(c) 810 cm^2 (d) 970 cm^2

122. The area of a triangle is 486 cm^2 and its sides are in the ratio 3:4:5. The perimeter of the triangle is

SSC CPO 29/06/2024 Shift-II

(a) 108 cm (b) 308 cm
(c) 218 cm (d) 105 cm

123. The breadth of a rectangular lawn is decreased by 8% and its length is increased by15%. Find the percentage change in the lawn area.

SSC CPO 29/06/2024 Shift-II

(a) 8.5% decrease (b) 8.5% increase
(c) 5.8% decrease (d) 5.8% increase

124. The in -radius of triangle is 8 cm and the sum of the lengths of its sides is 125 cm. The area of the triangle (in cm^2) is **SSC CPO 29/06/2024 Shift-II**

(a) 480 (b) 250
(c) 500 (d) 1000

125. The difference between the two perpendicular sides of a right-angled triangle is 2 cm and its area is 24 cm. What is the perimeter (in cm) of the triangle? **SSC CPO 29/06/2024 Shift-I**

(a) 18 (b) 16
(c) 14 (d) 24

126. A school has two rectangular playgrounds, which are similar in shape. If the length and the breadth of the first playground are given as 224 m and 160 m, respectively, then which of the following options cannot be the dimensions of the second playground?

SSC CPO 29/06/2024 Shift-I

(a) Length = 168 m; Breadth = 120 m
(b) Length = 343 m; Breadth = 255 m
(c) Length = 273 m; Breadth = 195 m
(d) Length = 210 m; Breadth = 150 m

127. A gear 15 cm in diameter is turning a gear 21 cm in diameter. When the smaller gear has 105 revolutions, how many has the larger one made?

SSC CPO 28/06/2024 Shift-III

(a) 100 (b) 75
(c) 85 (d) 90

128. Three circles each of radius 5 cm touch one another. The area (in cm^2) subtended between them is

SSC CPO 28/06/2024 Shift-III

(a) $25\left(\sqrt{3}+\frac{\pi}{2}\right)$ (b) $25\left(2\sqrt{3}-\frac{\pi}{2}\right)$
(c) $50\left(\sqrt{3}-\frac{\pi}{2}\right)$ (d) $25\left(\sqrt{3}-\frac{\pi}{2}\right)$

129. Find the perimeter of a triangle with sides equal to 13 cm, 12 cm and 5 cm. **SSC CPO 28/06/2024 Shift-III**

(a) 15 cm (b) 25 cm
(c) 30 cm (d) 15 cm

130. The distance between the parallel sides of a trapezium is 18 cm. If the area of the trapezium is 1188 cm^2, then what is the sum of the lengths of the parallel sides?

SSC CPO 28/06/2024 Shift-III

(a) 115 cm (b) 126 cm
(c) 132 cm (d) 150 cm

131. The area of a sector of a circle having radius 14 cm is 231 cm^2. Find the degree measure of the corresponding central angle. $\left(\text{Use } \pi = \frac{22}{7}\right)$ **SSC CPO 28/06/2024 Shift-II**

(a) 140° (b) 135°
(c) 150° (d) 125°

132. Find the area (in cm^2) of the sector of a circle of radius 21 cm with a central angle of 60°. $\left[\text{Use } \pi = \frac{22}{7}\right]$

SSC CPO 28/06/2024 Shift-I

(a) 302 (b) 289
(c) 231 (d) 245

133. Find the area of a minor sector of a circle whose circumference is 88 cm and the length of its minor arc is 22 cm $\left(\text{Use, } \pi = \frac{22}{7}\right)$.

SSC CPO 27/06/2024 Shift-II

(a) 415 cm^2 (b) 154 cm^2
(c) 451 cm^2 (d) 145 cm^2

134. What is the length of the arc of a circle whose radius is 35 cm and whose arc subtends an angle of 72° at the centre of the circle?

SSC CPO 27/06/2024 Shift-II

(a) 38 cm (b) 56 cm
(c) 44 cm (d) 28 cm

135. The base of a parallelogram is twice its height. If the area of the parallelogram is 338 cm^2, then find its height (in cm).

SSC CPO 27/06/2024 Shift-I

(a) 11 (b) 13
(c) 14 (d) 12

136. The chord length of a chord made on an arc of a circle is equal to the radius of the circle. The length of the arc is ....(in units), if the radius of the circle is 21 units. $\left(\text{take}\pi = \frac{22}{7}\right)$

SSC CPO 27/06/2024 Shift-I

(a) 21 (b) 24
(c) 22 (d) 20

137. Find the area of a triangle, whose length of two sides are 4 cm and 5 cm and the angle between them is 45°.

SSC CPO 04/10/2023 Shift-II

(a) $4\sqrt{2}$ cm^2 (b) $7\sqrt{2}$ cm^2
(c) $5\sqrt{2}$ cm^2 (d) $6\sqrt{2}$ cm^2

138. The area of a rectangular field is 480 m^2. If the length is 20% more than the breadth, then the length of the rectangular field is

SSC CPO 04/10/2023 Shift-II

(a) 30 m (b) 20 m
(c) 24 m (d) 27 m

139. The areas of the two triangles are in the ratio 4 : 3 and their heights are in the ratio 6 : 5. Find the ratio of their bases. **SSC CPO 03/10/2023 Shift-I**

(a) 5 : 6 (b) 10 : 9
(c) 6 : 5 (d) 9 : 10

140. The sides of a triangle are in the ratio 5 : 12 : 13 and its perimeter is 90 cm. Find its area (in cm^2).

SSC CPO 03/10/2023 Shift-I

(a) 150 (b) 270
(c) 30 (d) 60

141. What is the area of a triangle whose sides are of lengths 12 cm,13 cm and 5 cm? **SSC CPO 03/10/2023 Shift-I**

(a) 30 cm^2 (b) 15 cm^2
(c) 40 cm^2 (d) 70 cm^2

SSC CPO SI 2022-2020

142. If the arc of a circle of radius 30 cm has a length of 19 cm, then the angle (in degrees. rounded off to two decimal places) subtended at the centre of the circle is : $\left(\text{take} = \frac{22}{7}\right)$

SSC CPO 11/11/2022 Shift-I

(a) 51.25 (b) 16.27
(c) 36.27 (d) 46.25

143. If the sum of the diagonals of a rhombus is L and the perimeter is 4P, find the area of the rhombus?
SSC CPO 11/11/2022 Shift-I

(a) $\frac{1}{4}(L^2 - P^2)$
(b) $\frac{1}{4}(L^2 - 4P^2)$
(c) $\frac{1}{2}(L^2 - 4P^2)$
(d) $\frac{1}{4}(L^2 + 3P^2)$

144. As shown in the given figure inside the large semicircle, three semicircles (with equal radii) are drawn so that their diameters all sit on the large semicircles's diameter. What is the ratio between the shaded and unshaded areas ?
SSC CPO 10/11/2022 Shift-I

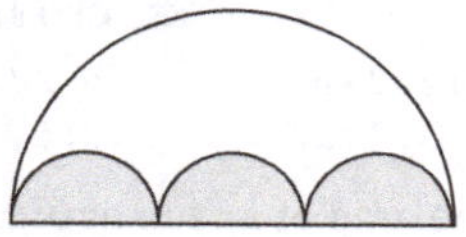

(a) 4 : 3 (b) 1 : 2
(c) 2 : 1 (d) 3 : 4

145. The base of a triangle is equal to the perimeter of a square whose diagonal is $9\sqrt{2}$ cm and its height is equal to the side of a square whose area is 144 cm^2. The area of the triangle (in cm^2) is
SSC CPO 25/11/2020 Shift-II

(a) 216 (b) 72
(c) 144 (d) 288

146. The perimeter of a square is half the perimeter of a rectangle. The perimeter of the square is 40 m. If rectangle's breadth is two-thirds of its length, then what is the area (in m^2) of the rectangle?
SSC CPO 25/11/2020 Shift-I

(a) 384 (b) 196
(c) 321 (d) 400

147. If each side of a square is decreased by 17%, then by what percentage does its area decrease?
SSC CPO 25/11/2020 Shift-I

(a) 25% (b) 30.79%
(c) 31.11% (d) 44.31%

148. One side of a rhombus is 13 cm and one of its diagonals is 24 cm. What is the area (in cm^2) of rhombus?
SSC CPO 25/11/2020 Shift-I

(a) 120 (b) 90 (c) 30 (d) 60

149. The sides of a triangle are 24 cm, 26 cm and 10 cm. At each of its vertex, circles of radius 4.2 cm are drawn. What is the area (in cm^2) of the portion covered by the three sectors of the circle? $\left(\pi = \frac{22}{7}\right)$
SSC CPO 25/11/2020 Shift-I

(a) 92.28 (b) 120
(c) 105.86 (d) 27.72

150. The area of a field in the shape of a hexagon is $1944\sqrt{3}$ m^2. What will be the cost (in ₹) of fencing it at the rate of ₹ 11.50 per metre?
SSC CPO 24/11/2020 Shift-I

(a) 2785 (b) 2484
(c) 3200 (d) 2256

151. The two parallel sides of a trapezium are 17 cm and 15 cm, respectively. If the height of the trapezium is 6 cm, then its area (in m^2) is **SSC CPO 24/11/2020 Shift-I**

(a) 9.6 (b) 960
(c) 0.96 (d) 0.0096

152. A rectangular lawn whose length is twice of its breadth is extended by having four semi-circular portions on its sides. What is the total area (in m^2) of the lawn if the smaller side of the rectangle is 12 m? (take $\pi = 3.14$) **SSC CPO 24/11/2020 Shift-I**

(a) 853.2 (b) 308.64
(c) 444 (d) 548.32

153. The perimeter of a square is the same as the perimeter of a rectangle. The perimeter of the square is 40 m. If rectangular's breadth is two-thirds of its length, then the area (in m^2) of the rectangle is **SSC CPO 23/11/2020 Shift-I**

(a) 121 (b) 96
(c) 100 (d) 84

154. If each side of a rectangle is decreased by 11%, then its area will decrease by **SSC CPO 23/11/2020 Shift-I**

(a) 25% (b) 21.13%
(c) 24.31% (d) 20.79%

155. One side of a rhombus is 13 cm and one of its diagonals is 10 cm. What is the area of the rhombus (in cm^2)?
SSC CPO 23/11/2020 Shift-I

(a) 60 (b) 90
(c) 30 (d) 120

156. The sides of a triangle are 24 cm, 26 cm and 10 cm. At each of its vertices, circles of radius 4.2 cm are drawn. What is the area (in cm^2) of the triangle, excluding the portion covered by the sectors of the circles? $\left(\pi = \frac{22}{7}\right)$ **SSC CPO 23/11/2020 Shift-I**

(a) 120 (b) 105.86
(c) 92.28 (d) 27.72

SSC CHSL 2024 (Tier I)

157. What is the area (in square units) of the sector if the radius of the circle is given to be 24 units and the arc length is 7.5 units?
SSC CHSL (Tier I) 11/07/2024 (Shift-IV)

(a) 135 (b) 180
(c) 45 (d) 90

158. A right angled triangle of area 600 m^2 is to be made such that the hypotenuse is double the base. For the triangle, the hypotenuse is .... more than the base.
SSC CHSL (Tier I) 11/07/2024 (Shift-IV)

(a) 20.36 m (b) 22.32 m
(c) 24.36 m (d) 26.32 m

159. If the area of a rhombus is 70 m^2 and its height is 5 m, its perimeter is .... **SSC CHSL (Tier I) 11/07/2024 Shift-II**

(a) 56 m (b) 35 m
(c) 64 m (d) 25 m

160. The measure of each side of an equilateral triangle is 16 cm. What is the ratio of its perimeter to the sum of its medians ?
SSC CHSL (Tier I) 11/07/2024 Shift-II

(a) $\sqrt{3} : 2$ (b) $1 : 2\sqrt{3}$
(c) $2\sqrt{3} : 1$ (d) $2 : \sqrt{3}$

161. What is the area of a quadrilateral *ABCD*, (shown below) in which sides *AB* and *BC* are equal sides *AD* and *CD* are of lengths 5 cm and 13 cm, respectively, and side *AD* is perpendicular to the diagonal *AC*?
SSC CHSL (Tier I) 11/07/2024 Shift-I

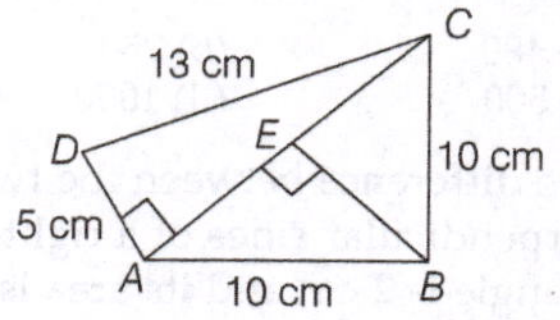

(a) 75 cm^2 (b) 78 cm^2
(c) 82 cm^2 (d) 80 cm^2

162. Let *ABCD* be a quadrilateral and *AC*, *BD* be diagonals. The length of *BD* = 20 cm and the heights of the triangles *ABD* and *BCD* are, 6 cm and 8 cm respectively. Find the area of the quadrilateral *ABCD* (in cm^2).
SSC CHSL (Tier I) 10/07/2024 Shift-III

(a) 140 (b) 120 (c) 148 (d) 1282

163. The ratio of the outer and the inner circumference of a circular path is 7:6. If the path is 45 m wide, then what is the radius (in m) of the inner circle? **SSC CHSL (Tier I) 10/07/2024 Shift-II**

(a) 240 (b) 120
(c) 150 (d) 270

164. A rectangle with the largest area is cut out of a circle with radius 5 units. What is the area of the remaining portion?
SSC CHSL (Tier I) 10/07/2024 Shift-I
(a) $25(2\pi - 3)$ (b) $25(\pi - 2)$
(c) $25(2\pi - 5)$ (d) $25(\pi - 3)$

165. If the radius of a circle is 48 cm and the length of the arc is 15 cm, then the area of the sector corresponding to that arc is
SSC CHSL (Tier I) 10/07/2024 Shift-I
(a) 36 m^2 (b) 360 cm^2
(c) 720 cm^2 (d) 7200 m^2

166. If three sides of a triangle are 6 cm, 8 cm and 10 cm, then the area of the triangle is
SSC CHSL (Tier I) 09/07/2024 Shift-IV
(a) 30cm^2 (b) $12\sqrt{3}$ cm^2
(c) 24 cm^2 (d) $24\sqrt{3}$ cm^2

167. The hypotenuse of a right triangle is 6m more than twice the shortest side. If the third side is 2 m less than the hypotenuse, find the area (in m^2) of the triangle.
SSC CHSL (Tier I) 09/07/2024 Shift-I
(a) 130 (b) 100
(c) 120 (d) 110

168. The length of a rectangular shaped park exceeds its breadth by 15 m. If the perimeter of the park is 110 m, find the length of the park (in m).
SSC CHSL (Tier I) 09/07/2024 Shift-I
(a) 20 (b) 35
(c) 25 (d) 40

169. Which of the following statements is incorrect about the circle?
SSC CHSL (Tier I) 08/07/2024 Shift-IV
(a) The area of a sector $= \frac{1}{2}(\text{arc length} \times R)$
(b) The length of an arc $= \frac{\text{Central angle made by the arc}}{360°} \times \pi r^2$.
(c) The radius of an incircle of an equilateral triangle of side '*s*' is $\frac{s}{2\sqrt{3}}$
(d) Circles are congruent if they have same radii while similar circles may have different radii

170. From a circular sheet of circumference 264 cm, two equal maximum-sized circular plates are cut off. What will be the circumference of each plate? $\left(\text{use } \pi = \frac{22}{7}\right)$
SSC CHSL (Tier I) 08/07/2024 Shift-III
(a) 264 cm (b) 135 cm
(c) 176 cm (d) 132 cm

171. The area of an isosceles right-angled triangle is 16 m^2. Its hypotenuse is
SSC CHSL (Tier I) 08/07/2024 Shift-III
(a) 0.8 m (b) 4 m
(c) 8 cm (d) 8 m

172. The perimeter of a square, whose area is the same as the area of a semi-circle of radius $2\sqrt{2}$ cm is
SSC CHSL (Tier I) 08/07/2024 Shift-II
(a) $4\sqrt{\pi}$ cm (b) $16\sqrt{\pi}$ cm
(c) $8\sqrt{2\pi}$ cm (d) $8\sqrt{\pi}$ cm

173. The perimeter of a rectangle is 70 cm and its diagonal is 25 cm. The area of the rectangle is
SSC CHSL (Tier I) 08/07/2024 Shift-I
(a) 425 cm^2 (b) 300 cm^2
(c) 625 cm^2 (d) 420 cm^2

174. The average of the areas of two similar triangles is 706.5 m^2 whose perimeters are in the ratio of 6 : 11. What is 20% of the difference (in m^2) in areas of both triangles?
SSC CHSL (Tier I) 08/07/2024 Shift-I
(a) 157 (b) 149
(c) 153 (d) 164

175. The altitude of an equilateral triangle is $3\sqrt{3}$ cm. Find its area.
SSC CHSL (Tier I) 05/07/2024 Shift-IV
(a) 9 sq cm (b) 27 sq cm
(c) $9\sqrt{3}$ sq cm (d) $3\sqrt{3}$ sq cm

176. Let *ABC* be a right-angled triangle such that $\angle C = 90°$. Let *D* be a point on *AB* such that *CD* is perpendicular to *AB*. If *AC* = 5 cm and *BC* = 12 cm, find the length of *CD* (in cm).
SSC CHSL (Tier I) 05/07/2024 Shift-IV
(a) $\frac{60}{13}$ (b) $\frac{40}{13}$ (c) $\frac{40}{23}$ (d) $\frac{50}{23}$

177. If the angle of the sector with radius 7 cm is 120°, then find the length of the sector (in cm). $\left(\text{Use } \pi = \frac{22}{7}\right)$
SSC CHSL (Tier I) 05/07/2024 Shift-III
(a) $\frac{67}{3}$ (b) $\frac{22}{3}$ (c) $\frac{47}{3}$ (d) $\frac{44}{3}$

178. What is the area (in cm^2) of an equilateral triangle, whose perimeter is 24 cm? (Round off to the nearest two decimal places)
SSC CHSL (Tier I) 05/07/2024 Shift-III
(a) 28.14 (b) 27.71
(c) 13.86 (d) 27.14

179. Find the height of the triangle whose base is two-thirds of its height and whose area is 363 cm^2.
SSC CHSL (Tier I) 05/07/2024 Shift-II
(a) 31 cm (b) 33 cm
(c) 29 cm (d) 27 cm

180. From a circle, a sector with a central angle of 30° is cut off. If the length of the arc of this sector is 5.5 cm, then find the radius (in cm) of the circle. $\left[\text{use } \pi = \frac{22}{7}\right]$
SSC CHSL (Tier I) 04/07/2024 Shift-IV
(a) 12 (b) 10 (c) 10.5 (d) 11

181. The perimeter of a semi-circle is 56.54 cm. What is its diameter (in cm)? (use $\pi = 3.14$)
SSC CHSL (Tier I) 04/07/2024 Shift-III
(a) 11 (b) 22 (c) 10 (d) 20

182. Find the area of a rhombus, whose diagonals are of lengths 10 cm and 8.2 cm. SSC CHSL (Tier I) 04/07/2024 Shift-II
(a) 43 cm^2 (b) 41 cm^2
(c) 40 cm^2 (d) 42 cm^2

183. If the area of a triangle, whose base measures 6 cm is 18 cm^2, then its height is
SSC CHSL (Tier I) 03/07/2024 Shift-IV
(a) 6 cm (b) 3.1 cm
(c) 2.2 cm (d) 9 cm

184. If the perimeter of a square is 64 cm, what would be its area?
SSC CHSL (Tier I) 03/07/2024 Shift-III
(a) 256 cm^2 (b) 206 cm^2
(c) 216 cm^2 (d) 266 cm^2

185. For a given circle of radius 4 cm, the angle of its sector is 45°. Find the area (in cm^2) of the sector. (Use $\pi = 3.14$)
SSC CHSL (Tier I) 03/07/2024 Shift-III
(a) 6.18 (b) 7.28
(c) 6.28 (d) 7.18

186. The area of a rectangular field is 3600 m^2. If the field is 45 m long, what is its perimeter ?
SSC CHSL (Tier I) 03/07/2024 Shift-II
(a) 260 m (b) 255 m
(c) 265 m (d) 250 m

187. The perimeter of a triangle is 36 units. Its area cannot be more than
SSC CHSL (Tier I) 02/07/2024 Shift-III
(a) $36\sqrt{2}$ (b) $36\sqrt{3}$
(c) $12\sqrt{7}$ (d) $18\sqrt{5}$

188. The perimeter of a minor sector of a circle of radius 4 units subtending an angle of 45° is
SSC CHSL (Tier I) 02/07/2024 Shift-I
(a) $4 - \pi$ units (b) $8 - \pi$ units
(c) $8 + \pi$ units (d) $4 + \pi$ units

189. Find the circumference of a circle, whose area is 154 m^2.
SSC CHSL (Tier I) 01/07/24 Shift-III
(a) 44 m (b) 29.5 m
(c) 39 m (d) 52 m

SSC CHSL 2023 (Tier I)

190. An arc of length 33 π cm subtends an angle of 132° at the centre of the circle. Find the radius of the circle.
SSC CHSL (Tier I) 17/08/2023 Shift-I
(a) 45 cm (b) 40 cm
(c) 30 cm (d) 35 cm

191. An equilateral triangle has sides of 18 cm each. The ratio of the inradius to circumradius of the triangle is
SSC CHSL (Tier I) 14/08/2023 Shift-IV
(a) 2 : 1 (b) 3 : 2
(c) 3 : 4 (d) 1 : 2

192. Find the circumfarence (in m) of the largest circle that can be inscribed in a rectanlge whose diamensions are given as 12 m and 7 m. (Take $\pi = 22/7$)
SSC CHSL (Tier I) 11/08/2023 Shift-I
(a) 22 (b) 19
(c) 11 (d) 37

193. The perimeter of a minor sector of a circle of radius 5 cm is 15.5 cm. Find the area of the minor sector (use $\pi = \frac{22}{7}$).
SSC CHSL (Tier I) 11/08/2023 Shift-I
(a) 17.53 cm^2 (b) 13.75 cm^2
(c) 13.57 cm^2 (d) 17.35 cm^2

194. The perimeter of a sector of a circle of radius 7.4 cm is 20.6 cm. The area of this sector is
SSC CHSL (Tier I) 10/08/2023 Shift-III
(a) 42.92 cm^2 (b) 5.8 cm^2
(c) 10.73 cm^2 (d) 21.46 cm^2

195. The sides of a triangle are 20 cm, 21 cm and 29 cm. The area of the triangle formed by joining the mid-points of the sides of triangle will be SSC CHSL (Tier I) 10/08/2023 Shift-III
(a) $67\frac{2}{3}$ cm^2 (b) $52\frac{1}{2}$ cm^2
(c) $47\frac{1}{2}$ cm^2 (d) $58\frac{1}{3}$ cm^2

196. If one diagonal of a rhombus is equal to its side, then the diagonals of the rhombus are in the ratio of
SSC CHSL (Tier I) 10/08/2023 Shift-III
(a) $\sqrt{3} : \sqrt{6}$ (b) $\sqrt{2} : 1$
(c) $\sqrt{2} : \sqrt{3}$ (d) $1 : \sqrt{3}$

197. The area of a sector of a circle is 616 cm^2 with a central angle of 10°. The radius of the circle is .... $\left(\text{Use } \pi = \frac{22}{7}\right)$
SSC CHSL (Tier I) 08/08/2023 Shift-II
(a) 84 cm (b) 21 cm
(c) 48 cm (d) 28 cm

198. The circumference of a circle is 132 cm. The area of circle is [Take $\pi = \frac{22}{7}$]
SSC CHSL (Tier I) 08/08/2023 Shift-II
(a) 1380 cm^2 (b) 1322 cm^2
(c) 1086 cm^2 (d) 1386 cm^2

199. Find the area of a circle whose radius is equal to the side of a square whose perimeter is 196 m.
SSC CHSL (Tier I) 20/03/2023 Shift-III
(a) 7457 m^2 (b) 7546 m^2
(c) 6477 m^2 (d) 8844 m^2

200. The ratio of areas of two circles is 81: 121. What will be the ratio of their circumferences?
SSC CHSL (Tier I) 20/03/2023 Shift-III
(a) 9 : 11 (b) 121 : 81
(c) 11 : 9 (d) 81 : 121

201. If the diagonals of a rhombus are 10 cm and 24 cm, then what is the perimeter of the rhombus?
SSC CHSL (Tier I) 16/03/2023 Shift-I
(a) 50 cm (b) 60 cm
(c) 56 cm (d) 52 cm

202. Radius of incircle of an equilateral triangle is $9\sqrt{3}$. What will be the perimeter of this equilateral triangle? SSC CHSL (Tier I) 14/03/2023 Shift-I
(a) 81 cm (b) 162 cm
(c) 108 cm (d) 54 cm

203. The length of the base of a triangle is 10 cm and its altitude from the same base is 8 cm. What will be the area of this triangle?
SSC CHSL (Tier I) 13/03/2023 Shift-III
(a) 30 cm^2 (b) 40 cm^2
(c) 50 cm^2 (d) 80 cm^2

204. The area (in cm^2) of biggest circle that could be drawn in a square of side 18 cm is
SSC CHSL (Tier I) 10/03/2023 Shift-II
(a) 91 π (b) 81 π (c) 49 π (d) 168 π

205. A wheel makes 500 revolutions in covering a distance of 44 km. Find the radius of the wheel.
SSC CHSL (Tier I) 10/03/2023 Shift-II
(a) 14 m (b) 21 m
(c) 28 m (d) 7 m

206. Find the area of a triangle whose length of each side is 13 inches, 15 inches and 14 inches.
SSC CHSL (Tier I) 09/03/2023 Shift-I
(a) 84 sq. inches (b) 81.2 sq. inches
(c) 42.1 sq. inches (d) 84.2 sq. inches

207. The radius of a wheel is 14 cm. How much distance will be travelled by the wheel in 10 revolutions?
SSC CHSL (Tier I) 09/03/2023 Shift-I
(a) 910 cm (b) 880 cm
(c) 800 cm (d) 820 cm

SSC CHSL 2022 & 2021 (Tier I)

208. What will be the area of a triangle whose sides are 13 cm, 5 cm and 12 cm? SSC CHSL (Tier I) 02/06/2022 Shift-I
(a) 50 cm^2 (b) 40 cm^2
(c) 35 cm^2 (d) 30 cm^2

209. The area of a triangle is 96 cm^2 and the length of one of its sides is 24 cm. What is the length of the perpendicular drawn to this side of the triangle from the opposite vertex? SSC CHSL (Tier I) 01/06/2022 Shift-I
(a) 16 cm (b) 8 cm
(c) 4 cm (d) 12 cm

210. If the length and the breadth of a rectangle are increased by 15% and 20%, respectively, then by how much per cent the area of the rectangle will increases?
SSC CHSL (Tier I) 31/05/2022 Shift-I
(a) 32% (b) 38%
(c) 36% (d) 48%

211. If the circumradius of an equilateral triangle is 18 cm, then the measure of its in-radius is:
SSC CHSL (Tier I) 27/05/2022 Shift-I
(a) 9 cm (b) 3 cm
(c) 10 cm (d) 12 cm

212. A rectangle with perimeter 50 cm has its sides in the ratio 1 : 4. What is the perimeter of a square whose area is the same as that of the rectangle?
SSC CHSL (Tier I) 12/05/2021 Shift-III
(a) 36 cm (b) 50 cm
(c) 40 cm (d) 45 cm

213. The sum of all the three sides of an equilateral triangle is $15\sqrt{3}$ cm. The height of the triangle is
SSC CHSL (Tier I) 12/08/2021 Shift-III
(a) 7 cm (b) 8 cm
(c) 7.5 cm (d) 9 cm

214. What is the perimeter (in cm) of an equilateral triangle whose height is 3.46 cm? (Take $\sqrt{3} = 1.73$)
SSC CHSL (Tier I) 04/08/2021 Shift-I
(a) 10.4 (b) 9 (c) 6 (d) 12

215. One-quarter of a circular pizza of diameter 28 cm was removed from the whole pizza. What is the perimeter (in cm) of the remaining pizza? (Take $\pi = \frac{22}{7}$)
SSC CHSL (Tier I) 04/08/2021 Shift-I
(a) 88 (b) 94
(c) 80 (d) 66

216. The length of the base of a triangle is 3 cm smaller than the length of its altitude. Its area is 104 cm^2. What is the length of the base?
SSC CHSL (Tier I) 19/04/2021 Shift-I
(a) 13 cm (b) 12 cm
(c) 14 cm (d) 14 cm

217. If the perimeter of a circle is 88 cm, then what is the area of the circle? $\left(\pi = \frac{22}{7}\right)$
SSC CHSL (Tier I) 19/04/2021 Shift-II
(a) 616 cm^2 (b) 566 cm^2
(c) 886 cm^2 (d) 446 cm^2

218. The length of a rectangle is five times of its breadth. If the area of the rectangle is 3125 cm^2, then what is the length of the rectangle?
SSC CHSL (Tier I) 12/04/2021 Shift-II
(a) 125 cm (b) 120 cm
(c) 135 cm (d) 130 cm

219. What is the area (in m^2, up to 1 place of decimal) of an equilateral triangular field of side 8.5 m?
SSC CHSL (Tier I) 12/04/2021 Shift-II
(a) $\frac{18.1}{\sqrt{3}}$ (b) $18.1\sqrt{3}$
(c) $\frac{72.25}{\sqrt{3}}$ (d) $72.25\sqrt{3}$

220. Find the area (in cm^2) and the diameter (in cm), respectively of a circle whose circumference is 40 π cm ?
SSC CHSL (Tier I) 12/04/2021 Shift-II
(a) 400 π and 40 (b) 40 and 400 π
(c) 400 and 40 (d) 40 and 400

SSC MTS 2024 & 2023

221. If a semi-circular plot has radius 100 m, find its perimeter. (Use π = 3.14)
SSC MTS 14/11/2024 Shift-III
(a) 414 m (b) 828 m
(c) 514 m (d) 500 m

222. If the length and breadth of a rectangle are 7 cm and 5 cm, respectively, the area of the rectangle is SSC MTS 13/11/2024 Shift-III
(a) 28 cm^2 (b) 35 cm^2
(c) 30 cm^2 (d) 12 cm^2

223. A trapezium has parallel sides 6 units and 10 units. Other two opposite sides are of same length 8 units and two diagonals are of equal length. What is the area of the trapezium (in square units)?
SSC MTS 05/11/2024 Shift-III
(a) $32\sqrt{5}$ (b) $16\sqrt{3}$
(c) $32\sqrt{3}$ (d) $16\sqrt{15}$

224. The length of a rectangle is four-fifths of the side of the square, whose area is 1225 $units^2$. What is the area (in $units^2$) of the rectangle if the breadth is 12 units?
SSC MTS 05/11/2024 Shift-III
(a) 336 (b) 225 (c) 300 (d) 425

225. The area of a right-angled triangle is 80 m^2. If its perpendicular is equal to 20 m, then find its base.
SSC MTS 04/11/2024 Shift-III
(a) 4 m (b) 3 m (c) 6 m (d) 8 m

226. The diagonals of two squares are in the ratio of 5 : 6. What is the ratio of their areas? SSC MTS 22/10/2024 Shift-II
(a) 18 : 20 (b) 25 : 36
(c) 23 : 18 (d) 2 : 3

227. Find the area of a parallelogram with a base of 12 m and a height of 20 m. SSC MTS 21/10/2024 Shift-II
(a) 120 m^2 (b) 144 m^2
(c) 240 m^2 (d) 210 m^2

228. If the diagonal of a rectangle is 16 cm long and its perimeter is 48 cm long, find the area of the rectangle. SSC MTS 15/10/2024 Shift-I
(a) 148 cm^2 (b) 120 cm^2
(c) 160 cm^2 (d) 140 cm^2

229. ABCDEF is a regular hexagon, and m($\overline{AD}$) = 12 cm. What is the area (in cm^2) of the given hexagon?
SSC MTS 09/10/2024 Shift-I
(a) $216\sqrt{3}$ (b) $54\sqrt{3}$
(c) $108\sqrt{3}$ (d) $162\sqrt{3}$

230. The area of a rectangular park of length 15 m and breadth 12 m is
SSC MTS 09/10/2024 Shift-I
(a) 54 m^2 (b) 180 m^2
(c) 144 m^2 (d) 170 m^2

231. The area of a rectangular field is 396 m^2, whose sides are in the ratio of 11 : 9. What is the perimeter of the rectangular field?
SSC MTS 08/10/2024 Shift-I
(a) 76 m (b) 80 m (c) 78 m (d) 74 m

232. What is the area of the remaining portion of a circle of radius 14 cm, when a square with maximum possible area inscribed in it, is removed from it? (Use $\pi = \frac{22}{7}$)
SSC MTS 07/10/2024 Shift-I
(a) 518 cm^2 (b) 520 cm^2
(c) 224 cm^2 (d) 616 cm^2

233. The area of a regular hexagon is $2048\sqrt{3}$ cm2 What is the length (in cm) of each side of the hexagon?
SSC MTS 30/09/2024 Shift-I
(a) $32\sqrt{3}$ (b) $\frac{64\sqrt{3}}{3}$ (c) $\frac{32\sqrt{3}}{3}$ (d) $64\sqrt{3}$

234. The area of an equilateral triangle is $\frac{\sqrt{5043}}{4}$ sq cm. The side of the equilateral triangle is
SSC MTS 30/09/2024 Shift-I
(a) $\sqrt{23}$ cm (b) $\sqrt{29}$ cm
(c) $\sqrt{47}$ cm (d) $\sqrt{41}$ cm

235. A path of uniform width 2.5 m runs around the outside of a rectangular field of dimensions 45 m × 35 m. What is the area of the path (in m^2)?
SSC MTS 08/09/2023 Shift-II
(a) 500 (b) 425 (c) 475 (d) 525

236. If the sides of a triangle are in the ratio 3 : 4 : 5 and its perimeter is 24 m, then find the area of the triangle.
SSC MTS 06/09/2023 Shift-I
(a) 32 m^2 (b) 37 m^2
(c) 16 m^2 (d) 24 m^2

237. Using the middle points of sides of a square with an area of 36 sq. units, another square is made. What is the area of a new square made in square units'? SSC MTS 05/09/2023 Shift-II
(a) 24 (b) 27 (c) 18 (d) 21

SSC MTS 2022 & 2021

238. The area of a square is 144 cm^2. What is the length of each of its diagonals? SSC MTS 15/07/2022 Shift-I
(a) $14\sqrt{2}$ cm (b) $6\sqrt{2}$ cm
(c) $12\sqrt{2}$ cm (d) 12 cm

239. 5 times of the perimeter of a square is 600 cm. What will be the area of this square ? SSC MTS 15/07/2022 Shift-I
(a) 900 cm^2 (b) 1150 cm^2
(c) 750 cm^2 (d) 480 cm^2

240. The perimeter of a rectangle is 68 cm. If the area of the rectangle is 240 cm^2, then what is the length of each of its diagonals?
SSC MTS 14/07/2022 Shift-I
(a) 25 cm (b) 27 cm
(c) 26 cm (d) 28 cm

241. The radius of a circular wheel of a toy car is 56 mm. In how many revolutions can it cover a distance of 176 cm ? $\left[\text{Use } \pi = \frac{22}{7}\right]$
SSC MTS 13/07/2022 Shift-I
(a) 6 (b) 3 (c) 5 (d) 4

242. The base of a triangle is 16 cm and its area is 144cm^2. Find its corresponding height, with respect to the given base.
SSC MTS 12/07/2022 Shift-I
(a) 18 cm (b) 9 cm (c) 24 cm (d) 12 cm

243. The area (in cm^2) of a sector of a circle of radius 2 cm is $\frac{4\pi}{5}$. What is the central angle (in degrees) of the sector? SSC MTS 02/11/2021 Shift-III

(a) 60 (b) 75
(c) 36 (d) 72

244. When a rectangle is divided into three equal parts, each of them turns out to be a square of area 16 cm^2. What is the perimeter (in cm) of the rectangle? SSC MTS 02/11/2021 Shift-III

(a) 64 (b) 16
(c) 32 (d) 48

245. The area of a trapezium whose parallel sides are 25 cm and 19 cm long is 330 cm^2. The distance between the sides (in cm) is SSC MTS 02/11/2021 Shift-II

(a) 10 (b) 12
(c) 30 (d) 15

246. A rectangle of dimensions 10 cm and 5 cm is placed adjacent to another rectangle of the same size to draw an *L* shape figure. Find the perimeter of the shape so formed. SSC MTS 02/11/2021 Shift-I

(a) 100 cm (b) 40 cm
(c) 50 cm (d) 60 cm

SSC GD Constable 2024 & 2023

247. Calculate the area of a right-angled triangle with a base of 22 cm and height corresponding to that base is 15 cm. SSC GD 24/02/2024 Shift-II

(a) 165 cm^2 (b) 140 cm^2
(c) 180 cm^2 (d) 150 cm^2

248. The diagonals of a rhombus are 10 cm and 30 cm, respectively. What is the area of the rhombus? SSC GD 23/02/2024 Shift-II

(a) 150 cm^2 (b) 105 cm^2
(c) 100 cm^2 (d) 75 cm^2

249. Three rectangular fields having areas of 70 m^2, 84 m^2 and 112 m^2 are to be divided into identical rectangular flower beds, each having a length of 7 m. Find the breadth of each flower bed. SSC GD 23/02/2024 Shift-I

(a) 6 m (b) 4 m
(c) 2 m (d) 3 m

250. The difference between circumference and the diameter of a circle is 12 cm. What is the area of the circle? SSC GD 22/02/2024 Shift-IV

(a) 18 cm^2 (b) 32.26 cm^2
(c) 25 cm^2 (d) 24.64 cm^2

251. Find the sides of an equilateral triangle whose area is $16\sqrt{3}$ cm^2. SSC GD 22/02/2024 Shift-III

(a) 8 cm (b) 6 cm (c) 12 cm (d) 4 cm

252. If the diagonals of a rhombus are 48 cm and 64 cm, then what is the perimeter of the rhombus? SSC GD 22/02/2024 Shift-I

(a) 120 cm (b) 75 cm
(c) 225 cm (d) 160 cm

253. Find the area of the right angled triangle if the longest side of a right angled triangle is 17 cm and the height is 15 cm. SSC GD 21/02/2024 Shift-III

(a) 54 cm^2 (b) 58 cm^2
(c) 60 cm^2 (d) 56 cm^2

254. Find the height of the triangle whose base is $\frac{5}{7}$ th of its height and whose area is 18.207 cm^2. SSC GD 21/02/2024 Shift-I

(a) 14.7 cm (b) 7.14 cm
(c) 2.25 cm (d) 8 cm

255. If the length of a rectangle is increased by 14.28%, then by how much percentage its breadth should be reduced to keep the area same? SSC GD 20/02/2024 Shift-I

(a) 14.28% (b) 12.5%
(c) 14% (d) 16.66%

256. An equilateral triangle with side a units is cut on the vertices to make it a regular hexagon. What is the area of the hexagon? SSC GD 06/02/2023 Shift-I

(a) $\frac{3a^2}{2\sqrt{3}}$ sq units (b) $\frac{2a^2}{3\sqrt{3}}$ sq units
(c) $\frac{2a^2}{\sqrt{3}}$ sq units (d) $\frac{a^2}{2\sqrt{3}}$ sq units

SSC Selection Post 2024-2022

257. Find the area (in cm^2) of a circle with a maximum radius that can be inscribed in a rectangle of length 18 cm and breadth 12 cm Graduate Level 20/06/2024 Shift-III

(a) 72π (b) 28π (c) 136π (d) 36π

258. The area of a sector of a circle is 88 cm^2 and the angle of the sector is 36°. Find the radius (in cm) of the circle. $\left[\text{use } \pi = \frac{22}{7}\right]$ Graduate Level 20/06/2024 Shift-III

(a) $3\sqrt{70}$ (b) $5\sqrt{70}$ (c) $\sqrt{70}$ (d) $2\sqrt{70}$

259. If the semi-perimeter and area of a rectangular field whose length and breadth are '*x*' and '*y*' is 12 cm and 28 cm^2, respectively. Then, find the value of $x^4 + x^2y^2 + y^4$. Graduate Level 20/06/2024 Shift-III

(a) 6690 (b) 6960
(c) 6609 (d) 6906

260. The area of the rhombus (in cm^2) having each side equal to 13 cm and one of its diagonals equal to 24 cm is Graduate Level 20/06/2024 Shift-III

(a) 110 (b) 120 (c) 60 (d) 130

261. The dimensions of a rectangular field, when extended by 6 m are in the ratio of 4 : 3 and when decreased by 6 m are in the ratio of 2 : 1. Find the dimensions of the field. Higher Secondary Level 20/06/2024 Shift-II

(a) 16 m, 12 m (b) 10 m, 6 m
(c) 18 m, 12 m (d) 14 m, 10 m

262. The radius of a circle is increased in such a way that its circumference increases by 7%. As a result, the area of the circle also increases by Higher Secondary Level 20/06/2024 Shift-II

(a) 18.69% (b) 10.28%
(c) 14.49% (d) 12.20%

263. Find the area of an equilateral triangle, whose sides are 16 cm each. Higher Secondary Level 20/06/2024 Shift-II

(a) $66\sqrt{3}$ cm^2 (b) $62\sqrt{3}$ cm^2
(c) $60\sqrt{3}$ cm^2 (d) $64\sqrt{3}$ cm^2

264. The radii of the two concentric circles are 27 cm and 18 cm. The area (in cm^2) of the closed figure bounded by the boundaries of the circle is Higher Secondary Level 20/06/2024 Shift-II

(a) 505π (b) 405π
(c) 288π (d) 504π

265. Let *A*, *B*, *C* be the mid-points of sides *XY*, *YZ* and *XZ*, respectively of ΔXYZ. If the area of ΔXYZ is 8464 cm^2, then find the area (in cm^2) of ΔABC. Higher Secondary Level 27/06/2023 Shift-III

(a) 2116 (b) 1812
(c) 1516 (d) 3112

266. If the perimeter of an equilateral triangle is 60 units, then its area is .... $unit^2$. Graduate Level 01-08-2022 Shift-IV

(a) $60\sqrt{3}$ (b) $200\sqrt{3}$
(c) $50\sqrt{3}$ (d) $100\sqrt{3}$

267. A regular hexagon is circumscribed by a circle of radius 4.5 cm. What is the area (in cm^2) of the hexagon? Matric Level 01-08-2022 Shift-I

(a) $\frac{135}{4}\sqrt{2}$ (b) $\frac{135}{4}\sqrt{3}$
(c) $\frac{243}{8}\sqrt{2}$ (d) $\frac{243}{8}\sqrt{3}$

Right Answers

1 (c)	2 (a)	3 (d)	4 (c)	5 (c)	6 (b)	7 (d)	8 (d)	9 (a)	10 (c)
11 (d)	12 (d)	13 (b)	14 (b)	15 (d)	16 (a)	17 (d)	18 (b)	19 (c)	20 (d)
21 (a)	22 (b)	23 (b)	24 (b)	25 (d)	26 (c)	27 (d)	28 (d)	29 (d)	30 (b)
31 (c)	32 (d)	33 (c)	34 (d)	35 (b)	36 (c)	37 (b)	38 (b)	39 (a)	40 (c)
41 (d)	42 (d)	43 (a)	44 (a)	45 (c)	46 (c)	47 (c)	48 (d)	49 (c)	50 (c)
51 (d)	52 (b)	53 (c)	54 (a)	55 (a)	56 (d)	57 (a)	58 (d)	59 (d)	60 (c)
61 (b)	62 (c)	63 (a)	64 (c)	65 (a)	66 (c)	67 (d)	68 (a)	69 (c)	70 (a)
71 (d)	72 (c)	73 (c)	74 (c)	75 (d)	76 (d)	77 (c)	78 (d)	79 (b)	80 (c)
81 (c)	82 (d)	83 (c)	84 (d)	85 (c)	86 (a)	87 (d)	88 (a)	89 (d)	90 (d)
91 (d)	92 (c)	93 (a)	94 (b)	95 (d)	96 (a)	97 (a)	98 (a)	99 (c)	100 (d)
101 (c)	102 (a)	103 (d)	104 (a)	105 (c)	106 (a)	107 (a)	108 (c)	109 (d)	110 (a)
111 (a)	112 (d)	113 (d)	114 (b)	115 (a)	116 (b)	117 (d)	118 (c)	119 (a)	120 (a)
121 (a)	122 (a)	123 (d)	124 (c)	125 (d)	126 (b)	127 (b)	128 (d)	129 (c)	130 (c)
131 (b)	132 (c)	133 (b)	134 (c)	135 (b)	136 (c)	137 (c)	138 (c)	139 (b)	140 (b)
141 (a)	142 (c)	143 (b)	144 (b)	145 (a)	146 (a)	147 (c)	148 (a)	149 (d)	150 (b)
151 (d)	152 (a)	153 (b)	154 (d)	155 (d)	156 (c)	157 (d)	158 (d)	159 (a)	160 (d)
161 (b)	162 (a)	163 (d)	164 (b)	165 (b)	166 (c)	167 (c)	168 (b)	169 (b)	170 (d)
171 (d)	172 (d)	173 (b)	174 (c)	175 (c)	176 (a)	177 (d)	178 (b)	179 (b)	180 (c)
181 (b)	182 (b)	183 (a)	184 (a)	185 (c)	186 (d)	187 (b)	188 (c)	189 (a)	190 (a)
191 (d)	192 (a)	193 (b)	194 (d)	195 (b)	196 (d)	197 (a)	198 (d)	199 (b)	200 (a)
201 (d)	202 (b)	203 (b)	204 (b)	205 (a)	206 (a)	207 (b)	208 (d)	209 (b)	210 (b)
211 (a)	212 (c)	213 (c)	214 (d)	215 (b)	216 (a)	217 (a)	218 (a)	219 (b)	220 (a)
221 (c)	222 (b)	223 (d)	224 (a)	225 (d)	226 (b)	227 (c)	228 (c)	229 (b)	230 (b)
231 (b)	232 (c)	233 (b)	234 (d)	235 (b)	236 (d)	237 (c)	238 (c)	239 (a)	240 (c)
241 (c)	242 (a)	243 (d)	244 (c)	245 (d)	246 (c)	247 (a)	248 (a)	249 (c)	250 (d)
251 (a)	252 (d)	253 (c)	254 (b)	255 (b)	256 (d)	257 (d)	258 (d)	259 (b)	260 (b)
261 (c)	262 (c)	263 (d)	264 (b)	265 (a)	266 (d)	267 (d)			

Solutions

1. (c) Given, diameter of identical rings $= 21$ cm

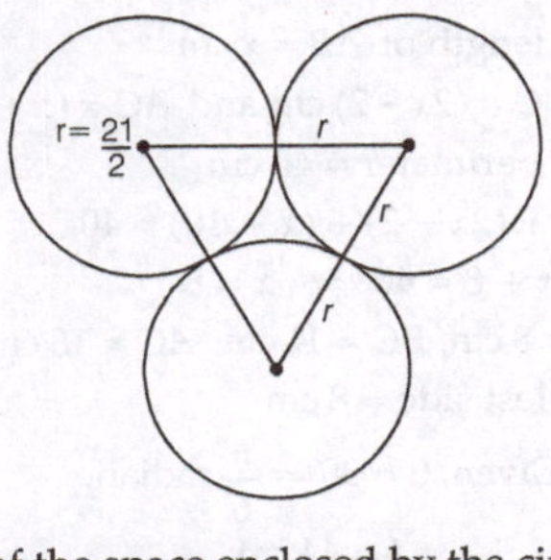

$\because$ Area of the space enclosed by the circles

$$= \frac{\sqrt{3}}{4} \times 4r^2 - \frac{\pi r^2}{2}$$

$$= r^2\left(\sqrt{3} - \frac{\pi}{2}\right)$$

$$= \left(\frac{21}{2}\right)^2 (1.732 - 1.57)$$

$$= 17.70 \text{ cm}^2$$

2. (a) According to the question,

$$\frac{l}{b} = \frac{3}{2} \Rightarrow 2l = 3b \quad \ldots\text{(i)}$$

and the perimeter of the park $= 120$ m

$\Rightarrow \quad 2l + 2b = 120$

$\Rightarrow \quad 3b + 2b = 120$ [from Eq. (i)]

$\Rightarrow \quad 5b = 120$

$\Rightarrow \quad b = 24$ m

$\therefore \quad l = \frac{3}{2}b = \frac{3}{2} \times 24 = 36$ m

Therefore, the area of the park $= l \times b$

$= 24 \times 36 = 864 \text{ m}^2$

3. (d) According to the question,

Length of arc $= 96\pi$

$$\frac{\theta}{360^\circ} \times 2\pi r = 96\pi$$

$$\Rightarrow \quad \frac{80^\circ}{360^\circ} \times 2r = 96$$

$$\Rightarrow \quad r = \frac{96 \times 360^\circ}{160^\circ} = 216 \text{ units}$$

4. (c) Given, $\frac{\text{Circumference of circle}}{\text{Diameter of circle}} = \frac{3}{5}$

Let circumference of circle $= 3x = 6$

$\Rightarrow \quad x = 2$ cm

and Diameter of circle $= 5x = 5 \times 2 = 10$ cm

$\therefore$ Radius $(r) = \frac{10}{2} = 5$ cm

5. (c) Perimeter of Sector $= 2\pi r \times \frac{45^\circ}{360^\circ} + 2r$

$$= 2 \times \frac{22}{7} \times 14 \times \frac{1}{8} + 2 \times 14$$

$$= 11 + 28 = 39 \text{ cm}$$

6. (b) Circumference of first circle $(C_1) = 2\pi r_1$

$C_1 = 24\pi$

Circumference of second circle $(C_2) = 2\pi r_2$

$C_2 = 32\pi$

Circumference third circle $(C_3) = C_1 + C_2$

$2\pi r_3 = 24\pi + 32\pi$

$\Rightarrow \quad 2\pi r_3 = 56\pi \Rightarrow r_3 = 28$ cm

$\therefore$ Diameter of third circle $= 28 \times 2 = 56$ cm

7. (d) Area of bigger circle $= \pi r^2 + \pi R^2$

$\pi R_1^2 = \pi \times 8^2 + \pi \times (15)^2$

$\Rightarrow \quad \pi R_1^2 = \pi(64 + 225)$

$\Rightarrow \quad \pi R_1^2 = \pi \times 289 \Rightarrow R_1^2 = 289$

$\Rightarrow R_1 = \sqrt{289} = 17 \Rightarrow$ (Radius of bigger circle)

Thus, perimeter $= 2\pi r = 2 \times \pi \times 17 = 34\pi$

8. (d) Side of equilateral triangle $= 37\sqrt{3}$ cm

Altitude $= \frac{1}{2} \times \sqrt{3}a = \frac{1}{2} \times \sqrt{3} \times 37\sqrt{3}$

$$= \frac{37 \times 3}{2} = \frac{111}{2} = 55.5 \text{ cm}$$

9. (a) Area of rectangle $= l \times b = 52 \times 9$

$= 468 \text{ m}^2$

10. (c) Given, Area $= 462 \text{ cm}^2$

Central angle $= 120°$

We know, Area of sector $= \pi r^2 \times \frac{\theta}{360°}$

$$462 = \pi r^2 \times \frac{120°}{360°} \Rightarrow 1386 = \frac{22}{7} r^2$$

$\Rightarrow \quad r^2 = 441 \Rightarrow r = 21 \text{ cm}$

11. (d) Given, $a + b = 9$ cm ...(i)

Area of rectangle $(ab) = 18 \text{ cm}^2$ ...(ii)

$\Rightarrow a - b = \sqrt{(a+b)^2 - 4ab} = \sqrt{81 - 4 \times 18}$

$\Rightarrow \quad a - b = 3$ ...(iii)

From Eq. (i) and (iii),

$a = 6$ cm and $b = 3$ cm

$\therefore \quad a^2 - ab + b^2 = (6)^2 + (3)^2 - 6 \times 3 = 27$ cm

12. (d) Base = 26 cm, Height = 18 cm

We know, Area of parallelogram $= b \times h$

$= 26 \times 18 = 468 \text{ cm}^2$

13. (b) We know, Length of Arc $= 2\pi r \times \frac{\theta}{360°}$

$$7 = 2\pi \times 24 \times \frac{\theta}{360°}$$

$\Rightarrow \quad \pi \frac{\theta}{360°} = \frac{7}{48}$

$\therefore$ Area of sector $= \pi r^2 \times \frac{\theta}{360°} = \frac{7}{48} \times 24 \times 24$

$= 84 \text{ cm}^2$

14. (b) Sides of an equilateral triangle

$(a) = 18$ cm

$\therefore$ Area $= \frac{\sqrt{3}}{4} \times a^2 = \frac{\sqrt{3}}{4} \times (18)^2 = 81\sqrt{3} \text{ cm}^2$

15. (d) We know,

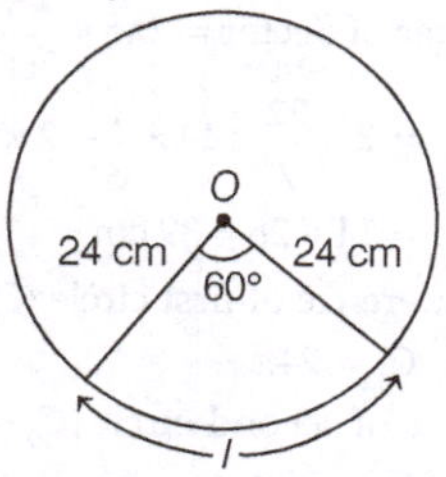

Perimeter of sector $= l + 2r = \frac{\theta}{360°} \times 2\pi r + 2r$

$= \frac{60°}{360°} \times 2 \times 3.14 \times 24 + 2 \times 24$

$= \frac{1}{6} \times 6.28 \times 24 + 48$

$= 6.28 \times 4 + 48 = 25.12 + 48 = 73.12$ cm

16. (a) Let breadth of rectangle be b m.

$\therefore$ Length of rectangle $(l) = (b + 6)$ m

As, perimeter of rectangle = 48 m

$\therefore \quad 2(l + b) = 48$

$\Rightarrow \quad 2(b + 6 + b) = 48$

$\Rightarrow \quad 2b + 6 = 24 \Rightarrow b = 9$ m

$\therefore \quad l = b + 6 = 15$ m

$\therefore$ Required area of rectangle

$= 15 \times 9 = 135 \text{ m}^2$

17. (d) Angle of sector $= 15°$

Radius of Arc = 14 m

Perimeter $= \frac{\theta}{360} \times 2\pi r + 2r$

$= \frac{15°}{360} \times 2 \times 3.14 \times 14 + 2 \times 14$

$= \frac{1}{24} \times 28 \times 3.14 + 28 = \frac{759.92}{24} = 31.66$ cm

18. (b) Length of arc $= \frac{\theta°}{360°} \times 2\pi r$

According to the question,

$$\frac{2\pi r}{2} = \frac{\theta°}{360} \times 2\pi r$$

$\Rightarrow \quad \theta° = 180°$

19. (c) In ΔABC,

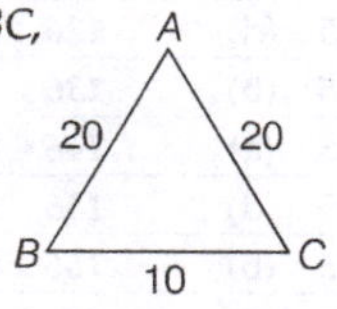

Semi-perimeter $(s) = \frac{20 + 20 + 10}{2} = 25$

Area of $\Delta ABC = \sqrt{s(s-a)(s-b)(s-c)}$

$= \sqrt{25 \times 5 \times 5 \times 15} = 25\sqrt{15}$

$= 25 \times 3.87 = 96.75 \text{ cm}^2$

By Pythagoras theorem,

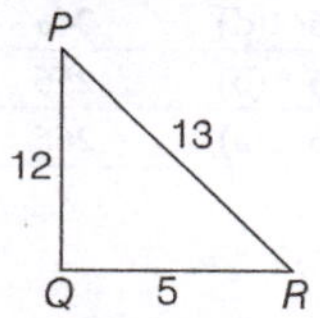

$QR^2 = 13^2 - 12^2 \Rightarrow QR^2 = 25 \times 1$

$\Rightarrow \quad QR = 5$

$\therefore$ Area of $\Delta PQR = \frac{1}{2} \times 5 \times 12 = 30 \text{ cm}^2$

Now, difference of area $= 96.75 - 30$

$= 66.75 \text{ cm}^2$

20. (d) Area of sector $= \frac{\theta}{360°} \times \pi r^2$

$\Rightarrow \quad 16\pi = \frac{\theta}{360} \times \pi \times 8 \times 8$

$\Rightarrow \quad \theta° = \frac{360°}{4} = 90°$

21. (a) Area of sector $= \frac{1}{2} \times l \times r$

Where, l is length of arc and r is radius.

$\therefore$ Area of sector $= \frac{1}{2} \times 7 \times 12 = 42 \text{ cm}^2$

22. (b) Radius $(r) = 21$ cm

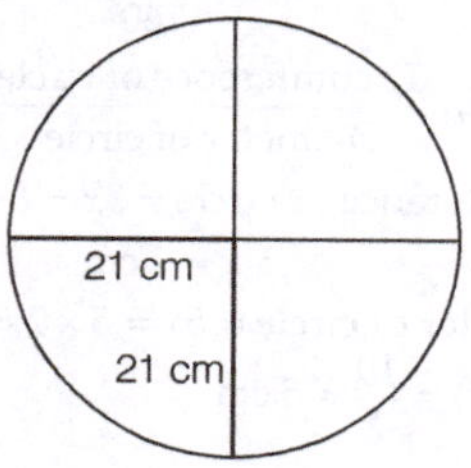

$\therefore$ Required perimeter $= \frac{3}{4} \times 2\pi r + 2r$

$= \frac{3\pi r}{2} + 2r = 3 \times \frac{22}{7} \times \frac{21}{2} + 2 \times 21$

$= 99 + 42 = 141$ cm

23. (b)

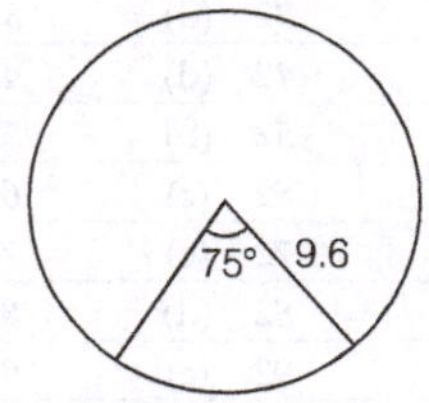

$\theta = 75°, \quad r = 9.6$

$\because \quad l = \frac{\theta}{360} \times 2\pi r$

$\therefore \quad \theta = \frac{75}{360} \times 2\pi \times \frac{9.6}{10} = 4\pi$

24. (b)

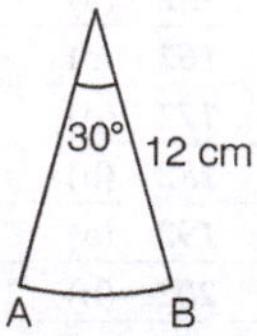

$\therefore$ Perimeter of sector $(AB) = 2\pi r \times \frac{30°}{360°} + 2r$

$= 2 \times 3.14 \times 12 \times \frac{1}{12} + 2 \times 12$

$= 6.28 + 24 = 30.28$ cm

25. (d)

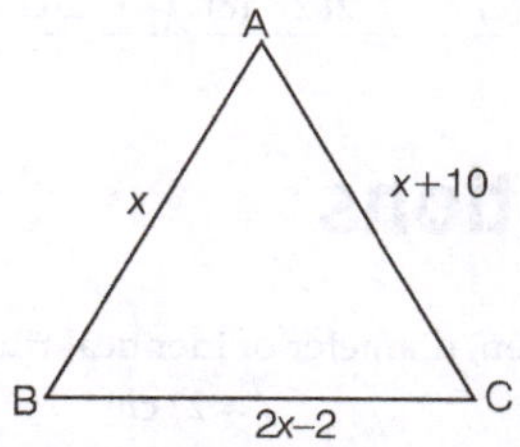

Let the length of $AB = x$ cm

Then, $BC = (2x - 2)$ cm and $AC = (x + 10)$ cm

Given, perimeter = 40 cm

$\Rightarrow \quad x + (2x - 2) + (x + 10) = 40$

$\Rightarrow \quad 4x + 8 = 40 \Rightarrow x = 8$

$\therefore$ $AB = 8$ cm, $BC = 14$ cm, $AC = 18$ cm

$\therefore$ Smallest side = 8 cm

26. (c) Given, $\theta = 30° = \frac{\pi}{6}$ radian.

$l = 44$ cm

$\therefore$ Area of sector $= \frac{\theta}{360°} \times \pi r^2$

$= \frac{30}{360} \times \pi \times \left(\frac{l}{\theta}\right)^2$

$= \frac{1}{12} \times \pi \times \frac{l^2}{\frac{\pi}{6} \times \frac{\pi}{6}} \qquad \left(\because r = \frac{l}{\theta}\right)$

$= \frac{1}{12} \times \frac{\pi \times l^2 \times 36}{\pi \times \pi}$

$= \frac{1}{12} \times \frac{44 \times 44 \times 36 \times 7}{22}$

$= 2 \times 44 \times 3 \times 7 = 1848 \text{ cm}^2$

27. (d) We know,

Diagonal of a square $= a\sqrt{2}$

[Here, a is the side of square]

$\therefore \quad 4.8 = a\sqrt{2} \Rightarrow \dfrac{24}{5} = a\sqrt{2}$

Squaring both sides, we get

$\Rightarrow \quad \dfrac{576}{25} = 2a^2 \Rightarrow \dfrac{576}{50} = a^2 \Rightarrow a^2 = 11.52\ m^2$

28. (d)

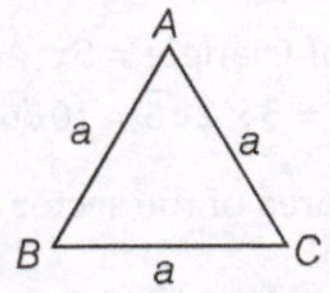

Let the sides of an equilateral triangle $= a$ unit

$\therefore$ Perimeter $= 3a = 36$ unit (given)

$\Rightarrow \quad a = 12$ unit

$\therefore$ Area $= \dfrac{\sqrt{3}}{4} \times a^2 = \dfrac{\sqrt{3}}{4} \times 12 \times 12$

$= 36\sqrt{3}$ sq unit.

29. (d) Area of the rectangular courtyard

$= 495 \times 1665\ cm^2$

Now, the HCF of 495 and 1665 = 45

$\therefore$ Area of one tile $= 45 \times 45\ cm^2 = 2025\ cm^2$

$\therefore$ Required number of tiles

$= \dfrac{495 \times 1665}{2025} = 407$

30. (b) Given, $r_1 = 28$ m, $r_2 = 25$ m

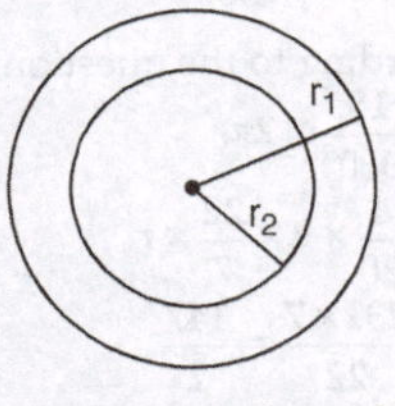

$\therefore$ Area of the track $= \pi(28^2 - 25^2)$

$= \pi(28 + 25)(28 - 25) = \pi \times 53 \times 3$

$\therefore$ Cost of levelling the track is

$= \dfrac{22}{7} \times 53 \times 3 \times 28 = ₹\ 13992$

31. (c) According to the question,

$l + 2r = 63 \quad$ ...(i)

Area of sector = 209

i.e., $\quad \dfrac{\theta}{360°} \times \pi r^2 = 209$

$\Rightarrow \quad \dfrac{\theta}{360°} = \dfrac{209}{\pi r^2} \quad$ ...(ii)

From Eqs. (i) and (ii),

$\dfrac{\theta}{360°} \times 2\pi r + 2r = 63$

$\Rightarrow \quad \dfrac{209}{\pi r^2} \times 2\pi r + 2r = 63$

$\Rightarrow \quad 418 + 2r^2 = 63r$

$\Rightarrow \quad 2r^2 - 63r + 418 = 0$

$\Rightarrow \quad r = \dfrac{63 \pm \sqrt{3969 - 3344}}{4}$

$= \dfrac{63 \pm \sqrt{625}}{4} = \dfrac{63 \pm 25}{4}$

$r = \dfrac{63 + 25}{4} = \dfrac{88}{4} = 22 \Rightarrow r = 22$ cm

$\therefore$ From Eq. (ii),

$\theta = \dfrac{209 \times 360 \times 7}{22 \times 484} = 49.5°$

32. (d) Given, area of square

$= 16x^2 + 40x + 25$

$= (4x)^2 + 2(4x)(5) + (5)^2$

$= (4x + 5)^2 = (4x + 5)(4x + 5)$

$\therefore$ Side of square $= (4x + 5)$ units

$\therefore$ Perimeter of square $= 4 \times$ Side

$= 4(4x + 5) = 2(8x + 10)$ units

33. (c) $\because$ Each angle in equilateral triangle is 60°.

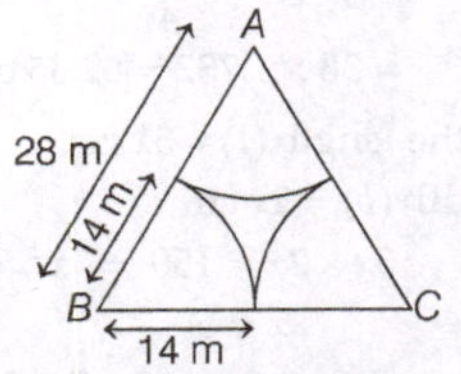

$\therefore$ Required area = Area of $\Delta - 3 \times$ Area of sector

$= \dfrac{\sqrt{3}}{4} \times 28 \times 28 - 3 \times \dfrac{22}{7} \times 14$

$\times 14 \times \dfrac{60°}{360°}$

$= 339.08 - 308 = 31.08\ m^2$

34. (d) Radius $(r) = 10$ cm

Angle of sector $\theta = 30°$

Length of arc $= \dfrac{\theta}{360°} \times 2\pi r$

$= \dfrac{30°}{360°} \times 2 \times 3.14 \times 10 = 5.23$

$\therefore$ Perimeter of sector of circle

= Length of arc + $2r$

$= 5.23 + 2 \times 10 = 25.23$

35. (b) Perimeter of the sector $= \dfrac{64}{3}$ cm

Central angle = 60°

Perimeter of the sector $= \dfrac{\theta}{360°} \times 2\pi r + 2r$

$\therefore \quad \dfrac{60°}{360°} \times 2 \times \dfrac{22}{7} \times r + 2r = \dfrac{64}{3}$

$\Rightarrow \quad \dfrac{22}{21}r + 2r = \dfrac{64}{3}$

$\Rightarrow \quad \dfrac{(42 + 22)r}{21} = \dfrac{64}{3} \Rightarrow \dfrac{64r}{21} = \dfrac{64}{3}$

$\therefore \quad r = 7$ cm

Area of sector $= \dfrac{\theta}{360°} \times \pi r^2$

$= \dfrac{60°}{360°} \times \dfrac{22}{7} \times 7 \times 7 = \dfrac{77}{3}\ cm^2$

36. (c) Let the equal side of an isosceles triangle be x.

We know, Area of triangle

$= \dfrac{1}{2} \times$ Base $\times$ Height

$\Rightarrow \quad \dfrac{1}{2} \times x \times x = 50 \Rightarrow x^2 = 100 \Rightarrow x = 10$

In ΔABC, using Pythagoras theorem, we get

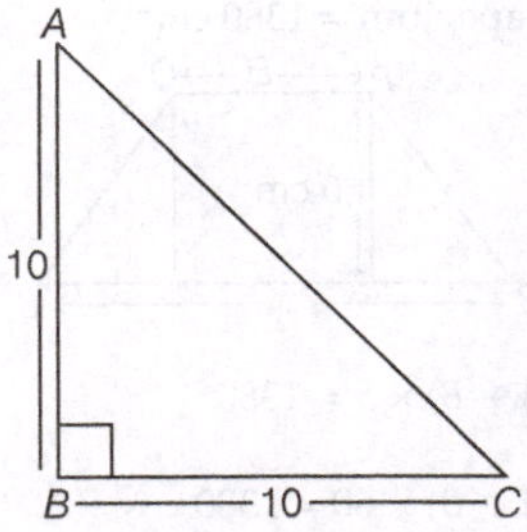

$P^2 + B^2 = H^2$

$\Rightarrow \quad (AC)^2 = (10)^2 + (10)^2$

$= 100 + 100 = 200$

$\Rightarrow \quad AC = 10\sqrt{2}$ cm

37. (b) We know,

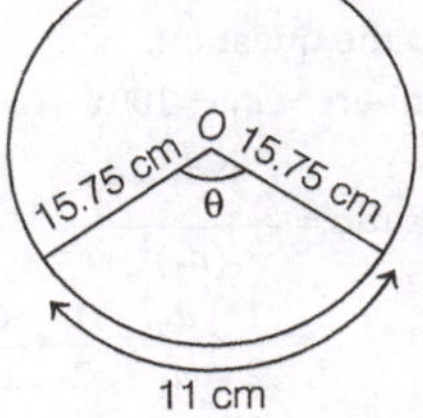

Given, $l = 11$ cm,

$r = 15.75$ cm

Area of sector $= \dfrac{1}{2} l.r$

$= \dfrac{1}{2} \times 11 \times 15.75$

$= 86.625\ cm^2$

38. (b) Given, trapezium $ABCD$,

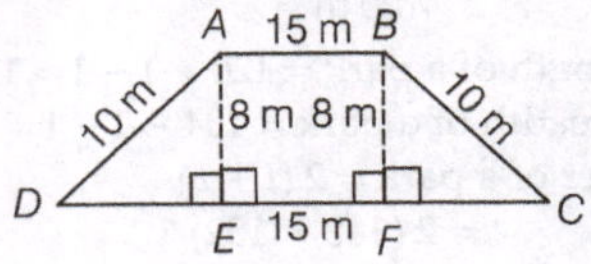

In ΔAED,

Applying Pythagoras theorem

$AD^2 = AE^2 + DE^2$

$(10)^2 = (8)^2 + (DE)^2$

$\Rightarrow \quad DE = \sqrt{100 - 64} \Rightarrow DE = 6$ m

$\therefore \quad DE = CF = 6$ m

Perimeter of a trapezium

$= AB + BC + CD + AD$

$= AB + BC + (DE + EF + FC) + AD$

$= 15 + 10 + 6 + 15 + 6 + 10 = 62$ m

39. (a) We know,

Diameter of a circle = Diagonal of a square

$10 = a\sqrt{2} \Rightarrow a = \dfrac{10}{\sqrt{2}} = 5\sqrt{2}$

$\therefore$ Perimeter of a square $= 4a$

$= 4 \times 5\sqrt{2} = 20\sqrt{2}$ cm

40. (c) Let the length of parallel sides be A and B $(A > B)$

Given, $A - B = 12 \quad$ ...(i)

Height $(h) = 60$ cm

Area of trapezium = 1380 cm^2

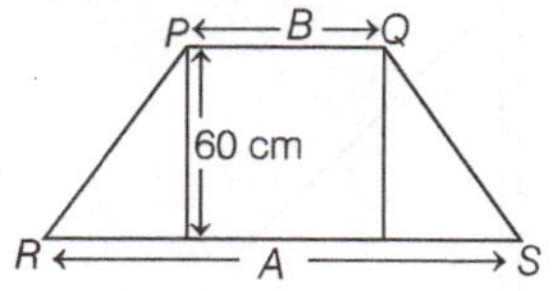

$\Rightarrow \quad \frac{1}{2}(A+B)\times h = 1380$

$\Rightarrow \quad \frac{1}{2}(A+B)\times 60 = 1380$

$\Rightarrow \quad A + B = 46 \quad \ldots(ii)$

Solving Eqs. (i) and (ii), we get
$A = 29$ and $B = 17$

41. (d) Let one diagonal of rhombus $(d_1) = 100x$

Then, other diagonal $(d_2) = 65x$

According to the question,

Side of the square = $d_1 = 100x$

$\therefore$ Required ratio $= \dfrac{\frac{1}{2}\times d_1 \times d_2}{(d_1)^2}$

$= \frac{1}{2}\times\frac{d_2}{d_1} = \frac{1}{2}\times\frac{65x}{100x}$

$= \frac{13}{40} = 13:40$

42. (d) According to the question,

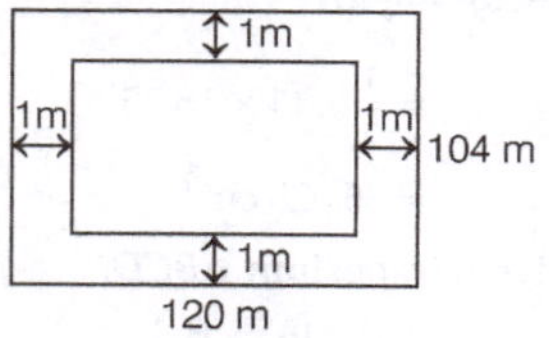

Inner length of a park = 120 − 1 − 1 = 118

Inner breadth of a park = 104 − 1 − 1 = 102

Perimeter of a park = $2(l + b)$
$= 2(118 + 102)$
$= 2 \times 220 = 440$ m

Cost of 1 m = ₹ 2.5

$\because$ Cost of 440 m = 2.5 × 440 = ₹ 1100

43. (a) Length of an arc $(l) = 2\pi r \times \frac{\theta}{360^\circ}$

$= 2\times\frac{22}{7}\times 4\times\frac{45^\circ}{360^\circ} \Rightarrow l = \frac{22}{7}$

$\therefore$ Perimeter of the sector $= l + r + r$

$= \frac{22}{7} + 4 + 4 = \frac{78}{7}$ cm

44. (a) Given, radius of circle = r

Then, length of arc $AB = 5r$

$5r = \frac{\theta}{360^\circ}\times 2\pi\times r \Rightarrow \frac{\theta}{360^\circ} = \frac{5}{2\pi}$

$\therefore$ Area of sector $= \frac{\theta}{360^\circ}\times\pi r^2$

$= \frac{5}{2\pi}\times\pi r^2 = 2.5r^2$

45. (c) Side of an equilateral triangle = 16 cm (given)

$\therefore$ Area of the triangle $= \frac{\sqrt{3}}{4}\times 16^2$

$= 64\sqrt{3}$ cm^2

46. (c) Area of sector $= \frac{1}{2} l \times r$

$= \frac{1}{2}\times 12\times 8 = 48$ cm^2

47. (c) Perimeter = 2(150 + 80) = 460 m

Diagonal $= \sqrt{150^2 + 80^2} = 170$ m

$\therefore$ Required ratio $= \frac{460}{170} = 2.7$

$\therefore$ Its perimeter is 2.7 times of its diagonal.

48. (d) $\frac{\text{Angle of arc at centre}}{360^\circ}\times\pi\times\text{Diameter}$
= Length of an arc

49. (c) Side of an equilateral triangle = 12 cm

$\therefore$ Area of the triangle $= \frac{\sqrt{3}}{4}\times 12^2$

$= 36 \times 1.732 = 62.35$ cm^2

50. (c) Let the length $(l) = 3x$ cm
and the width $(b) = 2x$ cm

$\therefore \quad 3x \times 2x = 150 \Rightarrow x^2 = 25$

$\Rightarrow \quad x = 5$

$\therefore$ Perimeter $= 2(3x + 2x) = 2\times 5\times 5 = 50$ cm

51. (d) Semi-perimeter $= \frac{\text{Perimeter}}{2}$

$= \frac{100}{2} = 50$ cm

52. (b) Let the length of the rectangle = l m

$\therefore$ Width $= (l - 2)$ m

$\therefore$ Perimeter = 68 m

$\because$ Perimeter = 2 (Length + Breadth)

$\Rightarrow \quad 2(l + l - 2) = 68 \Rightarrow 2(l - 1) = 34$

$\Rightarrow \quad l = 17 + 1 = 18$

$\therefore$ Length = 18 m

53. (c) Area of sector $= \frac{\theta}{360^\circ}\times\pi r^2$

Area of sector $= \frac{60^\circ}{360^\circ}\times\frac{22}{7}\times(7)^2 = \frac{77}{3}$ cm^2

54. (a) Diameter of the circle $(2r) = 7$ cm

Radius $= \frac{7}{2}$ cm

Length of an arc $= \frac{\theta}{360^\circ}\times 2\pi r$

$= \frac{108^\circ}{360^\circ}\times\frac{22}{7}\times 7 = 0.3\times 22 = 6.6$ cm

55. (a) According to the question,

$\frac{\theta}{360^\circ}\times\pi r^2 = 1848$

$\Rightarrow \quad r^2 = \frac{1848\times 360^\circ\times 7}{270^\circ\times 22}$

$\Rightarrow \quad r^2 = 28\times 28 \Rightarrow r = 28$ m

56. (d) Side of triangle $= \frac{48}{3} = 16$ cm

$\therefore$ Area of equilateral triangle

$= \frac{\sqrt{3}}{4}(\text{side})^2 = \frac{\sqrt{3}}{4}\times(16)^2 = 64\sqrt{3}$ cm^2

57. (a) Let the equal sides of triangle $= 3x = a$
and the third side of triangle $= 5x = b$

Given, area of triangle $= 30\sqrt{11}$ cm^2

$\frac{b}{4}\sqrt{4a^2 - b^2} = 30\sqrt{11}$

$\Rightarrow \quad \frac{5x}{4}\sqrt{4\times 9x^2 - 25x^2} = 30\sqrt{11}$

$\Rightarrow \quad \frac{5x}{4}\sqrt{11x^2} = 30\sqrt{11}$

$\Rightarrow \quad \frac{5x^2}{4} = 30 \Rightarrow x = 2\sqrt{6}$

So, third side of triangle = $5x$
$= 5\times 2\sqrt{6} = 10\sqrt{6}$ cm

58. (d) Given, area of the sector $= \frac{\pi r^2\theta}{360^\circ} = 32\pi$

Radius of the circle = 12 cm

Then, $32\pi = \frac{\pi}{360^\circ}\times 12\times 12\times\theta$

$\Rightarrow \quad \frac{\theta r}{360^\circ} = \frac{32}{12}$

Length of the arc $= \frac{2\pi r\theta}{360^\circ}$

$\therefore$ Length of the arc $= 2\pi\times\frac{32}{12} = \frac{16\pi}{3}$ cm

59. (d) Area of the sector

$= \frac{\theta}{360^\circ}\times\pi r^2 = \frac{60^\circ}{360^\circ}\times 3.14\times 10\times 10$

$= 52.33$ cm^2

60. (c) Area of a sector $= \pi r^2\left[\frac{\theta}{360^\circ}\right]$

$= \frac{22}{7}\times 5\times 5\times\frac{60^\circ}{360^\circ} = 13.09 \approx 13.1$ cm^2

61. (b) According to the question,

$23.1 = \frac{18^\circ}{360^\circ}\times 2\pi r$

$\Rightarrow \quad 23.1 = \frac{1}{20}\times 2\times\frac{22}{7}\times r$

$\Rightarrow \quad r = \frac{231\times 7}{22} = \frac{147}{2}$

$\therefore$ Area of circle $= \pi r^2$

$= \frac{22}{7}\times\frac{147}{2}\times\frac{147}{2} = 16978.50$ cm^2

62. (c) Increase in area $= \left(a + b + \frac{ab}{100}\right)\%$

Here, a and b = 34%

$= \left(34 + 34 + \frac{34\times 34}{100}\right)\%$

$= 68 + 11.56 = 79.56\%$

63. (a) Area of shaded portion

$= \frac{1}{2}\times\frac{\sqrt{3}}{4}(6)^2 - \frac{1}{4}\times\frac{22}{7}\times(1)^2$

$= \frac{9\sqrt{3}}{2} - \frac{11}{14} = \frac{1}{2}\left(9\sqrt{3} - \frac{11}{7}\right)$ unit^2

64. (c) Area of parallelogram
= Area of triangle

$\Rightarrow \quad 28\times 12 = \frac{1}{2}\times 28\times\text{Altitude}$

$\therefore$ Altitude = 24 cm

65. (a) Required area of sector

$= \frac{22\times 6\times 6\times 70^\circ}{7\times 360^\circ} = 22$ m^2

66. (c) Length of hour hand, $r = 6$ cm

Angle rounded in 4 h by hour hand,

$$\theta = 4 \times 30^\circ = 120^\circ$$

$\therefore$ Area of the sector covered by hour hand

$$= \frac{22 \times 36 \times 120^\circ}{7 \times 360^\circ} = \frac{264}{7} = 37.71 \text{ cm}^2$$

67. (d) Let the radii of circles be r_1 and r_2.

According to the question,

$$2\pi r_1 = 110 \quad \text{...(i)}$$

and $2\pi r_2 = 330 \quad$ ...(ii)

Subtracting Eq. (i) from Eq. (ii),

$$2\pi r_2 - 2\pi r_1 = 220$$

$\Rightarrow \quad 2\pi(r_2 - r_1) = 220$

$\Rightarrow \quad (r_2 - r_1) = \frac{220 \times 7}{2 \times 22} \Rightarrow r_2 - r_1 = 35$

68. (a) Ratio of sides of the triangle = 6:8:10

Let the sides are $6x, 8x$ and $10x$ (in cm)

Here, $(6x)^2 + (8x)^2 = (10x)^2$

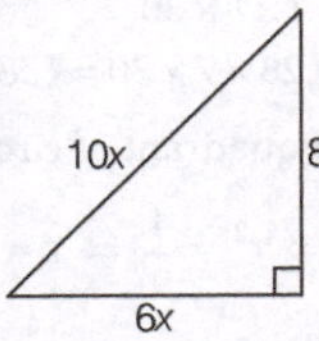

Now, area of a triangle $= \frac{1}{2} \times \text{base} \times \text{height}$

$\Rightarrow \quad 96 = \frac{1}{2} \times 6x \times 8x$

$\Rightarrow \quad x^2 = \frac{96 \times 2}{6 \times 8} = 2 \times 2$

$\therefore \quad x = 2$

Perimeter of the triangle $= (6x + 8x + 10x)$ cm

$= 24x$ cm $= 24 \times 2$ cm

$= 48$ cm

69. (c) Let the length of the tree $= r$ meter

According to the question,

$$44 = 2\pi r \times \frac{\theta}{360^\circ}$$

$\Rightarrow \quad 44 = 2 \times \frac{22}{7} \times r \times \frac{18^\circ}{360^\circ} \quad (\because \theta = 18^\circ)$

$\Rightarrow \quad r = \frac{44 \times 7 \times 360}{2 \times 22 \times 18} = 140$ m

70. (a) Length of minute hand of a clock,

$r = 20$ cm

Angle make by minute hand from 8:00 am to 8:45 am,

$$\theta = 45 \times 6^\circ = 270^\circ \quad (1 \text{ min} = 6^\circ)$$

$\therefore$ Area swept by minute hand

$$= \frac{22 \times (20)^2 \times 270^\circ}{7 \times 360^\circ} = \frac{6600}{7} \text{ cm}^2$$

71. (d) Let their radii be r_1 and r_2.

$\therefore \quad 2\pi r_2 - 2\pi r_1 = 396 - 264$

$\Rightarrow \quad (r_2 - r_1) = \frac{132 \times 7}{2 \times 22} = 21$

Hence, the difference between their radii is 21 cm.

72. (c) Given,

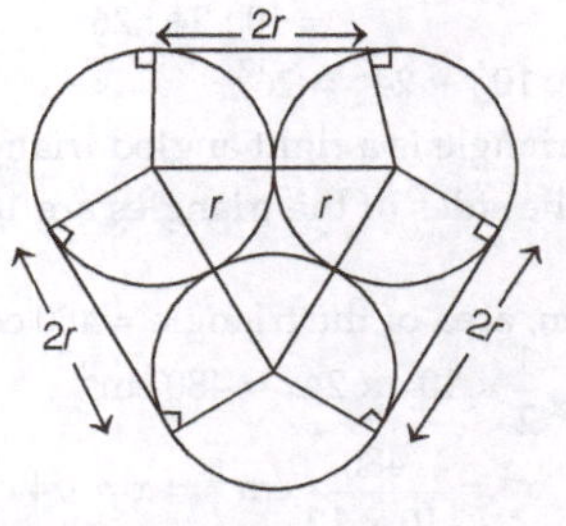

Since, radius of each circle = 7 cm

The length of the string not in contact with circle $= 2r + 2r + 2r = 6r$

$= 6 \times 7 = 42$ cm

By symmetry, the angles swiped by string on one circle is 120°.

$\therefore \quad \theta = 120^\circ$

$\Rightarrow$ Length of string touching circle

$$= \frac{2\pi r}{3} + \frac{2\pi r}{3} + \frac{2\pi r}{3}$$

$$\left(\because \text{length or arc} = \frac{\theta}{360^\circ} \times 2\pi r\right)$$

$$= 2\pi r = 2 \times \pi \times 7 = 14\pi$$

$\therefore$ Total length of the string $= (42 + 14\pi)$ cm

> **Speedy Method**
>
> Length of string $= 2r(\pi + n)$
>
> (where n is number of circle) $= 2 \times 7(\pi + 3)$
>
> $= (14\pi + 42)$ cm

73. (c) Area $= \frac{\sqrt{3}}{4} \times (8)^2 = \frac{1.732 \times 8 \times 8}{4} \text{ cm}^2$

$= 27.712 \text{ cm}^2 = 27.71 \text{ cm}^2$

74. (c) Here, $\frac{\sqrt{3}}{2} a = 6\sqrt{3}$ m $\Rightarrow a = 12$ m

Hence, perimeter of the equilateral triangle

$= 3a = 3 \times 12 = 36$ m

75. (d) Given, perimeter of square = 124 m

$\Rightarrow \quad 4 \times \text{side} = 124$ m

$\Rightarrow \quad \text{Side} = \frac{124}{4}$ m $= 31$ m

$\therefore$ Area of square $= (\text{Side})^2 = (31)^2 = 961 \text{ m}^2$

76. (d) According to the question,

$$9\sqrt{3} = \frac{\sqrt{3}}{2} a$$

$\Rightarrow \quad a = 18$ cm

Now, Area of triangle $= \frac{1}{2} \times \text{Base} \times \text{Height}$

$= \frac{1}{2} \times 18 \times 9\sqrt{3} = 81\sqrt{3} \text{ cm}^2$

77. (c) According to the question,

$$2\pi r = 220 \text{ cm} \Rightarrow r = \frac{220 \times 7}{2 \times 22}$$

$\therefore \quad r = 5 \times 7 = 35$ cm

78. (d) Let side of a square $= a$

Then, $\quad a\sqrt{2} = 8\sqrt{2} \quad$ (Given)

$\Rightarrow \quad a = 8$ cm

Area of square $= (8)^2 = 64 \text{ cm}^2$

Area of another square $= 3 \times 64 = 192 \text{ cm}^2$

$b^2 = 192$ (Side of this square $= b$)

$\Rightarrow \quad b = \sqrt{192} = 8\sqrt{3}$

$\therefore$ Diagonal of this square $= b\sqrt{2}$

$= 8\sqrt{3} \times \sqrt{2} = 8\sqrt{6}$ cm

79. (b) Let the length and breadth of the rectangle are $5x$ and $2x$, respectively.

Given, diagonal of square $= \sqrt{200}$ cm

$\therefore \quad \sqrt{2}(\text{side}) = 10\sqrt{2} \Rightarrow \text{side} = 10$ cm

According to the question,

Area of rectangle = Area of square

$\Rightarrow \quad 5x \times 2x = (10)^2 \Rightarrow 10x^2 = 100$

$\Rightarrow \quad x^2 = 10 \Rightarrow x = \sqrt{10}$

$\therefore$ Length of rectangle

$= 5x = 5\sqrt{10} = \sqrt{250}$ cm

80. (c) Let the radius of outer and inner circle be R and r respectively,

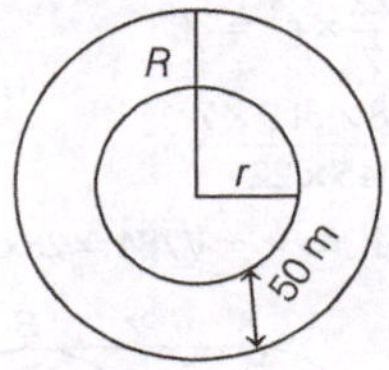

Then, $\frac{2\pi R}{2\pi r} = \frac{5}{4} \Rightarrow \frac{R}{r} = \frac{5}{4}$

$\Rightarrow \quad R = \frac{5r}{4} \quad$ ...(i)

According to the question,

$R - r = 50$

$\Rightarrow \quad \frac{5r}{4} - r = 50 \quad$ [from Eq. (i)]

$\Rightarrow \quad \frac{5r - 4r}{4} = 50 \Rightarrow r = 200$ m

81. (c) Area of sector $= \frac{\theta}{360^\circ} \times \pi r^2$

$= \frac{90^\circ}{360^\circ} \times \frac{22}{7} \times (10)^2 = 78.5 \text{ m}^2$

82. (d) Ratio of lengths of sides of triangle

$= \frac{1}{3} : \frac{1}{5} : \frac{1}{6} = 10 : 6 : 5$

Let the sides be $10x$ cm, $6x$ cm and $5x$ cm respectively,

Now, $10x + 6x + 5x = 147$

$\Rightarrow \quad 21x = 147 \Rightarrow x = 7$ cm

$\therefore$ Length of smallest side $= 5x = 5 \times 7 = 35$ cm

83. (c) According to the question,

$7\sqrt{3} = \frac{\sqrt{3}}{2} \times \text{Side} \Rightarrow \text{Side} = 14$ cm

Now, area of an equilateral triangle

$= \frac{\sqrt{3}}{4} \times 14 \times 14 = 49\sqrt{3} \text{ cm}^2$

84. (d) According to the question,

Perimeter of circle = Perimeter of square

$\Rightarrow \quad 2\pi r = 4 \times 11 \Rightarrow 2 \times \frac{22}{7} \times r = 44$

$\therefore \quad r = \frac{44 \times 7}{2 \times 22} = 7$ cm

85. (c) Here, required area $= \frac{\theta}{360^\circ} \times \pi r^2$

$= \frac{30^\circ}{360^\circ} \times 3.14 \times 4 \times 4 = 4.186 \text{ cm}^2$

86. (a)

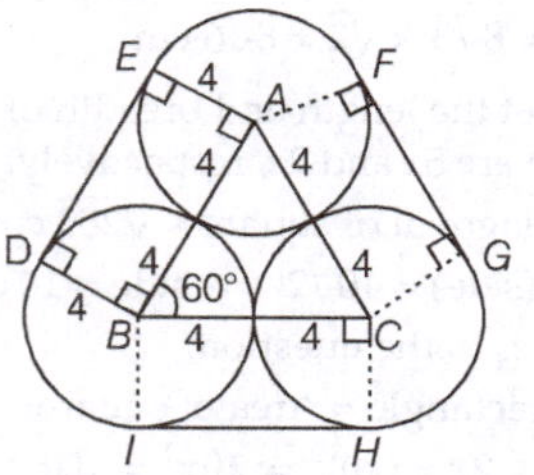

By formula

Length of string $= 2r(\pi + n) = 2r(\pi + 3)$

$= 2 \times 4(\pi + 3)$ $[\because r = 4 \text{ cm}]$

$= (8\pi + 24)$ cm

87. (d) Area of a sector $= 308 \text{ cm}^2$

$\Rightarrow \frac{45^\circ}{360^\circ} \times \frac{22}{7} \times r^2 = 308$

$\Rightarrow r^2 = \frac{308 \times 360 \times 7}{45 \times 22}$

$\Rightarrow r^2 = 784 \Rightarrow r = \sqrt{784} = 28$ cm

88. (a) Given,

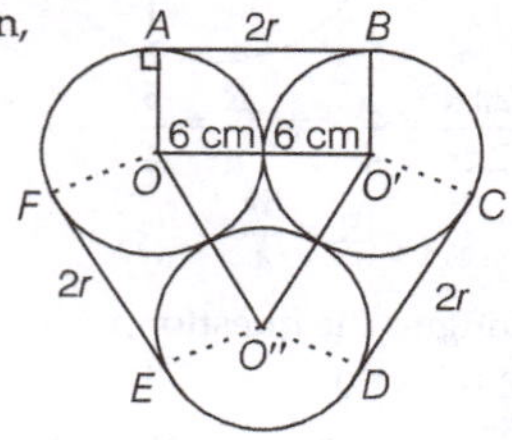

Length of string $= 2r(\pi + 3)$

$= 2 \times 6(\pi + 3) = (12\pi + 36)$ cm

89. (d) According to the question,

$\frac{\pi r^2 \theta}{360^\circ} = 66 \Rightarrow \frac{22 \times r^2 \times 60^\circ}{7 \times 360^\circ} = 66$

$\Rightarrow r^2 = \frac{6 \times 66 \times 7}{22} = 126$

$\Rightarrow r^2 = 126 \Rightarrow r = \sqrt{9 \times 14} = 3\sqrt{14}$ cm

90. (d) In the given figure,

Radius of $APCQ = 16\sqrt{2} \therefore r = 16\sqrt{2}$ cm

Now, the area of the shaded region

$= \frac{1}{4} \times \pi r^2 - (16)^2 = \frac{1}{4} \times (3.14)(16\sqrt{2})^2 - (16)^2$

$= (16)^2 \left[\frac{3.14 \times 2}{4} - 1\right]$

$= 256 \times 0.57 = 145.92 \text{ cm}^2$

91. (d) Area of an equilateral triangle

$= \frac{\sqrt{3}}{4}(\text{side})^2 = \frac{\sqrt{3}}{4} \times 20 \times 20 \text{ cm}^2$

$= 100\sqrt{3} \text{ cm}^2$

92. (c) Angle covered by hour hand from 9 pm to 3 am $= 6 \times 30^\circ = 180^\circ$

Length of hour hand $(r) = 6$ inch

$\therefore$ Distance covered by tip

$= \frac{\theta}{360^\circ} \times 2\pi r = \frac{180^\circ}{360^\circ} \times 2 \times \pi \times 6 = 6\pi$ inch

93. (a) Ratio of sides of the triangle

$= 10 : 24 : 26$

Here, $10^2 + 24^2 = 26^2$

So, triangle is a right angled triangle.

Let the sides of the triangles are $10x$, $24x$ and $26x$.

Given, area of the triangle $= 480 \text{ cm}^2$

$\Rightarrow \frac{1}{2} \times 10x \times 24x = 480 \text{ cm}^2$

$\Rightarrow x^2 = \frac{480}{10 \times 12} \text{ cm}^2 \Rightarrow x = \sqrt{4} \text{ cm} = 2$ cm

$\therefore$ Perimeter of the given triangle

$= 10x + 24x + 26x = 60x = 60 \times 2 = 120$ cm

94. (b) Required circum-radius

$= \frac{\text{Side}}{\sqrt{3}} = \frac{12}{\sqrt{3}} \times \frac{\sqrt{3}}{\sqrt{3}} = \frac{12\sqrt{3}}{3} = 4\sqrt{3}$ cm

95. (d) Since, the circumference of a circle $= 2\pi r$

According to the question,

Difference between their radii

$= \frac{(352 - 198)}{2\pi} = \frac{154 \times 7}{2 \times 22} = 24.5$ cm

96. (a) Required percentage

$= \left(x + y + \frac{xy}{100}\right)\% = \left(8 + 5 + \frac{8 \times 5}{100}\right)\%$

$[\because x = 8, y = 5]$

$= 13.4\%$

97. (a) Speed = 3 km/h or $\frac{3 \times 1000}{60} = 50$ m/min

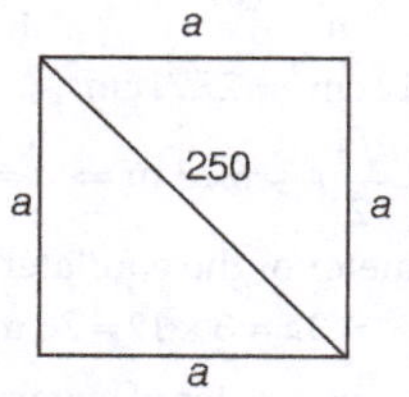

Time = 5 min

Distance $= 50 \times 5 = 250$ m (diagonal)

We know that, side of square

$= \frac{\text{Diagonal}}{\sqrt{2}} = \frac{250}{\sqrt{2}}$

$\therefore$ Area of square $= (\text{side})^2 = \frac{250}{\sqrt{2}} \times \frac{250}{\sqrt{2}}$

$= 31250 \text{ m}^2$

98. (a) According to the question,

$\frac{\sqrt{3}}{4}a^2 = 9\sqrt{3} \Rightarrow a^2 = 36$

$\Rightarrow a = 6$ cm

$\therefore$ Length of each side of table is 6 cm.

99. (c) According to the question,

$4a = 2\pi r$

$\Rightarrow 4a = 2 \times \frac{22}{7} \times 7$ $[\because r = 7 \text{ cm}]$

$\Rightarrow a = 11$ cm

$\therefore$ Area of circle : Area of square $= \pi r^2 : a^2$

$= \frac{22}{7} \times 7 \times 7 : 11^2 = 14 : 11$

100. (d) Let the inner radius $(r) = r$ cm

Then the outer radius $(R) = (r + 10)$ cm

According to the question,

$\pi(r + 10)^2 - \pi r^2 = 3080$

$\Rightarrow \pi(r^2 + 100 + 20r - r^2) = 3080$

$\Rightarrow (20r + 100) = \frac{3080}{22} \times 7$

$\Rightarrow 20r = 980 - 100 = 880$

$\therefore r = 44$ m

and $R = 44 + 10 = 54$ m

So, sum of two radii $= 54 + 44 = 98$ m

101. (c) Area of square $= 1764 \text{ m}^2$

$a^2 = 1764 \Rightarrow a = 42$ cm

According to the question,

Breadth $= \frac{1}{6} \times 42 = 7$ cm

Length is 4 times the breadth $= 4 \times 7 = 28$ cm

$\therefore$ Cost of levelling the park at ₹ 30/m² is

$= l \times b \times 30$

$= 28 \times 7 \times 30 = ₹5880$

102. (a) Area of quadrant of circle $= \frac{\pi}{9} \text{ m}^2$

$\Rightarrow \frac{\pi r^2}{4} = \frac{\pi}{9} \Rightarrow r^2 = \frac{4}{9} \Rightarrow r = \frac{2}{3}$ m

103. (d) General solution,

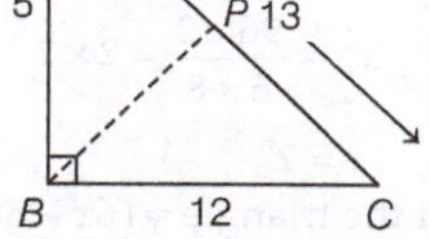

Area of $\Delta ABC = \frac{1}{2} \times 5 \times 12 = 30 \text{ cm}^2$

Again, area of ΔABC taking AC as base

$\frac{1}{2} \times AC \times PB = 30$

$\Rightarrow \frac{1}{2} \times 13 \times PB = 30 \Rightarrow PB = \frac{60}{13} = 4.6$ cm

Speedy Method

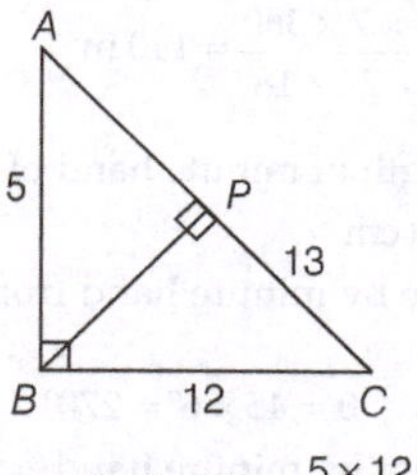

Smallest perpendicular $BP = \frac{5 \times 12}{13} = 4.6$ cm

104. (a) Given, perimeter of semi circle is

$= 25.7$ cm

$\Rightarrow \pi r + 2r = 25.7 \Rightarrow 3.14r + 2r = 25.7$

$\Rightarrow 5.14r = 25.7 \Rightarrow r = 5$ cm

$\therefore$ Diameter of semi-circle

$= 2r = 2 \times 5 = 10$ cm

105. (c) Area of square = 1764 m^2

$a^2 = 1764$

$\Rightarrow \quad a = 42$

Breadth $= \frac{1}{3} \times a \Rightarrow \frac{1}{3} \times 42 = 14$ m

Breadth = 14 m

Length = 2 × 14 = 28 m

∴ Cost of levelling the park at ₹ 15/m^2

$= 14 \times 28 \times 15 =$ ₹ 5880

106. (a) Given,

Area of circular park = 12474 m^2

$\pi r^2 = 12474$

$\Rightarrow \quad r^2 = \frac{12474}{22} \times 7 \Rightarrow r^2 = 3969$

$\Rightarrow \quad r = 63$

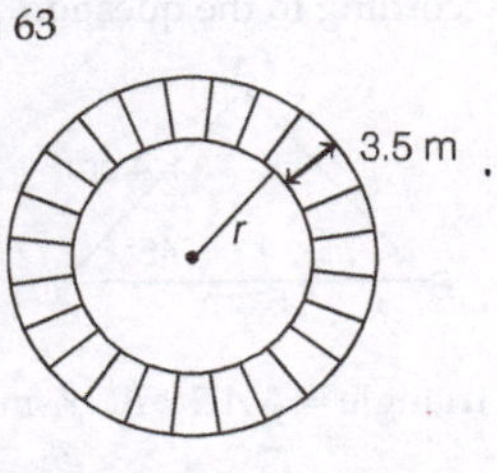

Width of path = 3.5 m

Now, new radius = 63 + 3.5 = 66.5 m = r

Total area including path $= \pi \times (66.5)^2$

$= 13898.5\ m^2$

∴ Area of path = 13898.5 − 12474 = 1424.5 m^2

107. (a) We know that,

$4a^2 = d_1^2 + d_2^2$

$\Rightarrow \quad 4(13)^2 = (24)^2 + d_2^2$

$\Rightarrow \quad d_2^2 = 676 - 576$

$\Rightarrow \quad d_2^2 = 100 \Rightarrow d_2 = 10$ cm

∴ Area of rhombus $= \frac{1}{2} d_1 \times d_2$

$= \frac{1}{2} \times 24 \times 10 = 120\ cm^2$

108. (c) Perimeter of rectangle = 50 units (given)

$2(l + b) = 50$

$\Rightarrow \quad l + b = 25 \quad$ ...(i)

Area of rectangle = 150 unit

$l \times b = 150 \quad$ ...(ii)

We can write

$(l - b)^2 = (l + b)^2 - 4lb = (25)^2 - 4 \times 150$

$= 625 - 600 = 25$

$\Rightarrow \quad (l - b) = \sqrt{25}$

$\Rightarrow \quad l - b = 5 \quad$ ...(iii)

From Eqs. (i) and (iii),

$l = 15$ units, $b = 10$ units

∴ Shorter side is 10 units.

109. (d) According to the question,

$2x + y = 50$

$2x + 18 = 50 \quad$ [given, base = 18 cm]

$\Rightarrow \quad 2x = 50 - 18 = 32$

$\Rightarrow \quad x = 16$

∴ The length of equal side is x = 16 cm.

110. (a) Net % change

$= -11 + (-11) + \frac{(-11 \times (-11))}{100}$

$= -22 + 1.21 = -20.79\%$

Thus, its area total decreases by 20.79%.

111. (a) Given, diagonal = 65 m

Length (l) = 63 m

∴ Breadth $(b) = \sqrt{(65)^2 - (63)^2} = \sqrt{256} = 16$ m

∴ Perimeter of the rectangular plot = 2(l + b)

= 2(63 + 16) = 2(79) = 158 m

112. (d) Area of circular track $= \pi(R^2 - r^2)$

$= \frac{22}{7} \times (29^2 - 23^2)$

$= \frac{22}{7} \times (29 + 23)(29 - 23) = \frac{22}{7} \times (52)(6)$

Cost of levelling $= \frac{22}{7} \times 6 \times 52 \times 7 =$ ₹ 6864

∴ The cost of levelling the track is ₹ 6864.

113. (d) Area of rhombus $= \frac{1}{2}(d_1 \times d_2)$

$= \frac{1}{2} \times 16 \times 12 = 16 \times 6 = 96\ cm^2$

114. (b) According to the question,

$\frac{\sqrt{3}}{4} a^2 = 36\sqrt{3}$

$\Rightarrow \quad a^2 = 36 \times 4 \quad \Rightarrow \quad a = 6 \times 2 = 12$

Perimeter of triangle = 3a

= 3 × 12 = 36 cm

115. (a) Area of disc = 0.64 π m^2

$\pi r^2 = 0.64\pi \Rightarrow r = \sqrt{0.64} = 0.8$ m

Circumference of disc = 2πr

$\Rightarrow \quad 2 \times \frac{22}{7} \times 0.8 = 5.02$ m

1.408 km = 1408 m

Number of revolutions disc makes

$= \frac{1408}{5.02} = 280$

116. (b) Perimeter of square = 4a

4a = 64 (given)

a = 16

Area of square $= a^2 = (16)^2 = 256\ cm^2$

117. (d) Area of square $A = (a + b)^2 / 2$

According to the question,

Area of square, $B = 2 \times \frac{(a + b)^2}{2} = (a + b)^2$

Side of square $(B) = \sqrt{(a + b)^2} = (a + b)$

Diagonal of square $B = \sqrt{2}(a + b)$

Area of square taking diagonal of square B as side Area $= [\sqrt{2}(a + b)]^2 = 2(a + b)^2$ sq. units

118. (c) Area of rectangular hexagon

$= \left(\frac{3\sqrt{3}}{2}\right)(\text{side})^2 = \frac{3\sqrt{3}}{2} s^2$

$\frac{3\sqrt{3}}{2} s^2 = 2400\sqrt{3}$

$\Rightarrow \quad s^2 = \frac{2400 \times 2}{3} \Rightarrow s^2 = 1600 \Rightarrow s = 40$ m

So, perimeter of that rectangular hexagon

= 6s = 6 × 40 = 240 m

∴ Required cost = 240 × 16.80 = ₹ 4032

119. (a) Longest chord of a circle will be Diameter.

Area of a circle $= \pi r^2$

$256\pi = \pi r^2$

$\Rightarrow \quad r^2 = 256 \Rightarrow r = 16$ cm

∴ Diameter = 2r = 32 cm

120. (a) Side of equilateral triangle

= a = 18 cm

Circum radius $(R) = \frac{a}{\sqrt{3}} = \frac{18}{\sqrt{3}}$

In radius $(r) = \frac{a}{2\sqrt{3}} = \frac{18}{2\sqrt{3}}$

Area of region in between $= \pi(R)^2 - \pi(r)^2$

$= \pi\left[\left(\frac{18}{\sqrt{3}}\right)^2 - \left(\frac{18}{2\sqrt{3}}\right)^2\right]$

$= \pi\left[\left(\frac{18 \times 18}{3}\right) - \left(\frac{18 \times 18}{4 \times 3}\right)\right]$

$= \pi(108 - 27) = 81\pi = 81 \times \frac{22}{7}$

$= \frac{1782}{7} = 254\frac{4}{7}\ cm^2$

121. (a) Given, Radius of the circle = 35 cm

Angle (θ) subtended by the arc = 72°

∴ Area of sector of the circle

$= \pi r^2 \times \frac{\theta}{360°} = \frac{22}{7} \times 35 \times 35 \times \frac{72°}{360°}$

$= 22 \times 35 = 770\ cm^2$

122. (a) Given,

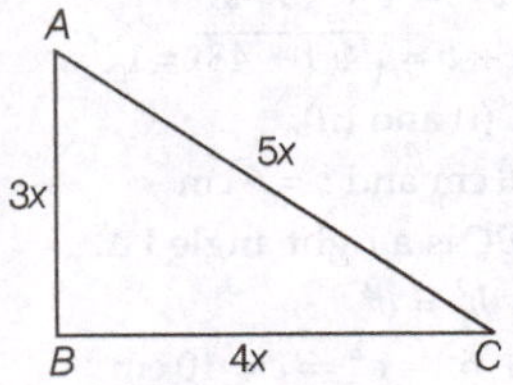

∴ Area of $\Delta ABC = \frac{1}{2} \times AB \times BC$

$\Rightarrow \quad 486 = \frac{1}{2} \times 3x \times 4x \Rightarrow 6x^2 = 486$

$\Rightarrow x^2 = 81 \Rightarrow x = 9$ cm

∴ Perimeter of $\Delta ABC = 3x + 4x + 5x = 12x$

= 12 × 9 = 108 cm

123. (d) Let the original length and breadth of rectangular lawn be 'l' and 'b', respectively.

Original area = lb

New length = 1.15l

New breadth = 0.92b

∴ New Area = 1.15l × 0.92b = 1.058 lb

Percentage change in the lawn area

$= \frac{1.058\ lb - lb}{lb} \times 100 = 0.058 \times 100$

= 5.8% increase

Speedy Method

Percentage change in area

$= 15 - 8 + \frac{(-8) \times 15}{100} = 7 - 1.2$

$= 5.8\%$ (increase)

124. (c) Let the sides of the triangle be a, b and c.

$\therefore a + b + c = 125$ cm

$\therefore$ Semi-perimeter $= \frac{a+b+c}{2} = \frac{125}{2}$ cm

We know that, In-radius

$= \frac{\text{Area of } \Delta}{\text{Semi - perimeter of } \Delta}$

$\Rightarrow 8 = \frac{\text{Area of } \Delta}{\frac{125}{2}} \Rightarrow \text{Area of } \Delta = \frac{125 \times 8}{2}$

$= 500 \text{ cm}^2$

125. (d) Given, $a - b = 2$ cm ...(i)

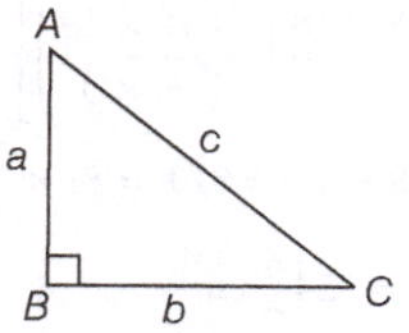

Area of triangle $= \frac{1}{2} \times \text{Base} \times \text{Height}$

$24 \text{ cm}^2 = \frac{1}{2} \times b \times a$

$ab = 48 \text{ cm}^2$

Since, $a - b = 2$

$(a+b)^2 = (a-b)^2 + 4ab$

$(a+b)^2 = 4 + 4 \times 48$

$a + b = \sqrt{4(1+48)} = 14$ ...(ii)

From Eqs. (i) and (ii),

$a = 8$ cm and $b = 6$ cm

Since, ΔABC is a right angled Δ.

$\therefore a^2 + b^2 = c^2$

$8^2 + 6^2 = c^2 \Rightarrow c = 10$ cm

$\therefore$ Perimeter of $\Delta ABC = 8 + 6 + 10 = 24$ cm

126. (b) Length of first playground = 224 m

Breadth of first playground = 160 m

Ratio of length to breadth of first play ground $= \frac{224}{160} = \frac{7}{5}$

$\therefore$ Ratio of length to breadth of 2nd playground should also be $\frac{7}{5}$.

$\therefore$ Length = 343 m and breadth = 255 m does not follow the ratio.

127. (b) $2\pi r_1 \times N_1 = 2\pi r_2 \times N_2$

$\Rightarrow r_1 \times N_1 = r_2 \times N_2$

$\Rightarrow \frac{15}{2} \times 105 = \frac{21}{2} \times N_2 \Rightarrow N_2 = 75$

Number of revolutions of larger gear = 75

128. (d) Center distance between the circle = Side of triangle = (5 + 5) = 10 cm

$\therefore$ Area subtended between the circles.

= Area of equilateral triangle − 3 × Area of sector

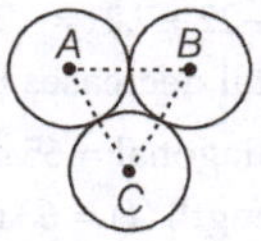

$= \frac{\sqrt{3}}{4}a^2 - 3 \times \frac{\theta}{360^\circ} \times \pi r^2$

$= \frac{\sqrt{3}}{4} \times (10)^2 - 3 \times \frac{60^\circ}{360^\circ} \times \pi(5)^2$

$= \frac{100\sqrt{3}}{4} - \frac{25\pi}{2} = 25\sqrt{3} - \frac{25\pi}{2}$

$= 25\left(\sqrt{3} - \frac{\pi}{2}\right)$

129. (c) Perimeter of triangle

$= (13 + 12 + 5)$ cm $= 30$ cm

130. (c) Area of trapezium =

$1188 = \frac{1}{2} \times \text{Sum of parallel sides} \times (18)$

$\Rightarrow \frac{1188 \times 2}{18} = \text{Sum of parallel sides}$

$\Rightarrow 66 \times 2 = \text{Sum of parallel sides}$

$\therefore$ Sum of parallel sides = 132 cm

131. (b) Given, Radius (r) of circle = 14 cm

Area of sector $= 231 \text{ cm}^2$

$\therefore 231 = \frac{\theta}{360} \times \pi r^2$

$\Rightarrow 231 = \frac{\theta}{360} \times \frac{22}{7} \times 14 \times 14$

$\Rightarrow 231 \times 360 = \theta \times 22 \times 2 \times 14$

$\therefore \theta = 135^\circ$

132. (c) Area of sector $= \frac{\theta}{360^\circ} \times \pi r^2$

$= \frac{60}{360} \times \frac{22}{7} \times 21 \times 21 = 231 \text{ cm}^2$

133. (b) Circumference of the circle

$= 2\pi r = 88$ cm

$\therefore r = 14$ cm

Now, length of minor arc

$= 2\pi r \times \frac{\theta}{360} = 22$ cm

$\Rightarrow 2 \times \frac{22}{7} \times 14 \times \frac{\theta}{360} = 22 \Rightarrow \theta = 90^\circ$

Now, area of minor sector $= \frac{\theta}{360} \times \pi r^2$

$= \frac{90}{360} \times \frac{22}{7} \times 14 \times 14 = 154 \text{ cm}^2$

Speedy Method

Area of minor sector

$= \frac{1}{2} \times l_{\text{minor}} \times r = \frac{1}{2} \times 22 \times 14 = 154$

134. (c) Length of the arc

$= 2 \times \frac{22}{7} \times 35 \times \frac{72^\circ}{360^\circ}$

$= 2 \times 22 \times 5 \times \frac{1}{5} = 44$ cm

135. (b) Given, base (b) of parallelogram $= 2 \times$ Height (h) of parallelogram

$\Rightarrow b = 2h$ ...(i)

$\because$ Area of parallelogram $= b \times h$

$\therefore 338 = b \times h \Rightarrow 338 = 2h \times h$ (by Eq. (i))

$\Rightarrow 169 = h^2 \Rightarrow h = 13$ cm

136. (c) Given, length of chord AB = Radius (r) of the circle

Hence, ΔAOB is an equilateral triangle.

$\therefore \angle AOB = 60^\circ$

Hence, length of arc $= 2\pi r \frac{\theta}{360^\circ}$

$= 2 \times \frac{22}{7} \times 21 \times \frac{60^\circ}{360^\circ} = 22$ units

137. (c) According to the question,

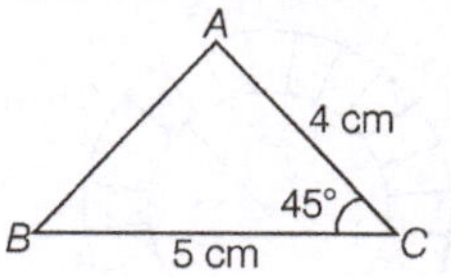

Area of a triangle $= \frac{1}{2} AC \times BC \times \sin 45^\circ$

$= \frac{1}{2} \times 4 \times 5 \times \sin 45^\circ = 2 \times 5 \times \frac{1}{\sqrt{2}}$

$= \sqrt{2} \times \sqrt{2} \times 5 \times \frac{1}{\sqrt{2}} = 5\sqrt{2} \text{ cm}^2$

138. (c) Let the breadth of the rectangular field $= x$ m

Then, the length of the rectangular field

$= x + 20\% \text{ of } x = \frac{6x}{5}$

According to the question,

$x \times \frac{6x}{5} = 480 \Rightarrow x = 20$ m

Thus, length of rectangle $= 6 \times \frac{20}{5} = 24$ m

139. (b) According to the question,

$\frac{\text{Area of triangles}(A_1)}{\text{Area of triangle}(A_2)} = \frac{\frac{1}{2} \times b_1 \times h_1}{\frac{1}{2} \times b_2 \times h_2}$

$\Rightarrow \frac{4}{3} = \frac{b_1 \times 6}{b_2 \times 5} \Rightarrow \frac{b_1}{b_2} = \frac{20}{18} = \frac{10}{9}$

$\therefore b_1 : b_2 = 10 : 9$

140. (b) Let sides of triangle be $= 5x$ cm, $12x$ and $13x$ cm respectively.

Then, perimeter

$\Rightarrow 5x + 12x + 13x = 90 \Rightarrow 30x = 90$

$\Rightarrow x = 3$ cm

Now, sides are 15, 36 and 39 cm.

Now, area of triangle $= \frac{1}{2} \times 15 \times 36$

$= 18 \times 15 = 270 \text{ cm}^2$

[15, 36, 39 are triplet

$\therefore$ It is right angle triangle]

141. (a) Since, 12, 13 and 5 are forming pythagorean triplets.

$\therefore$ Area $= \frac{1}{2} \times 12 \times 5 = 30 \text{ cm}^2$

142. (c) According to the question,

$$19 = 2 \times \frac{22}{7} \times 30 \times \frac{\theta}{360}$$

$$\Rightarrow \quad \theta = \frac{19 \times 7 \times 360}{2 \times 22 \times 30} = 36.27 \text{ (in degress)}$$

143. (b) Given, perimeter = $4P$

$\therefore$ Side = P

$\therefore$ In a rhombus

$$4p^2 = d_1^2 + d_2^2 \quad ....(i)$$

Also given, $d_1 + d_2 = L$

$$\Rightarrow \quad (d_1 + d_2)^2 = L^2$$

$$\Rightarrow \quad d_1^2 + d_2^2 + 2d_1d_2 = L^2$$

$$\Rightarrow \quad 2d_1d_2 = L^2 - (d_1^2 + d_2^2)$$

$$\therefore \quad d_1d_2 = \frac{L^2 - 4P^2}{2} \quad \text{[From Eq. (i)]}$$

$$\text{Area} = \frac{1}{2} \times d_1d_2 = \frac{1}{2}\left(\frac{L^2 - 4P^2}{2}\right)$$

$$= \frac{1}{4}(L^2 - 4P^2)$$

144. (b) Let the radius of large semi-circle be r.

$\therefore$ Radius of each small semi-circle $= \frac{r}{3}$

$\therefore$ Required ratio

= Shaded area : Unshaded area

$$= \left\{\frac{3}{2} \times \pi \times \left(\frac{r}{3}\right)^2 : \left(\frac{\pi r^2}{2} - \frac{\pi r^2}{6}\right)\right\}$$

$$= \frac{1}{6}\pi r^2 : \frac{\pi r^2}{3} = 1:2$$

145. (a) Diagonal of square = $9\sqrt{2}$ (given)

$$a\sqrt{2} = 9\sqrt{2}$$

$$a = 9$$

Perimeter of square = $4a = 4 \times 9 = 36$

$\Rightarrow$ Base of triangle = 36

Side of another square whose area is 144 cm^2.

$$a_2^2 = 144$$

$$a_2 = 12 = \text{Height of triangle}$$

$$\text{Area of triangle} = \frac{1}{2} \times \text{Base} \times \text{Height}$$

$$= \frac{1}{2} \times 36 \times 12 = 216 \text{ cm}$$

146. (a) Perimeter of the rectangle

$$= 2 \times 40 = 80 \text{ m}$$

Let the breadth of the rectangle = $2x$

Then the length of the rectangle = $3x$

Perimeter = $2 \times (2x + 3x) = 80$

$$\Rightarrow \quad 5x = 40$$

$$\Rightarrow \quad x = \frac{40}{5} \Rightarrow x = 8$$

$\therefore$ Area of the rectangle $= 2x \times 3x = 6x^2$

$$= 6 \times 8^2 = 384 \text{ m}^2$$

147. (c) Required percentage decrease

$$= \left(17 + 17 - \frac{17 \times 17}{100}\right)\%$$

$$= (34 - 2.89) = 31.11\%$$

148. (a) Given, $a = 13$ cm, $d_1 = 24$ cm

$$\therefore \quad 4a^2 = d_1^2 + d_2^2$$

$$\therefore \quad d_2 = \sqrt{4(13)^2 - (24)^2}$$

$$= \sqrt{676 - 576} = \sqrt{100} = 10 \text{ cm}$$

$$\therefore \text{Area of rhombus} = \frac{1}{2} \times d_1 \times d_2$$

$$= \frac{1}{2} \times 10 \times 24 = 120 \text{ cm}^2$$

149. (d) $(26)^2 = (24)^2 + (10)^2$

$\therefore$ Triangle is right angle triangle.

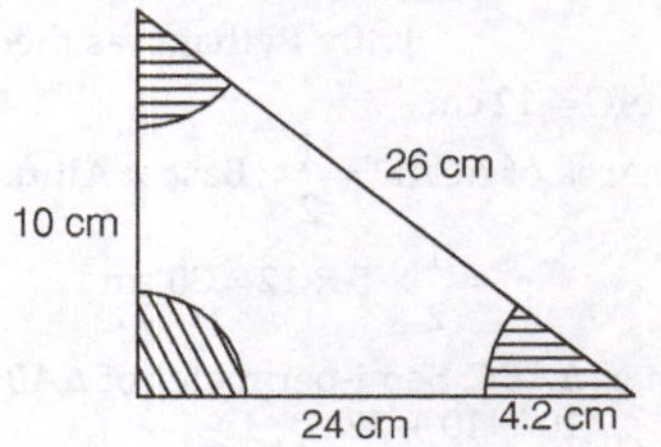

$$\therefore \text{Required area} = \frac{\pi r^2}{360°}(\theta_1 + \theta_2 + \theta_3)$$

$$= \frac{22 \times 4.2 \times 4.2}{7 \times 360°} \times 180°$$

$$[\because \theta_1 + \theta_2 + \theta_3 = 180°]$$

$$= 27.72 \text{ cm}^2$$

150. (b) Area of hexagonal field = $1944\sqrt{3}$

$$\Rightarrow \quad 6 \times \frac{\sqrt{3}}{4} \times a^2 = 1944\sqrt{3}$$

$$\Rightarrow \quad a^2 = \frac{1944 \times 4}{6} \Rightarrow a = 36$$

Now, the cost of fencing the hexagonal field

= $(6 \times 36) \times 11.50 =$ ₹ 2484

151. (d) Area of a trapezium

$$= \frac{1}{2} \times (17 + 15) \times 6$$

$$= \frac{1}{2} \times 32 \times 6$$

$$= 96 \text{ cm}^2 = 0.0096 \text{ m}^2$$

152. (a) Given, breadth = 12 m

Length = $2 \times 12 = 24$ m

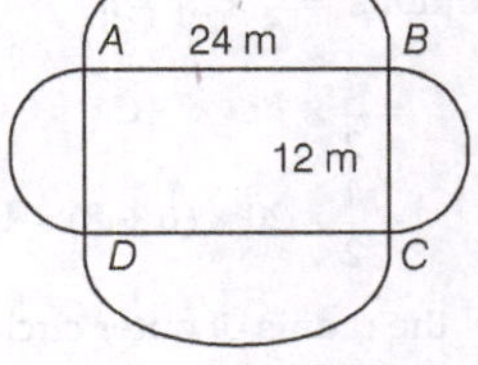

$$\text{Total area} = (24 \times 12) + 2 \times \left[\frac{1}{2} \times \pi \times \left(\frac{12}{2}\right)^2\right]$$

$$+ 2 \times \left[\frac{1}{2} \times \pi \times \left(\frac{24}{2}\right)^2\right]$$

$$= 288 + 36\pi + 144\pi = 288 + 180\pi$$

$$= 288 + 180 \times (3.14) = 853.2 \text{ m}^2$$

153. (b) Let the length of rectangle be $3x$.

$$\therefore \quad \text{Breadth} = \frac{2}{3} \text{ of } 3x = 2x$$

Perimeter = $2 \times$ (Length + Breadth)

$$40 = 2 \times (3x + 2x)$$

$$x = 4$$

Length = $3x$ = 12 m

Breadth = $2x$ = 8 m

$$\therefore \quad \text{Area} = \text{Length} \times \text{Breadth}$$

$$= 12 \times 8 = 96 \text{ m}^2$$

$\therefore$ Hence, area of rectangle is 96 m^2.

154. (d) Net % change

$$= -11 + (-11) + \frac{-11 \times (-11)}{100}$$

$$= -22 + 1.21 = -20.79\%$$

155. (d) $\because 4a^2 = d_1^2 + d_2^2$

$$\therefore \quad d_2^2 = \sqrt{4a^2 - d_1^2}$$

$$= \sqrt{4(13)^2 - (10)^2}$$

$$= \sqrt{676 - 100} = \sqrt{576} = 24 \text{ cm}$$

$$\therefore \quad \text{Area of rhombus} = \frac{1}{2} \times d_1 \times d_2$$

$$= \frac{1}{2} \times 10 \times 24 = 120 \text{ cm}^2$$

156. (c) Here, $(26)^2 = (24)^2 + (10)^2$

$\therefore$ Triangle is right angle triangle.

$$\text{Whose area} = \frac{1}{2} \times 24 \times 10 = 120 \text{ cm}^2$$

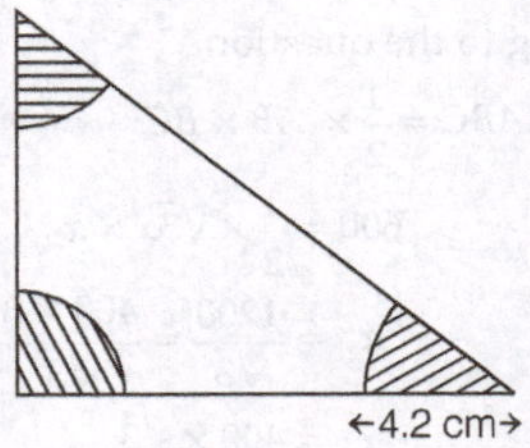

$\therefore$ The required area

$$= 120 - \left[\frac{\pi r^2}{360°}(\theta_1 + \theta_2 + \theta_3)\right]$$

$$= 120 - \left[\frac{22 \times 4.2 \times 4.2}{7 \times 360°} \times 180°\right]$$

$$= 120 - 27.72 = 92.28 \text{ cm}^2$$

157. (d) According to the question,

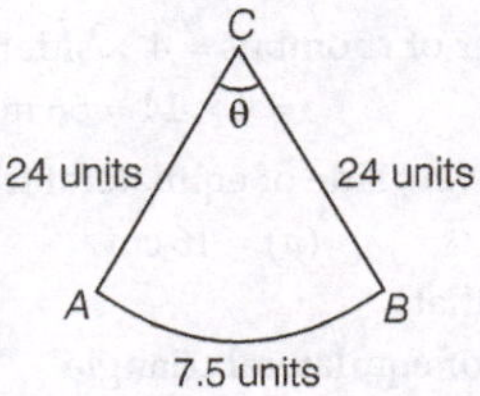

Radius of sector (r) = 24 units

Arc of sector (l) = 7.5 units

$$\because \quad l = r \times \theta$$

$$\Rightarrow \quad 7.5 = 24 \times \theta$$

$$\Rightarrow \quad \theta = \left(\frac{7.5}{24}\right) = \left(\frac{180}{\pi} \times \frac{7.5}{24}\right)^\circ$$

$$\therefore \text{Area of sector} = \frac{\theta}{360} \times \pi \times r^2$$

$$= \frac{\frac{180}{\pi} \times \frac{75}{240}}{360} \times \pi \times 24 \times 24$$

$$= \frac{180 \times 75}{360 \times 240 \times \pi} \times \pi \times 24 \times 24$$

$$= \frac{75}{10} \times 12 = 15 \times 6 = 90 \text{ sq units}$$

Speedy Method

Area of sector $= \frac{1}{2} \times$ Length of arc $\times$ Radius

$$= \frac{1}{2} \times 24 \times 7.5 = 12 \times 7.5 = 90 \text{ sq units}$$

158. (d) Let in right angled ΔABC, $BC = x$

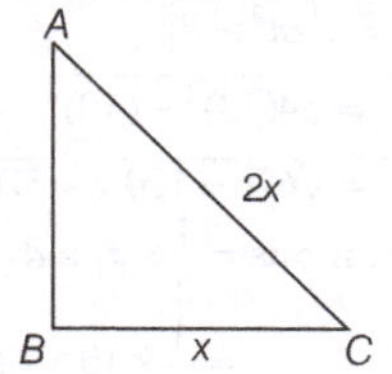

Then, $AC = 2x$

$\therefore \quad AC^2 = BC^2 + AB^2$

$\Rightarrow \quad (2x)^2 = x^2 + (AB)^2$

$\Rightarrow \quad AB^2 = 4x^2 - x^2 = 3x^2$

$\therefore \quad AB = \sqrt{3}x$

According to the question,

Area of $\Delta ABC = \frac{1}{2} \times AB \times BC$

$\Rightarrow \quad 600 = \frac{1}{2} \times \sqrt{3}x \times x$

$\Rightarrow \quad x^2 = \frac{1200}{\sqrt{3}} = \frac{400 \times 3}{\sqrt{3}}$

$\Rightarrow \quad x^2 = 400 \times \sqrt{3}$

$\Rightarrow \quad x = \sqrt{692.8} \Rightarrow x = 26.32$ m

Hence, hypotenuse is 26.32 m greater than base.

159. (a) Given, area $= 70 \text{ m}^2$, Height $= 5$ m

We know that,

Area of rhombus = Base × Height

$\Rightarrow \quad 70 = \text{Base} \times 5$

$\therefore \quad$ Side = Base = 14 m

$\therefore$ Perimeter of rhombus $= 4 \times$ side

$= 4 \times 14 = 56$ m

160. (d) Given, side of equilateral triangle

$(a) = 16$ cm

We know that,

Perimeter of equilateral triangle

$= 3a = 3 \times 16 = 48$ cm

In equilateral triangle,

Height = Median

$\therefore$ Median $= \frac{\sqrt{3}}{2}a = \frac{\sqrt{3}}{2} \times 16 = 8\sqrt{3}$ cm

$\therefore$ Sum of median $= 3(8\sqrt{3}) = 24\sqrt{3}$ cm

$\therefore \quad \frac{\text{Perimeter of triangle}}{\text{Sum of its median}} = \frac{48}{24\sqrt{3}} = \frac{2}{\sqrt{3}}$

$= 2 : \sqrt{3}$

161. (b) Given,

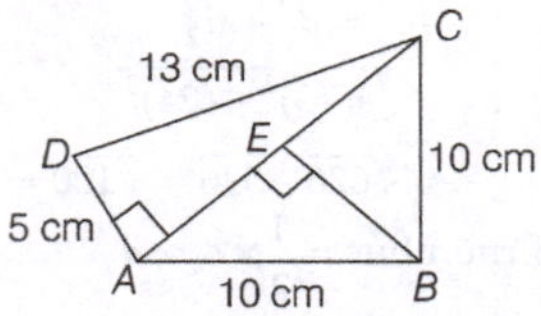

Here, $AD = 5$ cm, $DC = 13$ cm

$AB = 10$ cm, $CB = 10$ cm

ΔADC is right-angled triangle

$AC^2 = 13^2 - 5^2$

[$\because$ By Pythagoras theorem]

$AC = 12$ cm

Now, Area of $\Delta CAD = \frac{1}{2} \times$ Base $\times$ Altitude

$= \frac{1}{2} \times 5 \times 12 = 30 \text{ cm}^2 \quad \ldots(i)$

Again in ΔABC, Semi-perimeter of ΔABC

$s = \frac{10 + 10 + 12}{2} = 16$ cm

Area of $\Delta ABC = \sqrt{s \times (s-a)(s-b)(s-c)}$

$= \sqrt{16 \times 6 \times 6 \times 4} = 4 \times 6 \times 2$

$= 48 \text{ cm}^2$

Thus, total area of quadrilateral $ABCD$

$= 30 + 48 = 78 \text{ cm}^2$

162. (a) $ABCD$ is a quadrilateral.

AC and BD are diagonals.

$BD = 20$ cm

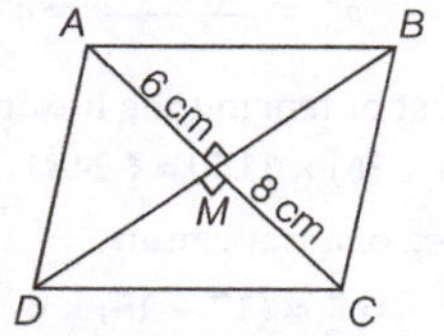

Let M be the intersecting point of BD and AC.

AM is the height of ΔABD.

$\therefore \; AM \perp BD$

Similarly, $CM \perp BD$

$\therefore \; \square ABCD$ is a rhombus.

Area of rhombus $= \frac{1}{2} \times d_1 \times d_2$

$= \frac{1}{2} \times BD \times AC$

$= \frac{1}{2} \times 20 \times (6 + 8) = 140 \text{ cm}^2$

163. (d) Let the radius of outer circle be R.

And radius of inner circle $= r$

According to the question,

$(R - r) = 45 \quad \ldots(i)$

and $\quad \frac{2\pi R}{2\pi r} = \frac{7}{6}$

$\therefore \quad R = \frac{7}{6} \times r$

Then, from Eq. (i),

$\frac{7}{6}r - r = 45 \Rightarrow \frac{r}{6} = 45$

$\Rightarrow \quad r = 270$ m

164. (b) According to the question,

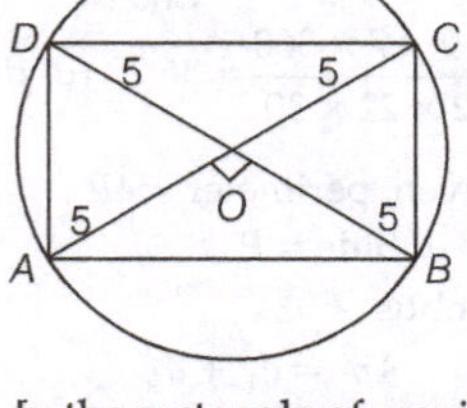

[$\because$ the rectangle of maximum area inscribed in a circle is a square]

In ΔOAB,

$AB^2 = 5^2 + 5^2 \Rightarrow AB^2 = 50$

$AB = 5\sqrt{2}$

Area $= 5\sqrt{2} \times 5\sqrt{2} = 50$ sq unit

Thus, remaining area $= \pi \times 5^2 - 50$

$= 25(\pi - 2)$

165. (b) Radius of circle = 48 cm

Length of arc = 15 cm

Angle of sector $(\theta) = \frac{\text{Arc}}{\text{Radius}} = \frac{15}{48} = \frac{5}{16}$

Radian

Now, area of sector $= \frac{\theta}{360^\circ} \times \pi r^2$

$\left[1R = \frac{180}{\pi} \text{ degree}\right]$

$= \frac{5}{16} \times \frac{180}{\pi} \times \frac{1}{360^\circ} \times \pi \times 48 \times 48$

$= 360 \text{ cm}^2$

Speedy Method

Area $= \frac{1}{2} l \times r = \frac{1}{2} 15 \times 48 = 360 \text{ cm}^2$

166. (c) Given, sides of triangle are 6 cm, 8 cm and 10 cm.

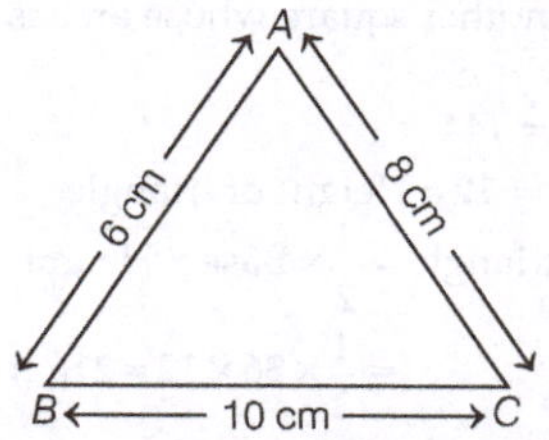

We know, Semi-perimeter $(s) = \frac{a + b + c}{2}$

$\therefore \quad s = \frac{6 + 8 + 10}{2}, s = \frac{24}{2} = 12$ cm

Using Heron's formula,

$\therefore$ Area $(\Delta ABC) = \sqrt{12(12-6)(12-8)(12-10)}$

$= \sqrt{12 \times 6 \times 4 \times 2}$

$= \sqrt{6 \times 2 \times 6 \times 2 \times 2 \times 2}$

$= 6 \times 2 \times 2 = 24 \text{ cm}^2$

Speedy Method

6, 8, 10 make a triplet so it is a right angle triangle. Area $= \frac{1}{2} \times$ Base $\times$ Height

$= \frac{1}{2} \times 6 \times 8 = 24 \text{ cm}^2$

167. (c) Let the shortest side be x m.
Then, hypotenuse of right triangle is $(2x + 6)$ m and third side $= 2x + 6 - 2$
$= (2x + 4)$ m

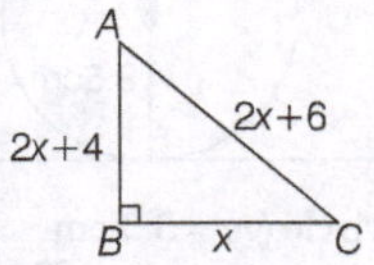

By Pythagoras theorem,

$$(2x + 6)^2 = (2x + 4)^2 + x^2$$
$$4x^2 + 36 + 24x = 4x^2 + 16 + 16x + x^2$$
$$x^2 - 8x - 20 = 0$$
$$\Rightarrow \quad (x - 10)(x + 2) = 0$$
$$x = 10, -2$$

Thus, $BC = 10$ m
and $AB = 2x + 4 = 20 + 4 = 24$

$\therefore$ Area of triangle $ABC = \frac{1}{2} \times BC \times AB$

$$= \frac{1}{2} \times 10 \times 24 = 120 \text{ m}^2$$

168. (b) Let the breadth of park be x m.
Then, length of rectangular shaped park
$= (x + 15)$ m
According to the question,
Perimeter of rectangular park = 110

$$2(l + b) = 110$$
$$\Rightarrow \quad 2(x + 15 + x) = 110$$
$$\Rightarrow \quad 2(2x + 15) = 110$$
$$\Rightarrow \quad 4x + 30 = 110$$
$$\Rightarrow \quad 4x = 80 \Rightarrow x = 20$$

Hence, length of park
$= x + 15 = 20 + 15 = 35$ m

169. (b) Incorrect option about the circle is option (b).

170. (d) Circumference of bigger circle
$= 264$ cm

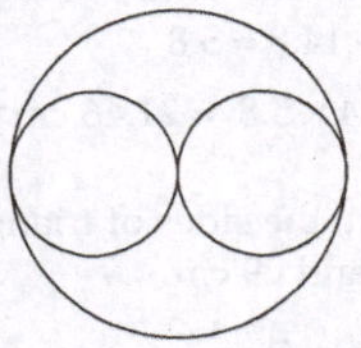

$$2\pi R = 264 \Rightarrow R = \frac{264}{2\pi}$$
$$\Rightarrow \quad R = \frac{264 \times 7}{2 \times 22} = 42 \text{ cm}$$

Then, radius of each smaller circular plates
$= \frac{42}{2} = 21$ cm

Then, circumference of each small plates
$= 2 \times \pi \times r = 2 \times \frac{22}{7} \times 21 = 132$ cm

171. (d) Suppose, ΔABC is an isosceles triangle.

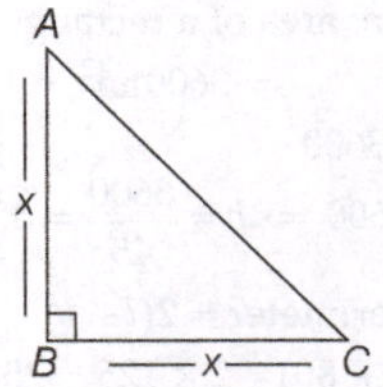

and let $BC = AB = x$ m
Then, by Pythagoras theorem,

$$AB^2 + BC^2 = AC^2$$
$$\Rightarrow \quad x^2 + x^2 = AC^2$$
$$\Rightarrow \quad 2x^2 = AC^2$$
$$\Rightarrow \quad AC = \sqrt{2}x \text{ m}$$

$\therefore$ Area of $\Delta ABC = \frac{1}{2} \times$ Base $\times$ Height

$$16 = \frac{1}{2} \times x \times x$$

$\Rightarrow 32 = x^2 \Rightarrow x = 4\sqrt{2}$ m
Hence, hypotenuse of ΔABC
$= \sqrt{2}x = \sqrt{2} \times 4\sqrt{2} = 8$ m

172. (d) Given,
Radius of semi-circle $(r) = 2\sqrt{2}$ cm
Also, assume the side of square be a cm.
According to the question,
Area of square = Area of semi-circle

$$a^2 = \frac{1}{2}\pi r^2 \Rightarrow a^2 = \frac{1}{2} \times \pi \times (2\sqrt{2})^2$$
$$a^2 = \frac{\pi}{2} \times 8 = 4\pi \Rightarrow a = 2\sqrt{\pi}$$

$\therefore$ Perimeter of square $= 4a$
$= 4(2\sqrt{\pi}) = 8\sqrt{\pi}$ cm

173. (b) Let length be l and breadth be b.
We know that,

$$\text{Diagonal} = \sqrt{l^2 + b^2} \Rightarrow (25)^2 = l^2 + b^2$$
$$\Rightarrow \quad l^2 + b^2 = 625 \quad \ldots\text{(i)}$$

We know that,
Perimeter of rectangle = 70 cm

$$\Rightarrow \quad 2(l + b) = 70$$
$$\Rightarrow \quad l + b = 35 \quad \ldots\text{(ii)}$$

We know that,
$(l - b)^2 + (l + b)^2 = 2(l^2 + b^2)$
Put the value from Eqs. (i) and (ii),
$(l - b)^2 + (35)^2 = 2(625) \Rightarrow (l - b)^2 = 25$

$$\Rightarrow \quad l - b = 5 \quad \ldots\text{(iii)}$$

On solving Eqs. (ii) and (iii),
$l = 20$ and $b = 15$

We know that,
Area of triangle $= l \times b = 20 \times 15 = 300 \text{ cm}^2$

174. (c) Given,
Average of the areas of two similar triangle
$= 706.5 \text{ m}^2$
Perimeter ratio = 6 : 11
In two similar triangle,
We know that,

$$\frac{\text{Area of first triangle}}{\text{Area of second triangle}} = \left(\frac{\text{Perimeter of first triangle}}{\text{Perimeter of second triangle}}\right)^2$$

$$\frac{\text{Area of first triangle}}{\text{Area of second triangle}} = \left(\frac{6}{11}\right)^2 = \frac{36}{121}$$

Let area of first triangle $= 36x \text{ m}^2$
and area of second triangle $= 121x \text{ m}^2$
We have, average of area $= 706.5 \text{ m}^2$

$$\Rightarrow \quad \frac{121x + 36x}{2} = 706.5$$
$$\Rightarrow \quad 157x = 706.5 \times 2 \Rightarrow x = 9$$

$\therefore$ Difference of area $= 121x - 36x$
$= 85x = 85 \times 9 = 765 \text{ m}^2$

$\therefore$ 20% of difference $= \frac{20}{100} \times 765 = 153 \text{ m}^2$

175. (c) Given, altitude $= 3\sqrt{3}$ cm
We know that,
Altitude of equilateral triangle $= \frac{\sqrt{3}}{2} \times$ Side

$$\therefore \quad 3\sqrt{3} = \frac{\sqrt{3}}{2} \times \text{side} \Rightarrow \text{Side} = 6 \text{ cm}$$
$$\therefore \quad \text{Area} = \frac{\sqrt{3}}{4} \times (\text{side})^2 = \frac{\sqrt{3}}{4} \times (6)^2$$
$$= 9\sqrt{3} \text{ sq cm}$$

176. (a) Given, $BC = 12$ cm, $AC = 5$ cm

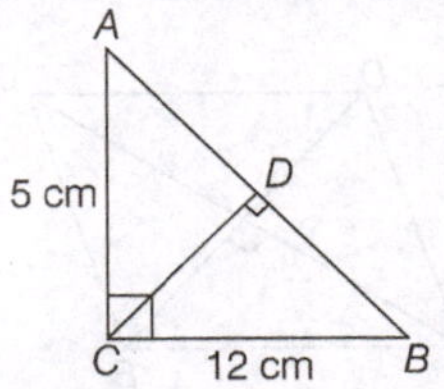

By Pythagoras theorem

$$(AB)^2 = (BC)^2 + (AC)^2 = 25 + 144$$
$$AB = \sqrt{169} = 13 \text{ cm}$$

We know that, $AB = 13$ cm
Area of $\Delta ABC = \frac{1}{2} \times$ Base $\times$ height

$$\Rightarrow \quad \frac{1}{2} \times 5 \times 12 = \frac{1}{2} \times CD \times AB$$
$$\Rightarrow \quad \frac{1}{2} \times 5 \times 12 = \frac{1}{2} \times CD \times 13 \Rightarrow CD = \frac{60}{13} \text{ cm}$$

177. (d) Given, radius of sector = 7 cm
Angle of sector $= 120°$

We know, length of an arc $= \frac{\theta}{360°} \times 2\pi r$

$$= \frac{120°}{360°} \times 2 \times \frac{22}{7} \times 7$$
$$= \frac{1}{3} \times 2 \times 22 = \frac{44}{3} \text{ cm}$$

178. (b) Let the side of an equilateral triangle be 'a' cm.
Given, Perimeter of triangle = 24 cm

$$a + a + a = 24 \Rightarrow 3a = 24$$
$$\Rightarrow \quad a = 8 \text{ cm}$$

Area of equilateral triangle

$$= \frac{\sqrt{3}}{4}(8)^2 = \frac{\sqrt{3}}{4} \times 64 = 16\sqrt{3}$$
$$= 16 \times 1.732 = 27.71 \text{ cm}^2$$

179. (b) Given, Base = $\frac{2}{3}$ Height

$$\frac{\text{Base}}{\text{Height}} = \frac{2}{3} = \frac{2x}{3x}$$

Area of triangle = $\frac{1}{2} \times$ Base $\times$ Height

$$\frac{1}{2} \times 2x \times 3x = 363 \Rightarrow x^2 = \frac{363}{3} = 121$$

$\therefore$ $x = 11$ cm

$\therefore$ Height of triangle = $3x = 3 \times 11 = 33$ cm

180. (c) Given, central angle = 30°,
Length of the arc = 5.5 cm

We know that,

Length of arc = $2\pi r \times \frac{\theta}{360°}$

$$\Rightarrow \quad 5.5 = 2 \times \frac{22}{7} \times r \times \frac{30°}{360°}$$

$$\Rightarrow 5.5 = 2 \times \frac{22}{7} \times r \times \frac{1}{12} \Rightarrow r = \frac{5.5 \times 7 \times 12}{2 \times 22}$$

$\therefore$ $r = 10.5$ cm

Hence, the radius of circle is 10.5 cm.

181. (b) Perimeter of a semi-circle = $\pi r + 2r$

$$56.54 = 3.14r + 2r$$

$\Rightarrow$ $5.14r = 56.54 \Rightarrow r = 11$ cm

Hence, diameter of a circle = $11 \times 2 = 22$ cm

182. (b)

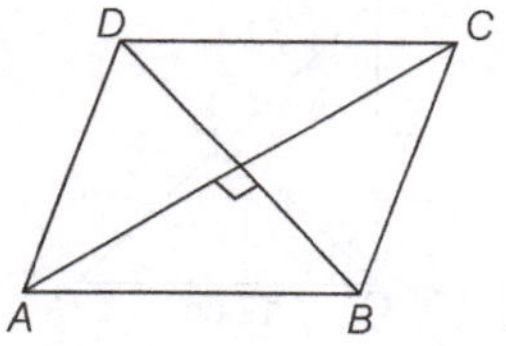

Area of rhombus = $\frac{1}{2} \times AC \times BD$

$$= \frac{1}{2} \times 10 \times 8.2 \text{ cm}^2 = 41 \text{ cm}^2$$

183. (a) We know that,

Area of triangle = $\frac{1}{2} \times$ Base $\times$ Height

$$18 = \frac{1}{2} \times 6 \times \text{Height}$$

$$\Rightarrow \text{Height} = \frac{18 \times 2}{6} \Rightarrow \text{Height} = 6 \text{ cm}$$

184. (a) According to the question,

Let area of square = a^2 cm^2

and side of square = a

$\therefore$ Perimeter of square, $4a = 64$ cm

$\Rightarrow$ $a = 16$ cm

$\therefore$ Area of square = $a^2 = 16 \times 16 = 256$ cm^2

185. (c) According to the question,

Radius of circle = 4 cm

Angle of its sector (θ) = 45°

$\therefore$ Area of the sector = $\frac{\theta}{360°} \times \pi r^2$

$$= \frac{45°}{360°} \times 3.14 \times 4 \times 4 \qquad [\pi = 3.14]$$

$$= 6.28 \text{ cm}^2$$

186. (d) Given, area of a rectangular field
= 3600 m^2

$$l \times b = 3600$$

$$45 \times b = 3600 \Rightarrow b = \frac{3600}{45} = 80 \text{ m}$$

Hence, the perimeter = $2(l + b)$

$$= 2(45 + 80) = 2 \times 125 = 250 \text{ m}$$

187. (b) Let given triangle is equilateral having sides 'a'.

$\therefore$ Perimeter of triangle = 36

$$a + a + a = 36$$

$$a = 12 \text{ units}$$

$\therefore$ Area of equilateral triangle

$$= \frac{\sqrt{3}}{4} \times 12 \times 12$$

$$= 36\sqrt{3} \text{ sq. units}$$

As we know, that equilateral triangle has maximum area among the other triangle i.e. scalene and isosceles, having the same perimeter.

Thus, area cannot be more than $36\sqrt{3}$.

188. (c) Given,

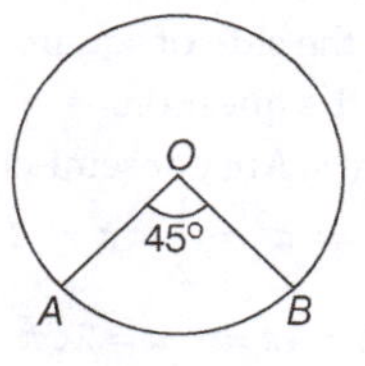

Given, $\theta = 45°$

We know that,

Perimeter of a sector = $2\pi r \frac{\theta}{360°} + 2r$

$$= 2\pi \times 4 \times \frac{45°}{360°} + 2 \times 4 = (\pi + 8) \text{ units}$$

189. (a) Given, area of circle = 154 m^2

$\Rightarrow$ $\pi r^2 = 154$

$\Rightarrow$ $\frac{22}{7} \times r^2 = 154$

$\Rightarrow$ $r^2 = 154 \times \frac{7}{22} = 49$

$\therefore$ $r = 7$ m

Now, circumference of circle = $2\pi r$

$$= 2 \times \frac{22}{7} \times 7 = 44 \text{ m}$$

190. (a) According to the question,

$$33\pi = \frac{2\pi r \times 132°}{360°}$$

$$\Rightarrow \quad r = \frac{33 \times 360°}{2 \times 132°} = 45 \text{ cm}$$

191. (d) Inradius of equilateral triangle

$$= \frac{18}{2\sqrt{3}} = \frac{9}{\sqrt{3}} = 3\sqrt{3}$$

Circumradius of equilateral triangle

$$= \frac{a}{\sqrt{3}} = \frac{18}{\sqrt{3}} \times \frac{\sqrt{3}}{\sqrt{3}} = \frac{18\sqrt{3}}{3} \text{ cm}$$

$$\text{Required ratio} = \frac{3\sqrt{3}}{\frac{18\sqrt{3}}{3}} = \frac{9}{18} = 1:2$$

192. (a) According to the question,

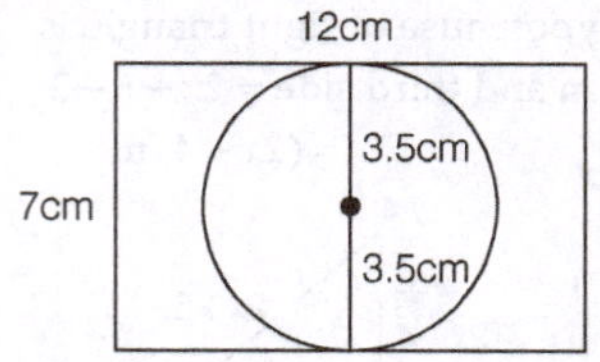

$\therefore$ Radius of circle (r) = 3.5 cm

$\therefore$ Circumference = $2\pi r = 2 \times \frac{22}{7} \times 3.5 = 22$ cm

193. (b) According to the question.

Let OAB be the given sector and arc $AB = l$

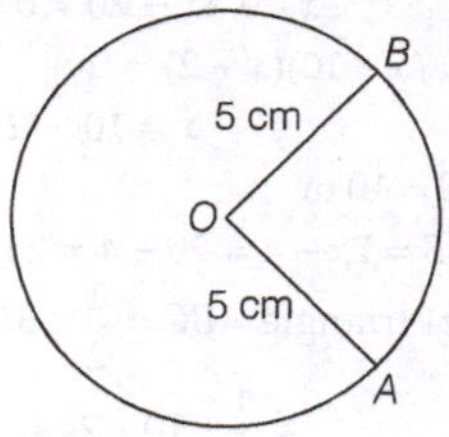

Perimeter of sector OAB

$$= OA + OB + \text{arc } AB$$

$\Rightarrow$ $15.5 = 5 + 5 + l$

$\therefore$ $l = 15.5 - 10 = 5.5$ cm

$$\text{Area} = \frac{1}{2} \times \text{arc} \times \text{radius} = \frac{1}{2} \times 5.5 \times 5$$

Area of OAB = 13.75 cm^2

194. (d) Let AOB be the sector with 'O' as center.

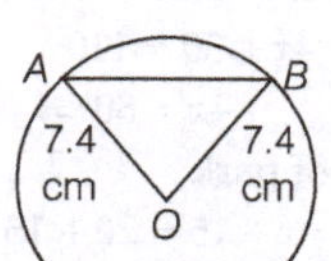

Here, $OB = OA = 7.4$ cm

Perimeter of sector = 20.6 cm (given)

$OA + OB +$ arc $AB = 20.6$

$\therefore$ $AB = 20.6 - 14.8 = 5.8$

$$\text{Area} = \frac{1}{2} \times 7.4 \times 5.8 = 21.46 \text{ cm}^2$$

195. (b) Given, the sides of triangle are 20 cm, 21 cm and 29 cm.

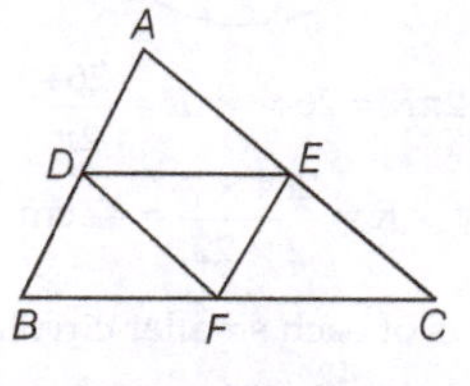

Since ABC is right angled triangle.

Area of triangle = $\frac{1}{2} \times 20 \times 21 = 210$ cm

$$\text{Area of } \Delta DEF = \frac{ar(\Delta ABC)}{4}$$

$$= \frac{210}{4} = \frac{105}{2} = 52\frac{1}{2} \text{ cm}^2$$

196. (d) Let side of the rhombus = a cm

$\therefore$ One diagonal $(d_1) = a$ cm

$\therefore \quad 4a^2 = d_1^2 + d_2^2 \Rightarrow d_2 = a\sqrt{3}$ cm

Now, $d_1 : d_2 = a : a\sqrt{3} = 1 : \sqrt{3}$

197. (a) According to the question,

$\Rightarrow \quad \frac{\theta}{360°} \times \pi r^2 = 616$

$\Rightarrow \quad \frac{10}{360°} \times \frac{22}{7} \times r^2 = 616$

$\Rightarrow \quad r = 84$ cm

198. (d) Given, $2\pi r = 132$

$2 \times \frac{22}{7} \times r = 132 \Rightarrow r = 21$

$\therefore$ Area of circle $= \pi r^2 = \frac{22}{7} \times (21)^2$

$= \frac{22}{7} \times 441 = 1386 \text{ cm}^2$

199. (b) Perimeter of square = $4a$ m

$\therefore \quad 4a = 196 \Rightarrow a = 49$ m

Given, $\quad r = a = 49$ m

Hence, area of circle $= \pi r^2$

$= \frac{22}{7} \times 49 \times 49 = 7546 \text{ m}^2$

200. (a) $\because \frac{\text{Area of 1st circle}}{\text{Area of 2nd circle}} = \frac{\pi r_1^2}{\pi r_2^2} = \frac{81}{121}$

$\Rightarrow \quad \frac{r_1^2}{r_2^2} = \frac{81}{121} \Rightarrow \frac{r_1}{r_2} = \frac{9}{11}$

$\therefore$ Required ratio $= \frac{2\pi r_1}{2\pi r_2} = \frac{r_1}{r_2} = \frac{9}{11} = 9 : 11$

201. (d) Let the side of rhombus be a.

$\because \quad 4a^2 = d_1^2 + d_2^2$

$\therefore \quad 4a^2 = 10^2 + 24^2$

$\Rightarrow \quad 4a^2 = 676 \Rightarrow a^2 = 169$

$\Rightarrow \quad a = 13$ cm

Then, perimeter of rhombus $= 4a = 4 \times 13$

$= 52$ cm

202. (b) Incircle radius of an equilateral triangle $= \frac{a}{2\sqrt{3}}$

Now, $\quad \frac{a}{2\sqrt{3}} = 9\sqrt{3}$ (given)

$\Rightarrow \quad a = 9\sqrt{3} \times 2\sqrt{3} = 54$

$\therefore$ Perimeter of triangle $= 3a = 3 \times 54 = 162$ cm

203. (b) Area of triangle

$= \frac{1}{2} \times 10 \times 8 = 40 \text{ cm}^2$

204. (b) Side of square = 18 cm

The biggest circle draw in square.

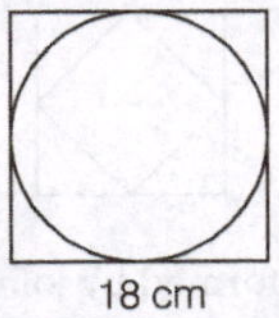

$\therefore$ Diameter of circle = 18 cm

Then, radius of circle, $r = \frac{18}{2} = 9$ cm

Hence, area of biggest circle $= \pi r^2$

$= \pi(9)^2 = 81\pi \text{ cm}^2$

205. (a) Distance covered in 500 revolutions

$= 44 \text{ km} = 44 \times 1000 \text{ m} = 44000$ m

So, Distance covered in 1 revolution

$= \frac{44000}{500} = \frac{440}{5}$ m

$\therefore$ Circumference of wheel = Distance covered in 1 revolution

$\Rightarrow \quad 2\pi r = \frac{440}{5}$ m

$\Rightarrow \quad \frac{2 \times 22 \times r}{7} = \frac{440}{5}$ cm

$\Rightarrow \quad r = \frac{440}{5} \times \frac{7}{2 \times 22} = 14$ cm

Hence, radius of the wheel is 14 m.

206. (a) Semi perimetre, $s = \frac{a + b + c}{2}$

$\Rightarrow \quad s = \frac{42}{2} = 21$

Area of scalene triangle

$= \sqrt{21(21 - 13)(21 - 15)(21 - 14)} = \sqrt{7056}$

= 84 sq. inches

207. (b) Given, radius $(r) = 14$ cm

$\therefore$ The required distance $= 10 \times 2\pi r$

$= 10 \times 2 \times \frac{22}{7} \times 14 \quad \left(\because \pi = \frac{22}{7}\right)$

$= 880$ cm

208. (d) So, the given triangle is a right angle triangle.

Area $= \frac{1}{2} \times 5 \times 12 = 30 \text{ cm}^2$

209. (b)

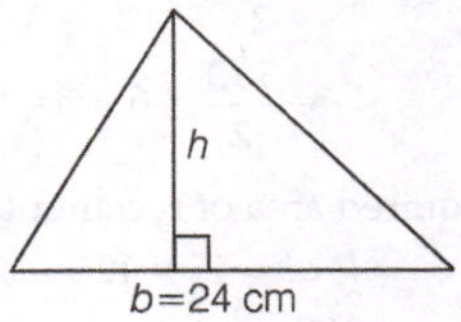

Area $= 96 = \frac{1}{2} \times 24 \times$ Height

$\therefore \quad$ Height = 8 cm

210. (b) Let length and breadth of a rectangle is x and y, respectively.

Area $= xy$

New length = 115% of $x = 1.15x$

New breadth = 120% of $y = 1.2y$

$\therefore$ New area $= 1.15x \times 1.2y = 1.38xy$

Increased area per cent $= \frac{1.38xy - xy}{xy} \times 100$

$= 38\%$

Speedy Method

Required per cent $= \left(15 + 20 + \frac{15 \times 20}{100}\right)\%$

$= (35 + 3)\% = 38\%$

211. (a) ΔABC is an equilateral triangle,

Circumradius = 2 × Inradius

18 = 2 × Inradius

Inradius = 9 cm

212. (c) Let the breadth of the rectangle be x cm.

and Length of the rectangle = $4x$ cm

Given, perimeter of rectangle = 50

$\therefore \quad 2(4x + x) = 50$

$10x = 50 \Rightarrow x = \frac{50}{10} = 5$ cm

According to the question,

Area of square = Area of rectangle

$\Rightarrow \quad a^2 = 4x \times x = 4 \times x^2$

$\therefore \quad a^2 = 4 \times (5)^2 = 100 \text{ cm}^2$

$\therefore \quad a = 10$ cm

According to the question,

$\therefore$ Perimeter of the square

$= 4 \times a = 4 \times 10 = 40$ cm

213. (c) Let the each side of the equilateral triangle be x cm.

$\Rightarrow \quad 3x = 15\sqrt{3}$

$\Rightarrow \quad x = \frac{15\sqrt{3}}{3} = 5\sqrt{3}$ cm

Now, height of the triangle

$= \frac{\sqrt{3}}{2} \times x = \frac{\sqrt{3}}{2} \times 5\sqrt{3} = \frac{15}{2} = 7.5$ cm

214. (d) According to the question,

$\frac{\sqrt{3}}{2} a = 3.46 \Rightarrow a = \frac{3.46 \times 2}{1.73}$

$a = 2 \times 2 = 4$ cm

Perimeter $= 4 \times 3 = 12$ cm

215. (b)

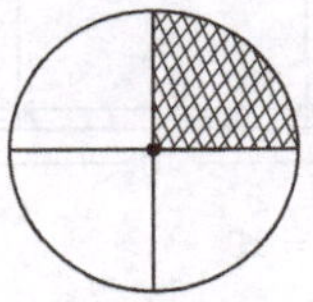

Diameter = 28 cm

Then, radius $(r) = 14$ cm

Since, one quarter is removed.

$\therefore$ Total perimeter of the remaining pizza

$= \frac{3\pi r}{2} + 2r = 3 \times \frac{22}{7} \times \frac{14}{2} + 2 \times 14$

$= 66 + 28 = 94$ cm

216. (a) Let the length of the base of the triangle be x cm.

$\therefore$ Length of altitude $= x + 3$

Area $\Rightarrow \frac{1}{2} \times x \times (x + 3) = 104$

$\Rightarrow \quad x^2 + 3x - 208 = 0$

$\Rightarrow \quad (x + 16)(x - 13)$

$\Rightarrow \quad x = 13$ and -16

Since, the length cannot be negative.

$\therefore$ Base $= x = 13$ cm.

217. (a) Given, $2\pi r = 88$

$\Rightarrow \quad r = \frac{88}{2} \times \frac{7}{22} = 14$ cm

$\therefore$ Area of the circle

$= \pi r^2 = \frac{22}{7} \times 14 \times 14 = 616 \text{ cm}^2$

218. (a) Let the length of the rectangle be x cm.

$$\text{Breadth} = \frac{x}{5} \text{ cm}$$

According to the question,

$$\text{Area} = x \times \frac{x}{5} = 3125$$

$$\Rightarrow \quad x^2 = 3125 \times 5 = 15625$$

$$\Rightarrow \quad x = \sqrt{15625} = 125 \text{ cm}$$

219. (b) Area of given equilateral triangular field $= \frac{\sqrt{3}}{4} \times (\text{side})^2$

$$= \frac{\sqrt{3}}{4} \times (8.5)^2 = \frac{\sqrt{3}}{4} \times 72.25$$

$$= 18.0625\sqrt{3} \approx 18.1\sqrt{3} \text{ m}^2$$

220. (a) Given, $2\pi r = 40\pi \Rightarrow r = 20$ cm

$\therefore$ Area of circle $= \pi(20)^2 = 400\pi \text{ cm}^2$

Diameter $= 2 \times 20 = 40$ cm

221. (c) Perimeter of semi-circular plot

$$= \pi r + 2r = 3.14 \times 100 + 2 \times 100$$

$$= 314 + 200 = 514 \text{ m}$$

222. (b) Area of rectangle = Length × Breadth

$$= 7 \times 5 = 35 \text{ cm}^2$$

223. (d) Height of trapezium

$$(h) = \sqrt{8^2 - 2^2} = \sqrt{60} = 2\sqrt{15}$$

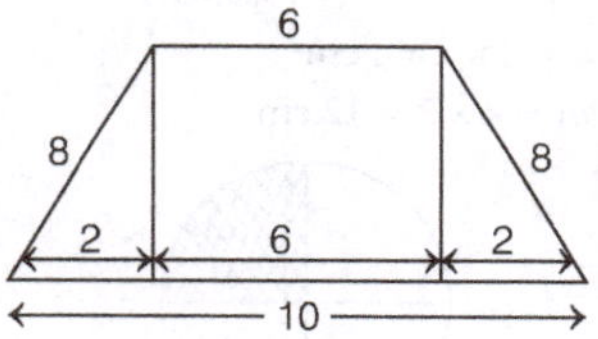

Here, $a = 6, b = 10$

$$\text{Area of trapezium} = \frac{1}{2}(a+b) \times h$$

$$= \frac{1}{2} \times (6+10) \times 2\sqrt{15}$$

$$= 16\sqrt{15}$$

224. (a) Let side of square be 'a' unit.

We know,

Area of square $= a^2$

$$1225 = a^2$$

$$\therefore \quad a = 35 \text{ unit}$$

Length of rectangle $(l) = 35 \times \frac{4}{5} = 28$ unit

Breadth of rectangle $(b) = 12$ unit

$\therefore$ Area of Rectangle $= l \times b = 12 \times 28$

$$= 336 \text{ unit}^2$$

225. (d) Area of right-angled triangle

$$= \frac{1}{2} \times \text{Base} \times \text{Height}$$

$$80 = \frac{1}{2} \times \text{Base} \times 20$$

$$\text{Base} = 8 \text{ m}$$

226. (b) Let d_1 = diagonal of Ist square, d_2 = diagonal of IInd square, a_1 = side of Ist circle and a_2 = side of IInd circle.

$$\frac{d_1}{d_2} = \frac{5}{6} \Rightarrow \frac{d_1^2}{d_2^2} = \frac{25}{36}$$

$$\Rightarrow \frac{2a_1^2}{2a_2^2} = \frac{25}{36}$$

$$\left[\because \text{Area of square} = (\text{side})^2 = \frac{(\text{diagonal})^2}{2}\right]$$

$$\frac{\text{Area of Ist square}}{\text{Area of IInd square}} = \frac{a_1^2}{a_1^2} = \frac{25}{36}$$

227. (c) Area of parallelogram

$$= \text{Base} \times \text{Height}$$

$$= 12 \times 20 = 240 \text{ m}^2$$

228. (c) Let length and breadth be l and b respectively.

We know,

$$\text{Perimeter} = 2(l+b)$$

$$\Rightarrow \quad 48 = 2(l+b)$$

$$\Rightarrow \quad (l+b) = 24 \quad \ldots\text{(i)}$$

Again, diagonal $= \sqrt{l^2 + b^2}$

$$16 = \sqrt{l^2 + b^2}$$

$$l^2 + b^2 = 256 \quad \ldots\text{(ii)}$$

We know,

$$2lb = (l+b)^2 - (l^2 + b^2)$$

$$\Rightarrow \quad 2lb = 576 - 256$$

$$\Rightarrow \quad 2lb = 320$$

Area $(lb) = 160 \text{ cm}^2$

229. (b) Side of regular hexagon $= \frac{12}{2} = 6$ cm

$$\text{Area of hexagon} = \frac{3\sqrt{3}}{2}(\text{Side})^2$$

$$= \frac{3\sqrt{3}}{2} \times 6 \times 6 = 54\sqrt{3} \text{ cm}^2$$

230. (b) Required area of rectangular park

$$= l \times b = 15 \times 12$$

$$= 180 \text{ m}^2$$

231. (b) Let length and breadth of rectangle be $11x$ and $9x$ respectively.

$$11x \times 9x = 396$$

$$\Rightarrow \quad x^2 = \frac{396}{99} = 4 \Rightarrow x = 2$$

$\therefore$ Perimeter of rectangle $= 2(11x + 9x)$

$$= 2 \times 20 \times 2 = 80 \text{ m}$$

232. (c) Diameter of circle $= 14 \times 2 = 28$ cm

Diagonal of square = side $\times\sqrt{2} = 28$

Side $= 14\sqrt{2}$

$$\text{Area of circle} = \frac{22}{7} \times 14 \times 14 = 616 \text{cm}^2$$

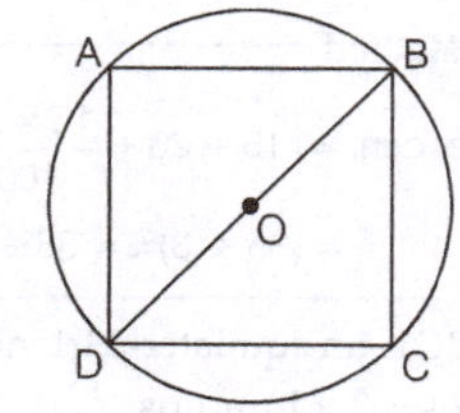

Area of square $= 14\sqrt{2} \times 14\sqrt{2} = 392 \text{cm}^2$

$\therefore$ Remaining Area $= 616 - 392 = 224 \text{cm}^2$

233. (b) Area of Regular hexagon

$$= \frac{3\sqrt{3}}{2}(\text{Side})^2$$

$$\Rightarrow \quad 2048\sqrt{3} = \frac{3\sqrt{3}}{2}(\text{Side})^2$$

$$\Rightarrow \quad \frac{4096}{3} = (\text{Side})^2 \Rightarrow \left(\frac{64}{\sqrt{3}}\right)^2 = (\text{Side})^2$$

$$\therefore \text{ Side} = \frac{64\sqrt{3}}{3} \text{ cm}$$

234. (d) Area of Triangle $= \frac{\sqrt{3}}{4}(\text{Side})^2$

$$\Rightarrow \quad \frac{\sqrt{5034}}{4} = \frac{\sqrt{3}}{4}(\text{Side})^2$$

$$\Rightarrow \quad \sqrt{1678} = (\text{Side})^2$$

$$\Rightarrow \quad 41 = (\text{Side})^2 \quad [\because \sqrt{1678} \approx 41]$$

$$\therefore \quad \text{Side} = \sqrt{41} \text{ cm}$$

235. (b) Area of the rectangular inner field

$$= l \times b = 45 \times 35 = 1575 \text{ m}^2$$

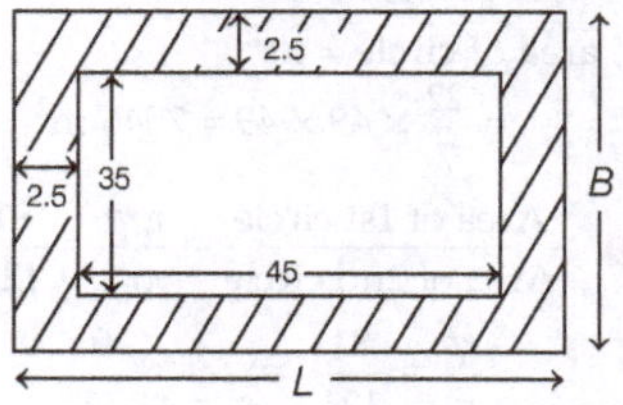

A uniform path of 2.5 m width runs around the outside of a field

$\therefore$ Length $(L) = 45 + 2.5 + 2.5 = 50$ m

Breadth $(B) = 35 + 2.5 + 2.5 = 40$ m

$\therefore$ Area of outer field $= L \times B = 50 \times 40$

$$= 2000 \text{ m}^2$$

$\therefore$ Area of path $= 2000 - 1575 = 425 \text{ m}^2$

236. (d) Let the sides of the triangle are $3x, 4x$ and $5x$ m.

According to the question,

$$3x + 4x + 5x = 24$$

$$\Rightarrow \quad x = \frac{24}{12} = 2$$

$\therefore$ Sides are $3x = 6, 4x = 8, 5x = 10$

So, the sides are 6 m, 8 m and 10 m.

Hence, triangle is a right angle triangle.

So, area of the given triangle

$$= \frac{1}{2} \times 6 \times 8 = 24 \text{m}^2$$

237. (c) Side of the square with an area of 36 sq units $= \sqrt{36} = 6$ units

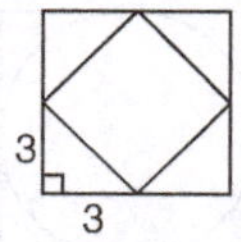

Area of square formed by joining mid-point of side of bigger square is half of the area of bigger square.

$\therefore$ Area of the square $= \frac{36}{2} = 18$ sq units

238. (c) Area of square $= a^2$

$\Rightarrow a^2 = 144 \Rightarrow a = 12$

$\therefore$ Diagonal $= a\sqrt{2} = 12\sqrt{2}$ cm

239. (a) Given,

$5 \times$ perimeter of square $= 600$ cm

$\therefore 5 \times 4 \times$ side of square $= 600$ cm

Side $= \frac{600}{20} = 30$ cm

$\therefore$ Area of the square $= (30)^2 = 900\text{ cm}^2$

240. (c) According to the question,

$2 \times (l + b) = 68$

$\Rightarrow l + b = \frac{68}{2} = 34$ ...(i)

and $l \times b = 240$ ...(ii)

From Eqs. (i) and (ii),

$(l + b)^2 = l^2 + b^2 + 2lb$

$l^2 + b^2 = (34)^2 - 2 \times 240$

$\Rightarrow l^2 + b^2 = 1156 - 480 = 676$

$\therefore$ Length of each diagonal of rectangle

$= \sqrt{l^2 + b^2}$

$= \sqrt{676} = 26$ cm

241. (c) Given, radius of wheel = 56 mm and distance = 176 cm = 1760 mm

According to the question,

Number of revolutions

$= \frac{\text{Total distance covered}}{\text{Distance covered in 1 revolution}}$

$= \frac{1760}{2 \times \frac{22}{7} \times 56} = \frac{1760}{352} = 5$

242. (a) $144\text{ cm}^2 = \frac{1}{2} \times 16\text{ cm} \times$ Height

$\Rightarrow$ Height = 18 cm

243. (d) According to the question,

$\frac{\theta}{360^\circ} \cdot \pi r^2 = \frac{4\pi}{5}$

$\Rightarrow \theta = \frac{4}{5} \times \frac{360^\circ}{2 \times 2} = 72^\circ$

244. (c) According to the question,

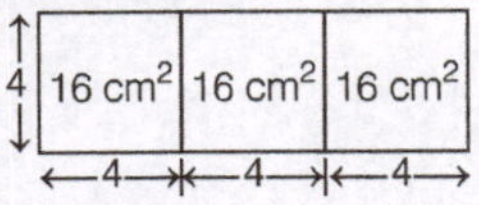

From the above figure,

Length of rectangle $(l) = 3 \times 4 = 12$ cm

Width of rectangle $(b) = 4$ cm

$\therefore$ Perimeter of rectangle $= 2(l + b)$

$= 2(12 + 4) = 32$ cm

245. (d) Since, area of trapezium

$= \frac{1}{2} \times$ sum of parallel sides $\times h$

$\therefore$ According to the question,

$330 = \frac{1}{2} \times (25 + 19) \times h$

$\therefore h = \frac{330 \times 2}{44} = 15$ cm

246. (c)

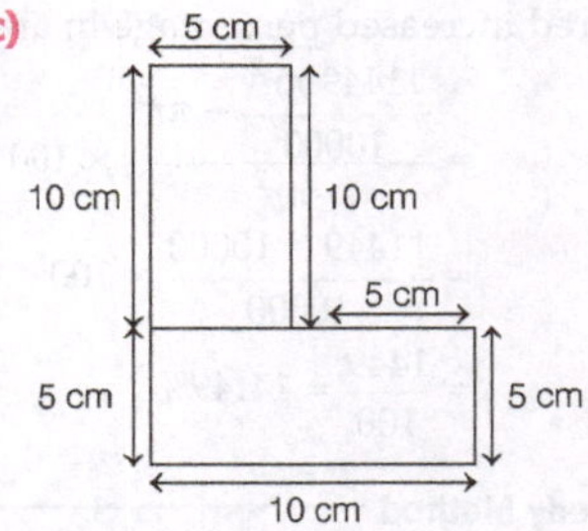

The perimeter of the figure is

$= 4 \times 5 + 3 \times 10$

$= 20 + 30 = 50$ cm

247. (a) Area of right-angled triangle

$= \frac{1}{2} \times$ Base $\times$ Height

$= \frac{1}{2} \times 22 \times 15 = 165\text{ cm}^2$

248. (a) $\because$ Area of rhombus $= \frac{1}{2} \times d_1 \times d_2$

$= \frac{1}{2} \times 10 \times 30 = 150\text{ cm}^2$

249. (c) According to the question,

Area of three rectangular field 70, 84, 112.

Now, HCF of (70, 84, 112) = 14

Maximum area of identical rectangular flower beds is 14 m^2.

Now, $L \times B = 14$

$\Rightarrow B = \frac{14}{7} = 2$ m [$\because L = 7$]

$\therefore$ Breadth = 2 m

250. (d) According to the given information,

$\Rightarrow 2\pi r - 2r = 12$ (where, r = radius)

$\Rightarrow 2r(\pi - 1) = 12$

$\Rightarrow r = \frac{12}{2 \times (\pi - 1)} = \frac{12}{2 \times \frac{15}{7}}$

$\Rightarrow r = \frac{12 \times 7}{30} = \frac{14}{5}$

So, area of circle $= \pi r^2 = \frac{22}{7} \times \left(\frac{14}{5}\right)^2 = \frac{616}{25}$

$= 24.64\text{ cm}^2$

251. (a) According to the question,

$\Rightarrow \frac{\sqrt{3}}{4}(\text{side})^2 = 16\sqrt{3} \Rightarrow (\text{side})^2 = 64$

$\therefore$ side = 8 cm

252. (d) As we know,

$4a^2 = d_1^2 + d_2^2$

$\Rightarrow 4a^2 = (48)^2 + (64)^2$

$\Rightarrow 4a^2 = 2304 + 4096$

$\Rightarrow 4a^2 = 6400$

$\Rightarrow a^2 = 1600$

$\Rightarrow a = 40$

Perimeter $= 4a = 4 \times 40 = 160$ cm

253. (c) Given, ILongest side of right-angled triangle = 17 cm

and height = 15 cm

$\therefore$ Base $= \sqrt{17^2 - 15^2} = \sqrt{289 - 225}$

$= \sqrt{64} = 8$ cm

$\because$ Area to triangle $= (8 \times 15)/2 = 60\text{ cm}^2$

254. (b) Let the height of triangle be x.

Base $= \frac{5}{7}x$

Then, Area $= \frac{1}{2} \times$ Base $\times$ Height

$\Rightarrow \frac{1}{2} \times x \times \frac{5}{7}x = 18.207$

$\Rightarrow 5x^2 = 254.898 \Rightarrow x^2 = 50.97$

$\Rightarrow x = 7.14$ cm

255. (b) Here, $a = 14.28\% = \frac{1}{7}$

$\therefore$ Required percentage decrease in breadth

$= L \rightarrow 7 : 8$

$B \rightarrow 8 : 7$ [to keep area same]

1

$= \frac{1}{8} \times 100 = 12.5\%$

256. (d) Side of the regular hexagon $= \frac{a}{3}$

$\therefore$ Area of a regular hexagon

$= \frac{3\sqrt{3}}{2} \times (\text{Side})^2$

$= \frac{3\sqrt{3}}{2} \times \frac{a^2}{3 \times 3} = \frac{a^2}{2\sqrt{3}}$ sq units

257. (d)

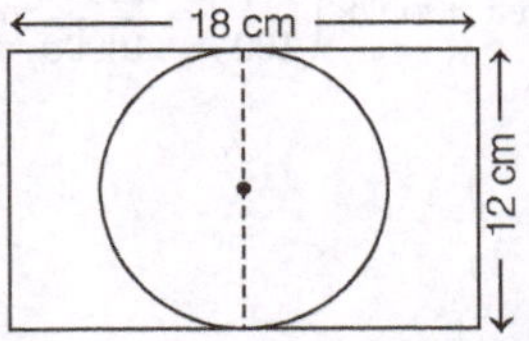

$\therefore$ Radius of required circle $= \frac{12}{2} = 6$ cm

$\therefore$ Area of circle $= \pi r^2 = \pi(6)^2 = 36\pi\text{ cm}^2$

258. (d) Let radius be r

$\therefore$ Area of a sector of a circle $= \frac{\pi r^2 \theta}{360^\circ}$

$\Rightarrow 88 = \frac{22 \times r^2 \times 36^\circ}{7 \times 360^\circ}$

$\Rightarrow 88 = \frac{22 \times r^2}{7 \times 10} \Rightarrow r^2 = 280$

$\Rightarrow r = \sqrt{280} = 2\sqrt{70}$ cm

259. (b) Semi perimeter of rectangular field

$= x + y$

$\Rightarrow 12 = x + y$ ...(i)

Area of rectangular field $= xy$.

$\Rightarrow 28 = xy$ ...(ii)

Now, $x^4 + x^2y^2 + y^4 = (x^2 + y^2)^2 - x^2y^2$

$= [(x + y)^2 - 2xy]^2 - (xy)^2$

$= [(12)^2 - 2 \times 28]^2 - (28)^2$

$= (144 - 56)^2 - 784$

$= (88)^2 - 784$

$= 7744 - 784 = 6960$

260. (b) Side of rhombus, $a = 13$ cm and one diagonal, $d_1 = 24$ cm

Let second diagonal be d_2

$\therefore \quad 4a^2 = d_1^2 + d_2^2$

$\Rightarrow \quad 4(13)^2 = (24)^2 + d_2^2$

$\Rightarrow \quad d_2^2 = 676 - 576 \Rightarrow d_2^2 = 100$

$\therefore \quad d_2 = 10$

Now, area of rhombus $= \dfrac{1}{2} \times d_1 \times d_2$

$= \dfrac{1}{2} \times 24 \times 10 = 120 \text{ cm}^2$

261. (c) Let the length and breadth of rectangular field be l and b, respectively.

According to the question,

$\dfrac{l+6}{b+6} = \dfrac{4}{3}$

$\Rightarrow \quad 3l - 4b = 6 \quad \ldots\text{(i)}$

and $\quad \dfrac{l-6}{b-6} = \dfrac{2}{1} \Rightarrow l - 2b = -6 \quad \ldots\text{(ii)}$

From Eqs. (i) and (ii),

$l = 18$ m, $b = 12$ m

262. (c) Let the radius of circle $= r$ then, area of circle $= \pi r^2$

If its circumference is increased by 7% then, its radius is also increased by 7%.

$\therefore$ New radius $= r \times \dfrac{107}{100}$

$\therefore$ New area $= \pi r^2 \times \left(\dfrac{107}{100}\right)^2 = \dfrac{11449}{10000} \pi r^2$

$\therefore$ Required increased percentage in area

$= \dfrac{\dfrac{11449 \pi r^2}{10000} - \pi r^2}{\pi r^2} \times 100$

$= \dfrac{11449 - 10000}{10000} \times 100$

$= \dfrac{1449}{100} = 14.49\%$

Speedy Method

Net percentage change $= a + b + \dfrac{ab}{100}$

$= 7 + 7 + \dfrac{7 \times 7}{100} = 14.49\%$

263. (d) Area of an equilateral triangle

$= \dfrac{\sqrt{3}}{4} a^2 = \dfrac{\sqrt{3}}{4} \times (16)^2$

$= \dfrac{\sqrt{3}}{4} \times 256 = 64\sqrt{3} \text{ cm}^2$

264. (b) Required area $= \pi(r_1^2 - r_2^2)$

$= \pi(27^2 - 18^2)$

$= \pi(27 + 18)(27 - 18)$

$= \pi \times 45 \times 9 = 405\pi$

265. (a) Area of $\Delta XYZ = 8464 \text{ cm}^2$

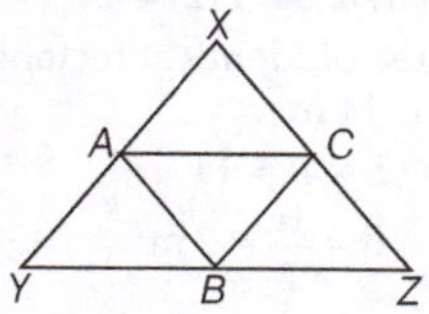

$\because$ A, B and C are mid-points of sides of XY, YZ and ZX of triangle XYZ.

$\therefore$ Area of $\Delta ABC = \dfrac{1}{4}$ (Area of ΔXYZ)

$= \dfrac{1}{4} \times 8464 = 2116 \text{ cm}^2$

266. (d) Let side of the equilateral triangle be a.

$\therefore$ Perimeter of triangle $= 3a = 60$ units

$\therefore \quad a = 20$ units

Now, area of equilateral triangle $= \dfrac{\sqrt{3}}{4} a^2$

$= \dfrac{\sqrt{3}}{4} (20)^2 = 100\sqrt{3}$ units.

267. (d) Given, radius of circle $= 4.5$ cm

$\therefore$ Area of hexagon circumscribed by a circle

$= 6\left(\dfrac{\sqrt{3}}{4} \times r^2\right)$

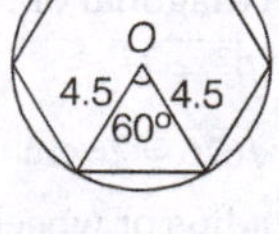

$= 6 \times \dfrac{\sqrt{3}}{4} \times 4.5 \times 4.5$

$= \dfrac{3}{2} \times \sqrt{3} \times \dfrac{45}{10} \times \dfrac{45}{10}$

$= \dfrac{243\sqrt{3}}{8} \text{ cm}^2$

23

Volume and Surface Area

Surface Area

The surface area of a solid object is a measurement of the total area that the surface of the object occupies and it is always measured in sq. unit Surface area is also known as total surface area.

Volume

The amount of space occupied by a three-dimensional objects is called volume of that particular object. It is always measured in cubic unit.

Cube

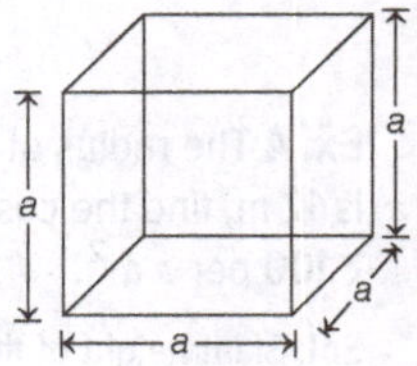

- Volume $= a^3$
- Total surface area $= 6a^2$
- Lateral surface area $= 4a^2$
- Diagonal $= a\sqrt{3}$

Where, a = Side (edge) of the cube

Cuboid

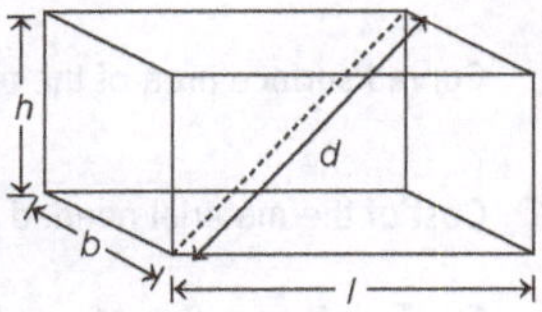

- Volume $= lbh$
- Total surface area $= 2(lb + bh + hl)$
- Lateral surface area $= 2(l + b)h$
- Diagonal $= \sqrt{l^2 + b^2 + h^2}$

Where, l = Length, b = Breadth and h = Height

Room

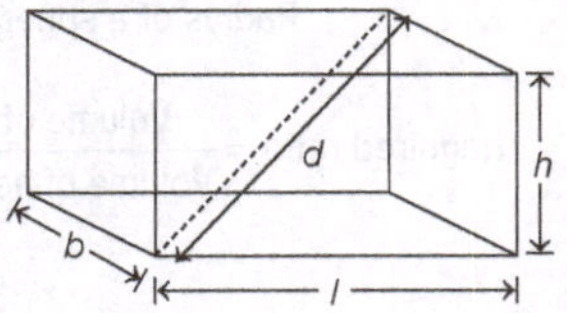

- Total area of walls $= 2(l + b) \times h$
- Total volume of the room $= lbh$
- Area of floor or roof $= lb$

Where, l = Length, b = Breadth and h = Height

Box

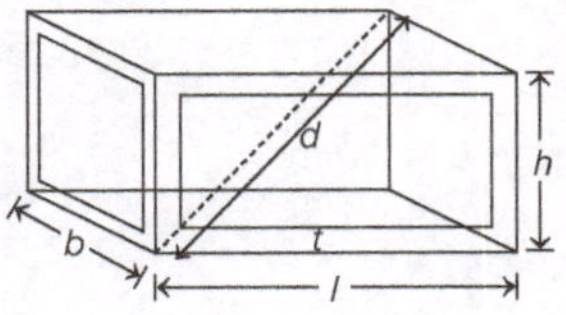

- Surface area of an open box $= 2(l + b)h + lb$
- Capacity of box $= (l - 2t)(b - 2t)(h - 2t)$
- Volume of the material of the box $= lbh - (l - 2t)(b - 2t)(h - 2t)$

Where, l = Length, b = Breadth, h = Height and t = Thickness of the box

Solid Cylinder

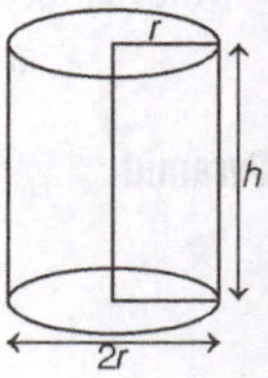

- Volume $= \pi r^2 h$
- Curved surface area $= 2\pi rh$
- Total surface area $= 2\pi r(h + r)$

Where, r = Radius of base and h = Height

Hollow Cylinder

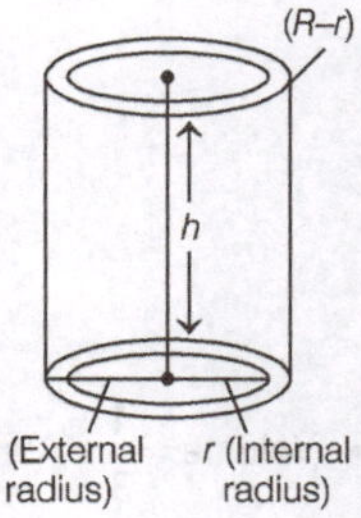

- Volume $= \pi h(R^2 - r^2)$
- Curved surface area $= 2\pi Rh + 2\pi rh = 2\pi h(R + r)$
- Total surface area $= 2\pi h(R + r) + 2\pi(R^2 - r^2)$

Where, R = External radius, r = Internal radius and h = Height

Right Circular Cone

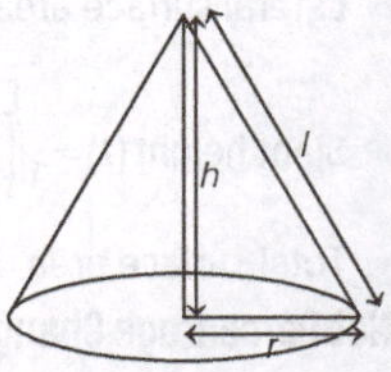

- Volume $= \frac{1}{3}\pi r^2 h$
- Slant height $(l) = \sqrt{r^2 + h^2}$
- Curved surface area $= \pi rl = \pi r\sqrt{r^2 + h^2}$
- Total surface area $= \pi r(l + r)$

Where, r = Radius of the base, h = Height and l = Slant height

Frustum of Right Circular Cone

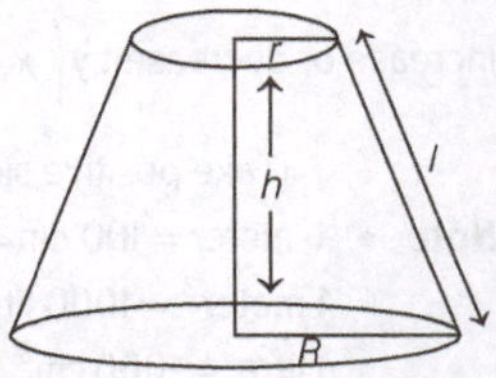

- Volume $= \frac{\pi h}{3}(r^2 + R^2 + rR)$
- Slant height $(l) = \sqrt{h^2 + (R - r)^2}$
- Curved surface area $= \pi(R + r)l$
- Total surface area $= \pi\{(r + R)l + r^2 + R^2\}$

Where, r = Radius of top, R = Radius of base h = Height and l = Slant height

Sphere

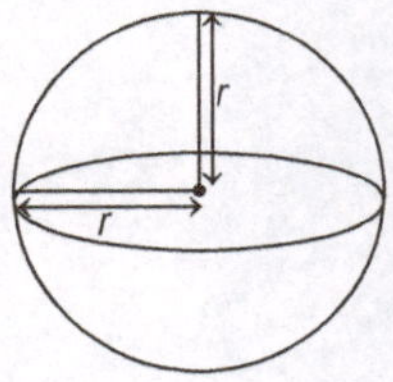

- Volume $= \frac{4}{3}\pi r^3$
- Total surface area $= 4\pi r^2$

Where, r = Radius

Hollow Sphere or Spherical Shell

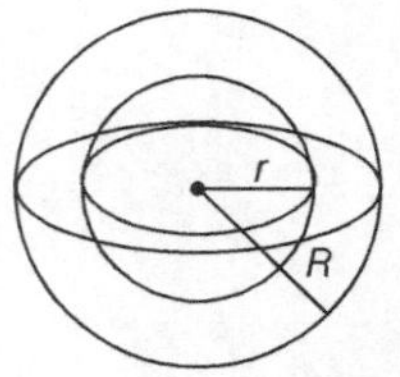

- Volume $= \frac{4}{3}\pi(R^3 - r^3)$
- Internal surface area $= 4\pi r^2$
- External surface area $= 4\pi R^2$

 Where, R = External radius and r = Internal radius

Hemisphere

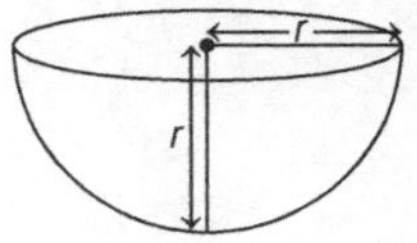

- Volume $= \frac{2}{3}\pi r^3$
- Curved surface area $= 2\pi r^2$

 Where, r = Radius
- Total surface area $= 3\pi r^2$

Prism

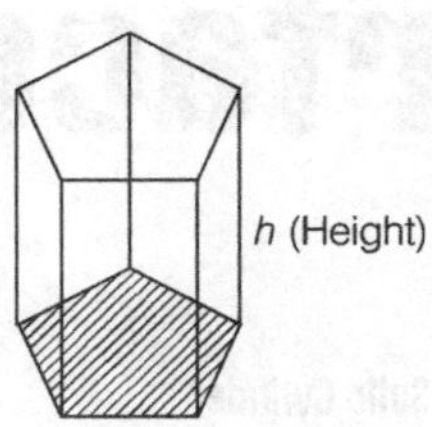

Base
(Pentagon prism)

- Volume = Area of base × Height
- Curved/Lateral surface area

 = Perimeter of base × Height
- Total surface area = Curved surface area + 2 × Area of base

Pyramid

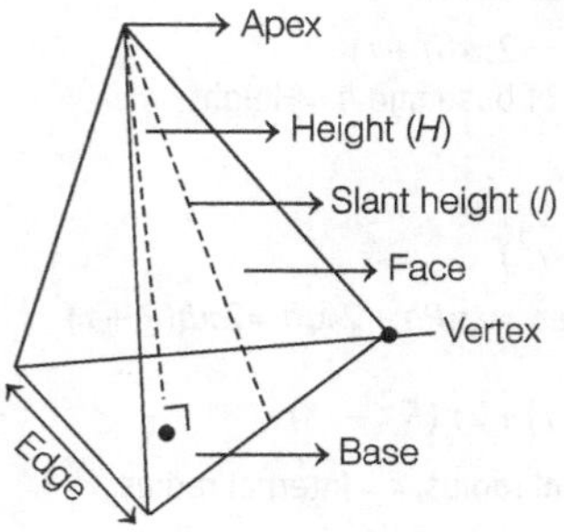

- Volume $= \frac{1}{3} \times$ Area of base × Height (vertical)
- Lateral surface area $= \frac{1}{2} \times$ Perimeter of the base × Slant height
- Slant height $(l) = \sqrt{\left(\frac{\text{Base}}{2}\right)^2 + (\text{Height})^2}$
- Total surface area = Lateral surface area + Area of the base

Net Percentage Change in Surface Area and Volume

If two measuring dimensions which are included in the surface area or volume of a cube, cuboid, sphere, cylinder or cone are increased or decreased by x% and y%, then the surface area or volume of the figure will increase or decrease by $\left(x + y + \frac{xy}{100}\right)$%.

[Take positive sign for increase and negative sign for decrease.]

Note
- 1 meter = 100 cm = 1000 millimeter
- 1 meter^3 = 1000 litre
- 1 litre = 1000 cm^3

Ex. 1 How many bricks will be required to build a wall of 1.6 m× 1 m× 20 cm, if the size of each brick is 10 cm× 8 cm× 4 cm?

Sol. Required number of bricks $= \frac{1.6 \times 100 \times 1 \times 100 \times 20}{10 \times 8 \times 4} = 1000$

[∵ 1 m = 100 cm]

Ex. 2 The length, the breadth and the height of a closed cuboidal box are 2.5 m, 2 m and 90 cm, respectively. What would be the cost of a canvas needed to cover this box completely, if the cost of the canvas is ₹ 80 per m^2?

Sol. Given, $l = 2.5$ m, $b = 2$ m and $h = 90$ cm $= 0.9$ m

Total surface area $= 2(lb + bh + hl)$

$= 2(2.5 \times 2 + 2 \times 0.9 + 0.9 \times 2.5)\,\text{m}^2$

$= 18.1\,\text{m}^2$

Cost of required canvas = ₹ (18.1 × 80) = ₹ 1448

Ex. 3 The height of a solid cylinder is 35 cm. The circumference of its base is 37 cm more than the radius. What will be the volume of this cylinder?

Sol. Circumference of base of cylinder $= 2\pi r$

$\Rightarrow \quad r + 37 = 2 \times \frac{22}{7} \times r$

$\Rightarrow \quad 7r + 37 \times 7 = 44r$

$\Rightarrow \quad 44r - 7r = 37 \times 7$

$\Rightarrow \quad r = 7$ cm

∴ Volume of cylinder $= \pi r^2 h$

$= \frac{22}{7} \times 7 \times 7 \times 35$

$= 5390\,\text{cm}^3$

Ex. 4 The radius of the base of the conical tent is 9 m and its height is 12 m, find the cost of the material needed to make it, if it costs ₹ 100 per π m^2.

Sol. Slant height of the conical tent $(l) = \sqrt{r^2 + h^2}$

$= \sqrt{9^2 + 12^2} = 15$ m

Curved surface area of the tent $= \pi rl$

$= \pi \times 9 \times 15 = 135\pi\,\text{m}^2$

Cost of the material needed $= 135\pi \times \frac{100}{\pi} =$ ₹ 13500

Ex. 5 If the radius of a sphere is thrice than the radius of a hemisphere, then what will be the respective ratio of their volumes?

Sol. Radius of a hemisphere $= r$

∴ Radius of a sphere $= 3r$

Required ratio $= \frac{\text{Volume of sphere}}{\text{Volume of hemisphere}} = \frac{\frac{4}{3}\pi(3r)^3}{\frac{2}{3}\pi r^3}$

$= \frac{2 \times 27}{1} = 54:1$

SSC Exam Scanner

SSC CGL 2024 (Tier I & II)

1. If the diameter of the base of a cone is 56 cm and its curved surface area is 3080 cm^2, then what will be its volume (in cm^3)? (Use $\pi = \frac{22}{7}$)
SSC CGL (Tier-II) 20/01/2025 Shift-I
(a) 17248 (b) 15391
(c) 14670 (d) 12250

2. The height of a right circular cone is 63 cm and the area of its curved surface is five times the area of its base. What is the volume (in cm^3) of the cone?
(Use $\pi = \frac{22}{7}$)
SSC CGL (Tier-II) 18/01/2025 Shift-I
(a) 12589.10 (b) 13540.25
(c) 11234.65 (d) 10914.75

3. Find the volume (in cm^3, rounded off to 2 decimal places) of a right circular cone of diameter 12 cm and height 5 cm. $\left[\text{Use } \pi = \frac{22}{7}\right]$
SSC CGL (Tier-II) 18/01/2025 Shift-I
(a) 188.57 (b) 197.25
(c) 147.23 (d) 156.39

4. A toy is in the form of a cone mounted on a hemisphere. The radius of the hemisphere and that of the cone is 36 cm and height of the cone is 105 cm. The total surface area (in cm^2) of the toy is
SSC CGL (Tier-II) 18/01/2025 Shift-I
(a) 6588 π (b) 5240 π
(c) 6025 π (d) 5799 π

5. Find the volume of a cone having base radius 3.5 cm and height 18 cm.
SSC CGL (Tier-I) 26/09/2024 Shift-III
(a) 241 cm^3 (b) 221 cm^3
(c) 201 cm^3 (d) 231 cm^3

6. If the radius and height of a right circular cylinder are 21 cm and 5 cm, respectively, then the total surface area of the cylinder is $\left(\text{Use } \pi = \frac{22}{7}\right)$
SSC CGL (Tier-I) 26/09/2024 Shift-II
(a) 4312 cm^2 (b) 3432 cm^2
(c) 5212 cm^2 (d) 3816 cm^2

7. What is the total surface area of a cone whose curved surface area is 550 cm^2 and radius is 7 cm? $\left(\text{Take } \pi = \frac{22}{7}\right)$
SSC CGL (Tier-I) 26/09/2024 Shift-I
(a) 764.71 cm^2 (b) 704.00 cm^2
(c) 682.60 cm^2 (d) 714.05 cm^2

8. A well with 14 cm radius is dug 23 cm deep. Find the volume of the earth taken out of it.
SSC CGL (Tier-I) 25/09/2024 Shift-III
(a) 14178 cm^3 (b) 14108 cm^3
(c) 14168 cm^3 (d) 15168 cm^3

9. A cylindrical tank of radius 14 cm is full of water. If 616 L of water are drawn out, then the water level in the tank is dropped by .... m. $\left(\text{Take } \pi = \frac{22}{7}\right)$
SSC CGL (Tier-I) 25/09/2024 Shift-II
(a) 1000 (b) 100 (c) 1 (d) 10

10. The circumference of the base of the cylindrical vessel is 154 cm and its height is 49 mm. How many litres of water can it hold? (correct to three places of decimals, use $\pi = \frac{22}{7}$)
SSC CGL (Tier-I) 25/09/2024 Shift-I
(a) 9.244 (b) 2.439
(c) 3.924 (d) 4.329

11. The ratio of the length, breadth and height of a solid cuboid is given as 3 : 2 : 1 and the breadth of this cuboid is given as 12 cm. Find the volume (in cm^3) of the cuboid.
SSC CGL (Tier-I) 24/09/2024 Shift-III
(a) 1250 (b) 1296 (c) 1200 (d) 1500

12. What is the length (in cm) of each side of a cube if the volume of a cube is 13824 cm^3?
SSC CGL (Tier-I) 24/09/2024 Shift-II
(a) 20.4 (b) 24 (c) 22 (d) 34

13. The volume of a right circular cylindrical box of radius 30 cm is 600 cm^3. Find the height of the box.
SSC CGL (Tier-I) 24/09/2024 Shift-I
(a) 0.61 cm (b) 0.31 cm
(c) 0.51 cm (d) 0.21 cm

14. The length, breadth and height of a room is 15 m, 9 m, and 5 m, respectively. From each can of paint 40 square metre of area is painted. How many cans paint will be needed to paint only the walls of the room?
SSC CGL (Tier-I) 23/09/2024 Shift-II
(a) 12 (b) 6 (c) 4 (d) 8

15. Find the length of the longest stick that can be fitted in a cubical vessel of edge 70 cm.
SSC CGL (Tier-I) 23/09/2024 Shift-I
(a) $35\sqrt{3}$ cm (b) $70\sqrt{3}$ cm
(c) $10\sqrt{3}$ cm (d) $70\sqrt{2}$ cm

16. The total surface area of a closed cube is given as 1152 cm^2. What is the length (in cm) of each side of the cube? SSC CGL (Tier-I) 19/09/2024 Shift-III
(a) $9\sqrt{2}$ (b) $4\sqrt{13}$
(c) $8\sqrt{3}$ (d) $8\sqrt{2}$

17. The base radius of a circular cylinder is 10.5 cm. If the area of its curved surface is 792 cm^2, then what is the volume of the cylinder?
SSC CGL (Tier-I) 19/09/2024 Shift-II
(a) 4185 cm^3 (b) 4518 cm^3
(c) 4152 cm^3 (d) 4158 cm^3

18. What is the volume of a cone (in cubic units) with radius 3 units and slant height $3\sqrt{2}$ units?
SSC CGL (Tier-I) 18/09/2024 Shift-III
(a) 18π (b) $\frac{10\pi}{3}$
(c) $\frac{9\pi}{2}$ (d) 9π

19. The radius of the base of a right circular cone is 9 cm and its slant height is 49 cm. Find the curved surface area of the cone.
SSC CGL (Tier-I) 18/09/2024 Shift-II
(a) 1386 cm^2 (b) 1265 cm^2
(c) 1262 cm^2 (d) 1490 cm^2

20. If three cubes of volume 512 cm^3 each are joined end to end, find the surface area of the resulting cuboid.
SSC CGL (Tier-I) 18/09/2024 Shift-I
(a) 896 cm^2 (b) 986 cm^2
(c) 895 cm^2 (d) 869 cm^2

21. Find the length of the longest diagonal (in cm) of a cuboidal box of dimensions 1.2 cm × 1.3 cm × 1.5 cm (correct to two decimal places).
SSC CGL (Tier-I) 17/09/2024 Shift-III
(a) 2.22 cm (b) 2.32 cm
(c) 2.23 cm (d) 2.35 cm

22. If the height and diameter of a cylinder are 12 cm and 28 cm, respectively, then find the ratio of the total surface area to the curved surface area.
SSC CGL (Tier-I) 17/09/2024 Shift-II
(a) 13 : 5 (b) 10 : 3
(c) 13 : 6 (d) 11 : 6

23. The circumference of the base of a cylindrical vessel is 44 cm and its height is 25 cm. How many liters of water can it hold? (Take $\pi = \frac{22}{7}$)
SSC CGL (Tier-I) 17/09/2024 Shift-I
(a) 38.5 (b) 3.58
(c) 3.85 (d) 83.5

24. If the curved surface area of a cylinder is 880 cm^2, then the product of its height and radius is
SSC CGL (Tier-I) 13/09/2024 Shift-III
(a) 90 cm^2 (b) 120 cm^2
(c) 220 cm^2 (d) 140 cm^2

25. What is the volume in cubic units of a cylinder with a height equal to the diameter and a radius is 4 units?
SSC CGL (Tier-I) 13/09/2024 Shift-II
(a) 128π (b) $\frac{64\pi}{3}$
(c) 32π (d) $\frac{32\pi}{3}$

26. What is the height (in m) of a conical water tank having radius of 70 m and volume of 46200 m^3?
(Take $\pi = \frac{22}{7}$)
SSC CGL (Tier-I) 13/09/2024 Shift-I
(a) 27 (b) 9 (c) 18 (d) 54

27. The circumference of the base of a conical tent of height 8 m is 32πm. Find its curved surface area.
SSC CGL (Tier-I) 12/09/2024 Shift-III
(a) $164\sqrt{5}\pi\ m^2$ (b) $162\sqrt{3}\pi\ m^2$
(c) $132\sqrt{3}\pi\ m^2$ (d) $128\sqrt{5}\pi\ m^2$

28. Two cylinders have the radii of their bases in the ratio 4 : 5 and their heights are in the ratio 5 : 7. Find the ratio of their curved surface areas.
SSC CGL (Tier-I) 12/09/2024 Shift-II
(a) 5 : 4 (b) 4 : 7 (c) 1 : 2 (d) 4 : 5

29. The height of a cylinder is 20 cm. The lateral surface area is 1760 cm^2. Its volume is
SSC CGL (Tier-I) 12/09/2024 Shift-I
(a) 12032 cm^3 (b) 12302 cm^3
(c) 12203 cm^3 (d) 12320 cm^3

30. A rectangular piece of paper is 50 cm long and 22 cm wide. If a cylinder is formed by rolling the paper along its breadth, then the volume of the cylinder is
SSC CGL (Tier-I) 10/09/2024 Shift-III
(a) 2125 cm^3 (b) 1925 cm^3
(c) 2025 cm^3 (d) 1825 cm^3

31. A cuboid of dimensions 50 cm, 150 cm, 175 cm can be divided into how many identical largest cubes?
SSC CGL (Tier-I) 11/09/2024 Shift-III
(a) 75 (b) 84 (c) 85 (d) 90

32. A right triangle with sides 3 cm, 4 cm and 5 cm is rotated about the sides of 3 cm to form a cone. The volume of the cone so formed is
SSC CGL (Tier-I) 10/09/2024 Shift-II
(a) $20\pi\ cm^3$ (b) $16\pi\ cm^3$
(c) $25\pi\ cm^3$ (d) $28\pi\ cm^3$

33. If a right circular cone of height 24 cm has a volume of 1232 cm^3, then the total surface area of the cone is $\left(\text{Use } \pi = \frac{22}{7}\right)$.
SSC CGL (Tier-I) 10/09/2024 Shift-I
(a) 806 cm^2 (b) 704 cm^2
(c) 904 cm^2 (d) 608 cm^2

34. If the length, breadth, and height of a cuboid is 8 cm, 4 cm and 6 cm, respectively, then the volume (in cm^3) of the cuboid is
SSC CGL (Tier-I) 09/09/2024 Shift-III
(a) 218 (b) 192
(c) 96 (d) 172

35. What is the volume (in cm^3) of a cylinder if the radius of the cylinder is 8 cm and height is 14 cm? (Take $\pi = \frac{22}{7}$)
SSC CGL (Tier-I) 09/09/2024 Shift-II
(a) 2686 (b) 2816
(c) 2784 (d) 2456

36. The radii of the two cones are in the ratio of 2 : 5 and their volumes are in the ratio of 3 : 5. What is the ratio of their heights?
SSC CGL (Tier-I) 09/09/2024 Shift-I
(a) 15 : 4 (b) 11 : 15
(c) 13 : 11 (d) 4 : 11

SSC CGL 2023 (Tier I & II)

37. The ratio of the length, width and height of a closed cuboid is given as 6 : 3 : 2. The total surface area of this cuboid is given as 1800 cm^2. Fing the volume (in cm^2) of this cuboid.
SSC CGL (Tier-II) 26/10/2023 Shift-I
(a) 4660 (b) 4800
(c) 4500 (d) 42000

38. A solid cube, whose each edge is of length 48 cm, is melted. Identical soild cubes, each of volume 64 cm^3, without any wastage. How many such small cubes are obtained?
SSC CGL (Tier-II) 26/10/2023 Shift-I
(a) 1728 (b) 1718
(c) 1748 (d) 1738

39. A prism and a pyramid have the same base and the same height. Find the ratio of the volumes of the prism and the pyramid.
SSC CGL (Tier-II) 7/3/2023 Shift-I
(a) 3 : 2 (b) 3 : 1
(c) 2 : 3 (d) 1 : 3

40. What is the volume of a cylinder if the radius of the cylinder is 10 cm and height is 20 cm? (Take, $\pi = 3.14$)
SSC CGL (Tier-II) 7/3/2023 Shift-I
(a) 5280 cm^3 (b) 6260 cm^3
(c) 6280 cm^3 (d) 5306 cm^3

41. A pyramid has an equilateral triangle as its base, of which each side is 8 cm. Its slant edge is 24 cm. The whole surface area of the pyramid (in cm^2) is SSC CGL (Tier-II) 6/3/2023 Shift-I
(a) $(16\sqrt{3} + 24\sqrt{35})$
(b) $(12\sqrt{3} + 24\sqrt{35})$
(c) $(24\sqrt{3} + 36\sqrt{35})$
(d) $(16\sqrt{3} + 48\sqrt{35})$

42. If the curved surface area of a cylinder is $126\pi\ cm^2$ and its height is 14 cm, what is the volume of the cylinder? SSC CGL (Tier-II) 6/3/2023 Shift-I
(a) $283\frac{1}{2}\pi\ cm^3$ (b) $137\frac{1}{2}\pi\ cm^3$
(c) $128\frac{1}{2}\pi\ cm^3$ (d) $125\frac{1}{2}\pi\ cm^3$

43. What is the total surface area of a pyramid whose base is a square with side 8 cm and height of the pyramid is 3 cm? SSC CGL (Tier-II) 3/3/2023 Shift-I
(a) 169 cm^2 (b) 121 cm^2
(c) 144 cm^2 (d) 184 cm^2

44. The breadth '*b*' of a room is twice its height and half of its length. Find the length of the longest diagonal of the room. SSC CGL (Tier-II) 3/3/2023 Shift-I
(a) $\frac{\sqrt{20b}}{2}$ (b) $\frac{b}{2}$ (c) $\frac{\sqrt{21b}}{2}$ (d) $\frac{\sqrt{19b}}{2}$

45. A hemispherical bowl of internal radius 18 cm is full of liquid. This liquid is to be filled in cylindrical bottles each of radius 3 cm and height 6 cm. How many bottles are required to empty the bowl?
SSC CGL (Tier-II) 3/3/2023 Shift-I
(a) 72 (b) 70 (c) 68 (d) 66

46. What is the volume of the largest sphere that can be carved out of a wooden cube of sides 21 cm? $\left(\pi = \frac{22}{7}\right)$
SSC CGL (Tier-II) 2/3/2023 Shift-I
(a) 3851 cm^3 (b) 6858 cm^3
(c) 4851 cm^3 (d) 5821 cm^3

47. If radius of a sphere is decreased by 48%, then by what per cent does its surface area decrease?
SSC CGL (Tier-II) 2/3/2023 Shift-I
(a) 82.91% (b) 72.96%
(c) 78.98% (d) 86.26%

48. The curved surface area of a right circular cylinder of height 56 cm is 1408 cm^2. Find the diameter of the base of the cylinder.
SSC CGL (Tier-I) 27/7/2023 Shift-III
(a) 8 m (b) 0.04 m
(c) 0.08 m (d) 0.008 m

49. A hemispherical bowl has a radius of 7 cm. It is to be painted from inside as well as outside. Find the cost of painting it at the rate of ₹ 40 per 20 cm^2? (Take thickness of the bowl as negligible).
SSC CGL (Tier-I) 27/7/2023 Shift-II
(a) ₹ 1232 (b) ₹ 1125
(c) ₹ 1432 (d) ₹ 1550

50. If the volume of a cube is 4096 cm^3, then what is the length of the side of the cube? SSC CGL (Tier-I) 26/7/2023 Shift-IV
(a) 12 cm (b) 18 cm (c) 16 cm (d) 14 cm

51. If the side of a cubical box is 12 cm, then find its total surface area.
SSC CGL (Tier-I) 26/7/2023 Shift-III
(a) 952 cm^2 (b) 864 cm^2
(c) 664 cm^2 (d) 792 cm^2

52. A petrol tank is of length 50 m, breadth 25 m, and depth 10 m. How many litres of petrol can be accommodated in the tank when it is completely filled?
SSC CGL (Tier-I) 26/7/2023 Shift-II
(a) 12500000 (b) 1250000
(c) 125000 (d) 12500

53. What is the surface area (in cm^2) of a spherical sculpture whose radius is 35 cm? $\left(\text{Take } \pi = \frac{22}{7}\right)$
SSC CGL (Tier-I) 26/7/2023 Shift-II
(a) 16540 (b) 15700
(c) 15400 (d) 14500

54. If the slant height of a cone is 60 cm and the radius of its base is 21 cm, then find its curved surface area. $\left(\text{use } \pi = \frac{22}{7}\right)$
SSC CGL (Tier-I) 26/7/2023 Shift-I
(a) 3880 cm^2 (b) 3820 cm^2
(c) 3960 cm^2 (d) 4020 cm^2

55. The curved surface area of a solid circular cylinder of height 12 cm is 2640 cm². What is the volume (in cm³) of the cylinder? (Take π = 22/7)
SSC CGL (Tier-I) 25/7/2023 Shift-III
(a) 46200 (b) 37900
(c) 42000 (d) 55200

56. The length, breadth and height of a hall are 10 m, 20 m and 15 m respectively. Find the cost of whitewashing the walls of the inside of the hall and ceiling at the rate of ₹ 10.20/m^2. **SSC CGL (Tier-I) 25/7/2023 Shift-II**
(a) ₹ 13394 (b) ₹ 11220
(c) ₹ 15320 (d) ₹ 16542

57. A metallic cube has each of its side of length 12 cm. It is melted and recast into three small cubes. Out of these cubes, two have their sides as 6 cm and 8 cm, respectively. The length of each side of the third cube is
SSC CGL (Tier-I) 25/7/2023 Shift-I
(a) 7 cm (b) 9 cm
(c) 10 cm (d) 5 cm

58. A ball is to be made with inner radius of 2 units and outside radius of 3 units. How much material is required to make the ball?
SSC CGL (Tier-I) 24/7/2023 Shift-IV
(a) $\frac{19}{3}\pi$ (b) 19π
(c) $\frac{76}{3}\pi$ (d) π

59. The length, breadth and height of a room are 10 m, 8 m and 6 m, respectively. Find the cost of white washing the walls of the room and the ceilling at the rate of ₹7.50 per m^2. **SSC CGL (Tier-I) 24/7/2023 Shift-II**
(a) ₹2220 (b) ₹ 1850
(c) ₹ 2150 (d) ₹ 2000

60. A one meter pipe is made with inner diameter equal to outer radius. How much material (in cubic units) is required to make the pipe, if it can hold $\frac{88}{7}$ cubic metres water in it?
SSC CGL (Tier-I) 24/7/2023 Shift-I
(a) 37.7 (b) 35.5
(c) 33.3 (d) 36.6

61. If the inner radius of a hemispherical bowl is 5 cm and its thickness is 0.25 cm, then find the volume of the material required in making the bowl. $\left(\text{Use } \pi = \frac{22}{7}\right)$ (Rounded up to two places of decimals).
SSC CGL (Tier-I) 21/7/2023 Shift-IV
(a) 34 cm^3 (b) 44 cm^3
(c) 45.34 cm^3 (d) 41.28 cm^3

62. If the volume of one brick is 0.0014 m^3, then how many bricks will be required to construct a wall of length 14 m, breadth 0.125 m and height 5 m? **SSC CGL (Tier-I) 21/7/2023 Shift-III**
(a) 5250 (b) 3250
(c) 6250 (d) 4250

63. Three solid metallic spheres of radii 1 cm, 6 cm and 8 cm, respectively, are melted and recast into a single solid sphere. The radius of the new sphere so formed is
SSC CGL (Tier-I) 21/7/2023 Shift-III
(a) 9 cm (b) 5.9 cm
(c) 7.7 cm (d) 8.5 cm

64. The volume of a cuboid is twice that of a cube. If the dimensions of the cuboid are (8 m × 8 m × 16 m), the total surface area of the cube is
SSC CGL (Tier-I) 21/7/2023 Shift-I
(a) 316 m^2 (b) 288 m^2
(c) 324 m^2 (d) 384 m^2

65. The length, breadth and height of a cuboid are in the ratio 1 : 2 : 3. The length, breadth and height of the cuboid are increased by 200%, 300% and 300%, respectively. Then compared to the original volume, the increase in the volume of the cuboid will be: **SSC CGL (Tier-I) 20/7/2023 Shift-IV**
(a) 47 times (b) 26 times
(c) 17 times (d) 15 times

66. The slant height of a cone is 10 cm and the radius is 6 cm. What is the total surface area of the cone? (Take π = 3.14)
SSC CGL (Tier-I) 20/7/2023 Shift-III
(a) 292.4 cm^2 (b) 312.2 cm^2
(c) 305.4 cm^2 (d) 301.44 cm^2

67. A solid cone with curved surface area twice its base area has slant height of $6\sqrt{3}$ cm. Its height is
SSC CGL (Tier-I) 20/7/2023 Shift-II
(a) $6\sqrt{2}$ cm (b) 9 cm
(c) 6 cm (d) $3\sqrt{6}$ cm

68. Find the total surface area (in cm^2) of a cuboid having dimensions 5 cm, 7 cm and 11 cm.
SSC CGL (Tier-I) 20/7/2023 Shift-II
(a) 385 (b) 334
(c) 343 (d) 167

69. Three cubes with sides in the ratio of 3 : 4 : 5 are melted to form a single cube whose diagonal is $18\sqrt{3}$ cm. The sides of the three cubes are
SSC CGL (Tier-I) 20/7/2023 Shift-I
(a) 21 cm, 28 cm and 35 cm
(b) 9 cm, 12 cm and 15 cm
(c) 18 cm, 24 cm and 30 cm
(d) 12 cm, 16 cm and 20 cm

70. If the surface area of a cube is 5046 cm^2, then the volume of the cube is **SSC CGL (Tier-I) 19/7/2023 Shift-IV**
(a) 26189 cm^3 (b) 25145 cm^3
(c) 22812 cm^3 (d) 24389 cm^3

71. To have a surface area of 9π square units of a ball, what should be the diameter (in units) of the ball?
SSC CGL (Tier-I) 19/7/2023 Shift-III
(a) 2.5 (b) 2 (c) 1.5 (d) 3

72. The lateral area of a cylinder is 3168 cm^2 and its height is 48 cm. Find the volume. **SSC CGL (Tier-I) 19/7/2023 Shift-II**
(a) 5244 cm^3 (b) 5544 cm^3
(c) 5644 cm^3 (d) 16632 cm^3

73. A conical tent has a radius of 7 m and a vertical height of 24 m. How many full bags of rice can be emptied in it if the space occupied by the rice in each bag is 2 m^3?
SSC CGL (Tier-I) 19/7/2023 Shift-I
(a) 566 (b) 616 (c) 716 (d) 650

74. A cone and a cylinder with equal radii have equal volumes. The ratio of their heights is
SSC CGL (Tier-I) 18/7/2023 Shift-IV
(a) 2 : 3 (b) 3 : 4 (c) 1 : 2 (d) 3 : 1

75. A conical tent with radius 6 units and height 8 unit is to be made by canvas. How much canvas is needed to make the tent? (Rounded off to two places of decimals)
SSC CGL (Tier-I) 18/7/2023 Shift-III
(a) 177.55 units (b) 166.57 units
(c) 188.57 units (d) 155.87 units

76. A conical tent of height 10 m and base diameter 48m was erected by a company in a park. Find the curved surface area of the tent (in m^2). SSC CGL (Tier-I) 18/7/2023 Shift-I
(a) 576π (b) 1248π
(c) 1152π (d) 624π

77. A spherical ball of lead, 3 cm in diameter, is melted and recast into three spherical balls. The diameters of two of these balls are $\frac{3}{2}$ cm and 2 cm, respectively. Find the diameter of the third ball.
SSC CGL (Tier-I) 17/7/2023 Shift-IV
(a) 2.1 cm (b) 3.3 cm
(c) 3 cm (d) 2.5 cm

78. What is the volume of a cube if the perimeter of one face of the cube is 40 cm? SSC CGL (Tier-I) 17/7/2023 Shift-III
(a) 1000 cm^3 (b) 820 cm^3
(c) 600 cm^3 (d) 800 cm^3

79. What is the whole surface area of a cone of base radius 6 cm and height 8 cm? SSC CGL (Tier-I) 17/7/2023 Shift-II
(a) 301.71 cm^2 (b) 350.51 cm^2
(c) 364.61 cm^2 (d) 354.50 cm^2

80. The volume of a cone with height equal to radius and slant height 5 cm is : SSC CGL (Tier-I) 17/7/2023 Shift-I
(a) $\frac{125\pi}{12\sqrt{3}}$ cm^3 (b) $\frac{125\pi}{6\sqrt{3}}$ cm^3
(c) $\frac{125\pi}{12\sqrt{2}}$ cm^3 (d) $\frac{125\pi}{6\sqrt{2}}$ cm^3

81. Ranu carries water to school in a cylindrical flask with diameter l2 cm and height 21 cm. Determine the amount of water that she can carry in the flask. (Use $\pi = \frac{22}{7}$)
SSC CGL (Tier-I) 14/7/2023 Shift-IV
(a) 2372 cm^3 (b) 2370 cm^3
(c) 2376 cm^3 (d) 2374 cm^3

82. The volume of a cone is 73920 cm^3. If the height of the cone is 160 cm, then find the diameter of its base.
SSC CGL (Tier-I) 14/7/2023 Shift-III
(a) 21 cm (b) 40 cm
(c) 22 cm (d) 42 cm

83. If the total surface area of a cube is 24 sq.units, then what is the volume of the cube ? SSC CGL (Tier-I) 14/7/2023 Shift-II
(a) 4 cu.units (b) 10 cu.units
(c) 8 cu.units (d) 16 cu.units

SSC CGL 2022-2020 (Tier I)

84. If the diameter of a solid hemisphere is 12.6 cm, then its volume is (take $\pi = \frac{22}{7}$) SSC CGL (Tier-I) 13/12/2022 Shift-III
(a) 1259 cm^3 (b) 987 cm^3
(c) 523.908 cm^3 (d) 1235.621 cm^3

85. If the numerical value of twice the curved surface area of a right circular cylinder is equal to the numerical value of its volume, then what is the numerical value of the radius of the base of the cylinder?
SSC CGL (Tier-I) 13/12/2022 Shift-I
(a) 2 (b) 3 (c) 5 (d) 4

86. A conical vessel, whose internal radius is 20 cm and height is 27 cm, is full of water. If this water is poured into a cylindrical vessel with internal radius 15 cm, what will be the height to which the water rises in it?
SSC CGL (Tier-I) 12/12/2022 Shift-IV
(a) 16 cm (b) 10 cm
(c) 12 cm (d) 14 cm

87. A solid metallic sphere of radius 12 cm is melted and recast into a cone having diameter of the base as 12 cm. What is the height of the cone?
SSC CGL (Tier-I) 12/12/2022 Shift-IV
(a) 258 cm (b) 192 cm
(c) 166 cm (d) 224 cm

88. The radii of the ends of a frustum of a cone 7 cm high are 5 cm and 3 cm. Find its volume correct to one decimal place. (Use $\pi = \frac{22}{7}$)
SSC CGL (Tier-I) 12/12/2022 Shift-II
(a) 345.6 cm^3 (b) 359.3 cm^3
(c) 379.3 cm^3 (d) 369.3 cm^3

89. The radius of a right circular cylinder is four times of its height. If the height of the cylinder is 14 cm , then what is the volume of cylinder?
SSC CGL (Tier-I) 12/12/2022 Shift-II
(a) 15468 cm^3 (b) 14262 cm^3
(c) 137984 cm^3 (d) 11296 cm^3

90. How many metres of 2 m wide cloth will be required to make a conical tent with the diameter of the base as 14 m and slant height as 9 m ignore wastage? SSC CGL (Tier-I) 12/12/2022 Shift-I
(a) 66 m (b) 88 m
(c) 99 m (d) 77 m

91. The number of solid spheres, each of diameter 6 cm, that could be moulded to form a solid metal cylinder of height 90 cm and diameter 4 cm is
SSC CGL (Tier-I) 9/12/2022 Shift-IV
(a) 10 (b) 14
(c) 16 (d) 13

92. The length of the side of a cube is 1.4 cm. What is the volume of the largest sphere that can be taken out of the cube? SSC CGL (Tier-I) 9/12/2022 Shift-IV
(a) 1.44 cm^3 (b) 3.26 cm^3
(c) 2.66 cm^3 (d) 5.64 cm^3

93. The curved surface area of a right circular cone of base radius 21 cm is 594 sq. cm. What is the slant height of the cone?
SSC CGL (Tier-I) 9/12/2022 Shift-III
(a) 15 cm (b) 11 cm
(c) 9 cm (d) 6 cm

94. The length of the side of a cube is 2.8 cm. What is the volume of the largest sphere that can be taken out of the cube? SSC CGL (Tier-I) 9/12/2022 Shift-II
(a) 11.50 cm^3 (b) 1.15 cm^3
(c) 11.55 cm^3 (d)115 cm^3

95. A conical vessel (solid) is made of iron. Its base radius is 7 cm and height is 15 cm. If the weight of the iron per cubic centimetre is 15 gm, what is the weight of the vessel?
SSC CGL (Tier-I) 9/12/2022 Shift-II
(a) 13.55 kg (b) 12.55 kg
(c) 14.55 kg (d) 11.55 kg

96. A cuboid of sides 12 cm, 18 cm and 27 cm is melted to form a cube. What is the ratio of the total surface area of the cuboid to that of the cube?
SSC CGL (Tier-I) 8/12/2022 Shift-IV
(a) 18 : 17 (b) 17 : 19
(c) 19 : 18 (d) 17 : 23

97. Find the total surface area of a cube whose volume is 343 m^3.
SSC CGL (Tier-I) 8/12/2022 Shift-III
(a) 186 m^2 (b) 294 m^2
(c) 196 m^2 (d) 210 m^2

98. A hollow sphere has an outer radius of 6 cm and inner radius of 3 cm. What is the volume of this hollow sphere? SSC CGL (Tier-I) 8/12/2022 Shift-III
(a) 252π cm^3 (b) 356π cm^3
(c) 144π cm^3 (d) 175π cm^3

99. An iron rod with diameter 4 cm and length 12 cm is drawn into a wire of length 12 m of uniform thickness. Determine the thickness of the wire.
SSC CGL (Tier-I) 8/12/2022 Shift-II
(a) 0.6 cm (b) 0.7 cm
(c) 0.3 cm (d) 0.4 cm

100. What is the area of the curved surface of a right circular cone with height 8 m and slant height 10 m?
SSC CGL (Tier-I) 8/12/2022 Shift-I
(a) 60 m^2 (b) 60π m^2
(c) 40 m^2 (d) 40π m^2

101. The radius of a hemisphere is 5.6 cm. What will be its volume?
SSC CGL (Tier-I) 7/12/2022 Shift-IV
(a) 367.95 cm^3 (b) 195.95 cm^3
(c) 380 cm^3 (d) 265.65 cm^3

102. The volume of the sphere is 38808 cm^3. What is the surface area of the sphere? SSC CGL (Tier-I) 7/12/2022 Shift-IV
(a) 4455 cm^2 (b) 4433 cm^2
(c) 5544 cm^2 (d) 3344 cm^2

103. A copper sphere of diameter 18 m is drawn into a cylindrical wire of length 12 m. What is the radius of the wire? SSC CGL (Tier-I) 7/12/2022 Shift-III

(a) 5 m (b) 9 m
(c) 3 m (d) 12 m

104. What is the total surface area of a cone, if the slant height and radius of a cone is 30 cm and 14 cm, respectively?
SSC CGL (Tier-I) 7/12/2022 Shift-III

(a) 1980 cm^2 (b) 1963 cm^2
(c) 1908 cm^2 (d) 1936 cm^2

105. Steel is used to make a hemispherical bowl that is 0.37 cm thick. The bowl's inner radius is 6 cm. Find the bowl's outside curved surface area $\left(\text{take } \pi = \frac{22}{7}\right)$
SSC CGL (Tier-I) 7/12/2022 Shift-I

(a) 532 cm^2 (b) 255.0548 cm^2
(c) 484 cm^2 (d) 523.4107 cm^2

106. If the diameter of a hemisphere is 35 cm, then what is the volume of hemisphere?
SSC CGL (Tier-I) 7/12/2022 Shift-I

(a) 11229.17 cm^3
(b) 15248.46 cm^3
(c) 17428.33 cm^3
(d) 9478.26 cm^3

107. The radius of a hemisphere is 6.3 cm. What will be its volume?
SSC CGL (Tier-I) 6/12/2022 Shift-IV

(a) 572.80 cm^3
(b) 643.50 cm^3
(c) 523.90 cm^3
(d) 353.38 cm^3

108. If the volume of a sphere is $179\frac{2}{3}$ m^3, what is its surface area?
SSC CGL (Tier-I) 6/12/2022 Shift-III

(a) 221 m^2 (b) 154 m^2
(c) 144 m^2 (d) 151 m^2

109. The external diameter of an iron pipe is 20 cm and its length is 12 cm. If the thickness of the pipe is 1 cm. Find the surface area of the pipe (take $\pi = \frac{22}{7}$) correct to two places of decimal.
SSC CGL (Tier-I) 6/12/2022 Shift-II

(a) 1662.67 cm^2 (b) 1552.57 cm^2
(c) 1442.48 cm^2 (d) 1772.76 cm^2

110. A solid hemisphere has radius 21 cm. It is melted to form a cylinder such that the ratio of its curved surface area to total surface area is 2 : 5. What is the radius (in cm) of its base (take $\pi = \frac{22}{7}$)?
SSC CGL (Tier-I) 6/12/2022 Shift-I

(a) 23 (b) 21 (c) 17 (d) 19

111. Three cubes of equal volume are joined end to end. Find the surface area of the resulting cuboid if the diagonal of the cube is $6\sqrt{3}$ cm.
SSC CGL (Tier-I) 5/12/2022 Shift-IV

(a) 509 cm^2 (b) 504 cm^2
(c) 516 cm^2 (d) 512 cm^2

112. The volume of the hemisphere is 19404 cm^3. The radius of the hemisphere is ....
SSC CGL (Tier-I) 5/12/2022 Shift-III

(a) 14 cm (b) 19 cm
(c) 21 cm (d) 17 cm

113. A hollow sphere has an outer radius of 4 cm and inner radius of 1 cm. What is the volume of this hollow sphere? SSC CGL (Tier-I) 5/12/2022 Shift-III

(a) 84π cm^3 (b) 68π cm^3
(c) 48π cm^3 (d) 92π cm^3

114. The total surface area of a cube is 1536 m^2.Find its volume.
SSC CGL (Tier-I) 5/12/2022 Shift-II

(a) 216 m^3 (b) 125 m^3
(c) 4096 m^3 (d) 729 m^3

115. The length of the side of a cube is 4.2 cm. What is the volume of the largest sphere that can be taken out of the cube?
SSC CGL (Tier-I) 5/12/2022 Shift-II

(a) 26.40 cm^3 (b) 20.50 cm^3
(c) 38.80 cm^3 (d) 48.60 cm^3

116. The curved surface area of the sphere is 154 cm^2. Find the volume of the sphere (rounded off to one digit after decimal). SSC CGL (Tier-I) 5/12/2022 Shift-I

(a) 179.7 cm^3 (b) 147.8 cm^3
(c) 161.1 cm^3 (d) 156.6 cm^3

117. The length of the side of a cube is 5.6 cm. What is the volume of the largest sphere that can be taken out of the cube? SSC CGL (Tier-I) 5/12/2022 Shift-I

(a) 91.98 cm^3 (b) 99.96 cm^3
(c) 96.98 cm^3 (d) 90.69 cm^3

118. If the length of the diagonal of a cube is $7\sqrt{3}$ cm, then the surface area of the cube is ....
SSC CGL (Tier-I) 3/12/2022 Shift-IV

(a) 216 cm^2 (b) 256 cm^2
(c) 284 cm^2 (d) 294 cm^2

119. A solid copper sphere of radius 9 cm is hammered and moulded into a wire of radius 2 cm. What is the length of this wire?
SSC CGL (Tier-I) 3/12/2022 Shift-III

(a) 224 cm (b) 183 cm
(c) 198 cm (d) 243 cm

120. The radius of a right circular cylinder is thrice of its height. If the height of the cylinder is 2.1 cm, then what is the volume of cylinder?
SSC CGL (Tier-I) 3/12/2022 Shift-III

(a) 224.65 cm^3 (b) 194.72 cm^3
(c) 324.86 cm^3 (d) 261.95 cm^3

121. The radii of two cylinders are in the ratio 1 : 4 and their heights are in the ratio 4 : 3. Their volumes will be in the ratio ....
SSC CGL (Tier-I) 3/12/2022 Shift-II

(a) 1 : 12 (b) 2 : 9
(c) 3 : 10 (d) 1 : 9

122. If the diameter of a sphere is 3.5 cm, then what is the total surface area of the sphere?
SSC CGL (Tier-I) 3/12/2022 Shift-I

(a) 45.75 cm^2 (b) 42.6 cm^2
(c) 38.5 cm^2 (d) 34.25 cm^2

123. A cuboid of length 36 m, breadth 18 m and height 9 m is melted and recast into a cube. Find the length of the diagonal of the cube.
SSC CGL (Tier-I) 2/12/2022 Shift-III

(a) $18\sqrt{3}$ m (b) $15\sqrt{3}$ m
(c) $12\sqrt{3}$ m (d) $17\sqrt{3}$ m

124. The radius of a right circular cylinder is five times of its height. If the height of the cylinder is 3.5 cm, then what is the volume of cylinder?
SSC CGL (Tier-I) 2/12/2022 Shift-III

(a) 3368.75 cm^3 (b) 3872.75 cm^3
(c) 3146.75 cm^3 (d) 3524.25 cm^3

125. The surface area of a cube is 864 cm^2. The volume of the cube is.........
SSC CGL (Tier-I) 2/12/2022 Shift-II

(a) 1728 cm^3 (b) 2197 cm^3
(c) 1331 cm^3 (d) 729 cm^3

126. If the diameter of a hemisphere is 28 cm, then what is the volume of hemisphere?
SSC CGL (Tier-I) 2/12/2022 Shift-II

(a) 5749.33 cm^3 (b) 6349.22 cm^3
(c) 6728.11 cm^3 (d) 5124.44 cm^3

127. Which of the following two will provide more volume?
SSC CGL (Tier-I) 2/12/2022 Shift-I

I. A cuboid of edges 6 cm, 7 cm and 8 cm.
II. A cube of edge 7 cm.
(a) Cube will have more volume
(b) Both will have equal volume
(c) Cuboid will have more volume
(d) Cannot be determined

128. A hemispherical bowl made of iron has inner diameter 84 cm. Find the cost of tin plating it on the inside at the rate of ₹ 21 per 100 cm^2 (take $\pi = \frac{22}{7}$) correct to two places of decimal. SSC CGL (Tier-I) 2/12/2022 Shift-I

(a) ₹ 2328.48 (b) ₹ 2425.48
(c) ₹ 2425.60 (d) ₹ 2355.48

129. If the diameter of a sphere is 63 cm, then what is the total surface area of the sphere?
SSC CGL (Tier-I) 2/12/2022 Shift-I

(a) 11824 cm^2 (b) 12836 cm^2
(c) 12474 cm^2 (d) 11248 cm^2

130. What is the edge of a cube whose volume is equal to the sum of the volumes of the cubes of edge 6 cm, 8 cm and 10 cm?
SSC CGL (Tier-I) 1/12/2022 Shift-IV

(a) 5 cm (b) 3 cm
(c) 6 cm (d) 12 cm

131. A copper sphere of diameter 18 cm is drawn into a wire of diameter 6 mm. Find the length of the wire.
SSC CGL (Tier-I) 1/12/2022 Shift-III

(a) 143 m (b) 108 m
(c) 324 m (d) 234 m

132. The radius of a sphere and the base radius of a cone both are equal to $3\sqrt{2}$ cm. If the surface area of the sphere is the same as the total surface area of the right circular cone, then the height of the cone will be
SSC CGL (Tier-I) 1/12/2022 Shift-III

(a) 8 cm (b) $9\sqrt{2}$ cm
(c) $8\sqrt{2}$ cm (d) 12 cm

133. A hemisphere of lead of radius 4 cm is cast into a right circular cone of height 72 cm. What is the radius of the base of the cone?
SSC CGL (Tier-I) 1/12/2022 Shift-II

(a) 1.63 cm (b) 1.35 cm
(c) 1.33 cm (d) 1.45 cm

134. How many spherical lead shots each of diameter 8.4 cm can be obtained from a rectangular solid of lead with dimension 88 cm, 63 cm and 42 cm (take $\pi = \frac{22}{7}$)?
SSC CGL (Tier-I) 1/12/2022 Shift-I

(a) 920 (b) 750 (c) 650 (d) 860

135. The surface area of a cube is 13.5 m^2. What is the length (in m) of its diagonal?
SSC CGL (Tier-I) 24/8/2021 Shift-III

(a) $2\sqrt{3}$ (b) $1.5\sqrt{3}$
(c) 1.5 (d) 2

136. The volume of a wall whose height is 10 times its width and whose length is 8 times its height is 51.2 m^3. What is the cost (in ₹) of painting the wall on one side at the rate of ₹ 100/m^2?
SSC CGL (Tier-I) 20/8/2021 Shift-II

(a) 12800 (b) 12750
(c) 12250 (d) 12500

137. The curved surface area of a cylinder is 462 cm^2 and its base area is 346.5 cm^2. What is the volume (in cm^3) of the cylinder? (use $\pi = \frac{22}{7}$)
SSC CGL (Tier-I) 17/8/2021 Shift-I

(a) 2400 (b) 2425.5
(c) 4800 (d) 4850

138. A metallic sphere of diameter 40 cm is melted into smaller spheres of radius 0.5 cm. How many such small balls can be made?
SSC CGL (Tier-I) 6/3/2020 Shift-I

(a) 32000 (b) 3200
(c) 64000 (d) 6400

139. If the radius of a right circular cylinder is decreased by 10% and the height is increased by 20%, then the percentage increase/decrease in its volume is **SSC CGL (Tier-I) 5/3/2020 Shift-II**

(a) increase by 2.8%
(b) decrease by 1.8%
(c) increase by 1.8%
(d) decrease by 2.8%

SSC CPO SI 2024

140. Two rectangular sheets of paper, each 60 cm × 36 cm are made into two right circular cylinders, one by rolling the paper along its length and the other along the breadth.The ratio of the volumes of the two cylinders, thus formed, is
SSC CPO 29/06/2024 Shift-III

(a) 5 : 6 (b) 5 : 3
(c) 8 : 3 (d) 7 : 4

141. The ratio of the slant height and the height of a cone is 4 : 3. If the curved surface area of the cone is $4\sqrt{7}\pi$ square units, then the radius of the cone is .... units.
SSC CPO 29/06/2024 Shift-III

(a) 7 (b) $7\sqrt{7}$
(c) $\frac{\sqrt{7}}{7}$ (d) $\sqrt{7}$

142. If the radius of a sphere is increased by 20%, then find the percentage increase in its volume.
SSC CPO 29/06/2024 Shift-III

(a) 68.5% (b) 72.8%
(c) 70.6% (d) 75.5%

143. If the length and breadth of a cuboid are increased by 6% and 8% respectively, then the percentage increase in its volume (correct to two decimal places) is
SSC CPO 29/06/2024 Shift-III

(a) 11.48% (b) 13.96%
(c) 12.96% (d) 14.48%

144. Find the volume (in cm^3) of a hemisphere of radius 18 cm. (Use $\pi = \frac{22}{7}$) (Rounded off to two decimal places.)
SSC CPO 29/06/2024 Shift-II

(a) 12200.43 (b) 12219.43
(c) 18750.23 (d) 11250.25

145. Find the surface area (in m^2) of a cuboid that is 11 m long, 7 m broad and 4 m high. **SSC CPO 29/06/2024 Shift-II**

(a) 249 (b) 289
(c) 298 (d) 320

146. The total percentage change in the volume of a cuboid if its length and breadth are decreased by 15% and 25%, respectively, while its height is increased by 60% is
SSC CPO 29/06/2024 Shift-II

(a) 5% decrease (b) 2% decrease
(c) 2% increase (d) 5% increase

147. Melting a metal ball of radius 3 units, 27 identical dice and a ball of radius 1 units are made. What is the side of dice? **SSC CPO 29/06/2024 Shift-II**

(a) 1.7 units
(b) 1.5 units
(c) 1.4 units
(d) 1.6 units

148. The height of a cylinder is 8 cm and its area of the base is 20 cm^2. Find its volume? **SSC CPO 29/06/2024 Shift-II**

(a) 80 cm^3 (b) 180 cm^3
(c) 160 cm^3 (d) 100 cm^3

149. The height and radius of a cone-shaped storage tank are 9 ft. and 7 ft., respectively. Find the volume of water the tank can hold? (use $\pi = \frac{22}{7}$) **SSC CPO 29/06/2024 Shift-I**

(a) 1423 cubic ft. (b) 462 cubic ft.
(c) 1386 cubic ft. (d) 527 cubic ft.

150. A cone of slant height 4.2 units has a lateral surface area 13.2 $unit^2$. The radius of the base is
SSC CPO 29/06/2024 Shift-I

(a) 2 units (b) 1.5 units
(c) 2.5 units (d) 1 unit

151. A woman working in a company was supplied a rectangular solid (cuboid shape) of wax with dimensions 70 cm, 44 cm and 20 cm to prepare cylindrical candles, each 14 cm in diameter and 20 cm of height. Find the number of candles.
SSC CPO 29/06/2024 Shift-I

(a) 20 (b) 15 (c) 10 (d) 30

152. Find the curved surface area (in cm^2) of a cone of radius 3 cm and height 4 cm. **SSC CPO 29/06/2024 Shift-I**

(a) 12π (b) 14π
(c) 15π (d) 7π

153. The breadth of a room is twice its height and half its length. The volume of the room is 1728 m^3. The length of the room is
SSC CPO 29/06/2024 Shift-I

(a) 28 m (b) 20 m
(c) 34 m (d) 24 m

154. The area of the canvas cloth needed to erect a right conical tent of height 20 ft and circular base of circumference 30π ft is
SSC CPO 28/06/2024 Shift-III

(a) 375π sq.ft. (b) 589π sq.ft.
(c) 470π sq.ft. (d) 455π sq.ft

155. The curved surface area of a cone is 308 cm^2 and its slant height is 28 cm. Find the radius of its base. $\left(\text{use } \pi = \frac{22}{7}\right)$
SSC CPO 28/06/2024 Shift-III

(a) 3.5 cm (b) 2.8 cm
(c) 3.0 cm (d) 2.5 cm

156. The volume of a right circular cone is 150π cm^3 and its height is 18 cm. Find its slant height (in cm) (correct to 2 decimal places).
SSC CPO 28/06/2024 Shift-III

(a) 28.68 (b) 25.35 (c) 15.25 (d) 18.68

157. A solid metal cylinder of 12 cm height and 7 cm radius is melted and recast into two cones in the proportion of 1 : 2 (volume), keeping the height 12 cm. What would be the percentage change in the flat surface area before and after? [use $\pi = \frac{22}{7}$]
SSC CPO 28/06/2024 Shift-III

(a) 45% (b) 20% (c) 50% (d) 35%

158. A spherical box has surface area 528 cm^2. Find the radius of the spherical box. SSC CPO 28/06/2024 Shift-II

(a) $\sqrt{35}$ cm (b) $\sqrt{42}$ cm
(c) $\sqrt{29}$ cm (d) $\sqrt{37}$ cm

159. A cylinder has a radius of 7 cm and the area of its curved surface is 396 cm^2. The volume of the cylinder is
SSC CPO 28/06/2024 Shift-II

(a) 1381 cm^3 (b) 1391 cm^3
(c) 1386 cm^3 (d) 1396 cm^3

160. A hollow sphere of external and internal diameters of 10 cm and 6 cm, respectively, is melted and made into another solid in the shape of a right circular cone of base diameter 10 cm. Find the height of the cone.
SSC CPO 28/06/2024 Shift-II

(a) 13.68 cm (b) 16.68 cm
(c) 14.68 cm (d) 15.68 cm

161. A cylinder of radius 7 cm has a curved surface area of 2200 cm^2. Find its total surface area. $\left(\text{Use } \pi = \frac{22}{7}\right)$
SSC CPO 28/06/2024 Shift-II

(a) 2508 cm^2 (b) 2260 cm^2
(c) 2550 cm^2 (d) 1580 cm^2

162. If the radius of a sphere is increased by 125%, then by what percentage will its surface area increase (correct to two decimal places)?
SSC CPO 28/06/2024 Shift-II

(a) 509.54% (b) 409.76%
(c) 406.25% (d) 506.25%

163. The cost of painting a spherical vessel of diameter 14 cm is ₹ 21560. What is the cost of painting (in ₹) per square centimeter? $\left(\text{Use } \pi = \frac{22}{7}\right)$
SSC CPO 28/06/2024 Shift-I

(a) 32 (b) 35
(c) 28 (d) 30

164. One laddoo with a radius of 5 cm belongs to a shopkeeper. How many laddoos of radius 2.5 cm may be created from the same one laddoo?
SSC CPO 28/06/2024 Shift-I

(a) 8 (b) 4 (c) 6 (d) 2

165. The length of the side of a cube is 8 cm. Find the volume of the cube?
SSC CPO 28/06/2024 Shift-I

(a) 664 cm^3 (b) 612 cm^3
(c) 512 cm^3 (d) 564 cm^3

166. The radius of a hemispherical bowl is 9 cm. The capacity of the bowls is $\left(\text{Use, } \pi = \frac{22}{7}\right)$
SSC CPO 28/06/2024 Shift-I

(a) 1625.37 cm^3
(b) 1821.47 cm^3
(c) 1428.78 cm^3
(d) 1527.43 cm^3

167. The radius of the base and height of a cone are 5 cm and 6 cm, respectively, whereas the radius of the base and height of a cylinder and 2.5 cm and 3 cm, respectively. The ratio of the volume of the cone to that of the cylinder is $\left(\text{Where, } \pi = \frac{22}{7}\right)$
SSC CPO 28/06/2024 Shift-I

(a) 8 : 5 (b) 3 : 5
(c) 9 : 4 (d) 8 : 3

168. If the surface areas of two spheres are in the ratio of 9 :49, then the ratio of their volumes is (where, $\pi = \frac{22}{7}$)
SSC CPO 27/06/2024 Shift-III

(a) 27 : 343 (b) 16 : 216
(c) 25 : 512 (d) 49 : 363

169. A drainage tile is a cylindrical shell 42 cm long. The inside and outside diameters are 8 cm and 14 cm, respectively. What is the volume (in cm^3) of clay required for the tile ? (Use $\pi = \frac{22}{7}$)
SSC CPO 27/06/2024 Shift-III

(a) 4125 (b) 4881
(c) 4356 (d) 5241

170. If the radius of a sphere is increased by 40%, then find the percentage increase in its surface area.
SSC CPO 27/06/2024 Shift-III

(a) 85% (b) 88% (c) 96% (d) 92%

171. Find the surface area (in cm^2) of a sphere of diameter 28 cm. (use $\pi = \frac{22}{7}$)
SSC CPO 27/06/2024 Shift-III

(a) 1731 (b) 2856]
(c) 1724 (d) 2464

172. A rectangular sheet of metal is 60 cm by 25 cm. Equal squares of side 5 cm are cut off at the corners and the remainder is folded up to form an open rectangular box. Find the volume of the box.
SSC CPO 27/06/2024 Shift-III

(a) 3750 cm^3 (b) 5750 cm^3
(c) 4750 cm^3 (d) 2750 cm^3

173. The volume of a cube is four times the volume of a cuboid. If the sides of the cuboid are 32 cm, 8 cm and 4 cm, then find the ratio of the total surface area of the cube to that of the cuboid. SSC CPO 27/06/2024 Shift-II

(a) 24 : 13 (b) 22 : 13
(c) 21 : 13 (d) 23 : 13

174. A copper sphere of diameter 12 cm is drawn into a wire of diameter 4 mm. What is the length (in cm) of the wire? $\left(\text{where, } \pi = \frac{22}{7}\right)$
SSC CPO 27/06/2024 Shift-II

(a) 7823 (b) 8342
(c) 9000 (d) 7200

175. The volumes of two spheres are in the ratio of 512 : 3375. The ratio of their surface areas is
SSC CPO 27/06/2024 Shift-II

(a) 27 : 144 (b) 68 : 125
(c) 49 : 325 (d) 64 : 225

176. The length of the largest possible rod that can be placed in a cubical room is $42\sqrt{3}$m. The surface area (in m^2) of the largest possible sphere that fit within the cubical room is $\left[\text{Use, } \pi = \frac{22}{7}\right]$
SSC CPO 27/06/2024 Shift-II

(a) 5544 (b) 2564
(c) 3590 (d) 4589

177. If the radius of a sphere is 2.1 cm, then the volume of sphere is equal to
SSC CPO 27/06/2024 Shift-I

(a) 38.088 cm^3
(b) 36.808 cm^3
(c) 38.808 cm^3
(d) 36.088 cm^3

178. A hemispherical bowl is 88 cm round the brim. Assuming it to be full, how many persons may be served from it in hemispherical glasses, 7 cm in diameter at the top? $\left(\text{where } \pi = \frac{22}{7}\right)$
SSC CPO 27/06/2024 Shift-I

(a) 68 (b) 64 (c) 74 (d) 70

179. How many metres of cloth will be required to make a conical tent, the radius of whose base is 21 m and height is 28 m. The width of the cloth is 5 m. $\left(\text{where } \pi = \frac{22}{7}\right)$ **SSC CPO 27/06/2024 Shift-I**

(a) 478 (b) 462
(c) 456 (d) 470

180. What is the total surface area of a cone, whose radius is $\frac{r}{4}$ and slant height is $4l$? **SSC CPO 27/06/2024 Shift-I**

(a) $4\pi r(l+r)$ (b) $\pi r\left(l+\frac{r}{4}\right)$
(c) $\pi r\left(l+\frac{r}{16}\right)$ (d) $8\pi r(l+r)$

181. Find the total surface area of a hemisphere with a radius of 11 cm? **SSC CPO 27/06/2024 Shift-II**

(a) $242\pi cm^2$ (b) $313\pi cm^2$
(c) $363\pi cm^2$ (d) $273\pi cm^2$

SSC CPO SI 2023-2020

182. The number of balls, each one is 4 cm in the diameter that can be made from a solid metallic sphere of diameter 32 cm is **SSC CPO 5/10/2023 Shift-III**

(a) 256 (b) 64
(c) 512 (d) 1024

183. If the slant height of a cone is 29 cm and its height is 20 cm, find the ratio between the magnitudes of total surface area and the volume. **SSC CPO 5/10/2023 Shift-III**

(a) 5 : 14 (b) 7 : 15
(c) 3 : 7 (d) 3 : 14

184. Some ice pieces, spherical in shape, of diameter 6 cm are dropped in a cylindrical container containing some juice and are fully submerged. If the diameter of the container is 18 cm and level of juice rises by 40 cm, then how many ice pieces are dropped in the container? **SSC CPO 5/10/2023 Shift-III**

(a) 95 (b) 85 (c) 80 (d) 90

185. The radius of a metallic spherical ball is 3 cm. If the metallic ball is melted and recast into x number of hemispheres of radius equal to half the radius of the metallic spherical ball, then find the value of x. **SSC CPO 5/10/2023 Shift-III**

(a) 15 (b) 14 (c) 16 (d) 13

186. A hollow cylindrical tube made of plastic is 3 cm thick. If the external diameter is 20 cm and length of the tube is 49 cm, find the volume of the plastic. **SSC CPO 5/10/2023 Shift-III**

(a) $7238 cm^3$ (b) $7644 cm^3$
(c) $7546 cm^3$ (d) $7854 cm^3$

187. Some medicine in liquid form is prepared in a hemispherical container of diameter 36 cm. When the container is full of medicine, the medicine is transferred to small cylindrical bottles of diameter 6 cm and height 6 cm. How many bottles are required to empty the container? **SSC CPO 4/10/2023 Shift-II**

(a) 76 (b) 72 (c) 70 (d) 75

188. If the diameter of a sphere is reduced to its half, then the volume would be **SSC CPO 4/10/2023 Shift-II**

(a) increased by $\frac{1}{4}$ of the former volume
(b) reduced by $\frac{1}{4}$ of the former volume
(c) increased by $\frac{1}{8}$ of the former volume
(d) reduced by $\frac{1}{8}$ of the former volume

189. The height of two cones are in the ratio 7:5 and their diameters are in the ratio 10:21. What is the ratio of their volumes? $\left(\text{Where } \pi = \frac{22}{7}\right)$. **SSC CPO 4/10/2023 Shift-II**

(a) 26 : 47 (b) 14 : 19
(c) 20 : 63 (d) 17 : 21

190. The radii of two cylinders are in the ratio of 4 : 5 and their heights are in the ratio of 5 : 2. The ratio of their volume is **SSC CPO 3/10/2023 Shift-I**

(a) 9 : 4 (b) 2 : 1 (c) 9 : 7 (d) 8 : 5

191. If the height of a cone is 7 cm and the diameter of the circular base is 12 cm, then its volume is (nearest to integer) **SSC CPO 3/10/2023 Shift-I**

(a) $254 cm^3$ (b) $284 cm^3$
(c) $264 cm^3$ (d) $274 cm^3$

192. The radii of the ends of a frustum of a solid right-circular cone 45 cm height are 28 cm and 7 cm. If this frustum is melted and reconstructed into a solid right circular cylinder whose radius of base and height are in the ratio 3 : 5, then find the curved surface area (in cm^2) of this cylinder. [use $\pi = \frac{22}{7}$] **SSC CPO 3/10/2023 Shift-I**

(a) 4580 (b) 4610 (c) 4640 (d) 4620

193. A cone-shaped storage tank's height and radius are 9 and 7 feet, respectively. Determine how much liquid the tank can contain. (Take $\pi = 3.14$) **SSC CPO 11/11/2022 Shift-I**

(a) 471 cubic feet
(b) 450 cubic feet
(c) 435.32 cubic feet
(d) 461.58 cubic feet

194. A hall of 10 m length, 5 m width and 6 m height is to be painted (one side only). Determine the total surface area to be painted. (neglect the area of windows and doors)(floor area is not to be painted) **SSC CPO 11/11/2022 Shift-I**

(a) $300 m^2$ (b) $280 m^2$
(c) $330 m^2$ (d) $230 m^2$

195. What is the length of the longest rod that can be placed in a room of dimensions 12 m × 9 m × 8 m? **SSC CPO 11/11/2022 Shift-I**

(a) 15 m (b) 17 m
(c) 16 m (d) 14 m

196. A cylindrical tank of capacity 64π L has equal height and radius. What would be the radius of the cylinder? ($1 L = 1000 cm^3$) **SSC CPO 11/11/2022 Shift-I**

(a) 5 cm (b) 40 cm
(c) 50 cm (d) 4 cm

197. What is the total surface area of a cuboid whose length, breadth and height are 7 cm, 5 cm and 9 cm, respectively? **SSC CPO 10/11/2022 Shift-I**

(a) $190 cm^2$ (b) $403 cm^2$
(c) $286 cm^2$ (d) $386 cm^2$

198. The volume of a wall, six times as high as its breadth and half as long as its height, is $23958 cm^3$. What is the breadth of the wall? **SSC CPO 10/11/2022 Shift-I**

(a) 21 cm (b) 15 cm
(c) 11 cm (d) 18 cm

199. The curved surface area and circumference at the base of a solid right circular cylinder are $2200 cm^2$ and 110 cm, respectively. Find the height of the cylinder. **SSC CPO 10/11/2022 Shift-I**

(a) 24 cm (b) 22 cm
(c) 20 cm (d) 18 cm

200. How many metallic spheres, each of diameter 6 cm can be melted to mould into a solid cylinder of diameter 8 cm and height of 18 cm? **SSC CPO 10/11/2022 Shift-I**

(a) 6 (b) 12
(c) 8 (d) 10

201. A sphere is of radius 5 cm. What is the surface area of the sphere? **SSC CPO 10/11/2022 Shift-I**

(a) $100\pi cm^2$ (b) $150\pi cm^2$
(c) $200\pi cm^2$ (d) $120\pi cm^2$

202. What is the length of the longest pole that can fit itself in a hall 60 feet long, 30 feet broad and 20 feet high? **SSC CPO 10/11/2022 Shift-I**

(a) 50 feet (b) 70 feet
(c) 30 feet (d) 20 feet

203. If the volume of a sphere is $4851\ cm^3$, then its surface area (in cm^2) is $\left(\text{take}\ \pi = \frac{22}{7}\right)$
SSC CPO 25/11/2020 Shift-II
(a) 1427 (b) 1386
(c) 1399 (d) 1268

204. The ratio of the total surface area and volume of a sphere is 2 : 7. Its radius is SSC CPO 25/11/2020 Shift-II
(a) 7.5 cm (b) 10.5 cm
(c) 10 cm (d) 7 cm

205. The internal length, breadth and height of a cuboidal room are 12 m, 8 m and 10 m, respectively. The total cost (in ₹) of whitewashing only all four walls of the room at the cost of ₹ 25 per m^2, is SSC CPO 25/11/2020 Shift-II
(a) 12600 (b) 10000
(c) 11400 (d) 18000

206. Let *A* and *B* be two cylinders such that the capacity of *A* is the same as the capacity of *B*. The ratio of the diameters of *A* and *B* is 1 : 4. What is the ratio of the heights of *A* and *B*?
SSC CPO 25/11/2020 Shift-II
(a) 16 : 1 (b) 16 : 3
(c) 3 : 16 (d) 1 : 16

207. The radius of the base of a cylinder is 14 cm and its volume is $6160\ cm^3$. The curved surface area (in cm^2) is $\left(\text{Take}\ \pi = \frac{22}{7}\right)$
SSC CPO 25/11/2020 Shift-I
(a) 778 (b) 880
(c) 660 (d) 940

208. A solid metallic cube of side 9 cm and a solid metallic cuboid having dimensions 5 cm, 13 cm, 31 cm are melted to form a single cube. How much (in ₹) is the cost to polish the new cube at a rate of ₹ 10 per cm^2?
SSC CPO 24/11/2020 Shift-I
(a) 8650 (b) 27440
(c) 13620 (d) 11760

209. A solid lead sphere of radius 11 cm is melted and recast into small solid spheres of radius 2 cm each. How many maximum number (in integer) of such spheres can be made?
SSC CPO 24/11/2020 Shift-I
(a) 125 (b) 166
(c) 30 (d) 100

210. The radius of the base of a cylinder is 14 cm and its curved surface area is $880\ cm^2$. Its volume (in cm^3) is $\left(\text{take}\ \pi = \frac{22}{7}\right)$ SSC CPO 23/11/2020 Shift-I
(a) 3080
(b) 1078
(c) 6160
(d) 9240

SSC CHSL 2024 (Tier I & II)

211. The surface area of a cube is $1728\ cm^3$. Find its volume.
SSC CHSL (Tier-II) 18/11/2024
(a) $4356\sqrt{2}\ cm^3$
(b) $3456\sqrt{2}\ cm^3$
(c) $6453\sqrt{2}\ cm^3$
(d) $5436\sqrt{2}\ cm^3$

212. A cylinder has a radius of $\frac{8}{\pi}$ cm and its volume is $448\ cm^3$. What is the height of the cylinder $\left(\text{take}\ \pi = \frac{22}{7}\right)$? SSC CHSL (Tier-II) 18/11/2024
(a) 21 cm (b) 23 cm
(c) 22 cm (d) 24 cm

213. For making a toy, a hemisphere is attached at one end of a cylinder and a cone is attached at the other end of the cylinder. The cylinder, the cone and the hemisphere have a common radius of 4.2 cm. The height of the cylinder and that of the cone is 7 cm. Find the volume (in cm^3) of the toy . $\left(\text{use}\ \pi = \frac{22}{7}\right)$ SSC CHSL (Tier-II) 18/11/2024
(a) 863.25 (b) 762.255
(c) 672.672 (d) 358.8

214. The radii of the two spheres are in the ratio 4 : 5. Their volume will be in the ratio
(a) 125 : 64 (b) 4 : 5
(c) 16 : 25 (d) 64 : 125

215. The volume of rectangular block is $12288\ m^3$. Its dimension are in the ratio of 4 : 3 : 2 . If the entire surface is polished at the rate 2 paise per m^2, then find the total cost of polishing.
SSC CHSL (Tier-I) 11/07/2024 Shift-IV
(a) ₹ 33.28 (b) ₹ 44.42
(c) ₹ 66.56 (d) ₹ 11.14

216. A cylindrical candle, 14 cm in diameter and length 2 cm is melted to form a cuboid candle of dimensions 7 cm × 11 cm × 2 cm. How many cuboidal candles can be obtained?
SSC CHSL (Tier-I) 11/07/2024 Shift-IV
(a) 4 (b) 5
(c) 2 (d) 3

217. The surface area of a spherical ball is $1386\ cm^2$. What will be its volume?
SSC CHSL (Tier-I) 11/07/2024 Shift-III
(a) $4825\ cm^3$ (b) $5000\ cm^3$
(c) $4851\ cm^3$ (d) $4800\ cm^3$

218. Find the whole surface area of a cuboid having a length of 19 cm, breadth of 9 cm and height of 4.5 cm.
SSC CHSL (Tier-I) 11/07/2024 Shift-III
(a) $619\ cm^2$ (b) $497\ cm^2$
(c) $917\ cm^2$ (d) $594\ cm^2$

219. A hemispherical bowl is made of silver and has an inner diameter of 4 cm, if the thickness of silver is 0.5 cm. Find the volume of silver used in making the bowl correct to two places of decimals (use π = 3.14)
SSC CHSL (Tier-I) 11/07/2024 Shift-II
(a) $15.96\ cm^3$ (b) $51.96\ cm^3$
(c) $15.69\ cm^3$ (d) $51.69\ cm^3$

220. Three cubes each of side 5 cm are joined end to end. The surface area of the resulting cuboid is
SSC CHSL (Tier-I) 11/07/2024 Shift-II
(a) $150\ cm^2$ (b) $175\ cm^2$
(c) $350\ cm^2$ (d) $75\ cm^2$

221. Find the surface area (in cm^2) of a cardboard box in th shape of a cuboid, whose length is 60 cm, breadth is half its length and height is one-third of its breadth.
SSC CHSL (Tier-I) 11/07/2024 Shift-I
(a) 2700 (b) 5400
(c) 10800 (d) 8100

222. A solid metallic sphere of radius 6 cm is melted and recast into spherical balls of radius 3 cm. The number of spherical balls thus obtained is
SSC CHSL (Tier-I) 11/07/2024 Shift-I
(a) 6 (b) 10 (c) 4 (d) 8

223. If the surface area of the sphere is $616\ cm^2$, then the radius of the sphere is equal to
SSC CHSL (Tier-I) 10/07/2024 Shift-IV
(a) 18.0 cm (b) 14.0 cm
(c) 7.0 cm (d) 3.5 cm

224. A solid metallic cube having surface area of $54\ cm^2$ is melted to form smaller cubes of surface area $\frac{8}{12}\ cm^2$ each. Find the number of smaller cubes. SSC CHSL (Tier-I) 10/07/2024 Shift-IV
(a) 729 (b) 216 (c) 343 (d) 512

225. If the surface areas of two spheres are in the ratio of 49 : 81, then find the ratio of their volumes.
SSC CHSL (Tier-I) 10/07/2024 Shift-IV
(a) 27 : 64 (b) 125 : 512
(c) 343 : 729 (d) 216 : 512

226. An article is of size 9 cm × 6 cm × 3 cm. The number of such articles that can be packed in a box measuring 63 cm × 42 cm × 21 cm is
SSC CHSL (Tier-I) 10/07/2024 Shift-III
(a) 343 (b) 243
(c) 49 (d) 196

227. A cuboid with dimensions 20 cm, 12 cm and 10 cm is cut into 8 identical pieces by 3 cuts. What will be the total surface area of all the pieces? SSC CHSL (Tier-I) 10/07/2024 Shift-III
(a) $1680\ cm^2$ (b) $3360\ cm^2$
(c) $2240\ cm^2$ (d) $1220\ cm^2$

228. The curved surface area of a right circular cone is 20π cm^2. If its radius is 4 cm, then find the volume of cone.
SSC CHSL (Tier-I) 10/07/2024 Shift-II
(a) 18π cm^3 (b) 21π cm^3
(c) 20π cm^3 (d) 16π cm^3

229. A cube of edge 4 cm is cut into cubes each of edge of 2 cm. The ratio of the total surface area of one of the small cubes to that of the large cube is equal to **SSC CHSL (Tier-I) 10/07/2024 Shift-II**
(a) 1 : 64 (b) 1 : 16
(c) 1 : 4 (d) 1 : 8

230. The volume of the hemisphere (to the nearest integer) with a radius of 5.5 cm is (use $\pi = 3.14$)
SSC CHSL (Tier-I) 10/07/2024 Shift-II
(a) 378 cm^3 (b) 325 cm^3
(c) 348 cm^3 (d) 362 cm^3

231. A cuboidal water purifier can carry 10 L of water. Its breadth is $\frac{1}{5}$ of its height and length is $\frac{1}{3}$ of the sum of the breadth and height. The height of the tank is
SSC CHSL (Tier-I) 10/07/2024 Shift-I
(a) 80 cm (b) 10 cm
(c) 20 cm (d) 50 cm

232. A patient in a hospital is given tea daily in a cylindrical cup of diameter 7 cm. If the cup is filled with tea to a height of 4 cm, how much tea the hospital has to prepare daily to serve 180 patients? $\left(\text{Use } \pi = \frac{22}{7}\right)$
SSC CHSL (Tier-I) 10/07/2024 Shift-I
(a) 22.27 L
(b) 22.77 L
(c) 27.27 L
(d) 27.72 L

233. A metallic sphere of volume 3136π cm^3 is melted and then, recast into smaller cones, each of radius 3.5 cm and height 4 cm. How many cones are obtained?
SSC CHSL (Tier-I) 09/07/2024 Shift-IV
(a) 148 (b) 192 (c) 196 (d) 172

234. Find the number of paper balls, each 2 cm in diameter, that can be made from a sphere of diameter 18 cm.
SSC CHSL (Tier-I) 09/07/2024 Shift-IV
(a) 1020 (b) 625
(c) 729 (d) 484

235. The area of three adjacent faces of a cuboidal box is 120 cm^2, 72 cm^2 and 60 cm^2, respectively. Find the volume (in cm^3) of the box.
SSC CHSL (Tier-I) 09/07/2024 Shift-III
(a) 425 (b) 650
(c) 720 (d) 864

236. If the radius of the base and slant height of the cone is 6 cm and 10 cm, respectively, then the volume of the cone is equal to
SSC CHSL (Tier-I) 09/07/2024 Shift-III
(a) 98π cm^3 (b) 106π cm^3
(c) 96π cm^3 (d) 108π cm^3

237. Two cubes have their volumes in the ratio 1 : 125. Find the ratio of their surface areas.
SSC CHSL (Tier-I) 09/07/2024 Shift-II
(a) 1 : 125 (b) 1 : 25
(c) 25 : 1 (d) 1 : 5

238. A closed cylindrical tank of radius 1.5 m and height 3 m is made from a sheet of metal, how much sheet of metal is required to do it?
SSC CHSL (Tier-I) 09/07/2024 Shift-II
(a) 42.24 m^2 (b) 22.42 m^2
(c) 42.42 m^2 (d) 24.24 m^2

239. How many cubes of edge 15 cm can be put in a cubical box of 3 m edge?
SSC CHSL (Tier-I) 09/07/2024 Shift-II
(a) 9000 (b) 1050
(c) 8000 (d) 2000

240. If the areas of three adjacent faces of a cuboid are 5 cm^2, 15 cm^2 and 27 cm^2, respectively, the surface area of the cuboid is
SSC CHSL (Tier-I) 09/07/2024 Shift-I
(a) 45 cm^2 (b) 75 cm^2
(c) 47 cm^2 (d) 94 cm^2

241. A cylinder has a curved surface area equal to 350% of the curved surface area of another cylinder. If their radii are in the ratio 3 : 1, then the volume of the smaller cylinder is approximately .... % of the larger cylinder (the smaller cylinder has its radius and height smaller, when compared to the larger).
SSC CHSL (Tier-I) 09/07/2024 Shift-I
(a) 9.52 (b) 8.86 (c) 7.28 (d) 10.16

242. If lateral surface area of a cube is 144 cm^2, then find its volume.
SSC CHSL (Tier-I) 09/07/2024 Shift-I
(a) 216 cm^3 (b) 117.58 cm^3
(c) 1728 cm^3 (d) 864 cm^3

243. A covered wooden box has the inner measures as 128 cm, 90 cm, 25 cm and the thickness of wood is 5.5 cm. Find the volume of the wood.
SSC CHSL (Tier-I) 09/07/2024 Shift-I
(a) 329431 cm^3 (b) 217404 cm^3
(c) 819832 cm^3 (d) 192392 cm

244. Two cubes, each of edge 5 cm, are joined face to face. Find the surface area of the cuboid thus formed.
SSC CHSL (Tier-I) 08/07/2024 Shift-IV
(a) 300 cm^2 (b) 125 cm^2
(c) 200 cm^2 (d) 250 cm^2

245. The inner and outer radii of a hemispherical wooden bowl are 6 cm and 8 cm, respectively. Its entire surface has to be polished and the cost of polishing π cm^2 is ₹ 50. How much will it cost to polish the bowl?
SSC CHSL (Tier-I) 08/07/2024 Shift-IV
(a) ₹ 12000 (b) ₹ 10000
(c) ₹ 11600 (d) ₹ 11400

246. Find the cost of painting a ball that is in the shape of a sphere with a radius of 14 cm. The painting cost of the ball is ₹ 5 per square centimetre $\left(\text{take } \pi = \frac{22}{7}\right)$.
SSC CHSL (Tier-I) 08/07/2024 Shift-IV
(a) ₹ 12320 (b) ₹ 13220
(c) ₹ 13022 (d) ₹ 12230

247. A solid metallic cylinder of base radius 6 cm and height 10 cm is melted to form small cylinders, each of height 2.5 cm and base radius 2 cm. Find the number of small cylinders.
SSC CHSL (Tier-I) 08/07/2024 Shift-III
(a) 32 (b) 36
(c) 80 (d) 360

248. If the radius of a sphere is increased by 3.5 cm, its surface area increases by 550 cm^2. What was the original radius of the sphere? $\left(\text{use } \pi = \frac{22}{7}\right)$
SSC CHSL (Tier-I) 08/07/2024 Shift-II
(a) 4.5 cm (b) 3.5 cm
(c) 4 cm (d) 6 cm

249. A metallic solid cuboid of dimensions 36 cm × 22 cm × 12 cm is melted and recast in the form of cubes of side 6 cm. Find the number of the cubes so formed.
SSC CHSL (Tier-I) 08/07/2024 Shift-II
(a) 46 (b) 43 (c) 45 (d) 44

250. If the radius of a sphere is increased by 5%, then by what percentage will the surface area of the sphere increase?
SSC CHSL (Tier-I) 08/07/2024 Shift-I
(a) 13.25% (b) 11.25%
(c) 10.25% (d) 15.25%

251. A solid sphere of radius 8 cm is melted and then recast into small spherical balls each of diameter 4 cm. Find the number of balls thus obtained $\left(\text{use } \pi = \frac{22}{7}\right)$.
SSC CHSL (Tier-I) 08/07/2024 Shift-I
(a) 48 (b) 64 (c) 24 (d) 32

252. The whole surface area of a cube is 294 cm^2. The volume of the cube is
SSC CHSL (Tier-I) 05/07/2024 Shift-IV
(a) 243 cm^3 (b) 343 cm^3
(c) 512 cm^3 (d) 216 cm^3

253. The diameter of a roller is 35 cm and its length is 100 cm. It takes 200 complete revolutions to level a playground. Find the area of the playground (in m^2).
SSC CHSL (Tier-I) 05/07/2024 Shift-IV

(a) 110000 (b) 110
(c) 22000000 (d) 220

254. If three spheres of radius 75 cm, 60 cm and 45 cm are melted into one big sphere, then the radius of the big sphere is
SSC CHSL (Tier-I) 05/07/2024 Shift-III

(a) 90 cm (b) 85 cm
(c) 95 cm (d) 80 cm

255. Find the percentage increase in surface area of a cube by triple each side. **SSC CHSL (Tier-I) 05/07/2024 Shift-III**

(a) 800% (b) 650%
(c) 700% (d) 500%

256. If the length, breadth and total surface area of a cuboid are 30 cm, 20 cm and 2600 cm^2, respectively, then find its height.
SSC CHSL (Tier-I) 05/07/2024 Shift-III

(a) 30 cm (b) 15 cm
(c) 50 cm (d) 14 cm

257. The diameter of the base of a cylindrical tank is 28 cm and its height is 42 cm. Find its curved surface area.
SSC CHSL (Tier-I) 05/07/2024 Shift-II

(a) 3680 cm^2
(b) 3690 cm^2
(c) 3696 cm^2
(d) 3686 cm^2

258. A solid copper sphere of radius 9 cm is drawn into a wire of radius 4 mm. Find the length of the wire.
SSC CHSL (Tier-I) 05/07/2024 Shift-II

(a) 60.75 m (b) 70.25 m
(c) 65.25 m (d) 20.75 m

259. Rajesh is playing with a football having diameter of 28 cm. He wants to get a photo of his favourite player painted on the entire ball. The painter charges ₹ 2/cm^2. What will be the cost (in ₹) of painting the ball $\left(\text{take } \pi = \frac{22}{7}\right)$?
SSC CHSL (Tier-I) 05/07/2024 Shift-I

(a) 4928 (b) 4828
(c) 2414 (d) 2464

260. A cylindrical oil tank has a radius of 5 m and a total surface area of 628 m^2, what would be its curved surface area? (round off to the second decimal place)
SSC CHSL (Tier-I) 05/07/2024 Shift-I

(a) 371.83 m^2 (b) 401.43 m^2
(c) 470.8 m^2 (d) 481.43 m^2

261. The length, breadth and height of a cuboid are in ratio of 3 : 4 : 5. If the volume of the cuboid is 1620 m^3, find the total surface area of the cuboid.
SSC CHSL (Tier-I) 05/07/2024 Shift-I

(a) 646 m^2 (b) 846 m^2
(c) 423 m^2 (d) 712 m^2

262. 3 solid spheres of diameters 6 cm, 8 cm and 10 cm are melted together to form a single solid sphere. Find its radius. **SSC CHSL (Tier-I) 04/07/2024 Shift-IV**

(a) 12 cm (b) 9 cm
(c) 3 cm (d) 6 cm

263. If the height of a solid right circular cylinder is 27 cm and diameter of its base is 30 cm, the total surface area (in cm^2) of the right circular cylinder is $\left(\text{Take } \pi = \frac{22}{7}\right)$
SSC CHSL (Tier-I) 04/07/2024 Shift-IV

(a) 3976 (b) 3964
(c) 3978 (d) 3960

264. The ratio of the lateral surface area to the total surface area of a cylinder with base diameter 60 cm and height 10 cm is
SSC CHSL (Tier-I) 04/07/2024 Shift-IV

(a) 1 : 9 (b) 1 : 7
(c) 1 : 4 (d) 1 : 3

265. Find the capacity of an overhead cylindrical water tank, in litres, whose radius is 2.1 m and height is 6.3 m. **SSC CHSL (Tier-I) 04/07/2024 Shift-III**

(a) 61802 (b) 87318
(c) 611726 (d) 65622

266. The total surface area of a solid hemisphere of diameter 28 cm is
SSC CHSL (Tier-I) 04/07/2024 Shift-III

(a) 1784 cm^2
(b) 1488 cm^2
(c) 1648 cm^2
(d) 1848 cm^2

267. The diameter of a cylinder is 14 cm and its height is 9 cm. Find the total surface area of the cylinder.
SSC CHSL (Tier-I) 04/07/2024 Shift-III

(a) 708 cm^2 (b) 714 cm^2
(c) 704 cm^2 (d) 700 cm^2

268. What is the curved surface area of cylinder, whose radius is 3 cm and height is 14 cm? $\left(\text{Take } \pi = \frac{22}{7}\right)$
SSC CHSL (Tier-I) 04/07/2024 Shift-II

(a) 262 cm^2 (b) 264 cm^2
(c) 263 cm^2 (d) 261 cm^2

269. The radius of a sphere is increased by 25%. What is the increase per cent in surface area?
SSC CHSL (Tier-I) 04/07/2024 Shift-II

(a) 56.25% (b) 36.45%
(c) 25.25% (d) 15.55%

270. If the diameter of the base and curved surfaced area of a cylinder are 14cm and 352 cm^2, respectively, then the total surface area of the cylinder is equal to
SSC CHSL (Tier-I) 04/07/2024 Shift-I

(a) 660 cm^2 (b) 760 cm^2
(c) 754 cm^2 (d) 654 cm^2

271. The edges of a rectangular box are in the ratio of 3 : 5 : 8, and its surface area is 632 cm^2. What will be the volume of the box?
SSC CHSL (Tier-I) 04/07/2024 Shift-I

(a) 801 cm^3 (b) 990 cm^3
(c) 510 cm^3 (d) 960 cm^3

272. Three solid cubes of metal have sides 6 cm, 8 cm and 10 cm, respectively. They are melted to form a new cube. What is the surface area of this new cube? **SSC CHSL (Tier-I) 04/07/2024 Shift-I**

(a) 915 cm^2 (b) 864 cm^2
(c) 950 cm^2 (d) 812 cm^2

273. A cylindrical rod of iron, whose height is 12 times its radius, is melted and cast into spherical balls, each of one-third the radius of the cylinder. Find the number of spherical balls.
SSC CHSL (Tier-I) 03/07/2024 Shift-IV

(a) 224 (b) 212 (c) 243 (d) 198

274. Four cubes each of volume 216 cubic cm are joined end to end to form a new solid. The surface area of the new solid is **SSC CHSL (Tier-I) 03/07/2024 Shift-IV**

(a) 1296 sq cm (b) 648 sq cm
(c) 672 sq cm (d) 324 sq cm

275. If the radius of a sphere is increased by 12 per cent, then the volume will be increased by approximately
SSC CHSL (Tier-I) 03/07/2024 Shift-III

(a) 42.5% (b) 45.49%
(c) 40.49% (d) 41.49%

276. If the height of a right circular cone is 24 cm and radius of its base is 10.5 cm, then the volume of right circular cone (in cm^3) is $\left(\text{Take } \pi = \frac{22}{7}\right)$
SSC CHSL (Tier-I) 03/07/2024 Shift-III

(a) 2772 (b) 2727 (c) 2237 (d) 2277

277. If the surface area of cuboid is 108 m^2, then find the height of the cuboid, whose length is 6 m and breadth is 3 m. **SSC CHSL (Tier-I) 03/07/2024 Shift-II**

(a) 4.5 m (b) 4 m (c) 5 m (d) 5.5 m

278. The curved surface area, of a right circular cylinder of height 14 cm, is 88 cm^2. Find the total surface area of the cylinder.
SSC CHSL (Tier-I) 03/07/2024 Shift-II

(a) $\frac{560}{7}$ cm^2 (b) $\frac{360}{7}$ cm^2
(c) $\frac{660}{7}$ cm^2 (d) $\frac{460}{7}$ cm^2

279. The heights of two cones are in the ratio of 5 : 3 and their radii are in the ratio 6 : 5. Find the ratio of their volumes. SSC CHSL (Tier-I) 03/07/2024 Shift-I

(a) 11 : 5 (b) 10 : 5
(c) 12 : 5 (d) 13 : 5

280. If the radius of a sphere is doubled, then the volume of the sphere becomes _____ times the previous volume. SSC CHSL (Tier-I) 03/07/2024 Shift-I

(a) eight (b) two
(c) four (d) one

281. The internal length, breadth and height of a cardboard box are 6 cm, 10 cm and 12 cm, respectively. How many boxes are needed in which cubes, whose volume is 2160 cm^3 can be packed?

SSC CHSL (Tier-I) 03/07/2024 Shift-I

(a) 4 (b) 3 (c) 6 (d) 5

282. The radius and height of a cylinder are in the ratio 6 : 7 and its volume is 792 cm^3. Calculate its curved surface area in cm^2.

SSC CHSL (Tier-I) 02/07/2024 Shift-IV

(a) 490 (b) 226
(c) 264 (d) 262

283. The outer surface of a sphere having diameter 10 m is painted at the rate of ₹ $\frac{80}{\pi}$ per m^2. What is the cost of painting?

SSC CHSL (Tier-I) 02/07/2024 Shift-IV

(a) ₹ 4000 (b) ₹ 6000
(c) ₹ 8000 (d) ₹ 9000

284. If the diameter of a hemisphere is 42 cm, then the volume of hemisphere (in cm^3) is $\left(\text{Take } \pi = \frac{22}{7}\right)$

SSC CHSL (Tier-I) 02/07/2024 Shift-III

(a) 19404 (b) 19254
(c) 19154 (d) 19444

285. Find the difference between the curved surface area and total surface area of a right circular cylinder having a length of 68 cm and base diameter of 28 cm.

SSC CHSL (Tier-I) 02/07/2024 Shift-III

(a) 1432 cm^2
(b) 1132 cm^2
(c) 1332 cm^2
(d) 1232 cm^2

286. An iron box with external dimensions 60 cm, 40 cm and 20 cm is made of 1 cm thick sheet. If 1 cm^3 of iron weighs 50 gm, the weight of the empty box is

SSC CHSL (Tier-I) 02/07/2024 Shift-III

(a) 214.05 kg (b) 240 kg
(c) 400 kg (d) 416.40 kg

287. If the brick size is 25 cm × 12 cm × 9 cm, then how many bricks are required to construct a wall of length 10 m, breadth 22.5 cm and height 6 m? SSC CHSL (Tier-I) 02/07/2024 Shift-II

(a) 6000 (b) 4500
(c) 5000 (d) 8000

288. A hemisphere has a radius of 6.2 cm. Find its total surface area (use $\pi = 3.14$) (round off to two decimal places). SSC CHSL (Tier-I) 02/07/2024 Shift-II

(a) 282.25 cm^2 (b) 358.52 cm^2
(c) 276.35 cm^2 (d) 362.10 cm^2

289. The capacity of a cylinder tank is 8316 cm^3 . If the radius of its base is 21 cm, then find the depth of the tank. SSC CHSL (Tier-I) 02/07/2024 Shift-I

(a) 4 cm (b) 8 cm
(c) 10 cm (d) 6 cm

290. If the diameter of a hemisphere is 21 cm, then the curved surface area (in cm^2) of the hemisphere is $\left(\text{Take } \pi = \frac{22}{7}\right)$

SSC CHSL (Tier-I) 02/07/2024 Shift-I

(a) 693 (b) 963
(c) 939 (d) 639

291. Find the diameter of a spherical ball, whose volume is 38.808 cm^3. $\left(\text{use } \pi = \frac{22}{7}\right)$

SSC CHSL (Tier-I) 01/07/2024 Shift-IV

(a) 4.2 cm (b) 4.8 cm
(c) 4.6 cm (d) 4.4 cm

292. If the side of a cube is 3 units,which of the following options is equal to the ratio between the surface area and the volume of the cube?

SSC CHSL (Tier-I) 01/07/2024 Shift-IV

(a) 2 : 5 (b) 2 : 7
(c) 2 : 1 (d) 2 : 3

293. The surface area of a sphere is 2464 cm^2. Find its volume.

SSC CHSL (Tier-I) 01/07/2024 Shift-IV

(a) $13121\frac{1}{3}$ cm^3 (b) $11892\frac{2}{3}$ cm^3

(c) $11498\frac{2}{3}$ cm^3 (d) $11621\frac{1}{3}$ cm^3

294. The radius of a roller is 49 cm and its length is 200 cm. It takes 700 complete revolutions to move once over to level a playground. Find the area of the playground. $\left(\text{use } \pi = \frac{22}{7}\right)$

SSC CHSL (Tier-I) 01/07/2024 Shift-III

(a) 4312×10^3 cm^2
(b) 4312×10^2 cm^2
(c) 4322×10^4 cm^2
(d) 4312×10^4 cm^3

295. The curved surface area of a cone is 2200 cm^2 and its radius is 28 cm, what is the slant height (in cm) of the cone? $\left(\text{use } \pi = \frac{22}{7}\right)$

SSC CHSL (Tier-I) 01/07/2024 Shift-III

(a) 25 (b) 24
(c) 22 (d) 23

296. The sides of a cuboid are in the ratio 3 : 4 : 5 and its surface area is equal to the surface area of the cube with side 6 units. What is the approximate volume of the cuboid?

SSC CHSL (Tier-I) 01/07/2024 Shift-II

(a) 210 (b) 150
(c) 240 (d) 180

297. The surface areas of two spheres are in the ratio 25 : 36. What is the ratio of their volumes?

SSC CHSL (Tier-I) 01/07/2024 Shift-II

(a) $\frac{25}{36}$ (b) $\frac{36}{115}$ (c) $\frac{125}{216}$ (d) $\frac{36}{125}$

298. The respective ratio between numerical values of the curved surface area and the volume of a right circular cylinder is 2 : 3. If the respective ratio between the radius and the height of the cylinder is 3 : 7, what is the total surface area of the cylinder?

SSC CHSL (Tier-I) 01/07/2024 Shift-II

(a) 62π cm^2 (b) 60π cm^2
(c) 45π cm^2 (d) 65π cm^2

299. The surface area of a cube is 486 cm^2. Find the volume.

SSC CHSL (Tier-I) 01/07/2024 Shift-I

(a) 486 cm^3 (b) 729 cm^3
(c) 625 cm^3 (d) 512 cm^3

300. The ratio of the diameters of two spheres is given as 1 : 4. The larger sphere is melted and 125 identical spheres are made out of the molten material. The smaller sphere is melted and 27 identical spheres are made out of the molten material. If the ratio of the volume of each of the 125 identical spheres to the volume of each of the 27 identical spheres is given as 1 : m, what is the value of m?

SSC CHSL (Tier-I) 01/07/2024 Shift-I

(a) $\frac{1728}{125}$ (b) $\frac{27}{8000}$
(c) $\frac{125}{1728}$ (d) $\frac{64}{3375}$

301. A largest possible sphere is carved from a cube of side 14 cm. What is its volume in cm^3?

SSC CHSL (Tier-I) 01/07/2024 Shift-I

(a) $1600\frac{1}{3}$ (b) $1437\frac{1}{3}$

(c) $205\frac{1}{3}$ (d) $1707\frac{1}{3}$

302. The base of a right prism is an equilateral triangle, whose each side is 4 cm. If the lateral surface area is 120 cm^2, then find the volume (in cm^3) of the prism
SSC CHSL (Tier-I) 01/07/2024 Shift-I
(a) $10\sqrt{3}$ (b) $20\sqrt{3}$
(c) $30\sqrt{3}$ (d) $40\sqrt{3}$

303. A right rectangular box's measurement are 1.6 m long, 90 cm wide, 60 cm in height. Soap cakes of measurement 6 cm × 5 cm × 40 mm are to be packed in the box, so that no space is left. How many cakes can be packed in the box?
SSC CHSL (Tier II) 10/1/2024 Shift-I
(a) 6000 (b) 5600
(c) 6500 (d) 7200

304. A hollow cube is made of paper to have a volume of 512 cubic units. How much paper in square units will be required to make the cube?
SSC CHSL (Tier II) 10/1/2024 Shift-I
(a) 328 (b) 348 (c) 288 (d) 384

SSC CHSL 2023-2021 (Tier I & II)

305. The diameter of a hemispherical bowl is 21 cm. The volume of the bowl is equal to $\left(\text{use } \pi = \frac{22}{7}\right)$
SSC CHSL (Tier II) 02/11/2023 Shift-I
(a) 2624.5 cm^3 (b) 2524.5 cm^3
(c) 2725.5 cm^3 (d) 2425.5 cm^3

306. The radius and height of a right circular cone is increased by 25%. Find the increase in percentage of the volume of the cone (rounded off to 2 decimal places).
SSC CHSL (Tier II) 2/11/2023 Shift-I
(a) 95.31% (b) 94.51%
(c) 93.51% (d) 94.31%

307. The diameter of a sphere is increased by 30%. What is the percentage increase in its volume?
SSC CHSL (Tier II) 2/11/2023 Shift-I
(a) 41.7% (b) 119.7%
(c) 69% (d) 90.5%

308. A hemispherical bowl is made of 1 cm thick steel. The inside radius of the bowl is 4 cm. The volume of the steel (in cm^2) used in making the bowl is SSC CHSL (Tier I) 17/8/2023 Shift-I
(a) $40\frac{2}{3}\pi$ (b) $27\frac{1}{3}\pi$
(c) $41\frac{1}{3}\pi$ (d) $35\frac{1}{3}\pi$

309. The curved surface area of a right circular cone of diameter 42 cm is 990 cm^2. What is the slant height (in cm) of the cone? $\left[\text{use } \pi = \frac{22}{7}\right]$
SSC CHSL (Tier I) 14/8/2023 Shift-IV
(a) 10 (b) 15 (c) 24 (d) 12

310. The total surface area of a solid hemisphere of diameter 14 cm is (use $\pi = \frac{22}{7}$)
SSC CHSL (Tier I) 11/8/2023 Shift-I
(a) 522 cm^2 (b) 462 cm^2
(c) 428 cm^2 (d) 584 cm^2

311. The volume of a solid sphere is 4500 π cm^3. The surface area of the solid sphere is SSC CHSL (Tier I) 9/8/2023 Shift-I
(a) 700π cm^2 (b) 850π cm^2
(c) 900π cm^2 (d) 810π cm^2

312. If the volume of a cube is 729 cm^3, then find the total surface area of the cube. SSC CHSL (Tier I) 8/8/2023 Shift-I
(a) 484 cm^2 (b) 482 cm^2
(c) 488 cm^2 (d) 486 cm^2

313. Find the volume of the largest right circular cone that can be cut out from a cube whose edge is $3\frac{1}{2}$ cm, correct to two places of decimals $\left(\text{use } \pi = \frac{22}{7}\right)$
SSC CHSL (Tier I) 7/8/2023 Shift-IV
(a) 13.21 cm^3 (b) 21.31 cm^3
(c) 11.23 cm^3 (d) 12.13 cm^3

314. The sides of the three cubes of metal are 15 cm, 18 cm and 25 cm, respectively. Find the side (in cm) of the new cube formed by melting these cubes together.
SSC CHSL (Tier I) 4/8/2023 Shift-II
(a) $9\sqrt[3]{388}$ (b) $6\sqrt[3]{388}$
(c) $7\sqrt[3]{388}$ (d) $4\sqrt[3]{388}$

315. If a right circular cone of height 24 cm has the circumference of its base 42π cm, then the volume of the cone is (Use $\pi = \frac{22}{7}$)
SSC CHSL (Tier I) 2/5/2023 Shift-I
(a) 15211 cm^3 (b) 11088 cm^3
(c) 12034 cm^3 (d) 21011 cm^3

316. A solid sphere of diameter 7 cm is cut into two equal halves. What will be the increase in its total surface area ?
SSC CHSL (Tier I) 21/3/2023 Shift-IV
(a) 77 cm^2 (b) 60.5 cm^2
(c) 65.5 cm^2 (d) 55 cm^2

317. What is the total surface area of a cylinder having radius of base as 7 cm and height as 5 cm?
SSC CHSL (Tier I) 21/3/2023 Shift-II
(a) 426 cm^2 (b) 528 cm^2
(c) 428 cm^2 (d) 572 cm^2

318. The length of a cuboid is 8 cm. If the breadth of the cuboid is twice of its length and height of the cuboid is half of its length, then what is the total surface area of the cuboid?
SSC CHSL (Tier I) 17/3/2023 Shift-II
(a) 448 cm^2 (b) 216 cm^2
(c) 188 cm^2 (d) 154 cm^2

319. The length of a cuboid is thrice of its breadth and the height of cuboid is twice of its breadth. If the breadth of the cuboid is 6 cm then what is the total surface area of cuboid?
SSC CHSL (Tier I) 15/3/2023 Shift-IV
(a) 844 cm^2 (b) 708 cm^2
(c) 762 cm^2 (d) 792 cm^2

320. If the radius of a sphere is thrice than the radius of a hemisphere, then what will be the respective ratio of their volumes?
SSC CHSL (Tier I) 14/3/2023 Shift-I
(a) 27 : 1 (b) 16 : 1
(c) 54 : 1 (d) 18 : 1

321. The length, breadth and height of a cubical box are 18 cm, 12 cm and 10 cm, respectively. What is the total surface area of this box?
SSC CHSL (Tier I) 13/3/2023 Shift-III
(a) 1120 cm^2 (b) 1000 cm^2
(c) 1032 cm^2 (d) 1048 cm^2

322. Find the volume of a cylinder whose diameter of base is 20 cm and height is two times that of the radius of its base. SSC CHSL (Tier I) 2/6/2022 Shift-I
(a) 4000 cm^3 (b) 2000π cm^3
(c) 6000π cm^3 (d) 3000 cm^3

323. The volume of a cube is 5832 cm^3. Find its total surface area.
SSC CHSL (Tier I) 2/6/2022 Shift-I
(a) 1672 cm^2 (b) 1944 cm^2
(c) 1536 cm^2 (d) 1824 cm^2

324. If the radii of two cylinders are in the ratio of 2 : 3 and their heights are in the ratio of 5 : 3, then the ratio of their volumes is
SSC CHSL (Tier I) 1/6/2022 Shift-I
(a) 22 : 15 (b) 20 : 27
(c) 3 : 4 (d) 16 : 23

325. What is the volume of a sphere whose diameter is 16.8 cm? [Use $\pi = \frac{22}{7}$]
SSC CHSL (Tier I) 1/6/2022 Shift-I
(a) 2487.312 cm^3 (b) 2473.812 cm^3
(c) 2483.712 cm^3 (d) 2483.172 cm^3

326. The sum of the length, breadth and depth of a cuboid is 23 cm and its diagonal is $5\sqrt{7}$ cm. Its surface area is
SSC CHSL (Tier I) 31/5/2022 Shift-I
(a) 144 cm^2 (b) 177 cm^2
(c) 188 cm^2 (d) 354 cm^2

327. What is the curved surface area of a cylinder with base radius 2 cm and height 6 cm? (Use π = 3.14)
SSC CHSL (Tier I) 31/5/2022 Shift-I
(a) 73 cm^2
(b) 88.24 cm^2
(c) 81 cm^2
(d) 75.36 cm^2

328. The curved surface area of a hemisphere is 1232 cm^2. Its radius will be (Take $\pi = 22/7$)
SSC CHSL (Tier I) 31/5/2022 Shift-I
(a) 12 cm (b) 14 cm
(c) 16 cm (d) 10 cm

329. The diagonal of a cube is 24 cm. Find its total surface area.
SSC CHSL (Tier I) 30/5/2022 Shift-I
(a) 1152 cm^2 (b) 1252 cm^2
(c) 1100 cm^2 (d) 1366 cm^2

330. Find the total surface area of a cuboid whose length is 20 cm, width is 15 cm, and height is 8 cm.
SSC CHSL (Tier I) 30/5/2022 Shift-I
(a) 1160 cm^2 (b) 990 cm^2
(c) 1120 cm^2 (d) 1080 cm^2

331. Find the surface area of a sphere of diameter 21 cm. $\left(\text{Use } \pi = \frac{22}{7}\right)$
SSC CHSL (Tier I) 30/5/2022 Shift-I
(a) 988 cm^2 (b) 1234 cm^2
(c) 1445 cm^2 (d) 1386 cm^2

332. As air is pumped into a spherical balloon, its radius increases from 7 cm to 14 cm. Find the ratio of volume of the balloon's in both circumstances.
SSC CHSL (Tier I) 27/5/2022 Shift-I
(a) 2 : 5 (b) 1 : 9 (c) 1 : 8 (d) 3 : 7

333. What is the surface area of a sphere whose diameter is 16.8 cm ? $\left[\text{Use } \pi = \frac{22}{7}\right]$
SSC CHSL (Tier I) 27/5/2022 Shift-I
(a) 877.04 cm^2 (b) 888.04 cm^2
(c) 878.04 cm^2 (d) 887.04 cm^2

334. A solid metallic sphere of radius 10 cm is melted and recast into spheres of radius 2 cm each. How many such spheres can be made?
SSC CHSL (Tier I) 10/8/2021 Shift-I
(a) 64 (b) 216
(c) 100 (d) 125

335. A solid metallic hemisphere of radius 6.3 cm is melted and recast into a right circular cylinder of radius 9 cm. What is the height (in cm, correct to one decimal place) of the cylinder?
SSC CHSL (Tier I) 4/8/2021 Shift-I
(a) 1.9 (b) 2.7
(c) 2.5 (d) 2.1

SSC MTS 2024

336. A solid hemisphere of radius 12 cm is melted into N identical cones, each of radius 6 cm and height 8 cm. What is the value of N?
SSC MTS 14/11/2024 Shift-III
(a) 12 (b) 8 (c) 10 (d) 15

337. The total surface area of a solid hemisphere is 1848 cm^2, then its volume (in cm^3) is $\left(\text{Use } \pi = \frac{22}{7}\right)$
SSC MTS 14/11/2024 Shift-III
(a) $5749\frac{1}{3}$ (b) $2640\frac{2}{3}$
(c) $6473\frac{1}{3}$ (d) $3370\frac{1}{3}$

338. The radius of a solid right circular cone is 36 cm and its height is 105 cm. The total surface area (in cm^2) of the cone is $\left(\text{Use } \pi = \frac{22}{7}\right)$
SSC MTS 13/11/2024 Shift-III
(a) 16632 (b) 14856
(c) 18821 (d) 17838

339. The diameter of the base of a right circular cylinder is 98 cm and its height is 42 cm. Find the total surface area of the cylinder. $\left(\text{Take } \pi = \frac{22}{7}\right)$
SSC MTS 13/11/2024 Shift-III
(a) 28082 cm^2 (b) 28028 cm^2
(c) 20828 cm^2 (d) 20882 cm^2

340. The height of a cylindrical pillar is 20 m. The diameter of its base is 350 cm. What will be the cost of painting the curved surface of the pillar at 40 / m^2? $\left(\text{Take } \pi = \frac{22}{7}\right)$
SSC MTS 12/11/2024 Shift-III
(a) ₹ 8600 (b) ₹ 8800
(c) ₹ 8000 (d) ₹ 8400

341. The curved surface of a right circular cylinder is to be coloured at the rate of ₹ 1.50 per sq. cm. If the radius of the circular base is 21 cm and height is 10 cm, then what will be the cost (in ₹) of colouring? $\left(\text{Take } \pi = \frac{22}{7}\right)$
SSC MTS 12/11/2024 Shift-III
(a) 1940 (b) 1980
(c) 1960 (d) 2000

342. The radius of the base of a right circular cone is 28 cm and its slant height is 13 cm. Find its lateral surface area. $\left(\text{Use } \pi = \frac{22}{7}\right)$
SSC MTS 12/11/2024 Shift-III
(a) 1044 cm^2 (b) 1144 cm^2
(c) 1140 cm^2 (d) 1122 cm^2

343. The total surface area of a solid cylinder of radius 8 cm, is 704 cm^2. Find the volume of the cylinder $\left(\text{Use } \pi = \frac{22}{7}\right)$
SSC MTS 11/11/2024 Shift-III
(a) $1106\frac{6}{7}$ cm^3 (b) $1026\frac{6}{7}$ cm^3
(c) $1206\frac{6}{7}$ cm^3 (d) $1602\frac{6}{7}$ cm^3

344. What is the height of a solid right circular cylinder of radius 21 cm if its total surface area is 3828 cm^2 $\left(\text{Use } \pi = \frac{22}{7}\right)$?
SSC MTS 11/11/2024 Shift-III
(a) 6 cm (b) 10 cm
(c) 12 cm (d) 8 cm

345. A solid sphere of radius 9 cm is melted to form a hollow, right circular cylindrical tube of length 12 cm and external radius 15 cm. The thickness (in cm) of the tube is
SSC MTS 11/11/2024 Shift-III
(a) 1 (b) 4 (c) 3 (d) 2

346. The circumference of a hemispherical oil container is 396 cm. One-third volume of the container is empty. The oil is to be transfered to a smaller hemispherical container of radius 2.1 cm. Find the number of smaller container required.
SSC MTS 5/11/2024 Shift-III
(a) 27000 (b) 18000
(c) 9000 (d) 900

347. The curved surface area of a solid cylinder is 605 cm^2. The circumference of its base is 22 cm. The total surface area is how many times the height of the cylinder? (Take $\pi = \frac{22}{7}$)
SSC MTS 4/11/2024 Shift-III
(a) 20.8 (b) 24.8 (c) 24.5 (d) 25

348. What fraction of space will a spherical ball of radius 2.1 cm take in a big spherical container of diameter of 84 cm? (Take $\pi = \frac{22}{7}$)
SSC MTS 4/11/2024 Shift-III
(a) $\frac{1}{400}$ (b) $\frac{1}{8000}$
(c) $\frac{1}{20}$ (d) $\frac{1}{64000}$

349. 12 solid spheres of the same size are made by melting a solid cylinder of 16 cm diameter and 4 cm height. The diameter of each sphere is
SSC MTS 30/10/2024 Shift-III
(a) $4 \times 2^{\frac{1}{3}}$ cm (b) $6 \times 2^{\frac{1}{3}}$ cm
(c) $8 \times 2^{\frac{1}{3}}$ cm (d) $12 \times 2^{\frac{1}{3}}$ cm

350. What will be the total surface area (in cm^2) of a right circular cone with base diameter 14 cm and height 24 cm? $\left(\text{Take } \pi = \frac{22}{7}\right)$
SSC MTS 30/10/2024 Shift-III
(a) 708 (b) 704
(c) 700 (d) 712

351. If the diameter of a hemisphere is 14 cm, then the total surface area of the hemisphere is
SSC MTS 30/10/2024 Shift-III
(a) 454 cm^2 (b) 624 cm^2
(c) 462 cm^2 (d) 554 cm^2

352. The curved surface area of a right circular cylinder is 8580 cm^2. If the height of the cylinder is 15 cm, then find the diameter (in cm) of the circular base. $\left(\text{Take } \pi = \frac{22}{7}\right)$
SSC MTS 29/10/2024 Shift-III
(a) 182 (b) 137
(c) 152 (d) 91

353. The radii of the bases of two cylinders and their heights are in the ratio 4 : 3 and 9 : 8, respectively. Find the ratio of their curved surface areas. SSC MTS 29/10/2024 Shift-III
(a) 3 : 2 (b) 4 : 5
(c) 2 : 3 (d) 5 : 6

354. The diameter of a hollow hemisphere is 30 cm. Water is filled in it up to its brim. When spherical lead shots each of radius 0.75 cm are dropped into the hemisphere, two-fifth of the water flows out. How many lead shots were dropped into the hemisphere?
SSC MTS 29/10/2024 Shift-III
(a) 1575 (b) 2250
(c) 1600 (d) 1380

355. What is the height of a solid cylinder whose radius is 7 cm and the total surface area is 704 cm^2? $\left(\text{Use } \pi = \frac{22}{7}\right)$
SSC MTS 28/10/2024 Shift-II
(a) 12 cm (b) 9 cm
(c) 8 cm (d) 7 cm

356. A well with an internal diameter of 8 m is dug to a depth of 12 m. The earth taken out of it is spread all around the well to a width of 8 m to form an embankment. What is the height (in m) of the embankment?
SSC MTS 28/10/2024 Shift-II
(a) 1.0 (b) 2.2
(c) 1.5 (d) 1.3

357. A hemispherical solid of radius 21 cm is melted and made into a cylinder whose height is 14 cm. The volume of the cylinder is given by $(a \times b^a \times c^b)\pi$ where *a*, *b* and *c* are prime. Then the value of $(a + b)c$ is
SSC MTS 28/10/2024 Shift-II
(a) 66 (b) 42
(c) 54 (d) 35

358. A metallic sphere with a radius of 35 cm is melted and subsequently transformed into several small solid cones, each having a diameter of 14 cm and a height of 4 cm. How many cones are formed as a result of this process?
SSC MTS 23/10/2024 Shift-II
(a) 825 (b) 875
(c) 900 (d) 850

359. A hemispherical bowl is made of 1 cm thick copper. The inner radius of the bowl is 6 cm. Find the cost to paint the outer curved surface area of the bowl, if the paint cost is ₹ 2 per cm^2? (Use $\pi = \frac{22}{7}$)
SSC MTS 23/10/2024 Shift-II
(a) ₹ 616 (b) ₹ 552
(c) ₹ 586 (d) ₹ 604

360. The expenses of painting the inner curved surface of a cylindrical vessel 20 m deep is ₹ 4400. If the painting rate is ₹ 40 per m^2, find the total surface area (in m^2) of the vessel correct to two places of decimals. (used $\pi = \frac{22}{7}$)
SSC MTS 23/10/2024 Shift-II
(a) 116.81 m^2
(b) 117.81 m^2
(c) 114.81 m^2
(d) 115.81 m^2

361. A hemispherical bowl of internal radius 24 cm contains liquid. The liquid is to be filled into cylindrical container of diameter 8 cm and height 12 cm. What is the number of containers that are necessary to empty the bowl?
SSC MTS 22/10/2024 Shift-II
(a) 45 (b) 50
(c) 48 (d) 39

362. Water in a conical flask with radius 7 cm and height 48 cm is poured into a cylindrical flask with radius 14 cm. The water level in the cylindrical flask is SSC MTS 22/10/2024 Shift-II
(a) 2 cm (b) 4 cm
(c) 3 cm (d) 5 cm

363. Find the volume of the largest right circular cone which is inscribed in a hollow cube of length 6 units and is standing on its base.
SSC MTS 21/10/2024 Shift-II
(a) 18π $units^3$ (b) 9π $units^3$
(c) 21π $units^3$ (d) 10π $units^3$

364. The total surface area of a right circular cylinder is $628\frac{4}{7}$ cm^2. If its radius is 4 cm, then the height (rounded off to the nearest whole number) of cylinder is equal to $\left(\text{Take } \pi = \frac{22}{7}\right)$
SSC MTS 21/10/2024 Shift-II
(a) 12 cm (b) 15 cm
(c) 21 cm (d) 18 cm

365. In a lead pipe 4.2 m long, the external diamter is 5.4 cm and the thickness of the pipe is 3 mm. Find the weight of the pipe, if 1 cm^3 of lead mass is 25 grams. $\left(\text{Use } \pi = \frac{22}{7}\right)$
SSC MTS 18/10/2024 Shift-II
(a) 54.90 kg (b) 45.09 kg
(c) 59.40 kg (d) 50.49 kg

366. The volume of an ice-cream cone is 66 cm^3. What will be the radius of base (in cm), if its height is 7 cm. $\left(\text{use } \pi = \frac{22}{7}\right)$
SSC MTS 18/10/2024 Shift-II
(a) 3 (b) 7
(c) 3.5 (d) 6

367. Anand wanted to make a cylindrical kaleidoscope of length 30 cm and radius 7 cm. If he is using handmade sheets to make it, then how much sheet will be required for this?
SSC MTS 18/10/2024 Shift-II
(a) 1520 cm^2 (b) 660 cm^2
(c) 1320 cm^2 (d) 1440 cm^2

368. The diameter of a right circular cone is 56 metres and its slant height is 35 metres.
Find its volume (rounded off to the nearest integer). $\left(\text{Take } \pi = \frac{22}{7}\right)$.
SSC MTS 17/10/2024 Shift-II
(a) 17,248 m^3 (b) 12,936 m^3
(c) 25,872 m^3 (d) 28,747 m^3

369. What is the cost of a tarpaulin required to make a conical tent with slant height 15 m and height 9 m, when one square meter tarpaulin costs ₹147?
SSC MTS 17/10/2024 Shift-II
(a) ₹ 67842 (b) ₹ 83160
(c) ₹ 62370 (d) ₹ 49896

370. A conical cavity is drilled in a solid circular cylinder of 7 cm height and 48 cm base diameter. The height and base diameter of the cone are the same as those of the cylinder. What is the total surface area of the remaining solid?
SSC MTS 17/10/2024 Shift-II
(a) 1512π cm^2 (b) 1076π cm^2
(c) 1420π cm^2 (d) 1654π cm^2

371. Find the ratio of the curved surface areas of two cones if the diameters of the bases are equal and slant heights are in the ratio 5 : 3.
SSC MTS 16/10/2024 Shift-II
(a) 2 : 3 (b) 7 : 5
(c) 3 : 2 (d) 5 : 3

372. The external and internal diameters of a hollow cylindrical pipe are 14 cm and 12 cm, respectively. What is the volume of iron used to make the pipe

if the height of the pipe is 21 cm ? $\left(\text{Use } \pi = \frac{22}{7}\right)$

SSC MTS 16/10/2024 Shift-II

(a) 462 cu.cm (b) 396 cu.cm
(c) 588 cu.cm (d) 858 cu.cm

373. A cylinder with a radius of 12 cm and height of 38 cm is cut parallel to the base into two pieces of different sizes. The total surface area of the larger piece formed is 60% of the total surface area of the given cylinder. The smaller piece is melted and used to create a sphere. Find the radius (in cm) of the sphere.

SSC MTS 16/10/2024 Shift-II

(a) $10 \times \sqrt[3]{6}$ (b) $6 \times \sqrt[3]{10}$
(c) $10 \times \sqrt[3]{5}$ (d) $5 \times \sqrt[3]{10}$

374. The radius and the height of a right circular cone are in the ratio of 7 : 24 and its volume is 1232 cm^3. Find the total surface area of the cone. $\left(\text{Use } \pi = \frac{22}{7}\right)$

SSC MTS 15/10/2024 Shift-I

(a) 704 cm^2 (b) 826 cm^2
(c) 862 cm^2 (d) 628 cm^2

375. The volume of a right circular cylinder is 2425.5 cm^3 and its base area is 346.5 cm^2. What is the curved surface area of the cylinder (in cm^2)?

SSC MTS 15/10/2024 Shift-I

(a) 462 (b) 284
(c) 364 (d) 588

376. If 2744 identical small spheres are made out of a big sphere of radius 7 cm, then what is the surface area of each small sphere?

SSC MTS 14/10/2024 Shift-I

(a) 2π cm^2 (b) 3π cm^2
(c) π cm^2 (d) 4π cm^2

377. A solid cuboid with dimensions 2 m × 4 m × 10 m is melted to form small solid cubes of side 8 cm. How many such cubes can be formed?

SSC MTS 14/10/2024 Shift-I

(a) 156250 (b) 160000
(c) 162250 (d) 158250

378. A rectangular sheet of paper of length 10π cm and width 5 cm is rolled along its length (width of the sheet becomes the height of the cylinder) to form a cylinder. What would be the radius of the cylinder?

SSC MTS 14/10/2024 Shift-I

(a) 10 cm (b) 6 cm
(c) 5 cm (d) 2.5 cm

379. The radius of solid right circular cone is 65 cm and its height is 72 cm. The total surface area (in cm^2) of the cone is $\left(\text{Use } \pi = \frac{22}{7}\right)$ SSC MTS 9/10/2024 Shift-I

(a) $38012\frac{1}{7}$ (b) $43051\frac{3}{7}$
(c) $33094\frac{2}{7}$ (d) $43084\frac{5}{7}$

380. A wooden toy is in the form of a sphere with diameter 28 cm. Find the cost of polishing its surface at the rate of 50 paise per cm^2. $\left(\text{Take } \pi = \frac{22}{7}\right)$

SSC MTS 08/10/2024 Shift-I

(a) ₹ 1234 (b) ₹ 1232
(c) ₹ 1236 (d) ₹ 1230

381. A hemispherical bowl of internal radius 15 cm contains a liquid. The liquid is to be filled into cylindrical shaped bottles of diameter 5 cm and height 6 cm. The number of bottles required to empty the bowl is

SSC MTS 08/10/2024 Shift-I

(a) 40 (b) 30 (c) 60 (d) 50

382. If the volume and surface area of a sphere are numerically the same, then find the volume (in cm^3) of its semi-sphere. (correct to two places of decimals, use $\pi = 3.14$)

SSC MTS 07/10/2024 Shift-I

(a) 65.25 (b) 65.52
(c) 56.25 (d) 56.52

383. A hemispherical bowl is 264 cm round at the brim. Suppose that the bowl is half-full of beverage. If the beverage is served in hemispherical glasses 6 cm in the diameter at the top, how many people would be served? SSC MTS 07/10/2024 Shift-I

(a) 1170 (b) 1372
(c) 1270 (d) 1470

384. A cylindrical tank of height 10 m and radius 5 m has a small circular cut of 0.5 m radius on its top surface. What would be the total surface area of the tank? SSC MTS 01/10/2024 Shift-I

(a) $\frac{599\pi}{4}m^2$ (b) $156\pi\,m^2$
(c) $\frac{299\pi}{2}m^2$ (d) $150\pi\,m^2$

385. A cylindrical disc of height 1 cm is made by melting two solid cylinders of radii 4 cm and 5 cm, and length 6 cm and 4 cm, respectively. The radius of the new cylinder is

SSC MTS 01/10/2024 Shift-I

(a) 7 cm (b) 21 cm
(c) 14 cm (d) 28 cm

386. 20 identical solid hemispheres of radius 3 cm are melted to form a big solid hemisphere. What is the radius (in cm) of the biggest hemisphere formed, if 20% of the solid is wasted during the process ?

SSC MTS 30/09/2024 Shift-I

(a) $3\sqrt{2}$ (b) 6
(c) $6\sqrt[3]{2}$ (d) 3

SSC MTS 2023-2021

387. The length, breadth and height of a cuboid are in the ratio of 6 : 4 : 3. If the total surface area of the cuboid is 972 cm^2. What is the length (in cm) of the diagonal of the cuboid?

SSC MTS 14/9/2023 Shift-I

(a) $5\sqrt{65}$ (b) $3\sqrt{61}$
(c) $3\sqrt{65}$ (d) $5\sqrt{61}$

388. The diameter of the base of a cylindrical vessel is 30 cm and its height is 56 cm. Find its curved surface area (in cm^2).

SSC MTS 14/9/2023 Shift-I

(a) 6080 (b) 6280 (c) 5280 (d) 5080

389. If the diameter of the base of a cone is 70 cm and its curved surface area is 4070 cm^2, then what will be its volume (in cm^3)? $\left(\text{use } \pi = \frac{22}{7}\right)$

SSC MTS 13/9/2023 Shift-I

(a) 1180 (b) 16300
(c) 15400 (d) 17600

390. The length of an edge of a cube is 3.5 cm. Find its total surface area.

SSC MTS 13/9/2023 Shift-I

(a) 73.5 cm^2 (b) 36 cm^2
(c) 27 cm^2 (d) 154 cm^2

391. If the length of the longest diagonal of a cubical box is $\sqrt{300}$ cm, then find its volume. SSC MTS 11/9/2023 Shift-II

(a) 10000 cm^3 (b) 400 cm^3
(c) 100 cm^3 (d) 1000 cm^3

392. A cone has base diameter 4m and height 1.5 m. Find the slant height of the cone (in m). SSC MTS 11/9/2023 Shift-II

(a) 2.1 (b) 2.3 (c) 2.7 (d) 2.5

393. The volume (in cm^3) of a sphere with diameter 7 cm is $\left[\text{Take } \pi = \frac{22}{7}\right]$

SSC MTS 11/9/2023 Shift-I

(a) 179.66 (b) 168.44
(c) 197.66 (d) 186.44

394. A hollow metal sphere of internal and external radii 5 cm and 6 cm respectively, is melted into a solid cone of base radius 5.2 cm. What is the height (in cm, rounded off to 1 decimal place) of the cone?

SSC MTS 11/9/2023 Shift-I

(a) 11.8 (b) 12.8
(c) 13.5 (d) 14.5

395. What is the total surface area (in cm^2) of a right circular cone of radius 10.5 cm and slant height 13 cm ? $\left(\text{taken } \pi = \frac{22}{7}\right)$

SSC MTS 8/9/2023 Shift-II

(a) 577.5 (b) 757.5
(c) 775.5 (d) 787.5

396. What is the length of the longest pole that can be placed in an indoor stadium 24 m long, 18 m wide and 16 m high? SSC MTS 6/9/2023 Shift-I

(a) 38 m (b) 34 m
(c) 42 m (d) 36 m

397. A right circular cone is 9.8 cm high with the radius of its base 4 cm. It is melted and recast into a right circular cone with the radius of its base 3.5 cm. Find its height $\left(\text{use } \pi = \frac{22}{7}\right)$.

SSC MTS 5/9/2023 Shift-II

(a) 21.8 cm (b) 28.1 cm
(c) 12.8 cm (d) 18.2 cm

398. A solid piece of metal, cuboidal in shape, with dimensions 12 cm, 9 cm and 2 cm is recast into a cube. What is the lateral surface area (in cm^2) of the cube? SSC MTS 4/9/2023 Shift-II

(a) 144 (b) 216
(c) 204 (d) 162

399. Find the total surface area of a cuboid whose dimensions are 18 m, 6 m and 3 m. SSC MTS 4/9/2023 Shift-II

(a) 90 m^2 (b) 180 m^2
(c) 324 m^2 (d) 360 m^2

400. From a cuboid of dimension of $8 \times 6 \times 6$ units, small cubes of dimension $0.5 \times 0.5 \times 0.5$ units are cut. How many small cubes can be cut form the big cuboid?

SSC MTS 1/9/2023 Shift-III

(a) 576 (b) 1152
(c) 2304 (d) 1552

401. The surface area of a sphere is 5544 cm^2. If the radius of the sphere is doubled, then find the surface area of the new sphere (in cm^2).

SSC MTS 1/9/2023 Shift-III

(a) 22176 (b) 22761
(c) 20761 (d) 20176

402. The diameter of a metallic sphere is 6 cm. It is melted and drawn into a wire having a diameter of the cross section as 0.4 cm. Find the length of the wire (in m). SSC MTS 1/9/2023 Shift-I

(a) 18 (b) 9 (c) 12 (d) 10

403. The surface area of a sphere is 616 cm^2, find its diameter $\left(\text{Take, } \pi = \frac{22}{7}\right)$ SSC MTS 1/9/2023 Shift-I

(a) 14 cm (b) 2 cm
(c) 4 cm (d) 3 cm

404. What is the height of a cylinder whose radius of base is 12 cm and volume is 19008 cm^3 ? $\left[\text{Use } \pi = \frac{22}{7}\right]$

SSC MTS 15/7/2022 Shift-I

(a) 6 cm^3 (b) 24 cm^3
(c) 38 cm^3 (d) 42 cm^3

405. The length of each side of a cube is 4 cm. What is the volume of the cube? SSC MTS 14/7/2022 Shift-I

(a) 128 cm^3 (b) 48 cm^3
(c) 64 cm^3 (d) 32 cm^3

406. Find the total cost of painting the outside of a closed cuboidal box, which is 7 m long, 5 m wide and 2 m high, at the rate of ₹ 2.4 per m^2.

SSC MTS 14/7/2022 Shift-I

(a) ₹ 296.30 (b) ₹ 263.40
(c) ₹ 283.20 (d) ₹ 251.20

407. The largest possible right circular cylinder is cut-out from a wooden cube of edge 7 cm. Find the volume of the cube left over after cutting the cylinder (in cm^3). $\left(\text{Use } \pi = \frac{22}{7}\right)$

SSC MTS 13/7/2022 Shift-I

(a) 73.5 (b) 63.5
(c) 87.5 (d) 67.5

408. The area of the base of a solid cone is 616 cm^2. If the height of the cone is 15 cm, then what is the volume of this cone ? SSC MTS 13/7/2022 Shift-I

(a) 2940 cm^3 (b) 3440 cm^3
(c) 3190 cm^3 (d) 3080 cm^3

409. The volume of a cone is 27720 cm^3. If the height of the cone is 20 cm, then what will be the area of the base ?

SSC MTS 12/7/2022 Shift-I

(a) 4158 cm^2 (b) 4272 cm^2
(c) 4626 cm^2 (d) 4836 cm^2

410. The length, the breadth, and the height of a cuboid are 40 cm, 20 cm and 10 cm, respectively. What is the volume of this cuboid ?

SSC MTS 12/7/2022 Shift-I

(a) 16000 cm^3
(b) 8000 cm^3
(c) 2000 cm^3
(d) 4000 cm^3

411. The radius of a sphere and that of the base of a cylinder are equal. The ratio of the radius of the base of the cylinder and the height of the cylinder is 3 : 4. What is the ratio of the volume of the sphere to that of the cylinder? SSC MTS 11/7/2022 Shift-I

(a) 27 : 64 (b) 1 : 2
(c) 1 : 1 (d) 9 : 16

412. The side of a square is equal to 40% of the radius of a sphere. If the volume of the sphere is $\frac{500\pi}{3}$ m^3, then what is the area of the square ? SSC MTS 11/7/2022 Shift-I

(a) 2 m^2 (b) 1 m^2
(c) 9 m^2 (d) 4 m^2

413. The total surface area of a closed cube is 128 cm^2 more than the area of a square. If the length of each side of the cube is 8 cm, then what is the length of each side of the square ? SSC MTS 11/7/2022 Shift-I

(a) 16 cm (b) 12 cm
(c) 18 cm (d) 9 cm

414. The total surface area of a hemisphere is very nearly equal to that of an equilateral triangle. The side of the triangle is how many times (approximately) of the radius of the hemisphere?

SSC MTS 2/11/2021 Shift-III

(a) $\left(\frac{8\pi}{\sqrt{3}}\right)^{0.5}$ (b) $\left(\frac{4\pi}{3}\right)^{0.5}$
(c) $(2\pi\sqrt{3})^{0.5}$ (d) $(4\pi\sqrt{3})^{0.5} \times r$

415. If the radius of the base of a right circular cylinder is 4 m and the area of the curved surface of the cylinder is 19.5 m^2, then its volume (in m^3) is SSC MTS 2/11/2021 Shift-II

(a) 65 (b) 42
(c) 36 (d) 39

416. A bucket in the shape of the frustum of a cone has its top and bottom radii as 20 cm and 10 cm, respectively. The depth of the bucket is 24 cm. The capacity of the bucket is $\left(\text{Take } \pi = \frac{22}{7}\right)$ SSC MTS 2/11/2021 Shift-I

(a) 8800 cm^3 (b) 13200 cm^3
(c) 17000 cm^3 (d) 17600 cm^3

417. A room has length 15 ft, width 12 ft and height 10 ft. It has one door of dimensions 8 ft and 3.5 ft and 2 windows of size 5 ft $\times$ 3 ft. Find the cost of painting the four walls and the ceiling at ₹ 50 per ft^2.

SSC MTS 2/11/2021 Shift-I

(a) ₹ 19600 (b) ₹ 21200
(c) ₹ 24100 (d) ₹ 33100

SSC GD Constable 2024 & 2023

418. Height of a cone is 24 cm and radius of its base is 10.5 cm. What is the volume of the cone ?

SSC GD 26/2/2024 Shift-I

(a) 2772 cm^3 (b) 2546 cm^3
(c) 2398 cm^3 (d) 2984 cm^3

419. The radius of a hemisphere is 2.1 cm. What will be its volume?

SSC GD 24/2/2024 Shift-III

(a) 24.6 cm^3 (b) 15.7 cm^3
(c) 19.4 cm^3 (d) 17.5 cm^3

420. The length and breadth of a cuboid are increased by 50% and 20%, respectively. If its height is decreased by 30% , then what will be percentage increase in the volume of cuboid? SSC GD 24/2/2024 Shift-III

(a) 25% (b) 26%
(c) 20% (d) 30%

421. The radius of a hemisphere is 3.5 cm. What will be its volume? **SSC GD 24/2/2024 Shift-I**

(a) 98.89 cm^3 (b) 62.38 cm^3
(c) 89.83 cm^3 (d) 79.24 cm^3

422. The length of the side of a cube is 13 cm. What is the lateral surface area of the cube? **SSC GD 23/2/2024 Shift-IV**

(a) 625 cm^2 (b) 576 cm^2
(c) 676 cm^2 (d) 484 cm^2

423. The height of a cone is 15 cm and radius of its base is 14 cm. What is the volume of the cone? **SSC GD 23/2/2024 Shift-III**

(a) 3420 cm^3 (b) 3080 cm^3
(c) 2860 cm^3 (d) 3240 cm^3

424. A solid metallic sphere of radius 15 cm is melted and recast into a cone having diameter of the base as 15 cm. What is the height of the cone? **SSC GD 23/2/2024 Shift-I**

(a) 284 cm (b) 186 cm
(c) 240 cm (d) 212 cm

425. How many spherical balls of radius 8 cm can be made by melting a hemisphere of radius 48 cm? **SSC GD 22/2/2024 Shift-II**

(a) 116 (b) 90 (c) 104 (d) 108

426. The diameter of a hemisphere is 21 cm. What is the total surface area of the hemisphere? **SSC GD 21/2/2024 Shift-IV**

(a) 1039.5 cm^2 (b) 790.5 cm^2
(c) 1238.5 cm^2 (d) 980.5 cm^2

427. The length of the side of a cube is 14 cm. What is the lateral surface area of the cube? **SSC GD 21/2/2024 Shift-II**

(a) 856 cm^2 (b) 624 cm^2
(c) 784 cm^2 (d) 512 cm^2

428. The radius of a sphere is 3.5 cm. What is the total surface area of the sphere? **SSC GD 20/2/2024 Shift-IV**

(a) 176 cm^2 (b) 128 cm^2
(c) 154 cm^2 (d) 196 cm^2

429. The radius of a sphere is 4.2 cm. What is the volume of the sphere? **SSC GD 20/2/2024 Shift-III**

(a) 348.21 cm^3 (b) 284.62 cm^3
(c) 329.32 cm^3 (d) 310.46 cm^3

430. Radius of a sphere is increased by 50%. What will be the percentage increase in its volume? **SSC GD 20/2/2024 Shift-II**

(a) 225.5% (b) 235.5%
(c) 237.5% (d) 150%

431. What is the curved surface area of a cylinder having radius of base as 70 cm and height as 14 cm? **SSC GD 20/2/2024 Shift-II**

(a) 6160 cm^2 (b) 6420 cm^2
(c) 5930 cm^2 (d) 6350 cm^2

432. If the length, breadth, and height of a cuboidal box are 24 cm, 16 cm and 12 cm respectively, then the volume of the box is **SSC GD 13/2/2023 Shift-IV**

(a) 4612 cm^3 (b) 4632 cm^3
(c) 4608 cm^3 (d) 4644 cm^3

433. What is the total surface area of a hemisphere of diameter 7 cm ? $\left(\text{take}, \pi = \frac{22}{7}\right)$ **SSC GD 13/2/2023 Shift-IV**

(a) 77 cm^2 (b) 98 cm^2
(c) 87.5 cm^2 (d) 115.5 cm^2

434. There is a cone with diameter 14 cm and height 12 cm. It is being filled with water at a rate of 4 cm^3 in every 10 s. How long will it take to fill the cone $\left(\text{use } \pi = \frac{22}{7}\right)$ **SSC GD 13/2/2023 Shift-II**

(a) 616 sec (b) 1540 sec
(c) 3080 sec (d) 6160 sec

435. A solid hemisphere has a volume of 1152 π cm^3. Find the curved surface area of the hemisphere. **SSC GD 13/2/2023 Shift-II**

(a) 344 cm^2 (b) 288 π cm^2
(c) 302 π cm^2 (d) 294 cm^2

436. What is the volume of a hemisphere with radius 2.8 cm? (Use, $\pi = \frac{22}{7}$) (Rounded up to three places of decimal) **SSC GD 9/2/2023 Shift-II**

(a) 41 cm^3 (b) 45.995 cm^3
(c) 28 cm^3 (d) 38.268 cm^3

437. A heap of wheat is in the form of a cone of diameter 30 m and height of 8 m. How much canvas cloth will be required to just cover the heap. (take, π = 3.14) **SSC GD 9/2/2023 Shift-II**

(a) 700.8 m^2 (b) 800.7 m^2
(c) 900.9 m^2 (d) 900.8 m^2

438. If the slant height and radius of a cone are 12 cm and 7 cm, respectively, then find the total surface area. **SSC GD 9/2/2023 Shift-I**

(a) 841 cm^2 (b) 481 cm^2
(c) 418 cm^2 (d) 448 cm^2

439. What is the radius of the base of a cylindrical container of volume 2640 cm^3 with height 21 cm? $\left(\text{take}, \pi = \frac{22}{7}\right)$ **SSC GD 9/2/2023 Shift-I**

(a) 1.64 cm (b) 5.24 cm
(c) 2.64 cm (d) 6.32 cm

440. If three solid spheres of metal whose radii are 1 cm, 6 cm and 8 cm are melted to form another solid sphere, then the surface area of new sphere (in cm^2) is **SSC GD 8/2/2023 Shift-I**

(a) 364π (b) 243π
(c) 324π (d) 642π

441. A cuboid has sides in the ratio 3 : 4 : 5 and its volume is 480 cubic units. The difference between the largest and the smallest side is ...... units. **SSC GD 8/2/2023 Shift-I**

(a) 3 (b) 4
(c) 5 (d) 6

442. If the volume of a solid right circular cone is v cm^3 and its height is h cm, then the radius of the cone is **SSC GD 7/2/2023 Shift-I**

(a) $\frac{v}{\pi h^2}$ cm (b) $\sqrt{\frac{3v}{\pi h}}$ cm
(c) $\frac{3v}{\pi h^2}$ cm (d) $\sqrt{\frac{v}{\pi h}}$ cm

443. A solid right-circular cylinder whose radius of the base is 22.5 cm and whose height is 24 cm is melted and moulded in the shape of a right circular cone whose radius of the base is 36 cm. What will be the height of this cone? **SSC GD 7/2/2023 Shift-I**

(a) 26.225 cm (b) 28.125 cm
(c) 29.105 cm (d) 30.25 cm

444. If the diameter of a sphere is 14 cm, find its volume (take $\pi = \frac{22}{7}$). **SSC GD 6/2/2023 Shift-I**

(a) 1437.33 cm^3 (b) 2437.34 cm^3
(c) 1637.13 cm^3 (d) 1537.23 cm^3

445. If each side of a cube is increased by 15%, then the volume of the cube will increase by : (Consider integral part only) **SSC GD 6/2/2023 Shift-I**

(a) 45% (b) 52% (c) 42% (d) 35%

446. What will be the volume of the largest sphere which can be carved out of a cube of side 6 cm ? **SSC GD 2/2/2023 Shift-I**

(a) 102.26 cm^3 (b) 113.14 cm^3
(c) 112.15 cm^3 (d) 115.13 cm^3

447. A hemispherical bowl is made of thick steel having thickness 0.5 cm. If the external diameter of the bowl is 43 cm, then the capacity of the bowl is (Use $\pi = \frac{22}{7}$) **SSC GD 2/2/2023 Shift-I**

(a) 19404 cm^3 (b) 38808 cm^3
(c) 77616 cm^3 (d) 3696 cm^3

448. The volume of a solid cone is 96π cm ^{3} and its height is 8 cm. What is the its total surface area (in cm^2)? **SSC GD 1/2/2023 Shift-I**

(a) 36π (b) 37π
(c) 96π (d) 23π

449. If a right circular cone of height 24 cm has a volume of 392 π cm^3, then the curved surface area is **SSC GD 1/2/2023 Shift-I**

(a) 163 π cm^2 (b) 191 π cm^2
(c) 175 π cm^2 (d) 185 π cm^2

SSC Selection Post 2024

450. The diagonal of a cube is $5\sqrt{3}$ cm. Find the surface area of the cube.
Matric Level 20/06/2024 Shift-IV
(a) 650cm^2 (b) 25 cm^2
(c) 250cm^2 (d) 150cm^2

451. The radius of a hemisphere is 9 cm. Its volume will be
Matric Level 20/06/2024 Shift-IV
(a) 712πcm^3
(b) 243πcm^3
(c) 486πcm^3
(d) 972πcm^3

452. If the cylinder height is 9 cm and the base area is 25πcm^2, then find the total surface area.
Matric Level 20/06/2024 Shift-IV
(a) 240 cm^2 (b) 140 cm^2
(c) 440 cm^2 (d) 340 cm^2

453. The dimensions of a cuboid are 8 cm, 12 cm and 14 cm. Find the total surface area.
Higher Secondary Level 20/06/2024 Shift-II
(a) 752 cm^2 (b) 754 cm^2
(c) 753 cm^2 (d) 751 cm^2

454. If the volume of a cube is given as 12167 cm^3, then the surface area of the cube will be
Graduate Level 27/06/2023 Shift-IV
(a) 3475 cm^2
(b) 4574 cm^2
(c) 3174 cm^2
(d) 5413 cm^2

455. Melting a hemisphere of radius 7 cm, four small identical spheres are made. What is the radius of these spheres?
Higher Secondary Level 27/06/2023 Shift-III
(a) 3 cm (b) 3.5 cm
(c) 4 cm (d) 4.5 cm

456. The internal and external diameters of a hollow hemispherical bowl are 6 cm and 10 cm, respectively. If it is melted and recast into a solid cylinder of diameter 14 cm, what is the height of the cylinder in cm?
Matric Level 27/06/2023 Shift-I
(a) 1.1 (b) 1.22
(c) 1.33 (d) 1

457. Find the length of a diagonal of a cuboid whose dimensions are 12 m, 10 m and 8 m. (up to one decimal point)
Matric Level 27/06/2023 Shift-I
(a) 18m (b) 16.5m
(c) 17m (d) 17.54m

458. The volumes of two cubes are in the ratio of 8 : 27. If the volume of the larger cube is 513 cm^3 more than that of the smaller cube,find the length of each side of the smaller cube.
Higher Secondary Level 01/08/2022 Shift-II
(a) 7 cm (b) 16 cm
(c) 27 cm (d) 6 cm

459. What is the volume of a hemisphere having a diameter of 16.8 cm? (take $\pi = \frac{22}{7}$)
Matric Level 01/08/2022 Shift-I
(a) 1241.856 cm^3 (b) 1249.404 cm^3
(c) 1218.804 cm^3 (d) 1239.960 cm^3

Right Answers

1	(a)	2	(d)	3	(a)	4	(a)	5	(d)	6	(b)	7	(b)	8	(c)	9	(d)	10	(a)
11	(b)	12	(b)	13	(d)	14	(b)	15	(b)	16	(c)	17	(d)	18	(d)	19	(a)	20	(a)
21	(b)	22	(c)	23	(c)	24	(d)	25	(a)	26	(b)	27	(d)	28	(b)	29	(d)	30	(b)
31	(b)	32	(b)	33	(b)	34	(b)	35	(b)	36	(a)	37	(c)	38	(a)	39	(b)	40	(c)
41	(d)	42	(a)	43	(c)	44	(c)	45	(a)	46	(c)	47	(b)	48	(c)	49	(a)	50	(c)
51	(b)	52	(a)	53	(c)	54	(c)	55	(a)	56	(b)	57	(c)	58	(c)	59	(a)	60	(a)
61	(d)	62	(c)	63	(a)	64	(d)	65	(a)	66	(d)	67	(b)	68	(b)	69	(b)	70	(d)
71	(d)	72	(d)	73	(b)	74	(d)	75	(c)	76	(d)	77	(d)	78	(a)	79	(a)	80	(d)
81	(c)	82	(d)	83	(c)	84	(c)	85	(d)	86	(a)	87	(b)	88	(b)	89	(c)	90	(c)
91	(a)	92	(a)	93	(c)	94	(a)	95	(d)	96	(c)	97	(b)	98	(a)	99	(d)	100	(b)
101	(a)	102	(c)	103	(b)	104	(d)	105	(b)	106	(a)	107	(c)	108	(b)	109	(b)	110	(b)
111	(b)	112	(c)	113	(a)	114	(c)	115	(c)	116	(a)	117	(a)	118	(d)	119	(d)	120	(d)
121	(a)	122	(c)	123	(a)	124	(a)	125	(a)	126	(a)	127	(a)	128	(a)	129	(c)	130	(d)
131	(b)	132	(d)	133	(c)	134	(b)	135	(b)	136	(a)	137	(b)	138	(c)	139	(d)	140	(b)
141	(d)	142	(b)	143	(d)	144	(b)	145	(c)	146	(c)	147	(d)	148	(c)	149	(b)	150	(d)
151	(a)	152	(c)	153	(d)	154	(a)	155	(a)	156	(d)	157	(c)	158	(b)	159	(c)	160	(d)
161	(a)	162	(c)	163	(b)	164	(a)	165	(c)	166	(d)	167	(d)	168	(a)	169	(c)	170	(c)
171	(d)	172	(a)	173	(a)	174	(d)	175	(d)	176	(a)	177	(c)	178	(b)	179	(b)	180	(c)
181	(c)	182	(c)	183	(a)	184	(d)	185	(c)	186	(d)	187	(b)	188	(d)	189	(c)	190	(d)
191	(c)	192	(d)	193	(d)	194	(d)	195	(b)	196	(b)	197	(c)	198	(c)	199	(c)	200	(c)
201	(a)	202	(b)	203	(b)	204	(b)	205	(b)	206	(a)	207	(b)	208	(d)	209	(b)	210	(c)
211	(b)	212	(c)	213	(c)	214	(d)	215	(c)	216	(c)	217	(c)	218	(d)	219	(a)	220	(c)
221	(b)	222	(d)	223	(c)	224	(a)	225	(c)	226	(a)	227	(c)	228	(d)	229	(c)	230	(c)
231	(d)	232	(d)	233	(b)	234	(c)	235	(c)	236	(c)	237	(b)	238	(c)	239	(c)	240	(d)
241	(a)	242	(a)	243	(b)	244	(d)	245	(d)	246	(a)	247	(b)	248	(a)	249	(d)	250	(c)
251	(b)	252	(b)	253	(d)	254	(a)	255	(a)	256	(d)	257	(c)	258	(a)	259	(a)	260	(c)
261	(b)	262	(d)	263	(d)	264	(c)	265	(b)	266	(d)	267	(c)	268	(b)	269	(a)	270	(a)
271	(d)	272	(b)	273	(c)	274	(b)	275	(c)	276	(a)	277	(b)	278	(c)	279	(c)	280	(a)
281	(b)	282	(c)	283	(c)	284	(a)	285	(d)	286	(d)	287	(c)	288	(d)	289	(d)	290	(a)
291	(a)	292	(c)	293	(c)	294	(d)	295	(a)	296	(a)	297	(c)	298	(b)	299	(b)	300	(c)
301	(b)	302	(d)	303	(d)	304	(d)	305	(d)	306	(a)	307	(b)	308	(a)	309	(b)	310	(b)
311	(c)	312	(d)	313	(c)	314	(d)	315	(b)	316	(a)	317	(b)	318	(a)	319	(d)	320	(c)
321	(c)	322	(b)	323	(b)	324	(b)	325	(c)	326	(d)	327	(d)	328	(b)	329	(a)	330	(a)
331	(d)	332	(c)	333	(d)	334	(d)	335	(d)	336	(a)	337	(a)	338	(a)	339	(b)	340	(b)
341	(b)	342	(b)	343	(c)	344	(d)	345	(c)	346	(b)	347	(b)	348	(b)	349	(a)	350	(b)
351	(c)	352	(a)	353	(a)	354	(c)	355	(b)	356	(c)	357	(d)	358	(b)	359	(a)	360	(c)
361	(c)	362	(b)	363	(a)	364	(c)	365	(d)	366	(a)	367	(c)	368	(a)	369	(b)	370	(a)
371	(d)	372	(d)	373	(b)	374	(a)	375	(a)	376	(c)	377	(a)	378	(c)	379	(c)	380	(b)
381	(c)	382	(d)	383	(b)	384	(a)	385	(c)	386	(c)	387	(b)	388	(c)	389	(c)	390	(a)
391	(d)	392	(d)	393	(a)	394	(c)	395	(c)	396	(b)	397	(c)	398	(a)	399	(d)	400	(c)
401	(a)	402	(b)	403	(a)	404	(d)	405	(c)	406	(c)	407	(a)	408	(d)	409	(a)	410	(b)
411	(c)	412	(d)	413	(a)	414	(d)	415	(d)	416	(d)	417	(d)	418	(a)	419	(c)	420	(b)
421	(c)	422	(c)	423	(b)	424	(c)	425	(d)	426	(a)	427	(c)	428	(c)	429	(d)	430	(c)
431	(a)	432	(c)	433	(d)	434	(b)	435	(b)	436	(b)	437	(b)	438	(c)	439	(d)	440	(c)
441	(b)	442	(b)	443	(b)	444	(a)	445	(b)	446	(b)	447	(a)	448	(c)	449	(c)	450	(d)
451	(c)	452	(c)	453	(a)	454	(c)	455	(b)	456	(c)	457	(d)	458	(d)	459	(a)		

Solutions

1. (a) We have, diameter of base of cone $= 56$ cm

and curved surface area $= 3080$ cm^2

$\because$ Curved surface area of cone $= \pi rl = 3080$

$\Rightarrow \quad l = 3080 \times \frac{7}{22} \times \frac{1}{28} = 35$ cm

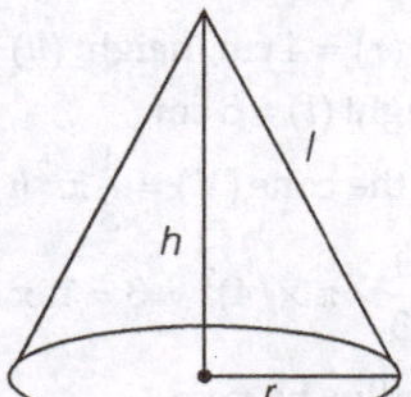

$r = \frac{56}{2} = 28$ cm

$\therefore \quad h = \sqrt{l^2 - r^2} = \sqrt{35^2 - 28^2} = 21$ cm

$\therefore$ Volume of cone $= \frac{1}{3}\pi r^2 h$

$= \frac{1}{3} \times \frac{22}{7} \times (28)^2 \times 21 = 17248$ cm^3

2. (d) $\because$ Area of curved surface $= 5 \times$ Area of base of cone

$\pi rl = 5 \times \pi r^2$

$l = 5r$

Now, $\quad l^2 = h^2 + r^2$

$\Rightarrow \quad (5r)^2 = (63)^2 + r^2$

$\Rightarrow \quad 24r^2 = 3969$

$\Rightarrow \quad r^2 = \frac{3969}{24}$

$\therefore$ Volume of cone $= \frac{1}{3}\pi r^2 h$

$= \frac{1}{3} \times \frac{22}{7} \times \frac{3969}{24} \times 63$

$= 10914.75$ cm^3

3. (a) Volume of right circular cone $= \frac{1}{3}\pi r^2 h$

$= \frac{1}{3} \times \frac{22}{7} \times 6 \times 6 \times 5$

$= \frac{3960}{21} = 188.57$ cm^3

4. (a) $\because$ Slant height (l) of cone

$= \sqrt{(105)^2 + (36)^2}$

$= \sqrt{11025 + 1296}$

$= \sqrt{12321} = 111$

$\therefore$ Total surface area of toy = Curved surface area of cone + Curved surface area of hemisphere

$= \pi rl + 2\pi r^2$

$= \pi \times 36 \times 111 + 2 \times \pi \times 36 \times 36$

$= 3996\pi + 2592\pi = 6588\pi$

5. (d) We know, Volume of cone $= \frac{1}{3}\pi r^2 h$

$= \frac{1}{3} \times \frac{22}{7} \times 3.5 \times 3.5 \times 18 = 231$ cm^3

6. (b) We know,

Total surface area of cylinder $= 2\pi r(r + h)$

$= 2 \times \frac{22}{7} \times 21 \times (21 + 5)$

$= 2 \times \frac{22}{7} \times 21 \times 26 = 3432$ cm^2

7. (b) Given, curved surface area $= 550$ cm^2

$\therefore \quad \pi rl = 550$

$\Rightarrow \quad \frac{22}{7} \times 7 \times l = 550 \Rightarrow l = 25$

$\therefore$ Total surface area $= \pi r(l + r)$

$= \frac{22}{7} \times 7(25 + 7) = 22(32) = 704$ cm^2

> **Speedy Method**
>
> Total surface area = Curved surface area + Area of base
>
> $= 550 + \pi r^2$
>
> $= 550 + \frac{22}{7} \times 7 \times 7 = 704$ cm^2

8. (c) Given, $r = 14$ cm, $h = 23$ cm

Volume of Earth taken out = Volume of cylinder $= \pi r^2 h = \frac{22}{7} \times 14 \times 14 \times 23$

$= 14168$ cm^3

9. (d) Let height of water in the cylinderical tank $= h$

Volume of cylindrical tank $= \pi r^2 h$

$616 \times 1000 = \frac{22}{7} \times 14 \times 14 \times h$

[$\because$ 1 litre = 1000 cm^3]

$h = 1000$ cm $= 10$ m $\quad$ [$\because$ 1 metre = 100 cm]

10. (a) Circumference of base $= 154$

$2\pi r = 154 \Rightarrow r = \frac{154 \times 7}{2 \times 22}$

$r = 24.5 = \frac{49}{2}$ cm

height $= 49$ mm $= 4.9$ cm

Volume of Cylinder $= \pi r^2 h$

$= \frac{22}{7} \times \frac{49}{2} \times \frac{49}{2} \times 4.9 = 9243.85$ cm^3

$= 9.244$ L $\quad$ [$\because$ 1 cm^3 = 0.001 × L]

11. (b) Ratio of length, breadth and height of cuboid $= 3 : 2 : 1$

Let l, b and h are $3x$, $2x$ and x.

Then, $2x = 12$, $\quad x = 6$ cm

Length $= 3x = 3 \times 6 = 18$ cm

Breadth $= 2x = 2 \times 6 = 12$ cm

Height $= x = 6$ cm

Volume of cuboid $= l \times b \times h = 18 \times 12 \times 6$

$= 1296$ cm^3

12. (b) Volume of cube $= 13824$

$(\text{side})^3 = 13824$

$\Rightarrow \quad \text{side} = \sqrt[3]{13824} = \sqrt[3]{24 \times 24 \times 24}$

$\Rightarrow \quad \text{side} = 24$ cm

$\therefore$ Side of cube is 24 cm.

13. (d)

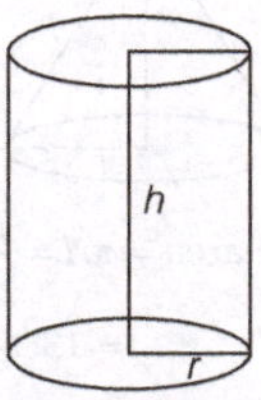

Given, radius $= 30$ cm

Volume of cylinder $= \pi r^2 h$

$\Rightarrow \quad 600 = \frac{22}{7} \times 30 \times 30 \times h$

$\Rightarrow \quad h = \frac{600 \times 7}{22 \times 900} = 0.21$ cm

14. (b) Length of room $= 15$ m

Breadth of room $= 9$ m

Height of room $= 5$ m

Area when only the walls of the room are painted $= 2(bh + hl)$

$= 2(9 \times 5 + 5 \times 15)$

$= 2(45 + 75) = 240$ m^2

Area per square meter $= 40$ m^2/cm

Number of cans of paint required $= \frac{240}{40} = 6$

15. (b) Length of longest stick = Diagonal of cube

$= \sqrt{(70)^2 + (70)^2 + (70)^2}$

$= \sqrt{3(70)^2} = 70\sqrt{3}$ cm

16. (c) Total surface area of cube $= 6a^2$

$\therefore \quad 1152 = 6a^2$

$\Rightarrow \quad a^2 = 192$

$\Rightarrow \quad a = 8\sqrt{3}$ cm

17. (d) We know,

Curved surface area of cylinder $= 792$ cm^2

$\therefore \quad 2\pi rh = 792$

$\Rightarrow \quad 2 \times \frac{22}{7} \times 10.5 \times h = 792$

$\Rightarrow \quad h = \frac{792 \times 7}{44 \times 10.5} = 12$ cm

$\therefore$ Volume of cylinder $= \pi r^2 h$

$= \frac{22}{7} \times 10.5 \times 10.5 \times 12$

$= 4158$ cm^3

> **Speedy Method**
>
> We know, volume $(\pi r^2 h) = 2\pi rh \times \frac{r}{2}$
>
> $= 792 \times \frac{10.5}{2} = 4158$ cm^3

18. (d) Height of cone $(h) = \sqrt{l^2 - r^2}$

$= \sqrt{(3\sqrt{2})^2 - (3)^2} = 3$ unit

$\therefore$ Volume of cone $= \frac{1}{3}\pi r^2 h = \frac{1}{3}\pi \times 3 \times 3 \times 3$

$= 9\pi$ cubic units

19. (a) Given, $r = 9$ cm, $l = 49$ cm

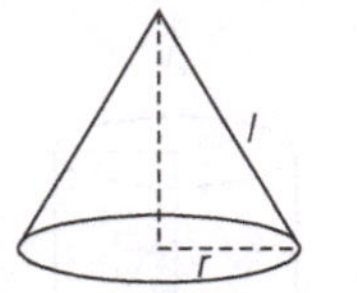

$\therefore$ Curved surface area $= \pi r l = \frac{22}{7} \times 9 \times 49$

$= 1386 \text{ cm}^2$

20. (a)

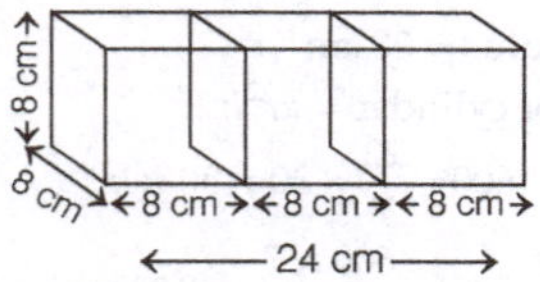

As, volume of each cube = 512

$\Rightarrow \quad (a)^3 = 512 \quad [\because \text{edge of cube} = a]$

$\Rightarrow \quad a = 8$ cm

$\therefore$ Length (l) of cuboid $= 8 + 8 + 8 = 24$ cm

Breadth (b) of cuboid = 8 cm

Height (h) of cuboid = 8 cm

$\therefore$ Surface area of cuboid

$= 2(24 \times 8 + 8 \times 8 + 8 \times 24)$

$= 896 \text{ cm}^2$

21. (b) Length = 1.2 cm

Breadth = 1.3 cm and Height = 1.5 cm

Diagonal of cuboid $= \sqrt{l^2 + b^2 + h^2}$

$= \sqrt{(1.2)^2 + (1.3)^2 + (1.5)^2}$

$= \sqrt{1.44 + 1.69 + 2.25} = \sqrt{5.38}$

Diagonal = 2.32 cm

22. (c) Height of cylinder = 12 cm

Diameter of cylinder = 28 cm

Radius of cylinder = 14 cm

Total surface area of cylinder

$= 2\pi r(h + r) = 2 \times \frac{22}{7} \times 14(12 + 14)$

$= 88 \times 26$

Curved surface area of cylinder

$= 2\pi r h = 2 \times \frac{22}{7} \times 14 \times 12$

$= 88 \times 12$

Ratio of TSA and CSA $= \frac{88 \times 26}{88 \times 12} = \frac{13}{6} = 13 : 6$

> **Speedy Method**
>
> TSA : CSA $= 2\pi r(h + r) : 2\pi r h$
>
> $= (h + r) : h$
>
> $= 26 : 12 = 13 : 6$

23. (c) Circumference of base = 44

$\therefore \quad 2\pi r = 44 \Rightarrow r = 44 \times \frac{1}{2 \times 22} \times 7$

$r = 7$ cm

Volume of cylinder $= \pi r^2 h = \frac{22}{7} \times 7 \times 7 \times 25$

$= 3850 \text{ cm}^3 = 3.850$ L

$[\because 1 \text{ litre} = 10^3 \text{cm}^3]$

24. (d) Curve surface of cylinder = 880

$2 \times \pi \times r \times h = 880 \Rightarrow r \times h = \frac{880 \times 7}{2 \times 22}$

$\Rightarrow \quad r \times h = 20 \times 7 = 140 \text{ cm}^2$

25. (a) Given, $r = 4$ unit, $h = 2r = 8$ unit

$\therefore$ Volume of cylinder $= \pi r^2 h$

$= \pi \times 8 \times 16 = 128\pi$ cubic units.

26. (b) $r = 70$ m

Let the height be h m

We know, volume of cone $= \frac{1}{3}\pi r^2 h$

$46200 = \frac{1}{3} \times \frac{22}{7} \times 70 \times 70 \times h$

$\Rightarrow \quad h = 9$ m

27. (d)

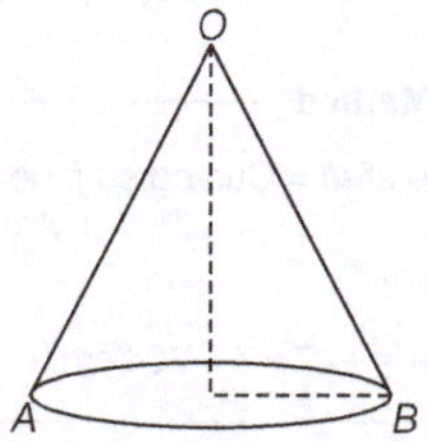

Let r be the radius of the conical tent

height = 8 m

$\therefore \quad 2\pi r = 32\pi \Rightarrow r = 16$ m

$\therefore \quad l = \sqrt{r^2 + h^2} = \sqrt{16^2 + 8^2}$

$= \sqrt{320} = 8\sqrt{5}$ m

$\therefore$ Curved surface area $= \pi r l = \pi \times 16 \times 8\sqrt{5}$

$= 128\sqrt{5}\pi \text{ m}^2$

28. (b) Given, $\frac{r_1}{r_2} = \frac{4}{5}$ and $\frac{h_1}{h_2} = \frac{5}{7}$

$\therefore$ The required ratio $= \frac{2\pi r_1 h_1}{2\pi r_2 h_2}$

$= \left(\frac{r_1}{r_2}\right) \times \left(\frac{h_1}{h_2}\right) = \frac{4}{5} \times \frac{5}{7} = \frac{4}{7} = 4 : 7$

29. (d) According to the question,

Lateral surface area $= 2\pi r h$

$\Rightarrow \quad 2\pi r h = 1760 \Rightarrow 2 \times \frac{22}{7} \times r \times 20 = 1760$

$\Rightarrow \quad r = \frac{1760 \times 7}{44 \times 20} = 14$

$\therefore$ Volume of cylinder $= \pi r^2 h$

$= \frac{22}{7} \times 14 \times 14 \times 20 = 12320 \text{ cm}^3$

30. (b) According to the question,

Circumference = Breadth

$\therefore \quad 2\pi r = 22 \Rightarrow 2 \times \frac{22}{7} \times r = 22 \Rightarrow r = \frac{7}{2}$

$\therefore$ Volume of cylinder $= \pi r^2 h$

$= \frac{22}{7} \times \frac{7}{2} \times \frac{7}{2} \times 50 = 1925 \text{ cm}^3$

31. (b) HCF of 50, 150 and 175 = 25 cm

Side of each cube = 25 cm

Total number of cubes $= \frac{\text{Volume of cuboid}}{\text{Volume of cube}}$

$= \frac{50 \times 150 \times 175}{25 \times 25 \times 25} = 2 \times 6 \times 7 = 84$

32. (b)

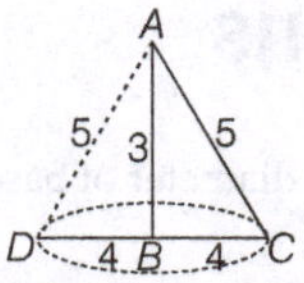

Let ΔABC is a right angled triangle.

Where $\angle B = 90°$ and $AB = 3$ cm

Triangle is rotated along AB to form a cone $ADBC$.

Here, radius $(r) = 4$ cm, height $(h) = 3$ cm and slant height $(l) = 5$ cm

$\therefore$ Volume of the cone $(V) = \frac{1}{3}\pi r^2 h$

$= \frac{1}{3} \times \pi \times (4)^2 \times 3 = 16\pi \text{ cm}^3$

33. (b) Let radius be r cm.

We know, Volume of cone $= \frac{1}{3}\pi r^2 h$

$1232 = \frac{1}{3} \times r^2 \times 24 \times \frac{22}{7}$

$r^2 = 49 \Rightarrow r = 7$ cm

We know, $l^2 = h^2 + r^2 = (24)^2 + (7)^2 = 625$

$\therefore \quad l = 25$ cm

Total surface area $= \pi r l + \pi r^2$

$= \pi r(l + r) = \frac{22}{7} \times 7\,(25 + 7)$

$= 22 \times 32 = 704 \text{ cm}^2$

34. (b) Length of cuboid = 8 cm

Breadth = 4 cm, Heigth = 6 cm

Volume of the cuboid $= l \times b \times h = 8 \times 4 \times 6$

$= 192 \text{ cm}^3$

35. (b) Given, radius $(r) = 8$ cm

Height $(h) = 14$ cm

We know,

$\therefore$ Volume of cylinder $= \pi r^2 h$

$= \frac{22}{7} \times 8 \times 8 \times 14 = 2816 \text{ cm}^3$

36. (a) Ratio of radii of cone is 2 : 5

Ratio of volume of cone is 3 : 5

$\frac{\text{Volume of first cone}}{\text{Volume of second cone}} = \frac{\frac{1}{3}\pi r_1^2 h_1}{\frac{1}{3}\pi r_2^2 h_2}$

$\Rightarrow \quad \frac{3}{5} = \left(\frac{2}{5}\right)^2 \times \frac{h_1}{h_2} \Rightarrow \frac{h_1}{h_2} = \frac{3}{5} \times \frac{25}{4}$

$\Rightarrow \quad \frac{h_1}{h_2} = \frac{15}{4}$ or 15 : 4

Hence, $h_1 : h_2 = 15 : 4$

37. (c) Let, length, width and height of cuboid is $6x$, $3x$ and $2x$ cm, respectively.

According to the question,

$2(6x \times 3x + 3x \times 2x + 2x \times 6x) = 1800$

$2 \times 36x^2 = 1800$

$x^2 = \frac{1800}{72} = 25 \Rightarrow x = 5$

Hence, volume of cuboid $= 6x \times 3x \times 2x$

$= 36x^3 = 36 \times 5 \times 5 \times 5 = 4500 \text{ cm}^3$

38. (a) Number of small cubes

$= \frac{\text{Volume of solid cube}}{\text{Volume of small cube}}$

$= \frac{48 \times 48 \times 48}{64} = 1728$

39. (b) $\because$ Prism and pyramid have same base and height

$\therefore$ Required ratio $= \frac{\text{Volume of prism}}{\text{Volume of pyramid}}$

$= \frac{\text{Area of base} \times \text{Height}}{\frac{1}{3} \times \text{Area of base} \times \text{Height}}$

$= \frac{3}{1} = 3 : 1$

40. (c) Volume of a cylinder $= \pi r^2 h$

$= 3.14 \times 10 \times 10 \times 20 = 6280 \text{ cm}^3$

41. (d) Area of base $= \frac{\sqrt{3}}{4}(\text{side})^2 = \frac{\sqrt{3}}{4} \times (8)^2$

$= 16\sqrt{3} \text{ cm}^2$

Clearly, the pyramid has 3 triangular faces each with sides 8 cm, 24 cm, 24 cm

So, $s = \frac{8 + 24 + 24}{2} = 28$

Area of each lateral face,

$= \sqrt{s(s-a)(s-b)(s-c)}$

$= \sqrt{28 \times (28-8)(28-24)(28-24)}$

$= \sqrt{28 \times 20 \times 4 \times 4} = 16\sqrt{35}$

$\therefore$ Whole surface area of the pyramid

$= 16\sqrt{3} + 3 \times 16\sqrt{35}$

$= (16\sqrt{3} + 48\sqrt{35}) \text{ cm}^2$

42. (a) Curved surface area of cylinder

$= 2\pi rh$

$\Rightarrow \quad 126\pi = 2\pi r \times 14$

$\Rightarrow \quad r = \frac{126}{14 \times 2} = \frac{9}{2} \text{ cm}$

Volume of cylinder $= \pi r^2 h$

$= \pi \times \frac{9}{2} \times \frac{9}{2} \times 14 = \frac{81 \times 7\pi}{2} = \frac{567\pi}{2}$

Volume of cylinder $= 283\frac{1}{2}\pi \text{ cm}^3$

43. (c) Side of a square base $(a) = 8$ cm

Height of a pyramid $(h) = 3$ cm

Slant height of a pyramid $(l) = \sqrt{\left(\frac{a}{2}\right)^2 + h^2}$

$= \sqrt{4^2 + 3^2} = \sqrt{16 + 9} = \sqrt{25} = 5 \text{ cm}$

Total surface area of a pyramid

$= \frac{1}{2} \times$ Perimeter of a base $\times$ Slant height of a pyramid + Area of a base

$= \frac{1}{2} \times 4a \times l + a^2 = 2al + a^2$

$= 2 \times 8 \times 5 + 8^2$

$= 80 + 64 = 144 \text{ cm}^2$

44. (c) Breadth of a room $(b) = b$

Height of a room $(h) = \frac{b}{2}$

Length of a room $(l) = 2b$

Length of the longest diagonal

$= \sqrt{l^2 + b^2 + h^2}$

$= \sqrt{(2b)^2 + b^2 + \left(\frac{b}{2}\right)^2}$

$= \sqrt{4b^2 + b^2 + \frac{b^2}{4}}$

$= \sqrt{\frac{16b^2 + 4b^2 + b^2}{4}} = \sqrt{\frac{21b^2}{4}} = \frac{\sqrt{21}b}{2}$

45. (a) According to the question,

Number of bottles

$= \frac{\text{Volume of hemispherical bowl}}{\text{Volume of cylindrical bottle}}$

$= \frac{\frac{2}{3}\pi r^3}{\pi r_c^2 h} \quad [r_c = \text{radius of bottle}]$

$= \frac{\frac{2}{3}\pi \times 18 \times 18 \times 18}{\pi \times 3 \times 3 \times 6}$

$= 2 \times 2 \times 18 = 72$

46. (c) Side of a cube = 21 cm

Diameter of a largest sphere = 21 cm

Radius of a largest sphere $= \frac{21}{2}$ cm

Volume of a sphere $= \frac{4}{3}\pi r^3$

$= \frac{4}{3} \times \frac{22}{7} \times \frac{21}{2} \times \frac{21}{2} \times \frac{21}{2}$

$= 4851 \text{ cm}^3$

47. (b) Let a radius of sphere be r.

Surface area of sphere $= 4\pi r^2$

New radius of sphere $= r \times \frac{100 - 48}{100}$

New radius of sphere $= \frac{52}{100} r$

Surface area of new sphere $= 4\pi \left(\frac{52r}{100}\right)^2$

Decreasing percentage

$= \frac{4\pi r^2 - 4\pi\left(\frac{52}{100}r\right)^2}{4\pi r^2} \times 100\%$

$= \frac{4\pi r^2 \left(\frac{100^2 - 52^2}{100^2}\right)}{4\pi r^2} \times 100\%$

$= \frac{10000 - 2704}{100 \times 100} \times 100\%$

$= \frac{7296}{100}\% = 72.96\%$

Speedy Method

Initial	:	Final
100		52
100		52
10000		2704
100	:	27.04

$\therefore$ Decrease in surface area

$= \frac{100 - 27.04}{100} \times 100 = 72.96\%$

48. (c) Curved surface area of cylinder

$= 1408 \text{ cm}^2$

$\Rightarrow \quad 2\pi rh = 1408$

$\Rightarrow \quad 2 \times \frac{22}{7} \times r \times 56 = 1408$

$\Rightarrow \quad 2r = 8 \text{ cm}$

Then, diameter of the base of cylinder

$= 2r = \frac{8}{100} = 0.08 \text{ m}$

49. (a) Total surface area of hemisphere

$= 4\pi r^2 = 4 \times \frac{22}{7} \times 7 \times 7 = 616 \text{ cm}^2$

$\therefore$ Cost of painting $= 616 \times \frac{40}{20} = ₹ 1232$

50. (c) Side of a cube $= \sqrt[3]{4096} = 16$ cm

51. (b) Total surface area of the box

$= 6 \times (\text{side})^2 = 6 \times 12^2 = 864 \text{ cm}^2$

52. (a) Volume of petrol tank

$= 50 \times 25 \times 10 \text{ m}^3 = 12500 \text{ m}^3$

$= 12500000 \text{ L} \quad [\because 1 \text{ m}^3 = 1000 \text{ L}]$

$\therefore$ 12500000 L of petrol can be accommodated, when the tank is completely filled.

53. (c) Surface area of the sculpture $= 4\pi r^2$

$= 4 \times \frac{22}{7} \times 35 \times 35 = 15400 \text{ cm}^2$

54. (c) CSA of cone $= \pi rl$

$= \frac{22}{7} \times 21 \times 60 = 3960 \text{ cm}^2$

55. (a) Height of the cylinder = 12 cm

Curved surface area = 2640 cm^2

Let radius of base = r cm

$2\pi r \times 12 = 2640$

$\Rightarrow \quad \frac{2 \times 22 \times 12 \times r}{7} = 2640$

$\Rightarrow \quad r = \frac{2640 \times 7}{44 \times 12} = 35 \text{ cm}$

$\therefore$ Volume of the cylinder $= \pi r^2 h$

$= \frac{22}{7} \times 35^2 \times 12 = 46200 \text{ cm}^3$

56. (b) Total area excluding the floor

$= 2(bh) + 2hl + (lb)$

$= 2(20 \times 15) + 2(10 \times 15) + 10 \times 20$

$= 600 + 300 + 200 = 1100\text{m}^2$

Total cost of white washing at the rate of ₹ 10.20 m^2 $= 1100 \times 10.20 = ₹ 11220$

57. (c) Length of the cube = 12 cm

Volume $= 12^3 = 1728 \text{ cm}^3$

Two smaller cubes having sides are 6 cm and 8 cm and their volumes are 216 cm^3 and 512 cm^3, respectively.

$\therefore$ Volume of the third cubes

$= 1728 - 216 - 512 = 1000 \text{ cm}^3$

$\therefore$ Side of the third cube $= \sqrt[3]{1000} = 10$ cm

58. (c) Material required $= \frac{4}{3}\pi(3^3 - 2^3)$

$= \frac{4}{3}\pi \times (27 - 8) = \frac{76\pi}{3}$ cubic unit

59. (a) Area of four walls of the room

$= 2h(l+b) = 2\times 6\times(8+10)$

$= 12\times 18 = 216\,m^2$

Area of ceiling $= l\times b = 10\times 8 = 80\,m^2$

Total area $= 80 + 216 = 296\,m^2$

Cost of white washing $= 296\times 7.50 =$ ₹ 2220.

60. (a) Given, inner diameter = outer radius

Volume of pipe $= \frac{88}{7}\,m^3$

and length of pipe = 1 m

$\therefore \quad \pi r^2 h = \frac{88}{7} \Rightarrow \frac{22}{7}\times r^2\times 1 = \frac{88}{7}$

$\Rightarrow \quad r^2 = 4 \Rightarrow r = 2$

Inner diameter $= 2\times 2 = 4$ cm

Then, outer radius, $R = 4$ m

Then, volume of outer pipe $= \pi(R^2 - r^2)h$

$= \pi(4^2 - 2^2)\times 1 = \frac{22}{7}\times 12\times 1 = 37.7\,m^3$

Hence, required material $= 37.7\,m^3$

61. (d) Given, inner radius of hemisphere

$= 5$ cm

and outer radius of hemisphere = 5.25 cm

So, volume of material $= \frac{2}{3}\pi(R^3 - r^3)$

$= \frac{2}{3}\times\frac{22}{7}\times(5.25^3 - 5^3)$

$= 41.28\,cm^3$

62. (c) Bricks required $= \frac{5\times 14\times 0.125}{0.0014} = 6250$

63. (a) Total volume of three sphere

$= \frac{4}{3}\pi\,\{(1^3 + 6^3 + 8^3)\}$

$= \frac{4}{3}\pi\,\{1 + 216 + 512\}$

$= \frac{4}{3}\pi\times 729$

According to the question,

$\frac{4}{3}\pi\times 729 = \frac{4}{3}\pi r^3 \Rightarrow 729 = r^3$

$\therefore$ Radius of the new sphere, $r = \sqrt[3]{729} = 9$ cm

64. (d) Volume of the cuboid $= 8\times 8\times 16\,m^3$

Volume of cube $= \frac{8\times 8\times 16}{2} = 8\times 8\times 8\,m^3$

$\therefore$Side of cube = 8

So, total surface area of cube $= 6a^2$

$[\because a = \text{side}]$

$= 6\times 8^2 = 384\,m^2$

65. (a) Given, length : breadth : height

$= 1:2:3$

Volume of cuboid $= lbh$

Volume = 6 cu. unit

After increasing

Length : Breadth : Height = 3 : 8 : 12

Volume = 288 cu. unit

Now, increase in volume $= 288 - 6 = 282$

$\therefore$Volume increased $= \frac{282}{6} = 47$ times

66. (d) $\therefore$ Total surface area of cone

$= \pi rl + \pi r^2 = \pi\times 6\times 10 + \pi\times 6^2$

$= 6(10\pi + 6\pi) = 6\times 16\times 3.14$

$= 301.44\,cm^2$

67. (b) Given, slant height $(l) = 6\sqrt{3}$ cm

According to the question,

Curved surface area of cone

$= 2\times$Base area of cone

$\Rightarrow \pi rl = 2\pi r^2 \Rightarrow r = \frac{l}{2} \Rightarrow r = \frac{6\sqrt{3}}{2} = 3\sqrt{3}$ cm

Then, $h = \sqrt{l^2 - r^2} = \sqrt{(6\sqrt{3})^2 - (3\sqrt{3})^2}$

$= \sqrt{108 - 27} = \sqrt{81} = 9$ cm

68. (b) Total surface area of cuboid

$= 2(lb + bh + lh)$

$= 2(5\times 7 + 7\times 11 + 5\times 11)$

$= 2(35 + 77 + 55)$

$= 2\times 167 = 334\,cm^2$

69. (b) Let the sides of three cubes be $3x$, $4x$ and $5x$ and the side of bigger cube be a.

$\therefore$ Sum of volume of three smaller cubes

= Volume of bigger cube

$\therefore\ 27x^3 + 64x^3 + 125x^3 = (a)^3$

$\Rightarrow \quad 216x^3 = (a)^3 \Rightarrow a = 6x$

We know, diagonal of cube $= a\sqrt{3}$

$\therefore$ Diagonal of bigger cube $= 6x\sqrt{3} = 18\sqrt{3}$

$\Rightarrow \quad 6x = 18 \Rightarrow x = 3$

$\therefore$ The sides of the smaller cubes

= 9 cm, 12 cm and 15 cm

70. (d) Given, surface area of a cube

$= 5046\,cm^2$

$\Rightarrow \quad 6a^2 = 5046 \Rightarrow a^2 = 841 \Rightarrow a = 29$ cm

Hence, volume of cube $= a^3$

$= (29)^3 = 24389\,cm^3$

71. (d) Surface area of the ball $= 9\pi$

$4\pi r^2 = 9\pi \Rightarrow r = \frac{3}{2}$

$\therefore$ Diameter of the ball $(D) = 2r$

$= \frac{3}{2}\times 2 = 3$ units

72. (d) Lateral surface area of cylinder

$= 3168\,cm^2$

$\Rightarrow \quad 2\pi rh = 3168$

$\Rightarrow \quad 2\times\frac{22}{7}\times r\times 48 = 3168$

$\Rightarrow \quad r = \frac{3168\times 7}{2\times 22\times 48} \Rightarrow r = \frac{21}{2}$ cm

Then, volume of cylinder $= \pi r^2 h$

$= \frac{22}{7}\times\frac{21}{2}\times\frac{21}{2}\times 48 = 16632\,cm^3$

73. (b) Volume of conical tent $= \frac{1}{3}\pi r^2 h$

$= \frac{1}{3}\times\frac{22}{7}\times 7^2\times 24 = 1232\,m^3$

Volume of each rice bag $= 2m^3$

$\therefore$ Number of rice bags $= \frac{1232}{2} = 616$

74. (d) $\because$ Volume of cone $= \frac{1}{3}\pi r^2 h_1$

Volume of cylinder $= \pi r^2 h_2$

If these are equals, then

$\Rightarrow \quad \frac{1}{3}\pi r^2 h_1 = \pi r^2 h_2 \Rightarrow \frac{h_1}{h_2} = \frac{3}{1}$

$\Rightarrow \quad h_1 : h_2 = 3:1$

75. (c) Surface area of cone $= \pi rl$

$= \pi r\sqrt{h^2 + r^2} = \frac{22}{7}\times 6\times\sqrt{64 + 36}$

$= \frac{22}{7}\times 6\times 10 = 188.57$ units

76. (d) Curved surface area of the tent $= \pi rl$

and $\quad l^2 = r^2 + h^2 \therefore l^2 = (24)^2 + (10)^2$

$l = \sqrt{676} = 26$ m

$\therefore$ Curved surface area of the tent $= \pi rl$

$= \pi\times 24\times 26 = 624\pi\,m^2$

77. (d) Let the radius of the third small ball be x cm.

A spherical ball of lead, 3 cm in diameter is melted and recasted into three spherical balls.

Radius of the ball $(r) = 1.5$ cm

Volume of the bigger spherical ball

$= \frac{4}{3}\pi r^3 = \frac{4}{3}\times\pi\times(1.5)^3 = \frac{9}{2}\pi\,cm^3$

The diameters of two smaller spherical balls are 1.5 cm and 2 cm respectively. So, the radius will be 0.75 cm and 1 cm respectively.

The volume of these two smaller spherical balls

$= \left\{\frac{4}{3}\pi\times(0.75)^3\right\} + \left\{\frac{4}{3}\pi\times(1)^3\right\}$

$= \frac{9\pi}{16} + \frac{4\pi}{3} = \frac{91\pi}{48}$

Volume of the third ball

$= \frac{9\pi}{2} - \frac{91\pi}{48} = \frac{125\pi}{48}\,cm^3$

$\Rightarrow \quad \frac{4}{3}\pi\times x^3 = \frac{125\pi}{48}$

$\Rightarrow \quad x^3 = \frac{125}{64} \Rightarrow x = \sqrt[3]{\frac{125}{64}}$

$x = \frac{5}{4} = 1.25$

$\therefore$Diameter of the third ball $= 1.25\times 2 = 2.5$ cm

78. (a) Given, Perimeter of one face of a cube

$= 40$ cm

$\therefore$Side of the cube $= \frac{40}{4} = 10$ cm

$\therefore$Volume of the cube $= 10^3 = 1000\,cm^3$

79. (a) Given, radius of a cone $(r) = 6$ cm

Height of a cone $(h) = 8$ cm

$\therefore \quad l = \sqrt{h^2 + r^2} = \sqrt{64 + 36} = 10$ cm

Then whole surface area of a cone

$= \pi r(r + l) = \frac{22}{7}\times 6(6 + 10)$

$= \frac{22}{7}\times 6\times 16 = 301.71\,cm^2$

80. (d) Given, slant height = 5 cm

Let the radius and height of cone = x cm

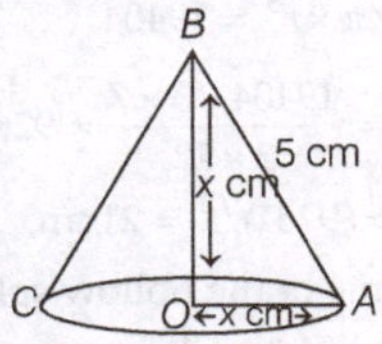

Then, $OA^2 + OB^2 = AB^2 \Rightarrow 2x^2 = (5)^2$

$x = \sqrt{\frac{25}{2}} \Rightarrow x = \frac{5}{\sqrt{2}}$ cm

Volume of cone $= \frac{1}{3}\pi r^2 h$

$= \frac{1}{3} \times \pi \times \left(\frac{5}{\sqrt{2}}\right)^2 \times \frac{5}{\sqrt{2}} = \frac{1}{3} \times \pi \times \frac{125}{2\sqrt{2}}$

$= \frac{125\pi}{6\sqrt{2}}$ cm^3

81. (c) Volume of cylindrical flask $= \pi r^2 h$

$= \frac{22}{7} \times (6)^2 \times 21$

$= 22 \times 36 \times 3 = 2376$ cm^3

82. (d) Volume of cone $= \frac{1}{3}\pi r^2 h$

$\Rightarrow \quad \frac{1}{3}\pi r^2 h = 73920$

$\Rightarrow \quad r^2 = \frac{73920 \times 3 \times 7}{22 \times 160}$

$\Rightarrow \quad r^2 = 441 \Rightarrow r = 21$ cm

Hence, diameter of the base $= 2r$

$= 2 \times 21 = 42$ cm

83. (c) Total surface area of a cube

$= 24$ sq. units

Let side of the cube = a unit

We know that,

Total surface area of cube $= 6a^2$

$\therefore \quad 6a^2 = 24 \Rightarrow a^2 = 4 \Rightarrow a = 2$

$\therefore$ Volume of the cube $= (\text{Side})^3$

$= 2^3 = 8$ cu. units

84. (c) Volume of solid hemisphere

$= \frac{2}{3} \times \frac{22}{7} \times \left(\frac{12.6}{2}\right)^3 = 523.908$ cm^3

85. (d) According to the question, 2 × Surface area of cylinder = Volume of cylinder

$\Rightarrow \quad 2 \times 2\pi rh = \pi r^2 h$

$\therefore \quad r = 4$

86. (a) Volume of water in conical vessel

$= \frac{1}{3} \times \pi \times r^2 \times h$

$= \frac{1}{3} \times \frac{22}{7} \times (20)^2 \times 27$

$= \frac{79200}{7}$ cm^3

Let the water rises by H cm into a cylindrical vessel.

$\pi \times (15)^2 \times H = \frac{79200}{7}$

$\therefore \quad H = \frac{79200}{7} \times \frac{7}{22} \times \frac{1}{225} = 16$ cm

87. (b) Let the height of the cone be h cm.

According to the question,

$\frac{1}{3} \times \pi \times 6 \times 6 \times h = \frac{4}{3} \times \pi \times 12 \times 12 \times 12$

$\therefore \quad h = 4 \times 48 = 192$ cm

88. (b) Given, $R = 5$ cm, $r = 3$ cm and $h = 7$ cm

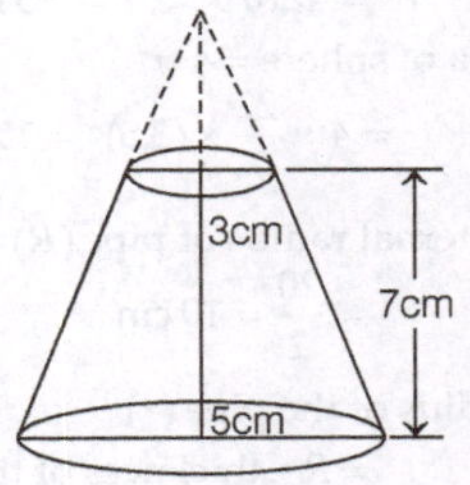

Volume of a frustum $= \frac{1}{3}\pi(R^2 + r^2 + Rr)h$

$= \frac{1}{3} \times \frac{22}{7}(25 + 9 + 15) \times 7$ cm^3

$= \frac{22 \times 49 \times 7}{3 \times 7}$ cm^3 $= 359.3$ cm^3

89. (c) Height of the cylinder (h) = 14 cm

Cylinder's radius (r) = 4 × 14 cm = 56 cm

Volume of the cylinder $= \pi r^2 h$

$= \frac{22}{7} \times 56 \times 56 \times 14$ cm^3

$= 137984$ cm^3

90. (c) Diameter of conical tent = 14 m

Then, Radius of conical tent, $r = \frac{14}{2} = 7$m

Slant height of conical tent, $l = 9$ m

Area of cloth to make in conical tent $= \pi rl$

$= \frac{22}{7} \times 7 \times 9 = 198$ m^2

$\therefore$ Length of cloth of 2 m width $= \frac{198}{2} = 99$ m

91. (a) According to the question,

Volume of cylinder = n × Volume of sphere

[n = Total number of solid spheres]

$\Rightarrow \quad \pi R^2 H = n \times \frac{4}{3}\pi r^3$

$[R = \frac{4}{2} = 2$ cm, $H = 90$ cm $r = \frac{6}{2} = 3$ cm$]$

$\Rightarrow \quad (2)^2 \times 90 = n \times \frac{4}{3} \times (3)^3$

$\Rightarrow \quad 4 \times 90 = n \times 4 \times 3 \times 3$

$\Rightarrow \quad n = \frac{4 \times 90}{4 \times 3 \times 3} \Rightarrow n = 10$

92. (a) Diameter of a sphere = Side of a cube

$= 1.4$ cm

Radius of a sphere $= \frac{14}{2} = 0.7$

Volume of a sphere $= \frac{4}{3}\pi r^3$

$= \frac{4}{3} \times \frac{22}{7} \times 0.7 \times 0.7 \times 0.7$

$= \frac{4}{3} \times \frac{22}{7} \times \frac{7}{10} \times \frac{7}{10} \times \frac{7}{10}$

$= 1.437 \approx 1.44$ cm^3

93. (c) Curved surface area of a cone $= \pi rl$

$594 = \frac{22}{7} \times 21 \times l \Rightarrow l = \frac{594 \times 7}{22 \times 21}$

$\therefore \quad l = 9$ cm

94. (a) According to the question, diameter of the sphere = Side of cube = 2.8 cm

Radius of the sphere $= \frac{2.8}{2} = 14$ cm

$\therefore$ Volume of largest sphere taken out of the cube $= \frac{4}{3} \times \pi \times r^3 = \frac{4}{3} \times \frac{22}{7} \times (1.4)^3$

$= 11.498$ cm^3 ≈ 11.50 cm^3

95. (d) Volume of vessel $= \frac{1}{3} \times \pi \times r^2 \times h$

$= \frac{1}{3} \times \frac{22}{7} \times 7 \times 7 \times 15 = 770$ cm^3

$\therefore$ Weight of vessel = 770 × 15 = 11550 gm

= 11.55 kg

96. (c) Let the side of the cube be a cm.

According to the question,

Volume of cuboid = Volume of cube

$\Rightarrow \quad l \times b \times h = (a)^3$

$\Rightarrow \quad 12 \times 18 \times 27 = a^3$

$\Rightarrow \quad a^3 = 5832 \Rightarrow a = \sqrt[3]{5832} \Rightarrow a = 18$ cm

Now, required ratio $= \frac{\text{Total surface of cuboid}}{\text{Total surface of cube}}$

$= \frac{2(lb + bh + hl)}{6a^2}$

$= \frac{2(12 \times 18 + 18 \times 27 + 12 \times 27)}{6 \times 18 \times 18}$

$= \frac{216 + 486 + 324}{3 \times 18 \times 18} = \frac{1026}{972} = \frac{19}{18}$

$= 19 : 18$

97. (b) We know that,

Volume of a cube $= (\text{side})^3$

$\Rightarrow \quad 343 = (\text{side})^3$

$\Rightarrow \quad$ Side of the cube $= \sqrt{343} = 7$ m

$\therefore$ Total surface area of the cube

$= 6\ (\text{side})^2 = 6 \times 7 \times 7 = 294$ m^2

98. (a) Volume of the hollow sphere

$= \frac{4}{3}\pi(R^3 - r^3) = \frac{4}{3}\pi(6^3 - 3^3)$ cm^3

$= \frac{4}{3}\pi(216 - 27)$ cm^3

$= \frac{4}{3} \times \pi \times 189$ cm^3 $= 252\pi$ cm^3

99. (d) Radius of the iron rod (R) = 2 cm

Length of the rod (L) = 12 cm

Wire's length (l) = 12 m = 1200 cm

[$\because$ 100 cm = 1 m]

Let radius of the wire (r) = x cm

Now, volume of the iron rod = Volume of the wire

$\pi R^2 L = \pi r^2 l$

$\Rightarrow \quad \pi \times 2 \times 2 \times 12 = \pi \times x \times x \times 1200$

$\Rightarrow \quad x^2 = \frac{4}{100} \Rightarrow x = \sqrt{\frac{4}{100}} = \frac{2}{10} = 0.2$

Thickness of the wire = Diameter of the wire

$= x \times 2$ cm

$[\because r = x = 0.2 \text{ cm}]$

$= 0.2 \times 2 \text{ cm} = 0.4$ cm

100. (b) Radius (r)

$= \sqrt{l^2 - h^2} = \sqrt{(10)^2 - (8)^2}$

$= \sqrt{100 - 64} = \sqrt{36} = 6$ m

$\therefore$ Curved surface area of cone

$= \pi rl = \pi \times 6 \times 10 = 60\pi \text{ m}^2$

101. (a) Volume of hemisphere $= \frac{2}{3}\pi r^3$

$= \frac{2}{3} \times \frac{22}{7} \times 5.6 \times 5.6 \times 5.6 \text{ cm}^3$

$= 367.95 \text{ cm}^3$

102. (c) Given, volume of sphere $= 38808 \text{ cm}^3$

$\Rightarrow \frac{4}{3}\pi r^3 = 38808 \Rightarrow \frac{4}{3} \times \frac{22}{7} \times r^3 = 38808$

$\Rightarrow r^3 = \frac{38808 \times 3 \times 7}{4 \times 22} \Rightarrow r^3 = 9261$

$\Rightarrow r = \sqrt[3]{9261} = 21$ cm

Hence, surface area of the sphere $= 4\pi r^2$

$= 4 \times \frac{22}{7} \times 21 \times 21 = 5544 \text{ cm}^2$

103. (b) Let radius of the wire be r m.

Since, sphere is drawn into a cylindrical wire. Then volume of sphere = volume of cylindrical wire

$\frac{4}{3}\pi R^3 = \pi(r)^2 h$

$\Rightarrow \frac{4}{3} \times \pi \times 9 \times 9 \times 9 = \pi \times r^2 \times 12$

$\Rightarrow r^2 = \frac{4 \times 9 \times 9 \times 9}{3 \times 12} \Rightarrow r^2 = 81$

$\Rightarrow r = \sqrt{81} = 9$ m

104. (d) Total surface area of cone

$= \pi r(l + r) = \frac{22}{7} \times 14 \times (30 + 14)$

$= 44 \times 44 = 1936 \text{ cm}^2$

105. (b) Inner radius of hemisphere bowl, $r = 6$ cm.

$\Rightarrow$ Outer radius of hemisphere bowl,

$R = (r + 0.37)$ cm $= (6 + 0.37)$ cm $= 6.37$ cm

Hence, outer curved surface area of hemisphere bowl $= 2\pi R^2$

$= 2 \times \frac{22}{7} \times 6.37 \times 6.37$

$= 255.0548 \text{ cm}^2$

106. (a) Volume of hemisphere $= \frac{2}{3}\pi r^3$

$= \frac{2}{3} \times \frac{22}{7} \times \frac{35}{2} \times \frac{35}{2} \times \frac{35}{2}$

$= 11229.166 \approx 11229.167 \text{ cm}^3$

107. (c) Volume of a hemisphere $= \frac{2}{3}\pi r^3$

$= \frac{2}{3} \times \frac{22}{7} \times (6.3)^3$

$= \frac{2}{3} \times \frac{22}{7} \times 6.3 \times 6.3 \times 6.3$

$= 523.908 \text{ cm}^3$

108. (b) Let radius of sphere be 'r' m.

Then, Volume of sphere $= 179\frac{2}{3} \text{ m}^3$

$\Rightarrow \frac{4}{3}\pi r^3 = \frac{539}{3} \Rightarrow 4 \times \frac{22}{7} \times r^3 = 539$

$\Rightarrow r^3 = \frac{539 \times 7}{4 \times 22}$

$\Rightarrow r^3 = 42.875 \Rightarrow r = 3.5$ m

Surface area of sphere $= 4\pi r^2$

$= 4 \times \frac{22}{7} \times (3.5)^2 = 154 \text{ m}^2$

109. (b) External radius of pipe (R)

$= \frac{20}{2} = 10$ cm

Internal radius of the pipe (r)

$= R -$ thickness of the pipe

$= (10 - 1)$ cm $= 9$ cm

Length of the pipe $(h) = 12$ cm

Total surface area of the pipe

$= 2\pi Rh + 2\pi rh + 2\pi(R^2 - r^2)$

$= \pi[2 \times 10 \times 12 + 2 \times 9 \times 12 + 2(10^2 - 9^2)]$

$= \pi[240 + 216 + 2 \times 19]$

$= \frac{22}{7} \times 494 = 1552.57 \text{ cm}^2$

110. (b) Radius of solid hemisphere,

$r = 21$ cm

Let, radius of base of cylinder $= R$ cm and height of cylinder $= H$ cm

$\Rightarrow$ Volume of hemisphere = Volume of cylinder

$\Rightarrow \frac{2}{3}\pi r^3 = \pi R^2 H \Rightarrow \frac{2}{3} \times 21 \times 21 \times 21 = R^2 H$

$\Rightarrow R^2 H = 6174 \Rightarrow H = \frac{6174}{R^2}$

Now, $\frac{\text{Curved surface area of cylinder}}{\text{Total surface area of cylinder}} = \frac{2}{5}$

$\Rightarrow \frac{2\pi RH}{2\pi R(H + R)} = \frac{2}{5} \Rightarrow \frac{H}{H + R} = \frac{2}{5}$

$\Rightarrow \frac{H + R}{H} = \frac{5}{2} \Rightarrow 1 + \frac{R}{H} = \frac{5}{2}$

$\Rightarrow \frac{R}{H} = \frac{5}{2} - 1 = \frac{3}{2} \Rightarrow \frac{R \times R^2}{6174} = \frac{3}{2}$

$\Rightarrow R^3 = \frac{3 \times 6174}{2} \Rightarrow R^3 = 9261$

$\Rightarrow R = \sqrt[3]{9261} = 21$ cm

111. (b) Given, diagonal of cube $= 6\sqrt{3}$ cm

Let side of cube $= a$

and diagonal of cube $= \sqrt{3}a$ cm

Side of cube $= a = 6$ cm

$\therefore$ Length of resulting cuboid

$= 6 + 6 + 6 = 18$ cm

Breadth of resulting cuboid = 6 cm

Height of resulting cuboid = 6 cm

Hence, surface area of resulting cuboid

$= 2(lb + bh + hl)$

$= 2(18 \times 6 + 6 \times 6 + 6 \times 18)$

$= 2(108 + 36 + 108) = 504 \text{ cm}^2$

112. (c) Volume of hemisphere $= \frac{2}{3} \times \pi \times r^3$

$\frac{2}{3} \times \pi \times r^3 = 19404$

$\Rightarrow r^3 = \frac{19404 \times 3 \times 7}{2 \times 22} = 9261$

$\Rightarrow r = (9261)^{1/3} = 21$ cm

113. (a) Volume of the hollow sphere

$= \frac{4}{3} \times \pi \times [(R)^3 - (r)^3] = \frac{4}{3} \times \pi \times [(4)^3 - (1)^3]$

$= \frac{4}{3} \times \pi \times [64 - 1] = \frac{4}{3} \times \pi \times 63 = 84\pi \text{ cm}^3$

114. (c) Total surface area of the cube

$= 1536 \text{ m}^2 \Rightarrow 6 \times (\text{Side})^2 = 1536$

$\Rightarrow (\text{Side})^2 = \frac{1536}{6} = 256$

Side $= \sqrt{256} = 16$ m

$\therefore$ Volume of the cube $= (\text{Side})^3$

$= (16)^3 = 4096 \text{ m}^3$

115. (c) Radius of the largest sphere

$= \frac{4.2}{2} = 2.1$ cm

$\therefore$ Volume of the largest sphere $= \frac{4}{3} \times \pi \times r^3$

$= \frac{4}{3} \times \frac{22}{7} \times (2.1)^3 = 38.808 \text{ cm}^3$

116. (a) Let the radius of sphere be r cm.

$\therefore$ Curved surface area of sphere $= 4\pi r^2$

$\Rightarrow 154 = 4 \times \frac{22}{7} \times r^2 \Rightarrow r^2 = \frac{154 \times 7}{4 \times 22}$

$\Rightarrow r^2 = \frac{7 \times 7}{4} \Rightarrow r = \frac{7}{2}$

$\therefore$ Volume of sphere $= \frac{4}{3}\pi r^3 = \frac{4}{3} \times \frac{22}{7} \times \left(\frac{7}{2}\right)^3$

$= 179.66 \text{ cm}^3 \approx 179.7 \text{ cm}^3$

117. (a) Length of the side of a cube = 5.6 cm

Radius of the largest sphere that can be taken out of the cube,

$r = \frac{5.6}{2} = 2.8$ cm

$\therefore$ Volume of sphere $= \frac{4}{3}\pi r^3$

$= \frac{4}{3} \times \frac{22}{7} \times (2.8)^3 = 91.98 \text{ cm}^3$

118. (d) Diagonal of a cube $= \sqrt{3}a$

$\sqrt{3}a = 7\sqrt{3} \Rightarrow a = 7$

Hence, surface area of the cube

$= 6 \times (a)^2 = 6 \times (7)^2$

$= 6 \times 49 = 294 \text{ cm}^2$

119. (d) $r = 9$ cm (radius of sphere)

$r' = 2$ cm (radius of wire)

Volume of sphere = Volume of wire

$\Rightarrow \frac{4\pi r^3}{3} = \pi(r')^2 h$

($\because$ wire is in the shape of cylinder)

$\Rightarrow \frac{4 \times 9 \times 9 \times 9}{3} = 2 \times 2 \times h$

$\Rightarrow h = 3 \times 81 = 243$ cm

120. (d) Given, height of the cylinder, $h = 2.1$ cm

Radius of the cylinder, $r = 3 \times 2.1$ cm $= 6.3$ cm

$\Rightarrow$ Volume of the cylinder $= \pi r^2 h$

$= \frac{22}{7} \times 6.3 \times 6.3 \times 2.1 = 261.95 \text{ cm}^3$

121. (a) The ratio of the radii of two cylinders $(r_1 : r_2) = 1:4$

and the ratio of their heights $(H_1 : H_2) = 4:3$

$\therefore$ Required ratio $= \frac{\pi r_1^2 H_1}{\pi r_2^2 H_2} = \left(\frac{r_1^2}{r_2^2}\right)\left(\frac{H_1}{H_2}\right)$

$= \left(\frac{1}{16}\right)\left(\frac{4}{3}\right) = \frac{1}{12} = 1:12$

122. (c) The total surface area of the sphere

$= 4\pi r^2 = 4 \times \frac{22}{7} \times \left(\frac{3.5}{2}\right)^2$

$= 4 \times \frac{22}{7} \times \frac{(3.5)^2}{4} = \frac{88}{7} \times \frac{12.25}{4}$

$= 38.5 \text{ cm}^2$

123. (a) Volume of the cuboid

$= 36 \times 18 \times 9 \text{ m}^3$

Volume of the cube $= (\text{side})^3$

Now, Volume of cuboid = Volume of cube

$\Rightarrow \quad 36 \times 18 \times 9 \text{ m}^3 = (\text{side})^3$

$\Rightarrow$ Side of the cube $= \sqrt[3]{36 \times 18 \times 9}$ m

$= \sqrt[3]{2 \times 2 \times 9 \times 2 \times 9 \times 9}$ m

$= 2 \times 9$ m $= 18$ m

Length of the diagonal of the cube

$= \sqrt{3} \times \text{side} = 18\sqrt{3}$ m.

124. (a) Height of the right circular cylinder $(h) = 3.5$ cm

Radius of the cylinder $= (r) = 5 \times 3.5$ cm

Volume of the cylinder $= \pi r^2 h$

$= \frac{22}{7} \times 5 \times 3.5 \times 5 \times 3.5 \times 3.5 \text{ cm}^3$

$= 22 \times 25 \times 6.125 = 3368.75 \text{ cm}^3$

125. (a) Surface area of cube = 864

$\Rightarrow \quad 6a^2 = 864 \Rightarrow a^2 = \frac{864}{6}$

$\Rightarrow \quad a^2 = 144 \quad a = \sqrt{144} = 12$ cm

$\therefore$ Volume of cube $= a^3 = (12)^3 = 1728 \text{ cm}^3$

126. (a) Radius of hemisphere

$(r) = \frac{28}{2} = 14$ cm

Volume of hemisphere $= \frac{2}{3}\pi r^3$

$= \frac{2}{3} \times \frac{22}{7} \times (14)^3 = 5749.33 \text{ cm}^3$

127. (a) I. Volume of the given cuboid

$6 \times 7 \times 8 = 336 \text{ cm}^3$

II. Volume of the given cube $= 7^3 = 343 \text{ cm}^3$

$\therefore$ Cube will have more volume.

128. (a) Radius (r) of hemispherical bowl

$= \frac{84}{2} = 42$ cm,

Curved Surface Area (CSA) of hemisphere

$= 2\pi r^2 = 2 \times \frac{22}{7} \times 42 \times 42$

$= 11088 \text{ cm}^2$

Cost of tin plating $= \frac{11088}{100} \times 21 =$ ₹ 2328.48

129. (c) Total surface area of sphere

$= 4\pi r^2 = 4 \times \frac{22}{7} \times \left(\frac{63}{2}\right)^2$

$= 12474 \text{ cm}^2$

130. (d) Volume of the resulted cube

= Sum of the volume of small cube

$= (6^3 + 8^3 + 10^3) \text{ cm}^3$

$= (216 + 512 + 1000) \text{ cm}^3 = 1728 \text{ cm}^3$

$= 12 \times 12 \times 12 \text{ cm}^3$

So, edge of the required cube $= \sqrt[3]{\text{Volume}}$

$= \sqrt[3]{12 \times 12 \times 12}$ cm $= 12$ cm

131. (b) Radius of the copper sphere

$(R) = \frac{18}{2}$ cm $= 9$ cm

Radius of the wire $(r) = \frac{6}{2}$ mm

$= 3$ mm $= 0.3$ cm [1cm = 10mm]

Let the length of the wire is h cm

Now, volume of copper sphere

= Volume of cylindrical wire

$\Rightarrow \quad \frac{4}{3}\pi R^3 = \pi r^2 h$

$\Rightarrow \quad \frac{4}{3} \times \pi \times 9 \times 9 \times 9 = \pi \times 0.3 \times 0.3 \times h$

$\Rightarrow \quad h = \frac{4 \times 3 \times 9 \times 9}{0.3 \times 0.3} = 4 \times 3 \times 9 \times 10 \times 10$

$= 10800$ cm $= 108$ m

[$\because$ 100 cm = 1 m]

132. (d) Given, radius of sphere

$(R) = 3\sqrt{2}$ cm

Base radius of cone $(r) = 3\sqrt{2}$ cm

If l be the slant height of the cone.

According to the question,

$4\pi R^2 = \pi r(l + r)$

$\Rightarrow \quad 4(3\sqrt{2})^2 = 3\sqrt{2}(l + 3\sqrt{2})$

$\Rightarrow \quad 12\sqrt{2} = l + 3\sqrt{2}$

$\therefore \quad l = 9\sqrt{2}$ cm

Now, height of the cone $(h) = \sqrt{l^2 - r^2}$

$h = \sqrt{(9\sqrt{2})^2 - (3\sqrt{2})^2}$

$= \sqrt{162 - 18} = \sqrt{144} = 12$ cm

133. (c) Let the radius of the cone be r cm.

According to the question,

$\frac{2}{3} \times \pi \times (4)^3 = \frac{1}{3} \times \pi \times r^2 \times 72$

$\Rightarrow \quad r^2 = \frac{2 \times 64}{72} = \frac{64}{36}$

$\Rightarrow \quad r = \sqrt{\frac{64}{36}} = \frac{8}{6} = 1.33$ cm

134. (b) Volume of rectangular solid

$= (88 \times 63 \times 42) \text{ cm}^3$

and volume of a spherical lead shot

$= \frac{4}{3} \times \frac{22}{7} \times \left(\frac{8.4}{2}\right)^3$

$\therefore$ Required number of shots

$= \frac{88 \times 63 \times 42}{\frac{4}{3} \times \frac{22}{7} \times \left(\frac{8.4}{2}\right)^3} = 750$

135. (b) Surface area of cube $= 6a^2$

$6a^2 = 13.5 \Rightarrow a^2 = 2.25$

$\Rightarrow \quad a = \sqrt{2.25} = 1.5$

Diagonal of cube $= a\sqrt{3} = 1.5\sqrt{3}$ m.

136. (a) Let the width of wall $= b$ m

Then height of wall $= 10\, b$ m

and length of wall $= 10b \times 8 = 80b$ m

Given volume of wall $= 51.2 \text{ m}^3$

$\Rightarrow \quad l \times b \times h = 51.2$

$\Rightarrow \quad 80b \times b \times 10b = 51.2$

$\Rightarrow \quad 800b^3 = 51.2 \Rightarrow b^3 = \frac{512}{8000}$

$\Rightarrow \quad b = \frac{8}{20} = \frac{2}{5}$ m

Now, area of one side of wall

$= l \times h = 80b \times 10b = 800 \times b^2$

$= 800 \times \frac{4}{25} = 128 \text{ m}^2$

$\therefore$ Required cost $= 128 \times 100 =$ ₹ 12800

137. (b) Area of base $= \pi r^2 = 346.5 \text{ cm}^2$

$\Rightarrow \quad r^2 = 110.25$ or $r = 10.5$ cm

Curved surface area $= 2\pi rh$

$2 \times \frac{22}{7} \times 10.5 \times h = 462$

$h = 7$ cm

Volume of cylinder $= \pi r^2 h = \frac{22}{7} \times 110.25 \times 7$

$= 2425.5 \text{ cm}^3$

138. (c) We know volume of sphere $= \frac{4}{3}\pi r^3$

Radius of bigger sphere $R = \frac{40}{2} = 20$ cm

Radius of smaller sphere $r = 0.5$ cm

Let number of smaller sphere be x,

According to the question,

$\Rightarrow x \times \frac{4}{3}\pi \times (0.5)^3 = \frac{4}{3} \times \pi \times (20)^3$

$x = \frac{8000}{0.125} = 64000$

139. (d) We know,

Volume = Base area × Height $= \pi r^2 \times h$

Net % change in base area

$= -10 + 10 + \frac{100}{100} = -19\%$

Net % change in volume

$= -19 + 20 - \frac{380}{100} = -2.8\%$

Hence, volume is decreased by 2.8%.

140. (b) Let the length of 1st rectangular sheet be 60 cm and breadth of 1st rectangular sheet be 36 cm.
Volume of cylinder (made by rolling along length) = $\pi r^2 h$

Now, $2\pi r_1 = 60 \Rightarrow r_1 = \frac{60}{2\pi}$

$\Rightarrow \quad V_1 = \pi\left(\frac{60}{2\pi}\right)^2 \times 36 \Rightarrow V_1 = \frac{3600}{4\pi} \times 36$

$\Rightarrow \quad V_1 = \frac{9 \times 3600}{\pi}$ cm^3

Similarly volume of cylinder (made by rolling along breadth) = $\pi r^2 h$

$\because \quad 2\pi r_2 = 36 \Rightarrow r_2 = \frac{36}{2\pi}$

$V_2 = \pi\left(\frac{36}{2\pi}\right)^2 \times 60 \Rightarrow V_2 = \frac{36 \times 36 \times 15}{\pi}$ cm^3

$\therefore$ Ratio of volumes $= \frac{V_1}{V_2}$

$= \frac{9 \times 3600}{\pi} \times \frac{\pi}{36 \times 36 \times 15}$

$\therefore \quad \frac{V_1}{V_2} = \frac{5}{3} \Rightarrow V_1 : V_2 = 5 : 3$

141. (d) Let slant height (l) of cone be $4x$ and height of cone (h) be $3x$ then
radius (r) of cone $= \sqrt{l^2 - h^2} = \sqrt{(4x)^2 - (3x)^2}$

$= \sqrt{16x^2 - 9x^2} = \sqrt{7}x$ unit

Now, CSA of cone $= 4\sqrt{7}\pi$

$\Rightarrow \quad \pi rl = 4\sqrt{7}\pi \Rightarrow \sqrt{7}x \times 4x = 4\sqrt{7}$

$\Rightarrow \quad x^2 = 1 \Rightarrow x = 1$

$\therefore$ Radius of cone $= \sqrt{7}x = \sqrt{7} \times 1 = \sqrt{7}$ units

142. (b) $\because$ Increment in the radius of sphere (r) = 20%

For two successive percentage, change in percentage $= \left(20 + 20 + \frac{20 \times 20}{100}\right)\% = 44\%$

Again, required change in volume

$= \left(44 + 20 + \frac{44 \times 20}{100}\right)$

$= (64 + 8.8)\ \% = 72.8\%$

Speedy Method

Volume of sphere $V_s = \frac{4}{3}\pi r^3$

$V_s \propto r^3$

Now, radius $\rightarrow +20\% = +\frac{1}{5}$

Initial	:	Final
5	:	6
5	:	6
5	:	6
125	:	216

+91

% Increase in volume $= \frac{91}{125} \times 100\% = +72.8\%$

143. (d) Required percentage change in volume $= \left(6 + 8 + \frac{6 \times 8}{100}\right)\% = 14.48\%$

144. (b) Volume of hemisphere $= \frac{2}{3}\pi r^3$

$= \frac{2}{3} \times \frac{22}{7} \times 18 \times 18 \times 18$

$= 12219.43$ cm^3

145. (c) Surface area of a cuboid

$= 2(lb + bh + hl)$

$= 2[(11 \times 7) + (7 \times 4) + (4 \times 11)]$

$= 2(77 + 28 + 44)$

$= 2 \times 149 = 298$ m^2

146. (c) Volume of cuboid $\propto lbh$

Initial	:	Final	
20	:	17	$\left(-15\% = \frac{-3}{20}\right)$
4	:	3	$\left(-25\% = \frac{-1}{4}\right)$
5	:	8	$\left(+60\% = \frac{+3}{5}\right)$
400	:	408	

% Increase in volume $= \frac{8}{400} \times 100\%$

$= 2\%$ (increase)

147. (d) Volume of the metal ball

$= \frac{4}{3}\pi r^3 = \frac{4}{3}\pi \times (3)^3$

Let the side of the cube formed be 'a'.
Volume of metal ball = Volume of dice formed + Volume of ball formed

$\Rightarrow \quad \frac{4}{3}\pi \times 3^3 = 27(a)^3 + \frac{4}{3}\pi \times 1^3$

$\Rightarrow \quad \frac{4}{3}\pi(27 - 1) = 27(a)^3$

$\Rightarrow \quad 27a^3 = \frac{4}{3} \times \frac{22}{7} \times 26 \Rightarrow a^3 = \frac{4 \times 22 \times 26}{3 \times 7 \times 27}$

$\Rightarrow \quad a^3 = 4.04$ units$^3 \Rightarrow a = 1.6$ units

148. (c) Area of the cylinder base,

$= \pi R^2 = 20$ cm^2

Volume of the cylinder $= \pi R^2 \times H$

$= 20 \times 8 = 160$ cm^3

149. (b) Given, Height of the cone, $h = 9$ ft.
Radius of the cone, $r = 7$ ft.
Volume of the cone-shaped storage

$= \frac{1}{3}\pi r^2 h = \frac{1}{3} \times \frac{22}{7} \times (7)^2 \times 9$

$= \frac{1}{3} \times \frac{22}{7} \times 49 \times 9 = 462$ cubic ft.

150. (d) $\pi rl = 13.2 \Rightarrow \frac{22}{7} \times r \times 4.2 = 13.2$

$\Rightarrow \quad r = \frac{13.2 \times 7}{22 \times 4.2} \Rightarrow r = 1$ unit

151. (a) Volume of wax (cuboid shape)

$= 70 \times 44 \times 20$ cm^3

Volume of 1 cylindrical candle

$= \frac{22}{7} \times 7 \times 7 \times 20$ cm^3

$= 22 \times 7 \times 20$ cm^3

$\therefore$ Total number of candles $= \frac{70 \times 44 \times 20}{22 \times 7 \times 20} = 20$

152. (c) Slant height of cone,

$l = \sqrt{9 + 16} = \sqrt{25} = 5$ cm

Curved surface area of cone $= \pi rl$

$= \pi \times 3 \times 5$ cm$^2 = 15\pi$ cm^2

153. (d) Let the breadth of the room be $2H$ m.

$\therefore$ The height of the room $= H$ m
the length of the room $= 4H$ m
Volume of the room $= 1728$ m^3

$\Rightarrow \quad (4H)(2H)(H) = 1728$

$\Rightarrow \quad 8H^3 = 1728$

$\therefore \quad H = 6$

$\therefore$ The length of the room is (6×4) m i.e., 24 m.

154. (a) Circumference $= 2\pi r = 30\pi$

$\Rightarrow \quad r = 15$ ft

Where, l is the slant height $= \sqrt{h^2 + r^2}$

$l = \sqrt{(20)^2 + (15)^2} = \sqrt{400 + 225}$

$= \sqrt{625} = 25$ ft

Thus, Area of canvas used for it $= \pi rl$

$= \pi \times 15 \times 25 = 375\pi$ sq ft

155. (a) Curved surface area of cone $= \pi rl$

$\therefore \quad 308 = \pi rl \Rightarrow 308 = \frac{22}{7} \times r \times 28$

$\Rightarrow \quad 308 = 22 \times r \times 4 \Rightarrow r = \frac{308}{22 \times 4}$

$\Rightarrow \quad r = 3.5$ cm

156. (d) volume of cone $= 150\pi$ cm^3

$\Rightarrow \frac{1}{3}\pi r^2 h = 150\pi \Rightarrow \frac{1}{3}\pi r^2 \times 18 = 150\pi$

$\Rightarrow \quad r^2 = \frac{150 \times 3}{18} \Rightarrow r^2 = 25 \Rightarrow r = 5$ cm

Slant height, $l = \sqrt{h^2 + r^2} = \sqrt{(18)^2 + (5)^2}$

$= \sqrt{324 + 25} = \sqrt{349}$

$\therefore \quad l = 18.68$ cm

157. (c) Let radius of cylinder, cone 1 and cone 2 be R, r_1 and r_2 respectively.
Let their volumes be V, V_1 and V_2 respectively.

$\therefore \ V = V_1 + V_2$

$V = x + 2x \quad [\because V_1 = x \text{ and } V_2 = 2x]$

$V = 3x$

Now, $\frac{22}{7} \times R^2 \times 12 : \frac{1}{3} \times \frac{22}{7} \times r_1^2 \times 12$

$: \frac{1}{3} \times \frac{22}{7} \times r_2^2 \times 12 = 3 : 1 : 2$

$\Rightarrow R^2 : r_1^2 : r_2^2 = 3 : 3 : 6$

Let R^2 be $3K$, r_1^2 be $3K$ and r_2^2 be $6K$.

Flat surface area of cylinder $= 2\pi R^2 = 6\pi K$

Flat surface area of two cones

$= \pi(r_1^2 + r_2^2) = 9\pi K$

Required percentage change

$= \frac{9\pi K - 6\pi K}{6\pi K} \times 100$

$= \frac{3\pi K}{6\pi K} \times 100 = 50\%$

158. (b) Surface area of spherical box $= 4\pi r^2$

$$528 = 4 \times \frac{22}{7} \times r^2 \Rightarrow r^2 = \frac{528 \times 7}{4 \times 22} = 42$$

$$\Rightarrow \quad r^2 = 42 \Rightarrow r = \sqrt{42}$$

159. (c) Radius (r) of cylinder = 7 cm

Curved surface area of cylinder $= 2\pi rh$

$$\Rightarrow \quad 396 = 2 \times \frac{22}{7} \times 7 \times h \Rightarrow h = \frac{396}{44} = 9$$

Now, Volume of cylinder $= \pi r^2 h$

$$= \frac{22}{7} \times 7 \times 7 \times 9 = 1386 \text{ cm}^3$$

160. (d) Now, according to the question,

Volume of hollow sphere = Volume of cone

$$\Rightarrow \quad \frac{4}{3}\pi [R^3 - r^3] = \frac{1}{3}\pi r_1^2 h$$

$$\Rightarrow \quad \frac{4}{3} \times \frac{22}{7}[(5)^3 - (3)^3] = \frac{1}{3} \times \frac{22}{7} \times (5)^2 \times h$$

$$\Rightarrow \quad 4[125 - 27] = 25 \times h$$

$$\Rightarrow \quad 4 \times 98 = 25h \Rightarrow h = 15.68 \text{ cm}$$

161. (a) CSA of cylinder $= 2200 \text{ cm}^2$

$$\Rightarrow \quad 2\pi rh = 2200$$

$$\Rightarrow \quad 2 \times \frac{22}{7} \times 7 \times h = 2200$$

$$\Rightarrow \quad h = 50 \text{ cm}$$

Now, TSA of cylinder $= 2\pi r(h + r)$

$$= 2 \times \frac{22}{7} \times 7(50 + 7) = 2 \times 22 \times 57$$

$$= 44 \times 57 = 2508 \text{ cm}^2$$

Speedy Method

Total surface area of cylinder = Curved surface area + $2\pi r^2$

$$= 2200 + 2 \times \frac{22}{7} \times 7 \times 7 = 2508$$

162. (c) Required change in surface area

$$= \left(125 + 125 + \frac{125 \times 125}{100}\right)\%$$

$$= (250 + 156.25)\% = 406.25\%$$

163. (b) Let the cost of painting per square centimeter = ₹ x

Now, according to the question,

$$4\pi r^2 \times x = 21560$$

$$\Rightarrow \quad 4 \times \frac{22}{7} \times \left(\frac{14}{2}\right)^2 \times x = 21560$$

$$\Rightarrow \quad 4 \times \frac{22}{7} \times \frac{14}{2} \times \frac{14}{2} \times x = 21560$$

$$\Rightarrow \quad x = \frac{21560}{616} \Rightarrow x = ₹\,35$$

164. (a) Let 'N' number of small laddoo be created from big laddoo.

$\therefore$ Volume of big laddoo = 'N' × Volume of small laddoo

$$\Rightarrow \quad \frac{4}{3}\pi R^3 = N \times \frac{4}{3}\pi r^3 \Rightarrow R^3 = N \times r^3$$

$$\Rightarrow \quad (5)^3 = N \times (2.5)^3 \Rightarrow N = 8$$

165. (c) Volume of cube $= a^3 = (8)^3$

$$= 512 \text{ cm}^3$$

166. (d) Capacity/volume of the bowl $= \frac{2}{3}\pi r^3$

$$= \frac{2}{3} \times \frac{22}{7} \times (9)^3 = 1527.43 \text{ cm}^3$$

167. (d) Volume of cone $= \frac{1}{3}\pi r^2 h$

$$= \frac{1}{3} \times \frac{22}{7} \times (5)^2 \times 6$$

Volume of cylinder $= \pi r^2 h = \frac{22}{7} \times (2.5)^2 \times 3$

$$\therefore \text{Required ratio} = \frac{\frac{1}{3} \times \frac{22}{7} \times 5 \times 5 \times 6}{\frac{22}{7} \times 2.5 \times 2.5 \times 3}$$

$$= \frac{2 \times 2 \times 2}{3} = \frac{8}{3} \text{ or } 8:3$$

168. (a) Given, $\frac{4\pi r_1^2}{4\pi r_2^2} = \frac{9}{49} \Rightarrow \frac{r_1}{r_2} = \frac{3}{7}$

$$\text{Ratio of volume} = \frac{\frac{4}{3}\pi(r_1)^3}{\frac{4}{3}\pi(r_2)^3} = \frac{(r_1)^3}{(r_2)^3} = \frac{(3)^3}{(7)^3}$$

$$= \frac{27}{343} = 27:343$$

169. (c) Length/Height of cylindrical shell

$$= 42 \text{ cm}$$

Volume of clay required $= \pi h(R^2 - r^2)$

$$= \frac{22}{7} \times 42[(7)^2 - (4)^2]$$

$$= 22 \times 6 \times (49 - 16) = 22 \times 6 \times 33$$

$$= 4356 \text{ cm}^3$$

170. (c) Let the radius of the sphere = r

New radius $= 1.4r$

Change in surface area $= 4\pi(1.4r)^2 - 4\pi r^2$

$$= 4\pi[1.96r^2 - r^2] = 4\pi r^2 \times 0.96$$

Now, Percentage increase in surface area

$$= \frac{4\pi r^2 \times 0.96 \times 100}{4\pi r^2}$$

$$= 0.96 \times 100 = 96\%$$

171. (d) Surface area of sphere

$$= 4 \times \frac{22}{7} \times 14 \times 14$$

$$= 4 \times 22 \times 2 \times 14$$

$$= 2464 \text{ cm}^2$$

172. (a) Now, length of the box formed

$$= 60 - (5 + 5) = 60 - 10 = 50 \text{ cm}$$

Breadth of the box formed

$$= 25 - (5 + 5) = 25 - 10 = 15 \text{ cm}$$

Height of the box formed = 5 cm

$\therefore$ Volume of the box $= l \times b \times h$

$$= 50 \times 15 \times 5 = 3750 \text{ cm}^3$$

173. (a) Volume of cube with side $a = a^3$

Volume of cuboid $= l \times b \times h$

Now, $\quad a^3 = 4(l \times b \times h)$

$$\Rightarrow \quad a^3 = 4(32 \times 8 \times 4)$$

$$a^2 = 4096 \Rightarrow a = 16 \text{ cm}$$

Now, total surface area of cube

$$= 6a^2 = 6 \times (16)^2$$

Total surface area of cuboid

$$= 2(lb + bh + hl)$$

$$= 2(32 \times 8 + 8 \times 4 + 4 \times 32)$$

$\therefore$ Required ratio

$$= \frac{6 \times 16 \times 16}{2(32 \times 8 + 8 \times 4 + 4 \times 32)}$$

$$= \frac{1536}{2 \times (256 + 32 + 128)}$$

$$= \frac{1536}{2 \times 416} = \frac{1536}{832} = 24:13$$

174. (d) Volume of sphere = Volume of wire

$$\Rightarrow \quad \frac{4}{3}\pi(6)^3 = \pi(0.2)^2 \times h$$

$\Rightarrow h$ (i.e., length of wire) = 7200 cm

175. (d) Volume of sphere $= \frac{4}{3}\pi r^3$

According to the question,

$$\frac{\frac{4}{3}\pi(r_1)^3}{\frac{4}{3}\pi(r_2)^3} = \frac{512}{3375}$$

$$\Rightarrow \quad \frac{(r_1)^3}{(r_2)^3} = \frac{512}{3375} \Rightarrow \frac{r_1}{r_2} = \frac{8}{15}$$

Now, surface area of sphere $= 4\pi r^2$

$\therefore$ Ratio of their surface areas

$$= \frac{4\pi(r_1)^2}{4\pi(r_2)^2} = \frac{(r_1)^2}{(r_2)^2} = \frac{64}{225} \text{ or } 64:225$$

176. (a) The largest possible rod that can be placed in a cubical room

$$= a\sqrt{3} = 42\sqrt{3} \Rightarrow a = 42 \text{ m}$$

The largest possible sphere that can fit inside the cubical room will have

$$2r = a \Rightarrow r = \frac{a}{2} = \frac{42}{2}$$

Now, its surface area $= 4\pi r^2$

$$= 4 \times \frac{22}{7} \times \frac{42}{2} \times \frac{42}{2} \quad (\because a = 42 \text{ m})$$

$$= 5544 \text{ m}^2$$

177. (c) Given, radius of sphere $(r) = 2.1$ cm

Volume of sphere $= \frac{4}{3}\pi r^3$

$$= \frac{4}{3} \times \frac{22}{7} \times 2.1 \times 2.1 \times 2.1$$

$$= 38.808 \text{ cm}^3$$

178. (b) Given, Circumference = 88 cm

$$\Rightarrow \quad 2\pi r = 88 \Rightarrow r = 14 \text{ cm}$$

Now, According to the question, let 'n' number of persons be served.

$\therefore$ Volume of hemispherical bowl

= n × Volume of hemispherical glass

$$\Rightarrow \quad \frac{2}{3}\pi(14)^3 = n \times \frac{2}{3}\pi\left(\frac{7}{2}\right)^3$$

$$\Rightarrow \quad (14)^3 = n \times \left(\frac{7}{2}\right)^3$$

$$\therefore \quad n = 64$$

179. (b) Slant height $(l) = \sqrt{(21)^2 + (28)^2}$

$$= \sqrt{441 + 784} = \sqrt{1225} = 35$$

Now, required cloths = Curved surface area of cone

$$= \pi rl = \frac{22}{7} \times 21 \times 35 = 2310\ m^2$$

Now, width of the cloth = 5 m

$\therefore$ Required length of cloth $= \frac{2310}{5} = 462$ m

180. (c) Given, $R = \frac{r}{4}$

and slant height = $L = 4l$

Total surface area of cone = $\pi R(R + L)$

$$\therefore \pi R(R + L) = \pi \times \frac{r}{4}\left(\frac{r}{4} + 4l\right) = \frac{\pi r^2}{16} + \frac{\pi r}{4} \times 4l$$

$$= \frac{\pi r^2}{16} + \pi rl = \pi r\left(\frac{r}{16} + l\right)$$

181. (c) Total surface area of hemisphere

$$= 3 \times \pi \times (11)^2 = 363\ \pi\ cm^2$$

182. (c) According to the question,

The number of balls,

$$n = \frac{\text{Volume of a solid metallic sphere}}{\text{Volume of a small ball}}$$

$$n = \frac{\frac{4}{3}\pi R^3}{\frac{4}{3}\pi r^3} \Rightarrow n = \frac{R^3}{r^3}$$

Here, R = radius of a solid metallic sphere

$$= \frac{32}{2} = 16\ cm$$

r = Radius of a solid ball $= \frac{4}{2} = 2$ cm

$$n = \frac{(16)^3}{(2)^3} \Rightarrow n = \frac{4096}{8} \Rightarrow n = 512$$

183. (a) We know that,

Radius $r^2 = l^2 - h^2$

$$r = \sqrt{(29)^2 - (20)^2} = \sqrt{441} = 21\ cm$$

According to the question,

$$\frac{\text{Total surface area of a cone}}{\text{Volume of a cone}}$$

$$= \frac{\pi r(r + l)}{\frac{1}{3}\pi r^2 h} = \frac{3(r + l)}{h \times r}$$

$$= \frac{3\,(21 + 29)}{20 \times 21} = \frac{5}{14} = 5:14$$

184. (d) The radius of a ice piece,

$$r = \frac{d}{2} = \frac{6}{2} = 3\ cm$$

The radius of a cylindrical container

$$R = \frac{d}{2} = \frac{18}{2} = 9\ cm$$

The height of a cylindrical container h = 40 cm

Formula used,

Number of ice pieces (n)

$$= \frac{\text{Volume of a cylindrical container}}{\text{Volume of an ice piece}}$$

$$n = \frac{\pi R^2 h}{\frac{4}{3}\pi r^3} \Rightarrow n = \frac{3 \times R^2 h}{4 \times r^3} = \frac{3 \times (9)^2 \times 40}{4 \times (3)^3}$$

$$n = \frac{3 \times 9 \times 9 \times 40}{4 \times 3 \times 3 \times 3} \Rightarrow n = 9 \times 10 \Rightarrow n = 90$$

185. (c) According to the question,

Number of hemisphere

$$(x) = \frac{\text{Volume of a metallic spherical ball}}{\text{Volume of a hemisphere}}$$

$$x = \frac{\frac{4}{3}\pi r^3}{\frac{2}{3}\pi R^3} \Rightarrow x = \frac{2r^3}{R^3}$$

Given, $\left(r = 3\text{ cm}, R = \frac{3}{2}\right)$

$$x = \frac{2(3)^3 \times (2)^3}{(3)^3} \Rightarrow x = 16$$

186. (d) Given, height of cylinder = 49 cm

And outer radius $= \frac{20}{2} = 10$ cm

And inner radius = 10 − 3 = 7 cm

$\therefore$ Volume of plastic = Volume of hollow cylinder = $\pi(R + r)(R - r)h$

$$= \frac{22}{7}(10 + 7)(10 - 7) \times 49$$

$$= 22 \times 17 \times 3 \times 7 = 7854\ cm^3$$

187. (b) Number of bottle required

$$= \frac{\text{Volume of hemispherical container}}{\text{Volume of a small cylindrical bottles}}$$

$$n = \frac{\frac{2}{3}\pi R^3}{\pi r^2 h} \Rightarrow n = \frac{2R^3}{3r^2 h}$$

$$D = 36, R = \frac{36}{2} = 18\ cm$$

(radius of hemispherical container)

$$d = 6, r = \frac{6}{2} = 3\ cm$$

(radius of a small cylindrical bottles)

$$h = 6\ cm$$

(height of a small cylindrical bottles)

$$n = \frac{2 \times 18 \times 18 \times 18}{3 \times 3 \times 3 \times 6} \Rightarrow n = 72$$

188. (d) Let diameter = x

Then, radius $= \frac{x}{2}$

Now, volume of a sphere $= \frac{4}{3} \times \pi \times r^3$

$$= \frac{4}{3} \times \pi \times \left(\frac{x}{2}\right)^3 = \frac{1}{6}x^3\pi$$

According to the questions, Diameter $= \frac{x}{2}$

Then, radius $= \frac{x}{4}$

Now, volume of a sphere $= \frac{4}{3}\pi r^3 = \frac{4}{3}\pi\left(\frac{x}{4}\right)^3$

$$= \frac{4}{3}\pi \times \frac{x}{4} \times \frac{x}{4} \times \frac{x}{4} = \frac{1}{48}x^3\pi = \frac{1}{8}\left(\frac{1}{6}x^3\pi\right)$$

We can clearly see that the volume reduced by $\frac{1}{8}$ of the former volume.

189. (c) Let their height be $7x$ and $5x$ and their diameter are $10y$ and $21y$.

So, their radius = $5y$ and $10.5y$ $\left[\because R = \frac{D}{2}\right]$

Now, their volumes $= \frac{1}{3}\pi r_1^2 h_1 : \frac{1}{3}\pi r_2^2 h_2$

$$= \frac{5y \times 5y \times 7x}{10.5 \times 10.5y \times 5x} = 20:63$$

190. (d) According to the question,

Ratio of volume of cylinders

$$= \frac{\pi r_1^2 h_1}{\pi r_2^2 h_2} = \frac{(4)^2 \times 5}{(5)^2 \times 2} = \frac{8}{5} = 8:5$$

191. (c) Volume of a cone $= \frac{1}{3}\pi r^2 h$

$$= \frac{1}{3} \times \frac{22}{7} \times 6 \times 6 \times 7 = 264\ cm^3$$

192. (d) Given, radius of frustum r_2 = 28 cm, r_1 = 7 cm

And height = 45 cm

Let radius of cylinder = $3x$

And height of cylinder = $5x$

Now,

Volume of frustum = Volume of cylinder

$$\frac{1}{3}\pi(r_1^2 + r_2^2 + r_1 \times r_2) \times h = \pi R^2 H$$

$$\Rightarrow \frac{1}{3}\{(7)^2 + (28)^2 + 7 \times 28\} \times 45 = 9x^2 \times 5x$$

$$\Rightarrow \frac{1}{3}(49 + 784 + 196) = \frac{45x^3}{45}$$

$$\Rightarrow \frac{1}{3} \times 1029 = x^3 \Rightarrow x^3 = 343 \Rightarrow x = 7$$

Radius of cylinder (R) = $3x = 3 \times 7 = 21$ cm

Height of cylinder (H) = $5x = 5 \times 7 = 35$ cm

Now, curved surface area of cylinder

$$= 2\pi RH = 2 \times \frac{22}{7} \times 21 \times 35 = 4620\ cm^2$$

193. (d) Capacity of the tank = Volume of cone

$$\Rightarrow \frac{1}{3}\pi r^2 h = \frac{1}{3} \times 3.14 \times 7 \times 7 \times 9 \text{ cubic feet}$$

$$= 461.58 \text{ cubic feet}$$

194. (d) Total surface area to be painted

= Area of 4 walls + Area of ceiling

$= [2(l + b)h + l \times b]$

[l = length, b = breadth, h = height]

$= [2(10 + 5)6 + 10 \times 5]\ m^2$

$= [180 + 50]\ m^2 = 230\ m^2$

195. (b) Length of the longest rod

= Length of the diagonal of the room

$$= \sqrt{(12)^2 + (9)^2 + (8)^2}\ m$$

$$= \sqrt{289}\ m = 17\ m$$

196. (b) Capacity of the cylindrical tank

$$= \pi r^2 h \Rightarrow 64\pi \times 1000\ cm^3 = \pi r^3$$

[Given, radius = height, 1L = 1000 cm^3]

$$\Rightarrow r = 4 \times 10\ cm = 40\ cm$$

197. (c) The total surface area of a cuboid

$= 2(l \times b + b \times h + l \times h)$

$= 2(7 \times 5 + 5 \times 9 + 7 \times 9)$

$= 2(35 + 45 + 63)$

$= 2(143) = 286\ cm^2$

198. (c) Given, The volume of a wall

$= 23958 \text{ cm}^3$

Let the breadth of the wall $= x$ cm

$\Rightarrow$ Height of the wall $= 6x$ cm

and Length of the wall $= 3x$ cm

According to the question,

$3x \times x \times 6x = 23958$

$\Rightarrow \quad x^3 = 1331 \Rightarrow x = 11 \text{ cm}$

199. (c) Given, the curved surface area of a solid right circular cylinder $= 2\pi rh$

$2\pi rh = 2200 \text{ cm}^2 \qquad \ldots\text{(i)}$

and the circumference of a solid right circular cylinder $2\pi r = 110 \qquad \ldots\text{(ii)}$

From Eqs. (i) and (ii),

$h = \dfrac{2200}{110} = 20 \text{ cm}$

200. (c) Required number of metallic spheres

$= \dfrac{\text{Volume of cylinder}}{\text{Volume of spheres}}$

$= \dfrac{\pi \times \left(\dfrac{8}{2}\right)^2 \times 18}{\dfrac{4}{3} \times \pi \times \left(\dfrac{6}{2}\right)^3} = \dfrac{4 \times 4 \times 18}{\dfrac{4}{3} \times 27} = \dfrac{72 \times 3}{27} = 8$

201. (a) Surface area of the sphere $= 4\pi r^2$

$= 4 \times \pi \times (5)^2 = 100\pi \text{ cm}^2$

202. (b) The length of the longest pole

$= \sqrt{l^2 + b^2 + h^2}$

$= \sqrt{(60)^2 + (30)^2 + (20)^2}$

$= \sqrt{3600 + 900 + 400}$

$= \sqrt{4900} = 70$ feet

203. (b) Volume of sphere $= \dfrac{4}{3}\pi r^3$

$\Rightarrow \quad \dfrac{4}{3}\pi r^3 = 4851 \Rightarrow r^3 = 4851 \times \dfrac{3}{4} \times \dfrac{7}{22}$

$\Rightarrow \quad r^3 = 1157.625 \Rightarrow r = 10.5 \text{ cm}$

Surface area $= 4\pi r^2 = 4 \times \dfrac{22}{7} \times (10.5)^2$

$= 1386 \text{ cm}^2$

204. (b) $\dfrac{\text{Total surface area of sphere}}{\text{Volume of sphere}} = \dfrac{2}{7}$

$\Rightarrow \quad \dfrac{4\pi r^2}{\dfrac{4}{3}\pi r^3} = \dfrac{2}{7} \Rightarrow \dfrac{3}{r} = \dfrac{2}{7} \Rightarrow r = 10.5 \text{ cm}$

205. (b) Area of four walls $= 2h(l + b)$

$= 2 \times 10(12 + 8) = 20(20) = 400 \text{ m}^2$

Cost of 400 m^2 wall painting

$= 25 \times 400 = 10000$

206. (a) Given, Capacity of cylinder *A* and *B* is same.

Ratio of diameters of *A* and *B* is 1 : 4 or radius $\dfrac{1}{2} : 2$

$\dfrac{\pi r_1^2 h_1}{\pi r_2^2 h_2} = \dfrac{1}{1} \Rightarrow \dfrac{h_1}{h_2} = \dfrac{(2)^2}{(1/2)^2}$

$\Rightarrow \quad \dfrac{h_1}{h_2} = \dfrac{16}{1} = 16 : 1$

207. (b) Volume of a cylinder $= \pi \times r^2 \times h$

$\pi r^2 h = 6160$

$h = \dfrac{6160}{\pi \times r^2} = \dfrac{6160 \times 7}{14 \times 14 \times 22} = 10 \text{ cm}$

Curved surface area $= 2\pi rh$

$= 2 \times \dfrac{22}{7} \times 14 \times 10 = 880 \text{ cm}^2$

208. (d) Let each side length of newly formed cube is x.

According to the question,

$x^3 = 9^3 + 5 \times 13 \times 31$

$\Rightarrow \quad x^3 = 729 + 2015$

$\Rightarrow \quad x^3 = 2744 = 14^3 \Rightarrow x = 14$

Total surface area of new cube

$= 6 \times 14^2 = 1176 \text{ cm}^2$

The total cost will be $= 1176 \times 10 =$ ₹ 11760

209. (b) Let, 'n' number of small solid sphere can be made.

So, $n \times$ Volume of small solid sphere

= Volume of bigger solid sphere

$\Rightarrow n \times \dfrac{4}{3} \times \pi \times 2^3 = \dfrac{4}{3} \times \pi \times 11^3$

$\Rightarrow \quad r = \dfrac{11 \times 11 \times 11}{2 \times 2 \times 2} = 166.37 \approx 166$

210. (c) Curved surface area of cylinder

$= 2\pi rh \Rightarrow 2\pi rh = 880$

$\Rightarrow 2 \times \left(\dfrac{22}{7}\right) \times 14 \times h = 880$

$\Rightarrow \quad 2 \times \dfrac{22}{7} \times 14 \times h = 880$

$\Rightarrow \quad h = \dfrac{880 \times 7}{2 \times 22 \times 14} = 10 \text{ cm}$

Now, volume of the cylinder $= \pi r^2 h$

$= \dfrac{22}{7} \times 14 \times 14 \times 10 = 22 \times 280 = 6160$

211. (b) Surface area of cube

$= 6a^2$ (a is side of cube)

$\Rightarrow \quad 1728 = 6a^2$

$\Rightarrow \quad a^2 = 288 \Rightarrow a = 12\sqrt{2}$

$\therefore$ Volume of cube $= (12\sqrt{2})^3 = 3456\sqrt{2}$

212. (c) Let the height be h.

Volume of Cylinder $= \pi r^2 h$

$448 = \dfrac{\pi \times 8 \times 8}{\pi \times \pi} \times h$

$\Rightarrow \quad h = \dfrac{448 \times \pi}{64} \Rightarrow h = \dfrac{448 \times 22}{64 \times 7} = 22 \text{ cm}$

213. (c) Volume of toy $= \dfrac{2}{3}\pi r^3 + \pi r^2 h + \dfrac{1}{3}\pi r^2 h$

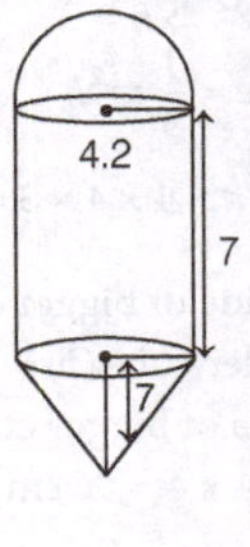

$= \pi r^2 \left(\dfrac{2}{3}r + h + \dfrac{h}{3}\right)$

$= \dfrac{22}{7} \times 4.2 \times 4.2 \left(\dfrac{2}{3} \times 4.2 + 7 + \dfrac{7}{3}\right)$

$= 55.44 \left(2.8 + \dfrac{28}{3}\right)$

$= 55.44 \times \dfrac{364}{30} = 672.672 \text{ cm}^3$

214. (d) Ratio of volume of sphere

$= \dfrac{\dfrac{4}{3}\pi r_1^3}{\dfrac{4}{3}\pi r_2^3} = \left(\dfrac{r_1}{r_2}\right)^3 = \left(\dfrac{4}{5}\right)^3 = \dfrac{64}{125}$

215. (c) Given, dimensions are in the ratio of 4 : 3 : 2.

Let length be $4x$ m, height be $2x$ m and breadth be $3x$ m.

We know that,

Volume = Length × Breadth × Height

$\Rightarrow \quad 12288 = 4x \times 3x \times 2x$

$\Rightarrow \quad 12288 = 24x^3 \Rightarrow x^3 = 512$

$\therefore \quad x = 8$

$\therefore$ Length $= 4x = 4 \times 8 = 32$ m

Breadth $= 3x = 3 \times 8 = 24$ m

Height $= 2x = 2 \times 8 = 16$ m

We know that, total surface area = 2 (length × breadth + breadth × height + height × length)

$= 2(32 \times 24 + 24 \times 16 + 16 \times 32)$

Total surface area $= 2(1664) = 3328 \text{ m}^2$

Rate of polish = 2 paise per m^2

$\therefore$ Total cost of polishing $= 2 \times 3328$ paise

= 6656 paise = ₹ 66.56

216. (c) According to the question, in cylinder

Radius $(r) = \dfrac{\text{Diameter}}{2} = \dfrac{14}{2} = 7 \text{ cm}$

Length $(h) = 2$ cm

Cylinder is melted to form cuboid hence volume will be same.

Volume of cylinder $= n \times$ Volume of cuboid

[Here, n is the number of cuboidal candles]

$\Rightarrow \quad \pi \times r^2 \times h = n \times 7 \times 11 \times 2$

$\Rightarrow \quad \dfrac{22}{7} \times 7 \times 7 \times 2 = n \times 7 \times 11 \times 2$

$\Rightarrow \quad n = \dfrac{22 \times 7 \times 2}{7 \times 11 \times 2} = 2$

$\therefore$ Total two cuboidal candles will be formed.

217. (c) Let the radius of spherical ball be 'r' cm, then surface area of sphere = 1386

$\Rightarrow \quad 4\pi r^2 = 1386$

$\Rightarrow \quad r^2 = \dfrac{1386}{4 \times \dfrac{22}{7}}$

$\Rightarrow \quad r^2 = 110.25 \Rightarrow r = \sqrt{110.25} = 10.5$

Now, volume of sphere $= \dfrac{4}{3}\pi r^3$

$= \dfrac{4}{3} \times \dfrac{22}{7} \times (10.5)^3 = 4851 \text{ cm}^3$

218. (d) Total surface area of cuboid
= 2 (Length × Breadth + Breadth × Height + Height × Length)
$= 2(19 \times 9 + 9 \times 4.5 + 4.5 \times 19)$
$= 2(171 + 40.5 + 85.5) = 2(297)$
$= 594\ cm^2$

219. (a) Given, diameter $(d) = 4$ cm
Inner radius $(r) = 2$ cm
Thickness = 0.5 cm
∴ Outer radius $(R) = 2.5$ cm
We know that,
Volume of silver used $= \frac{2}{3}\pi(R^3 - r^3)$
$= \frac{2}{3} \times 3.14 \times 7.625 = 15.96\ cm^3$

220. (c) Given, side of a cube is 5 cm.
When these are joined end to end to become cuboid of sides
$= (5 + 5 + 5), 5, 5 = 15, 5, 5$
∴ Length = 15 cm, breadth
= 5 cm and height = 5 cm
Cuboid surface area = 2 (Length × Breadth + Breadth × Height + Height × Length)
$= 2(15 \times 5 + 5 \times 5 + 15 \times 5)$
$= 2(75 + 25 + 75) = 350\ cm^2$

221. (b) Length of cuboid shaped cardboard
= 60 cm
Breadth of cardboard $= \frac{60}{2} = 30$ cm
Height of cardboard $= 30 \times \frac{1}{3} = 10$ cm
Thus, surface area of cardboard
$= 2(lb + bh + hl)$
$= 2(60 \times 30 + 30 \times 10 + 10 \times 60)$
$= 2(1800 + 300 + 600)$
$= 2(2700) = 5400\ cm^2$

222. (d) Let the number of small spherical balls be n.
Then, volume of bigger sphere
= Volume of small sphere × n
$\frac{4}{3}\pi R^3 = n \times \frac{4}{3}\pi r^3$
$\Rightarrow \frac{4}{3}\pi \times 6 \times 6 \times 6 = n \times \frac{4}{3} \times \pi \times 3 \times 3 \times 3$
$\Rightarrow n = \frac{\frac{4}{3} \times \pi \times 6 \times 6 \times 6}{\frac{4}{3}\pi \times 3 \times 3 \times 3}$
$\Rightarrow n = 2 \times 2 \times 2 = 8$
∴ Required number of small sphere = 8

223. (c) According to the question,
$4\pi r^2 = 616$
$\Rightarrow r^2 = 616 \times \frac{7}{22} \times \frac{1}{4} = 49$
$\therefore r = 7$ cm

224. (a) Let the number of smaller cubes be n.
Let the side of original and new cube be A cm and a cm, respectively.
As, surface area of original cube $= 54\ cm^2$
$\Rightarrow 6A^2 = 54 \Rightarrow A^2 = 9 \Rightarrow A = 3$ cm
Also, surface area of smaller cube $= \frac{8}{12}\ cm^2$
$\therefore 6a^2 = \frac{8}{12} \Rightarrow a^2 = \frac{8}{72} = \frac{1}{9} \Rightarrow a = \frac{1}{3}$
According to the question,
n × Volume of new cube = Volume of original cube
$\therefore n \times a^3 = A^3 \Rightarrow n \times \frac{1}{27} = 27$
$\Rightarrow n = 27 \times 27 = 729$

225. (c) We know, surface area of sphere
$= 4\pi r^2$
Let radii of two spheres be r_1 and r_2.
According to the question,
$\frac{4\pi r_1^2}{4\pi r_2^2} = \frac{49}{81} \Rightarrow \left(\frac{r_1}{r_2}\right)^2 = \frac{49}{81}$
$\Rightarrow \frac{r_1}{r_2} = \frac{7}{9} \Rightarrow r_1 : r_2 = 7 : 9$
∴ Ratio of their volumes $= \frac{\frac{4}{3}\pi r_1^3}{\frac{4}{3}\pi r_2^3} = \left(\frac{7}{9}\right)^3 = \frac{343}{729}$

226. (a) Given,
Article dimensions = 9 cm, 6 cm, 3 cm
and box dimensions = 63 cm, 42 cm, 21 cm
We know that,
Volume = length × breadth × height
∴ Number of articles $= \frac{63 \times 42 \times 21}{9 \times 6 \times 3}$
$= 7 \times 7 \times 7 = 343$

227. (c) Given, sides of cuboid = 20 cm, 12 cm and 10 cm
To divide a cuboid into 8 equal pieces, the cuboid must be cut through the middle of each surface.
∴ Sides of smaller cuboid $= \frac{20}{2}, \frac{12}{2}, \frac{10}{2}$
∴ = 10 cm, 6 cm, 5 cm
Total surface area of 8 smaller cuboid
$= 8 \times 2[10 \times 6 + 6 \times 5 + 5 \times 10]$
$= 16[60 + 30 + 50] = 2240\ cm^2$

228. (d) Given, Curved surface area of cone
$= 20\pi \Rightarrow \pi rl = 20\pi \Rightarrow rl = 20$
$\therefore l = 5$ cm [∵ $r = 4$]
Thus, we know,
$\Rightarrow 5^2 = 4^2 + h^2$
$\Rightarrow h^2 = 3^2 \Rightarrow h = 3$
∴ Volume of cone $= \frac{1}{3}\pi r^2 h$
$= \frac{1}{3} \times \pi \times 4 \times 4 \times 3 = 16\pi\ cm^3$

229. (c) Given, side of bigger cube $(a) = 4$ cm
and side of smaller cube $(b) = 2$ cm
Total surface area of bigger cube $= 6a^2$
$= 6 \times 4 \times 4 = 96\ cm^2$
Total surface area of smaller cube $= 6b^2$
$= 6 \times 2 \times 2 = 24\ cm^2$
∴ Required ratio $= \frac{24}{96} = \frac{1}{4}$

230. (c) According to the question,
Volume of hemisphere $= \frac{2}{3}\pi r^3$
$= \frac{2}{3}\pi \times (5.5)^3 = \frac{2}{3} \times 3.14 \times 5.5 \times 5.5 \times 5.5$
$= 348.27\ cm^3 \simeq 348\ cm^3$

231. (d) Let height be $5x$.
Then breadth $= 5x \times \frac{1}{5} = x$
and length of cuboid $= \frac{1}{3}(5x + x) = \frac{6x}{3} = 2x$
∴ Volume of cuboid $= l \times b \times h$
$10\ L = 2x \times x \times 5x$
$10 \times 1000\ cm^3 = 10x^3 \Rightarrow x^3 = 1000$
$\Rightarrow x = 10$ cm
Thus, height of cuboid $= 5x = 5 \times 10 = 50$ cm

232. (d) Diameter of cylindrical cup = 7 cm
Radius of cylindrical cup $= \frac{7}{2}$ cm
Height of cylindrical cup = 4 cm
Volume of each cylindrical cup $= \pi r^2 h$
$= \frac{22}{7} \times \frac{7}{2} \times \frac{7}{2} \times 4 = 154\ cm^3$
Thus, volume of cylindrical cup 180 patients,
$= 154 \times 180 = 27720\ cm^3$
$= 27.72$ L [∵ $1\ L = 1000\ cm^3$]

233. (b) Let the required number of cones be n.
According to the question,
n × Volume of smaller cone
= Volume of sphere
$\Rightarrow n \times \frac{1}{3}\pi(3.5)^2 \times (4) = 3136\pi$
$\Rightarrow n = \frac{3136 \times 3}{49} = 192$

234. (c) Let the number of paper balls be n.
Given, diameter of original sphere = 18 cm
∴ Radius of original sphere $(R) = \frac{18}{2} = 9$ cm
Also, diameter of paper ball = 2 cm
∴ Radius of paper ball $(r) = \frac{2}{2} = 1$ cm
According to the question,
$n \times \frac{4}{3}\pi r^3 = \frac{4}{3}\pi R^3 \Rightarrow n(1)^3 = (9)^3$
$\therefore n = 729$

235. (c) Given,
Area of first face $(lb) = 120\ cm^2$ ...(i)
Area of second face $(bh) = 72\ cm^2$ ...(ii)
Area of third face $(hl) = 60\ cm^2$ ...(iii)
From Eqs. (i), (ii) and (iii), we get
$(lb)(bh)(hl) = 120 \times 72 \times 60$
$\therefore (lbh)^2 = 120 \times 72 \times 60$
$\Rightarrow lbh = \sqrt{120 \times 72 \times 60} = \sqrt{518400}$
∴ Volume of cuboid $= 720\ cm^3$

236. (c) Given, Radius (r) of cone = 6 cm

Slant height (l) = 10 cm

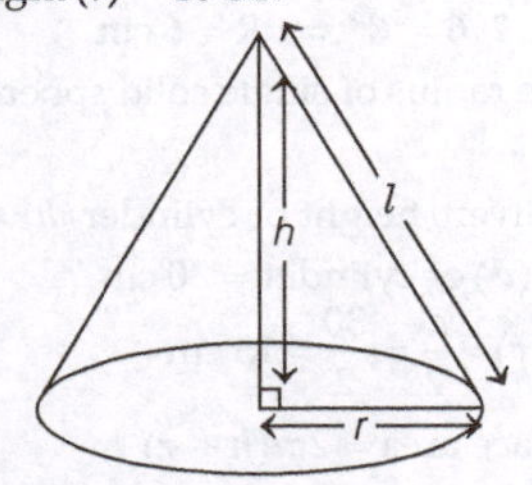

We know,

$\therefore$ Height (h) $= \sqrt{l^2 - r^2} = \sqrt{(10)^2 - (6)^2}$

$= \sqrt{100 - 36} = \sqrt{64}$

$h = 8$ cm

As, volume of cone $= \frac{1}{3}\pi r^2 h$

$= \frac{1}{3} \times \pi \times (6)^2 \times 8 = 96\,\pi\ \text{cm}^3$

237. (b) Given,

$$\frac{\text{Volume of first cube}}{\text{Volume of second cube}} = \frac{1}{125}$$

We know that, Volume of cube = $(\text{side})^3$

$$\therefore \frac{(\text{Side of first cube})^3}{(\text{Side of second cube})^3} = \frac{1}{125}$$

$$\frac{\text{Side of first cube}}{\text{Side of second cube}} = \frac{1}{5} \quad \ldots\text{(i)}$$

We know that,

Surface area of cube = $6\,(\text{side})^2$

$$\therefore \frac{\text{Surface area of first cube}}{\text{Surface area of second cube}} = \frac{6\,(\text{Side of first cube})^2}{6\,(\text{Side of second cube})^2}$$

$$= \left(\frac{1}{5}\right)^2 = \frac{1}{25} \quad \text{[From Eq. (i)]}$$

238. (c) Total sheet required

= Total surface area

We know that,

Total surface area of cylinder $= 2\pi r(r + h)$

$= 2 \times \frac{22}{7} \times 1.5\,(1.5 + 3)$

$= 2 \times \frac{22}{7} \times 1.5 \times 4.5 = 42.42\ \text{m}^2$

Hence, sheet of metal required = $42.42\ \text{m}^2$

239. (c) Given, Edge of cubical box

= 3 m = 300 cm

Edge of cube = 15 cm

We know that,

Volume of cubical box = $(\text{Side})^3 = (300)^3$

and volume of cube = $(\text{Side})^3 = (15)^3$

$\therefore$ Number of cube $= \frac{(300)^3}{(15)^3} = 8000$

240. (d) Area of adjacent faces are 5 cm^2, 15 cm^2 and 27 cm^2.

Surface area of cuboid $= 2(lb + bh + hl)$

$= 2(5 + 15 + 27) = 2 \times 47 = 94$

Surface area of cuboid = 94 cm^2

241. (a) Let for cylinder A, radius R and height H and for cylinder B, radius r and height = h

According to the question,

$$2\pi RH = 2\pi r \times h \times \frac{350}{100}$$

$$RH = rh \times \frac{7}{2} \quad \ldots\text{(i)}$$

and $R : r = 3 : 1$

Let radii are $3x$ and x.

Thus, $\frac{H}{h} = \frac{r}{R} \times \frac{7}{2} \Rightarrow \frac{H}{h} = \frac{1}{3} \times \frac{7}{2} = \frac{7}{6}$

Now, volume of cylinder A and cylinder B

$= \pi R^2 H : \pi r^2 h$

$= \pi \times 3^2 \times 7 : \pi \times 1^2 \times 6 = 63 : 6$

$\therefore$ Required percentage $= \frac{6}{63} \times 100 = 9.52\%$

242. (a) Lateral surface area of cube

= 144 cm^2

$4a^2 = 144 \Rightarrow a^2 = 36 \Rightarrow a = 6$ cm

Thus, side of cube is 6 cm.

Then, volume of cube $= a^3 = (6)^3 = 216\ \text{cm}^3$

243. (b) Volume of box with wood

$= (128 + 11) \times (90 + 11) \times (25 + 11)$

$= 139 \times 101 \times 36 = 505404\ \text{cm}^3$

Volume of wooden box without word

$= 128 \times 90 \times 25 = 288000\ \text{cm}^3$

Thus, volume of wood = 505404 − 288000

$= 217404\ \text{cm}^3$

244. (d) $\because$ Both cube joined,

$\therefore$ One of the sides = 5 + 5 = 10 cm

and remaining sides will be same.

$\therefore$ Side of cuboid = 5 cm, 5 cm and 10 cm.

We know that,

Total surface area of cuboid

= 2 (length × breadth + breadth × height + height 5 length)

$= 2\,(5 \times 5 + 5 \times 10 + 5 \times 10)$

$= 2\,(25 + 50 + 50)$

$= 2 \times 125 = 250\ \text{cm}^2$

245. (d) Given, Inner radius (r_1) = 6 cm

Outer radius (r_2) = 8 cm

Cost of polishing = ₹ 50/π cm^2

We know that,

Total surface area of a hemisphere

$= \pi\,(r_2^2 - r_1^2) + 2\pi\,(r_1^2 + r_2^2)$

$= \pi\,(8^2 - 6^2) + 2\pi\,(8^2 + 6^2)$

$= 28\pi + 200\pi = 228\pi$

$\therefore$ Total cost of polishing $= 228\pi \times \frac{50}{\pi}$

= ₹ 11400

246. (a) Given, radius (r) = 14 cm

and cost of painting = ₹ 5/cm^2

We know that, Surface area of sphere $= 4\pi r^2$

$= 4 \times \frac{22}{7} \times 14 \times 14 = 2464\ \text{cm}^2$

$\therefore$ Total cost of painting = Surface area of sphere × Cost

= 2464 × 5 = ₹ 12320

247. (b) Let the number of small cylinder be n.

According to the question,

Volume of bigger cylinder = n × Volume of smaller cylinder

$\pi \times R^2 H = n \times \pi r^2 h$

$\Rightarrow \pi \times 6 \times 6 \times 10 = n \times \pi \times 2 \times 2 \times 2.5$

$$n = \frac{\pi \times 6 \times 6 \times 10}{\pi \times 2 \times 2 \times 2.5} \Rightarrow n = 36$$

Hence, the required number of smaller cylinder = 36

248. (a) Let the original radius be r cm.

We know, Surface area of sphere $= 4\pi r^2$

According to the question,

$4\pi\,(r + 3.5)^2 = 4\pi r^2 + 550$

$\Rightarrow 4\pi\,(r^2 + 12.25 + 7r) = 4\pi r^2 + 550$

$\Rightarrow 4\pi r^2 + 49\pi + 28\pi r = 4\pi r^2 + 550$

$\Rightarrow 7\pi\,(7 + 4r) = 550$

$\Rightarrow 7 \times \frac{22}{7}(7 + 4r) = 550$

$\Rightarrow 22 \times 7 + 88r = 550$

$\Rightarrow 88r = 550 - 154 = 396$

$\Rightarrow r = \frac{396}{88} = 4.5$ cm

249. (d) Let the required number of cubes be n.

Given, dimensions of cuboid

= 36 cm × 22 cm × 12 cm

Dimension of cube = 6 cm

According to the question,

n × Volume of cube = Volume of cuboid

$\therefore \quad n \times (6)^3 = 36 \times 22 \times 12 \Rightarrow n = 44$

250. (c) Given, percentage increase = 5%

Effective percentage increase in surface area

$= \left(a + b + \frac{ab}{100}\right)\%$

$= \left(5 + 5 + \frac{5 \times 5}{100}\right)\% = 10.25\%$

251. (b) Given, radius of larger sphere

(R) = 8 cm

Radius of smaller sphere (r) $= \frac{4}{2}$ cm = 2 cm

We know that,

Volume of sphere $= \frac{4}{3}\pi\,(\text{radius})^3$

$\therefore$ Number of balls

$$= \frac{\text{Volume of larger sphere}}{\text{Volume of smaller sphere}}$$

$$= \frac{\frac{4}{3}\pi R^3}{\frac{4}{3}\pi r^3} = \frac{R^3}{r^3} = \frac{(8)^3}{(2)^3} = 64$$

252. (b) Total surface area = 294 cm^2

We know that,

Total surface area = $6a^2$ [where a = side]

$\Rightarrow 294 = 6a^2 \Rightarrow 49 = a^2 \Rightarrow a = 7$ cm

$\therefore$ Volume of cube = $a^3 = 7 \times 7 \times 7 = 343$ cm^3

253. (d) Given, diameter (d) = 35 cm

$\therefore$ Radius $(r) = \frac{35}{2}$ cm $= \frac{35}{200}$ m

Length (h) = 100 cm = 1 m

Revolution = 200

Surface area of roller = $2\pi rh$

$= 2 \times \frac{22}{7} \times \frac{35}{200} \times 1 = 1.1$ m^2

$\therefore$ Area of playground = Surface area × Number of revolutions

$= 1.1 \times 200 = 220$ m^2

254. (a) Let the radius of big sphere be 'R' cm.

Also, let the radii of three new circles be r_1, r_2 and r_3 cm.

We know, volume of sphere $= \frac{4}{3}\pi r^3$

According to the question,

$\frac{4}{3}\pi[r_1^3 + r_2^3 + r_3^3] = \frac{4}{3}\pi R^3$

$(75)^3 + (60)^3 + (45)^3 = R^3$

$\Rightarrow R^3 = (15)^3[(5)^3 + (4)^3 + (3)^3]$

$\Rightarrow R^3 = (15)^3[125 + 64 + 27]$

$\Rightarrow R^3 = (15)^3(216)$

$\Rightarrow R = \sqrt[3]{(15)^3 \times 216} = 15 \times 6 = 90$ cm

255. (a) Let the original side of cube be a cm.

$\because$ Original surface area = $6a^2$

New side of cube = $3a$ cm

$\therefore$ New surface area = $6(3a)^2 = 54a^2$

$\therefore$ Required percentage increase

$= \frac{54a^2 - 6a^2}{6a^2} \times 100 = \frac{48}{6} \times 100 = 800\%$

256. (d) Given, length = 30 cm

Breadth = 20 cm

Total surface area = 2600 cm^2

Let height of cuboid be 'h' cm.

According to the question,

$2(lb + bh + hl) = 2600$

$2(30 \times 20 + 20 \times h + h \times 30) = 2600$

$\Rightarrow 600 + 20h + 30h = 1300$

$\Rightarrow 50h = 700 \Rightarrow h = 14$ cm

257. (c) Given, diameter = 28 cm, height = 42 cm

We know, curved surface area $= 2\pi rh$

$= 2 \times \frac{22}{7} \times \frac{28}{2} \times 42 = 3696$ cm^2

258. (a) Given, radius of sphere (r_1) = 9 cm

Radius of wire (r_2) = 4 mm

According to the question,

Volume of sphere = Volume of wire

$\frac{4}{3}\pi \times \frac{9}{100} \times \frac{9}{100} \times \frac{9}{100} = \pi \times \frac{4}{1000} \times \frac{4}{1000} \times h$

$\Rightarrow h = \frac{4 \times \pi \times 9 \times 9 \times 9}{\pi \times 3 \times 4 \times 4} = 60.75$ m

259. (a) Given, diameter (d) of ball = 28 cm

$\therefore$ Radius (r) of ball $= \frac{d}{2} = \frac{28}{2} = 14$ cm

We know that,

Total surface area of ball = $4\pi r^2$

$= 4 \times \frac{22}{7} \times 14 \times 14 = 2464$ cm^2

$\therefore$ Cost of painting a ball = 2464 × 2 = ₹ 4928

260. (c) As, We know

Total surface area $= 2\pi r(h + r)$

$2 \times \frac{22}{7} \times 5(h + 5) = 628$

$h + 5 = \frac{628 \times 7}{2 \times 22 \times 5} \Rightarrow h + 5 = 19.98$

$h = 19.98 - 5 = 14.98$ m

Now, curved surface area $= 2\pi rh$

$= \left[2 \times \frac{22}{7} \times 5 \times 14.98\right] = 470.8$ m^2

> **Speedy Method**
>
> Total surface area
>
> = Curved surface area + $2\pi r^2$
>
> $\Rightarrow 628 = \text{CSA} + 2 \times \frac{22}{7} \times 25$ [$\because r = 5$ m]
>
> $\Rightarrow \text{CSA} = 628 - \frac{1100}{7} = 470.8$ m^2

261. (b) Let length (l), breadth (b) and height (h) of cuboid be $3x : 4x : 5x$.

According to the question,

$3x \times 4x \times 5x = 1620 \Rightarrow 60x^3 = 1620$

$x^3 = \frac{1620}{60} = 27 \Rightarrow x = 3$ m

$\therefore$ Length $(l) = 3x = 3(3) = 9$ m

Breadth $(b) = 4x = 4(3) = 12$ m

Height $(h) = 5x = 5(3) = 15$ m

Now, total surface area of cuboid

$= 2(lb + bh + hl)$

$= 2(9 \times 12 + 12 \times 15 + 15 \times 9)$

$= 2(108 + 180 + 135)$

$= 2 \times 423 = 846$ m^2

262. (d) Given, diameter$_1$ (d_1) = 6 cm

Diameter$_2$ (d_2) = 8 cm

Diameter$_3$ (d_3) = 10 cm

$\therefore$ Radius$_1$ $(r_1) = \frac{d_1}{2} = \frac{6}{2} = 3$ cm

Radius$_2$ $(r_2) = \frac{d_2}{2} = \frac{8}{2} = 4$ cm

Radius$_3$ $(r_3) = \frac{d_3}{2} = \frac{10}{2} = 5$ cm

Let the radius of single sphere = R

According to the question,

$\frac{4}{3}\pi r_1^3 + \frac{4}{3}\pi r_2^3 + \frac{4}{3}\pi r_3^3 = \frac{4}{3}\pi R^3$

$\Rightarrow \frac{4}{3}\pi(3)^3 + \frac{4}{3}\pi(4)^3 + \frac{4}{3}\pi(5)^3 = \frac{4}{3}\pi R^3$

$\Rightarrow \frac{4}{3}\pi[27 + 64 + 125] = \frac{4}{3}\pi R^3$

$\Rightarrow \frac{4}{3}\pi[216] = \frac{4}{3}\pi R^3$

$\Rightarrow 216 = R^3 \Rightarrow R = 6$ cm

Hence, the radius of single solid sphere is 6 cm.

263. (d) Given, height of cylinder (h) = 27 cm

Diameter (d) of cylinder = 30 cm

$\therefore$ Radius $(r) = \frac{d}{2} = \frac{30}{2} = 15$ cm

Total surface area $= 2\pi r(h + r)$

$= 2 \times \frac{22}{7} \times 15[27 + 15]$

$= 2 \times \frac{22}{7} \times 15 \times 42 = 3960$ cm^2

264. (c) Given, diameter (d) = 60 cm,

Height (h) = 10 cm

According to the question,

$\frac{2\pi rh}{2\pi r(h + r)} = \frac{h}{h + r} = \frac{10}{10 + \frac{60}{2}}$ $\left[\because r = \frac{d}{2}\right]$

$= \frac{10}{10 + 30} = \frac{10}{40}$

$\therefore$ Required ratio = 10 : 40 = 1 : 4

265. (b) Given, radius = 2.1 m = 210 cm

and height = 6.3 m = 630 cm

$\therefore$ Volume of tank/ capacity $= \pi r^2 h$

$= \frac{22}{7} \times 210 \times 210 \times 630$ cm^3

$= 87318000$ cm^3

$= 87318$ L $\left[\because 1\text{ L} = \frac{1}{1000}\text{ cm}^3\right]$

266. (d) Total surface area of a hemisphere

$= 3\pi r^2 = 3 \times \frac{22}{7} \times \left(\frac{28}{2}\right)^2$

$= 3 \times \frac{22}{7} \times 14 \times 14$

$= 1848$ cm^2

267. (c) Radius $(r) = \frac{14}{2} = 7$ cm

and height (h) = 9 cm

Total surface area of the cylinder

$= 2\pi r(r + h) = 2 \times \frac{22}{7} \times 7(7 + 9)$

$= 2 \times 22 \times 16 = 704$ cm^2

268. (b) According to the question,

Radius of cylinder = 3 cm

Height = 14 cm

$\therefore$ Curved surface area of cylinder

$= 2 \times \frac{22}{7} \times 3 \times 14 = 264$ cm^2

269. (a) Let radius of sphere = x

Radius of sphere is increased by 25%.

$\therefore$ Required per cent $= \left(x + x + \frac{x \times x}{100}\right)$

$= \left(25 + 25 + \frac{25 \times 25}{100}\right) = 56.25\%$

270. (a) Given, diameter $(d) = 14$ cm

Curved surface area $= 352\ cm^2$

Radius $= \frac{d}{2} = \frac{14}{2} = 7$ cm

According to the question,

$2\pi rh = 352\ cm^2$ [CSA $= 2\pi rh$]

$2 \times \frac{22}{7} \times 7 \times h = 352$ [$\because r = 7$ cm]

$\Rightarrow h = 8$ cm

Now, total surface area $= 2\pi r(h + r)$

$= 2 \times \frac{22}{7} \times 7[8 + 7]$

$= 44 \times 15 = 660\ cm^2$

Speedy Method

Total surface area

$=$ Curved surface area $+ 2\pi r^2$

$= 352 + 2 \times \frac{22}{7} \times 7 \times 7$ [$\because r = 7$]

$= 352 + 308 = 660$

271. (d) Let the edges of a rectangular box are $3x$, $5x$ and $8x$, respectively.

According to the question,

$2(3x \times 5x + 5x \times 8x + 3x \times 8x) = 632$

$\Rightarrow (15x^2 + 40x^2 + 24x^2) = 316$

$\Rightarrow 79x^2 = 316 \Rightarrow x^2 = 4 \Rightarrow x = 2$

$\therefore$ Edges of rectangular box are $3 \times 2, 5 \times 2, 8 \times 2 = 6, 10$ and 16

Now, volume of the box $= 6 \times 10 \times 16$

$= 960\ cm^3$ [$\because V = l \times b \times h$]

272. (b) Given, sides 6 cm, 8 cm and 10 cm.

According to the question,

$a^3 = 6^3 + 8^3 + 10^3 \Rightarrow a^3 = 1728 \Rightarrow a = 12$

Now, surface area of cube $= 6a^2$

$= 6 \times 12 \times 12 = 864\ cm^2$

273. (c) Let the radius of cylinder be r cm.

Then, radius of spherical ball will be $\frac{r}{3}$ cm.

Height of cylinder $(h) = 12r$

Let the number of spherical balls be n. Then, Volume of cylinder $= n \times$ Volume of each spherical ball

$\pi r^2 \times h = n \times \frac{4}{3}\pi\left(\frac{r}{3}\right)^3$

$\Rightarrow \pi r^2 \times (12r) = n \times \frac{4}{3}\pi \times \frac{r^3}{27}$

$\Rightarrow 12r^3 = n \times \frac{4}{3} \times \frac{r^3}{27}$

$\Rightarrow n = \frac{12 \times 27 \times 3}{4} = 243$

274. (b) Let the edge of each cube be a cm.

then, volume of cube $= 216\ cm^3$

$a^3 = 216 \Rightarrow a = \sqrt[3]{216} = 6$ cm

Length of new solid (cuboid) $= 4a$

$l = 4 \times 6 = 24$ cm

Width of new solid $(b) = a = 6$ cm

Height of new solid $(h) = a = 6$ cm

Total surface area of new solid

$= 2(lb + bh + hl)$

$= 2(24 \times 6 + 6 \times 6 + 6 \times 24)$

$= 2(144 + 36 + 144)$

$= 2 \times 324 = 648\ cm^2$

275. (c) According to the question,

Let radius of sphere $= 100$ units

$\therefore$ Volume $= \frac{4}{3}\pi \times (100)^3$

New radius of sphere $= 112$ units

$\therefore$ New volume $= \frac{4}{3}\pi \times (112)^3$

$\therefore$ Percentage increase in volume

$= \frac{4}{3}\pi(112)^3 - \frac{4}{3}\pi \times (100)^3$

$= \frac{4}{3}\pi((112)^3 - (100)^3)$

$= \frac{4}{3}\pi(1404928 - 1000000)$

$= \frac{4}{3}\pi \times 404928$

$\therefore$ Required increase in percentage

$= \frac{\frac{4}{3}\pi \times 404928}{\frac{4}{3}\pi \times 100 \times 100 \times 100} \times 100\%$

$= 40.49\%$

Speedy Method

Effective increased in volume

$= 12 + 12 + \frac{12 \times 12}{100}$

$= 24 + 1.44 = 25.44\%$

Again,

$= 25.44 + 12 + \frac{12 \times 25.44}{100}$

$= 37.44 + 3.0528 = 40.49\%$

276. (a) Given, Height of right circular cone $(h) = 24$ cm

Radius of its base $(r) = 10.5$ cm

$\therefore$ Volume of right circular cone $= \frac{1}{3} \times \pi r^2 h$

$= \frac{1}{3} \times \frac{22}{7} \times 10.5 \times 10.5 \times 24$

$= 2772\ cm^3$

277. (b) $\because$ Surface area of cuboid

$= 2(lb + bh + hl)$

$\therefore 2(6 \times 3 + 3 \times h + 6 \times h) = 108$

$\Rightarrow 9h + 18 = 54 \Rightarrow 9h = 54 - 18$

$\Rightarrow 9h = 36$

$\Rightarrow h = \frac{36}{9} = 4$ m

Hence, the height of cuboid is 4 m.

278. (c) The curved surface area of a cylinder

$= 2\pi rh \Rightarrow 2 \times \frac{22}{7} \times r \times 14 = 88$

$\Rightarrow r = \frac{88 \times 7}{44 \times 14} = 1$ cm

Hence, the total surface area of cylinder

$= 2\pi r(r + h)$

$= 2 \times \frac{22}{7} \times 1(1 + 14)$

$= \frac{2 \times 22 \times 15}{7} = \frac{660}{7}\ cm^2$

279. (c) Given, $\frac{h_1}{h_2} = \frac{5}{3}$ and $\frac{r_1}{r_2} = \frac{6}{5}$

As we know,

$\therefore$ Volume of cone $= \frac{1}{3}\pi r^2 h$

$\Rightarrow \frac{\frac{1}{3}\pi r_1^2 h_1}{\frac{1}{3}\pi r_2^2 h_2} = \frac{\pi \times (6)^2 \times 5}{\pi \times (5)^2 \times 3}$

$= \frac{\pi \times 36 \times 5}{\pi \times 25 \times 3} = \frac{12}{5}$

Hence, ratio of their volumes is 12 : 5.

280. (a) Let the initial radius $= r$

Let the final radius $= 2r$

Initial volume of sphere $= \frac{4}{3}\pi r^3$

Final volume of sphere $= \frac{4}{3}\pi(2r)^3$

$\therefore$ Then ratio of new and old sphere volume

$= \frac{\frac{4}{3}\pi(2r)^3}{\frac{4}{3}\pi r^3} = \frac{8}{1}$

$\therefore$ Required volume of sphere become 8 times the previous volume.

281. (b) Volume of cardboard box

$= l \times b \times h = 6 \times 10 \times 12 = 720\ cm^3$

According to the question,

Required boxes $= \frac{2160}{720} = 3$

Hence, 3 boxes are needed to pack $2160\ cm^3$.

282. (c) The radius and height of cylinder are in the ratio $= 6 : 7$

Let the radius $= 6x$

Let the height $= 7x$

$\therefore$ Volume of cylinder $= \pi r^2 h = 792\ cm^3$

$\Rightarrow \frac{22}{7} \times 6x \times 6x \times 7x = 792$

$x^3 = \frac{792 \times 7}{22 \times 6 \times 6 \times 7} = 1 \Rightarrow x = 1$

$\therefore$ Radius of cylinder $= 6 \times 1 = 6$

$\therefore$ Height of cylinder $= 7 \times 1 = 7$

Now, curved surface area $= 2\pi rh$

$= 2 \times \frac{22}{7} \times 6 \times 7 = 264$ cm

283. (c) Radius of sphere $(r) = \frac{10}{2} = 5$ cm

Total surface area of sphere $= 4\pi r^2$

$= 4 \times \pi \times 5 \times 5 = 100\pi$

Cost of paint $= \frac{80}{\pi} \times 100 \times \pi =$ ₹ 8000

284. (a) Given, diameter of hemisphere

$= 42$ cm

$\therefore$ Radius $(r) = \frac{42}{2} = 21$ cm

Volume of hemisphere $= \frac{2}{3}\pi r^3$

$= \frac{2}{3} \times \frac{22}{7} \times 21 \times 21 \times 21$

$= 19404$ cm^3

285. (d) Given, length = height (h) of cylinder = 68 cm

Base diameter (d) = 28 cm

$\therefore$ Radius $(r) = \frac{d}{2} = \frac{28}{2} = 14$ cm

Curved surface area $= 2\pi rh = 2 \times \frac{22}{7} \times 14 \times 68$

$= 5984$ cm^2

Total surface area $= 2\pi r(h + r)$

$= 2 \times \frac{22}{7} \times 14(68 + 14)$

$= 2 \times 22 \times 2 \times 82$

$= 7216$ cm^2

$\therefore$ Required difference = (7216 – 5984)

$= 1232$ cm^2

286. (d) Weight of empty box

= [External volume of box – Internal volume of box] $\times \frac{50}{1000}$

$= [60 \times 40 \times 20 - 58 \times 38 \times 18] \times \frac{50}{1000}$

$= [48000 - 39672] \times \frac{1}{20}$

$= 8328 \times \frac{1}{20} = 416.40$ kg

287. (c) Number of bricks

$= \frac{10 \text{ m} \times 22.5 \text{ cm} \times 6 \text{ m}}{25 \text{ cm} \times 12 \text{ cm} \times 9 \text{ cm}}$

$= \frac{10 \times 100 \times 22.5 \times 6 \times 100}{25 \times 12 \times 9} = 5000$

288. (d) Given, radius (r) = 6.2 cm

Total surface area $= 3\pi r^2 = 3 \times 3.14 \times (6.2)^2$

$= 9.42 \times 38.44 = 362.10$ cm^2

289. (d) As, we know that,

Capacity of a cylinder $= \pi r^2 h$

$\pi \times 21 \times 21 \times h = 8316$

$\Rightarrow \frac{22}{7} \times 21 \times 21 \times h = 8316$

$\Rightarrow h = 6$ cm

So, the depth of tank is 6 cm.

290. (a) Given, Diameter = 21 cm

Radius $= \frac{21}{2} = 10.5$ cm

$\therefore$ Curved surface area $= 2\pi r^2$ $\left[\because \pi = \frac{22}{7}\right]$

$= 2 \times \frac{22}{7} \times 10.5 \times 10.5 = \frac{4851}{7} = 693$

291. (a) $\because$ Volume of sphere $= \frac{4}{3}\pi r^3$

$\Rightarrow 38.808 = \frac{4}{3} \times \frac{22}{7} \times r^3$

$\Rightarrow r^3 = \frac{38.808 \times 21}{88} = 9.261 \Rightarrow r = 2.1$ cm

So, diameter of sphere = 2 × radius

$= 2 \times 2.1 = 4.2$ cm

292. (c) Given, side of a cube = 3 units

$\because$ Surface area of cube $= 6a^2$

Volume of cube $= a^3$

Hence, the required ratio between the surface area and the volume of the cube

$= \frac{6a^2}{a^3} = \frac{6}{a} = \frac{6}{3} = 2:1$

293. (c) $\because$ Surface area of sphere $= 4\pi r^2$

$\therefore 4\pi r^2 = 2464 \Rightarrow r^2 = \frac{2464 \times 7}{88} = 196$

$r = 14$ cm

So, volume of sphere $= \frac{4}{3}\pi r^3$

$= \frac{4}{3} \times \frac{22}{7} \times 14 \times 14 \times 14 = \frac{34496}{3}$

$= 11498\frac{2}{3}$ cm^3

294. (d) Given, radius = 49 cm,

length = 200 cm

We know that,

Area of playground = Curved surface area of roller × 700

$\Rightarrow 2\pi rh = 2 \times \frac{22}{7} \times 49 \times 200 = 61600$ sq. cm

In 700 revolutions, area covered

$= 61600 \times 700 = 4312 \times 10^4$ cm^2

295. (a) Given, curved surface area of cone

$= 2200$ cm^2

Radius (r) = 28 cm

We know that, curved surface area of cone

$= \pi rl \Rightarrow \frac{22}{7} \times 28 \times l = 2200$

$\therefore l = \frac{2200 \times 7}{22 \times 28} = 25$ cm

296. (a) Let the sides of cuboid be $3x$, $4x$ and $5x$.

Surface area of cuboid $= 2(lb + bh + hl)$

$= 2(3x \times 4x + 4x \times 5x + 5x \times 3x)$

$= 2(12x^2 + 20x^2 + 15x^2) = 94x^2$

and surface area of cube $= 6a^2 = 6 \times 6^2 = 216$

According to the question,

$94x^2 = 216 \Rightarrow x^2 = \frac{216}{94}$

$\Rightarrow x^2 \approx 2.3 \Rightarrow x \simeq 1.52$

$\therefore$ Volume of cuboid $= 3x \times 4x \times 5x = 60x^3$

$= 60 \times (1.52)^3 \approx 210.6$

297. (c) $\because$ Surface area of sphere $= 4\pi r^2$

According to the question,

$\frac{4\pi r_1^2}{4\pi r_2^2} = \frac{25}{36} \Rightarrow \frac{r_1}{r_2} = \frac{5}{6}$

$\therefore$ Ratio of volumes $= \frac{\frac{4}{3}\pi r_1^3}{\frac{4}{3}\pi r_2^3} = \left(\frac{r_1}{r_2}\right)^3 = \left(\frac{5}{6}\right)^3$

$= \frac{125}{216}$ $\left[\because \text{given, } \frac{r_1}{r_2} = \frac{5}{6}\right]$

298. (b) According to the question,

$\frac{2\pi rh}{\pi r^2 h} = \frac{2}{3} \Rightarrow r = 3$ unit

and ratio of radius to height = 3 : 7

So, height = 7 unit

Total surface area $= 2\pi r(r + h)$

$= 2\pi \times 3(3 + 7)$

$= 6\pi(10) = 60\pi$ cm^2

299. (b) Let the edge of cube be a cm. surface area of cube $= 6a^2$

$\Rightarrow 6a^2 = 486 \Rightarrow a^2 = \frac{486}{6} \Rightarrow a^2 = 81$

$\therefore a = \sqrt{81} = 9$ cm

$\therefore$ Volume of cube $= a^3 = 9^3 = 729$ cm^3

300. (c) Ratio of diameters = Ratio of radius

= 1 : 4

Let the radius of larger sphere be $4x$ cm and radius of smaller sphere be x cm.

Let the radius of each of the 125 identical spheres be y cm.

We know that,

Volume of sphere $= \frac{4}{3}\pi$ (radius)^3

Now, according to the question,

$\frac{4}{3}\pi(4x)^3 = 125 \times \frac{4}{3}\pi y^3$

$\Rightarrow 64x^3 = 125y^3$

$\Rightarrow y^3 = \frac{64x^3}{125} \Rightarrow y = \frac{4x}{5}$ cm

Let the radius of each of the 27 identical spheres be z cm, then

$\frac{4}{3}\pi x^3 = 27 \times \frac{4}{3}\pi z^3 \Rightarrow x^3 = 27z^3$

$z^3 = \frac{x^3}{27} \Rightarrow z = \frac{x}{3}$ cm

$\therefore$ Required ratio $= \frac{\frac{4}{3}\pi y^3}{\frac{4}{3}\pi z^3} = \frac{1}{m} \Rightarrow \frac{\left(\frac{4x}{5}\right)^3}{\left(\frac{x}{3}\right)^3} = \frac{1}{m}$

$\Rightarrow \frac{64}{125} \times 27 = \frac{1}{m} \Rightarrow \frac{1728}{125} = \frac{1}{m}$

$\therefore m = \frac{125}{1728}$

301. (b) Side of cube (a) = 14 cm

Radius of largest sphere carved out of the cube $(r) = \frac{a}{2} = \frac{14}{2} = 7$ cm

We know that,

Volume of sphere $= \frac{4}{3}\pi r^3 = \frac{4}{3} \times \frac{22}{7} \times (7)^3$

$= 1437\frac{1}{3}$ cm^3

302. (d) The perimeter of base

$= 3 \times 4 = 12$ cm

$\because$ Lateral surface area = Perimeter of base × Height

$\Rightarrow 120 = 12 \times$ Height

$\Rightarrow$ Height = 10 cm

Hence, volume of prism

$= \text{Area of base} \times \text{Height}$

$= \dfrac{\sqrt{3}}{4} \times 4 \times 4 \times 10 = 40\sqrt{3}\ \text{cm}^3$

303. (d) Number of soaps can be placed in box $= \dfrac{\text{Volume of box}}{\text{Volume of 1 soap}}$

$= \dfrac{160 \times 90 \times 60}{6 \times 5 \times 4} = 7200$

$[\because 1\ \text{m} = 100\ \text{cm and } 1\ \text{mm} = \dfrac{1}{10}\ \text{cm}]$

304. (d) Given that,

Volume of a cube = 512 cubic units

$\Rightarrow\ a^3 = 512$ cubic units

$\therefore$ Side of the cube, $a = \sqrt[3]{512} \Rightarrow a = 8$ units

$\therefore$ Paper required to make the cube

= Total surface area of cube

$\therefore$ Total surface area of cube $= 6a^2$

$= 6 \times 8^2 = 384$ sq. units

305. (d) Volume of hemispherical bowl

$= \dfrac{2}{3}\pi r^3$

$= \dfrac{2}{3} \times \dfrac{22}{7} \times \dfrac{21}{2} \times \dfrac{21}{2} \times \dfrac{21}{2}$

$= 2425.5\ \text{cm}^3$

Hence, volume of bowl $= 2425.5\ \text{cm}^3$

306. (a) Volume of cone $= \dfrac{1}{3}\pi r^2 h$

According to the question,

New radius $= r \times \dfrac{125}{100} = 1.25\ r$ cm

New height $= r \times \dfrac{125}{100} = 1.25\ h$ cm

$\therefore$ Volume of new cone $= \dfrac{1}{3}\pi (1.25\ r)^2\ (1.25\ h)$

$= \dfrac{1}{3}\pi r^2 h (1.25)^3$

$\therefore$ Percentage increase in the volume of cone

$= \dfrac{\frac{1}{3}\pi r^2 h (1.25)^3 - \frac{1}{3}\pi r^2 h}{\frac{1}{3}\pi r^2 h} \times 100$

$= \dfrac{\frac{1}{3}\pi r^2 h (1.9531 - 1)}{\frac{1}{3}\pi r^2 h} \times 100$

$= 95.31\%$

307. (b) Volume of sphere $= \dfrac{4}{3}\pi r^3$

$\left(30 + 30 + \dfrac{900}{100}\right)\% = 69\%$

and $\left(69 + 30 + \dfrac{69 \times 30}{100}\right)\% = 119.7\%$

Hence, increase % in volume = 119.7%

308. (a) The volume of the steel used in making the bowl

$= \dfrac{2}{3} \times \pi \times (5)^3 - \dfrac{2}{3} \times \pi \times (5-1)^3$

$= \pi\left[\left(\dfrac{2}{3} \times 125\right) - \left(\dfrac{2}{3} \times 64\right)\right]$

$= \pi\left[\dfrac{2}{3} \times 61\right] = \dfrac{122}{3}\pi = 40\dfrac{2}{3}\pi$

309. (b) Curved surface area of cone $= \pi r l$

$\dfrac{22}{7} \times 21 \times l = 990 \Rightarrow l = 15$ cm

310. (b) Total surface area of sphere $= 3\pi r^2$

$= 3 \times \dfrac{22}{7} \times 49 = 462\ \text{cm}^2$

311. (c) Volume of sphere $= 4500\ \pi\ \text{cm}^3$

$\Rightarrow\ \dfrac{4}{3}\pi r^3 = 4500\pi \Rightarrow r^3 = 3375$

$\Rightarrow\ r = 15$ cm

Surface area of sphere $= 4\pi r^2 = 4\pi \times 15 \times 15$

$= 900\ \pi\ \text{cm}^2$

312. (d) Volume of the cube $= 729\ \text{cm}^3$

$= a^3 = 729 \Rightarrow a = 9$

$\therefore$ Total surface area of cube $= 6a^2 = 6 \times (9)^2$

$= 6 \times 81 = 486\ \text{cm}^2$

313. (c) According to the given information, When the cube is converted into right circular cone whose edge is $3\dfrac{1}{2}$ cm, then

Volume of the cone $= \dfrac{1}{3} \times \pi \times \left(\dfrac{7}{4}\right)^2 \times \left(\dfrac{7}{2}\right)$

$= \dfrac{22}{7 \times 3} \times \left(\dfrac{7 \times 7 \times 7}{4 \times 4 \times 2}\right)$

$= \dfrac{49 \times 22}{3 \times 16 \times 2} = 11.23\ \text{cm}^3$

314. (d) Side of new cube

$= \sqrt[3]{(15)^3 + (18)^3 + (25)^3} = \sqrt[3]{24832}$

$= 4 \times \sqrt[3]{388}$

315. (b) Circumference $= 42\pi$

$\Rightarrow\ 2\pi r = 42\pi \Rightarrow r = 21$ cm

$\therefore$ Volume of cone $= \dfrac{1}{3}\pi r^2 h$

$= \dfrac{1}{3} \times \dfrac{22}{7} \times (21)^2 \times 24$

Volume of cone $= 11088\ \text{cm}^3$

316. (a) Total surface area of solid sphere

$= 4\pi r^2 = 4 \times \dfrac{22}{7} \times \dfrac{7}{2} \times \dfrac{7}{2} = 154\ \text{cm}^2$

When, a sphere is cut into two equal halves, then two hemisphere will be formed, then

Total surface area of two hemispheres

$= 2 \times 3\pi r^2 = 6\pi r^2 = 6 \times \dfrac{22}{7} \times \dfrac{7}{2} \times \dfrac{7}{2} = 231\ \text{cm}^2$

Increase in total surface area

$= 231 - 154 = 77\ \text{cm}^2$

317. (b) Total surface area of cylinder

$= 2\pi r(h + r) = 2 \times \dfrac{22}{7} \times 7(5 + 7)$

$= 2 \times \dfrac{22}{7} \times 7 \times 12 = 528\ \text{cm}^2$

318. (a) Length of cuboid $(l) = 8$ cm

Breadth of cuboid $(b) = 2 \times 8 = 16$ cm

and Height of cuboid $(h) = \dfrac{8}{2} = 4$ cm

Total surface area of cuboid

$= 2\,(lb + bh + hl) = 2[8 \times 16 + 16 \times 4 + 4 \times 8]$

$= 2[128 + 64 + 32] = 2 \times 224 = 448\ \text{cm}^2$

319. (d) Given, Breadth $(b) = 6$ cm

Length $(l) = 3 \times 6 = 18$ cm

Height $(h) = 2 \times 6 = 12$ cm

Total surface area of cuboid $= 2(lb + bh + hl)$

$= 2(18 \times 6 + 6 \times 12 + 12 \times 18)$

$= 2(108 + 72 + 216)$

$= 2(396) = 792\ \text{cm}^2$

320. (c) Let, radius of a hemisphere $= r$

$\therefore$ Radius of a sphere $= 3r$

$\therefore$ Required ratio $= \dfrac{\text{Volume of sphere}}{\text{Volume of hemisphere}}$

$= \dfrac{\frac{4}{3}\pi (3r)^3}{\frac{2}{3}\pi r^3} = \dfrac{2 \times 27}{1} = \dfrac{54}{1} = 54 : 1$

321. (c) Total surface area of cubical box

$= 2(lb + bh + hl)$

$= 2(18 \times 12 + 12 \times 10 + 10 \times 18)$

$= 2(216 + 120 + 180)$

$= 2 \times 516 = 1032\ \text{cm}^2$

322. (b) Volume of a cylinder $= \pi r^2 h$

$= \pi \times (10)^2 \times 20 = 2000\pi\ \text{cm}^3$

323. (b) Given, volume of a cube $= 5832\ \text{cm}^3$

Side $(a) = \sqrt[3]{5832} = 18$ cm

$\therefore$ Total surface area of a cube $= 6a^2$

$= 6 \times (18)^2 = 1944\ \text{cm}^2$

324. (b) Ratio of their volumes

$= \dfrac{\pi r_1^2 h_1}{\pi r_2^2 h_2} = \left(\dfrac{r_1}{r_2}\right)^2\left(\dfrac{h_1}{h_2}\right) = \left(\dfrac{2}{3}\right)^2\left(\dfrac{5}{3}\right)$

$= \dfrac{20}{27} = 20 : 27$

325. (c) Volume of sphere $= \dfrac{4}{3}\pi r^3$

$= \dfrac{4}{3} \times \dfrac{22}{7} \times \left(\dfrac{16.8}{2}\right)^3 = 2483.712\ \text{cm}^3$

326. (d) Let the length, breadth and depth of a cuboid are l, b and h cm, respectively.

Given, $l + b + h = 23$ cm

Diagonal of a cuboid $= \sqrt{l^2 + b^2 + h^2}$

$\Rightarrow\ 5\sqrt{7} = \sqrt{l^2 + b^2 + h^2}$

$\Rightarrow\ l^2 + b^2 + h^2 = 175$

Now, $(l + b + h)^2 = l^2 + b^2 + h^2 + 2(lb + bh + hl)$

$\Rightarrow\ (23)^2 = 175 + 2\,(lb + bh + hl)$

$\Rightarrow\ 2(lb + bh + hl) = (529 - 175)$

Total surface area $= 354\ \text{cm}^2$

327. (d) Surface area of a cylinder $= 2\pi rh$

$= 2 \times 3.14 \times 2 \times 6 = 75.36\ \text{cm}^2$

328. (b) Given, curved surface area of a hemisphere $= 1232\ \text{cm}^2$

$2\pi r^2 = 1232 \Rightarrow 2 \times \dfrac{22}{7} \times r^2 = 1232$

$\Rightarrow \quad r^2 = 28 \times 7$

$\therefore \quad r = 14$ cm

329. (a) Diagonal of a cube $= \sqrt{3}a$

$\Rightarrow \quad 24 \text{ cm} = \sqrt{3}a \Rightarrow a = 8\sqrt{3}$ cm

Total surface area of a cube $= 6a^2$

$= 6(8\sqrt{3})^2 \text{ cm}^2$

$= 6 \times 64 \times 3 \text{ cm}^2 = 1152 \text{ cm}^2$

330. (a) Total surface area of a cuboid

$= 2(lb + bh + hl)$

$= 2(20 \times 15 + 15 \times 8 + 8 \times 20) \text{ cm}^2$

$= 2 \times 580 \text{ cm}^2 = 1160 \text{ cm}^2$

331. (d) Surface area of sphere $= 4\pi r^2$

$= 4 \times \frac{22}{7} \times \frac{21}{2} \times \frac{21}{2} \text{ cm}^2 = 1386 \text{ cm}^2$

332. (c) Old radius $(r_1) = 7$ cm

New radius $(r_2) = 14$ cm

Ratio $= \frac{\text{Old volume}}{\text{New volume}}$

$= \frac{\frac{4}{3}\pi r_1^3}{\frac{4}{3}\pi r_2^3} = \frac{(7)^3}{(14)^3} = \frac{1}{8} = 1:8$

333. (d) Surface area of sphere $= 4\pi r^2$

$= 4 \times \frac{22}{7} \times (8.4)^2$

$= 4 \times \frac{22}{7} \times 8.4 \times 8.4$

$= 887.04 \text{ cm}^2$

334. (d) Let the number of required sphere be n.

According to the question,

$n \times \frac{4}{3} \times \pi \times (2)^3 = \frac{4}{3} \times \pi \times (10)^3$

$\Rightarrow \quad n = \frac{(10)^3}{(2)^3} = \frac{1000}{8} = 125$

335. (d) Let the height of the cylinder be h cm.

According to the question,

$\pi r^2 h = \frac{2}{3}\pi R^3$

$\pi \times (9)^2 \times h = \frac{2}{3} \times \pi \times (6.3)^3$

$\therefore \quad h = \frac{2}{3} \times \frac{6.3 \times 6.3 \times 6.3}{81} = 2.058$ cm

$\Rightarrow \quad h \approx 2.1$ cm

336. (a) Volume of solid hemisphere

$= N \times$ Volume of cone

$\Rightarrow \quad \frac{2}{3}\pi(12)^3 = N \times \frac{1}{3}\pi(6)^2 \times 8$

$\Rightarrow \quad N = \frac{2 \times 12 \times 12 \times 12}{6 \times 6 \times 8}$

$\Rightarrow \quad N = 12$

337. (a) Total surface area of solid hemisphere $= 3\pi r^2$

$3\pi r^2 = 1848$

$\Rightarrow \quad 3 \times \frac{22}{7} \times r^2 = 1848$

$\Rightarrow \quad r^2 = 28 \times 7 \Rightarrow r = 14$ cm

Now, volume of solid hemisphere $= \frac{2}{3}\pi r^3$

$= \frac{2}{3} \times \frac{22}{7} \times 14 \times 14 \times 14$

$= \frac{17248}{3} = 5749\frac{1}{3} \text{ cm}^3$

338. (a) Slant height of cone

$= \sqrt{(36)^2 + (105)^2}$

$= \sqrt{12321} = 111$ cm

Total surface area of cone $= \pi r(l + r)$

$= \frac{22}{7} \times 36\,(111 + 36)$

$= \frac{22}{7} \times 36 \times 147 = 16632 \text{ cm}^2$

339. (b) Total surface area of cylinder

$= 2\pi r(h + r)$

$= 2 \times \frac{22}{7} \times 49 \times 91 = 28028 \text{ cm}^2$

340. (b) CSA of piller $= 2\pi rh$

$= 2 \times \frac{22}{7} \times \frac{350}{2} \times \frac{1}{100} \times 20 = 220 \text{ m}^2$

$\therefore$ Cost of painting $= 220 \times 40 =$ ₹ 8800

341. (b) CSA of cylinder $= 2\pi rh$

$= 2 \times \frac{22}{7} \times 21 \times 10 = 1320 \text{ cm}^2$

Cost of colouring $= 1320 \times 1.5 =$ ₹ 1980

342. (b) Curved surface are a of cone $= \pi rl$

$= \frac{22}{7} \times 13 \times 28 = 1144 \text{ cm}^2$

343. (c) Total surface area of solid cylinder

$= 704 \text{cm}^2$

$\Rightarrow \quad 2\pi r(h + r) = 704$

$\Rightarrow \quad 2 \times \frac{22}{7} \times 8(h + 8) = 704$

$\Rightarrow \quad h + 8 = 14$

$\Rightarrow \quad h = 6$ cm

Now, Volume of solid cylinder $= \pi r^2 h$

$= \frac{22}{7} \times 8 \times 8 \times 6$

$= \frac{8448}{7} = 1206\frac{6}{7} \text{ cm}^3$

344. (d) Total surface area of cylinder

$= 3828 \text{cm}^2$

$2\pi r(h + r) = 3828$

$\Rightarrow \quad 2 \times \frac{22}{7} \times 21(h + 21) = 3828$

$\Rightarrow \quad 132(h + 21) = 3828$

$\Rightarrow \quad h + 21 = 29 \Rightarrow h = 8$ cm

345. (c) Let the internal radius of cylindrical tube be r cm.

According to the question,

$\frac{4}{3}\pi(9)^3 = \pi[(15)^2 - r^2]12$

$\Rightarrow \quad (15)^2 - r^2 = 81$

$\Rightarrow \quad r^2 = 144$

$\Rightarrow \quad r = 12$ cm

Thickness of tube $= 15 - 12 = 3$ cm

346. (b) Let radius of larger hemisphere

$= r$ cm

Given, circumference $= 2\pi r$

$396 = 2 \times \frac{22}{7} \times r \Rightarrow r = 63$ cm

Let n number of small hemisphere required.

According to the question,

$\left(1 - \frac{1}{3}\right) \times$ volume of larger hemisphere $= n \times$ volume of smaller hemisphere

$\frac{2}{3} \times \frac{2}{3} \times \pi \times (63)^3 = n \times \frac{2}{3} \times \pi \times (2.1)^3$

$n = 9000 \times 2 = 18000$

347. (b) Circumference of base of cylinder

$= 22$ cm

$\Rightarrow \quad 2\pi r = 22$ cm

$\Rightarrow \quad r = \frac{7}{2}$ cm

$\Rightarrow$ Curved surface area $= 2\pi rh$

$\Rightarrow \quad 605 = 22 \times h$

$\Rightarrow \quad h = \frac{605}{22} = \frac{55}{2}$ cm

Total surface area $= 2\pi r(h + r)$

$= 22\left(\frac{55}{2} + \frac{7}{2}\right) = 22 \times \frac{62}{2}$

Now, total surface area is n times of right of cylinder.

$22 \times \frac{62}{2} = n \times \frac{55}{2} \Rightarrow n = 24.8$ times

348. (b) Volume of spherical ball $= \frac{4}{3}\pi\,(2.1)^3$

Volume of spherical container $= \frac{4}{3}\pi\left(\frac{84}{2}\right)^3$

$\therefore$ Required fraction $= \frac{\frac{4}{3}\pi(2.1)^3}{\frac{4}{3}\pi(42)^3}$

$= \frac{21 \times 21 \times 21}{42 \times 42 \times 42 \times 1000} = \frac{1}{8000}$

349. (a) According to the question,

$12 \times \frac{4}{3} \times \pi \times r^3 = \pi \times \left(\frac{16}{2}\right)^2 \times 4$

$\Rightarrow \quad r^3 = 16 \Rightarrow r = 2 \times 2^{\frac{1}{3}}$

$\therefore$ Diameter $= 4 \times 2^{\frac{1}{3}}$ cm

350. (b) TSA of right circular cone

$= \pi r(r + l)$

$= \frac{22}{7} \times \frac{14}{2} \times \left(\frac{14}{2} + \sqrt{\left(\frac{14}{2}\right)^2 + (24)^2}\right)$

$= \frac{22}{7} \times \frac{14}{2} \times (7 + 25)$

$= \frac{22}{7} \times 7 \times 32 = 704 \text{ cm}^2$

351. (c) Radius $(r) = \frac{14}{2} = 7$ cm

TSA of hemisphere $= 3\pi r^2$

$= 3 \times \frac{22}{7} \times 7 \times 7 = 462 \text{ cm}^2$

352. (a) Let radius of cylinder be R.

$\therefore$ Curved surface area = 8580

$$2\pi Rh = 8580$$

$$\Rightarrow \quad R = \frac{8580 \times 7}{15 \times 2 \times 22} = 91 \text{ cm}$$

Thus, diameter = 2 × 91 = 182 cm

353. (a) Ratio of curved surface areas

$$= \frac{2\pi r_1 h_1}{2\pi r_2 h_2} = \frac{4 \times 9}{3 \times 8} = 3:2$$

354. (c) Let the number of lead shots be dropped = n

According to the question,

$n \times$ spherical lead volume $= \frac{2}{5} \times$ Volume of hemisphere

$$n \times \frac{4}{3}\pi(0.75)^3 = \frac{2}{5} \times \frac{2}{3} \times \pi \times (15)^3$$

$$\Rightarrow \quad n = \frac{2}{5} \times \frac{1}{2} \times \frac{(15)^3}{(0.75)^3} \Rightarrow n = 1600$$

355. (b) Let height of solid cylinder be 'h'.

Total surface area of cylinder = 704

$$2\pi r(h + r) = 704$$

$$\Rightarrow \quad 2 \times \frac{22}{7} \times 7(h + 7) = 704$$

$$\Rightarrow \quad h + 7 = 16 \Rightarrow h = 9 \text{ cm}$$

356. (c) Let the height of embankment be 'h'.

Volume of earth taken out from well = Volume of embankment

$$\pi \times 4 \times 4 \times 12 = \pi(12^2 - 4^2) \times h$$

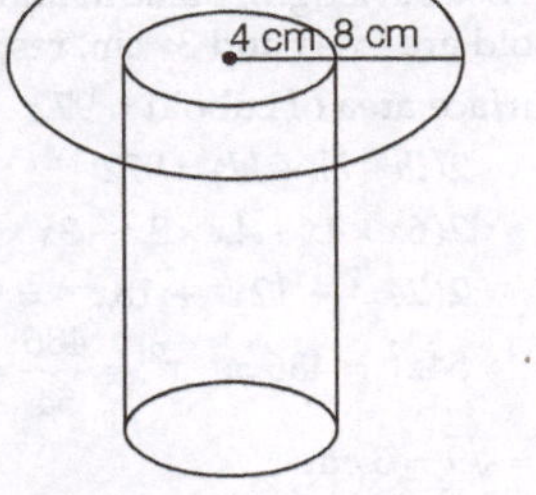

$$\Rightarrow \quad 16 \times 12 = 16 \times 8 \times h$$

$$\Rightarrow \quad h = \frac{3}{2} = 1.5 \text{ m}$$

357. (d) According to the question,

Volume of hemispherical solid = Volume of cylinder

$$\frac{2}{3}\pi \times 21 \times 21 \times 21 = \pi r^2 h$$

$$\Rightarrow \frac{2}{3} \times \pi \times 21 \times 21 \times 21 = \pi \times r^2 \times 14$$

$$\Rightarrow \quad r^2 = 441 \Rightarrow r = 21 \text{ cm}$$

$\therefore$ Volume of cylinder = $\pi \times 21 \times 21 \times 14$

$(a \times b^a \times c^b) \times \pi = \pi(7 \times 3 \times 7 \times 3 \times 7 \times 2)$

$(a \times (b)^a \times c^b)\pi = \pi((7)^3 \times (3)^2 \times (2)^1))$

On comparing $a = 2$, $b = 3$ and $c = 7$

$\therefore$ Thus, $(a + b)c = (2 + 3) \times 7 = 35$

358. (b) Let number of cones be x.

According to the question,

Volume of sphere = $x \times$ Volume of cone

$$\Rightarrow \frac{4}{3} \pi \times (35)^3 = x \times \frac{1}{3} \times \pi \times \left(\frac{14}{2}\right)^2 \times 4$$

$$x = 875$$

359. (a) Inner radius (r) = 6 cm

$\therefore$ Outer radius (R) = 6 + 1 = 7 cm

We know,

CSA of outer side

$$= 2\pi R^2 = 2 \times \frac{22}{7} \times 7 \times 7$$

$$= 308 \text{ cm}^2$$

$\therefore$ Total paint cost = 2 × 308 = ₹ 616

360. (c) Inner curved surface area

$$= \frac{4400}{40} = 110 \text{ m}^2$$

According to the question,

$$2 \times \pi \times r \times 20 = 110$$

$$r = \frac{7}{8}$$

TSA = CSA + Area of Top and bottom.

$$= 110 + 2 \times \frac{22}{7} \times \frac{7}{8} \times \frac{7}{8}$$

$$= 110 + 4.8125 = 114.81 \text{ m}^2$$

361. (c) Let n be the number of cylindrical container required.

According to the question,

Volume of bowl = $n \times$ Volume of Cylindrical container

$$\Rightarrow \quad \frac{2}{3} \times \pi (24)^3 = n \times \pi \times \left(\frac{8}{2}\right)^2 \times 12$$

$$\therefore \quad n = 48$$

362. (b) According to the question,

Volume of cone = Volume of cylinder

$$\frac{1}{3} \pi \times (7)^2 \times 48 = \pi \times (14)^2 \times h$$

[$\because$ Let height of cylinder be h]

$$h = 4 \text{ cm}$$

363. (a) Radius (r) = 3 unit

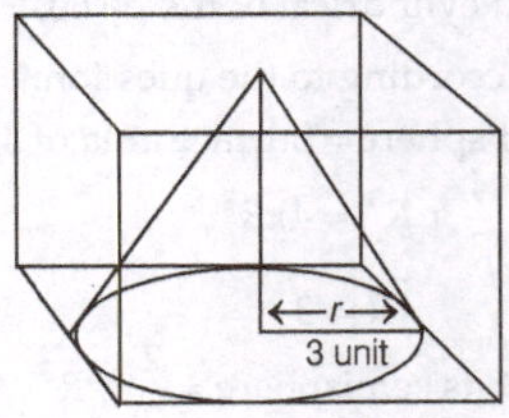

Volume of largest right circular cone

$$= \frac{1}{3}\pi r^2 h = \frac{1}{3} \pi \times (3)^2 \times 6 = 18\pi \text{ unit}^3$$

364. (c) Total surface area of cylinder $= 628\frac{4}{7}$

$$\Rightarrow \quad 2\pi r(h + r) = \frac{4400}{7}$$

$$\Rightarrow \quad 2 \times \frac{22}{7} \times 4(h + 4) = \frac{4400}{7}$$

$$\Rightarrow \quad (h + 4) = \frac{4400 \times 7}{7 \times 44 \times 4}$$

$$\Rightarrow \quad h + 4 = 25 \Rightarrow h = 21 \text{ cm}$$

365. (d) External radius (R) $= \frac{5.4}{2} = 2.7$ cm

Internal Radius (r) = 2.7 − 0.3 = 2.4 cm

$$h = 4.2 \text{ m} = 420 \text{ cm}$$

$\therefore$ Volume of pipe = $\pi h(R^2 - r^2)$

$$= \frac{22}{7} \times 420 \times [(2.7)^2 - (2.4)^2]$$

$$= \frac{22}{7} \times 420 \times 1.53 = 2019.6 \text{ cm}^3$$

$\therefore$ Weight of pipe = 2019.6 × 25 gram

$$= \frac{50490}{1000} = 50.49 \text{ kg}$$

366. (a) Let the radius of cone be r cm.

Volume of cone = 66 cm³

$$\frac{1}{3}\pi \times r^2 \times 7 = 66$$

$$\Rightarrow \quad r^2 = \frac{66 \times 3 \times 7}{22 \times 7}$$

$$\Rightarrow \quad r^2 = 9 \text{ cm}^2 \Rightarrow r = 3 \text{ cm}$$

367. (c) Required sheet = $2\pi rh$

$$= 2 \times \frac{22}{7} \times 30 \times 7 = 1320 \text{ cm}^2$$

368. (a) Radius of circular cone $= \frac{56}{2} = 28$ m

Slant height = 35 m

Height $= \sqrt{35^2 - 28^2} = \sqrt{441} = 21$ m

Volume of cone $= \frac{1}{3}\pi r^2 h$

$$= \frac{1}{3} \times \frac{22}{7} \times 28 \times 28 \times 21 = 17248 \text{ m}^3$$

369. (b) Radius of conical tent

$$= \sqrt{15^2 - 9^2} = 12 \text{ cm}$$

Surface area of conical tent = πrl

$$= \frac{22}{7} \times 12 \times 15 = \frac{3960}{7} \text{ m}^2$$

Cost of Tarpaulin $= \frac{3960}{7} \times 147$

$$= 3960 \times 21 = ₹ 83160$$

370. (a) Radius of cylinder $= \frac{48}{2} = 24$ cm

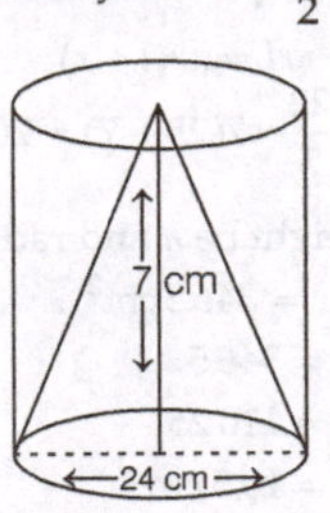

Surface area of cylinder = $2\pi rh$

$$= 2\pi \times 24 \times 7 = 336\pi$$

Slant height of cone $= \sqrt{(7)^2 + (24)^2}$

$$= \sqrt{625} = 25 \text{ cm}$$

Surface area of cone = πrl

$$= \pi \times 24 \times 25$$

$$= 600\pi$$

Area of one base $= \pi \times (24)^2 = 576\pi$

$\therefore$ Total surface area of remaining portion

$= 336\pi + 600\pi + 576\pi$

$= 1512\pi$

371. (d) Ratio of curved surface of cone

$= \frac{\pi r l_1}{\pi r l_2}$ [$\because$ radius is same]

$= \frac{\pi \times r}{\pi \times r} \times \frac{5}{3} = \frac{5}{3} = 5:3$

372. (d) Volume of hollow cylinder

$= \pi(R^2 - r^2) \times h$

$= \frac{22}{7}\left(\left(\frac{14}{2}\right)^2 - \left(\frac{12}{2}\right)^2\right) \times 21$

$= \frac{22}{7} \times 13 \times 21 = 858 \text{ cm}^3$

373. (b) Let height of larger part be h_1.

According to the question,

$2\pi r(h_1 + r) = 2\pi r(r + H) \times \frac{60}{100}$

$\Rightarrow 2\pi r(h_1 + 12) = 2\pi r(12 + 38) \times \frac{3}{5}$

$\Rightarrow h_1 + 12 = 30$

$\Rightarrow h_1 = 18 \text{ cm}$

Now, height of smaller piece

$= 38 - 18 = 20 \text{ cm}$

Now, volume of smaller piece

= Volume of sphere

$\pi r^2 \times 20 = \frac{4}{3}\pi R^3$

$\Rightarrow R^3 = \frac{12 \times 12 \times 20 \times 3}{4}$

$\Rightarrow R^3 = 3 \times 6 \times 2 \times 5 \times 4 \times 3$

$\Rightarrow R^3 = 6 \times 6 \times 6 \times 10$

$\Rightarrow R = \sqrt[3]{6 \times 6 \times 6 \times 10}$

$\therefore R = 6 \times \sqrt[3]{10}$

374. (a) Let radius be $7x$ and height be $24x$.

Volume of cone $= 1232\text{cm}^3$

$\frac{1}{3}\pi(7x)^2 \times (24x) = 1232$

$\Rightarrow x^3 = 1 \Rightarrow x = 1 \text{cm}$

Slant height $(l) = \sqrt{(24)^2 + (7)^2} = 25 \text{ cm}$

$\therefore$ TSA $= \pi r^2 + \pi r l = \pi r(l + r)$

$= \frac{22}{7} \times 7(25 + 7) = 704 \text{ cm}^2$

375. (a) Let height be h and radius be r.

Here, Base area $= 346.5 \text{cm}^2$

$\Rightarrow \pi r^2 = 346.5$

$\Rightarrow r^2 = 110.25$

$\Rightarrow r = 10.5 \text{ cm}$

We know,

Volume of right circular cylinder $= \pi r^2 h$

$2425.5 = 346.5 \times h$

$h = 7 \text{ cm}$

CSA $= 2\pi r h = 2 \times \frac{22}{7} \times 10.5 \times 7$

$= 462 \text{cm}^2$

376. (c) Volume of big sphere = 2744 × Volume of small sphere

$\Rightarrow \frac{4}{3}\pi(7)^3 = 2744 \times \frac{4}{3}\pi r^3$

$\Rightarrow \left(\frac{7}{14}\right)^3 = r^3 \Rightarrow r = \frac{1}{2} \text{ cm}$

Surface area of each small sphere $= 4\pi r^2$

$= 4\pi \times \frac{1}{4} = \pi \text{ cm}^2$

377. (a) Number of Cubes to be formed

$= \frac{2 \times 4 \times 10 \times 100 \times 100 \times 100}{8 \times 8 \times 8}$

$= 156250$

378. (c) $\because$ Length of rectangular sheet

= Circumference of base of cylinder

$\therefore 10\pi = 2\pi r$

$\Rightarrow r = 5 \text{ cm}$

379. (c) $l^2 = h^2 + r^2$

$\Rightarrow l^2 = (72)^2 + (65)^2$

$\Rightarrow l^2 = 5184 + 4225$

$\Rightarrow l^2 = 9409$

$\Rightarrow l = 97$

Total surface area $= \pi r(l + r)$

$= \frac{22}{7} \times 65 \times (97 + 65)$

$= \frac{22}{7} \times 65 \times 162$

$= 33094\frac{2}{7} \text{ cm}^2$

380. (b) Surface area of wooden toy

$= 4 \times \frac{22}{7} \times 14 \times 14 = 2464 \text{ cm}^2$

$\therefore$ Cost of polishing $= 2464 \times 0.50 =$ ₹ 1232

381. (c) Let number of cylindrical bottle be n.

According to the question,

$\frac{2}{3} \times \pi \times 15 \times 15 \times 15 = \pi \times \frac{5}{2} \times \frac{5}{2} \times 6 \times n$

$\Rightarrow n = \frac{2}{3} \times \frac{15 \times 15 \times 15 \times 2 \times 2}{5 \times 5 \times 6}$

$\Rightarrow n = 60$

$\therefore$ Required cylindrical bottle be 60.

382. (d) According to the question,

Volume of sphere = Surface area of sphere

$\frac{4}{3}\pi R^3 = 4\pi R^2$

$\Rightarrow R = 3$

Volume of its semisphere $= \frac{2}{3}\pi R^3$

$= \frac{2}{3} \times 3.14 \times (3)^3 = 56.52 \text{cm}^3$

383. (b) Let R be the radius of hemispherical bowl.

Circumference brim of hemispherical = 264

$\Rightarrow 2\pi R = 264$

$\Rightarrow R = \frac{264 \times 7}{2 \times 22} = 42 \text{ cm}$

Now, let n number of people would be served

Then, $\frac{1}{2} \times \frac{2}{3}\pi(42)^3 = \frac{2}{3}\pi(3)^3 \times n$

$\Rightarrow \frac{1}{3} \times \pi \times 42 \times 42 \times 42 = \frac{2}{3} \times \pi \times 27 \times n$

$\Rightarrow 74088 = 2 \times 27 \times n$

$\Rightarrow n = \frac{74088}{2 \times 27} = 1372$

384. (a) Outer radius, $(R) = 5\text{m}$,

Height, $(h) = 10\text{m}$,

Inner radius $(r) = 0.5 \text{ m} = \frac{1}{2} \text{ m}$

Total surface area of tank $= 2\pi R(R + h) - \pi r^2$

$= 5 \times 15 \times 2\pi - \frac{1}{4}\pi \Rightarrow = \frac{599\pi}{4} \text{m}^2$

385. (c) Let radius of new cylinder be x cm.

According to the question,

Total volume of old cylinder = Volume of new cylinder

$\therefore \pi \times (4)^2 \times 6 + \pi \times (5)^2 \times 4 = \pi x^2 \times 1$

$\Rightarrow 96\pi + 100\pi = \pi x^2$

$\Rightarrow 196\pi = \pi x^2$

$\Rightarrow x = 14 \text{ cm}$

386. (c) Total Volume of small hemisphere

$= 20 \times \frac{2}{3}\pi r^3$

$= 20 \times \frac{2}{3} \times \pi \times (3)^3 = 360\pi$

Volume of large hemisphere $= \frac{2}{3}\pi R^3$

$\Rightarrow 360\pi \times \frac{80}{100} = \frac{2}{3}\pi R^3$

$\Rightarrow R^3 = 432$

$\Rightarrow R = 6\sqrt[3]{2} \text{ cm}$

387. (b) Let the length, breadth and height of the cuboid are $6x$, $4x$ and $3x$ cm, respectively.

Total surface area of cuboid = 972

$\Rightarrow 2(lb + bh + hl) = 972$

$\Rightarrow 2(6x \times 4x + 4x \times 3x + 3x \times 6x) = 972$

$\Rightarrow 2(24x^2 + 12x^2 + 18x^2) = 972$

$\Rightarrow 54x^2 = 486 \Rightarrow x^2 = \frac{486}{54} = 9$

$\therefore x = \sqrt{9} = 3 \text{ cm}$

Length of cuboid $= 6 \times 3 = 18 \text{ cm}$

Breadth of cuboid $= 4 \times 3 = 12 \text{ cm}$

Height of cuboid $= 3 \times 3 = 9 \text{ cm}$

Diagonal of cuboid $= \sqrt{l^2 + b^2 + h^2}$

$= \sqrt{(18)^2 + (12)^2 + (9)^2}$

$= \sqrt{324 + 144 + 81}$

$= \sqrt{549} = 3\sqrt{61} \text{ cm}$

388. (c) Curved surface area of cylinder

$= 2\pi r h = 2 \times \frac{22}{7} \times 15 \times 56$

$= 5280 \text{ cm}^2$

389. (c) Curved surface area of cone

$= 4070 \text{ cm}^2$

$\Rightarrow \pi r l = 4070 \Rightarrow \frac{22}{7} \times \frac{70}{2} \times l = 4070$

$\Rightarrow l = 37 \text{ cm}$

$\therefore$ Height of cone,

$h = \sqrt{l^2 - r^2} = \sqrt{(37)^2 - (35)^2} = \sqrt{144}$

$\Rightarrow \quad h = 12$ cm

Volume of cone $= \frac{1}{3}\pi r^2 h$

$= \frac{1}{3} \times \frac{22}{7} \times 35 \times 35 \times 12 = 15400 \text{ cm}^3$

390. (a) Total surface area of cube

$= 6a^2 = 6(3.5)^2 = 73.5 \text{ cm}^2$

391. (d) Let the edge of cube be 'a'.

Given, length of diagonal

$= \sqrt{300}$ cm $\Rightarrow \sqrt{3}a = \sqrt{300}$

On squaring both sides,

$3a^2 = 300 \Rightarrow a^2 = 100 \Rightarrow a = 10$ cm

$\therefore$ Volume of cube $= (a)^3 = (10)^3 = 1000 \text{ cm}^3$

392. (d) Slant height, $l = \sqrt{r^2 + h^2}$

$= \sqrt{(2)^2 + (1.5)^2} = \sqrt{4 + 2.25} = \sqrt{6.25}$

$l = 2.5$ m

393. (a) Volume of sphere $= \frac{4}{3}\pi r^3$

$= \frac{4}{3} \times \frac{22}{7} \times \frac{7}{2} \times \frac{7}{2} \times \frac{7}{2} = \frac{1078}{6} = 179.66 \text{ cm}^3$

394. (c) Volume of hollow sphere

$= \frac{4}{3}\pi(R^3 - r^3) = \frac{4}{3}\pi[(6)^3 - (5)^3]$

Volume of cone $= \frac{1}{3}\pi r^2 h = \frac{1}{3}\pi(5.2)^2 h$

According to the question,

$\frac{4}{3}\pi(216 - 125) = \frac{1}{3}\pi(5.2)^2 h$

$\Rightarrow \quad \frac{4 \times 91}{(5.2)^2} = h \Rightarrow h = \frac{364}{27.04}$

$\Rightarrow \quad h = 13.46 \approx 13.5$ cm

395. (c) Total surface area of cone $= \pi r(l + r)$

$= \frac{22}{7} \times 10.5(13 + 10.5) = 775.5 \text{ cm}^2$

396. (b) The length of the longest pole

$= \sqrt{(24)^2 + (18)^2 + (16)^2}$

$= \sqrt{576 + 324 + 256}$

$= \sqrt{1156} = 34$ m

397. (c) Given, $H = 9.8$ cm, $R = 4$ cm,

and $r = 3.5$ cm,

Let height of new cone $= h$

Volume of the melted cone

$=$ Volume of the new cone

$\frac{1}{3}\pi R^2 H = \frac{1}{3}\pi r^2 h$

$\Rightarrow \quad \frac{1}{3}\pi(4)^2 \times 9.8 = \frac{1}{3}\pi(3.5)^2 \times h$

$\Rightarrow h = \frac{4 \times 4 \times 9.8}{3.5 \times 3.5}$ cm $= 12.8$ cm

398. (a) Volume of cube = Volume of cuboid

$\Rightarrow \quad a^3 = 12 \times 9 \times 2 \Rightarrow a^3 = 216 \Rightarrow a = 6$ cm

Side of cube = 6 cm

Lateral surface area of cube $= 4 \times (\text{side})^2$

$= 4(6)^2 = 144 \text{ cm}^2$

399. (d) Total surface area of cuboid

$= 2(lb + bh + hl)$

$= 2[(18 \times 6) + (6 \times 3) + (18 \times 3)]$

$= 2(108 + 18 + 54) = 360 \text{ m}^2$

400. (c) Volume of cuboid box

$= 8 \times 6 \times 6 = 288 \text{ units}^3$

Volume of small cube $= 0.5 \times 0.5 \times 0.5$

$= 0.125 \text{ units}^3$

Number of small cube $= \frac{288}{0.125} = 2304$

401. (a) Given, the surface area of sphere

$= 5544 \text{ cm}^2 \Rightarrow 4\pi r^2 = 5544$

$\Rightarrow \quad 4 \times \frac{22}{7} \times r^2 = 5544$

$\Rightarrow \quad r^2 = 441 \Rightarrow r = 21$ cm

Then, radius is double $= 21 \times 2 = 42$ cm

$\therefore$ Surface area of new sphere $= 4\pi r^2$

$= 4 \times \frac{22}{7} \times 42 \times 42 = 22176 \text{ cm}^2$

402. (b) Radius of metallic sphere $(r) = 3$ cm

Radius of cross section of cylindrical wire $(R) = 0.2$ cm

Let the length of the wire be h cm.

According to the question,

$\pi \times R^2 \times h = \frac{4}{3} \times \pi \times r^3$

$\Rightarrow \quad \pi \times (0.2)^2 \times h = \frac{4}{3} \times \pi \times 3^3$

$\Rightarrow \pi \times \left(\frac{2}{10}\right)^2 \times h = \frac{4}{3} \times \pi \times 27$

$\Rightarrow \quad \pi \times \frac{4}{100} \times h = 36\pi$

$\Rightarrow \quad h = \frac{36 \times 100}{4} = 900 \text{ cm} = 9 \text{ m}$

403. (a) Area of sphere $= 4\pi r^2$

$\Rightarrow \quad 4 \times \frac{22}{7} \times r^2 = 616 \Rightarrow \frac{616 \times 7}{22 \times 4} = r^2$

$\Rightarrow \quad r^2 = 49 \Rightarrow r = 7$

So, the diameter = 14 cm

404. (d) Volume of cylinder $= 19008 \text{ cm}^3$

$\Rightarrow \pi r^2 h = 19008 \Rightarrow \frac{22}{7} \times (12)^2 \times h = 19008$

$\Rightarrow \quad h = \frac{19008 \times 7}{144 \times 22} = 42$ cm

405. (c) Volume of the cube

$= (4)^3 = 4 \times 4 \times 4 = 64 \text{ cm}^3$

406. (c) Total cost

$= 2 \times (7 \times 5 + 5 \times 2 + 7 \times 2) \times 2.4$

$= 2 \times 59 \times 2.4 =$ ₹ 283.20

407. (a) Largest possible right circular cylinder from wooden cube has the same diameter and height as the edge of the cube.

$\therefore$ Volume left over after cutting the cylinder

$= [(7)^3 - \pi \times (3.5)^2 \times 7]$

$= \left[343 - \frac{22}{7} \times (3.5)^2 \times 7\right]$

$= [343 - 269.5] = 73.5 \text{ cm}^3$

408. (d) Volume of the cone $= \frac{1}{3} \times \pi r^2 h$

$= \frac{1}{3} \times 616 \times 15$

$= 616 \times 5 = 3080 \text{ cm}^3$

409. (a) Volume of a cone

$= \frac{1}{3} \times$ Area of base $\times$ Height

$\Rightarrow 27720 \text{ cm}^3 = \frac{1}{3} \times$ Area of base $\times 20$cm

$\therefore$ Area of the base $= \frac{27720 \times 3}{20} \text{ cm}^2$

$= 4158 \text{ cm}^2$

410. (b) Volume of cuboid

= Length $\times$ Breadth $\times$ Height

$= 40 \times 20 \times 10 \text{ cm}^3 = 8000 \text{ cm}^3$

411. (c) Let the radius of base of cylinder and sphere be 'r' cm.

Height of cylinder $(h) = \frac{4r}{3}$ cm.

$\therefore$ Required ratio $= \frac{\frac{4}{3}\pi r^3}{\pi r^2 \times \frac{4r}{3}} = 1:1$

412. (d) Let the radius of sphere be 'r' m and side of square be 'a' m respectively. Then,

Volume of sphere $= \frac{500\pi}{3}$

$\Rightarrow \quad \frac{4}{3}\pi r^3 = 500\frac{\pi}{3} \Rightarrow 4r^3 = 500$

$\Rightarrow \quad r^3 = 125 \Rightarrow r = 5$ m

$\therefore \quad a = \frac{40}{100} \times 5 \quad a = 2$ m

Area of square $= a^2 = 2^2 = 4 \text{ m}^2$

413. (a) Let the length of each side of square be 'a' cm.

Then, total surface area of cube $= 128 + a^2$

$6(8)^2 = 128 + a^2$

$\Rightarrow \quad 384 = 128 + a^2$

$\Rightarrow \quad a^2 = 256 \Rightarrow a = 16$ cm

414. (d) Let 'r' be the radius of hemisphere and 'a' be the side of equilateral triangle.

$\therefore$ Total surface area of hemisphere = Area of an equilateral triangle

$\Rightarrow \quad 3\pi r^2 = \frac{\sqrt{3}}{4}a^2$

$\Rightarrow \quad a^2 = \sqrt{3}\pi r^2 \times 4$

$\Rightarrow \quad a^2 = 4\pi\sqrt{3} \times r^2$

$\Rightarrow \quad a = (4\pi\sqrt{3})^{0.5} \times r$

415. (d) Curved surface area of cylinder

$= 2\pi rh \Rightarrow 19.5 = 2 \times \frac{22}{7} \times 4 \times h$

$\Rightarrow \quad h = \frac{19.5 \times 7}{2 \times 22 \times 4}$

Volume of cylinder $= \pi r^2 h$

$= \frac{22}{7} \times 16 \times \frac{19.5 \times 7}{2 \times 22 \times 4}$

$= 2 \times 19.5 = 39 \text{ m}^3$

416. (d) Given, $R = 20$ cm, $r = 10$ cm, $h = 24$ cm

Capacity of bucket $= \frac{\pi h}{3}(R^2 + r^2 + Rr)$

$= \frac{22}{7} \times \frac{24}{3}[(20)^2 + (10)^2 + 20 \times 10)]$

$= \frac{22 \times 8}{7}[400 + 100 + 200]$

$= \frac{22 \times 8}{7} \times 700 = 22 \times 8 \times 100$

$= 17600 \text{ cm}^3$

417. (d) Area of four walls excluding areas of door and two windows and including area of ceiling = Area of four walls + Area of ceiling – Area of doors – 2 × Area of windows

$= 2(15 + 12) \times 10 + 12 \times 15 - 8 \times 3.5 - 2 \times 5 \times 3$

$= 2 \times 27 \times 10 + 12 \times 15 - 28 - 30$

$= 540 + 180 - 58 = 662$

Total cost of painting = 50 × 662 = ₹ 33100

418. (a) Volume of cone $= \frac{1}{3}\pi r^2 h$

$= \frac{1}{3} \times \frac{22}{7} \times 10.5 \times 10.5 \times 24$

$= \frac{58212}{21} = 2772 \text{ cm}^3$

419. (c) ∵ Volume of hemisphere $= \frac{2}{3}\pi r^3$

$= \frac{2}{3} \times \frac{22}{7} \times 2.1 \times 2.1 \times 2.1 = 19.4 \text{ cm}^3$

420. (b) Let the length, breadth and height be l, b and h respectively in cuboid.

When the length and breadth are increased by 50% and 20%. Then, the new length and breadth

$l_1 = l + \frac{l \times 50}{100} = \frac{3}{2}l$ and $b_1 = b + \frac{b \times 20}{100} = \frac{6}{5}b$

When the height is decreased by 30%.

Then, the new height $h_1 = h - \frac{h \times 30}{100} = \frac{7}{10}h$

∴ Percentage increase in volume

$= \left(\frac{l_1 b_1 h_1 - lbh}{lbh}\right) \times 100$

$= \frac{\left(\frac{3}{2}l \times \frac{6}{5}b \times \frac{7}{10}h\right) - lbh}{lbh} \times 100$

$= \left(\frac{126}{100} - 1\right) \times 100$

$= \left(\frac{126 - 100}{100}\right) \times 100 = 26\%$

Speedy Method

Volume of cuboid = $l \times b \times h$

Net percentage increase in volume

$= \left(50 + 20 + \frac{1000}{100}\right)\% = 80\%$

and $\left(80 - 30 - \frac{2400}{100}\right)\% = 26\%$

Hence, percentage increase in volume = 26%

421. (c) Volume of the hemisphere

$= \frac{2}{3} \times \frac{22}{7} \times 3.5 \times 3.5 \times 3.5$

$= 89.83 \text{ cm}^3$

422. (c) Lateral surface area of cube

$= 4 \times (\text{Length})^2$

$= 4 \times (13)^2 = 676 \text{ cm}^2$

423. (b) Volume of cone $= \frac{1}{3}\pi r^2 h$

$= \frac{1}{3} \times \frac{22}{7} \times 14 \times 14 \times 15$

$= 22 \times 2 \times 14 \times 5 = 3080 \text{ cm}^3$

424. (c) According to the question,

Volume of cone = Volume of sphere

$\frac{1}{3}\pi(r)^2 h = \frac{4}{3}\pi(R)^3$

$\Rightarrow \frac{1}{3} \times \pi \times \left(\frac{15}{2}\right)^2 \times h = \frac{4}{3} \times \pi \times (15)^3$

$\Rightarrow h = \frac{4 \times 15 \times 15 \times 15}{\frac{15}{2} \times \frac{15}{2}}$

$\therefore h = 240$ cm

425. (d) According to the question,

∵ Number of balls $= \frac{\text{Volume of hemisphere}}{\text{Volume of sphere}}$

Number of balls $= \frac{\frac{2}{3}\pi R^3}{\left(\frac{4}{3}\pi r^3\right)}$

(Here, $R = 48$ cm, $r = 8$ cm)

$= \frac{\left(\frac{2}{3} \times \frac{22}{7} \times 48 \times 48 \times 48\right)}{\left(\frac{4}{3} \times \frac{22}{7} \times 8 \times 8 \times 8\right)}$

$= 3 \times 6 \times 6 = 108$

426. (a) Total surface area of hemisphere

$= 3\pi r^2 = 3 \times \frac{22}{7} \times \frac{21}{2} \times \frac{21}{2}$

$= 1039.5 \text{ cm}^2$

427. (c) Lateral surface area of the cube

$= 4 \times (\text{side})^2$

$= 4 \times 14 \times 14 = 784 \text{ cm}^2$

428. (c) Total surface area of sphere $= 4\pi r^2$

$= 4 \times \frac{22}{7} \times (3.5)^2$

$= 4 \times \frac{22}{7} \times \frac{35 \times 35}{100} = 154 \text{ cm}^2$

429. (d) Volume of sphere $= \frac{4}{3}\pi r^3$

$= \frac{4}{3} \times \frac{22}{7} \times (4.2)^3$

$= \frac{4}{3} \times \frac{22}{7} \times \frac{42}{10} \times \frac{42}{10} \times \frac{42}{10}$

$= 310.46 \text{ cm}^3$

430. (c) Let the radius of sphere = r

When the radius is increased by 50%,

then new radius $= r + \frac{r \times 50}{100} = r + \frac{1}{2}r = \frac{3}{2}r$

∴ Percentage increased volume

$= \left[\frac{\frac{4}{3}\pi\left(\frac{3}{2}r\right)^3 - \frac{4}{3}\pi(r)^3}{\frac{4}{3}\pi r^3}\right] \times 100$

$= \left[\frac{\frac{27}{8} - 1}{1}\right] \times 100$

$= \frac{19}{8} \times 100 = 237.5\%$

Speedy Method

Volume of sphere $= \frac{4}{3}\pi r^3$

$\left(50 + 50 + \frac{50 \times 50}{100}\right)\% = 125\%$

and $\left(125 + 50 + \frac{125 \times 50}{100}\right)\% = 237.5\%$

Hence, percentage increase in volume = 237.5%

431. (a) Curved surface area of cylinder $= 2\pi rh$

$= \left(2 \times \frac{22}{7} \times 70 \times 14\right) = 6160 \text{ cm}^2$

432. (c) Volume of cuboidal box

$= 24 \times 16 \times 12 = 4608 \text{ cm}^2$

433. (d) Total surface area of hemisphere

$= 3\pi r^2 = 3 \times \frac{22}{7} \times \frac{7}{2} \times \frac{7}{2} = 115.5 \text{cm}^2$

434. (b) Volume of cone $= \frac{1}{3}\pi r^2 h$

$= \frac{1}{3} \times \frac{22}{7} \times 7 \times 7 \times 12 = 616 \text{ cm}^3$

Water is filled at a rate of 4 cm^3 per 10 s.

So, time taken to fill the cone

$= \frac{616 \text{ cm}^3}{4 \text{ cm}^3} \times 10 = 1540$ s

435. (b) Volume of hemisphere $= 1152\pi \text{ cm}^3$

$\Rightarrow \frac{2}{3}\pi r^3 = 1152\pi \Rightarrow r^3 = \frac{1152 \times 3}{2} = 1728$

$\Rightarrow r = \sqrt[3]{1728} = 12$ cm

So, curved surface area of hemisphere $= 2\pi r^2$

$= 2 \times \pi \times (12)^2 = 288\pi \text{ cm}^2$

436. (b) Volume of hemisphere $= \frac{2}{3}\pi r^3$

$= \frac{2}{3} \times \frac{22}{7} \times 2.8 \times 2.8 \times 2.8$

$= 45.995 \text{ cm}^3$

437. (b) Slant height (l) $= \sqrt{r^2 + h^2}$

$= \sqrt{15^2 + 8^2} = 17$ m

∴ Required cloth $= \pi rl$

$= 3.14 \times 15 \times 17 = 800.7 \text{m}^2$

438. (c) Total surface area of cone

$= \pi r(l + r) = \frac{22}{7} \times 7 \times (12 + 7)$

$= 22 \times 19 = 418 \text{ cm}^2$

439. (d) Volume of cylinder $= \pi r^2 h$

$\Rightarrow \quad \frac{22}{7} \times r^2 \times 21 = 2640$

$\Rightarrow \quad r^2 = \frac{120 \times 7}{21} = 40$

$\Rightarrow \quad r^2 = 40 \Rightarrow r = 6.32$ cm

440. (c) Let the radius of new sphere $= R$ cm

According to the question, sum of volume of three small spheres = Volume of new sphere

$\frac{4}{3}\pi(1^3 + 6^3 + 8^3) = \frac{4}{3}\pi R^3$

$\Rightarrow \quad 1 + 216 + 512 = R^3$

$\Rightarrow \quad R^3 = 729 \Rightarrow R = 9$ cm

Hence, surface area of new sphere

$= 4\pi r^2 = 4 \times \pi \times 9 \times 9 = 324\pi$ cm^2

441. (b) Let the side of cuboid are $3x$, $4x$ and $5x$ units.

We know, volume of cuboid $= l \times b \times h$

According to the question,

$3x \times 4x \times 5x = 480 \Rightarrow 60x^3 = 480$

$x^3 = \frac{480}{60} = 8 \Rightarrow x = 2$

$\therefore$ Required difference $= (5 \times 2 - 3 \times 2)$

$= (10 - 6) = 4$ units

442. (b) Volume of solid circular cone

$= \frac{1}{3}\pi r^2 h \Rightarrow v \text{ cm}^3 = \frac{1}{3}\pi r^2 h$

$\Rightarrow 3v = \pi r^2 h \Rightarrow r^2 = \frac{3v}{\pi h} \Rightarrow r = \sqrt{\frac{3v}{\pi h}}$ cm

443. (b) Volume of cylinder = Volume of cone

$\because \quad \pi r^2 h = \frac{1}{3}\pi R^2 h$

$\pi \times (22.5)^2 \times 24 = \frac{1}{3} \times \pi \times (36)^2 \times h$

$\Rightarrow \quad \frac{50625}{100} \times 24 = \frac{1}{3} \times 1296 \times h$

$\Rightarrow \quad h = 28.125$

444. (a) Volume of sphere $= \frac{4}{3}\pi r^3$

$= \frac{4}{3} \times \frac{22}{7} \times (7)^3 = \frac{4}{3} \times \frac{22}{7} \times 343$

$= 1437.33$ cm^3

445. (b) Let the volume of the cube $= 100$ cm^3

$\therefore$ Required increased volume of cube

$= 100 \times \frac{115}{100} \times \frac{115}{100} \times \frac{115}{100} - 100$

$= 152.0875 - 100$

$= 52.0875\% \approx 52\%$

446. (b) $\because$ Diameter = Edge of the cube

$\Rightarrow$ 2 (radius) = 6 cm $\Rightarrow$ $r = 3$ cm

Volume of sphere $= \frac{4}{3}\pi r^3 = \frac{4}{3} \times \frac{22}{7} \times 3 \times 3 \times 3$

$= 113.14$ cm^3

$\therefore$ Volume of cube $= 113.14$ cm^3

447. (a) Given, external diameter = 43 cm

Radius $= \frac{43}{2} = 21.5$ cm

Inradius of hemisphere = Radius − thickness

$= 21.5 - 0.5 = 21$ cm

$\therefore$ Volume of hemisphere

$= \frac{2}{3} \times \frac{22}{7} \times 21 \times 21 \times 21$

$= 2 \times 22 \times 21 \times 21 = 19404$ cm^3

448. (c) According to the question,

Volume of cone $= 96\pi$

$\Rightarrow \quad \frac{1}{3}\pi r^2 h = 96\pi$

$\Rightarrow \quad r^2 = \frac{96 \times 3}{8} \quad [\because h = 8 \text{ cm, given}]$

$\Rightarrow r^2 = 36 \Rightarrow r = 6$ cm

Also, $l = \sqrt{h^2 + r^2} = \sqrt{8^2 + 6^2} = 10$ cm

Now, total surface area of cone $= \pi r(l + r)$

$= \pi \times 6(10 + 6) = 96\pi$ cm^2

449. (c) Volume of cone $= \frac{1}{3}\pi r^2 h$

$\Rightarrow 392\pi = \frac{1}{3}\pi \times r^2 \times 24 \Rightarrow r^2 = 49$

$r = 7$ cm $\Rightarrow$ $l = \sqrt{r^2 + h^2}$

$l = \sqrt{7^2 + 24^2} \Rightarrow l = 25$ cm

$\therefore$ Curved surface area $= \pi rl$

$= \pi \times 25 \times 7 = 175\pi$ cm^2

450. (d) Diagonal of cube $= \sqrt{3} \times$ (Side)

$5 \times \sqrt{3} = \sqrt{3} \times$ (Side)

Side = 5 cm

$\therefore$ Surface area $= 6 \times (\text{Side})^2 = 6 \times (5)^2$

$= 6 \times 25 = 150$ cm^2

451. (c) Volume of hemisphere $= \frac{2}{3} \times \pi r^3$

$= \frac{2}{3} \times \pi \times (9)^3 = 2\pi \times 243 = 486\pi$ cm^3

452. (c) Base area $= \pi r^2 \Rightarrow 25\pi = \pi r^2$

$r = 5$ cm

Total surface area of cylinder $= 2\pi r(h + r)$

$= 2 \times \frac{22}{7} \times 5(5 + 9) = 2 \times \frac{22}{7} \times 5 \times 14 = 440$ cm^2

453. (a) Given, $l = 8$ cm, $b = 12$ cm, $h = 14$ cm

Total surface area of cuboid $= 2(lb + bh + hl)$

$= 2(8 \times 12 + 12 \times 14 + 14 \times 8)$

$= 2(96 + 168 + 112)$

$= 2 \times 376 = 752$ cm^2

454. (c) Volume of cube $= (\text{Side})^3$

$\Rightarrow (\text{Side})^3 = 12167 \Rightarrow \text{Side} = \sqrt[3]{12167} = 23$ cm

$\therefore$ The surface area of the cube

$= 6 \times (\text{Side})^2 = 6 \times (23)^2 = 6 \times 529 = 3174$ cm^2

455. (b) Radius of hemisphere, $R = 7$ cm

Let radius of small sphere be r cm.

According to the question,

Volume of hemi-sphere $= 4 \times$ volume of a small sphere

$\Rightarrow \quad \frac{2}{3}\pi R^3 = 4 \times \frac{4}{3}\pi r^3 \Rightarrow 2(7)^3 = 16r^3$

$\Rightarrow \quad r^3 = \frac{(7)^3}{8} = \frac{(7)^3}{(2)^3} \Rightarrow r = \frac{7}{2} = 3.5$ cm

456. (c) Internal radius of hollow hemispherical bowl, $r_1 = \frac{6}{2} = 3$ cm

External radius of hollow hemispherical bowl, $r_2 = \frac{10}{2} = 5$ cm

Radius of solid cylinder, $R = \frac{14}{2} = 7$ cm

Let height of cylinder be h cm.

Volume of hollow hemispherical bowl

= Volume of cylinder

$\Rightarrow \quad \frac{2}{3}\pi(r_2^3 - r_1^3) = \pi R^2 h$

$\Rightarrow \quad \frac{2}{3}(125 - 27) = 49 \times h$

$\Rightarrow \quad h = \frac{2 \times 98}{3 \times 49} = 1.33$ cm

457. (d) Here, dimensions of cuboid,

$l = 12$ m, $b = 10$m, $h = 8$m

$\therefore$ Length of diagonal of cuboid

$= \sqrt{l^2 + b^2 + h^2} = \sqrt{144 + 100 + 64}$

$= \sqrt{308} = 17.54$ m

458. (d) Let length of each side of the smaller cube and larger cube be a_1 and a_2, respectively.

According to the question,

$\frac{\text{Volume of smaller cube}}{\text{Volume of larger cube}} = \frac{8}{27}$

$\Rightarrow \quad \frac{a_1^3}{a_2^3} = \left(\frac{2}{3}\right)^3 \Rightarrow \left(\frac{a_1}{a_2}\right)^3 = \left(\frac{2}{3}\right)^3$

$\Rightarrow \quad \frac{a_1}{a_2} = \frac{2}{3} \Rightarrow a_2 = \frac{3}{2}a_1 \quad \ldots(i)$

And volume of larger cube − volume of smaller cube = 513

$\Rightarrow \quad a_2^3 - a_1^3 = 513$

$\Rightarrow \quad \left(\frac{3}{2}a_1\right)^3 - a_1^3 = 513$ [from Eq. (i)]

$\Rightarrow \quad \frac{27}{8}a_1^3 - a_1^3 = 513 \Rightarrow \frac{19}{8}a_1^3 = 513$

$\Rightarrow \quad a_1^3 = \frac{513 \times 8}{19} \Rightarrow a_1^3 = 27 \times 8$

$\therefore \quad a_1 = 3 \times 2 = 6$ cm

459. (a) Radius of hemisphere $= \frac{16.8}{2} = 8.4$ cm

Volume of hemisphere $= \frac{2}{3}\pi r^3$

$= \frac{2}{3} \times \frac{22}{7} \times (8.4)^3$

$= \frac{44 \times 592.704}{21} = 1241.856$ cm^3

24

Trigonometry

Trigonometry is a branch of Mathematics in which we study right angled triangle and relationship between their sides and angles using trigonometric ratios.

Trigonometric Ratios

Trigonometric ratios for right angled ΔABC with respect to angle A are given below

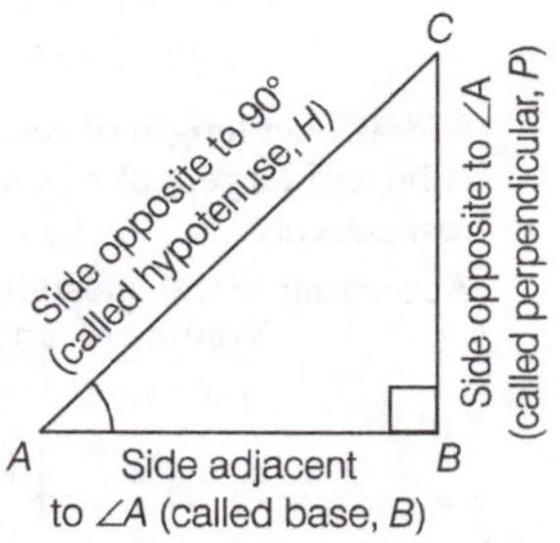

- $\sin A = \frac{BC}{AC} = \frac{P}{H}$
- $\cos A = \frac{AB}{AC} = \frac{B}{H}$
- $\tan A = \frac{BC}{AB} = \frac{P}{B}$

By Pythagoras theorem, $\boxed{H^2 = B^2 + P^2}$

Pythagorean Triplet

- (3, 4, 5) (5, 12, 13) (7, 24, 25)
- (8, 15, 17) (9, 40, 41) (11, 60, 61)
- (12, 35, 37) (13, 84, 85) (16, 63, 65)
- (20, 21, 29) (28, 45, 53) (33, 56, 65)

Inverse Relations

- $\sin A = \frac{1}{\text{cosec } A}$
- $\cos A = \frac{1}{\sec A}$
- $\tan A = \frac{\sin A}{\cos A}$
- $\tan A = \frac{1}{\cot A}$

Trigonometric Identities

In a right angled triangle, we have the following identities.

- $\sin^2 A + \cos^2 A = 1$
- $1 + \tan^2 A = \sec^2 A$
- $1 + \cot^2 A = \text{cosec}^2 A$

Trigonometric Ratios of Some Specific Angles

Trigonometric ratios	Angle (Degree)				
	0°	30°	45°	60°	90°
$\sin\theta$	0	$\frac{1}{2}$	$\frac{1}{\sqrt{2}}$	$\frac{\sqrt{3}}{2}$	1
$\cos\theta$	1	$\frac{\sqrt{3}}{2}$	$\frac{1}{\sqrt{2}}$	$\frac{1}{2}$	0
$\tan\theta$	0	$\frac{1}{\sqrt{3}}$	1	$\sqrt{3}$	∞
$\cot\theta$	∞	$\sqrt{3}$	1	$\frac{1}{\sqrt{3}}$	0
$\sec\theta$	1	$\frac{2}{\sqrt{3}}$	$\sqrt{2}$	2	∞
$\text{cosec}\,\theta$	∞	2	$\sqrt{2}$	$\frac{2}{\sqrt{3}}$	1

Sign of Trigonometric Functions

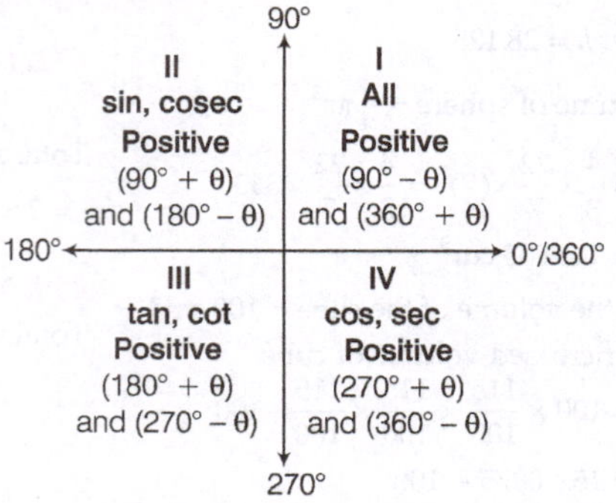

Trigonometric ratios of complementary and supplementary angles of angle θ are shown below

- $\sin(90° - \theta) = \cos\theta$
- $\cos(90° - \theta) = \sin\theta$
- $\tan(90° - \theta) = \cot\theta$
- $\cot(90° - \theta) = \tan\theta$
- $\sec(90° - \theta) = \text{cosec}\,\theta$
- $\text{cosec}(90° - \theta) = \sec\theta$
- $\sin(180° - \theta) = \sin\theta$,
- $\sin(90° + \theta) = \cos\theta$
- $\cos(90° + \theta) = -\sin\theta$
- $\tan 90° + \theta = -\cot\theta$
- $\cot(90° + \theta) = -\tan\theta$
- $\sec(90° + \theta) = -\text{cosec}\,\theta$
- $\text{cosec}(90° + \theta) = \sec\theta$
- $\sin(180° + \theta) = -\sin\theta$

- $\cos(180° - \theta) = -\cos\theta$
- $\tan(180° - \theta) = -\tan\theta$
- $\cot(180° - \theta) = -\cot\theta$
- $\sec(180° - \theta) = -\sec\theta$
- $\text{cosec}(180° - \theta) = \text{cosec}\,\theta$
- $\cos(180° + \theta) = -\cos\theta$
- $\tan(180° + \theta) = \tan\theta$
- $\cot(180° + \theta) = \cot\theta$
- $\sec(180° + \theta) = -\sec\theta$
- $\text{cosec}(180° + \theta) = -\text{cosec}\,\theta$

Negative Angles of Trigonometric Ratio

- $\sin(-\theta) = -\sin\theta$
- $\cos(-\theta) = \cos\theta$
- $\tan(-\theta) = -\tan\theta$
- $\text{cosec}(-\theta) = -\text{cosec}\,\theta$
- $\sec(-\theta) = \sec\theta$
- $\cot(-\theta) = -\cot\theta$

Trigonometric Ratios of Compound Angles

An angle made up of the algebraic sum of two or more angles is called a compound angle.

Sum and Difference Formulae

- $\sin(x \pm y) = \sin x \cos y \pm \cos x \sin y$
- $\cos(x \pm y) = \cos x \cos y \mp \sin x \sin y$
- $\tan(x \pm y) = \dfrac{\tan x \pm \tan y}{1 \mp \tan x \tan y}$
- $\cot(x + y) = \dfrac{\cot x \cot y - 1}{\cot x + \cot y}$
- $\cot(x - y) = \dfrac{\cot x \cot y + 1}{\cot y - \cot x}$
- $\sin(x + y)\sin(x - y) = (\sin^2 x - \sin^2 y)$ or $(\cos^2 y - \cos^2 x)$
- $\cos(x + y)\cos(x - y) = (\cos^2 x - \sin^2 y)$ or $(\cos^2 y - \sin^2 x)$

Product to Sum Formulae

- $2\sin A \cos B = \sin(A + B) + \sin(A - B)$
- $2\sin A \sin B = \cos(A - B) - \cos(A + B)$
- $2\cos A \sin B = \sin(A + B) - \sin(A - B)$
- $2\cos A \cos B = \cos(A + B) + \cos(A - B)$

Sum to Product Formulae

- $\sin C + \sin D = 2\sin\left(\dfrac{C+D}{2}\right)\cos\left(\dfrac{C-D}{2}\right)$
- $\sin C - \sin D = 2\cos\left(\dfrac{C+D}{2}\right)\sin\left(\dfrac{C-D}{2}\right)$
- $\cos C + \cos D = 2\cos\left(\dfrac{C+D}{2}\right)\cos\left(\dfrac{C-D}{2}\right)$
- $\cos C - \cos D = 2\sin\left(\dfrac{C+D}{2}\right)\sin\left(\dfrac{D-C}{2}\right)$

Trigonometric Ratios of Multiple of an Angle

- $\sin 2x = 2\sin x \cos x = \dfrac{2\tan x}{1 + \tan^2 x}$
- $\cos 2x = \cos^2 x - \sin^2 x = 2\cos^2 x - 1 = 1 - 2\sin^2 x = \dfrac{1 - \tan^2 x}{1 + \tan^2 x}$
- $\tan 2x = \dfrac{2\tan x}{1 - \tan^2 x}$ or $\cot 2x = \dfrac{\cot^2 x - 1}{2\cot x}$
- $\cos 3x = 4\cos^3 x - 3\cos x$
- $\sin 3x = 3\sin x - 4\sin^3 x$
- $\tan 3x = \dfrac{3\tan x - \tan^3 x}{1 - 3\tan^2 x}$
- $\cos x \cdot \cos 2x \cdot \cos 4x = \dfrac{1}{4}[\cos(4x - 2x + x)] = \dfrac{1}{4}\cos 3x$
- $\sin x \cdot \sin 2x \cdot \sin 4x = \dfrac{1}{4}[\sin(4x - 2x + x)] = \dfrac{1}{4}\sin 3x$
- $\tan x \cdot \tan 2x \cdot \tan 4x = \tan(4x - 2x + x) = \tan 3x$

Some Important Results

- $(\sin^4 x + \cos^4 x) = 1 - 2\sin^2 x \cos^2 x$
- $(\sin^6 x + \cos^6 x) = 1 - 3\sin^2 x \cos^2 x$
- If $\theta_1 + \theta_2 = 45°$, then $(1 + \tan\theta_1)(1 + \tan\theta_2) = 2$ and $(1 - \cot\theta_1)(1 - \cot\theta_2) = 2$
- If $\theta_1 + \theta_2 + \theta_3 = 90°$, then $\tan\theta_1 \cdot \tan\theta_2 + \tan\theta_2 \cdot \tan\theta_3 + \tan\theta_3 \cdot \tan\theta_1 = 1$ and $\cot\theta_1 + \cot\theta_2 + \cot\theta_3 = \cot\theta_1 \cdot \cot\theta_2 \cdot \cot\theta_3$
- If $\theta_1 + \theta_2 + \theta_3 = 180°$ then, $\tan\theta_1 + \tan\theta_2 + \tan\theta_3 = \tan\theta_1 \cdot \tan\theta_2 \cdot \tan\theta_3$ and $\cot\theta_1 \cdot \cot\theta_2 + \cot\theta_2 \cdot \cot\theta_3 + \cot\theta_3 \cdot \cot\theta_1 = 1$

Maximum and Minimum Values of Trigonometric Angles

- $-1 \le \sin\theta$ or $\cos\theta \le 1$
- $-\infty \le \tan\theta$ or $\cot\theta \le \infty$
- $\sec\theta$ or $\text{cosec}\,\theta \ge 1$
- $\sec\theta$ or $\text{cosec}\,\theta \le -1$
- $-\sqrt{m^2 + n^2} \le m\sin\theta \pm n\cos\theta \le \sqrt{m^2 + n^2}$

To obtain the maximum or minimum value of an expression try to convert it into $\sin\theta$ or $\cos\theta$.

Ex. 1 Find the maximum value of $4\tan\theta\cos\theta + 5\cos\theta$

Sol. $5\tan\theta\cos\theta + 4\cos\theta = \dfrac{5\sin\theta}{\cos\theta} \times \cos\theta + 4\cos\theta = 5\sin\theta + 4\cos\theta$

So, $m = 5$ and $n = 4$

$\therefore$ Maximum value $= \sqrt{4^2 + 5^2} = \sqrt{16 + 25} = \sqrt{41}$

Ex. 2 If $\cot\theta = \dfrac{7}{8}$, then evaluate $\dfrac{(1 + \sin\theta)(1 - \sin\theta)}{(1 + \cos\theta)(1 - \cos\theta)}$.

Sol. $\dfrac{(1 + \sin\theta)(1 - \sin\theta)}{(1 + \cos\theta)(1 - \cos\theta)} = \dfrac{(1)^2 - (\sin\theta)^2}{(1)^2 - (\cos\theta)^2}$

$= \dfrac{1 - \sin^2\theta}{1 - \cos^2\theta} = \dfrac{\cos^2\theta}{\sin^2\theta} = \left(\dfrac{\cos\theta}{\sin\theta}\right)^2$

$= (\cot\theta)^2 = \left(\dfrac{7}{8}\right)^2 = \dfrac{49}{64}$

Ex. 3 If $(1 + \tan A)(1 + \tan B) = 2$, then find the value of $(A + B)$.

Sol. Given, $(1 + \tan A)(1 + \tan B) = 2$

$\Rightarrow \tan A + \tan B = 1 - \tan A \tan B$

$\Rightarrow \dfrac{\tan A + \tan B}{1 - \tan A \tan B} = 1 = \tan 45°$

$\Rightarrow \tan(A + B) = \tan 45°$ $\left[\because \tan(A + B) = \dfrac{\tan A + \tan B}{1 - \tan A \tan B}\right]$

$\Rightarrow A + B = 45° = \dfrac{\pi}{4}$

SSC Exam Scanner

SSC CGL 2024 (Tier I & II)

1. If $\sin A = \frac{5}{13}$, then find the value of $\frac{\cos A - 2\tan A}{\sin A + 3\tan A}$.
SSC CGL (Tier-II) 20/01/2025 Shift-I
(a) $\frac{11}{255}$ (b) $\frac{12}{255}$ (c) $\frac{14}{255}$ (d) $\frac{13}{255}$

2. If $\cos 27° = \frac{p}{q}$, then find the value of $\operatorname{cosec} 27° - \cos 63°$.
SSC CGL (Tier-II) 20/01/2025 Shift-I
(a) $\frac{q^2}{p\sqrt{q^2 - p^2}}$ (b) $\frac{p^2}{q\sqrt{q^2 - p^2}}$
(c) $\frac{q}{p\sqrt{q^2 - p^2}}$ (d) $\frac{p}{q\sqrt{q^2 - p^2}}$

3. Let PQR be a right-angled triangle, right-angled at R. Let $PQ = 29$ cm, $QR = 21$ cm and $\angle Q = \theta$. Find the value of $\cos^2\theta - \sin^2\theta$.
SSC CGL (Tier-II) 20/01/2025 Shift-I
(a) $\frac{40}{840}$ (b) $\frac{840}{40}$
(c) $\frac{41}{841}$ (d) $\frac{841}{41}$

4. If $\frac{\sec\theta - \tan\theta}{\sec\theta + \tan\theta} = \frac{1}{9}$, θ lies in the first quadrant, then the value of $\frac{\sin\theta - \tan^2\theta}{\sin\theta + \tan^2\theta}$ is
SSC CGL (Tier-II) 18/01/2025 Shift-I
(a) $-\frac{13}{27}$ (b) $-\frac{11}{29}$
(c) $\frac{13}{27}$ (d) $\frac{11}{29}$

5. If $\tan(x + y)\tan(x - y) = 1$, then find the value of $\tan x$.
SSC CGL (Tier-II) 18/01/2025 Shift-I
(a) $\sqrt{3}$ (b) $\frac{1}{\sqrt{3}}$
(c) 1 (d) $\frac{1}{2\sqrt{3}}$

6. Let ABC be a right-angled triangle with a right angle at B. If $\tan A = \sqrt{3}$, then find the value of $\sin A\cos C + \cos A\sin C$ and $\cos A\cos C - \sin A\ \sin C$.
SSC CGL (Tier-II) 18/01/2025 Shift-I
(a) $\frac{\sqrt{3}}{2}, \frac{1}{2}$ (b) $\frac{\sqrt{3}}{2}, \frac{\sqrt{3}}{2}$
(c) $\frac{1}{2}, \frac{1}{2}$ (d) 1, 0

7. The greatest value of $\sin^4\theta + \cos^4\theta$ is
SSC CGL (Tier-I) 26/09/2024 Shift-III
(a) 2 (b) 1 (c) 3 (d) 4

8. If $x = a\sec\theta\cos\phi$, $y = b\sec\theta\sin\phi$ and $z = c\tan\theta$, then the value of $\left(\frac{x^2}{a^2} + \frac{y^2}{b^2} - \frac{z^2}{c^2}\right)$ is equal to
SSC CGL (Tier-I) 26/09/2024 Shift-III
(a) 2 (b) 1
(c) 3 (d) 0

9. If $\cot\theta = \sqrt{11}$, then the value of $\frac{\operatorname{cosec}^2\theta - \sec^2\theta}{\operatorname{cosec}^2\theta + \sec^2\theta}$ is
SSC CGL (Tier-I) 26/09/2024 Shift-III
(a) $\frac{3}{5}$ (b) $\frac{5}{6}$ (c) $\frac{4}{5}$ (d) $\frac{6}{7}$

10. If $8\cot\theta = 7$, then the value of $\frac{1 + \sin\theta}{\cos\theta}$ is
SSC CGL (Tier-I) 26/09/2024 Shift-II
(a) $\frac{8 + \sqrt{113}}{7}$ (b) $\frac{1 + \sqrt{113}}{8}$
(c) $\frac{7 + \sqrt{113}}{8}$ (d) $\frac{1 + \sqrt{113}}{7}$

11. In a ΔABC, a right angled at B if $\tan C = \sqrt{3}$, then find $\frac{\sin^2 C + \cos^2 C}{1 + \cot^2 C}$
SSC CGL (Tier-I) 26/09/2024 Shift-II
(a) $\frac{3}{4}$ (b) $\frac{16}{3}$ (c) $\frac{4}{15}$ (d) $\frac{3}{16}$

12. Evaluate the given expression. $\frac{5}{1 + \cot^2\theta} + \frac{3}{1 + \tan^2\theta} + 2\cos^2\theta$
SSC CGL (Tier-I) 26/09/2024 Shift-I
(a) 0 (b) 3
(c) 5 (d) 2

13. If A is an acute angle and $\tan A + \cot A = 2$, find the value of $7\tan^8 A - 6\cot^8 A + 8\sec^2 A$
SSC CGL (Tier-I) 26/09/2024 Shift-I
(a) 6 (b) 17
(c) 16 (d) 7

14. What is the value of $\left(\frac{5}{\sqrt{3}} - \operatorname{cosec} 60°\right)$?
SSC CGL (Tier-I) 25/09/2024 Shift-III
(a) $\sqrt{3}$ (b) $\frac{2}{\sqrt{3}}$ (c) $3\sqrt{3}$ (d) $\frac{1}{\sqrt{3}}$

15. If $\sec\theta + \tan\theta = x$, then find $\sin\theta$.
SSC CGL (Tier-I) 25/09/2024 Shift-III
(a) $\frac{x^2 + 1}{1 - x^2}$ (b) $\frac{x^2 - 1}{1 + 2x^2}$
(c) $\frac{x^2 - 1}{1 + x^2}$ (d) $\frac{1 - x^2}{1 + x^2}$

16. Find the value of $3\sin 15° - 4\sin^3 15°$
SSC CGL (Tier-I) 25/09/2024 Shift-III
(a) 2 (b) $\frac{1}{2}$
(c) $\frac{1}{\sqrt{2}}$ (d) $\sqrt{2}$

17. Find the value of $\tan 72° - \tan 27° - \tan 72° \tan 27°$.
SSC CGL (Tier-I) 25/09/2024 Shift-II
(a) – 1 (b) 1
(c) – 2 (d) 0

18. If $\cot^2\theta - 2\cos^2\theta = 0$, $(0° < \theta < 90°)$, then the value of θ is
SSC CGL (Tier-I) 25/09/2024 Shift-II
(a) 45° (b) 60°
(c) 90° (d) 30°

19. Find the value of $(\operatorname{cosec}\theta - \sin\theta)(\sec\theta - \cos\theta)(\tan\theta + \cot\theta)$.
SSC CGL (Tier-I) 25/09/2024 Shift-I
(a) 0 (b) $\frac{1}{2}$
(c) 1 (d) –1

20. Evaluate $2\frac{\tan 54°}{\cot 36°} - \frac{\cot 41°}{\tan 49°}$.
SSC CGL (Tier-I) 25/09/2024 Shift-I
(a) –1 (b) 1 (c) 0 (d) 2

21. If $m + 5 = \sec^2 A\operatorname{cosec}^2 A(1 - \cos^2 A)(1 - \sin^2 A) + 5$, then find the value of m
SSC CGL (Tier-I) 25/09/2024 Shift-I
(a) 10 (b) 0 (c) 1 (d) 5

22. If $10\sin^2\theta + 6\cos^2\theta = 7$, $0 < \theta < 90°$, then find the value of $\tan\theta$.
SSC CGL (Tier-I) 24/09/2024 Shift-III
(a) $\sqrt{3}$ (b) 1 (c) $\frac{1}{\sqrt{3}}$ (d) $\frac{1}{2}$

23. Simplify, $\frac{1 + \sin\theta - \cos\theta}{1 + \sin\theta + \cos\theta}$.
SSC CGL (Tier-I) 24/09/2024 Shift-III
(a) $\cos\frac{\theta}{2}$ (b) $\sin\frac{\theta}{2}$ (c) $\cot\frac{\theta}{2}$ (d) $\tan\frac{\theta}{2}$

24. If $A = 15°$, then what is the value of $\frac{11\sqrt{2}\cos 3A + 10\sin 2A}{7\sqrt{3}\sin 4A}$?
SSC CGL (Tier-I) 24/09/2024 Shift-III
(a) $\frac{11}{7}$ (b) $\frac{21}{32}$
(c) $\frac{32}{21}$ (d) $\frac{7}{11}$

25. If $3\tan A = 4$ and A is an acute angle, then the value of $4\sin A + 3\cos A$ is
SSC CGL (Tier-I) 24/09/2024 Shift-II
(a) 1 (b) 3
(c) 4 (d) 5

26. The value of $(\sin A + \operatorname{cosec} A)^2 + (\cos A + \sec A)^2$ is
SSC CGL (Tier-I) 24/09/2024 Shift-II
(a) $3 + \tan^2 A + \cot^2 A$
(b) $7 + \tan^2 A + \cot^2 A$
(c) $5 + \tan^2 A + \cot^2 A$
(d) $1 + \tan^2 A + \cot^2 A$

27. If $\tan A + \cot A = 2$, then the value of $\tan^2 A + \cot^2 A$ is
SSC CGL (Tier-I) 24/09/2024 Shift-II
(a) 16 (b) 2 (c) 8 (d) 4

28. If $\sin 3A = \cos(A - 26°)$, then $A =$ ...., where 3A is an acute angle.
SSC CGL (Tier-I) 24/09/2024 Shift-I
(a) 29° (b) 40°
(c) 26° (d) 78°

29. The value of $\dfrac{\sin^2\theta - 2\sin^4\theta}{2\cos^4\theta + \cos^2\theta}$ at $\theta = 45°$ is **SSC CGL (Tier-I) 23/09/2024 Shift-III**
(a) 1 (b) 0 (c) 3 (d) 2

30. If $\tan A = \dfrac{1}{\sqrt{10}}$, A is an acute angle, then the value of $\sin A + \operatorname{cosec} A$ is
SSC CGL (Tier-I) 23/09/2024 Shift-III
(a) $\dfrac{11}{\sqrt{10}}$ (b) $\dfrac{1}{\sqrt{10}}$
(c) $\dfrac{12}{\sqrt{11}}$ (d) $\dfrac{10}{\sqrt{22}}$

31. For what value of t is the value of $\sin^2(t)$, half of the value of $\tan(t)$?
SSC CGL (Tier-I) 23/09/2024 Shift-III
(a) 60° (b) 45°
(c) 30° (d) 22.5°

32. If $\sin A - \cos A = \dfrac{\sqrt{3} - \sqrt{2}}{2}$, then the value of $\sin A \cdot \cos A$ is
SSC CGL (Tier-I) 23/09/2024 Shift-II
(a) $\dfrac{2\sqrt{3} - 1}{4}$ (b) $\dfrac{2\sqrt{2} - 1}{8}$
(c) $\dfrac{2\sqrt{6} - 1}{8}$ (d) $\dfrac{3\sqrt{2} - 1}{4}$

33. The value of $\dfrac{1}{\operatorname{cosec}\theta - \cot\theta} - \dfrac{1}{\sin\theta}$ is equal to **SSC CGL (Tier-I) 23/09/2024 Shift-II**
(a) $\tan\theta$ (b) $\operatorname{cosec}\theta$
(c) $\cot\theta$ (d) $\sec\theta$

34. Let $x = r\cos(t)$, $y = r\sin(t)\cos(u)$, $z = r\sin(t)\sin(u)$. Then the value of $x^2 + y^2 + z^2$ is ....
SSC CGL (Tier-I) 23/09/2024 Shift-I
(a) $r^2\cos(u)$ (b) r^2
(c) $2r$ (d) $r^2\sin(t)$

35. The value of θ, when $\sqrt{3}\cos\theta + \sin\theta = 1 (1 \le \theta \le 90°)$, is
SSC CGL (Tier-I) 23/09/2024 Shift-I
(a) 20° (b) 60° (c) 90° (d) 30°

36. If $\tan\theta + \cot\theta = 2$ and θ is an acute angle, then the value of θ is
SSC CGL (Tier-I) 19/09/2024 Shift-III
(a) 30° (b) 15°
(c) 60° (d) 45°

37. If A is an acute angle, then $\sqrt{\dfrac{1 - \cos A}{1 + \cos A}} + \sqrt{\dfrac{1 + \cos A}{1 - \cos A}}$ is equal to
SSC CGL (Tier-I) 19/09/2024 Shift-III
(a) 2 cosec A (b) 2cos A
(c) 2 sec A (d) 2 sin A

38. If $\tan\theta = \dfrac{5}{8}$, then find the value of $\dfrac{(1 + \cos\theta)(1 - \cos\theta)}{(1 + \sin\theta)(1 - \sin\theta)}$
SSC CGL (Tier-I) 19/09/2024 Shift-III
(a) $\dfrac{5}{64}$ (b) $\dfrac{2}{25}$
(c) $\dfrac{25}{64}$ (d) $\dfrac{64}{25}$

39. The value of the expression $\dfrac{1 - \sin(2t)}{1 + \sin(2t)} \times \dfrac{\cos(t) + \sin(t)}{\cos(t) - \sin(t)}$ is
SSC CGL (Tier-I) 19/09/2024 Shift-II
(a) $\dfrac{1 - 2\tan(t)}{1 + 2\tan(t)}$ (b) $\dfrac{1 - \tan(t)}{1 + \tan(t)}$
(c) $\dfrac{1 + 2\tan(t)}{1 - 2\tan(t)}$ (d) $\dfrac{1 + \tan(t)}{1 - \tan(t)}$

40. Simplify : $\left[1 - \sin^2 32° + \dfrac{1}{1 + \tan^2 58°}\right]$.
SSC CGL (Tier-I) 19/09/2024 Shift-II
(a) $\dfrac{1}{2}$ (b) sin 32°
(c) 1 (d) $\sqrt{3}$

41. The maximum value of $(2\sin\theta + 3\cos\theta)$ is
SSC CGL (Tier-I) 19/09/2024 Shift-II
(a) $\sqrt{17}$ (b) $\sqrt{11}$
(c) 9 (d) $\sqrt{13}$

42. If $3\sin^2\theta + 5\cos^2\theta = 4$ and θ is an acute angle, then the value of tan θ is
SSC CGL (Tier-I) 19/09/2024 Shift-I
(a) $\dfrac{1}{\sqrt{2}}$ (b) $\dfrac{1}{\sqrt{3}}$ (c) $\dfrac{1}{2}$ (d) 1

43. The value of the expression $\sin x + \operatorname{cosec} x = 2$, then the value of $\sin^7 x + \operatorname{cosec}^7 x$ is
SSC CGL (Tier-I) 19/09/2024 Shift-I
(a) 0 (b) 1
(c) 2 (d) 4

44. If $\sin A + \cos A = \sqrt{3}$, then find the value of $\tan A + \cot A + 2\sin A\cos A$
SSC CGL (Tier-I) 19/09/2024 Shift-I
(a) 6 (b) 2
(c) 1 (d) 3

45. What is the value of $\sqrt{\dfrac{9\sin^2 26° + 9\sin^2 64° + 36}{32 - 7\cos^2 32° - 7\cos^2 58°}}$?
SSC CGL (Tier-I) 18/09/2024 Shift-III
(a) $\dfrac{3\sqrt{5}}{5}$ (b) $\dfrac{5\sqrt{3}}{3}$ (c) $\dfrac{5\sqrt{5}}{3}$ (d) $\dfrac{3\sqrt{3}}{5}$

46. $\sin A \sin B =$........
SSC CGL (Tier-I) 18/09/2024 Shift-III
(a) $\dfrac{1}{2}\{\sin(A + B) + \sin(A - B)\}$
(b) $\dfrac{1}{2}\{\sin(A + B) - \sin(A - B)\}$
(c) $\dfrac{1}{2}\{\cos(A + B) - \cos(A - B)\}$
(d) $\dfrac{1}{2}\{\cos(A - B) - \cos(A + B)\}$

47. The given expression is equivalent to $\sqrt{\dfrac{\sec\theta + 1}{\sec\theta - 1}} + \sqrt{\dfrac{\sec\theta - 1}{\sec\theta + 1}}$
SSC CGL (Tier-I) 18/09/2024 Shift-III
(a) 2 sin θ (b) 2 cosec θ
(c) 2 tan θ (d) 2 tan θ sec θ

48. If $\tan\theta = \dfrac{8}{15}$, and θ is an acute angle, then the value of $\dfrac{\sqrt{1 - \sin\theta}}{\sqrt{1 + \sin\theta}}$ is
SSC CGL (Tier-I) 18/09/2024 Shift-II
(a) $\dfrac{2}{5}$ (b) $\dfrac{3}{5}$
(c) $\dfrac{1}{5}$ (d) $\dfrac{4}{5}$

49. Simplify $\dfrac{\sin A}{1 + \cos A} + \cot A$, where A is an acute angle.
SSC CGL (Tier-I) 18/09/2024 Shift-II
(a) sin A (b) cos A
(c) sin A + cos A (d) cosec A

50. If $3\sin A + 4\cos A = 5$, then the value tan A is **SSC CGL (Tier-I) 18/09/2024 Shift-I**
(a) $\dfrac{3}{4}$ (b) $\dfrac{3}{5}$
(c) $\dfrac{5}{4}$ (d) $\dfrac{4}{5}$

51. If $\sec(t) = \dfrac{x}{y}$, then $\cot(t)$ is equal to
SSC CGL (Tier-I) 18/09/2024 Shift-I
(a) $\dfrac{y}{\sqrt{x^2 - y^2}}$ (b) $\dfrac{x}{\sqrt{x^2 + y^2}}$
(c) $\dfrac{x}{\sqrt{x^2 - y^2}}$ (d) $\dfrac{y}{\sqrt{x^2 + y^2}}$

52. If $\sin\theta + \cos\theta = \sqrt{3}\cos\theta$, then the value of cot θ is
SSC CGL (Tier-I) 17/09/2024 Shift-III
(a) $\sqrt{3} - 1$ (b) $\dfrac{(\sqrt{3} + 1)}{2}$
(c) $\dfrac{\sqrt{3} - 1}{2}$ (d) $\sqrt{3} + 1$

53. If $\operatorname{cosec} x = \frac{5}{4}$, then the value of $\frac{5\sin^2 x + 8\cot^2 x}{27\tan^2 x - 125\cos^2 x}$ is

SSC CGL (Tier-I) 17/09/2024 Shift-III

(a) $\frac{33}{91}$ (b) $\frac{77}{30}$ (c) $\frac{55}{87}$ (d) $\frac{99}{47}$

54. If $a = x\cos\theta + y\sin\theta$ and $b = x\sin\theta - y\cos\theta$, then $a^2 + b^2$ is equal to

SSC CGL (Tier-I) 17/09/2024 Shift-II

(a) $x + y$ (b) $x^2 - y^2$
(c) $x^2 + y^2$ (d) $x - y$

55. Find the value of $\left[\frac{4\cos(90-\theta)\sin^3(90+\theta) - 4\sin(90+\theta)\cos^3(90-\theta)}{\cos\left(\frac{180+8\theta}{2}\right)}\right]$

SSC CGL (Tier-I) 17/09/2024 Shift-II

(a) – 1 (b) 1
(c) 2 (d) 0

56. If $\sin A + \cos A = \frac{1}{2\sqrt{2}}$, then find the value of $\sin^4 A + \cos^4 A$.

SSC CGL (Tier-I) 17/09/2024 Shift-II

(a) $\frac{79}{128}$ (b) $\frac{7}{13}$ (c) $\frac{79}{126}$ (d) $\frac{5}{13}$

57. If $\cos 24° = \frac{m}{n}$, then the value of $(\operatorname{cosec}24° - \cos 66°)$ is

SSC CGL (Tier-I) 17/09/2024 Shift-I

(a) $\frac{m^2}{n\sqrt{m^2-n^2}}$ (b) $\frac{n^2}{m\sqrt{m^2-n^2}}$
(c) $\frac{n^2}{m\sqrt{n^2-m^2}}$ (d) $\frac{m^2}{n\sqrt{n^2-m^2}}$

58. If $\sec\theta = \frac{29}{20}$, where $0 < \theta < 90°$, then what is the value of $3\operatorname{cosec}\theta + 3\cot\theta$?

SSC CGL (Tier-I) 17/09/2024 Shift-I

(a) $\frac{7}{3}$ (b) 7 (c) 14 (d) 49

59. If $m = a\sec A$ and $y = b\tan A$, then find the value of $b^2m^2 - a^2y^2 + \frac{a^2y^2}{b^2m^2} + \cos^2 A$.

SSC CGL (Tier-I) 13/09/2024 Shift-III

(a) a^2b^2 (b) $1 - a^2b^2$
(c) $a^2b^2 + 2$ (d) $a^2b^2 + 1$

60. The value of $\left(\frac{\operatorname{cosec}A}{\operatorname{cosec}A - 1} + \frac{\operatorname{cosec}A}{\operatorname{cosec}A + 1}\right)\left(\frac{\sec A}{\sec A - 1} + \frac{\sec A}{\sec A + 1}\right)^{-1}$, When $A = 60°$ is

SSC CGL (Tier-I) 13/09/2024 Shift-III

(a) 4 (b) 3 (c) 1 (d) 2

61. If $\tan A = \frac{5}{7}$, then find the value of $\frac{7\sin A - 3\cos A}{7\sin A + 3\cos A} + 4$.

SSC CGL (Tier-I) 13/09/2024 Shift-II

(a) $4\frac{1}{4}$ (b) $3\frac{5}{7}$
(c) $3\frac{1}{5}$ (d) $7\frac{1}{3}$

62. If $\sin B = \frac{15}{17}$, what is the value of $\cos B(\sec B - \tan B)$? Given that $0 < B < \frac{\pi}{2}$

SSC CGL (Tier-I) 13/09/2024 Shift-II

(a) $\frac{1}{16}$ (b) $\frac{2}{15}$
(c) $\frac{8}{15}$ (d) $\frac{2}{17}$

63. If $\frac{\tan(x)}{\sec(x)} = \frac{1}{2}$, then the value of $(\sin(x) + \cos(x))^2$ is ....

SSC CGL (Tier-I) 13/09/2024 Shift-II

(a) $\frac{2+\sqrt{1}}{3}$ (b) $\frac{2+\sqrt{3}}{2}$
(c) $\frac{2-\sqrt{3}}{2}$ (d) $\frac{2-\sqrt{3}}{3}$

64. If $\frac{1}{1-\sin\theta} + \frac{1}{1+\sin\theta} = 4\sec\theta$, $(0 < \theta < 90°)$, then the value of $(\cot\theta + \operatorname{cosec}\theta)$ is

SSC CGL (Tier-I) 13/09/2024 Shift-I

(a) $\sqrt{3}$ (b) $\sqrt{6}$
(c) $\sqrt{2}$ (d) $\sqrt{5}$

65. If $p(\sqrt{3} + \cot 30°) = \tan^3 60° - 2\sin 60°$, then the value of p is

SSC CGL (Tier-I) 13/09/2024 Shift-I

(a) –1 (b) $2\sqrt{3}$ (c) 1 (d) $\sqrt{3}$

66. If $\tan 4\theta.\tan 6\theta = 1$, where 6θ is an acute angle, then find the value of $\cot 5\theta$.

SSC CGL (Tier-I) 12/09/2024 Shift-III

(a) $\sqrt{3}$ (b) $-\sqrt{3}$
(c) – 1 (d) 1

67. If $7\cos A = 6$, then the numerical value of $\frac{\operatorname{cosec} A + \cot A}{\operatorname{cosec} A - \cot A}$ is

SSC CGL (Tier-I) 12/09/2024 Shift-III

(a) 1 (b) 0
(c) 13 (d) –13

68. Find the exact value of $\sin 150°$.

SSC CGL (Tier-I) 12/09/2024 Shift-III

(a) 1.5 (b) 0.5
(c) 0.75 (d) –0.5

69. If $\cot^4\phi - \cot^2\phi = 1$, then the value of $\cos^4\phi + \cos^2\phi$ is

SSC CGL (Tier-I) 12/09/2024 Shift-II

(a) 2 (b) 1 (c) $\frac{1}{\sqrt{3}}$ (d) $\frac{3}{2}$

70. Solve the following $\frac{1}{1+\cos\theta} + \frac{1}{1-\cos\theta} = ?$

SSC CGL (Tier-I) 12/09/2024 Shift-II

(a) $2\operatorname{cosec}^2\theta$ (b) $2\sin^2\theta$
(c) $2\sec^2\theta$ (d) $2\tan^2\theta$

71. The value of $\left(\frac{\sin\theta - 2\sin^3\theta}{2\cos^3\theta - \cos\theta}\right)^3 \frac{1}{\tan\theta} - \sec^2\theta$ is

SSC CGL (Tier-I) 12/09/2024 Shift-I

(a) 2 (b) 1 (c) 0 (d) –1

72. $2\operatorname{cosec}^2\theta + 3\cot^2\theta = 17$, then the value of 'θ' when $0° \le \theta \le 90°$ is

SSC CGL (Tier-I) 12/09/2024 Shift-I

(a) 45° (b) 90°
(c) 30° (d) 75°

73. If $\tan A + \tan B = p$ and $\cot A + \cot B = q$, then $\cot(A + B)$ is

SSC CGL (Tier-I) 11/09/2024 Shift-III

(a) $\frac{p-q}{pq}$ (b) $\frac{q-p}{pq}$ (c) $\frac{pq}{p-q}$ (d) $\frac{pq}{p+q}$

74. Express $\sin 74° + \tan 74°$ in terms of trigonometric ratios of angles between 0° and 45°.

SSC CGL (Tier-I) 11/09/2024 Shift-III

(a) $\sec 16° + \cot 16°$
(b) $\operatorname{cosec} 16° + \sec 16°$
(c) $\operatorname{cosec} 16° + \cot 16°$
(d) $\cos 16° + \cot 16°$

75. If $P\sin A - \cos A = 1$, then $P^2 - (1 + P^2)\cos A$ equals

SSC CGL (Tier-I) 11/09/2024 Shift-III

(a) 1 (b) –1
(c) 2 (d) 0

76. In a triangle ΔABC, the $\angle ABC = 90°$. If $\sin(A) = \frac{1}{2}$, then $\cos(C)$ is equal to

SSC CGL (Tier-I) 11/09/2024 Shift-II

(a) $\frac{1}{\sqrt{2}}$ (b) 1 (c) $\frac{\sqrt{3}}{2}$ (d) $\frac{1}{2}$

77. Find the value of $\left[\frac{4}{3}\tan^2 60° + 3\cos^2 30° - 2\sec^2 30° - \frac{3}{4}\cot^2 60°\right] + [\sin 60°\cos 30° - \cos 60°\sin 30°]$

SSC CGL (Tier-I) 11/09/2024 Shift-II

(a) $6\frac{2}{3}$ (b) $3\frac{1}{2}$
(c) $4\frac{1}{3}$ (d) $6\frac{3}{2}$

78. Evaluate the value of $(\operatorname{cosec} 56° \cos 34° - \cos 59° \operatorname{cosec} 31°)$.

SSC CGL (Tier-I) 11/09/2024 Shift-II

(a) 1 (b) 2
(c) –1 (d) 0

79. If $a\sin^3 x + b\cos^3 x = \sin x\cos x$ and $a\sin x = b\cos x$, then find the value of $a^2 + b^2$, provided that x is neither 0° nor 90°. **SSC CGL (Tier-I) 11/09/2024 Shift-I**

(a) 0 (b) 1
(c) $a^2 - b^2$ (d) $a^2 + b^2$

80. Find the value of $\frac{\sec 35°}{\text{cosec } 55°} - \frac{\cos 25°}{\sin 65°}$. **SSC CGL (Tier-I) 11/09/2024 Shift-I**

(a) 0 (b) 1 (c) $\frac{1}{2}$ (d) 2

81. If $7\tan\theta = 3$, and θ is an acute angle, then $\frac{5\sin\theta - \cos\theta}{5\sin\theta + 2\cos\theta}$ is equal to **SSC CGL (Tier-I) 10/09/2024 Shift-III**

(a) $\frac{8}{29}$ (b) $\frac{11}{29}$ (c) $\frac{7}{29}$ (d) $\frac{9}{29}$

82. If $7\cos^2\theta + 5\sin^2\theta - 6 = 0$, $(0° < \theta < 90°)$, then what is the value of $1 + \sqrt{\frac{\sec\theta + \tan\theta}{\sec\theta - \tan\theta}}$? **SSC CGL (Tier-I) 10/09/2024 Shift-III**

(a) $\sqrt{2} + 2$ (b) $\sqrt{2} + 1$
(c) $\sqrt{2} - 1$ (d) $\sqrt{2} - 2$

83. $\frac{3\sin 58°}{5\cos 32°} + \frac{2\cos 62°}{5\sin 28°}$ is equal to **SSC CGL (Tier-I) 10/09/2024 Shift-III**

(a) 0 (b) 2
(c) 3 (d) 1

84. If $p\cos A = 2q\sin A$ and $2p\,\text{cosec } A - q\sec A = 3$, then the value of $p^2 + 4q^2$ is **SSC CGL (Tier-I) 10/09/2024 Shift-II**

(a) 2 (b) 4
(c) 1 (d) 3

85. If $\cot\theta = \frac{4}{3}$, then evaluate $(\sec\theta(1+\cot^2\theta)(\text{cosec}^2\theta - \cot^2\theta))/\text{cosec}^3\theta$. **SSC CGL (Tier-I) 10/09/2024 Shift-II**

(a) $\frac{3}{4}$ (b) $\frac{4}{5}$ (c) $\frac{4}{3}$ (d) $\frac{3}{5}$

86. Let $0° < t < 90°$. Then which of the followings is true? **SSC CGL (Tier-I) 10/09/2024 Shift-I**

(a) $\sin(t) \neq \cos(t)$ when $t = 45°$
(b) $\sin(t) > \cos(t)$ when $t < 45°$
(c) $\sin(t) < \cos(t)$ when $t < 45°$
(d) $\sin(t) < \cos(t)$ when $t > 45°$

87. $\frac{2 + \tan^2 2A + \cot^2 2A}{\sec 2A \cdot \text{cosec } 2A}$ is equal to .... **SSC CGL (Tier-I) 10/09/2024 Shift-I**

(a) $\sec 2A + \tan 2A$
(b) $\sec 2A \cdot \text{cosec } 2A$
(c) $\cot 2A - \text{cosec } 2A$
(d) $\sec 2A - \text{cosec } 2A$

88. If $\frac{7\sin\theta + 4\cos\theta}{9\sin\theta - 2\cos\theta} = \frac{5}{4}$, then the value of $\frac{\tan^2\theta + 5}{\tan^2\theta - 5}$ is **SSC CGL (Tier-I) 09/09/2024 Shift-III**

(a) $\frac{2121}{769}$ (b) $-\frac{2121}{769}$
(c) $\frac{769}{2121}$ (d) $-\frac{769}{2121}$

89. If A is an acute angle, which of the following is equal to $\frac{\sin A}{1+\cos A}$? **SSC CGL (Tier-I) 09/09/2024 Shift-III**

(a) $\frac{1-\cos A}{\sin A}$ (b) $\frac{1+\cos A}{\sin A}$
(c) $\frac{1-\sin A}{\cos A}$ (d) $\frac{1+\sin A}{\cos A}$

90. Simplify the following, $\frac{\sin^3 A - \cos^3 A}{\sin A - \cos A}$, where A is an acute angle. **SSC CGL (Tier-I) 09/09/2024 Shift-II**

(a) $1 + \sin A\cos A$ (b) $1 - 3\sin A$
(c) $3\cos A - 1$ (d) $\sin A + \cos A$

91. If $\text{cosec }\theta = \frac{5}{3}$, then evaluate $(\sec^2\theta - 1) \times \cot^2\theta \times (1 + \cot^2\theta)$. **SSC CGL (Tier-I) 09/09/2024 Shift-I**

(a) $\frac{25}{16}$ (b) $\frac{9}{16}$
(c) $\frac{25}{9}$ (d) $\frac{4}{5}$

92. The value of $\sin^2 30° - \sin^2 40° + \sin^2 45° - \sin^2 55° - \sin^2 35° + \sin^2 45° - \sin^2 50° + \sin^2 60°$ is **SSC CGL (Tier-I) 09/09/2024 Shift-I**

(a) 1 (b) 2 (c) 4 (d) 0

93. The value of $\cos^2 29° + \cos^2 61°$ is **SSC CGL (Tier-I) 09/09/2024 Shift-I**

(a) $\frac{\sqrt{3}}{2}$ (b) 2
(c) 1 (d) 0

SSC CGL 2023 (Tier I & II)

94. If $a\cot\theta + b\,\text{cosec}\theta = p$ and $b\cot\theta + a\,\text{cosec}\theta = q$, then $p^2 - q^2$ is equal to .... **SSC CGL (Tier-II) 07/03/2023 Shift-I**

(a) $a^2 - b^2$ (b) $b^2 - a^2$
(c) $a^2 + b^2$ (d) $b - a$

95. Select the incorrect formula from the following options. **SSC CGL (Tier-II) 03/03/2023 Shift-I**

(a) $\text{cosec}^2\theta - \cot^2\theta = 1$
(b) $\sin^2\theta + \cos^2\theta = 1$
(c) $\sec^2\theta + \cos^2\theta = 1$
(d) $\sec^2\theta - \tan^2\theta = 1$

96. Evaluate the following $\sin 25° \sin 65° - \cos 25° \cos 65°$ **SSC CGL (Tier-II) 02/03/2023 Shift-I**

(a) 4 (b) 1 (c) 0 (d) 40

97. If $\tan(A+B) = \sqrt{3}$ and $\tan(A-B) = \frac{1}{\sqrt{3}}$; $0° < (A+B) < 90°$; $A > B$, then the values of A and B are ...., respectively. **SSC CGL (Tier-II) 02/03/2023 Shift-I**

(a) 45° and 15° (b) 15° and 45°
(c) 30° and 30° (d) 60° and 30°

98. Evaluate the following : $\sqrt{2 + \sqrt{2 + \sqrt{2 + 2\cos 8\theta}}}$ **SSC CGL (Tier-I) 27/07/2023 Shift-III**

(a) $2\cos\theta$ (b) $2\cos 2\theta$
(c) $\sin 2\theta$ (d) $\cos 2\theta$

99. If $7\cot P = 24$, then find $\sin P$. **SSC CGL (Tier-I) 27/07/2023 Shift-III**

(a) $\frac{625}{7}$ (b) $\frac{24}{5}$ (c) $\frac{49}{625}$ (d) $\frac{7}{25}$

100. If $\tan^4\theta + \tan^2\theta = 1$, what is the value of $11(\cos^4\theta + \cos^2\theta)$? **SSC CGL (Tier-I) 27/07/2023 Shift-III**

(a) – 11 (b) 8
(c) 0 (d) 11

101. If $3x = \sec A$ and $\frac{3}{x} = \tan A$, then $9\left(x^2 - \frac{1}{x^2}\right)$ is .... **SSC CGL (Tier-I) 27/07/2023 Shift-II**

(a) 3 (b) 9 (c) 1 (d) $\frac{1}{9}$

102. If $\sec A + \tan A = 5$, then $\sin A$ is equal to **SSC CGL (Tier-I) 27/07/2023 Shift-II**

(a) $\frac{5}{13}$ (b) $\frac{5}{12}$ (c) $\frac{13}{12}$ (d) $\frac{12}{13}$

103. What is the value of given expression if $3\cot A = \frac{7}{3}$? $\frac{3\cos A + 2\sin A}{3\cos A - 2\sin A}$ **SSC CGL (Tier-I) 27/07/2023 Shift-I**

(a) $\frac{2}{3}$ (b) $\frac{1}{3}$ (c) 13 (d) 1

104. If $A = 22.5°$, what is the value of $(10\sqrt{2})\sin 2A - 7\sqrt{2}\cos 2A + 9\tan 2A$? **SSC CGL (Tier-I) 26/07/2023 Shift-IV**

(a) 12 (b) 15 (c) 10 (d) 6

105. What is $\tan\frac{\theta}{2}$? **SSC CGL (Tier-I) 26/07/2023 Shift-IV**

(a) $\frac{\cos\theta}{1-\sin\theta}$ (b) $\frac{\sin\theta}{1-\cos\theta}$
(c) $\frac{\cos\theta}{1-\cos\theta}$ (d) $\frac{\sin\theta}{1+\cos\theta}$

106. $\sin 600° \cos 750° + \sin 150° \cos 240° = ?$
SSC CGL (Tier-I) 26/07/2023 Shift-IV
(a) $\frac{2}{3}$ (b) 1 (c) $\frac{1}{2}$ (d) –1

107. $\tan 4384° + \cot 6814° = ?$
SSC CGL (Tier-I) 26/07/2023 Shift-III
(a) – 1 (b) 2
(c) 0 (d) 1

108. If $\cos x + \sec x = \frac{7}{2\sqrt{3}}$, then the value of $\cos^2 x + \sec^2 x$ will be ....
SSC CGL (Tier-I) 26/07/2023 Shift-III
(a) $\frac{15}{12}$ (b) $\frac{10}{12}$ (c) $\frac{25}{10}$ (d) $\frac{25}{12}$

109. Find the value of
$$\frac{\cos^2 15° - \sin^2 15°}{\cos^2 145° + \sin^2 145°}$$
SSC CGL (Tier-I) 26/07/2023 Shift-III
(a) $\frac{1}{\sqrt{3}}$ (b) $\frac{1}{1-\sqrt{3}}$
(c) $\frac{\sqrt{3}}{2}$ (d) $\frac{2}{\sqrt{3}}$

110. If $\tan A = \frac{3}{8}$, then the value of $\frac{3\sin A + 2\cos A}{3\sin A - 2\cos A}$ is
SSC CGL (Tier-I) 26/07/2023 Shift-III
(a) $-\frac{13}{25}$ (b) $-\frac{25}{7}$
(c) $\frac{28}{8}$ (d) $\frac{13}{21}$

111. ΔABC is right triangle. If $\angle B = 90°$ and $\tan A = \frac{1}{\sqrt{3}}$, then the value of $\sin A \cos C + \cos A \sin C$ is
SSC CGL (Tier-I) 26/07/2023 Shift-II
(a) 1 (b) 2
(c) $\frac{2}{3}$ (d) $\frac{1}{3}$

112. In a right triangle for an acute angle x, if $\sin x = \frac{3}{7}$, then find the value of $\cos x$.
SSC CGL (Tier-I) 26/07/2023 Shift-II
(a) $\frac{2}{7}$ (b) $\frac{3}{4}$
(c) $\frac{1}{\sqrt{3}}$ (d) $\frac{2\sqrt{10}}{7}$

113. The value of $\operatorname{cosec} 30° - \cos 60°$ is
SSC CGL (Tier-I) 26/07/2023 Shift-I
(a) 1 (b) $\frac{1}{2}$
(c) $\frac{3}{2}$ (d) $\frac{2\sqrt{2}-1}{\sqrt{2}}$

114. If $\cos A + \cos^2 A = 1$, then the value of $\sin^4 A + \sin^6 A$ is
SSC CGL (Tier-I) 26/07/2023 Shift-I
(a) 2 (b) cos A
(c) 1 (d) sin A

115. If $\cos(40° + x) = \sin 30°$, then the value of x is
SSC CGL (Tier-I) 25/07/2023 Shift-IV
(a) 22° (b) 20°
(c) 19° (d) 23°

116. The value of $\sqrt{\frac{1+\cos\theta}{1-\cos\theta}}$ is
SSC CGL (Tier-I) 25/07/2023 Shift-III
(a) $\sec\theta + \tan\theta$ (b) $\operatorname{cosec}\theta - \cot\theta$
(c) $\operatorname{cosec}\theta + \cot\theta$ (d) $\sec\theta - \tan\theta$

117. If $r = 15(\sin\theta + \cos\theta)$ and $s = 16(\sin\theta - \cos\theta)$, then the value of $\frac{r^2}{15^2} + \frac{s^2}{16^2}$ is ....
SSC CGL (Tier-I) 25/07/2023 Shift-III
(a) 8 (b) 6 (c) 4 (d) 2

118. What is the value of $5\sqrt{3}\cos 60° \tan 30° - 3\cos 0° + 3\cos^2 45° + 2\sin^2 60°$?
SSC CGL (Tier-I) 25/07/2023 Shift-III
(a) $2\sqrt{3}$ (b) 2.5
(c) 3.5 (d) $3\sqrt{2}$

119. If $\cos^2\theta = \frac{3}{4}$, where θ is an acute angle, then the value of $\sin(\theta + 30°)$ is
SSC CGL (Tier-I) 25/07/2023 Shift-III
(a) 1 (b) $\frac{1}{\sqrt{2}}$
(c) $\frac{1}{2}$ (d) $\frac{\sqrt{3}}{2}$

120. Find the value of $\tan(-1125°)$.
SSC CGL (Tier-I) 25/07/2023 Shift-II
(a) 1 (b) $\frac{1}{2}$ (c) – 1 (d) 0

121. If $\cot A = 1$, $\sin B = \frac{1}{\sqrt{2}}$, then find the value of $\sin(A + B) - \cot(A + B)$.
SSC CGL (Tier-I) 25/07/2023 Shift-I
(a) $1-\sqrt{2}$ (b) $\frac{1}{2}$
(c) 0 (d) 1

122. Using $\operatorname{cosec}(\alpha+\beta) = \frac{\sec\alpha \times \sec\beta \times \operatorname{cosec}\alpha \times \operatorname{cosec}\beta}{\sec\alpha \times \operatorname{cosec}\beta + \operatorname{cosec}\alpha \times \sec\beta}$, find the value of cosec 75°.
SSC CGL (Tier-I) 25/07/2023 Shift-I
(a) $\frac{\sqrt{6}+\sqrt{2}}{4}$ (b) $\frac{\sqrt{6}-\sqrt{2}}{4}$
(c) $\sqrt{6}-\sqrt{2}$ (d) $\sqrt{6}+\sqrt{2}$

123. If $a\cot\theta = b$, then what will be the value of $\frac{b\cos\theta - a\sin\theta}{b\cos\theta + a\sin\theta}$ is
SSC CGL (Tier-I) 24/07/2023 Shift-IV
(a) $\frac{b^2+a^2}{b^2-a^2}$ (b) $b^2 + a^2$
(c) $\frac{b^2-a^2}{b^2+a^2}$ (d) 0

124. Simplify the given expression.
$$\frac{1+\sin^4\theta + \cos^4\theta}{\cos^2\theta + \sin^4\theta}$$
SSC CGL (Tier-I) 24/07/2023 Shift-IV
(a) 3 (b) 1
(c) 2 (d) 4

125. If $\operatorname{cosec}\theta + \cot\theta = \frac{3}{2}$, then what is the value of cosec θ?
SSC CGL (Tier-I) 24/07/2023 Shift-III
(a) $\frac{13}{12}$ (b) $\frac{3}{2}$
(c) $\frac{11}{12}$ (d) $\frac{9}{12}$

126. If $\sin\theta + \operatorname{cosec}\theta = \sqrt{5}$, then the value of $\sin^3\theta + \operatorname{cosec}^3\theta =$
SSC CGL (Tier-I) 24/07/2023 Shift-III
(a) 0 (b) $3\sqrt{5}$
(c) $\frac{1}{\sqrt{5}}$ (d) $2\sqrt{5}$

127. If $\tan x = \frac{7}{5}$, then the value of $\frac{9\sin x - \frac{42}{5}\cos x}{15\sin x + 21\cos x}$ is
SSC CGL (Tier-I) 24/07/2023 Shift-III
(a) 0 (b) 1
(c) 0.1 (d) 0.5

128. If $\tan x = -\frac{12}{5}$, where x lies in the second quadrant, then what is the value of $\sin x - \cot x$?
SSC CGL (Tier-I) 24/07/2023 Shift-II
(a) $\frac{209}{156}$ (b) $\frac{169}{156}$ (c) $\frac{156}{209}$ (d) $\frac{144}{169}$

129. The value of $\tan 5° \tan 25° \tan 45° \tan 65° \tan 85°$ is equal to ......
SSC CGL (Tier-I) 24/07/2023 Shift-II
(a) 4 (b) 3 (c) 1 (d) 2

130. Which of the following options gives an expression equivalent to $\sin(A+B)$?
SSC CGL (Tier-I) 24/07/2023 Shift-II
(a) $\cos A\cos B - \sin A\sin B$
(b) $\sin A\cos B + \cos A\sin B$
(c) $\cos A\cos B + \sin A\sin B$
(d) $\sin A\cos B - \cos A\sin B$

131. If $2\cot\theta = 3$, then find the value of $\frac{\sqrt{13}\sin\theta - 3\tan\theta}{3\tan\theta + \sqrt{13}\cos\theta}$
SSC CGL (Tier-I) 24/07/2023 Shift-I
(a) $\frac{1}{\sqrt{13}}$ (b) $\frac{2}{\sqrt{13}}$ (c) 0 (d) $\frac{2}{3}$

132. Find the value of the given expression, $2 + \cos 49° \cos 41° - \sin 49° \sin 41°$
SSC CGL (Tier-I) 24/07/2023 Shift-I
(a) 2 (b) –1 (c) 0 (d) 1

133. Using the identity $\tan 2\alpha = \frac{2\tan\alpha}{1-\tan^2\alpha}$, find the value of $\tan 15°$, correct to three decimal places. [Use $\sqrt{3} = 1732$]
SSC CGL (Tier-I) 24/07/2023 Shift-I
(a) 0.268 (b) 0.27
(c) 0.267 (d) 0.269

134. Simplify $\frac{1+\sin t}{4-4\sin t} - \frac{1-\sin t}{4+4\sin t}$
SSC CGL (Tier-I) 21/07/2023 Shift-IV
(a) $4\tan t \cdot \sin t$ (b) $\tan t \cdot \sec t$
(c) $\tan t - \sin t$ (d) $\tan t + \sin t$

135. If $8\cot A = 7$, find $\sin A$.
SSC CGL (Tier-I) 21/07/2023 Shift-IV
(a) $\frac{7}{15}$ (b) $\frac{8}{\sqrt{113}}$ (c) $\frac{7}{8}$ (d) $\frac{8}{7}$

136. PQR is a triangle right angled at Q and $PQ : QR = 3 : 4$. What is the value of $\sin P + \sin Q + \sin R$?
SSC CGL (Tier-I) 21/07/2023 Shift-IV
(a) $\frac{4}{5}$ (b) $\frac{3}{5}$
(c) $\frac{12}{5}$ (d) $\frac{2}{5}$

137. In ΔXYZ, right angled at Y, if $\sin X = \frac{1}{2}$, find the value of $\cos X \cos Z + \sin X \sin Z$.
SSC CGL (Tier-I) 21/07/2023 Shift-III
(a) $\frac{\sqrt{3}}{2}$ (b) $\frac{\sqrt{3}}{4}$
(c) $\frac{2}{\sqrt{3}}$ (d) $\sqrt{3}$

138. If $\frac{\cos\alpha}{\sin\beta} = 10$ and $\frac{\cos\alpha}{\cos\beta} = 11$, then the value of $\cos^2\beta$ is
SSC CGL (Tier-I) 21/07/2023 Shift-III
(a) $\frac{121}{132}$ (b) $\frac{100}{221}$ (c) $\frac{88}{108}$ (d) $\frac{221}{121}$

139. Simplify the following expression.
$\frac{\sin\theta - 2\sin^3\theta}{2\cos^3\theta - \cos\theta}$
SSC CGL (Tier-I) 21/07/2023 Shift-III
(a) $\tan\theta$ (b) $\sin\theta$
(c) $\sec\theta$ (d) $\cos\theta$

140. Find the value of $\sqrt{\frac{1-\sin 3\theta}{1+\sin 3\theta}}$.
SSC CGL (Tier-I) 21/07/2023 Shift-II
(a) $\sec 3\theta - \tan 3\theta$
(b) $(\sec 3\theta - \tan 3\theta)^3$
(c) $(\sec 3\theta - \tan 3\theta)^2$
(d) $\sec 3\theta + \tan 3\theta$

141. The value of $\sec x - \cos x = ?$
SSC CGL (Tier-I) 21/07/2023 Shift-II
(a) $\tan x \sin x$ (b) $\sec x \tan x$
(c) $\tan x \cos x$ (d) $\sec x \cos x$

142. If $\sec A + \tan A = 3$, then $\cos A$ is equal to SSC CGL (Tier-I) 21/07/2023 Shift-I
(a) $\frac{4}{3}$ (b) $\frac{3}{5}$ (c) $\frac{3}{4}$ (d) $\frac{5}{3}$

143. Which of the following options is not a correct trigonometric identity?
SSC CGL (Tier-I) 21/07/2023 Shift-I
(a) $1+\cot^2\theta = \operatorname{cosec}^2\theta$
(b) $1+\tan^2\theta = \sec^2\theta$
(c) $1-\sin^2\theta = \cos^2\theta$
(d) $\cos^2\theta - \sin^2\theta = 1$

144. Find the value of $\frac{\cos 41°}{\sin 49°} + \frac{\sin 51°}{\cos 39°}$
SSC CGL (Tier-I) 20/07/2023 Shift-IV
(a) 4 (b) 2
(c) 3 (d) 1

145. In a right-angle triangle, the hypotenuse is 5 cm and the base is 3 cm. If one angle is θ, then $\tan\theta$ is equal to: SSC CGL (Tier-I) 20/07/2023 Shift-IV
(a) $\frac{4}{3}$ (b) $\frac{5}{3}$ (c) $\frac{3}{5}$ (d) $\frac{5}{4}$

146. The maximum value of $(\sin^{12}\theta + \cos^{20}\theta)$ for all the real values of θ is
SSC CGL (Tier-I) 20/07/2023 Shift-III
(a) 2 (b) 3
(c) 1 (d) 0

147. What is the value of $\sin(-405°)$?
SSC CGL (Tier-I) 20/07/2023 Shift-III
(a) $\frac{\sqrt{5}}{2}$ (b) $\frac{1}{2}$ (c) $\frac{-1}{2}$ (d) $\frac{-1}{\sqrt{2}}$

148. Find the value of $\frac{2}{3}\tan^2 60° + 3\cos^2 30° - 2\sec^2 30° - \frac{3}{4}\cot^2 60°$
SSC CGL (Tier-I) 20/07/2023 Shift-III
(a) 2.33 (b) 2.01
(c) 1.33 (d) 3.33

149. Find the value of $\sin(50° + \theta) - \cos(40° - \theta)$.
SSC CGL (Tier-I) 20/07/2023 Shift-II
(a) $\frac{1}{2}$ (b) −1
(c) 0 (d) 1

150. $\frac{2\tan A}{1+\tan^2 A} = ?$
SSC CGL (Tier-I) 20/07/2023 Shift-II
(a) $\cos 2A$ (b) $\sin A$
(c) $\cos A$ (d) $\sin 2A$

151. The following expression is equal to $\cot 85° + \cos 75°$
SSC CGL (Tier-I) 20/07/2023 Shift-II
(a) $\tan 85° + \sin 75°$
(b) $\tan 5° + \sin 15°$
(c) $\tan 85° - \sin 75°$
(d) $\tan 5° - \sin 15°$

152. Solve the given expression.
$\frac{\sec^2(90°-\theta) - \cot^2\theta}{2(\sin^2 35° + \sin^2 55°)}$
SSC CGL (Tier-I) 20/07/2023 Shift-I
(a) 0.5 (b) 2
(c) 1.5 (d) 1

153. $\operatorname{cosec} 2910° + \sec 4260° + \tan 2565° + \cot 1755° = ?$
SSC CGL (Tier-I) 20/07/2023 Shift-I
(a) 3 (b) 1 (c) 4 (d) 0

154. If $\sin x = \frac{3}{10}$, then what is the value of $\tan x + \cot x = ?$
SSC CGL (Tier-I) 20/07/2023 Shift-I
(a) $\frac{100}{3\sqrt{91}}$ (b) $\frac{100}{2\sqrt{83}}$
(c) $\frac{100}{7\sqrt{95}}$ (d) $\frac{100}{3\sqrt{85}}$

155. If $\cos x + \sin x = \sqrt{2}\cos x$, what is the value of $(\cos x - \sin x)^2 + (\cos x + \sin x)^2$?
SSC CGL (Tier-I) 19/07/2023 Shift-IV
(a) 2 (b) 1 (c) 0 (d) $\frac{1}{\sqrt{2}}$

156. If $2\cot x = 5$, then what is $\frac{2\cos x - \sin x}{2\cos x + \sin x}$ equal to?
SSC CGL (Tier-I) 19/07/2023 Shift-III
(a) $\frac{3}{4}$ (b) $\frac{1}{3}$ (c) $\frac{5}{6}$ (d) $\frac{2}{3}$

157. For any acute angle θ, $\sin\theta + \sin^2\theta = 1$, then the value of $\cos^2\theta + \cos^4\theta = \dots\dots$
SSC CGL (Tier-I) 19/07/2023 Shift-III
(a) 0 (b) 1
(c) 2 (d) −1

158. If $P\cos\alpha = 3$ and $4\tan\alpha = Q$, then what is the relation between P and Q, which is independent of α?
SSC CGL (Tier-I) 19/07/2023 Shift-II
(a) $\frac{9}{P^2} + \frac{16}{Q^2} = 1$ (b) $\frac{9}{P^2} - \frac{16}{Q^2} = 1$
(c) $\frac{P^2}{9} - \frac{Q^2}{16} = 1$ (d) $\frac{P^2}{9} + \frac{Q^2}{16} = 1$

159. If $\sec\theta = \frac{4}{3}$, what is the value of $\tan^2\theta + \tan^4\theta$?
SSC CGL (Tier-I) 19/07/2023 Shift-II
(a) $\frac{112}{81}$ (b) $\frac{256}{81}$ (c) $\frac{64}{27}$ (d) $\frac{16}{81}$

160. If $\frac{\sin x - \cos x}{\sin x + \cos x} = \frac{2}{5}$, then the value of $\frac{1+\cot^2 x}{1-\cot^2 x}$ is
SSC CGL (Tier-I) 19/07/2023 Shift-I
(a) 2.25 (b) 1.45
(c) 3.75 (d) 5.25

161. If $\left(\frac{\cos A}{1-\sin A}\right)+\left(\frac{\cos A}{1+\sin A}\right)=4$, then what will be the value of A? $(0^\circ<\theta<90^\circ)$

SSC CGL (Tier-I) 19/07/2023 Shift-I

(a) 90° (b) 45° (c) 60° (d) 30°

162. Find the value of the given expression.

$\frac{4}{3}\tan^2 45^\circ+3\cos^2 30^\circ-2\sec^2 30^\circ-\frac{3}{4}\cot^2 60^\circ$

SSC CGL (Tier-I) 18/07/2023 Shift-IV

(a) $\frac{3}{\sqrt{2}}$ (b) $\frac{3}{2}$ (c) $\frac{\sqrt{2}}{3}$ (d) $\frac{2}{3}$

163. Find the exact value of cos 120°.

SSC CGL (Tier-I) 18/07/2023 Shift-IV

(a) 1 (b) – 0.5
(c) 5.0 (d) 0.5

164. If $\sin(5x-25^\circ)=\cos(5y+25^\circ)$, where $5x-25^\circ$ and $5y+25^\circ$ are acute angles, then the value of $(x+y)$ is

SSC CGL (Tier-I) 18/07/2023 Shift-III

(a) 50° (b) 16° (c) 18° (d) 40°

165. Find the value of the following expression.

$12(\sin^4\theta+\cos^4\theta)+18(\sin^6\theta+\cos^6\theta)+78\sin^2\theta\cos^2\theta$

SSC CGL (Tier-I) 18/07/2023 Shift-III

(a) 10 (b) 20 (c) 40 (d) 30

166. The value of $\left(\frac{1}{\sin\theta}+\frac{1}{\tan\theta}\right)\left(\frac{1}{\sin\theta}-\frac{1}{\tan\theta}\right)$ is

SSC CGL (Tier-I) 18/07/2023 Shift-II

(a) 0 (b) 2
(c) 3 (d) 1

167. If $\sin A=-\frac{3}{5}$, A lies in III quadrant, the value of sec A is

SSC CGL (Tier-I) 18/07/2023 Shift-II

(a) $-\frac{4}{5}$ (b) $-\frac{5}{4}$
(c) $-\frac{3}{4}$ (d) $\frac{3}{4}$

168. Simplify the following

$\sin 2x+2\sin 4x+\sin 6x$

SSC CGL (Tier-I) 18/07/2023 Shift-II

(a) $4\cos^2 x\sin 4x$ (b) $4\cos^2 x\sin x$
(c) $2\cos^2 x\sin 4x$ (d) $4\sin^2 x\sin 4x$

169. If $\cot A=\frac{12}{5}$, then the value of $(\sin A+\cos A)\times\operatorname{cosec} A$ is ....

SSC CGL (Tier-I) 18/07/2023 Shift-I

(a) $\frac{13}{5}$ (b) $\frac{17}{5}$
(c) $\frac{14}{5}$ (d) 1

170. Using trigonometric formulas, find the value of $\left(\frac{\sin(x-y)}{\sin(x+y)}\right)\left(\frac{\tan x+\tan y}{\tan x-\tan y}\right)$

SSC CGL (Tier-I) 18/07/2023 Shift-I

(a) – 2 (b) 2
(c) 0 (d) 1

171. If $\tan\frac{A}{2}=x$, then find x

SSC CGL (Tier-I) 18/07/2023 Shift-I

(a) $\frac{\sqrt{1+\cos A}}{\sqrt{1-\cos A}}$ (b) $\frac{\sqrt{1-\sin A}}{\sqrt{1+\cos A}}$
(c) $\frac{\sqrt{1-\cos A}}{\sqrt{1+\cos A}}$ (d) $\frac{\sqrt{\cos A-1}}{\sqrt{1+\cos A}}$

172. $\frac{\sin^4\theta+\cos^4\theta}{1-2\sin^2\theta\cdot\cos^2\theta}=$......... .

SSC CGL (Tier-I) 17/07/2023 Shift-IV

(a) 1 (b) 2 (c) – 1 (d) 0

173. If $p\sin^2\beta+q\cos^2\beta=r$, then the value of $\cot^2\beta$ is

SSC CGL (Tier-I) 17/07/2023 Shift-III

(a) $\frac{r-q}{r-p}$ (b) $\frac{r-p}{r-q}$
(c) $\frac{p-r}{r-q}$ (d) $\frac{r-q}{p-r}$

174. Using $\cos(A+B)=\cos A\cos B-\sin A\sin B$, find the value of cos 75°.

SSC CGL (Tier-I) 17/07/2023 Shift-III

(a) $\frac{\sqrt{5}-1}{4}$ (b) $\frac{\sqrt{5}+1}{4}$
(c) $\frac{\sqrt{6}-\sqrt{2}}{4}$ (d) $\frac{\sqrt{6}+\sqrt{2}}{4}$

175. Find the value of $\cos 47^\circ\sec 133^\circ+\sin 44^\circ\operatorname{cosec}136^\circ$.

SSC CGL (Tier-I) 17/07/2023 Shift-II

(a) –1 (b) 0 (c) 1 (d) $\frac{1}{2}$

176. If $\tan\frac{\pi}{6}+\sec\frac{\pi}{6}=x$, then find x.

SSC CGL (Tier-I) 17/07/2023 Shift-II

(a) $\frac{-1}{\sqrt{3}}$ (b) $\frac{1}{\sqrt{3}}$
(c) $\sqrt{3}$ (d) $\frac{2}{\sqrt{3}}$

177. If $\sin\theta=\frac{4}{5}$, find the value of $\tan\theta-\cot\theta$.

SSC CGL (Tier-I) 17/07/2023 Shift-II

(a) $\frac{5}{12}$ (b) $\frac{7}{9}$ (c) $\frac{7}{8}$ (d) $\frac{7}{12}$

178. If $\sin t+\cos t=\frac{4}{5}$, then find $\sin t\cos t$.

SSC CGL (Tier-I) 17/07/2023 Shift-I

(a) $\frac{9}{50}$ (b) $\frac{-9}{50}$
(c) $\frac{9}{25}$ (d) $\frac{-9}{25}$

179. Find the value of $\sin^2 25^\circ+\sin^2 65^\circ$.

SSC CGL (Tier-I) 17/07/2023 Shift-I

(a) –1 (b) $\frac{1}{2}$ (c) 0 (d) 1

180. Simplify the following $\frac{\sin^3\alpha+\cos^3\alpha}{\sin\alpha+\cos\alpha}$

SSC CGL (Tier-I) 14/07/2023 Shift-IV

(a) $1+\sin\alpha\cos\alpha$ (b) $\tan\alpha$
(c) $1-\sin\alpha\cos\alpha$ (d) $\sec\alpha$

181. If $\sec\theta+\cos\theta=32$, then $\sec^2\theta+\cos^2\theta$ is ....

SSC CGL (Tier-I) 14/07/2023 Shift-IV

(a) 1000 (b) 1022 (c) 1024 (d) 1020

182. If $\frac{\cos\beta}{\sec\alpha}=15$ and $\frac{\sin\beta}{\sec\alpha}=16$, then the value of $\sin^2\beta$ is ....

SSC CGL (Tier-I) 14/07/2023 Shift-III

(a) $\frac{256}{481}$ (b) $-\frac{256}{481}$ (c) $\frac{481}{256}$ (d) $-\frac{481}{256}$

183. If $\sin 23^\circ=\frac{a}{b}$, then the value of $\sec 23^\circ-\sin 67^\circ$ is ....

SSC CGL (Tier-I) 14/07/2023 Shift-III

(a) $\frac{a^2}{\sqrt{b^2-a^2}}$ (b) $\frac{b^2-a^2}{ab}$
(c) $\frac{a^2}{b\sqrt{a^2-b^2}}$ (d) $\frac{a^2}{b\sqrt{b^2-a^2}}$

184. What is the value of $\sin 30^\circ+\cos 30^\circ+\tan 30^\circ$?

SSC CGL (Tier-I) 14/07/2023 Shift-III

(a) $\frac{5+\sqrt{3}}{2\sqrt{3}}$ (b) $\frac{5-\sqrt{3}}{2\sqrt{3}}$
(c) $\frac{5+\sqrt{3}}{\sqrt{3}}$ (d) $\frac{5-\sqrt{3}}{\sqrt{3}}$

185. If $\sec^2\theta+\tan^2\theta=\frac{25}{18}$, then the value of $\sec^4\theta-\tan^4\theta$ is

SSC CGL (Tier-I) 14/07/2023 Shift-III

(a) $\frac{18}{25}$ (b) $\frac{25}{12}$ (c) $\frac{25}{9}$ (d) $\frac{25}{18}$

186. Evaluate the following:

$\cos(36^\circ+A)\cos(36^\circ-A)+\cos(54^\circ+A)\cos(54^\circ-A)$.

SSC CGL (Tier-I) 14/07/2023 Shift-II

(a) cos A (b) sin 2 A
(c) sin A (d) cos 2A

187. What is the value of

$\sec^2 54^\circ-\cot^2 36^\circ+\frac{3}{2}\sin^2 37^\circ\times\sec^2 53^\circ+\frac{2}{\sqrt{3}}\tan 60^\circ$?

SSC CGL (Tier-I) 14/07/2023 Shift-II

(a) $\frac{3}{2}$ (b) $\frac{9}{2}$
(c) $\frac{7}{2}$ (d) $\frac{5}{2}$

188. If {(3 sin θ − cos θ) / (cos θ + sin θ)} = 1, then the value of cot θ is
SSC CGL (Tier-I) 14/07/2023 Shift-I
(a) 3 (b) 1 (c) 2 (d) 0

189. If sin(a + b) = 1 and cos (a − b) = $\frac{1}{2}$, then find a.
SSC CGL (Tier-I) 14/07/2023 Shift-I
(a) 30° (b) 45° (c) 75° (d) 15°

SSC CGL 2022 (Tier I)

190. If A is acute angle, the simplified form of
$$\frac{\cos(\pi - A)\cot\left(\frac{\pi}{2} + A\right)\cos(-A)}{\tan(\pi + A)\tan\left(\frac{3\pi}{2} + A\right)\sin(2\pi - A)}$$ is
SSC CGL (Tier-I) 13/12/2022 Shift-IV
(a) $\cos^2 A$ (b) sin A
(c) $\sin^2 A$ (d) cos A

191. If tan(α + β) = a, tan(α − β) = b, then the value of tan 2α is
SSC CGL (Tier-I) 13/12/2022 Shift-IV
(a) $\frac{a+b}{1-ab}$ (b) $\frac{a+b}{1+ab}$
(c) $\frac{a-b}{1+ab}$ (d) $\frac{a-b}{1-ab}$

192. If $\tan^2\theta + \tan^4\theta = 1$, then
SSC CGL (Tier-I) 13/12/2022 Shift-III
(a) $\cot^2\theta + \cot^4\theta = 1$
(b) $\cos^2\theta + \cos^4\theta = 1$
(c) $\sin^2\theta + \sin^4\theta = 1$
(d) $\text{cosec}^2\theta + \sec^4\theta = 1$

193. If tan 40° = α, then find $\frac{\tan 320° - \tan 310°}{1 + \tan 320° \cdot \tan 310°}$.
SSC CGL (Tier-I) 13/12/2022 Shift-II
(a) $\frac{1-\alpha^2}{\alpha}$ (b) $\frac{1+\alpha^2}{2\alpha}$
(c) $\frac{1-\alpha^2}{2\alpha}$ (d) $\frac{1+\alpha^2}{\alpha}$

194. If a = 45° and b = 15°, what is the value of $\frac{\cos(a-b) - \cos(a+b)}{\cos(a-b) + \cos(a+b)}$?
SSC CGL (Tier-I) 13/12/2022 Shift-II
(a) $3 - \sqrt{6}$ (b) $3 - \sqrt{2}$
(c) $2 - 2\sqrt{2}$ (d) $2 - \sqrt{3}$

195. If θ is an acute angle and tan θ + cot θ = 2, then the value of $\tan^{200}\theta + \cot^{200}\theta$ is
SSC CGL (Tier-I) 13/12/2022 Shift-I
(a) 1 (b) 2 (c) −1 (d) 0

196. If sec A = $\frac{5}{4}$, then the value of $\frac{\tan A}{1+\tan^2 A}$ $\frac{\sin A}{\sec A}$ is
SSC CGL (Tier-I) 12/12/2022 Shift-IV
(a) 2 (b) 1 (c) 0 (d) 3

197. If sin A = 4/5, then what is the value of $\sin^2 A$?
SSC CGL (Tier-I) 12/12/2022 Shift-IV
(a) 26/25 (b) 36/25
(c) 48/25 (d) 16/25

198. If $\cos\theta + \cos^2\theta = 1$, find the value of $\sqrt{\sin^4\theta + \cos^2\theta}$.
SSC CGL (Tier-I) 12/12/2022 Shift-III
(a) $\sqrt{2}\cos\theta$ (b) 2 cos θ
(c) $\sqrt{2}\sin\theta$ (d) 2 sin θ

199. If $2\sin\theta + 2\sin^2\theta = 2$, then the value of $2\cos^4\theta + 2\cos^2\theta$ is
SSC CGL (Tier-I) 12/12/2022 Shift-III
(a) 4 (b) 2 (c) 1 (d) 0

200. If tan 3θ · tan 7θ = 1, where 7θ is an acute angle, then find the value of cot15θ.
SSC CGL (Tier-I) 12/12/2022 Shift-III
(a) 1 (b) −1
(c) $-\sqrt{3}$ (d) $\sqrt{3}$

201. $\frac{1+\sin\theta}{\cos\theta}$ is equal to which of the following (where, $\theta \neq \frac{\pi}{2}$)?
SSC CGL (Tier-I) 12/12/2022 Shift-II
(a) $\frac{1+\cos\theta}{\sin\theta}$ (b) $\frac{\tan\theta+1}{\tan\theta-1}$
(c) $\frac{\tan\theta-1}{\tan\theta+1}$ (d) $\frac{\cos\theta}{1-\sin\theta}$

202. ΔABC is right-angle triangle at B and tan A = $\frac{3}{4}$, then sin A + sin B + sin C will be equal to
SSC CGL (Tier-I) 12/12/2022 Shift-II
(a) $2\frac{4}{5}$ (b) $2\frac{2}{5}$
(c) $3\frac{1}{5}$ (d) $1\frac{1}{5}$

203. If $\sin^2\theta - 3\sin\theta + 2 = 0$, then find the value of θ(0° ≤ θ ≤ 90°).
SSC CGL (Tier-I) 12/12/2022 Shift-II
(a) 45° (b) 0° (c) 60° (d) 90°

204. Find the value of tan 27° tan 34° + tan 34° tan 29° + tan 29° tan 27°.
SSC CGL (Tier-I) 12/12/2022 Shift-I
(a) 0 (b) −1
(c) $\sqrt{3}$ (d) 1

205. What is the value of the expression $\cos 2A \cdot \cos 2B + \sin^2(A-B) - \sin^2(A+B)$?
SSC CGL (Tier-I) 12/12/2022 Shift-I
(a) sin(2A − 2B) (b) sin(2A + 2B)
(c) cos(2A + 2B) (d) cos(2A − 2B)

206. If cosecθ + cot θ = P, then the value of $\frac{P^2-1}{P^2+1}$ is
SSC CGL (Tier-I) 12/12/2022 Shift-I
(a) cos θ (b) sin θ
(c) cot θ (d) cosec θ

207. If b cos θ = a, then cosecθ + cot θ = ...
SSC CGL (Tier-I) 09/12/2022 Shift-IV
(a) $\sqrt{\frac{1}{b+a}}$ (b) $\sqrt{\frac{b-a}{b+a}}$
(c) $\sqrt{\frac{b+a}{b-a}}$ (d) $\sqrt{\frac{1}{b\ a}}$

208. What is the value of sin 75° + sin 15°?
SSC CGL (Tier-I) 09/12/2022 Shift-IV
(a) $\frac{1}{\sqrt{2}}$ (b) $\frac{\sqrt{3}}{2}$ (c) $\sqrt{\frac{3}{2}}$ (d) $\frac{3}{\sqrt{2}}$

209. If $\frac{2(\cos^2 x - \sec^2 x)}{\tan^2 x} = a + b\cos 2x$, then a, b = ?
SSC CGL (Tier-I) 09/12/2022 Shift-III
(a) $\frac{-3}{2}, \frac{-1}{2}$ (b) $\frac{3}{2}, \frac{1}{2}$
(c) − 3, − 1 (d) 3, 1

210. If sin θ = $\frac{8}{17}$, where θ is an acute angle, then what is the value of tan θ + cot θ?
SSC CGL (Tier-I) 09/12/2022 Shift-III
(a) $\frac{217}{110}$ (b) $\frac{281}{190}$
(c) $\frac{289}{120}$ (d) $\frac{512}{321}$

211. If $\frac{\sin\theta + \cos\theta}{\sin\theta - \cos\theta} = \frac{3}{2}$, then the value of $\sin^4\theta - \cos^4\theta$ is
SSC CGL (Tier-I) 09/12/2022 Shift-II
(a) $\frac{5}{12}$ (b) $\frac{12}{13}$ (c) $\frac{11}{12}$ (d) $\frac{5}{13}$

212. If cos(A − B) = $\frac{\sqrt{3}}{2}$, and cos(A + B) = 0, where A and B are positive acute angles and A ≥ B, then the measures of A and B are
SSC CGL (Tier-I) 09/12/2022 Shift-I
(a) 80° and 10° (b) 60° and 30°
(c) 70° and 20° (d) 50° and 40°

213. What is the value of sin 28° sin 35° sin 45° sec 62° sec 55°?
SSC CGL (Tier-I) 09/12/2022 Shift-I
(a) 2 (b) $\frac{1}{\sqrt{2}}$
(c) $\sqrt{2}$ (d) $\frac{1}{2}$

214. If $5\sin^2 A + 3\cos^2 A = 4$, 0 < A < 90°, then what is the value of tan A?
SSC CGL (Tier-I) 09/12/2022 Shift-I
(a) 0 (b) 3
(c) 1 (d) 2

215. $\cos^3 60° - \cos^3 240° - \cos^3 360°$ = ...
SSC CGL (Tier-I) 09/12/2022 Shift-I
(a) $\frac{-3}{4}$ (b) $\frac{-7}{5}$
(c) $\frac{3}{5}$ (d) $\frac{-9}{7}$

216. If $\tan A \tan B + \dfrac{\cos x}{\cos A \cos B} = 1$, then $x = ?$ SSC CGL (Tier-I) 08/12/2022 Shift-IV

(a) B (b) A
(c) $A + B$ (d) $A - B$

217. If α is an acute angle, $\tan(4\alpha - 50°) = \cot(50° - \alpha)$, then find the value of α (in degrees).
SSC CGL (Tier-I) 08/12/2022 Shift-IV

(a) 60° (b) 45° (c) 30° (d) 90°

218. Evaluate the expression $\dfrac{\sin^2 63° + \sin^2 27°}{\cos^2 17° + \cos^2 73°}$.
SSC CGL (Tier-I) 08/12/2022 Shift-IV

(a) 0 (b) 3 (c) 1 (d) 2

219. If $\sec x - \cos x = 4$, then what will be the value of $\dfrac{(1+\cos^2 x)}{\cos x}$?
SSC CGL (Tier-I) 08/12/2022 Shift-III

(a) 9/4 (b) 1/4 (c) $2\sqrt{5}$ (d) $\sqrt{5}$

220. If $\theta = 135°$, $y = 15°$. What is the value of $2\cos(\theta)\sin(y)$?
SSC CGL (Tier-I) 08/12/2022 Shift-III

(a) $\dfrac{\sqrt{3}-1}{2}$ (b) $\dfrac{1-\sqrt{3}}{2}$
(c) $2-\sqrt{3}$ (d) $\sqrt{3}-2$

221. Which of the following will satisfy $a^2 = b^2 + (ab)^2$ for the values a and b?
SSC CGL (Tier-I) 08/12/2022 Shift-III

(a) $a = \sin x$, $b = \cot x$
(b) $a = \cos x$, $b = \tan x$
(c) $a = \cot x$, $b = \cos x$
(d) $a = \sin x$, $b = \tan x$

222. If $\tan(\alpha + \beta) = \sqrt{3}$, $\tan(\alpha - \beta) = 1$, where $(\alpha + \beta)$ and $(\alpha - \beta)$ are acute angles, then what is $\tan(6\alpha)$?
SSC CGL (Tier-I) 08/12/2022 Shift-II

(a) -1 (b) 0
(c) 1 (d) $\sqrt{2} - 1$

223. What is the value of $\tan 6° \times \tan 45° \times \tan 84°$?
SSC CGL (Tier-I) 08/12/2022 Shift-II

(a) 1
(b) $\tan 6° \times \tan 39°$
(c) 3
(d) $\tan 6° + \tan 45° + \tan 84°$

224. If $\cot A = \dfrac{12}{5}$, then the value of $\sin A = ?$ SSC CGL (Tier-I) 08/12/2022 Shift-II

(a) $\dfrac{5}{13}$ (b) $\dfrac{12}{13}$ (c) $\dfrac{5}{12}$ (d) $\dfrac{13}{12}$

225. If $x = 8(\sin\theta + \cos\theta)$ and $y = 9(\sin\theta - \cos\theta)$, then the value of $\dfrac{x^2}{8^2} + \dfrac{y^2}{9^2}$ is SSC CGL (Tier-I) 08/12/2022 Shift-I

(a) 4 (b) 6 (c) 8 (d) 2

226. If $A + B = C$, then $\tan A \tan B \tan C = ?$
SSC CGL (Tier-I) 08/12/2022 Shift-I

(a) $\tan C + \tan A - \tan B$
(b) $\tan C + \tan A + \tan B$
(c) $\tan A - \tan B - \tan C$
(d) $\tan C - \tan A - \tan B$

227. It $\tan A = 10/15$, then what will be the value of $\cos^2 A$?
SSC CGL (Tier-I) 07/12/2022 Shift-IV

(a) $\dfrac{3}{13}$ (b) $\dfrac{5}{13}$ (c) $\dfrac{9}{13}$ (d) $\dfrac{4}{13}$

228. If $4\tan\theta = 3$, then $\dfrac{4\sin\theta - \cos\theta + 1}{4\sin\theta + \cos\theta - 1} =$ ....
SSC CGL (Tier-I) 07/12/2022 Shift-IV

(a) $\dfrac{14}{11}$ (b) $\dfrac{12}{11}$ (c) $\dfrac{10}{11}$ (d) $\dfrac{13}{11}$

229. If $\sin\theta = \dfrac{3}{5}$, then what is $\tan\theta$?
SSC CGL (Tier-I) 07/12/2022 Shift-III

(a) $\dfrac{3}{5}$ (b) $\dfrac{4}{3}$
(c) $\dfrac{4}{5}$ (d) $\dfrac{3}{4}$

230. What will be the value of $\dfrac{\tan 45° - \tan 15°}{1 + \tan 45° \tan 15°}$?
SSC CGL (Tier-I) 07/12/2022 Shift-III

(a) $\sqrt{3}$ (b) $\dfrac{1}{\sqrt{2}}$
(c) $\dfrac{1}{\sqrt{3}}$ (d) $\sqrt{2}$

231. Find the value of the following expression.
$5(\sin^4\theta + \cos^4\theta) + 3(\sin^6\theta + \cos^6\theta) + 19\sin^2\theta\cos^2\theta$
SSC CGL (Tier-I) 07/12/2022 Shift-III

(a) 8 (b) 5 (c) 6 (d) 7

232. If $1 + \sin\theta = m\cos\theta$, then what is the value of $\sin\theta$?
SSC CGL (Tier-I) 07/12/2022 Shift-II

(a) $\dfrac{2m^2-1}{m^2+1}$ (b) $\dfrac{m^2-1}{m^2+1}$
(c) $\dfrac{m^2+1}{2m^2-1}$ (d) $\dfrac{m^2+1}{m^2-1}$

233. What is the value of $\cos 45° \cdot \sin 15°$?
SSC CGL (Tier-I) 07/12/2022 Shift-II

(a) $\dfrac{(\sqrt{3}-1)}{2}$ (b) $\dfrac{(\sqrt{3}-1)}{4}$
(c) $(\sqrt{3}+1)$ (d) $2\sqrt{3}-1$

234. If $\tan^2\alpha = 3 + Q^2$, then $\sec\alpha + \tan^3\alpha \operatorname{cosec}\alpha = ?$
SSC CGL (Tier-I) 07/12/2022 Shift-I

(a) $(3+Q^2)^{\frac{3}{2}}$ (b) $(7+Q^2)^{\frac{3}{2}}$
(c) $(5-Q^2)^{\frac{3}{2}}$ (d) $(4+Q^2)^{\frac{3}{2}}$

235. If $\tan A - \tan B - \tan C = \tan A \tan B \tan C$, what is the value of A in terms of B and C?
SSC CGL (Tier-I) 07/12/2022 Shift-I

(a) $A = B + C$ (b) $A = 2B + 2C$
(c) $A = B - C$ (d) $A = \dfrac{B-C}{2}$

236. In ΔXYZ, $\angle X = 90°$, $YZ = 15$ cm, and $XZ = 12$ cm. Then find $\cos Y$.
SSC CGL (Tier-I) 07/12/2022 Shift-I

(a) $\dfrac{2}{5}$ (b) $\dfrac{4}{5}$
(c) $\dfrac{3}{5}$ (d) $\dfrac{3}{4}$

237. What is the value of $\cos^2 15°$?
SSC CGL (Tier-I) 06/12/2022 Shift-IV

(a) $(2+\sqrt{3})$ (b) $\dfrac{(2+\sqrt{3})}{4}$
(c) $\dfrac{(2+\sqrt{3})}{2}$ (d) $\dfrac{(1+\sqrt{3})}{2}$

238. If $\sec\theta - 2\cos\theta = \dfrac{7}{2}$, where θ is a positive acute angle, then the value of $\sec\theta$ is SSC CGL (Tier-I) 06/12/2022 Shift-IV

(a) 6 (b) 8 (c) 5 (d) 4

239. If $\sin\theta = \dfrac{1}{2}$, then the value of $(3\cos\theta - 4\cos^3\theta)$ is
SSC CGL (Tier-I) 06/12/2022 Shift-III

(a) 0 (b) 1
(c) 2 (d) -1

240. Solve the following to find its value in terms of trigonometric ratios.
$(\sin A + \cos A)(1 - \sin A \cos A)$
SSC CGL (Tier-I) 06/12/2022 Shift-III

(a) $\sin^3 A + \cos^3 A$
(b) $\sin^2 A - \cos^2 A$
(c) $[\cos A - \sin A][\sin^2 A + \cos^2 A]$
(d) $\sin^3 A - \cos^3 A$

241. What is the value of $\cos\left(-\dfrac{17\pi}{3}\right)$
SSC CGL (Tier-I) 06/12/2022 Shift-II

(a) 1 (b) $\dfrac{\sqrt{3}}{2}$ (c) $\dfrac{1}{2}$ (d) 0

242. If $\cot A = \dfrac{15}{8}$, then what will be the value of $\tan 2A$?
SSC CGL (Tier-I) 06/12/2022 Shift-II

(a) 200/161 (b) 240/161
(c) 240/173 (d) 220/171

243. What will be the value of $\sin 10° - \dfrac{4}{3}\sin^3 10°$?
SSC CGL (Tier-I) 06/12/2022 Shift-I

(a) $\dfrac{1}{3\sqrt{3}}$ (b) $\dfrac{1}{6}$ (c) $\dfrac{1}{2\sqrt{3}}$ (d) $\dfrac{\sqrt{3}}{6}$

244. $\frac{\cos 20°}{\sin 70°}+\frac{\cos\theta}{\sin(90°-\theta)}=.....$
SSC CGL (Tier-I) 06/12/2022 Shift-I
(a) -2 (b) $\frac{1}{2}$ (c) $-\frac{1}{2}$ (d) 2

245. If $b\sin\theta=a$, then $\sec\theta+\tan\theta=?$
SSC CGL (Tier-I) 06/12/2022 Shift-I
(a) $\sqrt{\frac{b+a}{b-a}}$ (b) $\sqrt{\frac{1}{b+a}}$
(c) $\sqrt{\frac{1}{b-a}}$ (d) $\sqrt{\frac{b-a}{b+a}}$

246. If $8\cot\theta=6$, then the value of $\frac{\sin\theta+\cos\theta}{\sin\theta-\cos\theta}$ is
SSC CGL (Tier-I) 05/12/2022 Shift-IV
(a) 12 (b) 7
(c) 2 (d) 5

247. $\sqrt{\frac{1+\sin A}{1-\sin A}}=.......$
SSC CGL (Tier-I) 05/12/2022 Shift-IV
(a) $\operatorname{cosec} A-\cot A$ (b) $\sec A-\tan A$
(c) $\sec A+\tan A$ (d) $\sec A$

248. If θ is an acute angle and $\tan\theta+\cot\theta=2$, then the value of $\tan^2\theta+\cot^2\theta+2\tan^5\theta\cot^4\theta$ is
SSC CGL (Tier-I) 05/12/2022 Shift-III
(a) 3 (b) 4 (c) 1 (d) 2

249. If $\tan A=\frac{2}{3}$, then what is the value of the following ?
$(5\sin^2A-2\cos^2A)\div(15\sin^2A+3\cos^2A)$
SSC CGL (Tier-I) 05/12/2022 Shift-III
(a) $\frac{21}{47}$ (b) $\frac{2}{87}$ (c) $\frac{2}{5}$ (d) $\frac{3}{77}$

250. What will be the value of $\cos x\operatorname{cosec} x-\sin x\sec x$?
SSC CGL (Tier-I) 05/12/2022 Shift-II
(a) $\cot\frac{2x}{2}$ (b) $\tan 2x$
(c) $\cot 2x$ (d) $2\cot 2x$

251. $\sqrt{\frac{1+\cos\theta}{1-\cos\theta}}+\sqrt{\frac{1-\cos\theta}{1+\cos\theta}}=......$
SSC CGL (Tier-I) 05/12/2022 Shift-II
(a) $2\sin\theta$ (b) $2\cos\theta$
(c) $2\operatorname{cosec}\theta$ (d) $2\sec\theta$

252. $\cos^2 35°+\cos 55°\cdot\sin 35°+\frac{\tan 34°}{\cot 56°}=$ ....
SSC CGL (Tier-I) 05/12/2022 Shift-II
(a) 2 (b) 3 (c) 4 (d) 1

253. If $\sin\theta=\frac{8}{17}$, then find the value of $\tan\theta$.
SSC CGL (Tier-I) 05/12/2022 Shift-I
(a) $\frac{15}{8}$ (b) $\frac{15}{17}$ (c) $\frac{8}{15}$ (d) $\frac{17}{15}$

254. If $\sec 2\theta=\operatorname{cosec}(\theta-36°)$, where 2θ is an acute angle, find the value of θ.
SSC CGL (Tier-I) 05/12/2022 Shift-I
(a) 46 (b) 20 (c) 32 (d) 42

255. If $\sin\theta+\cos\theta=\frac{\sqrt{3}-1}{2\sqrt{2}}$, then what is the value of $\tan\theta+\cot\theta$?
SSC CGL (Tier-I) 05/12/2022 Shift-I
(a) $8(\sqrt{3}+2)$ (b) $12(\sqrt{3}-2)$
(c) $8(\sqrt{3}-2)$ (d) $12(\sqrt{3}+2)$

256. ΔABC is a right-angle triangle at B. If $\tan A=\frac{5}{12}$, then $\sin A+\sin B+\sin C$ will be equal to
SSC CGL (Tier-I) 03/12/2022 Shift-IV
(a) $1\frac{5}{13}$ (b) $2\frac{4}{13}$ (c) $3\frac{1}{13}$ (d) $2\frac{1}{13}$

257. Simplify the following $\frac{\cos x-\sqrt{3}\sin x}{2}$
SSC CGL (Tier-I) 03/12/2022 Shift-III
(a) $\cos\left(\frac{\pi}{3}-x\right)$ (b) $\sin\left(\frac{\pi}{3}+x\right)$
(c) $\cos\left(\frac{\pi}{3}+x\right)$ (d) $\sin\left(\frac{\pi}{3}-x\right)$

258. If $\cot B=9$, then what will be the value of $\sec^2 B$?
SSC CGL (Tier-I) 03/12/2022 Shift-III
(a) 98/81 (b) 92/81
(c) 42/81 (d) 82/81

259. If $\frac{k-k\cot^2 30°}{1+\cot^2 30°}=\sin^2 60°+4\tan^2 45°-\operatorname{cosec}^2 60°$, then the value of k (correct to two decimal places) is
SSC CGL (Tier-I) 03/12/2022 Shift-III
(a) 5.55 (b) -6.83 (c) -5.58 (d) 6.83

260. $\tan(\theta-14\pi)$ is equal to
SSC CGL (Tier-I) 03/12/2022 Shift-II
(a) $\tan\theta$ (b) $-\cot\theta$
(c) $\cot\theta$ (d) $-\tan\theta$

261. $\sin^4\theta+\cos^4\theta$ in terms of $\sin\theta$ can be written as
SSC CGL (Tier-I) 03/12/2022 Shift-II
(a) $2\sin^4\theta+2\sin^2\theta-1$
(b) $2\sin^4\theta-2\sin^2\theta$
(c) $2\sin^4\theta-2\sin^2\theta-1$
(d) $2\sin^4\theta-2\sin^2\theta+1$

262. If $(\cos q+\sin q)=\frac{31}{25}$, then what will be the value of $\cos 2q$?
SSC CGL (Tier-I) 03/12/2022 Shift-I
(a) $\frac{522}{625}$ (b) $\frac{512}{625}$ (c) $\frac{513}{625}$ (d) $\frac{527}{625}$

263. $\frac{1}{1+\cos(90°-\theta)}+\frac{1}{1-\cos(90°-\theta)}=.....$
SSC CGL (Tier-I) 03/12/2022 Shift-I
(a) $2\sec^2\theta$ (b) 1
(c) 0 (d) $2\tan^2\theta$

264. Simplify $\frac{\cos A}{1+\tan A}-\frac{\sin A}{1+\cot A}$
SSC CGL (Tier-I) 03/12/2022 Shift-I
(a) $\tan A$ (b) $\cos A-\sin A$
(c) $\cos A\sin A$ (d) $\cos A+\sin A$

265. If $\sin A=\frac{4}{5}$ and $\sin B=\frac{15}{17}$, what is the value of $\sin(A-B)$?
SSC CGL (Tier-I) 02/12/2022 Shift-IV
(a) $-\frac{32}{45}$ (b) $-\frac{13}{85}$
(c) $\frac{13}{85}$ (d) $\frac{32}{45}$

266. If $\frac{(1-\cos\theta)}{\sin\theta}=\frac{1}{5}$, then what will be the value of $\frac{(1+\cos\theta)}{\sin\theta}$?
SSC CGL (Tier-I) 02/12/2022 Shift-IV
(a) 5 (b) 2/5
(c) 4/5 (d) 1/5

267. If $\tan A+\cot A=2$, then the value of $2(\tan^2A+\cot^2A)$ is
SSC CGL (Tier-I) 02/12/2022 Shift-IV
(a) 1 (b) 4
(c) 2 (d) 3

268. The value of cot 15° cot 25° cot 45° cot 75° cot 65° is
SSC CGL (Tier-I) 02/12/2022 Shift-III
(a) 1 (b) $\sqrt{3}$ (c) 2 (d) $\sqrt{2}$

269. If $\operatorname{cosec}A-\cot A=\frac{1}{4}$, then the value of $\tan A$ is
SSC CGL (Tier-I) 02/12/2022 Shift-III
(a) $\frac{8}{15}$ (b) $\frac{8}{17}$
(c) $\frac{15}{17}$ (d) $\frac{17}{15}$

270. If $\sin\theta+\cos\theta=\sqrt{5}\sin(90°-\theta)$, find the value of $\cot\theta$.
SSC CGL (Tier-I) 02/12/2022 Shift-II
(a) $\frac{\sqrt{5}-1}{5}$ (b) $\frac{\sqrt{5}+1}{4}$
(c) $\frac{\sqrt{5}+1}{3}$ (d) $\frac{\sqrt{5}-1}{4}$

271. If $\sin(A+B)=\cos(A+B)$, what is the value of $\tan A$?
SSC CGL (Tier-I) 02/12/2022 Shift-I
(a) $\frac{1-\tan B}{1+\tan B}$ (b) $\frac{1+\tan B}{1-\tan B}$
(c) $\frac{1+\sec B}{1-\sec B}$ (d) $\frac{1-\operatorname{cosec} B}{1+\operatorname{cosec} B}$

272. If $\tan^2\theta=1-a^2$, then the value of $\sec\theta+\tan^3\theta\operatorname{cosec}\theta$ is
SSC CGL (Tier-I) 01/12/2022 Shift-IV
(a) $(2-a)^{\frac{3}{2}}$ (b) $(a^2-1)^{\frac{3}{2}}$
(c) $(2-a^2)^{\frac{3}{2}}$ (d) $a^{\frac{3}{2}}$

273. If $\cos A = \frac{9}{41}$, find cot A.
SSC CGL (Tier-I) 01/12/2022 Shift-IV
(a) $\frac{9}{40}$ (b) $\frac{41}{40}$ (c) $\frac{40}{9}$ (d) $\frac{9}{41}$

274. If $\tan\theta + \sec\theta = 7$, θ being acute, then the value of 5 sin θ is
SSC CGL (Tier-I) 01/12/2022 Shift-III
(a) $\frac{25}{24}$ (b) $\frac{24}{25}$
(c) $\frac{1}{24}$ (d) $\frac{24}{5}$

275. What is $\sin\alpha - \sin\beta$?
SSC CGL (Tier-I) 01/12/2022 Shift-II
(a) $2\cos\frac{\alpha+\beta}{2}\sin\frac{\alpha-\beta}{2}$
(b) $2\sin\frac{\alpha+\beta}{2}\sin\frac{\alpha-\beta}{2}$
(c) $2\cos\frac{\alpha-\beta}{2}\sin\frac{\alpha+\beta}{2}$
(d) $2\cos\frac{\alpha+\beta}{2}\cos\frac{\alpha-\beta}{2}$

276. The value of $(\sin 30°\cos 60° - \cos 30°\sin 60°)$ is equal to SSC CGL (Tier-I) 01/12/2022 Shift-II
(a) $-\cos 30°$ (b) $-\sin 30°$
(c) $\cos 30°$ (d) $\sin 30°$

277. What will be the value of $\frac{\sin 30°\sin 40°\sin 50°\sin 60°}{\cos 30°\cos 40°\cos 50°\cos 60°}$?
SSC CGL (Tier-I) 01/12/2022 Shift-II
(a) $\frac{1}{\sqrt{2}}$ (b) $\sqrt{3}$
(c) 1 (d) $\frac{1}{\sqrt{3}}$

278. The value of $\tan^2\theta + \cot^2\theta - \sec^2\theta\,\text{cosec}^2\theta$ is
SSC CGL (Tier-I) 01/12/2022 Shift-I
(a) 2 (b) – 2
(c) 0 (d) 1/2

279. Simplify $\frac{\cos 45°}{\sec 30° + \text{cosec}\,30°}$
SSC CGL (Tier-I) 01/12/2022 Shift-I
(a) $\frac{3\sqrt{2}+\sqrt{6}}{8}$ (b) $\frac{\sqrt{3}}{2\sqrt{2}-2\sqrt{6}}$
(c) $\frac{3\sqrt{2}-\sqrt{6}}{8}$ (d) $\frac{\sqrt{3}}{2\sqrt{6}-2\sqrt{2}}$

SSC CGL 2021 (Tier I)

280. If $\sec 31° = x$, then $\sin^2 59° + \frac{1}{\sec^2 31°} - \frac{1}{\sin^2 59°\,\text{cosec}^2 59°}$ is equal to
SSC CGL (Tier-I) 24/08/2021 Shift-III
(a) $\frac{x^2-2}{x^2}$ (b) $\frac{2-x^2}{x}$
(c) $\frac{2-x^2}{x^2}$ (d) $\frac{x^2-2}{x}$

281. If $\frac{\sin\theta+\cos\theta}{\sin\theta-\cos\theta} = 5$, then the value of $\frac{4\sin^2\theta+3}{2\cos^2\theta+2}$ is
SSC CGL (Tier-I) 24/08/2021 Shift-III
(a) $\frac{75}{17}$ (b) $\frac{75}{34}$ (c) $\frac{1}{2}$ (d) $\frac{3}{2}$

282. Simplify
$\frac{(\sin\theta+\sec\theta)^2+(\cos\theta+\text{cosec}\theta)^2}{(1+\sec\theta\,\text{cosec}\,\theta)^2}$,
$0° < \theta < 90°$.
SSC CGL (Tier-I) 24/08/2021 Shift-III
(a) 0 (b) 1 (c) –1 (d) 2

283. The value of
$\frac{\sec^2 60°\cos^2 45° + \text{cosec}^2 30°}{\cot 30°\sec^2 45° - \text{cosec}^2 30°\tan 45°}$ is
SSC CGL (Tier-I) 20/08/2021 Shift-II
(a) $-3(2+\sqrt{3})$ (b) $3(2-\sqrt{3})$
(c) $-3(2-\sqrt{3})$ (d) $3(2+\sqrt{3})$

284. If $\sin^2\theta = 2\sin\theta - 1$, $0° \le \theta \le 90°$, then find the value of $\frac{1+\text{cosec}\,\theta}{1-\cos\theta}$.
SSC CGL (Tier-I) 24/08/2021 Shift-II
(a) – 2 (b) 1 (c) 2 (d) – 1

285. If $\tan\theta + 3\cot\theta - 2\sqrt{3} = 0$, $0° < \theta < 90°$, then what is the value of $(\text{cosec}^2\theta + \cos^2\theta)$?
SSC CGL (Tier-I) 24/08/2021 Shift-I
(a) $\frac{2}{3}$ (b) $\frac{19}{12}$ (c) $\frac{14}{3}$ (d) $\frac{11}{12}$

286. Simplify
$\sec^2\alpha\left(1+\frac{1}{\text{cosec}\,\alpha}\right)\left(1-\frac{1}{\text{cosec}\,\alpha}\right)$.
SSC CGL (Tier-I) 24/08/2021 Shift-I
(a) $\tan^4\alpha$ (b) $\sin^2\alpha$ (c) 1 (d) –1

287. In ΔABC, right angled at B, if $\cot A = \frac{1}{2}$, then the value of $\frac{\sin A(\cos C+\cos A)}{\cos C(\sin C-\sin A)}$ is
SSC CGL (Tier-I) 24/08/2021 Shift-I
(a) 3 (b) –3 (c) –2 (d) 2

288. If $0° < \theta < 90°$, $\sqrt{\frac{\sec^2\theta+\text{cosec}^2\theta}{\tan^2\theta-\sin^2\theta}}$ is equal to SSC CGL (Tier-I) 23/08/2021 Shift-II
(a) $\sec^3\theta$ (b) $\text{cosec}^3\theta$
(c) $\sin^2\theta$ (d) $\sec^2\theta$

289. If $\frac{\sin^2\theta}{\tan^2\theta-\sin^2\theta} = 5$, θ is an acute angle, then the value of $\frac{24\sin^2\theta-15\sec^2\theta}{6\,\text{cosec}^2\theta-7\cot^2\theta}$ is
SSC CGL (Tier-I) 23/08/2021 Shift-II
(a) – 2 (b) 2
(c) – 14 (d) 14

290. If $\sin^2\theta - \cos^2\theta - 3\sin\theta + 2 = 0$, $0° < \theta < 90°$, then what is the value of $\frac{1}{\sqrt{\sec\theta-\tan\theta}}$ is
SSC CGL (Tier-I) 23/08/2021 Shift-I
(a) $\sqrt[2]{3}$ (b) $\sqrt[2]{2}$
(c) $\sqrt[4]{3}$ (d) $\sqrt[4]{2}$

291. Find the value of
$\frac{\tan^2 30°}{\sec^2 30°} + \frac{\text{cosec}^2 45°}{\cot^2 45°} - \frac{\sec^2 60°}{\text{cosec}^2 60°}$
SSC CGL (Tier-I) 23/08/2021 Shift-I
(a) $\frac{23}{12}$ (b) $\frac{13}{4}$
(c) $\frac{5}{4}$ (d) $-\frac{3}{4}$

292. If x is a real quantity, what is the minimum value of $(25\cos^2 x + 9\sec^2 x)$?
SSC CGL (Tier-I) 23/08/2021 Shift-I
(a) 30 (b) 15
(c) 20 (d) 40

293. If $\cos(2\theta + 54°) = \sin\theta$, $0° < (2\theta + 54°) < 90°$, then what is the value of $\frac{1}{\cot 5\theta + \sec\frac{5\theta}{2}}$?
SSC CGL (Tier-I) 20/08/2021 Shift-II
(a) $\frac{\sqrt{3}}{2}$ (b) $\frac{2\sqrt{3}}{3}$
(c) $\frac{\sqrt{3}}{3}$ (d) $\frac{1}{3}$

294. If $\cot\theta = \frac{15}{8}$, θ is an acute angle, then find the value of $\frac{(1-\cos\theta)(2+2\cos\theta)}{(2-2\sin\theta)(1+\sin\theta)}$.
SSC CGL (Tier-I) 20/08/2021 Shift-II
(a) $\frac{225}{64}$ (b) $\frac{64}{225}$
(c) $\frac{16}{15}$ (d) $\frac{8}{15}$

295. If $2\cos^2\theta - 5\cos\theta + 2 = 0$, $0° < \theta < 90°$, then the value of $(\sec\theta + \tan\theta)$ is
SSC CGL (Tier-I) 20/08/2021 Shift-II
(a) $2+\sqrt{3}$ (b) $1-\sqrt{3}$
(c) $1+\sqrt{3}$ (d) $2-\sqrt{3}$

296. If $\sec(5\alpha - 15°) = \text{cosec}(15° - 2\alpha)$, then the value of $\cos\alpha + \sin 2\alpha + \tan(1.5\alpha)$ is
SSC CGL (Tier-I) 20/08/2021 Shift-I
(a) $\sqrt{3}+1$ (b) $\sqrt{2}-1$
(c) $\sqrt{3}-1$ (d) $\sqrt{2}+1$

297. $(\sec\theta + \tan\theta)^2 + \frac{1+\text{cosec}\,\theta}{1-\text{cosec}\,\theta}$, $0° < \theta < 90°$ is
SSC CGL (Tier-I) 18/08/2021 Shift-III
(a) 0 (b) – 2 (c) 1 (d) 2

298. If $\sin^6\theta + \cos^6\theta = \frac{1}{3}$, $0° < \theta < 90°$, then what is the value of $\sin\theta\cos\theta$?
SSC CGL (Tier-I) 18/08/2021 Shift-III
(a) $\frac{\sqrt{2}}{3}$ (b) $\frac{\sqrt{6}}{6}$
(c) $\frac{\sqrt{2}}{\sqrt{3}}$ (d) $\frac{2}{9}$

299. If $\sin(A+B) = 1$ and $\cos(A-B) = \frac{\sqrt{3}}{2}$, $A + B \le 90°$ and $A > B$, then the value of $\frac{5\sin^2 B + 4\tan^2 A}{2\sin B\cos A}$ is
SSC CGL (Tier-I) 18/08/2021 Shift-III
(a) $16\frac{1}{2}$ (b) 18
(c) 20 (d) $26\frac{1}{2}$

300. Find the value of $\sin^4 30° + \cos^4 30° - \sin 25°\cos 65° - \sin 65°\cos 25°$.
SSC CGL (Tier-I) 18/08/2021 Shift-I
(a) $-\frac{3}{8}$ (b) 0
(c) $\frac{5}{8}$ (d) $\frac{13}{8}$

301. The value of $(\sin 37°\cos 53° + \cos 37°\sin 53°) - \frac{4\cos^2 37° - 7 + 4\cos^2 53°}{\tan^2 47° + 4 - \text{cosec}^2 43°}$ is
SSC CGL (Tier-I) 18/08/2021 Shift-I
(a) – 2 (b) 0 (c) 1 (d) 2

302. If $3\sin^2\theta - \cos\theta - 1 = 0$, $0° < \theta < 90°$, then what is the value of $\cot\theta + \text{cosec}\,\theta$?
SSC CGL (Tier-I) 18/08/2021 Shift-I
(a) $\frac{3\sqrt{2}}{2}$ (b) $2\sqrt{3}$
(c) $\sqrt{5}$ (d) $2\sqrt{5}$

303. The value of $\frac{\sqrt{2}\tan(60°-\theta)\tan(30°+\theta)}{\sin^2(45°+\theta)+\sin^2(45°-\theta)}$ is
SSC CGL (Tier-I) 17/08/2021 Shift-III
(a) $\sqrt{2}$ (b) 2
(c) 1 (d) $\frac{1}{\sqrt{2}}$

304. If $4\sin^2(2x-10)° = 3$, $0° \le (2x-10) \le 90°$, then find the value of $\frac{\sin^4(x-5)° + \cos^4(x-5)°}{1-2\sin^2(3x-15)°\cos^2(3x-15)°}$.
SSC CGL (Tier-I) 17/08/2021 Shift-III
(a) $\frac{5}{8}$ (b) –1
(c) 1 (d) $-\frac{5}{8}$

305. If $7\cos^2\theta + 5\sin^2\theta - 6 = 0$, $(0° < \theta < 90°)$, then what is the value of $\sqrt{\frac{\text{cosec}\,\theta + \tan\theta}{\sec\theta - \cot\theta}}$
SSC CGL (Tier-I) 17/08/2021 Shift-III
(a) $\sqrt{2}+1$ (b) $\sqrt{2}-1$
(c) $\sqrt{3}+1$ (d) $\sqrt{3}-1$

306. If $\cos(A-B) = \frac{\sqrt{3}}{2}$ and $\cot(A+B) = \frac{1}{\sqrt{3}}$, where $A - B$ and $A + B$ are acute angles, then $(2A - 3B)$ is equal to
SSC CGL (Tier-I) 17/08/2021 Shift-I
(a) 45° (b) 30° (c) 15° (d) 60°

307. $(\sqrt{\sec^2\theta + \text{cosec}^2\theta})\left(\frac{\sin\theta(1+\cos\theta)}{1+\cos\theta - \sin^2\theta}\right)$, $0° < \theta < 90°$
SSC CGL (Tier-I) 17/08/2021 Shift-I
(a) $\sec^2\theta$ (b) $\text{cosec}^2\theta$
(c) $\cot\theta$ (d) $\tan\theta$

308. The value of $\frac{\tan^2 30° + \sin^2 90° + \cot^2 60° + \sin^2 30°\cos^2 45°}{\sin 60°\cos 30° - \cos 60°\sin 30°}$ is
SSC CGL (Tier-I) 16/08/2021 Shift-III
(a) $\frac{47}{12}$ (b) $\frac{37}{12}$ (c) $\frac{43}{12}$ (d) $\frac{25}{12}$

309. The value of $4(\sin^4 30° + \cos^4 30°) - 3(\sin^2 45° - 2\cos^2 45°)$ is
SSC CGL (Tier-I) 16/08/2021 Shift-III
(a) 0 (b) 4 (c) 2 (d) 1

310. If $\sin\left(\frac{2A+B}{2}\right) = \cos\left(\frac{2A-B}{2}\right) = \frac{\sqrt{3}}{2}$, $0° < \frac{2A+B}{2} < 90°$ and $0° < \frac{2A+B}{2} < 90°$, then find the value of $\sin[3(A-B)]$.
SSC CGL (Tier-I) 16/08/2021 Shift-II
(a) $\frac{\sqrt{3}}{2}$ (b) $\frac{1}{\sqrt{2}}$ (c) $\frac{1}{2}$ (d) 1

311. If $3\cos^2\theta - 4\sin\theta + 1 = 0$, $0° < \theta < 90°$, then $\tan\theta + \sec\theta = ?$
SSC CGL (Tier-I) 16/08/2021 Shift-I
(a) $2\sqrt{5}$ (b) $2\sqrt{3}$
(c) $3\sqrt{3}$ (d) $\sqrt{5}$

312. If $\frac{\text{cosec}\,\theta + \cot\theta}{\text{cosec}\,\theta - \cot\theta} = 7$, then the value of $\frac{4\sin^2\theta - 1}{4\sin^2\theta + 5}$ is
SSC CGL (Tier-I) 16/08/2021 Shift-I
(a) $-\frac{1}{9}$ (b) $\frac{1}{3}$ (c) $-\frac{1}{3}$ (d) $\frac{1}{9}$

313. $1 + 2\tan^2\theta + 2\sin\theta\sec^2\theta$, $0° < \theta < 90°$, is equal to
SSC CGL (Tier-I) 16/08/2021 Shift-I
(a) $\frac{1-\cos\theta}{1+\cos\theta}$ (b) $\frac{1+\cos\theta}{1-\cos\theta}$
(c) $\frac{1-\sin\theta}{1+\sin\theta}$ (d) $\frac{1+\sin\theta}{1-\sin\theta}$

314. The value of $\frac{\tan(45°-\alpha)}{\cot(45°+\alpha)}$ $(\cos 19° + \sin 71°)$ $-\frac{(\sec 19° + \text{cosec}\,71°)}{\tan 12°\tan 24°\tan 66°\tan 78°}$ is
SSC CGL (Tier-I) 13/08/2021 Shift-III
(a) – 3 (b) 2 (c) – 2 (d) 0

315. If $3\sec\theta + 4\cos\theta - 4\sqrt{3} = 0$, where θ is an acute angle, then the value of θ is
SSC CGL (Tier-I) 13/08/2021 Shift-III
(a) 45° (b) 60° (c) 20° (d) 30°

316. If $3\tan\theta = 2\sqrt{3}\sin\theta$, $0° < \theta < 90°$, then find the value of $2\sin^2 2\theta - 3\cos^2 3\theta$.
SSC CGL (Tier-I) 13/08/2021 Shift-III
(a) $-\frac{3}{2}$ (b) $\frac{1}{2}$ (c) $\frac{3}{2}$ (d) 1

317. $\frac{\text{cosec}\theta}{\text{cosec}\,\theta - 1} + \frac{\text{cosec}\theta}{\text{cosec}\theta + 1} - \tan^2\theta$, $0° < \theta < 90°$, is equal to
SSC CGL (Tier-I) 13/08/2021 Shift-I
(a) $\sec^2\theta + 1$ (b) $\sec^2\theta$
(c) $2\sec^2\theta$ (d) $1 - \tan^2\theta$

318. If $\frac{\cos^2\theta}{\cot^2\theta + \sin^2\theta - 1} = 3$, $0° < \theta < 90°$, then the value of $(\tan\theta + \text{cosec}\,\theta)$ is
SSC CGL (Tier-I) 13/08/2021 Shift-I
(a) $\frac{5\sqrt{3}}{3}$ (b) $3\sqrt{3}$
(c) $2\sqrt{3}$ (d) $\frac{4\sqrt{3}}{3}$

SSC CGL 2020 (Tier I)

319. If $3\sec^2\theta + \tan\theta = 7$, $0° < \theta < 90°$, then the value of $\frac{\text{cosec}\,2\theta + \cos\theta}{\sin 2\theta + \cot\theta}$ is
SSC CGL (Tier-I) 07/03/2020 Shift-II
(a) $\frac{2+\sqrt{3}}{2}$ (b) $\frac{2+3\sqrt{2}}{4}$
(c) $\frac{2+\sqrt{2}}{4}$ (d) $\frac{3+\sqrt{2}}{4}$

320. If $\frac{\sin A + \cos A}{\cos A} = \frac{17}{12}$, then the value of $\frac{1-\cos A}{\sin A}$ is
SSC CGL (Tier-I) 07/03/2020 Shift-II
(a) $\frac{1}{5}$ (b) $\frac{5}{12}$
(c) – 5 (d) 1

321. In the given figure, $\cos\theta$ is equal to
SSC CGL (Tier-I) 07/03/2020 Shift-I

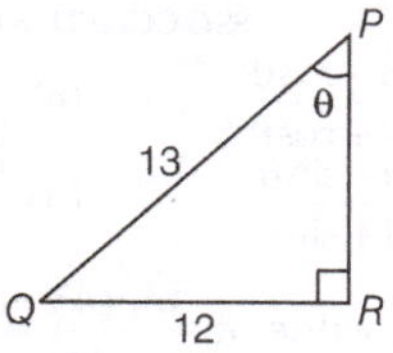

(a) $\frac{5}{13}$ (b) $\frac{12}{13}$
(c) $\frac{5}{12}$ (d) $\frac{12}{5}$

322. The value of $\frac{1-2\sin^2\theta\cos^2\theta}{\sin^4\theta+\cos^4\theta}-1$ is
SSC CGL (Tier-I) 07/03/2020 Shift-I

(a) -1 (b) 1
(c) $-2\sin^2\theta\cos^2\theta$ (d) 0

323. If A lies in third quadrant, and $20\tan A = 21$, then the value of $\frac{5\sin A - 2\cos A}{4\cos A - \frac{5}{7}\sin A}$ is
SSC CGL (Tier-I) 06/03/2020 Shift-III

(a) $\frac{5}{29}$ (b) $\frac{-65}{29}$
(c) 1 (d) $\frac{13}{12}$

324. If $0 < A, B < 45°$, $\cos(A+B) = \frac{24}{25}$ and $\sin(A-B) = \frac{15}{17}$, then $\tan 2A$ is
SSC CGL (Tier-I) 06/03/2020 Shift-III

(a) $\frac{213}{4}$ (b) 0 (c) 1 (d) $\frac{416}{87}$

325. The value of $4\left[\frac{(1-\sec A)^2+(1+\sec A)^2}{1+\sec^2 A}\right]$ is
SSC CGL (Tier-I) 06/03/2020 Shift-III

(a) 8 (b) 1
(c) 4 (d) 2

326. Solve the following
$\sin 0°\sin 30°\sin 45°\sin 60°\sin 90° = ?$
SSC CGL (Tier-I) 06/03/2020 Shift-II

(a) 1 (b) 0 (c) $\frac{\sqrt{6}}{8}$ (d) 4

327. If $(\cos^2\theta-1)(1+\tan^2\theta)+2\tan^2\theta=1$, $0° \le \theta \le 90°$, then θ is
SSC CGL (Tier-I) 06/03/2020 Shift-II

(a) 60° (b) 45°
(c) 90° (d) 30°

328. The value of $\frac{\sin 30°\sin 60°}{\cos 60°\cos 30°} - \tan 45°$ is
SSC CGL (Tier-I) 06/03/2020 Shift-II

(a) 0 (b) $\frac{2-\sqrt{2}}{2}$
(c) 5 (d) 2

329. If $(2\sin A + \operatorname{cosec} A) = 2\sqrt{2}$, $0° < A < 90°$, then the value of $2(\sin^4 A + \cos^4 A)$ is
SSC CGL (Tier-I) 06/03/2020 Shift-I

(a) 2 (b) 1 (c) 4 (d) 0

330. If $x\cos A - y\sin A = 1$ and $x\sin A + y\cos A = 4$, then the value of $17x^2+17y^2$ is
SSC CGL (Tier-I) 06/03/2020 Shift-I

(a) 0 (b) 7 (c) 49 (d) 289

331. If $\tan\theta - \cot\theta = \operatorname{cosec}\theta$, $0° < \theta < 90°$, then what is the value of $\frac{2\tan\theta-\cos\theta}{\sqrt{3}\cot\theta+\sec\theta}$?
SSC CGL (Tier-I) 05/03/2020 Shift-III

(a) $\frac{2(2\sqrt{3}-1)}{3}$ (b) $\frac{4\sqrt{3}-1}{6}$
(c) $\frac{3\sqrt{3}-1}{6}$ (d) $\frac{2\sqrt{3}-1}{3}$

332. If $11\sin^2\theta - \cos^2\theta + 4\sin\theta - 4 = 0$, $0° < \theta < 90°$, then what is the value of $\frac{\cos 2\theta + \cot 2\theta}{\sec 2\theta - \tan 2\theta}$?
SSC CGL (Tier-I) 05/03/2020 Shift-II

(a) $\frac{12+7\sqrt{3}}{6}$ (b) $\frac{12+5\sqrt{3}}{3}$
(c) $\frac{10+5\sqrt{3}}{3}$ (d) $\frac{10+7\sqrt{3}}{6}$

333. If $5\cos\theta - 12\sin\theta = 0$, then what is the value of $\frac{1+\sin\theta+\cos\theta}{1-\sin\theta+\cos\theta}$?
SSC CGL (Tier-I) 05/03/2020 Shift-II

(a) $\frac{5}{4}$ (b) $\frac{3}{2}$ (c) $\frac{3}{4}$ (d) $\frac{5}{2}$

334. What is the value of
$$\frac{\operatorname{cosec}(78°+\theta)-\sec(12°-\theta)-\tan(67°+\theta)+\cot(23°-\theta)}{\tan 13°\tan 37°\tan 45°\tan 53°\tan 77°}?$$
SSC CGL (Tier-I) 05/03/2020 Shift-II

(a) 1 (b) 0
(c) 2 (d) -1

335. If $12\cos^2\theta - 2\sin^2\theta + 3\cos\theta = 3$, $0° < \theta < 90°$, then what is the value of $\frac{\operatorname{cosec}\theta+\sec\theta}{\tan\theta+\cot\theta}$?
SSC CGL (Tier-I) 05/03/2020 Shift-I

(a) $\frac{1+2\sqrt{2}}{2}$ (b) $\frac{2+\sqrt{3}}{4}$
(c) $\frac{4+\sqrt{3}}{4}$ (d) $\frac{1+\sqrt{3}}{2}$

336. If $5\sin\theta = 4$, then the value of $\frac{\sec\theta+4\cot\theta}{4\tan\theta-5\cos\theta}$ is
SSC CGL (Tier-I) 05/03/2020 Shift-I

(a) 2 (b) 5/4
(c) 3/2 (d) 1

337. The value of $\frac{\sec^6\theta-\tan^6\theta-3\sec^2\theta\tan^2\theta+1}{\cos^4\theta-\sin^4\theta+2\sin^2\theta+2}$ is
SSC CGL (Tier-I) 05/03/2020 Shift-I

(a) 3/4 (b) 2/3 (c) 1/2 (d) 1

338. If $7\cos^2\theta + 3\sin^2\theta = 6$, $0° < \theta < 90°$, then the value of $\frac{\cot^2 2\theta+\sec^2 2\theta}{\tan^2 2\theta-\sin^2 2\theta}$ is
SSC CGL (Tier-I) 04/03/2020 Shift-III

(a) $\frac{52}{27}$ (b) $\frac{26}{15}$ (c) $\frac{28}{27}$ (d) $\frac{49}{45}$

339. If $\sec\theta + \tan\theta = p$, $0° < \theta < 90°$, then $\frac{p^2-1}{p^2+1}$ is equal to
SSC CGL (Tier-I) 04/03/2020 Shift-III

(a) $\operatorname{cosec}\theta$ (b) $\sin\theta$
(c) $\cos\theta$ (d) $2\operatorname{cosec}\theta$

SSC CPO SI 2024-2020

340. If $\cos A = \frac{4}{5}$, then find the value of $(8+\sin A)(3-\tan A)$.
SSC CPO 29/06/2024 Shift-III

(a) $\frac{373}{20}$ (b) $\frac{387}{20}$ (c) $\frac{381}{20}$ (d) $\frac{367}{20}$

341. The value of
$\sin^2 15° + \sin^2 25° + \sin^2 35° + \sin^2 45° + \sin^2 55° + \sin^2 65° + \sin^2 75°$ is
SSC CPO 29/06/2024 Shift-III

(a) 7 (b) $\frac{7}{2}$ (c) 4 (d) $\frac{7}{3}$

342. The value of $\frac{17}{\sec^2\theta} + 10\sin^2\theta + \frac{7}{1+\cot^2\theta}$ is .
SSC CPO 29/06/2024 Shift-III

(a) 34 (b) 19 (c) 17 (d) 20

343. What is the value of $\frac{[(\sin x+\sin y)(\sin y-\sin x)]}{[(\cos x+\cos y)(\cos y-\cos x)]}$?
SSC CPO 29/06/2024 Shift-III

(a) -1 (b) 0 (c) 2 (d) 1

344. Find the value of the following expression.
$(1+\tan\theta+\sec\theta)\times(1+\cot\theta-\operatorname{cosec}\theta)$
SSC CPO 29/06/2024 Shift-II

(a) $\cos\theta\sin\theta$ (b) 1
(c) 2 (d) $\tan\theta$

345. Simplify $\frac{\tan 71° + \tan 19°}{1-\tan 71°\tan 19°}$
SSC CPO 29/06/2024 Shift-II

(a) 0 (b) $\sqrt{3}$
(c) Not defined (d) 1

346. If $\sin^4\theta + \cos^4\theta = 2\sin^2\theta\cos^2\theta$, $0° < \theta < 90°$, then find the value of $\cot\theta$.
SSC CPO 29/06/2024 Shift-I

(a) $\frac{1}{\sqrt{2}}$ (b) $\frac{1}{3}$ (c) 1 (d) $\frac{1}{2}$

347. $\tan^4 A + \tan^2 A$ is equal to
SSC CPO 29/06/2024 Shift-I
(a) $\sec^4 A - \sec^2 A$
(b) $\sec^2 A - \sec^4 A$
(c) $\sec^4 A + \sec^2 A$
(d) $-(\sec^2 A + \sec^4 A)$

348. What is the least value of $15\cos^2\theta + 17\sin^2\theta$?
SSC CPO 29/06/2024 Shift-I
(a) 14 (b) 15
(c) 16 (d) 18

349. The value of $(\operatorname{cosec}\theta - \sin\theta)(\sec\theta - \cos\theta)(\tan\theta + \cot\theta)$ is
SSC CPO 29/06/2024 Shift-I
(a) 1 (b) $\sec\theta \cdot \operatorname{cosec}\theta$
(c) 3 (d) – 3

350. If A, B and C are the interior angles of ΔABC, then what is the value of $\left\{\tan\frac{A}{2} + \operatorname{cosec}\frac{B+C}{2}\right\}\left\{\tan\frac{A}{2} - \operatorname{cosec}\frac{B+C}{2}\right\}$?
SSC CPO 28/06/2024 Shift-III
(a) –1 (b) 2
(c) –2 (d) 1

351. Simplify $\dfrac{\sin^3 A + \cos^3 A}{\sin A + \cos A}$
SSC CPO 28/06/2024 Shift-III
(a) $1 - \cos A\cot A$ (b) $1 - \sin A\tan A$
(c) $1 - \sin A\cos A$ (d) $1 - \tan A\sec A$

352. The value of $\left(\dfrac{2\cos^3\theta - \cos\theta}{\sin\theta - 2\sin^3\theta}\right)^2 + 1, \theta \neq 45°$ is
SSC CPO 28/06/2024 Shift-III
(a) $\sec^2\theta$ (b) $\cot^2\theta$
(c) $\operatorname{cosec}^2\theta$ (d) $\sin^2\theta$

353. If $\sin(x+y) = 1$ and $\cos(x-y) = \dfrac{\sqrt{3}}{2}$, find the value of '$y$'.
SSC CPO 28/06/2024 Shift-III
(a) 90° (b) 30°
(c) 20° (d) 60°

354. If $\sin x + \cos x = \sqrt{2}\sin x$, then the value of $\sin x - \cos x$ is
SSC CPO 28/06/2024 Shift-II
(a) $\sqrt{2}\sin x$ (b) $2\sin x$
(c) $-\sqrt{2}\cos x$ (d) $\sqrt{2}\cos x$

355. If $4\sin^2\theta = 3(1+\cos\theta)$, $0° < \theta < 90°$, then what is the value of $\sqrt{15}\tan\theta + \dfrac{4}{\sqrt{15}}\sin\theta + 2\sec\theta$?
SSC CPO 28/06/2024 Shift-II
(a) 8 (b) 24
(c) $4\sqrt{15}$ (d) $\dfrac{8}{\sqrt{15}}$

356. If $\tan\theta + \cot\theta = 6$, then the value of $\tan^2\theta + \cot^2\theta$ is
SSC CPO 28/06/2024 Shift-II
(a) 20 (b) 24
(c) 34 (d) 22

357. Simplify $\dfrac{\cos 13° + \sin 13°}{\cos 13° - \sin 13°}$
SSC CPO 28/06/2024 Shift-I
(a) $\cot 58°$ (b) $\cos 26°$
(c) $\tan 32°$ (d) $\tan 58°$

358. Solve the equation for A (in degrees).
$2\cos^2 A + 3\cos A - 2 = 0, 0 < A < 90°$
SSC CPO 28/06/2024 Shift-I
(a) 45° (b) 60° (c) 80° (d) 30°

359. If $\dfrac{(\sec A + \tan A)}{(\sec A - \tan A)} = 2\dfrac{51}{79}$, then the value of sin A is equal to
SSC CPO 28/06/2024 Shift-I
(a) $\dfrac{87}{169}$ (b) $\dfrac{65}{144}$ (c) $\dfrac{77}{144}$ (d) $\dfrac{61}{169}$

360. Find the maximum value of $(19\sin\theta + 6\cot\theta\sin\theta)$.
SSC CPO 27/06/2024 Shift-III
(a) $\sqrt{197}$ (b) $\sqrt{397}$
(c) $\sqrt{497}$ (d) $\sqrt{297}$

361. Which of the following is true when $x = \sin A + \cos A$; $y = \sec A + \operatorname{cosec} A$?
SSC CPO 27/06/2024 Shift-III
(a) $y + 2x = x^2 y$ (b) $y(1 + x^2) = 2x$
(c) $y(1 - 2x^2) = x$ (d) $y - 2x = x^2 y$

362. If $\tan\theta = \dfrac{7}{24}$, then find the value of $(\cos^2\theta - \sin^2\theta)$ **SSC CPO 27/06/2024 Shift-III**
(a) 1 (b) $\dfrac{520}{625}$
(c) $\dfrac{576}{550}$ (d) $\dfrac{527}{625}$

363. If $(\sin x + \sin y) = a$ and $(\cos x + \cos y) = b$, then find the value of $(\sin x \cdot \sin y + \cos x \cdot \cos y)$.
SSC CPO 27/06/2024 Shift-II
(a) $\dfrac{a^2 + b^2 + 2}{2}$ (b) $\dfrac{a^2 - b^2 - 2}{2}$
(c) $\dfrac{a^2 + b^2 - 2}{2}$ (d) $\dfrac{a^2 + b^2 - 1}{2}$

364. If $\sin\alpha = \dfrac{5}{13}$, then the value of $\cos\alpha \cdot \operatorname{cosec}\alpha \cdot \cot\alpha$ is
SSC CPO 27/06/2024 Shift-II
(a) $\dfrac{12}{5}$ (b) $\dfrac{25}{144}$ (c) $\dfrac{144}{25}$ (d) $\dfrac{5}{12}$

365. Find the value of $(1 + \cot A - \operatorname{cosec} A)(1 + \tan A + \sec A) - 3(\sin^2 A + \cos^2 A)$.
SSC CPO 27/06/2024 Shift-II
(a) –1 (b) 1 (c) –2 (d) 2

366. Find the value of $\operatorname{cosec}\theta(1 - \cos\theta)(\operatorname{cosec}\theta + \cot\theta)$.
SSC CPO 27/06/2024 Shift-II
(a) 2 (b) –1
(c) 1 (d) 0

367. Simplify : $(1 + \tan^2 A) + \left(1 + \dfrac{1}{\tan^2 A}\right)$
SSC CPO 27/06/2024 Shift-I
(a) $\dfrac{1}{\cot^2 A - \tan^4 A}$ (b) $\dfrac{1}{\sin^2 A - \sin^4 A}$
(c) $\dfrac{1}{\sin^2 A - \cos^4 A}$ (d) $\dfrac{1}{\cos^2 A - \sin^4 A}$

368. If $\sec 6A = \text{coses}(A - 29°)$, where $2A$ is an acute angle, then the measure of $\angle A = ...°$ **SSC CPO 27/06/2024 Shift-I**
(a) 18 (b) 19
(c) 17 (d) 21

369. If $\tan(t) + \cot(t) = 1$, then one of the values of the expression $\dfrac{1}{\sin(t) + \cos(t)}$ is......
SSC CPO 27/06/2024 Shift-I
(a) $\dfrac{\sqrt{3}}{2}$ (b) $\dfrac{2}{\sqrt{3}}$
(c) $\dfrac{1}{\sqrt{3}}$ (d) $\sqrt{3}$

370. If $\sin\theta + \cos\theta = \sqrt{2}\cos\theta$, then find $\dfrac{\sin\theta - \cos\theta}{\sin\theta}$.
SSC CPO 05/10/2023 Shift-III
(a) $-\sqrt{2}$ (b) –1
(c) 1 (d) $\sqrt{2}$

371. The value of $2\tan^2 45° + \cos^2 30° - \sin^2 60°$ is
SSC CPO 05/10/2023 Shift-III
(a) 2 (b) 1
(c) –1 (d) –2

372. If $\dfrac{2\sin A - \cos A}{\sin A + \cos A} = 1$, then find the value of cot A. **SSC CPO 05/10/2023 Shift-III**
(a) 1 (b) $\dfrac{1}{2}$ (c) $\dfrac{1}{3}$ (d) 2

373. If $\cot^2\theta = 1 - e^2$, then the value of $\operatorname{cosec}\theta + \cot^3\theta\sec\theta$ is
SSC CPO 05/10/2023 Shift-III
(a) $(2 - e^2)^{\frac{1}{2}}$ (b) $(1 - e^2)^{\frac{3}{2}}$
(c) $(1 - e^2)$ (d) $(2 - e^2)^{\frac{3}{2}}$

374. $2(\sin 1° \times \sec 89°) + 3(\cos 11° \times \operatorname{cosec} 79°) + 5(\tan 21° \times \tan 69°) = ?$
SSC CPO 04/10/2023 Shift-II
(a) 11 (b) 12 (c) 20 (d) 10

375. $7\sin^2 A + 3\cos^2 A = 4$, then find cot A. **SSC CPO 04/10/2023 Shift-II**
(a) $\sqrt{3}$ (b) $\sqrt{2}$ (c) $\dfrac{1}{\sqrt{2}}$ (d) $\dfrac{1}{\sqrt{3}}$

376. Find the value of $\sqrt{\frac{1-\tan A}{1+\tan A}}$.
SSC CPO 04/10/2023 Shift-II
(a) $\sqrt{\frac{1+\sin 2A}{\cos 2A}}$ (b) $\sqrt{\frac{1-\sin 2A}{\cos 2A}}$
(c) $\sqrt{\frac{1+\sin A}{\cos A}}$ (d) $\sqrt{\frac{1-\sin A}{\cos A}}$

377. If $\cos\theta - \sin\theta = \sqrt{2}\sin\theta$, then $(\cos\theta + \sin\theta)$ is SSC CPO 03/10/2023 Shift-I
(a) $-\sqrt{2}\cos\theta$ (b) $\sqrt{2}\cos\theta$
(c) $\sqrt{2}\tan\theta$ (d) $-\sqrt{2}\sin\theta$

378. Find the value of $(\tan^2\theta + \tan^4\theta)$.
SSC CPO 03/10/2023 Shift-I
(a) $\cot^2\theta - \tan^2\theta$ (b) $\sec^4\theta - \sec^2\theta$
(c) $\sec^2\theta - \sec^4\theta$ (d) $\sec^4\theta + \sec^2\theta$

379. If θ is an acute angle and $\sin\theta + \text{cosec}\,\theta = 2$, then the value of $\sin^5\theta + \text{cosec}^5\theta$ is SSC CPO 03/10/2023 Shift-I
(a) 10 (b) 2 (c) 4 (d) 5

380. If $\tan A = \frac{4}{3}$, $0 \le A \ge 90°$, then find the value of $\sin A$.
SSC CPO 03/10/2023 Shift-I
(a) $\frac{3}{5}$ (b) 1 (c) $\frac{3}{4}$ (d) $\frac{4}{5}$

381. Simplify $\cos(36°-A)\cos(36°+A) + \cos(54°-A)\cos(54°+A)$ SSC CPO 11/11/2022
(a) $\cos A$ (b) $\sin 2A$
(c) $\cos 2A$ (d) $\sin A$

382. If $4\cos\theta + 3\sin\theta = x$ and $4\sin\theta - 3\cos\theta = y$, find the value of $x^2 + y^2$.
SSC CPO 11/11/2022
(a) 16 (b) 9 (c) 25 (d) 1

383. If $\cos A = \sin^2 A$, and $a\sin^{12} A + b\sin^{10} A + c\sin^8 A + \sin^6 A = 1$, then $a + b + c = ?$
SSC CPO 11/11/2022
(a) 7 (b) 8 (c) 9 (d) 6

384. If $\cos 48° = \frac{m}{n}$, then $\sec 48° - \cot 42°$ is equal to SSC CPO 10/11/2022
(a) $\frac{m-\sqrt{n^2-m^2}}{m}$ (b) $\frac{m-\sqrt{n^2-m^2}}{n}$
(c) $\frac{n-\sqrt{n^2-m^2}}{n}$ (d) $\frac{n-\sqrt{n^2-m^2}}{m}$

385. The value of $\frac{2\cos^3\theta - \cos\theta}{\sin\theta - 2\sin^3\theta}$ is
SSC CPO 10/11/2022
(a) $\sec\theta$ (b) $\sin\theta$
(c) $\cot\theta$ (d) $\tan\theta$

386. The value of the expression $\cos^2 45° + \cos^2 135° + \cos^2 225° + \cos^2 315°$ is SSC CPO 10/11/2022
(a) 2 (b) $\frac{1}{2}$ (c) $\frac{3}{2}$ (d) 1

387. Solve for θ, $\cos^2\theta - \sin^2\theta = \frac{1}{2}$, $0 < \theta < 90°$. SSC CPO 25/11/2020 Shift II
(a) 45° (b) 60°
(c) 30° (d) 40°

388. If $\cot\theta = \frac{1}{\sqrt{3}}$, $0° < \theta < 90°$, then the value of $\frac{2-\sin^2\theta}{1-\cos^2\theta} + (\text{cosec}^2\theta - \sec\theta)$ is
SSC CPO 25/11/2020 Shift II
(a) 0 (b) 2 (c) 5 (d) 1

389. If $4(\text{cosec}^2 57° - \tan^2 33°) - \cos 90° + y\tan^2 66° \tan^2 24° = \frac{y}{2}$, then the value of y is SSC CPO 25/11/2020 Shift-I
(a) 4 (b) – 4
(c) 8 (d) – 8

390. If $4 - 2\sin^2\theta - 5\cos\theta = 0$, $0° < \theta < 90°$, then the value of $\cos\theta - \tan\theta$ is
SSC CPO 25/11/2020 Shift-I
(a) $\frac{1+2\sqrt{3}}{2}$ (b) $\frac{2-\sqrt{3}}{2}$
(c) $\frac{2+\sqrt{3}}{2}$ (d) $\frac{1-2\sqrt{3}}{2}$

391. If $\sin 3x = \cos(3x - 45°)$, $0° < 3x < 90°$, then x is equal to
SSC CPO 24/11/2020 Shift-I
(a) 45° (b) 22.5°
(c) 35° (d) 27.5°

392. If $4 - 2\sin^2\theta - 5\cos\theta = 0$, $0° < \theta < 90°$, then the value of $\cos\theta + \tan\theta$ is SSC CPO 23/11/2020 Shift-I
(a) $\frac{2-\sqrt{3}}{2}$ (b) $\frac{1+2\sqrt{3}}{2}$
(c) $\frac{2+\sqrt{3}}{2}$ (d) $\frac{1-2\sqrt{3}}{2}$

393. If $4(\text{cosec}^2 57° - \tan^2 33°) - \cos 90° - y\tan^2 66° \tan^2 24° = \frac{y}{2}$, the value of y is SSC CPO 23/11/2020 Shift-I
(a) $\frac{8}{3}$ (b) $\frac{3}{8}$ (c) 8 (d) $\frac{1}{3}$

SSC CHSL 2024 (Tier I & II)

394. Find the value of $(\sin^6 A + \cos^6 A + 3\sin^2 A\cos^2 A) - (\sin^4 A - \cos^4 A + 1)\,\text{cosec}^2 A$.
SSC CHSL (Tier-II) 18/11/2024 Shift-I
(a) 0 (b) 3 (c) –3 (d) –1

395. Find the value of $3(\sec^2 A - 1)(\text{cosec}\,A - 1)(\text{cosec}\,A + 1) + 4(\text{cosec}^2 A - \cot^2 A)$.
SSC CHSL (Tier-II) 18/11/2024 Shift-I
(a) 10 (b) 3
(c) 7 (d) 12

396. If $\tan A + \sin A = x$, $\tan A - \sin A = y$, what is the value of $x^2 - y^2$?
SSC CHSL (Tier-I) 11/07/2024 Shift-IV
(a) $2\sqrt{\frac{x}{y}}$ (b) $4\sqrt{\frac{x}{y}}$
(c) $\sqrt{xy}$ (d) $4\sqrt{xy}$

397. What is the value of $\cos^{-1}\left(\frac{7}{25}\right) - \cos^{-1}\left(\frac{15}{17}\right)$?
SSC CHSL (Tier-I) 11/07/2024 Shift-II
(a) $\sin^{-1}\left(\frac{304}{425}\right)$ (b) $\cot^{-1}\left(\frac{297}{425}\right)$
(c) $\tan^{-1}\left(\frac{297}{425}\right)$ (d) $\cos^{-1}\left(\frac{304}{425}\right)$

398. The value of $\left(\frac{\sin\theta}{1+\cos\theta} + \frac{1+\cos\theta}{\sin\theta}\right)\left(\frac{1}{\tan\theta + \cot\theta}\right)$ is equal to
SSC CHSL (Tier-I) 11/07/2024 Shift-I
(a) $\tan\theta$ (b) 1
(c) $2\cos\theta$ (d) $2\sin\theta$

399. Evaluate $\frac{(9\sin\theta + 2\cos\theta)}{9\sin\theta - 2\cos\theta}$, if $3\tan\theta = 4$.
SSC CHSL (Tier-I) 10/07/2024 Shift-IV
(a) $\frac{9}{7}$ (b) $\frac{5}{7}$ (c) $\frac{7}{5}$ (d) $\frac{6}{5}$

400. If $4\sin^2\theta - 4\sqrt{3}\sin\theta + 3 = 0$, then find the value of θ. $(0 < \theta < 90°)$
SSC CHSL (Tier-I) 10/07/2024 Shift-III
(a) 30° (b) 75°
(c) 60° (d) 45°

401. If $f(p) = \sin^{p+2} x + \cos^{p+2} x$, then the value of $6f(2) - 4f(4) + 10f(0)$ is
SSC CHSL (Tier-I) 10/07/2024 Shift-II
(a) 14 (b) 10
(c) 12 (d) 11

402. If $\tan A = \sqrt{2} - 1$, then find the value of $\sin A\cos A + \tan A$.
SSC CHSL (Tier-I) 10/07/2024 Shift-I
(a) $\frac{24\sqrt{2}+15}{4}$ (b) $\frac{5\sqrt{2}-4}{4}$
(c) $\frac{24\sqrt{2}-15}{4}$ (d) $\frac{5\sqrt{2}+4}{4}$

403. What is the maximum value of $7\cos A + 24\sin A + 32$?
SSC CHSL (Tier-I) 09/07/2024 Shift-IV
(a) 57 (b) 32
(c) 25 (d) 39

404. If $\tan\theta = \frac{7}{4}$, then the value of $\frac{4\sin\theta - 3\cos\theta}{4\sin\theta + 3\cos\theta}$ is equal to
SSC CHSL (Tier-I) 09/07/2024 Shift-II
(a) $\frac{2}{5}$ (b) $\frac{1}{3}$ (c) $\frac{4}{5}$ (d) $\frac{3}{5}$

405. If $\cot\alpha = \frac{P}{Q}$, then find the value of $\frac{P\cos\alpha - Q\sin\alpha}{P\cos\alpha + Q\sin\alpha} - \frac{P^2 - Q^2}{P^2 + Q^2} + 3$.

SSC CHSL (Tier-I) 09/07/2024 Shift-I

(a) $\frac{P}{P^2 + Q^2}$ (b) $\frac{P}{Q}$
(c) 0 (d) 3

406. If $\cos^4\theta - \sin^4\theta = \frac{4}{5}$, then find the value of $\sin 4\theta$.

SSC CHSL (Tier-I) 08/07/2024 Shift-IV

(a) $\frac{24}{25}$ (b) $\frac{21}{25}$
(c) $\frac{16}{25}$ (d) $\frac{18}{25}$

407. If $\sin\theta = \frac{11}{12}$, then what will be the value of $(\tan\theta + \sec\theta)$?

SSC CHSL (Tier-I) 08/07/2024 Shift-III

(a) $\sqrt{23}$ (b) $\frac{11}{\sqrt{23}}$
(c) $\frac{12}{\sqrt{23}}$ (d) 23

408. If $\cot A = \frac{5}{12}$, then find the value of $\frac{\sqrt{\sec A - \text{cosec } A}}{\sqrt{\sec A + \text{cosec } A}} - \sqrt{\frac{17}{7}}$.

SSC CHSL (Tier-I) 08/07/2024 Shift-I

(a) $\frac{24}{\sqrt{119}}$ (b) 0
(c) $-\frac{10}{\sqrt{119}}$ (d) $\frac{10}{\sqrt{119}}$

409. $\left[\frac{\text{cosec } 31^\circ - \sec 59^\circ}{\sin 18^\circ + \cos 72^\circ} \times \frac{\tan 26^\circ}{\cot 64^\circ}\right] + \left[\frac{\tan 30^\circ + \tan 15^\circ}{1 - \tan 30^\circ \tan 15^\circ}\right] = \ldots\ldots\ldots$

SSC CHSL (Tier-I) 05/07/2024 Shift-IV

(a) 0 (b) −1
(c) 1 (d) 2

410. If $\sin(X - Y) = \sin X\cos Y - \cos X\sin Y$, then the value of $\frac{\sin(A-B)}{\cos A\cos B} + \frac{\sin(B-C)}{\cos B\cos C}$ is

SSC CHSL (Tier-I) 05/07/2024 Shift-II

(a) $\frac{\sin(C-A)}{\cos A\cos C}$ (b) $\frac{\sin(A-C)}{\cos A\cos C}$
(c) $\frac{\cos(A+C)}{\cos A\cos C}$ (d) $\frac{\cos(A+C)}{\sin A\sin C}$

411. If $\tan A = a\tan B$ and $\sin A = b\sin B$, then the value of $\cos^2 A$ is

SSC CHSL (Tier-I) 05/07/2024 Shift-I

(a) $\frac{b^2-1}{a^2-1}$ (b) $\frac{a^2-1}{b^2-1}$
(c) $\frac{b^2+1}{a^2+1}$ (d) $\frac{a^2+1}{b^2+1}$

412. If $\cot\theta = \frac{3}{4}$, θ is an acute angle, then $(\sin\theta + \cos\theta - \tan\theta)$ is equal to

SSC CHSL (Tier-I) 04/07/2024 Shift-IV

(a) $\frac{1}{11}$ (b) $\frac{1}{15}$
(c) $\frac{1}{13}$ (d) $\frac{1}{18}$

413. What is the value of $\frac{1}{\sin^4(90^\circ - 2\alpha)} + \frac{1}{\cos^2(90^\circ - 2\alpha) - 1}$?

SSC CHSL (Tier-I) 04/07/2024 Shift-II

(a) $\sin^2 2\alpha + \tan^2 2\alpha$
(b) $\sec^2 2\alpha\tan^2 2\alpha$
(c) $\sec^2 2\alpha + \cot^2 2\alpha$
(d) $\cos^2 2\alpha\cot^2 2\alpha$

414. What is the value of $\tan 570^\circ$?

SSC CHSL (Tier-I) 04/07/2024 Shift-I

(a) $-\frac{1}{\sqrt{3}}$ (b) $-\sqrt{3}$
(c) $\frac{1}{\sqrt{3}}$ (d) $\sqrt{3}$

415. If $\alpha + \beta = 45^\circ$ and $(\tan\alpha + 1)(\tan\beta + 1) = 2x$, then x is

SSC CHSL (Tier-I) 03/07/2024 Shift-IV

(a) 2 (b) −1
(c) 0 (d) 1

416. $\frac{3\cos^3\theta - 2\cos\theta}{\sin\theta - 3\sin^3\theta}$ is equal to

SSC CHSL (Tier-I) 03/07/2024 Shift-III

(a) $\tan\theta$ (b) $\cot^2\theta$
(c) $\cot\theta$ (d) $\tan^2\theta$

417. Find the value of the following expression. $\sin(30^\circ + \theta^\circ) - \cos(60^\circ - \theta)$

SSC CHSL (Tier-I) 03/07/2024 Shift-II

(a) $2\sin(30 + \theta)$ (b) 1
(c) $\frac{\sqrt{3}}{2}$ (d) 0

418. $(\cot\theta + \tan\theta)(\text{cosec }\theta - \sin\theta)(\cos\theta - \sec\theta) = \ldots\ldots\ldots$

SSC CHSL (Tier-I) 03/07/2024 Shift-I

(a) 0 (b) 1
(c) 2 (d) −1

419. If $\sqrt{13}\sin\theta = 2$, then the value of $\frac{3\tan\theta + \sqrt{13}\sin\theta}{\sqrt{13}\cos\theta - 3\tan\theta}$ is

SSC CHSL (Tier-I) 02/07/2024 Shift-IV

(a) 4 (b) 3
(c) 2 (d) 0

420. If θ is an acute angle and $\tan\theta + \cos\theta = 2$, then find the value of $\tan^3\theta + \cot^3\theta + 6\tan^3\theta\cot^2\theta$.

SSC CHSL (Tier-I) 02/07/2024 Shift-III

(a) 6 (b) 10
(c) 12 (d) 8

421. What is the value of $\cos(x + y) - \sin(x - y) + \tan(2z)$?

SSC CHSL (Tier-I) 02/07/2024 Shift-I

(a) $\cos x.\cos y - \sin x.\sin y - \sin x.\cos y - \cos x.\sin y + \frac{2\tan z}{1 - \tan^2 z}$
(b) $\cos x.\cos y - \sin x.\sin y - \sin x.\cos y + \cos x.\sin y + \frac{2\tan z}{1 - \tan^2 z}$
(c) $\cos x\cdot\cos y - \sin x\cdot\sin y - \cos x\cdot\sin y + \frac{\tan z}{1 - \tan^2 z}$
(d) $\sin x.\sin y + \frac{2\tan z}{1 - \tan^2 z}$

422. $12\sin^2 A + 2\cos^2 A = 7$, where $0 < A < 180^\circ$. Then, $\cot A$ is

SSC CHSL (Tier-I) 01/07/2024 Shift-IV

(a) ±1 (b) $\pm\frac{1}{2}$
(c) $\pm\frac{1}{\sqrt{2}}$ (d) $\pm\frac{1}{\sqrt{3}}$

423. If $\cot A = 7$, then the value of $\frac{5\cos A + 4\sin A}{\cos^3 A + 7\sin^3 A + 6\sin A}$ is

SSC CHSL (Tier-I) 01/07/2024 Shift-III

(a) 3 (b) 2
(c) 0 (d) 1

424. In right-angled triangle ABC, $\angle B = 90^\circ$ and $\angle A$ and $\angle C$ are acute angles. If $\text{cosec } A = 2\sqrt{2}$, then find the value of $\sin A\cdot\cos C + \cos A\cdot\sin C$.

SSC CHSL (Tier-I) 01/07/2024 Shift-I

(a) 0 (b) $2\sqrt{2}$
(c) 1 (d) $\sqrt{2}$

SSC CHSL 2023 (Tier I)

425. In a right-angled triangle PQR, $PQ = 5$ cm, $QR = 13$ cm and $\angle P = 90^\circ$. Find the value of $\tan Q - \tan R$.

SSC CHSL (Tier-I) 17/08/2023 Shift-I

(a) $\frac{5}{14}$ (b) $\frac{119}{60}$
(c) $\frac{60}{119}$ (d) $\frac{14}{5}$

426. If $\tan A = \frac{3}{4}$, find the value of the following expression. $\frac{6\sin A}{1 - \sin A}$

SSC CHSL (Tier-I) 17/08/2023 Shift-I

(a) 18 (b) 9 (c) 24 (d) 12

427. If $\text{cosec } A + \cot A = a\sqrt{b}$, then find the value of $\frac{(a^2b - 1)}{(a^2b + 1)}$.

SSC CHSL (Tier-I) 17/08/2023 Shift-I

(a) $\cos A$ (b) $\tan A$
(c) $\frac{1}{\sin A}$ (d) $\frac{1}{\cot A}$

428. If θ is an acute angle and $\sin\theta = \frac{43}{47}$, what is the value of cot θ?
SSC CHSL (Tier-I) 14/08/2023 Shift-IV

(a) $\frac{6\sqrt{10}}{47}$ (b) $\frac{43}{6\sqrt{10}}$
(c) $\frac{47}{6\sqrt{10}}$ (d) $\frac{6\sqrt{10}}{43}$

429. The given expression is equal to $(\cot B - \tan B).\sin B.\cos B$
SSC CHSL (Tier-I) 14/08/2023 Shift-IV

(a) $1 - 2\sec^2 B$
(b) $1 - 2\cos^2 B$
(c) $2\cos^2 B - 1$
(d) $2\sec^2 B - 1$

430. If $\operatorname{cosec}\theta - \cot\theta = \frac{7}{2}$, then the value of cosec θ will be
SSC CHSL (Tier-I) 11/08/2023 Shift-I

(a) $\frac{49}{28}$ (b) $\frac{21}{28}$
(c) $\frac{47}{28}$ (d) $\frac{53}{28}$

431. If $(4\sin\theta + 5\cos\theta) = 3$, then the value of $(4\cos\theta - 5\sin\theta)$ is
SSC CHSL (Tier-I) 11/08/2023 Shift-I

(a) $3\sqrt{2}$ (b) $4\sqrt{2}$
(c) $2\sqrt{3}$ (d) $2\sqrt{5}$

432. If $A = 60°$ and $B = 30°$, find the value of $\frac{(\tan A - \tan B)}{(1 + \tan A \tan B)}$.
SSC CHSL (Tier-I) 10/08/2023 Shift-IV

(a) 3 (b) $\frac{1}{\sqrt{3}}$
(c) $\sqrt{3}$ (d) 1

433. Δ*RMS* is right-angled at *M*. The length of the base, *RM* = 4 cm and the length of perpendicular *MS* = 3 cm. Find the value of sec *R*.
SSC CHSL (Tier-I) 10/08/2023 Shift-III

(a) $\frac{3}{4}$ (b) $\frac{5}{4}$
(c) $\frac{4}{5}$ (d) $\frac{2}{5}$

434. Evaluate the given expression
$\cos^2 36° + \cos 54°\cdot\sin 36° + \left(\frac{\tan 26°}{\cot 64°}\right)$.
SSC CHSL (Tier-I) 10/08/2023 Shift-III

(a) 4 (b) 3
(c) 1 (d) 2

435. If $\tan A = \frac{1}{2}$ and $\tan B = \frac{1}{3}$, then the value of *A* + *B* is
SSC CHSL (Tier-I) 09/08/2023 Shift-I

(a) 60° (b) 15°
(c) 30° (d) 45°

436. Δ*PQR* is right angled at *Q*. If *PQ* = 12 cm, *PR* = 13 cm, find tan *P* + cot *R*.
SSC CHSL (Tier-I) 09/08/2023 Shift-I

(a) $\frac{9}{10}$ (b) 0
(c) $\frac{10}{12}$ (d) $\frac{12}{10}$

437. If $\frac{\sin\theta - \cos\theta}{\sin\theta + \cos\theta} = \frac{4}{5}$, then the value of $\frac{\operatorname{cosec}^2\theta}{2 - \operatorname{cosec}^2\theta}$ is
SSC CHSL (Tier-I) 09/08/2023 Shift-I

(a) $\frac{16}{25}$ (b) $\frac{40}{41}$
(c) $\frac{41}{40}$ (d) $\frac{31}{30}$

438. If $\tan\theta + \sec\theta = a$, then what is sec θ equal to?
SSC CHSL (Tier-I) 08/08/2023 Shift-II

(a) $\frac{a+1}{2a^2}$ (b) $\frac{(a-1)}{2a^2}$
(c) $\frac{a^2-1}{2a}$ (d) $\frac{a^2+1}{2a}$

439. Simplify the given equation.
$\frac{\cot^3 A - 1}{\cot A - 1} = ?$
SSC CHSL (Tier-I) 08/08/2023 Shift-II

(a) $\operatorname{cosec}^2 A - \cot A$ (b) $\operatorname{cosec}^2 A + \cot A$
(c) $\cot^2 A + \operatorname{cosec} A$ (d) $\cot^2 A - \operatorname{cosec} A$

440. The value of $\frac{\sin 58°}{\cos 32°} + \frac{\sin 55° \sec 35°}{\tan 5° \tan 45° \tan 85°}$ is equal to
SSC CHSL (Tier-I) 07/08/2023 Shift-IV

(a) 2 (b) 1
(c) 0 (d) 3

441. The value of $\frac{1}{\sin\theta} - \frac{\cot^2\theta}{1 + \operatorname{cosec}\theta}$ is
SSC CHSL (Tier-I) 07/08/2023 Shift-IV

(a) 2 (b) 1
(c) –1 (d) 0

442. Simplify the given expression,
$\frac{\sin^2 32° + \sin^2 58°}{\cos^2 32° + \cos^2 58°} + \sin^2 53° + \cos 53° \sin 37°$.
SSC CHSL (Tier-I) 07/08/2023 Shift-IV

(a) 2 (b) –1
(c) –2 (d) 1

443. If *A* = 30°, then find the value of $\frac{(2\tan A)}{(1 - \tan^2 A)}$.
SSC CHSL (Tier-I) 04/08/2023 Shift-II

(a) $4\sqrt{3}$ (b) $\frac{3}{\sqrt{3}}$
(c) 3 (d) $2\sqrt{3}$

444. If $\tan\theta = \frac{4}{5}$, then sec θ is
SSC CHSL (Tier-I) 04/08/2023 Shift-II

(a) $\frac{\sqrt{41}}{5}$ (b) $\frac{\sqrt{41}}{4}$
(c) $\frac{5}{4}$ (d) $\frac{\sqrt{41}}{20}$

445. $\frac{\cos\theta}{\sec\theta - 1} + \frac{\cos\theta}{\sec\theta + 1}$ is equal to
SSC CHSL (Tier-I) 02/08/2023 Shift-I

(a) $2\sec^2\theta$ (b) $2\cot^2\theta$
(c) $2\cos^2\theta$ (d) $2\sin^2\theta$

446. If $\sin A + \sin^2 A = 1$, then the value of the expression $(\cos^2 A + \cos^4 A)$ is ……… **SSC CHSL (Tier-I) 02/08/2023 Shift-I**

(a) $\frac{3}{2}$ (b) 1
(c) 2 (d) $\frac{1}{2}$

447. Δ*ABC* is right angled triangle. ∠*C* = 90°, *AB* = 25 cm and *BC* = 20 cm. What is the value of sec *A* ?
SSC CHSL (Tier-I) 21/03/2023 Shift-IV

(a) 5/3 (b) 4/5
(c) 4/3 (d) 5/4

448. If $\tan\theta + \sin\theta = A$ and $\tan\theta - \sin\theta = B$, then what is the value of $A^2 - B^2$?
SSC CHSL (Tier-I) 21/03/2023 Shift-IV

(a) $\tan\theta\sin\theta$ (b) $4\cot\theta$
(c) $4\tan\theta\sin\theta$ (d) $2\tan\theta\sin\theta$

449. If $A = \cot 30° \tan 60° + \cot 60° \tan 30°$, then what is the value of *A*?
SSC CHSL (Tier-I) 21/03/2023 Shift-IV

(a) $\frac{1}{\sqrt{3}}$ (b) $\frac{10}{3}$
(c) $\frac{10}{\sqrt{3}}$ (d) $\frac{1}{3}$

450. If $\frac{2\cos^3 A - \cos A}{\sin A - 2\sin^3 A} = 1$, then what is the value of *A*?
SSC CHSL (Tier-I) 21/03/2023 Shift-II

(a) 90° (b) 30°
(c) 45° (d) 60°

451. If $\sin A = \frac{6}{7}$, then what is the value of sec *A*?
SSC CHSL (Tier-I) 21/03/2023 Shift-II

(a) $\frac{1}{\sqrt{13}}$ (b) $\frac{7}{\sqrt{13}}$
(c) $\frac{6}{\sqrt{13}}$ (d) $\frac{4}{\sqrt{13}}$

452. What is the value of $\operatorname{cosec} A(1 - \cos A)(\operatorname{cosec} A + \cot A)$?
SSC CHSL (Tier-I) 21/03/2023 Shift-II

(a) 2 (b) 1 (c) 0 (d) 3

453. If 6sec θ = 10, then find the value of (5cosecθ − 3cot θ) ÷ (4cos θ + 3sin θ).
SSC CHSL (Tier-I) 20/03/2023 Shift-III

(a) $\frac{2}{3}$ (b) $\frac{3}{2}$
(c) $\frac{5}{6}$ (d) $\frac{3}{6}$

454. If 3 tan θ = 4, then what is the value of 7sin θ − 2cos θ?
SSC CHSL (Tier-I) 20/03/2023 Shift-III

(a) $\frac{12}{5}$ (b) 4
(c) $\frac{22}{5}$ (d) $\frac{27}{5}$

455. If sin(θ + 30°) = cos 5θ, then what is the value of θ ?
SSC CHSL (Tier-I) 20/03/2023 Shift-III

(a) 30° (b) 10°
(c) 15° (d) 20°

456. If $\sec x + \cos x = 5/2$, where x lies between 0° and 90°, then what is the value of $\sin^2 x$?
SSC CHSL (Tier-I) 17/03/2023 Shift-II

(a) 3/4 (b) 1/2
(c) 1 (d) 1/4

457. What is the value of $\frac{1+\tan A}{\text{cosec } A}+\frac{1+\cot A}{\sec A}$?
SSC CHSL (Tier-I) 16/03/2023 Shift-I

(a) $2\sec^2 A$ (b) sec A + cosec A
(c) sec A − cosec A (d) $2\text{ cosec}^2 A$

458. If sin C = $\frac{9}{10}$, then what is the value of $\cos^2 C$?
SSC CHSL (Tier-I) 16/03/2023 Shift-I

(a) $\frac{19}{100}$ (b) $\frac{81}{\sqrt{19}}$
(c) $\frac{19}{10}$ (d) $\frac{\sqrt{19}}{100}$

459. If cos θ + sin θ = $\sqrt{2}$, then what is the value of sec θ cosec θ?
SSC CHSL (Tier-I) 16/03/2023 Shift-I

(a) 1/2 (b) 1
(c) 2 (d) 0

460. If $A = a\,\text{cosec}\,\theta + b\cot\theta$ and $B = a\cot\theta + b\,\text{cosec}\,\theta$, then what is the value of $A^2 - B^2$?
SSC CHSL (Tier-I) 15/03/2023 Shift-IV

(a) ab (b) $(a + b)$
(c) $(a^2 - b^2)$ (d) $(a - b)$

461. What is the value of $\frac{3\text{ cosec }42^\circ}{\sec 48^\circ}-\frac{5\cos 32^\circ}{\sin 58^\circ}$
SSC CHSL (Tier-I) 15/03/2023 Shift-IV

(a) −1 (b) 5
(c) 0 (d) −2

462. If sin θ = $\frac{3}{11}$, then what is the value of cot θ? **SSC CHSL (Tier-I) 15/03/2023 Shift-IV**

(a) $\frac{3\sqrt{7}}{11}$ (b) $\frac{4\sqrt{7}}{11}$
(c) $\frac{4\sqrt{7}}{3}$ (d) $\frac{3\sqrt{7}}{28}$

463. If tan θ + cot θ = 8, then what is the value of $\tan^2\theta + \cot^2\theta$?
SSC CHSL (Tier-I) 14/03/2023 Shift-I

(a) 36 (b) 64
(c) 62 (d) 16

464. ΔPQR is a right angled triangle. ∠Q = 90°, PQ = 9 cm and QR = 11 cm. What is the value of cot P?
SSC CHSL (Tier-I) 14/03/2023 Shift-I

(a) $\frac{9}{11}$ (b) $\frac{11}{9}$
(c) $\frac{9}{\sqrt{202}}$ (d) $\frac{\sqrt{202}}{9}$

465. What is the value of (sec A − tan A + 1) (sec A − tan A − 1) ?
SSC CHSL (Tier-I) 14/03/2023 Shift-I

(a) (1 + tan A)
(b) 2 tan A(tan A − sec A)
(c) 2 tan A
(d) 2 sec A

466. What is the value of θ in the following when $\cos^2\theta - 2 + \cos\theta = 0$
SSC CHSL (Tier-I) 13/03/2023 Shift-III

(a) 30° (b) 90°
(c) 60° (d) 0°

467. If tan α = $\frac{1}{\sqrt{3}}$ and tan β = $\sqrt{3}$, then what is the value of cos (α + β)?
SSC CHSL (Tier-I) 13/03/2023 Shift-III

(a) 1 (b) 0.5
(c) 0 (d) 0.2

468. ΔABC is a right angle triangle ∠A = 90°, AB = 4 cm, BC = 5 cm. What is the value of cos B + cot C ?
SSC CHSL (Tier-I) 13/03/2023 Shift-III

(a) 31/20 (b) 23/20
(c) 17/20 (d) 29/20

469. If sin $x = \frac{1}{2}$, then find the value of $(\sec^4 x + \text{cosec}^4 x) - (\tan^4 x + \cot^4 x)$
SSC CHSL (Tier-I) 10/03/2023 Shift-II

(a) 26/3 (b) 97/12
(c) 26/23 (d) 2

470. What is cosec 90°/(1 − $\cos^2$ 60°) ?
SSC CHSL (Tier-I) 10/03/2023 Shift-II

(a) 0 (b) 4/3
(c) 1/4 (d) 3/4

471. If tan θ + cot θ = 2, then what is the value of tan θ − cot θ?
SSC CHSL (Tier-I) 10/03/2023 Shift-II

(a) 0 (b) 5/8
(c) 1 (d) 3/4

472. If cot $y = \frac{12}{5}$, then what is the value of $\cos^2 y$? **SSC CHSL (Tier-I) 09/03/2023 Shift-I**

(a) $\frac{72}{143}$ (b) $\frac{72}{91}$
(c) $\frac{144}{169}$ (d) $\frac{84}{143}$

473. What is the value of $\left(\frac{1+\sec^2 A}{1+\cos^2 A}\right)\left(\frac{1+\sin^2 A}{1+\text{cosec}^2 A}\right)$?
SSC CHSL (Tier-I) 09/03/2023 Shift-I

(a) $\cos^2 A$ (b) $\text{cosec}^2 A$
(c) $\sec^2 A$ (d) $\tan^2 A$

474. If sec θ + tan θ = 5, then what is the value of sec θ − tan θ ?
SSC CHSL (Tier-I) 09/03/2023 Shift-I

(a) $\frac{1}{5}$ (b) $\frac{1}{3}$
(c) $\frac{1}{6}$ (d) $\frac{1}{2}$

SSC CHSL 2022 & 2021 (Tier I)

475. The value of sin 2θ(tan θ + cot θ) is
SSC CHSL (Tier-I) 01/06/2022 Shift-I

(a) $\frac{2}{3}$ (b) 1
(c) $\frac{1}{2}$ (d) 2

476. If $\sin x - 3\cos x = \sqrt{3}\cos x$, then the value of cot x is.
SSC CHSL (Tier-I) 31/05/2022 Shift-I

(a) $3 - \sqrt{3}$ (b) $3 + \sqrt{3}$
(c) $\sqrt{3}$ (d) $\frac{3-\sqrt{3}}{6}$

477. If tan θ + cot θ = 4, than find the value of $\tan^2\theta + \cot^2\theta$.
SSC CHSL (Tier-I) 30/05/2022 Shift-I

(a) 10 (b) 12
(c) 16 (d) 14

478. The value of $\frac{\sin 4\theta + \sin 2\theta}{\cos 4\theta + \cos 2\theta}$ is
SSC CHSL (Tier-I) 27/05/2022 Shift-I

(a) tan 3θ (b) cot 3θ
(c) tan θ (d) cot θ

479. If sec θ − cosec θ = 0 and θ is an acute angle, then what is the value of $\sec^2\theta + \text{cosec}^2\theta$?
SSC CHSL (Tier-I) 12/08/2021 Shift-III

(a) 4 (b) 1
(c) 2 (d) 0

480. If $\tan\theta = \frac{4}{3}$, then the value of $\frac{9\sin\theta + 12\cos\theta}{27\cos\theta - 20\sin\theta}$ will be equal to

SSC CHSL (Tier-I) 10/08/2021 Shift-I

(a) 72 (b) 36
(c) 18 (d) 100

481. For $\theta: 0° < \theta < 90°$ $3\sec\theta + 4\cos\theta = 4\sqrt{3}$, find the value of $(1-\sin\theta + \cos\theta)$.

SSC CHSL (Tier-I) 10/08/2021 Shift-I

(a) $\frac{1+2\sqrt{3}}{2}$ (b) $\frac{1+\sqrt{3}}{2}$
(c) $\frac{1-\sqrt{3}}{2}$ (d) $\frac{1-2\sqrt{3}}{2}$

482. Evaluate the following expression.

$$\frac{3(\cot^2 46° - \sec^2 44°)}{2(\sin^2 28° + \sin^2 62°)} + \frac{2\cos^2 60° \tan^2 33° \tan^2 57°}{\sec^2(90°-\theta) - \cot^2\theta}$$

SSC CHSL (Tier-I) 10/08/2021 Shift-I

(a) -1 (b) 1
(c) -2 (d) 2

483. If $\cos\theta = \frac{4x}{1+4x^2}$, then what is the value of $\sin\theta$?

SSC CHSL (Tier-I) 04/08/2021 Shift-I

(a) $\frac{1+4x^2}{1-4x^2}$ (b) $\frac{1+4x^2}{4x^2}$
(c) $\frac{1-4x^2}{1+4x^2}$ (d) $\frac{1-4x^2}{4x^2}$

484. If $\frac{\sin\theta + \cos\theta}{\sin\theta - \cos\theta} = 3$, then the value of $\sin^4\theta - \cos^4\theta$ is equal to

SSC CHSL (Tier-I) 19/04/2021 Shift-I

(a) $\frac{1}{5}$ (b) $\frac{2}{5}$
(c) $\frac{3}{5}$ (d) $\frac{4}{5}$

485. If $\sec\left(90° - \frac{3\theta}{2}\right) = \sqrt{2}, 0° < \theta < 90°$, then the value of $2\sin\theta + 4\cos 2\theta$ will be

SSC CHSL (Tier-I) 19/04/2021 Shift-I

(a) 4 (b) 2
(c) 3 (d) 6

486. Solve the following equation and find θ. $2\sqrt{3}\sin^2\theta + \cos\theta - \sqrt{3} = 0$, where θ is an acute angle.

SSC CHSL (Tier-I) 19/04/2021 Shift-I

(a) 30° (b) 45°
(c) 60° (d) 15°

487. If $2\tan x + 3\cot x = 5$, then the value of $4\tan^2 x + 9\cot^2 x$ is

SSC CHSL (Tier-I) 12/04/2021 Shift-II

(a) 11 (b) 15
(c) 17 (d) 13

488. If $3\cot^2 x - 7\,\text{cosec}^2 x + 7 = 0$, then the value of $x\ (0 \le x \le 90°)$ is

SSC CHSL (Tier-I) 12/04/2021 Shift-I

(a) 30° (b) 0°
(c) 90° (d) 60°

SSC Selection Post 2024-2022

489. If $\sin A + \cos A = \frac{4}{3}$, then find the value of $\tan A + \cot A$.

Graduate Level 20/06/2024 Shift-III

(a) $\frac{7}{18}$ (b) $\frac{3}{4}$
(c) $\frac{18}{7}$ (d) $\frac{4}{3}$

490. If $\tan\theta + \cot\theta = 2$, then find the value of $\tan^{53}\theta + \cot^{38}\theta$.

Graduate Level 20/06/2024 Shift-III

(a) -1 (b) 0
(c) 2 (d) 1

491. Evaluate

$$7\left(\frac{\text{cosec } 24°}{\sec 66°}\right)^3 + 8\left(\frac{\cot 37°}{\tan 53°}\right)^4 - \left(2\frac{\sec 14°}{\text{cosec } 76°}\right)^2 + \left(-3\frac{\tan 82°}{\cot 8°}\right)^3$$

Graduate Level 20/06/2024 Shift-II

(a) -16 (b) 40
(c) 10 (d) 2

492. The value of $\frac{32}{\sec^2\theta} - \frac{20}{1+\tan^2\theta} + 12\sin^2\theta$ is

Graduate Level 27/06/2023 Shift-IV

(a) 20 (b) 32
(c) 24 (d) 12

493. If $\sin\theta + \cos\theta = \frac{\sqrt{11}}{3}$, then what is $\tan\theta + \cot\theta$ equal to?

Graduate Level 27/06/2023 Shift-IV

(a) 5 (b) 9
(c) 7 (d) 11

494. If $4\tan A = 3$, then $\cos^2 A - \sin^2 A$ equals

Graduate Level 27/06/2023 Shift-III

(a) $\frac{1}{5}$ (b) $\frac{7}{25}$
(c) $\frac{9}{25}$ (d) $\frac{3}{5}$

495. If $\theta = 120°$ and $p = \cos\theta + \sin\theta$, then

Graduate Level 01/08/2022 Shift-IV

(a) $p < 0$ (b) $p \ge 0$
(c) $p > 0$ (d) $p \le 0$

496. If $\text{cosec}(A - B) = 2$ and $\cot(A + B) = 1/\sqrt{3}$, then what is the value of A?

Graduate Level 01/08/2022 Shift-IV

(a) 60° (b) 45°
(c) 90° (d) 30°

497. If $\tan 3\theta = \cot(\theta - 22°)$, where 3θ is an acute angle, find the value of θ.

Graduate Level 01/08/2022 Shift-II

(a) 27° (b) 26°
(c) 29° (d) 28°

Right Answers

1	(c)	2	(b)	3	(c)	4	(b)	5	(c)	6	(d)	7	(b)	8	(b)	9	(b)	10	(a)
11	(a)	12	(c)	13	(b)	14	(a)	15	(c)	16	(c)	17	(b)	18	(a)	19	(c)	20	(b)
21	(c)	22	(c)	23	(d)	24	(c)	25	(d)	26	(b)	27	(b)	28	(a)	29	(b)	30	(c)
31	(b)	32	(c)	33	(c)	34	(b)	35	(c)	36	(d)	37	(a)	38	(c)	39	(b)	40	(c)
41	(d)	42	(d)	43	(c)	44	(d)	45	(a)	46	(d)	47	(b)	48	(b)	49	(d)	50	(a)
51	(a)	52	(b)	53	(b)	54	(c)	55	(a)	56	(a)	57	(d)	58	(b)	59	(d)	60	(b)
61	(a)	62	(d)	63	(b)	64	(a)	65	(c)	66	(d)	67	(c)	68	(b)	69	(b)	70	(a)
71	(d)	72	(c)	73	(b)	74	(d)	75	(a)	76	(d)	77	(a)	78	(d)	79	(b)	80	(a)
81	(a)	82	(a)	83	(d)	84	(b)	85	(a)	86	(c)	87	(b)	88	(b)	89	(a)	90	(a)
91	(c)	92	(d)	93	(c)	94	(b)	95	(c)	96	(c)	97	(a)	98	(a)	99	(d)	100	(d)
101	(c)	102	(d)	103	(c)	104	(a)	105	(d)	106	(d)	107	(c)	108	(d)	109	(c)	110	(b)
111	(a)	112	(d)	113	(c)	114	(b)	115	(b)	116	(c)	117	(d)	118	(b)	119	(d)	120	(c)
121	(d)	122	(c)	123	(c)	124	(c)	125	(a)	126	(d)	127	(c)	128	(a)	129	(c)	130	(b)
131	(c)	132	(a)	133	(a)	134	(b)	135	(b)	136	(c)	137	(a)	138	(b)	139	(a)	140	(a)
141	(a)	142	(b)	143	(d)	144	(b)	145	(a)	146	(c)	147	(d)	148	(c)	149	(c)	150	(d)
151	(b)	152	(a)	153	(c)	154	(a)	155	(a)	156	(d)	157	(b)	158	(c)	159	(a)	160	(b)
161	(c)	162	(d)	163	(b)	164	(c)	165	(d)	166	(d)	167	(b)	168	(a)	169	(b)	170	(d)
171	(c)	172	(a)	173	(c)	174	(c)	175	(b)	176	(c)	177	(d)	178	(b)	179	(d)	180	(c)
181	(b)	182	(a)	183	(d)	184	(a)	185	(d)	186	(d)	187	(b)	188	(b)	189	(c)	190	(d)
191	(a)	192	(b)	193	(c)	194	(d)	195	(b)	196	(c)	197	(d)	198	(a)	199	(b)	200	(b)
201	(d)	202	(b)	203	(d)	204	(d)	205	(c)	206	(a)	207	(c)	208	(c)	209	(c)	210	(c)
211	(b)	212	(b)	213	(b)	214	(c)	215	(a)	216	(c)	217	(c)	218	(c)	219	(c)	220	(b)
221	(c)	222	(a)	223	(a)	224	(a)	225	(d)	226	(d)	227	(c)	228	(d)	229	(d)	230	(c)
231	(a)	232	(b)	233	(b)	234	(d)	235	(a)	236	(c)	237	(b)	238	(d)	239	(a)	240	(a)
241	(c)	242	(b)	243	(b)	244	(d)	245	(a)	246	(b)	247	(c)	248	(b)	249	(b)	250	(d)
251	(c)	252	(a)	253	(c)	254	(d)	255	(c)	256	(b)	257	(c)	258	(d)	259	(b)	260	(a)
261	(d)	262	(d)	263	(a)	264	(b)	265	(b)	266	(a)	267	(b)	268	(a)	269	(a)	270	(b)
271	(a)	272	(c)	273	(a)	274	(b)	275	(a)	276	(b)	277	(c)	278	(b)	279	(c)	280	(c)
281	(b)	282	(b)	283	(a)	284	(c)	285	(b)	286	(c)	287	(b)	288	(b)	289	(c)	290	(c)
291	(d)	292	(a)	293	(c)	294	(b)	295	(a)	296	(a)	297	(a)	298	(a)	299	(d)	300	(a)
301	(d)	302	(c)	303	(a)	304	(a)	305	(a)	306	(a)	307	(a)	308	(c)	309	(b)	310	(b)
311	(d)	312	(d)	313	(d)	314	(a)	315	(d)	316	(c)	317	(a)	318	(a)	319	(c)	320	(a)
321	(a)	322	(d)	323	(c)	324	(d)	325	(a)	326	(b)	327	(b)	328	(a)	329	(b)	330	(d)
331	(b)	332	(a)	333	(b)	334	(b)	335	(d)	336	(a)	337	(b)	338	(a)	339	(b)	340	(b)
341	(b)	342	(c)	343	(a)	344	(c)	345	(c)	346	(c)	347	(a)	348	(b)	349	(a)	350	(a)
351	(c)	352	(c)	353	(b)	354	(d)	355	(b)	356	(c)	357	(d)	358	(b)	359	(b)	360	(b)
361	(a)	362	(d)	363	(c)	364	(c)	365	(a)	366	(c)	367	(b)	368	(c)	369	(c)	370	(a)
371	(a)	372	(b)	373	(d)	374	(d)	375	(a)	376	(b)	377	(b)	378	(b)	379	(b)	380	(d)
381	(c)	382	(c)	383	(a)	384	(d)	385	(c)	386	(a)	387	(c)	388	(d)	389	(d)	390	(d)
391	(b)	392	(b)	393	(a)	394	(d)	395	(c)	396	(d)	397	(a)	398	(c)	399	(c)	400	(c)
401	(c)	402	(b)	403	(a)	404	(a)	405	(d)	406	(a)	407	(a)	408	(c)	409	(c)	410	(b)
411	(a)	412	(b)	413	(b)	414	(c)	415	(d)	416	(c)	417	(d)	418	(d)	419	(a)	420	(d)
421	(b)	422	(a)	423	(a)	424	(c)	425	(b)	426	(b)	427	(a)	428	(d)	429	(c)	430	(d)
431	(b)	432	(b)	433	(b)	434	(d)	435	(d)	436	(c)	437	(c)	438	(d)	439	(b)	440	(a)
441	(b)	442	(a)	443	(b)	444	(a)	445	(b)	446	(b)	447	(a)	448	(c)	449	(b)	450	(c)
451	(b)	452	(b)	453	(c)	454	(c)	455	(b)	456	(a)	457	(b)	458	(a)	459	(c)	460	(c)
461	(d)	462	(c)	463	(c)	464	(a)	465	(b)	466	(d)	467	(c)	468	(a)	469	(a)	470	(b)
471	(a)	472	(c)	473	(d)	474	(a)	475	(d)	476	(d)	477	(d)	478	(a)	479	(a)	480	(a)
481	(b)	482	(a)	483	(c)	484	(c)	485	(c)	486	(a)	487	(d)	488	(c)	489	(c)	490	(c)
491	(a)	492	(d)	493	(b)	494	(b)	495	(c)	496	(b)	497	(d)						

Solutions

1. (c) We have, $\sin A = \frac{5}{13}$

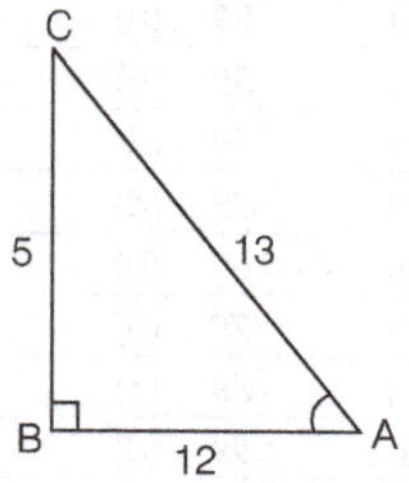

Trigonometric triplets (5, 12, 13)

$$\frac{\cos A - 2\tan A}{\sin A + 3\tan A} = \frac{\frac{12}{13} - 2\times\frac{5}{12}}{\frac{5}{13} + 3\times\frac{5}{12}}$$

$$= \frac{144-130}{60+195} = \frac{14}{255}$$

2. (b) We have, $\cos 27° = \frac{p}{q}$

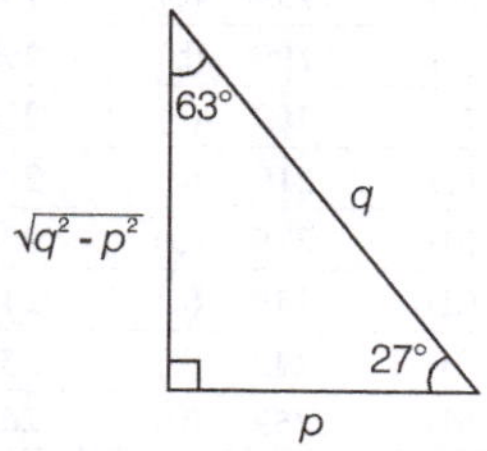

Now, cosec 27° − cos 63°

$$= \frac{q}{\sqrt{q^2-p^2}} - \frac{\sqrt{q^2-p^2}}{q}$$

$$= \frac{q^2-q^2+p^2}{q\sqrt{q^2-p^2}} = \frac{p^2}{q\sqrt{q^2-p^2}}$$

3. (c) Given, in a right-angled triangle PQR. $PQ = 29$ cm, $QR = 21$ cm and $\angle R = 90°$

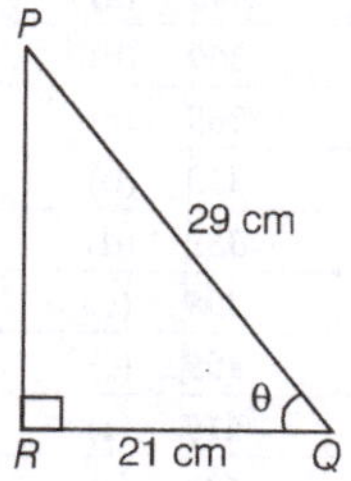

By Pythagoras theorem,

$$PR = \sqrt{(PQ)^2 - (QR)^2}$$

$$PR = \sqrt{(29)^2 - (21)^2}$$

$$PR = \sqrt{841-441} = \sqrt{400} = 20 \text{ cm}$$

Here, $\cos\theta = \frac{21}{29}$ and $\sin\theta = \frac{20}{29}$

$$\therefore \cos^2\theta - \sin^2\theta = \frac{441}{841} - \frac{400}{841} = \frac{41}{841}$$

4. (b) $\frac{\sec\theta - \tan\theta}{\sec\theta + \tan\theta} = \frac{1}{9}$

$\Rightarrow 9\sec\theta - 9\tan\theta = \sec\theta + \tan\theta$

$\Rightarrow \quad 8\sec\theta = 10\tan\theta$

$\Rightarrow \quad \sin\theta = \frac{8}{10} = \frac{4}{5}$

Now, $\frac{\sin\theta - \tan^2\theta}{\sin\theta + \tan^2\theta}$

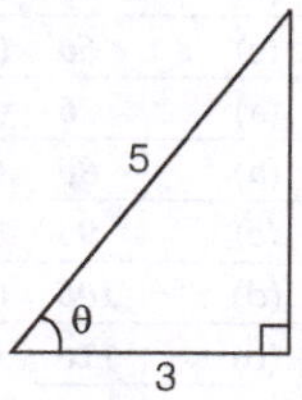

$$= \frac{\frac{4}{5} - \left(\frac{4}{3}\right)^2}{\frac{4}{5} + \left(\frac{4}{3}\right)^2} = \frac{36-80}{36+80} = \frac{-44}{116} = \frac{-11}{29}$$

5. (c) $\tan(x+y)\cdot\tan(x-y) = 1$

$$\tan(x+y) = \frac{1}{\tan(x-y)}$$

$\Rightarrow \tan(x+y) = \cot(x-y)$

$\Rightarrow \tan(x+y) = \tan\,[90° - (x-y)]$

$\Rightarrow \quad x + y = 90° - x + y$

$\Rightarrow \quad 2x = 90° \Rightarrow x = 45°$

$\therefore \quad \tan x = \tan 45° = 1$

> **Speedy Method**
>
> If $\tan A \times \tan B = 1$
>
> Then, $A + B = 90°$
>
> $\therefore\ x + y + x - y = 90° \Rightarrow x = 45°$
>
> $\therefore\ \tan x = \tan 45° = 1$

6. (d)

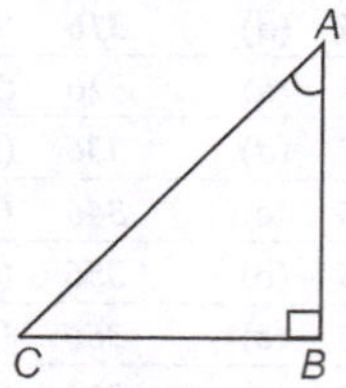

$\because \quad \tan A = \sqrt{3} = \tan 60°$

$\Rightarrow \quad \angle A = 60°$ and $\angle B = 90°$

$\therefore \quad \angle C = 180° - (90° + 60°)$

$\qquad = 180° - 150° = 30°$

Now, $\sin A\cdot\cos C + \cos A\cdot\sin C$

$\qquad = \sin(A+C) = \sin(60° + 30°) = \sin 90° = 1$

and $\cos A\cdot\cos C - \sin A\cdot\sin C$

$\qquad = \cos(A+C) = \cos(60° + 30°) = \cos 90° = 0$

7. (b) We know, $\sin^2\theta + \cos^2\theta = 1$

Squaring both sides, we get

$\sin^4\theta + \cos^4\theta + 2\sin^2\theta\cos^2\theta = 1$

$\sin^4\theta + \cos^4\theta = 1 - 2\sin^2\theta\cos^2\theta$

Now, to get Maximum value of $\sin^4\theta + \cos^4\theta$, $2\sin^2\theta\cos^2\theta$ should be '0'.

$\therefore$ Max value of $\sin^4\theta + \cos^4\theta = 1$

8. (b) We have,

$$x = a\sec\theta\cdot\cos\phi \Rightarrow \frac{x}{a} = \frac{\cos\phi}{\cos\theta} \Rightarrow \frac{x^2}{a^2} = \frac{\cos^2\phi}{\cos^2\theta}$$

$$y = b\sec\theta\sin\phi \Rightarrow \frac{y}{b} = \frac{\sin\phi}{\cos\theta} \Rightarrow \frac{y^2}{b^2} = \frac{\sin^2\phi}{\cos^2\theta}$$

$$z = c\tan\theta \Rightarrow \frac{z}{c} = \tan\theta \Rightarrow \frac{z^2}{c^2} = \tan^2\theta$$

$\therefore$ Required value i.e., $\left(\frac{x^2}{a^2} + \frac{y^2}{b^2} - \frac{z^2}{c^2}\right)$

$$= \frac{\cos^2\phi}{\cos^2\theta} + \frac{\sin^2\phi}{\cos^2\theta} - \tan^2\theta$$

$$= \frac{\cos^2\phi + \sin^2\phi}{\cos^2\theta} - \tan^2\theta$$

$$= \sec^2\theta - \tan^2\theta = 1$$

9. (b) Given, $\cot\theta = \sqrt{11} \Rightarrow \cot^2\theta = 11$

We know,

$\text{cosec}^2\theta - \cot^2\theta = 1 \Rightarrow \text{cosec}^2\theta = 12$

Now, As, $\cot\theta = \sqrt{11} \Rightarrow \tan\theta = \frac{1}{\sqrt{11}}$

$$\sec^2\theta = 1 + \tan^2\theta = 1 + \frac{1}{11} = \frac{12}{11}$$

$$\therefore \frac{\text{cosec}^2\theta - \sec^2\theta}{\text{cosec}^2\theta + \sec^2\theta} = \frac{12 - \frac{12}{11}}{12 + \frac{12}{11}} = \frac{11-1}{11+1}$$

$$= \frac{10}{12} = \frac{5}{6}$$

10. (a) Given, $\cot\theta = \frac{7}{8} = \frac{\text{Base}}{\text{Perpendicular}}$

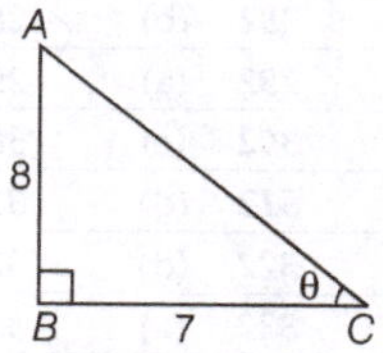

In ΔABC, $AC = \sqrt{AB^2 + BC^2}$

$$= \sqrt{(7)^2 + (8)^2} = \sqrt{113}$$

$\therefore$ Required value $= \frac{1+\sin\theta}{\cos\theta}$

$$= \frac{1 + \frac{8}{\sqrt{113}}}{\frac{7}{\sqrt{113}}} \qquad \left[\because \sin\theta = \frac{\text{Perpendicular}}{\text{Hypotenuse}},\ \cos\theta = \frac{\text{Base}}{\text{Hypotenuse}}\right]$$

$$= \frac{8+\sqrt{113}}{7}$$

11. (a) We have,

$$\frac{\sin^2 C + \cos^2 C}{1 + \cot^2 C} = \frac{1}{1 + \frac{1}{\tan^2 C}} = \frac{1}{1+\frac{1}{3}} = \frac{1}{\frac{4}{3}} = \frac{3}{4}$$

12. (c) $\frac{5}{1+\cot^2\theta} + \frac{3}{1+\tan^2\theta} + 2\cos^2\theta$

$$= \frac{5}{1 + \frac{1}{\tan^2\theta}} + \frac{3}{1+\tan^2\theta} + 2\cos^2\theta$$

$$\left[\because \cot\theta = \frac{1}{\tan\theta}\right]$$

$$= \frac{5\tan^2\theta}{\tan^2\theta+1} + \frac{3}{1+\tan^2\theta} + 2\cos^2\theta$$

$$= \frac{5\tan^2\theta+3}{1+\tan^2\theta} + 2\cos^2\theta$$

$$= \frac{5\sin^2\theta+3\cos^2\theta}{\sin^2\theta+\cos^2\theta} + 2\cos^2\theta \qquad \left[\because \tan\theta = \frac{\sin\theta}{\cos\theta}\right]$$

$$= \frac{2\sin^2\theta+3\sin^2\theta+3\cos^2\theta}{1} + 2\cos^2\theta$$

$$= 3(\sin^2\theta+\cos^2\theta) + 2(\sin^2\theta+\cos^2\theta)$$

$$= 3(1)+2(1) = 5$$

Speedy Method

$$\frac{5}{1+\cot^2\theta} + \frac{3}{1+\tan^2\theta} + 2\cos^2\theta$$

$$\Rightarrow \frac{5}{\text{cosec}^2\theta} + \frac{3}{\sec^2\theta} + 2\cos^2\theta$$

$$\Rightarrow 5\sin^2\theta + 3\cos^2\theta + 2\cos^2\theta$$

$$\Rightarrow 5(\sin^2\theta+\cos^2\theta) \Rightarrow 5\times 1 = 5$$

13. (b) Given, $\tan A + \cot A = 2$

$$\tan A + \frac{1}{\tan A} = 2$$

$$\Rightarrow \tan^2 A + 1 = 2\tan A$$

$$\Rightarrow \tan^2 A - 2\tan A + 1 = 0$$

$$\Rightarrow (\tan A - 1)^2 = 0 \Rightarrow \tan A = 1$$

$$\therefore 7\tan^8 A - 6\cot^8 A + 8\sec^2 A$$

$$= 7\tan^8 A - \frac{6}{\tan^8 A} + 8(1+\tan^2 A) \qquad \left[\because \cot A = \frac{1}{\tan A},\ \sec^2 A = 1+\tan^2 A\right]$$

$$= 7(1)^8 - \frac{6}{(1)^8} + 8(1+(1)^2)$$

$$= 7 - 6 + 16 = 17$$

Speedy Method

$\tan A + \cot A = 2$

Satisfy at $A = 45°$ [$\tan A = 1$ and $\cot A = 1$]

Then, $7\tan^8 A - 6\cot^8 A + 8\sec^2 A$

$= 7\times 1 - 6\times 1 + 8(\sqrt{2})^2 \Rightarrow 1 + 8\times 2 = 17$

14. (a) $\left(\frac{5}{\sqrt{3}} - \text{cosec } 60°\right)$

$$= \frac{5}{\sqrt{3}} - \frac{2}{\sqrt{3}} = \frac{3}{\sqrt{3}} = \sqrt{3}$$

15. (c) $\sec\theta + \tan\theta = x$ ...(i)

We know, $\sec\theta - \tan\theta = \frac{1}{x}$ ...(ii)

Adding both equations, we get

$$2\sec\theta = x + \frac{1}{x} \Rightarrow \frac{2}{\cos\theta} = \frac{x^2+1}{x}$$

$$\cos\theta = \frac{2x}{x^2+1}$$

$$\sin\theta = \sqrt{1-\cos^2\theta} = \sqrt{1-\left(\frac{2x}{x^2+1}\right)^2}$$

$$= \sqrt{\frac{x^4+1-2x^2}{(x^2+1)^2}} = \sqrt{\left(\frac{x^2-1}{x^2+1}\right)^2}$$

$$\sin\theta = \frac{x^2-1}{x^2+1}$$

16. (c) $3\sin 15° - 4\sin^3 15° = \sin(3\times 15°)$

$$[\because \sin 3A = 3\sin A - 4\sin^3 A]$$

$$= \sin 45° = \frac{1}{\sqrt{2}}$$

17. (b) We know that,

$$\tan 45° = \tan(72° - 27°)$$

$$1 = \frac{\tan 72° - \tan 27°}{1+\tan 27°\tan 72°} \qquad \left[\because \tan(A-B) = \frac{\tan A - \tan B}{1+\tan A\cdot\tan B}\right]$$

$$1 + \tan 27°\cdot\tan 72° = \tan 72° - \tan 27°$$

$$\tan 72° - \tan 27° - \tan 27°\cdot\tan 72° = 1$$

18. (a) $\cot^2\theta - 2\cos^2\theta = 0$

$$\frac{\cos^2\theta}{\sin^2\theta} - 2\cos^2\theta = 0$$

$$\frac{1}{\sin^2\theta} - 2 = 0$$

$$\frac{1}{\sin^2\theta} = 2 \Rightarrow \sin^2\theta = \frac{1}{2}$$

$$\Rightarrow \sin\theta = \frac{1}{\sqrt{2}}$$

$$\sin\theta = \sin 45° \Rightarrow \theta = 45°$$

19. (c) $(\text{cosec} - \sin\theta)(\sec\theta - \cos\theta)$

$$(\tan\theta + \cot\theta) = \left(\frac{1}{\sin\theta} - \sin\theta\right)\left(\frac{1}{\cos\theta} - \cos\theta\right)$$

$$\left(\frac{\sin\theta}{\cos\theta} + \frac{\cos\theta}{\sin\theta}\right) = \left(\frac{1-\sin^2\theta}{\sin\theta}\right)\left(\frac{1-\cos^2\theta}{\cos\theta}\right)$$

$$\left(\frac{\sin^2\theta+\cos^2\theta}{\sin\theta\cos\theta}\right) \qquad [\because \sin^2\theta + \cos^2\theta = 1]$$

$$= \frac{\cos^2\theta}{\sin\theta} \times \frac{\sin^2\theta}{\cos\theta} \times \frac{1}{\sin\theta\cos\theta} = 1$$

20. (b) $\frac{2\tan 54°}{\cot 36°} - \frac{\cot 41°}{\tan 49°}$

$$= 2\times\frac{\cot 36°}{\cot 36°} - \frac{\cot 41°}{\cot 41°} \qquad [\because \tan(90° - \theta) = \cot\theta]$$

$$= 2\times 1 - 1 = 1$$

21. (c) $m + 5 = \sec^2 A\,\text{cosec}^2 A(1-\cos^2 A)$

$$(1-\sin^2 A) + 5$$

$$\Rightarrow m + 5 = \left(\frac{1}{\cos^2 A\times\sin^2 A}\sin^2 A\cdot\cos^2 A\right) + 5$$

$$\left[\because 1-\sin^2 A = \cos^2 A,\ 1-\cos^2 A = \sin^2\right]$$

$$\Rightarrow m + 5 = 1 + 5$$

$$\Rightarrow m = 1$$

22. (c) $10\sin^2\theta + 6\cos^2\theta = 7$

$$\Rightarrow 10\sin^2\theta + 6(1-\sin^2\theta) = 7 \qquad [\because \sin^2\theta = 1-\cos^2\theta]$$

$$\Rightarrow 10\sin^2\theta + 6 - 6\sin^2\theta = 7$$

$$\Rightarrow 4\sin^2\theta = 1 \Rightarrow \sin\theta = \frac{1}{2}$$

$$\cos\theta = \sqrt{1-\left(\frac{1}{2}\right)^2} = \sqrt{1-\frac{1}{4}} = \frac{\sqrt{3}}{2}$$

$$\therefore \tan\theta = \frac{\sin\theta}{\cos\theta} = \frac{\frac{1}{2}}{\frac{\sqrt{3}}{2}} = \frac{1}{\sqrt{3}}$$

23. (d) $\frac{1+\sin\theta-\cos\theta}{1+\sin\theta+\cos\theta}$

$$= \frac{1+2\sin\frac{\theta}{2}\cos\frac{\theta}{2} - \left(1-2\sin^2\frac{\theta}{2}\right)}{1+2\sin\frac{\theta}{2}\cos\frac{\theta}{2} + 2\cos^2\frac{\theta}{2} - 1} \qquad \left[\because \sin 2\theta = 2\sin\theta\cos\theta,\ \cos 2\theta = 2\cos^2\theta - 1\right]$$

$$= \frac{1+2\sin\frac{\theta}{2}\cos\frac{\theta}{2} - 1 + 2\sin^2\frac{\theta}{2}}{1+2\sin\frac{\theta}{2}\cdot\cos\frac{\theta}{2} + 2\cos^2\frac{\theta}{2} - 1}$$

$$= \frac{2\sin\frac{\theta}{2}\left(\cos\frac{\theta}{2} + \sin\frac{\theta}{2}\right)}{2\cos\frac{\theta}{2}\left(\sin\frac{\theta}{2} + \cos\frac{\theta}{2}\right)} = \tan\frac{\theta}{2}$$

24. (c) $\frac{11\sqrt{2}\cos 3A + 10\sin 2A}{7\sqrt{3}\sin 4A}$

Where $A = 15°$ (given)

$$= \frac{11\sqrt{2}\cos 45° + 10\sin 30°}{7\sqrt{3}\sin 60°}$$

$$= \frac{11\sqrt{2}\times\frac{1}{\sqrt{2}} + 10\times\frac{1}{2}}{7\sqrt{3}\times\frac{\sqrt{3}}{2}} = \frac{11+5}{\frac{21}{2}} = \frac{32}{21}$$

25. (d) $3\tan A = 4 \Rightarrow \tan A = \frac{4}{3}$

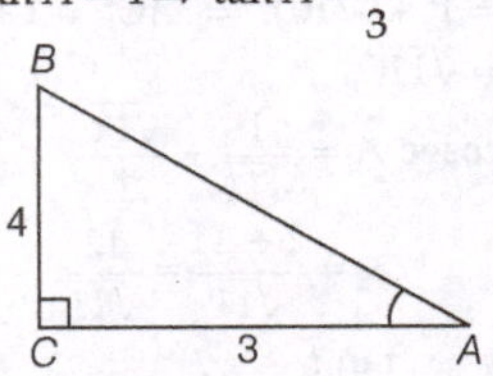

By Pythagoras theorem

$$\therefore (AB)^2 = 4^2 + 3^2 = 25 \Rightarrow AB = 5$$

$$\sin A = \frac{4}{5} \text{ and } \cos A = \frac{3}{5}$$

$$\therefore 4\sin A + 3\cos A = 4\times\frac{4}{5} + 3\times\frac{3}{5}$$

$$= \frac{16}{5} + \frac{9}{5} = \frac{25}{5} = 5$$

26. (b) $(\sin A + \text{cosec } A)^2 + (\cos A + \sec A)^2$

$$[\because (a+b)^2 = a^2 + b^2 + 2ab]$$

$$= \sin^2 A + \text{cosec}^2 A + 2 + \cos^2 A + \sec^2 A + 2$$

$$= 4 + \sin^2 A + \cos^2 A + \text{cosec}^2 A + \sec^2 A$$

$$[\because \sec^2 A - \tan^2 A = 1,\ \text{cosec}^2 A - \cot^2 = 1]$$

$$= 4 + 1 + 1 + \cot^2 A + 1 + \tan^2 A$$

$$= 7 + \cot^2 A + \tan^2 A$$

27. (b) Given, $\tan A + \cot A = 2$

On squaring both sides,

$$\Rightarrow (\tan A + \cot A)^2 = (2)^2$$

$$\Rightarrow \tan^2 A + \cot^2 A + 2 = 4$$

$$\Rightarrow \tan^2 A + \cot^2 A = 2$$

28. (a) $\sin 3A = \cos(A - 26^\circ)$

$\Rightarrow \cos(90^\circ - 3A) = \cos(A - 26^\circ)$

($\because 3A$ is an acute angle)

$\Rightarrow 90^\circ - 3A = A - 26^\circ$

$\Rightarrow 4A = 90^\circ + 26^\circ = 116^\circ \Rightarrow A = 29^\circ$

29. (b) $\dfrac{\sin^2\theta - 2\sin^4\theta}{2\cos^4\theta + \cos^2\theta}$

$\dfrac{\sin^2\theta(1 - 2\sin^2\theta)}{\cos^2\theta(2\cos^2\theta + 1)}$

$\left(\dfrac{\sin\theta}{\cos\theta}\right)^2\left(\dfrac{1 - 2\sin^2\theta}{2\cos^2\theta + 1}\right)$

At $\theta = 45^\circ$

$(\tan 45^\circ)^2\left(\dfrac{1 - 2\sin^2 45^\circ}{2\cos^2 45^\circ + 1}\right) = 1 \times \left(\dfrac{1 - 2\times\frac{1}{2}}{2\times\frac{1}{2} + 1}\right)$

$= 1 \times \left(\dfrac{0}{2}\right) = 0$

30. (c) $\tan A = \dfrac{1}{\sqrt{10}} = \dfrac{AB}{BC}$

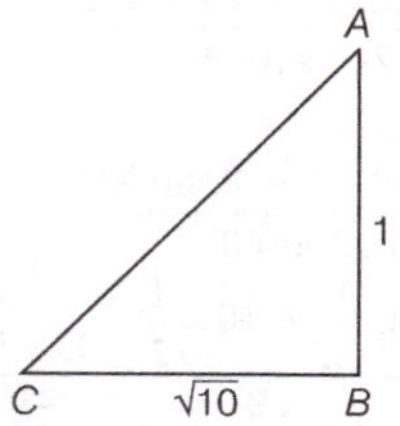

By Pythagoras theorem

$AC^2 = 1^2 + (\sqrt{10})^2 \Rightarrow AC^2 = 1 + 10$

$AC = \sqrt{11}$

$\therefore \sin A + \text{cosec } A = \dfrac{1}{\sqrt{11}} + \dfrac{\sqrt{11}}{1}$

$= \dfrac{1 + 11}{\sqrt{11}} = \dfrac{12}{\sqrt{11}}$

31. (b) $\sin^2 t = \dfrac{\tan t}{2} \Rightarrow \sin t \cos t = \dfrac{1}{2}$

Multiply by 2

$\Rightarrow 2\sin t \cos t = 1 \Rightarrow \sin 2t = \sin 90^\circ$

$\Rightarrow 2t = 90^\circ \Rightarrow t = 45^\circ$

32. (c) $\sin A - \cos A = \dfrac{\sqrt{3} - \sqrt{2}}{2}$

Squaring both sides,

$\Rightarrow (\sin A - \cos A)^2 = \left(\dfrac{\sqrt{3} - \sqrt{2}}{2}\right)^2$

$\Rightarrow \sin^2 A + \cos^2 A - 2\sin A\cos A = \dfrac{3 + 2 - 2\sqrt{6}}{4}$

$\Rightarrow 1 - 2\sin A\cos A = \dfrac{5 - 2\sqrt{6}}{4}$

$\Rightarrow 2\sin A\cos A = 1 - \left(\dfrac{5 - 2\sqrt{6}}{4}\right)$

$\Rightarrow 2\sin A\cos A = \dfrac{4 - 5 + 2\sqrt{6}}{4}$

$\Rightarrow \sin A\cos A = \dfrac{2\sqrt{6} - 1}{8}$

33. (c) $\dfrac{1}{\text{cosec }\theta - \cot\theta} \times \dfrac{\text{cosec }\theta + \cot\theta}{\text{cosec }\theta + \cot\theta} - \dfrac{1}{\sin\theta}$

$= \dfrac{\text{cosec }\theta + \cot\theta}{\text{cosec}^2\theta - \cot^2\theta} - \text{cosec }\theta$

$= \text{cosec }\theta + \cot\theta - \text{cosec }\theta = \cot\theta$

34. (b) Given,

$x = r\cos t,\ y = r\sin t\cos u,\ z = r\sin t\sin u$

$x^2 + y^2 + z^2 = r^2\cos^2 t + r^2\sin^2 t\cos^2 u + r^2\sin^2 t\sin^2 u$

$= r^2\cos^2 t + r^2\sin^2 t(\cos^2 u + \sin^2 u)$

$= r^2\cos^2 t + r^2\sin^2 t = r^2(\sin^2 t + \cos^2 t)$

$= r^2$

35. (c) $\sqrt{3}\cos\theta + \sin\theta = 1$

$\dfrac{\sqrt{3}}{2}\cos\theta + \dfrac{1}{2}\sin\theta = \dfrac{1}{2}$

$\cos 30^\circ\cos\theta + \sin 30^\circ.\sin\theta = \dfrac{1}{2}$

$\cos(\theta - 30)^\circ = \cos 60^\circ$

$[\because \cos(A - B) = \cos A\cdot\cos B + \sin A\cdot\sin B]$

$\theta - 30^\circ = 60^\circ \Rightarrow \theta = 90^\circ$

36. (d) $\tan\theta + \cot\theta = 2 \Rightarrow \tan\theta + \dfrac{1}{\tan\theta} = 2$

$\Rightarrow \tan^2\theta + 1 = 2\tan\theta$

$\Rightarrow \tan^2\theta - 2\tan\theta + 1 = 0$

$\Rightarrow (\tan\theta - 1)^2 = 0 \Rightarrow \tan\theta = 1$

$\Rightarrow \tan\theta = \tan 45^\circ \Rightarrow \theta = 45^\circ$

37. (a) $\sqrt{\dfrac{1 - \cos A}{1 + \cos A}} + \sqrt{\dfrac{1 + \cos A}{1 - \cos A}}$

$= \sqrt{\dfrac{(1 - \cos A)(1 - \cos A)}{1 - \cos^2 A}} + \sqrt{\dfrac{(1 + \cos A)(1 + \cos A)}{1 - \cos^2 A}}$

$= \sqrt{\dfrac{(1 - \cos A)^2}{(\sin A)^2}} + \sqrt{\dfrac{(1 + \cos A)^2}{(\sin A)^2}}$

$= \dfrac{1 - \cos A}{\sin A} + \dfrac{1 + \cos A}{\sin A} = \dfrac{2}{\sin A} = 2\,\text{cosec } A$

38. (c) Given, $\tan\theta = \dfrac{5}{8}$

So, $\dfrac{(1 + \cos\theta)(1 - \cos\theta)}{(1 + \sin\theta)(1 - \sin\theta)} = \dfrac{(1 - \cos^2\theta)}{(1 - \sin^2\theta)} = \dfrac{\sin^2\theta}{\cos^2\theta}$

$= \tan^2\theta = \left(\dfrac{5}{8}\right)^2 = \dfrac{25}{64}$

39. (b) We have, $\dfrac{1 - \sin 2t}{1 + \sin 2t} \times \dfrac{\cos(t) + \sin(t)}{\cos(t) - \sin(t)}$

$= \dfrac{\sin^2(t) + \cos^2(t) - 2\sin(t)\cos(t)}{\sin^2(t) + \cos^2(t) + 2\sin(t)\cos(t)} \times \dfrac{\cos(t) + \sin(t)}{\cos(t) - \sin(t)}$

$(\because \sin^2 t + \cos^2 t = 1)$

$= \dfrac{(\cos(t) - \sin(t))^2}{(\cos(t) + \sin(t))^2} \times \dfrac{(\cos(t) + \sin(t))}{(\cos(t) - \sin(t))}$

$= \dfrac{\cos(t) - \sin(t)}{\cos(t) + \sin(t)} = \dfrac{1 - \dfrac{\sin(t)}{\cos(t)}}{1 + \dfrac{\sin(t)}{\cos(t)}} = \dfrac{1 - \tan(t)}{1 + \tan(t)}$

40. (c) We have, $\left[1 - \sin^2 32^\circ + \dfrac{1}{1 + \tan^2 58^\circ}\right]$

$\left[\because \begin{array}{l}\cos^2\theta = 1 - \sin^2\theta \\ \sec^2\theta = 1 + \tan^2\theta\end{array}\right]$

$= \left[\cos^2 32^\circ + \dfrac{1}{\sec^2 58^\circ}\right]$

$= [\cos^2 32^\circ + \cos^2 58^\circ]$

$= [\cos^2 32^\circ + (\cos(90 - 32)^\circ)^2]$

$= \cos^2 32^\circ + \sin^2 32^\circ = 1$

$[\because \sin^2\theta + \cos^2\theta = 1]$

41. (d) We know, maximum value of

$m\sin\theta + n\cos\theta = \sqrt{m^2 + n^2}$

$\therefore$ Maximum value of $2\sin\theta + 3\cos\theta$

$= \sqrt{(2)^2 + (3)^2} = \sqrt{13}$

42. (d) $3\sin^2\theta + 5\cos^2\theta = 4$

$\Rightarrow 3\sin^2\theta + 3\cos^2\theta + 2\cos^2\theta = 4$

$\Rightarrow 3(\sin^2\theta + \cos^2\theta) + 2\cos^2\theta = 4$

$\Rightarrow 3 + 2\cos^2\theta = 4 \Rightarrow 2\cos^2\theta = 1$

$\Rightarrow \cos^2\theta = \dfrac{1}{2} \Rightarrow \cos\theta = \dfrac{1}{\sqrt{2}} \Rightarrow \cos\theta = \cos 45^\circ$

$\Rightarrow \theta = 45^\circ$

Then, $\tan\theta \Rightarrow \tan 45^\circ = 1$

43. (c) $\sin x + \text{cosec } x = 2$

$\Rightarrow \sin x + \dfrac{1}{\sin x} = 2 \Rightarrow \sin^2 x + 1 = 2\sin x$

$\Rightarrow \sin^2 x - 2\sin x + 1 = 0 \Rightarrow (\sin x - 1)^2 = 0$

$\Rightarrow (\sin x - 1) = 0 \Rightarrow \sin x = 1$

$\Rightarrow \sin x = \sin 90^\circ \Rightarrow x = 90^\circ$

Now, $\sin^7 x + \text{cosec}^7 x$

$(\sin 90^\circ)^7 + (\text{cosec } 90^\circ)^7 \Rightarrow 1 + 1 = 2$

44. (d) Given, $\sin A + \cos A = \sqrt{3}$

Squaring both sides,

$\Rightarrow \sin^2 A + \cos^2 A + 2\sin A\cos A = 3$

$\Rightarrow 1 + 2\sin A\cos A = 3 \Rightarrow 2\sin A\cos A = 2$

$\Rightarrow \sin A\cos A = 1$

Now, $\Rightarrow \tan A + \cot A + 2\sin A\cos A$

$\Rightarrow \dfrac{\sin A}{\cos A} + \dfrac{\cos A}{\sin A} + 2\sin A\cos A$

$\Rightarrow \dfrac{\sin^2 A + \cos^2 A}{\cos A\sin A} + 2\sin A\cos A$

$\Rightarrow \dfrac{1}{1} + 2\times 1 = 1 + 2 = 3$

45. (a) $\sqrt{\dfrac{9\sin^2 26^\circ + 9\sin^2 64^\circ + 36}{32 - 7\cos^2 32^\circ - 7\cos^2 58^\circ}}$

$\Rightarrow \sqrt{\dfrac{9[\sin^2 26^\circ + \sin^2(90^\circ - 26^\circ)] + 36}{32 - 7[\cos^2(90 - 58^\circ) + \cos^2 58^\circ]}}$

$\Rightarrow \sqrt{\dfrac{9(\sin^2 26^\circ + \cos^2 26^\circ) + 36}{32 - 7(\sin^2 58 + \cos^2 58^\circ)}}$

$\Rightarrow \sqrt{\dfrac{9 + 36}{32 - 7}} = \sqrt{\dfrac{45}{25}} = \dfrac{3\sqrt{5}}{5}$

46. (d) We know,

$2\sin A\cdot\sin B = \cos(A - B) - \cos(A + B)$

$\therefore \sin A\cdot\sin B = \dfrac{1}{2}[\cos(A - B) - \cos(A + B)]$

47. (b) $\sqrt{\dfrac{\sec\theta+1}{\sec\theta-1}}+\sqrt{\dfrac{\sec\theta-1}{\sec\theta+1}}$

$=\sqrt{\dfrac{1+\cos\theta}{1-\cos\theta}}+\sqrt{\dfrac{1-\cos\theta}{1+\cos\theta}}$

$=\sqrt{\dfrac{(1+\cos\theta)(1+\cos\theta)}{1-\cos^2\theta}}+\sqrt{\dfrac{(1-\cos\theta)(1-\cos\theta)}{1-\cos^2\theta}}$

$=\dfrac{1+\cos\theta}{\sin\theta}+\dfrac{1-\cos\theta}{\sin\theta}=\dfrac{2}{\sin\theta}=2\text{ cosec }\theta$

48. (b) Given, $\tan\theta=\dfrac{8}{15}$

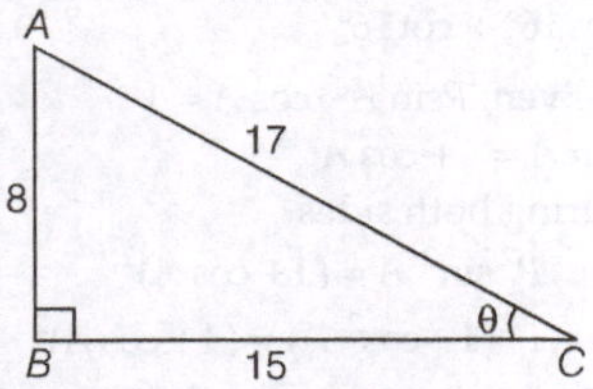

$\therefore\ AC=\sqrt{8^2+15^2}=\sqrt{64+225}=\sqrt{289}=17$

Now, $\dfrac{\sqrt{1-\sin\theta}}{\sqrt{1+\sin\theta}}\times\dfrac{\sqrt{1-\sin\theta}}{\sqrt{1-\sin\theta}}=\dfrac{1-\sin\theta}{\sqrt{1-\sin^2\theta}}$

$\Rightarrow\ \dfrac{1-\sin\theta}{\cos\theta}=\dfrac{1}{\cos\theta}-\tan\theta$

$=\dfrac{17}{15}-\dfrac{8}{15}=\dfrac{9}{15}=\dfrac{3}{5}\quad\left(\because\cos\theta=\dfrac{15}{17}\right)$

49. (d) $\dfrac{\sin A}{1+\cos A}+\cot A=\dfrac{\sin A}{1+\cos A}+\dfrac{\cos A}{\sin A}$

$=\dfrac{\sin^2 A+\cos A(1+\cos A)}{(1+\cos A)\sin A}=\dfrac{(1+\cos A)}{(1+\cos A)\sin A}$

$=\dfrac{1}{\sin A}=\text{cosec }A$

50. (a) Given, $3\sin A+4\cos A=5$

$\Rightarrow\ \dfrac{3}{5}\sin A+\dfrac{4}{5}\cos A=1$

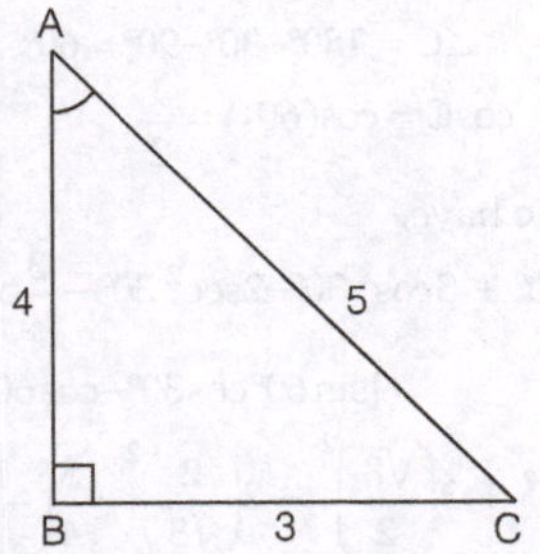

As, $\sin A\cdot\sin A+\cos A\cdot\cos A=1$

$\Rightarrow\ \sin^2 A+\cos^2 A=1$

$\therefore\ \sin A=\dfrac{3}{5}$ and $\cos A=\dfrac{4}{5}\Rightarrow\tan A=\dfrac{\frac{3}{5}}{\frac{4}{5}}=\dfrac{3}{4}$

51. (a) We know, $\tan(t)=\sqrt{\sec^2(t)-1}$

$=\sqrt{\left(\dfrac{x}{y}\right)^2-1}=\dfrac{\sqrt{x^2-y^2}}{y}$

As, $\cot(t)=\dfrac{1}{\tan(t)}=\dfrac{1}{\frac{\sqrt{x^2-y^2}}{y}}=\dfrac{y}{\sqrt{x^2-y^2}}$

52. (b) $\sin\theta+\cos\theta=\sqrt{3}\cos\theta$

$\sin\theta=(\sqrt{3}-1)\cos\theta$

$\dfrac{\cos\theta}{\sin\theta}=\dfrac{1}{\sqrt{3}-1}\Rightarrow\cot\theta=\dfrac{1}{\sqrt{3}-1}\times\dfrac{\sqrt{3}+1}{\sqrt{3}+1}$

$\cot\theta=\dfrac{\sqrt{3}+1}{2}$

53. (b) $\text{cosec }x=\dfrac{5}{4}$

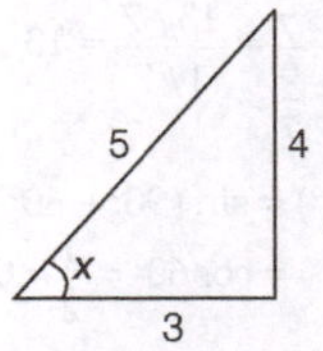

$\sin x=\dfrac{4}{5}$ and $\cos x=\dfrac{3}{5}$

$\dfrac{5\sin^2 x+8\cot^2 x}{27\tan^2 x-125\cos^2 x}=\dfrac{5\left(\frac{4}{5}\right)^2+8\left(\frac{3}{4}\right)^2}{27\left(\frac{4}{3}\right)^2-125\left(\frac{3}{5}\right)^2}$

$=\dfrac{5\times\frac{16}{25}+8\times\frac{9}{16}}{27\times\frac{16}{9}-125\times\frac{9}{25}}=\dfrac{\frac{16}{5}+\frac{9}{2}}{48-45}=\dfrac{\frac{32+45}{10}}{3}$

$=\dfrac{77}{30}$

54. (c) $a=x\cos\theta+y\sin\theta,\ b=x\sin\theta-y\cos\theta$

Then, $a^2+b^2=(x\cos\theta+y\sin\theta)^2+(x\sin\theta-y\cos\theta)^2$

$=x^2\cos^2\theta+y^2\sin^2\theta+2xy\cos\theta\sin\theta+x^2\sin^2\theta+y^2\cos^2\theta-2xy\sin\theta\cos\theta$

$=x^2\cos^2\theta+x^2\sin^2\theta+y^2\sin^2\theta+y^2\cos^2\theta$

$=x^2(\cos^2\theta+\sin^2\theta)+y^2(\sin^2\theta+\cos^2\theta)$

$=x^2+y^2$

55. (a) $\left[\dfrac{4\cos(90-\theta)\sin^3(90+\theta)-4\sin(90+\theta)\cos^3(90-\theta)}{\cos\left(\frac{180+8\theta}{2}\right)}\right]$

$\left[\dfrac{4\sin\theta\cos^3\theta-4\cos\theta\sin^3\theta}{\cos(90^\circ+4\theta)}\right]$

$\left[\dfrac{4\sin\theta\cos^3\theta-4\cos\theta\sin^3\theta}{-\sin4\theta}\right]$

$\left[\dfrac{4\sin\theta\cos^3\theta-4\cos\theta\sin^3\theta}{-2\sin2\theta\cos2\theta}\right]$

$\left[\dfrac{4\sin\theta\cos^3\theta-4\cos\theta\sin^3\theta}{-2(2\sin\theta\cos\theta)(\cos^2\theta-\sin^2\theta)}\right]$

$\left[\dfrac{4\sin\theta\cos\theta(\cos^2\theta-\sin^2\theta)}{-4\sin\theta\cos\theta(\cos^2\theta-\sin^2\theta)}\right]$

$=\dfrac{4}{-4}=-1$

56. (a) $\sin A+\cos A=\dfrac{1}{2\sqrt{2}}$

Squaring on both sides,

$(\sin A+\cos A)^2=\left(\dfrac{1}{2\sqrt{2}}\right)^2$

$\sin^2 A+\cos^2 A+2\sin A\cos A=\dfrac{1}{8}$

$1+2\sin A\cos A=\dfrac{1}{8}\Rightarrow2\sin A\cos A=\dfrac{1}{8}-1$

$\sin A\cos A=-\dfrac{7}{8\times2}\Rightarrow\sin A\cos A=-\dfrac{7}{16}$

Now, $\sin^4 A+\cos^4 A$

$\Rightarrow\ (\sin^2 A+\cos^2 A)^2=(1)^2$

$\Rightarrow\ \sin^4 A+\cos^4 A+2\sin^2\cos^2 A=(1)$

$\Rightarrow\ \sin^4 A+\cos^4 A+2\times\left(-\dfrac{7}{16}\right)^2=1$

$\Rightarrow\ \sin^4 A+\cos^4 A=1-2\times\dfrac{49}{256}$

$\Rightarrow\ \sin^4 A+\cos^4 A=\dfrac{79}{128}$

57. (d) $\cos24^\circ=\dfrac{m}{n}$

$\sin24^\circ=\sqrt{1-\dfrac{m^2}{n^2}}=\sqrt{\dfrac{n^2-m^2}{n^2}}$

$\sin24^\circ=\cos66^\circ=\dfrac{\sqrt{n^2-m^2}}{n}$

$\therefore\ (\text{cosec }24^\circ-\cos66^\circ)$

$=\dfrac{n}{\sqrt{n^2-m^2}}-\dfrac{\sqrt{n^2-m^2}}{n}=\dfrac{n^2-n^2+m^2}{n\sqrt{n^2-m^2}}$

$=\dfrac{m^2}{n\sqrt{n^2-m^2}}$

58. (b) $\sec\theta=\dfrac{29}{20}\Rightarrow\cos\theta=\dfrac{20}{29}$

$\sin\theta=\sqrt{1-\left(\dfrac{20}{29}\right)^2}=\sqrt{\dfrac{841-400}{29\times29}}$

$\sin\theta=\sqrt{\dfrac{441}{29\times29}}=\dfrac{21}{29}$

$\cot\theta=\dfrac{20}{29}\times\dfrac{29}{21}=\dfrac{20}{21}$

Thus, $3\text{ cosec }\theta+3\cot\theta$

$=3\times\dfrac{29}{21}+3\times\dfrac{20}{21}=\dfrac{29}{7}+\dfrac{20}{7}=\dfrac{49}{7}=7$

59. (d) $m=a\sec A,\ y=b\tan A$

$=b^2m^2-a^2y^2+\dfrac{a^2y^2}{b^2m^2}+\cos^2 A$

$=b^2a^2\sec^2 A-a^2b^2\tan^2 A+\dfrac{a^2b^2\tan^2 A}{b^2a^2\sec^2 A}+\cos^2 A$

$=a^2b^2(\sec^2 A-\tan^2 A)+\sin^2 A+\cos^2 A$

$=a^2b^2+1\quad\left[\begin{array}{l}\therefore\sec^2\theta-\tan^2\theta=1\\ \sin^2\theta+\cos^2\theta=1\end{array}\right]$

60. (b) $\left(\dfrac{\text{cosec }A}{\text{cosec }A-1}+\dfrac{\text{cosec }A}{\text{cosec }A+1}\right)\left(\dfrac{\sec A}{\sec A-1}+\dfrac{\sec A}{\sec A+1}\right)^{-1}$

$=\left(\dfrac{\text{cosec}^2 A+\text{cosec }A+\text{cosec}^2 A-\text{cosec}A}{\text{cosec}^2 A-1}\right)\left(\dfrac{\sec^2 A+\sec A+\sec^2 A-\sec A}{\sec^2 A-1}\right)^{-1}$

$$= \left(\frac{2\operatorname{cosec}^2 A}{\operatorname{cosec}^2 A - 1}\right) \times \left(\frac{2\sec^2 A}{\sec^2 A - 1}\right)^{-1}$$

$$= 2 \times \frac{\operatorname{cosec}^2 A}{\operatorname{cosec}^2 A - 1} \times \frac{\sec^2 A - 1}{2\sec^2 A}$$

$$= \cot^2 A \times \frac{\tan^2 A}{\cot^2 A} = \tan^2 A$$

$$= \tan^2 60^\circ = (\sqrt{3})^2 = 3 \quad [\because A = 60^\circ]$$

61. (a) $\dfrac{7\sin A - 3\cos A}{7\sin A + 3\cos A} + 4$

$$= \frac{7\tan A - 3}{7\tan A + 3} + 4 = \frac{7 \times \frac{5}{7} - 3}{7 \times \frac{5}{7} + 3} + 4$$

$$= \frac{5-3}{5+3} + 4 = \frac{2}{8} + 4 = 4\frac{1}{4}$$

62. (d) $\sin B = \dfrac{15}{17}$

$$\cos B = \sqrt{1 - \sin^2 B} = \sqrt{1 - \left(\frac{15}{17}\right)^2} = \frac{8}{17}$$

$\therefore \quad \sec B = \dfrac{17}{8} \Rightarrow \tan B = \dfrac{\sin B}{\cos B} = \dfrac{15}{8}$

$\therefore \quad \cos B(\sec B - \tan B)$

$$= \frac{8}{17}\left(\frac{17}{8} - \frac{15}{8}\right) = \frac{8}{17} \times \frac{2}{8} = \frac{2}{17}$$

Speedy Method

$\cos B(\sec B - \tan B) = 1 - \sin B$

$= 1 - \dfrac{15}{17} = \dfrac{2}{17}$

63. (b) $\dfrac{\tan x}{\sec x} = \dfrac{1}{2} \Rightarrow \dfrac{\sin x / \cos x}{1/\cos x} = \dfrac{1}{2}$

$$\sin x = \frac{1}{2} \Rightarrow \sin x = \sin 30^\circ \Rightarrow x = 30^\circ$$

$$(\sin x + \cos x)^2 = (\sin 30^\circ + \cos 30^\circ)^2$$

$$= \left(\frac{1}{2} + \frac{\sqrt{3}}{2}\right)^2 = \left(\frac{\sqrt{3}+1}{2}\right)^2$$

$$= \frac{3 + 1 + 2\sqrt{3}}{4} = \frac{\sqrt{3}+2}{2}$$

64. (a) Given, $\dfrac{1}{1-\sin\theta} + \dfrac{1}{1+\sin\theta} = 4\sec\theta$

$\Rightarrow \dfrac{1 + \sin\theta + 1 - \sin\theta}{1 - \sin^2\theta} = 4\sec\theta$

$\Rightarrow \dfrac{2}{\cos^2\theta} = 4\sec\theta \Rightarrow 2\sec^2\theta = 4\sec\theta$

$\Rightarrow \sec\theta = 2 \Rightarrow \sec\theta = \sec 60^\circ$

$\therefore \quad \theta = 60^\circ$

Now, $\cot 60^\circ + \operatorname{cosec} 60^\circ = \dfrac{1}{\sqrt{3}} + \dfrac{2}{\sqrt{3}}$

$$= \frac{3}{\sqrt{3}} = \sqrt{3}$$

65. (c) $p(\sqrt{3} + \cot 30^\circ) = \tan^3 60^\circ - 2\sin 60^\circ$

$$p(\sqrt{3} + \sqrt{3}) = (\sqrt{3})^3 - 2 \times \frac{\sqrt{3}}{2}$$

$$(2\sqrt{3})p = 3\sqrt{3} - \sqrt{3} = 2\sqrt{3}$$

$$p = 1$$

66. (d) $\tan 4\theta \cdot \tan 6\theta = 1$

$$\tan 4\theta = \frac{1}{\tan 6\theta} = \cot 6\theta$$

$$\tan 4\theta = \tan(90 - 6\theta) \Rightarrow 4\theta = 90 - 6\theta$$

$$10\theta = 90 \Rightarrow 5\theta = 45^\circ$$

$\Rightarrow \cot 45^\circ = 1$

67. (c) $7\cos A = 6 \Rightarrow \cos A = \dfrac{6}{7}$

Then, $\dfrac{\operatorname{cosec} A + \cot A}{\operatorname{cosec} A - \cot A} = \dfrac{(1 + \cos A)/\sin A}{1 - \cos A/\sin A}$

$$= \frac{1 + \frac{6}{7}}{1 - \frac{6}{7}} = \frac{13/7}{1/7} = 13$$

68. (b) $\sin(150^\circ) = \sin(90^\circ + 60^\circ)$

$$= \cos 60^\circ = \frac{1}{2} = 0.5$$

69. (b) Given, $\cot^4\phi - \cot^2\phi = 1$

$\Rightarrow \cot^4\phi = 1 + \cot^2\phi \Rightarrow \dfrac{\cos^4\phi}{\sin^4\phi} = \operatorname{cosec}^2\phi$

$\Rightarrow \dfrac{\cos^4\phi}{\sin^4\phi} = \dfrac{1}{\sin^2\phi}$

$\Rightarrow \cos^4\phi = \sin^2\phi \quad \ldots(i)$

Now, $\cos^4\phi + \cos^2\phi$

$= \sin^2\phi + 1 - \sin^2\phi \quad$ (from Eq. (i))

$= 1$

70. (a) $\dfrac{1}{1+\cos\theta} + \dfrac{1}{1-\cos\theta}$

$$= \frac{1 - \cos\theta + 1 + \cos\theta}{(1+\cos\theta)(1-\cos\theta)} = \frac{2}{1 - \cos^2\theta}$$

$$= \frac{2}{\sin^2\theta} = 2\operatorname{cosec}^2\theta$$

71. (d) $\left[\dfrac{\sin\theta - 2\sin^3\theta}{2\cos^3\theta - \cos\theta}\right]^3 \times \dfrac{1}{\tan\theta} - \sec^2\theta$

$$= \left[\frac{\sin\theta(1 - 2\sin^2\theta)}{\cos\theta(2\cos^2\theta - 1)}\right]^3 \times \frac{1}{\tan\theta} - \sec^2\theta$$

$$= \left[\frac{\sin\theta(1 - 2\sin^2\theta)}{\cos\theta[2(1 - \sin^2\theta) - 1]}\right]^3 \times \frac{1}{\tan\theta} - \sec^2\theta$$

$$= \left[\frac{\sin\theta(1 - 2\sin^2\theta)}{\cos\theta(1 - 2\sin^2\theta)}\right]^3 \times \frac{1}{\tan\theta} - \sec^2\theta$$

$$= \tan^3\theta \times \frac{1}{\tan\theta} - \sec^2\theta = \tan^2\theta - \sec^2\theta = -1$$

72. (c) According to the question,

$2\operatorname{cosec}^2\theta + 3\cot^2\theta = 17$

$\Rightarrow 2\operatorname{cosec}^2\theta + 3(\operatorname{cosec}^2\theta - 1) = 17$

$\Rightarrow 2\operatorname{cosec}^2\theta + 3\operatorname{cosec}^2\theta - 3 = 17$

$\Rightarrow 5\operatorname{cosec}^2\theta = 20 \Rightarrow \operatorname{cosec}^2\theta = 4$

$\Rightarrow \operatorname{cosec}\theta = 2 \quad (\because 0^\circ \le \theta \le 90^\circ)$

$\Rightarrow \operatorname{cosec}\theta = \operatorname{cosec} 30^\circ$

$\Rightarrow \theta = 30^\circ$

73. (b) Given, $\tan A + \tan B = p$

$\cot A + \cot B = q \quad \ldots(i)$

$\Rightarrow \dfrac{1}{\tan A} + \dfrac{1}{\tan B} = q$

$\Rightarrow \dfrac{\tan B + \tan A}{\tan A \cdot \tan B} = q$

$$\frac{p}{\tan A \cdot \tan B} = q$$

$\Rightarrow \cot A \cot B = \dfrac{q}{p} \quad \ldots(ii)$

Now, $\cot(A + B) = \dfrac{\cot A \cot B - 1}{\cot A + \cot B}$

$$= \frac{\frac{q}{p} - 1}{q} = \frac{q - p}{pq}$$

74. (d) $\sin 74^\circ + \tan 74^\circ$

$= \sin(90 - 16)^\circ + \tan(90 - 16)^\circ$

$[\because \sin(90^\circ - \theta) = \cos\theta, \tan(90^\circ - \theta) = \cot\theta]$

$= \cos 16^\circ + \cot 16^\circ$

75. (a) Given, $P\sin A - \cos A = 1$

$P\sin A = 1 + \cos A$

On squaring both sides

$P^2\sin^2 A = (1 + \cos A)^2$

$\Rightarrow P^2(1 - \cos^2 A) = (1 + \cos A)^2$

$\Rightarrow P^2(1 + \cos A)(1 - \cos A) = (1 + \cos A)^2$

$\Rightarrow P^2(1 - \cos A) = (1 + \cos A)$

$\Rightarrow P^2 - P^2\cos A - \cos A = 1$

$\Rightarrow P^2 - (P^2 + 1)\cos A = 1$

76. (d) According to the question,

$\angle ABC = 90^\circ$ and $\sin A = \dfrac{1}{2}$

$\Rightarrow \sin A = \sin 30^\circ \Rightarrow A = 30^\circ$

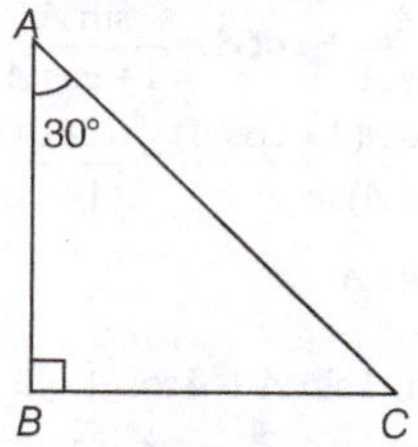

In ΔABC, $\angle C = 180^\circ - \angle A - \angle B$

$\Rightarrow \angle C = 180^\circ - 30^\circ - 90^\circ = 60^\circ$

$\therefore \cos C = \cos(60^\circ) = \dfrac{1}{2}$

77. (a) We have,

$$\left[\frac{4}{3}\tan^2 60^\circ + 3\cos^2 30^\circ - 2\sec^2 30^\circ - \frac{3}{4}\cot^2 60^\circ\right] + [\sin 60^\circ \cos 30^\circ - \cos 60^\circ \sin 30^\circ]$$

$$= \left[\frac{4}{3}(\sqrt{3})^2 + 3\left(\frac{\sqrt{3}}{2}\right)^2 - 2\left(\frac{2}{\sqrt{3}}\right)^2 - \frac{3}{4}\left(\frac{1}{\sqrt{3}}\right)^2\right] \div \left[\frac{\sqrt{3}}{2} \times \frac{\sqrt{3}}{2} - \frac{1}{2} \cdot \frac{1}{2}\right]$$

$$= \left[\frac{4}{3} \times 3 + 3\left(\frac{3}{4}\right) - 2\left(\frac{4}{3}\right) - \frac{3}{4}\left(\frac{1}{3}\right)\right] \div \left[\frac{3}{4} - \frac{1}{4}\right]$$

$$= \left[4 + \frac{9}{4} - \frac{8}{3} - \frac{1}{4}\right] \div \left[\frac{1}{2}\right]$$

$$= \left[4 + 2 - \frac{8}{3}\right] \div \left(\frac{1}{2}\right) = \left(\frac{18 - 8}{3}\right) \times 2$$

$$= \frac{10}{3} \times 2 = \frac{20}{3} = 6\frac{2}{3}$$

78. (d) According to the question,

$(\text{cosec } 56° \cos 34° - \cos 59° \text{ cosec } 31°)$

$= (\text{cosec } 56° \cos(90°-56°) - \cos(90°-31°) \text{ cosec } 31°)$

$= (\text{cosec } 56° \sin 56° - \sin 31° \text{cosec } 31°)$ $[\because \cos(90° - \theta) = \sin\theta]$

$= \left(\frac{1}{\sin 56°} \cdot \sin 56° - \sin 31° \cdot \frac{1}{\sin 31°}\right)$ $\left[\because \text{cosec } \theta = \frac{1}{\sin\theta}\right]$

$= (1 - 1) = 0$

79. (b) Given,

$a\sin^3 x + b\cos^3 x = \sin x \cos x$ ...(i)

and $a\sin x = b\cos x$ ...(ii)

From Eqs. (i) and (ii),

$b\cos x \times \sin^2 x + b\cos x \times \cos^2 x = \sin x \cdot \cos x$

$\Rightarrow b\cos x(\sin^2 x + \cos^2 x) = \sin x \cdot \cos x$

$\Rightarrow b\cos x = \sin x \cdot \cos x$

$\Rightarrow \sin x = b$ $(\because x \text{ is neither 0 nor } 90°)$

Put $\sin x = b$ in Eq. (ii),

$a \times b = b\cos x \Rightarrow \cos x = a$

$\therefore a^2 + b^2 = \sin^2 x + \cos^2 x = 1$

80. (a) $\frac{\sec 35°}{\text{cosec } 55°} - \frac{\cos 25°}{\sin 65°} = \frac{\sin 55°}{\cos 35°} - \frac{\cos 25°}{\sin 65°}$

$= \frac{\sin 55°}{\cos(90°-55°)} - \frac{\cos(90°-65°)}{\sin 65°}$

$= \frac{\sin 55°}{\sin 55°} - \frac{\sin 65°}{\sin 65°}$

$[\because \sin(90° - \theta) = \cos\theta \text{ and } \cos(90° - \theta) = \sin\theta]$

$= 1 - 1 = 0$

81. (a) Given, $7 \tan\theta = 3 \Rightarrow \tan\theta = \frac{3}{7}$

$\frac{5\sin\theta - \cos\theta}{5\sin\theta + 2\cos\theta}$

$= \frac{5\tan\theta - 1}{5\tan\theta + 2} = \frac{\left[5\left(\frac{3}{7}\right) - 1\right]}{\left[5\left(\frac{3}{7}\right) + 2\right]} = \frac{15 - 7}{15 + 14} = \frac{8}{29}$

82. (a) Given, $7\cos^2\theta + 5\sin^2\theta - 6 = 0$

$\Rightarrow 7(1 - \sin^2\theta) + 5\sin^2\theta - 6 = 0$

$\Rightarrow 7 - 7\sin^2\theta + 5\sin^2\theta - 6 = 0$

$\Rightarrow \sin\theta = \frac{1}{\sqrt{2}} \Rightarrow \theta = 45°$

$\therefore 1 + \sqrt{\frac{\sec 45° + \tan 45°}{\sec 45° - \tan 45°}}$

$= 1 + \sqrt{\frac{(\sqrt{2}+1)}{(\sqrt{2}-1)} \times \frac{(\sqrt{2}+1)}{(\sqrt{2}+1)}}$

$= 1 + \sqrt{\frac{(\sqrt{2}+1)^2}{1}} = 1 + \sqrt{2} + 1 = 2 + \sqrt{2}$

83. (d) According to the question,

$\frac{3\sin 58°}{5\cos 32°} + \frac{2\cos 62°}{5\sin 28°}$

$= \frac{3\sin(90° - 32°)}{5\cos 32°} + \frac{2\cos(90° - 28°)}{5\sin 28°}$

$= \frac{3\cos 32°}{5\cos 32°} + \frac{2\sin 28°}{5\sin 28°} = \frac{3}{5} + \frac{2}{5} = \frac{5}{5} = 1$

84. (b) Given, $p\cos A = 2q\sin A$

$2p\text{cosec } A = 4q\sec A$ ...(i)

$2p\text{cosec } A - q\sec A = 3$

$4q\sec A - q\sec A = 3$ [from Eq. (i)]

$3q\sec A = 3$

$q = \cos A$

Put the value of q in Eq. (i)

$p = 2\sin A$

$p^2 + 4q^2 = 4\sin^2 A + 4\cos^2 A = 4$

85. (a) Given, $\cot\theta = \frac{4}{3}$

Then, $\frac{[\sec\theta(1 + \cot^2\theta)(\text{cosec}^2\theta - \cot^2\theta]}{\text{cosec}^3\theta}$

$= \frac{(\sec\theta \times \text{cosec}^2\theta \times 1)}{(\text{cosec}^3\theta)}$ $(\because \text{cosec}^2\theta - \cot^2\theta = 1)$

$= \frac{\sec\theta}{\text{cosec }\theta} = \frac{\sin\theta}{\cos\theta} = \tan\theta = \frac{1}{\cot\theta} = \frac{1}{\frac{4}{3}} = \frac{3}{4}$

86. (c) For option (c),

Let $t = 30°$ $[\because 0° < t < 90°, t < 45°]$

$\sin 30° < \cos 30° \Rightarrow \frac{1}{2} < \frac{\sqrt{3}}{2}$ (True)

Hence, option (c) is correct.

87. (b) $\frac{2 + \tan^2 2A + \cot^2 2A}{\sec 2A \cdot \text{cosec } 2A}$

$\Rightarrow \frac{(\tan 2A + \cot 2A)^2}{\sec 2A \cdot \text{cosec} 2A} = \frac{\left(\frac{\sin 2A}{\cos 2A} + \frac{\cos 2A}{\sin 2A}\right)^2}{\sec 2A \text{cosec } 2A}$

$= \left(\frac{\sin^2 2A + \cos^2 2A}{\sin 2A \cdot \cos 2A}\right)^2 \times \cos 2A \cdot \sin 2A$

$= \frac{\cos 2A \times \sin 2A}{(\sin 2A \cdot \cos 2A)^2}$ $[\because \sin^2 A + \cos^2 A = 1]$

$= \frac{1}{\sin 2A \cdot \cos 2A} = \sec 2A \cdot \text{cosec } 2A$

88. (b) $\frac{7\sin\theta + 4\cos\theta}{9\sin\theta - 2\cos\theta} = \frac{5}{4}$

$\Rightarrow 4(7\sin\theta + 4\cos\theta) = 5(9\sin\theta - 2\cos\theta)$

$\Rightarrow 28\sin\theta + 16\cos\theta = 45\sin\theta - 10\cos\theta$

$\Rightarrow 45\sin\theta - 28\sin\theta = 16\cos\theta + 10\cos\theta$

$\Rightarrow 17\sin\theta = 26\cos\theta$

$\Rightarrow \frac{\sin\theta}{\cos\theta} = \frac{26}{17} \Rightarrow \tan\theta = \frac{26}{17}$

Now, $\frac{\tan^2\theta + 5}{\tan^2\theta - 5} = \frac{\left(\frac{26}{17}\right)^2 + 5}{\left(\frac{26}{17}\right)^2 - 5} = \frac{\frac{676}{289} + 5}{\frac{676}{289} - 5}$

$= \frac{676 + 289 \times 5}{676 - 289 \times 5} = \frac{676 + 1445}{676 - 1445} = \frac{-2121}{769}$

89. (a) $\frac{\sin A}{1 + \cos A}$ (where, A is an acute angle)

$= \frac{\sin A}{1 + \cos A}\left(\frac{1 - \cos A}{1 - \cos A}\right) = \frac{\sin A(1 - \cos A)}{1 - \cos^2 A}$

$= \frac{\sin A(1 - \cos A)}{\sin^2 A}$ $[\because 1 - \cos^2 A = \sin^2 A]$

$= \frac{1 - \cos A}{\sin A}$

90. (a) We have, $\frac{\sin^3 A - \cos^3 A}{\sin A - \cos A}$

$= \frac{(\sin A - \cos A)(\sin^2 A + \cos^2 A + \sin A\cos A)}{(\sin A - \cos A)}$

$[\because a^3 - b^3 = (a - b)(a^2 + b^2 + ab)]$

$= \sin^2 A + \cos^2 A + \sin A\cos A$

$= 1 + \sin A\cos A$ $[\because \sin^2 A + \cos^2 A = 1]$

91. (c) $\text{cosec }\theta = \frac{5}{3}$

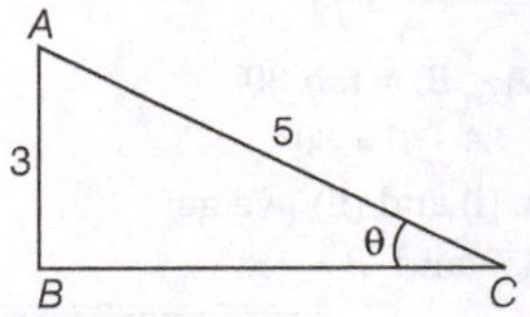

By Pythagoras theorem,

$BC^2 = AC^2 - AB^2$

$\Rightarrow BC^2 = 25 - 9 = 16$

$BC = 4$

$\cot\theta = \frac{4}{3}$

$\therefore (\sec^2\theta - 1) \times \cot^2\theta \times (1 + \cot^2\theta)$

$= \tan^2\theta \times \cot^2\theta \times \left(1 + \left(\frac{4}{3}\right)^2\right)$

$= 1 \times \left(\frac{25}{9}\right) = \frac{25}{9}$

92. (d) $\sin^2 30° - \sin^2 40° + \sin^2 45° - \sin^2 55° - \sin^2 35° + \sin^2 45° - \sin^2 50° + \sin^2 60°$

$= \cos^2 60° - \sin^2 40° + \sin^2 45° - \sin^2 55° - \sin^2 35° + \cos^2 45° - \cos^2 40° + \sin^2 60°$

$= (\cos^2 60° + \sin^2 60°) + (\sin^2 45° + \cos^2 45°) - (\cos^2 40° + \sin^2 40°) - (\sin^2 55° + \cos^2 55°)$

$\left[\because \sin^2(90° - \theta) = \cos^2\theta, \ \cos^2(90° - \theta) = \sin^2\theta\right]$

$= 1 + 1 - 1 - 1 = 0$ $[\because \sin^2\theta + \cos^2\theta = 1]$

93. (c) $\cos^2 29° + \cos^2 61°$

$= \cos^2(90° - 61°) + \cos^2 61°$

$[\because \sin^2\theta + \cos^2\theta = 1]$

$= \sin^2 61° + \cos^2 61° = 1$

94. (b) $p = a\cot\theta + b\text{cosec }\theta$ ...(i)

$q = b\cot\theta + a\text{ cosec }\theta$ ...(ii)

$p^2 - q^2 = (a\cot\theta + b\text{cosec }\theta)^2 - (b\cot\theta + a\text{ cosec }\theta)^2$

$= a^2\cot^2\theta + b^2\text{cosec}^2\theta + 2ab\cot\theta\text{cosec }\theta - b^2\cot^2\theta - a^2\text{cosec}^2\theta - 2ab\cot\theta\text{cosec }\theta$

$p^2 - q^2 = a^2(\cot^2\theta - \text{cosec}^2\theta) + b^2(\text{cosec}^2\theta - \cot^2\theta)$

$= a^2(-1) + b^2(1)$

$p^2 - q^2 = b^2 - a^2$

95. (c) (i) $\text{cosec}^2\theta - \cot^2\theta = 1$

(ii) $\sin^2\theta + \cos^2\theta = 1$

(iii) $\sec^2\theta + \cos^2\theta = 1$, $\sec^2\theta = 1 - \cos^2\theta$

$\sec^2\theta \neq \sin^2\theta$

So, incorrect option is (c).

96. (c) $\sin 25° \sin 65° - \cos 25° \cos 65°$

$= -(\cos 25° \cos 65° - \sin 25° \sin 65°)$

$= -\cos(25° + 65°) = -\cos 90°$

$= -1 \times 0 = 0$

$[\because \cos(A+B) = \cos A \cos B - \sin A \sin B]$

97. (a) $\tan(A+B) = \sqrt{3}$

$\tan(A+B) = \tan 60°$

$A + B = 60°$ ...(i)

$\tan(A-B) = \frac{1}{\sqrt{3}}$

$\tan(A-B) = \tan 30°$

$A - B = 30°$ ...(ii)

From Eqs. (i) and (ii), we get

$A = 45°$ and $B = 15°$

98. (a) Given, $\sqrt{2+\sqrt{2+\sqrt{2+2\cos 8\theta}}}$

$[\because \cos 2\theta = 2\cos^2\theta - 1]$

$= \sqrt{2+\sqrt{2+\sqrt{2+2(2\cos^2 4\theta - 1)}}}$

$= \sqrt{2+\sqrt{2+\sqrt{2+4\cos^2 4\theta - 2}}}$

$= \sqrt{2+\sqrt{2+2\cos 4\theta}}$

$= \sqrt{2+\sqrt{2+2(2\cos^2 2\theta - 1)}}$

$= \sqrt{2+\sqrt{2+4\cos^2 2\theta - 2}} = \sqrt{2+2\cos 2\theta}$

$= \sqrt{2+2(2\cos^2\theta - 1)} = \sqrt{2+4\cos^2\theta - 2}$

$= 2\cos\theta$

99. (d) Given, $7\cot P = 24 \Rightarrow \cot P = \frac{24}{7}$

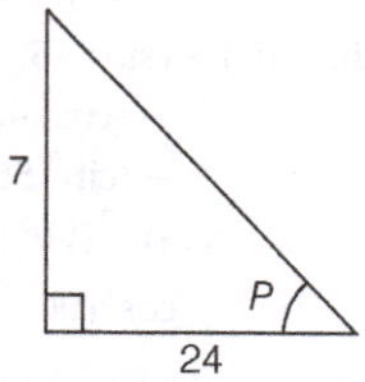

By Pythagoras theorem,

$(\text{Hypotenuse})^2 = (\text{Perpendicular})^2 + (\text{Base})^2$

$\text{Hypotenuse} = \sqrt{(7)^2 + (24)^2} = \sqrt{625}$

Hypotenuse = 25

Then, $\sin P = \frac{7}{25}$

100. (d) Given, $\tan^4\theta + \tan^2\theta = 1$

$\therefore \tan^2\theta(\tan^2\theta + 1) = 1$

$\therefore \tan^2\theta \sec^2\theta = 1$

$\frac{\sin^2\theta}{\cos^2\theta} \times \frac{1}{\cos^2\theta} = 1$

$\therefore \sin^2\theta = \cos^4\theta$

Now, $11(\cos^4\theta + \cos^2\theta) = 11(\sin^2\theta + \cos^2\theta)$

$= 11$

101. (c) Given, $3x = \sec A$ and $\frac{3}{x} = \tan A$

Then, $9\left(x^2 - \frac{1}{x^2}\right) = (3x)^2 - \left(\frac{3}{x}\right)^2$

$= (\sec A)^2 - (\tan A)^2 = 1$

$[\because \sec^2\theta - \tan^2\theta = 1]$

102. (d) Given, $\sec A + \tan A = 5$

$\Rightarrow \frac{1+\sin A}{\cos A} = 5$

On squaring both sides,

$1 + \sin^2 A + 2\sin A = 25\cos^2 A$

$1 + \sin^2 A + 2\sin A = 25 - 25\sin^2 A$

$26\sin^2 A + 2\sin A - 24 = 0$

$(26\sin A - 24)(\sin A + 1) = 0$

$\therefore \sin A = \frac{24}{26}, -1$

Hence, $\sin A = \frac{12}{13}$

Speedy Method

$\sec A + \tan A = 5$ ...(i)

$\sec A - \tan A = \frac{1}{5}$ ...(ii)

$[\because \sec^2 A - \tan^2 A = 1$

$(\sec A + \tan A)(\sec A - \tan A) = 1]$

Adding Eqs. (i) and (ii),

$2\sec A = 5 + \frac{1}{5}$

$\cos A = \frac{5\times 2}{26} = \frac{10}{26} = \frac{5}{13}$

$\sin A = \sqrt{1-\cos^2 A} = \sqrt{1-\left(\frac{5}{13}\right)^2}$

$= \sqrt{\frac{144}{169}} = \frac{12}{13}$

103. (c) Given, $3\cot A = \frac{7}{3}$

$\cot A = \frac{7}{9} \Rightarrow \frac{\cos A}{\sin A} = \frac{7}{9}$

Then, $\frac{3\cos A + 2\sin A}{3\cos A - 2\sin A} = \frac{3\times 7 + 2\times 9}{3\times 7 - 2\times 9}$

$= \frac{21+18}{21-18} = \frac{39}{3} = 13$

104. (a) Given, $A = 22.5°$

Then, $10\sqrt{2}\sin 2A - 7\sqrt{2}\cos 2A + 9\tan 2A$

$= 10\sqrt{2}\sin 45° - 7\sqrt{2}\cos 45° + 9\tan 45°$

$= 10\sqrt{2}\times\frac{1}{\sqrt{2}} - 7\sqrt{2}\times\frac{1}{\sqrt{2}} + 9\times 1$

$= 10 - 7 + 9 = 12$

105. (d) We know, By option (d), $\frac{\sin\theta}{1+\cos\theta}$

$[\because \sin 2\theta = 2\sin\theta\times\cos\theta, \cos 2\theta = 2\cos^2\theta - 1]$

$= \frac{2\sin\frac{\theta}{2}\cdot\cos\frac{\theta}{2}}{1 + 2\cos^2\frac{\theta}{2} - 1} = \frac{2\sin\frac{\theta}{2}\cdot\cos\frac{\theta}{2}}{2\cos^2\frac{\theta}{2}} = \tan\frac{\theta}{2}$

Hence, option (d) is correct.

106. (d) Given,

$\sin 600°\cos 750° + \sin 150°\cos 240°$

$= \sin(3\times 180° + 60°)\cos(4\times 180 + 30°)$

$+ \sin(180° - 30°)\cos(180° + 60°)$

$= -\sin(60°)\cos(30°) - \sin(30°)\cos(60°)$

$= \left(\frac{-\sqrt{3}}{2}\right)\left(\frac{\sqrt{3}}{2}\right) - \left(\frac{1}{2}\right)\left(\frac{1}{2}\right) = \frac{-3}{4} - \frac{1}{4} = \frac{-4}{4} = -1$

107. (c) $\tan 4384° + \cot 6814°$

$= \tan(24\times 180° + 64°) + \cot(75\times 90° + 64°)$

$[\because \tan(n\pi + \theta) = \tan\theta$ and $\cot\left(n\frac{\pi}{2} + \theta\right) = -\tan\theta]$

$= \tan 64° - \tan 64° = 0$

108. (d) Given, $\cos x + \sec x = \frac{7}{2\sqrt{3}}$

Squaring on both sides, we get

$\cos^2 x + 2\cos x \times \sec x + \sec^2 x = \frac{49}{12}$

$\Rightarrow \cos^2 x + \sec^2 x = \frac{49}{12} - 2$

$\therefore \cos^2 x + \sec^2 x = \frac{25}{12}$

109. (c) $\frac{\cos^2 15° - \sin^2 15°}{\cos^2 145° + \sin^2 145°}$

$= \frac{\cos(2\times 15°)}{1} = \cos 30°$

$\{\because \cos^2\theta - \sin^2\theta = \cos 2\theta$ and $\sin^2\theta + \cos^2\theta = 1\}$

$= \frac{\sqrt{3}}{2}$

110. (b) $\tan A = \frac{3}{8}$

ΔABC is right angle triangle, $\angle B = 90°$

$AC = \sqrt{8^2 + 3^2} = \sqrt{73}$ units

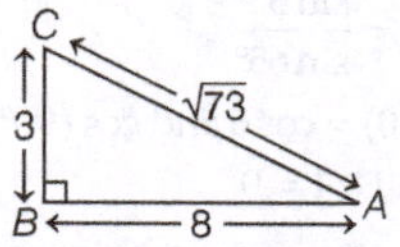

$\therefore \frac{3\sin A + 2\cos A}{3\sin A - 2\cos A} = \frac{\frac{3\times 3}{\sqrt{73}} + \frac{2\times 8}{\sqrt{73}}}{\frac{3\times 3}{\sqrt{73}} - \frac{2\times 8}{\sqrt{73}}} = -\frac{25}{7}$

Speedy Method

Given, $\tan A = \frac{3}{8}$,

Expression $= \frac{3\sin A + 2\cos A}{3\sin A - 2\cos A}$

On dividing numerator and denominator by $\cos A$, $= \frac{3\tan A + 2}{3\tan A - 2}$

$= \frac{3\times\frac{3}{8} + 2}{3\times\frac{3}{8} - 2} = \frac{9+16}{9-16} = -\frac{25}{7}$

111. (a) ΔABC is a right angled triangle at $\angle B = 90°$

Then, $\angle A + \angle C = 90°$

$\therefore \sin A\cos C + \cos A\sin C$

$= \sin(A + C) = \sin 90° = 1$

$[\because \sin(A+B) = \sin A\cos B + \cos A\sin B]$

112. (d) $\cos x = \sqrt{1 - \frac{9}{49}} = \sqrt{\frac{40}{49}} = \frac{2\sqrt{10}}{7}$

113. (c) $\text{cosec } 30° - \cos 60° = 2 - \frac{1}{2} = \frac{3}{2}$

114. (b) Given, $\cos A + \cos^2 A = 1$

$\cos A = 1 - \cos^2 A \Rightarrow \cos A = \sin^2 A$

Then, $\sin^4 A + \sin^6 A = (\sin^2 A)^2 + (\sin^2 A)^3$

$= \cos^2 A + \cos^3 A$

$[\because \cos A + \cos^2 A = 1 \text{ (given)}]$

$= \cos A (\cos A + \cos^2 A) = \cos A$

115. (b) $\cos(40° + x) = \sin 30°$

$\Rightarrow \cos(90° - 50° - x) = \sin 30°$

$\Rightarrow \sin(50° - x) = \sin 30° \; [\because \cos(90° - \theta) = \sin\theta]$

$\Rightarrow 50° - x = 30° \Rightarrow x = 50° - 30° \Rightarrow x = 20°$

116. (c) $\sqrt{\dfrac{1+\cos\theta}{1-\cos\theta}}$

Multiply by $\sqrt{1+\cos\theta}$ in numerator and in denominator

$= \sqrt{\dfrac{(1+\cos\theta)^2}{(1-\cos\theta)(1+\cos\theta)}}$

$= \dfrac{1+\cos\theta}{\sqrt{1-\cos^2\theta}} = \dfrac{1}{\sin\theta} + \dfrac{\cos\theta}{\sin\theta}$

$= \operatorname{cosec}\theta + \cot\theta$

117. (d) $r = 15(\sin\theta + \cos\theta)$;

$s = 16(\sin\theta - \cos\theta)$

$\therefore \dfrac{r^2}{15^2} + \dfrac{s^2}{16^2} = \dfrac{15^2(\sin\theta+\cos\theta)^2}{15^2} + \dfrac{16^2(\sin\theta-\cos\theta)^2}{16^2}$

$= (\sin\theta + \cos\theta)^2 + (\sin\theta - \cos\theta)^2$

$= 2(\sin^2\theta + \cos^2\theta) = 2$

118. (b) $5\sqrt{3}\cos 60° \tan 30° - 3\cos 0° + 3\cos^2 45° + 2\sin^2 60°$

$= 5\sqrt{3} \times \dfrac{1}{2} \times \dfrac{1}{\sqrt{3}} - 3 \times 1 + 3 \times \dfrac{1}{2} + 2 \times \dfrac{3}{4}$

$= \dfrac{5}{2} - 3 + \dfrac{3}{2} + \dfrac{3}{2} = \dfrac{5-6+3+3}{2} = \dfrac{5}{2} = 2.5$

119. (d) $\cos^2\theta = \dfrac{3}{4} \Rightarrow \cos\theta = \dfrac{\sqrt{3}}{2} \Rightarrow \theta = 30°$

$\therefore \sin(\theta + 30°) = \sin 60° = \dfrac{\sqrt{3}}{2}$

120. (c) Given, $\tan(-1125°)$

$[\because \tan(-\theta) = -\tan\theta]$

$= -\tan(3 \times 360° + 45°) = -\tan 45° = -1$

121. (d) $\sin B = \dfrac{1}{\sqrt{2}} \Rightarrow \angle B = 45°$

$\cot A = 1 \Rightarrow \angle A = 45°$

$\therefore \sin(A+B) - \cot(A+B)$

$= \sin 90° - \cot 90° = 1 - 0 = 1$

122. (c) $\operatorname{cosec} 75° = \operatorname{cosec}(45° + 30°)$

$= \dfrac{\sec 45° \times \sec 30° \times \operatorname{cosec} 45° \times \operatorname{cosec} 30°}{\sec 45° \times \operatorname{cosec} 30° + \operatorname{cosec} 45° \times \sec 30°}$

$= \dfrac{\sqrt{2} \times \dfrac{2}{\sqrt{3}} \times \sqrt{2} \times 2}{\sqrt{2} \times 2 + \sqrt{2} \times \dfrac{2}{\sqrt{3}}} = \dfrac{\dfrac{8}{\sqrt{3}}}{\dfrac{2\sqrt{6}+2\sqrt{2}}{\sqrt{3}}}$

$= \dfrac{8}{2(\sqrt{6}+\sqrt{2})} = \dfrac{4(\sqrt{6}-\sqrt{2})}{(\sqrt{6}+\sqrt{2})(\sqrt{6}-\sqrt{2})}$

$= \sqrt{6} - \sqrt{2}$

123. (c) $a\cot\theta = b$

$\Rightarrow \dfrac{\cos\theta}{\sin\theta} = \dfrac{b}{a} \Rightarrow \dfrac{a\cos\theta}{b\sin\theta} = 1$

$\Rightarrow \dfrac{b^2}{a^2} \cdot \dfrac{a\cos\theta}{b\sin\theta} = \dfrac{b^2}{a^2} \Rightarrow \dfrac{b\cos\theta}{a\sin\theta} = \dfrac{b^2}{a^2}$

By componendo and dividendo rule

$\Rightarrow \dfrac{b\cos\theta + a\sin\theta}{b\cos\theta - a\sin\theta} = \dfrac{b^2+a^2}{b^2-a^2}$

$\Rightarrow \dfrac{b\cos\theta - a\sin\theta}{b\cos\theta + a\sin\theta} = \dfrac{b^2-a^2}{b^2+a^2}$

Speedy Method

$a\cot\theta = b \Rightarrow \cot\theta = \dfrac{b}{a}$

$\dfrac{\sin\theta}{\sin\theta}\left(\dfrac{b\cot\theta - a}{b\cot\theta + a}\right) = \dfrac{b \times \dfrac{b}{a} - a}{b \times \dfrac{b}{a} + a} = \dfrac{\dfrac{b^2-a^2}{a}}{\dfrac{b^2+a^2}{a}}$

$= \dfrac{b^2-a^2}{b^2+a^2}$

124. (c) $\dfrac{1+\sin^4\theta+\cos^4\theta}{\cos^2\theta+\sin^4\theta}$

$= \dfrac{1+(\sin^2\theta+\cos^2\theta)^2 - 2\sin^2\theta\cos^2\theta}{1-\sin^2\theta+\sin^4\theta}$

$= \dfrac{2(1-\sin^2\theta\cos^2\theta)}{1-\sin^2\theta+\sin^4\theta}$

$= \dfrac{2\{1-(\sin^2\theta)(1-\sin^2\theta)\}}{1-\sin^2\theta+\sin^4\theta}$

$= \dfrac{2\{1-\sin^2\theta+\sin^4\theta\}}{(1-\sin^2\theta+\sin^4\theta)} = 2$

Speedy Method

Expression satistfy for all values of θ.

So, put $\theta = 0°$

$\dfrac{1+\sin^4\theta+\cos^4\theta}{\cos^2\theta+\sin^4\theta} = \dfrac{1+0+1}{1+0} = 2$

125. (a) Given, $\operatorname{cosec}\theta + \cot\theta = \dfrac{3}{2}$ ...(i)

$\because \operatorname{cosec}^2 - \cot^2\theta = 1$

$\therefore \operatorname{cosec}\theta - \cot\theta = \dfrac{2}{3}$ ...(ii)

From Eqs. (i) and (ii), we get

$\therefore \operatorname{cosec}\theta = \dfrac{13}{12}$

126. (d) Given, $\sin\theta + \operatorname{cosec}\theta = \sqrt{5}$

$\sin\theta + \dfrac{1}{\sin\theta} = \sqrt{5}$

Cubing both sides,

$\sin^3\theta + \dfrac{1}{\sin^3\theta} = (\sqrt{5})^3 - 3\sqrt{5}$

$= 5\sqrt{5} - 3\sqrt{5} = 2\sqrt{5}$

$\therefore \sin^3\theta + \operatorname{cosec}^3\theta = 2\sqrt{5}$

127. (c) Given, $\tan x = \dfrac{7}{5}$

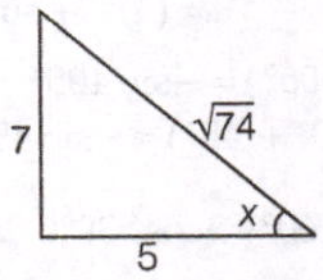

$\dfrac{9\sin x - \dfrac{42}{5}\cos x}{15\sin x + 21\cos x} = \dfrac{9 \times \dfrac{7}{\sqrt{74}} - \dfrac{42}{5} \times \dfrac{5}{\sqrt{74}}}{15 \times \dfrac{7}{\sqrt{74}} + 21 \times \dfrac{5}{\sqrt{74}}}$

$= \dfrac{\dfrac{21}{\sqrt{74}}}{\dfrac{210}{\sqrt{74}}} = \dfrac{21}{210} = 0.1$

128. (a) Given, $\tan x = \dfrac{-12}{5}, \cot x = \dfrac{-5}{12}$

$\therefore \sin x = \dfrac{12}{13}$

Then, $\sin x - \cot x = \dfrac{12}{13} - \left(\dfrac{-5}{12}\right) = \dfrac{209}{156}$

129. (c) Given, $\tan 5° \tan 25° \tan 45° \tan 65° \tan 85°$

$= \tan(90° - 85°) \cdot \tan(90° - 65) \tan 45° \cdot \tan 65° \cdot \tan 85°$

$[\because \tan 45° = 1, \tan(90° - \theta) = \cot\theta]$

$= \cot 85° \cdot \cot 65° \cdot \tan 65° \cdot \tan 85° = 1$

130. (b) We know,

$\sin(A+B) = \sin A \cdot \cos B + \cos A \sin B.$

131. (c) Given, $\cot\theta = \dfrac{3}{2} \Rightarrow \tan\theta = \dfrac{2}{3}$,

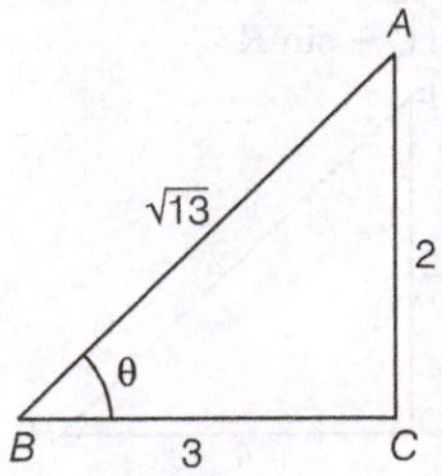

By Pythagoras theorem,

$AB = \sqrt{3^2 + 2^2} = \sqrt{13}$

$\therefore \dfrac{\sqrt{13}\sin\theta - 3\tan\theta}{3\tan\theta + \sqrt{13}\cos\theta} = \dfrac{\sqrt{13} \times \dfrac{2}{\sqrt{13}} - 3 \times \dfrac{2}{3}}{3 \times \dfrac{2}{3} + \sqrt{13} \times \dfrac{3}{\sqrt{13}}}$

$= \dfrac{2-2}{2+3} = 0$

132. (a) Given,

$2 + \cos 49° \cos 41° - \sin 49° \sin 41°$

$= 2 + \cos(49° + 41°) = 2 + \cos 90° = 2 + 0 = 2$

133. (a) Given, $\tan 2\alpha = \dfrac{2\tan\alpha}{1-\tan^2\alpha}$

If $\alpha = 15° \Rightarrow \tan 30° = \dfrac{2\tan 15°}{1-\tan^2 15°}$

$\dfrac{1}{\sqrt{3}} = \dfrac{2\tan 15°}{1-\tan^2 15°}$

Let $\tan 15° = x$

$1 - x^2 = 2x \times \sqrt{3}$

$x^2 + 2\sqrt{3}x - 1 = 0$

$x = \dfrac{-2\sqrt{3} \pm \sqrt{(2\sqrt{3})^2 - 4 \times 1 \times (-1)}}{2 \times 1}$

$= \dfrac{-2\sqrt{3} \pm \sqrt{12+4}}{2} = \dfrac{-2\sqrt{3} \pm 4}{2}$

$x = 2 - \sqrt{3}$

Then, $\tan 15° = 2 - 1.732 = 0 \cdot 268$

134. (b) $\dfrac{1+\sin t}{4-4\sin t}-\dfrac{1-\sin t}{4+4\sin t}$

$=\dfrac{1}{4}\left[\dfrac{(1+\sin t)^2-(1-\sin t)^2}{(1-\sin t)(1+\sin t)}\right]$

$=\dfrac{4\cdot 1\cdot \sin t}{4(1-\sin^2 t)}=\dfrac{\sin t}{\cos^2 t}=\tan t\cdot\sec t$

135. (b) $8\cot A=7\Rightarrow \cot A=\dfrac{7}{8}$

$AB=7, BC=8$

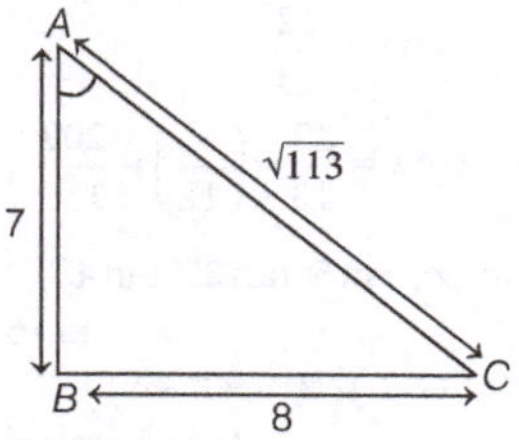

$AC=\sqrt{7^2+8^2}=\sqrt{49+64}=\sqrt{113}$

$\therefore \sin A=\dfrac{8}{\sqrt{113}}$

136. (c) In ΔPQR, $\angle Q=90°$

$PQ:QR=3:4$

Then, $QR:PR=4:5$

$\therefore \sin P+\sin Q+\sin R$

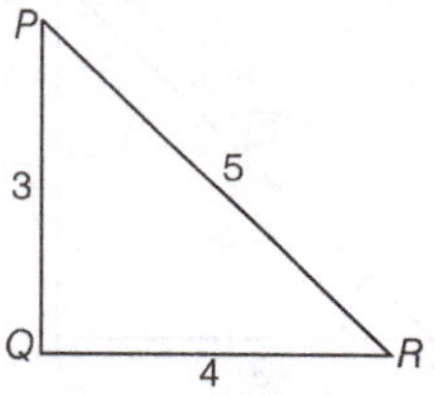

$=\dfrac{4}{5}+1+\dfrac{3}{5}=\dfrac{4+5+3}{5}=\dfrac{12}{5}$

137. (a) ΔXYZ, right angled at Y.

$\sin X=\dfrac{1}{2}$

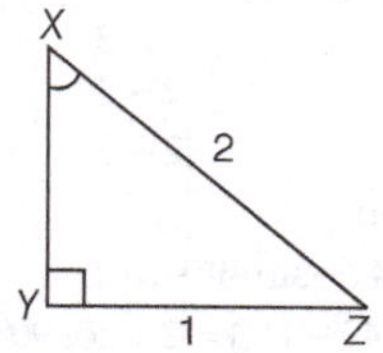

$XY=\sqrt{2^2-1^2}=\sqrt{4-1}=\sqrt{3}$

$\therefore \cos X\cos Z+\sin X\sin Z$

$=\dfrac{\sqrt{3}}{2}\times\dfrac{1}{2}+\dfrac{1}{2}\times\dfrac{\sqrt{3}}{2}=\dfrac{2\sqrt{3}}{4}=\dfrac{\sqrt{3}}{2}$

138. (b) $\dfrac{\cos\alpha}{\sin\beta}=10\Rightarrow\cos\alpha=10\sin\beta$ ... (i)

and $\dfrac{\cos\alpha}{\cos\beta}=11\Rightarrow\dfrac{10\sin\beta}{\cos\beta}=11$ [From Eq. (i)]

$\Rightarrow \tan\beta=\dfrac{11}{10}\Rightarrow\tan^2\beta=\dfrac{121}{100}$

[$\because \sec^2\beta=1+\tan^2\beta$]

$\Rightarrow \sec^2\beta=\dfrac{221}{100}$

$\therefore \cos^2\beta=\dfrac{100}{221}$

139. (a) $\dfrac{\sin\theta-2\sin^3\theta}{2\cos^3\theta-\cos\theta}=\dfrac{\sin\theta(1-2\sin^2\theta)}{\cos\theta(2\cos^2\theta-1)}$

$=\tan\theta\left(\dfrac{\cos 2\theta}{\cos 2\theta}\right)=\tan\theta$

140. (a) $\sqrt{\dfrac{1-\sin 3\theta}{1+\sin 3\theta}}$

$=\sqrt{\dfrac{(1-\sin 3\theta)^2}{(1+\sin 3\theta)(1-\sin 3\theta)}}$

$=\dfrac{1-\sin 3\theta}{\sqrt{1-\sin^2 3\theta}}=\dfrac{1}{\cos 3\theta}-\dfrac{\sin 3\theta}{\cos 3\theta}$

$=\sec 3\theta-\tan 3\theta$

141. (a) $\sec x-\cos x=\dfrac{1}{\cos x}-\cos x$

$=\dfrac{1-\cos^2 x}{\cos x}=\dfrac{\sin^2 x}{\cos x}=\tan x\sin x$

142. (b) Given, $\sec A+\tan A=3$ ...(i)

$\because \sec^2 A-\tan^2 A=1$

$\Rightarrow (\sec A+\tan A)(\sec A-\tan A)=1$

$\Rightarrow \sec A-\tan A=\dfrac{1}{3}$ ...(ii)

From Eqs. (i) and (ii), we get

$2\sec A=\dfrac{10}{3}\Rightarrow\sec A=\dfrac{5}{3}$

$\therefore \cos A=\dfrac{3}{5}$

143. (d) $\because \sin^2\theta+\cos^2\theta=1$

$\therefore \cos^2\theta-\sin^2\theta=1$, this identity is not correct.

144. (b) $\dfrac{\cos 41°}{\sin 49°}+\dfrac{\sin 51°}{\cos 39°}$

$=\dfrac{\cos 41°}{\sin(90°-41°)}+\dfrac{\sin 51°}{\cos(90°-51°)}$

$=\dfrac{\cos 41°}{\cos 41°}+\dfrac{\sin 51°}{\sin 51°}=1+1=2$

145. (a)

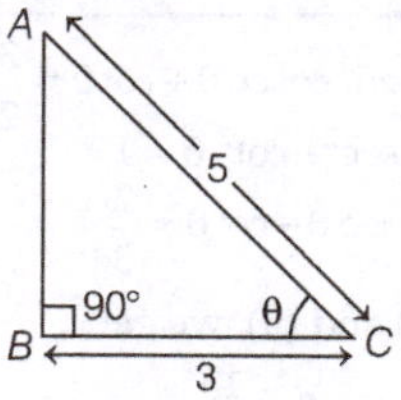

Perpendicular $=\sqrt{(5)^2-(3)^2}=\sqrt{16}=4$

$\therefore \tan\theta=\dfrac{P}{B}=\dfrac{4}{3}$

146. (c) $\sin^{12}\theta+\cos^{20}\theta$

$=\sin^{12}\theta+[\sin(90°-\theta)]^{20}$

$=\sin^{12}\theta+\sin^{20}(90°-\theta)$

Value of $\sin\theta$ is maximum for $\theta=90°$ and $\sin 90°=1$.

So, maximum value of $\sin^{12}\theta+\cos^{20}\theta$

$=\sin^{12}90°+\sin^{20}(90°-90°)$

$=(1)^{12}+\sin^{20}0°=1$

147. (d) $\sin(-405°)=-\sin 405°$

$=-\sin(360°+45°)=-\sin 45°=-\dfrac{1}{\sqrt{2}}$

148. (c) $\dfrac{2}{3}\tan^2 60°+3\cos^2 30°-2\sec^2 30°-\dfrac{3}{4}\cot^2 60°$

$=\dfrac{2}{3}\times 3+3\times\dfrac{3}{4}-2\times\dfrac{4}{3}-\dfrac{3}{4}\times\dfrac{1}{3}$

$=2+\dfrac{9}{4}-\dfrac{8}{3}-\dfrac{1}{4}=\dfrac{24+27-32-3}{12}$

$=\dfrac{16}{12}=\dfrac{4}{3}=1.33$

149. (c) Given, $\sin(50°+\theta)-\cos(40°-\theta)$

$=\sin[90°-(40°-\theta)]-\cos(40°-\theta)$

$=\cos(40°-\theta)-\cos(40°-\theta)=0$

150. (d) $\dfrac{2\tan A}{1+\tan^2 A}=\sin 2A$

151. (b) Given, $\cot 85°+\cos 75°$

$=\cot(90°-5°)+\cos(90°-15°)$

$=\tan 5°+\sin 15°$

152. (a) $\dfrac{\sec^2(90°-\theta)-\cot^2\theta}{2(\sin^2 35°+\sin^2 55°)}$

$=\dfrac{\operatorname{cosec}^2\theta-\cot^2\theta}{2\{\sin^2 35°+\sin^2(90°-35°)\}}$

$=\dfrac{1}{2(\sin^2 35°+\cos^2 35°)}=0.5$

153. (c) $\operatorname{cosec} 2910°+\sec 4260°+\tan 2565°+\cot 1755°$

$=\operatorname{cosec}(16\times 180°+30°)+\sec(24\times 180°-60°)+\tan(14\times 180°+45°)+\cot(10\times 180°-45°)$

$=\operatorname{cosec} 30°+\sec 60°+\tan 45°-\cot 45°$

$=2+2+1-1=4$

154. (a) $\sin x=\dfrac{3}{10}$

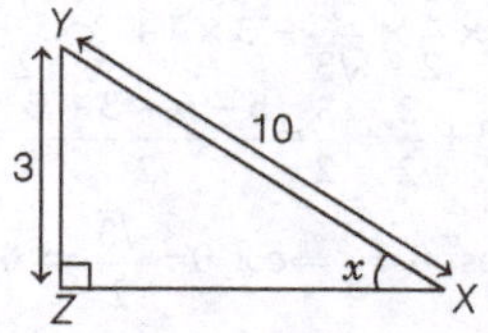

Let ΔYZX is right-angled triangle at $\angle Z=90°$

$\therefore ZX=\sqrt{10^2-3^2}=\sqrt{100-9}=\sqrt{91}$ unit

$\therefore \tan x+\cot x=\dfrac{3}{\sqrt{91}}+\dfrac{\sqrt{91}}{3}=\dfrac{9+91}{3\sqrt{91}}=\dfrac{100}{3\sqrt{91}}$

155. (a) Given, $\cos x+\sin x=\sqrt{2}\cos x$

Then, $(\cos x-\sin x)^2+(\cos x+\sin x)^2$

$=2\cos^2 x+2\sin^2 x=2(\sin^2 x+\cos^2 x)=2$

156. (d) Given, $2\cot x=5\Rightarrow\cot x=\dfrac{5}{2}$

We have, $\dfrac{2\cos x-\sin x}{2\cos x+\sin x}$

Divide numerator and denominator by $\sin x$

$\dfrac{2\cot x-1}{2\cot x+1}=\dfrac{2\left(\frac{5}{2}\right)-1}{2(5/2)+1}=\dfrac{5-1}{5+1}=\dfrac{4}{6}=\dfrac{2}{3}$

157. (b) $\because \theta$ is an acute angle.

$\therefore \sin\theta+\sin^2\theta=1\Rightarrow\sin\theta=1-\sin^2\theta$

$\Rightarrow \sin\theta=\cos^2\theta$

$\therefore \cos^2\theta+\cos^4\theta=\cos^2\theta+\sin^2\theta=1$

158. (c) Given, $P\cos\alpha=3$ and $4\tan\alpha=Q$

$\cos\alpha=\dfrac{3}{P}$, $\tan\alpha=\dfrac{Q}{4}$ and $\sec\alpha=\dfrac{P}{3}$

We know, $\sec^2\alpha - \tan^2\alpha = 1$

$$\left(\frac{P}{3}\right)^2 - \left(\frac{Q}{4}\right)^2 = 1$$

Hence, $\frac{P^2}{9} - \frac{Q^2}{16} = 1$

159. (a) Given, $\sec\theta = \frac{4}{3}, \tan\theta = \frac{\sqrt{7}}{3}$

Then, $\tan^2\theta + \tan^4\theta = \tan^2\theta(1+\tan^2\theta)$

$= \tan^2\theta\sec^2\theta$

$= \left(\frac{\sqrt{7}}{3}\right)^2\left(\frac{4}{3}\right)^2 = \frac{7}{9}\times\frac{16}{9} = \frac{112}{81}$

160. (b) $\frac{\sin x - \cos x}{\sin x + \cos x} = \frac{2}{5}$

$\Rightarrow \frac{\sin x - \cos x + \sin x + \cos x}{\sin x - \cos x - \sin x - \cos x} = \frac{2+5}{2-5}$

$\Rightarrow \frac{\sin x}{\cos x} = \frac{7}{3} \Rightarrow \cot x = \frac{3}{7}$

$\therefore \frac{1+\cot^2 x}{1-\cot^2 x} = \frac{1+\frac{9}{49}}{1-\frac{9}{49}} = \frac{\frac{58}{49}}{\frac{40}{49}} = \frac{58}{40} = 1.45$

161. (c) $\frac{\cos A}{1-\sin A} + \frac{\cos A}{1+\sin A} = 4$

$\Rightarrow \frac{\cos A + \sin A\cos A + \cos A - \sin A\cos A}{1-\sin^2 A} = 4$

$\Rightarrow \frac{2\cos A}{\cos^2 A} = 4 \Rightarrow \sec A = 2 \Rightarrow \sec A = \sec 60°$

$\therefore A = 60°$

162. (d) Given, $\frac{4}{3}\tan^2 45° + 3\cos^2 30°$

$- 2\sec^2 30° - \frac{3}{4}\cot^2 60°$

$= \frac{4}{3}\times 1 + 3\times\left(\frac{\sqrt{3}}{2}\right)^2 - 2\times\left(\frac{2}{\sqrt{3}}\right)^2 - \frac{3}{4}\times\left(\frac{1}{\sqrt{3}}\right)^2$

$= \frac{4}{3} + \frac{9}{4} - \frac{8}{3} - \frac{1}{4} = \frac{8}{12} = \frac{2}{3}$

163. (b) $\cos 120° = \cos(90° + 30°)$

$= -\sin 30° = -\frac{1}{2} = -0.5$

164. (c) Given,

$\sin(5x - 25°) = \cos(5y + 25°)$

$5x - 25° + 5y + 25° = 90°$

$5x + 5y = 90 \Rightarrow x + y = \frac{90°}{5}$

$\therefore \quad x + y = 18°$

165. (d) Given, $12(\sin^4\theta + \cos^4\theta)$

$+18(\sin^6\theta + \cos^6\theta) + 78\sin^2\theta\cos^2\theta$

$= 12 - 24\sin^2\theta\cos^2\theta + 18$

$(1 - 3\sin^2\theta\cos^2\theta) + 78\sin^2\theta\cos^2\theta$

$\left[\begin{array}{l}\because \sin^4\theta + \cos^4\theta = 1 - 2\sin^2\theta\cos^2\theta \\ \sin^6\theta + \cos^6\theta = 1 - 3\sin^2\theta\cos^2\theta\end{array}\right]$

$= 12 - 24\sin^2\theta\cos^2\theta + 18 - 54\sin^2\theta$

$\cos^2\theta + 78\sin^2\theta\cos^2\theta$

$= 30$

166. (d) Given, $\left(\frac{1}{\sin\theta} + \frac{1}{\tan\theta}\right)\left(\frac{1}{\sin\theta} - \frac{1}{\tan\theta}\right)$

$= \frac{1}{\sin^2\theta} - \frac{1}{\tan^2\theta} = \frac{1-\cos^2\theta}{\sin^2\theta} = \frac{\sin^2\theta}{\sin^2\theta} = 1$

167. (b) Given, $\sin A = -\frac{3}{5}$

$\cos A = \sqrt{1-\sin^2 A} = \sqrt{1-\frac{9}{25}}$

$\therefore \quad \cos A = -\frac{4}{5}$

Now, $\sec A = -\frac{5}{4}$

168. (a) Given, $\sin 2x + 2\sin 4x + \sin 6x$

$= 2\sin\left(\frac{6x+2x}{2}\right)\cos\left(\frac{6x-2x}{2}\right) + 2\sin 4x$

$= 2\sin 4x\cos 2x + 2\sin 4x$

$= 2\sin 4x(\cos 2x + 1) = 4\cos^2 x\sin 4x$

169. (b) Given, $\cot A = \frac{12}{5} = \frac{B}{P}$

$H = \sqrt{P^2 + B^2} = \sqrt{(12)^2 + (5)^2} = 13$

$\therefore \sin A = \frac{5}{13}, \cos A = \frac{12}{13}$ and $\text{cosec } A = \frac{13}{5}$

So, $(\sin A + \cos A)\times\text{cosec } A$

$= \left(\frac{5}{13} + \frac{12}{13}\right)\times\frac{13}{5} = \frac{17}{13}\times\frac{13}{5} = \frac{17}{5}$

170. (d) Given, $\frac{\sin(x-y)}{\sin(x+y)}\times\frac{\tan x + \tan y}{\tan x - \tan y}$

$= \frac{\sin(x-y)}{\sin(x+y)}\times\frac{\frac{\sin x}{\cos x} + \frac{\sin y}{\cos y}}{\frac{\sin x}{\cos x} - \frac{\sin y}{\cos y}}$

$= \frac{(\sin x\cos y - \cos x\sin y)\times(\sin x\cos y + \sin y\cos x)}{(\sin x\cos y + \cos x\sin y)\times(\sin x\cos y - \sin y\cos x)}$

$= 1$

171. (c) Given, $x = \tan\frac{A}{2} = \frac{\sin\frac{A}{2}}{\cos\frac{A}{2}}$

$= \frac{\sin\frac{A}{2}\times 2\sin\frac{A}{2}}{\cos\frac{A}{2}\times 2\sin\frac{A}{2}} = \frac{2\sin^2\frac{A}{2}}{2\sin\frac{A}{2}\cos\frac{A}{2}}$

$[\because \sin 2\theta = 2\sin\theta\cos\theta]$

$= \frac{1-\cos A}{\sin A} = \sqrt{\frac{(1-\cos A)^2}{\sin^2 A}}$

$= \frac{\sqrt{(1-\cos A)(1-\cos A)}}{\sqrt{(1-\cos^2 A)}}$

$= \frac{\sqrt{(1-\cos A)(1-\cos A)}}{\sqrt{(1-\cos A)(1+\cos A)}} \Rightarrow x = \sqrt{\frac{1-\cos A}{1+\cos A}}$

172. (a) Given, $\frac{\sin^4\theta + \cos^4\theta}{1-2\sin^2\theta\cos^2\theta}$

$= \frac{(\sin^4\theta + \cos^4\theta) + 2\sin^2\theta\cos^2\theta - 2\sin^2\theta\cos^2\theta}{1-2\sin^2\theta\cos^2\theta}$

$= \frac{(\sin^2\theta + \cos^2\theta)^2 - 2\sin^2\theta\cos^2\theta}{1-2\sin^2\theta\cdot\cos^2\theta}$

$= \frac{1-2\sin^2\theta\cos^2\theta}{1-2\sin^2\theta\cos^2\theta} = 1$

173. (c) Given, $p\sin^2\beta + q\cos^2\beta = r$

$p\sin^2\beta + q(1-\sin^2\beta) = r$

$p\sin^2\beta + q - q\sin^2\beta = r$

$\sin^2\beta(p-q) = r - q$

$\sin^2\beta = \frac{r-q}{p-q}$

$\therefore \quad \cot^2\beta = \text{cosec}^2\beta - 1$

$= \frac{p-q}{r-q} - 1 = \frac{p-q-r+q}{r-q}$

$\therefore \quad \cot^2\beta = \frac{p-r}{r-q}$

174. (c) $\because \cos 75° = \cos(45° + 30°)$

$= \cos 45°\cos 30° - \sin 45°\sin 30°$

$= \frac{1}{\sqrt{2}}.\frac{\sqrt{3}}{2} - \frac{1}{\sqrt{2}}.\frac{1}{2} = \frac{1}{\sqrt{2}}\left(\frac{\sqrt{3}-1}{2}\right)$

$= \frac{\sqrt{2}(\sqrt{3}-1)}{2\sqrt{2}\cdot\sqrt{2}} = \frac{\sqrt{6}-\sqrt{2}}{4}$

175. (b) Given,

$\cos 47°\sec 133° + \sin 44°\text{cosec} 136°$

$= \cos 47°\frac{1}{\cos 133°} + \sin 44°\frac{1}{\sin 136°}$

$= \frac{\cos(180°-133°)}{\cos 133°} + \frac{\sin(180°-136°)}{\sin 136°}$

$= \frac{-\cos 133°}{\cos 133°} + \frac{\sin 136°}{\sin 136°} = -1 + 1 = 0$

176. (c) Given, $\tan\frac{\pi}{6} + \sec\frac{\pi}{6} = x$

$\Rightarrow \frac{1}{\sqrt{3}} + \frac{2}{\sqrt{3}} = x \Rightarrow x = \frac{3}{\sqrt{3}}$

$\Rightarrow \quad x = \sqrt{3}$

177. (d) Given, $\sin\theta = \frac{4}{5} = \frac{p}{h}$

$b = \sqrt{5^2 - 4^2} = \sqrt{9} = 3$

$\therefore \tan\theta = \frac{4}{3}$ and $\cot\theta = \frac{3}{4}$

Now, $\tan\theta - \cot\theta = \frac{4}{3} - \frac{3}{4} = \frac{16-9}{12} = \frac{7}{12}$

178. (b) Given, $\sin t + \cos t = \frac{4}{5}$

On squaring both sides, we get

$\sin^2 t + \cos^2 t + 2\sin t\cos t = \frac{16}{25}$

$1 + 2\sin t\cos t = \frac{16}{25}$

$2\sin t\cos t = \frac{16}{25} - 1$

$\therefore \sin t\cos t = \left(\frac{16-25}{25}\right)\times\frac{1}{2}$

$\sin t\cos t = -\frac{9}{50}$

179. (d) Given, $\sin^2 25° + \sin^2 65°$

$= \sin^2 25° + \sin^2(90° - 25°)$

$= \sin^2 25° + \cos^2 25° = 1$

180. (c) Given, $\frac{\sin^3\alpha + \cos^3\alpha}{\sin\alpha + \cos\alpha}$

$= \frac{(\sin\alpha + \cos\alpha)(\sin^2\alpha + \cos^2\alpha - \sin\alpha\cos\alpha)}{(\sin\alpha + \cos\alpha)}$

$[\because a^3 + b^3 = (a+b)(a^2 + b^2 - ab)]$

$= 1 - \sin\alpha\cos\alpha$

181. (b) Given, $\sec\theta + \cos\theta = 32$

On squaring both sides,

$$(\sec\theta + \cos\theta)^2 = (32)^2$$
$$\sec^2\theta + \cos^2\theta + 2\sec\theta\cos\theta = 1024$$
$$\sec^2\theta + \cos^2\theta + 2\times\frac{1}{\cos\theta}\times\cos\theta = 1024$$
$$\sec^2\theta + \cos^2\theta = 1024 - 2 = 1022$$

182. (a) Given, $\frac{\cos\beta}{\sec\alpha} = 15$ ...(i)

and, $\frac{\sin\beta}{\sec\alpha} = 16$ ...(ii)

From Eq. (i), $\sec\alpha = \frac{\cos\beta}{15}$

Put in Eq. (ii), $\sin\beta = 16\times\frac{\cos\beta}{15}$

On squaring both sides,

$$(\sin\beta)^2 = \left(\frac{16}{15}\right)^2\times\cos^2\beta$$
$$225\sin^2\beta = 256(1-\sin^2\beta)$$
$$(225+256)\sin^2\beta = 256$$

Hence, $\sin^2\beta = \frac{256}{481}$

183. (d) Given, $\sin 23° = \frac{a}{b}$

$$\cos 23° = \sqrt{1-\left(\frac{a}{b}\right)^2} = \frac{\sqrt{b^2-a^2}}{b}$$

$\therefore$ $\sec 23° = \frac{b}{\sqrt{b^2-a^2}}$

$$\cos 23° = \cos(90° - 67°) = \frac{\sqrt{b^2-a^2}}{b}$$

$\therefore$ $\sin 67° = \frac{\sqrt{b^2-a^2}}{b}$

Then, value of $\sec 23° - \sin 67°$

$$= \frac{b}{\sqrt{b^2-a^2}} - \frac{\sqrt{b^2-a^2}}{b}$$
$$= \frac{b^2-b^2+a^2}{b\sqrt{b^2-a^2}} = \frac{a^2}{b\sqrt{b^2-a^2}}$$

184. (a) Given, $\sin 30° + \cos 30° + \tan 30°$

$$= \frac{1}{2} + \frac{\sqrt{3}}{2} + \frac{1}{\sqrt{3}} = \frac{\sqrt{3}+3+2}{2\sqrt{3}} = \frac{5+\sqrt{3}}{2\sqrt{3}}$$

185. (d) Given, $\sec^2\theta + \tan^2\theta = \frac{25}{18}$

Then, $\sec^4\theta - \tan^4\theta$

$$= (\sec^2\theta - \tan^2\theta)(\sec^2\theta + \tan^2\theta)$$
$$= 1\times\frac{25}{18} = \frac{25}{18}$$

186. (d) $\cos(36°+A)\cos(36°-A) + \cos(54°+A)\cos(54°-A)$

$$= \cos(36°+A)\cos(36°-A) + \cos(90°-(36°-A)), \cos[90°-(36°+A)]$$
$$= \cos(36°+A)\cos(36°-A) + \sin(36°-A)\sin(36°+A)$$
$$= \cos(36°+A-36°+A)$$

$[\because \cos(A-B) = \cos A\cos B + \sin A\sin B]$

$= \cos 2A$

187. (b) $\sec^2 54° - \cot^2 36° + \frac{3}{2}\sin^2 37° \times \sec^2 53° + \frac{2}{\sqrt{3}}\tan 60°$

$$= \sec^2 54° - \cot^2(90° - 54°) + \frac{3}{2}\times\frac{\sin^2 37°}{\cos^2(90° - 37°)} + \frac{2}{\sqrt{3}}\times\sqrt{3}$$
$$= \sec^2 54° - \tan^2 54° + \frac{3\sin^2 37°}{2\sin^2 37°} + 2$$
$$= 1 + \frac{3}{2} + 2 = \frac{2+3+4}{2} = \frac{9}{2}$$

188. (b) Given, $\frac{3\sin\theta - \cos\theta}{\cos\theta + \sin\theta} = 1$

$\therefore$ $3\sin\theta - \cos\theta = \cos\theta + \sin\theta$

$\Rightarrow$ $2\sin\theta = 2\cos\theta$

$\Rightarrow$ $1 = \frac{\cos\theta}{\sin\theta} \Rightarrow \cot\theta = 1$

189. (c) Given, $\sin(a+b) = 1$

and $\cos(a-b) = \frac{1}{2}$

Then, $\sin(a+b) = \sin 90°$

$a + b = 90°$ ...(i)

$\cos(a-b) = \cos 60°$

$a - b = 60°$ ...(ii)

From solving Eqs. (i) and (ii),

We have, $a = 75°$.

190. (d) $\frac{\cos(\pi - A)\cot(\frac{\pi}{2} + A)\cos(-A)}{\tan(\pi + A)\tan(\frac{3\pi}{2} + A)\sin(2\pi - A)}$

$$= \frac{-\cos A(-\tan A)\cos A}{\tan A(-\cot A)(-\sin A)}$$
$$= \frac{\cos^2 A}{\cot A\sin A} = \frac{\cot A}{\cot A}\cos A = \cos A$$

191. (a) Given, $\tan(\alpha+\beta) = a$,

and $\tan(\alpha-\beta) = b$

$\therefore$ $\tan 2\alpha = \tan[(\alpha+\beta)+(\alpha-\beta)]$

$$= \frac{\tan(\alpha+\beta)+\tan(\alpha-\beta)}{1-\tan(\alpha+\beta)\tan(\alpha-\beta)} = \frac{a+b}{1-ab}$$

192. (b) Given, $\tan^2\theta + \tan^4\theta = 1$

$\Rightarrow$ $\tan^2\theta(1+\tan^2\theta) = 1$

$\Rightarrow$ $\tan^2\theta\times\sec^2\theta = 1$

$\Rightarrow$ $\tan^2\theta = \frac{1}{\sec^2\theta} \Rightarrow \tan^2\theta = \cos^2\theta$

$\Rightarrow$ $\frac{\sin^2\theta}{\cos^2\theta} = \cos^2\theta \Rightarrow 1-\cos^2\theta = \cos^4\theta$

$\therefore$ $\cos^2\theta + \cos^4\theta = 1$

193. (c) We know that,

$$\tan(A-B) = \frac{\tan A - \tan B}{1+\tan A\tan B}$$

$\therefore$ $\frac{\tan 320° - \tan 310°}{1+\tan 320°\times\tan 310°}$

$$= \tan(320°-310°) = \tan 10° = \frac{1}{\cot 10°}$$
$$= \frac{1}{\cot(90°-80°)} = \frac{1}{\tan 80°} = \frac{1}{\tan 2\times(40°)}$$

Since, $\tan 2\theta = \frac{2\tan\theta}{1-\tan^2\theta}$

$\therefore$ $\frac{1}{\tan 2\times(40°)} = \frac{1-\tan^2 40°}{2\tan 40°} = \frac{1-\alpha^2}{2\alpha}$

194. (d) $\frac{\cos(a-b)-\cos(a+b)}{\cos(a-b)+\cos(a+b)}$

$$= \frac{\cos 30° - \cos 60°}{\cos 30° + \cos 60°}$$

$[\because a = 45° \text{ and } b = 15°]$

$$= \frac{\frac{\sqrt{3}}{2}-\frac{1}{2}}{\frac{\sqrt{3}}{2}+\frac{1}{2}} = \frac{\sqrt{3}-1}{\sqrt{3}+1}$$
$$= \frac{(\sqrt{3}-1)^2}{(\sqrt{3}+1)(\sqrt{3}-1)} = \frac{3+1-2\sqrt{3}}{3-1}$$
$$= \frac{2(2-\sqrt{3})}{2} = 2-\sqrt{3}$$

195. (b) Given, $\tan\theta + \cot\theta = 2$

$\Rightarrow \tan\theta + \frac{1}{\tan\theta} = 2 \Rightarrow \tan^2\theta + 1 = 2\tan\theta$

$\Rightarrow$ $\tan^2\theta - 2\tan\theta + 1 = 0 \Rightarrow (\tan\theta - 1)^2 = 0$

$\Rightarrow$ $\tan\theta - 1 = 0 \Rightarrow \tan\theta = 1 \Rightarrow \cot\theta = 1$

$\therefore$ $\tan^{200}\theta + \cot^{200}\theta = (1)^{200} + (1)^{200}$

$= 1 + 1 = 2$

> **Speedy Method**
>
> Let $\theta = 45° \Rightarrow \tan 45° + \cot 45° = 2$
>
> $\Rightarrow$ $1 + 1 = 2$
>
> $\therefore$ $\tan^{200}\theta + \cot^{200}\theta = 2$

196. (c) Given, $\sec A = \frac{5}{4} = \frac{H}{B}$

$\therefore$ By Pythagoras theorem,

$$P = \sqrt{(5)^2-(4)^2} = \sqrt{25-16} = \sqrt{9} = 3$$

$\therefore$ $\frac{\tan A}{1+\tan^2 A} - \frac{\sin A}{\sec A} = \frac{\frac{3}{4}}{1+\left(\frac{3}{4}\right)^2} - \frac{\frac{3}{5}}{\frac{5}{4}}$

$$= \frac{3}{4}\times\frac{16}{25} - \frac{3}{5}\times\frac{4}{5} = \frac{12}{25} - \frac{12}{25} = 0$$

197. (d) Given, $\sin A = \frac{4}{5}$

Squaring both sides, $(\sin A)^2 = \left(\frac{4}{5}\right)^2$

$$\sin^2 A = \frac{16}{25}$$

198. (a) Given, $\cos\theta + \cos^2\theta = 1$

$\Rightarrow$ $\cos\theta = 1 - \cos^2\theta = \sin^2\theta$

$\therefore$ $\cos^2\theta = \sin^4\theta$ ...(i)

Now, $\sqrt{\sin^4\theta + \cos^2\theta}$

$= \sqrt{\cos^2\theta + \cos^2\theta}$ [$\because$ From Eq. (i)]

$= \sqrt{2\cos^2\theta} = \sqrt{2}\times\cos\theta$

199. (b) Given, $2\sin\theta + 2\sin^2\theta = 2$ ...(i)

$\Rightarrow$ $2\sin\theta = 2 - 2\sin^2\theta = 2(1-\sin^2\theta) = 2\cos^2\theta$

$\Rightarrow$ $\sin\theta = \cos^2\theta$ ...(ii)

Now, $2\cos^4\theta + 2\cos^2\theta = 2(\cos^2\theta)^2 + 2\cos^2\theta$

$= 2(\sin\theta)^2 + 2\sin\theta$ [from Eq. (ii)]

$= 2\sin^2\theta + 2\sin\theta = 2$ [from Eq. (i)]

200. (b) Given, $\tan 3\theta \cdot \tan 7\theta = 1$

$\Rightarrow \quad \tan 3\theta = \dfrac{1}{\tan 7\theta} = \cot 7\theta$

$\Rightarrow \quad \tan 3\theta = \tan(90° - 7\theta)$

$\Rightarrow \quad 3\theta = 90° - 7\theta$

$\Rightarrow \quad 3\theta + 7\theta = 90° \Rightarrow 10\theta = 90°$

$\Rightarrow \quad \theta = \dfrac{90°}{10} = 9°$

$\therefore \ \cot 15\theta = \cot(15 \times 9°) = \cot 135°$

$= \cot(90° + 45°) = -\tan 45° = -1$

201. (d) $\dfrac{1+\sin\theta}{\cos\theta} = \dfrac{1+\sin\theta}{\cos\theta} \times \dfrac{1-\sin\theta}{1-\sin\theta}$

$= \dfrac{1-\sin^2\theta}{\cos\theta(1-\sin\theta)} = \dfrac{\cos^2\theta}{\cos\theta(1-\sin\theta)} = \dfrac{\cos\theta}{1-\sin\theta}$

202. (b) Given, $\tan A = \dfrac{3}{4} = \dfrac{P}{B}$ and $\angle B = 90°$

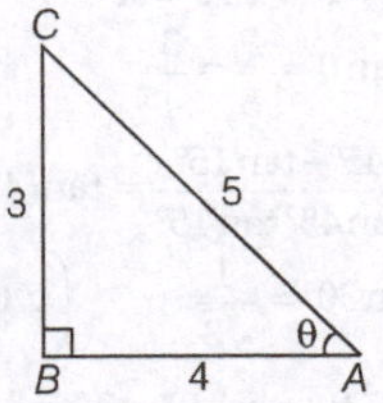

$H = \sqrt{3^2 + 4^2} = 5$

Now, $\sin A + \sin B + \sin C$

$= \dfrac{3}{5} + 1 + \dfrac{4}{5} = \dfrac{3+5+4}{5} = \dfrac{12}{5} = 2\dfrac{2}{5}$

203. (d) Given, $\sin^2\theta - 3\sin\theta + 2 = 0$

$\Rightarrow \ \sin^2\theta - 2\sin\theta - \sin\theta + 2 = 0$

$\Rightarrow \ \sin\theta(\sin\theta - 2) - 1(\sin\theta - 2) = 0$

$\Rightarrow \ (\sin\theta - 1)(\sin\theta - 2) = 0$

$\sin\theta = 1$ and $\sin\theta = 2$

$\because \ \theta = (0° \le \theta \le 90°)$ and $-1 \le \sin\theta \le 1$

$\therefore \ \sin\theta = 2$ Not possible

$\therefore \ \sin\theta = 1 = \sin 90°$

$\theta = 90°$

204. (d) $\tan 27° \tan 34° + \tan 34° \tan 29° + \tan 29° \tan 27°$

Let, $A = 27°, B = 34°, C = 29°$

$\therefore \quad A + B + C = 90°$

$\Rightarrow A + B = 90° - C$

Taking tan both sides,

$\Rightarrow \ \tan(A+B) = \tan(90° - C)$

$\Rightarrow \ \dfrac{\tan A + \tan B}{1 - \tan A \tan B} = \cot C$

$\Rightarrow \ \dfrac{\tan A + \tan B}{1 - \tan A \tan B} = \dfrac{1}{\tan C}$

$\Rightarrow \ \tan A \tan C + \tan B \tan C = 1 - \tan A \tan B$

$\Rightarrow \ \tan A \tan B + \tan B \tan C + \tan C \tan A = 1$

$\therefore \ \tan 27° \tan 34° + \tan 34° \tan 29° + \tan 29° \tan 27° = 1$

205. (c) $\cos 2A \cos 2B + \sin^2(A-B) - \sin^2(A+B)$

$= \cos 2A \cos 2B + \sin(A - B + A + B) \sin(A - B - A - B)$

$= \cos 2A \cos 2B + \sin 2A \sin(-2B)$

$= \cos 2A \cos 2B - \sin 2A \sin 2B = \cos(2A + 2B)$

206. (a) Given, $\operatorname{cosec}\theta + \cot\theta = P$

$\Rightarrow \quad \operatorname{cosec}\theta = P - \cot\theta$

Squaring on both sides,

$\operatorname{cosec}^2\theta = P^2 + \cot^2\theta - 2P\cot\theta$

$\Rightarrow \ \operatorname{cosec}^2\theta - \cot^2\theta = P^2 - 2P\cot\theta$

$\Rightarrow \quad 1 = P^2 - 2P\cot\theta$

$\Rightarrow \quad 2P\cot\theta = P^2 - 1 \qquad \ldots(i)$

Again, $\operatorname{cosec}\theta + \cot\theta = P$

$\Rightarrow \quad \cot\theta = P - \operatorname{cosec}\theta$

Squaring on both sides,

$\cot^2\theta = P^2 + \operatorname{cosec}^2\theta - 2P\operatorname{cosec}\theta$

$\Rightarrow \quad 2P\operatorname{cosec}\theta = P^2 + \operatorname{cosec}^2\theta - \cot^2\theta$

$\Rightarrow \quad 2P\operatorname{cosec}\theta = P^2 + 1 \qquad \ldots(ii)$

Now, $\dfrac{P^2 - 1}{P^2 + 1} = \dfrac{2P\cot\theta}{2P\operatorname{cosec}\theta}$

[From Eqs. (i) and (ii)]

$= \dfrac{\cot\theta}{\operatorname{cosec}\theta} = \dfrac{\cos\theta}{\sin\theta} \times \sin\theta = \cos\theta$

Speedy Method

$\operatorname{cosec}\theta + \cot\theta = P$

So, $\operatorname{cosec}\theta - \cot\theta = \dfrac{1}{P}$

$\dfrac{P^2 - 1}{P^2 + 1} = \dfrac{P\left(P - \dfrac{1}{P}\right)}{P\left(P + \dfrac{1}{P}\right)} = \dfrac{P - \dfrac{1}{P}}{P + \dfrac{1}{P}}$

$= \dfrac{2\cot\theta}{2\operatorname{cosec}\theta} = \dfrac{\cos\theta}{\sin\theta} . \sin\theta = \cos\theta$

207. (c) Given, $b\cos\theta = a \Rightarrow \cos\theta = \dfrac{a}{b}$

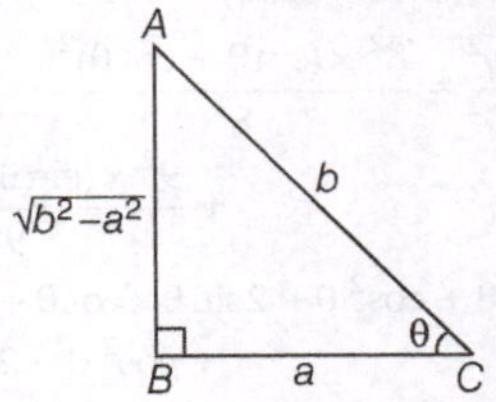

By applying Pythagoras theorem in ΔABC,

$\Rightarrow \ AB^2 = b^2 - a^2 \Rightarrow AB = \sqrt{b^2 - a^2}$

Now, $\operatorname{cosec}\theta = \dfrac{H}{P} = \dfrac{b}{\sqrt{b^2 - a^2}}$

and $\cot\theta = \dfrac{B}{P} = \dfrac{a}{\sqrt{b^2 - a^2}}$

$\therefore \operatorname{cosec}\theta + \cot\theta$

$= \dfrac{b}{\sqrt{b^2 - a^2}} + \dfrac{a}{\sqrt{b^2 - a^2}} = \dfrac{a + b}{\sqrt{b^2 - a^2}}$

$= \sqrt{\dfrac{(a+b)(a+b)}{(a+b)(b-a)}} = \sqrt{\dfrac{b+a}{b-a}}$

208. (c) $\sin 75° + \sin 15°$

We know that,

$\sin C + \sin D = 2\sin\left(\dfrac{C+D}{2}\right)\cos\left(\dfrac{C-D}{2}\right)$

$= 2\sin\left(\dfrac{75° + 15°}{2}\right)\cos\left(\dfrac{75° - 15°}{2}\right)$

$= 2\sin 45° \cos 30° = 2 \times \dfrac{1}{\sqrt{2}} \times \dfrac{\sqrt{3}}{2} = \sqrt{\dfrac{3}{2}}$

209. (c) Given, $\dfrac{2(\cos^2 x - \sec^2 x)}{\tan^2 x} = a + b\cos 2x$

$\text{LHS} = \dfrac{2\left(\cos^2 x - \dfrac{1}{\cos^2 x}\right)}{\dfrac{\sin^2 x}{\cos^2 x}} = \dfrac{2(\cos^4 x - 1)}{\sin^2 x}$

$= \dfrac{2(\cos^2 x + 1)(\cos^2 x - 1)}{\sin^2 x}$

$= \dfrac{-2(\cos^2 x + 1)(1 - \cos^2 x)}{\sin^2 x}$

$= \dfrac{-2(\cos^2 x + 1)(\sin^2 x)}{\sin^2 x}$

$= -2(\cos^2 x + 1) = -(2\cos^2 x - 1) - 3$

$= -(\cos 2x) - 3 = -3 - \cos 2x$

Compare it with $a + b\cos 2x$

$a = -3, \quad b = -1$

210. (c) Given, $\sin\theta = \dfrac{8}{17} = \dfrac{P}{H}$

In ΔABC, by applying Pythagoras theorem

$B = \sqrt{17^2 - 8^2} = 15$

$\therefore \quad \tan\theta + \cot\theta = \dfrac{8}{15} + \dfrac{15}{8} = \dfrac{64 + 225}{120} = \dfrac{289}{120}$

211. (b) Given, $\dfrac{\sin\theta + \cos\theta}{\sin\theta - \cos\theta} = \dfrac{3}{2}$

$\Rightarrow \ 2\sin\theta + 2\cos\theta = 3\sin\theta - 3\cos\theta$

$\Rightarrow \ \sin\theta = 5\cos\theta \Rightarrow \tan\theta = 5$

Now, $\sin^4\theta - \cos^4\theta$

$= (\sin^2\theta + \cos^2\theta)(\sin^2\theta - \cos^2\theta)$

$= -1 \times \cos 2\theta = -\left[\dfrac{1 - \tan^2\theta}{1 + \tan^2\theta}\right]$

$= \dfrac{(5)^2 - 1}{(5)^2 + 1} = \dfrac{24}{26} = \dfrac{12}{13}$

212. (b) Given, $\cos(A - B) = \dfrac{\sqrt{3}}{2}$

$\Rightarrow \quad \cos(A - B) = \cos 30°$

$\Rightarrow \quad A - B = 30° \qquad \ldots(i)$

and $\cos(A + B) = 0 = \cos 90°$

$A + B = 90° \qquad \ldots(ii)$

On adding Eqs. (i) and (ii),

$2A = 120 \Rightarrow A = \dfrac{120}{2} = 60°$

and $\quad B = 90° - 60° = 30°$

213. (b) $\sin 28° \sin 35° \sin 45° \sec 62° \sec 55°$

$= \sin(90° - 62°) \times \sin(90° - 55°) \times \dfrac{1}{\sqrt{2}} \times \sec 62° \times \sec 55°$

$= \cos 62° \times \cos 55° \times \dfrac{1}{\sqrt{2}} \times \dfrac{1}{\cos 62°} \times \dfrac{1}{\cos 55°}$

$= 1 \times 1 \times \dfrac{1}{\sqrt{2}} = \dfrac{1}{\sqrt{2}}$

214. (c) Given, $5\sin^2 A + 3\cos^2 A = 4$

$\Rightarrow 2\sin^2 A + 3\sin^2 A + 3\cos^2 A = 4$

$\Rightarrow 2\sin^2 A + 3(\sin^2 A + \cos^2 A) = 4$

$\Rightarrow 2\sin^2 A + 3 \times 1 = 4 \Rightarrow 2\sin^2 A = 4 - 3 = 1$

$\Rightarrow \sin^2 A = \frac{1}{2} \Rightarrow \sin A = \frac{1}{\sqrt{2}}$

$\Rightarrow \sin A = \sin 45^\circ$

Hence, $\tan A = \tan 45^\circ = 1$

215. (a) $\cos^3 60^\circ - \cos^3 240^\circ - \cos^3 360^\circ$

$= \left(\frac{1}{2}\right)^3 - \cos^3(180^\circ + 60^\circ) - \cos^3(270^\circ + 90^\circ)$

$= \frac{1}{8} - (-\cos^3 60^\circ) - (\sin^3 90^\circ)$

$= \frac{1}{8} + \frac{1}{8} - \sin^3 90^\circ = \frac{2}{8} - (1)^3$

$= \frac{1}{4} - 1 = \frac{1-4}{4} = -\frac{3}{4}$

216. (c) $\tan A \tan B + \frac{\cos x}{\cos A \cos B} = 1$

$\Rightarrow \frac{\sin A \sin B}{\cos A \cos B} + \frac{\cos x}{\cos A \cos B} = 1$

$\Rightarrow \frac{\sin A \sin B + \cos x}{\cos A \cos B} = 1$

$\Rightarrow \sin A \sin B + \cos x = \cos A \cos B$

$\Rightarrow \cos x = \cos A \cos B - \sin A \sin B$

$\Rightarrow \cos x = \cos(A + B) \Rightarrow x = A + B$

217. (c) Given, $\tan(4\alpha - 50^\circ) = \cot(50^\circ - \alpha)$

$\Rightarrow \tan[90^\circ - (140^\circ - 4\alpha)] = \cot(50^\circ - \alpha)$

$\Rightarrow \cot(140^\circ - 4\alpha) = \cot(50^\circ - \alpha)$

$\Rightarrow 140^\circ - 4\alpha = 50^\circ - \alpha$

$\Rightarrow 140^\circ - 50^\circ = -\alpha + 4\alpha \Rightarrow 90^\circ = 3\alpha$

$\therefore \alpha = \frac{90^\circ}{3} = 30^\circ$

218. (c) $\frac{\sin^2 63^\circ + \sin^2 27^\circ}{\cos^2 17^\circ + \cos^2 73^\circ}$

$= \frac{\sin^2(90^\circ - 27^\circ) + \sin^2 27^\circ}{\cos^2(90^\circ - 73^\circ) + \cos^2 73^\circ}$

$= \frac{\cos^2 27^\circ + \sin^2 27^\circ}{\sin^2 73^\circ + \cos^2 73^\circ} = \frac{1}{1} = 1$

219. (c) Given, $\sec x - \cos x = 4$

$\Rightarrow (\sec x - \cos x)^2 = 4^2$

$\Rightarrow (\sec x + \cos x)^2 - 4 \times \sec x \cdot \cos x = 16$

$[\because (a-b)^2 = (a+b)^2 - 4ab]$

$\Rightarrow (\sec x + \cos x)^2 = 16 + 4$

$\Rightarrow \sec x + \cos x = \sqrt{20} = 2\sqrt{5}$

$\Rightarrow \frac{1}{\cos x} + \cos x = 2\sqrt{5}$

$\therefore \frac{1 + \cos^2 x}{\cos x} = 2\sqrt{5}$

220. (b) $2\cos\theta \sin y = \sin(\theta + y) - \sin(\theta - y)$

$= \sin(135^\circ + 15^\circ) - \sin(135^\circ - 15^\circ)$

$= \sin 150^\circ - \sin 120^\circ$

$= \sin(90^\circ + 60^\circ) - \sin(90^\circ + 30^\circ)$

$= \cos 60^\circ - \cos 30^\circ = \frac{1}{2} - \frac{\sqrt{3}}{2} = \frac{1 - \sqrt{3}}{2}$

221. (c) Given, $a^2 = b^2 + (ab)^2$

$= b^2 + a^2b^2 = b^2(1 + a^2)$

$\Rightarrow b^2 = \frac{a^2}{1 + a^2}$

Now, from option (c),

$(\cos x)^2 = \frac{(\cot x)^2}{1 + (\cot x)^2} \Rightarrow \cos^2 x = \frac{\cot^2 x}{1 + \cot^2 x}$

$\Rightarrow \cos^2 x = \frac{\cot^2 x}{\operatorname{cosec}^2 x} \Rightarrow \cos^2 x = \sin^2 x \times \frac{\cos^2 x}{\sin^2 x}$

$\Rightarrow \cos^2 x = \cos^2 x$

So, the option (c) is the correct answer.

222. (a) Given, $\tan(\alpha + \beta) = \sqrt{3} = \tan 60^\circ$

$\Rightarrow \alpha + \beta = 60^\circ$ ...(i)

and $\tan(\alpha - \beta) = 1 = \tan 45^\circ$

$\Rightarrow \alpha - \beta = 45^\circ$ ...(ii)

From Eqs. (i) + (ii), we get

$2\alpha = 60^\circ + 45^\circ = 105^\circ$

$6\alpha = 3 \times 105^\circ = 315^\circ$

Now, $\tan 6\alpha = \tan 315^\circ = \tan(360^\circ - 45^\circ)$

$= -\tan 45^\circ = -1$

223. (a) $\tan 6^\circ \times \tan 45^\circ \times \tan 84^\circ$

$= \tan(90^\circ - 84^\circ) \times \tan 45^\circ \times \tan 84^\circ$

$= \cot 84^\circ \times \tan 45^\circ \times \tan 84^\circ$

$= \tan 45^\circ \times \cot 84^\circ \times \tan 84^\circ = 1 \times 1 = 1$

224. (a) Given,

$\cot A = \frac{12}{5} = \frac{\text{Base } (b)}{\text{Perpendicular } (p)}$

$h = \sqrt{12^2 + 5^2} = \sqrt{169} = 13$

Now, $\sin A = \frac{p}{h} = \frac{5}{13}$

225. (d) Given, $x = 8 \times (\sin\theta + \cos\theta)$

and $y = 9 \times (\sin\theta - \cos\theta)$

$\frac{x^2}{8^2} + \frac{y^2}{9^2} = \frac{8^2 \times (\sin\theta + \cos\theta)^2}{8^2} + \frac{9^2 \times (\sin\theta - \cos\theta)^2}{9^2}$

$= \sin^2\theta + \cos^2\theta + 2\sin\theta \times \cos\theta + \sin^2\theta + \cos^2\theta - 2\sin\theta\cos\theta$

$= 2$

226. (d) Given, $A + B = C$

Multiplying tan on both sides,

$\tan(A + B) = \tan C$

$\Rightarrow \frac{\tan A + \tan B}{1 - \tan A \tan B} = \tan C$

$\Rightarrow \tan A + \tan B = \tan C \times (1 - \tan A \tan B)$

$\Rightarrow \tan A + \tan B = \tan C - \tan A \tan B \tan C$

$\Rightarrow \tan A \tan B \tan C = \tan C - \tan A - \tan B$

227. (c) Given, $\tan A = \frac{10}{15} = \frac{P}{B}$

Using Pythagoras theorem,

$H = \sqrt{P^2 + B^2} = \sqrt{10^2 + 15^2}$

$= \sqrt{325} = 5\sqrt{13}$

Hence, $\cos^2 A = \left(\frac{15}{5\sqrt{13}}\right)^2 = \frac{9}{13}$

228. (d) Given, $4\tan\theta = 3$

$\Rightarrow \tan\theta = \frac{3}{4} = \frac{P}{B}$

Using Pythagoras theorem,

$H = \sqrt{P^2 + B^2} = \sqrt{3^2 + 4^2}$

$= \sqrt{9 + 16} = \sqrt{25} = 5$

$\therefore \frac{4\sin\theta - \cos\theta + 1}{4\sin\theta + \cos\theta - 1} = \frac{4 \times \frac{3}{5} - \frac{4}{5} + 1}{4 \times \frac{3}{5} + \frac{4}{5} - 1}$

$= \frac{12 - 4 + 5}{12 + 4 - 5} = \frac{13}{11}$

229. (d) Given, $\sin\theta = \frac{3}{5} = \frac{P}{H}$

We know, $H^2 = P^2 + B^2$

$\Rightarrow 5^2 = 3^2 + B^2 \Rightarrow B^2 = 25 - 9$

$\Rightarrow B^2 = 16 \Rightarrow B = \sqrt{16} = 4$

$\therefore \tan\theta = \frac{P}{B} = \frac{3}{4}$

230. (c) $\frac{\tan 45^\circ - \tan 15^\circ}{1 + \tan 45^\circ \tan 15^\circ} = \tan(45^\circ - 15^\circ)$

$= \tan 30^\circ = \frac{1}{\sqrt{3}}$ $\left(\because \tan 30^\circ = \frac{1}{\sqrt{3}}\right)$

231. (a) $5(\sin^4\theta + \cos^4\theta) + 3(\sin^6\theta + \cos^6\theta) + 19\sin^2\theta\cos^2\theta$

$= 5(1 - 2\sin^2\theta\cos^2\theta) + 3(1 - 3\sin^2\theta\cos^2\theta)$

$\left[\begin{array}{l}\therefore \sin^4\theta + \cos^4\theta = 1 - 2\sin^2\theta\cos^2\theta \\ \sin^6\theta + \cos^6\theta = 1 - 3\sin^2\theta\cos^2\theta\end{array}\right]$

$= 5 - 10\sin^2\theta\cos^2\theta + 3 - 9\sin^2\theta\cos^2\theta + 19\sin^2\theta\cos^2\theta$

$= 8$

232. (b) Given, $1 + \sin\theta = m\cos\theta$

$\Rightarrow \sin\theta = m\cos\theta - 1$

On squaring both sides,

$\sin^2\theta = (m\cos\theta - 1)^2$

$\Rightarrow \sin^2\theta = m^2\cos^2\theta + 1 - 2m\cos\theta$

$\Rightarrow 1 - \cos^2\theta = m^2\cos^2\theta + 1 - 2m\cos\theta$

$\Rightarrow 2m\cos\theta = m^2\cos^2\theta + \cos^2\theta$

$\Rightarrow 2m\cos\theta = \cos^2\theta(m^2 + 1)$

$\Rightarrow 2m = \cos\theta(m^2 + 1)$

$\Rightarrow \cos\theta = \frac{2m}{m^2 + 1}$

Hence, $\sin\theta = m\cos\theta - 1 = \frac{m \times 2m}{m^2 + 1} - 1$

$= \frac{2m^2 - m^2 - 1}{m^2 + 1} = \frac{m^2 - 1}{m^2 + 1}$

233. (b) $\cos 45^\circ \sin 15^\circ = \frac{2 \times \cos 45^\circ \sin 15^\circ}{2}$

$= \frac{\sin(45^\circ + 15^\circ) - \sin(45^\circ - 15^\circ)}{2}$

$[\because 2\cos A \sin B = \sin(A + B) - \sin(A - B)]$

$= \frac{\sin 60^\circ - \sin 30^\circ}{2} = \frac{\frac{\sqrt{3}}{2} - \frac{1}{2}}{2}$

$= \frac{\sqrt{3} - 1}{2 \times 2} = \frac{\sqrt{3} - 1}{4}$

234. (d) Given, $\tan^2\alpha = 3 + Q^2$

Now, $\sec\alpha + \tan^3\alpha \operatorname{cosec}\alpha$

$$= \sec\alpha + \frac{\sin^3\alpha}{\cos^3\alpha}\times\frac{1}{\sin\alpha}$$

$$= \frac{1}{\cos\alpha} + \frac{\sin^2\alpha}{\cos^3\alpha} = \frac{\cos^2\alpha + \sin^2\alpha}{\cos^3\alpha}$$

$$= \frac{1}{\cos^3\alpha} = \sec^3\alpha = (\sqrt{1+\tan^2\alpha})^3$$

$$= (1+3+Q^2)^{3/2} = (4+Q^2)^{3/2}$$

235. (a) $\tan A - \tan B - \tan C = \tan A \tan B \tan C$

$$\Rightarrow \frac{\sin A}{\cos A} - \frac{\sin B}{\cos B} - \frac{\sin C}{\cos C} = \frac{\sin A \sin B \sin C}{\cos A \cos B \cos C}$$

$$\Rightarrow \frac{\sin A \cos B \cos C - \sin B \cos A \cos C - \sin C \cos A \cos B}{\cos A \cos B \cos C} = \frac{\sin A \sin B \sin C}{\cos A \cos B \cos C}$$

$\Rightarrow \sin A \cos B \cos C - \sin B \cos A \cos C - \sin C \cos A \cos B = \sin A \sin B \sin C$

$\Rightarrow \sin A \cos B \cos C - \sin A \sin B \sin C = \cos A \sin B \cos C + \cos A \sin C \cos B$

$\Rightarrow \sin A(\cos B \cos C - \sin B \sin C) = \cos A(\sin B \cos C + \cos B \sin C)$

$$\Rightarrow \frac{\sin A}{\cos A} = \frac{\sin B \cos C + \cos B \sin C}{\cos B \cos C - \sin B \sin C}$$

$$\Rightarrow \tan A = \frac{\sin(B+C)}{\cos(B+C)}$$

$\Rightarrow \tan A = \tan(B+C) \Rightarrow A = B + C$

Speedy Method

Given, $\tan A - \tan B - \tan C = \tan A.\tan B.\tan C$

$\tan A - \tan A.\tan B.\tan C = \tan B + \tan C$

$\tan A(1 - \tan B.\tan C) = \tan B + \tan C$

$$\tan A = \frac{\tan B + \tan C}{1 - \tan B \tan C}$$

$\Rightarrow \tan A = \tan(B+C)$

So, $A = B + C$

236. (c)

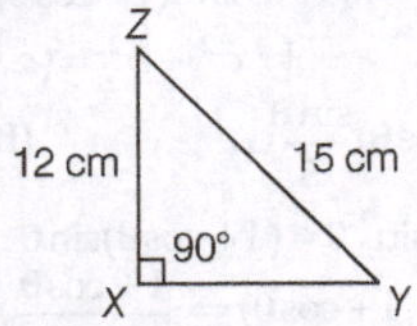

Here, by Pythagoras theorem,

$(YZ)^2 = (XZ)^2 + (XY)^2$

$\Rightarrow (15)^2 = (12)^2 + (XY)^2 \Rightarrow (XY)^2 = 81$

$\Rightarrow XY = 9$ cm

Now, $\cos Y = \frac{XY}{YZ} = \frac{9}{15} = \frac{3}{5}$

237. (b) $\cos^2 15° = \{\cos(60° - 45°)\}^2$

$$= (\cos 60° \cos 45° + \sin 60° \sin 45°)^2$$

$$= \left(\frac{1}{2}\times\frac{1}{\sqrt{2}} + \frac{\sqrt{3}}{2}\times\frac{1}{\sqrt{2}}\right)^2$$

$$= \left(\frac{1}{2\sqrt{2}} + \frac{\sqrt{3}}{2\sqrt{2}}\right)^2 = \left(\frac{1+\sqrt{3}}{2\sqrt{2}}\right)^2$$

$$= \frac{1+3+2\sqrt{3}}{8} = \frac{4+2\sqrt{3}}{8}$$

$$= \frac{2(2+\sqrt{3})}{8} = \frac{2+\sqrt{3}}{4}$$

238. (d) $\sec\theta - 2\cos\theta = \frac{7}{2}$

$\Rightarrow 2\sec\theta - 4\cos\theta = 7$

$\Rightarrow 2\times\frac{1}{\cos\theta} - 4\cos\theta = 7$

$\Rightarrow 2 - 4\cos^2\theta = 7\cos\theta$

$\Rightarrow 4\cos^2\theta + 7\cos\theta - 2 = 0$

$\Rightarrow 4\cos^2\theta + 8\cos\theta - \cos\theta - 2 = 0$

$\Rightarrow 4\cos\theta(\cos\theta + 2) - 1(\cos\theta + 2) = 0$

$\Rightarrow (4\cos\theta - 1)(\cos\theta + 2)$

$\cos\theta = \frac{1}{4}, \cos\theta = -2$ (not possible)

Hence, $\sec\theta = \frac{1}{\cos\theta} = \frac{1}{\frac{1}{4}} \Rightarrow 4$

239. (a) $\sin\theta = \frac{1}{2}$ and $\cos\theta = \sqrt{1-\sin^2\theta}$

$$= \sqrt{1-\left(\frac{1}{2}\right)^2} = \sqrt{1-\frac{1}{4}} = \frac{\sqrt{3}}{2}$$

Now, $3\cos\theta - 4\cos^3\theta = 3\times\frac{\sqrt{3}}{2} - 4\left(\frac{\sqrt{3}}{2}\right)^3$

$$= \frac{3\sqrt{3}}{2} - 4\times\frac{3\sqrt{3}}{8} = \frac{3\sqrt{3}}{2} - \frac{3\sqrt{3}}{2} = 0$$

Speedy Method

$\sin\theta = \frac{1}{2} \Rightarrow \sin\theta = \sin 30° \Rightarrow \theta = 30°$

Now, $3\cos\theta - 4\cos^3\theta = -\cos 3\theta$

$= -\cos 90° = 0$

240. (a) $(\sin A + \cos A)(1 - \sin A \cos A)$

$= (\sin A + \cos A)(\sin^2 A + \cos^2 A - \sin A \cos A)$

$= (\sin^3 A + \cos^3 A)$

241. (c) $\cos\left(-\frac{17\pi}{3}\right) = \cos\left(\frac{17\pi}{3}\right)$

$$= \cos\left(\frac{18\pi - \pi}{3}\right) = \cos\left(6\pi - \frac{\pi}{3}\right) = \cos\left(\frac{\pi}{3}\right) = \frac{1}{2}$$

242. (b) Given, $\cot A = \frac{15}{8}$ then,

$$\tan A = \frac{1}{\cot A} = \frac{8}{15}$$

Now, $\tan 2A = \frac{2\tan A}{1-\tan^2 A} = \frac{2\times\frac{8}{15}}{1-\left(\frac{8}{15}\right)^2}$

$$= \frac{16}{15}\times\frac{225}{161} = \frac{240}{161}$$

243. (b) Given, $\sin 10° - \frac{4}{3}\sin^3 10°$

$$= \frac{3\sin 10° - 4\sin^3 10°}{3}$$

$(\because \sin 3x = 3\sin x - 4\sin^3 x)$

$$= \frac{\sin 30°}{3} = \frac{1}{2\times 3} = \frac{1}{6}$$

244. (d) $\frac{\cos 20°}{\sin 70°} + \frac{\cos\theta}{\sin(90° - \theta)}$

$$= \frac{\cos 20°}{\sin(90° - 20°)} + \frac{\cos\theta}{\sin(90° - \theta)}$$

$$= \frac{\cos 20°}{\cos 20°} + \frac{\cos\theta}{\cos\theta} = 1 + 1 = 2$$

245. (a) $b\sin\theta = a \Rightarrow \frac{a}{b} = \sin\theta$

Now, $\sec\theta + \tan\theta = \frac{1}{\cos\theta} + \frac{\sin\theta}{\cos\theta}$

$$= \frac{1+\sin\theta}{\cos\theta} = \frac{1+\sin\theta}{\sqrt{1-\sin^2\theta}}$$

$(\because \sin^2\theta + \cos^2\theta = 1)$

$$= \frac{1+\frac{a}{b}}{\sqrt{1-\frac{a^2}{b^2}}} = \frac{\frac{b+a}{b}}{\sqrt{\frac{b^2-a^2}{b^2}}} = \frac{b+a}{\sqrt{(b-a)(b+a)}}$$

$$= \frac{\sqrt{b+a}\times\sqrt{b+a}}{\sqrt{b-a}\times\sqrt{b+a}} = \sqrt{\frac{b+a}{b-a}}$$

246. (b) Given, $8\cot\theta = 6 \Rightarrow \tan\theta = \frac{8}{6} = \frac{4}{3}$

Now, $\frac{\sin\theta + \cos\theta}{\sin\theta - \cos\theta} = \frac{\tan\theta + 1}{\tan\theta - 1} = \frac{\frac{4}{3}+1}{\frac{4}{3}-1}$

$$= \frac{4+3}{4-3} = \frac{7}{1} = 7$$

247. (c) $\sqrt{\frac{1+\sin A}{1-\sin A}} = \sqrt{\frac{1+\sin A}{1-\sin A}}\times\sqrt{\frac{1+\sin A}{1+\sin A}}$

$$= \frac{1+\sin A}{\sqrt{1-\sin^2 A}} = \frac{1+\sin A}{\sqrt{\cos^2 A}}$$

$$= \frac{1+\sin A}{\cos A} = \frac{1}{\cos A} + \frac{\sin A}{\cos A}$$

$= \sec A + \tan A$

248. (b) Given, $\tan\theta + \cot\theta = 2$

$$\Rightarrow \frac{\sin\theta}{\cos\theta} + \frac{\cos\theta}{\sin\theta} = 2 \Rightarrow \frac{\sin^2\theta + \cos^2\theta}{\sin\theta\cos\theta} = 2$$

$\Rightarrow 1 = 2\sin\theta\cos\theta \Rightarrow \sin 2\theta = \sin 90° \Rightarrow \theta = 45°$

Then, $\tan^2\theta + \cot^2\theta + 2\tan^5\theta\cot^4\theta$

$= \tan^2 45° + \cot^2 45° + 2\tan^5 45° \cot^4 45°$

$= (1)^2 + (1)^2 + 2\times(1)^5\times(1)^4 = 1 + 1 + 2 = 4$

249. (b) Given, $\tan A = \frac{2}{3} = \frac{P}{B}$

$$H = \sqrt{(3)^2 + (2)^2} = \sqrt{13}$$

$\therefore \sin A = \frac{2}{\sqrt{13}}$ and $\cos A = \frac{3}{\sqrt{13}}$

Then, $(5\sin^2 A - 2\cos^2 A) \div (15\sin^2 A + 3\cos^2 A)$

$$= \left(5\times\frac{4}{13} - 2\times\frac{9}{13}\right) \div \left(15\times\frac{4}{13} + 3\times\frac{9}{13}\right)$$

$$= \frac{2}{13} \div \frac{87}{13} = \frac{2}{87}$$

250. (d) $\cos x \operatorname{cosec} x - \sin x \sec x$

$$= \frac{\cos x}{\sin x} - \frac{\sin x}{\cos x} = \frac{\cos^2 x - \sin^2 x}{\sin x \cos x} = \frac{\cos 2x}{\frac{\sin 2x}{2}}$$

$$= 2\times\frac{\cos 2x}{\sin 2x} = 2\cot 2x$$

251. (c) Given, $\sqrt{\frac{(1+\cos\theta)}{(1-\cos\theta)}}+\sqrt{\frac{(1-\cos\theta)}{(1+\cos\theta)}}$

$=\frac{(1+\cos\theta)}{\sqrt{(1-\cos^2\theta)}}+\frac{(1-\cos\theta)}{\sqrt{(1-\cos^2\theta)}}$

$=\frac{1+\cos\theta}{\sin\theta}+\frac{1-\cos\theta}{\sin\theta}=\frac{1+\cos\theta+1-\cos\theta}{\sin\theta}$

$=\frac{2}{\sin\theta}=2\,\text{cosec}\,\theta$

252. (a) $\cos^2 35°+\cos 55°\times\sin 35°+\frac{\tan 34°}{\cot 56°}$

$=\cos^2 35°+\cos(90°-35°)\times\sin 35°+\frac{\tan(90°-56°)}{\cot 56°}$

$=\cos^2 35°+\sin 35°\times\sin 35°+\frac{\cot 56°}{\cot 56°}$

$=(\cos^2 35°+\sin^2 35°)+1=1+1=2$

253. (c) Given, $\sin\theta=\frac{8}{17}$

$\Rightarrow \text{cosec}\,\theta=\frac{17}{8} \Rightarrow \text{cosec}^2\theta=\frac{289}{64}$

$\Rightarrow 1+\cot^2\theta=\frac{289}{64} \Rightarrow \cot^2\theta=\frac{289}{64}-1$

$\Rightarrow \cot^2\theta=\frac{225}{64} \Rightarrow \tan^2\theta=\frac{64}{225}$

$\therefore \tan\theta=\frac{8}{15}$

254. (d) $\sec 2\theta=\text{cosec}(\theta-36°)$

$\Rightarrow \text{cosec}(90°-2\theta)=\text{cosec}(\theta-36°)$

$\Rightarrow 90°-2\theta=\theta-36° \Rightarrow 3\theta=90°+36°$

$\therefore \theta=\frac{126°}{3}=42°$

255. (c) Given, $\sin\theta+\cos\theta=\frac{\sqrt{3}-1}{2\sqrt{2}}$

Squaring both sides,

$\sin^2\theta+\cos^2\theta+2\sin\theta\cos\theta=\frac{3+1-2\sqrt{3}}{8}$

$\Rightarrow 1+2\sin\theta\cos\theta=\frac{4-2\sqrt{3}}{8}$

$\Rightarrow 2\sin\theta\cos\theta=\frac{4-2\sqrt{3}}{8}-1$

$\Rightarrow 2\sin\theta\cos\theta=\frac{4-2\sqrt{3}-8}{8}$

$\Rightarrow \sin\theta\cos\theta=\frac{-2\sqrt{3}-4}{8\times 2}$

$\Rightarrow \sin\theta\cos\theta=\frac{-(\sqrt{3}+2)}{8}$ ...(i)

$\therefore \tan\theta+\cot\theta=\frac{\sin\theta}{\cos\theta}+\frac{\cos\theta}{\sin\theta}$

$=\frac{\sin^2\theta+\cos^2\theta}{\sin\theta\cos\theta}=\frac{1}{\sin\theta\cos\theta}=\frac{-8}{(\sqrt{3}+2)}$ [from Eq. (i)]

$=\frac{-8}{\sqrt{3}+2}\times\frac{\sqrt{3}-2}{\sqrt{3}-2}=\frac{-8(\sqrt{3}-2)}{3-4}=8(\sqrt{3}-2)$

256. (b)

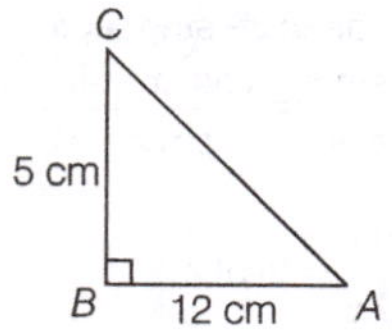

$\tan A=\frac{5}{12}=\frac{P}{B}$

Now, by Pythagoras theorem,

$H=\sqrt{P^2+B^2}=\sqrt{(5)^2+(12)^2}$

$=\sqrt{25+144}=\sqrt{169}=13$

Then, $\sin A+\sin B+\sin C$

$=\frac{BC}{AC}+\sin 90°+\frac{AB}{AC}$

$=\frac{5}{13}+1+\frac{12}{13}=1+\frac{17}{13}$

$=2+\frac{4}{13}=2\frac{4}{13}$

257. (c) $\frac{\cos x-\sqrt{3}\sin x}{2}=\frac{\cos x}{2}-\frac{\sqrt{3}\sin x}{2}$

$=\frac{1}{2}\cdot\cos x-\frac{\sqrt{3}}{2}\sin x$

$=\cos 60°\cos x-\sin 60°\sin x$

$=\cos(60°+x)=\cos\left(\frac{\pi}{3}+x\right)$

258. (d) Given, $\cot B=9 \Rightarrow \tan B=\frac{1}{9}$

$\Rightarrow \sec^2 B=1+\tan^2 B \Rightarrow \sec^2 B=1+\left(\frac{1}{9}\right)^2$

$\Rightarrow \sec^2 B=1+\frac{1}{81} \Rightarrow \sec^2 B=\frac{82}{81}$

259. (b) $\frac{k-k\cot^2 30°}{1+\cot^2 30°}$

$=\sin^2 60°+4\tan^2 45°-\text{cosec}^2 60°$

$\Rightarrow \frac{k-k(\sqrt{3})^2}{1+(\sqrt{3})^2}=\left(\frac{\sqrt{3}}{2}\right)^2+4\times(1)^2-\left(\frac{2}{\sqrt{3}}\right)^2$

$\Rightarrow \frac{k-3k}{1+3}=\frac{3}{4}+4-\frac{4}{3}$

$\Rightarrow \frac{-2k}{4}=\frac{3\times 3+4\times 12-4\times 4}{12}$

$\Rightarrow \frac{-k}{2}=\frac{9+48-16}{12} \Rightarrow -k=\frac{41}{6}$

$\Rightarrow k=-6.83$

260. (a) $\tan(\theta-14\pi)=-\tan(14\pi-\theta)$

$=-\tan\{(2\times 7\pi)-\theta\}=-(-\tan\theta)=\tan\theta$

261. (d) $\sin^4\theta+\cos^4\theta=\sin^4\theta+(1-\sin^2\theta)^2$

$=\sin^4\theta+1+\sin^4\theta-2\sin^2\theta$

$=2\sin^4\theta-2\sin^2\theta+1$

262. (d) Given; $(\cos q+\sin q)=\frac{31}{25}$

Squaring both sides,

$\cos^2 q+2\cos q\sin q+\sin^2 q=\left(\frac{31}{25}\right)^2$

$\Rightarrow (1+2\cos q\sin q)=\frac{961}{625}$

$\Rightarrow 1+\sin 2q=\frac{961}{625} \Rightarrow \sin 2q=\frac{336}{625}$

$\therefore \cos 2q=\sqrt{1-\sin^2 2q}=\sqrt{1-\left(\frac{336}{625}\right)^2}$

$=\sqrt{\frac{390625-112896}{(625)^2}}=\frac{527}{625}$

263. (a) Given, $\frac{1}{1+\cos(90°-\theta)}+\frac{1}{1-\cos(90°-\theta)}$

$=\frac{1}{1+\sin\theta}+\frac{1}{1-\sin\theta}$

$=\frac{1-\sin\theta+1+\sin\theta}{(1-\sin^2\theta)}$

$=\frac{2}{\cos^2\theta}=2\sec^2\theta$

264. (b) Given, $\frac{\cos A}{1+\tan A}-\frac{\sin A}{1+\cot A}$

$=\frac{\cos A}{1+\frac{\sin A}{\cos A}}-\frac{\sin A}{1+\frac{\cos A}{\sin A}}$

$=\frac{\cos^2 A}{\cos A+\sin A}-\frac{\sin^2 A}{\cos A+\sin A}$

$=\frac{(\cos A+\sin A)(\cos A-\sin A)}{\cos A+\sin A}$

$=\cos A-\sin A$

265. (b) Given, $\sin A=\frac{4}{5}$ and $\sin B=\frac{15}{17}$

Then, $\cos A=\sqrt{1-\sin^2 A}$

$=\sqrt{1-\left(\frac{4}{5}\right)^2}=\sqrt{\frac{9}{25}}=\frac{3}{5}$

and $\cos B=\sqrt{1-\sin^2 B}=\sqrt{1-\left(\frac{15}{17}\right)^2}=\frac{8}{17}$

Now, $\sin(A-B)=\sin A\cos B-\cos A\sin B$

$=\frac{4}{5}\times\frac{8}{17}-\frac{3}{5}\times\frac{15}{17}=\frac{32}{85}-\frac{45}{85}=-\frac{13}{85}$

266. (a) Given, $\frac{1-\cos\theta}{\sin\theta}=\frac{1}{5}$

$\Rightarrow 1-\cos\theta=\frac{\sin\theta}{5}$ ...(i)

By trigonometric formula,

$\sin^2\theta+\cos^2\theta=1$

$\Rightarrow \sin^2\theta=1-\cos^2\theta$

$=(1+\cos\theta)(1-\cos\theta)$

$[\because a^2-b^2=(a+b)(a-b)]$

$=(1+\cos\theta)\frac{\sin\theta}{5}$ [from Eq. (i)]

$\Rightarrow 5\sin^2\theta=(1+\cos\theta)\sin\theta$

$\Rightarrow 5\sin\theta=(1+\cos\theta) \Rightarrow \frac{1+\cos\theta}{\sin\theta}=5$

267. (b) Given, $\tan A+\cot A=2$

$\Rightarrow (\tan A+\cot A)^2=2^2$

$\Rightarrow \tan^2 A+\cot^2 A+2\cdot\tan A\cdot\cot A=4$

$\Rightarrow \tan^2 A+\cot^2 A+2=4$

$\Rightarrow \tan^2 A+\cot^2 A=4-2=2$

$\Rightarrow 2(\tan^2 A+\cot^2 A)=2\times 2=4$

268. (a) $\cot 15°\cot 25°\cot 45°\cot 75°\cot 65°$

$=\cot(90°-75°)\cdot\cot(90°-65°)\cdot\cot 45°\cot 75°\cot 65°$

$=\tan 75°\cdot\tan 65°\cot 75°\cot 65°$

$=1\times 1=1$

269. (a) We know that, $\operatorname{cosec}^2 A-\cot^2 A=1$

$\Rightarrow (\operatorname{cosec}A-\cot A)(\operatorname{cosec}A+\cot A)=1$

$\Rightarrow \frac{1}{4}(\operatorname{cosec}A+\cot A)=1$

$\operatorname{cosec}A+\cot A=4$ ...(i)

Now, $\operatorname{cosec}A-\cot A=\frac{1}{4}$ ...(ii)

Subtracting Eq. (ii) from Eq. (i), we get

$\operatorname{cosec}A+\cot A-\operatorname{cosec}A+\cot A=4-\frac{1}{4}$

$\Rightarrow 2\cot A=\frac{15}{4}\Rightarrow \cot A=\frac{15}{8}\Rightarrow \tan A=\frac{8}{15}$

270. (b) $\sin\theta+\cos\theta=\sqrt{5}\sin(90°-\theta)$

$\Rightarrow \sin\theta+\cos\theta=\sqrt{5}\cos\theta$

$\Rightarrow \sin\theta=\sqrt{5}\cos\theta-\cos\theta$

$\Rightarrow \sin\theta=\cos\theta(\sqrt{5}-1)$

$\Rightarrow \frac{\cos\theta}{\sin\theta}=\frac{1}{\sqrt{5}-1}\Rightarrow \cot\theta=\frac{1}{\sqrt{5}-1}\times\frac{\sqrt{5}+1}{\sqrt{5}+1}$

$\cot\theta=\frac{\sqrt{5}+1}{5-1}=\frac{\sqrt{5}+1}{4}$

271. (a) $\sin(A+B)=\cos(A+B)$

$\Rightarrow \frac{\sin(A+B)}{\cos(A+B)}=1\Rightarrow \tan(A+B)=1$

$\Rightarrow \frac{\tan A+\tan B}{1-\tan A\tan B}=1$

$\Rightarrow 1-\tan A\tan B=\tan A+\tan B$

$\Rightarrow 1-\tan B=\tan A(1+\tan B)$

$\Rightarrow \tan A=\frac{1-\tan B}{1+\tan B}$

272. (c) $\sec\theta+\tan^3\theta\operatorname{cosec}\theta$

$=\sec\theta\left(1+\frac{\tan^3\theta\cdot\operatorname{cosec}\theta}{\sec\theta}\right)$

$=\sec\theta\left(1+\tan^3\theta\cdot\frac{\cos\theta}{\sin\theta}\right)$

$=\sec\theta(1+\tan^3\theta\cdot\cot\theta)$

$=\sec\theta\,(1+\tan^2\theta)$

$=\sqrt{1+\tan^2\theta}(1+\tan^2\theta)$ $[\because \sec^2\theta=1+\tan^2\theta]$

$=\sqrt{1+1-a^2}\times(1+1-a^2)$

$=(2-a^2)^{\frac{1}{2}}(2-a^2)=(2-a^2)^{\frac{3}{2}}$

273. (a) $\cos A=\frac{9}{41}=\frac{b}{h}$

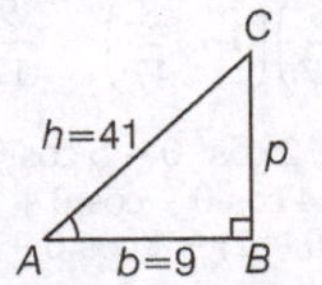

So, perpendicular $(p)=\sqrt{h^2-b^2}$

$=\sqrt{41^2-9^2}=\sqrt{1681-81}=\sqrt{1600}=40$

Now, $\cot A=\frac{b}{p}=\frac{9}{40}$

274. (b) $\tan\theta+\sec\theta=7$ ...(i)

$\sec\theta-\tan\theta=\frac{1}{7}$ ...(ii)

Add Eqs. (i) and (ii),

$2\sec\theta=\frac{50}{7}$

$\sec\theta=\frac{25}{7}\Rightarrow \cos\theta=\frac{7}{25}$

$\sin\theta=\sqrt{1-\frac{49}{625}}=\frac{24}{25}$

275. (a) Since, $\sin C-\sin D$

$=2\cos\frac{C+D}{2}\times\sin\frac{C-D}{2}$

$\therefore \sin\alpha-\sin\beta=2\cos\frac{\alpha+\beta}{2}\times\sin\frac{\alpha-\beta}{2}$

276. (b) Given,

$(\sin 30°\times\cos 60°-\cos 30°\times\sin 60°)$

$=\left(\frac{1}{2}\times\frac{1}{2}-\frac{\sqrt{3}}{2}\times\frac{\sqrt{3}}{2}\right)=\left(\frac{1}{4}-\frac{3}{4}\right)$

$=\frac{1-3}{4}=\frac{-2}{4}=-\frac{1}{2}=-\sin 30°$

277. (c) Given, $\frac{\sin 30°\sin 40°\sin 50°\sin 60°}{\cos 30°\cos 40°\cos 50°\cos 60°}$

$=\frac{\sin(90°-60°)\times\sin(90°-50°)\times\sin(90°-40°)\times\sin(90°-30°)}{\cos 30°\times\cos 40°\times\cos 50°\times\cos 60°}$

$=\frac{\cos 60°\times\cos 50°\times\cos 40°\times\cos 30°}{\cos 30°\times\cos 40°\times\cos 50°\times\cos 60°}=1$

278. (b) Value of

$\tan^2\theta+\cot^2\theta-\sec^2\theta\operatorname{cosec}^2\theta$

$=(\sec^2\theta-1)+(\operatorname{cosec}^2\theta-1)-\sec^2\theta\operatorname{cosec}^2\theta$

$=\sec^2\theta-\sec^2\theta\operatorname{cosec}^2\theta+\operatorname{cosec}^2\theta-2$

$=\sec^2\theta(1-\operatorname{cosec}^2\theta)+\operatorname{cosec}^2\theta\ 2$

$=\sec^2\theta\times-\cot^2\theta+\operatorname{cosec}^2\theta-2$

$=-\operatorname{cosec}^2\theta+\operatorname{cosec}^2\theta-2=-2$

Speedy Method

Put $\theta=45°$

$\tan^2 45°+\cot^2 45°-\sec^2 45°\cdot\operatorname{cosec}^2 45°$

$=1+1-2\times2=2-4=-2$

279. (c) Given, $\frac{\cos 45°}{\sec 30°+\operatorname{cosec} 30°}$

$=\frac{1/\sqrt{2}}{\frac{2}{\sqrt{3}}+2}=\frac{1/\sqrt{2}}{\frac{2\times(1+\sqrt{3})}{\sqrt{3}}}$

$=\frac{\sqrt{3}}{2(\sqrt{2}+\sqrt{6})}\times\frac{(\sqrt{6}-\sqrt{2})}{(\sqrt{6}-\sqrt{2})}$

$=\frac{3\sqrt{2}-\sqrt{6}}{2(6-2)}=\frac{3\sqrt{2}-\sqrt{6}}{8}$

280. (c) Given, $\sec 31°=x$.

Then, $\sin^2 59°+\frac{1}{\sec^2 31°}-\frac{1}{\sin^2 59°\operatorname{cosec}^2 59°}$

$=\sin^2 59°+\cos^2 31°-\frac{1}{\sin^2 59°\cdot\frac{1}{\sin^2 59°}}$ $\left(\because \cos\theta=\frac{1}{\sec\theta}\right)$

$=\sin^2 59°+\cos^2 31°-1$

$=\sin^2(90°-31°)+\cos^2 31°-1$ $[\because \sin(90°-\theta)=\cos\theta]$

$=\cos^2 31°+\cos^2 31°-1$

$=2\cos^2 31°-1=\frac{2}{\sec^2 31°}-1$

$=\frac{2}{x^2}-1=\frac{2-x^2}{x^2}$

281. (b) Given, $\frac{\sin\theta+\cos\theta}{\sin\theta-\cos\theta}=\frac{5}{1}$

$\Rightarrow \sin\theta+\cos\theta=5\sin\theta-5\cos\theta$

$\Rightarrow 5\sin\theta-\sin\theta=\cos\theta+5\cos\theta$

$\Rightarrow 4\sin\theta=6\cos\theta$

$\Rightarrow \frac{\sin\theta}{\cos\theta}=\frac{6}{4}=\frac{3}{2}\Rightarrow \tan\theta=\frac{3}{2}$ ...(i)

We know that, $\tan\theta=\frac{P}{B}=\frac{3}{2}$

By Pythagoras theorem,

$(H)^2=(3)^2+(2)^2=9+4$

$\Rightarrow (H)^2=13\Rightarrow H=\sqrt{13}$

Now, $\sin\theta=\frac{P}{H}=\frac{3}{\sqrt{13}}$ ...(ii)

$\cos\theta=\frac{B}{H}=\frac{2}{\sqrt{13}}$ ...(iii)

Then, $\frac{4\sin^2\theta+3}{2\cos^2\theta+2}=\frac{4\times\left(\frac{3}{\sqrt{13}}\right)^2+3}{2\times\left(\frac{2}{\sqrt{13}}\right)^2+2}$

$=\frac{4\times\frac{9}{13}+3}{2\times\frac{4}{13}+2}=\frac{\frac{36+39}{13}}{\frac{8+26}{13}}=\frac{75}{34}$

282. (b) Given,

$\frac{(\sin\theta+\sec\theta)^2+(\cos\theta+\operatorname{cosec}\theta)^2}{(1+\sec\theta\operatorname{cosec}\theta)^2}$

$=\frac{\left(\sin\theta+\frac{1}{\cos\theta}\right)^2+\left(\cos\theta+\frac{1}{\sin\theta}\right)^2}{\left(1+\frac{1}{\sin\theta\cos\theta}\right)^2}$

$=\frac{\frac{(\sin\theta\cos\theta+1)^2}{\cos^2\theta}+\frac{(\sin\theta\cos\theta+1)^2}{\sin^2\theta}}{\frac{(\sin\theta\cos\theta+1)^2}{\sin^2\theta\cos^2\theta}}$

$=\frac{\frac{1}{\cos^2\theta}+\frac{1}{\sin^2\theta}}{\frac{1}{\sin^2\theta\cos^2\theta}}=\sin^2\theta+\cos^2\theta=1$

Speedy Method

Put $\theta=45°$

$\frac{(\sin 45°+\sec 45°)^2+(\cos 45°+\operatorname{cosec} 45°)^2}{(1+\sec 45°\operatorname{cosec} 45°)^2}$

$=\frac{\left(\frac{1}{\sqrt{2}}+\sqrt{2}\right)^2+\left(\frac{1}{\sqrt{2}}+\sqrt{2}\right)^2}{(1+\sqrt{2}\times\sqrt{2})^2}$

$=\frac{\frac{1}{2}+2+2\times1+\frac{1}{2}+2+2\times1}{(3)^2}=\frac{9}{9}=1$

283. (a) $\dfrac{\sec^2 60^\circ \cos^2 45^\circ + \operatorname{cosec}^2 30^\circ}{\cot 30^\circ \times \sec^2 45^\circ - \operatorname{cosec}^2 30^\circ \tan 45^\circ}$

$= \dfrac{(2)^2 \times \left(\frac{1}{\sqrt{2}}\right)^2 + (2)^2}{(\sqrt{3}) \times (\sqrt{2})^2 - (2)^2 \times 1}$

$= \dfrac{2+4}{2\sqrt{3}-4} = \dfrac{6}{2(\sqrt{3}-2)} = \dfrac{3}{(\sqrt{3}-2)}$

$= -\dfrac{3}{(2-\sqrt{3})} \times \dfrac{(2+\sqrt{3})}{(2+\sqrt{3})} = -3(2+\sqrt{3})$

284. (c) $\sin^2\theta - 2\sin\theta + 1 = 0$

$\Rightarrow \sin^2\theta - \sin\theta - \sin\theta + 1 = 0$

$\Rightarrow (\sin\theta - 1)(\sin\theta - 1) = 0$

$\Rightarrow \sin\theta = 1 \Rightarrow \sin\theta = \sin 90^\circ$

$\therefore \theta = 90^\circ$

Now, $\dfrac{1+\operatorname{cosec}\theta}{1-\cos\theta} = \dfrac{1+\operatorname{cosec}90^\circ}{1-\cos 90^\circ}$

$= \dfrac{1+1}{1-0} = 2$

285. (b) Given, $\tan\theta + 3\cot\theta - 2\sqrt{3} = 0$

$\Rightarrow \tan\theta + \dfrac{3}{\tan\theta} - 2\sqrt{3} = 0$

$\Rightarrow \tan^2\theta - 2\sqrt{3}\tan\theta + 3 = 0$

$\Rightarrow \tan^2\theta - \sqrt{3}\tan\theta - \sqrt{3}\tan\theta + 3 = 0$

$\Rightarrow \tan\theta(\tan\theta - \sqrt{3}) - \sqrt{3}(\tan\theta - \sqrt{3}) = 0$

$\Rightarrow \tan\theta = \sqrt{3}$ or $\theta = 60^\circ$

$\therefore (\operatorname{cosec}^2\theta + \cos^2\theta) = (\operatorname{cosec}^2 60^\circ + \cos^2 60^\circ)$

$= \left(\dfrac{2}{\sqrt{3}}\right)^2 + \left(\dfrac{1}{2}\right)^2 = \dfrac{4}{3} + \dfrac{1}{4} = \dfrac{19}{12}.$

286. (c) $\sec^2\alpha\left(1+\dfrac{1}{\operatorname{cosec}\alpha}\right)\left(1-\dfrac{1}{\operatorname{cosec}\alpha}\right)$

$= \sec^2\alpha\left((1)^2 - \dfrac{1}{\operatorname{cosec}^2\alpha}\right)$

$= \sec^2\alpha - \dfrac{\sec^2\alpha}{\operatorname{cosec}^2\alpha}$

$= \sec^2\alpha - \dfrac{1}{\cos^2\alpha} \times \dfrac{\sin^2\alpha}{1}$

$= \sec^2\alpha - \tan^2\alpha = 1$

287. (b) Given, $\cot A = \dfrac{1}{2} = \dfrac{B}{P}$

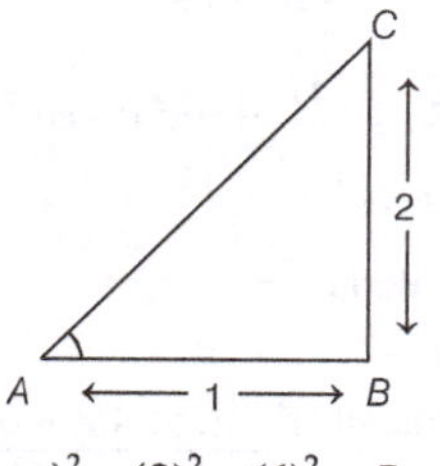

$\Rightarrow$ (Hypotenuse)$^2 = (2)^2 + (1)^2 = 5$

$\Rightarrow$ Hypotenuse $= \sqrt{5}$

Now, $\sin A = \dfrac{P}{H} = \dfrac{2}{\sqrt{5}}$

$\cos C = \dfrac{2}{\sqrt{5}}, \cos A = \dfrac{1}{\sqrt{5}}, \sin C = \dfrac{1}{\sqrt{5}}$

$\therefore \dfrac{\sin A(\cos C + \cos A)}{\cos C(\sin C - \sin A)} = \dfrac{\frac{2}{\sqrt{5}}\left(\frac{2}{\sqrt{5}} + \frac{1}{\sqrt{5}}\right)}{\frac{2}{\sqrt{5}}\left(\frac{1}{\sqrt{5}} - \frac{2}{\sqrt{5}}\right)}$

$= \dfrac{\frac{2}{\sqrt{5}} \times \frac{3}{\sqrt{5}}}{\frac{2}{\sqrt{5}} \times \left(-\frac{1}{\sqrt{5}}\right)} = -3$

288. (b) $\sqrt{\dfrac{\sec^2\theta + \operatorname{cosec}^2\theta}{\tan^2\theta - \sin^2\theta}}$

$= \sqrt{\dfrac{\frac{1}{\cos^2\theta} + \frac{1}{\sin^2\theta}}{\frac{\sin^2\theta}{\cos^2\theta} - \sin^2\theta}}$

$= \sqrt{\dfrac{\frac{\sin^2\theta + \cos^2\theta}{\sin^2\theta\cos^2\theta}}{\frac{\sin^2\theta - \sin^2\theta\cos^2\theta}{\cos^2\theta}}}\sqrt{\dfrac{\frac{1}{\sin^2\theta}}{\frac{\sin^2\theta(1-\cos^2\theta)}{1}}}$

$= \sqrt{\dfrac{1}{\sin^2\theta \times \sin^2\theta \times \sin^2\theta}} = \sqrt{\operatorname{cosec}^6\theta}$

$= \operatorname{cosec}^3\theta$

289. (c) Given, $\dfrac{\sin^2\theta}{\tan^2\theta - \sin^2\theta} = 5$

$\Rightarrow \sin^2\theta = 5\tan^2\theta - 5\sin^2\theta$

$\Rightarrow 6\sin^2\theta = 5\tan^2\theta$

$\Rightarrow 6\sin^2\theta = 5 \times \dfrac{\sin^2\theta}{\cos^2\theta} \Rightarrow \cos^2\theta = \dfrac{5}{6}$

We know that, $\sin^2\theta + \cos^2\theta = 1$

$\Rightarrow \sin^2\theta = 1 - \cos^2\theta = 1 - \dfrac{5}{6} \Rightarrow \sin^2\theta = \dfrac{1}{6}$

Now, $\sec^2\theta = \dfrac{1}{\cos^2\theta} = \dfrac{1}{\frac{5}{6}} \Rightarrow \sec^2\theta = \dfrac{6}{5}$

and $\operatorname{cosec}^2\theta = \dfrac{1}{\sin^2\theta} = \dfrac{1}{\frac{1}{6}} \Rightarrow \operatorname{cosec}^2\theta = 6$

$\Rightarrow \cot^2\theta = \dfrac{\cos^2\theta}{\sin^2\theta} = \dfrac{\frac{5}{6}}{\frac{1}{6}} \Rightarrow \cot^2\theta = 5$

$\therefore \dfrac{24\sin^2\theta - 15\sec^2\theta}{6\operatorname{cosec}^2\theta - 7\cot^2\theta}$

$= \dfrac{24 \times \left(\frac{1}{6}\right) - 15 \times \left(\frac{6}{5}\right)}{6 \times (6) - 7 \times 5} = \dfrac{4-18}{36-35} = -14$

290. (c) $\sin^2\theta - \cos^2\theta - 3\sin\theta + 2 = 0$

$\sin^2\theta - (1 - \sin^2\theta) - 3\sin\theta + 2 = 0$

$\Rightarrow \sin^2\theta - 1 + \sin^2\theta - 3\sin\theta + 2 = 0$

$\Rightarrow 2\sin^2\theta - 3\sin\theta + 1 = 0$

$\Rightarrow 2\sin^2\theta - 2\sin\theta - \sin\theta + 1 = 0$

$\Rightarrow (2\sin\theta - 1)(\sin\theta - 1) = 0$

$\Rightarrow \sin\theta = \dfrac{1}{2}, \sin\theta = 1$

$\sin\theta = \sin 30^\circ$

$\therefore \theta = 30^\circ$ [$\because 0^\circ < \theta < 90^\circ$]

Then, $\dfrac{1}{\sqrt{\sec\theta - \tan\theta}} = \dfrac{1}{\sqrt{(\sec 30^\circ - \tan 30^\circ)}}$

$= \dfrac{1}{\left(\frac{2}{\sqrt{3}} - \frac{1}{\sqrt{3}}\right)^{1/2}} = \dfrac{1}{\left[\frac{1}{\sqrt{3}}\right]^{1/2}} = (3)^{1/4}$ or $\sqrt[4]{3}$

291. (d) Given expression,

$\dfrac{\tan^2 30^\circ}{\sec^2 30^\circ} + \dfrac{\operatorname{cosec}^2 45^\circ}{\cot^2 45^\circ} - \dfrac{\sec^2 60^\circ}{\operatorname{cosec}^2 60^\circ}$

$= \dfrac{\left(\frac{1}{\sqrt{3}}\right)^2}{\left(\frac{2}{\sqrt{3}}\right)^2} + \dfrac{(\sqrt{2})^2}{(1)^2} - \dfrac{(2)^2}{\left(\frac{2}{\sqrt{3}}\right)^2} = \dfrac{\left(\frac{1}{3}\right)}{\frac{4}{3}} + \dfrac{2}{1} - \dfrac{4}{\frac{4}{3}}$

$= \dfrac{1}{4} + 2 - 3 = \dfrac{1}{4} - 1 = -\dfrac{3}{4}$

292. (a) If a and b both are positive then minimum value of $a\sec^2\theta + b\cos^2\theta = 2\sqrt{ab}$

here, $a = 9, b = 25$

$\therefore$ Minimum value

$= 2\sqrt{25 \times 9} = 2 \times 5 \times 3 = 30$

293. (c) Given, $\cos(2\theta + 54^\circ) = \sin\theta$

$\Rightarrow \cos(2\theta + 54^\circ) = \cos(90^\circ - \theta)$

$\Rightarrow 2\theta + 54^\circ = 90^\circ - \theta$

$\Rightarrow 3\theta = 36^\circ \Rightarrow \theta = 12^\circ$

$\therefore \dfrac{1}{\cot 5\theta + \sec\dfrac{5\theta}{2}}$

$= \dfrac{1}{\cot(5 \times 12^\circ) + \sec\left(\frac{5 \times 12^\circ}{2}\right)}$

$= \dfrac{1}{\cot 60^\circ + \sec 30^\circ} = \dfrac{1}{\left(\frac{1}{\sqrt{3}}\right) + \left(\frac{2}{\sqrt{3}}\right)} = \dfrac{\sqrt{3}}{3}$

294. (b) Given, $\cot\theta = \dfrac{15}{8} = \dfrac{B}{P}$

By Pythagoras theorem,

$\Rightarrow (H)^2 = (15)^2 + (8)^2 = 225 + 64$

$\Rightarrow (H)^2 = 289 \Rightarrow H = \sqrt{289} = 17$

$\therefore \dfrac{(1-\cos\theta)(2+2\cos\theta)}{(2-2\sin\theta)(1+\sin\theta)}$

$= \dfrac{\left(1-\frac{15}{17}\right) \times 2\left(1+\frac{15}{17}\right)}{2\left(1-\frac{8}{17}\right)\left(1+\frac{8}{17}\right)} = \dfrac{\frac{2}{17} \times \frac{32}{17}}{\frac{9}{17} \times \frac{25}{17}} = \dfrac{64}{225}$

295. (a) Given, $2\cos^2\theta - 5\cos\theta + 2 = 0$

$\Rightarrow 2\cos^2\theta - 4\cos\theta - \cos\theta + 2 = 0$

$\Rightarrow 2\cos\theta(\cos\theta - 2) - 1(\cos\theta - 2) = 0$

$\Rightarrow (2\cos\theta - 1)(\cos\theta - 2) = 0$

$\Rightarrow \cos\theta = \dfrac{1}{2}, \cos\theta = 2$ (Not taken)

$\Rightarrow \cos\theta = \cos 60^\circ$

$\Rightarrow \theta = 60^\circ$ [$\because 0 < \theta < 90^\circ$]

$\therefore \sec\theta + \tan\theta = \sec 60^\circ + \tan 60^\circ = 2 + \sqrt{3}$

296. (a) Given,

$$\sec(5\alpha - 15°) = \text{cosec}\,(15° - 2\alpha)$$
$$\Rightarrow \sec(5\alpha - 15°) = \sec[90° - (15° - 2\alpha)]$$
$$\Rightarrow 5\alpha - 15° = 90° - 15° + 2\alpha$$
$$\Rightarrow 3\alpha = 90° \Rightarrow \alpha = 30°$$
$$\therefore \cos\alpha + \sin 2\alpha + \tan(1.5\alpha)$$
$$= \cos 30° + \sin 60° + \tan 45°$$
$$= \frac{\sqrt{3}}{2} + \frac{\sqrt{3}}{2} + 1 = 2\left(\frac{\sqrt{3}}{2}\right) + 1 = (\sqrt{3} + 1)$$

297. (a) Given, $(\sec\theta + \tan\theta)^2 + \dfrac{(1 + \text{cosec}\theta)}{(1 - \text{cosec}\theta)}$

$$= \left(\frac{1}{\cos\theta} + \frac{\sin\theta}{\cos\theta}\right)^2 + \frac{(1 + \text{cosec}\theta)}{(1 - \text{cosec}\theta)}$$
$$= \frac{(1 + \sin\theta)^2}{\cos^2\theta} + \frac{(1 + \text{cosec}\theta)}{(1 - \text{cosec}\theta)}$$
$$= \frac{(1 + \sin\theta)(1 + \sin\theta)}{(1 - \sin^2\theta)} + \frac{(1 + \text{cosec}\theta)}{(1 - \text{cosec}\theta)}$$
$$= \frac{(1 + \sin\theta)(1 + \sin\theta)}{(1 + \sin\theta)(1 - \sin\theta)} + \frac{1 + \text{cosec}\theta}{1 - \text{cosec}\theta}$$
$$= \frac{(1 + \sin\theta)}{(1 - \sin\theta)} + \frac{(1 + \text{cosec}\theta)}{(1 - \text{cosec}\theta)}$$
$$= \frac{\left(1 + \dfrac{1}{\text{cosec}\,\theta}\right)}{\left(1 - \dfrac{1}{\text{cosec}\,\theta}\right)} + \frac{(1 + \text{cosec}\,\theta)}{(1 - \text{cosec}\,\theta)}$$
$$= \frac{\dfrac{\text{cosec}\,\theta + 1}{\text{cosec}\,\theta}}{\dfrac{\text{cosec} - 1}{\text{cosec}\,\theta}} + \frac{(1 + \text{cosec}\,\theta)}{(1 - \text{cosec}\,\theta)}$$
$$= \frac{(1 + \text{cosec}\theta)}{(\text{cosec}\theta - 1)} - \frac{(1 + \text{cosec}\,\theta)}{(\text{cosec}\theta - 1)} = 0$$

Speedy Method

Put $\theta = 45°$

$$(\sqrt{2} + 1)^2 + \frac{1 + \sqrt{2}}{1 - \sqrt{2}}$$
$$= (\sqrt{2} + 1)^2 - (\sqrt{2} + 1)^2 = 0$$

298. (a) Given, $\sin^6\theta + \cos^6\theta = \dfrac{1}{3}$

$$\Rightarrow (\sin^2\theta)^3 + (\cos^2\theta)^3 = \frac{1}{3}$$

We know that,

$$(a + b)^3 = a^3 + b^3 + 3ab(a + b)$$
$$\Rightarrow (\sin^2\theta + \cos^2\theta)^3 - 3\sin^2\theta\cos^2\theta$$
$$(\sin^2\theta + \cos^2\theta) = \frac{1}{3}$$
$$\Rightarrow 1 - 3\sin^2\theta\cos^2\theta = \frac{1}{3}$$
$$\Rightarrow 1 - \frac{1}{3} = 3\sin^2\theta\cos^2\theta$$
$$\Rightarrow \frac{2}{3} = 3\sin^2\theta\cos^2\theta$$
$$\Rightarrow \sin^2\theta \,.\, \cos^2\theta = \frac{2}{9}$$
$$\therefore \sin\theta\cos\theta = \frac{\sqrt{2}}{\sqrt{9}} = \frac{\sqrt{2}}{3}$$

299. (d) Given, $\sin(A + B) = 1$ and

$$\cos(A - B) = \frac{\sqrt{3}}{2}$$

Then, $\sin(A + B) = \sin 90°$

$$\Rightarrow A + B = 90° \quad \text{...(i)}$$

and $\cos(A - B) = \cos 30°$

$$\Rightarrow A - B = 30° \quad \text{...(ii)}$$

From Eqs. (i) and (ii)

$2A = 120° \Rightarrow A = 60°$ and $B = 30°$

$$\therefore \frac{5\sin^2 B + 4\tan^2 A}{2\sin B\cos A}$$
$$= \frac{5 \times \sin^2 30° + 4\tan^2 60°}{2\sin 30° \,.\, \cos 60°}$$
$$= \frac{5 \times \left(\dfrac{1}{2}\right)^2 + 4 \times (\sqrt{3})^2}{2 \times \left(\dfrac{1}{2}\right) . \dfrac{1}{2}}$$
$$= \frac{\dfrac{5}{4} + 4 \times 3}{1 \times \dfrac{1}{2}} = \frac{\dfrac{5 + 48}{4}}{\dfrac{1}{2}} = \frac{53}{4} \times 2 = \frac{53}{2} = 26\frac{1}{2}.$$

300. (a) $\sin^4 30° + \cos^4 30°$

$$- \sin 25° \cos 65° - \sin 65° \cos 25°$$
$$= \sin^4 30° + \cos^4 30° - \sin(65° + 25°)$$
$$[\because \sin(A + B) = \sin A\cos B + \cos A\sin B]$$
$$= \sin^4 30° + \cos^4 30° - \sin 90°$$
$$= \left(\frac{1}{2}\right)^4 + \left(\frac{\sqrt{3}}{2}\right)^4 - 1 = \frac{1}{16} + \frac{9}{16} - 1$$
$$= \frac{-6}{16} = -\frac{3}{8}$$

301. (d)
$$\left[\sin 37°\cos 53° + \cos 37°\sin 53° - \frac{4\cos^2 37° - 7 + 4\cos^2 53°}{\tan^2 47° + 4 - \text{cosec}^2 43°}\right]$$

$\because \sin(a + b) = \sin a\cos b + \cos a.\sin b$

$$= \left[\sin(37 + 53) - \frac{4(\sin^2 53° + \cos^2 53°) - 7}{\cot^2 43° - \text{cosec}^2 43° + 4}\right]$$
$$= 1 - \frac{4(1) - 7}{-[\text{cosec}^2 43° - \cot^2 43°] + 4}$$
$$= 1 - \frac{(-3)}{4 - 1} = 1 + \frac{3}{3} = 1 + 1 = 2$$

302. (c) Given, $3\sin^2\theta - \cos\theta - 1 = 0$

$$\Rightarrow 3(1 - \cos^2\theta) - \cos\theta - 1 = 0$$
$$\Rightarrow 3 - 3\cos^2\theta - \cos\theta - 1 = 0$$
$$\Rightarrow 3\cos^2\theta + \cos\theta - 2 = 0$$
$$\Rightarrow 3\cos^2\theta + 3\cos\theta - 2\cos\theta - 2 = 0$$
$$\Rightarrow (3\cos\theta - 2)(\cos\theta + 1) = 0$$
$$\Rightarrow \cos\theta = \frac{2}{3}, \cos\theta = -1 \quad [\because 0° < \theta < 90°]$$
$$\therefore \cos\theta = \frac{2}{3} = \frac{B}{H}$$

By Pythagoras theorem,

$$H^2 = P^2 + B^2$$
$$\Rightarrow (3)^2 = P^2 + (2)^2 \Rightarrow P^2 = 5 \Rightarrow P = \sqrt{5}$$
$$\Rightarrow \sin\theta = \frac{P}{H} = \frac{\sqrt{5}}{3}$$
$$\therefore \cot\theta + \text{cosec}\,\theta = \frac{\cos\theta}{\sin\theta} + \frac{1}{\sin\theta}$$
$$= \frac{\dfrac{2}{3}}{\dfrac{\sqrt{5}}{3}} + \frac{1}{\dfrac{\sqrt{5}}{3}} = \frac{2}{\sqrt{5}} + \frac{3}{\sqrt{5}} = \frac{5}{\sqrt{5}}$$
$$= \frac{\sqrt{5} \times \sqrt{5}}{\sqrt{5}} = \sqrt{5}$$

303. (a) $\dfrac{\sqrt{2}\tan(60° - \theta)\tan(30° + \theta)}{\sin^2(45° + \theta) + \sin^2(45° - \theta)}$

$$= \frac{\sqrt{2}\tan[90° - (30° + \theta)]\tan(30° + \theta)}{\sin^2(45° + \theta) + \sin^2(45° - \theta)}$$

$$\left[\begin{array}{ll} \because & \tan(90° - \theta) = \cot\theta \\ \text{If} & \sin^2 A + \sin^2 B = 1 \\ \text{Then,} & A + B = 90° \end{array}\right]$$

Here, $(45° + \theta + 45° - \theta) = 90°$

So, $\sin^2(45° + \theta) + \sin^2(45° - \theta) = 1$

$$= \frac{\sqrt{2}\cot(30° + \theta) \times \tan(30° + \theta)}{1}$$
$$= \frac{\sqrt{2} \times 1}{1} = \sqrt{2}$$

304. (a) Given, $4\sin^2(2x - 10)° = 3$

$$\Rightarrow \sin^2(2x - 10)° = \frac{3}{4} \Rightarrow \sin(2x - 10)° = \sqrt{\frac{3}{4}}$$
$$\Rightarrow \sin(2x - 10)° = \frac{\sqrt{3}}{2}$$
$$\Rightarrow \sin(2x - 10)° = \sin 60°$$
$$\Rightarrow 2x - 10° = 60°$$
$$\Rightarrow 2x = 70° \Rightarrow x = 35°$$
$$\therefore \frac{\sin^4(x - 5)° + \cos^4(x - 5)°}{1 - 2\sin^2(3x - 15)°\cos^2(3x - 15)°}$$
$$= \frac{\sin^4 30° + \cos^4 30°}{1 - 2\sin^2 90° . \cos^2 90°}$$
$$= \frac{\left(\dfrac{1}{2}\right)^4 + \left(\dfrac{\sqrt{3}}{2}\right)^4}{1 - 2 \times 1 \times 0} = \frac{\left(\dfrac{1}{2}\right)^4 + \left(\dfrac{\sqrt{3}}{2}\right)^4}{1}$$
$$= \frac{1}{16} + \frac{9}{16} = \frac{10}{16} = \frac{5}{8}.$$

305. (a) Given, $7\cos^2\theta + 5\sin^2\theta - 6 = 0$

$$\Rightarrow 5\sin^2\theta + 2\cos^2\theta + 5\cos^2\theta - 6 = 0$$
$$[\because \sin^2\theta + \cos^2\theta = 1]$$
$$\Rightarrow 5 + 2\cos^2\theta - 6 = 0 \Rightarrow \cos^2\theta = \frac{1}{2}$$
$$\Rightarrow \cos\theta = \frac{1}{\sqrt{2}}$$
$$\cos\theta = \cos 45° \Rightarrow \theta = 45°$$
$$\therefore \sqrt{\frac{\text{cosec}\theta + \tan\theta}{\sec\theta - \cot\theta}} = \sqrt{\frac{\text{cosec}45° + \tan 45°}{\sec 45° - \cot 45°}}$$
$$= \sqrt{\frac{\sqrt{2} + 1}{\sqrt{2} - 1}}$$

Divide and Multiply by $\sqrt{2} + 1$

$$= \sqrt{\frac{(\sqrt{2} + 1)^2}{(\sqrt{2})^2 - 1}} = \frac{(\sqrt{2} + 1)}{1} = \sqrt{2} + 1$$

306. (a) $\cos(A - B) = \dfrac{\sqrt{3}}{2}$

$$\cos(A - B) = \cos 30°$$
$$A - B = 30° \quad \text{...(i)}$$

and $\cot(A+B) = \frac{1}{\sqrt{3}}$

$\cot(A+B) = \cot 60°$

$(A+B) = 60°$ ...(ii)

Adding Eqs. (i) and (ii), $2A = 90$

$A = 45°$ and $B = 15°$

Now, $(2A - 3B) = 2 \times 45° - 3 \times 15°$

$= 90° - 45° = 45°$

307. (a) $\sqrt{\sec^2\theta + \operatorname{cosec}^2\theta} \times \left(\frac{\sin\theta(1+\cos\theta)}{1+\cos\theta - \sin^2\theta}\right)$

[$\because 0° < \theta < 90°$]

$= \sqrt{\left(\frac{1}{\cos^2\theta} + \frac{1}{\sin^2\theta}\right)} \times \left(\frac{\sin\theta + \sin\theta\cos\theta}{\cos^2\theta + \cos\theta}\right)$

$= \sqrt{\left(\frac{\sin^2\theta + \cos^2\theta}{\cos^2\theta\sin^2\theta}\right)} \times \left(\frac{\sin\theta(1+\cos\theta)}{\cos\theta(1+\cos\theta)}\right)$

$= \frac{1}{\cos\theta\sin\theta} \times \frac{\sin\theta}{\cos\theta} = \frac{1}{\cos^2\theta} = \sec^2\theta.$

308. (c) $\frac{\tan^2 30° + \sin^2 90° + \cot^2 60° + \sin^2 30°\cos^2 45°}{\sin 60°\cos 30° - \cos 60°\sin 30°}$

$= \frac{\left(\frac{1}{\sqrt{3}}\right)^2 + (1)^2 + \left(\frac{1}{\sqrt{3}}\right)^2 + \left(\frac{1}{2}\right)^2 \times \left(\frac{1}{\sqrt{2}}\right)^2}{\frac{\sqrt{3}}{2} \times \frac{\sqrt{3}}{2} - \frac{1}{2} \times \frac{1}{2}}$

$= \frac{\frac{1}{3} + 1 + \frac{1}{3} + \frac{1}{8}}{\frac{3}{4} - \frac{1}{4}} = \frac{\frac{8+24+8+3}{24}}{\frac{1}{2}} = \frac{43 \times 2}{24 \times 1} = \frac{43}{12}.$

309. (b) $4(\sin^4 30° + \cos^4 30°) - 3(\sin^2 45° - 2\cos^2 45°)$

$= 4\left[\left(\frac{1}{2}\right)^4 + \left(\frac{\sqrt{3}}{2}\right)^4\right] - 3\left[\left(\frac{1}{\sqrt{2}}\right)^2 - 2 \times \left(\frac{1}{\sqrt{2}}\right)^2\right]$

$= 4 \times \left[\frac{1}{16} + \frac{9}{16}\right] - 3\left[\frac{1}{2} - 2 \times \frac{1}{2}\right]$

$= 4 \times \frac{10}{16} - 3 \times \left(-\frac{1}{2}\right) = \frac{5}{2} + \frac{3}{2} = \frac{8}{2} = 4$

310. (b) Given,

$\sin\left(\frac{2A+B}{2}\right) = \cos\left(\frac{2A-B}{2}\right) = \frac{\sqrt{3}}{2},$

$0° < \frac{2A+B}{2} < 90°$

$\sin\left(\frac{2A+B}{2}\right) = \sin 60° \Rightarrow \frac{2A+B}{2} = 60°$

$\Rightarrow 2A + B = 120°$ ...(i)

$\Rightarrow \cos\left(\frac{2A-B}{2}\right) = \cos 30° \Rightarrow \frac{2A-B}{2} = 30°$

$2A - B = 60°$ ...(ii)

From Eq. (i) and Eq. (ii),

$A = 45°, B = 30°$

Then, $\sin[(3(A-B)] = \sin[3(45° - 30°)]$

$= \sin[45°] = \frac{1}{\sqrt{2}}$

311. (d) Given, $3\cos^2\theta - 4\sin\theta + 1 = 0$

$\Rightarrow 3(1 - \sin^2\theta) - 4\sin\theta + 1 = 0$

$\Rightarrow 3\sin^2\theta + 4\sin\theta - 4 = 0$

$\Rightarrow (3\sin\theta - 2)(\sin\theta + 2) = 0$

($\because \sin\theta = -2$ not possible)

$\therefore \sin\theta = \frac{2}{3} = \frac{P}{H}$

By Pythagoras theorem,

$P^2 + B^2 = H^2 \Rightarrow 4 + B^2 = 9$

$\Rightarrow B^2 = 5 \Rightarrow B = \sqrt{5}$

Now, $\sec\theta = \frac{1}{\cos\theta} = \frac{1}{\frac{\sqrt{5}}{3}} = \frac{3}{\sqrt{5}},$

And $\tan\theta = \frac{\sin\theta}{\cos\theta} = \frac{\frac{2}{3}}{\frac{\sqrt{5}}{3}} = \frac{2}{\sqrt{5}}$

$\therefore (\tan\theta + \sec\theta) = \left(\frac{2}{\sqrt{5}} + \frac{3}{\sqrt{5}}\right) = \frac{5}{\sqrt{5}} = \sqrt{5}$

312. (d) Given, $\frac{\operatorname{cosec}\theta + \cot\theta}{\operatorname{cosec}\theta - \cot\theta} = \frac{7}{1}$

$\Rightarrow \operatorname{cosec}\theta + \cot\theta = 7\operatorname{cosec}\theta - 7\cot\theta$

$\Rightarrow 7\operatorname{cosec}\theta - \operatorname{cosec}\theta = \cot\theta + 7\cot\theta$

$\Rightarrow 6\operatorname{cosec}\theta = 8\cot\theta$

$\Rightarrow 6 \times \frac{1}{\sin\theta} = 8 \times \frac{\cos\theta}{\sin\theta}$

$\Rightarrow \cos\theta = \frac{3}{4}$

$\because 4^2 = (3)^2 + AB^2$

$\therefore 7 = (AB)^2 \Rightarrow AB = \sqrt{7}$

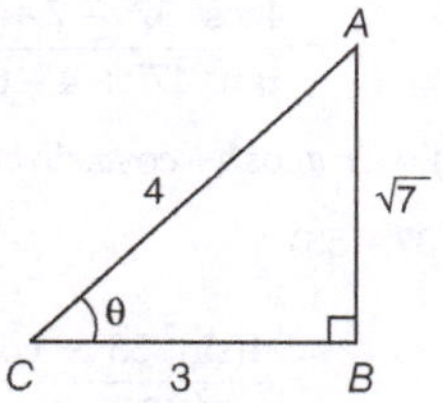

$\Rightarrow \sin\theta = \frac{\sqrt{7}}{4}$

$\therefore \frac{4\sin^2\theta - 1}{4\sin^2\theta + 5} = \frac{4 \times \frac{7}{16} - 1}{4 \times \frac{7}{16} + 5} = \frac{\frac{7}{4} - 1}{\frac{7}{4} + 5}$

$\Rightarrow \frac{\frac{3}{4}}{\frac{27}{4}} = \frac{3}{27} = \frac{1}{9}$

313. (d) $1 + 2\tan^2\theta + 2\sin\theta\sec^2\theta$

$= \sec^2\theta - \tan^2\theta + 2\tan^2\theta + 2 \times \sin\theta \times \frac{1}{\cos^2\theta}$

$= \sec^2\theta + \tan^2\theta + 2\tan\theta \cdot \sec\theta$

$= (\sec\theta + \tan\theta)^2$

$= \left(\frac{1}{\cos\theta} + \frac{\sin\theta}{\cos\theta}\right)^2 = \left(\frac{1+\sin\theta}{\cos\theta}\right)^2$

$= \frac{(1+\sin\theta)^2}{\cos^2\theta} = \frac{(1+\sin\theta)^2}{(1-\sin^2\theta)}$

$= \frac{(1+\sin\theta)^2}{(1-\sin\theta)(1+\sin\theta)} = \frac{(1+\sin\theta)}{(1-\sin\theta)}$

314. (a) Given, $\frac{\tan(45° - \alpha)}{\cot(45° + \alpha)} - \frac{(\cos 19° + \sin 71°)(\sec 19° + \operatorname{cosec} 71°)}{\tan 12° \cdot \tan 24° \cdot \tan 66° \cdot \tan 78°}$

$= \frac{\tan(45° - \alpha)}{\cot(45° + \alpha)} - \frac{[\cos 19° + \sin(90° - 19°)][\sec 19° + \operatorname{cosec}(90° - 19°)]}{\tan 12° \cdot \tan 24° \cdot \tan(90° - 24°) \cdot \tan(90° - 12°)}$

$= \frac{\tan(45° - \alpha)}{\cot(45° + \alpha)} - \frac{2\cos 19° \cdot 2\sec 19°}{\tan 12° \cdot \tan 24° \cdot \cot 24° \cdot \cot 12°}$

$= \frac{\tan[90° - (45° + \alpha)]}{\cot(45° + \alpha)} - 4 \cdot \cos 19° \times \frac{1}{\cos 19°}$

$= \frac{\cot(45° + \alpha)}{\cot(45° + \alpha)} - 4 = 1 - 4 = -3$

315. (d) Given, $3\sec\theta + 4\cos\theta - 4\sqrt{3} = 0$

$\Rightarrow \frac{3}{\cos\theta} + 4\cos\theta = 4\sqrt{3}$

$\Rightarrow 3 + 4\cos^2\theta = 4\sqrt{3}\cos\theta$

$\Rightarrow 4\cos^2\theta - 2\sqrt{3}\cos\theta - 2\sqrt{3}\cos\theta + 3 = 0$

$\Rightarrow 2\cos\theta(2\cos\theta - \sqrt{3}) - \sqrt{3}(2\cos\theta - \sqrt{3}) = 0$

$\Rightarrow (2\cos\theta - \sqrt{3})(2\cos\theta - \sqrt{3}) = 0$

$\Rightarrow \cos\theta = \frac{\sqrt{3}}{2} = \cos 30° \Rightarrow \theta = 30°$

316. (c) Given, $3\tan\theta = 2\sqrt{3}\sin\theta$

$\Rightarrow 3 \times \frac{\sin\theta}{\cos\theta} = 2\sqrt{3}\sin\theta$

$\Rightarrow \cos\theta = \frac{3}{2\sqrt{3}} = \frac{\sqrt{3}}{2} = \cos 30° \Rightarrow \theta = 30°$

Then, $2\sin^2 2\theta - 3\cos^2 3\theta$

$= 2 \times \sin^2(2 \times 30°) - 3\cos^2(3 \times 30°)$

$= 2 \times \sin^2 60° - 3\cos^2 90°$

$= 2 \times \left(\frac{\sqrt{3}}{2}\right)^2 - 0 = 2 \times \frac{3}{4} = \frac{3}{2}$

317. (a) $\frac{\operatorname{cosec}\theta}{\operatorname{cosec}\theta - 1} + \frac{\operatorname{cosec}\theta}{\operatorname{cosec}\theta + 1} - \tan^2\theta$

$= \frac{\operatorname{cosec}\theta(\operatorname{cosec}\theta + 1) + \operatorname{cosec}\theta(\operatorname{cosec}\theta - 1)}{\operatorname{cosec}^2\theta - 1} - \tan^2\theta$

$= \frac{\operatorname{cosec}^2\theta + \operatorname{cosec}\theta + \operatorname{cosec}^2\theta - \operatorname{cosec}\theta}{\cot^2\theta} - \tan^2\theta$

$= \frac{2\operatorname{cosec}^2\theta}{\cot^2\theta} - \tan^2\theta = \frac{\frac{2}{\sin^2\theta}}{\frac{\cos^2\theta}{\sin^2\theta}} - \tan^2\theta$

$= 2\sec^2\theta - \tan^2\theta = \sec^2\theta + \sec^2\theta - \tan^2\theta$

$= \sec^2\theta + 1$

318. (a) Given, $\frac{\cos^2\theta}{\cot^2\theta + \sin^2\theta - 1} = 3$

$\Rightarrow \frac{\cos^2\theta}{\cot^2\theta - \cos^2\theta} = 3 \Rightarrow \frac{\cos^2\theta}{\frac{\cos^2\theta}{\sin^2\theta} - \cos^2\theta} = 3$

$\Rightarrow \dfrac{\cos^2\theta}{\dfrac{\cos^2\theta-\sin^2\theta\cos^2\theta}{\sin^2\theta}}=3$

$\Rightarrow \dfrac{\cos^2\theta\sin^2\theta}{\cos^2\theta(1-\sin^2\theta)}=3 \Rightarrow \dfrac{\cos^2\theta\sin^2\theta}{\cos^2\theta\cos^2\theta}=3$

$\Rightarrow \quad \tan^2\theta = 3 \Rightarrow \tan\theta=\sqrt{3}$

$\Rightarrow \quad \tan\theta=\tan 60°$

$\Rightarrow \quad \theta = 60°$

$\therefore \tan\theta+\text{cosec}\,\theta=\tan 60°+\text{cosec}\,60°$

$=\sqrt{3}+\dfrac{2}{\sqrt{3}}=\dfrac{3+2}{\sqrt{3}}=\dfrac{5}{\sqrt{3}}$

$=\dfrac{5}{\sqrt{3}}\times\dfrac{\sqrt{3}}{\sqrt{3}}=\dfrac{5\sqrt{3}}{3}$

319. (c) Given, $3\sec^2\theta+\tan\theta=7$

$\Rightarrow 3(1+\tan^2\theta)+\tan\theta-7=0$

$\Rightarrow 3\tan^2\theta+\tan\theta-4=0$

$\Rightarrow [3\tan\theta+4][\tan\theta-1]=0$

$\Rightarrow \tan\theta=-\dfrac{4}{3}, \tan\theta=1$

$\because \quad 0°<\theta<90°$

$\therefore \tan\theta=1=\tan 45° \Rightarrow \theta=45°$

Now, $\dfrac{(\text{cosec}\,2\theta+\cos\theta)}{(\sin 2\theta+\cot\theta)}$

$\Rightarrow \dfrac{(\text{cosec}\,90°+\cos 45°)}{(\sin 90°+\cot 45°)}=\dfrac{\left(1+\dfrac{1}{\sqrt{2}}\right)}{(1+1)}=\dfrac{(\sqrt{2}+1)}{\sqrt{2}(2)}$

$=\dfrac{(\sqrt{2}+1)}{\sqrt{2}(2)}\times\dfrac{\sqrt{2}}{\sqrt{2}}=\dfrac{2+\sqrt{2}}{4}$

320. (a) $\dfrac{\sin A+\cos A}{\cos A}=\dfrac{17}{12}$

$\Rightarrow 12\sin A+12\cos A=17\cos A$

$\Rightarrow 12\sin A=5\cos A \Rightarrow \dfrac{\sin A}{\cos A}=\dfrac{5}{12}$

$\therefore \tan A=\dfrac{5}{12}=\dfrac{\text{Perpendicular}}{\text{Base}}$

By Pythagoras theorem,

$\Rightarrow \quad H^2=(5)^2+(12)^2$

$\Rightarrow \quad H=\sqrt{169}=13$

Then, $\sin A=\dfrac{5}{13}$ and $\cos A=\dfrac{12}{13}$

Now, $\dfrac{1-\cos A}{\sin A}=\dfrac{1-\dfrac{12}{13}}{\dfrac{5}{13}}=\dfrac{1}{13}\times\dfrac{13}{5}=\dfrac{1}{5}$

321. (a) Given,

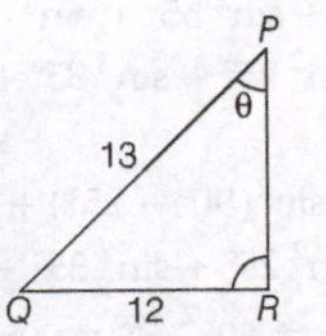

In ΔRPQ,

$\Rightarrow (13)^2=12^2+(\text{Base})^2 \Rightarrow (\text{Base})^2=25$

$\Rightarrow \quad \text{Base}=5$

$\therefore \quad \cos\theta=\dfrac{5}{13}$

322. (d) $\dfrac{1-2\sin^2\theta\cos^2\theta}{\sin^4\theta+\cos^4\theta}-1$

$=\dfrac{1-2\sin^2\theta\cos^2\theta-(\sin^4\theta+\cos^4\theta)}{\sin^4\theta+\cos^4\theta}$

$=\dfrac{1-2\sin^2\theta\cos^2\theta-\sin^4\theta-\cos^4\theta}{\sin^4\theta+\cos^4\theta}$

$=\dfrac{1-(\sin^4\theta+\cos^4\theta+2\sin^2\theta\cos^2\theta)}{\sin^4\theta+\cos^4\theta}$

$=\dfrac{1-(\sin^2\theta+\cos^2\theta)^2}{(\sin^4\theta+\cos^4\theta)}=\dfrac{1-1}{\sin^4\theta+\cos^4\theta}=0$

323. (c) $\tan A = 21/20$ (given)

$=\dfrac{5\sin A-2\cos A}{4\cos A-\dfrac{5}{7}\sin A}=\dfrac{5\dfrac{\sin A}{\cos A}-2}{4-\dfrac{5\sin A}{7\cos A}}$

$=\dfrac{5\tan A-2}{4-\dfrac{5}{7}\tan A}=\dfrac{5\times\left(\dfrac{21}{20}\right)-2}{4-\left(\dfrac{5}{7}\times\dfrac{21}{20}\right)}$

$=\dfrac{\left(\dfrac{21}{4}-2\right)}{\left(4-\dfrac{3}{4}\right)}=\dfrac{13}{13}=1$

324. (d) Given, $\cos(A+B)=\dfrac{24}{25}=\dfrac{B}{H}$

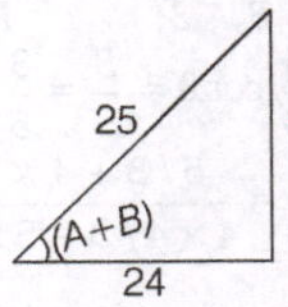

Using Pythagoras theorem,

$(25)^2=P^2+(24)^2 \Rightarrow 625-576=P^2$

$\Rightarrow \quad P^2=49 \Rightarrow P=7$

So, $\tan(A+B)=\dfrac{P}{B}=\dfrac{7}{24}$

Similarly, $\sin(A-B)=\dfrac{15}{17}=\dfrac{P}{H}$

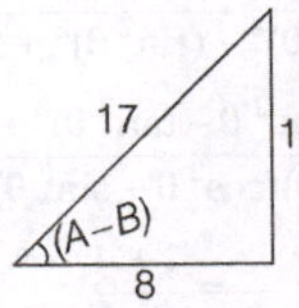

Using Pythagoras theorem,

$\therefore \quad 17^2=(15)^2+B^2$

$\Rightarrow \quad B^2=289-225=64 \Rightarrow B=8$

$\tan(A-B)=\dfrac{P}{B}=15/8$

$\tan[(A+B)+(A-B)]$

$=\dfrac{\tan(A+B)+\tan(A-B)}{1-\tan(A+B)\tan(A-B)}$

$\tan 2A=\dfrac{7/24+15/8}{1-7/24\times 15/8}$

$\tan 2A=\dfrac{\dfrac{7+45}{24}}{1-\dfrac{35}{64}}=\dfrac{52}{24}\times\dfrac{64}{29}=\dfrac{416}{87}$

325. (a) $4\left[\dfrac{(1-\sec A)^2+(1+\sec A)^2}{1+\sec^2 A}\right]$

$=\dfrac{4[1+\sec^2 A-2\sec A+1+\sec^2 A+2\sec A]}{(1+\sec^2 A)}$

$=\dfrac{4(2+2\sec^2 A)}{(1+\sec^2 A)}=\dfrac{4[2(1+\sec^2 A)]}{(1+\sec^2 A)}=4\times 2=8$

326. (b) $\sin 0°\cdot\sin 30°\cdot\sin 45°\cdot\sin 60°\cdot\sin 90°$

$=0\times\dfrac{1}{2}\times\dfrac{1}{\sqrt{2}}\times\dfrac{\sqrt{3}}{2}\times 1=0$

327. (b) Given,

$(\cos^2\theta-1)(1+\tan^2\theta)+2\tan^2\theta=1$

$\Rightarrow -\sin^2\theta\cdot\sec^2\theta+2\tan^2\theta=1$

$\Rightarrow \dfrac{-\sin^2\theta}{\cos^2\theta}+2\tan^2\theta=1$

$\Rightarrow -\tan^2\theta+2\tan^2\theta=1$

$\Rightarrow \tan^2\theta=1 \Rightarrow \tan\theta=1$

$\Rightarrow \quad \tan\theta=\tan 45°$

$\therefore \quad \theta=45°$

328. (a) $\dfrac{\sin 30°\sin 60°}{\cos 60°\cos 30°}-\tan 45°$

$=\dfrac{\dfrac{1}{2}\times\dfrac{\sqrt{3}}{2}}{\dfrac{1}{2}\times\dfrac{\sqrt{3}}{2}}-1=\dfrac{(\sqrt{3}/4)}{(\sqrt{3}/4)}-1=1-1=0$

329. (b) $2\sin A+\text{cosec}\,A=2\sqrt{2}$

$\Rightarrow 2\sin A+\dfrac{1}{\sin A}=2\sqrt{2}$

$\Rightarrow 2\sin^2 A+1=2\sqrt{2}\sin A$

$\Rightarrow 2\sin^2 A-2\sqrt{2}\sin A+1=0$

$\Rightarrow (\sqrt{2}\sin A)^2-2\sqrt{2}\sin A\times 1+1^2=0$

$\Rightarrow (\sqrt{2}\sin A-1)^2=0 \Rightarrow \sqrt{2}\sin A=1$

$\Rightarrow \sin A=\dfrac{1}{\sqrt{2}}=\sin 45°$

$\therefore \quad A=45°$

Now, $2(\sin^4 A+\cos^4 A)$

$=2(\sin^4 45°+\cos^4 45°)$

$=2\left[\left(\dfrac{1}{\sqrt{2}}\right)^4+\left(\dfrac{1}{\sqrt{2}}\right)^4\right]$

$=2\left[\dfrac{1}{4}+\dfrac{1}{4}\right]=2\times\dfrac{2}{4}=2\times\dfrac{1}{2}=1$

330. (d) $x\cos A-y\sin A=1$ ...(i)

$x\sin A+y\cos A=4$ ...(ii)

Add Eqs. (i) and (ii) after squaring,

$(x\cos A-y\sin A)^2+(x\sin A+y\cos A)^2=1^2+4^2$

$\Rightarrow x^2\cos^2 A+y^2\sin^2 A-2xy\sin A\cos A+x^2\sin^2 A+y^2\cos^2 A$

$+2xy\sin A\cos A=1+16$

$\Rightarrow x^2(\cos^2 A+\sin^2 A)+y^2(\sin^2 A+\cos^2 a)=17$

$\Rightarrow \quad x^2+y^2=17 \Rightarrow 17x^2+17y^2=289$

331. (b) Given, $\tan\theta-\cot\theta=\text{cosec}\,\theta$

$\Rightarrow \dfrac{\sin\theta}{\cos\theta}-\dfrac{\cos\theta}{\sin\theta}=\dfrac{1}{\sin\theta}$

$\Rightarrow \dfrac{\sin^2\theta-\cos^2\theta}{\sin\theta\cos\theta}=\dfrac{1}{\sin\theta}$

$\Rightarrow 1-\cos^2\theta-\cos^2\theta=\cos\theta$

$\Rightarrow 2\cos^2\theta+\cos\theta-1=0$

$\Rightarrow (\cos\theta+1)(2\cos\theta-1)=0$

$\Rightarrow 2\cos\theta-1=0 \Rightarrow 2\cos\theta=1$

$\Rightarrow \cos\theta=\dfrac{1}{2}=\cos 60^\circ$

$\therefore \theta=60^\circ$

$\therefore \dfrac{2\tan\theta-\cos\theta}{\sqrt{3}\cot\theta+\sec\theta}=\dfrac{2\tan 60^\circ-\cos 60^\circ}{\sqrt{3}\cot 60^\circ+\sec 60^\circ}$

$=\dfrac{2\times\sqrt{3}-\frac{1}{2}}{\sqrt{3}\times\frac{1}{\sqrt{3}}+2}=\dfrac{\frac{4\sqrt{3}-1}{2}}{1+2}=\dfrac{4\sqrt{3}-1}{6}$

332. (a) Given,

$11\sin^2\theta-\cos^2\theta+4\sin\theta-4=0$

$\Rightarrow 11\sin^2\theta-(1-\sin^2\theta)+4\sin\theta-4=0$

$\Rightarrow 11\sin^2\theta-1+\sin^2\theta+4\sin\theta-4=0$

$\Rightarrow 12\sin^2\theta+4\sin\theta-5=0$

$\Rightarrow (2\sin\theta-1)(6\sin\theta+5)=0$

$\Rightarrow \sin\theta=\dfrac{1}{2}=\sin 30^\circ \quad [\because 0^\circ<\theta<90^\circ]$

$\Rightarrow \theta=30^\circ$

$\therefore \dfrac{\cos 2\theta+\cot 2\theta}{\sec 2\theta-\tan 2\theta}=\dfrac{\cos 60^\circ+\cot 60^\circ}{\sec 60^\circ-\tan 60^\circ}$

$=\dfrac{\frac{1}{2}+\frac{1}{\sqrt{3}}}{2-\sqrt{3}}=\dfrac{\frac{\sqrt{3}+2}{2\sqrt{3}}}{2-\sqrt{3}}$

$=\dfrac{2+\sqrt{3}}{(2-\sqrt{3})\,2\sqrt{3}}\times\dfrac{(2+\sqrt{3})}{(2+\sqrt{3})}=\dfrac{(2+\sqrt{3})^2}{[2^2-(\sqrt{3})^2]\,2\sqrt{3}}$

$=\dfrac{4+3+4\sqrt{3}}{2\sqrt{3}}=\dfrac{7+4\sqrt{3}}{2\sqrt{3}}\times\dfrac{\sqrt{3}}{\sqrt{3}}$

$=\dfrac{7\sqrt{3}+12}{6}$

333. (b) Given, $5\cos\theta-12\sin\theta=0$

$\Rightarrow 5\cos\theta=12\sin\theta \Rightarrow \tan\theta=\dfrac{5}{12}=\dfrac{P}{B}$

In ΔABC, by Pythagoras theorem,

$H^2=P^2+B^2 \Rightarrow H^2=(12)^2+(5)^2$

$\Rightarrow H^2=169 \Rightarrow H=13$

$\therefore \sin\theta=\dfrac{P}{H}=\dfrac{5}{13}$ and $\cos\theta=\dfrac{B}{H}=\dfrac{12}{13}$

$\therefore \dfrac{1+\sin\theta+\cos\theta}{1-\sin\theta+\cos\theta}=\dfrac{1+\frac{5}{13}+\frac{12}{13}}{1-\frac{5}{13}+\frac{12}{13}}$

$=\dfrac{\frac{13+5+12}{13}}{\frac{13-5+12}{13}}=\dfrac{30}{20}=\dfrac{3}{2}$

334. (b) $\dfrac{\text{cosec}(78^\circ+\theta)-\sec(12^\circ-\theta)-\tan(67^\circ+\theta)+\cot(23^\circ-\theta)}{\tan 13^\circ\tan 37^\circ\tan 45^\circ\tan 53^\circ\tan 77^\circ}$

$=\dfrac{\text{cosec}[90^\circ-(12^\circ-\theta)]-\sec(12^\circ-\theta)-\tan[90^\circ-(23^\circ-\theta)]+\cot(23^\circ-\theta)}{\tan 13^\circ\tan 37^\circ\tan 45^\circ\tan 53^\circ\tan 77^\circ}$

$=\dfrac{-\cot(23^\circ-\theta)+\cot(23^\circ-\theta)}{\tan 13^\circ\tan 37^\circ\tan 45^\circ\tan 53^\circ\tan 77^\circ}$

$=\dfrac{0}{\tan 13^\circ\tan 37^\circ\tan 45^\circ\tan 53^\circ\tan 77^\circ}=0$

335. (d) Given,

$12\cos^2\theta-2\sin^2\theta+3\cos\theta=3$

$12\cos^2\theta-2(1-\cos^2\theta)+3\cos\theta-3=0$

$12\cos^2\theta-2+2\cos^2\theta+3\cos\theta-3=0$

$14\cos^2\theta+3\cos\theta-5=0$

$(7\cos\theta+5)(2\cos\theta-1)=0$

$\Rightarrow \cos\theta=\dfrac{1}{2},-\dfrac{5}{7} \quad [\because 0^\circ<\theta<90^\circ]$

$\therefore \cos\theta=\dfrac{1}{2}=\cos 60^\circ \Rightarrow \theta=60^\circ$

$\therefore \dfrac{\text{cosec}\,\theta+\sec\theta}{\tan\theta+\cot\theta}=\dfrac{\text{cosec}\,60^\circ+\sec 60^\circ}{\tan 60^\circ+\cot 60^\circ}$

$=\dfrac{\frac{2}{\sqrt{3}}+2}{\sqrt{3}+\frac{1}{\sqrt{3}}}=\dfrac{(2+2\sqrt{3})/\sqrt{3}}{(3+1)/\sqrt{3}}=\dfrac{(\sqrt{3}+1)}{2}$

336. (a) Given, $\sin\theta=\dfrac{4}{5}=\dfrac{P}{H}$

By Pythagoras theorem,

$(5)^2=(4)^2+B^2 \Rightarrow B^2=25-16=9$

$\Rightarrow B=3$

$\tan\theta=\dfrac{P}{B}=\dfrac{4}{3}, \cot\theta=\dfrac{B}{P}=\dfrac{3}{4}$

$\sec\theta=\dfrac{H}{B}=\dfrac{5}{3}, \cos\theta=\dfrac{B}{H}=\dfrac{3}{5}$

$=\dfrac{\sec\theta+4\cot\theta}{4\tan\theta-5\cos\theta}=\dfrac{5/3+4\times 3/4}{4\times 4/3-5\times 3/5}$

$=\dfrac{\frac{5}{3}+3}{\frac{16}{3}-3}=\dfrac{\frac{14}{3}}{\frac{7}{3}}=2$

337. (b) Given,

$\dfrac{\sec^6\theta-\tan^6\theta-3\sec^2\theta\tan^2\theta+1}{\cos^4\theta-\sin^4\theta+2\sin^2\theta+2}$

$=\dfrac{(\sec^2\theta)^3-(\tan^2\theta)^3-3\sec^2\theta\tan^2\theta+1}{(\cos^2\theta)^2-(\sin^2\theta)^2+2\sin^2\theta+2}$

$=\dfrac{(\sec^2\theta-\tan^2\theta)^3+1}{(\cos^2\theta+\sin^2\theta)(\cos^2\theta-\sin^2\theta)+2\sin^2\theta+2}$

$=\dfrac{1^3+1}{\cos^2\theta+\sin^2\theta+2}=\dfrac{1+1}{1+2}=\dfrac{2}{3}$

Speedy Method

$(\sec^2\theta-\tan^2\theta)^3=1$

$\sec^6\theta-\tan^6\theta-3\tan^2\theta\sec^2\theta=1$

$\sec^6\theta-\tan^6\theta-3\tan^2\theta\sec^2\theta+1=2 \quad \ldots(i)$

$\cos^2\theta=1-\sin^2\theta$

Squaring on both sides,

$\cos^4\theta=1+\sin^4\theta-2\sin^2\theta$

$\cos^4\theta-\sin^4\theta+2\sin^2\theta+2=3 \quad \ldots(ii)$

$\therefore$ Required value $=\dfrac{2}{3}$ [from Eqs. (i) and (ii)]

338. (a) Given, $7\cos^2\theta+3\sin^2\theta=6$

$\Rightarrow 4\cos^2\theta+3\cos^2\theta+3\sin^2\theta=6$

$\Rightarrow 4\cos^2\theta+3(\cos^2\theta+\sin^2\theta)=6$

$\Rightarrow 4\cos^2\theta+3=6$

$\Rightarrow \cos^2\theta=\dfrac{3}{4} \Rightarrow \cos\theta=\sqrt{\dfrac{3}{4}}=\dfrac{\sqrt{3}}{2}$

$\Rightarrow \cos\theta=\cos 30^\circ \Rightarrow \theta=30^\circ$

$\therefore \dfrac{\cot^2 2\theta+\sec^2 2\theta}{\tan^2 2\theta-\sin^2 2\theta}$

$=\dfrac{\cot^2 2(30^\circ)+\sec^2 2(30^\circ)}{\tan^2 2(30^\circ)-\sin^2 2(30^\circ)}$

$=\dfrac{\cot^2 60^\circ+\sec^2 60^\circ}{\tan^2 60^\circ-\sin^2 60^\circ}$

$=\dfrac{\left(\frac{1}{\sqrt{3}}\right)^2+(2)^2}{(\sqrt{3})^2-\left(\frac{\sqrt{3}}{2}\right)^2}=\dfrac{\frac{1}{3}+4}{3-\frac{3}{4}}=\dfrac{\frac{13}{3}}{\frac{9}{4}}$

$=\dfrac{13}{3}\times\dfrac{4}{9}=\dfrac{52}{27}$

339. (b) Given, $\sec\theta+\tan\theta=p$

$\therefore \dfrac{p^2-1}{p^2+1}=\dfrac{(\sec\theta+\tan\theta)^2-1}{(\sec\theta+\tan\theta)^2+1}$

$=\dfrac{(\sec^2\theta+2\sec\theta\tan\theta+\tan^2\theta)-1}{(\sec^2\theta+2\sec\theta\tan\theta+\tan^2\theta)+1}$

$=\dfrac{\sec^2\theta+2\sec\theta\tan\theta+\tan^2\theta-\sec^2\theta+\tan^2\theta}{\sec^2\theta+2\sec\theta\tan\theta+\tan^2\theta+\sec^2\theta-\tan^2\theta}$

$=\dfrac{2\sec\theta\tan\theta+2\tan^2\theta}{2\sec^2\theta+2\sec\theta\tan\theta}$

$=\dfrac{2\tan\theta(\sec\theta+\tan\theta)}{2\sec\theta(\sec\theta+\tan\theta)}=\dfrac{\tan\theta}{\sec\theta}=\dfrac{\frac{\sin\theta}{\cos\theta}}{\frac{1}{\cos\theta}}=\sin\theta$

340. (b) Given, $\cos A=\dfrac{4}{5}$

$\because \sin A=\sqrt{1-\cos^2 A}=\sqrt{1-\left(\dfrac{4}{5}\right)^2} \Rightarrow \sin A=\dfrac{3}{5}$

We also know, $\tan A=\dfrac{\sin A}{\cos A}=\dfrac{3\times 5}{5\times 4}=\dfrac{3}{4}$

Now, $(8+\sin A)(3-\tan A)$

$=\left(8+\dfrac{3}{5}\right)\left(3-\dfrac{3}{4}\right)=\dfrac{43}{5}\times\dfrac{9}{4}=\dfrac{387}{20}$

341. (b) We know that, $\sin^2\theta+\cos^2\theta=1$

Also, $\sin^2(90-\theta)=\cos^2\theta$

Now,

$\sin^2 15^\circ+\sin^2 25^\circ+\sin^2 35^\circ+\sin^2 45^\circ+\sin^2 55^\circ+\sin^2 65^\circ+\sin^2 75^\circ$

$=\sin^2 15^\circ+\sin^2 25^\circ+\sin^2 35^\circ+\sin^2 45^\circ+\sin^2(90^\circ-35^\circ)+\sin^2(90^\circ-25^\circ)+\sin^2(90^\circ-15^\circ)$

$=\sin^2 15^\circ+\sin^2 25^\circ+\sin^2 35^\circ+\sin^2 45^\circ+\cos^2 35^\circ+\cos^2 25^\circ+\cos^2 15^\circ$

$=(\sin^2 15^\circ+\cos^2 15^\circ)+(\sin^2 25^\circ+\cos^2 25^\circ)+(\sin^2 35^\circ+\cos^2 35^\circ)+\sin^2 45^\circ$

$=1+1+1+\dfrac{1}{2}=3+\dfrac{1}{2}=\dfrac{7}{2}$

342. (c) $\frac{17}{\sec^2\theta}+10\sin^2\theta+\frac{7}{1+\cot^2\theta}$

$=17\times\frac{1}{\sec^2\theta}+10\sin^2\theta+\frac{7}{\text{cosec}^2\theta}$

$\left[\because 1+\cot^2\theta=\text{cosec}^2\theta \text{ and } \frac{1}{\sec^2\theta}=\cos^2\theta\right]$

$=17\cos^2\theta+10\sin^2\theta+7\sin^2\theta$

$=17\cos^2\theta+17\sin^2\theta=17(\cos^2\theta+\sin^2\theta)$

$=17\times1=17$

343. (a) Expression

$=\frac{[(\sin x+\sin y)(\sin y-\sin x)]}{[(\cos x+\cos y)(\cos y-\cos x)]}$

$=\frac{\sin^2 y-\sin^2 x}{\cos^2 y-\cos^2 x}$

$=\frac{\sin^2 y-\sin^2 x}{(1-\sin^2 y)-(1-\sin^2 x)}$

$=\frac{(\sin^2 y-\sin^2 x)}{-(\sin^2 y-\sin^2 x)}=-1$

344. (c) $(1+\tan\theta+\sec\theta)\times(1+\cot\theta-\text{cosec}\,\theta)$

$=\left(1+\frac{\sin\theta}{\cos\theta}+\frac{1}{\cos\theta}\right)\times\left(1+\frac{\cos\theta}{\sin\theta}-\frac{1}{\sin\theta}\right)$

$=\frac{\cos\theta+\sin\theta+1}{\cos\theta}\times\frac{\sin\theta+\cos\theta-1}{\sin\theta}$

$=\frac{(\sin\theta+\cos\theta)^2-1^2}{\sin\theta.\cos\theta}$

$[\because (a+b)(a-b)=a^2-b^2]$

$=\frac{\sin^2\theta+\cos^2\theta+2\cos\theta.\sin\theta-1}{\sin\theta\cos\theta}$

$=\frac{1+2\sin\theta.\cos\theta-1}{\sin\theta.\cos\theta}=\frac{2\sin\theta.\cos\theta}{\sin\theta.\cos\theta}=2$

345. (c) $\frac{\tan 71^\circ+\tan 19^\circ}{1-\tan 71^\circ\cdot\tan 19^\circ}$

we know that, $\tan(A+B)=\frac{\tan A+\tan B}{1-\tan A\cdot\tan B}$

$\Rightarrow \frac{\tan 71^\circ+\tan 19^\circ}{1-\tan 71^\circ\cdot\tan 19^\circ}=\tan(71^\circ+19^\circ)$

$=\tan 90^\circ=\infty$ (undefined)

346. (c) $\sin^4\theta+\cos^4\theta=2\sin^2\theta\cdot\cos^2\theta$

$\Rightarrow(\sin^2\theta)^2+(\cos^2\theta)^2-2\sin^2\theta\cdot\cos^2\theta=0$

$\Rightarrow(\sin^2\theta-\cos^2\theta)^2=0\Rightarrow\sin^2\theta-\cos^2\theta=0$

$\Rightarrow \cos^2\theta=\sin^2\theta\Rightarrow\frac{\cos^2\theta}{\sin^2\theta}=1$

$\Rightarrow \cot^2\theta=1 \Rightarrow \cot\theta=1$

347. (a) $\tan^4 A+\tan^2 A=\tan^2 A[\tan^2 A+1]$

$=\tan^2 A[\sec^2 A]=[\sec^2 A-1][\sec^2 A]$

$=\sec^4 A-\sec^2 A$

348. (b) $15\cos^2\theta+17\sin^2\theta$

$=15\cos^2\theta+15\sin^2\theta+2\sin^2\theta$

$=15(\cos^2\theta+\sin^2\theta)+2\sin^2\theta$

$=15\times1+2\sin^2\theta=15+2\sin^2\theta$

$\therefore$ Minimum value = 15

349. (a) $(\text{cosec}\,\theta-\sin\theta)(\sec\theta-\cos\theta)(\tan\theta+\cot\theta)$

$=\left(\frac{1}{\sin\theta}-\sin\theta\right)\left(\frac{1}{\cos\theta}-\cos\theta\right)\left(\frac{\sin\theta}{\cos\theta}+\frac{\cos\theta}{\sin\theta}\right)$

$=\left(\frac{1-\sin^2\theta}{\sin\theta}\right)\left(\frac{1-\cos^2\theta}{\cos\theta}\right)\left(\frac{\sin^2\theta+\cos^2\theta}{\sin\theta\cdot\cos\theta}\right)$

$=\left(\frac{\cos^2\theta}{\sin\theta}\right)\left(\frac{\sin^2\theta}{\cos\theta}\right)\left(\frac{1}{\sin\theta\cdot\cos\theta}\right)$

$=\left(\frac{\cos\theta}{1}\right)\left(\frac{\sin\theta}{1}\right)\left(\frac{1}{\sin\theta\cdot\cos\theta}\right)=1$

350. (a) $\angle A+\angle B+\angle C=180^\circ$

$\Rightarrow \frac{\angle(A+B+C)}{2}=90^\circ$

Now, $\left\{\tan\frac{A}{2}+\text{cosec}\frac{B+C}{2}\right\}\left\{\tan\frac{A}{2}-\text{cosec}\frac{B+C}{2}\right\}$

$=\left\{\tan\frac{A}{2}+\text{cosec}\left(90^\circ-\frac{A}{2}\right)\right\}\left\{\tan\frac{A}{2}-\text{cosec}\left(90-\frac{A}{2}\right)\right\}$

$=\left\{\tan\frac{A}{2}+\sec\frac{A}{2}\right\}\left\{\tan\frac{A}{2}-\sec\frac{A}{2}\right\}$

So, $\tan^2\frac{A}{2}-\sec^2\frac{A}{2}=-1$

$[\because \sec^2\theta-\tan^2\theta=1]$

351. (c) We know that,

$a^3+b^3=(a+b)(a^2+b^2-ab)$

Now, $\frac{\sin^3 A+\cos^3 A}{\sin A+\cos A}$

$=\frac{(\sin A+\cos A)(\sin^2 A+\cos^2 A-\sin A\cos A)}{\sin A+\cos A}$

$=1-\sin A\cos A$

352. (c) $\left(\frac{2\cos^3\theta-\cos\theta}{\sin\theta-2\sin^3\theta}\right)^2+1$

$=\left[\frac{\cos\theta(2\cos^2\theta-1)}{\sin\theta(1-2\sin^2\theta)}\right]^2+1$

$=\left(\frac{\cos\theta\times\cos 2\theta}{\sin\theta\times\cos 2\theta}\right)^2+1$

$=\frac{\cos^2\theta}{\sin^2\theta}+1=\frac{\cos^2\theta+\sin^2\theta}{\sin^2\theta}$

$=\frac{1}{\sin^2\theta}=\text{cosec}^2\theta$

353. (b) $\sin(x+y)=1$

$\therefore \quad (x+y)=90^\circ$ ...(i)

And $\cos(x-y)=\frac{\sqrt{3}}{2}$

$\Rightarrow \quad (x-y)=30^\circ$ ...(ii)

Adding Eqs. (i) and (ii),

$2x=120^\circ\Rightarrow x=60^\circ$

$\therefore \quad y=90^\circ-60^\circ\Rightarrow y=30^\circ$

354. (d) $\sin x+\cos x=\sqrt{2}\sin x$

$\Rightarrow \quad \cos x=\sqrt{2}\sin x-\sin x$

$\Rightarrow \quad \cos x=(\sqrt{2}-1)\sin x.$

Multiplying both the sides by $(\sqrt{2}+1)$

$(\sqrt{2}+1)\cos x=(\sqrt{2}+1)(\sqrt{2}-1)\sin x$

$[\because a^2-b^2=(a+b)(a-b)]$

$\Rightarrow \sqrt{2}\cos x+\cos x=(2-1)\sin x$

$\Rightarrow \sqrt{2}\cos x=\sin x-\cos x$

$\therefore \quad \sin x-\cos x=\sqrt{2}\cos x$

355. (b) Given, $4\sin^2\theta=3(1+\cos\theta)$

$\Rightarrow 4(1-\cos^2\theta)=3+3\cos\theta$

$\Rightarrow 4-4\cos^2\theta=3+3\cos\theta$

$\Rightarrow 4\cos^2\theta+3\cos\theta-1=0$

$\Rightarrow 4\cos^2\theta+4\cos\theta-\cos\theta-1=0$

$\Rightarrow 4\cos\theta(\cos\theta+1)-1(\cos\theta+1)=0$

$\Rightarrow (4\cos\theta-1)(\cos\theta+1)=0$

$\Rightarrow \cos\theta=\frac{1}{4}$

$\sin\theta=\sqrt{1-\frac{1}{16}}=\frac{\sqrt{15}}{4}\Rightarrow\tan\theta=\sqrt{15}$

$\therefore \sqrt{15}\tan\theta+\frac{4}{\sqrt{15}}\sin\theta+2\sec\theta$

$\Rightarrow \sqrt{15}\times\sqrt{15}+\frac{4}{\sqrt{15}}\times\frac{\sqrt{15}}{4}+2\times4$

$=15+1+8=24$

356. (c) $\tan\theta+\cot\theta=6$

Squaring both the sides, $(\tan\theta+\cot\theta)^2=6^2$

$\Rightarrow \tan^2\theta+\cot^2\theta+2\tan\theta\cdot\cot\theta=36$

$\Rightarrow \tan^2\theta+\cot^2\theta+2=36$

$\therefore \tan^2\theta+\cot^2\theta=34$

357. (d) $\frac{\cos 13^\circ+\sin 13^\circ}{\cos 13^\circ-\sin 13^\circ}$

Dividing the numerator and denominator by $\cos 13^\circ$, we get

$\frac{1+\tan 13^\circ}{1-\tan 13^\circ}=\frac{1+\tan 13^\circ}{1-1\cdot\tan 13^\circ}$

$\left[\because \tan(x+y)=\frac{\tan x+\tan y}{1-\tan x\cdot\tan y}\right]$

$=\frac{\tan 45^\circ+\tan 13^\circ}{1-\tan 45^\circ-\tan 13^\circ}=\tan(45^\circ+13^\circ)$

$=\tan 58^\circ$

358. (b) Let $\cos A=x$

So, $2\cos^2 A+3\cos A-2=0$

$\Rightarrow \quad 2x^2+3x-2=0$

$\Rightarrow \quad 2x^2+4x-x-2=0$

$\Rightarrow \quad 2x(x+2)-1(x+2)=0$

$\Rightarrow (2x-1)(x+2)=0\Rightarrow x=-2;\ x=\frac{1}{2}$

Now, $x=-2=\cos A$, which is not possible.

$\therefore \quad \cos A=x=\frac{1}{2}$

$\therefore \quad A=60^\circ$

359. (b) $\frac{(\sec A+\tan A)}{(\sec A-\tan A)}=2\frac{51}{79}$

$\Rightarrow \frac{\left(\frac{1}{\cos A}+\frac{\sin A}{\cos A}\right)}{\left(\frac{1}{\cos A}-\frac{\sin A}{\cos A}\right)}=\frac{209}{79}$

$\Rightarrow \frac{1+\sin A}{1-\sin A}=\frac{209}{79}$

$\Rightarrow \frac{(1+\sin A)+(1-\sin A)}{(1+\sin A)-(1-\sin A)}=\frac{209+79}{209-79}$

$\Rightarrow \frac{2}{2\sin A}=\frac{288}{130} \Rightarrow \sin A=\frac{130}{288}=\frac{65}{144}$

360. (b) $(19\sin\theta+6\cot\theta\sin\theta)$

$=\left(19\sin\theta+\frac{6\cos\theta}{\sin\theta}\cdot\sin\theta\right)$

$=19\sin\theta+6\cos\theta=a\sin\theta+b\cos\theta$

Now, we know that,

Maximum value of

$(a\sin\theta+b\cos\theta)=\sqrt{a^2+b^2}$

$\therefore$ Maximum value of

$(19\sin\theta+6\cos\theta)=\sqrt{(19)^2+(6)^2}$

$=\sqrt{361+36}=\sqrt{397}$

361. (a) Let $A=45°$

Now, $x=\sin A+\cos A$

$\Rightarrow x=\sin 45°+\cos 45°;$

$y=\sec A+\operatorname{cosec} A$

$y=\sec 45°+\operatorname{cosec} 45°$

$\Rightarrow x=\frac{1}{\sqrt{2}}+\frac{1}{\sqrt{2}}\Rightarrow x=\sqrt{2}$

$\Rightarrow y=\sqrt{2}+\sqrt{2}\Rightarrow y=2\sqrt{2}$

Now, putting these values in the given options, we need to verify.

Option (a), $y+2x=x^2y$

$\Rightarrow 2\sqrt{2}+2\sqrt{2}=(\sqrt{2})^2\times 2\sqrt{2}$

$\Rightarrow 2\sqrt{2}+2\sqrt{2}=2\times 2\sqrt{2}$

$\Rightarrow 4\sqrt{2}=4\sqrt{2}$

Since LHS = RHS

Hence, $y+2x=x^2y$ is true.

362. (d) Given, $\tan\theta=\frac{7}{24}$

Now, $(\cos^2\theta-\sin^2\theta)=\cos 2\theta=\frac{1-\tan^2\theta}{1+\tan^2\theta}$

$=\frac{1-\left(\frac{7}{24}\right)^2}{1+\left(\frac{7}{24}\right)^2}=\frac{1-\frac{49}{576}}{1+\frac{49}{576}}=\frac{527}{625}$

363. (c) Given, $(\sin x+\sin y)=a$, $(\cos x+\cos y)=b$

On squaring and adding them,

$\sin^2 x+\sin^2 y+2\sin x\sin y$
$+\cos^2 x+\cos^2 y+2\cos x\cos y=b^2+a^2$

$\Rightarrow 2+2(\sin x\sin y+\cos x\cos y)=a^2+b^2$

$\Rightarrow \sin x\sin y+\cos x\cos y=\frac{a^2+b^2-2}{2}$

364. (c) Given, $\sin\alpha=\frac{5}{13}$

Now, 5, 12 and 13 form a Pythagoras triplet.

Value of $\cos\alpha\cdot\operatorname{cosec}\alpha\cdot\cot\alpha$

$=\frac{12}{13}\times\frac{13}{5}\times\frac{12}{5}=\frac{144}{25}$

365. (a) $(1+\cot A-\operatorname{cosec} A)(1+\tan A+\sec A)-3(\sin^2 A+\cos^2 A)$

$=\left(1+\frac{\cos A}{\sin A}-\frac{1}{\sin A}\right)\left(1+\frac{\sin A}{\cos A}+\frac{1}{\cos A}\right)-3\times 1$

$=\left(\frac{\sin A+\cos A-1}{\sin A}\right)\left(\frac{\cos A+\sin A+1}{\cos A}\right)-3$

$=\frac{(\sin A+\cos A)^2-1^2}{\sin A\cos A}-3$

$[\because a^2-b^2=(a+b)(a-b)]$

$=\frac{1+2\sin A\cos A-1}{\sin A\cos A}-3$

$=\frac{2\sin A\cos A}{\sin A\cos A}-3=2-3=-1$

366. (c) $\operatorname{cosec}\theta(1-\cos\theta)(\operatorname{cosec}\theta+\cot\theta)$

$=\operatorname{cosec}\theta(1-\cos\theta)\left(\frac{1}{\sin\theta}+\frac{\cos\theta}{\sin\theta}\right)$

$=\frac{1}{\sin\theta}(1-\cos\theta)\left(\frac{1+\cos\theta}{\sin\theta}\right)$

$=(1-\cos\theta)(1+\cos\theta)\times\frac{1}{\sin^2\theta}$

$=\frac{1-\cos^2\theta}{\sin^2\theta}=\frac{\sin^2\theta}{\sin^2\theta}=1$

367. (b) $(1+\tan^2 A)+\left(1+\frac{1}{\tan^2 A}\right)$

$=\sec^2 A+1+\cot^2 A$ $[\because \sec^2 A-\tan^2 A=1]$

$=\sec^2 A+\operatorname{cosec}^2 A$ $[\because \operatorname{cosec}^2 A-\cot^2 A=1]$

$=\frac{1}{\cos^2 A}+\frac{1}{\sin^2 A}=\frac{\sin^2 A+\cos^2 A}{\cos^2 A\sin^2 A}$

$=\frac{1}{(1-\sin^2 A)\sin^2 A}$ $(\because \sin^2\theta+\cos^2=1)$

$=\frac{1}{\sin^2 A-\sin^4 A}$

368. (c) $\sec 6A=\operatorname{cosec}(A-29°)$

$\therefore 6A+(A-29°)=90°\Rightarrow 7A-29°=90°$

$\therefore 7A=119°\Rightarrow A=17°$

369. (c) Given, $\tan(t)+\cot(t)=1$

$\Rightarrow \frac{\sin(t)}{\cos(t)}+\frac{\cos(t)}{\sin(t)}=1\Rightarrow\frac{\sin^2(t)+\cos^2(t)}{\sin(t)\cdot\cos(t)}=1$

$[\because \sin^2\theta+\cos^2\theta=1]$

$\Rightarrow \sin(t)\cdot\cos(t)=1$ ...(i)

Now, $[\sin(t)+\cos(t)]^2=\sin^2(t)+\cos^2(t)+2\sin(t)\cdot\cos(t)$

$=1+2\times 1=1+2=3$ [from Eq. (i)]

$\therefore \sin(t)+\cos(t)=\sqrt{3}$

Hence, $\frac{1}{\sin(t)+\cos(t)}=\frac{1}{\sqrt{3}}$

370. (a) Given,

$\sin\theta+\cos\theta=\sqrt{2}\cos\theta$ ...(i)

Squaring on both sides of Eq. (i),

$(\sin\theta+\cos\theta)^2=(\sqrt{2}\cos\theta)^2$

$\Rightarrow \sin^2\theta+\cos^2\theta+2\sin\theta\cos\theta=2\cos^2\theta$

$\Rightarrow 2\sin\theta\cos\theta=\cos^2\theta-\sin^2\theta$

$\Rightarrow 2\sin\theta\cos\theta=-(\sin\theta-\cos\theta)$
$(\sin\theta+\cos\theta)$

Put the value from Eq. (i),

$\frac{2\sin\theta\cos\theta}{\sqrt{2}\cos\theta}=-(\sin\theta-\cos\theta)$

$\therefore \frac{\sin\theta-\cos\theta}{\sin\theta}=-\sqrt{2}$

371. (a) $2\tan^2 45°+\cos^2 30°-\sin^2 60°$

$=2\times(1)^2+\left(\frac{\sqrt{3}}{2}\right)^2-\left(\frac{\sqrt{3}}{2}\right)^2=2$

372. (b) $\frac{2\sin A-\cos A}{\sin A+\cos A}=1$

$\Rightarrow 2\sin A-\cos A=\sin A+\cos A$

$\Rightarrow 2\sin A-\sin A=\cos A+\cos A$

$\Rightarrow \sin A=2\cos A$

$\Rightarrow \frac{\cos A}{\sin A}=\frac{1}{2}\Rightarrow \cot A=\frac{1}{2}$

373. (d) $\cot^2\theta=1-e^2\Rightarrow\operatorname{cosec}^2\theta-1=1-e^2$

$\Rightarrow \operatorname{cosec}^2\theta=2-e^2$

$\Rightarrow \operatorname{cosec}\theta=(2-e^2)^{\frac{1}{2}}$ ...(i)

$\therefore \operatorname{cosec}\theta+\cot^3\theta\sec\theta$

$=\operatorname{cosec}\theta+\frac{\cos^3\theta}{\sin^3\theta}\times\frac{1}{\cos\theta}$

$=\frac{1}{\sin\theta}+\frac{\cos^2\theta}{\sin^3\theta}=\frac{\sin^2\theta+\cos^2\theta}{\sin^3\theta}$

$=\frac{1}{\sin^3\theta}=\operatorname{cosec}^3\theta$

From Eq. (i), $=[(2-e^2)^{1/2}]^3=(2-e^2)^{3/2}$

374. (d) $2(\sin 1°\times\sec 89°)+3(\cos 11°\times\operatorname{cosec} 79°)+5(\tan 21°\times\tan 69°)$

$=2\left(\sin 1°\times\frac{1}{\cos 89°}\right)+3\left(\cos 11°\times\frac{1}{\sin 79°}\right)+5\left(\tan 21°\times\frac{1}{\cot 69°}\right)$

$=2\left(\sin 1°\times\frac{1}{\cos(90°-1°)}\right)+3\left(\cos 11°\times\frac{1}{\sin(90°-11)}\right)+5\left(\tan 21°\times\frac{1}{\cot(90°-21°)}\right)$

$=2+3+5=10$

375. (a) $7\sin^2 A+3\cos^2 A=4$

$7\sin^2 A+3(1-\sin^2 A)=4$

$7\sin^2 A+3-3\sin^2 A=4$

$\Rightarrow 4\sin^2 A=4-3$

$\Rightarrow \sin^2 A=\frac{1}{4}\Rightarrow\sin A=\frac{1}{2}$

$\therefore A=30°$

Now, $\cot A=\cot 30°=\sqrt{3}$

376. (b) $\sqrt{\frac{1-\tan A}{1+\tan A}}=\sqrt{\frac{1-\frac{\sin A}{\cos A}}{1+\frac{\sin A}{\cos A}}}$

$=\sqrt{\frac{\frac{\cos A-\sin A}{\cos A}}{\frac{\cos A+\sin A}{\cos A}}}$

$=\sqrt{\frac{\cos A-\sin A}{\cos A+\sin A}\times\frac{\cos A-\sin A}{\cos A-\sin A}}$

$=\sqrt{\frac{(\cos A-\sin A)^2}{\cos^2 A-\sin^2 A}}$

$=\sqrt{\frac{\cos^2 A+\sin^2 A-2\sin A\cos A}{\cos^2 A-\sin^2 A}}$

$=\sqrt{\frac{1-\sin 2A}{\cos 2A}}$

377. (b) Given, $\cos\theta-\sin\theta=\sqrt{2}\sin\theta$ ...(i)

On squaring on both sides,

$(\cos\theta-\sin\theta)^2=(\sqrt{2}\sin\theta)^2$

$\cos^2\theta+\sin^2\theta-2\sin\theta\cos\theta=2\sin^2\theta$

$1-2\sin^2\theta=2\cos\theta\sin\theta$ ...(ii)

Now, on squaring,

$(\cos\theta+\sin\theta)^2=\cos^2\theta+\sin^2\theta+2\sin\theta\cos\theta$

$=1+(1-2\sin^2\theta)=2-2\sin^2\theta=2\cos^2\theta$

$\cos\theta+\sin\theta=\sqrt{2\cos^2\theta}=\sqrt{2}\cos\theta$

378. (b) $\tan^2\theta+\tan^4\theta=\tan^2\theta(1+\tan^2\theta)$

$=(\sec^2\theta-1)[\sec^2\theta]=\sec^4\theta-\sec^2\theta$

379. (b) Given, $\sin\theta+\operatorname{cosec}\theta=2$

$\sin^2\theta+1=2\sin\theta$

$\Rightarrow \sin^2\theta-2\sin\theta+1=0$

$\Rightarrow (\sin\theta-1)^2=0\Rightarrow\sin\theta=1$

Now, $\sin^5\theta+\operatorname{cosec}^5\theta=\sin^5\theta+\frac{1}{\sin^5\theta}$

$=(1)^5+\frac{1}{(1)^5}=2$

380. (d) Given, $\tan A=\frac{4}{3}=\frac{\text{Perpendicular}}{\text{Base}}$

$(\text{Hypotenuse})^2=(4)^2+(3)^2=16+9=25$

$\therefore$ Hypotenuse $=\sqrt{25}=5$

Then, $\sin A=\frac{\text{Perpendicular}}{\text{Hypotenuse}}=\frac{4}{5}$

381. (c) Given,

$\cos(36^\circ-A)\cos(36^\circ+A)+\cos(54^\circ-A)\cos(54^\circ+A)$

$=\cos(36^\circ-A)\cos(36^\circ+A)+\cos[90^\circ-(36^\circ+A)]\cos[90^\circ-(36^\circ-A)]$

$=\cos(36^\circ-A)\cos(36^\circ+A)+\sin(36^\circ+A)\cdot\sin(36^\circ+A)$

$=\cos[(36^\circ-A)-(36^\circ+A)]$

$[\because\cos(a-b)=\cos a\cdot\cos b+\sin a\cdot\sin b]$

$=\cos[36^\circ-A-36^\circ-A]=\cos[-2A]=\cos 2A$

382. (c) Given, $4\cos\theta+3\sin\theta=x$

Squaring both sides,

$16\cos^2\theta+9\sin^2\theta+24\cos\theta\cdot\sin\theta=x^2$ ...(i)

Also, $4\sin\theta-3\cos\theta=y$

Squaring both side,

$16\sin^2\theta+9\cos^2\theta-24\sin\theta\cdot\cos\theta=y^2$ ...(ii)

Adding Eqs. (i) and (ii),

$x^2+y^2=16\cos^2\theta+9\sin^2\theta+24\cos\theta\cdot\sin\theta+16\sin^2\theta+9\cos^2\theta-24\sin\theta\cdot\cos\theta$

$=16(\cos^2\theta+\sin^2\theta)+9(\sin^2\theta+\cos^2\theta)$

$=16\times1+9\times1=25$

383. (a) Given, $\cos A=\sin^2 A$

Squaring both side, $\cos^2 A=\sin^4 A$

$\Rightarrow 1-\sin^2 A=\sin^4 A\Rightarrow\sin^4 A+\sin^2 A=1$

Taking cube both side,

$(\sin^4 A+\sin^2 A)^3=1^3$

$\Rightarrow \sin^{12}A+\sin^6 A+3\sin^4 A\cdot\sin^2 A(\sin^4 A+\sin^2 A)=1$

$\Rightarrow \sin^{12}A+\sin^6 A+3\sin^{10}A+3\sin^8 A=1$

$\Rightarrow \sin^{12}A+3\sin^{10}A+3\sin^8 A+\sin^6 A=1$ ...(i)

Also given, $a\sin^{12}A+b\sin^{10}A+c\sin^8 A+\sin^6 A=1$ ...(ii)

On comparing Eqs. (i) and (ii),

$a=1, b=3, c=3$

So, $a+b+c=1+3+3=7$

384. (d) Given, $\cos 48^\circ=\frac{m}{n}\Rightarrow\sec 48^\circ=\frac{n}{m}$

Again $\cos 48^\circ=\frac{m}{n}\Rightarrow\cos(90^\circ-42^\circ)=\frac{m}{n}$

$\Rightarrow \sin 42^\circ=\frac{m}{n}$

$\therefore \cos 42^\circ=\sqrt{1-\sin^2 42}$

$=\sqrt{1-\frac{m^2}{n^2}}=\frac{\sqrt{n^2-m^2}}{n}$

Then, $\cot 42^\circ=\frac{\cos 42^\circ}{\sin 42^\circ}=\frac{\sqrt{n^2-m^2}}{m}$

$\therefore \sec 48^\circ-\cot 42^\circ=\frac{n}{m}-\frac{\sqrt{n^2-m^2}}{m}$

$=\frac{n-\sqrt{n^2-m^2}}{m}$

385. (c) Given, $\frac{2\cos^3\theta-\cos\theta}{\sin\theta-2\sin^3\theta}$

$=\frac{\cos\theta(2\cos^2\theta-1)}{\sin\theta(1-2\sin^2\theta)}=\frac{\cos\theta\cdot\cos 2\theta}{\sin\theta\cdot\cos 2\theta}=\cot\theta$

386. (a) Given,

$\cos^2 45^\circ+\cos^2 135^\circ+\cos^2 225^\circ+\cos^2 315^\circ$

$=\cos^2 45^\circ+\cos^2(180^\circ-45^\circ)+\cos^2(180^\circ+45^\circ)+\cos^2(360^\circ-45^\circ)$

$=\cos^2 45^\circ+(-\cos 45^\circ)^2+(-\cos 45^\circ)^2+\cos^2 45^\circ$

$=\left(\frac{1}{\sqrt{2}}\right)^2+\left(-\frac{1}{\sqrt{2}}\right)^2+\left(-\frac{1}{\sqrt{2}}\right)^2+\left(\frac{1}{\sqrt{2}}\right)^2$

$=4\times\frac{1}{2}=2$

387. (c) $\cos^2\theta-\sin^2\theta=\frac{1}{2}$ (given) ...(i)

We know that,

$\cos^2\theta+\sin^2\theta=1$ ...(ii)

On adding Eqs. (i) and (ii),

$\Rightarrow 2\cos^2\theta=1+\frac{1}{2}\Rightarrow 2\cos^2\theta=\frac{3}{2}$

$\Rightarrow \cos^2\theta=\frac{3}{4}\Rightarrow\cos\theta=\frac{\sqrt{3}}{2}$

$\therefore \theta=30^\circ$

388. (d) Given, $\cot\theta=\frac{1}{\sqrt{3}}$

$\cot\theta=\cot 60^\circ\Rightarrow\theta=60^\circ$

$=\frac{2-\sin^2\theta}{1-\cos^2\theta}+(\operatorname{cosec}^2\theta-\sec\theta)$

$=\frac{2-\sin^2 60^\circ}{1-\cos^2 60^\circ}+(\operatorname{cosec}^2 60^\circ-\sec 60^\circ)$

$=\frac{2-(3/4)}{1-(1/4)}+[(2/\sqrt{3})^2-2]$

$=\frac{5/4}{3/4}+\left[\frac{4}{3}-2\right]=\frac{5}{3}+\left(-\frac{2}{3}\right)$

$=\frac{5}{3}-\frac{2}{3}=\frac{3}{3}=1$

389. (d) $4(\operatorname{cosec}^2 57^\circ-\tan^2 33^\circ)-\cos 90^\circ+y\times\tan^2 66^\circ\times\tan^2 24^\circ=\frac{y}{2}$

$\Rightarrow 4[\operatorname{cosec}^2 57^\circ-\cot^2(90^\circ-33^\circ)]-0+y\times\tan^2 66^\circ\times\cot^2(90^\circ-24^\circ)=\frac{y}{2}$

$\Rightarrow 4(\operatorname{cosec}^2 57^\circ-\cot^2 57^\circ)+y\times\tan^2 66^\circ\times\cot^2 66^\circ=\frac{y}{2}$

$\Rightarrow 4\times1+y\times\tan^2 66^\circ\times\frac{1}{\tan^2 66^\circ}=\frac{y}{2}$

$\Rightarrow 4+y=\frac{y}{2}\Rightarrow\frac{y}{2}=-4$

$\therefore y=-8$

390. (d) $4-2\sin^2\theta-5\cos\theta=0$

$\Rightarrow 4-2(1-\cos^2\theta)-5\cos\theta=0$

$\Rightarrow 2\cos^2\theta-5\cos\theta+2=0$

$\Rightarrow 2\cos^2\theta-4\cos\theta-\cos\theta+2=0$

$\Rightarrow 2\cos\theta(\cos\theta-2)-1(\cos\theta-2)=0$

$\Rightarrow (\cos\theta-2)(2\cos\theta-1)=0$

Since, $\cos\theta$ cannot be greater than 1, $(\cos\theta\neq2)$

$\Rightarrow \cos\theta=\frac{1}{2}\Rightarrow\theta=\frac{\pi}{3}$

Now, $\cos\theta-\tan\theta=\cos\frac{\pi}{3}-\tan\frac{\pi}{3}$

[substitute $\theta=\frac{\pi}{3}$ or 60°]

$=\frac{1}{2}-\sqrt{3}=\frac{1-2\sqrt{3}}{2}$

391. (b) $\sin 3x=\cos(3x-45^\circ)$

$\Rightarrow \sin 3x=\sin[90^\circ-(3x-45^\circ)]$ $\{\because 0<3x<90^\circ\}$

$\Rightarrow 3x=90^\circ-3x+45^\circ$

$\Rightarrow 6x=135^\circ\Rightarrow x=22.5$

392. (b) $4-2\sin^2\theta-5\cos\theta=0$

$\Rightarrow\quad 4-2(1-\cos^2\theta)-5\cos\theta=0$

$\Rightarrow\quad 2\cos^2\theta-5\cos\theta+2=0$

$\Rightarrow\quad (\cos\theta-2)(2\cos\theta-1)=0$

$\Rightarrow\quad \cos\theta=\frac{1}{2}=\cos 60^\circ$

$\therefore\quad \theta=60^\circ$

Hence, the value of $\cos\theta+\tan\theta$

$=\cos 60^\circ+\tan 60^\circ$

$=\frac{1}{2}+\sqrt{3}=\frac{1+2\sqrt{3}}{2}$

393. (a) $4(\text{cosec}^2 57^\circ-\tan^3 33^\circ)$

$-\cos 90^\circ-y\tan^2 66^\circ\tan^2 24^\circ=\frac{y}{2}$

$\Rightarrow 4(\text{cosec}^2(90-33)^\circ-\tan^2 33^\circ)$

$-0-y\tan^2(90-24)^\circ\tan^2 24^\circ=\frac{y}{2}$

$\Rightarrow 4(\sec^2 33^\circ-\tan^2 33^\circ)$

$-y\cot^2 24^\circ\tan^2 24^\circ=\frac{y}{2}$

$\Rightarrow\quad 4\times 1-y=\frac{y}{2}\Rightarrow y+\frac{y}{2}=4\quad\Rightarrow\frac{3y}{2}=4$

$\Rightarrow\quad y=\frac{8}{3}$

394. (d) $(\sin^6 A+\cos^6 A+3\sin^2 A\cos^2 A)$

$-(\sin^4 A-\cos^4 A+1)\,\text{cosec}^2 A$

$=(\sin^2 A+\cos^2 A)^3-(\sin^2 A+\cos^2 A)$

$(\sin^2 A-\cos^2 A+1)\,\text{cosec}^2 A$

$=1-(\sin^2 A-\cos^2 A+\sin^2 A+\cos^2 A)$

$\text{cosec}^2 A$

$=1-2\sin^2 A\,\text{cosec}^2 A=1-2=-1$

395. (c) $\dfrac{3(\sec^2 A-1)(\text{cosec}\,A-1)}{(\text{cosec}\,A+1)+4(\text{cosec}^2 A-\cot^2 A)}$

$=3(\sec^2 A-1)(\text{cosec}^2 A-1)$

$+4(\text{cosec}^2 A-\cot^2 A)$

$=3\tan^2 A\cot^2 A+4\times 1=3+4=7$

396. (d) Given, if $\tan A+\sin A=x$ ...(i)

and $\tan A-\sin A=y$ ...(ii)

Hence, $x^2-y^2=(\tan A+\sin A)^2$

$-(\tan A-\sin A)^2$

$x^2-y^2=\tan^2 A+\sin^2 A+2\tan A\sin A$

$-(\tan^2 A+\sin^2 A-2\sin A\tan A)$

$\Rightarrow x^2-y^2=\tan^2 A+\sin^2 A$

$+2\tan A\sin A-\tan^2 A$

$-\sin^2 A+2\tan A\cdot\sin A$

$\Rightarrow\quad x^2-y^2=4\tan A\cdot\sin A$ ... (iii)

Multiplying Eqs. (i) and (ii),

$(\tan A+\sin A)(\tan A-\sin A)=xy$

$\Rightarrow\quad \tan^2 A-\sin^2 A=xy$

$\Rightarrow\quad \frac{\sin^2 A}{\cos^2 A}-\sin^2 A=xy$

$\Rightarrow\quad \sin^2 A\left(\frac{1-\cos^2 A}{\cos^2 A}\right)=xy$

$\Rightarrow\quad \sin^2 A\times\tan^2 A=xy$

$\Rightarrow\quad \sin A\times\tan A=\sqrt{xy}$ ...(iv)

Now,

$\therefore\quad x^2-y^2=4\times\sin A\times\tan A$

$=4\sqrt{xy}$ [$\because$ from Eq. (iv)]

397. (a) Let $\cos^{-1}\left(\frac{7}{25}\right)=\theta_1$

and $\cos^{-1}\left(\frac{15}{17}\right)=\theta_2$

Let $\theta_1-\theta_2=\sin^{-1}x$ ... (i)

$\therefore\quad \frac{7}{25}=\cos\theta_1$ and $\frac{15}{17}=\cos\theta_2$

$\therefore\quad \sin\theta_1=\sqrt{1-\cos^2\theta_1}=\sqrt{1-\frac{49}{625}}$

$\sin\theta_1=\sqrt{\frac{576}{625}}=\frac{24}{25}$

and $\sin\theta_2=\sqrt{1-\cos^2\theta_2}=\sqrt{1-\frac{225}{289}}$

$\sin\theta_2=\sqrt{\frac{64}{289}}=\frac{8}{17}$

From Eq. (i), $(\theta_1-\theta_2)=\sin^{-1}x$

$\sin(\theta_1-\theta_2)=x$

$x=\sin\theta_1\cos\theta_2-\cos\theta_1\sin\theta_2$

[$\because\sin(A-B)=\sin A\cdot\cos B-\cos A\cdot\sin B$]

$=\frac{24}{25}\times\frac{15}{17}-\frac{7}{25}\times\frac{8}{17}$

$x=\frac{360}{425}-\frac{56}{425}=\frac{304}{425}$

From Eq. (i),

$\cos^{-1}\left(\frac{7}{25}\right)-\cos^{-1}\left(\frac{15}{17}\right)=\sin^{-1}\left(\frac{304}{425}\right)$

398. (c) Given,

$\left(\frac{\sin\theta}{1+\cos\theta}+\frac{1+\cos\theta}{\sin\theta}\right)\left(\frac{1}{\tan\theta+\cot\theta}\right)$

$=\left(\frac{\sin^2\theta+1+\cos^2\theta+2\cos\theta}{(1+\cos\theta)\sin\theta}\right)\left(\frac{1}{\frac{\sin\theta}{\cos\theta}+\frac{\cos\theta}{\sin\theta}}\right)$

$=\frac{2(1+\cos\theta)}{(1+\cos\theta)\sin\theta}\times\frac{\sin\theta\times\cos\theta}{(\sin^2\theta+\cos^2\theta)}$

$=\frac{2}{\sin\theta}\times\frac{\sin\theta\times\cos\theta}{1}$ [$\because\sin^2\theta+\cos^2\theta=1$]

$=2\cos\theta$

399. (c) Given, $3\tan\theta=4$

$\Rightarrow\quad \tan\theta=\frac{4}{3}$

$\Rightarrow\quad \frac{9\sin\theta+2\cos\theta}{9\sin\theta-2\cos\theta}$

Dividing numerator and denominator by $\cos\theta$, we get

$=\frac{9\tan\theta+2}{9\tan\theta-2}=\frac{9\left(\frac{4}{3}\right)+2}{9\left(\frac{4}{3}\right)-2}=\frac{12+2}{12-2}$

$=\frac{14}{10}=\frac{7}{5}$

400. (c) $4\sin^2\theta-4\sqrt{3}\sin\theta+3=0$

$\Rightarrow\quad (2\sin\theta-\sqrt{3})^2=0\Rightarrow\sin\theta=\frac{\sqrt{3}}{2}$

$\Rightarrow\quad \sin\theta=\sin 60^\circ$

$\Rightarrow\quad \theta=60^\circ$

401. (c) Given, $f(p)=\sin^{p+2}x+\cos^{p+2}x$

$f(2)=\sin^4 x+\cos^4 x$

[$\because\sin^4 x+\cos^4 x=1-2\sin^2 x\cos^2 x$]

$=1-2\sin^2 x\cos^2 x$

$f(4)=\sin^6 x+\cos^6 x$

[$\because\sin^6 x+\cos^6 x=1-3\sin^2 x\cos^2 x$]

$=1-3\sin^2 x\cos^2 x$

$f(0)=\sin^2 x+\cos^2 x=1$

Now, $6f(2)-4f(4)+10f(0)$

$=6(1-2\sin^2 x\cos^2 x)$

$-4(1-3\sin^2 x\cos^2 x)+10$

$=6-12\sin^2 x\cos^2 x-4$

$+12\sin^2 x\cos^2 x+10=12$

402. (b) $\tan A=\sqrt{2}-1$

$\tan^2 A=2+1-2\sqrt{2}=3-2\sqrt{2}$

$\sec^2 A-1=3-2\sqrt{2}$

$\sec^2 A=4-2\sqrt{2}$

$\cos^2 A=\frac{1}{4-2\sqrt{2}}\times\frac{4+2\sqrt{2}}{4+2\sqrt{2}}$

$=\frac{4+2\sqrt{2}}{16-8}=\frac{4+2\sqrt{2}}{8}$

Now, $\sin A\times\cos A+\tan A$

$=\sin A\times\cos A+\frac{\sin A}{\cos A}$

$=\sin A\left(\frac{\cos^2 A+1}{\cos A}\right)=\tan A(1+\cos^2 A)$

$=(\sqrt{2}-1)\left(1+\frac{4+2\sqrt{2}}{8}\right)$

$=(\sqrt{2}-1)\left(\frac{8+4+2\sqrt{2}}{8}\right)$

$=(\sqrt{2}-1)\left(\frac{2(6+\sqrt{2})}{8}\right)$

$=\frac{(\sqrt{2}-1)(6+\sqrt{2})}{4}$

$=\frac{6\sqrt{2}+2-6-\sqrt{2}}{4}=\frac{5\sqrt{2}-4}{4}$

403. (a) We know, maximum value of

$m\cos\theta+n\sin\theta\le\sqrt{m^2+n^2}$

$\therefore\quad 7\cos A+24\sin A\le\sqrt{(7)^2+(24)^2}$

$=\sqrt{49+576}=\sqrt{625}=25$

$\therefore$ Maximum value of

$7\cos A+24\sin A+32=25+32=57$

404. (a) Given, $\tan\theta=\frac{7}{4}$ ...(i)

$\frac{4\sin\theta-3\cos\theta}{4\sin\theta+3\cos\theta}=\frac{4\frac{\sin\theta}{\cos\theta}-3}{4\frac{\sin\theta}{\cos\theta}+3}=\frac{4\tan\theta-3}{4\tan\theta+3}$

[From Eq. (i)]

$=\frac{4\times\frac{7}{4}-3}{4\times\frac{7}{4}+3}=\frac{7-3}{7+3}=\frac{4}{10}=\frac{2}{5}$

405. (d) $\cot\alpha = \dfrac{P}{Q} \Rightarrow \tan\alpha = \dfrac{Q}{P}$

Thus, $\dfrac{P\cos\alpha - Q\sin\alpha}{P\cos\alpha + Q\sin\alpha} - \dfrac{P^2 - Q^2}{P^2 + Q^2} + 3$

$$= \frac{P\cos\alpha}{P\cos\alpha}\left[\frac{1 - \frac{Q}{P}\tan\alpha}{1 + \frac{Q}{P}\tan\alpha}\right] - \left(\frac{P^2 - Q^2}{P^2 + Q^2}\right) + 3$$

$$= \frac{\left(1 - \frac{Q}{P} \times \frac{Q}{P}\right)}{\left(1 + \frac{Q}{P} \times \frac{Q}{P}\right)} - \left(\frac{P^2 - Q^2}{P^2 + Q^2}\right) + 3$$

$$= \frac{P^2 - Q^2}{P^2} \times \frac{P^2}{(P^2 + Q^2)} - \left(\frac{P^2 - Q^2}{(P^2 + Q^2)}\right) + 3 = 3$$

406. (a) Given, $\cos^4\theta - \sin^4\theta = \dfrac{4}{5}$

$\Rightarrow (\cos^2\theta - \sin^2\theta)(\cos^2\theta + \sin^2\theta) = \dfrac{4}{5}$

$[\because a^4 - b^4 = (a^2 + b^2)(a^2 - b^2)]$

$\Rightarrow \cos^2\theta - \sin^2\theta = \dfrac{4}{5} \Rightarrow \cos 2\theta = \dfrac{4}{5}$

$[\because \cos 2\theta = \cos^2\theta - \sin^2\theta = 2\cos^2\theta - 1]$

We know that,

$\cos 4\theta = 2\cos^2 2\theta - 1$

$= 2 \times \dfrac{16}{25} - 1 = \dfrac{7}{25}$

$\sin 4\theta = \sqrt{1 - \cos^2 4\theta}$ $\quad [\because \sin\theta = \sqrt{1 - \cos^2\theta}]$

$= \sqrt{1 - \dfrac{49}{625}} = \sqrt{\dfrac{576}{625}}$

$\therefore \quad \sin 4\theta = \dfrac{24}{25}$

407. (a) $\sin\theta = \dfrac{11}{12} = \dfrac{P}{H}$

By Pythagoras theorem,

$H^2 = P^2 + B^2$

$(12)^2 = (11)^2 + B^2 \Rightarrow B^2 = 144 - 121$

$\Rightarrow \quad B^2 = 23 \Rightarrow B = \sqrt{23}$

$\therefore \tan\theta + \sec\theta = \dfrac{P}{B} + \dfrac{H}{B} = \dfrac{11}{\sqrt{23}} + \dfrac{12}{\sqrt{23}}$

$= \dfrac{23}{\sqrt{23}} = \sqrt{23}$

408. (c) Given, $\cot A = \dfrac{5}{12}$

$\dfrac{\sqrt{\sec A - \operatorname{cosec} A}}{\sqrt{\sec A + \operatorname{cosec} A}} - \sqrt{\dfrac{17}{7}}$

On dividing by $\sec A$ in first term, we get

$$= \sqrt{\frac{1 - \cot A}{1 + \cot A}} - \sqrt{\frac{17}{7}} = \frac{\sqrt{1 - \frac{5}{12}}}{\sqrt{1 + \frac{5}{12}}} - \sqrt{\frac{17}{7}}$$

$$= \sqrt{\frac{7}{17}} - \sqrt{\frac{17}{7}} = \frac{7 - 17}{\sqrt{119}} = \frac{-10}{\sqrt{119}}$$

409. (c) Given expression,

$$\left[\frac{\operatorname{cosec} 31^\circ - \sec 59^\circ}{(\sin 18^\circ + \cos 72^\circ)} \times \frac{\tan 26^\circ}{\cot 64^\circ}\right] + \left[\frac{\tan 30^\circ + \tan 15^\circ}{1 - \tan 30^\circ \cdot \tan 15^\circ}\right]$$

$$= \left[\frac{\sec(90 - 31)^\circ - \sec 59^\circ}{\cos(90 - 18)^\circ + \cos 72^\circ} \times \frac{\cot(90 - 26)^\circ}{\cot 64^\circ}\right] + \left[\frac{\tan 30^\circ + \tan 15^\circ}{1 - \tan 30^\circ \cdot \tan 15^\circ}\right]$$

$$= \left[\frac{\sec 59^\circ - \sec 59^\circ}{\cos 72^\circ + \cos 72^\circ} \times \frac{\cot 64^\circ}{\cot 64^\circ}\right] + \frac{\tan 30^\circ + \tan 15^\circ}{1 - \tan 15^\circ \cdot \tan 30^\circ}$$

$\left[\because \operatorname{cosec}(90 - \theta) = \sec\theta, \sin(90 - \theta) = \cos\theta, \tan(90 - \theta) = \cot\theta\right]$

$= 0 + \tan(15^\circ + 30^\circ)$

$\left[\because \tan(A + B) = \dfrac{\tan A + \tan B}{1 - \tan A \cdot \tan B}\right]$

$= 0 + \tan 45^\circ = 1$ $\quad (\because \tan 45^\circ = 1)$

410. (b) $\dfrac{\sin(A - B)}{\cos A\cos B} + \dfrac{\sin(B - C)}{\cos B\cos C}$

$$= \frac{\sin A\cos B - \cos A\sin B}{\cos A\cos B} + \frac{\sin B\cos C - \cos B\sin C}{\cos B \cdot \cos C}$$

$$= \frac{\cos C[\sin A \cdot \cos B - \cos A \cdot \sin B] + \cos A[\sin B \cdot \cos C - \cos B \sin C]}{\cos A \cdot \cos B \cdot \cos C}$$

$$= \frac{\sin A \cdot \cos B \cdot \cos C - \cos A\sin B\cos C + \sin B \cdot \cos C \cdot \cos A - \cos A \cdot \cos B \cdot \sin C}{\cos A \cdot \cos B \cdot \cos C}$$

$$= \frac{\sin(A - C)}{\cos A \cdot \cos C}$$

411. (a) Given, $\tan A = a\tan B$

$\therefore \quad \cot B = \dfrac{a}{\tan A}$

Also, $\sin A = b\sin B \Rightarrow \operatorname{cosec} B = \dfrac{b}{\sin A}$

Putting the values in

$\operatorname{cosec}^2 B - \cot^2 B = 1$, we get

$\Rightarrow \dfrac{b^2}{\sin^2 A} - \dfrac{a^2}{\tan^2 A} = 1$

$\Rightarrow \dfrac{b^2}{\sin^2 A} - \dfrac{a^2\cos^2 A}{\sin^2 A} = 1$

$\Rightarrow \dfrac{b^2 - a^2\cos^2 A}{\sin^2 A} = 1$

$\Rightarrow b^2 - a^2\cos^2 A = \sin^2 A$

$\Rightarrow b^2 - a^2\cos^2 A = 1 - \cos^2 A$

$\Rightarrow b^2 - 1 = a^2\cos^2 A - \cos^2 A$

$\Rightarrow b^2 - 1 = (a^2 - 1)\cos^2 A$

$\Rightarrow \dfrac{b^2 - 1}{a^2 - 1} = \cos^2 A$

412. (b) Given, $\cot\theta = \dfrac{3}{4} = \dfrac{AB}{AC}$

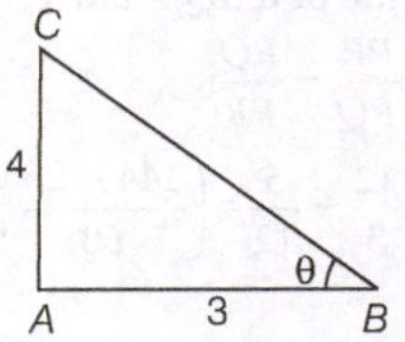

Now in ΔABC, using Pythagoras theorem,

$BC^2 = AC^2 + AB^2$

$\Rightarrow \quad BC^2 = (3)^2 + (4)^2 = 25$

$\therefore \quad BC = 5$

So, $\sin\theta = \dfrac{AC}{BC} = \dfrac{4}{5}$, $\cos\theta = \dfrac{AB}{BC} = \dfrac{3}{5}$ and

$\tan\theta = \dfrac{AC}{AB} = \dfrac{4}{3}$

Now, $\sin\theta + \cos\theta - \tan\theta = \dfrac{4}{5} + \dfrac{3}{5} - \dfrac{4}{3}$

$= \dfrac{7}{5} - \dfrac{4}{3} = \dfrac{21 - 20}{15} = \dfrac{1}{15}$

413. (b) $\dfrac{1}{\sin^4(90^\circ - 2\alpha)} + \dfrac{1}{\cos^2(90^\circ - 2\alpha) - 1}$

$= \dfrac{1}{\cos^4 2\alpha} + \dfrac{1}{\sin^2 2\alpha - 1}$

$= \dfrac{1}{\cos^4 2\alpha} - \dfrac{1}{1 - \sin^2 2\alpha} = \dfrac{1}{\cos^4 2\alpha} - \dfrac{1}{\cos^2 2\alpha}$

$= \dfrac{1}{\cos^2 2\alpha}\left(\dfrac{1}{\cos^2 2\alpha} - 1\right)$

$= \dfrac{1}{\cos^2 2\alpha} \dfrac{(1 - \cos^2 2\alpha)}{\cos^2 2\alpha}$

$= \dfrac{1}{\cos^2\alpha} \times \dfrac{\sin^2 2\alpha}{\cos^2 2\alpha} = \sec^2 2\alpha \times \tan^2 2\alpha$

414. (c) Given, $\tan 570^\circ$

$= \tan(540^\circ + 30^\circ) = \tan 30^\circ = \dfrac{1}{\sqrt{3}}$

415. (d) $(\tan\alpha + 1)(\tan\beta + 1) = 2x$

$\Rightarrow \tan\alpha\tan\beta + \tan\alpha + \tan\beta + 1 = 2x$ $\quad$ ...(i)

We know that,

$\tan(\alpha + \beta) = \dfrac{\tan\alpha + \tan\beta}{1 - \tan\alpha\tan\beta}$

$\tan 45^\circ = \dfrac{\tan\alpha + \tan\beta}{1 - \tan\alpha\tan\beta}$

$\Rightarrow \quad 1 = \dfrac{\tan\alpha + \tan\beta}{1 - \tan\alpha\tan\beta}$

$\Rightarrow 1 - \tan\alpha\tan\beta = \tan\alpha + \tan\beta$

Now, putting the value of $\tan\alpha + \tan\beta$ in Eq. (i), we get

$\tan\alpha\tan\beta + 1 - \tan\alpha\tan\beta + 1 = 2x$

$2x = 2 \Rightarrow x = \dfrac{2}{2} = 1$

416. (c) According to the question,

$\dfrac{3\cos^3\theta - 2\cos\theta}{\sin\theta - 3\sin^3\theta} = \dfrac{\cos\theta(3\cos^2\theta - 2)}{\sin\theta(1 - 3\sin^2\theta)}$

$= \dfrac{\cos\theta\{3(1 - \sin^2\theta) - 2\}}{\sin\theta(1 - 3\sin^2\theta)}$

$= \cot\theta\dfrac{(3 - 3\sin^2\theta - 2)}{(1 - 3\sin^2\theta)} = \cot\theta\dfrac{(1 - 3\sin^2\theta)}{(1 - 3\sin^2\theta)}$

$= \cot\theta$

417. (d) $\sin(30^\circ + \theta) - \cos(60^\circ - \theta)$

$= \sin(30^\circ + \theta) - \sin[90^\circ - (60^\circ - \theta)]$

$= \sin(30^\circ + \theta) - \sin(30^\circ + \theta) = 0$

418. (d) $(\cot\theta + \tan\theta)(\text{cosec}\,\theta - \sin\theta) \times (\cos\theta - \sec\theta)$

$$= \left(\frac{\cos\theta}{\sin\theta} + \frac{\sin\theta}{\cos\theta}\right)\left(\frac{1}{\sin\theta} - \sin\theta\right) \times \left(\cos\theta - \frac{1}{\cos\theta}\right)$$

$$= \left(\frac{\sin^2\theta + \cos^2\theta}{\sin\theta\cos\theta}\right)\left(\frac{1-\sin^2\theta}{\sin\theta}\right) \times \left(\frac{\cos^2\theta - 1}{\cos\theta}\right)$$

$$= \left(\frac{1}{\sin\theta \cdot \cos\theta}\right)\left(\frac{\cos^2\theta}{\sin\theta}\right)\left(\frac{-\sin^2\theta}{\cos\theta}\right) = -1$$

419. (a) According to the question,

$$\sqrt{13}\sin\theta = 2$$

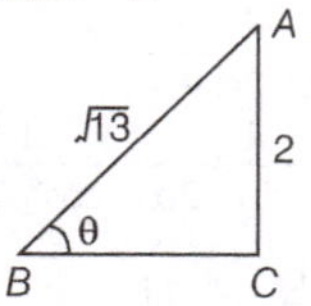

In ΔACB,

$$(BC)^2 = (AB)^2 - (AC)^2 = (\sqrt{13})^2 - (2)^2 = 9$$

$\therefore \quad BC = 3$

$$\therefore \frac{3\tan\theta + \sqrt{13}\sin\theta}{\sqrt{13}\cos\theta - 3\tan\theta}$$

$$= \frac{3 \times \frac{2}{3} + \sqrt{13} \times \frac{2}{\sqrt{13}}}{\sqrt{13} \times \frac{3}{\sqrt{13}} - 3 \times \frac{2}{3}} = \frac{2+2}{3-2} = 4$$

420. (d) $\tan\theta + \cot\theta = 2$

$\Rightarrow \quad \tan\theta + \frac{1}{\tan\theta} = 2$

$\Rightarrow \quad \frac{\tan^2\theta + 1}{\tan\theta} = 2$

$\Rightarrow \quad \tan^2\theta - 2\tan\theta + 1 = 0$

$\Rightarrow \quad (\tan^2\theta - 1)^2 = 0$

$\tan\theta = 1 \Rightarrow \theta = 45°$

Now, $\tan^3 45° + \cot^3 45° + 6\tan^3 45° \cot^2 45°$

$$= (1)^3 + (1)^3 + 6(1)^3 \cdot (1)^2 = 8$$

421. (b) Trigonometric expression,

$\cos(x+y) - \sin(x-y) + \tan(2z)$

$= (\cos x \,.\, \cos y - \sin x \,.\, \sin y)$

$- (\sin x \,.\, \cos y - \sin y \,.\, \cos x) + \frac{2\tan z}{1-\tan^2 z}$

$= \cos x \,.\, \cos y - \sin x \,.\, \sin y$

$- \sin x \,.\, \cos y + \sin y \,.\, \cos x + \frac{2\tan z}{1-\tan^2 z}$

422. (a) $12\sin^2 A + 2\cos^2 A = 7$

$12\sin^2 A + 2(1-\sin^2 A) = 7$

$12\sin^2 A + 2 - 2\sin^2 A = 7$

$10\sin^2 A = 5 \Rightarrow \sin^2 A = \frac{1}{2}$

$\therefore \quad \cos^2 A = 1 - \sin^2 A = 1 - \frac{1}{2} = \frac{1}{2}$

$\therefore \quad \cot^2 A = \frac{\cos^2 A}{\sin^2 A} = \frac{1}{2} \times \frac{2}{1} = 1$

$\therefore \quad \cot A = \pm 1$

423. (a) According to the question,

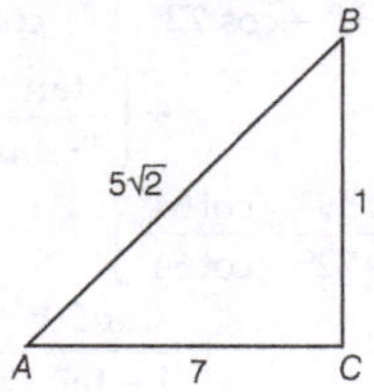

$$\cot A = \frac{7}{1} = \frac{B}{P}$$

Now, $(AB)^2 = 7^2 + 1^2 = 49 + 1$

$\therefore \quad AB = \sqrt{50} = 5\sqrt{2}$

Now,

$$5\cos A + 4\sin A = 5 \times \frac{7}{5\sqrt{2}} + 4 \times \frac{1}{5\sqrt{2}}$$

$$= \frac{35+4}{5\sqrt{2}} = \frac{39}{5\sqrt{2}}$$

and $\cos^3 A + 7\sin^3 A + 6\sin A$

$$= \left(\frac{7}{5\sqrt{2}}\right)^3 + 7 \times \left(\frac{1}{5\sqrt{2}}\right)^3 + 6 \times \frac{1}{5\sqrt{2}}$$

$$= \frac{343 + 7 + 300}{250\sqrt{2}} = \frac{650}{250\sqrt{2}}$$

Now, $$\frac{5\cos A + 4\sin A}{\cos^3 A + 7\sin^3 A + 6\sin A} = \frac{\frac{39}{5\sqrt{2}}}{\frac{650}{250\sqrt{2}}}$$

$$= \frac{39}{5\sqrt{2}} \times \frac{250\sqrt{2}}{650} = 3$$

424. (c) In right ΔABC, $\angle B = 90°$

$\angle A + \angle B + \angle C = 180°$

(∵ angles sum property of triangle)

$\angle A + \angle C = 180° - \angle B$

$\Rightarrow \quad \angle A + \angle C = 180° - 90°$

$\Rightarrow \quad \angle A + \angle C = 90°$

Now, $\sin A \cos C + \cos A \sin C = \sin(A + C)$

$[\because \sin x . \cos y + \cos x . \sin y = \sin(x+y)]$

$= \sin 90° = 1 \qquad (\because \angle A + \angle C = 90°)$

425. (b) In ΔPQR,

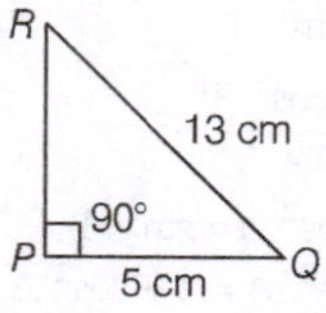

By Pythagoras theorem,

$(RQ)^2 = (PQ)^2 + (PR)^2$

$\Rightarrow (13)^2 = (5)^2 + (PR)^2$

$\Rightarrow \quad (PR)^2 = 169 - 25 = 144$

$\Rightarrow \quad PR = 12 \text{ cm}$

Then, the value of $\tan Q - \tan R$

$$= \frac{PR}{PQ} - \frac{PQ}{PR}$$

$$= \frac{12}{5} - \frac{5}{12} = \left(\frac{144 - 25}{60}\right) = \frac{119}{60}$$

426. (b) $\because \tan A = \frac{3}{4} = \frac{P}{B}$

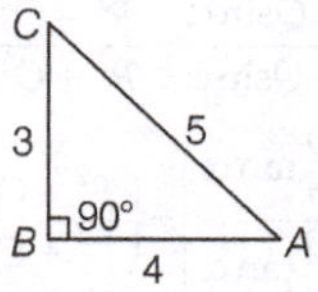

In ΔABC, $(AC)^2 = (AB)^2 + (BC)^2$

$\Rightarrow \quad (AC)^2 = (3)^2 + (4)^2 = 25 \Rightarrow AC = 5$

$$\therefore \quad \frac{6\sin A}{1 - \sin A} = \frac{6\left(\frac{3}{5}\right)}{1 - \left(\frac{3}{5}\right)} = \frac{\frac{18}{5}}{\frac{2}{5}} = 9$$

427. (a) $\text{cosec}\, A + \cot A = a\sqrt{b}$ ...(i)

Since, $\text{cosec}\, A - \cot A = \frac{1}{\text{cosec}A + \cot A}$

$= \frac{1}{a\sqrt{b}}$ ...(ii)

By Eqs. (i) and (ii),

$$2\text{cosec}A = a\sqrt{b} + \frac{1}{a\sqrt{b}}$$

$\Rightarrow \quad \frac{1}{\sin A} = \frac{1}{2}\left(a\sqrt{b} + \frac{1}{a\sqrt{b}}\right) = \frac{a^2b + 1}{2a\sqrt{b}}$ ...(iii)

Again Eqs. (i) − (ii),

$$2\cot A = a\sqrt{b} - \frac{1}{a\sqrt{b}} \Rightarrow \frac{2}{\tan A} = \left(\frac{a^2b - 1}{a\sqrt{b}}\right)$$

$\Rightarrow \quad \frac{1}{\tan A} = \left(\frac{a^2b-1}{2\sqrt{b}}\right)$ ...(iv)

Dividing Eqs. (iii) by (iv),

$$\left(\frac{1}{\sin A}\right)\left(\frac{\sin A}{\cos A}\right) = \frac{(a^2b+1)}{2a\sqrt{b}} \times \frac{2a\sqrt{b}}{(a^2b-1)}$$

$\Rightarrow \quad \left(\frac{a^2b+1}{a^2b-1}\right) = \frac{1}{\cos A}$

$\therefore \quad \cos A = \frac{a^2b - 1}{a^2b + 1}$

428. (d) Given, $\sin\theta = \frac{43}{47}$

$\because \cos^2\theta = 1 - \sin^2\theta$

$\Rightarrow \quad \cos^2\theta = 1 - \frac{1849}{2209} = \frac{360}{2209} \Rightarrow \cos\theta = \frac{6\sqrt{10}}{47}$

Now, $$\cot\theta = \frac{\cos\theta}{\sin\theta} = \frac{\frac{6\sqrt{10}}{47}}{\frac{43}{47}} = \frac{6\sqrt{10}}{43}$$

429. (c) Given, $(\cot B - \tan B).\sin B.\cos B$

$$= \left(\frac{\cos B}{\sin B} - \frac{\sin B}{\cos B}\right).\sin B.\cos B$$

$= \cos^2 B - \sin^2 B$

$= \cos^2 B - 1 + \cos^2 B = 2\cos^2 B - 1$

430. (d) Given, $\text{cosec}\,\theta - \cot\theta = \frac{7}{2}$ ...(i)

We know, $\text{cosec}^2\,\theta - \cot^2\theta = 1$

$\Rightarrow \quad (\text{cosec}\,\theta - \cot\theta)(\text{cosec}\,\theta + \cot\theta) = 1$

$\Rightarrow \left(\frac{7}{2}\right)(\text{cosec } \theta + \cot \theta) = 1$

$\Rightarrow (\text{cosec } \theta + \cot \theta) = \frac{2}{7}$ ...(ii)

On adding Eqs. (i) and (ii)

$\Rightarrow 2\text{cosec } \theta = \frac{7}{2} + \frac{2}{7} = \frac{53}{14} \Rightarrow \text{cosec } \theta = \frac{53}{28}$

431. (b) Given, $(4\sin\theta + 5\cos\theta) = 3$

On squaring both sides, we get

$16\sin^2 \theta + 25\cos^2 \theta + 2(4\sin\theta)(5\cos\theta) = 9$

$\Rightarrow 40 \sin\theta \cos\theta = 9 - 16\sin^2 \theta - 25\cos^2 \theta$ ...(i)

Now, $(4\cos\theta - 5\sin\theta)^2$

$= 16\cos^2 \theta + 25\sin^2 \theta - 40\cos\theta \sin\theta$

$= 16\cos^2 \theta + 25\sin^2 \theta - 9 + 16\sin^2 \theta + 25\cos^2 \theta$

$= 41(\sin^2 \theta + \cos^2 \theta) - 9 = 41 - 9 = 32$ [from Eq. (i)]

$\therefore 4\cos\theta - 5\sin\theta = 4\sqrt{2}$

432. (b) Given, $A = 60°, B = 30°$

$\tan(A - B) = \frac{\tan A - \tan B}{1 + \tan A \tan B}$

$\Rightarrow \tan(60° - 30°) = \frac{\tan A - \tan B}{1 + \tan A \tan B}$

$\therefore \frac{\tan A - \tan B}{1 + \tan A \cdot \tan B} = \tan 30° = \frac{1}{\sqrt{3}}$

433. (b) Given,

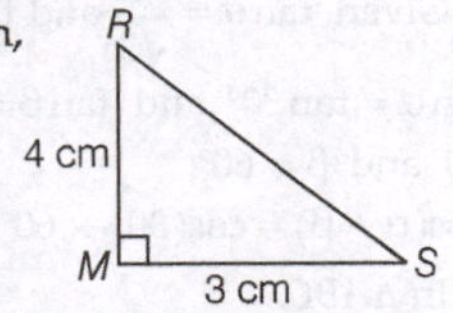

In ΔRMC, $RS = \sqrt{4^2 + 3^2} = \sqrt{25} = 5$ cm

$\therefore \sec R = \frac{RS}{RM} = \frac{5}{4}$

434. (d) Given expression,

$\cos^2 36° + \cos 54° \cdot \sin 36° + \left(\frac{\tan 26°}{\cot 64°}\right)$

$= \cos^2 36° + \cos(90° - 36°) \times \sin 36° + \frac{\tan 26°}{\cot(90° - 26°)}$

$= (\cos^2 36° + \sin^2 36°) + 1 = 1 + 1 = 2$

435. (d) Given, $\tan A = \frac{1}{2}$ and $\tan B = \frac{1}{3}$

$\Rightarrow \tan(A + B) = \frac{\tan A + \tan B}{1 - \tan A \cdot \tan B}$

$= \frac{\frac{1}{2} + \frac{1}{3}}{1 - \frac{1}{2} \times \frac{1}{3}} = \frac{\frac{5}{6}}{\frac{5}{6}} = 1 \Rightarrow \tan(A + B) = \tan 45°$

Hence, $A + B = 45°$

436. (c) Given,

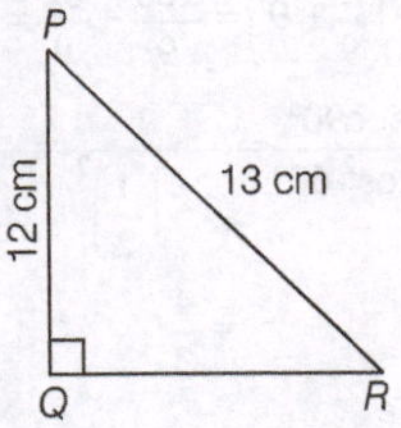

$QR = \sqrt{(13)^2 - (12)^2} = 5$ cm

$\therefore \tan P + \cot R = \frac{5}{12} + \frac{5}{12} = \frac{10}{12}$

437. (c) Given, $\frac{\sin\theta - \cos\theta}{\sin\theta + \cos\theta} = \frac{4}{5}$

$\Rightarrow 5\sin\theta - 5\cos\theta = 4\sin\theta + 4\cos\theta$

$\Rightarrow \sin\theta = 9\cos\theta$

$\Rightarrow \frac{\sin\theta}{\cos\theta} = 9 \Rightarrow \tan\theta = 9$

$\Rightarrow \cot\theta = \frac{1}{9}$ ...(i)

Now, $\frac{\text{cosec}^2 \theta}{2 - \text{cosec}^2 \theta} = \frac{1 + \cot^2 \theta}{2 - 1 - \cot^2 \theta}$

$= \frac{1 + \left(\frac{1}{9}\right)^2}{1 - \left(\frac{1}{9}\right)^2} = \frac{1 + \frac{1}{81}}{1 - \frac{1}{81}} = \frac{82}{80} = \frac{41}{40}$

438. (d) Given, $\tan\theta + \sec\theta = a$ ...(i)

Now $\sec^2 \theta - \tan^2 \theta = 1$

$\Rightarrow (\sec\theta - \tan\theta)(\sec\theta + \tan\theta) = 1$

$\Rightarrow (\sec\theta - \tan\theta) = \frac{1}{\sec\theta + \tan\theta}$

$\Rightarrow \sec\theta - \tan\theta = \frac{1}{a}$ ...(ii)

Adding Eqs. (i) and (ii),

$2\sec\theta = a + \frac{1}{a} \Rightarrow \sec\theta = \frac{a^2 + 1}{2a}$

439. (b) Given, $\frac{\cot^3 A - 1}{\cot A - 1} = ?$

Let $\cot A = a$

Now, $\frac{a^3 - 1}{a - 1} = \frac{(a - 1)(a^2 + 1 + a)}{a - 1}$

$= a^2 + 1 + a = \cot^2 A + 1 + \cot A$

$= \text{cosec}^2 A + \cot A$

440. (a) Trigonometry expression,

$\frac{\sin 58°}{\cos 32°} + \frac{\sin 55° \sec 35°}{\tan 5° \tan 45° \tan 85°}$

$= \frac{\cos(90° - 58°)}{\cos 32°} + \frac{\sin 55°}{\sin(90° - 35°)} \times \frac{1}{\tan 5° \cdot 1 \cdot \cot(90° - 85°)}$

$= \frac{\cos 32°}{\cos 32°} + \frac{\sin 55°}{\sin 55°} \times \frac{1}{\tan 5° \cdot 1 \cdot \cot 5°}$

$= 1 + 1 = 2$

441. (b) Trigonometry expression,

$\frac{1}{\sin\theta} - \frac{\cot^2 \theta}{1 + \text{cosec } \theta} = \frac{1}{\sin\theta} - \frac{(\text{cosec}^2 \theta - 1)}{(\text{cosec } \theta + 1)}$

$= \left(\frac{1}{\sin\theta}\right) - (\text{cosec } \theta - 1)$

$= \frac{1}{\sin\theta} - \left(\frac{1}{\sin\theta} - 1\right) = 1$

442. (a) Trigonometry expression,

$\frac{\sin^2 32° + \sin^2 58°}{\cos^2 32° + \cos^2 58°} + \sin^2 53° + \cos 53° \cdot \sin 37°$

$= \frac{\cos^2(90 - 32°) + \sin^2 58°}{\sin^2(90 - 32°) + \cos^2 58°} + \sin^2 53° + \cos 53° \cdot \cos(90 - 37°)$

$= \frac{\cos^2 58° + \sin^2 58°}{\sin^2 58° + \cos^2 58°} + \sin^2 53° + \cos^2 53°$ $[\because \sin^2 \theta + \cos^2 \theta = 1]$

$= \frac{1}{1} + 1 = 1 + 1 = 2$

443. (b) Given, $A = 30°$

$\therefore \frac{2\tan A}{1 - \tan^2 A} = \frac{2\tan 30°}{1 - \tan^2 30°}$

$= \frac{2 \times \frac{1}{\sqrt{3}}}{1 - \left(\frac{1}{\sqrt{3}}\right)^2} = \frac{\frac{2}{\sqrt{3}}}{\frac{3 - 1}{3}} = \frac{2}{\sqrt{3}} \times \frac{3}{2} = \frac{3}{\sqrt{3}}$

444. (a) Given, $\tan\theta = \frac{4}{5}$

$\therefore \sec\theta = \sqrt{1 + \tan^2 \theta} = \sqrt{1 + \left(\frac{4}{5}\right)^2} = \sqrt{1 + \frac{16}{25}}$

$= \frac{\sqrt{41}}{5}$

445. (b) $\frac{\cos\theta}{\sec\theta - 1} + \frac{\cos\theta}{\sec\theta + 1}$

$= \frac{\cos\theta[(\sec\theta + 1) + \sec\theta - 1]}{(\sec\theta - 1)(\sec\theta + 1)} = \frac{\cos\theta[2\sec\theta]}{\sec^2 \theta - 1}$

$= \frac{2}{\tan^2 \theta} = 2\cot^2 \theta$

446. (b) Given, $\sin A + \sin^2 A = 1$

$\therefore \sin A = 1 - \sin^2 A \Rightarrow \sin A = \cos^2 A$

$\sin^2 A = \cos^4 A$

$\therefore \cos^2 A + \cos^4 A = \sin A + \sin^2 A = 1$

447. (a)

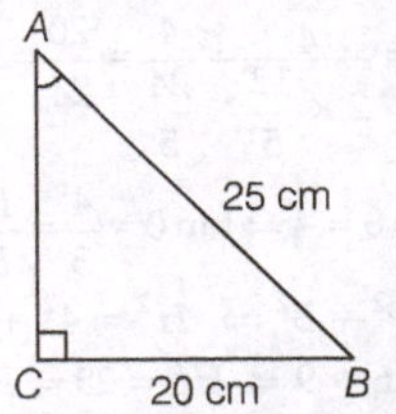

In ΔABC, by applying Pythagoras theorem,

$AB^2 = AC^2 + BC^2$

$\Rightarrow (25)^2 = (AC)^2 + (20)^2$

$\Rightarrow (AC)^2 = (25)^2 - (20)^2$

$\Rightarrow AC = \sqrt{225} \Rightarrow AC = 15$ cm

$\therefore \sec A = \frac{AB}{AC} = \frac{25}{15} = \frac{5}{3}$

448. (c) Given, $A = \tan\theta + \sin\theta$

and $B = \tan\theta - \sin\theta$

$\therefore A^2 - B^2 = (A + B)(A - B)$

$= (\tan\theta + \sin\theta + \tan\theta - \sin\theta)$

$(\tan\theta + \sin\theta - \tan\theta + \sin\theta)$

$= (2\tan\theta)(2\sin\theta) = 4\tan\theta\sin\theta$

449. (b) $A = \cot 30° \tan 60° + \cot 60° \tan 30°$

$\Rightarrow A = \sqrt{3} \times \sqrt{3} + \frac{1}{\sqrt{3}} \times \frac{1}{\sqrt{3}}$

$= 3 + \frac{1}{3} = \frac{10}{3}$

450. (c) $\dfrac{(2\cos^3 A - \cos A)}{(\sin A - 2\sin^3 A)} = 1$

$\Rightarrow \quad \dfrac{\cos A(2\cos^2 A - 1)}{\sin A(1 - 2\sin^2 A)} = 1$

$\Rightarrow \quad \dfrac{\cos A \cdot \cos 2A}{\sin A \cdot \cos 2A} = 1 \Rightarrow \dfrac{\cos A}{\sin A} = 1$

$\Rightarrow \quad \cot A = \cot 45^\circ \Rightarrow A = 45^\circ$

451. (b) Given, $\sin A = \dfrac{6}{7} = \left(\dfrac{P}{H}\right)$

$\because \ H^2 = P^2 + B^2$ [By Pythagoras theorem]

$\Rightarrow 7^2 = 6^2 + B^2 \Rightarrow 49 - 36 = B^2$

$\Rightarrow \quad B^2 = 13 \Rightarrow B = \sqrt{13}$

$\therefore \ \sec A = \dfrac{H}{B} = \dfrac{7}{\sqrt{13}}$

452. (b) $\text{cosec}\, A(1 - \cos A)(\text{cosec}\, A + \cot A)$

$= \dfrac{1}{\sin A}(1 - \cos A)\left(\dfrac{1}{\sin A} + \dfrac{\cos A}{\sin A}\right)$

$= \dfrac{1}{\sin A}(1 - \cos A)\left(\dfrac{1 + \cos A}{\sin A}\right)$

$= \dfrac{1}{\sin A}\dfrac{(1 - \cos^2 A)}{\sin A} = \dfrac{\sin^2 A}{\sin A \sin A} = 1$

453. (c) $6\sec\theta = 10$

$\sec\theta = \dfrac{10}{6} \Rightarrow \sec\theta = \dfrac{5}{3} = \dfrac{H}{B}$

$\therefore \quad P^2 = H^2 - B^2$

$P^2 = 25 - 9 = 16 \Rightarrow P = 4$

$\therefore \ \dfrac{(5\,\text{cosec}\,\theta - 3\cot\theta)}{(4\cos\theta + 3\sin\theta)} = \dfrac{5 \times \frac{5}{4} - 3 \times \frac{3}{4}}{4 \times \frac{3}{5} + 3 \times \frac{4}{5}}$

$= \dfrac{\frac{25}{4} - \frac{9}{4}}{\frac{12}{5} + \frac{12}{5}} = \dfrac{\frac{16}{4}}{2 \times \frac{12}{5}} = \dfrac{4}{\frac{24}{5}} = \dfrac{20}{24} = \dfrac{5}{6}$

454. (c) $3\tan\theta = 4 \Rightarrow \tan\theta = \dfrac{4}{3} = \dfrac{P}{B}$

Now, $H^2 = P^2 + B^2 \Rightarrow H^2 = 4^2 + 3^2$

$H^2 = 16 + 9 \Rightarrow H^2 = 25 \Rightarrow H = 5$

$\therefore 7\sin\theta - 2\cos\theta = 7 \times \dfrac{4}{5} - 2 \times \dfrac{3}{5}$

$= \dfrac{28}{5} - \dfrac{6}{5} = \dfrac{22}{5}$

455. (b) $\sin(\theta + 30^\circ) = \cos 5\theta$

$\Rightarrow \sin(\theta + 30^\circ) = \sin(90^\circ - 5\theta)$

$\Rightarrow \quad \theta + 30^\circ = 90^\circ - 5\theta$

$\Rightarrow \quad 6\theta = 60^\circ \Rightarrow \theta = 10^\circ$

456. (a) $\sec x + \cos x = \dfrac{5}{2}$

$\Rightarrow \quad \dfrac{1}{\cos x} + \cos x = \dfrac{5}{2} \Rightarrow \dfrac{1 + \cos^2 x}{\cos x} = \dfrac{5}{2}$

$\Rightarrow \ 2\cos^2 x - 5\cos x + 2 = 0$

$\Rightarrow \ (2\cos x - 1)(\cos x - 2) = 0$

$\Rightarrow \ \cos x = \dfrac{1}{2}$ and $\cos x = 2$ (impossible)

$\therefore \ \cos x = \dfrac{1}{2} = \cos 60^\circ \Rightarrow x = 60^\circ$

Now, $\sin^2 x = \sin^2 60^\circ = \left(\dfrac{\sqrt{3}}{2}\right)^2 = \dfrac{3}{4}$

457. (b) $\dfrac{1 + \tan A}{\text{cosec A}} + \dfrac{1 + \cot A}{\sec A}$

$= (1 + \tan A)\sin A + \left(1 + \dfrac{1}{\tan A}\right)\cos A$

$= (1 + \tan A)\sin A + \left(\dfrac{1 + \tan A}{\tan A}\right)\cos A$

$= (1 + \tan A)\left(\sin A + \dfrac{\cos A}{\tan A}\right)$

$= (1 + \tan A)\left(\sin A + \dfrac{\cos^2 A}{\sin A}\right)$

$= \left(1 + \dfrac{\sin A}{\cos A}\right)\left(\dfrac{1}{\sin A}\right) = \dfrac{1}{\sin A} + \dfrac{1}{\cos A}$

$= \text{cosec}\, A + \sec A$

458. (a) Given, $\sin C = \dfrac{9}{10}$

$\therefore \ \cos^2 C = 1 - \sin^2 C = 1 - \dfrac{81}{100} = \dfrac{19}{100}$

459. (c) $\cos\theta + \sin\theta = \sqrt{2}$ (Given)

Squaring both sides,

$\cos^2\theta + \sin^2\theta + 2\cos\theta\sin\theta = 2$

$\Rightarrow \ 1 + 2\cos\theta\sin\theta = 2 \Rightarrow 2\cos\theta\sin\theta = 1$

$\Rightarrow \ \cos\theta\sin\theta = \dfrac{1}{2} \Rightarrow \dfrac{1}{\sec\theta} \times \dfrac{1}{\text{cosec}\theta} = \dfrac{1}{2}$

$\Rightarrow \ \sec\theta\, \text{cosec}\,\theta = 2$

460. (c) Given, $A = a\,\text{cosec}\,\theta + b\cot\theta$

and $B = a\cot\theta + b\,\text{cosec}\,\theta$

Then, $A^2 - B^2 = (a\,\text{cosec}\,\theta + b\cot\theta)^2 - (a\cot\theta + b\,\text{cosec}\,\theta)^2$

$= a^2\,\text{cosec}^2\,\theta + b^2\cot^2\theta + 2ab\,\text{cosec}\,\theta\cot\theta - a^2\cot^2\theta - b^2\,\text{cosec}^2\,\theta - 2ab\cot\theta\,\text{cosec}\,\theta$

$= a^2\,\text{cosec}^2\,\theta - b^2\,\text{cosec}^2\,\theta - a^2\cot^2\theta + b^2\cot^2\theta$

$= \text{cosec}^2\,\theta(a^2 - b^2) - \cot^2\theta(a^2 - b^2)$

$= (\text{cosec}^2\,\theta - \cot^2\theta)(a^2 - b^2)$

$= (1)(a^2 - b^2) = (a^2 - b^2)$

461. (d) $\dfrac{3\,\text{cosec}\,42^\circ}{\sec 48^\circ} - \dfrac{5\cos 32^\circ}{\sin 58^\circ}$

$= \dfrac{3\,\text{cosec}\,42^\circ}{\sec(90^\circ - 42^\circ)} - \dfrac{5\cos 32^\circ}{\sin(90^\circ - 32^\circ)}$

$= \dfrac{3\,\text{cosec}\,42^\circ}{\text{cosec}\,42^\circ} - \dfrac{5\cos 32^\circ}{\cos 32^\circ} = 3 - 5 = -2$

462. (c) Given, $\sin\theta = \dfrac{3}{11} = \dfrac{P}{H}$

By using Pythagoras theorem,

$\Rightarrow \quad (B)^2 = (11)^2 - (3)^2 = 112$

$\Rightarrow \quad B = \sqrt{112} = 4\sqrt{7}$

$\therefore \quad \cot\theta = \dfrac{B}{P} = \dfrac{4\sqrt{7}}{3}$

463. (c) Given, $\tan\theta + \cot\theta = 8$

Squaring both sides,

$\tan^2\theta + \cot^2\theta + 2\tan\theta\cot\theta = 64$

$\Rightarrow \ \tan^2\theta + \cot^2\theta + 2 = 64$

$\Rightarrow \ \tan^2\theta + \cot^2\theta = 64 - 2 = 62$

464. (a) Given, in ΔPQR

$\angle Q = 90^\circ$, $PQ = 9$ cm, $QR = 11$ cm

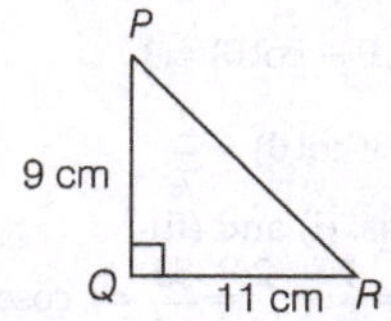

$\cot\theta = \dfrac{\text{Base}}{\text{Perpendicular}} \Rightarrow \cot P = \dfrac{PQ}{QR} = \dfrac{9}{11}$

465. (b) $(\sec A - \tan A + 1)(\sec A - \tan A - 1)$

$= [(\sec A - \tan A) + 1][(\sec A - \tan A) - 1]$

$= (\sec A - \tan A)^2 - (1)^2$

$= \sec^2 A + \tan^2 A - 2 \times \sec A \times \tan A - 1$

$= \sec^2 A + \tan^2 A - 2\sec A\tan A - \sec^2 A + \tan^2 A$

$= 2\tan^2 A - 2\sec A\tan A$

$= 2\tan A(\tan A - \sec A)$

466. (d) Given, $\cos^2\theta - 2 + \cos\theta = 0$

$\Rightarrow \quad \cos^2\theta + \cos\theta - 2 = 0$

$\Rightarrow \ \cos^2\theta + 2\cos\theta - \cos\theta - 2 = 0$

$\Rightarrow \cos\theta(\cos\theta + 2) - 1(\cos\theta + 2) = 0$

$\Rightarrow \ (\cos\theta + 2)(\cos\theta - 1) = 0$

$\Rightarrow \cos\theta = 1, \cos\theta = -2$ (not possible)

$\Rightarrow \ \cos\theta = \cos 0^\circ$

$\therefore \quad \theta = 0^\circ$

467. (c) Given, $\tan\alpha = \dfrac{1}{\sqrt{3}}$ and $\tan\beta = \sqrt{3}$

Then, $\tan\alpha = \tan 30^\circ$ and $\tan\beta = \tan 60^\circ$

$\therefore \ \alpha = 30^\circ$ and $\beta = 60^\circ$

Now, $\cos(\alpha + \beta) = \cos(30^\circ + 60^\circ) = \cos 90^\circ = 0$

468. (a) In ΔABC,

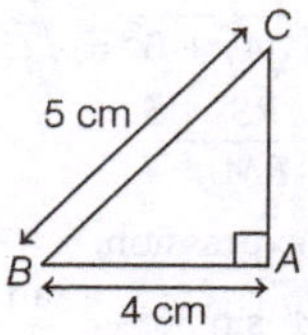

Now, $BC^2 = AB^2 + AC^2 \Rightarrow 5^2 = 4^2 + AC^2$

$\Rightarrow AC^2 = 25 - 16 = 9$

$\therefore \quad AC = 3$ cm

Hence, $\cos B + \cot C = \dfrac{AB}{BC} + \dfrac{AC}{AB} = \dfrac{4}{5} + \dfrac{3}{4} = \dfrac{31}{20}$

469. (a) Given, $\sin x = \dfrac{1}{2}$

$\Rightarrow \quad \sin x = \sin 30^\circ \Rightarrow x = 30^\circ$

So, $(\sec^4 x + \text{cosec}^4 x) - (\tan^4 x + \cot^4 x)$

$= [(\sec 30^\circ)^4 + (\text{cosec}\,30^\circ)^4] - [(\tan 30^\circ)^4 + (\cot 30^\circ)^4]$

$= \left(\left(\dfrac{2}{\sqrt{3}}\right)^4 + (2)^4\right) - \left(\left(\dfrac{1}{\sqrt{3}}\right)^4 + (\sqrt{3})^4\right)$

$= \left(\dfrac{16}{9} + 16\right) - \left(\dfrac{1}{9} + 9\right) = \dfrac{160}{9} - \dfrac{82}{9} = \dfrac{78}{9} = \dfrac{26}{3}$

470. (b) $\dfrac{\text{cosec}\,90^\circ}{1 - \cos^2 60^\circ} = \dfrac{1}{1 - \left(\frac{1}{2}\right)^2} = \dfrac{1}{1 - \frac{1}{4}} = \dfrac{1}{\frac{3}{4}}$

$= \dfrac{4}{3}$

471. (a) $\tan\theta + \cot\theta = 2$

$\Rightarrow \tan\theta + \dfrac{1}{\tan\theta} = 2 \Rightarrow \tan^2\theta - 2\tan\theta + 1 = 0$

$\Rightarrow (\tan\theta - 1)^2 = 0 \Rightarrow \tan\theta - 1 = 0$

$\Rightarrow \tan\theta = 1 = \tan 45^\circ \Rightarrow \theta = 45^\circ$

Now, $\tan\theta - \cot\theta = \tan 45^\circ - \cot 45^\circ = 1 - 1 = 0$

472. (c) Given, $\cot y = \dfrac{12}{5} = \dfrac{B}{P}$

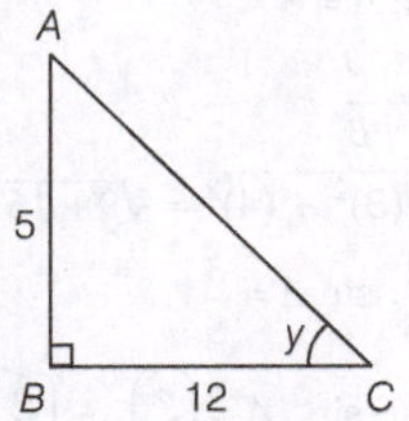

Now, $AC = \sqrt{12^2 + 5^2} = 13$

So, $\cos y = \dfrac{B}{H} = \dfrac{12}{13}$

$\Rightarrow \cos^2 y = \left(\dfrac{12}{13}\right)^2 = \dfrac{144}{169}$

473. (d) Given, $\left(\dfrac{1+\sec^2 A}{1+\cos^2 A}\right)\left(\dfrac{1+\sin^2 A}{1+\operatorname{cosec}^2 A}\right)$

$= \left(\dfrac{1+\dfrac{1}{\cos^2 A}}{1+\cos^2 A}\right)\left(\dfrac{1+\sin^2 A}{1+\dfrac{1}{\sin^2 A}}\right)$

$= \dfrac{\dfrac{1+\cos^2 A}{\cos^2 A}}{1+\cos^2 A} \times \left[\dfrac{1+\sin^2 A}{\dfrac{1+\sin^2 A}{\sin^2 A}}\right]$

$= \dfrac{1}{\cos^2 A} \times \sin^2 A = \tan^2 A$

474. (a) Given, $\sec\theta + \tan\theta = 5$

$\because \quad \sec^2\theta - \tan^2\theta = 1$

$(\sec\theta + \tan\theta)(\sec\theta - \tan\theta) = 1$

$(\sec\theta - \tan\theta)\cdot 5 = 1$

$\therefore \sec\theta - \tan\theta = \dfrac{1}{5}$

475. (d) Given, $\sin 2\theta(\tan\theta + \cot\theta)$

$= 2\sin\theta\cos\theta\left(\dfrac{\sin\theta}{\cos\theta} + \dfrac{\cos\theta}{\sin\theta}\right)$

$= 2\sin\theta\cdot\cos\theta\left(\dfrac{\sin^2\theta + \cos^2\theta}{\cos\theta\cdot\sin\theta}\right)$

$= 2\sin\theta\cdot\cos\theta \times \dfrac{1}{\cos\theta\cdot\sin\theta}$

$= 2$

476. (d) Given, $\sin x - 3\cos x = \sqrt{3}\cos x$

$\sin x = 3\cos x + \sqrt{3}\cos x = \cos x(3+\sqrt{3})$

$\Rightarrow \dfrac{\sin x}{\cos x} = 3 + \sqrt{3} \Rightarrow \tan x = 3 + \sqrt{3}$

$\Rightarrow \cot x = \dfrac{1}{3+\sqrt{3}} = \dfrac{3-\sqrt{3}}{(3+\sqrt{3})(3-\sqrt{3})}$

$= \dfrac{3-\sqrt{3}}{9-3} = \dfrac{3-\sqrt{3}}{6}$

477. (d) Given, $\tan\theta + \cot\theta = 4$

Squaring both side, we get

$\tan^2\theta + \cot^2\theta + 2\tan\theta\cdot\cot\theta = 16$

$\Rightarrow \tan^2\theta + \cot^2\theta + 2 = 16$

$\Rightarrow \tan^2\theta + \cot^2\theta = 16 - 2 = 14$

478. (a) $\dfrac{\sin 4\theta + \sin 2\theta}{\cos 4\theta + \cos 2\theta}$

$= \dfrac{2\sin\dfrac{(4\theta+2\theta)}{2}\cos\dfrac{(4\theta-2\theta)}{2}}{2\cos\dfrac{(4\theta+2\theta)}{2}\cos\dfrac{(4\theta-2\theta)}{2}}$

$\Rightarrow \dfrac{2\sin 3\theta\cos\theta}{2\cos 3\theta\cos\theta} = \dfrac{\sin 3\theta}{\cos 3\theta} = \tan 3\theta$

479. (a) Given, $\sec\theta - \operatorname{cosec}\theta = 0$

$\Rightarrow \sec\theta = \operatorname{cosec}\theta \Rightarrow \dfrac{1}{\cos\theta} = \dfrac{1}{\sin\theta}$

$\Rightarrow \dfrac{\sin\theta}{\cos\theta} = 1 \Rightarrow \tan\theta = 1$

Since, θ is an acute angle,

$\therefore \quad \tan\theta = \tan 45^\circ \Rightarrow \theta = 45^\circ$

Now, value of $\sec^2\theta + \operatorname{cosec}^2\theta$

$= \sec^2 45^\circ + \operatorname{cosec}^2 45^\circ = (\sqrt{2})^2 + (\sqrt{2})^2$

$= 2 + 2 = 4$

480. (a) Given, $\tan\theta = \dfrac{4}{3}$

$\therefore \dfrac{9\sin\theta + 12\cos\theta}{27\cos\theta - 20\sin\theta} = \dfrac{\cos\theta \times \left[\dfrac{9\sin\theta}{\cos\theta} + 12\right]}{\cos\theta \times \left[27 - 20\times\dfrac{\sin\theta}{\cos\theta}\right]}$

$= \dfrac{9\tan\theta + 12}{27 - 20\tan\theta} = \dfrac{9\times\dfrac{4}{3} + 12}{27 - 20\times\dfrac{4}{3}}$

$= \dfrac{24}{\dfrac{1}{3}} = 24 \times 3 = 72$

481. (b) Given, $0^\circ < \theta < 90^\circ$

and $3\sec\theta + 4\cos\theta = 4\sqrt{3}$

$\Rightarrow \quad \dfrac{3}{\cos\theta} + 4\cos\theta = 4\sqrt{3}$

$\Rightarrow \quad 4\cos^2\theta - 4\sqrt{3}\cos\theta + 3 = 0$

$\Rightarrow \quad (2\cos\theta - \sqrt{3})^2 = 0$

$\Rightarrow \quad (2\cos\theta - \sqrt{3}) = 0$

$\Rightarrow \quad \cos\theta = \dfrac{\sqrt{3}}{2} = \cos 30^\circ \quad [\because 0^\circ < \theta < 90^\circ]$

$\therefore (1 - \sin\theta + \cos\theta) = 1 - \sin 30^\circ + \cos 30^\circ$

$= 1 - \dfrac{1}{2} + \dfrac{\sqrt{3}}{2} = \dfrac{1}{2} + \dfrac{\sqrt{3}}{2} = \dfrac{1+\sqrt{3}}{2}$

482. (a) $\dfrac{3(\cot^2 46^\circ - \sec^2 44^\circ)}{2(\sin^2 28^\circ + \sin^2 62^\circ)} + \dfrac{2\cos^2 60^\circ \tan^2 33^\circ \tan^2 57^\circ}{\sec^2(90^\circ - \theta) - \cot^2\theta}$

$= \dfrac{3[\cot^2(90^\circ - 44^\circ) - \sec^2 44^\circ]}{2[\sin^2(90^\circ - 62^\circ) + \sin^2 62^\circ]} + \dfrac{2\cos^2 60^\circ \times \tan^2(90^\circ - 57^\circ) \times \tan^2 57^\circ}{\operatorname{cosec}^2\theta - \cot^2\theta}$

$= \dfrac{3(\tan^2 44^\circ - \sec^2 44^\circ)}{2(\cos^2 62^\circ + \sin^2 62^\circ)} + \dfrac{2\cos^2 60^\circ \times \cot^2 57^\circ \times \tan^2 57^\circ}{1}$

$= \dfrac{3\times(-1)}{2\times 1} + \dfrac{2\cos^2 60^\circ \times 1}{1} = \dfrac{-3}{2} + 2\times\left(\dfrac{1}{2}\right)^2$

$= \dfrac{-3}{2} + \dfrac{1}{2} = \dfrac{-3+1}{2} = \dfrac{-2}{2} = -1$

483. (c) Given,

$\cos\theta = \dfrac{4x}{1+4x^2} = \dfrac{\text{Base}}{\text{Hypotenuse}}$

$\therefore$ Perpendicular

$= \sqrt{(\text{Hypotenuse})^2 - (\text{Base})^2}$

$= \sqrt{(1+4x^2)^2 - (4x)^2}$

$= \sqrt{1 + 16x^4 + 8x^2 - 16x^2}$

$= \sqrt{1 + 16x^4 - 8x^2} = \sqrt{(1-4x^2)^2} = 1 - 4x^2$

$\therefore \sin\theta = \dfrac{\text{Perpendicular}}{\text{Hypotenuse}} = \dfrac{1-4x^2}{1+4x^2}$

484. (c) Given, $\dfrac{\sin\theta + \cos\theta}{\sin\theta - \cos\theta} = 3$

$\Rightarrow \sin\theta + \cos\theta = 3\sin\theta - 3\cos\theta$

$\Rightarrow 3\sin\theta - \sin\theta = \cos\theta + 3\cos\theta$

$\Rightarrow 2\sin\theta = 4\cos\theta \Rightarrow \dfrac{\sin\theta}{\cos\theta} = \dfrac{4}{2} = 2$

$\Rightarrow \tan\theta = 2 = \dfrac{\text{Perpendicular}}{\text{Base}}$

Now, Hypotenuse $= \sqrt{(2)^2 + (1)^2} = \sqrt{5}$

$\therefore \sin\theta = \dfrac{\text{Perpendicular}}{\text{Hypotenuse}} = \dfrac{2}{\sqrt{5}}$

and $\cos\theta = \dfrac{\text{Base}}{\text{Hypotenuse}} = \dfrac{1}{\sqrt{5}}$

Now, $\sin^4\theta - \cos^4\theta = \left(\dfrac{2}{\sqrt{5}}\right)^4 - \left(\dfrac{1}{\sqrt{5}}\right)^4$

$= \dfrac{16}{25} - \dfrac{1}{25} = \dfrac{16-1}{25} = \dfrac{15}{25} = \dfrac{3}{5}$

485. (c) Given, $\sec\left(90^\circ - \dfrac{3\theta}{2}\right) = \sqrt{2}$

$\Rightarrow \operatorname{cosec}\dfrac{3\theta}{2} = \sqrt{2} = \operatorname{cosec} 45^\circ$

$\Rightarrow \quad \dfrac{3\theta}{2} = 45^\circ \Rightarrow \theta = \dfrac{45^\circ}{3} \times 2 = 30^\circ$

$\therefore 2\sin\theta + 4\cos 2\theta = 2\sin 30^\circ + 4\cos(2\times 30^\circ)$

$= 2\sin 30^\circ + 4\cos 60^\circ = 2\times\dfrac{1}{2} + 4\times\dfrac{1}{2} = 1 + 2 = 3$

486. (a) $2\sqrt{3}\sin^2\theta + \cos\theta - \sqrt{3} = 0$

$\Rightarrow 2\sqrt{3}(1 - \cos^2\theta) + \cos\theta - \sqrt{3} = 0$

$\Rightarrow 2\sqrt{3} - 2\sqrt{3}\cos^2\theta + \cos\theta - \sqrt{3} = 0$

$\Rightarrow 2\sqrt{3}\cos^2\theta - \cos\theta - \sqrt{3} = 0$

Let $\cos\theta = x$,

Now, $\quad 2\sqrt{3}x^2 - x - \sqrt{3} = 0$

$\Rightarrow \quad 2\sqrt{3}x^2 - 3x + 2x - \sqrt{3} = 0$

$\Rightarrow \sqrt{3}x(2x - \sqrt{3}) + 1(2x - \sqrt{3}) = 0$

$\Rightarrow \quad (2x - \sqrt{3})(\sqrt{3}x + 1) = 0$

$\therefore \quad x = \dfrac{\sqrt{3}}{2}$ and $\dfrac{-1}{\sqrt{3}}$

So, $\cos\theta = \dfrac{\sqrt{3}}{2} = \cos 30^\circ$

$\therefore \quad \theta = 30^\circ$

487. (d) Given, $2\tan x + 3\cot x = 5$

On squaring both sides,

$$(2\tan x + 3\cot x)^2 = (5)^2$$

$$\Rightarrow 4\tan^2 x + 9\cot^2 x + 2 \times 2\tan x \times 3\cot x = 25$$

$$\Rightarrow 4\tan^2 x + 9\cot^2 x + 12 = 25$$

$$\therefore 4\tan^2 x + 9\cot^2 x = 25 - 12 = 13$$

488. (c) Given, $3\cot^2 x - 7\operatorname{cosec}^2 x + 7 = 0$

$$\Rightarrow 3(\operatorname{cosec}^2 x - 1) - 7\operatorname{cosec}^2 x + 7 = 0$$

$$\Rightarrow 3\operatorname{cosec}^2 x - 3 - 7\operatorname{cosec}^2 x + 7 = 0 \quad [\because \operatorname{cosec}^2\theta - \cot^2\theta = 1]$$

$$\Rightarrow -4\operatorname{cosec}^2 x = -4 \Rightarrow \operatorname{cosec}^2 x = 1$$

$$\Rightarrow \operatorname{cosec} x = \pm 1$$

Since, $0 \le x \le 90°$

$$\therefore \operatorname{cosec} x = 1$$

$$\Rightarrow \operatorname{cosec} x = \operatorname{cosec} 90°$$

$$\therefore x = 90°$$

489. (c) $\sin A + \cos A = \frac{4}{3}$

Squaring both sides, we get

$$\sin^2 A + \cos^2 A + 2\sin A\cos A = \frac{16}{9}$$

$$\Rightarrow 1 + \sin 2A = \frac{16}{9} \Rightarrow \sin 2A = \frac{16}{9} - 1$$

$$\Rightarrow \sin 2A = \frac{7}{9} \quad \text{....(i)}$$

Now, $\tan A + \cot A = \frac{\sin A}{\cos A} + \frac{\cos A}{\sin A}$

$$= \frac{\sin^2 A + \cos^2 A}{\sin A\cos A} = \frac{1}{\sin A\cos A}$$

$$= \frac{2}{2\sin A\cos A} = \frac{2}{\sin 2A}$$

$$= \frac{2 \times 9}{7} = \frac{18}{7} \quad \text{[from Eq. (i)]}$$

490. (c) $\tan\theta + \cot\theta = 2$

$$\Rightarrow (\sqrt{\tan\theta})^2 + (\sqrt{\cot\theta})^2 - 2\sqrt{\tan\theta}\sqrt{\cot\theta} = 0$$

$$\Rightarrow (\sqrt{\tan\theta} - \sqrt{\cot\theta})^2 = 0$$

$$\Rightarrow \sqrt{\tan\theta} - \sqrt{\cot\theta} = 0$$

$$\Rightarrow \tan\theta = \cot\theta \Rightarrow \tan^2\theta = 1$$

$$\Rightarrow \tan\theta = 1$$

$$\therefore \theta = 45° \text{ or } \frac{\pi}{4}$$

Now, $\tan^{53}\theta + \cot^{38}\theta$

$$= (\tan 45°)^{53} + (\cot 45°)^{38}$$

$$= (1)^{53} + (1)^{38} = 1 + 1 = 2$$

491. (a) $7\left(\frac{\operatorname{cosec} 24°}{\sec 66°}\right)^3 + 8\left(\frac{\cot 37°}{\tan 53°}\right)^4 - \left(\frac{2\sec 14°}{\operatorname{cosec} 76°}\right)^2 + \left(\frac{-3\tan 82°}{\cot 8°}\right)^3$

$$= 7\left(\frac{\operatorname{cosec}(90° - 66°)}{\sec 66°}\right)^3 + 8\left(\frac{\cot(90° - 53°)}{\tan 53°}\right)^4 - \left(\frac{2\sec(90° - 76°)}{\operatorname{cosec} 76°}\right)^2 + \left(\frac{-3\tan(90° - 8°)}{\cot 8°}\right)^3$$

$$= 7\left(\frac{\sec 66°}{\sec 66°}\right)^3 + 8\left(\frac{\tan 53°}{\tan 53°}\right)^4 - \left(\frac{2\operatorname{cosec} 76°}{\operatorname{cosec} 76°}\right)^2 + \left(\frac{-3\cot 8°}{\cot 8°}\right)^3$$

$$= 7 \times (1)^3 + 8(1)^4 - (2)^2 + (-3)^3$$

$$= 7 + 8 - 4 - 27 = 15 - 31 = -16$$

492. (d) $\frac{32}{\sec^2\theta} - \frac{20}{1 + \tan^2\theta} + 12\sin^2\theta$

$$= \frac{32}{\sec^2\theta} - \frac{20}{\sec^2\theta} + 12\sin^2\theta \quad [\because \sec^2\theta = 1 + \tan^2\theta]$$

$$= 32\cos^2\theta - 20\cos^2\theta + 12\sin^2\theta$$

$$= 12\cos^2\theta + 12\sin^2\theta = 12(\sin^2\theta + \cos^2\theta)$$

$$= 12 \quad (\because \sin^2\theta + \cos^2\theta = 1)$$

493. (b) $\sin\theta + \cos\theta = \frac{\sqrt{11}}{3}$

Squaring on both sides,

$$(\sin\theta + \cos\theta)^2 = \left(\frac{\sqrt{11}}{3}\right)^2$$

$$\Rightarrow \sin^2\theta + \cos^2\theta + 2\sin\theta \cdot \cos\theta = \frac{11}{9}$$

$$\Rightarrow 2\sin\theta \cdot \cos\theta = \frac{11}{9} - 1 \quad (\because \sin^2\theta + \cos^2\theta = 1)$$

$$\Rightarrow 2\sin\theta\cos\theta = \frac{2}{9}$$

$$\therefore \sin\theta \cdot \cos\theta = \frac{1}{9} \quad \text{...(i)}$$

Now, $\tan\theta + \cot\theta = \frac{\sin\theta}{\cos\theta} + \frac{\cos\theta}{\sin\theta}$

$$= \frac{\sin^2\theta + \cos^2\theta}{\sin\theta \cdot \cos\theta} = \frac{1}{\frac{1}{9}} = 9 \quad \text{[Eq. (i)]}$$

494. (b) $4\tan A = 3$

$$\therefore \tan A = \frac{3}{4} = \frac{P}{B}$$

$$\therefore H = \sqrt{(3)^2 + (4)^2} = \sqrt{9 + 16} = \sqrt{25} = 5$$

$$\therefore \cos A = \frac{4}{5}, \sin A = \frac{3}{5}$$

Now, $\cos^2 A - \sin^2 A = \left(\frac{4}{5}\right)^2 - \left(\frac{3}{5}\right)^2$

$$= \frac{16}{25} - \frac{9}{25} = \frac{7}{25}$$

495. (c) $\therefore p = \cos 120° + \sin 120° = -\frac{1}{2} + \frac{\sqrt{3}}{2}$

$$p = \frac{\sqrt{3} - 1}{2}$$

$$\therefore p > 0 \quad [\because \sqrt{3} > 1 \text{ or } \sqrt{3} - 1 > 0]$$

496. (b) $\operatorname{cosec}(A - B) = 2$

$$\Rightarrow \operatorname{cosec}(A - B) = \operatorname{cosec} 30°$$

$$\therefore A - B = 30° \quad \text{... (i)}$$

and $\cot(A + B) = \frac{1}{\sqrt{3}} \Rightarrow \cot(A + B) = \cot 60°$

$$\therefore A + B = 60° \quad \text{... (ii)}$$

Adding Eqs. (i) and (ii),

$$2A = 90°$$

$$\therefore A = 45°$$

497. (d) $\tan 3\theta = \cot(\theta - 22°)$

$$\Rightarrow \cot(90° - 3\theta) = \cot(\theta - 22°)$$

$$\Rightarrow 90° - 3\theta = \theta - 22° \Rightarrow 4\theta = 112°$$

$$\Rightarrow \theta = 28°$$

25

Height and Distance

Angle of Elevation

An angle of elevation is the angle between observer's line of sight and horizontal line, when the object which is being observed is above the horizontal level. This can be a balloon, a top of building, an airplane, etc.

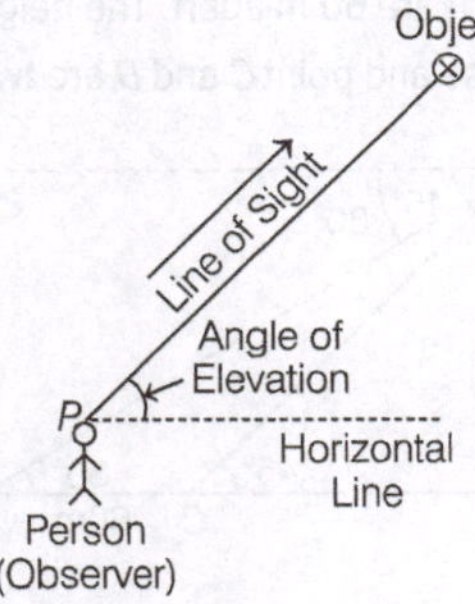

Angle of Depression

An angle of depression is the angle between line of sight and horizontal line, when line of sight is below the horizontal line. This can be a scenario, when a person observing a car on the road, standing on the top of a tower or any other such case.

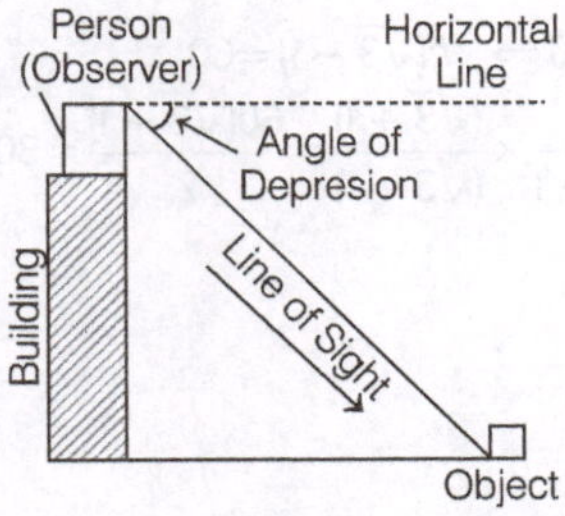

Note Angles of elevation and depression are always equal and acute angles.

Important Relation

(i)

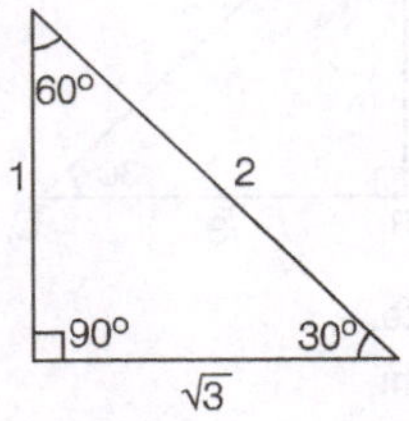

Here, angles are 30°, 60° and 90°.

If ratio of angles are 30° : 60° : 90°, then the ratio of sides are $1 : \sqrt{3} : 2$

(ii)

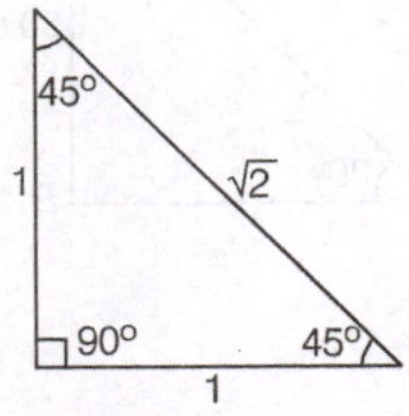

Here, angles are 45°, 45° and 90°.

If ratio of angles are 45° : 45° : 90°, then the ratio of sides are $1 : 1 : \sqrt{2}$.

Based on Angle of Elevation

Ex. 1 A ladder is resting against a wall. The angle between the foot of the ladder and the wall is 45° and the foot of the ladder is 7 m away from the wall. The length of the ladder (in m) is

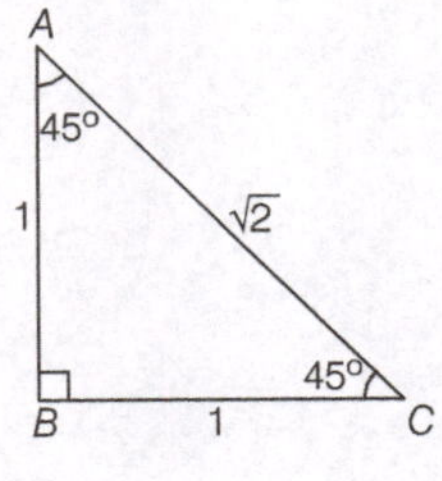

Sol. Let AC be the ladder.

We know that, $\cos\theta = \dfrac{\text{Base}}{\text{Hypotenuse}}$

$$\cos 45° = \frac{7}{AC}$$

$$\Rightarrow \quad \frac{1}{\sqrt{2}} = \frac{7}{AC}$$

$$\therefore \quad AC = 7\sqrt{2} \text{ m}$$

$\therefore$ Length of ladder $= 7 \times \sqrt{2}$ m

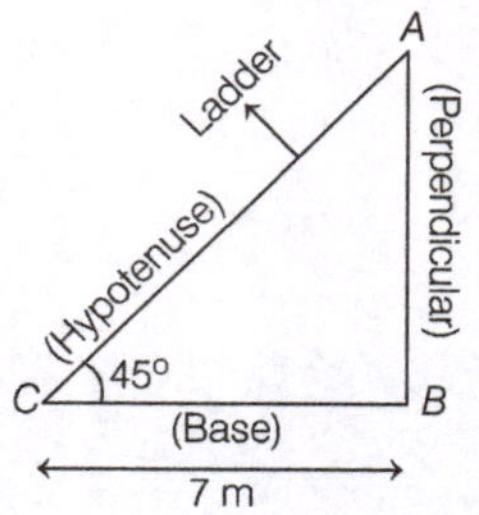

Speedy Method

$\because \quad 1 \rightarrow 7$

$\therefore \quad \sqrt{2} \rightarrow 7\sqrt{2}$

Hence, height of ladder $= 7\sqrt{2}$ m

Ex. 2 A kite is flying at height of 50 m. The thread attached to it assumed to be stretched straight and makes an angle of 30° with the level ground. The length of the string is

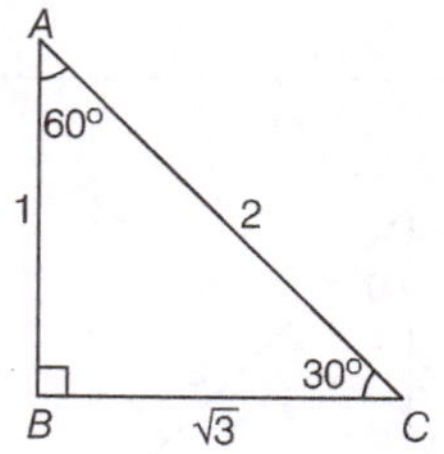

Sol. Let AC be thread of kite.

Then, $AB = 50$ m

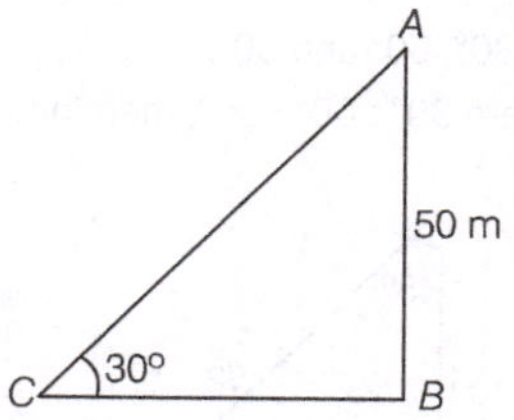

In ΔACB, $\sin 30° = \dfrac{AB}{AC}$

$$\Rightarrow \quad \frac{1}{2} = \frac{50}{AC}$$

$$\Rightarrow \quad AC = 100 \text{ m}$$

Speedy Method

$\because$ 1 → 50 m

$\therefore$ 2 → 100 m

Hence, length of string = 100 m

Based on Angle of Depression

Ex. 3 The horizontal distance between two towers is $40\sqrt{3}$ m. The angle of depression of the top of the first tower when seen from the top of the second tower is 30°. If the height of the second tower is 130 m. Find the height of the first tower.

Sol. Let BE be the first tower and AD be the second tower.

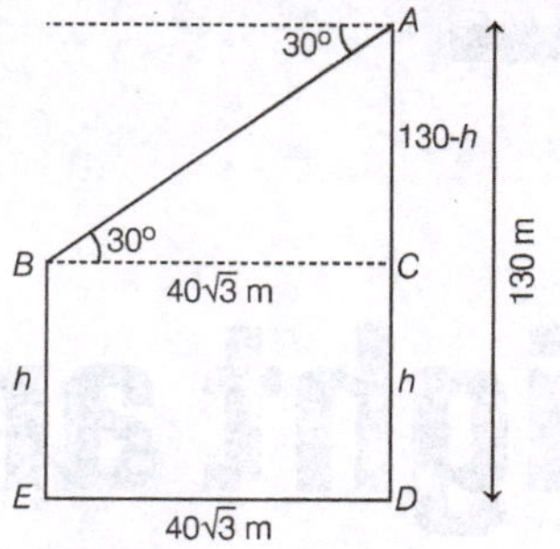

Also, let height of first tower be h.

$$\Rightarrow \quad CD = h \Rightarrow AC = AD - CD = (130 - h) \text{ m}$$

$\therefore$ In ΔABC, $\tan 30° = \dfrac{AC}{BC}$

$$\Rightarrow \quad \frac{1}{\sqrt{3}} = \frac{130 - h}{40\sqrt{3}} \Rightarrow 40 = 130 - h \Rightarrow h = 90 \text{ m}$$

Hence, height of first tower is 90 m.

Ex. 4 Angle of depression from the top of a light house of two boats are 45° and 30° due east which are 60 m apart. The height of the light house is

Sol. Here, AB is light house and point C and D are two boats.

Now, In ΔABC,

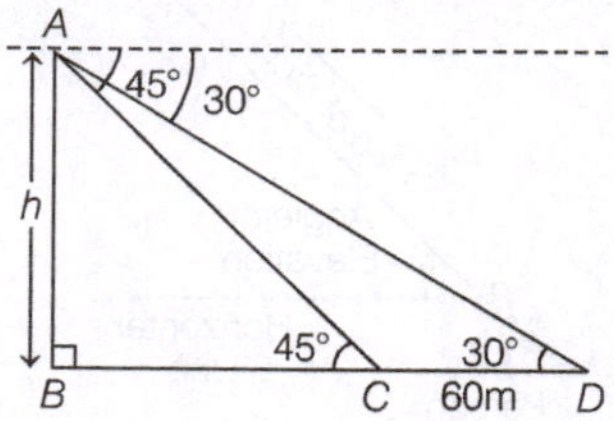

$$\tan 45° = \frac{AB}{BC} \Rightarrow 1 = \frac{AB}{BC}$$

$AB = BC \Rightarrow h = BC$ (given)

Again in ΔABD, $\tan 30° = \dfrac{AB}{BD} \Rightarrow \dfrac{1}{\sqrt{3}} = \dfrac{h}{BC + CD}$

$$\Rightarrow \quad \frac{1}{\sqrt{3}} = \frac{h}{h + 60} \qquad [\because BC = h]$$

$$\Rightarrow \quad \sqrt{3}h = h + 60 \Rightarrow h(\sqrt{3} - 1) = 60$$

$$\Rightarrow \quad h = \frac{60}{\sqrt{3} - 1} \times \frac{(\sqrt{3} + 1)}{(\sqrt{3} + 1)} = \frac{60(\sqrt{3} + 1)}{2} = 30(\sqrt{3} + 1) \text{ m}$$

SSC Exam Scanner

SSC CGL 2024-2023 (Tier I & II)

1. A pole 10 m long rests slantly against a vertical wall *AB* making an angle 30° with the horizontal (ground). Find how far the foot of the pole is from the wall (in metres). **SSC CGL (Tier-I) 10/09/2024 Shift-I**
(a) 15 (b) $\frac{5}{\sqrt{3}}$ (c) 10 (d) $5\sqrt{3}$

2. From the top of a tower, the angle of depression of the top of a 10 m high building is 60°. If the distance between the tower and the building is $50\sqrt{3}$m, find the height of the tower. **SSC CGL (Tier-II) 26/10/2023 Shift-I**
(a) 150 m (b) 100 m
(c) 160 m (d) 140 m

3. The angle of elevation of the top of a tower from the top of a building whose height is 680 m is 45° and the angle of elevation of the top of same tower from the foot of the same building is 60°. What is the height (in m) of the tower? **SSC CGL (Tier-II) 07/03/2023 Shift-I**
(a) $310(3+\sqrt{3})$ (b) $310(3-\sqrt{3})$
(c) $340(3-\sqrt{3})$ (d) $340(3+\sqrt{3})$

4. From the top of an upright pole $24\sqrt{3}$ feet high, the angle of elevation of the top of an upright tower was 60°. If the foot of the pole was 60 feet away from the foot of the tower, what tall (in feet) was the tower? **SSC CGL (Tier-II) 06/03/2023 Shift-I**
(a) $84\sqrt{3}$ (b) $36\sqrt{3}$ (c) $44\sqrt{3}$ (d) $60\sqrt{3}$

5. The angle of elevation of the top of a building at a distance of 70 m from its foot on a horizontal plane is found to be 60°. Find the height of the building. **SSC CGL (Tier-II) 03/03/2023 Shift-I**
(a) $70\sqrt{3}$ m (b) $60\sqrt{3}$ m
(c) $50\sqrt{3}$ m (d) $70\sqrt{2}$ m

6. From the top of an upright pole 17.75 m high, the angle of elevation of the top of an upright tower was 60°. If the tower was 57.75 m tall, how far away (in m) from the foot of the pole was the foot of the tower? **SSC CGL (Tier-II) 03/03/2023 Shift-I**
(a) $40\sqrt{3}$ (b) $\frac{151\sqrt{3}}{6}$
(c) $\frac{77}{4}\sqrt{3}$ (d) $\frac{40\sqrt{3}}{3}$

7. Two ships are on the opposite of a light house such that all three of them are collinear. The angles of depression of the two ships from the top of the light house are 30° and 60°. If the ships are $230\sqrt{3}$ m apart, then find the height of the light house (in m). **SSC CGL (Tier-II) 02/03/2023 Shift-I**
(a) 175.4 (b) 165.2
(c) 172.5 (d) 180.5

8. A person standing at a distance looks at a building having a height of 1000 m. The angle between the top of the building and the ground is 30°. At what approximate distance (in metres) is the person standing away from the building. **SSC CGL (Tier-I) 17/07/2023 Shift-IV**
(a) 1732 (b) 1000
(c) 1542 (d) 936

SSC CPO SI 2020

9. Let *A* and *B* be two towers with the same base. From the mid-point of the line joining their feet, the angles of elevation of the tops of *A* and *B* are 30° and 45°, respectively. The ratio of the heights of *A* and *B* is **SSC CPO SI 25/11/2020 Shift-II**
(a) 1 : 3 (b) $1:\sqrt{3}$
(c) $\sqrt{3}:1$ (d) 3 : 1

10. A ladder is resting against a wall. The angle between the foot of the ladder and the ground is 45° and the foot of the ladder is 6.6 m away from the wall. The length of the ladder (in m) is **SSC CPO 25/11/2020 Shift-II**
(a) $6.6\times\sqrt{2}$ (b) $3.3\times\sqrt{2}$
(c) $2.2\times\sqrt{2}$ (d) $3.6\times\sqrt{2}$

11. A person was standing on a road near a mall. He was 1215 m away from the mall and able to see the top of the mall from the road in such a way that the top of a tree, which is in between him and the mall, was exactly in line of sight with the top of the mall. The tree height is 20 m and it is 60 m away from him. How tall (in m) is the mall? **SSC CPO 25/11/2020 Shift-I**
(a) 300 (b) 375
(c) 405 (d) 250

12. A ladder leaning against a wall makes an angle θ with the horizontal ground such that $\tan\theta = \frac{12}{5}$. If the height of the top of the ladder from the ground is 24 m, then what is the distance (in m) of the foot of the ladder from the wall? **SSC CPO 25/11/2020 Shift-I**
(a) 18 (b) 19.5
(c) 7.5 (d) 10

13. The length of the shadow of a vertical pole on the ground is 36 m. If the angle of elevation of the sun at that time is θ, such that $\sec\theta = \frac{13}{12}$, then what is the height (in cm) of the pole? **SSC CPO 24/11/2020 Shift-I**
(a) 12 (b) 15
(c) 18 (d) 9

14. Asha and Suman's mud forts have heights 9 cm and 16 cm. If the fort tops are at 25 cm apart from each other, then the distance (in cm) between two forts is **SSC CPO 24/11/2020 Shift-I**
(a) 24 (b) 16
(c) 25 (d) 7

15. A ladder leaning against a wall makes an angle θ with the horizontal ground such that, $\cos\theta = \frac{5}{12}$. If the height of the top of the ladder from the ground is 18 m, then what is the distance (in m) of the foot of the ladder from the wall? **SSC CPO 23/11/2020 Shift-I**
(a) 18 (b) 7.5
(c) 13 (d) 19.5

16. A person was standing on a road near a mall. He was 1425 m away from the mall and able to see the top of the mall from the road in such a way that the top of a tree, which is in between him and the mall, was exactly in line of sight with the top of the mall. The tree heights is 10 m and it is 30 m away from him. How tall (in m) is the mall? **SSC CPO 23/11/2020 Shift-I**
(a) 475 (b) 300
(c) 425 (d) 525

SSC CHSL 2024-2021 (Tier I & II)

17. A vertical pole of length 6 m casts a 4 m long shadow on the ground. At the same time, a tower casts a 28 m long shadow. Find the height of the tower. **SSC CHSL (Tier I) 11/07/2024 Shift II**
(a) 42 m (b) 32 m
(c) 36 m (d) 48 m

18. A mirror is placed on the ground facing upwards. A man sees the top of a tower in the mirror, which is at a distance of 105 m from the mirror. The man is 0.5 m away from the mirror and his height is 1.5 m. Find the height of the tower (in metres).
SSC CHSL (Tier I) 10/07/2024 Shift I

(a) 315 (b) 115
(c) 210 (d) 280

19. A man looks at the reflection of the top of the lamp-post on the mirror that is 6.6 m away from the foot of the lamppost. The man's height is 1.25 m and he is standing 2 m away from the mirror. Assuming that the mirror is placed on the ground, facing the sky and the man, and that the mirror and the lamppost are in a same line, find the height of the lamppost (in m).
SSC CHSL (Tier I) 04/07/2024 Shift I

(a) 4.28 (b) 4.45
(c) 3.97 (d) 4.13

20. A man observed the top of an electric pole at angles of elevation of 60° and 30°, respectively, from two different observation points P and Q. If the distance between P and Q is 10 m, find the height of the pole (in m). **SSC CHSL (Tier-II) 10/01/2024 Shift-I**

(a) $5\sqrt{3}$ (b) 5
(c) 15 (d) $15\sqrt{3}$

21. The shadow of a tower standing on level ground is found to be 40 m longer, when the Sun's altitude is 30° than when it was 45°. Find the height (in meters) of the tower.
SSC CHSL (Tier-II) 10/01/2024 Shift-I

(a) $10(\sqrt{3}-1)$ (b) $20(\sqrt{3}-1)$
(c) $20(\sqrt{3}+1)$ (d) $10(\sqrt{3}+1)$

22. A pole stands vertically on the ground with the help of a 12 m steel wire tied to its top and affixed on the ground. If the steel wire makes an angle of 30° with the horizontal ground, then the height of the pole is equal to **SSC CHSL (Tier-II) 02/11/2023 Shift-I**

(a) 6 m (b) $6\sqrt{3}$ m
(c) 8 m (d) $8\sqrt{3}$ m

23. Suhas, a tree, and an 11.25 m tall building are positioned such that their feet on the ground are colinear and the tree is located between Suhas and the building. The tree is located at a distance of 7.5 m from Suhas and at a distance of 45 m from the building. Further, the eyes of Suhas, the top of the tree, and the top of the building fall in one line, and the eyes of Suhas are at a height of 1.8 m from the ground. Find the height (in m) of the tree.
SSC CHSL (Tier-I) 17/08/2023 Shift-I

(a) 3.00 (b) 3.30 (c) 3.15 (d) 3.45

24. A vertical pillar 42 cm long casts a 35 cm long shadow. At the same time, a tower casts a shadow 25 m long. Find the height of the tower.
SSC CHSL (Tier-I) 07/08/2023 Shift-IV

(a) 28 m (b) 35 m
(c) 32 m (d) 30 m

25. Suhas, a 3.15 m tall tree and an 11.25 m tall building are positioned such that their feet on the ground are collinear and the tree is located between suhas and the building. The tree is located at a distance of 45 m from the building. Further, the eyes of suhas, the top of the tree, and the top of the building fall in one line and the eyes of Suhas are at a height of 1.8 m from the ground. At what distance (in m) from Suhas is the tree located?
SSC CHSL (Tier-I) 02/08/2023 Shift-I

(a) 6 (b) 5 (c) 7.5 (d) 9

26. The string of a kite is 158 m long and it makes an angle of 30° with the horizontal. What is the height (in m) of the kite? Assume there is no slack in the string.
SSC CHSL (Tier-I) 04/08/2021 Shift-I

(a) 100 (b) 99
(c) 79 (d) 80

Right Answers

1 (d)	2 (c)	3 (d)	4 (a)	5 (a)	6 (d)	7 (c)	8 (a)	9 (b)	10 (a)
11 (c)	12 (d)	13 (b)	14 (a)	15 (b)	16 (a)	17 (a)	18 (a)	19 (d)	20 (a)
21 (c)	22 (a)	23 (c)	24 (d)	25 (c)	26 (c)				

Solutions

1. (d) Let, $BC = x$

In ΔABC,

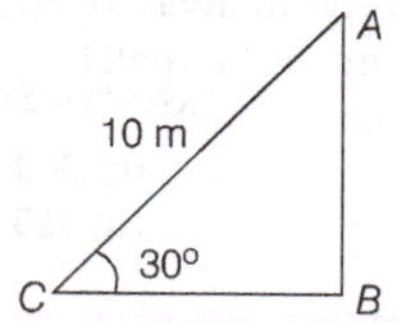

$$\cos C = \frac{BC}{AC}$$

$$\cos 30° = \frac{x}{10}$$

$$\frac{\sqrt{3}}{2} = \frac{x}{10}$$

$$x = 5\sqrt{3}$$

2. (c) Let AB and CD is tower and building respectively.

In $\angle AED$,

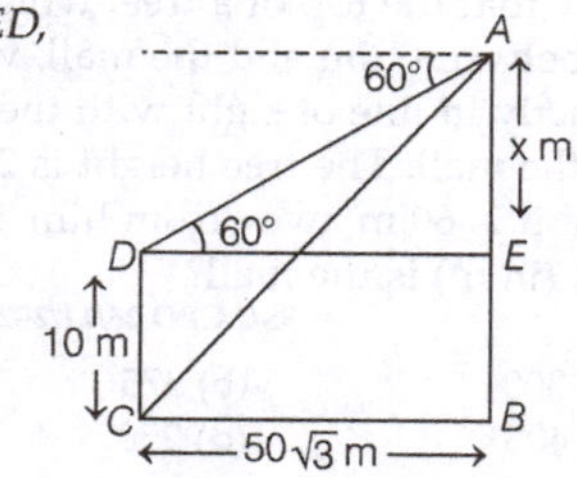

$$\tan 60° = \frac{AE}{DE}$$

$$\sqrt{3} = \frac{x}{50\sqrt{3}}$$

$\therefore$ $x = 150$m

Hence, height of tower = 150 + 10 = 160m

3. (d) Given,

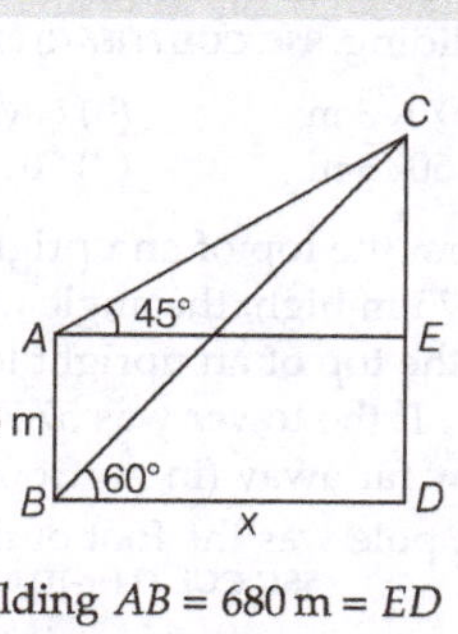

Height of building $AB = 680$ m $= ED$

Let, height of tower $CD = H$ m

$BD = x$ m

$BD = AE = x$ m

$CD = CE + ED$

$H = CE + 680$

$CE = H - 680$

In ΔACE, $\tan 45^\circ = \dfrac{CE}{AE}$

$1 = \dfrac{H-680}{x} \Rightarrow x = H - 680$

In ΔCBD, $\tan 60^\circ = \dfrac{CD}{BD} \Rightarrow \sqrt{3} = \dfrac{H}{x}$

$\Rightarrow \sqrt{3}(H-680) = H$

$\Rightarrow \sqrt{3}H - 680\sqrt{3} = H$

$\Rightarrow \sqrt{3}H - H = 680\sqrt{3}$

$\Rightarrow H(\sqrt{3}-1) = 680\sqrt{3}$

$\Rightarrow H = \dfrac{680\sqrt{3}}{(\sqrt{3}-1)} \times \dfrac{\sqrt{3}+1}{\sqrt{3}+1} = \dfrac{680(3+\sqrt{3})}{2}$

$\Rightarrow H = 340(3+\sqrt{3})$ m

4. (a) Let $CE = H$

Given, $AB = DE = 24\sqrt{3}$ ft

$AE = BD = 60$ ft

Find, $CD = H + 24\sqrt{3}$

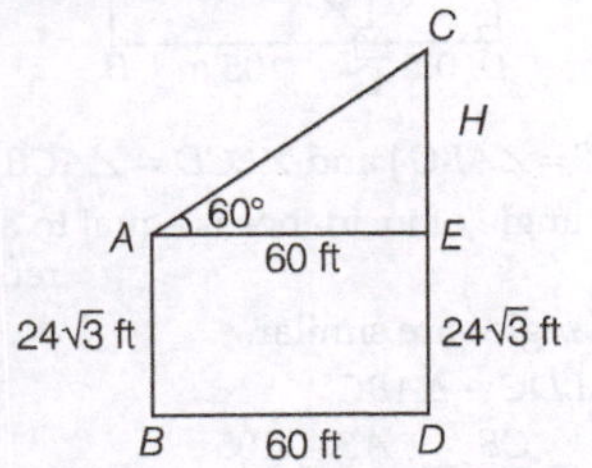

In ΔACE, $\tan 60^\circ = \dfrac{H}{60}$

$\sqrt{3} = \dfrac{H}{60} \Rightarrow H = 60\sqrt{3}$

$CD = CE + ED = 60\sqrt{3} + 24\sqrt{3}$

$CD = 84\sqrt{3}$ ft

5. (a) Let height of a building be H.

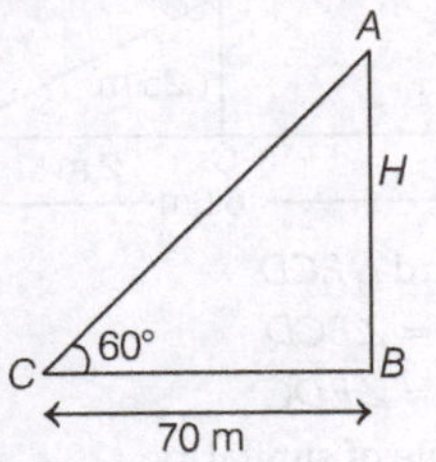

In ΔABC, $\tan 60^\circ = \dfrac{AB}{BC}$

$\Rightarrow \sqrt{3} = \dfrac{H}{70} \Rightarrow H = 70\sqrt{3}$ m

6. (d) Let AB is a pole and CD is a tower.

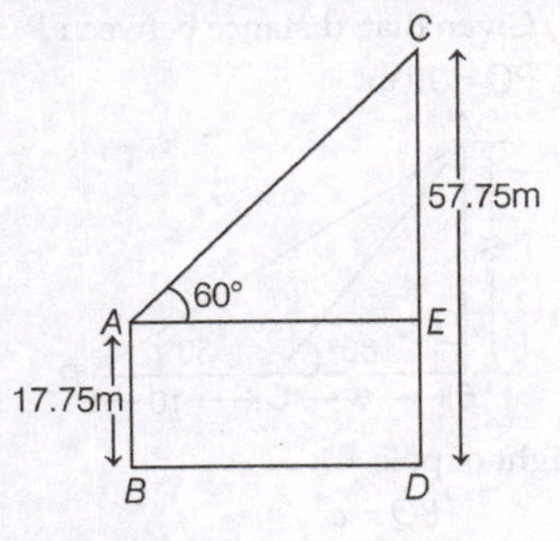

$AB = DE = 17.75$

$CE = CD - ED = 57.75 - 17.75$

$CE = 40$ m

In ΔAEC, $\tan 60^\circ = \dfrac{CE}{AE}$

$\sqrt{3} = \dfrac{40}{AE}$

$\Rightarrow AE = \dfrac{40}{\sqrt{3}} \times \dfrac{\sqrt{3}}{\sqrt{3}}$

$\Rightarrow AE = \dfrac{40\sqrt{3}}{3} = BD$

$\therefore$ Distance between foot of the pole and foot of the tower $= \dfrac{40\sqrt{3}}{3}$ m.

7. (c) Given,

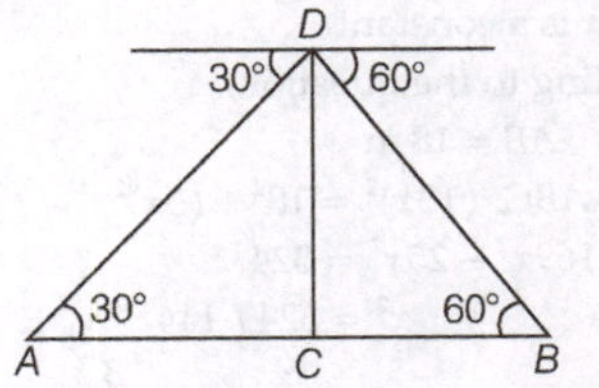

$AB = 230\sqrt{3}$

Let $CD = H$

$BC = x$

and $AC = 230\sqrt{3} - x$

In ΔBCD, $\tan 60^\circ = \dfrac{CD}{BC} = \dfrac{H}{x}$

$\sqrt{3} = \dfrac{H}{x}$

$x = \dfrac{H}{\sqrt{3}}$ ...(i)

In ΔACD, $\tan 30^\circ = \dfrac{CD}{AC}$

$\Rightarrow \dfrac{1}{\sqrt{3}} = \dfrac{H}{230\sqrt{3} - x}$

$\Rightarrow 230\sqrt{3} - x = \sqrt{3}H$

$\Rightarrow 230\sqrt{3} - \dfrac{H}{\sqrt{3}} = \sqrt{3}H$ [$\because$ from Eq. (i)]

$\Rightarrow 230\sqrt{3} = \sqrt{3}H + \dfrac{H}{\sqrt{3}}$

$\Rightarrow 230\sqrt{3} = \dfrac{3H + H}{\sqrt{3}}$

$\Rightarrow 4H = 230 \times 3 \Rightarrow 4H = 690$

$\therefore H = \dfrac{690}{4} = 172.5$ m

8. (a) Given,

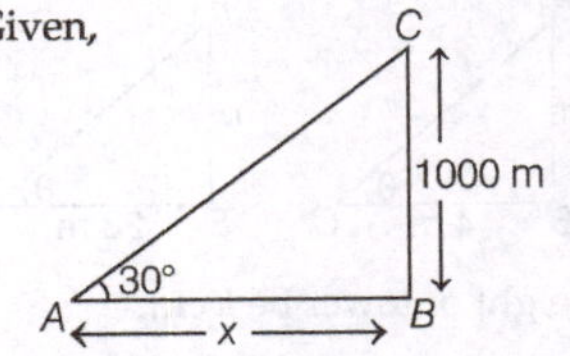

$\therefore \tan 30^\circ = \dfrac{1000}{x}$

$\dfrac{1}{\sqrt{3}} = \dfrac{1000}{x}$

$\Rightarrow x = 1000\sqrt{3} = 1000 \times 1.732 \Rightarrow x = 1732$ m

9. (b) Let the heights of A and B are h_1 and h_2, respectively.

$PM = MR$ .....(i)

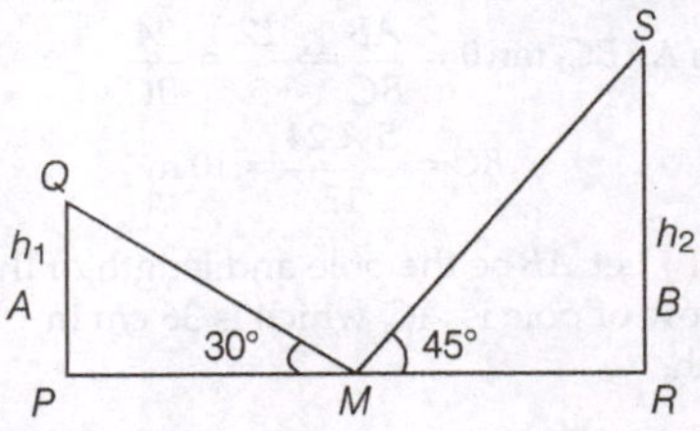

In ΔPQM, $\tan 30^\circ = \dfrac{PQ}{PM}$

$\Rightarrow \dfrac{1}{\sqrt{3}} = \dfrac{h_1}{PM} \Rightarrow PM = \sqrt{3}h_1$

In ΔRSM, $\tan 45^\circ = \dfrac{SR}{MR}$; $1 = \dfrac{h_2}{MR} \Rightarrow MR = h_2$

From Eq. (i), $\sqrt{3}h_1 = h_2$

$\therefore \dfrac{h_1}{h_2} = \dfrac{1}{\sqrt{3}} \Rightarrow h_1 : h_2 = 1 : \sqrt{3}$

10. (a) According to the question,

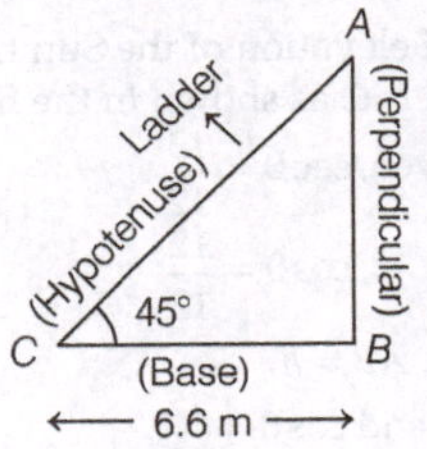

$\cos 45^\circ = \dfrac{6.6}{\text{Length of ladder}}$

$\Rightarrow \dfrac{1}{\sqrt{2}} = \dfrac{6.6}{\text{Length of ladder}}$

Length of ladder $= 6.6\sqrt{2}$

11. (c) According to the question,

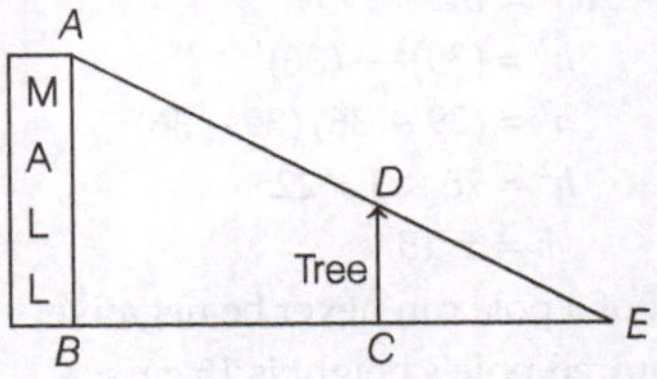

$BE = 1215$ m, $CE = 60$ m, $CD = 20$ m

As, $\Delta ABE \sim \Delta DCE$ [similar triangle]

$\therefore \dfrac{AB}{BE} = \dfrac{CD}{CE} \Rightarrow \dfrac{AB}{1215} = \dfrac{20}{60}$

$\Rightarrow AB = \dfrac{1215 \times 20}{60} = 405$ m

$\therefore$ The mall is 405 m tall.

12. (d) Given,

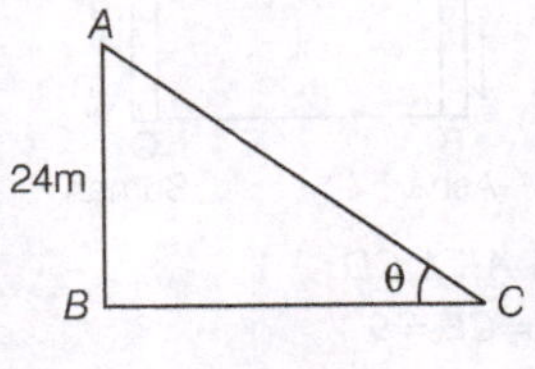

Let AC is a ladder and AB is the height of the wall.

Now, in ΔABC, $\tan\theta = \dfrac{12}{5}$

From ΔABC, $\tan\theta = \dfrac{AB}{BC} \Rightarrow \dfrac{12}{5} = \dfrac{24}{BC}$

$\therefore \quad BC = \dfrac{5 \times 24}{12} = 10$ m

13. (b) Let AB be the pole and length of the shadow of pole is AC, which is 36 cm in length.

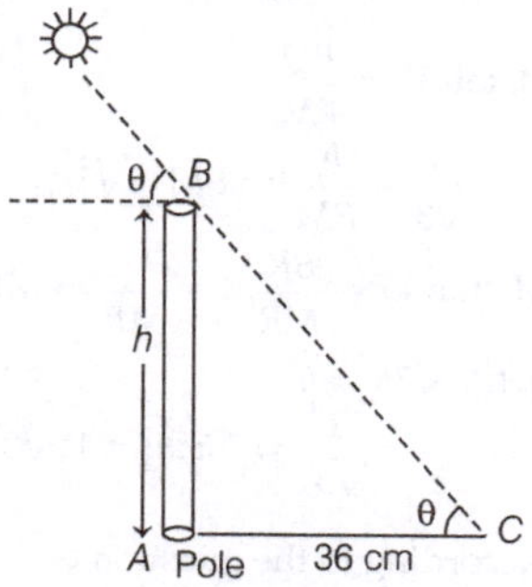

The angle of elevation of the Sun from the shadow end is θ, as shown in the figure.

And also given, $\sec\theta = \dfrac{13}{12}$

$\cos\theta = \dfrac{12}{13}$

From ΔABC, $AB = h$

$AC = 36$ and $\cos\theta = \dfrac{12}{13}$

$\Rightarrow \quad \dfrac{36}{BC} = \dfrac{12}{13}$

$\Rightarrow \quad BC = \dfrac{36 \times 13}{12} = 3 \times 13 = 39$

As $\angle BAC = 90°$,

According to the Pythagoras theorem,

$AB^2 + AC^2 = BC^2$

$\Rightarrow \quad h^2 = (39)^2 - (36)^2$

$\Rightarrow \quad h^2 = (39 + 36)(39 - 36)$

$\Rightarrow \quad h^2 = 75 \times 3 = 225$

$\Rightarrow \quad h = \pm 15$

Height of a pole can never be negative.

So, required pole's height is 15 cm.

14. (a) Let AB and CD are the height of Asha and Suman's mud forts.

So, $\quad AB = 9, \quad CD = 16$

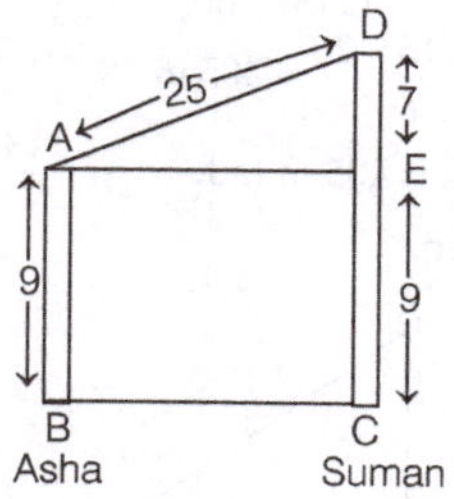

We draw, $AE \perp CD$

So, $\quad AB = CE = 9$

$DE = CD - CE = 16 - 9 = 7$

And, $BC = AE$, $AD = 25$ (distance between the two forts top)

Consider ΔAED, $\angle AED = 90°$

So, according to the Pythagorean,

$AE^2 + DE^2 = AD^2$

$\Rightarrow AE^2 = AD^2 - DE^2 = 25^2 - 7^2$

$\Rightarrow \quad AE = \sqrt{625 - 49} = \sqrt{576} = 24$

$\therefore$ Required distance $= BC = AE = 24$ cm

15. (b)

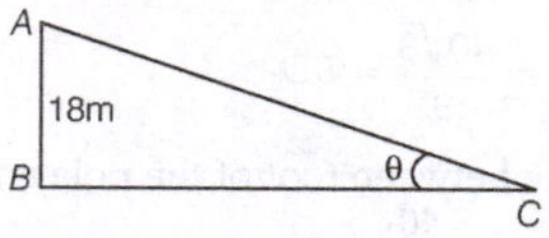

Let, Base $(BC) = 5x$ and

Hypotenuse $(AC) = 13x$,

where x is a constant.

According to the question,

$AB = 18$ m

From ΔABC, $(13x)^2 = 18^2 + (5x)^2$

$169x^2 - 25x^2 = 324$

$\Rightarrow \quad x^2 = 324 / 144$

$\Rightarrow \quad x = \sqrt{\dfrac{9}{4}} \Rightarrow x = \dfrac{3}{2}$

Base $(BC) = 5 \times \dfrac{3}{2} = \dfrac{15}{2} = 7.5$

The distance of the foot of the ladder from the wall is 7.5 m.

16. (a) Given,

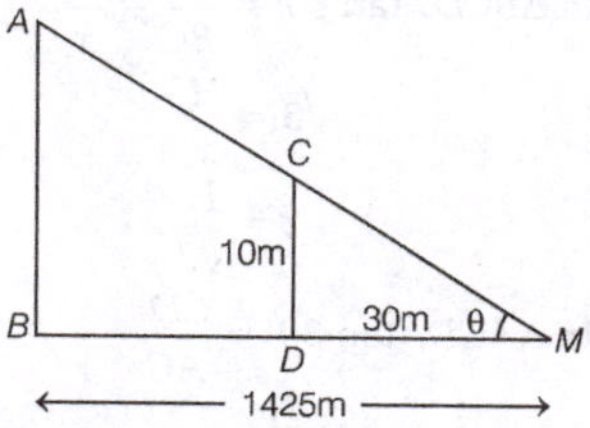

Let the height of the mall $AB = x$ m

From the figure,

$CD = 10$ m, $DM = 30$ m

$BM = 1425$ m

From ΔAMB and ΔCMD we get, [similar]

$\dfrac{AB}{1425} = \dfrac{CD}{DM} \Rightarrow \dfrac{AB}{1425} = \dfrac{10}{30}$

$\therefore \quad AB = \dfrac{1}{3} \times 1425 = 475$ m

The mall is 475 m tall.

17. (a) Given,

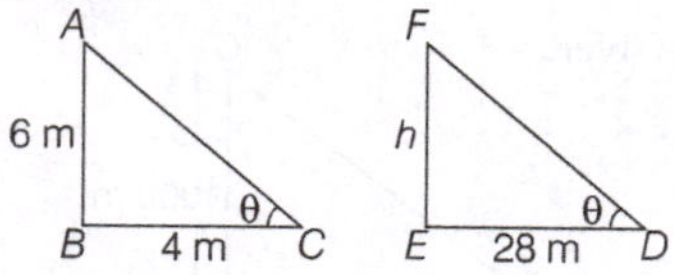

Let the height of tower be h cm.

In ΔABC,

$\tan\theta = \dfrac{\text{Perpendicular}}{\text{Base}}$

$\tan\theta = \dfrac{6}{4} = \dfrac{3}{2}$ ...(i)

In ΔDEF, $\tan\theta = \dfrac{\text{Perpendicular}}{\text{Base}}$

$\Rightarrow \quad \tan\theta = \dfrac{h}{28}$

$\Rightarrow \quad \dfrac{3}{2} = \dfrac{h}{28}$ [$\because$ From Eq. (i)]

$\therefore \quad h = 42$ m

Speedy Method

	Shadow		Actual height
Pole ⇒	4	$\xrightarrow{1.5}$	6
Tower ⇒	28	$\xrightarrow{\times 1.5}$	42

18. (a) Let LD and AB be height of man and tower, respectively and Point C be the mirror and point of incidence of tower in the mirror.

In ΔLDC and ΔABC [$\angle B = \angle D = 90°$

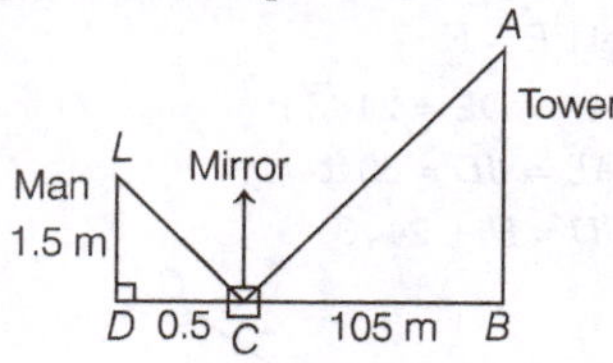

$\therefore \angle LDC = \angle ABC$] and $\angle LCD = \angle ACB$

($\because$ angle of incidence is equal to angle of reflection)

Both triangles are similar.

Then, $\Delta LDC \sim \Delta ABC$

$\dfrac{AB}{LD} = \dfrac{CB}{DC} \Rightarrow \dfrac{AB}{1.5} = \dfrac{105}{0.5}$

$\Rightarrow \quad AB = 315$ m

$\therefore$ Length of tower is 315 m.

19. (d) According to the question,

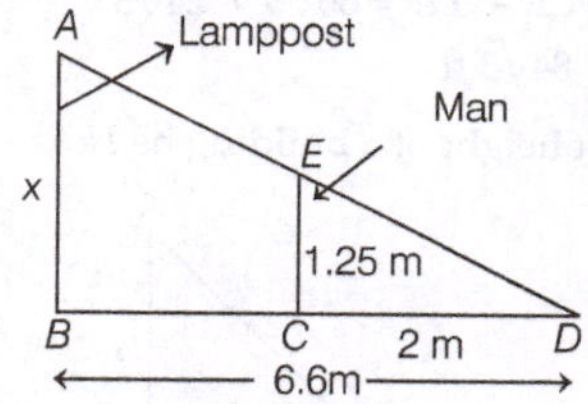

In ΔABD and ΔECD,

$\angle ABD = \angle ECD$

$\angle ADB = \angle EDC$

From the rule of similarity,

$\dfrac{AB}{EC} = \dfrac{BD}{CD} \Rightarrow \dfrac{x}{1.25} = \dfrac{6.6}{2}$

$\Rightarrow \quad x = \dfrac{6.6 \times 1.25}{2} \Rightarrow x = 4.125 \sim 4.13$ m

Hence, the height of lamp-post is 4.13 m.

20. (a) Given that, distance between P and Q, $PQ = 10$ m.

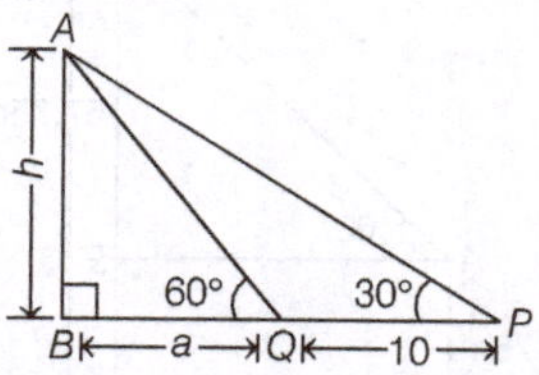

Let height of pole $= h$

Let $\quad BQ = a$

In ΔABQ, $\tan 60° = \frac{P}{B} = \frac{AB}{BQ}$

$\Rightarrow \quad \sqrt{3} = \frac{h}{a} \Rightarrow a = \frac{h}{\sqrt{3}}$

Now, in ΔABP, $\tan 30° = \frac{AB}{BP}$

$\frac{1}{\sqrt{3}} = \frac{h}{a+10} \Rightarrow \frac{1}{\sqrt{3}} = \frac{h}{\frac{h}{\sqrt{3}} + 10} \quad \left[\because a = \frac{h}{\sqrt{3}}\right]$

$\Rightarrow \frac{1}{\sqrt{3}} = \frac{h \times \sqrt{3}}{h + 10\sqrt{3}} \Rightarrow h\sqrt{3} \times \sqrt{3} = h + 10\sqrt{3}$

$\Rightarrow \quad 3h - h = 10\sqrt{3} \Rightarrow h = 5\sqrt{3}$

Hence, height of pole $= 5\sqrt{3}$ m

21. (c) According to the question,

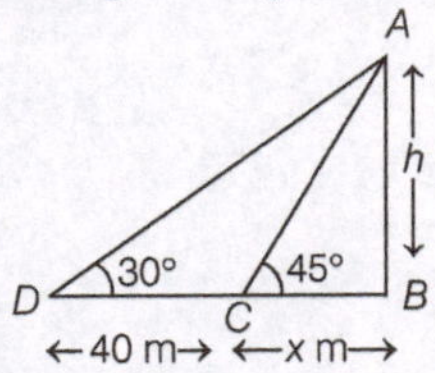

In ΔABC, $\tan 45° = \frac{h}{x}$

$\Rightarrow \quad 1 = \frac{h}{x}$

$\therefore \quad x = h$

Again in ΔABD,

$\tan 30° = \frac{h}{h+40}$

$\Rightarrow \quad \frac{1}{\sqrt{3}} = \frac{h}{h+40}$

$\Rightarrow \quad h = \frac{40}{\sqrt{3}-1} = 20(\sqrt{3}+1)$ m

$\therefore$ Height of tower $= 20(\sqrt{3}+1)$ m

22. (a)

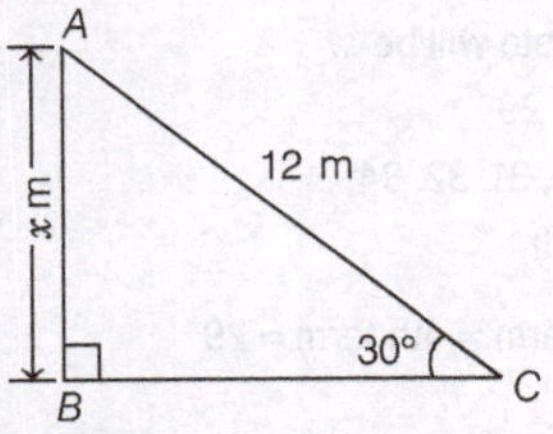

Let height of pole (AB) $= x$ (Perpendicular)

$\therefore \sin 30° = \frac{AB}{AC} \Rightarrow \frac{1}{2} = \frac{x}{12} \Rightarrow x = 6$ m

Hence, the length of pole $x = 6$ m

$\therefore$ Height of pole is 6 m.

23. (c) Let AF, BE and CD be the heights of suhas, tree and the building respectively.

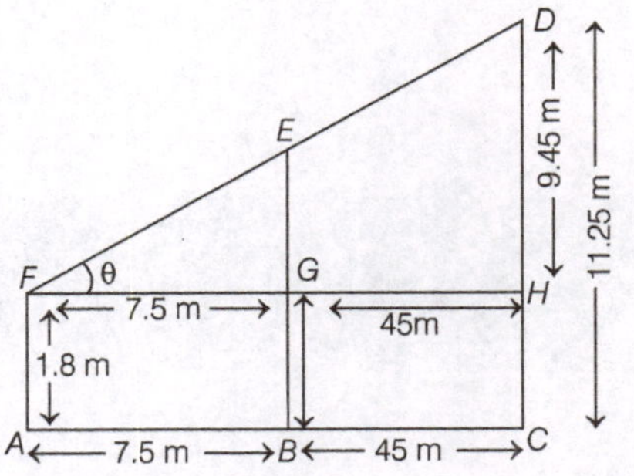

In ΔFGE, $\tan\theta = \frac{GE}{GF}$

$\Rightarrow \quad \tan\theta = \frac{GE}{7.5}$ ...(i)

Now, In ΔDFH $\tan\theta = \frac{DH}{HF}$

$\Rightarrow \quad \tan\theta = \frac{9.45}{52.5}$ ...(ii)

$[\because FH = FG + GH = 7.5 + 45 = 52.5]$

From (i) and (ii),

$\frac{GE}{7.5} = \frac{9.45}{52.5}$

$\Rightarrow \quad GE = \frac{9.45 \times 7.5}{52.5} = 1.35$ m

$\therefore$ Height of tree (BE) $= GE + BG$

$= 1.35 + 1.8 = 3.15$ m

> **Speedy Method**
>
> ΔFEG and ΔFDH are similar
>
> So, $\frac{EG}{9.45} = \frac{7.5}{52.5}$
>
> $\Rightarrow EG = \frac{7.5 \times 9.45}{52.5} \Rightarrow EG = 1.35$ m
>
> $\therefore$ Height of tree $= EG + GB$
>
> $= 1.35 + 1.8 = 3.15$ m

24. (d) According to the given information,

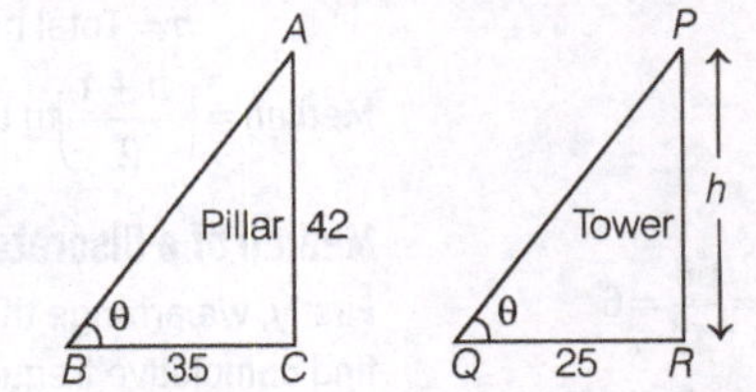

$\because$ Both pillar and tower are on same angle,

Then, $\tan\theta = \frac{AC}{BC} = \frac{PR}{QR}$

$\Rightarrow \frac{42}{35} = \frac{h}{25} \Rightarrow h = \frac{42 \times 25}{35} = \frac{42 \times 5}{7}$

$\therefore \quad h = 30$ m

So, the height of the tower is 30 m.

25. (c) Let FE, GD, AC be the heights of suhas tree and building, respectively. Also, let $FH = x$ m

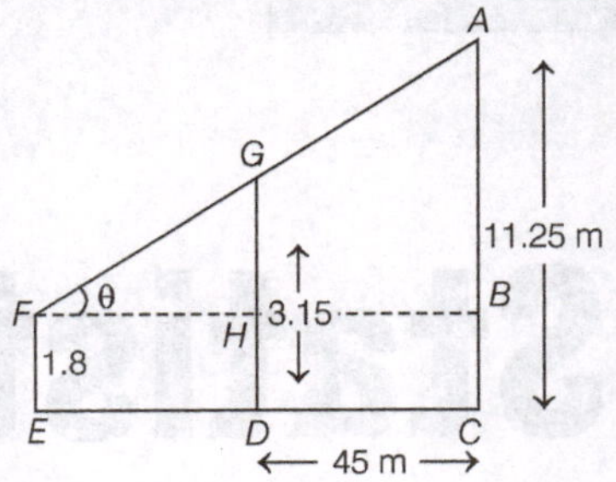

$\therefore FE = 1.8$ m, $GD = 3.15$ m,

$AC = 11.25$ m

Also, $GH = GD - DH = 3.15 - 1.8 = 1.35$ m

$AB = AC - BC = 11.25 - 1.8 = 9.45$ m

$\therefore$ In ΔGFH, $\tan\theta = \frac{GH}{FH}$

$\Rightarrow \quad \tan\theta = \frac{1.35}{x}$ ...(i)

In ΔABF, $\tan\theta = \frac{AB}{BF}$

$\Rightarrow \quad \tan\theta = \frac{9.45}{45+x}$ ...(ii)

From Eqs. (i) and (ii),

$\frac{1.35}{x} = \frac{9.45}{45+x}$

$\Rightarrow \quad 1.35 \times 45 + 1.35x = 9.45x$

$\Rightarrow \quad 60.75 = 8.1x$

$\Rightarrow \quad x = \frac{60.75}{8.1} = 7.5$ m

26. (c) Here, length of string $AB = 158$ m

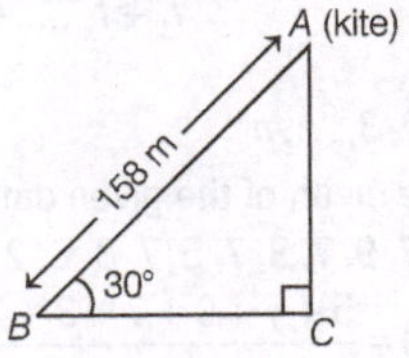

In ΔABC, $\sin 30° = \frac{AC}{AB}$

$\frac{1}{2} = \frac{AC}{158} \quad \left[\because \sin 30° = \frac{1}{2}\right]$

$\Rightarrow \quad AC = 79$

$\therefore$ Height of kite $= 79$ m

26

Statistics

Mean or Arithmetic Mean (AM)

The sum of all observations divided by the number of observations is called mean and it is denoted by $\bar{x}$.

$$\text{Mean}(\bar{x}) = \frac{\text{Sum of all observations}}{\text{Total number of observations}}$$

Mean of Ungrouped Data

If $x_1, x_2, x_3, \ldots, x_n$ are n observations, then mean is given by

$$\text{Mean}, \bar{x} = \frac{x_1 + x_2 + x_3 + \ldots + x_n}{n} = \frac{\sum_{i=1}^{n} x_i}{n} = \frac{\Sigma x_i}{n}$$

where, the Greek letter 'Σ' (sigma) means 'summation'.

Mean of Grouped Data

If $x_1, x_2, x_3, \ldots x_n$ are n observations with respective frequencies $f_1, f_2, f_3, \ldots, f_n$, then mean is given by

$$\text{Mean}, \bar{x} = \frac{f_1x_1 + f_2x_2 + \ldots + f_nx_n}{f_1 + f_2 \ldots\ldots + f_n} = \frac{\sum_{i=1}^{n} f_ix_i}{\sum_{i=1}^{n} f_i}$$

where, $i = 1, 2, 3, \ldots, n$

EX. 1 Find the mean of the given data.

5, 7, 9, 7, 3, 7, 5, 7, 8, 6, 2

Sol. $\text{Mean}(\bar{x}) = \frac{5+7+9+7+3+7+5+7+8+6+2}{11} = \frac{66}{11} = 6$

Ex. 2 If the mean of the following data is 18, then the value of x is

x_i	10	15	20	25
f_i	5	x	7	8

Sol.

x_i	f_i	x_if_i
10	5	50
15	x	$15x$
20	7	140
25	8	200
Total	$20 + x$	$390 + 15x$

$$\text{Mean} = \frac{\Sigma f_ix_i}{\Sigma f_i} = \frac{390 + 15x}{20 + x} = 18$$

$\Rightarrow \quad 18(20 + x) = 390 + 15x$

$\Rightarrow \quad 360 + 18x = 390 + 15x$

$\Rightarrow \quad 3x = 30 \Rightarrow x = 10$

Median

Median is defined as the middle most or the central value of the variable in a set of observations, when the observations are arranged either in ascending or descending order of their magnitudes.

Median of Ungrouped Data

Suppose there are n number of observations. Then, arrange the data in ascending or descending order.

(i) If n is odd, then median = Value of the $\left(\frac{n+1}{2}\right)$th observation

(ii) If n is even, then median

$$= \frac{\text{Value of the}\left[\left(\frac{n}{2}\right)\text{th} + \left(\frac{n}{2}+1\right)\text{th}\right]\text{observation}}{2}$$

Ex. 3 The median of the following data will be ...

31, 24, 32, 26, 34, 28 and 29

Sol. Ascending order 24, 26, 28, 29, 31, 32, 34

n = Total number = 7 (odd)

$$\text{Median} = \left(\frac{n+1}{2}\right)\text{th term} = \left(\frac{8}{2}\right)\text{th term} = \text{4th term} = 29$$

Median of a Discrete Frequency Data

Firstly, we arrange the data in the ascending or descending order, then we find cumulative frequencies of all the classes. Now, find $N/2$ where, $N = \Sigma f_i$. Look for the cumulative frequency just greater than $N/2$. The corresponding value of x is the median.

Cumulative Frequency

If the frequencies of the preceding classes intervals are added to the frequency of the succeeding class interval, then the frequencies so obtained are known as cumulative frequency.

Ex. 4

Average marks of students	Number of students (frequency)	Cumulative frequency
20-40	13	13
40-60	10	23
60-80	8	31
80-100	3	34
Total	34	

Median for Grouped Data

Median is given by the formula Median $= l + \left(\dfrac{\frac{N}{2} - cf}{f}\right) \times h$

where, l = Lower limit of median class

cf = Cumulative frequency of class preceding the median class

f = Frequency of median class and h = Class size.

Mode

Mode is that value of the variable, which occurs most frequently or we can say that the observation which has highest frequency is the mode.

Mode of Ungrouped Data

Mode is that value which is repeated maximum number of times.

Mode of Discrete Series

In this case, mode is the value of the variable corresponding to the maximum frequency.

Mode of Grouped Continuous Data

The mode is given by the formula,

$$\text{Mode} = l + \left(\frac{f_1 - f_0}{2f_1 - f_0 - f_2}\right) \times h$$

where, l = Lower limit of the modal class

h = Size of the class interval

f_0 = Frequency of the class preceding the modal class

f_1 = Frequency of the modal class

f_2 = Frequency of the class succeeding the modal class

Ex. 5 What is the mode of the given data?

6, 8, 9, 8, 3, 8, 5, 8, 8, 6, 8

Sol. 6, 8, 9, 8, 3, 8, 5, 8, 8, 6, 8

Mode = Highest repeated term = 8 (Repeat 6 times)

Range

The range is the difference of two extreme observation of data set.

Range = Highest observation − Lowest observation

Relation between Mean, Median and Mode

For moderately asymmetrical (not symmetrical distribution),

Mode = 3 Median − 2 Mean

For symmetrical distribution,

Mean = Median = Mode

Ex. 6 If the median and the mode of a set of data are 12 and 15 respectively, then find the value of thrice of the mean of the same data set.

Sol. Mode = 3 Median − 2 Mean

$\Rightarrow$ 15 = 3 × 12 − 2 Mean

$\Rightarrow$ 2 Mean = 36 − 15

$\Rightarrow$ Mean $= \dfrac{21}{2}$

$\Rightarrow$ 3 Mean $= 3 \times \dfrac{21}{2} = \dfrac{63}{2}$

SSC Exam Scanner

SSC CGL 2024-2022 (Tier I & II)

1. Find the median of the following data.

Class interval	0-20	20-40	40-60	60-80	80-100
Frequency	9	16	24	15	4

SSC CGL (Tier-II) 20/01/2025 Shift-I

(a) 55 (b) 58
(c) 47.5 (d) 50

2. The age of some students is given in years as 12, 13, 16, 18,14, 19, 13, 17, 15 and 11.

The median age (in years) of the students is SSC CGL (Tier-II) 20/01/2025 Shift-I

(a) 13.5 (b) 14
(c) 15 (d) 14.5

3. Using empirical formula, calculate the mode for the following data.

17, 20, 21, 18, 25, 28, 24, 22, 16, 24, 25, 24 SSC CGL (Tier-II) 18/01/2025 Shift-I

(a) 25.8 (b) 32
(c) 25 (d) 30.6

4. Find the median of the following data. (Rounded off to 2 decimal places) SSC CGL (Tier-II) 18/01/2025 Shift-I

Class interval	Frequency
0-5	3
5-10	5
10-15	4
15-20	2
20-25	7
25-30	6
30-35	5

(a) 21.43 (b) 23.40
(c) 20.53 (d) 18.64

5. The marks obtained by 15 students out of a maximum of 25 in a test are given as 13, 11, 16, 15, 18, 12, 13, 14, 10, 22, 15, 21, 20, 17 and 24. Find the product of the modes of this set of data. SSC CGL (Tier-II) 26/10/2023 Shift-I

(a) 192 (b) 210 (c) 182 (d) 195

6. The median of a set of 11 distinct observations is 73.2. If each of the largest five observations of the set is increased by 3, then the median of the new set SSC CGL (Tier-II) 07/03/2023 Shift-I

(a) is 3 times that of the original set
(b) is decreased by 3
(c) is increased by 3
(d) remains the same as that of the original set

7. What is the mode of the given data?
5, 7, 9, 7, 3, 7, 5, 7, 8, 6, 7 SSC CGL (Tier-II) 07/03/2023 Shift-I

(a) 5 (b) 3
(c) 6 (d) 7

8. The mode of the following data is ……… .
13, 15, 31, 12, 27, 13, 27, 30, 27, 28 and 16 SSC CGL (Tier-II) 06/03/2023 Shift-I

(a) 28 (b) 27
(c) 30 (d) 31

9. For a sample data, mean = 60 and median = 48. For this distribution, the mode is SSC CGL (Tier-II) 06/03/2023 Shift-I

(a) 18 (b) 48
(c) 36 (d) 24

10. The median of the following data will be ……… .
32, 25, 33, 27, 35, 29 and 30 SSC CGL (Tier-II) 03/03/2023 Shift-I

(a) 32 (b) 27 (c) 30 (d) 29

11. Find the standard deviation of the following data (rounded off to two decimal places).

5, 3, 4, 7 **SSC CGL (Tier-II) 03/03/2023 Shift-I**

(a) 1.48 (b) 3.21
(c) 4.12 (d) 2.45

12. Find the mode for the given distribution (rounded off to two decimal places).
SSC CGL (Tier-II) 02/03/2023 Shift-I

Class Interval	Frequency
5-10	8
10-15	7
15-20	6
20-25	9
25-30	11
30-35	10

(a) 35.25 (b) 40.25
(c) 30.33 (d) 28.33

13. The arithmetic mean of the following data is

23, 17, 20, 19, 21
SSC CGL (Tier-II) 02/03/2023 Shift-I

(a) 20 (b) 19
(c) 23 (d) 21

14. Study the given table and answer the question that follows.

The daily wages of 50 employees of a company is shown in the table.
SSC CGL (Tier-I) 03/12/2022 Shift-III

Daily wages Interval	Frequency (No. of Employee)
80-90	9
90-100	3
100-110	31
110-120	5
120-130	2

Select the correct statement from the following options.

(a) The average wage of the employees lie between 80-90
(b) The average wage of the employees lie between 110-120
(c) The average wage of the employees lie between 100-110
(d) The average wage of the employees lie between 90-100

15. Find the weighted arithmetic mean of the first n natural numbers, the weights being the corresponding numbers.
SSC CGL (Tier-I) 02/12/2022 Shift-II

(a) $\frac{[n(n+1)(2n+1)]}{6}$ (b) $\frac{\{n(n+1)\}}{2}$

(c) $\frac{(2n+1)}{3}$ (d) n

16. Calculate the mean from the following table.
SSC CGL (Tier-I) 09/12/2022 Shift-I

Scores	Frequencies
0-10	2
10-20	4
20-30	12
30-40	21
40-50	6
50-60	3
60-70	2

(a) 34.2 (b) 33.4
(c) 32.6 (d) 35.8

SSC CPO 2024

17. Find the mean from the following table (rounded off to two decimal places). **SSC CPO 29/06/2024 Shift-III**

Score	Frequencies
15	2
18	3
21	4
22	1
19	5
23	1
24	2

(a) 17.56 (b) 20.82
(c) 18.44 (d) 19.78

SSC CHSL 2024-2021 (Tier I & II)

18. If 88 is replaced by 93 and 41 is replaced by 47 in the following observations, 46, 48, 63, 76, 88, 41, 35, 55, 90, 56, 92, then what would be the difference between the new median and the previous median?
SSC CHSL (Tier-II) 18/11/2024 Shift-I

(a) 2 (b) 0
(c) 1 (d) 3

19. The weights (in kg) of 7 cousins in a family are 54, 62, 65, 70, 60, 59, 55.

Find the median weight.
SSC CHSL (Tier-II) 18/11/2024 Shift-I

(a) 60 kg (b) 61 kg
(c) 61.5 kg (d) 70 kg

20. Read the given information and answer the question that follows.

The following table gives the percentage of marks obtained by seven students in six different subjects in an examination.

The number in the brackets gives the maximum marks in each subject.

Students	Subjects (Max. Marks)					
	Maths	Chemistry	Physics	Geography	History	Computer Science
	(150)	(130)	(120)	(100)	(60)	(40)
Ayush	90	50	90	60	70	80
Aman	100	80	80	40	80	70
Sajal	90	60	70	70	90	70
Rohit	80	65	80	80	60	60
Muskan	80	65	85	95	50	90
Tanvi	70	75	65	85	40	60
Tarun	65	35	50	77	80	80

What is the median raw score of the marks obtained by the seven students in Chemistry?
SSC CHSL (Tier-I) 09/07/2024 Shift-III

(a) 65 (b) 81.25 (c) 84.5 (d) 62.5

21. Given below is the observed data of the ages of various children.
SSC CHSL (Tier-I) 09/07/2024 Shift-III

Ages (in year)	Number of children
6	8
7	3
8	7
9	2
10	20

What is the difference between the mean and mode of the ages?
SSC CHSL (Tier-I) 01/07/2024 Shift-III

(a) 4.425 yr (b) 2.425 yr
(c) 1.425 yr (d) 3.425 yr

22. The distribution of 100 workmen employed in a factory according to their monthly salary, showed an average salary of ₹ 4500 per month. If the median salary is found to be ₹ 4900, find the mode salary.
SSC CHSL (Tier-II) 10/01/2024 Shift-I

(a) ₹ 5600 (b) ₹ 5500
(c) ₹ 5700 (d) ₹ 5800

23. The runs scored by 11 players in the cricket match are as follows.

7, 16, 121, 51, 101, 81, 1, 16, 9, 11, 16.

Calculate the median of the data.
SSC CHSL (Tier-II) 10/01/2024 Shift-I

(a) 51 (b) 11 (c) 22 (d) 16

24. Find the mode of the given data.

21, 15, 16, 48, 6, 15, 44, 16, 6, 5, 15, 16, 21, 6, 15 and 43
SSC CHSL (Tier-II) 02/11/2023 Shift-I

(a) 21 (b) 16 (c) 15 (d) 6

25. Calculate the mode from the following data.
SSC CHSL (Tier-II) 02/11/2023 Shift-I

Days of confinement	6	7	8	9	10
Number of patients	4	6	7	5	3

(a) 8 (b) 7 (c) 5 (d) 6

26. The score in Maths of 50 students of a class is given in the following table. Calculate the mean score.
SSC CHSL (Tier-I) 31/05/2021 Shift-I

Interval	Frequencies
0-10	2
10-20	11
20-30	28
30-40	6
40-50	3

(a) 28.8
(b) 22.2
(c) 24.4
(d) 26.6

SSC MTS 2024-2021

27. Find the arithmetic mean of 5, 15, 25, 26 and 27. **SSC MTS 21/10/2024 Shift-II**
(a) 19.6 (b) 18.6 (c) 20.6 (d) 17.6

28. The mean of 23 observations is 36. If the mean of the first 12 observations is 32 and that of the last 12 observations is 39, then find the 12th observation. **SSC MTS 11/09/2023 Shift-II**
(a) 26 (b) 23 (c) 24 (d) 25

29. What is the range of the distribution of a variable which takes the ten values?
17, 18, 27, 11, 24, 21, 34, 21, 17, 32, ?
SSC MTS 02/11/2021 Shift-III
(a) 23 (b) 17 (c) 21 (d) 15

30. In a week, the prices of a bag of tea were ₹ 350, ₹ 280, ₹ 340, ₹ 270, ₹ 360, ₹ 310 and ₹ 300. The range (in ₹) is
SSC MTS 02/11/2021 Shift-II
(a) 100 (b) 80 (c) 70 (d) 90

SSC Selection Post 2022

31. A class of 68 students made a mean score of 60 marks and another class of 32 students made it exactly 52.5. What is the overall mean score?
Higher Secondary Level 01/08/2022 Shift-II
(a) 53.5 (b) 54.3
(c) 56.2 (d) 57.6

Right Answers

1 (c)	2 (d)	3 (c)	4 (a)	5 (d)	6 (d)	7 (d)	8 (b)	9 (d)	10 (c)
11 (a)	12 (d)	13 (a)	14 (c)	15 (c)	16 (b)	17 (d)	18 (b)	19 (a)	20 (c)
21 (c)	22 (c)	23 (d)	24 (c)	25 (a)	26 (c)	27 (a)	28 (c)	29 (a)	30 (d)
31 (d)									

Solutions

1. (c)

Class interval	Frequency	Cumulative frequency
0 - 20	9	9
20 - 40	16	25 (Cf)
40 - 60	24 (f)	49
60 - 80	15	64
80 - 100	4	68

Here, $\frac{N}{2} = \frac{68}{2} = 34$

$\because$ Median $= l + \left(\frac{\frac{N}{2} - Cf}{f}\right) \times h$

$= 40 + \left[\frac{34 - 25}{24}\right] \times 20 = 40 + \frac{3}{8} \times 20 = 47.5$

2. (d) Age of students (in ascending order)
11, 12, 13, 13, 14, 15, 16, 17, 18, 19
(Here, $n \rightarrow$ even)

$\therefore$ Median $= \frac{\left(\frac{n}{2}\right)^{th} \text{term} + \left(\frac{n}{2}+1\right)^{th} \text{term}}{2}$

$= \frac{14 + 15}{2} = 14.5$

3. (c) Ascending order,
16, 17, 18, 20, 21, 22, 24, 24, 24, 25, 25, 28

Mean ($\bar{x}$)

$= \frac{16 + 17 + 18 + 20 + 21 + 22 + 24 + 24 + 24 + 25 + 25 + 28}{12}$

$= \frac{264}{12} = 22$

Median $= \frac{\left(\frac{n}{2}\right)^{th} \text{term} + \left(\frac{n}{2}+1\right)^{th} \text{term}}{2}$

$= \frac{\left(\frac{12}{2}\right)^{th} \text{term} + \left(\frac{12}{2}+1\right)^{th} \text{term}}{2}$

$= \frac{6^{th} \text{term} + 7^{th} \text{term}}{2} = \frac{22 + 24}{2} = 23$

$\therefore$ Mode = 3 Median − 2 Mean
$= 3 \times 23 - 2 \times 22 = 69 - 44 = 25$

4. (a)

Class Interval	Frequency	Cumulative Frequency
0-5	3	3
5-10	5	8
10-15	4	12
15-20	2	14 ($c.f$)
20-25	7 (f)	21
25-30	6	27
30-35	5	32

$N = 32$

Here, $l = 20$, $c.f = 14$, $f = 7$, $h = 5$

Median $= l + \left(\frac{\frac{N}{2} - C.f}{f}\right) \times h$

$= 20 + \left(\frac{16 - 14}{7}\right) \times 5 = 20 + \frac{10}{7}$

$= 20 + 1.43 = 21.43$

5. (d) We know that, mode is the value that appear most frequently.
$\therefore$ Modes of this set of data = 15 and 13
Hence, required product $= 15 \times 13 = 195$

6. (d) Given, the median of a set of 11 distinct observation is 73.2
Since, median is the middle most term in given data, so if we have total 11 terms then middle most term is 6th term.
$\therefore$ 6th term = 73.2
If each of the largest 5 observation of the set are increased by 3, then 6th term of the data still remains same.
Therefore, median remains same as that of original set.

7. (d) 5, 7, 9, 7, 3, 7, 5, 7, 8, 6, 7
Mode = Highest repeated term = 7 (Repeat 5 times)

8. (b) 13, 15, 31, 12, 27, 13, 27, 30, 27, 28 and 16
Mode = Highest repeated term = 27 (repeat 3 times)

9. (d) Given, mean = 60, median = 48
Mode = 3 Median − 2 Mean $= 3 \times 48 - 2 \times 60$
= 144 − 120
$\Rightarrow$ Mode = 24

10. (c) 32, 25, 33, 27, 35, 29 and 30.
Ascending order, 25, 27, 29, 30, 32, 33, 35
n = total numbers = 7 (odd)

Median $= \left(\frac{n+1}{2}\right)$th term $= \left(\frac{8}{2}\right)$th term
= 4th term = 30

11. (a) Given, $x = 5, 3, 4, 7$ and $n = 4$

Mean $\bar{x} = \frac{\Sigma x}{n} = \frac{5+3+4+7}{4} = \frac{19}{4} = 4.75$

Value of Deviation $(x - \bar{x})$ are 0.25, – 1.75, – 0.75, 2.25

Variance $\sigma^2 = \frac{\Sigma(x_i - \bar{x})^2}{n}$

$$\sigma^2 = \frac{(0.25)^2 + (-1.75)^2 + (-0.75)^2 + (2.25)^2}{4}$$

$$\Rightarrow \sigma^2 = \frac{0.06 + 3.06 + 0.56 + 5.06}{4}$$

$$\Rightarrow \sigma^2 = \frac{8.74}{4} \Rightarrow \sigma^2 = 2.185$$

Taking square root on both sides, $\sigma = \sqrt{2.185} \Rightarrow \sigma = 1.477$

$\therefore \sigma = 1.48$

12. (d) Here, Maximum class frequency = 11

The class corresponding to maximum class frequency is the modal class.

So, Modal class = 25 -30,

Lower limit $(l) = 25$

Modal class size $(h) = 5$

Frequency of class preceding the modal class = $f_0 = 9$

Frequency of the modal class = $f_1 = 11$

Frequency of class succeeding the modal class = $f_2 = 10$

Mode formula is given by, Mode $= l + \left(\frac{f_1 - f_0}{2f_1 - f_0 - f_2}\right) \times h$

$$\text{Mode} = 25 + \left(\frac{11-9}{2(11)-9-10}\right) \times 5 = 25 + \left(\frac{2}{22-9-10}\right) \times 5$$

$$= 25 + \frac{2}{3} \times 5 = 25 + \frac{10}{3} = 28.33$$

13. (a) 23, 17, 20, 19, 21

Arithmetic mean $= \frac{23+17+20+19+21}{5} = \frac{100}{5} = 20$

$\left[\because \text{Mean} = \frac{\text{Total sum}}{\text{Total numbers}}\right]$

14. (c)

Daily wages Interval	Frequency (No. of employee)	Mean wages	Mean wages × Frequency
80-90	9	$\frac{80+90}{2} = 85$	$85 \times 9 = 765$
90-100	3	$\frac{90+100}{2} = 95$	$95 \times 3 = 285$
100-110	31	$\frac{100+110}{2} = 105$	$105 \times 31 = 3255$
110-120	5	$\frac{110+120}{2} = 115$	$115 \times 5 = 575$
120-130	2	$\frac{120+130}{2} = 125$	$125 \times 2 = 250$

Average wages of the employees $= \frac{\text{Sum of (Mean wages} \times \text{Frequency)}}{\text{Total number of employees}}$

$$= \frac{765 + 285 + 3255 + 575 + 250}{9 + 3 + 31 + 5 + 2}$$

$$= \frac{5130}{50} = 102.6$$

Hence, average of the employees lies between 100 – 110.

15. (c) Natural number are 1,2,3,.......... n

$\therefore$ Weighted mean $= \bar{x}_w = \sum_{i=1}^{n} \frac{w_i \cdot x_i}{w_i}$

$$= \frac{1 \times 1 + 2 \times 2 + 3 \times 3 + \ldots\ldots n \times n}{1 + 2 + 3 + \ldots n}$$

$$= \frac{1^2 + 2^2 + 3^2 + \ldots\ldots n^2}{1 + 2 + 3 + \ldots n} = \frac{\frac{1}{6}n(n+1)(2n+1)}{\frac{1}{2}n(n+1)} = \frac{1}{3}(2n+1)$$

$\left[\text{sum of squares of first } n \text{ natural numbers} = \frac{n(n+1)(2n+1)}{6}\right]$

16. (b)

Scores	Freqencies	Mean Score	Mean score × frequency
0-10	2	$\frac{0+10}{2} = 5$	$5 \times 2 = 10$
10-20	4	$\frac{10+20}{2} = 15$	$15 \times 4 = 60$
20-30	12	$\frac{20+30}{2} = 25$	$25 \times 12 = 300$
30-40	21	$\frac{30+40}{2} = 35$	$35 \times 21 = 735$
40-50	6	$\frac{40+50}{2} = 45$	$45 \times 6 = 270$
50-60	3	$\frac{50+60}{2} = 55$	$55 \times 3 = 165$
60-70	2	$\frac{60+70}{2} = 65$	$65 \times 2 = 130$

Now, Mean $= \frac{\text{Sum of all (mean score} \times \text{frequency)}}{\text{Sum of all frequencies}}$

$$= \frac{10 + 60 + 300 + 735 + 270 + 165 + 130}{2 + 4 + 12 + 21 + 6 + 3 + 2} = \frac{1670}{50} = 33.4$$

17. (d) Mean $= \frac{\Sigma n_i f_i}{\Sigma f_i}$ (Where, $f \rightarrow$ frequency $n \rightarrow$ score)

$$= \frac{(15 \times 2) + (18 \times 3) + (21 \times 4) + (22 \times 1) + (19 \times 5) + (23 \times 1) + (24 \times 2)}{2 + 3 + 4 + 1 + 5 + 1 + 2}$$

$$= \frac{356}{18} = 19.78$$

18. (b) Arranging the data in ascending order,

35, 41, 46, 48, 55, 56, 63 ,76, 88, 90, 92

Here, $n = 11$ (odd)

Median $= \frac{(n+1)}{2}$ th term $= \frac{(11+1)}{2}$ th term

= 6th term = 56

After replacement arranging the data in ascending order,

35, 46, 47, 48, 55, 56, 63, 76, 90, 92, 93

New Median $= \frac{(11+1)}{2}$ th term = 6th term = 56

$\therefore$ Required difference = 56 – 56 = 0

19. (a) Arrange the data in ascending order,

54, 55, 59, 60, 62, 65, 70

Here, $n = 7$ (odd)

$\therefore$ Median $= \frac{(n+1)}{2}$ th term $= \frac{(7+1)}{2}$ th item = 4th term = 60

20. (c) According to the question,

Arranging the percentage marks of Chemistry of all the students in ascending order, we get

35, 50, 60, 65, 65, 75, 80

As, Number of observations = 7 (odd)

$\therefore$ Median = $\left(\frac{n+1}{2}\right)$ th term = $\left(\frac{7+1}{2}\right)$ th term

= $\left(\frac{8}{2}\right)$ th term = 4 th term

$\therefore$ Required median = $\frac{65}{100} \times 130 = 84.5$ marks

21. (c) According to the question,

$$\text{Mean} = \frac{6 \times 8 + 7 \times 3 + 8 \times 7 + 9 \times 2 + 10 \times 20}{8 + 3 + 7 + 2 + 20}$$

$$= \frac{48 + 21 + 56 + 18 + 200}{40} = \frac{343}{40} = 8.575$$

Mode = 10

$\therefore$ Required difference = 10 − 8.575 = 1.425 yr

22. (c) We know that, Mode = 3 Median − 2 Mean

Here, Median = ₹ 4900 and Mean = ₹ 4500

$\therefore$ Mode = 3 × 4900 − 2 × 4500 = 14700 − 9000 = 5700

So, Mode salary of workman = ₹ 5700

23. (d) Arranging the runs scored by 11 players in ascending order,

1, 7, 9, 11, 16, 16, 16, 51, 81, 101, 121

$\therefore$ Median of data = Middle number of data

$= \left(\frac{n+1}{2}\right)$th [$\because$ n is odd]

$= \left(\frac{11+1}{2}\right)$ = 6th term = 16

$\therefore$ Median of data = 16

24. (c) Given data, 21, 15, 16, 48, 6, 15, 44, 16, 6, 5, 15, 16, 21, 6, 15, 43

Mode = Number of maximum frequency = 15

Hence, mode = 15

25. (a) Mode of the given data = Maximum frequency number = 8

$\therefore$ 8 days confinement has the maximum frequency 7.

26. (c)

Interval	Frequencies (f_i)	Mid-Point (x_i)	$f_i x_i$
0-10	2	$\frac{0+10}{2} = 5$	10
10-20	11	$\frac{10+20}{2} = 15$	165
20-30	28	$\frac{20+30}{2} = 25$	700
30-40	6	$\frac{30+40}{2} = 35$	210
40-50	3	$\frac{40+50}{2} = 45$	135
Total	50		1220

Here, $\Sigma f_i = 50$ and $\Sigma f_i x_i = 1220$

$\therefore$ Mean $(\bar{x}) = \frac{\Sigma f_i x_i}{\Sigma f_i} = \frac{1220}{50} = 24.4$

27. (a) Arithmetic mean = $\frac{5 + 15 + 25 + 26 + 27}{5} = \frac{98}{5} = 19.6$

28. (c) Given, Mean $(\bar{x}) = 36$

$\therefore$ $x_1 + x_2 + ...x_{23} = 36 \times 23 = 828$

Also, Mean of first 12 observations = 32

$\therefore$ $x_1 + x_2 + ...x_{12} = 32 \times 12 = 384$

$\Rightarrow$ $x_1 + x_2 + ...+ x_{11} = 384 - x_{12}$ ...(i)

Also, $x_{12} + x_{13} + ...+ x_{23} = 39 \times 12 = 468$ ...(ii)

$\therefore$ Total sum = 828

$384 - x_{12} + 468 = 828 \Rightarrow 852 - 828 = x_{12} \Rightarrow x_{12} = 24$

29. (a) Range = Highest observation − Lowest observation

= 34 − 11 = 23

30. (d) According to the question,

Range of the given data = 360 − 270 = ₹ 90

31. (d) Required mean = $\frac{68 \times 60 + 32 \times 52.5}{68 + 32} = \frac{4080 + 1680}{100}$

$= \frac{5760}{100} = 57.6$

27

Probability

Probability is the study of chances of occurrence of events.

Probability of occurrence of an event E

$$P(E)=\frac{\text{Number of favourable outcomes of events }(E)}{\text{Total number of outcomes}}$$

$$P(E)=\frac{n(E)}{n(S)}$$

The probability of an event E, then $0 \le P(E) \le 01$

Terms Related to Probability

- **Event** A probability event can be defined as set of outcomes of an experiment.
- **Elementary Events** The Event which have only one outcome. Sum of all possibilities of all elementary events is 1.
- **Sample Space** The set of all possible outcomes of an experiment is called sample space
- **Sure or Certain Events** The probability of such an event is 1.
- **Impossible Events** The probability of such an event is 0.
- **Complementary Events** Suppose probability of happening of an event is $P(E)$, then $P(\bar{E})$ is called complementary of events i.e.,

$$P(E)+P(\bar{E})=1$$

where, $\bar{E}$ denotes for "Not E".

- **Equally likely Events** Equally likely events means outcome is likely to occur as any other outcome.
- **Simple Events** If an event (E) has only one same point of a sample space, it is called simple event.
- **Compound Events** If an event has more than one sample point it is called compound events.

Mutually Exclusive and Exhaustive Events

- Two events E_1 and E_2 related to an experiment E, having sample space S are known as **mutually exclusiv**e, if the probability of occurrence of both events simultaneously is zero, i.e. $P(E \cap E_2)=0$.
- Two events E_1 and E_2 related to an experiment E, having sample space S are known as **mutually exhaustive**, if the probability of occurrence of event E_1, or E_2 is 1 i.e. $P(E_1 \cup E_2)=1$

Dependent and Independent Events

- **Dependent Events** Two events are called dependent, if the outcomes or occurrence of the first affects the outcomes or occurrence of the second, so that the probability is changed.
- **Independent Events** Two events A and B are called independent, if occurring or non-occurring of A does not affect the occurring or non-occurring of B.

If A and B are independent events, then

$$P(A \text{ and } B)=P(A \cap B)=P(A)\cdot P(B)$$

Rules/Theorems Related to Probability

The various theorems related to probability are discussed below

- **Addition Rule of Probability** When two events A and B are mutually exclusive.

$$P(A \cap B)=0 \text{ and } P(A \cup B)=P(A)+P(B)$$

But when two events A and B are non-mutually exclusive, the probability that A or B will occur, is $P(A \cup B)=P(A)+P(B)-P(A \cap B)$

- **Multiplication Theorem of Probability** When two events A and B are mutually exclusive, the probability that A and B will occur simultaneously is given as $P(A \cap B)=P(A)\cdot P(B/A)$

$$P(A \cap B)=P(A)\cdot P(B) \quad [\because A \text{ and } B \text{ are independent events}]$$

- **Conditional Probability** The conditional probability of an event B in relationship to an event A is the probability that event B occurs given that event A has already been occurred. Read as the probability of happening of an event B given that A has already been happened.

$$P(A/B)=\frac{P(A \cap B)}{P(B)} \text{ and } P(B/A)=\frac{P(A \cap B)}{P(A)}$$

Based on Coin

- When a coin is tossed, then we get two possible outcomes either a head (H) or tail (T).

Total outcomes $=\{H, T\}=2$

- When two coins are tossed the possible outcomes is $2^2=4$

Total outcomes $= HH, HT, TH, TT$

- When three coins are tossed then total outcomes is $2^3=8$ i.e. $\{HHH, HHT, HTH, THH, HTT, TTH, THT, TTT\}$

Ex.1 3 coins are tossed, then find the probability of exactly two heads.

Sol. Sample space of tossing three coins

$= \{HHH, HHT, HTH, THH, HTT, TTH, THT, TTT\}$

Total number of possible outcomes $= 8$

Number of favourable outcomes $= \{HTH, THH, HHT\} = 3$

$\therefore$ Required probability $= \frac{3}{8}$

Based on Cards

A deck of cards containing 52 cards is grouped into four parts and they are spade, club, heart and diamond.

(i) There are 13 cards of each suit, clubs, hearts, diamonds and spades.

(ii) There are 4 aces, 4 jacks, 4 queen and 4 kings

(iii) There are 26 red and 26 black cards.

(iv) There are 12 face cards i.e. king, queen, and jack in each suit.

Ex. 2 What is the probability that a card drawn at random from a pack of 52 cards is either a king or a spade?

Sol. Probability of getting a king, $P(A) = \frac{4}{52}$

Probability of getting a spade, $P(B) = \frac{13}{52}$

Probability of getting a king or spade, $P(A \cap B) = \frac{1}{52}$

$\therefore$ Probability of either a king or a spade,

$$P(A \cup B) = \frac{4}{52} + \frac{13}{52} - \frac{1}{52} = \frac{16}{52} = \frac{4}{13}$$

Based on Dice

- When we roll a dice once, we get 6 possible outcomes i.e., {1, 2, 3, 4, 5 and 6}.
- When two dice are rolled then we get $6^2 = 36$ possible outcomes.

Ex. 3 If two dice are rolled, then find the probability that the sum of outcomes is 12.

Sol. Total number of possible outcomes $= 6 \times 6 = 36$

Favourable outcomes $= (6, 6)$ i.e. 1

$\therefore$ Required probability $= \frac{1}{36}$

Based on Permutation and Combination

- Each of the different possible ways in which number of things can be arranged is called permutation.

  Number of permutation of n distinct object taken 'r' at a time is

$$^nP_r = \frac{n!}{(n-r)!}$$

- Each of the different selections made by taking some or all the number of objects irrespective of their order of arrangements is called combination

  Number of combination of n different things taken 'r' at a time is

$$^nC_r = \frac{n!}{r!(n-r)!}$$

Ex. 4 A bag contains 4 red balls, 6 green balls and 5 blue balls. If three balls are picked at random, what is the probability that two of them are green and one of them is blue?

Sol. Total number of balls in a bag $= 4R + 6G + 5B = 15$ balls

Total number of ways of drawing 3 balls $= {}^{15}C_3$

Probability that two of them are green and one of them is blue

$$= \frac{^6C_2 \times {}^5C_1}{^{15}C_3} = \frac{\frac{6!}{2! \times 4!} \times \frac{5!}{1! \times 4!}}{\frac{15!}{3! \times 12!}} = \frac{15}{91}$$

SSC Exam Scanner

SSC CGL 2024 & 2023 (Tier II)

1. If A and B are two events such that $P(A \cup B) = \frac{3}{4}$, $P(A \cap B) = \frac{1}{4}$ and $P(B) = \frac{1}{2}$, then the events A and B are ...... **SSC CGL (Tier-II) 20/01/2025 Shift-I**

(a) Not Mutually Exclusive
(b) Mutually Exclusive
(c) Independent
(d) Dependent

2. Let A and B be two players who are playing the game to hit the target. The probabilities of hitting the target by A and B is $\frac{2}{3}$ and $\frac{3}{4}$, respectively. What is the probability that exactly one of them hit the target? **SSC CGL (Tier-II) 18/01/2025 Shift-I**

(a) $\frac{7}{12}$ (b) $\frac{1}{4}$
(c) $\frac{1}{12}$ (d) $\frac{5}{12}$

3. If $P(A \cup B) = \frac{5}{9}$, $P(\overline{A} \cup \overline{B}) = \frac{13}{27}$, $P(A) = \frac{11}{18}$, then the odds against the event B are **SSC CGL (Tier-II) 26/10/2023 Shift-I**

(a) $\frac{38}{17}$ (b) $\frac{7}{57}$
(c) $\frac{29}{25}$ (d) $\frac{47}{7}$

4. Three cards are drawn one after another with replacement from a pack of cards. What is the probability of getting first card a jack, second card a black card, and third card an even numbered card? **SSC CGL (Tier-II) 26/10/2023 Shift-I**

(a) $\frac{5}{338}$ (b) $\frac{20}{338}$
(c) $\frac{25}{26}$ (d) $\frac{5}{169}$

5. A person can hit a target 5 times out of 8 shots. If he fires 10 shots, what is the probability that he will hit the target twice? **SSC CGL (Tier-II) 07/03/2023 Shift-I**

(a) $\frac{1165 \times 3^8}{8^{10}}$ (b) $\frac{1175 \times 3^8}{8^{10}}$
(c) $\frac{1125 \times 3^8}{8^{10}}$ (d) $\frac{1135 \times 3^8}{8^{10}}$

6. The probabilities of solving a problem by three students A, B and C are $\frac{3}{7}$, $\frac{5}{9}$ and $\frac{1}{5}$, respectively. The probability that problem will be solved is **SSC CGL (Tier-II) 06/03/2023 Shift-I**

(a) $\frac{155}{315}$ (b) $\frac{64}{315}$ (c) $\frac{251}{315}$ (d) $\frac{32}{315}$

7. A speaks the truth 5 out of 7 times and B speaks truth 8 out of 9 times. What is the probability that they contradict each other in stating the same fact? **SSC CGL (Tier-II) 03/03/2023 Shift-I**

(a) $\frac{1}{7}$ (b) $\frac{1}{9}$ (c) $\frac{1}{4}$ (d) $\frac{1}{3}$

8. A glass jar contains 6 white, 8 black, 4 red and 3 blue marbles. If a single marble is chosen at random from the jar, what is the probability that it is black or blue?

SSC CGL (Tier-II) 02/03/2023 Shift-I

(a) $\frac{8}{21}$ (b) $\frac{11}{21}$ (c) $\frac{5}{21}$ (d) $\frac{1}{7}$

SSC CHSL 2024 & 2023 (Tier II)

9. Sudarshan and Abraham appear for an interview for two vacancies. The probability of Sudarshan's selection is $\frac{1}{3}$ and that of Abraham's selection is $\frac{1}{5}$. Find the probability that none of them be selected.

SSC CHSL (Tier-II) 10/01/2024 Shift-I

(a) $\frac{8}{15}$ (b) $\frac{14}{15}$

(c) $\frac{1}{15}$ (d) $\frac{22}{15}$

10. If A and B are events with $P(A)=\frac{3}{8}$, $P(B)=\frac{1}{2}$ and $P(A\cap B)=\frac{1}{4}$. Find $P(\bar{A}\cap\bar{B})$.

SSC CHSL (Tier-II) 02/11/2023 Shift-I

(a) $\frac{1}{8}$ (b) $\frac{3}{8}$

(c) $\frac{7}{8}$ (d) $\frac{5}{8}$

Right Answers

1 (c)	2 (d)	3 (c)	4 (a)	5 (c)	6 (c)	7 (d)	8 (b)	9 (a)	10 (b)

Solutions

1. (c) $\because P(A\cup B)=P(A)+P(B)-P(A\cap B)$

$\Rightarrow \frac{3}{4}=P(A)+\frac{1}{2}-\frac{1}{4} \Rightarrow P(A)=\frac{2}{4}=\frac{1}{2}$

Now, $P(A\cap B)=P(A)\times P(B)$

$\Rightarrow \frac{1}{4}=\frac{1}{2}\times\frac{1}{2}$

Since, it's satisfy this condition.

Hence, it is independent.

2. (d) Given, probability of hitting the target by $A=\frac{2}{3}$

and probability of hitting the target by $B=\frac{3}{4}$

$\therefore$ The probability that exactly one of them hit the target

$=P_A\cdot\bar{P}_B+P_B\cdot\bar{P}_A=\frac{2}{3}\times\frac{1}{4}+\frac{3}{4}\times\frac{1}{3}$

$=\frac{2}{12}+\frac{3}{12}=\frac{5}{12}$

3. (c) Given, $P(A)=\frac{11}{18}$

$\therefore \quad P(\bar{A})=1-P(A)=1-\frac{11}{18}=\frac{7}{18}$

and $P(\bar{A}\cap\bar{B})=1-P(A\cup B)=1-\frac{5}{9}=\frac{4}{9}$

$\because \quad P(\bar{A}\cup\bar{B})=P(\bar{A})+P(\bar{B})-P(\bar{A}\cap\bar{B})$

$\frac{13}{27}=\frac{7}{18}+P(\bar{B})-\frac{4}{9}$

$P(\bar{B})=\frac{13}{27}-\frac{7}{18}+\frac{4}{9}=\frac{29}{54}$

$\therefore \quad P(B)=1-\frac{29}{54}=\frac{25}{54}$

Odds against the event B

$=\frac{P(\bar{B})}{P(B)}=\frac{29}{54}\times\frac{54}{25}=\frac{29}{25}$

4. (a) Total numbers of jack card in a pack of cards = 4

Total number of black card in a pack of cards = 26

Total number of even numbered card in a pack of cards = 20

Hence, required probability

$=\frac{4}{52}\times\frac{26}{52}\times\frac{20}{52}=\frac{5}{338}$

5. (c) Probability of hitting the target on a single shot $[P(H)]=\frac{5}{8}$

Probability of missing the target on a single shot $[P(H')]=1-P(H)=1-\frac{5}{8}=\frac{3}{8}$

The shooter fires 10 shots.

So, probability that the shooter hits the target twice from 10 shots.

$={}^{10}C_2\times[P(H)]^2\,[P(H')]^8$

$=\frac{10!}{2!(10-2)!}\times\left(\frac{5}{8}\right)^2\left(\frac{3}{8}\right)^8 \quad \left[\because {}^nC_r=\frac{n!}{r!\,n-r!}\right]$

$=45\times\frac{25}{8^2}\times\frac{3^8}{8^8}=\frac{1125\times3^8}{8^{10}}$

6. (c) Probabilities of solving a problem by three students A, B and C are $\frac{3}{7},\frac{5}{9},\frac{1}{5}$.

Probabilities of not solving a problem by three student A, B and C are $\frac{4}{7},\frac{4}{9},\frac{4}{5}$.

Probability that problem will not be solved

$=\frac{4}{7}\times\frac{4}{9}\times\frac{4}{5}=\frac{64}{315}$

$\therefore$ Probability that problem will be solved

$=1-\frac{64}{315}=\frac{251}{315}$

7. (d) Probability of A speaking truth $=\frac{5}{7}$

Probability of A speaking lie $=\frac{2}{7}$

Probability of B speaking truth $=\frac{8}{9}$

Probability of B speaking lie $=\frac{1}{9}$

Contradiction for same fact

$=\frac{5}{7}\times\frac{1}{9}+\frac{2}{7}\times\frac{8}{9}=\frac{5+16}{63}=\frac{21}{63}=\frac{1}{3}$

8. (b) Given, number of marbles

white = 6, black = 8, red = 4, blue = 3

Total number of marbles = 21

Favourable event (black or blue)

= 8 + 3 = 11

P (black or blue) $=\frac{\text{Favourable event}}{\text{Total number of event}}=\frac{11}{21}$

9. (a) Probability of selection of Sudarshan

$P(S)=\frac{1}{3}$

$\therefore$ Probability of Sudarshan not selecting

$P(S')=1-\frac{1}{3}=\frac{2}{3}$

$\therefore$ Probability of Abraham's selection

$P(A)=\frac{1}{5}$

and probability of Abraham's not selecting

$=P(A')=1-\frac{1}{5}=\frac{4}{5}$

Probability that none of them selected

$=\frac{2}{3}\times\frac{4}{5}=\frac{8}{15}$

10. (b) Given, $P(A)=\frac{3}{8}$; $P(B)=\frac{1}{2}$

$P(A\cap B)=\frac{1}{4}$

$\therefore P(A\cup B)=P(A)+P(B)-P(A\cap B)$

$P(A\cup B)=\frac{3}{8}+\frac{1}{2}-\frac{1}{4}=\frac{5}{8}$

$\therefore \; P(\bar{A}\cap\bar{B})=1-P(A\cup B)=1-\frac{5}{8}=\frac{3}{8}$

28

Data Interpretation

Data Interpretation is a process of understanding organising and interpreting the given data for making sense of and getting a meaningful conclusion. The collected data may be present in various forms like.

Tabular Graph

Statistical data are represented by tables. The data are placed in rows and columns. It allows for clear comparison and easy interpretation of information.

e.g. The given chart represents the import of various consumer goods (in lakh tons) during the years 2016-2020

Years	Electronics	Toys	Cosmetics
2016	27	30	35
2017	15	20	33
2018	35	25	32
2019	33	25	33
2020	12	20	25

Line graph

A line graph is a type of graph, which displays information as a series of data points connected by straight line segments.

e.g. The following line graph shows the annual profit percentage earned by a car manufacturing company during the period 2007-2012.

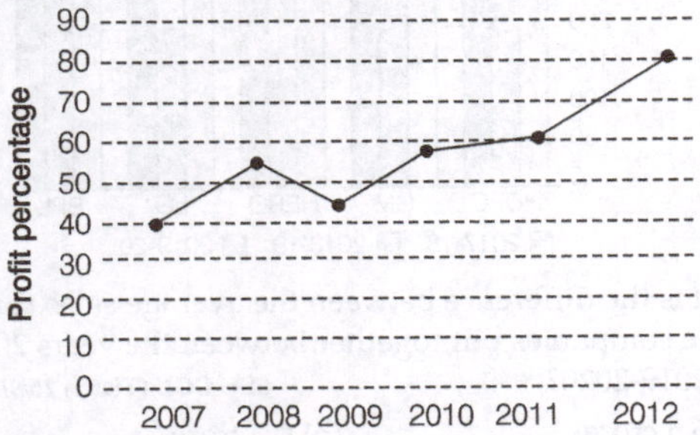

Bar Graph

A bar graph is a graph that represents data using rectangular bars, where the length of each bar is proportional to the value it represents.

e.g. The graph given below shows the units sold by two salesman, Mr. P and Mr. Q in 4 months and January to April.

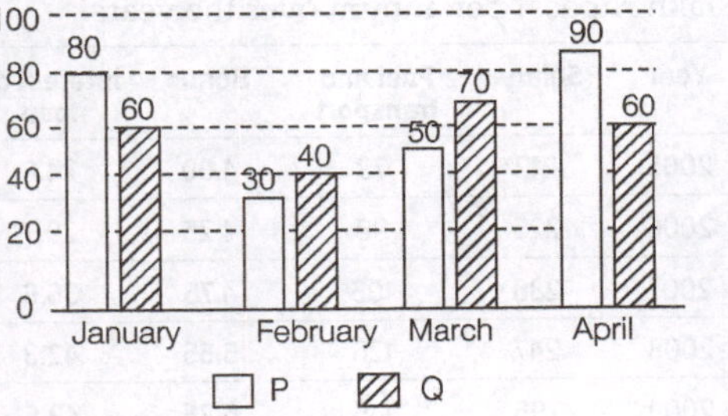

Pie Graph

Pie graph is a circular graph divided into segments that represent proportions or percentage of a whole.

The total quantity is distributed over a total angle of 360° or 100%.

Some Important Formulae

- If pie-chart is given in degree, then value of any sector

$$= \frac{\text{Angle of the sector}}{360°} \times \text{Total value}$$

- If pie-chart is given in percentage, then value of any sector

$$= \frac{\text{Percent of the sector}}{100} \times \text{Total value}$$

e.g. The given pie chart represents distribution of students by grades in class X board.

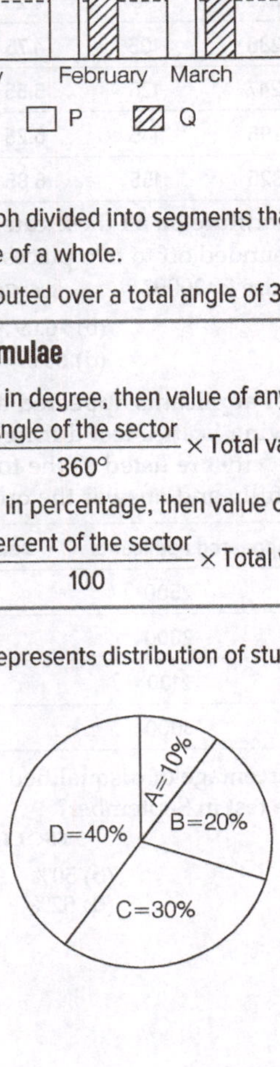

SSC Exam Scanner

SSC CGL 2024 (Tier I & II)

1. The following table shows the production (in units) and sales, of different items of a steel company. Study the table and answer the question that follows.

Item	Production (Units)	Sales (Units)
Plate	252	190
Bowl	356	307
Spoon	185	133
Pipe	220	155
Holder	458	419

In which item is there the least number of unsold items?
SSC CGL (Tier I) 26/9/2024 Shift-III

(a) Spoon (b) Holder
(c) Plate (d) Pipe

2. The given table shows the expenditure of a company (in lakh rupees) per annum over the years.

Year	Salary	Fuel and transport	Bonus	Interest on loan	Taxes
2005	212	78	4.00	24.6	88
2006	225	98	4.25	29.7	110
2007	236	105	4.75	36.8	125
2008	247	125	5.55	42.3	103
2009	295	145	6.25	49.6	118
2010	325	155	6.85	58.4	135

The total expenditure on all these categories in 2006 is what percentage (rounded off to two places of decimals) of the total expenditure in 2009? **SSC CGL (Tier I) 26/9/2024 Shift-III**

(a) 66.09% (b) 76.09%
(c) 76.07% (d) 66.07%

3. The number of applicants appeared and qualified in a 4-wheeler driving licence test during the last four months of 2022 from a city are listed in the following table. Study the table carefully and answer the question that follows.

Month	Appeared applicants	Qualified applicants
September	2500	1200
October	2000	1100
November	2100	900
December	3000	1500

What is the percentage of disqualified applicants for the driving licence test in September?
SSC CGL (Tier I) 26/9/2024 Shift-III

(a) 54% (b) 50%
(c) 48% (d) 52%

4. The table given below shows the distribution of employees in four different companies in 2022.

Company	Number of zones	Average number of employees per zone	Male : Female
A	30	300	3 : 5
B	35	400	5 : 3
C	27	500	4 : 5
D	25	450	5 : 4

Find the total number of male employees working in Company D in 2022. **SSC CGL (Tier I) 26/9/2024 Shift-II**

(a) 6000 (b) 6750
(c) 6250 (d) 6500

5. Study the below data and answer the question that follows.

Partners	Percentage of shares
Jeevan	10%
Kiran	15%
Lokesh	8%
Rasool	22%
Meera	45%

The company has issued 10 lakh shares between its five partners. If Jeevan offers to sell 20000 of his shares to Meera, how many shares will Meera have?
SSC CGL (Tier I) 26/9/2024 Shift-II

(a) 510000 (b) 480000
(c) 460000 (d) 470000

6. The given bar-graph shows the turnover of five companies (in crores).

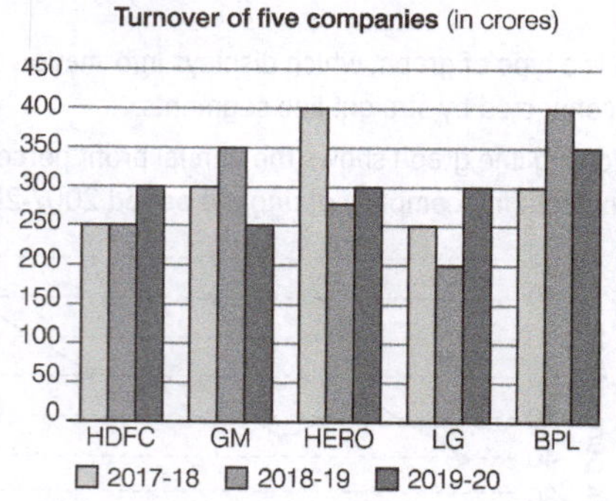

What is the difference between the average sales turnover of all the companies put together between the years 2018-2019 and 2019-2020? **SSC CGL (Tier I) 26/9/2024 Shift-II**

(a) ₹ 6.5 crore (b) ₹ 2 crore
(c) ₹ 5 crore (d) ₹ 3.5 crore

7. Annual income of five schools (in lakhs)

Source of Income	Schools				
	X	Y	Z	U	V
Tuition Fee	13	26	15	17	16
Semester Fee	43	56	39	89	59
Donation	14	17	14	50	19
Miscellaneous	25	18	29	13	23
Total	95	117	97	169	117

In case of how many schools, the income by semester fee, is less than three times of donation?
SSC CGL (Tier I) 26/9/2024 Shift-I

(a) 2
(b) 5
(c) 4
(d) 3

8. Study the below table and answer the question that follows.

	2017	2018	2019	2020	2021
Company P	2000	4000	2000	3000	4000
Company Q	1500	3000	1500	3000	3000
Company R	1400	2000	2000	3000	3000

For which of the following pairs of years are the total exports from the three companies together, equal?
SSC CGL (Tier I) 26/9/2024 Shift-I

(a) 2020 and 2021
(b) 2018 and 2019
(c) 2017 and 2018
(d) 2018 and 2020

9. Study the given table and answer the question that follows. The following table shows the percentage distribution of students in four different schools during the years 2021-22.

Year	Schools			
	School 1	School 2	School 3	School 4
2021	28	25	24	23
2022	27	28	23	22

If there was a total number of 16000 and 18,000 students during the years 2021 and 2022 respectively, then the difference in number of students in school 4 in 2022 with respect to 2021 is
SSC CGL (Tier I) 26/9/2024 Shift-I

(a) 240
(b) 280
(c) 180
(d) 380

10. The below table shows the number of 1 litre bottles of soft drink produced by three companies during 2016-2020. Study the given information carefully and answer the question that follows.

Year	A (in lakhs)	B (in lakhs)	C (in lakhs)
2016	38000	43000	51000
2017	41000	52000	57000
2018	53000	65000	63000
2019	30000	35000	32000
2020	20000	25000	28000

What is the difference in average production of A and C during 2016-2018 (in lakhs)?
SSC CGL (Tier I) 25/9/2024 Shift-III

(a) 7800
(b) 14000
(c) 13000
(d) 9500

11. The sales of two kinds of bicycles B1 and B2 (in lakhs) manufactured by a company over a period of three years are shown in the table below.

Year	B1	B2
2004	195	284
2005	230	300
2006	250	416

From 2004 to 2006, what is the ratio of the total sales of bicycles B1 to the total sales of bicycles B2?
SSC CGL (Tier I) 25/9/2024 Shift-III

(a) 27 : 40
(b) 9 : 10
(c) 10 : 9
(d) 40 : 27

12. Study the given table answer the question that follows. The following table shows the income of a person (in thousand rupees) per annum over the given years.

Year	School Salary	Coaching	Home tuition
2018	132	42	12
2019	148	55	18
2020	166	68	24
2021	178	74	28
2022	196	88	35

What is the average income from school as a salary per year earned by the person over the given years?
SSC CGL (Tier I) 25/9/2024 Shift-II

(a) ₹ 164000
(b) ₹ 174000
(c) ₹ 158000
(d) ₹ 148000

13. The given table shows the number of clerical and officer cadre employees recruited by four different banks A, B, C and D from 2011 to 2014.

Year	A		B		C		D	
	Officer	Clerk	Officer	Clerk	Officer	Clerk	Officer	Clerk
2011	260	458	255	460	205	428	265	470
2012	310	569	286	584	230	539	246	554
2013	350	730	321	725	340	740	361	725
2014	400	890	452	845	380	850	482	860

Compute the ratio of the number of officer cadre employees of bank A to the number of officer cadre employees of bank C.
SSC CGL (Tier I) 25/9/2024 Shift-II

(a) 6 : 5
(b) 7 : 8
(c) 5 : 6
(d) 8 : 7

14. Consider the following table for total exports of goods of 5 companies over 5 years (in lakhs).

Companies Year	R	S	T	U	V
2012	60	40	15	45	25
2013	30	60	70	15	90
2014	51	25	55	100	110
2015	45	51	20	70	65
2016	24	35	60	55	125

If the ratio of exports to the imports of companies S and U in the year 2015 is 3 : 2 and 1 : 2, respectively, then, the total imports (in ₹ lakhs) of companies S and U together in the year 2015 is
SSC CGL (Tier I) 25/9/2024 Shift-II

(a) 121
(b) 174
(c) 187
(d) 157

15. Study the given table and answer the question that follows. The given table shows the production of three types of cars (A, B and C) manufactured (in thousands) by an automobile company over the years.

Year	A	B	C
2015	840	680	890
2016	900	750	960
2017	760	620	1000
2018	800	540	1200

The total number of A-type cars produced by the company from 2015 to 2017 is what percentage (rounded off the nearest integer) is more or less than the total number of C-type cars produced by the compnay from 2016 to 2018?

SSC CGL (Tier I) 25/9/2024 Shift-I

(a) More, 24% (b) Less, 24%
(c) Less, 21% (d) More, 21%

16. The given bar graph shows sugar imports of a country (in thousand tonnes) over the years. Study the graph and answer the question that follows.

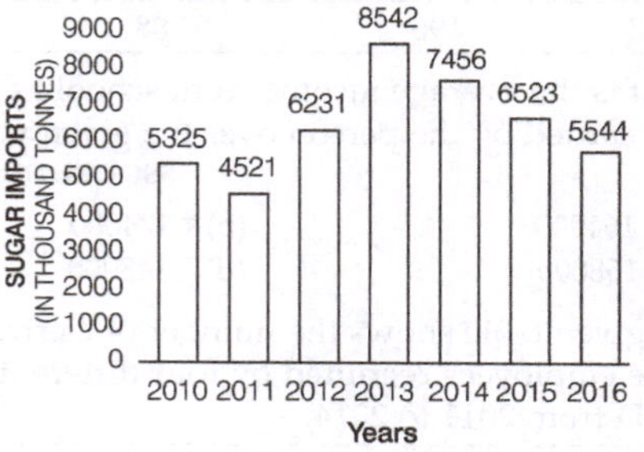

The average imports (in thousand tonnes) of all the years is

SSC CGL (Tier I) 25/9/2024 Shift-I

(a) 6306 (b) 6469
(c) 6433 (d) 6603

17. Study the given table and answer the question. The table displays the number of cars produced (in lakhs) by six different brands between 2018 and 2023.

Type	2018	2019	2020	2021	2022	2023
A	36	40	42	45	47	42
B	23	37	28	32	34	26
C	45	47	51	54	56	48
D	35	37	42	32	36	28
E	57	56	52	38	48	42
F	43	45	56	41	52	40

Find the difference in the average production of B and D during 2018-2022.

SSC CGL (Tier I) 25/9/2024 Shift-I

(a) 6 lakhs (b) 4 lakhs
(c) 5 lakhs (d) 5.5 lakhs

18. The following table shows the number of pages printed by 3 printers (P, Q and R) for 3 days.

Day	P	Q	R
Monday	100	130	200
Tuesday	120	145	160
Wednesday	180	85	120

What is the ratio of the total number of pages printed by printer P over the course of three days to the total number of pages printed by printer Q during the same three days?

SSC CGL (Tier I) 25/9/2024 Shift-I

(a) 9 : 10 (b) 11 : 10
(c) 10 : 11 (d) 10 : 9

19. Refer the below table and answer the question that follows.

India's exports in 2020	Value in million US$
Electronics	720
Cotton	680
Jewellery	500
Steel	450
Software	850

Jewellery was what percentage of the total exports ? (Rounded to two decimal places)

SSC CGL (Tier I) 24/9/2024 Shift-III

(a) 14.63% (b) 15.63%
(c) 15.78% (d) 14.34%

20. Study the given pie-chart carefully and answer the question that follows.
The given pie-chart depicts the expenditure incurred towards different hobby classes of an institute.

Expenditure in thousands

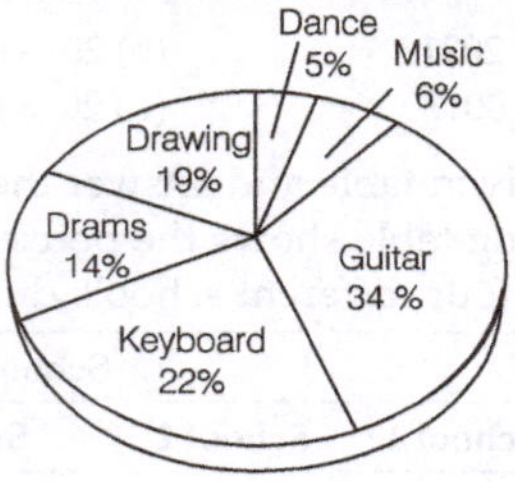

If the total expenditure is ₹1070000, then find the central angle of the sector representing 'drawing'.

SSC CGL (Tier I) 24/9/2024 Shift-III

(a) 19° (b) 90° (c) 68.4° (d) 70°

21. The given pie-chart shows the data on A, B, O, and AB blood groups of 240 donors. Study the chart and answer the question that follows.

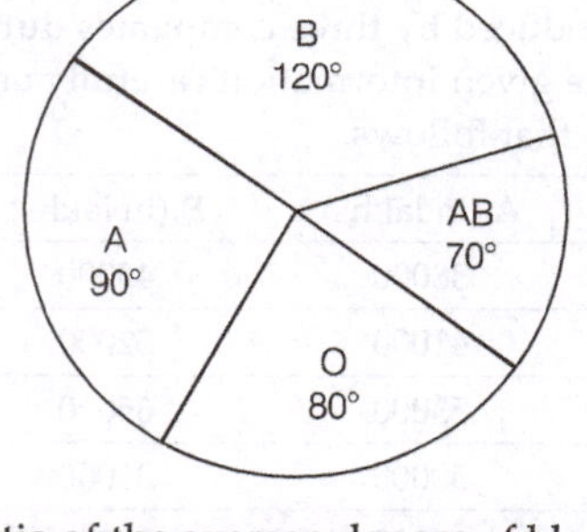

What is the ratio of the average donors of blood groups 'A', 'O' and 'AB' to the donors of blood group 'B'?

SSC CGL (Tier I) 24/9/2024 Shift-III

(a) 3 : 4 (b) 4 : 3
(c) 2 : 3 (d) 1 : 3

22. The number of students in a class who have answered correctly, incorrectly or not attempted each question in an examination is shown in the table below. The marks for each question are also listed. There is no negative or partial marking?

Q. No	Marks	Answered correctly	Answered incorrectly	Not attempted
1	1	20	10	10
2	2	15	15	10
3	5	20	20	0
4	10	12	15	13

Find the average of the marks obtained by the class in the examination. **SSC CGL (Tier I) 24/9/2024 Shift-III**

(a) 6.75 (b) 6.25 (c) 5.25 (d) 5.75

23. The following table gives zone wise survey report of the people of a country who take tea. Study the table and answer the question.

Take tea	Zone			
	East	West	North	South
More than 3 times a day	1732	1842	6045	2741
1 to 3 times a day	1462	2328	2584	4264
Twice a week	2280	2529	1123	3598
Only once a week	4059	1874	3169	7051
Never	317	127	223	293

The ratio of the total number of people surveyed who take tea more than 3 times a day to the number of people who do not take tea at all is **SSC CGL (Tier I) 24/9/2024 Shift-II**

(a) 103 : 8 (b) 8 : 103 (c) 101 : 5 (d) 5 : 107

24. Study the given table and answer the question that follows. The total money spent in advertisement (in ₹) and total number of advertisements in different newspapers given by a company for five years (2018 to 2022) is given in the below table.

Year	Total Money Spent in ₹ in Advertisement			Total No of Advertisements		
	NY Times	The Telegraph	Others	NY Times	The Tele-graph	Others
2018	350000	360000	210000	10	12	15
2019	480000	345000	289000	12	15	17
2020	615000	400000	576000	15	20	36
2021	760000	480000	440000	19	24	22
2022	1400000	350000	309000	38	18	30

What is the ratio of the money spent on each of the advertisements taken one from each of NY times, The Telegraph and Others for the year 2021 to that of the money spent on each of the advertisements taken one from each of NY times, The Telegraph and Others for the year 2018? **SSC CGL (Tier I) 24/9/2024 Shift-II**

(a) 80 : 79 (b) 80 : 71 (c) 71 : 80 (d) 79 : 80

25. The given table shows the expenditure (in crore ₹) of three companies A, B and C and the percentage profit of these companies in different years. Given that:

$$\text{Income} = \text{Expenditure} + \text{Expenditure} \times \frac{\text{Profit } \%}{100}$$

Year	Company A		Company B		Company C	
	Expen-diture	Profit	Expen diture	Profit	Expen-diture	Profit
2002	24	50%	20	40%	40	45%
2003	30	45%	15	25%	50	55%
2004	36	40%	25	35%	60	65%
2005	40	60%	35	48%	80	75%

What is the difference (in crore ₹) between the profits of Company A and Company B in the year 2005? **SSC CGL (Tier I) 24/9/2024 Shift-I**

(a) 7.2 (b) 12.5 (c) 10.4 (d) 8.3

26. The below figure shows the estimated expenses of a family whose total estimated expenditure was ₹ 250000. Study the figure and answer the question that follows.

Percentage Share of Estimated Expenses

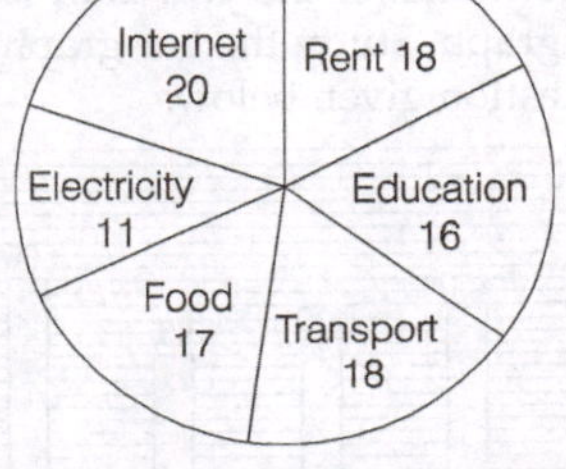

It was found that the actual expenditure on electricity was 10% more than the estimated expenditure, and the actual expenditure on rent was 20% less than estimated. All other expenses were same as that of the estimates. What was the total actual expenditure? **SSC CGL (Tier I) 24/9/2024 Shift-I**

(a) ₹ 252500 (b) ₹ 240750
(c) ₹ 243750 (d) ₹ 248750

27. Study the given table and answer the question.

Year	Rice gm/day	Wheat gm/day	Pulses gm/day	Vegetables gm/day
2019	450	55	160	280
2020	430	60	150	300
2021	380	65	140	320
2022	350	70	125	400
2023	350	80	120	350

For which year is the daily consumption equal to that of another given year? **SSC CGL (Tier I) 24/9/2024 Shift-I**

(a) 2019 and 2022 (b) 2019 and 2023
(c) 2021 and 2023 (d) 2020 and 2022

28. The following table represents the total number of students in different classes and the respective number of students who are vegetarian, in a school. Study the table carefully and answer the question that follows.

Class	Total number of students	Number of vegetarian students
XII	150	105
XI	165	100
X	125	80
IX	140	90

What is the percentage of non-vegetarian students in class XII? **SSC CGL (Tier I) 23/9/2024 Shift-III**

(a) 40% (b) 30%
(c) 35% (d) 25%

29. The following table shows the number of students admitted in to a university for higher education from 2010 to 2013.

Year	Number of Students
2010	450
2011	540
2012	370
2013	680

What is the average number of students admitted in to the university from 2010 to 2013? **SSC CGL (Tier I) 23/9/2024 Shift-III**

(a) 495 (b) 499 (c) 510 (d) 522

30. The monthly production of electric bulbs by a company during the second half of the year 2021 is shown by the following bar graph. Study the bar graph carefully and answer the question given below.

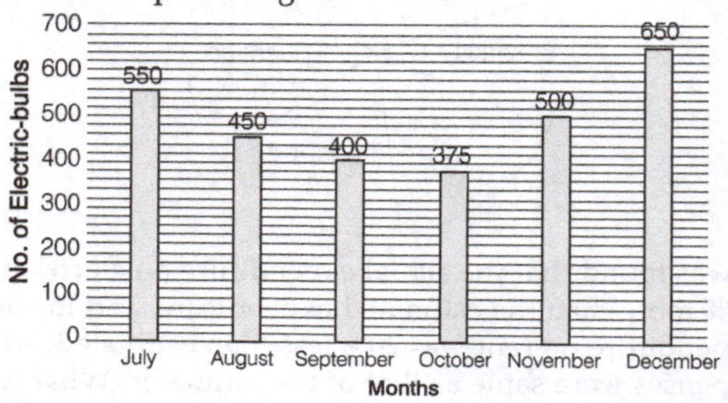

What is the percentage decrement in the production of electric bulbs in October as compared to the production in July? (Correct up to two decimal places.) **SSC CGL (Tier I) 23/9/2024 Shift-III**

(a) 30.28% (b) 31.82%
(c) 29.82% (d) 32.28%

31. The following bar chart shows the year-wise percentage hike in the fuel price with respect to the previous year.

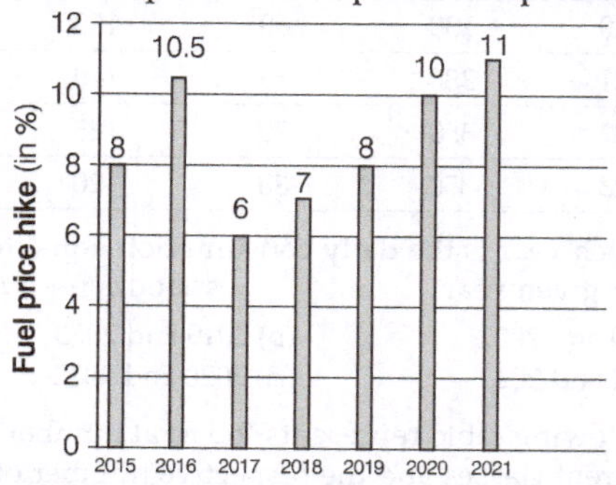

In how many years did the fuel prices not rise? **SSC CGL (Tier I) 23/9/2024 Shift-II**

(a) 0 (b) 1 (c) 2 (d) 5

32. The following pie-chart shows the percentage distribution of the expenditure incurred in publishing a book. Study the pie-chart and answer the question that follows.
Pie-chart shows that percentage distribution of the expenditure incurred in publishing a book.

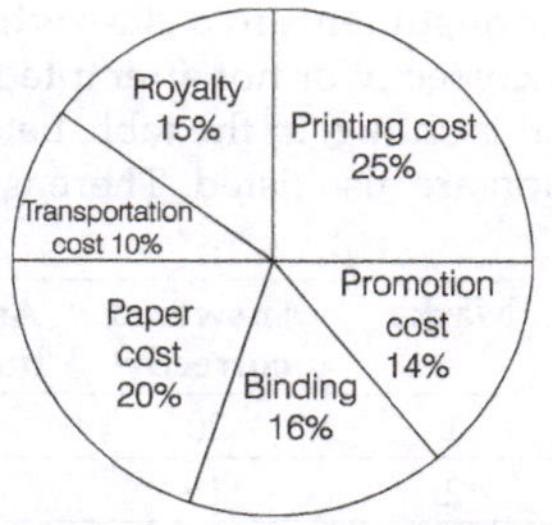

If the expenditure on royalty in publishing certain number of books be ₹ 43500, then what is the combined expenditure (in ₹) on transportation, binding and printing?

(a) 197900 (b) 179000
(c) 179000 (d) 147900

33. Study the below table and answer the question that follows.

Day of the weel	Distance jogged (in km)
Monday	6
Tuesday	5.5
Wednesday	5.5
Thursday	7
Friday	5
Saturday	3.5
Sunday	7.5

If 300 calories are burned by jogging 6 km, then how many calories were burnt in the given week? **SSC CGL (Tier I) 23/9/2024 Shift-II**

(a) 1600 (b) 2200
(c) 1800 (d) 2000

34. The bar graph shows the number of students present in a class on four days. The average number of students present on Monday, Tuesday and Wednesday is

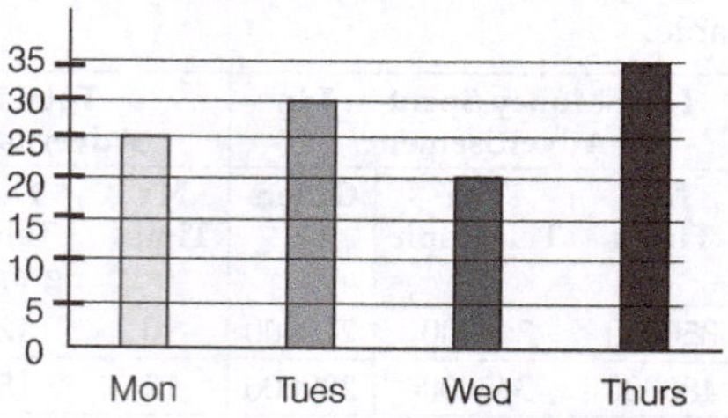

SSC CGL (Tier I) 23/9/2024 Shift-I

(a) 24 (b) 20 (c) 30 (d) 25

35. Study the given table and answer the question that follows.
The following table shows the production of printers by four plants of a company over the five years.

Year	Production (in thousands)			
	Plant 1	Plant 2	Plant 3	Plant 4
2018	35	25	40	45
2019	43	44	44	40
2020	48	39	36	30
2021	32	40	35	48
2022	42	44	30	42

What is the difference between the average production of plant 1 and plant 2 during five years?

SSC CGL (Tier I) 23/9/2024 Shift-I

(a) 1600 (b) 3000 (c) 3840 (d) 1400

36. The pie-chart below shows the expenditure (in ₹ lakh) of a country on various sports during a particular year. Study the graph carefully and answer the question given below it.

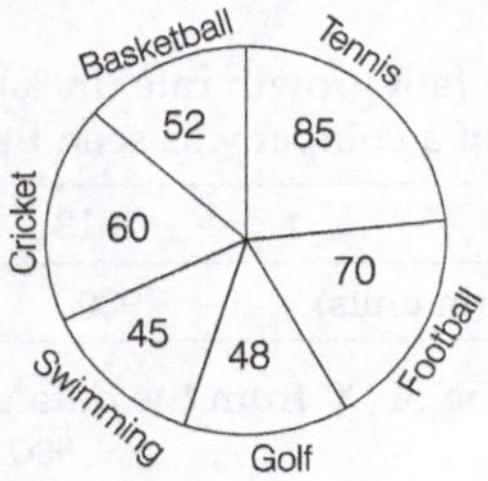

What is the average expenditure (in ₹ lakh) on tennis, golf, swimming and basketball, if the expenditure on cricket is ₹72 lakh?

SSC CGL (Tier I) 19/9/2024 Shift-III

(a) 138 (b) 44
(c) 69 (d) 120

37. Study the given table and answer the question that follows. The given table shows the number of candidates, who appeared (both male and female) in a Public Examination and the percentage of those, who qualified in the examination from two states X and Z. Few values are missing in the table (indicated by ……). You will be required to fill them up according to the question.

Year	State X		State Z	
	Number of appeared candidates	Percentage of qualified candidates	Number of appeared candidates	Percentage of qualified candidates
2008	480	70%	……	70%
2009	560	75%	……	80%
2010	……	60%	650	50%
2011	450	89%	720	72%
2012	790	……	660	……

The number of appeared candidates from State Z increased by 100% from 2008 to 2009. If the total number of qualified candidates from State Z in 2008 and 2009 together is 552, what is the number of appeared candidates from State Z in 2009?

SSC CGL (Tier I) 19/9/2024 Shift-III

(a) 360 (b) 240 (c) 480 (d) 600

38. Study the given bar-graph and answer the question that follows.

The following bar-graph shows the quarterly profit (in lakhs) of a departmental store from 1997 to 2000.

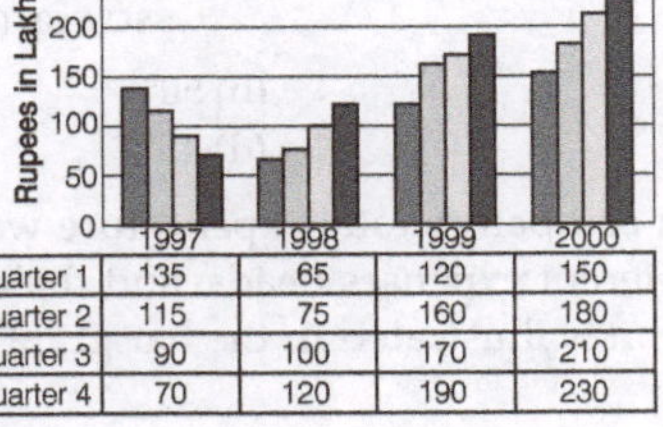

	1997	1998	1999	2000
Quarter 1	135	65	120	150
Quarter 2	115	75	160	180
Quarter 3	90	100	170	210
Quarter 4	70	120	190	230

What was the percentage increase in annual profit of the departmental store from 1997 to 2000?

SSC CGL (Tier I) 19/9/2024 Shift-II

(a) $85\frac{33}{41}\%$ (b) $84\frac{33}{41}\%$ (c) $87\frac{33}{41}\%$ (d) $83\frac{33}{41}\%$

39. The given pie-chart shows the number of students admitted in to different classes of a school in the academic year 2022-23.

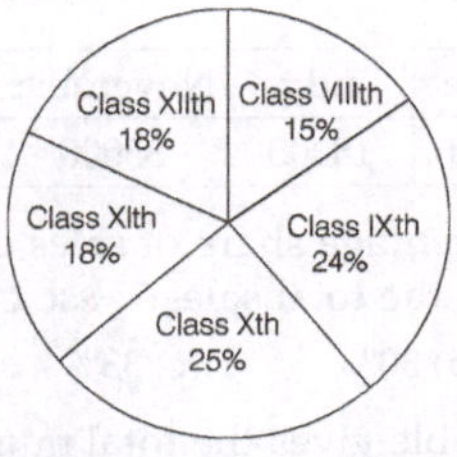

How many students were more in class 10 than in class 12 if 600 students were admitted in to class 8?

SSC CGL (Tier I) 19/9/2024 Shift-II

(a) 280 (b) 298 (c) 240 (d) 295

40. The following bar graph shows the sales of a company (in ₹ crore) in different years. Study the graph and answer the question.

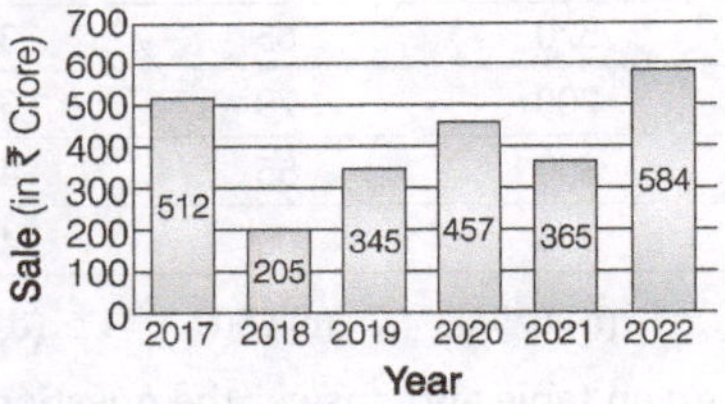

The mean of the highest and lowest sales (in ₹ crore) is.

SSC CGL (Tier I) 19/9/2024 Shift-II

(a) 326.7 (b) 394.5 (c) 484.2 (d) 412.3

41. The marks of 6 students are given. All the marks are out of 100.

Student	English	Hindi	Maths	Physics	Chemistry	Biology
A	70	60	99	80	80	75
B	75	65	85	75	75	70
C	80	80	70	60	70	60
D	72	63	65	70	60	60
E	70	60	60	60	55	55
F	60	60	70	70	60	50

Find the percentage scored by C. **SSC CGL (Tier I) 19/9/2024 Shift-I**

(a) 75% (b) 70% (c) 68% (d) 65%

42. The table given below shows the marks obtained by four students in 4 different subjects. Maximum marks for each subject is 175.

Student	Subject			
	Mathematics	Physics	Chemistry	English
Amit	105	98	109	86
Gunja	112	119	99	97
Arpit	103	121	94	100
Kavya	108	102	104	120

What is the aggregate percentage of marks obtained by Gunja in all the four subjects? **SSC CGL (Tier I) 19/9/2024 Shift-I**

(a) 67 (b) 61 (c) 58 (d) 71

43. The following table shows the sales during two seasons of a company. Study the table and answer the question that follow.

Sales in summer season (in ₹)			Sales in winter season (in ₹)		
May	June	July	November	December	January
25000	24000	18000	35000	26000	22000

What is the percentage share of sales during months of June and July to the total sales? **SSC CGL (Tier I) 19/9/2024 Shift-I**

(a) 28% (b) 30% (c) 33% (d) 24%

44. The following table gives the total number of employees in 5 different companies A, B, C, D and E and the percentage of males and females. Study the table carefully and answer the question. Find the number of females in companies A, C and E put together. **SSC CGL (Tier I) 18/9/2024 Shift-III**

Companies	Total No. of Employees	Percentage of males	Percentage of females
A	600	75	25
B	570	65	35
C	700	70	30
D	800	55	45
E	850	60	40

(a) 700 (b) 675 (c) 650 (d) 725

45. Study the given table and answer the question that follows. The table represents the number of scooters (in thousands) manufactured by four companies A, B, C and D from the period 2012 to 2015.

Year	A	B	C	D
2012	360	420	380	520
2013	580	940	570	980
2014	1000	780	1020	1090
2015	1240	950	1180	1660

The average number of scooters produced by company D is what per cent (rounded off to 2 decimal places) more than the combined average number of scooters produced by the three companies A, B, and C? **SSC CGL (Tier I) 18/9/2024 Shift-III**

(a) 52.75% (b) 27.25% (c) 44.66% (d) 35.35%

46. The following table shows the expenditure of a company (in ₹ lakh) per annum over the given years. Study the table and answer the question that follows.

Year	Salary	Bonus	Interest on Loans	Fuel and Transport	Taxes
2005	348	3.00	25.0	110	75
2006	405	4.25	28.5	145	90
2007	458	4.50	30.5	120	120
2008	389	4.85	38.0	168	100
2009	425	4.90	48.5	190	140

The total amount of bonus paid by the company during the given period is what percentage of the total amount of fuels and transport paid during this period (correct to two places of decimals)? **SSC CGL (Tier I) 18/9/2024 Shift-III**

(a) 3.92%
(b) 2.39%
(c) 3.29%
(d) 2.93%

47. There is constant growth rate (in %) every year in the production of a company as seen the given table.

Year	2018	2019	2020
Production (in units)	9000	10800	X

Find the value of 'X' from the data given in the table. **SSC CGL (Tier I) 18/9/2024 Shift-III**

(a) 12600
(b) 11880
(c) 12000
(d) 12960

48. The given pie chart shows the amount of money (in ₹) spent (in degrees) on various sports by a sports academy in a particular year. Study the pie-chart and answer the question that follows.
Amount of money (₹) spent (in degrees) on various sports by a sports academy in a particular year.

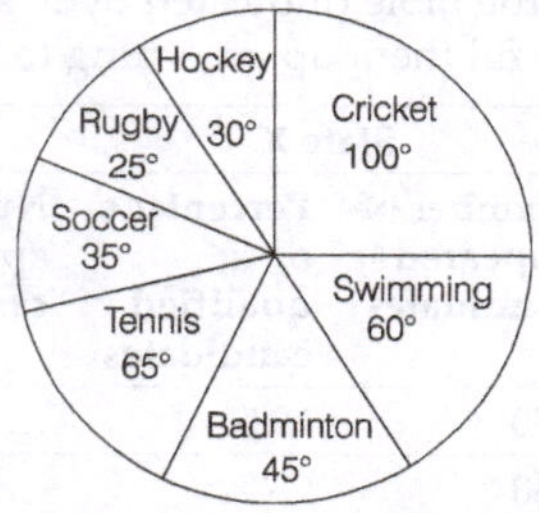

If ₹ 42000 were spent on Soccer, then the money spent on Badminton, Tennis and Rugby taken together is what percentage (rounded off to 2 decimal places) more/less than the money spent on Cricket, Swimming and Hockey taken together? **SSC CGL (Tier I) 18/9/2024 Shift-II**

(a) Less, 34.87%
(b) More, 28.95%
(c) More, 34.87%
(d) Less, 28.95%

49. Refer the below table and answer the question that follows.

Discipline	Boys	Girls
Engineering	120	80
Medical	80	120

What percentage of students, who chose medical are boys? **SSC CGL (Tier I) 18/9/2024 Shift-II**

(a) 30% (b) 50%
(c) 40% (d) 45%

50. In 2010, a company's total expenditure was categorised under different expenses heads, and their percentage distribution is illustrated in the bar graph given below.

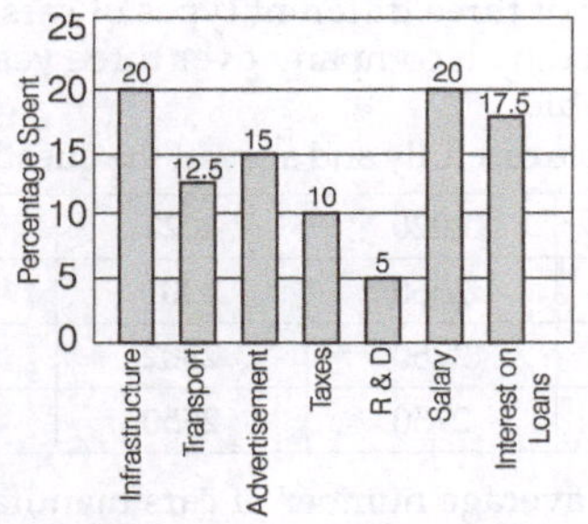

If the expenditure on an advertisement is ₹ 2.1 crore, then the difference between the expenditure on transport and taxes is? **SSC CGL (Tier I) 18/9/2024 Shift-I**

(a) ₹ 32 lakh
(b) ₹ 42 lakh
(c) ₹ 30 lakh
(d) ₹ 35 lakh

51. The given table shows the number of televisions that were sold by different showrooms in years 2015 to 2019.

Year/Showroom	A	B	C	D
2015	212	200	205	208
2016	210	215	225	220
2017	190	204	212	205
2018	198	212	222	224
2019	218	192	205	203

Find the difference between the sale of televisions from showrooms A, B and C in 2017 and the sale of televisions from showrooms B, C and D in 2019? **SSC CGL (Tier I) 18/9/2024 Shift-I**

(a) 8
(b) 5
(c) 6
(d) 3

52. The following table shows the expenditure of a factory (in ₹ lakh) per annum on different heads over the given years.

Year/ Expenditure Head	Salary	Transport	Bonus	Loan Interest
1998	125	38	8	25
1999	135	45	18	37
2000	149	57	37	39
2001	153	63	50	43

What was the average expenditure (in ₹ lakh) on transport per year that the factory had to pay during the given period? **SSC CGL (Tier I) 17/9/2024 Shift-III**

(a) 56.63
(b) 48.75
(c) 50.75
(d) 45.58

53. The following bar graph shows the number of students who passed the exam of GATE in the given years.

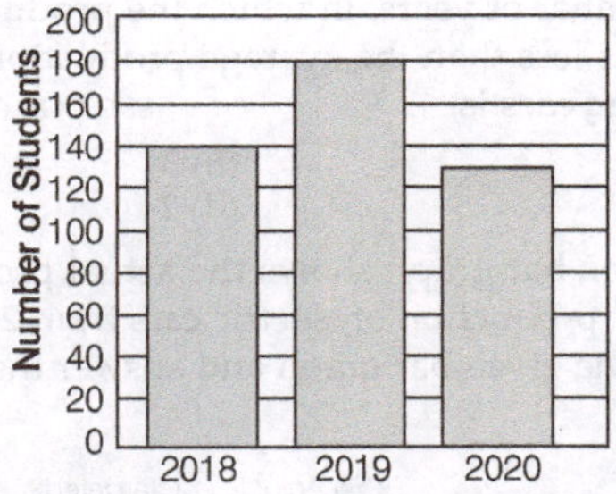

What was the percentage increase in the number of students in 2019 over 2018 (rounded off to two decimal places)? **SSC CGL (Tier I) 17/9/2024 Shift-III**

(a) 35.79% (b) 29.52%
(c) 28.57% (d) 32.25%

54. The below table gives shares traded on Hyderabad, Mumbai, and Bengaluru stock exchanges (in ₹). Study the table and answer the question that follows.

Name of the company	Hyderabad		Mumbai		Bengaluru	
	High	Low	High	Low	High	Low
A	150	140	180	165	160	155
B	250	225	325	315	300	290
C	180	175	195	180	190	185
D	350	325	410	395	390	375

For C, the low rates of shares are less than average of low rates of shares of the same company in stock exchanges at .... **SSC CGL (Tier I) 17/9/2024 Shift-III**

(a) Mumbai (b) Bengaluru
(c) Hyderabad (d) Hyderabad and Mumbai

55. The below table shows the sales of motorbikes of four manufactures from 2016 to 2020 (All the figures are in thousands). Study the table and answer the question that follows.

Manufacturer	2016	2017	2018	2019	2020
P	220	225	235	240	260
Q	280	290	310	310	330
R	350	375	385	390	400
S	400	420	430	440	450

Find the ratio of the total number of sales of the motorbikes of manufacturer Q to the total number of sales of the motorbikes of manufacturer S from 2016 to 2020. **SSC CGL (Tier I) 17/9/2024 Shift-III**

(a) 72 : 105 (b) 76 : 107 (c) 74 : 103 (d) 78 : 107

56. The table shows the production of different types of bikes (in thousands).

Years / Bikes	2015	2016	2017	2018
A	157	194	271	290
B	138	225	146	206
C	255	227	213	239
D	196	304	162	224

The number of years, in which the production of bikes of type C is less than the average production of type A bikes over the years is **SSC CGL (Tier I) 17/9/2024 Shift-II**

(a) 4 (b) 3
(c) 1 (d) 2

57. The given bar graph shows the actual production and targeted production of electric cars from 2019 to 2022. Study the given bar graph and answer the question that follows.

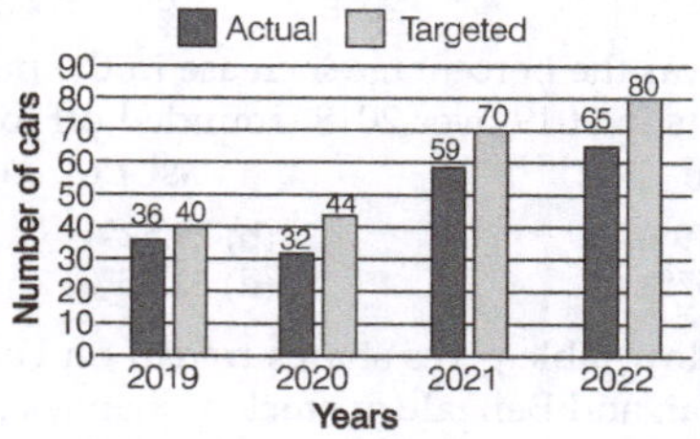

What is the ratio of the total targeted production of cars in 2021 and 2022 to the actual production of cars from 2019 to 2022 taken together? **SSC CGL (Tier I) 17/9/2024 Shift-II**

(a) 32 : 25 (b) 25 : 36
(c) 36 : 25 (d) 25 : 32

58. Study the given graph and answer the question that follows. The graph shows the sales of three products: P, Q and R by four companies: A, B, C and D.

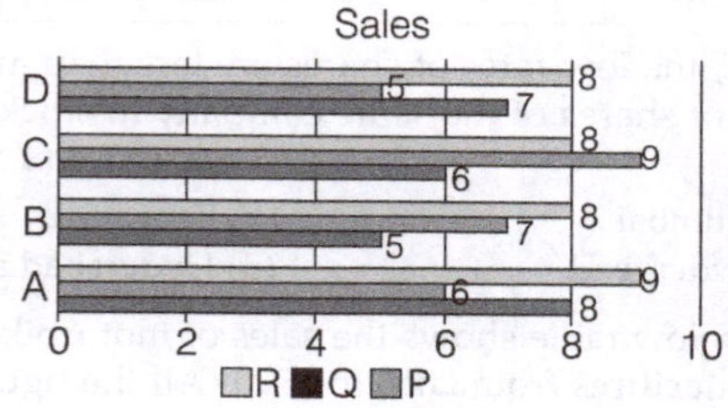

What percentage is the total production by company C, of the total production by company A? **SSC CGL (Tier-I) 17/9/2024 Shift-I**

(a) 110% (b) 90%
(c) 100% (d) 105%

59. A shopkeeper sold the following items to Arushi earning profit on it. How much total profit (in ₹) did he earn on the basis of the given date? **SSC CGL (Tier-I) 17/9/2024 Shift-I**

Item	Cost Price per unit (₹)	Profit on cost (%)
Mobile	20000	10
Laptop	72000	20
Mobile covers	300	12

(a) 16436
(b) 34760
(c) 16760
(d) 16636

60. The number of three different types of cars, X, Y, Z manufactured by a company over three years is given in the below table.
Study the table carefully and answer the question that follows.

Cars/Years	2020	2021	2022
X	2560	3201	3551
Y	2250	2802	3020
Z	2750	2550	2600

What is the average number of cars manufactured by the company in the year 2022? **SSC CGL (Tier-I) 17/9/2024 Shift-I**

(a) 3227
(b) 2851
(c) 3057
(d) 2720

61. The table shows the percentage distribution of the population (only male and female) according to Gender and Literacy.

State	Percentage literate	Gender	
		Literate	Illiterate
		M : F	M : F
A	55	5 : 6	4 : 5
B	72	1 : 1	3 : 2
C	78	4 : 3	3 : 2

If the literate male population of state A is 500000 then the total population of the state is **SSC CGL (Tier-I) 13/9/2024 Shift-III**

(a) 3000000
(b) 4000000
(c) 1600000
(d) 2000000

62. The following table shows the percentage population of four states below poverty line, and the male to female ratios both above and below the poverty line.

State	Percentage of population below poverty line	Ratio of male to female	
		Below poverty line	Above poverty line
		Male : Female	Male : Female
P	13	1 : 2	1 : 4
Q	19	2 : 5	3 : 5
R	11	3 : 4	2 : 9
S	15	1 : 6	7 : 4

If the population of states Q and S is 14700 each, then what is the total number of males below poverty line in these states? **SSC CGL (Tier-I) 13/9/2024 Shift-III**

(a) 1276 (b) 1479
(c) 1113 (d) 1364

63. Study the given graph carefully and answer the question that follows.
The given graph shows the number of male and female volunteers for helping handicapped people from four different districts A, B, C and D.

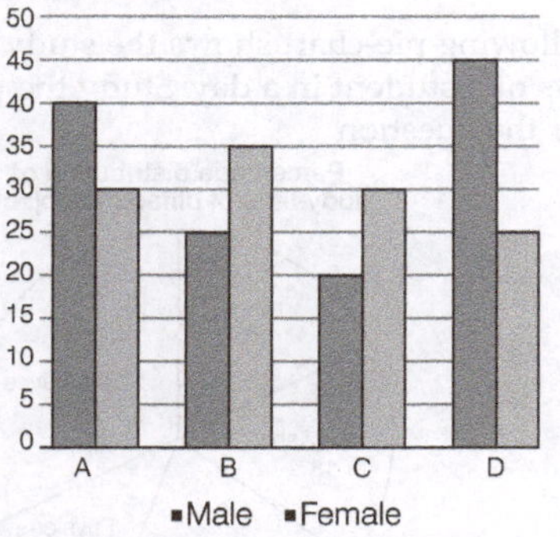

Find the number of volunteers altogether.
SSC CGL (Tier-I) 13/9/2024 Shift-III

(a) 230 (b) 250 (c) 240 (d) 260

64. The following table indicates the number of students studying in three subjects in four colleges.

Subjects	Colleges			
	W	X	Y	Z
Physics	420	435	412	285
Chemistry	380	340	315	420
Mathematics	256	310	295	345

What is the ratio of the total number of students studying in the Physics to that of studying in Mathematics in all four colleges taken together? **SSC CGL (Tier-I) 13/9/2024 Shift-II**

(a) 781 : 585 (b) 775 : 601 (c) 576 : 731 (d) 776 : 603

65. The given table shows the marks obtained by a student in class 9.

Subjects	Marks (out of 100)
Social Science	93
Science	90
Hindi	90
English	95
Mathematics	78

What is the percentage of marks obtained by the student?
SSC CGL (Tier-I) 13/9/2024 Shift-I

(a) 89.2% (b) 88.8% (c) 90% (d) 88%

66. The pie-chart below shows the per-cent sale of different fruits in a day for a shop.
If the total number of fruits sold by a fruit seller in a day is 1200, what is the combined central angle in the pie-chart for oranges and apples? **SSC CGL (Tier-I) 13/9/2024 Shift-I**

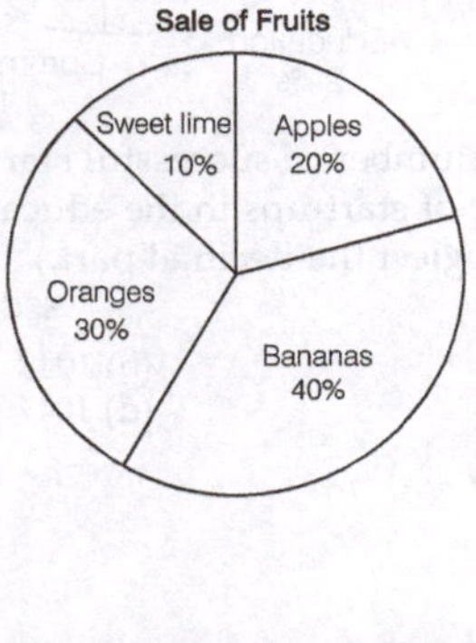

(a) 220° (b) 90°
(c) 180° (d) 160°

67. The following table shows the scale (in lakh rupees) of six commodities in a provision store from August 2012 to October 2012.

Commodity / Month	Dry Fruits	Tea	Pulses	Sugar	Flour	Rice
August	27	24	45	48	55	42
September	32	15	34	42	33	23
October	25	30	42	47	49	27

The total combined sale of dry fruits, sugar and rice for the period from August 2012 to October 2012 is what percentage (rounded off to the nearest whole number) of the total combined sale of tea, pulses and flour.
SSC CGL (Tier-I) 13/9/2024 Shift-I

(a) 94% (b) 98%
(c) 95% (d) 96%

68. The following pie chart shows the percentage distribution of a total of 1600 employees in different departments of a company. The table shows the ratio of male to female employees in different departments. Study the information and answer the question that follows.

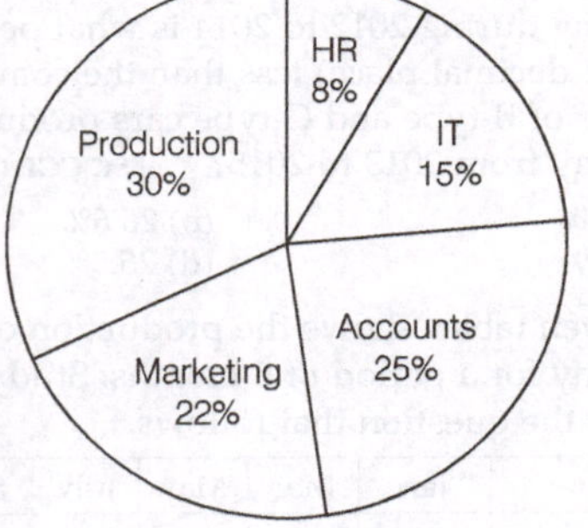

Departments	Male : Female
HR	3 : 5
IT	2 : 3
Accounts	3 : 7
Marketing	7 : 4
Production	5 : 3

What is the percentage of the number of employees in production department to the number of female employees of all the departments taken together? (correct to one decimal place) **SSC CGL (Tier-I) 12/9/2024 Shift-III**

(a) 64.3% (b) 50.7%
(c) 44.9% (d) 59.1%

69. Study the given chart and answer the question that follows.
The following chart shows the production of textbooks in thousands in the years 2018, 2020 and 2022 from the print houses A, B and C, respectively ....

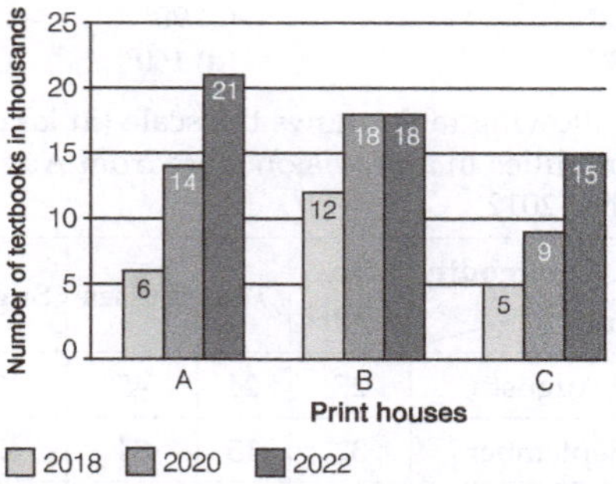

The ratio of textbooks produced by Print house B in the year 2018 to the textbooks produced by Print house C in the year 2020 is **SSC CGL (Tier-I) 12/9/2024 Shift-III**

(a) 4 : 5 (b) 3 : 4 (c) 4 : 3 (d) 2 : 3

70. The table below shows the production of three types of cars (A, B and C) manufactured (in thousands) by an automobile company over the years.

Year	A	B	C
2012	1750	1880	1900
2013	1800	2950	2070
2014	2950	3020	3150
2015	3100	3240	3290

The average number of A-type cars produced by the company during 2012 to 2014 is what percent (rounded off to the 1 decimal place) less than the combined average number of B-type and C-type cars produced by the company from 2013 to 2015? **SSC CGL (Tier-I) 12/9/2024 Shift-III**

(a) 36.6% (b) 26.6%
(c) 28.4% (d) 25.5%

71. The given tables shows the production of iron rods by a company for a period of 6 months. Study the table and answer the question that follows.

Month	Jan	Mar	May	July	Sep	Nov
Produ-ction	60	75	45	85	90	108

What is the ratio of the month having the highest production to the month having the least production? **SSC CGL (Tier-I) 12/9/2024 Shift-II**

(a) 9 : 5 (b) 12 : 5
(c) 1 : 2 (d) 5 : 12

72. The given pie-chart shows the percentage distribution of 20000 employees in a company.

Percentage distribution of employees in different department of a company

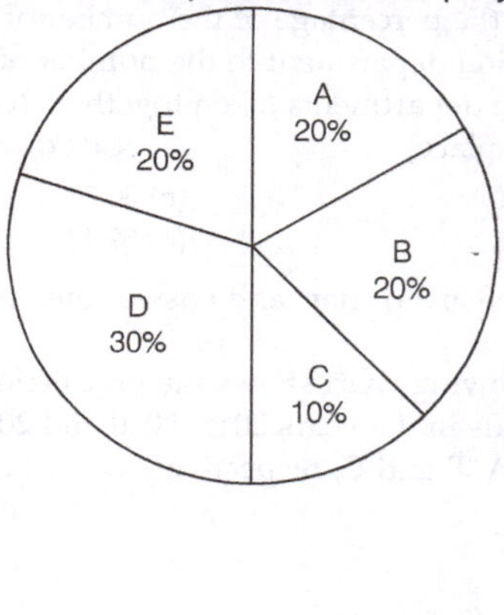

If 30% of the employees in department D are females, then how many male employees are there in that department? **SSC CGL (Tier-I) 12/9/2024 Shift-II**

(a) 4200 (b) 4500
(c) 5000 (d) 4000

73. The following pie-chart shows the study time of different subjects of a student in a day. Study the pie-chart and answer the question

Percentage distribution of study-time of different subjects

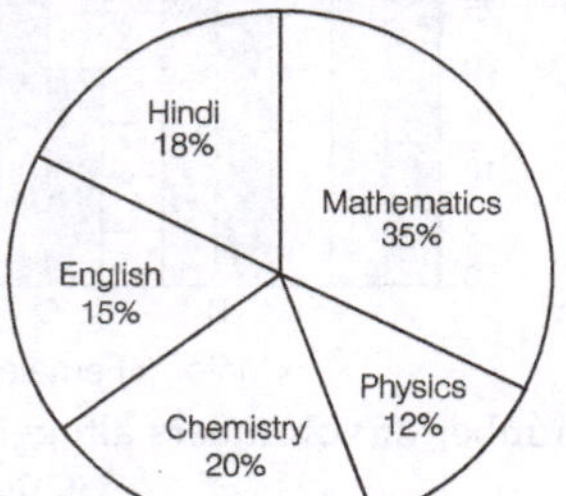

If the student studied English for 3 h, then he studied Mathematics for **SSC CGL (Tier-I) 12/9/2024 Shift-II**

(a) 2 h (b) 1 h
(c) 7 h (d) 5 h

74. The given table shows the number of soaps sold by four different companies in 4 different months.

Company \ Month	May	June	July	August
P	1924	1780	1820	1490
Q	1540	1245	1648	2450
R	2035	1485	1350	1650
S	1736	1855	1470	1180

The total number of soaps sold by Companies Q and S together in May, is what percentage more than the number of soaps sold by Company P in July? **SSC CGL (Tier-I) 12/9/2024 Shift-I**

(a) 75% (b) 90%
(c) 65% (d) 80%

75. Study the given pie-chart carefully and answer the question that follows. The given pie-chart shows the number of successful start-ups in different sectors in a particular year.

Start-ups in the different sectors

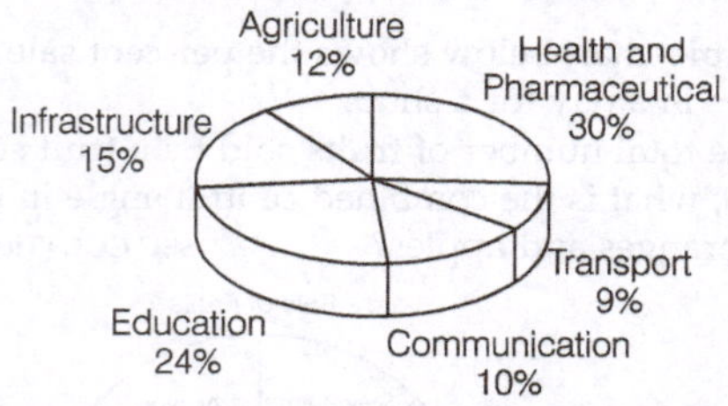

If the total number of successful start-ups is 2910, then find the number of start-ups in the education and agriculture sectors. (Neglect the decimal part.) **SSC CGL (Tier-I) 12/9/2024 Shift-I**

(a) 698 (b) 1048
(c) 1074 (d) 1047

76. The given table shows the number of banans produced by five farms over 4 years.

Year	Farm				
	L	M	N	O	P
2020	17500	14180	16300	17405	15805
2021	11200	13900	14600	15304	16207
2022	12300	17652	14800	15150	16404
2023	14650	15558	17465	14185	15450

What is the respectivce ratio of the dozens of bananas produced by farm M to farm P in the year 2022?

SSC CGL (Tier-I) 11/9/2024 Shift-III

(a) 1471 : 1367 (b) 1230 : 1331 (c) 1367 : 1471 (d) 1331 : 1230

77. The percentage distribution of expenditure over various items of Saloni's monthly income is given in the following table. Study the table carefully and answer the question that follows.

Item	Rent	Food	Education	Bills	Miscellaneous
Percentage distribution	30%	20%	25%	20%	5%

If Saloni's monthly income is ₹ 75000, how much money (in ₹) does she spend on rent and education?

SSC CGL (Tier-I) 11/9/2024 Shift-III

(a) 42150 (b) 43250 (c) 40150 (d) 41250

78. The following bar graph shows the circulation growth of a magazine ABC from July 2022 to December 2022.

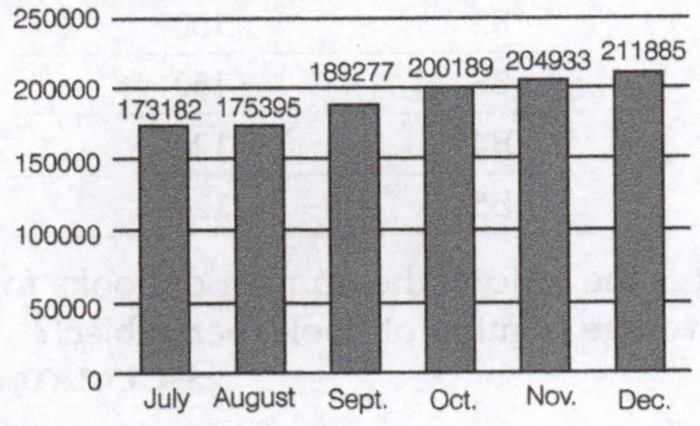

During October to December there was an even growth rate, the average of which, is (correct up to one decimal place).

SSC CGL (Tier-I) 11/9/2024 Shift-II

(a) 3.2% (b) 2.4%
(c) 2.9% (d) 3.8%

79. The following table shows the sales of cars of five manufactures from 2016 to 2020.
(All the figures are in hundreds)

Manufacturer	2016	2017	2018	2019	2020
M_1	180	190	200	210	220
M_2	160	170	180	190	200
M_3	190	200	210	220	230
M_4	200	210	220	230	240
M_5	210	220	230	240	250

What is the difference between the total number of sales of manufacturer M_2 and the total number of sales of manufacturer M_4 during the years 2016 to 2019?

SSC CGL (Tier-I) 11/9/2024 Shift-II

(a) 12000 (b) 18000
(c) 14000 (d) 16000

80. The following table shows scores in different subjects obtained by Akshay in school. Study the table and answer the question that follows.

Subject	Marks obtained	Total Marks
English	73	100
Hindi	56	80
Science	45	75
Mathematics	90	125
IT	45	60

In which subject did he score the highest marks (in %)?

SSC CGL (Tier-I) 11/9/2024 Shift-II

(a) IT (b) English
(c) Hindi (d) Mathematics

81. Five different companies, P, Q, R, S and T, manufacture plastic and wooden bats. These bats are labelled as Brand A or Brand B. The given table shows the number of wooden bats as a percentage of the total bats manufactured by each company. It also shows the ratio of plastic bats labelled as Brand A to Brand B. Each company manufactures 100000 bats. Study the table carefully and answer the question that follows.

Company	Wooden bats	Brand A : Brand B
P	65%	3:7
Q	70%	7:8
R	60%	19:6
S	70%	7:8
T	50%	2:3

Taking all companies together, how many plastic bats of Brand B have been manufactured?

SSC CGL (Tier-I) 11/9/2024 Shift-II

(a) 86100 (b) 96100
(c) 90500 (d) 80500

82. The bar graph below shows the production of coffee (in lakh tons) by four companies *A, B, C* and *D* over a period of four years from 2010 to 2013. Study the graph and answer the question that follows.

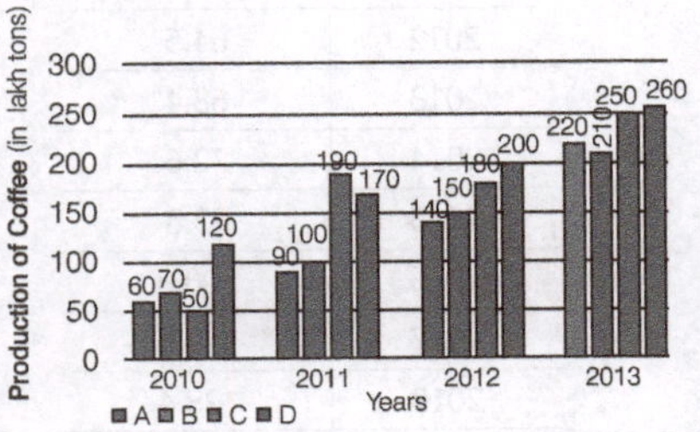

The combined average production for four years of companies A and C is what percentage (rounded off to 2 decimal places) more/less than the combined average production for four years of companies B and D?

SSC CGL (Tier-I) 11/9/2024 Shift-I

(a) Less, 7.81% (b) More, 10.51%
(c) More, 7.81% (d) Less, 10.51%

83. The following pie-chart shows the distribution of the percentage of students in various courses at the university. The total number of students (boys and girls only) in the university is 7000.

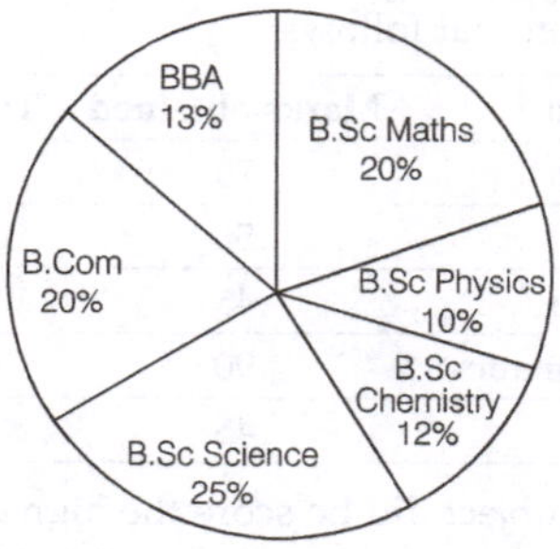

In B.Com, there are 60% girls and in B.Sc. Science, there are 40% boys. The total number of girls who took admission in B.Sc Science and B.Com courses is what percentage of the total students admitted to the university?

SSC CGL (Tier-I) 11/9/2024 Shift-I

(a) 25% (b) 29%
(c) 23% (d) 27%

84. The table below shows incomes (in rupees) earned by five employees of a company during the month of March 2019 and the income sources.

Source/Name of Employee	Reeta	Seeta	Geeta	Neeta	Aneeta
Overtime	2500	2800	2300	2200	2600
Arrears	4500	4800	4900	5300	5600
Bonus	2300	2100	2500	2700	2800
Salary	24000	30000	29000	32000	34000

The total amount of arrears paid by the company during the given period is what percentage of the total amount of bonus paid during the given period?

SSC CGL (Tier-I) 10/9/2024 Shift-III

(a) 302.42% (b) 402.42%
(c) 102.42% (d) 202.42%

85. Study the given table and answer the question that follow. The following table show the population of a city at the end of the years mentioned.

Year	Population
2012	64.5
2013	68.4
2014	72.6
2015	83.8
2016	100.6
2017	112.8
2018	128.4
2019	134.6
2020	156.8
2021	176.4

Which of the following years has the highest rate of increase compared to the previous year?

SSC CGL (Tier-I) 10/9/2024 Shift-III

(a) 2019 (b) 2018 (c) 2015 (d) 2016

86. The pie-chart given below shows the number of hours spent by a student for different activities on a working day. The percentage of hours spent at school in a day is …… .

SSC CGL (Tier-I) 10/9/2024 Shift-III

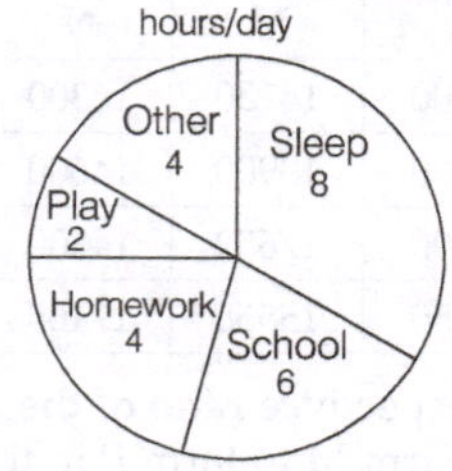

(a) 25% (b) 35%
(c) 40% (d) 30%

87. Akshay purchased pens and notebooks from a shop for a total sum of ₹180. From the following data, what is the value of 'X'?

Items	Price per unit (in ₹)	Quantity
Pens	10	X
Notebooks	20	6

SSC CGL (Tier-I) 10/9/2024 Shift-II

(a) 4 (b) 6
(c) 5 (d) 7

88. The given table shows the number of books on different subjects.

Subjects	Number of books
B1	120
B2	150
B3	150
B4	120
B5	120

What is the ratio of the number of books for subject B1 to the average number of books per subject?

SSC CGL (Tier-I) 10/9/2024 Shift-II

(a) 3 : 5 (b) 10 : 11
(c) 4 : 5 (d) 2 : 5

89. The given bar-graph shows the production of bikes by a company (in thousands) over the years.

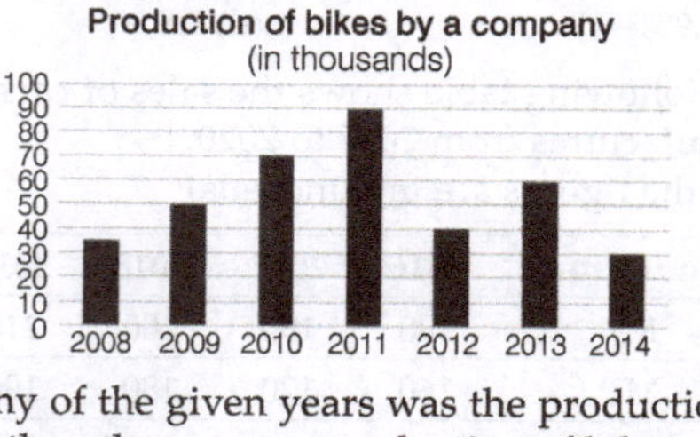

In how many of the given years was the production of bikes more than the average production of bikes over the years?

SSC CGL (Tier-I) 10/9/2024 Shift-II

(a) 1 yr (b) 2 yr
(c) 3 yr (d) 4 yr

90. Study the given table and answer the question that follows.
The given table shows the production of three types of cars (A, B and C) manufactured (in thousands) by an automobile company over the years.

Year	A	B	C
2015	840	680	890
2016	900	750	960
2017	760	620	1000
2018	800	540	1200

For all the years from 2015 to 2018, the average production of B-type cars is how much less (in thousands) than that of the combined average production of A-type and C-type cars? **SSC CGL (Tier-I) 10/9/2024 Shift-I**

(a) 238.5
(b) 271.25
(c) 314.75
(d) 284.55

91. The bar graph given below shows the sales of books from six schools during two consecutive years, 2013 and 2014.

What percentage of the average sales of the schools A, B and C in 2014 is the average sales of schools A, C and F in 2013? **SSC CGL (Tier-I) 10/9/2024 Shift-I**

(a) 81.08%
(b) 81%
(c) 80%
(d) 80.08%

92. The following table represents the total number of research scholars and the respective number of female research scholars in various departments of a university. Study the table carefully and answer the question that follows.

Department	Total number of research scholars	Number of female research scholars
Physics	35	12
Chemistry	40	28
Mathematics	18	4
Statistics	12	3

What is the ratio of male research scholars in Mathematics to Statistics? **SSC CGL (Tier-I) 10/9/2024 Shift-I**

(a) 14 : 9
(b) 7 : 6
(c) 6 : 7
(d) 9 : 14

93. Study the given table and answer the question that follows. The given table shows the production of T-shirts by four companies i.e., C_1, C_2, C_3 and C_4 over the four years.

Year	Production (in thousands)			
	C_1	C_2	C_3	C_4
2019	243	244	244	240
2020	248	239	236	230
2021	232	240	235	248
2022	242	244	230	242

Which company had the maximum average production of T-shirts during these four years? **SSC CGL (Tier-I) 9/9/2024 Shift-III**

(a) C_1
(b) C_3
(c) C_2
(d) C_4

94. The given table shows the number of pages printed by four printers in the three days.

Days	Printers			
	L	M	N	O
Friday	10230	9580	7560	9600
Saturday	8540	11230	6580	7890
Sunday	9235	8264	7546	10325

If the total number of pages printed by all the given printers together on Wednesday was 15% more than the total number of pages printed by all the given printers together on Saturday, what was the total number of pages printed by all the given printers together on Wednesday? **SSC CGL (Tier-I) 9/9/2024 Shift-III**

(a) 38450 (b) 42577 (c) 40263 (d) 39376

95. The following table shows the sale (in thousands) of different types of helmets by a shop over the given years.

Types of Helmet/Year	1998	1999	2000	2001	2002
A	78	45	56	63	88
B	58	64	78	60	68
C	46	54	58	64	68
D	76	65	72	78	82
E	87	66	74	80	84

What was the percentage increase in the sale of Helmets C in 2002 as compared to that in 1999? **SSC CGL (Tier-I) 9/9/2024 Shift-III**

(a) 25.93% (b) 26.39% (c) 28.26% (d) 27.62%

96. The monthly wages (in ₹) of three mess workers, Rahul, Sunil and Vipin, of a boy's hostel for three months are given in the following table. Study the table carefully and answer the question given below.

Mess workers/Month	October	November	December
Rahul	10800	11500	12000
Sunil	10000	10500	11500
Vipin	10400	11600	12200

In November, the wages of Sunil is what percentage of the wages of Rahul? (Correct up to two decimal places.) **SSC CGL (Tier-I) 9/9/2024 Shift-II**

(a) 90.23%
(b) 89.30%
(c) 88.23%
(d) 91.30%

97. The given table shows the percentage of marks obtained by three students in three different subjects in an institute. (maximum marks are given in brackets)

Subject/ Student	History (175)	Geography (200)	Botany (125)
Ram	54	87	71
Mohan	51	79	78
Shyam	75	49	76

If in order to pass the exam, a maximum of 105 marks are needed in History, how many students pass in the exam? **SSC CGL (Tier-I) 9/9/2024 Shift-I**

(a) 3 (b) 1 (c) 0 (d) 2

98. The following table shows the total candidates appeared and number of candidates present, in different exam centres – P, Q and R.
Study the table and answer the question that follows.

Year	P		Q		R	
	Total	Present	Total	Present	Total	Present
2016	45	42	56	45	55	50
2017	50	45	75	55	45	40
2018	64	60	65	45	65	55
2019	80	69	84	72	70	62
2020	55	44	80	66	90	85

'Total' denotes total candidates applied for the centre, 'Present' denotes the candidates appeared.
In which year was the number of absentees the second highest in total of all centres? **SSC CGL (Tier-I) 9/9/2024 Shift-I**

(a) 2018 (b) 2017 (c) 2020 (d) 2019

99. Read the given information and answer the question that follows.
The following table gives the percentage of marks obtained by seven students in six different subjects in an examination. The number in the brackets give the maximum marks in each subject.

Students	Subject (Max. Marks)					
	Maths	Chemistry	Physics	Geography	History	Computer Science
	(150)	(130)	(120)	(100)	(60)	(40)
Ayush	90	50	90	60	70	80
Aman	100	80	80	40	80	70
Sajal	90	60	70	70	90	70
Rohit	80	65	80	80	60	60
Muskan	80	65	85	95	50	90
Tanvi	70	75	65	85	40	60
Tarun	65	35	50	77	80	80

If someone secured all the highest scores that have been obtained by some students or the other in the six subjects as given in the table above, which would be the exact overall percentage score obtained by that student? **SSC CGL (Tier-I) 9/9/2024 Shift-I**

(a) $91\frac{1}{6}\%$ (b) 95.16% (c) 91% (d) $90\frac{5}{6}\%$

100. The following table shows the marks (out of 100) obtained by five students in five different subjects.

Student/ Subject	Maths	Physics	Chemistry	English	Physical Education
Tarun	65	80	75	85	90
Rohit	69	76	80	88	94
Mohit	73	84	77	90	95
Shobhit	76	85	76	86	78
Sumit	90	88	78	82	68

Who obtained 79% marks in all the subjects taken together? **SSC CGL (Tier-I) 9/9/2024 Shift-I**

(a) Sumit (b) Mohit
(c) Rohit (d) Tarun

SSC CGL 2023 (Tier I & II)

101. The following pie-charts show the data of the number of appeared and passed students of class 12 in sections A, B, C, D and E. **SSC CGL (Tier-I) 27/07/2023 Shift-III**

Appeared students = 1800

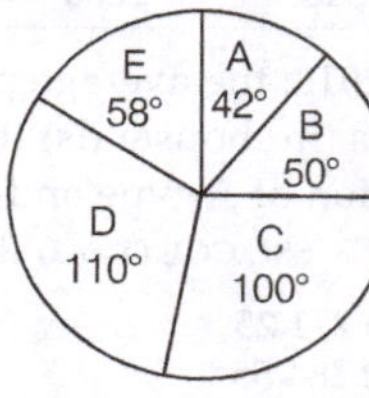

Passed students = 800

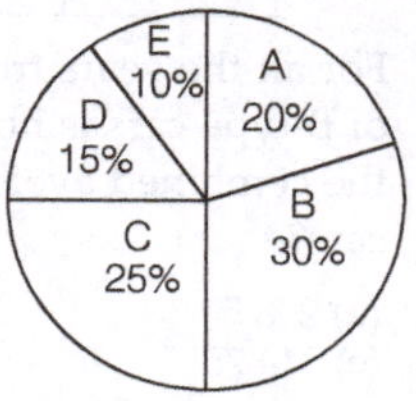

How many students failed in Section C?
(a) 250 (b) 200
(c) 300 (d) 400

102. The distribution of monthly expenditure of Ramesh on various items is shown in the following pie-chart.

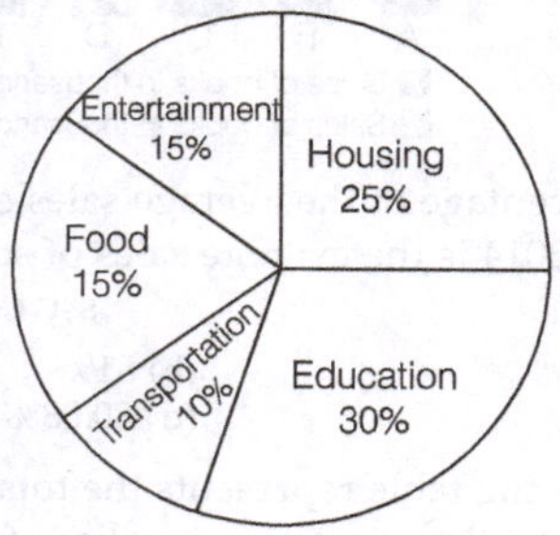

If the monthly income of Ramesh is ₹ 45000, then find his total monthly expenditure (in ₹) on housing and transportation. **SSC CGL (Tier-I) 27/07/2023 Shift-III**

(a) 16800 (b) 15750
(c) 11250 (d) 13500

103. The following shows the number of delivery partners (in thousands) who joined five difference companies during six different years.

Years	Companies				
	Emazon	Clipkart	Twiggy	Tomato	Pyatra
2016	2.4	4.5	1.2	0.9	4.2
2017	1.8	5.4	1.5	1.2	5.6
2018	3.2	7.2	2.4	2.1	6.3
2019	3.9	5.6	2.8	2.7	6.5
2020	4.2	6.4	3.2	3.3	7.0
2021	5.0	7.2	3.6	3.6	7.2

Find the ratio of the number of delivery partners who joined Clipkart (in 2019 and 2020) to the number of delivery partners who joined Tomato (in 2019 and 2020). **SSC CGL (Tier-I) 27/07/2023 Shift-II**

(a) 4 : 3
(b) 3 : 2
(c) 1 : 2
(d) 2 : 1

104. Study the graph carefully.

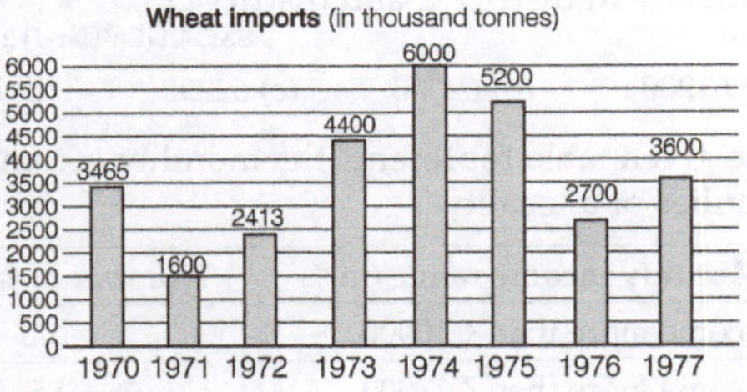

The imports in 1974 were approximately how many times that of the year 1971? **SSC CGL (Tier-I) 27/07/2023 Shift-I**

(a) 3.75 (b) 3 (c) 2.5 (d) 3.5

105. The following data shows the number of boys and girls in Class VII, Class VIII, Class IX and Class X of a school. Study the data and answer the question. **SSC CGL (Tier-I) 27/07/2023 Shift-I**

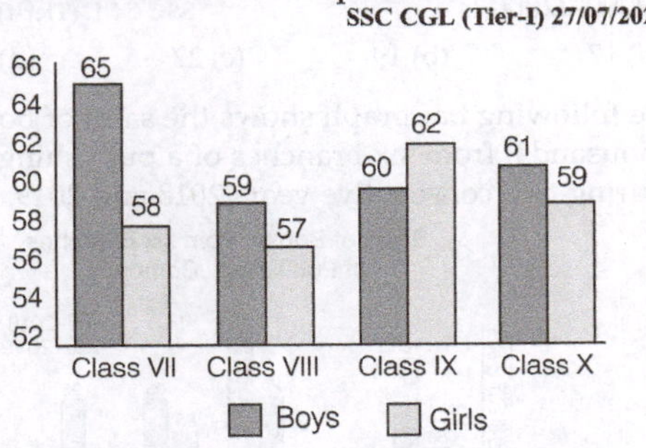

Which class has the maximum number of students?

(a) Class VII (b) Class IX
(c) Class X (d) Class VIII

106. Study the given table and answer the question that follows. The table shows the marks distribution among the students in a class.

Marks	Number of Students
Less than 10	2
Less than 20	5
Less than 30	6
Less than 40	8
Less than 50	10

How many students scored more than 40 marks? **SSC CGL (Tier-I) 26/07/2023 Shift-IV**

(a) 2 (b) 4 (c) 5 (d) 3

107. Study the given bar-chart and answer the question that follows. The bar-chart shows the production of maize by a state (in 1000 tonnes) over the years.

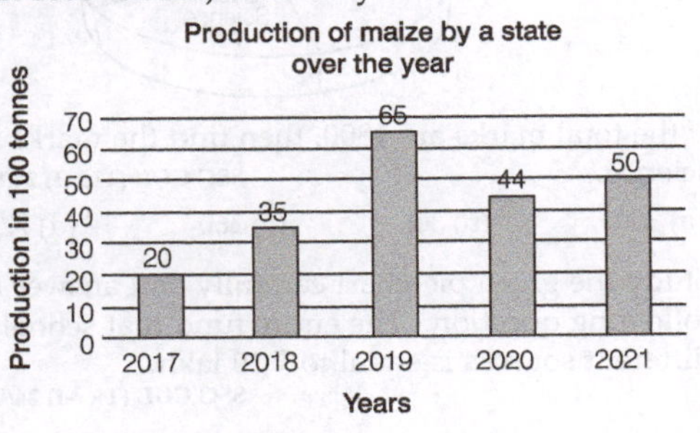

What was the percentage increase in the production of maize in 2019 compared to that in 2017? **SSC CGL (Tier-I) 26/07/2023 Shift-III**

(a) 220% (b) 225% (c) 230% (d) 200%

108. Study the given table and answer the question that follows. The table gives the number of graduate students enrolled in 4 different colleges, A, B, C and D in a city over the years 2010 to 2014 and also the number of students who passed in the final examination during these years.

Year	2010	2010	2011	2011	2012	2012	2013	2013	2014	2014
College	Enrolled	Pass	Enrolled	Pass	Enrolled	Pass	Enrolled	Pass	Enrolled	Pass
A	680	620	600	560	720	700	800	760	750	700
B	550	530	450	420	600	550	650	620	700	680
C	480	450	520	500	580	550	620	600	720	700
D	710	650	750	710	680	640	720	690	740	710

Find the percentage of students who passed from college B for all the years put together to the number of students from college B during all the years (rounded to 2 decimals). **SSC CGL (Tier-I) 26/07/2023 Shift-III**

(a) 94.92% (b) 94.98% (c) 94.95% (d) 94.96%

109. The following graph shows the number of illiterates in different states of a country in the year 2021.

Total Illiterates in 4 States = 450000

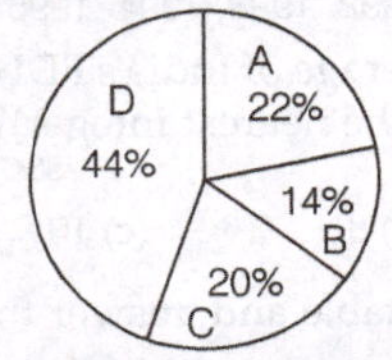

Number of Illiterates in different in 2021

What is the percentage of the total number of illiterates in A, B and C to the illiterates in D in 2021? **SSC CGL (Tier-I) 26/07/2023 Shift-III**

(a) 126.78% (b) 127.27%
(c) 150.57% (d) 110.24%

110. The following table shows the percentage distribution of employees in five different department 1-5 in a company during the years 2020 and 2021.

The total number of employees in 2020 and 2021 is 1200 and 1600, respectively.

Year	Departments				
	Department 1	Department 2	Department 3	Department 4	Department 5
2020	24	21	20	19	16
2021	21	22	18	19	20

In which department is the variation in strength of employees maximum in 2021 in comparison to that in 2020? **SSC CGL (Tier-I) 26/07/2023 Shift-II**

(a) Department 1 (b) Department 4
(c) Department 5 (d) Department 2

111. The following table shows the percentage of population of five states below poverty line and the proportion of males and females below and above poverty line.

State	Percentage of Population Below Poverty Line	Proportion of Males and Females	
		Below Poverty Line	Above Poverty Line
		Males : Females	Males : Females
A	25%	7 : 3	1 : 5
B	13%	8 : 5	1 : 7
C	26%	9 : 4	2 : 11
D	11%	4 : 3	13 : 4
E	17%	5 : 9	3 : 2

If the population of State B and State C is 6000 each, then what is the total number of females below poverty line in these two states?
SSC CGL (Tier-I) 26/07/2023 Shift-I

(a) 720 (b) 780 (c) 740 (d) 750

112. The following bar-chart shows the trends of Foreign Direct Investment (FDI) into India from all over the world.

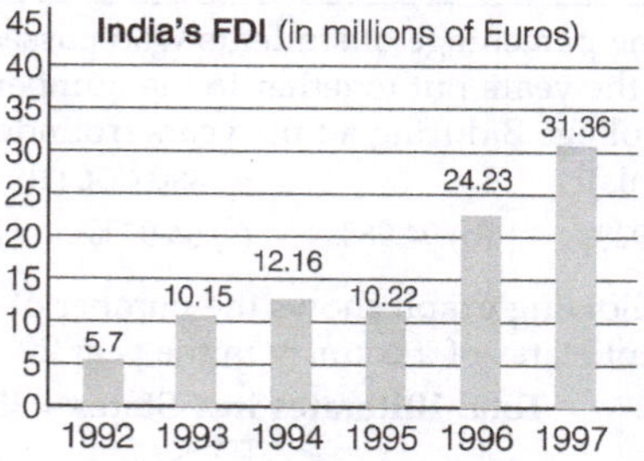

What was the average of India's FDI over the years 1992-1995 (rounded-off to the nearest integer)?
SSC CGL (Tier-I) 26/07/2023 Shift-I

(a) 7 (b) 8 (c) 10 (d) 9

113. Study the given table and answer the question that follows. The table represents the expenditure of a company (in thousand rupees) per annum over the given year.

Year	Expenditure			
	Salary	Transport	Interest	Tax
2018	200	90	3	80
2019	250	100	2.5	100
2020	300	120	3	70
2021	350	130	3.5	80

What is the average amount of salary per year, which the company has to pay during these four years?
SSC CGL (Tier-I) 25/07/2023 Shift-IV

(a) ₹ 280000 (b) ₹ 300000 (c) ₹ 200000 (d) ₹ 275000

114. The pie-chart below shows the distribution of female employees working in a company in five different districts (A, B, C, D and E).

Total number of female employees in five districts = 136000

Distribution of total number of female employees working in a company in five different districts

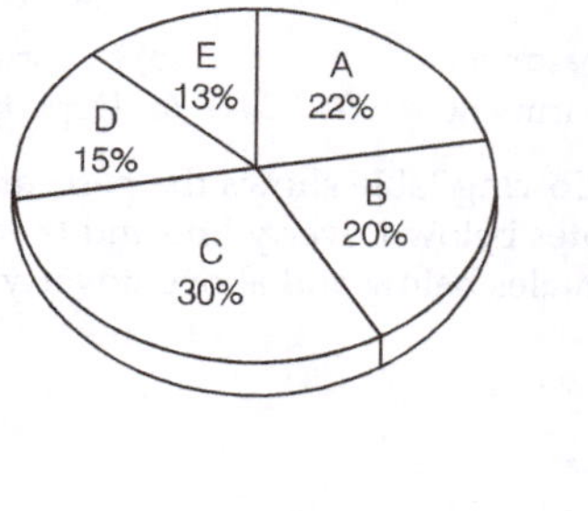

What is the total number of female employees working in a company in district C and district D?
SSC CGL (Tier-I) 25/07/2023 Shift-III

(a) 61200 (b) 62000 (c) 62290 (d) 61000

115. The given table represents the monthly income of 100 families of a locality

Monthly income range (in ₹)	Number of families
Income more than ₹ 10000	100
Income more than ₹ 13000	85
Income more than ₹ 16000	69
Income more than ₹ 19000	50
Income more than ₹ 22000	33
Income more than ₹ 25000	15

The number of families having income range (in ₹) 19000-22000 is
SSC CGL (Tier-I) 25/07/2023 Shift-II

(a) 17 (b) 19 (c) 22 (d) 24

116. The following bar graph shows the sales of books (in thousands) from six branches of a publishing company during two consecutive years 2018 and 2019.

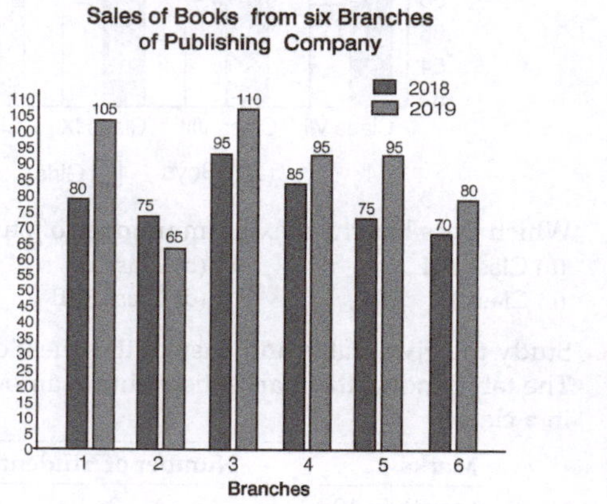

Total sales of 6th branch for both the years is what percentage of the total sales of 3rd branch for both the years? (rounded off to two decimal places)
SSC CGL (Tier-I) 25/07/2023 Shift-I

(a) 73.17% (b) 65.29%
(c) 68.25% (d) 62.23%

117. The given chart shows the marks scored by a class X student in different subject.

Class X marks of a student (Values are in Degree)

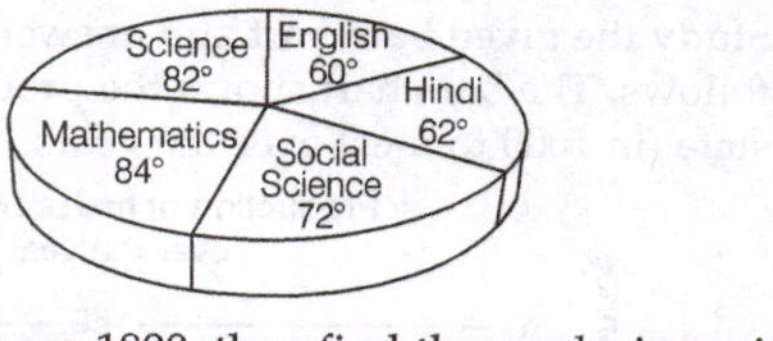

If the total marks are 1800, then find the marks in social science.
SSC CGL (Tier-I) 24/07/2023 Shift-IV

(a) 350 (b) 306 (c) 360 (d) 72

118. Study the given pie-chart carefully and answer the following question. The entire fund that school gets from different sources is equal to ₹ 10 lakh.
SSC CGL (Tier-I) 24/07/2023 Shift-IV

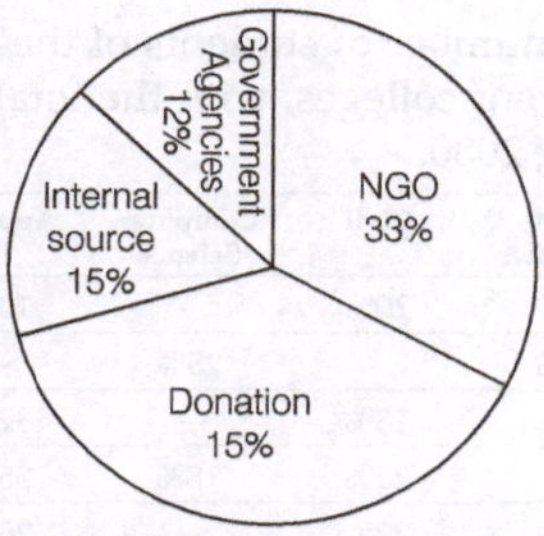

Source of Funds in School

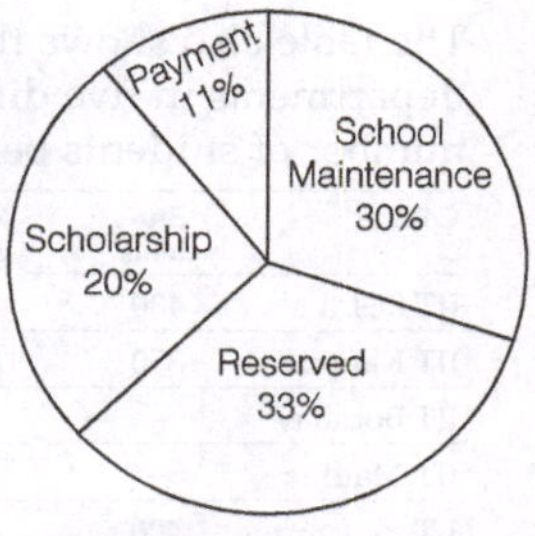

Uses of Funds by School

What is the total amount (in ₹) used by the school for the payment?

(a) 120000 (b) 310000 (c) 110000 (d) 210000

119. Study the given pie-chart and answer the question that follows.

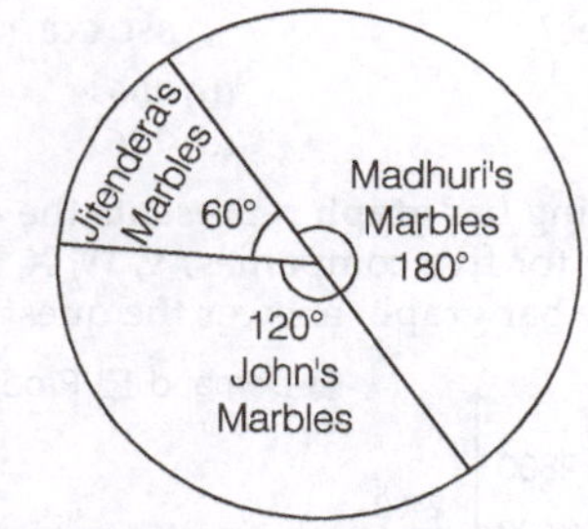

If the pie-chart shows the distribution of 36 marbles among 3 persons, then the number of marbles Madhuri SSC CGL (Tier-I) 24/07/2023 Shift-III

(a) 12 (b) 8 (c) 16 (d) 18

120. Study the given bar graph carefully and answer the following question. What is the difference between the average demand and the average production of the three companies taken together? **SSC CGL (Tier-I) 24/07/2023 Shift-III**

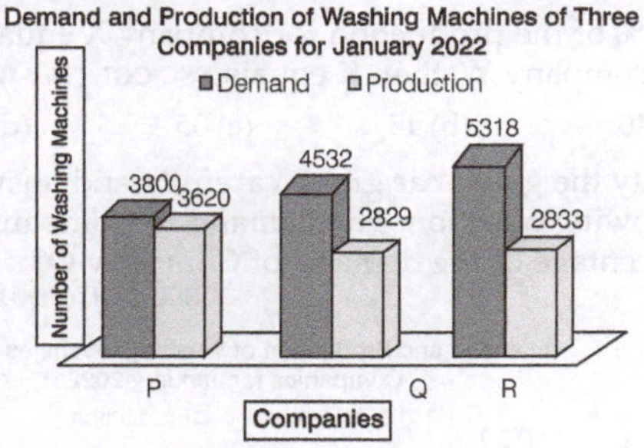

(a) 1272 (b) 1530 (c) 1850 (d) 1456

121. Study the given table and answer the question that follows. The table shows the number of students studying in six different classes of six different schools.

School	Class V	Class VI	Class VII	Class VIII	Class IX	Class X
P	152	160	145	156	147	144
Q	148	166	150	155	157	143
R	161	152	140	145	143	165
S	159	142	149	140	142	168
T	147	144	158	163	154	150
U	150	160	162	160	161	140
Total	917	924	904	919	904	910

What is the respective ratio of students studying in class IX of schools Q and R together to those studying in class VI of schools S and T together? **SSC CGL (Tier-I) 24/07/2023 Shift-II**

(a) 181 : 127 (b) 143 : 150 (c) 150 : 143 (d) 127 : 181

122. The number of students in different classes of a school is shown in the following bar graph.

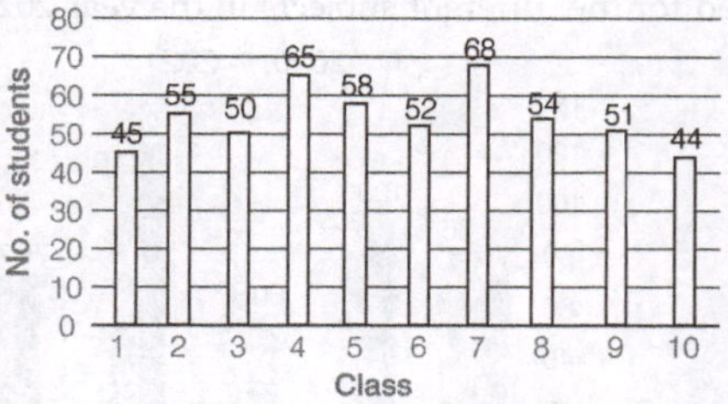

The maximum difference in the number of students in any two classes is what percentage of the number of students in Class 7 (correct to two decimal places)?

SSC CGL (Tier-I) 24/07/2023 Shift-I

(a) 35.29% (b) 34.29% (c) 33.48% (d) 36.48%

123. The following pie-chart represents the percentage distribution of girls in five girls' colleges A, B, C, D and E. The total number of girls in all the five colleges is 2500.

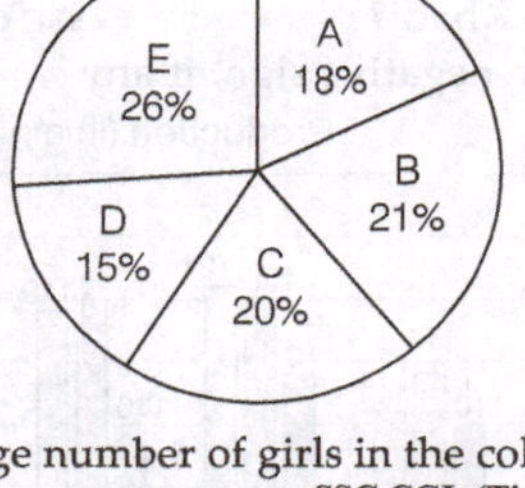

What is the average number of girls in the colleges C and E?

SSC CGL (Tier-I) 24/07/2023 Shift-I

(a) 500 (b) 650 (c) 700 (d) 575

124. Study the given data and answer the question that follows. Data regarding population of different states in the year 2015 is shown in the pie-chart and table.

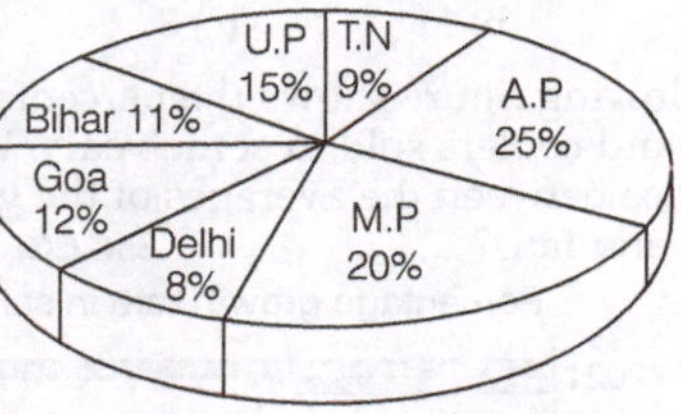

States	Sex and Literacy-wise Population Ratio			
	Sex		Literacy	
	M	F	Literate	Illiterate
AP	5	3	2	7
MP	3	1	1	4
Delhi	2	3	2	1
Goa	3	5	3	2
Bihar	3	4	4	1
UP	3	2	7	2
TN	3	4	9	4

If the total population of the given states is 315000, then what was the total number of illiterate people in Goa and MP? SSC CGL (Tier-I) 21/07/2023 Shift-III

(a) 65520 (b) 81900
(c) 120500 (d) 90870

125. The following bar diagram shows the number of students who opted for the different subjects in the year 2020 and 2021.

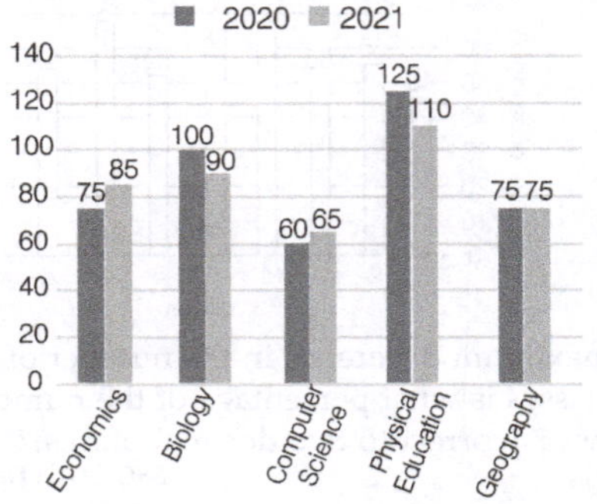

Out of all 5 subjects, what percentage (rounded up to two decimals) of students opted for Biology in 2021? SSC CGL (Tier-I) 21/07/2023 Shift-II

(a) 23.14% (b) 22.34% (c) 21.18% (d) 24.31%

126. What is the difference between the total production of Cotton and Khadi? SSC CGL (Tier-I) 21/07/2023 Shift-I

Note Ignore negative sign, if any

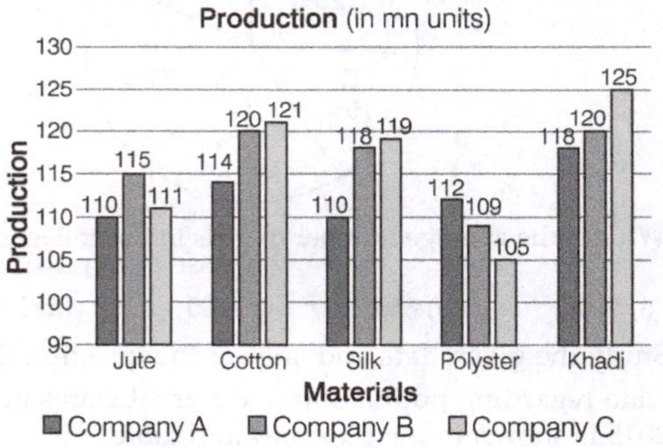

(a) 10 (b) 11 (c) 8 (d) 7

127. The following figure shows the percentage growth in units of fans and coolers sold in some years. What is the difference between the averages of the growth rate in coolers and fans? SSC CGL (Tier-I) 21/07/2023 Shift-I

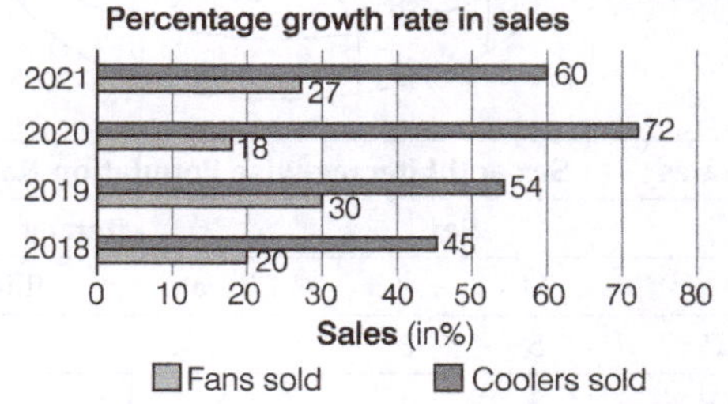

(a) 34% (b) 30% (c) 32% (d) 42%

128. Study the given table carefully and answer the following question.

The table shows the percentage of students of four departments - Mechanical, Civil, Computer Science and Applied - with each student being in only one department. The table also shows the number of students of these four departments in five different colleges, with the total number of students being 2080.

College	Students	Mechanical	Civil	Computer Science	Applied
IIT Delhi	430	–	20%	–	10%
IIT Kanpur	350	20%	–	25%	–
IIT Bombay	–	20%	18%	–	32%
IIT Madras	–	–	25%	18%	35%
IIT Guwahati	400	20%	22%	–	20%

If the number of students in IIT Bombay is 20% less than the number of students in IIT Madras, then what is the difference between the total number of students who study in the Applied department in these two colleges and that of the students who study in the Civil department in these two colleges? SSC CGL (Tier-I) 20/07/2023 Shift-IV

(a) 106 (b) 206
(c) 116 (d) 126

129. The following bar graph represents the demand and production for five companies, V, W, X, Y and Z. On the basis of the bar graph, answer the question.

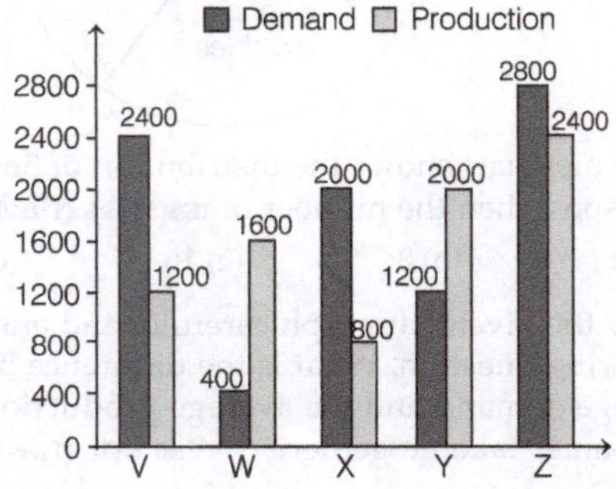

If K% of the production for company X equals the demand for company W, then K equals SSC CGL (Tier-I) 20/07/2023 Shift-III

(a) 40 (b) 45 (c) 35 (d) 50

130. Study the given bar graph carefully and answer the following question. The demand of Company P is what percentage of the demand of Company Q? SSC CGL (Tier-I) 20/07/2023 Shift-II

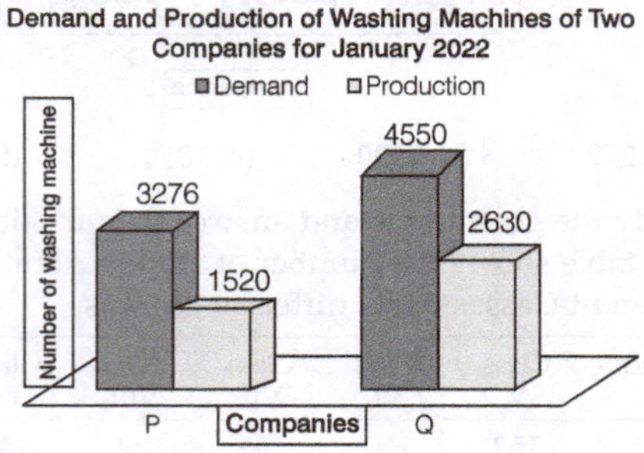

(a) 68% (b) 65%
(c) 70% (d) 72%

131. Study the given table and answer the question that follows.

The table shows the number of candidates who appeared (App), qualified (Qual) and were selected (Sel) in a competitive examination from four states Delhi, Goa, Karnataka and Maharashtra over the years 2012 to 2016.

Years	Delhi			Goa			Karnataka			Maharashtra		
	App	Qual	Sel	App	Qual	Sel	App	Qual	Sel	App	Qual	Sel
2012	8000	850	94	7800	810	82	7500	720	78	8200	680	85
2013	4800	500	48	7500	800	65	5600	620	85	6800	600	70
2014	9500	850	90	8800	920	86	7000	650	70	7800	720	84
2015	9000	800	70	7200	850	75	8500	950	80	5700	485	60
2016	7500	640	82	7400	560	70	4800	400	48	6500	525	65

The percentage of candidates that qualified from Goa over those that appeared from Goa is highest in the year ....

SSC CGL (Tier-I) 20/07/2023 Shift-I

(a) 2013 (b) 2014 (c) 2012 (d) 2015

132. Study the bar-graph carefully and answer the question that follows.

The following bar-graph shows the sale of Bluetooth earphones on online market places over the years.

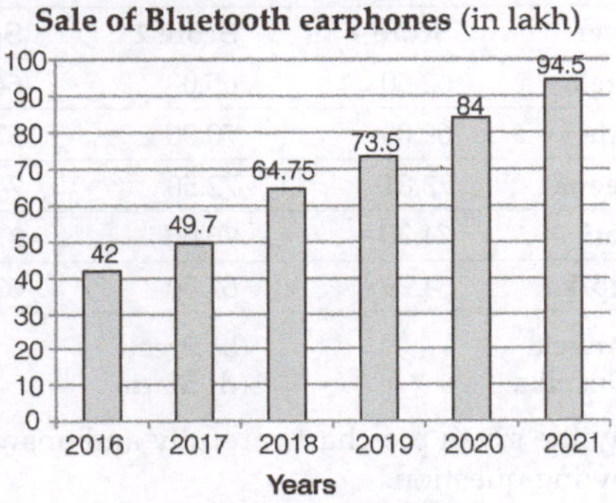

Find the approx percentage increase in the sale of earphones from 2017 to 2020. **SSC CGL (Tier-I) 20/07/2023 Shift-I**

(a) 69% (b) 57%
(c) 78% (d) 71%

133. Study the given bar graph carefully and answer the following question.

What is the ratio of the number of companies with more demand than production to the number of companies with more production than demand?

SSC CGL (Tier-I) 19/07/2023 Shift-IV

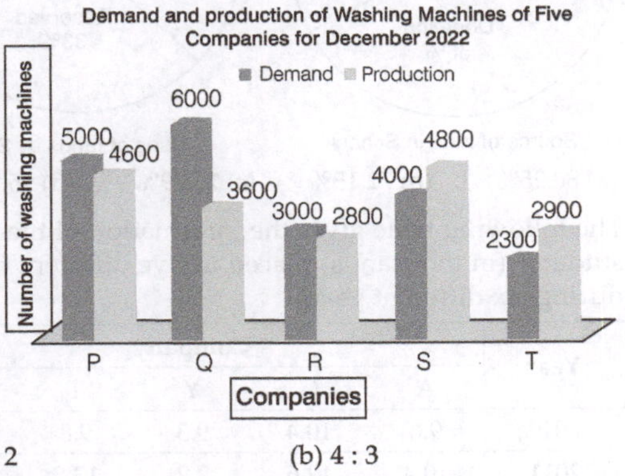

(a) 3 : 2 (b) 4 : 3
(c) 3 : 5 (d) 2 : 3

134. The following figure shows the different expenses that are incurred in manufacturing toys. If the total expenditure is ₹ 300000, then how much expenditure was incurred on Material Cost and Selling Expenses (in ₹)?

SSC CGL (Tier-I) 19/07/2023 Shift-IV

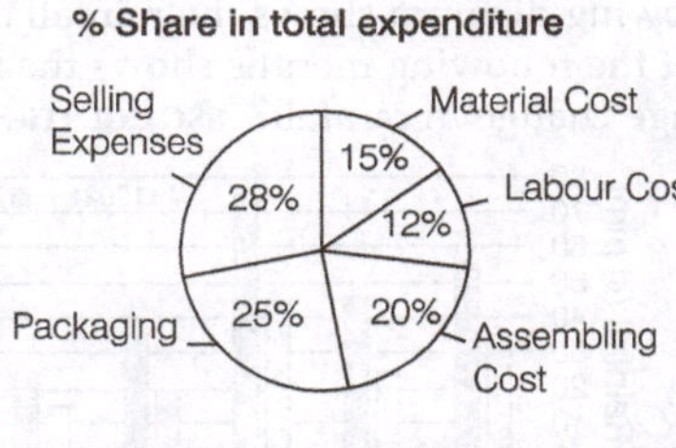

(a) 120000 (b) 115000 (c) 129000 (d) 84000

135. The wages (in ₹) earned by a labourer in twelve months of a year are shown in the following bar-graph.

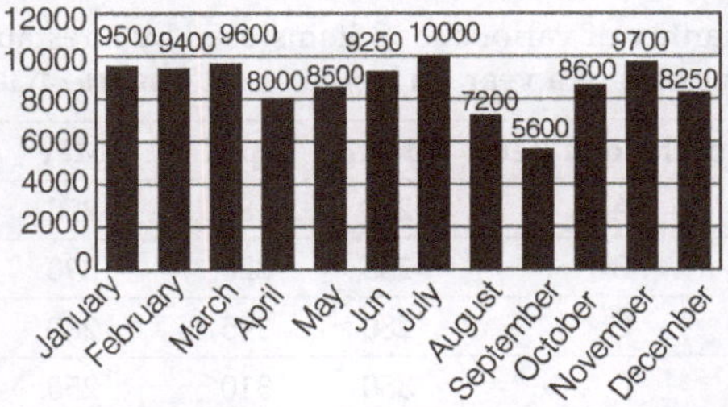

What is the average wage (in ₹) received by the labourer in the first five months of the year? **SSC CGL (Tier-I) 19/07/2023 Shift-II**

(a) 9300 (b) 9000 (c) 9100 (d) 9200

136. The following figure shows the scores of students in three tests organised by a coaching institution. Who scored the best on average? **SSC CGL (Tier-I) 19/07/2023 Shift-I**

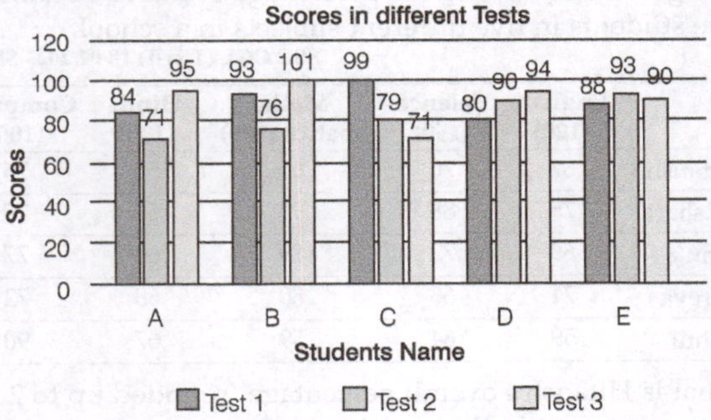

(a) D (b) C
(c) E (d) B

137. Study the given pie-chart and answer the question that follows.

The pie-chart displays the percentage of fruits sold (in kg) by a fruit seller in one month.

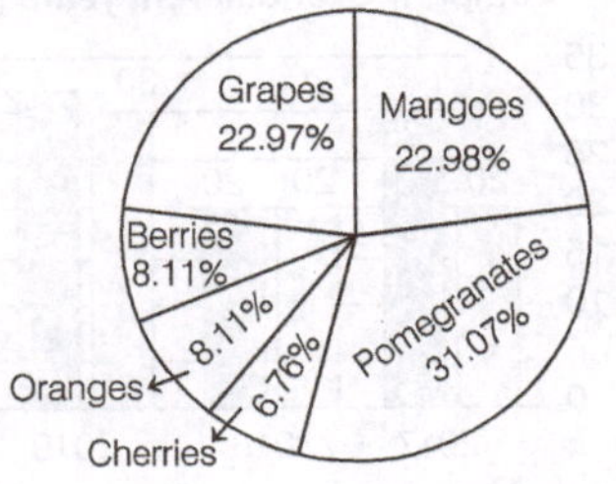

If the total fruits sold by a fruit seller in one month was 50000 kg, find the approximate difference of the quantity (in kg) of pomegranates and that of berries.

SSC CGL (Tier-I) 19/07/2023 Shift-I

(a) 11480 (b) 13535
(c) 21408 (d) 12465

138. The following diagram shows the rainfall over two years. Which of the following months shows the highest percentage change in rainfall? **SSC CGL (Tier-I) 18/07/2023 Shift-IV**

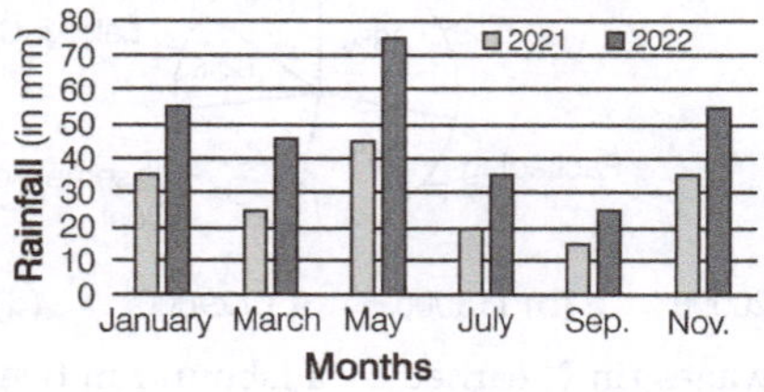

(a) March (b) January (c) May (d) September

139. Quantity of various food items used by a restaurent during 4 months of a year (in kg) **SSC CGL (Tier-I) 18/07/2023 Shift-IV**

Month/Food Item	March	April	May	June
A	220	180	270	320
B	255	320	390	420
C	280	295	280	315
D	350	310	250	280
E	308	340	350	365

What is the average of food item C used during all the 4 months together?

(a) 211.8 kg (b) 253.6 kg
(c) 303.7 kg (d) 292.5 kg

140. The given table shows the percentage of marks obtained by five students in five different subjects in a school. **SSC CGL (Tier-I) 18/07/2023 Shift-III**

	English (100)	Science (150)	Mathe matics (100)	Hindi (100)	Computer (100)
Hitansh	67	70	64	55	75
Akshara	75	88	95	60	75
Pihu	69	72	89	64	77
Shreya	71	66	80	68	72
Rahul	59	64	59	67	90

What is Hitansh's overall percentage (rounded up to 2 decimal places) in the examination?

(a) 64.89% (b) 75.11% (c) 66.55% (d) 65.31%

141. A toffee company prepares toffee of two different flavours X and Y. The production of two flavours over a period of 4 yrs is expressed in the bar graph given below.

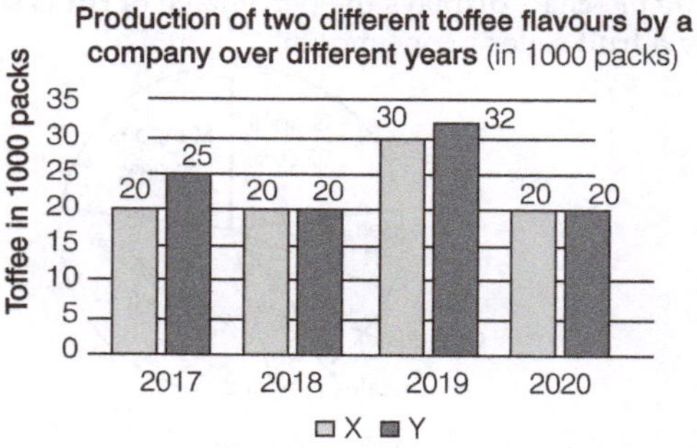

What is the difference between the average production of flavour X in 2017 and 2018 and the average production of flavour Y in 2019 and 2020? **SSC CGL (Tier-I) 18/07/2023 Shift-III**

(a) 6000 packs (b) 6400 packs
(c) 7500 packs (d) 7000 packs

142. Study the following table and answer the question below.

School name	Total number of students enrolled	Percentage of enrolled students who opted for Biology	Ratio of male to female students who opted for Biology
A	900	30%	7 : 8
B	400	38%	9 : 10
C	1000	24%	5 : 19
D	800	18%	5 : 7

What is the ratio of the total number of male students to that of female students who opted for Biology in schools A and D together? **SSC CGL (Tier-I) 18/07/2023 Shift-I**

(a) 38 : 31 (b) 21 : 38 (c) 31 : 28 (d) 31 : 38

143. The following table shows the scores of three attempts of Archery players in a tournament. The player scoring the highest average score was declared the best player. Who was the best player? **SSC CGL (Tier-I) 17/07/2023 Shift-IV**

Player	Score 1	Score 2	Score 3
Angela	62.50	65.00	64.50
Maria	69.05	70.00	67.52
Sareena	73.81	72.50	74.20
Preeti	74.30	75.00	77.50
Deepika	64.29	67.50	63.28

(a) Angela (b) Preeti
(c) Deepika (d) Maria

144. Study the given pie-chart carefully and answer the following question.
If scholarship has to be paid out of the donation fund, then what is the percentage of donation fund used for this purpose (rounded off to two decimal places)?
The entire fund that school gets from different sources is equal to ₹ 10 lakh. **SSC CGL (Tier-I) 17/07/2023 Shift-IV**

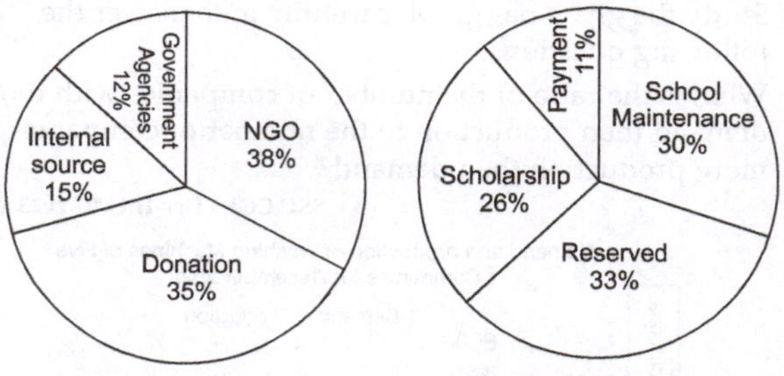

Source of fund in School Uses of funds by School

(a) 80.25% (b) 72.15% (c) 74.29% (d) 75.25%

145. The following table gives the information of the number of students (in thousands) placed in five different companies during six different years.

Year	Company				
	A	G	Y	T	F
2010	9.6	10.4	9.3	9.8	8.7
2011	10.4	12.6	7.2	13.8	6.2
2012	12.6	9.8	10.4	14.9	9.8
2013	16.8	15.4	11.4	16.3	11.3
2014	19.3	13.4	13.4	11.8	7.8
2015	18.7	16.7	12.7	15.7	13.7

What is the difference (in thousands) between the students placed in all companies in the year 2014 and 2012?

SSC CGL (Tier-I) 17/07/2023 Shift-III

(a) 9000 (b) 7800
(c) 8200 (d) 7500

146. Select the correct statement with respect to the below bar graph.

SSC CGL (Tier-I) 17/07/2023 Shift-I

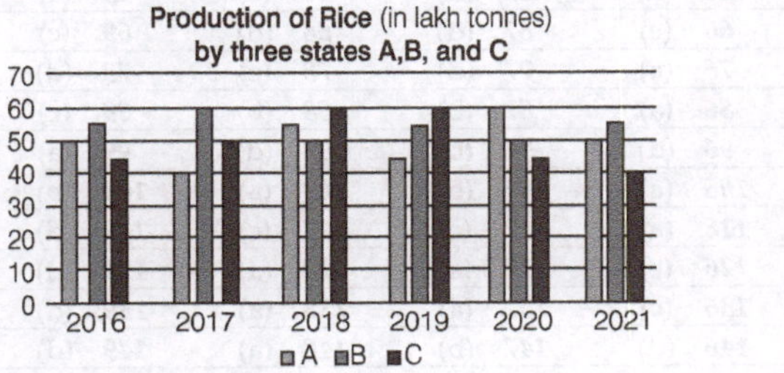

(a) Rice production by A in 2016 is less than the rice production by C in 2020.
(b) B produced more rice than A and C is 2018
(c) The highest production of rice was in the year 2017.
(d) Rice production by B in 2017 is equal to the rice production by A in 2020.

147. The following pie-chart shows the monthly sale of laptops of five companies A, B, C, D and E in a store.

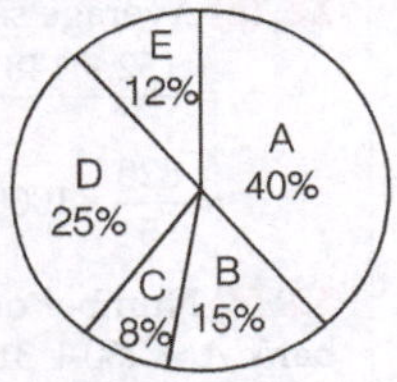

If 2500 laptops were sold by the store in a month, then what is the difference between the number of laptops sold of Company A and that of Company C?

SSC CGL (Tier-I) 14/07/2023 Shift-IV

(a) 650 (b) 800 (c) 700 (d) 750

148. The following table shows the number of sweets manufactured by six factories.

Year	Factory					
	P	Q	R	S	T	U
1996	196	145	254	169	291	220
1997	172	233	141	125	167	189
1998	178	240	150	130	177	192
1999	180	260	160	140	188	195

What is the respective ratio of sweets manufactured by factories P, Q and R together in the year 1998, to the sweets manufactured by factories S, T and U together in the same year ?

SSC CGL (Tier-I) 14/07/2023 Shift-IV

(a) 568 : 499 (b) 61 : 72 (c) 61 : 42 (d) 40 : 51

149. What is the central angle corresponding to the sector indicating the expenses incurred on Health?

SSC CGL (Tier-I) 14/07/2023 Shift-III

Amount spent on various expenses (in ₹)

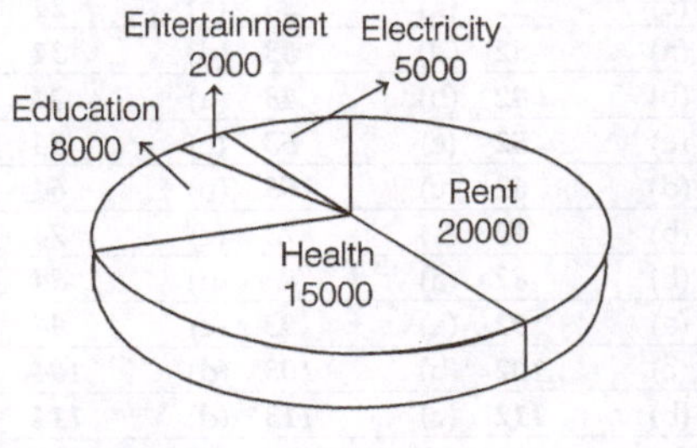

(a) 72° (b) 54°
(c) 110° (d) 108°

150. Study the given pie chart and answer the question that follows.

Population of six villages in 2020

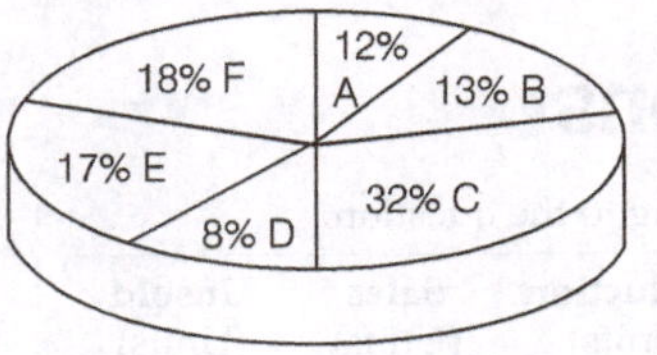

The population of village D in 2020 was 10500. What was the population of village A in 2020? Total population of these six villages is 100%.

SSC CGL (Tier-I) 14/07/2023 Shift-II

(a) 15570
(b) 17550
(c) 15750
(d) 7875

151. The following bar chart represents the gross amount (in ₹ crores) and total cost (in ₹ crores) of a firm.

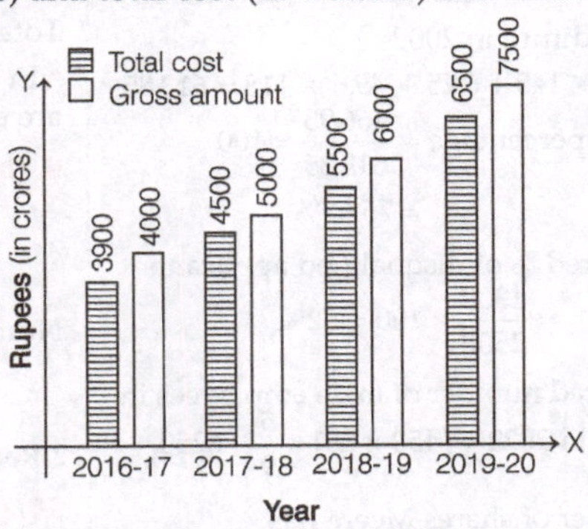

In order to make a profit of 25%, what should be gross amount have been (in ₹ crores) in 2019-2020, if the total cost remained the same?

SSC CGL (Tier-I) 14/07/2023 Shift-I

(a) 8250 (b) 8125
(c) 7800 (d) 8000

Right Answers

1 (b)	2 (c)	3 (d)	4 (c)	5 (d)	6 (c)	7 (a)	8 (d)	9 (b)	10 (c)
11 (a)	12 (a)	13 (d)	14 (b)	15 (c)	16 (a)	17 (c)	18 (d)	19 (b)	20 (c)
21 (c)	22 (a)	23 (a)	24 (a)	25 (a)	26 (c)	27 (a)	28 (b)	29 (c)	30 (b)
31 (a)	32 (d)	33 (d)	34 (d)	35 (a)	36 (c)	37 (c)	38 (c)	39 (a)	40 (b)
41 (b)	42 (b)	43 (a)	44 (a)	45 (d)	46 (d)	47 (d)	48 (d)	49 (c)	50 (d)
51 (c)	52 (c)	53 (c)	54 (c)	55 (b)	56 (d)	57 (d)	58 (c)	59 (a)	60 (c)
61 (d)	62 (c)	63 (b)	64 (d)	65 (a)	66 (c)	67 (d)	68 (d)	69 (c)	70 (b)
71 (b)	72 (a)	73 (c)	74 (d)	75 (d)	76 (a)	77 (d)	78 (c)	79 (d)	80 (a)
81 (b)	82 (a)	83 (d)	84 (d)	85 (d)	86 (a)	87 (b)	88 (b)	89 (c)	90 (b)
91 (a)	92 (a)	93 (c)	94 (d)	95 (a)	96 (d)	97 (b)	98 (d)	99 (a)	100 (d)
101 (c)	102 (b)	103 (d)	104 (a)	105 (a)	106 (a)	107 (b)	108 (a)	109 (b)	110 (c)
111 (b)	112 (c)	113 (d)	114 (a)	115 (a)	116 (a)	117 (c)	118 (c)	119 (d)	120 (d)
121 (c)	122 (a)	123 (d)	124 (a)	125 (c)	126 (c)	127 (a)	128 (a)	129 (d)	130 (d)
131 (d)	132 (a)	133 (a)	134 (c)	135 (b)	136 (c)	137 (a)	138 (a)	139 (d)	140 (c)
141 (a)	142 (d)	143 (b)	144 (c)	145 (c)	146 (d)	147 (b)	148 (a)	149 (d)	150 (c)
151 (b)									

Solutions

1. (b) According to the question,

Item	Production (Units)	Sales (Units)	Unsold (Units)
Plate	252	190	62
Bowl	356	307	49
Spoon	185	133	52
Pipe	220	155	65
Holder	458	419	39

∴ Least number of unsold items 'Holder'.

2. (c) Total expenditure in 2006

$= 225 + 98 + 4.25 + 29.7 + 110 = 466.95$

Total expenditure in 2009

$= 295 + 145 + 6.25 + 49.6 + 118 = 613.85$

∴ Required percentage $= \frac{466.95}{613.85} \times 100$

$= 76.07\%$

3. (d) Required % of disqualified applicants

$= \frac{1300}{2500} \times 100 = 52\%$

4. (c) Required number of male employees in company D in 2022 $= (450 \times 25) \times \frac{5}{9} = 6250$

5. (d) Number of shares Meera has

$= \frac{45}{100} \times 1000000 = 450000$

∴ After acquiring shares from Jeevan.

Number of shares Meera will have

$= 450000 + 20000 = 470000$

6. (c) In 2018-19, average sales turnover

$= \frac{250 + 350 + 275 + 200 + 400}{5} = \frac{1475}{5} = 295$

In 2019-20, average sales turnover

$= \frac{300 + 250 + 300 + 300 + 350}{5}$

$= \frac{1500}{5} = 300$

∴ Required difference $= 300 - 295$

$= ₹\,5$ (in crores)

7. (a) School Z

Semester fee $= 39 < 3$ (Donation)

i.e., $39 < 3(14) \rightarrow 39 < 42$

School U

Semester fee $= 89$ (Donation)

i.e., $89 < 3(50) \Rightarrow 89 < 150$

∴ Required number of school = 2

8. (d) In 2018

Total exports $= 4000 + 3000 + 2000 = 9000$

In 2020

Total exports $= 3000 + 3000 + 3000 = 9000$

∴ In the years, 2018 and 2020, total exports are equal.

9. (b) Number of students in schooll – 4 (2021)

$= 23\% \times 16000 = \frac{23}{100} \times 16000 = 3680$

Number of students in school – 4 (2022)

$= 22\% \times 18000 = \frac{22}{100} \times 18000 = 3960$

∴ Required difference $= 3960 - 3680 = 280$

10. (c) Average production of A during 2016-2018

$= \frac{38000 + 41000 + 53000}{3} = \frac{132000}{3} = 44000$

Average production of C during 2016-2018

$= \frac{51000 + 57000 + 63000}{3}$

$= \frac{171000}{3} = 57000$

∴ Required difference

$= 57000 - 44000 = 13000$

11. (a) Total sales of bicycle B_1

$= 195 + 230 + 250 = 675$

Total sales of bicycle B_2

$= 284 + 300 + 416 = 1000$

∴ Required ratio $= 675 : 1000 = 27 : 40$

12. (a) Average salary from school

$= \frac{132 + 148 + 166 + 178 + 196}{5} \times 1000$

$= \frac{820}{5} \times 1000 = ₹164000$

13. (d) Number of officer cadre employees of bank A $= 260 + 310 + 350 + 400 = 1320$

Number of officer cadre employees of bank C $= 205 + 230 + 340 + 380 = 1155$

∴ Required ratio $= 1320 : 1155 = 8 : 7$

14. (b) Exports to import of companies S and U in year 2015 = 3 : 2 and 1 : 2

∵ Exports of company S in year 2015 = 51

∴ Imports of company S in year 2015

$= \frac{51}{3} \times 2 = 34$

∵ Exports of company U in year 2015 = 70

∴ Imports of company U in year 2015

$= \frac{70}{1} \times 2 = 140$

∴ Total import $= 140 + 34 = 174$

15. (c) Total number of car produced by A from 2015 to 2017 $= 840 + 900 + 760 = 2500$

Total number of Car Produced by C from 2016 to 2018

$= 960 + 1000 + 1200 = 3160$

∴ Required percentage $= \frac{3160 - 2500}{3160} \times 100$

$= \frac{660}{3160} \times 100 = 20.88 \approx 21\%$

16. (a) Average of imports of all years

$= \frac{\text{Sum of all imports of all year}}{\text{Number of year}}$

$= \frac{5325 + 4521 + 6231 + 8542 + 7456 + 6523 + 5544}{7}$

$= \frac{44142}{7} = 6306$

17. (c) Average production by Brand B in 2018-2023 $= \frac{23 + 37 + 28 + 32 + 34 + 26}{6}$

$= \frac{180}{6} = 30$ lakh

Average Production by Brand D during 2018-2023 $= \frac{35 + 37 + 42 + 32 + 36 + 28}{6}$

$= \frac{210}{6} = 35$ lakh

$\therefore$ Required difference = 35 – 30 = 5 lakh

18. (d) Total number of pages printed by printer P = 100 + 120 + 180 = 400

Total number of pages printed by printer Q = 130 + 145 + 85 = 360

$\therefore$Required ratio = 400 : 360 = 10 : 9

19. (b) Total exports = 720 + 680 + 500 + 450 + 850 = 3200

$\therefore$Required Percentage $= \frac{500}{3200} \times 100$

$= \frac{500}{32} = 15.63\%$

20. (c) Central angle of drawing

$= \frac{\theta}{360} \times 100 = 19$

$\Rightarrow \theta = \frac{19 \times 360}{100} = 68.4°$

21. (c) Average donors of blood of A, O and AB group $= \frac{240 \times (90 + 80 + 70)}{3 \times 360} = \frac{240 \times 240}{3 \times 360°}$

Donors of blood group B $= 240 \times \frac{120}{360}$

Required ratio $= \frac{240 \times 240}{3 \times 360} : \frac{240 \times 120}{360}$

$= 80 : 120 = 2 : 3$

22. (a) Total number of students in a class 20 + 20 = 40 student

Total marks $= 20 \times 1 + 15 \times 2 + 20 \times 5 + 10 \times 12$

$= 20 + 30 + 100 + 120 = 270$

Average of class $= \frac{270}{40} = 6.75$

23. (a) Number of people who take tea more than 3 times = 1732 + 1842 + 6045 + 2741 = 12360

Number of people who never take tea at all = 317 + 127 + 223 + 293 = 960

Required ratio = 12360 : 960 = 103 : 8

24. (a) Total money spent on each from NY, telegraph and others for 2018

$\frac{350000}{10} + \frac{360000}{12} + \frac{210000}{15}$

= 35000 + 30000 + 14000 = 79000

Total money spent on each from NY, telegraph and others for 2021

$= \frac{760000}{19} + \frac{480000}{24} + \frac{440000}{22}$

= 40000 + 20000 + 20000 = 80000

$\therefore$ Thus required ratio = 80000 : 79000 = 80 : 79

25. (a) Income of company A in 2005

$= 40 + 40 \times \frac{60}{100} =$ ₹64 crore

Income of company B in 2005

$= 35 + 35 \times \frac{48}{100} =$ ₹51.8 crore

$\therefore$Profit of company A in 2005 = 64 – 40 = ₹ 24 crore

and profit of company B in 2005 = 51.8 – 35 = ₹16.8 crore

The required difference = 24 – 16.8 = ₹7.2 crore

26. (c) Increased expenditure on electricity

$= 2{,}50{,}000 \times \frac{11}{100} \times \frac{10}{100}$

= ₹ 27,50

Decreasing expenditure on rent

$= 2{,}50{,}000 \times \frac{18}{100} \times \frac{20}{100} =$ ₹ 9000

Hence, required expenditure = 250000 + 2750 – 9000 = ₹ 243750

27. (a) Daily consumption in 2019

450 + 55 + 160 + 280 = 945

For 2020, 430 + 60 + 150 + 300 = 940

For 2021, 380 + 65 + 140 + 320 = 905

For 2022, 350 + 70 + 125 + 400 = 945

For 2023, 350 + 80 + 120 + 350 = 900

$\therefore$In 2019 and 2022 daily consumption is equal.

28. (b) Total number of students in class XII = 150

Total number of vegetarian students = 105

Total number of non-vegetarian students = 150 – 105 = 45

Percentage of non-vegetarian students

$= \frac{45}{150} \times 100 = 30\%$

29. (c) Total number of students admitted in to the university from 2010 to 2013 = 450 + 540 + 370 + 680 = 2040

Average number of students $= \frac{2040}{4} = 510$

30. (b) Production of electric bulbs in October = 375

Production of electric bulls in July = 550

Percentage decrement $= \frac{550 - 375}{550} \times 100$

$= \frac{17500}{550} = 31.82\%$

31. (a) From the given bar graph it is very clear that their is price rise in every year.

32. (d) Let the total expenditure = ₹ x

Expenditure on royalty = ₹ 43500

So, $x \times \frac{15}{100} = 43500$

$\Rightarrow x = \frac{43500 \times 100}{15} =$ ₹ 290000

Combined expenditure on transportation, binding and printing

$= 290000 \times (10 + 16 + 25)\%$

$= 290000 \times \frac{51}{100} =$ ₹ 147900

33. (d) Total distance covered in a week

= 6 + 5.5 + 5.5 + 7 + 5 + 3.5 + 7.5 = 40

Calories burned by jogging 6 km = 300

Calories burned by jogging 1 km = 50

Calories burned by jogging 40 km = 40 × 50 = 2000

34. (d) Average number of students present on Monday, Tuesday and Wednesday

$= \frac{25 + 30 + 20}{3} = \frac{75}{3} = 25$

35. (a) Average production of plant 1 during five years

$= \frac{35 + 43 + 48 + 32 + 42}{5} = 40$ thousand

Average production of plant 2 during five years $= \frac{25 + 44 + 39 + 40 + 44}{5}$

$= \frac{192}{5} = 38.4$ thousand

$\therefore$Required difference = 40 – 38.4 = 1.6 thousand = 1600

36. (c) According to the question, 60° → 72

$\therefore (85° + 48° + 45° + 52°) \rightarrow \frac{72}{60} \times 230$

= 276 lakh

$\therefore$Average expenditure $= \frac{276}{4} = 69$ lakh

37. (c) Let number of appeared candidates from states in year 2008 = x

$\therefore$Number of appeared candidates from state Z in year 2009 $= x \times \frac{200}{100} = 2x$

According to the question,

$x \times \frac{70}{100} + 2x \times \frac{80}{100} = 552$

$\Rightarrow \frac{7x}{10} + \frac{16x}{10} = 552 \Rightarrow 23x = 552 \times 10 \Rightarrow x = 240$

$\therefore$Number of appeared candidates from state Z in 2009 $= 2 \times 240 = 480$

38. (c) In 1997,

Total profit = 135 + 115 + 90 + 70 = 410

In 2000,

Total profit = 150 + 180 + 210 + 230 = 770

$\therefore$ Required percentage $= \frac{770 - 410}{410} \times 100$

$= \frac{360}{410} \times 100 = 87\frac{33}{41}\%$

39. (a) According to the question,

15% of total student = 600

$\Rightarrow$ Total number of student

$$= 600 \times \frac{100}{15} = 4000$$

$\therefore$ Total number of student in X

$$= \frac{25}{100} \times 4000 = 1000$$

Total number of students in XII

$$= \frac{18}{100} \times 4000 = 720$$

$\therefore$ Required difference = 1000 − 720 = 280

Speedy Method

According to the question,

Students in class 8, 15% $\rightarrow$ 600

$\therefore$ 1% $\rightarrow$ 40

$\therefore$ Required difference = (25 − 18%)

= 7% $\rightarrow$ 7 × 40 = 280

40. (b) Required mean $= \frac{584 + 205}{2}$

$$= \frac{789}{2} = 394.5$$

41. (b) Total marks of all subjects

= 100 + 100 + 100 + 100 + 100 + 100 = 600

Total marks scored by C

= 80 + 80 + 70 + 60 + 70 + 60 = 420

Percentage scored by C $= \frac{420}{600} \times 100 = 70\%$

42. (b) Total maximum marks of all four subjects = 175 + 175 + 175 + 175 = 700

Total marks obtained by Gunja

= 112 + 119 + 99 + 97 = 427

Aggregate percentage $= \frac{427}{700} \times 100 = 61\%$

43. (a) Total sales

= 25000 + 24000 + 18000 + 35000 + 26000 + 22000

= 150000

Total sales during the month of June and July = 24000 + 18000 = 42000

Percentage shares during months of June and July $= \frac{42000}{150000} \times 100 = 28\%$

44. (a) Female in company A

$$= 600 \times \frac{25}{100} = 150$$

Female in company C $= 700 \times \frac{30}{100} = 210$

Female in company E $= 850 \times \frac{40}{100} = 340$

$\therefore$ Required total = 150 + 210 + 340 = 700

45. (d) Average number of scooters produced by company D

$$= \frac{520 + 980 + 1090 + 1660}{4}$$

$$= \frac{4250}{4} = 1062.5 \text{ thousand}$$

Average number of scooter produced by company A, B and C together

$$= \frac{360 + 580 + 1000 + 1240 + 420 + 940 + 780 + 950 + 380 + 570 + 1020 + 1180}{12}$$

$$= \frac{9420}{12} = 785 \text{ thousand}$$

$\therefore$ Required percentage $= \frac{1062.5 - 785}{785} \times 100$

$$= \frac{277.5}{785} \times 100 = 35.35\%$$

46. (d) Amount paid for Bonus

= 3 + 4.25 + 4.5 + 4.85 + 4.9 = 21.5 lakh

and amount paid for fuel and transport together = 110 + 145 + 120 + 168 + 190

= 733 lakh

$\therefore$ Required percentage $= \frac{21.5}{733} \times 100 = 2.93\%$

47. (d) Growth rate $= \frac{10800}{9000} \times 100 = 120\%$

$\therefore$ Value of 'X' $= 10800 \times \frac{120}{100} = 12960$

48. (d) Net angle made by Badminton, Tennis and Rugby on pie-chart

= (45 + 65 + 25)° = 135°

and net angle made by Cricket, Swimming and Hockey on Pie-chart

= (100 + 60 + 30)° = 190°

$\therefore$ Required% $= \frac{190 - 135°}{190} \times 100$

$$= \frac{55°}{190°} \times 100 = 28.95\% \text{ less}$$

49. (c) Number of students who choose medical = 80 + 120 = 200

and the number of boys who choose medical = 80

$\therefore$ Required% $= \frac{80}{200} \times 100 = 40\%$

50. (d) According to the question,

15% × Total expenditure = 2.1 cr

$\therefore$ Total expenditure $= \frac{2.1 \times 100}{15} = 14$ cr

$\therefore$ Required difference = (12.5 − 10)% × 14

$$= \frac{2.5}{100} \times 14 = 0.35 \text{ cr} = 35 \text{ lakhs}$$

51. (c) Required difference

= (190 + 204 + 212) − (192 + 205 + 203) = 6

52. (c) Average expenditure on transport

$$= \frac{38 + 45 + 57 + 63}{4} = 50.75$$

53. (c) Percentage increase in the number of students in 2019 over 2018

$$= \frac{180 - 140}{140} \times 100 = \frac{40}{140} \times 100 = 28.57\%$$

54. (c) Average of low rates of shares of company C $= \frac{175 + 180 + 185}{3} = \frac{540}{3} = 180$

Low rates of shares of company C less than (180) < (175)

Low rate of share of Hyderabad.

55. (b) Total number of sales of bikes of manufacturer Q from 2016 to 2020

= 280 + 290 + 310 + 310 + 330 = 1520

Total number of sales of bikes of manufacturer S from 2016 to 2020

= 400 + 420 + 430 + 440 + 450 = 2140

$\therefore$ Required ratio = 1520 : 2140 = 76 : 107

56. (d) Total production of type A bikes

= 157 + 194 + 271 + 290 = 912

Average production of type A bikes

$$= \frac{912}{4} = 228$$

Number of years in which production of type C bikes less than 228 = 2

57. (d) Total targeted production of cars in 2021 and 2022 = 70 + 80 = 150

Total actual production of cars from 2019 to 2022 = 36 + 32 + 59 + 65 = 192

Ratio $= \frac{150}{192} = \frac{25}{32} = 25 : 32$

58. (c) Total production of company C

= 8 + 9 + 6 = 23

Total production of company A

= 9 + 6 + 8 = 23

$\therefore$ Required percentage $= \frac{23}{23} \times 100 = 100\%$

59. (a) Profit earn on mobile

$$= 20000 \times \frac{10}{100} = ₹\ 2000$$

Profit earn on laptop $= 72000 \times \frac{20}{100} = ₹\ 14400$

Profit earn on mobile covers

$$= 300 \times \frac{12}{100} = ₹\ 36$$

Thus, total profit = 2000 + 14400 + 36

= ₹ 16436

60. (c) Average of car manufactured in 2022

$$= \frac{3551 + 3020 + 2600}{3} = \frac{9171}{3} = 3057$$

61. (d) Let total population of state A be *P*.

According to the question,

$$\frac{55}{100} \times P \times \frac{5}{(5+6)} = 500000$$

$$\Rightarrow \frac{5 \times P \times 5}{100} = 500000 \Rightarrow P = 2000000$$

62. (c) Male below poverty line for state Q

$$= 14700 \times \frac{19}{100} \times \frac{2}{7} = 798$$

Male below poverty line for state S

$$= 14700 \times \frac{15}{100} \times \frac{1}{7} = 315$$

Thus, total male below poverty line in state Q and S = 798 + 315 = 1113

63. (b) Volunteers at district A = 40 + 30 = 70

Volunteers at district B = 25 + 35 = 60

Volunteers at district C = 20 + 30 = 50

Volunteers at district D = 45 + 25 = 70

Total volunteers = 70 + 60 + 50 + 70 = 250

64. (d) Total number of student studying in the Physics $= 420 + 435 + 412 + 285 = 1552$

Total number of students studying in the Maths $= 256 + 310 + 295 + 345 = 1206$

$\therefore$ Required ratio $= 1552 : 1206 = 776 : 603$

65. (a) Percentage of marks obtained

$$= \frac{93 + 90 + 90 + 95 + 78}{500} \times 100 = 89.2\%$$

66. (c) Total fruits sold = 100%

Fruits sold (oranges + Apples)

$$= 30\% + 20\% = 50\%$$

$$\therefore \text{Required angle} = \frac{50}{100} \times 360° = 180°$$

67. (d) Combined sale of dry fruits sugar and rice $= (27 + 32 + 25) + (48 + 42 + 47) + (42 + 23 + 27)$

$= 84 + 137 + 92 = 313$

Combined sale of tea, pulses and flour

$= (24 + 15 + 30) + (45 + 34 + 42) + (55 + 33 + 49)$

$= 69 + 121 + 137 = 327$

$$\therefore \text{Required percentage} = \frac{313}{327} \times 100 = 96\%$$

68. (d) Number of employees in production department $= 1600 \times \frac{30}{100} = 480$

Number of females employees in all

$$\text{department} = 1600 \times \frac{8}{100} \times \frac{5}{8} + 1600 \times \frac{15}{100} \times \frac{3}{5} + 1600 \times \frac{25}{100} \times \frac{7}{10} + 1600 \times \frac{22}{100} \times \frac{4}{11} + 1600 \times \frac{30}{100} \times \frac{3}{8}$$

$= 80 + 144 + 280 + 128 + 180 = 812$

$$\therefore \text{Required percentage} = \frac{480}{812} \times 100 = 59.1\%$$

69. (c) Number of textbooks produced by print house B in the year 2018 = 12000

Number of textbooks produced by print house C in the year 2020 = 9000

$$\text{Required ratio} = \frac{12000}{9000} = \frac{4}{3} = 4 : 3$$

70. (b) Average number of A type car

$$= \frac{1750 + 1800 + 2950}{3} = 2166.67$$

Average number of B and C type car

$$= \frac{\frac{3240 + 3020 + 2950}{3} + \frac{2070 + 3150 + 3290}{3}}{2}$$

$$= \frac{3070 + 2836.67}{2} = 2953.335$$

$$\therefore \text{Required (\%)} = \frac{2953.335 - 2166.67}{2953.335} \times 100$$

$$= \frac{786.665}{2953.335} \times 100 = 26.6\%$$

71. (b) Month having the highest production = 108 (November)

and month having the least production = 45 (May)

$\therefore$ The required ratio $= 108 : 45 = 12 : 5$

72. (a) Number of employees in

$$\text{Department D} = 20000 \times \frac{30}{100} = 6000$$

Percentage of male employees in Department D = 100% − 30% = 70%

$\therefore$ Number of male employees

$$= 6000 \times \frac{70}{100} = 4200$$

73. (c) The percentage hour distribution for English = 15%

Given, total time for English = 3 h.

$\therefore$ 15% is equivalent to 3 h.

$\therefore$ 1% is equivalent to $\frac{3}{15}$ h.

$\therefore$ 35% (for mathematics) is equivalent to

$$= \frac{3}{15} \times 35\,\text{h} = 7\,\text{h}$$

74. (d) Total number of soaps sold by companies Q ans S together in May

$= 1540 + 1736 = 3276$

Total number of soaps sold by company P in July = 1820

$$\therefore \text{Required percentage} = \frac{3276 - 1820}{1820} \times 100$$

$$= \frac{1456}{1820} \times 100 = 80\%$$

75. (d) Total number of startups in the education and agriculture sector

$= 2910 \times (24\% + 12\%)$

$$= 2910 \times \frac{36}{100} = 1047$$

76. (a) Number of dozens of bananas by farm *M* in 2022 $= \frac{17652}{12}$

Number of dozens of bananas by farm *P* in 2022 $= \frac{16404}{12}$

$$\therefore \text{Required ratio} = \frac{17652}{12} : \frac{16404}{12} = 1471 : 1367$$

77. (d) Let total expenses/monthly income be $100x$.

Expenses on rent and education

$$= 100x \times \frac{30}{100} + 100x \times \frac{25}{100} = 55x$$

$\because \quad 100x = 75000$

$\therefore$ Expenses on rent and education

$$(55x) = \frac{75000}{100x} \times 55x = ₹\,41250$$

78. (c) Percentage growth rate from October-November

$$= \frac{204933 - 200189}{200189} \times 100 = 2.36\%$$

Percentage growth rate from November-December

$$= \frac{211885 - 204933}{204933} \times 100 = 3.39\%$$

$$\therefore \text{Required average} = \frac{2.36\% + 3.39\%}{2}$$

$= 2.875\% \approx 2.9\%$

79. (d) From 2016 to 2019

Total sales of Manufacturer M_2

$= 160 + 170 + 180 + 190 = 700$

Total sales of Manufacturer M_4

$= 200 + 210 + 220 + 230 = 860$

$\therefore$ Required difference

$= 860 - 700 = 160$ (in hundred) $= 16000$

80. (a)

Subject	Marks obtained	Total Marks	Percentage
English	73	100	73%
Hindi	56	80	70%
Science	45	75	60%
Mathematics	90	125	72%
IT	45	60	75%

$\therefore$ Student scored highest marks in IT.

81. (b)

Com-pany	Wooden Bats	Plastic Bats	Brand A : Brand B	Brand B (Plastic Bats Manufactured)
P	65%	35%	3 : 7	$35000 \times \frac{7}{10} = 24500$
Q	70%	30%	7 : 8	$30000 \times \frac{8}{15} = 16{,}000$
R	60%	40%	19 : 6	$40000 \times \frac{6}{25} = 9600$
S	70%	30%	7 : 8	$30000 \times \frac{8}{15} = 16{,}000$
T	50%	50%	2 : 3	$50{,}000 \times \frac{3}{5} = 30{,}000$

$\therefore$ Total plastic bats of brand B manufactured

$= 24500 + 16000 + 9600 + 16000 + 30000$

$= 96100$

82. (a) Combined average production for four years of companies B and D

$$= \frac{[(70 + 100 + 150 + 210) + (120 + 170 + 200 + 260)]}{8} = 160$$

and combined average production for four years of companies A and C

$$= \frac{[(60 + 90 + 140 + 220) + (50 + 190 + 180 + 250)]}{8} = 147.5$$

$\therefore$ Difference $(160 - 147.5) = 12.5$

$\therefore$ Required less percentage

$$= \frac{12.5}{160} \times 100\% = 7.81\%$$

83. (d) Total students = 7000

Girls in B.Sc. Computer Science

$$= 7000 \times \frac{25}{100} \times \frac{60}{100} = 1050$$

Girls in B.Com = $7000 \times \frac{20}{100} \times \frac{60}{100} = 840$

Total girls in B.Sc Computer Science and B.Com = 1050 + 840 = 1890

The required% = $\frac{1890}{7000} \times 100\% = 27\%$

84. (d) Total arrears

$= 4500 + 4800 + 4900 + 5300 + 5600$

$=$ ₹ 25100

Total bonus

$= 2300 + 2100 + 2500 + 2700 + 2800$

$=$ ₹ 12400

∴ Required percentage = $\frac{25100}{12400} \times 100\%$

$= 202.42\%$

85. (d) From the options,

$2019 \rightarrow \left[\frac{134.6 - 128.4}{128.4}\right] \times 100 = 4.82\%$

$2018 \rightarrow \left[\frac{128.4 - 112.8}{112.8}\right] \times 100 = 13.82\%$

$2015 \rightarrow \left[\frac{83.8 - 72.6}{72.6}\right] \times 100 = 15.42\%$

$2016 \rightarrow \left[\frac{100.6 - 83.8}{83.8}\right] \times 100 = 20.04\%$

86. (a) Required percentage

$= \frac{6}{24} \times 100 = 25\%$

87. (b) For pens, price = ₹ 10 /unit

Quantity = X

For notebooks, price = ₹ 20/units

Quantity = 6

According to the question,

$10X + 20 \times 6 = 180$

$\Rightarrow \quad 10X + 120 = 180$

$\Rightarrow \quad X = \frac{60}{10} = 6 \Rightarrow X = 6$

88. (b) Average number of books per subject

$= \frac{120 + 150 + 150 + 120 + 120}{5}$

$= \frac{660}{5} = 132$

And the number of books of subject B1 = 120

∴ Required ratio = 120 : 132 = 10: 11

89. (c) Average production of bikes over the years = $\frac{35 + 50 + 70 + 90 + 40 + 60 + 30}{7}$

$= \frac{375}{7} = 53.57$

∴ In years 2010, 2011 and 2013 the production of bikes is more than the average production.

90. (b) Average production of B type cars from 2015-18 = $\frac{680 + 620 + 750 + 540}{4} = 647.5$

Average production of A type and C type cars from 2015-18

$= \frac{\frac{840 + 900 + 760 + 800}{4} + \frac{890 + 960 + 1000 + 1200}{4}}{2}$

$= \frac{825 + 1012.5}{2} = 918.75$

∴ Required difference = 918.75 − 647.5 = 271.25

91. (a) Average sales in schools A, B and C in 2014 $= \frac{70 + 35 + 80}{3} = \frac{185}{3}$

Average sales in schools A, C and F in 2013

$= \frac{50 + 60 + 40}{3} = \frac{150}{3}$

∴ Required% = $\frac{\frac{150}{3} \times 100}{\frac{185}{3}} = 81.08\%$

92. (a) Male research scholar in Mathematics

$= 18 - 4 = 14$

Male research scholar in Statistics

$= 12 - 3 = 9$

∴ Required ratio = 14 : 9

93. (c) According to the given table

Total production of T- shirts by C_1

$= 243 + 248 + 232 + 242 = 965$

Average production of t-shirts by C_1

$= \frac{965}{4} = 241.25$

Total production of t-shirts by C_2

$= 244 + 239 + 240 + 244 = 967$

Average production of t-shirts by C_2

$= \frac{967}{4} = 241.75$

Total production of t-shirts by C_3

$= 244 + 236 + 235 + 230 = 945$

Average production of t-shirts by C_3

$= \frac{945}{4} = 236.25$

Total production of t-shirts by C_4

$= 240 + 230 + 248 + 242 = 960$

Average production of t-shirts by C_4

$= \frac{960}{4} = 240$

So, C_2 had the maximum average production of t-shirts during these 4 yrs.

94. (d) Total pages printed on Saturday

$= 8540 + 11230 + 6580 + 7890 = 34240$

Total pages printed on Wednesday

$= 34240 + 34240 \times \frac{15}{100}$

$= 34240\left(1 + \frac{15}{100}\right) = 34240 \times \frac{115}{100} = 39376$

95. (a) Sale of helmets C in 2002 = 68

Sales of helmets C in 1999 = 54

Percentage increase = $\left(\frac{68 - 54}{54}\right) \times 100$

$= \frac{14}{54} \times 100$

∴ Percentage increase = 25.93%

96. (d) Required ratio = $\frac{10500}{11500} \times 100$

$= 91.30\%$

97. (b) Maximum marks in History = 175

Passing marks in History is 105 marks.

Marks obtained by Ram = $175 \times \frac{54}{100} = 94.5$

Marks obtained by Mohan

$= 175 \times \frac{51}{100} = 89.25$

Marks obtained by Shyam

$= 175 \times \frac{75}{100} = 131.25$

Thus, it is very clear that only Shyam passed the exam.

98. (d) Total absent at center P, Q and R in 2016 = (45 − 42) + (56 − 45) + (55 − 50)

$= 3 + 11 + 5 = 19$

Total absent at center P, Q and R in 2017

$= (50 - 45) + (75 - 55) + (45 - 40)$

$= 5 + 20 + 5 = 30$

Total absent at center P, Q and R in 2018

$= (64 - 60) + (65 - 45) + (65 - 55)$

$= 4 + 20 + 10 = 34$

Total absent at center P, Q and R in 2019

$= (80 - 69) + (84 - 72) + (70 - 62)$

$= 11 + 12 + 8 = 31$

Total absent at center P, Q and R in 2020

$= (55 - 44) + (80 - 66) + (90 - 85)$

$= 11 + 14 + 5 = 30$

Thus, second highest absentees are in 2019.

99. (a) Highest scored marks in Maths 150 (100%).

Highest marks in Chemistry

$= 130 \times \frac{80}{100} = 104$

Highest marks in Physics = $120 \times \frac{90}{100} = 108$

Highest marks in Geography

$= 100 \times \frac{95}{100} = 95$

Highest marks in History = $60 \times \frac{90}{100} = 54$

Highest marks in Computer Science

$= 40 \times \frac{90}{100} = 36$

∴ Over all percentage

$= \frac{150 + 104 + 108 + 95 + 54 + 36}{150 + 130 + 120 + 100 + 60 + 40} \times 100$

$= \frac{547}{600} \times 100 = 91\frac{1}{6}\%$

100. (d) Total marks obtained by Sumit

$= 90 + 88 + 78 + 82 + 68 = 406$

Percentage of marks obtained by Sumit

$= \frac{406}{500} \times 100 = 81.2\%$

Percentage of marks obtained by Rohit

$= \frac{69 + 76 + 80 + 88 + 94}{500} \times 100$

$= \frac{407}{5} = 81.4\%$

Percentage of marks obtained by Tarun

$= \frac{65+80+75+85+90}{500} \times 100 = \frac{395}{5} = 79\%$

Thus, 79% marks obtained by Tarun.

101. (c) Appeared students in Section C

$= \frac{100°}{360°} \times 1800 = 500$

Passed students in Section C

$= \frac{25}{100} \times 800 = 200$

$\therefore$ Failed students = 500 − 200 = 300

102. (b) Ramesh expend on housing and transportation $= ₹\ 45000 \times \frac{25+10}{100} = ₹\ 15750$

103. (d) Number of delivery partners joined Clipkart in 2019 and 2020 = 5.6 + 6.4 = 12.0

Number of delivery partners joined Tomato in 2019 and 2020 = 2.7 + 3.3 = 6.0

$\therefore$ Ratio $= \frac{12}{6} = \frac{2}{1} = 2:1$

104. (a) Required times $= \frac{6000}{1600} = \frac{15}{4} = 3.75$

105. (a) Total students In Class VII

= 58 + 65 = 123

In Class VIII = 59 + 57 = 116

In Class IX = 60 + 62 = 122

In Class X = 61 + 59 = 120

Hence, Class VII has the maximum number of students.

106. (a) Number of students who scored less than 50 marks = 10

Number of students who scored less than 40 marks = 8

Number of students who scored more than 40 marks = 10 − 8 = 2

107. (b) Required % $= \frac{65-20}{20} \times 100$

$= \frac{45}{20} \times 100 = 225\%$

108. (a) Total students passed from B

= 530 + 420 + 550 + 620 + 680 = 2800

Total students enrolled from B

= 550 + 450 + 600 + 650 + 700 = 2950

$\therefore$ Required % $= \frac{2800}{2950} \times 100\% = 94.92\%$

109. (b) Total illiterates in A, B, C altogether

= 22 + 14 + 20 = 56%

Illiterates in D = 44%

$\therefore$ Required % $= \frac{56}{44} \times 100\% = 127.27\%$

110. (c) Variation in strength in Department 1 = |24 − 21| = 3

Department 2 = |22 − 21| = 1

Department 3 = |20 − 18| = 2

Department 4 = |19 − 19| = 0

Department 5 = |20 − 16| = 4

$\therefore$ In department 5 variation is maximum.

111. (b) Total number of people below poverty line in State B = 13% of 6000

$= \frac{13 \times 6000}{100} = 780$

Then, number of females $= \frac{5}{13} \times 780 = 300$

Total number of people below poverty line in State C = 26% of 6000 $= \frac{26}{100} \times 6000 = 1560$

Then, number of females $= \frac{4}{13} \times 1560 = 480$

Total number of females below poverty line in both states = 480 + 300 = 780

112. (c) Average $= \frac{\text{Sum of all numbers}}{\text{Total quantities}}$

$= \frac{5.7 + 10.15 + 12.16 + 10.22}{4}$

$= \frac{38.23}{4} = 9.56 = 10$ (approx.)

113. (d) Total salary in 4 yr

= (200 + 250 + 300 + 350) × 1000

= 1100 × 1000

$\therefore$ Average salary $= \frac{1100 \times 1000}{4} = 11 \times 25000$

= ₹ 275000

114. (a) Total female employees = 136000

$\therefore$ Female employees in district C and D

= 136000 × (30% + 15%)

= 136000 × 45% = 61200

115. (a) According to the table number of families having income range ₹ 19000-22000

= 50 − 33 = 17

116. (a) Total sales of 6th branch

= 70 + 80 = 150

Total sales of 3rd branch = 110 + 95 = 205

$\therefore$ Required% $= \frac{150}{205} \times 100 = 73.17\%$

117. (c) Marks in social science

$= \frac{1800}{360°} \times 72° = 360$

118. (c) Total amount used by the school for the payment $= 1000000 \times \frac{11}{100} = ₹\ 110000$

119. (d) Madhuri has marbles $= \frac{180°}{360°} \times 36° = 18$

120. (d) Average production of three companies $= \frac{3620+2829+2833}{3}$

$= \frac{9282}{3} = 3094$

Average demand of three companies

$= \frac{3800+4532+5318}{3} = 4550$

$\therefore$ Required difference = 4550 − 3094 = 1456

121. (c) Students in Class IX of school (Q + R) = 157 + 143 = 300

Students in Class VI of school (S + T) = 142 + 144 = 286

$\therefore$ Required ratio = 300 : 286 = 150 : 143

122. (a) Maximum difference in number of students = 68 − 44 = 24

$\therefore$ Required percentage $= \frac{24}{68} \times 100 = 35.29\%$

123. (d) Number of girls in college C

= 20% of 2500 = 500

Number of girls in college E

= 26% of 2500 = 650

Hence, required average

$= \frac{500+650}{2} = \frac{1150}{2} = 575$

124. (a) People in Goa $= \frac{315000 \times 12}{100} = 37800$

People in MP = 20% of 315000

= 3150 × 20 = 63000

Illiterate people in Goa $= \frac{2}{5} \times 37800 = 15120$

Illiterate people in MP $= \frac{4}{5} \times 63000 = 50400$

$\therefore$ Total illiterate people in Goa andMP

= 15120 + 50400 = 65520

125. (c) Total students in 2021

= 85 + 90 + 65 + 110 + 75 = 425

Students opted for biology = 90

$\therefore$ Percentage of students opted for biology in 2021 $= \frac{90}{425} \times 100 = 21.18\%$

126. (c) Total production of Khadi

= 118 + 120 + 125 = 363

Total production of Cotton

= 114 + 120 + 121 = 355

$\therefore$ Required difference = |363 − 355| = 8

127. (a) Average growth rate in cooler

$= \frac{60+72+54+45}{4} = \frac{231}{4} = 57.75\%$

Average growth rate in fans

$= \frac{27+18+30+20}{4} = \frac{95}{4} = 23.75\%$

$\therefore$ Required difference = 57.75 − 23.75 = 34%

128. (a) Given,

Total number of students = 2080

Let total number of students in IIT Madras be x.

$\therefore$ Total number of students in IIT Bombay

$= x - 20\% \text{ of } x = \frac{4x}{5}$

$\therefore$ According to the question,

$430 + 350 + \frac{4x}{5} + x + 400 = 2080$

$\Rightarrow \frac{9x}{5} = 2080 - 1180 = 900 \Rightarrow x = 500$

Total students in IIT Madras = 500

and total students in IIT Bombay = 400

Total number of students who study in applied department

$= 32\% \text{ of } 400 + 35\% \text{ of } 500$

$= 128 + 175 = 303$

Also, total number of students who study civil $= 18\% \text{ of } 400 + 25\% \text{ of } 500$

$= 72 + 125 = 197$

$\therefore$ Required difference $= 303 - 197 = 106$

129. (d) Production of company X is = 800

Demand of company W is = 400

$K\%$ of 800 = 400 $\quad K \times \frac{800}{100} = 400 \Rightarrow K = 50$

$\therefore$ Value of $K = 50$

130. (d) Demand of company P = 3276

Demand of company Q = 4550

$\therefore$ Required percentage $= \frac{3276}{4550} \times 100 = 72\%$

131. (d) From Goa,

Percentage of qualified candidates in 2012

$= \frac{810}{7800} \times 100 = 10.38\%$

Qualified candidates in 2013

$= \frac{800}{7500} \times 100 = 10.66\%$

Qualified candidates in 2014

$= \frac{920}{8800} \times 100 = 10.45\%$

Qualified candidates in 2015

$= \frac{850}{7200} \times 100 = 11.80\%$

$\therefore$ Percentage of qualified candidates in 2015 is the highest.

132. (a) Sale of earphones in 2017 = 49.7 lakhs

Sale of earphones in 2020 = 84 lakhs

Increase = 84 – 49.7 = 34.3 lakhs

$\therefore$ Required % $= \frac{34.3}{49.7} \times 100 = 69\%$

133. (a) Number of companies with more demand = 3

Number of companies with more production = 2

Hence, required ratio = 3 : 2

134. (c) Total expenditure on material cost and selling expenses

$= (28 + 15)\% \text{ of } 300000$

$= 43\% \times 300000 = ₹\,129000$

135. (b) Average of five months

$= \frac{9500 + 9400 + 9600 + 8000 + 8500}{5}$

$= \frac{45000}{5} = ₹\,9000$

136. (c) Average of A $= \frac{84 + 71 + 95}{3} = 83.33$

Average of B $= \frac{93 + 76 + 101}{3} = 90$

Average of C $= \frac{99 + 79 + 71}{3} = 83$

Average of D $= \frac{80 + 90 + 94}{3} = 88$

Average of E $= \frac{88 + 93 + 90}{3} = 90.33$

$\therefore$ E scored the best on average.

137. (a) Difference between pomegranates and berries = 31.07 – 8.11 = 22.96%

$\therefore$ Required difference

$= 50000 \times \frac{22.96}{100} = 11480$

138. (a) For January $= \frac{55 - 35}{35} \times 100$

$= \frac{20}{35} \times 100 = 57.1\%$

For March $= \frac{45 - 25}{25} \times 100 = \frac{20}{25} \times 100 = 80\%$

For May $= \frac{75 - 45}{45} \times 100 = \frac{30}{45} \times 100 = 66.6\%$

For September

$= \frac{25 - 15}{15} \times 100 = \frac{10}{15} \times 100 = 66.6\%$

Hence, highest rainfall difference is in March.

139. (d) Average quantity of food item C

$= \frac{280 + 295 + 280 + 315}{4} = \frac{1170}{4} = 292.5 \text{ kg}$

140. (c) Total marks obtained by Hitansh in all 5 subjects

$= 100 \times \frac{67}{100} + 150 \times \frac{70}{100} + 100 \times \frac{64}{100} + 100 \times \frac{55}{100} + 100 \times \frac{75}{100}$

$= 67 + 105 + 64 + 55 + 75 = 366$

and total marks

$= 100 + 150 + 100 + 100 + 100 = 550$

So, required % $= \frac{366}{550} \times 100 = 66.55\%$

141. (a) Average production of flavour X in 2017 and 2018 $= \frac{20 + 20}{2} = 20$

Average production of flavour Y in 2019 and 2020 $= \frac{32 + 20}{2} = 26$

$\therefore$ Required difference $= (26 - 20) \times 1000$

= 6000 packs

142. (d) Total number of male students who opted for Biology in school A

$= 900 \times \frac{30}{100} \times \frac{7}{15} = 126$

Total number of female students who opted for biology in school A $= 900 \times \frac{30}{100} \times \frac{8}{15} = 144$

In school D number of males

$= \frac{800 \times 18}{100} \times \frac{5}{12} = 60$

and in school D number of females

$= \frac{800 \times 18}{100} \times \frac{7}{12} = 84$

Then total number of male in both schools

$= 126 + 60 = 186$

and total number of female in both schools

$= 144 + 84 = 228$

Hence, required ratio $= \frac{186}{228} = \frac{31}{38} = 31 : 38$

143. (b) Average score of Angela

$= \frac{69.5 + 65 + 64.5}{3} = 64$

Average score of Maria

$= \frac{69.05 + 70 + 67.52}{3} = 68.8$

Average score of Sareena

$= \frac{73.81 + 72.5 + 74.3}{3} = 73.5$

Average score of Preeti

$= \frac{74.3 + 75 + 77.5}{3} = 75.6$

Preeti had highest average score.

Hence, Preeti was the best player.

144. (c) Given, donation = 35 %

Scholarship = 26 %

$\therefore$ Required percentage $= \frac{26}{35} \times 100\%$

$= 74.2857\% \approx 74.29$

145. (c) Placed students in 2014

$= 19.3 + 13.4 + 13.4 + 11.8 + 7.8$

$= 65.7$ thousand

Placed students in 2012

$= 12.6 + 9.8 + 10.4 + 14.9 + 9.8$

$= 57.5$ thousand

$\therefore$ Required difference $= 65.7 - 57.5$

$= 8.2 \times 1000 = 8200$

146. (d) We get from the bar graph that rice production by B in 2017 is equal to the rice production by A in 2020.

So, only Statement (d) is correct.

147. (b) Difference between laptop sold by company A and C

$= (40 - 8)\% \times 2500$

$= \frac{32}{100} \times 2500 = 800$

148. (a) Total sweet manufactured by P, Q and R in 1998 = 178 + 240 + 150 = 568

Total sweet manufactured by S, T and U in 1998 = 130 + 177 + 192 = 499

Hence, required ratio = 568 : 499

149. (d) Expenses on health = ₹ 15000

Total expenses

$= 15000 + 20000 + 5000 + 2000 + 8000$

$= ₹\,50000$

Then, central angle $= \frac{15000}{50000} \times 360° = 108°$

150. (c) **151. (b)**

Scan Given QR Code for Remaining Questions & Solutions(152-696) of this Chapter

POWER PACK

arihant
SUCCESS AND NOTHING LESS

Imp.

Maths Formulae

HIGHLY USEFUL FOR ALL SSC EXAMS

Free Booklet with POWER PACK

SSC Maths

Chapterwise 7000+ TCS MCQs

Important Maths Formulae

Number System

Decimal System

We use 10 digits 0, 1, 2, 3, 4, 5, 6, 7, 8, 9 for writing a number. These digits are called numeral.

Roman System

We use some special digits for writing a number.

$1 \rightarrow$ I, $2 \rightarrow$ II, $3 \rightarrow$ III, $5 \rightarrow$ V, $10 \rightarrow$ X

L $\rightarrow 50$, C $\rightarrow 100$, D $\rightarrow 500$, M $\rightarrow 1000$.

Divisibility Rules

1. **Divisibility Rule of 2, 4, 8**
   - $2 \rightarrow$ Last digit should be divisible by 2.
   - $4 \rightarrow$ The number formed by last 2 digits should be divisible by 4.
   - $8 \rightarrow$ The number formed by last 3 digits should be divisible by 8.
2. **Divisibility Rule of 3 and 9**
   - $3 \rightarrow$ Sum of digits should be divisible by 3.
   - $9 \rightarrow$ Sum of digits should be divisible by 9.
3. **Divisibility Rule of 5**
   - $5 \rightarrow$ Last digit should be either 0 or 5.
4. **Divisibility Rule of 6**
   - $6 \rightarrow$ If a number is divisible by 2 and 3 both, then that number will also be divisible by 6.
5. **Divisibility Rule of 7**
   - Multiply last digit by 2 and subtract from remaining number. Repeat this process untill number become less than check divisibility of 7.
6. **Divisibility Rule of 11**
   - If the difference between the sum of the digits at odd places and sum of the digits at even places is either zero or multiple of 11.

Division Rules

1. **Division Algorithm**

   Dividend = Divisor × Quotient + Remainder

2. (i) $a^n + b^n$ is divisible by $(a + b)$, if n is odd

   (ii) $a^n + b^n$ is not divisible by $(a + b)$ and $(a - b)$, if n is even.

   (iii) $a^n - b^n$ is divisible by $(a - b)$, if n is odd.

   (iv) $a^n - b^n$ is divisible by $(a + b)$ and $(a - b)$, if n is even.

Unit Digit

1. (i) $5 \times \text{Odd} \rightarrow$ Unit digit $= 5$ (ii) $5 \times \text{Even} \rightarrow$ Unit digit $= 0$
2. Any power of 0, 1, 5, 6 $\rightarrow$ Unit digit = same.
3. $(9)^{\text{odd}} \rightarrow$ Unit digit $= 9$; $(9)^{\text{even}} \rightarrow$ Unit digit $= 1$
4. Rule of 2, 3, 7, 8 $\rightarrow$ Unit digit repeat after four power.

HCF and LCM

Some Special Cases Based on HCF and LCM

(i) The greatest number which divides the number x, y, and z leaving remainders a, b and c respectively is given by HCF $[(x-a),(y-b),(z-c)]$.

(ii) The greatest number which divides the numbers x, y, z...... leaving the same remainder in each case is given by HCF $[|x-y|,|y-z|,|z-x|, ...]$

(iii) The least number which when divided by x, y, z leaves the same remainder 'k' in each case is given by LCM $(x, y, z) + k$.

(iv) The least number which when divided by x, y, and z leaves the remainders a, b and c respectively is given by LCM $[(x, y, z)] - k$

Where, $k = (x-a) = (y-b) = (z-c)$.

Relations based on HCF and LCM

(i) Product of two numbers = HCF $\times$ LCM

(ii) HCF of fractions $= \dfrac{\text{HCF of numerators}}{\text{LCM of denominators}}$

(iii) LCM of fractions $= \dfrac{\text{LCM of numerators}}{\text{HCF of denominators}}$

Simplification

V	B	O	D	M	A	S
↓	↓	↓	↓	↓	↓	↓
Vinculum	Brackets	Of	Divide	Multiply	Addition	Subtraction

(i) Small $\longrightarrow$ ( ) (ii) Middle $\longrightarrow$ { }

(iii) Large $\longrightarrow$ [ ]

The operation have to be carried out in this order.

Average

(i) Average $= \dfrac{\text{Sum of all quantities}}{\text{Total number of quantities}}$

(ii) If the average of n_1 numbers is a_1 and the average of n_2 numbers is a_2, then average of total numbers n_1 and n_2 is $= \dfrac{n_1 a_1 + n_2 a_2}{n_1 + n_2}$

Average of Consecutive Numbers

(i) Average of first 'n' natural numbers
$$= \frac{n+1}{2}$$

(ii) Average of square of first 'n' natural numbers
$$= \frac{(n+1)(2n+1)}{6}$$

(iii) Average of cubes of first 'n' consecutive natural numbers $= \frac{n(n+1)^2}{4}$

(iv) Average of certain numbers or average of numbers in AP
$$= \frac{\text{First number} + \text{Last number}}{2}$$

(v) Average of first 'n' multiples of certain number 'x' $= \frac{x(n+1)}{2}$

(vi) Average of first n odd numbers $= n$

(vii) Average of first n even numbers $= n + 1$

(viii) Average of 1 to n odd numbers $= \frac{\text{Last odd number} + 1}{2}$

(ix) Average of 1 to n even numbers $= \frac{\text{Last even number} + 2}{2}$

Ratio and Proportion

1. If an amount R is to be divided between A and B in the ratio $m : n$, then

(i) Part of $A = \frac{m}{m+n} \times R$

(ii) Part of $B = \frac{n}{m+n} \times R$

2. (i) Duplicate ratio of $a : b$ is $a^2 : b^2$.

(ii) The subduplicate ratio of $a : b = \sqrt{a} : \sqrt{b}$

(iii) The triplicate ratio of $a : b = a^3 : b^3$

(iv) The subtriplicate ratio of $a : b = \sqrt[3]{a} : \sqrt[3]{b}$

3. (i) **Componendo Rule** If $a : b :: c : d$, then, $(a + b) : b :: (c + d) : d$

(ii) **Dividendo Rule** If $a : b :: c : d$, then, $(a - b) : b :: (c - d) : d$

(iii) **Componendo and Dividendo Rule**
If $a : b :: c : d$, then $(a + b) : (a - b) :: (c + d) : (c - d)$

4. (i) Mean proportional of a and $b = \sqrt{ab}$

(ii) Third proportional of a and $b = \frac{b^2}{a}$

(iii) Fourth proportional of a, b and $c = \frac{bc}{a}$.

5. If $A:B=m:n, B:C=p:q$
   Then, $\boldsymbol{A:B:C=pm:pn:nq}$
6. If $A:B=m:n, B:C=p:q, C:D=r:s$
   Then, $\boldsymbol{A:B:C:D=mpr:npr:nqr:nqs}$

$$\boldsymbol{A:D=\frac{m}{n}\times\frac{p}{q}\times\frac{r}{s}}$$

Percentage

1. $x\%$ of $y=\dfrac{xy}{100}$
2. If the population/cost of a certain town/article is P and annual increment rate is $r\%$, then
   (i) After t years population/cost $=\boldsymbol{P\left(1+\frac{r}{100}\right)^t}$
   (ii) Before t years population/cost $=\dfrac{\boldsymbol{P}}{\boldsymbol{\left(1+\frac{r}{100}\right)^t}}$
3. If the population of a town/cost of article is P and it decreases/reduces at the rate of $r\%$ annually, then
   (i) After t years population/cost $=\boldsymbol{P\left(1-\frac{r}{100}\right)^t}$
   (ii) Before t years population/cost $=\dfrac{\boldsymbol{P}}{\boldsymbol{\left(1-\frac{r}{100}\right)^t}}$
4. If the present population of a town is P and the population increases or decreases at the rate of $R_1\%$, $R_2\%$ and $R_3\%$ in first, second and third year, respectively. Then, the population of town after 3 yr $=\boldsymbol{P\left(1\pm\frac{R_1}{100}\right)\left(1\pm\frac{R_2}{100}\right)\left(1\pm\frac{R_3}{100}\right)}$
   '+' →, Increase '–' → Decrease
5. If an amount is increased by $x\%$ and then it is reduced by $x\%$ again, then percentage change will be decrease of $\boldsymbol{\dfrac{x^2}{100}}\%$.
6. If a number is increased/decreased by $a\%$ and, then it is increased/decreased by $b\%$, then resultant change in percentage will be $=\boldsymbol{\left[\pm a\pm b+\frac{(\pm a)(\pm b)}{100}\right]}\%$
   [where '+' → Increase and '–' → Decrease]
7. If the cost of an article is increased by $x\%$, then how much to decrease the consumption of article so that expenditure remains same is given by $=\boldsymbol{\left(\frac{x}{100+x}\times 100\right)}\%$

8. If the cost of an article is decreased by x%, then the increase in consumption of article so that expenditure remains same is given by $= \left(\dfrac{x}{100 - x} \times 100\right)\%$

Profit and Loss

1. If SP > CP, then Profit = SP − CP
2. If SP < CP, then Loss = CP − SP
3. If an article is sold on r % profit, then

$$SP = CP\left[\frac{100 + \text{Profit\%}}{100}\right] \text{ Or } CP = SP\left[\frac{100}{100 + \text{Profit\%}}\right]$$

4. If an object is sold on r% loss, then

$$SP = CP\left[\frac{100 - \text{Loss\%}}{100}\right] \text{ Or } CP = SP\left[\frac{100}{100 - \text{Loss\%}}\right]$$

5. If A sells an article to B at a% profit (or loss) and B sells it to C at b% profit (or loss), then **Total profit** (or loss) $= \left[(\pm a) + (\pm b) + \dfrac{(\pm a)(\pm b)}{100}\right]\%$

6. If A sold an article to B at a profit (or loss) of x% and B sold this article to C at a profit (or loss) of y% then cost price for C = Cost price for $A\left(1 \pm \dfrac{x}{100}\right)\left(1 \pm \dfrac{y}{100}\right)$.

   Here, (+) → profit, (−) → loss

7. If cost price of x articles is equal to selling price of y articles, then $= \dfrac{x - y}{y} \times 100\%$

8. On selling 'x' articles, the profit or loss is equal to selling of 'y' articles, then

$$\text{Profit \%} = \frac{y \times 100}{x - y}\%; \quad \text{Loss \%} = \frac{y}{x + y} \times 100\%$$

9. If a man sells two similar objects, one at a loss of x% and another at a gain of x%, then he always incures loss in this transaction and loss% $= \dfrac{x^2}{100}\%$

Discount

1. Discount = MP − SP
2. Discount % $= \dfrac{\text{Discount}}{\text{MP}} \times 100\%$
3. $\dfrac{CP}{MP} = \dfrac{100 - d\%}{100 + P\%}$, where, d = Discount, P = Profit
4. $SP = \dfrac{MP(100 - d\%)}{100}$ or $MP = \dfrac{SP \times 100}{(100 - d\%)}$, where d → Discount

Successive Discount

If successive discount → x%, y% ∴ Net discount $= \left(x + y - \dfrac{xy}{100}\right)\%$

Partnership

1. Profit $=$ Capital $\times$ Time
2. If the money invested by partner is different as $I_1, I_2, I_3, \ldots\ldots$ for the same time period then profit $P_1, P_2, P_3 \ldots\ldots\ldots$ is distributed among partners in the ratio of their investments
   i.e. $P_1 : P_2 : P_3 : \ldots\ldots\ldots = I_1 : I_2 : I_3 : \ldots\ldots$
3. If the money invested by partners is different as $I_1, I_2, I_3, \ldots\ldots$ for different time periods, t_1, t_2, t_3 ... in a business, then
   Ratio of their profits $=$ Ratio of products of money invested and respective time period.
   i.e., $P_1 : P_2 : P_3 : \ldots\ldots = I_1 \times t_1 : I_2 \times t_2 : I_3 \times t_3 : \ldots\ldots\ldots$.

Mixture and Alligation

Mixture

If from x litre of liquid A, p litre is withdrawn and same quantity of liquid B is added. Again from mixture, q litre mixture is withdrawn and same quantity of liquid B is added. Again from mixture, r litre mixture is withdrawn and same quantity of liquid B is added, then

In final mixture, liquid $A = x\left(\frac{x-p}{x}\right)\left(\frac{x-q}{x}\right)\left(\frac{x-r}{x}\right)\ldots$

If only one process is repeated n times, then A in final mixture $A = x\left(1-\frac{p}{x}\right)^n$

Alligation

If a substance priced at ₹ D per unit (dearer price) is mixed with another substance priced at ₹ C per unit (cheaper price) to form a mixture with a mean price of ₹ M per unit, then

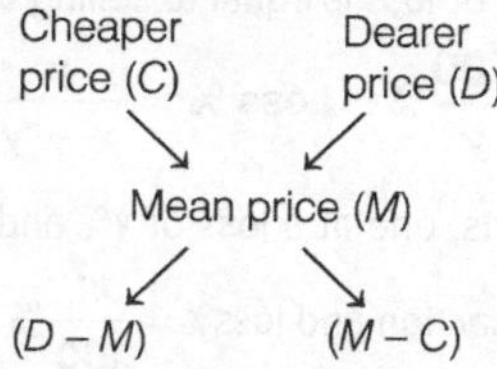

$$\frac{\text{Quantity of cheaper substance}}{\text{Quantity dearer substance}} = \frac{D-M}{M-C}$$

Simple Interest

1. Interest $=$ Amount $-$ Principal
2. Amount $=$ Principal $+$ Interest
3. (i) $\text{SI} = \frac{P \times R \times T}{100}$; SI $\rightarrow$ Simple Interest; $R \rightarrow$ Rate of Interest; $T \rightarrow$ Time

   or $R = \frac{\text{SI} \times 100}{P \times T}$ or $T = \frac{\text{SI} \times 100}{P \times R}$

   (ii) When interest is payable half-yearly, then $R = \frac{R}{2}\%, T = 2n$

   (iii) When interest is payable quarterly, then $R = \frac{R}{4}\%, T = 4n$

If amount A is borrowed at r % rate of simple interest to be based in t yr through equal annual installments then,

$$\text{Annual installment} = \frac{100A}{100 \times t + \frac{r \times t(t-1)}{2}}$$

Compound Interest

1. (i) $\text{CI} = A - P = P\left[\left(1 + \frac{r}{100}\right)^t - 1\right]$ (ii) $A = P\left(1 + \frac{r}{100}\right)^t$

   where, $A \to$ Amount $P \to$ Principal; $r \to$ Rate, $t \to$ Time

2. If the time is in fraction form, i.e. (Let time $= n\frac{a}{b}$)

$$A = P\left(1 + \frac{r}{100}\right)^n \left(1 + \frac{r \times \frac{a}{b}}{100}\right)$$

3. Difference between SI and CI at the rate of R% on amount P

   (i) For 2 years $= P\left(\frac{R}{100}\right)^2 = \frac{\text{SI} \times R}{200}$

   (ii) For 3 years $= P\left(\frac{R}{100}\right)^2\left(3 + \frac{R}{100}\right)$

4. Each annual installment for $n = \dfrac{P}{\left(\frac{100}{100+r}\right) + \left(\frac{100}{100+r}\right)^2 + \ldots + \left(\frac{100}{100+r}\right)^n}$

5. A certain sum at CI becomes x times in n_1 year and y times in n_2 years, then $x^{\frac{1}{n_1}} = y^{\frac{1}{n_2}}$

Time and Work

1. If A completes a piece of work in x days and B completes the same work in y days, then total time taken to complete the work by A and B both $= \dfrac{xy}{x+y}$ days.

2. If A, B and C can do a piece of work in x, y and z days respectively, then total time taken to complete the work by A, B and $C = \dfrac{xyz}{xy + yz + zx}$ days.

3. If A and B can do a work in x days, B and C can do the same work in y days, C and A can do the same work in z days, then total time taken when A, B and C work together $= \dfrac{2xyz}{xy + yz + zx}$

4. If M_1 men finish W_1 work in D_1 days, working T_1 time each day and M_2 men finish W_2 work in D_2 days, working T_2 time each day, then $\dfrac{M_1 D_1 T_1}{W_1} = \dfrac{M_2 D_2 T_2}{W_2}$

Pipe and Cistern

1. Two taps A and B can fill a tank in x h and y h, respectively. If both the taps are opened together, then time taken to fill the tank $= \left(\frac{xy}{x+y}\right)$ h
2. If a pipe fills a tank in x h but it takes t more hours to fill due to leakage in tank. If tank is filled completely, then it will be empty in Time $= \frac{x(x+t)}{t}$
3. Tap A can fill a tank in x h and tap B can empty the tank in y h, then Time taken to fill the empty tank $= \frac{xy}{y-x}\ (y > x)$

Time, Speed and Distance

1. Distance (D) = Speed (S) × Time (T)

   1 km/h $= \frac{5}{18}$ m/s ; 1 m/s $= \frac{18}{5}$ km/h
2. If A and B starts walking towards each other. After meeting each other, A covered his remaining distance in t_1 time and B covered his remaining distance in t_2 time. Then the ratio of their speed $\frac{A}{B} = \sqrt{\frac{t_2}{t_1}}$

   If they meet after t h, then, $t = \sqrt{t_1 t_2}$

Average Speed Average speed $= \frac{\text{Total distance}}{\text{Total time}}$

If a bus travels from A to B with the speed of x km/h and returns from B to A with the speed of y km/h, then the average speed will be $\left(\frac{2xy}{x+y}\right)$ **km/h.**

Relative Speed

- When two objects travel in same direction, then Relative speed = Difference of speeds
- When two objects travel in opposite direction, then Relative speed = Sum of speeds

Train

- When train passes a pole or stationary man, then Covered distance = Length of train
- When train passes a bridge/platform...etc, then Covered distance = Length of train + Length of bridge

Boat and Stream

If speed of boat in still water = x km/h and speed of current/stream = y km/h, then

(i) Downstream speed, $D = x + y$

(ii) Upstream speed $U = x - y$

Also, Speed of boat $= \frac{D+U}{2}$; Speed of current $= \frac{D-U}{2}$

Race

If in a race of L m, 1st contestant beats 2nd contestant and 3rd contestant by distances of a_{12} and a_{13} respectively and the 2nd contestant beats the 3rd contestant by a distance of a_{23}, then we get the relation $(L - a_{12})a_{23} = L(a_{13} - a_{12})$

1. If A beats B by x m,

   then, Distance covered by A(winner) = Lm

   Distance covered by B(Loser) = $(L - x)m$
2. If B starts x m ahead of A (or A gives B a start of x m) then distance covered by $B = (L - x)$ m (A starts from point M and B starts from point Z).
3. If A beats B by T sec, then A and B both start from point M then

   Time taken by A (winner) = Time taken by (loser) $- T$.

Line and Angle

When two parallel lines are intersected by a transversal line, then

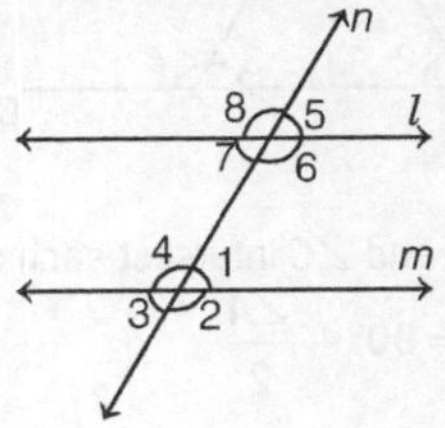

(i) **Corresponding Angles**

$$\angle 1 = \angle 5, \angle 4 = \angle 8; \angle 3 = \angle 7, \angle 2 = \angle 6$$

(ii) **Alternate Interior Angles**

$$\angle 6 = \angle 4, \angle 7 = \angle 1$$

(iii) **Alternate Exterior Angles**

$$\angle 5 = \angle 3, \angle 8 = \angle 2$$

(iv) **Consecutive Interior Angles**

$$\angle 6 + \angle 1 = 180°; \angle 7 + \angle 4 = 180°$$

(v) **Vertically Opposite Angles**

$$\angle 1 = \angle 3, \angle 2 = \angle 4 \;\; ; \angle 5 = \angle 7, \angle 6 = \angle 8$$

Triangle

Identification of Triangle

There are three conditions for identification of triangle.

If a, b and c are the sides of a triangle with also $a < b < c$; then

(i) If $c^2 < a^2 + b^2$, then triangle is an acute angle triangle.

(ii) If $c^2 = a^2 + b^2$, then triangle is a right angle triangle.

(iii) If $c^2 > a^2 + b^2$, then triangle is an obtuse angle triangle.

Main Properties of Triangle

(i) Sum of three angles of a triangle is 180°

$$\angle A + \angle B + \angle C = 180°$$

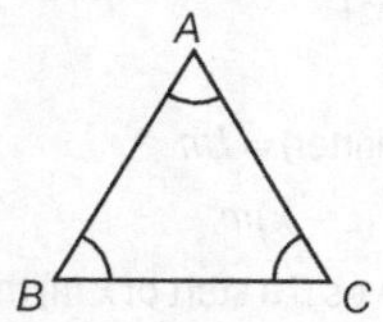

(ii) If a side of triangle is produced, then the exterior angle so formed is equal to the sum of two interior opposite angles.

$$\angle ACD = \angle CAB + \angle ABC$$

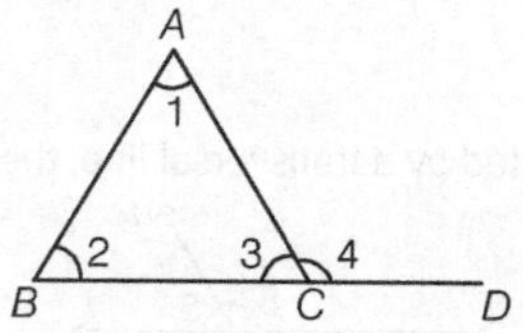

or $\angle 4 = \angle 1 + \angle 2$

(iii) In a ΔABC, the bisector of $\angle B$ and $\angle C$ intersect each other at a point O, then

$$\angle BOC = 90° + \frac{\angle A}{2}$$

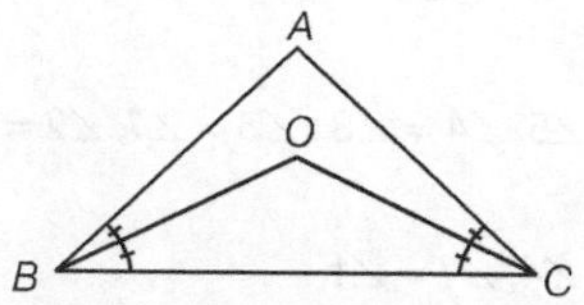

In a ΔABC the side AB and AC are produced to P and Q respectively. The bisectors of $\angle PBC$ and $\angle QCB$ interest at a point O.

Then, $\angle BOC = 90° - \frac{1}{2}\angle A$

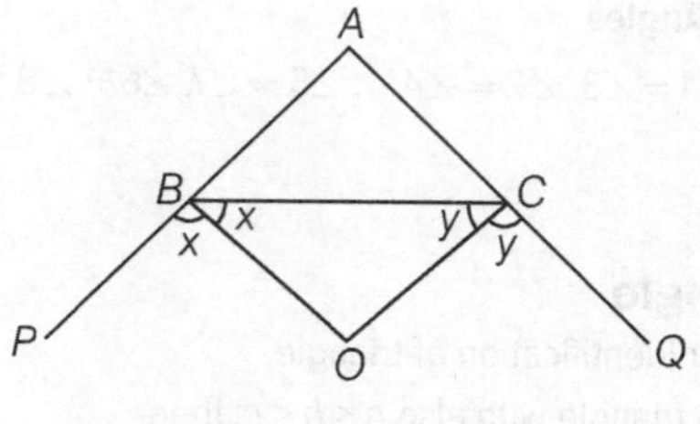

Areas of Similar Triangles

If ΔABC and ΔPQR are similar triangles

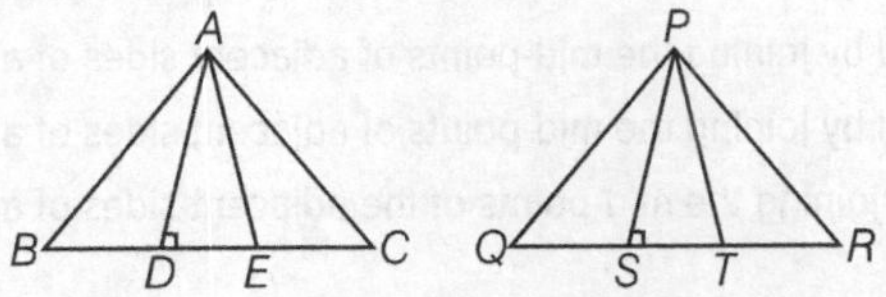

(i) Ratio of area of triangles = (Ratio of corresponding sides)^2

$$\frac{ar(\Delta ABC)}{ar(\Delta PQR)} = \frac{AB^2}{PQ^2} = \frac{BC^2}{QR^2} = \frac{AC^2}{PR^2}$$

(ii) Ratio of area of triangles = (Ratio of corresponding altitudes)^2

$$\frac{ar(\Delta ABC)}{ar(\Delta PQR)} = \frac{AD^2}{PS^2}$$

(iii) Ratio of area of triangles = (Ratio of corresponding medians)^2

$$\frac{ar(\Delta ABC)}{ar(\Delta PQR)} = \frac{AE^2}{PT^2}$$

Theorems Based on Triangle

Pythagoras Theorem

In a right angled triangle, the square of the hypotenuse is equal to the sum of the square of the other two sides.

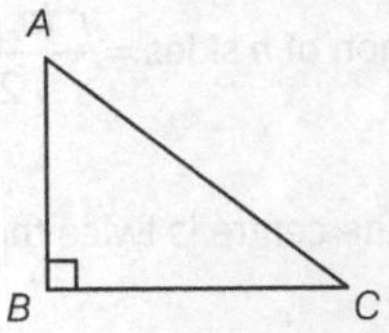

If, $\angle B = 90°$ Then, $AB^2 + BC^2 = AC^2$

Basic Proportionality Theorem (Thales Theorem)

A line drawn parallel to one side of a triangle divides other two sides in the same ratio.

If $DE \parallel BC$,

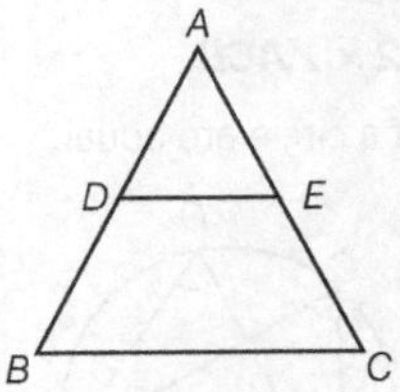

Then, $\dfrac{AD}{DB} = \dfrac{AE}{EC}$

Quadrilateral

(i) Line joining the mid-points of the adjacent sides of a quadrilateral form a parallelogram.

(ii) The figure formed by joining the mid-points of adjacent sides of a rectangle is a rhombus.

(iii) The figure formed by joining the mid-points of adjacent sides of a square is a square.

(iv) Figure formed by joining the mid-points of the adjacent sides of a rhombus is a rectangle.

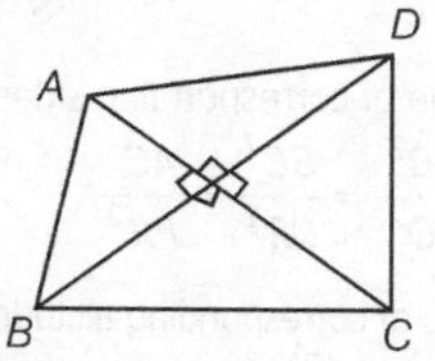

(v) If diagonals of the quadrilateral intersect each other at 90°, then

$$AB^2 + CD^2 = BC^2 + AD^2$$

Polygons

(i) Sum of all interior angles of a polygon of n sides $= (n-2) \times 180°$

(ii) Sum of all exterior angles of a polygon of n sides $= 360°$

(iii) Each interior angle of a regular polygon of n sides $= \dfrac{(n-2) \times 180°}{n}$

(iv) Each exterior angle of a regular polygon of n sides $\dfrac{360°}{n}$

(v) Number of diagonals in a polygon of n sides $= \dfrac{n(n-3)}{2}$

Circle

(i) Angle subtended by an arc at the centre is twice the angle subtended by the same arc at any point on the circumference.

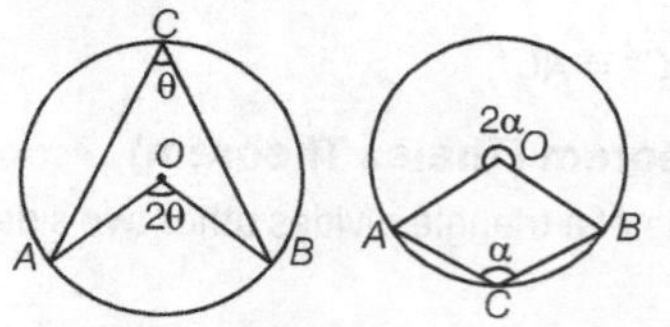

$$\angle AOB = 2 \times \angle ACB$$

(ii) Angles in the same segment of a circle are equal.

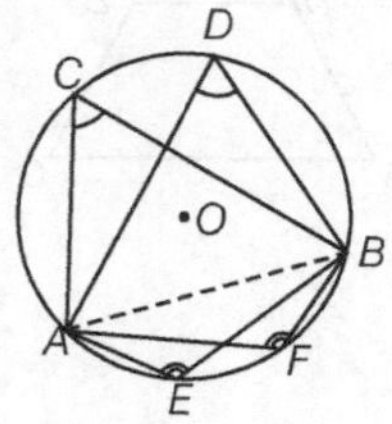

$$\angle ACB = \angle ADB$$

(iii) Angle made in semi-circle is right angle.

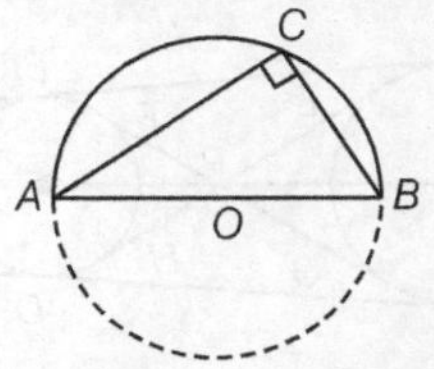

$\angle ACB = 90°$

(iv) Two chords AB and CD of a circle intersect each other at point P internally.

$$PA \times PB = PC \times PD$$

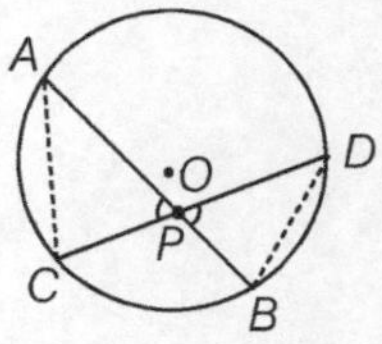

(v) Two chords AB and CD of a circle intersect each other at point P externally.

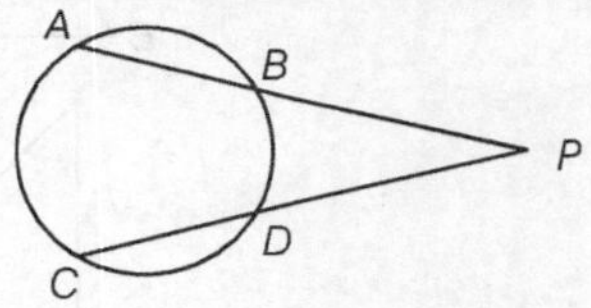

$$PB \times PA = PD \times PC$$

(vi) If a chord and a tangent of a circle intersect each other at a point P externally, then

$$PA \times PB = PT^2$$

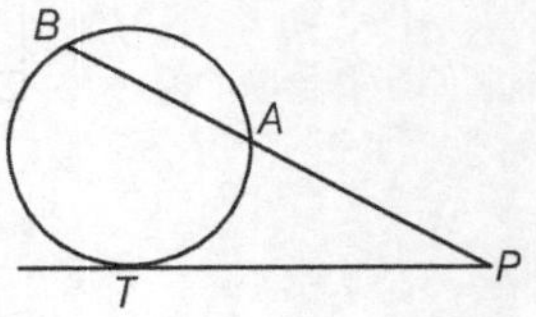

Lengths of Tangents

(i) The lengths of two tangents drawn from the external point to the circle are equal

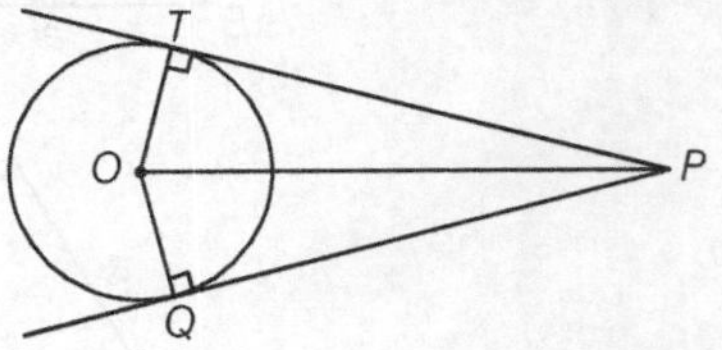

$$PT \text{ or } PQ = \sqrt{(OP)^2 - (OT)^2}$$

(ii) If draw two tangents of two circles then

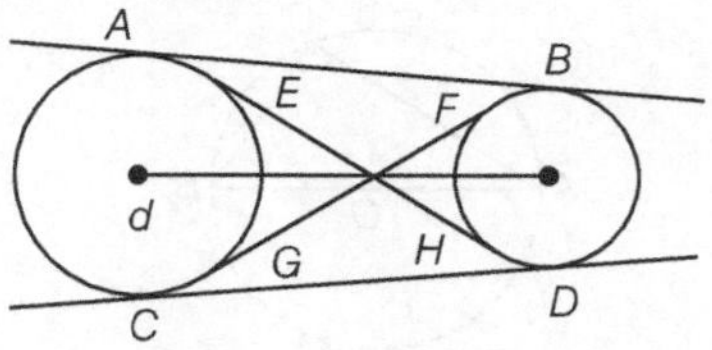

Length of the direct common tangent $= \sqrt{d^2 - (r_1 - r_2)^2}$

Length of the transverse tangent $= \sqrt{d^2 - (r_1 + r_2)^2}$

where, d is the distance between their centres.

Mensuration 2D

Scalene Triangle

- Perimeter $= a + b + c$
- Area $= \sqrt{s(s-a)(s-b)(s-c)}$,

  where. $s = \dfrac{a+b+c}{2}$

  ($s \rightarrow$ Semi-perimeter)

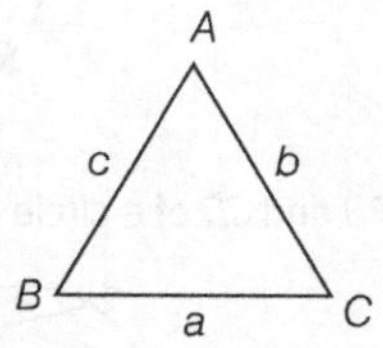

Right Angle Triangle

- Perimeter $= P + B + H$
- Area $= \dfrac{1}{2} PB$

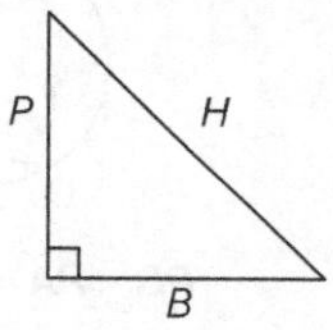

Isosceles Right Angle Triangle

- Perimeter $= H + \sqrt{2}H$
- Area $= \dfrac{H^2}{4}$

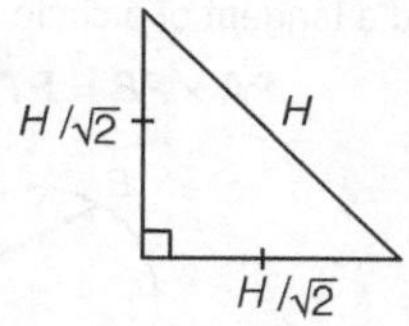

Equilateral Triangle

- Perimeter $= 3a$
- Area $= \dfrac{\sqrt{3}}{4} a^2$
- Height $= \dfrac{\sqrt{3}}{2} a$

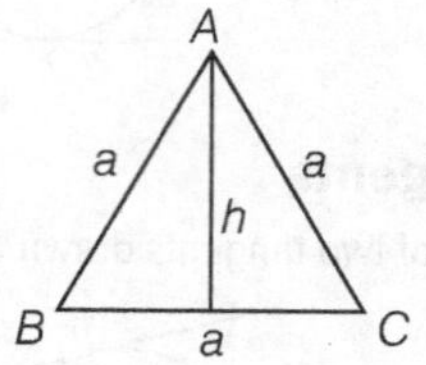

Isosceles Triangle

- Perimeter $= 2a + b$
- Area $= \dfrac{b}{4}\sqrt{4a^2 - b^2}$
- Height $= \dfrac{1}{2}\sqrt{4a^2 - b^2}$

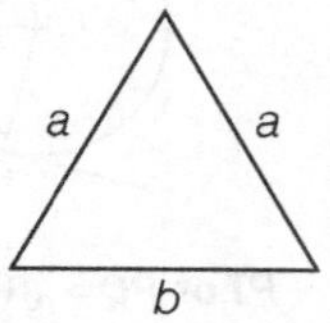

Quadrilateral

Area $= \frac{1}{2} \times AC \times (h_1 + h_2) = \frac{1}{2} \times$ Diagonal $\times$ (Sum of perpendiculars drawn on this diagonal)

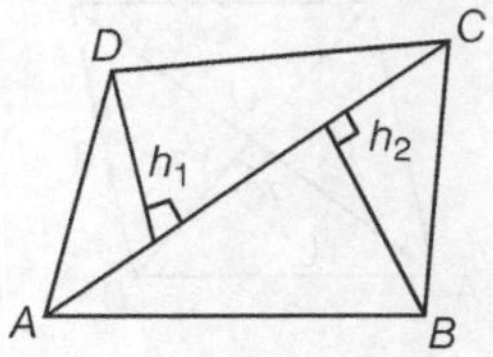

Square

If the side of a square is a, then

- Perimeter $= 4a$
- Area $= a^2$
- Diagonal $= a\sqrt{2}$

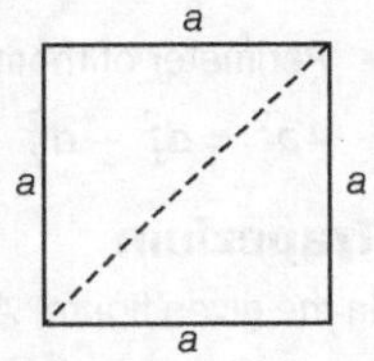

Rectangle

If the length and breadth of a rectangle is a and b, respectively.

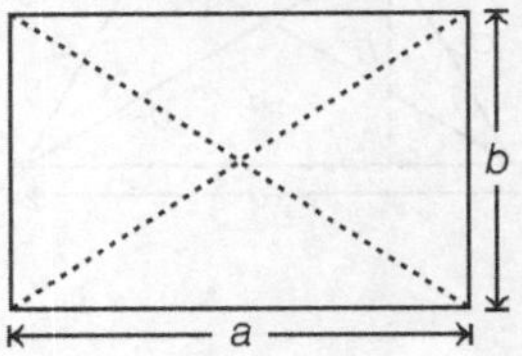

- Perimeter $= 2(a + b) = 2$(Length + Breadth)
- Area $= ab =$ Length $\times$ Breadth
- Diagonal $= \sqrt{a^2 + b^2} = \sqrt{(\text{Length})^2 + (\text{Breadth})^2}$

Parallelogram

In a parallelogram $ABCD$, let side $AB = a$ cm and $BC = b$ cm, then

- Area = Base $\times$ Height $= ah_1 = bh_2$
- Perimeter $= 2(a + b)$

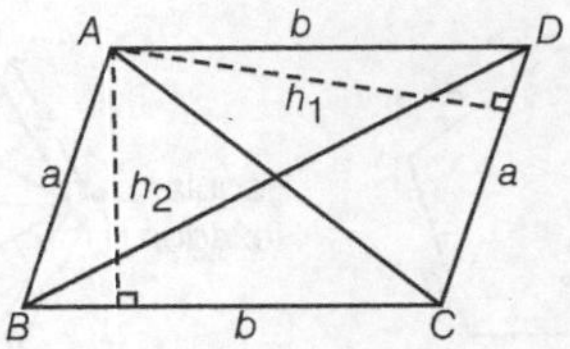

- The length of one diagonal is d, then

  Area of parallelogram $ABCD = 2\sqrt{s(s-a)(s-b)(s-d)}$

  where, $s = \frac{a+b+d}{2}$

Rhombus

In rhombus *ABCD*, let each side is *a* and diagonals $AC = d_1$ and $BD = d_2$, then

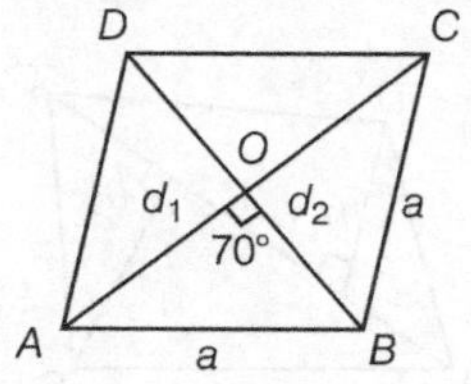

- Area of rhombus $= \frac{1}{2} \times d_1 \times d_2$
- Perimeter of rhombus $= 4a$
- $4a^2 = d_1^2 + d_2^2$

Trapezium

In the given figure, *ABCD* is a trapezium, then

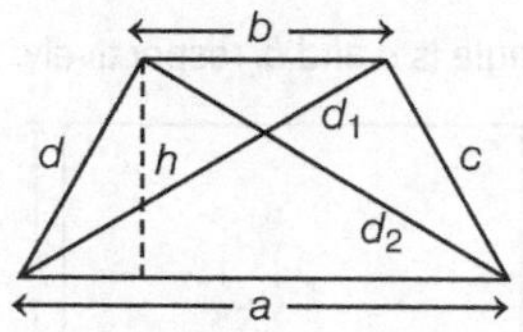

- Perimeter $= a + b + c + d$
- Area $= \frac{1}{2}$ (Sum of parallel sides) $\times$ Distance between them $= \frac{1}{2}(a + b) \times h$

Polygon

- Area of regular pentagon$= \frac{1}{4}\sqrt{5(5 + 2\sqrt{5})}a^2$
- Perimeter $= 5a$
- Area of regular hexagon $= \frac{6\sqrt{3}a^2}{4}$
- Perimeter $= 6a$

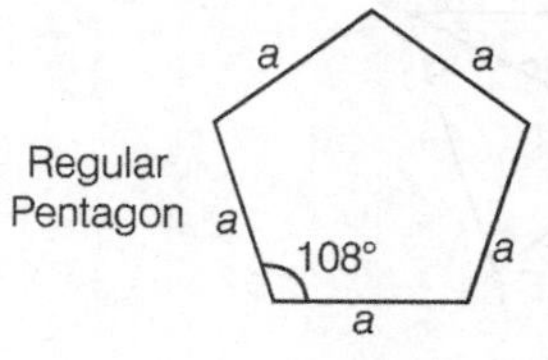

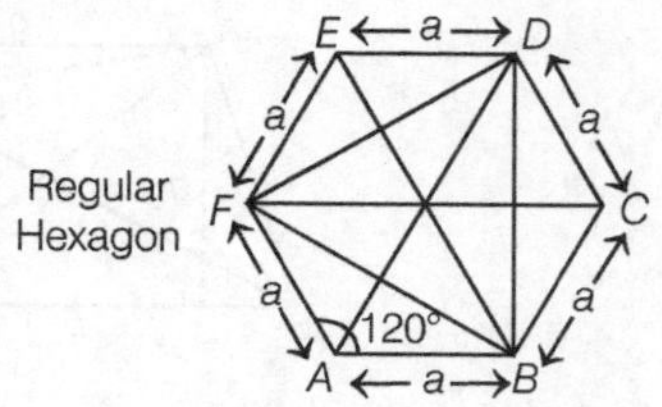

Circle

In the given figure, radius of circle $= r$, then

- Circumference $= 2\pi r$
- Area $= \pi r^2$

Sector of a Circle

In the given figure

- $\theta =$ Central angle $= \frac{l}{r}$
- Area of sector $= \frac{\theta}{360°} \times \pi r^2$
  $= \frac{lr}{2}$
- Length of $\widehat{AB} = l = \frac{\theta}{360°} \times 2\pi r$

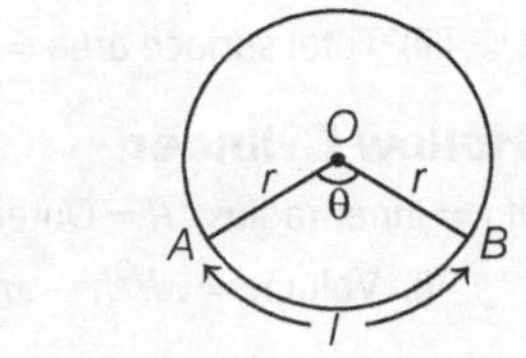

- Area of major segment
  = Area of sector $OAQB$ + Area of ΔAOB
- Area of major segment
  = Area of circle − Area of minor segment

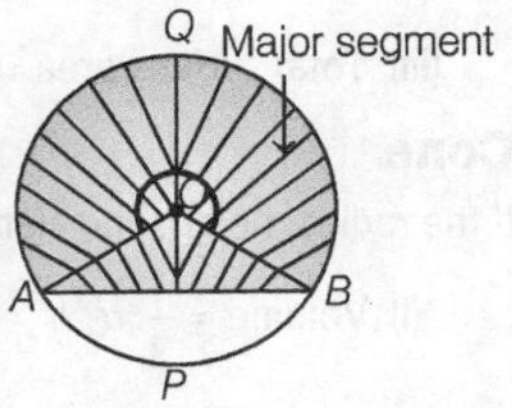

Semi-circle

In the given figure, there is a semi-circle with radius r.

- Perimeter $= \pi r +$ Diameter $= \pi r + 2r$
- Area $= \frac{\pi r^2}{2}$

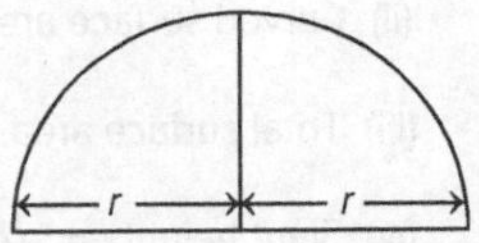

Mensuration 3D

Cube

If a is the side of a cube, then

(i) Lateral surface area $= 4a^2$
(ii) Total surface area $= 6a^2$
(iii) Volume $= a^3$
(iv) Diagonal $= \sqrt{3}a$

Note There are 6 faces, 8 vertices and 12 edges in a cube.
[Here V = Vertices, F = Faces, E = Edges]

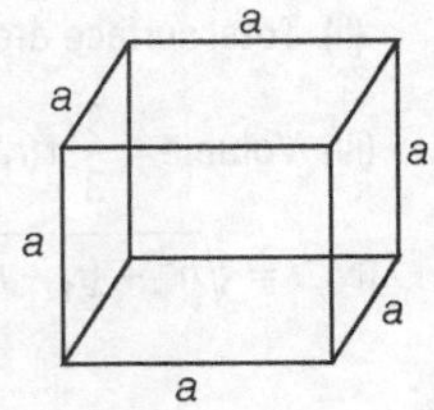

Cuboid

If l, b and h are the length, breadth and height of a cuboid respectively, then

(i) Lateral surface area $= 2(l + b)h$
(ii) Area of four walls = Perimeter of floor × Height
$= 2(l + b) \times h$
(iii) Total surface area $= 2(lb + bh + hl)$
(iv) Volume $= lbh$
(v) Diagonal $= \sqrt{l^2 + b^2 + h^2}$

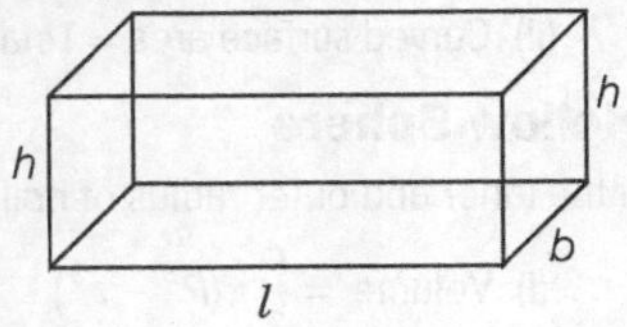

Cylinder

If radius of cylinder is r and height of cylinder is h.

(i) Volume $= \pi r^2 h$

(ii) Curved surface area or lateral surface area $= 2\pi rh$

(iii) Total surface area $= 2\pi rh + 2\pi r^2 = 2\pi r(h + r)$

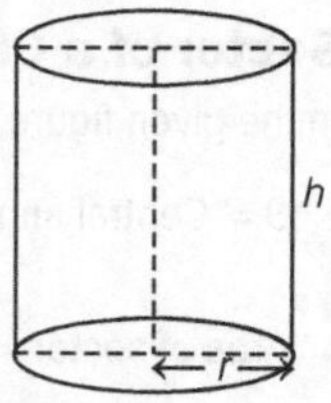

Hollow Cylinder

If r = Inner radius, R = Outer radius, h = Height

(i) Volume $= \pi R^2 h - \pi r^2 h = \pi(R^2 - r^2)h$

(ii) Curved surface area $= 2\pi(R + r)h$

(iii) Total surface area $= 2\pi(R + r)(h + R - r)$

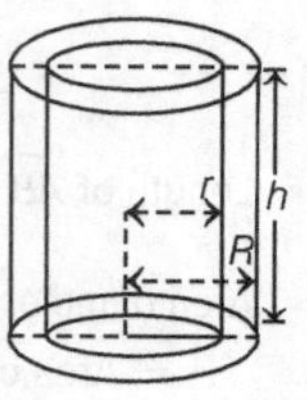

Cone

If the radius, height and slant height of the cone are r, h and l respectively, then

(i) Volume $= \frac{1}{3}\pi r^2 h$

(ii) Curved surface area $= \frac{1}{2} \times 2\pi r \times l = \pi rl$

(iii) Total surface area $= \pi rl + \pi r^2 = \pi r(l + r)$

(iv) Slant height $l = \sqrt{h^2 + r^2}$

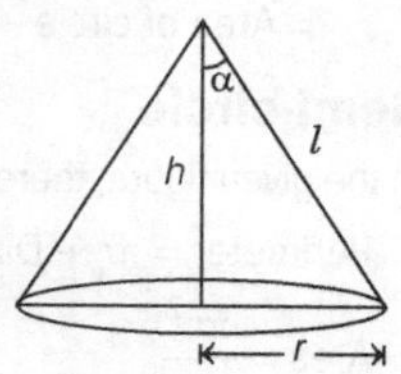

Frustum of Cone

(i) Curved surface area $= \pi(r_1 + r_2)l$

(ii) Total surface area $= \pi(r_1 + r_2)\,l + \pi(r_1^2 + r_2^2)$

(iii) Volume $= \frac{1}{3}\pi(r_1^2 + r_2^2 + r_1 r_2) \times h$

(iv) $l = \sqrt{h^2 + (r_1 - r_2)^2}$

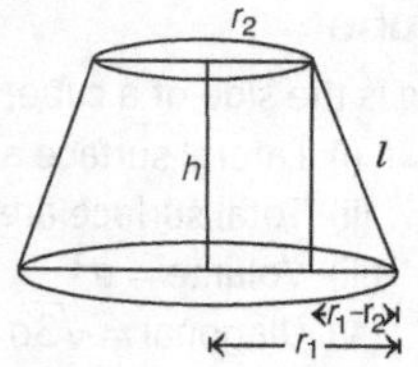

Sphere

(i) Volume $= \frac{4}{3}\pi r^3$

(ii) Curved surface area = Total surface area

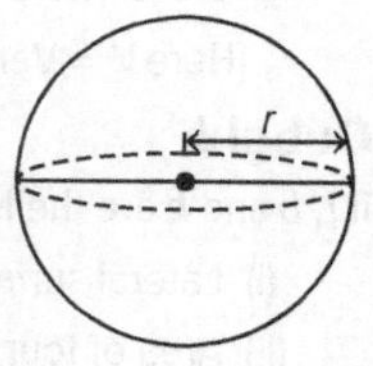

Hollow Sphere

If the inner and outer radius of hollow sphere are r and R respectively, then

(i) Volume $= \frac{4}{3}\pi(R^3 - r^3)$

(ii) Internal surface area of hollow sphere $= 4\pi r^2$

(iii) External surface area of hollow sphere $= 4\pi R^2$

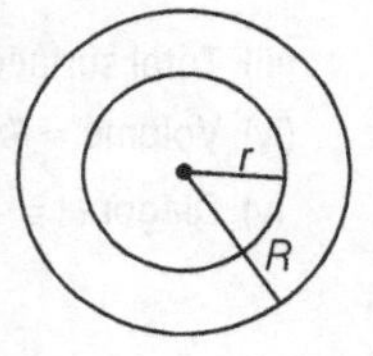

Hemi-Sphere

If the radius of hemi-sphere is r, then

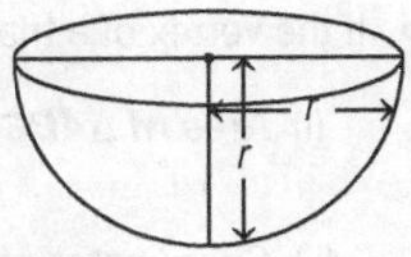

(i) Volume $= \frac{2}{3}\pi r^3$

(ii) Curved surface area $= 2\pi r^2$

(iii) Total surface area $= 3\pi r^2$

Coordinate Geometry

Distance Formula

Distance between two points $A(x_1, y_1)$ and $B(x_2, y_2)$,

$$AB = \sqrt{(x_2 - x_1)^2 + (y_2 - y_1)^2}$$

- Distance between the point (x, y) and origin *i.e.*, (0, 0)

$$d = \sqrt{x^2 + y^2}$$

Section Formula

(i) The coordinate of a point which internally divides the line PQ joined by the point $P(x_1, y_1)$ and $Q(x_2, y_2)$ in the ratio $m : n$, is

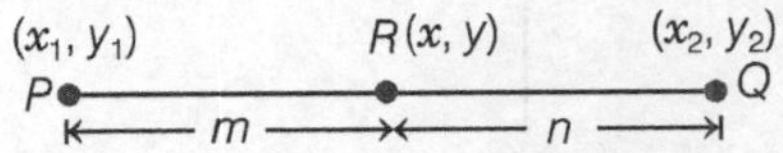

$$x = \frac{mx_2 + nx_1}{m + n}, y = \frac{my_2 + ny_1}{m + n}$$

(ii) If $R(x, y)$ divides the line segment PQ externally in the ratio $m : n$, then

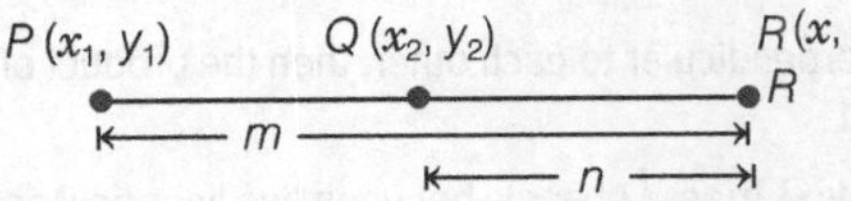

$$x = \frac{mx_2 - nx_1}{m - n}, y = \frac{my_2 - ny_1}{m - n}$$

(iii) **Mid-Point Formula** If $m = n = 1$, then R is the mid point of PQ.

Then,

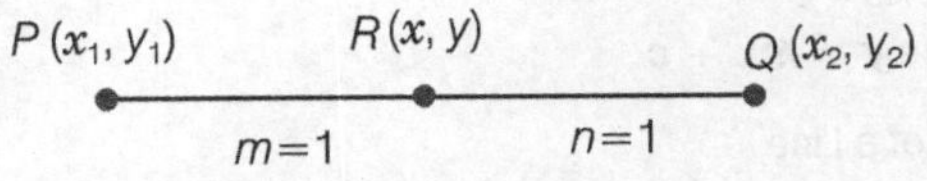

$$x = \frac{x_1 + x_2}{2}, y = \frac{y_1 + y_2}{2}$$

Some Points Related to Triangle

- If the vertex of a triangle ABC are $A(x_1, y_1)$, $B(x_2, y_2)$ and $C(x_3, y_3)$, then

  (i) **Area of ΔABC** $= \frac{1}{2}|x_1(y_2 - y_3) + x_2(y_3 - y_1) + x_3(y_1 - y_2)|$

  (ii) Coordinates of centroid of $\Delta ABC = \left(\frac{x_1 + x_2 + x_3}{3}, \frac{y_1 + y_2 + y_3}{3}\right)$

Area of Quadrilateral

If the vertices of the quadrilateral are given as

$$A(x_1, y_1), B(x_2, y_2), C(x_3, y_3), D(x_4, y_4)$$

Then, $\quad \text{Area} = \frac{1}{2}|(x_1y_2 + x_2y_3 + x_3y_4 + x_4\,y_1) - (x_2y_1 + x_3y_2 + x_4y_3 + x_1y_4)|$

Straight Line

(i) **Slope of a Line The slope of a line is a measure of its steepness.**

Slope of a line, $m = \tan\theta = \frac{y_2 - y_1}{x_2 - x_1}$

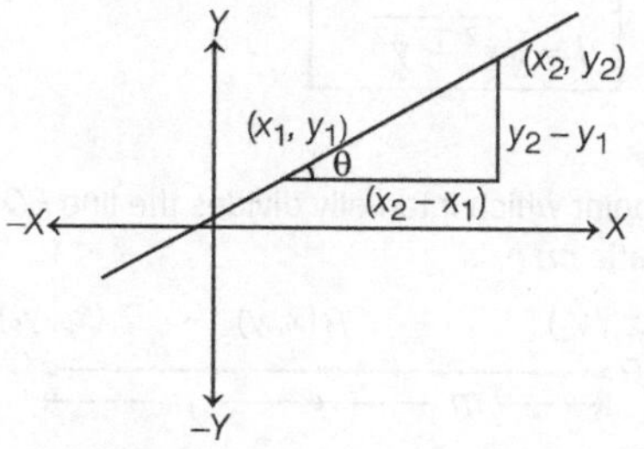

If standard equation of line is $ax + by + c = 0$, then

$$\textbf{Slope} = \frac{-\textbf{Coefficient of } x}{\textbf{Coefficient of } y} = \frac{-a}{b}$$

- If two lines are parallel to each other, then their slopes will be equal. $m_1 = m_2$
- If two lines are perpendicular to each other, then the product of their slopes be equal to -1. $m_1m_2 = -1$

(ii) **Angle Between Two Lines** Let angle between two lines be θ and their slopes are m_1 and m_2, then

$$\tan\theta = \left|\frac{m_1 - m_2}{1 + m_1m_2}\right| \quad \text{or} \quad \theta = \tan^{-1}\left|\frac{m_1 - m_2}{1 + m_1m_2}\right|$$

(iii) **Equation of Straight Line in Various Form**

- Intercept on Y-axis $= c$

  Equation of line $y = mx + c$

- Intercept Form of a Line

  Intercept at X-axis $= a$ and Intercept at Y-axis $= b$

  $\therefore$ Equation of line, $\frac{x}{a} + \frac{y}{b} = 1$

- The equation of a line passing through point (x_1, y_1) and (x_2, y_2)

$$y - y_1 = \frac{y_2 - y_1}{x_2 - x_1}(x - x_1)$$

- The equation of a straight line passing through (x_1, y_1) and its slope is m.

$$y - y_1 = m(x - x_1)$$

- Equation of line parallel to line $ax + by + c = 0$,

$$ax + by = k$$

- Equation of line perpendicular to line $ax + by + c = 0$,

$$bx - ay = k$$

(iv) Perpendicular distance of a line $ax + by + c = 0$ from a point (x, y)

$$= \left|\frac{ax_1 + by_1 + c}{\sqrt{a^2 + b^2}}\right|$$

(v) The perpendicular distance between two parallel lines $ax + by + c_1 = 0$ and

$ax + by + c_2 = 0$ is $\left|\frac{c_1 - c_2}{\sqrt{a^2 + b^2}}\right|$

Algebra

Square Formulae

1. $a^2 - b^2 = (a + b)(a - b)$
2. $(a + b)^2 = a^2 + b^2 + 2ab$
3. $(a - b)^2 = a^2 + b^2 - 2ab$
4. $(a + b + c)^2 = a^2 + b^2 + c^2 + 2(ab + bc + ca)$

Cube Formulae

1. $(a + b)^3 = a^3 + 3a^2b + 3ab^2 + b^3 = a^3 + b^3 + 3ab(a + b)$
2. $a^3 + b^3 = (a + b)^3 - 3ab(a + b)$
3. $a^3 - b^3 = (a - b)^3 + 3ab(a - b)$
4. $a^3 - b^3 = (a - b)(a^2 + b^2 + ab)$

Linear Equation

The equation which has degree 1, is called a linear equation.

- **Conditions for Solution of Equations**

A system of linear equations is $a_1x + b_1y + c_1 = 0$ and $a_2x + b_2y + c_2 = 0$

(i) If $\frac{a_1}{a_2} \neq \frac{b_1}{b_2}$, then system has unique solution. (Consistent)

(ii) If $\frac{a_1}{a_2} = \frac{b_1}{b_2} = \frac{c_1}{c_2}$, then system has infinite solutions. (Consistent)

(iii) If $\frac{a_1}{a_2} = \frac{b_1}{b_2} \neq \frac{c_1}{c_2}$, then system has no solution. (Inconsistent)

Quadratic Equation

- **Solution of Quadratic Equation**

(i) Factorisation method

Let $ax^2 + bx + c = (x - \alpha)(x - \beta) = 0$, then $x = \alpha$ and $x = \beta$ will satisfy the given equation.

(ii) Quadratic Formula

Quadratic equation $ax^2 + bx + c = 0 \, (a \neq 0)$ has two roots, given by

$$\alpha = \frac{-b \pm \sqrt{b^2 - 4ac}}{2a}$$

it is also called Sridharacharya formula.

(iii) Discriminant (D) of quadratic equation $ax^2 + bx + c = 0$ is

$$D = b^2 - 4ac$$

Nature of Roots

If D is discriminant of the quadratic equation $ax^2 + bx + c = 0 \, (a \neq 0)$, then

(i) If $D = 0$, then roots are real and equal.

(ii) If $D > 0$ and perfect square, then roots are real, unequal and rational.

(iii) If $D > 0$ and is not perfect square, then roots are real, unequal and irrational.

(iv) If $D < 0$, then roots are imaginary.

Relation Between Roots and Coefficients

(i) If roots of quadratic equation $ax^2 + bx + c = 0$, are α, β, then

- Sum of roots $= \alpha + \beta = \dfrac{-b}{a} = \dfrac{-\text{ Coefficient of } x}{\text{Coefficient of } x^2}$
- Product of roots $= \alpha\beta = \dfrac{c}{a} = \dfrac{\text{Constant term}}{\text{Coefficient of } x^2}$

(ii) If α and β be two roots of a quadratic equation, then quadratic equation is

$= x^2 -$ (Sum of roots) $x +$ (Product of roots) $= 0$ Or $x^2 - (\alpha + \beta)x + \alpha\,\beta = 0$

Indices and Surds

Law of Indices

1. $a \times a \times a \times \ldots . n \text{ times} = a^n$
2. $a^m \times a^n = (a)^{m+n}$
3. $a^m \times a^n \times a^p \times .. = (a)^{m+n+p+\ldots}$
4. $\dfrac{a^m}{a^n} = (a)^{m-n}$
5. $(a^m)^n = (a)^{mn}$
6. $(abc)^n = a^n \times b^n \times c^n$
7. $\left(\dfrac{a}{b}\right)^n = \dfrac{a^n}{b^n}$
8. $a^0 = 1$
9. $a^{-1} = \dfrac{1}{a}$
10. $\left(\dfrac{a}{b}\right)^m = \left(\dfrac{b}{a}\right)^{-m}$

Laws of Surds

1. $\sqrt[n]{a} = a^{1/n}$ 2. $\sqrt[n]{ab} = \sqrt[n]{a} \times \sqrt[n]{b} = a^{1/n} \times b^{1/n} = (ab)^{1/n}$

3. $\sqrt[n]{\frac{a}{b}} = \frac{\sqrt[n]{a}}{\sqrt[n]{b}} = \left(\frac{a}{b}\right)^{\frac{1}{n}}$ 4. $(\sqrt[n]{a})^m = a^{\frac{m}{n}} = \sqrt[n]{a^m}$ 5. $(\sqrt[n]{a})^n = a$

Progressions

Arithmetic Progression (AP)

Sequence $a, a+d, a+2d, ...$ is an AP.

(i) nth term of AP, $a_n = a + (n-1)d$. (ii) nth term of AP from last $= l - (n-1)d$

(iii) Sum of first n terms of AP

$$S_n = \frac{n}{2}[2a + (n-1)d] = \frac{n}{2}[a + l]$$, where, $a \rightarrow$ First term, $d \rightarrow$ Common ratio, $l \rightarrow$ Last term

Arithmetic Mean

If a, b, c are in AP, then b is called arithmetic mean of a and c. *i.e.* $b = \frac{a+c}{2}$

Geometric Progression (GP)

Sequence $a, ar, ar^2, ...$ is a GP.

(i) nth term of a GP $a_n = ar^{n-1}$

(ii) The sum of the first n terms of a GP, $S_n = \frac{a(1-r^n)}{1-r}; r < 1$

$$S_n = \frac{a(r^n - 1)}{r-1}; r > 1; S_n = n \cdot a, r = 1$$

where, $a \rightarrow$ First term ; $r \rightarrow$ Common ratio

(iii) The sum of infinite terms of a GP, $S_\infty = \frac{a}{1-r}; |r| < 1$

(iv) If a, b and c are in GP, then b is called Geometric Mean of a and c. *i.e.*, $b = \sqrt{ac}$

Note Geometric mean of a and b

$$G = \sqrt{ab}$$

Permutation and Combination

Permutation

The systematic arrangement of r objects by selecting it from 'n' different object is called as permutation. It is denoted by '${}^nP_r$'

$${}^nP_r = \frac{n!}{(n-r)!}$$

Number of Permutation in Special Cases

1. The number of permutation of n different objects taken 'r' at a time where repetition is allowed $= n^r$
2. The number of permutation of n objects, where p objects are of same kind, and rest are all different $\frac{n!}{p!}$
3. The number of permutation of n objects, where p_1 objects are of one kind, p_2 are of second kind, ...p_k are of kth kind and the rest if any are of different kind $= \frac{n!}{p_1!\,p_2!....p_k!}$

Combination

The number of combinations of n different things taken r at a time $= C(n, r)$

Or $${}^nC_r = \frac{n!}{r!(n-r)!}, 0 \le r \le n$$

Some Other Results based on Permutation and Combination

- ${}^nP_0 = 1$
- ${}^nP_1 = n$
- ${}^nP_n = n! = {}^nP_{n-1}$
- ${}^nP_r = {}^nC_r \times r!$
- ${}^nC_r = {}^nC_{n-r}$
- ${}^nC_n = {}^nC_0 = 1$
- ${}^nC_1 = {}^nC_{n-1} = n$
- ${}^nC_{r-1} + {}^nC_r = {}^{n+1}C_r$

Probability

(i) $P(E) = \frac{\text{Number of favourable outcomes}}{\text{Total number of outcomes}}$

(ii) Probability of an event (E) + Probability of the event not $E = 1$

$$P(E) + P(\bar{E}) = 1$$

Tossing a coin : A coin has two sides i.e., Heads (H) and Tails (T).

If a coin is tossed n times then possible outcomes $= 2^n$

Rolling a Dice A dice has six faces marked as 1,2,3,4,5,6.

If a dice is rolled n times then possible outcomes $= 6^n$

Cards: A deck of playing cards consists of 52 cards

Black (26)		**Red** (26)	
Club (13)	Spade (13)	Diamond (13)	Heart (13)

Trigonometry

Trigonometric Ratios

In a right angle triangle

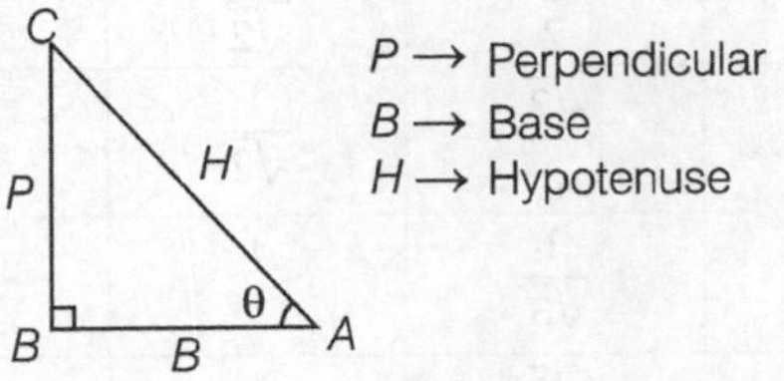

(i) $\sin\theta = \frac{P}{H}$ (ii) $\cos\theta = \frac{B}{H}$ (iii) $\tan\theta = \frac{P}{B}$

(iv) $\cot\theta = \frac{B}{P}$ (v) $\sec\theta = \frac{H}{B}$ (vi) $\text{cosec}\,\theta = \frac{H}{P}$

Relation between Trigonometric Ratios

(i) $\sin\theta = \frac{1}{\text{cosec}\,\theta}$; $\text{cosec}\,\theta = \frac{1}{\sin\theta}$; $\sin\theta \cdot \text{cosec}\,\theta = 1$

(ii) $\cos\theta = \frac{1}{\sec\theta}$; $\sec\theta = \frac{1}{\cos\theta}$; $\cos\theta \cdot \sec\theta = 1$

(iii) $\tan\theta = \frac{1}{\cot\theta}$; $\cot\theta = \frac{1}{\tan\theta}$; $\tan\theta \cdot \cot\theta = 1$

(iv) $\tan\theta = \frac{\sin\theta}{\cos\theta}$; $\sin\theta = \tan\theta \cdot \cos\theta$; $\cos\theta = \frac{\sin\theta}{\tan\theta}$

(v) $\cot\theta = \frac{\cos\theta}{\sin\theta}$; $\cos\theta = \cot\theta \cdot \sin\theta$; $\sin\theta = \frac{\cos\theta}{\cot\theta}$

Trigonometric Identities

(i) $\sin^2\theta + \cos^2\theta = 1$, $\sin^2\theta = 1 - \cos^2\theta$; $\cos^2\theta = 1 - \sin^2\theta$

(ii) $\sec^2\theta - \tan^2\theta = 1$, $\sec^2\theta = 1 + \tan^2\theta$; $\tan^2\theta = \sec^2\theta - 1$

If $\sec\theta + \tan\theta = k$, then $\sec\theta - \tan\theta = \frac{1}{k}$

(iii) $\text{cosec}^2\theta - \cot^2\theta = 1$, $\text{cosec}^2\theta = 1 + \cot^2\theta$; $\cot^2\theta = \text{cosec}^2\theta - 1$

If $\text{cosec}\,\theta + \cot\theta = p$, then $\text{cosec}\,\theta - \cot\theta = \frac{1}{p}$

Values of some Specific Angles of Trigonometric Ratios

Angle → **T-Ratio ↓**	0°	$30°/\frac{\pi}{6}$	$45°/\frac{\pi}{4}$	$60°/\frac{\pi}{3}$	$90°/\frac{\pi}{2}$
$\sin\theta$	0	$\frac{1}{2}$	$\frac{1}{\sqrt{2}}$	$\frac{\sqrt{3}}{2}$	1
$\cos\theta$	1	$\frac{\sqrt{3}}{2}$	$\frac{1}{\sqrt{2}}$	$\frac{1}{2}$	0
$\tan\theta$	0	$\frac{1}{\sqrt{3}}$	1	$\sqrt{3}$	∞
$\cot\theta$	∞	$\sqrt{3}$	1	$\frac{1}{\sqrt{3}}$	0
$\sec\theta$	1	$\frac{2}{\sqrt{3}}$	$\sqrt{2}$	2	∞
$\operatorname{cosec}\theta$	∞	2	$\sqrt{2}$	$\frac{2}{\sqrt{3}}$	1

Trigonometric ratios of Sum and Difference of two Angles

- $\sin(A+B) = \sin A\cos B + \cos A\sin B$
- $\tan(A+B) = \dfrac{\tan A + \tan B}{1 - \tan A\tan B}$
- $\sin(A-B) = \sin A\cos B - \cos A\sin B$
- $\tan(A-B) = \dfrac{\tan A - \tan B}{1 + \tan A\tan B}$
- $\sin(A+B)\sin(A-B) = \sin^2 A - \sin^2 B$
- $\cos(A+B) = \cos A\cos B - \sin A\sin B$
- $\cot(A+B) = \dfrac{\cot A\cot B - 1}{\cot B + \cot A}$
- $\cos(A-B) = \cos A\cos B + \sin A\sin B$
- $\cot(A-B) = \dfrac{\cot A\cot B + 1}{\cot B - \cot A}$
- $\cos(A+B)\cos(A-B) = \cos^2 A - \sin^2 B$

Conversion of Trigonometric Ratios from product to Sum and Difference

- $2\sin A\cos B = \sin(A+B) + \sin(A-B), (A>B)$
- $2\cos A\sin B = \sin(A+B) - \sin(A-B), (A>B)$
- $2\cos A\cos B = \cos(A+B) + \cos(A-B)$
- $2\sin A\sin B = \cos(A-B) - \cos(A+B)$

Conversion of Trigonometric Ratios, Sum and Difference into Product

- $\sin C + \sin D = 2\sin\dfrac{C+D}{2}\cos\dfrac{C-D}{2}$
- $\sin C - \sin D = 2\cos\dfrac{C+D}{2}\sin\dfrac{C-D}{2}$
- $\cos C + \cos D = 2\cos\dfrac{C+D}{2}\cos\dfrac{C-D}{2}$
- $\cos C - \cos D = 2\sin\dfrac{C+D}{2}\sin\dfrac{D-C}{2}$

Trigonometric Ratios of multiple of an Angle

- $\sin 2\theta = 2\sin\theta\cos\theta = \dfrac{2\tan\theta}{1+\tan^2\theta}$
- $\cos 2\theta = \cos^2\theta - \sin^2\theta = 2\cos^2\theta - 1 = 1 - 2\sin^2\theta = \dfrac{1-\tan^2\theta}{1+\tan^2\theta}$
- $\cot 2\theta = \dfrac{\cot^2\theta - 1}{2\cot\theta}$
- $\sin 3\theta = 3\sin\theta - 4\sin^3\theta$
- $\cos 3\theta = 4\cos^3\theta - 3\cos\theta$
- $\tan 3\theta = \dfrac{3\tan\theta - \tan^3\theta}{1 - 3\tan^2\theta}$

Trigonometric Ratios of Sub-Multiple Angles

- $\sin\theta = 2\sin\dfrac{\theta}{2}\cos\dfrac{\theta}{2} = \dfrac{2\tan\theta/2}{1+\tan^2\theta/2}$
- $\cos\theta = \cos^2(\theta/2) - \sin^2(\theta/2) = 2\cos^2(\theta/2) - 1$
  $= 1 - 2\sin^2(\theta/2) = \dfrac{1-\tan^2(\theta/2)}{1+\tan^2(\theta/2)}$
- $\tan\theta = \dfrac{2\tan(\theta/2)}{1-\tan^2(\theta/2)}$

Values of Trigonometric Ratios for Some Special Angles

- $\sin 18° = \dfrac{\sqrt{5}-1}{4} = \cos 72°$
- $\cos 18° = \dfrac{\sqrt{10+2\sqrt{5}}}{4} = \sin 72°$
- $\cos 36° = \dfrac{\sqrt{5}+1}{4} = \sin 54°$
- $\sin 36° = \dfrac{\sqrt{10-2\sqrt{5}}}{4} = \cos 54°$

Relations between Angles and Sides of a Triangle in Trigonometric Ratio Form

1. Sine Rule

$$\frac{a}{\sin A} = \frac{b}{\sin B} = \frac{c}{\sin C} = k \text{ (constant)}$$

$a : b : c = k\sin A : k\sin B : k\sin C$

$a : b : c = \sin A : \sin B : \sin C$

$h = c\sin B = b\sin C$

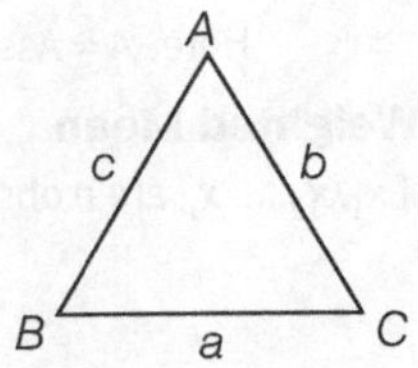

2. Cosine Rule

$$\cos A = \frac{b^2 + c^2 - a^2}{2bc}$$

$$a^2 = b^2 + c^2 - 2bc\cos A$$

$$\cos B = \frac{c^2 + a^2 - b^2}{2ca}; \quad b^2 = a^2 + c^2 - 2ac\cos B$$

$$\cos C = \frac{a^2 + b^2 - c^2}{2ab}; \quad c^2 = a^2 + b^2 - 2ab\cos C$$

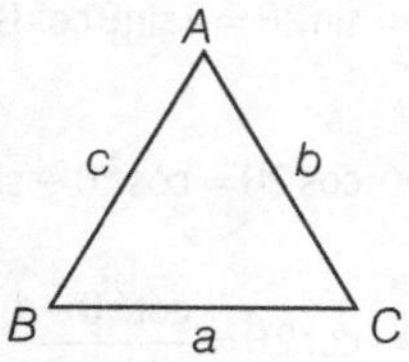

Statistics

Class Mark It is the mid-point of the class interval. *i.e.* Class mark $= \frac{\text{Lower limit} + \text{Upper limit}}{2}$

Mean

1. Mean $(\bar{x}) = \frac{\text{Sum of all observations}}{\text{Total number of observations}}$

2. **Mean of Ungrouped Data**

   If $x_1, x_2, x_3, \ldots x_n$ are n observations, then

   (i) **Mean** $(\bar{x}) = \frac{x_1 + x_2 + x_3 + \ldots + x_n}{n} = \frac{\sum_{i=1}^{n} x_i}{n}$

3. **Mean of Grouped Data**

   If $x_1, x_2, x_3, \ldots x_n$ are n observations with respective frequencies $f_1, f_2, f_3, \ldots f_n$, then

   (i) Mean $(\bar{x}) = \frac{f_1x_1 + f_2x_2 + f_3x_3 + \ldots + f_nx_n}{f_1 + f_2 + f_3 + \ldots + f_n} = \frac{\sum_{i=1}^{n} f_i x_i}{\sum_{i=1}^{n} f_i}$

   (ii) Mean $(\bar{x}) = A + \frac{\sum_{i=1}^{n} f_i d_i}{\sum_{i=1}^{n} f_i}$, where $d = x - A$

   Here, $A =$ Assumed mean

Weighted Mean

If $x_1, x_2 \ldots x_n$ are n observations to which respective weights attached are $w_1, w_2, w_3 \ldots w_n$ then

$$\text{Weighted Mean } (\bar{x}) = \frac{x_1w_1 + x_2w_2 + \ldots + x_nw_n}{w_1 + w_2 + \ldots + w_n}$$

Median

1. Median of Ungrouped Data

Suppose there are n number of observations. Then arrange the data in ascending or descending order.

(i) If n is odd, then

$$\text{Median} = \text{Value of}\left(\frac{n+1}{2}\right)\text{th observation}$$

(ii) If n is even, then

$$\text{Median} = \frac{\text{Value of}\left[\frac{n}{2}\text{th} + \left(\frac{n}{2}+1\right)\text{th}\right]\text{observation}}{2}$$

2. Median of Grouped Data

Firstly we find commulative frequencies of all the classes and find median class. Then,

$$\text{Median} = l + \frac{\frac{N}{2} - C_f}{f} \times h$$

where, l = Lower limit of median class

C_f = Commulative frequency of class preceding the median class

f = Frequency of median class, h = Class size

Mode

1. Mode of Ungrouped Data

Mode is that value which is repeated maximum number of times.

2. Mode of Grouped Data

$$\text{Mode} = l + \left(\frac{f_1 - f_0}{2f_1 - f_0 - f_2}\right) \times h$$

Where

l = Lower limit of modal class

h = Size of the class interval

f_0 = Frequency of the class preceding the modal class

f_1 = Frequency of the modal class

f_2 = Frequency of the class succeeding the modal class

Relation between Mean, Median and Mode

If distribution is not symmetric.

$$\text{Mode} = 3\,\text{Median} - 2\,\text{Mean}$$

- If distribution is symmetric

$$\text{Mean} = \text{Median} = \text{Mode}$$

Range

Range is the difference of the extreme observations of the data set.

i.e. **Range = Highest – Observation – Lowest observation**

Mean Deviation

1. **Mean Deviation for Ungrouped Data**

   Let $x_1, x_2, \ldots x_n$ be n observations, then

$$\textbf{Mean deviation} = \frac{\sum_{i=1}^{n} |x_i - \bar{x}|}{n}, \text{ where, } \bar{x} \rightarrow \text{Mean}$$

2. **Mean Deviation for Grouped Data**

   Let $x_1, x_2, \ldots x_n$ be n observations and $f_1, f_2, \ldots f_n$ are their corresponding frequencies. Then,

$$\textbf{Mean deviation} = \frac{\sum_{i=1}^{n} f_i |x_i - \bar{x}|}{N}, \text{ where, } \bar{x} \rightarrow \text{Mean}$$

$$N = \sum_{i=1}^{n} f_i = \text{Total frequency}$$

Variance

- Variance $(\sigma^2) = \dfrac{\sum_{i=1}^{n} (x_i - \bar{x})^2}{n}$

  Here, x_i = Value of observation

  $\bar{x}$ = Mean

  n = Total number of observations

- Standard Deviation $(\sigma) = \sqrt{\text{Variance}}$